Get Connected.

Interactive Presentations

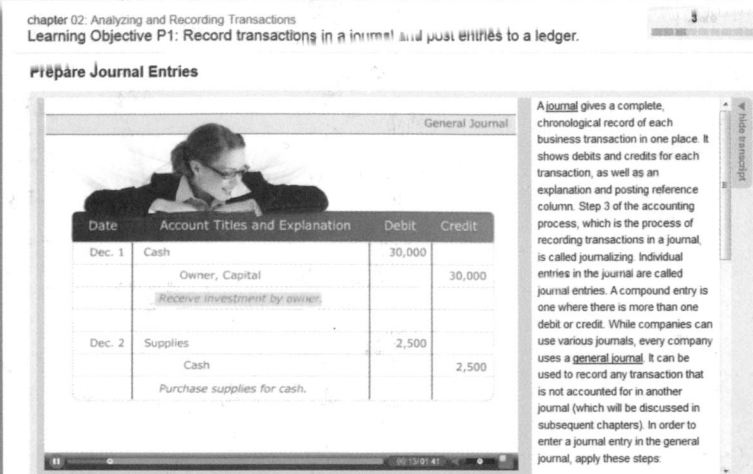

chapter 02: Analyzing and Recording Transactions
Learning Objective P1: Record transactions in a journal and post entries to a ledger.

Connect Accounting's **Interactive Presentations** teach each chapter's core learning objectives and concepts through an engaging, hands-on presentation, bringing the text content to life. Interactive Presentations harness the full power of technology to truly engage and appeal to all learning styles. Interactive Presentations are ideal in all class formats—online, face-to-face, or hybrid.

Intelligent Response Technology

Intelligent Response Technology (IRT) is Connect Accounting's new student interface for end-of-chapter assessment content. Intelligent Response Technology provides a general journal application that looks and feels more like what you would find in a general ledger software package, improves answer acceptance to reduce student frustration with formatting issues (such as rounding), and, for select questions, provides an expanded table that guides students through the process of solving the problem.

view transaction list   view general journal

Journal Entry Worksheet

1 2 3 4 5 6 7

Two-thirds of the work related to $12,000 cash received in advance is performed this period.

Transaction	General Journal	Debit	Credit
a.	Unearned fee revenue	12,000	
	fe		12,000
	Fee revenue		
	Unearned fee revenue		

*Enter debits before credits

done   clear transaction   record transaction

Get Engaged.

eBooks

Connect Plus includes a media-rich eBook that allows you to share your notes with your students. Your students can insert and review their own notes, highlight the text, search for specific information, and interact with media resources. Using an eBook with Connect Plus gives your students a complete digital solution that allows them to access their materials from any computer.

Lecture Capture

Make your classes available anytime, anywhere. With simple, one-click recording, students can search for a word or phrase and be taken to the exact place in your lecture that they need to review.

Fundamental
Accounting Principles

21st edition

John J. Wild

University of Wisconsin at Madison

Ken W. Shaw

University of Missouri at Columbia

Barbara Chiappetta

Nassau Community College

McGraw-Hill Irwin

McGraw-Hill
Irwin

To my students and family, especially **Kimberly, Jonathan, Stephanie,** and **Trevor.**
To my wife **Linda** and children, **Erin, Emily,** and **Jacob.**
To my mother, husband **Bob,** and sons **Michael** and **David.**

FUNDAMENTAL ACCOUNTING PRINCIPLES, TWENTY-FIRST EDITION
Published by McGraw-Hill/Irwin, a business unit of The McGraw-Hill Companies, Inc., 1221 Avenue of the Americas, New York, NY, 10020. Copyright © 2013 by The McGraw-Hill Companies, Inc. All rights reserved. Printed in the United States of America. Previous editions © 2011, 2009, and 2007. No part of this publication may be reproduced or distributed in any form or by any means, or stored in a database or retrieval system, without the prior written consent of The McGraw-Hill Companies, Inc., including, but not limited to, in any network or other electronic storage or transmission, or broadcast for distance learning.

Some ancillaries, including electronic and print components, may not be available to customers outside the United States.

This book is printed on acid-free paper.

1 2 3 4 5 6 7 8 9 0 DOW/DOW 1 0 9 8 7 6 5 4 3 2

ISBN-13: 978-0-07-802558-7 (combined edition)
ISBN-10: 0-07-802558-3 (combined edition)
ISBN-13: 978-0-07-752528-6 (volume 1, chapters 1-12)
ISBN-10: 0-07-752528-0 (volume 1, chapters 1-12)
ISBN-13: 978-0-07-752527-9 (volume 2, chapters 12-25)
ISBN-10: 0-07-752527-2 (volume 2, chapters 12-25)
ISBN-13: 978-0-07-752526-2 (principles, chapters 1-17)
ISBN-10: 0-07-752526-4 (principles, chapters 1-17)

Senior Vice President, Products & Markets: *Kurt L. Strand*
Vice President, General Manager, Products
 & Markets: *Brent Gordon*
Vice President, Content Production & Technology
 Services: *Kimberly Meriwether David*
Director: *Tim Vertovec*
Executive Brand Manager: *Steve Schuetz*
Executive Director of Development: *Ann Torbert*
Managing Development Editor: *Christina A. Sanders*
Director of Digital Content: *Patricia Plumb*
Digital Development Editor: *Julie Hankins*
Senior Marketing Manager: *Michelle Heaster*

Lead Project Manager: *Lori Koetters*
Senior Buyer: *Carol A. Bielski*
Lead Designer: *Matthew Baldwin*
Cover Designer: *Laurie Entringer*
Cover Image: © *Getty Images*
Senior Content Licensing Specialist: *Jeremy Cheshareck*
Photo researcher: *Sarah Evertson*
Lead Media Project Manager: *Brian Nacik*
Media Project Manager: *Ron Nelms*
Typeface: *10.5/12 Times Roman*
Compositor: *Aptara®, Inc.*
Printer: *R. R. Donnelley*

All credits appearing on page or at the end of the book are considered to be an extension of the copyright page.

Library of Congress Cataloging-in-Publication Data
Wild, John J.
 Fundamental accounting principles / John J. Wild, Ken W. Shaw, Barbara Chiappetta.—21st ed.
  p. cm.
 Includes index.
 ISBN 978-0-07-802558-7 (combined ed. : alk. paper)—ISBN 0-07-802558-3 (combined ed. : alk. paper)—
 ISBN 978-0-07-752528-6 (vol. 1, chapters 1-12 : alk. paper)—ISBN 0-07-752528-0 (vol. 1, chapters 1-12 : alk. paper)—
 ISBN 978-0-07-752527-9 (vol. 2, chapters 12-25 : alk. paper)—ISBN 0-07-752527-2 (vol. 2, chapters 12-25 : alk. paper)—
 ISBN 978-0-07-752526-2 (principles, chapters 1-17 : alk. paper)—ISBN 0-07-752526-4 (principles, chapters 1-17 :
 alk. paper)
  1. Accounting. I. Shaw, Ken W. II. Chiappetta, Barbara. III. Title.
 HF5636.W675 2013
 657—dc23
                                                                                          2012027838

The Internet addresses listed in the text were accurate at the time of publication. The inclusion of a website does not indicate an endorsement by the authors or McGraw-Hill, and McGraw-Hill does not guarantee the accuracy of the information presented at these sites.

www.mhhe.com

Adapting to the Needs of Today's Students

Fundamental Accounting Principles 21e

Enhancements in technology have changed the spectrum of how we live and learn in the world today. Being able to download and work with learning tools on smart phones, tablets, or laptop computers empowers students to drive their own learning by putting increasingly intelligent technology into their hands.

No two students are alike, and whether the goal is to become an accountant or a businessperson or simply to be an informed consumer of accounting information, *Fundamental Accounting Principles (FAP)* has helped generations of students succeed by giving them support in the form of leading-edge accounting content that engages students, paired with state-of-the-art technology that elevates their understanding of key accounting principles.

With *FAP* on your side, you'll be provided with **engaging content** in a **motivating style** to help students see the relevance of accounting. Students are motivated when reading materials that are clear and pertinent. *FAP* excels at engaging students. Its chapter-opening vignettes showcase dynamic, successful entrepreneurial individuals and companies guaranteed to **interest and excite students, and highlights the usefulness of accounting to those business owners**. This edition's featured companies—**Polaris, Arctic Cat, KTM,** and **Piaggio**—captivate students with their products and annual reports, which are a pathway for learning financial statements. Further, this book's coverage of the accounting cycle fundamentals is widely praised for its clarity and effectiveness.

FAP also delivers innovative technology to help student performance. ***Connect Accounting*** provides students with instant grading and feedback for assignments that are completed online. With our new **Intelligent Response Technology,** we are taking our accounting content to the next level, delivering assessment material in a **more intuitive, less restrictive** format that adapts to the needs of today's students.

Our new content features:

- **a general journal interface** that looks and feels more like that found in practice
- **an auto-calculation** feature that allows students to focus on concepts rather than rote tasks.
- **a smart (auto-fill) drop-down design**.

The end result is content that better prepares students for the real world. *Connect Accounting* also includes digitally based, interactive adaptive learning tools that provide an opportunity to engage students more effectively by offering varied instructional methods and more personalized learning paths that build on different learning styles, interests, and abilities, allowing students to work at their own pace.

McGraw-Hill LearnSmart™ is an intelligent learning system that uses a series of adaptive questions to pinpoint each student's knowledge gaps. LearnSmart then provides an optimal learning path for each student, so that they spend less time in areas they already know and more time in areas they don't. The result is LearnSmart's adaptive learning path that helps students retain more knowledge, learn faster, and study more efficiently.

Our **Interactive Presentations** teach each chapter's core learning objectives in a rich multimedia format, bringing the content to life. Your students will come to class prepared when you assign Interactive Presentations. Students can also review the Interactive Presentations as they study.

Guided Examples provide students with narrated, animated, step-by-step walkthroughs of algorithmic versions of assigned exercises. Students appreciate the Guided Examples because they can help students learn accounting and complete assignments when outside of class.

Connect Plus Accounting integrates a media-rich online version of the textbook with *Connect Accounting.*

> "I believe that FAP is the best intro accounting text on the market—clear, concise, complete... Additionally, it is clear that the authors stay in touch with the 'times'."
> — **JAMES L . LOCK, Northern Virginia Community College**

About the Authors

JOHN J. WILD is a distinguished professor of accounting at the University of Wisconsin at Madison. He previously held appointments at Michigan State University and the University of Manchester in England. He received his BBA, MS, and PhD from the University of Wisconsin.

Professor Wild teaches accounting courses at both the undergraduate and graduate levels. He has received numerous teaching honors, including the Mabel W. Chipman Excellence-in-Teaching Award, the departmental Excellence-in-Teaching Award, and the Teaching Excellence Award from the 2003 and 2005 business graduates at the University of Wisconsin. He also received the Beta Alpha Psi and Roland F. Salmonson Excellence-in-Teaching Award from Michigan State University. Professor Wild has received several research honors and is a past KPMG Peat Marwick National Fellow and is a recipient of fellowships from the American Accounting Association and the Ernst and Young Foundation.

Professor Wild is an active member of the American Accounting Association and its sections. He has served on several committees of these organizations, including the Outstanding Accounting Educator Award, Wildman Award, National Program Advisory, Publications, and Research Committees. Professor Wild is author of *Financial Accounting*, *Managerial Accounting*, and *College Accounting*, each published by McGraw-Hill/Irwin. His research articles on accounting and analysis appear in *The Accounting Review*, *Journal of Accounting Research*, *Journal of Accounting and Economics*, *Contemporary Accounting Research*, *Journal of Accounting, Auditing and Finance*, *Journal of Accounting and Public Policy*, and other journals. He is past associate editor of *Contemporary Accounting Research* and has served on several editorial boards including *The Accounting Review*.

In his leisure time, Professor Wild enjoys hiking, sports, travel, people, and spending time with family and friends.

KEN W. SHAW is an associate professor of accounting and the Deloitte Professor of Accounting at the University of Missouri. He previously was on the faculty at the University of Maryland at College Park. He received an accounting degree from Bradley University and an MBA and PhD from the University of Wisconsin. He is a Certified Public Accountant with work experience in public accounting.

Professor Shaw teaches financial accounting at the undergraduate and graduate levels. He received the Williams-Keepers LLC Teaching Excellence award in 2007, was voted the "Most Influential Professor" by three School of Accountancy graduating classes, and is a two-time recipient of the O'Brien Excellence in Teaching Award. He is the advisor to his School's chapter of the Association of Certified Fraud Examiners.

Professor Shaw is an active member of the American Accounting Association and its sections. He has served on many committees of these organizations and presented his research papers at national and regional meetings. Professor Shaw's research appears in the *Journal of Accounting Research*; *Contemporary Accounting Research*; *Journal of Financial and Quantitative Analysis*; *Journal of the American Taxation Association*; *Strategic Management Journal; Journal of Accounting, Auditing, and Finance*; *Journal of Financial Research*; and other journals. He has served on the editorial boards of *Issues in Accounting Education* and the *Journal of Business Research*. Professor Shaw is co-author of *Financial and Managerial Accounting* and *College Accounting*, both published by McGraw-Hill.

In his leisure time, Professor Shaw enjoys tennis, cycling, music, and coaching his children's sports teams.

BARBARA CHIAPPETTA received her BBA in Accountancy and MS in Education from Hofstra University and is a tenured full professor at Nassau Community College. For the past two decades, she has been an active executive board member of the Teachers of Accounting at Two-Year Colleges (TACTYC), serving 10 years as vice president and as president from 1993 through 1999. As an active member of the American Accounting Association, she has served on the Northeast Regional Steering Committee, chaired the Curriculum Revision Committee of the Two-Year Section, and participated in numerous national committees. Professor Chiappetta has been inducted into the American Accounting Association Hall of Fame for the Northeast Region. She had also received the Nassau Community College dean of instruction's Faculty Distinguished Achievement Award. Professor Chiappetta was honored with the State University of New York Chancellor's Award for Teaching Excellence in 1997. As a confirmed believer in the benefits of the active learning pedagogy, Professor Chiappetta has authored Student Learning Tools, an active learning workbook for a first-year accounting course, published by McGraw-Hill/Irwin.

In her leisure time, Professor Chiappetta enjoys tennis and participates on a U.S.T.A. team. She also enjoys the challenge of bridge. Her husband, Robert, is an entrepreneur in the leisure sport industry. She has two sons—Michael, a lawyer, specializing in intellectual property law in New York, and David, a composer, pursuing a career in music for film in Los Angeles.

Dear Colleagues/Friends,

As we roll out the new edition of *Fundamental Accounting Principles*, we thank each of you who provided suggestions to improve our textbook. As teachers, we know how important it is to select the right book for our course. This new edition reflects the advice and wisdom of many dedicated reviewers, symposium and workshop participants, students, and instructors. Our book consistently rates number one in customer loyalty because of you. Together, we have created the most readable, concise, current, accurate, and innovative accounting book available today.

Throughout the writing process, we steered this book in the manner you directed. Reviewers, instructors, and students say this book's enhanced presentation, graphics, and technology cater to different learning styles and helps students better understand accounting. *Connect Plus Accounting* offers new features to improve student learning and to assist instructor teaching and grading. You and your students will find all these tools easy to apply.

We owe the success of this book to you and other instructors who graciously took time to help us focus on the changing needs of today's students and their learning needs. We feel fortunate to have witnessed our profession's extraordinary devotion to teaching. Your feedback and suggestions are reflected in everything we write. Please accept our heartfelt thanks for your dedication in helping today's students learn, understand, and appreciate accounting.

With kindest regards,

John J. Wild   *Ken W. Shaw*   *Barbara Chiappetta*

McGraw-Hill *Connect Plus Accounting* is a complete online assignment, learning, and textbook assessment solution that connects your students with the tools and resources needed to achieve success through faster learning, more efficient studying, and higher retention of knowledge. Key features found in *Connect Plus Accounting* include:

Intelligent Response Technology Intelligent Response Technology is *Connect Accounting's* new student interface for end-of-chapter assessment content. Intelligent Response Technology provides a general journal application that looks and feels more like what you would find in a general ledger software package, improves answer acceptance to reduce student frustration with formatting issues (such as rounding), and, for select questions, provides an expanded table that guides students through the process of solving the problem.

> "I like that this system was formatted like real-world accounting is."
>
> **—Student, Rose State College**

> "I love how the general journal was set up. It felt like what I would be filling out if I had an accounting job."
>
> **—Student, Chabot Community College**

Today's Students!

1. Complete the table to determine the cost assigned to ending inventory and cost of goods sold using specific identification.

Specific Identification

| | | Available for Sale | | Cost of Goods Sold | | | Ending Inventory | | |
Date	Activity	Units	Unit Cost	Units Sold	Unit Cost	COGS	Ending Inventory-Units	Cost Per Unit	Ending Inventory-Cost
Mar. 1	Beginning Inventory	150							
Mar. 20	Purchase	220							
Mar. 30	Purchase	90							
		460				$ 0			$ 0

contact MH Publishing   check my work   View Hint #1   references   ebook & resources

BIZKID COMPANY
Income Statement
For Year Ended August 31, 2011

Sales	✓		$ 218,880 ✓
Less: Sales discounts	✓ $	3,349 ✓	
Less: Sales returns and allowances	✓	14,446 ✓	17,795
Net sales	✓		201,085
Cost of goods sold	✓		85,312 ✓
Gross profit	✓		115,773
Expenses			
Selling expenses			
Sales salaries expense	✓	29,987 ✓	
Rent expense-selling space	✓	10,287 ✓	
Store supplies expense	✓	2,627 ✓	
Advertising expense	✓	18,605 ✓	
Total selling expenses			61,506
General and administrative expenses			
Accounts payable	✗	876 ✓	
Accum-depreciation - store equipment	✗	9,785 ✗	
Total general and administrative expenses			10,661
Total expenses			72,167

BIZKID COMPANY
Income Statement
For Year Ended August 31, 2011

Sales		$ 218,880
Less: Sales discounts	$ 3,349	
Less: Sales returns and allowances	14,446	17,795
Net sales		201,085
Cost of goods sold		85,312
Gross profit		115,773
Expenses		
Selling expenses		
Sales salaries expense	29,987	
Rent expense-selling space	10,287	
Store supplies expense	2,627	
Advertising expense	18,605	
Total selling expenses		61,506
General and administrative expenses		
Office salaries expense	876	
Rent expense-office space	2,627	
of		
		3,503
		65,009

Cost of goods sold
Office salaries expense
Office supplies expense
Rent expense-office space

ask your instructor a question   report a content issue   check my work   references

Connect Accounting helps students learn more efficiently by providing feedback and practice material when they need it, where they need it. *Connect* grades homework automatically and gives immediate feedback on any questions students may have missed.

> "This system has improved the journal entry and T-account set-up processes to more accurately resemble the way it is done in class."
>
> —Student, Tallahassee Community College

Interactive Presentations *Connect Accounting's* Interactive Presentations teach each chapter's core learning objectives and concepts through an engaging, hands-on presentation, bringing the text content to life. Interactive Presentations harness the full power of technology to truly engage and appeal to all learning styles. Interactive Presentations are ideal in all class formats—online, face-to-face, or hybrid.

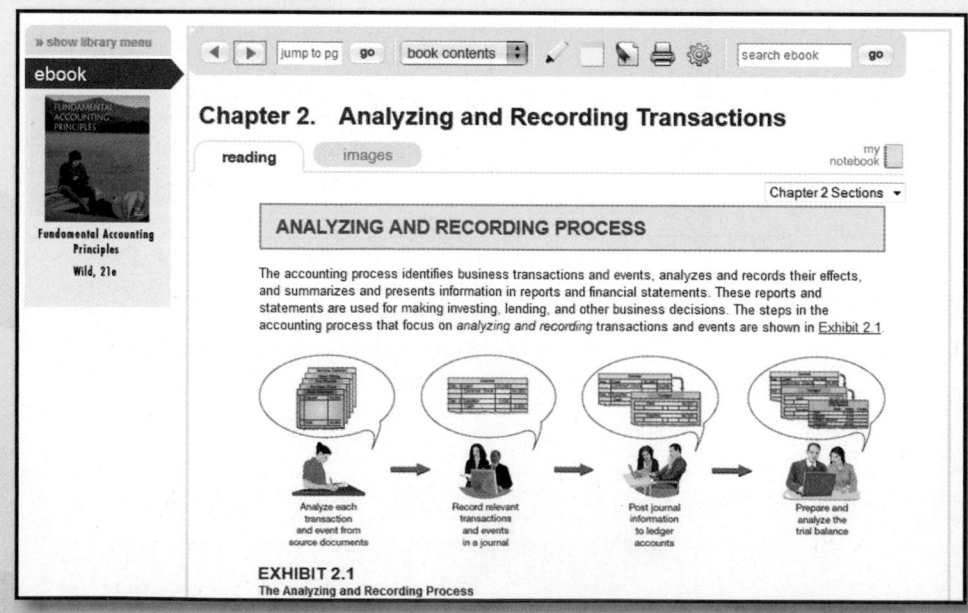

Integrated eBooks *Connect Plus* includes a media-rich eBook. With it, you can share your notes with your students, and they can insert their own notes, highlight the text, search for specific information, and review their materials. Using an eBook with *Connect* gives your students a complete digital solution that allows them to access their materials from any computer. And over time, as more and more students use mobile devices, our eBooks will even enable them to learn on the go.

Today's Students!

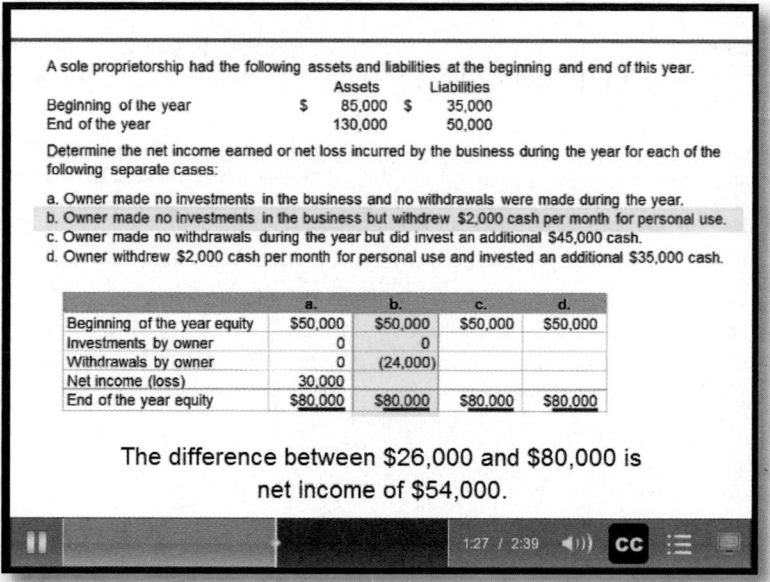

Guided Examples Guided Examples provide narrated, animated, and step-by-step walkthroughs of algorithmic versions of assigned exercises in *Connect Accounting*, allowing the student to identify, review, or reinforce the concepts and activities covered in class. Guided Examples provide immediate feedback and focus on the areas where students need the most guidance.

LearnSmart No two students are alike. McGraw-Hill LearnSmart™ is an intelligent learning system that uses a series of adaptive questions to pinpoint each student's knowledge gaps. LearnSmart then provides an optimal learning path for each student, so that they spend less time in areas they already know and more time in areas they don't. The result is that LearnSmart's adaptive learning path helps students retain more knowledge, learn faster, and study more efficiently.

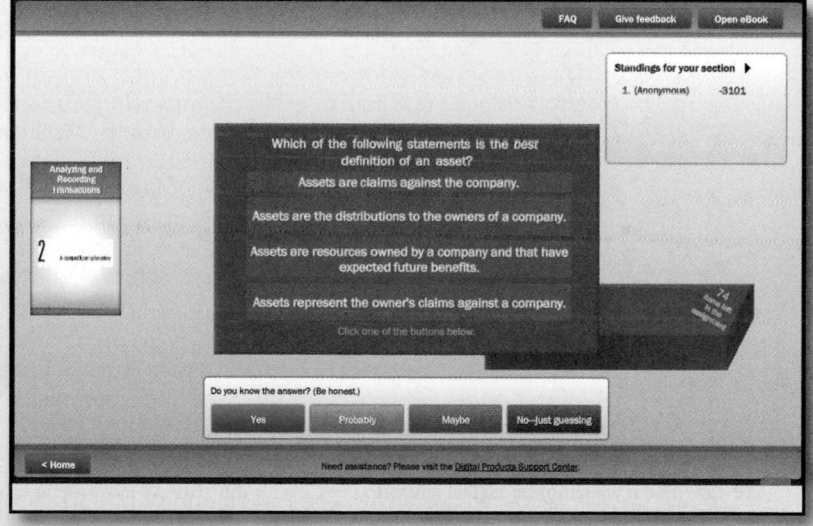

Student Resource Library The *Connect Accounting* Student Study Center gives access to additional resources such as recorded lectures, online practice materials, an eBook, and more.

Adapting to the Needs of

McGraw-Hill's solutions are proven to improve student performance. With *Connect Accounting*, students can access a wealth of engaging resources to help them study more effectively and perform at a higher level on homework and exams. *Connect Accounting* also allows instructors to assign McGraw-Hill's world class content and assess student performance.

The integrated solutions for *Fundamental Accounting Principles* have been specifically designed to help you achieve your course goals of improving student readiness, enhancing student engagement, and increasing their comprehension of content. McGraw-Hill's adaptive learning component, LearnSmart, provides assignable modules that help students master chapter core content and come to class more prepared. In addition, Interactive Presentations deliver learning objectives in an interactive environment, giving students access to course-critical content anytime, anywhere. Known for its engaging style, the FAP solution employs the use of current companies, LearnSmart, and our instant feedback on practice problems to help students engage with our materials, comprehend the content, and achieve higher outcomes in the course.

Simple Assignment Management and Smart Grading

With *Connect Plus Accounting*, creating assignments is easier than ever, so you can spend more time teaching and less time managing. *Connect Accounting* enables you to:

• Create and deliver assignments easily with select end-of-chapter questions and test bank items.
• Go paperless with the eBook and online submission and grading of student assignments.
• Have assignments scored automatically, giving students immediate feedback on their work and side-by-side comparisons with correct answers.
• Reinforce classroom concepts with practice tests and instant quizzes.

Today's Instructors

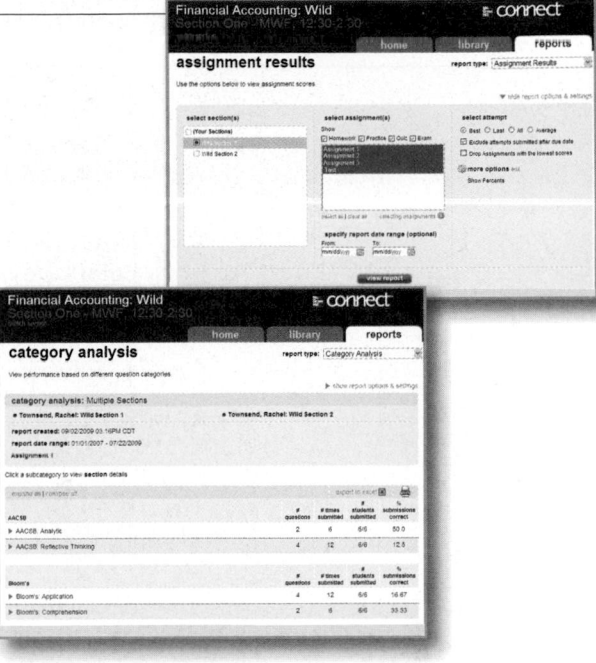

Student Reporting

Connect Accounting keeps instructors informed about how each student, section, and class is performing, allowing for more productive use of lecture and office hours. The reporting function enables you to:

- View scored work immediately and track individual or group performance with assignment and grade reports.
- Access an instant view of student or class performance relative to learning objectives.
- Collect data and generate reports required by many accreditation organizations, such as AACSB and AICPA.
- Identify low-performance students with the "At Risk" student report.

Instructor Library

The *Connect Accounting* Instructor Library is your repository for additional resources to improve student engagement in and out of class. You can select and use any asset that enhances your lecture. The *Connect Accounting* Instructor Library includes: access to the eBook version of the text, PowerPoint files, Solutions Manual, Instructor Resource Manual, and Test Bank.

Tegrity: Lectures 24/7

Make your classes available anytime, anywhere. With simple one-click recording, instructors can record lectures, presentations, and step-by-step problem solutions with Tegrity. Using Tegrity with *Connect Accounting*, instructors can post recordings directly to *Connect* for student viewing. Students can also search for a word or phrase and be taken to the exact place in your lecture that they need to review.

To learn more about Tegrity watch a two-minute Flash demo at **http://tegritycampus.mhhe.com**.

McGraw-Hill Customer Experience Group Contact Information

At McGraw-Hill, we understand that getting the most from new technology can be challenging. That's why our services don't stop after you purchase our products. You can e-mail our Product Specialists 24 hours a day to get product training online. Or you can search our knowledge bank of Frequently Asked Questions on our support Website. For Customer Support, call 800-331-5094 or visit **www.mhhe.com/support**. One of our Technical Support Analysts will be able to assist you in a timely fashion.

How Can Text-Related Web Resources Enrich My Course?

Online Learning Center (OLC)

We offer an Online Learning Center (OLC) that follows *Fundamental Accounting Principles* chapter by chapter. It doesn't require any building or maintenance on your part. It's ready to go the moment you and your students type in the URL: *www.mhhe.com/wildFAP21e*

As students study and learn from *Fundamental Accounting Principles*, they can visit the Student Edition of the OLC Website to work with a multitude of helpful tools:

- Generic Template Working Papers
- Chapter Learning Objectives
- Interactive Chapter Quizzes
- PowerPoint® Presentations
- Excel Template Assignments

A secured Instructor Edition stores essential course materials to save you prep time before class. Everything you need to run a lively classroom and an efficient course is included. All resources available to students, plus . . .

- Instructor's Resource Manual
- Solutions Manual
- Solutions to Excel Template Assignments
- Test Bank
- Solutions to Sage 50 Complete Accounting and QuickBooks templates

The OLC Website also serves as a doorway to other technology solutions, like course management systems.

Online Course Management

The **Best** of **Both Worlds**

McGraw-Hill Higher Education and Blackboard have teamed up. What does this mean for you?

1. Single sign-on. Now you and your students can access McGraw-Hill's *Connect*™ and Create™ right from within your Blackboard course—all with one single sign-on.

2. Deep integration of content and tools. You get single sign-on with *Connect* and Create, you also get integration of McGraw-Hill content and content engines right in Blackboard. Whether you're choosing a book for your course or building *Connect* assignments, all the tools you need are right where you want them—inside Blackboard.

3. One grade book. Keeping several grade books and manually synchronizing grades in Blackboard is no longer necessary. When a student completes an integrated *Connect* assignment, the grade for that assignment automatically (and instantly) feeds your Blackboard grade center.

4. A solution for everyone. Whether your institution is already using Blackboard or you just want to try Blackboard on your own, we have a solution for you. McGraw-Hill and Blackboard can now offer you easy access to industry-leading technology and content, whether your campus hosts it, or we do. Be sure to ask your local McGraw-Hill representative for details.

McGraw-Hill Campus™

McGraw-Hill Campus™ is a new one-stop teaching and learning experience available to users of any learning management system. This complimentary integration allows faculty and students to enjoy single sign-on (SSO) access to all McGraw-Hill Higher Education materials and synchronized grade-book with our award-winning McGraw-Hill Connect platform. McGraw-Hill Campus provides faculty with instant access to all McGraw-Hill Higher Education teaching materials (eTextbooks, test banks, PowerPoint slides, animations and learning objects, and so on), allowing them to browse, search, and use any instructor ancillary content in our vast library at no additional cost to instructor or students. Students enjoy SSO access to a variety of free (quizzes, flash cards, narrated presentations, and so on) and subscription-based products (McGraw-Hill *Connect*). With this integration enabled, faculty and students will never need to create another account to access McGraw-Hill products and services. For more information on McGraw-Hill Campus please visit our website at **www.mhcampus.com**.

CourseSmart

CourseSmart is a new way to find and buy eTextbooks. CourseSmart has the largest selection of eTextbooks available anywhere, offering thousands of the most commonly adopted textbooks from a wide variety of higher education publishers. CourseSmart eTextbooks are available in one standard online reader with full text search, notes, highlighting, and email tools for sharing between classmates. Visit **www.CourseSmart.com** for more information on ordering.

How Can Adaptive Online Learning Improve Student Performance?

ALEKS®

Significantly Increase Student Success and Retention

"After I adopted ALEKS for my Principles of Accounting course, I got fewer and shorter lines for my office hours, and the class average jumped 10-15 percent overall. It's a win-win situation."

—**Professor Fatma Cebenoyan,
Hunter College, NY**

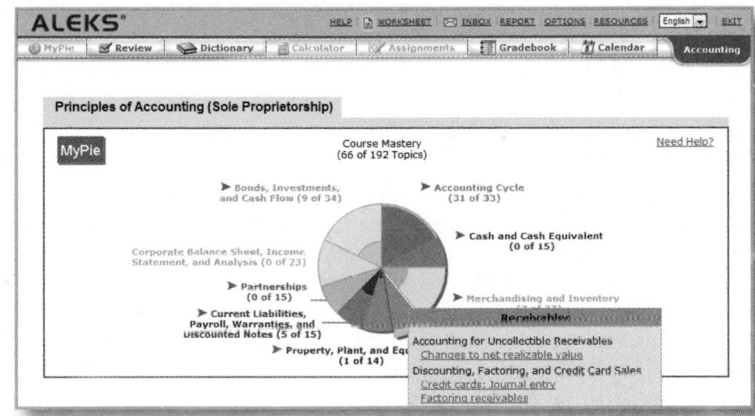

ALEKS: A Superior, Student-Friendly Accounting Experience:

- **Artificial Intelligence** Fills Individual Student Knowledge Gaps
- **Cycle of Learning & Assessment** Increases Learning Momentum & Engages Students
- **Adaptive, Open-Response Environment** Avoids Multiple-Choice Questions
- **Customizable Curriculum** Aligns with Your Course Syllabi and Textbooks
- **Dynamic, Automated Reports** Monitor Detailed Student & Class Progress

To learn more, visit: **www.aleks.com/highered/business**

ALEKS is a registered trademark of ALEKS Corporation.

Innovative Textbook Features

Using Accounting for Decisions

Whether we prepare, analyze, or apply accounting information, one skill remains essential: decision-making. To help develop good decision-making habits and to illustrate the relevance of accounting, our book uses a unique pedagogical framework we call the Decision Center. This framework comprises a variety of approaches and subject areas, giving students insight into every aspect of business decision-making; see three examples to the right and one below. Answers to Decision Maker and Ethics boxes are at the end of each chapter.

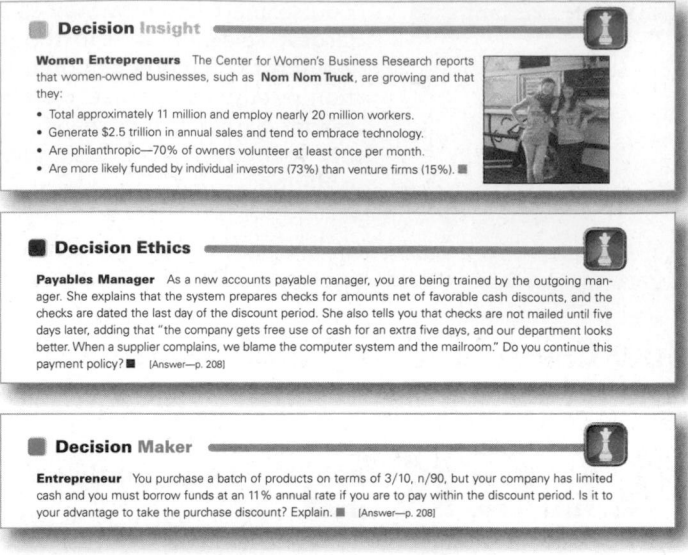

Decision Insight

Women Entrepreneurs The Center for Women's Business Research reports that women-owned businesses, such as **Nom Nom Truck**, are growing and that they:
- Total approximately 11 million and employ nearly 20 million workers.
- Generate $2.5 trillion in annual sales and tend to embrace technology.
- Are philanthropic—70% of owners volunteer at least once per month.
- Are more likely funded by individual investors (73%) than venture firms (15%). ■

Decision Ethics

Payables Manager As a new accounts payable manager, you are being trained by the outgoing manager. She explains that the system prepares checks for amounts net of favorable cash discounts, and the checks are dated the last day of the discount period. She also tells you that checks are not mailed until five days later, adding that "the company gets free use of cash for an extra five days, and our department looks better. When a supplier complains, we blame the computer system and the mailroom." Do you continue this payment policy? ■ [Answer—p. 208]

Decision Maker

Entrepreneur You purchase a batch of products on terms of 3/10, n/90, but your company has limited cash and you must borrow funds at an 11% annual rate if you are to pay within the discount period. Is it to your advantage to take the purchase discount? Explain. ■ [Answer—p. 208]

Decision Analysis Current Ratio

A1 Compute the current ratio and describe what it reveals about a company's financial condition.

An important use of financial statements is to help assess a company's ability to pay its debts in the near future. Such analysis affects decisions by suppliers when allowing a company to buy on credit. It also affects decisions by creditors when lending money to a company, including loan terms such as interest rate, due date, and collateral requirements. It can also affect a manager's decisions about using cash to pay debts when they come due. The **current ratio** is one measure of a company's ability to pay its short-term obligations. It is defined in Exhibit 4.10 as current assets divided by current liabilities.

EXHIBIT 4.10
Current Ratio

$$\text{Current ratio} = \frac{\text{Current assets}}{\text{Current liabilities}}$$

CAP Model

The Conceptual/Analytical/Procedural (CAP) Model allows courses to be specially designed to meet your teaching needs or those of a diverse faculty. This model identifies learning objectives, textual materials, assignments, and test items by C, A, or P, allowing different instructors to teach from the same materials, yet easily customize their courses toward a conceptual, analytical, or procedural approach (or a combination thereof) based on personal preferences.

Learning Objectives

CONCEPTUAL

C1 Explain the steps in processing transactions and the role of source documents. (p. 50)

C2 Describe an account and its use in recording transactions. (p. 51)

C3 Describe a ledger and a chart of accounts. (p. 54)

C4 Define *debits* and *credits* and explain double-entry accounting. (p. 55)

ANALYTICAL

A1 Analyze the impact of transactions on accounts and financial statements. (p. 59)

A2 Compute the debt ratio and describe its use in analyzing financial condition. (p. 69)

PROCEDURAL

P1 Record transactions in a journal and post entries to a ledger. (p. 56)

P2 Prepare and explain the use of a trial balance. (p. 65)

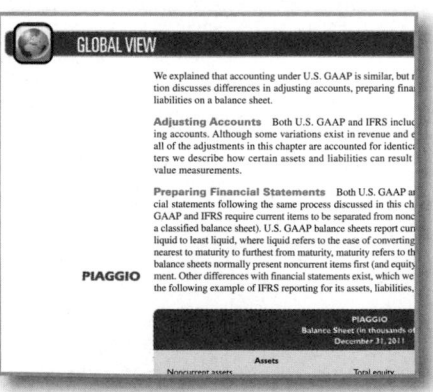

GLOBAL VIEW

We explained that accounting under U.S. GAAP is similar, but this section discusses differences in adjusting accounts, preparing financial liabilities on a balance sheet.

Adjusting Accounts Both U.S. GAAP and IFRS include ing accounts. Although some variations exist in revenue and all of the adjustments in this chapter are accounted for identically. We describe how certain assets and liabilities can result value measurements.

Preparing Financial Statements Both U.S. GAAP and cial statements following the same process discussed in this chapter. GAAP and IFRS require current items to be separated from noncurrent a classified balance sheet). U.S. GAAP balance sheets report current liquid to least liquid, where liquid refers to the ease of converting nearest to maturity to furthest from maturity, maturity refers to the balance sheets normally present noncurrent items first (and equity ment. Other differences with financial statements exist, which we the following example of IFRS reporting for its assets, liabilities,

PIAGGIO

PIAGGIO
Balance Sheet (in thousands of
December 31, 2011

Assets

Noncurrent assets   Total equity

Global View

This section explains international accounting practices relating to the material covered in that chapter. This section is purposefully located at the end of each chapter so that each instructor can decide what emphasis, if at all, is to be assigned to it. The aim of this Global View section is to describe accounting practices and to identify the similarities and differences in international accounting practices versus that in the United States. As we move toward global convergence in accounting practices, and as we witness the likely conversion of U.S. GAAP to IFRS, the importance of student familiarity with international accounting grows. This innovative section helps us begin down that path of learning and teaching global accounting practices.

> "Authors do a good job of relating material to real-life situations and putting students in the decision-maker role."
>
> —**Morgan Rockett, Moberly Area Community College**

Bring Accounting To Life

Chapter Preview With Flowchart

This feature provides a handy textual/visual guide at the start of every chapter. Students can now begin their reading with a clear understanding of what they will learn and when, allowing them to stay more focused and organized along the way.

Quick Check

These short question/answer features reinforce the material immediately preceding them. They allow the reader to pause and reflect on the topics described, then receive immediate feedback before going on to new topics. Answers are provided at the end of each chapter.

> "High quality book that provides coverage of essential content to aid student learning in a manner that students understand."
>
> **—Steve Ludwig , Northwest Missouri State University**

Point: Prepaid accounts that apply to current and future periods are assets. These assets are adjusted at the end of each period to reflect only those amounts that have not yet expired, and to record as expenses those amounts that have expired.

when an insurance fee, called a *premium*, is pa[i]
account Prepaid Insurance. Over time, the ex[
this asset account and reported in expenses on [
in Prepaid Insurance and is reported on the bal[
accounts that will expire or be used before the[
statements are prepared. In this case, the prepa[

Marginal Student Annotations

These annotations provide students with additional hints, tips, and examples to help them more fully understand the concepts and retain what they have learned. The annotations also include notes on global implications of accounting and further examples.

Outstanding Assignment Material

Once a student has finished reading the chapter, how well he or she retains the material can depend greatly on the questions, exercises, and problems that reinforce it. This book leads the way in comprehensive, accurate assignments.

Demonstration Problems present both a problem and a complete solution, allowing students to review the entire problem-solving process and achieve success.

Chapter Summaries provide students with a review organized by learning objectives. Chapter Summaries are a component of the CAP model (see page xiv), which recaps each conceptual, analytical, and procedural objective.

Key Terms are bolded in the text and repeated at the end of the chapter with page numbers indicating their location. The book also includes a complete Glossary of Key Terms.

Multiple Choice Quiz questions quickly test chapter knowledge before a student moves on to complete Quick Studies, Exercises, and Problems.

Quick Study assignments are short exercises that often focus on one learning objective. Most are included in *Connect Accounting*. There are usually 8-10 Quick Study assignments per chapter.

Exercises are one of this book's many strengths and a competitive advantage. There are about 10-15 per chapter and most are included in *Connect Accounting*.

Problem Sets A & B are proven problems that can be assigned as homework or for in-class projects. All problems are coded according to the CAP model (see page xiv), and Set A is included in *Connect Accounting*.

Helps Students Master Key Concepts

Beyond the Numbers exercises ask students to use accounting figures and understand their meaning. Students also learn how accounting applies to a variety of business situations. These creative and fun exercises are all new or updated, and are divided into sections:

- Reporting in Action
- Comparative Analysis
- Ethics Challenge
- Communicating in Practice
- Taking It To The Net
- Teamwork in Action
- Hitting the Road
- Entrepreneurial Decision
- Global Decision

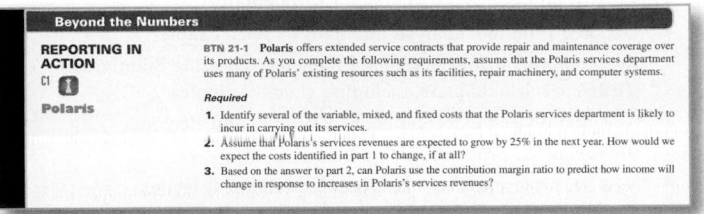

Serial Problem uses a continuous running case study to illustrate chapter concepts in a familiar context. The Serial Problem can be followed continuously from the first chapter or picked up at any later point in the book; enough information is provided to ensure students can get right to work.

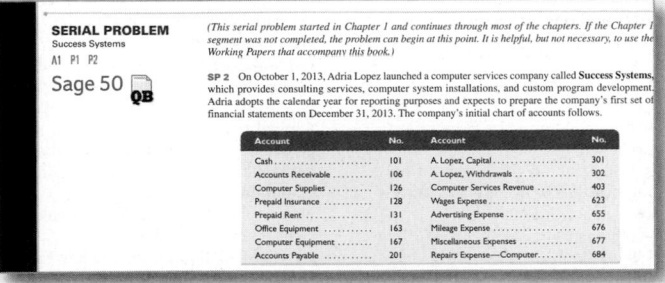

> "I have used many editions of this text and have been very happy with the text and all of the supplementary materials. The textbook is kept current, is straight-forward, and very usable by students. The online resources get better with each edition."
>
> **— Susan Cordes, Johnson County Community College**

The End of the Chapter Is Only the Beginning Our valuable and proven assignments aren't just confined to the book. From problems that require technological solutions to materials found exclusively online, this book's end-of-chapter material is fully integrated with its technology package.

 • Quick Studies, Exercises, and Problems available in *Connect* are marked with an icon.

 • Problems supported by the Sage 50 Complete Accounting or Quickbooks are marked with an icon.

mhhe.com/wildFAP21e • Problems supported with Microsoft Excel template assignments are marked with an icon.

 • Assignments that focus on global accounting practices and companies are often identified with an icon.

Enhancements in This Edition

This edition's revisions are driven by instructors and students. General revisions to the entire book follow (including chapter-by-chapter revisions):

- Revised and updated assignments throughout
- Updated ratio/tool analysis and data for each chapter
- New material on International Financial Reporting Standards (IFRS) in most chapters, including global examples
- New and revised entrepreneurial examples and elements
- Revised serial problem through nearly all chapters
- New art program, visual info-graphics, and text layout

- New Polaris (maker of ATVs, snowmobiles, motorcycles, and electric vehicles) annual report with comparisons to Arctic Cat, KTM (IFRS), and Piaggio (IFRS) with new assignments
- Updated graphics added to each chapter's analysis section
- New technology content integrated and referenced in the book
- Updated Global View section in each chapter referencing international accounting including examples using global companies
- New innovative assignments sprinkled throughout the book

Chapter 1
Twitter NEW opener with new entrepreneurial assignment
Streamlined and reorganized discussion of the users of accounting information
Updated salary information and new margin notes on the value of education
New presentation on the 'fraud triangle' and its relevance to accounting and internal control
New discussion on the joint role of the FASB and IASB in standard setting
Revised layout for accounting principles and assumptions
New information on the Dodd-Frank act and its relevance to accounting
New survey data from executives on the impact of fraud in the economic downturn
New world map on the adoption of IFRS or a variant of IFRS across countries
New company (Dell) for the return on assets section of Decision Analysis

Chapter 2
Nom Nom Truck NEW opener with new entrepreneurial assignment
Reorganized discussion and presentation of assets, liabilities, and equity accounts
Revised description of journalizing and posting of transactions
New headings on each general journal for this chapter's major illustration introducing our unique four-step transaction analysis
Revised global view and new Piaggio's (abbreviated) balance sheet
Updated debt ratio discussion using recent Skechers's information

Chapter 3
ash&dans NEW opener with new entrepreneurial assignment
New layout for the types of adjustments
New example of unearned revenues using USA Today
Enhanced and emphasized the innovative three-step process for adjusting accounts
Updated IFRS and FASB revenue recognition convergence

Added six new Quick Studies to directly apply the three-step adjustment process

Chapter 4
Girl Team Mobile NEW opener with new entrepreneurial assignment
Introduced Google Docs and Office Web Apps as ways to share accounting work sheets
Revised and clarified several steps in preparing an accounting work sheet
Expanded explanation of temporary and permanent accounts
Revised visual display of four-step closing process
Enhanced display of general ledger for ease in learning

Chapter 5
Faithful Fish NEW opener with new entrepreneurial assignment
Enhanced exhibit on transportation costs and FOB terms, with inclusion of entries
New discussion of online ordering, tracking numbers, RFID, and FOB
Revised the two-step explanation of recording merchandise sales
New discussion on the importance and risks of accounting for sales returns
Revised visual display of a sales invoice
Revised discussion of merchandising purchases and sales
New Volkswagen example of IFRS income statement

Chapter 6
Feverish Ice Cream NEW opener with new entrepreneurial assignment
Enhanced exhibit that visually shows cost flows from inventory to financial statements, with superior info-graphics
Added new discussion on inventory controls
New explanatory boxes added to selected exhibits as learning aids
Expanded assignments covering perpetual and periodic inventory measurement
New material on IFRS and inventory methods

Chapter 7
Happy Family Brands NEW opener with new entrepreneurial assignment
Expanded discussion and examples of hackers and internal controls
New pneumonic tool for system principles
Enhanced exhibit on system components
New discussion on voice recognition controls
New discussion on cloud computing, its implications to accounting, and its risks
New references to XBRL, Great Plains, and QuickBooks in accounting
Updated discussion and examples for ERP
Streamlined chapter by moving Appendix 7A, 'Special Journals under a Periodic System' and its assignments, to the textbook Website

Chapter 8
CHEESEBOY NEW opener with new entrepreneurial assignment
New discussion of payroll controls
Expanded presentation of 'Hacker's Guide'
New discussion of the lock box and its purpose
New data on sources of fraud complaints
New evidence on methods to override controls
New visual on document to bond (insure) an employee
New example of MLB controls, or lack thereof

Chapter 9
Under Armour NEW opener with new entrepreneurial assignment
Added explanation of credit card sales
New discussion of mobile payment systems using mini-card-readers and iPads
New illustration comparing bad debts recognition under the allowance method versus the direct write-off method
Revised exhibit on aging of accounts receivable, including all detailed accounts
New illustration on why the banker's rule is commonly applied

Chapter 10
BizChair.com NEW opener with new entrepreneurial assignment
New learning boxes added to selected exhibits identifying salvage value
New explanation on how asset purchases occurring on different days of the month are commonly processed
New example of extraordinary repairs applied to the stealth bomber
New notes added to emphasize that depreciation is cost allocation, and not valuation
New explanation on how drugmakers fight patent expirations
New information on the Mickey Mouse Protection Act for intangibles
New goodwill example using Google's purchase of YouTube

Chapter 11
SmartIT Staffing NEW opener with new entrepreneurial assignment
Revised unearned revenues example based on Rihanna ticket sales
Added explanation on the role of sellers as tax collection 'agents' for the government
New information on franchise costs and how they are accounted for
Added select formulas to enhance the exhibit on payroll deductions
Updated payroll rates to 2012 with discussion on likely adjustments for 2013 and 2014
Added discussion on maximum withholding allowances claimed
New discussion on IRS actions against companies that fail to pay employment taxes
New evidence on payroll fraud, its median loss, and time taken to uncover such frauds

Chapter 12
College Hunks Hauling Junk NEW opener with new entrepreneurial assignment
New examples of LLPs and their prevalence among professional services
New discussion of the potential for multiple drawing accounts in practice
Revised and streamlined three-step process to liquidate a partnership

For Better Learning

Chapter 13

Groupon NEW opener with new entrepreneurial assignment
New discussion of Facebook's IPO and the role of accounting information
New reference to corporate governance
New reference to state laws and where companies incorporate
New examples using Target for stock quotes and Google for stock splits
New discussion of fraudulent information dissemination and stock prices
Updated the global view on equity accounting

Chapter 14

barley & birch NEW opener with new entrepreneurial assignment
New explanation on why debt (credit) financing is less costly than equity financing
New margin graphics (four) illustrating how a debt's carrying value is periodically adjusted until it equals maturity value at the end of its life
New margin boxes on calculator functions to compute the price of bonds
New explanation of what is investment grade debt
New discussion on the role of unreported liabilities and the 2008-2009 financial crisis
Reference to changes in lease accounting
New discussion of collateral and its role in debt financing
New separate appendix learning objectives on amortizing a discount or a premium using effective interest

Chapter 15

myYearbook (MeetMe Inc.) NEW opener with new entrepreneurial assignment
New discussion of the two optional presentations for comprehensive income per FASB guidance in 2012
Revised discussion of accounting for securities
New reference to Greek debt in the context of international operations

Chapter 16

TOMS NEW opener with new entrepreneurial assignment
Revised graphics to better illustrate cash inflows and outflows for operating, investing, and financing activities
Revised graphic to better reflect cash and cash equivalents
Added discussion on the use of T-accounts for reconstructing transactions impacting cash
New margin clarification for computing free cash flow
New discussion on the potential for IASB and FASB to issue guidance for the statement of cash flow that would require the direct method... stay tuned

Chapter 17

Motley Fool REVISED opener with new entrepreneurial assignment
New companies—Polaris, Arctic Cat, KTM and Piaggio—data throughout the chapter, exhibits, and illustrations
New boxed discussion on the role of financial statement analysis to fight and prevent fraud
Enhanced horizontal, vertical, ratio analysis using new companies and industry data
Streamlined global view section

Chapter 18

Back to the Roots NEW opener with new entrepreneurial assignment
New analytical learning objective
Updated ACFE statistics on fraud costs
New exhibit and discussion on fraud occurrence and average fraud loss by industry
Revised discussion of direct and indirect costs and related exhibit for added clarity
New summary of cost classifications and associated managerial decisions
New Decision Analysis to focus on raw materials inventory turnover and days' sales in raw materials inventory
Moved discussion of types of manufacturing costs to appear before presentation of manufacturer's financial statements
Expanded discussion of financial statements for service companies
New end of chapter assignments on raw materials inventory management and cost classification for service companies
Moved cycle time discussion to Chapter 24

Chapter 19

Astor and Black NEW opener with new entrepreneurial assignment
Reorganized discussion of job order costing for service companies
New discussion of accounting for nonmanufacturing costs and their role in pricing decisions
Added new journal entries for indirect materials and indirect labor for improved learning

Chapter 20

Three Twins Ice Cream NEW opener with new entrepreneurial assignment
Revised comparison of job order and process costing systems
New comparison of reports produced from job order and process costing systems
Added details for accounts used in the entry to record sales in process costing
Added new process costing assignments
Revisions to two learning objectives

Chapter 21

Leather Head Sports NEW opener with new entrepreneurial assignment
(Was Chapter 22 in prior edition)
New graphics on relations between per-unit fixed and variable costs and volume
Revised discussion of per-unit fixed and variable costs
Moved discussion of margin of safety to section on break-even
Revised discussion of assumptions in CVP analysis
Enhanced the formatting and layout of several key exhibits
New discussion and examples of using the contribution margin income statement to perform sensitivity analyses and compute sales needed for target income
Revised data for estimating cost behavior
New discussion on the use of RFID tags to control inventory costs and for error-reduction

Chapter 22

Freshii NEW opener with new entrepreneurial assignment
(Was Chapter 23 in prior edition)
New discussion on incentive compensation and budgeting
Expanded global view on foreign currency exchange rates and budgeting
Updated discussion on Apple's cash cushion
Added new end of chapter assignments

Chapter 23

Folsom Custom Skis NEW opener with new entrepreneurial assignment
(Was Chapter 24 in prior edition)
New discussion on budgeting for service providers
Revised several exhibits for learning clarity
Revised discussion of predicting activity levels
New enhanced exhibit on framework for understanding total overhead variance, including formulas
Revised discussion of controllable and volume variances

Chapter 24

United By Blue NEW opener with new entrepreneurial assignment
(Was Chapter 21 in prior edition)
Moved section on two-stage allocation and activity based costing methods to (new) Appendix C
Revised discussion linking direct and indirect expenses to controllable and uncontrollable costs
Highlighted four-step process to prepare departmental income statements
Moved discussion and illustration of profit margin and investment turnover to main body of chapter
Added discussion on cycle time and cycle efficiency
New exhibit on how to prepare departmental performance reports
Edited discussion of example on preparing departmental performance reports
New discussion on issues in computing return on (assets) investment and residual income
New discussion on the link between executive compensation and company performance
Updated global view on division reporting and its explanation for added clarity

Chapter 25

Charlie's Brownies NEW opener with new entrepreneurial assignment
Updated graphic on industry cost of capital estimates
New discussion on outsourcing of information and technology services
New presentation on payback periods for health care providers
New discussion on link between CEO compensation and IRR
Simplified computation of the accounting rate of return
New example showing calculation of net present value with salvage value
New exhibit showing formula for computing average investment
Simplified discussions and exhibits for several examples of managerial decisions
Enhanced graphics on NPV and IRR decision rules

Appendix C

New appendix; consisting of selected materials from Chapter 21 in prior edition
Replaced two-stage cost allocation discussion with single plantwide rate method
Streamlined examples and several exhibits
New end of chapter assignments

Instructor Supplements

Instructor's Resource CD-ROM
Chapters 1-25
ISBN13: 9780077525118
ISBN10: 0077525116

This is your all-in-one resource. It allows you to create custom presentations from your own materials or from the following text-specific materials provided in the CD's asset library:

- **Instructor's Resource Manual**
  Written by Barbara Chiappetta, Nassau Community College, and Patricia Walczak, Lansing Community College.

This manual contains (for each chapter) a Lecture Outline, a chart linking all assignment materials to Learning Objectives, and additional visuals with transparency masters.

- **Solutions Manual**
  Written by John J. Wild, Ken W. Shaw, and Anita Kroll, University of Wisconsin–Madison.
- **Test Bank, Computerized Test Bank**
  Revised by Jeanine Metzler, Northampton Community College.

- **PowerPoint® Presentations**
  Prepared by Jon Booker, Charles Caldwell, Cindy Rooney, and Susan Galbreth.

  Presentations allow for revision of lecture slides, and includes a viewer, allowing screens to be shown with or without the software.

Student Supplements

Excel Working Papers CD
ISBN13: 9780077525101
ISBN10: 0077525108

Written by John J. Wild.

Working Papers (for Chapters 1-25) delivered in Excel spreadsheets. These Excel Working Papers are available on CD-ROM and can be bundled with the printed Working Papers; see your representative for information.

Working Papers
Vol. 1, Chapters 1-12
ISBN13: 9780077525231
ISBN10: 007752523X

Vol. 2, Chapters 12-25
ISBN13: 9780077525217
ISBN10: 0077525213

Principles of Financial Accounting Chapters 1-17
ISBN13: 9780077525224
ISBN10: 0077525221

Written by John J. Wild.

Study Guide
Vol. 1, Chapters 1-12
ISBN13: 9780077525187
ISBN10: 0077525183

Vol. 2, Chapters 12-25
ISBN13: 9780077525200
ISBN10: 0077525205

Written by Barbara Chiappetta, Nassau Community College, and Patricia Walczak, Lansing Community College.

Covers each chapter and appendix with reviews of the learning objectives, outlines of the chapters, summaries of chapter materials, and additional problems with solutions.

Connect Accounting with LearnSmart Two Semester Access Code Card
ISBN13: 9780077525064
ISBN10: 007752506X

Connect Plus Accounting with LearnSmart Two Semester Access Code Card
ISBN13: 9780077525088
ISBN10: 0077525086

Carol Yacht's Sage 50 Complete Accounting 2013 Student Guide and Templates
ISBN13: 9780077778972
ISBN10: 0077778979

Prepared by Carol Yacht.

To better prepare students for accounting in the real world, selected end-of-chapter material in the text is tied to Sage 50 Complete Accounting 2013 software (formerly Peachtree). The accompanying student guide provides a step-by-step walkthrough for students on how to complete the problem in the software.

QuickBooks Pro 2013 Student Guide and Templates
ISBN13: 9780077525156
ISBN10: 0077525159

Prepared by Carol Yacht.

To better prepare students for accounting in the real world, selected end-of-chapter material in the text is tied to QuickBooks software. The accompanying student guide provides a step-by-step walkthrough for students on how to complete the problem in the software.

Assurance of Learning Ready

Many educational institutions today are focused on the notion of assurance of learning, an important element of some accreditation standards. *Fundamental Accounting Principles* is designed specifically to support your assurance of learning initiatives with a simple, yet powerful solution. Each test bank question for *Fundamental Accounting Principles* maps to a specific chapter learning objective listed in the text. You can use our test bank software, EZ Test Online or *Connect Accounting* to easily query for learning objectives that directly relate to the learning objectives for your course. You can then use the reporting features of EZ Test to aggregate student results in similar fashion, making the collection and presentation of assurance of learning data simple and easy.

"FAP... is an old friend, dependable and true over time, with enough pizazz and modernity to keep the relationship interesting and ongoing. The authors and publisher are dedicated to producing quality instructional materials in a variety of formats to meet the educational requirements and learning styles of a diverse audience. Hooray for them!"

— **Beverly R. Beatty, Anne Arundel Community College**

AACSB Statement

The McGraw-Hill Companies is a proud corporate member of AACSB International. Understanding the importance and value of AACSB accreditation, *Fundamental Accounting Principles* recognizes the curricula guidelines detailed in the AACSB standards for business accreditation by connecting selected questions in the test bank to the six general knowledge and skill guidelines in the AACSB standards. The statements contained in *Fundamental Accounting Principles* are provided only as a guide for the users of this textbook. The AACSB leaves content coverage and assessment within the purview of individual schools, the mission of the school, and the faculty. While *Fundamental Accounting Principles* and the teaching package make no claim of any specific AACSB qualification or evaluation, we have within *Fundamental Accounting Principles* labeled select questions according to the six general knowledge and skills areas.

Acknowledgments

John J. Wild, Ken W. Shaw, Barbara Chiappetta, and McGraw-Hill/Irwin would like to recognize the following instructors for their valuable feedback and involvement in the development of *Fundamental Accounting Principles* 21e. We are thankful for their suggestions, counsel, and encouragement.

Khaled Abdou, Penn State University - Berks

Anne Marie Anderson, Raritan Valley Community College

Elaine Anes, Heald College -Fresno

Jerome Apple, University of Akron

Jack Aschkenazi, American Intercontinental University

Sidney Askew, Borough of Manhattan Community College

Lawrence Awopetu, University of Arkansas -Pine Bluff

Jon Backman, Spartanburg Community College

Charles Baird, University of Wisconsin-Stout

Richard Barnhart, Grand Rapids Community College

Beverly R. Beatty, Anne Arundel Community College

Judy Benish, Fox Valley Tech College

Patricia Bentley, Keiser University

Teri Bernstein, Santa Monica College

Jaswinder Bhangal, Chabot College

Susan Blizzard, San Antonio College

Marvin Blye, Wor-Wic Community College

Patrick Borja, Citrus College

Anna Boulware, St. Charles Community College

Gary Bower, Community College of Rhode Island-Flanagan

Leslee Brock, Southwest Mississippi Community College

Gregory Brookins, Santa Monica College

Regina Brown, Eastfield College

Tracy L. Bundy, University of Louisiana at Lafayette

Roy Carson, Anne Arundel Community College

Deborah Carter, Coahoma Community College

Roberto Castaneda, DeVry University Online

Amy Chataginer, Mississippi Gulf Coast Community College

Gerald Childs, Waukesha County Technical College

Colleen Chung, Miami Dade College- Kendall

Shifei Chung, Rowan University

Robert Churchman, Harding University

Marilyn Ciolino, Delgado Community College

Thomas Clement, University of North Dakota

Oyinka Coakley, Broward College

Susan Cockrell, Birmingham-Southern College

Lisa Cole, Johnson County Community College

Robbie R. Coleman, Northeast Mississippi Community College

Christie Comunale, Long Island University – C.W. Post Campus

Jackie Conrecode, Florida Gulf Coast University

Debora Constable, Georgia Perimeter College

Susan Cordes, Johnson County Community College

Anne Cordozo, Broward College

Cheryl Corke, Genesse Community College

James Cosby, John Tyler Community College

Ken Couvillion, Delta College

Loretta Darche, Southwest Florida College

Judy Daulton, Piedmont Technical College

Dorothy Davis, University of Louisiana-Monroe

Walter DeAguero, Saddleback College

Mike Deschamps, MiraCosta College

Pamela Donahue, Northern Essex Community College

Steve Doster, Shawnee State University

Larry Dragosavac, Edison Community College

Samuel Duah, Bowie State University

Robert Dunlevy, Montgomery County Community College

Jerrilyn Eisenhauer, Tulsa Community College-Southeast

Ronald Elders, Virginia College

Terry Elliott, Morehead State University

Patricia Feller, Nashville State Community College

Annette Fisher, Glendale Community College

Ron Fitzgerald, Santa Monica College

David Flannery, Bryant and Stratton College

Hollie Floberg, Tennessee Wesleyan College

Linda Flowers, Houston Community College

Jeannie Folk, College of DuPage

Rebecca Foote, Middle Tennessee State University

Paul Franklin, Kaplan University

Tim Garvey, Westwood College

Barbara Gershman, Northern Virginia Community College-Woodbridge

Barbara Gershowitz, Nashville State Technical Community College

Mike Glasscock, Amarillo College

Diane Glowacki, Tarrant County College

Ernesto Gonzalez, Florida National College

Gloria Grayless, Sam Houston State University

Ann Gregory, South Plains College

Rameshwar Gupta, Jackson State University

Amy Haas, Kingsborough Community College

Pat Halliday, Santa Monica College

Keith Hallmark, Calhoun Community College

Rebecca Hancock, El Paso Community College-Valley Verde

Mechelle Harris, Bossier Parish Community College

Tracey Hawkins, University of Cincinnati-Clermont College

Thomas Hayes, University of Arkansas-Ft. Smith

Laurie Hays, Western Michigan University

Roger Hehman, University of Cincinnati-Clermont College

Cheri Hernandez, Des Moines Area Community College

Margaret Hicks, Howard University

Melanie Hicks, Liberty University

James Higgins, Holy Family University

Patricia Holmes, Des Moines Area Community College

Barbara Hopkins, Northern Virginia Community College-Manassas

Wade Hopkins, Heald College

Aileen Huang, Santa Monica College

Les Hubbard, Solano College

Deborah Hudson, Gaston College

James Hurst, National College

Constance Hylton, George Mason University

Christine Irujo, Westfield State University

Fred Jex, Macomb Community College

Gina M. Jones, Aims Community College

Jeff Jones, College of Southern Nevada

Rita Jones, Columbus State University

Dmitriy Kalyagin, Chabot College

Thomas Kam, Hawaii Pacific University

Naomi Karolinski, Monroe Community College

Shirly A. Kleiner, Johnson County Community College

Kenneth A. Koerber, Bucks County Community College

Tamara Kowalczyk, Appalachian State University

Anita Kroll, University of Wisconsin-Madison

David Krug, Johnson County Community College

Christopher Kwak, DeAnza College

Jeanette Landin, Empire College

Beth Lasky, Delgado Community College

Neal Leviton, Santa Monica College

Danny Litt, University of California Los Angeles

James L. Lock, Northern Virginia Community College

Steve Ludwig, Northwest Missouri State University

Debra Luna, El Paso Community College

Amado Mabul, Heald College

Lori Major, Luzerne County Community College

Jennifer Malfitano, Delaware County Community College

Maria Mari, Miami Dade College-Kendall

Thomas S. Marsh, Northern Virginia Community College-Annandale

Karen Martinson, University of Wisconsin-Stout

Brenda Mattison, Tri-County Technical College

Stacie Mayes, Rose State College

Jeanine Metzler, Northampton Community College

Theresa Michalow, Moraine Valley Community College

Kathleen Michele, WECA – Madison

Julie Miller, Chippewa Valley Tech College

Tim Miller, El Camino College

John Minchin, California Southern University

Edna C. Mitchell, Polk State College

Jill Mitchell, Northern Virginia Community College

Lynn Moore, Aiken Technical College

Angela Mott, Northeast Mississippi Community College

Timothy Murphy, Diablo Valley College

Kenneth F. O'Brien, Farmingdale State College

Kathleen O'Donnell, Onondaga Community College

Ahmed Omar, Burlington County College

Robert A. Pacheco, Massasoit Community College

Margaret Parilo, Cosumnes River College

Paige Paulsen, Salt Lake Community College

Yvonne Phang, Borough of Manhattan Community College

Gary Pieroni, Diablo Valley College

David Ravetch, University of California Los Angeles

Ruthie Reynolds, Howard University

Cecile Roberti, Community College of Rhode Island

Morgan Rockett, Moberly Area Community College

Patrick Rogan, Cosumnes River College

Paul Rogers, Community College of Beaver County

Helen Roybark, Radford University

Alphonse Ruggiero, Suffolk County Community College

Arjan Sadhwani, South University

Gary K. Sanborn, Northwestern Michigan College

Kin Kin Sandhu, Heald College

Marcia Sandvold, Des Moines Area Community College

Gary Schader, Kean University

Darlene Schnuck, Waukesha County Technical College

Elizabeth Serapin, Columbia Southern University

Geeta Shankhar, University of Dayton

Regina Shea, Community College of Baltimore County—Essex

James Shelton, Liberty University

Jay Siegel, Union County College

Gerald Singh, New York City College of Technology

Lois Slutsky, Broward College-South

Gerald Smith, University of Northern Iowa

Kathleen Sobieralski, University of Maryland University College

Charles Spector, State University of New York at Oswego

Diane Stark, Phoenix College

Thomas Starks, Heald College

Carolyn L. Strauch, Crowder College

Latazia Stuart, Fortis University Online

Gene Sullivan, Liberty University

David Sulzen, Ferrum College

Dominique Svarc, William Rainey Harper College

Linda Sweeney, Sam Houston State University

Margaret Tanner, University of Arkansas—Ft. Smith

Ulysses Taylor, Fayetteville State University

Anthony Teng, Saddleback College

Paula Thomas, Middle Tennessee State University

Teresa Thompson, Chaffey Community College

Leslie Thysell, John Tyler Community College

Melanie Torborg, Globe University

Shafi Ullah, Broward College

Bob Urell, Irvine Valley College

Adam Vitalis, University of Wisconsin-Madison

Patricia Walczak, Lansing Community College

Terri Walsh, Seminole State College-Oviedo

Shunda Ware, Atlanta Technical College

Dave Welch, Franklin University

Jean Wells-Jessup, Howard University

Christopher Widmer, Tidewater Community College

Andrew Williams, Edmonds Community College

Kenneth L. Wild, University of London

John Woodward, Polk State College

Gail E. Wright, Stevenson University

Wanda Wong, Chabot College

Patricia Worsham, Norco College, Riverside Community College

Lynnette Yerbury, Salt Lake Community College

Judy Zander, Grossmont College

Mary Zenner, College of Lake County

Jane Zlojutro, Northwestern Michigan College

The authors extend a special thank you to our contributing and technology supplement authors:

Contributing Authors: Anita Kroll, University of Wisconsin; Kathleen O'Donnell, Onondaga Community College

Accuracy Checkers: Dave Krug, Johnson County Community College; Thomas Marsh, Northern Virginia Community College-Annandale; Mark McCarthy, East Carolina University; Helen Roybark, Radford University; and Regina Shea, Community College of Baltimore County-Essex

LearnSmart Authors: April Mohr, Jefferson Community and Technical College, SW; Anna Boulware, St. Charles Community College; Brenda Mattison, Tri County Technical College; and Dominique Svarc, William Rainey Harper College

Online Quizzes: Gina Jones, Aims Community College

Interactive Presentations: Jeannie Folk, College of DuPage

PowerPoint: Jon Booker, Charles Caldwell, Cindy Rooney, and Susan Galbreth

Instructor Resource Manual and Study Guide: Barbara Chiappetta, Nassau Community College; and Patricia Walczak, Lansing Community College

QuickBooks and **Sage 50 Complete Accounting:** Carol Yacht

Excel Templates: Jack Terry

"I am always impressed with the simplicity, accuracy, and elegance of the writing of the... Fundamental Accounting Principles text. I can always count on the text to be properly updated and the overall attention to detail is appreciated as well. Thank you"

— **Patricia Feller, Nashville State Community College**

In addition to the helpful and generous colleagues listed above, we thank the entire McGraw-Hill/Irwin *Fundamental Accounting Principles* 21e team, including Tim Vertovec, Steve Schuetz, Christina Sanders, Aaron Downey of Matrix Productions, Lori Koetters, Matthew Baldwin, Carol Bielski, Patricia Plumb, Jeremy Cheshareck, Ron Nelms, Xin Lin, and Brian Nacik. We also thank the great marketing and sales support staff, including Michelle Heaster and Kathleen Klehr. Many talented educators and professionals worked hard to create the supplements for this book, and for their efforts we're grateful. Finally, many more people we either did not meet or whose efforts we did not personally witness nevertheless helped to make this book everything that it is, and we thank them all.

John J. Wild   Ken W. Shaw   Barbara Chiappetta

Brief Contents

Contents

11 Current Liabilities and Payroll Accounting 436

12 Accounting for Partnerships 480

13 Accounting for Corporations 508

**17 Analysis of Financial
Statements 686**

**18 Managerial Accounting
Concepts and Principles 732**

**19 Job Order Cost
Accounting 776**

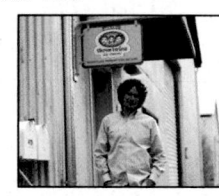

**20 Process Cost
Accounting 814**

Fundamental
Accounting Principles

Accounting in Business

Learning Objectives are classified as conceptual, analytical, or procedural.

A Look at This Chapter

Accounting is crucial in our information age. In this chapter, we discuss the importance of accounting to different types of organizations and describe its many users and uses. We explain that ethics are essential to accounting. We also explain business transactions and how they are reflected in financial statements.

A Look Ahead

Chapter 2 describes and analyzes business transactions. We explain the analysis and recording of transactions, the ledger and trial balance, and the double-entry system. More generally, Chapters 2 through 4 use the accounting cycle to show how financial statements reflect business activities.

Learning Objectives

CONCEPTUAL

C1 Explain the purpose and importance of accounting. (p. 4)

C2 Identify users and uses of, and opportunities in, accounting. (p. 5)

C3 Explain why ethics are crucial to accounting. (p. 7)

C4 Explain generally accepted accounting principles and define and apply several accounting principles. (p. 9)

C5 *Appendix 1B*—Identify and describe the three major activities of organizations. (p. 27)

ANALYTICAL

A1 Define and interpret the accounting equation and each of its components. (p. 15)

A2 Compute and interpret return on assets. (p. 23)

A3 *Appendix 1A*—Explain the relation between return and risk. (p. 27)

PROCEDURAL

P1 Analyze business transactions using the accounting equation. (p. 16)

P2 Identify and prepare basic financial statements and explain how they interrelate. (p. 20)

Decision Insight

*A **Decision Feature** launches each chapter showing the relevance of accounting for a real entrepreneur. An **Entrepreneurial Decision** problem at the end of the assignments returns to this feature with a mini-case.*

Accounting for Twitter

"There is so much going on here . . ."
—BIZ STONE (CENTER)

SAN FRANCISCO—"We came across the word 'twitter,' and it was just perfect," recalls Jack Dorsey (right of photo). "The definition was 'a short burst of inconsequential information,' and 'chirps from birds,' and that's exactly what the product was." Today, Twitter boasts over 200 million users. Founded by Jack, along with Biz Stone and Evan Williams (left), **Twitter (Twitter.com)** is "facilitating connections between businesses and individuals in meaningful and relevant ways," says Jack. Along the way, the young entrepreneurs had to learn accounting and the details of preparing and interpreting financial statements.

"There is so much going on here," explains Biz when describing Twitter's business model. However, admits Evan, "We did a poor job of communicating." Important questions involving business formation, transaction analysis, and financial reporting arose. The entrepreneurs eventually met those challenges and, in the process, set Twitter apart. "If you stand pat," says Evan, "you risk being stagnant."

Information is the focus within Twitter's accounting records and systems. Jack recalls that when they launched Twitter, there were all these reasons why they would not succeed. He applied their similar "can-do" approach to accounting information. "My whole philosophy is making tech [and accounting] more accessible and human," says Jack. This includes using accounting information to make key business decisions.

Twitter is the language of micro-blogging, and accounting is the language of business. "Twitter is so many things: a messaging service, a customer service tool, a real-time search," explains Biz, and the accounting system had to capture those things. Biz adds that Twitter is exploring additional "interesting ways to generate revenue." That revenue-stream is reflected in its financial statements, which are based on transaction analysis and accounting concepts.

Twitter's revenues exhibit growth and reflect what experts call the *monetizing* of its business. A recent study by the marketing firm SocialTwist found that the click-through rate was 19 for Twitter, which is the number of clicks on an embedded link. This compares with 3 clicks for Facebook links. Twitter's revenues in the recent year were estimated at $45 million, which are projected to exceed $100 million next year. Twitter also tracks its expenses and asset purchases. Twitter owners have an estimated valuation of between $5 and $10 billion!

The three entrepreneurs emphasize that accounting records must be in order for Twitter to realize its full potential. Many experts predict a public offering of its stock within the next two years, which could generate untold wealth. Still, Evan recognizes that "so many people here [at Twitter] contribute to that success." He also emphasizes that learning is a key to their business success. "I realized," insists Evan, "I could buy accounting books and learn something that people spent years learning."

[Sources: Twitter Website, January 2013; *Entrepreneur*, December 2010; *USA Today*, May 2009; Smedio.com, June 2011; *San Francisco Chronicle*, March 2011; SocialTwist.com, October 2010; *The Wall Street Journal*, February 2011]

*A **Preview** opens each chapter with a summary of topics covered.*

Today's world is one of information—its preparation, communication, analysis, and use. Accounting is at the core of this information age. Knowledge of accounting gives us career opportunities and the insight to take advantage of them. This book introduces concepts, procedures, and analyses that help us make better decisions, including career choices. In this chapter we describe accounting, the users and uses of accounting information, the forms and activities of organizations, and several accounting principles. We also introduce transaction analysis and financial statements.

Accounting in Business

Importance of Accounting	Fundamentals of Accounting	Transaction Analysis	Financial Statements
• Accounting information users • Opportunities in accounting	• Ethics—key concept • Generally accepted accounting principles • International standards	• Accounting equation • Transaction analysis—illustrated	• Income statement • Statement of owner's equity • Balance sheet • Statement of cash flows

IMPORTANCE OF ACCOUNTING

C1 Explain the purpose and importance of accounting.

Why is accounting so popular on campus? Why are there so many openings for accounting jobs? Why is accounting so important to companies? Why do politicians and business leaders focus on accounting regulations? The answer is that we live in an information age, where that information, and its reliability, impacts us all.

Accounting is an information and measurement system that identifies, records, and communicates relevant, reliable, and comparable information about an organization's business activities. *Identifying* business activities requires that we select relevant transactions and events. Examples are the sale of iPhones by **Apple** and the receipt of ticket money by **TicketMaster**. *Recording* business activities requires that we keep a chronological log of transactions and events measured in dollars. *Communicating* business activities requires that we prepare accounting reports such as financial statements, which we analyze and interpret. (The financial statements and notes of **Polaris** are shown in Appendix A near the end of this book. This appendix also shows the financial statements of **Arctic Cat**, **KTM**, and **Piaggio**.) Exhibit 1.1 summarizes accounting activities.

Real company names are printed in bold magenta.

Accounting is part of our everyday lives. Our most common contact with accounting is through credit approvals, checking accounts, tax forms, and payroll. These experiences tend to focus on the recordkeeping parts of accounting. **Recordkeeping,** or **bookkeeping,** is the recording of transactions and events, either manually or electronically. This is just one part of accounting. Accounting also identifies and communicates information on transactions and events, and it includes the crucial processes of analysis and interpretation.

Technology is a key part of modern business and plays a major role in accounting. Technology reduces the time, effort, and cost of recordkeeping while improving clerical accuracy. Some small organizations continue to perform various accounting tasks manually, but even they are impacted

EXHIBIT 1.1

Accounting Activities

Identifying	Recording	Communicating
Select transactions and events	Input, measure, and log	Prepare, analyze, and interpret

by technology. As technology makes more information available, the demand for accounting increases and so too the skills for applying that information. Consulting, planning, and other financial services are now closely linked to accounting. These services require sorting through data, interpreting their meaning, identifying key factors, and analyzing their implications.

Users of Accounting Information

Accounting is called the *language of business* because all organizations set up an accounting information system to communicate data to help people make better decisions. Exhibit 1.2 shows that accounting serves many users (this is a partial listing) who can be divided into two groups: external users and internal users.

EXHIBIT 1.2

Users of Accounting Information

External users

- Lenders
- Shareholders
- Governments
- Consumer groups
- External auditors
- Customers

Internal users

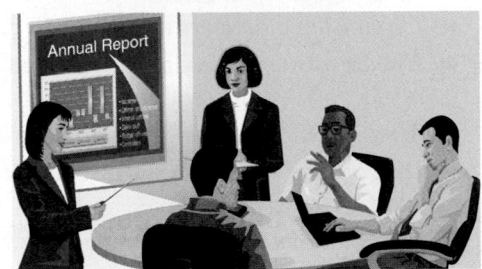

- Officers
- Managers
- Internal auditors
- Sales staff
- Budget officers
- Controllers

C2 Identify users and uses of, and opportunities in, accounting.

External Information Users **External users** of accounting information are *not* directly involved in running the organization. They include shareholders (investors), lenders, directors, customers, suppliers, regulators, lawyers, brokers, and the press. External users have limited access to an organization's information. Yet their business decisions depend on information that is reliable, relevant, and comparable. **Financial accounting** is the area of accounting aimed at serving external users by providing them with *general-purpose financial statements*. The term *general-purpose* refers to the broad range of purposes for which external users rely on these statements. Following is a partial list of external users and some decisions they make with accounting information.

- *Lenders* (creditors) loan money or other resources to an organization. Banks, savings and loans, co-ops, and mortgage and finance companies are lenders. Lenders look for information to help them assess whether an organization is likely to repay its loans with interest.

- *Shareholders* (*investors*) are the owners of a corporation. They use accounting reports in deciding whether to buy, hold, or sell stock.

- *Directors* are typically elected to a *board of directors* to oversee their interests in an organization. Since directors are responsible to shareholders, their information needs are similar.

- *External* (independent) *auditors* examine financial statements to verify that they are prepared according to generally accepted accounting principles.

- *Nonexecutive employees* and *labor unions* use financial statements to judge the fairness of wages, assess job prospects, and bargain for better wages.

- *Regulators* often have legal authority over certain activities of organizations. For example, the Internal Revenue Service (IRS) and other tax authorities require organizations to file accounting reports in computing taxes. Other regulators include utility boards that use accounting information to set utility rates and securities regulators that require reports for companies that sell their stock to the public.

- *Voters, legislators,* and *government officials* use accounting information to monitor and evaluate government receipts and expenses.

- *Contributors* to nonprofit organizations use accounting information to evaluate the use and impact of their donations.

- *Suppliers* use accounting information to judge the soundness of a customer before making sales on credit.
- *Customers* use financial reports to assess the staying power of potential suppliers.

Internal Information Users   **Internal users** of accounting information are those directly involved in managing and operating an organization. They use the information to help improve the efficiency and effectiveness of an organization. **Managerial accounting** is the area of accounting that serves the decision-making needs of internal users. Internal reports are not subject to the same rules as external reports and instead are designed with the special needs of internal users in mind. Following is a partial list of internal users and some decisions they make with accounting information.

- *Research and development managers* need information about projected costs and revenues of any proposed changes in products and services.
- *Purchasing managers* need to know what, when, and how much to purchase.
- *Human resource managers* need information about employees' payroll, benefits, performance, and compensation.
- *Production managers* depend on information to monitor costs and ensure quality.
- *Distribution managers* need reports for timely, accurate, and efficient delivery of products and services.
- *Marketing managers* use reports about sales and costs to target consumers, set prices, and monitor consumer needs, tastes, and price concerns.
- *Service managers* require information on the costs and benefits of looking after products and services.

Opportunities in Accounting

Accounting information is in all aspects of our lives. When we earn money, pay taxes, invest savings, budget earnings, and plan for the future, we use accounting. Accounting has four broad areas of opportunities: financial, managerial, taxation, and accounting-related. Exhibit 1.3 lists selected opportunities in each area.

EXHIBIT 1.3

Accounting Opportunities

Exhibit 1.4 shows that the majority of opportunities are in *private accounting,* which are employees working for businesses. *Public accounting* offers the next largest number of opportunities, which involve services such as auditing and tax advice. Still other opportunities exist in government and not-for-profit agencies, including business regulation and investigation of law violations.

EXHIBIT 1.4

Accounting Jobs by Area

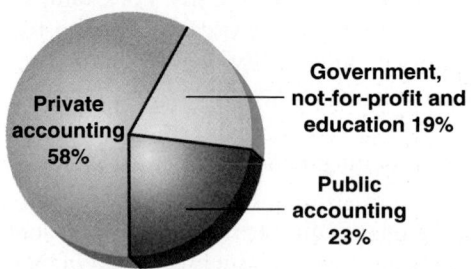

Accounting specialists are highly regarded. Their professional standing often is denoted by a certificate. Certified public accountants (CPAs) must meet education and experience requirements, pass an examination, and exhibit ethical character. Many accounting specialists hold certificates in addition to or instead of the CPA. Two of the most common are the certificate in management accounting (CMA) and the certified internal auditor (CIA). Employers also look for specialists with designations such as certified bookkeeper (CB), certified payroll professional (CPP), personal financial specialist (PFS), certified fraud examiner (CFE), and certified forensic accountant (CrFA).

Point: The largest accounting firms are Deloitte, Ernst & Young, KPMG, and PricewaterhouseCoopers.

Demand for accounting specialists is strong. Exhibit 1.5 reports average annual salaries for several accounting positions. Salary variation depends on location, company size, professional designation, experience, and other factors. For example, salaries for chief financial officers (CFO) range from under $100,000 to more than $1 million per year. Likewise, salaries for bookkeepers range from under $30,000 to more than $80,000.

Point: Census Bureau (2011) reports that for workers 25 and over, higher education yields higher average pay:
Advanced degree $81,568
Bachelor's degree.   57,326
High school degree   36,876
No high school degree.   26,124

Field	Title (experience)	2011 Salary	2016 Estimate*
Public Accounting	Partner.	$202,000	$223,000
	Manager (6–8 years)	97,500	107,500
	Senior (3–5 years).	75,000	83,000
	Junior (0–2 years)	57,500	63,500
Private Accounting	CFO	242,000	267,000
	Controller/Treasurer	157,500	174,000
	Manager (6–8 years)	91,500	101,000
	Senior (3–5 years).	74,500	82,000
	Junior (0–2 years)	53,000	58,500
Recordkeeping	Full-charge bookkeeper	59,500	65,500
	Accounts manager	52,000	57,500
	Payroll manager	55,500	61,000
	Accounting clerk (0–2 years)	38,500	42,500

EXHIBIT 1.5

Accounting Salaries for Selected Fields

Point: For updated salary information:
Abbott-Langer.com
www.AICPA.org
Kforce.com

* Estimates assume a 2% compounded annual increase over current levels (rounded to nearest $500).

Quick Check

Answers — p. 29

1. What is the purpose of accounting?
2. What is the relation between accounting and recordkeeping?
3. Identify some advantages of technology for accounting.
4. Who are the internal and external users of accounting information?
5. Identify at least five types of managers who are internal users of accounting information.

Quick Check is a chance to stop and reflect on key points.

Point: U.S. Bureau of Labor (June 2011) reports higher education is linked to a lower unemployment rate:
Bachelor's degree or more 4.4%
High school degree 10.0%
No high school degree. 14.3%

FUNDAMENTALS OF ACCOUNTING

Accounting is guided by principles, standards, concepts, and assumptions. This section describes several of these key fundamentals of accounting.

Ethics—A Key Concept

The goal of accounting is to provide useful information for decisions. For information to be useful, it must be trusted. This demands ethics in accounting. **Ethics** are beliefs that distinguish right from wrong. They are accepted standards of good and bad behavior.

C3 Explain why ethics are crucial to accounting.

Identifying the ethical path is sometimes difficult. The preferred path is a course of action that avoids casting doubt on one's decisions. For example, accounting users are less likely to trust an auditor's report if the auditor's pay depends on the client's success . To avoid such concerns, ethics rules are often set. For example, auditors are banned from direct investment in their

Point: Sarbanes-Oxley Act requires each issuer of securities to disclose whether it has adopted a code of ethics for its senior officers and the contents of that code.

EXHIBIT 1.6

Guidelines for Ethical
Decision Making

Identify ethical concerns	Analyze options	Make ethical decision
Use personal ethics to recognize an ethical concern.	Consider all good and bad consequences.	Choose best option after weighing all consequences.

client and cannot accept pay that depends on figures in the client's reports. Exhibit 1.6 gives guidelines for making ethical decisions.

Accountants face many ethical choices as they prepare financial reports. These choices can affect the price a buyer pays and the wages paid to workers. They can even affect the success of products and services. Misleading information can lead to a wrongful closing of a division that harms workers, customers, and suppliers. There is an old saying: *Good ethics are good business.*

Some people extend ethics to *social responsibility,* which refers to a concern for the impact of actions on society. An organization's social responsibility can include donations to hospitals, colleges, community programs, and law enforcement. It also can include programs to reduce pollution, increase product safety, improve worker conditions, and support continuing education. These programs are not limited to large companies. For example, many small businesses offer discounts to students and senior citizens. Still others help sponsor events such as the Special Olympics and summer reading programs.

Point: The American Institute of Certified Public Accountants' *Code of Professional Conduct* is available at **www.AICPA.org**.

Decision Insight boxes highlight relevant items from practice.

Decision Insight

Virtuous Returns Virtue is not always its own reward. Compare the S&P 500 with the Domini Social Index (DSI), which covers 400 companies that have especially good records of social responsibility. We see that returns for companies with socially responsible behavior are roughly on par with those of the S&P 500 for the past 10-year period (Domini.com, 2011 Annual Report). Copyright © 2005 by KLD Research & Analytics, Inc. The "Domini 400 Social Index" is a service mark of KLD Research & Analytics. ■

Fraud Triangle

The fraud triangle is a model created by a criminologist that asserts the following *three* factors must exist for a person to commit fraud: opportunity, pressure, and rationalization.

Opportunity is one side of the fraud triangle. A person must envision a way to commit fraud with a low perceived risk of getting caught. Employers can directly reduce this risk. An example of some control on opportunity is a pre-employment background check. *Pressure,* or incentive, is another side of the fraud triangle. A person must have some pressure to commit fraud. Examples are unpaid bills and addictions. *Rationalization,* or attitude, is the third side of the fraud triangle. A person who rationalizes fails to see the criminal nature of the fraud or justifies the action.

It is important to recognize that all three factors of the fraud triangle must usually exist for fraud to occur. The absence of one or more factors suggests fraud is unlikely.

The key to dealing with fraud is to focus on prevention. It is less expensive and more effective to prevent fraud from happening than it is to try to detect the crime. By the time the fraud is discovered, the money is gone and chances are slim that it will be recovered. Additionally, it is costly and time consuming to investigate a fraud.

Both internal and external users rely on internal controls to reduce the likelihood of fraud. *Internal controls* are procedures set up to protect company property and equipment, ensure reliable accounting reports, promote efficiency, and encourage adherence to company policies. Examples are good records, physical controls (locks, passwords, guards), and independent reviews.

■ Decision Insight

They Fought the Law   Our economic and social welfare depends on reliable accounting. Some individuals forgot that and are now paying their dues. They include Raj Rajaratnam (in photo), an investor, convicted of trading stocks using inside information; Bernard Madoff of **Madoff Investment Securities**, convicted of falsifying securities records; Bernard Ebbers of **WorldCom**, convicted of an $11 billion accounting scandal; Andrew Fastow of **Enron**, guilty of hiding debt and inflating income; and Ramalinga Raju of **Satyam Computers**, accused of overstating assets by $1.5 billion. ■

Generally Accepted Accounting Principles

Financial accounting is governed by concepts and rules known as **generally accepted accounting principles (GAAP).** We must understand these principles to best use accounting data. GAAP aims to make information *relevant, reliable,* and *comparable.* Relevant information affects decisions of users. Reliable information is trusted by users. Comparable information is helpful in contrasting organizations.

In the United States, the **Securities and Exchange Commission (SEC),** a government agency, has the legal authority to set GAAP. The SEC also oversees proper use of GAAP by companies that raise money from the public through issuances of their stock and debt. Those companies that issue their stock on U.S. exchanges include both *U.S. SEC registrants* (companies incorporated in the United States) and *non-U.S. SEC registrants* (companies incorporated under non-U.S. laws). The SEC has largely delegated the task of setting U.S. GAAP to the **Financial Accounting Standards Board (FASB),** which is a private-sector group that sets both broad and specific principles.

C4 Explain generally accepted accounting principles and define and apply several accounting principles.

Point: State ethics codes require CPAs who audit financial statements to disclose areas where those statements fail to comply with GAAP. If CPAs fail to report noncompliance, they can lose their licenses and be subject to criminal and civil actions and fines.

International Standards

In today's global economy, there is increased demand by external users for comparability in accounting reports. This demand often arises when companies wish to raise money from lenders and investors in different countries. To that end, the **International Accounting Standards Board (IASB),** an independent group (consisting of individuals from many countries), issues **International Financial Reporting Standards (IFRS)** that identify preferred accounting practices.

If standards are harmonized, one company can potentially use a single set of financial statements in all financial markets. Differences between U.S. GAAP and IFRS are decreasing as the FASB and IASB pursue a *convergence* process aimed to achieve a single set of accounting standards for global use. More than 115 countries now require or permit companies to prepare financial reports following IFRS. Further, non-U.S. SEC registrants can use IFRS in financial reports filed with the SEC (with no reconciliation to U.S. GAAP). This means there are *two* sets of accepted accounting principles in the United States: (1) U.S. GAAP for U.S. SEC registrants and (2) either IFRS or U.S. GAAP for non-U.S. SEC registrants.

The SEC is encouraging the FASB to change U.S. GAAP over a period of several years by endorsing, and thereby incorporating, individual IFRS standards into U.S. GAAP. This endorsement process would still allow the FASB to modify IFRS when necessary. The SEC would:

- Maintain its statutory oversight of the FASB, including authority to prescribe accounting principles and standards for U.S. issuers.

- Contribute to oversight and governance of the IASB through its involvement on the IFRS Foundation Monitoring Board.

The FASB would continue, but its role would be to provide input and support to the IASB in crafting high-quality, global standards. The FASB is to develop a transition plan to effect these changes over the next five years or so. For updates on this roadmap, we can check with the AICPA (**IFRS.com**), FASB (**FASB.org**), and IASB (**ifrs.org**).

IFRS

Like the FASB, the IASB uses a conceptual framework to aid in revising or drafting new standards. However, unlike the FASB, the IASB's conceptual framework is used as a reference when specific guidance is lacking. The IASB also requires that transactions be accounted for according to their substance (not only their legal form), and that financial statements give a fair presentation, whereas the FASB narrows that scope to fair presentation *in accordance with U.S. GAAP.* ■

Conceptual Framework and Convergence

The FASB and IASB are attempting to converge and enhance the **conceptual framework** that guides standard setting. The FASB framework consists broadly of the following:

- **Objectives**—to provide information useful to investors, creditors, and others.
- **Qualitative Characteristics**—to require information that is *relevant, reliable,* and *comparable.*
- **Elements**—to define items that financial statements can contain.
- **Recognition and Measurement**—to set criteria that an item must meet for it to be recognized as an element; and how to measure that element.

For updates on this joint FASB and IASB conceptual framework convergence we can check with **FASB.org** or **ifrs.org** Websites. We must remember that U.S. GAAP and IFRS are two similar, but not identical, systems. However, their similarities greatly outweigh any differences. The remainder of this section describes key principles and assumptions of accounting.

■ Decision Insight

Principles and Scruples   Auditors, directors, and lawyers are using principles to improve accounting reports. Examples include accounting restatements at **Navistar**, financial restatements at **Nortel**, accounting reviews at **Echostar**, and expense adjustments at **Electronic Data Systems**. Principles-based accounting has led accounting firms to drop clients deemed too risky. Examples include **Grant Thornton**'s resignation as auditor of **Fremont General** due to alleged failures in providing information when promised, and **Ernst and Young**'s resignation as auditor of **Catalina Marketing** due to alleged accounting errors. ■

Principles and Assumptions of Accounting   Accounting principles (and assumptions) are of two types. *General principles* are the basic assumptions, concepts, and guidelines for preparing financial statements. *Specific principles* are detailed rules used in reporting business transactions and events. General principles stem from long-used accounting practices. Specific principles arise more often from the rulings of authoritative groups.

We need to understand both general and specific principles to effectively use accounting information. Several general principles are described in this section that are relied on in later chapters. General principles (in purple font with white shading) and assumptions (in red font with white shading) are portrayed

EXHIBIT 1.7

Building Blocks for GAAP

as building blocks of GAAP in Exhibit 1.7. The specific principles are described as we encounter them in the book.

Accounting Principles   General principles consist of at least four basic principles, four assumptions, and two constraints.

The **measurement principle,** also called the **cost principle,** usually prescribes that accounting information is based on actual cost (with a potential for subsequent adjustments to market). Cost is measured on a cash or equal-to-cash basis. This means if cash is given for a service, its cost is measured as the amount of cash paid. If something besides cash is exchanged (such as a car traded for a truck), cost is measured as the cash value of what is given up or received. The cost principle emphasizes reliability and verifiability, and information based on cost is considered objective. *Objectivity* means that information is supported by independent, unbiased evidence; it demands more than a person's opinion. To illustrate, suppose a company pays $5,000 for equipment. The cost principle requires that this purchase be recorded at $5,000. It makes no difference if the owner thinks this equipment is worth $7,000. Later in the book we introduce *fair value* measures.

Revenue (sales) is the amount received from selling products and services. The **revenue recognition principle** provides guidance on when a company must recognize revenue. To *recognize* means to record it. If revenue is recognized too early, a company would look more profitable than it is. If revenue is recognized too late, a company would look less profitable than it is.

Three concepts are important to revenue recognition. (1) *Revenue is recognized when earned.* The earnings process is normally complete when services are performed or a seller transfers ownership of products to the buyer. (2) *Proceeds from selling products and services need not be in cash.* A common noncash proceed received by a seller is a customer's promise to pay at a future date, called *credit sales.* (3) *Revenue is measured by the cash received plus the cash value of any other items received.*

The **expense recognition principle,** also called the **matching principle,** prescribes that a company record the expenses it incurred to generate the revenue reported. The principles of matching and revenue recognition are key to modern accounting.

The **full disclosure principle** prescribes that a company report the details behind financial statements that would impact users' decisions. Those disclosures are often in footnotes to the statements.

Point: The cost principle is also called the *historical cost principle.*

Example: When a bookstore sells a textbook on credit is its earnings process complete? *Answer:* A bookstore can record sales for these books minus an amount expected for returns.

■ **Decision** Insight ▬▬▬▬▬▬▬▬▬▬▬▬▬▬▬▬▬▬▬

Revenues for the **Green Bay Packers, New England Patriots, New York Giants,** and other professional football teams include ticket sales, television and cable broadcasts, radio rights, concessions, and advertising. Revenues from ticket sales are earned when the NFL team plays each game. Advance ticket sales are not revenues; instead, they represent a liability until the NFL team plays the game for which the ticket was sold. At that point, the liability is removed and revenues are reported. ■

Accounting Assumptions   There are four accounting assumptions: the going concern assumption, the monetary unit assumption, the time period assumption, and the business entity assumption.

The **going-concern assumption** means that accounting information reflects a presumption that the business will continue operating instead of being closed or sold. This implies, for example, that property is reported at cost instead of, say, liquidation values that assume closure.

Point: For currency conversion: xe.com

The **monetary unit assumption** means that we can express transactions and events in monetary, or money, units. Money is the common denominator in business. Examples of monetary units are the dollar in the United States, Canada, Australia, and Singapore; and the peso in Mexico, the Philippines, and Chile. The monetary unit a company uses in its accounting reports usually depends on the country where it operates, but many companies today are expressing reports in more than one monetary unit.

The **time period assumption** presumes that the life of a company can be divided into time periods, such as months and years, and that useful reports can be prepared for those periods.

Point: Abuse of the entity assumption was a main culprit in **Enron's** collapse.

The **business entity assumption** means that a business is accounted for separately from other business entities, including its owner. The reason for this assumption is that separate information about each business is necessary for good decisions. A business entity can take one of three legal forms: *proprietorship, partnership,* or *corporation.*

1. A **sole proprietorship,** or simply **proprietorship,** is a business owned by one person. No special legal requirements must be met to start a proprietorship. It is a separate entity for accounting purposes, but it is *not* a separate legal entity from its owner. This means, for example, that a court can order an owner to sell personal belongings to pay a proprietorship's debt. This *unlimited liability* of a proprietorship is a disadvantage. However, an advantage is that a proprietorship's income is not subject to a business income tax but is instead reported and taxed on the owner's personal income tax return. Proprietorship attributes are summarized in Exhibit 1.8, including those for partnerships and corporations.

EXHIBIT 1.8

Attributes of Businesses

Attribute Present	Proprietorship	Partnership	Corporation
One owner allowed...........	yes	no	yes
Business taxed	no	no	yes
Limited liability...............	no*	no*	yes
Business entity	yes	yes	yes
Legal entity...................	no	no	yes
Unlimited life	no	no	yes

* Proprietorships and partnerships that are set up as LLCs provide limited liability.

2. A **partnership** is a business owned by two or more people, called *partners.* Like a proprietorship, no special legal requirements must be met in starting a partnership. The only requirement is an agreement between partners to run a business together. The agreement can be either oral or written and usually indicates how income and losses are to be shared. A partnership, like a proprietorship, is *not* legally separate from its owners. This means that each partner's share of profits is reported and taxed on that partner's tax return. It also means *unlimited liability* for its partners. However, at least three types of partnerships limit liability. A *limited partnership* (*LP*) includes a general partner(s) with unlimited liability and a limited partner(s) with liability restricted to the amount invested. A *limited liability partnership* (*LLP*) restricts partners' liabilities to their own acts and the acts of individuals under their control. This protects an innocent partner from the negligence of another partner, yet all partners remain responsible for partnership debts. A *limited liability company* (*LLC*) offers the limited liability of a corporation and the tax treatment of a partnership (and proprietorship). Most proprietorships and partnerships are now organized as LLCs.

Point: Proprietorships and partnerships are usually managed by their owners. In a corporation, the owners (shareholders) elect a board of directors who appoint managers to run the business.

3. A **corporation** is a business legally separate from its owners, meaning it is responsible for its own acts and its own debts. Separate legal status means that a corporation can conduct

business with the rights, duties, and responsibilities of a person. A corporation acts through its managers, who are its legal agents. Separate legal status also means that its owners, who are called **shareholders** (or **stockholders**), are not personally liable for corporate acts and debts. This limited liability is its main advantage. A main disadvantage is what's called *double taxation*—meaning that (1) the corporation income is taxed and (2) any distribution of income to its owners through dividends is taxed as part of the owners' personal income, usually at the 15% rate. (For lower income taxpayers, the dividend tax is less than 15%, and in some cases zero.) An *S corporation,* a corporation with special attributes, does not owe corporate income tax. Owners of S corporations report their share of corporate income with their personal income. Ownership of all corporations is divided into units called **shares** or **stock.** When a corporation issues only one class of stock, we call it **common stock** (or *capital stock*).

> *Decision Ethics* boxes are role-playing exercises that stress ethics in accounting and business.

Decision Ethics

Entrepreneur   You and a friend develop a new design for in-line skates that improves speed by 25% to 30%. You plan to form a business to manufacture and market those skates. You and your friend want to minimize taxes, but your prime concern is potential lawsuits from individuals who might be injured on these skates. What form of organization do you set up? ∎ [Answer—p. 28]

Accounting Constraints   There are two basic constraints on financial reporting. The **materiality constraint** prescribes that only information that would influence the decisions of a reasonable person need be disclosed. This constraint looks at both the importance and relative size of an amount. The **cost-benefit constraint** prescribes that only information with benefits of disclosure greater than the costs of providing it need be disclosed. Additionally, *conservatism* and *industry practices* are sometimes referred to as accounting constraints.

Sarbanes–Oxley (SOX)

Congress passed the **Sarbanes–Oxley Act,** also called *SOX,* to help curb financial abuses at companies that issue their stock to the public. SOX requires that these public companies apply both accounting oversight and stringent internal controls. The desired results include more transparency, accountability, and truthfulness in reporting transactions.

Compliance with SOX requires documentation and verification of internal controls and increased emphasis on internal control effectiveness. Failure to comply can yield financial penalties, stock market delisting, and criminal prosecution of executives. Management must issue a report stating that internal controls are effective. CEOs and CFOs who knowingly sign off on bogus accounting reports risk millions of dollars in fines and years in prison. **Auditors** also must verify the effectiveness of internal controls.

A listing of some of the more publicized accounting scandals in recent years follows.

> **Point:** An **audit** examines whether financial statements are prepared using GAAP. It does *not* attest to absolute accuracy of the statements.

> **Point:** *BusinessWeek* reports that external audit costs run about $35,000 for start-ups, up from $15,000 pre-SOX.

Company	Alleged Accounting Abuses
Enron	Inflated income, hid debt, and bribed officials
WorldCom	Understated expenses to inflate income and hid debt
Fannie Mae	Inflated income
Adelphia Communications	Understated expenses to inflate income and hid debt
AOL Time Warner	Inflated revenues and income
Xerox	Inflated income
Bristol-Myers Squibb	Inflated revenues and income
Nortel Networks	Understated expenses to inflate income
Global Crossing	Inflated revenues and income
Tyco	Hid debt, and CEO evaded taxes
Halliburton	Inflated revenues and income
Qwest Communications	Inflated revenues and income

To reduce the risk of accounting fraud, companies set up *governance systems*. A company's governance system includes its owners, managers, employees, board of directors, and other important stakeholders, who work together to reduce the risk of accounting fraud and increase confidence in accounting reports.

The impact of SOX regulations for accounting and business is discussed throughout this book. Ethics and investor confidence are key to company success. Lack of confidence in accounting numbers impacts company value as evidenced by huge stock price declines for **Enron**, **WorldCom**, **Tyco**, and **ImClone** after accounting misconduct was uncovered.

Decision Insight

Economic Downturn, Fraud Upturn? Executives polled show that 80% believe that the economic downturn has or will have a significant impact on fraud control in their companies (Deloitte 2010). The top three responses to the question "What activity would best counter this increased fraud risk?" are tallied in the graphic to the right. ■

Dodd-Frank

Congress recently passed the **Dodd-Frank Wall Street Reform and Consumer Protection Act**, or *Dodd-Frank*, in a desire to (1) promote accountability and transparency in the financial system, (2) put an end to the notion of "too big to fail," (3) protect the taxpayer by ending bailouts, and (4) protect consumers from abusive financial services. It includes provisions whose impacts are unknown until regulators set detailed rules. However, a few proposals are notable and include the following:

- Exemption from Section 404(b) of SOX for smaller public entities (whose public value is less than $75 million) from the requirement to obtain an external audit on the effectiveness of internal control over financial reporting.
- Independence for all members of the compensation committee (including additional disclosures); in the event of an accounting restatement, an entity must set policies mandating recovery ("clawback") of excess incentive compensation.
- Requires the SEC, when sanctions exceed $1 million, to pay whistle-blowers between 10% and 30% of the sanction.

Quick Check   Answers — p. 29

6. What are internal controls and why are they important?

7. What three-step guidelines can help people make ethical decisions?

8. Why are ethics and social responsibility valuable to organizations?

9. Why are ethics crucial in accounting?

10. Who sets U.S. accounting rules?

11. How are U.S. companies affected by international accounting standards?

12. How are the objectivity concept and cost principle related?

13. Why is the business entity assumption important?

14. Why is the revenue recognition principle important?

15. What are the three basic forms of business organization?

16. Identify the owners of corporations and the terminology for ownership units.

TRANSACTION ANALYSIS AND THE ACCOUNTING EQUATION

To understand accounting information, we need to know how an accounting system captures relevant data about transactions, and then classifies, records, and reports data.

Accounting Equation

The accounting system reflects two basic aspects of a company: what it owns and what it owes. *Assets* are resources a company owns or controls. Examples are cash, supplies, equipment, and land, where each carries expected benefits. The claims on a company's assets—what it owes—are separated into owner and nonowner claims. *Liabilities* are what a company owes its nonowners (creditors) in future payments, products, or services. *Equity* (also called owner's equity or capital) refers to the claims of its owner(s). Together, liabilities and equity are the source of funds to acquire assets. The relation of assets, liabilities, and equity is reflected in the following **accounting equation:**

A1 Define and interpret the accounting equation and each of its components.

$$\text{Assets} = \text{Liabilities} + \text{Equity}$$

Liabilities are usually shown before equity in this equation because creditors' claims must be paid before the claims of owners. (The terms in this equation can be rearranged; for example, Assets − Liabilities = Equity.) The accounting equation applies to all transactions and events, to all companies and forms of organization, and to all points in time. For example, **Apple**'s assets equal \$116,371, its liabilities equal \$39,756, and its equity equals \$76,615 (\$ in millions). Let's now look at the accounting equation in more detail.

Assets   Assets are resources a company owns or controls. These resources are expected to yield future benefits. Examples are Web servers for an online services company, musical instruments for a rock band, and land for a vegetable grower. The term *receivable* is used to refer to an asset that promises a future inflow of resources. A company that provides a service or product on credit is said to have an account receivable from that customer.

Point: The phrases "on credit" and "on account" imply that cash payment will occur at a future date.

Liabilities   Liabilities are creditors' claims on assets. These claims reflect company obligations to provide assets, products or services to others. The term *payable* refers to a liability that promises a future outflow of resources. Examples are wages payable to workers, accounts payable to suppliers, notes payable to banks, and taxes payable to the government.

Equity   Equity is the owner's claim on assets, and is equal to assets minus liabilities. This is the reason equity is also called *net assets* or *residual equity*.

   Equity for a noncorporate entity—commonly called owner's equity—increases and decreases as follows: owner investments and revenues *increase* equity, whereas owner withdrawals and expenses *decrease* equity. **Owner investments** are resources such as cash that an owner puts into the company and are included under the generic account **Owner, Capital. Revenues** are sales of products or services to customers. Revenues increase equity (via net income) and result from a company's earnings activities. Examples of revenues are consulting services, sales of products, rentals to others, and commissions from services. **Owner withdrawals** are resources such as cash that an owner takes from the company for personal use. **Expenses** are the costs necessary to earn revenues. Expenses decrease equity. Examples of expenses are costs of employee time, use of supplies, and advertising, utilities, and insurance services from others. In sum, the breakdown of equity yields the following **expanded accounting equation:**

Key **terms** are printed in bold and defined again in the end-of-book **glossary.**

$$\text{Assets} = \text{Liabilities} + \underbrace{\underset{\text{Capital}}{\text{Owner,}} - \underset{\text{Withdrawals}}{\text{Owner,}} + \text{Revenues} - \text{Expenses}}_{\text{Equity}}$$

Net income occurs when revenues exceed expenses. Net income increases equity. A **net loss** occurs when expenses exceed revenues, which decreases equity.

Decision Insight

Web Info Most organizations maintain Websites that include accounting data—see **Polaris Industries (Polaris.com)** as an example. Polaris makes off-road vehicles such as all-terrain vehicles (ATV) and snowmobiles; it also makes on-road vehicles such as motorcycles and small electric vehicles. The SEC keeps an online database called **EDGAR (www.sec.gov/edgar.shtml),** which has accounting information for thousands of companies that issue stock to the public. The annual report filing for most publicly traded U.S. companies is known as Form 10-K, and the quarterly filing is Form 10-Q. Information services such as **Finance.Google.com** and **Finance.Yahoo.com** offer online data and analysis. ∎

Transaction Analysis

P1 Analyze business transactions using the accounting equation.

Business activities can be described in terms of transactions and events. **External transactions** are exchanges of value between two entities, which yield changes in the accounting equation. An example is the sale of ad space by **Twitter**. **Internal transactions** are exchanges within an entity, which may or may not affect the accounting equation. An example is Twitter's use of its supplies, which are reported as expenses when used. **Events** refer to happenings that affect the accounting equation *and* are reliably measured. They include business events such as changes in the market value of certain assets and liabilities and natural events such as floods and fires that destroy assets and create losses. They do not include, for example, the signing of service or product contracts, which by themselves do not impact the accounting equation.

This section uses the accounting equation to analyze 11 selected transactions and events of FastForward, a start-up consulting (service) business, in its first month of operations. Remember that each transaction and event leaves the equation in balance and that assets *always* equal the sum of liabilities and equity.

Point: There are 3 basic types of company operations: (1) **Services**—providing customer services for profit, (2) **Merchandisers**—buying products and re-selling them for profit, and (3) **Manufacturers**—creating products and selling them for profit.

Transaction 1: Investment by Owner On December 1, Chas Taylor forms a consulting business, named FastForward and set up as a proprietorship, that focuses on assessing the performance of footwear and accessories. Taylor owns and manages the business. The marketing plan for the business is to focus primarily on publishing online reviews and consulting with clubs, athletes, and others who place orders for footwear and accessories with manufacturers. Taylor personally invests $30,000 cash in the new company and deposits the cash in a bank account opened under the name of FastForward. After this transaction, the cash (an asset) and the owner's equity each equal $30,000. The source of increase in equity is the owner's investment, which is included in the column titled C. Taylor, Capital. (Owner investments are always included under the title *'Owner name,' Capital.*) The effect of this transaction on FastForward is reflected in the accounting equation as follows (we label the equity entries):

	Assets	=	Liabilities	+	Equity
	Cash	=			**C. Taylor, Capital**
(1)	**+$30,000**	=			**+$30,000** owner investment

Transaction 2: Purchase Supplies for Cash FastForward uses $2,500 of its cash to buy supplies of brand name footwear for performance testing over the next few months. This transaction is an exchange of cash, an asset, for another kind of asset, supplies. It merely changes the form of assets from cash to supplies. The decrease in cash is exactly equal to the increase in supplies. The supplies of footwear are assets because of the expected future benefits from the test results of their performance. This transaction is reflected in the accounting equation as follows:

	Assets			=	Liabilities	+	Equity
	Cash	+	**Supplies**	=			**C. Taylor, Capital**
Old Bal.	$30,000			=			$30,000
(2)	**−2,500**	+	**$2,500**				
New Bal.	$27,500	+	$ 2,500	=			$30,000
		$30,000				$30,000	

Transaction 3: Purchase Equipment for Cash FastForward spends $26,000 to acquire equipment for testing footwear. Like transaction 2, transaction 3 is an exchange of one asset, cash, for another asset, equipment. The equipment is an asset because of its expected future benefits from testing footwear. This purchase changes the makeup of assets but does not change the asset total. The accounting equation remains in balance.

	Assets				=	Liabilities	+	Equity
	Cash	+	**Supplies**	+	**Equipment**	=		**C. Taylor, Capital**
Old Bal.	$27,500	+	$2,500			=		$30,000
(3)	26,000			+	$26,000			
New Bal.	$ 1,500	+	$2,500	+	$ 26,000	=		$30,000
			$30,000					$30,000

Transaction 4: Purchase Supplies on Credit Taylor decides more supplies of footwear and accessories are needed. These additional supplies total $7,100, but as we see from the accounting equation in transaction 3, FastForward has only $1,500 in cash. Taylor arranges to purchase them on credit from CalTech Supply Company. Thus, FastForward acquires supplies in exchange for a promise to pay for them later. This purchase increases assets by $7,100 in supplies, and liabilities (called *accounts payable* to CalTech Supply) increase by the same amount. The effects of this purchase follow:

Example: If FastForward pays $500 cash in transaction 4, how does this partial payment affect the liability to CalTech? What would be FastForward's cash balance? *Answers:* The liability to CalTech would be reduced to $6,600 and the cash balance would be reduced to $1,000.

	Assets				=	Liabilities	+	Equity
	Cash	+	**Supplies**	+	**Equipment**	=	**Accounts Payable**	+	**C. Taylor, Capital**
Old Bal.	$1,500	+	$2,500	+	$26,000	=			$30,000
(4)		+	7,100				+$7,100		
New Bal.	$1,500	+	$9,600	+	$26,000	=	$ 7,100	+	$30,000
			$37,100					$37,100	

Transaction 5: Provide Services for Cash FastForward earns revenues by selling online ad space to manufacturers and by consulting with clients about test results on footwear and accessories. It earns net income only if its revenues are greater than its expenses incurred in earning them. In one of its first jobs, FastForward provides consulting services to a power-walking club and immediately collects $4,200 cash. The accounting equation reflects this increase in cash of $4,200 and in equity of $4,200. This increase in equity is identified in the far right column under Revenues because the cash received is earned by providing consulting services.

	Assets						=	Liabilities	+		Equity		
	Cash	+	**Supplies**	+	**Equipment**		=	**Accounts Payable**	+	**C. Taylor, Capital**	+	**Revenues**
Old Bal.	$1,500	+	$9,600	+	$26,000		=	$7,100	+	$30,000		
(5)	+4,200										+	$4,200 consulting
New Bal.	$5,700	+	$9,600	+	$26,000		=	$7,100	+	$30,000	+	$ 4,200
			$41,300							$41,300		

Transactions 6 and 7: Payment of Expenses in Cash FastForward pays $1,000 rent to the landlord of the building where its facilities are located. Paying this amount allows FastForward to occupy the space for the month of December. The rental payment is reflected in the following accounting equation as transaction 6. FastForward also pays the biweekly $700 salary of the company's only employee. This is reflected in the accounting equation as transaction 7. Both transactions 6 and 7 are December expenses for FastForward. The costs of both rent and salary are expenses, as opposed to assets, because their benefits are used in December (they

By definition, increases in expenses yield decreases in equity.

have no future benefits after December). These transactions also use up an asset (cash) in carrying out FastForward's operations. The accounting equation shows that both transactions reduce cash and equity. The far right column identifies these decreases as Expenses.

	Assets				=	Liabilities	+			Equity			
	Cash	+	Supplies	+	Equipment	=	Accounts Payable	+	C. Taylor, Capital	+	Revenues	−	Expenses
Old Bal.	$5,700	+	$9,600	+	$26,000	=	$7,100	+	$30,000	+	$4,200		
(6)	−1,000											−	$1,000 rent
Bal.	4,700	+	9,600	+	26,000	=	7,100	+	30,000	+	4,200	−	1,000
(7)	− 700											−	700 salaries
New Bal.	$4,000	+	$9,600	+	$26,000	=	$7,100	+	$30,000	+	$4,200	−	$ 1,700
			$39,600						$39,600				

Transaction 8: Provide Services and Facilities for Credit   FastForward provides consulting services of $1,600 and rents its test facilities for $300 to a podiatric services center. The rental involves allowing members to try recommended footwear and accessories at FastForward's testing area. The center is billed for the $1,900 total. This transaction results in a new asset, called *accounts receivable,* from this client. It also yields an increase in equity from the two revenue components reflected in the Revenues column of the accounting equation:

	Assets								=	Liabilities	+			Equity			
	Cash	+	Accounts Receivable	+	Supplies	+	Equipment	=	Accounts Payable	+	C. Taylor, Capital	+	Revenues	−	Expenses
Old Bal.	$4,000	+			$9,600	+	$26,000	=	$7,100	+	$30,000	+	$4,200	−	$1,700
(8)		+	$1,900									+	1,600 consulting		
												+	300 rental		
New Bal.	$4,000	+	$ 1,900	+	$9,600	+	$26,000	=	$7,100	+	$30,000	+	$6,100	−	$1,700
			$41,500								$41,500				

Transaction 9: Receipt of Cash from Accounts Receivable   The client in transaction 8 (the podiatric center) pays $1,900 to FastForward 10 days after it is billed for consulting services. This transaction 9 does not change the total amount of assets and does not affect liabilities or equity. It converts the receivable (an asset) to cash (another asset). It does not create new revenue. Revenue was recognized when FastForward rendered the services in transaction 8, not when the cash is now collected. This emphasis on the earnings process instead of cash flows is a goal of the revenue recognition principle and yields useful information to users. The new balances follow:

Point: Receipt of cash is not always a revenue.

	Assets								=	Liabilities	+			Equity			
	Cash	+	Accounts Receivable	+	Supplies	+	Equipment	=	Accounts Payable	+	C. Taylor, Capital	+	Revenues	−	Expenses
Old Bal.	$4,000	+	$1,900	+	$9,600	+	$26,000	=	$7,100	+	$30,000	+	$6,100	−	$1,700
(9)	+1,900	−	1,900												
New Bal.	$5,900	+	$ 0	+	$9,600	+	$26,000	=	$7,100	+	$30,000	+	$6,100	−	$1,700
			$41,500								$41,500				

Transaction 10: Payment of Accounts Payable   FastForward pays CalTech Supply $900 cash as partial payment for its earlier $7,100 purchase of supplies (transaction 4), leaving $6,200 unpaid. The accounting equation shows that this transaction decreases FastForward's cash by $900 and decreases its liability to CalTech Supply by $900. Equity does not change. This event does not create an expense even though cash flows out of FastForward (instead the expense is recorded when FastForward derives the benefits from these supplies).

	Assets					=	Liabilities	+		Equity		
	Cash	+	Accounts Receivable	+	Supplies	+	Equipment	=	Accounts Payable	+	C. Taylor, Capital	+	Revenues	−	Expenses

	Cash	+	Accounts Receivable	+	Supplies	+	Equipment	=	Accounts Payable	+	C. Taylor, Capital	+	Revenues	−	Expenses
Old Bal.	$5,900	+	$ 0	+	$9,600	+	$26,000	=	$7,100	+	$30,000	+	$6,100	−	$1,700
(10)	− 900								− 900						
New Bal.	$5,000	+	$ 0	+	$9,600	+	$26,000	=	$6,200	+	$30,000	+	$6,100	−	$1,700
			$40,600								$40,600				

Transaction 11: Withdrawal of Cash by Owner

The owner of FastForward withdraws $200 cash for personal use. Withdrawals (decreases in equity) are not reported as expenses because they are not part of the company's earnings process. Since withdrawals are not company expenses, they are not used in computing net income.

By definition, increases in withdrawals yield decreases in equity.

	Assets					=	Liabilities	+			Equity		

	Cash	+	Accounts Receivable	+	Supplies	+	Equipment	=	Accounts Payable	+	C. Taylor, Capital	−	C. Taylor, Withdrawals	+	Revenues	−	Expenses
Old Bal.	$5,000	+	$ 0	+	$9,600	+	$26,000	=	$6,200	+	$30,000			+	$6,100	−	$1,700
(11)	− 200											−	$200 owner withdrawal				
New Bal.	$4,800	+	$ 0	+	$9,600	+	$26,000	=	$6,200	+	$30,000	−	$200	+	$6,100	−	$1,700
			$40,400										$40,400				

Summary of Transactions

We summarize in Exhibit 1.9 the effects of these 11 transactions of FastForward using the accounting equation. First, we see that the accounting equation remains in balance after each transaction. Second, transactions can be analyzed by their effects on components of the

EXHIBIT 1.9

Summary of Transactions Using the Accounting Equation

	Assets							=	Liabilities	+		Equity			
	Cash	+	Accounts Receivable	+	Supplies	+	Equipment	=	Accounts Payable	+	C. Taylor, Capital	−	C. Taylor, Withdrawals	+	Revenues	−	Expenses
(1)	$30,000							=			$30,000					
(2)	− 2,500			+	$2,500											
Bal.	27,500			+	2,500			=			30,000					
(3)	−26,000					+	$26,000									
Bal.	1,500			+	2,500	+	26,000	=			30,000					
(4)				+	7,100				+$7,100							
Bal.	1,500			+	9,600	+	26,000	=	7,100	+	30,000					
(5)	+ 4,200													+	$4,200	
Bal.	5,700			+	9,600	+	26,000	=	7,100	+	30,000			+	4,200	
(6)	− 1,000															− $1,000
Bal.	4,700			+	9,600	+	26,000	=	7,100	+	30,000			+	4,200	−	1,000
(7)	− 700															− 700
Bal.	4,000			+	9,600	+	26,000	=	7,100	+	30,000			+	4,200	−	1,700
(8)		+	$1,900											+	1,600	
														+	300	
Bal.	4,000	+	1,900	+	9,600	+	26,000	=	7,100	+	30,000			+	6,100	−	1,700
(9)	+ 1,900	−	1,900													
Bal.	5,900	+	0	+	9,600	+	26,000	=	7,100	+	30,000			+	6,100	−	1,700
(10)	− 900								− 900							
Bal.	5,000	+	0	+	9,600	+	26,000	=	6,200	+	30,000			+	6,100	−	1,700
(11)	− 200											−	$200			
Bal.	$ 4,800	+	$ 0	+	$ 9,600	+	$ 26,000	=	$ 6,200	+	$ 30,000	−	$ 200	+	$6,100	−	$1,700

Point: Knowing how financial statements are prepared improves our analysis of them. We develop the skills for analysis of financial statements throughout the book. Chapter 17 focuses on financial statement analysis.

accounting equation. For example, in transactions 2, 3, and 9, one asset increased while another asset decreased by equal amounts.

Quick Check

Answers — p. 29

17. When is the accounting equation in balance, and what does that mean?
18. How can a transaction not affect any liability and equity accounts?
19. Describe a transaction increasing equity and one decreasing it.
20. Identify a transaction that decreases both assets and liabilities.

FINANCIAL STATEMENTS

P2 Identify and prepare basic financial statements and explain how they interrelate.

This section introduces us to how financial statements are prepared from the analysis of business transactions. The four financial statements and their purposes are:

1. **Income statement**—describes a company's revenues and expenses along with the resulting net income or loss over a period of time due to earnings activities.
2. **Statement of owner's equity**—explains changes in equity from net income (or loss) and from any owner investments and withdrawals over a period of time.
3. **Balance sheet**—describes a company's financial position (types and amounts of assets, liabilities, and equity) at a point in time.
4. **Statement of cash flows**—identifies cash inflows (receipts) and cash outflows (payments) over a period of time.

We prepare these financial statements, in this order, using the 11 selected transactions of Fast-Forward. (These statements are technically called *unadjusted*—we explain this in Chapters 2 and 3.)

Income Statement

FastForward's income statement for December is shown at the top of Exhibit 1.10. Information about revenues and expenses is conveniently taken from the Equity columns of Exhibit 1.9. Revenues are reported first on the income statement. They include consulting revenues of $5,800 from transactions 5 and 8 and rental revenue of $300 from transaction 8. Expenses are reported after revenues. (For convenience in this chapter, we list larger amounts first, but we can sort expenses in different ways.) Rent and salary expenses are from transactions 6 and 7. Expenses reflect the costs to generate the revenues reported. Net income (or loss) is reported at the bottom of the statement and is the amount earned in December. Owner's investments and withdrawals are *not* part of income.

Point: Net income is sometimes called *earnings* or *profit.*

Statement of Owner's Equity

Point: The statement of owner's equity is also called the *statement of changes in owner's equity.* Note: Beg. Capital + Net Income − Withdrawals = Ending Capital

The statement of owner's equity reports information about how equity changes over the reporting period. This statement shows beginning capital, events that increase it (owner investments and net income), and events that decrease it (withdrawals and net loss). Ending capital is computed in this statement and is carried over and reported on the balance sheet. FastForward's statement of owner's equity is the second report in Exhibit 1.10. The beginning capital balance is measured as of the start of business on December 1. It is zero because FastForward did not exist before then. An existing business reports a beginning balance equal to that as of the end of the prior reporting period (such as from November 30). FastForward's statement of owner's equity shows that Taylor's initial investment created $30,000 of equity. It also shows the $4,400 of net income earned during the period. This links the income statement to the statement of owner's equity (see line ①). The statement also reports Taylor's $200 cash withdrawal and FastForward's end-of-period capital balance.

Balance Sheet

FastForward's balance sheet is the third report in Exhibit 1.10. This statement refers to Fast-Forward's financial condition at the close of business on December 31. The left side of the balance

EXHIBIT 1.10

Financial Statements and
Their Links

FASTFORWARD
Income Statement
For Month Ended December 31, 2013

Revenues		
Consulting revenue ($4,200 + $1,600).............	$ 5,800	
Rental revenue......................................	300	
Total revenues		$ 6,100
Expenses		
Rent expense	1,000	
Salaries expense	700	
Total expenses		1,700
Net income		$ 4,400

Point: A statement's heading identifies the company, the statement title, and the date or time period.

FASTFORWARD
Statement of Owner's Equity
For Month Ended December 31, 2013

C. Taylor, Capital, December 1, 2013	$ 0	
Plus: Investments by owner	$30,000	
Net income	4,400	34,400
		34,400
Less: Withdrawals by owner		200
C. Taylor, Capital, December 31, 2013		$34,200

Point: Arrow lines show how the statements are linked. ① Net income is used to compute equity. ② Owner capital is used to prepare the balance sheet. ③ Cash from the balance sheet is used to reconcile the statement of cash flows.

FASTFORWARD
Balance Sheet
December 31, 2013

Assets		Liabilities	
Cash	$ 4,800	Accounts payable.............	$ 6,200
Supplies	9,600	Total liabilities	6,200
Equipment........	26,000		
		Equity	
		C. Taylor, Capital.............	34,200
Total assets	$ 40,400	Total liabilities and equity	$ 40,400

Point: The income statement, the statement of owner's equity, and the statement of cash flows are prepared for a *period* of time. The balance sheet is prepared as of a *point* in time.

FASTFORWARD
Statement of Cash Flows
For Month Ended December 31, 2013

Cash flows from operating activities		
Cash received from clients ($4,200 + $1,900)..........	$ 6,100	
Cash paid for supplies ($2,500 + $900)...............	(3,400)	
Cash paid for rent	(1,000)	
Cash paid to employee	(700)	
Net cash provided by operating activities		$ 1,000
Cash flows from investing activities		
Purchase of equipment	(26,000)	
Net cash used by investing activities		(26,000)
Cash flows from financing activities		
Investments by owner	30,000	
Withdrawals by owner.............................	(200)	
Net cash provided by financing activities		29,800
Net increase in cash		$ 4,800
Cash balance, December 1, 2013		0
Cash balance, December 31, 2013		$ 4,800

Point: A single ruled line denotes an addition or subtraction. Final totals are double underlined. Negative amounts are often in parentheses.

sheet lists FastForward's assets: cash, supplies, and equipment. The upper right side of the balance sheet shows that FastForward owes $6,200 to creditors. Any other liabilities (such as a bank loan) would be listed here. The equity (capital) balance is $34,200. Line ② shows the link between the ending balance of the statement of owner's equity and the equity balance on the balance sheet. (This presentation of the balance sheet is called the *account form:* assets on the left and liabilities and equity on the right. Another presentation is the *report form:* assets on top, followed by liabilities and then equity at the bottom. Either presentation is acceptable.) As always, we see the accounting equation applies: Assets of $40,400 = Liabilities of $6,200 + Equity of $34,200.

Statement of Cash Flows

Point: Statement of cash flows has three main sections: operating, investing, and financing.

Point: Payment for supplies is an operating activity because supplies are expected to be used up in short-term operations (typically less than one year).

Point: Investing activities refer to long-term asset investments by the company, *not* to owner investments.

FastForward's statement of cash flows is the final report in Exhibit 1.10. The first section reports cash flows from *operating activities*. It shows the $6,100 cash received from clients and the $5,100 cash paid for supplies, rent, and employee salaries. Outflows are in parentheses to denote subtraction. Net cash provided by operating activities for December is $1,000. If cash paid exceeded the $5,100 cash received, we would call it "cash used by operating activities." The second section reports *investing activities,* which involve buying and selling assets such as land and equipment that are held for *long-term use* (typically more than one year). The only investing activity is the $26,000 purchase of equipment. The third section shows cash flows from *financing activities,* which include the *long-term* borrowing and repaying of cash from lenders and the cash investments from, and withdrawals by, the owner. FastForward reports $30,000 from the owner's initial investment and the $200 cash withdrawal. The net cash effect of all financing transactions is a $29,800 cash inflow. The final part of the statement shows FastForward increased its cash balance by $4,800 in December. Since it started with no cash, the ending balance is also $4,800—see line ③. We see that cash flow numbers are different from income statement (*accrual*) numbers, which is common.

Quick Check   Answers – p. 29

21. Explain the link between the income statement and the statement of owner's equity.
22. Describe the link between the balance sheet and the statement of owner's equity.
23. Discuss the three major sections of the statement of cash flows.

GLOBAL VIEW

Accounting according to U.S. GAAP is similar, but not identical, to IFRS. Throughout the book we use this last section to identify major similarities and differences between IFRS and U.S. GAAP for the materials in each chapter.

Basic Principles   Both U.S. GAAP and IFRS include broad and similar guidance for accounting. However, neither system specifies particular account names nor the detail required. (A typical *chart of accounts* is shown near the end of this book.) IFRS does require certain minimum line items be reported in the balance sheet along with other minimum disclosures that U.S. GAAP does not. On the other hand, U.S. GAAP requires disclosures for the current and prior two years for the income statement, statement of cash flows, and statement of retained earnings (equity), while IFRS requires disclosures for the current and prior year. Still, the basic principles behind these two systems are similar.

Transaction Analysis   Both U.S. GAAP and IFRS apply transaction analysis identically as shown in this chapter. Although some variations exist in revenue and expense recognition and other principles, all of the transactions in this chapter are accounted for identically under these two systems. It is often said that U.S. GAAP is more *rules-based* whereas IFRS is more *principles-based*. The main difference on the rules versus principles focus is with the approach in deciding how to account for certain transactions. Under U.S. GAAP, the approach is more focused on strictly following the accounting rules; under IFRS, the approach is more focused on a review of the situation and how accounting can best reflect it. This difference typically impacts advanced topics beyond the introductory course.

PIAGGIO

Financial Statements   Both U.S. GAAP and IFRS prepare the same four basic financial statements. To illustrate, a condensed version of **Piaggio**'s income statement follows (numbers are in Euros thousands).

Piaggio manufactures two-, three- and four-wheel vehicles, and is Europe's leading manufacturer of motorcycles and scooters. Similar condensed versions can be prepared for the other three statements (see Appendix A).

PIAGGIO **Income Statement (in € thousands)** **For Year Ended December 31, 2011**	
Net revenues	1,516,463
Cost for materials	904,060
Cost for services, leases, employees, depreciation, and other expenses.........	533,045
Taxes	32,305
Net income (profit)	47,053

Status of IFRS Accounting impacts companies across the world, which requires us to take a global view. IFRS is now adopted or accepted in over 115 countries, including over 30 member-states of the EU (see gold and light tan shading in the map below). Teal shading in the map reflects a system other than IFRS. The FASB and IASB continue to work on the convergence of IFRS and U.S. GAAP. Further, the SEC has a "roadmap" for ultimate use of IFRS by U.S. companies. Currently, the roadmap extends out over the next several years.

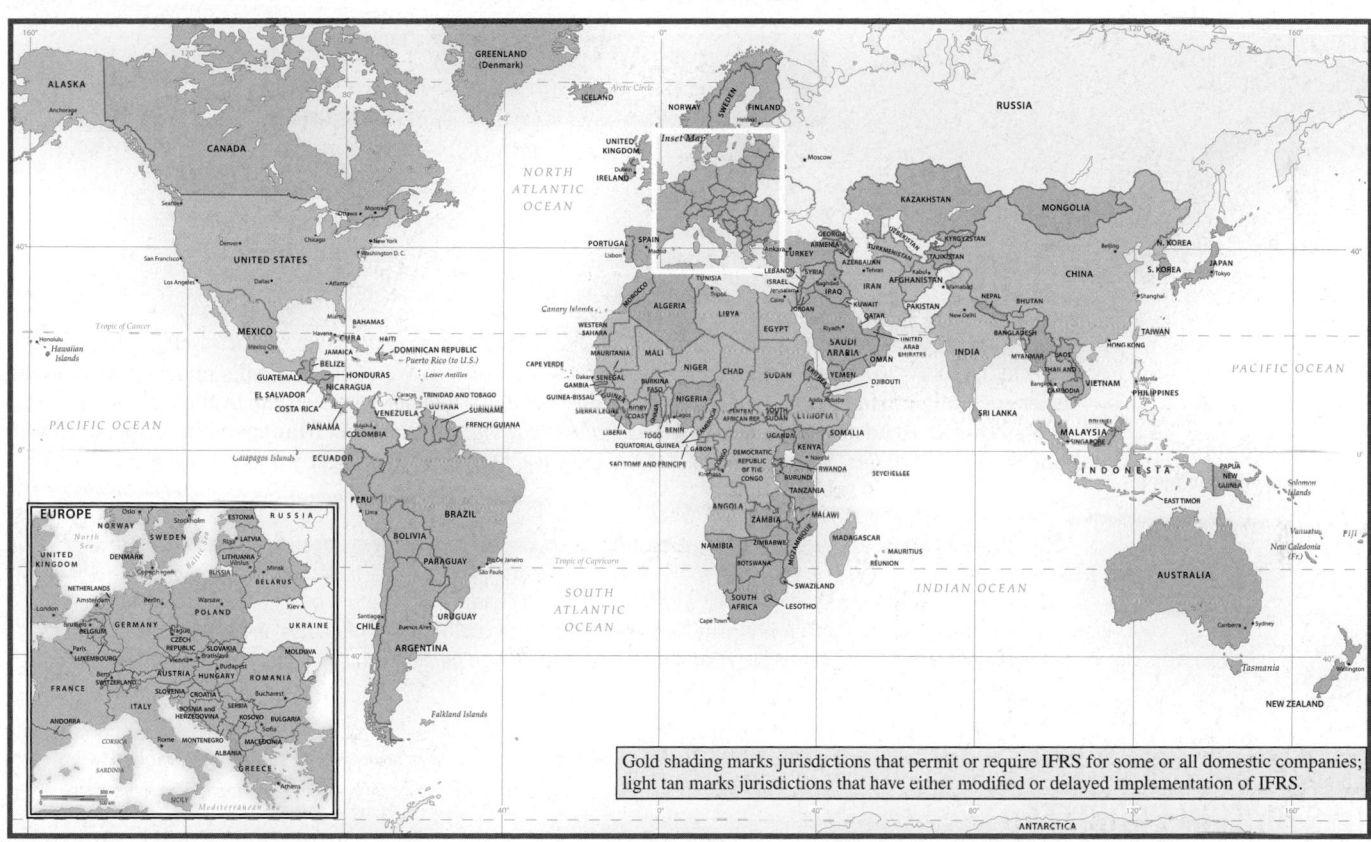

Gold shading marks jurisdictions that permit or require IFRS for some or all domestic companies; light tan marks jurisdictions that have either modified or delayed implementation of IFRS.

Decision Analysis (a section at the end of each chapter) introduces and explains ratios helpful in decision making using real company data. Instructors can skip this section and cover all ratios in Chapter 17. ———→

Return on Assets ▢▢▢ **Decision Analysis**

A *Decision Analysis* section at the end of each chapter is devoted to financial statement analysis. We organize financial statement analysis into four areas: (1) liquidity and efficiency, (2) solvency, (3) profitability, and (4) market prospects—Chapter 17 has a ratio listing with definitions and groupings by area. When analyzing ratios, we need benchmarks to identify good, bad, or average levels. Common benchmarks include the company's prior levels and those of its competitors.

A2 Compute and interpret return on assets.

This chapter presents a profitability measure: return on assets. Return on assets is useful in evaluating management, analyzing and forecasting profits, and planning activities. **Dell** has its marketing department compute return on assets for *every* order. **Return on assets (ROA),** also called *return on investment* (*ROI*), is defined in Exhibit 1.11.

EXHIBIT 1.11

Return on Assets

$$\text{Return on assets} = \frac{\text{Net income}}{\text{Average total assets}}$$

Net income is from the annual income statement, and average total assets is computed by adding the beginning and ending amounts for that same period and dividing by 2. To illustrate, **Dell** reports net income of $3,492 million for fiscal year 2012. At the beginning of fiscal 2012, its total assets are $38,599 million and at the end of fiscal 2012, they total $44,533 million. Dell's return on assets for fiscal 2012 is:

$$\text{Return on assets} = \frac{\$3,492 \text{ million}}{(\$38,599 \text{ million} + \$44,533 \text{ million})/2} = 8.4\%$$

Is an 8.4% return on assets good or bad for Dell? To help answer this question, we compare (benchmark) Dell's return with its prior performance, the returns of competitors (such as **Hewlett-Packard**, **IBM**, and **Lenovo**), and the returns from alternative investments. Dell's return for each of the prior five years is in the second column of Exhibit 1.12, which ranges from 4.8% to 11.1%.

EXHIBIT 1.12

Dell and Industry Returns

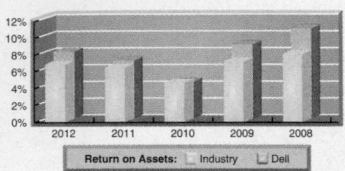

| | Return on Assets | |
Fiscal Year	Dell	Industry
2012	8.4%	6.9%
2011	7.3	6.5
2010	4.8	4.7
2009	9.2	7.2
2008	11.1	8.1

Dell shows a fairly stable pattern of good returns that reflect its productive use of assets. There is a decline in its 2009–2010 returns reflecting the recessionary period. We compare Dell's return to the normal return for similar manufacturers of computers (third column). Industry averages are available from services such as **Dun & Bradstreet**'s *Industry Norms and Key Ratios* and **The Risk Management Association** *Annual Statement Studies*. When compared to the industry, Dell performs slightly above average.

Each Decision Analysis section ends with a role-playing scenario to show the usefulness of ratios.

■ **Decision Maker** ══════════════════════════════════════

Business Owner   You own a small winter ski resort that earns a 21% return on its assets. An opportunity to purchase a winter ski equipment manufacturer is offered to you. This manufacturer earns a 19% return on its assets. The industry return for this manufacturer is 14%. Do you purchase this manufacturer? ■   [Answer—p. 29]

*The **Demonstration Problem** is a review of key chapter content. The Planning the Solution offers strategies in solving the problem.*

DEMONSTRATION PROBLEM

After several months of planning, Jasmine Worthy started a haircutting business called Expressions. The following events occurred during its first month of business.

a. On August 1, Worthy invested $3,000 cash and $15,000 of equipment in Expressions.

b. On August 2, Expressions paid $600 cash for furniture for the shop.

c. On August 3, Expressions paid $500 cash to rent space in a strip mall for August.

d. On August 4, it purchased $1,200 of equipment on credit for the shop (using a long-term note payable).

e. On August 5, Expressions opened for business. Cash received from haircutting services in the first week and a half of business (ended August 15) was $825.

f. On August 15, it provided $100 of haircutting services on account.

g. On August 17, it received a $100 check for services previously rendered on account.

h. On August 17, it paid $125 cash to an assistant for hours worked during the grand opening.

i. Cash received from services provided during the second half of August was $930.

j. On August 31, it paid a $400 installment toward principal on the note payable entered into on August 4.

k. On August 31, Worthy made a $900 cash withdrawal from the company for personal use.

Required

1. Arrange the following asset, liability, and equity titles in a table similar to the one in Exhibit 1.9: Cash; Accounts Receivable; Furniture; Store Equipment; Note Payable; J. Worthy, Capital; J. Worthy, Withdrawals; Revenues; and Expenses. Show the effects of each transaction using the accounting equation.

2. Prepare an income statement for August.

3. Prepare a statement of owner's equity for August.

4. Prepare a balance sheet as of August 31.

5. Prepare a statement of cash flows for August.

6. Determine the return on assets ratio for August.

PLANNING THE SOLUTION

- Set up a table like Exhibit 1.9 with the appropriate columns for accounts.
- Analyze each transaction and show its effects as increases or decreases in the appropriate columns. Be sure the accounting equation remains in balance after each transaction.
- Prepare the income statement, and identify revenues and expenses. List those items on the statement, compute the difference, and label the result as *net income* or *net loss*.
- Use information in the Equity columns to prepare the statement of owner's equity.
- Use information in the last row of the transactions table to prepare the balance sheet.
- Prepare the statement of cash flows; include all events listed in the Cash column of the transactions table. Classify each cash flow as operating, investing, or financing.
- Calculate return on assets by dividing net income by average assets.

SOLUTION TO DEMONSTRATION PROBLEM

1.

	Assets								=	Liabilities	+			Equity					
	Cash	+	Accounts Receivable	+	Furniture	+	Store Equipment	=	Note Payable	+	J. Worthy, Capital	−	J. Worthy, Withdrawals	+	Revenues	−	Expenses
a.	$3,000						$15,000				$18,000						
b.	− 600				+ $600												
Bal.	2,400	+			+ 600	+	15,000	=			18,000						
c.	− 500															−	$500
Bal.	1,900	+			+ 600	+	15,000	=			18,000					−	500
d.						+	1,200		+$1,200								
Bal.	1,900	+			+ 600	+	16,200	=	1,200	+	18,000					−	500
e.	+ 825													+	$ 825		
Bal.	2,725	+			+ 600	+	16,200	=	1,200	+	18,000			+	825	−	500
f.		+	$100											+	100		
Bal.	2,725	+	100	+	600	+	16,200	=	1,200	+	18,000			+	925	−	500
g.	+ 100	−	100														
Bal.	2,825	+	0	+	600	+	16,200	=	1,200	+	18,000			+	925	−	500
h.	− 125															−	125
Bal.	2,700	+	0	+	600	+	16,200	=	1,200	+	18,000			+	925	−	625
i.	+ 930													+	930		
Bal.	3,630	+	0	+	600	+	16,200	=	1,200	+	18,000			+	1,855	−	625
j.	− 400								− 400								
Bal.	3,230	+	0	+	600	+	16,200	=	800	+	18,000			+	1,855	−	625
k.	− 900											−	$900				
Bal.	$ 2,330	+	0	+	$600	+	$ 16,200	=	$ 800	+	$ 18,000	−	$900	+	$1,855	−	$625

2.

EXPRESSIONS
Income Statement
For Month Ended August 31

Revenues
    Haircutting services revenue $1,855
Expenses
    Rent expense $500
    Wages expense . . . . <u>125</u>
    Total expenses . . . . <u>625</u>
Net Income . . . . <u>$1,230</u>

3.

EXPRESSIONS
Statement of Owner's Equity
For Month Ended August 31

J. Worthy, Capital, August 1* . . . . $ 0
Plus: Investments by owner $18,000
          Net income. . . . . <u>1,230</u>   <u>19,230</u>
                                    19,230
Less: Withdrawals by owner. . . . .   <u>900</u>
J. Worthy, Capital, August 31. . . . .   <u>$18,330</u>

* If Expressions had been an existing business from a prior period, the beginning capital balance would equal the Capital account balance from the end of the prior period.

4.

EXPRESSIONS
Balance Sheet
August 31

Assets		**Liabilities**	
Cash	$ 2,330	Note payable	$ 800
Furniture	600	**Equity**	
Store equipment	<u>16,200</u>	J. Worthy, Capital	<u>18,330</u>
Total assets	<u>$19,130</u>	Total liabilities and equity	<u>$19,130</u>

5.

EXPRESSIONS
Statement of Cash Flows
For Month Ended August 31

Cash flows from operating activities
    Cash received from customers $1,855
    Cash paid for rent . . . . (500)
    Cash paid for wages . . . . <u>(125)</u>
    Net cash provided by operating activities $1,230
Cash flows from investing activities
    Cash paid for furniture . . . .   (600)
Cash flows from financing activities
    Cash investments by owner. 3,000
    Cash withdrawals by owner . . . . (900)
    Partial repayment of (long-term) note payable . . . . <u>(400)</u>
    Net cash provided by financing activities . . . .   <u>1,700</u>
Net increase in cash. $2,330
Cash balance, August 1 . . . .   <u>0</u>
Cash balance, August 31. . . . .   <u>$2,330</u>

6. Return on assets $= \dfrac{\text{Net income}}{\text{Average assets}} = \dfrac{\$1,230}{(\$18,000^* + \$19,130)/2} = \dfrac{\$1,230}{\$18,565} = \underline{\underline{6.63\%}}$

   * Uses the initial $18,000 investment as the beginning balance for the *start-up period only.*

Return and Risk Analysis

A3 Explain the relation between return and risk.

This appendix explains return and risk analysis and its role in business and accounting.

Net income is often linked to **return.** Return on assets (ROA) is stated in ratio form as income divided by assets invested. For example, banks report return from a savings account in the form of an interest return such as 4%. If we invest in a savings account or in U.S. Treasury bills, we expect a return of around 2% to 7%. We could also invest in a company's stock, or even start our own business. How do we decide among these investment options? The answer depends on our trade-off between return and risk.

Risk is the uncertainty about the return we will earn. All business investments involve risk, but some investments involve more risk than others. The lower the risk of an investment, the lower is our expected return. The reason that savings accounts pay such a low return is the low risk of not being repaid with interest (the government guarantees most savings accounts from default). If we buy a share of eBay or any other company, we might obtain a large return. However, we have no guarantee of any return; there is even the risk of loss.

The bar graph in Exhibit 1A.1 shows recent returns for 10-year bonds with different risks. *Bonds* are written promises by organizations to repay amounts loaned with interest. U.S. Treasury bonds provide a low expected return, but they also offer low risk since they are backed by the U.S. government. High-risk corporate bonds offer a much larger potential return but with much higher risk.

The trade-off between return and risk is a normal part of business. Higher risk implies higher, but riskier, expected returns. To help us make better decisions, we use accounting information to assess both return and risk.

EXHIBIT 1A.1

Average Returns for Bonds with Different Risks

Business Activities and the Accounting Equation

This appendix explains how the accounting equation is derived from business activities.

There are three major types of business activities: financing, investing, and operating. Each of these requires planning. *Planning* involves defining an organization's ideas, goals, and actions. Most public corporations use the *Management Discussion and Analysis* section in their annual reports to communicate plans. However, planning is not cast in stone. This adds *risk* to both setting plans and analyzing them.

C5 Identify and describe the three major activities of organizations.

Financing   *Financing activities* provide the means organizations use to pay for resources such as land, buildings, and equipment to carry out plans. Organizations are careful in acquiring and managing financing activities because they can determine success or failure. The two sources of financing are owner and nonowner. *Owner financing* refers to resources contributed by the owner along with any income the owner leaves in the organization. *Nonowner* (or *creditor*) *financing* refers to resources contributed by creditors (lenders). *Financial management* is the task of planning how to obtain these resources and to set the right mix between owner and creditor financing.

Point: Management must understand accounting data to set financial goals, make financing and investing decisions, and evaluate operating performance.

Investing   *Investing activities* are the acquiring and disposing of resources (assets) that an organization uses to acquire and sell its products or services. Assets are funded by an organization's financing. Organizations differ on the amount and makeup of assets. Some require land and factories to operate. Others need only an office. Determining the amount and type of assets for operations is called *asset management*. Invested

Point: Investing (assets) and financing (liabilities plus equity) totals are *always* equal.

amounts are referred to as *assets*. Financing is made up of creditor and owner financing, which hold claims on assets. Creditors' claims are called *liabilities*, and the owner's claim is called *equity*. This basic equality is called the *accounting equation* and can be written as: Assets = Liabilities + Equity.

EXHIBIT 1B.1

Activities of Organizations

Operating   *Operating activities* involve using resources to research, develop, purchase, produce, distribute, and market products and services. Sales and revenues are the inflow of assets from selling products and services. Costs and expenses are the outflow of assets to support operating activities. *Strategic management* is the process of determining the right mix of operating activities for the type of organization, its plans, and its market.

Exhibit 1B.1 summarizes business activities. Planning is part of each activity and gives them meaning and focus. Investing (assets) and financing (liabilities and equity) are set opposite each other to stress their balance. Operating activities are below investing and financing activities to show that operating activities are the result of investing and financing.

Summary   *← A **Summary** organized by learning objectives concludes each chapter.*

C1   **Explain the purpose and importance of accounting.** Accounting is an information and measurement system that aims to identify, record, and communicate relevant, reliable, and comparable information about business activities. It helps assess opportunities, products, investments, and social and community responsibilities.

C2   **Identify users and uses of, and opportunities in, accounting.** Users of accounting are both internal and external. Some users and uses of accounting include (a) managers in controlling, monitoring, and planning; (b) lenders for measuring the risk and return of loans; (c) shareholders for assessing the return and risk of stock; (d) directors for overseeing management; and (e) employees for judging employment opportunities. Opportunities in accounting include financial, managerial, and tax accounting. They also include accounting-related fields such as lending, consulting, managing, and planning.

C3   **Explain why ethics are crucial to accounting.** The goal of accounting is to provide useful information for decision making. For information to be useful, it must be trusted. This demands ethical behavior in accounting.

C4   **Explain generally accepted accounting principles and define and apply several accounting principles.** Generally accepted accounting principles are a common set of standards applied by accountants. Accounting principles aid in producing relevant, reliable, and comparable information. Four principles underlying financial statements were introduced: cost, revenue recognition, matching, and full disclosure. Financial statements also reflect four assumptions: going-concern, monetary unit, time period, and business entity.

C5[B]   **Identify and describe the three major activities of organizations.** Organizations carry out three major activities: financing, investing, and operating. Financing is the means used to pay for resources such as land, buildings, and machines. Investing

refers to the buying and selling of resources used in acquiring and selling products and services. Operating activities are those necessary for carrying out the organization's plans.

A1   **Define and interpret the accounting equation and each of its components.** The accounting equation is: Assets = Liabilities + Equity. Assets are resources owned by a company. Liabilities are creditors' claims on assets. Equity is the owner's claim on assets (*the residual*). The expanded accounting equation is: Assets = Liabilities + [Owner Capital − Owner Withdrawals + Revenues − Expenses].

A2   **Compute and interpret return on assets.** Return on assets is computed as net income divided by average assets. For example, if we have an average balance of $100 in a savings account and it earns $5 interest for the year, the return on assets is $5/$100, or 5%.

A3[A]   **Explain the relation between return and risk.** *Return* refers to income, and *risk* is the uncertainty about the return we hope to make. All investments involve risk. The lower the risk of an investment, the lower is its expected return. Higher risk implies higher, but riskier, expected return.

P1   **Analyze business transactions using the accounting equation.** A *transaction* is an exchange of economic consideration between two parties. Examples include exchanges of products, services, money, and rights to collect money. Transactions always have at least two effects on one or more components of the accounting equation. This equation is always in balance.

P2   **Identify and prepare basic financial statements and explain how they interrelate.** Four financial statements report on an organization's activities: balance sheet, income statement, statement of owner's equity, and statement of cash flows.

Guidance Answers to Decision Maker and Decision Ethics

Entrepreneur   (p. 13) You should probably form the business as a corporation if potential lawsuits are of prime concern. The corporate form of organization protects your personal property from lawsuits

directed at the business and places only the corporation's resources at risk. A downside of the corporate form is double taxation: The corporation must pay taxes on its income, and you normally must pay taxes on any money distributed to you from the business (even though the corporation already paid taxes on this money). You should also examine the ethical and socially responsible aspects of starting a business in which you anticipate injuries to others. Formation as an LLC or S corp. should also be explored.

Business Owner   (p. 24) The 19% return on assets for the manufacturer exceeds the 14% industry return (and many others). This is a positive factor for a potential purchase. Also, the purchase of this manufacturer is an opportunity to spread your risk over two businesses as opposed to one. Still, you should hesitate to purchase a business whose return of 19% is lower than your current resort's return of 21%. You are probably better off directing efforts to increase investment in your resort, assuming you can continue to earn a 21% return.

Guidance Answers to Quick Checks

1. Accounting is an information and measurement system that identifies, records, and communicates relevant information to help people make better decisions.

2. Recordkeeping, also called *bookkeeping,* is the recording of financial transactions and events, either manually or electronically. Recordkeeping is essential to data reliability; but accounting is this and much more. Accounting includes identifying, measuring, recording, reporting, and analyzing business events and transactions.

3. Technology offers increased accuracy, speed, efficiency, and convenience in accounting.

4. External users of accounting include lenders, shareholders, directors, customers, suppliers, regulators, lawyers, brokers, and the press. Internal users of accounting include managers, officers, and other internal decision makers involved with strategic and operating decisions.

5. Internal users (managers) include those from research and development, purchasing, human resources, production, distribution, marketing, and servicing.

6. Internal controls are procedures set up to protect assets, ensure reliable accounting reports, promote efficiency, and encourage adherence to company policies. Internal controls are crucial for relevant and reliable information.

7. Ethical guidelines are threefold: (1) identify ethical concerns using personal ethics, (2) analyze options considering all good and bad consequences, and (3) make ethical decisions after weighing all consequences.

8. Ethics and social responsibility yield good behavior, and they often result in higher income and a better working environment.

9. For accounting to provide useful information for decisions, it must be trusted. Trust requires ethics in accounting.

10. Two major participants in setting rules include the SEC and the FASB. (*Note:* Accounting rules reflect society's needs, not those of accountants or any other single constituency.)

11. Most U.S. companies are not directly affected by international accounting standards. International standards are put forth as preferred accounting practices. However, stock exchanges and other parties are increasing the pressure to narrow differences in worldwide accounting practices. International accounting standards are playing an important role in that process.

12. The objectivity concept and cost principle are related in that most users consider information based on cost as objective. Information prepared using both is considered highly reliable and often relevant.

13. Users desire information about the performance of a specific entity. If information is mixed between two or more entities, its usefulness decreases.

14. The revenue recognition principle gives preparers guidelines on when to recognize (record) revenue. This is important; for example, if revenue is recognized too early, the statements report revenue sooner than it should and the business looks more profitable than it is. The reverse is also true.

15. The three basic forms of business organization are sole proprietorships, partnerships, and corporations.

16. Owners of corporations are called *shareholders* (or *stockholders*). Corporate ownership is divided into units called *shares* (or *stock*). The most basic of corporate shares is common stock (or capital stock).

17. The accounting equation is: Assets = Liabilities + Equity. This equation is always in balance, both before and after each transaction.

18. A transaction that changes the makeup of assets would not affect liability and equity accounts. FastForward's transactions 2 and 3 are examples. Each exchanges one asset for another.

19. Earning revenue by performing services, as in FastForward's transaction 5, increases equity (and assets). Incurring expenses while servicing clients, such as in transactions 6 and 7, decreases equity (and assets). Other examples include owner investments that increase equity and withdrawals that decrease equity.

20. Paying a liability with an asset reduces both asset and liability totals. One example is FastForward's transaction 10 that reduces a payable by paying cash.

21. An income statement reports a company's revenues and expenses along with the resulting net income or loss. A statement of owner's equity shows changes in equity, including that from net income or loss. Both statements report transactions occurring over a period of time.

22. The balance sheet describes a company's financial position (assets, liabilities, and equity) at a point in time. The equity amount in the balance sheet is obtained from the statement of owner's equity.

23. Cash flows from operating activities report cash receipts and payments from the primary business the company engages in. Cash flows from investing activities involve cash transactions from buying and selling long-term assets. Cash flows from financing activities include long-term cash borrowings and repayments to lenders and the cash investments from and withdrawals by the owner.

A list of key terms with page references concludes each chapter (a complete glossary is at the end of the book).

Key Terms

Accounting (p. 4)

Accounting equation (p. 15)

Assets (p. 15)

Audit (p. 13)

Auditors (p. 13)

Balance sheet (p. 20)

Bookkeeping (p. 4)

Business entity assumption (p. 12)

Common stock (p. 13)

Conceptual framework (p. 10)

Corporation (p. 12)

Cost-benefit constraint (p. 13)

Cost principle (p. 11)

Dodd-Frank Wall Street Reform and Consumer Protection Act (p. 14)

Equity (p. 15)

Ethics (p. 7)

Events (p. 16)

Expanded accounting equation (p. 15)

Expense recognition principle (p. 11)

Expenses (p. 15)

External transactions (p. 16)

External users (p. 5)

Financial accounting (p. 5)

Financial Accounting Standards Board (FASB) (p. 9)

Full disclosure principle (p. 11)

Generally accepted accounting principles (GAAP) (p. 9)

Going-concern assumption (p. 12)

Income statement (p. 20)

Internal transactions (p. 16)

Internal users (p. 6)

International Accounting Standards Board (IASB) (p. 9)

International Financial Reporting Standards (IFRS) (p. 9)

Liabilities (p. 15)

Managerial accounting (p. 6)

Matching principle (p. 11)

Materiality constraint (p. 13)

Measurement principle (p. 11)

Monetary unit assumption (p. 12)

Net income (p. 15)

Net loss (p. 15)

Owner, Capital (p. 15)

Owner investment (p. 15)

Owner withdrawals (p. 15)

Partnership (p. 12)

Proprietorship (p. 12)

Recordkeeping (p. 4)

Return (p. 27)

Return on assets (p. 24)

Revenue recognition principle (p. 11)

Revenues (p. 15)

Risk (p. 27)

Sarbanes–Oxley Act (p. 13)

Securities and Exchange Commission (SEC) (p. 9)

Shareholders (p. 13)

Shares (p. 13)

Sole proprietorship (p. 12)

Statement of cash flows (p. 20)

Statement of owner's equity (p. 20)

Stock (p. 13)

Stockholders (p. 13)

Time period assumption (p. 12)

Withdrawals (p. 15)

Multiple Choice Quiz   Answers on p. 47   mhhe.com/wildFAP21e

Additional Quiz Questions are available at the book's Website.

1. A building is offered for sale at $500,000 but is currently assessed at $400,000. The purchaser of the building believes the building is worth $475,000, but ultimately purchases the building for $450,000. The purchaser records the building at:
   a. $50,000
   b. $400,000
   c. $450,000
   d. $475,000
   e. $500,000

2. On December 30, 2012, **KPMG** signs a $150,000 contract to provide accounting services to one of its clients in 2013. KPMG has a December 31 year-end. Which accounting principle or assumption requires KPMG to record the accounting services revenue from this client in 2013 and not 2012?
   a. Business entity assumption
   b. Revenue recognition principle
   c. Monetary unit assumption
   d. Cost principle
   e. Going-concern assumption

3. If the assets of a company increase by $100,000 during the year and its liabilities increase by $35,000 during the same year, then the change in equity of the company during the year must have been:
   a. An increase of $135,000.
   b. A decrease of $135,000.
   c. A decrease of $65,000.
   d. An increase of $65,000.
   e. An increase of $100,000.

4. **Brunswick** borrows $50,000 cash from Third National Bank. How does this transaction affect the accounting equation for Brunswick?
   a. Assets increase by $50,000; liabilities increase by $50,000; no effect on equity.
   b. Assets increase by $50,000; no effect on liabilities; equity increases by $50,000.
   c. Assets increase by $50,000; liabilities decrease by $50,000; no effect on equity.
   d. No effect on assets; liabilities increase by $50,000; equity increases by $50,000.
   e. No effect on assets; liabilities increase by $50,000; equity decreases by $50,000.

5. **Geek Squad** performs services for a customer and bills the customer for $500. How would Geek Squad record this transaction?
   a. Accounts receivable increase by $500; revenues increase by $500.
   b. Cash increases by $500; revenues increase by $500.
   c. Accounts receivable increase by $500; revenues decrease by $500.
   d. Accounts receivable increase by $500; accounts payable increase by $500.
   e. Accounts payable increase by $500; revenues increase by $500.

A(B) *Superscript letter A (B) denotes assignments based on Appendix 1A (1B).*
🔔 Icon denotes assignments that involve decision making.

Discussion Questions

1. What is the purpose of accounting in society?
2. Technology is increasingly used to process accounting data. Why then must we study and understand accounting?
3. 🔔 Identify four kinds of external users and describe how they use accounting information.
4. 🔔 What are at least three questions business owners and managers might be able to answer by looking at accounting information?
5. Identify three actual businesses that offer services and three actual businesses that offer products.
6. 🔔 Describe the internal role of accounting for organizations.
7. Identify three types of services typically offered by accounting professionals.
8. 🔔 What type of accounting information might be useful to the marketing managers of a business?
9. Why is accounting described as a service activity?
10. What are some accounting-related professions?
11. How do ethics rules affect auditors' choice of clients?
12. What work do tax accounting professionals perform in addition to preparing tax returns?
13. What does the concept of *objectivity* imply for information reported in financial statements? Why?
14. A business reports its own office stationery on the balance sheet at its $400 cost, although it cannot be sold for more than $10 as scrap paper. Which accounting principle and/or assumption justifies this treatment?
15. Why is the revenue recognition principle needed? What does it demand?
16. Describe the three basic forms of business organization and their key attributes.
17. Define (a) assets, (b) liabilities, (c) equity, and (d) net assets.
18. What events or transactions change equity?
19. Identify the two main categories of accounting principles.
20. What do accountants mean by the term *revenue?*
21. Define *net income* and explain its computation.
22. Identify the four basic financial statements of a business.
23. 🔔 What information is reported in an income statement?
24. Give two examples of expenses a business might incur.
25. What is the purpose of the statement of owner's equity?
26. 🔔 What information is reported in a balance sheet?
27. The statement of cash flows reports on what major activities?
28. 🔔 Define and explain return on assets.
29.A🔔 Define return and risk. Discuss the trade-off between them.
30.B Describe the three major business activities in organizations.
31.B Explain why investing (assets) and financing (liabilities and equity) totals are always equal.
32. Refer to the financial statements of **Polaris** in Appendix A near the end of the book. To what level of significance are dollar amounts rounded? What time period does its income statement cover?   **Polaris**
33. Identify the dollar amounts of **Arctic Cat**'s 2011 assets, liabilities, and equity as reported in its statements in Appendix A near the end of the book.   **Arctic Cat**
34. Refer to **KTM**'s 2011 balance sheet in Appendix A near the end of the book. Confirm that its total assets equal its total liabilities plus total equity.   **KTM**
35. 🔔 Access the SEC EDGAR database (**www.sec.gov**) and retrieve **Polaris**' 2011 10-K (filed February 27, 2012). Identify its auditor. What responsibility does its independent auditor claim regarding Polaris' financial statements?   **Polaris**

Connect reproduces assignments online, in static or algorithmic mode, which allows instructors to monitor, promote, and assess student learning. It can be used for practice, homework, or exams.

Quick Study exercises give readers a brief test of key elements.

🅼🅶🅷 **connect** ──────────────────────────

Reading and interpreting accounting reports requires some knowledge of accounting terminology. (a) Identify the meaning of these accounting-related acronyms: GAAP, SEC, FASB, IASB and IFRS. (b) Briefly explain the importance of the knowledge base or organization that is referred to for each of the accounting-related acronyms.

QUICK STUDY

QS 1-1
Identifying accounting terms   C1

QS 1-2

Identifying accounting users

C2

Identify the following users as either external users (E) or internal users (I).

a. Customers	**d.** Business press	**g.** Shareholders	**j.** FBI and IRS
b. Suppliers	**e.** Managers	**h.** Lenders	**k.** Consumer group
c. Brokers	**f.** District attorney	**i.** Controllers	**l.** Sales staff

---

QS 1-3

Explaining internal control

C1

An important responsibility of many accounting professionals is to design and implement internal control procedures for organizations. Explain the purpose of internal control procedures. Provide two examples of internal controls applied by companies.

QS 1-4

Accounting opportunities   C2

There are many job opportunities for those with accounting knowledge. Identify at least three main areas of opportunities for accounting professionals. For each area, identify at least three job possibilities linked to accounting.

QS 1-5

Identifying ethical concerns   C3

This icon highlights assignments that enhance decision-making skills.

Accounting professionals must sometimes choose between two or more acceptable methods of accounting for business transactions and events. Explain why these situations can involve difficult matters of ethical concern.

QS 1-6

Identifying accounting principles

C4

Identify which accounting principle or assumption best describes each of the following practices:

a. In December 2012, Chavez Landscaping received a customer's order and cash prepayment to install sod at a new house that would not be ready for installation until March 2013. Chavez should record the revenue from the customer order in March 2013, not in December 2012.

b. If $51,000 cash is paid to buy land, the land is reported on the buyer's balance sheet at $51,000.

c. Jo Keene owns both Sailing Passions and Dockside Supplies. In preparing financial statements for Dockside Supplies, Keene makes sure that the expense transactions of Sailing Passions are kept separate from Dockside's transactions and financial statements.

QS 1-7

Applying the accounting equation   A1

a. Total assets of Charter Company equal $700,000 and its equity is $420,000. What is the amount of its liabilities?

b. Total assets of Martin Marine equal $500,000 and its liabilities and equity amounts are equal to each other. What is the amount of its liabilities? What is the amount of its equity?

QS 1-8

Applying the accounting equation

A1

Use the accounting equation to compute the missing financial statement amounts (*a*), (*b*), and (*c*).

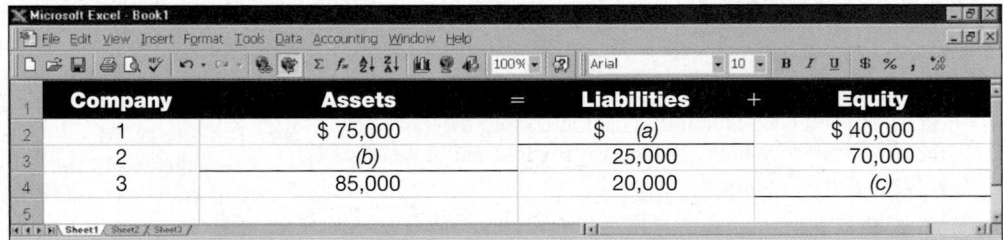

Company	Assets	=	Liabilities	+	Equity
1	$ 75,000		$ *(a)*		$ 40,000
2	*(b)*		25,000		70,000
3	85,000		20,000		*(c)*

QS 1-9

Identifying transactions and events   P1

Accounting provides information about an organization's business transactions and events that both affect the accounting equation and can be reliably measured. Identify at least two examples of both (*a*) business transactions and (*b*) business events that meet these requirements.

QS 1-10

Identifying and computing assets, liabilities, and equity   P1

Polaris

Use **Polaris'** December 31, 2011, financial statements, in Appendix A near the end of the book, to answer the following:

a. Identify the dollar amounts of Polaris' 2011 (1) assets, (2) liabilities, and (3) equity.

b. Using Polaris' amounts from part *a*, verify that Assets = Liabilities + Equity.

QS 1-11

Identifying items with financial statements

P2

Indicate in which financial statement each item would most likely appear: income statement (I), balance sheet (B), statement of owner's equity (E), or statement of cash flows (CF).

a. Assets	**d.** Equipment	**g.** Net decrease (or increase) in cash
b. Cash from operating activities	**e.** Expenses	**h.** Revenues
c. Withdrawals	**f.** Liabilities	**i.** Total liabilities and equity

In a recent year's financial statements, **Home Depot** reported the following results. Compute and interpret Home Depot's return on assets (assume competitors average a 8.0% return on assets).

Sales	$67,997 million
Net income	3,338 million
Average total assets	40,501 million

QS 1-12
Computing and interpreting return on assets

A2

Answer each of the following questions related to international accounting standards.

a. The International Accounting Standards Board (IASB) issues preferred accounting practices that are referred to as what?

b. The FASB and IASB are working on a convergence process for what purpose?

c. The SEC has proposed a roadmap for use of IFRS by U.S. companies. What is the proposed time period (as suggested by the SEC) for the FASB to endorse IFRS (with necessary exceptions) as U.S. GAAP?

QS 1-13
International accounting standards C4

 ← *This icon highlights assignments that focus on IFRS-related content.*

connect

Many accounting professionals work in one of the following three areas:

A. Managerial accounting   **B.** Financial accounting   **C.** Tax accounting

Identify the area of accounting that is most involved in each of the following responsibilities:

_____ **1.** Internal auditing.   _____ **5.** Investigating violations of tax laws.

_____ **2.** External auditing.   _____ **6.** Planning transactions to minimize taxes.

_____ **3.** Cost accounting.   _____ **7.** Preparing external financial statements.

_____ **4.** Budgeting.   _____ **8.** Reviewing reports for SEC compliance.

EXERCISES

Exercise 1-1
Describing accounting responsibilities

C2

Accounting is an information and measurement system that identifies, records, and communicates relevant, reliable, and comparable information about an organization's business activities. Classify the following activities as part of the identifying (I), recording (R), or communicating (C) aspects of accounting.

_____ **1.** Analyzing and interpreting reports.

_____ **2.** Presenting financial information.

_____ **3.** Maintaining a log of service costs.

_____ **4.** Measuring the costs of a product.

_____ **5.** Preparing financial statements.

_____ **6.** Establishing revenues generated from a product.

_____ **7.** Determining employee tasks behind a service.

Exercise 1-2
Classifying activities reflected in the accounting system

C1

Part A. Identify the following users of accounting information as either an internal (I) or an external (E) user.

_____ **1.** Research and development director

_____ **2.** Human resources director

_____ **3.** Nonexecutive employee

_____ **4.** Shareholders

_____ **5.** Distribution managers

_____ **6.** Creditors

_____ **7.** Production supervisors

_____ **8.** Purchasing manager

Exercise 1-3
Identifying accounting users and uses

C2

Part B. Identify the following questions as most likely to be asked by an internal (I) or an external (E) user of accounting information.

_____ **1.** What are reasonable payroll benefits and wages?

_____ **2.** Should we make a five-year loan to that business?

_____ **3.** What are the costs of our product's ingredients?

_____ **4.** Do income levels justify the current stock price?

_____ **5.** Should we spend further research on our product?

_____ **6.** Which firm reports the highest sales and income?

_____ **7.** What are the costs of our service to customers?

Assume the following role and describe a situation in which ethical considerations play an important part in guiding your decisions and actions:

a. You are a student in an introductory accounting course.

b. You are a manager with responsibility for several employees.

c. You are an accounting professional preparing tax returns for clients.

d. You are an accounting professional with audit clients that are competitors in business.

Exercise 1-4
Identifying ethical concerns

C3

Exercise 1-5
Identifying accounting principles and assumptions
C4

Match each of the numbered descriptions with the principle or assumption it best reflects. Enter the letter for the appropriate principle or assumption in the blank space next to each description.

A. General accounting principle   **E.** Specific accounting principle
B. Cost principle   **F.** Matching principle
C. Business entity assumption   **G.** Going-concern assumption
D. Revenue recognition principle   **H.** Full disclosure principle

_____ **1.** Usually created by a pronouncement from an authoritative body.
_____ **2.** Financial statements reflect the assumption that the business continues operating.
_____ **3.** Derived from long-used and generally accepted accounting practices.
_____ **4.** Every business is accounted for separately from its owner or owners.
_____ **5.** Revenue is recorded only when the earnings process is complete.
_____ **6.** Information is based on actual costs incurred in transactions.
_____ **7.** A company records the expenses incurred to generate the revenues reported.
_____ **8.** A company reports details behind financial statements that would impact users' decisions.

Exercise 1-6
Learning the language of business
C1–C3

Match each of the numbered descriptions with the term or phrase it best reflects. Indicate your answer by writing the letter for the term or phrase in the blank provided.

A. Audit   **C.** Ethics   **E.** SEC   **G.** Net income
B. GAAP   **D.** Tax accounting   **F.** Public accountants   **H.** IASB

_____ **1.** Principles that determine whether an action is right or wrong.
_____ **2.** Accounting professionals who provide services to many clients.
_____ **3.** An accounting area that includes planning future transactions to minimize taxes paid.
_____ **4.** An examination of an organization's accounting system and records that adds credibility to financial statements.
_____ **5.** Amount a business earns after paying all expenses and costs associated with its sales and revenues.

Exercise 1-7
Distinguishing business organizations
C4

The following describe several different business organizations. Determine whether the description refers to a sole proprietorship, partnership, or corporation.

a. Ownership of Zander Company is divided into 1,000 shares of stock.
b. Wallingford is owned by Trent Malone, who is personally liable for the company's debts.
c. Micah Douglas and Nathan Logan own Financial Services, a financial services provider. Neither Douglas nor Logan has personal responsibility for the debts of Financial Services.
d. Riley and Kay own Speedy Packages, a courier service. Both are personally liable for the debts of the business.
e. IBC Services does not have separate legal existence apart from the one person who owns it.
f. Physio Products does not pay income taxes and has one owner.
g. AJ pays its own income taxes and has two owners.

Exercise 1-8
Using the accounting equation
A1 P1

Check (c) Beg. equity, $60,000

Answer the following questions. (*Hint:* Use the accounting equation.)

a. Office Store has assets equal to $123,000 and liabilities equal to $47,000 at year-end. What is the total equity for Office Store at year-end?
b. At the beginning of the year, Addison Company's assets are $300,000 and its equity is $100,000. During the year, assets increase $80,000 and liabilities increase $50,000. What is the equity at the end of the year?
c. At the beginning of the year, Quaker Company's liabilities equal $70,000. During the year, assets increase by $60,000, and at year-end assets equal $190,000. Liabilities decrease $5,000 during the year. What are the beginning and ending amounts of equity?

Exercise 1-9
Using the accounting equation
A1

Determine the missing amount from each of the separate situations *a*, *b*, and *c* below.

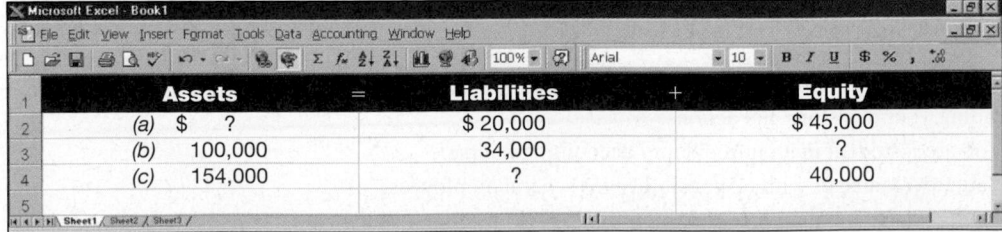

	Assets	=	Liabilities	+	Equity
(a)	$?		$ 20,000		$ 45,000
(b)	100,000		34,000		?
(c)	154,000		?		40,000

Provide an example of a transaction that creates the described effects for the separate cases *a* through *g*.

a. Decreases an asset and decreases equity.
b. Increases an asset and increases a liability.
c. Decreases a liability and increases a liability.
d. Decreases an asset and decreases a liability.
e. Increases an asset and decreases an asset.
f. Increases a liability and decreases equity.
g. Increases an asset and increases equity.

Exercise 1-10
Identifying effects of transactions on the accounting equation

P1

Lena Holden began a professional practice on June 1 and plans to prepare financial statements at the end of each month. During June, Holden (the owner) completed these transactions:

a. Owner invested $60,000 cash in the company along with equipment that had a $15,000 market value.
b. The company paid $1,500 cash for rent of office space for the month.
c. The company purchased $10,000 of additional equipment on credit (payment due within 30 days).
d. The company completed work for a client and immediately collected the $2,500 cash earned.
e. The company completed work for a client and sent a bill for $8,000 to be received within 30 days.
f. The company purchased additional equipment for $6,000 cash.
g. The company paid an assistant $3,000 cash as wages for the month.
h. The company collected $5,000 cash as a partial payment for the amount owed by the client in transaction *e*.
i. The company paid $10,000 cash to settle the liability created in transaction *c*.
j. Owner withdrew $1,000 cash from the company for personal use.

Exercise 1-11
Identifying effects of transactions using the accounting equation

P1

Required

Create a table like the one in Exhibit 1.9, using the following headings for columns: Cash; Accounts Receivable; Equipment; Accounts Payable; L. Holden, Capital; L. Holden, Withdrawals; Revenues; and Expenses. Then use additions and subtractions to show the effects of the transactions on individual items of the accounting equation. Show new balances after each transaction.

Check   Net income, $6,000

Zen began a new consulting firm on January 5. The accounting equation showed the following balances after each of the company's first five transactions. Analyze the accounting equation for each transaction and describe each of the five transactions with their amounts.

Exercise 1-12
Analysis using the accounting equation

P1

	Assets									=	Liabilities	+		Equity		
Trans-action	Cash	+	Accounts Receivable	+	Office Supplies	+	Office Furniture	=	Accounts Payable	+	Zen, Capital	+	Revenues
a.	$40,000	+	$ 0	+	$ 0	+	$ 0	=	$ 0	+	$40,000	+	$ 0
b.	38,000	+	0	+	3,000	+	0	=	1,000	+	40,000	+	0
c.	30,000	+	0	+	3,000	+	8,000	=	1,000	+	40,000	+	0
d.	30,000	+	6,000	+	3,000	+	8,000	=	1,000	+	40,000	+	6,000
e.	31,000	+	6,000	+	3,000	+	8,000	=	1,000	+	40,000	+	7,000

The following table shows the effects of five transactions (*a* through *e*) on the assets, liabilities, and equity of Trista's Boutique. Write short descriptions of the probable nature of each transaction.

Exercise 1-13
Identifying effects of transactions on accounting equation

P1

	Cash	+	Accounts Receivable	+	Office Supplies	+	Land	=	Accounts Payable	+	Trista, Capital	+	Revenues
	$ 21,000	+	$ 0	+	$3,000	+	$19,000	=	$ 0	+	$43,000	+	$ 0
a.	− 4,000					+	4,000						
b.				+	1,000				+1,000				
c.		+	1,900									+	1,900
d.	− 1,000								−1,000				
e.	+ 1,900	−	1,900										
	$ 17,900	+	$ 0	+	$4,000	+	$23,000	=	$ 0	+	$43,000	+	$1,900

Exercise 1-14
Preparing an income statement
P2

On October 1, Keisha King organized Real Answers, a new consulting firm; on October 3, the owner contributed $84,000 cash. On October 31, the company's records show the following items and amounts. Use this information to prepare an October income statement for the business.

Cash.....................	$11,360		Cash withdrawals by owner.........	$ 2,000
Accounts receivable	14,000		Consulting fees earned.............	14,000
Office supplies	3,250		Rent expense	3,550
Land.....................	46,000		Salaries expense	7,000
Office equipment	18,000		Telephone expense................	760
Accounts payable...........	8,500		Miscellaneous expenses	580
Owner investments.........	84,000			

Check Net income, $2,110

Exercise 1-15
Preparing a statement of owner's equity P2

Use the information in Exercise 1-14 to prepare an October statement of owner's equity for Real Answers.

Exercise 1-16
Preparing a balance sheet P2

Use the information in Exercise 1-14 (if completed, you can also use your solution to Exercise 1-15) to prepare an October 31 balance sheet for Real Answers.

Exercise 1-17
Preparing a statement of cash flows

P2

Use the information in Exercise 1-14 to prepare an October 31 statement of cash flows for Real Answers. Also assume the following:

a. The owner's initial investment consists of $38,000 cash and $46,000 in land.

b. The company's $18,000 equipment purchase is paid in cash.

c. The accounts payable balance of $8,500 consists of the $3,250 office supplies purchase and $5,250 in employee salaries yet to be paid.

d. The company's rent, telephone, and miscellaneous expenses are paid in cash.

Check Net increase in cash, $11,360   **e.** No cash has been collected on the $14,000 consulting fees earned.

Exercise 1-18
Analysis of return on assets
A2

Swiss Group reports net income of $40,000 for 2013. At the beginning of 2013, Swiss Group had $200,000 in assets. By the end of 2013, assets had grown to $300,000. What is Swiss Group's 2013 return on assets? How would you assess its performance if competitors average a 10% return on assets?

Exercise 1-19
Identifying sections of the statement of cash flows

P2

Indicate the section where each of the following would appear on the statement of cash flows.

O. Cash flows from operating activity
I. Cash flows from investing activity
F. Cash flows from financing activity

_____ **1.** Cash paid for advertising   _____ **5.** Cash paid for rent
_____ **2.** Cash paid for wages   _____ **6.** Cash paid on an account payable
_____ **3.** Cash withdrawal by owner   _____ **7.** Cash investment by owner
_____ **4.** Cash purchase of equipment   _____ **8.** Cash received from clients

Exercise 1-20ᴮ
Identifying business activities

C5

Match each transaction or event to one of the following activities of an organization: financing activities (F), investing activities (I), or operating activities (O).

a. _____ An owner contributes resources to the business.

b. _____ An organization sells some of its land.

c. _____ An organization purchases equipment.

d. _____ An organization advertises a new product.

e. _____ The organization borrows money from a bank.

Exercise 1-21
Preparing an income statement for a global company

P2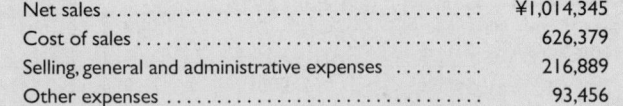

Nintendo Company reports the following income statement accounts for the year ended March 31, 2011. (Japanese yen in millions.)

Net sales.......................................	¥1,014,345
Cost of sales...................................	626,379
Selling, general and administrative expenses	216,889
Other expenses	93,456

Use this information to prepare Nintendo's income statement for the year ended March 31, 2011.

Problem Set B located at the end of Problem Set A is provided for each problem to reinforce the learning process.

connect

The following financial statement information is from five separate companies:

PROBLEM SET A

Problem 1-1A
Computing missing information using accounting knowledge

A1 P1

	Company A	Company B	Company C	Company D	Company E
December 31, 2012					
Assets....................	$55,000	$34,000	$24,000	$60,000	$119,000
Liabilities	24,500	21,500	9,000	40,000	?
December 31, 2013					
Assets....................	58,000	40,000	?	85,000	113,000
Liabilities	?	26,500	29,000	24,000	70,000
During year 2013					
Owner investments.............	6,000	1,400	9,750	?	6,500
Net income (loss)	8,500	?	8,000	14,000	20,000
Owner cash withdrawals	3,500	2,000	5,875	0	11,000

Required

1. Answer the following questions about Company A:
   a. What is the amount of equity on December 31, 2012?
   b. What is the amount of equity on December 31, 2013?
   c. What is the amount of liabilities on December 31, 2013?
2. Answer the following questions about Company B:
   a. What is the amount of equity on December 31, 2012?
   b. What is the amount of equity on December 31, 2013?
   c. What is net income for year 2013?
3. Calculate the amount of assets for Company C on December 31, 2013.
4. Calculate the amount of owner investments for Company D during year 2013.
5. Calculate the amount of liabilities for Company E on December 31, 2012.

Check   (1*b*) $41,500

(2*c*) $1,600
(3) $55,875

Identify how each of the following separate transactions affects financial statements. For the balance sheet, identify how each transaction affects total assets, total liabilities, and total equity. For the income statement, identify how each transaction affects net income. For the statement of cash flows, identify how each transaction affects cash flows from operating activities, cash flows from financing activities, and cash flows from investing activities. For increases, place a "+" in the column or columns. For decreases, place a "−" in the column or columns. If both an increase and a decrease occur, place a "+/−" in the column or columns. The first transaction is completed as an example.

Problem 1-2A
Identifying effects of transactions on financial statements

A1 P1

		Balance Sheet			Income Statement	Statement of Cash Flows		
	Transaction	Total Assets	Total Liab.	Total Equity	Net Income	Operating Activities	Financing Activities	Investing Activities
1	Owner invests cash in business	+		+			+	
2	Receives cash for services provided							
3	Pays cash for employee wages							
4	Incurs legal costs on credit							
5	Borrows cash by signing long-term note payable							
6	Owner withdraws cash							
7	Buys land by signing note payable							
8	Provides services on credit							
9	Buys office equipment for cash							
10	Collects cash on receivable from (8)							

Problem 1-3A
Preparing an income statement
P2

The following is selected financial information for Elko Energy Company for the year ended December 31, 2013: revenues, $55,000; expenses, $40,000; net income, $15,000.

Required

Prepare the 2013 calendar-year income statement for Elko Energy Company.

Problem 1-4A
Preparing a balance sheet
P2

The following is selected financial information for Amity Company as of December 31, 2013: liabilities, $44,000; equity, $46,000; assets, $90,000.

Required

Prepare the balance sheet for Amity Company as of December 31, 2013.

Problem 1-5A
Preparing a statement of cash flows
P2

Following is selected financial information of ABM Company for the year ended December 31, 2013.

Cash used by investing activities	$(2,000)
Net increase in cash	1,200
Cash used by financing activities	(2,800)
Cash from operating activities	6,000
Cash, December 31, 2012	2,300

Check   Cash balance, Dec. 31, 2013, $3,500

Required

Prepare the 2013 statement of cash flows for ABM Company.

Problem 1-6A
Preparing a statement of owner's equity
P2

Following is selected financial information for Kasio Co. for the year ended December 31, 2013.

K. Kasio, Capital, Dec. 31, 2013	$14,000	K. Kasio, Withdrawals.	$1,000
Net income	8,000	K. Kasio, Capital, Dec. 31, 2012.	7,000

Required

Prepare the 2013 statement of owner's equity for Kasio.

Problem 1-7A
Analyzing transactions and preparing financial statements
C4 P1 P2

mhhe.com/wildFAP21e

Holden Graham started The Graham Co., a new business that began operations on May 1. The Graham Co. completed the following transactions during its first month of operations.

May 1   H. Graham invested $40,000 cash in the company.
1   The company rented a furnished office and paid $2,200 cash for May's rent.
3   The company purchased $1,890 of office equipment on credit.
5   The company paid $750 cash for this month's cleaning services.
8   The company provided consulting services for a client and immediately collected $5,400 cash.
12   The company provided $2,500 of consulting services for a client on credit.
15   The company paid $750 cash for an assistant's salary for the first half of this month.
20   The company received $2,500 cash payment for the services provided on May 12.
22   The company provided $3,200 of consulting services on credit.
25   The company received $3,200 cash payment for the services provided on May 22.
26   The company paid $1,890 cash for the office equipment purchased on May 3.
27   The company purchased $80 of advertising in this month's (May) local paper on credit; cash payment is due June 1.
28   The company paid $750 cash for an assistant's salary for the second half of this month.
30   The company paid $300 cash for this month's telephone bill.
30   The company paid $280 cash for this month's utilities.
31   H. Graham withdrew $1,400 cash from the company for personal use.

Required

1. Arrange the following asset, liability, and equity titles in a table like Exhibit 1.9: Cash; Accounts Receivable; Office Equipment; Accounts Payable; H. Graham, Capital; H. Graham, Withdrawals; Revenues; and Expenses.

2. Show effects of the transactions on the accounts of the accounting equation by recording increases and decreases in the appropriate columns. Do not determine new account balances after each transaction. Determine the final total for each account and verify that the equation is in balance.

3. Prepare an income statement for May, a statement of owner's equity for May, a May 31 balance sheet, and a statement of cash flows for May.

Check (2) Ending balances: Cash, $42,780; Expenses, $5,110

(3) Net income, $5,990; Total assets, $44,670

Helga Ander started a new business and completed these transactions during December.

Problem 1-8A
Analyzing transactions and preparing financial statements

C4 P1 P2

mhhe.com/wildFAP21e

Dec. 1 Helga Ander transferred $65,000 cash from a personal savings account to a checking account in the name of Ander Electric.
2 The company rented office space and paid $1,000 cash for the December rent.
3 The company purchased $13,000 of electrical equipment by paying $4,800 cash and agreeing to pay the $8,200 balance in 30 days.
5 The company purchased office supplies by paying $800 cash.
6 The company completed electrical work and immediately collected $1,200 cash for these services.
8 The company purchased $2,530 of office equipment on credit.
15 The company completed electrical work on credit in the amount of $5,000.
18 The company purchased $350 of office supplies on credit.
20 The company paid $2,530 cash for the office equipment purchased on December 8.
24 The company billed a client $900 for electrical work completed; the balance is due in 30 days.
28 The company received $5,000 cash for the work completed on December 15.
29 The company paid the assistant's salary of $1,400 cash for this month.
30 The company paid $540 cash for this month's utility bill.
31 H. Ander withdrew $950 cash from the company for personal use.

Required

1. Arrange the following asset, liability, and equity titles in a table like Exhibit 1.9: Cash; Accounts Receivable; Office Supplies; Office Equipment; Electrical Equipment; Accounts Payable; H. Ander, Capital; H. Ander, Withdrawals; Revenues; and Expenses.

2. Use additions and subtractions to show the effects of each transaction on the accounts in the accounting equation. Show new balances after each transaction.

3. Use the increases and decreases in the columns of the table from part 2 to prepare an income statement, a statement of owner's equity, and a statement of cash flows—each of these for the current month. Also prepare a balance sheet as of the end of the month.

Check (2) Ending balances: Cash, $59,180, Accounts Payable, $8,550

(3) Net income, $4,160; Total assets, $76,760

Analysis Component

4. Assume that the owner investment transaction on December 1 was $49,000 cash instead of $65,000 and that Ander Electric obtained another $16,000 in cash by borrowing it from a bank. Explain the effect of this change on total assets, total liabilities, and total equity.

Isabel Lopez started Biz Consulting, a new business, and completed the following transactions during its first year of operations.

Problem 1-9A
Analyzing effects of transactions

C4 P1 P2 A1

a. I. Lopez invests $70,000 cash and office equipment valued at $10,000 in the company.

b. The company purchased a $150,000 building to use as an office. Biz paid $20,000 in cash and signed a note payable promising to pay the $130,000 balance over the next ten years.

c. The company purchased office equipment for $15,000 cash.

d. The company purchased $1,200 of office supplies and $1,700 of office equipment on credit.

e. The company paid a local newspaper $500 cash for printing an announcement of the office's opening.

f. The company completed a financial plan for a client and billed that client $2,800 for the service.

g. The company designed a financial plan for another client and immediately collected an $4,000 cash fee.

h. Lopez withdrew $3,275 cash from the company for personal use.

i. The company received $1,800 cash as partial payment from the client described in transaction f.

j. The company made a partial payment of $700 cash on the equipment purchased in transaction d.

k. The company paid $1,800 cash for the office secretary's wages for this period.

Required

1. Create a table like the one in Exhibit 1.9, using the following headings for the columns: Cash; Accounts Receivable; Office Supplies; Office Equipment; Building; Accounts Payable; Notes Payable; I. Lopez, Capital; I. Lopez, Withdrawals; Revenues; and Expenses.

Check   (2) Ending balances: Cash, $34,525; Expenses, $2,300; Notes Payable, $130,000

          (3) Net income, $4,500

2. Use additions and subtractions within the table created in part *1* to show the dollar effects of each transaction on individual items of the accounting equation. Show new balances after each transaction.

3. Once you have completed the table, determine the company's net income.

Problem 1-10A
Computing and interpreting return on assets

A2

Coca-Cola and PepsiCo both produce and market beverages that are direct competitors. Key financial figures (in $ millions) for these businesses over the past year follow.

Key Figures ($ millions)	Coca-Cola	PepsiCo
Sales	$46,542	$66,504
Net income	8,634	6,462
Average assets	76,448	70,518

Required

Check   (1*a*) 11.3%; (1*b*) 9.2%

1. Compute return on assets for (*a*) Coca-Cola and (*b*) PepsiCo.

2. Which company is more successful in its total amount of sales to consumers?

3. Which company is more successful in returning net income from its assets invested?

Analysis Component

4. Write a one-paragraph memorandum explaining which company you would invest your money in and why. (Limit your explanation to the information provided.)

Problem 1-11A
Determining expenses, liabilities, equity, and return on assets

A1   A2

Kyzera manufactures, markets, and sells cellular telephones. The average total assets for Kyzera is $250,000. In its most recent year, Kyzera reported net income of $65,000 on revenues of $475,000.

Required

1. What is Kyzera's return on assets?

2. Does return on assets seem satisfactory for Kyzera given that its competitors average a 12% return on assets?

Check   (3) $410,000
        (4) $250,000

3. What are total expenses for Kyzera in its most recent year?

4. What is the average total amount of liabilities plus equity for Kyzera?

Problem 1-12A[A]
Identifying risk and return

A3

All business decisions involve aspects of risk and return.

Required

Identify both the risk and the return in each of the following activities:

1. Investing $2,000 in a 5% savings account.

2. Placing a $2,500 bet on your favorite sports team.

3. Investing $10,000 in Yahoo! stock.

4. Taking out a $7,500 college loan to earn an accounting degree.

Problem 1-13A[B]
Describing organizational activities

C5

A start-up company often engages in the following transactions in its first year of operations. Classify those transactions in one of the three major categories of an organization's business activities.

F. Financing   **I.** Investing   **O.** Operating

_____ **1.** Owner investing land in business.   _____ **5.** Purchasing equipment.

_____ **2.** Purchasing a building.   _____ **6.** Selling and distributing products.

_____ **3.** Purchasing land.   _____ **7.** Paying for advertising.

_____ **4.** Borrowing cash from a bank.   _____ **8.** Paying employee wages.

Problem 1-14A[B]
Describing organizational activities   C5

An organization undertakes various activities in pursuit of business success. Identify an organization's three major business activities, and describe each activity.

The following financial statement information is from five separate companies.

PROBLEM SET B

	Company V	Company W	Company X	Company Y	Company Z
December 31, 2012					
Assets......................	$54,000	$80,000	$141,500	$92,500	$144,000
Liabilities	25,000	60,000	68,500	51,500	?
December 31, 2013					
Assets......................	59,000	100,000	186,500	?	170,000
Liabilities	36,000	?	65,800	42,000	42,000
During year 2013					
Owner investments	5,000	20,000	?	48,100	60,000
Net income or (loss)............	?	40,000	18,500	24,000	32,000
Owner cash withdrawals.........	5,500	2,000	0	20,000	8,000

Problem 1-1B
Computing missing information using accounting knowledge

A1 P1

Required

1. Answer the following questions about Company V:
   a. What is the amount of equity on December 31, 2012?
   b. What is the amount of equity on December 31, 2013?
   c. What is the net income or loss for the year 2013?
2. Answer the following questions about Company W:
   a. What is the amount of equity on December 31, 2012?
   b. What is the amount of equity on December 31, 2013?
   c. What is the amount of liabilities on December 31, 2013?
3. Calculate the amount of owner investments for Company X during 2013.
4. Calculate the amount of assets for Company Y on December 31, 2013.
5. Calculate the amount of liabilities for Company Z on December 31, 2012.

Check (1*b*) $23,000

(2*c*) $22,000

(4) $135,100

Identify how each of the following separate transactions affects financial statements. For the balance sheet, identify how each transaction affects total assets, total liabilities, and total equity. For the income statement, identify how each transaction affects net income. For the statement of cash flows, identify how each transaction affects cash flows from operating activities, cash flows from financing activities, and cash flows from investing activities. For increases, place a "+" in the column or columns. For decreases, place a "−" in the column or columns. If both an increase and a decrease occur, place "+/−" in the column or columns. The first transaction is completed as an example.

Problem 1-2B
Identifying effects of transactions on financial statements A1 P1

		Balance Sheet			Income Statement	Statement of Cash Flows		
	Transaction	**Total Assets**	**Total Liab.**	**Total Equity**	**Net Income**	**Operating Activities**	**Financing Activities**	**Investing Activities**
1	Owner invests cash in business	+		+			+	
2	Buys building by signing note payable							
3	Pays cash for salaries incurred							
4	Provides services for cash							
5	Pays cash for rent incurred							
6	Incurs utilities costs on credit							
7	Buys store equipment for cash							
8	Owner withdraws cash							
9	Provides services on credit							
10	Collects cash on receivable from (9)							

Problem 1-3B
Preparing an income
statement
P2

Selected financial information for Offshore Co. for the year ended December 31, 2013, follows.

Revenues	$68,000	Expenses	$40,000	Net income	$28,000

Required

Prepare the 2013 income statement for Offshore Company.

Problem 1-4B
Preparing a balance sheet
P2

The following is selected financial information for TLC Company as of December 31, 2013.

Liabilities	$64,000	Equity	$50,000	Assets	$114,000

Required

Prepare the balance sheet for TLC Company as of December 31, 2013.

Problem 1-5B
Preparing a statement of
cash flows
P2

Selected financial information of HalfLife Co. for the year ended December 31, 2013, follows.

Cash from investing activities	$1,600
Net increase in cash	400
Cash from financing activities	1,800
Cash used by operating activities	(3,000)
Cash, December 31, 2012	1,300

Required

Prepare the 2013 statement of cash flows for HalfLife Company.

Problem 1-6B
Preparing a statement of
owner's equity
P2

Following is selected financial information of ATV Company for the year ended December 31, 2013.

A.T. Vee, Capital, Dec. 31, 2013	$47,000	A.T. Vee, Withdrawals	$ 7,000
Net income	5,000	A.T. Vee, Capital, Dec. 31, 2012.	49,000

Required

Prepare the 2013 statement of owner's equity for ATV Company.

Problem 1-7B
Analyzing transactions and
preparing financial statements
C4 P1 P2

Holly Nikolas launched a new business, Holly's Maintenance Co., that began operations on June 1. The
following transactions were completed by the company during that first month.

June 1 H. Nikolas invested $130,000 cash in the company.
     2 The company rented a furnished office and paid $6,000 cash for June's rent.
     4 The company purchased $2,400 of equipment on credit.
     6 The company paid $1,150 cash for this month's advertising of the opening of the business.
     8 The company completed maintenance services for a customer and immediately collected $850
        cash.
    14 The company completed $7,500 of maintenance services for City Center on credit.
    16 The company paid $800 cash for an assistant's salary for the first half of the month.
    20 The company received $7,500 cash payment for services completed for City Center on June 14.
    21 The company completed $7,900 of maintenance services for Paula's Beauty Shop on credit.
    24 The company completed $675 of maintenance services for Build-It Coop on credit.
    25 The company received $7,900 cash payment from Paula's Beauty Shop for the work completed on
        June 21.
    26 The company made payment of $2,400 cash for equipment purchased on June 4.
    28 The company paid $800 cash for an assistant's salary for the second half of this month.
    29 H. Nikolas withdrew $4,000 cash from the company for personal use.
    30 The company paid $150 cash for this month's telephone bill.
    30 The company paid $890 cash for this month's utilities.

Required

1. Arrange the following asset, liability, and equity titles in a table like Exhibit 1.9: Cash; Accounts Receivable; Equipment; Accounts Payable; H. Nikolas, Capital; H. Nikolas, Withdrawals; Revenues; and
Expenses.

2. Show the effects of the transactions on the accounts of the accounting equation by recording increases and decreases in the appropriate columns. Do not determine new account balances after each transaction. Determine the final total for each account and verify that the equation is in balance.

3. Prepare a June income statement, a June statement of owner's equity, a June 30 balance sheet, and a June statement of cash flows.

Check (2) Ending balances: Cash, $130,060; Expenses, $9,790

(3) Net income, $7,135; Total assets, $133,135

Truro Excavating Co., owned by Raul Truro, began operations in July and completed these transactions during that first month of operations.

July 1   R. Truro invested $80,000 cash in the company.
     2   The company rented office space and paid $700 cash for the July rent.
     3   The company purchased excavating equipment for $5,000 by paying $1,000 cash and agreeing to pay the $4,000 balance in 30 days.
     6   The company purchased office supplies for $600 cash.
     8   The company completed work for a customer and immediately collected $7,600 cash for the work.
    10   The company purchased $2,300 of office equipment on credit.
    15   The company completed work for a customer on credit in the amount of $8,200.
    17   The company purchased $3,100 of office supplies on credit.
    23   The company paid $2,300 cash for the office equipment purchased on July 10.
    25   The company billed a customer $5,000 for work completed; the balance is due in 30 days.
    28   The company received $8,200 cash for the work completed on July 15.
    30   The company paid an assistant's salary of $1,560 cash for this month.
    31   The company paid $295 cash for this month's utility bill.
    31   R. Truro withdrew $1,800 cash from the company for personal use.

Problem 1-8B
Analyzing transactions and preparing financial statements
C4 P1 P2

Required

1. Arrange the following asset, liability, and equity titles in a table like Exhibit 1.9: Cash; Accounts Receivable; Office Supplies; Office Equipment; Excavating Equipment; Accounts Payable; R. Truro, Capital; R. Truro, Withdrawals; Revenues; and Expenses.

2. Use additions and subtractions to show the effects of each transaction on the accounts in the accounting equation. Show new balances after each transaction.

3. Use the increases and decreases in the columns of the table from part 2 to prepare an income statement, a statement of owner's equity, and a statement of cash flows—each of these for the current month. Also prepare a balance sheet as of the end of the month.

Check (2) Ending balances: Cash, $87,545; Accounts Payable, $7,100

(3) Net income, $18,245; Total assets, $103,545

Analysis Component

4. Assume that the $5,000 purchase of excavating equipment on July 3 was financed from an owner investment of another $5,000 cash in the business (instead of the purchase conditions described in the transaction). Explain the effect of this change on total assets, total liabilities, and total equity.

Nico Mitchell started a new business, Nico's Solutions, and completed the following transactions during its first year of operations.

a. N. Mitchell invests $90,000 cash and office equipment valued at $20,000 in the company.
b. The company purchased a $150,000 building to use as an office. It paid $40,000 in cash and signed a note payable promising to pay the $110,000 balance over the next ten years.
c. The company purchased office equipment for $25,000 cash.
d. The company purchased $1,200 of office supplies and $1,700 of office equipment on credit.
e. The company paid a local newspaper $750 cash for printing an announcement of the office's opening.
f. The company completed a financial plan for a client and billed that client $2,800 for the service.
g. The company designed a financial plan for another client and immediately collected a $4,000 cash fee.
h. N. Mitchell withdrew $11,500 cash from the company for personal use.
i. The company received $1,800 cash from the client described in transaction f.
j. The company made a payment of $700 cash on the equipment purchased in transaction d.
k. The company paid $2,500 cash for the office secretary's wages.

Problem 1-9B
Analyzing effects of transactions
C4 P1 P2 A1

Required

1. Create a table like the one in Exhibit 1.9, using the following headings for the columns: Cash; Accounts Receivable; Office Supplies; Office Equipment; Building; Accounts Payable; Notes Payable; N. Mitchell, Capital; N. Mitchell, Withdrawals; Revenues; and Expenses.

2. Use additions and subtractions within the table created in part *1* to show the dollar effects of each transaction on individual items of the accounting equation. Show new balances after each transaction.

3. Once you have completed the table, determine the company's net income.

Problem 1-10B
Computing and interpreting return on assets

A2

AT&T and **Verizon** produce and market telecommunications products and are competitors. Key financial figures (in $ millions) for these businesses over the past year follow.

Key Figures ($ millions)	AT&T	Verizon
Sales	$126,723	$110,875
Net income	4,184	10,198
Average assets	269,868	225,233

Required

1. Compute return on assets for (*a*) AT&T and (*b*) Verizon.

2. Which company is more successful in the total amount of sales to consumers?

3. Which company is more successful in returning net income from its assets invested?

Analysis Component

4. Write a one-paragraph memorandum explaining which company you would invest your money in and why. (Limit your explanation to the information provided.)

Problem 1-11B
Determining expenses, liabilities, equity, and return on assets

A1 A2

Carbondale Company manufactures, markets, and sells snowmobile and snowmobile equipment and accessories. The average total assets for Carbondale is $3,000,000. In its most recent year, Carbondale reported net income of $201,000 on revenues of $1,400,000.

Required

1. What is Carbondale Company's return on assets?

2. Does return on assets seem satisfactory for Carbondale given that its competitors average a 9.5% return on assets?

3. What are the total expenses for Carbondale Company in its most recent year?

4. What is the average total amount of liabilities plus equity for Carbondale Company?

Problem 1-12B^A
Identifying risk and return

A3

All business decisions involve aspects of risk and return.

Required

Identify both the risk and the return in each of the following activities:

1. Stashing $500 cash under your mattress.

2. Placing a $250 bet on a horse running in the Kentucky Derby.

3. Investing $20,000 in Nike stock.

4. Investing $35,000 in U.S. Savings Bonds.

Problem 1-13B^B
Describing organizational activities

C5

A start-up company often engages in the following activities during its first year of operations. Classify each of the following activities into one of the three major activities of an organization.

F. Financing   **I.** Investing   **O.** Operating

_____ **1.** Providing client services.   _____ **5.** Supervising workers.

_____ **2.** Obtaining a bank loan.   _____ **6.** Owner investing money in business.

_____ **3.** Purchasing machinery.   _____ **7.** Renting office space.

_____ **4.** Research for its products.   _____ **8.** Paying utilities expenses.

Identify in outline format the three major business activities of an organization. For each of these activities, identify at least two specific transactions or events normally undertaken by the business's owners or its managers.

Problem 1-14B[B]
Describing organizational
activities C5

This serial problem starts in this chapter and continues throughout most chapters of the book. It is most readily solved if you use the Working Papers that accompany this book (but working papers are not required).

SP 1 On October 1, 2013, Adria Lopez launched a computer services company, **Success Systems,** that is organized as a proprietorship and provides consulting services, computer system installations, and custom program development. Lopez adopts the calendar year for reporting purposes and expects to prepare the company's first set of financial statements on December 31, 2013.

SERIAL PROBLEM
Success Systems
C4 P1

Required

Create a table like the one in Exhibit 1.9 using the following headings for columns: Cash; Accounts Receivable; Computer Supplies; Computer System; Office Equipment; Accounts Payable; A. Lopez, Capital; A. Lopez, Withdrawals; Revenues; and Expenses. Then use additions and subtractions within the table created to show the dollar effects for each of the following October transactions for Success Systems on the individual items of the accounting equation. Show new balances after each transaction.

Oct. 1 A. Lopez invested $55,000 cash, a $20,000 computer system, and $8,000 of office equipment in the company.
3 The company purchased $1,420 of computer supplies on credit from Harris Office Products.
6 The company billed Easy Leasing $4,800 for services performed in installing a new Web server.
8 The company paid $1,420 cash for the computer supplies purchased from Harris Office Products on October 3.
10 The company hired Lyn Addie as a part-time assistant for $125 per day, as needed.
12 The company billed Easy Leasing another $1,400 for services performed.
15 The company received $4,800 cash from Easy Leasing as partial payment toward its account.
17 The company paid $805 cash to repair computer equipment damaged when moving it.
20 The company paid $1,940 cash for advertisements published in the local newspaper.
22 The company received $1,400 cash from Easy Leasing toward its account.
28 The company billed IFM Company $5,208 for services performed.
31 The company paid $875 cash for Lyn Addie's wages for seven days of work this month.
31 A. Lopez withdrew $3,600 cash from the company for personal use.

Check Ending balances: Cash, $52,560, Revenues, $11,408; Expenses, $3,620

Beyond the Numbers (BTN) *is a special problem section aimed to refine communication, conceptual, analysis, and research skills. It includes many activities helpful in developing an active learning environment.*

Beyond the Numbers

BTN 1-1 Key financial figures for **Polaris'** fiscal year ended December 31, 2011, follow.

Key Figure	In Thousands
Liabilities + Equity.........	$1,228,024
Net income	227,575
Revenues	2,656,949

REPORTING IN ACTION
A1 A2 A3

Polaris

Required

1. What is the total amount of assets invested in Polaris?
2. What is Polaris' return on assets for 2011? Its assets at December 31, 2010, equal $1,061,647 (in thousands).
3. How much are total expenses for Polaris for the year ended December 31, 2011?
4. Does Polaris' return on assets for 2011 seem satisfactory if competitors average an 18% return?

Check (2) 19.9%

Fast Forward

5. Access Polaris' financial statements (Form 10-K) for years ending after December 31, 2011, from its Website (**Polaris.com**) or from the SEC Website (**www.SEC.gov**) and compute its return on assets for those years. Compare the December 31, 2011, year-end return on assets to any subsequent years' returns you are able to compute, and interpret the results.

COMPARATIVE ANALYSIS

A1 A2 A3

Polaris

Arctic Cat

BTN 1-2 Key comparative figures ($ thousands) for both **Polaris** and **Arctic Cat** follow.

Key Figure	Polaris	Arctic Cat
Liabilities + Equity..........	$1,228,024	$272,906
Net income	227,575	13,007
Revenues and sales	2,656,949	464,651

Required

Check (2b) 5.0%

1. What is the total amount of assets invested in (*a*) Polaris and (*b*) Arctic Cat?
2. What is the return on assets for (*a*) Polaris and (*b*) Arctic Cat? Polaris' beginning-year assets equal $1,061,647 (in thousands) and Arctic Cat's beginning-year assets equal $246,084 (in thousands).
3. How much are expenses for (*a*) Polaris and (*b*) Arctic Cat?
4. Is return on assets satisfactory for (*a*) Polaris and (*b*) Arctic Cat? (Assume competitors average an 18% return.)
5. What can you conclude about Polaris and Arctic Cat from these computations?

ETHICS CHALLENGE

C3 C4

BTN 1-3 Craig Thorne works in a public accounting firm and hopes to eventually be a partner. The management of Allnet Company invites Thorne to prepare a bid to audit Allnet's financial statements. In discussing the audit fee, Allnet's management suggests a fee range in which the amount depends on the reported profit of Allnet. The higher its profit, the higher will be the audit fee paid to Thorne's firm.

Required

1. Identify the parties potentially affected by this audit and the fee plan proposed.
2. What are the ethical factors in this situation? Explain.
3. Would you recommend that Thorne accept this audit fee arrangement? Why or why not?
4. Describe some ethical considerations guiding your recommendation.

COMMUNICATING IN PRACTICE

A1 C2

BTN 1-4 Refer to this chapter's opening feature about **Twitter**. Assume that the owners desire to expand their online services to meet people's demands regarding online services. They eventually decide to meet with their banker to discuss a loan to allow Twitter to expand.

Required

1. Prepare a half-page report outlining the information you would request from the owners if you were the loan officer.
2. Indicate whether the information you request and your loan decision are affected by the form of business organization for Twitter.

TAKING IT TO THE NET

A2

BTN 1-5 Visit the EDGAR database at (**www.SEC.gov**). Access the Form 10-K report of **Rocky Mountain Chocolate Factory** (ticker RMCF) filed on **May 24, 2011**, covering its 2011 fiscal year.

Required

1. Item 6 of the 10-K report provides comparative financial highlights of RMCF for the years 2007–2011. How would you describe the revenue trend for RMCF over this five-year period?
2. Has RMCF been profitable (see net income) over this five-year period? Support your answer.

TEAMWORK IN ACTION

C1

BTN 1-6 Teamwork is important in today's business world. Successful teams schedule convenient meetings, maintain regular communications, and cooperate with and support their members. This assignment aims to establish support/learning teams, initiate discussions, and set meeting times.

Required

1. Form teams and open a team discussion to determine a regular time and place for your team to meet between each scheduled class meeting. Notify your instructor via a memorandum or e-mail message as to when and where your team will hold regularly scheduled meetings.
2. Develop a list of telephone numbers and/or e-mail addresses of your teammates.

BTN 1-7   Refer to this chapter's opening feature about **Twitter**. Assume that the owners decide to open a new Website devoted to micro-blogging for accountants and those studying accounting. This new company will be called **AccounTwit**.

Required

1. AccounTwit obtains a $500,000 loan and the three owners contribute $250,000 in total from their own savings in exchange for common stock in the new company.
   a. What is the new company's total amount of liabilities plus equity?
   b. What is the new company's total amount of assets?

2. If the new company earns $80,250 in net income in the first year of operation, compute its return on assets (assume average assets equal $750,000). Assess its performance if competitors average a 10% return.

Check   (2) 10.7%

BTN 1-8   You are to interview a local business owner. (This can be a friend or relative.) Opening lines of communication with members of the business community can provide personal benefits of business networking. If you do not know the owner, you should call ahead to introduce yourself and explain your position as a student and your assignment requirements. You should request a 30-minute appointment for a face-to-face or phone interview to discuss the form of organization and operations of the business. Be prepared to make a good impression.

Required

1. Identify and describe the main operating activities and the form of organization for this business.
2. Determine and explain why the owner(s) chose this particular form of organization.
3. Identify any special advantages and/or disadvantages the owner(s) experiences in operating with this form of business organization.

BTN 1-9   KTM (**KTM.com**) is a leading manufacturer of offroad and street motorcycles, and it competes to some extent with both **Polaris** and **Arctic Cat**. Key financial figures for KTM follow.

Key Figure*	Euro in Thousands
Average assets.....................	465,550
Net income......................	20,818
Revenue..........................	526,801
Return on assets.................	4.5%

* Figures prepared in accordance with International Financial Reporting Standards.

Required

1. Identify any concerns you have in comparing KTM's income and revenue figures to those of Polaris and Arctic Cat (in BTN 1-2) for purposes of making business decisions.
2. Identify any concerns you have in comparing KTM's return on assets ratio to those of Polaris and Arctic Cat (computed for BTN 1-2) for purposes of making business decisions.

ANSWERS TO MULTIPLE CHOICE QUIZ

1. c; $450,000 is the actual cost incurred.   **4.** a
2. b; revenue is recorded when earned.   **5.** a
3. d;

Assets	=	Liabilities	+	Equity
+$100,000	=	+35,000	+	?

Change in equity = $100,000 − $35,000 = $65,000

Analyzing and Recording Transactions

2

A Look Back

Chapter 1 defined accounting and introduced financial statements. We described forms of organizations and identified users and uses of accounting. We defined the accounting equation and applied it to transaction analysis.

A Look at This Chapter

This chapter focuses on the accounting process. We describe transactions and source documents, and we explain the analysis and recording of transactions. The accounting equation, T-account, general ledger, trial balance, and debits and credits are key tools in the accounting process.

A Look Ahead

Chapter 3 extends our focus on processing information. We explain the importance of adjusting accounts and the procedures in preparing financial statements.

Learning Objectives

CONCEPTUAL

C1 Explain the steps in processing transactions and the role of source documents. (p. 50)

C2 Describe an account and its use in recording transactions. (p. 51)

C3 Describe a ledger and a chart of accounts. (p. 54)

C4 Define *debits* and *credits* and explain double-entry accounting. (p. 55)

ANALYTICAL

A1 Analyze the impact of transactions on accounts and financial statements. (p. 59)

A2 Compute the debt ratio and describe its use in analyzing financial condition. (p. 69)

PROCEDURAL

P1 Record transactions in a journal and post entries to a ledger. (p. 56)

P2 Prepare and explain the use of a trial balance. (p. 65)

P3 Prepare financial statements from business transactions. (p. 66)

Some Like It Hot

"You can still excel if you work really hard and follow your dreams!"

—**MISA CHIEN** (ON LEFT)

LOS ANGELES—"We call our customers Nomsters!" exclaims Misa. "There's an entire Nom Nom movement." **Nom Nom Truck (NomNomTruck.com)** is a mobile food business and the brainchild of Misa Chien and Jennifer Green. (Nom Nom is drawn from the sound "nom nom nom" when eating something "oh so tasty.") Their specialty is the Vietnamese baguette sandwich, called *banh mi*, a sort of Vietnamese subsandwich. "It's portable, it's fast, and has a fresh taste that you can't get from a burrito or hamburger," states Jennifer.

To pursue their business ambitions, Misa and Jennifer took business courses. They learned about recordkeeping processes, transaction analysis, inventory accounting, and financial statement reporting. "We did lose a lot of money initially," explains Misa. "We didn't have the right pricing structure." With careful analysis of their accounting reports, Misa and Jennifer solved the problem. Their business is now profitable and they have a reliable accounting system to help them make good business decisions.

"We had to account for product expenses, trucking expenses, supplier payments, and other expenses such as salaries, rent and insurance," explains Misa. At the same time, the two have grown sales and expanded their food offerings. "Sales have definitely increased," says Misa. "People totally embraced us!"

The two insist that it is crucial to track and account for all revenues and expenses, including what is invested in the business. They maintain that success requires proper accounting for and analysis of the financial side. "There was a point when we couldn't keep up," recounts Misa. Given the importance of accounting, "we [now] have a bookkeeper and an accountant!" The women emphasize the value of a great business model along with a sound accounting system. "It's really easy to balance both now that we've been in the business for awhile," explains Misa.

"The bigger message of our company", says Jennifer, "is that each of us can succeed no matter what our starting point". "You have to be responsible for yourself," adds Misa. "We want to make people happy through our food!"

[Sources: *Nom Nom Truck Website,* January 2013; *Inc.,* June 2011; *Bundle.com,* October 2010; *VirgoBlue.net,* September 2011; *CNNMoney,* October 2011.]

Financial statements report on the financial performance and condition of an organization. Knowledge of their preparation, organization, and analysis is important. A main goal of this chapter is to illustrate how transactions are recorded, how they are reflected in financial statements, and how they impact analysis of financial statements. Debits and credits are introduced and identified as a tool in helping analyze and process transactions.

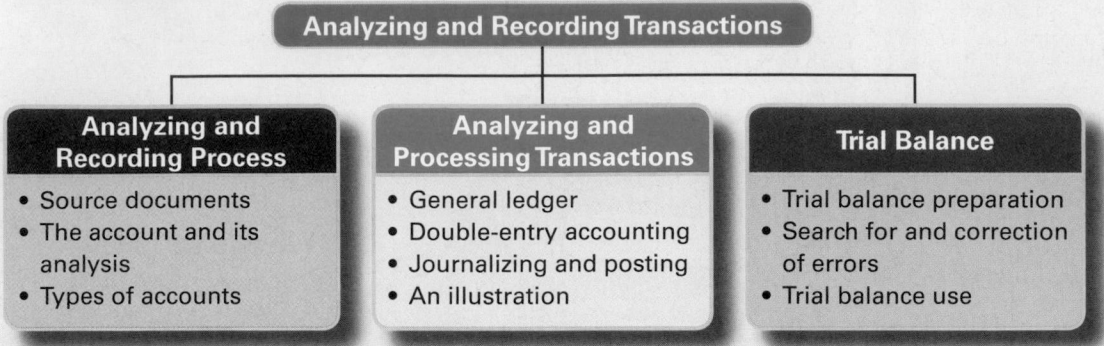

Analyzing and Recording Transactions

Analyzing and Recording Process	Analyzing and Processing Transactions	Trial Balance
• Source documents • The account and its analysis • Types of accounts	• General ledger • Double-entry accounting • Journalizing and posting • An illustration	• Trial balance preparation • Search for and correction of errors • Trial balance use

ANALYZING AND RECORDING PROCESS

The accounting process identifies business transactions and events, analyzes and records their effects, and summarizes and presents information in reports and financial statements. These reports and statements are used for making investing, lending, and other business decisions. The steps in the accounting process that focus on *analyzing and recording* transactions and events are shown in Exhibit 2.1.

EXHIBIT 2.1

The Analyzing and Recording Process

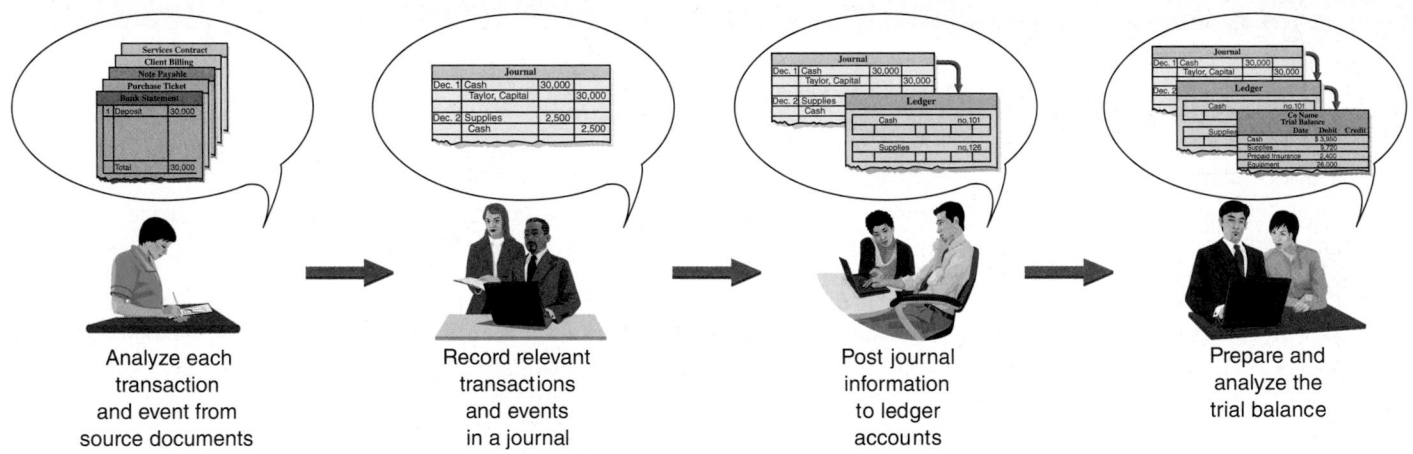

Analyze each transaction and event from source documents → Record relevant transactions and events in a journal → Post journal information to ledger accounts → Prepare and analyze the trial balance

C1 Explain the steps in processing transactions and the role of source documents.

Business transactions and events are the starting points. Relying on source documents, the transactions and events are analyzed using the accounting equation to understand how they affect company performance and financial position. These effects are recorded in accounting records, informally referred to as the *accounting books*, or simply the *books*. Additional steps such as posting and then preparing a trial balance help summarize and classify the effects of transactions and events. Ultimately, the accounting process provides information in useful reports or financial statements to decision makers.

Source Documents

Source documents identify and describe transactions and events entering the accounting process. They are the sources of accounting information and can be in either hard copy or electronic form. Examples are sales tickets, checks, purchase orders, bills from suppliers, employee earnings records, and bank statements. To illustrate, when an item is purchased on credit, the seller usually prepares at least two copies of a sales invoice. One copy is given to the buyer. Another copy, often sent electronically, results in an entry in the seller's information system to record the sale. Sellers use invoices for recording sales and for control; buyers use them for recording purchases and for monitoring purchasing activity. Many cash registers record information for each sale on a tape or electronic file locked inside the register. This record can be used as a source document for recording sales in the accounting records. Source documents, especially if obtained from outside the organization, provide objective and reliable evidence about transactions and events and their amounts.

Point: To ensure that all sales are rung up on the register, most sellers require customers to have their receipts to exchange or return purchased items.

■ Decision Ethics

Cashier   Your manager requires that you, as cashier, immediately enter each sale. Recently, lunch hour traffic has increased and the assistant manager asks you to avoid delays by taking customers' cash and making change without entering sales. The assistant manager says she will add up cash and enter sales after lunch. She says that, in this way, the register will always match the cash amount when the manager arrives at three o'clock. What do you do? ■ [Answer—p. 74]

The Account and Its Analysis

An **account** is a record of increases and decreases in a specific asset, liability, equity, revenue, or expense item. Information from an account is analyzed, summarized, and presented in reports and financial statements. The **general ledger,** or simply **ledger,** is a record containing all accounts used by a company. The ledger is often in electronic form. While most companies' ledgers contain similar accounts, a company often uses one or more unique accounts because of its type of operations. As shown in Exhibit 2.2, accounts are classified into three general categories based on the accounting equation: asset, liability, or equity.

C2 Describe an account and its use in recording transactions.

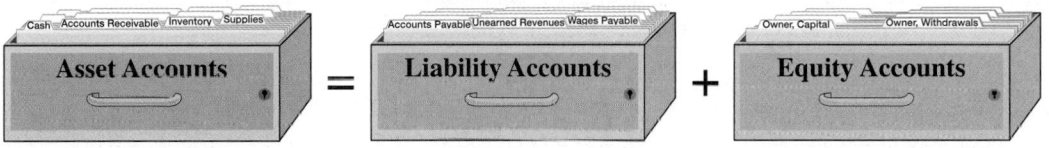

EXHIBIT 2.2

Accounts Organized by the Accounting Equation

Asset Accounts   Assets are resources owned or controlled by a company and that have expected future benefits. Most accounting systems include (at a minimum) separate accounts for the assets described here.

Cash   A *Cash* account reflects a company's cash balance. All increases and decreases in cash are recorded in the Cash account. It includes money and any medium of exchange that a bank accepts for deposit (coins, checks, money orders, and checking account balances).

Accounts Receivable   *Accounts receivable* are held by a seller and refer to promises of payment from customers to sellers. These transactions are often called *credit sales* or *sales on account* (or *on credit*). Accounts receivable are increased by credit sales and are decreased by customer payments. A company needs a separate record for each customer, but for now, we use the simpler practice of recording all increases and decreases in receivables in a single account called Accounts Receivable.

Point: Customers and others who owe a company are called its **debtors.**

Note Receivable   A *note receivable,* or promissory note, is a written promise of another entity to pay a definite sum of money on a specified future date to the holder of the note. A company holding a promissory note signed by another entity has an asset that is recorded in a Note (or Notes) Receivable account.

Prepaid Accounts   *Prepaid accounts* (also called *prepaid expenses*) are assets that represent prepayments of future expenses (*not* current expenses). When the expenses are later incurred, the amounts in prepaid accounts are transferred to expense accounts. Common examples of prepaid accounts include prepaid insurance, prepaid rent, and prepaid services (such as club memberships). Prepaid accounts expire with the passage of time (such as with rent) or through use (such as with prepaid meal tickets). When financial statements are prepared, prepaid accounts are adjusted so that (1) all expired and used prepaid accounts are recorded as regular expenses and (2) all unexpired and unused prepaid accounts are recorded as assets (reflecting future use in future periods). To illustrate,

Point: A college parking fee is a prepaid account from the student's standpoint. At the beginning of the term, it represents an asset that entitles a student to park on or near campus. The benefits of the parking fee expire as the term progresses. At term-end, prepaid parking (asset) equals zero as it has been entirely recorded as parking expense.

Point: Prepaid accounts that apply to current and future periods are assets. These assets are adjusted at the end of each period to reflect only those amounts that have not yet expired, and to record as expenses those amounts that have expired.

when an insurance fee, called a *premium,* is paid in advance, the cost is typically recorded in the asset account Prepaid Insurance. Over time, the expiring portion of the insurance cost is removed from this asset account and reported in expenses on the income statement. Any unexpired portion remains in Prepaid Insurance and is reported on the balance sheet as an asset. (An exception exists for prepaid accounts that will expire or be used before the end of the current accounting period when financial statements are prepared. In this case, the prepayments *can* be recorded immediately as expenses.)

Supplies Accounts   *Supplies* are assets until they are used. When they are used up, their costs are reported as expenses. The costs of unused supplies are recorded in a Supplies asset account. Supplies are often grouped by purpose—for example, office supplies and store supplies. *Office supplies* include stationery, paper, toner, and pens. *Store supplies* include packaging materials, plastic and paper bags, gift boxes and cartons, and cleaning materials. The costs of these unused supplies can be recorded in an Office Supplies or a Store Supplies asset account. When supplies are used, their costs are transferred from the asset accounts to expense accounts.

Point: Some assets are described as *intangible* because they do not have physical existence or their benefits are highly uncertain. A recent balance sheet for **Coca-Cola Company** shows nearly $1 billion in intangible assets.

Equipment Accounts   *Equipment* is an asset. When equipment is used and gets worn down, its cost is gradually reported as an expense (called depreciation). Equipment is often grouped by its purpose—for example, office equipment and store equipment. *Office equipment* includes computers, printers, desks, chairs, and shelves. Costs incurred for these items are recorded in an Office Equipment asset account. The Store Equipment account includes the costs of assets used in a store, such as counters, showcases, ladders, hoists, and cash registers.

Buildings Accounts   *Buildings* such as stores, offices, warehouses, and factories are assets because they provide expected future benefits to those who control or own them. Their costs are recorded in a Buildings asset account. When several buildings are owned, separate accounts are sometimes kept for each of them.

Land   The cost of *land* owned by a business is recorded in a Land account. The cost of buildings located on the land is separately recorded in one or more building accounts.

■ Decision Insight

Women Entrepreneurs   The Center for Women's Business Research reports that women-owned businesses, such as **Nom Nom Truck**, are growing and that they:

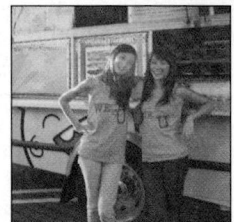

- Total approximately 11 million and employ nearly 20 million workers.
- Generate $2.5 trillion in annual sales and tend to embrace technology.
- Are philanthropic—70% of owners volunteer at least once per month.
- Are more likely funded by individual investors (73%) than venture firms (15%). ■

Liability Accounts   Liabilities are claims (by creditors) against assets, which means they are obligations to transfer assets or provide products or services to others. **Creditors** are individuals and organizations that have rights to receive payments from a company. If a company fails to pay its obligations, the law gives creditors a right to force the sale of that company's assets to obtain the money to meet creditors' claims. When assets are sold under these conditions, creditors are paid first, but only up to the amount of their claims. Any remaining money, the residual, goes to the owners of the company. Creditors often use a balance sheet to help decide whether to loan money to a company. A loan is less risky if the borrower's liabilities are small in comparison to assets because this means there are more resources than claims on resources. Common liability accounts are described here.

Point: Accounts payable are also called *trade payables.*

Accounts Payable   *Accounts payable* refer to oral or implied promises to pay later, which usually arise from purchases of merchandise. Payables can also arise from purchases of supplies, equipment, and services. Accounting systems keep separate records about each creditor. We describe these individual records in Chapter 5.

Note Payable   A *note payable* refers to a formal promise, usually denoted by the signing of a promissory note, to pay a future amount. It is recorded in either a short-term Note Payable account or a long-term Note Payable account, depending on when it must be repaid. We explain details of short- and long-term classification in Chapter 3.

Unearned Revenue Accounts   **Unearned revenue** refers to a liability that is settled in the future when a company delivers its products or services. When customers pay in advance for products or services (before revenue is earned), the revenue recognition principle requires that the seller consider this payment as unearned revenue. Examples of unearned revenue include magazine subscriptions collected in advance by a publisher, sales of gift certificates by stores, and season ticket sales by sports teams. The seller would record these in liability accounts such as Unearned Subscriptions, Unearned Store Sales, and Unearned Ticket Revenue. When products and services are later delivered, the earned portion of the unearned revenue is transferred to revenue accounts such as Subscription Fees, Store Sales, and Ticket Sales.[1]

Point: If a subscription is canceled, the publisher is expected to refund the unused portion to the subscriber.

Accrued Liabilities   Accrued liabilities are amounts owed that are not yet paid. Examples are wages payable, taxes payable, and interest payable. These are often recorded in separate liability accounts by the same title. If they are not large in amount, one or more ledger accounts can be added and reported as a single amount on the balance sheet. (Financial statements often have amounts reported that are a summation of several ledger accounts.)

Decision Insight

Revenue Spread   The **New York Giants** have *Unearned Revenues* of about $100 million in advance ticket sales. When the team plays its home games, it settles this liability to its ticket holders and then transfers the amount earned to *Ticket Revenues.* ∎

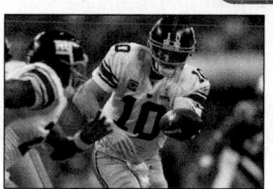

Equity Accounts   The owner's claim on a company's assets is called *equity* or *owner's equity*. Equity is the owner's *residual interest* in the assets of a business after deducting liabilities. Equity is impacted by four types of accounts: owner's capital, owner's withdrawals, revenues, and expenses. We show this visually in Exhibit 2.3 by expanding the accounting equation.

Point: Equity is also called *net assets*.

EXHIBIT 2.3

Expanded Accounting Equation

Owner Investments   When an owner invests in a company, the invested amount is recorded in an account titled Owner, Capital (where the owner's name is inserted in place of "owner"). The account titled *C. Taylor, Capital* is used for FastForward. Any further owner investments are recorded in this account.

Owner Withdrawals   When an owner withdraws assets for personal use it decreases both company assets and total equity. Withdrawals are not expenses of the business; they are simply the opposite of owner investments. The Owner, Withdrawals account is used to record asset distributions to the owner. The account titled *C. Taylor, Withdrawals* is used for FastForward. (Owners of proprietorships cannot receive company salaries because they are not legally separate from their companies; and they cannot enter into company contracts with themselves.)

Point: The Owner's Withdrawals account is a *contra equity* account because it reduces the normal balance of equity.

Point: The withdrawal of assets by the owners of a corporation is called a *dividend*.

Revenue Accounts   Revenues and expenses also impact equity. Examples of revenue accounts are Sales, Commissions Earned, Professional Fees Earned, Rent Revenue, and Interest Revenue. *Revenues increase equity* and result from products and services provided to customers.

---

[1] In practice, account titles vary. As one example, Subscription Fees is sometimes called Subscription Fees Revenue, Subscription Fees Earned, or Earned Subscription Fees. As another example, Rent Earned is sometimes called Rent Revenue, Rental Revenue, or Earned Rent Revenue. We must use good judgment when reading financial statements because titles can differ even within the same industry. For example, product sales are called *sales* at **Polaris**, *net sales* at **Arctic Cat**, and *net revenues* at **Piaggio**. Generally, the term *revenues* or *fees* is more commonly used with service businesses, and *net sales* or *sales* with product businesses.

Expense Accounts Examples of expense accounts are Advertising Expense, Store Supplies Expense, Office Salaries Expense, Office Supplies Expense, Rent Expense, Utilities Expense, and Insurance Expense. *Expenses decrease equity* and result from assets and services used in a company's operations. The variety of revenues and expenses can be seen by looking at the *chart of accounts* that follows the index at the back of this book. (Different companies sometimes use different account titles than those in this book's chart of accounts. For example, some might use Interest Revenue instead of Interest Earned, or Rental Expense instead of Rent Expense. It is important only that an account title describe the item it represents.)

■ Decision Insight

Sporting Accounts The **Miami Heat**, **Los Angeles Lakers**, and the other NBA teams have the following major revenue and expense accounts:

Revenues	Expenses
Basketball ticket sales	Team salaries
TV & radio broadcast fees	Game costs
Advertising revenues	NBA franchise costs
Basketball playoff receipts	Promotional costs ■

ANALYZING AND PROCESSING TRANSACTIONS

This section explains several tools and processes that comprise an accounting system. These include a ledger, T-account, debits and credits, double-entry accounting, journalizing, and posting.

Ledger and Chart of Accounts

C3 Describe a ledger and a chart of accounts.

The collection of all accounts and their balances for an information system is called a *ledger* (or *general ledger*). If accounts are in files on a hard drive, the sum of those files is the ledger. If the accounts are pages in a file, that file is the ledger. A company's size and diversity of operations affect the number of accounts needed. A small company can get by with as few as 20 or 30 accounts; a large company can require several thousand. The **chart of accounts** is a list of all ledger accounts and includes an identification number assigned to each account. A small business might use the following numbering system for its accounts:

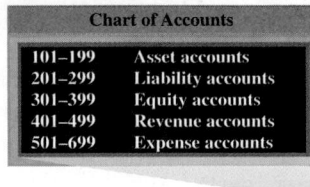

Chart of Accounts	
101–199	Asset accounts
201–299	Liability accounts
301–399	Equity accounts
401–499	Revenue accounts
501–699	Expense accounts

These numbers provide a three-digit code that is useful in recordkeeping. In this case, the first digit assigned to asset accounts is a 1, the first digit assigned to liability accounts is a 2, and so on. The second and third digits relate to the accounts' subcategories. Exhibit 2.4 shows a partial

EXHIBIT 2.4

Partial Chart of Accounts for FastForward

Chart of Accounts							
Acct. No.	**Account Name**		**Acct. No.**	**Account Name**		**Acct. No.**	**Account Name**
101	Cash		236	Unearned consulting revenue		622	Salaries expense
106	Accounts receivable					637	Insurance expense
126	Supplies		301	C. Taylor, Capital		640	Rent expense
128	Prepaid insurance		302	C. Taylor, Withdrawals		652	Supplies expense
167	Equipment		403	Consulting revenue		690	Utilities expense
201	Accounts payable		406	Rental revenue			

chart of accounts for FastForward, the focus company of Chapter 1. (Please review the more complete chart of accounts that follows the index at the back of this book.)

Debits and Credits

A **T-account** represents a ledger account and is a tool used to understand the effects of one or more transactions. Its name comes from its shape like the letter **T**. The layout of a T-account, shown in Exhibit 2.5, is (1) the account title on top, (2) a left, or debit side, and (3) a right, or credit, side.

The left side of an account is called the **debit** side, often abbreviated *Dr*. The right side is called the **credit** side, abbreviated *Cr*.[2] To enter amounts on the left side of an account is to *debit* the account. To enter amounts on the right side is to *credit* the account. Do not make the error of thinking that the terms *debit* and *credit* mean increase or decrease. Whether a debit or a credit is an increase or decrease depends on the account. For an account where a debit is an increase, the credit is a decrease; for an account where a debit is a decrease, the credit is an increase. The difference between total debits and total credits for an account, including any beginning balance, is the **account balance.** When the sum of debits exceeds the sum of credits, the account has a *debit balance*. It has a *credit balance* when the sum of credits exceeds the sum of debits. When the sum of debits equals the sum of credits, the account has a *zero balance*.

Account Title	
(Left side) **Debit**	(Right side) **Credit**

C4 Define *debits* and *credits* and explain double-entry accounting.

EXHIBIT 2.5

The T-Account

Point: Think of *debit* and *credit* as accounting directions for left and right.

Double-Entry Accounting

Double-entry accounting requires that for each transaction:

- At least two accounts are involved, with at least one debit and one credit.
- The total amount debited must equal the total amount credited.
- The accounting equation must not be violated.

This means the sum of the debits for all entries must equal the sum of the credits for all entries, and the sum of debit account balances in the ledger must equal the sum of credit account balances.

The system for recording debits and credits follows from the usual accounting equation—see Exhibit 2.6. Two points are important here. First, like any simple mathematical relation, net increases or decreases on one side have equal net effects on the other side. For example, a net increase in assets must be accompanied by an identical net increase on the liabilities and equity

"Total debits equal total credits for each entry."

Assets		=	Liabilities		+	Equity	
Debit for increases	Credit for decreases		Debit for decreases	Credit for increases		Debit for decreases	Credit for increases
+	**−**		**−**	**+**		**−**	**+**
Normal				**Normal**			**Normal**

EXHIBIT 2.6

Debits and Credits in the Accounting Equation

side. Recall that some transactions affect only one side of the equation, meaning that two or more accounts on one side are affected, but their net effect on this one side is zero. Second, the left side is the *normal balance* side for assets, and the right side is the *normal balance* side for liabilities and equity. This matches their layout in the accounting equation where assets are on the left side of this equation, and liabilities and equity are on the right.

Recall that equity increases from revenues and owner investments and it decreases from expenses and owner withdrawals. These important equity relations are conveyed by expanding the accounting equation to include debits and credits in double-entry form as shown in Exhibit 2.7.

Increases (credits) to owner's capital and revenues *increase* equity; increases (debits) to withdrawals and expenses *decrease* equity. The normal balance of each account (asset, liability, capital, withdrawals, revenue, or expense) refers to the left or right (debit or credit) side where

Point: Debits and credits do not mean favorable or unfavorable. A debit to an asset increases it, as does a debit to an expense. A credit to a liability increases it, as does a credit to a revenue.

---

[2] These abbreviations are remnants of 18th-century English recordkeeping practices where the terms *debitor* and *creditor* were used instead of *debit* and *credit*. The abbreviations use the first and last letters of these terms, just as we still do for Saint (St.) and Doctor (Dr.).

EXHIBIT 2.7

Debit and Credit Effects for
Component Accounts

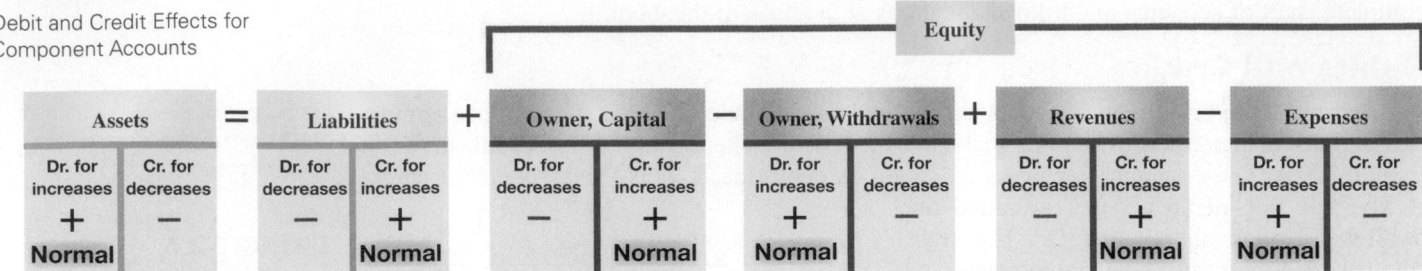

increases are recorded. Understanding these diagrams and rules is required to prepare, analyze, and interpret financial statements.

The T-account for FastForward's Cash account, reflecting its first 11 transactions (from Exhibit 1.9), is shown in Exhibit 2.8. The total increases in its Cash account are $36,100, the total decreases are $31,300, and the account's debit balance is $4,800. (We illustrate use of T-accounts later in this chapter.)

EXHIBIT 2.8

Computing the Balance for
a T-Account

Point: The ending balance is on the side with the larger dollar amount. Also, a plus (+) and minus (−) are not used in a T-account.

Cash			
Receive investment by owner	30,000	Purchase of supplies	2,500
Consulting services revenue earned	4,200	Purchase of equipment	26,000
Collection of account receivable	1,900	Payment of rent	1,000
		Payment of salary	700
		Payment of account payable	900
		Withdrawal by owner	200
Balance	**4,800**		

Quick Check

Answers — p. 75

1. Identify examples of accounting source documents.
2. Explain the importance of source documents.
3. Identify each of the following as either an asset, a liability, or equity: (*a*) Prepaid Rent, (*b*) Unearned Fees, (*c*) Building, (*d*) Wages Payable, and (*e*) Office Supplies.
4. What is an account? What is a ledger?
5. What determines the number and types of accounts a company uses?
6. Does *debit* always mean increase and *credit* always mean decrease?
7. Describe a chart of accounts.

Journalizing and Posting Transactions

Processing transactions is a crucial part of accounting. The four usual steps of this process are depicted in Exhibit 2.9. Steps 1 and 2—involving transaction analysis and the accounting equation—were introduced in prior sections. This section extends that discussion and focuses on steps 3 and 4 of the accounting process. Step 3 is to record each transaction chronologically in a journal. A **journal** gives a complete record of each transaction in one place. It also shows debits and credits for each transaction. The process of recording transactions in a journal is called **journalizing.** Step 4 is to transfer (or *post*) entries from the journal to the ledger. The process of transferring journal entry information to the ledger is called **posting.**

Journalizing Transactions   The process of journalizing transactions requires an understanding of a journal. While companies can use various journals, every company uses a **general journal.** It can be used to record any transaction and includes the following information about each transaction: ⓐ date of transaction, ⓑ titles of affected accounts, ⓒ dollar amount of each

Step 1: Identify transactions and source documents.

Step 2: Analyze transactions using the accounting equation.

Step 3: Record journal entry.

Step 4: Post entry to ledger.

EXHIBIT 2.9

Steps in Processing Transactions

debit and credit, and ⓓ explanation of the transaction. Exhibit 2.10 shows how the first two transactions of FastForward are recorded in a general journal. This process is similar for manual and computerized systems. Computerized journals are often designed to look like a manual journal page, and also include error-checking routines that ensure debits equal credits for each entry. Shortcuts allow recordkeepers to select account names and numbers from pull-down menus.

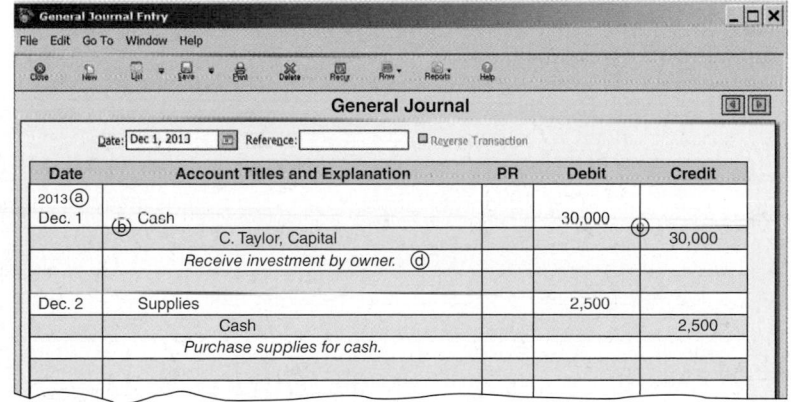

EXHIBIT 2.10

Partial General Journal for FastForward

To record entries in a general journal, apply these steps; refer to the entries in Exhibit 2.10 when reviewing these steps.

a. Date the transaction: Enter the year at the top of the first column and the month and day on the first line of each journal entry.

b. Enter titles of accounts debited and then enter amounts in the Debit column on the same line. Account titles are taken from the chart of accounts and are aligned with the left margin of the Account Titles and Explanation column.

c. Enter titles of accounts credited and then enter amounts in the Credit column on the same line. Account titles are from the chart of accounts and are indented from the left margin of the Account Titles and Explanation column to distinguish them from debited accounts.

d. Enter a brief explanation of the transaction on the line below the entry (it often references a source document). This explanation is indented about half as far as the credited account titles to avoid confusing it with accounts, and it is italicized.

Point: There are no exact rules for writing journal entry explanations. An explanation should be short yet describe why an entry is made.

A blank line is left between each journal entry for clarity. When a transaction is first recorded, the **posting reference (PR) column** is left blank (in a manual system). Later, when posting entries to the ledger, the identification numbers of the individual ledger accounts are entered in the PR column.

 IFRS

IFRS requires that companies report the following four basic financial statements with explanatory notes:

- Balance sheet
- Income statement
- Statement of changes in equity (or statement of recognized revenue and expense)
- Statement of cash flows

IFRS does not prescribe specific formats; and comparative information is required for the preceding period only. ∎

Balance Column Account   T-accounts are simple and direct means to show how the accounting process works. However, actual accounting systems need more structure and therefore use **balance column accounts,** such as that in Exhibit 2.11.

EXHIBIT 2.11

Cash Account in Balance Column Format

General Ledger					
Cash					**Account No. 101**
Date	**Explanation**	**PR**	**Debit**	**Credit**	**Balance**
2013 Dec. 1		G1	30,000		30,000
Dec. 2		G1		2,500	27,500
Dec. 3		G1		26,000	1,500
Dec. 10		G1	4,200		5,700

The balance column account format is similar to a T-account in having columns for debits and credits. It is different in including transaction date and explanation columns. It also has a column with the balance of the account after each entry is recorded. To illustrate, FastForward's Cash account in Exhibit 2.11 is debited on December 1 for the $30,000 owner investment, yielding a $30,000 debit balance. The account is credited on December 2 for $2,500, yielding a $27,500 debit balance. On December 3, it is credited again, this time for $26,000, and its debit balance is reduced to $1,500. The Cash account is debited for $4,200 on December 10, and its debit balance increases to $5,700; and so on.

Point: Explanations are typically included in ledger accounts only for unusual transactions or events.

EXHIBIT 2.12

Posting an Entry to the Ledger

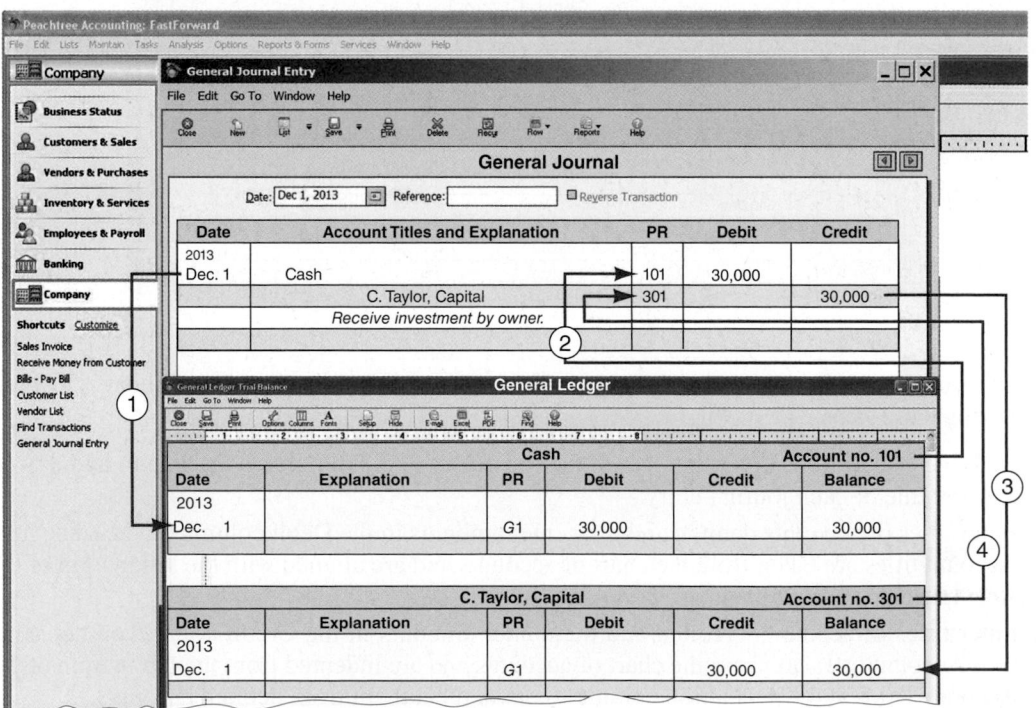

Point: The fundamental concepts of a manual (pencil-and-paper) system are identical to those of a computerized information system.

Key: (1) Identify debit account in Ledger: enter date, journal page, amount, and balance.
   (2) Enter the debit account number from the Ledger in the PR column of the journal.
   (3) Identify credit account in Ledger: enter date, journal page, amount, and balance.
   (4) Enter the credit account number from the Ledger in the PR column of the journal.

The heading of the Balance column does not show whether it is a debit or credit balance. Instead, an account is assumed to have a *normal balance*. Unusual events can sometimes temporarily give an account an abnormal balance. An *abnormal balance* refers to a balance on the side where decreases are recorded. For example, a customer might mistakenly overpay a bill. This gives that customer's account receivable an abnormal (credit) balance. An abnormal balance is often identified by circling it or by entering it in red or some other unusual color. A zero balance for an account is usually shown by writing zeros or a dash in the Balance column to avoid confusion between a zero balance and one omitted in error.

Posting Journal Entries   Step 4 of processing transactions is to post journal entries to ledger accounts (see Exhibit 2.9). To ensure that the ledger is up-to-date, entries are posted as soon as possible. This might be daily, weekly, or when time permits. All entries must be posted to the ledger before financial statements are prepared to ensure that account balances are up-to-date. When entries are posted to the ledger, the debits in journal entries are transferred into ledger accounts as debits, and credits are transferred into ledger accounts as credits. Exhibit 2.12 shows the *four steps to post a journal entry*. First, identify the ledger account that is debited in the entry; then, in the ledger, enter the entry date, the journal and page in its PR column, the debit amount, and the new balance of the ledger account. (The letter *G* shows it came from the General Journal.) Second, enter the ledger account number in the PR column of the journal. Steps 3 and 4 repeat the first two steps for credit entries and amounts. The posting process creates a link between the ledger and the journal entry. This link is a useful cross-reference for tracing an amount from one record to another.

Analyzing Transactions — An Illustration

We return to the activities of FastForward to show how double-entry accounting is useful in analyzing and processing transactions. Analysis of each transaction follows the four steps of Exhibit 2.9.

A1 Analyze the impact of transactions on accounts and financial statements.

|Step 1| Identify the transaction and any source documents.

|Step 2| Analyze the transaction using the accounting equation.

|Step 3| Record the transaction in journal entry form applying double-entry accounting.

|Step 4| Post the entry (for simplicity, we use T-accounts to represent ledger accounts).

Study each transaction thoroughly before proceeding to the next. The first 11 transactions are from Chapter 1, and we analyze five additional December transactions of FastForward (numbered 12 through 16) that were omitted earlier.

FAST~~Forward~~

1. Receive investment by Owner

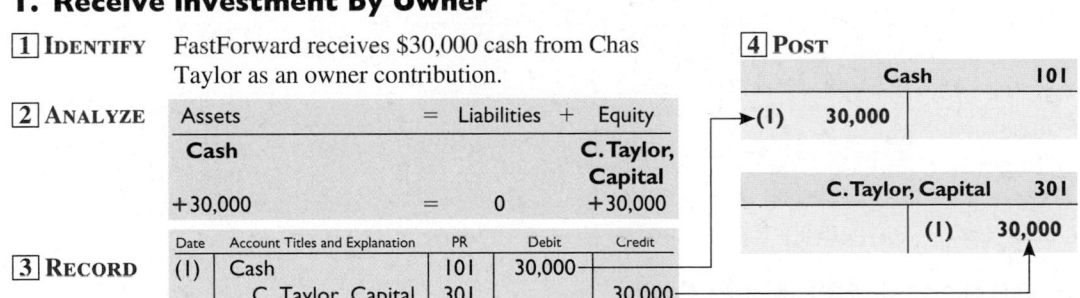

|1| **IDENTIFY**   FastForward receives $30,000 cash from Chas Taylor as an owner contribution.

|2| **ANALYZE**

Assets	=	Liabilities	+	Equity
Cash				**C. Taylor, Capital**
+30,000	=	0		+30,000

|3| **RECORD**

Date	Account Titles and Explanation	PR	Debit	Credit
(1)	Cash	101	30,000	
	C. Taylor, Capital	301		30,000

|4| **POST**

Cash		101
(1) 30,000		

C. Taylor, Capital		301
	(1)	30,000

2. Purchase Supplies for Cash

|1| **IDENTIFY**   FastForward pays $2,500 cash for supplies.

|2| **ANALYZE**

Assets		=	Liabilities	+	Equity
Cash	**Supplies**				
−2,500	+2,500	=	0	+	0

Changes the composition of assets but not the total.

|3| **RECORD**

Date	Account Titles and Explanation	PR	Debit	Credit
(2)	Supplies	126	2,500	
	Cash	101		2,500

|4| **POST**

Supplies		126
(2) 2,500		

Cash		101
(1) 30,000	(2)	2,500

3. Purchase Equipment for Cash

1 IDENTIFY   FastForward pays $26,000 cash for equipment.

2 ANALYZE

Assets		=	Liabilities	+	Equity
Cash	**Equipment**				
−26,000	+26,000	=	0	+	0

Changes the composition of assets but not the total.

3 RECORD

Date	Account Titles and Explanation	PR	Debit	Credit
(3)	Equipment	167	26,000	
	Cash	101		26,000

4 POST

Equipment		167
(3)	26,000	

Cash			101
(1)	30,000	(2)	2,500
		(3)	26,000

4. Purchase Supplies on Credit

1 IDENTIFY   FastForward purchases $7,100 of supplies on credit from a supplier.

2 ANALYZE

Assets	=	Liabilities	+	Equity
Supplies		**Accounts Payable**		
+7,100	=	+7,100	+	0

3 RECORD

Date	Account Titles and Explanation	PR	Debit	Credit
(4)	Supplies	126	7,100	
	Accounts Payable	201		7,100

4 POST

Supplies		126
(2)	2,500	
(4)	7,100	

Accounts Payable		201
	(4)	7,100

5. Provide Services for Cash

1 IDENTIFY   FastForward provides consulting services and immediately collects $4,200 cash.

2 ANALYZE

Assets	=	Liabilities	+	Equity
Cash				**Consulting Revenue**
+4,200	=	0		+4,200

3 RECORD

Date	Account Titles and Explanation	PR	Debit	Credit
(5)	Cash	101	4,200	
	Consulting Revenue	403		4,200

4 POST

Cash			101
(1)	30,000	(2)	2,500
(5)	4,200	(3)	26,000

Consulting Revenue		403
	(5)	4,200

6. Payment of Expense in Cash

1 IDENTIFY   FastForward pays $1,000 cash for December rent.

2 ANALYZE

Assets	=	Liabilities	+	Equity
Cash				**Rent Expense**
−1,000	=	0		−1,000

3 RECORD

Date	Account Titles and Explanation	PR	Debit	Credit
(6)	Rent Expense	640	1,000	
	Cash	101		1,000

4 POST

Rent Expense		640
(6)	1,000	

Cash			101
(1)	30,000	(2)	2,500
(5)	4,200	(3)	26,000
		(6)	1,000

7. Payment of Expense in Cash

Point: *Salary* usually refers to compensation for an employee who receives a fixed amount for a given time period, whereas *wages* usually refers to compensation based on time worked.

1 IDENTIFY   FastForward pays $700 cash for employee salary.

2 ANALYZE

Assets	=	Liabilities	+	Equity
Cash				**Salaries Expense**
−700	=	0		−700

3 RECORD

Date	Account Titles and Explanation	PR	Debit	Credit
(7)	Salaries Expense	622	700	
	Cash	101		700

4 POST

Salaries Expense		622
(7)	700	

Cash			101
(1)	30,000	(2)	2,500
(5)	4,200	(3)	26,000
		(6)	1,000
		(7)	700

8. Provide Consulting and Rental Services on Credit

1 IDENTIFY FastForward provides consulting services of $1,600 and rents its test facilities for $300. The customer is billed $1,900 for these services.

2 ANALYZE

Assets	=	Liabilities	+	Equity	
Accounts Receivable				**Consulting Revenue**	**Rental Revenue**
+1,900	=	0		+1,600	+300

3 RECORD

Date	Account Titles and Explanation	PR	Debit	Credit
(8)	Accounts Receivable	106	1,900	
	Consulting Revenue	403		1,600
	Rental Revenue	406		300

4 POST

Accounts Receivable		106
(8)	1,900	

Consulting Revenue		403
	(5)	4,200
	(8)	1,600

Rental Revenue		406
	(8)	300

Point: Transaction 8 is a **compound journal entry,** which affects three or more accounts.

9. Receipt of Cash on Account

1 IDENTIFY FastForward receives $1,900 cash from the client billed in transaction 8.

2 ANALYZE

Assets		=	Liabilities	+	Equity
Cash	**Accounts Receivable**				
+1,900	−1,900	=	0	+	0

3 RECORD

Date	Account Titles and Explanation	PR	Debit	Credit
(9)	Cash	101	1,900	
	Accounts Receivable	106		1,900

4 POST

Cash			101
(1)	30,000	(2)	2,500
(5)	4,200	(3)	26,000
(9)	1,900	(6)	1,000
		(7)	700

Accounts Receivable			106
(8)	1,900	(9)	1,900

Point: The *revenue recognition principle* requires revenue to be recognized when earned, which is when the company provides products and services to a customer. This is not necessarily the same time that the customer pays. A customer can pay before or after products or services are provided.

10. Partial Payment of Accounts Payable

1 IDENTIFY FastForward pays CalTech Supply $900 cash toward the payable of transaction 4.

2 ANALYZE

Assets	=	Liabilities	+	Equity
Cash		**Accounts Payable**		
−900	=	−900	+	0

3 RECORD

Date	Account Titles and Explanation	PR	Debit	Credit
(10)	Accounts Payable	201	900	
	Cash	101		900

4 POST

Accounts Payable			201
(10)	900	(4)	7,100

Cash			101
(1)	30,000	(2)	2,500
(5)	4,200	(3)	26,000
(9)	1,900	(6)	1,000
		(7)	700
		(10)	900

11. Withdrawal of Cash by Owner

1 IDENTIFY Chas Taylor withdraws $200 cash from FastForward for personal use.

2 ANALYZE

Assets	=	Liabilities	+	Equity
Cash				**C. Taylor, Withdrawals**
−200	=	0		−200

3 RECORD

Date	Account Titles and Explanation	PR	Debit	Credit
(11)	C. Taylor, Withdrawals	302	200	
	Cash	101		200

4 POST

C. Taylor, Withdrawals		302
(11)	200	

Cash			101
(1)	30,000	(2)	2,500
(5)	4,200	(3)	26,000
(9)	1,900	(6)	1,000
		(7)	700
		(10)	900
		(11)	200

12. Receipt of Cash for Future Services

1 IDENTIFY   FastForward receives $3,000 cash in advance of providing consulting services to a customer.

2 ANALYZE

Assets	=	Liabilities	+	Equity
		Unearned		
Cash		**Consulting Revenue**		
+3,000	=	+3,000	+	0

Accepting $3,000 cash obligates FastForward to perform future services and is a liability. No revenue is earned until services are provided.

3 RECORD

Date	Account Titles and Explanation	PR	Debit	Credit
(12)	Cash	101	3,000	
	Unearned Consulting Revenue	236		3,000

4 POST

Cash			101
(1)	30,000	(2)	2,500
(5)	4,200	(3)	26,000
(9)	1,900	(6)	1,000
(12)	3,000	(7)	700
		(10)	900
		(11)	200

Unearned Consulting Revenue			236
		(12)	3,000

13. Pay Cash for Future Insurance Coverage

1 IDENTIFY   FastForward pays $2,400 cash (insurance premium) for a 24-month insurance policy. Coverage begins on December 1.

2 ANALYZE

Assets		=	Liabilities	+	Equity
	Prepaid				
Cash	**Insurance**				
−2,400	+2,400	=	0	+	0

Changes the composition of assets from cash to prepaid insurance. Expense is incurred as insurance coverage expires.

3 RECORD

Date	Account Titles and Explanation	PR	Debit	Credit
(13)	Prepaid Insurance	128	2,400	
	Cash	101		2,400

4 POST

Prepaid Insurance			128
(13)	2,400		

Cash			101
(1)	30,000	(2)	2,500
(5)	4,200	(3)	26,000
(9)	1,900	(6)	1,000
(12)	3,000	(7)	700
		(10)	900
		(11)	200
		(13)	2,400

14. Purchase Supplies for Cash

1 IDENTIFY   FastForward pays $120 cash for supplies.

2 ANALYZE

Assets		=	Liabilities	+	Equity
Cash	**Supplies**				
−120	+120	=	0	+	0

3 RECORD

Date	Account Titles and Explanation	PR	Debit	Credit
(14)	Supplies	126	120	
	Cash	101		120

4 POST

Supplies			126
(2)	2,500		
(4)	7,100		
(14)	120		

Cash			101
(1)	30,000	(2)	2,500
(5)	4,200	(3)	26,000
(9)	1,900	(6)	1,000
(12)	3,000	(7)	700
		(10)	900
		(11)	200
		(13)	2,400
		(14)	120

15. Payment of Expense in Cash

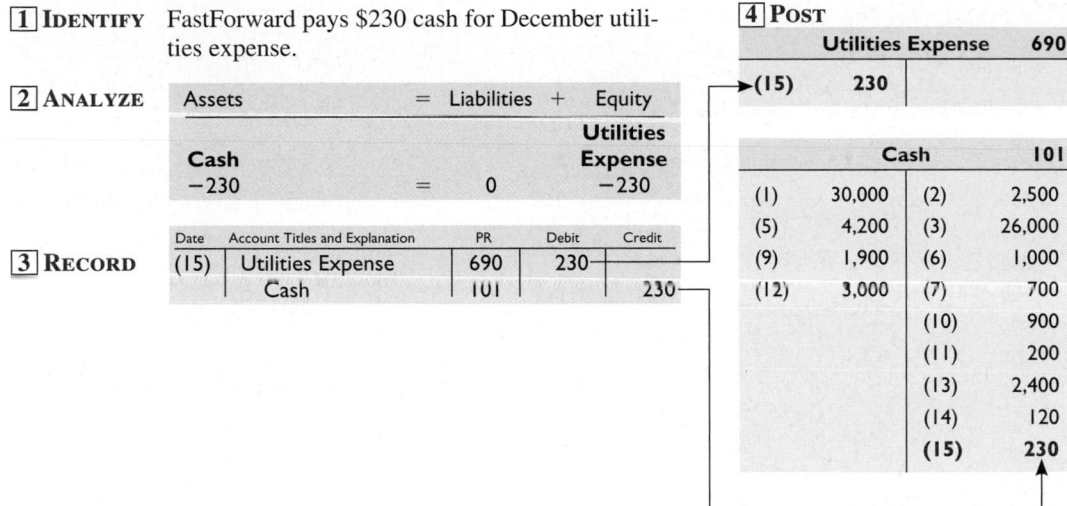

1 IDENTIFY FastForward pays $230 cash for December utilities expense.

16. Payment of Expense in Cash

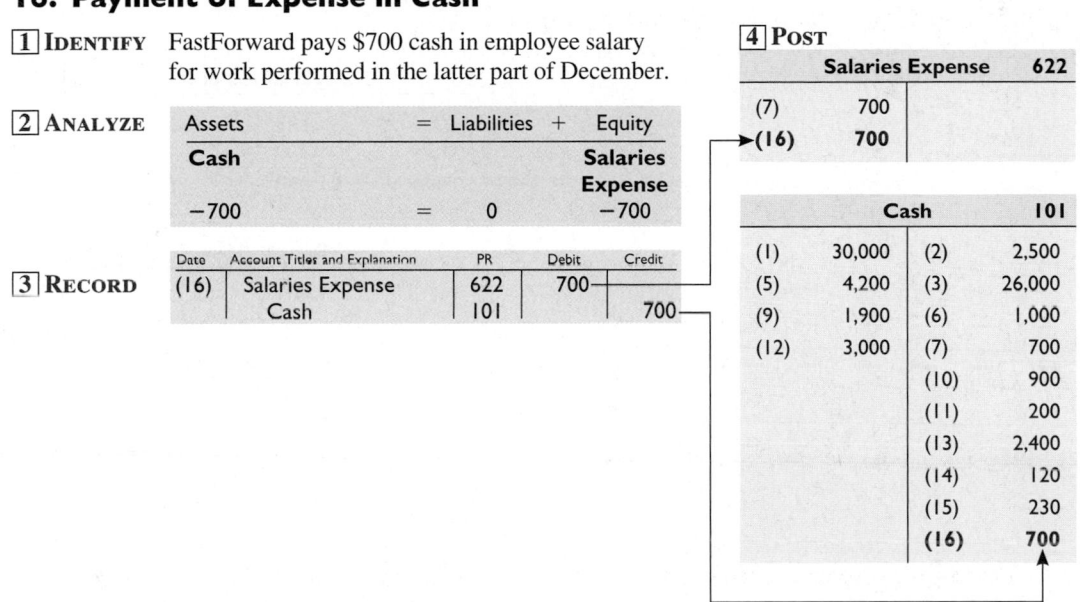

1 IDENTIFY FastForward pays $700 cash in employee salary for work performed in the latter part of December.

Point: We could merge transactions 15 and 16 into one *compound entry*.

Accounting Equation Analysis

Exhibit 2.13 shows the ledger accounts (in T-account form) of FastForward after all 16 transactions are recorded and posted and the balances computed. The accounts are grouped into three major columns corresponding to the accounting equation: assets, liabilities, and equity. Note several important points. First, as with each transaction, the totals for the three columns must obey the accounting equation. Specifically, assets equal $42,470 ($4,350 + $0 + $9,720 + $2,400 + $26,000); liabilities equal $9,200 ($6,200 + $3,000); and equity equals $33,270 ($30,000 − $200 + $5,800 + $300 − $1,400 − $1,000 − $230). These numbers prove the accounting equation: Assets of $42,470 = Liabilities of $9,200 + Equity of $33,270. Second, the capital, withdrawals, revenue, and expense accounts reflect the transactions that change equity. These account categories underlie the statement of owner's equity. Third, the revenue and expense account balances will be summarized and reported in the income statement. Fourth, increases and decreases in the cash account make up the elements reported in the statement of cash flows.

Debit and Credit Rules		
Accounts	**Increase (normal bal.)**	**Decrease**
Asset	Debit	Credit
Liability	Credit	Debit
Capital	Credit	Debit
Withdrawals	Debit	Credit
Revenue	Credit	Debit
Expense	Debit	Credit

Point: Technology does not provide the judgment required to analyze most business transactions. Analysis requires the expertise of skilled and ethical professionals.

EXHIBIT 2.13

Ledger for FastForward (in T-Account Form)

General Ledger

	Assets			=		Liabilities			+		Equity	

Cash   101

(1)	30,000	(2)	2,500
(5)	4,200	(3)	26,000
(9)	1,900	(6)	1,000
(12)	3,000	(7)	700
		(10)	900
		(11)	200
		(13)	2,400
		(14)	120
		(15)	230
		(16)	700
Balance	**4,350**		

Accounts Receivable   106

(8)	1,900	(9)	1,900
Balance	**0**		

Supplies   126

(2)	2,500	
(4)	7,100	
(14)	120	
Balance	**9,720**	

Prepaid Insurance   128

(13)	**2,400**

Equipment   167

(3)	**26,000**

Accounts Payable   201

(10)	900	(4)	7,100
		Balance	**6,200**

Unearned Consulting Revenue   236

		(12)	**3,000**

C. Taylor, Capital   301

		(1)	30,000

C. Taylor, Withdrawals   302

(11)	200

Consulting Revenue   403

		(5)	4,200
		(8)	1,600
		Balance	**5,800**

Rental Revenue   406

		(8)	**300**

Salaries Expense   622

(7)	700	
(16)	700	
Balance	**1,400**	

Rent Expense   640

(6)	**1,000**

Utilities Expense   690

(15)	**230**

Accounts in this white area reflect those reported on the income statement.

$42,470	=	**$9,200**	+	**$33,270**	

Quick Check

Answers — p. 75

8. What types of transactions increase equity? What types decrease equity?

9. Why are accounting systems called *double-entry?*

10. For each transaction, double-entry accounting requires which of the following? (*a*) Debits to asset accounts must create credits to liability or equity accounts, (*b*) a debit to a liability account must create a credit to an asset account, or (*c*) total debits must equal total credits.

11. An owner invests $15,000 cash along with equipment having a market value of $23,000 in a company. Prepare the necessary journal entry.

12. Explain what a compound journal entry is.

13. Why are posting reference numbers entered in the journal when entries are posted to ledger accounts?

TRIAL BALANCE

Double-entry accounting requires the sum of debit account balances to equal the sum of credit account balances. A trial balance is used to confirm this. A **trial balance** is a list of accounts and their balances at a point in time. Account balances are reported in their appropriate debit or credit columns of a trial balance. A trial balance can be used to confirm this and to follow up on any abnormal or unusual balances. Exhibit 2.14 shows the trial balance for FastForward after its 16 entries have been posted to the ledger. (This is an *unadjusted* trial balance—Chapter 3 explains the necessary adjustments.)

EXHIBIT 2.14

Trial Balance (Unadjusted)

Peachtree Accounting: FastForward
File Edit Lists Maintain Tasks Analysis Options Reports & Forms Services Window Help

Company
Business Status
Customers & Sales
Vendors & Purchases
Inventory & Services
Employees & Payroll
Banking
Company

Shortcuts Customize
Sales Invoice
Receive Money from Customer
Bills - Pay Bill
Customer List
Vendor List
Find Transactions
General Journal Entry

FASTFORWARD
Trial Balance
December 31, 2013

	Debit	Credit
Cash	$ 4,350	
Accounts receivable	0	
Supplies	9,720	
Prepaid insurance	2,400	
Equipment	26,000	
Accounts payable		$ 6,200
Unearned consulting revenue		3,000
C. Taylor, Capital		30,000
C. Taylor, Withdrawals	200	
Consulting revenue		5,800
Rental revenue		300
Salaries expense	1,400	
Rent expense	1,000	
Utilities expense	230	
Totals	$ 45,300	$ 45,300

Point: The ordering of accounts in a trial balance typically follows their identification number from the chart of accounts.

Preparing a Trial Balance

Preparing a trial balance involves three steps:

P2 Prepare and explain the use of a trial balance.

1. List each account title and its amount (from ledger) in the trial balance. If an account has a zero balance, list it with a zero in its normal balance column (or omit it entirely).
2. Compute the total of debit balances and the total of credit balances.
3. Verify (*prove*) total debit balances equal total credit balances.

The total of debit balances equals the total of credit balances for the trial balance in Exhibit 2.14. Equality of these two totals does not guarantee that no errors were made. For example, the column totals still will be equal when a debit or credit of a correct amount is made to a wrong account. Another error that does not cause unequal column totals occurs when equal debits and credits of an incorrect amount are entered.

Searching for and Correcting Errors If the trial balance does not balance (when its columns are not equal), the error (or errors) must be found and corrected. An efficient way to search for an error is to check the journalizing, posting, and trial balance preparation

Point: A trial balance is *not* a financial statement but a mechanism for checking equality of debits and credits in the ledger. Financial statements do not have debit and credit columns.

Example: If a credit to Unearned Revenue was incorrectly posted from the journal as a credit to the Revenue ledger account, would the ledger still balance? Would the financial statements be correct? *Answers:* The ledger would balance, but liabilities would be understated, equity would be overstated, and income would be overstated (all because of overstated revenues).

Point: The IRS requires companies to keep records that can be audited.

P3   Prepare financial statements from business transactions.

EXHIBIT 2.15

Links between Financial Statements across Time

in *reverse order.* Step 1 is to verify that the trial balance columns are correctly added. If step 1 fails to find the error, step 2 is to verify that account balances are accurately entered from the ledger. Step 3 is to see whether a debit (or credit) balance is mistakenly listed in the trial balance as a credit (or debit). A clue to this error is when the difference between total debits and total credits equals twice the amount of the incorrect account balance. If the error is still undiscovered, Step 4 is to recompute each account balance in the ledger. Step 5 is to verify that each journal entry is properly posted. Step 6 is to verify that the original journal entry has equal debits and credits. At this point, the errors should be uncovered.[3]

If an error in a journal entry is discovered before the error is posted, it can be corrected in a manual system by drawing a line through the incorrect information. The correct information is written above it to create a record of change for the auditor. Many computerized systems allow the operator to replace the incorrect information directly.

If an error in a journal entry is not discovered until after it is posted, we do not strike through both erroneous entries in the journal and ledger. Instead, we correct this error by creating a *correcting entry* that removes the amount from the wrong account and records it to the correct account. As an example, suppose a $100 purchase of supplies is journalized with an incorrect debit to Equipment, and then this incorrect entry is posted to the ledger. The Supplies ledger account balance is understated by $100, and the Equipment ledger account balance is overstated by $100. The correcting entry is: debit Supplies and credit Equipment (both for $100).

Using a Trial Balance to Prepare Financial Statements

This section shows how to prepare *financial statements* from the trial balance in Exhibit 2.14 and from information on the December transactions of FastForward. These statements differ from those in Chapter 1 because of several additional transactions. These statements are also more precisely called *unadjusted statements* because we need to make some further accounting adjustments (described in Chapter 3).

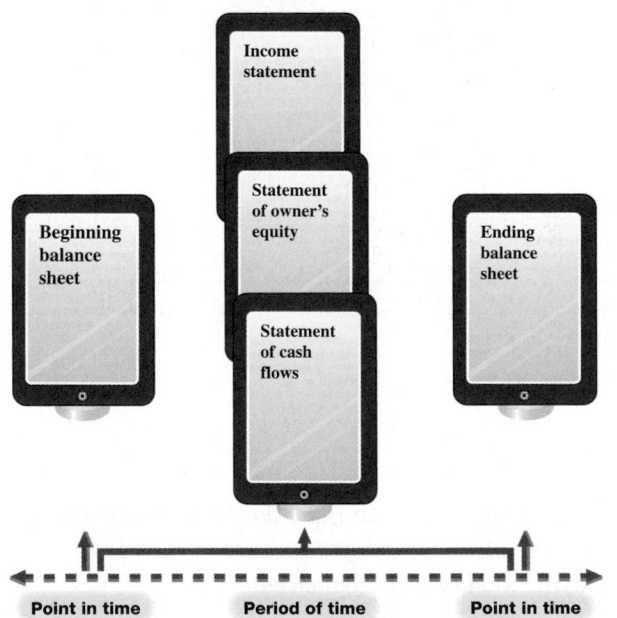

Point in time   Period of time   Point in time

How financial statements are linked in time is illustrated in Exhibit 2.15. A balance sheet reports on an organization's financial position at a *point in time.* The income statement, statement of owner's equity, and statement of cash flows report on financial performance over a *period of time.* The three statements in the middle column of Exhibit 2.15 link balance sheets from the beginning to the end of a reporting period. They explain how financial position changes from one point to another.

Preparers and users (including regulatory agencies) determine the length of the reporting period. A one-year, or annual, reporting period is common, as are semiannual, quarterly, and monthly periods. The one-year reporting period

---

[3] *Transposition* occurs when two digits are switched, or transposed, within a number. If transposition is the only error, it yields a difference between the two trial balance totals that is evenly divisible by 9. For example, assume that a $691 debit in an entry is incorrectly posted to the ledger as $619. Total credits in the trial balance are then larger than total debits by $72 ($691 − $619). The $72 error is *evenly* divisible by 9 (72/9 = 8). The first digit of the quotient (in our example it is 8) equals the difference between the digits of the two transposed numbers (the 9 and the 1). The number of digits in the quotient also tells the location of the transposition, starting from the right. The quotient in our example had only one digit (8), so it tells us the transposition is in the first digit. Consider another example where a transposition error involves posting $961 instead of the correct $691. The difference in these numbers is $270, and its quotient is 30 (270/9). The quotient has two digits, so it tells us to check the second digit from the right for a transposition of two numbers that have a difference of 3.

is known as the *accounting,* or *fiscal, year.* Businesses whose accounting year begins on January 1 and ends on December 31 are known as *calendar-year* companies. **Polaris** is a calendar-year company. Many companies choose a fiscal year ending on a date other than December 31. **Arctic Cat** is a *noncalendar-year* company as reflected in the headings of its March 31 year-end financial statements in Appendix A near the end of the book.

Point: A statement's heading lists the 3 W's: **W**ho—name of organization, **W**hat—name of statement, **W**hen— statement's point in time or period of time.

Income Statement   An income statement reports the revenues earned less the expenses incurred by a business over a period of time. FastForward's income statement for December is shown at the top of Exhibit 2.16. Information about revenues and expenses is conveniently taken from the trial balance in Exhibit 2.14. Net income of $3,470 is reported at the bottom of the statement. Owner investments and withdrawals are *not* part of income.

Statement of Owner's Equity   The statement of owner's equity reports information about how equity changes over the reporting period. FastForward's statement of owner's equity is the second report in Exhibit 2.16. It shows the $30,000 owner investment, the $3,470 of net income, the $200 withdrawal, and the $33,270 end-of-period (capital) balance. (The beginning

EXHIBIT 2.16

Financial Statements and Their Links

FASTFORWARD
Income Statement
For Month Ended December 31, 2013

Revenues		
Consulting revenue ($4,200 + $1,600)	$ 5,800	
Rental revenue	300	
Total revenues		$ 6,100
Expenses		
Rent expense	1,000	
Salaries expense	1,400	
Utilities expense	230	
Total expenses		2,630
Net income		$ 3,470 ◄

FASTFORWARD
Statement of Owner's Equity
For Month Ended December 31, 2013

C. Taylor, Capital, December 1, 2013		$ 0
Plus: Investments by owner	$30,000	
Net income	**3,470**	33,470
		33,470
Less: Withdrawals by owner		200
C. Taylor, Capital, December 31, 2013		$33,270 ◄

Point: Arrow lines show how the statements are linked.

FASTFORWARD
Balance Sheet
December 31, 2013

Assets		Liabilities	
Cash	$ 4,350	Accounts payable	$ 6,200
Supplies	9,720	Unearned revenue	3,000
Prepaid insurance . .	2,400	Total liabilities	9,200
Equipment	26,000	**Equity**	
		C. Taylor, Capital	33,270 ◄
Total assets	$42,470	Total liabilities and equity . .	$ 42,470

Point: To *foot* a column of numbers is to add them.

balance in the statement of owner's equity is rarely zero; an exception is for the first period of operations. The beginning capital balance in January 2014 is $33,270, which is December's ending balance.)

Balance Sheet   The balance sheet reports the financial position of a company at a point in time, usually at the end of a month, quarter, or year. FastForward's balance sheet is the third report in Exhibit 2.16. This statement refers to financial condition at the close of business on December 31. The left side of the balance sheet lists its assets: cash, supplies, prepaid insurance, and equipment. The upper right side of the balance sheet shows that it owes $6,200 to creditors and $3,000 in services to customers who paid in advance. The equity section shows an ending balance of $33,270. Note the link between the ending balance of the statement of owner's equity and the capital balance. (Recall that this presentation of the balance sheet is called the *account form:* assets on the left and liabilities and equity on the right. Another presentation is the *report form:* assets on top, followed by liabilities and then equity. Either presentation is acceptable.)

▮ Decision Maker

Entrepreneur   You open a wholesale business selling entertainment equipment to retail outlets. You find that most of your customers demand to buy on credit. How can you use the balance sheets of these customers to decide which ones to extend credit to? ▮   [Answer—p. 74]

Presentation Issues   Dollar signs are not used in journals and ledgers. They do appear in financial statements and other reports such as trial balances. The usual practice is to put dollar signs beside only the first and last numbers in a column. **Polaris**'s financial statements in Appendix A show this. When amounts are entered in a journal, ledger, or trial balance, commas are optional to indicate thousands, millions, and so forth. However, commas are always used in financial statements. Companies also commonly round amounts in reports to the nearest dollar, or even to a higher level. Polaris is typical of many companies in that it rounds its financial statement amounts to the nearest thousand (or million). This decision is based on the perceived impact of rounding for users' business decisions.

off the mark.com   by Mark Parisi
                          offthemark.com

HE CONTINUED ACCOUNTING RIGHT THROUGH HIS COFFEE BREAK... THEN HIS LUNCH BREAK. CLEARLY, MYRON WAS "IN THE ZONE."

Quick Check   Answers — p. 75

14. Where are dollar signs typically entered in financial statements?
15. If a $4,000 debit to Equipment in a journal entry is incorrectly posted to the ledger as a $4,000 credit, and the ledger account has a resulting debit balance of $20,000, what is the effect of this error on the Trial Balance column totals?
16. Describe the link between the income statement and the statement of owner's equity.
17. Explain the link between the balance sheet and the statement of owner's equity.
18. Define and describe revenues and expenses.
19. Define and describe assets, liabilities, and equity.

GLOBAL VIEW

Financial accounting according to U.S. GAAP is similar, but not identical, to IFRS. This section discusses differences in analyzing and recording transactions, and with the preparation of financial statements.

Analyzing and Recording Transactions   Both U.S. GAAP and IFRS include broad and similar guidance for financial accounting. As the FASB and IASB work toward a common conceptual framework over the next few years, even those differences will fade. Further, both U.S. GAAP and IFRS apply transaction analysis and recording as shown in this chapter—using the same debit and credit system and accrual accounting. Although some variations exist in revenue and expense recognition and other accounting principles, all of the transactions in this chapter are accounted for identically under these two systems.

Financial Statements   Both U.S. GAAP and IFRS prepare the same four basic financial statements. A few differences within each statement do exist and we will discuss those throughout the book. For example, both U.S. GAAP and IFRS require balance sheets to separate current items from noncurrent items. However, while U.S. GAAP balance sheets report current items first, IFRS balance sheets normally (but are not required to) present noncurrent items first, and equity before liabilities. To illustrate, a condensed version of **Piaggio**'s balance sheet follows (numbers using Euros in thousands).

PIAGGIO

PIAGGIO				
Balance Sheet (in thousands of Euros)				
December 31, 2011				
Assets		**Equity and Liabilities**		
Noncurrent assets	1,010,476	Total equity	446,218
Current assets	509,708	Noncurrent liabilities	429,689
		Current liabilities	644,277
Total assets	1,520,184	Total equity and liabilities	1,520,184

Accounting Controls and Assurance   Accounting systems depend on control procedures that assure the proper principles were applied in processing accounting information. The passage of SOX legislation strengthened U.S. control procedures in recent years. However, global standards for control are diverse and so are enforcement activities. Consequently, while global accounting standards are converging, their application in different countries can yield different outcomes depending on the quality of their auditing standards and enforcement.

■ **Decision** Insight

Accounting Control Recording valid transactions, and not recording fraudulent transactions, enhances the quality of financial statements. The graph here shows the percentage of employees in information technology that report observing specific types of misconduct within the past year [Source: KPMG 2009]. ■

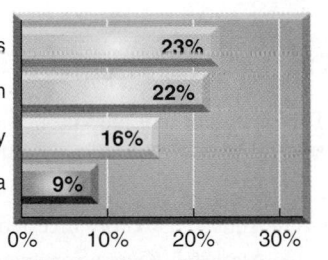

Breaching database controls	23%
Mishandling private information	22%
Breaching customer privacy	16%
Falsifying accounting data	9%

0%   10%   20%   30%
Percent Citing Misconduct

Debt Ratio ▢▢▢   **Decision Analysis**

An important business objective is gathering information to help assess a company's risk of failing to pay its debts. Companies finance their assets with either liabilities or equity. A company that finances a relatively large portion of its assets with liabilities is said to have a high degree of *financial leverage*. Higher financial leverage involves greater risk because liabilities must be repaid and often require regular interest payments (equity financing does not). The risk that a company might not be able to meet such required payments is higher if it has more liabilities (is more highly leveraged). One way to assess the risk associated with a company's use of liabilities is to compute the **debt ratio** as in Exhibit 2.17.

A2 Compute the debt ratio and describe its use in analyzing financial condition.

$$\text{Debt ratio} = \frac{\text{Total liabilities}}{\text{Total assets}}$$

EXHIBIT 2.17

Debt Ratio

Point: Compare the equity amount to the liability amount to assess the extent of owner versus nonowner financing.

To see how to apply the debt ratio, let's look at **Skechers**'s liabilities and assets. The company designs, markets, and sells footwear for men, women, and children under the Skechers brand. Exhibit 2.18 computes and reports its debt ratio at the end of each year from 2006 to 2011.

EXHIBIT 2.18

Computation and Analysis of Debt Ratio

$ in millions	2011	2010	2009	2008	2007	2006
Total liabilities	$ 389	$ 359	$246	$204	$201	$288
Total assets	$1,282	$1,305	$996	$876	$828	$737
Debt ratio	**0.30**	**0.28**	**0.25**	**0.23**	**0.24**	**0.39**
Industry debt ratio	0.47	0.49	0.51	0.50	0.46	0.48

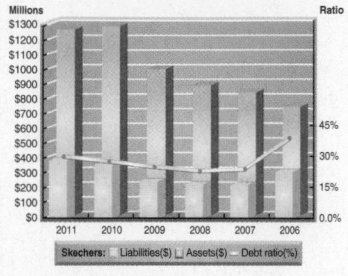

Skechers's debt ratio ranges from a low of 0.23 to a high of 0.39—also, see graph in margin. Its ratio is lower, compared with the industry ratio. This analysis implies a low risk from its financial leverage. Is financial leverage good or bad for Skechers? To answer that question we need to compare the company's return on the borrowed money to the rate it is paying creditors. If the company's return is higher, it is successfully borrowing money to make more money. A company's success with making money from borrowed money can quickly turn unprofitable if its own return drops below the rate it is paying creditors.

■ **Decision** Maker ══════════════════════

Investor   You consider buying stock in **Converse**. As part of your analysis, you compute its debt ratio for 2011, 2012, and 2013 as: 0.35, 0.74, and 0.94, respectively. Based on the debt ratio, is Converse a low-risk investment? Has the risk of buying Converse stock changed over this period? (The industry debt ratio averages 0.40.) ■ [Answer—p. 75]

DEMONSTRATION PROBLEM

(This problem extends the demonstration problem of Chapter 1.) After several months of planning, Jasmine Worthy started a haircutting business called Expressions. The following events occurred during its first month.

a. On August 1, Worthy invested $3,000 cash and $15,000 of equipment in Expressions.

b. On August 2, Expressions paid $600 cash for furniture for the shop.

c. On August 3, Expressions paid $500 cash to rent space in a strip mall for August.

d. On August 4, it purchased $1,200 of equipment on credit for the shop (using a long-term note payable).

e. On August 5, Expressions opened for business. Cash received from haircutting services in the first week and a half of business (ended August 15) was $825.

f. On August 15, it provided $100 of haircutting services on account.

g. On August 17, it received a $100 check for services previously rendered on account.

h. On August 17, it paid $125 to an assistant for hours worked during the grand opening.

i. Cash received from services provided during the second half of August was $930.

j. On August 31, it paid a $400 installment toward principal on the note payable entered into on August 4.

k. On August 31, Worthy withdrew $900 cash for personal use.

Required

1. Open the following ledger accounts in balance column format (account numbers are in parentheses): Cash (101); Accounts Receivable (102); Furniture (161); Store Equipment (165); Note Payable (240); J. Worthy, Capital (301); J. Worthy, Withdrawals (302); Haircutting Services Revenue (403); Wages Expense (623); and Rent Expense (640). Prepare general journal entries for the transactions.

2. Post the journal entries from (1) to the ledger accounts.

3. Prepare a trial balance as of August 31.

4. Prepare an income statement for August.

5. Prepare a statement of owner's equity for August.

6. Prepare a balance sheet as of August 31.

7. Determine the debt ratio as of August 31.

Extended Analysis

8. In the coming months, Expressions will experience a greater variety of business transactions. Identify which accounts are debited and which are credited for the following transactions. (*Hint:* We must use some accounts not opened in part 1.)

   a. Purchase supplies with cash.

   b. Pay cash for future insurance coverage.

   c. Receive cash for services to be provided in the future.

   d. Purchase supplies on account.

PLANNING THE SOLUTION

- Analyze each transaction and use the debit and credit rules to prepare a journal entry for each.
- Post each debit and each credit from journal entries to their ledger accounts and cross-reference each amount in the posting reference (PR) columns of the journal and ledger.
- Calculate each account balance and list the accounts with their balances on a trial balance.
- Verify that total debits in the trial balance equal total credits.
- To prepare the income statement, identify revenues and expenses. List those items on the statement, compute the difference, and label the result as *net income* or *net loss*.
- Use information in the ledger to prepare the statement of owner's equity.
- Use information in the ledger to prepare the balance sheet.
- Calculate the debt ratio by dividing total liabilities by total assets.
- Analyze the future transactions to identify the accounts affected and apply debit and credit rules.

SOLUTION TO DEMONSTRATION PROBLEM

1. General journal entries:

General Journal

Page 1

Date	Account Titles and Explanation	PR	Debit	Credit
Aug. 1	Cash	101	3,000	
	Store Equipment	165	15,000	
	J. Worthy, Capital	301		18,000
	Owner's investment.			
2	Furniture	161	600	
	Cash	101		600
	Purchased furniture for cash.			
3	Rent Expense	640	500	
	Cash	101		500
	Paid rent for August.			
4	Store Equipment	165	1,200	
	Note Payable	240		1,200
	Purchased additional equipment on credit.			
15	Cash	101	825	
	Haircutting Services Revenue	403		825
	Cash receipts from first half of August.			

[continued on next page]

[continued from previous page]

15	Accounts Receivable	102	100	
	Haircutting Services Revenue	403		100
	To record revenue for services provided on account.			
17	Cash	101	100	
	Accounts Receivable	102		100
	To record cash received as payment on account.			
17	Wages Expense....................................	623	125	
	Cash	101		125
	Paid wages to assistant.			
31	Cash	101	930	
	Haircutting Services Revenue	403		930
	Cash receipts from second half of August.			
31	Note Payable	240	400	
	Cash	101		400
	Paid an installment on the note payable.			
31	J. Worthy, Withdrawals	302	900	
	Cash	101		900
	Cash withdrawal by owner.			

2. Post journal entries from part 1 to the ledger accounts:

General Ledger

Cash Account No. 101

Date	PR	Debit	Credit	Balance
Aug. 1	G1	3,000		3,000
2	G1		600	2,400
3	G1		500	1,900
15	G1	825		2,725
17	G1	100		2,825
17	G1		125	2,700
31	G1	930		3,630
31	G1		400	3,230
31	G1		900	2,330

Accounts Receivable Account No. 102

Date	PR	Debit	Credit	Balance
Aug. 15	G1	100		100
17	G1		100	0

Furniture Account No. 161

Date	PR	Debit	Credit	Balance
Aug. 2	G1	600		600

Store Equipment Account No. 165

Date	PR	Debit	Credit	Balance
Aug. 1	G1	15,000		15,000
4	G1	1,200		16,200

Note Payable Account No. 240

Date	PR	Debit	Credit	Balance
Aug. 4	G1		1,200	1,200
31	G1	400		800

J. Worthy, Capital Account No. 301

Date	PR	Debit	Credit	Balance
Aug. 1	G1		18,000	18,000

J. Worthy, Withdrawals Account No. 302

Date	PR	Debit	Credit	Balance
Aug. 31	G1	900		900

Haircutting Services Revenue Account No. 403

Date	PR	Debit	Credit	Balance
Aug. 15	G1		825	825
15	G1		100	925
31	G1		930	1,855

Wages Expense Account No. 623

Date	PR	Debit	Credit	Balance
Aug. 17	G1	125		125

Rent Expense Account No. 640

Date	PR	Debit	Credit	Balance
Aug. 3	G1	500		500

3. Prepare a trial balance from the ledger:

EXPRESSIONS Trial Balance August 31		
	Debit	**Credit**
Cash	$ 2,330	
Accounts receivable	0	
Furniture	600	
Store equipment	16,200	
Note payable		$ 800
J. Worthy, Capital		18,000
J. Worthy, Withdrawals	900	
Haircutting services revenue		1,855
Wages expense	125	
Rent expense	500	
Totals	$20,655	$20,655

4.

EXPRESSIONS Income Statement For Month Ended August 31		
Revenues		
Haircutting services revenue		$1,855
Operating expenses		
Rent expense	$500	
Wages expense	125	
Total operating expenses		625
Net income		$1,230

5.

EXPRESSIONS Statement of Owner's Equity For Month Ended August 31		
J. Worthy, Capital, August 1		$ 0
Plus: Investments by owner	$18,000	
Net income	1,230	19,230
		19,230
Less: Withdrawals by owner		900
J. Worthy, Capital, August 31		$18,330

6.

EXPRESSIONS Balance Sheet August 31			
Assets		**Liabilities**	
Cash	$ 2,330	Note payable	$ 800
Furniture	600	**Equity**	
Store equipment	16,200	J. Worthy, Capital	18,330
Total assets	$19,130	Total liabilities and equity	$19,130

7. Debt ratio $= \dfrac{\text{Total liabilities}}{\text{Total assets}} = \dfrac{\$800}{\$19,130} = \underline{\underline{\textbf{4.18}\%}}$

8a. Supplies *debited*   **8c.** Cash *debited*
       Cash *credited*   Unearned Services Revenue *credited*

8b. Prepaid Insurance *debited*   **8d.** Supplies *debited*
       Cash *credited*   Accounts Payable *credited*

Summary

C1 Explain the steps in processing transactions and the role of source documents. The accounting process identifies business transactions and events, analyzes and records their effects, and summarizes and prepares information useful in making decisions. Transactions and events are the starting points in the accounting process. Source documents identify and describe transactions and events. Examples are sales tickets, checks, purchase orders, bills, and bank statements. Source documents provide objective and reliable evidence, making information more useful. The effects of transactions and events are recorded in journals. Posting along with a trial balance helps summarize and classify these effects.

C2 Describe an account and its use in recording transactions. An account is a detailed record of increases and decreases in a specific asset, liability, equity, revenue, or expense. Information from accounts is analyzed, summarized, and presented in reports and financial statements for decision makers.

C3 Describe a ledger and a chart of accounts. The ledger (or general ledger) is a record containing all accounts used by a company and their balances. It is referred to as the *books*. The chart of accounts is a list of all accounts and usually includes an identification number assigned to each account.

C4 Define *debits* and *credits* and explain double-entry accounting. *Debit* refers to left, and *credit* refers to right. Debits increase assets, expenses, and withdrawals while credits decrease them. Credits increase liabilities, owner capital, and revenues; debits decrease them. Double-entry accounting means each transaction affects at least two accounts and has at least one debit and one credit. The system for recording debits and credits follows from the accounting equation. The left side of an account is the normal balance for assets, withdrawals, and expenses, and the right side is the normal balance for liabilities, capital, and revenues.

A1 Analyze the impact of transactions on accounts and financial statements. We analyze transactions using concepts of double-entry accounting. This analysis is performed by determining a transaction's effects on accounts. These effects are recorded in journals and posted to ledgers.

A2 Compute the debt ratio and describe its use in analyzing financial condition. A company's debt ratio is computed as total liabilities divided by total assets. It reveals how much of the assets are financed by creditor (nonowner) financing. The higher this ratio, the more risk a company faces because liabilities must be repaid at specific dates.

P1 Record transactions in a journal and post entries to a ledger. Transactions are recorded in a journal. Each entry in a journal is posted to the accounts in the ledger. This provides information that is used to produce financial statements. Balance column accounts are widely used and include columns for debits, credits, and the account balance.

P2 Prepare and explain the use of a trial balance. A trial balance is a list of accounts from the ledger showing their debit or credit balances in separate columns. The trial balance is a summary of the ledger's contents and is useful in preparing financial statements and in revealing recordkeeping errors.

P3 Prepare financial statements from business transactions. The balance sheet, the statement of owner's equity, the income statement, and the statement of cash flows use data from the trial balance (and other financial statements) for their preparation.

Guidance Answers to Decision Maker and Decision Ethics

Cashier   The advantages to the process proposed by the assistant manager include improved customer service, fewer delays, and less work for you. However, you should have serious concerns about internal control and the potential for fraud. In particular, the assistant manager could steal cash and simply enter fewer sales to match the remaining cash. You should reject her suggestion without the manager's approval. Moreover, you should have an ethical concern about the assistant manager's suggestion to ignore store policy.

Entrepreneur   We can use the accounting equation (Assets = Liabilities + Equity) to help us identify risky customers to whom we would likely not want to extend credit. A balance sheet provides amounts for each of these key components. The lower a customer's equity is relative to liabilities, the less likely you would extend credit. A low equity means the business has little value that does not already have creditor claims to it.

Investor   The debt ratio suggests the stock of Converse is of higher risk than normal and that this risk is rising. The average industry ratio of 0.40 further supports this conclusion. The 2013 debt ratio for Converse is twice the industry norm. Also, a debt ratio approaching 1.0 indicates little to no equity.

Guidance Answers to Quick Checks

1. Examples of source documents are sales tickets, checks, purchase orders, charges to customers, bills from suppliers, employee earnings records, and bank statements.

2. Source documents serve many purposes, including record-keeping and internal control. Source documents, especially if obtained from outside the organization, provide objective and reliable evidence about transactions and their amounts.

3.
Assets	Liabilities	Equity
a,c,e	b,d	—

4. An account is a record in an accounting system that records and stores the increases and decreases in a specific asset, liability, equity, revenue, or expense. The ledger is a collection of all the accounts of a company.

5. A company's size and diversity affect the number of accounts in its accounting system. The types of accounts depend on information the company needs to both effectively operate and report its activities in financial statements.

6. No. Debit and credit both can mean increase or decrease. The particular meaning in a circumstance depends on the *type of account*. For example, a debit increases the balance of asset, withdrawals, and expense accounts, but it decreases the balance of liability, capital, and revenue accounts.

7. A chart of accounts is a list of all of a company's accounts and their identification numbers.

8. Equity is increased by revenues and by owner investments. Equity is decreased by expenses and owner withdrawals.

9. The name *double-entry* is used because all transactions affect at least two accounts. There must be at least one debit in one account and at least one credit in another account.

10. The answer is (c).

11.
Cash	15,000	
Equipment	23,000	
Owner, Capital		38,000
Investment by owner of cash and equipment.		

12. A compound journal entry affects three or more accounts.

13. Posting reference numbers are entered in the journal when posting to the ledger as a cross-reference that allows the record-keeper or auditor to trace debits and credits from one record to another.

14. At a minimum, dollar signs are placed beside the first and last numbers in a column. It is also common to place dollar signs beside any amount that appears after a ruled line to indicate that an addition or subtraction has occurred.

15. The Equipment account balance is incorrectly reported at $20,000—it should be $28,000. The effect of this error understates the trial balance's Debit column total by $8,000. This results in an $8,000 difference between the column totals.

16. An income statement reports a company's revenues and expenses along with the resulting net income or loss. A statement of owner's equity reports changes in equity, including that from net income or loss. Both statements report transactions occurring over a period of time.

17. The balance sheet describes a company's financial position (assets, liabilities, and equity) at a point in time. The capital amount in the balance sheet is obtained from the statement of owner's equity.

18. Revenues are inflows of assets in exchange for products or services provided to customers as part of the main operations of a business. Expenses are outflows or the using up of assets that result from providing products or services to customers.

19. Assets are the resources a business owns or controls that carry expected future benefits. Liabilities are the obligations of a business, representing the claims of others against the assets of a business. Equity reflects the owner's claims on the assets of the business after deducting liabilities.

Key Terms

Account (p. 51)

Account balance (p. 55)

Balance column account (p. 58)

Chart of accounts (p. 54)

Compound journal entry (p. 61)

Credit (p. 55)

Creditors (p. 52)

Debit (p. 55)

Double-entry accounting (p. 55)

General journal (p. 56)

General ledger (p. 51)

Journal (p. 56)

Journalizing (p. 56)

Posting (p. 56)

Posting reference (PR) column (p. 58)

Source documents (p. 50)

T-accounts (p. 54)

Trial balance (p. 65)

Unearned revenue (p. 53)

Additional Quiz Questions are available at the book's Website.

1. Amalia Company received its utility bill for the current period of $700 and immediately paid it. Its journal entry to record this transaction includes a
   a. Credit to Utility Expense for $700.
   b. Debit to Utility Expense for $700.
   c. Debit to Accounts Payable for $700.
   d. Debit to Cash for $700.
   e. Credit to capital for $700.

2. On May 1, Mattingly Lawn Service collected $2,500 cash from a customer in advance of five months of lawn service. Mattingly's journal entry to record this transaction includes a
   a. Credit to Unearned Lawn Service Fees for $2,500.
   b. Debit to Lawn Service Fees Earned for $2,500.
   c. Credit to Cash for $2,500.
   d. Debit to Unearned Lawn Service Fees for $2,500.
   e. Credit to capital for $2,500.

3. Liang Shue contributed $250,000 cash and land worth $500,000 to open his new business, Shue Consulting. Which of the following journal entries does Shue Consulting make to record this transaction?

   a. Cash Assets 750,000
         L. Shue, Capital   750,000
   b. L. Shue, Capital 750,000
         Assets   750,000
   c. Cash 250,000
      Land 500,000
         L. Shue, Capital   750,000

   d. L. Shue, Capital 750,000
         Cash   250,000
         Land   500,000

4. A trial balance prepared at year-end shows total credits exceed total debits by $765. This discrepancy could have been caused by
   a. An error in the general journal where a $765 increase in Accounts Payable was recorded as a $765 decrease in Accounts Payable.
   b. The ledger balance for Accounts Payable of $7,650 being entered in the trial balance as $765.
   c. A general journal error where a $765 increase in Accounts Receivable was recorded as a $765 increase in Cash.
   d. The ledger balance of $850 in Accounts Receivable was entered in the trial balance as $85.
   e. An error in recording a $765 increase in Cash as a credit.

5. Bonaventure Company has total assets of $1,000,000, liabilities of $400,000, and equity of $600,000. What is its debt ratio (rounded to a whole percent)?
   a. 250%
   b. 167%
   c. 67%
   d. 150%
   e. 40%

⚏ Icon denotes assignments that involve decision making.

Discussion Questions

1. Provide the names of two (a) asset accounts, (b) liability accounts, and (c) equity accounts.

2. What is the difference between a note payable and an account payable?

3. ⚏ Discuss the steps in processing business transactions.

4. What kinds of transactions can be recorded in a general journal?

5. Are debits or credits typically listed first in general journal entries? Are the debits or the credits indented?

6. Should a transaction be recorded first in a journal or the ledger? Why?

7. If assets are valuable resources and asset accounts have debit balances, why do expense accounts also have debit balances?

8. ⚏ Why does the recordkeeper prepare a trial balance?

9. If an incorrect amount is journalized and posted to the accounts, how should the error be corrected?

10. Identify the four financial statements of a business.

11. ⚏ What information is reported in a balance sheet?

12. ⚏ What information is reported in an income statement?

13. ⚏ Why does the user of an income statement need to know the time period that it covers?

14. Define (a) assets, (b) liabilities, (c) equity, and (d) net assets.

15. Which financial statement is sometimes called the statement of financial position?

16. ⚏ Review the **Polaris** balance sheet in Appendix A. Identify three accounts on its balance sheet that carry debit balances and three accounts on its balance sheet that carry credit balances.   **Polaris**

17. Review the **Arctic Cat** balance sheet in Appendix A. Identify an asset with the word receivable in its account title and a liability with the word payable in its account title.   **Arctic Cat**

18. Locate **KTM**'s income statement in Appendix A. What is the title of its revenue account?   **KTM**

19. Refer to **Piaggio**'s balance sheet in Appendix A. What does Piaggio title its current asset referring to merchandise available for sale?   **PIAGGIO**

connect

Identify the items from the following list that are likely to serve as source documents.

a. Sales ticket
b. Income statement
c. Trial balance
d. Telephone bill
e. Invoice from supplier
f. Company revenue account
g. Balance sheet
h. Prepaid insurance
i. Bank statement

Identify the financial statement(s) where each of the following items appears. Use I for income statement, E for statement of owner's equity, and D for balance sheet.

a. Office equipment
b. Cash withdrawal by owner
c. Revenue
d. Prepaid insurance
e. Office supplies
f. Rent expense
g. Cash
h. Unearned rent revenue
i. Accounts payable

Identify the normal balance (debit or credit) for each of the following accounts.

a. Office Supplies
b. Owner Withdrawals
c. Fees Earned
d. Wages Expense
e. Accounts Receivable
f. Prepaid Rent
g. Wages Payable
h. Building
i. Owner Capital

Indicate whether a debit or credit *decreases* the normal balance of each of the following accounts.

a. Service Revenue
b. Interest Payable
c. Accounts Receivable
d. Salaries Expense
e. Owner Capital
f. Prepaid Insurance
g. Buildings
h. Interest Revenue
i. Owner Withdrawals
j. Unearned Revenue
k. Accounts Payable
l. Land

Identify whether a debit or credit yields the indicated change for each of the following accounts.

a. To increase Land
b. To decrease Cash
c. To increase Office Expense
d. To increase Fees Earned
e. To decrease Unearned Revenue
f. To decrease Prepaid Rent
g. To increase Notes Payable
h. To decrease Accounts Receivable
i. To increase Owner Capital
j. To increase Store Equipment

Prepare journal entries for each of the following selected transactions.

a. On May 15, DeShawn Tyler opens a landscaping company called Elegant Lawns by investing $70,000 cash along with equipment having a $30,000 value.
b. On May 21, Elegant Lawns purchases office supplies on credit for $280.
c. On May 25, Elegant Lawns receives $7,800 cash for performing landscaping services.
d. On May 30, Elegant Lawns receives $1,000 cash in advance of providing landscaping services to a customer.

A trial balance has total debits of $20,000 and total credits of $24,500. Which one of the following errors would create this imbalance? Explain.

a. A $2,250 debit to Utilities Expense in a journal entry is incorrectly posted to the ledger as a $2,250 credit, leaving the Utilities Expense account with a $3,000 debit balance.
b. A $4,500 debit to Salaries Expense in a journal entry is incorrectly posted to the ledger as a $4,500 credit, leaving the Salaries Expense account with a $750 debit balance.
c. A $2,250 credit to Consulting Fees Earned in a journal entry is incorrectly posted to the ledger as a $2,250 debit, leaving the Consulting Fees Earned account with a $6,300 credit balance.
d. A $2,250 debit posting to Accounts Receivable was posted mistakenly to Land.
e. A $4,500 debit posting to Equipment was posted mistakenly to Cash.
f. An entry debiting Cash and crediting Accounts Payable for $4,500 was mistakenly not posted.

QS 2-8

Classifying accounts in
financial statements

P3

Indicate the financial statement on which each of the following items appears. Use I for income statement,
E for statement of owner's equity, and B for balance sheet.

a. Services Revenue	**e.** Equipment	**i.** Owner Withdrawals
b. Interest Payable	**f.** Prepaid Insurance	**j.** Office Supplies
c. Accounts Receivable	**g.** Buildings	**k.** Interest Expense
d. Salaries Expense	**h.** Rental Revenue	**l.** Insurance Expense

QS 2-9

International accounting
standards

C4

Answer each of the following questions related to international accounting standards.

a. What type of entry system is applied when accounting follows IFRS?

b. Identify the number and usual titles of the financial statements prepared under IFRS.

c. How do differences in accounting controls and enforcement impact accounting reports prepared across
different countries?

☰ connect

EXERCISES

Exercise 2-1

Steps in analyzing and recording
transactions C1

Order the following steps in the accounting process that focus on analyzing and recording transactions.

_____ **a.** Analyze each transaction from source documents.

_____ **b.** Prepare and analyze the trial balance.

_____ **c.** Record relevant transactions in a journal.

_____ **d.** Post journal information to ledger accounts.

Exercise 2-2

Identifying and classifying
accounts

C2

Enter the number for the item that best completes each of the descriptions below.

1. Asset	**3.** Account	**5.** Three
2. Equity	**4.** Liability	

a. An _____ is a record of increases and decreases in a specific asset, liability, equity, revenue, or
expense item.

b. Accounts payable, unearned revenue, and note payable are examples of _____ accounts.

c. Accounts receivable, prepaid accounts, supplies, and land are examples of _____ accounts.

d. Accounts are arranged into _____ general categories.

e. Owner, capital and owner, withdrawals are examples of _____ accounts.

Exercise 2-3

Identifying a ledger and chart
of accounts

C3

Enter the number for the item that best completes each of the descriptions below.

1. Chart   **2.** General ledger

a. The _____ is a record containing all accounts used by a company.

b. A _____ of accounts is a list of all accounts a company uses.

Exercise 2-4

Identifying type and normal
balances of accounts

C4

For each of the following (1) identify the type of account as an asset, liability, equity, revenue, or expense,
(2) identify the normal balance of the account, and (3) enter *debit* (*Dr.*) or *credit* (*Cr.*) to identify the kind of
entry that would increase the account balance.

a. Cash	**e.** Accounts Receivable	**i.** Fees Earned
b. Legal Expense	**f.** Owner Withdrawals	**j.** Equipment
c. Prepaid Insurance	**g.** License Fee Revenue	**k.** Notes Payable
d. Land	**h.** Unearned Revenue	**l.** Owner Capital

Exercise 2-5

Analyzing account entries
and balances

A1

Use the information in each of the following separate cases to calculate the unknown amount.

a. Corentine Co. had $152,000 of accounts payable on September 30 and $132,500 on October 31. Total
purchases on account during October were $281,000. Determine how much cash was paid on accounts
payable during October.

b. On September 30, Valerian Co. had a $102,500 balance in Accounts Receivable. During October, the
company collected $102,890 from its credit customers. The October 31 balance in Accounts Receivable was $89,000. Determine the amount of sales on account that occurred in October.

c. During October, Alameda Company had $102,500 of cash receipts and $103,150 of cash disbursements. The October 31 Cash balance was $18,600. Determine how much cash the company had at the
close of business on September 30.

Groro Co. bills a client $62,000 for services provided and agrees to accept the following three items in full payment: (1) $10,000 cash, (2) computer equipment worth $80,000, and (3) to assume responsibility for a $28,000 note payable related to the computer equipment. The entry Groro makes to record this transaction includes which one or more of the following?

a. $28,000 increase in a liability account

d. $62,000 increase in an asset account

b. $10,000 increase in the Cash account

e. $62,000 increase in a revenue account

c. $10,000 increase in a revenue account

f. $62,000 increase in an equity account

Exercise 2-6
Analyzing effects of transactions on accounts

A1

Prepare general journal entries for the following transactions of a new company called Pose-for-Pics.

Aug. 1   Madison Harris, the owner, invested $6,500 cash and $33,500 of photography equipment in the company.
      2   The company paid $2,100 cash for an insurance policy covering the next 24 months.
      5   The company purchased office supplies for $880 cash.
     20   The company received $3,331 cash in photography fees earned.
     31   The company paid $675 cash for August utilities.

Exercise 2-7
Preparing general journal entries

P1

Use the information in Exercise 2-7 to prepare an August 31 trial balance for Pose-for-Pics. Begin by opening these T-accounts: Cash; Office Supplies; Prepaid Insurance; Photography Equipment; M. Harris, Capital; Photography Fees Earned; and Utilities Expense. Then, post the general journal entries to these T-accounts (which will serve as the ledger), and prepare the trial balance.

Exercise 2-8
Preparing T-accounts (ledger) and a trial balance   P2

Prepare general journal entries to record the transactions below for Spade Company by using the following accounts: Cash; Accounts Receivable; Office Supplies; Office Equipment; Accounts Payable; K. Spade, Capital; K. Spade, Withdrawals; Fees Earned; and Rent Expense. Use the letters beside each transaction to identify entries. After recording the transactions, post them to T-accounts, which serves as the general ledger for this assignment. Determine the ending balance of each T-account.

a. Kacy Spade, owner, invested $100,750 cash in the company.

b. The company purchased office supplies for $1,250 cash.

c. The company purchased $10,050 of office equipment on credit.

d. The company received $15,500 cash as fees for services provided to a customer.

e. The company paid $10,050 cash to settle the payable for the office equipment purchased in transaction c.

f. The company billed a customer $2,700 as fees for services provided.

g. The company paid $1,225 cash for the monthly rent.

h. The company collected $1,125 cash as partial payment for the account receivable created in transaction f.

i. Kacy Spade withdrew $10,000 cash from the company for personal use.

Exercise 2-9
Recording effects of transactions in T-accounts

A1

Check   Cash ending balance, $94,850

After recording the transactions of Exercise 2-9 in T-accounts and calculating the balance of each account, prepare a trial balance. Use May 31, 2013, as its report date.

Exercise 2-10
Preparing a trial balance   P2

Examine the following transactions and identify those that create revenues for Valdez Services, a company owned by Brina Valdez. Prepare general journal entries to record those revenue transactions and explain why the other transactions did not create revenues.

a. Brina Valdez invests $39,350 cash in the company.

b. The company provided $2,300 of services on credit.

c. The company provided services to a client and immediately received $875 cash.

d. The company received $10,200 cash from a client in payment for services to be provided next year.

e. The company received $3,500 cash from a client in partial payment of an account receivable.

f. The company borrowed $120,000 cash from the bank by signing a promissory note.

Exercise 2-11
Analyzing and journalizing revenue transactions

A1 P1

Exercise 2-12

Analyzing and journalizing expense transactions

A1   P1

Examine the following transactions and identify those that create expenses for Valdez Services. Prepare general journal entries to record those expense transactions and explain why the other transactions did not create expenses.

a. The company paid $12,200 cash for payment on a 16-month old liability for office supplies.

b. The company paid $1,233 cash for the just completed two-week salary of the receptionist.

c. The company paid $39,200 cash for equipment purchased.

d. The company paid $870 cash for this month's utilities.

e. Owner (Valdez) withdrew $4,500 cash from the company for personal use.

Exercise 2-13

Preparing an income statement

C3   P3

Carmen Camry operates a consulting firm called Help Today. On August 31, the company's records show the following accounts and amounts for the month of August. Use this information to prepare an August income statement for the business.

Cash	$25,360	C. Camry, Withdrawals	$ 6,000
Accounts receivable	22,360	Consulting fees earned	27,000
Office supplies	5,250	Rent expense	9,550
Land	44,000	Salaries expense.	5,600
Office equipment	20,000	Telephone expense	860
Accounts payable	10,500	Miscellaneous expenses.	520
C. Camry, Capital, July 31.	2,000	Owner investment made on August 4	100,000

Check   Net income, $10,470

Exercise 2-14

Preparing a statement of owner's equity   P3

Check   End. Capital, $106,470

Use the information in Exercise 2-13 to prepare an August statement of owner's equity for Help Today. (The owner invested $100,000 cash in the company during the first week of August.)

Exercise 2-15

Preparing a balance sheet   P3

Use the information in Exercise 2-13 (if completed, you can also use your solution to Exercise 2-14) to prepare an August 31 balance sheet for Help Today.

Exercise 2-16

Computing net income

A1

A sole proprietorship had the following assets and liabilities at the beginning and end of this year.

	Assets	Liabilities
Beginning of the year	$ 60,000	$20,000
End of the year	105,000	36,000

Determine the net income earned or net loss incurred by the business during the year for each of the following *separate* cases:

a. Owner made no investments in the business and no withdrawals were made during the year.

b. Owner made no investments in the business but withdrew $1,250 cash per month for personal use.

c. Owner made no withdrawals during the year but did invest an additional $55,000 cash.

d. Owner withdrew $1,250 cash per month for personal use and invested an additional $35,000 cash.

Exercise 2-17

Analyzing changes in a company's equity

P3

Compute the missing amount for each of the following separate companies *a* through *d*.

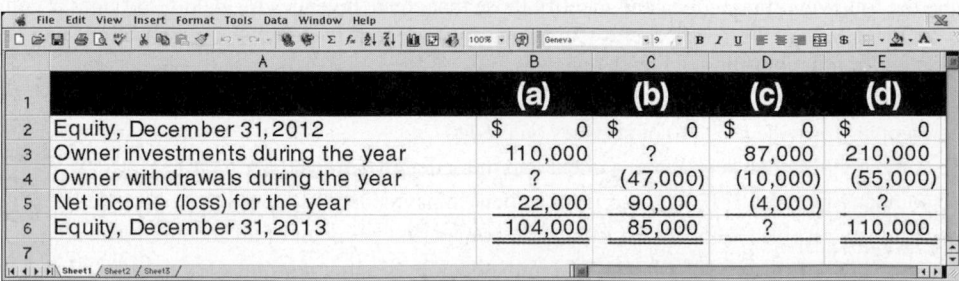

	(a)	(b)	(c)	(d)
Equity, December 31, 2012	$ 0	$ 0	$ 0	$ 0
Owner investments during the year	110,000	?	87,000	210,000
Owner withdrawals during the year	?	(47,000)	(10,000)	(55,000)
Net income (loss) for the year	22,000	90,000	(4,000)	?
Equity, December 31, 2013	104,000	85,000	?	110,000

Assume the following T-accounts reflect Belle Co.'s general ledger and that seven transactions *a* through *g* are posted to them. Provide a short description of each transaction. Include the amounts in your descriptions.

Cash			
(a)	6,000	(b)	4,800
(e)	4,500	(c)	900
		(f)	1,600
		(g)	820

Office Supplies	
(c)	900
(d)	300

Prepaid Insurance	
(b)	4,800

Equipment	
(a)	7,600
(d)	9,700

Automobiles	
(a)	12,000

Accounts Payable			
(f)	1,600	(d)	10,000

D. Belle, Capital			
		(a)	25,600

Delivery Services Revenue			
		(e)	4,500

Gas and Oil Expense	
(g)	820

Use information from the T-accounts in Exercise 2-18 to prepare general journal entries for each of the seven transactions *a* through *g*.

Posting errors are identified in the following table. In column (1), enter the amount of the difference between the two trial balance columns (debit and credit) due to the error. In column (2), identify the trial balance column (debit or credit) with the larger amount if they are not equal. In column (3), identify the account(s) affected by the error. In column (4), indicate the amount by which the account(s) in column (3) is under- or overstated. Item (a) is completed as an example.

	Description of Posting Error	(1) Difference between Debit and Credit Columns	(2) Column with the Larger Total	(3) Identify Account(s) Incorrectly Stated	(4) Amount that Account(s) Is Over- or Understated
a.	$3,600 debit to Rent Expense is posted as a $1,340 debit.	$2,260	Credit	Rent Expense	Rent Expense understated $2,260
b.	$6,500 credit to Cash is posted twice as two credits to Cash.				
c.	$10,900 debit to the Withdrawals account is debited to Owner's Capital.				
d.	$2,050 debit to Prepaid Insurance is posted as a debit to Insurance Expense.				
e.	$38,000 debit to Machinery is posted as a debit to Accounts Payable.				
f.	$5,850 credit to Services Revenue is posted as a $585 credit.				
g.	$1,390 debit to Store Supplies is not posted.				

You are told the column totals in a trial balance are not equal. After careful analysis, you discover only one error. Specifically, a correctly journalized credit purchase of an automobile for $18,950 is posted from the journal to the ledger with a $18,950 debit to Automobiles and another $18,950 debit to Accounts Payable. The Automobiles account has a debit balance of $37,100 on the trial balance. Answer each of the following questions and compute the dollar amount of any misstatement.

a. Is the debit column total of the trial balance overstated, understated, or correctly stated?

b. Is the credit column total of the trial balance overstated, understated, or correctly stated?

c. Is the Automobiles account balance overstated, understated, or correctly stated in the trial balance?

d. Is the Accounts Payable account balance overstated, understated, or correctly stated in the trial balance?

e. If the debit column total of the trial balance is $200,000 before correcting the error, what is the total of the credit column before correction?

Exercise 2-22

Interpreting the debt ratio and return on assets

A2

a. Calculate the debt ratio and the return on assets using the year-end information for each of the following six separate companies ($ thousands).

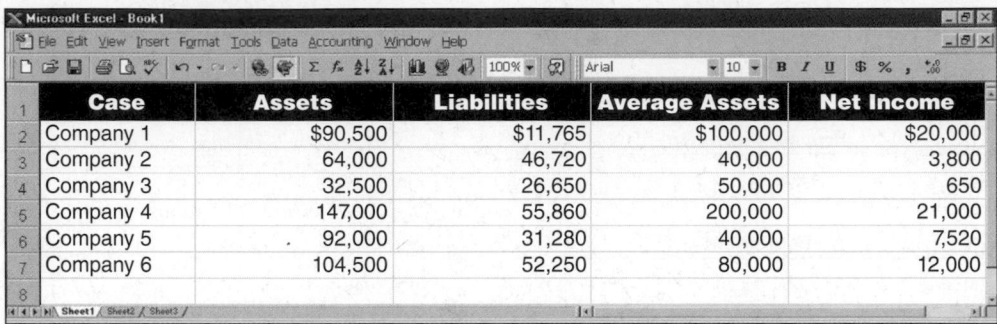

Case	Assets	Liabilities	Average Assets	Net Income
Company 1	$90,500	$11,765	$100,000	$20,000
Company 2	64,000	46,720	40,000	3,800
Company 3	32,500	26,650	50,000	650
Company 4	147,000	55,860	200,000	21,000
Company 5	92,000	31,280	40,000	7,520
Company 6	104,500	52,250	80,000	12,000

b. Of the six companies, which business relies most heavily on creditor financing?

c. Of the six companies, which business relies most heavily on equity financing?

d. Which two companies indicate the greatest risk?

e. Which two companies earn the highest return on assets?

f. Which one company would investors likely prefer based on the risk–return relation?

Exercise 2-23

Preparing a balance sheet following IFRS

P3

BMW reports the following balance sheet accounts for the year ended December 31, 2011 (euro in millions). Prepare the balance sheet for this company as of December 31, 2011, following the usual IFRS formats.

Current liabilities	€11,519	Noncurrent liabilities	€7,767
Current assets	17,682	Noncurrent assets	9,826
Total equity	8,222		

connect

PROBLEM SET A

Problem 2-1A

Preparing and posting journal entries; preparing a trial balance

C3 C4 A1 P1 P2

Aracel Engineering completed the following transactions in the month of June.

a. Jenna Aracel, the owner, invested $100,000 cash, office equipment with a value of $5,000, and $60,000 of drafting equipment to launch the company.

b. The company purchased land worth $49,000 for an office by paying $6,300 cash and signing a long-term note payable for $42,700.

c. The company purchased a portable building with $55,000 cash and moved it onto the land acquired in *b*.

d. The company paid $3,000 cash for the premium on an 18-month insurance policy.

e. The company completed and delivered a set of plans for a client and collected $6,200 cash.

f. The company purchased $20,000 of additional drafting equipment by paying $9,500 cash and signing a long-term note payable for $10,500.

g. The company completed $14,000 of engineering services for a client. This amount is to be received in 30 days.

h. The company purchased $1,150 of additional office equipment on credit.

i. The company completed engineering services for $22,000 on credit.

j. The company received a bill for rent of equipment that was used on a recently completed job. The $1,333 rent cost must be paid within 30 days.

k. The company collected $7,000 cash in partial payment from the client described in transaction *g*.

l. The company paid $1,200 cash for wages to a drafting assistant.

m. The company paid $1,150 cash to settle the account payable created in transaction *h*.

n. The company paid $925 cash for minor maintenance of its drafting equipment.

o. Jenna Aracel withdrew $9,480 cash from the company for personal use.

p. The company paid $1,200 cash for wages to a drafting assistant.

q. The company paid $2,500 cash for advertisements on the Web during June.

Required

1. Prepare general journal entries to record these transactions (use the account titles listed in part 2).

2. Open the following ledger accounts—their account numbers are in parentheses (use the balance column format): Cash (101); Accounts Receivable (106); Prepaid Insurance (108); Office Equipment (163); Drafting Equipment (164); Building (170); Land (172); Accounts Payable (201); Notes Payable (250); J. Aracel, Capital (301); J. Aracel, Withdrawals (302); Engineering Fees Earned (402); Wages Expense (601); Equipment Rental Expense (602); Advertising Expense (603); and Repairs Expense (604). Post the journal entries from part 1 to the accounts and enter the balance after each posting.

3. Prepare a trial balance as of the end of June.

Check (2) Ending balances: Cash, $22,945; Accounts Receivable, $29,000; Accounts Payable, $1,333

(3) Trial balance totals, $261,733

Denzel Brooks opens a Web consulting business called Venture Consultants and completes the following transactions in March.

March 1 Brooks invested $150,000 cash along with $22,000 in office equipment in the company.
       2 The company prepaid $6,000 cash for six months' rent for an office. (*Hint:* Debit Prepaid Rent for $6,000.)
       3 The company made credit purchases of office equipment for $3,000 and office supplies for $1,200. Payment is due within 10 days.
       6 The company completed services for a client and immediately received $4,000 cash.
       9 The company completed a $7,500 project for a client, who must pay within 30 days.
      12 The company paid $4,200 cash to settle the account payable created on March 3.
      19 The company paid $5,000 cash for the premium on a 12-month insurance policy. (*Hint:* Debit Prepaid Insurance for $5,000.)
      22 The company received $3,500 cash as partial payment for the work completed on March 9.
      25 The company completed work for another client for $3,820 on credit.
      29 Brooks withdrew $5,100 cash from the company for personal use.
      30 The company purchased $600 of additional office supplies on credit.
      31 The company paid $500 cash for this month's utility bill.

Problem 2-2A
Preparing and posting journal entries; preparing a trial balance
C3 C4 A1 P1 P2

mhhe.com/wildFAP21e

Sage 50

Required

1. Prepare general journal entries to record these transactions (use the account titles listed in part 2).

2. Open the following ledger accounts—their account numbers are in parentheses (use the balance column format): Cash (101); Accounts Receivable (106); Office Supplies (124); Prepaid Insurance (128); Prepaid Rent (131); Office Equipment (163); Accounts Payable (201); D. Brooks, Capital (301); D. Brooks, Withdrawals (302); Services Revenue (403); and Utilities Expense (690). Post the journal entries from part 1 to the ledger accounts and enter the balance after each posting.

3. Prepare a trial balance as of the end of March.

Check (2) Ending balances: Cash, $136,700; Accounts Receivable, $7,820; Accounts Payable, $600

(3) Total debits, $187,920

Karla Tanner opens a Web consulting business called Linkworks and completes the following transactions in its first month of operations.

April 1 Tanner invests $80,000 cash along with office equipment valued at $26,000 in the company.
       2 The company prepaid $9,000 cash for twelve months' rent for office space. (*Hint:* Debit Prepaid Rent for $9,000.)
       3 The company made credit purchases for $8,000 in office equipment and $3,600 in office supplies. Payment is due within 10 days.
       6 The company completed services for a client and immediately received $4,000 cash.
       9 The company completed a $6,000 project for a client, who must pay within 30 days.
      13 The company paid $11,600 cash to settle the account payable created on April 3.
      19 The company paid $2,400 cash for the premium on a 12-month insurance policy. (*Hint:* Debit Prepaid Insurance for $2,400.)
      22 The company received $4,400 cash as partial payment for the work completed on April 9.
      25 The company completed work for another client for $2,890 on credit.
      28 Tanner withdrew $5,500 cash from the company for personal use.
      29 The company purchased $600 of additional office supplies on credit.
      30 The company paid $435 cash for this month's utility bill.

Problem 2-3A
Preparing and posting journal entries; preparing a trial balance
C3 C4 A1 P1 P2

Sage 50

Required

1. Prepare general journal entries to record these transactions (use account titles listed in part 2).

2. Open the following ledger accounts—their account numbers are in parentheses (use the balance column format): Cash (101); Accounts Receivable (106); Office Supplies (124); Prepaid Insurance (128); Prepaid Rent (131); Office Equipment (163); Accounts Payable (201); K. Tanner, Capital (301); K. Tanner, Withdrawals (302); Services Revenue (403); and Utilities Expense (690). Post journal entries from part 1 to the ledger accounts and enter the balance after each posting.

3. Prepare a trial balance as of April 30.

Problem 2-4A
Computing net income from equity analysis, preparing a balance sheet, and computing the debt ratio

C2 A1 A2 P3

mhhe.com/wildFAP21e

The accounting records of Nettle Distribution show the following assets and liabilities as of December 31, 2012 and 2013.

December 31	2012	2013
Cash	$ 64,300	$ 15,640
Accounts receivable	26,240	19,390
Office supplies	3,160	1,960
Office equipment	44,000	44,000
Trucks	148,000	157,000
Building	0	80,000
Land	0	60,000
Accounts payable	3,500	33,500
Note payable	0	40,000

Late in December 2013, the business purchased a small office building and land for $140,000. It paid $100,000 cash toward the purchase and a $40,000 note payable was signed for the balance. Mr. Nettle had to invest $35,000 cash in the business to enable it to pay the $100,000 cash. Mr. Nettle withdraws $3,000 cash per month for personal use.

Required

1. Prepare balance sheets for the business as of December 31, 2012 and 2013. (*Hint:* Report only total equity on the balance sheet and remember that total equity equals the difference between assets and liabilities.)

2. By comparing equity amounts from the balance sheets and using the additional information presented in this problem, prepare a calculation to show how much net income was earned by the business during 2013.

3. Compute the 2013 year-end debt ratio (in percent and rounded to one decimal).

Problem 2-5A
Analyzing account balances and reconstructing transactions

C1 C3 A1 P2

Yi Min started an engineering firm called Min Engineering. He began operations and completed seven transactions in May, which included his initial investment of $18,000 cash. After those seven transactions, the ledger included the following accounts with normal balances.

Cash	$37,641
Office supplies	890
Prepaid insurance	4,600
Office equipment	12,900
Accounts payable	12,900
Y. Min, Capital	18,000
Y. Min, Withdrawals	3,329
Engineering fees earned	36,000
Rent expense	7,540

Required

1. Prepare a trial balance for this business as of the end of May.

Analysis Components

2. Analyze the accounts and their balances and prepare a list that describes each of the seven most likely transactions and their amounts.

3. Prepare a report of cash received and cash paid showing how the seven transactions in part 2 yield the $37,641 ending Cash balance.

Business transactions completed by Hannah Venedict during the month of September are as follows.

a. Venedict invested $60,000 cash along with office equipment valued at $25,000 in a new sole proprietorship named HV Consulting.

b. The company purchased land valued at $40,000 and a building valued at $160,000. The purchase is paid with $30,000 cash and a long-term note payable for $170,000.

c. The company purchased $2,000 of office supplies on credit.

d. Venedict invested her personal automobile in the company. The automobile has a value of $16,500 and is to be used exclusively in the business.

e. The company purchased $5,600 of additional office equipment on credit.

f. The company paid $1,800 cash salary to an assistant.

g. The company provided services to a client and collected $8,000 cash.

h. The company paid $635 cash for this month's utilities.

i. The company paid $2,000 cash to settle the account payable created in transaction *c.*

j. The company purchased $20,300 of new office equipment by paying $20,300 cash.

k. The company completed $6,250 of services for a client, who must pay within 30 days.

l. The company paid $1,800 cash salary to an assistant.

m. The company received $4,000 cash in partial payment on the receivable created in transaction *k.*

n. Venedict withdrew $2,800 cash from the company for personal use.

Required

1. Prepare general journal entries to record these transactions (use account titles listed in part 2).

2. Open the following ledger accounts—their account numbers are in parentheses (use the balance column format): Cash (101); Accounts Receivable (106); Office Supplies (108); Office Equipment (163); Automobiles (164); Building (170); Land (172); Accounts Payable (201); Notes Payable (250); H. Venedict, Capital (301); H. Venedict, Withdrawals (302); Fees Earned (402); Salaries Expense (601); and Utilities Expense (602). Post the journal entries from part 1 to the ledger accounts and enter the balance after each posting.

3. Prepare a trial balance as of the end of September.

At the beginning of April, Bernadette Grechus launched a custom computer solutions company called Softworks. The company had the following transactions during April.

a. Bernadette Grechus invested $65,000 cash, office equipment with a value of $5,750, and $30,000 of computer equipment in the company.

b. The company purchased land worth $22,000 for an office by paying $5,000 cash and signing a long-term note payable for $17,000.

c. The company purchased a portable building with $34,500 cash and moved it onto the land acquired in *b.*

d. The company paid $5,000 cash for the premium on a two-year insurance policy.

e. The company provided services to a client and immediately collected $4,600 cash.

f. The company purchased $4,500 of additional computer equipment by paying $800 cash and signing a long-term note payable for $3,700.

g. The company completed $4,250 of services for a client. This amount is to be received within 30 days.

h. The company purchased $950 of additional office equipment on credit.

i. The company completed client services for $10,200 on credit.

j. The company received a bill for rent of a computer testing device that was used on a recently completed job. The $580 rent cost must be paid within 30 days.

k. The company collected $5,100 cash in partial payment from the client described in transaction *i.*

l. The company paid $1,800 cash for wages to an assistant.

m. The company paid $950 cash to settle the payable created in transaction *h.*

n. The company paid $608 cash for minor maintenance of the company's computer equipment.

o. B. Grechus withdrew $6,230 cash from the company for personal use.

p. The company paid $1,800 cash for wages to an assistant.

q. The company paid $750 cash for advertisements on the Web during April.

Problem 2-6A
Recording transactions; posting to ledger; preparing a trial balance
C3 A1 P1 P2

Check (2) Ending balances: Cash, $12,665; Office Equipment, $50,900

(3) Trial balance totals, $291,350

PROBLEM SET B

Problem 2-1B
Preparing and posting journal entries; preparing a trial balance
C3 C4 A1 P1 P2

Required

1. Prepare general journal entries to record these transactions (use account titles listed in part 2).

2. Open the following ledger accounts—their account numbers are in parentheses (use the balance column format): Cash (101); Accounts Receivable (106); Prepaid Insurance (108); Office Equipment (163); Computer Equipment (164); Building (170); Land (172); Accounts Payable (201); Notes Payable (250); B. Grechus, Capital (301); B. Grechus, Withdrawals (302); Fees Earned (402); Wages Expense (601); Computer Rental Expense (602); Advertising Expense (603); and Repairs Expense (604). Post the journal entries from part 1 to the accounts and enter the balance after each posting.

3. Prepare a trial balance as of the end of April.

Problem 2-2B
Preparing and posting journal entries; preparing a trial balance
C3 C4 A1 P1 P2

Zucker Management Services opens for business and completes these transactions in November.

Nov. 1   Matt Zucker, the owner, invested $30,000 cash along with $15,000 of office equipment in the company.
  2   The company prepaid $4,500 cash for six months' rent for an office. (*Hint:* Debit Prepaid Rent for $4,500.)
  4   The company made credit purchases of office equipment for $2,500 and of office supplies for $600. Payment is due within 10 days.
  8   The company completed work for a client and immediately received $3,400 cash.
  12   The company completed a $10,200 project for a client, who must pay within 30 days.
  13   The company paid $3,100 cash to settle the payable created on November 4.
  19   The company paid $1,800 cash for the premium on a 24-month insurance policy.
  22   The company received $5,200 cash as partial payment for the work completed on November 12.
  24   The company completed work for another client for $1,750 on credit.
  28   M. Zucker withdrew $5,300 cash from the company for personal use.
  29   The company purchased $249 of additional office supplies on credit.
  30   The company paid $831 cash for this month's utility bill.

Required

1. Prepare general journal entries to record these transactions (use account titles listed in part 2).

2. Open the following ledger accounts—their account numbers are in parentheses (use the balance column format): Cash (101); Accounts Receivable (106); Office Supplies (124); Prepaid Insurance (128); Prepaid Rent (131); Office Equipment (163); Accounts Payable (201); M. Zucker, Capital (301); M. Zucker, Withdrawals (302); Services Revenue (403); and Utilities Expense (690). Post the journal entries from part 1 to the ledger accounts and enter the balance after each posting.

3. Prepare a trial balance as of the end of November.

Problem 2-3B
Preparing and posting journal entries; preparing a trial balance
C3 C4 A1 P1 P2

Humble Management Services opens for business and completes these transactions in September.

Sept. 1   Henry Humble, the owner, invests $38,000 cash along with office equipment valued at $15,000 in the company.
  2   The company prepaid $9,000 cash for 12 months' rent for office space. (*Hint:* Debit Prepaid Rent for $9,000.)
  4   The company made credit purchases for $8,000 in office equipment and $2,400 in office supplies. Payment is due within 10 days.
  8   The company completed work for a client and immediately received $3,280 cash.
  12   The company completed a $15,400 project for a client, who must pay within 30 days.
  13   The company paid $10,400 cash to settle the payable created on September 4.
  19   The company paid $1,900 cash for the premium on an 18-month insurance policy. (*Hint:* Debit Prepaid Insurance for $1,900.)
  22   The company received $7,700 cash as partial payment for the work completed on September 12.
  24   The company completed work for another client for $2,100 on credit.
  28   Henry Humble withdrew $5,300 cash from the company for personal use.
  29   The company purchased $550 of additional office supplies on credit.
  30   The company paid $860 cash for this month's utility bill.

Required

1. Prepare general journal entries to record these transactions (use account titles listed in part 2).

2. Open the following ledger accounts—their account numbers are in parentheses (use the balance column format): Cash (101); Accounts Receivable (106); Office Supplies (124); Prepaid Insurance (128); Prepaid Rent (131); Office Equipment (163); Accounts Payable (201); H. Humble, Capital (301); H. Humble, Withdrawals (302); Service Fees Earned (401); and Utilities Expense (690). Post journal entries from part 1 to the ledger accounts and enter the balance after each posting.

Check (2) Ending balances: Cash, $21,520; Accounts Receivable, $9,800; Accounts Payable, $550

3. Prepare a trial balance as of the end of September.

(3) Total debits, $74,330

The accounting records of Tama Co. show the following assets and liabilities as of December 31, 2012 and 2013.

Problem 2-4B
Computing net income from equity analysis, preparing a balance sheet, and computing the debt ratio

C2 A1 A2 P3

December 31	2012	2013
Cash	$20,000	$ 5,000
Accounts receivable	35,000	25,000
Office supplies	8,000	13,500
Office equipment	40,000	40,000
Machinery	28,500	28,500
Building	0	250,000
Land	0	50,000
Accounts payable	4,000	12,000
Note payable	0	250,000

Late in December 2013, the business purchased a small office building and land for $300,000. It paid $50,000 cash toward the purchase and a $250,000 note payable was signed for the balance. Joe Tama, the owner, had to invest an additional $15,000 cash to enable it to pay the $50,000 cash toward the purchase. The owner withdraws $250 cash per month for personal use.

Required

1. Prepare balance sheets for the business as of December 31, 2012 and 2013. (*Hint:* Report only total equity on the balance sheet and remember that total equity equals the difference between assets and liabilities.)

Check (2) Net income, $10,500

2. By comparing equity amounts from the balance sheets and using the additional information presented in the problem, prepare a calculation to show how much net income was earned by the business during 2013.

(3) Debt ratio, 63.6%

3. Calculate the December 31, 2013, debt ratio (in percent and rounded to one decimal).

Roshaun Gould started a Web consulting firm called Gould Solutions. He began operations and completed seven transactions in April that resulted in the following accounts, which all have normal balances.

Problem 2-5B
Analyzing account balances and reconstructing transactions

C1 C3 A1 P2

Cash	$19,982
Office supplies	760
Prepaid rent	1,800
Office equipment	12,250
Accounts payable	12,250
R. Gould, Capital	15,000
R. Gould, Withdrawals	5,200
Consulting fees earned	20,400
Operating expenses	7,658

Required

1. Prepare a trial balance for this business as of the end of April.

Check (1) Trial balance total, $47,650

Analysis Component

2. Analyze the accounts and their balances and prepare a list that describes each of the seven most likely transactions and their amounts.

3. Prepare a report of cash received and cash paid showing how the seven transactions in part 2 yield the $19,982 ending Cash balance.

(3) Cash paid, $15,418

Problem 2-6B
Recording transactions;
posting to ledger; preparing
a trial balance
C3 A1 P1 P2

Nuncio Consulting completed the following transactions during June.

   a. Armand Nuncio, the owner, invested $35,000 cash along with office equipment valued at $11,000 in the new company.

   b. The company purchased land valued at $7,500 and a building valued at $40,000. The purchase is paid with $15,000 cash and a long-term note payable for $32,500.

   c. The company purchased $500 of office supplies on credit.

   d. A. Nuncio invested his personal automobile in the company. The automobile has a value of $8,000 and is to be used exclusively in the business.

   e. The company purchased $1,200 of additional office equipment on credit.

   f. The company paid $1,000 cash salary to an assistant.

   g. The company provided services to a client and collected $3,200 cash.

   h. The company paid $540 cash for this month's utilities.

   i. The company paid $500 cash to settle the payable created in transaction *c*.

   j. The company purchased $3,400 of new office equipment by paying $3,400 cash.

   k. The company completed $4,200 of services for a client, who must pay within 30 days.

   l. The company paid $1,000 cash salary to an assistant.

   m. The company received $2,200 cash in partial payment on the receivable created in transaction *k*.

   n. A. Nuncio withdrew $1,100 cash from the company for personal use.

Required

1. Prepare general journal entries to record these transactions (use account titles listed in part 2).

Check (2) Ending balances: Cash,
$17,860; Office Equipment, $15,600

2. Open the following ledger accounts—their account numbers are in parentheses (use the balance column format): Cash (101); Accounts Receivable (106); Office Supplies (108); Office Equipment (163); Automobiles (164); Building (170); Land (172); Accounts Payable (201); Notes Payable (250); A. Nuncio, Capital (301); A. Nuncio, Withdrawals (302); Fees Earned (402); Salaries Expense (601); and Utilities Expense (602). Post the journal entries from part 1 to the ledger accounts and enter the balance after each posting.

(3) Trial balance totals,
$95,100

3. Prepare a trial balance as of the end of June.

SERIAL PROBLEM
Success Systems
A1 P1 P2

Sage 50

(This serial problem started in Chapter 1 and continues through most of the chapters. If the Chapter 1 segment was not completed, the problem can begin at this point. It is helpful, but not necessary, to use the Working Papers that accompany this book.)

SP 2   On October 1, 2013, Adria Lopez launched a computer services company called **Success Systems,** which provides consulting services, computer system installations, and custom program development. Adria adopts the calendar year for reporting purposes and expects to prepare the company's first set of financial statements on December 31, 2013. The company's initial chart of accounts follows.

Account	No.	Account	No.
Cash.....................	101	A. Lopez, Capital...................	301
Accounts Receivable.........	106	A. Lopez, Withdrawals..............	302
Computer Supplies..........	126	Computer Services Revenue.........	403
Prepaid Insurance...........	128	Wages Expense....................	623
Prepaid Rent...............	131	Advertising Expense...............	655
Office Equipment...........	163	Mileage Expense...................	676
Computer Equipment........	167	Miscellaneous Expenses............	677
Accounts Payable...........	201	Repairs Expense—Computer........	684

Required

1. Prepare journal entries to record each of the following transactions for Success Systems.

Oct. 1   Adria Lopez invested $55,000 cash, a $20,000 computer system, and $8,000 of office equipment in the company.

   2   The company paid $3,300 cash for four months' rent. (*Hint:* Debit Prepaid Rent for $3,300.)

   3   The company purchased $1,420 of computer supplies on credit from Harris Office Products.

   5   The company paid $2,220 cash for one year's premium on a property and liability insurance policy. (*Hint:* Debit Prepaid Insurance for $2,220.)

6   The company billed Easy Leasing $4,800 for services performed in installing a new Web server.

8   The company paid $1,420 cash for the computer supplies purchased from Harris Office Products on October 3.

10   The company hired Lyn Addie as a part-time assistant for $125 per day, as needed.

12   The company billed Easy Leasing another $1,400 for services performed.

15   The company received $4,800 cash from Easy Leasing as partial payment on its account.

17   The company paid $805 cash to repair computer equipment that was damaged when moving it.

20   The company paid $1,940 cash for advertisements published in the local newspaper.

22   The company received $1,400 cash from Easy Leasing on its account.

28   The company billed IFM Company $5,208 for services performed.

31   The company paid $875 cash for Lyn Addie's wages for seven days' work.

31   Adria Lopez withdrew $3,600 cash from the company for personal use.

Nov. 1   The company reimbursed Adria Lopez in cash for business automobile mileage allowance (Lopez logged 1,000 miles at $0.32 per mile).

2   The company received $4,633 cash from Liu Corporation for computer services performed.

5   The company purchased computer supplies for $1,125 cash from Harris Office Products.

8   The company billed Gomez Co. $5,668 for services performed.

13   The company received notification from Alex's Engineering Co. that Success Systems' bid of $3,950 for an upcoming project is accepted.

18   The company received $2,208 cash from IFM Company as partial payment of the October 28 bill.

22   The company donated $250 cash to the United Way in the company's name.

24   The company completed work for Alex's Engineering Co. and sent it a bill for $3,950.

25   The company sent another bill to IFM Company for the past-due amount of $3,000.

28   The company reimbursed Adria Lopez in cash for business automobile mileage (1,200 miles at $0.32 per mile).

30   The company paid $1,750 cash for Lyn Addie's wages for 14 days' work.

30   Adria Lopez withdrew $2,000 cash from the company for personal use.

2. Open ledger accounts (in balance column format) and post the journal entries from part 1 to them.

3. Prepare a trial balance as of the end of November.

Check (2) Cash, Nov. 30 bal., $48,052

(3) Trial bal. totals, $108,659

Beyond the Numbers

BTN 2-1 Refer to **Polaris'** financial statements in Appendix A for the following questions.

Required

1. What amount of total liabilities does it report for each of the fiscal years ended December 31, 2011 and 2010?

2. What amount of total assets does it report for each of the fiscal years ended December 31, 2011 and 2010?

3. Compute its debt ratio for each of the fiscal years ended December 31, 2011 and 2010. (Report ratio in percent and round it to one decimal.)

4. In which fiscal year did it employ more financial leverage (December 31, 2011 or 2010)? Explain.

Fast Forward

5. Access its financial statements (10-K report) for a fiscal year ending after December 31, 2011, from its Website (**Polaris.com**) or the SEC's EDGAR database (**www.sec.gov**). Recompute its debt ratio for any subsequent year's data and compare it with the debt ratio for 2010 and 2011.

REPORTING IN ACTION

A1 A2

Polaris

BTN 2-2 Key comparative figures for **Polaris** and **Arctic Cat** follow.

COMPARATIVE ANALYSIS

A1 A2

Polaris

Arctic Cat

($ thousands)	Polaris		Arctic Cat	
	Current Year	Prior Year	Current Year	Prior Year
Total liabilities	$ 727,968	$ 690,656	$ 89,870	$ 78,745
Total assets	1,228,024	1,061,647	272,906	246,084

1. What is the debt ratio for Polaris in the current year and for the prior year?
2. What is the debt ratio for Arctic Cat in the current year and for the prior year?
3. Which of the two companies has the higher degree of financial leverage? What does this imply?

ETHICS CHALLENGE

C1

BTN 2-3   Review the *Decision Ethics* case from the first part of this chapter involving the cashier. The guidance answer suggests that you should not comply with the assistant manager's request.

Required

Propose and evaluate two other courses of action you might consider, and explain why.

COMMUNICATING IN PRACTICE

C1 C2 A1 P3

BTN 2-4   Lila Corentine is an aspiring entrepreneur and your friend. She is having difficulty understanding the purposes of financial statements and how they fit together across time.

Required

Write a one-page memorandum to Corentine explaining the purposes of the four financial statements and how they are linked across time.

TAKING IT TO THE NET

A1

BTN 2-5   Access EDGAR online (www.SEC.gov) and locate the 2011 year 10-K report of **Amazon.com** (ticker AMZN) filed on February 1, 2012. Review its financial statements reported for years ended 2011, 2010, and 2009 to answer the following questions.

Required

1. What are the amounts of its net income or net loss reported for each of these three years?
2. Does Amazon's operating activities provide cash or use cash for each of these three years?
3. If Amazon has a 2011 net income of more than $600 million and 2011 operating cash flows of nearly $4,000 million, how is it possible that its cash balance at December 31, 2011, increases by less than $1,500 million relative to its balance at December 31, 2010?

TEAMWORK IN ACTION

C1 C2 C4 A1

BTN 2-6   The expanded accounting equation consists of assets, liabilities, capital, withdrawals, revenues, and expenses. It can be used to reveal insights into changes in a company's financial position.

Required

1. Form *learning teams* of six (or more) members. Each team member must select one of the six components and each team must have at least one expert on each component: (*a*) assets, (*b*) liabilities, (*c*) capital, (*d*) withdrawals, (*e*) revenues, and (*f*) expenses.
2. Form *expert teams* of individuals who selected the same component in part 1. Expert teams are to draft a report that each expert will present to his or her learning team addressing the following:
   a. Identify for its component the (i) increase and decrease side of the account and (ii) normal balance side of the account.
   b. Describe a transaction, with amounts, that increases its component.
   c. Using the transaction and amounts in (*b*), verify the equality of the accounting equation and then explain any effects on the income statement and statement of cash flows.
   d. Describe a transaction, with amounts, that decreases its component.
   e. Using the transaction and amounts in (*d*), verify the equality of the accounting equation and then explain any effects on the income statement and statement of cash flows.
3. Each expert should return to his/her learning team. In rotation, each member presents his/her expert team's report to the learning team. Team discussion is encouraged.

ENTREPRENEURIAL DECISION

A1 A2 P3

BTN 2-7   Assume Misa Chien and Jennifer Green of **Nom Nom Truck** plan on expanding their business to accommodate more product lines. They are considering financing their expansion in one of two ways: (1) contributing more of their own funds to the business or (2) borrowing the funds from a bank.

Required

Identify at least two issues that Misa and Jennifer should consider when trying to decide on the method for financing their expansion.

BTN 2-8 Angel Martin is a young entrepreneur who operates Martin Music Services, offering singing lessons and instruction on musical instruments. Martin wishes to expand but needs a $30,000 loan. The bank requests Martin to prepare a balance sheet and key financial ratios. Martin has not kept formal records but is able to provide the following accounts and their amounts as of December 31, 2013.

Cash	$ 3,600	Accounts Receivable	$ 9,600	Prepaid Insurance	$ 1,500
Prepaid Rent	9,400	Store Supplies	6,600	Equipment	50,000
Accounts Payable	2,200	Unearned Lesson Fees . . .	15,600	Total Equity*	62,900
Annual net income . . .	40,000				

* The total equity amount reflects all owner investments, withdrawals, revenues, and expenses as of December 31, 2013.

Required

1. Prepare a balance sheet as of December 31, 2013, for Martin Music Services. (Report only the total equity amount on the balance sheet.)
2. Compute Martin's debt ratio and its return on assets (the latter ratio is defined in Chapter 1). Assume average assets equal its ending balance.
3. Do you believe the prospects of a $30,000 bank loan are good? Why or why not?

BTN 2-9 Obtain a recent copy of the most prominent newspaper distributed in your area. Research the classified section and prepare a report answering the following questions (attach relevant classified clippings to your report). Alternatively, you may want to search the Web for the required information. One suitable Website is **CareerOneStop** (**www.CareerOneStop.org**). For documentation, you should print copies of Websites accessed.

1. Identify the number of listings for accounting positions and the various accounting job titles.
2. Identify the number of listings for other job titles, with examples, that require or prefer accounting knowledge/experience but are not specifically accounting positions.
3. Specify the salary range for the accounting and accounting-related positions if provided.
4. Indicate the job that appeals to you, the reason for its appeal, and its requirements.

BTN 2-10 KTM (**www.KTM.com**) is a leading manufacturer of offroad and street motorcycles, and it competes to some extent with both **Polaris** and **Arctic Cat**. Key financial ratios for the current fiscal year follow.

Key Figure	KTM	Polaris	Arctic Cat
Return on assets	4.3%	18.5%	4.8%
Debt ratio	54.8%	59.3%	32.9%

Required

1. Which company is most profitable according to its return on assets?
2. Which company is most risky according to the debt ratio?
3. Which company deserves increased investment based on a joint analysis of return on assets and the debt ratio? Explain.

ANSWERS TO MULTIPLE CHOICE QUIZ

1. b; debit Utility Expense for $700, and credit Cash for $700.
2. a; debit Cash for $2,500, and credit Unearned Lawn Service Fees for $2,500.
3. c; debit Cash for $250,000, debit Land for $500,000, and credit L. Shue, Capital for $750,000.
4. d
5. e; Debt ratio = $400,000/$1,000,000 = <u>40%</u>

Adjusting Accounts and Preparing Financial Statements

3

A Look Back

Chapter 2 explained the analysis and recording of transactions. We showed how to apply and interpret company accounts, T-accounts, double-entry accounting, ledgers, postings, and trial balances.

A Look at This Chapter

This chapter explains the timing of reports and the need to adjust accounts. Adjusting accounts is important for recognizing revenues and expenses in the proper period. We describe the adjusted trial balance and how it is used to prepare financial statements.

A Look Ahead

Chapter 4 highlights the completion of the accounting cycle. We explain the important final steps in the accounting process. These include closing procedures, the post-closing trial balance, and reversing entries.

Learning Objectives

CONCEPTUAL

C1 Explain the importance of periodic reporting and the time period assumption. (p. 94)

C2 Explain accrual accounting and how it improves financial statements. (p. 95)

C3 Identify the types of adjustments and their purpose. (p. 96)

ANALYTICAL

A1 Explain how accounting adjustments link to financial statements. (p. 105)

A2 Compute profit margin and describe its use in analyzing company performance. (p. 109)

PROCEDURAL

P1 Prepare and explain adjusting entries. (p. 97)

P2 Explain and prepare an adjusted trial balance. (p. 106)

P3 Prepare financial statements from an adjusted trial balance. (p. 106)

P4 *Appendix 3A*—Explain the alternatives in accounting for prepaids. (p. 113)

Dorm Roomies to Fashion Divas

"Do what you love and love what you do."
ASHLEY COOK (ON RIGHT)

NEW YORK—"Never in a million years did I think that just three months after graduation I would already have my own business," recalls Ashley Cook. "It is a lot of work, but a dream come true!" Ashley, along with Danielle Dankner, launched **ash&dans (ashanddans.com)**, an affordable line of scarves and embellished jersey pieces, including tops and dresses. "We learn something new everyday," explains Ashley. "We enjoy both the business side and the creative side and fill each day with equal amounts of both."

Ashley and Danielle explain how they set up an accounting system early on to account for all business activities, including cash, revenues, receivables, and payables. They also had to learn about the deferral and accrual of revenues and expenses. Setting up an accounting system was an important part of their success, explains Ashley. "The reason we were able to make things work was because we were extremely prudent with our money. We kept our costs down to a minimum . . . [and] because we were so careful with our buying, we were able to cover our costs by selling our product and keeping very little inventory."

"It is amazing how much we have developed our business savvy," says Ashley. This includes monitoring the adjusting of accounts so that revenues and expenses are properly reported

so that good decisions are made. Adds Ashley, "We do everything inhouse . . . from design to marketing to PR to sales to accounting."

Financial statement preparation and analysis are tasks that Ashley and Danielle emphasize. Although they insist on timely and accurate accounting reports, Ashley says "we are very happy with how our business started and how it has grown." To achieve that growth, Ashley and Danielle took time to understand accounting adjustments and their effects. It is part of the larger picture. "People love our story." For that to continue, they insist that a reliable accounting system is necessary . . . otherwise the business side would fail.

"We look forward to growing our brand, continually challenging ourselves and coming up with innovative designs," says Ashley. She also offers a little advice: "Educate yourself and surround yourself with people who know more than you do. Never be afraid to ask questions or take risks." Adds Danielle, "The most difficult part was simply learning to block out the non-believers."

[Sources: *ash&dans Website*, January 2013; *Under30CEO*, March 2010; *ClosetVanity.com*, December 2011; *Washington Magazine*, October 2010; *YHP*, December 2009]

Financial statements reflect revenues when earned and expenses when incurred. This is known as *accrual accounting,* which was the focus of Chapter 2. We showed how companies use accounting systems to collect information about *external* transactions and events. We also explained how journals, ledgers, and other tools are useful in preparing financial statements.

This chapter describes the accounting process for producing useful information involving *internal* transactions and events. An important part of this process is adjusting the account balances so that financial statements at the end of a reporting period reflect the effects of all transactions. We then explain the important steps in preparing financial statements.

Adjusting Accounts and Preparing Financial Statements

Timing and Reporting	**Adjusting Accounts**	**Preparing Financial Statements**
• Accounting period • Accrual versus cash • Recognition of revenues and expenses	• Prepaid expenses • Unearned revenues • Accrued expenses • Accrued revenues • Adjusted trial balance	• Income statement • Statement of owner's equity • Balance sheet

TIMING AND REPORTING

This section describes the importance of reporting accounting information at regular intervals and its impact for recording revenues and expenses.

The Accounting Period

C1 Explain the importance of periodic reporting and the time period assumption.

The value of information is often linked to its timeliness. Useful information must reach decision makers frequently and promptly. To provide timely information, accounting systems prepare reports at regular intervals. This results in an accounting process impacted by the time period (or periodicity) assumption. The **time period assumption** presumes that an organization's activities can be divided into specific time periods such as a month, a three-month quarter, a six-month interval, or a year. Exhibit 3.1 shows various **accounting,** or *reporting,* **periods.** Most organizations use a year as their primary accounting period. Reports covering a one-year period are known as **annual financial statements.** Many organizations also prepare **interim financial statements** covering one, three, or six months of activity.

"Polaris announces annual income of . . ."

EXHIBIT 3.1

Accounting Periods

The annual reporting period is not always a calendar year ending on December 31. An organization can adopt a **fiscal year** consisting of any 12 consecutive months. It is also acceptable to adopt an annual reporting period of 52 weeks. For example, **Gap**'s fiscal year consistently ends the final week of January or the first week of February each year.

Companies with little seasonal variation in sales often choose the calendar year as their fiscal year. **Facebook, Inc.**, uses calendar year reporting. However, the financial statements of **The Kellogg Company** (the company that controls characters such as Tony the Tiger, Snap! Crackle! Pop!, and Keebler Elf) reflect a fiscal year that ends on the Saturday nearest December 31. Companies experiencing seasonal variations in sales often choose a **natural business year** end, which is when sales activities are at their lowest level for the year. The natural business year for retailers such as **Walmart**, **Target**, and **Macy's** usually ends around January 31, after the holiday season.

Accrual Basis versus Cash Basis

After external transactions and events are recorded, several accounts still need adjustments before their balances appear in financial statements. This need arises because internal transactions and events remain unrecorded. **Accrual basis accounting** uses the adjusting process to recognize revenues when earned and expenses when incurred (matched with revenues).

Cash basis accounting recognizes revenues when cash is received and records expenses when cash is paid. This means that cash basis net income for a period is the difference between cash receipts and cash payments. Cash basis accounting is not consistent with generally accepted accounting principles (neither U.S. GAAP nor IFRS).

It is commonly held that accrual accounting better reflects business performance than information about cash receipts and payments. Accrual accounting also increases the *comparability* of financial statements from one period to another. Yet cash basis accounting is useful for several business decisions—which is the reason companies must report a statement of cash flows.

To see the difference between these two accounting systems, let's consider FastForward's Prepaid Insurance account. FastForward paid $2,400 for 24 months of insurance coverage that began on December 1, 2013. Accrual accounting requires that $100 of insurance expense be reported on December 2013's income statement. Another $1,200 of expense is reported in year 2014, and the remaining $1,100 is reported as expense in the first 11 months of 2015. Exhibit 3.2 illustrates this allocation of insurance cost across these three years. Any unexpired premium is reported as a Prepaid Insurance asset on the accrual basis balance sheet.

> **C2** Explain accrual accounting and how it improves financial statements.

EXHIBIT 3.2

Accrual Accounting for Allocating Prepaid Insurance to Expense

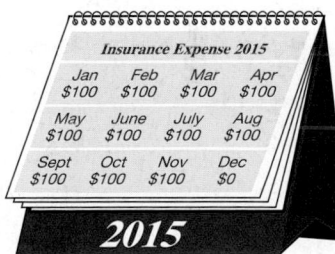

Alternatively, a cash basis income statement for December 2013 reports insurance expense of $2,400, as shown in Exhibit 3.3. The cash basis income statements for years 2014 and 2015 report no insurance expense. The cash basis balance sheet never reports an insurance asset because it is immediately expensed. This shows that cash basis income for 2013–2015 fails to match the cost of insurance with the insurance benefits received for those years and months.

EXHIBIT 3.3

Cash Accounting for Allocating Prepaid Insurance to Expense

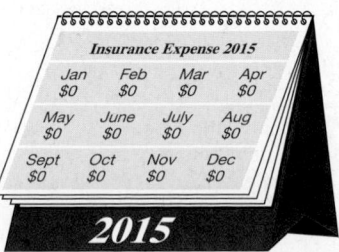

Recognizing Revenues and Expenses

We use the time period assumption to divide a company's activities into specific time periods, but not all activities are complete when financial statements are prepared. Thus, adjustments often are required to get correct account balances.

We rely on two principles in the adjusting process: revenue recognition and expense recognition (the latter is often referred to as matching). Chapter 1 explained that the *revenue recognition principle* requires that revenue be recorded when earned, not before and not after. Most companies earn revenue when they provide services and products to customers. A major goal of the adjusting process is to have revenue recognized (reported) in the time period when it is earned. The **expense recognition** (or **matching**) **principle** aims to record expenses in the same accounting period as the revenues that are earned as a result of those expenses. This matching of expenses with the revenue benefits is a major part of the adjusting process.

Matching expenses with revenues often requires us to predict certain events. When we use financial statements, we must understand that they require estimates and therefore include measures that are not precise. **Walt Disney**'s annual report explains that its production costs from movies, such as its *Pirates of the Caribbean* series, are matched to revenues based on a ratio of current revenues from the movie divided by its predicted total revenues.

Decision Insight

Diamond Foods, Inc., a popular snack maker, was recently investigated for postponing expenses related to payments to its walnut growers. This alleged late expense recognition caused income to be overstated in 2011. Further, this misstatement threatened completion of its recent acquisition of **Pringles** (for more details, see *BusinessWeek*, January 17, 2012). ■

Quick Check

Answers — p. 116

1. Describe a company's annual reporting period.
2. Why do companies prepare interim financial statements?
3. What two accounting principles most directly drive the adjusting process?
4. Is cash basis accounting consistent with the matching principle? Why or why not?
5. If your company pays a $4,800 premium on April 1, 2013, for two years' insurance coverage, how much insurance expense is reported in 2014 using cash basis accounting?

ADJUSTING ACCOUNTS

Adjusting accounts is a 3-step process:

> ***Step 1:*** **Determine what the current account balance *equals*.**
>
> ***Step 2:*** **Determine what the current account balance *should equal*.**
>
> ***Step 3:*** **Record an adjusting entry to get from step *1* to step *2*.**

Framework for Adjustments

Adjustments are necessary for transactions and events that extend over more than one period. It is helpful to group adjustments by the timing of cash receipt or cash payment in relation to the recognition of the related revenues or expenses. Exhibit 3.4 identifies four types of adjustments.

The left half of this exhibit shows prepaid expenses (including depreciation) and unearned revenues, which reflect transactions when cash is paid or received *before* a related expense or

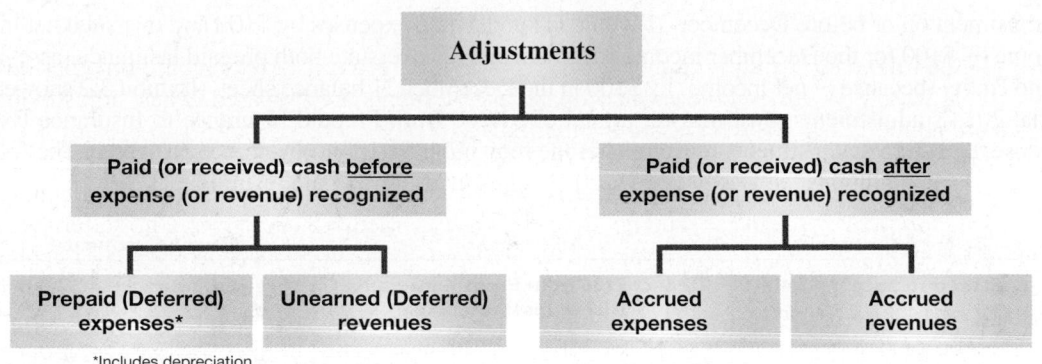

EXHIBIT 3.4

Types of Adjustments

revenue is recognized. They are also called *deferrals* because the recognition of an expense (or revenue) is *deferred* until after the related cash is paid (or received). The right half of this exhibit shows accrued expenses and accrued revenues, which reflect transactions when cash is paid or received *after* a related expense or revenue is recognized. Adjusting entries are necessary for each of these so that revenues, expenses, assets, and liabilities are correctly reported. Specifically, an **adjusting entry** is made at the end of an accounting period to reflect a transaction or event that is not yet recorded. Each adjusting entry affects one or more income statement accounts *and* one or more balance sheet accounts (but never the Cash account).

Point: Source documents provide information for most daily transactions, and in many businesses the recordkeepers record them. Adjustments require more knowledge and are usually handled by senior accounting professionals.

Prepaid (Deferred) Expenses

Prepaid expenses refer to items *paid for* in advance of receiving their benefits. Prepaid expenses are assets. When these assets are used, their costs become expenses. Adjusting entries for prepaids increase expenses and decrease assets as shown in the T-accounts of Exhibit 3.5. Such adjustments reflect transactions and events that use up prepaid expenses (including passage of time). To illustrate the accounting for prepaid expenses, we look at prepaid insurance, supplies, and depreciation.

P1 Prepare and explain adjusting entries.

EXHIBIT 3.5

Adjusting for Prepaid Expenses

Prepaid Insurance   We use our 3-step process for this and all accounting adjustments.

Step 1:   We determine that the current balance of FastForward's prepaid insurance is equal to its $2,400 payment for 24 months of insurance benefits that began on December 1, 2013.

Step 2:   With the passage of time, the benefits of the insurance gradually expire and a portion of the Prepaid Insurance asset becomes expense. For instance, one month's insurance coverage expires by December 31, 2013. This expense is $100, or 1/24 of $2,400, which leaves $2,300.

Step 3:   The adjusting entry to record this expense and reduce the asset, along with T-account postings, follows:

Assets = Liabilities + Equity
−100   −100

Explanation   After adjusting and posting, the $100 balance in Insurance Expense and the $2,300 balance in Prepaid Insurance are ready for reporting in financial statements. *Not* making the

Point: Many companies record adjusting entries only at the end of each year because of the time and cost necessary.

adjustment on or before December 31 would (1) understate expenses by $100 and overstate net income by $100 for the December income statement and (2) overstate both prepaid insurance (assets) and equity (because of net income) by $100 in the December 31 balance sheet. (Exhibit 3.2 showed that 2014's adjustments must transfer a total of $1,200 from Prepaid Insurance to Insurance Expense, and 2015's adjustments must transfer the remaining $1,100 to Insurance Expense.) The following table highlights the December 31, 2013, adjustment for prepaid insurance.

Before Adjustment	Adjustment	After Adjustment
Prepaid Insurance = $2,400	Deduct $100 from Prepaid Insurance Add $100 to Insurance Expense	Prepaid Insurance = $2,300
Reports $2,400 policy for 24-months' coverage.	Record current month's $100 insurance expense and $100 reduction in prepaid amount.	Reports $2,300 in coverage for remaining 23 months.

Supplies   Supplies are a prepaid expense requiring adjustment.

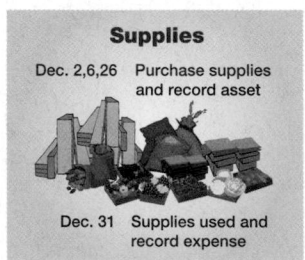

Supplies

Dec. 2,6,26   Purchase supplies and record asset

Dec. 31   Supplies used and record expense

Step 1:   FastForward purchased $9,720 of supplies in December and some of them were used during this month. When financial statements are prepared at December 31, the cost of supplies used during December must be recognized.

Step 2:   When FastForward computes (takes physical count of) its remaining unused supplies at December 31, it finds $8,670 of supplies remaining of the $9,720 total supplies. The $1,050 difference between these two amounts is December's supplies expense.

Step 3:   The adjusting entry to record this expense and reduce the Supplies asset account, along with T-account postings, follows:

Assets = Liabilities + Equity
−1,050   −1,050

Adjustment (b)		
Dec. 31 Supplies Expense	1,050	
Supplies		1,050
To record supplies used.		

Supplies Expense	652
Dec. 31 1,050	

	Supplies		126
Dec. 2	2,500	Dec. 31	1,050
6	7,100		
26	120		
Balance	8,670		

Explanation   The balance of the Supplies account is $8,670 after posting—equaling the cost of the remaining supplies. *Not* making the adjustment on or before December 31 would (1) understate expenses by $1,050 and overstate net income by $1,050 for the December income statement and (2) overstate both supplies and equity (because of net income) by $1,050 in the December 31 balance sheet. The following table highlights the adjustment for supplies.

Before Adjustment	Adjustment	After Adjustment
Supplies = $9,720	Deduct $1,050 from Supplies Add $1,050 to Supplies Expense	Supplies = $8,670
Reports $9,720 in supplies.	Record $1,050 in supplies used and $1,050 as supplies expense.	Reports $8,670 in supplies.

Other Prepaid Expenses   Other prepaid expenses, such as Prepaid Rent, are accounted for exactly as Insurance and Supplies are. We should note that some prepaid expenses are both paid for and fully used up within a single accounting period. One example is when a company pays monthly rent on the first day of each month. This payment creates a prepaid expense on the first day of each month that fully expires by the end of the month. In these special cases, we can record the cash paid with a debit to an expense account instead of an asset account. This practice is described more completely later in the chapter.

Point: We assume that prepaid and unearned items are recorded in balance sheet accounts. An alternative is to record them in income statement accounts; Appendix 3A discusses this alternative. The adjusted financial statements are identical.

■ **Decision Maker**

Depreciation   A special category of prepaid expenses is **plant assets,** which refers to long-term tangible assets used to produce and sell products and services. Plant assets are expected to provide benefits for more than one period. Examples of plant assets are buildings, machines, vehicles, and fixtures. All plant assets, with a general exception for land, eventually wear out or decline in usefulness. The costs of these assets are deferred but are gradually reported as expenses in the income statement over the assets' useful lives (benefit periods). **Depreciation** is the process of allocating the costs of these assets over their expected useful lives. Depreciation expense is recorded with an adjusting entry similar to that for other prepaid expenses.

Point: Plant assets are also called *Plant & Equipment,* or *Property, Plant & Equipment.*

Point: Depreciation does not necessarily measure decline in market value.

Point: An asset's expected value at the end of its useful life is called *salvage value.*

Step 1:   Recall that FastForward purchased equipment for $26,000 in early December to use in earning revenue. This equipment's cost must be depreciated.

Step 2:   The equipment is expected to have a useful life (benefit period) of four years and to be worth about $8,000 at the end of four years. This means the *net* cost of this equipment over its useful life is $18,000 ($26,000 − $8,000). We can use any of several methods to allocate this $18,000 net cost to expense. FastForward uses a method called **straight-line depreciation,** which allocates equal amounts of the asset's net cost to depreciation during its useful life. Dividing the $18,000 net cost by the 48 months in the asset's useful life gives a monthly cost of $375 ($18,000/48).

Depreciation

Dec. 3   Purchase equipment and record asset

Dec. 31   Allocate asset cost and record depreciation

Step 3:   The adjusting entry to record monthly depreciation expense, along with T-account postings, follows:

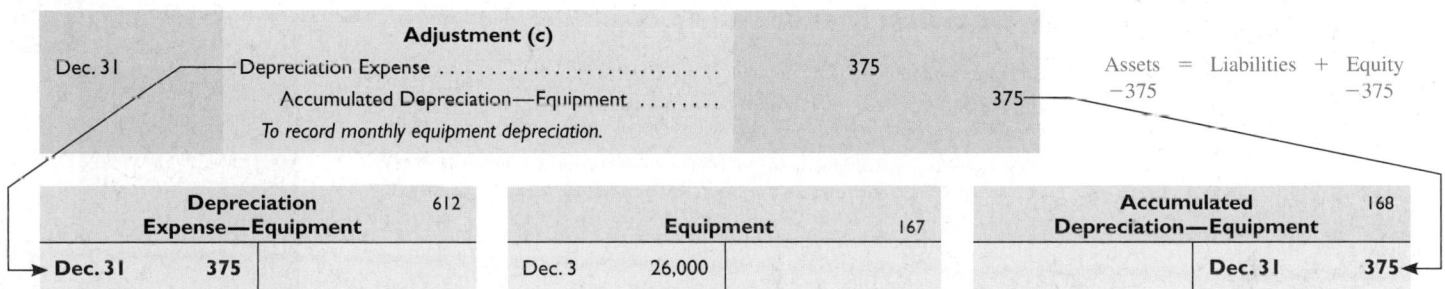

	Adjustment (c)		
Dec. 31	Depreciation Expense	375	
	Accumulated Depreciation—Equipment		375
	To record monthly equipment depreciation.		

Assets = Liabilities + Equity
−375   −375

Depreciation Expense—Equipment	612		**Equipment**	167		**Accumulated Depreciation—Equipment**	168
Dec. 31 375			Dec. 3 26,000				Dec. 31 375

Explanation   After posting the adjustment, the Equipment account ($26,000) less its Accumulated Depreciation ($375) account equals the $25,625 net cost (made up of $17,625 for the 47 remaining months in the benefit period plus the $8,000 value at the end of that time). The $375 balance in the Depreciation Expense account is reported in the December income statement. *Not* making the adjustment at December 31 would (1) understate expenses by $375 and overstate net income by $375 for the December income statement and (2) overstate both assets and equity (because of income) by $375 in the December 31 balance sheet. The following table highlights the adjustment for depreciation.

Before Adjustment	Adjustment	After Adjustment
Equipment, net = $26,000	Deduct $375 from Equipment, net Add $375 to Depreciation Expense	Equipment, net = $25,625
Reports $26,000 in equipment.	Record $375 in depreciation and $375 as accumulated depreciation, which is deducted from equipment.	Reports $25,625 in equipment, net of accumulated depreciation.

Accumulated depreciation is kept in a separate contra account. A **contra account** is an account linked with another account, it has an opposite normal balance, and it is reported as a subtraction from that other account's balance. For instance, FastForward's contra account of Accumulated Depreciation—Equipment is subtracted from the Equipment account in the balance sheet (see Exhibit 3.7). This contra account allows balance sheet readers to know both the full costs of assets and the total depreciation.

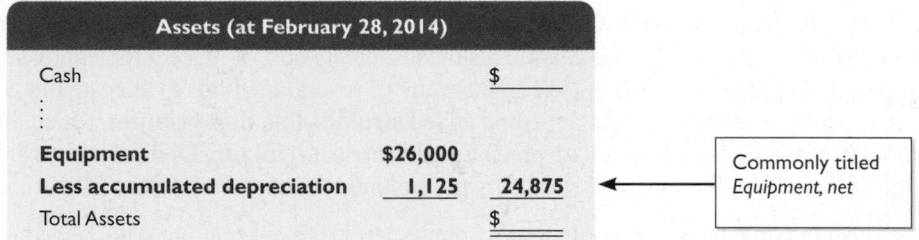

Equipment	167
Dec. 3 26,000	

Accumulated Depreciation—Equipment	168
Dec. 31	375
Jan. 31	375
Feb. 28	375
Balance	**1,125**

Point: The cost principle requires an asset to be initially recorded at acquisition cost. Depreciation causes the asset's book value (cost less accumulated depreciation) to decline over time.

Point: The net cost of equipment is also called the *depreciable basis.*

The title of the contra account, *Accumulated Depreciation,* reveals that this account includes total depreciation expense for all prior periods for which the asset was used. To illustrate, the Equipment and the Accumulated Depreciation accounts appear as in Exhibit 3.6 on February 28, 2014, after three months of adjusting entries. The $1,125 balance in the accumulated depreciation account can be subtracted from its related $26,000 asset cost. The difference ($24,875) between these two balances is the cost of the asset that has not yet been depreciated. This difference is called the **book value,** or the *net amount,* which equals the asset's costs less its accumulated depreciation.

These account balances are reported in the assets section of the February 28 balance sheet in Exhibit 3.7.

EXHIBIT 3.7

Equipment and Accumulated Depreciation on February 28 Balance Sheet

Assets (at February 28, 2014)		
Cash		$ _____
⋮		
Equipment	$26,000	
Less accumulated depreciation	1,125	24,875
Total Assets		$ _____

Commonly titled *Equipment, net*

■ **Decision Maker** ━━━━━━━━━━━━━━━━━━━━━━━━━━━━━━━━

Entrepreneur You are preparing an offer to purchase a skate board shop. The depreciation schedule for the shop's building and equipment shows costs of $175,000 and accumulated depreciation of $155,000. This leaves a net for building and equipment of $20,000. Is this information useful in helping you decide on a purchase offer? ■ [Answer—p. 116]

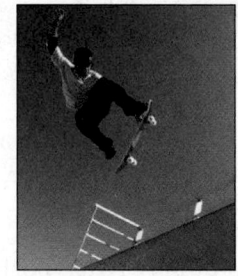

Unearned (Deferred) Revenues

Point: To *defer* is to postpone. We postpone reporting amounts received as revenues until they are earned.

The term **unearned revenues** refers to cash received in advance of providing products and services. Unearned revenues, also called *deferred revenues,* are liabilities. When cash is accepted, an obligation to provide products or services is accepted. As products or services are provided, the unearned revenues become *earned* revenues. Adjusting entries for unearned revenues involve increasing revenues and decreasing unearned revenues, as shown in Exhibit 3.8.

EXHIBIT 3.8

Adjusting for Unearned Revenues

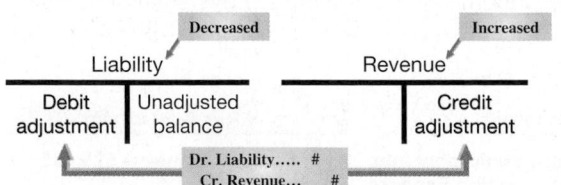

Decreased		Increased
Liability		Revenue
Debit adjustment	Unadjusted balance	Credit adjustment

Dr. Liability..... #
Cr. Revenue... #

An example of unearned revenues is from **Gannett Co., Inc.**, publisher of USATODAY, which reports unexpired (unearned subscriptions) of $224 million: "Revenue is recognized in the period in which it is earned (as newspapers are delivered)." Unearned revenues are nearly 25% of the current liabilities for Gannett. Another example comes from the **Boston Celtics**. When the Celtics receive cash from advance ticket sales and broadcast fees, they record it in an unearned revenue account called *Deferred Game Revenues.* The Celtics recognize this unearned revenue with adjusting entries on a game-by-game basis. Since the NBA regular season begins in October and ends in April, revenue recognition is mainly limited to this period. For a recent season, the Celtics' quarterly revenues were $0 million for July–September; $34 million for October–December; $48 million for January–March; and $17 million for April–June.

Unearned Revenues

Dec. 26   Cash received in advance and record liability

Thanks for cash in advance. I'll work now through Feb. 24

Dec. 31   Provided services and record revenue

Returning to FastForward, it also has unearned revenues. It agreed on December 26 to provide consulting services to a client for a fixed fee of $3,000 for 60 days.

Step 1: On December 26, the client paid the 60-day fee in advance, covering the period December 27 to February 24. The entry to record the cash received in advance is

Dec. 26	Cash	3,000	
	Unearned Consulting Revenue		3,000
	Received advance payment for services over the next 60 days.		

Assets = Liabilities + Equity
+3,000   +3,000

This advance payment increases cash and creates an obligation to do consulting work over the next 60 days.

Step 2: As time passes, FastForward earns this payment through consulting. By December 31, it has provided five days' service and earned 5/60 of the $3,000 unearned revenue. This amounts to $250 ($3,000 × 5/60). The *revenue recognition principle* implies that $250 of unearned revenue must be reported as revenue on the December income statement.

Step 3: The adjusting entry to reduce the liability account and recognize earned revenue, along with T-account postings, follows:

Assets = Liabilities + Equity
−250   +250

Explanation The adjusting entry transfers $250 from unearned revenue (a liability account) to a revenue account. *Not* making the adjustment (1) understates revenue and net income by $250 in the December income statement and (2) overstates unearned revenue and understates equity by $250 on the December 31 balance sheet. The following highlights the adjustment for unearned revenue.

Before Adjustment	Adjustment	After Adjustment
Unearned Consulting Revenue = $3,000	**Deduct $250 from Unearned Consulting Revenue Add $250 to Consulting Revenue**	**Unearned Consulting Revenue = $2,750**
Reports $3,000 in unearned revenue for consulting services promised for 60 days.	Record 5 days of earned consulting revenue, which is 5/60 of unearned amount.	Reports $2,750 in unearned revenue for consulting services owed over next 55 days.

Accounting for unearned revenues is crucial to many companies. For example, the **National Retail Federation** reports that gift card sales, which are unearned revenues for sellers, exceed $20 billion annually. Gift cards are now the top selling holiday gift; 57.3% of all gift givers planned to give at least one gift card in 2011 (source: NRF Website).

Accrued Expenses

Accrued expenses refer to costs that are incurred in a period but are both unpaid and unrecorded. Accrued expenses must be reported on the income statement for the period when incurred. Adjusting entries for recording accrued expenses involve increasing expenses and

Point: Accrued expenses are also called accrued liabilities.

EXHIBIT 3.9

Adjusting for Accrued Expenses

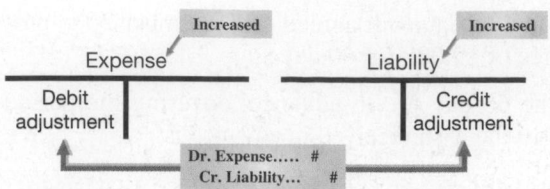

increasing liabilities as shown in Exhibit 3.9. This adjustment recognizes expenses incurred in a period but not yet paid. Common examples of accrued expenses are salaries, interest, rent, and taxes. We use salaries and interest to show how to adjust accounts for accrued expenses.

Accrued Salaries Expense FastForward's employee earns $70 per day, or $350 for a five-day workweek beginning on Monday and ending on Friday.

Step 1: Its employee is paid every two weeks on Friday. On December 12 and 26, the wages are paid, recorded in the journal, and posted to the ledger.

Step 2: The calendar in Exhibit 3.10 shows three working days after the December 26 payday (29, 30, and 31). This means the employee has earned three days' salary by the close of business

EXHIBIT 3.10

Salary Accrual and Paydays

Point: An employer records salaries expense and a vacation pay liability when employees earn vacation pay.

on Wednesday, December 31, yet this salary cost has not been paid or recorded. The financial statements would be incomplete if FastForward fails to report the added expense and liability to the employee for unpaid salary from December 29, 30, and 31.

Step 3: The adjusting entry to account for accrued salaries, along with T-account postings, follows:

Assets = Liabilities + Equity
    +210   −210

Adjustment (e)		
Dec. 31 Salaries Expense	210	
Salaries Payable		210
To record three days' accrued salary (3 × $70).		

Salaries Expense		622
Dec. 12	700	
26	700	
31	210	
Balance	1,610	

Salaries Payable		209
	Dec. 31	210

Explanation Salaries expense of $1,610 is reported on the December income statement and $210 of salaries payable (liability) is reported in the balance sheet. *Not* making the adjustment (1) understates salaries expense and overstates net income by $210 in the December income statement and (2) understates salaries payable (liabilities) and overstates equity by $210 on the December 31 balance sheet. The following highlights the adjustment for salaries incurred.

Before Adjustment	Adjustment	After Adjustment
Salaries Payable = $0	**Add $210 to Salaries Payable** **Add $210 to Salaries Expense**	**Salaries Payable = $210**
Reports $0 from employee salaries incurred but not yet paid in cash.	Record 3 days' salaries owed to employee, but not yet paid, at $70 per day.	Reports $210 salaries payable to employee but not yet paid.

Accrued Interest Expense Companies commonly have accrued interest expense on notes payable and other long-term liabilities at the end of a period. Interest expense is incurred with the passage of time. Unless interest is paid on the last day of an accounting period, we need to adjust for interest expense incurred but not yet paid. This means we must accrue interest cost from the most recent payment date up to the end of the period. The formula for computing accrued interest is:

Principal amount owed × Annual interest rate × Fraction of year since last payment date.

To illustrate, if a company has a $6,000 loan from a bank at 6% annual interest, then 30 days' accrued interest expense is $30—computed as $6,000 × 0.06 × 30/360. The adjusting entry would be to debit Interest Expense for $30 and credit Interest Payable for $30.

Point: Interest computations assume a 360-day year; known as the *bankers' rule.*

Future Payment of Accrued Expenses Adjusting entries for accrued expenses foretell cash transactions in future periods. Specifically, accrued expenses at the end of one accounting period result in *cash payment* in a *future period*(s). To illustrate, recall that FastForward recorded accrued salaries of $210. On January 9, the first payday of the next period, the following entry settles the accrued liability (salaries payable) and records salaries expense for seven days of work in January:

Jan. 9	Salaries Payable (3 days at $70 per day)	210	
	Salaries Expense (7 days at $70 per day)	490	
	Cash		700
	Paid two weeks' salary including three days accrued in December.		

Assets = Liabilities + Equity
−700   −210   −490

The $210 debit reflects the payment of the liability for the three days' salary accrued on December 31. The $490 debit records the salary for January's first seven working days (including the New Year's Day holiday) as an expense of the new accounting period. The $700 credit records the total amount of cash paid to the employee.

Accrued Revenues

The term **accrued revenues** refers to revenues earned in a period that are both unrecorded and not yet received in cash (or other assets). An example is a technician who bills customers only when the job is done. If one-third of a job is complete by the end of a period, then the technician must record one-third of the expected billing as revenue in that period—even though there is no billing or collection. The adjusting entries for accrued revenues increase assets and increase revenues as shown in Exhibit 3.11. Accrued revenues commonly arise from services, products, interest, and rent. We use service fees and interest to show how to adjust for accrued revenues.

Point: Accrued revenues are also called *accrued assets.*

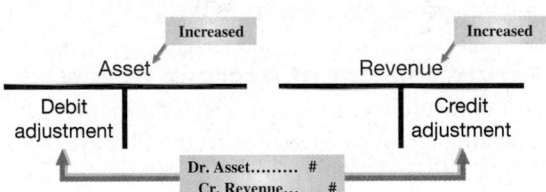

EXHIBIT 3.11

Adjusting for Accrued Revenues

Accrued Services Revenue Accrued revenues are not recorded until adjusting entries are made at the end of the accounting period. These accrued revenues are earned but unrecorded because either the buyer has not yet paid for them or the seller has not yet billed the buyer. FastForward provides an example.

Step 1: In the second week of December, it agreed to provide 30 days of consulting services to a local fitness club for a fixed fee of $2,700. The terms of the initial agreement call for FastForward to provide services from December 12, 2013, through January 10, 2014, or 30 days of service. The club agrees to pay FastForward $2,700 on January 10, 2014, when the service period is complete.

Step 2: At December 31, 2013, 20 days of services have already been provided. Since the contracted services have not yet been entirely provided, FastForward has neither billed the club nor recorded the services already provided. Still, FastForward has earned two-thirds of the 30-day fee, or $1,800 ($2,700 × 20/30). The *revenue recognition principle* implies that it must report the $1,800 on the December income statement. The balance sheet also must report that the club owes FastForward $1,800.

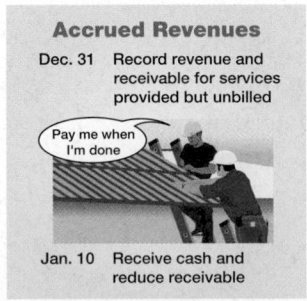

Accrued Revenues

Dec. 31 Record revenue and receivable for services provided but unbilled

Jan. 10 Receive cash and reduce receivable

Step 3:   The year-end adjusting entry to account for accrued services revenue is

Assets = Liabilities + Equity
+1,800   +1,800

Adjustment (f)		
Dec. 31 Accounts Receivable	1,800	
Consulting Revenue		1,800
To record 20 days' accrued revenue.		

Accounts Receivable			106
Dec. 12	1,900	Dec. 22	1,900
31	**1,800**		
Balance	1,800		

Consulting Revenue		403
	Dec. 5	4,200
	12	1,600
	31	250
	31	**1,800**
	Balance	7,850

Example: What is the adjusting entry if the 30-day consulting period began on December 22? *Answer:* One-third of the fee is earned:
Accounts Receivable 900
    Consulting Revenue.... 900

Explanation   Accounts receivable are reported on the balance sheet at $1,800, and the $7,850 total of consulting revenue is reported on the income statement. *Not* making the adjustment would understate (1) both consulting revenue and net income by $1,800 in the December income statement and (2) both accounts receivable (assets) and equity by $1,800 on the December 31 balance sheet. The following table highlights the adjustment for accrued revenue.

Before Adjustment	Adjustment	After Adjustment
Accounts Receivable = $0	**Add $1,800 to Accounts Receivable** **Add $1,800 to Consulting Revenue**	**Accounts Receivable = $1,800**
Reports $0 from revenue earned but not yet received in cash.	Record 20 days of earned consulting revenue, which is 20/30 of total contract amount.	Reports $1,800 in accounts receivable from consulting services provided.

Accrued Interest Revenue   In addition to the accrued interest expense we described earlier, interest can yield an accrued revenue when a debtor owes money (or other assets) to a company. If a company is holding notes or accounts receivable that produce interest revenue, we must adjust the accounts to record any earned and yet uncollected interest revenue. The adjusting entry is similar to the one for accruing services revenue. Specifically, we debit Interest Receivable (asset) and credit Interest Revenue.

Future Receipt of Accrued Revenues   Accrued revenues at the end of one accounting period result in *cash receipts* in a *future period*(s). To illustrate, recall that FastForward made an adjusting entry for $1,800 to record 20 days' accrued revenue earned from its consulting contract. When FastForward receives $2,700 cash on January 10 for the entire contract amount, it makes the following entry to remove the accrued asset (accounts receivable) and recognize the revenue earned in January. The $2,700 debit reflects the cash received. The $1,800 credit reflects the removal of the receivable, and the $900 credit records the revenue earned in January.

Assets = Liabilities + Equity
+2,700   +900
−1,800

Jan. 10	Cash	2,700	
	Accounts Receivable (20 days at $90 per day)		1,800
	Consulting Revenue (10 days at $90 per day)		900
	Received cash for the accrued asset and recorded earned consulting revenue for January.		

■ Decision Maker

Loan Officer   The owner of a custom audio, video, and home theater store applies for a business loan. The store's financial statements reveal large increases in current-year revenues and income. Analysis shows that these increases are due to a promotion that let consumers buy now and pay nothing until January 1 of next year. The store recorded these sales as accrued revenue. Does your analysis raise any concerns? ■   [Answer—p. 116]

Links to Financial Statements

The process of adjusting accounts is intended to bring an asset or liability account balance to its correct amount. It also updates a related expense or revenue account. These adjustments are necessary for transactions and events that extend over more than one period. (Adjusting entries are posted like any other entry.)

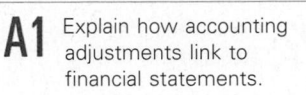

A1 Explain how accounting adjustments link to financial statements.

Exhibit 3.12 summarizes the four types of transactions requiring adjustment. Understanding this exhibit is important to understanding the adjusting process and its importance to financial statements. Remember that each adjusting entry affects one or more income statement accounts *and* one or more balance sheet accounts (but never cash).

EXHIBIT 3.12

Summary of Adjustments and Financial Statement Links

	BEFORE Adjusting		
Category	Balance Sheet	Income Statement	Adjusting Entry
Prepaid expenses†	Asset overstated	Expense understated	**Dr. Expense**
	Equity overstated		**Cr. Asset***
Unearned revenues†	Liability overstated	Revenue understated	Dr. Liability
	Equity understated		Cr. Revenue
Accrued expenses	Liability understated	Expense understated	**Dr. Expense**
	Equity overstated		**Cr. Liability**
Accrued revenues	Asset understated	Revenue understated	Dr. Asset
	Equity understated		Cr. Revenue

* For depreciation, the credit is to Accumulated Depreciation (contra asset).

† Exhibit assumes that prepaid expenses are initially recorded as assets and that unearned revenues are initially recorded as liabilities.

Information about some adjustments is not always available until several days or even weeks after the period-end. This means that some adjusting and closing entries are recorded later than, but dated as of, the last day of the period. One example is a company that receives a utility bill on January 10 for costs incurred for the month of December. When it receives the bill, the company records the expense and the payable as of December 31. Other examples include long-distance phone usage and costs of many Web billings. The December income statement reflects these additional expenses incurred, and the December 31 balance sheet includes these payables, although the amounts were not actually known on December 31.

Point: CFOs often feel pressure to pursue fraudulent accounting due to pressure applied by their superiors, such as overbearing CEOs or aggressive boards.

■ Decision Ethics

Financial Officer At year-end, the president instructs you, the financial officer, not to record accrued expenses until next year because they will not be paid until then. The president also directs you to record in current-year sales a recent purchase order from a customer that requires merchandise to be delivered two weeks after the year-end. Your company would report a net income instead of a net loss if you carry out these instructions. What do you do? ■ [Answer—p. 116]

Quick Check

Answers — p. 116

6. If an adjusting entry for accrued revenues of $200 at year-end is omitted, what is this error's effect on the year-end income statement and balance sheet?

7. What is a contra account? Explain its purpose.

8. What is an accrued expense? Give an example.

9. Describe how an unearned revenue arises. Give an example.

Adjusted Trial Balance

An **unadjusted trial balance** is a list of accounts and balances prepared *before* adjustments are recorded. An **adjusted trial balance** is a list of accounts and balances prepared *after* adjusting entries have been recorded and posted to the ledger.

Exhibit 3.13 shows both the unadjusted and the adjusted trial balances for FastForward at December 31, 2013. The order of accounts in the trial balance is usually set up to match the order in the chart of accounts. Several new accounts arise from the adjusting entries.

EXHIBIT 3.13

Unadjusted and Adjusted Trial Balances

Acct. No.	Account Title	Unadjusted Trial Balance Dr.	Unadjusted Trial Balance Cr.	Adjustments Dr.	Adjustments Cr.	Adjusted Trial Balance Dr.	Adjusted Trial Balance Cr.
		FASTFORWARD Trial Balances December 31, 2013					
101	Cash	$ 4,350				$ 4,350	
106	Accounts receivable	0		(f) $1,800		1,800	
126	Supplies	9,720			(b) $1,050	8,670	
128	Prepaid insurance	2,400			(a) 100	2,300	
167	Equipment	26,000				26,000	
168	Accumulated depreciation—Equip.		$ 0		(c) 375		$ 375
201	Accounts payable		6,200				6,200
209	Salaries payable		0		(e) 210		210
236	Unearned consulting revenue		3,000	(d) 250			2,750
301	C. Taylor, Capital		30,000				30,000
302	C. Taylor, Withdrawals	200				200	
403	Consulting revenue		5,800		(d) 250		7,850
					(f) 1,800		
406	Rental revenue		300				300
612	Depreciation expense—Equip.	0		(c) 375		375	
622	Salaries expense	1,400		(e) 210		1,610	
637	Insurance expense	0		(a) 100		100	
640	Rent expense	1,000				1,000	
652	Supplies expense	0		(b) 1,050		1,050	
690	Utilities expense	230				230	
	Totals	$45,300	$45,300	$3,785	$3,785	$47,685	$47,685

Each adjustment (see middle columns) is identified by a letter in parentheses that links it to an adjusting entry explained earlier. Each amount in the Adjusted Trial Balance columns is computed by taking that account's amount from the Unadjusted Trial Balance columns and adding or subtracting any adjustment(s). To illustrate, Supplies has a $9,720 Dr. balance in the unadjusted columns. Subtracting the $1,050 Cr. amount shown in the adjustments columns yields an adjusted $8,670 Dr. balance for Supplies. An account can have more than one adjustment, such as for Consulting Revenue. Also, some accounts might not require adjustment for this period, such as Accounts Payable.

PREPARING FINANCIAL STATEMENTS

We can prepare financial statements directly from information in the *adjusted* trial balance. An adjusted trial balance (see the right-most columns in Exhibit 3.13) includes all accounts and balances appearing in financial statements, and is easier to work from than the entire ledger when preparing financial statements.

Exhibit 3.14 shows how revenue and expense balances are transferred from the adjusted trial balance to the income statement (red lines). The net income and the withdrawals amount are then used to prepare the statement of owner's equity (black lines). Asset and liability balances on the adjusted trial balance are then transferred to the balance sheet (blue lines). The ending capital is determined on the statement of owner's equity and transferred to the balance sheet (green lines).

EXHIBIT 3.14

Preparing Financial Statements (Adjusted Trial Balance from Exhibit 3.13)

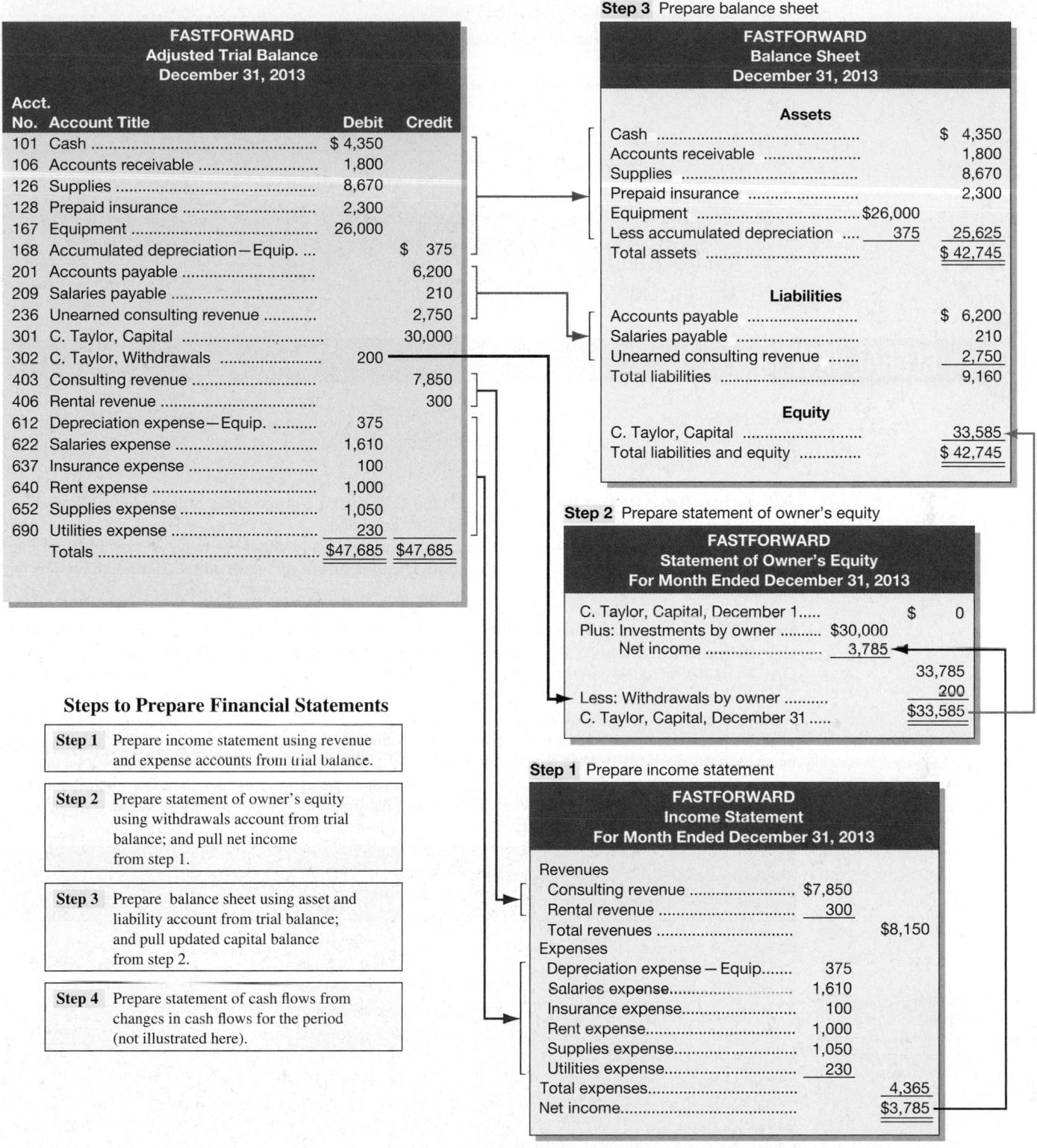

FASTFORWARD
Adjusted Trial Balance
December 31, 2013

Acct. No.	Account Title	Debit	Credit
101	Cash	$ 4,350	
106	Accounts receivable	1,800	
126	Supplies	8,670	
128	Prepaid insurance	2,300	
167	Equipment	26,000	
168	Accumulated depreciation—Equip.		$ 375
201	Accounts payable		6,200
209	Salaries payable		210
236	Unearned consulting revenue		2,750
301	C. Taylor, Capital		30,000
302	C. Taylor, Withdrawals	200	
403	Consulting revenue		7,850
406	Rental revenue		300
612	Depreciation expense—Equip.	375	
622	Salaries expense	1,610	
637	Insurance expense	100	
640	Rent expense	1,000	
652	Supplies expense	1,050	
690	Utilities expense	230	
	Totals	$47,685	$47,685

Step 3 Prepare balance sheet

FASTFORWARD
Balance Sheet
December 31, 2013

Assets

Cash		$ 4,350
Accounts receivable		1,800
Supplies		8,670
Prepaid insurance		2,300
Equipment	$26,000	
Less accumulated depreciation	375	25,625
Total assets		$ 42,745

Liabilities

Accounts payable	$ 6,200
Salaries payable	210
Unearned consulting revenue	2,750
Total liabilities	9,160

Equity

C. Taylor, Capital	33,585
Total liabilities and equity	$ 42,745

Step 2 Prepare statement of owner's equity

FASTFORWARD
Statement of Owner's Equity
For Month Ended December 31, 2013

C. Taylor, Capital, December 1		$ 0
Plus: Investments by owner	$30,000	
Net income	3,785	
		33,785
Less: Withdrawals by owner		200
C. Taylor, Capital, December 31		$33,585

Steps to Prepare Financial Statements

Step 1	Prepare income statement using revenue and expense accounts from trial balance.
Step 2	Prepare statement of owner's equity using withdrawals account from trial balance; and pull net income from step 1.
Step 3	Prepare balance sheet using asset and liability account from trial balance; and pull updated capital balance from step 2.
Step 4	Prepare statement of cash flows from changes in cash flows for the period (not illustrated here).

Step 1 Prepare income statement

FASTFORWARD
Income Statement
For Month Ended December 31, 2013

Revenues		
Consulting revenue	$7,850	
Rental revenue	300	
Total revenues		$8,150
Expenses		
Depreciation expense—Equip.	375	
Salaries expense	1,610	
Insurance expense	100	
Rent expense	1,000	
Supplies expense	1,050	
Utilities expense	230	
Total expenses		4,365
Net income		$3,785

We prepare financial statements in the following order: income statement, statement of owner's equity, and balance sheet. This order makes sense because the balance sheet uses information from the statement of owner's equity, which in turn uses information from the income statement. The statement of cash flows is usually the final statement prepared.

Point: Each trial balance amount is used in only *one* financial statement and, when financial statements are completed, each account will have been used once.

Quick Check Answers — p. 116

10. Music-Mart records $1,000 of accrued salaries on December 31. Five days later, on January 5 (the next payday), salaries of $7,000 are paid. What is the January 5 entry?

11. Jordan Air has the following information in its unadjusted and adjusted trial balances. What are the adjusting entries that Jordan Air likely recorded?

	Unadjusted		Adjusted	
	Debit	Credit	Debit	Credit
Prepaid insurance	$6,200		$5,900	
Salaries payable		$ 0		$1,400

12. What accounts are taken from the adjusted trial balance to prepare an income statement?

13. In preparing financial statements from an adjusted trial balance, what statement is usually prepared second?

GLOBAL VIEW

We explained that accounting under U.S. GAAP is similar, but not identical, to that under IFRS. This section discusses differences in adjusting accounts, preparing financial statements, and reporting assets and liabilities on a balance sheet.

Adjusting Accounts   Both U.S. GAAP and IFRS include broad and similar guidance for adjusting accounts. Although some variations exist in revenue and expense recognition and other principles, all of the adjustments in this chapter are accounted for identically under the two systems. In later chapters we describe how certain assets and liabilities can result in different adjusted amounts using fair value measurements.

Preparing Financial Statements   Both U.S. GAAP and IFRS prepare the same four basic financial statements following the same process discussed in this chapter. Chapter 2 explained how both U.S. GAAP and IFRS require current items to be separated from noncurrent items on the balance sheet (yielding a classified balance sheet). U.S. GAAP balance sheets report current items first. Assets are listed from most liquid to least liquid, where liquid refers to the ease of converting an asset to cash. Liabilities are listed from nearest to maturity to furthest from maturity, maturity refers to the nearness of paying off the liability. IFRS balance sheets normally present noncurrent items first (and equity before liabilities), but this is not a requirement. Other differences with financial statements exist, which we identify in later chapters. **Piaggio** provides the following example of IFRS reporting for its assets, liabilities, and equity within the balance sheet:

PIAGGIO

PIAGGIO
Balance Sheet (in thousands of Euro)
December 31, 2011

Assets		Equity and Liabilities	
Noncurrent assets		Total equity	446,218
Intangible assets	649,420	Noncurrent liabilities	
Property, plant and equipment....	274,871	Financial liabilities falling due after one year......	329,200
Other noncurrent assets	86,185	Other long-term liabilities	100,489
Total noncurrent assets	1,010,476	Total noncurrent liabilities	429,689
Current assets		Current liabilities	
Trade receivables	65,560	Financial liabilities falling due within one year	170,261
Other receivables	28,028	Trade payables	375,263
Short-term tax receivables	27,245	Tax payables	20,920
Inventories	236,988	Other short-term payables	64,718
Cash and cash equivalents	151,887	Current portion of other long-term provisions ...	13,115
Total current assets	509,708	Total current liabilities	644,277
Total assets	1,520,184	Total equity and liabilities	1,520,184

Point: IASB and FASB are working to improve financial statements. One proposal would reorganize the balance sheet to show assets and liabilities classified as operating, investing, or financing.

IFRS: New revenue recognition rules proposed by the FASB and the IASB reduce variation between U.S. GAAP and IFRS when accounting for revenue.

IFRS

Revenue and expense recognition are key to recording accounting adjustments. IFRS tends to be more *principles-based* relative to U.S. GAAP, which is viewed as more *rules-based*. A principles-based system depends heavily on control procedures to reduce the potential for fraud or misconduct. Failure in judgment led to improper accounting adjustments at **Fannie Mae**, **Xerox**, **WorldCom**, and others. A KPMG survey of accounting and finance employees found that more than 10% of them had witnessed falsification or manipulation of accounting data within the past year. Internal controls and governance processes are directed at curtailing such behavior. Yet, a 2011 KPMG fraud survey found that one in seven frauds was uncovered by chance, which emphasizes our need to improve internal controls and governance. ■

Profit Margin ▢▢▢ **Decision Analysis**

A useful measure of a company's operating results is the ratio of its net income to net sales. This ratio is called **profit margin,** or *return on sales,* and is computed as in Exhibit 3.15.

A2 Compute profit margin and describe its use in analyzing company performance.

$$\text{Profit margin} = \frac{\text{Net income}}{\text{Net sales}}$$

EXHIBIT 3.15

Profit Margin

This ratio is interpreted as reflecting the percent of profit in each dollar of sales. To illustrate how we compute and use profit margin, let's look at the results of **Limited Brands, Inc.**, in Exhibit 3.16 for its fiscal years 2007 through 2011.

$ in millions	2011	2010	2009	2008	2007
Net income	$ 805	$ 448	$ 220	$ 718	$ 676
Net sales	$9,613	$8,632	$9,043	$10,134	$10,671
Profit margin	8.4%	5.2%	2.4%	7.1%	6.3%
Industry profit margin	2.1%	0.9%	0.3%	1.1%	1.6%

EXHIBIT 3.16

Limited Brands' Profit Margin

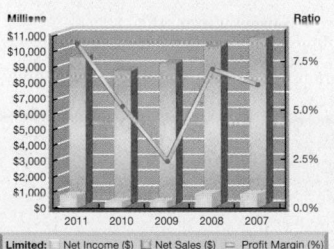

The Limited's average profit margin is 5.9% during this 5-year period. This favorably compares to the average industry profit margin of 1.2%. However, Limited's profit margin has rebounded in the most recent two years—from 2.4% in 2009 to 5.2% and 8.4% for the recent recovery periods (see margin graph). Future success depends on Limited maintaining its market share and increasing its profit margin.

DEMONSTRATION PROBLEM 1

The following information relates to Fanning's Electronics on December 31, 2013. The company, which uses the calendar year as its annual reporting period, initially records prepaid and unearned items in balance sheet accounts (assets and liabilities, respectively).

a. The company's weekly payroll is $8,750, paid each Friday for a five-day workweek. Assume December 31, 2013, falls on a Monday, but the employees will not be paid their wages until Friday, January 4, 2014.

b. Eighteen months earlier, on July 1, 2012, the company purchased equipment that cost $20,000. Its useful life is predicted to be five years, at which time the equipment is expected to be worthless (zero salvage value).

c. On October 1, 2013, the company agreed to work on a new housing development. The company is paid $120,000 on October 1 in advance of future installation of similar alarm systems in 24 new homes. That amount was credited to the Unearned Services Revenue account. Between October 1 and December 31, work on 20 homes was completed.

d. On September 1, 2013, the company purchased a 12-month insurance policy for $1,800. The transaction was recorded with an $1,800 debit to Prepaid Insurance.

e. On December 29, 2013, the company completed a $7,000 service that has not been billed and not recorded as of December 31, 2013.

Required

1. Prepare any necessary adjusting entries on December 31, 2013, in relation to transactions and events *a* through *e*.

2. Prepare T-accounts for the accounts affected by adjusting entries, and post the adjusting entries. Determine the adjusted balances for the Unearned Revenue and the Prepaid Insurance accounts.

3. Complete the following table and determine the amounts and effects of your adjusting entries on the year 2013 income statement and the December 31, 2013, balance sheet. Use up (down) arrows to indicate an increase (decrease) in the Effect columns.

Entry	Amount in the Entry	Effect on Net Income	Effect on Total Assets	Effect on Total Liabilities	Effect on Total Equity

PLANNING THE SOLUTION

- Analyze each situation to determine which accounts need to be updated with an adjustment.
- Calculate the amount of each adjustment and prepare the necessary journal entries.
- Show the amount of each adjustment in the designated accounts, determine the adjusted balance, and identify the balance sheet classification of the account.
- Determine each entry's effect on net income for the year and on total assets, total liabilities, and total equity at the end of the year.

SOLUTION TO DEMONSTRATION PROBLEM 1

1. Adjusting journal entries.

(a) Dec. 31	Wages Expense	1,750	
	Wages Payable		1,750
	To accrue wages for the last day of the year ($8,750 × 1/5).		
(b) Dec. 31	Depreciation Expense—Equipment	4,000	
	Accumulated Depreciation—Equipment		4,000
	To record depreciation expense for the year ($20,000/5 years = $4,000 per year).		
(c) Dec. 31	Unearned Services Revenue	100,000	
	Services Revenue		100,000
	To recognize services revenue earned ($120,000 × 20/24).		
(d) Dec. 31	Insurance Expense	600	
	Prepaid Insurance		600
	To adjust for expired portion of insurance ($1,800 × 4/12).		
(e) Dec. 31	Accounts Receivable	7,000	
	Services Revenue		7,000
	To record services revenue earned.		

2. T-accounts for adjusting journal entries *a* through *e*.

Wages Expense		
(a)	1,750	

Wages Payable		
	(a)	1,750

Depreciation Expense—Equipment		
(b)	4,000	

Accumulated Depreciation—Equipment		
	(b)	4,000

Unearned Revenue			
	Unadj. Bal.	120,000	
(c)	100,000		
	Adj. Bal.	20,000	

Services Revenue			
	(c)	100,000	
	(e)	7,000	
	Adj. Bal.	107,000	

Insurance Expense		
(d)	600	

Prepaid Insurance			
Unadj. Bal.	1,800		
		(d)	600
Adj. Bal.	1,200		

Accounts Receivable		
(e)	7,000	

3. Financial statement effects of adjusting journal entries.

Entry	Amount in the Entry	Effect on Net Income	Effect on Total Assets	Effect on Total Liabilities	Effect on Total Equity
a	$ 1,750	$ 1,750 ↓	No effect	$ 1,750 ↑	$ 1,750 ↓
b	4,000	1,000 ↓	$4,000 ↓	No effect	4,000 ↓
c	100,000	100,000 ↑	No effect	$100,000 ↓	100,000 ↑
d	600	600 ↓	$ 600 ↓	No effect	600 ↓
e	7,000	7,000 ↑	$7,000 ↑	No effect	7,000 ↑

DEMONSTRATION PROBLEM 2

Use the following adjusted trial balance to answer questions 1–3.

CHOI COMPANY Adjusted Trial Balance December 31		
	Debit	Credit
Cash	$ 3,050	
Accounts receivable	400	
Prepaid insurance	830	
Supplies	80	
Equipment	217,200	
Accumulated depreciation—Equipment		$ 29,100
Wages payable		880

[continued on next page]

[continued from previous page]

Interest payable		3,600
Unearned rent		460
Long-term notes payable		150,000
M. Choi, Capital		40,340
M. Choi, Withdrawals	21,000	
Rent earned		57,500
Wages expense	25,000	
Utilities expense	1,900	
Insurance expense	3,200	
Supplies expense	250	
Depreciation expense—Equipment	5,970	
Interest expense	3,000	
Totals	$281,880	$281,880

1. Prepare the annual income statement from the adjusted trial balance of Choi Company.

Answer:

CHOI COMPANY		
Income Statement		
For Year Ended December 31		
Revenues		
Rent earned		$57,500
Expenses		
Wages expense	$25,000	
Utilities expense	1,900	
Insurance expense	3,200	
Supplies expense	250	
Depreciation expense—Equipment	5,970	
Interest expense	3,000	
Total expenses		39,320
Net income		$18,180

2. Prepare a statement of owner's equity from the adjusted trial balance of Choi Company. Choi's capital account balance of $40,340 consists of a $30,340 balance from the prior year-end, plus a $10,000 owner investment during the current year.

Answer:

CHOI COMPANY		
Statement of Owner's Equity		
For Year Ended December 31		
M. Choi, Capital, December 31 prior year-end		$30,340
Plus: Owner investments	$10,000	
Net income	18,180	28,180
		58,520
Less: Withdrawals by owner		21,000
M. Choi, Capital, December 31 current year-end		$37,520

3. Prepare a balance sheet from the adjusted trial balance of Choi Company.

Answer:

CHOI COMPANY
Balance Sheet
December 31

Assets

Cash		$ 3,050
Accounts receivable		400
Prepaid insurance		830
Supplies		80
Equipment	$217,200	
Less accumulated depreciation	29,100	188,100
Total assets		$192,460

Liabilities

Wages payable		$ 880
Interest payable		3,600
Unearned rent		460
Long-term notes payable		150,000
Total liabilities		154,940

Equity

M. Choi, Capital		37,520
Total liabilities and equity		$192,460

APPENDIX

Alternative Accounting for Prepayments

3A

This appendix explains an alternative in accounting for prepaid expenses and unearned revenues.

RECORDING PREPAYMENT OF EXPENSES **IN EXPENSE ACCOUNTS**

An alternative method is to record *all* prepaid expenses with debits to expense accounts. If any prepaids remain unused or unexpired at the end of an accounting period, then adjusting entries must transfer the cost of the unused portions from expense accounts to prepaid expense (asset) accounts. This alternative method is acceptable. The financial statements are identical under either method, but the adjusting entries are different. To illustrate the differences between these two methods, let's look at FastForward's cash payment of December 6 for 24 months of insurance coverage beginning on December 1. FastForward recorded that payment with a debit to an asset account, but it could have recorded a debit to an expense account. These alternatives are shown in Exhibit 3A.1.

P4 Explain the alternatives in accounting for prepaids.

		Payment Recorded as Asset	Payment Recorded as Expense
Dec. 6	Prepaid Insurance	2,400	
	Cash	2,400	
Dec. 6	Insurance Expense		2,400
	Cash		2,400

EXHIBIT 3A.1

Alternative Initial Entries for Prepaid Expenses

At the end of its accounting period on December 31, insurance protection for one month has expired. This means $100 ($2,400/24) of insurance coverage expired and is an expense for December. The adjusting entry depends on how the original payment was recorded. This is shown in Exhibit 3A.2.

EXHIBIT 3A.2

Adjusting Entry for Prepaid Expenses for the Two Alternatives

			Payment Recorded as Asset	Payment Recorded as Expense
Dec. 31	Insurance Expense		100	
	Prepaid Insurance		100	
Dec. 31	Prepaid Insurance			2,300
	Insurance Expense			2,300

When these entries are posted to the accounts in the ledger, we can see that these two methods give identical results. The December 31 adjusted account balances in Exhibit 3A.3 show Prepaid Insurance of $2,300 and Insurance Expense of $100 for both methods.

EXHIBIT 3A.3

Account Balances under Two Alternatives for Recording Prepaid Expenses

Payment Recorded as Asset			
Prepaid Insurance			128
Dec. 6	2,400	Dec. 31	100
Balance	**2,300**		

Insurance Expense		637
Dec. 31	100	

Payment Recorded as Expense			
Prepaid Insurance			128
Dec. 31	**2,300**		

Insurance Expense			637
Dec. 6	2,400	Dec. 31	2,300
Balance	**100**		

RECORDING PREPAYMENT OF REVENUES IN REVENUE ACCOUNTS

As with prepaid expenses, an alternative method is to record *all* unearned revenues with credits to revenue accounts. If any revenues are unearned at the end of an accounting period, then adjusting entries must transfer the unearned portions from revenue accounts to unearned revenue (liability) accounts. This alternative method is acceptable. The adjusting entries are different for these two alternatives, but the financial statements are identical. To illustrate the accounting differences between these two methods, let's look at FastForward's December 26 receipt of $3,000 for consulting services covering the period December 27 to February 24. FastForward recorded this transaction with a credit to a liability account. The alternative is to record it with a credit to a revenue account, as shown in Exhibit 3A.4.

EXHIBIT 3A.4

Alternative Initial Entries for Unearned Revenues

			Receipt Recorded as Liability	Receipt Recorded as Revenue
Dec. 26	Cash		3,000	
	Unearned Consulting Revenue		3,000	
Dec. 26	Cash			3,000
	Consulting Revenue			3,000

By the end of its accounting period on December 31, FastForward has earned $250 of this revenue. This means $250 of the liability has been satisfied. Depending on how the initial receipt is recorded, the adjusting entry is as shown in Exhibit 3A.5.

EXHIBIT 3A.5

Adjusting Entry for Unearned Revenues for the Two Alternatives

			Receipt Recorded as Liability	Receipt Recorded as Revenue
Dec. 31	Unearned Consulting Revenue		250	
	Consulting Revenue		250	
Dec. 31	Consulting Revenue			2,750
	Unearned Consulting Revenue			2,750

After adjusting entries are posted, the two alternatives give identical results. The December 31 adjusted account balances in Exhibit 3A.6 show unearned consulting revenue of $2,750 and consulting revenue of $250 for both methods.

EXHIBIT 3A.6

Account Balances under Two Alternatives for Recording Unearned Revenues

Receipt Recorded as Liability			
Unearned Consulting Revenue			236
Dec. 31	250	Dec. 26	3,000
		Balance	**2,750**

Consulting Revenue			403
		Dec. 31	**250**

Receipt Recorded as Revenue			
Unearned Consulting Revenue			236
		Dec. 31	**2,750**

Consulting Revenue			403
Dec. 31	2,750	Dec. 26	3,000
		Balance	**250**

Summary

C1 **Explain the importance of periodic reporting and the time period assumption.** The value of information is often linked to its timeliness. To provide timely information, accounting systems prepare periodic reports at regular intervals. The time period assumption presumes that an organization's activities can be divided into specific time periods for periodic reporting.

C2 **Explain accrual accounting and how it improves financial statements.** Accrual accounting recognizes revenue when earned and expenses when incurred—not necessarily when cash inflows and outflows occur. This information is valuable in assessing a company's financial position and performance.

C3 **Identify the types of adjustments and their purpose.** Adjustments can be grouped according to the timing of cash receipts and cash payments relative to when they are recognized as revenues or expenses as follows: prepaid expenses, unearned revenues, accrued expenses, and accrued revenues. Adjusting entries are necessary so that revenues, expenses, assets, and liabilities are correctly reported.

A1 **Explain how accounting adjustments link to financial statements.** Accounting adjustments bring an asset or liability account balance to its correct amount. They also update related expense or revenue accounts. Every adjusting entry affects one or more income statement accounts *and* one or more balance sheet accounts. An adjusting entry never affects cash.

A2 **Compute profit margin and describe its use in analyzing company performance.** *Profit margin* is defined as the reporting period's net income divided by its net sales. Profit margin reflects on a company's earnings activities by showing how much income is in each dollar of sales.

P1 **Prepare and explain adjusting entries.** *Prepaid expenses* refer to items paid for in advance of receiving their benefits.

Prepaid expenses are assets. Adjusting entries for prepaids involve increasing (debiting) expenses and decreasing (crediting) assets. *Unearned* (or *prepaid*) *revenues* refer to cash received in advance of providing products and services. Unearned revenues are liabilities. Adjusting entries for unearned revenues involve increasing (crediting) revenues and decreasing (debiting) unearned revenues. *Accrued expenses* refer to costs incurred in a period that are both unpaid and unrecorded. Adjusting entries for recording accrued expenses involve increasing (debiting) expenses and increasing (crediting) liabilities. *Accrued revenues* refer to revenues earned in a period that are both unrecorded and not yet received in cash. Adjusting entries for recording accrued revenues involve increasing (debiting) assets and increasing (crediting) revenues.

P2 **Explain and prepare an adjusted trial balance.** An adjusted trial balance is a list of accounts and balances prepared after recording and posting adjusting entries. Financial statements are often prepared from the adjusted trial balance.

P3 **Prepare financial statements from an adjusted trial balance.** Revenue and expense balances are reported on the income statement. Asset, liability, and equity balances are reported on the balance sheet. We usually prepare statements in the following order: income statement, statement of owner's equity, balance sheet, and statement of cash flows.

P4A **Explain the alternatives in accounting for prepaids.** Charging all prepaid expenses to expense accounts when they are purchased is acceptable. When this is done, adjusting entries must transfer any unexpired amounts from expense accounts to asset accounts. Crediting all unearned revenues to revenue accounts when cash is received is also acceptable. In this case, the adjusting entries must transfer any unearned amounts from revenue accounts to unearned revenue accounts.

Guidance Answers to Decision Maker **and Decision Ethics**

Investor Prepaid expenses are items paid for in advance of receiving their benefits. They are assets and are expensed as they are used up. The publishing company's treatment of the signing bonus is

acceptable provided future book sales can at least match the $500,000 expense. As an investor, you are concerned about the risk of future book sales. The riskier the likelihood of future book sales is, the more likely your analysis is to treat the $500,000, or a portion of it, as an expense, not a prepaid expense (asset).

Entrepreneur Depreciation is a process of cost allocation, not asset valuation. Knowing the depreciation schedule is not especially useful in your estimation of what the building and equipment are currently worth. Your own assessment of the age, quality, and usefulness of the building and equipment is more important.

Loan Officer Your concern in lending to this store arises from analysis of current-year sales. While increased revenues and income are fine, your concern is with collectibility of these promotional sales. If the owner sold products to customers with poor records of

paying bills, then collectibility of these sales is low. Your analysis must assess this possibility and recognize any expected losses.

Financial Officer Omitting accrued expenses and recognizing revenue early can mislead financial statement users. One action is to request a second meeting with the president so you can explain that accruing expenses when incurred and recognizing revenue when earned are required practices. If the president persists, you might discuss the situation with legal counsel and any auditors involved. Your ethical action might cost you this job, but the potential pitfalls for falsification of statements, reputation and personal integrity loss, and other costs are too great.

Guidance Answers to Quick Checks

1. An annual reporting (or accounting) period covers one year and refers to the preparation of annual financial statements. The annual reporting period is not always a calendar year that ends on December 31. An organization can adopt a fiscal year consisting of any consecutive 12 months or 52 weeks.

2. Interim financial statements (covering less than one year) are prepared to provide timely information to decision makers.

3. The revenue recognition principle and the matching principle lead most directly to the adjusting process.

4. No. Cash basis accounting is not consistent with the matching principle because it reports revenue when received, not necessarily when earned, and expenses when paid, not necessarily in the period when the expenses were incurred as a result of the revenues earned.

5. No expense is reported in 2014. Under cash basis accounting, the entire $4,800 is reported as an expense in April 2013 when the premium is paid.

6. If the accrued revenues adjustment of $200 is not made, then both revenues and net income are understated by $200 on the current year's income statement, and both assets and equity are understated by $200 on the balance sheet.

7. A contra account is an account that is subtracted from the balance of a related account. Use of a contra account provides more information than simply reporting a net amount.

8. An accrued expense is a cost incurred in a period that is both unpaid and unrecorded prior to adjusting entries. One example is salaries earned but not yet paid at period-end.

9. An unearned revenue arises when a firm receives cash (or other assets) from a customer before providing the services or products to the customer. A magazine subscription paid in advance is one example; season ticket sales is another.

10. Salaries Payable 1,000
    Salaries Expense 6,000
        Cash 7,000
    Paid salary including accrual from December.

11. The probable adjusting entries of Jordan Air are:
    Insurance Expense 300
        Prepaid Insurance 300
    To record insurance expired.
    Salaries Expense 1,400
        Salaries Payable 1,400
    To record accrued salaries.

12. Revenue accounts and expense accounts.

13. Statement of owner's equity.

Key Terms

Accounting periods (p. 94)	Cash basis accounting (p. 95)	Plant assets (p. 99)
Accrual basis accounting (p. 95)	Contra account (p. 99)	Prepaid expenses (p. 97)
Accrued expenses (p. 101)	Depreciation (p. 99)	Profit margin (p. 109)
Accrued revenues (p. 103)	Expense recognition (or **matching**)	Straight-line depreciation method (p. 99)
Adjusted trial balance (p. 106)	principle (p. 96)	Time period assumption (p. 94)
Adjusting entry (p. 97)	Fiscal year (p. 95)	Unadjusted trial balance (p. 106)
Annual financial statements (p. 94)	Interim financial statements (p. 94)	Unearned revenues (p. 100)
Book value (p. 100)	Natural business year (p. 95)	

Multiple Choice Quiz   Answers on p. 137   mhhe.com/wildFAP21e

Additional Quiz Questions are available at the book's Website.

1. A company forgot to record accrued and unpaid employee wages of $350,000 at period-end. This oversight would
   a. Understate net income by $350,000.
   b. Overstate net income by $350,000.
   c. Have no effect on net income.
   d. Overstate assets by $350,000.
   e. Understate assets by $350,000.

2. Prior to recording adjusting entries, the Supplies account has a $450 debit balance. A physical count of supplies shows $125 of unused supplies still available. The required adjusting entry is:
   a. Debit Supplies $125; Credit Supplies Expense $125.
   b. Debit Supplies $325; Credit Supplies Expense $325.
   c. Debit Supplies Expense $325; Credit Supplies $325.
   d. Debit Supplies Expense $325; Credit Supplies $125.
   e. Debit Supplies Expense $125; Credit Supplies $125.

3. On May 1, 2013, a two-year insurance policy was purchased for $24,000 with coverage to begin immediately. What is the amount of insurance expense that appears on the company's income statement for the year ended December 31, 2013?
   a. $4,000
   b. $8,000

   c. $12,000
   d. $20,000
   e. $24,000

4. On November 1, 2013, Stockton Co. receives $3,600 cash from Hans Co. for consulting services to be provided evenly over the period November 1, 2013, to April 30, 2014—at which time Stockton credited $3,600 to Unearned Consulting Fees. The adjusting entry on December 31, 2013 (Stockton's year-end) would include a
   a. Debit to Unearned Consulting Fees for $1,200.
   b. Debit to Unearned Consulting Fees for $2,400.
   c. Credit to Consulting Fees Earned for $2,400.
   d. Debit to Consulting Fees Earned for $1,200.
   e. Credit to Cash for $3,600.

5. If a company had $15,000 in net income for the year, and its sales were $300,000 for the same year, what is its profit margin?
   a. 20%
   b. 2,000%
   c. $285,000
   d. $315,000
   e. 5%

^A Superscript letter A denotes assignments based on Appendix 3A.

🄸 Icon denotes assignments that involve decision making.

Discussion Questions

1. What is the difference between the cash basis and the accrual basis of accounting?

2. 🄸 Why is the accrual basis of accounting generally preferred over the cash basis?

3. What type of business is most likely to select a fiscal year that corresponds to its natural business year instead of the calendar year?

4. What is a prepaid expense and where is it reported in the financial statements?

5. 🄸 What type of assets require adjusting entries to record depreciation?

6. 🄸 What contra account is used when recording and reporting the effects of depreciation? Why is it used?

7. 🌐 Assume **Piaggio** has unearned revenue. **PIAGGIO** What is unearned revenue and where is it reported in financial statements?

8. What is an accrued revenue? Give an example.

9.^A If a company initially records prepaid expenses with debits to expense accounts, what type of account is debited in the adjusting entries for those prepaid expenses?

10. 🄸 Review the balance sheet of **Polaris** in **Polaris** Appendix A. Identify one asset account that requires adjustment before annual financial statements can be prepared. What would be the effect on the income statement if this asset account were not adjusted? (Number not required, but comment on over- or understating of net income.)

11. 🄸 Review the balance sheet of **Arctic Cat** in **Arctic Cat** Appendix A. Identify the amount for property and equipment. What adjusting entry is necessary (no numbers required) for this account when preparing financial statements?

12. 🌐 Refer to **KTM**'s balance sheet in Appendix A. If it made an adjustment for unpaid wages at year-end, **KTM** where would the accrued wages be reported on its balance sheet?

🄼 connect

a. On July 1, 2013, Lamis Company paid $1,200 for six months of insurance coverage. No adjustments have been made to the Prepaid Insurance account, and it is now December 31, 2013. Prepare the journal entry to reflect expiration of the insurance as of December 31, 2013.

b. Shandi Company has a Supplies account balance of $5,000 on January 1, 2013. During 2013, it purchased $2,000 of supplies. As of December 31, 2013, a supplies inventory shows $800 of supplies available. Prepare the adjusting journal entry to correctly report the balance of the Supplies account and the Supplies Expense account as of December 31, 2013.

QUICK STUDY

QS 3-1
Adjusting prepaid expenses
P1

QS 3-2
Adjusting for depreciation
P1

a. Bargains Company purchases $20,000 of equipment on January 1, 2013. The equipment is expected to last five years and be worth $2,000 at the end of that time. Prepare the entry to record one year's depreciation expense of $3,600 for the equipment as of December 31, 2013.

b. Welch Company purchases $10,000 of land on January 1, 2013. The land is expected to last indefinitely. What depreciation adjustment, if any, should be made with respect to the Land account as of December 31, 2013?

QS 3-3
Identifying accounting adjustments
P1

Classify the following adjusting entries as involving prepaid expenses (PE), unearned revenues (UR), accrued expenses (AE), or accrued revenues (AR).

a. _____ To record expiration of prepaid insurance.

b. _____ To record revenue earned but not yet billed (nor recorded).

c. _____ To record wages expense incurred but not yet paid (nor recorded).

d. _____ To record annual depreciation expense.

e. _____ To record revenue earned that was previously received as cash in advance.

QS 3-4
Accruing salaries
A1 P1

Jasmine Culpepper employs one college student every summer in her coffee shop. The student works the five weekdays and is paid on the following Monday. (For example, a student who works Monday through Friday, June 1 through June 5, is paid for that work on Monday, June 8.) Culpepper adjusts her books monthly, if needed, to show salaries earned but unpaid at month-end. The student works the last week of July—Friday is August 1. If the student earns $100 per day, what adjusting entry must Culpepper make on July 31 to correctly record accrued salaries expense for July?

QS 3-5
Adjusting for unearned revenues
A1 P1

a. Tao Co. receives $10,000 cash in advance for 4 months of legal services on October 1, 2013, and records it by debiting Cash and crediting Unearned Revenue both for $10,000. It is now December 31, 2013, and Tao has provided legal services as planned. What adjusting entry should Tao make to account for the work performed from October 1 through December 31, 2013?

b. A. Caden started a new publication called *Contest News*. Its subscribers pay $24 to receive 12 monthly issues. With every new subscriber, Caden debits Cash and credits Unearned Subscription Revenue for the amounts received. The company has 100 new subscribers as of July 1, 2013. It sends *Contest News* to each of these subscribers every month from July through December. Assuming no changes in subscribers, prepare the journal entry that Caden must make as of December 31, 2013, to adjust the Subscription Revenue account and the Unearned Subscription Revenue account.

QS 3-6
Computing accrual and cash income   P1 C2

In its first year of operations, Roma Co. earned $45,000 in revenues and received $37,000 cash from these customers. The company incurred expenses of $25,500 but had not paid $5,250 of them at year-end. The company also prepaid $6,750 cash for expenses that would be incurred the next year. Calculate the first year's net income under both the cash basis and the accrual basis of accounting.

QS 3-7
Recording and analyzing adjusting entries
A1

Adjusting entries affect at least one balance sheet account and at least one income statement account. For the following entries, identify the account to be debited and the account to be credited. Indicate which of the accounts is the income statement account and which is the balance sheet account.

a. Entry to record revenue earned that was previously received as cash in advance.

b. Entry to record wage expenses incurred but not yet paid (nor recorded).

c. Entry to record revenue earned but not yet billed (nor recorded).

d. Entry to record expiration of prepaid insurance.

e. Entry to record annual depreciation expense.

QS 3-8
Preparing adjusting entries
C3 P1

During the year, Sereno Co. recorded prepayments of expenses in asset accounts, and cash receipts of unearned revenues in liability accounts. At the end of its annual accounting period, the company must make three adjusting entries: (1) accrue salaries expense, (2) adjust the Unearned Services Revenue account to recognize earned revenue, and (3) record services revenue earned for which cash will be received the following period. For each of these adjusting entries (1), (2), and (3), indicate the account from *a* through *i* to be debited and the account to be credited.

a. Prepaid Salaries

b. Cash

c. Salaries Payable

d. Unearned Services Revenue

e. Salaries Expense

f. Services Revenue

g. Accounts Receivable

h. Accounts Payable

i. Equipment

The following information is taken from Brooke Company's unadjusted and adjusted trial balances.

	Unadjusted		Adjusted	
	Debit	Credit	Debit	Credit
Prepaid insurance.........	$4,100		$3,700	
Interest payable		$ 0		$800

QS 3-9
Interpreting adjusting entries
C2 P2

Given this information, which of the following is likely included among its adjusting entries?

a. A $400 debit to Insurance Expense and an $800 debit to Interest Payable.

b. A $400 debit to Insurance Expense and an $800 debit to Interest Expense.

c. A $400 credit to Prepaid Insurance and an $800 debit to Interest Payable.

In making adjusting entries at the end of its accounting period, Chao Consulting failed to record $3,200 of insurance coverage that had expired. This $3,200 cost had been initially debited to the Prepaid Insurance account. The company also failed to record accrued salaries expense of $2,000. As a result of these two oversights, the financial statements for the reporting period will [choose one] (1) understate assets by $3,200; (2) understate expenses by $5,200; (3) understate net income by $2,000; or (4) overstate liabilities by $2,000.

QS 3-10
Determining effects of
adjusting entries
C3 A1

Deklin Company reported net income of $48,025 and net sales of $425,000 for the current year. Calculate the company's profit margin and interpret the result. Assume that its competitors earn an average profit margin of 15%.

QS 3-11
Analyzing profit margin
A2

Calvin Consulting initially records prepaid and unearned items in income statement accounts. Given this company's accounting practices, which of the following applies to the preparation of adjusting entries at the end of its first accounting period?

a. Unearned fees (on which cash was received in advance earlier in the period) are recorded with a debit to Consulting Fees Earned and a credit to Unearned Consulting Fees.

b. Unpaid salaries are recorded with a debit to Prepaid Salaries and a credit to Salaries Expense.

c. The cost of unused office supplies is recorded with a debit to Supplies Expense and a credit to Office Supplies.

d. Earned but unbilled (and unrecorded) consulting fees are recorded with a debit to Unearned Consulting Fees and a credit to Consulting Fees Earned.

QS 3-12ᴬ
Preparing adjusting entries
C3 P4

Answer each of the following questions related to international accounting standards.

a. Do financial statements prepared under IFRS normally present assets from least liquid to most liquid or vice-versa?

b. Do financial statements prepared under IFRS normally present liabilities from furthest from maturity to nearest to maturity or vice versa?

QS 3-13
International accounting
standards
P3

For each separate case below, follow the 3-step process for adjusting the prepaid asset account: Step 1: Determine what the current account balance equals. Step 2: Determine what the current account balance should equal. Step 3: Record an adjusting entry to get from step 1 to step 2. *Assume no other adjusting entries are made during the year.*

a. Prepaid Insurance. The Prepaid Insurance account has a $4,700 debit balance to start the year. A review of insurance policies and payments shows that $900 of unexpired insurance remains at year-end.

b. Prepaid Insurance. The Prepaid Insurance account has a $5,890 debit balance at the start of the year. A review of insurance policies and payments shows $1,040 of insurance has expired by year-end.

c. Prepaid Rent. On September 1 of the current year, the company prepaid $24,000 for 2 years of rent for facilities being occupied that day. The company debited Prepaid Rent and credited Cash for $24,000.

QS 3-14
Prepaid (deferred) expenses
adjustments
P1

QS 3-15
Prepaid (deferred) expenses adjustments
P1

For each separate case below, follow the 3-step process for adjusting the supplies asset account: Step 1: Determine what the current account balance equals. Step 2: Determine what the current account balance should equal. Step 3: Record an adjusting entry to get from step 1 to step 2. *Assume no other adjusting entries are made during the year.*

a. Supplies. The Supplies account has a $300 debit balance to start the year. No supplies were purchased during the current year. A December 31 physical count shows $110 of supplies remaining.

b. Supplies. The Supplies account has an $800 debit balance to start the year. Supplies of $2,100 were purchased during the current year and debited to the Supplies account. A December 31 physical count shows $650 of supplies remaining.

c. Supplies. The Supplies account has a $4,000 debit balance to start the year. During the current year, supplies of $9,400 were purchased and debited to the Supplies account. The inventory of supplies available at December 31 totaled $2,660.

QS 3-16
Accumulated depreciation adjustments
P1

For each separate case below, follow the 3-step process for adjusting the accumulated depreciation account: Step 1: Determine what the current account balance equals. Step 2: Determine what the current account balance should equal. Step 3: Record an adjusting entry to get from step 1 to step 2. *Assume no other adjusting entries are made during the year.*

a. Accumulated Depreciation. The Krug Company's Accumulated Depreciation account has a $13,500 balance to start the year. A review of depreciation schedules reveals that $14,600 of depreciation expense must be recorded for the year.

b. Accumulated Depreciation. The company has only one fixed asset (truck) that it purchased at the start of this year. That asset had cost $44,000, had an estimated life of 5 years, and is expected to have zero value at the end of the 5 years.

c. Accumulated Depreciation. The company has only one fixed asset (equipment) that it purchased at the start of this year. That asset had cost $32,000, had an estimated life of 7 years, and is expected to be valued at $4,000 at the end of the 7 years.

QS 3-17
Unearned (deferred) revenues adjustments
P1

For each separate case below, follow the 3-step process for adjusting the unearned revenue liability account: Step 1: Determine what the current account balance equals. Step 2: Determine what the current account balance should equal. Step 3: Record an adjusting entry to get from step 1 to step 2. *Assume no other adjusting entries are made during the year.*

a. Unearned Rent Revenue. The Krug Company collected $6,000 rent in advance on November 1, debiting Cash and crediting Unearned Rent Revenue. The tenant was paying twelve months rent in advance and occupancy began November 1.

b. Unearned Services Revenue. The company charges $75 per month to spray a house for insects. A customer paid $300 on October 1 in advance for four treatments, which was recorded with a debit to Cash and a credit to Unearned Services Revenue. At year-end, the company has applied three treatments for the customer.

c. Unearned Rent Revenue. On September 1, a client paid the company $24,000 cash for six months of rent in advance (the client leased a building and took occupancy immediately). The company recorded the cash as Unearned Rent Revenue.

QS 3-18
Accrued expenses adjustments
P1

For each separate case below, follow the 3-step process for adjusting the accrued expense account: Step 1: Determine what the current account balance equals. Step 2: Determine what the current account balance should equal. Step 3: Record an adjusting entry to get from step 1 to step 2. *Assume no other adjusting entries are made during the year.*

a. Salaries Payable. At year-end, salaries expense of $15,500 has been incurred by the company, but is not yet paid to employees.

b. Interest Payable. At its December 31 year-end, the company owes $250 of interest on a line-of-credit loan. That interest will not be paid until sometime in January of the next year.

c. Interest Payable. At its December 31 year-end, the company holds a mortgage payable that has incurred $875 in annual interest that is neither recorded nor paid. The company intends to pay the interest on January 7 of the next year.

QS 3-19
Accrued revenues adjustments
P1

For each separate case below, follow the 3-step process for adjusting the accrued revenue account: Step 1: Determine what the current account balance equals. Step 2: Determine what the current account balance should equal. Step 3: Record an adjusting entry to get from step 1 to step 2. *Assume no other adjusting entries are made during the year.*

a. Accounts Receivable. At year-end, the Krug Company has completed services of $19,000 for a client, but the client has not yet been billed for those services.

b. Interest Receivable. At year-end, the company has earned, but not yet recorded, $390 of interest earned from its investments in government bonds.

c. Accounts Receivable. A painting company collects fees when jobs are complete. The work for one customer, whose job was bid at $1,300, has been completed, but the customer has not yet been billed.

Mc Graw Hill connect _____

In the blank space beside each adjusting entry, enter the letter of the explanation *A* through *F* that most closely describes the entry.

EXERCISES

Exercise 3-1
Classifying adjusting entries
C3

A. To record this period's depreciation expense.

D. To record accrued interest revenue.

B. To record accrued salaries expense.

E. To record accrued interest expense.

C. To record this period's use of a prepaid expense.

F. To record the earning of previously unearned income.

_____ 1.	Interest Expense	2,208	
	Interest Payable		2,208
_____ 2.	Insurance Expense	3,180	
	Prepaid Insurance		3,180
_____ 3.	Unearned Professional Fees	19,250	
	Professional Fees Earned		19,250
_____ 4.	Interest Receivable	3,300	
	Interest Revenue		3,300
_____ 5.	Depreciation Expense	38,217	
	Accumulated Depreciation		38,217
_____ 6.	Salaries Expense	13,280	
	Salaries Payable		13,280

Prepare adjusting journal entries for the year ended (date of) December 31, 2013, for each of these separate situations. Assume that prepaid expenses are initially recorded in asset accounts. Also assume that fees collected in advance of work are initially recorded as liabilities.

Exercise 3-2
Preparing adjusting entries
P1

a. Depreciation on the company's equipment for 2013 is computed to be $18,000.

b. The Prepaid Insurance account had a $6,000 debit balance at December 31, 2013, before adjusting for the costs of any expired coverage. An analysis of the company's insurance policies showed that $1,100 of unexpired insurance coverage remains.

c. The Office Supplies account had a $700 debit balance on December 31, 2012; and $3,480 of office supplies were purchased during the year. The December 31, 2013, physical count showed $298 of supplies available.

Check   (c) Dr. Office Supplies Expense, $3,882; (e) Dr. Insurance Expense, $5,800

d. Two-thirds of the work related to $15,000 of cash received in advance was performed this period.

e. The Prepaid Insurance account had a $6,800 debit balance at December 31, 2013, before adjusting for the costs of any expired coverage. An analysis of insurance policies showed that $5,800 of coverage had expired.

f. Wage expenses of $3,200 have been incurred but are not paid as of December 31, 2013.

For each of the following separate cases, prepare adjusting entries required of financial statements for the year ended (date of) December 31, 2013. (Assume that prepaid expenses are initially recorded in asset accounts and that fees collected in advance of work are initially recorded as liabilities.)

Exercise 3-3
Preparing adjusting entries
P1

a. One-third of the work related to $15,000 cash received in advance is performed this period.

b. Wages of $8,000 are earned by workers but not paid as of December 31, 2013.

c. Depreciation on the company's equipment for 2013 is $18,531.

d. The Office Supplies account had a $240 debit balance on December 31, 2012. During 2013, $5,239 of office supplies are purchased. A physical count of supplies at December 31, 2013, shows $487 of supplies available.

e. The Prepaid Insurance account had a $4,000 balance on December 31, 2012. An analysis of insurance policies shows that $1,200 of unexpired insurance benefits remain at December 31, 2013.

Check   (e) Dr. Insurance Expense, $2,800; (f) Cr. Interest Revenue, $1,050

f. The company has earned (but not recorded) $1,050 of interest from investments in CDs for the year ended December 31, 2013. The interest revenue will be received on January 10, 2014.

g. The company has a bank loan and has incurred (but not recorded) interest expense of $2,500 for the year ended December 31, 2013. The company must pay the interest on January 2, 2014.

Exercise 3-4
Adjusting and paying
accrued wages

C1 P1

Pablo Management has five part-time employees, each of whom earns $250 per day. They are normally paid on Fridays for work completed Monday through Friday of the same week. Assume that December 28, 2013, was a Friday, and that they were paid in full on that day. The next week, the five employees worked only four days because New Year's Day was an unpaid holiday. (*a*) Assuming that December 31, 2013, was a Monday, prepare the adjusting entry that would be recorded at the close of that day. (*b*) Assuming that January 4, 2014, was a Friday, prepare the journal entry that would be made to record payment of the employees' wages.

Exercise 3-5
Adjusting and paying
accrued expenses

A1 P1

Check (*b*) May 20 Dr. Interest
Expense, $6,000

The following three separate situations require adjusting journal entries to prepare financial statements as of April 30. For each situation, present both the April 30 adjusting entry and the subsequent entry during May to record the payment of the accrued expenses.

a. On April 1, the company retained an attorney for a flat monthly fee of $3,500. Payment for April legal services was made by the company on May 12.

b. A $900,000 note payable requires 10% annual interest, or $9,000 to be paid at the 20th day of each month. The interest was last paid on April 20 and the next payment is due on May 20. As of April 30, $3,000 of interest expense has accrued.

c. Total weekly salaries expense for all employees is $10,000. This amount is paid at the end of the day on Friday of each five-day workweek. April 30 falls on Tuesday of this year, which means that the employees had worked two days since the last payday. The next payday is May 3.

Exercise 3-6
Determining cost flows
through accounts

C1 A1 P1

Determine the missing amounts in each of these four separate situations *a* through *d*.

	a	b	c	d
Supplies available—prior year-end	$ 400	$1,200	$1,260	?
Supplies purchased during the current year	2,800	6,500	?	$3,000
Supplies available—current year-end	650	?	1,350	700
Supplies expense for the current year	?	1,200	8,400	4,588

Exercise 3-7
Analyzing and preparing
adjusting entries

A1 P1 P3

Following are two income statements for Alexis Co. for the year ended December 31. The left column is prepared before any adjusting entries are recorded, and the right column includes the effects of adjusting entries. The company records cash receipts and payments related to unearned and prepaid items in balance sheet accounts. Analyze the statements and prepare the eight adjusting entries that likely were recorded. (*Note:* 30% of the $7,000 adjustment for Fees Earned has been earned but not billed, and the other 70% has been earned by performing services that were paid for in advance.)

ALEXIS CO. Income Statements For Year Ended December 31		
	Unadjusted	**Adjusted**
Revenues		
Fees earned	$18,000	$25,000
Commissions earned	36,500	36,500
Total revenues	$54,500	61,500
Expenses		
Depreciation expense—Computers	0	1,600
Depreciation expense—Office furniture	0	1,850
Salaries expense	13,500	15,750
Insurance expense	0	1,400
Rent expense	3,800	3,800
Office supplies expense	0	580
Advertising expense	2,500	2,500
Utilities expense	1,245	1,335
Total expenses	21,045	28,815
Net income	$33,455	$32,685

On March 1, 2011, a company paid a $18,000 premium on a 36-month insurance policy for coverage beginning on that date. Refer to that policy and fill in the blanks in the following table.

	Balance Sheet Prepaid Insurance Asset Using			Insurance Expense Using	
	Accrual Basis	Cash Basis		Accrual Basis	Cash Basis
Dec. 31, 2011	$_____	$_____	2011	$_____	$_____
Dec. 31, 2012	_____	_____	2012	_____	_____
Dec. 31, 2013	_____	_____	2013	_____	_____
Dec. 31, 2014	_____	_____	2014	_____	_____
			Total	$_____	$_____

Exercise 3-8
Determining assets and expenses for accrual and cash accounting
C2

Check 2013 insurance expense: Accrual, $6,000; Cash, $0.
Dec. 31, 2013, asset: Accrual, $1,000; Cash, $0.

Use the following information to compute profit margin for each separate company *a* through *e*.

	Net Income	Net Sales			Net Income	Net Sales
a.	$ 4,361	$ 44,500		d.	$65,646	$1,458,800
b.	97,706	398,800		e.	80,142	435,500
c.	111,281	257,000				

Which of the five companies is the most profitable according to the profit margin ratio? Interpret that company's profit margin ratio.

Exercise 3-9
Computing and interpreting profit margin
A2

Ricardo Construction began operations on December 1. In setting up its accounting procedures, the company decided to debit expense accounts when it prepays its expenses and to credit revenue accounts when customers pay for services in advance. Prepare journal entries for items *a* through *d* and the adjusting entries as of its December 31 period-end for items *e* through *g*.

a. Supplies are purchased on December 1 for $2,000 cash.

b. The company prepaid its insurance premiums for $1,540 cash on December 2.

c. On December 15, the company receives an advance payment of $13,000 cash from a customer for remodeling work.

d. On December 28, the company receives $3,700 cash from another customer for remodeling work to be performed in January.

e. A physical count on December 31 indicates that the Company has $1,840 of supplies available.

f. An analysis of the insurance policies in effect on December 31 shows that $340 of insurance coverage had expired.

g. As of December 31, only one remodeling project has been worked on and completed. The $5,570 fee for this project had been received in advance.

Exercise 3-10^A
Adjusting for prepaids recorded as expenses and unearned revenues recorded as revenues
P4

Check (*f*) Cr. Insurance Expense, $1,200; (*g*) Dr. Remodeling Fees Earned, $11,130

Costanza Company experienced the following events and transactions during July.

July 1 Received $3,000 cash in advance of performing work for Vivian Solana.
6 Received $7,500 cash in advance of performing work for Iris Haru.
12 Completed the job for Solana.
18 Received $8,500 cash in advance of performing work for Amina Jordan.
27 Completed the job for Haru.
31 None of the work for Jordan has been performed.

a. Prepare journal entries (including any adjusting entries as of the end of the month) to record these events using the procedure of initially crediting the Unearned Fees account when payment is received from a customer in advance of performing services.

Exercise 3-11^A
Recording and reporting revenues received in advance
P4

b. Prepare journal entries (including any adjusting entries as of the end of the month) to record these events using the procedure of initially crediting the Fees Earned account when payment is received from a customer in advance of performing services.

Check (c) Fees Earned—using entries from part b, $10,500

c. Under each method, determine the amount of earned fees reported on the income statement for July and the amount of unearned fees reported on the balance sheet as of July 31.

Exercise 3-12
Preparing a balance sheet following IFRS

P3

adidas AG reports the following balance sheet accounts for the year ended December 31, 2011 (euros in millions). Prepare the balance sheet for this company as of December 31, 2011, following usual IFRS practices.

Tangible and other assets	€ 255		Intangible assets	€ 154
Total equity	2,322		Total current liabilities	345
Receivables and other assets	1,767		Inventories	30
Total noncurrent liabilities	3,379		Total liabilities	3,724
Cash and cash equivalents	383		Other current assets	28
Total current assets	2,208		Total noncurrent assets	3,838
Other noncurrent assets	3,429			

═ connect

PROBLEM SET A

Problem 3-1A
Identifying adjusting entries with explanations

C3   P1

For each of the following entries, enter the letter of the explanation that most closely describes it in the space beside each entry. (You can use letters more than once.)

A. To record receipt of unearned revenue.

B. To record this period's earning of prior unearned revenue.

C. To record payment of an accrued expense.

D. To record receipt of an accrued revenue.

E. To record an accrued expense.

F. To record an accrued revenue.

G. To record this period's use of a prepaid expense.

H. To record payment of a prepaid expense.

I. To record this period's depreciation expense.

____ 1.	Interest Expense	1,000	
	Interest Payable		1,000
____ 2.	Depreciation Expense	4,000	
	Accumulated Depreciation		4,000
____ 3.	Unearned Professional Fees	3,000	
	Professional Fees Earned		3,000
____ 4.	Insurance Expense	4,200	
	Prepaid Insurance		4,200
____ 5.	Salaries Payable	1,400	
	Cash		1,400
____ 6.	Prepaid Rent	4,500	
	Cash		4,500
____ 7.	Salaries Expense	6,000	
	Salaries Payable		6,000
____ 8.	Interest Receivable	5,000	
	Interest Revenue		5,000
____ 9.	Cash	9,000	
	Accounts Receivable (from consulting)		9,000
____ 10.	Cash	7,500	
	Unearned Professional Fees		7,500
____ 11.	Cash	2,000	
	Interest Receivable		2,000
____ 12.	Rent Expense	2,000	
	Prepaid Rent		2,000

Arnez Co. follows the practice of recording prepaid expenses and unearned revenues in balance sheet accounts. The company's annual accounting period ends on December 31, 2013. The following information concerns the adjusting entries to be recorded as of that date.

a. The Office Supplies account started the year with a $4,000 balance. During 2013, the company purchased supplies for $13,400, which was added to the Office Supplies account. The inventory of supplies available at December 31, 2013, totaled $2,554.

b. An analysis of the company's insurance policies provided the following facts.

Policy	Date of Purchase	Months of Coverage	Cost
A	April 1, 2011	24	$14,400
B	April 1, 2012	36	12,960
C	August 1, 2013	12	2,400

The total premium for each policy was paid in full (for all months) at the purchase date, and the Prepaid Insurance account was debited for the full cost. (Year-end adjusting entries for Prepaid Insurance were properly recorded in all prior years.)

c. The company has 15 employees, who earn a total of $1,960 in salaries each working day. They are paid each Monday for their work in the five-day workweek ending on the previous Friday. Assume that December 31, 2013, is a Tuesday, and all 15 employees worked the first two days of that week. Because New Year's Day is a paid holiday, they will be paid salaries for five full days on Monday, January 6, 2014.

d. The company purchased a building on January 1, 2013. It cost $960,000 and is expected to have a $45,000 salvage value at the end of its predicted 30-year life. Annual depreciation is $30,500.

e. Since the company is not large enough to occupy the entire building it owns, it rented space to a tenant at $3,000 per month, starting on November 1, 2013. The rent was paid on time on November 1, and the amount received was credited to the Rent Earned account. However, the tenant has not paid the December rent. The company has worked out an agreement with the tenant, who has promised to pay both December and January rent in full on January 15. The tenant has agreed not to fall behind again.

f. On November 1, the company rented space to another tenant for $2,800 per month. The tenant paid five months' rent in advance on that date. The payment was recorded with a credit to the Unearned Rent account.

Required

1. Use the information to prepare adjusting entries as of December 31, 2013.
2. Prepare journal entries to record the first subsequent cash transaction in 2014 for parts *c* and *e*.

Problem 3-2A
Preparing adjusting and subsequent journal entries
C1 A1 P1

Check   (1*b*) Dr. Insurance Expense, $11,440 (1*d*) Dr. Depreciation Expense, $30,500

Wells Technical Institute (WTI), a school owned by Tristana Wells, provides training to individuals who pay tuition directly to the school. WTI also offers training to groups in off-site locations. Its unadjusted trial balance as of December 31, 2013, follows. WTI initially records prepaid expenses and unearned revenues in balance sheet accounts. Descriptions of items *a* through *h* that require adjusting entries on December 31, 2013, follow.

Additional Information Items

a. An analysis of WTI's insurance policies shows that $2,400 of coverage has expired.

b. An inventory count shows that teaching supplies costing $2,800 are available at year-end 2013.

c. Annual depreciation on the equipment is $13,200.

d. Annual depreciation on the professional library is $7,200.

e. On November 1, WTI agreed to do a special six-month course (starting immediately) for a client. The contract calls for a monthly fee of $2,500, and the client paid the first five months' fees in advance. When the cash was received, the Unearned Training Fees account was credited. The fee for the sixth month will be recorded when it is collected in 2014.

Problem 3-3A
Preparing adjusting entries, adjusted trial balance, and financial statements
A1 P1 P2 P3

mhhe.com/wildFAP21e

f. On October 15, WTI agreed to teach a four-month class (beginning immediately) for an individual for $3,000 tuition per month payable at the end of the class. The class started on October 15, but no payment has yet been received. (WTI's accruals are applied to the nearest half-month; for example, October recognizes one-half month accrual.)

g. WTI's two employees are paid weekly. As of the end of the year, two days' salaries have accrued at the rate of $100 per day for each employee.

h. The balance in the Prepaid Rent account represents rent for December.

WELLS TECHNICAL INSTITUTE Unadjusted Trial Balance December 31, 2013	Debit	Credit
Cash	$ 34,000	
Accounts receivable	0	
Teaching supplies	8,000	
Prepaid insurance	12,000	
Prepaid rent	3,000	
Professional library	35,000	
Accumulated depreciation—Professional library		$ 10,000
Equipment	80,000	
Accumulated depreciation—Equipment		15,000
Accounts payable		26,000
Salaries payable		0
Unearned training fees		12,500
T. Wells, Capital		90,000
T. Wells, Withdrawals	50,000	
Tuition fees earned		123,900
Training fees earned		40,000
Depreciation expense—Professional library	0	
Depreciation expense—Equipment	0	
Salaries expense	50,000	
Insurance expense	0	
Rent expense	33,000	
Teaching supplies expense	0	
Advertising expense	6,000	
Utilities expense	6,400	
Totals	$ 317,400	$ 317,400

Required

1. Prepare T-accounts (representing the ledger) with balances from the unadjusted trial balance.

2. Prepare the necessary adjusting journal entries for items *a* through *h* and post them to the T-accounts. Assume that adjusting entries are made only at year-end.

3. Update balances in the T-accounts for the adjusting entries and prepare an adjusted trial balance.

4. Prepare Watson Technical Institute's income statement and statement of owner's equity for the year 2013 and prepare its balance sheet as of December 31, 2013.

Check (2e) Cr. Training Fees Earned, $5,000; (2f) Cr. Tuition Fees Earned, $7,500; (3) Adj. Trial balance totals, $345,700; (4) Net income, $49,600; Ending T. Wells, Capital $89,600

Problem 3-4A

Interpreting unadjusted and adjusted trial balances, and preparing financial statements

C3 A1 P1 P2 P3

mhhe.com/wildFAP21e

A six-column table for JKL Company follows. The first two columns contain the unadjusted trial balance for the company as of July 31, 2013. The last two columns contain the adjusted trial balance as of the same date.

Required

Analysis Component

1. Analyze the differences between the unadjusted and adjusted trial balances to determine the eight adjustments that likely were made. Show the results of your analysis by inserting these adjustment amounts in the table's two middle columns. Label each adjustment with a letter *a* through *h* and provide a short description of it at the bottom of the table.

Preparation Component

2. Use the information in the adjusted trial balance to prepare the company's (*a*) income statement and its statement of owner's equity for the year ended July 31, 2013 (*Note:* J. Logan, Capital at July 31, 2012, was $40,000, and the current-year withdrawals were $5,000), and (*b*) the balance sheet as of July 31, 2013.

Check (2) Net income, $4,960; J. Logan, Capital (7/31/2013), $39,960; Total assets, $124,960

	Unadjusted Trial Balance		Adjustments		Adjusted Trial Balance	
Cash	$ 34,000				$ 34,000	
Accounts receivable	14,000				22,000	
Office supplies	16,000				2,000	
Prepaid insurance	8,540				2,960	
Office equipment	84,000				84,000	
Accum. depreciation— Office equip.		$ 14,000				$ 20,000
Accounts payable		9,100				10,000
Interest payable		0				1,000
Salaries payable		0				7,000
Unearned consulting fees		18,000				15,000
Long-term notes payable		52,000				52,000
J. Logan, Capital		40,000				40,000
J. Logan, Withdrawals	5,000				5,000	
Consulting fees earned		123,240				134,240
Depreciation expense— Office equip.	0				6,000	
Salaries expense	67,000				74,000	
Interest expense	1,200				2,200	
Insurance expense	0				5,580	
Rent expense	14,500				14,500	
Office supplies expense	0				14,000	
Advertising expense	12,100				13,000	
Totals	$256,340	$256,340			$279,240	$279,240

The adjusted trial balance for Chiara Company as of December 31, 2013, follows.

Problem 3-5A
Preparing financial statements from the adjusted trial balance and calculating profit margin

P3 A1 A2

	Debit	Credit
Cash	$ 30,000	
Accounts receivable	52,000	
Interest receivable	18,000	
Notes receivable (due in 90 days)	168,000	
Office supplies	16,000	
Automobiles	168,000	
Accumulated depreciation—Automobiles		$ 50,000
Equipment	138,000	
Accumulated depreciation—Equipment		18,000
Land	78,000	
Accounts payable		96,000
Interest payable		20,000
Salaries payable		19,000
Unearned fees		30,000
Long-term notes payable		138,000

[continued on next page]

[continued from previous page]

R. Chiara, Capital		255,800
R. Chiara, Withdrawals	46,000	
Fees earned		484,000
Interest earned		24,000
Depreciation expense—Automobiles	26,000	
Depreciation expense—Equipment	18,000	
Salaries expense	188,000	
Wages expense	40,000	
Interest expense	32,000	
Office supplies expense	34,000	
Advertising expense	58,000	
Repairs expense—Automobiles	24,800	
Totals	$1,134,800	$1,134,800

Required

Check   (1) Total assets, $600,000

1. Use the information in the adjusted trial balance to prepare (*a*) the income statement for the year ended December 31, 2013; (*b*) the statement of owner's equity for the year ended December 31, 2013; and (*c*) the balance sheet as of December 31, 2013.

2. Calculate the profit margin for year 2013.

Problem 3-6A[A]

Recording prepaid expenses and unearned revenues

P1 P4

Gomez Co. had the following transactions in the last two months of its year ended December 31.

Nov.   1   Paid $1,800 cash for future newspaper advertising.
      1   Paid $2,460 cash for 12 months of insurance through October 31 of the next year.
    30   Received $3,600 cash for future services to be provided to a customer.
Dec.   1   Paid $3,000 cash for a consultant's services to be received over the next three months.
    15   Received $7,950 cash for future services to be provided to a customer.
    31   Of the advertising paid for on November 1, $1,200 worth is not yet used.
    31   A portion of the insurance paid for on November 1 has expired. No adjustment was made in November to Prepaid Insurance.
    31   Services worth $1,500 are not yet provided to the customer who paid on November 30.
    31   One-third of the consulting services paid for on December 1 have been received.
    31   The company has performed $3,300 of services that the customer paid for on December 15.

Required

1. Prepare entries for these transactions under the method that records prepaid expenses as assets and records unearned revenues as liabilities. Also prepare adjusting entries at the end of the year.

2. Prepare entries for these transactions under the method that records prepaid expenses as expenses and records unearned revenues as revenues. Also prepare adjusting entries at the end of the year.

Analysis Component

3. Explain why the alternative sets of entries in requirements 1 and 2 do not result in different financial statement amounts.

PROBLEM SET B

Problem 3-1B

Identifying adjusting entries with explanations

C3 P1

For each of the following entries, enter the letter of the explanation that most closely describes it in the space beside each entry. (You can use letters more than once.)

A. To record payment of a prepaid expense.

B. To record this period's use of a prepaid expense.

C. To record this period's depreciation expense.

D. To record receipt of unearned revenue.

E. To record this period's earning of prior unearned revenue.

F. To record an accrued expense.

G. To record payment of an accrued expense.

H. To record an accrued revenue.

I. To record receipt of accrued revenue.

_____	1.	Interest Receivable	3,500	
		Interest Revenue		3,500
_____	2.	Salaries Payable	9,000	
		Cash		9,000
_____	3.	Depreciation Expense	8,000	
		Accumulated Depreciation		8,000
_____	4.	Cash	9,000	
		Unearned Professional Fees		9,000
_____	5.	Insurance Expense	4,000	
		Prepaid Insurance		4,000
_____	6.	Interest Expense	5,000	
		Interest Payable		5,000
_____	7.	Cash	1,500	
		Accounts Receivable (from services)		1,500
_____	8.	Salaries Expense	7,000	
		Salaries Payable		7,000
_____	9.	Cash	1,000	
		Interest Receivable		1,000
_____	10.	Prepaid Rent	3,000	
		Cash		3,000
_____	11.	Rent Expense	7,500	
		Prepaid Rent		7,500
_____	12.	Unearned Professional Fees	6,000	
		Professional Fees Earned		6,000

Natsu Co. follows the practice of recording prepaid expenses and unearned revenues in balance sheet accounts. The company's annual accounting period ends on October 31, 2013. The following information concerns the adjusting entries that need to be recorded as of that date.

Problem 3-2B
Preparing adjusting and subsequent journal entries

C1 A1 P1

a. The Office Supplies account started the fiscal year with a $600 balance. During the fiscal year, the company purchased supplies for $4,570, which was added to the Office Supplies account. The supplies available at October 31, 2013, totaled $800.

b. An analysis of the company's insurance policies provided the following facts.

Policy	Date of Purchase	Months of Coverage	Cost
A	April 1, 2012	24	$6,000
B	April 1, 2013	36	7,200
C	August 1, 2013	12	1,320

The total premium for each policy was paid in full (for all months) at the purchase date, and the Prepaid Insurance account was debited for the full cost. (Year-end adjusting entries for Prepaid Insurance were properly recorded in all prior fiscal years.)

c. The company has four employees, who earn a total of $1,000 for each workday. They are paid each Monday for their work in the five-day workweek ending on the previous Friday. Assume that October 31, 2013, is a Monday, and all four employees worked the first day of that week. They will be paid salaries for five full days on Monday, November 7, 2013.

d. The company purchased a building on November 1, 2010, that cost $175,000 and is expected to have a $40,000 salvage value at the end of its predicted 25-year life. Annual depreciation is $5,400.

e. Since the company does not occupy the entire building it owns, it rented space to a tenant at $1,000 per month, starting on September 1, 2013. The rent was paid on time on September 1, and the amount received was credited to the Rent Earned account. However, the October rent has not been paid. The company has worked out an agreement with the tenant, who has promised to pay both October and November rent in full on November 15. The tenant has agreed not to fall behind again.

f. On September 1, the company rented space to another tenant for $725 per month. The tenant paid five months' rent in advance on that date. The payment was recorded with a credit to the Unearned Rent account.

Required

1. Use the information to prepare adjusting entries as of October 31, 2013.

2. Prepare journal entries to record the first subsequent cash transaction in November 2013 for parts *c* and *e*.

Problem 3-3B
Preparing adjusting entries, adjusted trial balance, and financial statements

A1 P1 P2 P3

Following is the unadjusted trial balance for Augustus Institute as of December 31, 2013, which initially records prepaid expenses and unearned revenues in balance sheet accounts. The Institute provides one-on-one training to individuals who pay tuition directly to the business and offers extension training to groups in off-site locations. Shown after the trial balance are items *a* through *h* that require adjusting entries as of December 31, 2013.

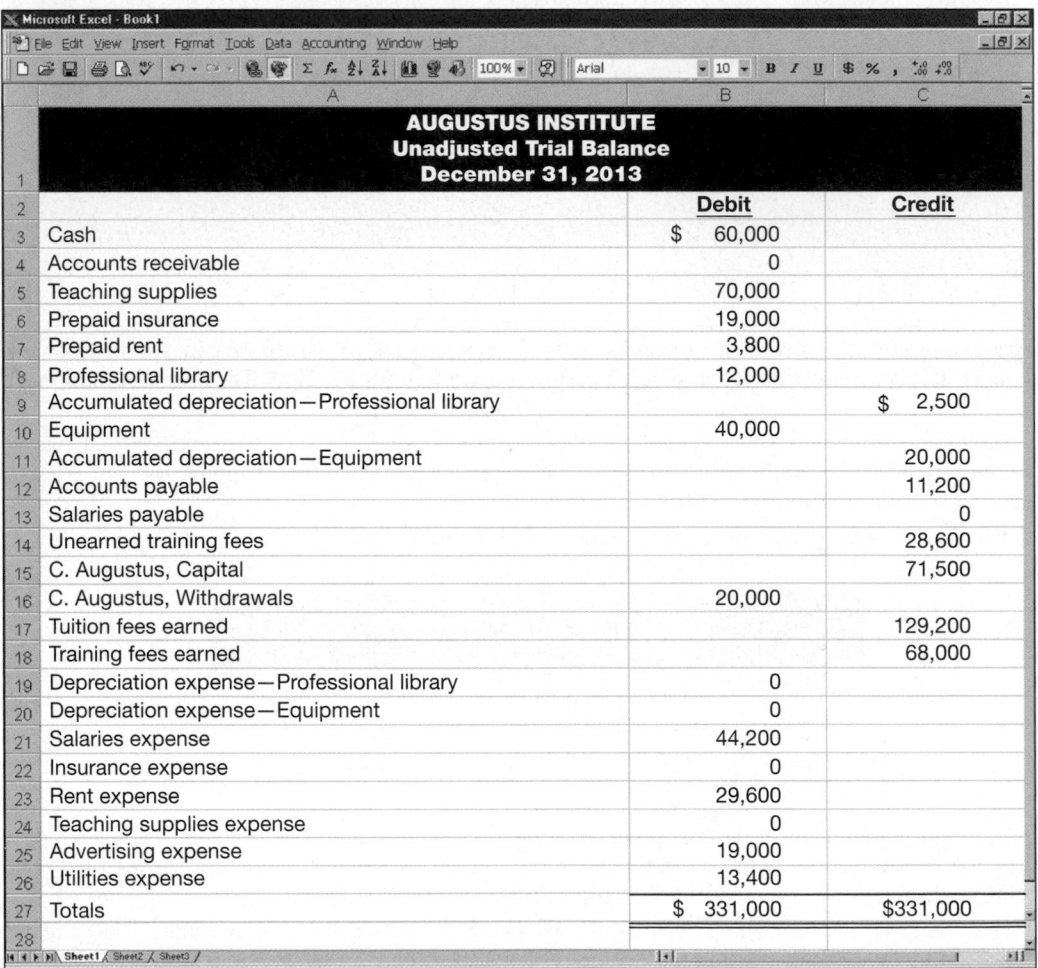

AUGUSTUS INSTITUTE
Unadjusted Trial Balance
December 31, 2013

		Debit	Credit
3	Cash	$ 60,000	
4	Accounts receivable	0	
5	Teaching supplies	70,000	
6	Prepaid insurance	19,000	
7	Prepaid rent	3,800	
8	Professional library	12,000	
9	Accumulated depreciation—Professional library		$ 2,500
10	Equipment	40,000	
11	Accumulated depreciation—Equipment		20,000
12	Accounts payable		11,200
13	Salaries payable		0
14	Unearned training fees		28,600
15	C. Augustus, Capital		71,500
16	C. Augustus, Withdrawals	20,000	
17	Tuition fees earned		129,200
18	Training fees earned		68,000
19	Depreciation expense—Professional library	0	
20	Depreciation expense—Equipment	0	
21	Salaries expense	44,200	
22	Insurance expense	0	
23	Rent expense	29,600	
24	Teaching supplies expense	0	
25	Advertising expense	19,000	
26	Utilities expense	13,400	
27	Totals	$ 331,000	$331,000

Additional Information Items

a. An analysis of the Institute's insurance policies shows that $9,500 of coverage has expired.

b. An inventory count shows that teaching supplies costing $20,000 are available at year-end 2013.

c. Annual depreciation on the equipment is $5,000.

d. Annual depreciation on the professional library is $2,400.

e. On November 1, the Institute agreed to do a special five-month course (starting immediately) for a client. The contract calls for a $14,300 monthly fee, and the client paid the first two months' fees in advance. When the cash was received, the Unearned Training Fees account was credited. The last two month's fees will be recorded when collected in 2014.

f. On October 15, the Institute agreed to teach a four-month class (beginning immediately) to an individual for $2,300 tuition per month payable at the end of the class. The class started on October 15, but no payment has yet been received. (The Institute's accruals are applied to the nearest half-month; for example, October recognizes one-half month accrual.)

g. The Institute's only employee is paid weekly. As of the end of the year, three days' salaries have accrued at the rate of $150 per day.

h. The balance in the Prepaid Rent account represents rent for December.

Required

1. Prepare T-accounts (representing the ledger) with balances from the unadjusted trial balance.

2. Prepare the necessary adjusting journal entries for items *a* through *h*, and post them to the T-accounts. Assume that adjusting entries are made only at year-end.

3. Update balances in the T-accounts for the adjusting entries and prepare an adjusted trial balance.

4. Prepare the company's income statement and statement of owner's equity for the year 2013, and prepare its balance sheet as of December 31, 2013.

Check (2*e*) Cr. Training Fees Earned, $28,600; (2*f*) Cr. Tuition Fees Earned, $5,750; (3) Adj. trial balance totals, $344,600; (4) Net income, $54,200; Ending C. Augustus, Capital, $105,700

A six-column table for Yan Consulting Company follows. The first two columns contain the unadjusted trial balance for the company as of December 31, 2013, and the last two columns contain the adjusted trial balance as of the same date.

Problem 3-4B
Interpreting unadjusted and adjusted trial balances, and preparing financial statements

C3 A1 P1 P2 P3

	Unadjusted Trial Balance		Adjustments		Adjusted Trial Balance	
Cash	$ 45,000				$ 45,000	
Accounts receivable	60,000				66,660	
Office supplies	40,000				17,000	
Prepaid insurance	8,200				3,600	
Office equipment	120,000				120,000	
Accumulated depreciation— Office equip.		$ 20,000				$ 30,000
Accounts payable		26,000				32,000
Interest payable		0				2,150
Salaries payable		0				16,000
Unearned consulting fees		40,000				27,800
Long-term notes payable		75,000				75,000
Z. Yan, Capital		80,200				80,200
Z. Yan, Withdrawals	20,000				20,000	
Consulting fees earned		234,600				253,460
Depreciation expense— Office equip.	0				10,000	
Salaries expense	112,000				128,000	
Interest expense	8,600				10,750	
Insurance expense	0				4,600	
Rent expense	20,000				20,000	
Office supplies expense	0				23,000	
Advertising expense	42,000				48,000	
Totals	$475,800	$475,800			$516,610	$516,610

Required

Analysis Component

1. Analyze the differences between the unadjusted and adjusted trial balances to determine the eight adjustments that likely were made. Show the results of your analysis by inserting these adjustment amounts in the table's two middle columns. Label each adjustment with a letter *a* through *h* and provide a short description of it at the bottom of the table.

Preparation Component

Check (2) Net income, $9,110; Z. Yan, Capital (12/31/13), $69,310; Total assets, $222,260

2. Use the information in the adjusted trial balance to prepare this company's (*a*) income statement and its statement of owner's equity for the year ended December 31, 2013 (*Note:* Z. Yan, Capital at December 31, 2012, was $80,200, and the current-year withdrawals were $20,000), and (*b*) the balance sheet as of December 31, 2013.

Problem 3-5B
Preparing financial statements from the adjusted trial balance and calculating profit margin
P3 A1 A2

The adjusted trial balance for Speedy Courier as of December 31, 2013, follows.

	Debit	Credit
Cash	$ 58,000	
Accounts receivable	120,000	
Interest receivable	7,000	
Notes receivable (due in 90 days)	210,000	
Office supplies	22,000	
Trucks	134,000	
Accumulated depreciation—Trucks		$ 58,000
Equipment	270,000	
Accumulated depreciation—Equipment		200,000
Land	100,000	
Accounts payable		134,000
Interest payable		20,000
Salaries payable		28,000
Unearned delivery fees		120,000
Long-term notes payable		200,000
L. Horace, Capital		125,000
L. Horace, Withdrawals	50,000	
Delivery fees earned		611,800
Interest earned		34,000
Depreciation expense—Trucks	29,000	
Depreciation expense—Equipment	48,000	
Salaries expense	74,000	
Wages expense	300,000	
Interest expense	15,000	
Office supplies expense	31,000	
Advertising expense	27,200	
Repairs expense—Trucks	35,600	
Totals	$1,530,800	$1,530,800

Required

Check (1) Total assets, $663,000

1. Use the information in the adjusted trial balance to prepare (*a*) the income statement for the year ended December 31, 2013, (*b*) the statement of owner's equity for the year ended December 31, 2013, and (*c*) the balance sheet as of December 31, 2013.

2. Calculate the profit margin for year 2013.

Tremor Co. had the following transactions in the last two months of its fiscal year ended May 31.

Problem 3-6B^A
Recording prepaid expenses and unearned revenues

P1 P4

Apr. 1 Paid $2,450 cash to an accounting firm for future consulting services.
     1 Paid $3,600 cash for 12 months of insurance through March 31 of the next year.
    30 Received $8,500 cash for future services to be provided to a customer.
May 1 Paid $4,450 cash for future newspaper advertising.
    23 Received $10,450 cash for future services to be provided to a customer.
    31 Of the consulting services paid for on April 1, $2,000 worth has been performed.
    31 A portion of the insurance paid for on April 1 has expired. No adjustment was made in April to Prepaid Insurance.
    31 Services worth $4,600 are not yet provided to the customer who paid on April 30.
    31 Of the advertising paid for on May 1, $2,050 worth is not yet used.
    31 The company has performed $5,500 of services that the customer paid for on May 23.

Required

1. Prepare entries for these transactions under the method that records prepaid expenses and unearned revenues in balance sheet accounts. Also prepare adjusting entries at the end of the year.

2. Prepare entries for these transactions under the method that records prepaid expenses and unearned revenues in income statement accounts. Also prepare adjusting entries at the end of the year.

Analysis Component

3. Explain why the alternative sets of entries in parts 1 and 2 do not result in different financial statement amounts.

This serial problem began in Chapter 1 and continues through most of the book. If previous chapter segments were not completed, the serial problem can still begin at this point. It is helpful, but not necessary, to use the Working Papers that accompany the book.

SERIAL PROBLEM
Success Systems

P1 P2 P3

Sage 50
QB

SP 3   After the success of the company's first two months, Adria Lopez continues to operate Success Systems. (Transactions for the first two months are described in the serial problem of Chapter 2.) The November 30, 2013, unadjusted trial balance of Success Systems (reflecting its transactions for October and November of 2013) follows.

No.	Account Title	Debit	Credit
101	Cash	$ 48,052	
106	Accounts receivable	12,618	
126	Computer supplies	2,545	
128	Prepaid insurance	2,220	
131	Prepaid rent	3,300	
163	Office equipment	8,000	
164	Accumulated depreciation—Office equipment		$ 0
167	Computer equipment	20,000	
168	Accumulated depreciation—Computer equipment		0
201	Accounts payable		0
210	Wages payable		0
236	Unearned computer services revenue		0
301	A. Lopez, Capital		83,000
302	A. Lopez, Withdrawals	5,600	
403	Computer services revenue		25,659
612	Depreciation expense—Office equipment	0	
613	Depreciation expense—Computer equipment	0	
623	Wages expense	2,625	
637	Insurance expense	0	
640	Rent expense	0	

[continued on next page]

[continued from previous page]

652	Computer supplies expense	0	
655	Advertising expense	1,940	
676	Mileage expense	704	
677	Miscellaneous expenses	250	
684	Repairs expense—Computer	805	
	Totals	$108,659	$108,659

Success Systems had the following transactions and events in December 2013.

Dec. 2   Paid $1,025 cash to Hillside Mall for Success Systems' share of mall advertising costs.
      3   Paid $500 cash for minor repairs to the company's computer.
      4   Received $3,950 cash from Alex's Engineering Co. for the receivable from November.
     10   Paid cash to Lyn Addie for six days of work at the rate of $125 per day.
     14   Notified by Alex's Engineering Co. that Success Systems' bid of $7,000 on a proposed project has been accepted. Alex's paid a $1,500 cash advance to Success Systems.
     15   Purchased $1,100 of computer supplies on credit from Harris Office Products.
     16   Sent a reminder to Gomez Co. to pay the fee for services recorded on November 8.
     20   Completed a project for Liu Corporation and received $5,625 cash.
  22–26   Took the week off for the holidays.
     28   Received $3,000 cash from Gomez Co. on its receivable.
     29   Reimbursed A. Lopez for business automobile mileage (600 miles at $0.32 per mile).
     31   A. Lopez withdrew $1,500 cash from the company for personal use.

The following additional facts are collected for use in making adjusting entries prior to preparing financial statements for the company's first three months:

a. The December 31 inventory count of computer supplies shows $580 still available.

b. Three months have expired since the 12-month insurance premium was paid in advance.

c. As of December 31, Lyn Addie has not been paid for four days of work at $125 per day.

d. The company's computer is expected to have a four-year life with no salvage value.

e. The office equipment is expected to have a five-year life with no salvage value.

f. Three of the four months' prepaid rent has expired.

Required

1. Prepare journal entries to record each of the December transactions and events for Success Systems. Post those entries to the accounts in the ledger.

2. Prepare adjusting entries to reflect *a* through *f.* Post those entries to the accounts in the ledger.

Check (3) Adjusted trial balance totals, $119,034

3. Prepare an adjusted trial balance as of December 31, 2013.

4. Prepare an income statement for the three months ended December 31, 2013.

5. Prepare a statement of owner's equity for the three months ended December 31, 2013.

(6) Total assets, $93,248

6. Prepare a balance sheet as of December 31, 2013.

Beyond the Numbers

REPORTING IN ACTION

C1 C2 A1 A2

Polaris

BTN 3-1   Refer to **Polaris'** financial statements in Appendix A to answer the following.

1. Identify and write down the revenue recognition principle as explained in the chapter.

2. Review Polaris' footnotes to discover how it applies the revenue recognition principle and when it recognizes revenue. Report what you discover.

3. What is Polaris' profit margin for fiscal years ended December 31, 2011 and 2010.

Fast Forward

4. Access Polaris' annual report (10-K) for fiscal years ending after December 31, 2011, at its Website (**Polaris.com**) or the SEC's EDGAR database (**www.SEC.gov**). Assess and compare the December 31, 2011, fiscal year profit margin to any subsequent year's profit margin that you compute.

BTN 3-2   Key figures for the recent two years of both **Polaris** and **Arctic Cat** follow.

($ thousands)	Polaris		Arctic Cat	
	Current Year	Prior Year	Current Year	Prior Year
Net income	$ 227,575	$ 147,138	$ 13,007	$ 1,875
Net sales	2,656,949	1,991,139	363,015	350,871
Current assets	878,676	808,145	232,040	201,015
Current liabilities	615,531	584,210	87,444	75,320

Required

1. Compute profit margins for (*a*) Polaris and (*b*) Arctic Cat for the two years of data shown.
2. Which company is more successful on the basis of profit margin? Explain.

BTN 3-3   Jessica Boland works for Sea Biscuit Co. She and Farah Smith, her manager, are preparing adjusting entries for annual financial statements. Boland computes depreciation and records it as

Depreciation Expense—Equipment	123,000	
Accumulated Depreciation—Equipment		123,000

Smith agrees with her computation but says the credit entry should be directly to the Equipment account. Smith argues that while accumulated depreciation is technically correct, "it is less hassle not to use a contra account and just credit the Equipment account directly. And besides, the balance sheet shows the same amount for total assets under either method."

Required

1. How should depreciation be recorded? Do you support Boland or Smith?
2. Evaluate the strengths and weaknesses of Smith's reasons for preferring her method.
3. Indicate whether the situation Boland faces is an ethical problem. Explain.

BTN 3-4   The class should be divided into teams. Teams are to select an industry (such as automobile manufacturing, airlines, defense contractors), and each team member is to select a different company in that industry. Each team member is to acquire the annual report of the company selected. Annual reports can be downloaded from company Websites or from the SEC's EDGAR database at (**www.sec.gov**).

Required

1. Use the annual report to compute the return on assets, debt ratio, and profit margin.
2. Communicate with team members via a meeting, e-mail, or telephone to discuss the meaning of the ratios, how different companies compare to each other, and the industry norm. The team must prepare a single memo reporting the ratios for each company and identifying the conclusions or consensus of opinion reached during the team's discussion. The memo is to be copied and distributed to the instructor and all classmates.

BTN 3-5   Access EDGAR online (**www.sec.gov**) and locate the 10-K report of **The Gap, Inc.**, (ticker GPS) filed on March 26, 2012. Review its financial statements reported for the year ended January 28, 2012, to answer the following questions.

Required

1. What are Gap's main brands?
2. What is Gap's fiscal year-end?
3. What is Gap's net sales for the period ended January 28, 2012?
4. What is Gap's net income for the period ended January 28, 2012?
5. Compute Gap's profit margin for the year ended January 28, 2012.
6. Do you believe Gap's decision to use a year-end of late January or early February relates to its natural business year? Explain.

TEAMWORK IN ACTION

C3 A1 P1

BTN 3-6   Four types of adjustments are described in the chapter: (1) prepaid expenses, (2) unearned revenues, (3) accrued expenses, and (4) accrued revenues.

Required

1. Form *learning teams* of four (or more) members. Each team member must select one of the four adjustments as an area of expertise (each team must have at least one expert in each area).
2. Form *expert teams* from the individuals who have selected the same area of expertise. Expert teams are to discuss and write a report that each expert will present to his or her learning team addressing the following:
   a. Description of the adjustment and why it's necessary.
   b. Example of a transaction or event, with dates and amounts, that requires adjustment.
   c. Adjusting entry(ies) for the example in requirement *b*.
   d. Status of the affected account(s) before and after the adjustment in requirement *c*.
   e. Effects on financial statements of not making the adjustment.
3. Each expert should return to his or her learning team. In rotation, each member should present his or her expert team's report to the learning team. Team discussion is encouraged.

ENTREPRENEURIAL DECISION

A2

BTN 3-7   Review the opening feature of this chapter dealing with **ash&dans** and the entrepreneurial owners, Ashley Cook and Danielle Dankner.

Required

1. Assume that ash&dans sells a $300 gift certificate to a customer, collecting the $300 cash in advance. Prepare the journal entry for the (*a*) collection of the cash for delivery of the gift certificate to the customer and (*b*) revenue from the subsequent delivery of merchandise when the gift certificate is used.
2. How can keeping less inventory help to improve ash&dans's profit margin?
3. Ashley Cook and Danielle Dankner understand that many companies carry considerable inventory, and they are thinking of carrying additional inventory of merchandise for sale. Ashley and Danielle desire your advice on the pros and cons of carrying such inventory. Provide at least one reason for and one reason against carrying additional inventory.

HITTING THE ROAD

C1

BTN 3-8   Visit the Website of a major company that interests you. Use the Investor Relations link at the Website to obtain the toll-free telephone number of the Investor Relations Department. Call the company, ask to speak to Investor Relations, and request a copy of the company's most recent annual report (a company will sometimes send a pre-packaged *investor packet,* which includes the annual report plus other relevant information). You should receive the requested report within one to two weeks. Once you have received your report, use it throughout the term to see that the principles you are learning in class are being applied in practice.

BTN 3-9 **Piaggio (Piaggio.com)** manufactures two-, three- and four-wheel vehicles, and is Europe's leading manufacturer of motorcycles and scooters.

GLOBAL DECISION

A2 C1 C2

PIAGGIO

Required

1. Locate the notes to its December 31, 2011, financial statements at the company's Website, and read note *2.2 Accounting Principles—Recognition of Revenues,* first paragraph only. When is revenue recognized by Piaggio?

2. Refer to Piaggio's financials in Appendix A. What is Piaggio's profit margin for the year ended December 31, 2011?

ANSWERS TO MULTIPLE CHOICE QUIZ

1. b; the forgotten adjusting entry is: *dr.* Wages Expense, *cr.* Wages Payable.

2. c; Supplies used = $450 − $125 = $325

3. b; Insurance expense = $24,000 × (8/24) = $8,000; adjusting entry is: *dr.* Insurance Expense for $8,000, *cr.* Prepaid Insurance for $8,000.

4. a; Consulting fees earned = $3,600 × (2/6) = $1,200; adjusting entry is: *dr.* Unearned Consulting Fee for $1,200, *cr.* Consulting Fees Earned for $1,200.

5. e; Profit margin = $15,000/$300,000 = 5%

Completing the Accounting Cycle

A Look Back

Chapter 3 explained the timing of reports. We described why adjusting accounts is key for recognizing revenues and expenses in the proper period. We prepared an adjusted trial balance and used it to prepare financial statements.

A Look at This Chapter

This chapter emphasizes the final steps in the accounting process and reviews the entire accounting cycle. We explain the closing process, including accounting procedures and the use of a post-closing trial balance. We show how a work sheet aids in preparing financial statements.

A Look Ahead

Chapter 5 looks at accounting for merchandising activities. We describe the sale and purchase of merchandise and their implications for preparing and analyzing financial statements.

Learning Objectives

CONCEPTUAL

C1 Explain why temporary accounts are closed each period. (p. 144)

C2 Identify steps in the accounting cycle. (p. 148)

C3 Explain and prepare a classified balance sheet. (p. 149)

ANALYTICAL

A1 Compute the current ratio and describe what it reveals about a company's financial condition. (p. 152)

PROCEDURAL

P1 Prepare a work sheet and explain its usefulness. (p. 140)

P2 Describe and prepare closing entries. (p. 145)

P3 Explain and prepare a post-closing trial balance. (p. 146)

P4 *Appendix 4A*—Prepare reversing entries and explain their purpose. (p. 156)

Decision Insight

An Inspiring Account

"Learn as you go . . . always trust your instinct."
—ARYNETTA FLOYZELLE

SAN DIEGO—"I wanted to write a story which entertained kids while they learned about diversity," explains Arynetta Floyzelle. "I wanted to encourage . . . and start a movement of kids embracing that which makes them different." The result is **Girl Team Mobile (GirlTeamMobile.com)**, launched by Arynetta, which is "an App Development Studio and Independent Publishing House whose goal is to educate while encouraging positive values, exploring diversity, and inspiring confidence."

Success, however, requires Arynetta to monitor and control costs. "Publishing was proving to be expensive," recalls Arynetta. She set up an accounting system to track costs and match them with revenues. Arynetta explains, "I let everyone I was working with know upfront that I preferred a payment plan option." Her effective use of accrued expenses to preserve much needed cash is good management. Further, she explains that properly applying the accounting cycle, preparing classified financial statements, and acting on that information all increase the chances of success.

To date, Arynetta has successfully controlled costs while monitoring both revenue flows and customer needs. "Owning

a business and realizing a vision takes good old fashion discipline and work," asserts Arynetta. "I went ahead and jumped in head first and learned that much of fear is in the unknown." She explains that applying the accounting cycle, including closing entries, to help identify and match costs with revenues improves information for business decisions. She adds that classified balance sheets are useful to plan payment schedules. Still, what keeps her going, admits Arynetta, is "the creation of empowering, entertaining, and educational interactive children's e-books."

Arynetta is on a mission. "Our goal is to encourage positive values, explore diversity, and inspire confidence." To make that happen, she tracks accounting numbers to be sure her dream is realized. "When you're an entrepreneur you are taking control of your destiny. You're taking ownership of your ideas." Arynetta adds: "Living full, creative lives is an extraordinary blessing."

[Sources: *Girl Team Mobile Website*, January 2013; *Young Female Entrepreneurs*, November 2011; *Black Like Moi*, February 2012; *PRLog (Press Release)*, December 2011; *ThankfulForAMillion.com*, December 2011.]

Many of the important steps leading to financial statements were explained in earlier chapters. We described how transactions and events are analyzed, journalized, and posted. This chapter explains the closing process that readies revenue, expense, and withdrawal accounts for the next reporting period and updates the capital account. A work sheet is shown to be a useful tool for these final steps and in preparing financial statements. It also explains how accounts are classified on a balance sheet to increase their usefulness to decision makers.

Completing the Accounting Cycle

Work Sheet	Closing Process	Accounting Cycle	Classified Balance Sheet
• Benefits of a work sheet • Use of a work sheet	• Temporary and permanent accounts • Closing entries • Post-closing trial balance	• Definition of accounting cycle • Review of accounting cycle	• Classification structure • Classification categories

WORK SHEET AS A TOOL

Information preparers use various analyses and internal documents when organizing information for internal and external decision makers. Internal documents are often called **working papers.** One widely used working paper is the **work sheet,** which is a useful tool for preparers in working with accounting information. It is usually not available to external decision makers.

Benefits of a Work Sheet (Spreadsheet)

P1 Prepare a work sheet and explain its usefulness.

A work sheet is *not* a required report, yet using a manual or electronic work sheet has several potential benefits. Specifically, a work sheet

- Aids the preparation of financial statements.
- Reduces the possibility of errors when working with many accounts and adjustments.
- Links accounts and adjustments to their impacts in financial statements.
- Assists in planning and organizing an audit of financial statements—as it can be used to reflect any adjustments necessary.
- Helps in preparing interim (monthly and quarterly) financial statements when the journalizing and posting of adjusting entries are postponed until year-end.
- Shows the effects of proposed or "what-if" transactions.

Decision Insight

High-Tech Work Sheet An electronic work sheet using spreadsheet software such as Excel allows us to easily change numbers, assess the impact of alternative strategies, and quickly prepare financial statements at less cost. **Google Docs** (or **Microsoft Office Web Apps** or **Zoho Docs**) allows the sharing of a spreadsheet so that team members can work on the same work sheet simultaneously. Electronic work sheets can also increase the available time for analysis and interpretation. ■

Use of a Work Sheet

Point: Since a work sheet is *not* a required report or an accounting record, its format is flexible and can be modified by its user to fit his/her preferences.

When a work sheet is used to prepare financial statements, it is constructed at the end of a period before the adjusting process. The complete work sheet includes a list of the accounts, their balances and adjustments, and their sorting into financial statement columns. It provides two columns each for the unadjusted trial balance, the adjustments, the adjusted trial balance, the income statement, and the balance sheet (including the statement of owner's equity). To describe and interpret the work sheet, we use the information from FastForward. Preparing the work sheet has five important steps. Each step, 1 through 5, is color-coded and explained with reference to Exhibits 4.1 and 4.2.

① Step 1. Enter Unadjusted Trial Balance

Refer to Exhibit 4.1. The first step in preparing a work sheet is to list the title of every account and its account number that is expected to appear on its financial statements. This includes all accounts in the ledger plus any new ones from adjusting entries. Most adjusting entries—including expenses from salaries, supplies, depreciation, and insurance—are predictable and recurring. The unadjusted balance for each account is then entered in the appropriate Debit or Credit column of the unadjusted trial balance columns. The totals of these two columns must be equal. Exhibit 4.1 shows FastForward's work sheet after completing this first step. Sometimes blank lines are left on the work sheet based on past experience to indicate where lines will be needed for adjustments to certain accounts. Exhibit 4.1 shows Consulting Revenue as one example. An alternative is to squeeze adjustments on one line or to combine the effects of two or more adjustments in one amount. In the unusual case when an account is not predicted, we can add a new line for such an account following the *Totals* line.

② Step 2. Enter Adjustments

Refer to Exhibit 4.1A (turn over first transparency). The second step in preparing a work sheet is to enter adjustments in the Adjustments columns. The adjustments shown are the same ones shown in Exhibit 3.13. An identifying letter links the debit and credit of each adjustment. This is called *keying* the adjustments. After preparing a work sheet, adjustments must still be entered in the journal and posted to the ledger. The Adjustments columns provide the information for adjusting entries in the journal.

Point: A recordkeeper often can complete the procedural task of journalizing and posting adjusting entries by using a work sheet and the guidance that *keying* provides.

③ Step 3. Prepare Adjusted Trial Balance

Refer to Exhibit 4.1B (turn over second transparency). The adjusted trial balance is prepared by combining the adjustments with the unadjusted balances for each account. As an example, the Prepaid Insurance account has a $2,400 debit balance in the Unadjusted Trial Balance columns. This $2,400 debit is combined with the $100 credit in the Adjustments columns to give Prepaid Insurance a $2,300 debit in the Adjusted Trial Balance columns. The totals of the Adjusted Trial Balance columns confirm the equality of debits and credits.

Point: To avoid omitting the transfer of an account balance, start with the first line (cash) and continue in account order.

④ Step 4. Sort Adjusted Trial Balance Amounts to Financial Statements

Refer to Exhibit 4.1C (turn over third transparency). This step involves sorting account balances from the adjusted trial balance to their proper financial statement columns. Expenses go to the Income Statement Debit column and revenues to the Income Statement Credit column. Assets and withdrawals go to the Balance Sheet & Statement of Owner's Equity Debit column. Liabilities and owner's capital go to the Balance Sheet & Statement of Owner's Equity Credit column.

⑤ Step 5. Total Statement Columns, Compute Income or Loss, and Balance Columns

Refer to Exhibit 4.1D (turn over fourth transparency). Each financial statement column (from Step 4) is totaled. The difference between the totals of the Income Statement columns is net income or net loss. This occurs because revenues are entered in the Credit column and expenses in the Debit column. If the Credit total exceeds the Debit total, there is net income. If the Debit total exceeds the Credit total, there is a net loss. For FastForward, the Credit total exceeds the Debit total, giving a $3,785 net income.

The net income from the Income Statement columns is then entered in the Balance Sheet & Statement of Owner's Equity Credit column. Adding net income to the last Credit column implies that it is to be added to owner's capital. If a loss occurs, it is added to the Debit column. This implies that it is to be subtracted from owner's capital. The ending balance of owner's capital does not appear in the last two columns as a single amount, but it is computed in the statement of owner's equity using these account balances. When net income or net loss is added

[continued on p. 144]

EXHIBIT 4.1

Work Sheet with Unadjusted Trial Balance

File Edit View Insert Format Tools Data Window Help

		FastForward Work Sheet For Month Ended December 31, 2013									
			Unadjusted Trial Balance		Adjustments		Adjusted Trial Balance		Income Statement		Balance Sheet & Statement of Owner's Equity	
No.	Account		Dr.	Cr.	Dr.	Cr.	Dr.	Cr.	Dr.	Cr.	Dr.	Cr.
101	Cash		4,350									
126	Supplies		9,720									
128	Prepaid insurance		2,400									
167	Equipment		26,000									
201	Accounts payable			6,200								
236	Unearned consulting revenue			3,000								
301	C. Taylor, Capital			30,000								
302	C. Taylor, Withdrawals		200									
403	Consulting revenue			5,800								
406	Rental revenue			300								
622	Salaries expense		1,400									
640	Rent expense		1,000									
690	Utilities expense		230									
	Totals		45,300	45,300								

Sheet1 Sheet2 Sheet3

List all accounts from the ledger (can include those expected to arise from accounting adjustments).

Enter all amounts available from ledger accounts. Column totals must be equal.

A work sheet collects and summarizes information used to prepare adjusting entries, financial statements, and closing entries.

EXHIBIT 4.2

Financial Statements Prepared from the Work Sheet

FASTFORWARD
Income Statement
For Month Ended December 31, 2013

Revenues		
Consulting revenue	$ 7,850	
Rental revenue	300	
Total revenues		$ 8,150
Expenses		
Depreciation expense—Equipment	375	
Salaries expense	1,610	
Insurance expense	100	
Rent expense	1,000	
Supplies expense	1,050	
Utilities expense	230	
Total expenses		4,365
Net income		$ 3,785

FASTFORWARD
Statement of Owner's Equity
For Month Ended December 31, 2013

C. Taylor, Capital, December 1		$ 0
Add: Investment by owner	$30,000	
Net income	3,785	33,785
		33,785
Less: Withdrawals by owner		200
C. Taylor, Capital, December 31		$33,585

FASTFORWARD
Balance Sheet
December 31, 2013

Assets		
Cash		$ 4,350
Accounts receivable		1,800
Supplies		8,670
Prepaid insurance		2,300
Equipment	$26,000	
Accumulated depreciation—Equipment	(375)	25,625
Total assets		$42,745
Liabilities		
Accounts payable		$ 6,200
Salaries payable		210
Unearned consulting revenue		2,750
Total liabilities		9,160
Equity		
C. Taylor, Capital		33,585
Total liabilities and equity		$42,745

to the proper Balance Sheet & Statement of Owner's Equity column, the totals of the last two columns must balance. If they do not, one or more errors have been made. The error can either be mathematical or involve sorting one or more amounts to incorrect columns.

 Decision Maker ══

Entrepreneur　You make a printout of the electronic work sheet used to prepare financial statements. There is no depreciation adjustment, yet you own a large amount of equipment. Does the absence of depreciation adjustment concern you? ■　[Answer—p. 158]

Work Sheet Applications and Analysis

A work sheet does not substitute for financial statements. It is a tool we can use at the end of an accounting period to help organize data and prepare financial statements. FastForward's financial statements are shown in Exhibit 4.2. Its income statement amounts are taken from the Income Statement columns of the work sheet. Similarly, amounts for its balance sheet and its statement of owner's equity are taken from the Balance Sheet & Statement of Owner's Equity columns of the work sheet.

　Information from the Adjustments columns of a work sheet can be used to journalize adjusting entries. It is important to remember that a work sheet is not a journal. This means that even when a work sheet is prepared, it is necessary to both journalize adjustments and post them to the ledger.

　Work sheets are also useful in analyzing the effects of proposed, or what-if, transactions. This is done by entering financial statement amounts in the Unadjusted (what-if) columns. Proposed transactions are then entered in the Adjustments columns. We then compute "adjusted" amounts from these proposed transactions. The extended amounts in the financial statement columns show the effects of these proposed transactions. These financial statement columns yield **pro forma financial statements** because they show the statements *as if* the proposed transactions occurred.

Quick Check　　　　　　　　　　　　　　　Answers — p. 158　

1. Where do we get the amounts to enter in the Unadjusted Trial Balance columns of a work sheet?
2. What are the advantages of using a work sheet to help prepare adjusting entries?
3. What are the overall benefits of a work sheet?

CLOSING PROCESS

 C1　Explain why temporary accounts are closed each period.

The **closing process** is an important step at the end of an accounting period *after* financial statements have been completed. It prepares accounts for recording the transactions and the events of the *next* period. In the closing process we must (1) identify accounts for closing, (2) record and post the closing entries, and (3) prepare a post-closing trial balance. The purpose of the closing process is twofold. First, it resets revenue, expense, and withdrawals account balances to zero at the end of each period. This is done so that these accounts can properly measure income and withdrawals for the next period. Second, it helps in summarizing a period's revenues and expenses. This section explains the closing process.

Temporary Accounts
(closed at period-end)

Revenues
Expenses
Owner Withdrawals
Income Summary

Permanent Accounts
(not closed at period-end)

Assets
Liabilities
Owner Capital

Temporary and Permanent Accounts

Temporary (or *nominal*) **accounts** accumulate data related to one accounting period. They include all income statement accounts, the withdrawals account, and the Income Summary account. They are temporary because the accounts are opened at the beginning of a period, used to record transactions and events for that period, and then closed at the end of the period. *The closing process applies only to temporary accounts.* **Permanent** (or *real*) **accounts** report on activities related to one or more future accounting periods. They carry their ending balances into the next period and generally consist of all balance sheet accounts. These asset, liability, and equity accounts are not closed.

Recording Closing Entries

To record and post **closing entries** is to transfer the end-of-period balances in revenue, expense, and withdrawals accounts to the permanent capital account. Closing entries are necessary at the end of each period after financial statements are prepared because

- Revenue, expense, and withdrawals accounts must begin each period with zero balances.
- Owner's capital must reflect prior periods' revenues, expenses, and withdrawals.

An income statement aims to report revenues and expenses for a *specific accounting period*. The statement of owner's equity reports similar information, including withdrawals. Since revenue, expense, and withdrawals accounts must accumulate information separately for each period, they must start each period with zero balances. To close these accounts, we transfer their balances first to an account called *Income Summary*. **Income Summary** is a temporary account (only used for the closing process) that contains a credit for the sum of all revenues (and gains) and a debit for the sum of all expenses (and losses). Its balance equals net income or net loss and it is transferred to the capital account. Next the withdrawals account balance is transferred to the capital account. After these closing entries are posted, the revenue, expense, withdrawals, and Income Summary accounts have zero balances. These accounts are then said to be *closed* or *cleared*.

Exhibit 4.3 uses the adjusted account balances of FastForward (from the Adjusted Trial Balance columns of Exhibit 4.1 or from the left side of Exhibit 4.4) to show the four steps necessary to close its temporary accounts. We explain each step.

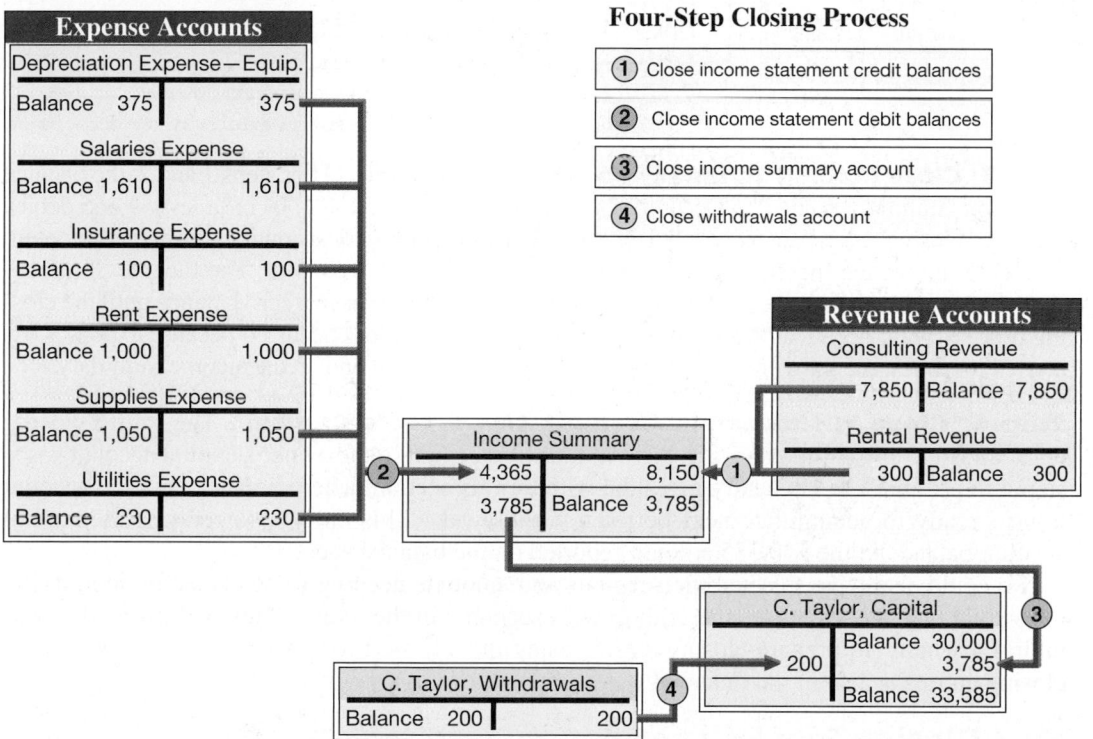

EXHIBIT 4.3

Four-Step Closing Process

Step 1: Close Credit Balances in Revenue Accounts to Income Summary The first closing entry transfers credit balances in revenue (and gain) accounts to the Income Summary account. We bring accounts with credit balances to zero by debiting them. For FastForward, this journal entry is step 1 in Exhibit 4.4. This entry closes revenue accounts and leaves them with zero balances. The accounts are now ready to record revenues when they occur in the next period. The $8,150 credit entry to Income Summary equals total revenues for the period.

Step 2: Close Debit Balances in Expense Accounts to Income Summary The second closing entry transfers debit balances in expense (and loss) accounts to the Income Summary account. We bring expense accounts' debit balances to zero by crediting them. With a balance of zero, these accounts are ready to accumulate a record of expenses for the next period. This second closing entry for FastForward is step 2 in Exhibit 4.4. Exhibit 4.3 shows that posting this entry gives each expense account a zero balance.

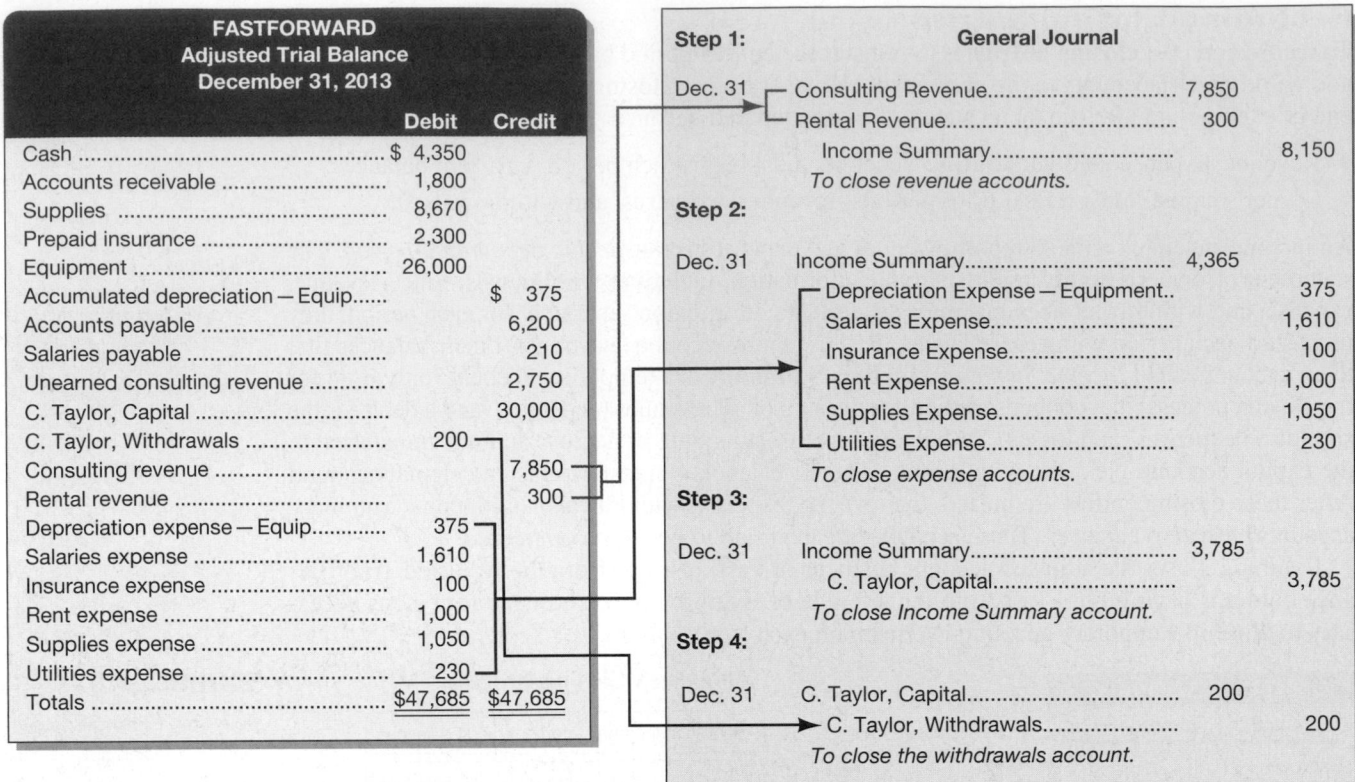

EXHIBIT 4.4

Preparing Closing Entries

Step 3: Close Income Summary to Owner's Capital   After steps 1 and 2, the balance of Income Summary is equal to December's net income of $3,785 ($8,150 credit less $4,365 debit). The third closing entry transfers the balance of the Income Summary account to the capital account. This entry closes the Income Summary account–see step 3 in Exhibit 4.4. The Income Summary account has a zero balance after posting this entry. It continues to have a zero balance until the closing process again occurs at the end of the next period. (If a net loss occurred because expenses exceeded revenues, the third entry is reversed: debit Owner Capital and credit Income Summary.)

Step 4: Close Withdrawals Account to Owner's Capital   The fourth closing entry transfers any debit balance in the withdrawals account to the owner's capital account—see step 4 in Exhibit 4.4. This entry gives the withdrawals account a zero balance, and the account is now ready to accumulate next period's withdrawals. This entry also reduces the capital account balance to the $33,585 amount reported on the balance sheet.

We could also have selected the accounts and amounts needing to be closed by identifying individual revenue, expense, and withdrawals accounts in the ledger. This is illustrated in Exhibit 4.4 where we prepare closing entries using the adjusted trial balance.[1] (Information for closing entries is also in the financial statement columns of a work sheet.)

Post-Closing Trial Balance

P3 Explain and prepare a post-closing trial balance.

Exhibit 4.5 shows the entire ledger of FastForward as of December 31 after adjusting and closing entries are posted. (The transaction and adjusting entries are in Chapters 2 and 3.) The temporary accounts (revenues, expenses, and withdrawals) have ending balances equal to zero.

A **post-closing trial balance** is a list of permanent accounts and their balances from the ledger after all closing entries have been journalized and posted. It lists the balances for all accounts not closed. These accounts comprise a company's assets, liabilities, and equity, which are identical to those in the balance sheet. The aim of a post-closing trial balance is to verify that

---

[1] The closing process has focused on proprietorships. It is identical for partnerships with the exception that each owner has separate capital and withdrawals accounts (for steps 3 and 4). The closing process for a corporation is similar with the exception that it uses a Retained Earnings account instead of a Capital account, and a Dividend account instead of a Withdrawals account.

EXHIBIT 4.5

General Ledger after the Closing Process for FastForward

Asset Accounts

Cash — Acct. No. 101

Date	Explan.	PR	Debit	Credit	Balance
2012					
Dec. 1	(1)	G1	30,000		30,000
2	(2)	G1		2,500	27,500
3	(3)	G1		26,000	1,500
5	(5)	G1	4,200		5,700
6	(13)	G1		2,400	3,300
12	(6)	G1		1,000	2,300
12	(7)	G1		700	1,600
22	(9)	G1	1,900		3,500
24	(10)	G1		900	2,600
24	(11)	G1		200	2,400
26	(12)	G1	3,000		5,400
26	(14)	G1		120	5,280
26	(15)	G1		230	5,050
26	(16)	G1		700	4,350

Accounts Receivable — Acct. No. 106

Date	Explan.	PR	Debit	Credit	Balance
2013					
Dec. 12	(8)	G1	1,900		1,900
22	(9)	G1		1,900	0
31	Adj.(f)	G1	1,800		1,800

Supplies — Acct. No. 126

Date	Explan.	PR	Debit	Credit	Balance
2013					
Dec. 2	(2)	G1	2,500		2,500
6	(4)	G1	7,100		9,600
26	(14)	G1	120		9,720
31	Adj.(b)	G1		1,050	8,670

Prepaid Insurance — Acct. No. 128

Date	Explan.	PR	Debit	Credit	Balance
2013					
Dec. 6	(13)	G1	2,400		2,400
31	Adj.(a)	G1		100	2,300

Equipment — Acct. No. 167

Date	Explan.	PR	Debit	Credit	Balance
2013					
Dec. 3	(3)	G1	26,000		26,000

Accumulated Depreciation—Equipment — Acct. No. 168

Date	Explan.	PR	Debit	Credit	Balance
2013					
Dec. 31	Adj.(c)	G1		375	375

Liability and Equity Accounts

Accounts Payable — Acct. No. 201

Date	Explan.	PR	Debit	Credit	Balance
2013					
Dec. 6	(4)	G1		7,100	7,100
24	(10)	G1	900		6,200

Salaries Payable — Acct. No. 209

Date	Explan.	PR	Debit	Credit	Balance
2013					
Dec. 31	Adj.(e)	G1		210	210

Unearned Consulting Revenue — Acct. No. 236

Date	Explan.	PR	Debit	Credit	Balance
2013					
Dec. 26	(12)	G1		3,000	3,000
31	Adj.(d)	G1	250		2,750

C. Taylor, Capital — Acct. No. 301

Date	Explan.	PR	Debit	Credit	Balance
2013					
Dec. 1	(1)	G1		30,000	30,000
31	Clos.(3)	G1		3,785	33,785
31	Clos.(4)	G1	200		33,585

C. Taylor, Withdrawals — Acct. No. 302

Date	Explan.	PR	Debit	Credit	Balance
2013					
Dec. 24	(11)	G1	200		200
31	Clos.(4)	G1		200	0

Revenue and Expense Accounts (Including Income Summary)

Consulting Revenue — Acct. No. 403

Date	Explan.	PR	Debit	Credit	Balance
2013					
Dec. 5	(5)	G1		4,200	4,200
12	(8)	G1		1,600	5,800
31	Adj.(d)	G1		250	6,050
31	Adj.(f)	G1		1,800	7,850
31	Clos.(1)	G1	7,850		0

Rental Revenue — Acct. No. 406

Date	Explan.	PR	Debit	Credit	Balance
2013					
Dec. 12	(8)	G1		300	300
31	Clos.(1)	G1	300		0

Depreciation Expense—Equipment — Acct. No. 612

Date	Explan.	PR	Debit	Credit	Balance
2013					
Dec. 31	Adj.(c)	G1	375		375
31	Clos.(2)	G1		375	0

Salaries Expense — Acct. No. 622

Date	Explan.	PR	Debit	Credit	Balance
2013					
Dec. 12	(7)	G1	700		700
26	(16)	G1	700		1,400
31	Adj.(e)	G1	210		1,610
31	Clos.(2)	G1		1,610	0

Insurance Expense — Acct. No. 637

Date	Explan.	PR	Debit	Credit	Balance
2013					
Dec. 31	Adj.(a)	G1	100		100
31	Clos.(2)	G1		100	0

Rent Expense — Acct. No. 640

Date	Explan.	PR	Debit	Credit	Balance
2013					
Dec. 12	(6)	G1	1,000		1,000
31	Clos.(2)	G1		1,000	0

Supplies Expense — Acct. No. 652

Date	Explan.	PR	Debit	Credit	Balance
2013					
Dec. 31	Adj.(b)	G1	1,050		1,050
31	Clos.(2)	G1		1,050	0

Utilities Expense — Acct. No. 690

Date	Explan.	PR	Debit	Credit	Balance
2013					
Dec. 26	(15)	G1	230		230
31	Clos.(2)	G1		230	0

Income Summary — Acct. No. 901

Date	Explan.	PR	Debit	Credit	Balance
2013					
Dec. 31	Clos.(1)	G1		8,150	8,150
31	Clos.(2)	G1	4,365		3,785
31	Clos.(3)	G1	3,785		0

(1) total debits equal total credits for permanent accounts and (2) all temporary accounts have zero balances. FastForward's post-closing trial balance is shown in Exhibit 4.6. The post-closing trial balance usually is the last step in the accounting process.

EXHIBIT 4.6

Post-Closing Trial Balance

FASTFORWARD Post-Closing Trial Balance December 31, 2013		
	Debit	Credit
Cash	$ 4,350	
Accounts receivable	1,800	
Supplies	8,670	
Prepaid insurance	2,300	
Equipment	26,000	
Accumulated depreciation—Equipment		$ 375
Accounts payable		6,200
Salaries payable		210
Unearned consulting revenue		2,750
C. Taylor, Capital		33,585
Totals	$43,120	$43,120

■ **Decision Maker**

Colleague   A friend shows you the post-closing trial balance she is working on as part of a class assignment. You review the statement quickly and see a line item for rent expense. You immediately tell your friend, "I see that you have an error." How did you conclude so quickly that an error exists? ■   [Answer—p. 158]

ACCOUNTING CYCLE

 C2   Identify steps in the accounting cycle.

The term **accounting cycle** refers to the steps in preparing financial statements. It is called a *cycle* because the steps are repeated each reporting period. Exhibit 4.7 shows the 10 steps in the cycle, beginning with analyzing transactions and ending with a post-closing trial balance or

EXHIBIT 4.7

Steps in the Accounting Cycle*

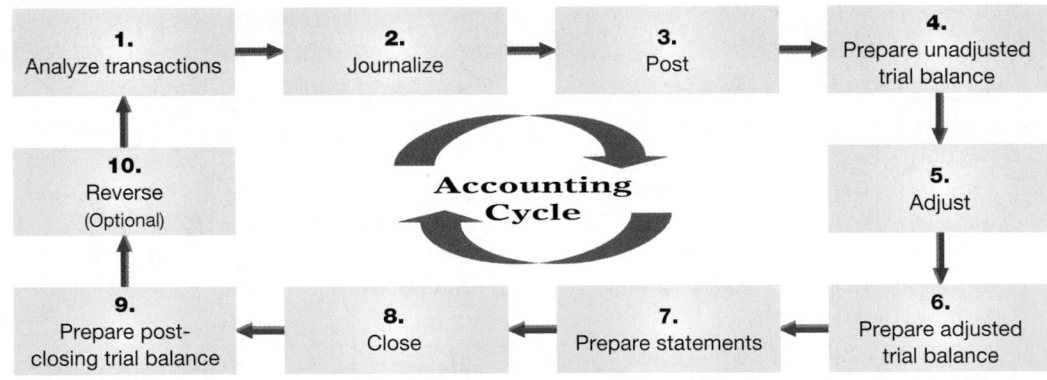

Explanations

1. Analyze transactions	Analyze transactions to prepare for journalizing.
2. Journalize	Record accounts, including debits and credits, in a journal.
3. Post	Transfer debits and credits from the journal to the ledger.
4. Prepare unadjusted trial balance	Summarize unadjusted ledger accounts and amounts.
5. Adjust	Record adjustments to bring account balances up to date; journalize and post adjustments.
6. Prepare adjusted trial balance	Summarize adjusted ledger accounts and amounts.
7. Prepare statements	Use adjusted trial balance to prepare financial statements.
8. Close	Journalize and post entries to close temporary accounts.
9. Prepare post-closing trial balance	Test clerical accuracy of the closing procedures.
10. Reverse (optional)	Reverse certain adjustments in the next period—optional step; see Appendix 4A.

* Steps 4, 6, and 9 can be done on a work sheet. A work sheet is useful in planning adjustments, but adjustments (step 5) must always be journalized and posted. Steps 3, 4, 6, and 9 are automatic with a computerized system.

reversing entries. Steps 1 through 3 usually occur regularly as a company enters into transactions. Steps 4 through 9 are done at the end of a period. *Reversing entries* in step 10 are optional and are explained in Appendix 4A.

CLASSIFIED BALANCE SHEET

Our discussion to this point has been limited to unclassified financial statements. This section describes a classified balance sheet. The next chapter describes a classified income statement. An **unclassified balance sheet** is one whose items are broadly grouped into assets, liabilities, and equity. One example is FastForward's balance sheet in Exhibit 4.2. A **classified balance sheet** organizes assets and liabilities into important subgroups that provide more information to decision makers.

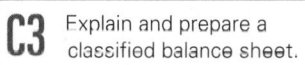

C3 Explain and prepare a classified balance sheet.

Classification Structure

A classified balance sheet has no required layout, but it usually contains the categories in Exhibit 4.8. One of the more important classifications is the separation between current and noncurrent items for both assets and liabilities. Current items are those expected to come due (either collected or owed) within one year or the company's operating cycle, whichever is longer. The **operating cycle** is the time span from when *cash is used* to acquire goods and services until *cash is received* from the sale of goods and services. "Operating" refers to company operations and "cycle" refers to the circular flow of cash used for company inputs and then cash received from its outputs. The length of a company's operating cycle depends on its activities. For a service company, the operating cycle is the time span between (1) paying employees who perform the services and (2) receiving cash from customers. For a merchandiser selling products, the operating cycle is the time span between (1) paying suppliers for merchandise and (2) receiving cash from customers.

Assets	Liabilities and Equity
Current assets	Current liabilities
Noncurrent assets	Noncurrent liabilities
Long-term investments	Equity
Plant assets	
Intangible assets	

EXHIBIT 4.8

Typical Categories in a Classified Balance Sheet

Most operating cycles are less than one year. This means most companies use a one-year period in deciding which assets and liabilities are current. A few companies have an operating cycle longer than one year. For instance, producers of certain beverages (wine) and products (ginseng) that require aging for several years have operating cycles longer than one year. A balance sheet lists current assets before noncurrent assets and current liabilities before noncurrent liabilities. This consistency in presentation allows users to quickly identify current assets that are most easily converted to cash and current liabilities that are shortly coming due. Items in current assets and current liabilities are listed in the order of how quickly they will be converted to, or paid in, cash.

EXHIBIT 4.9

Example of a Classified
Balance Sheet

SNOWBOARDING COMPONENTS			
Balance Sheet			
January 31, 2013			
Assets			
Current assets			
Cash		$ 6,500	
Short-term investments		2,100	
Accounts receivable, net		4,400	
Merchandise inventory		27,500	
Prepaid expenses		2,400	
Total current assets			$ 42,900
Long-term investments			
Notes receivable		1,500	
Investments in stocks and bonds		18,000	
Land held for future expansion		48,000	
Total long-term investments			67,500
Plant assets			
Equipment and buildings		203,200	
Less accumulated depreciation		53,000	
Equipment and buildings, net			150,200
Land			73,200
Total plant assets			223,400
Intangible assets			10,000
Total assets			$343,800
Liabilities			
Current liabilities			
Accounts payable		$ 15,300	
Wages payable		3,200	
Notes payable		3,000	
Current portion of long-term liabilities		7,500	
Total current liabilities			$ 29,000
Long-term liabilities (net of current portion)			150,000
Total liabilities			179,000
Equity			
T. Hawk, Capital			164,800
Total liabilities and equity			$343,800

Classification Categories

This section describes the most common categories in a classified balance sheet. The balance sheet for Snowboarding Components in Exhibit 4.9 shows the typical categories. Its assets are classified as either current or noncurrent. Its noncurrent assets include three main categories: long-term investments, plant assets, and intangible assets. Its liabilities are classified as either current or long-term. Not all companies use the same categories of assets and liabilities for their balance sheets. **K2 Sports**, a manufacturer of snowboards, reported a balance sheet with only three asset classes: current assets; property, plant and equipment; and other assets.

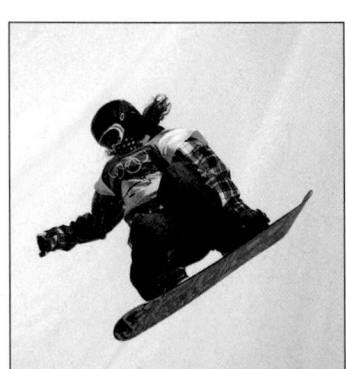

Current Assets   **Current assets** are cash and other resources that are expected to be sold, collected, or used within one year or the company's operating cycle, whichever is longer. Examples are cash, short-term investments, accounts receivable, short-term notes receivable, goods for sale (called *merchandise* or *inventory*), and prepaid expenses. The individual prepaid expenses of a company are usually small in amount compared to many other assets and are often combined and shown as a single item. The prepaid expenses in Exhibit 4.9 likely include items such as prepaid insurance, prepaid rent, office supplies, and store supplies. Prepaid expenses are usually listed last because they will not be converted to cash (instead, they are used).

Long-Term Investments A second major balance sheet classification is **long-term** (or *noncurrent*) **investments.** Notes receivable and investments in stocks and bonds are long-term assets when they are expected to be held for more than the longer of one year or the operating cycle. Land held for future expansion is a long-term investment because it is *not* used in operations.

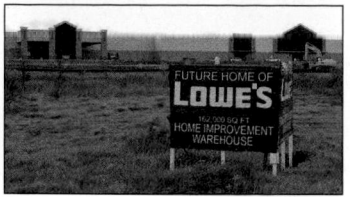

Point: Current is also called *short-term*, and noncurrent is also called *long-term*.

Plant Assets Plant assets are tangible assets that are both *long-lived* and *used to produce* or *sell products and services.* Examples are equipment, machinery, buildings, and land that are used to produce or sell products and services. The order listing for plant assets is usually from most liquid to least liquid such as equipment and machinery to buildings and land.

Point: Plant assets are also called *fixed assets; property, plant and equipment;* or *long-lived assets.*

Intangible Assets **Intangible assets** are long-term resources that benefit business operations, usually lack physical form, and have uncertain benefits. Examples are patents, trademarks, copyrights, franchises, and goodwill. Their value comes from the privileges or rights granted to or held by the owner. **K2 Sports**, reported intangible assets of $228 million, which is nearly 20 percent of its total assets. Its intangibles included trademarks, patents, and licensing agreements.

Point: Furniture and fixtures are referred to as F&F, which are classified as noncurrent assets.

Current Liabilities **Current liabilities** are obligations due to be paid or settled within one year or the operating cycle, whichever is longer. They are usually settled by paying out current assets such as cash. Current liabilities often include accounts payable, notes payable, wages payable, taxes payable, interest payable, and unearned revenues. Also, any portion of a long-term liability due to be paid within one year or the operating cycle, whichever is longer, is a current liability. Unearned revenues are current liabilities when they will be settled by delivering products or services within one year or the operating cycle, whichever is longer. Current liabilities are reported in the order of those to be settled first.

Point: Many financial ratios are distorted if accounts are not classified correctly.

Long-Term Liabilities **Long-term liabilities** are obligations *not* due within one year or the operating cycle, whichever is longer. Notes payable, mortgages payable, bonds payable, and lease obligations are common long-term liabilities. If a company has both short- and long-term items in each of these categories, they are commonly separated into two accounts in the ledger.

Point: Only assets and liabilities are classified as current or noncurrent.

Equity Equity is the owner's claim on assets. For a proprietorship, this claim is reported in the equity section with an owner's capital account. (For a partnership, the equity section reports a capital account for each partner. For a corporation, the equity section is divided into two main subsections, common stock and retained earnings.)

Quick Check   Answers – p. 158

7. Classify the following assets as (1) current assets, (2) plant assets, or (3) intangible assets:
   (a) land used in operations, (b) office supplies, (c) receivables from customers due in 10 months, (d) insurance protection for the next 9 months, (e) trucks used to provide services to customers, (f) trademarks.
8. Cite at least two examples of assets classified as investments on the balance sheet.
9. Explain the operating cycle for a service company.

GLOBAL VIEW

We explained that accounting under U.S. GAAP is similar, but not identical, to that under IFRS. This section discusses differences in the closing process and in reporting assets and liabilities on a balance sheet.

Closing Process   The closing process is identical under U.S. GAAP and IFRS. Although unique accounts can arise under either system, the closing process remains the same.

Reporting Assets and Liabilities   The definition of an asset is similar under U.S. GAAP and IFRS and involves three basic criteria: (1) the company owns or controls the right to use the item, (2) the right arises from a past transaction or event, and (3) the item can be reliably measured. Both systems define the initial asset value as historical cost for nearly all assets. After acquisition, one of two asset measurement systems is applied: historical cost or fair value. Generally, U.S. GAAP defines fair value as the amount to be received in an orderly sale. IFRS defines fair value as *exchange value*—either replacement cost or selling price. We describe these differences, and the assets to which they apply, in later chapters.

The definition of a liability is similar under U.S. GAAP and IFRS and involves three basic criteria: (1) the item is a *present* obligation requiring a probable future resource outlay, (2) the obligation arises from a past transaction or event, and (3) the obligation can be reliably measured. As with assets, both systems apply one of two measurement systems to liabilities: historical cost or fair value. Later chapters discuss specific differences.

Decision Analysis Current Ratio

A1   Compute the current ratio and describe what it reveals about a company's financial condition.

An important use of financial statements is to help assess a company's ability to pay its debts in the near future. Such analysis affects decisions by suppliers when allowing a company to buy on credit. It also affects decisions by creditors when lending money to a company, including loan terms such as interest rate, due date, and collateral requirements. It can also affect a manager's decisions about using cash to pay debts when they come due. The **current ratio** is one measure of a company's ability to pay its short-term obligations. It is defined in Exhibit 4.10 as current assets divided by current liabilities.

EXHIBIT 4.10

Current Ratio

$$\text{Current ratio} = \frac{\text{Current assets}}{\text{Current liabilities}}$$

Using financial information from **Limited Brands, Inc.**, we compute its current ratio for the recent five-year period. The results are in Exhibit 4.11.

EXHIBIT 4.11

Limited Brands' Current Ratio

$ in millions	2012	2011	2010	2009	2008	2007
Current assets	$2,368	$2,592	$3,250	$2,867	$2,919	$2,771
Current liabilities	$1,526	$1,504	$1,322	$1,255	$1,374	$1,709
Current ratio	**1.6**	**1.7**	**2.5**	**2.3**	**2.1**	**1.6**
Industry current ratio	1.6	1.7	1.9	2.0	2.1	2.3

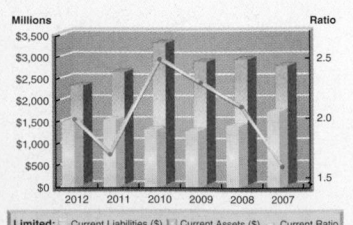

Limited Brands' current ratio averaged 2.0 for its fiscal years 2007 through 2012. The current ratio for each of these years suggests that the company's short-term obligations can be covered with its short-term assets. However, if its ratio would approach 1.0, Limited would expect to face challenges in covering liabilities. If the ratio were *less* than 1.0, current liabilities would exceed current assets, and the company's ability to pay short-term obligations could be in doubt. Limited Brand's liquidity, as evidenced by its current ratio, declines in 2011 and 2012, after growing steadily from 2008–2010.

■ **Decision Maker** ═══════════════════════════════════

Analyst   You are analyzing the financial condition of a company to assess its ability to meet upcoming loan payments. You compute its current ratio as 1.2. You also find that a major portion of accounts receivable is due from one client who has not made any payments in the past 12 months. Removing this receivable from current assets lowers the current ratio to 0.7. What do you conclude? ■   [Answer p. 168]

DEMONSTRATION PROBLEM

The partial work sheet of Midtown Repair Company at December 31, 2013, follows.

	Adjusted Trial Balance		Income Statement		Balance Sheet and Statement of Owner's Equity	
	Debit	**Credit**	**Debit**	**Credit**	**Debit**	**Credit**
Cash	95,600					
Notes receivable (current)	50,000					
Prepaid insurance	16,000					
Prepaid rent	4,000					
Equipment	170,000					
Accumulated depreciation—Equipment		57,000				
Accounts payable		52,000				
Long-term notes payable		63,000				
C. Trout, Capital		178,500				
C. Trout, Withdrawals	30,000					
Repair services revenue		180,800				
Interest revenue		7,500				
Depreciation expense—Equipment	28,500					
Wages expense	85,000					
Rent expense	48,000					
Insurance expense	6,000					
Interest expense	5,700					
Totals	538,800	538,800				

Required

1. Complete the work sheet by extending the adjusted trial balance totals to the appropriate financial statement columns.

2. Prepare closing entries for Midtown Repair Company.

3. Set up the Income Summary and the C. Trout, Capital account in the general ledger (in balance column format) and post the closing entries to these accounts.

4. Determine the balance of the C. Trout, Capital account to be reported on the December 31, 2013, balance sheet.

5. Prepare an income statement, statement of owner's equity, and classified balance sheet (in report form) as of December 31, 2013.

PLANNING THE SOLUTION

● Extend the adjusted trial balance account balances to the appropriate financial statement columns.
● Prepare entries to close the revenue accounts to Income Summary, to close the expense accounts to Income Summary, to close Income Summary to the capital account, and to close the withdrawals account to the capital account.

- Post the first and second closing entries to the Income Summary account. Examine the balance of income summary and verify that it agrees with the net income shown on the work sheet.
- Post the third and fourth closing entries to the capital account.
- Use the work sheet's two right-most columns and your answer in part 4 to prepare the classified balance sheet.

SOLUTION TO DEMONSTRATION PROBLEM

1. Completing the work sheet.

	Adjusted Trial Balance		Income Statement		Balance Sheet and Statement of Owner's Equity	
	Debit	Credit	Debit	Credit	Debit	Credit
Cash	95,600				95,600	
Notes receivable (current)	50,000				50,000	
Prepaid insurance	16,000				16,000	
Prepaid rent	4,000				4,000	
Equipment	170,000				170,000	
Accumulated depreciation—Equipment ...		57,000				57,000
Accounts payable		52,000				52,000
Long-term notes payable		63,000				63,000
C. Trout, Capital		178,500				178,500
C. Trout, Withdrawals	30,000				30,000	
Repair services revenue		180,800		180,800		
Interest revenue		7,500		7,500		
Depreciation expense—Equipment	28,500		28,500			
Wages expense	85,000		85,000			
Rent expense	48,000		48,000			
Insurance expense	6,000		6,000			
Interest expense	5,700		5,700			
Totals	538,800	538,800	173,200	188,300	365,600	350,500
Net income			15,100			15,100
Totals			188,300	188,300	365,600	365,600

2. Closing entries.

Dec. 31	Repair Services Revenue	180,800	
	Interest Revenue	7,500	
	Income Summary		188,300
	To close revenue accounts.		
Dec. 31	Income Summary	173,200	
	Depreciation Expense—Equipment		28,500
	Wages Expense		85,000
	Rent Expense		48,000
	Insurance Expense		6,000
	Interest Expense		5,700
	To close expense accounts.		
Dec. 31	Income Summary	15,100	
	C. Trout, Capital		15,100
	To close the Income Summary account.		
Dec. 31	C. Trout, Capital	30,000	
	C. Trout, Withdrawals		30,000
	To close the withdrawals account.		

3. Set up the Income Summary and the capital ledger accounts and post the closing entries.

Income Summary					Account No. 901
Date	Explanation	PR	Debit	Credit	Balance
2013					
Jan. 1	Beginning balance				0
Dec. 31	Close revenue accounts			188,300	188,300
31	Close expense accounts		173,200		15,100
31	Close income summary		15,100		0

C. Trout, Capital					Account No. 301
Date	Explanation	PR	Debit	Credit	Balance
2013					
Jan. 1	Beginning balance				178,500
Dec. 31	Close Income Summary			15,100	193,600
31	Close C. Trout, Withdrawals		30,000		163,600

4. The final capital balance of $163,600 (from part 3) will be reported on the December 31, 2013, balance sheet. The final capital balance reflects the increase due to the net income earned during the year and the decrease for the owner's withdrawals during the year.

5.

MIDTOWN REPAIR COMPANY
Income Statement
For Year Ended December 31, 2013

Revenues		
Repair services revenue	$180,800	
Interest revenue	7,500	
Total revenues		$188,300
Expenses		
Depreciation expense—Equipment	28,500	
Wages expense	85,000	
Rent expense	48,000	
Insurance expense	6,000	
Interest expense	5,700	
Total expenses		173,200
Net income		$ 15,100

MIDTOWN REPAIR COMPANY
Statement of Owner's Equity
For Year Ended December 31, 2013

C. Trout, Capital, December 31, 2012		$178,500
Add: Investment by owner	$ 0	
Net income	15,100	15,100
		193,600
Less: Withdrawals by owner		30,000
C. Trout, Capital, December 31, 2013		$163,600

MIDTOWN REPAIR COMPANY
Balance Sheet
December 31, 2013

Assets

Current assets

Cash		$ 95,600
Notes receivable		50,000
Prepaid insurance		16,000
Prepaid rent		4,000
Total current assets		165,600

Plant assets

Equipment	$170,000	
Less: Accumulated depreciation—Equipment	(57,000)	
Total plant assets		113,000
Total assets		$278,600

Liabilities

Current liabilities

Accounts payable		$ 52,000

Long-term liabilities

Long-term notes payable		63,000
Total liabilities		115,000

Equity

C. Trout, Capital		163,600
Total liabilities and equity		$278,600

4A

Reversing Entries

Point: As a general rule, adjusting entries that create new asset or liability accounts are likely candidates for reversing.

Reversing entries are optional. They are recorded in response to accrued assets and accrued liabilities that were created by adjusting entries at the end of a reporting period. The purpose of reversing entries is to simplify a company's recordkeeping. Exhibit 4A.1 shows an example of FastForward's reversing entries. The top of the exhibit shows the adjusting entry FastForward recorded on December 31 for its employee's earned but unpaid salary. The entry recorded three days' salary of $210, which increased December's total salary expense to $1,610. The entry also recognized a liability of $210. The expense is reported on December's income statement. The expense account is then closed. The ledger on January 1, 2014, shows a $210 liability and a zero balance in the Salaries Expense account. At this point, the choice is made between using or not using reversing entries.

Accounting *without* Reversing Entries   The path down the left side of Exhibit 4A.1 is described in the chapter. To summarize here, when the next payday occurs on January 9, we record payment with a compound entry that debits both the expense and liability accounts and credits Cash. Posting that entry creates a $490 balance in the expense account and reduces the liability account balance to zero because the debt has been settled. The disadvantage of this approach is the slightly more complex entry required on January 9. Paying the accrued liability means that this entry differs from the routine entries made on all other paydays. To construct the proper entry on January 9, we must recall the effect of the December 31 adjusting entry. Reversing entries overcome this disadvantage.

Point: Firms that use reversing entries hope that this simplification will reduce errors.

Accounting *with* Reversing Entries   The right side of Exhibit 4A.1 shows how a reversing entry on January 1 overcomes the disadvantage of the January 9 entry when not using reversing entries. A reversing entry is the exact opposite of an adjusting entry. For FastForward, the Salaries Payable liability account is debited for $210, meaning that this account now has a zero balance after the entry is posted. The Salaries Payable account temporarily understates the liability, but this is not a problem since

P4 Prepare reversing entries and explain their purpose.

Accrue salaries expense on December 31, 2013

Salaries Expense 210
    Salaries Payable 210

Salaries Expense

Date	Expl.	Debit	Credit	Balance
2013				
Dec. 12	(7)	700		700
26	(16)	700		1,400
31	(e)	210		1,610

Salaries Payable

Date	Expl.	Debit	Credit	Balance
2013				
Dec. 31	(e)		210	210

WITHOUT Reversing Entries	— OR —	**WITH Reversing Entries**
No reversing entry recorded on January 1, 2014		*Reversing entry recorded on January 1, 2014*

WITHOUT Reversing Entries

NO ENTRY

Salaries Expense

Date	Expl.	Debit	Credit	Balance
2014				

Salaries Payable

Date	Expl.	Debit	Credit	Balance
2013				
Dec. 31	(e)		210	210
2014				

WITH Reversing Entries

Salaries Payable 210
    Salaries Expense 210

Salaries Expense*

Date	Expl.	Debit	Credit	Balance
2014				
Jan. 1			210	(210)

Salaries Payable

Date	Expl.	Debit	Credit	Balance
2013				
Dec. 31	(e)		210	210
2014				
Jan. 1		210		0

Pay the accrued and current salaries on January 9, the first payday in 2014

WITHOUT Reversing Entries

Salaries Expense 490
Salaries Payable 210
    Cash 700

Salaries Expense

Date	Expl.	Debit	Credit	Balance
2014				
Jan. 9		490		**490**

Salaries Payable

Date	Expl.	Debit	Credit	Balance
2013				
Dec. 31	(e)		210	210
2014				
Jan. 9		210		**0**

WITH Reversing Entries

Salaries Expense 700
    Cash 700

Salaries Expense*

Date	Expl.	Debit	Credit	Balance
2014				
Jan. 1			210	(210)
Jan. 9		700		**490**

Salaries Payable

Date	Expl.	Debit	Credit	Balance
2013				
Dec. 31	(e)		210	210
2014				
Jan. 1		210		**0**

Under both approaches, the expense and liability accounts have
identical balances after the cash payment on January 9.

Salaries Expense $490
Salaries Payable .... $ 0

*Circled numbers in the *Balance* column indicate abnormal balances.

financial statements are not prepared before the liability is settled on January 9. The credit to the Salaries Expense account is unusual because it gives the account an *abnormal credit balance*. We highlight an abnormal balance by circling it. Because of the reversing entry, the January 9 entry to record payment is straightforward. This entry debits the Salaries Expense account and credits Cash for the full $700 paid. It is the same as all other entries made to record 10 days' salary for the employee. Notice that after the payment entry is posted, the Salaries Expense account has a $490 balance that reflects seven days' salary of $70 per day (see the lower right side of Exhibit 4A.1). The zero balance in the Salaries Payable account is now correct. The lower section of Exhibit 4A.1 shows that the expense and liability accounts have exactly the same balances whether reversing entries are used or not. This means that both approaches yield identical results.

Summary

C1   **Explain why temporary accounts are closed each period.** Temporary accounts are closed at the end of each accounting period for two main reasons. First, the closing process updates the capital account to include the effects of all transactions and events recorded for the period. Second, it prepares revenue, expense, and withdrawals accounts for the next reporting period by giving them zero balances.

C2   **Identify steps in the accounting cycle.** The accounting cycle consists of 10 steps: (1) analyze transactions, (2) journalize, (3) post, (4) prepare an unadjusted trial balance, (5) adjust accounts, (6) prepare an adjusted trial balance, (7) prepare statements, (8) close, (9) prepare a post-closing trial balance, and (10) prepare (optional) reversing entries.

C3   **Explain and prepare a classified balance sheet.** Classified balance sheets report assets and liabilities in two categories: current and noncurrent. Noncurrent assets often include long-term investments, plant assets, and intangible assets. Owner's equity for proprietorships (and partnerships) report the capital account balance. A corporation separates equity into common stock and retained earnings.

A1   **Compute the current ratio and describe what it reveals about a company's financial condition.** A company's current ratio is defined as current assets divided by current liabilities. We use it to evaluate a company's ability to pay its current liabilities out of current assets.

P1   **Prepare a work sheet and explain its usefulness.** A work sheet can be a useful tool in preparing and analyzing financial statements. It is helpful at the end of a period in preparing adjusting entries, an adjusted trial balance, and financial statements. A work sheet usually contains five pairs of columns: Unadjusted Trial Balance, Adjustments, Adjusted Trial Balance, Income Statement, and Balance Sheet & Statement of Owner's Equity.

P2   **Describe and prepare closing entries.** Closing entries involve four steps: (1) close credit balances in revenue (and gain) accounts to Income Summary, (2) close debit balances in expense (and loss) accounts to Income Summary, (3) close Income Summary to the capital account, and (4) close withdrawals account to owner's capital.

P3   **Explain and prepare a post-closing trial balance.** A post-closing trial balance is a list of permanent accounts and their balances after all closing entries have been journalized and posted. Its purpose is to verify that (1) total debits equal total credits for permanent accounts and (2) all temporary accounts have zero balances.

P4^A   **Prepare reversing entries and explain their purpose.** Reversing entries are an optional step. They are applied to accrued expenses and revenues. The purpose of reversing entries is to simplify subsequent journal entries. Financial statements are unaffected by the choice to use or not use reversing entries.

Guidance Answers to Decision Maker and Decision Ethics

Entrepreneur   Yes, you are concerned about the absence of a depreciation adjustment. Equipment does depreciate, and financial statements must recognize this occurrence. Its absence suggests an error or a misrepresentation (there is also the possibility that equipment is fully depreciated).

Colleague   The error is readily spotted in your friend's post-closing trial balance as you know that rent expense is a temporary account. Post-closing trial balances only show permanent accounts.

Analyst   A current ratio of 1.2 suggests that current assets are sufficient to cover current liabilities, but it implies a minimal buffer in case of errors in measuring current assets or current liabilities. Removing the past due receivable reduces the current ratio to 0.7. Your assessment is that the company will have some difficulty meeting its loan payments.

Guidance Answers to Quick Checks

1. Amounts in the Unadjusted Trial Balance columns are taken from current account balances in the ledger. The balances for new accounts expected to arise from adjusted entries can be left blank or set at zero.

2. A work sheet offers the advantage of listing on one page all necessary information to make adjusting entries.

3. A work sheet can help in (a) accounting efficiency and avoiding errors, (b) linking transactions and events to their effects in financial statements, (c) showing adjustments for audit purposes, (d) preparing interim financial statements, and (e) showing effects from proposed, or what-if, transactions.

4. The major steps in preparing closing entries are to close (1) credit balances in revenue accounts to Income Summary, (2) debit balances in expense accounts to Income Summary,

(3) Income Summary to owner's capital, and (4) any withdrawals account to owner's capital.

5. Revenue (and gain) and expense (and loss) accounts are called *temporary* because they are opened and closed each period. The Income Summary and owner's withdrawals accounts are also temporary.

6. Permanent accounts make up the post-closing trial balance, which consist of asset, liability, and equity accounts.

7. Current assets: (b), (c), (d). Plant assets: (a), (e). Item (f) is an intangible asset.

8. Investment in common stock, investment in bonds, and land held for future expansion.

9. For a service company, the operating cycle is the usual time between (1) paying employees who do the services and (2) receiving cash from customers for services provided.

Key Terms

Accounting cycle (p. 148)
Classified balance sheet (p. 149)
Closing entries (p. 145)
Closing process (p. 144)
Current assets (p. 150)
Current liabilities (p. 151)
Current ratio (p. 152)

Income summary (p. 145)
Intangible assets (p. 151)
Long-term investments (p. 151)
Long-term liabilities (p. 151)
Operating cycle (p. 149)
Permanent accounts (p. 144)
Post-closing trial balance (p. 146)

Pro forma financial statements (p. 144)
Reversing entries (p. 156)
Temporary accounts (p. 144)
Unclassified balance sheet (p. 149)
Working papers (p. 140)
Work sheet (p. 140)

Multiple Choice Quiz   Answers on p. 179   mhhe.com/wildFAP21e

Additional Quiz Questions are available at the book's Website.

1. G. Venda, owner of Venda Services, withdrew $25,000 from the business during the current year. The entry to close the withdrawals account at the end of the year is:

a.	G. Venda, Withdrawals	25,000	
	G. Venda, Capital		25,000
b.	Income Summary	25,000	
	G. Venda, Capital		25,000
c.	G. Venda, Withdrawals	25,000	
	Cash		25,000
d.	G. Venda, Capital	25,000	
	Salary Expense		25,000
e.	G. Venda, Capital	25,000	
	G. Venda, Withdrawals		25,000

2. The following information is available for the R. Kandamil Company before closing the accounts. After all of the closing entries are made, what will be the balance in the R. Kandamil, Capital account?

Total revenues	$300,000
Total expenses	195,000
R. Kandamil, Capital	100,000
R. Kandamil, Withdrawals	45,000

a. $360,000   **d.** $150,000
b. $250,000   **e.** $60,000
c. $160,000

3. Which of the following errors would cause the balance sheet and statement of owner's equity columns of a work sheet to be out of balance?
   a. Entering a revenue amount in the balance sheet and statement of owner's equity debit column.

b. Entering a liability amount in the balance sheet and statement of owner's equity credit column.
c. Entering an expense account in the balance sheet and statement of owner's equity debit column.
d. Entering an asset account in the income statement debit column.
e. Entering a liability amount in the income statement credit column.

4. The temporary account used only in the closing process to hold the amounts of revenues and expenses before the net difference is added or subtracted from the owner's capital account is called the
   a. Closing account.
   b. Nominal account.
   c. Income Summary account.
   d. Balance Column account.
   e. Contra account.

5. Based on the following information from Repicor Company's balance sheet, what is Repicor Company's current ratio?

Current assets	$ 75,000
Investments	30,000
Plant assets	300,000
Current liabilities	50,000
Long-term liabilities	60,000
D. Repicor, Capital	295,000

a. 2.10   **d.** 0.95
b. 1.50   **e.** 0.67
c. 1.00

^A *Superscript letter A denotes assignments based on Appendix 4A.*

🔘 Icon denotes assignments that involve decision making.

Discussion Questions

1. What are the steps in recording closing entries?

2. What accounts are affected by closing entries? What accounts are not affected?

3. 🔘 What two purposes are accomplished by recording closing entries?

4. What is the purpose of the Income Summary account?

5. 🔘 Explain whether an error has occurred if a post-closing trial balance includes a Depreciation Expense account.

6. What tasks are aided by a work sheet?

7. Why are the debit and credit entries in the Adjustments columns of the work sheet identified with letters?

8. What is a company's operating cycle?

9. What classes of assets and liabilities are shown on a typical classified balance sheet?

10. How is unearned revenue classified on the balance sheet?

11. What are the characteristics of plant assets?

12.^A How do reversing entries simplify recordkeeping?

13.^A If a company recorded accrued salaries expense of $500 at the end of its fiscal year, what reversing entry could be made? When would it be made?

14. 🔘 Refer to the most recent balance sheet for **Polaris** in Appendix A. What five main noncurrent asset categories are used on its classified balance sheet?   **Polaris**

15. Refer to **KTM**'s most recent balance sheet in Appendix A. Identify and list its 7 current assets.   **KTM**

16. 🔘 Refer to **Arctic Cat**'s most recent balance sheet in Appendix A. Identify the three accounts listed as current liabilities.   **Arctic Cat**

17. 🔘 Refer to **Piaggio**'s financial statements in Appendix A. What journal entry was likely recorded as of December 31, 2011, to close its Income Summary account?   **PIAGGIO**

Mc Graw Hill connect

QUICK STUDY

QS 4-1

Explaining temporary and permanent accounts

C1

Complete the following descriptions related to temporary and permanent accounts.

1. Permanent accounts report on activities related to _____ future accounting periods, and they carry their ending balances into the next period.

2. _____ accounts include all income statement accounts, the withdrawals account, and the Income Summary account.

3. _____ accounts generally consist of all balance sheet accounts, and these accounts are not closed.

4. Temporary accounts accumulate data related to _____ accounting period.

QS 4-2

Identifying the accounting cycle

C2

List the following steps of the accounting cycle in their proper order.

a. Posting the journal entries.

b. Journalizing and posting adjusting entries.

c. Preparing the adjusted trial balance.

d. Journalizing and posting closing entries.

e. Analyzing transactions and events.

f. Preparing the financial statements.

g. Preparing the unadjusted trial balance.

h. Journalizing transactions and events.

i. Preparing the post-closing trial balance.

QS 4-3

Classifying balance sheet items

C3

The following are common categories on a classified balance sheet.

A. Current assets

B. Long-term investments

C. Plant assets

D. Intangible assets

E. Current liabilities

F. Long-term liabilities

For each of the following items, select the letter that identifies the balance sheet category where the item typically would appear.

_____ 1. Land not currently used in operations

_____ 2. Notes payable (due in five years)

_____ 3. Accounts receivable

_____ 4. Trademarks

_____ 5. Accounts payable

_____ 6. Store equipment

_____ 7. Wages payable

_____ 8. Cash

Compute Chavez Company's current ratio using the following information.

Accounts receivable	$18,000	Long-term notes payable	$21,000
Accounts payable	11,000	Office supplies	2,800
Buildings	45,000	Prepaid insurance	3,560
Cash	7,000	Unearned services revenue	3,000

QS 4-4
Identifying current accounts and computing the current ratio
A1

List the following steps in preparing a work sheet in their proper order by writing numbers 1–5 in the blank spaces provided.

a. _____ Total the statement columns, compute net income (loss), and complete work sheet.
b. _____ Extend adjusted balances to appropriate financial statement columns.
c. _____ Prepare an unadjusted trial balance on the work sheet.
d. _____ Prepare an adjusted trial balance on the work sheet.
e. _____ Enter adjustments data on the work sheet.

QS 4-5
Ordering work sheet steps
P1

In preparing a work sheet, indicate the financial statement Debit column to which a normal balance in the following accounts should be extended. Use IS for the Income Statement Debit column and BS for the Balance Sheet and Statement of Owner's Equity Debit column.

_____ **a.** Equipment   _____ **d.** Depreciation expense—Equipment
_____ **b.** Owner, Withdrawals   _____ **e.** Accounts receivable
_____ **c.** Prepaid rent   _____ **f.** Insurance expense

QS 4-6
Applying a work sheet
P1

The ledger of Claudell Company includes the following unadjusted normal balances: Prepaid Rent $1,000, Services Revenue $55,600, and Wages Expense $5,000. Adjusting entries are required for **(a)** prepaid rent expense used, $200; **(b)** accrued services revenue $900; and **(c)** accrued wages expense $700. Enter these unadjusted balances and the necessary adjustments on a work sheet and complete the work sheet for these accounts. *Note:* Also include the following accounts: Accounts Receivable, Wages Payable, and Rent Expense.

QS 4-7
Preparing a partial work sheet
P1

The following selected information is taken from the work sheet for Warton Company as of December 31, 2013. Using this information, determine the amount for B. Warton, Capital, that should be reported on its December 31, 2013, balance sheet.

QS 4-8
Interpreting a work sheet
P1

	Income Statement		Balance Sheet and Statement of Owner's Equity	
	Dr.	Cr.	Dr.	Cr.
⋮				
B. Warton, Capital				72,000
B. Warton, Withdrawals			39,000	
⋮				
Totals	122,000	181,000		

The ledger of Mai Company includes the following accounts with normal balances: D. Mai, Capital $9,000; D. Mai, Withdrawals $800; Services Revenue $13,000; Wages Expense $8,400; and Rent Expense $1,600. Prepare the necessary closing entries from the available information at December 31.

QS 4-9
Prepare closing entries from the ledger **P2**

Identify the accounts listed in QS 4-9 that would be included in a post-closing trial balance.

QS 4-10
Identify post-closing accounts **P3**

On December 31, 2012, Yates Co. prepared an adjusting entry for $12,000 of earned but unrecorded management fees. On January 16, 2013, Yates received $26,700 cash in management fees, which included the accrued fees earned in 2012. Assuming the company uses reversing entries, prepare the January 1, 2013, reversing entry and the January 16, 2013, cash receipt entry.

QS 4-11[A]
Reversing entries
P4

QS 4-12
International accounting
standards   P2

Answer each of the following questions related to international accounting standards.

a. Explain how the closing process is different between accounting under IFRS versus U.S. GAAP.

b. What basic principle do U.S. GAAP and IFRS rely upon in recording the initial acquisition value for nearly all assets?

EXERCISES

Exercise 4-1
Preparing and posting
closing entries
P2

Check   M. Muncel, Capital (ending
balance), $46,200

Use the May 31 fiscal year-end information from the following ledger accounts (assume that all accounts have normal balances) to prepare closing journal entries and then post those entries to the appropriate ledger accounts.

General Ledger

M. Muncel, Capital   Acct. No. 301

Date	PR	Debit	Credit	Balance
May 31	G2			40,000

M. Muncel, Withdrawals   Acct. No. 302

Date	PR	Debit	Credit	Balance
May 31	G2			22,000

Services Revenue   Acct. No. 401

Date	PR	Debit	Credit	Balance
May 31	G2			76,000

Depreciation Expense   Acct. No. 603

Date	PR	Debit	Credit	Balance
May 31	G2			15,000

Salaries Expense   Acct. No. 622

Date	PR	Debit	Credit	Balance
May 31	G2			20,000

Insurance Expense   Acct. No. 637

Date	PR	Debit	Credit	Balance
May 31	G2			4,400

Rent Expense   Acct. No. 640

Date	PR	Debit	Credit	Balance
May 31	G2			8,400

Income Summary   Acct. No. 901

Date	PR	Debit	Credit	Balance

Exercise 4-2
Preparing closing entries and a
post-closing trial balance
P2   P3

Check   (2) T. Cruz, Capital (ending),
$51,500; Total debits, $59,000

The following adjusted trial balance contains the accounts and balances of Cruz Company as of December 31, 2013, the end of its fiscal year. (1) Prepare the December 31, 2013, closing entries for Cruz Company. Assume the account number for Income Summary is 901. (2) Prepare the December 31, 2013, post-closing trial balance for Cruz Company.

No.	Account Title	Debit	Credit
101	Cash	$19,000	
126	Supplies	13,000	
128	Prepaid insurance	3,000	
167	Equipment	24,000	
168	Accumulated depreciation—Equipment		$ 7,500
301	T. Cruz, Capital		47,600
302	T. Cruz, Withdrawals	7,000	
404	Services revenue		44,000
612	Depreciation expense—Equipment	3,000	
622	Salaries expense	22,000	
637	Insurance expense	2,500	
640	Rent expense	3,400	
652	Supplies expense	2,200	
	Totals	$99,100	$99,100

The adjusted trial balance for Salonika Marketing Co. follows. Complete the four right-most columns of the table by first entering information for the four closing entries (keyed *1* through *4*) and second by completing the post-closing trial balance.

Exercise 4-3

Preparing closing entries and a post-closing trial balance P2 P3

No.	Account Title	Adjusted Trial Balance Dr.	Adjusted Trial Balance Cr.	Closing Entry Information Dr.	Closing Entry Information Cr.	Post-Closing Trial Balance Dr.	Post-Closing Trial Balance Cr.
101	Cash	$ 9,200					
106	Accounts receivable	25,000					
153	Equipment	42,000					
154	Accumulated depreciation—Equipment		$ 17,500				
193	Franchise	31,000					
201	Accounts payable		15,000				
209	Salaries payable		4,200				
233	Unearned fees		3,600				
301	E. Salonika, Capital		68,500				
302	E. Salonika, Withdrawals	15,400					
401	Marketing fees earned		80,000				
611	Depreciation expense—Equipment	12,000					
622	Salaries expense	32,500					
640	Rent expense	13,000					
677	Miscellaneous expenses	8,700					
901	Income summary						
	Totals	$188,800	$188,800				

Use the following adjusted trial balance of Wilson Trucking Company to prepare the (1) income statement and (2) statement of owner's equity, for the year ended December 31, 2013. The K. Wilson, Capital, account balance is $175,000 at December 31, 2012.

Exercise 4-4

Preparing the financial statements

C2

Account Title	Debit	Credit
Cash	$ 8,000	
Accounts receivable	17,500	
Office supplies	3,000	
Trucks	172,000	
Accumulated depreciation—Trucks		$ 36,000
Land	85,000	
Accounts payable		12,000
Interest payable		4,000
Long-term notes payable		53,000
K. Wilson, Capital		175,000
K. Wilson, Withdrawals	20,000	
Trucking fees earned		130,000
Depreciation expense—Trucks	23,500	
Salaries expense	61,000	
Office supplies expense	8,000	
Repairs expense—Trucks	12,000	
Totals	$410,000	$410,000

Use the information in the adjusted trial balance reported in Exercise 4-4 to prepare Wilson Trucking Company's classified balance sheet as of December 31, 2013.

Exercise 4-5

Preparing a classified balance sheet C3

Check Total assets, $249,500; K. Wilson, Capital, $180,500

Exercise 4-6
Computing the current ratio

A1

Use the information in the adjusted trial balance reported in Exercise 4-4 to compute the current ratio as of the balance sheet date (round the ratio to two decimals). Interpret the current ratio for the Wilson Trucking Company. (Assume that the industry average for the current ratio is 1.5.)

Exercise 4-7
Computing and analyzing the current ratio

A1

Calculate the current ratio in each of the following separate cases (round the ratio to two decimals). Identify the company case with the strongest liquidity position. (These cases represent competing companies in the same industry.)

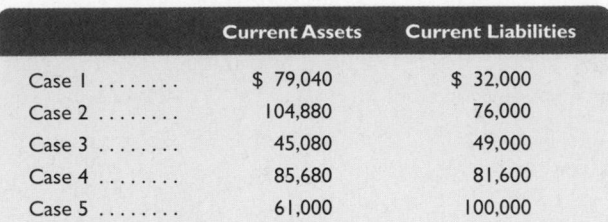

	Current Assets	Current Liabilities
Case 1	$ 79,040	$ 32,000
Case 2	104,880	76,000
Case 3	45,080	49,000
Case 4	85,680	81,600
Case 5	61,000	100,000

Exercise 4-8
Extending adjusted account balances on a work sheet

P1

These 16 accounts are from the Adjusted Trial Balance columns of a company's 10-column work sheet. In the blank space beside each account, write the letter of the appropriate financial statement column (A, B, C, or D) to which a normal account balance is extended.

A. Debit column for the Income Statement columns.

B. Credit column for the Income Statement columns.

C. Debit column for the Balance Sheet and Statement of Owner's Equity columns.

D. Credit column for the Balance Sheet and Statement of Owner's Equity columns.

_____	**1.** Interest Revenue		_____	**9.** Accounts Receivable
_____	**2.** Machinery		_____	**10.** Accumulated Depreciation
_____	**3.** Owner, Withdrawals		_____	**11.** Office Supplies
_____	**4.** Depreciation Expense		_____	**12.** Insurance Expense
_____	**5.** Accounts Payable		_____	**13.** Interest Receivable
_____	**6.** Service Fees Revenue		_____	**14.** Cash
_____	**7.** Owner, Capital		_____	**15.** Rent Expense
_____	**8.** Interest Expense		_____	**16.** Wages Payable

Exercise 4-9
Extending accounts in a work sheet   P1

The Adjusted Trial Balance columns of a 10-column work sheet for Planta Company follow. Complete the work sheet by extending the account balances into the appropriate financial statement columns and by entering the amount of net income for the reporting period.

	A	B	C	D	E	F	G	H	I	J	K	L
1											Balance Sheet and	
2			Unadjusted				Adjusted		Income		Statement of	
3			Trial Balance		Adjustments		Trial Balance		Statement		Owner's Equity	
4	No.	Account Title	Dr.	Cr.	Dr.	Cr.	Dr.	Cr.	Dr.	Cr.	Dr.	Cr.
5	101	Cash					$ 7,000					
6	106	Accounts receivable					27,200					
7	153	Trucks					42,000					
8	154	Accumulated depreciation—Trucks						$ 17,500				
9	183	Land					32,000					
10	201	Accounts payable						15,000				
11	209	Salaries payable						4,200				
12	233	Unearned fees						3,600				
13	301	F. Planta, Capital						65,500				
14	302	F. Planta, Withdrawals					15,400					
15	401	Plumbing fees earned						84,000				
16	611	Depreciation expense—Trucks					6,500					
17	622	Salaries expense					38,000					
18	640	Rent expense					13,000					
19	677	Miscellaneous expenses					8,700					
20		Totals					$189,800	$189,800				
21												

Check Net income, $17,800

Use the following information from the Adjustments columns of a 10-column work sheet to prepare the necessary adjusting journal entries (*a*) through (*e*).

Exercise 4-10
Preparing adjusting entries from a work sheet
P1

	A	B	C	D	E	F	G	H	I	J	K	L
1											Balance Sheet	
2			Unadjusted Trial Balance		Adjustments		Adjusted Trial Balance		Income Statement		and Statement of Owner's Equity	
3												
4	No.	Account Title	Dr.	Cr.	Dr.	Cr.	Dr.	Cr.	Dr.	Cr.	Dr.	Cr.
5	109	Interest receivable			(d) $ 880							
6	124	Office supplies				(b) $1,750						
7	128	Prepaid insurance				(a) 900						
8	164	Accumulated depreciation—Office equipment				(c) 2,200						
9	209	Salaries payable				(e) 560						
10	409	Interest revenue				(d) 880						
11	612	Depreciation expense—Office equipment			(c) 2,200							
12	620	Office salaries expense			(e) 560							
13	636	Insurance expense—Office equipment			(a) 332							
14	637	Insurance expense—Store equipment			(a) 568							
15	650	Office supplies expense			(b) 1,750							
16		Totals			$6,290	$6,290						
17												

These partially completed Income Statement columns from a 10-column work sheet are for Brown's Bike Rental Company. (1) Use the information to determine the amount that should be entered on the net income line of the work sheet. (2) Prepare the company's closing entries. The owner, H. Brown, did not make any withdrawals this period.

Exercise 4-11
Completing the income statement columns and preparing closing entries
P1   P2

Account Title	Debit	Credit
Rent earned		120,000
Salaries expense	46,300	
Insurance expense	7,400	
Office supplies expense	16,000	
Bike repair expense	4,200	
Depreciation expense—Bikes	20,500	
Totals	_____	_____
Net income	_____	_____
Totals	══════	══════

Check   Net income, $25,600

The following unadjusted trial balance contains the accounts and balances of Dylan Delivery Company as of December 31, 2013, its first year of operations.

(1) Use the following information about the company's adjustments to complete a 10-column work sheet.

a. Unrecorded depreciation on the trucks at the end of the year is $40,000.

b. The total amount of accrued interest expense at year-end is $6,000.

c. The cost of unused office supplies still available at the year-end is $2,000.

(2) Prepare the year-end closing entries for this company, and determine the capital amount to be reported on its year-end balance sheet.

Exercise 4-12
Preparing a work sheet and recording closing entries
P1   P2

A		B	C
1		Unadjusted Trial Balance	
2	**Account Title**	**Debit**	**Credit**
3	Cash	$ 16,000	
4	Accounts receivable	34,000	
5	Office supplies	5,000	
6	Trucks	350,000	
7	Accumulated depreciation—Trucks		$ 80,000
8	Land	160,000	
9	Accounts payable		24,000
10	Interest payable		5,000
11	Long-term notes payable		100,000
12	S. Dylan, Capital		307,000
13	S. Dylan, Withdrawals	34,000	
14	Delivery fees earned		263,000
15	Depreciation expense—Truck	40,000	
16	Salaries expense	110,000	
17	Office supplies expense	15,000	
18	Interest expense	5,000	
19	Repairs expense—Trucks	10,000	
20	Totals	$779,000	$779,000
21			

Check Adj. trial balance totals, $820,000; Net income, $39,000

Exercise 4-13^A

Preparing reversing entries

P4

The following two events occurred for Trey Co. on October 31, 2013, the end of its fiscal year.

a. Trey rents a building from its owner for $2,800 per month. By a prearrangement, the company delayed paying October's rent until November 5. On this date, the company paid the rent for both October and November.

b. Trey rents space in a building it owns to a tenant for $850 per month. By prearrangement, the tenant delayed paying the October rent until November 8. On this date, the tenant paid the rent for both October and November.

Required

1. Prepare adjusting entries that the company must record for these events as of October 31.

2. Assuming Trey does *not* use reversing entries, prepare journal entries to record Trey's payment of rent on November 5 and the collection of the tenant's rent on November 8.

3. Assuming that the company uses reversing entries, prepare reversing entries on November 1 and the journal entries to record Trey's payment of rent on November 5 and the collection of the tenant's rent on November 8.

Exercise 4-14^A

Preparing reversing entries

P4

Hawk Company records prepaid assets and unearned revenues in balance sheet accounts. The following information was used to prepare adjusting entries for the company as of August 31, the end of the company's fiscal year.

a. The company has earned $6,000 in service fees that were not yet recorded at period-end.

b. The expired portion of prepaid insurance is $3,700.

c. The company has earned $2,900 of its Unearned Service Fees account balance.

d. Depreciation expense for office equipment is $3,300.

e. Employees have earned but have not been paid salaries of $3,400.

Prepare any necessary reversing entries for the accounting adjustments *a* through *e* assuming that the company uses reversing entries in its accounting system.

Exercise 4-15

Determining effects of closing entries

C1

Capri Company began the current period with a $20,000 credit balance in the K. Capri, Capital account. At the end of the period, the company's adjusted account balances include the following temporary accounts with normal balances.

Service fees earned	$70,000	Interest revenue	$ 7,000
Salaries expense	38,000	K. Capri, Withdrawals	12,000
Depreciation expense	8,000	Utilities expense	4,600

After closing the revenue and expense accounts, what will be the balance of the Income Summary account? After all closing entries are journalized and posted, what will be the balance of the K. Capri, Capital account?

Following are **Nintendo**'s revenue and expense accounts for a recent calendar year (yen in millions). Prepare the company's closing entries for its revenues and its expenses.

Exercise 4-16
Preparing closing entries

P2

Net sales	¥1,014,345
Cost of sales	626,379
Advertising expense	96,359
Other expense, net	213,986

The following data are taken from the unadjusted trial balance of the Westcott Company at December 31, 2013. Each account carries a normal balance and the accounts are shown here in alphabetical order.

Exercise 4-17
Completing a worksheet

P1

Accounts Payable	$ 6	Prepaid Insurance	$18	W. Westcott, Withdrawals ...	$ 6
Accounts Receivable...............	12	Revenue	75	Unearned Revenue	12
Accumulated Depreciation—Equip....	15	Salaries Expense......	18	Utilities Expense	12
Cash............................	21	Supplies	24		
Equipment......................	39	W. Westcott, Capital...	42		

1. Use the data above to prepare a worksheet. Enter the accounts in proper order and enter their balances in the correct debit or credit column.

2. Use the following adjustment information to complete the worksheet.

   a. Depreciation on equipment, $3   **d.** Supplies available at December 31, 2013, $15

   b. Accrued salaries, $6   **e.** Expired insurance, $15

   c. The $12 of unearned revenue has been earned

connect

In the blank space beside each numbered balance sheet item, enter the letter of its balance sheet classification. If the item should not appear on the balance sheet, enter a Z in the blank.

A. Current assets   **D.** Intangible assets   **F.** Long-term liabilities
B. Long-term investments   **E.** Current liabilities   **G.** Equity
C. Plant assets

PROBLEM SET A

Problem 4-1A
Determining balance sheet classifications

C3

    _____ **1.** Long-term investment in stock   _____ **12.** Accumulated depreciation—Trucks
    _____ **2.** Depreciation expense—Building   _____ **13.** Cash
    _____ **3.** Prepaid rent   _____ **14.** Buildings
    _____ **4.** Interest receivable   _____ **15.** Store supplies
    _____ **5.** Taxes payable   _____ **16.** Office equipment
    _____ **6.** Automobiles   _____ **17.** Land (used in operations)
    _____ **7.** Notes payable (due in 3 years)   _____ **18.** Repairs expense
    _____ **8.** Accounts payable   _____ **19.** Office supplies
    _____ **9.** Prepaid insurance   _____ **20.** Current portion of long-term
    _____ **10.** Owner, Capital   note payable
    _____ **11.** Unearned services revenue

On April 1, 2013, Jiro Nozomi created a new travel agency, Adventure Travel. The following transactions occurred during the company's first month.

Problem 4-2A
Applying the accounting cycle

C1 C2 P2 P3

mhhe.com/wildFAP21e

April 1   Nozomi invested $30,000 cash and computer equipment worth $20,000 in the company.
      2   The company rented furnished office space by paying $1,800 cash for the first month's (April) rent.
      3   The company purchased $1,000 of office supplies for cash.
    10   The company paid $2,400 cash for the premium on a 12-month insurance policy. Coverage begins on April 11.
    14   The company paid $1,600 cash for two weeks' salaries earned by employees.
    24   The company collected $8,000 cash on commissions from airlines on tickets obtained for customers.
    28   The company paid $1,600 cash for two weeks' salaries earned by employees.
    29   The company paid $350 cash for minor repairs to the company's computer.
    30   The company paid $750 cash for this month's telephone bill.
    30   Nozomi withdrew $1,500 cash from the company for personal use.

The company's chart of accounts follows:

101	Cash	405	Commissions Earned
106	Accounts Receivable	612	Depreciation Expense—Computer Equip.
124	Office Supplies	622	Salaries Expense
128	Prepaid Insurance	637	Insurance Expense
167	Computer Equipment	640	Rent Expense
168	Accumulated Depreciation—Computer Equip.	650	Office Supplies Expense
209	Salaries Payable	684	Repairs Expense
301	J. Nozomi, Capital	688	Telephone Expense
302	J. Nozomi, Withdrawals	901	Income Summary

Required

Check (3) Unadj. trial balance totals, $58,000

1. Use the balance column format to set up each ledger account listed in its chart of accounts.
2. Prepare journal entries to record the transactions for April and post them to the ledger accounts. The company records prepaid and unearned items in balance sheet accounts.
3. Prepare an unadjusted trial balance as of April 30.
4. Use the following information to journalize and post adjusting entries for the month:

(4a) Dr. Insurance Expense, $133

   a. Two-thirds (or $133) of one month's insurance coverage has expired.
   b. At the end of the month, $600 of office supplies are still available.
   c. This month's depreciation on the computer equipment is $500.
   d. Employees earned $420 of unpaid and unrecorded salaries as of month-end.
   e. The company earned $1,750 of commissions that are not yet billed at month-end.

(5) Net income, $2,197; J. Nozomi, Capital (4/30/2013), $50,697; Total assets, $51,117

5. Prepare the adjusted trial balance as of April 30. Prepare the income statement and the statement of owner's equity for the month of April and the balance sheet at April 30, 2013.

(7) P-C trial balance totals, $51,617

6. Prepare journal entries to close the temporary accounts and post these entries to the ledger.
7. Prepare a post-closing trial balance.

Problem 4-3A

Preparing a work sheet, adjusting and closing entries, and financial statements

C3 P1 P2

The following unadjusted trial balance is for Ace Construction Co. as of the end of its 2013 fiscal year. The June 30, 2012, credit balance of the owner's capital account was $53,660, and the owner invested $35,000 cash in the company during the 2013 fiscal year.

	A	B	C	D
1		**ACE CONSTRUCTION CO.**		
2		**Unadjusted Trial Balance**		
3		**June 30, 2013**		
4	**No.**	**Account Title**	**Debit**	**Credit**
5	101	Cash	$ 18,500	
6	126	Supplies	9,900	
7	128	Prepaid insurance	7,200	
8	167	Equipment	132,000	
9	168	Accumulated depreciation—Equipment		$ 26,250
10	201	Accounts payable		6,800
11	203	Interest payable		0
12	208	Rent payable		0
13	210	Wages payable		0
14	213	Property taxes payable		0
15	251	Long-term notes payable		25,000
16	301	V. Ace, Capital		88,660
17	302	V. Ace, Withdrawals	33,000	
18	401	Construction fees earned		132,100
19	612	Depreciation expense—Equipment	0	
20	623	Wages expense	46,860	
21	633	Interest expense	2,750	
22	637	Insurance expense	0	
23	640	Rent expense	12,000	
24	652	Supplies expense	0	
25	683	Property taxes expense	7,800	
26	684	Repairs expense	2,910	
27	690	Utilities expense	5,890	
28		Totals	$278,810	$278,810
29				

Required

1. Prepare and complete a 10-column work sheet for fiscal year 2013, starting with the unadjusted trial balance and including adjustments based on these additional facts.

   a. The supplies available at the end of fiscal year 2013 had a cost of $3,300.

   b. The cost of expired insurance for the fiscal year is $3,800.

   c. Annual depreciation on equipment is $8,400.

   d. The June utilities expense of $650 is not included in the unadjusted trial balance because the bill arrived after the trial balance was prepared. The $650 amount owed needs to be recorded.

   e. The company's employees have earned $1,800 of accrued wages at fiscal year-end.

   f. The rent expense incurred and not yet paid or recorded at fiscal year-end is $500.

   g. Additional property taxes of $1,000 have been assessed for this fiscal year but have not been paid or recorded in the accounts.

   h. The long-term note payable bears interest at 12% per year. The unadjusted Interest Expense account equals the amount paid for the first 11 months of the 2013 fiscal year. The $250 accrued interest for June has not yet been paid or recorded. (The company is required to make a $5,000 payment toward the note payable during the 2014 fiscal year.)

2. Using information from the completed 10-column work sheet in part 1, journalize the adjusting entries and the closing entries.

3. Prepare the income statement and the statement of owner's equity for the year ended June 30 and the classified balance sheet at June 30, 2013.

Check (3) Total assets, $122,550; Current liabilities, $16,000; Net income, $30,890

Analysis Component

4. Analyze the following separate errors and describe how each would affect the 10-column work sheet. Explain whether the error is likely to be discovered in completing the work sheet and, if not, the effect of the error on the financial statements.

   a. Assume that the adjustment for supplies used consisted of a credit to Supplies and a debit to Supplies Expense for $3,300, when the correct amount was $6,600.

   b. When the adjusted trial balance in the work sheet is completed, assume that the $18,500 Cash balance is incorrectly entered in the Credit column.

The adjusted trial balance of Karise Repairs on December 31, 2013, follows.

Problem 4-4A
Preparing trial balances, closing entries, and financial statements

C3 P2 P3

Sage 50

mhhe.com/wildFAP21e

No.	Account Title	Debit	Credit
	KARISE REPAIRS		
	Adjusted Trial Balance		
	December 31, 2013		
101	Cash	$ 14,000	
124	Office supplies	1,300	
128	Prepaid insurance	2,050	
167	Equipment	50,000	
168	Accumulated depreciation—Equipment		$ 5,000
201	Accounts payable		14,000
210	Wages payable		600
301	C. Karise, Capital		33,000
302	C. Karise, Withdrawals	16,000	
401	Repair fees earned		90,950
612	Depreciation expense—Equipment	5,000	
623	Wages expense	37,500	
637	Insurance expense	800	
640	Rent expense	10,600	
650	Office supplies expense	3,600	
690	Utilities expense	2,700	
	Totals	$143,550	$143,550

Required

1. Prepare an income statement and a statement of owner's equity for the year 2013, and a classified balance sheet at December 31, 2013. There are no owner investments in 2013.

Check (1) Ending capital balance, $47,750; net income, $30,750

(2) P-C trial balance totals,
$67,350

2. Enter the adjusted trial balance in the first two columns of a six-column table. Use columns three and four for closing entry information and the last two columns for a post-closing trial balance. Insert an Income Summary account as the last item in the trial balance.

3. Enter closing entry information in the six-column table and prepare journal entries for it.

Analysis Component

4. Assume for this part only that

    a. None of the $800 insurance expense had expired during the year. Instead, assume it is a prepayment of the next period's insurance protection.

    b. There are no earned and unpaid wages at the end of the year. (*Hint:* Reverse the $600 wages payable accrual.)

Describe the financial statement changes that would result from these two assumptions.

Problem 4-5A
Preparing closing entries,
financial statements, and ratios

C3 A1 P2

Sage 50

The adjusted trial balance for Tybalt Construction as of December 31, 2013, follows.

No.	Account Title	Debit	Credit
	TYBALT CONSTRUCTION		
	Adjusted Trial Balance		
	December 31, 2013		
101	Cash	$ 5,000	
104	Short-term investments	23,000	
126	Supplies	8,100	
128	Prepaid insurance	7,000	
167	Equipment	40,000	
168	Accumulated depreciation—Equipment		$ 20,000
173	Building	150,000	
174	Accumulated depreciation—Building		50,000
183	Land	55,000	
201	Accounts payable		16,500
203	Interest payable		2,500
208	Rent payable		3,500
210	Wages payable		2,500
213	Property taxes payable		900
233	Unearned professional fees		7,500
251	Long-term notes payable		67,000
301	O. Tybalt, Capital		126,400
302	O. Tybalt, Withdrawals	13,000	
401	Professional fees earned		97,000
406	Rent earned		14,000
407	Dividends earned		2,000
409	Interest earned		2,100
606	Depreciation expense—Building	11,000	
612	Depreciation expense—Equipment	6,000	
623	Wages expense	32,000	
633	Interest expense	5,100	
637	Insurance expense	10,000	
640	Rent expense	13,400	
652	Supplies expense	7,400	
682	Postage expense	4,200	
683	Property taxes expense	5,000	
684	Repairs expense	8,900	
688	Telephone expense	3,200	
690	Utilities expense	4,600	
	Totals	$411,900	$411,900

O. Tybalt invested $5,000 cash in the business during year 2013 (the December 31, 2012, credit balance of the O. Tybalt, Capital account was $121,400). Tybalt Construction is required to make a $7,000 payment on its long-term notes payable during 2014.

Required

1. Prepare the income statement and the statement of owner's equity for the calendar year 2013 and the classified balance sheet at December 31, 2013.

2. Prepare the necessary closing entries at December 31, 2013.

3. Use the information in the financial statements to compute these ratios: (*a*) return on assets (total assets at December 31, 2012, was $200,000), (*b*) debt ratio, (*c*) profit margin ratio (use total revenues as the denominator), and (*d*) current ratio. Round ratios to three decimals for parts *a* and *c*, and to two decimals for parts *b* and *d*.

Check (1) Total assets (12/31/2013), $218,100; Net income, $4,300

The following six-column table for Hawkeye Ranges includes the unadjusted trial balance as of December 31, 2013.

Problem 4-6A[A]
Preparing adjusting, reversing, and next period entries

P4

	A	B	C	D	E	F	G
1		HAWKEYE RANGES					
2		December 31, 2013					
3		Unadjusted				Adjusted	
4		Trial Balance		Adjustments		Trial Balance	
5	Account Title	Dr.	Cr.	Dr.	Cr.	Dr.	Cr.
6	Cash	$ 14,000					
7	Accounts receivable	0					
8	Supplies	6,500					
9	Equipment	135,000					
10	Accumulated depreciation—Equipment		$ 30,000				
11	Interest payable		0				
12	Salaries payable		0				
13	Unearned member fees		15,000				
14	Notes payable		75,000				
15	P. Hawkeye, Capital		50,250				
16	P. Hawkeye, Withdrawals	21,125					
17	Member fees earned		42,000				
18	Depreciation expense—Equipment	0					
19	Salaries expense	30,000					
20	Interest expense	5,625					
21	Supplies expense	0					
22	Totals	$212,250	$212,250				
23							

Required

1. Complete the six-column table by entering adjustments that reflect the following information.

   a. As of December 31, 2013, employees had earned $1,200 of unpaid and unrecorded salaries. The next payday is January 4, at which time $1,500 of salaries will be paid.

   b. The cost of supplies still available at December 31, 2013, is $3,000.

   c. The notes payable requires an interest payment to be made every three months. The amount of unrecorded accrued interest at December 31, 2013, is $1,875. The next interest payment, at an amount of $2,250, is due on January 15, 2014.

   d. Analysis of the unearned member fees account shows $5,800 remaining unearned at December 31, 2013.

   e. In addition to the member fees included in the revenue account balance, the company has earned another $9,300 in unrecorded fees that will be collected on January 31, 2014. The company is also expected to collect $10,000 on that same day for new fees earned in January 2014.

   f. Depreciation expense for the year is $15,000.

2. Prepare journal entries for the adjustments entered in the six-column table for part 1.

3. Prepare journal entries to reverse the effects of the adjusting entries that involve accruals.

4. Prepare journal entries to record the cash payments and cash collections described for January.

Check (1) Adjusted trial balance totals, $239,625

PROBLEM SET B

Problem 4-1B
Determining balance sheet classifications

C3

In the blank space beside each numbered balance sheet item, enter the letter of its balance sheet classification. If the item should not appear on the balance sheet, enter a Z in the blank.

A. Current assets
B. Long-term investments
C. Plant assets
D. Intangible assets

E. Current liabilities
F. Long-term liabilities
G. Equity

_____ **1.** Commissions earned
_____ **2.** Interest receivable
_____ **3.** Long-term investment in stock
_____ **4.** Prepaid insurance
_____ **5.** Machinery
_____ **6.** Notes payable (due in 15 years)
_____ **7.** Copyrights
_____ **8.** Current portion of long-term
         note payable
_____ **9.** Accumulated depreciation—Trucks
_____ **10.** Office equipment

_____ **11.** Rent receivable
_____ **12.** Salaries payable
_____ **13.** Income taxes payable
_____ **14.** Owner, Capital
_____ **15.** Office supplies
_____ **16.** Interest payable
_____ **17.** Rent revenue
_____ **18.** Notes receivable (due in 120 days)
_____ **19.** Land (used in operations)
_____ **20.** Depreciation expense—Trucks

Problem 4-2B
Applying the accounting cycle

C1 C2 P2 P3

On July 1, 2013, Lula Plume created a new self-storage business, Safe Storage Co. The following transactions occurred during the company's first month.

July 1 Plume invested $30,000 cash and buildings worth $150,000 in the company.
      2 The company rented equipment by paying $2,000 cash for the first month's (July) rent.
      5 The company purchased $2,400 of office supplies for cash.
     10 The company paid $7,200 cash for the premium on a 12-month insurance policy. Coverage begins on July 11.
     14 The company paid an employee $1,000 cash for two weeks' salary earned.
     24 The company collected $9,800 cash for storage fees from customers.
     28 The company paid $1,000 cash for two weeks' salary earned by an employee.
     29 The company paid $950 cash for minor repairs to a leaking roof.
     30 The company paid $400 cash for this month's telephone bill.
     31 Plume withdrew $2,000 cash from the company for personal use.

The company's chart of accounts follows:

101	Cash		401	Storage Fees Earned
106	Accounts Receivable		606	Depreciation Expense—Buildings
124	Office Supplies		622	Salaries Expense
128	Prepaid Insurance		637	Insurance Expense
173	Buildings		640	Rent Expense
174	Accumulated Depreciation—Buildings		650	Office Supplies Expense
209	Salaries Payable		684	Repairs Expense
301	L. Plume, Capital		688	Telephone Expense
302	L. Plume, Withdrawals		901	Income Summary

Required

1. Use the balance column format to set up each ledger account listed in its chart of accounts.
2. Prepare journal entries to record the transactions for July and post them to the ledger accounts. Record prepaid and unearned items in balance sheet accounts.
3. Prepare an unadjusted trial balance as of July 31.

Check (3) Unadj. trial balance totals, $189,800

4. Use the following information to journalize and post adjusting entries for the month:

   a. Two-thirds of one month's insurance coverage has expired.

   b. At the end of the month, $1,525 of office supplies are still available.

   c. This month's depreciation on the buildings is $1,500.

   d. An employee earned $100 of unpaid and unrecorded salary as of month-end.

   e. The company earned $1,150 of storage fees that are not yet billed at month-end.

5. Prepare the adjusted trial balance as of July 31. Prepare the income statement and the statement of owner's equity for the month of July and the balance sheet at July 31, 2013.

6. Prepare journal entries to close the temporary accounts and post these entries to the ledger.

7. Prepare a post-closing trial balance.

(4*a*) Dr. Insurance Expense, $400

(5) Net income, $2,725; L. Plume, Capital (7/31/2013), $180,725; Total assets, $180,825

(7) P-C trial balance totals, $182,325

The following unadjusted trial balance is for Power Demolition Company as of the end of its April 30, 2013, fiscal year. The April 30, 2012, credit balance of the owner's capital account was $46,900, and the owner invested $40,000 cash in the company during the 2013 fiscal year.

Problem 4-3B
Preparing a work sheet, adjusting and closing entries, and financial statements

C3 P1 P2

	A	B	C	
1		POWER DEMOLITION COMPANY		
2		Unadjusted Trial Balance		
3		April 30, 2013		
4	**No.**	**Account Title**	**Debit**	**Credit**
5	101	Cash	$ 7,000	
6	126	Supplies	16,000	
7	128	Prepaid insurance	12,600	
8	167	Equipment	200,000	
9	168	Accumulated depreciation—Equipment		$ 14,000
10	201	Accounts payable		6,800
11	203	Interest payable		0
12	208	Rent payable		0
13	210	Wages payable		0
14	213	Property taxes payable		0
15	251	Long-term notes payable		30,000
16	301	J. Bonn, Capital		86,900
17	302	J. Bonn, Withdrawals	12,000	
18	401	Demolition fees earned		187,000
19	612	Depreciation expense—Equipment	0	
20	623	Wages expense	41,400	
21	633	Interest expense	3,300	
22	637	Insurance expense	0	
23	640	Rent expense	13,200	
24	652	Supplies expense	0	
25	683	Property taxes expense	9,700	
26	684	Repairs expense	4,700	
27	690	Utilities expense	4,800	
28		Totals	$324,700	$324,700
29				

Required

1. Prepare and complete a 10-column work sheet for fiscal year 2013, starting with the unadjusted trial balance and including adjustments based on these additional facts.

   a. The supplies available at the end of fiscal year 2013 had a cost of $7,900.

   b. The cost of expired insurance for the fiscal year is $10,600.

   c. Annual depreciation on equipment is $7,000.

   d. The April utilities expense of $800 is not included in the unadjusted trial balance because the bill arrived after the trial balance was prepared. The $800 amount owed needs to be recorded.

   e. The company's employees have earned $2,000 of accrued wages at fiscal year-end.

   f. The rent expense incurred and not yet paid or recorded at fiscal year-end is $3,000.

   g. Additional property taxes of $550 have been assessed for this fiscal year but have not been paid or recorded in the accounts.

   h. The long-term note payable bears interest at 12% per year. The unadjusted Interest Expense account equals the amount paid for the first 11 months of the 2013 fiscal year. The $300 accrued interest for April has not yet been paid or recorded. (Note that the company is required to make a $10,000 payment toward the note payable during the 2014 fiscal year.)

Check (3) Total assets, $195,900; current liabilities, $23,450; Net income, $77,550

2. Using information from the completed 10-column work sheet in part 1, journalize the adjusting entries and the closing entries.

3. Prepare the income statement and the statement of owner's equity for the year ended April 30 and the classified balance sheet at April 30, 2013.

Analysis Component

4. Analyze the following separate errors and describe how each would affect the 10-column work sheet. Explain whether the error is likely to be discovered in completing the work sheet and, if not, the effect of the error on the financial statements.

    a. Assume the adjusting entry to reflect expiration of insurance coverage for the period was recorded with a $2,000 credit to Prepaid Insurance and a $2,000 debit to Insurance Expense. The adjustment should have been for $10,600.

    b. When the adjusted trial balance in the work sheet was completed, assume that the $4,700 Repairs Expense account balance is extended to the Debit column of the balance sheet columns.

Problem 4-4B
Preparing trial balances, closing entries, and financial statements

C3 P2 P3

Santo Company's adjusted trial balance on December 31, 2013, follows.

No.	Account Title	Debit	Credit
	SANTO COMPANY Adjusted Trial Balance December 31, 2013		
101	Cash	$ 14,450	
125	Store supplies	5,140	
128	Prepaid insurance	1,200	
167	Equipment	31,000	
168	Accumulated depreciation—Equipment		$ 8,000
201	Accounts payable		1,500
210	Wages payable		2,700
301	P. Santo, Capital		35,650
302	P. Santo, Withdrawals	15,000	
401	Repair fees earned		54,700
612	Depreciation expense—Equipment	2,000	
623	Wages expense	26,400	
637	Insurance expense	600	
640	Rent expense	3,600	
651	Store supplies expense	1,200	
690	Utilities expense	1,960	
	Totals	$102,550	$102,550

Check (1) Ending capital balance, $39,590

(2) P-C trial balance totals, $51,790

Required

1. Prepare an income statement and a statement of owner's equity for the year 2013, and a classified balance sheet at December 31, 2013. There are no owner investments in 2013.

2. Enter the adjusted trial balance in the first two columns of a six-column table. Use the middle two columns for closing entry information and the last two columns for a post-closing trial balance. Insert an Income Summary account (No. 901) as the last item in the trial balance.

3. Enter closing entry information in the six-column table and prepare journal entries for it.

Analysis Component

4. Assume for this part only that

    a. None of the $600 insurance expense had expired during the year. Instead, assume it is a prepayment of the next period's insurance protection.

    b. There are no earned and unpaid wages at the end of the year. (*Hint:* Reverse the $2,700 wages payable accrual.)

Describe the financial statement changes that would result from these two assumptions.

The adjusted trial balance for Anara Co. as of December 31, 2013, follows.

Problem 4-5B
Preparing closing entries,
financial statements, and ratios

C3 A1 P2

No.	Account Title	Debit	Credit
	ANARA COMPANY		
	Adjusted Trial Balance		
	December 31, 2013		
101	Cash	$ 7,400	
104	Short-term investments	11,200	
126	Supplies	4,600	
128	Prepaid insurance	1,000	
167	Equipment	24,000	
168	Accumulated depreciation—Equipment		$ 4,000
173	Building	100,000	
174	Accumulated depreciation—Building		10,000
183	Land	30,500	
201	Accounts payable		3,500
203	Interest payable		1,750
208	Rent payable		400
210	Wages payable		1,280
213	Property taxes payable		3,330
233	Unearned professional fees		750
251	Long-term notes payable		40,000
301	P. Anara, Capital		92,800
302	P. Anara, Withdrawals	8,000	
401	Professional fees earned		59,600
406	Rent earned		4,500
407	Dividends earned		1,000
409	Interest earned		1,320
606	Depreciation expense—Building	2,000	
612	Depreciation expense—Equipment	1,000	
623	Wages expense	18,500	
633	Interest expense	1,550	
637	Insurance expense	1,525	
640	Rent expense	3,600	
652	Supplies expense	1,000	
682	Postage expense	410	
683	Property taxes expense	4,825	
684	Repairs expense	679	
688	Telephone expense	521	
690	Utilities expense	1,920	
	Totals	$224,230	$224,230

P. Anara invested $40,000 cash in the business during year 2013 (the December 31, 2012, credit balance of the P. Anara, Capital account was $52,800). Anara Company is required to make a $8,400 payment on its long-term notes payable during 2014.

Required

1. Prepare the income statement and the statement of owner's equity for the calendar year 2011 and the classified balance sheet at December 31, 2013.

2. Prepare the necessary closing entries at December 31, 2013.

3. Use the information in the financial statements to calculate these ratios: (*a*) return on assets (total assets at December 31, 2012, were $160,000), (*b*) debt ratio, (*c*) profit margin ratio (use total revenues as the denominator), and (*d*) current ratio. Round ratios to three decimals for parts *a* and *c,* and to two decimals for parts *b* and *d.*

Check (1) Total assets (12/31/2013),
$164,700; Net income, $28,890

Problem 4-6B^A

Preparing adjusting, reversing, and next period entries

P4

The following six-column table for Solutions Co. includes the unadjusted trial balance as of December 31, 2013.

	A	B	C	D	E	F	G
1		**SOLUTIONS COMPANY**					
2		**December 31, 2013**					
3		**Unadjusted**				**Adjusted**	
4		**Trial Balance**		**Adjustments**		**Trial Balance**	
5	**Account Title**	**Dr.**	**Cr.**	**Dr.**	**Cr.**	**Dr.**	**Cr.**
6	Cash	$ 10,000					
7	Accounts receivable	0					
8	Supplies	7,600					
9	Machinery	50,000					
10	Accumulated depreciation — Machinery		$ 20,000				
11	Interest payable		0				
12	Salaries payable		0				
13	Unearned rental fees		7,200				
14	Notes payable		30,000				
15	G. Clay, Capital		14,200				
16	G. Clay, Withdrawals	9,500					
17	Rental fees earned		32,450				
18	Depreciation expense — Machinery	0					
19	Salaries expense	24,500					
20	Interest expense	2,250					
21	Supplies expense	0					
22	Totals	$103,850	$103,850				
23							

Required

1. Complete the six-column table by entering adjustments that reflect the following information:

   a. As of December 31, 2013, employees had earned $400 of unpaid and unrecorded wages. The next payday is January 4, at which time $1,200 in wages will be paid.

   b. The cost of supplies still available at December 31, 2013, is $3,450.

   c. The notes payable requires an interest payment to be made every three months. The amount of unrecorded accrued interest at December 31, 2013, is $800. The next interest payment, at an amount of $900, is due on January 15, 2014.

   d. Analysis of the unearned rental fees shows that $3,200 remains unearned at December 31, 2013.

   e. In addition to the machinery rental fees included in the revenue account balance, the company has earned another $2,450 in unrecorded fees that will be collected on January 31, 2014. The company is also expected to collect $5,400 on that same day for new fees earned in January 2014.

Check (1) Adjusted trial balance totals, $111,300

   f. Depreciation expense for the year is $3,800.

2. Prepare journal entries for the adjustments entered in the six-column table for part 1.

3. Prepare journal entries to reverse the effects of the adjusting entries that involve accruals.

4. Prepare journal entries to record the cash payments and cash collections described for January.

SERIAL PROBLEM

Success Systems

P2 P3

Sage 50

(This serial problem began in Chapter 1 and continues through most of the book. If previous chapter segments were not completed, the serial problem can begin at this point. It is helpful, but not necessary, to use the Working Papers that accompany the book.)

SP 4 The December 31, 2013, adjusted trial balance of Success Systems (reflecting its transactions from October through December of 2013) follows.

No.	Account Title	Debit	Credit
101	Cash	$ 58,160	
106	Accounts receivable	5,668	
126	Computer supplies	580	
128	Prepaid insurance	1,665	

[continued on next page]

[continued from previous page]

131	Prepaid rent	825	
163	Office equipment	8,000	
164	Accumulated depreciation—Office equipment		$ 400
167	Computer equipment	20,000	
168	Accumulated depreciation—Computer equipment		1,250
201	Accounts payable		1,100
210	Wages payable		500
236	Unearned computer services revenue		1,500
301	A. Lopez, Capital		83,000
302	A. Lopez, Withdrawals	7,100	
403	Computer services revenue		31,284
612	Depreciation expense—Office equipment	400	
613	Depreciation expense—Computer equipment	1,250	
623	Wages expense	3,875	
637	Insurance expense	555	
640	Rent expense	2,475	
652	Computer supplies expense	3,065	
655	Advertising expense	2,965	
676	Mileage expense	896	
677	Miscellaneous expenses	250	
684	Repairs expense—Computer	1,305	
901	Income summary		0
	Totals	$119,034	$119,034

Required

1. Record and post the necessary closing entries for Success Systems.
2. Prepare a post-closing trial balance as of December 31, 2013.

Check   Post-closing trial balance totals, $94,898

Beyond the Numbers

BTN 4-1   Refer to **Polaris**'s financial statements in Appendix A to answer the following.

REPORTING IN ACTION

C1 P2

Polaris

Required

1. For the year ended December 31, 2011, what amount is credited to Income Summary to summarize its revenues earned?
2. For the year ended December 31, 2011, what amount is debited to Income Summary to summarize its expenses incurred?
3. For the year ended December 31, 2011, what is the balance of its Income Summary account before it is closed?
4. In its statement of cash flows for the year ended December 31, 2011, what amount of cash is paid in dividends to common stockholders?

Fast Forward

5. Access Polaris's annual report for years ending after December 31, 2011, at its Website (**Polaris.com**) or the SEC's EDGAR database (**www.SEC.gov**). How has the amount of net income closed to Income Summary changed in the years ending after December 31, 2011? How has the amount of cash paid as dividends changed in the years ending after December 31, 2011?

BTN 4-2   Key figures for the recent two years of **Polaris** and **Arctic Cat** follow.

Key Figures ($ thousands)	Polaris		Arctic Cat	
	Current Year	Prior Year	Current Year	Prior Year
Current assets	$878,676	$808,145	$232,040	$201,015
Current liabilities	615,531	584,210	87,444	75,320

COMPARATIVE ANALYSIS

A1

Polaris

Arctic Cat

Required

1. Compute the current ratio for both years for both companies.
2. Which company has the better ability to pay short-term obligations according to the current ratio?
3. Analyze and comment on each company's current ratios for the past two years.
4. How do Polaris's and Arctic Cat's current ratios compare to their industry (assumed) average ratio of 2.4?

ETHICS CHALLENGE

C2

BTN 4-3   On January 20, 2013, Tamira Nelson, the accountant for Picton Enterprises, is feeling pressure to complete the annual financial statements. The company president has said he needs up-to-date financial statements to share with the bank on January 21 at a dinner meeting that has been called to discuss Picton's obtaining loan financing for a special building project. Tamira knows that she will not be able to gather all the needed information in the next 24 hours to prepare the entire set of adjusting entries. Those entries must be posted before the financial statements accurately portray the company's performance and financial position for the fiscal period ended December 31, 2012. Tamira ultimately decides to estimate several expense accruals at the last minute. When deciding on estimates for the expenses, she uses low estimates because she does not want to make the financial statements look worse than they are. Tamira finishes the financial statements before the deadline and gives them to the president without mentioning that several account balances are estimates that she provided.

Required

1. Identify several courses of action that Tamira could have taken instead of the one she took.
2. If you were in Tamira's situation, what would you have done? Briefly justify your response.

COMMUNICATING IN PRACTICE

C1   P2

BTN 4-4   Assume that one of your classmates states that a company's books should be ongoing and therefore not closed until that business is terminated. Write a half-page memo to this classmate explaining the concept of the closing process by drawing analogies between (1) a scoreboard for an athletic event and the revenue and expense accounts of a business or (2) a sports team's record book and the capital account. (*Hint:* Think about what would happen if the scoreboard is not cleared before the start of a new game.)

TAKING IT TO THE NET

A1

BTN 4-5   Access **Motley Fool**'s discussion of the current ratio at **Fool.com/School/Valuation/ CurrentAndQuickRatio.htm**. (If the page changed, search that site for the *current ratio*.)

Required

1. What level for the current ratio is generally regarded as sufficient to meet near-term operating needs?
2. Once you have calculated the current ratio for a company, what should you compare it against?
3. What are the implications for a company that has a current ratio that is too high?

TEAMWORK IN ACTION

P1   P2   P3

BTN 4-6   The unadjusted trial balance and information for the accounting adjustments of Noseworthy Investigators follow. Each team member involved in this project is to assume one of the four responsibilities listed. After completing each of these responsibilities, the team should work together to prove the accounting equation utilizing information from teammates (1 and 4). If your equation does not balance, you are to work as a team to resolve the error. The team's goal is to complete the task as quickly and accurately as possible.

Unadjusted Trial Balance		
Account Title	Debit	Credit
Cash	$16,000	
Supplies	12,000	
Prepaid insurance	3,000	
Equipment	25,000	
Accumulated depreciation—Equipment		$ 7,000
Accounts payable		3,000
D. Noseworthy, Capital		34,000
D. Noseworthy, Withdrawals	6,000	
Investigation fees earned		33,000
Rent expense	15,000	
Totals	$77,000	$77,000

Additional Year-End Information

a. Insurance that expired in the current period amounts to $2,200.

b. Equipment depreciation for the period is $4,000.

c. Unused supplies total $5,000 at period-end.

d. Services in the amount of $800 have been provided but have not been billed or collected.

Responsibilities for Individual Team Members

1. Determine the accounts and adjusted balances to be extended to the balance sheet columns of the work sheet for Noseworthy. Also determine total assets and total liabilities.

2. Determine the adjusted revenue account balance and prepare the entry to close this account.

3. Determine the adjusted account balances for expenses and prepare the entry to close these accounts.

4. Prepare T-accounts for both D. Noseworthy, Capital (reflecting the unadjusted trial balance amount) and Income Summary. Prepare the third and fourth closing entries. Ask teammates assigned to parts 2 and 3 for the postings for Income Summary. Obtain amounts to complete the third closing entry and post both the third and fourth closing entries. Provide the team with the ending capital account balance.

5. The entire team should prove the accounting equation using post-closing balances.

BTN 4-7 Review this chapter's opening feature involving Arynetta Floyzelle and her **Girl Team Mobile** business.

1. Explain how a classified balance sheet can help Arynetta Floyzelle know what bills are due when, and whether she has the resources to pay those bills.

2. Why is it important for Arynetta Floyzelle to match costs and revenues in a specific time period? How do closing entries help her in this regard?

3. What objectives are met when Arynetta Floyzelle applies closing procedures each fiscal year-end?

**ENTREPRENEURIAL
DECISION**

A1 C3 P2

BTN 4-8 Select a company that you can visit in person or interview on the telephone. Call ahead to the company to arrange a time when you can interview an employee (preferably an accountant) who helps prepare the annual financial statements. Inquire about the following aspects of its *accounting cycle:*

1. Does the company prepare interim financial statements? What time period(s) is used for interim statements?

2. Does the company use the cash or accrual basis of accounting?

3. Does the company use a work sheet in preparing financial statements? Why or why not?

4. Does the company use a spreadsheet program? If so, which software program is used?

5. How long does it take after the end of its reporting period to complete annual statements?

**HITTING THE
ROAD**

C2

BTN 4-9 **Piaggio (www.Piaggio.com)** manufactures two-, three- and four-wheel vehicles, and is Europe's leading manufacturer of motorcycles and scooters. The following selected information is available from Piaggio's financial statements.

GLOBAL DECISION

A1

PIAGGIO

(Euro thousands)	Current Year	Prior Year
Current assets	509,708	575,897
Current liabilities	644,277	616,166

Required

1. Compute Piaggio's current ratio for both the current year and the prior year.

2. Comment on any change from the prior year to the current year for the current ratio.

ANSWERS TO MULTIPLE CHOICE QUIZ

1. e

2. c

3. a

4. c

5. b

Accounting for Merchandising Operations

5

A Look Back

Chapters 3 and 4 focused on the final steps of the accounting process. We explained the importance of proper revenue and expense recognition and described the adjusting and closing processes. We also prepared financial statements.

A Look at This Chapter

This chapter emphasizes merchandising activities. We explain how reporting merchandising activities differs from reporting service activities. We also analyze and record merchandise purchases and sales transactions, and explain the adjustments and closing process for merchandisers.

A Look Ahead

Chapter 6 extends our analysis of merchandising activities and focuses on the valuation of inventory. Topics include the items in inventory, costs assigned, costing methods used, and inventory estimation techniques.

Learning Objectives

CONCEPTUAL

C1 Describe merchandising activities and identify income components for a merchandising company. (p. 182)

C2 Identify and explain the inventory asset and cost flows of a merchandising company. (p. 183)

ANALYTICAL

A1 Compute the acid-test ratio and explain its use to assess liquidity. (p. 198)

A2 Compute the gross margin ratio and explain its use to assess profitability. (p. 198)

PROCEDURAL

P1 Analyze and record transactions for merchandise purchases using a perpetual system. (p. 184)

P2 Analyze and record transactions for merchandise sales using a perpetual system. (p. 189)

P3 Prepare adjustments and close accounts for a merchandising company. (p. 192)

P4 Define and prepare multiple-step and single-step income statements. (p. 194)

P5 *Appendix 5A*—Record and compare merchandising transactions using both periodic and perpetual inventory systems. (p. 203)

Decision Insight

Faithful Business

"I have a vision, a BIG vision, a HUGE vision!"
—**CHELSEA EUBANK**

ATLANTA—"I have a learning disability," explains Chelsea Eubank. "I went to LD schools and attend Beacon College, the only accredited LD college in America. It will always be with me." However, Chelsea uses her LD as an opportunity. "It [LD] has made me take risks and focus on what my gifts are." Explains Chelsea, "I always tell them that everyone has a talent and everyone has a disability. They just need to figure out what their talent is!"

For Chelsea, her "goal is to create a clothing line that gives to charity and to become a role model for students with challenges." That goal has led her to launch **Faithful Fish (FaithfulFish.com)**. Our mission, explains Chelsea, is to develop a "clothing line that expresses the customers positive values and lifestyle." She adds, "We are offering something that is not in the marketplace."

Still, her start-up was a struggle. "We had to go through our business plan and then . . . give a summary of the company," explains Chelsea. She recalls how the business required a merchandising accounting system to account for purchases and sales transactions and to effectively track merchandise. Inventory was especially important to account for and monitor.

Chelsea admits, "I don't really know what I am doing, so I have made mistakes."

To succeed, Chelsea made smart business decisions. She set up an accounting system to capture and communicate costs and sales information. Tracking merchandising activities was necessary to set prices and to manage discounts, allowances, and returns of both sales and purchases. A perpetual inventory system enabled her to stock the right kind and amount of merchandise and to avoid the costs of out-of-stock and excess inventory. Chelsea stresses that one must "ask people for advice." To help with the accounting for merchandise, Chelsea admits, "I have a financial manager."

Mastering accounting for merchandising is about more than profits and losses—it is a means to an end for Chelsea. "Faithful Fish gives a portion of all sales to charities." Adds Chelsea, "I want Faithful Fish to get big enough that I will be able to give over $1,000,000 a year away!"

[Sources: *Faithful Fish Website,* January 2013; *YHP,* October 2009; *FBEnow.com,* August 2009; *Entrepreneur Girl,* January 2012; *EmbracingBeauty.com,* March 2011]

Buyers of merchandise expect many products, discount prices, inventory on demand, and high quality. This chapter introduces the accounting practices used by companies engaged in merchandising. We show how financial statements reflect merchandising activities and explain the new financial statement items created by merchandising activities. We also analyze and record merchandise purchases and sales, and explain the adjustments and the closing process for these companies.

Accounting for Merchandising Operations

Merchandising Activities	Merchandising Purchases	Merchandising Sales	Accounting Cycle	Financial Statement Formats
• Reporting income • Reporting inventory • Operating cycles • Inventory systems	• Purchase discounts • Purchase returns and allowances • Transportation costs	• Sales of merchandise • Sales discounts • Sales returns and allowances	• Adjusting entries • Preparing financial statements • Closing entries	• Multiple-step income statement • Single-step income statement • Classified balance sheet

MERCHANDISING ACTIVITIES

C1 Describe merchandising activities and identify income components for a merchandising company.

Previous chapters emphasized the accounting and reporting activities of service companies. A merchandising company's activities differ from those of a service company. **Merchandise** consists of products, also called *goods,* that a company acquires to resell to customers. A **merchandiser** earns net income by buying and selling merchandise. Merchandisers are often identified as either wholesalers or retailers. A **wholesaler** is an *intermediary* that buys products from manufacturers or other wholesalers and sells them to retailers or other wholesalers. A **retailer** is an intermediary that buys products from manufacturers or wholesalers and sells them to consumers. Many retailers sell both products and services.

Reporting Income for a Merchandiser

Net income for a merchandiser equals revenues from selling merchandise minus both the cost of merchandise sold to customers and the cost of other expenses for the period, see Exhibit 5.1. The

EXHIBIT 5.1

Computing Income for a Merchandising Company versus a Service Company

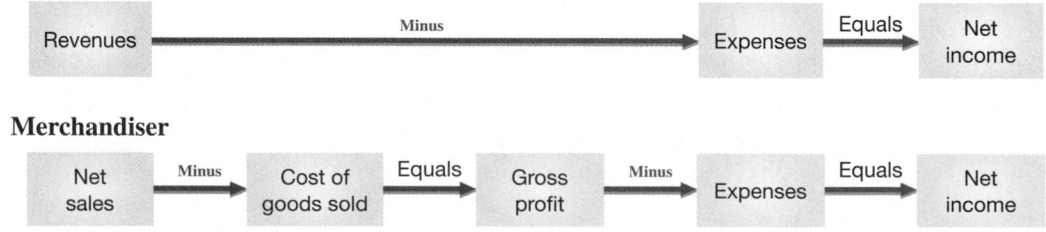

Service Company

Revenues —— Minus ——→ Expenses —— Equals ——→ Net income

Merchandiser

Net sales —— Minus ——→ Cost of goods sold —— Equals ——→ Gross profit —— Minus ——→ Expenses —— Equals ——→ Net income

Point: Fleming, SuperValu, and **SYSCO** are wholesalers. **Aeropostale, Coach, Target,** and **Walmart** are retailers.

usual accounting term for revenues from selling merchandise is *sales,* and the term used for the expense of buying and preparing the merchandise is **cost of goods sold.** (Some service companies use the term *sales* instead of revenues; and cost of goods sold is also called *cost of sales.*)

The income statement for Z-Mart in Exhibit 5.2 illustrates these key components of a merchandiser's net income. The first two lines show that products are acquired at a cost of $230,400 and sold for $314,700. The third line shows an $84,300 **gross profit,** also called

Z-MART Income Statement For Year Ended December 31, 2013	
Net sales	$314,700
Cost of goods sold	**230,400**
Gross profit	**84,300**
Expenses	71,400
Net income	$ 12,900

EXHIBIT 5.2

Merchandiser's Income Statement

gross margin, which equals net sales less cost of goods sold. Additional expenses of $71,400 are reported, which leaves $12,900 in net income.

Reporting Inventory for a Merchandiser

A merchandiser's balance sheet includes a current asset called *merchandise inventory,* an item not on a service company's balance sheet. **Merchandise inventory,** or simply *inventory,* refers to products that a company owns and intends to sell. The cost of this asset includes the cost incurred to buy the goods, ship them to the store, and make them ready for sale.

> **C2** Identify and explain the inventory asset and cost flows of a merchandising company.

Operating Cycle for a Merchandiser

A merchandising company's operating cycle begins by purchasing merchandise and ends by collecting cash from selling the merchandise. The length of an operating cycle differs across the types of businesses. Department stores often have operating cycles of two to five months. Operating cycles for grocery merchants usually range from two to eight weeks. A grocer has more operating cycles in a year than, say, clothing or electronics retailers.

EXHIBIT 5.3

Merchandiser's Operating Cycle

Exhibit 5.3 illustrates an operating cycle for a merchandiser with credit sales. The cycle moves from (*a*) cash purchases of merchandise to (*b*) inventory for sale to (*c*) credit sales to (*d*) accounts receivable to (*e*) cash. Companies try to keep their operating cycles short because assets tied up in inventory and receivables are not productive. Cash sales shorten operating cycles.

Inventory Systems

Cost of goods sold is the cost of merchandise sold to customers during a period. It is often the largest single expense on a merchandiser's income statement. **Inventory** refers to products a company owns and expects to sell in its normal operations. Exhibit 5.4 shows that a company's merchandise available for sale consists of what it begins with (beginning inventory) and what it

EXHIBIT 5.4

Merchandiser's Cost Flow for a Single Time Period

Point: Mathematically, Exhibit 5.4 says
$$BI + NP = MAS,$$
where BI is beginning inventory, NP is net purchases, and MAS is merchandise available for sale. Exhibit 5.4 also says
$$MAS = EI + COGS,$$
which can be rewritten as MAS − EI = COGS or MAS − COGS = EI, where EI is ending inventory and COGS is cost of goods sold. In both equations above, if we know two of the three values, we can solve for the third.

purchases (net purchases). The merchandise available is either sold (cost of goods sold) or kept for future sales (ending inventory).

Two alternative inventory accounting systems can be used to collect information about cost of goods sold and cost of inventory: *perpetual system* or *periodic system*. The **perpetual inventory system** continually updates accounting records for merchandising transactions—specifically, for those records of inventory available for sale and inventory sold. The **periodic inventory system** updates the accounting records for merchandise transactions only at the *end of a period*. Technological advances and competitive pressures have dramatically increased the use of the perpetual system. It gives managers immediate access to detailed information on sales and inventory levels, where they can strategically react to sales trends, cost changes, consumer tastes, and so forth, to increase gross profit. (Some companies use a *hybrid* system where the perpetual system is used for tracking units available and the periodic system is used to compute cost of sales.)

Point: Growth of superstores such as **Costco** and **Sam's** is fueled by efficient use of perpetual inventory. Such large stores evolved only after scannable UPC codes to help control inventory were invented.

Quick Check

Answers — p. 209

1. Describe a merchandiser's cost of goods sold.
2. How do we compute gross profit for a merchandising company?
3. Explain why use of the perpetual inventory system has dramatically increased.

> The following sections, consisting of the next 10 pages on purchasing, selling, and adjusting merchandise, use the perpetual system. Appendix 5A uses the periodic system (with the perpetual results on the side). An instructor can choose to cover either one or both inventory systems.

ACCOUNTING FOR MERCHANDISE PURCHASES

P1 Analyze and record transactions for merchandise purchases using a perpetual system.

The cost of merchandise purchased for resale is recorded in the Merchandise Inventory asset account. To illustrate, Z-Mart records a $1,200 cash purchase of merchandise on November 2 as follows:

Assets = Liabilities + Equity
+1,200
−1,200

Nov. 2	Merchandise Inventory	1,200	
	Cash		1,200
	Purchased merchandise for cash.		

The invoice for this merchandise is shown in Exhibit 5.5. The buyer usually receives the original invoice, and the seller keeps a copy. This *source document* serves as the purchase invoice of Z-Mart (buyer) and the sales invoice for Trex (seller). The amount recorded for merchandise inventory includes its purchase cost, shipping fees, taxes, and any other costs necessary to make it ready for sale. This section explains how we compute the recorded cost of merchandise purchases.

Point: The Merchandise Inventory account reflects the cost of goods available for resale. Costs recorded in Merchandise Inventory are sometimes called *inventoriable costs.*

■ **Decision** Insight

Trade Discounts When a manufacturer or wholesaler prepares a catalog of items it has for sale, it usually gives each item a **list price,** also called a *catalog price.* However, an item's intended *selling price* equals list price minus a given percent called a **trade discount.** The amount of trade discount usually depends on whether a buyer is a wholesaler, retailer, or final consumer. A wholesaler buying in large quantities is often granted a larger discount than a retailer buying in smaller quantities. A buyer records the net amount of list price minus trade discount. For example, in the November 2 purchase of merchandise by Z-Mart, the merchandise was listed in the seller's catalog at $2,000 and Z-Mart received a 40% trade discount. This meant that Z-Mart's purchase price was $1,200, computed as $2,000 − (40% × $2,000). ■

Point: Lowes and **Home Depot** offer trade discounts to construction companies and contractors. Trade discounts help create loyalty among customers.

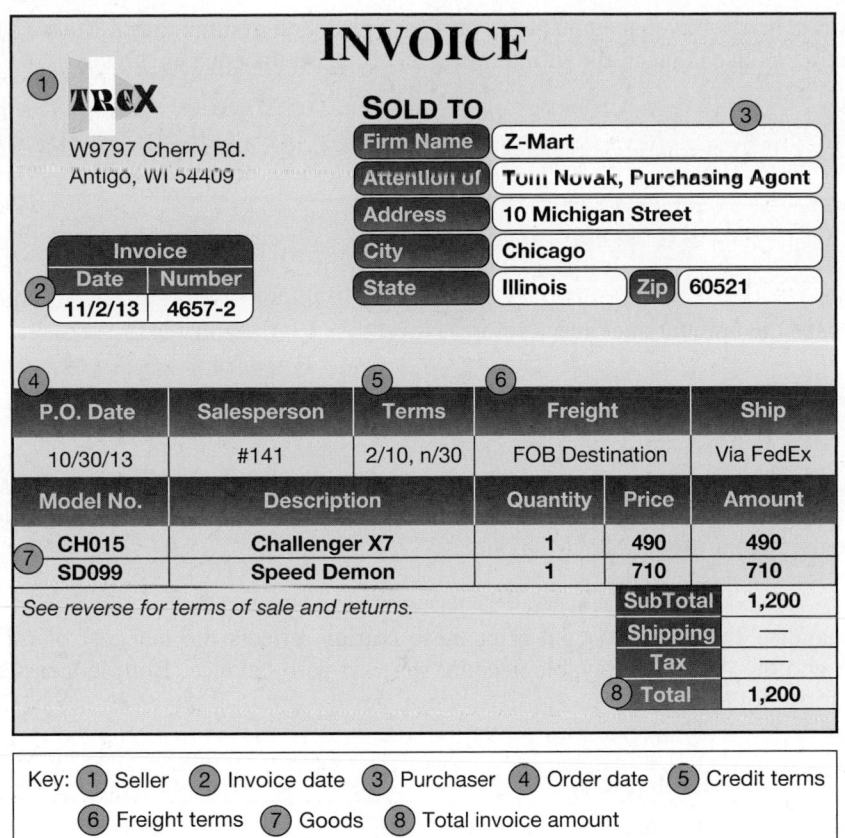

EXHIBIT 5.5

Invoice

Purchase Discounts

The purchase of goods on credit requires a clear statement of expected future payments and dates to avoid misunderstandings. **Credit terms** for a purchase include the amounts and timing of payments from a buyer to a seller. Credit terms usually reflect an industry's practices. To illustrate, when sellers require payment within 10 days after the end of the month of the invoice date, the invoice will show credit terms as "n/10 EOM," which stands for net 10 days after end of month (**EOM**). When sellers require payment within 30 days after the invoice date, the invoice shows credit terms of "n/30," which stands for *net 30 days*.

Exhibit 5.6 portrays credit terms. The amount of time allowed before full payment is due is called the **credit period.** Sellers can grant a **cash discount** to encourage buyers to pay earlier. A buyer views a cash discount as a **purchase discount.** A seller views a cash discount as a **sales discount.** Any cash discounts are described in the credit terms on the invoice. For example, credit terms of "2/10, n/60" mean that full payment is due within a 60-day credit period, but the buyer can deduct 2% of the invoice amount if payment is made within 10 days of the invoice date. This reduced payment applies only for the **discount period.**

Point: Since both the buyer and seller know the invoice date, this date is used in setting the discount and credit periods.

EXHIBIT 5.6

Credit Terms

Point: Appendix 5A repeats journal entries *a* through *f* using a periodic inventory system.

To illustrate how a buyer accounts for a purchase discount, assume that Z-Mart's $1,200 purchase of merchandise is on credit with terms of 2/10, n/30. Its entry is

Assets = Liabilities + Equity
+1,200   +1,200

(a) Nov. 2	Merchandise Inventory	1,200	
	Accounts Payable		1,200
	Purchased merchandise on credit, invoice		
	dated Nov. 2, terms 2/10, n/30.		

If Z-Mart pays the amount due on (or before) November 12, the entry is

Assets = Liabilities + Equity
−24   −1,200
−1,176

(b) Nov. 12	Accounts Payable	1,200	
	Merchandise Inventory		24
	Cash		1,176
	Paid for the $1,200 purchase of Nov. 2 less the		
	discount of $24 (2% × $1,200).		

Point: These entries illustrate what is called the *gross method* of accounting for purchases with discount terms.

The Merchandise Inventory account after these entries reflects the net cost of merchandise purchased, and the Accounts Payable account shows a zero balance. Both ledger accounts, in T-account form, follow:

Merchandise Inventory					Accounts Payable			
Nov. 2	1,200	Nov. 12	24		Nov. 12	1,200	Nov. 2	1,200
Balance	1,176						Balance	0

A buyer's failure to pay within a discount period can be expensive. To illustrate, if Z-Mart does not pay within the 10-day 2% discount period, it can delay payment by 20 more days. This delay costs Z-Mart $24, computed as 2% × $1,200. Most buyers take advantage of a purchase discount because of the usually high interest rate implied from not taking it.[1] Also, good cash management means that no invoice is paid until the last day of the discount or credit period.

■ Decision Maker

Entrepreneur   You purchase a batch of products on terms of 3/10, n/90, but your company has limited cash and you must borrow funds at an 11% annual rate if you are to pay within the discount period. Is it to your advantage to take the purchase discount? Explain. ■   [Answer—p. 208]

Purchase Returns and Allowances

Purchase returns refer to merchandise a buyer acquires but then returns to the seller. A *purchase allowance* is a reduction in the cost of defective or unacceptable merchandise that a buyer acquires. Buyers often keep defective but still marketable merchandise if the seller grants an acceptable allowance. When a buyer returns or takes an allowance on merchandise, the buyer issues a **debit memorandum** to inform the seller of a debit made to the seller's account payable in the buyer's records.

Point: The sender (maker) of a *debit memorandum* will debit the account payable of the memo's receiver. The memo's receiver will credit the sender's account receivable.

---

[1] The *implied annual interest rate* formula is:

[365 days ÷ (Credit period − Discount period)] × Cash discount rate.

For terms of 2/10, n/30, missing the 2% discount for an additional 20 days is equal to an annual interest rate of 36.5%, computed as [365 days/(30 days − 10 days)] × 2% discount rate. *Favorable purchase discounts* are those with implied annual interest rates that exceed the purchaser's annual rate for borrowing money.

Purchase Allowances   To illustrate purchase allowances, assume that on November 15, Z-Mart (buyer) issues a $300 debit memorandum for an allowance from Trex for defective merchandise. Z-Mart's November 15 entry to update its Merchandise Inventory account to reflect the purchase allowance is

(c) Nov. 15	Accounts Payable..............................	300	
	Merchandise Inventory		300
	Allowance for defective merchandise.		

Assets = Liabilities + Equity
−300   −300

The buyer's allowance for defective merchandise is usually offset against the buyer's current account payable balance to the seller. When cash is refunded, the Cash account is debited instead of Accounts Payable.

Purchase Returns   Returns are recorded at the net costs charged to buyers. To illustrate the accounting for returns, suppose Z-Mart purchases $1,000 of merchandise on June 1 with terms 2/10, n/60. Two days later, Z-Mart returns $100 of goods before paying the invoice. When Z-Mart later pays on June 11, it takes the 2% discount only on the $900 remaining balance. When goods are returned, a buyer can take a purchase discount on only the remaining balance of the invoice. The resulting discount is $18 (2% × $900) and the cash payment is $882 ($900 − $18). The following entries reflect this illustration.

Point: In the perpetual system, all purchases, purchase discounts, purchase returns, and cost of sales are recorded in the Merchandise Inventory account. This is different from the periodic system as explained in Appendix 5A.

June 1	Merchandise Inventory	1,000	
	Accounts Payable		1,000
	Purchased merchandise, invoice dated June 1,		
	terms 2/10, n/60.		
June 3	Accounts Payable..............................	100	
	Merchandise Inventory		100
	Returned merchandise to seller.		
June 11	Accounts Payable..............................	900	
	Merchandise Inventory		18
	Cash		882
	Paid for $900 merchandise ($1,000 − $100)		
	less $18 discount (2% × $900).		

Example: Assume Z-Mart pays $980 cash for $1,000 of merchandise purchased within its 2% discount period. Later, it returns $100 of the original $1,000 merchandise. The return entry is
Cash 98
    Merchandise Inventory 98

 Decision Ethics ▬▬▬▬▬▬▬▬▬▬▬▬▬▬▬▬▬▬▬▬▬▬▬▬▬

Payables Manager   As a new accounts payable manager, you are being trained by the outgoing manager. She explains that the system prepares checks for amounts net of favorable cash discounts, and the checks are dated the last day of the discount period. She also tells you that checks are not mailed until five days later, adding that "the company gets free use of cash for an extra five days, and our department looks better. When a supplier complains, we blame the computer system and the mailroom." Do you continue this payment policy? ■ [Answer—p. 208]

Transportation Costs and Ownership Transfer

The buyer and seller must agree on who is responsible for paying any freight costs and who bears the risk of loss during transit for merchandising transactions. This is essentially the same as asking at what point ownership transfers from the seller to the buyer. The point of transfer is called the **FOB** (*free on board*) point, which determines who pays transportation costs (and often other incidental costs of transit such as insurance).

Exhibit 5.7 identifies two alternative points of transfer. (1) *FOB shipping point,* also called *FOB factory,* means the buyer accepts ownership when the goods depart the seller's place of business. The buyer is then responsible for paying shipping costs and bearing the risk of damage or loss when goods are in transit. The goods are part of the buyer's inventory when they are in transit since ownership has transferred to the buyer. **1-800-FLOWERS.COM**, a floral and gift

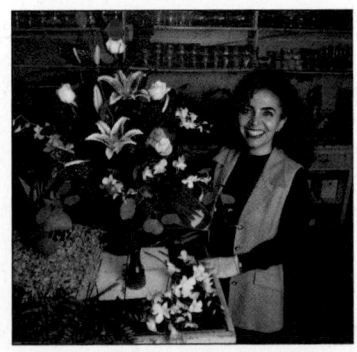

EXHIBIT 5.7

Ownership Transfer and
Transportation Costs

Seller		Buyer
Shipping point	Carrier	Destination

	Ownership Transfers When Goods Passed to	Transportation Costs Paid by
FOB shipping point	Carrier	**Buyer** Merchandise Inventory... # Cash .... #
FOB destination	Buyer	**Seller** Delivery Expense .... # Cash .... #

Point: If we place an order online and receive free shipping, we have terms FOB destination.

Point: The party not responsible for shipping costs sometimes pays the carrier. In these cases, the party paying these costs either bills the party responsible or, more commonly, adjusts its account payable or account receivable with the other party. For example, a buyer paying a carrier when terms are FOB destination can decrease its account payable to the seller by the amount of shipping cost.

merchandiser, and **Bare Escentuals**, a cosmetic manufacturer, both use FOB shipping point. (2) *FOB destination* means ownership of goods transfers to the buyer when the goods arrive at the buyer's place of business. The seller is responsible for paying shipping charges and bears the risk of damage or loss in transit. The seller does not record revenue from this sale until the goods arrive at the destination because this transaction is not complete before that point. **Kyocera**, a manufacturer, uses FOB destination.

Z-Mart's $1,200 purchase on November 2 is on terms of FOB destination. This means Z-Mart is not responsible for paying transportation costs. When a buyer is responsible for paying transportation costs, the payment is made to a carrier or directly to the seller depending on the agreement. The cost principle requires that any necessary transportation costs of a buyer (often called *transportation-in* or *freight-in*) be included as part of the cost of purchased merchandise. To illustrate, Z-Mart's entry to record a $75 freight charge from an independent carrier for merchandise purchased FOB shipping point is

Assets = Liabilities + Equity
+75
−75

(d) Nov. 24	Merchandise Inventory	75	
	Cash		75
	Paid freight costs on purchased merchandise.		

A seller records the costs of shipping goods to customers in a Delivery Expense account when the seller is responsible for these costs. Delivery Expense, also called *transportation-out* or *freight-out,* is reported as a selling expense in the seller's income statement.

In summary, purchases are recorded as debits to Merchandise Inventory. Any later purchase discounts, returns, and allowances are credited (decreases) to Merchandise Inventory. Transportation-in is debited (added) to Merchandise Inventory. Z-Mart's itemized costs of merchandise purchases for year 2013 are in Exhibit 5.8.

Point: With *tracking numbers* it is possible to know the exact time shipped goods arrive at their destination.

EXHIBIT 5.8

Itemized Costs of
Merchandise Purchases

Z-MART **Itemized Costs of Merchandise Purchases** **For Year Ended December 31, 2013**	
Invoice cost of merchandise purchases	$235,800
Less: Purchase discounts received	(4,200)
Purchase returns and allowances	(1,500)
Add: Costs of transportation-in	2,300
Total cost of merchandise purchases	**$232,400**

Point: Some companies have separate accounts for purchase discounts, returns and allowances, and transportation-in. These accounts are then transferred to Merchandise Inventory at period-end. This is a *hybrid system* of perpetual and periodic. That is, Merchandise Inventory is updated on a perpetual basis but only for purchases and cost of goods sold.

The accounting system described here does not provide separate records (accounts) for total purchases, total purchase discounts, total purchase returns and allowances, and total transportation-in. Yet nearly all companies collect this information in supplementary records because managers need this information to evaluate and control each of these cost elements. **Supplementary records,** also called *supplemental records,* refer to information outside the usual general ledger accounts.

4. How long are the credit and discount periods when credit terms are 2/10, n/60?

5. Identify which items are subtracted from the *list* amount and not recorded when computing purchase price: (*a*) freight-in; (*b*) trade discount; (*c*) purchase discount; (*d*) purchase return.

6. What does *FOB* mean? What does *FOB destination* mean?

ACCOUNTING FOR MERCHANDISE SALES

Merchandising companies also must account for sales, sales discounts, sales returns and allowances, and cost of goods sold. A merchandising company such as Z-Mart reflects these items in its gross profit computation, as shown in Exhibit 5.9. This section explains how this information is derived from transactions.

P2 Analyze and record transactions for merchandise sales using a perpetual system.

EXHIBIT 5.9

Gross Profit Computation

Z-MART Computation of Gross Profit For Year Ended December 31, 2013		
Sales.		$321,000
Less: Sales discounts	$4,300	
Sales returns and allowances	2,000	6,300
Net sales		314,700
Cost of goods sold		230,400
Gross profit		**$ 84,300**

Sales of Merchandise

Each sales transaction for a seller of merchandise involves two parts.

1. Revenue received in the form of an asset from the customer.
2. Cost recognized for the merchandise sold to the customer.

Accounting for a sales transaction under the perpetual system requires recording information about both parts. This means that each sales transaction for merchandisers, whether for cash or on credit, requires *two entries:* one for revenue and one for cost. To illustrate, Z-Mart sold $2,400 of merchandise on credit on November 3. The revenue part of this transaction is recorded as

(e) Nov. 3	Accounts Receivable	2,400	
	Sales		2,400
	Sold merchandise on credit.		

Assets = Liabilities + Equity
+2,400   +2,400

This entry reflects an increase in Z-Mart's assets in the form of accounts receivable. It also shows the increase in revenue (Sales). If the sale is for cash, the debit is to Cash instead of Accounts Receivable.

The cost part of each sales transaction ensures that the Merchandise Inventory account under a perpetual inventory system reflects the updated cost of the merchandise available for sale. For example, the cost of the merchandise Z-Mart sold on November 3 is $1,600, and the entry to record the cost part of this sales transaction is

(e) Nov. 3	Cost of Goods Sold	1,600	
	Merchandise Inventory		1,600
	To record the cost of Nov. 3 sale.		

Assets = Liabilities + Equity
−1,600   −1,600

■ Decision Insight ●━━━━━━━━━━━━━━━━━━━━━━━━━━━

Suppliers and Demands Large merchandising companies often bombard suppliers with demands. These include discounts for bar coding and technology support systems, and fines for shipping errors. Merchandisers' goals are to reduce inventories, shorten lead times, and eliminate errors. Many colleges now offer programs in supply chain management and logistics to train future employees that can help merchandisers meet such goals. ■

Sales Discounts

Sales discounts on credit sales can benefit a seller by decreasing the delay in receiving cash and reducing future collection efforts. At the time of a credit sale, a seller does not know whether a customer will pay within the discount period and take advantage of a discount. This means the seller usually does not record a sales discount until a customer actually pays within the discount period. To illustrate, Z-Mart completes a credit sale for $1,000 on November 12 with terms of 2/10, n/60. The entry to record the revenue part of this sale is

Point: Radio-frequency identification (RFID) tags attach to objects for tracking purposes. Such tags help find items in a store, monitor shipments, and help check on production progress.

Assets = Liabilities + Equity
+1,000   +1,000

Nov. 12	Accounts Receivable	1,000	
	Sales		1,000
	Sold merchandise under terms of 2/10, n/60.		

This entry records the receivable and the revenue as if the customer will pay the full amount. The customer has two options, however. One option is to wait 60 days until January 11 and pay the full $1,000. In this case, Z-Mart records that payment as

Assets = Liabilities + Equity
+1,000
−1,000

Jan. 11	Cash	1,000	
	Accounts Receivable		1,000
	Received payment for Nov. 12 sale.		

The customer's second option is to pay $980 within a 10-day period ending November 22. If the customer pays on (or before) November 22, Z-Mart records the payment as

Assets = Liabilities + Equity
+980   −20
−1,000

Nov. 22	Cash	980	
	Sales Discounts	20	
	Accounts Receivable		1,000
	Received payment for Nov. 12 sale less discount.		

Sales Discounts is a contra revenue account, meaning the Sales Discounts account is deducted from the Sales account when computing a company's net sales (see Exhibit 5.9). Management monitors Sales Discounts to assess the effectiveness and cost of its discount policy.

Sales Returns and Allowances

Point: Published income statements rarely disclose sales discounts, returns and allowances.

Sales returns refer to merchandise that customers return to the seller after a sale. Many companies allow customers to return merchandise for a full refund. *Sales allowances* refer to reductions in the selling price of merchandise sold to customers. This can occur with damaged or defective merchandise that a customer is willing to purchase with a decrease in selling price. Sales returns and allowances usually involve dissatisfied customers and the possibility of lost future sales, and managers monitor information about returns and allowances.

Sales Returns To illustrate, recall Z-Mart's sale of merchandise on November 3 for $2,400 that had cost $1,600. Assume that the customer returns part of the merchandise on

November 6, and the returned items sell for $800 and cost $600. The revenue part of this transaction must reflect the decrease in sales from the customer's return of merchandise as follows:

(f) Nov. 6	Sales Returns and Allowances	800	
	Accounts Receivable		800
	Customer returns merchandise of Nov. 3 sale.		

Assets = Liabilities + Equity
−800   −800

If the merchandise returned to Z-Mart is not defective and can be resold to another customer, Z-Mart returns these goods to its inventory. The entry to restore the cost of such goods to the Merchandise Inventory account is

Nov. 6	Merchandise Inventory	600	
	Cost of Goods Sold		600
	Returned goods added to inventory.		

Assets = Liabilities + Equity
+600   +600

This entry changes if the goods returned are defective. In this case the returned inventory is re-corded at its estimated value, not its cost. To illustrate, if the goods (costing $600) returned to Z-Mart are defective and estimated to be worth $150, the following entry is made: Dr. Merchan-dise Inventory for $150, Dr. Loss from Defective Merchandise for $450, and Cr. Cost of Goods Sold for $600.

Point: Some sellers charge buyers a re-stocking fee for returns.

Decision Insight

Reversing Returns.   On May 3, 2011, **Green Mountain Coffee Roasters** beat analysts' earnings estimates by $0.10 per share for the 13-week period ended March 26, 2011. The next day the stock price rose $11.91 per share to close at $75.98 per share, an 18.5% increase over the prior day's closing price. In the weeks that followed, some analysts raised questions about the quality of Green Mountain's earnings because of its ac-counting for sales returns. They allege that a large part of that earnings increase was due to an accounting adjustment that reversed much of a reserve that was set up for sales returns in prior periods. ■

Sales Allowances   To illustrate sales allowances, assume that $800 of the merchandise Z-Mart sold on November 3 is defective but the buyer decides to keep it because Z-Mart of-fers a $100 price reduction. Z-Mart records this allowance as follows:

Nov. 6	Sales Returns and Allowances	100	
	Accounts Receivable		100
	To record sales allowance on Nov. 3 sale.		

Assets = Liabilities + Equity
−100   −100

The seller usually prepares a credit memorandum to confirm a buyer's return or allowance. A seller's **credit memorandum** informs a buyer of the seller's credit to the buyer's Account Re-ceivable (on the seller's books).

Point: The sender (maker) of a credit memorandum will *credit* the account of the receiver. The receiver of a credit memorandum will *debit* the sender's account.

Quick Check   Answers — p. 209

7. Why are sales discounts and sales returns and allowances recorded in contra revenue accounts instead of directly in the Sales account?

8. Under what conditions are two entries necessary to record a sales return?

9. When merchandise is sold on credit and the seller notifies the buyer of a price allowance, does the seller create and send a credit memorandum or a debit memorandum?

COMPLETING THE ACCOUNTING CYCLE

Exhibit 5.10 shows the flow of merchandising costs during a period and where these costs are reported at period-end. Specifically, beginning inventory plus the net cost of purchases is the merchandise available for sale. As inventory is sold, its cost is recorded in cost of goods sold on the income statement; what remains is ending inventory on the balance sheet. A period's ending inventory is the next period's beginning inventory.

EXHIBIT 5.10

Merchandising Cost Flow in the Accounting Cycle

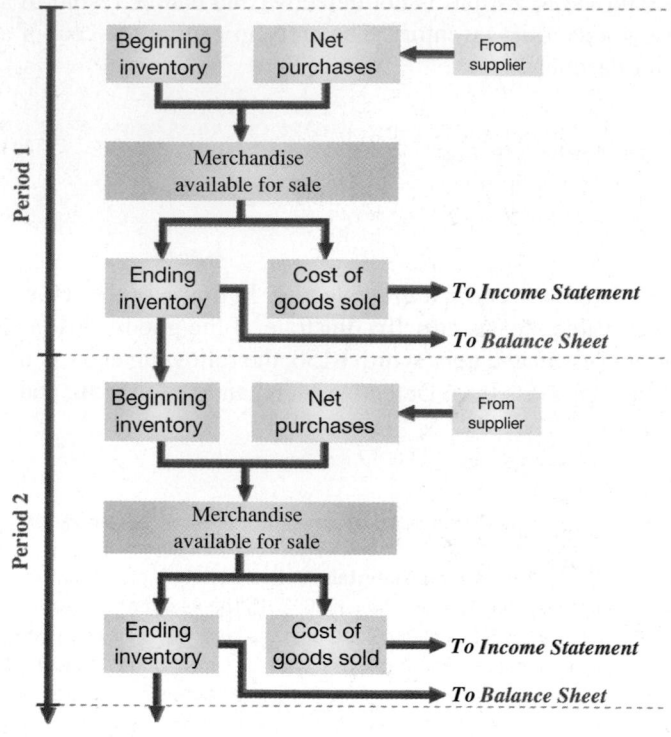

Adjusting Entries for Merchandisers

> **P3** Prepare adjustments and close accounts for a merchandising company.

Each of the steps in the accounting cycle described in the prior chapter for a service company applies to a merchandiser. This section and the next two further explain three steps of the accounting cycle for a merchandiser—adjustments, statement preparation, and closing.

Adjusting entries are generally the same for merchandising companies and service companies, including those for prepaid expenses (including depreciation), accrued expenses, unearned revenues, and accrued revenues. However, a merchandiser using a perpetual inventory system is usually required to make another adjustment to update the Merchandise Inventory account to reflect any loss of merchandise, including theft and deterioration. **Shrinkage** is the term used to refer to the loss of inventory and it is computed by comparing a physical count of inventory with recorded amounts. A physical count is usually performed at least annually.

To illustrate, Z-Mart's Merchandise Inventory account at the end of year 2013 has a balance of $21,250, but a physical count reveals that only $21,000 of inventory exists. The adjusting entry to record this $250 shrinkage is

Point: About two-thirds of shoplifting losses are thefts by employees.

Assets = Liabilities + Equity
−250   −250

Dec. 31	Cost of Goods Sold	250	
	Merchandise Inventory		250
	To adjust for $250 shrinkage revealed by a physical count of inventory.		

Preparing Financial Statements

The financial statements of a merchandiser, and their preparation, are similar to those for a service company described in Chapters 2 through 4. The income statement mainly differs by the inclusion of *cost of goods sold* and *gross profit*. Also, net sales is affected by discounts, returns, and allowances, and some additional expenses are possible such as delivery expense and loss from defective merchandise. The balance sheet mainly differs by the inclusion of *merchandise inventory* as part of current assets. The statement of owner's equity is unchanged. A work sheet can be used to help prepare these statements, and one is illustrated in Appendix 5B for Z-Mart.

Point: Staples's costs of shipping merchandise to its stores is included in its costs of inventories as required by the cost principle.

Closing Entries for Merchandisers

Closing entries are similar for service companies and merchandising companies using a perpetual system. The difference is that we must close some new temporary accounts that arise from merchandising activities. Z-Mart has several temporary accounts unique to merchandisers: Sales (of goods), Sales Discounts, Sales Returns and Allowances, and Cost of Goods Sold. Their existence in the ledger means that the first two closing entries for a merchandiser are slightly different from the ones described in the prior chapter for a service company. These differences are set in **red boldface** in the closing entries of Exhibit 5.11.

Point: The Inventory account is not affected by the closing process under a perpetual system.

EXHIBIT 5.11

Closing Entries for a Merchandiser

Step 1: Close Credit Balances in Temporary Accounts to Income Summary.

Dec. 31	Sales	321,000	
	Income Summary		321,000
	To close credit balances in temporary accounts.		

Step 2: Close Debit Balances in Temporary Accounts to Income Summary.

Dec. 31	Income Summary	308,100	
	Sales Discounts		**4,300**
	Sales Returns and Allowances		**2,000**
	Cost of Goods Sold		**230,400**
	Depreciation Expense		3,700
	Salaries Expense		43,800
	Insurance Expense		600
	Rent Expense		9,000
	Supplies Expense		3,000
	Advertising Expense		11,300
	To close debit balances in temporary accounts.		

Step 3: Close Income Summary to Owner's Capital.

The third closing entry is identical for a merchandising company and a service company. The $12,900 amount is net income reported on the income statement.

Dec. 31	Income Summary	12,900	
	K. Marty, Capital		12,900
	To close the Income Summary account.		

Step 4: Close Withdrawals Account to Owner's Capital.

The fourth closing entry is identical for a merchandising company and a service company. It closes the Withdrawals account and adjusts the Owner's Capital account to the amount shown on the balance sheet.

Dec. 31	K. Marty, Capital	4,000	
	K. Marty, Withdrawals		4,000
	To close the Withdrawals account.		

Summary of Merchandising Entries

Exhibit 5.12 summarizes the key adjusting and closing entries of a merchandiser (using a perpetual inventory system) that are different from those of a service company described in prior chapters (the Demonstration Problem 2 illustrates these merchandising entries).

EXHIBIT 5.12

Summary of Merchandising Entries

Merchandising Transactions		Merchandising Entries	Dr.	Cr.
Purchases	Purchasing merchandise for resale.	Merchandise Inventory .... Cash or Accounts Payable	#	#
	Paying freight costs on purchases; FOB shipping point.	Merchandise Inventory .... Cash	#	#

	Paying within discount period.	Accounts Payable ....
		    Merchandise Inventory ....
		    Cash ....
			#	#
				#

	Recording purchase returns or allowances.	Cash or Accounts Payable............. Merchandise Inventory	#	#
Sales	Selling merchandise.	Cash or Accounts Receivable .... Sales	#	#
		Cost of Goods Sold .... Merchandise Inventory	#	#
	Receiving payment within discount period.	Cash .... Sales Discounts .... Accounts Receivable	# #	#
	Granting sales returns or allowances.	Sales Returns and Allowances........... Cash or Accounts Receivable	#	#
		Merchandise Inventory .... Cost of Goods Sold	#	#
	Paying freight costs on sales; FOB destination.	Delivery Expense .... Cash	#	#

Merchandising Events		Adjusting and Closing Entries		
Adjusting	Adjusting due to shrinkage (occurs when recorded amount larger than physical inventory).	Cost of Goods Sold .... Merchandise Inventory	#	#
Closing	Closing temporary accounts with credit balances.	Sales .... Income Summary	#	#

	Closing temporary accounts with debit balances.	Income Summary ....
		    Sales Returns and Allowances ....
		    Sales Discounts ....
		    Cost of Goods Sold ....
		    Delivery Expense ....
		    "Other Expenses" ....
			#	#
				#
				#
				#
				#

Quick Check

Answers — p. 209

10. When a merchandiser uses a perpetual inventory system, why is it sometimes necessary to adjust the Merchandise Inventory balance with an adjusting entry?

11. What temporary accounts do you expect to find in a merchandising business but not in a service business?

12. Describe the closing entries normally made by a merchandising company.

FINANCIAL STATEMENT FORMATS

P4 Define and prepare multiple-step and single-step income statements.

Generally accepted accounting principles do not require companies to use any one presentation format for financial statements so we see many different formats in practice. This section describes two common income statement formats: multiple-step and single-step. The classified balance sheet of a merchandiser is also explained.

Multiple-Step Income Statement

A **multiple-step income statement** format shows detailed computations of net sales and other costs and expenses, and reports subtotals for various classes of items. Exhibit 5.13 shows a multiple-step income statement for Z-Mart. The statement has three main parts: (1) *gross profit,* determined by net sales less cost of goods sold, (2) *income from operations,* determined by gross profit less operating expenses, and (3) *net income,* determined by income from operations adjusted for nonoperating items.

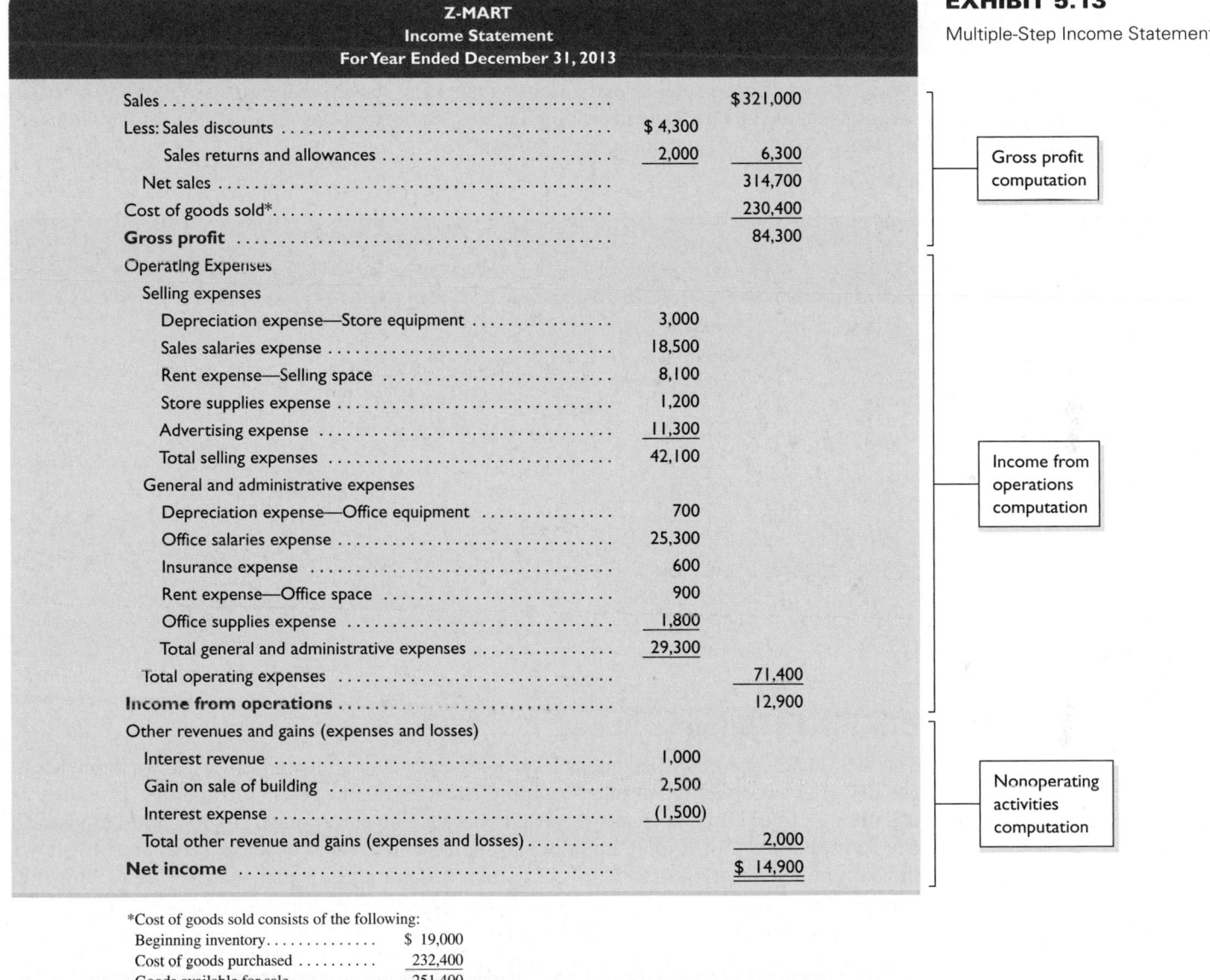

EXHIBIT 5.13

Multiple-Step Income Statement

*Cost of goods sold consists of the following:

Beginning inventory	$ 19,000
Cost of goods purchased	232,400
Goods available for sale	251,400
Less ending inventory	21,000
Cost of goods sold	$230,400

Operating expenses are classified into two sections. **Selling expenses** include the expenses of promoting sales by displaying and advertising merchandise, making sales, and delivering goods to customers. **General and administrative expenses** support a company's overall operations and include expenses related to accounting, human resource management, and financial management. Expenses are allocated between sections when they contribute to more than one. Z-Mart allocates rent expense of $9,000 from its store building between two sections: $8,100 to selling expense and $900 to general and administrative expense.

Nonoperating activities consist of other expenses, revenues, losses, and gains that are unrelated to a company's operations. *Other revenues and gains* commonly include interest revenue,

Point: Z-Mart did not have any non-operating activities; however, Exhibit 5.13 includes some for illustrative purposes.

Point: Many companies report interest expense and interest revenue in separate categories after operating income and before subtracting income tax expense. As one example, see **Arctic Cat's** and **KTM's** income statements in Appendix A.

Example: Sometimes interest revenue and interest expense are reported on the income statement as *interest, net.* To illustrate, if a company has $1,000 of interest expense and $600 of interest revenue, it might report $400 as *interest, net.*

dividend revenue, rent revenue, and gains from asset disposals. *Other expenses and losses* commonly include interest expense, losses from asset disposals, and casualty losses. When a company has no reportable nonoperating activities, its income from operations is simply labeled net income.

Single-Step Income Statement

A **single-step income statement** is another widely used format and is shown in Exhibit 5.14 for Z-Mart. It lists cost of goods sold as another expense and shows only one subtotal for total expenses. Expenses are grouped into very few, if any, categories. Many companies use formats that combine features of both the single- and multiple-step statements. Provided that income statement items are shown sensibly, management can choose the format. (In later chapters, we describe some items, such as extraordinary gains and losses, that must be reported in certain locations on the income statement.) Similar presentation options are available for the statement of owner's equity and statement of cash flows.

EXHIBIT 5.14

Single-Step Income Statement

Z-MART Income Statement For Year Ended December 31, 2013		
Revenues		
Net sales		$314,700
Interest revenue		1,000
Gain on sale of building		2,500
Total revenues		318,200
Expenses		
Cost of goods sold	$230,400	
Selling expenses	42,100	
General and administrative expenses	29,300	
Interest expense	1,500	
Total expenses		303,300
Net income		$ 14,900

Classified Balance Sheet

The merchandiser's classified balance sheet reports merchandise inventory as a current asset, usually after accounts receivable according to an asset's nearness to liquidity. Inventory is usually less liquid than accounts receivable because inventory must first be sold before cash can be received; but it is more liquid than supplies and prepaid expenses. Exhibit 5.15 shows the current asset section of Z-Mart's classified balance sheet (other sections are as shown in Chapter 4).

EXHIBIT 5.15

Classified Balance Sheet (partial) of a Merchandiser

Z-MART Balance Sheet (partial) December 31, 2013	
Current assets	
Cash	$ 8,200
Accounts receivable	11,200
Merchandise inventory	**21,000**
Office supplies	550
Store supplies	250
Prepaid insurance	300
Total current assets	$ 41,500

Decision Insight

Merchandising Shenanigans Accurate invoices are important to both sellers and buyers. Merchandisers rely on invoices to make certain they receive all monies for products provided—no more, no less. To achieve this, controls are set up. Still, failures arise. A survey reports that 9% of employees in sales and marketing witnessed false or misleading invoices sent to customers. Another 14% observed employees violating contract terms with customers (KPMG 2009). ■

GLOBAL VIEW

This section discusses similarities and differences between U.S. GAAP and IFRS in accounting and reporting for merchandise purchases and sales, and for the income statement.

Accounting for Merchandise Purchases and Sales   Both U.S. GAAP and IFRS include broad and similar guidance for the accounting of merchandise purchases and sales. Specifically, all of the transactions presented and illustrated in this chapter are accounted for identically under the two systems. The closing process for merchandisers also is identical for U.S. GAAP and IFRS. In the next chapter we describe how inventory valuation can, in some cases, be different for the two systems.

Income Statement Presentation   We explained that net income, profit, and earnings refer to the same (*bottom line*) item. However, IFRS tends to use the term *profit* more than any other term, whereas U.S. statements tend to use *net income* more than any other term. Both U.S. GAAP and IFRS income statements begin with the net sales or net revenues (*top line*) item. For merchandisers and manufacturers, this is followed by cost of goods sold. The presentation is similar for the remaining items with the following differences.

- U.S. GAAP offers little guidance about the presentation or order of expenses. IFRS requires separate disclosures for financing costs (interest expense), income tax expense, and some other special items.
- Both systems require separate disclosure of items when their size, nature, or frequency are important.
- IFRS permits expenses to be presented by their function or their nature. U.S. GAAP provides no direction but the SEC requires presentation by function.
- Neither U.S. GAAP nor IFRS define *operating* income, which results in latitude in reporting.
- IFRS permits alternative income measures on the income statement; U.S. GAAP does not.

Volkswagen Group provides the following example of income statement reporting. We see the separate disclosure of finance costs, taxes, and other items. We also see the unusual practice of using the minus symbol in an income statement.

VOLKSWAGEN

VOLKSWAGEN GROUP Income Statement (in Euros million) For Year Ended December 31, 2011	
Sales revenue	159,337
Cost of sales	−131,371
Gross profit	27,966
Distribution expenses	−14,582
Administrative expenses	−4,384
Other operating income (net of other expenses)	2,271
Operating profit	11,271
Finance costs	−2,047
Other financial results (including equity investments)	9,702
Profit before tax	18,926
Income tax	−3,127
Profit	15,799

Balance Sheet Presentation   Chapters 2 and 3 explained how both U.S. GAAP and IFRS require current items to be separated from noncurrent items on the balance sheet (yielding a *classified balance sheet*). As discussed, U.S. GAAP balance sheets report current items first. Assets are listed from most liquid to least liquid, whereas liabilities are listed from nearest to maturity to furthest from maturity. IFRS balance sheets normally present noncurrent items first (and equity before liabilities), but this is *not* a requirement. **Piaggio** provides an example of IFRS reporting for the balance sheet in Appendix A.

PIAGGIO

Decision Analysis   Acid-Test and Gross Margin Ratios

Acid-Test Ratio

 A1 Compute the acid-test ratio and explain its use to assess liquidity.

For many merchandisers, inventory makes up a large portion of current assets. Inventory must be sold and any resulting accounts receivable must be collected before cash is available. Chapter 4 explained that the current ratio, defined as current assets divided by current liabilities, is useful in assessing a company's ability to pay current liabilities. Because it is sometimes unreasonable to assume that inventories are a source of payment for current liabilities, we look to other measures.

One measure of a merchandiser's ability to pay its current liabilities (referred to as its *liquidity*) is the acid-test ratio. It differs from the current ratio by excluding less liquid current assets such as inventory and prepaid expenses that take longer to be converted to cash. The **acid-test ratio,** also called *quick ratio,* is defined as *quick assets* (cash, short-term investments, and current receivables) divided by current liabilities—see Exhibit 5.16.

EXHIBIT 5.16

Acid-Test (Quick) Ratio

$$\text{Acid-test ratio} = \frac{\text{Cash and cash equivalents} + \text{Short-term investments} + \text{Current receivables}}{\text{Current liabilities}}$$

Exhibit 5.17 shows both the acid-test and current ratios of retailer **JCPenney** for fiscal years 2008 through 2012—also see margin graph. JCPenney's acid-test ratio reveals a general increase from 2008 through 2011 that exceeds the industry average, and then a marked decline in 2012. Further, JCPenney's current ratio shows a marked decline in 2012 to 1.84, which suggests that its short-term obligations are less confidently covered with short-term assets compared with prior years.

EXHIBIT 5.17

JCPenney's Acid-Test and Current Ratios

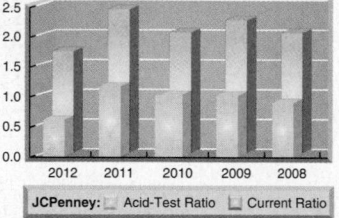

JCPenney: ☐ Acid-Test Ratio ☐ Current Ratio

($ millions)	2012	2011	2010	2009	2008
Total quick assets	$1,920	$2,956	$3,406	$2,704	$2,845
Total current assets	5,081	$6,370	$6,652	$6,220	$6,751
Total current liabilities	2,756	$2,647	$3,249	$2,794	$3,338
Acid-test ratio	**0.70**	**1.12**	**1.05**	**0.97**	**0.85**
Current ratio	**1.84**	**2.41**	**2.05**	**2.23**	**2.02**
Industry acid-test ratio	0.54	0.61	0.59	0.63	0.62
Industry current ratio	2.01	2.27	2.15	2.31	2.39

An acid-test ratio less than 1.0 means that current liabilities exceed quick assets. A rule of thumb is that the acid-test ratio should have a value near, or higher than, 1.0 to conclude that a company is unlikely to face near-term liquidity problems. A value much less than 1.0 raises liquidity concerns unless a company can generate enough cash from inventory sales or if much of its liabilities are not due until late in the next period. Similarly, a value slightly larger than 1.0 can hide a liquidity problem if payables are due shortly and receivables are not collected until late in the next period. Analysis of JCPenney shows some need for concern regarding its liquidity as its acid-test ratio is less than one. However, retailers such as JCPenney pay many current liabilities from inventory sales and in all years, JCPenney's acid-test ratios exceed the industry norm (and its inventory is fairly liquid).

Point: Successful use of a just-in-time inventory system can narrow the gap between the acid-test ratio and the current ratio.

 Decision Maker ━━━━━━━━━━━━━━━━━━━━━━━━

Supplier   A retailer requests to purchase supplies on credit from your company. You have no prior experience with this retailer. The retailer's current ratio is 2.1, its acid-test ratio is 0.5, and inventory makes up most of its current assets. Do you extend credit? ■   [Answer—p. 208]

Gross Margin Ratio

 A2 Compute the gross margin ratio and explain its use to assess profitability.

The cost of goods sold makes up much of a merchandiser's expenses. Without sufficient gross profit, a merchandiser will likely fail. Users often compute the gross margin ratio to help understand this relation. It differs from the profit margin ratio in that it excludes all costs except cost of goods sold. The **gross margin ratio** (also called *gross profit ratio*) is defined as *gross margin* (net sales minus cost of goods sold) divided by net sales—see Exhibit 5.18.

EXHIBIT 5.18

Gross Margin Ratio

$$\text{Gross margin ratio} = \frac{\text{Net sales} - \text{Cost of goods sold}}{\text{Net sales}}$$

Exhibit 5.19 shows the gross margin ratio of **JCPenney** for fiscal years 2008 through 2012. For JCPenney, each $1 of sales in 2012 yielded about 36.0¢ in gross margin to cover all other expenses and still produce a net income. This 36.0¢ margin is down from 38.6¢ in 2008. This decrease is not a favorable development. Success for merchandisers such as JCPenney depends on adequate gross margin. For example, the 2.60¢ decrease in the gross margin ratio, computed as 36.0¢ − 38.6¢, means that JCPenney has $448.76 million less in gross margin! (This is computed as net sales of $17,260 million multiplied by the 2.6% decrease in gross margin.) Management's discussion in its annual report attributes this decline to "softer than expected selling environment and the resulting increased promotional activity and the costs associated with implementing our new pricing strategy."

Point: The power of a ratio is often its ability to identify areas for more detailed analysis.

($ millions)	2012	2011	2010	2009	2008
Gross margin	$ 6,218	$ 6,960	$ 6,910	$ 6,915	$ 7,671
Net sales	$17,260	$17,759	$17,556	$18,486	$19,860
Gross margin ratio	36.0%	39.2%	39.4%	37.4%	38.6%

EXHIBIT 5.19

JCPenney's Gross Margin Ratio

■ **Decision Maker** ━━━━━━━━━━━━━━━━━━━━━━━━

Financial Officer   Your company has a 36% gross margin ratio and a 17% net profit margin ratio. Industry averages are 44% for gross margin and 16% for net profit margin. Do these comparative results concern you? ■   [Answer—p. 209]

DEMONSTRATION PROBLEM 1

Use the following adjusted trial balance and additional information to complete the requirements.

KC ANTIQUES Adjusted Trial Balance December 31, 2013	Debit	Credit
Cash	$ 7,000	
Accounts receivable	13,000	
Merchandise inventory	60,000	
Store supplies	1,500	
Equipment	45,600	
Accumulated depreciation—Equipment		$ 16,600
Accounts payable		9,000
Salaries payable		2,000
K. Carter, Capital		79,000
K. Carter, Withdrawals	10,000	
Sales		343,250
Sales discounts	5,000	
Sales returns and allowances	6,000	
Cost of goods sold	159,900	
Depreciation expense—Store equipment	4,100	
Depreciation expense—Office equipment	1,600	
Sales salaries expense	30,000	
Office salaries expense	34,000	
Insurance expense	11,000	
Rent expense (70% is store, 30% is office)	24,000	
Store supplies expense	5,750	
Advertising expense	31,400	
Totals	$449,850	$449,850

KC Antiques' *supplementary records* for 2013 reveal the following itemized costs for merchandising activities:

Invoice cost of merchandise purchases	$150,000
Purchase discounts received	2,500
Purchase returns and allowances	2,700
Cost of transportation-in	5,000

Required

1. Use the supplementary records to compute the total cost of merchandise purchases for 2013.

2. Prepare a 2013 multiple-step income statement. (Inventory at December 31, 2012, is $70,100.)

3. Prepare a single-step income statement for 2013.

4. Prepare closing entries for KC Antiques at December 31, 2013.

5. Compute the acid-test ratio and the gross margin ratio. Explain the meaning of each ratio and interpret them for KC Antiques.

PLANNING THE SOLUTION

- Compute the total cost of merchandise purchases for 2013.
- To prepare the multiple-step statement, first compute net sales. Then, to compute cost of goods sold, add the net cost of merchandise purchases for the year to beginning inventory and subtract the cost of ending inventory. Subtract cost of goods sold from net sales to get gross profit. Then classify expenses as selling expenses or general and administrative expenses.
- To prepare the single-step income statement, begin with net sales. Then list and subtract the expenses.
- The first closing entry debits all temporary accounts with credit balances and opens the Income Summary account. The second closing entry credits all temporary accounts with debit balances. The third entry closes the Income Summary account to the capital account, and the fourth entry closes the withdrawals account to the capital account.
- Identify the quick assets on the adjusted trial balance. Compute the acid-test ratio by dividing quick assets by current liabilities. Compute the gross margin ratio by dividing gross profit by net sales.

SOLUTION TO DEMONSTRATION PROBLEM 1

1.

Invoice cost of merchandise purchases	$150,000
Less: Purchases discounts received	2,500
Purchase returns and allowances	2,700
Add: Cost of transportation-in	5,000
Total cost of merchandise purchases	$149,800

2. Multiple-step income statement

KC ANTIQUES
Income Statement
For Year Ended December 31, 2013

Sales		$343,250
Less: Sales discounts	$ 5,000	
Sales returns and allowances	6,000	11,000
Net sales		332,250
Cost of goods sold*		159,900
Gross profit		172,350
Expenses		
Selling expenses		
Depreciation expense—Store equipment	4,100	
Sales salaries expense	30,000	
Rent expense—Selling space	16,800	
Store supplies expense	5,750	
Advertising expense	31,400	
Total selling expenses	88,050	

[continued on next page]

[continued from previous page]

General and administrative expenses		
Depreciation expense—Office equipment	1,600	
Office salaries expense.........................	34,000	
Insurance expense	11,000	
Rent expense—Office space	7,200	
Total general and administrative expenses	53,800	
Total operating expenses		141,850
Net income..		$ 30,500

* Cost of goods sold can also be directly computed (applying concepts from Exhibit 5.4):

Merchandise inventory, December 31, 2012	$ 70,100
Total cost of merchandise purchases (from part 1)	149,800
Goods available for sale	219,900
Merchandise inventory, December 31, 2013	60,000
Cost of goods sold	$159,900

3. Single-step income statement

KC ANTIQUES		
Income Statement		
For Year Ended December 31, 2013		
Net sales		$332,250
Expenses		
Cost of goods sold	$159,900	
Selling expenses	88,050	
General and administrative expenses	53,800	
Total expenses		301,750
Net income		$ 30,500

4.

Dec. 31	Sales	343,250	
	Income Summary		343,250
	To close credit balances in temporary accounts.		
Dec. 31	Income Summary	312,750	
	Sales Discounts		5,000
	Sales Returns and Allowances		6,000
	Cost of Goods Sold		159,900
	Depreciation Expense—Store Equipment		4,100
	Depreciation Expense—Office Equipment		1,600
	Sales Salaries Expense		30,000
	Office Salaries Expense		34,000
	Insurance Expense		11,000
	Rent Expense		24,000
	Store Supplies Expense		5,750
	Advertising Expense		31,400
	To close debit balances in temporary accounts.		
Dec. 31	Income Summary	30,500	
	K. Carter, Capital		30,500
	To close the Income Summary account.		
Dec. 31	K. Carter, Capital	10,000	
	K. Carter, Withdrawals		10,000
	To close the Withdrawals account.		

5. Acid-test ratio = (Cash and equivalents + Short-term investments + Current receivables)/
        Current liabilities

= (Cash + Accounts receivable/(Accounts payable + Salaries payable)

= ($7,000 + $13,000)/($9,000 + $2,000) = $20,000/$11,000 = 1.82

Gross margin ratio = Gross profit/Net sales = $172,350/$332,250 = 0.52 (or 52%)

KC Antiques has a healthy acid-test ratio of 1.82. This means it has more than $1.80 in liquid assets to satisfy each $1.00 in current liabilities. The gross margin of 0.52 shows that KC Antiques spends 48¢ ($1.00 − $0.52) of every dollar of net sales on the costs of acquiring the merchandise it sells. This leaves 52¢ of every dollar of net sales to cover other expenses incurred in the business and to provide a net profit.

DEMONSTRATION PROBLEM 2

Prepare journal entries to record the following merchandising transactions for both the seller (BMX) and buyer (Sanuk).

May 4   BMX sold $1,500 of merchandise on account to Sanuk, terms FOB shipping point, n/45, invoice dated May 4. The cost of the merchandise was $900.

May 6   Sanuk paid transportation charges of $30 on the May 4 purchase from BMX.

May 8   BMX sold $1,000 of merchandise on account to Sanuk, terms FOB destination, n/30, invoice dated May 8. The cost of the merchandise was $700.

May 10   BMX paid transportation costs of $50 for delivery of merchandise sold to Sanuk on May 8.

May 16   BMX issued Sanuk a $200 credit memorandum for merchandise returned. The merchandise was purchased by Sanuk on account on May 8. The cost of the merchandise returned was $140.

May 18   BMX received payment from Sanuk for purchase of May 8.

May 21   BMX sold $2,400 of merchandise on account to Sanuk, terms FOB shipping point, 2/10, n/EOM. BMX prepaid transportation costs of $100, which were added to the invoice. The cost of the merchandise was $1,440.

May 31   BMX received payment from Sanuk for purchase of May 21, less discount (2% × $2,400).

SOLUTION TO DEMONSTRATION PROBLEM 2

	BMX (Seller)				Sanuk (Buyer)		
May 4	Accounts Receivable—Sanuk	1,500			Merchandise Inventory	1,500	
	Sales		1,500		Accounts Payable—BMX		1,500
	Cost of Goods Sold	900					
	Merchandise Inventory		900				
6	No entry.				Merchandise Inventory	30	
					Cash		30
8	Accounts Receivable—Sanuk	1,000			Merchandise Inventory	1,000	
	Sales		1,000		Accounts Payable—BMX		1,000
	Cost of Goods Sold	700					
	Merchandise Inventory		700				
10	Delivery Expense	50			No entry.		
	Cash		50				
16	Sales Returns & Allowances	200			Accounts Payable—BMX	200	
	Accounts Receivable—Sanuk		200		Merchandise Inventory		200
	Merchandise Inventory	140					
	Cost of Goods Sold		140				
18	Cash	800			Accounts Payable—BMX	800	
	Accounts Receivable—Sanuk		800		Cash		800
21	Accounts Receivable—Sanuk	2,400			Merchandise Inventory	2,500	
	Sales		2,400		Accounts Payable—BMX		2,500
	Accounts Receivable—Sanuk	100					
	Cash		100				
	Cost of Goods Sold	1,440					
	Merchandise Inventory		1,440				
31	Cash	2,452			Accounts Payable—BMX	2,500	
	Sales Discounts	48			Merchandise Inventory		48
	Accounts Receivable—Sanuk		2,500		Cash		2,452

Periodic Inventory System

5A

A periodic inventory system requires updating the inventory account only at the *end of a period* to reflect the quantity and cost of both the goods available and the goods sold. Thus, during the period, the Merchandise Inventory balance remains unchanged. It reflects the beginning inventory balance until it is updated at the end of the period. During the period the cost of merchandise is recorded in a temporary *Purchases* account. When a company sells merchandise, it records revenue **but not the cost of the goods sold.** At the end of the period when a company prepares financial statements, it takes a *physical count of inventory* by counting the quantities and costs of merchandise available. The cost of goods sold is then computed by subtracting the ending inventory amount from the cost of merchandise available for sale.

Recording Merchandise Transactions Under a periodic system, purchases, purchase returns and allowances, purchase discounts, and transportation-in transactions are recorded in separate temporary accounts. At period-end, each of these temporary accounts is closed and the Merchandise Inventory account is updated. To illustrate, journal entries under the periodic inventory system are shown for the most common transactions (codes *a* through *f* link these transactions to those in the chapter, and we drop explanations for simplicity). For comparison, perpetual system journal entries are shown to the right of each periodic entry, where differences are in green font.

> **P5** Record and compare merchandising transactions using both periodic and perpetual inventory systems.

Purchases The periodic system uses a temporary *Purchases* account that accumulates the cost of all purchase transactions during each period. Z-Mart's November 2 entry to record the purchase of merchandise for $1,200 on credit with terms of 2/10, n/30 is

(a)

Periodic			Perpetual		
Purchases	1,200		Merchandise Inventory	1,200	
Accounts Payable		1,200	Accounts Payable		1,200

Purchase Discounts The periodic system uses a temporary *Purchase Discounts* account that accumulates discounts taken on purchase transactions during the period. If payment in (*a*) is delayed until after the discount period expires, the entry is to debit Accounts Payable and credit Cash for $1,200 each. However, if Z-Mart pays the supplier for the previous purchase in (*a*) within the discount period, the required payment is $1,176 ($1,200 × 98%) and is recorded as

(b)

Periodic			Perpetual		
Accounts Payable	1,200		Accounts Payable	1,200	
Purchase Discounts		24	Merchandise Inventory		24
Cash		1,176	Cash		1,176

Purchase Returns and Allowances Z-Mart returned merchandise purchased on November 2 because of defects. In the periodic system, the temporary *Purchase Returns and Allowances* account accumulates the cost of all returns and allowances during a period. The recorded cost (including discounts) of the defective merchandise is $300, and Z-Mart records the November 15 return with this entry:

> **Point:** Purchase Discounts and Purchase Returns and Allowances are both classified as contra-purchases accounts *and* have normal credit balances.

(c)

Periodic			Perpetual		
Accounts Payable	300		Accounts Payable	300	
Purchase Returns and Allowances		300	Merchandise Inventory		300

Transportation-In Z-Mart paid a $75 freight charge to transport merchandise to its store. In the periodic system, this cost is charged to a temporary *Transportation-In* account.

(d)

Periodic			Perpetual		
Transportation-In	75		Merchandise Inventory	75	
Cash		75	Cash		75

Sales   Under the periodic system, the cost of goods sold is *not* recorded at the time of each sale. (We later show how to compute total cost of goods sold at the end of a period.) Z-Mart's November 3 entry to record sales of $2,400 in merchandise on credit (when its cost is $1,600) is:

(e)

Periodic			Perpetual		
Accounts Receivable	2,400		Accounts Receivable	2,400	
Sales		2,400	Sales		2,400
			Cost of Goods Sold	1,600	
			Merchandise Inventory		1,600

Sales Returns   A customer returned part of the merchandise from the transaction in (e), where the returned items sell for $800 and cost $600. (*Recall:* The periodic system records only the revenue effect, not the cost effect, for sales transactions.) Z-Mart restores the merchandise to inventory and records the November 6 return as

(f)

Periodic			Perpetual		
Sales Returns and Allowances	800		Sales Returns and Allowances	800	
Accounts Receivable ...		800	Accounts Receivable		800
			Merchandise Inventory	600	
			Cost of Goods Sold		600

Sales Discounts   To illustrate sales discounts, assume that the remaining $1,600 of receivables (computed as $2,400 from *e* less $800 for *f*) has credit terms of 3/10, n/90 and that customers all pay within the discount period. Z-Mart records this payment as

Periodic			Perpetual		
Cash	1,552		Cash	1,552	
Sales Discounts ($1,600 × .03)	48		Sales Discounts ($1,600 × .03) ...	48	
Accounts Receivable ...		1,600	Accounts Receivable		1,600

Adjusting and Closing Entries   The periodic and perpetual inventory systems have slight differences in adjusting and closing entries. The period-end Merchandise Inventory balance (unadjusted) is $19,000 under the periodic system and $21,250 under the perpetual system. Since the periodic system does not update the Merchandise Inventory balance during the period, the $19,000 amount is the beginning inventory. However, the $21,250 balance under the perpetual system is the recorded ending inventory before adjusting for any inventory shrinkage.

A physical count of inventory taken at the end of the period reveals $21,000 of merchandise available. The adjusting and closing entries for the two systems are shown in Exhibit 5A.1. The periodic system records the ending inventory of $21,000 in the Merchandise Inventory account (which includes

EXHIBIT 5A.1

Comparison of Adjusting and Closing Entries—Periodic and Perpetual

PERIODIC			PERPETUAL		
Adjusting Entry—Shrinkage			**Adjusting Entry—Shrinkage**		
None			Cost of Goods Sold	250	
			Merchandise Inventory		250

[continued on next page]

[continued from previous page]

PERIODIC		
Closing Entries		
(1) Sales	321,000	
Merchandise Inventory	**21,000**	
Purchase Discounts	**4,200**	
Purchase Returns and Allowances	**1,500**	
Income Summary		347,700
(2) Income Summary	334,800	
Sales Discounts		4,300
Sales Returns and Allowances		2,000
Merchandise Inventory		**19,000**
Purchases		**235,800**
Transportation-In		**2,300**
Depreciation Expense		3,700
Salaries Expense		43,800
Insurance Expense		600
Rent Expense		9,000
Supplies Expense		3,000
Advertising Expense		11,300
(3) Income Summary	12,900	
K. Marty, Capital		12,900
(4) K. Marty, Capital	4,000	
K. Marty, Withdrawals		4,000

PERPETUAL		
Closing Entries		
(1) Sales	321,000	
Income Summary		321,000
(2) Income Summary	308,100	
Sales Discounts		4,300
Sales Returns and Allowances		2,000
Cost of Goods Sold		**230,400**
Depreciation Expense		3,700
Salaries Expense		43,800
Insurance Expense		600
Rent Expense		9,000
Supplies Expense		3,000
Advertising Expense		11,300
(3) Income Summary	12,900	
K. Marty, Capital		12,900
(4) K. Marty, Capital	4,000	
K. Marty, Withdrawals		4,000

shrinkage) in the first closing entry and removes the $19,000 beginning inventory balance from the account in the second closing entry.[2]

By updating Merchandise Inventory and closing Purchases, Purchase Discounts, Purchase Returns and Allowances, and Transportation-In, the periodic system transfers the cost of goods sold amount to Income Summary. Review the periodic side of Exhibit 5A.1 and notice that the **boldface** items affect Income Summary as follows.

Credit to Income Summary in the first closing entry includes amounts from:	
Merchandise inventory (ending)	$ 21,000
Purchase discounts	4,200
Purchase returns and allowances	1,500
Debit to Income Summary in the second closing entry includes amounts from:	
Merchandise inventory (beginning)	(19,000)
Purchases	(235,800)
Transportation-in	(2,300)
Net effect on Income Summary	**$(230,400)**

This $230,400 effect on Income Summary is the cost of goods sold amount. The periodic system transfers cost of goods sold to the Income Summary account but without using a Cost of Goods Sold account. Also, the periodic system does not separately measure shrinkage. Instead, it computes cost of goods available

---

[2] This approach is called the *closing entry method.* An alternative approach, referred to as the *adjusting entry method,* would not make any entries to Merchandise Inventory in the closing entries of Exhibit 5A.1, but instead would make two adjusting entries. Using Z-Mart data, the two adjusting entries would be: (1) Dr. Income Summary and Cr. Merchandise Inventory for $19,000 each, and (2) Dr. Merchandise Inventory and Cr. Income Summary for $21,000 each. The first entry removes the beginning balance of Merchandise Inventory, and the second entry records the actual ending balance.

for sale, subtracts the cost of ending inventory, and defines the difference as cost of goods sold, which includes shrinkage.

Preparing Financial Statements   The financial statements of a merchandiser using the periodic system are similar to those for a service company described in prior chapters. The income statement mainly differs by the inclusion of *cost of goods sold* and *gross profit*—of course, net sales is affected by discounts, returns, and allowances. The cost of goods sold section under the periodic system follows

Calculation of Cost of Goods Sold For Year Ended December 31, 2013	
Beginning inventory	$ 19,000
Cost of goods purchased	232,400
Cost of goods available for sale	251,400
Less ending inventory	21,000
Cost of goods sold	$230,400

The balance sheet mainly differs by the inclusion of *merchandise inventory* in current assets—see Exhibit 5.15. The statement of owner's equity is unchanged. A work sheet can be used to help prepare these statements. The only differences under the periodic system from the work sheet illustrated in Appendix 5B using the perpetual system are highlighted as follows in blue boldface font.

File Edit View Insert Format Tools Data Accounting Window Help

	No.	Account	Unadjusted Trial Balance Dr.	Cr.	Adjustments Dr.	Cr.	Adjusted Trial Balance Dr.	Cr.	Income Statement Dr.	Cr.	Balance Sheet Dr.	Cr.
3	101	Cash	8,200				8,200				8,200	
4	106	Accounts receivable	11,200				11,200				11,200	
5	119	**Merchandise Inventory**	19,000				19,000		19,000	21,000	21,000	
6	126	Supplies	3,800			(b) 3,000	800				800	
7	128	Prepaid insurance	900			(a) 600	300				300	
8	167	Equipment	34,200				34,200				34,200	
9	168	Accumulated depr.—Equip.		3,700		(c) 3,700		7,400				7,400
10	201	Accounts payable		16,000				16,000				16,000
11	209	Salaries payable				(d) 800		800				800
12	301	K. Marty, Capital		42,600				42,600				42,600
13	302	K. Marty, Withdrawals	4,000				4,000				4,000	
14	413	Sales		321,000				321,000		321,000		
15	414	Sales returns and allowances	2,000				2,000		2,000			
16a	415	Sales discounts	4,300				4,300		4,300			
16b	505	**Purchases**	235,800				235,800		235,800			
16c	506	**Purchases returns & allowance**		1,500				1,500		1,500		
16d	507	**Purchases discounts**		4,200				4,200		4,200		
17	508	**Transportation-in**	2,300				2,300		2,300			
18	612	Depreciation expense—Equip.			(c) 3,700		3,700		3,700			
19	622	Salaries expense	43,000		(d) 800		43,800		43,800			
20	637	Insurance expense			(a) 600		600		600			
21	640	Rent expense	9,000				9,000		9,000			
22	652	Supplies expense			(b) 3,000		3,000		3,000			
23	655	Advertising expense	11,300				11,300		11,300			
24		Totals	389,000	389,000	8,100	8,100	393,500	393,500	334,800	347,700	79,700	66,800
25		Net income							12,900			12,900
26		Totals							347,700	347,700	79,700	79,700

Sheet1 / Sheet2 / Sheet3 /

Quick Check

Answers – p. 209

13. What account is used in a perpetual inventory system but not in a periodic system?

14. Which of the following accounts are temporary accounts under a periodic system?
(a) Merchandise Inventory; (b) Purchases; (c) Transportation-In.

15. How is cost of goods sold computed under a periodic inventory system?

16. Do reported amounts of ending inventory and net income differ if the adjusting entry method of recording the change in inventory is used instead of the closing entry method?

APPENDIX

Work Sheet—Perpetual System

5B

Exhibit 5B.1 shows the work sheet for preparing financial statements of a merchandiser. It differs slightly from the work sheet layout in Chapter 4—the differences are in **red boldface**. Also, the adjustments in the work sheet reflect the following: (a) Expiration of $600 of prepaid insurance. (b) Use of $3,000 of supplies. (c) Depreciation of $3,700 for equipment. (d) Accrual of $800 of unpaid salaries. (e) Inventory shrinkage of $250. Once the adjusted amounts are extended into the financial statement columns, the information is used to develop financial statements.

EXHIBIT 5B.1

Work Sheet for Merchandiser (using a perpetual system)

No.	Account	Unadjusted Trial Balance Dr.	Cr.	Adjustments Dr.	Cr.	Adjusted Trial Balance Dr.	Cr.	Income Statement Dr.	Cr.	Balance Sheet Dr.	Cr.
101	Cash	8,200				8,200				8,200	
106	Accounts receivable	11,200				11,200				11,200	
119	**Merchandise Inventory**	21,250			(e) 250	21,000				**21,000**	
126	Supplies	3,800			(b) 3,000	800				800	
128	Prepaid insurance	900			(a) 600	300				300	
167	Equipment	34,200				34,200				34,200	
168	Accumulated depr.—Equip.		3,700		(c) 3,700		7,400				7,400
201	Accounts payable		16,000				16,000				16,000
209	Salaries payable				(d) 800		800				800
301	K. Marty, Capital		42,600				42,600				42,600
302	K. Marty, Withdrawals	4,000				4,000				4,000	
413	**Sales**		321,000				321,000		321,000		
414	**Sales returns and allowances**	2,000				2,000		2,000			
415	**Sales discounts**	4,300				4,300		4,300			
502	**Cost of goods sold**	230,150		(e) 250		230,400		230,400			
612	Depreciation expense—Equip.			(c) 3,700		3,700		3,700			
622	Salaries expense	43,000		(d) 800		43,800		43,800			
637	Insurance expense			(a) 600		600		600			
640	Rent expense	9,000				9,000		9,000			
652	Supplies expense			(b) 3,000		3,000		3,000			
655	Advertising expense	11,300				11,300		11,300			
	Totals	383,300	383,300	8,350	8,350	387,800	387,800	308,100	321,000	79,700	66,800
	Net income							12,900			12,900
	Totals							321,000	321,000	79,700	79,700

Summary

C1 **Describe merchandising activities and identify income components for a merchandising company.** Merchandisers buy products and resell them. Examples of merchandisers include Walmart, Home Depot, The Limited, and Barnes & Noble. A merchandiser's costs on the income statement include an amount for cost of goods sold. Gross profit, or gross margin, equals sales minus cost of goods sold.

C2 **Identify and explain the inventory asset and cost flows of a merchandising company.** The current asset section of a merchandising company's balance sheet includes *merchandise inventory,* which refers to the products a merchandiser sells and are available for sale at the balance sheet date. Cost of merchandise purchases flows into Merchandise Inventory and from there to Cost of Goods Sold on the income statement. Any remaining inventory is reported as a current asset on the balance sheet.

A1 **Compute the acid-test ratio and explain its use to assess liquidity.** The acid-test ratio is computed as quick assets (cash, short-term investments, and current receivables) divided by current liabilities. It indicates a company's ability to pay its current liabilities with its existing quick assets. An acid-test ratio equal to or greater than 1.0 is often adequate.

A2 **Compute the gross margin ratio and explain its use to assess profitability.** The gross margin ratio is computed as gross margin (net sales minus cost of goods sold) divided by net sales. It indicates a company's profitability before considering other expenses.

P1 **Analyze and record transactions for merchandise purchases using a perpetual system.** For a perpetual inventory system, purchases of inventory (net of trade discounts) are added to the Merchandise Inventory account. Purchase discounts and purchase returns and allowances are subtracted from Merchandise Inventory, and transportation-in costs are added to Merchandise Inventory.

P2 **Analyze and record transactions for merchandise sales using a perpetual system.** A merchandiser records sales at list price less any trade discounts. The cost of items sold is transferred from Merchandise Inventory to Cost of Goods Sold. Refunds or credits given to customers for unsatisfactory merchandise are recorded in Sales Returns and Allowances, a contra account to Sales. If merchandise is returned and restored to inventory, the cost of this merchandise is removed from Cost of Goods Sold and transferred back to Merchandise Inventory. When cash discounts from the sales price are offered and customers pay within the discount period, the seller records Sales Discounts, a contra account to Sales.

P3 **Prepare adjustments and close accounts for a merchandising company.** With a perpetual system, it is often necessary to make an adjustment for inventory shrinkage. This is computed by comparing a physical count of inventory with the Merchandise Inventory balance. Shrinkage is normally charged to Cost of Goods Sold. Temporary accounts closed to Income Summary for a merchandiser include Sales, Sales Discounts, Sales Returns and Allowances, and Cost of Goods Sold.

P4 **Define and prepare multiple-step and single-step income statements.** Multiple-step income statements include greater detail for sales and expenses than do single-step income statements. They also show details of net sales and report expenses in categories reflecting different activities.

P5^A **Record and compare merchandising transactions using both periodic and perpetual inventory systems.** A perpetual inventory system continuously tracks the cost of goods available for sale and the cost of goods sold. A periodic system accumulates the cost of goods purchased during the period and does not compute the amount of inventory or the cost of goods sold until the end of a period. Transactions involving the sale and purchase of merchandise are recorded and analyzed under both the periodic and perpetual inventory systems. Adjusting and closing entries for both inventory systems are illustrated and explained.

Guidance Answers to Decision Maker and Decision Ethics

Entrepreneur For terms of 3/10, n/90, missing the 3% discount for an additional 80 days equals an implied annual interest rate of 13.69%, computed as (365 days ÷ 80 days) × 3%. Since you can borrow funds at 11% (assuming no other processing costs), it is better to borrow and pay within the discount period. You save 2.69% (13.69% − 11%) in interest costs by paying early.

Payables Manager Your decision is whether to comply with prior policy or to create a new policy and not abuse discounts offered by suppliers. Your first step should be to meet with your superior to find out if the late payment policy is the actual policy and, if so, its rationale. If it is the policy to pay late, you must apply your own sense of ethics. One point of view is that the late payment policy is unethical. A deliberate plan to make late payments means the company lies when it pretends to make payment within the discount period. Another view is that the late payment policy is acceptable. In some markets, attempts to take discounts through late payments are

accepted as a continued phase of "price negotiation." Also, your company's suppliers can respond by billing your company for the discounts not accepted because of late payments. However, this is a dubious viewpoint, especially since the prior manager proposes that you dishonestly explain late payments as computer or mail problems and since some suppliers have complained.

Supplier A current ratio of 2.1 suggests sufficient current assets to cover current liabilities. An acid-test ratio of 0.5 suggests, however, that quick assets can cover only about one-half of current liabilities. This implies that the retailer depends on money from sales of inventory to pay current liabilities. If sales of inventory decline or profit margins decrease, the likelihood that this retailer will default on its payments increases. Your decision is probably not to extend credit. If you do extend credit, you are likely to closely monitor the retailer's financial condition. (It is better to hold unsold inventory than uncollectible receivables.)

Financial Officer Your company's net profit margin is about equal to the industry average and suggests typical industry performance. However, gross margin reveals that your company is paying far more in cost of goods sold or receiving far less in sales price than competitors. Your attention must be directed to finding the problem with cost of goods sold, sales, or both. One positive note is that your company's expenses make up 19% of sales (36% − 17%). This favorably compares with competitors' expenses that make up 28% of sales (44% − 16%).

Guidance Answers to Quick Checks

1. Cost of goods sold is the cost of merchandise purchased from a supplier that is sold to customers during a specific period.

2. Gross profit (or gross margin) is the difference between net sales and cost of goods sold.

3. Widespread use of computing and related technology has dramatically increased the use of the perpetual inventory system.

4. Under credit terms of 2/10, n/60, the credit period is 60 days and the discount period is 10 days.

5. (*b*) trade discount.

6. *FOB* means "free on board." It is used in identifying the point when ownership transfers from seller to buyer. *FOB destination* means that the seller transfers ownership of goods to the buyer when they arrive at the buyer's place of business. It also means that the seller is responsible for paying shipping charges and bears the risk of damage or loss during shipment.

7. Recording sales discounts and sales returns and allowances separately from sales gives useful information to managers for internal monitoring and decision making.

8. When a customer returns merchandise *and* the seller restores the merchandise to inventory, two entries are necessary. One entry records the decrease in revenue and credits the customer's account. The second entry debits inventory and reduces cost of goods sold.

9. Credit memorandum—seller credits accounts receivable from buyer.

10. Merchandise Inventory may need adjusting to reflect shrinkage.

11. Sales (of goods), Sales Discounts, Sales Returns and Allowances, and Cost of Goods Sold (and maybe Delivery Expense).

12. Four closing entries: (1) close credit balances in temporary accounts to Income Summary, (2) close debit balances in temporary accounts to Income Summary, (3) close Income Summary to owner's capital, and (4) close withdrawals account to owner's capital.

13. Cost of Goods Sold.

14. (*b*) Purchases and (*c*) Transportation-In.

15. Under a periodic inventory system, the cost of goods sold is determined at the end of an accounting period by adding the net cost of goods purchased to the beginning inventory and subtracting the ending inventory.

16. Both methods report the same ending inventory and income.

Key Terms

Acid-test ratio (p. 198)

Cash discount (p. 185)

Cost of goods sold (p. 182)

Credit memorandum (p. 191)

Credit period (p. 185)

Credit terms (p. 185)

Debit memorandum (p. 186)

Discount period (p. 185)

EOM (p. 185)

FOB (p. 187)

General and administrative expenses (p. 195)

Gross margin (p. 183)

Gross margin ratio (p. 198)

Gross profit (p. 182)

Inventory (p. 183)

List price (p. 184)

Merchandise (p. 182)

Merchandise inventory (p. 183)

Merchandiser (p. 182)

Multiple-step income statement (p. 195)

Periodic inventory system (p. 184)

Perpetual inventory system (p. 184)

Purchase discount (p. 185)

Retailer (p. 182)

Sales discount (p. 185)

Selling expenses (p. 195)

Shrinkage (p. 192)

Single-step income statement (p. 196)

Supplementary records (p. 188)

Trade discount (p. 184)

Wholesaler (p. 182)

Multiple Choice Quiz   Answers on p. 227   mhhe.com/wildFAP21e

Additional Quiz Questions are available at the book's Website.

1. A company has $550,000 in net sales and $193,000 in gross profit. This means its cost of goods sold equals
   a. $743,000
   b. $550,000
   c. $357,000
   d. $193,000
   e. $(193,000)

2. A company purchased $4,500 of merchandise on May 1 with terms of 2/10, n/30. On May 6, it returned $250 of that merchandise. On May 8, it paid the balance owed for merchandise, taking any discount it is entitled to. The cash paid on May 8 is
 a. $4,500
 b. $4,250
 c. $4,160
 d. $4,165
 e. $4,410

3. A company has cash sales of $75,000, credit sales of $320,000, sales returns and allowances of $13,700, and sales discounts of $6,000. Its net sales equal
 a. $395,000
 b. $375,300
 c. $300,300
 d. $339,700
 e. $414,700

4. A company's quick assets are $37,500, its current assets are $80,000, and its current liabilities are $50,000. Its acid-test ratio equals
 a. 1.600
 b. 0.750
 c. 0.625
 d. 1.333
 e. 0.469

5. A company's net sales are $675,000, its costs of goods sold are $459,000, and its net income is $74,250. Its gross margin ratio equals
 a. 32%
 b. 68%
 c. 47%
 d. 11%
 e. 34%

A(B) *Superscript letter A (B) denotes assignments based on Appendix 5A (5B).*

 Icon denotes assignments that involve decision making.

Discussion Questions

1. What items appear in financial statements of merchandising companies but not in the statements of service companies?

2. In comparing the accounts of a merchandising company with those of a service company, what additional accounts would the merchandising company likely use, assuming it employs a perpetual inventory system?

3. Explain how a business can earn a positive gross profit on its sales and still have a net loss.

4. Why do companies offer a cash discount?

5. How does a company that uses a perpetual inventory system determine the amount of inventory shrinkage?

6. Distinguish between cash discounts and trade discounts. Is the amount of a trade discount on purchased merchandise recorded in the accounts?

7. What is the difference between a sales discount and a purchase discount?

8. Why would a company's manager be concerned about the quantity of its purchase returns if its suppliers allow unlimited returns?

9. Does the sender (maker) of a debit memorandum record a debit or a credit in the recipient's account? What entry (debit or credit) does the recipient record?

10. What is the difference between the single-step and multiple-step income statement formats?

11. Refer to the balance sheet and income statement for **Polaris** in Appendix A. What does the company title its inventory account? Does the company present a detailed calculation of its cost of sales? **Polaris**

12. Refer to **Arctic Cat**'s income statement in Appendix A. What title does it use for cost of goods sold? **Arctic Cat**

13. Refer to the income statement for **Piaggio** in Appendix A. What does Piaggio title its cost of goods sold account? **PIAGGIO**

14. Refer to the income statement of **KTM** in Appendix A. Does its income statement report a gross profit figure? If yes, what is the amount? **KTM**

15. Buyers negotiate purchase contracts with suppliers. What type of shipping terms should a buyer attempt to negotiate to minimize freight-in costs?

 connect

QUICK STUDY

QS 5-1

Applying merchandising terms

C1

Enter the letter for each term in the blank space beside the definition that it most closely matches.

 A. Sales discount
 B. Credit period
 C. Discount period
 D. FOB destination
 E. FOB shipping point
 F. Gross profit
 G. Merchandise inventory
 H. Purchase discount
 I. Cash discount
 J. Trade discount

_____ **1.** Goods a company owns and expects to sell to its customers.

_____ **2.** Time period that can pass before a customer's payment is due.

_____ **3.** Seller's description of a cash discount granted to buyers in return for early payment.

_____ **4.** Reduction below list or catalog price that is negotiated in setting the price of goods.

_____ **5.** Ownership of goods is transferred when the seller delivers goods to the carrier.

_____ **6.** Purchaser's description of a cash discount received from a supplier of goods.

_____ **7.** Reduction in a receivable or payable if it is paid within the discount period.

_____ **8.** Difference between net sales and the cost of goods sold.

_____ **9.** Time period in which a cash discount is available.

_____ **10.** Ownership of goods is transferred when delivered to the buyer's place of business.

The cost of merchandise inventory includes which of the following:

a. Costs incurred to make the goods ready for sale. **d.** Both b and c.

b. Costs incurred to ship the goods to the store(s). **e.** a, b, and c.

c. Costs incurred to buy the goods.

QS 5-2
Identifying inventory costs
C2

Prepare journal entries to record each of the following purchases transactions of a merchandising company. Show supporting calculations and assume a perpetual inventory system.

Nov. 5   Purchased 600 units of product at a cost of $10 per unit. Terms of the sale are 2/10, n/60; the invoice is dated November 5.

Nov. 7   Returned 25 defective units from the November 5 purchase and received full credit.

Nov. 15   Paid the amount due from the November 5 purchase, less the return on November 7.

QS 5-3
Recording purchases—
perpetual system
P1

Prepare journal entries to record each of the following sales transactions of a merchandising company. Show supporting calculations and assume a perpetual inventory system.

Apr. 1   Sold merchandise for $3,000, granting the customer terms of 2/10, EOM; invoice dated April 1. The cost of the merchandise is $1,800.

Apr. 4   The customer in the April 1 sale returned merchandise and received credit for $600. The merchandise, which had cost $360, is returned to inventory.

Apr. 11   Received payment for the amount due from the April 1 sale less the return on April 4.

QS 5-4
Recording sales—
perpetual system
P2

Compute net sales, gross profit, and the gross margin ratio for each separate case *a* through *d*. Interpret the gross margin ratio for case *a*.

	a	b	c	d
Sales	$150,000	$550,000	$38,700	$255,700
Sales discounts	5,000	17,500	600	4,800
Sales returns and allowances	20,000	6,000	5,100	900
Cost of goods sold	79,750	329,589	24,453	126,500

QS 5-5
Computing and analyzing
gross margin
A2

Nix'It Company's ledger on July 31, its fiscal year-end, includes the following selected accounts that have normal balances (Nix'It uses the perpetual inventory system).

Merchandise inventory	$ 37,800	Sales returns and allowances	$ 6,500
T. Nix, Capital	115,300	Cost of goods sold	105,000
T. Nix, Withdrawals	7,000	Depreciation expense	10,300
Sales	160,200	Salaries expense	32,500
Sales discounts	4,700	Miscellaneous expenses	5,000

QS 5-6
Accounting for shrinkage—
perpetual system
P3

A physical count of its July 31 year-end inventory discloses that the cost of the merchandise inventory still available is $35,900. Prepare the entry to record any inventory shrinkage.

QS 5-7

Closing entries   P3

Refer to QS 5-6 and prepare journal entries to close the balances in temporary revenue and expense accounts. Remember to consider the entry for shrinkage that is made to solve QS 5-6.

QS 5-8

Computing and interpreting acid-test ratio

A1

Use the following information on current assets and current liabilities to compute and interpret the acid-test ratio. Explain what the acid-test ratio of a company measures.

Cash	$1,490	Prepaid expenses	$ 700
Accounts receivable	2,800	Accounts payable	5,750
Inventory	6,000	Other current liabilities	850

QS 5-9

Contrasting liquidity ratios   A1

Identify similarities and differences between the acid-test ratio and the current ratio. Compare and describe how the two ratios reflect a company's ability to meet its current obligations.

QS 5-10

Multiple-step income statement

P4

The multiple-step income statement normally includes which of the following:

a. Operating expenses are usually classified into (1) selling expenses and (2) general and administrative expenses.

b. Detailed computations of expenses, including subtotals for various expense categories.

c. Detailed computations of net sales.

d. Both a and c.

e. a, b, and c.

QS 5-11[A]

Contrasting periodic and perpetual systems

P5

Identify whether each description best applies to a periodic or a perpetual inventory system.

a. Updates the inventory account only at period-end.

b. Requires an adjusting entry to record inventory shrinkage.

c. Markedly increased in frequency and popularity in business within the past decade.

d. Records cost of goods sold each time a sales transaction occurs.

e. Provides more timely information to managers.

QS 5-12[A]

Recording purchases—periodic system   P5

Refer to QS 5-3 and prepare journal entries to record each of the merchandising transactions assuming that the periodic inventory system is used.

QS 5-13[A]

Recording purchases—periodic system   P5

Refer to QS 5-4 and prepare journal entries to record each of the merchandising transactions assuming that the periodic inventory system is used.

QS 5-14

IFRS income statement presentation

P4

Income statement information for **adidas Group**, a German footwear, apparel, and accessories manufacturer, for the year ended December 31, 2011, follows. The company applies IFRS, as adopted by the European Union, and reports its results in millions of Euros. Prepare its calendar year 2011 (1) multiple-step income statement and (2) single-step income statement.

Net income	€ 670
Financial income	31
Financial expenses	115
Operating profit	1,011
Cost of sales	7,000
Income taxes	257
Income before taxes	927
Gross profit	6,344
Royalty and commission income	93
Other operating income	98
Other operating expenses	5,524
Net sales	13,344

Answer each of the following questions related to international accounting standards.

a. Explain how the accounting for merchandise purchases and sales is different between accounting under IFRS versus U.S. GAAP.

b. Income statements prepared under IFRS usually report an item titled *finance costs*. What do finance costs refer to?

c. U.S. GAAP prohibits alternative measures of income reported on the income statement. Does IFRS permit such alternative measures on the income statement?

QS 5-15
International accounting standards
C1

On August 1, Gilmore Company purchased merchandise from Hendren with an invoice price of $60,000 and credit terms of 2/10, n/30. Gilmore Company paid Hendren on August 11. Prepare any required journal entry(ies) for Gilmore Company (the purchaser) on: (*a*) August 1, and (*b*) August 11. Assume Gilmore uses the perpetual inventory method.

QS 5-16
Recording discounts taken—perpetual   P1

On September 15, Krug Company purchased merchandise inventory from Makarov with an invoice price of $35,000 and credit terms of 2/10, n/30. Schneider Company paid Makarov on September 28. Prepare any required journal entry(ies) for Schneider Company (the purchaser) on: (*a*) September 15, and (*b*) September 28. Assume Krug uses the perpetual inventory method.

QS 5-17
Recording discounts missed—perpetual   P1

Use the following information (in alphabetical order) from a service company and from a merchandiser to compute net income. For the merchandiser, also compute gross profit, the goods available for sale, and the cost of goods sold. *Hint:* Not all information may be necessary.

QS 5-18
Merchandise equations and flows
C2

Krug Service Company		Kleiner Merchandising Company	
Expenses.	$ 8,500	Accumulated Depreciation	$ 700
Revenues	14,000	Beginning Inventory	5,000
Owner, Withdrawals.	1,600	Owner, Capital	950
Cash	700	Ending Inventory	1,700
Prepaid Rent	800	Operating Expenses.	1,450
Accounts Payable	200	Purchases	3,900
Owner, Capital	3,000	Sales	9,500
Equipment	1,300	Owner, Withdrawals	1,600

---

connect

The operating cycle of a merchandiser with credit sales includes the following five activities. Starting with merchandise acquisition, identify the chronological order of these five activities.

a. _____ inventory made available for sale.

b. _____ cash collections from customers.

c. _____ credit sales to customers.

d. _____ purchases of merchandise.

e. _____ accounts receivable accounted for.

EXERCISES

Exercise 5-1
Operating cycle for merchandiser
C2

Prepare journal entries to record the following transactions for a retail store. Assume a perpetual inventory system.

Apr. 2   Purchased merchandise from Lyon Company under the following terms: $4,600 price, invoice dated April 2, credit terms of 2/15, n/60, and FOB shipping point.
  3   Paid $300 for shipping charges on the April 2 purchase.
  4   Returned to Lyon Company unacceptable merchandise that had an invoice price of $600.
  17   Sent a check to Lyon Company for the April 2 purchase, net of the discount and the returned merchandise.
  18   Purchased merchandise from Frist Corp. under the following terms: $8,500 price, invoice dated April 18, credit terms of 2/10, n/30, and FOB destination.
  21   After negotiations, received from Frist a $1,100 allowance on the April 18 purchase.
  28   Sent check to Frist paying for the April 18 purchase, net of the discount and allowance.

Exercise 5-2
Recording entries for merchandise purchases
P1

Check   April 28, Cr. Cash $7,252

Exercise 5-3

Analyzing and recording
merchandise transactions—
both buyer and seller

P1 P2

Check (3) $465 savings

Santa Fe Company purchased merchandise for resale from Mesa Company with an invoice price of $24,000 and credit terms of 3/10, n/60. The merchandise had cost Mesa $16,000. Santa Fe paid within the discount period. Assume that both buyer and seller use a perpetual inventory system.

1. Prepare entries that the buyer should record for (*a*) the purchase and (*b*) the cash payment.

2. Prepare entries that the seller should record for (*a*) the sale and (*b*) the cash collection.

3. Assume that the buyer borrowed enough cash to pay the balance on the last day of the discount period at an annual interest rate of 8% and paid it back on the last day of the credit period. Compute how much the buyer saved by following this strategy. (Assume a 365-day year and round dollar amounts to the nearest cent, including computation of interest per day.)

Exercise 5-4

Recording sales returns and
allowances   P2

Check (c) Dr. Merchandise
Inventory $400

Allied Parts was organized on May 1, 2013, and made its first purchase of merchandise on May 3. The purchase was for 2,000 units at a price of $10 per unit. On May 5, Allied Parts sold 1,500 of the units for $14 per unit to Baker Co. Terms of the sale were 2/10, n/60. Prepare entries for Allied Parts to record the May 5 sale and each of the following separate transactions *a* through *c* using a perpetual inventory system.

a. On May 7, Baker returns 200 units because they did not fit the customer's needs. Allied Parts restores the units to its inventory.

b. On May 8, Baker discovers that 300 units are damaged but are still of some use and, therefore, keeps the units. Allied Parts sends Baker a credit memorandum for $600 to compensate for the damage.

c. On May 15, Baker discovers that 100 units are the wrong color. Baker keeps 60 of these units because Allied Parts sends a $120 credit memorandum to compensate. Baker returns the remaining 40 units to Allied Parts. Allied Parts restores the 40 returned units to its inventory.

Exercise 5-5

Recording purchase returns
and allowances   P1

Refer to Exercise 5-4 and prepare the appropriate journal entries for Baker Co. to record the May 5 purchase and each of the three separate transactions *a* through *c*. Baker is a retailer that uses a perpetual inventory system and purchases these units for resale.

Exercise 5-6

Sales returns and allowances

C1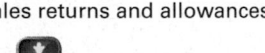

Business decision makers desire information on sales returns and allowances. (1) Explain why a company's manager wants the accounting system to record customers' returns of unsatisfactory goods in the Sales Returns and Allowances account instead of the Sales account. (2) Explain whether this information would be useful for external decision makers.

Exercise 5-7

Analyzing and recording
merchandise transactions—
both buyer and seller

P1 P2

Check (1) May 20, Cr. Cash $37,442

On May 11, Sydney Co. accepts delivery of $40,000 of merchandise it purchases for resale from Troy Corporation. With the merchandise is an invoice dated May 11, with terms of 3/10, n/90, FOB shipping point. The goods cost Troy $30,000. When the goods are delivered, Sydney pays $345 to Express Shipping for delivery charges on the merchandise. On May 12, Sydney returns $1,400 of goods to Troy, who receives them one day later and restores them to inventory. The returned goods had cost Troy $800. On May 20, Sydney mails a check to Troy Corporation for the amount owed. Troy receives it the following day. (Both Sydney and Troy use a perpetual inventory system.)

1. Prepare journal entries that Sydney Co. records for these transactions.

2. Prepare journal entries that Troy Corporation records for these transactions.

Exercise 5-8

Recording effects of
merchandising activities

P1 P2

Check Year-End Merchandise
Inventory Dec. 31, $20,000

The following supplementary records summarize Tosca Company's merchandising activities for year 2013. Set up T-accounts for Merchandise Inventory and Cost of Goods Sold. Then record the summarized activities in those T-accounts and compute account balances.

Cost of merchandise sold to customers in sales transactions	$196,000
Merchandise inventory, December 31, 2012	25,000
Invoice cost of merchandise purchases	192,500
Shrinkage determined on December 31, 2013	800
Cost of transportation-in	2,900
Cost of merchandise returned by customers and restored to inventory	2,100
Purchase discounts received	1,700
Purchase returns and allowances	4,000

The following list includes selected permanent accounts and all of the temporary accounts from the December 31, 2013, unadjusted trial balance of Emiko Co., a business owned by Kumi Emiko. Use these account balances along with the additional information to journalize (a) adjusting entries and (b) closing entries. Emiko Co. uses a perpetual inventory system.

Exercise 5-9
Preparing adjusting and closing entries for a merchandiser
P3

	Debit	Credit
Merchandise inventory	$ 30,000	
Prepaid selling expenses	5,600	
K. Emiko, Withdrawals	33,000	
Sales		$529,000
Sales returns and allowances	17,500	
Sales discounts	5,000	
Cost of goods sold	212,000	
Sales salaries expense	48,000	
Utilities expense	15,000	
Selling expenses	36,000	
Administrative expenses	105,000	

Additional Information

Accrued sales salaries amount to $1,700. Prepaid selling expenses of $3,000 have expired. A physical count of year-end merchandise inventory shows $28,450 of goods still available.

Check Entry to close Income Summary: Cr. K. Emiko, Capital $84,250

Using your accounting knowledge, fill in the blanks in the following separate income statements a through e. Identify any negative amount by putting it in parentheses.

Exercise 5-10
Computing revenues, expenses, and income
C1 C2

	a	b	c	d	e
Sales	$62,000	$43,500	$46,000	$?	$25,600
Cost of goods sold					
Merchandise inventory (beginning)	8,000	17,050	7,500	8,000	4,560
Total cost of merchandise purchases	38,000	?	?	32,000	6,600
Merchandise inventory (ending)	?	(3,000)	(9,000)	(6,600)	?
Cost of goods sold	34,050	16,000	?	?	7,000
Gross profit	?	?	3,750	45,600	?
Expenses	10,000	10,650	12,150	3,600	6,000
Net income (loss)	$?	$16,850	$ (8,400)	$42,000	$?

A retail company recently completed a physical count of ending merchandise inventory to use in preparing adjusting entries. In determining the cost of the counted inventory, company employees failed to consider that $3,000 of incoming goods had been shipped by a supplier on December 31 under an FOB shipping point agreement. These goods had been recorded in Merchandise Inventory as a purchase, but they were not included in the physical count because they were in transit. Explain how this overlooked fact affects the company's financial statements and the following ratios: return on assets, debt ratio, current ratio, and acid-test ratio.

Exercise 5-11
Interpreting a physical count error as inventory shrinkage
A1

Refer to the information in Exercise 5-11 and explain how the error in the physical count affects the company's gross margin ratio and its profit margin ratio.

Exercise 5-12
Physical count error and profits
A2

Exercise 5-13
Computing and analyzing
acid-test and current ratios

A1

Compute the current ratio and acid-test ratio for each of the following separate cases. (Round ratios to two decimals.) Which company case is in the best position to meet short-term obligations? Explain.

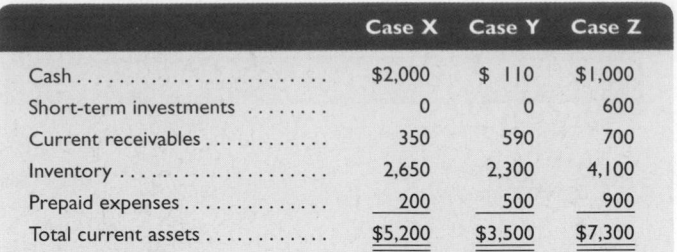

	Case X	Case Y	Case Z
Cash........................	$2,000	$ 110	$1,000
Short-term investments	0	0	600
Current receivables............	350	590	700
Inventory	2,650	2,300	4,100
Prepaid expenses..............	200	500	900
Total current assets	$5,200	$3,500	$7,300
Current liabilities..............	$2,200	$1,200	$3,750

Exercise 5-14
Preparing journal entries—
perpetual system

P1 P2

Journalize the following merchandising transactions for Chilton Systems assuming it uses a perpetual inventory system.

1. On November 1, Chilton Systems purchases merchandise for $1,500 on credit with terms of 2/5, n/30, FOB shipping point; invoice dated November 1.

2. On November 5, Chilton Systems pays cash for the November 1 purchase.

3. On November 7, Chilton Systems discovers and returns $200 of defective merchandise purchased on November 1 for a cash refund.

4. On November 10, Chilton Systems pays $90 cash for transportation costs with the November 1 purchase.

5. On November 13, Chilton Systems sells merchandise for $1,600 on credit. The cost of the merchandise is $800.

6. On November 16, the customer returns merchandise from the November 13 transaction. The returned items sell for $300 and cost $130. The merchandise is returned to inventory.

Exercise 5-15
Multiple-step income statement

P4

A company reports the following sales related information: Sales (gross) of $200,000; Sales discounts of $4,000; Sales returns and allowances of $16,000; Sales salaries expense of $10,000. Prepare the net sales portion only of this company's multiple-step income statement.

Exercise 5-16ᴬ
Recording purchases—
periodic system   P5

Refer to Exercise 5-2 and prepare journal entries to record each of the merchandising transactions assuming that the periodic inventory system is used.

Exercise 5-17ᴬ
Recording purchases and sales—
periodic system   P5

Refer to Exercise 5-3 and prepare journal entries to record each of the merchandising transactions assuming that the periodic inventory system is used by both the buyer and the seller. (Skip the part 3 requirement.)

Exercise 5-18ᴬ
Buyer and seller transactions—
periodic system   P5

Refer to Exercise 5-7 and prepare journal entries to record each of the merchandising transactions assuming that the periodic inventory system is used by both the buyer and the seller.

Exercise 5-19ᴬ
Recording purchases—
periodic system   P5

Refer to Exercise 5-14 and prepare journal entries to record each of the merchandising transactions assuming that the periodic inventory system is used.

L'Oréal reports the following income statement accounts for the year ended December 31, 2011 (euros in millions). Prepare the income statement for this company for the year ended December 31, 2011, following usual IFRS practices.

Exercise 5-20
Preparing an income statement following IFRS

P4

Net profit	€ 2,440.9	Income tax expense	€1,025.8
Finance costs	19.6	Profit before tax expense	3,466.7
Net sales	20,343.1	Research and development expense	720.5
Gross profit	14,491.6	Selling, general and administrative expense	4,186.9
Other income	193.7	Advertising and promotion expense	6,291.6
Cost of sales	5,851.5		

connect

Prepare journal entries to record the following merchandising transactions of Blink Company, which applies the perpetual inventory system. (*Hint:* It will help to identify each receivable and payable; for example, record the purchase on July 1 in Accounts Payable—Boden.)

PROBLEM SET A

Problem 5-1A
Preparing journal entries for merchandising activities—perpetual system

P1 P2 Sage 50 QB

July 1 Purchased merchandise from Boden Company for $6,000 under credit terms of 1/15, n/30, FOB shipping point, invoice dated July 1.
2 Sold merchandise to Creek Co. for $900 under credit terms of 2/10, n/60, FOB shipping point, invoice dated July 2. The merchandise had cost $500.
3 Paid $125 cash for freight charges on the purchase of July 1.
8 Sold merchandise that had cost $1,300 for $1,700 cash.
9 Purchased merchandise from Leight Co. for $2,200 under credit terms of 2/15, n/60, FOB destination, invoice dated July 9.
11 Received a $200 credit memorandum from Leight Co. for the return of part of the merchandise purchased on July 9.
12 Received the balance due from Creek Co. for the invoice dated July 2, net of the discount.
16 Paid the balance due to Boden Company within the discount period.
19 Sold merchandise that cost $800 to Art Co. for $1,200 under credit terms of 2/15, n/60, FOB shipping point, invoice dated July 19.
21 Issued a $200 credit memorandum to Art Co. for an allowance on goods sold on July 19.
24 Paid Leight Co. the balance due after deducting the discount.
30 Received the balance due from Art Co. for the invoice dated July 19, net of discount.
31 Sold merchandise that cost $4,800 to Creek Co. for $7,000 under credit terms of 2/10, n/60, FOB shipping point, invoice dated July 31.

Check July 12, Dr. Cash $882
July 16, Cr. Cash $5,940

July 24, Cr. Cash $1,960
July 30, Dr. Cash $980

Prepare journal entries to record the following merchandising transactions of Sheng Company, which applies the perpetual inventory system. (*Hint:* It will help to identify each receivable and payable; for example, record the purchase on August 1 in Accounts Payable—Arotek.)

Problem 5-2A
Preparing journal entries for merchandising activities—perpetual system

P1 P2

Aug. 1 Purchased merchandise from Arotek Company for $7,500 under credit terms of 1/10, n/30, FOB destination, invoice dated August 1.
4 At Arotek's request, Sheng paid $200 cash for freight charges on the August 1 purchase, reducing the amount owed to Abilene.
5 Sold merchandise to Laird Corp. for $5,200 under credit terms of 2/10, n/60, FOB destination, invoice dated August 5. The merchandise had cost $4,000.
8 Purchased merchandise from Waters Corporation for $5,400 under credit terms of 1/10, n/45, FOB shipping point, invoice dated August 8. The invoice showed that at Sheng's request, Waters paid the $140 shipping charges and added that amount to the bill. (*Hint:* Discounts are not applied to freight and shipping charges.)
9 Paid $125 cash for shipping charges related to the August 5 sale to Laird Corp.
10 Laird returned merchandise from the August 5 sale that had cost Sheng $400 and been sold for $600. The merchandise was restored to inventory.
12 After negotiations with Waters Corporation concerning problems with the merchandise purchased on August 8, Sheng received a credit memorandum from Waters granting a price reduction of $700.

Check Aug. 9, Dr. Delivery Expense, $125

Aug. 18, Cr. Cash $4,793

15 Received balance due from Laird Corp. for the August 5 sale less the return on August 10.
18 Paid the amount due Waters Corporation for the August 8 purchase less the price reduction granted.
19 Sold merchandise to Tux Co. for $4,800 under credit terms of 1/10, n/30, FOB shipping point, invoice dated August 19. The merchandise had cost $2,400.
22 Tux requested a price reduction on the August 19 sale because the merchandise did not meet specifications. Sheng sent Tux a $500 credit memorandum to resolve the issue.

Aug. 29, Dr. Cash $4,257

29 Received Tux's cash payment for the amount due from the August 19 sale.
30 Paid Arotek Company the amount due from the August 1 purchase.

Problem 5-3A

Preparing adjusting entries and income statements; and computing gross margin, acid-test, and current ratios

A1 A2 P3 P4

mhhe.com/wildFAP21e

The following unadjusted trial balance is prepared at fiscal year-end for Nelson Company.

File Edit View Insert Format Tools Data Accounting Window Help		
NELSON COMPANY **Unadjusted Trial Balance** **January 31, 2013**		
	Debit	**Credit**
Cash	$ 1,000	
Merchandise inventory	12,500	
Store supplies	5,800	
Prepaid insurance	2,400	
Store equipment	42,900	
Accumulated depreciation—Store equipment		$ 15,250
Accounts payable		10,000
J. Nelson, Capital		32,000
J. Nelson, Withdrawals	2,200	
Sales		111,950
Sales discounts	2,000	
Sales returns and allowances	2,200	
Cost of goods sold	38,400	
Depreciation expense—Store equipment	0	
Salaries expense	35,000	
Insurance expense	0	
Rent expense	15,000	
Store supplies expense	0	
Advertising expense	9,800	
Totals	$169,200	$169,200

Sheet1 / Sheet2 / Sheet3 /

Rent expense and salaries expense are equally divided between selling activities and the general and administrative activities. Nelson Company uses a perpetual inventory system.

Required

1. Prepare adjusting journal entries to reflect each of the following:
   a. Store supplies still available at fiscal year-end amount to $1,750.
   b. Expired insurance, an administrative expense, for the fiscal year is $1,400.
   c. Depreciation expense on store equipment, a selling expense, is $1,525 for the fiscal year.
   d. To estimate shrinkage, a physical count of ending merchandise inventory is taken. It shows $10,900 of inventory is still available at fiscal year-end.

Check (2) Gross profit, $67,750; (3) Total expenses, $106,775; Net income, $975

2. Prepare a multiple-step income statement for fiscal year 2013.
3. Prepare a single-step income statement for fiscal year 2013.
4. Compute the current ratio, acid-test ratio, and gross margin ratio as of January 31, 2013. (Round ratios to two decimals.)

Valley Company's adjusted trial balance on August 31, 2013, its fiscal year-end, follows.

Problem 5-4A
Computing merchandising
amounts and formatting
income statements

C2   P4

	Debit	Credit
Merchandise inventory	$ 41,000	
Other (noninventory) assets	130,400	
Total liabilities		$ 25,000
K.Valley, Capital		104,550
K.Valley, Withdrawals	8,000	
Sales		225,600
Sales discounts	2,250	
Sales returns and allowances	12,000	
Cost of goods sold	74,500	
Sales salaries expense	32,000	
Rent expense—Selling space	8,000	
Store supplies expense	1,500	
Advertising expense	13,000	
Office salaries expense	28,500	
Rent expense—Office space	3,600	
Office supplies expense	400	
Totals	$355,150	$355,150

On August 31, 2012, merchandise inventory was $25,400. Supplementary records of merchandising activities for the year ended August 31, 2013, reveal the following itemized costs.

Invoice cost of merchandise purchases	$92,000
Purchase discounts received	2,000
Purchase returns and allowances	4,500
Costs of transportation-in	4,600

Required

1. Compute the company's net sales for the year.
2. Compute the company's total cost of merchandise purchased for the year.
3. Prepare a multiple-step income statement that includes separate categories for selling expenses and for general and administrative expenses.
4. Prepare a single-step income statement that includes these expense categories: cost of goods sold, selling expenses, and general and administrative expenses.

Check   (2) $90,100;

(3) Gross profit, $136,850;
Net income, $49,850;

(4) Total expenses, $161,500

Use the data for Valley Company in Problem 5-4A to complete the following requirements.

Problem 5-5A
Preparing closing entries and
interpreting information about
discounts and returns

C2   P3

Required

1. Prepare closing entries as of August 31, 2013 (the perpetual inventory system is used).

Analysis Component

2. The company makes all purchases on credit, and its suppliers uniformly offer a 3% sales discount. Does it appear that the company's cash management system is accomplishing the goal of taking all available discounts? Explain.
3. In prior years, the company experienced a 4% returns and allowance rate on its sales, which means approximately 4% of its gross sales were eventually returned outright or caused the company to grant allowances to customers. How do this year's results compare to prior years' results?

Sage 50
QB

Check   (1) $49,850 Dr. to close
Income Summary
(3) Current-year rate, 5.3%

Problem 5-6A^B

Preparing a work sheet for a merchandiser

P3

Refer to the data and information in Problem 5-3A.

Required

Prepare and complete the entire 10-column work sheet for Nelson Company. Follow the structure of Exhibit 5B.1 in Appendix 5B.

PROBLEM SET B

Problem 5-1B

Preparing journal entries for merchandising activities— perpetual system

P1   P2

Prepare journal entries to record the following merchandising transactions of Yarvelle Company, which applies the perpetual inventory system. (*Hint:* It will help to identify each receivable and payable; for example, record the purchase on May 2 in Accounts Payable—Havel.)

May	2	Purchased merchandise from Havel Co. for $10,000 under credit terms of 1/15, n/30, FOB shipping point, invoice dated May 2.
	4	Sold merchandise to Heather Co. for $11,000 under credit terms of 2/10, n/60, FOB shipping point, invoice dated May 4. The merchandise had cost $5,600.
	5	Paid $250 cash for freight charges on the purchase of May 2.
	9	Sold merchandise that had cost $2,000 for $2,500 cash.
	10	Purchased merchandise from Duke Co. for $3,650 under credit terms of 2/15, n/60, FOB destination, invoice dated May 10.
	12	Received a $400 credit memorandum from Duke Co. for the return of part of the merchandise purchased on May 10.
	14	Received the balance due from Heather Co. for the invoice dated May 4, net of the discount.
	17	Paid the balance due to Havel Co. within the discount period.
	20	Sold merchandise that cost $1,450 to Tameron Co. for $2,800 under credit terms of 2/15, n/60, FOB shipping point, invoice dated May 20.
	22	Issued a $400 credit memorandum to Tameron Co. for an allowance on goods sold from May 20.
	25	Paid Duke Co. the balance due after deducting the discount.
	30	Received the balance due from Tameron Co. for the invoice dated May 20, net of discount and allowance.
	31	Sold merchandise that cost $3,600 to Heather Co. for $7,200 under credit terms of 2/10, n/60, FOB shipping point, invoice dated May 31.

Check   May 14, Dr. Cash $10,780
May 17, Cr. Cash $9,900

May 30, Dr. Cash $2,352

Problem 5-2B

Preparing journal entries for merchandising activities— perpetual system

P1   P2

Prepare journal entries to record the following merchandising transactions of Mason Company, which applies the perpetual inventory system. (*Hint:* It will help to identify each receivable and payable; for example, record the purchase on July 3 in Accounts Payable—OLB.)

July	3	Purchased merchandise from OLB Corp. for $15,000 under credit terms of 1/10, n/30, FOB destination, invoice dated July 3.
	4	At OLB's request, Mason paid $150 cash for freight charges on the July 3 purchase, reducing the amount owed to OLB.
	7	Sold merchandise to Brill Co. for $11,500 under credit terms of 2/10, n/60, FOB destination, invoice dated July 7. The merchandise had cost $7,750.
	10	Purchased merchandise from Rupert Corporation for $14,200 under credit terms of 1/10, n/45, FOB shipping point, invoice dated July 10. The invoice showed that at Mason's request, Rupert paid the $500 shipping charges and added that amount to the bill. (*Hint:* Discounts are not applied to freight and shipping charges.)
	11	Paid $300 cash for shipping charges related to the July 7 sale to Brill Co.
	12	Brill returned merchandise from the July 7 sale that had cost Mason $1,450 and been sold for $1,850. The merchandise was restored to inventory.
	14	After negotiations with Rupert Corporation concerning problems with the merchandise purchased on July 10, Mason received a credit memorandum from Rupert granting a price reduction of $2,000.
	17	Received balance due from Brill Co. for the July 7 sale less the return on July 12.
	20	Paid the amount due Rupert Corporation for the July 10 purchase less the price reduction granted.
	21	Sold merchandise to Brown for $11,000 under credit terms of 1/10, n/30, FOB shipping point, invoice dated July 21. The merchandise had cost $7,000.
	24	Brown requested a price reduction on the July 21 sale because the merchandise did not meet specifications. Mason sent Brown a credit memorandum for $1,300 to resolve the issue.
	30	Received Brown's cash payment for the amount due from the July 21 sale.
	31	Paid OLB Corp. the amount due from the July 3 purchase.

Check   July 17, Dr. Cash $9,457
July 20, Cr. Cash $12,578

July 30, Dr. Cash $9,603

The following unadjusted trial balance is prepared at fiscal year-end for Foster Products Company.

Problem 5-3B
Preparing adjusting entries
and income statements; and
computing gross margin,
acid-test, and current ratios

A1 A2 P3 P4

File Edit View Insert Format Tools Data Accounting Window Help

FOSTER PRODUCTS COMPANY
Unadjusted Trial Balance
October 31, 2013

		Debit	Credit
2	Cash	$ 7,400	
3	Merchandise inventory	24,000	
4	Store supplies	9,700	
5	Prepaid insurance	6,600	
6	Store equipment	81,800	
7	Accumulated depreciation—Store equipment		$ 32,000
8	Accounts payable		18,000
9	D. Foster, Capital		43,000
10	D. Foster, Withdrawals	2,000	
11	Sales		227,100
12	Sales discounts	1,000	
13	Sales returns and allowances	5,000	
14	Cost of goods sold	75,800	
15	Depreciation expense—Store equipment	0	
16	Salaries expense	63,000	
17	Insurance expense	0	
18	Rent expense	26,000	
19	Store supplies expense	0	
20	Advertising expense	17,800	
21	Totals	$ 320,100	$ 320,100

Sheet1 / Sheet2 / Sheet3 /

Rent expense and salaries expense are equally divided between selling activities and the general and administrative activities. Foster Products Company uses a perpetual inventory system.

Required

1. Prepare adjusting journal entries to reflect each of the following.
   a. Store supplies still available at fiscal year-end amount to $3,700.
   b. Expired insurance, an administrative expense, for the fiscal year is $2,800.
   c. Depreciation expense on store equipment, a selling expense, is $3,000 for the fiscal year.
   d. To estimate shrinkage, a physical count of ending merchandise inventory is taken. It shows $21,300 of inventory is still available at fiscal year-end.
2. Prepare a multiple-step income statement for fiscal year 2013.
3. Prepare a single-step income statement for fiscal year 2013.
4. Compute the current ratio, acid-test ratio, and gross margin ratio as of October 31, 2013. (Round ratios to two decimals.)

Check (2) Gross profit, $142,600;
(3) Total expenses, $197,100;
Net income, $24,000

Barkley Company's adjusted trial balance on March 31, 2013, its fiscal year-end, follows.

Problem 5-4B
Computing merchandising
amounts and formatting
income statements

C1 C2 P4

	Debit	Credit
Merchandise inventory	$ 56,500	
Other (noninventory) assets	202,600	
Total liabilities		$ 42,500
C. Barkley, Capital		164,425
C. Barkley, Withdrawals	3,000	

[continued on next page]

[continued from previous page]

Sales		332,650
Sales discounts	5,875	
Sales returns and allowances	20,000	
Cost of goods sold	115,600	
Sales salaries expense	44,500	
Rent expense—Selling space	16,000	
Store supplies expense ....:........	3,850	
Advertising expense	26,000	
Office salaries expense	40,750	
Rent expense—Office space	3,800	
Office supplies expense	1,100	
Totals	$539,575	$539,575

On March 31, 2012, merchandise inventory was $37,500. Supplementary records of merchandising activities for the year ended March 31, 2013, reveal the following itemized costs.

Invoice cost of merchandise purchases	$138,500
Purchase discounts received	2,950
Purchase returns and allowances	6,700
Costs of transportation-in	5,750

Required

1. Calculate the company's net sales for the year.

Check (2) $134,600;

2. Calculate the company's total cost of merchandise purchased for the year.

(3) Gross profit, $191,175; Net income, $55,175;

3. Prepare a multiple-step income statement that includes separate categories for selling expenses and for general and administrative expenses.

(4) Total expenses, $251,600

4. Prepare a single-step income statement that includes these expense categories: cost of goods sold, selling expenses, and general and administrative expenses.

Problem 5-5B
Preparing closing entries and interpreting information about discounts and returns

C2 P3

Use the data for Barkley Company in Problem 5-4B to complete the following requirements.

Required

1. Prepare closing entries as of March 31, 2013 (the perpetual inventory system is used).

Analysis Component

Check (1) $55,175 Dr. to close Income Summary

2. The company makes all purchases on credit, and its suppliers uniformly offer a 3% sales discount. Does it appear that the company's cash management system is accomplishing the goal of taking all available discounts? Explain.

(3) Current-year rate, 6.0%

3. In prior years, the company experienced a 5% returns and allowance rate on its sales, which means approximately 5% of its gross sales were eventually returned outright or caused the company to grant allowances to customers. How do this year's results compare to prior years' results?

Problem 5-6B[B]
Preparing a work sheet for a merchandiser

P3

Refer to the data and information in Problem 5-3B.

Required

Prepare and complete the entire 10-column work sheet for Foster Products Company. Follow the structure of Exhibit 5B.1 in Appendix 5B.

(This serial problem began in Chapter 1 and continues through most of the book. If previous chapter segments were not completed, the serial problem can begin at this point. It is helpful, but not necessary, to use the Working Papers that accompany the book.)

SP 5   Adria Lopez created Success Systems on October 1, 2013. The company has been successful, and its list of customers has grown. To accommodate the growth, the accounting system is modified to set up separate accounts for each customer. The following chart of accounts includes the account number used for each account and any balance as of December 31, 2013. Adria Lopez decided to add a fourth digit with a decimal point to the 106 account number that had been used for the single Accounts Receivable account. This change allows the company to continue using the existing chart of accounts.

No.	Account Title	Dr.	Cr.
101	Cash	$58,160	
106.1	Alex's Engineering Co.	0	
106.2	Wildcat Services	0	
106.3	Easy Leasing	0	
106.4	IFM Co.	3,000	
106.5	Liu Corp.	0	
106.6	Gomez Co.	2,668	
106.7	Delta Co.	0	
106.8	KC, Inc.	0	
106.9	Dream, Inc.	0	
119	Merchandise inventory	0	
126	Computer supplies	580	
128	Prepaid insurance	1,665	
131	Prepaid rent	825	
163	Office equipment	8,000	
164	Accumulated depreciation—Office equipment		$ 400
167	Computer equipment	20,000	
168	Accumulated depreciation—Computer equipment		1,250
201	Accounts payable		1,100

No.	Account Title	Dr.	Cr.
210	Wages payable		$ 500
236	Unearned computer services revenue		1,500
301	A. Lopez, Capital		90,148
302	A. Lopez, Withdrawals	$0	
403	Computer services revenue		0
413	Sales		0
414	Sales returns and allowances	0	
415	Sales discounts	0	
502	Cost of goods sold	0	
612	Depreciation expense—Office equipment	0	
613	Depreciation expense—Computer equipment	0	
623	Wages expense	0	
637	Insurance expense	0	
640	Rent expense	0	
652	Computer supplies expense	0	
655	Advertising expense	0	
676	Mileage expense	0	
677	Miscellaneous expenses	0	
684	Repairs expense—Computer	0	

In response to requests from customers, A. Lopez will begin selling computer software. The company will extend credit terms of 1/10, n/30, FOB shipping point, to all customers who purchase this merchandise. However, no cash discount is available on consulting fees. Additional accounts (Nos. 119, 413, 414, 415, and 502) are added to its general ledger to accommodate the company's new merchandising activities. Also, Success Systems does not use reversing entries and, therefore, all revenue and expense accounts have zero beginning balances as of January 1, 2014. Its transactions for January through March follow:

Jan. 4   The company paid cash to Lyn Addie for five days' work at the rate of $125 per day. Four of the five days relate to wages payable that were accrued in the prior year.
5   Adria Lopez invested an additional $25,000 cash in the company.
7   The company purchased $5,800 of merchandise from Kansas Corp. with terms of 1/10, n/30, FOB shipping point, invoice dated January 7.
9   The company received $2,668 cash from Gomez Co. as full payment on its account.
11   The company completed a five-day project for Alex's Engineering Co. and billed it $5,500, which is the total price of $7,000 less the advance payment of $1,500.
13   The company sold merchandise with a retail value of $5,200 and a cost of $3,560 to Liu Corp., invoice dated January 13.
15   The company paid $600 cash for freight charges on the merchandise purchased on January 7.
16   The company received $4,000 cash from Delta Co. for computer services provided.
17   The company paid Kansas Corp. for the invoice dated January 7, net of the discount.
20   Liu Corp. returned $500 of defective merchandise from its invoice dated January 13. The returned merchandise, which had a $320 cost, is discarded. (The policy of Success Systems is to leave the cost of defective products in cost of goods sold.)

Check   Jan. 11, Dr. Unearned Computer Services Revenue $1,500

Check   Jan. 20, No entry to Cost of Goods Sold

	22	The company received the balance due from Liu Corp., net of both the discount and the credit for the returned merchandise.
	24	The company returned defective merchandise to Kansas Corp. and accepted a credit against future purchases. The defective merchandise invoice cost, net of the discount, was $496.
	26	The company purchased $9,000 of merchandise from Kansas Corp. with terms of 1/10, n/30, FOB destination, invoice dated January 26.
	26	The company sold merchandise with a $4,640 cost for $5,800 on credit to KC, Inc., invoice dated January 26.
	29	The company received a $496 credit memorandum from Kansas Corp. concerning the merchandise returned on January 24.
	31	The company paid cash to Lyn Addie for 10 days' work at $125 per day.
Feb.	1	The company paid $2,475 cash to Hillside Mall for another three months' rent in advance.
	3	The company paid Kansas Corp. for the balance due, net of the cash discount, less the $496 amount in the credit memorandum.
	5	The company paid $600 cash to the local newspaper for an advertising insert in today's paper.
	11	The company received the balance due from Alex's Engineering Co. for fees billed on January 11.
	15	Adria Lopez withdrew $4,800 cash from the company for personal use.
	23	The company sold merchandise with a $2,660 cost for $3,220 on credit to Delta Co., invoice dated February 23.
	26	The company paid cash to Lyn Addie for eight days' work at $125 per day.
	27	The company reimbursed Adria Lopez for business automobile mileage (600 miles at $0.32 per mile).
Mar.	8	The company purchased $2,730 of computer supplies from Harris Office Products on credit, invoice dated March 8.
	9	The company received the balance due from Delta Co. for merchandise sold on February 23.
	11	The company paid $960 cash for minor repairs to the company's computer.
	16	The company received $5,260 cash from Dream, Inc., for computing services provided.
	19	The company paid the full amount due to Harris Office Products, consisting of amounts created on December 15 (of $1,100) and March 8.
	24	The company billed Easy Leasing for $8,900 of computing services provided.
	25	The company sold merchandise with a $2,002 cost for $2,800 on credit to Wildcat Services, invoice dated March 25.
	30	The company sold merchandise with a $1,100 cost for $2,220 on credit to IFM Company, invoice dated March 30.
	31	The company reimbursed Adria Lopez for business automobile mileage (400 miles at $0.32 per mile).

The following additional facts are available for preparing adjustments on March 31 prior to financial statement preparation:

a. The March 31 amount of computer supplies still available totals $2,005.

b. Three more months have expired since the company purchased its annual insurance policy at a $2,220 cost for 12 months of coverage.

c. Lyn Addie has not been paid for seven days of work at the rate of $125 per day.

d. Three months have passed since any prepaid rent has been transferred to expense. The monthly rent expense is $825.

e. Depreciation on the computer equipment for January 1 through March 31 is $1,250.

f. Depreciation on the office equipment for January 1 through March 31 is $400.

g. The March 31 amount of merchandise inventory still available totals $704.

Required

1. Prepare journal entries to record each of the January through March transactions.

Check (2) Ending balances at March 31: Cash, $77,845; Sales, $19,240;

(3) Unadj. totals, $161,198; Adj. totals, $163,723;

(4) Net income, $18,686;

2. Post the journal entries in part 1 to the accounts in the company's general ledger. (*Note:* Begin with the ledger's post-closing adjusted balances as of December 31, 2013.)

3. Prepare a partial work sheet consisting of the first six columns (similar to the one shown in Exhibit 5B.1) that includes the unadjusted trial balance, the March 31 adjustments (*a*) through (*g*), and the adjusted trial balance. Do not prepare closing entries and do not journalize the adjustments or post them to the ledger.

4. Prepare an income statement (from the adjusted trial balance in part 3) for the three months ended March 31, 2014. Use a single-step format. List all expenses without differentiating between selling expenses and general and administrative expenses.

5. Prepare a statement of owner's equity (from the adjusted trial balance in part 3) for the three months ended March 31, 2014.

6. Prepare a classified balance sheet (from the adjusted trial balance) as of March 31, 2014.

(5) A. Lopez, Capital (at March 31), $129,034;

(6) Total assets, $129,909

Beyond the Numbers

BTN 5-1 Refer to **Polaris'** financial statements in Appendix A to answer the following.

REPORTING IN ACTION

A1

Polaris

Required

1. Assume that the amounts reported for inventories and cost of sales reflect items purchased in a form ready for resale. Compute the net cost of goods purchased for the year ended December 31, 2011.

2. Compute the current ratio and acid-test ratio as of December 31, 2011 and 2010. Interpret and comment on the ratio results. How does Polaris compare to the industry average of 1.5 for the current ratio and 1.25 for the acid-test ratio?

Fast Forward

3. Access Polaris' financial statements (form 10-K) for fiscal years ending after December 31, 2011, from its Website (**Polaris.com**) or the SEC's EDGAR database (**www.sec.gov**). Recompute and interpret the current ratio and acid-test ratio for these current fiscal years.

BTN 5-2 Key comparative figures for both **Polaris** and **Arctic Cat** follow.

COMPARATIVE ANALYSIS

A2

Polaris

Arctic Cat

($ thousands)	Polaris		Arctic Cat	
	Current Year	Prior Year	Current Year	Prior Year
Net sales	$2,656,949	$1,991,139	$464,651	$450,728
Cost of sales	1,916,366	1,460,926	363,142	367,492

Required

1. Compute the dollar amount of gross margin and the gross margin ratio for the two years shown for each of these companies.

2. Which company earns more in gross margin for each dollar of net sales? How do they compare to the industry average of 25.0%?

3. Did the gross margin ratio improve or decline for these companies?

BTN 5-3 Amy Martin is a student who plans to attend approximately four professional events a year at her college. Each event necessitates a financial outlay of $100 to $200 for a new suit and accessories. After incurring a major hit to her savings for the first event, Amy developed a different approach. She buys the suit on credit the week before the event, wears it to the event, and returns it the next week to the store for a full refund on her charge card.

ETHICS CHALLENGE

C1   P2

Required

1. Comment on the ethics exhibited by Amy and possible consequences of her actions.

2. How does the merchandising company account for the suits that Amy returns?

BTN 5-4 You are the financial officer for Music Plus, a retailer that sells goods for home entertainment needs. The business owner, Vic Velakturi, recently reviewed the annual financial statements you prepared and sent you an e-mail stating that he thinks you overstated net income. He explains that although he has invested a great deal in security, he is sure shoplifting and other forms of inventory shrinkage have occurred, but he does not see any deduction for shrinkage on the income statement. The store uses a perpetual inventory system.

COMMUNICATING IN PRACTICE

C2   P3   P5

Required

Prepare a brief memorandum that responds to the owner's concerns.

TAKING IT TO THE NET

A2 C1

BTN 5-5 Access the SEC's EDGAR database (**www.SEC.gov**) and obtain the March 19, 2012, filing of its fiscal 2012 10-K report (for year ended January 28, 2012) for **J. Crew Group, Inc.** (ticker: JCG).

Required

Prepare a table that reports the gross margin ratios for J. Crew using the revenues and cost of goods sold data from J. Crew's income statement for each of its most recent three years. Analyze and comment on the trend in its gross margin ratio.

TEAMWORK IN ACTION

C1 C2

BTN 5-6 Official Brands' general ledger and supplementary records at the end of its current period reveal the following.

Sales	$600,000	Merchandise inventory (beginning of period)		$ 98,000
Sales returns	20,000	Invoice cost of merchandise purchases		360,000
Sales discounts	13,000	Purchase discounts received		9,000
Cost of transportation-in	22,000	Purchase returns and allowances		11,000
Operating expenses	50,000	Merchandise inventory (end of period)		84,000

Required

Point: In teams of four, assign the same student *a* and *e*. Rotate teams for reporting on a different computation and the analysis in step 3.

1. *Each* member of the team is to assume responsibility for computing *one* of the following items. You are not to duplicate your teammates' work. Get any necessary amounts to compute your item from the appropriate teammate. Each member is to explain his or her computation to the team in preparation for reporting to the class.

    a. Net sales   **d.** Gross profit

    b. Total cost of merchandise purchases   **e.** Net income

    c. Cost of goods sold

2. Check your net income with the instructor. If correct, proceed to step 3.

3. Assume that a physical inventory count finds that actual ending inventory is $76,000. Discuss how this affects previously computed amounts in step 1.

ENTREPRENEURIAL DECISION

C1 C2 P4

BTN 5-7 Refer to the opening feature about **Faithful Fish**. Assume that Chelsea Eubank reports current annual sales at approximately $1 million and discloses the following income statement.

FAITHFUL FISH Income Statement For Year Ended January 31, 2012	
Net sales	$1,000,000
Cost of sales	610,000
Expenses (other than cost of sales)	200,000
Net income	$ 190,000

Chelsea Eubank sells to various individuals and retailers, ranging from small shops to large chains. Assume that she currently offers credit terms of 1/15, n/60, and ships FOB destination. To improve her cash flow, she is considering changing credit terms to 3/10, n/30. In addition, she proposes to change shipping terms to FOB shipping point. She expects that the increase in discount rate will increase net sales by 9%, but the gross margin ratio (and ratio of cost of sales divided by net sales) is expected to remain unchanged. She also expects that delivery expenses will be zero under this proposal; thus, expenses other than cost of sales are expected to increase only 6%.

Required

1. Prepare a forecasted income statement for the year ended January 31, 2013, based on the proposal.

2. Based on the forecasted income statement alone (from your part 1 solution), do you recommend that Chelsea implement the new sales policies? Explain.

3. What else should Chelsea consider before deciding whether or not to implement the new policies? Explain.

BTN 5-8   Arrange an interview (in person or by phone) with the manager of a retail shop in a mall or in the downtown area of your community. Explain to the manager that you are a student studying merchandising activities and the accounting for sales returns and sales allowances. Ask the manager what the store policy is regarding returns. Also find out if sales allowances are ever negotiated with customers. Inquire whether management perceives that customers are abusing return policies and what actions management takes to counter potential abuses. Be prepared to discuss your findings in class.

HITTING THE ROAD

C1 💡

Point: This activity complements the Ethics Challenge assignment.

BTN 5-9   **KTM** (**www.KTM.com**), **Polaris**, and **Arctic Cat** are competitors in the global marketplace. Key comparative figures for each company follow.

GLOBAL DECISION

A2 P4

KTM
Polaris
Arctic Cat

	Net Sales	Cost of Sales
KTM*	526,801	371,752
Polaris†	$2,656,949	$1,916,366
Arctic Cat†	$ 464,651	$ 363,142

* EUR thousands for KTM.

† $ thousands for Polaris and Arctic Cat.

Required

1. Rank the three companies (highest to lowest) based on the gross margin ratio.
2. Which of the companies uses a multiple-step income statement format? (These companies' income statements are in Appendix A.)

ANSWERS TO MULTIPLE CHOICE QUIZ

1. c; Gross profit = $550,000 − $193,000 = $357,000
2. d; ($4,500 − $250) × (100% − 2%) = $4,165
3. b; Net sales = $75,000 + $320,000 − $13,700 − $6,000 = $375,300

4. b; Acid-test ratio = $37,500/$50,000 = 0.750
5. a; Gross margin ratio = ($675,000 − $459,000)/$675,000 = 32%

Inventories and Cost of Sales

6

A Look Back

Chapter 5 focused on merchandising activities and how they are reported. We analyzed and recorded purchases and sales and explained accounting adjustments and closing for merchandisers.

A Look at This Chapter

This chapter emphasizes accounting for inventory. We describe methods for assigning costs to inventory and we explain the items and costs making up merchandise inventory. We also discuss methods of estimating and measuring inventory.

A Look Ahead

Chapter 7 emphasizes accounting information systems. We describe system principles, the system components, use of special journals and subsidiary ledgers, and technology-based systems.

Learning Objectives

CONCEPTUAL

C1 Identify the items making up merchandise inventory. (p. 230)

C2 Identify the costs of merchandise inventory. (p. 231)

ANALYTICAL

A1 Analyze the effects of inventory methods for both financial and tax reporting. (p. 238)

A2 Analyze the effects of inventory errors on current and future financial statements. (p. 240)

A3 Assess inventory management using both inventory turnover and days' sales in inventory. (p. 243)

PROCEDURAL

P1 Compute inventory in a perpetual system using the methods of specific identification, FIFO, LIFO, and weighted average. (p. 233)

P2 Compute the lower of cost or market amount of inventory. (p. 239)

P3 *Appendix 6A*—Compute inventory in a periodic system using the methods of specific identification, FIFO, LIFO, and weighted average. (p. 249)

P4 *Appendix 6B*—Apply both the retail inventory and gross profit methods to estimate inventory. (p. 254)

Decision Insight

Cool Company

MIAMI—"America is, and will always be, a place of unlimited opportunity for all who dream," insists Derick Pearson. Derick, along with his soon to be-wife Felecia Hatcher, launched **Feverish Ice Cream (FeverishIceCream.com)** after losing their jobs. Their company sells gourmet ice pops and ice cream concocted in their production facility, and the two sell them using ecofriendly, acid green carts and a Scion. Felecia explains that they focus on venues that attract young adults such as music events, campuses, skate parks, and farmers' markets. Their travels are posted on Twitter and Facebook.

The company launch, however, was a challenge. "We purchased two tricycle carts that we found on Craigslist," explains Felecia. "As the business grew, we were able to reinvest more money into it, buy more equipment." The couple also had to confront inventory production and sales planning, and had to deal with discounts and allowances.

A major challenge was identifying the appropriate inventories while controlling costs. "In the beginning it was just a lot of trial and error," says Felecia. "We had a lot of melted ice cream!" Applying inventory management, and old fashioned trial-and-error, Felecia and Derick learned to fill orders, collect money, and maintain the right level and mix of inventory. To help, they set up an inventory system to account for sales and purchases in real time.

The two insist that while it is important to serve customers' needs, business success demands sound inventory management. Further, that success requires more than good products and perpetual inventory management. Felecia explains that it requires commitment, patience, energy, faith, and maybe some luck. "It was a crazy idea but we really didn't have anything to lose," recalls Felecia. "Loving ice cream fueled a lot of our madness!"

While Derick and Felecia continue to measure, monitor, and manage inventories and costs, their success and growth are pushing them into new products and opportunities. "[We are] always about growing as organically as possible," asserts Felecia. "[Including] sustaining that growth." Their inventory procedures and accounting systems contribute to their lean business model. "[We] budget every cent, along with saving for future expenses," explains Derick. "There's nothing wrong with living simple," says Felecia. "Spend money on things that will last, and make do with what you have." Adds Derick, "We are living examples that dreams do come true!"

[Sources: Feverish Ice Cream Website, January 2013; *South Florida Times,* November 2011; *Palm Beach Post,* July 2011; Graves Publishing Company, February 2010; *Miami New Times,* November 2011]

Merchandisers' activities include the purchasing and reselling of merchandise. We explained accounting for merchandisers in Chapter 5, including that for purchases and sales. In this chapter, we extend the study and analysis of inventory by explaining the methods used to assign costs to merchandise inventory *and* to cost of goods sold. Retailers, wholesalers, and other merchandising companies that purchase products for resale use the principles and methods described here. Understanding inventory accounting helps in the analysis and interpretation of financial statements and helps people run their businesses.

INVENTORY BASICS

This section identifies the items and costs making up merchandise inventory. It also describes the importance of internal controls in taking a physical count of inventory.

Determining Inventory Items

C1 Identify the items making up merchandise inventory.

Merchandise inventory includes all goods that a company owns and holds for sale. This rule holds regardless of where the goods are located when inventory is counted. Certain inventory items require special attention, including goods in transit, goods on consignment, and goods that are damaged or obsolete.

Goods in Transit   Does a purchaser's inventory include goods in transit from a supplier? The answer is that if ownership has passed to the purchaser, the goods are included in the purchaser's inventory. We determine this by reviewing the shipping terms: *FOB destination* or *FOB shipping point.* If the purchaser is responsible for paying freight, ownership passes when goods are loaded on the transport vehicle. If the seller is responsible for paying freight, ownership passes when goods arrive at their destination.

Point: FOB shipping point is also called *FOB origin* or *FOB supplier's warehouse.*

Goods on Consignment   Goods on consignment are goods shipped by the owner, called the **consignor,** to another party, the **consignee.** A consignee sells goods for the owner. The consignor continues to own the consigned goods and reports them in its inventory. **Upper Deck**, for instance, pays sports celebrities such as Aaron Rodgers of the Green Bay Packers to sign memorabilia, which are offered to shopping networks on consignment. Upper Deck, the consignor, must report these items in its inventory until sold.

Goods Damaged or Obsolete   Damaged and obsolete (and deteriorated) goods are not counted in inventory if they cannot be sold. If these goods can be sold at a reduced price, they are included in inventory at a conservative estimate of their **net realizable value.** Net realizable value is sales price minus the cost of making the sale. The period when damage or obsolescence (or deterioration) occurs is the period when the loss in value is reported.

■ **Decision** Insight

A wireless portable device with a two-way radio allows clerks to quickly record inventory by scanning bar codes and to instantly send and receive inventory data. It gives managers access to up-to-date information on inventory and its location. ■

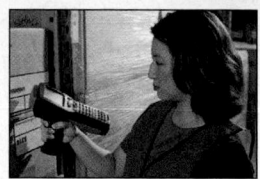

Determining Inventory Costs

Merchandise inventory includes costs of expenditures necessary, directly or indirectly, to bring an item to a salable condition and location. This means that the cost of an inventory item includes its invoice cost minus any discount, and plus any incidental costs necessary to put it in a place and condition for sale. Incidental costs can include import tariffs, freight, storage, insurance, and costs incurred in an aging process (for example, aging wine or cheese).

> **C2** Identify the costs of merchandise inventory.

Accounting principles prescribe that incidental costs be added to inventory. Also, the *matching (expense recognition) principle* states that inventory costs should be recorded against revenue in the period when inventory is sold. However, some companies use the *materiality constraint (cost-to-benefit constraint)* to avoid assigning some incidental costs of acquiring merchandise to inventory. Instead, they expense them to cost of goods sold when incurred. These companies argue either that those incidental costs are immaterial or that the effort in assigning them outweighs the benefit.

Internal Controls and Taking a Physical Count

Events can cause the Inventory account balance to differ from the actual inventory available. Such events include theft, loss, damage, and errors. Thus, nearly all companies take a *physical count of inventory* at least once each year—informally called *taking an inventory*. This often occurs at the end of a fiscal year or when inventory amounts are low. This physical count is used to adjust the Inventory account balance to the actual inventory available.

> **Fraud:** Auditors commonly observe employees as they take a physical inventory. Auditors take their own test counts to monitor the accuracy of a company's count.

A company applies internal controls when taking a physical count of inventory that usually include the following procedures to minimize fraud and to increase reliability:

- *Prenumbered inventory tickets* are prepared and distributed to the *counters*—each ticket must be accounted for.
- Counters of inventory are assigned and do not include those responsible for inventory.
- Counters confirm the validity of inventory, including its existence, amount, and quality.
- A second count is taken by a different counter.
- A manager confirms that all inventories are ticketed once, and only once.

> **Point:** The Inventory account is a controlling account for the inventory subsidiary ledger. This *subsidiary ledger* contains a separate record (units and costs) for each separate product, and it can be in electronic or paper form. Subsidiary records assist managers in planning and monitoring inventory.

Quick Check

Answers — p. 257

1. What accounting principle most guides the allocation of cost of goods available for sale between ending inventory and cost of goods sold?
2. If **Skechers** sells goods to **Famous Footwear** with terms FOB shipping point, which company reports these goods in its inventory while they are in transit?
3. An art gallery purchases a painting for $11,400 on terms FOB shipping point. Additional costs in obtaining and offering the artwork for sale include $130 for transportation-in, $150 for import tariffs, $100 for insurance during shipment, $180 for advertising, $400 for framing, and $800 for office salaries. In computing inventory, what cost is assigned to the painting?

INVENTORY COSTING UNDER A PERPETUAL SYSTEM

Accounting for inventory affects both the balance sheet and the income statement. A major goal in accounting for inventory is to properly match costs with sales. We use the *expense recognition* (or *matching*) *principle* to decide how much of the cost of the goods available for sale is deducted from sales and how much is carried forward as inventory and matched against future sales.

Management decisions in accounting for inventory involve the following:

- Items included in inventory and their costs.
- Costing method (specific identification, FIFO, LIFO, or weighted average).
- Inventory system (perpetual or periodic).
- Use of market values or other estimates.

The first point was explained on the prior two pages. The second and third points will be addressed now. The fourth point is the focus at the end of this chapter. Decisions on these points affect the reported amounts for inventory, cost of goods sold, gross profit, income, current assets, and other accounts.

One of the most important issues in accounting for inventory is determining the per unit costs assigned to inventory items. When all units are purchased at the same unit cost, this process is simple. When identical items are purchased at different costs, however, a question arises as to which amounts to record in cost of goods sold and which amounts remain in inventory.

Four methods are commonly used to assign costs to inventory and to cost of goods sold: (1) specific identification; (2) first-in, first-out; (3) last-in, first-out; and (4) weighted average. Exhibit 6.1 shows the frequency in the use of these methods.

EXHIBIT 6.1

Frequency in Use of Inventory Methods

Other* 3%

FIFO 50%

Weighted Average 20%

LIFO 27%

*Includes specific identification.

Each method assumes a particular pattern for how costs flow through inventory. Each of these four methods is acceptable whether or not the actual physical flow of goods follows the cost flow assumption. Physical flow of goods depends on the type of product and the way it is stored. (Perishable goods such as fresh fruit demand that a business attempt to sell them in a first-in, first-out physical flow. Other products such as crude oil and minerals such as coal, gold, and decorative stone can be sold in a last-in, first-out physical flow.) **Physical flow and cost flow need not be the same**.

Inventory Cost Flow Assumptions

This section introduces inventory cost flow assumptions. For this purpose, assume that three identical units are purchased separately at the following three dates and costs: May 1 at $45, May 3 at $65, and May 6 at $70. One unit is then sold on May 7 for $100. Exhibit 6.2 gives a visual layout of the flow of costs to either the gross profit section of the income statement or the inventory reported on the balance sheet for FIFO, LIFO, and weighted average.

(1) *FIFO assumes costs flow in the order incurred.* The unit purchased on May 1 for $45 is the earliest cost incurred—it is sent to cost of goods sold on the income statement first. The remaining two units ($65 and $70) are reported in inventory on the balance sheet.

(2) *LIFO assumes costs flow in the reverse order incurred.* The unit purchased on May 6 for $70 is the most recent cost incurred—it is sent to cost of goods sold on the income statement. The remaining two units ($45 and $65) are reported in inventory on the balance sheet.

(3) *Weighted average assumes costs flow at an average of the costs available.* The units available at the May 7 sale average $60 in cost, computed as ($45 + $65 + $70)/3. One unit's $60 average cost is sent to cost of goods sold on the income statement. The remaining two units' average costs are reported in inventory at $120 on the balance sheet.

Cost flow assumptions can markedly impact gross profit and inventory numbers. Exhibit 6.2 shows that gross profit as a percent of net sales ranges from 30% to 55% due to nothing else but the cost flow assumption.

Point: It is helpful to recall the cost flow of inventory from Exhibit 5.4.

Beginning inventory + Net purchases

= Merchandise available for sale

Ending inventory + Cost of goods sold

The following sections on inventory costing use the perpetual system. Appendix 6A uses the periodic system. An instructor can choose to cover either one or both systems. If the perpetual system is skipped, then read Appendix 6A and return to the Decision Maker box (on page 238) titled "Cost Analyst."

EXHIBIT 6.2

Cost Flow Assumptions

Inventory Costing Illustration

This section provides a comprehensive illustration of inventory costing methods. We use information from Trekking, a sporting goods store. Among its many products, Trekking carries one type of mountain bike whose sales are directed at resorts that provide inexpensive mountain bikes for complimentary guest use. Its customers usually purchase in amounts of 10 or more bikes. We use Trekking's data from August. Its mountain bike (unit) inventory at the beginning of August and its purchases and sales during August are shown in Exhibit 6.3. It ends August with 12 bikes remaining in inventory.

P1 Compute inventory in a perpetual system using the methods of specific identification, FIFO, LIFO, and weighted average.

EXHIBIT 6.3

Purchases and Sales of Goods

Date	Activity	Units Acquired at Cost	Units Sold at Retail	Unit Inventory
Aug. 1	Beginning inventory	10 units @ $ 91 = $ 910		10 units
Aug. 3	Purchases	15 units @ $106 = $ 1,590		25 units
Aug. 14	Sales		20 units @ $130	5 units
Aug. 17	Purchases	20 units @ $115 = $ 2,300		25 units
Aug. 28	Purchases	10 units @ $119 = $ 1,190		35 units
Aug. 31	Sales		23 units @ $150	**12 units**
	Totals	**55 units** **$5,990**	**43 units**	

Units available for sale | Goods available for sale | Units sold | Units left

Trekking uses the perpetual inventory system, which means that its merchandise inventory account is continually updated to reflect purchases and sales. **(Appendix 6A describes the assignment of costs to inventory using a periodic system.)** Regardless of what inventory method or system is used, cost of goods available for sale must be allocated between cost of goods sold and ending inventory.

Point: The perpetual inventory system is the most dominant system for U.S. businesses.

Point: Beginning inventory units plus purchased units equals units available for sale (UAFS).

Specific Identification

When each item in inventory can be identified with a specific purchase and invoice, we can use **specific identification** (also called *specific invoice inventory pricing*) to assign costs. We also need sales records that identify exactly which items were sold and when. Trekking's internal documents reveal the following specific unit sales:

August 14 Sold 8 bikes costing $91 each and 12 bikes costing $106 each
August 31 Sold 2 bikes costing $91 each, 3 bikes costing $106 each, 15 bikes costing $115 each, and 3 bikes costing $119 each

Point: Three key variables determine the dollar value of ending inventory: (1) inventory quantity, (2) costs of inventory, and (3) cost flow assumption.

Applying specific identification, and using the information above and from Exhibit 6.3, we prepare Exhibit 6.4. This exhibit starts with 10 bikes at $91 each in beginning inventory. On August 3, 15 more bikes are purchased at $106 each for $1,590. Inventory available now consists of 10 bikes at $91 each and 15 bikes at $106 each, for a total of $2,500. On August 14 (see sales data on previous page), 20 bikes costing $2,000 are sold—leaving 5 bikes costing $500 in inventory. On August 17, 20 bikes costing $2,300 are purchased, and on August 28, another 10 bikes costing $1,190 are purchased, for a total of 35 bikes costing $3,990 in inventory. On August 31 (see sales data on previous page), 23 bikes costing $2,582 are sold, which leaves 12 bikes costing $1,408 in ending inventory. Carefully study this exhibit and the boxed explanations to see the flow of costs both in and out of inventory. Each unit, whether sold or remaining in inventory, has its own specific cost attached to it.

EXHIBIT 6.4

Specific Identification Computations

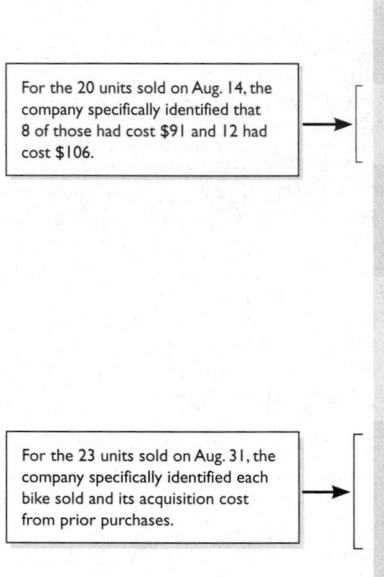

"goods in"   "goods out"   "what's left"

Date	Goods Purchased	Cost of Goods Sold	Inventory Balance
Aug. 1	Beginning balance		10 @ $ 91 = $ 910
Aug. 3	15 @ $106 = $1,590		10 @ $ 91 ⎫ 15 @ $106 ⎬ = $2,500
Aug. 14		8 @ $ 91 = $ 728 ⎫ 12 @ $106 = $1,272 ⎬ = $2,000*	2 @ $ 91 ⎫ 3 @ $106 ⎬ = $ 500
Aug. 17	20 @ $115 = $2,300		2 @ $ 91 ⎫ 3 @ $106 ⎬ = $2,800 20 @ $115 ⎭
Aug. 28	10 @ $119 = $1,190		2 @ $ 91 ⎫ 3 @ $106 ⎪ 20 @ $115 ⎬ = $3,990 10 @ $119 ⎭
Aug. 31		2 @ $ 91 = $ 182 ⎫ 3 @ $106 = $ 318 ⎪ 15 @ $115 = $1,725 ⎬ = $2,582* 3 @ $119 = $ 357 ⎭ $4,582	5 @ $115 ⎫ 7 @ $119 ⎬ = $1,408

For the 20 units sold on Aug. 14, the company specifically identified that 8 of those had cost $91 and 12 had cost $106.

For the 23 units sold on Aug. 31, the company specifically identified each bike sold and its acquisition cost from prior purchases.

* Identification of items sold (and their costs) is obtained from internal documents that track each unit from its purchase to its sale.

When using specific identification, Trekking's cost of goods sold reported on the income statement totals **$4,582**, the sum of $2,000 and $2,582 from the third column of Exhibit 6.4. Trekking's ending inventory reported on the balance sheet is **$1,408**, which is the final inventory balance from the fourth column of Exhibit 6.4.

The purchases and sales entries for Exhibit 6.4 follow (the colored boldface numbers are those impacted by the cost flow assumption):

Point: Specific identification is usually practical for companies with expensive or custom-made inventory. Examples include car dealerships, implement dealers such as John Deere, jewelers, and fashion designers.

Purchases

Aug. 3	Merchandise Inventory	1,590	
	Accounts Payable		1,590
17	Merchandise Inventory	2,300	
	Accounts Payable		2,300
28	Merchandise Inventory	1,190	
	Accounts Payable		1,190

Sales

Aug. 14	Accounts Receivable	2,600	
	Sales		2,600
14	Cost of Goods Sold	**2,000**	
	Merchandise Inventory		**2,000**
31	Accounts Receivable	3,450	
	Sales		3,450
31	Cost of Goods Sold	**2,582**	
	Merchandise Inventory		**2,582**

Point: The assignment of costs to the goods sold and to inventory using specific identification is the same for both the perpetual and periodic systems.

First-In, First-Out

The **first-in, first-out (FIFO)** method of assigning costs to both inventory and cost of goods sold assumes that inventory items are sold in the order acquired. When sales occur, the costs of the earliest units acquired are charged to cost of goods sold. This leaves the costs from the most recent purchases in ending inventory. Use of FIFO for computing the cost of inventory and cost of goods sold is shown in Exhibit 6.5.

This exhibit starts with beginning inventory of 10 bikes at $91 each. On August 3, 15 more bikes costing $106 each are bought for $1,590. Inventory now consists of 10 bikes at $91 each and 15 bikes at $106 each, for a total of $2,500. On August 14, 20 bikes are sold—applying FIFO, the first 10 sold cost $91 each and the next 10 sold cost $106 each, for a total cost of $1,970. This leaves 5 bikes costing $106 each, or $530, in inventory. On August 17, 20 bikes costing $2,300 are purchased, and on August 28, another 10 bikes costing $1,190 are purchased, for a total of 35 bikes costing $4,020 in inventory. On August 31, 23 bikes are sold—applying FIFO, the first 5 bikes sold cost $530 and the next 18 sold cost $2,070, which leaves 12 bikes costing $1,420 in ending inventory.

Point: The "Goods Purchased" column is identical for all methods. Data are taken from Exhibit 6.3.

Date	Goods Purchased	Cost of Goods Sold	Inventory Balance
Aug. 1	Beginning balance		10 @ $ 91 = $ 910
Aug. 3	15 @ $106 = $1,590		10 @ $ 91 } 15 @ $106 } = $2,500
Aug. 14		10 @ $ 91 = $ 910 } 10 @ $106 = $1,060 } = **$1,970**	5 @ $106 = $ 530
Aug. 17	20 @ $115 = $2,300		5 @ $106 } 20 @ $115 } = $2,830
Aug. 28	10 @ $119 = $1,190		5 @ $106 } 20 @ $115 } = $4,020 10 @ $119 }
Aug. 31		5 @ $106 = $ 530 } 18 @ $115 = $2,070 } = **$2,600** **$4,570**	2 @ $115 } 10 @ $119 } = **$1,420**

EXHIBIT 6.5

FIFO Computations—
Perpetual System

For the 20 units sold on Aug. 14, the first 10 sold are assigned the earliest cost of $91 (from beg. bal.). The next 10 sold are assigned the next earliest cost of $106.

For the 23 units sold on Aug. 31, the first 5 sold are assigned the earliest available cost of $106 (from Aug. 3 purchase). The next 18 sold are assigned the next earliest cost of $115 (from Aug. 17 purchase).

Trekking's FIFO cost of goods sold reported on its income statement (reflecting the 43 units sold) is **$4,570** ($1,970 + $2,600), and its ending inventory reported on the balance sheet (reflecting the 12 units unsold) is **$1,420**.

The purchases and sales entries for Exhibit 6.5 follow (the colored boldface numbers are those affected by the cost flow assumption).

Point: Under FIFO, a unit sold is assigned the earliest (oldest) cost from inventory. This leaves the most recent costs in ending inventory.

Point: *LOSH (last ones still here)* can help remember what costs are in FIFO ending inventory.

Purchases		
Aug. 3	Merchandise Inventory 1,590	
	Accounts Payable	1,590
17	Merchandise Inventory 2,300	
	Accounts Payable	2,300
28	Merchandise Inventory 1,190	
	Accounts Payable	1,190

Sales		
Aug. 14	Accounts Receivable 2,600	
	Sales	2,600
14	Cost of Goods Sold **1,970**	
	Merchandise Inventory	**1,970**
31	Accounts Receivable 3,450	
	Sales	3,450
31	Cost of Goods Sold **2,600**	
	Merchandise Inventory	**2,600**

Last-In, First-Out

The **last-in, first-out (LIFO)** method of assigning costs assumes that the most recent purchases are sold first. These more recent costs are charged to the goods sold, and the costs of the earliest purchases are assigned to inventory. As with other methods, LIFO is acceptable even when the physical flow of goods does not follow a last-in, first-out pattern. One appeal of LIFO is that by assigning costs from the most recent purchases to cost of goods sold, LIFO comes closest to matching current costs of goods sold with revenues (compared to FIFO or weighted average).

Exhibit 6.6 shows the LIFO computations. It starts with beginning inventory of 10 bikes at $91 each. On August 3, 15 more bikes costing $106 each are bought for $1,590. Inventory now consists of 10 bikes at $91 each and 15 bikes at $106 each, for a total of $2,500. On August 14, 20 bikes are sold—applying LIFO, the first 15 sold are from the most recent purchase costing $106 each, and the next 5 sold are from the next most recent purchase costing $91 each, for a total cost of $2,045. This leaves 5 bikes costing $91 each, or $455, in inventory. On August 17, 20 bikes costing $2,300 are purchased, and on August 28, another 10 bikes costing $1,190 are purchased, for a total of 35 bikes costing $3,945 in inventory. On August 31, 23 bikes are sold—applying LIFO, the first 10 bikes sold are from the most recent purchase costing $1,190, and the next 13 sold are from the next most recent purchase costing $1,495, which leaves 12 bikes costing $1,260 in ending inventory.

EXHIBIT 6.6

LIFO Computations—
Perpetual System

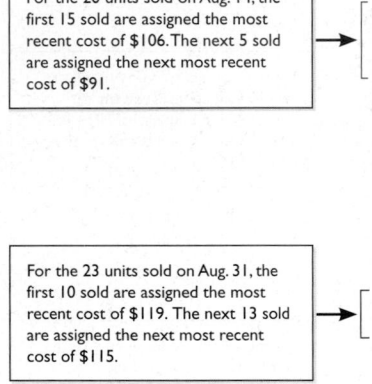

For the 20 units sold on Aug. 14, the first 15 sold are assigned the most recent cost of $106. The next 5 sold are assigned the next most recent cost of $91.

For the 23 units sold on Aug. 31, the first 10 sold are assigned the most recent cost of $119. The next 13 are assigned the next most recent cost of $115.

Date	Goods Purchased	Cost of Goods Sold	Inventory Balance
Aug. 1	Beginning balance		10 @ $ 91 = $ 910
Aug. 3	15 @ $106 = $1,590		10 @ $ 91 ⎱ = $ 2,500 15 @ $106 ⎰
Aug. 14		15 @ $106 = $1,590 ⎱ = $2,045 5 @ $ 91 = $ 455 ⎰	5 @ $ 91 = $ 455
Aug. 17	20 @ $115 = $2,300		5 @ $ 91 ⎱ = $ 2,755 20 @ $115 ⎰
Aug. 28	10 @ $119 = $1,190		5 @ $ 91 ⎱ 20 @ $115 ⎬ = $ 3,945 10 @ $119 ⎰
Aug. 31		10 @ $119 = $1,190 ⎱ = $2,685 13 @ $115 = $1,495 ⎰	5 @ $ 91 ⎱ = $1,260 7 @ $115 ⎰
		$4,730	

Trekking's LIFO cost of goods sold reported on the income statement is **$4,730** ($2,045 + $2,685), and its ending inventory reported on the balance sheet is **$1,260**.

The purchases and sales entries for Exhibit 6.6 follow (the colored boldface numbers are those affected by the cost flow assumption).

	Purchases		
Aug. 3	Merchandise Inventory	1,590	
	Accounts Payable		1,590
17	Merchandise Inventory	2,300	
	Accounts Payable		2,300
28	Merchandise Inventory	1,190	
	Accounts Payable		1,190

	Sales		
Aug. 14	Accounts Receivable	2,600	
	Sales		2,600
14	Cost of Goods Sold	**2,045**	
	Merchandise Inventory		**2,045**
31	Accounts Receivable	3,450	
	Sales		3,450
31	Cost of Goods Sold	**2,685**	
	Merchandise Inventory		**2,685**

Weighted Average

The **weighted average** (also called **average cost**) method of assigning cost requires that we use the weighted average cost per unit of inventory at the time of each sale. Weighted average cost per unit at the time of each sale equals the cost of goods available for sale divided by the units available. The results using weighted average (WA) for Trekking are shown in Exhibit 6.7.

This exhibit starts with beginning inventory of 10 bikes at $91 each. On August 3, 15 more bikes costing $106 each are bought for $1,590. Inventory now consists of 10 bikes at $91 each and 15 bikes at $106 each, for a total of $2,500. The average cost per bike for that inventory is $100, computed as $2,500/(10 bikes + 15 bikes). On August 14, 20 bikes are sold—applying

Date	Goods Purchased	Cost of Goods Sold	Inventory Balance	
Aug. 1	Beginning balance		10 @ $ 91 = $ 910	
Aug. 3	15 @ $106 = $1,590		10 @ $ 91 ⎱ 15 @ $106 ⎰ = $2,500 (or $100 per unit)[a]	
Aug. 14		20 @ $100 = **$2,000**	5 @ $100 = $ 500 (or $100 per unit)[b]	
Aug. 17	20 @ $115 = $2,300		5 @ $100 ⎱ 20 @ $115 ⎰ = $2,800 (or $112 per unit)[c]	
Aug. 28	10 @ $119 = $1,190		5 @ $100 ⎱ 20 @ $115 ⎬ = $3,990 (or $114 per unit)[d] 10 @ $119 ⎰	
Aug. 31		23 @ $114 = **$2,622**	12 @ $114 = **$1,368** (or $114 per unit)[e]	
		$4,622		

EXHIBIT 6.7

Weighted Average
Computations—Perpetual System

> For the 20 units sold on Aug. 14, the cost assigned is the $100 *average cost* per unit from the inventory balance column at the time of sale.

> For the 23 units sold on Aug. 31, the cost assigned is the $114 *average cost* per unit from the inventory balance column at the time of sale.

[a] $100 per unit = ($2,500 inventory balance ÷ 25 units in inventory).
[b] $100 per unit = ($500 inventory balance ÷ 5 units in inventory).
[c] $112 per unit = ($2,800 inventory balance ÷ 25 units in inventory).
[d] $114 per unit = ($3,990 inventory balance ÷ 35 units in inventory).
[e] $114 per unit = ($1,368 inventory balance ÷ 12 units in inventory).

WA, the 20 sold are assigned the $100 average cost, for a total cost of $2,000. This leaves 5 bikes with an average cost of $100 each, or $500, in inventory. On August 17, 20 bikes costing $2,300 are purchased, and on August 28, another 10 bikes costing $1,190 are purchased, for a total of 35 bikes costing $3,990 in inventory at August 28. The average cost per bike for the August 28 inventory is $114, computed as $3,990/(5 bikes + 20 bikes + 10 bikes). On August 31, 23 bikes are sold—applying WA, the 23 sold are assigned the $114 average cost, for a total cost of $2,622. This leaves 12 bikes costing $1,368 in ending inventory.

Trekking's cost of goods sold reported on the income statement (reflecting the 43 units sold) is **$4,622** ($2,000 + $2,622), and its ending inventory reported on the balance sheet (reflecting the 12 units unsold) is **$1,368**.

The purchases and sales entries for Exhibit 6.7 follow (the colored boldface numbers are those affected by the cost flow assumption).

Point: Under weighted average, a unit sold is assigned the average cost of all items currently available for sale at the date of each sale. This means a new average cost is computed after each purchase.

Purchases				Sales		
Aug. 3	Merchandise Inventory	1,590		Aug. 14	Accounts Receivable	2,600
	Accounts Payable		1,590		Sales		2,600
17	Merchandise Inventory	2,300		14	Cost of Goods Sold	**2,000**
	Accounts Payable		2,300		Merchandise Inventory		**2,000**
28	Merchandise Inventory	1,190		31	Accounts Receivable	3,450
	Accounts Payable		1,190		Sales		3,450
				31	Cost of Goods Sold	**2,622**
					Merchandise Inventory		**2,622**

This completes computations under the four most common perpetual inventory costing methods. Advances in technology have greatly reduced the cost of a perpetual inventory system. Many companies now ask whether they can afford *not* to have a perpetual inventory system because timely access to inventory information is a competitive advantage and it can help reduce the amount of inventory, which reduces costs.

Point: Cost of goods available for sale (COGAFS), units available for sale (UAFS), and units in ending inventory are identical for all methods.

 Decision Insight

Inventory Control   Inventory safeguards include restricted access, use of authorized requisitions, security measures, and controlled environments to prevent damage. Proper accounting includes matching inventory received with purchase order terms and quality requirements, preventing misstatements, and controlling access to inventory records. A study reports that 23% of employees in purchasing and procurement observed inappropriate kickbacks or gifts from suppliers. Another study reports that submission of fraudulent supplier invoices is now common, and perpetrators are often employees (KPMG 2011). ■

Financial Statement Effects of Costing Methods

A1 Analyze the effects of inventory methods for both financial and tax reporting.

When purchase prices do not change, each inventory costing method assigns the same cost amounts to inventory and to cost of goods sold. When purchase prices are different, however, the methods nearly always assign different cost amounts. We show these differences in Exhibit 6.8 using Trekking's data.

EXHIBIT 6.8

Financial Statement Effects of Inventory Costing Methods

TREKKING COMPANY For Month Ended August 31				
	Specific Identification	FIFO	LIFO	Weighted Average
Income Statement				
Sales	$ 6,050	$ 6,050	$ 6,050	$ 6,050
Cost of goods sold	4,582	4,570	4,730	4,622
Gross profit	1,468	1,480	1,320	1,428
Expenses	450	450	450	450
Income before taxes	1,018	1,030	870	978
Income tax expense (30%)	305	309	261	293
Net income	$ 713	$ 721	$ 609	$ 685
Balance Sheet				
Inventory	$1,408	$1,420	$1,260	$1,368

This exhibit reveals two important results. First, when purchase costs *regularly rise,* as in Trekking's case, the following occurs:

Point: Managers prefer FIFO when costs are rising *and* incentives exist to report higher income for reasons such as bonus plans, job security, and reputation.

- FIFO assigns the lowest amount to cost of goods sold—yielding the highest gross profit and net income.
- LIFO assigns the highest amount to cost of goods sold—yielding the lowest gross profit and net income, which also yields a temporary tax advantage by postponing payment of some income tax.
- Weighted average yields results between FIFO and LIFO.
- Specific identification always yields results that depend on which units are sold.

Point: LIFO inventory is often less than the inventory's replacement cost because LIFO inventory is valued using the oldest inventory purchase costs.

Second, when costs *regularly decline,* the reverse occurs for FIFO and LIFO. Namely, FIFO gives the highest cost of goods sold—yielding the lowest gross profit and income. However, LIFO then gives the lowest cost of goods sold—yielding the highest gross profit and income.

All four inventory costing methods are acceptable. However, a company must disclose the inventory method it uses in its financial statements or notes. Each method offers certain advantages as follows:

- FIFO assigns an amount to inventory on the balance sheet that approximates its current cost; it also mimics the actual flow of goods for most businesses.
- LIFO assigns an amount to cost of goods sold on the income statement that approximates its current cost; it also better matches current costs with revenues in computing gross profit.
- Weighted average tends to smooth out erratic changes in costs.
- Specific identification exactly matches the costs of items with the revenues they generate.

■ Decision Maker

Cost Analyst   Your supervisor says she finds managing product costs easier if the balance sheet reflects inventory values that closely reflect replacement cost. Which inventory costing method do you advise adopting? ■ [Answer—p. 256]

Tax Effects of Costing Methods   Trekking's segment income statement in Exhibit 6.8 includes income tax expense (at a rate of 30%) because it was formed as a corporation. Since inventory costs affect net income, they have potential tax effects. Trekking gains a temporary tax advantage by using LIFO. Many companies use LIFO for this reason.

Companies can and often do use different costing methods for financial reporting and tax reporting. *The only exception is when LIFO is used for tax reporting; in this case, the IRS requires that it also be used in financial statements*—called the LIFO conformity rule.

Point: *LIFO conformity rule* may be revised if IFRS is adopted for U.S. companies as IFRS currently does not permit LIFO (see Global View).

Consistency in Using Costing Methods

The **consistency concept** prescribes that a company use the same accounting methods period after period so that financial statements are comparable across periods—the only exception is when a change from one method to another will improve its financial reporting. The *full-disclosure principle* prescribes that the notes to the statements report this type of change, its justification, and its effect on income.

The consistency concept does *not* require a company to use one method exclusively. For example, it can use different methods to value different categories of inventory.

◼ Decision Ethics

Inventory Manager   Your compensation as inventory manager includes a bonus plan based on gross profit. Your superior asks your opinion on changing the inventory costing method from FIFO to LIFO. Since costs are expected to continue to rise, your superior predicts that LIFO would match higher current costs against sales, thereby lowering taxable income (and gross profit). What do you recommend? ◼   [Answer—p. 256]

Quick Check   Answers — p. 257

4. Describe one advantage for each of the inventory costing methods: specific identification, FIFO, LIFO, and weighted average.
5. When costs are rising, which method reports higher net income—LIFO or FIFO?
6. When costs are rising, what effect does LIFO have on a balance sheet compared to FIFO?
7. A company takes a physical count of inventory at the end of 2012 and finds that ending inventory is understated by $10,000. Would this error cause cost of goods sold to be overstated or understated in 2012? In year 2013? If so, by how much?

VALUING INVENTORY AT LCM AND THE EFFECTS OF INVENTORY ERRORS

This section examines the role of market costs in determining inventory on the balance sheet and also the financial statement effects of inventory errors.

Lower of Cost or Market

We explained how to assign costs to ending inventory and cost of goods sold using one of four costing methods (FIFO, LIFO, weighted average, or specific identification). However, *accounting principles require that inventory be reported at the market value (cost) of replacing inventory when market value is lower than cost.* Merchandise inventory is then said to be reported on the balance sheet at the **lower of cost or market (LCM).**

P2 Compute the lower of cost or market amount of inventory.

Computing the Lower of Cost or Market   *Market* in the term *LCM* is defined as the current replacement cost of purchasing the same inventory items in the usual manner. A decline in replacement cost reflects a loss of value in inventory. When the recorded cost of inventory is higher than the replacement cost, a loss is recognized. When the recorded cost is lower, no adjustment is made.

LCM is applied in one of three ways: (1) to each individual item separately, (2) to major categories of items, or (3) to the whole of inventory. The less similar the items that make up inventory, the more likely companies are to apply LCM to individual items or categories. With the increasing application of technology and inventory tracking, companies increasingly apply

EXHIBIT 6.9

Lower of Cost or Market
Computations

Inventory Items	Units	Per Unit Cost	Per Unit Market	Total Cost	Total Market	LCM Applied to Items
Cycles						
Roadster	20	$8,000	$7,000	$160,000	$140,000	$ 140,000
Sprint	10	5,000	6,000	50,000	60,000	50,000
Off-Road						
Trax-4	8	5,000	6,500	40,000	52,000	40,000
Blazer	5	9,000	7,000	45,000	35,000	35,000
Totals				$295,000		$265,000

> $140,000 is the lower of $160,000 or $140,000

> Market amount of $265,000 is lower than the $295,000 recorded cost

LCM to each individual item separately. Accordingly, we show that method only; however, advanced courses cover the other two methods. To illustrate LCM, we apply it to the ending inventory of a motorsports retailer in Exhibit 6.9.

LCM Applied to Individual Items   When LCM is applied to individual *items* of inventory, the number of comparisons equals the number of items. For Roadster, $140,000 is the lower of the $160,000 cost and the $140,000 market. For Sprint, $50,000 is the lower of the $50,000 cost and the $60,000 market. For Trax-4, $40,000 is the lower of the $40,000 cost and the $52,000 market. For Blazer, $35,000 is the lower of the $45,000 cost and the $35,000 market. This yields a $265,000 reported inventory, computed from $140,000 for Roadster plus $50,000 for Sprint plus $40,000 for Trax-4 plus $35,000 for Blazer.

The retailer **The Buckle** applies LCM and reports that its "inventory is stated at the lower of cost or market. Cost is determined using the average cost method."

Recording the Lower of Cost or Market   Inventory must be adjusted downward when market is less than cost. To illustrate, if LCM is applied to the individual items of inventory in Exhibit 6.9, the Merchandise Inventory account must be adjusted from the $295,000 recorded cost down to the $265,000 market amount as follows.

Cost of Goods Sold	30,000	
Merchandise Inventory		30,000
To adjust inventory cost to market.		

Accounting rules require that inventory be adjusted to market when market is less than cost, but inventory normally cannot be written up to market when market exceeds cost. If recording inventory down to market is acceptable, why are companies not allowed to record inventory up to market? One view is that a gain from a market increase should not be realized until a sales transaction verifies the gain. However, this view also applies when market is less than cost. A second and primary reason is the **conservatism constraint,** which prescribes the use of the less optimistic amount when more than one estimate of the amount to be received or paid exists and these estimates are about equally likely.

Financial Statement Effects of Inventory Errors

A2 Analyze the effects of inventory errors on current and future financial statements.

Companies must take care in both taking a physical count of inventory and in assigning a cost to it. An inventory error causes misstatements in cost of goods sold, gross profit, net income, current assets, and equity. It also causes misstatements in the next period's statements because ending inventory of one period is the beginning inventory of the next. As we consider the financial statement effects in this section, it is helpful if we recall the following *inventory relation.*

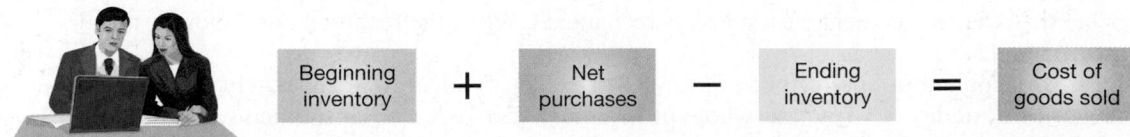

Income Statement Effects   Exhibit 6.10 shows the effects of inventory errors on key amounts in the current and next periods' income statements. Let's look at row 1 and year 1. We

> **Point:** Advances in technology encourage the individual-item approach for LCM.

> **Global:** IFRS requires LCM applied to individual items; this results in the most conservative inventory amount.

see that understating ending inventory overstates cost of goods sold. This can be seen from the above inventory relation where we subtract a smaller ending inventory amount in computing cost of goods sold. Then a higher cost of goods sold yields a lower income.

To understand year 2 of row 1, remember that an understated ending inventory for year 1 becomes an understated beginning inventory for year 2. Using the above inventory relation, we see that if beginning inventory is understated, then cost of goods sold is understated (because we are starting with a smaller amount). A lower cost of goods sold yields a higher income.

Turning to overstatements, let's look at row 2 and year 1. If ending inventory is overstated, we use the inventory relation to see that cost of goods sold is understated. A lower cost of goods sold yields a higher income.

For year 2 of row 2, we again recall that an overstated ending inventory for year 1 becomes an overstated beginning inventory for year 2. If beginning inventory is overstated, we use the inventory relation to see that cost of goods sold is overstated. A higher cost of goods sold yields a lower income.

EXHIBIT 6.10

Effects of Inventory Errors on the Income Statement

	Year 1		Year 2	
Ending Inventory	Cost of Goods Sold	Net Income	Cost of Goods Sold	Net Income
Understated⬇	Overstated⬆	Understated⬇	Understated⬇	Overstated⬆
Overstated*⬆	Understated⬇	Overstated⬆	Overstated⬆	Understated⬇

* This error is less likely under a perpetual system versus a periodic because it implies more inventory than is recorded (or less shrinkage than expected). Management will normally follow up and discover and correct this error before it impacts any accounts.

To illustrate, consider an inventory error for a company with $100,000 in sales for each of the years 2012, 2013, and 2014. If this company maintains a steady $20,000 inventory level during this period and makes $60,000 in purchases in each of these years, its cost of goods sold is $60,000 and its gross profit is $40,000 each year.

Ending Inventory Understated—Year 1 Assume that this company errs in computing its 2012 ending inventory and reports $16,000 instead of the correct amount of $20,000. The effects of this error are shown in Exhibit 6.11. The $4,000 understatement of 2012 ending inventory causes a $4,000 overstatement in 2012 cost of goods sold and a $4,000 understatement in both gross profit and net income for 2012. We see that these effects match the effects predicted in Exhibit 6.10.

EXHIBIT 6.11

Effects of Inventory Errors on Three Periods' Income Statements

Income Statements	2012		2013		2014	
Sales		$100,000		$100,000		$100,000
Cost of goods sold						
Beginning inventory	$20,000		→$16,000*		→$20,000	
Cost of goods purchased	60,000		60,000		60,000	
Goods available for sale	80,000		76,000		80,000	
Ending inventory	16,000*		20,000		20,000	
Cost of goods sold		64,000†		56,000†		60,000
Gross profit		36,000		44,000		40,000
Expenses		10,000		10,000		10,000
Net income		$ 26,000		$ 34,000		$ 30,000

Correct income is $30,000 for each year

* Correct amount is $20,000.   † Correct amount is $60,000.

Ending Inventory Understated—Year 2 The 2012 understated ending inventory becomes the 2013 understated *beginning* inventory. We see in Exhibit 6.11 that this error causes an understatement in 2013 cost of goods sold and a $4,000 overstatement in both gross profit and net income for 2013.

Ending Inventory Understated—Year 3 Exhibit 6.11 shows that the 2012 ending inventory error affects only that period and the next. It does not affect 2014 results or any period thereafter. An inventory error is said to be *self-correcting* because it always yields an offsetting error in the next period. This does not reduce the severity of inventory errors. Managers, lenders, owners, and others make important decisions from analysis of income and costs.

Example: If 2012 ending inventory in Exhibit 6.11 is overstated by $3,000 (not understated by $4,000), what is the effect on cost of goods sold, gross profit, assets, and equity? *Answer:* Cost of goods sold is understated by $3,000 in 2012 and overstated by $3,000 in 2013. Gross profit and net income are overstated in 2012 and understated in 2013. Assets and equity are overstated in 2012.

Point: A former internal auditor at **Coca-Cola** alleges that just before midnight at a prior calendar year-end, fully loaded Coke trucks were ordered to drive about 2 feet away from the loading dock so that Coke could record millions of dollars in extra sales.

We can also do an analysis of beginning inventory errors. The income statement effects are the opposite of those for ending inventory.

Balance Sheet Effects   Balance sheet effects of an inventory error can be seen by considering the accounting equation: Assets = Liabilities + Equity. For example, understating ending inventory understates both current and total assets. An understatement in ending inventory also yields an understatement in equity because of the understatement in net income. Exhibit 6.12 shows the effects of inventory errors on the current period's balance sheet amounts. Errors in *beginning* inventory do not yield misstatements in the end-of-period balance sheet, but they do affect that current period's income statement.

EXHIBIT 6.12

Effects of Inventory Errors on Current Period's Balance Sheet

Ending Inventory	Assets	Equity
Understated ⬇	Understated ⬇	Understated ⬇
Overstated ⬆	Overstated ⬆	Overstated ⬆

Quick Check   Answers — p. 257

8. Use LCM applied separately to the following individual items to compute ending inventory.

Product	Units	Unit Recorded Cost	Unit Market Cost
A	20	$ 6	$ 5
B	40	9	8
C	10	12	15

GLOBAL VIEW

This section discusses differences between U.S. GAAP and IFRS in the items and costs making up merchandise inventory, in the methods to assign costs to inventory, and in the methods to estimate inventory values.

Items and Costs Making Up Inventory   Both U.S. GAAP and IFRS include broad and similar guidance for the items and costs making up merchandise inventory. Specifically, under both accounting systems, merchandise inventory includes all items that a company owns and holds for sale. Further, merchandise inventory includes costs of expenditures necessary, directly or indirectly, to bring those items to a salable condition and location.

Assigning Costs to Inventory   Both U.S. GAAP and IFRS allow companies to use specific identification in assigning costs to inventory. Further, both systems allow companies to apply a *cost flow assumption*. The usual cost flow assumptions are: FIFO, Weighted Average, and LIFO. However, IFRS does not (currently) allow use of LIFO. As the convergence project progresses, this prohibition may or may not persist.

Estimating Inventory Costs   The value of inventory can change while it awaits sale to customers. That value can decrease or increase.

Decreases in Inventory Value   Both U.S. GAAP and IFRS require companies to write down (reduce the cost recorded for) inventory when its value falls below the cost recorded. This is referred to as the *lower of cost or market* method explained in this chapter. U.S. GAAP prohibits any later increase in the recorded value of that inventory even if that decline in value is reversed through value increases in later periods. However, IFRS allows reversals of those write downs up to the original acquisition cost. For example, if **Polaris** wrote down its 2011 inventory from $298 million to $250 million, it could not reverse this in future periods even if its value increased to more than $298 million. However, if Polaris applied IFRS, it could reverse that previous loss. (Another difference is that value refers to *replacement cost* under U.S. GAAP, but *net realizable value* under IFRS.)

Increases in Inventory Value   Neither U.S. GAAP nor IFRS allow inventory to be adjusted upward beyond the original cost. (One exception is that IFRS requires agricultural assets such as animals, forests, and plants to be measured at fair value less point-of-sale costs.)

Nokia provides the following description of its inventory valuation procedures: **NOKIA**

> Inventories are stated at the lower of cost or net realizable value. Cost . . . approximates actual cost on a FIFO (First-in First-out) basis. Net realizable value is the amount that can be realized from the sale of the inventory in the normal course of business after allowing for the costs of realization.

Inventory Turnover and Days' Sales in Inventory ▢▢▢ **Decision Analysis**

Inventory Turnover

Earlier chapters described two important ratios useful in evaluating a company's short-term liquidity: current ratio and acid-test ratio. A merchandiser's ability to pay its short-term obligations also depends on how quickly it sells its merchandise inventory. **Inventory turnover,** also called *merchandise inventory turnover* or, simply, *turns,* is one ratio used to assess this and is defined in Exhibit 6.13.

> **A3** Assess inventory management using both inventory turnover and days' sales in inventory.

EXHIBIT 6.13

Inventory Turnover

$$\text{Inventory turnover} = \frac{\text{Cost of goods sold}}{\text{Average inventory}}$$

This ratio reveals how many *times* a company turns over (sells) its inventory during a period. If a company's inventory greatly varies within a year, average inventory amounts can be computed from interim periods such as quarters or months.

Users apply inventory turnover to help analyze short-term liquidity and to assess whether management is doing a good job controlling the amount of inventory available. A low ratio compared to that of competitors suggests inefficient use of assets. The company may be holding more inventory than it needs to support its sales volume. Similarly, a very high ratio compared to that of competitors suggests inventory might be too low. This can cause lost sales if customers must back-order merchandise. Inventory turnover has no simple rule except to say *a high ratio is preferable provided inventory is adequate to meet demand.*

> **Point:** We must take care when comparing turnover ratios across companies that use different costing methods (such as FIFO and LIFO).

Days' Sales in Inventory

To better interpret inventory turnover, many users measure the adequacy of inventory to meet sales demand. **Days' sales in inventory,** also called *days' stock on hand,* is a ratio that reveals how much inventory is available in terms of the number of days' sales. It can be interpreted as the number of days one can sell from inventory if no new items are purchased. This ratio is often viewed as a measure of the buffer against out-of-stock inventory and is useful in evaluating liquidity of inventory. It is defined in Exhibit 6.14.

> **Point:** Inventory turnover is higher and days' sales in inventory is lower for industries such as foods and other perishable products. The reverse holds for nonperishable product industries.

EXHIBIT 6.14

Days' Sales in Inventory

$$\text{Days' sales in inventory} = \frac{\text{Ending inventory}}{\text{Cost of goods sold}} \times 365$$

Days' sales in inventory focuses on ending inventory and it estimates how many days it will take to convert inventory at the end of a period into accounts receivable or cash. Days' sales in inventory focuses on *ending* inventory whereas inventory turnover focuses on *average* inventory.

> **Point:** Days' sales in inventory for many Ford models has risen: Freestyle, 122 days; Montego, 109 days; Five Hundred, 118 days. The industry average is 73 days. (*BusinessWeek*)

 Decision Insight ━━━━━━━━━━━━━━━━━━━━━━━

Short Shelf Life   Whole Foods Market, Inc., is committed to foods that are fresh, wholesome, and safe to eat. To fulfill those values, Whole Foods Market focuses on inventory management. It turns its inventory 20 times a year with days' sales in inventory of 19 days. ∎

Analysis of Inventory Management

Inventory management is a major emphasis for merchandisers. They must both plan and control inventory purchases and sales. **Toys "R" Us** is one of those merchandisers. Its inventory in fiscal year 2011 was $2,104 million. This inventory constituted 58% of its current assets and 24% of its total assets. We apply the analysis tools in this section to Toys "R" Us, as shown in Exhibit 6.15—also see margin graph.

EXHIBIT 6.15

Inventory Turnover and Days'
Sales in Inventory for Toys "R" Us

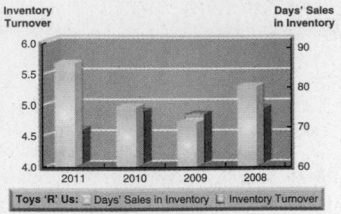

($ millions)	2011	2010	2009	2008
Cost of goods sold	$8,939	$8,790	$8,976	$8,987
Ending inventory	$2,104	$1,810	$1,781	$1,998
Inventory turnover	**4.6** times	**4.9** times	**4.8** times	**4.9** times
Industry inventory turnover	3.3 times	3.5 times	3.2 times	3.4 times
Days' sales in inventory	**86** days	**75** days	**72** days	**81** days
Industry days' sales in inventory	132 days	129 days	124 days	135 days

Its 2011 inventory turnover of 4.6 times means that Toys "R" Us turns over its inventory 4.6 times per year, or once every 79 days (365 days ÷ 4.6). We prefer inventory turnover to be high provided inventory is not out of stock and the company is not losing customers. The second metric, the 2011 days' sales in inventory of 86 days, reveals that it is carrying 86 days of sales in inventory. This inventory buffer seems more than adequate. The increased days' sales in inventory suggests that Toys "R" Us would benefit from further management efforts to increase inventory turnover and reduce inventory levels.

■ Decision Maker

Entrepreneur　Analysis of your retail store yields an inventory turnover of 5.0 and a days' sales in inventory of 73 days. The industry norm for inventory turnover is 4.4 and for days' sales in inventory is 74 days. What is your assessment of inventory management? ■　[Answer—p. 256]

DEMONSTRATION PROBLEM 1—PERPETUAL METHOD

Information: Craig Company buys and sells one product. Its beginning inventory, purchases, and sales during calendar year 2013 follow:

Date	Activity	Units Acquired at Cost	Units Sold at Retail	Unit Inventory
Jan. 1	Beg. Inventory	400 units @ $14 = $ 5,600		400 units
Jan. 15	Sale		200 units @ $30	200 units
March 10	Purchase	200 units @ $15 = $ 3,000		400 units
April 1	Sale		200 units @ $30	200 units
May 9	Purchase	300 units @ $16 = $ 4,800		500 units
Sept. 22	Purchase	250 units @ $20 = $ 5,000		750 units
Nov. 1	Sale		300 units @ $35	450 units
Nov. 28	Purchase	100 units @ $21 = $ 2,100		550 units
	Totals	1,250 units $20,500	700 units	

Additional tracking data for specific identification: (1) January 15 sale—200 units @ $14, (2) April 1 sale—200 units @ $15, and (3) November 1 sale—200 units @ $14 and 100 units @ $20.

Required

1. Calculate the cost of goods available for sale.
2. Apply the four different methods of inventory costing (FIFO, LIFO, weighted average, and specific identification) to calculate ending inventory and cost of goods sold under each method using the perpetual system.
3. Compute gross profit earned by the company for each of the four costing methods in part 2. Also, report the inventory amount reported on the balance sheet for each of the four methods.

4. In preparing financial statements for year 2013, the financial officer was instructed to use FIFO but failed to do so and instead computed cost of goods sold according to LIFO, which led to a $1,400 overstatement in cost of goods sold from using LIFO. Determine the impact on year 2013's income from the error. Also determine the effect of this error on year 2014's income. Assume no income taxes.

5. Management wants a report that shows how changing from FIFO to another method would change net income. Prepare a table showing (1) the cost of goods sold amount under each of the four methods, (2) the amount by which each cost of goods sold total is different from the FIFO cost of goods sold, and (3) the effect on net income if another method is used instead of FIFO.

PLANNING THE SOLUTION

- Compute cost of goods available for sale by multiplying the units of beginning inventory and each purchase by their unit costs to determine the total cost of goods available for sale.
- Prepare a perpetual FIFO table starting with beginning inventory and showing how inventory changes after each purchase and after each sale (see Exhibit 6.5).
- Prepare a perpetual LIFO table starting with beginning inventory and showing how inventory changes after each purchase and after each sale (see Exhibit 6.6).
- Make a table of purchases and sales recalculating the average cost of inventory prior to each sale to arrive at the weighted average cost of ending inventory. Total the average costs associated with each sale to determine cost of goods sold (see Exhibit 6.7).
- Prepare a table showing the computation of cost of goods sold and ending inventory using the specific identification method (see Exhibit 6.4).
- Compare the year-end 2013 inventory amounts under FIFO and LIFO to determine the misstatement of year 2013 income that results from using LIFO. The errors for year 2013 and 2014 are equal in amount but opposite in effect.
- Create a table showing cost of goods sold under each method and how net income would differ from FIFO net income if an alternate method is adopted.

SOLUTION TO DEMONSTRATION PROBLEM

1. Cost of goods available for sale (this amount is the same for all methods).

Date		Units	Unit Cost	Cost
Jan. 1	Beg. Inventory	400	$14	$ 5,600
March 10	Purchase	200	15	3,000
May 9	Purchase	300	16	4,800
Sept. 22	Purchase	250	20	5,000
Nov. 28	Purchase	100	21	2,100
	Total goods available for sale	1,250		$20,500

2a. FIFO perpetual method.

Date	Goods Purchased	Cost of Goods Sold	Inventory Balance
Jan. 1	Beginning balance		400 @ $14 = $ 5,600
Jan. 15		200 @ $14 = $2,800	200 @ $14 = $ 2,800
Mar. 10	200 @ $15 = $3,000		200 @ $14 200 @ $15 } = $ 5,800
April 1		200 @ $14 = $2,800	200 @ $15 = $ 3,000
May 9	300 @ $16 = $4,800		200 @ $15 300 @ $16 } = $ 7,800
Sept. 22	250 @ $20 = $5,000		200 @ $15 300 @ $16 250 @ $20 } = $12,800
Nov. 1		200 @ $15 = $3,000 100 @ $16 = $1,600	200 @ $16 250 @ $20 } = $ 8,200
Nov. 28	100 @ $21 = $2,100		200 @ $16 250 @ $20 100 @ $21 } = **$10,300**
Total cost of goods sold		**$10,200**	

Point: Students often mistakenly assume that the costing acronym refers to what remains in inventory. For example, it is important to realize that FIFO refers to costs that are assumed to flow into COGS; namely, the first units purchased are assumed to be the first ones to flow out to cost of goods sold. For FIFO, this means that the goods purchased most recently are assumed to be in ending inventory.

Note to students: **In a classroom situation,** once we compute cost of goods available for sale, we can compute the amount for either cost of goods sold or ending inventory—it is a matter of preference. **In practice,** the costs of items sold are identified as sales are made and immediately transferred from the inventory account to the cost of goods sold account. The previous solution showing the line-by-line approach illustrates actual application in practice. The following alternate solutions illustrate that, once the concepts are understood, other solution approaches are available. Although this is only shown for FIFO, it could be shown for all methods.

Alternate Methods to Compute FIFO Perpetual Numbers

[FIFO Alternate No. 1: Computing cost of goods sold first]

Cost of goods available for sale (from part 1)				$ 20,500
Cost of goods sold				
Jan. 15	Sold (200 @ $14)	$2,800		
April 1	Sold (200 @ $14)	2,800		
Nov. 1	Sold (200 @ $15 and 100 @ $16)	4,600	10,200	
Ending inventory				**$10,300**

[FIFO Alternate No. 2: Computing ending inventory first]

Cost of goods available for sale (from part 1)				$ 20,500
Ending inventory*				
Nov. 28	Purchase (100 @ $21)	$2,100		
Sept. 22	Purchase (250 @ $20)	5,000		
May 9	Purchase (200 @ $16)	3,200		
Ending inventory			10,300	
Cost of goods sold			**$10,200**	

* Since FIFO assumes that the earlier costs are the first to flow out, we determine ending inventory by assigning the most recent costs to the remaining items.

2b. LIFO perpetual method.

Date	Goods Purchased	Cost of Goods Sold	Inventory Balance	
Jan. 1	Beginning balance		400 @ $14	= $ 5,600
Jan. 15		200 @ $14 = $2,800	200 @ $14	= $ 2,800
Mar. 10	200 @ $15 = $3,000		200 @ $14 ⎱ 200 @ $15 ⎰	= $ 5,800
April 1		200 @ $15 = $3,000	200 @ $14	= $ 2,800
May 9	300 @ $16 = $4,800		200 @ $14 ⎱ 300 @ $16 ⎰	= $ 7,600
Sept. 22	250 @ $20 = $5,000		200 @ $14 ⎱ 300 @ $16 ⎱ 250 @ $20 ⎰	= $12,600
Nov. 1		250 @ $20 = $5,000 ⎱ 50 @ $16 = $ 800	200 @ $14 ⎱ 250 @ $16 ⎰	= $ 6,800
Nov. 28	100 @ $21 = $2,100		200 @ $14 ⎱ 250 @ $16 ⎱ 100 @ $21 ⎰	= $ 8,900
Total cost of goods sold		**$11,600**		

2c. Weighted average perpetual method.

Date	Goods Purchased	Cost of Goods Sold	Inventory Balance
Jan. 1	Beginning balance		400 @ $14 = $ 5,600
Jan. 15		200 @ $14 = $2,800	200 @ $14 = $ 2,800
Mar. 10	200 @ $15 = $3,000		200 @ $14 200 @ $15 } = $ 5,800 (avg. cost is $14.5)
April 1		200 @ $14.5 = $2,900	200 @ $14.5 = $ 2,900
May 9	300 @ $16 = $4,800		200 @ $14.5 300 @ $16 } = $ 7,700 (avg. cost is $15.4)
Sept. 22	250 @ $20 = $5,000		200 @ $14.5 300 @ $16 } = $ 12,700 250 @ $20 (avg. cost is $16.93)
Nov. 1		300 @ $16.93 = $5,079	450 @ $16.93 = $ 7,618.5
Nov. 28	100 @ $21 = $2,100		450 @ $16.93 100 @ $21 } = **$9,718.5**
Total cost of goods sold*		**$10,779**	

* The cost of goods sold ($10,779) plus ending inventory ($9,718.5) is $2.5 less than the cost of goods available for sale ($20,500) due to rounding.

2d. Specific identification method.

Date	Goods Purchased	Cost of Goods Sold	Inventory Balance
Jan. 1	Beginning balance		400 @ $14 = $ 5,600
Jan. 15		200 @ $14 = $2,800	200 @ $14 = $ 2,800
Mar. 10	200 @ $15 = $3,000		200 @ $14 200 @ $15 } = $ 5,800
April 1		200 @ $15 = $3,000	200 @ $14 = $ 2,800
May 9	300 @ $16 = $4,800		200 @ $14 300 @ $16 } = $ 7,600
Sept. 22	250 @ $20 = $5,000		200 @ $14 300 @ $16 } = $ 12,600 250 @ $20
Nov. 1		200 @ $14 = $2,800 100 @ $20 = $2,000	300 @ $16 150 @ $20 } = $ 7,800
Nov. 28	100 @ $21 = $2,100		300 @ $16 150 @ $20 } = **$ 9,900** 100 @ $21
Total cost of goods sold		**$10,600**	

3.

	FIFO	LIFO	Weighted Average	Specific Identification
Income Statement				
Sales*	$ 22,500	$22,500	$ 22,500	$22,500
Cost of goods sold	10,200	11,600	10,779	10,600
Gross profit	$ 12,300	$10,900	$ 11,721	$11,900
Balance Sheet				
Inventory	$10,300	$ 8,900	$9,718.5	$ 9,900

* Sales = (200 units × $30) + (200 units × $30) + (300 units × $35) = $22,500

4. Mistakenly using LIFO when FIFO should have been used overstates cost of goods sold in year 2013 by $1,400, which is the difference between the FIFO and LIFO amounts of ending inventory. It understates income in 2013 by $1,400. In year 2014, income is overstated by $1,400 because of the understatement in beginning inventory.

5. Analysis of the effects of alternative inventory methods.

	Cost of Goods Sold	Difference from FIFO Cost of Goods Sold	Effect on Net Income If Adopted Instead of FIFO
FIFO	$10,200	—	—
LIFO	11,600	+$1,400	$1,400 lower
Weighted average	10,779	+ 579	579 lower
Specific identification	10,600	+ 400	400 lower

DEMONSTRATION PROBLEM 2—PERIODIC METHOD

Refer to the information in Demonstration Problem 1 to answer the following requirements.

Required

1. Calculate the cost of goods available for sale.
2. Apply the four different methods of inventory costing (FIFO, LIFO, weighted average, and specific identification) to calculate ending inventory and cost of goods sold under each method using the periodic system.
3. Compute gross profit earned by the company for each of the four costing methods in part 2. Also, report the inventory amount reported on the balance sheet for each of the four methods.
4. In preparing financial statements for year 2013, the financial officer was instructed to use FIFO but failed to do so and instead computed cost of goods sold according to LIFO. Determine the impact of the error on year 2013's income. Also determine the effect of this error on year 2014's income. Assume no income taxes.

SOLUTION TO DEMONSTRATION PROBLEM

1. The solution is identical to the solution for part 1 of Demonstration Problem 1.
2a. FIFO periodic method (FIFO under periodic and perpetual yields identical results).

Cost of goods available for sale (from part 1)			$ 20,500
Ending inventory*			
Nov. 28	Purchase (100 @ $21)	$2,100	
Sept. 22	Purchase (250 @ $20)	5,000	
May 9	Purchase (200 @ $16)	3,200	
Ending inventory			10,300
Cost of goods sold			$10,200

* Since FIFO assumes that the earlier costs are the first to flow out, we determine ending inventory by assigning the most recent costs to the remaining items.

2b. LIFO periodic method.

Cost of goods available for sale (from part 1)		$ 20,500
Ending inventory*		
January 1 Purchase (400 @ $14)	$5,600	
March 10 Purchase (150 @ $15)	2,250	
Ending inventory		**7,850**
Cost of goods sold		**$12,650**

* Since LIFO assumes that the most recent (newest) costs are the first to flow out, we determine ending inventory by assigning the earliest (oldest) costs to the remaining items.

2c. Weighted average periodic method.

Step 1:	400 units @ $14 =	$ 5,600	
	200 units @ $15 =	3,000	
	300 units @ $16 =	4,800	
	250 units @ $20 =	5,000	
	100 units @ $21 =	2,100	
	1,250	**$20,500**	
Step 2:	$20,500/1,250 units = **$16.40** weighted average cost per unit		
Step 3:	Total cost of 1,250 units available for sale	$20,500	
	Less **ending inventory** priced on a weighted average cost basis: 550 units at $16.40 each	**9,020**	
	Cost of goods sold	**$11,480**	

2d. Specific identification method.

The solution is identical to the solution shown in part 2d of Demonstration Problem 1. This is because specific identification is *not* a cost flow assumption; instead, this method specifically identifies each item in inventory and each item that is sold.

3.

	FIFO	LIFO	Weighted Average	Specific Identification
Income Statement				
Sales*	$ 22,500	$22,500	$ 22,500	$22,500
Cost of goods sold	10,200	12,650	11,480	10,600
Gross profit	$ 12,300	$ 9,850	$ 11,020	$11,900
Balance Sheet				
Inventory	**$10,300**	**$7,850**	**$ 9,020**	**$9,900**

* Sales = (200 units × $30) + (200 units × $30) + (300 units × $35) = $22,500

4. The solution is identical to the solution for part 4 of Demonstration Problem 1.

APPENDIX

Inventory Costing under a Periodic System

6A

This section illustrates inventory costing methods. We use information from Trekking, a sporting goods store. Among its products, Trekking carries one type of mountain bike whose sales are directed at resorts that provide inexpensive mountain bikes for complimentary guest use. These resorts usually purchase in amounts of 10 or more bikes. We use Trekking's data from August. Its mountain bike (unit) inventory at the beginning of August and its purchases and sales during August are in Exhibit 6A.1. It ends August with 12 bikes in inventory. Trekking uses the **periodic inventory system**, which means that its

P3 Compute inventory in a periodic system using the methods of specific identification, FIFO, LIFO, and weighted average.

EXHIBIT 6A.1

Purchases and Sales of Goods

Date	Activity	Units Acquired at Cost	Units Sold at Retail	Unit Inventory
Aug. 1	Beginning inventory	10 units @ $ 91 = $ 910		10 units
Aug. 3	Purchases	15 units @ $106 = $1,590		25 units
Aug. 14	Sales		20 units @ $130	5 units
Aug. 17	Purchases	20 units @ $115 = $2,300		25 units
Aug. 28	Purchases	10 units @ $119 = $1,190		35 units
Aug. 31	Sales		23 units @ $150	12 units
	Totals	55 units $5,990	43 units	

Units available for sale   Goods available for sale   Units sold   Units left

merchandise inventory account is updated at the end of each period (monthly for Trekking) to reflect purchases and sales. Regardless of what inventory method or system is used, cost of goods available for sale must be allocated between cost of goods sold and ending inventory.

Specific Identification
When each item in inventory can be identified with a specific purchase and invoice, we can use **specific identification** (also called *specific invoice inventory pricing*) to assign costs. We also need sales records that identify exactly which items were sold and when. Trekking's internal data reveal the following specific unit sales:

August 14   Sold 8 bikes costing $91 each and 12 bikes costing $106 each

August 31   Sold 2 bikes costing $91 each, 3 bikes costing $106 each, 15 bikes costing $115 each, and 3 bikes costing $119 each

Point: Three key variables determine the dollar value of ending inventory: (1) inventory quantity, (2) costs of inventory, and (3) cost flow assumption.

Applying specific identification and using the information above, we prepare Exhibit 6A.2. This exhibit starts with 10 bikes at $91 each in beginning inventory. On August 3, 15 more bikes are purchased at $106 each for $1,590. Inventory available now consists of 10 bikes at $91 each and 15 bikes at $106 each, for a total of $2,500. On August 14 (see sales data above), 20 bikes costing $2,000 are sold—leaving

EXHIBIT 6A.2

Specific Identification Computations

"goods in"   "goods out"   "what's left"

Date	Goods Purchased	Cost of Goods Sold	Inventory Balance
Aug. 1	Beginning balance		10 @ $ 91 = $ 910
Aug. 3	15 @ $106 = $1,590		10 @ $ 91 } 15 @ $106 } = $2,500
Aug. 14		8 @ $ 91 = $ 728 } 12 @ $106 = $1,272 } = $2,000*	2 @ $ 91 } 3 @ $106 } = $ 500
Aug. 17	20 @ $115 = $2,300		2 @ $ 91 } 3 @ $106 } 20 @ $115 } = $2,800
Aug. 28	10 @ $119 = $1,190		2 @ $ 91 } 3 @ $106 } 20 @ $115 } 10 @ $119 } = $3,990
Aug. 31		2 @ $ 91 = $ 182 } 3 @ $106 = $ 318 } 15 @ $115 = $1,725 } 3 @ $119 = $ 357 } = $2,582*	5 @ $115 } 7 @ $119 } = $1,408
		$4,582	

For the 20 units sold on Aug. 14, the company specifically identified that 8 of those had cost $91 and 12 had cost $106.

For the 23 units sold on Aug. 31, the company specifically identified each bike sold and its acquisition cost from prior purchases.

* Identification of items sold (and their costs) is obtained from internal documents that track each unit from its purchase to its sale.

5 bikes costing $500 in inventory. On August 17, 20 bikes costing $2,300 are purchased, and on August 28, another 10 bikes costing $1,190 are purchased, for a total of 35 bikes costing $3,990 in inventory. On August 31 (see sales data above), 23 bikes costing $2,582 are sold, which leaves 12 bikes costing $1,408 in ending inventory. Carefully study Exhibit 6A.2 to see the flow of costs both in and out of inventory. Each unit, whether sold or remaining in inventory, has its own specific cost attached to it.

When using specific identification, Trekking's cost of goods sold reported on the income statement totals **$4,582**, the sum of $2,000 and $2,582 from the third column of Exhibit 6A.2. Trekking's ending inventory reported on the balance sheet is **$1,408**, which is the final inventory balance from the fourth column. The purchases and sales entries for Exhibit 6A.2 follow (the colored boldface numbers are those impacted by the cost flow assumption):

Point: The assignment of costs to the goods sold and to inventory using specific identification is the same for both the perpetual and periodic systems.

Point: Specific identification is usually practical only for companies with expensive, custom-made inventory. Examples include car dealerships, implement dealers such as John Deere, jewelers, and fashion designers.

Purchases

Aug.	3	Purchases	1,590	
		Accounts Payable		1,590
	17	Purchases	2,300	
		Accounts Payable		2,300
	28	Purchases	1,190	
		Accounts Payable		1,190

Sales

Aug.	14	Accounts Receivable	2,600	
		Sales....................		2,600
	31	Accounts Receivable	3,450	
		Sales....................		3,450

Adjusting Entry

	31	Merchandise Inventory	**1,408**	
		Income Summary.........		498
		Merchandise Inventory		910

First-In, First-Out The first-in, first-out (FIFO) method of assigning costs to both inventory and cost of goods sold assumes that inventory items are sold in the order acquired. When sales occur, the costs of the earliest units acquired are charged to cost of goods sold. This leaves the costs from the most recent purchases in ending inventory. Use of FIFO for computing the cost of inventory and cost of goods sold is shown in Exhibit 6A.3.

This exhibit starts with computing $5,990 in total units available for sale—this is from Exhibit 6A.1. Applying FIFO, we know that the 12 units in ending inventory will be reported at the cost of the most recent 12 purchases. Reviewing purchases in reverse order, we assign costs to the 12 bikes in ending inventory as follows: $119 cost to 10 bikes and $115 cost to 2 bikes. This yields 12 bikes costing $1,420 in ending inventory. We then subtract this $1,420 in ending inventory from $5,990 in cost of goods available to get $4,570 in cost of goods sold.

EXHIBIT 6A.3

FIFO Computations—
Periodic System

Total cost of 55 units available for sale (from Exhibit 6A.1)		$5,990
Less ending inventory priced using FIFO		
10 units from August 28 purchase at $119 each	$1,190	
2 units from August 17 purchase at $115 each	230	
Ending inventory		1,420
Cost of goods sold		$4,570

> Exhibit 6A.1 shows that the 12 units in ending inventory consist of 10 units from the latest purchase on Aug. 28 and 2 units from the next latest purchase on Aug. 17.

Trekking's ending inventory reported on the balance sheet is **$1,420**, and its cost of goods sold reported on the income statement is **$4,570**. These amounts are the same as those computed using the perpetual system. This always occurs because the most recent purchases are in ending inventory under both systems. The purchases and sales entries for Exhibit 6A.3 follow (the colored boldface numbers are those affected by the cost flow assumption).

Point: The assignment of costs to the goods sold and to inventory using FIFO is the same for both the perpetual and periodic systems.

Purchases

Aug.	3	Purchases....................	1,590	
		Accounts Payable..........		1,590
	17	Purchases....................	2,300	
		Accounts Payable..........		2,300
	28	Purchases....................	1,190	
		Accounts Payable..........		1,190

Sales

Aug.	14	Accounts Receivable	2,600	
		Sales		2,600
	31	Accounts Receivable	3,450	
		Sales		3,450

Adjusting Entry

	31	Merchandise Inventory	**1,420**	
		Income Summary		510
		Merchandise Inventory		910

Last-In, First-Out   The last-in, first-out (LIFO) method of assigning costs assumes that the most recent purchases are sold first. These more recent costs are charged to the goods sold, and the costs of the earliest purchases are assigned to inventory. LIFO results in costs of the most recent purchases being assigned to cost of goods sold, which means that LIFO comes close to matching current costs of goods sold with revenues. Use of LIFO for computing cost of inventory and cost of goods sold is shown in Exhibit 6A.4.

This exhibit starts with computing $5,990 in total units available for sale—this is from Exhibit 6A.1. Applying LIFO, we know that the 12 units in ending inventory will be reported at the cost of the earliest 12 purchases. Reviewing the earliest purchases in order, we assign costs to the 12 bikes in ending inventory as follows: $91 cost to 10 bikes and $106 cost to 2 bikes. This yields 12 bikes costing $1,122 in ending inventory. We then subtract this $1,122 in ending inventory from $5,990 in cost of goods available to get $4,868 in cost of goods sold.

EXHIBIT 6A.4

LIFO Computations—
Periodic System

Exhibit 6A.1 shows that the 12 units in ending inventory consist of 10 units from the earliest purchase (beg. inv.) and 2 units from the next earliest purchase on Aug. 3.

Total cost of 55 units available for sale (from Exhibit 6A.1)		$5,990
Less ending inventory priced using LIFO		
10 units in beginning inventory at $91 each	$910	
2 units from August 3 purchase at $106 each	212	
Ending inventory		1,122
Cost of goods sold		$4,868

Trekking's ending inventory reported on the balance sheet is **$1,122**, and its cost of goods sold reported on the income statement is **$4,868**. When LIFO is used with the periodic system, cost of goods sold is assigned costs from the most recent purchases for the period. With a perpetual system, cost of goods sold is assigned costs from the most recent purchases at the point of *each sale*. The purchases and sales entries for Exhibit 6A.4 follow (the colored boldface numbers are those affected by the cost flow assumption).

Purchases			
Aug. 3	Purchases	1,590	
	Accounts Payable		1,590
17	Purchases	2,300	
	Accounts Payable		2,300
28	Purchases	1,190	
	Accounts Payable		1,190

Sales			
Aug. 14	Accounts Receivable	2,600	
	Sales		2,600
31	Accounts Receivable	3,450	
	Sales		3,450
	Adjusting Entry		
31	Merchandise Inventory	1,122	
	Income Summary		212
	Merchandise Inventory		910

Weighted Average   The **weighted average** or **WA** (also called **average cost**) method of assigning cost requires that we use the average cost per unit of inventory at the end of the period. Weighted average cost per unit equals the cost of goods available for sale divided by the units available. The weighted average method of assigning cost involves three important steps. The first two steps are shown in Exhibit 6A.5. First, multiply the per unit cost for beginning inventory and each particular purchase by the corresponding number of units (from Exhibit 6A.1). Second, add these amounts and divide by the total number of units available for sale to find the weighted average cost per unit.

EXHIBIT 6A.5

Weighted Average Cost per Unit

Example: In Exhibit 6A.5, if 5 more units had been purchased at $120 each, what would be the weighted average cost per unit?
Answer: $109.83 ($6,590/60)

Step 1:	10 units @ $ 91 =	$ 910	
	15 units @ $106 =	1,590	
	20 units @ $115 =	2,300	
	10 units @ $119 =	1,190	
	55	$5,990	
Step 2:	$5,990/55 units = **$108.91** weighted average cost per unit		

The third step is to use the weighted average cost per unit to assign costs to inventory and to the units sold as shown in Exhibit 6A.6.

Step 3:	Total cost of 55 units available for sale (from Exhibit 6A.1)		$ 5,990
	Less **ending inventory** priced on a weighted average		
	cost basis: 12 units at $108.91 each (from Exhibit 6A.5)		**1,307**
	Cost of goods sold		**$4,683**

EXHIBIT 6A.6

Weighted Average
Computations—Periodic

Trekking's ending inventory reported on the balance sheet is **$1,307**, and its cost of goods sold reported on the income statement is **$4,683** when using the weighted average (periodic) method. The purchases and sales entries for Exhibit 6A.6 follow (the colored boldface numbers are those affected by the cost flow assumption).

Point: Weighted average usually yields different results for the perpetual and the periodic systems because under a perpetual system it recomputes the per unit cost prior to each sale, whereas under a periodic system, the per unit cost is computed only at the end of a period.

Purchases

Aug. 3	Purchases	1,590	
	Accounts Payable		1,590
17	Purchases	2,300	
	Accounts Payable		2,300
28	Purchases	1,190	
	Accounts Payable		1,190

Sales

Aug. 14	Accounts Receivable	2,600	
	Sales		2,600
31	Accounts Receivable	3,450	
	Sales		3,450
	Adjusting Entry		
31	Merchandise Inventory	**1,307**	
	Income Summary		397
	Merchandise Inventory		**910**

Point: LIFO inventory is often less than the inventory's replacement cost because LIFO inventory is valued using the oldest inventory purchase costs.

Financial Statement Effects When purchase prices do not change, each inventory costing method assigns the same cost amounts to inventory and to cost of goods sold. When purchase prices are different, however, the methods nearly always assign different cost amounts. We show these differences in Exhibit 6A.7 using Trekking's data.

TREKKING COMPANY For Month Ended August 31				
	Specific Identification	FIFO	LIFO	Weighted Average
Income Statement				
Sales	$ 6,050	$ 6,050	$ 6,050	$ 6,050
Cost of goods sold	**4,582**	**4,570**	**4,868**	**4,683**
Gross profit	1,468	1,480	1,182	1,367
Expenses	450	450	450	450
Income before taxes	1,018	1,030	732	917
Income tax expense (30%)	305	309	220	275
Net income	**$ 713**	**$ 721**	**$ 512**	**$ 642**
Balance Sheet				
Inventory	**$1,408**	**$1,420**	**$1,122**	**$1,307**

EXHIBIT 6A.7

Financial Statement Effects of Inventory Costing Methods

This exhibit reveals two important results. First, when purchase costs *regularly rise,* as in Trekking's case, observe the following:

- FIFO assigns the lowest amount to cost of goods sold—yielding the highest gross profit and net income.
- LIFO assigns the highest amount to cost of goods sold—yielding the lowest gross profit and net income, which also yields a temporary tax advantage by postponing payment of some income tax.
- Weighted average yields results between FIFO and LIFO.
- Specific identification always yields results that depend on which units are sold.

Second, when costs *regularly decline,* the reverse occurs for FIFO and LIFO. FIFO gives the highest cost of goods sold—yielding the lowest gross profit and income. And LIFO gives the lowest cost of goods sold—yielding the highest gross profit and income.

All four inventory costing methods are acceptable in practice. A company must disclose the inventory method it uses. Each method offers certain advantages as follows:

- FIFO assigns an amount to inventory on the balance sheet that approximates its current cost; it also mimics the actual flow of goods for most businesses.
- LIFO assigns an amount to cost of goods sold on the income statement that approximates its current cost; it also better matches current costs with revenues in computing gross profit.
- Weighted average tends to smooth out erratic changes in costs.
- Specific identification exactly matches the costs of items with the revenues they generate.

APPENDIX

6B

Inventory Estimation Methods

P4 Apply both the retail inventory and gross profit methods to estimate inventory.

Inventory sometimes requires estimation for two reasons. First, companies often require **interim statements** (financial statements prepared for periods of less than one year), but they only annually take a physical count of inventory. Second, companies may require an inventory estimate if some casualty such as fire or flood makes taking a physical count impossible. Estimates are usually only required for companies that use the periodic system. Companies using a perpetual system would presumably have updated inventory data.

This appendix describes two methods to estimate inventory.

Point: When a retailer takes a physical inventory, it can restate the retail value of inventory to a cost basis by applying the cost-to-retail ratio. It can also estimate the amount of shrinkage by comparing the inventory computed with the amount from a physical inventory.

Retail Inventory Method   To avoid the time-consuming and expensive process of taking a physical inventory each month or quarter, some companies use the **retail inventory method** to estimate cost of goods sold and ending inventory. Some companies even use the retail inventory method to prepare the annual statements. **Home Depot**, for instance, says in its annual report: "Inventories are stated at the lower of cost (first-in, first-out) or market, as determined by the retail inventory method." A company may also estimate inventory for audit purposes or when inventory is damaged or destroyed.

The retail inventory method uses a three-step process to estimate ending inventory. We need to know the amount of inventory a company had at the beginning of the period in both *cost* and *retail* amounts. We already explained how to compute the cost of inventory. The *retail amount of inventory* refers to its dollar amount measured using selling prices of inventory items. We also need to know the net amount of goods purchased (minus returns, allowances, and discounts) in the period, both at cost and at retail. The amount of net sales at retail is also needed. The process is shown in Exhibit 6B.1.

The reasoning behind the retail inventory method is that if we can get a good estimate of the cost-to-retail ratio, we can multiply ending inventory at retail by this ratio to estimate ending in-

EXHIBIT 6B.1

Retail Inventory Method of Inventory Estimation

ventory at cost. We show in Exhibit 6B.2 how these steps are applied to estimate ending inventory for a typical company. First, we find that $100,000 of goods (at retail selling prices) were available for sale. We see that $70,000 of these goods were sold, leaving $30,000 (retail value) of merchandise in ending inventory. Second, the cost of these goods is 60% of the $100,000 retail value. Third, since cost for these goods is 60% of retail, the estimated cost of ending inventory is $18,000.

Example: What is the cost of ending inventory in Exhibit 6B.2 if the cost of beginning inventory is $22,500 and its retail value is $34,500? *Answer:*
$30,000 × 62% = $18,600

EXHIBIT 6B.2

Estimated Inventory Using the
Retail Inventory Method

	At Cost	At Retail
Goods available for sale		
Beginning inventory	$ 20,500	$ 34,500
Cost of goods purchased	39,500	65,500
Step 1: { Goods available for sale	60,000	100,000
Step 1: { Deduct net sales at retail		70,000
Step 1: { Ending inventory at retail		$ 30,000
Step 2: Cost-to-retail ratio: ($60,000 ÷ $100,000) = 60%		
Step 3: Estimated ending inventory at cost ($30,000 × 60%)	$18,000	

Point: A retailer such as Target can speed up its year-end physical count by using the retail inventory method. Inventory counters can record the item's retail price without having to look up the cost of each item.

Gross Profit Method   The **gross profit method** estimates the cost of ending inventory by applying the gross profit ratio to net sales (at retail). This type of estimate often is needed when inventory is destroyed, lost, or stolen. These cases require an inventory estimate so that a company can file a claim with its insurer. Users also apply this method to see whether inventory amounts from a physical count are reasonable. This method uses the historical relation between cost of goods sold and net sales to estimate the proportion of cost of goods sold making up current sales. This cost of goods sold estimate is then subtracted from cost of goods available for sale to estimate the ending inventory at cost. These two steps are shown in Exhibit 6B.3.

To illustrate, assume that a company's inventory is destroyed by fire in March 2013. When the fire occurs, the company's accounts show the following balances for January through March: sales, $31,500; sales returns, $1,500; inventory (January 1, 2013), $12,000; and cost of goods purchased, $20,500. If this company's gross profit ratio is 30%, then 30% of each net sales dollar is gross profit and 70% is cost of goods sold. We show in Exhibit 6B.4 how this 70% is used to estimate lost inventory of $11,500. To understand this exhibit, think of subtracting the cost of goods sold from the goods available for sale to get the ending inventory.

EXHIBIT 6B.3

Gross Profit Method of
Inventory Estimation

Point: A fire or other catastrophe can result in an insurance claim for lost inventory or income. Backup and off-site storage of data help ensure coverage for such losses.

Point: Reliability of the gross profit method depends on an accurate and stable estimate of the gross profit ratio.

EXHIBIT 6B.4

Estimated Inventory Using the
Gross Profit Method

Goods available for sale	
Inventory, January 1, 2013	$12,000
Cost of goods purchased	20,500
Goods available for sale (at cost)	32,500
Net sales at retail ($31,500 − $1,500)	$30,000
Step 1: Estimated cost of goods sold ($30,000 × 70%)	(21,000) ← × 0.70
Step 2: Estimated March inventory at cost	$11,500

9. Using the retail method and the following data, estimate the cost of ending inventory.

	Cost	Retail
Beginning inventory	$324,000	$530,000
Cost of goods purchased	195,000	335,000
Net sales		320,000

Summary

C1 **Identify the items making up merchandise inventory.** Merchandise inventory refers to goods owned by a company and held for resale. Three special cases merit our attention. Goods in transit are reported in inventory of the company that holds ownership rights. Goods on consignment are reported in the consignor's inventory. Goods damaged or obsolete are reported in inventory at their net realizable value.

C2 **Identify the costs of merchandise inventory.** Costs of merchandise inventory include expenditures necessary to bring an item to a salable condition and location. This includes its invoice cost minus any discount plus any added or incidental costs necessary to put it in a place and condition for sale.

A1 **Analyze the effects of inventory methods for both financial and tax reporting.** When purchase costs are rising or falling, the inventory costing methods are likely to assign different costs to inventory. Specific identification exactly matches costs and revenues. Weighted average smooths out cost changes. FIFO assigns an amount to inventory closely approximating current replacement cost. LIFO assigns the most recent costs incurred to cost of goods sold and likely better matches current costs with revenues.

A2 **Analyze the effects of inventory errors on current and future financial statements.** An error in the amount of ending inventory affects assets (inventory), net income (cost of goods sold), and equity for that period. Since ending inventory is next period's beginning inventory, an error in ending inventory affects next period's cost of goods sold and net income. Inventory errors in one period are offset in the next period.

A3 **Assess inventory management using both inventory turnover and days' sales in inventory.** We prefer a high inventory turnover, provided that goods are not out of stock and customers are not turned away. We use days' sales in inventory to assess the likelihood of goods being out of stock. We prefer a small number of days' sales in inventory if we can serve customer needs and provide a buffer for uncertainties.

P1 **Compute inventory in a perpetual system using the methods of specific identification, FIFO, LIFO, and weighted average.** Costs are assigned to the cost of goods sold account *each time* a sale occurs in a perpetual system. Specific identification assigns a cost to each item sold by referring to its actual cost (for example, its net invoice cost). Weighted average assigns a cost to items sold by dividing the current balance in the inventory account by the total items available for sale to determine cost per unit. We then multiply the number of units sold by this cost per unit to get the cost of each sale. FIFO assigns cost to items sold assuming that the earliest units purchased are the first units sold. LIFO assigns cost to items sold assuming that the most recent units purchased are the first units sold.

P2 **Compute the lower of cost or market amount of inventory.** Inventory is reported at market cost when market is *lower* than recorded cost, called the *lower of cost or market (LCM) inventory.* Market is typically measured as replacement cost. Lower of cost or market can be applied separately to each item, to major categories of items, or to the entire inventory.

P3A **Compute inventory in a periodic system using the methods of specific identification, FIFO, LIFO, and weighted average.** Periodic inventory systems allocate the cost of goods available for sale between cost of goods sold and ending inventory *at the end of a period.* Specific identification and FIFO give identical results whether the periodic or perpetual system is used. LIFO assigns costs to cost of goods sold assuming the last units purchased for the period are the first units sold. The weighted average cost per unit is computed by dividing the total cost of beginning inventory and net purchases for the period by the total number of units available. Then, it multiplies cost per unit by the number of units sold to give cost of goods sold.

P4B **Apply both the retail inventory and gross profit methods to estimate inventory.** The retail inventory method involves three steps: (1) goods available at retail minus net sales at retail equals ending inventory at retail, (2) goods available at cost divided by goods available at retail equals the cost-to-retail ratio, and (3) ending inventory at retail multiplied by the cost-to-retail ratio equals estimated ending inventory at cost. The gross profit method involves two steps: (1) net sales at retail multiplied by 1 minus the gross profit ratio equals estimated cost of goods sold, and (2) goods available at cost minus estimated cost of goods sold equals estimated ending inventory at cost.

Guidance Answers to Decision Maker and Decision Ethics

Cost Analyst Explain to your supervisor that when inventory costs are increasing, FIFO results in an inventory valuation that approximates replacement cost. The most recently purchased goods are assigned to ending inventory under FIFO and are likely closer to replacement values than earlier costs that would be assigned to inventory if LIFO were used.

Inventory Manager It seems your company can save (or at least postpone) taxes by switching to LIFO, but the switch is likely to reduce bonus money that you think you have earned and deserve. Since the U.S. tax code requires companies that use LIFO for tax reporting also to use it for financial reporting, your options are further constrained. Your best decision is to tell your superior about the tax savings with

LIFO. You also should discuss your bonus plan and how this is likely to hurt you unfairly. You might propose to compute inventory under the LIFO method for reporting purposes but use the FIFO method for your bonus calculations. Another solution is to revise the bonus plan to reflect the company's use of the LIFO method.

Entrepreneur Your inventory turnover is markedly higher than the norm, whereas days' sales in inventory approximates the norm. Since your turnover is already 14% better than average, you are probably best served by directing attention to days' sales in inventory. You should see whether you can reduce the level of inventory while maintaining service to customers. Given your higher turnover, you should be able to hold less inventory.

Guidance Answers to Quick Checks

1. The matching principle.
2. Famous Footwear reports these goods in its inventory.
3. Total cost assigned to the painting is $12,180, computed as $11,400 + $130 + $150 + $100 + $400.
4. Specific identification exactly matches costs and revenues. Weighted average tends to smooth out cost changes. FIFO assigns an amount to inventory that closely approximates current replacement cost. LIFO assigns the most recent costs incurred to cost of goods sold and likely better matches current costs with revenues.
5. FIFO—it gives a lower cost of goods sold, a higher gross profit, and a higher net income when costs are rising.
6. When costs are rising, LIFO gives a lower inventory figure on the balance sheet as compared to FIFO. FIFO's inventory amount approximates current replacement costs.

7. Cost of goods sold would be overstated by $10,000 in 2012 and understated by $10,000 in year 2013.
8. The reported LCM inventory amount (using items) is $540, computed as $[(20 \times \$5) + (40 \times \$8) + (10 \times \$12)]$.
9.[B] Estimated ending inventory (at cost) is $327,000. It is computed as follows:

Step 1:   ($530,000 + $335,000) − $320,000 = $545,000

Step 2: $\dfrac{\$324,000 + \$195,000}{\$530,000 + \$335,000} = 60\%$

Step 3: $545,000 \times 60\% = \underline{\$327,000}$

Key Terms

Average cost (p. 236, 252)	**First-in, first-out (FIFO)** (p. 235)	**Net realizable value** (p. 230)
Conservatism constraint (p. 240)	**Gross profit method** (p. 255)	**Retail inventory method** (p. 254)
Consignee (p. 230)	**Interim statements** (p. 254)	**Specific identification** (p. 233, 250)
Consignor (p. 230)	**Inventory turnover** (p. 243)	**Weighted average** (p. 236, 252)
Consistency concept (p. 239)	**Last-in, first-out (LIFO)** (p. 235)	
Days' sales in inventory (p. 243)	**Lower of cost or market (LCM)** (p. 239)	

Multiple Choice Quiz   Answers on p. 274   mhhe.com/wildFAP21e

Additional Quiz Questions are available at the book's Website.

Use the following information from Marvel Company for the month of July to answer questions 1 through 4.

July 1	Beginning inventory	75 units @ $25 each
July 3	Purchase	348 units @ $27 each
July 8	Sale	300 units
July 15	Purchase	257 units @ $28 each
July 23	Sale	275 units

1. **Perpetual:** Assume that Marvel uses a perpetual FIFO inventory system. What is the dollar value of its ending inventory?
   a. $2,940   d. $2,852
   b. $2,685   e. $2,705
   c. $2,625

2. **Perpetual:** Assume that Marvel uses a perpetual LIFO inventory system. What is the dollar value of its ending inventory?
   a. $2,940   d. $2,852
   b. $2,685   e. $2,705
   c. $2,625

3. **Perpetual:** Assume that Marvel uses a perpetual specific identification inventory system. Its ending inventory consists of 20 units from beginning inventory, 40 units from the July 3 purchase, and 45 units from the July 15 purchase. What is the dollar value of its ending inventory?
   a. $2,940   d. $2,852
   b. $2,685   e. $2,840
   c. $2,625

4. **Periodic:** Assume that Marvel uses a *periodic* FIFO inventory system. What is the dollar value of its ending inventory?
   a. $2,940   d. $2,852
   b. $2,685   e. $2,705
   c. $2,625

5. **Periodic:** A company reports the following beginning inventory and purchases, and it ends the period with 30 units in inventory.

Beginning inventory	100 units at $10 cost per unit
Purchase 1.................	40 units at $12 cost per unit
Purchase 2.................	20 units at $14 cost per unit

   a. Compute ending inventory using the FIFO periodic system.
   b. Compute cost of goods sold using the LIFO periodic system.

6. A company has cost of goods sold of $85,000 and ending inventory of $18,000. Its days' sales in inventory equals:
   a. 49.32 days   d. 77.29 days
   b. 0.21 days   e. 1,723.61 days
   c. 4.72 days

^B *Superscript letter A (B) denotes assignments based on Appendix 6A (6B).*

🔋 Icon denotes assignments that involve decision making.

Discussion Questions

1. Describe how costs flow from inventory to cost of goods sold for the following methods: (*a*) FIFO and (*b*) LIFO.

2. Where is the amount of merchandise inventory disclosed in the financial statements?

3. Why are incidental costs sometimes ignored in inventory costing? Under what accounting constraint is this permitted?

4. 🔋 If costs are declining, will the LIFO or FIFO method of inventory valuation yield the lower cost of goods sold? Why?

5. What does the full-disclosure principle prescribe if a company changes from one acceptable accounting method to another?

6. Can a company change its inventory method each accounting period? Explain.

7. 🔋 Does the accounting concept of consistency preclude any changes from one accounting method to another?

8. 🔋 If inventory errors are said to correct themselves, why are accounting users concerned when such errors are made?

9. Explain the following statement: "Inventory errors correct themselves."

10. What is the meaning of *market* as it is used in determining the lower of cost or market for inventory?

11. 🔋 What guidance does the accounting constraint of conservatism offer?

12. What factors contribute to (or cause) inventory shrinkage?

13.^B When preparing interim financial statements, what two methods can companies utilize to estimate cost of goods sold and ending inventory?

14. Refer to **Polaris**' financial statements in Appendix A. On December 31, 2011, what percent of current assets are represented by inventory?   **Polaris**

15. Refer to **Arctic Cat**'s financial statements in Appendix A and compute its cost of goods available for sale for the year ended March 31, 2011.   **Arctic Cat**

16. Refer to **KTM**'s financial statements in Appendix A. Compute its cost of goods available for sale for the year ended December 31, 2011.   **KTM**

17. Refer to **Piaggio**'s financial statements in Appendix A. What percent of its current assets are inventory as of December 31, 2011 and 2010?   **PIAGGIO**

───

🅜 **connect**·

QUICK STUDY

QS 6-1

Perpetual: Inventory costing with FIFO

P1

Information: A company reports the following beginning inventory and purchases for the month of January. On January 26, the company sells 350 units. 150 units remain in ending inventory at January 31.

	Units	Unit Cost
Beginning inventory on January 1	320	$3.00
Purchase on January 9	80	3.20
Purchase on January 25	100	3.34

Required

Assume the perpetual inventory system is used and then determine the costs assigned to ending inventory when costs are assigned based on the FIFO method. (Round per unit costs and inventory amounts to dollars and cents.)

QS 6-2

Perpetual: Inventory costing with LIFO   P1

Refer to the information in QS 6-1 and assume the perpetual inventory system is used. Determine the costs assigned to ending inventory when costs are assigned based on LIFO. (Round per unit costs and inventory amounts to dollars and cents.)

QS 6-3

Perpetual: Inventory costing with weighted average   P1

Check $465

Refer to the information in QS 6-1 and assume the perpetual inventory system is used. Determine the costs assigned to ending inventory when costs are assigned based on the weighted average method. (Round per unit costs and inventory amounts to dollars and cents.)

QS 6-4^A

Periodic: Inventory costing with FIFO   P3

Refer to the **information** in QS 6-1 and assume the periodic inventory system is used. Determine the costs assigned to ending inventory when costs are assigned based on the FIFO method. (Round per unit costs and inventory amounts to dollars and cents.)

Refer to the **information** in QS 6-1 and assume the periodic inventory system is used. Determine the costs assigned to ending inventory when costs are assigned based on the LIFO method. (Round per unit costs and inventory amounts to dollars and cents.)

QS 6-5^A
Periodic: Inventory costing with LIFO P3

Refer to the **information** in QS 6-1 and assume the periodic inventory system is used. Determine the costs assigned to ending inventory when costs are assigned based on the weighted average method. (Round per unit costs and inventory amounts to dollars and cents.)

QS 6-6^A
Periodic: Inventory costing with weighted average P3

Wattan Company reports beginning inventory of 10 units at $60 each. Every week for four weeks it purchases an additional 10 units at respective costs of $61, $62, $65 and $70 per unit for weeks 1 through 4. Calculate the cost of goods available for sale and the units available for sale for this four-week period. Assume that no sales occur during those four weeks.

QS 6-7
Computing goods available for sale P1

Information: Trey Monson starts a merchandising business on December 1 and enters into the following three inventory purchases. During December, Monson sells 15 units for $20 each on December 15.

QS 6-8
Perpetual: Assigning costs with FIFO

P1

Purchases on December 7	10 units @ $ 6.00 cost
Purchases on December 14	20 units @ $12.00 cost
Purchases on December 21	15 units @ $14.00 cost

Required

Monson uses a perpetual inventory system. Determine the costs assigned to the December 31 ending inventory based on the FIFO method. (Round per unit costs and inventory amounts to dollars and cents.)

Refer to the information in QS 6-8 and assume the perpetual inventory system is used. Determine the costs assigned to ending inventory when costs are assigned based on the LIFO method. (Round per unit costs and inventory amounts to dollars and cents.)

QS 6-9
Perpetual: Inventory costing with LIFO P1

Refer to the information in QS 6-8 and assume the perpetual inventory system is used. Determine the costs assigned to ending inventory when costs are assigned based on the weighted average method. (Round per unit costs and inventory amounts to dollars and cents.)

QS 6-10
Perpetual: Inventory costing with weighted average P1

Check End. Inv. = $360

Refer to the information in QS 6-8 and assume the perpetual inventory system is used. Determine the costs assigned to ending inventory when costs are assigned based on specific identification. Of the units sold, eight are from the December 7 purchase and seven are from the December 14 purchase. (Round per unit costs and inventory amounts to dollars and cents.)

QS 6-11
Perpetual: Inventory costing with specific identification P1

Refer to the **information** in QS 6-8 and assume the periodic inventory system is used. Determine the costs assigned to ending inventory when costs are assigned based on the FIFO method. (Round per unit costs and inventory amounts to dollars and cents.)

QS 6-12^A
Periodic: Inventory costing with FIFO P3

Refer to the **information** in QS 6-8 and assume the periodic inventory system is used. Determine the costs assigned to ending inventory when costs are assigned based on the LIFO method. (Round per unit costs and inventory amounts to dollars and cents.)

QS 6-13
Periodic: Inventory costing with LIFO P3

Refer to the **information** in QS 6-8 and assume the periodic inventory system is used. Determine the costs assigned to ending inventory when costs are assigned based on the weighted average method. (Round per unit costs and inventory amounts to dollars and cents.)

QS 6-14^A
Periodic: Inventory costing with weighted average P3

Refer to the **information** in QS 6-8 and assume the periodic inventory system is used. Determine the costs assigned to ending inventory when costs are assigned based on specific identification. Of the units sold, eight are from the December 7 purchase and seven are from the December 14 purchase. (Round per unit costs and inventory amounts to dollars and cents.)

QS 6-15^A
Periodic: Inventory costing with specific identification P3

QS 6-16
Contrasting inventory
costing methods
A1

Identify the inventory costing method best described by each of the following separate statements. Assume a period of increasing costs.
1. Yields a balance sheet inventory amount often markedly less than its replacement cost.
2. Results in a balance sheet inventory amount approximating replacement cost.
3. Provides a tax advantage (deferral) to a corporation when costs are rising.
4. Recognizes (matches) recent costs against net sales.
5. The preferred method when each unit of product has unique features that markedly affect cost.

QS 6-17
Inventory ownership
C1

Homestead Crafts, a distributor of handmade gifts, operates out of owner Emma Finn's house. At the end of the current period, Emma reports she has 1,300 units (products) in her basement, 20 of which were damaged by water and cannot be sold. She also has another 350 units in her van, ready to deliver per a customer order, terms FOB destination, and another 80 units out on consignment to a friend who owns a retail store. How many units should Emma include in her company's period-end inventory?

QS 6-18
Inventory costs
C2

A car dealer acquires a used car for $14,000, terms FOB shipping point. Additional costs in obtaining and offering the car for sale include $250 for transportation-in, $900 for import duties, $300 for insurance during shipment, $150 for advertising, and $1,250 for sales staff salaries. For computing inventory, what cost is assigned to the used car?

QS 6-19
Applying LCM to inventories
P2

Ames Trading Co. has the following products in its ending inventory. Compute lower of cost or market for inventory applied separately to each product.

Product	Quantity	Cost per Unit	Market per Unit
Mountain bikes	11	$600	$550
Skateboards	13	350	425
Gliders	26	800	700

QS 6-20
Inventory errors
A2

In taking a physical inventory at the end of year 2013, Grant Company forgot to count certain units. Explain how this error affects the following: (*a*) 2013 cost of goods sold, (*b*) 2013 gross profit, (*c*) 2013 net income, (*d*) 2014 net income, (*e*) the combined two-year income, and (*f*) income for years after 2014.

QS 6-21
Analyzing inventory   A3

Endor Company begins the year with $150,000 of goods in inventory. At year-end, the amount in inventory has increased to $180,000. Cost of goods sold for the year is $1,200,000. Compute Endor's inventory turnover and days' sales in inventory. Assume that there are 365 days in the year.

QS 6-22ᴮ
Estimating inventories—gross
profit method
P4

Kauai Store's inventory is destroyed by a fire on September 5, 2013. The following data for year 2013 are available from the accounting records. Estimate the cost of the inventory destroyed.

Jan. 1 inventory	$190,000
Jan. 1 through Sept. 5 purchases (net)	$352,000
Jan. 1 through Sept. 5 sales (net)	$685,000
Year 2013 estimated gross profit rate	44%

QS 6-23
International accounting
standards
C1   C2   P2

Answer each of the following questions related to international accounting standards.
a. Explain how the accounting for items and costs making up merchandise inventory is different between IFRS and U.S. GAAP.
b. Can companies reporting under IFRS apply a cost flow assumption in assigning costs to inventory? If yes, identify at least two acceptable cost flow assumptions.
c. Both IFRS and U.S. GAAP apply the lower of cost or market method for reporting inventory values. If inventory is written down from applying the lower of cost or market method, explain in general terms how IFRS and U.S. GAAP differ in accounting for any subsequent period reversal of that reported decline in inventory value.

■ connect

1. Harris Company has shipped $20,000 of goods to Harlow Co., and Harlow Co. has arranged to sell the goods for Harris. Identify the consignor and the consignee. Which company should include any unsold goods as part of its inventory?

2. At year-end, Harris Co. had shipped $12,500 of merchandise FOB destination to Harlow Co. Which company should include the $12,500 of merchandise in transit as part of its year-end inventory?

Exercise 6-1
Inventory ownership   C1

Walberg Associates, antique dealers, purchased the contents of an estate for $75,000. Terms of the purchase were FOB shipping point, and the cost of transporting the goods to Walberg Associates' warehouse was $2,400. Walberg Associates insured the shipment at a cost of $300. Prior to putting the goods up for sale, they cleaned and refurbished them at a cost of $980. Determine the cost of the inventory acquired from the estate.

Exercise 6-2
Inventory costs
C2

Information: Laker Company reported the following January purchases and sales data for its only product.

Exercise 6-3
Perpetual: Inventory costing methods
P1

Date	Activities	Units Acquired at Cost	Units Sold at Retail
Jan. 1	Beginning inventory	140 units @ $6.00 = $ 840	
Jan. 10	Sales		100 units @ $15
Jan. 20	Purchase	60 units @ $5.00 = 300	
Jan. 25	Sales		80 units @ $15
Jan. 30	Purchase	180 units @ $4.50 = 810	
	Totals	380 units $1,950	180 units

Required

The Company uses a perpetual inventory system. Determine the cost assigned to ending inventory and to cost of goods sold using (*a*) specific identification, (*b*) weighted average, (*c*) FIFO, and (*d*) LIFO. (Round per unit costs and inventory amounts to dollars and cents.) For specific identification, ending inventory consists of 200 units, where 180 are from the January 30 purchase, 5 are from the January 20 purchase, and 15 are from beginning inventory.

Check   Ending inventory: LIFO, $930; WA, $918

Use the data in Exercise 6-3 to prepare comparative income statements for the month of January for Laker Company similar to those shown in Exhibit 6.8 for the four inventory methods. Assume expenses are $1,250, and that the applicable income tax rate is 40%. (Round amounts to dollars and cents.)

1. Which method yields the highest net income?

2. Does net income using weighted average fall between that using FIFO and LIFO?

3. If costs were rising instead of falling, which method would yield the highest net income?

Exercise 6-4
Perpetual: Income effects of inventory methods

A1

Refer to the information in Exercise 6-3 and assume the periodic inventory system is used. Determine the costs assigned to ending inventory and to cost of goods sold using (*a*) specific identification, (*b*) weighted average, (*c*) FIFO, and (*d*) LIFO. (Round per unit costs and inventory amounts to dollars and cents.)

Exercise 6-5^A
Periodic: Inventory costing   P3

Use the data in Exercise 6-5 to prepare comparative income statements for the month of January for the company similar to those shown in Exhibit 6.8 for the four inventory methods. Assume expenses are $1,250, and that the applicable income tax rate is 40%. (Round amounts to dollars and cents.)

Exercise 6-6^A
Periodic: Income effects of inventory methods

A1

Required

1. Which method yields the highest net income?

2. Does net income using weighted average fall between that using FIFO and LIFO?

3. If costs were rising instead of falling, which method would yield the highest net income?

Exercise 6-7

Perpetual: Inventory costing methods—FIFO and LIFO

P1

Information: Hemming Co. reported the following current-year purchases and sales for its only product.

Date	Activities	Units Acquired at Cost	Units Sold at Retail
Jan. 1	Beginning inventory	200 units @ $10 = $ 2,000	
Jan. 10	Sales		150 units @ $40
Mar. 14	Purchase	350 units @ $15 = 5,250	
Mar. 15	Sales		300 units @ $40
July 30	Purchase	450 units @ $20 = 9,000	
Oct. 5	Sales		430 units @ $40
Oct. 26	Purchase	100 units @ $25 = 2,500	
	Totals	1,100 units $18,750	880 units

Required

Check Ending inventory: LIFO, $4,150

Hemming uses a perpetual inventory system. Determine the costs assigned to ending inventory and to cost of goods sold using (*a*) FIFO and (*b*) LIFO. Compute the gross margin for each method. (Round amounts to dollars and cents.)

Exercise 6-8

Specific identification   P1

Refer to the information in Exercise 6-7. Ending inventory consists of 45 units from the March 14 purchase, 75 units from the July 30 purchase, and all 100 units from the October 26 purchase. Using the specific identification method, calculate (*a*) the cost of goods sold and (*b*) the gross profit. (Round amounts to dollars and cents.)

Exercise 6-9[A]

Periodic: Inventory costing

P3

Refer to the **information** in Exercise 6-7 and assume the periodic inventory system is used. Determine the costs assigned to ending inventory and to cost of goods sold using (*a*) FIFO and (*b*) LIFO. Then (*c*) compute the gross margin for each method.

Exercise 6-10

Lower of cost or market

P2

Martinez Company's ending inventory includes the following items. Compute the lower of cost or market for ending inventory applied separately to each product.

		Per Unit	
Product	Units	Cost	Market
Helmets	24	$50	$54
Bats	17	78	72
Shoes	38	95	91
Uniforms	42	36	36

Check LCM = $7,394

Exercise 6-11

Comparing LIFO numbers to FIFO numbers; ratio analysis

A1 A3

Cruz Company uses LIFO for inventory costing and reports the following financial data. It also recomputed inventory and cost of goods sold using FIFO for comparison purposes.

	2013	2012
LIFO inventory	$160	$110
LIFO cost of goods sold	740	680
FIFO inventory	240	145
FIFO cost of goods sold	660	645
Current assets (using LIFO)	220	180
Current liabilities	200	170

Check (1) FIFO: Current ratio, 1.5; Inventory turnover, 3.4 times

1. Compute its current ratio, inventory turnover, and days' sales in inventory for 2013 using (*a*) LIFO numbers and (*b*) FIFO numbers. (Round answers to one decimal.)

2. Comment on and interpret the results of part 1.

Vibrant Company had $850,000 of sales in each of three consecutive years 2012–2014, and it purchased merchandise costing $500,000 in each of those years. It also maintained a $250,000 physical inventory from the beginning to the end of that three-year period. In accounting for inventory, it made an error at the end of year 2012 that caused its year-end 2012 inventory to appear on its statements as $230,000 rather than the correct $250,000.

1. Determine the correct amount of the company's gross profit in each of the years 2012–2014.
2. Prepare comparative income statements as in Exhibit 6.11 to show the effect of this error on the company's cost of goods sold and gross profit for each of the years 2012–2014.

Exercise 6-12
Analysis of inventory errors
A2

Check   2012 reported gross profit, $330,000

Use the following information for Palmer Co. to compute inventory turnover for 2013 and 2012, and its days' sales in inventory at December 31, 2013 and 2012. (Round answers to one decimal.) Comment on Palmer's efficiency in using its assets to increase sales from 2012 to 2013.

Exercise 6-13
Inventory turnover and days' sales in inventory
A3

	2013	2012	2011
Cost of goods sold	$643,825	$426,650	$391,300
Ending inventory	97,400	87,750	92,500

Martinez Co. reported the following current-year data for its only product. The company uses a periodic inventory system, and its ending inventory consists of 150 units—50 from each of the last three purchases. Determine the cost assigned to ending inventory and to cost of goods sold using (a) specific identification, (b) weighted average, (c) FIFO, and (d) LIFO. (Round per unit costs and inventory amounts to dollars and cents.) Which method yields the highest net income?

Exercise 6-14ᴬ
Periodic: Cost flow assumptions
P3

Jan.	1	Beginning inventory	96 units @ $2.00 = $	192
Mar.	7	Purchase	220 units @ $2.25 =	495
July	28	Purchase	544 units @ $2.50 =	1,360
Oct.	3	Purchase	480 units @ $2.80 =	1,344
Dec.	19	Purchase	160 units @ $2.90 =	464
		Totals	1,500 units	$3,855

Check   Inventory; LIFO, $313.50; FIFO, $435.00

Flora's Gifts reported the following current-monthly data for its only product. The company uses a periodic inventory system, and its ending inventory consists of 60 units—50 units from the January 6 purchase, and 10 units from the January 25 purchase. Determine the cost assigned to ending inventory and to cost of goods sold using (a) specific identification, (b) weighted average, (c) FIFO, and (d) LIFO. (Round per unit costs and inventory amounts to dollars and cents.) Which method yields the lowest net income?

Exercise 6-15
Cost flow assumptions
P3

Jan.	1	Beginning inventory	138 units @ $3.00 = $	414
Jan.	6	Purchase	300 units @ $2.80 =	840
Jan.	17	Purchase	540 units @ $2.30 =	1,242
Jan.	25	Purchase	22 units @ $2.00 −	44
		Totals	1,000 units	$2,540

Check   Inventory: LIFO, $180.00; FIFO, $131.40

In 2013, Dakota Company had net sales (at retail) of $260,000. The following additional information is available from its records at the end of 2013. Use the retail inventory method to estimate Dakota's 2013 ending inventory at cost.

Exercise 6-16ᴮ
Estimating ending inventory— retail method
P4

	At Cost	At Retail
Beginning inventory	$ 63,800	$128,400
Cost of goods purchased	115,060	196,800

Check   End. Inventory, $35,860

Exercise 6-17ᴮ
Estimating ending inventory—
gross profit method
P4

On January 1, JKR Shop had $225,000 of inventory at cost. In the first quarter of the year, it purchased $795,000 of merchandise, returned $11,550, and paid freight charges of $18,800 on purchased merchandise, terms FOB shipping point. The company's gross profit averages 30%, and the store had $1,000,000 of net sales (at retail) in the first quarter of the year. Use the gross profit method to estimate its cost of inventory at the end of the first quarter.

Exercise 6-18
Accounting for inventory
following IFRS
P2

Samsung Electronics reports the following regarding its accounting for inventories.

> Inventories are stated at the lower of cost or net realizable value. Cost is determined using the average cost method, except for materials-in-transit. Inventories are reduced for the estimated losses arising from excess, obsolescence, and the decline in value. This reduction is determined by estimating market value based on future customer demand. The losses on inventory obsolescence are recorded as a part of cost of sales.

1. What cost flow assumption(s) does Samsung apply in assigning costs to its inventories?

2. If at year-end 2011 there was an increase in the value of its inventories such that there was a reversal of ₩550 (₩ is Korean won) million for the 2010 write-down, how would Samsung account for this under IFRS? Would Samsung's accounting be different for this reversal if it reported under U.S. GAAP? Explain.

PROBLEM SET A

Problem 6-1A
Perpetual: Alternative cost flows
P1

Information: Warnerwoods Company uses a perpetual inventory system. It entered into the following purchases and sales transactions for March. (For specific identification, the March 9 sale consisted of 80 units from beginning inventory and 340 units from the March 5 purchase; the March 29 sale consisted of 40 units from the March 18 purchase and 120 units from the March 25 purchase.)

Date	Activities	Units Acquired at Cost	Units Sold at Retail
Mar. 1	Beginning inventory	100 units @ $50.00 per unit	
Mar. 5	Purchase....................	400 units @ $55.00 per unit	
Mar. 9	Sales		420 units @ $85.00 per unit
Mar. 18	Purchase...................	120 units @ $60.00 per unit	
Mar. 25	Purchase..................	200 units @ $62.00 per unit	
Mar. 29	Sales		160 units @ $95.00 per unit
	Totals	820 units	580 units

Required

1. Compute cost of goods available for sale and the number of units available for sale.

2. Compute the number of units in ending inventory.

Check (3) Ending Inventory: FIFO, $14,800; LIFO, $13,680, WA, $14,352
(4) LIFO gross profit, $17,980

3. Compute the cost assigned to ending inventory using (*a*) FIFO, (*b*) LIFO, (*c*) weighted average, and (*d*) specific identification. (Round all amounts to dollars and cents.)

4. Compute gross profit earned by the company for each of the four costing methods in part 3.

Problem 6-2Aᴬ
Periodic: Alternative cost flows
P1

Refer to the **information** in Problem 6-1A and assume the periodic inventory system is used.

Required

1. Compute cost of goods available for sale and the number of units available for sale.

2. Compute the number of units in ending inventory.

3. Compute the cost assigned to ending inventory using (*a*) FIFO, (*b*) LIFO, (*c*) weighted average, and (*d*) specific identification. (Round all amounts to dollars and cents.)

4. Compute gross profit earned by the company for each of the four costing methods in part 3.

Problem 6-3A
Perpetual: Alternative cost flows
P1

Information: Montoure Company uses a perpetual inventory system. It entered into the following calendar-year 2013 purchases and sales transactions. (For specific identification, units sold consist of 600 units from beginning inventory, 300 from the February 10 purchase, 200 from the March 13 purchase, 50 from the August 21 purchase, and 250 from the September 5 purchase.)

Date	Activities	Units Acquired at Cost	Units Sold at Retail
Jan. 1	Beginning inventory	600 units @ $45.00 per unit	
Feb. 10	Purchase.	400 units @ $42.00 per unit	
Mar. 13	Purchase.	200 units @ $27.00 per unit	
Mar. 15	Sales		800 units @ $75.00 per unit
Aug. 21	Purchase.	100 units @ $50.00 per unit	
Sept. 5	Purchase.	500 units @ $46.00 per unit	
Sept. 10	Sales		600 units @ $75.00 per unit
	Totals	1,800 units	1,400 units

Required

1. Compute cost of goods available for sale and the number of units available for sale.
2. Compute the number of units in ending inventory.
3. Compute the cost assigned to ending inventory using (*a*) FIFO, (*b*) LIFO, (*c*) weighted average, and (*d*) specific identification. (Round all amounts to dollars and cents.)
4. Compute gross profit earned by the company for each of the four costing methods in part 3.

Check (3) Ending inventory: FIFO, $18,400; LIFO, $18,000; WA, $17,760; (4) LIFO gross profit, $45,800

Analysis Component

5. If the company's manager earns a bonus based on a percent of gross profit, which method of inventory costing will the manager likely prefer?

Refer to the **information** in Problem 6-3A and assume the periodic inventory system is used.

Problem 6-4A^A

Problem 6-4A[A]
Periodic: Alternative cost flows
P1

Required

1. Compute cost of goods available for sale and the number of units available for sale.
2. Compute the number of units in ending inventory.
3. Compute the cost assigned to ending inventory using (*a*) FIFO, (*b*) LIFO, (*c*) weighted average, and (*d*) specific identification. (Round all amounts to dollars and cents.)
4. Compute gross profit earned by the company for each of the four costing methods in part 3.

Analysis Component

5. If the company's manager earns a bonus based on a percentage of gross profit, which method of inventory costing will the manager likely prefer?

A physical inventory of Liverpool Company taken at December 31 reveals the following.

Problem 6-5A
Lower of cost or market
P2

		Per Unit	
Item	Units	Cost	Market
Audio equipment			
Receivers	345	$ 90	$ 98
CD players	260	111	100
MP3 players	326	86	95
Speakers	204	52	41
Video equipment			
Handheld LCDs	480	150	125
VCRs	291	93	84
Camcorders	212	310	322
Car audio equipment			
Satellite radios	185	70	84
CD/MP3 radios	170	97	105

Required

1. Calculate the lower of cost or market for the inventory applied separately to each item.
2. If the market amount is less than the recorded cost of the inventory, then record the LCM adjustment to the Merchandise Inventory account.

Check (1) $273,054

Problem 6-6A
Analysis of inventory errors

A2

mhhe.com/wildFAP21e

Navajo Company's financial statements show the following. The company recently discovered that in making physical counts of inventory, it had made the following errors: Inventory on December 31, 2012, is understated by $56,000, and inventory on December 31, 2013, is overstated by $20,000.

For Year Ended December 31		2012	2013	2014
(a)	Cost of goods sold	$ 615,000	$ 957,000	$ 780,000
(b)	Net income........................	230,000	285,000	241,000
(c)	Total current assets	1,255,000	1,365,000	1,200,000
(d)	Total equity	1,387,000	1,530,000	1,242,000

Required

1. For each key financial statement figure—(a), (b), (c), and (d) above—prepare a table similar to the following to show the adjustments necessary to correct the reported amounts.

Figure: _____	2012	2013	2014
Reported amount	_____	_____	_____
Adjustments for: 12/31/2012 error	_____	_____	_____
12/31/2013 error	_____	_____	_____
Corrected amount	_____	_____	_____

Check (1) Corrected net income:
2012, $286,000; 2013, $209,000;
2014, $261,000

Analysis Component

2. What is the error in total net income for the combined three-year period resulting from the inventory errors? Explain.

3. Explain why the understatement of inventory by $56,000 at the end of 2012 results in an understatement of equity by the same amount in that year.

Problem 6-7A[A]
Periodic: Alternative cost flows

P3

mhhe.com/wildFAP21e

Information: Seminole Company began year 2013 with 23,000 units of product in its January 1 inventory costing $15 each. It made successive purchases of its product in year 2013 as follows. The company uses a periodic inventory system. On December 31, 2013, a physical count reveals that 40,000 units of its product remain in inventory.

Mar. 7	30,000 units @ $18.00 each
May 25	39,000 units @ $20.00 each
Aug. 1	23,000 units @ $25.00 each
Nov. 10	35,000 units @ $26.00 each

Required

Check (2) Cost of goods sold:
FIFO, $2,115,000; LIFO, $2,499,000;
WA, $2,310,000

1. Compute the number and total cost of the units available for sale in year 2013.

2. Compute the amounts assigned to the 2013 ending inventory and the cost of goods sold using (a) FIFO, (b) LIFO, and (c) weighted average. (Round all amounts to dollars and cents.)

Problem 6-8A[A]
Periodic: Income comparisons
and cost flows

A1 P3

Information: QP Corp. sold 4,000 units of its product at $50 per unit in year 2013 and incurred operating expenses of $5 per unit in selling the units. It began the year with 700 units in inventory and made successive purchases of its product as follows.

Jan. 1	Beginning inventory	700 units @ $18.00 per unit
Feb. 20	Purchase	1,700 units @ $19.00 per unit
May 16	Purchase	800 units @ $20.00 per unit
Oct. 3	Purchase	500 units @ $21.00 per unit
Dec. 11	Purchase	2,300 units @ $22.00 per unit
	Total	6,000 units

Required

1. Prepare comparative income statements similar to Exhibit 6.8 for the three inventory costing methods of FIFO, LIFO, and weighted average. (Round all amounts to dollars and cents.) Include a detailed cost of goods sold section as part of each statement. The company uses a periodic inventory system, and its income tax rate is 40%.

2. How would the financial results from using the three alternative inventory costing methods change if the Company had been experiencing declining costs in its purchases of inventory?

3. What advantages and disadvantages are offered by using (*a*) LIFO and (*b*) FIFO? Assume the continuing trend of increasing costs.

Check (1) Net income: FIFO, $61,200; LIFO, $57,180; WA, $59,196

The records of Alaska Company provide the following information for the year ended December 31.

Problem 6-9A[B]
Retail inventory method

P4

	At Cost	At Retail
January 1 beginning inventory	$ 469,010	$ 928,950
Cost of goods purchased	3,376,050	6,381,050
Sales		5,595,800
Sales returns		42,800

Required

1. Use the retail inventory method to estimate the company's year-end inventory at cost.

2. A year-end physical inventory at retail prices yields a total inventory of $1,686,900. Prepare a calculation showing the company's loss from shrinkage at cost and at retail.

Check (1) Inventory, $924,182 cost; (2) Inventory shortage at cost, $36,873

Wayward Company wants to prepare interim financial statements for the first quarter. The company wishes to avoid making a physical count of inventory. Wayward's gross profit rate averages 34%. The following information for the first quarter is available from its records.

Problem 6-10A[B]
Gross profit method

P4

January 1 beginning inventory	$ 302,580
Cost of goods purchased	941,040
Sales	1,211,160
Sales returns	8,410

Required

Use the gross profit method to estimate the company's first quarter ending inventory.

Check Estimated ending inventory, $449,805

Information: TDS Company uses a perpetual inventory system. It entered into the following purchases and sales transactions for April. (For specific identification, the April 9 sale consisted of 8 units from beginning inventory and 27 units from the April 6 purchase; the April 30 sale consisted of 12 units from beginning inventory 3 units from the April 6 purchase and 10 units from the April 25 purchase.)

PROBLEM SET B

Problem 6-1B
Perpetual: Alternative cost flows

P1

Date	Activities	Units Acquired at Cost	Units Sold at Retail
Apr. 1	Beginning inventory	20 units @ $3,000.00 per unit	
Apr. 6	Purchase	30 units @ $3,500.00 per unit	
Apr. 9	Sales		35 units @ $12,000.00 per unit
Apr. 17	Purchase	5 units @ $4,500.00 per unit	
Apr. 25	Purchase	10 units @ $4,800.00 per unit	
Apr. 30	Sales		25 units @ $14,000.00 per unit
	Total	65 units	60 units

Required

1. Compute cost of goods available for sale and the number of units available for sale.
2. Compute the number of units in ending inventory.
3. Compute the cost assigned to ending inventory using (*a*) FIFO, (*b*) LIFO, (*c*) weighted average, and (*d*) specific identification. (Round all amounts to dollars and cents.)
4. Compute gross profit earned by the company for each of the four costing methods in part 3.

Problem 6-2B[A]
Periodic: Alternative cost flows

P1

Refer to the **information** in Problem 6-1B and assume the periodic inventory system is used.

Required

1. Compute cost of goods available for sale and the number of units available for sale.
2. Compute the number of units in ending inventory.
3. Compute the cost assigned to ending inventory using (*a*) FIFO, (*b*) LIFO, (*c*) weighted average, and (*d*) specific identification. (Round all amounts to dollars and cents.)
4. Compute gross profit earned by the company for each of the four costing methods in part 3.

Problem 6-3B
Perpetual: Alternative cost flows

P1

Information: Aloha Company uses a perpetual inventory system. It entered into the following calendar-year 2013 purchases and sales transactions. (For specific identification, the May 9 sale consisted of 80 units from beginning inventory and 100 units from the May 6 purchase; the May 30 sale consisted of 200 units from the May 6 purchase and 100 units from the May 25 purchase.)

Date	Activities	Units Acquired at Cost	Units Sold at Retail
May 1	Beginning inventory	150 units @ $300.00 per unit	
May 6	Purchase	350 units @ $350.00 per unit	
May 9	Sales		180 units @ $1,200.00 per unit
May 17	Purchase	80 units @ $450.00 per unit	
May 25	Purchase	100 units @ $458.00 per unit	
May 30	Sales	_____	300 units @ $1,400.00 per unit
	Total	680 units	480 units

Required

1. Compute cost of goods available for sale and the number of units available for sale.
2. Compute the number of units in ending inventory.

3. Compute the cost assigned to ending inventory using (*a*) FIFO, (*b*) LIFO, (*c*) weighted average, and (*d*) specific identification. (Round all amounts to dollars and cents.)
4. Compute gross profit earned by the company for each of the four costing methods in part 3.

Analysis Component

5. If the company's manager earns a bonus based on a percent of gross profit, which method of inventory costing will the manager likely prefer?

Problem 6-4B[A]
Periodic: Alternative cost flows

P1

Refer to the **information** in Problem 6-3B and assume the periodic inventory system is used.

Required

1. Compute cost of goods available for sale and the number of units available for sale.
2. Compute the number of units in ending inventory.
3. Compute the cost assigned to ending inventory using (*a*) FIFO, (*b*) LIFO, (*c*) weighted average, and (*d*) specific identification. (Round all amounts to dollars and cents.)
4. Compute gross profit earned by the company for each of the four costing methods in part 3.

Analysis Component

5. If the company's manager earns a bonus based on a percentage of gross profit, which method of inventory costing will the manager likely prefer?

A physical inventory of Office Necessities taken at December 31 reveals the following.

Problem 6-5B
Lower of cost or market
P2

File Edit View Insert Format Tools Data Accounting Window Help			

		Per Unit	
Item	**Units**	**Cost**	**Market**
Office furniture			
Desks	536	$261	$305
Credenzas	395	227	256
Chairs	687	49	43
Bookshelves	421	93	82
Filing cabinets			
Two-drawer	114	81	70
Four-drawer	298	135	122
Lateral	75	104	118
Office equipment			
Fax machines	370	168	200
Copiers	475	317	288
Telephones	302	125	117

Required

1. Compute the lower of cost or market for the inventory applied separately to each item.
2. If the market amount is less than the recorded cost of the inventory, then record the LCM adjustment to the Merchandise Inventory account.

Check   (1) $580,054

Hallam Company's financial statements show the following. The company recently discovered that in making physical counts of inventory, it had made the following errors: Inventory on December 31, 2012, is overstated by $18,000, and inventory on December 31, 2013, is understated by $26,000.

Problem 6-6B
Analysis of inventory errors
A2

For Year Ended December 31	2012	2013	2014
(a) Cost of goods sold	$207,200	$213,800	$197,030
(b) Net income	175,800	212,270	184,910
(c) Total current assets	276,000	277,500	272,950
(d) Total equity	314,000	315,000	346,000

Required

1. For each key financial statement figure—(a), (b), (c), and (d) above—prepare a table similar to the following to show the adjustments necessary to correct the reported amounts.

Figure: _____	2012	2013	2014
Reported amount	_____	_____	_____
Adjustments for: 12/31/2012 error	_____	_____	_____
12/31/2013 error	_____	_____	_____
Corrected amount	_____	_____	_____

Check   (1) Corrected net income: 2012, $157,800; 2013, $256,270; 2014, $158,910

Analysis Component

2. What is the error in total net income for the combined three-year period resulting from the inventory errors? Explain.
3. Explain why the overstatement of inventory by $18,000 at the end of 2012 results in an overstatement of equity by the same amount in that year.

Problem 6-7B[A]
Periodic: Alternative cost flows
P3

Information: Seneca Co. began year 2013 with 6,500 units of product in its January 1 inventory costing $35 each. It made successive purchases of its product in year 2013 as follows. The company uses a periodic inventory system. On December 31, 2013, a physical count reveals that 8,500 units of its product remain in inventory.

Jan. 4	11,500 units @ $33 each
May 18	13,400 units @ $32 each
July 9	11,000 units @ $29 each
Nov. 21	7,600 units @ $27 each

Required

Check (2) Cost of goods sold:
FIFO, $1,328,700; LIFO, $1,266,500;
WA, $1,294,800

1. Compute the number and total cost of the units available for sale in year 2013.
2. Compute the amounts assigned to the 2013 ending inventory and the cost of goods sold using (a) FIFO, (b) LIFO, and (c) weighted average. (Round all amounts to dollars and cents.)

Problem 6-8B[A]
Periodic: Income comparisons
and cost flows
A1 P3

Information: Shepard Company sold 4,000 units of its product at $100 per unit in year 2013 and incurred operating expenses of $15 per unit in selling the units. It began the year with 840 units in inventory and made successive purchases of its product as follows.

Jan. 1	Beginning inventory	840 units @ $58 per unit
April 2	Purchase	600 units @ $59 per unit
June 14	Purchase	1,205 units @ $61 per unit
Aug. 29	Purchase	700 units @ $64 per unit
Nov. 18	Purchase	1,655 units @ $65 per unit
	Total	5,000 units

Required

Check (1) Net income: LIFO,
$52,896; FIFO, $57,000; WA, $55,200

1. Prepare comparative income statements similar to Exhibit 6.8 for the three inventory costing methods of FIFO, LIFO, and weighted average. (Round all amounts to dollars and cents.) Include a detailed cost of goods sold section as part of each statement. The company uses a periodic inventory system, and its income tax rate is 40%.
2. How would the financial results from using the three alternative inventory costing methods change if the company had been experiencing decreasing prices in its purchases of inventory?
3. What advantages and disadvantages are offered by using (a) LIFO and (b) FIFO? Assume the continuing trend of increasing costs.

Problem 6-9B[B]
Retail inventory method
P4

The records of Macklin Co. provide the following information for the year ended December 31.

	At Cost	At Retail
January 1 beginning inventory	$ 90,022	$115,610
Cost of goods purchased	502,250	761,830
Sales		782,300
Sales returns		3,460

Required

Check (1) Inventory, $66,555 cost;
(2) Inventory shortage at
cost, $12,251.25

1. Use the retail inventory method to estimate the company's year-end inventory.
2. A year-end physical inventory at retail prices yields a total inventory of $80,450. Prepare a calculation showing the company's loss from shrinkage at cost and at retail.

Problem 6-10B[B]
Gross profit method
P4

Otingo Equipment Co. wants to prepare interim financial statements for the first quarter. The company wishes to avoid making a physical count of inventory. Otingo's gross profit rate averages 35%. The following information for the first quarter is available from its records.

January 1 beginning inventory	$ 802,880
Cost of goods purchased	2,209,636
Sales	3,760,260
Sales returns	79,300

Required

Use the gross profit method to estimate the company's first quarter ending inventory.

Check Estim. ending inventory, $619,892

(This serial problem began in Chapter 1 and continues through most of the book. If previous chapter segments were not completed, the serial problem can begin at this point.)

SERIAL PROBLEM
Success Systems

P2 A3

SP 6

Part A

Adria Lopez of Success Systems is evaluating her inventory to determine whether it must be adjusted based on lower of cost or market rules. Her company has three different types of software in its inventory and the following information is available for each.

		Per Unit	
Inventory Items	Units	Cost	Market
Office productivity	3	$ 76	$ 74
Desktop publishing	2	103	100
Accounting	3	90	96

Required

1. Compute the lower of cost or market for ending inventory assuming Lopez applies the lower of cost or market rule to inventory as a whole. Must Lopez adjust the reported inventory value? Explain.
2. Assume that Lopez had instead applied the lower of cost or market rule to each product in inventory. Under this assumption, must Lopez adjust the reported inventory value? Explain.

Part B

Selected accounts and balances for the three months ended March 31, 2014, for Success Systems follow.

January 1 beginning inventory	$ 0
Cost of goods sold	14,052
March 31 ending inventory	704

Required

1. Compute inventory turnover and days' sales in inventory for the three months ended March 31, 2014.
2. Assess the company's performance if competitors average 15 times for inventory turnover and 29 days for days' sales in inventory.

Beyond the Numbers

BTN 6-1 Refer to **Polaris**' financial statements in Appendix A to answer the following.

REPORTING IN ACTION

C2 A3

Polaris

Required

1. What amount of inventories did Polaris report as a current asset on December 31, 2011? On December 31, 2010?
2. Inventories represent what percent of total assets on December 31, 2011? On December 31, 2010?
3. Comment on the relative size of Polaris' inventories compared to its other types of assets.
4. What accounting method did Polaris use to compute inventory amounts on its balance sheet?
5. Compute inventory turnover for fiscal year ended December 31, 2011, and days' sales in inventory as of December 31, 2011.

Fast Forward

6. Access Polaris' financial statements for fiscal years ended after December 31, 2011, from its Website (**Polaris.com**) or the SEC's EDGAR database (**www.SEC.gov**). Answer questions 1 through 5 using the current Polaris information and compare results to those prior years.

COMPARATIVE ANALYSIS

A3

Polaris

Arctic Cat

BTN 6-2   Comparative figures for **Polaris** and **Arctic Cat** follow.

($ thousands)	Polaris			Arctic Cat		
	Current Year	One Year Prior	Two Years Prior	Current Year	One Year Prior	Two Years Prior
Inventory	$ 298,042	$ 235,927	$ 179,315	$ 61,478	$ 81,361	$ 120,804
Cost of sales	1,916,366	1,460,926	1,172,668	363,142	367,492	480,441

Required

1. Compute inventory turnover for each company for the most recent two years shown.

2. Compute days' sales in inventory for each company for the three years shown.

3. Comment on and interpret your findings from parts 1 and 2. Assume an industry average for inventory turnover of 5.

ETHICS CHALLENGE

A1

BTN 6-3   Golf Challenge Corp. is a retail sports store carrying golf apparel and equipment. The store is at the end of its second year of operation and is struggling. A major problem is that its cost of inventory has continually increased in the past two years. In the first year of operations, the store assigned inventory costs using LIFO. A loan agreement the store has with its bank, its prime source of financing, requires the store to maintain a certain profit margin and current ratio. The store's owner is currently looking over Golf Challenge's preliminary financial statements for its second year. The numbers are not favorable. The only way the store can meet the required financial ratios agreed on with the bank is to change from LIFO to FIFO. The store originally decided on LIFO because of its tax advantages. The owner recalculates ending inventory using FIFO and submits those numbers and statements to the loan officer at the bank for the required bank review. The owner thankfully reflects on the available latitude in choosing the inventory costing method.

Required

1. How does Golf Challenge's use of FIFO improve its net profit margin and current ratio?

2. Is the action by Golf Challenge's owner ethical? Explain.

COMMUNICATING IN PRACTICE

A1

BTN 6-4   You are a financial adviser with a client in the wholesale produce business that just completed its first year of operations. Due to weather conditions, the cost of acquiring produce to resell has escalated during the later part of this period. Your client, Javonte Gish, mentions that because her business sells perishable goods, she has striven to maintain a FIFO flow of goods. Although sales are good, the increasing cost of inventory has put the business in a tight cash position. Gish has expressed concern regarding the ability of the business to meet income tax obligations.

Required

Prepare a memorandum that identifies, explains, and justifies the inventory method you recommend your client, Ms. Gish, adopt.

BTN 6-5   Access the September 24, 2011, 10-K report for **Apple, Inc.** (Ticker AAPL), filed on October 26, 2011, from the EDGAR filings at **www.sec.gov**.

Required

1. What products are manufactured by Apple?

2. What inventory method does Apple use? (*Hint:* See the Note 1 to its financial statements.)

3. Compute its gross margin and gross margin ratio for the 2011 fiscal year. Comment on your computations—assume an industry average of 40% for the gross margin ratio.

4. Compute its inventory turnover and days' sales in inventory for the year ended September 24, 2011. Comment on your computations—assume an industry average of 40 for inventory turnover and 9 for days' sales in inventory.

BTN 6-6   Each team member has the responsibility to become an expert on an inventory method. This expertise will be used to facilitate teammates' understanding of the concepts relevant to that method.

TEAMWORK IN ACTION

A1 P1

1. Each learning team member should select an area for expertise by choosing one of the following inventory methods: specific identification, LIFO, FIFO, or weighted average.

2. Form expert teams made up of students who have selected the same area of expertise. The instructor will identify where each expert team will meet.

Point: Step 1 allows four choices or areas for expertise. Larger teams will have some duplication of choice, but the specific identification method should not be duplicated.

3. Using the following data, each expert team must collaborate to develop a presentation that illustrates the relevant concepts and procedures for its inventory method. Each team member must write the presentation in a format that can be shown to the learning team.

Data

The company uses a perpetual inventory system. It had the following beginning inventory and current year purchases of its product.

Jan. 1	Beginning inventory........	50 units @ $100 =	$ 5,000
Jan. 14	Purchase	150 units @ $120 =	18,000
Apr. 30	Purchase	200 units @ $150 =	30,000
Sept. 26	Purchase	300 units @ $200 =	60,000

The company transacted sales on the following dates at a $350 per unit sales price.

Jan. 10	30 units	(specific cost: 30 @ $100)
Feb. 15	100 units	(specific cost: 100 @ $120)
Oct. 5	350 units	(specific cost: 100 @ $150 and 250 @ $200)

Concepts and Procedures to Illustrate in Expert Presentation

a. Identify and compute the costs to assign to the units sold. (Round per unit costs to three decimals.)

b. Identify and compute the costs to assign to the units in ending inventory. (Round inventory balances to the dollar.)

c. How likely is it that this inventory costing method will reflect the actual physical flow of goods? How relevant is that factor in determining whether this is an acceptable method to use?

d. What is the impact of this method versus others in determining net income and income taxes?

e. How closely does the ending inventory amount reflect replacement cost?

4. Re-form learning teams. In rotation, each expert is to present to the team the presentation developed in part 3. Experts are to encourage and respond to questions.

ENTREPRENEURIAL DECISION

A3

BTN 6-7   Review the chapter's opening feature highlighting Derick Pearson and Felecia Hatcher and their company, **Feverish Ice Cream**. Assume that Feverish Ice Cream consistently maintains an inventory level of $30,000, meaning that its average and ending inventory levels are the same. Also assume its annual cost of sales is $120,000. To cut costs, Derick and Felecia propose to slash inventory to a constant level of $15,000 with no impact on cost of sales. They plan to work with suppliers to get quicker deliveries and to order smaller quantities more often.

Required

1. Compute the company's inventory turnover and its days' sales in inventory under (*a*) current conditions and (*b*) proposed conditions.
2. Evaluate and comment on the merits of their proposal given your analysis for part 1. Identify any concerns you might have about the proposal.

HITTING THE ROAD

C1 C2

BTN 6-8   Visit four retail stores with another classmate. In each store, identify whether the store uses a bar-coding system to help manage its inventory. Try to find at least one store that does not use bar-coding. If a store does not use bar-coding, ask the store's manager or clerk whether he or she knows which type of inventory method the store employs. Create a table that shows columns for the name of store visited, type of merchandise sold, use or nonuse of bar-coding, and the inventory method used if bar-coding is not employed. You might also inquire as to what the store's inventory turnover is and how often physical inventory is taken.

GLOBAL DECISION

A3

PIAGGIO
Polaris
Arctic Cat

BTN 6-9   Following are key figures (Euro in thousands) for **Piaggio** (**www.piaggio.com**), which is a leading manufacturer of two-, three- and four-wheel vehicles, and is Europe's leading manufacturer of motorcycles and scooters.

Euro in thousands	Current Year	One Year Prior	Two Years Prior
Inventory	236,988	240,066	252,496
Cost of sales	1,061,900	1,023,100	1,019,800

Required

1. Use these data and those from BTN 6-2 to compute (*a*) inventory turnover and (*b*) days' sales in inventory for the most recent two years shown for **Piaggio**, **Polaris**, and **Arctic Cat**.
2. Comment on and interpret your findings from part 1.

ANSWERS TO MULTIPLE CHOICE QUIZ

1. a; FIFO perpetual

Date	Goods Purchased	Cost of Goods Sold	Inventory Balance
July 1			75 units @ $25 = $ 1,875
July 3	348 units @ $27 = $9,396		75 units @ $25 ⎫ 348 units @ $27 ⎭ = $ 11,271
July 8		75 units @ $25 ⎫ 225 units @ $27 ⎭ = $ 7,950	123 units @ $27 = $ 3,321
July 15	257 units @ $28 = $7,196		123 units @ $27 ⎫ 257 units @ $28 ⎭ = $ 10,517
July 23		123 units @ $27 ⎫ 152 units @ $28 ⎭ = $ 7,577	105 units @ $28 = **$ 2,940**
		$15,527	

2. b; LIFO perpetual

Date	Goods Purchased	Cost of Goods Sold	Inventory Balance
July 1			75 units @ $25 = $ 1,875
July 3	348 units @ $27 = $9,396		75 units @ $25 ⎫ 348 units @ $27 ⎭ = $ 11,271
July 8		300 units @ $27 = $ 8,100	75 units @ $25 ⎫ 48 units @ $27 ⎭ = $ 3,171
July 15	257 units @ $28 = $7,196		75 units @ $25 ⎫ 48 units @ $27 ⎬ = $ 10,367 257 units @ $28 ⎭
July 23		257 units @ $28 ⎫ 18 units @ $27 ⎭ = $ 7,682 $15,782	75 units @ $25 ⎫ 30 units @ $27 ⎭ = $ **2,685**

3. e; Specific identification (perpetual & periodic are identical)—Ending inventory computation.

20 units @ $25	$ 500
40 units @ $27	1,080
45 units @ $28	1,260
105 units	$2,840

4. a; FIFO periodic—Ending inventory computation.

105 units @ $28 each = $2,940; The FIFO periodic inventory computation is identical to the FIFO perpetual inventory computation (see question 1).

5. a; FIFO periodic inventory = $(20 \times \$14) + (10 \times \$12)$
$$= \$400$$

a; LIFO periodic cost of goods sold = $(20 \times \$14) + (40 \times \$12) + (70 \times \$10)$
$$= \$1,460$$

6. d; Days' sales in inventory = (Ending inventory/Cost of goods sold × 365)
$$= (\$18,000/\$85,000) \times 365 = \underline{77.29 \text{ days}}$$

Accounting Information Systems

A Look Back

Chapters 5 and 6 focused on merchandising activities and accounting for inventory. We explained inventory systems, accounting for inventory transactions, and assigning costs to inventory.

A Look at This Chapter

This chapter emphasizes accounting information systems. We describe fundamental system principles, the system's components, use of special journals and subsidiary ledgers, and technology-based systems.

A Look Ahead

Chapter 8 focuses on internal controls and accounting for cash and cash equivalents. We explain good internal control procedures and their importance.

Happy Times

"We let our investors see, and share, our passion."
—**SHAZI VISRAM**

NEW YORK—Shazi Visram grew up in Alabama but she felt entrepreneurship was her calling. "I always knew that I wanted to be my own boss," recalls Shazi. "I had this idea to make baby food the way moms would." However, entrepreneurship had its challenges. "There was an evening when I got to the subway with nothing in my wallet but maxed out credit cards and no way to pay for my ride home," admits Shazi. "The path of entrepreneurship isn't smooth . . . it's a rollercoaster!" From these modest beginnings, Shazi created **Happy Family Brands (HappyBabyFood.com),** which is committed to quality foods for the entire family.

"We are an authentic mom-run company; we are real people behind this business who care about the quality of our products," explains Shazi. "I made the first recipes in my kitchen, using the best organic ingredients. Then, I subjected these recipes to the critics; hundreds of babies, including my own!" Along the way, Shazi set up an accounting system to measure, track, summarize, and report on operations. "We are a small business with a big vision and a big heart," says Shazi. That vision fundamentally shapes Shazi's accounting system and controls.

"Quality is of the utmost concern," explains Shazi. That focus on quality includes applying internal controls, special journals, accounting ledgers, and systems technology. Shazi maintains special journals for sales, cash receipts, purchases, and cash disbursements. Developing her accounting system to capture all aspects of her operations is no easy task, but well worth the effort. "We've grown exponentially . . . now we're in over 17,000 stores," says Shazi. "What's important [in both business and accounting] is . . . being adaptable!" Shazi explains that this in turn helps shape the special journals for her company, including the appropriate control procedures.

Shazi's company is riding high with the right accounting systems and controls for long-run success. "What an incredible opportunity to build a meaningful brand," says Shazi. "[We] make a difference in a child's life." Shazi adds, "We have been really blessed!"

[Sources: Happy Family Brands *Website*, January 2013; *INC.*, August 2011 and March 2012; *New Hope 360*, March 2011; *FOXBusiness*, November 2011]

With increases in the number and complexity of business activities, the demands placed on accounting information systems increase. Accounting information systems must meet this challenge in an efficient and effective manner. In this chapter, we learn about fundamental principles guiding information systems, and we study components making up these systems. We also explain procedures that use special journals and subsidiary ledgers to make accounting information systems more efficient. An understanding of the details of accounting reports makes us better decision makers when using financial information, and it improves our ability to analyze and interpret financial statements.

Accounting Information Systems

System Principles	System Components	Special Journals	System Technology
• Control • Relevance • Compatibility • Flexibility • Cost-Benefit	• Source documents • Input devices • Processors • Storage • Output devices	• Subsidiary ledgers • Sales journal • Cash receipts journal • Purchases journal • Cash disbursements journal	• Computers • Data processing • Networks • Enterprise resource planning (ERP)

FUNDAMENTAL SYSTEM PRINCIPLES

C1 Identify the principles and components of accounting information systems.

Accounting information systems collect and process data from transactions and events, organize them in useful reports, and communicate results to decision makers. With the increasing complexity of business and the growing need for information, accounting information systems are more important than ever. All decision makers need to have a basic knowledge of how accounting information systems work. This knowledge gives decision makers a competitive edge as they gain a better understanding of information constraints, measurement limitations, and potential applications. It allows them to make more informed decisions and to better balance the risks and returns of different strategies. This section explains five basic principles of accounting information systems, shown in Exhibit 7.1.

EXHIBIT 7.1

System Principles

Circular diagram with "System Principles" at center surrounded by: Control, Relevance, Compatibility, Flexibility, Cost-Benefit Principle

Control Principle

Managers need to control and monitor business activities. The **control principle** prescribes that an accounting information system have internal controls. **Internal controls** are methods and procedures allowing managers to control and monitor business activities. They include policies to direct operations toward common goals, procedures to ensure reliable financial reports, safeguards to protect company assets, and methods to achieve compliance with laws and regulations.

Point: Hackers stole 45 million debit and credit card numbers from **T.J. Maxx.** The security breach is estimated to have cost the company $100 per card or $4.5 billion.

Relevance Principle

Decision makers need relevant information to make informed decisions. The **relevance principle** prescribes that an accounting information system report useful, understandable, timely, and pertinent information for effective decision making. The system must be designed to capture data that make a difference in decisions. To ensure this, we must consider all decision makers when identifying relevant information for disclosure.

Compatibility Principle

Accounting information systems must be consistent with the aims of a company. The **compatibility principle** prescribes that an accounting information system conform with a company's activities, personnel, and structure. It also must adapt to a company's unique characteristics. The system must not be intrusive but must work in harmony with and be driven by company goals. Most start-up entrepreneurs require only a simple information system. **Starbucks**, on the other hand, demands both a merchandising and a manufacturing information system able to assemble data from its global operations.

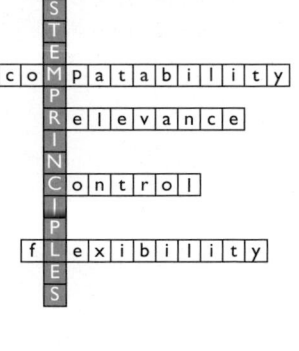

Flexibility Principle

Accounting information systems must be able to adjust to changes. The **flexibility principle** prescribes that an accounting information system be able to adapt to changes in the company, business environment, and needs of decisions makers. Technological advances, competitive pressures, consumer tastes, regulations, and company activities constantly evolve. A system must be designed to adapt to these changes.

Cost-Benefit Principle

The **cost-benefit principle** prescribes that the benefits from an activity in an accounting information system outweigh the costs of that activity. The costs and benefits of an activity such as producing a specific report will impact the decisions of both external and internal users. Decisions regarding other systems principles (control, relevance, compatibility, and flexibility) are also affected by the cost-benefit principle.

Point: Law requires that *all* employers destroy credit-check and other employee records *before* tossing them. A cross-cut shredder is the tool of choice.

 Decision Insight

Digitals Are Forever   E-communications have helped bring down many employees, including the former CEO of **Boeing**. To comply with Sarbanes-Oxley, more and more companies now archive and monitor e-mails, instant messages, blog postings, and Net-based phone calls. Using natural-language software, companies sift through digital communications in milliseconds, checking for trade secrets, bad language, porn, and pirated files. Also, employers should draft policies for employee use and access to electronic media to preserve company property interest and access rights to electronic data. ■

COMPONENTS OF ACCOUNTING SYSTEMS

Accounting information systems consist of people, records, methods, and equipment. The systems are designed to capture information about a company's transactions and to provide output including financial, managerial, and tax reports. All accounting information systems have these same goals, and thus share some basic components. These components apply whether or not a system is heavily computerized, yet the components of computerized systems usually provide more accuracy, speed, efficiency, and convenience than those of manual systems.

The five basic **components of accounting systems** are source documents, input devices, information processors, information storage, and output devices. Exhibit 7.2 shows these components as a series of steps, yet we know that much two-way communication occurs between many of these components. We briefly describe each of these key components in this section.

EXHIBIT 7.2

Accounting System Components

| Source Document | Input Devices | Information Processor | Information Storage | Output Devices |

Source Documents

We introduced source documents in Chapters 1 and 2 and explained their importance for both business transactions and information collection. Source documents provide the basic information processed by an accounting system. Examples of source documents include bank statements and checks, invoices from suppliers, billings to customers, cash register files, and employee earnings records. Source documents can be paper, although they increasingly are taking the form of electronic files and Web communications. A growing number of companies are sending documents directly from their systems to their customers' and suppliers' systems. The Web is playing a major role in this transformation from paper-based to *paperless* systems.

Accurate source documents are crucial to accounting information systems. Input of faulty or incomplete information seriously impairs the reliability and relevance of the information system. We commonly refer to this as "garbage in, garbage out." Information systems are set up with attention on control procedures to limit the possibility of entering faulty data in the system.

Input Devices

Point: Understanding a manual accounting system is useful in understanding an electronic system.

Input devices capture information from source documents and enable its transfer to the system's information processing component. These devices often involve converting data on source documents from written or electronic form to a form usable for the system. Journal entries, both electronic and paper based, are a type of input device. Keyboards, scanners, and modems are some of the most common input devices in practice today. For example, bar code readers capture code numbers and transfer them to the organization's computer for processing. Moreover, a scanner can capture writing samples and other input directly from source documents. Cell phone cameras also can serve as input devices via bar codes.

Controls are used to ensure that only authorized individuals input data to the system. Controls increase the system's reliability and allow information to be traced back to its source.

▊ Decision Insight ━━━━━━━━━━━━━━━━━━━━━━━━

Siri Exposure Siri (Speech Interpretation and Recognition Interface) is an intelligent personal assistant and knowledge navigator that works as an application for Apple's iOS. The latest iPhones include Siri, including its voice recognition capabilities. Companies should ask: *Siri, do we have adequate controls for inputs to our system via voice recognition?* ▪

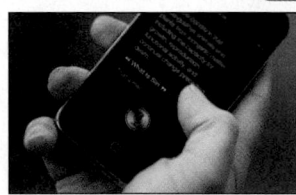

Information Processors

Point: *BusinessWeek* reported that 75% of all e-mail traffic is spam.

Information processors are systems that interpret, transform, and summarize information for use in analysis and reporting. An important part of an information processor in accounting systems is professional judgment. Accounting principles are never so structured that they limit the need for professional judgment. Other parts of an information processor include journals, ledgers, working papers, and posting procedures. Each assists in transforming raw data to useful information.

Increasingly, computer technology (both computing hardware and software) is assisting manual information processors. This assistance is freeing accounting professionals to take on increased analysis, interpretive, and managerial roles. Web-based application service providers (ASPs) offer another type of information processor.

Information Storage

Point: Well-designed accounting software includes a report generator that allows accountants to design and customize internal reports.

Information storage is the accounting system component that keeps data in a form accessible to information processors. After being input and processed, data are stored for use in future analyses and reports. The database must be accessible to preparers of periodic financial reports. Auditors rely on this database when they audit both financial statements and a company's controls. Companies also maintain files of source documents.

Older systems consisted almost exclusively of paper documents, but most modern systems depend on electronic storage devices or, increasingly, cloud storage. Advances in information storage enable accounting systems to increasingly store more detailed data. This means managers have more data to access and work with in planning and controlling business activities. Information storage can be online, meaning that data can be accessed whenever, and from wherever, it is needed. Off-line storage means access often requires assistance and authorization. Information storage is increasingly augmented by Web sources such as SEC databases, benchmarking services, and financial and product markets. Also, audit technology allows external auditors 365-day real-time access to client records from remote locations.

Decision Insight

Virtual Output A screenless computer display, called *virtual retinal display* (VRD), scans rows of pixels directly onto the user's retina by means of a laser. VRDs can simulate three-dimensional virtual worlds, including 3D financial graphics. ■

Output Devices

Output devices are the means to take information out of an accounting system and make it available to users. Common output devices are printers, monitors, projectors, and Web communications. Output devices provide users a variety of items including graphics, analysis reports, bills to customers, checks to suppliers, employee paychecks, financial statements, and internal reports. When requests for output occur, an information processor takes the needed data from a database and prepares the necessary report, which is then sent to an output device. A special type of output is an electronic funds transfer (EFT). One example is the transfer of payroll from the company's bank account to its employees' bank accounts. This requires an interface to allow a company's accounting system to send payroll data directly to the bank's accounting system. This interface can involve a company recording its payroll data in an encrypted zip file and forwarding it to the bank. The bank then uses this output to transfer wages earned to employees' accounts.

Point: The SEC database now allows searchable data fields in required company filings. The software that facilitates this capability is XBRL (eXtensible Business Reporting Language).

Decision Ethics

Accountant Your client requests advice in purchasing software for its accounting system. You have been offered a 10% commission by a software company for each purchase of its system by one of your clients. Does this commission arrangement affect your evaluation of software? Do you tell your client about the commission arrangement? ■ [Answer—p. 300]

Quick Check   Answers — p. 300

1. Identify the five primary components of an accounting information system.
2. What is the aim of information processors in an accounting system?
3. How are data in the information storage component of an accounting system used?

SPECIAL JOURNALS IN ACCOUNTING

This section describes the underlying records of accounting information systems. Designed correctly, these records support efficiency in processing transactions and events. They are part of all systems in various forms and are increasingly electronic. Even in technologically advanced systems, a basic understanding of the records we describe in this section aids in using, interpreting, and applying accounting information. It also improves our knowledge of computer-based systems. Remember that all accounting systems have common purposes and internal workings whether or not they depend on technology. (Popular accounting software that utilizes special journals includes *Great Plains* and *QuickBooks*.)

C2 Explain the goals and uses of special journals.

This section focuses on special journals and subsidiary ledgers that are an important part of accounting systems. We describe how special journals are used to capture transactions, and we explain how subsidiary ledgers are set up to capture details of accounts. This section uses a *perpetual* inventory system, and the special journals are set up using this system. We include a note at the bottom of each of the special journals explaining the change required if a company uses a periodic system.

Basics of Special Journals

A **general journal** is an all-purpose journal in which we can record any transaction. Use of a general journal for all transactions is usually more costly for a business *and* is a less effective control procedure. Moreover, for less technologically advanced systems, use of a general journal requires that each debit and each credit entered be individually posted to its respective ledger account. To enhance internal control and reduce costs, transactions are organized into common groups. A **special journal** is used to record and post transactions of similar type. Most transactions of a merchandiser, for instance, can be categorized into the journals shown in Exhibit 7.3. This section assumes the use of these four special journals along with the general journal. The general journal continues to be used for transactions not covered by special journals and for adjusting, closing, and correcting entries. We show in the following discussion that special journals are *efficient tools in helping journalize and post transactions.* This is done, for instance, by accumulating debits and credits of similar transactions, which allows posting of amounts as column *totals* rather than as individual amounts. The advantage of this system increases as the number of transactions increases. Special journals allow an *efficient division of labor,* which is also an effective control procedure.

Point: Companies can use as many special journals as necessary given their unique business activities.

Point: A specific transaction is recorded in only *one* journal.

EXHIBIT 7.3

Using Special Journals with a General Journal

    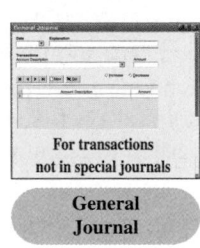

For recording credit sales	For recording cash receipts	For recording credit purchases	For recording cash payments	For transactions not in special journals
Sales Journal	**Cash Receipts Journal**	**Purchases Journal**	**Cash Disbursements Journal**	**General Journal**

It is important to note that special journals and subsidiary ledgers *are designed in a manner that is best suited for each business.* The most likely candidates for special journal status are recurring transactions—for many businesses those are sales, cash receipts, purchases, and cash disbursements. However, good systems design for a business could involve collapsing sales and cash receipts in one journal, or purchases and cash disbursements in another. It could also involve adding more special journals or additional subsidiary ledgers for other recurring transactions. This design decision extends to journal and ledger format. That is, the selection on number of columns, column headings, and so forth is based on what is best suited for each business. Thus, read the following sections as one example of a common systems design, but not the only design. (Proprietary software is internally developed by companies to meet system needs not met by off-the-shelf accounting software.)

Subsidiary Ledgers

 Describe the use of controlling accounts and subsidiary ledgers.

To understand special journals, it is necessary to understand the workings of a **subsidiary ledger,** which is a list of individual accounts with a common characteristic. A subsidiary ledger contains detailed information on specific accounts in the general ledger. Information systems often include several subsidiary ledgers. Two of the most important are:

- *Accounts receivable ledger*—stores transaction data of individual customers.
- *Accounts payable ledger*—stores transaction data of individual suppliers.

Individual accounts in subsidiary ledgers are often arranged alphabetically, which is the approach taken here. We describe accounts receivable and accounts payable ledgers in this section. Our discussion of special journals uses these ledgers.

Accounts Receivable Ledger When we recorded credit sales in prior chapters, we debited (increased) Accounts Receivable. When a company has more than one credit customer, the accounts receivable records must show how much *each* customer purchased, paid, and has yet to pay. This information is collected by keeping a separate account receivable for each credit customer. A separate account for each customer *could* be kept in the general ledger with the other financial statement accounts, but this is uncommon. Instead, the general ledger usually has a single Accounts Receivable account, and a *subsidiary ledger* is set up to keep a separate account for each customer. This subsidiary ledger is called the **accounts receivable ledger** (also called *accounts receivable subsidiary ledger* or *customers ledger*), and it can exist in electronic or paper form.

Exhibit 7.4 shows the relation between the Accounts Receivable account and its individual accounts in the subsidiary ledger. After all items are posted, the balance in the Accounts Receivable account must equal the sum of all balances of its customers' accounts. The Accounts Receivable account is said to control the accounts receivable ledger and is called a **controlling account.** Since the accounts receivable ledger is a supplementary record controlled by an account in the general ledger, it is called a *subsidiary* ledger.

Point: When a general ledger account has a subsidiary ledger, any transaction that impacts one of them also impacts the other—some refer to this as *general and subsidiary ledgers kept in tandem.*

EXHIBIT 7.4

Accounts Receivable Controlling Account and Its Subsidiary Ledger

Point: A **control account** refers to any general ledger account that summarizes subsidiary ledger data.

Accounts Payable Ledger There are other controlling accounts and subsidiary ledgers. We know, for example, that many companies buy on credit from several suppliers. This means that companies must keep a separate account for each supplier by keeping an Accounts Payable controlling account in the general ledger and a separate account for each supplier (creditor) in an **accounts payable ledger** (also called *accounts payable subsidiary ledger* or *creditors ledger*).

Other Subsidiary Ledgers Subsidiary ledgers are common for several other accounts. A company with many classes of equipment, for example, might keep only one Equipment account in its general ledger, but its Equipment account would control a subsidiary ledger in which each class of equipment is recorded in a separate account. Similar treatment is common for investments, inventory, and any accounts needing separate detailed records. **Genmar Holdings**, which manufactures boats by Champion, Glastron, Four Winns, and Larson, reports sales information by product line in its report. Yet its accounting system keeps much more detailed sales records. Genmar Holdings, for instance, sells hundreds of different products and must be able to analyze the sales performance of each. This detail can be captured by many different general ledger sales accounts but is instead captured by using supplementary records that function like subsidiary ledgers. Overall, subsidiary ledgers are applied in many different ways to ensure that the accounting system captures sufficient details to support analyses that decision makers need. At least four benefits derive from subsidiary ledgers:

1. Removal of excessive details, and detailed accounts, from the general ledger.
2. Up-to-date information readily available on specific customers and suppliers.
3. Aid in error identification for specific accounts.
4. Potential efficiencies in recordkeeping through division of labor in posting.

Sales Journal

A typical **sales journal** is used to record sales of inventory *on credit.* Sales of inventory for cash are not recorded in a sales journal but in a cash receipts journal. Sales of noninventory assets on credit are recorded in the general journal.

Journalizing   Credit sale transactions are recorded with information about each sale entered separately in a sales journal. This information is often taken from a copy of the sales ticket or invoice prepared at the time of sale. The top portion of Exhibit 7.5 shows a typical sales journal from a merchandiser. It has columns for recording the date, customer's name, invoice number, posting reference, and the retail and cost amounts of each credit sale. The sales journal in this exhibit is called a **columnar journal,** which is any journal with more than one column.

Point: Each transaction in the sales journal includes a debit to accounts receivable and a credit to sales.

Each transaction recorded in the sales journal yields an entry in the "Accounts Receivable Dr., Sales Cr." column. We usually need only one column for these two accounts. (An exception is when managers need more information about taxes, returns, and other sales details.) Each transaction in the sales journal also yields an entry in the "Cost of Goods Sold Dr., Inventory Cr." column. This entry reflects the perpetual inventory system of tracking costs with each sale. To illustrate, on February 2, this company sold merchandise on account to Jason Henry for $450. The invoice number is 307, and the cost of this merchandise is $315. This information is

EXHIBIT 7.5

Sales Journal with Posting*

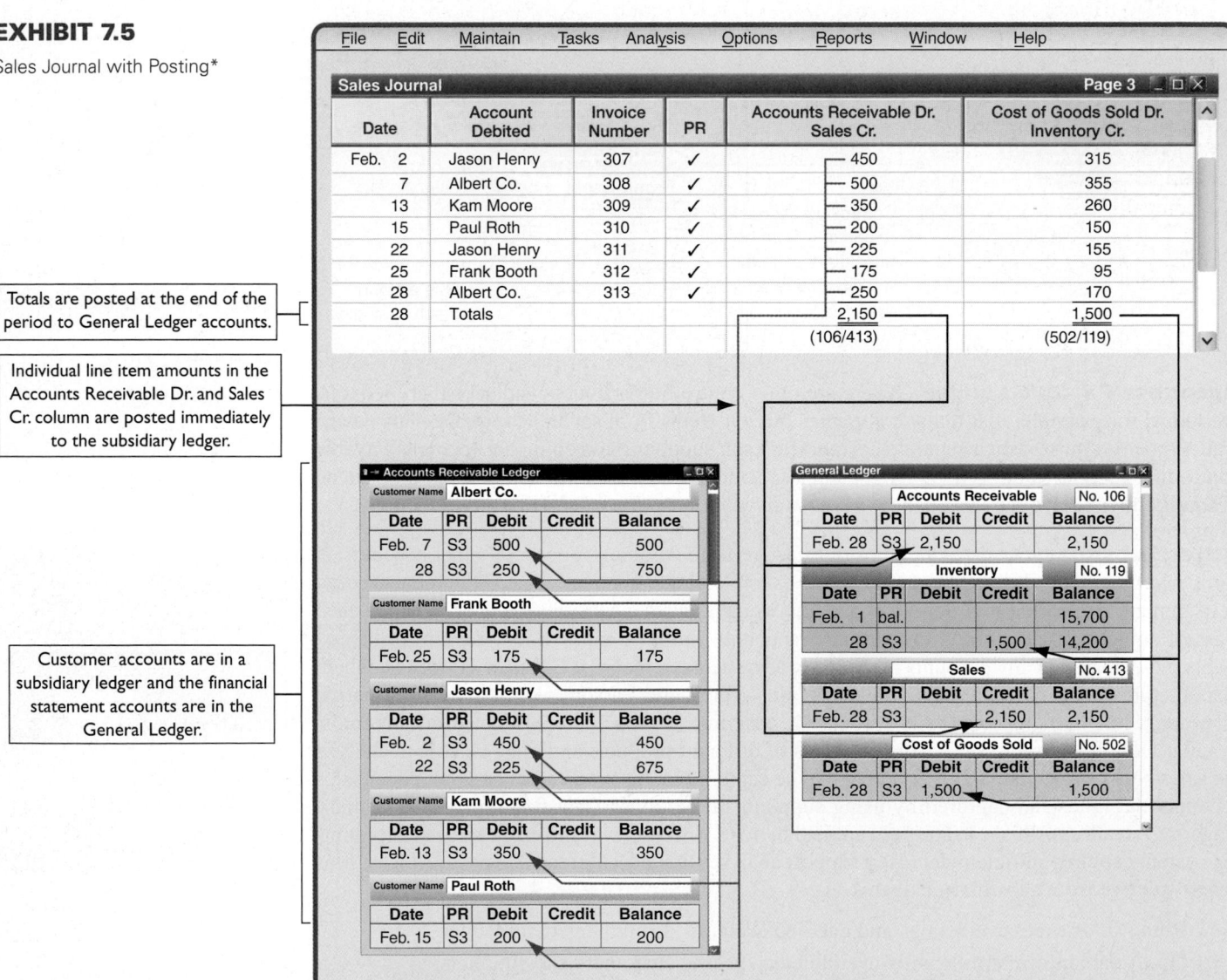

Totals are posted at the end of the period to General Ledger accounts.

Individual line item amounts in the Accounts Receivable Dr. and Sales Cr. column are posted immediately to the subsidiary ledger.

Customer accounts are in a subsidiary ledger and the financial statement accounts are in the General Ledger.

*The Sales Journal in a *periodic* system would exclude the column on the far right titled "Cost of Goods Sold Dr., Inventory Cr."

captured on one line in the sales journal. No further explanations or entries are necessary, saving time and effort. Moreover, this sales journal is consistent with most inventory systems that use bar codes to record both sales and costs with each sale transaction. Note that the Posting Reference (PR) column is not used when entering transactions but instead is used when posting.

Posting   A sales journal is posted as reflected in the arrow lines of Exhibit 7.5. Two types of posting can be identified: (1) posting to the subsidiary ledger(s) and (2) posting to the general ledger.

Posting to subsidiary ledger.   Individual transactions in the sales journal are posted regularly (typically concurrently) to customer accounts in the accounts receivable ledger. These postings keep customer accounts up-to-date, which is important for the person granting credit to customers. When sales recorded in the sales journal are individually posted to customer accounts in the accounts receivable ledger, check marks are entered in the sales journal's PR column. Check marks are used rather than account numbers because customer accounts usually are arranged alphabetically in the accounts receivable ledger. Note that posting debits to Accounts Receivable twice—once to Accounts Receivable and once to the customer's subsidiary account—does not violate the accounting equation of debits equal credits. The equality of debits and credits is always maintained in the general ledger.

Posting to general ledger.   The sales journal's account columns are totaled at the end of each period (the month of February in this case). For the "sales" column, the $2,150 total is debited to Accounts Receivable and credited to Sales in the general ledger (see Exhibit 7.5). For the "cost" column, the $1,500 total is debited to Cost of Goods Sold and credited to Inventory in the general ledger. When totals are posted to accounts in the general ledger, the account numbers are entered below the column total in the sales journal for tracking. For example, we enter (106/413) below the total in the sales column after this amount is posted to account number 106 (Accounts Receivable) and account number 413 (Sales).

A company identifies in the PR column of its subsidiary ledgers the journal and page number from which an amount is taken. We identify a journal by using an initial. Items posted from the sales journal carry the initial *S* before their journal page numbers in a PR column. Likewise, items from the cash receipts journal carry the initial *R*; items from the cash disbursements journal carry the initial *D*; items from the purchases journal carry the initial *P*; and items from the general journal carry the initial *G*.

Proving the Ledgers   Account balances in the general ledger and subsidiary ledgers are periodically proved (or reviewed) for accuracy after posting. To do this we first prepare a trial balance of the general ledger to confirm that debits equal credits. Second, we test a subsidiary ledger by preparing a *schedule* of individual accounts and amounts. A **schedule of accounts receivable** lists each customer and the balance owed. If this total equals the balance of the Accounts Receivable controlling account, the accounts in the accounts receivable ledger are assumed correct. Exhibit 7.6 shows a schedule of accounts receivable drawn from the accounts receivable ledger of Exhibit 7.5. (Accountants may use the expression "tie out" when checking whether the balance of the accounts receivable control account matches the total balance on the subsidiary listing of accounts receivable.)

Schedule of Accounts Receivable February 28	
Albert Co.	$ 750
Frank Booth	175
Jason Henry	675
Kam Moore	350
Paul Roth	200
Total accounts receivable	$2,150

EXHIBIT 7.6

Schedule of Accounts Receivable

Additional Issues   We consider three additional issues with the sales journal: (1) recording sales taxes, (2) recording sales returns and allowances, and (3) using actual sales invoices as a journal.

Point: Continuously updated customer accounts provide timely information for customer inquiries on those accounts and on current amounts owed.

Point: PR column is only checked *after* the amount(s) is posted.

Point: Postings are automatic in a computerized system.

P2 Prepare and prove the accuracy of subsidiary ledgers.

Point: In accounting, the word *schedule* generally means a list.

Sales taxes. Governmental agencies such as cities and states often require sellers to collect sales taxes from customers and to periodically send these taxes to the appropriate agency. When using a columnar sales journal, we can keep a record of taxes collected by adding a Sales Taxes Payable column as follows.

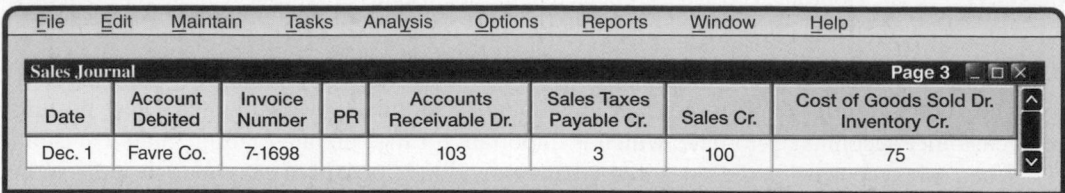

Individual amounts in the Accounts Receivable column would continue to be posted immediately to customer accounts in the accounts receivable ledger. Individual amounts in the Sales Taxes Payable and Sales columns are not posted. Column totals would continue to be posted as usual. (A company that collects sales taxes on its cash sales can also use a Sales Taxes Payable column in its cash receipts journal.)

Sales returns and allowances. A company with only a few sales returns and allowances can record them in a general journal with an entry such as the following:

Assets = Liabilities + Equity
−175   −175

May 17	Sales Returns and Allowances	414	175	
	Accounts Receivable—Ray Ball	106/✓		175
	Customer returned merchandise.			

The debit in this entry is posted to the Sales Returns and Allowances account (no. 414). The credit is posted to both the Accounts Receivable controlling account (no. 106) and to the customer's account. When we enter the account number and the check mark, 106/✓, in the PR column on the credit line, this means both the Accounts Receivable controlling account in the general ledger and the Ray Ball account in the accounts receivable ledger are credited for $175. [*Note:* If the returned goods can be resold to another customer, the company would debit (increase) the Inventory account and credit (decrease) the Cost of Goods Sold account. If the returned goods are defective (worthless), the company could simply leave their costs in the Cost of Goods Sold account (see Chapter 5).] A company with a large number of sales returns and allowances can save time by recording them in a separate sales returns and allowances journal.

Sales invoices as a sales journal. To save costs, some small companies avoid using a sales journal for credit sales and instead post each sales invoice amount directly to the customer's account in the accounts receivable ledger. They then put copies of invoices in a file. At the end of the period, they total all invoices for that period and make a general journal entry to debit Accounts Receivable and credit Sales for the total amount. The file of invoice copies acts as a sales journal. This is called *direct posting of sales invoices*.

Quick Check   Answers — p. 300

4. When special journals are used, where are cash payments by check recorded?
5. How does a columnar journal save posting time and effort?
6. How do debits and credits remain equal when credit sales are posted twice (once to Accounts Receivable and once to the customer's subsidiary account)?
7. How do we identify the journal from which an amount in a ledger account was posted?
8. How are sales taxes recorded in the context of special journals?
9. What is direct posting of sales invoices?

Cash Receipts Journal

A **cash receipts journal** is typically used to record all receipts of cash. Exhibit 7.7 shows one common form of the cash receipts journal.

Journalizing and Posting   Cash receipts can be separated into one of three types: (1) cash from credit customers in payment of their accounts, (2) cash from cash sales, and (3) cash from other sources. The cash receipts journal in Exhibit 7.7 has a separate credit column for each of

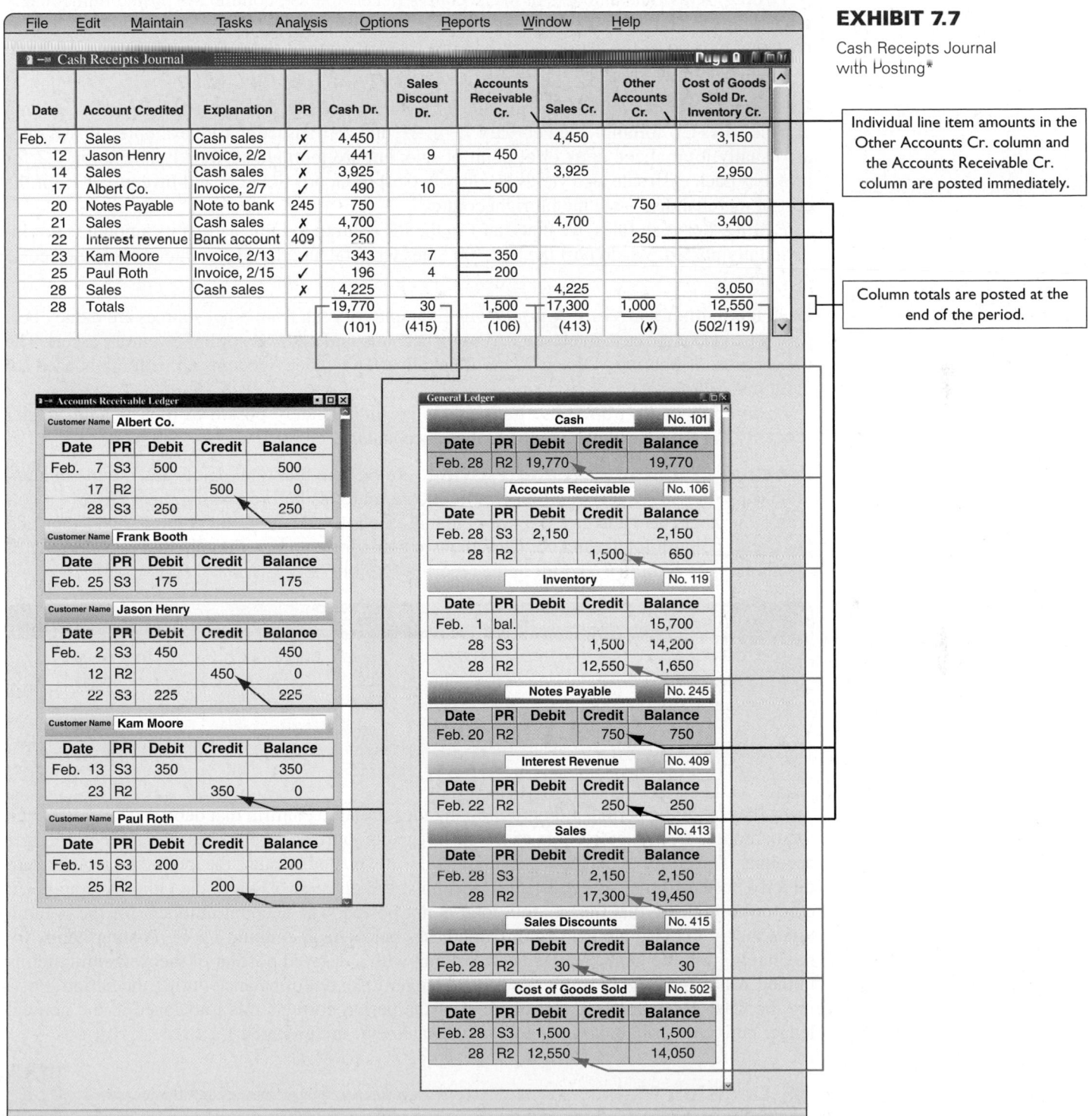

EXHIBIT 7.7

Cash Receipts Journal with Posting*

Individual line item amounts in the Other Accounts Cr. column and the Accounts Receivable Cr. column are posted immediately.

Column totals are posted at the end of the period.

*The Cash Receipts Journal in a *periodic* system would exclude the column on the far right titled "Cost of Goods Sold Dr., Inventory Cr."

these three sources. We describe how to journalize transactions from each of these three sources. (An Explanation column is included in the cash receipts journal to identify the source.)

Cash from credit customers.   *Journalizing.* To record cash received in payment of a customer's account, the customer's name is first entered in the Account Credited column—see transactions dated February 12, 17, 23, and 25. Then the amounts debited to both Cash and the Sales Discount (if any) are entered in their respective columns, and the amount credited to the customer's account is entered in the Accounts Receivable Cr. column.

Posting. Individual amounts in the Accounts Receivable Cr. column are posted immediately to customer accounts in the subsidiary accounts receivable ledger. The $1,500 column total is posted at the end of the period (month in this case) as a credit to the Accounts Receivable controlling account in the general ledger.

Cash sales.   *Journalizing.* The amount for each cash sale is entered in the Cash Dr. column and the Sales Cr. column. The February 7, 14, 21, and 28 transactions are examples. (Cash sales are usually journalized daily or at point of sale, but are journalized weekly in Exhibit 7.7 for brevity.) Each cash sale also yields an entry to Cost of Goods Sold Dr. and Inventory Cr. for the cost of merchandise—see the far right column.

Posting. For cash sales, we place an *x* in the PR column to indicate that its amount is not individually posted. We do post the $17,300 Sales Cr. total and the $12,550 total from the "cost" column.

Cash from other sources.   *Journalizing.* Examples of cash from other sources are money borrowed from a bank, cash interest received on account, and cash sale of noninventory assets. The transactions of February 20 and 22 are illustrative. The Other Accounts Cr. column is used for these transactions.

Posting. Amounts from these transactions are immediately posted to their general ledger accounts and the PR column identifies those accounts.

Footing, Crossfooting, and Posting   To be sure that total debits and credits in a columnar journal are equal, we often crossfoot column totals before posting them. To *foot* a column of numbers is to add it. To *crossfoot* in this case is to add the Debit column totals, then add the Credit column totals, and compare the two sums for equality. Footing and crossfooting of the numbers in Exhibit 7.7 result in the report in Exhibit 7.8.

EXHIBIT 7.8

Footing and Crossfooting
Journal Totals

Debit Columns		Credit Columns	
Cash Dr.	$19,770	Accounts Receivable Cr.	$ 1,500
Sales Discounts Dr.	30	Sales Cr.	17,300
Cost of Goods Sold Dr.	12,550	Other Accounts Cr.	1,000
		Inventory Cr.	12,550
Total	$32,350	Total	$32,350

At the end of the period, after crossfooting the journal to confirm that debits equal credits, the total amounts from the columns of the cash receipts journal are posted to their general ledger accounts. The Other Accounts Cr. column total is not posted because the individual amounts are directly posted to their general ledger accounts. We place an *x* below the Other Accounts Cr. column to indicate that this column total is not posted. The account numbers for the column totals that are posted are entered in parentheses below each column. (*Note:* Posting items immediately from the Other Accounts Cr. column with a delayed posting of their offsetting items in the Cash column total causes the general ledger to be out of balance during the period. Posting the Cash Dr. column total at the end of the period corrects this imbalance in the general ledger before the trial balance and financial statements are prepared.)

◼ Decision Maker ━━━━━━━━━━━━━━━━━━━━━━━━━

Entrepreneur You want to know how promptly customers are paying their bills. This information can help you decide whether to extend credit and to plan your cash payments. Where do you find this information? ◼ [Answer—p. 300]

Purchases Journal

A **purchases journal** is typically used to record all credit purchases, including those for inventory. Purchases for cash are recorded in the Cash Disbursements Journal.

Journalizing Entries in the purchases journal in Exhibit 7.9 reflect purchase invoices or other source documents. We use the invoice date and terms to compute the date when payment for each purchase is due. The Accounts Payable Cr. column is used to record the amounts owed to each creditor. Inventory purchases are recorded in the Inventory Dr. column.

    To illustrate, inventory costing $200 is purchased from Ace Manufacturing on February 5. The creditor's name (Ace) is entered in the Account column, the invoice date is entered in the Date of Invoice column, the purchase terms are entered in the Terms column, and the $200 amount is entered in the Accounts Payable Cr. and the Inventory Dr. columns. When a purchase involves an amount recorded in the Other Accounts Dr. column, we use the Account column to identify the general ledger account debited. For example, the February 28 transaction involves purchases of inventory, office supplies, and store supplies from ITT. The journal has no column for store supplies, so the Other Accounts Dr. column is used. In this case, Store Supplies is entered in the Account column along with the creditor's name (ITT). This purchases journal also includes a separate column for credit purchases of office supplies. A separate column such as this is useful when several transactions involve debits to the same account. Each company uses its own judgment in deciding on the number of separate columns necessary.

Posting The amounts in the Accounts Payable Cr. column are immediately posted to individual creditor accounts in the accounts payable subsidiary ledger. Individual amounts in the Other Accounts Dr. column are immediately posted to their general ledger accounts. At the end

Point: The number of special journals and the design of each are based on a company's specific needs.

Point: Each transaction in the purchases journal has a credit to Accounts Payable. Debit accounts will vary.

Point: The Other Accounts Dr. column allows the purchases journal to be used for any purchase on credit.

EXHIBIT 7.9

Purchases Journal with Posting*

Individual amounts in the Other Accounts Dr. column and the Accounts Payable Cr. column are posted immediately.

Column totals, except for Other Accounts Dr. column, are posted at the end of the period.

*The Purchases Journal in a *periodic* system replaces "Inventory Dr." with "Purchases Dr."

of the period, all column totals except the Other Accounts Dr. column are posted to their general ledger accounts.

Proving the Ledger Accounts payable balances in the subsidiary ledger can be periodically proved after posting. We prove the subsidiary ledger by preparing a **schedule of accounts payable,** which is a list of accounts from the accounts payable ledger with their balances and the total. If this total of the individual balances equals the balance of the Accounts Payable controlling account, the accounts in the accounts payable ledger are assumed correct. Exhibit 7.10 shows a schedule of accounts payable drawn from the accounts payable ledger of Exhibit 7.9. (This schedule can be done after any posting; for example, we could prepare another schedule of accounts payable after the postings in Exhibit 7.11.)

EXHIBIT 7.10

Schedule of Accounts Payable

Schedule of Accounts Payable February 28	
Ace Mfg. Company	$ 300
Horning Supply Company	350
ITT Company	225
Smite Company	300
Wynet & Company	150
Total accounts payable	$1,325

Cash Disbursements Journal

A **cash disbursements journal,** also called a *cash payments journal,* is typically used to record all cash payments.

Journalizing The cash disbursements journal shown in Exhibit 7.11 illustrates repetitive entries to the Cash Cr. column of this journal (reflecting cash payments). Also note the frequent credits to Inventory (which reflect purchase discounts) and the debits to Accounts Payable. For example, on February 15, the company pays Ace on account (credit terms of 2/10, n/30—see February 5 transaction in Exhibit 7.9). Since payment occurs in the discount period, the company pays $196 ($200 invoice less $4 discount). The $4 discount is credited to Inventory. Note that when this company purchases inventory for cash, it is recorded using the Other Accounts Dr. column and the Cash Cr. column as illustrated in the February 3 and 12 transactions. Generally, the Other Accounts column is used to record cash payments on items for which no column exists. For example, on February 15, the company pays salaries expense of $250. The title of the account debited (Salaries Expense) is entered in the Account Debited column.

The cash disbursements journal has a column titled Ck. No. (check number). For control over cash disbursements, all payments except for those of small amounts are made by check. Checks should be prenumbered and each check's number entered in the journal in numerical order in the column headed Ck. No. This makes it possible to scan the numbers in the column for omitted checks. When a cash disbursements journal has a column for check numbers, it is sometimes called a **check register.**

Posting Individual amounts in the Other Accounts Dr. column of a cash disbursements journal are immediately posted to their general ledger accounts. Individual amounts in the Accounts Payable Dr. column are also immediately posted to creditors' accounts in the subsidiary Accounts Payable ledger. At the end of the period, we crossfoot column totals and post the Accounts Payable Dr. column total to the Accounts Payable controlling account. Also, the Inventory Cr. column total is posted to the Inventory account, and the Cash Cr. column total is posted to the Cash account.

 Decision Maker

Controller You wish to analyze your company's cash payments to suppliers and its purchases discounts. Where do you find this information? ■ [Answer—p. 300]

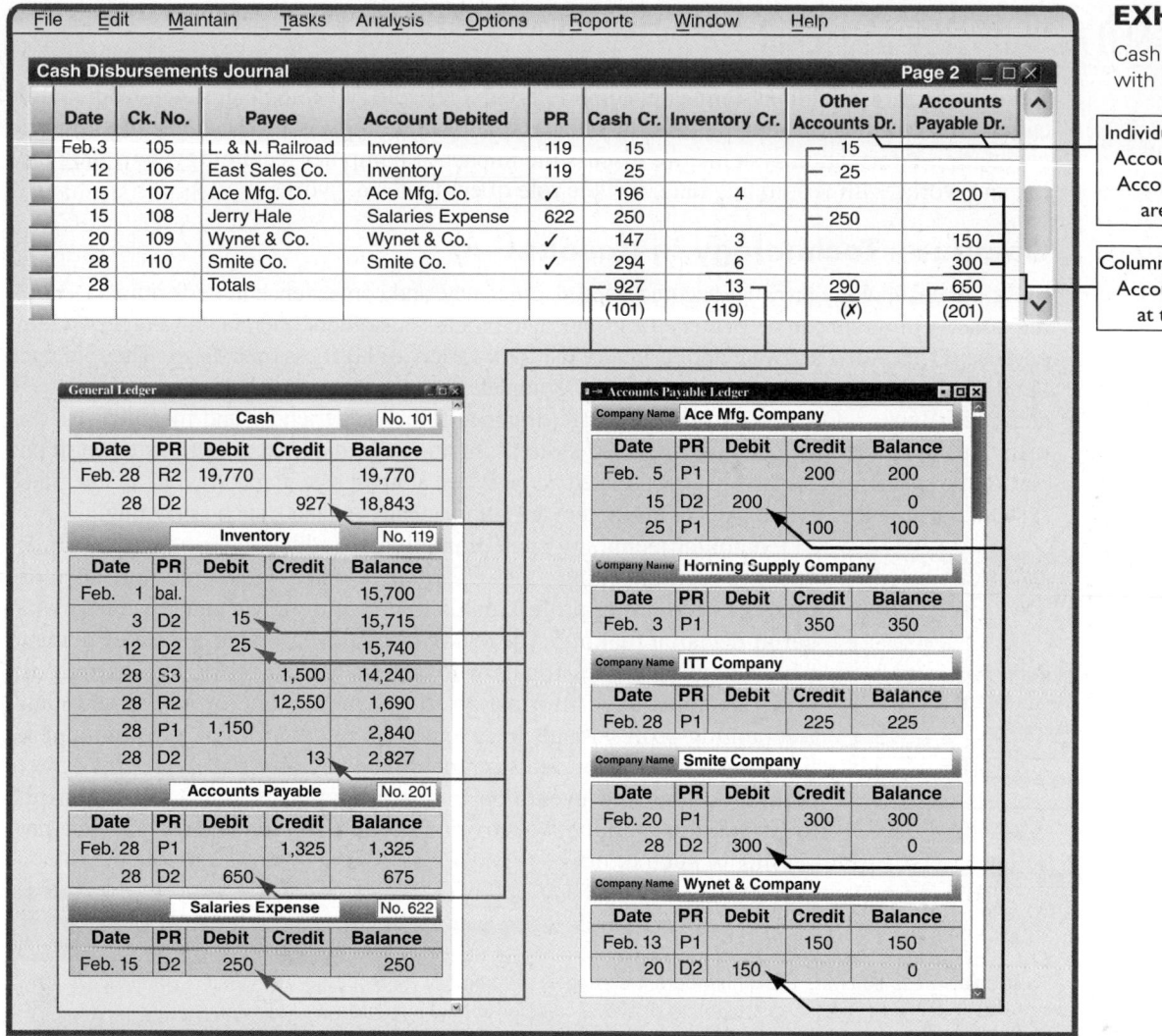

EXHIBIT 7.11

Cash Disbursements Journal with Posting*

*The Cash Disbursements Journal in a *periodic* system replaces "Inventory Cr." with "Purchases Discounts Cr."

General Journal Transactions

When special journals are used, we still need a general journal for adjusting, closing, and any other transactions for which no special journal has been set up. Examples of these other transactions might include purchases returns and allowances, purchases of plant assets by issuing a note payable, sales returns if a sales returns and allowances journal is not used, and receipt of a note receivable from a customer. We described the recording of transactions in a general journal in Chapters 2 and 3.

Quick Check   Answers — p. 300

10. What are the normal recording and posting procedures when using special journals and controlling accounts with subsidiary ledgers?

11. What is the process for posting to a subsidiary ledger and its controlling account?

12. How do we prove the accuracy of account balances in the general ledger and subsidiary ledgers after posting?

13. Why does a company need a general journal when using special journals for sales, purchases, cash receipts, and cash disbursements?

TECHNOLOGY-BASED ACCOUNTING SYSTEMS

Accounting information systems are supported with technology, which can range from simple calculators to advanced computerized systems. Since technology is increasingly important in accounting information systems, we discuss the impact of computer technology, how data processing works with accounting data, and the role of computer networks.

Computer Technology in Accounting

Computer technology provides accuracy, speed, efficiency, and convenience in performing accounting tasks. A program can be written, for instance, to process customers' merchandise orders. Multipurpose off-the-shelf software applications exist for a variety of business operations. These include familiar accounting programs such as Sage 50 Complete Accounting (formerly known as Peachtree®) and QuickBooks®. Off-the-shelf programs are designed to be user friendly and menu driven, and many operate more efficiently as *integrated* systems. In an integrated system, actions taken in one part of the system automatically affect related parts. When a credit sale is recorded in an integrated system, for instance, several parts of the system are automatically updated, such as posting.

Point: Companies that have reported missing or stolen employee data such as Social Security numbers include Time Warner, Polo Ralph Lauren, Lexis/Nexis, ChoicePoint, and DSW Shoes.

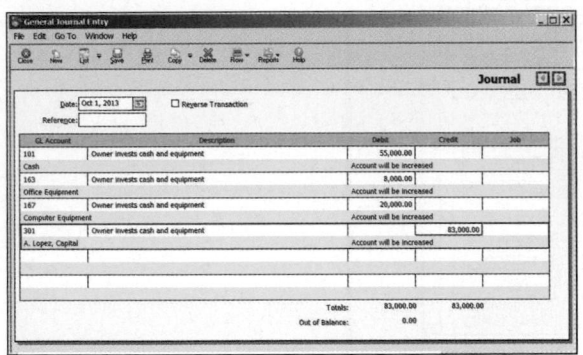

Computer technology can dramatically reduce the time and effort devoted to recordkeeping. Less effort spent on recordkeeping means more time for accounting professionals to concentrate on analysis and managerial decision making. These advances have created a greater demand for accounting professionals who understand financial reports and can draw insights and information from mountains of processed data. Accounting professionals have expertise in determining relevant and reliable information for decision making. They also can assess the effects of transactions and events on a company and its financial statements. (The IRS allows individuals to enter tax info online and receive free processing of such returns.)

■ Decision Insight ━━━━━━━━━━━━━━

Middleware is software allowing different computer programs in a company or across companies to work together. It allows transfer of purchase orders, invoices, and other electronic documents between accounting systems. For example, suppliers can monitor inventory levels of their buyers for production and shipping purposes. ■

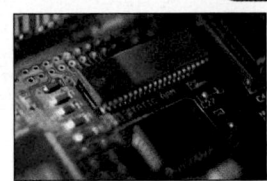

Data Processing in Accounting

Accounting systems differ with regard to how input is entered and processed. **Online processing** enters and processes data as soon as source documents are available. This means that databases are immediately updated. **Batch processing** accumulates source documents for a period of time and then processes them all at once such as daily, weekly, or monthly. The advantage of online processing is timeliness. This often requires additional costs related to both software and hardware requirements. Companies such as **Intuit** (**Intuit.com**) are making online processing of accounting data a reality for many businesses. The advantage of batch processing is that it requires only periodic updating of databases. Records used to send bills to customers, for instance, might require updating only once a month. The disadvantage of batch processing is the lack of updated databases for management to use when making business decisions. (Businesses and individuals can now deposit checks into bank accounts using scanners with capabilities of reading amounts, ensuring that each item passes a specified image quality standard, and reducing the risk that the scanned image is a duplicate of a previously scanned check.)

Computer Networks in Accounting

Networking, or linking computers with each other, can create information advantages (and cost efficiencies). **Computer networks** are links among computers giving different users and different computers access to common databases, programs, and hardware. Many college computer labs, for instance, are networked. A small computer network is called a *local area network (LAN);* it links machines with *hard-wire* hookups. Large computer networks extending over long distances often rely on *modem* or *wireless* communication.

Demand for information sometimes requires advanced networks such as the systems **Federal Express** and **UPS** use to track packages and bill customers and the system **Walmart** uses to monitor inventory levels in its stores. These networks include many computers and satellite communications to gather information and to provide ready access to its databases from all locations.

Enterprise Resource Planning Software

Enterprise resource planning (ERP) software includes the programs that manage a company's vital operations. They extend from order taking to manufacturing to accounting. (Your college likely relies on ERP software to track its budget and student records information.) When working properly, these integrated programs can speed decision making, identify costs for reduction, and give managers control over operations with the click of a mouse. For many managers, ERP software allows them to scrutinize business, identify where inventories are piling up, and see what plants are most efficient. The software is designed to link every part of a company's operations. This software allowed **Butterball**, one of America's leading poultry brands, to reduce costs, enable rapid acquisitions, realize return on IT investment, and drive business improvements.

ERP has several suppliers. **SAP** leads the market, with **Oracle**, which gobbled up PeopleSoft and J. D. Edwards, a distant second (*AMR Research*). SAP software is used by more than half of the world's 500 largest companies. It links ordering, inventory, production, purchasing, planning, tracking, and human resources. A transaction or event triggers an immediate chain reaction of events throughout the enterprise. It is making companies more efficient and profitable. **Tasty Baking Company**, a leading U.S. producer of snack cakes and other baked goods, uses SAP solutions to access real-time information, gain greater efficiencies, plan and respond to business needs, and achieve measurable results.

Total ERP Market: About $30 Billion

Other 23%
SAP 35%
Oracle Applications 21%
Infor (SSA) 7%
Microsoft Dynamics 6%
Sage Group 8%

ERP is pushing into cyberspace and customer relationship management (CRM). Now companies can share data with customers and suppliers. Applesauce maker **Mott's** is using SAP so that distributors can check the status of orders and place them over the Net, and the **Coca-Cola Company** uses it to ship soda on time. ERP is also increasingly used by small business. One-third of Oracle's sales in North America are to companies with less than $500 million in annual revenue. Worldwide, small and midsize companies are 25% to 30% of Oracle's sales. For example, **NetSuite**'s accounting services to small and medium businesses are powered by Oracle's system. Jeff Johanson, director of channel operations of SAP's practice for small and midsize businesses asserts that: "Small and medium businesses don't have different needs from larger companies, but they generally can't afford customized solutions."

 Decision Insight

A new generation of accounting support is available. With the touch of a key, users can create real-time inventory reports showing all payments, charges, and credit limits at any point in the accounting cycle. Many services also include "alert signals" notifying the company when, for example, a large order exceeds a customer's credit limit or when purchases need to be made or when a bank balance is running low. These alerts occur via e-mail, fax, PDA, or phone. ∎

Cloud Computing

Cloud computing is the delivery of computing as a service rather than a product. Many argue that its introduction will revolutionize information systems applications. Cloud computing uses applications via the Web instead of installing them on individual computers. This means that companies lease, rather than purchase, those applications, which also means that the user does not need to update applications as that is the job of the computing service provider. Thus, as tax laws change or when rates are revised, the service provider takes on that responsibility (and cost).

When a company transfers computing applications to a provider, there is much less risk if a user's computers crash or are stolen. Further, many users and their clients can access the same applications and share data. Accountants, lawyers, and analysts can similarly access data for quicker and easier processing and analysis. For example, all invoices could be offloaded to a Web-based bill management system, where documentation, disbursement, and record keeping could all be handled in the cloud. However, the user does lose control over the data and is dependent on the provider's control system. Today, many companies are exploring cloud computing and often begin with applications that are independent of other systems so that if problems arise, they are concentrated within that application only. Examples are training programs and workflow systems. Further, many argue that the gains of cloud computing are great for small and medium-sized companies, which do not have large IT departments or require unique information systems.

Cloud computing has enormous potential for greater efficiency and effectiveness with information systems applications. The future will reveal whether or not that potential will be achieved. Cloud computing has the potential to improve controls due to data centralization and the enhanced security from providers who can spread that cost over many customers. Still, some users worry about exposure to sensitive data. Users should consider the following factors when looking at providers of cloud computing:

- Provider's knowledge of the user's business.
- Security of the provider's cloud, including firewalls.
- Provider's history, reputation, and references.
- Service level agreement for hardware and software.
- Provider's cloud compatibility with user's system.

Quick Check
Answers — p. 300

14. Identify an advantage of an integrated computer-based accounting system.
15. What advantages do computer systems offer over manual systems?
16. Identify an advantage of computer networks.
17. Describe ERP software and its potential advantages to businesses.

GLOBAL VIEW

This section discusses similarities and differences between U.S. GAAP and IFRS regarding system principles and components, and special journals.

System Principles and Components   Both U.S. GAAP and IFRS aim for high-quality financial reporting. That aim implies that sound information system principles and components are applied worldwide. However, while system principles and components are fundamentally similar across the globe, culture and other realities often mean different emphases are placed on the mix of system controls. **BMW** provides the following description of its system controls:

> The internal control system ensures that all the information needed to achieve the objectives set for the internal control system is made available to those responsible in an appropriate and timely manner. Controls are carried out with the aid of the IT applications, thus reducing the incidence of process risks.

Special Journals   Accounting systems for recording sales, purchases, cash receipts, and cash disbursements are similar worldwide. Although the exact structure of special journals is unique to each company, the basic structure is identical. Companies desire to apply accounting in an efficient manner. Accordingly, systems that employ special journals are applied worldwide.

Good accounting information systems collect financial data for a company's various segments. A *segment* refers to a part of a company that is separately identified by its products or services, or by the geographic market it serves. **Callaway Golf Company** reports that it operates in two business segments: (1) golf clubs and (2) golf balls. Users of financial statements are especially interested in segment information to better understand a company's activities because segments often vary on profitability, risk, and growth.

> **A1** Compute segment return on assets and use it to evaluate segment performance.

Companies must report segment information, including their sales, operating income, identifiable assets, capital expenditures, and depreciation. However, managers are reluctant to release information that can harm competitive position. Exhibit 7.12 shows survey results on the number of companies with different (reported) segments.

*Total exceeds 100% because companies can report more than one segment.

EXHIBIT 7.12

Companies Reporting Operations by Types of Segments*

One measure of success for business segments is the **segment return on assets** ratio defined as follows.

$$\text{Segment return on assets} = \frac{\text{Segment operating income}}{\text{Segment average assets}}$$

EXHIBIT 7.13

Callaway Golf's Segment Return on Assets

This ratio reflects on the profitability of a segment. Exhibit 7.13 shows the segments' operating income, average assets, and return on assets for Callaway Golf Company.

Golf Segment* ($ thousands)	2011 Clubs	2011 Balls	2010 Clubs	2010 Balls	2009 Clubs	2009 Balls	2008 Clubs	2008 Balls
Operating income	$ (3,899)	$(12,655)	$ 39,176	$ 2,559	$ 34,502	$ (9,427)	$134,018	$ 6,903
Average assets	$423,538	$ 107,214	$422,419	$125,972	$418,003	$138,326	$421,261	$143,793
Segment return on assets ...	n.a.	n.a.	9%	2%	8%	n.a.	32%	5%

*A segment's operating income is usually measured as pretax income, and assets is usually measured as identifiable assets.

The trend in Callaway's segment return on assets is up-and-down for its golf club segment, and similarly mixed for its golf balls segment. Importantly, its golf clubs segment makes up a much greater portion of its operations; for example, 2010 income of $39,176 from golf clubs make up 94% of its total income of $41,735 from both segments. 2011 was a poor year for Callaway as both segments reported losses, which meant its returns for 2011 were not applicable (n.a.) for analysis. Still, those negative returns must return to positive levels as losses are not sustainable in the long run. Callaway should continue its emphasis on its golf club segment vis-a-vis its golf balls segment given the greater returns and larger total income from that segment. Analysis can also be extended to geographical segments and any other segments that companies report.

■ **Decision** Maker ━━━━━━━━━━━━━━━━━━━━━━━━

Banker A soccer equipment merchandiser requests a loan from you to expand operations. Its net income is $220,000, reflecting a 10% increase over the prior year. You ask about segment results. The owner reports that $160,000 of net income is from Cuban operations, reflecting a 60% increase over the prior year. The remaining $60,000 of net income is from U.S. operations, reflecting a 40% decrease. Does this segment information impact your loan decision? ■ [Answer—p. 300]

DEMONSTRATION PROBLEM—PERPETUAL SYSTEM

Pepper Company completed the following selected transactions and events during March of this year. (Terms of all credit sales for the company are 2/10, n/30.)

Mar. 4   Sold merchandise on credit to Jennifer Nelson, Invoice No. 954, for $16,800 (cost is $12,200).

      6   Purchased $1,220 of office supplies on credit from Mack Company. Invoice dated March 3, terms n/30.

      6   Sold merchandise on credit to Dennie Hoskins, Invoice No. 955, for $10,200 (cost is $8,100).

   11   Purchased $52,600 of merchandise, invoice dated March 6, terms 2/10, n/30, from Defore Industries.

   12   Borrowed $26,000 cash by giving Commerce Bank a long-term promissory note payable.

   14   Received cash payment from Jennifer Nelson for the March 4 sale less the discount (Invoice No. 954).

   16   Received a $200 credit memorandum from Defore Industries for unsatisfactory merchandise Pepper purchased on March 11 and later returned.

   16   Received cash payment from Dennie Hoskins for the March 6 sale less the discount (Invoice No. 955).

   18   Purchased $22,850 of store equipment on credit from Schmidt Supply, invoice dated March 15, terms n/30.

   20   Sold merchandise on credit to Marjorie Allen, Invoice No. 956, for $5,600 (cost is $3,800).

   21   Sent Defore Industries Check No. 516 in payment of its March 6 dated invoice less the return and the discount.

   22   Purchased $41,625 of merchandise, invoice dated March 18, terms 2/10, n/30, from Welch Company.

   26   Issued a $600 credit memorandum to Marjorie Allen for defective merchandise Pepper sold on March 20 and Allen later returned.

   31   Issued Check No. 517, payable to Payroll, in payment of $15,900 sales salaries for the month. Cashed the check and paid the employees.

   31   Cash sales for the month are $134,680 (cost is $67,340). (Cash sales are recorded daily but are recorded only once here to reduce repetitive entries.)

Required

1. Open the following selected general ledger accounts: Cash (101), Accounts Receivable (106) Inventory (119), Office Supplies (124), Store Equipment (165), Accounts Payable (201), Long-Term Notes Payable (251), Sales (413), Sales Returns and Allowances (414), Sales Discounts (415), Cost of Goods Sold (502), and Sales Salaries Expense (621). Open the following accounts receivable ledger accounts: Marjorie Allen, Dennie Hoskins, and Jennifer Nelson. Open the following accounts payable ledger accounts: Defore Industries, Mack Company, Schmidt Supply, and Welch Company.

2. Enter the transactions using a sales journal, a purchases journal, a cash receipts journal, a cash disbursements journal, and a general journal similar to the ones illustrated in the chapter. Regularly post to the individual customer and creditor accounts. Also, post any amounts that should be posted as individual amounts to general ledger accounts. Foot and crossfoot the journals and make the month-end postings. *Pepper Co. uses the perpetual inventory system.*

3. Prepare a trial balance for the selected general ledger accounts in part 1 and prove the accuracy of subsidiary ledgers by preparing schedules of accounts receivable and accounts payable.

PLANNING THE SOLUTION

- Set up the required general ledger, the subsidiary ledger accounts, and the five required journals as illustrated in the chapter.
- Read and analyze each transaction and decide in which special journal (or general journal) the transaction is recorded.
- Record each transaction in the proper journal (and post the appropriate individual amounts).
- Once you have recorded all transactions, total the journal columns. Post from each journal to the appropriate ledger accounts.
- Prepare a trial balance to prove the equality of the debit and credit balances in your general ledger.
- Prepare schedules of accounts receivable and accounts payable. Compare the totals of these schedules to the Accounts Receivable and Accounts Payable controlling account balances, making sure that they agree.

SOLUTION TO DEMONSTRATION PROBLEM—PERPETUAL SYSTEM

Sales Journal — Page 2

Date	Account Debited	Invoice Number	PR	Accounts Receivable Dr. Sales Cr.	Cost of Goods Sold Dr. Inventory Cr.
Mar. 4	Jennifer Nelson	954	✓	16,800	12,200
6	Dennie Hoskins	955	✓	10,200	8,100
20	Marjorie Allen	956	✓	5,600	3,800
31	Totals			32,600	24,100
				(106/413)	(502/119)

Cash Receipts Journal — Page 3

Date	Account Credited	Explanation	PR	Cash Dr.	Sales Discount Dr.	Accounts Receivable Cr.	Sales Cr.	Other Accounts Cr.	Cost of Goods Sold Dr. Inventory Cr.
Mar. 12	L.T. Notes Payable	Note to bank	251	26,000				26,000	
14	Jennifer Nelson	Invoice 954, 3/4	✓	16,464	336	16,800			
16	Dennie Hoskins	Invoice 955, 3/6	✓	9,996	204	10,200			
31	Sales	Cash sales	x	134,680			134,680		67,340
31	Totals			187,140	540	27,000	134,680	26,000	67,340
				(101)	(415)	(106)	(413)	(x)	(502/119)

Purchases Journal — Page 3

Date	Account	Date of Invoice	Terms	PR	Accounts Payable Cr.	Inventory Dr.	Office Supplies Dr.	Other Accounts Dr.
Mar. 6	Office Supplies/Mack Co	3/3	n/30	✓	1,220		1,220	
11	Defore Industries	3/6	2/10, n/30	✓	52,600	52,600		
18	Store Equipment/Schmidt Supp	3/15	n/30	165/✓	22,850			22,850
22	Welch Company	3/18	2/10, n/30	✓	41,625	41,625		
31	Totals				118,295	94,225	1,220	22,850
					(201)	(119)	(124)	(x)

Cash Disbursements Journal — Page 3

Date	Ck. No.	Payee	Account Debited	PR	Cash Cr.	Inventory Cr.	Other Accounts Dr.	Accounts Payable Dr.
Mar. 21	516	Defore Industries	Defore Industries	✓	51,352	1,048		52,400
31	517	Payroll	Sales Salaries Expense	621	15,900		15,900	
31		Totals			67,252	1,048	15,900	52,400
					(101)	(119)	(x)	(201)

General Journal — Page 2

Mar. 16	Accounts Payable—Defore Industries	201/✓	200	
	Inventory	119		200
	To record credit memorandum received.			
26	Sales Returns and Allowances	414	600	
	Accounts Receivable—Marjorie Allen	106/✓		600
	To record credit memorandum issued.			

Accounts Receivable Ledger

Marjorie Allen

Date	PR	Debit	Credit	Balance
Mar. 20	S2	5,600		5,600
26	G2		600	5,000

Dennie Hoskins

Date	PR	Debit	Credit	Balance
Mar. 6	S2	10,200		10,200
16	R3		10,200	0

Jennifer Nelson

Date	PR	Debit	Credit	Balance
Mar. 4	S2	16,800		16,800
14	R3		16,800	0

Accounts Payable Ledger

Defore Industries

Date	PR	Debit	Credit	Balance
Mar. 11	P3		52,600	52,600
16	G2	200		52,400
21	D3	52,400		0

Mack Company

Date	PR	Debit	Credit	Balance
Mar. 6	P3		1,220	1,220

Schmidt Supply

Date	PR	Debit	Credit	Balance
Mar. 18	P3		22,850	22,850

Welch Company

Date	PR	Debit	Credit	Balance
Mar. 22	P3		41,625	41,625

General Ledger (Partial Listing)

Cash   Acct. No. 101

Date	PR	Debit	Credit	Balance
Mar. 31	R3	187,140		187,140
31	D3		67,252	119,888

Accounts Receivable   Acct. No. 106

Date	PR	Debit	Credit	Balance
Mar. 26	G2		600	(600)
31	S2	32,600		32,000
31	R3		27,000	5,000

Inventory   Acct. No. 119

Date	PR	Debit	Credit	Balance
Mar. 16	G2		200	(200)
21	D3		1,048	(1,248)
31	P3	94,225		92,977
31	S2		24,100	68,877
31	R3		67,340	1,537

Office Supplies   Acct. No. 124

Date	PR	Debit	Credit	Balance
Mar. 31	P3	1,220		1,220

Store Equipment   Acct. No. 165

Date	PR	Debit	Credit	Balance
Mar. 18	P3	22,850		22,850

Accounts Payable   Acct. No. 201

Date	PR	Debit	Credit	Balance
Mar. 16	G2	200		(200)
31	P3		118,295	118,095
31	D3	52,400		65,695

Long-Term Notes Payable   Acct. No. 251

Date	PR	Debit	Credit	Balance
Mar. 12	R3		26,000	26,000

Sales   Acct. No. 413

Date	PR	Debit	Credit	Balance
Mar. 31	S2		32,600	32,600
31	R3		134,680	167,280

Sales Returns and Allowances   Acct. No. 414

Date	PR	Debit	Credit	Balance
Mar. 26	G2	600		600

Sales Discounts   Acct. No. 415

Date	PR	Debit	Credit	Balance
Mar. 31	R3	540		540

Cost of Goods Sold   Acct. No. 502

Date	PR	Debit	Credit	Balance
Mar. 31	R3	67,340		67,340
31	S2	24,100		91,440

Sales Salaries Expense   Acct. No. 621

Date	PR	Debit	Credit	Balance
Mar. 31	D3	15,900		15,900

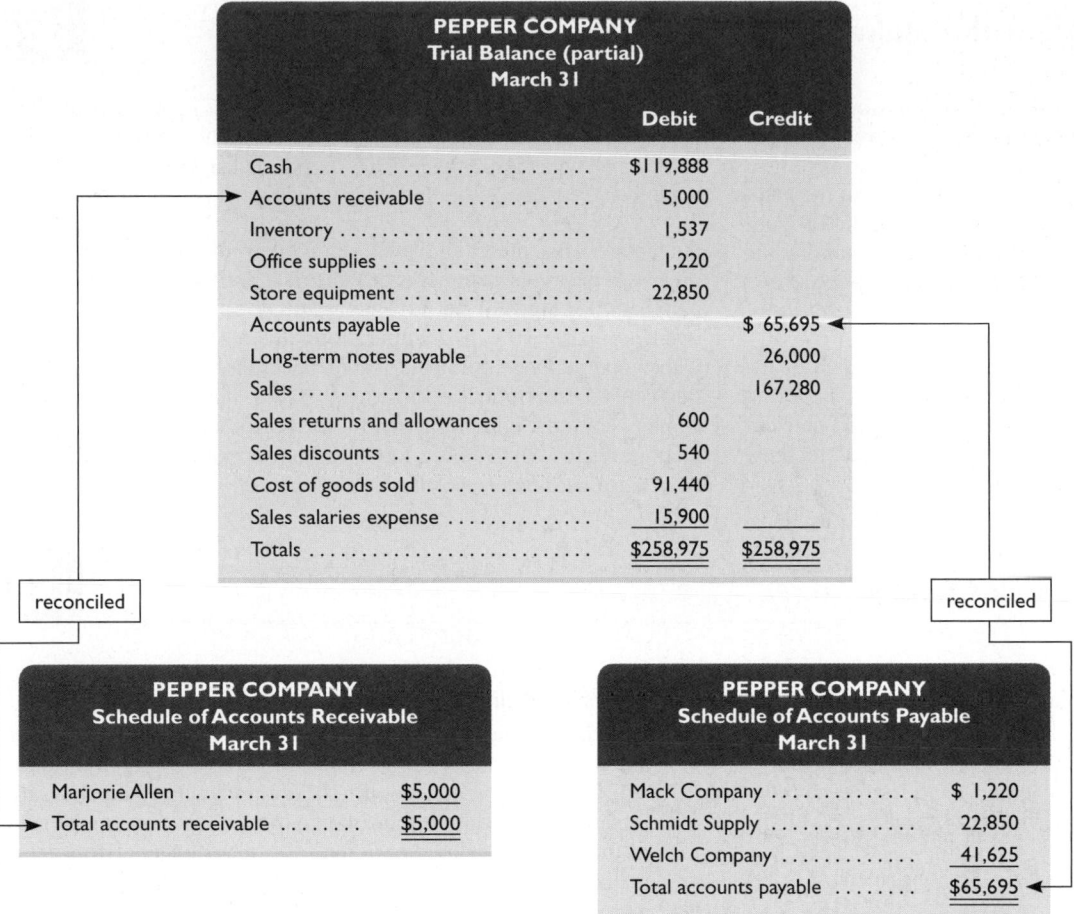

PEPPER COMPANY
Trial Balance (partial)
March 31

	Debit	Credit
Cash	$119,888	
Accounts receivable	5,000	
Inventory	1,537	
Office supplies	1,220	
Store equipment	22,850	
Accounts payable		$ 65,695
Long-term notes payable		26,000
Sales		167,280
Sales returns and allowances	600	
Sales discounts	540	
Cost of goods sold	91,440	
Sales salaries expense	15,900	
Totals	$258,975	$258,975

reconciled

reconciled

PEPPER COMPANY
Schedule of Accounts Receivable
March 31

Marjorie Allen	$5,000
Total accounts receivable	$5,000

PEPPER COMPANY
Schedule of Accounts Payable
March 31

Mack Company	$ 1,220
Schmidt Supply	22,850
Welch Company	41,625
Total accounts payable	$65,695

Summary

C1 Identify the principles and components of accounting information systems. Accounting information systems are governed by five fundamental principles: control, relevance, compatibility, flexibility, and cost-benefit. The five basic components of an accounting information system are source documents, input devices, information processors, information storage, and output devices.

C2 Explain the goals and uses of special journals. Special journals are used for recording transactions of similar type, each meant to cover one kind of transaction. Four of the most common special journals are the sales journal, cash receipts journal, purchases journal, and cash disbursements journal. Special journals are efficient and cost-effective tools in the journalizing and posting processes.

C3 Describe the use of controlling accounts and subsidiary ledgers. A general ledger keeps controlling accounts such as Accounts Receivable and Accounts Payable, but details on individual accounts making up the controlling account are kept in subsidiary ledgers (such as an accounts receivable ledger). The balance in a controlling account must equal the sum of its subsidiary account balances after posting is complete.

A1 Compute segment return on assets and use it to evaluate segment performance. A business segment is a part of a company that is separately identified by its products or services or by the geographic market it serves. Analysis of a company's

segments is aided by the segment return on assets (segment operating income divided by segment average assets).

P1 Journalize and post transactions using special journals. Each special journal is devoted to similar kinds of transactions. Transactions are journalized on one line of a special journal, with columns devoted to specific accounts, dates, names, posting references, explanations, and other necessary information. Posting is threefold: (1) individual amounts in the Other Accounts column are posted to their general ledger accounts on a regular (daily) basis, (2) individual amounts in a column whose total is *not* posted to a controlling account at the end of a period (month) are posted regularly (daily) to their general ledger accounts, and (3) total amounts for all columns except the Other Accounts column are posted at the end of a period (month) to their column's account title in the general ledger.

P2 Prepare and prove the accuracy of subsidiary ledgers. Account balances in the general ledger and its subsidiary ledgers are tested for accuracy after posting is complete. This procedure is twofold: (1) prepare a trial balance of the general ledger to confirm that debits equal credits and (2) prepare a schedule to confirm that the controlling account's balance equals the subsidiary ledger's balance.

Guidance Answers to Decision Maker and Decision Ethics

Accountant   The main issue is whether commissions have an actual or perceived impact on the integrity and objectivity of your advice. You probably should not accept a commission arrangement (the AICPA Code of Ethics prohibits it when you perform the audit or a review). In any event, you should tell the client of your commission arrangement. Also, you need to seriously examine the merits of agreeing to a commission arrangement when you are in a position to exploit it.

Entrepreneur   The accounts receivable ledger has much of the information you need. It lists detailed information for each customer's account, including the amounts, dates for transactions, and dates of payments. It can be reorganized into an "aging schedule" to show how long customers wait before paying their bills.

Controller   Much of the information you need is in the accounts payable ledger. It contains information for each supplier, the amounts due, and when payments are made. This subsidiary ledger along with information on credit terms should enable you to conduct your analyses.

Banker   This merchandiser's segment information is likely to greatly impact your loan decision. The risks associated with the company's two sources of net income are quite different. While net income is up by 10%, U.S. operations are performing poorly and Cuban operations are subject to many uncertainties. These uncertainties depend on political events, legal issues, business relationships, Cuban economic conditions, and a host of other risks. Overall, net income results suggested a low-risk loan opportunity, but the segment information reveals a high-risk situation.

Guidance Answers to Quick Checks

1. The five components are source documents, input devices, information processors, information storage, and output devices.

2. Information processors interpret, transform, and summarize the recorded accounting information so that it can be used in analysis, interpretation, and decision making.

3. Data saved in information storage are used to prepare periodic financial reports and special-purpose internal reports as well as source documentation for auditors.

4. All cash payments by check are recorded in the cash disbursements journal.

5. Columnar journals allow us to accumulate repetitive debits and credits and post them as column totals rather than as individual amounts from each entry.

6. The equality of debits and credits is kept within the general ledger. The subsidiary ledger keeps the customer's individual account and is used only for supplementary information.

7. An initial and the page number of the journal from which the amount was posted are entered in the PR column next to the amount.

8. A separate column for Sales Taxes Payable can be included in both the cash receipts journal and the sales journal.

9. This refers to a procedure of using copies of sales invoices as a sales journal. Each invoice amount is posted directly to the customer's account. All invoices are totaled at period-end for posting to the general ledger accounts.

10. The normal recording and posting procedures are threefold. First, transactions are entered in a special journal if applicable. Second, individual amounts are posted to any subsidiary ledger

accounts. Third, column totals are posted to general ledger accounts if not already individually posted.

11. Controlling accounts are debited periodically for an amount or amounts equal to the sum of their respective debits in the subsidiary ledgers (equals journal column totals), and they are credited periodically for an amount or amounts equal to the sum of their respective credits in the subsidiary ledgers (from journal column totals).

12. Tests for accuracy of account balances in the general ledger and subsidiary ledgers are twofold. First, we prepare a trial balance of the general ledger to confirm that debits equal credits. Second, we prove the subsidiary ledgers by preparing schedules of accounts receivable and accounts payable.

13. The general journal is still needed for adjusting, closing, and correcting entries and for special transactions such as sales returns, purchases returns, and certain asset purchases.

14. Integrated systems can save time and minimize errors. This is so because actions taken in one part of the system automatically affect and update related parts.

15. Computer systems offer increased accuracy, speed, efficiency, and convenience.

16. Computer networks can create advantages by linking computers, and giving different users and different computers access to common databases, programs, and hardware.

17. ERP software involves integrated programs, from order taking to manufacturing to accounting. It can speed decision making, help identify costs for reduction, and aid managers in controlling operations.

Key Terms

Accounting information systems (p. 278)

Accounts payable ledger (p. 283)

Accounts receivable ledger (p. 283)

Batch processing (p. 292)

Cash disbursements journal (p. 290)

Cash receipts journal (p. 287)

Check register (p. 290)

Columnar journal (p. 284)

Compatibility principle (p. 279)

Components of accounting systems (p. 279)

Computer network (p. 292)

Control principle (p. 278)	Information processor (p. 280)	Relevance principle (p. 278)
Controlling account (p. 283)	Information storage (p. 280)	Sales journal (p. 284)
Cost-benefit principle (p. 279)	Input device (p. 280)	Schedule of accounts payable (p. 290)
Enterprise resource planning (ERP) software (p. 293)	Internal controls (p. 278)	Schedule of accounts receivable (p. 285)
	Online processing (p. 292)	Segment return on assets (p. 295)
Flexibility principle (p. 279)	Output devices (p. 281)	Special journal (p. 282)
General journal (p. 282)	Purchases journal (p. 289)	Subsidiary ledger (p. 282)

Multiple Choice Quiz Answers on p. 315 mhhe.com/wildFAP21e

Additional Quiz Questions are available at the book's Website.

1. The sales journal is used to record
   a. Credit sales
   b. Cash sales
   c. Cash receipts
   d. Cash purchases
   e. Credit purchases

2. The purchases journal is used to record
   a. Credit sales
   b. Cash sales
   c. Cash receipts
   d. Cash purchases
   e. Credit purchases

3. The ledger that contains the financial statement accounts of a company is the
   a. General journal
   b. Column balance journal

   c. Special ledger
   d. General ledger
   e. Special journal

4. A subsidiary ledger that contains a separate account for each supplier (creditor) to the company is the
   a. Controlling account
   b. Accounts payable ledger
   c. Accounts receivable ledger
   d. General ledger
   e. Special journal

5. Enterprise resource planning software
   a. Refers to programs that help manage company operations.
   b. Is another name for spreadsheet programs.
   c. Uses batch processing of business information.
   d. Is substantially declining in use.
   e. Is another name for database programs.

🔲 Icon denotes assignments that involve decision making.

Discussion Questions

1. What are five basic components of an accounting system?
2. What are source documents? Give two examples.
3. What are the five fundamental principles of accounting information systems?
4. What is the purpose of an input device? Give examples of input devices for computer systems.
5. What is the difference between data that are stored off-line and data that are stored online?
6. What purpose is served by the output devices of an accounting system?
7. When special journals are used, they are usually used to record each of four different types of transactions. What are these four types of transactions?
8. What notations are entered into the Posting Reference column of a ledger account?
9. 🔲 When a general journal entry is used to record sales returns, the credit of the entry must be posted twice. Does this cause the trial balance to be out of balance? Explain.
10. Describe the procedures involving the use of copies of a company's sales invoices as a sales journal.

11. Credits to customer accounts and credits to Other Accounts are individually posted from a cash receipts journal such as the one in Exhibit 7.7. Why not put both types of credits in the same column and save journal space?
12. 🔲 Why should sales to and receipts of cash from credit customers be recorded and posted immediately?
13. 🔲 Locate the annual report note that discusses **Polaris**'s operations by segments in Appendix A. In what segment does it predominantly operate?
14. 🔲 Does the income statement of **Arctic Cat** in Appendix A indicate the net income earned by its business segments? If so, list them.
15. Locate the note that discusses **KTM**'s segments from its 2011 annual report on its Website. What three reportable segments does KTM have?
16. 🔲 Does the balance sheet of **Piaggio** in Appendix A indicate the identifiable assets owned by its business segments? If so, list them.

QUICK STUDY

For account titles and numbers, use the Chart of Accounts at the end of the book.

QS 7-1

Accounting information
system principles

C1

Enter the letter of each system principle in the blank next to its best description.

A. Control principle   **D.** Flexibility principle

B. Relevance principle   **E.** Cost-benefit principle

C. Compatibility principle

1. _____ The principle prescribes the accounting information system to help monitor activities.

2. _____ The principle prescribes the accounting information system to adapt to the unique characteristics of the company.

3. _____ The principle prescribes the accounting information system to change in response to technological advances and competitive pressures.

4. _____ The principle that affects all other accounting information system principles.

5. _____ The principle prescribes the accounting information system to provide timely information for
effective decision making.

QS 7-2

Accounting information system

C1

Fill in the blanks to complete the following descriptions.

1. With _____ processing, source documents are accumulated for a period and then processed all at the
same time, such as once a day, week, or month.

2. A computer _____ allows different computer users to share access to data and programs.

3. A _____ is an input device that captures writing and other input directly from source documents.

4. _____ _____ _____ software comprises programs that help manage a company's vital operations,
from manufacturing to accounting.

QS 7-3

Accounting information
system components

C1

Identify the most likely role in an accounting system played by each of the numbered items 1 through 12 by
assigning a letter from the list A through E on the left.

A. Source documents   _____   **1.** Computer keyboard

B. Input devices   _____   **2.** Computer printer

C. Information processors   _____   **3.** Computer monitor

D. Information storage   _____   **4.** MP3 player

E. Output devices   _____   **5.** Bank statement

                                 _____   **6.** Computer software

                                 _____   **7.** Bar code reader

                                 _____   **8.** Digital camera

                                 _____   **9.** Invoice from a supplier

                                 _____   **10.** Zip drive

                                 _____   **11.** Computer scanner

                                 _____   **12.** Filing cabinet

QS 7-4

Identifying the special journal
of entry

C2

Wilcox Electronics uses a sales journal, a purchases journal, a cash receipts journal, a cash disbursements
journal, and a general journal as illustrated in this chapter. Wilcox recently completed the following transactions *a* through *h*. Identify the journal in which each transaction should be recorded.

a. Sold merchandise on credit.   **e.** Sold merchandise for cash.

b. Purchased shop supplies on credit.   **f.** Purchased merchandise on credit.

c. Paid an employee's salary in cash.   **g.** Purchased inventory for cash.

d. Borrowed cash from the bank.   **h.** Paid cash to a creditor.

QS 7-5

Entries in the general journal

C2

Biloxi Gifts uses a sales journal, a purchases journal, a cash receipts journal, a cash disbursements journal,
and a general journal as illustrated in this chapter. Journalize its November transactions that should be recorded in the general journal. For those not recorded in the general journal, identify the special journal
where each should be recorded.

Nov. 2   The company purchased $2,600 of merchandise on credit from the Midland Co., terms 2/10, n/30.

    12   The owner, T. Biloxi, contributed an automobile worth $17,000 to the company.

    16   The company sold $1,200 of merchandise (cost is $800) on credit to K. Myer, terms n/30.

    19   K. Myer returned $175 of (worthless) merchandise to the company originally purchased on
         November 16 (assume the cost of this merchandise is left in cost of goods sold).

Following is information from Fredrickson Company for its initial month of business. (1) Identify the balances listed in the accounts receivable subsidiary ledger. (2) Identify the accounts receivable balance listed in the general ledger at month's end.

QS 7-6
Controlling accounts and subsidiary ledgers
C3

Credit Sales			Cash Collections		
Jan. 10	Stern Company	$4,000	Jan. 20	Stern Company	$2,000
19	Diaz Brothers	1,600	28	Diaz Brothers	1,600
23	Rex Company	2,500	31	Rex Company	1,300

Peachtree Company uses a sales journal, a purchases journal, a cash receipts journal, a cash disbursements journal, and a general journal. The following transactions occur in the month of May.

QS 7-7
Purchases journal—perpetual
P1

May   1   Purchased $10,100 of merchandise on credit from Krause, Inc., terms n/30.
    8   Sold merchandise costing $900 on credit to G. Seles for $1,500 subject to a $30 sales discount if paid by the end of the month.
   14   Purchased $240 of store supplies from Chang Company on credit, terms n/30.
   17   Purchased $260 of office supplies on credit from Monder Company, terms n/30.
   24   Sold merchandise costing $400 to D. Air for $650 cash.
   28   Purchased store supplies from Porter's for $90 cash.
   29   Paid Krause, Inc., $10,100 cash for the merchandise purchased on May 1.

Prepare headings for a purchases journal like the one in Exhibit 7.9. Journalize the May transactions that should be recorded in the purchases journal.

Refer to QS 7-7 and for each of the May transactions identify the journal in which it would be recorded. Assume the company uses a sales journal, purchases journal, cash receipts journal, cash disbursements journal, and general journal as illustrated in this chapter.

QS 7-8
Identifying journal of entry   C2

Warton Company posts its sales invoices directly and then binds them into a Sales Journal. The company had the following credit sales to these customers during July.

QS 7-9
Accounts receivable ledger; posting from sales journal
P2

July	2	Mary Mack	$ 8,600
	8	Eric Horner	11,100
	10	Troy Wilson	13,400
	14	Hong Jiang	20,500
	20	Troy Wilson	11,200
	29	Mary Mack	7,300
		Total credit sales	$72,100

Required

1. Open an accounts receivable subsidiary ledger having a T-account for each customer. Post the invoices to the subsidiary ledger.

2. Open an Accounts Receivable controlling T-account and a Sales T-account to reflect general ledger accounts. Post the end-of-month total from the sales journal to these accounts.

3. Prepare a schedule of accounts receivable and prove that its total equals the Accounts Receivable controlling account balance.

Apple reports the following operating income (and average assets in parentheses) in a recent year for each of its geographic segments—$ millions: Americas, $13,538 ($3,308); Europe, $11,528 ($2,456); and Japan, $2,481 ($898). Apple also reports the following sales (only) by product segments: iPhone, $47,057; iPad, $20,358; iPod, $7,453; Desktops, $6,439; Portables, $15,344; Other, $11,598. Compute Apple's return on assets for each of its geographic segments, and assess the relative performance of these segments. Compute the percentage of total sales for each of its five product segments.

QS 7-10
Analyzing segment reports
A1

Apple

QS 7-11

International accounting and special journals

C2

Nestlé, a Switzerland-based company, uses a sales journal, a purchases journal, a cash receipts journal, a cash disbursements journal, and a general journal in a manner similar to that explained in this chapter. Journalize the following summary transactions of Nestlé transactions that should be recorded in the general journal. For those not recorded in the general journal, identify only the special journal where each should be recorded. (All amounts in millions of Swiss franc, CHF.)

1. Assume Nestlé purchased CHF 17,000 of merchandise on credit from the suppliers.

2. Assume Nestlé sold CHF 94,000 of merchandise (cost is CHF 42,300) on credit to customers.

3. Assume a key customer returned CHF 2,400 of (worthless) merchandise to Nestlé (assume the cost of this merchandise is left in cost of goods sold).

Mc Graw Hill connect

EXERCISES

For account titles and numbers, use the Chart of Accounts at the end of the book.

Exercise 7-1

Sales journal—perpetual

P1

Finer Company uses a sales journal, a purchases journal, a cash receipts journal, a cash disbursements journal, and a general journal. The following transactions occur in the month of May.

May	2	Sold merchandise costing $300 to B. Facer for $450 cash, invoice no. 5703.
	5	Purchased $2,400 of merchandise on credit from Marchant Corp.
	7	Sold merchandise costing $800 to J. Dryer for $1,250, terms 2/10, n/30, invoice no. 5704.
	8	Borrowed $9,000 cash by signing a note payable to the bank.
	12	Sold merchandise costing $200 to R. Lamb for $340, terms n/30, invoice no. 5705.
	16	Received $1,225 cash from J. Dryer to pay for the purchase of May 7.
	19	Sold used store equipment for $900 cash to Golf, Inc.
	25	Sold merchandise costing $500 to T. Taylor for $750, terms n/30, invoice no. 5706.

Prepare headings for a sales journal like the one in Exhibit 7.5. Journalize the May transactions that should be recorded in this sales journal.

Exercise 7-2

Identifying journal of entry   C2

Refer to Exercise 7-1 and for each of the May transactions identify the journal in which it would be recorded. Assume the company uses a sales journal, purchases journal, cash receipts journal, cash disbursements journal, and general journal as illustrated in this chapter.

Exercise 7-3

Cash receipts journal—perpetual

P1

Ali Co. uses a sales journal, a purchases journal, a cash receipts journal, a cash disbursements journal, and a general journal. The following transactions occur in the month of November.

Nov.	3	The company purchased $3,200 of merchandise on credit from Hart Co., terms n/20.
	7	The company sold merchandise costing $840 on credit to J. Than for $1,000, subject to an $20 sales discount if paid by the end of the month.
	9	The company borrowed $3,750 cash by signing a note payable to the bank.
	13	J. Ali, the owner, contributed $5,000 cash to the company.
	18	The company sold merchandise costing $250 to B. Cox for $330 cash.
	22	The company paid Hart Co. $3,200 cash for the merchandise purchased on November 3.
	27	The company received $980 cash from J. Than in payment of the November 7 purchase.
	30	The company paid salaries of $1,650 in cash.

Prepare headings for a cash receipts journal like the one in Exhibit 7.7. Journalize the November transactions that should be recorded in the cash receipts journal.

Exercise 7-4

Identifying journal of entry   C2

Refer to Exercise 7-3 and for each of the November transactions identify the journal in which it would be recorded. Assume the company uses a sales journal, purchases journal, cash receipts journal, cash disbursements journal, and general journal as illustrated in this chapter.

Exercise 7-5

Controlling accounts and subsidiary ledgers

C3

Following is information from Jesper Company for its initial month of business. (1) Identify the balances listed in the accounts payable subsidiary ledger. (2) Identify the accounts payable balance listed in the general ledger at month's end.

Credit Purchases			Cash Paid		
Jan. 9	Bailey Company	$14,000	Jan. 19	Bailey Company	$10,100
18	Johnson Brothers	6,600	27	Johnson Brothers	6,600
22	Preston Company	6,200	31	Preston Company	5,400

Marx Supply uses a sales journal, a purchases journal, a cash receipts journal, a cash disbursements journal, and a general journal. The following transactions occur in the month of April.

Apr.   3   Purchased merchandise for $2,950 on credit from Seth, Inc., terms 2/10, n/30.
   9   Issued check no. 210 to Kitt Corp. to buy store supplies for $650.
   12   Sold merchandise costing $500 on credit to C. Myrs for $770, terms n/30.
   17   Issued check no. 211 for $1,400 to pay off a note payable to City Bank.
   20   Purchased merchandise for $4,500 on credit from Lite, terms 2/10, n/30.
   28   Issued check no. 212 to Lite to pay the amount due for the purchase of April 20, less the discount.
   29   Paid salary of $1,800 to B. Dock by issuing check no. 213.
   30   Issued check no. 214 to Seth, Inc., to pay the amount due for the purchase of April 3.

Prepare headings for a cash disbursements journal like the one in Exhibit 7.11. Journalize the April transactions that should be recorded in the cash disbursements journal.

Exercise 7-6
Cash disbursements
journal—perpetual
P1

Refer to Exercise 7-6 and for each of the April transactions identify the journal in which it would be recorded. Assume the company uses a sales journal, purchases journal, cash receipts journal, cash disbursements journal, and general journal as illustrated in this chapter.

Exercise 7-7
Identifying journal of entry   C2

A company that records credit purchases in a purchases journal and records purchases returns in a general journal made the following errors. Indicate when each error should be discovered.

1. Made an addition error in totaling the Office Supplies column of the purchases journal.
2. Made an addition error in determining the balance of a creditor's subsidiary account.
3. Posted a purchases return to the Accounts Payable account and to the creditor's subsidiary account but did not post the purchases return to the Inventory account.
4. Correctly recorded a $8,000 purchase in the purchases journal but posted it to the creditor's subsidiary account as a $800 purchase.
5. Posted a purchases return to the Inventory account and to the Accounts Payable account but did not post to the creditor's subsidiary account.

Exercise 7-8
Purchases journal and
error identification

P1

Post Pharmacy uses the following journals: sales journal, purchases journal, cash receipts journal, cash disbursements journal, and general journal. On June 5, Post purchased merchandise priced at $14,000, subject to credit terms of 2/10, n/30. On June 14, the pharmacy paid the net amount due for the merchandise. In journalizing the payment, the pharmacy debited Accounts Payable for $14,000 but failed to record the cash discount on the purchases. Cash was properly credited for the actual $13,720 paid. (a) In what journals would the June 5 and the June 14 transactions be recorded? (b) What procedure is likely to discover the error in journalizing the June 14 transaction?

Exercise 7-9
Special journal transactions and
error discovery

P1

At the end of May, the sales journal of Mountain View appears as follows.

Exercise 7-10
Posting to subsidiary ledger
accounts; preparing a schedule
of accounts receivable

P2

Sales Journal					Page 2	
Date	Account Debited	Invoice Number	PR	Accounts Receivable Dr. Sales Cr.	Cost of Goods Sold Dr. Inventory Cr.	
May 6	Aaron Reckers	190		3,880	3,120	
10	Sara Reed	191		2,940	2,325	
17	Anna Page	192		1,850	1,480	
25	Sara Reed	193		1,340	1,075	
31	Totals			10,010	8,000	

Mountain View also recorded the return of defective merchandise with the following entry.

May 20	Sales Returns and Allowances	350	
	Accounts Receivable—Anna Page		350
	Customer returned (worthless) merchandise.		

Required

1. Open an accounts receivable subsidiary ledger that has a T-account for each customer listed in the sales journal. Post to the customer accounts the entries in the sales journal and any portion of the general journal entry that affects a customer's account.
2. Open a general ledger that has T-accounts for Accounts Receivable, Inventory, Sales, Sales Returns and Allowances, and Cost of Goods Sold. Post the sales journal and any portion of the general journal entry that affects these accounts.
[continued on next page]

Check (3) Ending Accounts
Receivable, $9,660

3. Prepare a schedule of accounts receivable and prove that its total equals the balance in the Accounts Receivable controlling account.

Exercise 7-11
Computing and analyzing
segment return on assets

A1

Refer to Exhibit 7.13 and complete the segment return on assets table for Teton Company (round ratios to three decimals, or one decimal if shown in percent form). Analyze your findings and identify the segment with the highest, and that with the lowest, segment return on assets.

	Segment Operating Income (in $ mil.)		Segment Assets (in $ mil.)		Segment Return on Assets
Segment	2013	2012	2013	2012	2013
Specialty					
Skiing Group	$ 72	$ 68	$ 591	$450	
Skating Group	19	16	63	52	
Specialty Footwear	32	29	165	146	
Other Specialty	21	14	47	34	
Subtotal	144	127	866	682	
General Merchandise					
South America	42	46	315	284	
United States	17	18	62	45	
Europe	15	13	24	22	
Subtotal	74	77	401	351	
Total	$218	$204	$1,267	$1,033	

Check Europe segment return,
65.2%

McGraw Hill **connect**

PROBLEM SET A

For account titles and numbers, use the Chart of Accounts at the end of the book.

Problem 7-1A
Special journals, subsidiary
ledgers, and schedule of
accounts receivable—perpetual

C3 P1 P2

Sage 50 📄
QB

Wiset Company completes these transactions during April of the current year (the terms of all its credit sales are 2/10, n/30).

Apr. 2 Purchased $14,300 of merchandise on credit from Noth Company, invoice dated April 2, terms 2/10, n/60.
3 Sold merchandise on credit to Page Alistair, Invoice No. 760, for $4,000 (cost is $3,000).
3 Purchased $1,480 of office supplies on credit from Custer, Inc. Invoice dated April 2, terms n/10 EOM.
4 Issued Check No. 587 to *World View* for advertising expense, $899.
5 Sold merchandise on credit to Paula Kohr, Invoice No. 761, for $8,000 (cost is $6,500).
6 Received an $80 credit memorandum from Custer, Inc., for the return of some of the office supplies received on April 3.
9 Purchased $12,125 of store equipment on credit from Hal's Supply, invoice dated April 9, terms n/10 EOM.
11 Sold merchandise on credit to Nic Nelson, Invoice No 762, for $10,500 (cost is $7,000).
12 Issued Check No. 588 to Noth Company in payment of its April 2 invoice, less the discount.
13 Received payment from Page Alistair for the April 3 sale, less the discount.
13 Sold $5,100 of merchandise on credit to Page Alistair (cost is $3,600), Invoice No. 763.
14 Received payment from Paula Kohr for the April 5 sale, less the discount.
16 Issued Check No. 589, payable to Payroll, in payment of sales salaries expense for the first half of the month, $10,750. Cashed the check and paid employees.
16 Cash sales for the first half of the month are $52,840 (cost is $35,880). (Cash sales are recorded daily from cash register data but are recorded only twice in this problem to reduce repetitive entries.)
17 Purchased $13,750 of merchandise on credit from Grant Company, invoice dated April 17, terms 2/10, n/30.
18 Borrowed $60,000 cash from First State Bank by signing a long-term note payable.
20 Received payment from Nic Nelson for the April 11 sale, less the discount.
20 Purchased $830 of store supplies on credit from Hal's Supply, invoice dated April 19, terms n/10 EOM.
23 Received a $750 credit memorandum from Grant Company for the return of defective merchandise received on April 17.
23 Received payment from Page Alistair for the April 13 sale, less the discount.

25 Purchased $11,375 of merchandise on credit from Noth Company, invoice dated April 24, terms 2/10, n/60.

26 Issued Check No. 590 to Grant Company in payment of its April 17 invoice, less the return and the discount.

27 Sold $3,170 of merchandise on credit to Paula Kohr, Invoice No. 764 (cost is $2,520).

27 Sold $6,700 of merchandise on credit to Nic Nelson, Invoice No. 765 (cost is $4,305).

30 Issued Check No. 591, payable to Payroll, in payment of the sales salaries expense for the last half of the month, $10,750.

30 Cash sales for the last half of the month are $73,975 (cost is $58,900).

Required

1. Prepare a sales journal like that in Exhibit 7.5 and a cash receipts journal like that in Exhibit 7.7. Number both journal pages as page 3. Then review the transactions of Wiset Company and enter those that should be journalized in the sales journal and those that should be journalized in the cash receipts journal. Ignore any transactions that should be journalized in a purchases journal, a cash disbursements journal, or a general journal.

2. Open the following general ledger accounts: Cash, Accounts Receivable, Inventory, Long-Term Notes Payable, B. Wiset, Capital, Sales, Sales Discounts, and Cost of Goods Sold. Enter the March 31 balances for Cash ($85,000), Inventory ($125,000), Long-Term Notes Payable ($110,000), and B. Wiset, Capital ($100,000). Also open accounts receivable subsidiary ledger accounts for Paula Kohr, Page Alistair, and Nic Nelson.

3. Verify that amounts that should be posted as individual amounts from the journals have been posted. (Such items are immediately posted.) Foot and crossfoot the journals and make the month-end postings.

4. Prepare a trial balance of the general ledger and prove the accuracy of the subsidiary ledger by preparing a schedule of accounts receivable.

Check Trial balance totals, $434,285

Analysis Component

5. Assume that the total for the schedule of Accounts Receivable does not equal the balance of the controlling account in the general ledger. Describe steps you would take to discover the error(s).

The April transactions of Wiset Company are described in Problem 7-1A.

Required

1. Prepare a general journal, a purchases journal like that in Exhibit 7.9, and a cash disbursements journal like that in Exhibit 7.11. Number all journal pages as page 3. Review the April transactions of Wiset Company and enter those transactions that should be journalized in the general journal, the purchases journal, or the cash disbursements journal. Ignore any transactions that should be journalized in a sales journal or cash receipts journal.

2. Open the following general ledger accounts: Cash, Inventory, Office Supplies, Store Supplies, Store Equipment, Accounts Payable, Long-Term Notes Payable, B. Wiset, Capital, Sales Salaries Expense, and Advertising Expense. Enter the March 31 balances of Cash ($85,000), Inventory ($125,000), Long-Term Notes Payable ($110,000), and B. Wiset, Capital ($100,000). Also open accounts payable subsidiary ledger accounts for Hal's Supply, Noth Company, Grant Company, and Custer, Inc.

3. Verify that amounts that should be posted as individual amounts from the journals have been posted. (Such items are immediately posted.) Foot and crossfoot the journals and make the month-end postings.

4. Prepare a trial balance of the general ledger and a schedule of accounts payable.

Problem 7-2A
Special journals, subsidiary ledgers, and schedule of accounts payable—perpetual

C3 P1 P2

Check Trial balance totals, $235,730

Church Company completes these transactions and events during March of the current year (terms for all its credit sales are 2/10, n/30).

Mar. 1 Purchased $43,600 of merchandise from Van Industries, invoice dated March 1, terms 2/15, n/30.

2 Sold merchandise on credit to Min Cho, Invoice No. 854, for $16,800 (cost is $8,400).

3 Purchased $1,230 of office supplies on credit from Gabel Company, invoice dated March 3, terms n/10 EOM.

3 Sold merchandise on credit to Linda Witt, Invoice No. 855, for $10,200 (cost is $5,800).

6 Borrowed $82,000 cash from Federal Bank by signing a long-term note payable.

9 Purchased $21,850 of office equipment on credit from Spell Supply, invoice dated March 9, terms n/10 EOM.

10 Sold merchandise on credit to Jovita Albany, Invoice No. 856, for $5,600 (cost is $2,900).

Problem 7-3A
Special journals, subsidiary ledgers, trial balance—perpetual

C3 P1 P2

mhhe.com/wildFAP21e

Sage 50 QB

12 Received payment from Min Cho for the March 2 sale less the discount.

13 Sent Van Industries Check No. 416 in payment of the March 1 invoice less the discount.

13 Received payment from Linda Witt for the March 3 sale less the discount.

14 Purchased $32,625 of merchandise from the CD Company, invoice dated March 13, terms 2/10, n/30.

15 Issued Check No. 417, payable to Payroll, in payment of sales salaries expense for the first half of the month, $18,300. Cashed the check and paid the employees.

15 Cash sales for the first half of the month are $34,680 (cost is $20,210). (Cash sales are recorded daily, but are recorded only twice here to reduce repetitive entries.)

16 Purchased $1,770 of store supplies on credit from Gabel Company, invoice dated March 16, terms n/10 EOM.

17 Received a $2,425 credit memorandum from CD Company for the return of unsatisfactory merchandise purchased on March 14.

19 Received a $630 credit memorandum from Spell Supply for office equipment received on March 9 and returned for credit.

20 Received payment from Jovita Albany for the sale of March 10 less the discount.

23 Issued Check No. 418 to CD Company in payment of the invoice of March 13 less the March 17 return and the discount.

27 Sold merchandise on credit to Jovita Albany, Invoice No. 857, for $14,910 (cost is $7,220).

28 Sold merchandise on credit to Linda Witt, Invoice No. 858, for $4,315 (cost is $3,280).

31 Issued Check No. 419, payable to Payroll, in payment of sales salaries expense for the last half of the month, $18,300. Cashed the check and paid the employees.

31 Cash sales for the last half of the month are $30,180 (cost is $16,820).

31 Verify that amounts impacting customer and creditor accounts were posted and that any amounts that should have been posted as individual amounts to the general ledger accounts were posted. Foot and crossfoot the journals and make the month-end postings.

Required

1. Open the following general ledger accounts: Cash; Accounts Receivable; Inventory (March 1 beg. bal. is $10,000); Office Supplies; Store Supplies; Office Equipment; Accounts Payable; Long-Term Notes Payable; Z. Church, Capital (March 1 beg. bal. is $10,000); Sales; Sales Discounts; Cost of Goods Sold; and Sales Salaries Expense. Open the following accounts receivable subsidiary ledger accounts: Jovita Albany, Min Cho, and Linda Witt. Open the following accounts payable subsidiary ledger accounts: Gabel Company, Van Industries, Spell Supply, and CD Company.

2. Enter these transactions in a sales journal like Exhibit 7.5, a purchases journal like Exhibit 7.9, a cash receipts journal like Exhibit 7.7, a cash disbursements journal like Exhibit 7.11, or a general journal. Number all journal pages as page 2.

Check Trial balance totals, $232,905 **3.** Prepare a trial balance of the general ledger and prove the accuracy of the subsidiary ledgers by preparing schedules of both accounts receivable and accounts payable.

PROBLEM SET B

For account titles and numbers, use the Chart of Accounts at the end of the book.

Problem 7-1B
Special journals, subsidiary ledgers, schedule of accounts receivable—perpetual

C3 P1 P2

Acorn Industries completes these transactions during July of the current year (the terms of all its credit sales are 2/10, n/30).

July 1 Purchased $6,500 of merchandise on credit from Teton Company, invoice dated June 30, terms 2/10, n/30.

3 Issued Check No. 300 to *The Weekly* for advertising expense, $625.

5 Sold merchandise on credit to Kim Nettle, Invoice No. 918, for $19,200 (cost is $10,500).

6 Sold merchandise on credit to Ruth Blake, Invoice No. 919, for $7,500 (cost is $4,300).

7 Purchased $1,250 of store supplies on credit from Plaine, Inc., invoice dated July 7, terms n/10 EOM.

8 Received a $250 credit memorandum from Plaine, Inc., for the return of store supplies received on July 7.

9 Purchased $38,220 of store equipment on credit from Charm's Supply, invoice dated July 8, terms n/10 EOM.

10 Issued Check No. 301 to Teton Company in payment of its June 30 invoice, less the discount.

13 Sold merchandise on credit to Ashton Moore, Invoice No. 920, for $8,550 (cost is $5,230).

14 Sold merchandise on credit to Kim Nettle, Invoice No. 921, for $5,100 (cost is $3,800).

15 Received payment from Kim Nettle for the July 5 sale, less the discount.
15 Issued Check No. 302, payable to Payroll, in payment of sales salaries expense for the first half of the month, $31,850. Cashed the check and paid employees.
15 Cash sales for the first half of the month are $118,350 (cost is $76,330). (Cash sales are recorded daily using data from the cash registers but are recorded only twice in this problem to reduce repetitive entries.)
16 Received payment from Ruth Blake for the July 6 sale, less the discount.
17 Purchased $7,200 of merchandise on credit from Drake Company, invoice dated July 17, terms 2/10, n/30.
20 Purchased $650 of office supplies on credit from Charm's Supply, invoice dated July 19, terms n/10 EOM.
21 Borrowed $15,000 cash from College Bank by signing a long-term note payable.
23 Received payment from Ashton Moore for the July 13 sale, less the discount.
24 Received payment from Kim Nettle for the July 14 sale, less the discount.
24 Received a $2,400 credit memorandum from Drake Company for the return of defective merchandise received on July 17.
26 Purchased $9,770 of merchandise on credit from Teton Company, invoice dated July 26, terms 2/10, n/30.
27 Issued Check No. 303 to Drake Company in payment of its July 17 invoice, less the return and the discount.
29 Sold merchandise on credit to Ruth Blake, Invoice No. 922, for $17,500 (cost is $10,850).
30 Sold merchandise on credit to Ashton Moore, Invoice No. 923, for $16,820 (cost is $9,840).
31 Issued Check No. 304, payable to Payroll, in payment of the sales salaries expense for the last half of the month, $31,850.
31 Cash sales for the last half of the month are $80,244 (cost is $53,855).

Required

1. Prepare a sales journal like that in Exhibit 7.5 and a cash receipts journal like that in Exhibit 7.7. Number both journals as page 3. Then review the transactions of Acorn Industries and enter those transactions that should be journalized in the sales journal and those that should be journalized in the cash receipts journal. Ignore any transactions that should be journalized in a purchases journal, a cash disbursements journal, or a general journal.

2. Open the following general ledger accounts: Cash, Accounts Receivable, Inventory, Long-Term Notes Payable, R. Acorn, Capital, Sales, Sales Discounts, and Cost of Goods Sold. Enter the June 30 balances for Cash ($100,000), Inventory ($200,000), Long-Term Notes Payable ($200,000), and R. Acorn, Capital ($100,000). Also open accounts receivable subsidiary ledger accounts for Kim Nettle, Ashton Moore, and Ruth Blake.

3. Verify that amounts that should be posted as individual amounts from the journals have been posted. (Such items are immediately posted.) Foot and crossfoot the journals and make the month-end postings.

4. Prepare a trial balance of the general ledger and prove the accuracy of the subsidiary ledger by preparing a schedule of accounts receivable.

Check Trial balance totals, $588,264

Analysis Component

5. Assume that the total for the schedule of Accounts Receivable does not equal the balance of the controlling account in the general ledger. Describe steps you would take to discover the error(s).

The July transactions of Acorn Industries are described in Problem 7-1B.

Required

1. Prepare a general journal, a purchases journal like that in Exhibit 7.9, and a cash disbursements journal like that in Exhibit 7.11. Number all journal pages as page 3. Review the July transactions of Acorn Industries and enter those transactions that should be journalized in the general journal, the purchases journal, or the cash disbursements journal. Ignore any transactions that should be journalized in a sales journal or cash receipts journal.

2. Open the following general ledger accounts: Cash, Inventory, Office Supplies, Store Supplies, Store Equipment, Accounts Payable, Long-Term Notes Payable, R. Acorn, Capital, Sales Salaries Expense, and Advertising Expense. Enter the June 30 balances of Cash ($100,000), Inventory

Problem 7-2B
Special journals, subsidiary ledgers, and schedule of accounts payable—perpetual

C3 P1 P2

($200,000), Long-Term Notes Payable ($200,000), and R. Acorn, Capital ($100,000). Also open accounts payable subsidiary ledger accounts for Charm's Supply, Teton Company, Drake Company, and Plaine, Inc.

3. Verify that amounts that should be posted as individual amounts from the journals have been posted. (Such items are immediately posted.) Foot and crossfoot the journals and make the month-end postings.

Check   Trial balance totals, $349,640   **4.** Prepare a trial balance of the general ledger and a schedule of accounts payable.

Problem 7-3B
Special journals, subsidiary
ledgers, trial balance—perpetual

C3 P2 P3

Grassley Company completes these transactions during November of the current year (terms for all its credit sales are 2/10, n/30).

Nov. 1   Purchased $5,058 of office equipment on credit from Brun Supply, invoice dated November 1, terms n/10 EOM.

     2   Borrowed $88,500 cash from Wisconsin Bank by signing a long-term note payable.

     4   Purchased $33,500 of merchandise from BLR Industries, invoice dated November 3, terms 2/10, n/30.

     5   Purchased $1,040 of store supplies on credit from Grebe Company, invoice dated November 5, terms n/10 EOM.

     8   Sold merchandise on credit to Cyd Rounder, Invoice No. 439, for $6,550 (cost is $3,910).

   10   Sold merchandise on credit to Carlos Mantel, Invoice No. 440, for $13,500 (cost is $8,500).

   11   Purchased $2,557 of merchandise from Lo Company, invoice dated November 10, terms 2/10, n/30.

   12   Sent BLR Industries Check No. 633 in payment of its November 3 invoice less the discount.

   15   Issued Check No. 634, payable to Payroll, in payment of sales salaries expense for the first half of the month, $6,585. Cashed the check and paid the employees.

   15   Cash sales for the first half of the month are $18,170 (cost is $9,000). (Cash sales are recorded daily but are recorded only twice in this problem to reduce repetitive entries.)

   15   Sold merchandise on credit to Tori Tripp, Invoice No. 441, for $5,250 (cost is $2,450).

   16   Purchased $459 of office supplies on credit from Grebe Company, invoice dated November 16, terms n/10 EOM.

   17   Received a $557 credit memorandum from Lo Company for the return of unsatisfactory merchandise purchased on November 11.

   18   Received payment from Cyd Rounder for the November 8 sale less the discount.

   19   Received payment from Carlos Mantel for the November 10 sale less the discount.

   19   Issued Check No. 635 to Lo Company in payment of its invoice of November 10 less the return and the discount.

   22   Sold merchandise on credit to Carlos Mantel, Invoice No. 442, for $3,695 (cost is $2,060).

   24   Sold merchandise on credit to Tori Tripp, Invoice No. 443, for $4,280 (cost is $2,130).

   25   Received payment from Tori Tripp for the sale of November 15 less the discount.

   26   Received a $922 credit memorandum from Brun Supply for the return of office equipment purchased on November 1.

   30   Issued Check No. 636, payable to Payroll, in payment of sales salaries expense for the last half of the month, $6,585. Cashed the check and paid the employees.

   30   Cash sales for the last half of the month are $16,703 (cost is $10,200).

   30   Verify that amounts impacting customer and creditor accounts were posted and that any amounts that should have been posted as individual amounts to the general ledger accounts were posted. Foot and crossfoot the journals and make the month-end postings.

Required

1. Open the following general ledger accounts: Cash; Accounts Receivable; Inventory (November 1 beg. bal. is $40,000); Office Supplies; Store Supplies; Office Equipment; Accounts Payable; Long-Term Notes Payable; C. Grassley, Capital (Nov. 1 beg. bal. is $40,000); Sales; Sales Discounts; Cost of Goods Sold; and Sales Salaries Expense. Open the following accounts receivable subsidiary ledger accounts: Carlos Mantel, Tori Tripp, and Cyd Rounder. Open the following accounts payable subsidiary ledger accounts: Grebe Company, BLR Industries, Brun Supply, and Lo Company.

2. Enter these transactions in a sales journal like that in Exhibit 7.5, a purchases journal like that in Exhibit 7.9, a cash receipts journal like that in Exhibit 7.7, a cash disbursements journal like that in Exhibit 7.11, or a general journal. Number all journal pages as page 2.

3. Prepare a trial balance of the general ledger and prove the accuracy of the subsidiary ledgers by preparing schedules of both accounts receivable and accounts payable.

Check   Trial balance totals, $202,283

(This serial problem began in Chapter 1 and continues through most of the book. If previous chapter segments were not completed, the serial problem can begin at this point. It is helpful, but not necessary, to use the Working Papers that accompany the book.)

SP 7   Assume that Adria Lopez expands Success Systems' accounting system to include special journals.

SERIAL PROBLEM

Success Systems   P1

Sage 50

Required

1. Locate the transactions related to January through March 2014 for Success Systems in Chapter 5.

2. Enter the Success Systems transactions for January through March in a sales journal like that in Exhibit 7.5 (insert "n/a" in the Invoice column), a cash receipts journal like that in Exhibit 7.7, a purchases journal like that in Exhibit 7.9 (use Computer Supplies heading instead of Office Supplies), and a cash disbursements journal like that in Exhibit 7.11 (insert "n/a" in the Check Number column), or a general journal. Number journal pages as page 2. If the transaction does not specify the name of the payee, state "not specified" in the Payee column of the cash disbursements journal.

3. The transactions on the following dates should be journalized in the general journal: January 5, 11, 20, 24, and 29 (no entry required) and March 24. Do not record and post the adjusting entries for the end of March.

(If the Working Papers that accompany this book are not available, omit this comprehensive problem.)
Assume it is Monday, May 1, the first business day of the month, and you have just been hired as the accountant for Colo Company, which operates with monthly accounting periods. All of the company's accounting work is completed through the end of April and its ledgers show April 30 balances. During your first month on the job, the company experiences the following transactions and events (terms for all its credit sales are 2/10, n/30 unless stated differently):

COMPREHENSIVE PROBLEM

Colo Company

mhhe.com/wildFAP21e

Sage 50

| May | 1 | Issued Check No. 3410 to S&P Management Co. in payment of the May rent, $3,710. (Use two lines to record the transaction. Charge 80% of the rent to Rent Expense—Selling Space and the balance to Rent Expense—Office Space.) |

May 1   Issued Check No. 3410 to S&P Management Co. in payment of the May rent, $3,710. (Use two lines to record the transaction. Charge 80% of the rent to Rent Expense—Selling Space and the balance to Rent Expense—Office Space.)

2   Sold merchandise on credit to Hensel Company, Invoice No. 8785, for $6,100 (cost is $4,100).

2   Issued a $175 credit memorandum to Knox Co., for defective (worthless) merchandise sold on April 28 and returned for credit. The total selling price (gross) was $4,725.

3   Received a $798 credit memorandum from Peyton Products for the return of merchandise purchased on April 29.

4   Purchased the following on credit from Gear Supply Co.: merchandise, $37,072; store supplies, $574; and office supplies, $83. Invoice dated May 4, terms n/10 EOM.

5   Received payment from Knox Co., for the balance from the April 28 sale less the May 2 return and the discount.

8   Issued Check No. 3411 to Peyton Products to pay for the $7,098 of merchandise purchased on April 29 less the May 3 return and a 2% discount.

9   Sold store supplies to the merchant next door at their cost of $350 cash.

10   Purchased $4,074 of office equipment on credit from Gear Supply Co., invoice dated May 10, terms n/10 EOM.

11   Received payment from Hensel Company for the May 2 sale less the discount.

11   Purchased $8,800 of merchandise from Garcia, Inc., invoice dated May 10, terms 2/10, n/30.

12   Received an $854 credit memorandum from Gear Supply Co. for the return of defective office equipment received on May 10.

15   Issued Check No. 3412, payable to Payroll, in payment of sales salaries, $5,320, and office salaries, $3,150. Cashed the check and paid the employees.

15   Cash sales for the first half of the month are $59,220 (cost is $38,200). (Cash sales are recorded daily but are recorded only twice here to reduce repetitive entries.)

15   Post to the customer and creditor accounts. Also post individual items that are not included in column totals at the end of the month to the general ledger accounts. (Such items are posted daily but are posted only twice each month because they are few in number.)

16   Sold merchandise on credit to Hensel Company, Invoice No. 8786, for $3,990 (cost is $1,890).

17   Purchased $13,650 of merchandise from Fink Corp., invoice dated May 14, terms 2/10, n/60.

19   Issued Check No. 3413 to Garcia, Inc., in payment of its May 10 invoice less the discount.

22   Sold merchandise to Lee Services, Invoice No. 8787, for $6,850 (cost is $4,990), terms 2/10, n/60.

23   Issued Check No. 3414 to Fink Corp. in payment of its May 14 invoice less the discount.

24   Purchased the following on credit from Gear Supply Co.: merchandise, $8,120; store supplies, $630; and office supplies, $280. Invoice dated May 24, terms n/10 EOM.

25   Purchased $3,080 of merchandise from Peyton Products, invoice dated May 23, terms 2/10, n/30.

26   Sold merchandise on credit to Crane Corp., Invoice No. 8788, for $14,210 (cost is $8,230).

26   Issued Check No. 3415 to Perennial Power in payment of the May electric bill, $1,283.

29   The owner of Colo Company, Jenny Colo, used Check No. 3416 to withdraw $7,000 cash from the business for personal use.

30   Received payment from Lee Services for the May 22 sale less the discount.

30   Issued Check No. 3417, payable to Payroll, in payment of sales salaries, $5,320, and office salaries, $3,150. Cashed the check and paid the employees.

31   Cash sales for the last half of the month are $66,052 (cost is $42,500).

31   Post to the customer and creditor accounts. Also post individual items that are not included in column totals at the end of the month to the general ledger accounts. Foot and crossfoot the journals and make the month-end postings.

Required

1. Enter these transactions in a sales journal, a purchases journal, a cash receipts journal, a cash disbursements journal, or a general journal as illustrated in this chapter (number all journal pages as page 2). Post when instructed to do so. Assume a perpetual inventory system.

Check   (2) Unadjusted trial balance totals, $545,020; Adjustments column totals, $2,407

2. Prepare a trial balance in the Trial Balance columns of the work sheet form provided with the working papers. Complete the work sheet using the following information for accounting adjustments.

 a. Expired insurance, $553.

 b. Ending store supplies inventory, $2,632.

 c. Ending office supplies inventory, $504.

 d. Depreciation of store equipment, $567.

 e. Depreciation of office equipment, $329.

 Prepare and post adjusting and closing entries.

(3) Net income, $31,647; Total assets, $385,791

3. Prepare a May 2013 multiple-step income statement, a May 2013 statement of owner's equity, and a May 31, 2013, classified balance sheet.

4. Prepare a post-closing trial balance. Also prove the accuracy of subsidiary ledgers by preparing schedules of both accounts receivable and accounts payable.

Beyond the Numbers

REPORTING IN ACTION

A1

Polaris

BTN 7-1   Refer to **Polaris**'s financial statements in Appendix A to answer the following.

1. Identify the note that reports on Polaris' business segments.

2. Describe the focus and activities of each of Polaris' business segments.

Fast Forward

3. Access Polaris' annual report for fiscal years ending after December 31, 2011, from its Website (**Polaris.com**) or the SEC's EDGAR database (**www.sec.gov**). Has Polaris changed its reporting policy regarding segment information? Explain.

BTN 7-2 Key figures for **Polaris** and **Arctic Cat** follow ($ thousands).

Polaris Segment	Current Year		One Year Prior		Two Years Prior	
	Segment Revenue	Segment Assets	Segment Revenue	Segment Assets	Segment Revenue	Segment Assets
Domestic	$1,864,099	$957,497	$1,405,966	$873,183	$1,074,228	$630,420
International	792,850	270,527	585,173	188,464	491,659	133,233

Arctic Cat Segment	Current Year		One Year Prior		Two Years Prior	
	Segment Revenue	Segment Assets	Segment Revenue	Segment Assets	Segment Revenue	Segment Assets
Domestic	$218,560	$271,163	$215,460	$244,020	$292,295	$248,625
International	246,091	1,743	235,268	2,064	271,318	2,540

COMPARATIVE ANALYSIS

A1

Polaris

Arctic Cat

Required

1. Compute the ratio of segment revenue divided by segment assets for each of the segments of Polaris and Arctic Cat for each of the two most recent years shown. (We do not compute the segment return on assets as these companies did not report their segment income.)
2. Interpret and comment on your results of part 1.

BTN 7-3 Erica Gray, CPA, is a sole practitioner. She has been practicing as an auditor for 10 years. Recently a long-standing audit client asked Gray to design and implement an integrated computer-based accounting information system. The fees associated with this additional engagement with the client are very attractive. However, Gray wonders if she can remain objective on subsequent audits in her evaluation of the client's accounting system and its records if she was responsible for its design and implementation. Gray knows that professional auditing standards require her to remain independent in fact and appearance from her auditing clients.

ETHICS CHALLENGE

C1

Required

1. What do you believe auditing standards are mainly concerned with when they require independence in fact? In appearance?
2. Why is it important that auditors remain independent of their clients?
3. Do you think Gray can accept this engagement and remain independent? Justify your response.

BTN 7-4 Your friend, Wendy Geiger, owns a small retail store that sells candies and nuts. Geiger acquires her goods from a few select vendors. She generally makes purchase orders by phone and on credit. Sales are primarily for cash. Geiger keeps her own manual accounting system using a general journal and a general ledger. At the end of each business day, she records one summary entry for cash sales. Geiger recently began offering items in creative gift packages. This has increased sales substantially, and she is now receiving orders from corporate and other clients who order large quantities and prefer to buy on credit. As a result of increased credit transactions in both purchases and sales, keeping the accounting records has become extremely time consuming. Geiger wants to continue to maintain her own manual system and calls you for advice. Write a memo to her advising how she might modify her current manual accounting system to accommodate the expanded business activities. Geiger is accustomed to checking her ledger by using a trial balance. Your memo should explain the advantages of what you propose and of any other verification techniques you recommend.

COMMUNICATING IN PRACTICE

C2 C3

BTN 7-5 Access the March 13, 2012, filing of the fiscal 2012 10-K report for **Dell** (ticker DELL) at www.SEC.gov. Read its Note 14 that details Dell's segment information and answer the following.

1. Dell's operations are divided among which four global business segments?
2. In fiscal year 2012, which segment had the largest dollar amount of operating income? Which had the largest amount of assets?

[continued on next page]

TAKING IT TO THE NET

A1

3. Compute the return on assets for each segment for fiscal year 2012. Use operating income and average total assets by segment for your calculation. Which segment has the highest return on assets?

4. For what product groups does Dell provide segment data? What percent of Dell's net revenue is earned by each product group?

TEAMWORK IN ACTION

C3   P1   P2

BTN 7-6   Each member of the team is to assume responsibility for one of the following tasks:

a. Journalizing in the purchases journal.

b. Journalizing in the cash disbursements journal.

c. Maintaining and verifying the Accounts Payable ledger.

d. Journalizing in the sales journal and the general journal.

e. Journalizing in the cash receipts journal.

f. Maintaining and verifying the Accounts Receivable ledger.

The team should abide by the following procedures in carrying out responsibilities.

Required

1. After tasks *a–f* are assigned, each team member is to quickly read the list of transactions in Problem 7-3A, identifying with initials the journal in which each transaction is to be recorded. Upon completion, the team leader is to read transaction dates, and the appropriate team member is to vocalize responsibility. Any disagreement between teammates must be resolved.

2. Journalize and continually update subsidiary ledgers. Journal recorders should alert teammates assigned to subsidiary ledgers when an entry must be posted to their subsidiary.

3. Team members responsible for tasks *a*, *b*, *d*, and *e* are to summarize and prove journals; members responsible for tasks *c* and *f* are to prepare both payables and receivables schedules.

4. The team leader is to take charge of the general ledger, rotating team members to obtain amounts to be posted. The person responsible for a journal must complete posting references in that journal. Other team members should verify the accuracy of account balance computations. To avoid any abnormal account balances, post in the following order: P, S, G, R, D. (*Note:* Posting any necessary individual general ledger amounts is also done at this time.)

5. The team leader is to read out general ledger account balances while another team member fills in the trial balance form. Concurrently, one member should keep a running balance of debit account balance totals and another credit account balance totals. Verify the final total of the trial balance and the schedules. If necessary, the team must resolve any errors. Turn in the trial balance and schedules to the instructor.

ENTREPRENEURIAL DECISION

P1

BTN 7-7   Refer to the chapter's opening feature about Shazi Visram and her company, **Happy Family**. Her organic food company deals with numerous suppliers and customers.

Required

1. Identify the special journals that Happy Family would be likely to use in its operations. Also identify any subsidiary ledgers that it would likely use.

2. Happy Family hopes to double yearly sales within five years hence from its current $100 million annual amount. Assume that its sales growth projections are as follows.

Year	One Year Hence	Two Years Hence	Three Years Hence	Four Years Hence	Five Years Hence
Projected growth in sales (from the preceding year)	0%	20%	15%	25%	20%

Estimate Happy Family's projected sales for each year (round to the nearest dollar). If this pattern of sales growth holds, will Happy Family achieve its goal of doubling sales in five years?

BTN 7-8   Access and refer to the December 31, 2011, annual report for **KTM** at <u>www.KTM.com</u>.

Required

1. Identify its 'Enclosure to the Notes to the Financial Statements' (Segment Information) to its financial statements and locate its information relating to KTM's operating and reportable segments. List its three segments.
2. What accounting information does it disclose for each segment? (Answers need only list titles for the accounting line items, not numbers, disclosed for each segment.)
3. Does KTM have a dominant segment (from a financial perspective)? Explain.

GLOBAL DECISION

A1

KTM

ANSWERS TO MULTIPLE CHOICE QUIZ

1. a

2. e

3. d

4. b

5. a

Cash and Internal Controls

8

A Look Back

Chapter 7 focused on accounting information systems. We explained the principles and components of information systems, the use of special journals and subsidiary ledgers, and technology-based systems.

A Look at This Chapter

This chapter extends our study of accounting to internal control and the analysis of cash. We describe procedures that are good for internal control. We also explain the control of and the accounting for cash, including control features of banking activities.

A Look Ahead

Chapter 9 focuses on receivables. We explain how to account and report on receivables and their related accounts. This includes estimating uncollectible receivables and computing interest earned.

Learning Objectives

CONCEPTUAL

C1 Define internal control and identify its purpose and principles. (p. 318)

C2 Define cash and cash equivalents and explain how to report them. (p. 323)

ANALYTICAL

A1 Compute the days' sales uncollected ratio and use it to assess liquidity. (p. 337)

PROCEDURAL

P1 Apply internal control to cash receipts and disbursements. (p. 324)

P2 Explain and record petty cash fund transactions. (p. 328)

P3 Prepare a bank reconciliation. (p. 333)

P4 *Appendix 8A*—Describe the use of documentation and verification to control cash disbursements. (p. 340)

P5 *Appendix 8B—Apply the net method to control purchase discounts.* (p. 343)

Decision Insight

Cheese Wiz

"Entrepreneurship is the antithesis of stability."
—MICHAEL INWALD

BOSTON—Michael Inwald did his research: 2.2 billion grilled cheese sandwiches are consumed by Americans each year. His conclusion: The country is one big cheeseball! Given the cheese wiz he is, Michael, known to his friends as *Cheeseboy*, opened a fast-food grilled cheese take-out joint named **CHEESEBOY (CheeseBoy.com).** "I'm somewhat obsessed with cheese!" admits Michael. That obsession has led to several CHEESEBOY locations, and he is readying for a national franchise program.

"Giving our customers an amazing grilled cheese experience, all-around, is very critical to us," insists Michael. He currently offers customers a grilled cheese experience with four bread options, five cheese options, and a range of toppings. He also provides the classic tomato soup combo, along with other soup options. "The most challenging part of my business is . . . to create the perfect experience," explains Michael.

Although the grilled cheese experience is key to his success, Michael's management of internal controls and cash is equally impressive. Several control procedures monitor business activities and safeguard assets. An example is his inventory control system. Explains Michael, quality ingredients are crucial to

customer satisfaction, and monitoring controls ensure the quality of his ingredients. Similar controls are applied throughout his store. Michael explains that such controls raise productivity, cut expenses, and enhance the customer experience.

His store's cash management practices are equally impressive, including controls over cash receipts, disbursements, and petty cash. The use of bank reconciliations further helps with his store's control and management of cash. "Take basic accounting," explains Michael, "I was able to say, 'I'm going to need to know how to balance my books.'" Michael explains that he takes advantage of available banking services to enhance controls over cash.

Internal controls are crucial when on a busy day his stores bring in thousands of customers, and their cash. "We have put the infrastructure in place to ensure that (the growth) goes as smoothly as possible," explains Michael. "We're definitely going to be moving at what feels like light speed."

[Sources: *CHEESEBOY Website,* January 2013; *CNNMoney,* July 2011; *BOLDFACERS,* August 2011; *The Patriot Ledger,* November 2011; *Boston Business Journal,* December 2011; *The New Journal,* February 2012.]

We all are aware of theft and fraud. They affect us in several ways: We lock doors, chain bikes, review credit card statements, and acquire alarm systems. A company also takes actions to safeguard, control, and manage what it owns. Experience tells us that small companies are most vulnerable, usually due to weak internal controls. It is management's responsibility to set up policies and procedures to safeguard a company's assets, especially cash. To do so, management *and* employees must understand and apply principles of internal control. This chapter describes these principles and how to apply them. It focuses special attention on cash because it is easily transferable and is often at high risk of loss.

Cash and Internal Controls

Internal Control
- Purpose of controls
- Principles of controls
- Technology and controls
- Limitations of controls

Control of Cash
- Cash, cash equivalents, and liquidity
- Control of receipts
- Control of disbursements

Banking Activities as Controls
- Basic bank services
- Bank statement
- Bank reconciliation

INTERNAL CONTROL

This section describes internal control and its fundamental principles. We also discuss the impact of technology on internal control and the limitations of control procedures.

Purpose of Internal Control

C1 Define internal control and identify its purpose and principles.

Managers (or owners) of small businesses often control the entire operation. These managers usually purchase all assets, hire and manage employees, negotiate all contracts, and sign all checks. They know from personal contact and observation whether the business is actually receiving the assets and services paid for. Most companies, however, cannot maintain this close personal supervision. They must delegate responsibilities and rely on formal procedures rather than personal contact in controlling business activities.

Internal Control System Managers use an internal control system to monitor and control business activities. An **internal control system** consists of the policies and procedures managers use to

- Protect assets.
- Ensure reliable accounting.
- Promote efficient operations.
- Urge adherence to company policies.

A properly designed internal control system is a key part of systems design, analysis, and performance. Managers place a high priority on internal control systems because they can prevent avoidable losses, help managers plan operations, and monitor company and employee performance. For example, internal controls for health care must protect patient records and privacy. Internal controls do not provide guarantees, but they lower the company's risk of loss.

Sarbanes-Oxley Act (SOX) The **Sarbanes-Oxley Act (SOX)** requires the managers and auditors of companies whose stock is traded on an exchange (called *public companies*) to document and certify the system of internal controls. Following are some of the specific requirements:

- Auditors must evaluate internal controls and issue an internal control report.
- Auditors of a client are restricted as to what consulting services they can provide that client.
- The person leading an audit can serve no more than seven years without a two-year break.
- Auditors' work is overseen by the *Public Company Accounting Oversight Board* (PCAOB).
- Harsh penalties exist for violators—sentences up to 25 years in prison with severe fines.

SOX has markedly impacted companies, and the costs of its implementation are high. Importantly, **Section 404** of SOX requires that managers document and assess the effectiveness of all internal control processes that can impact financial reporting. The benefits include greater confidence in accounting systems and their related reports. However, the public continues to debate the costs versus the benefits of SOX as nearly all business activities of these companies are impacted by SOX. Section 404 of SOX requires that managers document and assess their internal controls *and* that auditors provide an opinion on managers' documentation and assessment. Costs of complying with Section 404 for companies is reported to average $4 million (source: Financial Executives Institute).

Principles of Internal Control

Internal control policies and procedures vary from company to company according to such factors as the nature of the business and its size. Certain fundamental internal control principles apply to all companies. The **principles of internal control** are to

1. Establish responsibilities.
2. Maintain adequate records.
3. Insure assets and bond key employees.
4. Separate recordkeeping from custody of assets.
5. Divide responsibility for related transactions.
6. Apply technological controls.
7. Perform regular and independent reviews.

...a control system is only as strong as its weakest link

This section explains these seven principles and describes how internal control procedures minimize the risk of fraud and theft. These procedures also increase the reliability and accuracy of accounting records. A framework for how these seven principles improve the quality of financial reporting is provided by the **Committee of Sponsoring Organizations (COSO)** (**www.COSO.org**). Specifically, these principles link to five aspects of internal control: control activities, control environment, risk assessment, monitoring, and communication.

Point: Sarbanes-Oxley Act (SOX) requires that each annual report contain an *internal control report,* which must: (1) state managers' responsibility for establishing and maintaining adequate internal controls for financial reporting; and (2) assess the effectiveness of those controls.

Establish Responsibilities Proper internal control means that responsibility for a task is clearly established and assigned to one person. When a problem occurs in a company where responsibility is not identified, determining who is at fault is difficult. For instance, if two sales-clerks share the same cash register and there is a cash shortage, neither clerk can be held accountable. To prevent this problem, one clerk might be given responsibility for handling all cash sales. Alternately, a company can use a register with separate cash drawers for each clerk. Most of us have waited at a retail counter during a shift change while employees swap cash drawers.

Point: Many companies have a mandatory vacation policy for employees who handle cash. When another employee must cover for the one on vacation, it is more difficult to hide cash frauds.

Maintain Adequate Records Good recordkeeping is part of an internal control system. It helps protect assets and ensures that employees use prescribed procedures. Reliable records are also a source of information that managers use to monitor company activities. When detailed records of equipment are kept, for instance, items are unlikely to be lost or stolen without detection. Similarly, transactions are less likely to be entered in wrong accounts if a chart of accounts is set up and carefully used. Many preprinted forms and internal documents are also designed for use in a good internal control system. When sales slips are properly designed, for instance, sales personnel can record needed information efficiently with less chance of errors or delays to customers. When sales slips are prenumbered and controlled, each one issued is the responsibility of one salesperson, preventing the salesperson from pocketing cash by making a sale and destroying the sales slip. Computerized point-of-sale systems achieve the same control results.

Insure Assets and Bond Key Employees Good internal control means that assets are adequately insured against casualty and that employees handling large amounts of cash and easily transferable assets are bonded. An employee is *bonded* when a company purchases an insurance policy, or a bond, against losses from theft by that employee. Bonding reduces the risk of loss. It also discourages theft because bonded employees know an independent bonding company will be involved when theft is uncovered and is unlikely to be sympathetic with an employee involved in theft. (A common question on job applications is whether you are bonded or bondable.)

■ **Decision** Insight ━━━━━━━━━━━━━━━━━━━━━━━━━━━━━━━━━━━━▶

Tagging Assets   A novel technique exists for marking physical assets. It involves embedding a less than one-inch-square tag of fibers that creates a unique optical signature recordable by scanners. Manufacturers hope to embed tags in everything from compact discs and credit cards to designer clothes for purposes of internal control and efficiency. ■

Point: The Association of Certified Fraud Examiners (**acfe.com**) estimates that employee fraud costs small companies more than $100,000 per incident.

Separate Recordkeeping from Custody of Assets
A person who controls or has access to an asset must not keep that asset's accounting records. This principle reduces the risk of theft or waste of an asset because the person with control over it knows that another person keeps its records. Also, a recordkeeper who does not have access to the asset has no reason to falsify records. This means that to steal an asset and hide the theft from the records, two or more people must *collude*—or agree in secret to commit the fraud. Some payroll cash checking services require fingerprint ID before the payroll check is cashed.

Divide Responsibility for Related Transactions
Good internal control divides responsibility for a transaction or a series of related transactions between two or more individuals or departments. This is to ensure that the work of one individual acts as a check on the other. This principle, often called *separation of duties,* is not a call for duplication of work. Each employee or department should perform unduplicated effort. Examples of transactions with divided responsibility are placing purchase orders, receiving merchandise, and paying vendors. These tasks should not be given to one individual or department. Assigning responsibility for two or more of these tasks to one party increases mistakes and perhaps fraud. Having an independent person, for example, check incoming goods for quality and quantity encourages more care and attention to detail than having the person who placed the order do the checking. Added protection can result from identifying a third person to approve payment of the invoice. A company can even designate a fourth person with authority to write checks as another protective measure.

Point: There's a new security device—a person's ECG (electrocardiogram) reading—that is as unique as a fingerprint and a lot harder to lose or steal than a PIN. ECGs can be read through fingertip touches. An ECG also shows that a living person is actually there, whereas fingerprint and facial recognition software can be fooled.

Apply Technological Controls
Cash registers, check protectors, time clocks, and personal identification scanners are examples of devices that can improve internal control. Technology often improves the effectiveness of controls. A cash register with a locked-in tape or electronic file makes a record of each cash sale. A check protector perforates the amount of a check into its face and makes it difficult to alter the amount. A time clock registers the exact time an employee both arrives at and departs from the job. Mechanical change and currency counters quickly and accurately count amounts, and personal scanners limit access to only authorized individuals. Each of these and other technological controls are an effective part of many internal control systems. Some companies video record workers as they clock in and out, which discourages them from clocking in or out for others.

■ **Decision** Insight ━━━━━━━━━━━━━━━━━━━━━━━━━━━━━━━━━

Face Reading   Face-recognition software snaps a digital picture of the face and converts key facial features—say, the distance between the eyes—into a series of numerical values. These can be stored on an ID or ATM card as a simple bar code to prohibit unauthorized access. ■

Perform Regular and Independent Reviews
Changes in personnel, stress of time pressures, and technological advances present opportunities for shortcuts and lapses. To counter these factors, regular reviews of internal control systems are needed to ensure that procedures are followed. These reviews are preferably done by internal auditors not directly involved in the activities. Their impartial perspective encourages an evaluation of the efficiency as well as the effectiveness of the internal control system. Many companies also pay for audits by independent, external auditors. These external auditors test the company's financial records to give an opinion as to whether its financial statements are presented fairly. Before external auditors decide on how much testing is needed, they evaluate the effectiveness of the internal control system. This evaluation is often helpful to a client. Independent, external audits are usually performed by auditors who work for public accounting firms.

Point: COSO organizes control components into five types:
- Control environment
- Control activities
- Risk assessment
- Monitoring
- Information and communication

■ Decision Maker

Entrepreneur   As owner of a start-up information services company, you hire a systems analyst. The analyst sees that your company only employs two workers. She recommends you improve controls and says that as owner you must serve as a compensating control. What does the analyst mean? ■   [Answer—p. 345]

Technology and Internal Control

The fundamental principles of internal control are relevant no matter what the technological state of the accounting system, from purely manual to fully automated systems. Technology impacts an internal control system in several important ways. Perhaps the most obvious is that technology allows us quicker access to databases and information. Used effectively, technology greatly improves managers' abilities to monitor and control business activities. This section describes some technological impacts we must be alert to.

Reduced Processing Errors   Technologically advanced systems reduce the number of errors in processing information. Provided the software and data entry are correct, the risk of mechanical and mathematical errors is nearly eliminated. However, we must remember that erroneous software or data entry does exist. Also, less human involvement in data processing can cause data entry errors to go undiscovered. Moreover, errors in software can produce consistent but erroneous processing of transactions. Continually checking and monitoring all types of systems are important.

More Extensive Testing of Records   A company's review and audit of electronic records can include more extensive testing when information is easily and rapidly accessed. When accounting records are kept manually, auditors and others likely select only small samples of data to test. When data are accessible with computer technology, however, auditors can quickly analyze large samples or even the entire database.

Limited Evidence of Processing   Many data processing steps are increasingly done by computer. Accordingly, fewer hard-copy items of documentary evidence are available for review. Yet technologically advanced systems can provide new evidence. They can, for instance, record who made the entries, the date and time, the source of the entry, and so on. Technology can also be designed to require the use of passwords or other identification before access to the system is granted. This means that internal control depends more on the design and operation of the information system and less on the analysis of its resulting documents.

Crucial Separation of Duties   Technological advances in accounting information systems often yield some job eliminations or consolidations. While those who remain have the special skills necessary to operate advanced programs and equipment, a company with a reduced workforce risks losing its crucial separation of duties. The company must establish ways to control and monitor employees to minimize risk of error and fraud. For instance, the person who designs and programs the information system must not be the one who operates it. The company must also separate control over programs and files from the activities related to cash receipts and disbursements. For instance, a computer operator should not control check-writing activities. Achieving acceptable separation of duties can be especially difficult and costly in small companies with few employees.

Increased E-Commerce   Technology has encouraged the growth of e-commerce. **Amazon.com** and **eBay** are examples of companies that have successfully exploited e-commerce. Most companies have some e-commerce transactions. All such transactions involve at least three risks. (1) *Credit card number theft* is a risk of using, transmitting, and storing such data online. This increases the cost of e-commerce. (2) *Computer viruses* are malicious programs that attach themselves to innocent files for purposes of infecting and harming other files and programs. (3) *Impersonation* online can result in charges of sales to bogus accounts, purchases of inappropriate materials, and the unknowing giving up of confidential information to hackers. Companies use both firewalls and encryption to

Point: Information on Internet fraud can be found at these Websites: **sec.gov/investor/pubs/cyberfraud.htm ftc.gov/bcp/consumer.shtm www.fraud.org**

Point: Evidence of any internal control failure for a company reduces user confidence in its financial statements.

Point: We look to several sources when assessing a company's internal controls. Sources include the auditor's report, management report on controls (if available), management discussion and analysis, and financial press.

"Worst case of identity theft I've ever seen!"

Copyright 2004 by Randy Glasbergen. www.glasbergen.com

combat some of these risks—firewalls are points of entry to a system that require passwords to continue, and encryption is a mathematical process to rearrange contents that cannot be read without the process code. Nearly 5% of Americans already report being victims of identity theft, and roughly 10 million say their privacy has been compromised.

■ **Decision** Insight

Winnings and Controls   Certified Fraud Examiners Website reports the following: Andrew Cameron stole Jacqueline Boanson's credit card. Cameron headed to the racetrack and promptly charged two bets for $150 on the credit card—winning $400. Unfortunately for Cameron the racetrack refused to pay him cash as its internal control policy is to credit winnings from bets made on a credit card to that same card. Cameron was later nabbed; and the racetrack let Ms. Boanson keep the winnings. ■

Limitations of Internal Control

All internal control policies and procedures have limitations that usually arise from either (1) the human element or (2) the cost–benefit principle.

Internal control policies and procedures are applied by people. This human element creates several potential limitations that we can categorize as either (1) human error or (2) human fraud. *Human error* can occur from negligence, fatigue, misjudgment, or confusion. *Human fraud* involves intent by people to defeat internal controls, such as *management override,* for personal gain. Fraud also includes collusion to thwart the separation of duties. The human element highlights the importance of establishing an *internal control environment* to convey management's commitment to internal control policies and procedures. Human fraud is driven by the *triple-threat* of fraud:

- **Opportunity**—refers to internal control deficiencies in the workplace.
- **Pressure**—refers to financial, family, society, and other stresses to succeed.
- **Rationalization**—refers to employees justifying fraudulent behavior.

The second major limitation on internal control is the *cost–benefit principle,* which dictates that the costs of internal controls must not exceed their benefits. Analysis of costs and benefits must consider all factors, including the impact on morale. Most companies, for instance, have a legal right to read employees' e-mails, yet companies seldom exercise that right unless they are confronted with evidence of potential harm to the company. The same holds for drug testing, phone tapping, and hidden cameras. The bottom line is that managers must establish internal control policies and procedures with a net benefit to the company.

Point: Cybercrime.gov pursues computer and intellectual property crimes, including that of e-commerce.

Hacker's Guide to Cyberspace

Pharming Viruses attached to e-mails and Websites load software onto your PC that monitors keystrokes; when you sign on to financial Websites, it steals your passwords.

Phishing Hackers send e-mails to you posing as banks; you are asked for information using fake Websites where they reel in your passwords and personal data.

WI-Phishing Cybercrooks set up wireless networks hoping you use them to connect to the Web; your passwords and data are stolen as you use their network.

Bot-Networking Hackers send remote-control programs to your PC that take control to send out spam and viruses; they even rent your bot to other cybercrooks.

Typo-Squatting Hackers set up Websites with addresses similar to legit outfits; when you make a typo and hit their sites, they infect your PC with viruses or take them over as bots.

Hackers also have their own self-identification system...
- *Hackers,* or *external attackers,* crack systems and take data for illicit gains (as unauthorized users).
- *Rogue insiders,* or *internal attackers,* crack systems and take data for illicit gains or revenge (as authorized users).
- *Ethical hackers,* or *good-guys* or *white-hat hackers,* crack systems and reveal vulnerabilities to enhance controls.
- *Crackers,* or *criminal hackers,* crack systems illegally for illicit gains, fame, or revenge.

Decision Insight

Ball Control   Ryan Braun of the Milwaukee Brewers won an appeal of a 50-game Major League Baseball (MLB) suspension for a positive drug test. Ryan maintained that MLB did not maintain control over his sample through the testing process and raised the risk that his sample was tainted. This control failure led to dismissal of that particular test result and him winning the appeal. Controls are crucial when people's livelihoods and reputations are on the line. ■

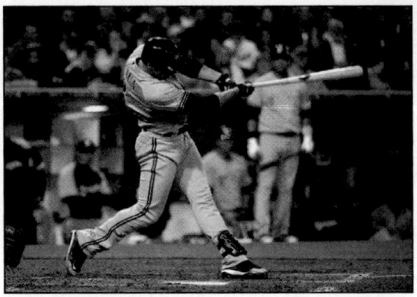

Quick Check   Answers — p. 345

1. Principles of internal control suggest that (choose one): (*a*) Responsibility for a series of related transactions (such as placing orders, receiving and paying for merchandise) should be assigned to one employee; (*b*) Responsibility for individual tasks should be shared by more than one employee so that one serves as a check on the other; or (*c*) Employees who handle considerable cash and easily transferable assets should be bonded.
2. What are some impacts of computing technology on internal control?
3. Many companies require each employee to take at least one week (five consecutive days) of vacation per year. Why is a "forced vacation" policy good for internal control?

CONTROL OF CASH

Cash is a necessary asset of every company. Most companies also own *cash equivalents* (defined below), which are assets similar to cash. Cash and cash equivalents are the most liquid of all assets and are easily hidden and moved. Cash is also the most desired asset as other assets must be *fenced* (sold in a secondary market). An effective system of internal controls protects cash assets and it should meet three basic guidelines:

1. Handling cash is separate from recordkeeping of cash.
2. Cash receipts are promptly deposited in a bank.
3. Cash disbursements are made by check.

The first guideline applies separation of duties to minimize errors and fraud. When duties are separated, two or more people must collude to steal cash and conceal this action in the accounting records. The second guideline uses immediate (say, daily) deposits of all cash receipts to produce a timely independent record of the cash received. It also reduces the likelihood of cash theft (or loss) and the risk that an employee could personally use the money before depositing it. The third guideline uses payments by check to develop an independent bank record of cash disbursements. This guideline also reduces the risk of cash theft (or loss).

This section begins with definitions of cash and cash equivalents. Discussion then focuses on controls and accounting for both cash receipts and disbursements. The exact procedures used to achieve control over cash vary across companies. They depend on factors such as company size, number of employees, volume of cash transactions, and sources of cash.

Cash, Cash Equivalents, and Liquidity

Good accounting systems help in managing the amount of cash and controlling who has access to it. Cash is the usual means of payment when paying for assets, services, or liabilities. **Liquidity** refers to a company's ability to pay for its near-term obligations. Cash and similar assets are called **liquid assets** because they can be readily used to settle such obligations. A company needs liquid assets to effectively operate.

Cash includes currency and coins along with the amounts on deposit in bank accounts, checking accounts (called *demand deposits*), and many savings accounts (called *time deposits*). Cash also

C2   Define cash and cash equivalents and explain how to report them.

includes items that are acceptable for deposit in these accounts such as customer checks, cashier's checks, certified checks, and money orders. **Cash equivalents** are short-term, highly liquid investment assets meeting two criteria: (1) readily convertible to a known cash amount and (2) sufficiently close to their due date so that their market value is not sensitive to interest rate changes. Only investments purchased within three months of their due date usually satisfy these criteria. Examples of cash equivalents are short-term investments in assets such as U.S. Treasury bills and money market funds. To increase their return, many companies invest idle cash in cash equivalents. Most companies combine cash equivalents with cash as a single item on the balance sheet.

Cash Management

When companies fail, one of the most common causes is their inability to manage cash. Companies must plan both cash receipts and cash payments. The goals of cash management are twofold:

1. Plan cash receipts to meet cash payments when due.
2. Keep a minimum level of cash necessary to operate.

The *treasurer* of the company is responsible for cash management. Effective cash management involves applying the following cash management principles.

- **Encourage collection of receivables.** The more quickly customers and others pay the company, the more quickly that company can use the money. Some companies have cash-only sales policies. Others might offer discounts for payments received early.
- **Delay payment of liabilities.** The more delayed a company is in paying others, the more time it has to use the money. Some companies regularly wait to pay their bills until the last possible day allowed—although, a company must take care not to hurt its credit standing.
- **Keep only necessary levels of assets.** The less money tied up in idle assets, the more money to invest in productive assets. Some companies maintain *just-in-time* inventory; meaning they plan inventory to be available at the same time orders are filled. Others might lease out excess warehouse space or rent equipment instead of buying it.
- **Plan expenditures.** Money should be spent only when it is available. Companies must look at seasonal and business cycles to plan expenditures.
- **Invest excess cash.** Excess cash earns no return and should be invested. Excess cash from seasonal cycles can be placed in a bank account or other short-term investment for income. Excess cash beyond what's needed for regular business should be invested in productive assets like factories and inventories.

 Decision Insight

Days' Cash Expense Coverage The ratio of *cash (and cash equivalents) to average daily cash expenses* indicates the number of days a company can operate without additional cash inflows. It reflects on company liquidity and on the potential of excess cash. ■

Control of Cash Receipts

 P1 Apply internal control to cash receipts and disbursements.

Internal control of cash receipts ensures that cash received is properly recorded and deposited. Cash receipts can arise from transactions such as cash sales, collections of customer accounts, receipts of interest earned, bank loans, sales of assets, and owner investments. This section explains internal control over two important types of cash receipts: over-the-counter and by mail.

Over-the-Counter Cash Receipts For purposes of internal control, over-the-counter cash receipts from sales should be recorded on a cash register at the time of each sale. To help ensure that correct amounts are entered, each register should be located so customers can read the amounts entered. Clerks also should be required to enter each sale before wrapping merchandise and to give the customer a receipt for each sale. The design of each cash register should provide a permanent, locked-in record of each transaction. In many systems, the register is directly linked with computing and accounting services. Less advanced registers simply print a record of each transaction on a paper tape or electronic file locked inside the register.

Proper internal control prescribes that custody over cash should be separate from its recordkeeping. For over-the-counter cash receipts, this separation begins with the cash sale. The clerk who has access to cash in the register should not have access to its locked-in record. At the end of the clerk's work period, the clerk should count the cash in the register, record the amount, and turn over the cash and a record of its amount to the company cashier. The cashier, like the clerk, has access to the cash but should not have access to accounting records (or the register tape or file). A third employee, often a supervisor, compares the record of total register transactions (or the register tape or file) with the cash receipts reported by the cashier. This record is the basis for a journal entry recording over-the-counter cash receipts. The third employee has access to the records for cash but not to the actual cash. The clerk and the cashier have access to cash but not to the accounting records. None of them can make a mistake or divert cash without the difference being revealed—see the following diagram.

Point: Convenience stores sometimes display a sign: *Cashier has no access to cash in locked floor (or wall) safe.* Such signs help thwart theft and holdups because of lack of access to the floor (or wall) safe.

Sales Department

Clerk rings up cash sales on register; clerk prepares cash count sheet (and keeps copy) and sends to company cashier along with the cash

Supervisor reads register data, prepares register sheet (and keeps copy), and sends both to company cashier

Cashier Department

Cashier prepares cash records, deposit slip, and journal entry

Cash over and short.   Sometimes errors in making change are discovered from differences between the cash in a cash register and the record of the amount of cash receipts. Although a clerk is careful, one or more customers can be given too much or too little change. This means that at the end of a work period, the cash in a cash register might not equal the record of cash receipts. This difference is reported in the **Cash Over and Short** account, also called *Cash Short and Over,* which is an income statement account recording the income effects of cash overages and cash shortages. To illustrate, if a cash register's record shows $550 but the count of cash in the register is $555, the entry to record cash sales and its overage is

Point: Retailers often require cashiers to restrictively endorse checks immediately on receipt by stamping them "For deposit only."

Cash	555	
Cash Over and Short		5
Sales		550
To record cash sales and a cash overage.		

Assets = Liabilities + Equity
+555   + 5
               +550

On the other hand, if a cash register's record shows $625 but the count of cash in the register is $621, the entry to record cash sales and its shortage is

Cash	621	
Cash Over and Short	4	
Sales		625
To record cash sales and a cash shortage.		

Assets = Liabilities + Equity
+621   − 4
               +625

Since customers are more likely to dispute being shortchanged than being given too much change, the Cash Over and Short account usually has a debit balance at the end of an accounting period. A debit balance reflects an expense. It is reported on the income statement as part of general and administrative expenses. (Since the amount is usually small, it is often combined

Point: Merchants begin a business day with a *change fund* in their cash register. The accounting for a change fund is similar to that for petty cash, including that for cash shortages or overages.

with other small expenses and reported as part of *miscellaneous expenses*—or as part of *miscellaneous revenues* if it has a credit balance.)

Cash Receipts by Mail   Control of cash receipts that arrive through the mail starts with the person who opens the mail. Preferably, two people are assigned the task of, and are present for, opening the mail. In this case, theft of cash receipts by mail requires collusion between these two employees. Specifically, the person(s) opening the mail enters a list (in triplicate) of money received. This list should contain a record of each sender's name, the amount, and an explanation of why the money is sent. The first copy is sent with the money to the cashier. A second copy is sent to the recordkeeper in the accounting area. A third copy is kept by the clerk(s) who opened the mail. The cashier deposits the money in a bank, and the recordkeeper records the amounts received in the accounting records.

Point: Collusion implies that two or more individuals are knowledgeable or involved with the activities of the other(s).

This process reflects good internal control. That is, when the bank balance is reconciled by another person (explained later in the chapter), errors or acts of fraud by the mail clerks, the cashier, or the recordkeeper are revealed. They are revealed because the bank's record of cash deposited must agree with the records from each of the three. Moreover, if the mail clerks do not report all receipts correctly, customers will question their account balances. If the cashier does not deposit all receipts, the bank balance does not agree with the recordkeeper's cash balance. The recordkeeper and the person who reconciles the bank balance do not have access to cash and therefore have no opportunity to divert cash to themselves. This system makes errors and fraud highly unlikely. The exception is employee collusion.

Decision Insight

Perpetual Accounting   **Walmart** uses a network of information links with its point-of-sale cash registers to coordinate sales, purchases, and distribution. Its supercenters, for instance, ring up 15,000 separate sales on heavy days. By using cash register information, the company can fix pricing mistakes quickly and capitalize on sales trends. Interestingly, Sam Walton, the founder, was a self-described distruster of computers. ■

Control of Cash Disbursements

Control of cash disbursements is especially important as most large thefts occur from payment of fictitious invoices. One key to controlling cash disbursements is to require all expenditures to be made by check. The only exception is small payments made from petty cash. Another key is to deny access to the accounting records to anyone other than the owner who has the authority to sign checks. A small business owner often signs checks and knows from personal contact that the items being paid for are actually received. This arrangement is impossible in large businesses. Instead, internal control procedures must be substituted for personal contact. Such procedures are designed to assure the check signer that the obligations recorded are properly incurred and should be paid. This section describes these and other internal control procedures, including the voucher system and petty cash system. A method for management of cash disbursements for purchases is described in Appendix 8B.

Cash Budget   Projected cash receipts and cash disbursements are often summarized in a *cash budget*. Provided that sufficient cash exists for effective operations, companies wish to minimize the cash they hold because of its risk of theft and its low return versus other investment opportunities.

Decision Insight

Lock Box   Some companies do not receive cash in the mail but, instead, elect to have customers send deposits directly to the bank using a *lock box* system. Bank employees are charged with receipting the cash and depositing it in the correct business bank account. ■

Voucher System of Control   A **voucher system** is a set of procedures and approvals designed to control cash disbursements and the acceptance of obligations. The voucher system of control establishes procedures for

- Verifying, approving, and recording obligations for eventual cash disbursement.
- Issuing checks for payment of verified, approved, and recorded obligations.

A reliable voucher system follows standard procedures for every transaction. This applies even when multiple purchases are made from the same supplier.

A voucher system's control over cash disbursements begins when a company incurs an obligation that will result in payment of cash. A key factor in this system is that only approved departments and individuals are authorized to incur such obligations. The system often limits the type of obligations that a department or individual can incur. In a large retail store, for instance, only a purchasing department should be authorized to incur obligations for merchandise inventory. Another key factor is that procedures for purchasing, receiving, and paying for merchandise are divided among several departments (or individuals). These departments include the one requesting the purchase, the purchasing department, the receiving department, and the accounting department. To coordinate and control responsibilities of these departments, a company uses several different business documents. Exhibit 8.1 shows how documents are accumulated in a **voucher,** which is an internal document (or file) used to accumulate information to control cash disbursements and to ensure that a transaction is properly recorded. This specific example begins with a *purchase requisition* and concludes with a *check* drawn against cash. Appendix 8A describes the documentation and verification necessary for a voucher system of control. It also describes the internal control objective served by each document.

Point: MCI, formerly **WorldCom,** paid a whopping $500 million in SEC fines for accounting fraud. Among the charges were that it inflated earnings by as much as $10 billion. Its CEO, Bernard Ebbers, was sentenced to 25 years.

Sender		Receiver(s)
Cashier	→	Supplier (vendor)
Accounting	→	Cashier
Receiving	→	Accounting; Requesting; and Purchasing
Supplier (vendor)	→	Accounting
Purchasing	→	Supplier; Requesting; Receiving; and Accounting
Requesting	→	Purchasing; and Accounting

EXHIBIT 8.1

Document Flow in a Voucher System

A voucher system should be applied not only to purchases of inventory but to all expenditures. To illustrate, when a company receives a monthly telephone bill, it should review and verify the charges, prepare a voucher (file), and insert the bill. This transaction is then recorded with a journal entry. If the amount is currently due, a check is issued. If not, the voucher is filed for payment on its due date. If no voucher is prepared, verifying the invoice and its amount after several days or weeks can be difficult. Also, without records, a dishonest employee could collude with a dishonest supplier to get more than one payment for an obligation, payment for excessive amounts, or payment for goods and services not received. An effective voucher system helps prevent such frauds.

Point: A *voucher* is an internal document (or file).

Point: The basic purposes of paper and electronic documents are similar. However, the internal control system must change to reflect different risks, including confidential and competitive-sensitive information that is at greater risk in electronic systems.

■ Decision Insight ▶

Cyber Setup   The FTC is on the cutting edge of cybersleuthing. Opportunists in search of easy money are lured to **WeMarket4U. net/SundaeStation** and **WeMarket4U.net/FatFoe**. Take the bait and you get warned. The top 5 fraud complaints as compiled by the Federal Trade Commission are shown to the right. ■

P2 Explain and record petty cash fund transactions.

Petty Cash System of Control   A basic principle for controlling cash disbursements is that all payments must be made by check. An exception to this rule is made for *petty cash disbursements,* which are the small payments required for items such as postage, courier fees, minor repairs, and low-cost supplies. To avoid the time and cost of writing checks for small amounts, a company sets up a petty cash fund to make small payments. (**Petty cash** activities are part of an *imprest system,* which designates advance money to establish the fund, to withdraw from the fund, and to reimburse the fund.)

Operating a petty cash fund.   Establishing a petty cash fund requires estimating the total amount of small payments likely to be made during a short period such as a week or month. A check is then drawn by the company cashier for an amount slightly in excess of this estimate. This check is recorded with a debit to the Petty Cash account (an asset) and a credit to Cash. The check is cashed, and the currency is given to an employee designated as the *petty cashier* or *petty cash custodian.* The petty cashier is responsible for keeping this cash safe, making payments from the fund, and keeping records of it in a secure place referred to as the *petty cashbox.*

When each cash disbursement is made, the person receiving payment should sign a prenumbered *petty cash receipt,* also called *petty cash ticket*—see Exhibit 8.2. The petty cash receipt is then placed in the petty cashbox with the remaining money. Under this system, the sum of all receipts plus the remaining cash equals the total fund amount. A $100 petty cash fund, for instance, contains any combination of cash and petty cash receipts that totals $100 (examples are $80 cash plus $20 in receipts, or $10 cash plus $90 in receipts). Each disbursement reduces cash and increases the amount of receipts in the petty cashbox.

Point: A petty cash fund is used only for business expenses.

EXHIBIT 8.2

Petty Cash Receipt

Z-Mart   No. 9
PETTY CASH RECEIPT

For _Freight charges_
Date _November 5, 2013_   Approved by _fl Gull_
Charge to _Merchandise Inventory_
Amount _$6.75_   Received by _Dl. Fll_

Point: Petty cash receipts with either no signature or a forged signature usually indicate misuse of petty cash. Companies respond with surprise petty cash counts for verification.

The petty cash fund should be reimbursed when it is nearing zero and at the end of an accounting period when financial statements are prepared. For this purpose, the petty cashier sorts the paid receipts by the type of expense or account and then totals the receipts. The petty cashier presents all paid receipts to the company cashier, who stamps all receipts *paid* so they cannot be reused, files them for recordkeeping, and gives the petty cashier a check for their sum. When this check is cashed and the money placed in the cashbox, the total money in the cashbox is restored to its original amount. The fund is now ready for a new cycle of petty cash payments.

Illustrating a petty cash fund.   To illustrate, assume Z-Mart establishes a petty cash fund on November 1 and designates one of its office employees as the petty cashier. A $75 check is drawn, cashed, and the proceeds given to the petty cashier. The entry to record the setup of this petty cash fund is

Nov. 1	Petty Cash	75	
	Cash		75
	To establish a petty cash fund.		

Assets = Liabilities + Equity
+75
−75

After the petty cash fund is established, the Petty Cash account is not debited or credited again unless the amount of the fund is changed. (A fund should be increased if it requires reimbursement too frequently. On the other hand, if the fund is too large, some of its money should be redeposited in the Cash account.)

Next, assume that Z-Mart's petty cashier makes several November payments from petty cash. Each person who received payment is required to sign a receipt. On November 27, after making a $26.50 cash payment for tile cleaning, only $3.70 cash remains in the fund. The petty cashier then summarizes and totals the petty cash receipts as shown in Exhibit 8.3.

Point: Reducing or eliminating a petty cash fund requires a credit to Petty Cash.

Point: Although *individual* petty cash disbursements are not evidenced by a check, the initial petty cash fund is evidenced by a check, and later petty cash expenditures are evidenced by a check to replenish them *in total.*

EXHIBIT 8.3

Petty Cash Payments Report

Z-MART
Petty Cash Payments Report

Miscellaneous Expenses
| Nov. 2 | Cleaning of LCD panels .... | $20.00 | |
| Nov. 27 | Tile cleaning .... | 26.50 | $ 46.50 |

Merchandise Inventory (transportation-in)
| Nov. 5 | Transport of merchandise purchased .... | 6.75 | |
| Nov. 20 | Transport of merchandise purchased .... | 8.30 | 15.05 |

Delivery Expense
| Nov. 18 | Customer's package delivered .... | | 5.00 |

Office Supplies Expense
| Nov. 15 | Purchase of office supplies immediately used .... | | 4.75 |
| **Total** .... | | | **$71.30** |

Point: This report can also include receipt number and names of those who approved and received cash payment (see Demo Problem 2).

The petty cash payments report and all receipts are given to the company cashier in exchange for a $71.30 check to reimburse the fund. The petty cashier cashes the check and puts the $71.30 cash in the petty cashbox. The company records this reimbursement as follows.

Nov. 27	Miscellaneous Expenses	46.50	
	Merchandise Inventory	15.05	
	Delivery Expense	5.00	
	Office Supplies Expense	4.75	
	Cash		71.30
	To reimburse petty cash.		

Assets = Liabilities + Equity
−71.30   −46.50
             −15.05
             − 5.00
             − 4.75

A petty cash fund is usually reimbursed at the end of an accounting period so that expenses are recorded in the proper period, even if the fund is not low on money. If the fund is not reimbursed at the end of a period, the financial statements would show both an overstated cash asset and understated expenses (or assets) that were paid out of petty cash. Some companies do not reimburse the petty cash fund at the end of each period under the notion that this amount is immaterial to users of financial statements.

Point: To avoid errors in recording petty cash reimbursement, follow these steps: (1) prepare payments report, (2) compute cash needed by subtracting cash remaining from total fund amount, (3) record entry, and (4) check "Dr. = Cr." in entry. Any difference is Cash Over and Short.

Increasing or decreasing a petty cash fund. A decision to increase or decrease a petty cash fund is often made when reimbursing it. To illustrate, assume Z-Mart decides to *increase* its petty cash fund from $75 to $100 on November 27 when it reimburses the fund. The entries required are to (1) reimburse the fund as usual (see the preceding November 27 entry) and (2) increase the fund amount as follows.

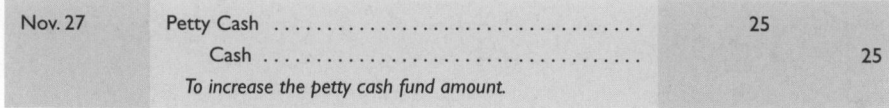

Nov. 27	Petty Cash	25	
	Cash		25
	To increase the petty cash fund amount.		

Alternatively, if Z-Mart *decreases* the petty cash fund from $75 to $55 on November 27, the entry is to (1) credit Petty Cash for $20 (decreasing the fund from $75 to $55) and (2) debit Cash for $20 (reflecting the $20 transfer from Petty Cash to Cash).

Cash over and short.   Sometimes a petty cashier fails to get a receipt for payment or overpays for the amount due. When this occurs and the fund is later reimbursed, the petty cash payments report plus the cash remaining will not total to the fund balance. This mistake causes the fund to be *short*. This shortage is recorded as an expense in the reimbursing entry with a debit to the Cash Over and Short account. (An overage in the petty cash fund is recorded with a credit to Cash Over and Short in the reimbursing entry.) To illustrate, prepare the June 1 entry to reimburse a $200 petty cash fund when its payments report shows $178 in miscellaneous expenses and $15 cash remains.

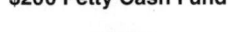

Summary of Petty Cash Accounting

Event	Petty Cash	Cash	Expenses
Set up fund	Dr.	Cr.	—
Reimburse fund..	—	Cr.	Dr.
Increase fund....	Dr.	Cr.	—
Decrease fund...	Cr.	Dr.	—

$200 Petty Cash Fund

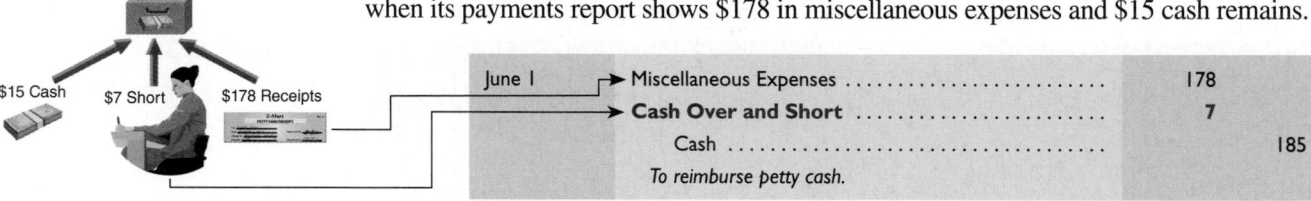

$15 Cash $7 Short $178 Receipts

June 1	➤ Miscellaneous Expenses	178	
	➤ **Cash Over and Short**	7	
	Cash		185
	To reimburse petty cash.		

 Decision Insight

Warning Signs   There are clues to internal control violations. Warning signs from accounting include (1) an increase in customer refunds—could be fake, (2) missing documents—could be used for fraud, (3) differences between bank deposits and cash receipts—could be cash embezzled, and (4) delayed recording—could reflect fraudulent records. Warning signs from employees include (1) lifestyle change—could be embezzlement, (2) too close with suppliers—could signal fraudulent transactions, and (3) failure to leave job, even for vacations—could conceal fraudulent activities. ■

Quick Check   Answers — p. 345

   9. Why are some cash payments made from a petty cash fund and not by check?
  10. Why should a petty cash fund be reimbursed at the end of an accounting period?
  11. Identify at least two results of reimbursing a petty cash fund.
  12. Assume that we are auditing a company for the first time. Our audit procedures for petty cash require a surprise audit of the petty cash fund. We approach the petty cash custodian to conduct the audit and she says: "I'm busy right now. Can we do this after lunch?" Do we accommodate the request?

BANKING ACTIVITIES AS CONTROLS

Banks (and other financial institutions) provide many services, including helping companies control cash. Banks safeguard cash, provide detailed and independent records of cash transactions, and are a source of cash financing. This section describes these services and the documents provided by banking activities that increase managers' control over cash.

Basic Bank Services

This section explains basic bank services—such as the bank account, the bank deposit, and checking—that contribute to the control of cash.

Bank Account, Deposit, and Check A *bank account* is a record set up by a bank for a customer. It permits a customer to deposit money for safekeeping and helps control withdrawals. To limit access to a bank account, all persons authorized to write checks on the account must sign a **signature card,** which bank employees use to verify signatures on checks. Many companies have more than one bank account to serve different needs and to handle special transactions such as payroll.

Each bank deposit is supported by a **deposit ticket,** which lists items such as currency, coins, and checks deposited along with their corresponding dollar amounts. The bank gives the customer a copy of the deposit ticket or a deposit receipt as proof of the deposit. Exhibit 8.4 shows one type of deposit ticket.

Point: Online banking services include the ability to stop payment on a check, move money between accounts, get up-to-date balances, and identify cleared checks and deposits.

EXHIBIT 8.4

Deposit Ticket

To withdraw money from an account, the depositor can use a **check,** which is a document signed by the depositor instructing the bank to pay a specified amount of money to a designated recipient. A check involves three parties: a *maker* who signs the check, a *payee* who is the recipient, and a *bank* (or *payer*) on which the check is drawn. The bank provides a depositor the checks that are serially numbered and imprinted with the name and address of both the depositor and bank. Both checks and deposit tickets are imprinted with identification codes in magnetic ink for computer processing. Exhibit 8.5 shows one type of check. It is accompanied with an optional *remittance advice* explaining the payment. When a remittance advice is unavailable, the *memo* line is often used for a brief explanation.

Electronic Funds Transfer **Electronic funds transfer (EFT)** is the electronic transfer of cash from one party to another. No paper documents are necessary. Banks simply transfer cash from one account to another with a journal entry. Companies are increasingly using EFT because of its convenience and low cost. For instance, it can cost up to 50 cents to process a check through the banking system, whereas EFT cost is near zero. We now commonly see items such as payroll, rent, utilities, insurance, and interest payments being handled by EFT. The bank statement lists cash withdrawals by EFT with the checks and other deductions. Cash receipts by EFT are listed with deposits and other additions. A bank statement is sometimes a depositor's only notice of an EFT. *Automated teller machines (ATMs)* are one form of EFT, which allows bank customers to deposit, withdraw, and transfer cash.

EXHIBIT 8.5

Check with Remittance Advice

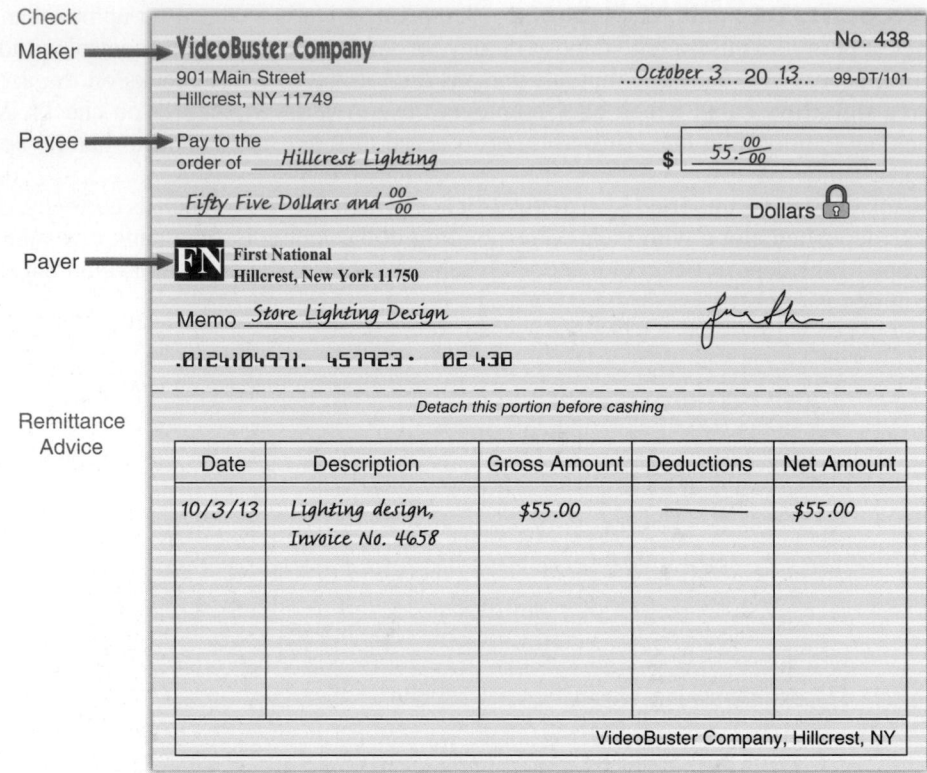

Check Maker ⟶

Payee ⟶

Payer ⟶

Remittance Advice

Bank Statement

Point: Good internal control is to deposit all cash receipts daily and make all payments for goods and services by check. This controls access to cash and creates an independent record of all cash activities.

Usually once a month, the bank sends each depositor a **bank statement** showing the activity in the account. Although a monthly statement is common, companies often regularly access information on their banking transactions. (Companies can choose to record any accounting adjustments required from the bank statement immediately or later, say, at the end of each day, week, month, or when reconciling a bank statement.) Different banks use different formats for their bank statements, but all of them include the following items of information:

1. Beginning-of-period balance of the depositor's account.
2. Checks and other debits decreasing the account during the period.
3. Deposits and other credits increasing the account during the period.
4. End-of-period balance of the depositor's account.

This information reflects the bank's records. Exhibit 8.6 shows one type of bank statement. Identify each of these four items in that statement. Part Ⓐ of Exhibit 8.6 summarizes changes in the account. Part Ⓑ lists paid checks along with other debits. Part Ⓒ lists deposits and credits to the account, and part Ⓓ shows the daily account balances.

In reading a bank statement note that a depositor's account is a liability on the bank's records. This is so because the money belongs to the depositor, not the bank. When a depositor increases the account balance, the bank records it with a *credit* to that liability account. This means that debit memos from the bank produce *credits* on the depositor's books, and credit memos from the bank produce *debits* on the depositor's books.

Enclosed with a bank statement is a list of the depositor's canceled checks (or the actual canceled checks) along with any debit or credit memoranda affecting the account. Increasingly, banks are showing canceled checks electronically via online access to accounts. **Canceled checks** are checks the bank has paid and deducted from the customer's account during the period. Other deductions that can appear on a bank statement include (1) service charges and fees assessed by the bank, (2) checks deposited that are uncollectible, (3) corrections of previous errors, (4) withdrawals through automated teller machines (ATMs), and (5) periodic payments arranged in advance by a depositor. (Most company checking accounts do not allow ATM withdrawals because of the company's desire to make all disbursements by check.) Except for service charges, the bank notifies the depositor of each deduction with a debit memorandum when the bank

Global: If cash is in more than one currency, a company usually translates these amounts into U.S. dollars using the exchange rate as of the balance sheet date. Also, a company must disclose any restrictions on cash accounts located outside the U.S.

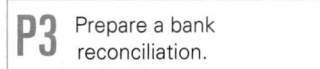

reduces the balance. A copy of each debit memorandum is usually sent with the statement (again, this information is often available earlier via online access and notifications).

Transactions that increase the depositor's account include amounts the bank collects on behalf of the depositor and the corrections of previous errors. Credit memoranda notify the depositor of all increases when they are recorded. A copy of each credit memorandum is often sent with the bank statement. Banks that pay interest on checking accounts often compute the amount of interest earned on the average cash balance and credit it to the depositor's account each period. In Exhibit 8.6, the bank credits $8.42 of interest to the account.

Bank Reconciliation

When a company deposits all cash receipts and makes all cash payments (except petty cash) by check, it can use the bank statement for proving the accuracy of its cash records. This is done using a **bank reconciliation,** which is a report explaining any differences between the checking account balance according to the depositor's records and the balance reported on the bank statement. The figure below reflects this process, which we describe in the following sections.

P3 Prepare a bank reconciliation.

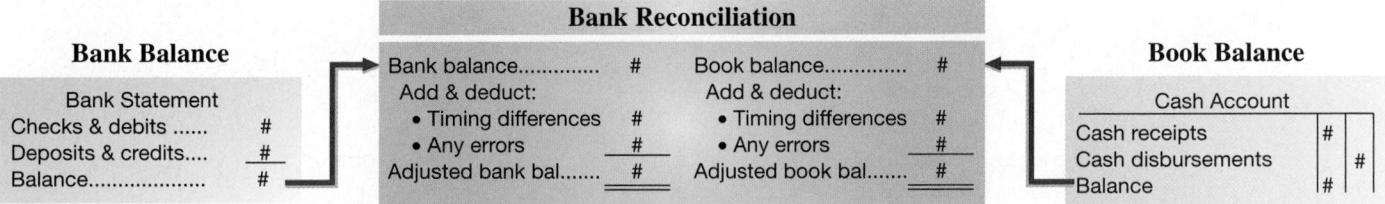

Purpose of Bank Reconciliation The balance of a checking account reported on the bank statement rarely equals the balance in the depositor's accounting records. This is usually due to information that one party has that the other does not. We must therefore prove the accuracy of both the depositor's records and those of the bank. This means we must *reconcile* the two balances and explain or account for any differences in them. Among the factors causing the bank statement balance to differ from the depositor's book balance are these:

- **Outstanding checks. Outstanding checks** are checks written (or drawn) by the depositor, deducted on the depositor's records, and sent to the payees but not yet received by the bank for payment at the bank statement date.

- **Deposits in transit** (also called **outstanding deposits**). **Deposits in transit** are deposits made and recorded by the depositor but not yet recorded on the bank statement. For example, companies can make deposits (in the night depository) at the end of a business day after the bank is closed. If such a deposit occurred on a bank statement date, it would not appear on this period's statement. The bank would record such a deposit on the next business day, and it would appear on the next period's bank statement. Deposits mailed to the bank near the end of a period also can be in transit and unrecorded when the statement is prepared.

- **Deductions for uncollectible items and for services.** A company sometimes deposits another party's check that is uncollectible (usually meaning the balance in that party's account is not large enough to cover the check). This check is called a *nonsufficient funds (NSF)* check. The bank would have initially credited the depositor's account for the amount of the check. When the bank learns the check is uncollectible, it debits (reduces) the depositor's account for the amount of that check. The bank may also charge the depositor a fee for processing an uncollectible check and notify the depositor of the deduction by sending a debit memorandum. The depositor should record each deduction when a debit memorandum is received, but an entry is sometimes not made until the bank reconciliation is prepared. Other possible bank charges to a depositor's account that are first reported on a bank statement include printing new checks and service fees.

- **Additions for collections and for interest.** Banks sometimes act as collection agents for their depositors by collecting notes and other items. Banks can also receive electronic funds transfers to the depositor's account. When a bank collects an item, it is added to the depositor's account, less any service fee. The bank also sends a credit memorandum to notify the depositor of the transaction. When the memorandum is received, the depositor should record it; yet it sometimes remains unrecorded until the bank reconciliation is prepared. The bank statement also includes a credit for any interest earned.

- **Errors.** Both banks and depositors can make errors. Bank errors might not be discovered until the depositor prepares the bank reconciliation. Also, depositor errors are sometimes discovered when the bank balance is reconciled. Error testing includes: (a) comparing deposits on the bank statement with deposits in the accounting records and (b) comparing canceled checks on the bank statement with checks recorded in the accounting records.

Illustration of a Bank Reconciliation   We follow nine steps in preparing the bank reconciliation. It is helpful to refer to the bank reconciliation in Exhibit 8.7 when studying steps ① through ⑨.

Forms of Check Fraud (CkFraud.org)

- Forged signatures—legitimate blank checks with fake payer signature
- Forged endorsements—stolen check that is endorsed and cashed by someone other than the payee
- Counterfeit checks—fraudulent checks with fake payer signature
- Altered checks—legitimate check altered (such as changed payee or amount) to benefit perpetrator
- Check kiting—deposit check from one bank account (without sufficient funds) into a second bank account

Point: Small businesses with few employees often allow recordkeepers to both write checks and keep the general ledger. If this is done, it is essential that the owner do the bank reconciliation.

Point: The person preparing the bank reconciliation should not be responsible for processing cash receipts, managing checks, or maintaining cash records.

EXHIBIT 8.7

Bank Reconciliation

	VIDEOBUSTER Bank Reconciliation October 31, 2013					
①	Bank statement balance		$ 2,050.00	⑤	Book balance		$ 1,404.58
②	Add			⑥	Add		
	Deposit of Oct. 31 in transit		145.00		Collect $500 note less $15 fee	$485.00	
			2,195.00		Interest earned	8.42	493.42
							1,898.00
③	Deduct			⑦	Deduct		
	Outstanding checks				Check printing charge	23.00	
	No. 124	$150.00			NSF check plus service fee	30.00	53.00
	No. 126	200.00	350.00				
④	**Adjusted bank balance**		**$1,845.00**	⑧	**Adjusted book balance**		**$1,845.00**

⑨ Balances are equal (reconciled)

① Identify the bank statement balance of the cash account (*balance per bank*). VideoBuster's bank balance is $2,050.

② Identify and list any unrecorded deposits and any bank errors understating the bank balance. Add them to the bank balance. VideoBuster's $145 deposit placed in the bank's night depository on October 31 is not recorded on its bank statement.

③ Identify and list any outstanding checks and any bank errors overstating the bank balance. Deduct them from the bank balance. VideoBuster's comparison of canceled checks with its books shows two checks outstanding: No. 124 for $150 and No. 126 for $200.

④ Compute the *adjusted bank balance*, also called the *corrected* or *reconciled balance*.

⑤ Identify the company's book balance of the cash account (*balance per book*). VideoBuster's book balance is $1,404.58.

⑥ Identify and list any unrecorded credit memoranda from the bank, any interest earned, and errors understating the book balance. Add them to the book balance. VideoBuster's bank statement includes a credit memorandum showing the bank collected a note receivable for the company on October 23. The note's proceeds of $500 (minus a $15 collection fee) are credited to the company's account. VideoBuster's bank statement also shows a credit of $8.42 for interest earned on the average cash balance. There was no prior notification of this item, and it is not yet recorded.

⑦ Identify and list any unrecorded debit memoranda from the bank, any service charges, and errors overstating the book balance. Deduct them from the book balance. Debits on VideoBuster's bank statement that are not yet recorded include (a) a $23 charge for check printing and (b) an NSF check for $20 plus a related $10 processing fee. (The NSF check is dated October 16 and was included in the book balance.)

⑧ Compute the *adjusted book balance*, also called *corrected* or *reconciled balance*.

⑨ Verify that the two adjusted balances from steps 4 and 8 are equal. If so, they are reconciled. If not, check for accuracy and missing data to achieve reconciliation.

Point: Outstanding checks are identified by comparing canceled checks on the bank statement with checks recorded. This includes identifying any outstanding checks listed on the *previous* period's bank reconciliation that are not included in the canceled checks on this period's bank statement.

Point: Adjusting entries can be combined into one compound entry.

Adjusting Entries from a Bank Reconciliation

A bank reconciliation often identifies unrecorded items that need recording by the company. In VideoBuster's reconciliation, the adjusted balance of $1,845 is the correct balance as of October 31. But the company's accounting records show a $1,404.58 balance. We must prepare journal entries to adjust the book balance to the correct balance. It is important to remember that only the items reconciling the *book balance* require adjustment. A review of Exhibit 8.7 indicates that four entries are required for VideoBuster.

Collection of note.   The first entry is to record the proceeds of its note receivable collected by the bank less the expense of having the bank perform that service.

Oct. 31	Cash	485	
	Collection Expense	15	
	Notes Receivable		500
	To record the collection fee and proceeds		
	for a note collected by the bank.		

Assets = Liabilities + Equity
+485   −15
−500

Interest earned.   The second entry records interest credited to its account by the bank.

Oct. 31	Cash	8.42	
	Interest Revenue		8.42
	To record interest earned on the cash		
	balance in the checking account.		

Assets = Liabilities + Equity
+8.42   +8.42

Check printing.   The third entry records expenses for the check printing charge.

Oct. 31	Miscellaneous Expenses	23	
	Cash		23
	Check printing charge.		

Assets = Liabilities + Equity
−23   −23

NSF check.   The fourth entry records the NSF check that is returned as uncollectible. The $20 check was originally received from T. Woods in payment of his account and then deposited. The bank charged $10 for handling the NSF check and deducted $30 total from VideoBuster's account. This means the entry must reverse the effects of the original entry made when the check was received and must record (add) the $10 bank fee.

Oct. 31	Accounts Receivable—T. Woods	30	
	Cash		30
	To charge Woods' account for $20 NSF check		
	and $10 bank fee.		

Cash			
Unadj. bal.	1,404.58		
⑥	485.00	⑦	23.00
⑥	8.42	⑦	30.00
Adj. bal.	1,845.00		

After these four entries are recorded, the book balance of cash is adjusted to the correct amount of $1,845 (computed as $1,404.58 + $485 + $8.42 − $23 − $30). The Cash T-account to the side shows the same computation, where entries are keyed to the numerical codes in Exhibit 8.7.

Decision Insight

Fraud   A survey reports that 74% of employees had 'personally seen' or had 'firsthand knowledge of' fraud or misconduct within the past year. Another survey found that fraudsters exploited weak internal controls in 74% of the frauds—up from 47% four years earlier—see graphic (KPMG 2011). ∎

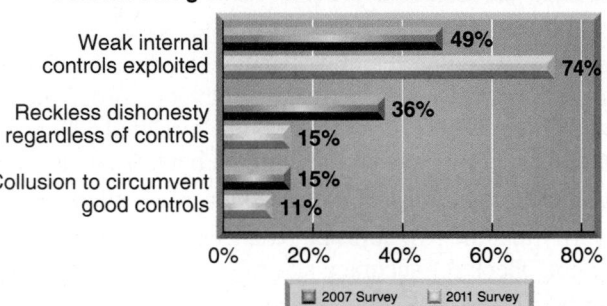

Percent Citing These Root Causes to Override Controls

Weak internal controls exploited — 49% / 74%
Reckless dishonesty regardless of controls — 36% / 15%
Collusion to circumvent good controls — 15% / 11%

☐ 2007 Survey   ☐ 2011 Survey

Quick Check
Answers — p. 346

13. What is a bank statement?

14. What is the meaning of the phrase *to reconcile a bank balance?*

15. Why do we reconcile the bank statement balance of cash and the depositor's book balance of cash?

16. List at least two items affecting the *bank balance* side of a bank reconciliation and indicate whether the items are added or subtracted.

17. List at least three items affecting the *book balance* side of a bank reconciliation and indicate whether the items are added or subtracted.

 ## GLOBAL VIEW

This section discusses similarities and differences between U.S. GAAP and IFRS regarding internal controls and in the accounting and reporting of cash.

Internal Control Purposes, Principles, and Procedures   Both U.S. GAAP and IFRS aim for high-quality financial reporting. That aim translates into enhanced internal controls worldwide. Specifically, the purposes and principles of internal control systems are fundamentally the same across the globe. However, culture and other realities suggest different emphases on the mix of control procedures, and some sensitivity to different customs and environments when establishing that mix. Nevertheless, the discussion in this chapter applies internationally. **Nokia** provides the following description of its control activities.

NOKIA

Nokia has an internal audit function that acts as an independent appraisal function by examining and evaluating the adequacy and effectiveness of the company's system of internal control.

Control of Cash Accounting definitions for cash are similar for U.S. GAAP and IFRS. The need for control of cash is universal and applies globally. This means that companies worldwide desire to apply cash management procedures as explained in this chapter and aim to control both cash receipts and disbursements. Accordingly, systems that employ tools such as cash monitoring mechanisms, verification of documents, and petty cash processes are applied worldwide. The basic techniques explained in this chapter are part of those control procedures.

Banking Activities as Controls There is a global demand for banking services, bank statements, and bank reconciliations. To the extent feasible, companies utilize banking services as part of their effective control procedures. Further, bank statements are similarly used along with bank reconciliations to control and monitor cash.

 IFRS

Internal controls are crucial to companies that convert from U.S. GAAP to IFRS. Major risks include misstatement of financial information and fraud. Other risks are ineffective communication of the impact of this change for investors, creditors and others, and management's inability to certify the effectiveness of controls over financial reporting. ■

Days' Sales Uncollected **Decision Analysis**

An important part of cash management is monitoring the receipt of cash from receivables. If customers and others who owe money to a company are delayed in payment, then that company can find it difficult to pay its obligations when they are due. A company's customers are crucial partners in its cash management. Many companies attract customers by selling to them on credit. This means that cash receipts from customers are delayed until accounts receivable are collected.

> **A1** Compute the days' sales uncollected ratio and use it to assess liquidity.

One measure of how quickly a company can convert its accounts receivable into cash is the **days' sales uncollected,** also called *days' sales in receivables*. This measure is computed by dividing the current balance of receivables by net credit sales over the year just completed and then multiplying by 365 (number of days in a year). Since net credit sales usually are not reported to external users, the net sales (or revenues) figure is commonly used in the computation as in Exhibit 8.8.

$$\text{Days' sales uncollected} = \frac{\text{Accounts receivable}}{\text{Net sales}} \times 365$$

EXHIBIT 8.8

Days' Sales Uncollected

We use days' sales uncollected to estimate how much time is likely to pass before the current amount of accounts receivable is received in cash. For evaluation purposes, we need to compare this estimate to that for other companies in the same industry. We also make comparisons between current and prior periods.

To illustrate, we select data from the annual reports of two toy manufacturers, **Hasbro** and **Mattel**. Their days' sales uncollected figures are shown in Exhibit 8.9.

EXHIBIT 8.9

Analysis Using Days' Sales Uncollected

Company	Figure ($ millions)	2011	2010	2009	2008	2007
Hasbro	Accounts receivable	$1,035	$961	$1,039	$612	$655
	Net sales	$4,286	$4,002	$4,068	$4,022	$3,838
	Days' sales uncollected	**88 days**	**88 days**	**93 days**	**56 days**	**62 days**
Mattel	Accounts receivable	$1,247	$1,146	$749	$874	$991
	Net sales	$6,266	$5,856	$5,431	$5,918	$5,970
	Days' sales uncollected	**73 days**	**71 days**	**50 days**	**54 days**	**61 days**

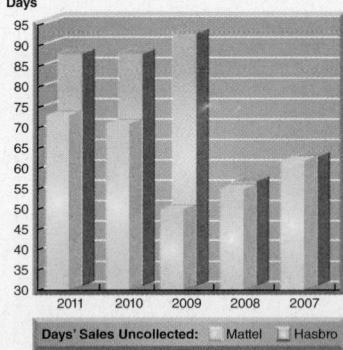

Days' sales uncollected for Hasbro in 2011 is computed as ($1,035/$4,286) × 365 days = 88 days. This means that it will take about 88 days to collect cash from ending accounts receivable. This number reflects one or more of the following factors: a company's ability to collect receivables, customer financial health, customer payment strategies, and discount terms. To further assess days' sales uncollected for Hasbro, we compare it to four prior years and to those of Mattel. We see that Hasbro's days' sales uncollected has worsened since 2008 as it takes much longer to collect its receivables relative to 2007 and 2008. In comparison, Mattel has also worsened from 50 days in 2009 up to 73 days in 2011. For all years, Mattel is superior to Hasbro on this measure of cash management. The less time that money is tied up in receivables often translates into increased profitability.

■ **Decision Maker**

Sales Representative The sales staff is told to take action to help reduce days' sales uncollected for cash management purposes. What can you, a salesperson, do to reduce days' sales uncollected? ■ [Answer—p. 345]

DEMONSTRATION PROBLEM 1

Prepare a bank reconciliation for Jamboree Enterprises for the month ended November 30, 2013. The following information is available to reconcile Jamboree Enterprises' book balance of cash with its bank statement balance as of November 30, 2013:

a. After all posting is complete on November 30, the company's book balance of Cash has a $16,380 debit balance, but its bank statement shows a $38,520 balance.

b. Checks No. 2024 for $4,810 and No. 2026 for $5,000 are outstanding.

c. In comparing the canceled checks on the bank statement with the entries in the accounting records, it is found that Check No. 2025 in payment of rent is correctly drawn for $1,000 but is erroneously entered in the accounting records as $880.

Point: Generally, the party that is not the initial recorder of an item, but is later informed, includes that item on its "book" of the bank reconciliation. For example, the bank records an NSF check and then informs the company. The company, as not the initial recorder of the item, reports it on the book side of its reconciliation.

d. The November 30 deposit of $17,150 was placed in the night depository after banking hours on that date, and this amount does not appear on the bank statement.

e. In reviewing the bank statement, a check written by Jumbo Enterprises in the amount of $160 was erroneously drawn against Jamboree's account.

f. A credit memorandum enclosed with the bank statement indicates that the bank collected a $30,000 note and $900 of related interest on Jamboree's behalf. This transaction was not recorded by Jamboree prior to receiving the statement.

g. A debit memorandum for $1,100 lists a $1,100 NSF check received from a customer, Marilyn Welch. Jamboree had not recorded the return of this check before receiving the statement.

h. Bank service charges for November total $40. These charges were not recorded by Jamboree before receiving the statement.

PLANNING THE SOLUTION

- Set up a bank reconciliation with a bank side and a book side (as in Exhibit 8.7). Leave room to both add and deduct items. Each column will result in a reconciled, equal balance.
- Examine each item *a* through *h* to determine whether it affects the book or the bank balance and whether it should be added or deducted from the bank or book balance.
- After all items are analyzed, complete the reconciliation and arrive at a reconciled balance between the bank side and the book side.
- For each reconciling item on the book side, prepare an adjusting entry. Additions to the book side require an adjusting entry that debits Cash. Deductions on the book side require an adjusting entry that credits Cash.

SOLUTION TO DEMONSTRATION PROBLEM 1

JAMBOREE ENTERPRISES Bank Reconciliation November 30, 2013					
Bank statement balance		$ 38,520	Book balance		$ 16,380
Add			Add		
Deposit of Nov. 30	$17,150		Collection of note	$30,000	
Bank error (Jumbo)	160	17,310	Interest earned	900	30,900
		55,830			47,280
Deduct			Deduct		
Outstanding checks			NSF check (M. Welch)	1,100	
No. 2024	4,810		Recording error (# 2025) ...	120	
No. 2026	5,000	9,810	Service charge	40	1,260
Adjusted bank balance ...		**$46,020**	**Adjusted book balance**		**$46,020**

Required Adjusting Entries for Jamboree

Nov. 30	Cash	30,900	
	Notes Receivable		30,000
	Interest Earned		900
	To record collection of note with interest.		
Nov. 30	Accounts Receivable—M. Welch	1,100	
	Cash		1,100
	To reinstate account due from an NSF check.		
Nov. 30	Rent Expense	120	
	Cash		120
	To correct recording error on check no. 2025.		
Nov. 30	Bank Service Charges	40	
	Cash		40
	To record bank service charges.		

Point: Error correction can alternatively involve (1) reversing the error entry, and (2) recording the correct entry.

DEMONSTRATION PROBLEM 2

Bacardi Company established a $150 petty cash fund with Eminem as the petty cashier. When the fund balance reached $19 cash, Eminem prepared a petty cash payment report, which follows.

	Petty Cash Payments Report			
Receipt No.	**Account Charged**		**Approved by**	**Received by**
12	Delivery Expense	$ 29	Eminem	A. Smirnoff
13	Merchandise Inventory	18	Eminem	J. Daniels
15	(Omitted)	32	Eminem	C. Carlsberg
16	Miscellaneous Expense	41	(Omitted)	J. Walker
	Total	$120		

Required

1. Identify four internal control weaknesses from the payment report.

2. Prepare general journal entries to record:
   a. Establishment of the petty cash fund.
   b. Reimbursement of the fund. (Assume for this part only that petty cash receipt no. 15 was issued for miscellaneous expenses.)

3. What is the Petty Cash account balance immediately before reimbursement? Immediately after reimbursement?

SOLUTION TO DEMONSTRATION PROBLEM 2

1. Four internal control weaknesses are

   a. Petty cash ticket no. 14 is missing. Its omission raises questions about the petty cashier's management of the fund.

   b. The $19 cash balance means that $131 has been withdrawn ($150 − $19 = $131). However, the total amount of the petty cash receipts is only $120 ($29 + $18 + $32 + $41). The fund is $11 short of cash ($131 − $120 = $11). Was petty cash receipt no. 14 issued for $11? Management should investigate.

   c. The petty cashier (Eminem) did not sign petty cash receipt no. 16. This omission could have been an oversight on his part or he might not have authorized the payment. Management should investigate.

   d. Petty cash receipt no. 15 does not indicate which account to charge. This omission could have been an oversight on the petty cashier's part. Management could check with C. Carlsberg and the petty cashier (Eminem) about the transaction. Without further information, debit Miscellaneous Expense.

2. Petty cash general journal entries.

a. Entry to establish the petty cash fund.

Petty Cash	150	
Cash		150

b. Entry to reimburse the fund.

Delivery Expense	29	
Merchandise Inventory	18	
Miscellaneous Expense ($41 + $32)	73	
Cash Over and Short	11	
Cash		131

3. The Petty Cash account balance *always* equals its fund balance, in this case $150. This account balance does not change unless the fund is increased or decreased.

APPENDIX

8A

Documentation and Verification

This appendix describes the important business documents of a voucher system of control.

P4 Describe the use of documentation and verification to control cash disbursements.

Purchase Requisition   Department managers are usually not allowed to place orders directly with suppliers for control purposes. Instead, a department manager must inform the purchasing department of its needs by preparing and signing a **purchase requisition,** which lists the merchandise needed and requests that it be purchased—see Exhibit 8A.1. Two copies of the purchase requisition are sent to the purchasing department, which then sends one copy to the accounting department. When the accounting department receives a purchase requisition, it creates and maintains a voucher for this transaction. The requesting department keeps the third copy.

EXHIBIT 8A.1

Purchase Requisition

Z-Mart

PURCHASE REQUISITION   No. 917

From *Sporting Goods Department*   Date *October 28, 2013*
To *Purchasing Department*   Preferred Vendor *Trex*

Request purchase of the following item(s):

MODEL NO.	DESCRIPTION	QUANTITY
CH 015	*Challenger X7*	*1*
SD 099	*SpeedDemon*	*1*

Reason for Request _____ *Replenish inventory* _____
Approval for Request _____ *T.Z.* _____

For Purchasing Department use only: Order Date *10/30/13*   P.O. No. _____ *P98* _____

Point: A voucher system is designed to uniquely meet the needs of a specific business. Thus, we should read this appendix as one example of a common voucher system design, but *not* the only design.

Purchase Order   A **purchase order** is a document the purchasing department uses to place an order with a **vendor** (seller or supplier). A purchase order authorizes a vendor to ship ordered merchandise at the stated price and terms—see Exhibit 8A.2. When the purchasing department receives a purchase requisition, it prepares at least five copies of a purchase order. The copies are distributed as follows: *copy 1* to the vendor as a purchase request and as authority to ship merchandise; *copy 2,* along with a copy of the purchase requisition, to the accounting department, where it is entered in the voucher and used in approving payment of the invoice; *copy 3* to the requesting department to inform its manager that action is being taken; *copy 4* to the receiving department without order quantity so it can compare with goods received and provide independent count of goods received; and *copy 5* retained on file by the purchasing department.

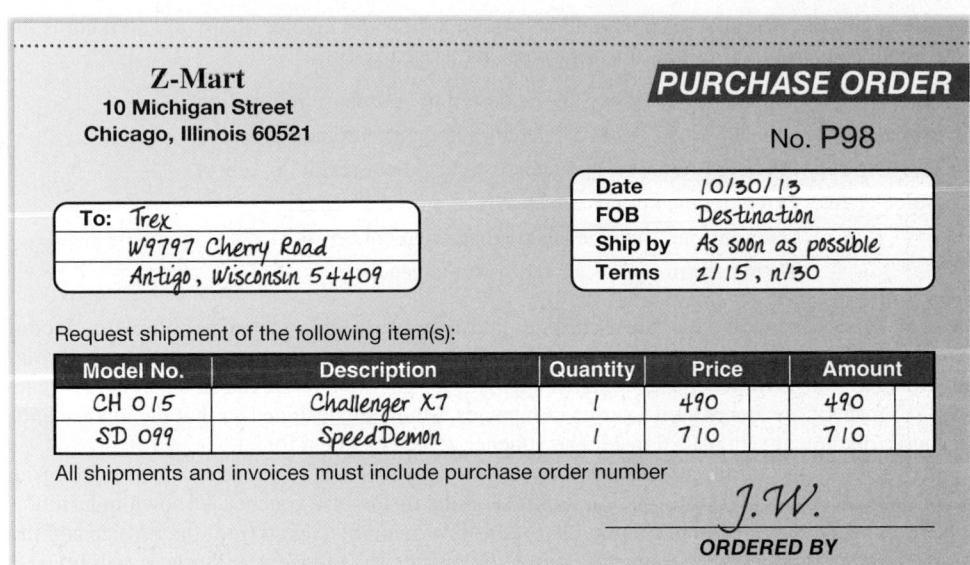

EXHIBIT 8A.2

Purchase Order

Point: Shipping terms and credit terms are shown on the purchase order.

Invoice An **invoice** is an itemized statement of goods prepared by the vendor listing the customer's name, items sold, sales prices, and terms of sale. An invoice is also a bill sent to the buyer from the supplier. From the vendor's point of view, it is a *sales invoice*. The buyer, or **vendee,** treats it as a *purchase invoice.* When receiving a purchase order, the vendor ships the ordered merchandise to the buyer and includes or mails a copy of the invoice covering the shipment to the buyer. The invoice is sent to the buyer's accounting department where it is placed in the voucher. (Refer back to Exhibit 5.5, which shows Z-Mart's purchase invoice.)

Receiving Report Many companies maintain a separate department to receive all merchandise and purchased assets. When each shipment arrives, this receiving department counts the goods and checks them for damage and agreement with the purchase order. It then prepares four or more copies of a **receiving report,** which is used within the company to notify the appropriate persons that ordered goods have been received and to describe the quantities and condition of the goods. One copy is sent to accounting and placed in the voucher. Copies are also sent to the requesting department and the purchasing department to notify them that the goods have arrived. The receiving department retains a copy in its files.

Invoice Approval When a receiving report arrives, the accounting department should have copies of the following documents in the voucher: purchase requisition, purchase order, and invoice. With the information in these documents, the accounting department can record the purchase and approve its payment. In approving an invoice for payment, it checks and compares information across all documents. To facilitate this checking and to ensure that no step is omitted, it often uses an **invoice approval,** also called *check authorization*—see Exhibit 8A.3. An invoice approval is a checklist of steps necessary for approving an invoice for recording and payment. It is a separate document either filed in the voucher or preprinted (or stamped) on the voucher.

EXHIBIT 8A.3

Invoice Approval

INVOICE APPROVAL				
DOCUMENT			**BY**	**DATE**
Purchase requisition		917	TZ	10/28/13
Purchase order		P98	JW	10/30/13
Receiving report		R85	SK	11/03/13
Invoice:		4657		11/12/13
Price			JK	11/12/13
Calculations			JK	11/12/13
Terms			JK	11/12/13
Approved for payment			BC	

Point: Recording a purchase is initiated by an invoice approval, not an invoice. An invoice approval verifies that the amount is consistent with that requested, ordered, and received. This controls and verifies purchases and related liabilities.

Point: Auditors, when auditing inventory, check a sampling of purchases by reviewing the purchase order, receiving report, and invoice.

As each step in the checklist is approved, the person initials the invoice approval and records the current date. Final approval implies the following steps have occurred:

1. **Requisition check:** Items on invoice are requested per purchase requisition.
2. **Purchase order check:** Items on invoice are ordered per purchase order.
3. **Receiving report check:** Items on invoice are received per receiving report.
4. **Invoice check: Price:** Invoice prices are as agreed with the vendor.
    Calculations: Invoice has no mathematical errors.
    Terms: Terms are as agreed with the vendor.

Voucher   Once an invoice has been checked and approved, the voucher is complete. A complete voucher is a record summarizing a transaction. Once the voucher certifies a transaction, it authorizes recording an obligation. A voucher also contains approval for paying the obligation on an appropriate date. The physical form of a voucher varies across companies. Many are designed so that the invoice and other related source documents are placed inside the voucher, which can be a folder.

Completion of a voucher usually requires a person to enter certain information on both the inside and outside of the voucher. Typical information required on the inside of a voucher is shown in Exhibit 8A.4, and that for the outside is shown in Exhibit 8A.5. This information is taken from the invoice and the supporting documents filed in the voucher. A complete voucher is sent to an authorized individual (often called an *auditor*). This person performs a final review, approves the accounts and amounts for debiting (called the *accounting distribution*), and authorizes recording of the voucher.

EXHIBIT 8A.4

Inside of a Voucher

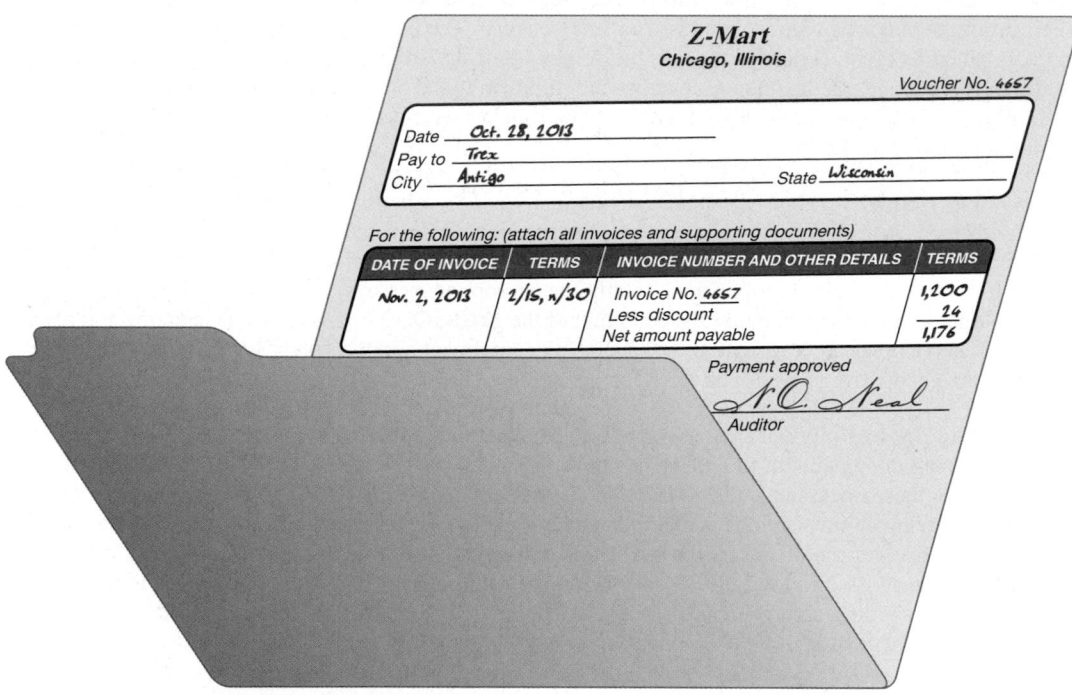

After a voucher is approved and recorded (in a journal called a **voucher register**), it is filed by its due date. A check is then sent on the payment date from the cashier, the voucher is marked "paid," and the voucher is sent to the accounting department and recorded (in a journal called the **check register**). The person issuing checks relies on the approved voucher and its signed supporting documents as proof that an obligation has been incurred and must be paid. The purchase requisition and purchase order confirm the purchase was authorized. The receiving report shows that items have been received, and the invoice approval form verifies that the invoice has been checked for errors. There is little chance for error and even less chance for fraud without collusion unless all the documents and signatures are forged.

EXHIBIT 8A.5
Outside of a Voucher

Voucher No. *4657*

Accounting Distribution

ACCOUNT DEBITED	AMOUNT
Merch. Inventory	1,200
Store Supplies	
Office Supplies	
Sales Salaries	
Other	
Total Vouch. Pay. Cr.	1,200

Due Date ___*November 12, 2013*___
Pay to ___*Trex*___
City ___*Antigo*___
State ___*Wisconsin*___

Summary of charges:
Total charges ___1,200___
Discount ___24___
Net payment ___1,176___

Record of payment:
Paid _____
Check No. _____

EXHIBIT 8A.5

Outside of a Voucher

Control of Purchase Discounts

8B

This appendix explains how a company can better control its cash *disbursements* to take advantage of favorable purchases discounts. Chapter 5 described the entries to record the receipt and payment of an invoice for a merchandise purchase with and without discount terms. Those entries were prepared under what is called the **gross method** of recording purchases, which initially records the invoice at its *gross* amount ignoring any cash discount.

> **P5** Apply the net method to control purchase discounts.

The **net method** is another means of recording purchases, which initially records the invoice at its *net* amount of any cash discount. The net method gives management an advantage in controlling and monitoring cash payments involving purchase discounts.

To explain, when invoices are recorded at *gross* amounts, the amount of any discounts taken is deducted from the balance of the Merchandise Inventory account when cash payment is made. This means that the amount of any discounts lost is not reported in any account or on the income statement. Lost discounts recorded in this way are unlikely to come to the attention of management. When purchases are recorded at *net* amounts, a **Discounts Lost** expense account is recorded and brought to management's attention. Management can then seek to identify the reason for discounts lost such as oversight, carelessness, or unfavorable terms. (Chapter 5 explains how managers assess whether a discount is favorable or not.)

Perpetual Inventory System To illustrate, assume that a company purchases merchandise on November 2 at a $1,200 invoice price with terms of 2/10, n/30. Its November 2 entries under the gross and net methods are

Gross Method—Perpetual		
Merchandise Inventory	1,200	
Accounts Payable		1,200

Net Method—Perpetual		
Merchandise Inventory	1,176	
Accounts Payable		1,176

If the invoice is paid on November 12 within the discount period, it records the following:

Gross Method—Perpetual		
Accounts Payable	1,200	
Merchandise Inventory		24
Cash		1,176

Net Method—Perpetual		
Accounts Payable	1,176	
Cash		1,176

If the invoice is *not* paid within the discount period, it records the following November 12 entry (which is the date corresponding to the end of the discount period):

Gross Method—Perpetual			Net Method—Perpetual		
No entry			Discounts Lost	24	
			Accounts Payable		24

Then, when the invoice is later paid on December 2, outside the discount period, it records the following:

Gross Method—Perpetual			Net Method—Perpetual		
Accounts Payable	1,200		Accounts Payable	1,200	
Cash		1,200	Cash		1,200

(The discount lost can be recorded when the cash payment is made with a single entry. However, in this case, when financial statements are prepared after a discount is lost and before the cash payment is made, an adjusting entry is required to recognize any unrecorded discount lost in the period when incurred.)

Periodic Inventory System   The preceding entries assume a perpetual inventory system. If a company is using a periodic system, its November 2 entries under the gross and net methods are

Gross Method—Periodic			Net Method—Periodic		
Purchases	1,200		Purchases	1,176	
Accounts Payable		1,200	Accounts Payable		1,176

If the invoice is paid on November 12 within the discount period, it records the following:

Gross Method—Periodic			Net Method—Periodic		
Accounts Payable	1,200		Accounts Payable	1,176	
Purchases Discounts		24	Cash		1,176
Cash		1,176			

If the invoice is *not* paid within the discount period, it records the following November 12 entry:

Gross Method—Periodic			Net Method—Periodic		
No entry			Discounts Lost	24	
			Accounts Payable		24

Then, when the invoice is later paid on December 2, outside the discount period, it records the following:

Gross Method—Periodic			Net Method—Periodic		
Accounts Payable	1,200		Accounts Payable	1,200	
Cash		1,200	Cash		1,200

Summary

C1 Define internal control and identify its purpose and principles. An internal control system consists of the policies and procedures managers use to protect assets, ensure reliable accounting, promote efficient operations, and urge adherence to company policies. It can prevent avoidable losses and help managers both plan operations and monitor company and human performance. Principles of good internal control include establishing responsibilities, maintaining adequate records, insuring assets and bonding employees, separating recordkeeping from custody of assets, dividing responsibilities for related transactions, applying technological controls, and performing regular independent reviews.

C2 Define cash and cash equivalents and explain how to report them. Cash includes currency, coins, and amounts on (or acceptable for) deposit in checking and savings accounts. Cash equivalents are short-term, highly liquid investment assets readily convertible to a known cash amount and sufficiently close to their maturity date so that market value is not sensitive to interest rate changes. Cash and cash equivalents are liquid assets because they are readily converted into other assets or can be used to pay for goods, services, or liabilities.

A1 Compute the days' sales uncollected ratio and use it to assess liquidity. Many companies attract customers by selling to them on credit. This means that cash receipts from customers are delayed until accounts receivable are collected. Users want to know how quickly a company can convert its accounts receivable into cash. The days' sales uncollected ratio, one measure reflecting company liquidity, is computed by dividing the ending balance of receivables by annual net sales, and then multiplying by 365.

P1 **Apply internal control to cash receipts and disbursements.** Internal control of cash receipts ensures that all cash received is properly recorded and deposited. Attention focuses on two important types of cash receipts: over-the-counter and by mail. Good internal control for over-the-counter cash receipts includes use of a cash register, customer review, use of receipts, a permanent transaction record, and separation of the custody of cash from its record-keeping. Good internal control for cash receipts by mail includes at least two people assigned to open mail and a listing of each sender's name, amount, and explanation. (Banks offer several services that promote the control and safeguarding of cash.)

P2 **Explain and record petty cash fund transactions.** Petty cash disbursements are payments of small amounts for items such as postage, courier fees, minor repairs, and supplies. A company usually sets up one or more petty cash funds. A petty cash fund cashier is responsible for safekeeping the cash, making payments from this fund, and keeping receipts and records. A Petty Cash account is debited only when the fund is established or increased in amount. When the fund is replenished, petty cash disbursements are recorded with debits to expense (or asset) accounts and a credit to cash.

P3 **Prepare a bank reconciliation.** A bank reconciliation proves the accuracy of the depositor's and the bank's records. The bank statement balance is adjusted for items such as outstanding checks and unrecorded deposits made on or before the bank statement date but not reflected on the statement. The book balance is adjusted for items such as service charges, bank collections for the depositor, and interest earned on the account.

P4^A **Describe the use of documentation and verification to control cash disbursements.** A voucher system is a set of procedures and approvals designed to control cash disbursements and acceptance of obligations. The voucher system of control relies on several important documents, including the voucher and its supporting files. A key factor in this system is that only approved departments and individuals are authorized to incur certain obligations.

P5^B **Apply the net method to control purchase discounts.** The net method aids management in monitoring and controlling purchase discounts. When invoices are recorded at gross amounts, the amount of discounts taken is deducted from the balance of the Inventory account. This means that the amount of any discounts lost is not reported in any account and is unlikely to come to the attention of management. When purchases are recorded at net amounts, a Discounts Lost account is brought to management's attention as an operating expense. Management can then seek to identify the reason for discounts lost, such as oversight, carelessness, or unfavorable terms.

Guidance Answers to Decision Maker and Decision Ethics

Entrepreneur To achieve proper separation of duties, a minimum of three employees are required. Transaction authorization, recording, and asset custody are ideally handled by three employees. Many small businesses do not employ three workers. In such cases, an owner must exercise more oversight to make sure that the lack of separation of duties does not result in fraudulent transactions.

Sales Representative A salesperson can take several steps to reduce days' sales uncollected. These include (1) decreasing the ratio of sales on account to total sales by encouraging more cash sales, (2) identifying customers most delayed in their payments and encouraging earlier payments or cash sales, and (3) applying stricter credit policies to eliminate credit sales to customers that never pay.

Guidance Answers to Quick Checks

1. (*c*)
2. Technology reduces processing errors. It also allows more extensive testing of records, limits the amount of hard evidence, and highlights the importance of separation of duties.
3. When employees are forced to take vacations, their ability to hide any fraudulent behavior decreases because others must perform the vacationers' duties. A replacement employee potentially can uncover fraudulent behavior or falsified records. A forced vacation policy is especially important for employees in sensitive positions of handling money or in control of easily transferable assets.
4. A company holds liquid assets so that it can purchase other assets, buy services, and pay obligations.
5. It owns cash equivalents because they yield a return greater than what cash earns (and are readily exchanged for cash).
6. Examples of cash equivalents are 90-day (or less) U.S. Treasury bills, money market funds, and commercial paper (notes).

7. (*a*)
8. A voucher system is used when an owner/manager can no longer control purchasing procedures through personal supervision and direct participation.
9. If all cash payments are made by check, numerous checks for small amounts must be written. Since this practice is expensive and time-consuming, a petty cash fund is often established for making small (immaterial) cash payments.
10. If the petty cash fund is not reimbursed at the end of an accounting period, the transactions involving petty cash are not yet recorded and the petty cash asset is overstated.
11. First, petty cash transactions are recorded when the petty cash fund is reimbursed. Second, reimbursement provides cash to allow the fund to continue being used. Third, reimbursement identifies any cash shortage or overage in the fund.

12. If we accommodate the custodian's request, we reduce effectiveness of this audit procedure. If the custodian uses the lunch period to fix any shortages or irregularities in the petty cash fund, we risk not discovering such problems when we defer our audit.

13. A bank statement is a report prepared by the bank describing the activities in a depositor's account.

14. To reconcile a bank balance means to explain the difference between the cash balance in the depositor's accounting records and the cash balance on the bank statement.

15. The purpose of the bank reconciliation is to determine whether the bank or the depositor has made any errors and whether the bank has entered any transactions affecting the account that the depositor has not recorded.

16. Unrecorded deposits—added
Outstanding checks—subtracted

17. Interest earned—added   Debit memos—subtracted
Credit memos—added   NSF checks—subtracted
                                 Bank service charges—subtracted

Key Terms

Bank reconciliation (p. 333)	Deposits in transit (p. 334)	Principles of internal control (p. 319)
Bank statement (p. 332)	Discounts lost (p. 343)	Purchase order (p. 340)
Canceled checks (p. 332)	Electronic funds transfer (EFT) (p. 331)	Purchase requisition (p. 340)
Cash (p. 323)	Gross method (p. 343)	Receiving report (p. 341)
Cash equivalents (p. 323)	Internal control system (p. 318)	Sarbanes-Oxley Act (p. 318)
Cash Over and Short (p. 325)	Invoice (p. 341)	Section 404 (of SOX) (p. 319)
Check (p. 331)	Invoice approval (p. 341)	Signature card (p. 331)
Check register (p. 342)	Liquid assets (p. 323)	Vendee (p. 341)
Committee of Sponsoring Organizations (COSO) (p. 319)	Liquidity (p. 323)	Vendor (p. 340)
Days' sales uncollected (p. 337)	Net method (p. 343)	Voucher (p. 327)
Deposit ticket (p. 341)	Outstanding checks (p. 334)	Voucher register (p. 342)
	Petty cash (p. 328)	Voucher system (p. 326)

Multiple Choice Quiz   Answers on p. 359   mhhe.com/wildFAP21e

Additional Quiz Questions are available at the book's Website.

1. A company needs to replenish its $500 petty cash fund. Its petty cash box has $75 cash and petty cash receipts of $420. The journal entry to replenish the fund includes
  a. A debit to Cash for $75.
  b. A credit to Cash for $75.
  c. A credit to Petty Cash for $420.
  d. A credit to Cash Over and Short for $5.
  e. A debit to Cash Over and Short for $5.

2. The following information is available for Hapley Company:
- The November 30 bank statement shows a $1,895 balance.
- The general ledger shows a $1,742 balance at November 30.
- A $795 deposit placed in the bank's night depository on November 30 does not appear on the November 30 bank statement.
- Outstanding checks amount to $638 at November 30.
- A customer's $335 note was collected by the bank in November. A collection fee of $15 was deducted by the bank and the difference deposited in Hapley's account.
- A bank service charge of $10 is deducted by the bank and appears on the November 30 bank statement.

How will the customer's note appear on Hapley's November 30 bank reconciliation?
  a. $320 appears as an addition to the book balance of cash.
  b. $320 appears as a deduction from the book balance of cash.
  c. $320 appears as an addition to the bank balance of cash.
  d. $320 appears as a deduction from the bank balance of cash.
  e. $335 appears as an addition to the bank balance of cash.

3. Using the information from question 2, what is the reconciled balance on Hapley's November 30 bank reconciliation?
  a. $2,052
  b. $1,895
  c. $1,742
  d. $2,201
  e. $1,184

4. A company had net sales of $84,000 and accounts receivable of $6,720. Its days' sales uncollected is
  a. 3.2 days
  b. 18.4 days
  c. 230.0 days
  d. 29.2 days
  e. 12.5 days

5.[B] A company records its purchases using the net method. On August 1, it purchases merchandise on account for $6,000 with terms of 2/10, n/30. The August 1 journal entry to record this transaction includes a
  a. Debit to Merchandise Inventory for $6,000.
  b. Debit to Merchandise Inventory for $5,880.
  c. Debit to Merchandise Inventory for $120.
  d. Debit to Accounts Payable for $5,880.
  e. Credit to Accounts Payable for $6,000.

^{A(B)} *Superscript letter A(B) denotes assignments based on Appendix 8A (8B).*

🛈 Icon denotes assignments that involve decision making.

Discussion Questions

1. List the seven broad principles of internal control.
2. 🛈 Internal control procedures are important in every business, but at what stage in the development of a business do they become especially critical?
3. 🛈 Why should responsibility for related transactions be divided among different departments or individuals?
4. 🛈 Why should the person who keeps the records of an asset not be the person responsible for its custody?
5. 🛈 When a store purchases merchandise, why are individual departments not allowed to directly deal with suppliers?
6. What are the limitations of internal controls?
7. Which of the following assets is most liquid? Which is least liquid? Inventory, building, accounts receivable, or cash.
8. What is a petty cash receipt? Who should sign it?
9. Why should cash receipts be deposited on the day of receipt?
10. **Polaris'** statement of cash flows in Appendix A **Polaris** describes changes in cash and cash equivalents for the year ended December 31, 2011. What total amount is

provided (used) by investing activities? What amount is provided (used) by financing activities?

11. Refer to **Arctic Cat**'s financial statements in **Arctic Cat** Appendix A. Identify Arctic Cat's net earnings (income) for the year ended March 31, 2011. Is its net earnings equal to the increase in cash and cash equivalents for the year? Explain the difference between net earnings and the increase in cash and cash equivalents.
12. 🛈 Refer to **KTM**'s balance sheet in Appendix A. **KTM** How does its cash (titled "liquid assets") compare with its other current assets (both in amount and percent) as of December 31, 2011? Compare and assess its cash at December 31, 2011, with·its cash at December 31, 2010.
13. 🛈 **Piaggio**'s balance sheet in Appendix A re- **PIAGGIO** ports that cash and equivalents decreased during the year ended December 31, 2011. Identify the cash generated (or used) by operating activities, by investing activities, and by financing (funding) activities.

Mc Graw Hill connect

An internal control system consists of all policies and procedures used to protect assets, ensure reliable accounting, promote efficient operations, and urge adherence to company policies.

1. What is the main objective of internal control procedures? How is that objective achieved?
2. Why should recordkeeping for assets be separated from custody over those assets?
3. Why should the responsibility for a transaction be divided between two or more individuals or departments?

QUICK STUDY

QS 8-1
Internal control objectives
C1

Good accounting systems help in managing cash and controlling who has access to it.

1. What items are included in the category of cash?
2. What items are included in the category of cash equivalents?
3. What does the term *liquidity* refer to?

QS 8-2
Cash and equivalents
C2

A good system of internal control for cash provides adequate procedures for protecting both cash receipts and cash disbursements.

1. What are three basic guidelines that help achieve this protection?
2. Identify two control systems or procedures for cash disbursements.

QS 8-3
Internal control for cash
P1 🛈

---

1. For each of the following items, indicate whether its amount (i) affects the bank or book side of a bank reconciliation and (ii) represents an addition or a subtraction in a bank reconciliation.

   a. Interest on cash balance   **d.** Outstanding checks   **g.** Outstanding deposits
   b. Bank service charges   **e.** Credit memos
   c. Debit memos   **f.** NSF checks

2. Which of the items in part 1 require an adjusting journal entry?

QS 8-4
Bank reconciliation
P3

---

1. The petty cash fund of the Brooks Agency is established at $150. At the end of the current period, the fund contained $28 and had the following receipts: film rentals, $24, refreshments for meetings, $46 (both expenditures to be classified as Entertainment Expense); postage, $30; and printing, $22. Prepare journal entries to record (*a*) establishment of the fund and (*b*) reimbursement of the fund at the end of the current period.
2. Identify the two events that cause a Petty Cash account to be credited in a journal entry.

QS 8-5
Petty cash accounting
P2

QS 8-6
Bank reconciliation
P3

Nolan Company deposits all cash receipts on the day when they are received and it makes all cash payments by check. At the close of business on June 30, 2013, its Cash account shows an $22,352 debit balance. Nolan's June 30 bank statement shows $21,332 on deposit in the bank. Prepare a bank reconciliation for the Company using the following information.

a. Outstanding checks as of June 30 total $3,713.

b. The June 30 bank statement included a $41 debit memorandum for bank services; the company has not yet recorded the cost of these services.

c. In reviewing the bank statement, a $90 check written by the Company was mistakenly recorded in the company's books at $99.

d. June 30 cash receipts of $4,724 were placed in the bank's night depository after banking hours and were not recorded on the June 30 bank statement.

e. The bank statement included a $23 credit for interest earned on the cash in the bank.

QS 8-7
Reviewing bank statements
P3

An entrepreneur commented that a bank reconciliation may not be necessary as she regularly reviews her online bank statement for any unusual items and errors.

a. Describe how a bank reconciliation and an online review (or reading) of the bank statement are not equivalent.

b. Identify and explain at least two frauds or errors that would be uncovered through a bank reconciliation and that would *not* be uncovered through an online review of the bank statement.

QS 8-8
Days' sales uncollected
A1

The following annual account balances are taken from Armour Sports at December 31.

	2013	2012
Accounts receivable	$ 85,692	$ 80,485
Net sales	2,691,855	2,396,858

What is the change in the number of days' sales uncollected between years 2012 and 2013? (Round the number of days to one decimal.) According to this analysis, is the company's collection of receivables improving? Explain.

QS 8-9^A
Documents in a voucher system
P4

Management uses a voucher system to help control and monitor cash disbursements. Identify and describe at least four key documents that are part of a voucher system of control.

QS 8-10^B
Purchase discounts   P5

An important part of cash management is knowing when, and if, to take purchase discounts.

a. Which accounting method uses a Discounts Lost account?

b. What is the advantage of this method for management?

QS 8-11
International accounting and internal controls
C1   P1

Answer each of the following related to international accounting standards.

a. Explain how the purposes and principles of internal controls are different between accounting systems reporting under IFRS versus U.S. GAAP.

b. Cash presents special internal control challenges. How do internal controls for cash differ for accounting systems reporting under IFRS versus U.S. GAAP? How do the procedures applied differ across those two accounting systems?

connect

EXERCISES

Exercise 8-1
Analyzing internal control
C1

Franco Company is a rapidly growing start-up business. Its recordkeeper, who was hired six months ago, left town after the company's manager discovered that a large sum of money had disappeared over the past three months. An audit disclosed that the recordkeeper had written and signed several checks made payable to her fiancé and then recorded the checks as salaries expense. The fiancé, who cashed the checks but never worked for the company, left town with the recordkeeper. As a result, the company incurred an uninsured loss of $184,000. Evaluate Franco's internal control system and indicate which principles of internal control appear to have been ignored.

Some of Crown Company's cash receipts from customers are received by the company with the regular mail. The company's recordkeeper opens these letters and deposits the cash received each day. (*a*) Identify any internal control problem(s) in this arrangement. (*b*) What changes to its internal control system do you recommend?

Exercise 8-2
Control of cash receipts by mail
P1

What internal control procedures would you recommend in each of the following situations?

1. A concession company has one employee who sells towels, coolers, and sunglasses at the beach. Each day, the employee is given enough towels, coolers, and sunglasses to last through the day and enough cash to make change. The money is kept in a box at the stand.

2. An antique store has one employee who is given cash and sent to garage sales each weekend. The employee pays cash for any merchandise acquired that the antique store resells.

Exercise 8-3
Internal control recommendations
C1

Good accounting systems help with the management and control of cash and cash equivalents.

1. Define and contrast the terms *liquid asset* and *cash equivalent*.

2. Why would companies invest their idle cash in cash equivalents?

3. Identify five principles of effective cash management.

Exercise 8-4
Cash, liquidity, and return
C2

Palmona Co. establishes a $200 petty cash fund on January 1. On January 8, the fund shows $38 in cash along with receipts for the following expenditures: postage, $74; transportation-in, $29; delivery expenses, $16; and miscellaneous expenses, $43. Palmona uses the perpetual system in accounting for merchandise inventory. Prepare journal entries to (1) establish the fund on January 1, (2) reimburse it on January 8, and (3) both reimburse the fund and increase it to $450 on January 8, assuming no entry in part 2. (*Hint*: Make two separate entries for part 3.)

Exercise 8-5
Petty cash fund accounting
P2

Check   (3) Cr. Cash $162 (total)

Waupaca Company establishes a $350 petty cash fund on September 9. On September 30, the fund shows $104 in cash along with receipts for the following expenditures: transportation-in, $40; postage expenses, $123; and miscellaneous expenses, $80. The petty cashier could not account for a $3 shortage in the fund. The company uses the perpetual system in accounting for merchandise inventory. Prepare (1) the September 9 entry to establish the fund, (2) the September 30 entry to reimburse the fund, and (3) an October 1 entry to increase the fund to $400.

Exercise 8-6
Petty cash fund with a shortage
P2

Check   (2) Cr. Cash $246 and (3) Cr. Cash $50

Prepare a table with the following headings for a monthly bank reconciliation dated September 30.

Exercise 8-7
Bank reconciliation and adjusting entries
P3

Bank Balance		Book Balance			Not Shown on the Reconciliation
Add	Deduct	Add	Deduct	Adjust	Reconciliation

For each item 1 through 12, place an *x* in the appropriate column to indicate whether the item should be added to or deducted from the book or bank balance, or whether it should not appear on the reconciliation. If the book balance is to be adjusted, place a *Dr.* or *Cr.* in the Adjust column to indicate whether the Cash balance should be debited or credited. At the left side of your table, number the items to correspond to the following list.

1. NSF check from customer is returned on September 25 but not yet recorded by this company.

2. Interest earned on the September cash balance in the bank.

3. Deposit made on September 5 and processed by the bank on September 6.

4. Checks written by another depositor but charged against this company's account.

5. Bank service charge for September.

6. Checks outstanding on August 31 that cleared the bank in September.

7. Check written against the company's account and cleared by the bank; erroneously not recorded by the company's recordkeeper.

8. Principal and interest on a note receivable to this company is collected by the bank but not yet recorded by the company.

9. Checks written and mailed to payees on October 2.

10. Checks written by the company and mailed to payees on September 30.

11. Night deposit made on September 30 after the bank closed.

12. Special bank charge for collection of note in part 8 on this company's behalf.

Exercise 8-8
Voucher system
P1

The voucher system of control is designed to control cash disbursements and the acceptance of obligations.
1. The voucher system of control establishes procedures for what two processes?
2. What types of expenditures should be overseen by a voucher system of control?
3. When is the voucher initially prepared? Explain.

Exercise 8-9
Bank reconciliation
P3

Wright Company deposits all cash receipts on the day when they are received and it makes all cash payments by check. At the close of business on May 31, 2013, its Cash account shows a $27,500 debit balance. The company's May 31 bank statement shows $25,800 on deposit in the bank. Prepare a bank reconciliation for the company using the following information.

  a. The May 31 bank statement included a $100 debit memorandum for bank services; the company has not yet recorded the cost of these services.

  b. Outstanding checks as of May 31 total $5,600.

  c. May 31 cash receipts of $6,200 were placed in the bank's night depository after banking hours and were not recorded on the May 31 bank statement.

  d. In reviewing the bank statement, a $400 check written by Smith Company was mistakenly drawn against Wright's account.

Check   Reconciled bal., $26,800

  e. A debit memorandum for $600 refers to a $600 NSF check from a customer; the company has not yet recorded this NSF check.

Exercise 8-10
Bank reconciliation
P3

Del Gato Clinic deposits all cash receipts on the day when they are received and it makes all cash payments by check. At the close of business on June 30, 2013, its Cash account shows a $11,589 debit balance. Del Gato Clinic's June 30 bank statement shows $10,555 on deposit in the bank. Prepare a bank reconciliation for Del Gato Clinic using the following information:

  a. Outstanding checks as of June 30 total $1,829.

  b. The June 30 bank statement included a $16 debit memorandum for bank services.

  c. Check No. 919, listed with the canceled checks, was correctly drawn for $467 in payment of a utility bill on June 15. Del Gato Clinic mistakenly recorded it with a debit to Utilities Expense and a credit to Cash in the amount of $476.

Check   Reconciled bal., $11,582

  d. The June 30 cash receipts of $2,856 were placed in the bank's night depository after banking hours and were not recorded on the June 30 bank statement.

Exercise 8-11
Adjusting entries from bank reconciliation   P3

Prepare the adjusting journal entries that Del Gato Clinic must record as a result of preparing the bank reconciliation in Exercise 8-10.

Exercise 8-12
Liquid assets and accounts receivable

A1

Bargains Co. reported annual net sales for 2012 and 2013 of $665,000 and $747,000, respectively. Its year-end balances of accounts receivable follow: December 31, 2012, $61,000; and December 31, 2013, $93,000. (a) Calculate its days' sales uncollected at the end of each year. Round the number of days to one decimal. (b) Evaluate and comment on any changes in the amount of liquid assets tied up in receivables.

Exercise 8-13[A]
Documents in a voucher system
P4

Match each document in a voucher system in column one with its description in column two.

Document	Description
1. Purchase requisition	**A.** An itemized statement of goods prepared by the vendor listing the customer's name, items sold, sales prices, and terms of sale.
2. Purchase order	
3. Invoice	**B.** An internal file used to store documents and information to control cash disbursements and to ensure that a transaction is properly authorized and recorded.
4. Receiving report	
5. Invoice approval	
6. Voucher	**C.** A document used to place an order with a vendor that authorizes the vendor to ship ordered merchandise at the stated price and terms.
	D. A checklist of steps necessary for the approval of an invoice for recording and payment; also known as a check authorization.
	E. A document used by department managers to inform the purchasing department to place an order with a vendor.
	F. A document used to notify the appropriate persons that ordered goods have arrived, including a description of the quantities and condition of goods.

Piere Imports uses the perpetual system in accounting for merchandise inventory and had the following transactions during the month of October. Prepare entries to record these transactions assuming that Piere Imports records invoices (*a*) at gross amounts and (*b*) at net amounts.

Oct. 2 Purchased merchandise at a $3,000 price, invoice dated October 2, terms 2/10, n/30.
10 Received a $500 credit memorandum (at full invoice price) for the return of merchandise that it purchased on October 2.
17 Purchased merchandise at a $5,400 price, invoice dated October 16, terms 2/10, n/30.
26 Paid for the merchandise purchased on October 17, less the discount.
31 Paid for the merchandise purchased on October 2. Payment was delayed because the invoice was mistakenly filed for payment today. This error caused the discount to be lost.

Exercise 8-14[B]

Record invoices at gross or net amounts

P5

---

connect

For each of these five separate cases, identify the principle(s) of internal control that is violated. Recommend what the business should do to ensure adherence to principles of internal control.

1. Chi Han records all incoming customer cash receipts for her employer and posts the customer payments to their respective accounts.

2. At Tico Company, Julia and Justine alternate lunch hours. Julia is the petty cash custodian, but if someone needs petty cash when he is at lunch, Jose fills in as custodian.

3. Nori Nozumi posts all patient charges and payments at the Hopeville Medical Clinic. Each night Nori backs up the computerized accounting system to a tape and stores the tape in a locked file at her desk.

4. Benedict Shales prides himself on hiring quality workers who require little supervision. As office manager, Benedict gives his employees full discretion over their tasks and for years has seen no reason to perform independent reviews of their work.

5. Carla Farah's manager has told her to reduce costs. Cala decides to raise the deductible on the plant's property insurance from $5,000 to $10,000. This cuts the property insurance premium in half. In a related move, she decides that bonding the plant's employees is a waste of money since the company has not experienced any losses due to employee theft. Cala saves the entire amount of the bonding insurance premium by dropping the bonding insurance.

PROBLEM SET A

Problem 8-1A
Analyzing internal control

C1

Nakashima Gallery had the following petty cash transactions in February of the current year.

Feb. 2 Wrote a $400 check, cashed it, and gave the proceeds and the petty cashbox to Chloe Addison, the petty cashier.
5 Purchased bond paper for the copier for $14.15 that is immediately used.
9 Paid $32.50 COD shipping charges on merchandise purchased for resale, terms FOB shipping point. Nakashima uses the perpetual system to account for merchandise inventory.
12 Paid $7.95 postage to express mail a contract to a client.
14 Reimbursed Adina Sharon, the manager, $68 for business mileage on her car.
20 Purchased stationery for $67.77 that is immediately used.
23 Paid a courier $20 to deliver merchandise sold to a customer, terms FOB destination.
25 Paid $13.10 COD shipping charges on merchandise purchased for resale, terms FOB shipping point.
27 Paid $54 for postage expenses.
28 The fund had $120.42 remaining in the petty cash box. Sorted the petty cash receipts by accounts affected and exchanged them for a check to reimburse the fund for expenditures.
28 The petty cash fund amount is increased by $100 to a total of $500.

Problem 8-2A
Establish, reimburse, and increase petty cash

P2

Required

1. Prepare the journal entry to establish the petty cash fund.

2. Prepare a petty cash payments report for February with these categories: delivery expense, mileage expense, postage expense, merchandise inventory (for transportation-in), and office supplies expense. Sort the payments into the appropriate categories and total the expenditures in each category.

3. Prepare the journal entries (in dollars and cents) for part 2 to both (*a*) reimburse and (*b*) increase the fund amount.

Check (3a & 3b) Total Cr. to Cash $379.58

Problem 8-3A
Establish, reimburse, and adjust petty cash

P2 Sage 50

Kiona Co. set up a petty cash fund for payments of small amounts. The following transactions involving the petty cash fund occurred in May (the last month of the company's fiscal year).

May 1   Prepared a company check for $300 to establish the petty cash fund.
     15   Prepared a company check to replenish the fund for the following expenditures made since May 1.
          a.   Paid $88 for janitorial services.
          b.   Paid $53.68 for miscellaneous expenses.
          c.   Paid postage expenses of $53.50.
          d.   Paid $47.15 to *The County Gazette* (the local newspaper) for an advertisement.
          e.   Counted $62.15 remaining in the petty cash box.
     16   Prepared a company check for $200 to increase the fund to $500.
     31   The petty cashier reports that $288.20 cash remains in the fund. A company check is drawn to replenish the fund for the following expenditures made since May 15.
          f.   Paid postage expenses of $147.36.
          g.   Reimbursed the office manager for business mileage, $23.50.
          h.   Paid $34.75 to deliver merchandise to a customer, terms FOB destination.
     31   The company decides that the May 16 increase in the fund was too large. It reduces the fund by $100, leaving a total of $400.

Required

Check   (1) Cr. to Cash: May 15, $237.85; May 16, $200.00

1. Prepare journal entries (in dollars and cents) to establish the fund on May 1, to replenish it on May 15 and on May 31, and to reflect any increase or decrease in the fund balance on May 16 and May 31.

Analysis Component

2. Explain how the company's financial statements are affected if the petty cash fund is not replenished and no entry is made on May 31.

Problem 8-4A
Prepare a bank reconciliation and record adjustments

P3

mhhe.com/wildFAP21e

The following information is available to reconcile Branch Company's book balance of cash with its bank statement cash balance as of July 31, 2013.

a. On July 31, the company's Cash account has a $27,497 debit balance, but its July bank statement shows a $27,233 cash balance.

b. Check No. 3031 for $1,482 and Check No. 3040 for $558 were outstanding on the June 30 bank reconciliation. Check No. 3040 is listed with the July canceled checks, but Check No. 3031 is not. Also, Check No. 3065 for $382 and Check No. 3069 for $2,281, both written in July, are not among the canceled checks on the July 31 statement.

c. In comparing the canceled checks on the bank statement with the entries in the accounting records, it is found that Check No. 3056 for July rent was correctly written and drawn for $1,270 but was erroneously entered in the accounting records as $1,250.

d. A credit memorandum enclosed with the July bank statement indicates the bank collected $8,000 cash on a non-interest-bearing note for Branch, deducted a $45 collection fee, and credited the remainder to its account. Branch had not recorded this event before receiving the statement.

e. A debit memorandum for $805 lists a $795 NSF check plus a $10 NSF charge. The check had been received from a customer, Evan Shaw. Branch has not yet recorded this check as NSF.

f. Enclosed with the July statement is a $25 debit memorandum for bank services. It has not yet been recorded because no previous notification had been received.

g. Branch's July 31 daily cash receipts of $11,514 were placed in the bank's night depository on that date, but do not appear on the July 31 bank statement.

Required

Check   (1) Reconciled balance, $34,602; (2) Cr. Note Receivable $8,000

1. Prepare the bank reconciliation for this company as of July 31, 2013.

2. Prepare the journal entries necessary to bring the company's book balance of cash into conformity with the reconciled cash balance as of July 31, 2013.

Analysis Component

3. Assume that the July 31, 2013, bank reconciliation for this company is prepared and some items are treated incorrectly. For each of the following errors, explain the effect of the error on (i) the adjusted bank statement cash balance and (ii) the adjusted cash account book balance.

   a. The company's unadjusted cash account balance of $27,497 is listed on the reconciliation as $27,947.

   b. The bank's collection of the $8,000 note less the $45 collection fee is added to the bank statement cash balance on the reconciliation.

Chavez Company most recently reconciled its bank statement and book balances of cash on August 31 and it reported two checks outstanding, No. 5888 for $1,028.05 and No. 5893 for $494.25. The following information is available for its September 30, 2013, reconciliation.

Problem 8-5A
Prepare a bank reconciliation and record adjustments

P3

mhhe.com/wildFAP21e

Sage 50

From the September 30 Bank Statement

PREVIOUS BALANCE	TOTAL CHECKS AND DEBITS	TOTAL DEPOSITS AND CREDITS	CURRENT BALANCE
16,800.45	9,620.05	11,272.85	18,453.25

CHECKS AND DEBITS			DEPOSITS AND CREDITS		DAILY BALANCE	
Date	No.	Amount	Date	Amount	Date	Amount
09/03	5888	1,028.05	09/05	1,103.75	08/31	16,800.45
09/04	5902	719.90	09/12	2,226.90	09/03	15,772.40
09/07	5901	1,824.25	09/21	4,093.00	09/04	15,052.50
09/17		600.25 NSF	09/25	2,351.70	09/05	16,156.25
09/20	5905	937.00	09/30	12.50 IN	09/07	14,332.00
09/22	5903	399.10	09/30	1,485.00 CM	09/12	16,558.90
09/22	5904	2,090.00			09/17	15,958.65
09/28	5907	213.85			09/20	15,021.65
09/29	5909	1,807.65			09/21	19,114.65
					09/22	16,625.55
					09/25	18,977.25
					09/28	18,763.40
					09/29	16,955.75
					09/30	18,453.25

From Chavez Company's Accounting Records

Cash Receipts Deposited		
Date		Cash Debit
Sept.	5	1,103.75
	12	2,226.90
	21	4,093.00
	25	2,351.70
	30	1,682.75
		11,458.10

Cash Disbursements		
Check No.		Cash Credit
5901		1,824.25
5902		719.90
5903		399.10
5904		2,060.00
5905		937.00
5906		982.30
5907		213.85
5908		388.00
5909		1,807.65
		9,332.05

Cash						Acct. No. 101
Date		Explanation	PR	Debit	Credit	Balance
Aug.	31	Balance				15,278.15
Sept.	30	Total receipts	R12	11,458.10		26,736.25
	30	Total disbursements	D23		9,332.05	17,404.20

Additional Information

Check No. 5904 is correctly drawn for $2,090 to pay for computer equipment; however, the recordkeeper misread the amount and entered it in the accounting records with a debit to Computer Equipment and a credit to Cash of $2,060. The NSF check shown in the statement was originally received from a customer, S. Nilson, in payment of her account. Its return has not yet been recorded by the company. The credit memorandum is from the collection of a $1,500 note for Chavez Company by the bank. The bank deducted a $15 collection fee. The collection and fee are not yet recorded.

Required

1. Prepare the September 30, 2013, bank reconciliation for this company.

2. Prepare the journal entries (in dollars and cents) to adjust the book balance of cash to the reconciled balance.

Analysis Component

3. The bank statement reveals that some of the prenumbered checks in the sequence are missing. Describe three situations that could explain this.

PROBLEM SET B

Problem 8-1B
Analyzing internal control

C1

For each of these five separate cases, identify the principle(s) of internal control that is violated. Recommend what the business should do to ensure adherence to principles of internal control.

1. Latisha Tally is the company's computer specialist and oversees its computerized payroll system. Her boss recently asked her to put password protection on all office computers. Latisha has put a password in place that allows only the boss access to the file where pay rates are changed and personnel are added or deleted from the payroll.

2. Marker Theater has a computerized order-taking system for its tickets. The system is active all week and backed up every Friday night.

3. Sutton Company has two employees handling acquisitions of inventory. One employee places purchase orders and pays vendors. The second employee receives the merchandise.

4. The owner of Super Pharmacy uses a check protector to perforate checks, making it difficult for anyone to alter the amount of the check. The check protector is on the owner's desk in an office that contains company checks and is normally unlocked.

5. Lavina Company is a small business that has separated the duties of cash receipts and cash disbursements. The employee responsible for cash disbursements reconciles the bank account monthly.

Problem 8-2B
Establish, reimburse, and increase petty cash

P2

Blues Music Center had the following petty cash transactions in March of the current year.

March 5 Wrote a $250 check, cashed it, and gave the proceeds and the petty cashbox to Jen Rouse, the petty cashier.

6 Paid $12.50 COD shipping charges on merchandise purchased for resale, terms FOB shipping point. Blues uses the perpetual system to account for merchandise inventory.

11 Paid $10.75 delivery charges on merchandise sold to a customer, terms FOB destination.

12 Purchased file folders for $14.13 that are immediately used.

14 Reimbursed Bob Geldof, the manager, $11.65 for office supplies purchased and used.

18 Purchased printer paper for $20.54 that is immediately used.

27 Paid $45.10 COD shipping charges on merchandise purchased for resale, terms FOB shipping point.

28 Paid postage expenses of $18.

30 Reimbursed Geldof $56.80 for business car mileage.

31 Cash of $61.53 remained in the fund. Sorted the petty cash receipts by accounts affected and exchanged them for a check to reimburse the fund for expenditures.

31 The petty cash fund amount is increased by $50 to a total of $300.

Required

1. Prepare the journal entry to establish the petty cash fund.

2. Prepare a petty cash payments report for March with these categories: delivery expense, mileage expense, postage expense, merchandise inventory (for transportation-in), and office supplies expense. Sort the payments into the appropriate categories and total the expenses in each category.

3. Prepare the journal entries (in dollars and cents) for part 2 to both (*a*) reimburse and (*b*) increase the fund amount.

Problem 8-3B
Establishing, reimbursing, and adjusting petty cash

P2

Moya Co. establishes a petty cash fund for payments of small amounts. The following transactions involving the petty cash fund occurred in January (the last month of the company's fiscal year).

Jan. 3 A company check for $150 is written and made payable to the petty cashier to establish the petty cash fund.

14   A company check is written to replenish the fund for the following expenditures made since
     January 3.
     a.   Purchased office supplies for $14.29 that are immediately used up.
     b.   Paid $19.60 COD shipping charges on merchandise purchased for resale, terms FOB ship-
          ping point. Moya uses the perpetual system to account for inventory.
     c.   Paid $38.57 to All-Tech for minor repairs to a computer.
     d.   Paid $12.82 for items classified as miscellaneous expenses.
     e.   Counted $62.28 remaining in the petty cash box.
15   Prepared a company check for $50 to increase the fund to $200.
31   The petty cashier reports that $17.35 remains in the fund. A company check is written to replen-
     ish the fund for the following expenditures made since January 14.
     f.   Paid $50 to *The Smart Shopper* for an advertisement in January's newsletter.
     g.   Paid $48.19 for postage expenses.
     h.   Paid $78 to Smooth Delivery for delivery of merchandise, terms FOB destination.
31   The company decides that the January 15 increase in the fund was too little. It increases the fund
     by another $50, leaving a total of $250.

Required

1. Prepare journal entries (in dollars and cents) to establish the fund on January 3, to replenish it on
January 14 and January 31, and to reflect any increase or decrease in the fund balance on January 15
and 31.

Check (1) Cr. to Cash: Jan. 14,
$87.72; Jan. 31 (total), $232.65

Analysis Component

2. Explain how the company's financial statements are affected if the petty cash fund is not replenished
and no entry is made on January 31.

The following information is available to reconcile Severino Co.'s book balance of cash with its bank
statement cash balance as of December 31, 2013.

a. The December 31 cash balance according to the accounting records is $32,878.30, and the bank state-
ment cash balance for that date is $46,822.40.

b. Check No. 1273 for $4,589.30 and Check No. 1282 for $400, both written and entered in the accounting records in December, are not among the canceled checks. Two checks, No. 1231 for $2,289 and
No. 1242 for $410.40, were outstanding on the most recent November 30 reconciliation. Check No. 1231
is listed with the December canceled checks, but Check No. 1242 is not.

c. When the December checks are compared with entries in the accounting records, it is found that
Check No. 1267 had been correctly drawn for $3,456 to pay for office supplies but was erroneously
entered in the accounting records as $3,465.

d. Two debit memoranda are enclosed with the statement and are unrecorded at the time of the reconciliation. One debit memorandum is for $762.50 and dealt with an NSF check for $745 received from a
customer, Titus Industries, in payment of its account. The bank assessed a $17.50 fee for processing
it. The second debit memorandum is a $99 charge for check printing. Severino did not record these
transactions before receiving the statement.

e. A credit memorandum indicates that the bank collected $19,000 cash on a note receivable for the
company, deducted a $20 collection fee, and credited the balance to the company's Cash account.
Severino did not record this transaction before receiving the statement.

f. Severino's December 31 daily cash receipts of $9,583.10 were placed in the bank's night depository
on that date, but do not appear on the December 31 bank statement.

Problem 8-4B
Prepare a bank reconciliation
and record adjustments

P3

Required

1. Prepare the bank reconciliation for this company as of December 31, 2013.

2. Prepare the journal entries (in dollars and cents) necessary to bring the company's book balance of
cash into conformity with the reconciled cash balance as of December 31, 2013.

Check (1) Reconciled balance,
$51,005.80; (2) Cr. Note Receivable
$19,000.00

Analysis Component

3. Explain the nature of the communications conveyed by a bank when the bank sends the depositor
(*a*) a debit memorandum and (*b*) a credit memorandum.

Problem 8-5B
Prepare a bank reconciliation and record adjustments

P3

Shamara Systems most recently reconciled its bank balance on April 30 and reported two checks outstanding at that time, No. 1771 for $781 and No. 1780 for $1,425.90. The following information is available for its May 31, 2013, reconciliation.

From the May 31 Bank Statement

PREVIOUS BALANCE	TOTAL CHECKS AND DEBITS	TOTAL DEPOSITS AND CREDITS	CURRENT BALANCE
18,290.70	13,094.80	16,566.80	21,762.70

CHECKS AND DEBITS			DEPOSITS AND CREDITS		DAILY BALANCE	
Date	No.	Amount	Date	Amount	Date	Amount
05/01	1771	781.00	05/04	2,438.00	04/30	18,290.70
05/02	1783	382.50	05/14	2,898.00	05/01	17,509.70
05/04	1782	1,285.50	05/22	1,801.80	05/02	17,127.20
05/11	1784	1,449.60	05/25	7,350.00 CM	05/04	18,279.70
05/18		431.80 NSF	05/26	2,079.00	05/11	16,830.10
05/25	1787	8,032.50			05/14	19,728.10
05/26	1785	63.90			05/18	19,296.30
05/29	1788	654.00			05/22	21,098.10
05/31		14.00 SC			05/25	20,415.60
					05/26	22,430.70
					05/29	21,776.70
					05/31	21,762.70

From Shamara Systems' Accounting Records

Cash Receipts Deposited				Cash Disbursements		
Date			Cash Debit	Check No.		Cash Credit
May	4		2,438.00	1782		1,285.50
	14		2,898.00	1783		382.50
	22		1,801.80	1784		1,449.60
	26		2,079.00	1785		63.90
	31		2,727.30	1786		353.10
			11,944.10	1787		8,032.50
				1788		644.00
				1789		639.50
						12,850.60

Cash						Acct. No. 101
Date		Explanation	PR	Debit	Credit	Balance
Apr.	30	Balance				16,083.80
May	31	Total receipts	R7	11,944.10		28,027.90
	31	Total disbursements	D8		12,850.60	15,177.30

Additional Information

Check No. 1788 is correctly drawn for $654 to pay for May utilities; however, the recordkeeper misread the amount and entered it in the accounting records with a debit to Utilities Expense and a credit to Cash for $644. The bank paid and deducted the correct amount. The NSF check shown in the statement was originally received from a customer, W. Sox, in payment of her account. The company has not yet recorded its return. The credit memorandum is from a $7,400 note that the bank collected for the company.

The bank deducted a $50 collection fee and deposited the remainder in the company's account. The collection and fee have not yet been recorded.

Required

1. Prepare the May 31, 2013, bank reconciliation for Shamara Systems.
2. Prepare the journal entries (in dollars and cents) to adjust the book balance of cash to the reconciled balance.

Check (1) Reconciled balance, $22,071.50; (2) Cr. Note Receivable $7,400.00

Analysis Component

3. The bank statement reveals that some of the prenumbered checks in the sequence are missing. Describe three possible situations to explain this.

(This serial problem began in Chapter 1 and continues through most of the book. If previous chapter segments were not completed, the serial problem can begin at this point. It is helpful, but not necessary, to use the Working Papers that accompany the book.)

SERIAL PROBLEM
Success Systems
P3

Sage 50

SP 8   Adria Lopez receives the March bank statement for Success Systems on April 11, 2014. The March 31 bank statement shows an ending cash balance of $77,354. A comparison of the bank statement with the general ledger Cash account, No. 101, reveals the following.

a. A. Lopez notices that the bank erroneously cleared a $500 check against her account in March that she did not issue. The check documentation included with the bank statement shows that this check was actually issued by a company named Sierra Systems.

b. On March 25, the bank issued a $50 debit memorandum for the safety deposit box that Success Systems agreed to rent from the bank beginning March 25.

c. On March 26, the bank issued a $102 debit memorandum for printed checks that Success Systems ordered from the bank.

d. On March 31, the bank issued a credit memorandum for $33 interest earned on Success Systems' checking account for the month of March.

e. A. Lopez notices that the check she issued for $128 on March 31, 2014, has not yet cleared the bank.

f. A. Lopez verifies that all deposits made in March do appear on the March bank statement.

g. The general ledger Cash account, No. 101, shows an ending cash balance per books of $77,845 as of March 31 (prior to any reconciliation).

Required

1. Prepare a bank reconciliation for Success Systems for the month ended March 31, 2014.
2. Prepare any necessary adjusting entries. Use Miscellaneous Expenses, No. 677, for any bank charges. Use Interest Revenue, No. 404, for any interest earned on the checking account for the month of March.

Check (1) Adj. bank bal. $77,726

Beyond the Numbers

BTN 8-1   Refer to **Polaris'** financial statements in Appendix A to answer the following.

1. For both years ended December 31, 2011 and 2010, identify the total amount of cash and cash equivalents. Determine the percent (rounded to one decimal) that this amount represents of total current assets, total current liabilities, total shareholders' equity, and total assets for both years. Comment on any trends.

2. For years ended December 31, 2011 and 2010, use the information in the statement of cash flows to determine the percent change (rounded to one decimal) between the beginning and ending year amounts of cash and cash equivalents.

3. Compute the days' sales uncollected (rounded to two decimals) as of December 31, 2011 and 2010. Has the collection of receivables improved? Are accounts receivable an important asset for Polaris? Explain.

REPORTING IN ACTION
C2 A1

Polaris

Fast Forward

4. Access Polaris' financial statements for fiscal years ending after December 31, 2011, from its Website (**Polaris.com**) or the SEC's EDGAR database (**www.sec.gov**). Recompute its days' sales uncollected for years ending after December 31, 2011. Compare this to the days' sales uncollected for 2011 and 2010.

COMPARATIVE ANALYSIS

A1

Polaris

Arctic Cat

BTN 8-2   Key comparative figures for **Polaris** and **Arctic Cat** follow.

($ thousands)	Polaris		Arctic Cat	
	Current Year	Prior Year	Current Year	Prior Year
Accounts receivable	$ 115,302	$ 89,294	$ 23,732	$ 29,227
Net sales	2,656,949	1,991,139	363,015	350,871

Required

Compute days' sales uncollected (rounded to two decimals) for these companies for each of the two years shown. Comment on any trends for the companies. Which company has the largest percent change (rounded to two decimals) in days' sales uncollected?

ETHICS CHALLENGE

C1

BTN 8-3   Harriet Knox, Ralph Patton, and Marcia Diamond work for a family physician, Dr. Gwen Conrad, who is in private practice. Dr. Conrad is knowledgeable about office management practices and has segregated the cash receipt duties as follows. Knox opens the mail and prepares a triplicate list of money received. She sends one copy of the list to Patton, the cashier, who deposits the receipts daily in the bank. Diamond, the recordkeeper, receives a copy of the list and posts payments to patients' accounts. About once a month the office clerks have an expensive lunch they pay for as follows. First, Patton endorses a patient's check in Dr. Conrad's name and cashes it at the bank. Knox then destroys the remittance advice accompanying the check. Finally, Diamond posts payment to the customer's account as a miscellaneous credit. The three justify their actions by their relatively low pay and knowledge that Dr. Conrad will likely never miss the money.

Required

1. Who is the best person in Dr. Conrad's office to reconcile the bank statement?
2. Would a bank reconciliation uncover this office fraud?
3. What are some procedures to detect this type of fraud?
4. Suggest additional internal controls that Dr. Conrad could implement.

COMMUNICATING IN PRACTICE

P5

BTN 8-4[B]   Assume you are a business consultant. The owner of a company sends you an e-mail expressing concern that the company is not taking advantage of its discounts offered by vendors. The company currently uses the gross method of recording purchases. The owner is considering a review of all invoices and payments from the previous period. Due to the volume of purchases, however, the owner recognizes that this is time-consuming and costly. The owner seeks your advice about monitoring purchase discounts in the future. Provide a response in memorandum form.

TAKING IT TO THE NET

C1 P1

BTN 8-5   Visit the Association of Certified Fraud Examiners Website at **acfe.com**. Find and open the file "2010 Report to the Nation." Read the two-page Executive Summary and fill in the following blanks. (The report is under its *Fraud Resources* tab or under its *About the ACFE* tab [under Press Room]; we can also use the *Search* tab.)

1. The median loss caused by occupational frauds was $_____.
2. Nearly _____ of fraud cases involved losses of at least $1 million in losses.
3. Companies lose ___% of their annual revenues to fraud; this figure translates to a potential total fraud loss of more than $_____ trillion.
4. The typical length of fraud schemes was _____ months from the time the fraud began until it was detected.
5. Less than ___% of victim organizations conducted surprise audits, however these organizations have lower fraud losses and detect fraud more quickly than those without surprise audits.
6. Asset misappropriation schemes were most common at ___% of cases with a median loss of $_____.
7. Financial statement fraud schemes made up less than ___% of cases with a median loss of more than $_____ million.
8. Corruption schemes comprised ___% of cases with a median loss of $_____.
9. Less than ___% of the perpetrators had convictions prior to committing their frauds.

BTN 8-6   Organize the class into teams. Each team must prepare a list of 10 internal controls a consumer could observe in a typical retail department store. When called upon, the team's spokesperson must be prepared to share controls identified by the team that have not been shared by another team's spokesperson.

TEAMWORK IN ACTION

C1

BTN 8-7   Review the opening feature of this chapter that highlights Michael Inwald and his company **CHEESEBOY**.

Required

1. List the seven principles of internal control and explain how Michael could implement each of them in his stores.
2. Do you believe that Michael will need to add controls as his business expands? Explain.

ENTREPRENEURIAL DECISION

C1   P1

BTN 8-8   Visit an area of your college that serves the student community with either products or services. Some examples are food services, libraries, and bookstores. Identify and describe between four and eight internal controls being implemented.

HITTING THE ROAD

C1

BTN 8-9   The following information is from **Piaggio** (**www.Piaggio.com**), which manufactures two-, three- and four-wheel vehicles, and is Europe's leading manufacturer of motorcycles and scooters.

GLOBAL DECISION

C2   A1

🌐 **PIAGGIO**

Euro in thousands	Current Year	Prior Year
Cash	151,887	154,859
Accounts receivable	65,560	90,421
Current assets	509,708	575,897
Total assets	1,520,184	1,545,722
Current liabilities	644,277	616,166
Shareholders' equity	446,218	442,890
Net sales	1,516,463	1,485,351

Required

1. For each year, compute the percentage (rounded to one decimal) that cash represents of current assets, total assets, current liabilities, and shareholders' equity. Comment on any trends in these percentages.
2. Determine the percentage change (rounded to one decimal) between the current and prior year cash balances.
3. Compute the days' sales uncollected (rounded to one decimal) at the end of both the current year and the prior year. Has the collection of receivables improved? Explain.

ANSWERS TO MULTIPLE CHOICE QUIZ

1. e; The entry follows.

Debits to expenses (or assets)	420	
Cash Over and Short	5	
Cash		425

2. a; recognizes cash collection of note by bank.
3. a; the bank reconciliation follows.

4. d; ($6,720/$84,000) × 365 = <u>29.2 days</u>
5. b; The entry follows.

Merchandise Inventory*	5,880	
Accounts Payable		5,880

*$6,000 × 98%

Bank Reconciliation November 30			
Balance per bank statement	$1,895	Balance per books	$1,742
Add: Deposit in transit	795	Add: Note collected less fee	320
Deduct: Outstanding checks	(638)	Deduct: Service charge	(10)
Reconciled balance	$2,052	Reconciled balance	$2,052

Accounting for Receivables

9

A Look Back

Chapter 8 focused on internal control and reporting for cash. We described internal control procedures and the accounting for and management of cash.

A Look at This Chapter

This chapter emphasizes receivables. We explain that they are liquid assets and describe how companies account for and report them. We also discuss the importance of estimating uncollectibles.

A Look Ahead

Chapter 10 focuses on plant assets, natural resources, and intangible assets. We explain how to account for, report, and analyze these long-term assets.

Learning Objectives

CONCEPTUAL

C1 Describe accounts receivable and how they occur and are recorded. (p. 362)

C2 Describe a note receivable, the computation of its maturity date, and the recording of its existence. (p. 372)

C3 Explain how receivables can be converted to cash before maturity. (p. 375)

ANALYTICAL

A1 Compute accounts receivable turnover and use it to help assess financial condition. (p. 377)

PROCEDURAL

P1 Apply the direct write-off method to account for accounts receivable. (p. 366)

P2 Apply the allowance method and estimate uncollectibles based on sales and accounts receivable. (p. 368)

P3 Record the honoring and dishonoring of a note and adjustments for interest. (p. 374)

Decision Insight

Sweat Equity

BALTIMORE, MD—"There was a void in apparel and I decided to fill it," says Kevin Plank, the founder of **Under Armour (UnderArmour.com),** which is a manufacturer of athletic apparel. Kevin invested his life savings of $20,000 and began by working out of his grandma's basement.

As sales grew, Kevin partnered with a factory in Ohio and hit it off with the factory manager, Sal Fasciana. Sal spent many evenings and weekends teaching Kevin about accounting and cost controls. "I said, 'OK, kid. This is the way it's going to be done,'" recalls Sal. That attention to details carried over to where Kevin learned to monitor receivables. Decisions on credit sales and policies for extending credit can make or break a start-up.

Kevin applied well what Sal taught him. He ensured that credit sales were extended to customers in good credit standing. Kevin knows his clients, including who pays and when. Says Kevin, we understand our customers—inside and out—including cash payment patterns that allow us to estimate uncollectibles and minimize bad debts. His financial report says, "We make ongoing estimates relating to the collectibility of our accounts receivable and maintain a reserve for estimated losses resulting from the inability of our customers to make required payments."

A commitment to quality customers is propelling Under Armour's sales and shattering Kevin's most optimistic goals. "It's about educating consumers . . . investing in the product." Kevin has also issued notes receivable to select employees. Both accounts and notes receivables receive his attention. His financial report states that they "review the allowance for doubtful accounts monthly."

"When I first started . . . I was a young punk who thought he knew everything," explains Kevin. While he admits that insight and ingenuity are vital, he knows accounting reports must show profits for long-term success. "Most people out there are saying we're going to trip up at some point," says Kevin. "Our job is to prove them wrong." His evolving fabrics continue to lead the industry in removing perspiration. He also gives us a new perspective on Thomas Edison's assertion that: genius is 99 percent perspiration and 1 percent inspiration.

[Sources: *Under Armour Website,* January 2013; *Under Armour 10-K Report,* Filed February 2012; *FastCompany,* 2005; *USA Today,* December 2004; *Inc.com,* 2003 and 2004; *Entrepreneur's Journey,* November 2007; *Fortune,* October 2011; *Forbes,* December 2011]

This chapter focuses on accounts receivable and short-term notes receivable. We describe each of these assets, their uses, and how they are accounted for and reported in financial statements. This knowledge helps us use accounting information to make better business decisions. It can also help in predicting future company performance and financial condition as well as in managing one's own business.

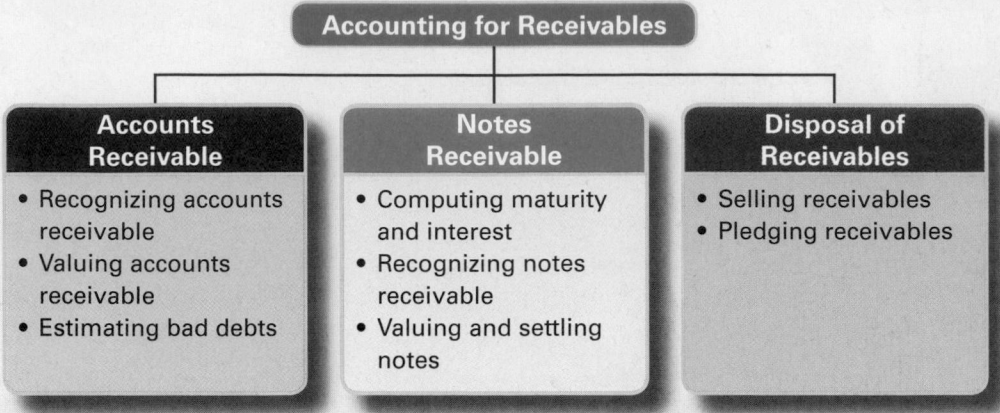

Accounting for Receivables

Accounts Receivable	Notes Receivable	Disposal of Receivables
• Recognizing accounts receivable • Valuing accounts receivable • Estimating bad debts	• Computing maturity and interest • Recognizing notes receivable • Valuing and settling notes	• Selling receivables • Pledging receivables

ACCOUNTS RECEIVABLE

A *receivable* is an amount due from another party. The two most common receivables are accounts receivable and notes receivable. Other receivables include interest receivable, rent receivable, tax refund receivable, and receivables from employees. **Accounts receivable** are amounts due from customers for credit sales. This section begins by describing how accounts receivable occur. It includes receivables that occur when customers use credit cards issued by third parties and when a company gives credit directly to customers. When a company does extend credit directly to customers, it (1) maintains a separate account receivable for each customer and (2) accounts for bad debts from credit sales.

Recognizing Accounts Receivable

C1 Describe accounts receivable and how they occur and are recorded.

Accounts receivable occur from credit sales to customers. The amount of credit sales has increased in recent years, reflecting several factors including an efficient financial system. Retailers such as **Costco** and **Best Buy** hold millions of dollars in accounts receivable. Similar amounts are held by wholesalers such as **SUPERVALU** and **SYSCO**. Exhibit 9.1 shows recent dollar amounts of receivables and their percent of total assets for four well-known companies.

EXHIBIT 9.1

Accounts Receivable for Selected Companies

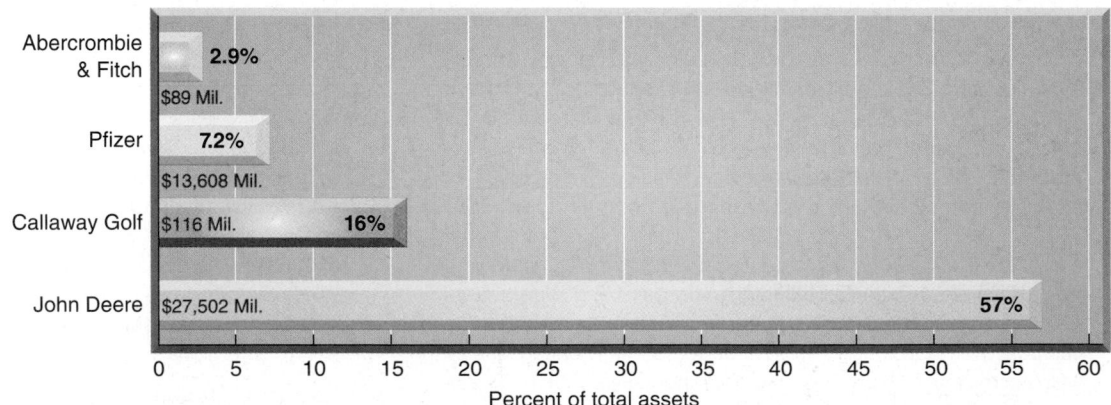

Sales on Credit Credit sales are recorded by increasing (debiting) Accounts Receivable. A company must also maintain a separate account for each customer that tracks how much that customer purchases, has already paid, and still owes. This information provides the basis for sending bills to customers and for other business analyses. To maintain this information, companies that extend credit directly to their customers keep a separate account receivable for each one of them.

The general ledger continues to have a single Accounts Receivable account (called a *control* account) along with the other financial statement accounts, but a supplementary record is created to maintain a separate account for each customer. This supplementary record is called the *accounts receivable ledger* (or *accounts receivable subsidiary ledger*).

Exhibit 9.2 shows the relation between the Accounts Receivable account in the general ledger and its individual customer accounts in the accounts receivable ledger for TechCom, a small electronics wholesaler. This exhibit reports a $3,000 ending balance of TechCom's accounts receivable for June 30. TechCom's transactions are mainly in cash, but it has two major credit customers: CompStore and RDA Electronics. Its *schedule of accounts receivable* shows that the $3,000 balance of the Accounts Receivable account in the general ledger equals the total of its two customers' balances in the accounts receivable ledger.

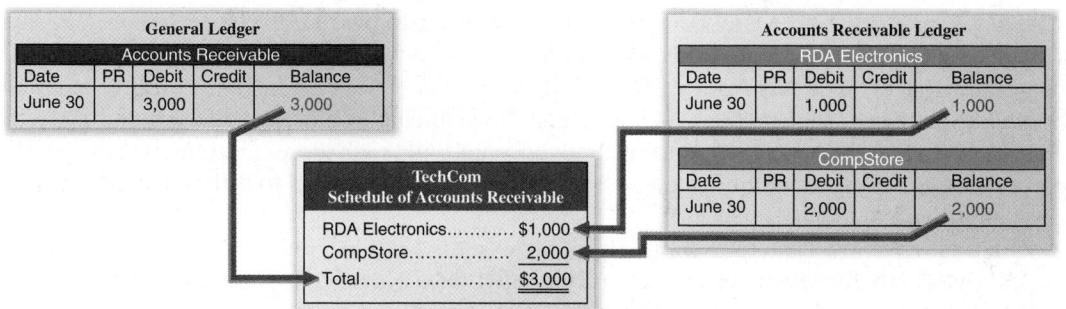

EXHIBIT 9.2

General Ledger and the Accounts Receivable Ledger (before July 1 transactions)

To see how accounts receivable from credit sales are recognized in the accounting records, we look at two transactions on July 1 between TechCom and its credit customers—see Exhibit 9.3. The first is a credit sale of $950 to CompStore. A credit sale is posted with both a debit to the Accounts Receivable account in the general ledger and a debit to the customer account in the accounts receivable ledger. The second transaction is a collection of $720 from RDA Electronics from a prior credit sale. Cash receipts from a credit customer are posted with a credit to the Accounts Receivable account in the general ledger and flow through to credit the customer account in the accounts receivable ledger. (Posting debits or credits to Accounts Receivable in two separate ledgers does not violate the requirement that debits equal credits. The equality of debits and credits is maintained in the general ledger. The accounts receivable ledger is a *supplementary* record providing information on each customer.)

EXHIBIT 9.3

Accounts Receivable Transactions

July 1	Accounts Receivable—CompStore	950	
	Sales		950
	*To record credit sales**		
July 1	Cash	720	
	Accounts Receivable—RDA Electronics		720
	To record collection of credit sales.		

Assets = Liabilities + Equity
+ 950   +950

Assets = Liabilities + Equity
+720
−720

* We omit the entry to Dr. Cost of Sales and Cr. Merchandise Inventory to focus on sales and receivables.

Exhibit 9.4 shows the general ledger and the accounts receivable ledger after recording the two July 1 transactions. The general ledger shows the effects of the sale, the collection, and the resulting balance of $3,230. These events are also reflected in the individual customer accounts:

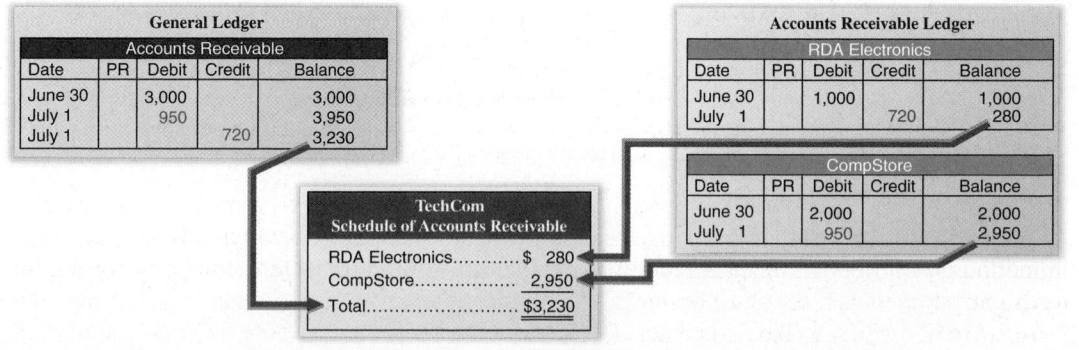

EXHIBIT 9.4

General Ledger and the Accounts Receivable Ledger (after July 1 transactions)

RDA Electronics has an ending balance of $280, and CompStore's ending balance is $2,950. The $3,230 sum of the individual accounts equals the debit balance of the Accounts Receivable account in the general ledger.

Like TechCom, many large retailers such as **Target** and **JCPenney** sell on credit. Many also maintain their own credit cards to grant credit to approved customers and to earn interest on any balance not paid within a specified period of time. This allows them to avoid the fee charged by credit card companies. The entries in this case are the same as those for TechCom except for the possibility of added interest revenue. If a customer owes interest on a bill, we debit Interest Receivable and credit Interest Revenue for that amount. (Many retailers require clerks to ask customers during checkout if they wish to apply for a store credit card—sweeteners are often used such as: *save 10% off today's purchases if you apply now.*)

Point: Visa USA now transacts more than $1 trillion from its credit, debit, and prepaid cards.

Credit Card Sales   Many companies allow their customers to pay for products and services using third-party credit cards such as **Visa**, **MasterCard**, or **American Express**, and debit cards (also called ATM or bank cards). This practice gives customers the ability to make purchases without cash or checks. Once credit is established with a credit card company or bank, the customer does not have to open an account with each store. Customers using these cards can make single monthly payments instead of several payments to different creditors and can defer their payments.

Many sellers allow customers to use third-party credit cards and debit cards instead of granting credit directly for several reasons. First, the seller does not have to evaluate each customer's credit standing or make decisions about who gets credit and how much. Second, the seller avoids the risk of extending credit to customers who cannot or do not pay. This risk is transferred to the card company. Third, the seller typically receives cash from the card company sooner than had it granted credit directly to customers. Fourth, a variety of credit options for customers offers a potential increase in sales volume. **Sears** historically offered credit only to customers using a Sears card but later changed its policy to permit customers to charge purchases to third-party credit card companies in a desire to increase sales. It reported: "SearsCharge increased its share of Sears retail sales even as the company expanded the payment options available to its customers with the acceptance . . . of Visa, MasterCard, and American Express in addition to the [Sears] Card."

There are guidelines in how companies account for credit card and debit card sales. Some credit cards, but nearly all debit cards, credit a seller's Cash account immediately upon deposit. In this case the seller deposits a copy of each card sales receipt in its bank account just as it deposits a customer's check. The majority of credit cards, however, require the seller to remit a copy (often electronically) of each receipt to the card company. Until payment is received, the seller has an account receivable from the card company. In both cases, the seller pays a fee for services provided by the card company, often ranging from 1% to 5% of card sales. This charge is deducted from the credit to the seller's account or the cash payment to the seller. (Many retailers accept MasterCard and Visa, but not American Express. The reason is that American Express usually charges retailers a higher percentage fee than other credit card companies.)

🔲 **Decision** Insight ══════════════════════════════════

Debit Card vs. Credit Card   A buyer's debit card purchase reduces the buyer's cash account balance at the card company, which is often a bank. Since the buyer's cash account balance is a liability (with a credit balance) for the card company to the buyer, the card company would debit that account for a buyer's purchase—hence, the term *debit card*. A credit card reflects authorization by the card company of a line of credit for the buyer with preset interest rates and payment terms—hence, the term *credit card*. Most card companies waive interest charges if the buyer pays its balance each month. ∎

Point: Web merchants pay twice as much in credit card association fees as other retailers because they suffer 10 times as much fraud.

The procedures used in accounting for credit card sales depend on whether cash is received immediately on deposit or cash receipt is delayed until the credit card company makes the payment.

Cash Received Immediately on Deposit   To illustrate, if TechCom has $100 of credit card sales with a 4% fee, and its $96 cash is received immediately on deposit, the entry is

July 15	Cash	96	
	Credit Card Expense	4	
	Sales		100
	*To record credit card sales less a 4% credit card expense.**		

Assets = Liabilities + Equity
+96   +100
                             −4

* We omit the entry to Dr. Cost of Sales and Cr. Merchandise Inventory to focus on credit card expense.

Cash Received Some Time after Deposit   However, if instead TechCom must remit electronically the credit card sales receipts to the credit card company and wait for the $96 cash payment, the entry on the date of sale is

July 15	**Accounts Receivable—Credit Card Co.**	96	
	Credit Card Expense	4	
	Sales		100
	*To record credit card sales less 4% credit card expense.**		

Assets = Liabilities + Equity
+96   +100
                             −4

* We omit the entry to Dr. Cost of Sales and Cr. Merchandise Inventory to focus on credit card expense.

When cash is later received from the credit card company, usually through electronic funds transfer, the entry is

July 20	Cash	96	
	Accounts Receivable—Credit Card Co.		96
	To record cash receipt.		

Assets = Liabilities + Equity
+96
−96

Some firms report credit card expense in the income statement as a type of discount deducted from sales to get net sales. Other companies classify it as a selling expense or even as an administrative expense. Arguments can be made for each approach.

Point: Third-party credit card costs can be large. JCPenney reported third-party credit card costs exceeding $10 million.

■ Decision Insight

Cabbie Credit Card Sales   Thirty New York cabs rolled out the first phase of a new mobile payment system for taxis. These 30 cabs are equipped with an iPad encased in a metal housing that includes a credit card reader. The iPad allows fares to swipe their card, sign their name on the screen with their finger, and then receive a receipt on their phone either by text or email. Taxi drivers are also able to interact with the system, dubbed "Checker," using their own iPhone app. ■

Installment Sales and Receivables   Many companies allow their credit customers to make periodic payments over several months. For example, **Ford Motor Company** reports more than $70 billion in installment receivables. The seller refers to such assets as *installment accounts* (or *finance*) *receivable,* which are amounts owed by customers from credit sales for which payment is required in periodic amounts over an extended time period. Source documents for installment accounts receivable include sales slips or invoices describing the sales transactions. The customer is usually charged interest. Although installment accounts receivable can have credit periods of more than one year, they are classified as current assets if the seller regularly offers customers such terms.

■ Decision Maker

Entrepreneur   As a small retailer, you are considering allowing customers to buy merchandise using credit cards. Until now, your store accepted only cash and checks. What analysis do you use to make this decision? ■   [Answer—p. 380]

Quick Check   Answers — p. 381

1. In recording credit card sales, when do you debit Accounts Receivable and when do you debit Cash?
2. A company accumulates sales receipts and remits them to the credit card company for payment. When are the credit card expenses recorded? When are these expenses incurred?

Valuing Accounts Receivable—Direct Write-Off Method

When a company directly grants credit to its customers, it expects that some customers will not pay what they promised. The accounts of these customers are *uncollectible accounts,* commonly called **bad debts.** The total amount of uncollectible accounts is an expense of selling on credit. Why do companies sell on credit if they expect some accounts to be uncollectible? The answer is that companies believe that granting credit will increase total sales and net income enough to offset bad debts. Companies use two methods to account for uncollectible accounts: (1) direct write-off method and (2) allowance method. We describe both.

Point: Managers realize that some portion of credit sales will be uncollectible, but which credit sales are uncollectible is unknown.

Recording and Writing Off Bad Debts The **direct write-off method** of accounting for bad debts records the loss from an uncollectible account receivable when it is determined to be uncollectible. No attempt is made to predict bad debts expense. To illustrate, if TechCom determines on January 23 that it cannot collect $520 owed to it by its customer J. Kent, it recognizes the loss using the direct write-off method as follows:

Assets = Liabilities + Equity
−520   −520

Jan. 23	Bad Debts Expense	520	
	Accounts Receivable—J. Kent		520
	To write off an uncollectible account.		

The debit in this entry charges the uncollectible amount directly to the current period's Bad Debts Expense account. The credit removes its balance from the Accounts Receivable account in the general ledger (and its subsidiary ledger).

Point: If a customer fails to pay within the credit period, most companies send out repeated billings and make other efforts to collect.

Recovering a Bad Debt Although uncommon, sometimes an account written off is later collected. This can be due to factors such as continual collection efforts or a customer's good fortune. If the account of J. Kent that was written off directly to Bad Debts Expense is later collected in full, the following two entries record this recovery:

Assets = Liabilities + Equity
+520   +520

Assets = Liabilities + Equity
+520
−520

Mar. 11	Accounts Receivable—J. Kent	520	
	Bad Debts Expense		520
	To reinstate account previously written off.		
Mar. 11	Cash	520	
	Accounts Receivable—J. Kent		520
	To record full payment of account.		

Assessing the Direct Write-Off Method Examples of companies that use the direct write-off method include **Rand Medical Billing, Gateway Distributors, Microwave Satellite Technologies, First Industrial Realty, New Frontier Energy**, and **Sub Surface Waste Management.** The following disclosure by **Pharma-Bio Serv** is typical of the justification for this method: Bad debts are accounted for using the direct write-off method whereby an expense is recognized only when a specific account is determined to be uncollectible. The effect of using this method approximates that of the allowance method. Companies must weigh at least two accounting concepts when considering the use of the direct write-off method: the (1) matching principle and (2) materiality constraint.

Matching principle applied to bad debts. The **matching (expense recognition) principle** requires expenses to be reported in the same accounting period as the sales they helped produce. This means that if extending credit to customers helped produce sales, the bad debts expense linked to those sales is matched and reported in the same period. The direct write-off method usually does *not* best match sales and expenses because bad debts expense is not recorded until an account becomes uncollectible, which often occurs in a period after that of the credit sale. To match bad debts expense with the sales it produces therefore requires a company to estimate future uncollectibles.

Point: **Harley-Davidson** reports $150 million of credit losses matched against $4,962 million of finance receivables.

Materiality constraint applied to bad debts. The **materiality constraint** states that an amount can be ignored if its effect on the financial statements is unimportant to users' business decisions. The materiality constraint permits the use of the direct write-off method when bad debts expenses are very small in relation to a company's other financial statement items such as sales and net income.

Valuing Accounts Receivable—Allowance Method

The **allowance method** of accounting for bad debts matches the *estimated* loss from uncollectible accounts receivable against the sales they helped produce. We must use estimated losses because when sales occur, management does not know which customers will not pay their bills. This means that at the end of each period, the allowance method requires an estimate of the total bad debts expected to result from that period's sales. This method has two advantages over the direct write-off method: (1) it records estimated bad debts expense in the period when the related sales are recorded and (2) it reports accounts receivable on the balance sheet at the estimated amount of cash to be collected.

Point: Under direct write-off, expense is recorded each time an account is written off. Under the allowance method, expense is recorded with an adjusting entry equal to the total estimated uncollectibles for that period's sales.

Recording Bad Debts Expense   The allowance method estimates bad debts expense at the end of each accounting period and records it with an adjusting entry. TechCom, for instance, had credit sales of $300,000 during its first year of operations. At the end of the first year, $20,000 of credit sales remained uncollected. Based on the experience of similar businesses, TechCom estimated that $1,500 of its accounts receivable would be uncollectible. This estimated expense is recorded with the following adjusting entry:

	Bad Debts Expense Recognized in
Direct write-off method	The future when account is deemed uncollectible
Allowance method	Current period to yield realizable Accts. Rec. bal.

Dec. 31	Bad Debts Expense	1,500	
	Allowance for Doubtful Accounts		1,500
	To record estimated bad debts.		

Assets = Liabilities + Equity
−1,500   −1,500

The estimated Bad Debts Expense of $1,500 is reported on the income statement (as either a selling expense or an administrative expense) and offsets the $300,000 credit sales it helped produce. The **Allowance for Doubtful Accounts** is a contra asset account. A contra account is used instead of reducing accounts receivable directly because at the time of the adjusting entry, the company does not know which customers will not pay. After the bad debts adjusting entry is posted, TechCom's account balances (in T-account form) for Accounts Receivable and its Allowance for Doubtful Accounts are as shown in Exhibit 9.5.

Point: Credit approval is usually not assigned to the selling dept. because its goal is to increase sales, and it may approve customers at the cost of increased bad debts. Instead, approval is assigned to a separate credit-granting or administrative dept.

Accounts Receivable				**Allowance for Doubtful Accounts**		
Dec. 31	20,000				Dec. 31	1,500

EXHIBIT 9.5

General Ledger Entries after Bad Debts Adjusting Entry

The Allowance for Doubtful Accounts credit balance of $1,500 has the effect of reducing accounts receivable to its estimated realizable value. **Realizable value** refers to the expected proceeds from converting an asset into cash. Although credit customers owe $20,000 to TechCom, only $18,500 is expected to be realized in cash collections from these customers. In the balance sheet, the Allowance for Doubtful Accounts is subtracted from Accounts Receivable and is often reported as shown in Exhibit 9.6.

Point: Bad Debts Expense is also called *Uncollectible Accounts Expense.* The Allowance for Doubtful Accounts is also called *Allowance for Uncollectible Accounts.*

Current assets		
Accounts receivable	$20,000	
Less allowance for doubtful accounts	1,500	$18,500

EXHIBIT 9.6

Balance Sheet Presentation of the Allowance for Doubtful Accounts

Sometimes the Allowance for Doubtful Accounts is not reported separately. This alternative presentation is shown in Exhibit 9.7 (also see Appendix A).

Current assets	
Accounts receivable (net of $1,500 doubtful accounts)	$18,500

EXHIBIT 9.7

Alternative Presentation of the Allowance for Doubtful Accounts

Writing Off a Bad Debt   When specific accounts are identified as uncollectible, they are written off against the Allowance for Doubtful Accounts. To illustrate, TechCom decides that J. Kent's $520 account is uncollectible and makes the following entry to write it off.

Jan. 23	Allowance for Doubtful Accounts	520	
	Accounts Receivable—J. Kent		520
	To write off an uncollectible account.		

Assets = Liabilities + Equity
+520
−520

Point: The Bad Debts Expense account is not debited in the write-off entry because it was recorded in the period when sales occurred.

Posting this write-off entry to the Accounts Receivable account removes the amount of the bad debt from the general ledger (it is also posted to the accounts receivable subsidiary ledger). The general ledger accounts now appear as in Exhibit 9.8 (assuming no other transactions affecting these accounts).

EXHIBIT 9.8

General Ledger Entries after Write-Off

Accounts Receivable				Allowance for Doubtful Accounts			
Dec. 31	20,000					Dec. 31	1,500
		Jan. 23	520	Jan. 23	520		

Point: In posting a write-off, the ledger's Explanation column indicates the reason for this credit so it is not misinterpreted as payment in full.

The write-off does *not* affect the realizable value of accounts receivable as shown in Exhibit 9.9. Neither total assets nor net income is affected by the write-off of a specific account. Instead, both assets and net income are affected in the period when bad debts expense is predicted and recorded with an adjusting entry.

EXHIBIT 9.9

Realizable Value before and after Write-Off of a Bad Debt

	Before Write-Off	After Write-Off
Accounts receivable	$ 20,000	$ 19,480
Less allowance for doubtful accounts	1,500	980
Estimated realizable accounts receivable	**$18,500**	**$18,500**

Recovering a Bad Debt   When a customer fails to pay and the account is written off as uncollectible, his or her credit standing is jeopardized. To help restore credit standing, a customer sometimes volunteers to pay all or part of the amount owed. A company makes two entries when collecting an account previously written off by the allowance method. The first is to reverse the write-off and reinstate the customer's account. The second entry records the collection of the reinstated account. To illustrate, if on March 11 Kent pays in full his account previously written off, the entries are

Assets = Liabilities + Equity
+520
−520

Assets = Liabilities + Equity
+520
−520

Mar. 11	Accounts Receivable—J. Kent	520	
	Allowance for Doubtful Accounts		520
	To reinstate account previously written off.		
Mar. 11	Cash	520	
	Accounts Receivable—J. Kent		520
	To record full payment of account.		

Example: If TechCom used a collection agency and paid a 35% commission on $520 collected from Kent, how is this recorded? *Answer:*
Cash 338
Collection Expense 182
   Accts. Recble.—J. Kent 520

In this illustration, Kent paid the entire amount previously written off, but sometimes a customer pays only a portion of the amount owed. A question then arises as to whether the entire balance of the account or just the amount paid is returned to accounts receivable. This is a matter of judgment. If we believe this customer will later pay in full, we return the entire amount owed to accounts receivable, but if we expect no further collection, we return only the amount paid.

Decision Insight

PayPal   PayPal is legally just a money transfer agent, but it is increasingly challenging big credit card brands—see chart. PayPal is successful because: (1) online credit card processing fees often exceed $0.15 per dollar, but PayPal's fees are under $0.10 per dollar. (2) PayPal's merchant fraud losses are under 0.2% of revenues, which compares to nearly 2% for online merchants using credit cards. ∎

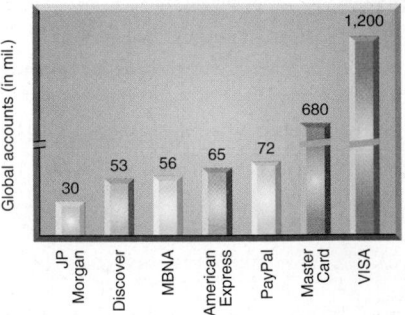

P2   Apply the allowance method and estimate uncollectibles based on sales and accounts receivable.

Estimating Bad Debts—Percent of Sales Method

The allowance method requires an estimate of bad debts expense to prepare an adjusting entry at the end of each accounting period. There are two common methods. One is based on the income statement relation between bad debts expense and sales. The second is based on the balance sheet relation between accounts receivable and the allowance for doubtful accounts.

The *percent of sales method,* also referred to as the *income statement method,* is based on the idea that a given percent of a company's credit sales for the period is uncollectible. To illustrate, assume that Musicland has credit sales of $400,000 in year 2013. Based on past experience, Musicland estimates 0.6% of credit sales to be uncollectible. This implies that Musicland expects $2,400 of bad debts expense from its sales (computed as $400,000 × 0.006). The adjusting entry to record this estimated expense is

Dec. 31	Bad Debts Expense	2,400	
	Allowance for Doubtful Accounts		2,400
	To record estimated bad debts.		

Assets = Liabilities + Equity
−2,400   −2,400

The allowance account ending balance on the balance sheet for this method would rarely equal the bad debts expense on the income statement. This is so because unless a company is in its first period of operations, its allowance account has a zero balance only if the prior amounts written off as uncollectible *exactly* equal the prior estimated bad debts expenses. (When computing bad debts expense as a percent of sales, managers monitor and adjust the percent so it is not too high or too low.)

Estimating Bad Debts—Percent of Receivables Method

The *accounts receivable methods,* also referred to as *balance sheet methods,* use balance sheet relations to estimate bad debts—mainly the relation between accounts receivable and the allowance amount. The goal of the bad debts adjusting entry for these methods is to make the Allowance for Doubtful Accounts balance equal to the portion of accounts receivable that is estimated to be uncollectible. The estimated balance for the allowance account is obtained in one of two ways: (1) computing the percent uncollectible from the total accounts receivable or (2) aging accounts receivable.

The *percent of accounts receivable method* assumes that a given percent of a company's receivables is uncollectible. This percent is based on past experience and is impacted by current conditions such as economic trends and customer difficulties. The total dollar amount of all receivables is multiplied by this percent to get the estimated dollar amount of uncollectible accounts—reported in the balance sheet as the Allowance for Doubtful Accounts.

To illustrate, assume that Musicland has $50,000 of accounts receivable on December 31, 2013. Experience suggests 5% of its receivables is uncollectible. This means that *after* the adjusting entry is posted, we want the Allowance for Doubtful Accounts to show a $2,500 credit balance (5% of $50,000). We are also told that its beginning balance is $2,200, which is 5% of the $44,000 accounts receivable on December 31, 2012—see Exhibit 9.10.

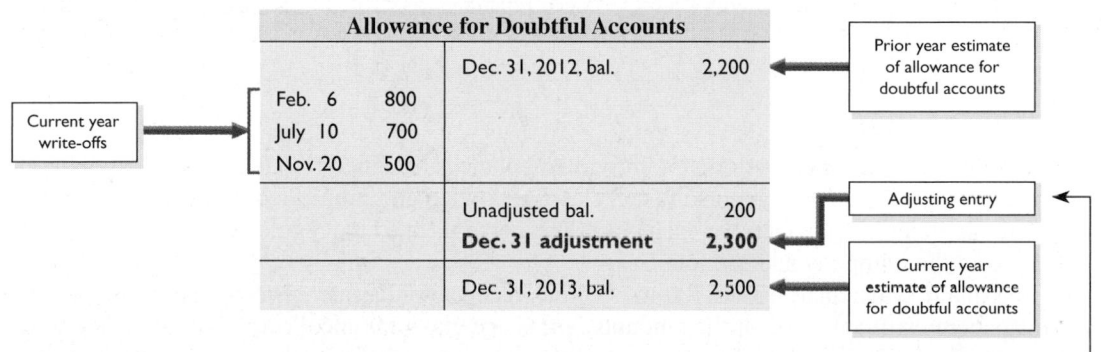

During 2013, accounts of customers are written off on February 6, July 10, and November 20. Thus, the account has a $200 credit balance *before* the December 31, 2013, adjustment. The adjusting entry to give the allowance account the estimated $2,500 balance is

Dec. 31	Bad Debts Expense	2,300	
	Allowance for Doubtful Accounts		2,300
	To record estimated bad debts.		

Assets = Liabilities + Equity
−2,300   −2,300

■ **Decision Insight** ●━━━━━━━━━━━━━━━━━━━━━━━━━━━

Aging Pains   Unlike wine, accounts receivable do not improve with age. Experience shows that the longer a receivable is past due, the lower is the likelihood of its collection. An *aging schedule* uses this knowledge to estimate bad debts. The chart here is from a survey that reported estimates of bad debts for receivables grouped by how long they were past their due dates. Each company sets its own estimates based on its customers and its experiences with those customers' payment patterns. ■

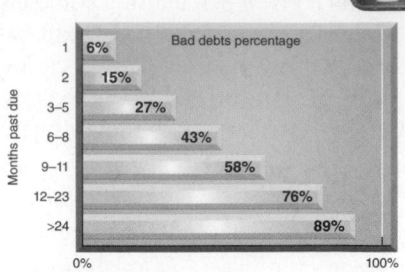

Estimating Bad Debts—Aging of Receivables Method

The **aging of accounts receivable** method uses both past and current receivables information to estimate the allowance amount. Specifically, each receivable is classified by how long it is past its due date. Then estimates of uncollectible amounts are made assuming that the longer an amount is past due, the more likely it is to be uncollectible. Classifications are often based on 30-day periods. After the amounts are classified (or aged), experience is used to estimate the percent of each uncollectible class. These percents are applied to the amounts in each class and then totaled to get the estimated balance of the Allowance for Doubtful Accounts. This computation is performed by setting up a schedule such as Exhibit 9.11.

EXHIBIT 9.11

Aging of Accounts Receivable

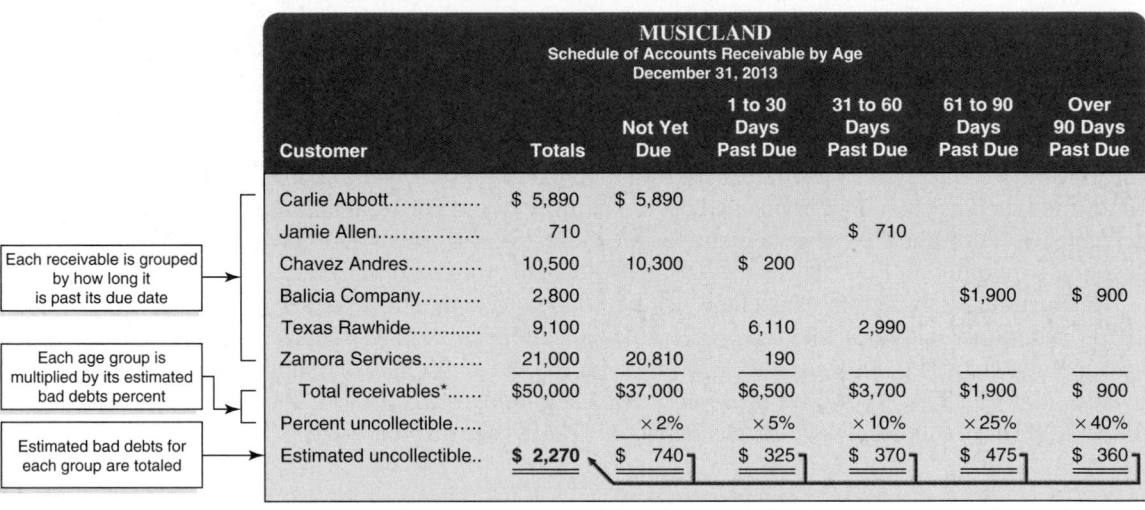

Customer	Totals	Not Yet Due	1 to 30 Days Past Due	31 to 60 Days Past Due	61 to 90 Days Past Due	Over 90 Days Past Due
Carlie Abbott..............	$ 5,890	$ 5,890				
Jamie Allen.................	710			$ 710		
Chavez Andres............	10,500	10,300	$ 200			
Balicia Company..........	2,800				$1,900	$ 900
Texas Rawhide.............	9,100		6,110	2,990		
Zamora Services..........	21,000	20,810	190			
Total receivables*......	$50,000	$37,000	$6,500	$3,700	$1,900	$ 900
Percent uncollectible.....		× 2%	× 5%	× 10%	× 25%	× 40%
Estimated uncollectible..	$ 2,270	$ 740	$ 325	$ 370	$ 475	$ 360

Each receivable is grouped by how long it is past its due date

Each age group is multiplied by its estimated bad debts percent

Estimated bad debts for each group are totaled

Exhibit 9.11 lists each customer's individual balances assigned to one of five classes based on its days past due. The amounts in each class are totaled and multiplied by the estimated percent of uncollectible accounts for each class. The percents used are regularly reviewed to reflect changes in the company and economy.

To explain, Musicland has $3,700 in accounts receivable that are 31 to 60 days past due. Its management estimates 10% of the amounts in this age class are uncollectible, or a total of $370 (computed as $3,700 × 10%). Similar analysis is done for each of the other four classes. The final total of $2,270 ($740 + $325 + 370 + $475 + $360) shown in the first column is the estimated balance for the Allowance for Doubtful Accounts. Exhibit 9.12 shows that since the allowance

EXHIBIT 9.12

Computation of the Required Adjustment for the Accounts Receivable Method

Unadjusted balance	$ 200 credit
Estimated balance	2,270 credit
Required adjustment	**$2,070 credit**

account has an unadjusted credit balance of $200, the required adjustment to the Allowance for Doubtful Accounts is $2,070. (We could also use a T-account for this analysis as shown in the margin.) This yields the following end-of-period adjusting entry:

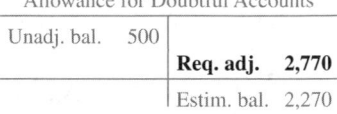

Allowance for Doubtful Accounts	
	Unadj. bal. 200
	Req. adj. 2,070
	Estim. bal. 2,270

Dec. 31	Bad Debts Expense	2,070	
	Allowance for Doubtful Accounts		2,070
	To record estimated bad debts.		

Assets = Liabilities + Equity
−2,070   −2,070

Alternatively, if the allowance account had an unadjusted *debit* balance of $500 (instead of the $200 credit balance), its required adjustment would be computed as follows. (Again, a T-account can be used for this analysis as shown in the margin.)

Point: A debit balance implies that write-offs for that period exceed the total allowance.

Allowance for Doubtful Accounts	
Unadj. bal. 500	
	Req. adj. 2,770
	Estim. bal. 2,270

The entry to record the end-of-period adjustment for this alternative case is

Dec. 31	Bad Debts Expense	2,770	
	Allowance for Doubtful Accounts		2,770
	To record estimated bad debts.		

Assets − Liabilities + Equity
−2,770   −2,770

The aging of accounts receivable method is an examination of specific accounts and is usually the most reliable of the estimation methods.

Estimating Bad Debts—Summary of Methods Exhibit 9.13 summarizes the principles guiding all three estimation methods and their focus of analysis. Percent of sales, with its income statement focus, does a good job at matching bad debts expense with sales. The accounts receivable methods, with their balance sheet focus, do a better job at reporting accounts receivable at realizable value.

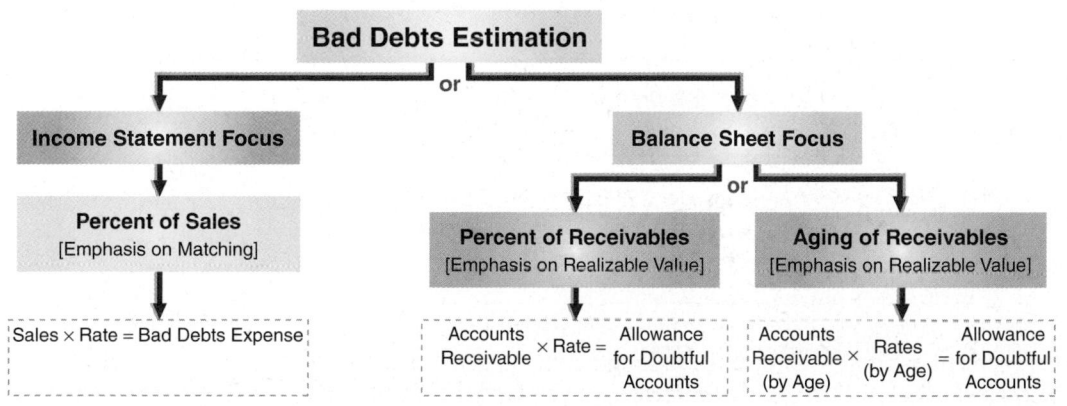

EXHIBIT 9.13

Methods to Estimate Bad Debts

 Decision Maker

Labor Union Chief One week prior to labor contract negotiations, financial statements are released showing no income growth. A 10% growth was predicted. Your analysis finds that the company increased its allowance for uncollectibles from 1.5% to 4.5% of receivables. Without this change, income would show a 9% growth. Does this analysis impact negotiations? ■ [Answer—p. 381]

3. Why must bad debts expense be estimated if such an estimate is possible?

4. What term describes the balance sheet valuation of Accounts Receivable less the Allowance for Doubtful Accounts?

5. Why is estimated bad debts expense credited to a contra account (Allowance for Doubtful Accounts) rather than to the Accounts Receivable account?

6. SnoBoard Company's year-end balance in its Allowance for Doubtful Accounts is a credit of $440. By aging accounts receivable, it estimates that $6,142 is uncollectible. Prepare SnoBoard's year-end adjusting entry for bad debts.

7. Record entries for these transactions assuming the allowance method is used:

   Jan. 10   The $300 account of customer Cool Jam is determined uncollectible.

   April 12   Cool Jam unexpectedly pays in full the account deemed uncollectible on Jan. 10.

NOTES RECEIVABLE

C2 Describe a note receivable, the computation of its maturity date, and the recording of its existence.

A **promissory note** is a written promise to pay a specified amount of money, usually with interest, either on demand or at a definite future date. Promissory notes are used in many transactions, including paying for products and services, and lending and borrowing money. Sellers sometimes ask for a note to replace an account receivable when a customer requests additional time to pay a past-due account. For legal reasons, sellers generally prefer to receive notes when the credit period is long and when the receivable is for a large amount. If a lawsuit is needed to collect from a customer, a note is the buyer's written acknowledgment of the debt, its amount, and its terms.

Exhibit 9.14 shows a simple promissory note dated July 10, 2013. For this note, Julia Browne promises to pay TechCom or to its order (according to TechCom's instructions) a specified amount of money ($1,000), called the **principal of a note,** at a definite future date (October 8, 2013). As the one who signed the note and promised to pay it at maturity, Browne is the **maker of the note.** As the person to whom the note is payable, TechCom is the **payee of the note.** To Browne, the note is a liability called a *note payable*. To TechCom, the same note is an asset called a *note receivable*. This note bears interest at 12%, as written on the note. **Interest** is the charge for using the money until its due date. To a borrower, interest is an expense. To a lender, it is revenue.

EXHIBIT 9.14

Promissory Note

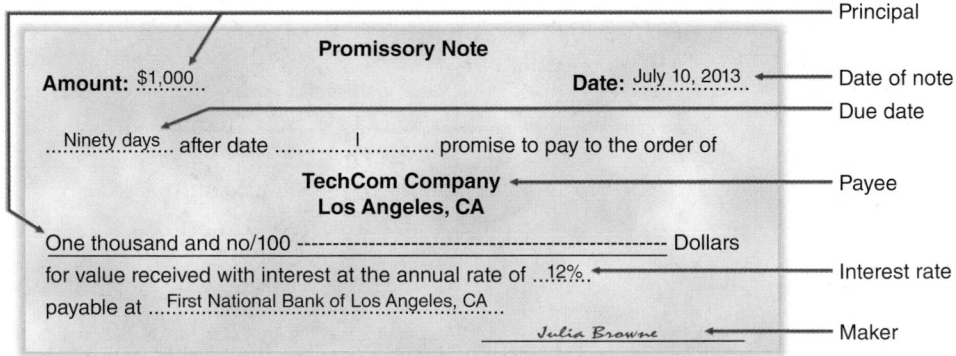

Computing Maturity and Interest

This section describes key computations for notes including the determination of maturity date, period covered, and interest computation.

Maturity Date and Period   The **maturity date of a note** is the day the note (principal and interest) must be repaid. The *period* of a note is the time from the note's (contract) date to its maturity date. Many notes mature in less than a full year, and the period they cover is often expressed in days. When the time of a note is expressed in days, its maturity date is the specified number of days after the note's date. As an example, a five-day note dated June 15 matures and is due on June 20. A 90-day note dated July 10 matures on October 8. This October 8 due date is computed as shown in Exhibit 9.15. The period of a note is sometimes expressed in months or years. When months are used, the note matures and is payable in the month of its maturity on the *same day of the month* as its original date. A nine-month note dated July 10, for instance, is payable on April 10. The same analysis applies when years are used.

Days in July	31
Minus the date of the note	10
Days remaining in July	21 ← July 11–31
Add days in August	31 ← Aug. 1–31
Add days in September	30 ← Sept. 1–30
Days to equal 90 days, or **maturity date of October 8**	8 ← Oct. 1–8
Period of the note in days	90

EXHIBIT 9.15

Maturity Date Computation

Interest Computation   *Interest* is the cost of borrowing money for the borrower or, alternatively, the profit from lending money for the lender. Unless otherwise stated, the rate of interest on a note is the rate charged for the use of the principal for one year. The formula for computing interest on a note is shown in Exhibit 9.16.

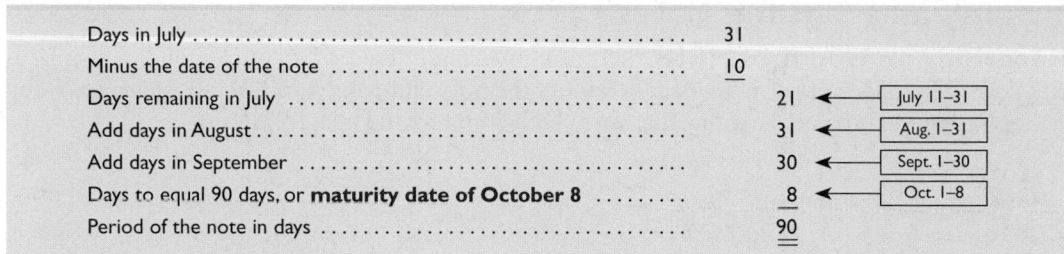

$$\frac{\textbf{Principal}}{\textbf{of the note}} \times \frac{\textbf{Annual}}{\textbf{interest rate}} \times \frac{\textbf{Time expressed}}{\textbf{in fraction of year}} = \textbf{Interest}$$

EXHIBIT 9.16

Computation of Interest Formula

To simplify interest computations, a year is commonly treated as having 360 days (called the *banker's rule* in the business world and widely used in commercial transactions). **We treat a year as having 360 days for interest computations in the examples and assignments**. Using the promissory note in Exhibit 9.14 where we have a 90-day, 12%, $1,000 note, the total interest is computed as follows:

$$\$1,000 \times 12\% \times \frac{90}{360} = \$1,000 \times 0.12 \times 0.25 = \$30$$

Point: If the *banker's rule* is not followed, interest is computed as:

$1,000 × 12% × 90/365 = $29.589041

The *banker's rule* would yield $30, which is easier to account for than $29.589041.

Recognizing Notes Receivable

Notes receivable are usually recorded in a single Notes Receivable account to simplify record-keeping. The original notes are kept on file, including information on the maker, rate of interest, and due date. (When a company holds a large number of notes, it sometimes sets up a controlling account and a subsidiary ledger for notes. This is similar to the handling of accounts receivable.) To illustrate the recording for the receipt of a note, we use the $1,000, 90-day, 12% promissory note in Exhibit 9.14. TechCom received this note at the time of a product sale to Julia Browne. This transaction is recorded as follows:

July 10*	Notes Receivable	1,000	
	Sales		1,000
	Sold goods in exchange for a 90-day, 12% note.		

Assets = Liabilities + Equity
+1,000   +1,000

* We omit the entry to Dr. Cost of Sales and Cr. Merchandise Inventory to focus on sales and receivables.

When a seller accepts a note from an overdue customer as a way to grant a time extension on a past-due account receivable, it will often collect part of the past-due balance in cash. This partial payment forces a concession from the customer, reduces the customer's debt (and the seller's risk), and produces a note for a smaller amount. To illustrate, assume that Tech-Com agreed to accept $232 in cash along with a $600, 60-day, 15% note from Jo Cook to

Point: Notes receivable often are a major part of a company's assets. Likewise, notes payable often are a large part of a company's liabilities.

settle her $832 past-due account. TechCom made the following entry to record receipt of this cash and note:

Assets = Liabilities + Equity
+232
+600
−832

Oct. 5	Cash	232	
	Notes Receivable	600	
	Accounts Receivable—J. Cook		832
	Received cash and note to settle account.		

Valuing and Settling Notes

Recording an Honored Note   The principal and interest of a note are due on its maturity date. The maker of the note usually *honors* the note and pays it in full. To illustrate, when J. Cook pays the note above on its due date, TechCom records it as follows:

Assets = Liabilities + Equity
+615   +15
−600

Dec. 4	Cash	615	
	Notes Receivable		600
	Interest Revenue		15
	Collect note with interest of $600 × 15% × 60/360.		

Interest Revenue, also called *Interest Earned,* is reported on the income statement.

Recording a Dishonored Note   When a note's maker is unable or refuses to pay at maturity, the note is *dishonored.* The act of dishonoring a note does not relieve the maker of the obligation to pay. The payee should use every legitimate means to collect. How do companies report this event? The balance of the Notes Receivable account should include only those notes that have not matured. Thus, when a note is dishonored, we remove the amount of this note from the Notes Receivable account and charge it back to an account receivable from its maker. To illustrate, TechCom holds an $800, 12%, 60-day note of Greg Hart. At maturity, Hart dishonors the note. TechCom records this dishonoring of the note as follows:

Point: When posting a dishonored note to a customer's account, an explanation is included so as not to misinterpret the debit as a sale on account.

Assets = Liabilities + Equity
+816   +16
−800

Oct. 14	Accounts Receivable—G. Hart	816	
	Interest Revenue		16
	Notes Receivable		800
	To charge account of G. Hart for a dishonored note and interest of $800 × 12% × 60/360.		

Point: Reporting the details of notes is consistent with the **full disclosure principle,** which requires financial statements (including footnotes) to report all relevant information.

Charging a dishonored note back to the account of its maker serves two purposes. First, it removes the amount of the note from the Notes Receivable account and records the dishonored note in the maker's account. Second, and more important, if the maker of the dishonored note applies for credit in the future, his or her account will reveal all past dealings, including the dishonored note. Restoring the account also reminds the company to continue collection efforts from Hart for both principal and interest. The entry records the full amount, including interest, to ensure that it is included in collection efforts.

Recording End-of-Period Interest Adjustment   When notes receivable are outstanding at the end of a period, any accrued interest earned is computed and recorded. To illustrate, on December 16, TechCom accepts a $3,000, 60-day, 12% note from a customer in granting an extension on a past-due account. When TechCom's accounting period ends on December 31, $15 of interest has accrued on this note ($3,000 × 12% × 15/360). The following adjusting entry records this revenue:

Assets = Liabilities + Equity
+15   +15

Dec. 31	Interest Receivable	15	
	Interest Revenue		15
	To record accrued interest earned.		

Interest Revenue appears on the income statement, and Interest Receivable appears on the balance sheet as a current asset. When the December 16 note is collected on February 14, TechCom's entry to record the cash receipt is

Feb. 14	Cash	3,060	
	Interest Revenue		45
	Interest Receivable		15
	Notes Receivable		3,000
	Received payment of note and its interest.		

Assets = Liabilities + Equity
+3,060   +45
−15
−3,000

Total interest earned on the 60-day note is $60. The $15 credit to Interest Receivable on February 14 reflects the collection of the interest accrued from the December 31 adjusting entry. The $45 interest earned reflects TechCom's revenue from holding the note from January 1 to February 14 of the current period.

Quick Check   Answers — p. 381

8. Irwin purchases $7,000 of merchandise from Stamford on December 16, 2013. Stamford accepts Irwin's $7,000, 90-day, 12% note as payment. Stamford's accounting period ends on December 31, and it does not make reversing entries. Prepare entries for Stamford on December 16, 2013, and December 31, 2013.

9. Using the information in Quick Check 8, prepare Stamford's March 16, 2014, entry if Irwin dishonors the note.

10. What is the maturity date of a 60-day note signed by the maker on September 15?

DISPOSAL OF RECEIVABLES

Companies can convert receivables to cash before they are due. Reasons for this include the need for cash or the desire not to be involved in collection activities. Converting receivables is usually done either by (1) selling them or (2) using them as security for a loan. A recent survey shows that about 20% of companies obtain cash from either selling receivables or pledging them as security. In some industries such as textiles, apparel and furniture, this is common practice.

C3 Explain how receivables can be converted to cash before maturity.

Selling Receivables

A company can sell all or a portion of its receivables to a finance company or bank. The buyer, called a *factor,* charges the seller a *factoring fee* and then the buyer takes ownership of the receivables and receives cash when they come due. By incurring a factoring fee, the seller receives cash earlier and can pass the risk of bad debts to the factor. The seller can also choose to avoid costs of billing and accounting for the receivables. To illustrate, if TechCom sells $20,000 of its accounts receivable and is charged a 4% factoring fee, it records this sale as follows:

Global: Firms in export sales increasingly sell their receivables to factors.

Aug. 15	Cash	19,200	
	Factoring Fee Expense	800	
	Accounts Receivable		20,000
	Sold accounts receivable for cash, less 4% fee.		

Assets − Liabilities + Equity
+19,200   −800
−20,000

The accounting for sales of notes receivable is similar to that for accounts receivable. The detailed entries are covered in advanced courses. Remember: When factoring receivables, the company selling receivables always receives less cash than the amount of receivables sold due to factoring fees.

Pledging Receivables

A company can raise cash by borrowing money and *pledging* its receivables as security for the loan. Pledging receivables does not transfer the risk of bad debts to the lender because the borrower retains ownership of the receivables. If the borrower defaults on the loan, the lender has a right to be paid from the cash receipts of the receivable when collected. To illustrate, when TechCom borrows $35,000 and pledges its receivables as security, it records this transaction as follows:

Assets = Liabilities + Equity
+35,000   +35,000

Aug. 20	Cash	35,000	
	Notes Payable		35,000
	Borrowed money with a note secured by pledging receivables.		

Since pledged receivables are committed as security for a specific loan, the borrower's financial statements disclose the pledging of them. TechCom, for instance, includes the following note with its statements: Accounts receivable of $40,000 are pledged as security for a $35,000 note payable. Inventory and accounts receivable are two assets commonly demanded by bankers as collateral when making business loans.

 Decision Maker ━━━━━━━━━━━━━━━━━━━━━━

Analyst/Auditor: What's the Proper Allowance? You are reviewing accounts receivable. Over the past five years, the allowance account as a percentage of gross accounts receivable shows a steady downward trend. What does this finding suggest? ■ [Answer—p. 381]

 GLOBAL VIEW

This section discusses similarities and differences between U.S. GAAP and IFRS regarding the recognition, measurement, and disposition of receivables.

Recognition of Receivables Both U.S. GAAP and IFRS have similar asset criteria that apply to recognition of receivables. Further, receivables that arise from revenue-generating activities are subject to broadly similar criteria for U.S. GAAP and IFRS. Specifically, both refer to the realization principle and an earnings process. The realization principle under U.S. GAAP implies an *arm's-length transaction* occurs, whereas under IFRS this notion is applied in terms of reliable measurement and likelihood of economic benefits. Regarding U.S. GAAP's reference to an earnings process, IFRS instead refers to risk transfer and ownership reward. While these criteria are broadly similar, differences do exist, and they arise mainly from industry-specific guidance under U.S. GAAP, which is very limited under IFRS.

Valuation of Receivables Both U.S. GAAP and IFRS require that receivables be reported net of estimated uncollectibles. Further, both systems require that the expense for estimated uncollectibles be recorded in the same period when any revenues from those receivables are recorded. This means that for accounts receivable, both U.S. GAAP and IFRS require the allowance method for uncollectibles (unless uncollectibles are immaterial). The allowance method using percent of sales, percent of receivables, and aging was explained in this chapter. **Nokia** reports the following for its allowance for uncollectibles:

NOKIA

Management specifically analyzes accounts receivables and historical bad debt, customer concentrations, customer creditworthiness, current economic trends and changes in our customer payment terms when evaluating the adequacy of the allowance.

Disposition of Receivables Both U.S. GAAP and IFRS apply broadly similar rules in recording dispositions of receivables. Those rules are discussed in this chapter. We should be aware of an important difference in terminology. Companies reporting under U.S. GAAP disclose Bad Debts Expense, which is also referred to as Provision for Bad Debts or the Provision for Uncollectible Accounts. For U.S. GAAP, *provision* here refers to expense. Under IFRS, the term *provision* usually refers to a liability whose amount or timing (or both) is uncertain.

For a company selling on credit, we want to assess both the quality and liquidity of its accounts receivable. *Quality* of receivables refers to the likelihood of collection without loss. Experience shows that the longer receivables are outstanding beyond their due date, the lower the likelihood of collection. *Liquidity* of receivables refers to the speed of collection. **Accounts receivable turnover** is a measure of both the quality and liquidity of accounts receivable. It indicates how often, on average, receivables are received and collected during the period. The formula for this ratio is shown in Exhibit 9.17.

A1 Compute accounts receivable turnover and use it to help assess financial condition.

$$\text{Accounts receivable turnover} = \frac{\text{Net sales}}{\text{Average accounts receivable, net}}$$

EXHIBIT 9.17

Accounts Receivable Turnover

We prefer to use net *credit* sales in the numerator because cash sales do not create receivables. However, since financial statements rarely report net credit sales, our analysis uses net sales. The denominator is the *average* accounts receivable balance, computed as (Beginning balance + Ending balance) ÷ 2. TechCom has an accounts receivable turnover of 5.1. This indicates its average accounts receivable balance is converted into cash 5.1 times during the period. Exhibit 9.18 shows graphically this turnover activity for TechCom.

5.1 times per year

Jan.   Feb.   March   Apr.   May   June   July   Aug.   Sept.   Oct.   Nov.   Dec.

EXHIBIT 9.18

Rate of Accounts Receivable Turnover for TechCom

Accounts receivable turnover also reflects how well management is doing in granting credit to customers in a desire to increase sales. A high turnover in comparison with competitors suggests that management should consider using more liberal credit terms to increase sales. A low turnover suggests management should consider stricter credit terms and more aggressive collection efforts to avoid having its resources tied up in accounts receivable.

Point: Credit risk ratio is computed by dividing the Allowance for Doubtful Accounts by Accounts Receivable. The higher this ratio, the higher is credit risk.

To illustrate, we take fiscal year data from two competitors: **Dell** and **Apple**. Exhibit 9.19 shows accounts receivable turnover for both companies.

Company	Figure ($ millions)	2011	2010	2009	2008
Dell	Net sales	$ 61,494	$52,902	$61,101	$61,133
	Average accounts receivable, net	$ 6,165	$ 5,284	$ 5,346	$ 5,292
	Accounts receivable turnover	10.0	10.0	11.4	11.6
Apple	Net sales	$108,249	$65,225	$42,905	$37,491
	Average accounts receivable, net	$ 5,440	$ 4,436	$ 2,892	$ 2,030
	Accounts receivable turnover	19.9	14.7	14.8	18.5

EXHIBIT 9.19

Analysis Using Accounts Receivable Turnover

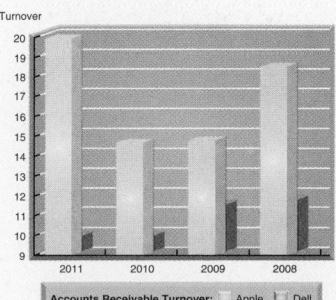

Dell's 2011 turnover is 10.0, computed as $61,494/$6,165 ($ millions). This means that Dell's average accounts receivable balance was converted into cash 10.0 times in 2011. Its turnover was flat in 2011, but it had been slightly declining in recent years. Apple's turnover exceeds that for Dell in each of the past 4 years. Is either company's turnover too high? Since sales are stable or markedly growing over this time period, each company's turnover rate does not appear to be too high. Instead, both Dell and Apple seem to be doing well in managing receivables. This is especially true given the recent recessionary period. Turnover for competitors is generally in the range of 7 to 12 for this same period.[1]

 Decision Maker

Family Physician   Your medical practice is barely profitable, so you hire a health care analyst. The analyst highlights several points including the following: *"Accounts receivable turnover is too low. Tighter credit policies are recommended along with discontinuing service to those most delayed in payments."* How do you interpret these recommendations? What actions do you take? ■   [Answer—p. 381]

DEMONSTRATION PROBLEM

Clayco Company completes the following selected transactions during year 2013.

July 14   Writes off a $750 account receivable arising from a sale to Briggs Company that dates to 10 months ago. (Clayco Company uses the allowance method.)

30   Clayco Company receives a $1,000, 90-day, 10% note in exchange for merchandise sold to Sumrell Company (the merchandise cost $600).

Aug. 15   Receives $2,000 cash plus a $10,000 note from JT Co. in exchange for merchandise that sells for $12,000 (its cost is $8,000). The note is dated August 15, bears 12% interest, and matures in 120 days.

Nov. 1   Completed a $200 credit card sale with a 4% fee (the cost of sales is $150). The cash is received immediately from the credit card company.

3   Sumrell Company refuses to pay the note that was due to Clayco Company on October 28. Prepare the journal entry to charge the dishonored note plus accrued interest to Sumrell Company's accounts receivable.

5   Completed a $500 credit card sale with a 5% fee (the cost of sales is $300). The payment from the credit card company is received on Nov. 9.

15   Received the full amount of $750 from Briggs Company that was previously written off on July 14. Record the bad debts recovery.

Dec. 13   Received payment of principal plus interest from JT for the August 15 note.

Required

1. Prepare journal entries to record these transactions on Clayco Company's books.

2. Prepare an adjusting journal entry as of December 31, 2013, assuming the following:

a. Bad debts are estimated to be $20,400 by aging accounts receivable. The unadjusted balance of the Allowance for Doubtful Accounts is $1,000 debit.

b. Alternatively, assume that bad debts are estimated using the percent of sales method. The Allowance for Doubtful Accounts had a $1,000 debit balance before adjustment, and the company estimates bad debts to be 1% of its credit sales of $2,000,000.

PLANNING THE SOLUTION

● Examine each transaction to determine the accounts affected, and then record the entries.

● For the year-end adjustment, record the bad debts expense for the two approaches.

---

[1] As an estimate of *average days' sales uncollected,* we compute how many days (*on average*) it takes to collect receivables as follows: 365 days ÷ accounts receivable turnover. An increase in this *average collection period* can signal a decline in customers' financial condition.

SOLUTION TO DEMONSTRATION PROBLEM

1.

July 14	Allowance for Doubtful Accounts	750	
	Accounts Receivable—Briggs Co.		750
	Wrote off an uncollectible account.		
July 30	Notes Receivable—Sumrell Co.	1,000	
	Sales		1,000
	Sold merchandise for a 90-day, 10% note.		
July 30	Cost of Goods Sold	600	
	Merchandise Inventory		600
	To record the cost of July 30 sale.		
Aug. 15	Cash	2,000	
	Notes Receivable—JT Co.	10,000	
	Sales		12,000
	Sold merchandise to customer for $2,000 cash and $10,000 note.		
Aug. 15	Cost of Goods Sold	8,000	
	Merchandise Inventory		8,000
	To record the cost of Aug. 15 sale.		
Nov. 1	Cash	192	
	Credit Card Expense	8	
	Sales		200
	To record credit card sale less a 4% credit card expense.		
Nov. 1	Cost of Goods Sold	150	
	Merchandise Inventory		150
	To record the cost of Nov. 1 sale.		
Nov. 3	Accounts Receivable—Sumrell Co.	1,025	
	Interest Revenue		25
	Notes Receivable—Sumrell Co.		1,000
	To charge account of Sumrell Company for a $1,000 dishonored note and interest of $1,000 × 10% × 90/360.		
Nov. 5	Accounts Receivable—Credit Card Co.	475	
	Credit Card Expense	25	
	Sales		500
	To record credit card sale less a 5% credit card expense.		
Nov. 5	Cost of Goods Sold	300	
	Merchandise Inventory		300
	To record the cost of Nov. 5 sale.		
Nov. 9	Cash	475	
	Accounts Receivable—Credit Card Co.		475
	To record cash receipt from Nov. 5 sale.		
Nov. 15	Accounts Receivable—Briggs Co.	750	
	Allowance for Doubtful Accounts		750
	To reinstate the account of Briggs Company previously written off.		
Nov. 15	Cash	750	
	Accounts Receivable—Briggs Co.		750
	Cash received in full payment of account.		
Dec. 13	Cash	10,400	
	Interest Revenue		400
	Note Receivable—JT Co.		10,000
	Collect note with interest of $10,000 × 12% × 120/360.		

2a. Aging of accounts receivable method.

Dec. 31	Bad Debts Expense	21,400	
	Allowance for Doubtful Accounts		21,400
	To adjust allowance account from a $1,000 debit balance to a $20,400 credit balance.		

2b. Percent of sales method.*

Dec. 31	Bad Debts Expense	20,000	
	Allowance for Doubtful Accounts		20,000
	To provide for bad debts as 1% × $2,000,000 in credit sales.		

* For the income statement approach, which requires estimating bad debts as a percent of sales or credit sales, the Allowance account balance is *not* considered when making the adjusting entry.

Summary

C1 Describe accounts receivable and how they occur and are recorded. Accounts receivable are amounts due from customers for credit sales. A subsidiary ledger lists amounts owed by each customer. Credit sales arise from at least two sources: (1) sales on credit and (2) credit card sales. *Sales on credit* refers to a company's granting credit directly to customers. Credit card sales involve customers' use of third-party credit cards.

C2 Describe a note receivable, the computation of its maturity date, and the recording of its existence. A note receivable is a written promise to pay a specified amount of money at a definite future date. The maturity date is the day the note (principal and interest) must be repaid. Interest rates are normally stated in annual terms. The amount of interest on the note is computed by expressing time as a fraction of one year and multiplying the note's principal by this fraction and the annual interest rate. A note received is recorded at its principal amount by debiting the Notes Receivable account. The credit amount is to the asset, product, or service provided in return for the note.

C3 Explain how receivables can be converted to cash before maturity. Receivables can be converted to cash before maturity in three ways. First, a company can sell accounts receivable to a factor, who charges a factoring fee. Second, a company can borrow money by signing a note payable that is secured by pledging the accounts receivable. Third, notes receivable can be discounted at (sold to) a financial institution.

A1 Compute accounts receivable turnover and use it to help assess financial condition. Accounts receivable turnover is a measure of both the quality and liquidity of accounts receivable.

The accounts receivable turnover measure indicates how often, on average, receivables are received and collected during the period. Accounts receivable turnover is computed as net sales divided by average accounts receivable.

P1 Apply the direct write-off method to account for accounts receivable. The direct write-off method charges Bad Debts Expense when accounts are written off as uncollectible. This method is acceptable only when the amount of bad debts expense is immaterial.

P2 Apply the allowance method and estimate uncollectibles based on sales and accounts receivable. Under the allowance method, bad debts expense is recorded with an adjustment at the end of each accounting period that debits the Bad Debts Expense account and credits the Allowance for Doubtful Accounts. The uncollectible accounts are later written off with a debit to the Allowance for Doubtful Accounts. Uncollectibles are estimated by focusing on either (1) the income statement relation between bad debts expense and credit sales or (2) the balance sheet relation between accounts receivable and the allowance for doubtful accounts. The first approach emphasizes the matching principle using the income statement. The second approach emphasizes realizable value of accounts receivable using the balance sheet.

P3 Record the honoring and dishonoring of a note and adjustments for interest. When a note is honored, the payee debits the money received and credits both Notes Receivable and Interest Revenue. Dishonored notes are credited to Notes Receivable and debited to Accounts Receivable (to the account of the maker in an attempt to collect), and Interest Revenue is recorded for interest earned for the time the note is held.

Guidance Answers to Decision Maker and Decision Ethics

Entrepreneur　Analysis of credit card sales should weigh the benefits against the costs. The primary benefit is the potential to increase sales by attracting customers who prefer the convenience of credit cards. The primary cost is the fee charged by the credit card company for providing this service. Analysis should therefore esti-mate the expected increase in dollar sales from allowing credit card sales and then subtract (1) the normal costs and expenses and (2) the credit card fees associated with this expected increase in dollar sales. If your analysis shows an increase in profit from allowing credit card sales, your store should probably accept them.

Labor Union Chief Yes, this information is likely to impact your negotiations. The obvious question is why the company markedly increased this allowance. The large increase in this allowance means a substantial increase in bad debts expense *and* a decrease in earnings. This change (coming immediately prior to labor contract discussions) also raises concerns since it reduces the union's bargaining power for increased compensation. You want to ask management for supporting documentation justifying this increase. You also want data for two or three prior years and similar data from competitors. These data should give you some sense of whether the change in the allowance for uncollectibles is justified.

Analyst/Auditor The downward trend suggests the company is reducing the relative amount charged to bad debts expense each year. This may reflect the company's desire to increase net income. On the other hand, it might be that collections have improved and the lower provision for bad debts is justified. If this is not the case, the lower allowances might be insufficient for bad debts.

Family Physician The recommendations are twofold. First, the analyst suggests more stringent screening of patients' credit standing. Second, the analyst suggests dropping patients who are most overdue in payments. You are likely bothered by both suggestions. They are probably financially wise recommendations, but you are troubled by eliminating services to those less able to pay. One alternative is to follow the recommendations while implementing a care program directed at patients less able to pay for services. This allows you to continue services to patients less able to pay and lets you discontinue services to patients able but unwilling to pay.

Guidance Answers to Quick Checks

1. If cash is immediately received when credit card sales receipts are deposited, the company debits Cash at the time of sale. If the company does not receive payment until after it submits receipts to the credit card company, it debits Accounts Receivable at the time of sale. (Cash is later debited when payment is received from the credit card company.)

2. Credit card expenses are usually *recorded* and *incurred* at the time of their related sales, not when cash is received from the credit card company.

3. If possible, bad debts expense must be matched with the sales that gave rise to the accounts receivable. This requires that companies estimate future bad debts at the end of each period before they learn which accounts are uncollectible.

4. Realizable value (also called *net realizable value*).

5. The estimated amount of bad debts expense cannot be credited to the Accounts Receivable account because the specific customer accounts that will prove uncollectible cannot yet be identified and removed from the accounts receivable subsidiary ledger. Moreover, if only the Accounts Receivable account is credited, its balance would not equal the sum of its subsidiary account balances.

6.
| Dec. 31 | Bad Debts Expense | 5,702 | |
| | Allowance for Doubtful Accounts | | 5,702 |

7.
Jan. 10	Allowance for Doubtful Accounts	300	
	Accounts Receivable—Cool Jam		300
Apr. 12	Accounts Receivable—Cool Jam	300	
	Allowance for Doubtful Accounts		300
Apr. 12	Cash	300	
	Accounts Receivable—Cool Jam		300

8.
Dec. 16	Note Receivable—Irwin	7,000	
	Sales		7,000
Dec. 31	Interest Receivable	35	
	Interest Revenue		35
	($7,000 × 12% × 15/360)		

9.
Mar. 16	Accounts Receivable—Irwin	7,210	
	Interest Revenue		175
	Interest Receivable		35
	Notes Receivable—Irwin		7,000

10. The note matures on November 14, computed as follows:

Days in September	30
Minus the date of the note	(15)
Days remaining in September	15
Add days in October	31
Add days in November to equal 60 days	14
Period of the note in days	60

Key Terms

Accounts receivable (p. 362)
Accounts receivable turnover (p. 377)
Aging of accounts receivable (p. 370)
Allowance for Doubtful Accounts (p. 367)
Allowance method (p. 367)
Bad debts (p. 366)

Direct write-off method (p. 366)   Materiality constraint (p. 366)   Promissory note (or note) (p. 372)

Interest (p. 372)   Maturity date of a note (p. 372)   Realizable value (p. 367)

Maker of the note (p. 372)   Payee of the note (p. 372)

Matching (expense recognition) principle (p. 366)   Principal of a note (p. 372)

Multiple Choice Quiz   Answers on p. 393   mhhe.com/wildFAP21e

Additional Quiz Questions are available at the book's Website.

1. A company's Accounts Receivable balance at its December 31 year-end is $125,650, and its Allowance for Doubtful Accounts has a credit balance of $328 before year-end adjustment. Its net sales are $572,300. It estimates that 4% of outstanding accounts receivable are uncollectible. What amount of Bad Debts Expense is recorded at December 31?
   a. $5,354
   b. $328
   c. $5,026
   d. $4,698
   e. $34,338

2. A company's Accounts Receivable balance at its December 31 year-end is $489,300, and its Allowance for Doubtful Accounts has a debit balance of $554 before year-end adjustment. Its net sales are $1,300,000. It estimates that 6% of outstanding accounts receivable are uncollectible. What amount of Bad Debts Expense is recorded at December 31?
   a. $29,912
   b. $28,804
   c. $78,000
   d. $29,358
   e. $554

3. Total interest to be earned on a $7,500, 5%, 90-day note is
   a. $93.75
   b. $375.00
   c. $1,125.00
   d. $31.25
   e. $125.00

4. A company receives a $9,000, 8%, 60-day note. The maturity value of the note is
   a. $120
   b. $9,000
   c. $9,120
   d. $720
   e. $9,720

5. A company has net sales of $489,600 and average accounts receivable of $40,800. What is its accounts receivable turnover?
   a. 0.08
   b. 30.41
   c. 1,341.00
   d. 12.00
   e. 111.78

🔲 Icon denotes assignments that involve decision making.

Discussion Questions

1. 🔲 How do sellers benefit from allowing their customers to use credit cards?

2. 🔲 Why does the direct write-off method of accounting for bad debts usually fail to match revenues and expenses?

3. Explain the accounting constraint of materiality.

4. Why might a business prefer a note receivable to an account receivable?

5. Explain why writing off a bad debt against the Allowance for Doubtful Accounts does not reduce the estimated realizable value of a company's accounts receivable.

6. 🔲 Why does the Bad Debts Expense account usually not have the same adjusted balance as the Allowance for Doubtful Accounts?

7. 🔲 Refer to the financial statements and notes of **Polaris** in Appendix A. In its presentation of accounts receivable on the balance sheet, how does it title

accounts receivable? What does it report for its allowance as of December 31, 2011?

8. 🔲 Refer to the balance sheet of **Arctic Cat** in Appendix A. Does it use the direct write-off method or allowance method in accounting for its accounts receivable? What is the realizable value of its receivable's balance as of March 31, 2011?

9. Refer to the financial statements of **KTM** in Appendix A. What does KTM title its accounts receivable on its consolidated balance sheet? What are KTM's accounts receivable at December 31, 2011?

10. Refer to the December 31, 2011, financial statements of **Piaggio** in Appendix A. What does it title its accounts receivable on its statement of financial position? Does Piaggio report its accounts receivable as current or non-current asset?

⛰connect

Prepare journal entries for the following credit card sales transactions (the company uses the perpetual inventory system).

1. Sold $20,000 of merchandise, that cost $15,000, on MasterCard credit cards. The net cash receipts from sales are immediately deposited in the seller's bank account. MasterCard charges a 5% fee.

2. Sold $5,000 of merchandise, that cost $3,000, on an assortment of credit cards. Net cash receipts are received 5 days later, and a 4% fee is charged.

QUICK STUDY

QS 9-1
Credit card sales
C1

Gomez Corp. uses the allowance method to account for uncollectibles. On January 31, it wrote off a $800 account of a customer, C. Green. On March 9, it receives a $300 payment from Green.

1. Prepare the journal entry or entries for January 31.

2. Prepare the journal entry or entries for March 9; assume no additional money is expected from Green.

QS 9-2
Allowance method for bad debts
P2

Warner Company's year-end unadjusted trial balance shows accounts receivable of $99,000, allowance for doubtful accounts of $600 (credit), and sales of $280,000. Uncollectibles are estimated to be 1.5% of accounts receivable.

1. Prepare the December 31 year-end adjusting entry for uncollectibles.

2. What amount would have been used in the year-end adjusting entry if the allowance account had a year-end unadjusted debit balance of $300?

QS 9-3
Percent of accounts receivable method
P2

Assume the same facts as in QS 9-3, except that Warner estimates uncollectibles as 0.5% of sales. Prepare the December 31 year-end adjusting entry for uncollectibles.

QS 9-4
Percent of sales method P2

On August 2, 2013, Jun Co. receives a $6,000, 90-day, 12% note from customer Ryan Albany as payment on his $6,000 account. (1) Compute the maturity date for this note. (2) Prepare Jun's journal entry for August 2.

QS 9-5
Note receivable C2

Refer to the information in QS 9-5 and prepare the journal entry assuming the note is honored by the customer on October 31, 2013.

QS 9-6
Note receivable P3

Dominika Company's December 31 year-end unadjusted trial balance shows a $10,000 balance in Notes Receivable. This balance is from one 6% note dated December 1, with a period of 45 days. Prepare any necessary journal entries for December 31 and for the note's maturity date assuming it is honored.

QS 9-7
Note receivable P3

Record the sale by Balus Company of $125,000 in accounts receivable on May 1. Balus is charged a 2.5% factoring fee.

QS 9-8
Disposing receivables C3

Solstice Company determines on October 1 that it cannot collect $50,000 of its accounts receivable from its customer P. Moore. Apply the direct write-off method to record this loss as of October 1.

QS 9-9
Direct write-off method P1

Refer to the information in QS 9-9. On October 30, P. Moore unexpectedly paid his account in full to Solstice Company. Record Solstice's entry(ies) to reflect this recovery of this bad debt.

QS 9-10
Recovering a bad debt P1

The following data are taken from the comparative balance sheets of Ruggers Company. Compute and interpret its accounts receivable turnover for year 2013 (competitors average a turnover of 7.5).

	2013	2012
Accounts receivable, net	$153,400	$138,500
Net sales	861,105	910,600

QS 9-11
Accounts receivable turnover

A1

Answer each of the following related to international accounting standards.

a. Explain (in general terms) how the accounting for recognition of receivables is different between IFRS and U.S. GAAP.

b. Explain (in general terms) how the accounting for valuation of receivables is different between IFRS and U.S. GAAP.

QS 9-12
International accounting standards

C1

EXERCISES

Exercise 9-1
Accounts receivable subsidiary ledger; schedule of accounts receivable

C1

Morales Company recorded the following selected transactions during November 2013.

Nov. 5	Accounts Receivable—Ski Shop	4,615	
	Sales		4,615
10	Accounts Receivable—Welcome Enterprises	1,350	
	Sales		1,350
13	Accounts Receivable—Zia Natara	832	
	Sales		832
21	Sales Returns and Allowances	209	
	Accounts Receivable—Zia Natara		209
30	Accounts Receivable—Ski Shop	2,713	
	Sales		2,713

1. Open a general ledger having T-accounts for Accounts Receivable, Sales, and Sales Returns and Allowances. Also open an accounts receivable subsidiary ledger having a T-account for each customer. Post these entries to both the general ledger and the accounts receivable ledger.

Check Accounts Receivable ending balance, $9,301

2. Prepare a schedule of accounts receivable (see Exhibit 9.4) and compare its total with the balance of the Accounts Receivable controlling account as of November 30.

Exercise 9-2
Accounting for credit card sales

C1

Levine Company uses the perpetual inventory system and allows customers to use two credit cards in charging purchases. With the Suntrust Bank Card, Levine receives an immediate credit to its account when it deposits sales receipts. Suntrust assesses a 4% service charge for credit card sales. The second credit card that Levine accepts is the Continental Card. Levine sends its accumulated receipts to Continental on a weekly basis and is paid by Continental about a week later. Continental assesses a 2.5% charge on sales for using its card. Prepare journal entries to record the following selected credit card transactions of Levine Company.

Apr. 8 Sold merchandise for $8,400 (that had cost $6,000) and accepted the customer's Suntrust Bank Card. The Suntrust receipts are immediately deposited in Levine's bank account.
   12 Sold merchandise for $5,600 (that had cost $3,500) and accepted the customer's Continental Card. Transferred $5,600 of credit card receipts to Continental, requesting payment.
   20 Received Continental's check for the April 12 billing, less the service charge.

Exercise 9-3
Direct write-off method

P1

Dexter Company applies the direct write-off method in accounting for uncollectible accounts. Prepare journal entries to record the following selected transactions of Dexter.

March 11 Dexter determines that it cannot collect $45,000 of its accounts receivable from its customer Lester Company.
     29 Lester Company unexpectedly pays its account in full to Dexter Company. Dexter records its recovery of this bad debt.

Exercise 9-4
Percent of sales method; write-off

P2

At year-end (December 31), Chan Company estimates its bad debts as 0.5% of its annual credit sales of $975,000. Chan records its Bad Debts Expense for that estimate. On the following February 1, Chan decides that the $580 account of P. Park is uncollectible and writes it off as a bad debt. On June 5, Park unexpectedly pays the amount previously written off. Prepare the journal entries of Chan to record these transactions and events of December 31, February 1, and June 5.

Exercise 9-5
Percent of accounts receivable method

P2

At each calendar year-end, Mazie Supply Co. uses the percent of accounts receivable method to estimate bad debts. On December 31, 2013, it has outstanding accounts receivable of $55,000, and it estimates that 2% will be uncollectible. Prepare the adjusting entry to record bad debts expense for year 2013 under the assumption that the Allowance for Doubtful Accounts has (a) a $415 credit balance before the adjustment and (b) a $291 debit balance before the adjustment.

Exercise 9-6
Aging of receivables method

P2

Daley Company estimates uncollectible accounts using the allowance method at December 31. It prepared the following aging of receivables analysis.

| | | | | Days Past Due | | |
	Total	0	1 to 30	31 to 60	61 to 90	Over 90
Accounts receivable	$570,000	$396,000	$90,000	$36,000	$18,000	$30,000
Percent uncollectible		1%	2%	5%	7%	10%

a. Estimate the balance of the Allowance for Doubtful Accounts using the aging of accounts receivable method.

b. Prepare the adjusting entry to record Bad Debts Expense using the estimate from part *a*. Assume the unadjusted balance in the Allowance for Doubtful Accounts is a $3,600 credit.

c. Prepare the adjusting entry to record Bad Debts Expense using the estimate from part *a*. Assume the unadjusted balance in the Allowance for Doubtful Accounts is a $100 debit.

Refer to the information in Exercise 9-6 to complete the following requirements.

a. Estimate the balance of the Allowance for Doubtful Accounts assuming the company uses 4.5% of total accounts receivable to estimate uncollectibles, instead of the aging of receivables method.

b. Prepare the adjusting entry to record Bad Debts Expense using the estimate from part *a*. Assume the unadjusted balance in the Allowance for Doubtful Accounts is a $12,000 credit.

c. Prepare the adjusting entry to record Bad Debts Expense using the estimate from part *a*. Assume the unadjusted balance in the Allowance for Doubtful Accounts is a $1,000 debit.

Exercise 9-7
Percent of receivables method
P2

Refer to the information in Exercise 9-6 to complete the following requirements.

a. On February 1 of the next period, the company determined that $6,800 in customer accounts is uncollectible; specifically, $900 for Oakley Co. and $5,900 for Brookes Co. Prepare the journal entry to write off those accounts.

b. On June 5 of that next period, the company unexpectedly received a $900 payment on a customer account, Oakley Company, that had previously been written off in part *a*. Prepare the entries necessary to reinstate the account and to record the cash received.

Exercise 9-8
Writing off receivables
P2

At December 31, Folgeys Coffee Company reports the following results for its calendar year.

Cash sales	$900,000
Credit sales	300,000

Its year-end unadjusted trial balance includes the following items.

Accounts receivable	$125,000 debit
Allowance for doubtful accounts	5,000 debit

a. Prepare the adjusting entry to record Bad Debts Expense assuming uncollectibles are estimated to be 1.5% of credit sales.

b. Prepare the adjusting entry to record Bad Debts Expense assuming uncollectibles are estimated to be 0.5% of total sales.

c. Prepare the adjusting entry to record Bad Debts Expense assuming uncollectibles are estimated to be 6% of year-end accounts receivable.

Exercise 9-9
Estimating bad debts
P2

Check   Dr. Bad Debts Expense:
(a) $4,500

(c) $12,500

On June 30, Petrov Co. has $128,700 of accounts receivable. Prepare journal entries to record the following selected July transactions. Also prepare any footnotes to the July 31 financial statements that result from these transactions. (The company uses the perpetual inventory system.)

July   4   Sold $7,245 of merchandise (that had cost $5,000) to customers on credit.
      9   Sold $20,000 of accounts receivable to Main Bank. Main charges a 4% factoring fee.
    17   Received $5,859 cash from customers in payment on their accounts.
    27   Borrowed $10,000 cash from Main Bank, pledging $12,500 of accounts receivable as security for the loan.

Exercise 9-10
Selling and pledging accounts receivable
C3

Prepare journal entries to record these selected transactions for Vitalo Company.

Nov.   1   Accepted a $6,000, 180-day, 8% note dated November 1 from Kelly White in granting a time extension on her past-due account receivable.
Dec. 31   Adjusted the year-end accounts for the accrued interest earned on the White note.
Apr. 30   White honors her note when presented for payment; February has 28 days for the current year.

Exercise 9-11
Honoring a note
P3

Exercise 9-12

Dishonoring a note

P3

Prepare journal entries to record the following selected transactions of Ridge Company.

Mar. 21   Accepted a $9,500, 180-day, 8% note dated March 21 from Tamara Jackson in granting a time extension on her past-due account receivable.

Sept. 17   Jackson dishonors her note when it is presented for payment.

Dec. 31   After exhausting all legal means of collection, Ridge Company writes off Jackson's account against the Allowance for Doubtful Accounts.

Exercise 9-13

Notes receivable transactions

C2

Check Dec. 31, Cr. Interest
Revenue $38

Prepare journal entries for the following selected transactions of Dulcinea Company for 2012.

2012

Dec. 13   Accepted a $9,500, 60-day, 8% note dated December 13 in granting Miranda Lee a time extension on her past-due account receivable.

    31   Prepared an adjusting entry to record the accrued interest on the Lee note.

Exercise 9-14

Notes receivable transactions

P3

Check Jan. 27, Dr. Cash $9,627

June 1, Dr. Cash $5,125

Refer to the information in Exercise 9-13 and prepare the journal entries for the following selected transactions of Dulcinea Company for 2013.

2013

Jan. 27   Received Lee's payment for principal and interest on the note dated December 13.

Mar. 3   Accepted a $5,000, 10%, 90-day note dated March 3 in granting a time extension on the past-due account receivable of Tomas Company.

    17   Accepted a $2,000, 30-day, 9% note dated March 17 in granting Hiroshi Cheng a time extension on his past-due account receivable.

Apr. 16   Cheng dishonors his note when presented for payment.

May   1   Wrote off the Cheng account against the Allowance for Doubtful Accounts.

June 1   Received the Tomas payment for principal and interest on the note dated March 3.

Exercise 9-15

Accounts receivable turnover

A1

The following information is from the annual financial statements of Raheem Company. Compute its accounts receivable turnover for 2012 and 2013. Compare the two years results and give a possible explanation for any change (competitors average a turnover of 11).

	2013	2012	2010
Net sales	$405,140	$335,280	$388,000
Accounts receivable, net (year-end)	44,800	41,400	34,800

Exercise 9-16

Accounting for bad debts following IFRS

P2

Hitachi, Ltd., reports total revenues of ¥9,315,807 million for its fiscal year ending March 31, 2011, and its March 31, 2011, unadjusted trial balance reports a debit balance for trade receivables (gross) of ¥2,127,682 million.

a. Prepare the adjusting entry to record its Bad Debts Expense assuming uncollectibles are estimated to be 0.4% of total revenues and its unadjusted trial balance reports a credit balance of ¥10,000 million.

b. Prepare the adjusting entry to record Bad Debts Expense assuming uncollectibles are estimated to be 2.1% of year-end trade receivables (gross) and its unadjusted trial balance reports a credit balance of ¥10,000 million.

M Graw Hill connect

PROBLEM SET A

Problem 9-1A

Sales on account and credit card sales

C1 **Sage 50**

Mayfair Co. allows select customers to make purchases on credit. Its other customers can use either of two credit cards: Zisa or Access. Zisa deducts a 3% service charge for sales on its credit card and credits the bank account of Mayfair immediately when credit card receipts are deposited. Mayfair deposits the Zisa credit card receipts each business day. When customers use Access credit cards, Mayfair accumulates the receipts for several days before submitting them to Access for payment. Access deducts a 2% service charge and usually pays within one week of being billed. Mayfair completes the following transactions in June. (The terms of all credit sales are 2/15, n/30, and all sales are recorded at the gross price.)

June 4   Sold $650 of merchandise (that had cost $400) on credit to Natara Morris.

     5   Sold $6,900 of merchandise (that had cost $4,200) to customers who used their Zisa cards.

6   Sold $5,850 of merchandise (that had cost $3,800) to customers who used their Access cards.

8   Sold $4,350 of merchandise (that had cost $2,900) to customers who used their Access cards.

10   Submitted Access card receipts accumulated since June 6 to the credit card company for payment.

13   Wrote off the account of Abigail McKee against the Allowance for Doubtful Accounts. The $429 balance in McKee's account stemmed from a credit sale in October of last year.

17   Received the amount due from Access.

18   Received Morris's check in full payment for the purchase of June 4.

Check   June 17, Dr. Cash $9,996

Required

Prepare journal entries to record the preceding transactions and events. (The company uses the perpetual inventory system. Round amounts to the nearest dollar.)

Liang Company began operations on January 1, 2012. During its first two years, the company completed a number of transactions involving sales on credit, accounts receivable collections, and bad debts. These transactions are summarized as follows:

Problem 9-2A
Accounts receivable transactions and bad debts adjustments

C1   P2

2012

a. Sold $1,345,434 of merchandise (that had cost $975,000) on credit, terms n/30.

b. Wrote off $18,300 of uncollectible accounts receivable.

c. Received $669,200 cash in payment of accounts receivable.

d. In adjusting the accounts on December 31, the company estimated that 1.5% of accounts receivable will be uncollectible.

Check   (d) Dr. Bad Debts Expense $28,169

2013

e. Sold $1,525,634 of merchandise (that had cost $1,250,000) on credit, terms n/30.

f. Wrote off $27,800 of uncollectible accounts receivable.

g. Received $1,204,600 cash in payment of accounts receivable.

h. In adjusting the accounts on December 31, the company estimated that 1.5% of accounts receivable will be uncollectible.

(h) Dr. Bad Debts Expense $32,198

Required

Prepare journal entries to record Liang's 2012 and 2013 summarized transactions and its year-end adjustments to record bad debts expense. (The company uses the perpetual inventory system and it applies the allowance method for its accounts receivable. Round amounts to the nearest dollar.)

At December 31, 2013, Hawke Company reports the following results for its calendar year.

Cash sales	$1,905,000
Credit sales	5,682,000

Problem 9-3A
Estimating and reporting bad debts

P2

In addition, its unadjusted trial balance includes the following items.

Accounts receivable	$1,270,100 debit
Allowance for doubtful accounts	16,580 debit

Required

1. Prepare the adjusting entry for this company to recognize bad debts under each of the following independent assumptions.

   a. Bad debts are estimated to be 1.5% of credit sales.

   b. Bad debts are estimated to be 1% of total sales.

   c. An aging analysis estimates that 5% of year-end accounts receivable are uncollectible.

2. Show how Accounts Receivable and the Allowance for Doubtful Accounts appear on its December 31, 2013, balance sheet given the facts in part 1a.

3. Show how Accounts Receivable and the Allowance for Doubtful Accounts appear on its December 31, 2013, balance sheet given the facts in part 1c.

Check   Bad Debts Expense:
(1a) $85,230, (1c) $80,085

Problem 9-4A

Aging accounts receivable and accounting for bad debts

P2

Jarden Company has credit sales of $3.6 million for year 2013. On December 31, 2013, the company's Allowance for Doubtful Accounts has an unadjusted credit balance of $14,500. Jarden prepares a schedule of its December 31, 2013, accounts receivable by age. On the basis of past experience, it estimates the percent of receivables in each age category that will become uncollectible. This information is summarized here.

| | File Edit View Insert Format Tools Data Accounting Window Help | | | | _ | ||| Arial ▼ 10 ▼ B *I* U | | | |

December 31, 2013 Accounts Receivable	Age of Accounts Receivable	Expected Percent Uncollectible
$830,000	Not yet due	1.25%
254,000	1 to 30 days past due	2.00
86,000	31 to 60 days past due	6.50
38,000	61 to 90 days past due	32.75
12,000	Over 90 days past due	68.00

Required

1. Estimate the required balance of the Allowance for Doubtful Accounts at December 31, 2013, using the aging of accounts receivable method.

Check (2) Dr. Bad Debts Expense $27,150

2. Prepare the adjusting entry to record bad debts expense at December 31, 2013.

Analysis Component

3. On June 30, 2014, Jarden Company concludes that a customer's $4,750 receivable (created in 2013) is uncollectible and that the account should be written off. What effect will this action have on Jarden's 2014 net income? Explain.

Problem 9-5A

Analyzing and journalizing notes receivable transactions

C2 C3 P3

 Sage 50

Check Feb. 14, Cr. Interest Revenue $108

June 2, Cr. Interest Revenue $122

Nov. 2, Cr. Interest Revenue $35

The following selected transactions are from Ohlmeyer Company.

2012

Dec. 16   Accepted a $10,800, 60-day, 8% note dated this day in granting Danny Todd a time extension on his past-due account receivable.

     31   Made an adjusting entry to record the accrued interest on the Todd note.

2013

Feb. 14   Received Todd's payment of principal and interest on the note dated December 16.

Mar. 2   Accepted an $6,100, 8%, 90-day note dated this day in granting a time extension on the past-due account receivable from Midnight Co.

    17   Accepted a $2,400, 30-day, 7% note dated this day in granting Ava Privet a time extension on her past-due account receivable.

Apr. 16   Privet dishonored her note when presented for payment.

June 2   Midnight Co. refuses to pay the note that was due to Ohlmeyer Co. on May 31. Prepare the journal entry to charge the dishonored note plus accrued interest to Midnight Co.'s accounts receivable.

July 17   Received payment from Midnight Co. for the maturity value of its dishonored note plus interest for 46 days beyond maturity at 8%.

Aug. 7   Accepted an $7,450, 90-day, 10% note dated this day in granting a time extension on the past-due account receivable of Mulan Co.

Sept. 3   Accepted a $2,100, 60-day, 10% note dated this day in granting Noah Carson a time extension on his past-due account receivable.

Nov. 2   Received payment of principal plus interest from Carson for the September 3 note.

Nov. 5   Received payment of principal plus interest from Mulan for the August 7 note.

Dec. 1   Wrote off the Privet account against Allowance for Doubtful Accounts.

Required

1. Prepare journal entries to record these transactions and events. (Round amounts to the nearest dollar.)

Analysis Component

2. What reporting is necessary when a business pledges receivables as security for a loan and the loan is still outstanding at the end of the period? Explain the reason for this requirement and the accounting principle being satisfied.

Archer Co. allows select customers to make purchases on credit. Its other customers can use either of two credit cards: Commerce Bank or Aztec. Commerce Bank deducts a 3% service charge for sales on its credit card and immediately credits the bank account of Archer when credit card receipts are deposited. Archer deposits the Commerce Bank credit card receipts each business day. When customers use the Aztec card, Archer accumulates the receipts for several days and then submits them to Aztec for payment. Aztec deducts a 2% service charge and usually pays within one week of being billed. Archer completed the following transactions in August (terms of all credit sales are 2/10, n/30; and all sales are recorded at the gross price).

Aug. 4   Sold $3,700 of merchandise (that had cost $2,000) on credit to McKenzie Carpenter.
     10   Sold $5,200 of merchandise (that had cost $2,800) to customers who used their Commerce Bank credit cards.
     11   Sold $1,250 of merchandise (that had cost $900) to customers who used their Aztec cards.
     14   Received Carpenter's check in full payment for the purchase of August 4.
     15   Sold $3,240 of merchandise (that had cost $1,758) to customers who used their Aztec cards.
     18   Submitted Aztec card receipts accumulated since August 11 to the credit card company for payment.
     22   Wrote off the account of Craw Co. against the Allowance for Doubtful Accounts. The $498 balance in Craw City's account stemmed from a credit sale in November of last year.
     25   Received the amount due from Aztec.

Required

Prepare journal entries to record the preceding transactions and events. (The company uses the perpetual inventory system. Round amounts to the nearest dollar.)

Sherman Co. began operations on January 1, 2012, and completed several transactions during 2012 and 2013 that involved sales on credit, accounts receivable collections, and bad debts. These transactions are summarized as follows.

2012

a. Sold $685,350 of merchandise (that had cost $500,000) on credit, terms n/30.
b. Received $482,300 cash in payment of accounts receivable.
c. Wrote off $9,350 of uncollectible accounts receivable.
d. In adjusting the accounts on December 31, the company estimated that 1% of accounts receivable will be uncollectible.

2013

e. Sold $870,220 of merchandise (that had cost $650,000) on credit, terms n/30.
f. Received $990,800 cash in payment of accounts receivable.
g. Wrote off $11,090 of uncollectible accounts receivable.
h. In adjusting the accounts on December 31, the company estimated that 1% of accounts receivable will be uncollectible.

Required

Prepare journal entries to record Sherman's 2012 and 2013 summarized transactions and its year-end adjusting entry to record bad debts expense. (The company uses the perpetual inventory system and it applies the allowance method for its accounts receivable. Round amounts to the nearest dollar.)

At December 31, 2013, Ingleton Company reports the following results for the year:

Cash sales	$1,025,000
Credit sales	1,342,000

In addition, its unadjusted trial balance includes the following items:

Accounts receivable	$575,000 debit
Allowance for doubtful accounts	7,500 credit

PROBLEM SET B

Problem 9-1B
Sales on account and credit card sales

C1

Check Aug. 25, Dr. Cash $4,400

Problem 9-2B
Accounts receivable transactions and bad debts adjustments

C1 P2

Check (d) Dr. Bad Debts Expense $11,287

(h) Dr. Bad Debts Expense $9,773

Problem 9-3B
Estimating and reporting bad debts

P2

Required

1. Prepare the adjusting entry for Ingleton Co. to recognize bad debts under each of the following independent assumptions.

   a. Bad debts are estimated to be 2.5% of credit sales.

   b. Bad debts are estimated to be 1.5% of total sales.

   c. An aging analysis estimates that 6% of year-end accounts receivable are uncollectible.

2. Show how Accounts Receivable and the Allowance for Doubtful Accounts appear on its December 31, 2013, balance sheet given the facts in part 1a.

3. Show how Accounts Receivable and the Allowance for Doubtful Accounts appear on its December 31, 2013, balance sheet given the facts in part 1c.

Check Bad debts expense:
(1b) $35,505, (1c) $27,000

Problem 9-4B

Aging accounts receivable and accounting for bad debts

P2

Hovak Company has credit sales of $4.5 million for year 2013. At December 31, 2013, the company's Allowance for Doubtful Accounts has an unadjusted debit balance of $3,400. Hovak prepares a schedule of its December 31, 2013, accounts receivable by age. On the basis of past experience, it estimates the percent of receivables in each age category that will become uncollectible. This information is summarized here.

December 31, 2013 Accounts Receivable	Age of Accounts Receivable	Expected Percent Uncollectible
$396,400	Not yet due	2.0%
277,800	1 to 30 days past due	4.0
48,000	31 to 60 days past due	8.5
6,600	61 to 90 days past due	39.0
2,800	Over 90 days past due	82.0

Required

1. Compute the required balance of the Allowance for Doubtful Accounts at December 31, 2013, using the aging of accounts receivable method.

2. Prepare the adjusting entry to record bad debts expense at December 31, 2013.

Check (2) Dr. Bad Debts Expense
$31,390

Analysis Component

3. On July 31, 2014, Hovak concludes that a customer's $3,455 receivable (created in 2013) is uncollectible and that the account should be written off. What effect will this action have on Hovak's 2014 net income? Explain.

Problem 9-5B

Analyzing and journalizing notes receivable transactions

C2 C3 P3

The following selected transactions are from Springer Company.

2012

Nov. 1   Accepted a $4,800, 90-day, 8% note dated this day in granting Steve Julian a time extension on his past-due account receivable.

Dec. 31   Made an adjusting entry to record the accrued interest on the Julian note.

2013

Jan. 30   Received Julian's payment for principal and interest on the note dated November 1.

Feb. 28   Accepted a $12,600, 8%, 30-day note dated this day in granting a time extension on the past-due account receivable from King Co.

Mar. 1   Accepted a $6,200, 60-day, 12% note dated this day in granting Myron Shelley a time extension on his past-due account receivable.

     30   The King Co. dishonored its note when presented for payment.

April 30   Received payment of principal plus interest from M. Shelley for the March 1 note.

June 15   Accepted a $2,000, 72-day, 8% note dated this day in granting a time extension on the past-due account receivable of Ryder Solon.

     21   Accepted a $9,500, 90-day, 8% note dated this day in granting J. Felton a time extension on his past-due account receivable.

Aug. 26   Received payment of principal plus interest from R. Solon for the note of June 15.

Sep. 19   Received payment of principal plus interest from J. Felton for the June 21 note.

Nov. 30   Wrote off King's account against Allowance for Doubtful Accounts.

Check Jan. 30, Cr. Interest
Revenue $32

April 30, Cr. Interest
Revenue $124

Sep. 19, Cr. Interest
Revenue $190

Required

1. Prepare journal entries to record these transactions and events. (Round amounts to the nearest dollar.)

Analysis Component

2. What reporting is necessary when a business pledges receivables as security for a loan and the loan is still outstanding at the end of the period? Explain the reason for this requirement and the accounting principle being satisfied.

(This serial problem began in Chapter 1 and continues through most of the book. If previous chapter segments were not completed, the serial problem can begin at this point. It is helpful, but not necessary, to use the Working Papers that accompany the book.)

SP 9 Adria Lopez, owner of Success Systems, realizes that she needs to begin accounting for bad debts expense. Assume that Success Systems has total revenues of $43,853 during the first three months of 2014, and that the Accounts Receivable balance on March 31, 2014, is $22,720.

Required

1. Prepare the adjusting entry needed for Success Systems to recognize bad debts expense on March 31, 2014, under each of the following independent assumptions (assume a zero unadjusted balance in the Allowance for Doubtful Accounts at March 31).

  a. Bad debts are estimated to be 1% of total revenues. (Round amounts to the dollar.)

  b. Bad debts are estimated to be 2% of accounts receivable. (Round amounts to the dollar.)

2. Assume that Success Systems' Accounts Receivable balance at June 30, 2014, is $20,250 and that one account of $100 has been written off against the Allowance for Doubtful Accounts since March 31, 2014. If Adria Lopez uses the method prescribed in Part 1*b*, what adjusting journal entry must be made to recognize bad debts expense on June 30, 2014?

3. Should Adria Lopez consider adopting the direct write-off method of accounting for bad debts expense rather than one of the allowance methods considered in part 1? Explain.

SERIAL PROBLEM
Success Systems
P1 P2

Sage 50

Check (2) Bad Debts Expense, $51

Beyond the Numbers

BTN 9-1 Refer to **Polaris'** financial statements in Appendix A to answer the following.

1. What is the amount of Polaris' accounts receivable as of December 31, 2011?

2. Compute Polaris' accounts receivable turnover as of December 31, 2011.

3. How long does it take, *on average,* for the company to collect receivables? Do you believe that customers actually pay the amounts due within this short period? Explain.

4. Polaris' most liquid assets include (*a*) cash and cash equivalents, (*b*) receivables, and (*c*) inventory. Compute the percentage that these liquid assets make up of current liabilities as of December 31, 2011. Do the same computations for December 31, 2010. Comment on the company's ability to satisfy its current liabilities as of its 2011 year-end compared to its 2010 year-end.

5. What criteria did Polaris use to classify items as cash equivalents?

REPORTING IN ACTION

A1

Polaris

Fast Forward

6. Access Polaris' financial statements for fiscal years after December 31, 2011, at its Website (**www.Polaris.com**) or the SEC's EDGAR database (**www.sec.gov**). Recompute parts 2 and 4 and comment on any changes since December 31, 2011.

BTN 9-2 Comparative figures for **Polaris** and **Arctic Cat** follow.

COMPARATIVE ANALYSIS

A1 P2

Polaris
Arctic Cat

($ thousands)	Polaris			Arctic Cat		
	Current Year	One Year Prior	Two Years Prior	Current Year	One Year Prior	Two Years Prior
Accounts receivable, net	$ 115,302	$ 89,294	$ 90,405	$ 23,732	$ 29,227	$ 38,231
Net sales	2,659,949	1,991,139	1,565,887	464,651	450,728	563,613

Required

Hint: Average collection period equals 365 divided by the accounts receivable turnover.

1. Compute the accounts receivable turnover for Polaris and Arctic Cat for each of the two most recent years using the data shown.

2. Using results from part 1, compute how many days it takes each company, *on average,* to collect receivables. Compare the collection periods for Polaris and Arctic Cat, and suggest at least one explanation for the difference.

3. Which company is more efficient in collecting its accounts receivable? Explain.

ETHICS CHALLENGE
P2

BTN 9-3   Anton Blair is the manager of a medium-size company. A few years ago, Blair persuaded the owner to base a part of his compensation on the net income the company earns each year. Each December he estimates year-end financial figures in anticipation of the bonus he will receive. If the bonus is not as high as he would like, he offers several recommendations to the accountant for year-end adjustments. One of his favorite recommendations is for the controller to reduce the estimate of doubtful accounts.

Required

1. What effect does lowering the estimate for doubtful accounts have on the income statement and balance sheet?

2. Do you believe Blair's recommendation to adjust the allowance for doubtful accounts is within his right as manager, or do you believe this action is an ethics violation? Justify your response.

3. What type of internal control(s) might be useful for this company in overseeing the manager's recommendations for accounting changes?

COMMUNICATING IN PRACTICE
P2

BTN 9-4   As the accountant for Pure-Air Distributing, you attend a sales managers' meeting devoted to a discussion of credit policies. At the meeting, you report that bad debts expense is estimated to be $59,000 and accounts receivable at year-end amount to $1,750,000 less a $43,000 allowance for doubtful accounts. Sid Omar, a sales manager, expresses confusion over why bad debts expense and the allowance for doubtful accounts are different amounts. Write a one-page memorandum to him explaining why a difference in bad debts expense and the allowance for doubtful accounts is not unusual. The company estimates bad debts expense as 2% of sales.

TAKING IT TO THE NET
C1

BTN 9-5   Access **eBay**'s, January 31, 2012, filing of its 10-K report for the year ended December 31, 2011, at **www.SEC.gov**.

Required

1. What is the amount of eBay's net accounts receivable at December 31, 2011, and at December 31, 2010?

2. "Financial Statement Schedule II" to its financial statements lists eBay's allowance for doubtful accounts (including authorized credits). For the two years ended December 31, 2011 and 2010, compute its allowance for doubtful accounts (including authorized credits) as a percent of gross accounts receivable.

3. Do you believe that these percentages are reasonable based on what you know about eBay? Explain.

TEAMWORK IN ACTION
P2

BTN 9-6   Each member of a team is to participate in estimating uncollectibles using the aging schedule and percents shown in Problem 9-4A. The division of labor is up to the team. Your goal is to accurately complete this task as soon as possible. After estimating uncollectibles, check your estimate with the instructor. If the estimate is correct, the team then should prepare the adjusting entry and the presentation of accounts receivable (net) for the December 31, 2013, balance sheet.

ENTREPRENEURIAL DECISION
C1

BTN 9-7   Kevin Plank of **Under Armour** is introduced in the chapter's opening feature. Kevin currently sells his products through multiple outlets. Assume that he is considering two new selling options.

Plan A. Under Armour would begin selling additional products online directly to customers, which are only currently sold directly to stores. These new online customers would use their credit cards. It currently has the capability of selling through its Website with no additional investment in hardware or software. Credit sales are expected to increase by $250,000 per year. Costs associated with this plan are: cost of these sales will be $135,500, credit card fees will be 4.75% of sales, and additional recordkeeping and shipping costs will be 6% of sales. These online sales will reduce the sales to stores by $35,000 because some customers will now purchase items online. Sales to stores have a 25% gross margin percentage.

Plan B. Under Armour would expand its market to more stores. It would make additional credit sales of $500,000 to those stores. Costs associated with those sales are: cost of sales will be $375,000, additional recordkeeping and shipping will be 4% of sales, and uncollectible accounts will be 6.2% of sales.

Required

1. Compute the additional annual net income or loss expected under (a) Plan A and (b) Plan B.
2. Should Under Armour pursue either plan? Discuss both the financial and nonfinancial factors relevant to this decision.

Check (1*b*) Additional net income, $74,000

BTN 9-8 Many commercials include comments similar to the following: "We accept **VISA**" or "We do not accept **American Express**." Conduct your own research by contacting at least five companies via interviews, phone calls, or the Internet to determine the reason(s) companies discriminate in their use of credit cards. Collect information on the fees charged by the different cards for the companies contacted. (The instructor can assign this as a team activity.)

HITTING THE ROAD

C1

BTN 9-9 Key information from **Piaggio** (www.Piaggio.com), which manufactures two-, three- and four-wheel vehicles, and is Europe's leading manufacturer of motorcycles and scooters, follows.

Euro in thousands	Current Year	Prior Year
Accounts receivable, net*	65,560	90,421
Sales	1,516,463	1,485,351

*Piaggio refers to it as "Trade receivables."

1. Compute the accounts receivable turnover for the current year.
2. How long does it take on average for Piaggio to collect receivables?
3. Refer to BTN 9-2. How does Piaggio compare to Polaris and Arctic Cat in terms of its accounts receivable turnover and its collection period?

GLOBAL DECISION

C1 P2

PIAGGIO
Polaris
Arctic Cat

ANSWERS TO MULTIPLE CHOICE QUIZ

1. d; Desired balance in Allowance for Doubtful Accounts = $ 5,026 cr.
   ($125,650 × 0.04)
   Current balance in Allowance for Doubtful Accounts = ___(328) cr.
   Bad Debts Expense to be recorded = $ 4,698

2. a; Desired balance in Allowance for Doubtful Accounts = $29,358 cr.
   ($489,300 × 0.06)
   Current balance in Allowance for Doubtful Accounts = ___554 dr.
   Bad Debts Expense to be recorded = $29,912

3. a; $7,500 × 0.05 × 90/360 = $93.75

4. c; Principal amount $9,000
   Interest accrued ....   ___120 ($9,000 × 0.08 × 60/360)
   Maturity value $9,120

5. d; $489,600/$40,800 = 12

Plant Assets, Natural Resources, and Intangibles

A Look Back

Chapters 8 and 9 focused on short-term assets: cash, cash equivalents, and receivables. We explained why they are known as liquid assets and described how companies account and report for them.

A Look at This Chapter

This chapter introduces us to long-term assets. We explain how to account for a long-term asset's cost, the allocation of an asset's cost to periods benefiting from it, the recording of additional costs after an asset is purchased, and the disposal of an asset.

A Look Ahead

Chapter 11 focuses on current liabilities. We explain how they are computed, recorded, and reported in financial statements. We also explain the accounting for company payroll and contingencies.

Learning Objectives

CONCEPTUAL

C1 Explain the cost principle for computing the cost of plant assets. (p. 397)

C2 Explain depreciation for partial years and changes in estimates. (p. 404)

C3 Distinguish between revenue and capital expenditures, and account for them. (p. 406)

ANALYTICAL

A1 Compute total asset turnover and apply it to analyze a company's use of assets. (p. 415)

PROCEDURAL

P1 Compute and record depreciation using the straight-line, units-of-production, and declining-balance methods. (p. 400)

P2 Account for asset disposal through discarding or selling an asset. (p. 408)

P3 Account for natural resource assets and their depletion. (p. 410)

P4 Account for intangible assets. (p. 411)

P5 *Appendix 10A—Account for asset exchanges.* (p. 418)

Sitting Pretty

Don't be afraid to take risks . . . [but] not careless risks."
—**SEAN BELNICK**

CANTON, GA—"It is never too early to start," explains Sean Belnick. "Just do the research and find a way." Sean's way was to create **BizChair.com** to sell office chairs more efficiently. "I was inspired to create BizChair.com through my fascination with selling things on the Internet," admits Sean. "Before selling office chairs, I would sell Pokemon cards . . . on eBay. I started with $500 advertising and $100 for Website hosting . . . I was 14 at the time."

From those modest beginnings Sean has continued to expand his business beyond office chairs and now sells stack chairs, folding chairs, recliners, and a range of office, home, and medical equipment. "Business has been really good," says Sean. However, long-term assets such as warehousing facilities, office structures, packing equipment, and delivery and conveyor systems are expensive. Sean explains that financing equipment, machinery, and similar assets is a challenge. "Most likely [because of asset funding limitations] we stayed in the office chair market for a while before expanding into office furniture and home furniture as well as some other segments," explains Sean. "If we had done that faster, we could have cemented a larger position as a market leader." Further, Sean had to work out depreciation schedules and estimate payback for different asset purchases as his business grew.

BizChair.com is now sitting pretty—employing over 150 workers, offering greater product selection, and generating tens of millions in annual sales. Still, a constant challenge for Sean is maintaining the right kind and amount of assets to meet business demands and be profitable. Sean admits he had to learn how "to properly read and create a balance sheet and income statement, and how to create pro-forma financial statements [which] have helped me ultimately run the company better."

Sean says BizChair.com's success depends on continued monitoring and control of asset costs. Each of his tangible and intangible assets commands Sean's attention. He accounts for, manages, and focuses on recovering all costs of those long-term assets. "I love the excitement, the future growth prospects, as well as watching the company grow and prosper," explains Sean. He recently oversaw a 150,000-square-foot warehouse expansion to make room for more inventory. His success in asset management permits BizChair.com "to focus on growth and continued expansion of the business." Adds Sean, "I'm like any other kid!"

[Sources: *BizChair.com Website,* January 2013; *Cherokee Tribune,* June 2011; *Goizueta Magazine,* Winter 2009 and October 2010; *Retire@21* June 2010; *Under30CEO,* January 2011]

This chapter focuses on long-term assets, which can be grouped into plant assets, natural resource assets, and intangible assets. Plant assets make up a large part of assets on most balance sheets, and they yield depreciation, often one of the largest expenses on income statements. The acquisition or building of a plant asset is often referred to as a *capital expenditure*. Capital expenditures are important events because they impact both the short- and long-term success of a company. Natural resource assets and intangible assets have similar impacts. This chapter describes the purchase and use of these assets. We also explain what distinguishes these assets from other types of assets, how to determine their cost, how to allocate their costs to periods benefiting from their use, and how to dispose of them.

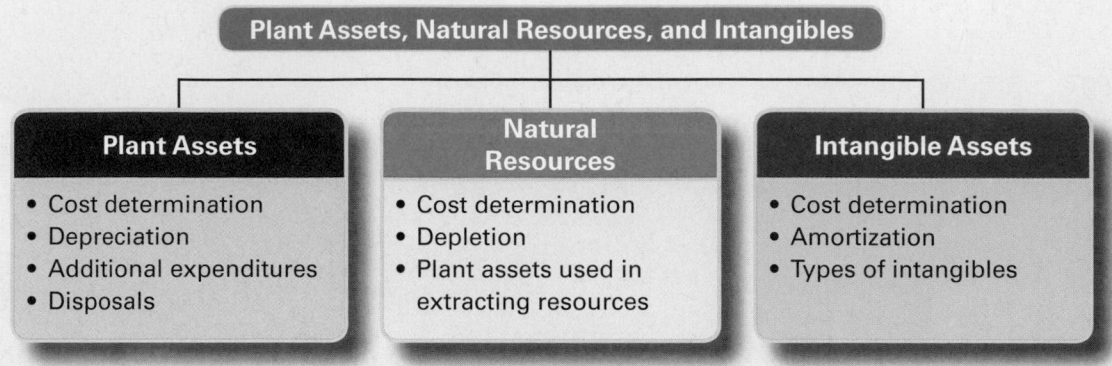

Plant Assets, Natural Resources, and Intangibles

Plant Assets
- Cost determination
- Depreciation
- Additional expenditures
- Disposals

Natural Resources
- Cost determination
- Depletion
- Plant assets used in extracting resources

Intangible Assets
- Cost determination
- Amortization
- Types of intangibles

Section 1—Plant Assets

Plant assets are tangible assets used in a company's operations that have a useful life of more than one accounting period. Plant assets are also called *plant and equipment; property, plant, and equipment;* or *fixed assets.* For many companies, plant assets make up the single largest class of assets they own. Exhibit 10.1 shows plant assets as a percent of total assets for several companies. Not only do they make up a large percent of many companies' assets, but their dollar values are large. **McDonald's** plant assets, for instance, are reported at more than $22 billion, and **Walmart** reports plant assets of more than $107 billion.

EXHIBIT 10.1

Plant Assets of Selected Companies

eBay	$1,986 mil. **7%**
Boston Beer	$144 mil. **53%**
Walmart	$107,878 mil. **60%**
McDonald's	$22,835 mil. **69%**

As a Percent of Total Assets

Plant assets are set apart from other assets by two important features. First, *plant assets are used in operations.* This makes them different from, for instance, inventory that is held for sale and not used in operations. The distinctive feature here is use, not type of asset. A company that purchases a computer to resell it reports it on the balance sheet as inventory. If the same company purchases this computer to use in operations, however, it is a plant asset. Another example is land held for future expansion, which is reported as a long-term investment. However, if this land holds a factory used in operations, the land is part of plant assets. Another example is equipment held for use in the event of a breakdown or for peak periods of production, which is reported in plant assets. If this same equipment is removed from use and held for sale, however, it is not reported in plant assets.

The second important feature is that *plant assets have useful lives extending over more than one accounting period.* This makes plant assets different from current assets such as supplies that are normally consumed in a short time period after they are placed in use.

Point: The phrase *capital-intensive* refers to companies with large amounts invested in plant assets. Exhibit 10.1 reveals that McDonalds is more capital-intensive than eBay.

The accounting for plant assets reflects these two features. Since plant assets are used in operations, we try to match their costs against the revenues they generate. Also, since their useful lives extend over more than one period, our matching of costs and revenues must extend over several periods. Specifically, we value plant assets (balance sheet effect) and then, for many of them, we allocate their costs to periods benefiting from their use (income statement effect). An important exception is land; land cost is not allocated to expense when we expect it to have an indefinite life.

Exhibit 10.2 shows four main issues in accounting for plant assets: (1) computing the costs of plant assets, (2) allocating the costs of most plant assets (less any salvage amounts) against revenues for the periods they benefit, (3) accounting for expenditures such as repairs and improvements to plant assets, and (4) recording the disposal of plant assets. The following sections discuss these issues.

Point: It can help to view plant assets as prepaid expenses that benefit several future accounting periods.

EXHIBIT 10.2

Issues in Accounting for Plant Assets

COST DETERMINATION

Plant assets are recorded at cost when acquired. This is consistent with the *cost principle.* **Cost** includes all normal and reasonable expenditures necessary to get the asset in place and ready for its intended use. The cost of a factory machine, for instance, includes its invoice cost less any cash discount for early payment, plus any necessary freight, unpacking, assembling, installing, and testing costs. Examples are the costs of building a base or foundation for a machine, providing electrical hookups, and testing the asset before using it in operations.

C1 Explain the cost principle for computing the cost of plant assets.

To be recorded as part of the cost of a plant asset, an expenditure must be normal, reasonable, and necessary in preparing it for its intended use. If an asset is damaged during unpacking, the repairs are not added to its cost. Instead, they are charged to an expense account. Nor is a paid traffic fine for moving heavy machinery on city streets without a proper permit part of the machinery's cost; but payment for a proper permit is included in the cost of machinery. Charges are sometimes incurred to modify or customize a new plant asset. These charges are added to the asset's cost. We explain in this section how to determine the cost of plant assets for each of its four major classes.

Land

When land is purchased for a building site, its cost includes the total amount paid for the land, including any real estate commissions, title insurance fees, legal fees, and any accrued property taxes paid by the purchaser. Payments for surveying, clearing, grading, and draining also are included in the cost of land. Other costs include government assessments, whether incurred at the time of purchase or later, for items such as public roadways, sewers, and sidewalks. These assessments are included because they permanently add to the land's value. Land purchased as a building site sometimes includes structures that must be removed. In such cases, the total purchase price is charged to the Land account as is the cost of removing the structures, less any amounts recovered through sale of salvaged materials. To illustrate, assume that **Starbucks** paid $167,000 cash to acquire land for a retail store. This land had an old service garage that was removed at a net cost of

EXHIBIT 10.3

Computing Cost of Land

Cash price of land	$ 167,000
Net cost of garage removal	13,000
Closing costs	10,000
Cost of land	**$190,000**

$13,000 ($15,000 in costs less $2,000 proceeds from salvaged materials). Additional closing costs total $10,000, consisting of brokerage fees ($8,000), legal fees ($1,500), and title costs ($500). The cost of this land to Starbucks is $190,000 and is computed as shown in Exhibit 10.3.

Land Improvements

Land has an indefinite (unlimited) life and is not usually used up over time. **Land improvements** such as parking lot surfaces, driveways, fences, shrubs, and lighting systems, however, have limited useful lives and are used up. While the costs of these improvements increase the usefulness of the land, they are charged to a separate Land Improvement account so that their costs can be allocated to the periods they benefit.

Buildings

A Building account is charged for the costs of purchasing or constructing a building that is used in operations. When purchased, a building's costs usually include its purchase price, brokerage fees, taxes, title fees, and attorney fees. Its costs also include all expenditures to ready it for its intended use, including any necessary repairs or renovations such as wiring, lighting, flooring, and wall coverings. When a company constructs a building or any plant asset for its own use, its costs include materials and labor plus a reasonable amount of indirect overhead cost. Overhead includes the costs of items such as heat, lighting, power, and depreciation on machinery used to construct the asset. Costs of construction also include design fees, building permits, and insurance during construction. However, costs such as insurance to cover the asset *after* it is placed in use are operating expenses.

Machinery and Equipment

The costs of machinery and equipment consist of all costs normal and necessary to purchase them and prepare them for their intended use. These include the purchase price, taxes, transportation charges, insurance while in transit, and the installing, assembling, and testing of the machinery and equipment.

Lump-Sum Purchase

Example: If appraised values in Exhibit 10.4 are land, $24,000; land improvements, $12,000; and building, $84,000, what cost is assigned to the building? *Answer:*
(1) $24,000 + $12,000 + $84,000 = $120,000 (total appraisal)
(2) $84,000/$120,000 = 70% (building's percent of total)
(3) 70% × $90,000 = $63,000 (building's apportioned cost)

Plant assets sometimes are purchased as a group in a single transaction for a lump-sum price. This transaction is called a *lump-sum purchase,* or *group, bulk,* or *basket purchase.* When this occurs, we allocate the cost of the purchase among the different types of assets acquired based on their *relative market values,* which can be estimated by appraisal or by using the tax-assessed valuations of the assets. To illustrate, assume **CarMax** paid $90,000 cash to acquire a group of items consisting of land appraised at $30,000, land improvements appraised at $10,000, and a building appraised at $60,000. The $90,000 cost is allocated on the basis of these appraised values as shown in Exhibit 10.4.

EXHIBIT 10.4

Computing Costs in a Lump-Sum Purchase

	Appraised Value	Percent of Total	Apportioned Cost
Land	$ 30,000	30% ($30,000/$100,000)	**$27,000** ($90,000 × 30%)
Land improvements	10,000	10 ($10,000/$100,000)	**9,000** ($90,000 × 10%)
Building	60,000	60 ($60,000/$100,000)	**54,000** ($90,000 × 60%)
Totals	$100,000	100%	$ 90,000

Quick Check   Answers — p. 421

1. Identify the asset class for each of the following: (*a*) supplies, (*b*) office equipment, (*c*) inventory, (*d*) land for future expansion, and (*e*) trucks used in operations.
2. Identify the account charged for each of the following: (*a*) the purchase price of a vacant lot to be used in operations and (*b*) the cost of paving that same vacant lot.
3. Compute the amount recorded as the cost of a new machine given the following payments related to its purchase: gross purchase price, $700,000; sales tax, $49,000; purchase discount taken, $21,000; freight cost—terms FOB shipping point, $3,500; normal assembly costs, $3,000; cost of necessary machine platform, $2,500; cost of parts used in maintaining machine, $4,200.

DEPRECIATION

Depreciation is the process of allocating the cost of a plant asset to expense in the accounting periods benefiting from its use. Depreciation does not measure the decline in the asset's market value each period, nor does it measure the asset's physical deterioration. Since depreciation reflects the cost of using a plant asset, depreciation charges are only recorded when the asset is actually in service. This section describes the factors we must consider in computing depreciation, the depreciation methods used, revisions in depreciation, and depreciation for partial periods.

Point: Depreciation is cost allocation, not asset valuation.

Factors in Computing Depreciation

Factors that determine depreciation are (1) cost, (2) salvage value, and (3) useful life.

Cost   The **cost** of a plant asset consists of all necessary and reasonable expenditures to acquire it and to prepare it for its intended use.

Salvage Value   The total amount of depreciation to be charged off over an asset's benefit period equals the asset's cost minus its salvage value. **Salvage value,** also called *residual value* or *scrap value,* is an estimate of the asset's value at the end of its benefit period. This is the amount the owner expects to receive from disposing of the asset at the end of its benefit period. If the asset is expected to be traded in on a new asset, its salvage value is the expected trade-in value.

Point: If we expect additional costs in preparing a plant asset for disposal, the salvage value equals the expected amount from disposal less any disposal costs.

Useful Life   The **useful life** of a plant asset is the length of time it is productively used in a company's operations. Useful life, also called *service life,* might not be as long as the asset's total productive life. For example, the productive life of a computer can be eight years or more. Some companies, however, trade in old computers for new ones every two years. In this case, these computers have a two-year useful life, meaning the cost of these computers (less their expected trade-in values) is charged to depreciation expense over a two-year period.

Point: Useful life and salvage value are estimates. Estimates require judgment based on all available information.

Several variables often make the useful life of a plant asset difficult to predict. A major variable is the wear and tear from use in operations. Two other variables, inadequacy and obsolescence, also require consideration. **Inadequacy** refers to the insufficient capacity of a company's plant assets to meet its growing productive demands. **Obsolescence** refers to the condition of a plant asset that is no longer useful in producing goods or services with a competitive advantage because of new inventions and improvements. Both inadequacy and obsolescence are difficult to predict because of demand changes, new inventions, and improvements. A company usually disposes of an inadequate or obsolete asset before it wears out.

A company is often able to better predict a new asset's useful life when it has past experience with a similar asset. When it has no such experience, a company relies on the experience of others or on engineering studies and judgment. In note 1 of its annual report, **Tootsie Roll**, a snack food manufacturer, reports the following useful lives:

Point: Land is recorded at cost but not depreciated because it normally retains its value over time.

Buildings	20–35 years
Machinery and Equipment	5–20 years

■ **Decision** Insight ━━━━━━━━━━━━━━━━━━━━━━━━━━━━━━━━━━━━━

Life Line Life expectancy of plant assets is often in the eye of the beholder. For instance, **Hershey Foods** and **Tootsie Roll** are competitors and apply similar manufacturing processes, yet their equipment's life expectancies are different. Hershey depreciates equipment over 3 to 15 years, but Tootsie Roll depreciates them over 5 to 20 years. Such differences markedly impact financial statements. ■

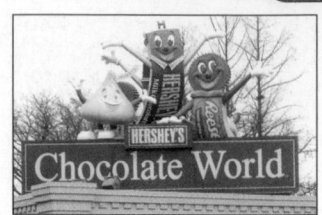

Depreciation Methods

P1	Compute and record depreciation using the straight-line, units-of-production, and declining-balance methods.

Depreciation methods are used to allocate a plant asset's cost over the accounting periods in its useful life. The most frequently used method of depreciation is the straight-line method. Another common depreciation method is the units-of-production method. We explain both of these methods in this section. This section also describes accelerated depreciation methods, with a focus on the declining-balance method.

The computations in this section use information about a machine that inspects athletic shoes before packaging. Manufacturers such as **Converse**, **Reebok**, **adidas**, and **Fila** use this machine. Data for this machine are in Exhibit 10.5.

EXHIBIT 10.5

Data for Athletic Shoe-Inspecting Machine

Cost	$10,000
Salvage value	1,000
Depreciable cost	$ 9,000
Useful life	
Accounting periods	5 years
Units inspected	36,000 shoes

Straight-Line Method **Straight-line depreciation** charges the same amount of expense to each period of the asset's useful life. A two-step process is used. We first compute the *depreciable cost* of the asset, also called the *cost to be depreciated.* It is computed by subtracting the asset's salvage value from its total cost. Second, depreciable cost is divided by the number of accounting periods in the asset's useful life. The formula for straight-line depreciation, along with its computation for the inspection machine just described, is shown in Exhibit 10.6.

EXHIBIT 10.6

Straight-Line Depreciation Formula and Example

$$\frac{\text{Cost} - \text{Salvage value}}{\text{Useful life in periods}} = \frac{\$10,000 - \$1,000}{5 \text{ years}} = \$1,800 \text{ per year}$$

If this machine is purchased on December 31, 2012, and used throughout its predicted useful life of five years, the straight-line method allocates an equal amount of depreciation to each of the years 2013 through 2017. We make the following adjusting entry at the end of each of the five years to record straight-line depreciation of this machine.

Assets = Liabilities + Equity
−1,800   −1,800

Dec. 31	Depreciation Expense	1,800	
	Accumulated Depreciation—Machinery		1,800
	To record annual depreciation.		

Example: If the salvage value of the machine is $2,500, what is the annual depreciation? *Answer:* ($10,000 − $2,500)/5 years = $1,500

The $1,800 Depreciation Expense is reported on the income statement among operating expenses. The $1,800 Accumulated Depreciation is a contra asset account to the Machinery account in the balance sheet. The graph on the left in Exhibit 10.7 shows the $1,800 per year expenses reported in each of the five years. The graph on the right shows the amounts reported on each of the six December 31 balance sheets.

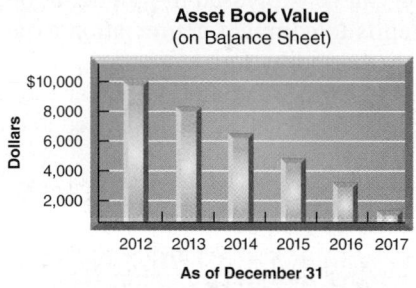

EXHIBIT 10.7

Financial Statement Effects of Straight-Line Depreciation

The net balance sheet amount is the **asset book value,** or simply *book value,* and is computed as the asset's total cost less its accumulated depreciation. For example, at the end of year 2 (December 31, 2014), its book value is $6,400 and is reported in the balance sheet as follows:

Book value = Cost − Accumulated depreciation

Machinery	$10,000	
Less accumulated depreciation	3,600	$6,400 ◄── Book value

The book value of this machine declines by $1,800 each year due to depreciation. The left-side graphic in Exhibit 10.7 reveals why this method is called straight-line.

We also can compute the *straight-line depreciation rate,* defined as 100% divided by the number of periods in the asset's useful life. For the inspection machine, this rate is 20% (100% ÷ 5 years, or 1/5 per period). We use this rate, along with other information, to compute the machine's *straight-line depreciation schedule* shown in Exhibit 10.8. Note three points in this exhibit. First, depreciation expense is the same each period. Second, accumulated depreciation is the sum of current and prior periods' depreciation expense. Third, book value declines each period until it equals salvage value at the end of the machine's useful life.

Point: Depreciation requires estimates for salvage value and useful life. Ethics are relevant when managers might be tempted to choose estimates to achieve desired results on financial statements.

Annual Period	Depreciation for the Period			End of Period	
	Depreciable Cost*	Depreciation Rate	Depreciation Expense	Accumulated Depreciation	Book Value†
2012	—	—	—	—	$10,000
2013	$9,000	20%	**$1,800**	$1,800	8,200
2014	9,000	20	**1,800**	3,600	6,400
2015	9,000	20	**1,800**	5,400	4,600
2016	9,000	20	**1,800**	7,200	2,800
2017	9,000	20	**1,800**	9,000	**1,000** ◄── Salvage value (not depreciated)

EXHIBIT 10.8

Straight-Line Depreciation Schedule

* $10,000 − $1,000.   † Book value is total cost minus accumulated depreciation.

Units-of-Production Method   The straight-line method charges an equal share of an asset's cost to each period. If plant assets are used up in about equal amounts each accounting period, this method produces a reasonable matching of expenses with revenues. However, the use of some plant assets varies greatly from one period to the next. A builder, for instance, might use a piece of construction equipment for a month and then not use it again for several months. When equipment use varies from period to period, the units-of-production depreciation method can better match expenses with revenues. **Units-of-production depreciation** charges a varying amount to expense for each period of an asset's useful life depending on its *usage.*

A two-step process is used to compute units-of-production depreciation. We first compute *depreciation per unit* by subtracting the asset's salvage value from its total cost and then dividing by the total number of units expected to be produced during its useful life. Units of production can be expressed in product or other units such as hours used or miles driven. The second step is to compute depreciation expense for the period by multiplying the units produced in the period by the depreciation per unit. The formula for units-of-production depreciation, along with its computation for the machine described in Exhibit 10.5, is shown in Exhibit 10.9. (7,000 shoes are inspected and sold in its first year.)

EXHIBIT 10.9

Units-of-Production Depreciation Formula and Example

Step 1

$$\text{Depreciation per unit} = \frac{\text{Cost} - \text{Salvage value}}{\text{Total units of production}} = \frac{\$10,000 - \$1,000}{36,000 \text{ shoes}} = \$0.25 \text{ per shoe}$$

Step 2

$$\text{Depreciation expense} = \text{Depreciation per unit} \times \text{Units produced in period}$$
$$\$0.25 \text{ per shoe} \times 7,000 \text{ shoes} = \$1,750$$

Using data on the number of shoes inspected by the machine, we can compute the *units-of-production depreciation schedule* shown in Exhibit 10.10. For example, depreciation for the first year is $1,750 (7,000 shoes at $0.25 per shoe). Depreciation for the second year is $2,000 (8,000 shoes at $0.25 per shoe). Other years are similarly computed. Exhibit 10.10 shows that (1) depreciation expense depends on unit output, (2) accumulated depreciation is the sum of current and prior periods' depreciation expense, and (3) book value declines each period until it equals salvage value at the end of the asset's useful life. **Deltic Timber** is one of many companies using the units-of-production depreciation method. It reports that depreciation "is calculated over the estimated useful lives of the assets by using the units of production method for machinery and equipment."

Example: Refer to Exhibit 10.10. If the number of shoes inspected in 2017 is 5,500, what is depreciation for 2017? *Answer:* $1,250 (never depreciate below salvage value)

EXHIBIT 10.10

Units-of-Production Depreciation Schedule

Annual Period	Depreciation for the Period			End of Period	
	Number of Units	Depreciation per Unit	Depreciation Expense	Accumulated Depreciation	Book Value
2012	—	—	—	—	$10,000
2013	7,000	$0.25	**$1,750**	$1,750	8,250
2014	8,000	0.25	**2,000**	3,750	6,250
2015	9,000	0.25	**2,250**	6,000	4,000
2016	7,000	0.25	**1,750**	7,750	2,250
2017	5,000	0.25	**1,250**	9,000	**1,000**

Salvage value (not depreciated)

Declining-Balance Method An **accelerated depreciation method** yields larger depreciation expenses in the early years of an asset's life and less depreciation in later years. The most common accelerated method is the **declining-balance method** of depreciation, which uses a depreciation rate that is a multiple of the straight-line rate and applies it to the asset's beginning-of-period book value. The amount of depreciation declines each period because book value declines each period.

A common depreciation rate for the declining-balance method is double the straight-line rate. This is called the *double-declining-balance (DDB)* method. This method is applied in three steps: (1) compute the asset's straight-line depreciation rate, (2) double the straight-line rate, and (3) compute depreciation expense by multiplying this rate by the asset's beginning-of-period book value. To illustrate, let's return to the machine in Exhibit 10.5 and apply the double-declining-balance method to compute depreciation expense. Exhibit 10.11 shows the first-year depreciation computation for the machine. The three-step process is to (1) divide 100% by five years to determine the straight-line rate of 20%, or 1/5, per year, (2) double this 20% rate to get the

Point: In the DDB method, *double* refers to the rate and *declining balance* refers to book value. The rate is applied to beginning book value each period.

declining-balance rate of 40%, or 2/5, per year, and (3) compute depreciation expense as 40%, or 2/5, multiplied by the beginning-of-period book value.

EXHIBIT 10.11

Double-Declining-Balance
Depreciation Formula*

Step 1
Straight-line rate = 100% ÷ Useful life = 100% ÷ 5 years = 20%

Step 2
Double-declining-balance rate = 2 × Straight-line rate = 2 × 20% = 40%

Step 3
Depreciation expense = Double-declining-balance rate × Beginning-period book value
40% × $10,000 = $4,000 (for 2013)

* To simplify: DDB depreciation = (2 × Beginning-period book value)/Useful life.

The *double-declining-balance depreciation schedule* is shown in Exhibit 10.12. The schedule follows the formula except for year 2017, when depreciation expense is $296. This $296 is not equal to 40% × $1,296, or $518.40. If we had used the $518.40 for depreciation expense in 2017, the ending book value would equal $777.60, which is less than the $1,000 salvage value. Instead, the $296 is computed by subtracting the $1,000 salvage value from the $1,296 book value at the beginning of the fifth year (the year when DDB depreciation cuts into salvage value).

EXHIBIT 10.12

Double-Declining-Balance
Depreciation Schedule

Annual Period	Depreciation for the Period			End of Period	
	Beginning of Period Book Value	Depreciation Rate	Depreciation Expense	Accumulated Depreciation	Book Value
2012	—	—	—	—	$10,000
2013	$10,000	40%	**$4,000**	$4,000	6,000
2014	6,000	40	**2,400**	6,400	3,600
2015	3,600	40	**1,440**	7,840	2,160
2016	2,160	40	**864**	8,704	1,296
2017	1,296	40	**296***	9,000	1,000

Salvage value (not depreciated)

* Year 2017 depreciation is $1,296 − $1,000 = $296 (never depreciate book value below salvage value).

Comparing Depreciation Methods   Exhibit 10.13 shows depreciation expense for each year of the machine's useful life under each of the three depreciation methods. While depreciation expense per period differs for different methods, total depreciation expense of $9,000 is the same over the machine's useful life.

EXHIBIT 10.13

Depreciation Expense for the
Different Methods

File Edit View Insert Format Tools Data Accounting Window Help

Period	Straight-Line	Units-of-Production	Double-Declining-Balance
2013	$1,800	$1,750	$4,000
2014	1,800	2,000	2,400
2015	1,800	2,250	1,440
2016	1,800	1,750	864
2017	1,800	1,250	296
Totals	**$9,000**	**$9,000**	**$9,000**

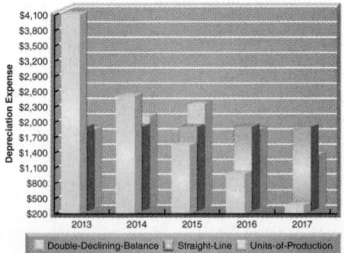

Each method starts with a total cost of $10,000 and ends with a salvage value of $1,000. The difference is the pattern in depreciation expense over the useful life. The book value of the asset when using straight-line is always greater than the book value from using double-declining-balance, except at the beginning and end of the asset's useful life, when it is the same. Also, the straight-line method yields a steady pattern of depreciation expense while the units-of-production depreciation depends on the number of units produced. Each of these methods is acceptable because it allocates cost in a systematic and rational manner.

Decision Insight

In Vogue   About 87% of companies use straight-line depreciation for plant assets, 4% use units-of-production, and 4% use declining-balance. Another 5% use an unspecified accelerated method—most likely declining-balance. ∎

Straight-line, 87%

Accelerated and other, 5%

Declining-balance, 4%

Units-of-production, 4%

Depreciation for Tax Reporting   The records a company keeps for financial accounting purposes are usually separate from the records it keeps for tax accounting purposes. This is so because financial accounting aims to report useful information on financial performance and position, whereas tax accounting reflects government objectives in raising revenues. Differences between these two accounting systems are normal and expected. Depreciation is a common example of how the records differ. For example, many companies use accelerated depreciation in computing taxable income. Reporting higher depreciation expense in the early years of an asset's life reduces the company's taxable income in those years and increases it in later years, when the depreciation expense is lower. The company's goal here is to *postpone* its tax payments.

The U.S. federal income tax law has rules for depreciating assets. These rules include the **Modified Accelerated Cost Recovery System (MACRS),** which allows straight-line depreciation for some assets but requires accelerated depreciation for most kinds of assets. MACRS separates depreciable assets into different classes and defines the depreciable life and rate for each class. MACRS is *not* acceptable for financial reporting because it often allocates costs over an arbitrary period that is less than the asset's useful life and it fails to estimate salvage value. Details of MACRS are covered in tax accounting courses.

Point: Understanding depreciation for financial accounting will help in learning MACRS for tax accounting. Rules for MACRS are available from www.IRS.gov.

Partial-Year Depreciation

C2 Explain depreciation for partial years and changes in estimates.

Plant assets are purchased and disposed of at various times. When an asset is purchased (or disposed of) at a time other than the beginning or end of an accounting period, depreciation is recorded for part of a year. This is done so that the year of purchase or the year of disposal is charged with its share of the asset's depreciation.

To illustrate, assume that the machine in Exhibit 10.5 is purchased and placed in service on October 8, 2012, and the annual accounting period ends on December 31. Since this machine is purchased and used for nearly three months in 2012, the calendar-year income statement should report depreciation expense on the machine for that part of the year. Normally, depreciation assumes that the asset is purchased on the first day of the month nearest the actual date of purchase. In this case, since the purchase occurred on October 8, we assume an October 1 purchase date. This means that three months' depreciation is recorded in 2012. Using straight-line depreciation, we compute three months' depreciation of $450 as follows.

Point: Assets purchased on days 1 through 15 of a month are usually recorded as purchased on the 1st of that month. Assets purchased on days 16 to the month-end are recorded as if purchased on the 1st of the next month.

$$\frac{\$10,000 - \$1,000}{5 \text{ years}} \times \frac{3}{12} = \$450$$

A similar computation is necessary when an asset disposal occurs during a period. To illustrate, assume that the machine is sold on June 24, 2017. Depreciation is recorded for the period January 1 through June 24 when it is disposed of. This partial year's depreciation, computed to the nearest whole month, is

Example: If the machine's salvage value is zero and purchase occurs on Oct. 8, 2012, how much depreciation is recorded at Dec. 31, 2012?
Answer: $10,000/5 × 3/12 = $500

$$\frac{\$10,000 - \$1,000}{5 \text{ years}} \times \frac{6}{12} = \$900$$

Change in Estimates for Depreciation

Depreciation is based on estimates of salvage value and useful life. During the useful life of an asset, new information may indicate that these estimates are inaccurate. If our estimate of an asset's useful life and/or salvage value changes, what should we do? The answer is to use the new estimate to compute depreciation for current and future periods. This means that we revise the depreciation expense computation by spreading the cost yet to be depreciated over the remaining useful life. This approach is used for all depreciation methods.

Point: Remaining depreciable cost equals book value less revised salvage value at the point of revision.

Let's return to the machine described in Exhibit 10.8 using straight-line depreciation. At the beginning of this asset's third year, its book value is $6,400, computed as $10,000 minus $3,600. Assume that at the beginning of its third year, the estimated number of years remaining in its useful life changes from three to four years *and* its estimate of salvage value changes from $1,000 to $400. Straight-line depreciation for each of the four remaining years is computed as shown in Exhibit 10.14.

Point: Income is overstated (and depreciation understated) when useful life is too high; when useful life is too low, the opposite results.

$$\frac{\text{Book value} - \text{Revised salvage value}}{\text{Revised remaining useful life}} = \frac{\$6,400 - \$400}{4 \text{ years}} = \$1,500 \text{ per year}$$

EXHIBIT 10.14

Computing Revised
Straight-Line Depreciation

Thus, $1,500 of depreciation expense is recorded for the machine at the end of the third through sixth years—each year of its remaining useful life. Since this asset was depreciated at $1,800 per year for the first two years, it is tempting to conclude that depreciation expense was overstated in the first two years. However, these expenses reflected the best information available at that time. We do not go back and restate prior years' financial statements for this type of new information. Instead, we adjust the current and future periods' statements to reflect this new information. Revising an estimate of the useful life or salvage value of a plant asset is referred to as a **change in an accounting estimate** and is reflected in current and future financial statements, not in prior statements.

Example: If at the beginning of its second year the machine's remaining useful life changes from four to three years and salvage value from $1,000 to $400, how much straight-line depreciation is recorded in remaining years?
Answer: Revised depreciation = ($8,200 − $400)/3 = $2,600.

Reporting Depreciation

Both the cost and accumulated depreciation of plant assets are reported on the balance sheet or in its notes. **Dale Jarrett Racing Adventure**, for instance, reports the following.

Office furniture and equipment	$ 54,593
Shop and track equipment	202,973
Race vehicles and other	975,084
Property and equipment, gross	1,232,650
Less accumulated depreciation	628,355
Property and equipment, net	$ 604,295

Many companies also show plant assets on one line with the net amount of cost less accumulated depreciation. When this is done, the amount of accumulated depreciation is disclosed in a note. **Apple** reports only the net amount of its property, plant and equipment in its balance sheet. To satisfy the full-disclosure principle, Apple describes its depreciation methods in its Note 1 and the amounts comprising plant assets in its Note 5—see its 10-K at www.SEC.gov.

Point: A company usually keeps records for each asset showing its cost and depreciation to date. The combined records for individual assets are a type of *plant asset subsidiary ledger*.

Reporting both the cost and accumulated depreciation of plant assets helps users compare the assets of different companies. For example, a company holding assets costing $50,000 and accumulated depreciation of $40,000 is likely in a situation different from a company with new assets costing $10,000. While the net undepreciated cost of $10,000 is the same in both cases, the first company may have more productive capacity available but likely is facing the need to replace older assets. These insights are not provided if the two balance sheets report only the $10,000 book values.

Users must remember that plant assets are reported on a balance sheet at their undepreciated costs (book value), not at fair (market) values. This emphasis on costs rather than fair values is based on the *going-concern assumption* described in Chapter 1. This assumption states that, unless there is evidence to the contrary, we assume that a company continues in business. This implies that plant assets are held and used long enough to recover their cost through the sale of products and services. Because plant assets are not for sale, their fair values are not reported. An exception is

Example: Assume equipment carries a book value of $800 ($900 cost less $100 accumulated depreciation) and a fair (market) value of $750, *and* this $50 decline in value meets the 2-step impairment test. The entry to record this impairment is:

Impairment Loss $50
  Accum Depr-Equip. $50

when there is a *permanent decline* in the fair value of an asset relative to its book value, called an asset **impairment.** In this case the company writes the asset down to this fair value (details for the two-step process for assessing and computing the impairment loss are in advanced courses).

Accumulated Depreciation is a contra asset account with a normal credit balance. It does *not* reflect funds accumulated to buy new assets when the assets currently owned are replaced. If a company has funds available to buy assets, the funds are shown on the balance sheet among liquid assets such as Cash or Investments.

Decision Ethics

Controller You are the controller for a struggling company. Its operations require regular investments in equipment, and depreciation is its largest expense. Its competitors frequently replace equipment—often depreciated over three years. The company president instructs you to revise useful lives of equipment from three to six years and to use a six-year life on all new equipment. What actions do you take? ■ [Answer—p. 420]

Quick Check
Answers — p. 421

4. On January 1, 2013, a company pays $77,000 to purchase office furniture with a zero salvage value. The furniture's useful life is somewhere between 7 and 10 years. What is the year 2013 straight-line depreciation on the furniture using (*a*) a 7-year useful life and (*b*) a 10-year useful life?

5. What does the term *depreciation* mean in accounting?

6. A company purchases a machine for $96,000 on January 1, 2013. Its useful life is five years or 100,000 units of product, and its salvage value is $8,000. During 2013, 10,000 units of product are produced. Compute the book value of this machine on December 31, 2013, assuming (*a*) straight-line depreciation and (*b*) units-of-production depreciation.

7. In early January 2013, a company acquires equipment for $3,800. The company estimates this equipment to have a useful life of three years and a salvage value of $200. Early in 2015, the company changes its estimates to a total four-year useful life and zero salvage value. Using the straight-line method, what is depreciation for the year ended 2015?

ADDITIONAL EXPENDITURES

 C3 Distinguish between revenue and capital expenditures, and account for them.

Financial Statement Effect		
	Accounting	**Expense Timing**
Revenue expenditure	Income stmt. account debited	Expensed currently
Capital expenditure	Balance sheet account debited	Expensed in future

After a company acquires a plant asset and puts it into service, it often makes additional expenditures for that asset's operation, maintenance, repair, and improvement. In recording these expenditures, it must decide whether to capitalize or expense them (to capitalize an expenditure is to debit the asset account). The issue is whether these expenditures are reported as current period expenses or added to the plant asset's cost and depreciated over its remaining useful life.

Revenue expenditures, also called *income statement expenditures,* are additional costs of plant assets that do not materially increase the asset's life or productive capabilities. They are recorded as expenses and deducted from revenues in the current period's income statement. Examples of revenue expenditures are cleaning, repainting, adjustments, and lubricants. **Capital expenditures,** also called *balance sheet expenditures,* are additional costs of plant assets that provide benefits extending beyond the current period. They are debited to asset accounts and reported on the balance sheet. Capital expenditures increase or improve the type or amount of service an asset provides. Examples are roofing replacement, plant expansion, and major overhauls of machinery and equipment.

Financial statements are affected for several years by the accounting choice of recording costs as either revenue expenditures or capital expenditures. This decision is based on whether the expenditures are identified as ordinary repairs or as betterments and extraordinary repairs.

Decision Maker

Entrepreneur Your start-up Internet services company needs cash, and you are preparing financial statements to apply for a short-term loan. A friend suggests that you treat as many expenses as possible as capital expenditures. What are the impacts on financial statements of this suggestion? What do you think is the aim of this suggestion? ■ [Answer—p. 421]

Ordinary Repairs

Ordinary repairs are expenditures to keep an asset in normal, good operating condition. They are necessary if an asset is to perform to expectations over its useful life. Ordinary repairs do not extend an asset's useful life beyond its original estimate or increase its productivity beyond original expectations. Examples are normal costs of cleaning, lubricating, adjusting, oil changing, and replacing small parts of a machine. Ordinary repairs are treated as *revenue expenditures*. This means their costs are reported as expenses on the current period income statement. Following this rule, **Brunswick** reports that "maintenance and repair costs are expensed as incurred." If Brunswick's current year repair costs are $9,500, it makes the following entry.

Point: Many companies apply the *materiality constraint* to treat *low-cost plant assets* (say, less than $500) as revenue expenditures. This practice is referred to as a "capitalization policy."

Dec. 31	Repairs Expense	9,500	
	Cash		9,500
	To record ordinary repairs of equipment.		

Assets = Liabilities + Equity
−9,500   −9,500

Betterments and Extraordinary Repairs

Accounting for betterments and extraordinary repairs is similar—both are treated as *capital expenditures*.

Betterments (Improvements)   **Betterments,** also called *improvements,* are expenditures that make a plant asset more efficient or productive. A betterment often involves adding a component to an asset or replacing one of its old components with a better one and does not always increase an asset's useful life. An example is replacing manual controls on a machine with automatic controls. One special type of betterment is an *addition,* such as adding a new wing or dock to a warehouse. Since a betterment benefits future periods, it is debited to the asset account as a capital expenditure. The new book value (less salvage value) is then depreciated over the asset's remaining useful life. To illustrate, suppose a company pays $8,000 for a machine with an eight-year useful life and no salvage value. After three years and $3,000 of depreciation, it adds an automated control system to the machine at a cost of $1,800. This results in reduced labor costs in future periods. The cost of the betterment is added to the Machinery account with this entry.

Example: Assume a firm owns a Web server. Identify each cost as a revenue or capital expenditure: (1) purchase price, (2) necessary wiring, (3) platform for operation, (4) circuits to increase capacity, (5) cleaning after each month of use, (6) repair of a faulty switch, and (7) replaced a worn fan. *Answer:* Capital expenditures: 1, 2, 3, 4; revenue expenditures: 5, 6, 7.

Jan. 2	Machinery	1,800	
	Cash		1,800
	To record installation of automated system.		

Assets = Liabilities + Equity
+1,800
−1,800

After the betterment is recorded, the remaining cost to be depreciated is $6,800, computed as $8,000 − $3,000 + $1,800. Depreciation expense for the remaining five years is $1,360 per year, computed as $6,800/5 years.

Point: Both extraordinary repairs and betterments require revising future depreciation.

Extraordinary Repairs (Replacements)   **Extraordinary repairs** are expenditures extending the asset's useful life beyond its original estimate. Extraordinary repairs are *capital expenditures* because they benefit future periods. Their costs are debited to the asset account (or to accumulated depreciation). For example, **Delta Air Lines** reports, "modifications that . . . extend the useful lives of airframes or engines are capitalized and amortized [depreciated] over the remaining estimated useful life of the asset."

Decision Insight

Extraordinary Bombers If we owned a 20-year-old truck and planned to use it in our work for another 40 years, we would expect some extraordinary repairs in future years. A similar situation confronts Whiteman Air Force Base, home to the B-2 stealth bomber, which rolled out of a Northrop Grumman hangar in the 1980s. The plan is to keep those bat-winged bombers flying until 2058. The Pentagon is moving forward with a $2 billion, 10-year effort to modernize the bombers' defensive capabilities. ■

DISPOSALS OF PLANT ASSETS

Plant assets are disposed of for several reasons. Some are discarded because they wear out or become obsolete. Others are sold because of changing business plans. Regardless of the reason, disposals of plant assets occur in one of three basic ways: discarding, sale, or exchange. The general steps in accounting for a disposal of plant assets are described in Exhibit 10.15.

EXHIBIT 10.15

Accounting for Disposals of Plant Assets

1. Record depreciation up to the date of disposal—this also updates Accumulated Depreciation.
2. Record the removal of the disposed asset's account balances—including its Accumulated Depreciation.
3. Record any cash (and/or other assets) received or paid in the disposal.
4. Record any gain or loss—computed by comparing the disposed asset's book value with the market value of any assets received.*

* An exception to step 4 is the case of an exchange that lacks *commercial substance*—see Appendix 10A.

Discarding Plant Assets

P2 Account for asset disposal through discarding or selling an asset.

A plant asset is *discarded* when it is no longer useful to the company and it has no market value. To illustrate, assume that a machine costing $9,000 with accumulated depreciation of $9,000 is discarded. When accumulated depreciation equals the asset's cost, it is said to be *fully depreciated* (zero book value). The entry to record the discarding of this asset is

Assets = Liabilities + Equity
+9,000
−9,000

June 5	Accumulated Depreciation—Machinery	9,000	
	Machinery		9,000
	To discard fully depreciated machinery.		

This entry reflects all four steps of Exhibit 10.15. Step 1 is unnecessary since the machine is fully depreciated. Step 2 is reflected in the debit to Accumulated Depreciation and credit to Machinery. Since no other asset is involved, step 3 is irrelevant. Finally, since book value is zero and no other asset is involved, no gain or loss is recorded in step 4.

How do we account for discarding an asset that is not fully depreciated or one whose depreciation is not up-to-date? To answer this, consider equipment costing $8,000 with accumulated depreciation of $6,000 on December 31 of the prior fiscal year-end. This equipment is being depreciated using the straight-line method over eight years with zero salvage. On July 1 of the current year it is discarded. Step 1 is to bring depreciation up-to-date.

Point: Recording depreciation expense up-to-date gives an up-to-date book value for determining gain or loss.

Assets = Liabilities + Equity
−500 −500

July 1	Depreciation Expense	500	
	Accumulated Depreciation—Equipment		500
	To record 6 months' depreciation ($1,000 × 6/12).		

Steps 2 through 4 of Exhibit 10.15 are reflected in the second (and final) entry.

Assets = Liabilities + Equity
+6,500 −1,500
−8,000

July 1	Accumulated Depreciation—Equipment	6,500	
	Loss on Disposal of Equipment	1,500	
	Equipment		8,000
	To discard equipment with a $1,500 book value.		

Point: Gain or loss is determined by comparing "value given" (book value) to "value received."

This loss is computed by comparing the equipment's $1,500 book value ($8,000 − $6,000 − $500) with the zero net cash proceeds. The loss is reported in the Other Expenses and Losses section of the income statement. Discarding an asset can sometimes require a cash payment that would increase the loss.

Selling Plant Assets

Companies often sell plant assets when they restructure or downsize operations. To illustrate the accounting for selling plant assets, we consider BTO's March 31 sale of equipment that cost $16,000 and has accumulated depreciation of $12,000 at December 31 of the prior calendar year-end. Annual depreciation on this equipment is $4,000 computed using straight-line depreciation. Step 1 of this sale is to record depreciation expense and update accumulated depreciation to March 31 of the current year.

March 31	Depreciation Expense	1,000	
	Accumulated Depreciation—Equipment		1,000
	To record 3 months' depreciation ($4,000 × 3/12).		

Assets = Liabilities + Equity
−1,000   −1,000

Steps 2 through 4 of Exhibit 10.15 can be reflected in one final entry that depends on the amount received from the asset's sale. We consider three different possibilities.

Sale at Book Value   If BTO receives $3,000 cash, an amount equal to the equipment's book value as of March 31 (book value = $16,000 − $12,000 − $1,000), no gain or loss occurs on disposal. The entry is

Sale price = Book value → No gain or loss

March 31	Cash	3,000	
	Accumulated Depreciation—Equipment	13,000	
	Equipment		16,000
	To record sale of equipment for no gain or loss.		

Assets = Liabilities + Equity
+3,000
+13,000
−16,000

Sale above Book Value   If BTO receives $7,000, an amount that is $4,000 above the equipment's $3,000 book value as of March 31, a gain on disposal occurs. The entry is

Sale price > Book value → Gain

March 31	Cash	7,000	
	Accumulated Depreciation—Equipment	13,000	
	Gain on Disposal of Equipment		4,000
	Equipment		16,000
	To record sale of equipment for a $4,000 gain.		

Assets = Liabilities + Equity
+7,000   +4,000
+13,000
−16,000

Sale below Book Value   If BTO receives $2,500, an amount that is $500 below the equipment's $3,000 book value as of March 31, a loss on disposal occurs. The entry is

Sale price < Book value → Loss

March 31	Cash	2,500	
	Loss on Disposal of Equipment	500	
	Accumulated Depreciation—Equipment	13,000	
	Equipment		16,000
	To record sale of equipment for a $500 loss.		

Assets = Liabilities + Equity
+2,500   −500
+13,000
−16,000

 IFRS

Unlike U.S. GAAP, IFRS requires an annual review of useful life and salvage value estimates. IFRS also permits revaluation of plant assets to market value if market value is reliably determined. ∎

Quick Check   Answers — p. 421

8. Early in the fifth year of a machine's six-year useful life, it is overhauled, and its useful life is extended to nine years. This machine originally cost $108,000 and the overhaul cost is $12,000. Prepare the entry to record the overhaul cost.

9. Explain the difference between revenue expenditures and capital expenditures and how both are recorded.

10. What is a betterment? How is a betterment recorded?

11. A company acquires equipment on January 10, 2013, at a cost of $42,000. Straight-line depreciation is used with a five-year life and $7,000 salvage value. On June 27, 2014, the company sells this equipment for $32,000. Prepare the entry(ies) for June 27, 2014.

Section 2—Natural Resources

<table>
<tr><td>

P3 Account for natural resource assets and their depletion.

</td></tr>
</table>

Natural resources are assets that are physically consumed when used. Examples are standing timber, mineral deposits, and oil and gas fields. Since they are consumed when used, they are often called *wasting assets*. These assets represent soon-to-be inventories of raw materials that will be converted into one or more products by cutting, mining, or pumping. Until that conversion takes place, they are noncurrent assets and are shown in a balance sheet using titles such as timberlands, mineral deposits, or oil reserves. Natural resources are reported under either plant assets or their own separate category. **Alcoa**, for instance, reports its natural resources under the balance sheet title *Properties, plants and equipment*. In a note to its financial statements, Alcoa reports a separate amount for *Land and land rights, including mines*. **Weyerhaeuser**, on the other hand, reports its timber holdings in a separate balance sheet category titled *Timber and timberlands*.

Cost Determination and Depletion

Natural resources are recorded at cost, which includes all expenditures necessary to acquire the resource and prepare it for its intended use. **Depletion** is the process of allocating the cost of a natural resource to the period when it is consumed. Natural resources are reported on the balance sheet at cost less *accumulated depletion*. The depletion expense per period is usually based on units extracted from cutting, mining, or pumping. This is similar to units-of-production depreciation. **Exxon Mobil** uses this approach to amortize the costs of discovering and operating its oil wells.

To illustrate depletion of natural resources, let's consider a mineral deposit with an estimated 250,000 tons of available ore. It is purchased for $500,000, and we expect zero salvage value. The depletion charge per ton of ore mined is $2, computed as $500,000 ÷ 250,000 tons. If 85,000 tons are mined and sold in the first year, the depletion charge for that year is $170,000. These computations are detailed in Exhibit 10.16.

EXHIBIT 10.16

Depletion Formula and Example

Step 1

$$\text{Depletion per unit} = \frac{\text{Cost} - \text{Salvage value}}{\text{Total units of capacity}} = \frac{\$500,000 - \$0}{250,000 \text{ tons}} = \$2 \text{ per ton}$$

Step 2

$$\text{Depletion expense} = \text{Depletion per unit} \times \text{Units extracted and sold in period}$$
$$= \$2 \times 85,000 = \$170,000$$

Depletion expense for the first year is recorded as follows.

Assets	= Liabilities +	Equity
−170,000		−170,000

Dec. 31	Depletion Expense—Mineral Deposit	170,000	
	Accumulated Depletion—Mineral Deposit		170,000
	To record depletion of the mineral deposit.		

The period-end balance sheet reports the mineral deposit as shown in Exhibit 10.17.

EXHIBIT 10.17

Balance Sheet Presentation of Natural Resources

Mineral deposit	$500,000	
Less accumulated depletion	**170,000**	$330,000

Since all 85,000 tons of the mined ore are sold during the year, the entire $170,000 of depletion is reported on the income statement. If some of the ore remains unsold at year-end, however, the depletion related to the unsold ore is carried forward on the balance sheet and reported as

Ore Inventory, a current asset. To illustrate, and continuing with our example, assume that 40,000 tons are mined in the second year, but only 34,000 tons are sold. We record depletion of $68,000 (34,000 tons × $2 depletion per unit) and the remaining Ore Inventory of $12,000 (6,000 tons × $2 depletion per unit) as follows.

Dec. 31	Depletion Expense—Mineral Deposit	68,000	
	Ore Inventory	12,000	
	Accumulated Depletion—Mineral Deposit		80,000
	To record depletion and inventory of mineral deposit.		

Assets = Liabilities + Equity
−80,000   −68,000
+12,000

Plant Assets Used in Extracting

The conversion of natural resources by mining, cutting, or pumping usually requires machinery, equipment, and buildings. When the usefulness of these plant assets is directly related to the depletion of a natural resource, their costs are depreciated using the units-of-production method in proportion to the depletion of the natural resource. For example, if a machine is permanently installed in a mine and 10% of the ore is mined and sold in the period, then 10% of the machine's cost (less any salvage value) is allocated to depreciation expense. The same procedure is used when a machine is abandoned once resources have been extracted. If, however, a machine will be moved to and used at another site when extraction is complete, the machine is depreciated over its own useful life.

■ Decision Insight

Asset Control   Long-term assets must be safeguarded against theft, misuse, and other damages. Controls take many forms depending on the asset, including use of security tags, the legal monitoring of rights infringements, and approvals of all asset disposals. A study reports that 43% of employees in operations and service areas witnessed the wasting, mismanaging, or abusing of assets in the past year (KPMG 2011). ■

Section 3—Intangible Assets

Intangible assets are nonphysical assets (used in operations) that confer on their owners long-term rights, privileges, or competitive advantages. Examples are patents, copyrights, licenses, leaseholds, franchises, goodwill, and trademarks. Lack of physical substance does not necessarily imply an intangible asset. Notes and accounts receivable, for instance, lack physical substance, but they are not intangibles. This section identifies the more common types of intangible assets and explains the accounting for them.

P4 Account for intangible assets.

Cost Determination and Amortization

An intangible asset is recorded at cost when purchased. Intangibles are then separated into those with limited lives or indefinite lives. If an intangible has a **limited life,** its cost is systematically allocated to expense over its estimated useful life through the process of **amortization.** If an intangible asset has an **indefinite life**—meaning that no legal, regulatory, contractual, competitive, economic, or other factors limit its useful life—it should not be amortized. (If an intangible with an indefinite life is later judged to have a limited life, it is amortized over that limited life.) Amortization of intangible assets is similar to depreciation of plant assets and the depletion of natural resources in that it is a process of cost allocation. However, only the straight-line method is used for amortizing intangibles *unless* the company can show that another method is preferred. The effects of amortization are recorded in a contra account (Accumulated Amortization). The gross acquisition cost of intangible assets is disclosed in the balance sheet along with their accumulated amortization (these disclosures are new). The eventual disposal of an intangible asset involves removing its book value, recording any other asset(s) received or given up, and recognizing any gain or loss for the difference.

Point: Depreciation, depletion, and amortization are related in that each describes cost allocation.

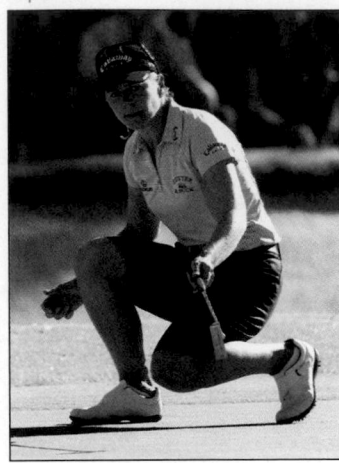

Many intangibles have limited lives due to laws, contracts, or other asset characteristics. Examples are patents, copyrights, and leaseholds. Other intangibles such as goodwill, trademarks, and trade names have lives that cannot be easily determined. The cost of intangible assets is amortized over the periods expected to benefit by their use, but in no case can this period be longer than the asset's legal existence. The values of some intangible assets such as goodwill continue indefinitely into the future and are not amortized. (An intangible asset that is not amortized is tested annually for **impairment**—if necessary, an impairment loss is recorded. Details for this test are in advanced courses.)

Intangible assets are often shown in a separate section of the balance sheet immediately after plant assets. **Callaway Golf**, for instance, follows this approach in reporting over $120 million of intangible assets in its balance sheet. Companies usually disclose their amortization periods for intangibles. The remainder of our discussion focuses on accounting for specific types of intangible assets.

Types of Intangibles

Patents The federal government grants patents to encourage the invention of new technology, mechanical devices, and production processes. A **patent** is an exclusive right granted to its owner to manufacture and sell a patented item or to use a process for 20 years. When patent rights are purchased, the cost to acquire the rights is debited to an account called Patents. If the owner engages in lawsuits to successfully defend a patent, the cost of lawsuits is debited to the Patents account. However, the costs of research and development leading to a new patent are expensed when incurred.

A patent's cost is amortized over its estimated useful life (not to exceed 20 years). If we purchase a patent costing $25,000 with a useful life of 10 years, we make the following adjusting entry at the end of each of the 10 years to amortize one-tenth of its cost.

Assets = Liabilities + Equity
−2,500   −2,500

Dec. 31	Amortization Expense—Patents	2,500	
	Accumulated Amortization—Patents		2,500
	To amortize patent costs over its useful life.		

The $2,500 debit to Amortization Expense appears on the income statement as a cost of the product or service provided under protection of the patent. The Accumulated Amortization—Patents account is a contra asset account to Patents.

■ Decision Insight

Mention "drug war" and most people think of illegal drug trade. But another drug war is under way: Brand-name drugmakers are fighting to stop generic copies of their products from hitting the market once patents expire. Delaying a generic rival can yield millions in extra sales. One way drugmakers fight patent expirations is to alter *drug delivery.* The first patent might require a patient to take a pill 4×/day. When that patent expires, the drugmaker can "improve" the drug's delivery release system to 2×/day, and then 1×/day, and so forth. ■

Prescriptions That Specify Generics (60%, 40%, 20%, 0%; 1980 1990 2000 2010)

Copyrights A **copyright** gives its owner the exclusive right to publish and sell a musical, literary, or artistic work during the life of the creator plus 70 years, although the useful life of most copyrights is much shorter. The costs of a copyright are amortized over its useful life. The only identifiable cost of many copyrights is the fee paid to the Copyright Office of the federal government or international agency granting the copyright. If this fee is immaterial, it is charged directly to an expense account; but if the identifiable costs of a copyright are material, they are capitalized (recorded in an asset account) and periodically amortized by debiting an account called Amortization Expense—Copyrights.

■ **Decision** Insight ━━━━━━━━━━━━━━━━━━━━━

Mickey Mouse Protection Act   The Walt Disney Company successfully lobbied Congress to extend copyright protection from the life of the creator plus 50 years to life of the creator plus 70 years. This extension allows the company to protect its characters for 20 additional years before the right to use them enters the public domain. Mickey Mouse is now protected by copyright law until 2023. The law is officially termed the Copyright Term Extension Act (CTEA) but it is also known as the Mickey Mouse Protection Act. ■

Franchises and Licenses   **Franchises** and **licenses** are rights that a company or government grants an entity to deliver a product or service under specified conditions. Many organizations grant franchise and license rights—**McDonald's**, **Pizza Hut**, and **Major League Baseball** are just a few examples. The costs of franchises and licenses are debited to a Franchises and Licenses asset account and are amortized over the lives of the agreements. If an agreement is for an indefinite or perpetual period, those costs are not amortized.

Trademarks and Trade Names   Companies often adopt unique symbols or select unique names and brands in marketing their products. A **trademark** or **trade (brand) name** is a symbol, name, phrase, or jingle identified with a company, product, or service. Examples are Nike swoosh, Marlboro Man, Big Mac, Coca-Cola, and Corvette. Ownership and exclusive right to use a trademark or trade name is often established by showing that one company used it before another. Ownership is best established by registering a trademark or trade name with the government's Patent Office. The cost of developing, maintaining, or enhancing the value of a trademark or trade name (such as advertising) is charged to expense when incurred. If a trademark or trade name is purchased, however, its cost is debited to an asset account and then amortized over its expected life. If the company plans to renew indefinitely its right to the trademark or trade name, the cost is not amortized.

Point: McDonald's "golden arches" are one of the world's most valuable trademarks, yet this asset is not shown on McDonald's balance sheet.

Goodwill   **Goodwill** has a specific meaning in accounting. Goodwill is the amount by which a company's value exceeds the value of its individual assets and liabilities. This usually implies that the company as a whole has certain valuable attributes not measured among its individual assets and liabilities. These can include superior management, skilled workforce, good supplier or customer relations, quality products or services, good location, or other competitive advantages.

To keep accounting information from being too subjective, goodwill is not recorded unless an entire company or business segment is purchased. Purchased goodwill is measured by taking the purchase price of the company and subtracting the market value of its individual net assets (excluding goodwill). For instance, **Google** paid $1.19 billion to acquire **YouTube**; about $1.13 of the $1.19 billion was for goodwill.

Goodwill is measured as the excess of the cost of an acquired entity over the value of the acquired net assets. Goodwill is recorded as an asset, and it is *not* amortized. Instead, goodwill is annually tested for impairment. If the book value of goodwill does not exceed its fair (market) value, goodwill is not impaired. However, if the book value of goodwill does exceed its fair value, an impairment loss is recorded equal to that excess. (Details of this test are in advanced courses.)

Point: Amortization of goodwill is different for financial accounting and tax accounting. The IRS requires the amortization of goodwill over 15 years.

Example: Assume goodwill carries a book value of $500 and has an implied fair value of $475, *and* this $25 decline in value meets the 2-step impairment test. The entry to record this impairment is:
Impairment Loss $25
    Goodwill $25

Leaseholds   Property is rented under a contract called a **lease.** The property's owner, called the **lessor,** grants the lease. The one who secures the right to possess and use the property is called the **lessee.** A **leasehold** refers to the rights the lessor grants to the lessee under the terms of the lease. A leasehold is an intangible asset for the lessee.

Certain leases require no advance payment from the lessee but require monthly rent payments. In this case, we do not set up a Leasehold account. Instead, the monthly payments are debited to a Rent Expense account. If a long-term lease requires the lessee to pay the final period's rent in advance when the lease is signed, the lessee records this advance payment with a debit to the Leasehold account. Since the advance payment is not used until the final period, the Leasehold account balance remains intact until that final period when its balance is transferred to Rent Expense. (Some long-term leases give the lessee essentially the same rights as a purchaser. This results in a tangible asset and a liability reported by the lessee. Chapter 14 describes these so-called *capital leases*.)

Point: A leasehold account implies existence of future benefits that the lessee controls because of a prepayment. It also meets the definition of an asset.

A long-term lease can increase in value when current rental rates for similar property rise while the required payments under the lease remain constant. This increase in value of a lease is not reported on the lessee's balance sheet. However, if the property is subleased and the new tenant makes a cash payment to the original lessee for the rights under the old lease, the new tenant debits this payment to a Leasehold account, which is amortized to Rent Expense over the remaining life of the lease.

Leasehold Improvements   A lessee sometimes pays for alterations or improvements to the leased property such as partitions, painting, and storefronts. These alterations and improvements are called **leasehold improvements,** and the lessee debits these costs to a Leasehold Improvements account. Since leasehold improvements become part of the property and revert to the lessor at the end of the lease, the lessee amortizes these costs over the life of the lease or the life of the improvements, whichever is shorter. The amortization entry debits Amortization Expense— Leasehold Improvements and credits Accumulated Amortization—Leasehold Improvements.

Other Intangibles   There are other types of intangible assets such as *software, noncompete covenants, customer lists,* and so forth. Our accounting for them is the same. First, we record the intangible asset's costs. Second, we determine whether the asset has a limited or indefinite life. If limited, we allocate its costs over that period. If indefinite, its costs are not amortized.

Quick Check
Answers — p. 421

12. Give an example of a natural resource and of an intangible asset.
13. A company pays $650,000 for an ore deposit. The deposit is estimated to have 325,000 tons of ore that will be mined over the next 10 years. During the first year, it mined, processed, and sold 91,000 tons. What is that year's depletion expense?
14. On January 6, 2013, a company pays $120,000 for a patent with a remaining 17-year legal life to produce a toy expected to be marketable for three years. Prepare entries to record its acquisition and the December 31, 2013, amortization entry.

 GLOBAL VIEW

This section discusses similarities and differences between U.S. GAAP and IFRS in accounting and reporting for plant assets and intangible assets.

Accounting for Plant Assets   Issues involving cost determination, depreciation, additional expenditures, and disposals of plant assets are subject to broadly similar guidance for both U.S. GAAP and IFRS. Although differences exist, the similarities vastly outweigh the differences. **Nokia** describes its accounting for plant assets as follows:

NOKIA

> Property, plant and equipment are stated at cost less accumulated depreciation. Depreciation is recorded on a straight-line basis over the expected useful lives of the assets. Maintenance, repairs and renewals are generally charged to expense during the financial period in which they are incurred. However, major renovations are capitalized and included in the carrying amount of the asset ... Major renovations are depreciated over the remaining useful life of the related asset.

One area where notable differences exist is in accounting for changes in the value of plant assets (between the time they are acquired and when disposed of). Namely, how does IFRS and U.S. GAAP treat decreases and increases in the value of plant assets subsequent to acquisition?

Decreases in the Value of Plant Assets   When the value of plant assets declines after acquisition, but before disposition, both U.S. GAAP and IFRS require companies to record those decreases as *impairment losses*. While the *test for impairment* uses a different base between U.S. GAAP and IFRS, a more fundamental difference is that U.S. GAAP revalues impaired plant assets to *fair value* whereas IFRS revalues them to a *recoverable amount* (defined as fair value less costs to sell).

Increases in the Value of Plant Assets   U.S. GAAP prohibits companies from recording increases in the value of plant assets. However, IFRS permits upward *asset revaluations*. Namely, under IFRS, if an impairment was previously recorded, a company would reverse that impairment to the extent necessary and record that increase in income. If the increase is beyond the original cost, that increase is recorded in comprehensive income.

Accounting for Intangible Assets   For intangible assets, the accounting for cost determination, amortization, additional expenditures, and disposals is subject to broadly similar guidance for U.S. GAAP and IFRS. Although differences exist, the similarities vastly outweigh differences. Again, and consistent with the accounting for plant assets, U.S. GAAP and IFRS handle decreases and increases in the value of intangible assets differently. However, IFRS requirements for recording increases in the value of intangible assets are so restrictive that such increases are rare. **Nokia** describes its accounting for intangible assets as follows:

> [Intangible assets] are capitalized and amortized using the straight-line method over their useful lives. Where an indication of impairment exists, the carrying amount of any intangible asset is assessed and written down to its recoverable amount.

NOKIA

Total Asset Turnover   **Decision Analysis**

A company's assets are important in determining its ability to generate sales and earn income. Managers devote much attention to deciding what assets a company acquires, how much it invests in assets, and how to use assets most efficiently and effectively. One important measure of a company's ability to use its assets is **total asset turnover,** defined in Exhibit 10.18.

A1 Compute total asset turnover and apply it to analyze a company's use of assets.

EXHIBIT 10.18

Total Asset Turnover

$$\text{Total asset turnover} = \frac{\text{Net sales}}{\text{Average total assets}}$$

The numerator reflects the net amounts earned from the sale of products and services. The denominator reflects the average total resources devoted to operating the company and generating sales.

To illustrate, let's look at total asset turnover in Exhibit 10.19 for two competing companies: **Molson Coors** and **Boston Beer**.

EXHIBIT 10.19

Analysis Using Total Asset Turnover

Company	Figure ($ millions)	2011	2010	2009	2008	2007
Molson Coors	Net sales	$ 3,515.7	$ 3,254.4	$ 3,032.4	$ 4,774.3	$ 6,190.6
	Average total assets	$12,560.7	$12,359.4	$11,203.9	$11,934.1	$12,527.5
	Total asset turnover	0.28	0.26	0.27	0.40	0.49
Boston Beer	Net sales	$ 513.000	$ 463.798	$ 415.053	$ 398.400	$ 341.647
	Average total assets	$ 265.509	$ 260.733	$ 241.347	$ 208.856	$ 176.215
	Total asset turnover	1.93	1.78	1.72	1.91	1.94

To show how we use total asset turnover, let's look at Molson Coors. We express Molson Coors's use of assets in generating net sales by saying "it turned its assets over 0.28 times during 2011." This means that each $1.00 of assets produced $0.28 of net sales. Is a total asset turnover of 0.28 good or bad? It is safe to say that all companies desire a high total asset turnover. Like many ratio analyses, however, a company's total asset turnover must be interpreted in comparison with those of prior years and of its competitors. Interpreting the total asset turnover also requires an understanding of the company's operations. Some operations are capital intensive, meaning that a relatively large amount is invested in assets to generate sales. This suggests a relatively lower total asset turnover. Other companies' operations are labor intensive, meaning that they generate sales more by the efforts of people than the use of assets. In that case, we expect a higher total asset turnover. Companies with low total asset turnover require higher profit margins (examples are hotels and real estate); companies with high total asset turnover can succeed with lower profit margins (examples are food stores and toy merchandisers). Molson Coors's turnover recently declined and is now much lower than that for Boston Beer and many other competitors. Total asset turnover for Molson Coors's competitors, available in industry publications such as Dun & Bradstreet, is generally in the range of 0.5 to 1.0 over this same period. Overall, Molson Coors must improve relative to its competitors on total asset turnover.

Point: An estimate of **plant asset useful life** equals the plant asset cost divided by depreciation expense.

Point: The **plant asset age** is estimated by dividing accumulated depreciation by depreciation expense. Older plant assets can signal needed asset replacements; they may also signal less efficient assets.

Decision Maker

Environmentalist A paper manufacturer claims it cannot afford more environmental controls. It points to its low total asset turnover of 1.9 and argues that it cannot compete with companies whose total asset turnover is much higher. Examples cited are food stores (5.5) and auto dealers (3.8). How do you respond? ■ [Answer—p. 421]

DEMONSTRATION PROBLEM

On July 14, 2013, Tulsa Company pays $600,000 to acquire a fully equipped factory. The purchase involves the following assets and information.

Asset	Appraised Value	Salvage Value	Useful Life	Depreciation Method
Land	$160,000			Not depreciated
Land improvements	80,000	$ 0	10 years	Straight-line
Building	320,000	100,000	10 years	Double-declining-balance
Machinery	240,000	20,000	10,000 units	Units-of-production*
Total	$800,000			

* The machinery is used to produce 700 units in 2013 and 1,800 units in 2014.

Required

1. Allocate the total $600,000 purchase cost among the separate assets.

2. Compute the 2013 (six months) and 2014 depreciation expense for each asset, and compute the company's total depreciation expense for both years.

3. On the last day of calendar year 2015, Tulsa discarded machinery that had been on its books for five years. The machinery's original cost was $12,000 (estimated life of five years) and its salvage value was $2,000. No depreciation had been recorded for the fifth year when the disposal occurred. Journalize the fifth year of depreciation (straight-line method) and the asset's disposal.

4. At the beginning of year 2015, Tulsa purchased a patent for $100,000 cash. The company estimated the patent's useful life to be 10 years. Journalize the patent acquisition and its amortization for the year 2015.

5. Late in the year 2015, Tulsa acquired an ore deposit for $600,000 cash. It added roads and built mine shafts for an additional cost of $80,000. Salvage value of the mine is estimated to be $20,000. The company estimated 330,000 tons of available ore. In year 2015, Tulsa mined and sold 10,000 tons of ore. Journalize the mine's acquisition and its first year's depletion.

6.^A On the first day of 2015, Tulsa exchanged the machinery that was acquired on July 14, 2013, along with $5,000 cash for machinery with a $210,000 market value. Journalize the exchange of these assets assuming the exchange lacked commercial substance. (Refer to background information in parts 1 and 2.)

PLANNING THE SOLUTION

● Complete a three-column table showing the following amounts for each asset: appraised value, percent of total value, and apportioned cost.

● Using allocated costs, compute depreciation for 2013 (only one-half year) and 2014 (full year) for each asset. Summarize those computations in a table showing total depreciation for each year.

● Remember that depreciation must be recorded up-to-date before discarding an asset. Calculate and record depreciation expense for the fifth year using the straight-line method. Since salvage value is not received at the end of a discarded asset's life, the amount of any salvage value becomes a loss on disposal. Record the loss on the disposal as well as the removal of the discarded asset and its related accumulated depreciation.

● Record the patent (an intangible asset) at its purchase price. Use straight-line amortization over its useful life to calculate amortization expense.

● Record the ore deposit (a natural resource asset) at its cost, including any added costs to ready the mine for use. Calculate depletion per ton using the depletion formula. Multiply the depletion per ton by the amount of tons mined and sold to calculate depletion expense for the year.

● Remember that gains and losses on asset exchanges that lack commercial substance are not recognized. Make a journal entry to add the acquired machinery to the books and to remove the old machinery, along with its accumulated depreciation, and to record the cash given in the exchange.

SOLUTION TO DEMONSTRATION PROBLEM

1. Allocation of the total cost of $600,000 among the separate assets.

Asset	Appraised Value	Percent of Total Value	Apportioned Cost
Land	$160,000	20%	**$120,000** ($600,000 × 20%)
Land improvements	80,000	10	**60,000** ($600,000 × 10%)
Building	320,000	40	**240,000** ($600,000 × 40%)
Machinery	240,000	30	**180,000** ($600,000 × 30%)
Total	$800,000	100%	$ 600,000

2. Depreciation for each asset. (Land is not depreciated.)

Land Improvements

Cost	$ 60,000
Salvage value	0
Depreciable cost	$ 60,000
Useful life	10 years
Annual depreciation expense ($60,000/10 years)	$ 6,000
2013 depreciation ($6,000 × 6/12)	**$ 3,000**
2014 depreciation	**$ 6,000**

Building

Straight-line rate = 100%/10 years = 10%
Double-declining-balance rate = 10% × 2 = 20%

2013 depreciation ($240,000 × 20% × 6/12)	**$ 24,000**
2014 depreciation [($240,000 − $24,000) × 20%]	**$ 43,200**

Machinery

Cost	$180,000
Salvage value	20,000
Depreciable cost	$160,000
Total expected units of production	10,000 units
Depreciation per unit ($160,000/10,000 units)	$ 16
2013 depreciation ($16 × 700 units)	**$ 11,200**
2014 depreciation ($16 × 1,800 units)	**$ 28,800**

Total depreciation expense for each year:

	2013	2014
Land improvements	$ 3,000	$ 6,000
Building	24,000	43,200
Machinery	11,200	28,800
Total	$38,200	$78,000

3. Record the depreciation up-to-date on the discarded asset.

Depreciation Expense—Machinery	2,000	
Accumulated Depreciation—Machinery		2,000
To record depreciation on date of disposal: ($12,000 − $2,000)/5		

Record the removal of the discarded asset and its loss on disposal.

Accumulated Depreciation—Machinery	10,000	
Loss on Disposal of Machinery	2,000	
Machinery		12,000
To record the discarding of machinery with a $2,000 book value.		

4.

Patent	100,000	
Cash		100,000
To record patent acquisition.		

Amortization Expense—Patent	10,000	
Accumulated Amortization—Patent		10,000
To record amortization expense: $100,000/10 years = $10,000.		

5.

Ore Deposit	680,000	
Cash		680,000
To record ore deposit acquisition and its related costs.		

Depletion Expense—Ore Deposit	20,000	
Accumulated Depletion—Ore Deposit		20,000
To record depletion expense: ($680,000 − $20,000)/330,000 tons =		
$2 per ton. 10,000 tons mined and sold × $2 = $20,000 depletion.		

6. Record the asset exchange: The book value on the exchange date is $180,000 (cost) − $40,000 (accumulated depreciation). The book value of the machinery given up in the exchange ($140,000) plus the $5,000 cash paid is less than the $210,000 value of the machine acquired. The entry to record this exchange of assets that lacks commercial substance does not recognize the $65,000 "gain."

Machinery (new)	145,000*	
Accumulated Depreciation—Machinery (old)	40,000	
Machinery (old)		180,000
Cash		5,000
To record asset exchange that lacks commercial substance.		

* Market value of the acquired asset of $210,000 minus $65,000 "gain."

10A

Exchanging Plant Assets

P5A Account for asset exchanges.

Many plant assets such as machinery, automobiles, and office equipment are disposed of by exchanging them for newer assets. In a typical exchange of plant assets, a *trade-in allowance* is received on the old asset and the balance is paid in cash. Accounting for the exchange of assets depends on whether the transaction has *commercial substance* (per *SFAS 153,* commercial substance implies that it alters the company's future cash flows). If an asset exchange has commercial substance, a gain or loss is recorded based on the difference between the book value of the asset(s) given up and the market value of the asset(s) received. If an asset exchange lacks commercial substance, no gain or loss is recorded, and the asset(s) received is recorded based on the book value of the asset(s) given up. An exchange has commercial substance if the company's future cash flows change as a result of the transaction. This section describes the accounting for the exchange of assets.

Exchange with Commercial Substance: A Loss   A company acquires $42,000 in new equipment. In exchange, the company pays $33,000 cash and trades in old equipment. The old equipment originally cost $36,000 and has accumulated depreciation of $20,000, which implies a $16,000 book value at the time of exchange. We are told this exchange has commercial substance and that the old equipment has a trade-in allowance of $9,000. This exchange yields a loss as computed in the middle (Loss) columns of Exhibit 10A.1; the loss is computed as Asset received − Assets given = $42,000 − $49,000 = $(7,000). We can also compute the loss as Trade-in allowance − Book value of asset given = $9,000 − $16,000 = $(7,000).

EXHIBIT 10A.1

Computing Gain or Loss on Asset Exchange with Commercial Substance

Asset Exchange Has Commercial Substance	Loss		Gain	
Market value of asset received		$42,000		$52,000
Book value of assets given:				
Equipment ($36,000 − $20,000)	$16,000		$16,000	
Cash	33,000	49,000	33,000	49,000
Gain (loss) on exchange		$(7,000)		$3,000

The entry to record this asset exchange is

Jan. 3	Equipment (new)	42,000	
	Loss on Exchange of Assets	7,000	
	Accumulated Depreciation—Equipment (old)	20,000	
	Equipment (old)		36,000
	Cash		33,000
	To record exchange (with commercial substance) of old equipment and cash for new equipment.		

Assets = Liabilities + Equity
+42,000   −7,000
+20,000
−36,000
−33,000

Point: Parenthetical notes to "new" and "old" equipment are for illustration only. Both the debit and credit are to the same Equipment account.

Exchange with Commercial Substance: A Gain   Let's assume the same facts as in the preceding asset exchange *except* that the new equipment received has a market value of $52,000 instead of $42,000. We are told that this exchange has commercial substance and that the old equipment has a trade-in allowance of $19,000. This exchange yields a gain as computed in the right-most (Gain) columns of Exhibit 10A.1; the gain is computed as Asset received − Assets given = $52,000 − $49,000 = $3,000. We can also compute the gain as Trade-in allowance − Book value of asset given = $19,000 − $16,000 = $3,000. The entry to record this asset exchange is

Jan. 3	Equipment (new)	52,000	
	Accumulated Depreciation—Equipment (old)	20,000	
	Equipment (old)		36,000
	Cash		33,000
	Gain on Exchange of Assets		3,000
	To record exchange (with commercial substance) of old equipment and cash for new equipment.		

Assets = Liabilities + Equity
+52,000   +3,000
+20,000
−36,000
−33,000

Exchanges without Commercial Substance   Let's assume the same facts as in the preceding asset exchange involving new equipment received with a market value of $52,000, but let's instead assume the transaction *lacks commercial substance.* The entry to record this asset exchange is

Jan. 3	Equipment (new)	49,000	
	Accumulated Depreciation—Equipment (old)	20,000	
	Equipment (old)		36,000
	Cash		33,000
	To record exchange (without commercial substance) of old equipment and cash for new equipment.		

Assets = Liabilities + Equity
+49,000
+20,000
−36,000
−33,000

The $3,000 gain recorded when the transaction has commercial substance is *not* recognized in this entry because of the rule prohibiting recording a gain or loss on asset exchanges without commercial substance. The $49,000 recorded for the new equipment equals its cash price ($52,000) less the unrecognized gain ($3,000) on the exchange. The $49,000 cost recorded is called the *cost basis* of the new machine. This cost basis is the amount we use to compute depreciation and its book value. The cost basis of the new asset also can be computed by summing the book values of the assets given up as shown in Exhibit 10A.2. The same analysis and approach are taken for a loss on an asset exchange without commercial substance.

Point: No gain or loss is recorded for exchanges *without* commercial substance.

EXHIBIT 10A.2

Cost Basis of New Asset When Gain Not Recorded on Asset Exchange without Commercial Substance

Cost of old equipment	$ 36,000
Less accumulated depreciation	20,000
Book value of old equipment	16,000
Cash paid in the exchange	33,000
Cost recorded for new equipment	**$49,000**

15. A company trades an old Web server for a new one. The cost of the old server is $30,000, and its accumulated depreciation at the time of the trade is $23,400. The new server has a cash price of $45,000. Prepare entries to record the trade under two different assumptions where the company receives a trade-in allowance of (a) $3,000 and the exchange has commercial substance, and (b) $7,000 and the exchange lacks commercial substance.

Summary

C1 **Explain the cost principle for computing the cost of plant assets.** Plant assets are set apart from other tangible assets by two important features: use in operations and useful lives longer than one period. Plant assets are recorded at cost when purchased. Cost includes all normal and reasonable expenditures necessary to get the asset in place and ready for its intended use. The cost of a lump-sum purchase is allocated among its individual assets.

C2 **Explain depreciation for partial years and changes in estimates.** Partial-year depreciation is often required because assets are bought and sold throughout the year. Depreciation is revised when changes in estimates such as salvage value and useful life occur. If the useful life of a plant asset changes, for instance, the remaining cost to be depreciated is spread over the remaining (revised) useful life of the asset.

C3 **Distinguish between revenue and capital expenditures, and account for them.** Revenue expenditures expire in the current period and are debited to expense accounts and matched with current revenues. Ordinary repairs are an example of revenue expenditures. Capital expenditures benefit future periods and are debited to asset accounts. Examples of capital expenditures are extraordinary repairs and betterments.

A1 **Compute total asset turnover and apply it to analyze a company's use of assets.** Total asset turnover measures a company's ability to use its assets to generate sales. It is defined as net sales divided by average total assets. While all companies desire a high total asset turnover, it must be interpreted in comparison with those for prior years and its competitors.

P1 **Compute and record depreciation using the straight-line, units-of-production, and declining-balance methods.** *Depreciation* is the process of allocating to expense the cost of a plant asset over the accounting periods that benefit from its use. Depreciation does not measure the decline in a plant asset's market value or its physical deterioration. Three factors determine depreciation:

cost, salvage value, and useful life. Salvage value is an estimate of the asset's value at the end of its benefit period. Useful (service) life is the length of time an asset is productively used. The straight-line method divides cost less salvage value by the asset's useful life to determine depreciation expense per period. The units-of-production method divides cost less salvage value by the estimated number of units the asset will produce over its life to determine depreciation per unit. The declining-balance method multiplies the asset's beginning-of-period book value by a factor that is often double the straight-line rate.

P2 **Account for asset disposal through discarding or selling an asset.** When a plant asset is discarded or sold, its cost and accumulated depreciation are removed from the accounts. Any cash proceeds from discarding or selling an asset are recorded and compared to the asset's book value to determine gain or loss.

P3 **Account for natural resource assets and their depletion.** The cost of a natural resource is recorded in a noncurrent asset account. Depletion of a natural resource is recorded by allocating its cost to depletion expense using the units-of-production method. Depletion is credited to an Accumulated Depletion account.

P4 **Account for intangible assets.** An intangible asset is recorded at the cost incurred to purchase it. The cost of an intangible asset with a definite useful life is allocated to expense using the straight-line method, and is called *amortization*. Goodwill and intangible assets with an indefinite useful life are not amortized—they are annually tested for impairment. Intangible assets include patents, copyrights, leaseholds, goodwill, and trademarks.

P5[A] **Account for asset exchanges.** For an asset exchange with commercial substance, a gain or loss is recorded based on the difference between the book value of the asset given up and the market value of the asset received. For an asset exchange without commercial substance, no gain or loss is recorded, and the asset received is recorded based on the book value of the asset given up.

Guidance Answers to Decision Maker and Decision Ethics

Controller The president's instructions may reflect an honest and reasonable prediction of the future. Since the company is struggling financially, the president may have concluded that the normal pattern of replacing assets every three years cannot continue. Perhaps the strategy is to avoid costs of frequent replacements and stretch use of equipment a few years longer until financial conditions improve.

However, if you believe the president's decision is unprincipled, you might confront the president with your opinion that it is unethical to change the estimate to increase income. Another possibility is to wait and see whether the auditor will prohibit this change in estimate. In either case, you should insist that the statements be based on reasonable estimates.

Entrepreneur Treating an expense as a capital expenditure means that reported expenses will be lower and income higher in the short run. This is so because a capital expenditure is not expensed immediately but is spread over the asset's useful life. Treating an expense as a capital expenditure also means that asset and equity totals are reported at larger amounts in the short run. This continues until the asset is fully depreciated. Your friend is probably trying to help, but the suggestion is misguided. Only an expenditure benefiting future periods is a capital expenditure.

Environmentalist The paper manufacturer's comparison of its total asset turnover with food stores and auto dealers is misdirected. These other industries' turnovers are higher because their profit margins are lower (about 2%). Profit margins for the paper industry are usually 3% to 3.5%. You need to collect data from competitors in the paper industry to show that a 1.9 total asset turnover is about the norm for this industry. You might also want to collect data on this company's revenues and expenses, along with compensation data for its high-ranking officers and employees.

Guidance Answers to Quick Checks

1. a. Supplies—current assets
   b. Office equipment—plant assets
   c. Inventory—current assets
   d. Land for future expansion—long-term investments
   e. Trucks used in operations—plant assets

2. a. Land   **b.** Land Improvements

3. $700,000 + $49,000 − $21,000 + $3,500 + $3,000 + $2,500 = $737,000

4. a. Straight-line with 7-year life: ($77,000/7) = $11,000
   b. Straight-line with 10-year life: ($77,000/10) = $7,700

5. Depreciation is a process of allocating the cost of plant assets to the accounting periods that benefit from the assets' use.

6. a. Book value using straight-line depreciation:
   $96,000 − [($96,000 − $8,000)/5] = $78,400
   b. Book value using units of production:
   $96,000 − [($96,000 − $8,000) × (10,000/100,000)]
   = $87,200

7. ($3,800 − $200)/3 = $1,200 (original depreciation per year)
   $1,200 × 2 = $2,400 (accumulated depreciation)
   ($3,800 − $2,400)/2 = $700 (revised depreciation)

8.

Machinery	12,000	
Cash		12,000

9. A revenue expenditure benefits only the current period and should be charged to expense in the current period. A capital expenditure yields benefits that extend beyond the end of the current period and should be charged to an asset.

10. A betterment involves modifying an existing plant asset to make it more efficient, usually by replacing part of the asset with an improved or superior part. The cost of a betterment is debited to the asset account.

11.

Depreciation Expense	3,500	
Accumulated Depreciation		3,500
Cash	32,000	
Accumulated Depreciation	10,500	
Gain on Sale of Equipment		500
Equipment		42,000

12. Examples of natural resources are timberlands, mineral deposits, and oil reserves. Examples of intangible assets are patents, copyrights, leaseholds, leasehold improvements, goodwill, trademarks, and licenses.

13. ($650,000/325,000 tons) × 91,000 tons = $182,000

14.

Jan. 6	Patents	120,000	
	Cash		120,000
Dec. 31	Amortization Expense	40,000*	
	Accumulated Amortization—Patents		40,000

* $120,000/3 years = $40,000.

15.

(a)	Equipment (new)	45,000	
	Loss on Exchange of Assets	3,600	
	Accumulated Depreciation—Equipment (old)	23,400	
	Equipment (old)		30,000
	Cash ($45,000 − $3,000)		42,000

(b)	Equipment (new)*	44,600	
	Accumulated Depreciation—Equipment (old)	23,400	
	Equipment (old)		30,000
	Cash ($45,000 − $7,000)		38,000

* Includes $400 unrecognized gain.

Key Terms

Accelerated depreciation method (p. 402)	**Copyright** (p. 412)	**Franchises** (p. 413)
Amortization (p. 411)	**Cost** (pp. 397, 399)	**Goodwill** (p. 413)
Asset book value (p. 401)	**Declining-balance method** (p. 402)	**Impairment** (pp. 406, 412)
Betterments (p. 407)	**Depletion** (p. 410)	**Inadequacy** (p. 399)
Capital expenditures (p. 406)	**Depreciation** (p. 399)	**Indefinite life** (p. 411)
Change in an accounting estimate (p. 405)	**Extraordinary repairs** (p. 407)	**Intangible assets** (p. 411)

Land improvements (p. 398)	**Modified Accelerated Cost Recovery**	**Revenue expenditures** (p. 406)
Lease (p. 413)	**System (MACRS)** (p. 404)	**Salvage value** (p. 399)
Leasehold (p. 413)	**Natural resources** (p. 410)	**Straight-line depreciation** (p. 400)
Leasehold improvements (p. 414)	**Obsolescence** (p. 399)	**Total asset turnover** (p. 415)
Lessee (p. 413)	**Ordinary repairs** (p. 407)	**Trademark** or **trade (brand) name** (p. 413)
Lessor (p. 413)	**Patent** (p. 412)	**Units-of-production depreciation** (p. 401)
Licenses (p. 413)	**Plant asset age** (p. 415)	**Useful life** (p. 399)
Limited life (p. 411)	**Plant assets** (p. 396)	

Multiple Choice Quiz   Answers on p. 435   mhhe.com/wildFAP21e

Additional Quiz Questions are available at the book's Website.

1. A company paid $326,000 for property that included land, land improvements, and a building. The land was appraised at $175,000, the land improvements were appraised at $70,000, and the building was appraised at $105,000. What is the allocation of property costs to the three assets purchased?
   a. Land, $150,000; Land Improvements, $60,000; Building, $90,000
   b. Land, $163,000; Land Improvements, $65,200; Building, $97,800
   c. Land, $150,000; Land Improvements, $61,600; Building, $92,400
   d. Land, $159,000; Land Improvements, $65,200; Building, $95,400
   e. Land, $175,000; Land Improvements, $70,000; Building, $105,000

2. A company purchased a truck for $35,000 on January 1, 2013. The truck is estimated to have a useful life of four years and an estimated salvage value of $1,000. Assuming that the company uses straight-line depreciation, what is the depreciation expense on the truck for the year ended December 31, 2014?
   a. $8,750
   b. $17,500
   c. $8,500
   d. $17,000
   e. $25,500

3. A company purchased machinery for $10,800,000 on January 1, 2013. The machinery has a useful life of 10 years and an estimated salvage value of $800,000. What is the depreciation expense on the machinery for the year ended December 31, 2014, assuming that the double-declining-balance method is used?
   a. $2,160,000
   b. $3,888,000
   c. $1,728,000
   d. $2,000,000
   e. $1,600,000

4. A company sold a machine that originally cost $250,000 for $120,000 when accumulated depreciation on the machine was $100,000. The gain or loss recorded on the sale of this machine is
   a. $0 gain or loss.
   b. $120,000 gain.
   c. $30,000 loss.
   d. $30,000 gain.
   e. $150,000 loss.

5. A company had average total assets of $500,000, gross sales of $575,000, and net sales of $550,000. The company's total asset turnover is
   a. 1.15
   b. 1.10
   c. 0.91
   d. 0.87
   e. 1.05

---

^A *Superscript letter A denotes assignments based on Appendix 10A.*
🄸 Icon denotes assignments that involve decision making.

Discussion Questions

1. 🄸 What characteristics of a plant asset make it different from other assets?
2. What is the general rule for cost inclusion for plant assets?
3. What is different between land and land improvements?
4. Why is the cost of a lump-sum purchase allocated to the individual assets acquired?

5. 🄸 Does the balance in the Accumulated Depreciation—Machinery account represent funds to replace the machinery when it wears out? If not, what does it represent?
6. Why is the Modified Accelerated Cost Recovery System not generally accepted for financial accounting purposes?

7. [I] What accounting concept justifies charging low-cost plant asset purchases immediately to an expense account?

8. What is the difference between ordinary repairs and extraordinary repairs? How should each be recorded?

9. [I] Identify events that might lead to disposal of a plant asset.

10. What is the process of allocating the cost of natural resources to expense as they are used?

11. Is the declining-balance method an acceptable way to compute depletion of natural resources? Explain.

12. What are the characteristics of an intangible asset?

13. What general procedures are applied in accounting for the acquisition and potential cost allocation of intangible assets?

14. [I] When do we know that a company has goodwill? When can goodwill appear in a company's balance sheet?

15. [I] Assume that a company buys another business and pays for its goodwill. If the company plans to incur costs each year to maintain the value of the goodwill, must it also amortize this goodwill?

16. [I] How is total asset turnover computed? Why would a financial statement user be interested in total asset turnover?

17. On its recent balance sheet in Appendix A, **Polaris** lists its plant assets as "Property and equipment, net." What does "net" mean in this title?

18. Refer to **Arctic Cat**'s recent balance sheet in Appendix A. What property, plant and equipment assets does Arctic Cat list on its balance sheet? What is the book value of its total net property, plant and equipment assets at March 31, 2011?

19. [I] Refer to **KTM**'s balance sheet in Appendix A. What does it title its plant assets? What is the book value of its plant assets at December 31, 2011?

20. Refer to the December 31, 2011, balance sheet of **Piaggio** in Appendix A. What long-term assets discussed in this chapter are reported by the company?

▩ connect

Identify the main difference between (1) plant assets and current assets, (2) plant assets and inventory, and (3) plant assets and long-term investments.

QUICK STUDY

QS 10-1
Defining assets C1

Kegler Bowling installs automatic scorekeeping equipment with an invoice cost of $190,000. The electrical work required for the installation costs $20,000. Additional costs are $4,000 for delivery and $13,700 for sales tax. During the installation, a component of the equipment is carelessly left on a lane and hit by the automatic lane-cleaning machine. The cost of repairing the component is $1,850. What is the total recorded cost of the automatic scorekeeping equipment?

QS 10-2
Cost of plant assets C1

On January 2, 2013, the Cerritos Band acquires sound equipment for concert performances at a cost of $65,800. The band estimates it will use this equipment for four years, during which time it anticipates performing about 200 concerts. It estimates that after four years it can sell the equipment for $2,000. During year 2013, the band performs 45 concerts. Compute the year 2013 depreciation using the straight-line method.

QS 10-3
Straight-line depreciation
P1

Refer to the information in QS 10-3. Compute the year 2013 depreciation using the units-of-production method.

QS 10-4
Units-of-production depreciation
P1

Refer to the facts in QS 10-3. Assume that the Cerritos Band uses straight-line depreciation but realizes at the start of the second year that due to concert bookings beyond expectations, this equipment will last only a total of three years. The salvage value remains unchanged. Compute the revised depreciation for both the second and third years.

QS 10-5
Computing revised depreciation
C2

A fleet of refrigerated delivery trucks is acquired on January 5, 2013, at a cost of $830,000 with an estimated useful life of eight years and an estimated salvage value of $75,000. Compute the depreciation expense for the first three years using the double-declining-balance method.

QS 10-6
Double-declining-balance
method P1

Assume a company's equipment carries a book value of $16,000 ($16,500 cost less $500 accumulated depreciation) and a fair value of $14,750, *and* that the $1,250 decline in fair value in comparison to the book value meets the 2-step impairment test. Prepare the entry to record this $1,250 impairment.

QS 10-7
Recording plant asset
impairment C2

QS 10-8
Revenue and capital expenditures

C3

1. Classify the following as either revenue or capital expenditures.
   a. Paid $40,000 cash to replace a compressor on a refrigeration system that extends its useful life by four years.
   b. Paid $200 cash per truck for the cost of their annual tune-ups.
   c. Paid $175 for the monthly cost of replacement filters on an air-conditioning system.
   d. Completed an addition to an office building for $225,000 cash.
2. Prepare the journal entries to record transactions a and d of part 1.

QS 10-9
Disposal of assets P2

Hortez Co. owns equipment that cost $76,800, with accumulated depreciation of $40,800. Hortez sells the equipment for cash. Record the sale of the equipment assuming Hortez sells the equipment for (1) $47,000 cash, (2) $36,000 cash, and (3) $31,000 cash.

QS 10-10
Natural resources and depletion
P3

Corentine Company acquires an ore mine at a cost of $1,400,000. It incurs additional costs of $400,000 to access the mine, which is estimated to hold 1,000,000 tons of ore. The estimated value of the land after the ore is removed is $200,000.

1. Prepare the entry(ies) to record the cost of the ore mine.
2. Prepare the year-end adjusting entry if 180,000 tons of ore are mined and sold the first year.

QS 10-11
Classify assets

P3 P4

Which of the following assets are reported on the balance sheet as intangible assets? Which are reported as natural resources? (a) Oil well, (b) trademark, (c) leasehold, (d) gold mine, (e) building, (f) copyright, (g) franchise, (h) timberland.

QS 10-12
Intangible assets and amortization P4

On January 4 of this year, Freckles Boutique incurs a $105,000 cost to modernize its store. Improvements include new floors, ceilings, wiring, and wall coverings. These improvements are estimated to yield benefits for 10 years. Freckles leases its store and has eight years remaining on the lease. Prepare the entry to record (1) the cost of modernization and (2) amortization at the end of this current year.

QS 10-13
Computing total asset turnover

A1

Aneko Company reports the following ($ 000s): net sales of $14,800 for 2013 and $13,990 for 2012; end-of-year total assets of $19,100 for 2013 and $17,900 for 2012. Compute its total asset turnover for 2013, and assess its level if competitors average a total asset turnover of 2.0 times.

QS 10-14[A]
Asset exchange
P5

Caleb Co. owns a machine that costs $42,400 with accumulated depreciation of $18,400. Caleb exchanges the machine for a newer model that has a market value of $52,000. (1) Record the exchange assuming Caleb paid $30,000 cash and the exchange has commercial substance. (2) Record the exchange assuming Caleb pays $22,000 cash and the exchange lacks commercial substance.

QS 10-15
International accounting standards

C1 C3

Answer each of the following related to international accounting standards.
a. Accounting for plant assets involves cost determination, depreciation, additional expenditures, and disposals. Is plant asset accounting broadly similar or dissimilar between IFRS and U.S. GAAP? Identify one notable difference between IFRS and U.S. GAAP in accounting for plant assets.
b. Describe how IFRS and U.S. GAAP treat increases in the value of plant assets subsequent to their acquisition (but before their disposition).

McGraw Hill **connect**

EXERCISES

Exercise 10-1
Cost of plant assets

C1

Rizio Co. purchases a machine for $12,500, terms 2/10, n/60, FOB shipping point. The seller prepaid the $360 freight charges, adding the amount to the invoice and bringing its total to $12,860. The machine requires special steel mounting and power connections costing $895. Another $475 is paid to assemble the machine and get it into operation. In moving the machine to its steel mounting, $180 in damages occurred. Materials costing $40 are used in adjusting the machine to produce a satisfactory product. The adjustments are normal for this machine and are not the result of the damages. Compute the cost recorded for this machine. (Rizio pays for this machine within the cash discount period.)

Cala Manufacturing purchases a large lot on which an old building is located as part of its plans to build a new plant. The negotiated purchase price is $280,000 for the lot plus $110,000 for the old building. The company pays $33,500 to tear down the old building and $47,000 to fill and level the lot. It also pays a total of $1,540,000 in construction costs—this amount consists of $1,452,200 for the new building and $87,800 for lighting and paving a parking area next to the building. Prepare a single journal entry to record these costs incurred by Cala, all of which are paid in cash.

Exercise 10-2
Recording costs of assets
C1

Liltua Company pays $375,280 for real estate plus $20,100 in closing costs. The real estate consists of land appraised at $157,040; land improvements appraised at $58,890; and a building appraised at $176,670. Allocate the total cost among the three purchased assets and prepare the journal entry to record the purchase.

Exercise 10-3
Lump-sum purchase of plant assets   C1

In early January 2013, NewTech purchases computer equipment for $154,000 to use in operating activities for the next four years. It estimates the equipment's salvage value at $25,000. Prepare a table showing depreciation and book value for each of the four years assuming straight-line depreciation.

Exercise 10-4
Straight-line depreciation   P1

Refer to the information in Exercise 10-4. Prepare a table showing depreciation and book value for each of the four years assuming double-declining-balance depreciation.

Exercise 10-5
Double-declining-balance depreciation   P1

Ramircz Company installs a computerized manufacturing machine in its factory at the beginning of the year at a cost of $43,500. The machine's useful life is estimated at 10 years, or 385,000 units of product, with a $5,000 salvage value. During its second year, the machine produces 32,500 units of product. Determine the machine's second-year depreciation under the straight-line method.

Exercise 10-6
Straight-line depreciation
P1

Refer to the information in Exercise 10-6. Determine the machine's second-year depreciation using the units-of-production method.

Exercise 10-7
Units-of-production depreciation
P1

Refer to the information in Exercise 10-6. Determine the machine's second-year depreciation using the double-declining-balance method.

Exercise 10-8
Double-declining-balance depreciation   P1

On April 1, 2012, Cyclone's Backhoe Co. purchases a trencher for $280,000. The machine is expected to last five years and have a salvage value of $40,000. Compute depreciation expense for both 2012 and 2013 assuming the company uses the straight-line method.

Exercise 10-9
Straight-line, partial-year depreciation   C2

Refer to the information in Exercise 10-9. Compute depreciation expense for both 2012 and 2013 assuming the company uses the double-declining-balance method.

Exercise 10-10
Double-declining-balance, partial-year depreciation   C2

Apex Fitness Club uses straight-line depreciation for a machine costing $23,860, with an estimated four-year life and a $2,400 salvage value. At the beginning of the third year, Apex determines that the machine has three more years of remaining useful life, after which it will have an estimated $2,000 salvage value. Compute (1) the machine's book value at the end of its second year and (2) the amount of depreciation for each of the final three years given the revised estimates.

Exercise 10-11
Revising depreciation
C2

Check   (2) $3,710

Tory Enterprises pays $238,400 for equipment that will last five years and have a $43,600 salvage value. By using the equipment in its operations for five years, the company expects to earn $88,500 annually, after deducting all expenses except depreciation. Prepare a table showing income before depreciation, depreciation expense, and net (pretax) income for each year and for the total five-year period, assuming straight-line depreciation.

Exercise 10-12
Straight-line depreciation and income effects   P1

Refer to the information in Exercise 10-12. Prepare a table showing income before depreciation, depreciation expense, and net (pretax) income for each year and for the total five-year period, assuming double-declining-balance depreciation is used.

Exercise 10-13
Double-declining-balance depreciation   P1

Check   Year 3 NI, $54,170

Exercise 10-14
Extraordinary repairs;
plant asset age

C3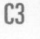

Check   (3) $211,350

Veradis Company owns a building that appears on its prior year-end balance sheet at its original $572,000 cost less $429,000 accumulated depreciation. The building is depreciated on a straight-line basis assuming a 20-year life and no salvage value. During the first week in January of the current calendar year, major structural repairs are completed on the building at a $68,350 cost. The repairs extend its useful life for 5 years beyond the 20 years originally estimated.

1. Determine the building's age (plant asset age) as of the prior year-end balance sheet date.
2. Prepare the entry to record the cost of the structural repairs that are paid in cash.
3. Determine the book value of the building immediately after the repairs are recorded.
4. Prepare the entry to record the current calendar year's depreciation.

Exercise 10-15
Ordinary repairs, extraordinary
repairs and betterments

C3

Oki Company pays $264,000 for equipment expected to last four years and have a $29,000 salvage value. Prepare journal entries to record the following costs related to the equipment.

1. During the second year of the equipment's life, $22,000 cash is paid for a new component expected to increase the equipment's productivity by 10% a year.
2. During the third year, $6,250 cash is paid for normal repairs necessary to keep the equipment in good working order.
3. During the fourth year, $14,870 is paid for repairs expected to increase the useful life of the equipment from four to five years.

Exercise 10–16
Disposal of assets

P2

Diaz Company owns a milling machine that cost $250,000 and has accumulated depreciation of $182,000. Prepare the entry to record the disposal of the milling machine on January 3 under each of the following independent situations.

1. The machine needed extensive repairs, and it was not worth repairing. Diaz disposed of the machine, receiving nothing in return.
2. Diaz sold the machine for $35,000 cash.
3. Diaz sold the machine for $68,000 cash.
4. Diaz sold the machine for $80,000 cash.

Exercise 10-17
Partial-year depreciation;
disposal of plant asset

P2

Rayya Co. purchases and installs a machine on January 1, 2013, at a total cost of $105,000. Straight-line depreciation is taken each year for four years assuming a seven-year life and no salvage value. The machine is disposed of on July 1, 2017, during its fifth year of service. Prepare entries to record the partial year's depreciation on July 1, 2017, and to record the disposal under the following separate assumptions: (1) the machine is sold for $45,500 cash and (2) Rayya receives an insurance settlement of $25,000 resulting from the total destruction of the machine in a fire.

Exercise 10-18
Depletion of natural resources

P1   P3

On April 2, 2013, Montana Mining Co. pays $3,721,000 for an ore deposit containing 1,525,000 tons. The company installs machinery in the mine costing $213,500, with an estimated seven-year life and no salvage value. The machinery will be abandoned when the ore is completely mined. Montana begins mining on May 1, 2013, and mines and sells 166,200 tons of ore during the remaining eight months of 2013. Prepare the December 31, 2013, entries to record both the ore deposit depletion and the mining machinery depreciation. Mining machinery depreciation should be in proportion to the mine's depletion.

Exercise 10-19
Amortization of intangible assets

P4

Milano Gallery purchases the copyright on an oil painting for $418,000 on January 1, 2013. The copyright legally protects its owner for 10 more years. The company plans to market and sell prints of the original for 11 years. Prepare entries to record the purchase of the copyright on January 1, 2013, and its annual amortization on December 31, 2013.

Exercise 10-20
Goodwill

P4

On January 1, 2013, Robinson Company purchased Franklin Company at a price of $2,500,000. The fair market value of the net assets purchased equals $1,800,000.

1. What is the amount of goodwill that Robinson records at the purchase date?
2. Explain how Robinson would determine the amount of goodwill amortization for the year ended December 31, 2013.
3. Robinson Company believes that its employees provide superior customer service, and through their efforts, Robinson Company believes it has created $900,000 of goodwill. How would Robinson Company record this goodwill?

Refer to the statement of cash flows for **Arctic Cat** in Appendix A for the fiscal year ended March 31, 2011, to answer the following.

1. What amount of cash is used to purchase property and equipment?

2. How much depreciation and amortization are recorded?

3. What total amount of net cash is used in investing activities?

Exercise 10-21
Cash flows related to assets

C1

Arctic Cat

Lok Co. reports net sales of $5,856,480 for 2012 and $8,679,690 for 2013. End-of-year balances for total assets are 2011, $1,686,000; 2012, $1,800,000; and 2013, $1,982,000. (*a*) Compute Lok's total asset turnover for 2012 and 2013. (*b*) Comment on Lok's efficiency in using its assets if its competitors average a total asset turnover of 3.0.

Exercise 10-22
Evaluating efficient use of assets

A1

Gilly Construction trades in an old tractor for a new tractor, receiving a $29,000 trade-in allowance and paying the remaining $83,000 in cash. The old tractor had cost $96,000, and straight-line accumulated depreciation of $52,500 had been recorded to date under the assumption that it would last eight years and have a $12,000 salvage value. Answer the following questions assuming the exchange has commercial substance.

1. What is the book value of the old tractor at the time of exchange?

2. What is the loss on this asset exchange?

3. What amount should be recorded (debited) in the asset account for the new tractor?

Exercise 10-23[A]
Exchanging assets

P5

Check (2) $14,500

On January 2, 2013, Bering Co. disposes of a machine costing $44,000 with accumulated depreciation of $24,625. Prepare the entries to record the disposal under each of the following separate assumptions.

1. The machine is sold for $18,250 cash.

2. The machine is traded in for a newer machine having a $60,200 cash price. A $25,000 trade-in allowance is received, and the balance is paid in cash. Assume the asset exchange lacks commercial substance.

3. The machine is traded in for a newer machine having a $60,200 cash price. A $15,000 trade-in allowance is received, and the balance is paid in cash. Assume the asset exchange has commercial substance.

Exercise 10-24[A]
Recording plant asset disposals

P2 P5

Check (2) Dr. Machinery (new), $54,575

Volkswagen Group reports the following information for property, plant and equipment as of December 31, 2010, along with additions, disposals, depreciation, and impairments for the year ended December 31, 2010 (euros in millions):

Property, plant and equipment, net	€25,847
Additions to property, plant and equipment	5,634
Disposals of property, plant and equipment	2,522
Depreciation on property, plant and equipment	4,731
Impairments to property, plant and equipment	451

1. Prepare Volkswagen's journal entry to record its depreciation for 2010.

2. Prepare Volkswagen's journal entry to record its additions for 2010 assuming they are paid in cash and are treated as "betterments (improvements)" to the assets.

3. Prepare Volkswagen's journal entry to record its €2,522 in disposals for 2010 assuming it receives €700 cash in return and the accumulated depreciation on the disposed assets totals €1,322.

4. Volkswagen reports €451 of impairments. Do these impairments increase or decrease the property, plant and equipment account? And, by what amount?

Exercise 10-25
Accounting for plant assets under IFRS

C2 P1 P2

⬛ connect

Timberly Construction negotiates a lump-sum purchase of several assets from a company that is going out of business. The purchase is completed on January 1, 2013, at a total cash price of $900,000 for a building, land, land improvements, and four vehicles. The estimated market values of the assets are building, $508,800; land, $297,600; land improvements, $28,800; and four vehicles, $124,800. The company's fiscal year ends on December 31.

PROBLEM SET A

Problem 10-1A
Plant asset costs; depreciation methods C1 P1

Required

1. Prepare a table to allocate the lump-sum purchase price to the separate assets purchased (round percents to the nearest 1%). Prepare the journal entry to record the purchase.

Check (2) $30,000

(3) $10,800

2. Compute the depreciation expense for year 2013 on the building using the straight-line method, assuming a 15-year life and a $27,000 salvage value.

3. Compute the depreciation expense for year 2013 on the land improvements assuming a five-year life and double-declining-balance depreciation.

Analysis Component

4. Defend or refute this statement: Accelerated depreciation results in payment of less taxes over the asset's life.

Problem 10-2A
Asset cost allocation;
straight-line depreciation

C1 P1

mhhe.com/wildFAP21e

In January 2013, Mitzu Co. pays $2,600,000 for a tract of land with two buildings on it. It plans to demolish Building 1 and build a new store in its place. Building 2 will be a company office; it is appraised at $644,000, with a useful life of 20 years and an $60,000 salvage value. A lighted parking lot near Building 1 has improvements (Land Improvements 1) valued at $420,000 that are expected to last another 12 years with no salvage value. Without the buildings and improvements, the tract of land is valued at $1,736,000. The company also incurs the following additional costs:

Cost to demolish Building 1	$ 328,400
Cost of additional land grading	175,400
Cost to construct new building (Building 3), having a useful life of 25 years and a $392,000 salvage value	2,202,000
Cost of new land improvements (Land Improvements 2) near Building 2 having a 20-year useful life and no salvage value	164,000

Required

Check (1) Land costs, $2,115,800; Building 2 costs, $598,000

1. Prepare a table with the following column headings: Land, Building 2, Building 3, Land Improvements 1, and Land Improvements 2. Allocate the costs incurred by Mitzu to the appropriate columns and total each column (round percents to the nearest 1%).

2. Prepare a single journal entry to record all the incurred costs assuming they are paid in cash on January 1, 2013.

(3) Depr.—Land Improv. 1 and 2, $32,500 and $8,200

3. Using the straight-line method, prepare the December 31 adjusting entries to record depreciation for the 12 months of 2013 when these assets were in use.

Problem 10-3A
Computing and revising
depreciation; revenue and
capital expenditures

C1 C2 C3

Champion Contractors completed the following transactions and events involving the purchase and operation of equipment in its business.

2012

Jan. 1 Paid $287,600 cash plus $11,500 in sales tax and $1,500 in transportation (FOB shipping point) for a new loader. The loader is estimated to have a four-year life and a $20,600 salvage value. Loader costs are recorded in the Equipment account.

Jan. 3 Paid $4,800 to enclose the cab and install air conditioning in the loader to enable operations under harsher conditions. This increased the estimated salvage value of the loader by another $1,400.

Check Dec. 31, 2012, Dr. Depr. Expense—Equip., $70,850

Dec. 31 Recorded annual straight-line depreciation on the loader.

2013

Jan. 1 Paid $5,400 to overhaul the loader's engine, which increased the loader's estimated useful life by two years.

Feb. 17 Paid $820 to repair the loader after the operator backed it into a tree.

Check Dec. 31, 2013, Dr. Depr. Expense—Equip., $43,590

Dec. 31 Recorded annual straight-line depreciation on the loader.

Required

Prepare journal entries to record these transactions and events.

Problem 10-4A
Computing and revising
depreciation; selling plant assets

C2 P1 P2

Yoshi Company completed the following transactions and events involving its delivery trucks.

2012

Jan. 1 Paid $20,515 cash plus $1,485 in sales tax for a new delivery truck estimated to have a five-year life and a $2,000 salvage value. Delivery truck costs are recorded in the Trucks account.

Dec. 31 Recorded annual straight-line depreciation on the truck.

2013

Dec. 31   Due to new information obtained earlier in the year, the truck's estimated useful life was changed from five to four years, and the estimated salvage value was increased to $2,400. Recorded annual straight-line depreciation on the truck.

Check Dec. 31, 2013, Dr. Depr. Expense—Trucks, $5,200

2014

Dec. 31   Recorded annual straight-line depreciation on the truck.
Dec. 31   Sold the truck for $5,300 cash.

Dec. 31, 2014, Dr. Loss on Disposal of Trucks, $2,300

Required

Prepare journal entries to record these transactions and events.

A machine costing $257,500 with a four-year life and an estimated $20,000 salvage value is installed in Luther Company's factory on January 1. The factory manager estimates the machine will produce 475,000 units of product during its life. It actually produces the following units: year 1, 220,000; year 2, 124,600; year 3, 121,800; and year 4, 15,200. The total number of units produced by the end of year 4 exceeds the original estimate—this difference was not predicted. (The machine must not be depreciated below its estimated salvage value.)

Problem 10-5A
Depreciation methods
P1

Required

Prepare a table with the following column headings and compute depreciation for each year (and total depreciation of all years combined) for the machine under each depreciation method.

Year	Straight-Line	Units-of-Production	Double-Declining-Balance

Check Year 4: units-of-production depreciation, $4,300; DDB depreciation, $12,187

Onslow Co. purchases a used machine for $178,000 cash on January 2 and readies it for use the next day at an $2,840 cost. On January 3, it is installed on a required operating platform costing $1,160, and it is further readied for operations. The company predicts the machine will be used for six years and have a $14,000 salvage value. Depreciation is to be charged on a straight-line basis. On December 31, at the end of its fifth year in operations, it is disposed of.

Problem 10-6A
Disposal of plant assets
C1 P1 P2

Required

1. Prepare journal entries to record the machine's purchase and the costs to ready and install it. Cash is paid for all costs incurred.

2. Prepare journal entries to record depreciation of the machine at December 31 of (a) its first year in operations and (b) the year of its disposal.

Check (2b) Depr. Exp., $28,000

3. Prepare journal entries to record the machine's disposal under each of the following separate assumptions: (a) it is sold for $15,000 cash; (b) it is sold for $50,000 cash; and (c) it is destroyed in a fire and the insurance company pays $30,000 cash to settle the loss claim.

(3c) Dr. Loss from Fire, $12,000

On July 23 of the current year, Dakota Mining Co. pays $4,715,000 for land estimated to contain 5,125,000 tons of recoverable ore. It installs machinery costing $410,000 that has a 10-year life and no salvage value and is capable of mining the ore deposit in eight years. The machinery is paid for on July 25, seven days before mining operations begin. The company removes and sells 480,000 tons of ore during its first five months of operations ending on December 31. Depreciation of the machinery is in proportion to the mine's depletion as the machinery will be abandoned after the ore is mined.

Problem 10-7A
Natural resources
P3

Required

Prepare entries to record (a) the purchase of the land, (b) the cost and installation of machinery, (c) the first five months' depletion assuming the land has a net salvage value of zero after the ore is mined, and (d) the first five months' depreciation on the machinery.

Check (c) Depletion, $441,600
(d) Depreciation, $38,400

Analysis Component

Describe both the similarities and differences in amortization, depletion, and depreciation.

Problem 10-8A
Intangible assets

P4

Sage 50

On July 1, 2008, Falk Company signed a contract to lease space in a building for 15 years. The lease contract calls for annual (prepaid) rental payments of $80,000 on each July 1 throughout the life of the lease and for the lessee to pay for all additions and improvements to the leased property. On June 25, 2013, Falk decides to sublease the space to Ryan & Associates for the remaining 10 years of the lease—Ryan pays $200,000 to Falk for the right to sublease and it agrees to assume the obligation to pay the $80,000 annual rent to the building owner beginning July 1, 2013. After taking possession of the leased space, Ryan pays for improving the office portion of the leased space at a $130,000 cost. The improvements are paid for by Ryan on July 5, 2013, and are estimated to have a useful life equal to the 16 years remaining in the life of the building.

Required

1. Prepare entries for Ryan to record (*a*) its payment to Falk for the right to sublease the building space, (*b*) its payment of the 2013 annual rent to the building owner, and (*c*) its payment for the office improvements.

Check   Dr. Rent Expense for (2*a*) $10,000, (2*c*) $40,000

2. Prepare Ryan's year-end adjusting entries required at December 31, 2013, to (*a*) amortize the $200,000 cost of the sublease, (*b*) amortize the office improvements, and (*c*) record rent expense.

PROBLEM SET B

Problem 10-1B
Plant asset costs; depreciation methods

C1 P1

Nagy Company negotiates a lump-sum purchase of several assets from a contractor who is relocating. The purchase is completed on January 1, 2013, at a total cash price of $1,800,000 for a building, land, land improvements, and five trucks. The estimated market values of the assets are building, $890,000; land, $427,200; land improvements, $249,200; and five trucks, $213,600. The company's fiscal year ends on December 31.

Required

1. Prepare a table to allocate the lump-sum purchase price to the separate assets purchased (round percents to the nearest 1%). Prepare the journal entry to record the purchase.

Check   (2) $65,000

2. Compute the depreciation expense for year 2013 on the building using the straight-line method, assuming a 12-year life and a $120,000 salvage value.

     (3) $50,400

3. Compute the depreciation expense for year 2013 on the land improvements assuming a 10-year life and double-declining-balance depreciation.

Analysis Component

4. Defend or refute this statement: Accelerated depreciation results in payment of more taxes over the asset's life.

Problem 10-2B
Asset cost allocation; straight-line depreciation

C1 P1

In January 2013, ProTech Co. pays $1,550,000 for a tract of land with two buildings. It plans to demolish Building A and build a new shop in its place. Building B will be a company office; it is appraised at $482,800, with a useful life of 15 years and a $99,500 salvage value. A lighted parking lot near Building B has improvements (Land Improvements B) valued at $142,000 that are expected to last another five years with no salvage value. Without the buildings and improvements, the tract of land is valued at $795,200. The company also incurs the following additional costs.

Cost to demolish Building A	$ 122,000
Cost of additional land grading	174,500
Cost to construct new building (Building C), having a useful life of 20 years and a $258,000 salvage value	1,458,000
Cost of new land improvements (Land Improvements C) near Building C, having a 10-year useful life and no salvage value	103,500

Required

Check   (1) Land costs, $1,164,500; Building B costs, $527,000

1. Prepare a table with the following column headings: Land, Building B, Building C, Land Improvements B, and Land Improvements C. Allocate the costs incurred by ProTech to the appropriate columns and total each column (round percents to the nearest 1%).

2. Prepare a single journal entry to record all incurred costs assuming they are paid in cash on January 1, 2013.

     (3) Depr.—Land Improv. B and C, $31,000 and $10,350

3. Using the straight-line method, prepare the December 31 adjusting entries to record depreciation for the 12 months of 2013 when these assets were in use.

Mercury Delivery Service completed the following transactions and events involving the purchase and operation of equipment for its business.

2012

Jan. 1   Paid $25,860 cash plus $1,810 in sales tax for a new delivery van that was estimated to have a five-year life and a $3,670 salvage value. Van costs are recorded in the Equipment account.

Jan. 3   Paid $1,850 to install sorting racks in the van for more accurate and quicker delivery of packages. This increases the estimated salvage value of the van by another $230.

Dec. 31   Recorded annual straight-line depreciation on the van.

2013

Jan. 1   Paid $2,064 to overhaul the van's engine, which increased the van's estimated useful life by two years.

May 10   Paid $800 to repair the van after the driver backed it into a loading dock.

Dec. 31   Record annual straight-line depreciation on the van. (Round to the nearest dollar.)

Required

Prepare journal entries to record these transactions and events.

Problem 10-3B
Computing and revising depreciation; revenue and capital expenditures

C1   C2   C3

Check   Dec. 31, 2012, Dr. Depr. Expense—Equip., $5,124

Check   Dec. 31, 2013, Dr. Depr. Expense—Equip., $3,760

York Instruments completed the following transactions and events involving its machinery.

2012

Jan. 1   Paid $107,800 cash plus $6,470 in sales tax for a new machine. The machine is estimated to have a six-year life and a $9,720 salvage value.

Dec. 31   Recorded annual straight-line depreciation on the machinery.

2013

Dec. 31   Due to new information obtained earlier in the year, the machine's estimated useful life was changed from six to four years, and the estimated salvage value was increased to $14,345. Recorded annual straight-line depreciation on the machinery.

2014

Dec. 31   Recorded annual straight-line depreciation on the machinery.

Dec. 31   Sold the machine for $25,240 cash.

Required

Prepare journal entries to record these transactions and events.

Problem 10-4B
Computing and revising depreciation; selling plant assets

C2   P1   P2

Check   Dec. 31, 2013, Dr. Depr. Expense—Machinery, $27,500

Dec. 31, 2014, Dr. Loss on Disposal of Machinery, $16,605

On January 2, Manning Co. purchases and installs a new machine costing $324,000 with a five-year life and an estimated $30,000 salvage value. Management estimates the machine will produce 1,470,000 units of product during its life. Actual production of units is as follows: year 1, 355,600; year 2, 320,400; year 3, 317,000; year 4, 343,600; and year 5, 138,500. The total number of units produced by the end of year 5 exceeds the original estimate—this difference was not predicted. (The machine must not be depreciated below its estimated salvage value.)

Required

Prepare a table with the following column headings and compute depreciation for each year (and total depreciation of all years combined) for the machine under each depreciation method.

Year	Straight-Line	Units-of-Production	Double-Declining-Balance

Problem 10-5B
Depreciation methods

P1

Check   DDB Depreciation, Year 3, $46,656; U-of-P Depreciation, Year 4, $68,720

On January 1, Walker purchases a used machine for $150,000 and readies it for use the next day at a cost of $3,510. On January 4, it is mounted on a required operating platform costing $4,600, and it is further readied for operations. Management estimates the machine will be used for seven years and have an $18,110 salvage value. Depreciation is to be charged on a straight-line basis. On December 31, at the end of its sixth year of use, the machine is disposed of.

Problem 10-6B
Disposal of plant assets

C1   P1   P2

Required

1. Prepare journal entries to record the machine's purchase and the costs to ready and install it. Cash is paid for all costs incurred.

Check   (2*b*) Depr. Exp., $20,000

2. Prepare journal entries to record depreciation of the machine at December 31 of (*a*) its first year in operations and (*b*) the year of its disposal.

(3*c*) Dr. Loss from Fire, $13,110

3. Prepare journal entries to record the machine's disposal under each of the following separate assumptions: (*a*) it is sold for $28,000 cash; (*b*) it is sold for $52,000 cash; and (*c*) it is destroyed in a fire and the insurance company pays $25,000 cash to settle the loss claim.

Problem 10-7B
Natural resources
P3

On February 19 of the current year, Quartzite Co. pays $5,400,000 for land estimated to contain 4 million tons of recoverable ore. It installs machinery costing $400,000 that has a 16-year life and no salvage value and is capable of mining the ore deposit in 12 years. The machinery is paid for on March 21, eleven days before mining operations begin. The company removes and sells 254,000 tons of ore during its first nine months of operations ending on December 31. Depreciation of the machinery is in proportion to the mine's depletion as the machinery will be abandoned after the ore is mined.

Required

Check   (*c*) Depletion, $342,900;
(*d*) Depreciation, $25,400

Prepare entries to record (*a*) the purchase of the land, (*b*) the cost and installation of the machinery, (*c*) the first nine months' depletion assuming the land has a net salvage value of zero after the ore is mined, and (*d*) the first nine months' depreciation on the machinery.

Analysis Component

Describe both the similarities and differences in amortization, depletion, and depreciation.

Problem 10-8B
Intangible assets
P4

On January 1, 2006, Mason Co. entered into a 12-year lease on a building. The lease contract requires (1) annual (prepaid) rental payments of $36,000 each January 1 throughout the life of the lease and (2) for the lessee to pay for all additions and improvements to the leased property. On January 1, 2013, Mason decides to sublease the space to Stewart Co. for the remaining five years of the lease—Stewart pays $40,000 to Mason for the right to sublease and agrees to assume the obligation to pay the $36,000 annual rent to the building owner beginning January 1, 2013. After taking possession of the leased space, Stewart pays for improving the office portion of the leased space at a $20,000 cost. The improvements are paid for by Stewart on January 3, 2013, and are estimated to have a useful life equal to the 13 years remaining in the life of the building.

Required

1. Prepare entries for Stewart to record (*a*) its payment to Mason for the right to sublease the building space, (*b*) its payment of the 2013 annual rent to the building owner, and (*c*) its payment for the office improvements.

Check   Dr. Rent Expense:
(2*a*) $8,000, (2*c*) $36,000

2. Prepare Stewart's year-end adjusting entries required on December 31, 2013, to (*a*) amortize the $40,000 cost of the sublease, (*b*) amortize the office improvements, and (*c*) record rent expense.

SERIAL PROBLEM
Success Systems
P1 A1

(This serial problem began in Chapter 1 and continues through most of the book. If previous chapter segments were not completed, the serial problem can begin at this point. It is helpful, but not necessary, to use the Working Papers that accompany the book.)

SP 10   Selected ledger account balances for Success Systems follow.

	For Three Months Ended December 31, 2013	For Three Months Ended March 31, 2014
Office equipment	$ 8,000	$ 8,000
Accumulated depreciation— Office equipment	400	800
Computer equipment	20,000	20,000
Accumulated depreciation— Computer equipment	1,250	2,500
Total revenue	31,284	43,853
Total assets	93,248	129,909

Required

1. Assume that Success Systems does not acquire additional office equipment or computer equipment in 2014. Compute amounts for *the year ended* December 31, 2014, for Depreciation Expense—Office Equipment and for Depreciation Expense—Computer Equipment (assume use of the straight-line method).

2. Given the assumptions in part 1, what is the book value of both the office equipment and the computer equipment as of December 31, 2014?

3. Compute the three-month total asset turnover for Success Systems as of March 31, 2014. Use total revenue for the numerator and average the December 31, 2013, total assets and the March 31, 2014, total assets for the denominator. Interpret its total asset turnover if competitors average 2.5 for annual periods. (Round turnover to two decimals.)

Check   (3) Three-month (annual) turnover = 0.393 (1.572 annual)

Beyond the Numbers

BTN 10-1   Refer to the financial statements of **Polaris** in Appendix A to answer the following.

1. What percent of the original cost of Polaris' property and equipment remains to be depreciated as of December 31, 2011, and at December 31, 2010? Assume these assets have no salvage value.

2. Over what length(s) of time is Polaris depreciating its major categories of property and equipment?

3. What is the change in total property and equipment (before accumulated depreciation) for the year ended December 31, 2011? What is the amount of cash provided (used) by investing activities for property and equipment for the year ended December 31, 2011? What is one possible explanation for the difference between these two amounts?

4. Compute its total asset turnover for the year ended December 31, 2011, and the year ended December 31, 2010. Assume total assets at December 31, 2008, are $763,653 ($ thousands).

REPORTING IN ACTION

A1 🔖

Polaris

Fast Forward

5. Access Polaris' financial statements for fiscal years ending after December 31, 2011, at its Website (**Polaris.com**) or the SEC's EDGAR database (**www.SEC.gov**). Recompute Polaris' total asset turnover for the additional years' data you collect. Comment on any differences relative to the turnover computed in part 4.

BTN 10-2   Comparative figures for **Polaris** and **Arctic Cat** follow.

COMPARATIVE ANALYSIS

A1

Polaris

Arctic Cat

($ thousands)	Polaris			Arctic Cat		
	Current Year	One Year Prior	Two Years Prior	Current Year	One Year Prior	Two Years Prior
Total assets	$1,228,024	$1,061,647	$ 763,653	$272,906	$246,084	$251,165
Net sales	2,656,949	1,991,139	1,565,887	464,651	450,728	563,613

Required

1. Compute total asset turnover for the most recent two years for Polaris and Arctic Cat using the data shown.

2. Which company is more efficient in generating net sales given the total assets it employs? Assume an industry average of 1.0 for asset turnover.

BTN 10-3   Flo Choi owns a small business and manages its accounting. Her company just finished a year in which a large amount of borrowed funds was invested in a new building addition as well as in equipment and fixture additions. Choi's banker requires her to submit semiannual financial statements so he can monitor the financial health of her business. He has warned her that if profit margins erode, he might raise the interest rate on the borrowed funds to reflect the increased loan risk from the bank's point of view. Choi knows profit margin is likely to decline this year. As she prepares year-end adjusting entries, she decides to apply the following depreciation rule: All asset additions are considered to be in use on the first day of the following month. (The previous rule assumed assets are in use on the first day of the month nearest to the purchase date.)

ETHICS CHALLENGE

C1

Required

1. Identify decisions that managers like Choi must make in applying depreciation methods.
2. Is Choi's rule an ethical violation, or is it a legitimate decision in computing depreciation?
3. How will Choi's new depreciation rule affect the profit margin of her business?

COMMUNICATING IN PRACTICE
A1

BTN 10-4   Teams are to select an industry, and each team member is to select a different company in that industry. Each team member is to acquire the financial statements (Form 10-K) of the company selected—see the company's Website or the SEC's EDGAR database (www.sec.gov). Use the financial statements to compute total asset turnover. Communicate with teammates via a meeting, e-mail, or telephone to discuss the meaning of this ratio, how different companies compare to each other, and the industry norm. The team must prepare a one-page report that describes the ratios for each company and identifies the conclusions reached during the team's discussion.

TAKING IT TO THE NET
P4

BTN 10-5   Access the **Yahoo!** (ticker: YHOO) 10-K report for the year ended December 31, 2011, filed on February 29, 2012, at www.sec.gov.

Required

1. What amount of goodwill is reported on Yahoo!'s balance sheet? What percentage of total assets does its goodwill represent? Is goodwill a major asset for Yahoo!? Explain.
2. Locate Note 5 to its financial statements. Identify the change in goodwill from December 31, 2010, to December 31, 2011. Comment on the change in goodwill over this period.
3. Locate Note 6 to its financial statements. What are the three categories of intangible assets that Yahoo! reports at December 31, 2011? What proportion of total assets do the intangibles represent?
4. What does Yahoo! indicate is the life of "Trade names, trademarks, and domain names" according to its Note 6? Comment on the difference between the estimated useful life and the legal life of Yahoo!'s trademark.

TEAMWORK IN ACTION
P1

BTN 10-6   Each team member is to become an expert on one depreciation method to facilitate teammates' understanding of that method. Follow these procedures:

a. Each team member is to select an area for expertise from one of the following depreciation methods: straight-line, units-of-production, or double-declining-balance.
b. Expert teams are to be formed from those who have selected the same area of expertise. The instructor will identify the location where each expert team meets.
c. Using the following data, expert teams are to collaborate and develop a presentation answering the requirements. Expert team members must write the presentation in a format they can show to their learning teams.

Data and Requirements On January 8, 2011, Whitewater Riders purchases a van to transport rafters back to the point of departure at the conclusion of the rafting adventures they operate. The cost of the van is $44,000. It has an estimated salvage value of $2,000 and is expected to be used for four years and driven 60,000 miles. The van is driven 12,000 miles in 2011, 18,000 miles in 2012, 21,000 in 2013, and 10,000 in 2014.

   1. Compute the annual depreciation expense for each year of the van's estimated useful life.
   2. Explain when and how annual depreciation is recorded.
   3. Explain the impact on income of this depreciation method versus others over the van's life.
   4. Identify the van's book value for each year of its life and illustrate the reporting of this amount for any one year.

d. Re-form original learning teams. In rotation, experts are to present to their teams the results from part *c*. Experts are to encourage and respond to questions.

Point: This activity can follow an overview of each method. Step 1 allows for three areas of expertise. Larger teams will have some duplication of areas, but the straight-line choice should not be duplicated. Expert teams can use the book and consult with the instructor.

ENTREPRENEURIAL DECISION
A1

BTN 10-7   Review the chapter's opening feature involving **BizChair.com**. Assume that the company currently has net sales of $8,000,000, and that it is planning an expansion that will increase net sales by $4,000,000. To accomplish this expansion, BizChair.com must increase its average total assets from $2,500,000 to $3,000,000.

Required

1. Compute the company's total asset turnover under (*a*) current conditions and (*b*) proposed conditions.
2. Evaluate and comment on the merits of the proposal given your analysis in part 1. Identify any concerns you would express about the proposal.

BTN 10-8   Team up with one or more classmates for this activity. Identify companies in your community or area that must account for at least one of the following assets: natural resource; patent; lease; leasehold improvement; copyright; trademark; or goodwill. You might find a company having more than one type of asset. Once you identify a company with a specific asset, describe the accounting this company uses to allocate the cost of that asset to the periods benefited from its use.

HITTING THE ROAD

P3 P4

BTN 10-9   **Piaggio** (**www.Piaggio.com**), **Polaris**, and **Arctic Cat** are all competitors in the global marketplace. Comparative figures for these companies' recent annual accounting periods follow.

GLOBAL DECISION

A1

PIAGGIO
Polaris
Arctic Cat

(in thousands, except turnover)	Piaggio (Euro thousands)			Polaris		Arctic Cat	
	Current Year	Prior Year	Two Years Prior	Current Year	Prior Year	Current Year	Prior Year
Total assets	1,520,184	1,545,722	1,564,820	$1,228,024	$1,061,647	$272,906	$246,084
Net sales	1,516,463	1,485,351	1,486,882	2,656,949	1,991,139	464,651	450,728
Total asset turnover	?	?	—	2.32	2.18	1.79	1.81

Required

1. Compute total asset turnover for the most recent two years for Piaggio using the data shown.
2. Which company is most efficient in generating net sales given the total assets it employs?

ANSWERS TO MULTIPLE CHOICE QUIZ

1. b;

	Appraisal Value	%	Total Cost	Allocated
Land	$175,000	50%	$326,000	$163,000
Land improvements	70,000	20	326,000	65,200
Building	105,000	30	326,000	97,800
Totals	$350,000			$326,000

2. c; ($35,000 − $1,000)/4 years = $8,500 per year.
3. c; 2013: $10,800,000 × (2 × 10%) = $2,160,000
   2014: ($10,800,000 − $2,160,000) × (2 × 10%) = $1,728,000
4. c;

Cost of machine	$250,000
Accumulated depreciation	100,000
Book value	150,000
Cash received	120,000
Loss on sale	$ 30,000

5. b; $550,000/$500,000 = 1.10

Current Liabilities and Payroll Accounting

A Look Back

Chapter 10 focused on long-term assets including plant assets, natural resources, and intangibles. We showed how to account for and analyze those assets.

A Look at This Chapter

This chapter explains how to identify, compute, record, and report current liabilities in financial statements. We also analyze and interpret these liabilities, including those related to employee costs.

A Look Ahead

Chapter 12 explains the partnership form of organization. It also describes the accounting concepts and procedures for partnership transactions.

Learning Objectives

CONCEPTUAL

C1 Describe current and long-term liabilities and their characteristics. (p. 438)

C2 Identify and describe known current liabilities. (p. 440)

C3 Explain how to account for contingent liabilities. (p. 450)

ANALYTICAL

A1 Compute the times interest earned ratio and use it to analyze liabilities. (p. 452)

PROCEDURAL

P1 Prepare entries to account for short-term notes payable. (p. 441)

P2 Compute and record *employee* payroll deductions and liabilities. (p. 444)

P3 Compute and record *employer* payroll expenses and liabilities. (p. 445)

P4 Account for estimated liabilities, including warranties and bonuses. (p. 447)

P5 *Appendix 11A*—Identify and describe the details of payroll reports, records, and procedures. (p. 455)

Decision Insight

Basement to Boardroom

"Provide the highest level of service, value, and integrity."

—KAREN COOPER

INDIANAPOLIS—Karen Cooper had labored for several years in the industry and saw a demand for information technology (IT) workers. "I felt," insists Karen, "that I could build a model company that would provide the highest level of [IT] services." Launched from her basement in 2005, Karen started **SmartIT Staffing (Smart-ITstaffing.com).** "With more than 15 years of staffing experience and a passion for recruiting," explains Karen, "I decided to start an IT staffing company" to serve the human resource needs of modern businesses.

Karen's commitment to help businesses use information wisely carries over to her own financial house. "When we started," recalls Karen, "there were just a handful of faithful clients who believed in us." To increase her odds of success, she focused on the important task of managing liabilities for payroll, supplies, employee wages, training, and taxes. Karen insists that effective management of liabilities, especially payroll and employee benefits, is crucial. She stresses that monitoring and controlling liabilities is a must.

To help control liabilities, Karen points to how she began by working out of her basement to limit liabilities. "Now," says Karen, "we're at a point where I feel we're on the verge of some really significant growth." By controlling liabilities, she is able to grow her company and increase the odds of financial success. Creative reduction of liabilities, such as launching from one's basement, can mean success or failure.

Karen continues to monitor liabilities and payment patterns. "I'm so glad to be part of the [accounting success stories]," explains Karen, and to use that knowledge "to help me manage this growth." She insists that accounting for and monitoring liabilities are a key to a successful start-up. Her company now generates sufficient income to pay for liabilities and produces revenue growth for expansion. And, Karen no longer works from her basement! "Our growth and success is a testament," explains Karen, "to the service, quality, execution, and overall value we bring to clients."

[Sources: *SmartIT Staffing Website,* January 2013; *INC.* (Top Ten Black Entrepreneurs), September 2010; *Black Web,* September 2010; *Inside Indiana Business,* July 2010; *Business Courier,* January 2011; *Cincinnati USA Regional Chamber,* February 2011.]

Previous chapters introduced liabilities such as accounts payable, notes payable, wages payable, and unearned revenues. This chapter further explains these liabilities and additional ones such as warranties, taxes, payroll, vacation pay, and bonuses. It also describes contingent liabilities and introduces long-term liabilities. The focus is on how to define, classify, measure, report, and analyze these liabilities so that this information is useful to business decision makers.

Current Liabilities and Payroll Accounting

Liability Characteristics	Known Liabilities	Estimated Liabilities	Contingent Liabilities
• Definition • Classification • Uncertainty	• Accounts payable • Sales taxes payable • Unearned revenues • Short-term notes • Payroll liabilities	• Health and pension benefits • Vacation benefits • Bonus plans • Warranty liabilities	• Accounting for contingencies • Reasonably possible contingencies

CHARACTERISTICS OF LIABILITIES

This section discusses important characteristics of liabilities and how liabilities are classified and reported.

Defining Liabilities

C1 Describe current and long-term liabilities and their characteristics.

A *liability* is a probable future payment of assets or services that a company is presently obligated to make as a result of past transactions or events. This definition includes three crucial factors:

1. A past transaction or event.
2. A present obligation.
3. A future payment of assets or services.

These three important elements are portrayed visually in Exhibit 11.1. Liabilities reported in financial statements exhibit those characteristics. No liability is reported when one or more of those characteristics is absent. For example, most companies expect to pay wages to their employees in upcoming months and years, but these future payments are *not* liabilities because no past event such as employee work resulted in a present obligation. Instead, such liabilities arise when employees perform their work and earn the wages.

EXHIBIT 11.1

Characteristics of a Liability

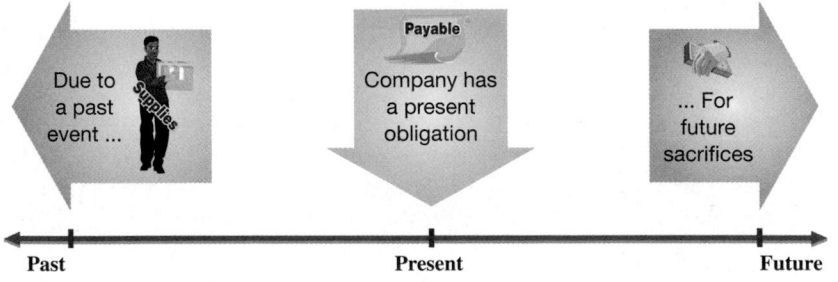

| Past | Present | Future |

Due to a past event ...

Company has a present obligation

... For future sacrifices

Classifying Liabilities

Point: Account titles using "payable" refer to liabilities.

Information about liabilities is more useful when the balance sheet identifies them as either current or long term. Decision makers need to know when obligations are due so they can plan for them and take appropriate action.

Current Liabilities   **Current liabilities,** also called *short-term liabilities,* are obligations due within one year or the company's operating cycle, whichever is longer. They are expected to be paid using current assets or by creating other current liabilities. Common examples of current liabilities are accounts payable, short-term notes payable, wages payable, warranty liabilities, lease liabilities, taxes payable, and unearned revenues.

Current liabilities differ across companies because they depend on the type of company operations. **MGM Mirage**, for instance, included the following current liabilities related to its gaming, hospitality and entertainment operations ($000s):

Advance deposits and ticket sales	$ 97,753
Casino outstanding chip liability	290,238
Casino front money deposits	111,763

Harley-Davidson reports a much different set of current liabilities. It discloses current liabilities made up of items such as warranty, recall, and dealer incentive liabilities.

Long-Term Liabilities   A company's obligations not expected to be paid within the longer of one year or the company's operating cycle are reported as **long-term liabilities.** They can include long-term notes payable, warranty liabilities, lease liabilities, and bonds payable. They are sometimes reported on the balance sheet in a single long-term liabilities total or in multiple categories. **Domino's Pizza**, for instance, reports long-term liabilities of $1,485 million. They are reported after current liabilities. A single liability also can be divided between the current and noncurrent sections if a company expects to make payments toward it in both the short and long term. Domino's reports long-term debt, $1,451,000,000; and current portion of long-term debt, $835,000, which is less than 1%. The second item is reported in current liabilities. We sometimes see liabilities that do not have a fixed due date but instead are payable on the creditor's demand. These are reported as current liabilities because of the possibility of payment in the near term. Exhibit 11.2 shows amounts of current liabilities and as a percent of total liabilities for selected companies.

Point: Improper classification of liabilities can distort ratios used in financial statement analysis and business decisions.

Point: The current ratio is overstated if a company fails to classify any portion of long-term debt due next period as a current liability.

EXHIBIT 11.2

Current Liabilities of Selected Companies

Uncertainty in Liabilities

Accounting for liabilities involves addressing three important questions: Whom to pay? When to pay? How much to pay? Answers to these questions are often decided when a liability is incurred. For example, if a company has a $100 account payable to a specific individual, payable on March 15, the answers are clear. The company knows whom to pay, when to pay, and how much to pay. However, the answers to one or more of these questions are uncertain for some liabilities.

Uncertainty in Whom to Pay   Liabilities can involve uncertainty in whom to pay. For instance, a company can create a liability with a known amount when issuing a note that is payable to its holder. In this case, a specific amount is payable to the note's holder at a specified date, but the company does not know who the holder is until that date. Despite this uncertainty, the company reports this liability on its balance sheet.

Point: An *accrued expense* is an unpaid expense, and is also called an *accrued liability.*

Uncertainty in When to Pay A company can have an obligation of a known amount to a known creditor but not know when it must be paid. For example, a legal services firm can accept fees in advance from a client who plans to use the firm's services in the future. This means that the firm has a liability that it settles by providing services at an unknown future date. Although this uncertainty exists, the legal firm's balance sheet must report this liability. These types of obligations are reported as current liabilities because they are likely to be settled in the short term.

Uncertainty in How Much to Pay A company can be aware of an obligation but not know how much will be required to settle it. For example, a company using electrical power is billed only after the meter has been read. This cost is incurred and the liability created before a bill is received. A liability to the power company is reported as an estimated amount if the balance sheet is prepared before a bill arrives.

 IFRS

IFRS records a contingent liability when an obligation exists from a past event if there is a 'probable' outflow of resources and the amount can be estimated reliably. However, IFRS defines probable as 'more likely than not' while U.S. GAAP defines it as 'likely to occur.' ■

Quick Check   Answers — p. 463

1. What is a liability? Identify its crucial characteristics.
2. Is every expected future payment a liability?
3. If a liability is payable in 15 months, is it classified as current or long term?

KNOWN LIABILITIES

 C2 Identify and describe known current liabilities.

Most liabilities arise from situations with little uncertainty. They are set by agreements, contracts, or laws and are measurable. These liabilities are **known liabilities,** also called *definitely determinable liabilities.* Known liabilities include accounts payable, notes payable, payroll, sales taxes, unearned revenues, and leases. We describe how to account for these known liabilities in this section.

Accounts Payable

Accounts payable, or trade accounts payable, are amounts owed to suppliers, also called *vendors,* for products or services purchased on credit. Accounting for accounts payable is primarily explained and illustrated in our discussion of merchandising activities in Chapters 5 and 6.

Sales Taxes Payable

Nearly all states and many cities levy taxes on retail sales. Sales taxes are stated as a percent of selling prices. The seller collects sales taxes from customers when sales occur and remits these collections (often monthly) to the proper government agency. Since sellers currently owe these collections to the government, this amount is a current liability. **Home Depot,** for instance, reports sales taxes payable of $391 million in its recent annual report. To illustrate, if Home Depot sells materials on August 31 for $6,000 cash that are subject to a 5% sales tax, the revenue portion of this transaction is recorded as follows:

Assets = Liabilities + Equity
+6,300   +300   +6,000

Aug. 31	Cash	6,300	
	Sales		6,000
	Sales Taxes Payable ($6,000 × 0.05)		300
	To record cash sales and 5% sales tax.		

Sales Taxes Payable is debited and Cash credited when it remits these collections to the government. Sales Taxes Payable is not an expense. It arises because laws require sellers to collect this cash from customers for the government.[1]

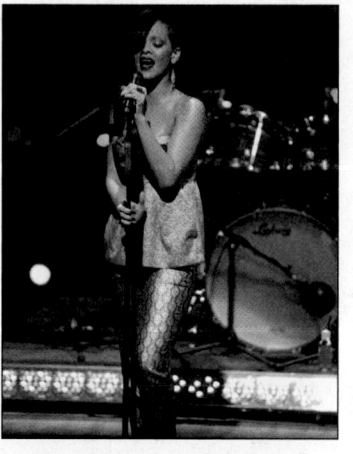

Unearned Revenues

Unearned revenues (also called *deferred revenues, collections in advance,* and *prepayments*) are amounts received in advance from customers for future products or services. Advance ticket sales for sporting events or music concerts are examples. **Rihanna**, for instance, has "deferred revenues" from advance ticket sales. To illustrate, assume that Rihanna sells $5 million in tickets for eight concerts; the entry is

Point: To *defer* a revenue means to postpone recognition of a revenue collected in advance until it is earned. Sport teams must defer recognition of ticket sales until games are played.

June 30	Cash	5,000,000	
	Unearned Ticket Revenue		5,000,000
	To record sale of concert tickets.		

Assets = Liabilities + Equity
+5,000,000   +5,000,000

When a concert is played, Rihanna would record revenue for the portion earned.

Oct. 31	Unearned Ticket Revenue	625,000	
	Ticket Revenue		625,000
	To record concert ticket revenues earned.		

Assets = Liabilities + Equity
−625,000   +625,000

Unearned Ticket Revenue is an unearned revenue account and is reported as a current liability. Unearned revenues also arise with airline ticket sales, magazine subscriptions, construction projects, hotel reservations, and custom orders.

Decision Insight

Reward Programs Gift card sales now exceed $100 billion annually, and reward (also called loyalty) programs are growing. There are no exact rules for how retailers account for rewards. When **Best Buy** launched its "Reward Zone," shoppers earned $5 on each $125 spent and had 90 days to spend it. Retailers make assumptions about how many reward program dollars will be spent and how to report it. Best Buy sets up a liability and reduces revenue by the same amount. **Talbots** does not reduce revenue but instead increases selling expense. **Men's Wearhouse** records rewards in cost of goods sold, whereas **Neiman Marcus** subtracts them from revenue. The FASB continues to review reward programs. ■

Short-Term Notes Payable

A **short-term note payable** is a written promise to pay a specified amount on a definite future date within one year or the company's operating cycle, whichever is longer. These promissory notes are negotiable (as are checks), meaning they can be transferred from party to party by endorsement. The written documentation provided by notes is helpful in resolving disputes and for pursuing legal actions involving these liabilities. Most notes payable bear interest to compensate for use of the money until payment is made. Short-term notes payable can arise from many transactions. A company that purchases merchandise on credit can sometimes extend the credit period by signing a note to replace an account payable. Such notes also can arise when money is borrowed from a bank. We describe both of these cases.

P1 Prepare entries to account for short-term notes payable.

Point: Required characteristics for negotiability of a note: (1) unconditional promise, (2) in writing, (3) specific amount, and (4) definite due date.

---

[1] Sales taxes can be computed from total sales receipts when sales taxes are not separately identified on the register. To illustrate, assume a 5% sales tax and $420 in total sales receipts (which includes sales taxes). Sales are computed as follows:

$$\text{Sales} = \text{Total sales receipts}/(1 + \text{Sales tax percentage}) = \$420/1.05 = \$400$$

Thus, the sales tax amount equals total sales receipts minus sales, or $420 − $400 = $20. Sellers are required to act as "agents" for the government and collect sales tax. This extra work can be offset by the sellers' ability to use or invest that cash until it must be paid to the government.

Note Given to Extend Credit Period   A company can replace an account payable with a note payable. A common example is a creditor that requires the substitution of an interest-bearing note for an overdue account payable that does not bear interest. A less common situation occurs when a debtor's weak financial condition motivates the creditor to accept a note, sometimes for a lesser amount, and to close the account to ensure that this customer makes no additional credit purchases.

To illustrate, let's assume that on August 23, Brady Company asks to extend its past-due $600 account payable to McGraw. After some negotiations, McGraw agrees to accept $100 cash and a 60-day, 12%, $500 note payable to replace the account payable. Brady records the transaction with this entry:

Assets = Liabilities + Equity
−100   −600
          +500

Aug. 23	Accounts Payable—McGraw	600	
	Cash		100
	Notes Payable—McGraw		500
	Gave $100 cash and a 60-day, 12% note for		
	payment on account.		

Point: Accounts payable are detailed in a subsidiary ledger, but notes payable are sometimes not. A file with copies of notes can serve as a subsidiary ledger.

Signing the note does not resolve Brady's debt. Instead, the form of debt is changed from an account payable to a note payable. McGraw prefers the note payable over the account payable because it earns interest and it is written documentation of the debt's existence, term, and amount. When the note comes due, Brady pays the note and interest by giving McGraw a check for $510. Brady records that payment with this entry:

Assets = Liabilities + Equity
−510   −500   −10

Oct. 22	Notes Payable—McGraw	500	
	Interest Expense	10	
	Cash		510
	Paid note with interest ($500 × 12% × 60/360).		

Point: Commercial companies commonly compute interest using a 360-day year. This is known as the *banker's rule.*

Interest expense is computed by multiplying the principal of the note ($500) by the annual interest rate (12%) for the fraction of the year the note is outstanding (60 days/360 days).

Note Given to Borrow from Bank   A bank nearly always requires a borrower to sign a promissory note when making a loan. When the note matures, the borrower repays the note with an amount larger than the amount borrowed. The difference between the amount borrowed and the amount repaid is *interest*. This section considers a type of note whose signer promises to pay *principal* (the amount borrowed) plus interest. In this case, the *face value* of the note equals principal. Face value is the value shown on the face (front) of the note. To illustrate, assume that a company needs $2,000 for a project and borrows this money from a bank at 12% annual interest. The loan is made on September 30, 2013, and is due in 60 days. Specifically, the borrowing company signs a note with a face value equal to the amount borrowed. The note includes a statement similar to this: *"I promise to pay $2,000 plus interest at 12% within 60 days after September 30."* This simple note is shown in Exhibit 11.3.

Point: When money is borrowed from a bank, the loan is reported as an asset (receivable) on the bank's balance sheet.

EXHIBIT 11.3

Note with Face Value Equal to Amount Borrowed

Promissory Note

$2,000   *Sept. 30, 2013*
Face Value   **Date**

Sixty days after date, ___*I*___ promise to pay to the order of
National Bank
Boston, MA
Two thousand and no/100 ------------------------- **Dollars**

plus interest at the annual rate of _12%_.

_____
Janet Lee

The borrower records its receipt of cash and the new liability with this entry:

Sept. 30	Cash	2,000	
	Notes Payable		2,000
	Borrowed $2,000 cash with a 60-day, 12%, $2,000 note.		

Assets = Liabilities + Equity
+2,000   +2,000

When principal and interest are paid, the borrower records payment with this entry:

Nov. 29	Notes Payable	2,000	
	Interest Expense	40	
	Cash		2,040
	Paid note with interest ($2,000 × 12% × 60/360).		

Assets = Liabilities + Equity
−2,040   −2,000   −40

End-of-period interest adjustment.   When the end of an accounting period occurs between the signing of a note payable and its maturity date, the *expense recognition (matching) principle* requires us to record the accrued but unpaid interest on the note. To illustrate, let's return to the note in Exhibit 11.3, but assume that the company borrows $2,000 cash on December 16, 2013, instead of September 30. This 60-day note matures on February 14, 2014, and the company's fiscal year ends on December 31. Thus, we need to record interest expense for the final 15 days in December. This means that one-fourth (15 days/60 days) of the $40 total interest is an expense of year 2013. The borrower records this expense with the following adjusting entry:

2013 Dec. 31	Interest Expense	10	
	Interest Payable		10
	To record accrued interest on note ($2,000 × *12% × 15/360).*		

Assets = Liabilities + Equity
            +10   −10

When this note matures on February 14, the borrower must recognize 45 days of interest expense for year 2014 and remove the balances of the two liability accounts:

2014 Feb. 14	Interest Expense*	30	
	Interest Payable	10	
	Notes Payable	2,000	
	Cash		2,040
	Paid note with interest. *($2,000 × 12% × 45/360)		

Example: If this note is dated Dec. 1 instead of Dec. 16, how much expense is recorded on Dec. 31? *Answer:* $2,000 × 12% × 30/360 = $20

Assets = Liabilities + Equity
−2,040   −10   −30
                −2,000

■ **Decision** Insight ━━━━━━━━━━━━━━━━━━━━━━━━━━━━━━━

Many franchisors such as **Baskin-Robbins**, **Dunkin' Donuts**, and **Cold Stone Creamery**, use notes to help entrepreneurs acquire their own franchises, including using notes to pay for the franchise fee and any equipment. Payments on these notes are usually collected monthly and often are secured by the franchisees' assets. For example, a **McDonald's** franchise can cost from under $200,000 to over $2 million, depending on the type selected, see **FranchiseFoundations.com.** ■

Payroll Liabilities

An employer incurs several expenses and liabilities from having employees. These expenses and liabilities are often large and arise from salaries and wages earned, from employee benefits, and from payroll taxes levied on the employer. **Boston Beer**, for instance, reports payroll-related current liabilities of more than $9.6 million from accrued "employee wages, benefits and reimbursements." We discuss payroll liabilities and related accounts in this section. Appendix 11A describes details about payroll reports, records, and procedures.

Employee Payroll Deductions   **Gross pay** is the total compensation an employee earns including wages, salaries, commissions, bonuses, and any compensation earned before deductions

P2 Compute and record *employee* payroll deductions and liabilities.

Point: Deductions at some companies, such as those for insurance coverage, are "required" under its own labor contracts.

such as taxes. (*Wages* usually refer to payments to employees at an hourly rate. *Salaries* usually refer to payments to employees at a monthly or yearly rate.) **Net pay,** also called *take-home pay,* is gross pay less all deductions. **Payroll deductions,** commonly called *withholdings,* are amounts withheld from an employee's gross pay, either required or voluntary. Required deductions result from laws and include income taxes and Social Security taxes. Voluntary deductions, at an employee's option, include pension and health contributions, health and life insurance premiums, union dues, and charitable giving. Exhibit 11.4 shows the typical payroll deductions of an employee. The employer withholds payroll deductions from employees' pay and is obligated to transmit this money to the designated organization. The employer records payroll deductions as current liabilities until these amounts are transmitted. This section discusses the major payroll deductions.

EXHIBIT 11.4

Payroll Deductions

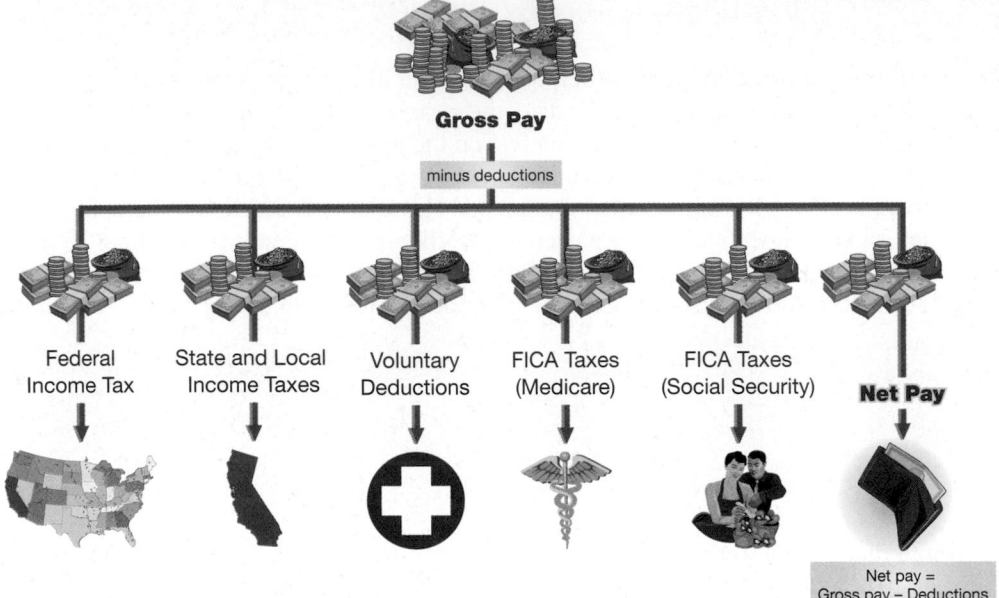

Gross Pay

minus deductions

| Federal Income Tax | State and Local Income Taxes | Voluntary Deductions | FICA Taxes (Medicare) | FICA Taxes (Social Security) | **Net Pay** |

Net pay = Gross pay − Deductions

Employee FICA taxes.   The federal Social Security system provides retirement, disability, survivorship, and medical benefits to qualified workers. Laws *require* employers to withhold **Federal Insurance Contributions Act (FICA) taxes** from employees' pay to cover costs of the system. Employers usually separate FICA taxes into two groups: (1) retirement, disability, and survivorship and (2) medical. For the first group, the Social Security system provides monthly cash payments to qualified retired workers for the rest of their lives. These payments are often called *Social Security benefits.* Taxes related to this group are often called *Social Security taxes.* For the second group, the system provides monthly payments to deceased workers' surviving families and to disabled workers who qualify for assistance. These payments are commonly called *Medicare benefits;* like those in the first group, they are paid with *Medicare taxes* (part of FICA taxes).

Law requires employers to withhold FICA taxes from each employee's salary or wages on each payday. The taxes for Social Security and Medicare are computed separately. For example, for 2012, the amount scheduled to be withheld from each employee's pay for Social Security tax is 6.2% of the first $110,100 the employee earns in the calendar year, or a maximum of $6,826.20. The Medicare tax is 1.45% of *all* amounts the employee earns; there is no maximum limit to Medicare tax. (Politicians could pass a 2013 or 2014 adjustment; for example, politicians reduced the 2012 *employee* share from 6.2% to 4.2%.)

Point: The sources of U.S. tax receipts are roughly as follows:

50%	Personal income tax
35	FICA and FUTA taxes
10	Corporate income tax
5	Other taxes

Employers must pay withheld taxes to the Internal Revenue Service (IRS) on specific filing dates during the year. Employers who fail to send the withheld taxes to the IRS on time can be assessed substantial penalties. Until all the taxes are sent to the IRS, they are included in employers' current liabilities. For any changes in rates or with the maximum earnings level, check the IRS Website at **www.IRS.gov** or the SSA Website at **www.SSA.gov**.

Point: Part-time employees may claim "exempt from withholding" if they did not have any income tax liability in the prior year and do not expect any in the current year.

Employee income tax.   Most employers are required to withhold federal income tax from each employee's paycheck. The amount withheld is computed using tables published by the IRS. The amount depends on the employee's annual earnings rate and the number of *withholding* *allowances* the employee claims. Allowances reduce the amount of taxes one owes the government. The more allowances one claims, the less tax the employer will withhold. Employees can claim allowances for themselves and their dependents. They also can claim additional allowances if they expect major declines in their taxable income for medical expenses. (An employee who claims more allowances than appropriate is subject to a fine.) Most states and many local governments require employers to withhold income taxes from employees' pay and to remit them promptly to the proper government agency. Until they are paid, withholdings are reported as a current liability on the employer's balance sheet.

Point: IRS withholding tables are based on projecting weekly (or other period) pay into an annual figure.

Point: Is there a maximum to the withholding allowances one can claim? Recall, the more allowances, the lower the withholding. However, an employee that claims, say, over 10 allowances on the W-4 is likely to receive an IRS inquiry asking to justify the number of allowances.

Employee voluntary deductions. Beyond Social Security, Medicare, and income taxes, employers often withhold other amounts from employees' earnings. These withholdings arise from employee requests, contracts, unions, or other agreements. They can include amounts for charitable giving, medical and life insurance premiums, pension contributions, and union dues. Until they are paid, such withholdings are reported as part of employers' current liabilities.

Recording employee payroll deductions. Employers must accrue payroll expenses and liabilities at the end of each pay period. To illustrate, assume that an employee earns a salary of $2,000 per month. At the end of January, the employer's entry to accrue payroll expenses and liabilities for this employee is

Jan. 31	Salaries Expense	2,000	
	FICA—Social Security Taxes Payable (6.2%)		124
	FICA—Medicare Taxes Payable (1.45%)		29
	Employee Federal Income Taxes Payable*		213
	Employee Medical Insurance Payable*		85
	Employee Union Dues Payable*		25
	Salaries Payable		1,524
	To record accrued payroll for January.		

Assets	=	Liabilities	+	Equity
		+124		−2,000
		+29		
		+213		
		+85		
		+25		
		+1,524		

* Amounts taken from employer's accounting records.

Salaries Expense (debit) shows that the employee earns a gross salary of $2,000. The first five payables (credits) show the liabilities the employer owes on behalf of this employee to cover FICA taxes, income taxes, medical insurance, and union dues. The Salaries Payable account (credit) records the $1,524 net pay the employee receives from the $2,000 gross pay earned. When the employee is paid, another entry (or a series of entries) is required to record the check written and distributed (or funds transferred). The entry to record cash payment to this employee is to debit Salaries Payable and credit Cash for $1,524.

Salaries Payable	1,524	
Cash		1,524

■ Decision Insight ◄

Pay or Else "Failure to pay employment taxes is stealing from the employees of the business," said IRS Commissioner Mark W. Everson. "The IRS pursues business owners who don't follow the law, and those who embrace these schemes face civil or criminal sanctions." There are many reasons employers do not withhold or pay employment taxes. For some, they attempt to use the government as a "bank to borrow money for a short time," some others collect the taxes and keep it, and still others object to U.S. tax laws. Regardless, federal law requires employment tax withholding and payment by employers. (IRS.gov/newsroom).

Employer Payroll Taxes Employers must pay payroll taxes in addition to those required of employees. Employer taxes include FICA and unemployment taxes.

P3 Compute and record *employer* payroll expenses and liabilities.

Employer FICA tax. Employers must pay FICA taxes on their payroll to employees. For 2012, the employer must pay Social Security tax of 6.2% on the first $110,100 earned by each employee, and 1.45% Medicare tax on all earnings of each employee. An employer's tax is credited to the same FICA Taxes Payable accounts used to record the Social Security and Medicare taxes withheld from employees. (A self-employed person must pay both the employee and employer FICA taxes.)

Federal and state unemployment taxes. The federal government participates with states in a joint federal and state unemployment insurance program. Each state administers its program. These programs provide unemployment benefits to qualified workers. The federal government approves state programs and pays a portion of their administrative expenses.

Federal Unemployment Taxes (FUTA). Employers are subject to a federal unemployment tax on wages and salaries paid to their employees. For the year 2012, employers were required to pay FUTA taxes of as much as 6.2% of the first $7,000 earned by each employee. This federal tax can be reduced by a credit of up to 5.4% for taxes paid to a state program. As a result, the net federal unemployment tax is often only 0.8%.

State Unemployment Taxes (SUTA). All states support their unemployment insurance programs by placing a payroll tax on employers. (A few states require employees to make a contribution. In the book's assignments, we assume that this tax is only on the employer.) In most states, the base rate for SUTA taxes is 5.4% of the first $7,000 paid each employee. This base rate is adjusted according to an employer's merit rating. The state assigns a **merit rating** that reflects a company's stability or instability in employing workers. A good rating reflects stability in employment and means an employer can pay less than the 5.4% base rate. A low rating reflects high turnover or seasonal hirings and layoffs. To illustrate, an employer with 50 employees each of whom earns $7,000 or more per year saves $15,400 annually if it has a merit rating of 1.0% versus 5.4%. This is computed by comparing taxes of $18,900 at the 5.4% rate to only $3,500 at the 1.0% rate.

Recording employer payroll taxes. Employer payroll taxes are an added expense beyond the wages and salaries earned by employees. These taxes are often recorded in an entry separate from the one recording payroll expenses and deductions. To illustrate, assume that the $2,000 recorded salaries expense from the previous example is earned by an employee whose earnings have not yet reached $5,000 for the year. This means the entire salaries expense for this period is subject to tax because year-to-date pay is under $7,000. Also assume that the federal unemployment tax rate is 0.8% and the state unemployment tax rate is 5.4%. Consequently, the FICA portion of the employer's tax is $153, computed by multiplying both the 6.2% and 1.45% by the $2,000 gross pay. Moreover, state unemployment (SUTA) taxes are $108 (5.4% of the $2,000 gross pay), and federal unemployment (FUTA) taxes are $16 (0.8% of $2,000). The entry to record the employer's payroll tax expense and related liabilities is

Example: If the employer's merit rating in this example reduces its SUTA rate to 2.9%, what is its SUTA liability? *Answer:* SUTA payable = $2,000 × 2.9% = $58

Assets = Liabilities + Equity
　　　　+124　　　−277
　　　　+29
　　　　+108
　　　　+16

Jan. 31	Payroll Taxes Expense	277	
	FICA—Social Security Taxes Payable (6.2%)		124
	FICA—Medicare Taxes Payable (1.45%)		29
	State Unemployment Taxes Payable		108
	Federal Unemployment Taxes Payable		16
	To record employer payroll taxes.		

Point: Internal control is important for payroll accounting. Managers must monitor (1) employee hiring, (2) time-keeping, (3) payroll listings, and (4) payroll payments. Poor controls led the U.S. Army to pay nearly $10 million to deserters, fictitious soldiers, and other unauthorized entities.

■ Decision Ethics

Web Designer You take a summer job working for a family friend who runs a small IT service. On your first payday, the owner slaps you on the back, gives you full payment in cash, winks, and adds: "No need to pay those high taxes, eh." What action, if any, do you take? ■ [Answer—p. 462]

Multi-Period Known Liabilities

Point: If *Sports Illustrated* offers you a sweatshirt of your favorite team if you subscribe, it must account for the sweatshirts using a *promotions liability account*.

Many known liabilities extend over multiple periods. These often include unearned revenues and notes payable. For example, if **Sports Illustrated** sells a four-year magazine subscription, it records amounts received for this subscription in an Unearned Subscription Revenues account. Amounts in this account are liabilities, but are they current or long term? They are *both.* The portion of the Unearned Subscription Revenues account that will be fulfilled in the next year is reported as a current liability. The remaining portion is reported as a long-term liability.

　　The same analysis applies to notes payable. For example, a borrower reports a three-year note payable as a long-term liability in the first two years it is outstanding. In the third year, the borrower reclassifies this note as a current liability since it is due within one year or the operating cycle, whichever is longer. The **current portion of long-term debt** refers to that part of long-term debt due within one year or the operating cycle, whichever is longer. Long-term debt is reported under long-term liabilities, but the *current portion due* is reported under current liabilities. To illustrate, assume that a $7,500 debt is paid in installments of $1,500 per year for five years. The $1,500 due within the year is reported as a current liability. No journal entry is necessary for this reclassification. Instead, we simply classify the amounts for debt as either current or long term when the balance sheet is prepared.

Some known liabilities are rarely reported in long-term liabilities. These include accounts payable, sales taxes, and wages and salaries.

> **Point:** Some accounting systems do make an entry to transfer the current amount due out of Long-Term Debt and into the Current Portion of Long-Term Debt as follows:
>
> Long-Term Debt 1,500
>   Current Portion of L-T Debt . . . 1,500

Decision Insight

Liability Limits   Probably the greatest number of frauds involve payroll. Companies must safeguard payroll activities. Controls include proper approvals and processes for employee additions, deletions, and pay rate changes. A common fraud is a manager adding a fictitious employee to the payroll and then cashing the fictitious employee's check. A study reports that 28% of employees in operations and service areas witnessed violations of employee wage, overtime, or benefit rules in the past year (KPMG 2009). Another 21% observed falsifying of time and expense reports. ■

> *Ceridian Connection* (Oct. 2010) reports:
> **8.5%** of workplace fraud is tied to payroll.
> **$72,000** is median loss per payroll fraud.
> **24 months** is median time to uncover payroll fraud.

Quick Check   Answers — p. 463 ☑

4. Why does a creditor prefer a note payable to a past-due account payable?

5. A company pays its one employee $3,000 per month. This company's FUTA rate is 0.8% on the first $7,000 earned; its SUTA rate is 4.0% on the first $7,000; its Social Security tax rate is 6.2% of the first $110,100; and its Medicare tax rate is 1.45% of all amounts earned. The entry to record this company's March payroll includes what amount for total payroll taxes expense?

6. Identify whether the employer or employee or both incurs each of the following: (*a*) FICA taxes, (*b*) FUTA taxes, (*c*) SUTA taxes, and (*d*) withheld income taxes.

ESTIMATED LIABILITIES

An **estimated liability** is a known obligation that is of an uncertain amount but that can be reasonably estimated. Common examples are employee benefits such as pensions, health care and vacation pay, and warranties offered by a seller. We discuss each of these in this section. Other examples of estimated liabilities include property taxes and certain contracts to provide future services.

> **P4** Account for estimated liabilities, including warranties and bonuses.

Health and Pension Benefits

Many companies provide **employee benefits** beyond salaries and wages. An employer often pays all or part of medical, dental, life, and disability insurance. Many employers also contribute to *pension plans,* which are agreements by employers to provide benefits (payments) to employees after retirement. Many companies also provide medical care and insurance benefits to their retirees. When payroll taxes and charges for employee benefits are totaled, payroll cost often exceeds employees' gross earnings by 25% or more.

To illustrate, assume that an employer agrees to (1) pay an amount for medical insurance equal to $8,000 and (2) contribute an additional 10% of the employees' $120,000 gross salary to a retirement program. The entry to record these accrued benefits is

Dec. 31	Employee Benefits Expense	20,000	
	Employee Medical Insurance Payable		8,000
	Employee Retirement Program Payable		12,000
	To record costs of employee benefits.		

Assets = Liabilities + Equity
        +8,000   −20,000
        +12,000

Decision Insight

Postgame Spoils Baseball was the first pro sport to set up a pension, originally up to $100 per month depending on years played. Many former players now take home six-figure pensions. Cal Ripken Jr.'s pension when he reaches 62 is estimated at $160,000 per year (he played 21 seasons). The requirement is only 43 games for a full pension and just one game for full medical benefits. ■

Vacation Benefits

Many employers offer paid vacation benefits, also called *paid absences* or *compensated absences.* To illustrate, assume that salaried employees earn 2 weeks' vacation per year. This benefit increases employers' payroll expenses because employees are paid for 52 weeks but work for only 50 weeks. Total annual salary is the same, but the cost per week worked is greater than the amount paid per week. For example, if an employee is paid $20,800 for 52 weeks but works only 50 weeks, the total weekly expense to the employer is $416 ($20,800/50 weeks) instead of the $400 cash paid weekly to the employee ($20,800/52 weeks). The $16 difference between these two amounts is recorded weekly as follows:

Assets = Liabilities + Equity
          +16   −16

Vacation Benefits Expense	16	
Vacation Benefits Payable		16
To record vacation benefits accrued.		

Vacation Benefits Payable . . . . #
   Cash . . . . #

Vacation Benefits Expense is an operating expense, and Vacation Benefits Payable is a current liability. When the employee takes a vacation, the employer reduces (debits) the Vacation Benefits Payable and credits Cash (no additional expense is recorded).

Bonus Plans

Many companies offer bonuses to employees, and many of the bonuses depend on net income. To illustrate, assume that an employer offers a bonus to its employees equal to 5% of the company's annual pre-bonus net income (to be equally shared by all). The company's expected annual pre-bonus net income is $210,000. The year-end adjusting entry to record this benefit is

Assets = Liabilities + Equity
         +10,000   −10,000

Dec. 31	Employee Bonus Expense*	10,000	
	Bonus Payable		10,000
	To record expected bonus costs.		

* Bonus Expense (B) equals 5% of pre-bonus net income, which equals $210,000 minus the bonus; this is computed as:

$$B = 0.05 (\$210{,}000 - B)$$
$$B = \$10{,}500 - 0.05B$$
$$1.05B = \$10{,}500$$
$$\mathbf{B = \$10{,}500/1.05 = \$10{,}000}$$

When the bonus is paid, Bonus Payable is debited and Cash is credited for $10,000.

Warranty Liabilities

Point: Kodak recently reported $46 million in warranty obligations.

A **warranty** is a seller's obligation to replace or correct a product (or service) that fails to perform as expected within a specified period. Most new cars, for instance, are sold with a warranty covering parts for a specified period of time. **Ford Motor Company** reported almost $7 billion in "dealer and customer allowances and claims" in its annual report. To comply with the *full disclosure* and *matching principles,* the seller reports the expected warranty expense in the period when revenue from the sale of the product or service is reported. The seller reports this warranty obligation as a liability, although the existence, amount, payee, and date of future sacrifices are uncertain. This is because such warranty costs are probable and the amount can be estimated using, for instance, past experience with warranties.

To illustrate, a dealer sells a used car for $16,000 on December 1, 2013, with a maximum one-year or 12,000-mile warranty covering parts. This dealer's experience shows that warranty

expense averages about 4% of a car's selling price, or $640 in this case ($16,000 × 4%). The
dealer records the estimated expense and liability related to this sale with this entry:

2013			
Dec. 1	Warranty Expense	640	
	Estimated Warranty Liability		640
	To record estimated warranty expense.		

Assets = Liabilities + Equity
+640   −640

This entry alternatively could be made as part of end-of-period adjustments. Either way, the
estimated warranty expense is reported on the 2013 income statement and the warranty
liability on the 2013 balance sheet. To further extend this example, suppose the customer
returns the car for warranty repairs on January 9, 2014. The dealer performs this work by
replacing parts costing $200. The entry to record partial settlement of the estimated warranty
liability is

Point: Recognition of warranty liabilities is necessary to comply with the matching and full disclosure principles.

2014			
Jan. 9	Estimated Warranty Liability	200	
	Auto Parts Inventory		200
	To record costs of warranty repairs.		

Assets = Liabilities + Equity
−200   −200

This entry reduces the balance of the estimated warranty liability. Warranty expense was previously recorded in 2013, the year the car was sold with the warranty. Finally, what happens
if total warranty expenses are more or less than the estimated 4%, or $640? The answer is that
management should monitor actual warranty expenses to see whether the 4% rate is accurate.
If experience reveals a large difference from the estimate, the rate for current and future sales
should be changed. Differences are expected, but they should be small.

Point: Both U.S. GAAP and IFRS account for restructuring costs in a manner similar to accounting for warranties.

Decision Insight

Guaranteed Profits   When we purchase a new
laptop at **Best Buy**, a sales clerk commonly asks:
Want the Black Tie Protection Plan?" Best Buy
earns about a 60% profit margin on such warranty
contracts, and those contracts are a large part of its
profit—see table to the side [*BusinessWeek*]. ■

Warranty contracts as a percentage of sales	4%
Warranty contracts as a percentage	
of operating profit	45%
Profit margin on warranty contracts	60%

Multi-Period Estimated Liabilities

Estimated liabilities can be both current and long term. For example, pension liabilities to employees are long term to workers who will not retire within the next period. For employees who
are retired or will retire within the next period, a portion of pension liabilities is current. Other
examples include employee health benefits and warranties. Specifically, many warranties are for
30 or 60 days in length. Estimated costs under these warranties are properly reported in current
liabilities. Many other automobile warranties are for three years or 36,000 miles. A portion of
these warranties is reported as long term.

Quick Check   Answers — p. 463

7. Estimated liabilities involve an obligation to pay which of these? (*a*) An uncertain but
   reasonably estimated amount owed on a known obligation or (*b*) A known amount to a
   specific entity on an uncertain due date.

8. A car is sold for $15,000 on June 1, 2013, with a one-year warranty on parts. Warranty
   expense is estimated at 1.5% of selling price at each calendar year-end. On March 1, 2014,
   the car is returned for warranty repairs costing $135. The amount recorded as warranty
   expense on March 1 is (*a*) $0; (*b*) $60; (*c*) $75; (*d*) $135; (*e*) $225.

CONTINGENT LIABILITIES

C3 Explain how to account for contingent liabilities.

A **contingent liability** is a potential obligation that depends on a future event arising from a past transaction or event. An example is a pending lawsuit. Here, a past transaction or event leads to a lawsuit whose result depends on the outcome of the suit. Future payment of a contingent liability depends on whether an uncertain future event occurs.

Accounting for Contingent Liabilities

Accounting for contingent liabilities depends on the likelihood that a future event will occur and the ability to estimate the future amount owed if this event occurs. Three different possibilities are identified in the following chart: record liability, disclose in notes, or no disclosure.

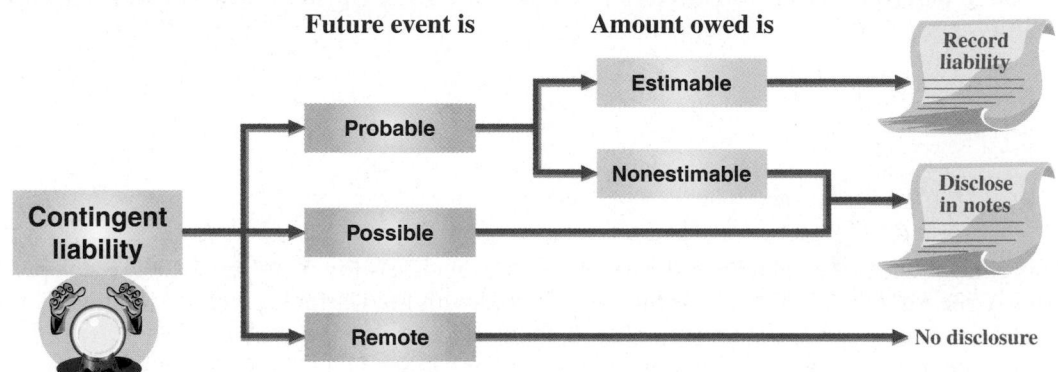

The conditions that determine each of these three possibilities follow:

1. The future event is *probable* (likely) and the amount owed can be *reasonably estimated*. We then record this amount as a liability. Examples are the estimated liabilities described earlier such as warranties, vacation pay, and income taxes.
2. The future event is *reasonably possible* (could occur). We disclose information about this type of contingent liability in notes to the financial statements.
3. The future event is *remote* (unlikely). We do not record or disclose information on remote contingent liabilities.

Point: A contingency is an *if*. Namely, if a future event occurs, then financial consequences are likely for the entity.

Reasonably Possible Contingent Liabilities

This section identifies and discusses contingent liabilities that commonly fall in the second category—when the future event is reasonably possible. Disclosing information about contingencies in this category is motivated by the *full-disclosure principle,* which requires information relevant to decision makers be reported and not ignored.

Point: A sale of a note receivable is often a contingent liability. It becomes a liability if the original signer of the note fails to pay it at maturity.

Potential Legal Claims   Many companies are sued or at risk of being sued. The accounting issue is whether the defendant should recognize a liability on its balance sheet or disclose a contingent liability in its notes while a lawsuit is outstanding and not yet settled. The answer is that a potential claim is recorded in the accounts *only* if payment for damages is probable and the amount can be reasonably estimated. If the potential claim cannot be reasonably estimated or is less than probable but reasonably possible, it is disclosed. **Ford Motor Company**, for example, includes the following note in its annual report: "Various legal actions, governmental investigations and proceedings and claims are pending . . . arising out of alleged defects in our products."

Debt Guarantees   Sometimes a company guarantees the payment of debt owed by a supplier, customer, or another company. The guarantor usually discloses the guarantee in its financial statement notes as a contingent liability. If it is probable that the debtor will default, the guarantor needs to record and report the guarantee in its financial statements as a liability. The **Boston Celtics** report a unique guarantee when it comes to coaches and players: "Certain of the contracts provide for guaranteed payments which must be paid even if the employee [player] is injured or terminated."

Other Contingencies Other examples of contingencies include environmental damages, possible tax assessments, insurance losses, and government investigations. **Sunoco**, for instance, reports that "federal, state and local laws . . . result in liabilities and loss contingencies. Sunoco accrues . . . cleanup costs [that] are probable and reasonably estimable. Management believes it is reasonably possible (i.e., less than probable but greater than remote) that additional . . . losses will be incurred." Many of Sunoco's contingencies are revealed only in notes.

Decision Insight

Pricing Priceless What's it worth to see from one side of the Grand Canyon to the other? What's the cost when gulf coast beaches are closed due to an oil well disaster? A method to measure environmental liabilities is *contingent valuation*, by which people answer such questions. Regulators use their answers to levy fines and assess punitive damages. ■

Uncertainties that Are Not Contingencies

All organizations face uncertainties from future events such as natural disasters and the development of new competing products or services. These uncertainties are not contingent liabilities because they are future events *not* arising from past transactions. Accordingly, they are not disclosed.

Quick Check
Answers — p. 463

9. A future payment is reported as a liability on the balance sheet if payment is contingent on a future event that (*a*) is reasonably possible but the payment cannot be reasonably estimated; (*b*) is probable and the payment can be reasonably estimated; or (*c*) is not probable but the payment is known.

10. Under what circumstances is a future payment reported in the notes to the financial statements as a contingent liability?

GLOBAL VIEW

This section discusses similarities and differences between U.S. GAAP and IFRS in accounting and reporting for current liabilities.

Characteristics of Liabilities The definitions and characteristics of current liabilities are broadly similar for both U.S. GAAP and IFRS. Although differences exist, the similarities vastly outweigh any differences. Remembering that "provision" is typically used under IFRS to refer to what is titled "liability" under U.S. GAAP, **Nokia** describes its recognition of liabilities as follows:

> Provisions are recognized when the Group has a present legal or constructive obligation as a result of past events, it is probable that an outflow of resources will be required to settle the obligation and a reliable estimate of the amount can be made.

NOKIA

Known (Determinable) Liabilities When there is little uncertainty surrounding current liabilities, both U.S. GAAP and IFRS require companies to record them in a similar manner. This correspondence in accounting applies to accounts payable, sales taxes payable, unearned revenues, short-term notes, and payroll liabilities. Of course, tax regulatory systems of countries are different, which implies use of different rates and levels. Still, the basic approach is the same.

Estimated Liabilities   When there is a known current obligation that involves an uncertain amount, but one that can be reasonably estimated, both U.S. GAAP and IFRS require similar treatment. This treatment extends to many obligations such as those arising from vacations, warranties, restructurings, pensions, and health care. Both accounting systems require that companies record estimated expenses related to these obligations when they can reasonably estimate the amounts. **Nokia** reports wages, salaries and bonuses of €6,284 million. It also reports pension expenses of €445 million.

 Decision Analysis   Times Interest Earned Ratio

| A1 | Compute the times interest earned ratio and use it to analyze liabilities. |

A company incurs interest expense on many of its current and long-term liabilities. Examples extend from its short-term notes and the current portion of long-term liabilities to its long-term notes and bonds. Interest expense is often viewed as a *fixed expense* because the amount of these liabilities is likely to remain in one form or another for a substantial period of time. This means that the amount of interest is unlikely to vary due to changes in sales or other operating activities. While fixed expenses can be advantageous when a company is growing, they create risk. This risk stems from the possibility that a company might be unable to pay fixed expenses if sales decline. To illustrate, consider Diego Co.'s results for 2013 and two possible outcomes for year 2014 in Exhibit 11.5.

EXHIBIT 11.5

Actual and Projected Results

| ($ thousands) | 2013 | 2014 Projections | |
		Sales Increase	Sales Decrease
Sales	$600	$900	$300
Expenses (75% of sales)	450	675	225
Income before interest	150	225	75
Interest expense (fixed)	60	60	60
Net income	$ 90	$165	$ 15

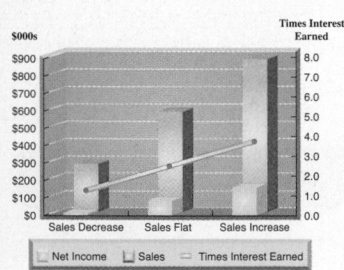

Expenses excluding interest are at, and expected to remain at, 75% of sales. Expenses such as these that change with sales volume are called *variable expenses*. However, interest expense is at, and expected to remain at, $60,000 per year due to its fixed nature.

The middle numerical column of Exhibit 11.5 shows that Diego's income increases by 83% to $165,000 if sales increase by 50% to $900,000. In contrast, the far right column shows that income decreases by 83% if sales decline by 50%. These results reveal that the amount of fixed interest expense affects a company's risk of its ability to pay interest, which is numerically reflected in the **times interest earned** ratio in Exhibit 11.6.

EXHIBIT 11.6

Times Interest Earned

$$\text{Times interest earned} = \frac{\text{Income before interest expense and income taxes}}{\text{Interest expense}}$$

For 2013, Diego's times interest earned is computed as $150,000/$60,000, or 2.5 times. This ratio suggests that Diego faces low to moderate risk because its sales must decline sharply before it would be unable to cover its interest expenses. (Diego is an LLC and does not pay income taxes.)

Experience shows that when times interest earned falls below 1.5 to 2.0 and remains at that level or lower for several periods, the default rate on liabilities increases sharply. This reflects increased risk for companies and their creditors. We also must interpret the times interest earned ratio in light of information about the variability of a company's income before interest. If income is stable from year to year or if it is growing, the company can afford to take on added risk by borrowing. If its income greatly varies from year to year, fixed interest expense can increase the risk that it will not earn enough income to pay interest.

Decision Maker

DEMONSTRATION PROBLEM

The following transactions and events took place at Kern Company during its recent calendar-year reporting period (Kern does not use reversing entries).

a. In September 2013, Kern sold $140,000 of merchandise covered by a 180-day warranty. Prior experience shows that costs of the warranty equal 5% of sales. Compute September's warranty expense and prepare the adjusting journal entry for the warranty liability as recorded at September 30. Also prepare the journal entry on October 8 to record a $300 cash expenditure to provide warranty service on an item sold in September.

b. On October 12, 2013, Kern arranged with a supplier to replace Kern's overdue $10,000 account payable by paying $2,500 cash and signing a note for the remainder. The note matures in 90 days and has a 12% interest rate. Prepare the entries recorded on October 12, December 31, and January 10, 2014, related to this transaction.

c. In late December, Kern learns it is facing a product liability suit filed by an unhappy customer. Kern's lawyer advises that although it will probably suffer a loss from the lawsuit, it is not possible to estimate the amount of damages at this time.

d. Sally Bline works for Kern. For the pay period ended November 30, her gross earnings are $3,000. Bline has $800 deducted for federal income taxes and $200 for state income taxes from each paycheck. Additionally, a $35 premium for her health care insurance and a $10 donation for the United Way are deducted. Bline pays FICA Social Security taxes at a rate of 6.2% and FICA Medicare taxes at a rate of 1.45%. She has not earned enough this year to be exempt from any FICA taxes. Journalize the accrual of salaries expense of Bline's wages by Kern.

e. On November 1, Kern borrows $5,000 cash from a bank in return for a 60-day, 12%, $5,000 note. Record the note's issuance on November 1 and its repayment with interest on December 31.

f.[B] Kern has estimated and recorded its quarterly income tax payments. In reviewing its year-end tax adjustments, it identifies an additional $5,000 of income tax expense that should be recorded. A portion of this additional expense, $1,000, is deferrable to future years. Record this year-end income taxes expense adjusting entry.

g. For this calendar-year, Kern's net income is $1,000,000, its interest expense is $275,000, and its income taxes expense is $225,000. Calculate Kern's times interest earned ratio.

PLANNING THE SOLUTION

● For *a,* compute the warranty expense for September and record it with an estimated liability. Record the October expenditure as a decrease in the liability.

● For *b,* eliminate the liability for the account payable and create the liability for the note payable. Compute interest expense for the 80 days that the note is outstanding in 2013 and record it as an additional liability. Record the payment of the note, being sure to include the interest for the 10 days in 2014.

● For *c,* decide whether the company's contingent liability needs to be disclosed or accrued (recorded) according to the two necessary criteria: probable loss and reasonably estimable.

● For *d,* set up payable accounts for all items in Bline's paycheck that require deductions. After deducting all necessary items, credit the remaining amount to Salaries Payable.

● For *e,* record the issuance of the note. Calculate 60 days' interest due using the 360-day convention in the interest formula.

● For *f,* determine how much of the income taxes expense is payable in the current year and how much needs to be deferred.

● For *g,* apply and compute times interest earned.

SOLUTION TO DEMONSTRATION PROBLEM

a. Warranty expense = 5% × $140,000 = $7,000

Sept. 30	Warranty Expense	7,000	
	Estimated Warranty Liability		7,000
	To record warranty expense for the month.		
Oct. 8	Estimated Warranty Liability	300	
	Cash		300
	To record the cost of the warranty service.		

b. Interest expense for 2013 = 12% × $7,500 × 80/360 = $200
Interest expense for 2014 = 12% × $7,500 × 10/360 = $25

Oct. 12	Accounts Payable	10,000	
	Notes Payable		7,500
	Cash		2,500
	Paid $2,500 cash and gave a 90-day, 12% note to extend the due date on the account.		
Dec. 31	Interest Expense	200	
	Interest Payable		200
	To accrue interest on note payable.		
Jan. 10	Interest Expense	25	
	Interest Payable	200	
	Notes Payable	7,500	
	Cash		7,725
	Paid note with interest, including the accrued interest payable.		

c. Disclose the pending lawsuit in the financial statement notes. Although the loss is probable, no liability can be accrued since the loss cannot be reasonably estimated.

d.

Nov. 30	Salaries Expense	3,000.00	
	FICA—Social Security Taxes Payable (6.2%)		186.00
	FICA—Medicare Taxes Payable (1.45%)		43.50
	Employee Federal Income Taxes Payable		800.00
	Employee State Income Taxes Payable		200.00
	Employee Medical Insurance Payable		35.00
	Employee United Way Payable		10.00
	Salaries Payable		1,725.50
	To record Bline's accrued payroll.		

e.

Nov. 1	Cash	5,000	
	Notes Payable		5,000
	Borrowed cash with a 60-day, 12% note.		

When the note and interest are paid 60 days later, Kern Company records this entry:

Dec. 31	Notes Payable	5,000	
	Interest Expense	100	
	Cash		5,100
	Paid note with interest ($5,000 × 12% × 60/360).		

f.

Dec. 31	Income Taxes Expense	5,000	
	Income Taxes Payable		4,000
	Deferred Income Tax Liability		1,000
	To record added income taxes expense and the		
	deferred tax liability.		

g. Times interest earned $= \dfrac{\$1{,}000{,}000 + \$275{,}000 + \$225{,}000}{\$275{,}000} = \underline{\underline{5.45 \text{ times}}}$

APPENDIX

Payroll Reports, Records, and Procedures

11A

Understanding payroll procedures and keeping adequate payroll reports and records are essential to a company's success. This appendix focuses on payroll accounting and its reports, records, and procedures.

Payroll Reports   Most employees and employers are required to pay local, state, and federal payroll taxes. Payroll expenses involve liabilities to individual employees, to federal and state governments, and to other organizations such as insurance companies. Beyond paying these liabilities, employers are required to prepare and submit reports explaining how they computed these payments.

P5 Identify and describe the details of payroll reports, records, and procedures.

Reporting FICA Taxes and Income Taxes   The Federal Insurance Contributions Act (FICA) requires each employer to file an Internal Revenue Service (IRS) **Form 941,** the *Employer's Quarterly Federal Tax Return,* within one month after the end of each calendar quarter. A sample Form 941 is shown in Exhibit 11A.1 for Phoenix Sales & Service, a landscape design company. Accounting information and software are helpful in tracking payroll transactions and reporting the accumulated information on Form 941. Specifically, the employer reports total wages subject to income tax withholding on line 2 of Form 941. (For simplicity, this appendix uses *wages* to refer to both wages and salaries.) The income tax withheld is reported on line 3. The combined amount of employee and employer FICA (Social Security) taxes for Phoenix Sales & Service is reported on line 5a (taxable Social Security wages, $36,599 × 12.4% = $4,538.28). The 12.4% is the sum of the Social Security tax withheld, computed as 6.2% tax withheld from the employee wages for the quarter plus the 6.2% tax levied on the employer. The combined amount of employee Medicare wages is reported on line 5c. The 2.9% is the sum of 1.45% withheld from employee wages for the quarter plus 1.45% tax levied on the employer. Total FICA taxes are reported on line 5d and are added to the total income taxes withheld of $3,056.47 to yield a total of $8,656.12. For this year, assume that income up to $110,100 is subject to Social Security tax. There is no income limit on amounts subject to Medicare tax. Congress sets annual limits on the amount owed for Social Security tax.

Federal depository banks are authorized to accept deposits of amounts payable to the federal government. Deposit requirements depend on the amount of tax owed. For example, when the sum of FICA taxes plus the employee income taxes is less than $2,500 for a quarter, the taxes can be paid when Form 941 is filed. Companies with large payrolls are often required to pay monthly or even semiweekly.

Reporting FUTA Taxes and SUTA Taxes   An employer's federal unemployment taxes (FUTA) are reported on an annual basis by filing an *Annual Federal Unemployment Tax Return,* IRS **Form 940.** It must be mailed on or before January 31 following the end of each tax year. Ten more days are allowed if all required tax deposits are filed on a timely basis and the full amount of tax is paid on or before January 31. FUTA payments are made quarterly to a federal depository bank if the total amount due exceeds $500. If $500 or less is due, the taxes are remitted annually. Requirements for paying and reporting state unemployment taxes (SUTA) vary depending on the laws of each state. Most states require quarterly payments and reports.

Point: Line 5a shows the matching nature of the FICA tax as 6.2% × 2, or 12.4%; which is shown as 0.124.

Point: Auditors rely on the four 941 forms filed during a year when auditing a company's annual wage and salaries expense account.

Form **941**

Employer's QUARTERLY Federal Tax Return

Department of the Treasury — Internal Revenue Service

(EIN) Employer identification number: 8 6 – 3 2 1 4 5 8 7

Name (not your trade name): *Phoenix Sales & Service*

Trade name (if any):

Address: *1214* Number *Mill Road* Street   Suite or room number

Phoenix City *AZ* State *85621* ZIP code

Report for this Quarter ... (Check one.)

- [ ] 1: January, February, March
- [ ] 2: April, May, June
- [ ] 3: July, August, September
- [X] 4: October, November, December

Part 1: Answer these questions for this quarter.

1 Number of employees who received wages, tips, or other compensation for the pay period including: *Mar. 12 (Quarter 1), June 12 (Quarter 2), Sept. 12 (Quarter 3), Dec. 12 (Quarter 4)* — **1** | *1*

2 Wages, tips, and other compensation — **2** | 36,599.00

3 Total income tax withheld from wages, tips, and other compensation — **3** | 3,056.47

4 If no wages, tips, and other compensation are subject to social security or Medicare tax . [ ] Check and go to line 6.

5 Taxable social security and Medicare wages and tips:

	Column 1		Column 2
5a Taxable social security wages	36,599.00	× .124 =	4,538.28
5b Taxable social security tips	.	× .124 =	.
5c Taxable Medicare wages & tips	36,599.00	× .029 =	1,061.37

5d Total social security and Medicare taxes (*Column 2, lines 5a + 5b + 5c = line 5d*) — **5d** | 5,599.65

6 Total taxes before adjustments (lines 3 + 5d = line 6) — **6** | 8,656.12

7 TAX ADJUSTMENTS (Read the instructions for line 7 before completing lines 7a through 7h.):

7a Current quarter's fractions of cents — .

7b Current quarter's sick pay — .

7c Current quarter's adjustments for tips and group-term life insurance — .

7d Current year's income tax withholding (attach Form 941c) — .

7e Prior quarters' social security and Medicare taxes (attach Form 941c) — .

7f Special additions to federal income tax (attach Form 941c) — .

7g Special additions to social security and Medicare (attach Form 941c) — .

7h TOTAL ADJUSTMENTS (Combine all amounts: lines 7a through 7g.) — **7h** | 0.00

8 Total taxes after adjustments (Combine lines 6 and 7h.) — **8** | 8,656.12

9 Advance earned income credit (EIC) payments made to employees — **9** | .

10 Total taxes after adjustment for advance EIC (lines 8 – line 9 = line 10) — **10** | 8,656.12

11 Total deposits for this quarter, including overpayment applied from a prior quarter — **11** | 8,656.12

12 Balance due (If line 10 is more than line 11, write the difference here.) — **12** | 0.00
Make checks payable to *United States Treasury.*

13 Overpayment (If line 11 is more than line 10, write the difference here.) | 0.00 Check one [ ] Apply to next return. [ ] Send a refund.

Part 2: Tell us about your deposit schedule and tax liability for this quarter.

If you are unsure about whether you are a monthly schedule depositor or a semiweekly schedule depositor, see *Pub. 15 (Circular E),* section 11.

14 [A][Z] Write the state abbreviation for the state where you made your deposits OR write "MU" if you made your deposits in *multiple* states.

15 Check one: [ ] Line 10 is less than $2,500. Go to Part 3.

[X] You were a monthly schedule depositor for the entire quarter. Fill out your tax liability for each month. Then go to Part 3.

Tax liability:	Month 1	3,079.11
	Month 2	2,049.77
	Month 3	3,527.24
	Total liability for quarter	8,656.12	Total must equal line 10.

[ ] You were a semiweekly schedule depositor for any part of this quarter. Fill out *Schedule B (Form 941): Report of Tax Liability for Semiweekly Schedule Depositors,* and attach it to this form.

Part 3: Tell us about your business. If a question does NOT apply to your business, leave it blank.

16 If your business has closed or you stopped paying wages — . [ ] Check here, and enter the final date you paid wages   /   / .

17 If you are a seasonal employer and you do not have to file a return for every quarter of the year. [ ] Check here.

Part 4: May we speak with your third-party designee?

Do you want to allow an employee, a paid tax preparer, or another person to discuss this return with the IRS? See the instructions for details.

[ ] Yes. Designee's name

Phone ( ) –   Personal Identification Number (PIN) [ ][ ][ ][ ][ ]

[X] No.

Part 5: Sign here. You MUST fill out both sides of this form and SIGN it.

Under penalties of perjury, I declare that I have examined this return, including accompanying schedules and statements, and to the best of my knowledge and belief, it is true, correct, and complete.

X Sign your name here

Print name and title

Date   /   /   Phone ( ) –

Reporting Wages and Salaries   Employers are required to give each employee an annual report of his or her wages subject to FICA and federal income taxes along with the amounts of these taxes withheld. This report is called a *Wage and Tax Statement,* or **Form W-2.** It must be given to employees before January 31 following the year covered by the report. Exhibit 11A.2 shows Form W-2 for one of the employees at Phoenix Sales & Service. Copies of the W-2 Form must be sent to the Social Security Administration, where the amount of the employee's wages subject to FICA taxes and FICA taxes withheld are posted to each employee's Social Security account. These posted amounts become the basis for determining an employee's retirement and survivors' benefits. The Social Security Administration also transmits to the IRS the amount of each employee's wages subject to federal income taxes and the amount of taxes withheld.

EXHIBIT 11A.2

Form W-2

Payroll Records   Employers must keep payroll records in addition to reporting and paying taxes. These records usually include a payroll register and an individual earnings report for each employee.

Payroll Register   A **payroll register** usually shows the pay period dates, hours worked, gross pay, deductions, and net pay of each employee for each pay period. Exhibit 11A.3 shows a payroll register for Phoenix Sales & Service. It is organized into nine columns:

Col. 1   Employee identification (ID); Employee name; Social Security number (SS No.); Reference (check number); and Date (date check issued)

Col. 2   Pay Type (regular and overtime)

Col. 3   Pay Hours (number of hours worked as regular and overtime)

Col. 4   Gross Pay (amount of gross pay)[2]

Col. 5   FIT (federal income taxes withheld); FUTA (federal unemployment taxes)

Col. 6   SIT (state income taxes withheld); SUTA (state unemployment taxes)

Col. 7   FICA-SS_EE (social security taxes withheld, employee); FICA-SS_ER (social security taxes, employer)

Col. 8   FICA-Med_EE (medicare tax withheld, employee); FICA-Med_ER (medicare tax, employer)

Col. 9   Net pay (Gross pay less amounts withheld from employees)

---

[2] The Gross Pay column shows regular hours worked on the first line multiplied by the regular pay rate—this equals regular pay. Overtime hours multiplied by the overtime premium rate equals overtime premium pay reported on the second line. If employers are engaged in interstate commerce, federal law sets a minimum overtime rate of pay to employees. For this company, workers earn 150% of their regular rate for hours in excess of 40 per week.

EXHIBIT 11A.3

Payroll Register

Accounting System: Exhibit A.3								

File Edit Maintain Tasks Analysis Options Reports Window Help

Phoenix Sales & Service
Payroll Register
For Week Ended Oct. 8, 2013

Employee ID Employee SS No. Refer., Date	Gross Pay			FIT [blank] FUTA	SIT [blank] SUTA	FICA-SS_EE [blank] FICA-SS_ER	FICA-Med_EE [blank] FICA-Med_ER	Net Pay
	Pay Type	Pay Hours	Gross Pay					
AR101	Regular	40.00	400.00	−28.99	−2.32	−24.80	−5.80	338.09
Robert Austin	Overtime	0.00	0.00					
333-22-9999			400.00	−3.20	−10.80	−24.80	−5.80	
9001, 10/8/13								
CJ102	Regular	40.00	560.00	−52.97	−4.24	−36.02	−8.42	479.35
Judy Cross	Overtime	1.00	21.00					
299-11-9201			581.00	−4.65	−15.69	−36.02	−8.42	
9002, 10/8/13								
DJ103	Regular	40.00	560.00	−48.33	−3.87	−37.32	−8.73	503.75
John Diaz	Overtime	2.00	42.00					
444-11-9090			602.00	−4.82	−16.25	−37.32	−8.73	
9003, 10/8/13								
KK104	Regular	40.00	560.00	−68.57	−5.49	−34.72	−8.12	443.10
Kay Keife	Overtime	0.00	0.00					
909-11-3344			560.00	−4.48	−15.12	−34.72	−8.12	
9004, 10/8/13								
ML105	Regular	40.00	560.00	−34.24	−2.74	−34.72	−8.12	480.18
Lee Miller	Overtime	0.00	0.00					
444-56-3211			560.00	−4.48	−15.12	−34.72	−8.12	
9005, 10/8/13								
SD106	Regular	40.00	560.00	−68.57	−5.49	−34.72	−8.12	443.10
Dale Sears	Overtime	0.00	0.00					
909-33-1234			560.00	−4.48	−15.12	−34.72	−8.12	
9006, 10/8/13								
Totals	Regular	240.00	3,200.00	−301.67	−24.15	−202.30	−47.31	2,687.57
	Overtime	3.00	63.00					
			3,263.00	−26.11	−88.10	−202.30	−47.31	

Sales   Purchases   General Ledger   Payroll   Inventory   Company   Analysis

Net pay for each employee is computed as gross pay minus the items on the first line of columns 5–8. The employer's payroll tax for each employee is computed as the sum of items on the third line of columns 5–8. A payroll register includes all data necessary to record payroll. In some software programs the entries to record payroll are made in a special *payroll journal.*

Payroll Check Payment of payroll is usually done by check or electronic funds transfer. Exhibit 11A.4 shows a *payroll check* for a Phoenix employee. This check is accompanied with a detachable *statement of earnings* (at top) showing gross pay, deductions, and net pay.

Employee Earnings Report An **employee earnings report** is a cumulative record of an employee's hours worked, gross earnings, deductions, and net pay. Payroll information on this report is taken from the payroll register. The employee earnings report for R. Austin at Phoenix Sales & Service is shown in Exhibit 11A.5. An employee earnings report accumulates information that can show when an employee's earnings reach the tax-exempt points for FICA, FUTA, and SUTA taxes. It also gives data an employer needs to prepare Form W-2.

Payroll Procedures Employers must be able to compute federal income tax for payroll purposes. This section explains how we compute this tax and how to use a payroll bank account.

Computing Federal Income Taxes To compute the amount of taxes withheld from each employee's wages, we need to determine both the employee's wages earned and the employee's number of *withholding*

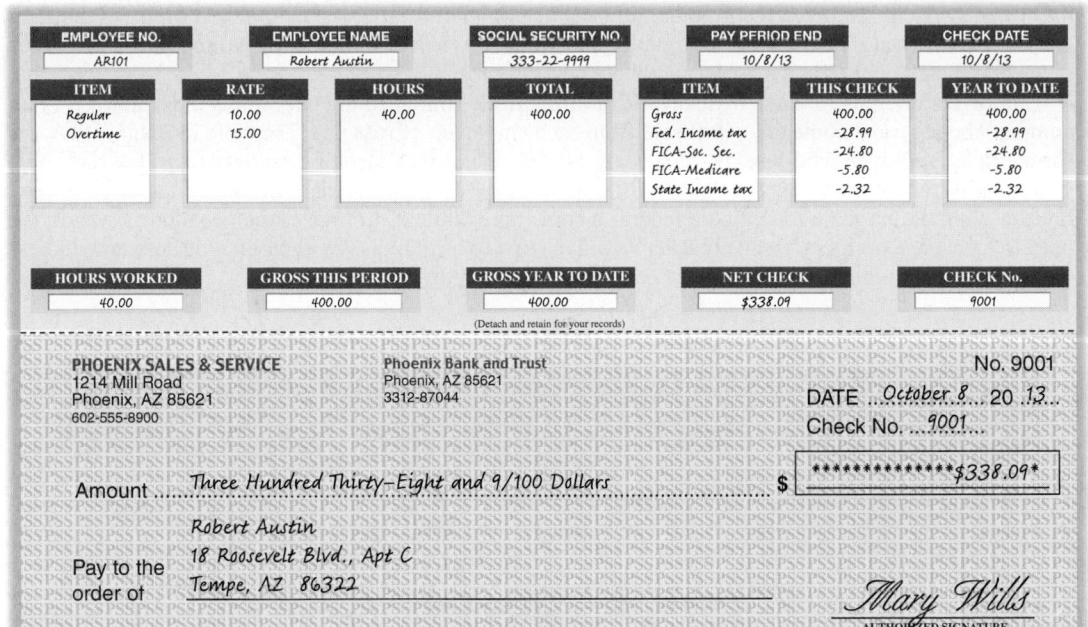

EXHIBIT 11A.4

Check and Statement of Earnings

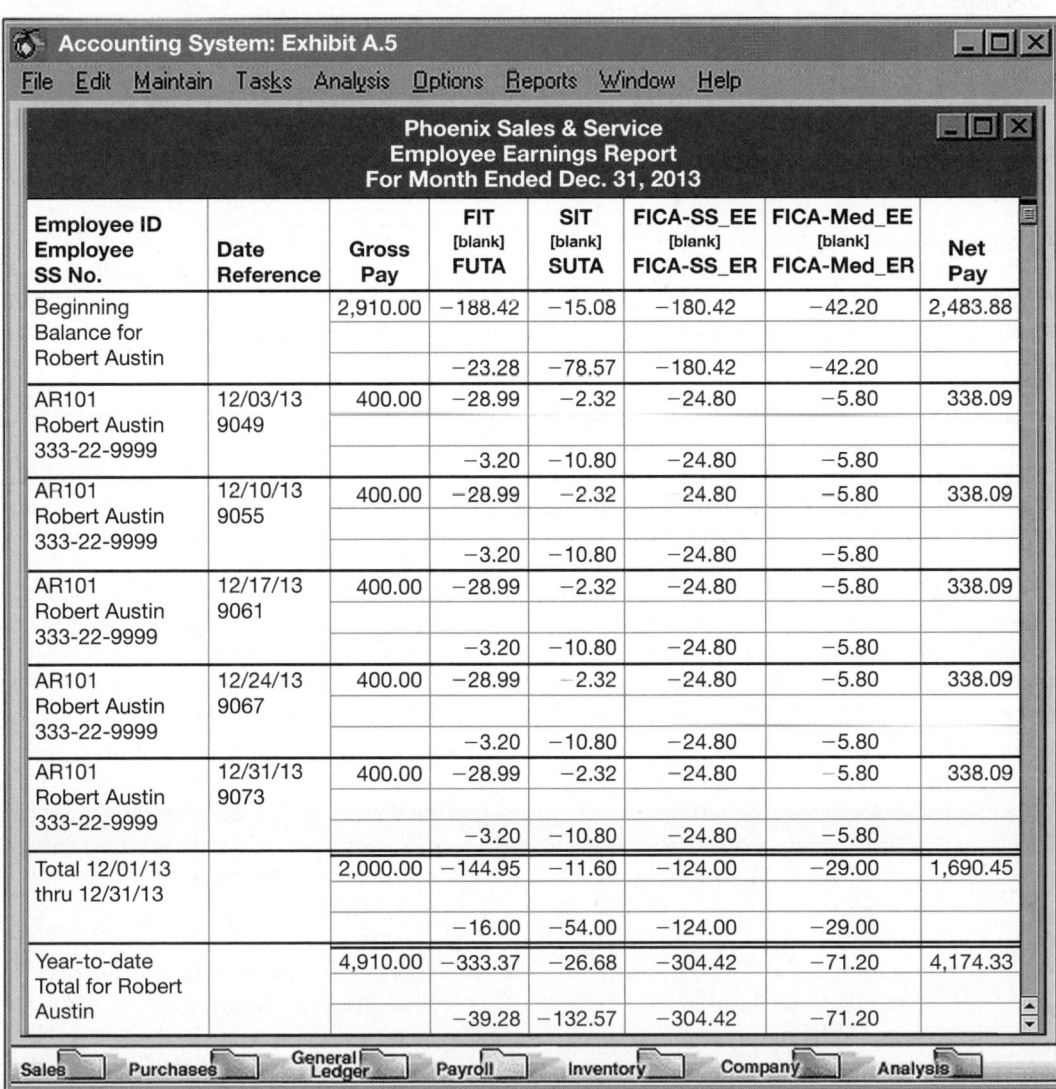

EXHIBIT 11A.5

Employee Earnings Report

allowances. Each employee records the number of withholding allowances claimed on a withholding allowance certificate, **Form W-4,** filed with the employer. When the number of withholding allowances increases, the amount of income taxes withheld decreases.

Employers often use a **wage bracket withholding table** similar to the one shown in Exhibit 11A.6 to compute the federal income taxes withheld from each employee's gross pay. The table in Exhibit 11A.6 is for a single employee paid weekly. Tables are also provided for married employees and for biweekly, semimonthly, and monthly pay periods (most payroll software includes these tables). When using a wage bracket withholding table to compute federal income tax withheld from an employee's gross wages, we need to locate an employee's wage bracket within the first two columns. We then find the amount withheld by looking in the withholding allowance column for that employee.

EXHIBIT 11A.6

Wage Bracket Withholding Table

SINGLE Persons—WEEKLY Payroll Period

If the wages are—		And the number of withholding allowances claimed is—										
At least	But less than	0	1	2	3	4	5	6	7	8	9	10
		The amount of income tax to be withheld is—										
$600	$610	$76	$67	$58	$49	$39	$30	$21	$12	$6	$0	$0
610	620	79	69	59	50	41	32	22	13	7	1	0
620	630	81	70	61	52	42	33	24	15	8	2	0
630	640	84	72	62	53	44	35	25	16	9	3	0
640	650	86	73	64	55	45	36	27	18	10	4	0
650	660	89	75	65	56	47	38	28	19	11	5	0
660	670	91	76	67	58	48	39	30	21	12	6	0
670	680	94	78	68	59	50	41	31	22	13	7	1
680	690	96	81	70	61	51	42	33	24	14	8	2
690	700	99	83	71	62	53	44	34	25	16	9	3
700	710	101	86	73	64	54	45	35	27	17	10	4
710	720	104	88	74	65	56	47	37	28	19	11	5
720	730	106	91	76	67	57	48	39	30	20	12	6
730	740	109	93	78	68	59	50	40	31	22	13	7
740	750	111	96	80	70	60	51	42	33	23	14	8

Payroll Bank Account   Companies with few employees often pay them with checks drawn on the company's regular bank account. Companies with many employees often use a special **payroll bank account** to pay employees. When this account is used, a company either (1) draws one check for total payroll on the regular bank account and deposits it in the payroll bank account or (2) executes an *electronic funds transfer* to the payroll bank account. Individual payroll checks are then drawn on this payroll bank account. Since only one check for the total payroll is drawn on the regular bank account each payday, use of a special payroll bank account helps with internal control. It also helps in reconciling the regular bank account. When companies use a payroll bank account, they usually include check numbers in the payroll register. The payroll register in Exhibit 11A.3 shows check numbers in column 1. For instance, Check No. 9001 is issued to Robert Austin. With this information, the payroll register serves as a supplementary record of wages earned by and paid to employees.

Who Pays What Payroll Taxes and Benefits   We conclude this appendix with the following table identifying who pays which payroll taxes and which common employee benefits such as medical, disability, pension, charitable, and union costs. Who pays which employee benefits, and what portion, is subject to agreements between companies and their workers. Also, self-employed workers must pay both the employer and employee FICA taxes for Social Security and Medicare.

Employer Payroll Taxes and Costs	Employee Payroll Deductions
• FICA—Social Security Taxes	• FICA—Social Security taxes
• FICA—Medicare Taxes	• FICA—Medicare taxes
• FUTA (Federal Unemployment Taxes)	• Federal Income taxes
• SUTA (State Unemployment Taxes)	• State and local income taxes
• Share of medical coverage, if any	• Share of medical coverage, if any
• Share of pension coverage, if any	• Share of pension coverage, if any
• Share of other benefits, if any	• Share of other benefits, if any

Point: IRS Statistics of Income Bulletin (Winter 2012) reports the following average (effective) income tax rate for different categories of U.S. income earners:

Top 1%	24%
Top 5%	20%
Top 10%	18%
Bottom 50%	1.85%

11. What three items determine the amount deducted from an employee's wages for federal income taxes?

12. What amount of income tax is withheld from the salary of an employee who is single with three withholding allowances and earnings of $675 in a week? (*Hint:* Use the wage bracket withholding table in Exhibit 11A.6.)

13. Which of the following steps are executed when a company draws one check for total payroll and deposits it in a special payroll bank account? (*a*) Write a check to the payroll bank account for the total payroll and record it with a debit to Salaries Payable and a credit to Cash. (*b*) Deposit a check (or transfer funds) for the total payroll in the payroll bank account. (*c*) Issue individual payroll checks drawn on the payroll bank account. (*d*) All of the above.

APPENDIX

Corporate Income Taxes

11B

This appendix explains current liabilities involving income taxes for corporations.

Income Tax Liabilities   Corporations are subject to income taxes and must estimate their income tax liability when preparing financial statements. Since income tax expense is created by earning income, a liability is incurred when income is earned. This tax must be paid quarterly under federal regulations. To illustrate, consider a corporation that prepares monthly financial statements. Based on its income in January 2013, this corporation estimates that it owes income taxes of $12,100. The following adjusting entry records this estimate:

Jan. 31	Income Taxes Expense	12,100	
	Income Taxes Payable		12,100
	To accrue January income taxes.		

Assets = Liabilities + Equity
       +12,100   −12,100

The tax liability is recorded each month until the first quarterly payment is made. If the company's estimated taxes for this first quarter total $30,000, the entry to record its payment is

Apr. 10	Income Taxes Payable	30,000	
	Cash		30,000
	Paid estimated quarterly income taxes based on		
	first quarter income.		

Assets = Liabilities + Equity
−30,000   −30,000

This process of accruing and then paying estimated income taxes continues through the year. When annual financial statements are prepared at year-end, the corporation knows its actual total income and the actual amount of income taxes it must pay. This information allows it to properly record income taxes expense for the fourth quarter so that the total of the four quarters' expense amounts equals the actual taxes paid to the government.

Deferred Income Tax Liabilities   An income tax liability for corporations can arise when the amount of income before taxes that the corporation reports on its income statement is not the same as the amount of income reported on its income tax return. This difference occurs because income tax laws and GAAP measure income differently. (Differences between tax laws and GAAP arise because Congress uses tax laws to generate receipts, stimulate the economy, and influence behavior, whereas GAAP are intended to provide financial information useful for business decisions. Also, tax accounting often follows the cash basis, whereas GAAP follows the accrual basis.)

Some differences between tax laws and GAAP are temporary. *Temporary differences* arise when the tax return and the income statement report a revenue or expense in different years. As an example, companies are often able to deduct higher amounts of depreciation in the early years of an asset's life and smaller amounts in later years for tax reporting in comparison to GAAP. This means that in the early years, depreciation for tax reporting is often more than depreciation on the income statement. In later years, depreciation for tax reporting is often less than depreciation on the income statement. When temporary differences exist between taxable income on the tax return and the income before taxes on the income statement, corporations compute income taxes expense based on the income reported on the income statement. The result is that income taxes expense reported in the income statement is often different from the amount of income taxes payable to the government. This difference is the **deferred income tax liability.**

To illustrate, assume that in recording its usual quarterly income tax payments, a corporation computes $25,000 of income taxes expense. It also determines that only $21,000 is currently due and $4,000 is deferred to future years (a timing difference). The entry to record this end-of-period adjustment is

Assets = Liabilities + Equity
    +21,000   −25,000
    +4,000

Dec. 31	Income Taxes Expense	25,000	
	Income Taxes Payable		21,000
	Deferred Income Tax Liability		4,000
	To record tax expense and deferred tax liability.		

The credit to Income Taxes Payable reflects the amount currently due to be paid. The credit to Deferred Income Tax Liability reflects tax payments deferred until future years when the temporary difference reverses.

Temporary differences also can cause a company to pay income taxes *before* they are reported on the income statement as expense. If so, the company reports a *Deferred Income Tax Asset* on its balance sheet.

Summary

C1   **Describe current and long-term liabilities and their characteristics.** Liabilities are probable future payments of assets or services that past transactions or events obligate an entity to make. Current liabilities are due within one year or the operating cycle, whichever is longer. All other liabilities are long term.

C2   **Identify and describe known current liabilities.** Known (determinable) current liabilities are set by agreements or laws and are measurable with little uncertainty. They include accounts payable, sales taxes payable, unearned revenues, notes payable, payroll liabilities, and the current portion of long-term debt.

C3   **Explain how to account for contingent liabilities.** If an uncertain future payment depends on a probable future event and the amount can be reasonably estimated, the payment is recorded as a liability. The uncertain future payment is reported as a contingent liability (in the notes) if (*a*) the future event is reasonably possible but not probable or (*b*) the event is probable but the payment amount cannot be reasonably estimated.

A1   **Compute the times interest earned ratio and use it to analyze liabilities.** Times interest earned is computed by dividing a company's net income before interest expense and income taxes by the amount of interest expense. The times interest earned ratio reflects a company's ability to pay interest obligations.

P1   **Prepare entries to account for short-term notes payable.** Short-term notes payable are current liabilities; most bear interest. When a short-term note's face value equals the amount borrowed, it identifies a rate of interest to be paid at maturity.

P2   **Compute and record *employee* payroll deductions and liabilities.** Employee payroll deductions include FICA taxes, income taxes, and voluntary deductions such as for pensions and charities. They make up the difference between gross and net pay.

P3   **Compute and record *employer* payroll expenses and liabilities.** An employer's payroll expenses include employees' gross earnings, any employee benefits, and the payroll taxes levied on the employer. Payroll liabilities include employees' net pay amounts, withholdings from employee wages, any employer-promised benefits, and the employer's payroll taxes.

P4   **Account for estimated liabilities, including warranties and bonuses.** Liabilities for health and pension benefits, warranties, and bonuses are recorded with estimated amounts. These items are recognized as expenses when incurred and matched with revenues generated.

P5ᴬ   **Identify and describe the details of payroll reports, records, and procedures.** Employers report FICA taxes and federal income tax withholdings using Form 941. FUTA taxes are reported on Form 940. Earnings and deductions are reported to each employee and the federal government on Form W-2. An employer's payroll records often include a payroll register for each pay period, payroll checks and statements of earnings, and individual employee earnings reports.

Guidance Answers to Decision Maker and Decision Ethics

Web Designer   You need to be concerned about being an accomplice to unlawful payroll activities. Not paying federal and state taxes on wages earned is illegal and unethical. Such payments also will not provide the employee with Social Security and some Medicare credits. The best course of action is to request payment by check. If this fails to change the owner's payment practices, you must consider quitting this job.

Entrepreneur   Risk is partly reflected by the times interest earned ratio. This ratio for the first franchise is 1.5 [($100,000 +

$200,000)/$200,000], whereas the ratio for the second franchise is 3.5 [($100,000 + $40,000)/$40,000]. This analysis shows that the first franchise is more at risk of incurring a loss if its sales decline. The second question asks about variability of income. If income greatly varies, this increases the risk an owner will not earn sufficient income to cover interest. Since the first franchise has the greater variability, it is a riskier investment.

Guidance Answers to Quick Checks

1. A liability involves a probable future payment of assets or services that an entity is presently obligated to make as a result of past transactions or events.

2. No, an expected future payment is not a liability unless an existing obligation was created by a past event or transaction.

3. In most cases, a liability due in 15 months is classified as long term. It is classified as a current liability if the company's operating cycle is 15 months or longer.

4. A creditor prefers a note payable instead of a past-due account payable so as to (a) charge interest and/or (b) have evidence of the debt and its terms for potential litigation or disputes.

5. $1,000* × (.008) + $1,000* × (.04) + $3,000 × (.062) + $3,000 × (.0145) = $277.50

---

* $1,000 of the $3,000 March pay is subject to FUTA and SUTA—the entire $6,000 pay from January and February was subject to them.

6. (a) FICA taxes are incurred by both employee and employer.
   (b) FUTA taxes are incurred by the employer.
   (c) SUTA taxes are incurred by the employer.
   (d) Withheld income taxes are incurred by the employee.

7. (a)

8. (a) Warranty expense was previously estimated and recorded.

9. (b)

10. A future payment is reported in the notes as a contingent liability if (a) the uncertain future event is probable but the amount of payment cannot be reasonably estimated or (b) the uncertain future event is not probable but has a reasonable possibility of occurring.

11. An employee's marital status, gross earnings and number of withholding allowances determine the deduction for federal income taxes.

12. $59

13. (d)

Key Terms

Multiple Choice Quiz   Answers on p. 479   mhhe.com/wildFAP21e

Additional Quiz Questions are available at the book's Website.

1. On December 1, a company signed a $6,000, 90-day, 5% note payable, with principal plus interest due on March 1 of the following year. What amount of interest expense should be accrued at December 31 on the note?
   a. $300
   b. $25
   c. $100
   d. $75
   e. $0

2. An employee earned $50,000 during the year. FICA tax for social security is 6.2% and FICA tax for Medicare is 1.45%. The employer's share of FICA taxes is
   a. Zero, since the employee's pay exceeds the FICA limit.
   b. Zero, since FICA is not an employer tax.
   c. $3,100
   d. $725
   e. $3,825

3. Assume the FUTA tax rate is 0.8% and the SUTA tax rate is 5.4%. Both taxes are applied to the first $7,000 of an employee's pay. What is the total unemployment tax an employer must pay on an employee's annual wages of $40,000?
   a. $2,480
   b. $434
   c. $56
   d. $378
   e. Zero; the employee's wages exceed the $7,000 maximum.

4. A company sells big screen televisions for $3,000 each. Each television has a two-year warranty that covers the replacement of defective parts. It is estimated that 1% of all televisions sold will be returned under warranty at an average cost of $250 each. During July, the company sold 10,000 big screen televisions, and 80 were serviced under the warranty during July at a total cost of $18,000. The credit balance in the Estimated

Warranty Liability account at July 1 was $26,000. What is the company's warranty expense for the month of July?
a. $51,000
b. $1,000
c. $25,000
d. $33,000
e. $18,000

5. Employees earn vacation pay at the rate of 1 day per month. During October, 150 employees qualify for one vacation day

each. Their average daily wage is $175 per day. What is the amount of vacation benefit expense for October?
a. $26,250
b. $175
c. $2,100
d. $63,875
e. $150

A(B) *Superscript letter A (B) denotes assignments based on Appendix 11A (11B).*

🛡 Icon denotes assignments that involve decision making.

Discussion Questions

1. 🛡 What is the difference between a current and a long-term liability?
2. What is an estimated liability?
3. 🛡 What are the three important questions concerning the uncertainty of liabilities?
4. If $988 is the total of a sale that includes its sales tax of 4%, what is the selling price of the item only?
5. What is the combined amount (in percent) of the employee and employer Social Security tax rate?
6. What is the current Medicare tax rate? This rate is applied to what maximum level of salary and wages?
7. Which payroll taxes are the employee's responsibility and which are the employer's responsibility?
8. What determines the amount deducted from an employee's wages for federal income taxes?
9. What is an employer's unemployment merit rating? How are these ratings assigned to employers?
10. 🛡 Why are warranty liabilities usually recognized on the balance sheet as liabilities even when they are uncertain?
11. 🛡 Suppose that a company has a facility located where disastrous weather conditions often occur. Should it report a probable

loss from a future disaster as a liability on its balance sheet? Explain.
12.A What is a wage bracket withholding table?
13.A What amount of income tax is withheld from the salary of an employee who is single with two withholding allowances and earning $725 per week? What if the employee earned $625 and has no withholding allowances? (Use Exhibit 11A.6.)
14. 🛡 Refer to **Polaris**' balance sheet in Appendix A. What accrued expenses (liabilities) does Polaris report at December 31, 2011? **Polaris**
15. Refer to **Arctic Cat**'s balance sheet in Appendix A. What is the amount of Arctic Cat's accounts payable as of March 31, 2011? **Arctic Cat**
16. 🛡 Refer to **KTM**'s balance sheet in Appendix A. List KTM's current liabilities as of December 31, 2011. **KTM**
17. 🛡 Refer to **Piaggio**'s recent balance sheet in Appendix A. What current liabilities related to income taxes are on its balance sheet? Explain the meaning of each income tax account identified. **PIAGGIO**

Mc Graw Hill **connect**

QUICK STUDY

QS 11-1
Classifying liabilities C1

Which of the following items are normally classified as a current liability for a company that has a 15-month operating cycle?
1. Note payable due in 18 months.
2. Note payable maturing in 2 years.
3. Portion of long-term note due in 15 months.
4. Salaries payable.
5. FICA taxes payable.
6. Note payable due in 11 months.

QS 11-2
Unearned revenue C2

Ticketsales, Inc., receives $5,000,000 cash in advance ticket sales for a four-date tour of Bon Jovi. Record the advance ticket sales on October 31. Record the revenue earned for the first concert date of November 5, assuming it represents one-fourth of the advance ticket sales.

QS 11-3
Accounting for sales taxes
C2

Dextra Computing sells merchandise for $6,000 cash on September 30 (cost of merchandise is $3,900). The sales tax law requires Dextra to collect 5% sales tax on every dollar of merchandise sold. Record the entry for the $6,000 sale and its applicable sales tax. Also record the entry that shows the remittance of the 5% tax on this sale to the state government on October 15.

The following legal claims exist for Huprey Co. Identify the accounting treatment for each claim as either (*a*) a liability that is recorded or (*b*) an item described in notes to its financial statements.

1. Huprey (defendant) estimates that a pending lawsuit could result in damages of $1,250,000; it is reasonably possible that the plaintiff will win the case.

2. Huprey faces a probable loss on a pending lawsuit; the amount is not reasonably estimable.

3. Huprey estimates damages in a case at $3,500,000 with a high probability of losing the case.

QS 11-4
Accounting for contingent liabilities

C3

On November 7, 2013, Mura Company borrows $160,000 cash by signing a 90-day, 8% note payable with a face value of $160,000. (1) Compute the accrued interest payable on December 31, 2013, (2) prepare the journal entry to record the accrued interest expense at December 31, 2013, and (3) prepare the journal entry to record payment of the note at maturity.

QS 11-5
Interest-bearing note transactions   P1

On January 15, the end of the first biweekly pay period of the year, North Company's payroll register showed that its employees earned $35,000 of sales salaries. Withholdings from the employees' salaries include FICA Social Security taxes at the rate of 6.2%, FICA Medicare taxes at the rate of 1.45%, $6,500 of federal income taxes, $772.50 of medical insurance deductions, and $120 of union dues. No employee earned more than $7,000 in this first period. Prepare the journal entry to record North Company's January 15 (employee) payroll expenses and liabilities. (Round amounts to cents.)

QS 11-6
Record employee payroll taxes
P2

Merger Co. has ten employees, each of whom earns $2,000 per month and has been employed since January 1. FICA Social Security taxes are 6.2% of the first $110,100 paid to each employee, and FICA Medicare taxes are 1.45% of gross pay. FUTA taxes are 0.8% and SUTA taxes are 5.4% of the first $7,000 paid to each employee. Prepare the March 31 journal entry to record the March payroll taxes expenses. (Round amounts to cents.)

QS 11-7
Record employer payroll taxes
P3

Noura Company offers an annual bonus to employees if the company meets certain net income goals. Prepare the journal entry to record a $15,000 bonus owed to its workers (to be shared equally) at calendar year-end.

QS 11-8
Accounting for bonuses   P4

Chavez Co.'s salaried employees earn four weeks vacation per year. It pays $312,000.00 in total employee salaries for 52 weeks but its employees work only 48 weeks. This means Chavez's total weekly expense is $6,500 ($312,000/48 weeks) instead of the $6,000 cash paid weekly to the employees ($312,000/52 weeks). Record Chavez's weekly vacation benefits expense.

QS 11-9
Accounting for vacations
P4

On September 11, 2012, Home Store sells a mower for $500 with a one-year warranty that covers parts. Warranty expense is estimated at 8% of sales. On July 24, 2013, the mower is brought in for repairs covered under the warranty requiring $35 in materials taken from the Repair Parts Inventory. Prepare the September 11, 2012, entry to record the mower sale, and the July 24, 2013, entry to record the warranty repairs.

QS 11-10
Recording warranty repairs
P4

Compute the times interest earned for Park Company, which reports income before interest expense and income taxes of $1,885,000, and interest expense of $145,000. Interpret its times interest earned (assume that its competitors average a times interest earned of 4.0).

QS 11-11
Times interest earned   A1

The payroll records of Speedy Software show the following information about Marsha Gottschalk, an employee, for the weekly pay period ending September 30, 2013. Gottschalk is single and claims one allowance. Compute her Social Security tax (6.2%), Medicare tax (1.45%), federal income tax withholding, state income tax (1.0%), and net pay for the current pay period. (Use the withholding table in Exhibit 11A.6 and round tax amounts to the nearest cent.)

Total (gross) earnings for current pay period	$ 740
Cumulative earnings of previous pay periods	$9,700

QS 11-12[A]
Net pay and tax computations
P5

Check   Net pay, $579.99

Sera Corporation has made and recorded its quarterly income tax payments. After a final review of taxes for the year, the company identifies an additional $40,000 of income tax expense that should be recorded. A portion of this additional expense, $6,000, is deferred for payment in future years. Record Sera's year-end adjusting entry for income tax expense.

QS 11-13[B]
Record deferred income tax liability   P4

Answer each of the following related to international accounting standards.

a. In general, how similar or different are the definitions and characteristics of current liabilities between IFRS and U.S. GAAP?

b. Companies reporting under IFRS often reference a set of current liabilities with the title *financial liabilities*. Identify two current liabilities that would be classified under financial liabilities per IFRS. (*Hint:* **Nokia** provides examples in this chapter.)

QS 11-14
International accounting standards

C1   C2

connect

EXERCISES

Exercise 11-1
Classifying liabilities

C1

The following items appear on the balance sheet of a company with a two-month operating cycle. Identify the proper classification of each item as follows: *C* if it is a current liability, *L* if it is a long-term liability, or *N* if it is not a liability.

_____	**1.** Notes payable (due in 120 days).	_____	**6.** Sales taxes payable.
_____	**2.** Notes payable (mature in five years).	_____	**7.** Accounts receivable.
_____	**3.** Notes payable (due in 6 to 12 months).	_____	**8.** Wages payable.
_____	**4.** Current portion of long-term debt.	_____	**9.** FUTA taxes payable.
_____	**5.** Notes payable (due in 13 to 24 months).	_____	**10.** Salaries payable.

Exercise 11-2
Recording known
current liabilities

C2

Prepare any necessary adjusting entries at December 31, 2013, for Piper Company's year-end financial statements for each of the following separate transactions and events.

1. Piper Company records an adjusting entry for $10,000,000 of previously unrecorded cash sales (costing $5,000,000) and its sales taxes at a rate of 4%.

2. The company earned $50,000 of $125,000 previously received in advance for services.

Exercise 11-3
Accounting for contingent
liabilities

C3

Prepare any necessary adjusting entries at December 31, 2013, for Melbourn Company's year-end financial statements for each of the following separate transactions and events.

1. Melbourn Company guarantees the $100,000 debt of a supplier. The supplier will probably not default on the debt.

2. A disgruntled employee is suing Melbourn Company. Legal advisers believe that the company will probably need to pay damages, but the amount cannot be reasonably estimated.

Exercise 11-4
Accounting for note payable

P1

Check (2b) Interest expense, $2,200

Sylvestor Systems borrows $110,000 cash on May 15, 2013, by signing a 60-day, 12% note.

1. On what date does this note mature?

2. Suppose the face value of the note equals $110,000, the principal of the loan. Prepare the journal entries to record (*a*) issuance of the note and (*b*) payment of the note at maturity.

Exercise 11-5
Interest-bearing notes payable
with year-end adjustments

P1

Check (2) $3,000
      (3) $1,500

Keesha Co. borrows $200,000 cash on November 1, 2013, by signing a 90-day, 9% note with a face value of $200,000.

1. On what date does this note mature? (Assume that February of 2013 has 28 days.)

2. How much interest expense results from this note in 2013? (Assume a 360-day year.)

3. How much interest expense results from this note in 2014? (Assume a 360-day year.)

4. Prepare journal entries to record (*a*) issuance of the note, (*b*) accrual of interest at the end of 2013, and (*c*) payment of the note at maturity.

Exercise 11-6
Computing payroll taxes

P2 P3

Check (*a*) FUTA, $4.80; SUTA,
      $17.40

BMX Company has one employee. FICA Social Security taxes are 6.2% of the first $110,100 paid to its employee, and FICA Medicare taxes are 1.45% of gross pay. For BMX, its FUTA taxes are 0.8% and SUTA taxes are 2.9% of the first $7,000 paid to its employee. Compute BMX's amounts for each of these four taxes as applied to the employee's gross earnings for September under each of three separate situations (*a*), (*b*), and (*c*). (Round amounts to cents.)

	Gross Pay through August	Gross Pay for September
a.	$ 6,400	$ 800
b.	18,200	2,100
c.	103,800	8,000

Exercise 11-7
Payroll-related journal entries P2

Using the data in situation *a* of Exercise 11-6, prepare the employer's September 30 journal entries to record salary expense and its related payroll liabilities for this employee. The employee's federal income taxes withheld by the employer are $80 for this pay period. (Round amounts to cents.)

Exercise 11-8
Payroll-related journal entries P3

Using the data in situation *a* of Exercise 11-6, prepare the employer's September 30 journal entries to record the *employer's* payroll taxes expense and its related liabilities. (Round amounts to cents.)

Exercise 11-9
Warranty expense and liability
computations and entries P4

Hitzu Co. sold a copier costing $4,800 with a two-year parts warranty to a customer on August 16, 2013, for $6,000 cash. Hitzu uses the perpetual inventory system. On November 22, 2014, the copier requires on-site repairs that are completed the same day. The repairs cost $209 for materials taken from the Repair Parts Inventory.

These are the only repairs required in 2014 for this copier. Based on experience, Hitzu expects to incur warranty costs equal to 4% of dollar sales. It records warranty expense with an adjusting entry at the end of each year.

1. How much warranty expense does the company report in 2013 for this copier?

2. How much is the estimated warranty liability for this copier as of December 31, 2013?

3. How much warranty expense does the company report in 2014 for this copier?

4. How much is the estimated warranty liability for this copier as of December 31, 2014?

5. Prepare journal entries to record (*a*) the copier's sale; (*b*) the adjustment on December 31, 2013, to recognize the warranty expense; and (*c*) the repairs that occur in November 2014.

Check   (1) $240

(4) $31

For the year ended December 31, 2013, Lopez Company has implemented an employee bonus program equal to 3% of Lopez's net income, which employees will share equally. Lopez's net income (prebonus) is expected to be $500,000, and bonus expense is deducted in computing net income.

1. Compute the amount of the bonus payable to the employees at year-end (use the method described in the chapter and round to the nearest dollar).

2. Prepare the journal entry at December 31, 2013, to record the bonus due the employees.

3. Prepare the journal entry at January 19, 2014, to record payment of the bonus to employees.

Exercise 11-10
Computing and recording bonuses   P4

Check   (1) $14,563

Prepare any necessary adjusting entries at December 31, 2013, for Maxum Company's year-end financial statements for each of the following separate transactions and events.

1. Employees earn vacation pay at a rate of one day per month. During December, 20 employees qualify for one vacation day each. Their average daily wage is $160 per employee.

2. During December, Maxum Company sold 12,000 units of a product that carries a 60-day warranty. December sales for this product total $460,000. The company expects 10% of the units to need warranty repairs, and it estimates the average repair cost per unit will be $15.

Exercise 11-11
Accounting for estimated liabilities
P4

Use the following information from separate companies *a* through *f* to compute times interest earned. Which company indicates the strongest ability to pay interest expense as it comes due? (Round ratios to two decimals.)

Exercise 11-12
Computing and interpreting times interest earned

A1

	Net Income (Loss)	Interest Expense	Income Taxes
a.	$115,000	$44,000	$ 35,000
b.	110,000	16,000	50,000
c.	100,000	12,000	70,000
d.	235,000	14,000	130,000
e.	59,000	14,000	30,000
f.	(5,000)	10,000	0

Check   (b) 11.00

Nishi Corporation prepares financial statements for each month-end. As part of its accounting process, estimated income taxes are accrued each month for 30% of the current month's net income. The income taxes are paid in the first month of each quarter for the amount accrued for the prior quarter. The following information is available for the fourth quarter of year 2013. When tax computations are completed on January 20, 2014, Nishi determines that the quarter's Income Taxes Payable account balance should be $28,300 on December 31, 2013 (its unadjusted balance is $24,690).

Exercise 11-13ᴮ
Accounting for income taxes
P4

October 2013 net income	$28,600
November 2013 net income	19,100
December 2013 net income	34,600

1. Determine the amount of the accounting adjustment (dated as of December 31, 2013) to produce the proper ending balance in the Income Taxes Payable account.

2. Prepare journal entries to record (*a*) the December 31, 2013, adjustment to the Income Taxes Payable account and (*b*) the January 20, 2014, payment of the fourth-quarter taxes.

Check   (1) $3,610

Lenny Florita, an unmarried employee, works 48 hours in the week ended January 12. His pay rate is $14 per hour, and his wages are subject to no deductions other than FICA—Social Security, FICA— Medicare, and federal income taxes. He claims two withholding allowances. Compute his regular pay, overtime pay (for this company, workers earn 150% of their regular rate for hours in excess of 40 per week), and gross pay. Then compute his FICA tax deduction (use 6.2% for the Social Security portion and 1.45% for the Medicare portion), income tax deduction (use the wage bracket withholding table of Exhibit 11A.6), total deductions, and net pay. (Round tax amounts to the nearest cent.)

Exercise 11-14ᴬ
Gross and net pay computation
P5

Check   Net pay, $596.30

Exercise 11-15
Recording payroll
P2 P3

The following monthly data are taken from Ramirez Company at July 31: Sales salaries, $300,000; Office salaries, $60,000; Federal income taxes withheld, $90,000; State income taxes withheld, $20,000; Social security taxes withheld, $22,320; Medicare taxes withheld, $5,220; Medical insurance premiums, $7,000; Life insurance premiums, $4,000; Union dues deducted, $1,000; and Salaries subject to unemployment taxes, $50,000. The employee pays forty percent of medical and life insurance premiums.

Prepare journal entries to record: (1) accrued payroll, including employee deductions, for July; (2) cash payment of the net payroll (salaries payable) for July; (3) accrued employer payroll taxes, and other related employment expenses, for July—assume that FICA taxes are identical to those on employees and that SUTA taxes are 5.4% and FUTA taxes are 0.8%; and (4) cash payment of all liabilities related to the July payroll.

Exercise 11-16
Computing payroll taxes
P2 P3

Mester Company has 10 employees. FICA Social Security taxes are 6.2% of the first $110,100 paid to each employee, and FICA Medicare taxes are 1.45% of gross pay. FUTA taxes are 0.8% and SUTA taxes are 5.4% of the first $7,000 paid to each employee. Cumulative pay for the current year for each of its employees follows.

Employee	Cumulative Pay	Employee	Cumulative Pay	Employee	Cumulative Pay
Steve S.	$ 6,000	Christina S.	$156,600	Lori K.	$116,600
Tim V.	60,000	Kathleen K.	106,900	Matt B.	36,800
Brent G.	87,000	Michelle H.	110,100	Sankha B.	4,000

a. Prepare a table with the following column headings: Employee; Cumulative Pay; Pay Subject to FICA Social Security Taxes; Pay Subject to FICA Medicare Taxes; Pay Subject to FUTA Taxes; Pay Subject to SUTA Taxes. Compute the amounts in this table for each employee and total the columns.

b. For the company, compute each total for: FICA Social Security taxes, FICA Medicare taxes, FUTA taxes, and SUTA taxes. (*Hint:* Remember to include in those totals any employee share of taxes that the company must collect.) (Round amounts to cents.)

Exercise 11-17
Preparing payroll register and related entries P5

Stark Company has five employees. Employees paid by the hour receive a $10 per hour pay rate for the regular 40-hour work week plus one and one-half times the hourly rate for each overtime hour beyond the 40-hours per week. Hourly employees are paid every two weeks, but salaried employees are paid monthly on the last biweekly payday of each month. FICA Social Security taxes are 6.2% of the first $110,100 paid to each employee, and FICA Medicare taxes are 1.45% of gross pay. FUTA taxes are 0.8% and SUTA taxes are 5.4% of the first $7,000 paid to each employee. The company has a benefits plan that includes medical insurance, life insurance, and retirement funding for employees. Under this plan, employees must contribute 5 percent of their gross income as a payroll withholding, which the company matches with double the amount. Following is the partially completed payroll register for the biweekly period ending August 31, which is the last payday of August.

Employee	Cumulative Pay (Excludes Current Period)	Pay Type	Pay Hours	Gross Pay	FIT / SIT	FUTA / SUTA	FICA-SS_EE / FICA-SS_ER	FICA-Med_EE / FICA-Med_ER	EE-Ben_Plan Withholding / ER-Ben_Plan Withholding	Employee Net Pay
Kathleen	$108,300.00	Salary	---	$7,000.00	$2,000.00 300.00					
Anthony	6,800.00	Salary	---	500.00	80.00 20.00					
Nichole	15,000.00	Regular Overtime	80 8		110.00 25.00					
Zoey	6,500.00	Regular Overtime	80 4		100.00 22.00					
Gracie	5,000.00	Regular Overtime	74 0	740.00 0.00	90.00 21.00					
Totals	141,600.00				2,380.00 388.00					

* Table abbreviations follow those in Exhibit 11A.3 (see pages 457–458); and, "Ben_Plan" refers to employee (EE) or employer (ER) withholding for the benefits plan.

a. Complete this payroll register by filling in all cells for the pay period ended August 31. *Hint:* See Exhibit 11A.5 for guidance. (Round amounts to cents.)

b. Prepare the August 31 journal entry to record the accrued biweekly payroll and related liabilities for deductions.

c. Prepare the August 31 journal entry to record the employer's cash payment of the net payroll of part *b*.

d. Prepare the August 31 journal entry to record the employer's payroll taxes including the contribution to the benefits plan.

e. Prepare the August 31 journal entry to pay all liabilities (expect net payroll in part *c*) for this biweekly period.

Volvo Group reports the following information for its product warranty costs as of December 31, 2011, along with provisions and utilizations of warranty liabilities for the year ended December 31, 2011 (SEK in millions).

Exercise 11-18
Accounting for current liabilities under IFRS

P4

Provision for product warranty Warranty provisions are estimated with consideration of historical claims statistics, the warranty period, the average time-lag between faults occurring and claims to the company and anticipated changes in quality indexes. Estimated costs for product warranties are charged to cost of sales when the products are sold. Differences between actual warranty claims and the estimated claims generally affect the recognized expense and provisions in future periods. Refunds from suppliers, that decrease Volvo's warranty costs, are recognized to the extent these are considered to be certain. At December 31, 2011 (2010) warranty cost provisions amounted to 8,652 (7,841).

Product warranty liabilities, December 31, 2010	SEK 7,841
Additional provisions to product warranty liabilities	7,749
Utilizations and reductions of product warranty liabilities	(6,938)
Product warranty liabilities, December 31, 2011	8,652

1. Prepare Volvo's journal entry to record its estimated warranty liabilities (provisions) for 2011.

2. Prepare Volvo's journal entry to record its costs (utilizations) related to its warranty program for 2011. Assume those costs involve replacements taken out of Inventory, with no cash involved.

3. How much warranty expense does Volvo report for 2011?

connect

Tyrell Co. entered into the following transactions involving short-term liabilities in 2012 and 2013.

PROBLEM SET A

2012

Apr. 20   Purchased $40,250 of merchandise on credit from Locust, terms are 1/10, n/30. Tyrell uses the perpetual inventory system.

May 19   Replaced the April 20 account payable to Locust with a 90-day, $35,000 note bearing 10% annual interest along with paying $5,250 in cash.

July 8   Borrowed $80,000 cash from National Bank by signing a 120-day, 9% interest-bearing note with a face value of $80,000.

____?____   Paid the amount due on the note to Locust at the maturity date.

____?____   Paid the amount due on the note to National Bank at the maturity date.

Nov. 28   Borrowed $42,000 cash from Fargo Bank by signing a 60-day, 8% interest-bearing note with a face value of $42,000.

Dec. 31   Recorded an adjusting entry for accrued interest on the note to Fargo Bank.

Problem 11-1A
Short-term notes payable transactions and entries

P1

mhhe.com/wildFAP21e

Sage 50

2013

____?____   Paid the amount due on the note to Fargo Bank at the maturity date.

Required

1. Determine the maturity date for each of the three notes described.

2. Determine the interest due at maturity for each of the three notes. (Assume a 360-day year.)

3. Determine the interest expense to be recorded in the adjusting entry at the end of 2012.

4. Determine the interest expense to be recorded in 2013.

5. Prepare journal entries for all the preceding transactions and events for years 2012 and 2013.

Check (2) Locust, $875
(3) $308
(4) $252

Paloma Co. Stars has four employees. FICA Social Security taxes are 6.2% of the first $110,100 paid to each employee, and FICA Medicare taxes are 1.45% of gross pay. Also, for the first $7,000 paid to each employee, the company's FUTA taxes are 0.8% and SUTA taxes are 2.15%. The company is preparing its payroll calculations for the week ended August 25. Payroll records show the following information for the company's four employees.

Problem 11-2A
Payroll expenses, withholdings, and taxes P2 P3

mhhe.com/wildFAP21e

	Gross Pay	Current Week	
Name	through 8/18	Gross Pay	Income Tax Withholding
Dahlia	$109,000	$2,000	$284
Trey	36,650	900	145
Kiesha	7,100	450	39
Chee	1,050	400	30

In addition to gross pay, the company must pay one-half of the $60 per employee weekly health insurance; each employee pays the remaining one-half. The company also contributes an extra 8% of each employee's gross pay (at no cost to employees) to a pension fund.

Required

Compute the following for the week ended August 25 (round amounts to the nearest cent):

1. Each employee's FICA withholdings for Social Security.

2. Each employee's FICA withholdings for Medicare.

Check (3) $176.70

3. Employer's FICA taxes for Social Security.

(4) $54.38

4. Employer's FICA taxes for Medicare.

(5) $3.20

5. Employer's FUTA taxes.

6. Employer's SUTA taxes.

(7) Total net pay, $2,900.92

7. Each employee's net (take-home) pay.

8. Employer's total payroll-related expense for each employee.

Problem 11-3A
Entries for payroll transactions
P2 P3

On January 8, the end of the first weekly pay period of the year, Regis Company's payroll register showed that its employees earned $22,760 of office salaries and $65,840 of sales salaries. Withholdings from the employees' salaries include FICA Social Security taxes at the rate of 6.2%, FICA Medicare taxes at the rate of 1.45%, $12,860 of federal income taxes, $1,340 of medical insurance deductions, and $840 of union dues. No employee earned more than $7,000 in this first period.

Required

Check (1) Cr. Salaries Payable, $66,782.10

1. Calculate FICA Social Security taxes payable and FICA Medicare taxes payable. Prepare the journal entry to record Regis Company's January 8 (employee) payroll expenses and liabilities. (Round amounts to cents.)

(2) Dr. Payroll Taxes Expense, $11,030.70

2. Prepare the journal entry to record Regis's (employer) payroll taxes resulting from the January 8 payroll. Regis's merit rating reduces its state unemployment tax rate to 4% of the first $7,000 paid each employee. The federal unemployment tax rate is 0.8%. (Round amounts to cents.)

Problem 11-4A
Warranty expense and
liability estimation
P4

Sage 50 QB

On October 29, 2012, Lobo Co. began operations by purchasing razors for resale. Lobo uses the perpetual inventory method. The razors have a 90-day warranty that requires the company to replace any nonworking razor. When a razor is returned, the company discards it and mails a new one from Merchandise Inventory to the customer. The company's cost per new razor is $20 and its retail selling price is $75 in both 2012 and 2013. The manufacturer has advised the company to expect warranty costs to equal 8% of dollar sales. The following transactions and events occurred.

2012

Nov. 11 Sold 105 razors for $7,875 cash.
   30 Recognized warranty expense related to November sales with an adjusting entry.
Dec. 9 Replaced 15 razors that were returned under the warranty.
   16 Sold 220 razors for $16,500 cash.
   29 Replaced 30 razors that were returned under the warranty.
   31 Recognized warranty expense related to December sales with an adjusting entry.

2013

Jan. 5 Sold 150 razors for $11,250 cash.
   17 Replaced 50 razors that were returned under the warranty.
   31 Recognized warranty expense related to January sales with an adjusting entry.

Required

1. Prepare journal entries to record these transactions and adjustments for 2012 and 2013.

2. How much warranty expense is reported for November 2012 and for December 2012?

3. How much warranty expense is reported for January 2013?

4. What is the balance of the Estimated Warranty Liability account as of December 31, 2012?

5. What is the balance of the Estimated Warranty Liability account as of January 31, 2013?

Check (3) $900
(4) $1,050 Cr.
(5) $950 Cr.

Shown here are condensed income statements for two different companies (both are organized as LLCs and pay no income taxes).

Problem 11-5A
Computing and analyzing times interest earned

A1

Miller Company	
Sales	$1,000,000
Variable expenses (80%)	800,000
Income before interest	200,000
Interest expense (fixed)	60,000
Net income	$ 140,000

Weaver Company	
Sales	$1,000,000
Variable expenses (60%)	600,000
Income before interest	400,000
Interest expense (fixed)	260,000
Net income	$ 140,000

Required

1. Compute times interest earned for Miller Company.

2. Compute times interest earned for Weaver Company.

3. What happens to each company's net income if sales increase by 30%?

4. What happens to each company's net income if sales increase by 50%?

5. What happens to each company's net income if sales increase by 80%?

6. What happens to each company's net income if sales decrease by 10%?

7. What happens to each company's net income if sales decrease by 20%?

8. What happens to each company's net income if sales decrease by 40%?

Check (3) Miller net income,
$200,000 (43% increase)

(6) Weaver net income,
$100,000 (29% decrease)

Analysis Component

9. Comment on the results from parts 3 through 8 in relation to the fixed-cost strategies of the two companies and the ratio values you computed in parts 1 and 2.

Francisco Company has 10 employees, each of whom earns $2,800 per month and is paid on the last day of each month. All 10 have been employed continuously at this amount since January 1. Francisco uses a payroll bank account and special payroll checks to pay its employees. On March 1, the following accounts and balances exist in its general ledger:

Problem 11-6A^A
Entries for payroll transactions

P2 P3 P5

a. FICA—Social Security Taxes Payable, $3,472; FICA—Medicare Taxes Payable, $812. (The balances of these accounts represent total liabilities for *both* the employer's and employees' FICA taxes for the February payroll only.)

b. Employees' Federal Income Taxes Payable, $4,000 (liability for February only).

c. Federal Unemployment Taxes Payable, $448 (liability for January and February together).

d. State Unemployment Taxes Payable, $2,240 (liability for January and February together).

During March and April, the company had the following payroll transactions.

Mar. 15 Issued check payable to Swift Bank, a federal depository bank authorized to accept employers' payments of FICA taxes and employee income tax withholdings. The $8,284 check is in payment of the February FICA and employee income taxes.

31 Recorded the March payroll and transferred funds from the regular bank account to the payroll bank account. Issued checks payable to each employee in payment of the March payroll. The payroll register shows the following summary totals for the March pay period.

Check March 31: Salaries Payable,
$21,858

Salaries				Federal	
Office Salaries	Shop Salaries	Gross Pay	FICA Taxes*	Income Taxes	Net Pay
$11,200	$16,800	$28,000	$1,736	$4,000	$21,858
			$ 406		

* FICA taxes are Social Security and Medicare, respectively.

<table>
<tr><td>

March 31: Dr. Payroll Taxes
Expenses, $2,814

April 15: Cr. Cash, $8,284
(Swift Bank)

</td></tr>
</table>

31   Recorded the employer's payroll taxes resulting from the March payroll. The company has a merit rating that reduces its state unemployment tax rate to 4.0% of the first $7,000 paid each employee. The federal rate is 0.8%.

Apr. 15   Issued check to Swift Bank in payment of the March FICA and employee income taxes.

15   Issued check to the State Tax Commission for the January, February, and March state unemployment taxes. Mailed the check and the first quarter tax return to the Commission.

30   Issued check payable to Swift Bank in payment of the employer's FUTA taxes for the first quarter of the year.

30   Mailed Form 941 to the IRS, reporting the FICA taxes and the employees' federal income tax withholdings for the first quarter.

Required

Prepare journal entries to record the transactions and events for both March and April.

PROBLEM SET B

Problem 11-1B

Short-term notes payable transactions and entries

P1

Warner Co. entered into the following transactions involving short-term liabilities in 2012 and 2013.

2012

Apr. 22   Purchased $5,000 of merchandise on credit from Fox Products, terms are 1/10, n/30. Warner uses the perpetual inventory system.

May 23   Replaced the April 22 account payable to Fox Products with a 60-day, $4,600 note bearing 15% annual interest along with paying $400 in cash.

July 15   Borrowed $12,000 cash from Spring Bank by signing a 120-day, 10% interest-bearing note with a face value of $12,000.

___?___   Paid the amount due on the note to Fox Products at maturity.

___?___   Paid the amount due on the note to Spring Bank at maturity.

Dec. 6   Borrowed $8,000 cash from City Bank by signing a 45-day, 9% interest-bearing note with a face value of $8,000.

31   Recorded an adjusting entry for accrued interest on the note to City Bank.

2013

___?___   Paid the amount due on the note to City Bank at maturity.

Required

1. Determine the maturity date for each of the three notes described.

2. Determine the interest due at maturity for each of the three notes. (Assume a 360-day year.)

3. Determine the interest expense to be recorded in the adjusting entry at the end of 2012.

4. Determine the interest expense to be recorded in 2013.

5. Prepare journal entries for all the preceding transactions and events for years 2012 and 2013.

Check   (2) Fox, $115
(3) $50
(4) $40

Problem 11-2B

Payroll expenses, withholdings, and taxes

P2   P3

Fishing Guides Co. has four employees. FICA Social Security taxes are 6.2% of the first $110,100 paid to each employee, and FICA Medicare taxes are 1.45% of gross pay. Also, for the first $7,000 paid to each employee, the company's FUTA taxes are 0.8% and SUTA taxes are 1.75%. The company is preparing its payroll calculations for the week ended September 30. Payroll records show the following information for the company's four employees.

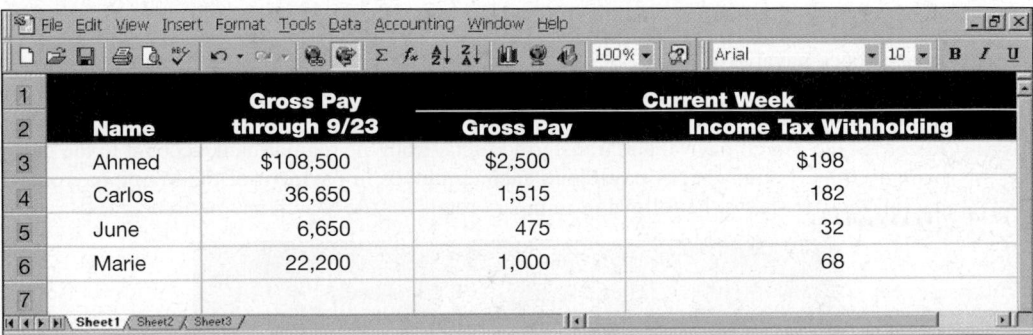

Name	Gross Pay through 9/23	Current Week Gross Pay	Current Week Income Tax Withholding
Ahmed	$108,500	$2,500	$198
Carlos	36,650	1,515	182
June	6,650	475	32
Marie	22,200	1,000	68

In addition to gross pay, the company must pay one-half of the $50 per employee weekly health insurance; each employee pays the remaining one-half. The company also contributes an extra 5% of each employee's gross pay (at no cost to employees) to a pension fund.

Required

Compute the following for the week ended September 30 (round amounts to the nearest cent):

1. Each employee's FICA withholdings for Social Security.
2. Each employee's FICA withholdings for Medicare.
3. Employer's FICA taxes for Social Security.
4. Employer's FICA taxes for Medicare.
5. Employer's FUTA taxes.
6. Employer's SUTA taxes.
7. Each employee's net (take-home) pay.
8. Employer's total payroll-related expense for each employee.

Check (3) $284.58
(4) $79.61
(5) $2.80
(7) Total net pay, $4,545.81

Tavella Company's first weekly pay period of the year ends on January 8. On that date, the column totals in Tavella's payroll register indicate its sales employees earned $34,745, its office employees earned $21,225, and its delivery employees earned $1,030 in salaries. The employees are to have withheld from their salaries FICA Social Security taxes at the rate of 6.2%, FICA Medicare taxes at the rate of 1.45%, $8,625 of federal income taxes, $1,160 of medical insurance deductions, and $138 of union dues. No employee earned more than $7,000 in the first pay period.

Problem 11-3B
Entries for payroll transactions
P2 P3

Required

1. Calculate FICA Social Security taxes payable and FICA Medicare taxes payable. Prepare the journal entry to record Tavella Company's January 8 (employee) payroll expenses and liabilities. (Round amounts to cents.)

2. Prepare the journal entry to record Tavella's (employer) payroll taxes resulting from the January 8 payroll. Tavella's merit rating reduces its state unemployment tax rate to 3.4% of the first $7,000 paid each employee. The federal unemployment tax rate is 0.8%. (Round amounts to cents.)

Check (1) Cr. Salaries Payable, $42,716.50

(2) Dr. Payroll Taxes Expense, $6,754.50

On November 10, 2013, Lee Co. began operations by purchasing coffee grinders for resale. Lee uses the perpetual inventory method. The grinders have a 60-day warranty that requires the company to replace any nonworking grinder. When a grinder is returned, the company discards it and mails a new one from Merchandise Inventory to the customer. The company's cost per new grinder is $24 and its retail selling price is $50 in both 2013 and 2014. The manufacturer has advised the company to expect warranty costs to equal 10% of dollar sales. The following transactions and events occurred.

Problem 11-4B
Warranty expense and liability estimation
P4

2013

Nov. 16 Sold 50 grinders for $2,500 cash.
    30 Recognized warranty expense related to November sales with an adjusting entry.
Dec. 12 Replaced six grinders that were returned under the warranty.
    18 Sold 200 grinders for $10,000 cash.
    28 Replaced 17 grinders that were returned under the warranty.
    31 Recognized warranty expense related to December sales with an adjusting entry.

2014

Jan. 7 Sold 40 grinders for $2,000 cash.
   21 Replaced 36 grinders that were returned under the warranty.
   31 Recognized warranty expense related to January sales with an adjusting entry.

Required

1. Prepare journal entries to record these transactions and adjustments for 2013 and 2014.
2. How much warranty expense is reported for November 2013 and for December 2013?
3. How much warranty expense is reported for January 2014?
4. What is the balance of the Estimated Warranty Liability account as of December 31, 2013?
5. What is the balance of the Estimated Warranty Liability account as of January 31, 2014?

Check (3) $200
(4) $698 Cr.
(5) $34 Cr.

Shown here are condensed income statements for two different companies (both are organized as LLCs and pay no income taxes).

Problem 11-5B
Computing and analyzing times interest earned
A1

Ellis Company	
Sales	$240,000
Variable expenses (50%)	120,000
Income before interest	120,000
Interest expense (fixed)	90,000
Net income	$ 30,000

Seidel Company	
Sales	$240,000
Variable expenses (75%)	180,000
Income before interest	60,000
Interest expense (fixed)	30,000
Net income	$ 30,000

Required

1. Compute times interest earned for Ellis Company.
2. Compute times interest earned for Seidel Company.
3. What happens to each company's net income if sales increase by 10%?
4. What happens to each company's net income if sales increase by 40%?
5. What happens to each company's net income if sales increase by 90%?
6. What happens to each company's net income if sales decrease by 20%?
7. What happens to each company's net income if sales decrease by 50%?
8. What happens to each company's net income if sales decrease by 80%?

Check (4) Ellis net income, $78,000 (160% increase)

(6) Seidel net income, $18,000 (40% decrease)

Analysis Component

9. Comment on the results from parts 3 through 8 in relation to the fixed-cost strategies of the two companies and the ratio values you computed in parts 1 and 2.

Problem 11-6B[A]
Entries for payroll transactions
P2 P3 P5

MLS Company has five employees, each of whom earns $1,600 per month and is paid on the last day of each month. All five have been employed continuously at this amount since January 1. MLS uses a payroll bank account and special payroll checks to pay its employees. On June 1, the following accounts and balances exist in its general ledger:

a. FICA—Social Security Taxes Payable, $992; FICA—Medicare Taxes Payable, $232. (The balances of these accounts represent total liabilities for *both* the employer's and employees' FICA taxes for the May payroll only.)
b. Employees' Federal Income Taxes Payable, $1,050 (liability for May only).
c. Federal Unemployment Taxes Payable, $88 (liability for April and May together).
d. State Unemployment Taxes Payable, $440 (liability for April and May together).

During June and July, the company had the following payroll transactions.

June 15 Issued check payable to Security Bank, a federal depository bank authorized to accept employers' payments of FICA taxes and employee income tax withholdings. The $2,274 check is in payment of the May FICA and employee income taxes.

30 Recorded the June payroll and transferred funds from the regular bank account to the payroll bank account. Issued checks payable to each employee in payment of the June payroll. The payroll register shows the following summary totals for the June pay period.

Check June 30: Cr. Salaries Payable, $6,338

Salaries				Federal	
Office Salaries	Shop Salaries	Gross Pay	FICA Taxes*	Income Taxes	Net Pay
$3,800	$4,200	$8,000	$496	$1,050	$6,338
			$116		

* FICA taxes are Social Security and Medicare, respectively.

Check June 30: Dr. Payroll Taxes Expenses, $612

30 Recorded the employer's payroll taxes resulting from the June payroll. The company has a merit rating that reduces its state unemployment tax rate to 4.0% of the first $7,000 paid each employee. The federal rate is 0.8%.

July 15 Issued check payable to Security Bank in payment of the June FICA and employee income taxes.

July 15: Cr. Cash $2,274 (Security Bank)

15 Issued check to the State Tax Commission for the April, May and June state unemployment taxes. Mailed the check and the second quarter tax return to the State Tax Commission.

31 Issued check payable to Security Bank in payment of the employer's FUTA taxes for the first quarter of the year.

31 Mailed Form 941 to the IRS, reporting the FICA taxes and the employees' federal income tax withholdings for the second quarter.

Required

Prepare journal entries to record the transactions and events for both June and July.

(This serial problem began in Chapter 1 and continues through most of the book. If previous chapter segments were not completed, the serial problem can begin at this point. It is helpful, but not necessary, to use the Working Papers that accompany the book.)

SP 11   Review the February 26 and March 25 transactions for Success Systems (SP 5) from Chapter 5.

Required

1. Assume that Lyn Addie is an unmarried employee. Her $1,000 of wages are subject to no deductions other than FICA Social Security taxes, FICA Medicare taxes, and federal income taxes. Her federal income taxes for this pay period total $159. Compute her net pay for the eight days' work paid on February 26. (Round amounts to the nearest cent.)

2. Record the journal entry to reflect the payroll payment to Lyn Addie as computed in part 1.

3. Record the journal entry to reflect the (employer) payroll tax expenses for the February 26 payroll payment. Assume Lyn Addie has not met earnings limits for FUTA and SUTA—the FUTA rate is 0.8% and the SUTA rate is 4% for Success Systems. (Round amounts to the nearest cent.)

4. Record the entry(ies) for the merchandise sold on March 25 if a 4% sales tax rate applies.

SERIAL PROBLEM
Success Systems
P2 P3 C2

CP 11   Bug-Off Exterminators provides pest control services and sells extermination products manufactured by other companies. The following six-column table contains the company's unadjusted trial balance as of December 31, 2013.

COMPREHENSIVE PROBLEM
Bug-Off Exterminators
(Review of Chapters 1–11)

BUG-OFF EXTERMINATORS December 31, 2013					
	Unadjusted Trial Balance		Adjustments	Adjusted Trial Balance	
Cash	$ 17,000				
Accounts receivable	4,000				
Allowance for doubtful accounts		$ 828			
Merchandise inventory	11,700				
Trucks	32,000				
Accum. depreciation—Trucks		0			
Equipment	45,000				
Accum. depreciation—Equipment		12,200			
Accounts payable...................		5,000			
Estimated warranty liability		1,400			
Unearned services revenue		0			
Interest payable		0			
Long-term notes payable		15,000			
D. Buggs, Capital		59,700			
D. Buggs, Withdrawals	10,000				
Extermination services revenue		60,000			
Interest revenue		872			
Sales (of merchandise)		71,026			
Cost of goods sold	46,300				
Depreciation expense—Trucks	0				
Depreciation expense—Equipment	0				
Wages expense	35,000				
Interest expense	0				
Rent expense	9,000				
Bad debts expense	0				
Miscellaneous expense	1,226				
Repairs expense	8,000				
Utilities expense	6,800				
Warranty expense	0				
Totals	$226,026	$226,026			

The following information in *a* through *h* applies to the company at the end of the current year.

a. The bank reconciliation as of December 31, 2013, includes the following facts.

Cash balance per bank	$15,100
Cash balance per books	17,000
Outstanding checks	1,800
Deposit in transit	2,450
Interest earned (on bank account)	52
Bank service charges (miscellaneous expense)	15

Reported on the bank statement is a canceled check that the company failed to record. (Information from the bank reconciliation allows you to determine the amount of this check, which is a payment on an account payable.)

b. An examination of customers' accounts shows that accounts totaling $679 should be written off as uncollectible. Using an aging of receivables, the company determines that the ending balance of the Allowance for Doubtful Accounts should be $700.

c. A truck is purchased and placed in service on January 1, 2013. Its cost is being depreciated with the straight-line method using the following facts and estimates.

Original cost	$32,000
Expected salvage value	8,000
Useful life (years)	4

d. Two items of equipment (a sprayer and an injector) were purchased and put into service in early January 2011. They are being depreciated with the straight-line method using these facts and estimates.

	Sprayer	Injector
Original cost	$27,000	$18,000
Expected salvage value	3,000	2,500
Useful life (years)	8	5

e. On August 1, 2013, the company is paid $3,840 cash in advance to provide monthly service for an apartment complex for one year. The company began providing the services in August. When the cash was received, the full amount was credited to the Extermination Services Revenue account.

f. The company offers a warranty for the services it sells. The expected cost of providing warranty service is 2.5% of the extermination services revenue of $57,760 for 2013. No warranty expense has been recorded for 2013. All costs of servicing warranties in 2013 were properly debited to the Estimated Warranty Liability account.

g. The $15,000 long-term note is an 8%, five-year, interest-bearing note with interest payable annually on December 31. The note was signed with First National Bank on December 31, 2013.

h. The ending inventory of merchandise is counted and determined to have a cost of $11,700. Bug-Off uses a perpetual inventory system.

Required

1. Use the preceding information to determine amounts for the following items.

a. Correct (reconciled) ending balance of Cash, and the amount of the omitted check.

b. Adjustment needed to obtain the correct ending balance of the Allowance for Doubtful Accounts.

c. Depreciation expense for the truck used during year 2013.

d. Depreciation expense for the two items of equipment used during year 2013.

e. The adjusted 2013 ending balances of the Extermination Services Revenue and Unearned Services Revenue accounts.

f. The adjusted 2013 ending balances of the accounts for Warranty Expense and Estimated Warranty Liability.

g. The adjusted 2013 ending balances of the accounts for Interest Expense and Interest Payable. (Round amounts to nearest whole dollar.)

Check (1*a*) Cash bal. $15,750
(1*b*) $551 credit

(1*f*) Estim. warranty liability, $2,844 Cr.

2. Use the results of part 1 to complete the six-column table by first entering the appropriate adjustments for items *a* through *g* and then completing the adjusted trial balance columns. (*Hint:* Item *b* requires two adjustments.)

3. Prepare journal entries to record the adjustments entered on the six-column table. Assume Bug-Off's adjusted balance for Merchandise Inventory matches the year-end physical count.

4. Prepare a single-step income statement, a statement of owner's equity (cash withdrawals during 2013 were $10,000), and a classified balance sheet.

(2) Adjusted trial balance totals, $238,207

(4) Net income, $9,274; Total assets, $82,771

Beyond the Numbers

BTN 11-1   Refer to the financial statements of **Polaris** in Appendix A to answer the following.

1. Compute times interest earned for the fiscal years ended 2011, 2010, and 2009. Comment on Polaris' ability to cover its interest expense for this period. Assume an industry average of 20 for times interest earned.

2. Polaris' current liabilities include "Sales promotions and incentives"; assume that this account reflects "Loyalty reward liabilities." Is this a known or an estimated liability? Explain how this liability is created.

3. Does Polaris have any commitments or contingencies? If yes, then briefly explain them.

Fast Forward

4. Access Polaris' financial statements for fiscal years ending after December 31, 2011, at its Website (**Polaris.com**) or the SEC's EDGAR database (**www.sec.gov**). Compute its times interest earned for years ending after December 31, 2011, and compare your results to those in part 1.

REPORTING IN ACTION

A1 P4 🛡

Polaris

BTN 11-2   Key figures for **Polaris** and **Arctic Cat** follow.

($ thousands)	Polaris			Arctic Cat		
	Current Year	One Year Prior	Two Years Prior	Current Year	One Year Prior	Two Years Prior
Net income	$227,575	$147,138	$101,017	$13,007	$1,875	$(9,508)
Income taxes	119,051	71,403	50,157	5,224	(777)	(6,247)
Interest expense	3,987	2,680	4,111	11	250	1,015

COMPARATIVE ANALYSIS

A1 🛡

Polaris

Arctic Cat

Required

1. Compute times interest earned for the three years' data shown for each company.

2. Comment on which company appears stronger in its ability to pay interest obligations if income should decline. Assume an industry average of 20.

BTN 11-3   Cameron Bly is a sales manager for an automobile dealership. He earns a bonus each year based on revenue from the number of autos sold in the year less related warranty expenses. Actual warranty expenses have varied over the prior 10 years from a low of 3% of an automobile's selling price to a high of 10%. In the past, Bly has tended to estimate warranty expenses on the high end to be conservative. He must work with the dealership's accountant at year-end to arrive at the warranty expense accrual for cars sold each year.

1. Does the warranty accrual decision create any ethical dilemma for Bly?

2. Since warranty expenses vary, what percent do you think Bly should choose for the current year? Justify your response.

ETHICS CHALLENGE

P4 🛡

BTN 11-4   Dusty Johnson is the accounting and finance manager for a manufacturer. At year-end, he must determine how to account for the company's contingencies. His manager, Tom Pretti, objects to Johnson's proposal to recognize an expense and a liability for warranty service on units of a new product introduced in the fourth quarter. Pretti comments, "There's no way we can estimate this warranty cost. We don't owe anyone anything until a product fails and it is returned. Let's report an expense if and when we do any warranty work."

COMMUNICATING IN PRACTICE

C3 🛡

Required

Prepare a one-page memorandum for Johnson to send to Pretti defending his proposal.

TAKING IT TO THE NET

C1 A1

BTN 11-5 Access the February 24, 2012, filing of the December 31, 2011, annual 10-K report of **McDonald's Corporation** (Ticker: MCD), which is available from **www.SEC.gov**.

Required

1. Identify the current liabilities on McDonald's balance sheet as of December 31, 2011.
2. What portion (in percent) of McDonald's long-term debt matures within the next 12 months?
3. Use the consolidated statement of income for the year ended December 31, 2011, to compute McDonald's times interest earned ratio. Comment on the result. Assume an industry average of 15.0.

TEAMWORK IN ACTION

C2 P1

BTN 11-6 Assume that your team is in business and you must borrow $6,000 cash for short-term needs. You have been shopping banks for a loan, and you have the following two options.
A. Sign a $6,000, 90-day, 10% interest-bearing note dated June 1.
B. Sign a $6,000, 120-day, 8% interest-bearing note dated June 1.

Required

1. Discuss these two options and determine the best choice. Ensure that all teammates concur with the decision and understand the rationale.
2. Each member of the team is to prepare *one* of the following journal entries.
   a. Option A—at date of issuance.
   b. Option B—at date of issuance.
   c. Option A—at maturity date.
   d. Option B—at maturity date.
3. In rotation, each member is to explain the entry he or she prepared in part 2 to the team. Ensure that all team members concur with and understand the entries.
4. Assume that the funds are borrowed on December 1 (instead of June 1) and your business operates on a calendar-year reporting period. Each member of the team is to prepare *one* of the following entries.
   a. Option A—the year-end adjustment.
   b. Option B—the year-end adjustment.
   c. Option A—at maturity date.
   d. Option B—at maturity date.
5. In rotation, each member is to explain the entry he or she prepared in part 4 to the team. Ensure that all team members concur with and understand the entries.

ENTREPRENEURIAL DECISION

A1

BTN 11-7 Review the chapter's opening feature about Karen Cooper, and her start-up company, **SmartIT Staffing**. Assume that she is considering expanding her business to open an office in Europe. Assume her current income statement is as follows.

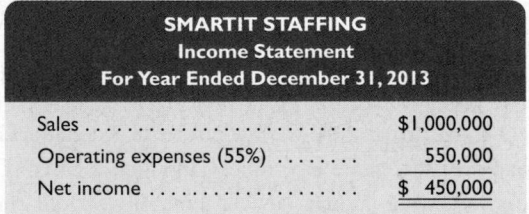

SMARTIT STAFFING Income Statement For Year Ended December 31, 2013	
Sales	$1,000,000
Operating expenses (55%)	550,000
Net income	$ 450,000

SmartIT Staffing currently has no interest-bearing debt. If it expands to open a European location, it will require a $300,000 loan. SmartIT Staffing has found a bank that will loan it the money on a 7% note payable. The company believes that, at least for the first few years, sales at its European location will be $250,000, and that all expenses will follow the same patterns as its current locations.

Required

1. Prepare an income statement (showing three separate columns for current operations, European, and total) for the company assuming that it borrows the funds and expands to Europe. Annual revenues for current operations are expected to remain at $1,000,000.

2. Compute the company's times interest earned under the expansion assumptions in part 1.

3. Assume sales at its European location are $400,000. Prepare an income statement (with columns for current operations, European, and total) for the company and compute times interest earned.

4. Assume sales at its European location are $100,000. Prepare an income statement (with columns for current operations, European, and total) for the company and compute times interest earned.

5. Comment on your results from parts 1 through 4.

BTN 11-8 Check your phone book or the Social Security Administration Website (www.ssa.gov) to locate the Social Security office near you. Visit the office to request a personal earnings and estimate form. Fill out the form and mail according to the instructions. You will receive a statement from the Social Security Administration regarding your earnings history and future Social Security benefits you can receive. (Formerly the request could be made online. The online service has been discontinued and is now under review by the Social Security Administration due to security concerns.) It is good to request an earnings and benefit statement every 5 to 10 years to make sure you have received credit for all wages earned and for which you and your employer have paid taxes into the system.

HITTING THE ROAD

P2

BTN 11-9 **KTM**, **Polaris**, and **Arctic Cat** are all competitors in the global marketplace. Comparative figures for KTM (www.KTM.com), along with selected figures from Polaris and Arctic Cat, follow.

GLOBAL DECISION

A1

KTM
Polaris
Arctic Cat

Key Figures	KTM (EUR thousands) Current Year	KTM (EUR thousands) Prior Year	Polaris Current Year	Polaris Prior Year	Arctic Cat Current Year	Arctic Cat Prior Year
Net income	20,818	2,660	—	—	—	—
Income taxes	1,709*	(229)	—	—	—	—
Interest expense	9,693	4,256	—	—	—	—
Times interest earned	?	?	87.9	82.5	1,658.4	5.4

*KTM's income taxes is a "positive" for the current year, which is not normal and occurs because of tax loss carryforwards that are explained in advanced courses.

Required

1. Compute the times interest earned ratio for the most recent two years for KTM using the data shown.

2. Which company of the three presented provides the best coverage of interest expense? Explain.

ANSWERS TO MULTIPLE CHOICE QUIZ

1. b; $6,000 × 0.05 × 30/360 = $25

2. e; $50,000 × (.062 + .0145) = $3,825

3. b; $7,000 × (.008 + .054) = $434

4. c; 10,000 television sets × .01 × $250 = $25,000

5. a; 150 employees × $175 per day × 1 vacation day earned = $26,250

Accounting for Partnerships

A Look Back

Chapter 11 focused on how current liabilities are identified, computed, recorded, and reported. Attention was directed at notes, payroll, sales taxes, warranties, employee benefits, and contingencies.

A Look at This Chapter

This chapter explains the partnership form of organization. Important partnership characteristics are described along with the accounting concepts and procedures for its most fundamental transactions.

A Look Ahead

Chapter 13 extends our discussion to the corporate form of organization. We describe the accounting and reporting for stock issuances, dividends, and other equity transactions.

Learning Objectives

CONCEPTUAL

C1 Identify characteristics of partnerships and similar organizations. (p. 482)

ANALYTICAL

A1 Compute partner return on equity and use it to evaluate partnership performance. (p. 494)

PROCEDURAL

P1 Prepare entries for partnership formation. (p. 485)

P2 Allocate and record income and loss among partners. (p. 485)

P3 Account for the admission and withdrawal of partners. (p. 488)

P4 Prepare entries for partnership liquidation. (p. 491)

Hunks and Junk

"Start with a vision, create a strategic plan, and live by it."
—NICK FRIEDMAN

TAMPA—"I never said that I wanted to be a 'trash-man' when I was growing up," laughs Omar Soliman. "But I had a natural interest in entrepreneurship and starting my own business." That interest led Omar, along with Nick Friedman, to launch **College Hunks Hauling Junk LLC (CollegeHunksHaulingJunk.com).** "We are like a dumpster service," admits Omar, "but we provide the labor. We haul away and remove junk and trash."

Although the young partners must focus on the trashy side of the business, they also focus on the accounting and financial side. Nick explains that to save costs and help the bottom line, the partners began with a "beat up cargo van from Omar's mom . . . [and by] operating the business out of my parents' house." Adds Nick, "A light bulb went off in our heads: We could borrow the van and go around town cleaning out basements, garages and attics and also help deliver and move items."

The young owners set up a partnership arrangement. Nick describes how they set up their business as a limited liability company (LLC), which is a partnership with some protection against liability claims. Both partners stress the importance of attending to partnership formation, partnership agreements, and financial reports to stay afloat, especially in the early stages.

They refer to the partners' return on equity and establishing the proper organizational form as key inputs to partnership strategies and decisions.

Success is causing their partnership to evolve. Nick explains that "the company now has over 40 franchises nationwide, and our vision is to become the largest employer of college students." Adds Omar, "The toughest hurdle was to get out of the mind frame that I was creating my own job, but rather I was creating something bigger." To aid in that growth, the partners joined with **1-800-Junk-USA** to further expand their opportunities. Omar explains that he and Nick sit on the boards of both companies and now hold ownership in both companies.

The partners continue to watch the accounting fundamentals. Both Omar and Nick insist that the partnership cannot survive unless it is profitable. To that end, both partners review their accounting results and regularly assess the partnership's costs and revenues. Nevertheless, Nick advises, "Don't chase the money, chase the vision, and the money will eventually come."

[Sources: *College Hunks Hauling Junk Website,* January 2013; *Time,* October 2011; *CareerCreator.com,* May 2009; *The Wall Street Journal,* September 2011; *YES Magazine,* November 2011]

The three basic types of business organizations are proprietorships, partnerships, and corporations. Partnerships are similar to proprietorships, except they have more than one owner. This chapter explains partnerships and looks at several variations of them such as limited partnerships, limited liability partnerships, S corporations, and limited liability companies. Understanding the advantages and disadvantages of the partnership form of business organization is important for making informed business decisions.

Accounting for Partnerships			
Partnership Organization	**Basic Partnership Accounting**	**Partner Admission and Withdrawal**	**Partnership Liquidation**
• Characteristics • Organizations with partnership characteristics • Choice of business form	• Organizing a partnership • Dividing income or loss • Partnership financial statements	• Admission of partner • Withdrawal of partner • Death of partner	• No capital deficiency • Capital deficiency

PARTNERSHIP FORM OF ORGANIZATION

C1 Identify characteristics of partnerships and similar organizations.

A **partnership** is an unincorporated association of two or more people to pursue a business for profit as co-owners. Many businesses are organized as partnerships. They are especially common in small retail and service businesses. Many professional practitioners, including physicians, lawyers, investors, and accountants, also organize their practices as partnerships.

Characteristics of Partnerships

Partnerships are an important type of organization because they offer certain advantages with their unique characteristics. We describe these characteristics in this section.

Voluntary Association   A partnership is a voluntary association between partners. Joining a partnership increases the risk to one's personal financial position. Some courts have ruled that partnerships are created by the actions of individuals even when there is no *express agreement* to form one.

Partnership Agreement   Forming a partnership requires that two or more legally competent people (who are of age and of sound mental capacity) agree to be partners. Their agreement becomes a **partnership contract,** also called *articles of copartnership.* Although it should be in writing, the contract is binding even if it is only expressed verbally. Partnership agreements normally include details of the partners' (1) names and contributions, (2) rights and duties, (3) sharing of income and losses, (4) withdrawal arrangement, (5) dispute procedures, (6) admission and withdrawal of partners, and (7) rights and duties in the event a partner dies.

Point: When a new partner is admitted, all parties usually must agree to the admission.

Point: The end of a partnership is referred to as its *dissolution.*

Point: Partners are taxed on their share of partnership income, not on their withdrawals. Partners receive a "K-1" form each year showing their share of income they must report on their personal tax return.

Limited Life   The life of a partnership is limited. Death, bankruptcy, or any event taking away the ability of a partner to enter into or fulfill a contract ends a partnership. Any one of the partners can also terminate a partnership at will.

Taxation   A partnership is not subject to taxes on its income. The income or loss of a partnership is allocated to the partners according to the partnership agreement, and it is included in determining the taxable income for each partner's tax return. Partnership income or loss is allocated each year whether or not cash is distributed to partners.

Mutual Agency   Mutual agency implies that each partner is a fully authorized agent of the partnership. As its agent, a partner can commit or bind the partnership to any contract within the scope of the partnership business. For instance, a partner in a merchandising business can sign contracts binding the partnership to buy merchandise, lease a store building, borrow money, or hire cmployees. These activities are all within the scope of a merchandising firm. A partner in a law firm, acting alone, however, cannot bind the other partners to a contract to buy snowboards for resale or rent an apartment for parties. These actions are outside the normal scope of a law firm's business. Partners also can agree to limit the power of any one or more of the partners to negotiate contracts for the partnership. This agreement is binding on the partners and on outsiders who know it exists. It is not binding on outsiders who do not know it exists. Outsiders unaware of the agreement have the right to assume each partner has normal agency powers for the partnership. Mutual agency exposes partners to the risk of unwise actions by any one partner.

Unlimited Liability   **Unlimited liability** implies that each partner can be called on to pay a partnership's debts. When a partnership cannot pay its debts, creditors usually can apply their claims to partners' *personal* assets. If a partner does not have enough assets to meet his or her share of the partnership debt, the creditors can apply their claims to the assets of the other partners. A partnership in which all partners have *mutual agency* and *unlimited liability* is called a **general partnership.** Mutual agency and unlimited liability are two main reasons that most general partnerships have only a few members.

Point: The majority of states adhere to the Uniform Partnership Act for the basic rules of partnership formation, operation, and dissolution.

Co-Ownership of Property   Partnership assets are owned jointly by all partners. Any investment by a partner becomes the joint property of all partners. Partners have a claim on partnership assets based on their capital account and the partnership contract.

Point: Limited life, mutual agency, and unlimited liability are disadvantages of a partnership.

Organizations with Partnership Characteristics

Organizations exist that combine certain characteristics of partnerships with other forms of organizations. We discuss several of these forms in this section.

Limited Partnerships   Some individuals who want to invest in a partnership are unwilling to accept the risk of unlimited liability. Their needs can be met with a **limited partnership.** This type of organization is identified in its name with the words "Limited Partnership" or "Ltd." or "LP." A limited partnership has two classes of partners, general and limited. At least one partner must be a **general partner,** who assumes management duties and unlimited liability for the debts of the partnership. The **limited partners** have no personal liability beyond the amounts they invest in the partnership. Limited partners have no active role except as specified in the partnership agreement. A limited partnership agreement often specifies unique procedures for allocating income and losses between general and limited partners. The accounting procedures are similar for both limited and general partnerships.

Limited Liability Partnerships   Most states allow individuals to form a **limited liability partnership.** This is identified in its name with the words "Limited Liability Partnership" or by "LLP." This type of partnership is designed to protect innocent partners from malpractice or negligence claims resulting from the acts of another partner. When a partner provides service resulting in a malpractice claim, that partner has personal liability for the claim. The remaining partners who were not responsible for the actions resulting in the claim are not personally liable for it. However, most states hold all partners personally liable for other partnership debts. Accounting for a limited liability partnership is the same as for a general partnership.

Point: Many accounting, law, consulting, and architectural firms are set up as LLPs.

Decision Insight

Pencil Pushing Partners   Most states allow any business to form as a limited liability partnership (LLP); however, some states only allow approved professional service companies to form them. Of the four largest CPA firms in the United States (KPMG, Deloitte, PricewaterhouseCoopers, and Ernst & Young), all are set up as LLPs. ∎

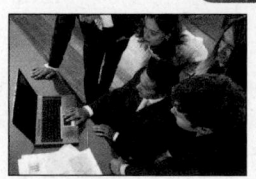

S Corporations   Certain corporations with 100 or fewer stockholders can elect to be treated as a partnership for income tax purposes. These corporations are called *Sub-Chapter S* or simply **S corporations.** This distinguishes them from other corporations, called *Sub-Chapter C* or

Global: Forms of business organizations allowed vary by country.

simply **C corporations.** S corporations provide stockholders the same limited liability feature that C corporations do. The advantage of an S corporation is that it does not pay income taxes. If stockholders work for an S corporation, their salaries are treated as expenses of the corporation. The remaining income or loss of the corporation is allocated to stockholders for inclusion on their personal tax returns. Except for C corporations having to account for income tax expenses and liabilities, the accounting procedures are the same for both S and C corporations.

Point: The majority of proprietorships and partnerships that are organized today are set up as LLCs.

Limited Liability Companies   A relatively new form of business organization is the **limited liability company.** The names of these businesses usually include the words "Limited Liability Company" or an abbreviation such as "LLC" or "LC." This form of business has certain features similar to a corporation and others similar to a limited partnership. The owners, who are called *members,* are protected with the same limited liability feature as owners of corporations. While limited partners cannot actively participate in the management of a limited partnership, the members of a limited liability company can assume an active management role. A limited liability company usually has a limited life. For income tax purposes, a limited liability company is typically treated as a partnership. This treatment depends on factors such as whether the members' equity interests are freely transferable and whether the company has continuity of life. A limited liability company's accounting system is designed to help management comply with the dictates of the articles of organization and company regulations adopted by its members. The accounting system also must provide information to support the company's compliance with state and federal laws, including taxation.

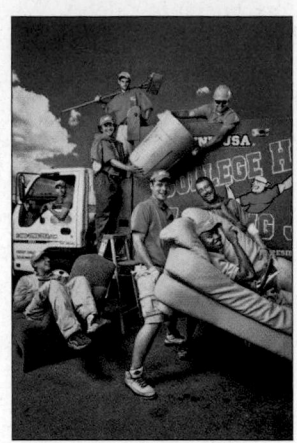

Point: Accounting for LLCs is similar to that for partnerships (and proprietorships). One difference is that Owner (Partner), Capital is usually called *Members, Capital* for LLCs.

Choosing a Business Form

Choosing the proper business form is crucial. Many factors should be considered, including taxes, liability risk, tax and fiscal year-end, ownership structure, estate planning, business risks, and earnings and property distributions. The following table summarizes several important characteristics of business organizations:

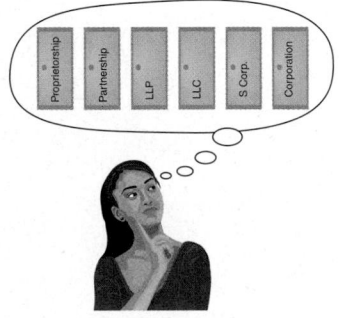

	Proprietorship	Partnership	LLP	LLC	S Corp.	Corporation
Business entity	Yes	Yes	Yes	Yes	Yes	Yes
Legal entity	No	No	No	Yes	Yes	Yes
Limited liability	No	No	Limited*	Yes	Yes	Yes
Business taxed	No	No	No	No	No	Yes
One owner allowed	Yes	No	No	Yes	Yes	Yes

* A partner's personal liability for LLP debts is limited. Most LLPs carry insurance to protect against malpractice.

Point: The Small Business Administration provides suggestions and information on setting up the proper form for your organization—see **SBA.gov**.

We must remember that this table is a summary, not a detailed list. Many details underlie each of these business forms, and several details differ across states. Also, state and federal laws change, and a body of law is still developing around LLCs. Business owners should look at these details and consider unique business arrangements such as organizing various parts of their businesses in different forms.

Quick Check

Answers — p. 497

1. A partnership is terminated in the event (*a*) a partnership agreement is not in writing, (*b*) a partner dies, (*c*) a partner exercises mutual agency.
2. What does the term *unlimited liability* mean when applied to a general partnership?
3. Which of the following forms of organization do not provide limited liability to *all* of its owners? (*a*) S corporation, (*b*) limited liability company, (*c*) limited partnership.

BASIC PARTNERSHIP ACCOUNTING

Since ownership rights in a partnership are divided among partners, partnership accounting

- Uses a capital account for each partner.
- Uses a withdrawals account for each partner.
- Allocates net income or loss to partners according to the partnership agreement.

This section describes partnership accounting for organizing a partnership, distributing income and loss, and preparing financial statements.

Organizing a Partnership

When partners invest in a partnership, their capital accounts are credited for the invested amounts. Partners can invest both assets and liabilities. Each partner's investment is recorded at an agreed-on value, normally the market values of the contributed assets and liabilities at the date of contribution. To illustrate, Kayla Zayn and Hector Perez organize a partnership on January 11 called BOARDS that offers year-round facilities for skateboarding and snowboarding. Zayn's initial net investment in BOARDS is $30,000, made up of cash ($7,000), boarding facilities ($33,000), and a note payable reflecting a bank loan for the new business ($10,000). Perez's initial investment is cash of $10,000. These amounts are the values agreed on by both partners. The entries to record these investments follow.

P1 | Prepare entries for partnership formation.

Zayn's Investment

Jan. 11	Cash	7,000	
	Boarding facilities	33,000	
	Note payable		10,000
	K. Zayn, Capital		30,000
	To record the investment of Zayn.		

Assets   = Liabilities +   Equity
+7,000   +10,000   +30,000
+33,000

Perez's Investment

Jan. 11	Cash	10,000	
	H. Perez, Capital		10,000
	To record the investment of Perez.		

Assets   = Liabilities +   Equity
+10,000   +10,000

In accounting for a partnership, the following additional relations hold true: (1) Partners' withdrawals are debited to their own separate withdrawals accounts. (2) Partners' capital accounts are credited (or debited) for their shares of net income (or net loss) when closing the accounts at the end of a period. (3) Each partner's withdrawals account is closed to that partner's capital account. Separate capital and withdrawals accounts are kept for each partner.

Point: Both equity and cash are reduced when a partner withdraws cash from a partnership.

■ **Decision** Insight ━━━━━━━━━━━━━━━━━━━━━━━━

Broadway Partners   Big River Productions is a partnership that owns the rights to the play *Big River*. The play is performed on tour and periodically on Broadway. For a recent year-end, its Partners' Capital was approximately $300,000, and it was distributed in its entirety to the partners. ■

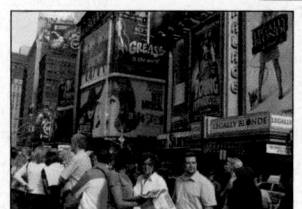

Dividing Income or Loss

Partners are not employees of the partnership but are its owners. If partners devote their time and services to their partnership, they are understood to do so for profit, not for salary. This means there are no salaries to partners that are reported as expenses on the partnership income statement. However, when net income or loss of a partnership is allocated among partners, the partners can agree to allocate "salary allowances" reflecting the relative value of services

P2 | Allocate and record income and loss among partners.

provided. Partners also can agree to allocate "interest allowances" based on the amount invested. For instance, since Zayn contributes three times the investment of Perez, it is only fair that this be considered when allocating income between them. Like salary allowances, these interest allowances are not expenses on the income statement.

Partners can agree to any method of dividing income or loss. In the absence of an agreement, the law says that the partners share income or loss of a partnership equally. If partners agree on how to share income but say nothing about losses, they share losses the same way they share income. Three common methods to divide income or loss use (1) a stated ratio basis, (2) the ratio of capital balances, or (3) salary and interest allowances and any remainder according to a fixed ratio. We explain each of these methods in this section.

Allocation on Stated Ratios

The *stated ratio* (also called the *income-and-loss-sharing ratio,* the *profit and loss ratio,* or the *P&L ratio*) method of allocating partnership income or loss gives each partner a fraction of the total. Partners must agree on the fractional share each receives. To illustrate, assume the partnership agreement of K. Zayn and H. Perez says Zayn receives two-thirds and Perez one-third of partnership income and loss. If their partnership's net income is $60,000, it is allocated to the partners when the Income Summary account is closed as follows.

Dec. 31	Income Summary	60,000	
	K. Zayn, Capital		40,000
	H. Perez, Capital		20,000
	To allocate income and close Income Summary.		

Allocation on Capital Balances

The *capital balances* method of allocating partnership income or loss assigns an amount based on the ratio of each partner's relative capital balance. If Zayn and Perez agree to share income and loss on the ratio of their beginning capital balances—Zayn's $30,000 and Perez's $10,000—Zayn receives three-fourths of any income or loss ($30,000/$40,000) and Perez receives one-fourth ($10,000/$40,000). The journal entry follows the same format as that using stated ratios (see the preceding entries).

Allocation on Services, Capital, and Stated Ratios

The *services, capital, and stated ratio* method of allocating partnership income or loss recognizes that service and capital contributions of partners often are not equal. Salary allowances can make up for differences in service contributions. Interest allowances can make up for unequal capital contributions. Also, the allocation of income and loss can include *both* salary and interest allowances. To illustrate, assume that the partnership agreement of K. Zayn and H. Perez reflects differences in service and capital contributions as follows: (1) annual salary allowances of $36,000 to Zayn and $24,000 to Perez, (2) annual interest allowances of 10% of a partner's beginning-year capital balance, and (3) equal share of any remaining balance of income or loss. These salaries and interest allowances are *not* reported as expenses on the income statement. They are simply a means of dividing partnership income or loss. The remainder of this section provides two illustrations using this three-point allocation agreement.

Illustration when income exceeds allowance.   If BOARDS has first-year net income of $70,000, and Zayn and Perez apply the three-point partnership agreement described in the prior paragraph, income is allocated as shown in Exhibit 12.1. Zayn gets $42,000 and Perez gets $28,000 of the $70,000 total.

Illustration when allowances exceed income.   The sharing agreement between Zayn and Perez must be followed even if net income is less than the total of the allowances. For example, if BOARDS' first-year net income is $50,000 instead of $70,000, it is allocated to the partners as shown in Exhibit 12.2. Computations for salaries and interest are identical to those in Exhibit 12.1. However, when we apply the total allowances against income, the balance of income is negative. This $(14,000) negative balance is allocated equally to the partners per their sharing agreement. This means that a negative $(7,000) is allocated to each partner. In this case, Zayn ends up with $32,000 and Perez with $18,000. If BOARDS had experienced a net loss, Zayn and Perez would share it in the same manner as the $50,000 income. The only difference is that they would have begun with a negative amount because of the loss. Specifically, the partners would still have been

	Zayn	Perez	Total
Net income			$70,000
Salary allowances			
Zayn	$ 36,000		
Perez		$ 24,000	
Interest allowances			
Zayn (10% × $30,000)	3,000		
Perez (10% × $10,000)		1,000	
Total salaries and interest	39,000	25,000	64,000
Balance of income			6,000
Balance allocated equally			
Zayn	3,000 ←		
Perez		3,000 ←	
Total allocated			6,000
Balance of income			$ 0
Income of each partner	**$42,000**	**$28,000**	

EXHIBIT 12.1

Dividing Income When Income Exceeds Allowances

	Zayn	Perez	Total
Net income			$50,000
Salary allowances			
Zayn	$ 36,000		
Perez		$ 24,000	
Interest allowances			
Zayn (10% × $30,000)	3,000		
Perez (10% × $10,000)		1,000	
Total salaries and interest	39,000	25,000	64,000
Balance of income			(14,000)
Balance allocated equally			
Zayn	(7,000) ←		
Perez		(7,000) ←	
Total allocated			(14,000)
Balance of income			$ 0
Income of each partner	**$32,000**	**$18,000**	

EXHIBIT 12.2

Dividing Income When Allowances Exceed Income

allocated their salary and interest allowances, further adding to the negative balance of the loss. This *total* negative balance *after* salary and interest allowances would have been allocated equally between the partners. These allocations would have been applied against the positive numbers from any allowances to determine each partner's share of the loss.

Point: When a loss occurs, it is possible for a specific partner's capital to increase (when closing income summary) if that partner's allowance is in excess of his or her share of the negative balance. This implies that decreases to the capital balances of other partners exceed the partnership's loss amount.

Quick Check

Answer — p. 497

4. Denzel and Shantell form a partnership by contributing $70,000 and $35,000, respectively. They agree to an interest allowance equal to 10% of each partner's capital balance at the beginning of the year, with the remaining income shared equally. Allocate first-year income of $40,000 to each partner.

Partnership Financial Statements

Partnership financial statements are similar to those of other organizations. The **statement of partners' equity,** also called *statement of partners' capital,* is one exception. It shows *each* partner's beginning capital balance, additional investments, allocated income or loss, withdrawals, and ending capital balance. To illustrate, Exhibit 12.3 shows the statement of partners' equity for BOARDS prepared using the sharing agreement of Exhibit 12.1. Recall that BOARDS' income was $70,000; also, assume that Zayn withdrew $20,000 and Perez $12,000 at year-end.

EXHIBIT 12.3

Statement of Partners' Equity

BOARDS				
Statement of Partners' Equity				
For Year Ended December 31, 2013				
	Zayn		**Perez**	**Total**
Beginning capital balances		$ 0	$ 0	$ 0
Plus				
Investments by owners		30,000	10,000	40,000
Net income				
Salary allowances	$36,000		$24,000	
Interest allowances	3,000		1,000	
Balance allocated	3,000		3,000	
Total net income		42,000	28,000	70,000
		72,000	38,000	110,000
Less partners' withdrawals		(20,000)	(12,000)	(32,000)
Ending capital balances		**$52,000**	**$26,000**	**$78,000**

The equity section of the balance sheet of a partnership usually shows the separate capital account balance of each partner. In the case of BOARDS, both K. Zayn, Capital, and H. Perez, Capital, are listed in the equity section along with their balances of $52,000 and $26,000, respectively.

Decision Insight

Double Draw   Partnerships sometimes use two accounts to reflect a partner's withdrawal of cash from a partnership. For example, a "Drawing" account might be used for regular withdrawals such as for a monthly salary allowance. A second "Withdrawals" account might be used for infrequent or personal draws such as to help pay for a daughter/son's wedding or a lake home. ■

ADMISSION AND WITHDRAWAL OF PARTNERS

P3 | Account for the admission and withdrawal of partners.

A partnership is based on a contract between individuals. When a partner is admitted or withdraws, the present partnership ends. Still, the business can continue to operate as a new partnership consisting of the remaining partners. This section considers how to account for the admission and withdrawal of partners.

Admission of a Partner

A new partner is admitted in one of two ways: by purchasing an interest from one or more current partners or by investing cash or other assets in the partnership.

Purchase of Partnership Interest   The purchase of partnership interest is a *personal transaction between one or more current partners and the new partner.* To become a partner, the current partners must accept the purchaser. Accounting for the purchase of partnership interest involves reallocating current partners' capital to reflect the transaction. To illustrate, at the end of BOARDS' first year, H. Perez sells one-half of his partnership interest to Tyrell Rasheed for $18,000. This means that Perez gives up a $13,000 recorded interest ($26,000 × 1/2) in the partnership (see the ending capital balance in Exhibit 12.3). The partnership records this January 4 transaction as follows.

Assets = Liabilities + Equity
          −13,000
          +13,000

Jan. 4	H. Perez, Capital	13,000	
	T. Rasheed, Capital		13,000
	To record admission of Rasheed by purchase.		

After this entry is posted, BOARDS' equity shows K. Zayn, Capital; H. Perez, Capital; and T. Rasheed, Capital, and their respective balances of $52,000, $13,000, and $13,000.

Two aspects of this transaction are important. First, the partnership does *not* record the $18,000 Rasheed paid Perez. The partnership's assets, liabilities, and *total equity* are unaffected by this transaction among partners. Second, Zayn and Perez must agree that Rasheed is to become a partner. If they agree to accept Rasheed, a new partnership is formed and a new contract with a new income-and-loss-sharing agreement is prepared. If Zayn or Perez refuses to accept Rasheed as a partner, then (under the Uniform Partnership Act) Rasheed gets Perez's sold share of partnership income and loss. If the partnership is liquidated, Rasheed gets Perez's sold share of partnership assets. Rasheed gets no voice in managing the company unless Rasheed is admitted as a partner.

Point: Partners' withdrawals are not constrained by the partnership's annual income or loss.

Investing Assets in a Partnership   Admitting a partner by accepting assets is a *transaction between the new partner and the partnership*. The invested assets become partnership property. To illustrate, if Zayn (with a $52,000 interest) and Perez (with a $26,000 interest) agree to accept Rasheed as a partner in BOARDS after an investment of $22,000 cash, this is recorded as follows.

Jan. 4	Cash	22,000	
	T. Rasheed, Capital		22,000
	To record admission of Rasheed by investment.		

Assets = Liabilities + Equity
+22,000   +22,000

After this entry is posted, both assets (cash) and equity (T. Rasheed, Capital) increase by $22,000. Rasheed now has a 22% equity in the assets of the business, computed as $22,000 divided by the entire partnership equity ($52,000 + $26,000 + $22,000). Rasheed does not necessarily have a right to 22% of income. Dividing income and loss is a separate matter on which partners must agree.

Bonus to old partners.   When the current value of a partnership is greater than the recorded amounts of equity, the partners usually require a new partner to pay a bonus for the privilege of joining. To illustrate, assume that Zayn and Perez agree to accept Rasheed as a partner with a 25% interest in BOARDS if Rasheed invests $42,000. Recall that the partnership's accounting records show that Zayn's recorded equity in the business is $52,000 and Perez's recorded equity is $26,000 (see Exhibit 12.3). Rasheed's equity is determined as follows.

Equities of existing partners ($52,000 + $26,000)	$ 78,000
Investment of new partner	42,000
Total partnership equity	$120,000
Equity of Rasheed (25% × $120,000)	$ 30,000

Although Rasheed invests $42,000, the equity attributed to Rasheed in the new partnership is only $30,000. The $12,000 difference is called a *bonus* and is allocated to existing partners (Zayn and Perez) according to their income-and-loss-sharing agreement. A bonus is shared in this way because it is viewed as reflecting a higher value of the partnership that is not yet reflected in income. The entry to record this transaction follows.

Jan. 4	Cash	42,000	
	T. Rasheed, Capital		30,000
	K. Zayn, Capital ($12,000 × ½)		6,000
	H. Perez, Capital ($12,000 × ½)		6,000
	To record admission of Rasheed and bonus.		

Assets = Liabilities + Equity
+42,000   +30,000
                            +6,000
                            +6,000

Bonus to new partner.   Alternatively, existing partners can grant a bonus to a new partner. This usually occurs when they need additional cash or the new partner has exceptional talents. The bonus to the new partner is in the form of a larger share of equity than the amount invested. To illustrate, assume that Zayn and Perez agree to accept Rasheed as a partner with a

25% interest in the partnership, but they require Rasheed to invest only $18,000. Rasheed's equity is determined as follows.

Equities of existing partners ($52,000 + $26,000)	$78,000
Investment of new partner	18,000
Total partnership equity	$96,000
Equity of Rasheed (25% × $96,000)	$24,000

The old partners contribute the $6,000 bonus (computed as $24,000 minus $18,000) to Rasheed according to their income-and-loss-sharing ratio. Moreover, Rasheed's 25% equity does not necessarily entitle Rasheed to 25% of future income or loss. This is a separate matter for agreement by the partners. The entry to record the admission and investment of Rasheed is

Assets = Liabilities + Equity
+18,000   −3,000
                         −3,000
                         +24,000

Jan. 4	Cash	18,000	
	K. Zayn, Capital ($6,000 × ½)	3,000	
	H. Perez, Capital ($6,000 × ½)	3,000	
	T. Rasheed, Capital		24,000
	To record Rasheed's admission and bonus.		

Withdrawal of a Partner

A partner generally withdraws from a partnership in one of two ways. (1) First, the withdrawing partner can sell his or her interest to another person who pays for it in cash or other assets. For this, we need only debit the withdrawing partner's capital account and credit the new partner's capital account. (2) The second case is when cash or other assets of the partnership are distributed to the withdrawing partner in settlement of his or her interest. To illustrate these cases, assume that Perez withdraws from the partnership of BOARDS in some future period. The partnership shows the following capital balances at the date of Perez's withdrawal: K. Zayn, $84,000; H. Perez, $38,000; and T. Rasheed, $38,000. The partners (Zayn, Perez, and Rasheed) share income and loss equally. Accounting for Perez's withdrawal depends on whether a bonus is paid. We describe three possibilities.

No Bonus If Perez withdraws and takes cash equal to Perez's capital balance, the entry is

Assets = Liabilities + Equity
−38,000   −38,000

Oct. 31	H. Perez, Capital	38,000	
	Cash		38,000
	To record withdrawal of Perez from partnership		
	with no bonus.		

Perez can take any combination of assets to which the partners agree to settle Perez's equity. Perez's withdrawal creates a new partnership between the remaining partners. A new partnership contract and a new income-and-loss-sharing agreement are required.

Bonus to Remaining Partners A withdrawing partner is sometimes willing to take less than the recorded value of his or her equity to get out of the partnership or because the recorded value is overstated. Whatever the reason, when this occurs, the withdrawing partner in effect gives the remaining partners a bonus equal to the equity left behind. The remaining partners share this unwithdrawn equity according to their income-and-loss-sharing ratio. To illustrate, if Perez withdraws and agrees to take $34,000 cash in settlement of Perez's capital balance, the entry is

Assets = Liabilities + Equity
−34,000   −38,000
                         +2,000
                         +2,000

Oct. 31	H. Perez, Capital	38,000	
	Cash		34,000
	K. Zayn, Capital		2,000
	T. Rasheed, Capital		2,000
	To record withdrawal of Perez and bonus to		
	remaining partners.		

Perez withdrew $4,000 less than Perez's recorded equity of $38,000. This $4,000 is divided between Zayn and Rasheed according to their income-and-loss-sharing ratio.

Bonus to Withdrawing Partner A withdrawing partner may be able to receive more than his or her recorded equity for at least two reasons. First, the recorded equity may be understated. Second, the remaining partners may agree to remove this partner by giving assets of greater value than this partner's recorded equity. In either case, the withdrawing partner receives a bonus. The remaining partners reduce their equity by the amount of this bonus according to their income-and-loss-sharing ratio. To illustrate, if Perez withdraws and receives $40,000 cash in settlement of Perez's capital balance, the entry is

Oct. 31	H. Perez, Capital	38,000	
	K. Zayn, Capital	1,000	
	T. Rasheed, Capital	1,000	
	Cash		40,000
	To record Perez's withdrawal from partnership with a bonus to Perez.		

Assets = Liabilities + Equity
-40,000   -38,000
                        -1,000
                        -1,000

Falcon Cable Communications set up a partnership withdrawal agreement. Falcon owns and operates cable television systems and had two managing general partners. The partnership agreement stated that either partner "can offer to sell to the other partner the offering partner's entire partnership interest . . . for a negotiated price. If the partner receiving such an offer rejects it, the offering partner may elect to cause [the partnership] . . . to be liquidated and dissolved."

Death of a Partner

A partner's death dissolves a partnership. A deceased partner's estate is entitled to receive his or her equity. The partnership contract should contain provisions for settlement in this case. These provisions usually require (1) closing the books to determine income or loss since the end of the previous period and (2) determining and recording current market values for both assets and liabilities. The remaining partners and the deceased partner's estate then must agree to a settlement of the deceased partner's equity. This can involve selling the equity to remaining partners or to an outsider, or it can involve withdrawing assets.

■ Decision Ethics

Financial Planner You are hired by the two remaining partners of a three-member partnership after the third partner's death. The partnership agreement states that a deceased partner's estate is entitled to a "share of partnership assets equal to the partner's relative equity balance" (partners' equity balances are equal). The estate argues that it is entitled to one-third of the current value of partnership assets. The remaining partners say the distribution should use asset book values, which are 75% of current value. They also point to partnership liabilities, which equal 40% of total asset book value and 30% of current value. How would you resolve this situation? ■ [Answer—p. 497]

LIQUIDATION OF A PARTNERSHIP

When a partnership is liquidated, its business ends and three concluding steps are required.

P4 Prepare entries for partnership liquidation.

1. Record the sale of noncash assets for cash, and any gain or loss from liquidation is allocated to partners *using their income-and-loss-sharing agreement.*
2. Pay or settle all partner liabilities.
3. Distribute any remaining cash to partners *based on their capital balances.*

Partnership liquidation usually falls into one of two cases, as described in this section.

No Capital Deficiency

No capital deficiency means that all partners have a zero or credit balance in their capital accounts for final distribution of cash. To illustrate, assume that Zayn, Perez, and Rasheed operate their partnership in BOARDS for several years, sharing income and loss equally. The partners then decide to liquidate. On the liquidation date, the current period's income or loss is transferred to the partners' capital accounts according to the sharing agreement. After that transfer, assume the partners' recorded account balances (immediately prior to liquidation) are:

Cash	$178,000	Accounts payable	$20,000	H. Perez, Capital	$66,000
Land	40,000	K. Zayn, Capital	70,000	T. Rasheed, Capital	62,000

We apply three steps for liquidation. ① *The partnership sells its noncash assets, and any losses or gains from liquidation are shared among partners according to their income-and-loss-sharing agreement* (equal for these partners). Assume that BOARDS sells its noncash assets consisting of $40,000 in land for $46,000 cash, yielding a net gain of $6,000. In a liquidation, gains or losses usually result from the sale of noncash assets, which are called *losses and gains from liquidation*. The entry to sell its assets for $46,000 follows.

Assets = Liabilities + Equity
−40,000   +6,000
+46,000

Jan. 15	Cash	46,000	
	Land		40,000
	Gain from Liquidation		6,000
	Sold noncash assets at a gain.		

Allocation of the gain from liquidation per the partners' income-and-loss-sharing agreement follows.

Assets = Liabilities + Equity
                     −6,000
                     +2,000
                     +2,000
                     +2,000

Jan. 15	Gain from Liquidation	6,000	
	K. Zayn, Capital		2,000
	H. Perez, Capital		2,000
	T. Rasheed, Capital		2,000
	To allocate liquidation gain to partners.		

② *The partnership pays its liabilities, and any losses or gains from liquidation of liabilities are shared among partners according to their income-and-loss-sharing agreement.* BOARDS' only liability is $20,000 in accounts payable, and no gain or loss occurred.

Assets = Liabilities + Equity
−20,000   −20,000

Jan. 15	Accounts Payable	20,000	
	Cash		20,000
	To pay claims of creditors.		

After step 2, we have the following capital balances along with the remaining cash balance.

K. Zayn			H. Perez, Capital			T. Rasheed, Capital			Cash			
	Bal.	70,000		Bal.	66,000		Bal.	62,000	Bal.	178,000	(3)	20,000
	(2)	2,000		(2)	2,000		(2)	2,000	(1)	46,000		
	Bal.	72,000		Bal.	68,000		Bal.	64,000	Bal.	204,000		

③ *Any remaining cash is divided among the partners **according to their capital account balances.*** The entry to record the final distribution of cash to partners follows.

Assets   = Liabilities + Equity
−204,000   −72,000
                             −68,000
                             −64,000

Jan. 15	K. Zayn, Capital	72,000	
	H. Perez, Capital	68,000	
	T. Rasheed, Capital	64,000	
	Cash		204,000
	To distribute remaining cash to partners.		

It is important to remember that the final cash payment is distributed to partners according to their capital account balances, whereas gains and losses from liquidation are allocated according to the income-and-loss-sharing ratio. The following *statement of liquidation* summarizes the three steps in this section.

Statement of Liquidation	Cash	Noncash Assets	=	Liabilities	K. Zayn, Capital	H. Perez, Capital	T. Rasheed, Capital
Balances prior to liquidation....	$178,000	$ 40,000		$ 20,000	$ 70,000	$66,000	$62,000
① Sale of noncash assets	46,000	(40,000)			2,000	2,000	2,000
② Payment of liabilities	(20,000)			(20,000)	0	0	0
Balances for distribution	204,000	$ 0		$ 0	72,000	68,000	64,000
③ Distribution of cash to partners	(204,000)				(72,000)	(68,000)	(64,000)
	$ 0				$ 0	$ 0	$ 0

Capital Deficiency

Capital deficiency means that at least one partner has a debit balance in his or her capital account at the point of final cash distribution (during step ③ as explained in the prior section). This can arise from liquidation losses, excessive withdrawals before liquidation, or recurring losses in prior periods. A partner with a capital deficiency must, if possible, cover the deficit by paying cash into the partnership.

To illustrate, assume that Zayn, Perez, and Rasheed operate their partnership in BOARDS for several years, sharing income and losses equally. The partners then decide to liquidate. Immediately prior to the final distribution of cash, the partners' recorded capital balances are Zayn, $19,000; Perez, $8,000; and Rasheed, $(3,000). Rasheed's capital deficiency means that Rasheed owes the partnership $3,000. Both Zayn and Perez have a legal claim against Rasheed's personal assets. The final distribution of cash in this case depends on how this capital deficiency is handled. Two possibilities exist: the partner pays the deficiency or the partner cannot pay the deficiency.

Partner Pays Deficiency   Rasheed is obligated to pay $3,000 into the partnership to cover the deficiency. If Rasheed is willing and able to pay, the entry to record receipt of payment from Rasheed follows.

Jan. 15	Cash	3,000	
	T. Rasheed, Capital		3,000
	To record payment of deficiency by Rasheed.		

Assets = Liabilities + Equity
+3,000   +3,000

After the $3,000 payment, the partners' capital balances are Zayn, $19,000; Perez, $8,000; and Rasheed, $0. The entry to record the final cash distributions to partners is

Jan. 15	K. Zayn, Capital	19,000	
	H. Perez, Capital	8,000	
	Cash		27,000
	To distribute remaining cash to partners.		

Assets = Liabilities + Equity
−27,000   −19,000
                   −8,000

Partner Cannot Pay Deficiency   The remaining partners with credit balances absorb any partner's unpaid deficiency according to their income-and-loss-sharing ratio. To illustrate, if Rasheed is unable to pay the $3,000 deficiency, Zayn and Perez absorb it. Since they share income and loss equally, Zayn and Perez each absorb $1,500 of the deficiency. This is recorded as follows.

Jan. 15	K. Zayn, Capital	1,500	
	H. Perez, Capital	1,500	
	T. Rasheed, Capital		3,000
	To transfer Rasheed deficiency to Zayn and Perez.		

Assets = Liabilities + Equity
                   −1,500
                   −1,500
                   +3,000

After Zayn and Perez absorb Rasheed's deficiency, the capital accounts of the partners are Zayn, $17,500; Perez, $6,500; and Rasheed, $0. The entry to record the final cash distribution to the partners is

Jan. 15	K. Zayn, Capital	17,500	
	H. Perez, Capital	6,500	
	Cash		24,000
	To distribute remaining cash to partners.		

Assets = Liabilities + Equity
−24,000   −17,500
                   −6,500

Rasheed's inability to cover this deficiency does not relieve Rasheed of the liability. If Rasheed becomes able to pay at a future date, Zayn and Perez can each collect $1,500 from Rasheed.

GLOBAL VIEW

Partnership accounting according to U.S. GAAP is similar, but not identical, to that under IFRS. This section discusses broad differences in partnership accounting, organization, admission, withdrawal, and liquidation.

Both U.S. GAAP and IFRS include broad and similar guidance for partnership accounting. Further, partnership organization is similar worldwide; however, different legal and tax systems dictate different implications and motivations for how a partnership is effectively set up.

The accounting for partnership admission, withdrawal, and liquidation is likewise similar worldwide. Specifically, procedures for admission, withdrawal, and liquidation depend on the partnership agreements constructed by all parties involved. However, different legal and tax systems impact those agreements and their implications to the parties.

Decision Analysis Partner Return on Equity

A1 Compute partner return on equity and use it to evaluate partnership performance.

An important role of partnership financial statements is to aid current and potential partners in evaluating partnership success compared with other opportunities. One measure of this success is the **partner return on equity** ratio:

$$\text{Partner return on equity} = \frac{\text{Partner net income}}{\text{Average partner equity}}$$

This measure is separately computed for each partner. To illustrate, Exhibit 12.4 reports selected data from the **Boston Celtics LP**. The return on equity for the *total* partnership is computed as $216/[(\$85 + \$253)/2] = 127.8\%$. However, return on equity is quite different across the partners. For example, the **Boston Celtics LP I** partner return on equity is computed as $44/[(\$122 + \$166)/2] = 30.6\%$, whereas the **Celtics LP** partner return on equity is computed as $111/[(\$270 + \$333)/2] = 36.8\%$. Partner return on equity provides *each* partner an assessment of its return on its equity invested in the partnership. A specific partner often uses this return to decide whether additional investment or withdrawal of resources is best for that partner. Exhibit 12.4 reveals that the year shown produced good returns for all partners (the Boston Celtics LP II return is not computed because its average equity is negative due to an unusual and large distribution in the prior year).

EXHIBIT 12.4

Selected Data from Boston Celtics LP

($ thousands)	Total*	Boston Celtics LP I	Boston Celtics LP II	Celtics LP
Beginning-year balance	$ 85	$122	$(307)	$270
Net income (loss) for year	216	44	61	111
Cash distribution	(48)	—	—	(48)
Ending-year balance	$253	$166	$(246)	$333
Partner return on equity	127.8%	30.6%	n.a.	36.8%

* Totals may not add up due to rounding.

DEMONSTRATION PROBLEM

The following transactions and events affect the partners' capital accounts in several successive partnerships. Prepare a table with six columns, one for each of the five partners along with a total column to show the effects of the following events on the five partners' capital accounts.

Part 1

4/13/2011   Ries and Bax create R&B Company. Each invests $10,000, and they agree to share income and losses equally.

12/31/2011   R&B Co. earns $15,000 in income for its first year. Ries withdraws $4,000 from the partnership, and Bax withdraws $7,000.

1/1/2012   Royce is made a partner in RB&R Company after contributing $12,000 cash. The partners agree that a 10% interest allowance will be given on each partner's beginning-year capital balance. In addition, Bax and Royce are to receive $5,000 salary allowances. The remainder of the income or loss is to be divided evenly.

12/31/2012 The partnership's income for the year is $40,000, and withdrawals at year-end are Ries, $5,000; Bax, $12,500; and Royce, $11,000.

1/1/2013 Ries sells her interest for $20,000 to Murdock, whom Bax and Royce accept as a partner in the new BR&M Co. Income or loss is to be shared equally after Bax and Royce receive $25,000 salary allowances.

12/31/2013 The partnership's income for the year is $35,000, and year-end withdrawals are Bax, $2,500, and Royce, $2,000.

1/1/2014 Elway is admitted as a partner after investing $60,000 cash in the new Elway & Associates partnership. He is given a 50% interest in capital after the other partners transfer $3,000 to his account from each of theirs. A 20% interest allowance (on the beginning-year capital balances) will be used in sharing any income or loss, there will be no salary allowances, and Elway will receive 40% of the remaining balance—the other three partners will each get 20%.

12/31/2014 Elway & Associates earns $127,600 in income for the year, and year-end withdrawals are Bax, $25,000; Royce, $27,000; Murdock, $15,000; and Elway, $40,000.

1/1/2015 Elway buys out Bax and Royce for the balances of their capital accounts after a revaluation of the partnership assets. The revaluation gain is $50,000, which is divided in using a 1:1:1:2 ratio (Bax:Royce:Murdock:Elway). Elway pays the others from personal funds. Murdock and Elway will share income on a 1:9 ratio.

2/28/2015 The partnership earns $10,000 of income since the beginning of the year. Murdock retires and receives partnership cash equal to her capital balance. Elway takes possession of the partnership assets in his own name, and the partnership is dissolved.

Part 2

Journalize the events affecting the partnership for the year ended December 31, 2012.

PLANNING THE SOLUTION

- Evaluate each transaction's effects on the capital accounts of the partners.
- Each time a new partner is admitted or a partner withdraws, allocate any bonus based on the income-or-loss-sharing agreement.
- Each time a new partner is admitted or a partner withdraws, allocate subsequent net income or loss in accordance with the new partnership agreement.
- Prepare entries to (1) record Royce's initial investment; (2) record the allocation of interest, salaries, and remainder; (3) show the cash withdrawals from the partnership; and (4) close the withdrawal accounts on December 31, 2012.

SOLUTION TO DEMONSTRATION PROBLEM

Part 1

Event	Ries	Bax	Royce	Murdock	Elway	Total
4/13/2011						
Initial investment	$10,000	$10,000				$ 20,000
12/31/2011						
Income (equal)	7,500	7,500				15,000
Withdrawals	(4,000)	(7,000)				(11,000)
Ending balance	$13,500	$10,500				$ 24,000
1/1/2012						
New investment			$12,000			$ 12,000
12/31/2012						
10% interest	1,350	1,050	1,200			3,600
Salaries		5,000	5,000			10,000
Remainder (equal)	8,800	8,800	8,800			26,400
Withdrawals	(5,000)	(12,500)	(11,000)			(28,500)
Ending balance	$18,650	$12,850	$16,000			$ 47,500

[continued on next page]

[continued from previous page]

Event	Ries	Bax	Royce	Murdock	Elway	Total
1/1/2013						
Transfer interest	(18,650)			$18,650		$ 0
12/31/2013						
Salaries		25,000	25,000			50,000
Remainder (equal)		(5,000)	(5,000)	(5,000)		(15,000)
Withdrawals		(2,500)	(2,000)			(4,500)
Ending balance	$ 0	$30,350	$34,000	$13,650		$ 78,000
1/1/2014						
New investment					$ 60,000	60,000
Bonuses to Elway		(3,000)	(3,000)	(3,000)	9,000	0
Adjusted balance		$27,350	$31,000	$10,650	$ 69,000	$138,000
12/31/2014						
20% interest..............		5,470	6,200	2,130	13,800	27,600
Remainder (1:1:1:2)		20,000	20,000	20,000	40,000	100,000
Withdrawals..............		(25,000)	(27,000)	(15,000)	(40,000)	(107,000)
Ending balance		$27,820	$30,200	$17,780	$ 82,800	$158,600
1/1/2015						
Gain (1:1:1:2)		10,000	10,000	10,000	20,000	50,000
Adjusted balance		$37,820	$40,200	$27,780	$102,800	$208,600
Transfer interests		(37,820)	(40,200)		78,020	0
Adjusted balance		$ 0	$ 0	$27,780	$180,820	$208,600
2/28/2015						
Income (1:9)..............				1,000	9,000	10,000
Adjusted balance				$28,780	$189,820	$218,600
Settlements				(28,780)	(189,820)	(218,600)
Final balance..............				$ 0	$ 0	$ 0

Part 2

2012			
Jan. 1	Cash	12,000	
	Royce, Capital		12,000
	To record investment of Royce.		
Dec. 31	Income Summary	40,000	
	Ries, Capital		10,150
	Bax, Capital		14,850
	Royce, Capital		15,000
	To allocate interest, salaries, and remainders.		
Dec. 31	Ries, Withdrawals	5,000	
	Bax, Withdrawals	12,500	
	Royce, Withdrawals	11,000	
	Cash		28,500
	To record cash withdrawals by partners.		
Dec. 31	Ries, Capital	5,000	
	Bax, Capital	12,500	
	Royce, Capital	11,000	
	Ries, Withdrawals		5,000
	Bax, Withdrawals		12,500
	Royce, Withdrawals		11,000
	To close withdrawal accounts.		

Summary

C1 **Identify characteristics of partnerships and similar organizations.** Partnerships are voluntary associations, involve partnership agreements, have limited life, are not subject to income tax, include mutual agency, and have unlimited liability. Organizations that combine selected characteristics of partnerships and corporations include limited partnerships, limited liability partnerships, S corporations, and limited liability companies.

A1 **Compute partner return on equity and use it to evaluate partnership performance.** Partner return on equity provides each partner an assessment of his or her return on equity invested in the partnership.

P1 **Prepare entries for partnership formation.** A partner's initial investment is recorded at the market value of the assets contributed to the partnership.

P2 **Allocate and record income and loss among partners.** A partnership agreement should specify how to allocate partnership income or loss among partners. Allocation can be based on a stated ratio, capital balances, or salary and interest allowances to compensate partners for differences in their service and capital contributions.

P3 **Account for the admission and withdrawal of partners.** When a new partner buys a partnership interest directly from one or more existing partners, the amount of cash paid from one partner to another does not affect the partnership total recorded equity. When a new partner purchases equity by investing additional assets in the partnership, the new partner's investment can yield a bonus either to existing partners or to the new partner. The entry to record a withdrawal can involve payment from either (1) the existing partners' personal assets or (2) partnership assets. The latter can yield a bonus to either the withdrawing or remaining partners.

P4 **Prepare entries for partnership liquidation.** When a partnership is liquidated, losses and gains from selling partnership assets are allocated to the partners according to their income-and-loss-sharing ratio. If a partner's capital account has a deficiency that the partner cannot pay, the other partners share the deficit according to their relative income-and-loss-sharing ratio.

Guidance Answers to Decision Ethics

Financial Planner The partnership agreement apparently fails to mention liabilities or use the term *net assets*. To give the estate one-third of total assets is not fair to the remaining partners because if the partner had lived and the partners had decided to liquidate, the liabilities would need to be paid out of assets before any liquidation. Also, a settlement based on the deceased partner's recorded equity would fail to recognize excess of current value over book value. This value increase would be realized if the partnership were liquidated. A fair settlement would seem to be a payment to the estate for the balance of the deceased partner's equity based on the *current value of net assets*.

Guidance Answers to Quick Checks

1. (*b*)

2. *Unlimited liability* means that the creditors of a partnership require each partner to be personally responsible for all partnership debts.

3. (*c*)

4.

	Denzel	Shantell	Total
Net income			$40,000
Interest allowance (10%)	$ 7,000	$ 3,500	10,500
Balance of income			$29,500
Balance allocated equally	14,750	14,750	29,500
Balance of income			$ 0
Income of partners	**$21,750**	**$18,250**	

Key Terms

Additional Quiz Questions are available at the book's Website.

1. Stokely and Leder are forming a partnership. Stokely invests a building that has a market value of $250,000; and the partnership assumes responsibility for a $50,000 note secured by a mortgage on that building. Leder invests $100,000 cash. For the partnership, the amounts recorded for the building and for Stokely's Capital account are these:
   a. Building, $250,000; Stokely, Capital, $250,000.
   b. Building, $200,000; Stokely, Capital, $200,000.
   c. Building, $200,000; Stokely, Capital, $100,000.
   d. Building, $200,000; Stokely, Capital, $250,000.
   e. Building, $250,000; Stokely, Capital, $200,000.

2. Katherine, Alliah, and Paulina form a partnership. Katherine contributes $150,000, Alliah contributes $150,000, and Paulina contributes $100,000. Their partnership agreement calls for the income or loss division to be based on the ratio of capital invested. If the partnership reports income of $90,000 for its first year of operations, what amount of income is credited to Paulina's capital account?
   a. $22,500
   b. $25,000
   c. $45,000
   d. $30,000
   e. $90,000

3. Jamison and Blue form a partnership with capital contributions of $600,000 and $800,000, respectively. Their partnership agreement calls for Jamison to receive $120,000 per year in salary. Also, each partner is to receive an interest allowance equal to 10% of the partner's beginning capital contributions, with any remaining income or loss divided equally. If net income for its initial year is $270,000, then Jamison's and Blue's respective shares are
   a. $135,000; $135,000.
   b. $154,286; $115,714.
   c. $120,000; $150,000.
   d. $185,000; $85,000.
   e. $85,000; $185,000.

4. Hansen and Fleming are partners and share equally in income or loss. Hansen's current capital balance in the partnership is $125,000 and Fleming's is $124,000. Hansen and Fleming agree to accept Black with a 20% interest. Black invests $75,000 in the partnership. The bonus granted to Hansen and Fleming equals
   a. $13,000 each.
   b. $5,100 each.
   c. $4,000 each.
   d. $5,285 to Hansen; $4,915 to Fleming.
   e. $0; Hansen and Fleming grant a bonus to Black.

5. Mee Su is a partner in Hartford Partners, LLC. Her partnership capital balance at the beginning of the current year was $110,000, and her ending balance was $124,000. Her share of the partnership income is $10,500. What is her partner return on equity?
   a. 8.97%
   b. 1060.00%
   c. 9.54%
   d. 1047.00%
   e. 8.47%

🔘 Icon denotes assignments that involve decision making.

Discussion Questions

1. 🔘 If a partnership contract does not state the period of time the partnership is to exist, when does the partnership end?
2. What does the term *mutual agency* mean when applied to a partnership?
3. How does a general partnership differ from a limited partnership?
4. 🔘 Can partners limit the right of a partner to commit their partnership to contracts? Would such an agreement be binding (a) on the partners and (b) on outsiders?
5. 🔘 Assume that Amey and Lacey are partners. Lacey dies, and her son claims the right to take his mother's place in the partnership. Does he have this right? Why or why not?
6. 🔘 Assume that the Barnes and Ardmore partnership agreement provides for a two-third/one-third sharing of income but says nothing about losses. The first year of partnership operation resulted in a loss, and Barnes argues that the loss should be shared equally because the partnership agreement said nothing about sharing losses. Is Barnes correct? Explain.
7. Allocation of partnership income among the partners appears on what financial statement?
8. What does the term *unlimited liability* mean when it is applied to partnership members?
9. 🔘 George, Burton, and Dillman have been partners for three years. The partnership is being dissolved. George is leaving the firm, but Burton and Dillman plan to carry on the business. In the final settlement, George places a $75,000 salary claim against the partnership. He contends that he has a claim for a salary of $25,000 for each year because he devoted all of his time for three years to the affairs of the partnership. Is his claim valid? Why or why not?
10. 🔘 Kay, Kat, and Kim are partners. In a liquidation, Kay's share of partnership losses exceeds her capital account balance. Moreover, she is unable to meet the deficit from her personal assets, and her partners shared the excess losses. Does this relieve Kay of liability?
11. After all partnership assets have been converted to cash and all liabilities paid, the remaining cash should equal the sum of the balances of the partners' capital accounts. Why?
12. Assume a partner withdraws from a partnership and receives assets of greater value than the book value of his equity. Should the remaining partners share the resulting reduction in their equities in the ratio of their relative capital balances or according to their income-and-loss-sharing ratio?

connect

Amy and Lester are partners in operating a store. Without consulting Amy, Lester enters into a contract to purchase merchandise for the store. Amy contends that she did not authorize the order and refuses to pay for it. The vendor sues the partners for the contract price of the merchandise. (*a*) Must the partnership pay for the merchandise? Why? (*b*) Does your answer differ if Amy and Lester are partners in a public accounting firm? Explain.

QUICK STUDY

QS 12-1
Partnership liability

C1

Ann Stolton and Susie Bright are partners in a business they started two years ago. The partnership agreement states that Stolton should receive a salary allowance of $15,000 and that Bright should receive a $20,000 salary allowance. Any remaining income or loss is to be shared equally. Determine each partner's share of the current year's net income of $52,000.

QS 12-2
Partnership income allocation

P2

Blake and Matthew are partners who agree that Blake will receive a $100,000 salary allowance and that any remaining income or loss will be shared equally. If Matthew's capital account is credited for $2,000 as his share of the net income in a given period, how much net income did the partnership earn in that period?

QS 12-3
Partnership income allocation

P2

Fancher organized a limited partnership and is the only general partner. Carley invested $20,000 in the partnership and was admitted as a limited partner with the understanding that she would receive 10% of the profits. After two unprofitable years, the partnership ceased doing business. At that point, partnership liabilities were $85,000 larger than partnership assets. How much money can the partnership's creditors obtain from Carley's personal assets to satisfy the unpaid partnership debts?

QS 12-4
Liability in limited partnerships

P1

Stein agrees to pay Choi and Amal $10,000 each for a one-third (33⅓%) interest in the Choi and Amal partnership. Immediately prior to Stein's admission, each partner had a $30,000 capital balance. Make the journal entry to record Stein's purchase of the partners' interest.

QS 12-5
Partner admission through purchase of interest

P3

Jules and Johnson are partners, each with $40,000 in their partnership capital accounts. Kwon is admitted to the partnership by investing $40,000 cash. Make the entry to show Kwon's admission to the partnership.

QS 12-6
Admission of a partner

P3

The Field, Brown & Snow partnership was begun with investments by the partners as follows: Field, $131,250; Brown, $165,000; and Snow, $153,750. The operations did not go well, and the partners eventually decided to liquidate the partnership, sharing all losses equally. On May 31, after all assets were converted to cash and all creditors were paid, only $45,000 in partnership cash remained.

1. Compute the capital account balance of each partner after the liquidation of assets and the payment of creditors.

2. Assume that any partner with a deficit agrees to pay cash to the partnership to cover the deficit. Present the journal entries on May 31 to record (*a*) the cash receipt from the deficient partner(s) and (*b*) the final disbursement of cash to the partners.

3. Assume that any partner with a deficit is not able to reimburse the partnership. Present journal entries (*a*) to transfer the deficit of any deficient partners to the other partners and (*b*) to record the final disbursement of cash to the partners.

QS 12-7
Liquidation of partnership

P4

Check (1) Field, $(3,750)

Howe and Duley's company is organized as a partnership. At the prior year-end, partnership equity totaled $150,000 ($100,000 from Howe and $50,000 from Duley). For the current year, partnership net income is $24,990 ($20,040 allocated to Howe and $4,950 allocated to Duley), and year-end total partnership equity is $200,000 ($140,000 from Howe and $60,000 from Duley). Compute the total partnership return on equity *and* the individual partner return on equity ratios.

QS 12-8
Partner return on equity

A1

EXERCISES

Exercise 12-1
Characteristics of partnerships
C1

Next to the following list of eight characteristics of business organizations, enter a brief description of how each characteristic applies to general partnerships.

Characteristic	Application to General Partnerships
1. Life	
2. Owners' liability	
3. Legal status	
4. Tax status of income	
5. Owners' authority	
6. Ease of formation	
7. Transferability of ownership	
8. Ability to raise large amounts of capital	

Exercise 12-2
Forms of organization
C1

For each of the following separate cases, recommend a form of business organization. With each recommendation, explain how business income would be taxed if the owners adopt the form of organization recommended. Also list several advantages that the owners will enjoy from the form of business organization that you recommend.

a. Sharif, Henry and Korb are recent college graduates in computer science. They want to start a Website development company. They all have college debts and currently do not own any substantial computer equipment needed to get the company started.

b. Dr. Ward and Dr. Liu are recent graduates from medical residency programs. Both are family practice physicians and would like to open a clinic in an underserved rural area. Although neither has any funds to bring to the new venture, an investor has expressed interest in making a loan to provide start-up funds for their practice.

c. Munson has been out of school for about five years and has become quite knowledgeable about the residential real estate market. He would like to organize a company that buys and sells real estate. Munson believes he has the expertise to manage the company but needs funds to invest in residential property.

Exercise 12-3
Journalizing partnership transactions
P2

On March 1, 2013, Eckert and Kelley formed a partnership. Eckert contributed $82,500 cash and Kelley contributed land valued at $60,000 and a building valued at $100,000. The partnership also assumed responsibility for Kelley's $92,500 long-term note payable associated with the land and building. The partners agreed to share income as follows: Eckert is to receive an annual salary allowance of $25,000, both are to receive an annual interest allowance of 10% of their beginning-year capital investment, and any remaining income or loss is to be shared equally. On October 20, 2013, Eckert withdrew $34,000 cash and Kelley withdrew $20,000 cash. After the adjusting and closing entries are made to the revenue and expense accounts at December 31, 2013, the Income Summary account had a credit balance of $90,000.

1. Prepare journal entries to record (*a*) the partners' initial capital investments, (*b*) their cash withdrawals, and (*c*) the December 31 closing of both the Withdrawals and Income Summary accounts.

Check (2) Kelley, $79,250

2. Determine the balances of the partners' capital accounts as of December 31, 2013.

Exercise 12-4
Journalizing partnership formation
P2

Angela Moss and Autumn Barber organize a partnership on January 1. Moss's initial net investment is $75,000, consisting of cash ($17,500), equipment ($82,500), and a note payable reflecting a bank loan for the new business ($25,000). Barber's initial investment is cash of $31,250. These amounts are the values agreed on by both partners. Prepare journal entries to record (1) Moss's investment and (2) Barber's investment.

Exercise 12-5
Income allocation in a partnership
P2

Kramer and Knox began a partnership by investing $60,000 and $80,000, respectively. During its first year, the partnership earned $160,000. Prepare calculations showing how the $160,000 income should be allocated to the partners under each of the following three separate plans for sharing income and loss: (1) the partners failed to agree on a method to share income; (2) the partners agreed to share income and loss in proportion to their initial investments (round amounts to the nearest dollar); and (3) the partners agreed to share income by granting a $50,000 per year salary allowance to Kramer, a $40,000 per year salary allowance to Knox, 10% interest on their initial capital investments, and the remaining balance shared equally.

Check Plan 3, Kramer, $84,000

Assume that the partners of Exercise 12-5 agreed to share net income and loss by granting annual salary allowances of $50,000 to Kramer and $40,000 to Knox, 10% interest allowances on their investments, and any remaining balance shared equally.

1. Determine the partners' shares of Kramer and Knox given a first-year net income of $98,800.

2. Determine the partners' shares of Kramer and Knox given a first-year net loss of $16,800.

Exercise 12-6
Income allocation in
a partnership
P2

Check   (2) Kramer, $(4,400)

The Struter Partnership has total partners' equity of $510,000, which is made up of Main, Capital, $400,000, and Frist, Capital, $110,000. The partners share net income and loss in a ratio of 80% to Main and 20% to Frist. On November 1, Madison is admitted to the partnership and given a 15% interest in equity and a 15% share in any income and loss. Prepare the journal entry to record the admission of Madison under each of the following separate assumptions: Madison invests cash of (1) $90,000; (2) $120,000; and (3) $80,000.

Exercise 12-7
Admission of new partner
P3

Hunter, Folgers, and Tulip have been partners while sharing net income and loss in a 5:3:2 ratio. On January 31, the date Tulip retires from the partnership, the equities of the partners are Hunter, $150,000; Folgers, $90,000; and Tulip, $60,000. Present journal entries to record Tulip's retirement under each of the following separate assumptions: Tulip is paid for her equity using partnership cash of (1) $60,000; (2) $80,000; and (3) $30,000.

Exercise 12-8
Retirement of partner
P3

The partners in the Biz Partnership have agreed that partner Mandy may sell her $100,000 equity in the partnership to Brittney, for which Brittney will pay Mandy $85,000. Present the partnership's journal entry to record the sale of Mandy's interest to Brittney on September 30.

Exercise 12-9
Sale of partnership interest
P3

Turner, Roth, and Lowe are partners who share income and loss in a 1:4:5 ratio. After lengthy disagreements among the partners and several unprofitable periods, the partners decide to liquidate the partnership. Immediately before liquidation, the partnership balance sheet shows total assets, $126,000; total liabilities, $78,000; Turner, Capital, $2,500; Roth, Capital, $14,000; and Lowe, Capital, $31,500. The cash proceeds from selling the assets were sufficient to repay all but $28,000 to the creditors. (*a*) Calculate the loss from selling the assets. (*b*) Allocate the loss to the partners. (*c*) Determine how much of the remaining liability should be paid by each partner.

Exercise 12-10
Liquidation of partnership
P4

Check   (b) Lowe, Capital after
allocation, $(6,500)

Assume that the Turner, Roth, and Lowe partnership of Exercise 12-10 is a limited partnership. Turner and Roth are general partners and Lowe is a limited partner. How much of the remaining $28,000 liability should be paid by each partner? (Round amounts to the nearest dollar.)

Exercise 12-11
Liquidation of limited partnership
P4

Rugged Sports Enterprises LP is organized as a limited partnership consisting of two individual partners: Hockey LP and Football LP. Both partners separately operate a minor league hockey team and a semipro football team. Compute partner return on equity for each limited partnership (and the total) for the year ended June 30, 2013, using the following selected data on partner capital balances from Rugged Sports Enterprises LP.

Exercise 12-12
Partner return on equity
A1

	Hockey LP	Football LP	Total
Balance at 6/30/2012	$189,000	$ 758,000	$ 947,000
Annual net income	22,208	445,473	468,032
Cash distribution	—	(50,000)	(50,000)
Balance at 6/30/2013	$211,134	$1,153,898	$1,365,032

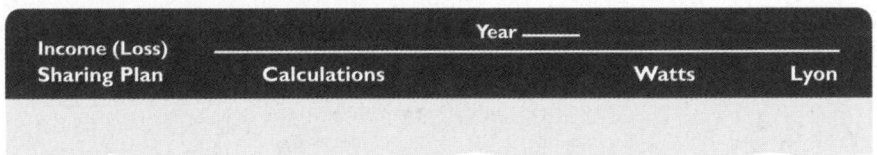

PROBLEM SET A

Problem 12-1A
Allocating partnership income

P2 **Sage 50**

Check (3) Thomas, Capital, $97,800

Kara Ries, Tammy Bax, and Joe Thomas invested $80,000, $112,000, and $128,000, respectively, in a partnership. During its first calendar year, the firm earned $249,000.

Required

Prepare the entry to close the firm's Income Summary account as of its December 31 year-end and to allocate the $249,000 net income to the partners under each of the following separate assumptions: The partners (1) have no agreement on the method of sharing income and loss; (2) agreed to share income and loss in the ratio of their beginning capital investments; and (3) agreed to share income and loss by providing annual salary allowances of $66,000 to Ries, $56,000 to Bax, and $80,000 to Thomas; granting 10% interest on the partners' beginning capital investments; and sharing the remainder equally.

Problem 12-2A
Allocating partnership income and loss; sequential years

P2

mhhe.com/wildFAP21e

Irene Watts and John Lyon are forming a partnership to which Watts will devote one-half time and Lyon will devote full time. They have discussed the following alternative plans for sharing income and loss: (a) in the ratio of their initial capital investments, which they have agreed will be $42,000 for Watts and $63,000 for Lyon; (b) in proportion to the time devoted to the business; (c) a salary allowance of $6,000 per month to Lyon and the balance in accordance with the ratio of their initial capital investments; or (d) a salary allowance of $6,000 per month to Lyon, 10% interest on their initial capital investments, and the balance shared equally. The partners expect the business to perform as follows: year 1, $36,000 net loss; year 2, $90,000 net income; and year 3, $150,000 net income.

Required

Prepare three tables with the following column headings.

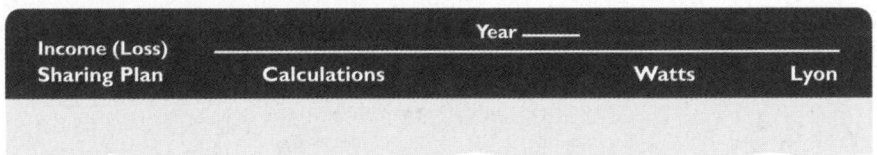

Income (Loss) Sharing Plan	Calculations	Year ____	
		Watts	Lyon

Check Plan d, year 1, Lyon's share, $19,050

Complete the tables, one for each of the first three years, by showing how to allocate partnership income or loss to the partners under each of the four plans being considered. (Round answers to the nearest whole dollar.)

Problem 12-3A
Partnership income allocation, statement of partners' equity, and closing entries

P2

mhhe.com/wildFAP21e

Bill Beck, Bruce Beck, and Barb Beck formed the BBB Partnership by making capital contributions of $67,500, $262,500, and $420,000, respectively. They predict annual partnership net income of $450,000 and are considering the following alternative plans of sharing income and loss: (a) equally; (b) in the ratio of their initial capital investments; or (c) salary allowances of $80,000 to Bill, $60,000 to Bruce, and $90,000 to Barb; interest allowances of 10% on their initial capital investments; and the balance shared as follows: 20% to Bill, 40% to Bruce, and 40% to Barb..

Required

1. Prepare a table with the following column headings.

Income (Loss) Sharing Plan	Calculations	Bill	Bruce	Barb	Total

Check (2) Barb, Ending Capital, $449,600

Use the table to show how to distribute net income of $450,000 for the calendar year under each of the alternative plans being considered. (Round answers to the nearest whole dollar.)

2. Prepare a statement of partners' equity showing the allocation of income to the partners assuming they agree to use plan (c), that income earned is $209,000, and that Bill, Bruce, and Barb withdraw $34,000, $48,000, and $64,000, respectively, at year-end.

3. Prepare the December 31 journal entry to close Income Summary assuming they agree to use plan (c) and that net income is $209,000. Also close the withdrawals accounts.

Part 1. Meir, Benson, and Lau are partners and share income and loss in a 3:2:5 ratio. The partnership's capital balances are as follows: Meir, $168,000; Benson, $138,000; and Lau, $294,000. Benson decides to withdraw from the partnership, and the partners agree to not have the assets revalued upon Benson's retirement. Prepare journal entries to record Benson's February 1 withdrawal from the partnership under each of the following separate assumptions: Benson (*a*) sells her interest to North for $160,000 after Meir and Lau approve the entry of North as a partner; (*b*) gives her interest to a son-in-law, Schmidt, and thereafter Meir and Lau accept Schmidt as a partner; (*c*) is paid $138,000 in partnership cash for her equity; (*d*) is paid $214,000 in partnership cash for her equity; and (*e*) is paid $30,000 in partnership cash plus equipment recorded on the partnership books at $70,000 less its accumulated depreciation of $23,200.

Part 2. Assume that Benson does not retire from the partnership described in Part 1. Instead, Rhode is admitted to the partnership on February 1 with a 25% equity. Prepare journal entries to record Rhode's entry into the partnership under each of the following separate assumptions: Rhode invests (*a*) $200,000; (*b*) $145,000; and (*c*) $262,000.

Problem 12-4A
Partner withdrawal and admission
P3

Check (1*e*) Cr. Lau, Capital, $38,250

(2*c*) Cr. Benson, Capital, $9,300

Kendra, Cogley, and Mei share income and loss in a 3:2:1 ratio. The partners have decided to liquidate their partnership. On the day of liquidation their balance sheet appears as follows.

Problem 12-5A
Liquidation of a partnership
P4

KENDRA, COGLEY, AND MEI Balance Sheet May 31			
Assets		**Liabilities and Equity**	
Cash	$180,800	Accounts payable	$245,500
Inventory	537,200	Kendra, Capital	93,000
		Cogley, Capital	212,500
		Mei, Capital	167,000
Total assets	$718,000	Total liabilities and equity	$718,000

Required

Prepare journal entries for (*a*) the sale of inventory, (*b*) the allocation of its gain or loss, (*c*) the payment of liabilities at book value, and (*d*) the distribution of cash in each of the following separate cases: Inventory is sold for (1) $600,000; (2) $500,000; (3) $320,000 and any partners with capital deficits pay in the amount of their deficits; and (4) $250,000 and the partners have no assets other than those invested in the partnership. (Round to the nearest dollar.)

Check (4) Cash distribution: Mei, $102,266

Mark Albin, Roland Peters and Sam Ramsey invested $164,000, $98,400 and $65,600, respectively, in a partnership. During its first calendar year, the firm earned $270,000.

PROBLEM SET B

Problem 12-1B
Allocating partnership income
P2

Required

Prepare the entry to close the firm's Income Summary account as of its December 31 year-end and to allocate the $270,000 net income to the partners under each of the following separate assumptions. (Round answers to whole dollars.) The partners (1) have no agreement on the method of sharing income and loss; (2) agreed to share income and loss in the ratio of their beginning capital investments; and (3) agreed to share income and loss by providing annual salary allowances of $96,000 to Albin, $72,000 to Peters, and $50,000 to Ramsey; granting 10% interest on the partners' beginning capital investments; and sharing the remainder equally.

Check (3) Ramsey, Capital, $62,960

Maria Bell and J.R. Green are forming a partnership to which Bell will devote one-third time and Green will devote full time. They have discussed the following alternative plans for sharing income and loss: (*a*) in the ratio of their initial capital investments, which they have agreed will be $104,000 for Bell and $156,000 for Green; (*b*) in proportion to the time devoted to the business; (*c*) a salary allowance of $4,000 per month to Green and the balance in accordance with the ratio of their initial capital investments; or

Problem 12-2B
Allocating partnership income and loss; sequential years
P2

(*d*) a salary allowance of $4,000 per month to Green, 10% interest on their initial capital investments, and the balance shared equally. The partners expect the business to perform as follows: year 1, $36,000 net loss; year 2, $76,000 net income; and year 3, $188,000 net income.

Required

Prepare three tables with the following column headings.

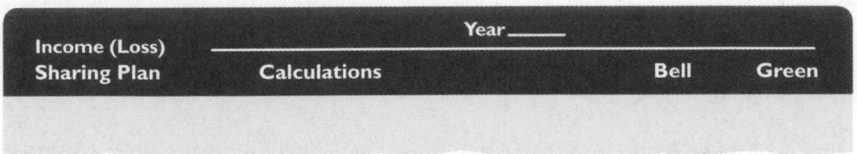

Income (Loss) Sharing Plan	Calculations	Year_____	Bell	Green

Check Plan d, year 1, Green's share, $8,600

Complete the tables, one for each of the first three years, by showing how to allocate partnership income or loss to the partners under each of the four plans being considered. (Round answers to the nearest whole dollar.)

Problem 12-3B
Partnership income allocation, statement of partners' equity, and closing entries

P2

Sally Cook, Lin Xi, and Ken Schwartz formed the CXS Partnership by making capital contributions of $144,000, $216,000, and $120,000, respectively. They predict annual partnership net income of $240,000 and are considering the following alternative plans of sharing income and loss: (*a*) equally; (*b*) in the ratio of their initial capital investments; or (*c*) salary allowances of $40,000 to Cook, $30,000 to Xi, and $80,000 to Schwartz; interest allowances of 12% on their initial capital investments; and the balance shared equally.

Required

1. Prepare a table with the following column headings.

Income (Loss) Sharing Plan	Calculations	Cook	Xi	Schwartz	Total

Use the table to show how to distribute net income of $240,000 for the calendar year under each of the alternative plans being considered. (Round answers to the nearest whole dollar.)

Check (2) Schwartz, Ending Capital, $150,400

2. Prepare a statement of partners' equity showing the allocation of income to the partners assuming they agree to use plan (*c*), that income earned is $87,600, and that Cook, Xi, and Schwartz withdraw $18,000, $38,000, and $24,000, respectively, at year-end.

3. Prepare the December 31 journal entry to close Income Summary assuming they agree to use plan (*c*) and that net income is $87,600. Also close the withdrawals accounts.

Problem 12-4B
Partner withdrawal and admission

P3

Part 1. Gibbs, Cook, and Chan are partners and share income and loss in a 5:1:4 ratio. The partnership's capital balances are as follows: Gibbs, $606,000; Cook, $148,000; and Chan, $446,000. Gibbs decides to withdraw from the partnership, and the partners agree not to have the assets revalued upon Gibbs's retirement. Prepare journal entries to record Gibbs's April 30 withdrawal from the partnership under each of the following separate assumptions: Gibbs (*a*) sells her interest to Brady for $250,000 after Cook and Chan approve the entry of Brady as a partner; (*b*) gives her interest to a daughter-in-law, Cannon, and thereafter Cook and Chan accept Cannon as a partner; (*c*) is paid $606,000 in partnership cash for her equity; (*d*) is paid $350,000 in partnership cash for her equity; and (*e*) is paid $200,000 in partnership cash plus manufacturing equipment recorded on the partnership books at $538,000 less its accumulated depreciation of $336,000.

Check (1e) Cr. Chan, Capital, $163,200

Part 2. Assume that Gibbs does not retire from the partnership described in Part 1. Instead, Chip is admitted to the partnership on April 30 with a 20% equity. Prepare journal entries to record the entry of Brise under each of the following separate assumptions: Chip invests (*a*) $300,000; (*b*) $196,000; and (*c*) $426,000.

Check (2c) Cr. Cook, Capital, $10,080

Lasure, Ramirez, and Toney, who share income and loss in a 2:1:2 ratio, plan to liquidate their partnership. At liquidation, their balance sheet appears as follows.

LASURE, RAMIREZ, AND TONEY Balance Sheet January 18			
Assets		**Liabilities and Equity**	
Cash	$348,600	Accounts payable	$342,600
Equipment	617,200	Lasure, Capital	300,400
		Ramirez, Capital	195,800
		Toney, Capital	127,000
Total assets	$965,800	Total liabilities and equity	$965,800

Required

Prepare journal entries for (*a*) the sale of equipment, (*b*) the allocation of its gain or loss, (*c*) the payment of liabilities at book value, and (*d*) the distribution of cash in each of the following separate cases: Equipment is sold for (1) $650,000; (2) $530,000; (3) $200,000 and any partners with capital deficits pay in the amount of their deficits; and (4) $150,000 and the partners have no assets other than those invested in the partnership. (Round amounts to the nearest dollar.)

(This serial problem began in Chapter 1 and continues through most of the book. If previous chapter segments were not completed, the serial problem can begin at this point. It is helpful, but not necessary, to use the Working Papers that accompany the book.)

SP 12 At the start of 2014, Adria Lopez is considering adding a partner to her business. She envisions the new partner taking the lead in generating sales of both services and merchandise for Success Systems. A. Lopez's equity in Success Systems as of January 1, 2014, is reflected in the following capital balance.

A. Lopez, Capital. $90,148

Required

1. A. Lopez is evaluating whether the prospective partner should be an equal partner with respect to capital investment and profit sharing (1:1) or whether the agreement should be 4:1 with Lopez retaining four-fifths interest with rights to four-fifths of the net income or loss. What factors should she consider in deciding which partnership agreement to offer?

2. Prepare the January 1, 2014, journal entry(ies) necessary to admit a new partner to Success Systems through the purchase of a partnership interest for each of the following two separate cases: (*a*) 1:1 sharing agreement and (*b*) 4:1 sharing agreement.

3. Prepare the January 1, 2014, journal entry(ies) required to admit a new partner if the new partner invests cash of $22,537.

4. After posting the entry in part 3, what would be the new partner's equity percentage?

BTN 12-1 Take a step back in time and imagine **Polaris** in its infancy as a company. The year is 1954.

Required

1. Read the history of Polaris at **www.Polaris.com**. Identify the founder of the company.

2. Assume that Polaris was originally organized as a partnership. Polaris' income statement in Appendix A varies in several key ways from what it would look like for a partnership. Identify at least two ways in which a corporate income statement differs from a partnership income statement.

3. Compare the Polaris balance sheet in Appendix A to what a partnership balance sheet would have shown. Identify and explain any account differences we would anticipate.

COMPARATIVE ANALYSIS

C1

Polaris

Arctic Cat

BTN 12-2   Over the years **Polaris** and **Arctic Cat** have evolved into large corporations. Today it is difficult to imagine them as fledgling start-ups. Research each company's history online.

Required

1. Which company is older?
2. In what years did each company have its first public offering of stock?
3. Which stock exchange is each company listed under?

ETHICS CHALLENGE

P2

BTN 12-3   Doctors Mobey, Oak, and Chesterfield have been in a group practice for several years. Mobey and Oak are family practice physicians, and Chesterfield is a general surgeon. Chesterfield receives many referrals for surgery from his family practice partners. Upon the partnership's original formation, the three doctors agreed to a two-part formula to share income. Every month each doctor receives a salary allowance of $3,000. Additional income is divided according to a percent of patient charges the doctors generate for the month. In the current month, Mobey generated 10% of the billings, Oak 30%, and Chesterfield 60%. The group's income for this month is $50,000. Chesterfield has expressed dissatisfaction with the income-sharing formula and asks that income be split entirely on patient charge percents.

Required

1. Compute the income allocation for the current month using the original agreement.
2. Compute the income allocation for the current month using Chesterfield's proposed agreement.
3. Identify the ethical components of this partnership decision for the doctors.

COMMUNICATING IN PRACTICE

C1

BTN 12-4   Assume that you are studying for an upcoming accounting exam with a good friend. Your friend says that she has a solid understanding of general partnerships but is less sure that she understands organizations that combine certain characteristics of partnerships with other forms of business organization. You offer to make some study notes for your friend to help her learn about limited partnerships, limited liability partnerships, S corporations, and limited liability companies. Prepare a one-page set of well-organized, complete study notes on these four forms of business organization.

TAKING IT TO THE NET

P1   P2

BTN 12-5   Access the March 14, 2011, filing of the December 31, 2010, 10-K of **America First Tax Exempt Investors LP**. This company deals with tax-exempt mortgage revenue bonds that, among other things, finance student housing properties.

1. Locate its December 31, 2010, balance sheet and list the account titles reported in the equity section of the balance sheet.
2. Locate its statement of partners' capital and comprehensive income (loss). How many units of limited partnership (known as "beneficial unit certificate holders") are outstanding at December 31, 2010?
3. What is the partnership's largest asset and its amount at December 31, 2010?

TEAMWORK IN ACTION

P2

BTN 12-6   This activity requires teamwork to reinforce understanding of accounting for partnerships.

Required

1. Assume that Baker, Warner, and Rice form the BWR Partnership by making capital contributions of $200,000, $300,000, and $500,000, respectively. BWR predicts annual partnership net income of $450,000. The partners are considering various plans for sharing income and loss. Assign a different team member to compute how the projected $450,000 income would be shared under each of the following separate plans:

     a. Shared equally.

     b. In the ratio of the partners' initial capital investments.

     c. Salary allowances of $50,000 to Baker, $60,000 to Warner, and $70,000 to Rice, with the remaining balance shared equally.

     d. Interest allowances of 10% on the partners' initial capital investments, with the remaining balance shared equally.

2. In sequence, each member is to present his or her income-sharing calculations with the team.

3. As a team, identify and discuss at least one other possible way that income could be shared.

BTN 12-7   Recall the chapter's opening feature involving Omar Soliman and Nick Friedman, and their company, **College Hunks Hauling Junk LLC**. Assume that Omar and Nick, partners in the company, decide to expand their business with the help of general partners.

ENTREPRENEURIAL DECISION

C1

Required

1. What details should Omar, Nick, and their future partners specify in the general partnership agreements?

2. What advantages should Omar, Nick, and their future partners be aware of with respect to organizing as a general partnership?

3. What disadvantages should Omar, Nick, and their future partners be aware of with respect to organizing as a general partnership?

BTN 12-8   Access **KTM**'s Website (**www.KTM.com**) and research the company's history (profile).

1. When did the company go public?

2. What stock exchange is the company listed under?

3. What are the companies that are part of KTM?

GLOBAL DECISION

C1

KTM

ANSWERS TO MULTIPLE CHOICE QUIZ

1. e; Capital = $250,000 − $50,000

2. a; $90,000 × [$100,000/($150,000 + $150,000 + $100,000)]
   = $22,500

3. d;

	Jamison	Blue	Total
Net income			$ 270,000
Salary allowance	$120,000		(120,000)
Interest allowance	60,000	$80,000	(140,000)
Balance of income			10,000
Balance divided equally	5,000	5,000	(10,000)
Totals	$185,000	$85,000	$ 0

4. b; Total partnership equity = $125,000 + $124,000 + $75,000
   = $324,000
   Equity of Black = $324,000 × 20% = $64,800
   Bonus to old partners = $75,000 − $64,800 = $10,200, split equally

5. a; $10,500/[($110,000 + $124,000)/2] = 8.97%

Accounting for Corporations

13

A Look Back

Chapter 12 focused on the partnership form of organization. We described crucial characteristics of partnerships and the accounting and reporting of their important transactions.

A Look at This Chapter

This chapter emphasizes details of the corporate form of organization. The accounting concepts and procedures for equity transactions are explained. We also describe how to report and analyze income, earnings per share, and retained earnings.

A Look Ahead

Chapter 14 focuses on long-term liabilities. We explain how to value, record, amortize, and report these liabilities in financial statements.

Learning Objectives

CONCEPTUAL

C1 Identify characteristics of corporations and their organization. (p. 510)

C2 Explain characteristics of, and distribute dividends between, common and preferred stock. (p. 520)

C3 Explain the items reported in retained earnings. (p. 526)

ANALYTICAL

A1 Compute earnings per share and describe its use. (p. 529)

A2 Compute price-earnings ratio and describe its use in analysis. (p. 529)

A3 Compute dividend yield and explain its use in analysis. (p. 530)

A4 Compute book value and explain its use in analysis. (p. 530)

PROCEDURAL

P1 Record the issuance of corporate stock. (p. 514)

P2 Record transactions involving cash dividends, stock dividends, and stock splits. (p. 517)

P3 Record purchases and sales of treasury stock and the retirement of stock. (p. 524)

The Groupon Clipper

"Focus on trying to make the product awesome for consumers."

—ANDREW MASON

CHICAGO—"I've never been driven to create a huge company and make a lot of money or run my own business," insists Andrew Mason. "I've always just been motivated to be working on interesting things." What interested Andrew was the launch of a Website called **Groupon (Groupon.com).** "A Groupon is, essentially, a voucher that's worth money that you can take into a business and use like cash," explains Andrew. "It's a great way to explore your city and find out about really cool, local things to do."

Andrew explains that his success would not have been possible without equity financing and knowledge of business operations. To make it happen, says Andrew, he studied corporate formation, equity issuance, stock types, retaining earnings, and dividend policies. After that analysis, Andrew set up Groupon as a corporation, which had several benefits given his business goals and strategies. With his corporate structure in place, Andrew was ready to attack the market. "We found a way to make e-commerce work for local businesses online," asserts Andrew. "We found a way to deliver effective marketing results for brick and mortar businesses."

The success of Andrew's corporate structure and his equity financing brings both opportunities and challenges. The positive is being part of empowering consumers. "We get crazy emails that feel like they're written by a PR company or something, from our customers about how their marriage was at its end and then Groupon came along and they started going out more," says Andrew. "Now they're happier than ever. We're affecting people's lives in real ways."

The challenge is effectively using accounting as a tool to achieve those objectives. That includes his knowledge of corporate formation, stock types, and equity transactions. The SEC, for instance, has raised some questions about Groupon's revenue and expense recognition policies. Admits Andrew, "There are things we would've done differently and we would've loved to avoid."

Nevertheless, Groupon had the largest initial public stock offering of any Internet company since Google. Its value skyrocketed to $18 billion on the first day of trading. "It caught me by surprise," says Andrew. "It was just this rocket ship ride that you couldn't let go. And, you didn't want to let go either!"

[Sources: *Groupon Website,* January 2013; *Mixergy.com,* July 2010; *The Wall Street Journal,* December 2010; *Time,* February 2011; *CBS News, 60 Minutes,* January 2012]

This chapter focuses on equity transactions. The first part of the chapter describes the basics of the corporate form of organization and explains the accounting for common and preferred stock. We then focus on several special financing transactions, including cash and stock dividends, stock splits, and treasury stock. The final section considers accounting for retained earnings, including prior period adjustments, retained earnings restrictions, and reporting guidelines.

Accounting for Corporations

Corporations	Common Stock	Dividends	Preferred Stock	Treasury Stock	Reporting on Equity
• Characteristics • Organization and management • Stockholders • Stock basics	• Par value • No-par value • Stated value • Stock for non-cash assets	• Cash dividends • Stock dividends • Stock splits	• Issuance • Dividend preferences • Convertible preferred • Callable preferred	• Purchasing treasury stock • Reissuing treasury stock • Retiring stock	• Statement of retained earnings • Statement of stockholders' equity • Stock options

CORPORATE FORM OF ORGANIZATION

C1 Identify characteristics of corporations and their organization.

A **corporation** is an entity created by law that is separate from its owners. It has most of the rights and privileges granted to individuals. Owners of corporations are called *stockholders* or *shareholders*. Corporations can be separated into two types. A *privately held* (or *closely held*) corporation does not offer its stock for public sale and usually has few stockholders. A *publicly held* corporation offers its stock for public sale and can have thousands of stockholders. *Public sale* usually refers to issuance and trading on an organized stock market.

Characteristics of Corporations

Corporations represent an important type of organization. Their unique characteristics offer advantages and disadvantages.

Advantages of Corporate Characteristics

- **Separate legal entity:** A corporation conducts its affairs with the same rights, duties, and responsibilities of a person. It takes actions through its agents, who are its officers and managers.

- **Limited liability of stockholders:** Stockholders are liable for neither corporate acts nor corporate debt.

Point: The *business entity assumption* requires a corporation to be accounted for separately from its owners (shareholders).

Global: U.S., U.K., and Canadian corporations finance much of their operations with stock issuances, but companies in countries such as France, Germany, and Japan finance mainly with note and bond issuances.

- **Transferable ownership rights:** The transfer of shares from one stockholder to another usually has no effect on the corporation or its operations except when this causes a change in the directors who control or manage the corporation.

- **Continuous life:** A corporation's life continues indefinitely because it is not tied to the physical lives of its owners.

- **Lack of mutual agency for stockholders:** A corporation acts through its agents, who are its officers and managers. Stockholders, who are not its officers and managers, do not have the power to bind the corporation to contracts—referred to as *lack of mutual agency*.

- **Ease of capital accumulation:** Buying stock is attractive to investors because (1) stockholders are not liable for the corporation's acts and debts, (2) stocks usually are transferred easily, (3) the life of the corporation is unlimited, and (4) stockholders are not corporate agents. These advantages enable corporations to accumulate large amounts of capital from the combined investments of many stockholders.

Disadvantages of Corporate Characteristics

- **Government regulation:** A corporation must meet requirements of a state's incorporation laws, which subject the corporation to state regulation and control. Proprietorships and partnerships avoid many of these regulations and governmental reports.

- **Corporate taxation:** Corporations are subject to the same property and payroll taxes as proprietorships and partnerships plus *additional* taxes. The most burdensome of these are federal and state income taxes that together can take 40% or more of corporate pretax income. Moreover, corporate income is usually taxed a second time as part of stockholders' personal income when they receive cash distributed as dividends. This is called *double taxation*. (The usual dividend tax is 15%; however, it is less than 15% for lower income taxpayers, and in some cases zero.)

Point: Proprietorships and partnerships are not subject to income taxes. Their income is taxed as the personal income of their owners.

Point: Double taxation is less severe when a corporation's owner-manager collects a salary that is taxed only once as part of his or her personal income.

Decision Insight

Stock Financing Mark Zuckerberg took his company, **Facebook**, public by issuing its first shares on the Nasdaq exchange in 2012. This initial public offering (IPO) of Facebook shares raised billions in equity financing. It also raised the importance of accounting reports versus market hype. The IPO of Facebook shares comes 8 years after the company was founded by Zuckerberg in his college dorm room. ■

Corporate Organization and Management

This section describes the incorporation, costs, and management of corporate organizations.

Incorporation A corporation is created by obtaining a charter from a state government. A charter application usually must be signed by the prospective stockholders called *incorporators* or *promoters* and then filed with the proper state official. When the application process is complete and fees paid, the charter is issued and the corporation is formed. Investors then purchase the corporation's stock, meet as stockholders, and elect a board of directors. Directors oversee a corporation's affairs.

Point: A corporation is not required to have an office in its state of incorporation. Delaware is viewed as having favorable corporate laws and about half of all corporations listed on the NYSE are incorporated there.

Organization Expenses **Organization expenses** (also called *organization costs*) are the costs to organize a corporation; they include legal fees, promoters' fees, and amounts paid to obtain a charter. The corporation records (debits) these costs to an expense account called *Organization Expenses*. Organization costs are expensed as incurred because it is difficult to determine the amount and timing of their future benefits.

Management of a Corporation The ultimate control of a corporation rests with stockholders who control a corporation by electing its *board of directors,* or simply, *directors.* Each stockholder usually has one vote for each share of stock owned. This control relation is shown in Exhibit 13.1. Directors are responsible for and have final authority for managing corporate activities. A board can act only as a collective body and usually limits its actions to setting general policy.

A corporation usually holds a stockholder meeting at least once a year to elect directors and transact business as its bylaws require. A group of stockholders owning or controlling votes of more than a 50% share of a corporation's stock can elect the board and control the corporation. Stockholders who do not attend stockholders' meetings must have an opportunity to delegate their voting rights to an agent by signing a **proxy,** a document that gives a designated agent the right to vote the stock.

Day-to-day direction of corporate business is delegated to executive officers appointed by the board. A corporation's chief executive officer (CEO) is often its president. Several vice presidents, who report to the president, are commonly assigned specific areas of management responsibility such as finance, production, and marketing. One person often has the dual role of chairperson of the board of directors and CEO. In this case, the president is usually designated the chief operating officer (COO).

EXHIBIT 13.1

Corporate Structure

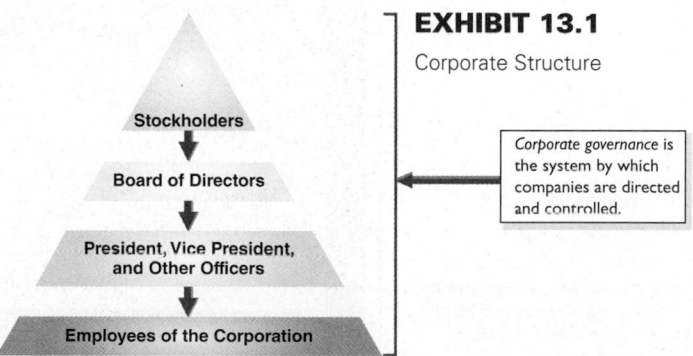

Corporate governance is the system by which companies are directed and controlled.

Point: *Bylaws* are guidelines that govern the behavior of individuals employed by and managing the corporation.

Global: Some corporate labels are:

Country	Label
United States	Inc.
France	SA
United Kingdom	
Public	PLC
Private	Ltd
Germany & Austria	
Public	AG
Private	GmbH
Sweden & Finland	AB
Italy	SpA
Netherlands	NV
Australia	AG
Mexico	SA
Bahamas	IBC

■ Decision Insight

Seed Money   Sources for start-up money include (1) "angel" investors such as family, friends, or anyone who believes in a company, (2) employees, investors, and even suppliers who can be paid with stock, and (3) venture capitalists (investors) who have a record of entrepreneurial success. See the National Venture Capital Association (**NVCA.org**) for information. ■

Stockholders of Corporations

This section explains stockholder rights, stock purchases and sales, and the role of registrar and transfer agents.

Rights of Stockholders   When investors buy stock, they acquire all *specific* rights the corporation's charter grants to stockholders. They also acquire *general* rights granted stockholders by the laws of the state in which the company is incorporated. When a corporation has only one class of stock, it is identified as **common stock.** State laws vary, but common stockholders usually have the general right to

1. Vote at stockholders' meetings (or register proxy votes electronically).
2. Sell or otherwise dispose of their stock.
3. Purchase their proportional share of any common stock later issued by the corporation. This **preemptive right** protects stockholders' proportionate interest in the corporation. For example, a stockholder who owns 25% of a corporation's common stock has the first opportunity to buy 25% of any new common stock issued.
4. Receive the same dividend, if any, on each common share of the corporation.
5. Share in any assets remaining after creditors and preferred stockholders are paid when, and if, the corporation is liquidated. Each common share receives the same amount.

Stockholders also have the right to receive timely financial reports.

Stock Certificates and Transfer   Investors who buy a corporation's stock, sometimes receive a *stock certificate* as proof of share ownership. Many corporations issue only one certificate for each block of stock purchased. A certificate can be for any number of shares. Exhibit 13.2 shows a stock certificate of the **Green Bay Packers**. A certificate shows the company name, stockholder name, number of shares, and other crucial information. Issuance of certificates is becoming less common. Instead, many stockholders maintain accounts with the corporation or their stockbrokers and never receive actual certificates.

EXHIBIT 13.2

Stock Certificate

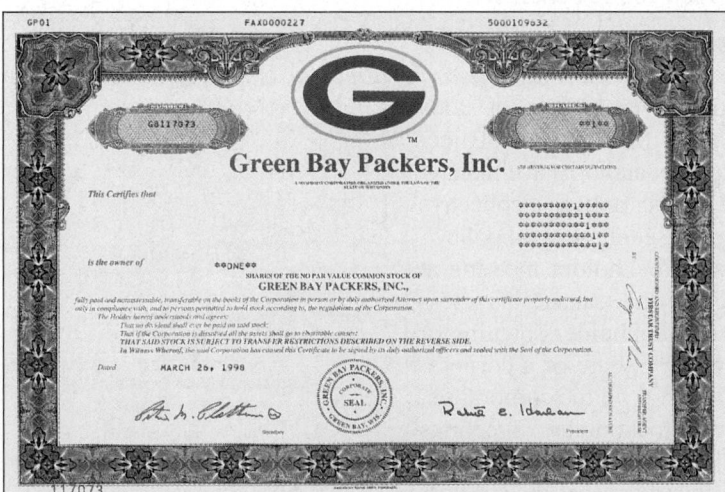

Point: The Green Bay Packers is the only nonprofit, community-owned major league professional sports team. The NFL now prohibits any other teams from becoming community-owned.

Registrar and Transfer Agents   If a corporation's stock is traded on a major stock exchange, the corporation must have a registrar and a transfer agent. A *registrar* keeps stockholder records and prepares official lists of stockholders for stockholder meetings and dividend payments. A *transfer agent* assists with purchases and sales of shares by receiving and issuing certificates as necessary. Registrars and transfer agents are usually large banks or trust companies with computer facilities and staff to do this work.

Decision Insight

Pricing Stock   A prospectus accompanies a stock's initial public offering (IPO), giving financial information about the company issuing the stock. A prospectus should help answer these questions to price an IPO: (1) Is the underwriter reliable? (2) Is there growth in revenues, profits, and cash flows? (3) What is management's view of operations? (4) Are current owners selling? (5) What are the risks? ■

Basics of Capital Stock

Capital stock is a general term that refers to any shares issued to obtain capital (owner financing). This section introduces terminology and accounting for capital stock.

Authorized Stock   **Authorized stock** is the number of shares that a corporation's charter **Subcategories of Authorized Stock**
allows it to sell. The number of authorized shares usually exceeds the number of shares issued (and outstanding), often by a large amount. (*Outstanding stock* refers to issued stock held by stockholders.) No formal journal entry is required for stock authorization. A corporation must apply to the state for a change in its charter if it wishes to issue more shares than previously authorized. A corporation discloses the number of shares authorized in the equity section of its balance sheet or notes. **Apple**'s balance sheet reports 1.8 billion common shares authorized as of the start of its 2012 fiscal year.

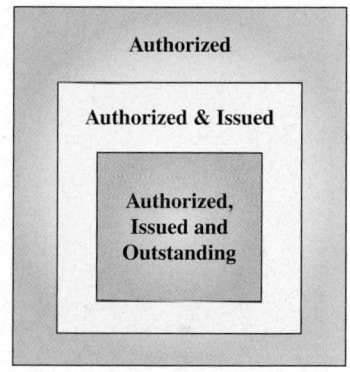

The inner-most box shows that shares issued decline if a company buys back its stock previously issued.

Selling (Issuing) Stock   A corporation can sell stock directly or indirectly. To *sell directly*, it advertises its stock issuance to potential buyers. This type of issuance is most common with privately held corporations. To *sell indirectly*, a corporation pays a brokerage house (investment banker) to issue its stock. Some brokerage houses *underwrite* an indirect issuance of stock; that is, they buy the stock from the corporation and take all gains or losses from its resale.

Market Value of Stock   **Market value per share** is the price at which a stock is bought and sold. Expected future earnings, dividends, growth, and other company and economic factors influence market value. Traded stocks' market values are available daily in newspapers such as *The Wall Street Journal* and online. The current market value of previously issued shares (for example, the price of stock in trades between investors) does not impact the issuing corporation's stockholders' equity.

Classes of Stock   When all authorized shares have the same rights and characteristics, the stock is called *common stock*. A corporation is sometimes authorized to issue more than one class of stock, including preferred stock and different classes of common stock. **American Greetings**, for instance, has two types of common stock: Class A stock has 1 vote per share and Class B stock has 10 votes per share.

Par Value Stock   **Par value stock** is stock that is assigned a **par value,** which is an amount assigned per share by the corporation in its charter. For example, **Monster Worldwide, Inc.**'s common stock has a par value of $0.001. Other commonly assigned par values are $10, $5, $1 and $0.01. There is no restriction on the assigned par value. In many states, the par value of a stock establishes **minimum legal capital,** which refers to the least amount that the buyers of stock must contribute to the corporation or be subject to paying at a future date. For example, if a corporation issues 1,000 shares of $10 par value stock, the corporation's minimum legal capital in these states would be $10,000. Minimum legal capital is intended to protect a corporation's creditors. Since creditors cannot demand payment from stockholders' personal assets, their claims are limited to the corporation's assets and any minimum legal capital. At liquidation, creditor claims are paid before any amounts are distributed to stockholders.

Point: Managers are motivated to set a low par value when minimum legal capital or state issuance taxes are based on par value.

Point: Minimum legal capital was intended to protect creditors by requiring a minimum level of net assets.

No-Par Value Stock   **No-par value stock,** or simply *no-par stock,* is stock *not* assigned a value per share by the corporate charter. Its advantage is that it can be issued at any price without the possibility of a minimum legal capital deficiency.

Point: Par, no-par, and stated value do *not* set the stock's market value.

EXHIBIT 13.3

Equity Composition

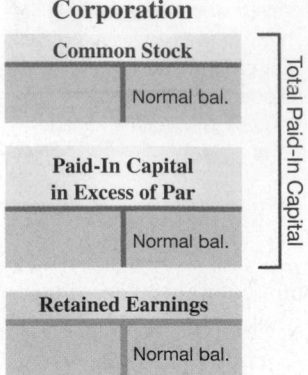

Corporation

Point: Paid-in capital comes from stock-related transactions, whereas retained earnings comes from operations; if retained earnings has a debit balance, it is often titled Accumulated Deficit.

Stated Value Stock   Stated value stock is no-par stock to which the directors assign a "stated" value per share. Stated value per share becomes the minimum legal capital per share in this case.

Stockholders' Equity   A corporation's equity is known as **stockholders' equity,** also called *shareholders' equity* or *corporate capital*. Stockholders' equity consists of (1) paid-in (or contributed) capital and (2) retained earnings; see Exhibit 13.3. **Paid-in capital** is the total amount of cash and other assets the corporation receives from its stockholders in exchange for its stock. **Retained earnings** is the cumulative net income (and loss) not distributed as dividends to its stockholders.

■ **Decision Insight** ━━━━━━━━━━━━━━━━━━━━━━━━━━━━━━

Stock Quote   The **Target** stock quote is interpreted as (left to right): **Hi,** highest price in past 52 weeks; **Lo,** lowest price in past 52 weeks;

52 Weeks				Yld		Vol				Net
Hi	Lo	Sym	Div	%	PE	mil.	Hi	Lo	Close	Chg
58.95	45.28	TGT	1.20	2.07	13.5	668	58.06	57.40	57.63	−0.30

Sym, company exchange symbol; **Div,** dividends paid per share in past year; **Yld %,** dividend divided by closing price; **PE,** stock price per share divided by earnings per share; **Vol mil.,** number (in millions) of shares traded; **Hi,** highest price for the day; **Lo,** lowest price for the day; **Close,** closing price for the day; **Net Chg,** change in closing price from prior day. ■

Quick Check   Answers — p. 535

1. Which of the following is *not* a characteristic of the corporate form of business? (*a*) Ease of capital accumulation, (*b*) Stockholder responsibility for corporate debts, (*c*) Ease in transferability of ownership rights, or (*d*) Double taxation.
2. Why is a corporation's income said to be taxed twice?
3. Is it more common for a company to issue common stock with a par value of $10 or $.001? Explain why.

COMMON STOCK

 P1   Record the issuance of corporate stock.

Accounting for the issuance of common stock affects only paid-in (contributed) capital accounts; no retained earnings accounts are affected.

Issuing Par Value Stock

Par value stock can be issued at par, at a premium (above par), or at a discount (below par). In each case, stock can be exchanged for either cash or noncash assets.

Issuing Par Value Stock at Par   When common stock is issued at par value, we record amounts for both the asset(s) received and the par value stock issued. To illustrate, the entry to record Dillon Snowboards' issuance of 30,000 shares of $10 par value stock for $300,000 cash on June 5, 2013, follows:

Assets = Liabilities + Equity
+300,000   +300,000

$10 par value × 30,000 shares

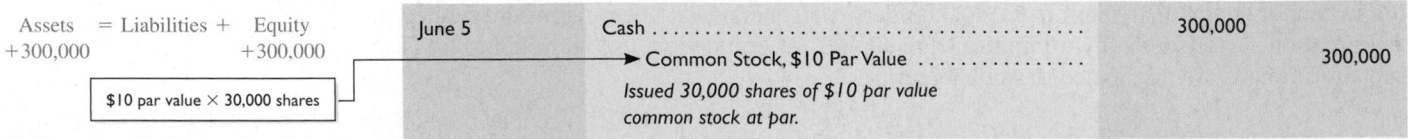

June 5	Cash	300,000	
	→ Common Stock, $10 Par Value		300,000
	Issued 30,000 shares of $10 par value		
	common stock at par.		

Exhibit 13.4 shows the stockholders' equity of Dillon Snowboards at year-end 2013 (its first year of operations) after income of $65,000 and no dividend payments.

Stockholders' Equity	
Common Stock—$10 par value; 50,000 shares authorized;	
30,000 shares issued and outstanding	$300,000
Retained earnings	65,000
Total stockholders' equity	$365,000

EXHIBIT 13.4

Stockholders' Equity for Stock Issued at Par

Issuing Par Value Stock at a Premium   A **premium on stock** occurs when a corporation sells its stock for more than par (or stated) value. To illustrate, if Dillon Snowboards issues its $10 par value common stock at $12 per share, its stock is sold at a $2 per share premium. The premium, known as **paid-in capital in excess of par value,** is reported as part of equity; it is not revenue and is not listed on the income statement. The entry to record Dillon Snowboards' issuance of 30,000 shares of $10 par value stock for $12 per share on June 5, 2013, follows:

Point: A *premium* is the amount by which issue price exceeds par (or stated) value. It is recorded in the "Paid-In Capital in Excess of Par Value, Common Stock" account; also called "Additional Paid-In Capital, Common Stock."

The Paid-In Capital in Excess of Par Value account is added to the par value of the stock in the equity section of the balance sheet as shown in Exhibit 13.5.

Point: The *Paid-In Capital* terminology is interchangeable with *Contributed Capital.*

Stockholders' Equity	
Common Stock—$10 par value; 50,000 shares authorized;	
30,000 shares issued and outstanding	$300,000
Paid-in capital in excess of par value, common stock	60,000
Retained earnings	65,000
Total stockholders' equity	$425,000

EXHIBIT 13.5

Stockholders' Equity for Stock Issued at a Premium

Issuing Par Value Stock at a Discount   A **discount on stock** occurs when a corporation sells its stock for less than par (or stated) value. Most states prohibit the issuance of stock at a discount. In states that allow stock to be issued at a discount, its buyers usually become contingently liable to creditors for the discount. If stock is issued at a discount, the amount by which issue price is less than par is debited to a *Discount on Common Stock* account, a contra to the common stock account, and its balance is subtracted from the par value of stock in the equity section of the balance sheet. This discount is not an expense and does not appear on the income statement.

Point: Retained earnings can be negative, reflecting accumulated losses. **Pandora Media** had an accumulated deficit of $101 million at the start of 2012.

Issuing No-Par Value Stock

When no-par stock is issued and is not assigned a stated value, the amount the corporation receives becomes legal capital and is recorded as Common Stock. This means that the entire proceeds are credited to a no-par stock account. To illustrate, a corporation records its October 20 issuance of 1,000 shares of no-par stock for $40 cash per share as follows:

Frequency of Stock Types

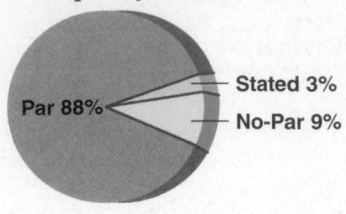

Par 88%

Stated 3%

No-Par 9%

Issuing Stated Value Stock

When no-par stock is issued and assigned a stated value, its stated value becomes legal capital and is credited to a stated value stock account. Assuming that stated value stock is issued at an amount in excess of stated value (the usual case), the excess is credited to Paid-In Capital in Excess of Stated Value, Common Stock, which is reported in the stockholders' equity section. To illustrate, a corporation that issues 1,000 shares of no-par common stock having a stated value of $40 per share in return for $50 cash per share records this as follows:

Assets = Liabilities + Equity
+50,000   +40,000
                    +10,000

$40 stated value × 1,000 shares

[$50 issue price − $40 stated value] × 1,000 shares

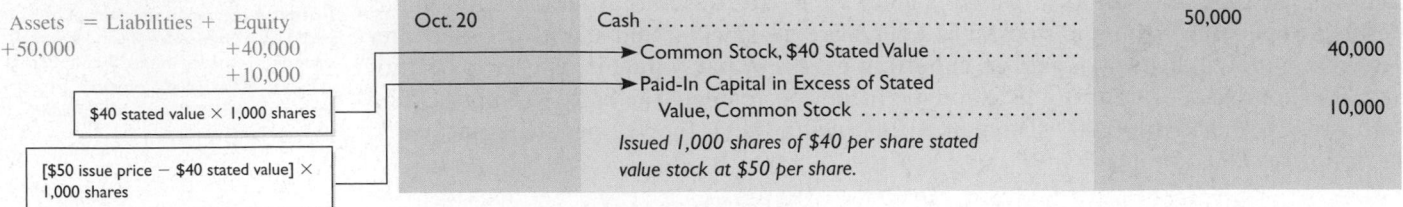

Oct. 20	Cash	50,000	
	► Common Stock, $40 Stated Value		40,000
	► Paid-In Capital in Excess of Stated		
	Value, Common Stock		10,000
	Issued 1,000 shares of $40 per share stated		
	value stock at $50 per share.		

Issuing Stock for Noncash Assets

A corporation can receive assets other than cash in exchange for its stock. (It can also assume liabilities on the assets received such as a mortgage on property received.) The corporation records the assets received at their market values as of the date of the transaction. The stock given in exchange is recorded at its par (or stated) value with any excess recorded in the Paid-In Capital in Excess of Par (or Stated) Value account. (If no-par stock is issued, the stock is recorded at the assets' market value.) To illustrate, the entry to record receipt of land valued at $105,000 in return for issuance of 4,000 shares of $20 par value common stock on June 10 is

Point: Stock issued for noncash assets should be recorded at the market value of either the stock or the noncash asset, whichever is more clearly determinable.

Assets = Liabilities + Equity
+105,000   +80,000
                   +25,000

$20 par value × 4,000 shares

$105,000 asset value − $80,000 stock value

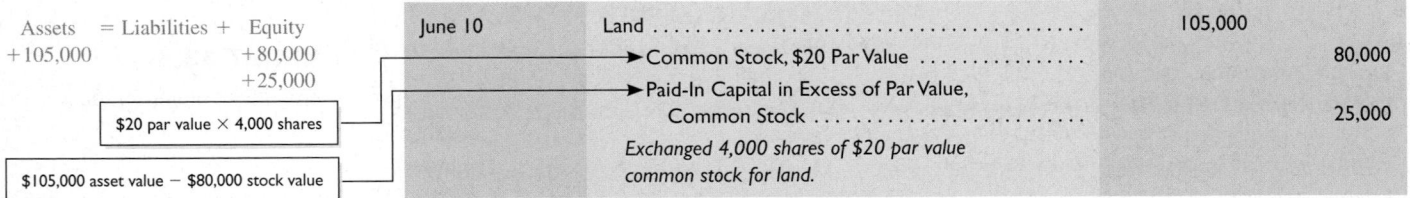

June 10	Land	105,000	
	► Common Stock, $20 Par Value		80,000
	► Paid-In Capital in Excess of Par Value,		
	Common Stock		25,000
	Exchanged 4,000 shares of $20 par value		
	common stock for land.		

A corporation sometimes gives shares of its stock to promoters in exchange for their services in organizing the corporation, which the corporation records as Organization Expenses. The entry to record receipt of services valued at $12,000 in organizing the corporation in return for 600 shares of $15 par value common stock on June 5 is

Point: Any type of stock can be issued for noncash assets.

Assets = Liabilities + Equity
                     −12,000
                     +9,000
                     +3,000

$15 par value × 600 shares

$12,000 services value − $9,000 stock value

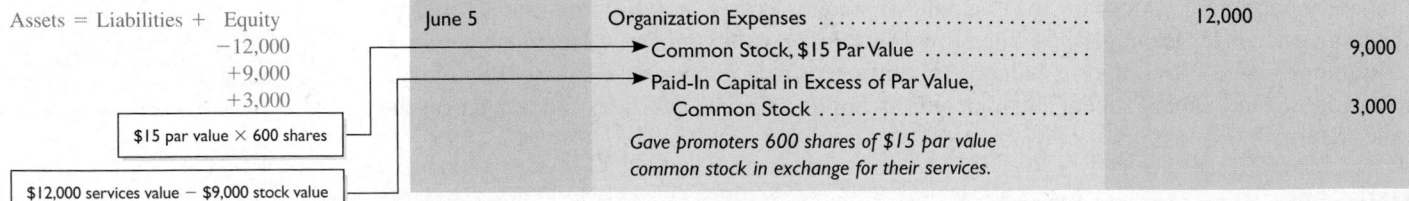

June 5	Organization Expenses	12,000	
	► Common Stock, $15 Par Value		9,000
	► Paid-In Capital in Excess of Par Value,		
	Common Stock		3,000
	Gave promoters 600 shares of $15 par value		
	common stock in exchange for their services.		

Quick Check   Answers — p. 535

4. A company issues 7,000 shares of its $10 par value common stock in exchange for equipment valued at $105,000. The entry to record this transaction includes a credit to (*a*) Paid-In Capital in Excess of Par Value, Common Stock, for $35,000. (*b*) Retained Earnings for $35,000. (*c*) Common Stock, $10 Par Value, for $105,000.

5. What is a premium on stock issuance?

6. Who is protected by the minimum legal capital requirement?

DIVIDENDS

This section describes both cash and stock dividend transactions.

Cash Dividends

The decision to pay cash dividends rests with the board of directors and involves more than evaluating the amounts of retained earnings and cash. The directors, for instance, may decide to keep the cash to invest in the corporation's growth, to meet emergencies, to take advantage of unexpected opportunities, or to pay off debt. Alternatively, many corporations pay cash dividends to their stockholders at regular dates. These cash flows provide a return to investors and almost always affect the stock's market value.

P2 Record transactions involving cash dividends, stock dividends, and stock splits.

Accounting for Cash Dividends Dividend payment involves three important dates: declaration, record, and payment. **Date of declaration** is the date the directors vote to declare and pay a dividend. This creates a legal liability of the corporation to its stockholders. **Date of record** is the future date specified by the directors for identifying those stockholders listed in the corporation's records to receive dividends. The date of record usually follows the date of declaration by at least two weeks. Persons who own stock on the date of record receive dividends. **Date of payment** is the date when the corporation makes payment; it follows the date of record by enough time to allow the corporation to arrange checks, money transfers, or other means to pay dividends.

Percent of Corporations Paying Dividends

To illustrate, the entry to record a January 9 declaration of a $1 per share cash dividend by the directors of Z-Tech, Inc., with 5,000 outstanding shares is

Date of Declaration

Jan. 9	Retained Earnings	5,000	
	Common Dividend Payable		5,000
	Declared $1 per common share cash dividend.[1]		

Assets = Liabilities + Equity
       +5,000   −5,000

$1 per share declared dividend × 5,000 shares

Common Dividend Payable is a current liability. The date of record for the Z-Tech dividend is January 22. *No formal journal entry is needed on the date of record.* The February 1 date of payment requires an entry to record both the settlement of the liability and the reduction of the cash balance, as follows:

Date of Payment

Feb. 1	Common Dividend Payable	5,000	
	Cash		5,000
	Paid $1 per common share cash dividend.		

Assets = Liabilities + Equity
−5,000   −5,000

Deficits and Cash Dividends A corporation with a debit (abnormal) balance for retained earnings is said to have a **retained earnings deficit,** which arises when a company incurs cumulative losses and/or pays more dividends than total earnings from current and prior years. A deficit is reported as a deduction on the balance sheet, as shown in Exhibit 13.6. Most states prohibit a corporation with a deficit from paying a cash dividend to its stockholders. This legal restriction is designed to protect creditors by preventing distribution of assets to stockholders when the company may be in financial difficulty.

Point: It is often said a dividend is a distribution of retained earnings, but it is more precise to describe a dividend as a distribution of assets to satisfy stockholder claims.

Point: The Retained Earnings Deficit account is also called *Accumulated Deficit.*

---

[1] An alternative entry is to debit Dividends instead of Retained Earnings. The balance in Dividends is then closed to Retained Earnings at the end of the reporting period. The effect is the same: Retained Earnings is decreased and a Dividend Payable is increased. For simplicity, all assignments in this chapter use the Retained Earnings account to record dividend declarations.

EXHIBIT 13.6

Stockholders' Equity
with a Deficit

Common stock—$10 par value, 5,000 shares authorized, issued, and outstanding	$50,000
Retained earnings deficit	**(6,000)**
Total stockholders' equity	$44,000

Point: Amazon.com has never
declared a cash dividend.

Some state laws allow cash dividends to be paid by returning a portion of the capital contributed by stockholders. This type of dividend is called a **liquidating cash dividend,** or simply *liquidating dividend,* because it returns a part of the original investment back to the stockholders. This requires a debit entry to one of the contributed capital accounts instead of Retained Earnings at the declaration date.

Quick Check

Answers — p. 536

7. What type of an account is the Common Dividend Payable account?
8. What three crucial dates are involved in the process of paying a cash dividend?
9. When does a dividend become a company's legal obligation?

Stock Dividends

A **stock dividend,** declared by a corporation's directors, is a distribution of additional shares of the corporation's own stock to its stockholders without the receipt of any payment in return. Stock dividends and cash dividends are different. A stock dividend does not reduce assets and equity but instead transfers a portion of equity from retained earnings to contributed capital.

Reasons for Stock Dividends   Stock dividends exist for at least two reasons. First, directors are said to use stock dividends to keep the market price of the stock affordable. For example, if a corporation continues to earn income but does not issue cash dividends, the price of its common stock likely increases. The price of such a stock may become so high that it discourages some investors from buying the stock (especially in lots of 100 and 1,000). When a corporation has a stock dividend, it increases the number of outstanding shares and lowers the per share stock price. Another reason for a stock dividend is to provide evidence of management's confidence that the company is doing well and will continue to do well.

Accounting for Stock Dividends   A stock dividend affects the components of equity by transferring part of retained earnings to contributed capital accounts, sometimes described as *capitalizing* retained earnings. Accounting for a stock dividend depends on whether it is a small or large stock dividend. A **small stock dividend** is a distribution of 25% or less of previously outstanding shares. It is recorded by capitalizing retained earnings for an amount equal to the market value of the shares to be distributed. A **large stock dividend** is a distribution of more than 25% of previously outstanding shares. A large stock dividend is recorded by capitalizing retained earnings for the minimum amount required by state law governing the corporation. Most states require capitalizing retained earnings equal to the par or stated value of the stock.

To illustrate stock dividends, we use the equity section of Quest's balance sheet shown in Exhibit 13.7 just *before* its declaration of a stock dividend on December 31.

EXHIBIT 13.7

Stockholders' Equity *before*
Declaring a Stock Dividend

Stockholders' Equity (before dividend)	
Common stock—$10 par value, 15,000 shares authorized, 10,000 shares issued and outstanding	$100,000
Paid-in capital in excess of par value, common stock	8,000
Retained earnings	35,000
Total stockholders' equity	$143,000

Recording a small stock dividend.   Assume that Quest's directors declare a 10% stock dividend on December 31. This stock dividend of 1,000 shares, computed as 10% of its 10,000 issued and outstanding shares, is to be distributed on January 20 to the stockholders of record on January 15. Since the market price of Quest's stock on December 31 is $15 per share, this small stock dividend declaration is recorded as follows:

Date of Declaration—Small Stock Dividend

Dec. 31	Retained Earnings	15,000	
	Common Stock Dividend Distributable		10,000
	Paid-In Capital in Excess of Par Value,		
	Common Stock		5,000
	Declared a 1,000-share (10%) stock dividend.		

Assets = Liabilities + Equity
−15,000
+10,000
+5,000

10% dividend × 10,000 issued shares × $10 par value

10% dividend × 10,000 issued shares × [$15 market price − $10 par value]

The $10,000 credit in the declaration entry equals the par value of the shares and is recorded in *Common Stock Dividend Distributable,* an equity account. Its balance exists only until the shares are issued. The $5,000 credit equals the amount by which market value exceeds par value. This amount increases the Paid-In Capital in Excess of Par Value account in anticipation of the issuance of shares. In general, the balance sheet changes in three ways when a stock dividend is declared. First, the amount of equity attributed to common stock increases; for Quest, from $100,000 to $110,000 for 1,000 additional declared shares. Second, paid-in capital in excess of par increases by the excess of market value over par value for the declared shares. Third, retained earnings decreases, reflecting the transfer of amounts to both common stock and paid-in capital in excess of par. The stockholders' equity of Quest is shown in Exhibit 13.8 *after* its 10% stock dividend is declared on December 31—the items impacted are in bold.

Point: Small stock dividends are recorded at market value.

Point: The term *Distributable* (not *Payable*) is used for stock dividends. A stock dividend is never a liability because it never reduces assets.

Point: The credit to Paid-In Capital in Excess of Par Value is recorded when the stock dividend is declared. This account is not affected when stock is later distributed.

EXHIBIT 13.8

Stockholders' Equity *after* Declaring a Stock Dividend

Stockholders' Equity (after dividend)	
Common stock—$10 par value, 15,000 shares authorized,	
10,000 shares issued and outstanding	$100,000
Common stock dividend distributable—1,000 shares	**10,000**
Paid-in capital in excess of par value, common stock	**13,000**
Retained earnings	**20,000**
Total stockholders' equity	$143,000

No entry is made on the date of record for a stock dividend. On January 20, the date of payment, Quest distributes the new shares to stockholders and records this entry:

Date of Payment—Small Stock Dividend

Jan. 20	Common Stock Dividend Distributable	10,000	
	Common Stock, $10 Par Value		10,000
	To record issuance of common stock dividend.		

Assets = Liabilities + Equity
−10,000
+10,000

The combined effect of these stock dividend entries is to transfer (or capitalize) $15,000 of retained earnings to paid-in capital accounts. The amount of capitalized retained earnings equals the market value of the 1,000 issued shares ($15 × 1,000 shares). A stock dividend has no effect on the ownership percent of individual stockholders.

Recording a large stock dividend.   A corporation capitalizes retained earnings equal to the minimum amount required by state law for a large stock dividend. For most states, this amount is the par or stated value of the newly issued shares. To illustrate, suppose Quest's board declares a stock dividend of 30% instead of 10% on December 31. Since this dividend is more

Point: A stock dividend does not affect assets.

Point: Large stock dividends are recorded at par or stated value.

than 25%, it is treated as a large stock dividend. Thus, the par value of the 3,000 dividend shares is capitalized at the date of declaration with this entry:

Date of Declaration—Large Stock Dividend

Assets = Liabilities + Equity
            −30,000
            +30,000

30% dividend × 10,000 issued shares × $10 par value

Dec. 31	Retained Earnings	30,000	
	► Common Stock Dividend Distributable		30,000
	Declared a 3,000-share (30%) stock dividend.		

This transaction decreases retained earnings and increases contributed capital by $30,000. On the date of payment the company debits Common Stock Dividend Distributable and credits Common Stock for $30,000. The effects from a large stock dividend on balance sheet accounts are similar to those for a small stock dividend except for the absence of any effect on paid-in capital in excess of par.

Stock Splits

Before 5:1 Split: 1 share, $50 par

After 5:1 Split: 5 shares, $10 par

A **stock split** is the distribution of additional shares to stockholders according to their percent owner-ship. When a stock split occurs, the corporation "calls in" its outstanding shares and issues more than one new share in exchange for each old share. Splits can be done in any ratio, including 2-for-1, 3-for-1, or higher. In 2012, Google directors approved a 2-for-1 stock split. Stock splits reduce the par or stated value per share. The reasons for stock splits are similar to those for stock dividends.

To illustrate, CompTec has 100,000 outstanding shares of $20 par value common stock with a current market value of $88 per share. A 2-for-1 stock split cuts par value in half as it replaces 100,000 shares of $20 par value stock with 200,000 shares of $10 par value stock. Market value is reduced from $88 per share to about $44 per share. The split does not affect any equity amounts reported on the balance sheet or any individual stockholder's percent ownership. Both the Paid-In Capital and Retained Earnings accounts are unchanged by a split, and *no journal entry is made*. The only effect on the accounts is a change in the stock account description. CompTec's 2-for-1 split on its $20 par value stock means that after the split, it changes its stock account title to Com-mon Stock, $10 Par Value. This stock's description on the balance sheet also changes to reflect the additional authorized, issued, and outstanding shares and the new par value.

Point: Berkshire Hathaway has resisted a stock split. Its recent stock price was $120,000 per share.

Point: A reverse stock split is the opposite of a stock split. It increases both the market value per share and the par or stated value per share with a split ratio less than 1-for-1, such as 1-for-2. A reverse split results in fewer shares. Markets often read bad news into reverse splits.

The difference between stock splits and large stock dividends is often blurred. Many companies report stock splits in their financial statements without calling in the original shares by simply changing their par value. This type of "split" is really a large stock dividend and results in additional shares issued to stockholders by capitalizing retained earnings or transferring other paid-in capital to Common Stock. This approach avoids administrative costs of splitting the stock. **Harley-Davidson** recently declared a 2-for-1 stock split executed in the form of a 100% stock dividend.

■ Decision Maker

Entrepreneur   A company you cofounded and own stock in announces a 50% stock dividend. Has the value of your stock investment increased, decreased, or remained the same? Would it make a difference if it was a 3-for-2 stock split executed in the form of a dividend? ■   [Answer—p. 535]

Quick Check   Answers — p. 536

10. How does a stock dividend impact assets and retained earnings?
11. What distinguishes a large stock dividend from a small stock dividend?
12. What amount of retained earnings is capitalized for a small stock dividend?

PREFERRED STOCK

C2   Explain characteristics of, and distribute dividends between, common and preferred stock.

A corporation can issue two basic kinds of stock, common and preferred. **Preferred stock** has special rights that give it priority (or senior status) over common stock in one or more areas. Spe-cial rights typically include a preference for receiving dividends and for the distribution of assets if the corporation is liquidated. Preferred stock carries all rights of common stock unless the corporate charter nullifies them. Most preferred stock, for instance, does not confer the right to vote. Exhibit 13.9 shows that preferred stock is issued by about one-fourth of corporations. All corporations issue common stock. (While rare, not all common stock carries voting rights; Google's C class common shares are non-voting.)

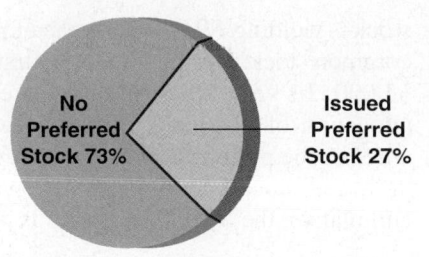

EXHIBIT 13.9

Corporations and Preferred Stock

Issuance of Preferred Stock

Preferred stock usually has a par value. Like common stock, it can be sold at a price different from par. Preferred stock is recorded in its own separate capital accounts. To illustrate, if Dillon Snowboards issues 50 shares of $100 par value preferred stock for $6,000 cash on July 1, 2013, the entry is

The equity section of the year-end balance sheet for Dillon Snowboards, including preferred stock, is shown in Exhibit 13.10. (This exhibit assumes that common stock was issued at par.) Issuing no-par preferred stock is similar to issuing no-par common stock. Also, the entries for issuing preferred stock for noncash assets are similar to those for common stock.

Stockholders' Equity	
Common stock—$10 par value; 50,000 shares authorized; 30,000 shares issued and outstanding	$300,000
Preferred stock—$100 par value; 1,000 shares authorized; 50 shares issued and outstanding	5,000
Paid-in capital in excess of par value, preferred stock	1,000
Retained earnings	65,000
Total stockholders' equity	$371,000

EXHIBIT 13.10

Stockholders' Equity with Common and Preferred Stock

Dividend Preference of Preferred Stock

Preferred stock usually carries a preference for dividends, meaning that preferred stockholders are allocated their dividends before any dividends are allocated to common stockholders. The dividends allocated to preferred stockholders are usually expressed as a dollar amount per share or a percent applied to par value. A preference for dividends does *not* ensure dividends. If the directors do not declare a dividend, neither the preferred nor the common stockholders receive one.

Cumulative or Noncumulative Dividend   Most preferred stocks carry a cumulative dividend right. **Cumulative preferred stock** has a right to be paid both the current and all prior periods' unpaid dividends before any dividend is paid to common stockholders. When preferred stock is cumulative and the directors either do not declare a dividend to preferred stockholders or declare one that does not cover the total amount of cumulative dividend, the unpaid dividend amount is called **dividend in arrears.** Accumulation of dividends in arrears on cumulative preferred stock does not guarantee they will be paid. **Noncumulative preferred stock** confers no right to prior periods' unpaid dividends if they were not declared in those prior periods.

To illustrate the difference between cumulative and noncumulative preferred stock, assume that a corporation's outstanding stock includes (1) 1,000 shares of $100 par, 9% preferred

Point: Dividend preference does not imply that preferred stockholders receive more dividends than common stockholders, nor does it guarantee a dividend.

stock—yielding $9,000 per year in potential dividends, and (2) 4,000 shares of $50 par value common stock. During 2012, the first year of operations, the directors declare cash dividends of $5,000. In year 2013, they declare cash dividends of $42,000. See Exhibit 13.11 for the allocation of dividends for these two years. Allocation of year 2013 dividends depends on whether the preferred stock is noncumulative or cumulative. With noncumulative preferred, the preferred stockholders never receive the $4,000 skipped in 2012. If the preferred stock is cumulative, the $4,000 in arrears is paid in 2013 before any other dividends are paid.

EXHIBIT 13.11

Allocation of Dividends (noncumulative vs. cumulative preferred stock)

Example: What dividends do cumulative preferred stockholders receive in 2013 if the corporation paid only $2,000 of dividends in 2012? How does this affect dividends to common stockholders in 2013? *Answers:* $16,000 ($7,000 dividends in arrears, plus $9,000 current preferred dividends). Dividends to common stockholders decrease to $26,000.

	Preferred	Common
Preferred Stock Is Noncumulative		
Year 2012	$ 5,000	$ 0
Year 2013		
Step 1: Current year's preferred dividend	$ 9,000	
Step 2: Remainder to common		$33,000
Preferred Stock Is Cumulative		
Year 2012	$ 5,000	$ 0
Year 2013		
Step 1: Dividend in arrears	$ 4,000	
Step 2: Current year's preferred dividend	9,000	
Step 3: Remainder to common		$29,000
Totals for year 2013	$13,000	$29,000

A liability for a dividend does not exist until the directors declare a dividend. If a preferred dividend date passes and the corporation's board fails to declare the dividend on its cumulative preferred stock, the dividend in arrears is not a liability. The *full-disclosure principle* requires a corporation to report (usually in a note) the amount of preferred dividends in arrears as of the balance sheet date.

Participating or Nonparticipating Dividend   **Nonparticipating preferred stock** has a feature that limits dividends to a maximum amount each year. This maximum is often stated as a percent of the stock's par value or as a specific dollar amount per share. Once preferred stockholders receive this amount, the common stockholders receive any and all additional dividends. **Participating preferred stock** has a feature allowing preferred stockholders to share with common stockholders in any dividends paid in excess of the percent or dollar amount stated on the preferred stock. This participation feature does not apply until common stockholders receive dividends equal to the preferred stock's dividend percent. Many corporations are authorized to issue participating preferred stock but rarely do, and most managers never expect to issue it.[2]

Convertible Preferred Stock

Preferred stock is more attractive to investors if it carries a right to exchange preferred shares for a fixed number of common shares. **Convertible preferred stock** gives holders the option to

---

[2] Participating preferred stock is usually authorized as a defense against a possible corporate *takeover* by an "unfriendly" investor (or a group of investors) who intends to buy enough voting common stock to gain control. Taking a term from spy novels, the financial world refers to this type of plan as a *poison pill* that a company swallows if enemy investors threaten its capture. A poison pill usually works as follows: A corporation's common stockholders on a given date are granted the right to purchase a large amount of participating preferred stock at a very low price. This right to purchase preferred shares is *not* transferable. If an unfriendly investor buys a large block of common shares (whose right to purchase participating preferred shares does *not* transfer to this buyer), the board can issue preferred shares at a low price to the remaining common shareholders who retained the right to purchase. Future dividends are then divided between the newly issued participating preferred shares and the common shares. This usually transfers value from common shares to preferred shares, causing the unfriendly investor's common stock to lose much of its value and reduces the potential benefit of a hostile takeover.

exchange their preferred shares for common shares at a specified rate. When a company prospers and its common stock increases in value, convertible preferred stockholders can share in this success by converting their preferred stock into more valuable common stock.

Callable Preferred Stock

Callable preferred stock gives the issuing corporation the right to purchase (retire) this stock from its holders at specified future prices and dates. The amount paid to call and retire a preferred share is its **call price,** or *redemption value,* and is set when the stock is issued. The call price normally includes the stock's par value plus a premium giving holders additional return on their investment. When the issuing corporation calls and retires a preferred stock, the terms of the agreement often require it to pay the call price *and* any dividends in arrears.

Point: The issuing corporation has the right, or option, to retire its callable preferred stock.

 IFRS

Like U.S. GAAP, IFRS requires that preferred stocks be classified as debt or equity based on analysis of the stock's contractual terms. However, IFRS uses different criteria for such classification. ■

Reasons for Issuing Preferred Stock

Corporations issue preferred stock for several reasons. One is to raise capital without sacrificing control. For example, suppose a company's organizers have $100,000 cash to invest and organize a corporation that needs $200,000 of capital to start. If they sell $200,000 worth of common stock (with $100,000 to the organizers), they would have only 50% control and would need to negotiate extensively with other stockholders in making policy. However, if they issue $100,000 worth of common stock to themselves and sell outsiders $100,000 of 8%, cumulative preferred stock with no voting rights, they retain control.

A second reason to issue preferred stock is to boost the return earned by common stockholders. To illustrate, suppose a corporation's organizers expect to earn an annual after-tax income of $24,000 on an investment of $200,000. If they sell and issue $200,000 worth of common stock, the $24,000 income produces a 12% return on the $200,000 of common stockholders' equity. However, if they issue $100,000 of 8% preferred stock to outsiders and $100,000 of common stock to themselves, their own return increases to 16% per year, as shown in Exhibit 13.12.

EXHIBIT 13.12

Return to Common Stockholders When Preferred Stock Is Issued

Net (after-tax) income	$24,000
Less preferred dividends at 8%	(8,000)
Balance to common stockholders	$16,000
Return to common stockholders ($16,000/$100,000)	16%

Common stockholders earn 16% instead of 12% because assets contributed by preferred stockholders are invested to earn $12,000 while the preferred dividend is only $8,000. Use of preferred stock to increase return to common stockholders is an example of **financial leverage** (also called *trading on the equity*). As a general rule, when the dividend rate on preferred stock is less than the rate the corporation earns on its assets, the effect of issuing preferred stock is to increase (or *lever*) the rate earned by common stockholders.

Point: Financial leverage also occurs when debt is issued and the interest rate paid on it is less than the rate earned from using the assets the creditors lend the company.

Other reasons for issuing preferred stock include its appeal to some investors who believe that the corporation's common stock is too risky or that the expected return on common stock is too low.

■ **Decision Maker** ━━━━━━━━━━━━━━━━━━━━━━━

Concert Organizer   Assume that you alter your business strategy from organizing concerts targeted at under 1,000 people to those targeted at between 5,000 to 20,000 people. You also incorporate because of increased risk of lawsuits and a desire to issue stock for financing. It is important that you control the company for decisions on whom to schedule. What types of stock do you offer? ■   [Answer—p. 535]

13. In what ways does preferred stock often have priority over common stock?

14. Increasing the return to common stockholders by issuing preferred stock is an example of (*a*) Financial leverage. (*b*) Cumulative earnings. (*c*) Dividend in arrears.

15. A corporation has issued and outstanding (i) 9,000 shares of $50 par value, 10% cumulative, nonparticipating preferred stock and (ii) 27,000 shares of $10 par value common stock. No dividends have been declared for the two prior years. During the current year, the corporation declares $288,000 in dividends. The amount paid to common shareholders is (*a*) $243,000. (*b*) $153,000. (*c*) $135,000.

TREASURY STOCK

P3   Record purchases and sales of treasury stock and the retirement of stock.

Corporations acquire shares of their own stock for several reasons: (1) to use their shares to acquire another corporation, (2) to purchase shares to avoid a hostile takeover of the company, (3) to reissue them to employees as compensation, and (4) to maintain a strong market for their stock or to show management confidence in the current price.

Corporations and Treasury Stock

With Treasury Stock 62%

No Treasury Stock 38%

A corporation's reacquired shares are called **treasury stock,** which is similar to unissued stock in several ways: (1) neither treasury stock nor unissued stock is an asset, (2) neither receives cash dividends or stock dividends, and (3) neither allows the exercise of voting rights. However, treasury stock does differ from unissued stock in one major way: The corporation can resell treasury stock at less than par without having the buyers incur a liability, provided it was originally issued at par value or higher. Treasury stock purchases also require management to exercise ethical sensitivity because funds are being paid to specific stockholders instead of all stockholders. Managers must be sure the purchase is in the best interest of all stockholders. These concerns cause companies to fully disclose treasury stock transactions.

Purchasing Treasury Stock

Purchasing treasury stock reduces the corporation's assets and equity by equal amounts. (We describe the *cost method* of accounting for treasury stock, which is the most widely used method. The *par value* method is another method explained in advanced courses.) To illustrate, Exhibit 13.13 shows Cyber Corporation's account balances *before* any treasury stock purchase (Cyber has no liabilities).

EXHIBIT 13.13

Account Balances *before* Purchasing Treasury Stock

Assets		Stockholders' Equity	
Cash	$ 30,000	Common stock—$10 par; 10,000 shares	
Other assets	95,000	authorized, issued, and outstanding	$100,000
		Retained earnings	25,000
Total assets	$125,000	Total stockholders' equity	$125,000

Cyber then purchases 1,000 of its own shares for $11,500 on May 1, which is recorded as follows:

Assets = Liabilities + Equity
−11,500   −11,500

$11.50 cost per share × 1,000 shares

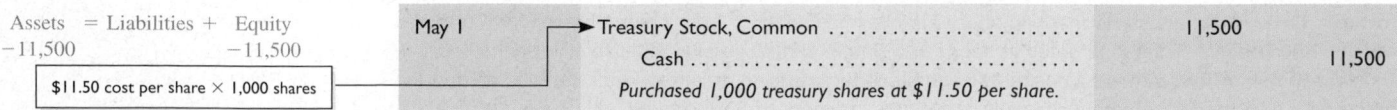

May 1	Treasury Stock, Common	11,500	
	Cash		11,500
	Purchased 1,000 treasury shares at $11.50 per share.		

This entry reduces equity through the debit to the Treasury Stock account, which is a contra equity account. Exhibit 13.14 shows account balances *after* this transaction.

Assets		Stockholders' Equity	
Cash	$ 18,500	Common stock—$10 par; 10,000 shares authorized and issued; 1,000 shares in treasury	$100,000
Other assets	95,000	Retained earnings, $11,500 restricted by treasury stock purchase	25,000
		Less cost of treasury stock	**(11,500)**
Total assets	$113,500	Total stockholders' equity	$113,500

EXHIBIT 13.14

Account Balances *after* Purchasing Treasury Stock

The treasury stock purchase reduces Cyber's cash, total assets, and total equity by $11,500 but does not reduce the balance of either the Common Stock or the Retained Earnings account. The equity reduction is reported by deducting the cost of treasury stock in the equity section. Also, two disclosures are evident. First, the stock description reveals that 1,000 issued shares are in treasury, leaving only 9,000 shares still outstanding. Second, the description for retained earnings reveals that it is partly restricted.

Point: The Treasury Stock account is *not* an asset. Treasury stock does not carry voting or dividend rights.

Point: A treasury stock purchase is also called a *stock buyback*.

Reissuing Treasury Stock

Treasury stock can be reissued by selling it at cost, above cost, or below cost.

Selling Treasury Stock at Cost If treasury stock is reissued at cost, the entry is the reverse of the one made to record the purchase. For instance, if on May 21 Cyber reissues 100 of the treasury shares purchased on May 1 at the same $11.50 per share cost, the entry is

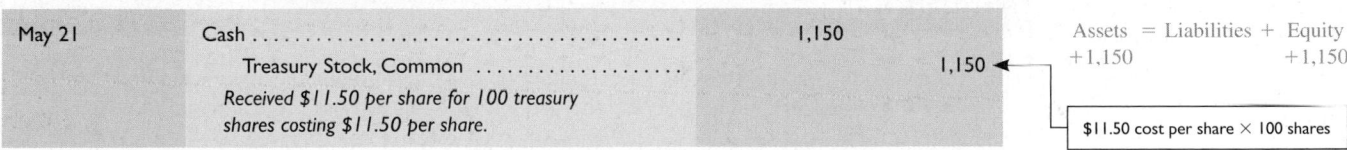

May 21	Cash	1,150	
	Treasury Stock, Common		1,150
	Received $11.50 per share for 100 treasury shares costing $11.50 per share.		

Assets = Liabilities + Equity
+1,150   +1,150

$11.50 cost per share × 100 shares

Selling Treasury Stock *above* Cost If treasury stock is sold for more than cost, the amount received in excess of cost is credited to the Paid-In Capital, Treasury Stock account. This account is reported as a separate item in the stockholders' equity section. No gain is ever reported from the sale of treasury stock. To illustrate, if Cyber receives $12 cash per share for 400 treasury shares costing $11.50 per share on June 3, the entry is

Point: Treasury stock does not represent ownership. A company cannot own a part of itself.

June 3	Cash	4,800	
	Treasury Stock, Common		4,600
	Paid-In Capital, Treasury Stock		200
	Received $12 per share for 400 treasury shares costing $11.50 per share.		

Assets = Liabilities + Equity
+4,800   +4,600
                  +200

$11.50 cost per share × 400 shares

[$12 issue price − $11.50 cost per share] × 400 shares

Selling Treasury Stock *below* Cost When treasury stock is sold below cost, the entry to record the sale depends on whether the Paid-In Capital, Treasury Stock account has a credit balance. If it has a zero balance, the excess of cost over the sales price is debited to Retained Earnings. If the Paid-In Capital, Treasury Stock account has a credit balance, it is debited for the excess of the cost over the selling price but not to exceed the balance in this account. When the credit balance in this paid-in capital account is eliminated, any remaining difference between the cost and selling price is debited to Retained Earnings. To illustrate, if Cyber sells its remaining 500 shares of treasury stock at $10 per share on July 10, equity is

Point: The phrase *treasury stock* is believed to arise from the fact that reacquired stock is held in a corporation's treasury.

Point: The Paid-In Capital, Treasury Stock account can have a zero or credit balance but never a debit balance.

reduced by $750 (500 shares × $1.50 per share excess of cost over selling price), as shown in this entry:

Assets = Liabilities + Equity
+5,000   −200
                          −550
                        +5,750

[$10 issue price − $11.50 cost per share] × 500 shares; not to exceed $200

For any amount exceeding $200

$11.50 cost per share × 500 shares

July 10	Cash	5,000	
	Paid-In Capital, Treasury Stock	200	
	Retained Earnings	550	
	Treasury Stock, Common		5,750
	Received $10 per share for 500 treasury shares costing $11.50 per share.		

This entry eliminates the $200 credit balance in the paid-in capital account created on June 3 and then reduces the Retained Earnings balance by the remaining $550 excess of cost over selling price. A company never reports a loss (or gain) from the sale of treasury stock.

Retiring Stock

Point: Recording stock retirement results in canceling the equity from the original issuance of the shares.

A corporation can purchase its own stock and retire it. Retiring stock reduces the number of issued shares. Retired stock is the same as authorized and unissued shares. Purchases and retirements of stock are permissible under state law only if they do not jeopardize the interests of creditors and stockholders. When stock is purchased for retirement, we remove all capital amounts related to the retired shares. If the purchase price exceeds the net amount removed, this excess is debited to Retained Earnings. If the net amount removed from all capital accounts exceeds the purchase price, this excess is credited to the Paid-In Capital from Retirement of Stock account. A company's assets and equity are always reduced by the amount paid for the retiring stock.

Quick Check   Answers — p. 536

16. Purchase of treasury stock (*a*) has no effect on assets; (*b*) reduces total assets and total equity by equal amounts; or (*c*) is recorded with a debit to Retained Earnings.

17. Southern Co. purchases shares of Northern Corp. Should either company classify these shares as treasury stock?

18. How does treasury stock affect the authorized, issued, and outstanding shares?

19. When a company purchases treasury stock, (*a*) retained earnings are restricted by the amount paid; (*b*) Retained Earnings is credited; or (*c*) it is retired.

REPORTING OF EQUITY

C3 Explain the items reported in retained earnings.

Statement of Retained Earnings

Retained earnings generally consist of a company's cumulative net income less any net losses and dividends declared since its inception. Retained earnings are part of stockholders' claims on the company's net assets, but this does *not* imply that a certain amount of cash or other assets is available to pay stockholders. For example, **Abercrombie & Fitch** has $2,320,571 thousand in retained earnings, but only $583,495 thousand in cash. This section describes events and transactions affecting retained earnings and how retained earnings are reported.

Restrictions and Appropriations   The term **restricted retained earnings** refers to both statutory and contractual restrictions. A common *statutory* (or *legal*) *restriction* is to limit treasury stock purchases to the amount of retained earnings. The balance sheet in Exhibit 13.14 provides an example. A common *contractual restriction* involves loan agreements that restrict paying dividends beyond a specified amount or percent of retained earnings. Restrictions are usually described in the notes. The term **appropriated retained earnings** refers to a voluntary transfer of amounts from the Retained Earnings account to the Appropriated Retained Earnings account to inform users of special activities that require funds.

Prior Period Adjustments   **Prior period adjustments** are corrections of material errors in prior period financial statements. These errors include arithmetic mistakes, unacceptable accounting, and missed facts. Prior period adjustments are reported in the *statement of retained earnings* (or the statement of stockholders' equity), net of any income tax effects. Prior period adjustments result in changing the beginning balance of retained earnings for events occurring prior to the earliest period reported in the current set of financial statements. To illustrate, assume that ComUS makes an error in a 2011 journal entry for the purchase of land by incorrectly debiting an expense account. When this is discovered in 2013, the statement of retained earnings includes a prior period adjustment, as shown in Exhibit 13.15. This exhibit also shows the usual format of the statement of retained earnings.

EXHIBIT 13.15

Statement of Retained Earnings with a Prior Period Adjustment

ComUS Statement of Retained Earnings For Year Ended December 31, 2013	
Retained earnings, Dec. 31, 2012, as previously reported	$4,745,000
Prior period adjustment	
Cost of land incorrectly expensed (net of $63,000 income taxes)	**147,000**
Retained earnings, Dec. 31, 2012, as adjusted	4,892,000
Plus net income	1,224,300
Less cash dividends declared	(301,800)
Retained earnings, Dec. 31, 2013	$5,814,500

Many items reported in financial statements are based on estimates. Future events are certain to reveal that some of these estimates were inaccurate even when based on the best data available at the time. These inaccuracies are *not* considered errors and are *not* reported as prior period adjustments. Instead, they are identified as **changes in accounting estimates** and are accounted for in current and future periods. To illustrate, we know that depreciation is based on estimated useful lives and salvage values. As time passes and new information becomes available, managers may need to change these estimates and the resulting depreciation expense for current and future periods.

Closing Process   The closing process was explained earlier in the book as: (1) Close credit balances in revenue accounts to Income Summary, (2) Close debit balances in expense accounts to Income Summary, and (3) Close Income Summary to Retained Earnings. If dividends are recorded in a Dividends account, and not as an immediate reduction to Retained Earnings (as shown in this chapter), a fourth step is necessary to close the Dividends account to Retained Earnings.

Statement of Stockholders' Equity

Instead of a separate statement of retained earnings, companies commonly report a statement of stockholders' equity that includes changes in retained earnings. A **statement of stockholders' equity** lists the beginning and ending balances of key equity accounts and describes the changes that occur during the period. The companies in Appendix A report such a statement. The usual format is to provide a column for each component of equity and use the rows to describe events occurring in the period. Exhibit 13.16 shows a condensed statement for **Apple**.

Reporting Stock Options

The majority of corporations whose shares are publicly traded issue **stock options,** which are rights to purchase common stock at a fixed price over a specified period. As the stock's price rises, the option's value increases. **Starbucks** and **Home Depot** offer stock options to both full- and part-time employees. Stock options are said to motivate managers and employees to (1) focus on company performance, (2) take a long-run perspective, and (3) remain with the company. A stock option is like having an investment with no risk ("a carrot with no stick").

EXHIBIT 13.16

Statement of Stockholders' Equity

Apple

APPLE Statement of Stockholders' Equity					
($ millions, shares in thousands)	Common Stock Shares	Common Stock Amount	Retained Earnings	Other	Total Equity
Balance, Sept. 25, 2010	915,970	$10,668	$37,169	$ (46)	$47,791
Net income	—	—	25,922	—	25,922
Issuance of Common Stock	13,307	1,729	(250)	—	1,479
Other	—	934	—	489	1,423
Cash Dividends ($0.00 per share)	—	—	—	—	—
Balance, Sept. 24, 2011	929,277	$13,331	$62,841	$443	$76,615

To illustrate, Quantum grants each of its employees the option to purchase 100 shares of its $1 par value common stock at its current market price of $50 per share anytime within the next 10 years. If the stock price rises to $70 per share, an employee can exercise the option at a gain of $20 per share (acquire a $70 stock at the $50 option price). With 100 shares, a single employee would have a total gain of $2,000, computed as $20 × 100 shares. Companies report the cost of stock options in the income statement. Measurement of this cost is explained in advanced courses.

■ **Decision** Insight

Pump 'n Dump   Fraudulent information can be used by the owners of a company's stock to pump it up and claim it is undervalued, which causes naïve investors to seek to acquire the stock and drive up its price. After that, those behind the release of fraudulent information dump the stock at an inflated price. When later information reveals that the stock is overvalued, its price declines and investors still holding the stock lose value. This scheme is called *pump 'n dump*. Jonathan Lebed, at 15 years old, is one of the most infamous cases of pump 'n dump, in which he allegedly made about $1 million. ■

GLOBAL VIEW

This section discusses similarities and differences between U.S. GAAP and IFRS in accounting and reporting for equity.

Accounting for Common Stock   The accounting for and reporting of common stock under U.S. GAAP and IFRS are similar. Specifically, procedures for issuing common stock at par, at a premium, at a discount, and for noncash assets are similar across the two systems. However, we must be aware of legal and cultural differences across the world that can impact the rights and responsibilities of common share-

PIAGGIO   holders. **Piaggio**'s terminology is a bit different as it uses the phrase "share capital" in reference to what U.S. GAAP would title "common shares" (see Appendix A).

Accounting for Dividends   Accounting for and reporting of dividends under U.S. GAAP and IFRS are consistent. This applies to cash dividends, stock dividends, and stock splits. For **Piaggio**, a "the company will pay a dividend equal to 0.082 Euro . . . for all ordinary shares." Piaggio, like many other companies, follows a dividend policy set by management and its board.

Accounting for Preferred Stock   Accounting and reporting for preferred stock are similar for U.S. GAAP and IFRS, but there are some important differences. First, preferred stock that is redeemable at the option of the preferred stockholders is reported *between* liabilities and equity in U.S. GAAP balance sheets. However, that same stock is reported as a liability in IFRS balance sheets. Second, the issue price of convertible preferred stock (and bonds) is recorded entirely under preferred stock (or bonds) *and none is assigned to the conversion feature* under U.S. GAAP. However, IFRS requires that a portion of the issue price be allocated to the conversion feature when it exists. Piaggio has no preferred stock.

Accounting for Treasury Stock   Both U.S. GAAP and IFRS apply the principle that companies do not record gains or losses on transactions involving their own stock. This applies to purchases, reissuances, and retirements of treasury stock. Consequently, the accounting for treasury stock explained in this chapter is consistent with that under IFRS. However, IFRS in this area is less detailed than that of U.S. GAAP.

Earnings per Share

The income statement reports **earnings per share,** also called *EPS* or *net income per share,* which is the amount of income earned per each share of a company's outstanding common stock. The **basic earnings per share** formula is shown in Exhibit 13.17. When a company has no preferred stock, then preferred dividends are zero. The weighted-average common shares outstanding is measured over the income reporting period; its computation is explained in advanced courses.

 A1 Compute earnings per share and describe its use.

$$\text{Basic earnings per share} = \frac{\text{Net income} - \text{Preferred dividends}}{\text{Weighted-average common shares outstanding}}$$

EXHIBIT 13.17

Basic Earnings per Share

To illustrate, assume that Quantum Co. earns $40,000 net income in 2013 and declares dividends of $7,500 on its noncumulative preferred stock. (If preferred stock is *non*cumulative, the income available [numerator] is the current period net income less any preferred dividends *declared* in that same period. If preferred stock is cumulative, the income available [numerator] is the current period net income less the preferred dividends whether declared or not.) Quantum has 5,000 weighted-average common shares outstanding during 2013. Its basic EPS[3] is

$$\text{Basic earnings per share} = \frac{\$40,000 - \$7,500}{5,000 \text{ shares}} = \$6.50$$

Price-Earnings Ratio

A stock's market value is determined by its *expected* future cash flows. A comparison of a company's EPS and its market value per share reveals information about market expectations. This comparison is traditionally made using a **price-earnings** (or **PE) ratio,** expressed also as *price earnings, price to earnings,* or *PE.* Some analysts interpret this ratio as what price the market is willing to pay for a company's current earnings stream. Price-earnings ratios can differ across companies that have similar earnings because of either higher or lower expectations of future earnings. The price-earnings ratio is defined in Exhibit 13.18.

A2 Compute price-earnings ratio and describe its use in analysis.

Point: The average PE ratio of stocks in the 1950–2012 period is about 14.

$$\text{Price-earnings ratio} = \frac{\text{Market value (price) per share}}{\text{Earnings per share}}$$

EXHIBIT 13.18

Price-Earnings Ratio

This ratio is often computed using EPS from the most recent period (for Amazon, its PE is 138; for Altria, its PE is 19). However, many users compute this ratio using *expected* EPS for the next period.

Some analysts view stocks with high PE ratios (higher than 20 to 25) as more likely to be overpriced and stocks with low PE ratios (less than 5 to 8) as more likely to be underpriced. These investors prefer to sell or avoid buying stocks with high PE ratios and to buy or hold stocks with low PE ratios. However, investment decision making is rarely so simple as to rely on a single ratio. For instance, a stock with a high PE ratio can prove to be a good investment if its earnings continue to increase beyond current expectations. Similarly, a stock with a low PE ratio can prove to be a poor investment if its earnings decline below expectations.

Point: Average PE ratios for U.S. stocks increased over the past two decades. Some analysts interpret this as a signal the market is overpriced. But higher ratios can at least partly reflect accounting changes that have reduced reported earnings.

---

[3] A corporation can be classified as having either a simple or complex capital structure. The term **simple capital structure** refers to a company with only common stock and nonconvertible preferred stock outstanding. The term **complex capital structure** refers to companies with dilutive securities. **Dilutive securities** include options, rights to purchase common stock, and any bonds or preferred stock that are convertible into common stock. A company with a complex capital structure must often report two EPS figures: basic and diluted. **Diluted earnings per share** is computed by adding all dilutive securities to the denominator of the basic EPS computation. It reflects the decrease in basic EPS *assuming* that all dilutive securities are converted into common shares.

Decision Maker

Money Manager You plan to invest in one of two companies identified as having identical future prospects. One has a PE of 19 and the other a PE of 25. Which do you invest in? Does it matter if your *estimate* of PE for these two companies is 29 as opposed to 22? ■ [Answer—p. 535]

Dividend Yield

A3	Compute dividend yield and explain its use in analysis.

Investors buy shares of a company's stock in anticipation of receiving a return from either or both cash dividends and stock price increases. Stocks that pay large dividends on a regular basis, called *income stocks,* are attractive to investors who want recurring cash flows from their investments. In contrast, some stocks pay little or no dividends but are still attractive to investors because of their expected stock price increases. The stocks of companies that distribute little or no cash but use their cash to finance expansion are called *growth stocks.* One way to help identify whether a stock is an income stock or a growth stock is to analyze its dividend yield. **Dividend yield,** defined in Exhibit 13.19, shows the annual amount of cash dividends distributed to common shares relative to their market value.

EXHIBIT 13.19

Dividend Yield

$$\text{Dividend yield} = \frac{\text{Annual cash dividends per share}}{\text{Market value per share}}$$

Dividend yield can be computed for current and prior periods using actual dividends and stock prices and for future periods using expected values. Exhibit 13.20 shows recent dividend and stock price data for **Amazon** and **Altria Group** to compute dividend yield.

EXHIBIT 13.20

Dividend and Stock Price Information

Company	Cash Dividends per Share	Market Value per Share	Dividend Yield
Amazon	$0.00	$189	0.0%
Altria Group.	1.64	32	5.3

Point: The *payout ratio* equals cash dividends declared on common stock divided by net income. A low payout ratio suggests that a company is retaining earnings for future growth.

Dividend yield is zero for Amazon, implying it is a growth stock. An investor in Amazon would look for increases in stock prices (and eventual cash from the sale of stock). Altria has a dividend yield of 5.3%, implying it is an income stock for which dividends are important in assessing its value.

Book Value per Share

A4	Compute book value and explain its use in analysis.

Case 1: Common Stock (Only) Outstanding. **Book value per common share,** defined in Exhibit 13.21, reflects the amount of equity applicable to *common* shares on a per share basis. To illustrate, we use Dillon Snowboards' data from Exhibit 13.4. Dillon has 30,000 outstanding common shares, and the stockholders' equity applicable to common shares is $365,000. Dillon's book value per common share is $12.17, computed as $365,000 divided by 30,000 shares.

EXHIBIT 13.21

Book Value per Common Share

$$\text{Book value per common share} = \frac{\text{Stockholders' equity applicable to common shares}}{\text{Number of common shares outstanding}}$$

Point: Book value per share is also referred to as *stockholders' claim to assets on a per share basis.*

Case 2: Common and Preferred Stock Outstanding. To compute book value when both common and preferred shares are outstanding, we allocate total equity between the two types of shares. The **book value per preferred share** is computed first; its computation is shown in Exhibit 13.22.

EXHIBIT 13.22

Book Value per Preferred Share

$$\text{Book value per preferred share} = \frac{\text{Stockholders' equity applicable to preferred shares}}{\text{Number of preferred shares outstanding}}$$

The equity applicable to preferred shares equals the preferred share's call price (or par value if the preferred is not callable) plus any cumulative dividends in arrears. The remaining equity is the portion applicable to common shares. To illustrate, consider LTD's equity in Exhibit 13.23. Its preferred stock is callable at $108 per share, and two years of cumulative preferred dividends are in arrears.

EXHIBIT 13.23

Stockholders' Equity with
Preferred and Common Stock

Stockholders' Equity

Preferred stock—$100 par value, 7% cumulative,	
2,000 shares authorized, 1,000 shares issued and outstanding	$100,000
Common stock—$25 par value, 12,000 shares authorized,	
10,000 shares issued and outstanding	250,000
Paid-in capital in excess of par value, common stock	15,000
Retained earnings	82,000
Total stockholders' equity	$447,000

The book value computations are in Exhibit 13.24. Equity is first allocated to preferred shares before the book value of common shares is computed.

EXHIBIT 13.24

Computing Book Value per
Preferred and Common Share

Total stockholders' equity		$447,000
Less equity applicable to preferred shares		
Call price (1,000 shares × $108)	$108,000	
Dividends in arrears ($100,000 × 7% × 2 years)	14,000	(122,000)
Equity applicable to common shares		$325,000
Book value per preferred share ($122,000/1,000 shares)		**$ 122.00**
Book value per common share ($325,000/10,000 shares)		**$ 32.50**

Book value per share reflects the value per share if a company is liquidated at balance sheet amounts. Book value is also the starting point in many stock valuation models, merger negotiations, price setting for public utilities, and loan contracts. The main limitation in using book value is the potential difference between recorded value and market value for assets and liabilities. Investors often adjust their analysis for estimates of these differences.

■ **Decision Maker** ════════════════════════════════════

Investor You are considering investing in **BMX**, whose book value per common share is $4 and price per common share on the stock exchange is $7. From this information, are BMX's net assets priced higher or lower than its recorded values? ■ [Answer—p. 535]

DEMONSTRATION PROBLEM 1

Barton Corporation began operations on January 1, 2012. The following transactions relating to stockholders' equity occurred in the first two years of the company's operations.

2012

Jan. 1 Authorized the issuance of 2 million shares of $5 par value common stock and 100,000 shares of $100 par value, 10% cumulative, preferred stock.
Jan. 2 Issued 200,000 shares of common stock for $12 cash per share.
Jan. 3 Issued 100,000 shares of common stock in exchange for a building valued at $820,000 and merchandise inventory valued at $380,000.
Jan. 4 Paid $10,000 cash to the company's founders for organization activities.
Jan. 5 Issued 12,000 shares of preferred stock for $110 cash per share.

2013

June 4 Issued 100,000 shares of common stock for $15 cash per share.

Required

1. Prepare journal entries to record these transactions.

2. Prepare the stockholders' equity section of the balance sheet as of December 31, 2012, and December 31, 2013, based on these transactions.

3. Prepare a table showing dividend allocations and dividends per share for 2012 and 2013 assuming Barton declares the following cash dividends: 2012, $50,000, and 2013, $300,000.

4. Prepare the January 2, 2012, journal entry for Barton's issuance of 200,000 shares of common stock for $12 cash per share assuming

a. Common stock is no-par stock without a stated value.

b. Common stock is no-par stock with a stated value of $10 per share.

PLANNING THE SOLUTION

- Record journal entries for the transactions for 2012 and 2013.
- Determine the balances for the 2012 and 2013 equity accounts for the balance sheet.
- Prepare the contributed capital portion of the 2012 and 2013 balance sheets.
- Prepare a table similar to Exhibit 13.11 showing dividend allocations for 2012 and 2013.
- Record the issuance of common stock under both specifications of no-par stock.

SOLUTION TO DEMONSTRATION PROBLEM 1

1. Journal entries.

2012			
Jan. 2	Cash	2,400,000	
	Common Stock, $5 Par Value		1,000,000
	Paid-In Capital in Excess of Par Value, Common Stock		1,400,000
	Issued 200,000 shares of common stock.		
Jan. 3	Building	820,000	
	Merchandise Inventory	380,000	
	Common Stock, $5 Par Value		500,000
	Paid-In Capital in Excess of Par Value, Common Stock		700,000
	Issued 100,000 shares of common stock.		
Jan. 4	Organization Expenses	10,000	
	Cash		10,000
	Paid founders for organization costs.		
Jan. 5	Cash	1,320,000	
	Preferred Stock, $100 Par Value		1,200,000
	Paid-In Capital in Excess of Par Value, Preferred Stock		120,000
	Issued 12,000 shares of preferred stock.		
2013			
June 4	Cash	1,500,000	
	Common Stock, $5 Par Value		500,000
	Paid-In Capital in Excess of Par Value, Common Stock		1,000,000
	Issued 100,000 shares of common stock.		

2. Balance sheet presentations (at December 31 year-end).

	2013	2012
Stockholders' Equity		
Preferred stock—$100 par value, 10% cumulative, 100,000 shares authorized, 12,000 shares issued and outstanding	$1,200,000	$1,200,000
Paid-in capital in excess of par value, preferred stock	120,000	120,000
Total paid-in capital by preferred stockholders	1,320,000	1,320,000
Common stock—$5 par value, 2,000,000 shares authorized, 300,000 shares issued and outstanding in 2012, and 400,000 shares issued and outstanding in 2013	2,000,000	1,500,000
Paid-in capital in excess of par value, common stock	3,100,000	2,100,000
Total paid-in capital by common stockholders	5,100,000	3,600,000
Total paid-in capital	$6,420,000	$4,920,000

3. Dividend allocation table.

	Common	Preferred
2012 ($50,000)		
Preferred—current year (12,000 shares × $10 = $120,000)	$ 0	$ 50,000
Common—remainder (300,000 shares outstanding)	0	0
Total for the year	$ 0	$ 50,000
2013 ($300,000)		
Preferred—dividend in arrears from 2012 ($120,000 − $50,000)	$ 0	$ 70,000
Preferred—current year	0	120,000
Common—remainder (400,000 shares outstanding)	110,000	0
Total for the year	$110,000	$190,000
Dividends per share		
2012	$ 0.00	$ 4.17
2013	$ 0.28	$ 15.83

4. Journal entries.

a. For 2012 (no-par stock without a stated value):

Jan. 2	Cash	2,400,000	
	Common Stock, No-Par Value		2,400,000
	Issued 200,000 shares of no-par common stock at $12 per share.		

b. For 2012 (no-par stock with a stated value):

Jan. 2	Cash	2,400,000	
	Common Stock, $10 Stated Value		2,000,000
	Paid-In Capital in Excess of Stated Value, Common Stock		400,000
	Issued 200,000 shares of $10 stated value common stock at $12 per share.		

DEMONSTRATION PROBLEM 2

Precision Company began year 2013 with the following balances in its stockholders' equity accounts.

Common stock—$10 par, 500,000 shares authorized, 200,000 shares issued and outstanding	$2,000,000
Paid-in capital in excess of par, common stock	1,000,000
Retained earnings	5,000,000
Total	$8,000,000

All outstanding common stock was issued for $15 per share when the company was created. Prepare journal entries to account for the following transactions during year 2013.

Jan. 10 The board declared a $0.10 cash dividend per share to shareholders of record Jan. 28.
Feb. 15 Paid the cash dividend declared on January 10.
Mar. 31 Declared a 20% stock dividend. The market value of the stock is $18 per share.
May 1 Distributed the stock dividend declared on March 31.
July 1 Purchased 30,000 shares of treasury stock at $20 per share.
Sept. 1 Sold 20,000 treasury shares at $26 cash per share.
Dec. 1 Sold the remaining 10,000 shares of treasury stock at $7 cash per share.

PLANNING THE SOLUTION

- Calculate the total cash dividend to record by multiplying the cash dividend declared by the number of shares as of the date of record.
- Decide whether the stock dividend is a small or large dividend. Then analyze each event to determine the accounts affected and the appropriate amounts to be recorded.

SOLUTION TO DEMONSTRATION PROBLEM 2

Jan. 10	Retained Earnings	20,000	
	Common Dividend Payable		20,000
	Declared a $0.10 per share cash dividend.		
Feb. 15	Common Dividend Payable	20,000	
	Cash		20,000
	Paid $0.10 per share cash dividend.		
Mar. 31	Retained Earnings	720,000	
	Common Stock Dividend Distributable		400,000
	Paid-In Capital in Excess of		
	Par Value, Common Stock		320,000
	Declared a small stock dividend of 20% or		
	40,000 shares; market value is $18 per share.		
May 1	Common Stock Dividend Distributable	400,000	
	Common Stock		400,000
	Distributed 40,000 shares of common stock.		
July 1	Treasury Stock, Common	600,000	
	Cash		600,000
	Purchased 30,000 common shares at $20 per share.		
Sept. 1	Cash	520,000	
	Treasury Stock, Common		400,000
	Paid-In Capital, Treasury Stock		120,000
	Sold 20,000 treasury shares at $26 per share.		
Dec. 1	Cash	70,000	
	Paid-In Capital, Treasury Stock	120,000	
	Retained Earnings	10,000	
	Treasury Stock, Common		200,000
	Sold 10,000 treasury shares at $7 per share.		

Summary

C1 **Identify characteristics of corporations and their organization.** Corporations are legal entities whose stockholders are not liable for its debts. Stock is easily transferred, and the life of a corporation does not end with the incapacity of a stockholder. A corporation acts through its agents, who are its officers and managers. Corporations are regulated and subject to income taxes. Authorized stock is the stock that a corporation's charter authorizes it to sell. Issued stock is the portion of authorized shares sold. Par value stock is a value per share assigned by the charter. No-par value stock is stock *not* assigned a value per share by the charter. Stated value stock is no-par stock to which the directors assign a value per share.

C2 **Explain characteristics of, and distribute dividends between, common and preferred stock.** Preferred stock has a priority (or senior status) relative to common stock in one or more areas, usually (1) dividends and (2) assets in case of liquidation. Preferred stock usually does not carry voting rights and can be convertible or callable. Convertibility permits the holder to convert preferred to common. Callability permits the issuer to buy back preferred stock under specified conditions. Preferred stockholders usually hold the right to dividend distributions before common stockholders. When preferred stock is cumulative and in arrears, the amount in arrears must be distributed to preferred before any dividends are distributed to common.

C3 **Explain the items reported in retained earnings.** Stockholders' equity is made up of (1) paid-in capital and (2) retained earnings. Paid-in capital consists of funds raised by stock issuances. Retained earnings consists of cumulative net income (losses) not distributed. Many companies face statutory and contractual restrictions on retained earnings. Corporations can voluntarily appropriate retained earnings to inform others about their disposition. Prior period adjustments are corrections of errors in prior financial statements.

A1 **Compute earnings per share and describe its use.** A company with a simple capital structure computes basic EPS by dividing net income less any preferred dividends by the weighted-average number of outstanding common shares. A company with a complex capital structure must usually report both basic and diluted EPS.

A2 **Compute price-earnings ratio and describe its use in analysis.** A common stock's price-earnings (PE) ratio is computed by dividing the stock's market value (price) per share by its EPS. A stock's PE is based on expectations that can prove to be better or worse than eventual performance.

A3 **Compute dividend yield and explain its use in analysis.** Dividend yield is the ratio of a stock's annual cash dividends per share to its market value (price) per share. Dividend yield can be compared with the yield of other companies to determine whether the stock is expected to be an income or growth stock.

A4 **Compute book value and explain its use in analysis.** Book value per common share is equity applicable to common shares divided by the number of outstanding common shares. Book value per preferred share is equity applicable to preferred shares divided by the number of outstanding preferred shares.

P1 **Record the issuance of corporate stock.** When stock is issued, its par or stated value is credited to the stock account and any excess is credited to a separate contributed capital account. If a stock has neither par nor stated value, the entire proceeds are credited to the stock account. Stockholders must contribute assets equal to minimum legal capital or be potentially liable for the deficiency.

P2 **Record transactions involving cash dividends, stock dividends, and stock splits.** Cash dividends involve three events. On the date of declaration, the directors bind the company to pay the dividend. A dividend declaration reduces retained earnings and creates a current liability. On the date of record, recipients of the dividend are identified. On the date of payment, cash is paid to stockholders and the current liability is removed. Neither a stock dividend nor a stock split alters the value of the company. However, the value of each share is less due to the distribution of additional shares. The distribution of additional shares is according to individual stockholders' ownership percent. Small stock dividends ($\leq 25\%$) are recorded by capitalizing retained earnings equal to the market value of distributed shares. Large stock dividends ($> 25\%$) are recorded by capitalizing retained earnings equal to the par or stated value of distributed shares. Stock splits do not necessitate journal entries but do necessitate changes in the description of stock.

P3 **Record purchases and sales of treasury stock and the retirement of stock.** When a corporation purchases its own previously issued stock, it debits the cost of these shares to Treasury Stock. Treasury stock is subtracted from equity in the balance sheet. If treasury stock is reissued, any proceeds in excess of cost are credited to Paid-In Capital, Treasury Stock. If the proceeds are less than cost, they are debited to Paid-In Capital, Treasury Stock to the extent a credit balance exists. Any remaining amount is debited to Retained Earnings. When stock is retired, all accounts related to the stock are removed.

Guidance Answers to Decision Maker and Decision Ethics

Entrepreneur   The 50% stock dividend provides you no direct income. A stock dividend often reveals management's optimistic expectations about the future and can improve a stock's marketability by making it affordable to more investors. Accordingly, a stock dividend usually reveals "good news" and because of this, it likely increases (slightly) the market value for your stock. The same conclusions apply to the 3-for-2 stock split.

Concert Organizer   You have two basic options: (1) different classes of common stock or (2) common and preferred stock. Your objective is to issue to yourself stock that has all or a majority of the voting power. The other class of stock would carry limited or no voting rights. In this way, you maintain control and are able to raise the necessary funds.

Money Manager   Since one company requires a payment of $19 for each $1 of earnings, and the other requires $25, you would prefer the stock with the PE of 19; it is a better deal given identical prospects. You should make sure these companies' earnings computations are roughly the same, for example, no extraordinary items, unusual events, and so forth. Also, your PE estimates for these companies do matter. If you are willing to pay $29 for each $1 of earnings for these companies, you obviously expect both to exceed current market expectations.

Investor   Book value reflects recorded values. BMX's book value is $4 per common share. Stock price reflects the market's expectation of net asset value (both tangible and intangible items). BMX's market value is $7 per common share. Comparing these figures suggests BMX's market value of net assets is higher than its recorded values (by an amount of $7 versus $4 per share).

Guidance Answers to Quick Checks

1. (*b*)

2. A corporation pays taxes on its income, and its stockholders normally pay personal income taxes (at the 15% rate or lower) on any cash dividends received from the corporation.

3. Companies desire to minimize the amount of legal capital. It is more likely that the par value of common stock will be $0.001 per share than $10 per share.

4. (*a*)

5. A stock premium is an amount in excess of par (or stated) value paid by purchasers of newly issued stock.

6. Minimum legal capital intends to protect creditors of a corporation by obligating stockholders to some minimum level of equity financing and by constraining a corporation from excessive payments to stockholders.

7. Common Dividend Payable is a current liability account.

8. The date of declaration, date of record, and date of payment.

9. A dividend is a legal liability at the date of declaration, on which date it is recorded as a liability.

10. A stock dividend does not transfer assets to stockholders, but it does require an amount of retained earnings to be transferred to a contributed capital account(s).

11. A small stock dividend is 25% or less of the previous outstanding shares. A large stock dividend is more than 25%.

12. Retained earnings equal to the distributable shares' market value should be capitalized for a small stock dividend.

13. Typically, preferred stock has a preference in receipt of dividends and in distribution of assets.

14. (a)

15. (b)

Total cash dividend	$288,000
To preferred shareholders	135,000*
Remainder to common shareholders	$153,000

* 9,000 × $50 × 10% × 3 years = $135,000.

16. (b)

17. No. The shares are an investment for Southern Co. and are issued and outstanding shares for Northern Corp.

18. Treasury stock does not affect the number of authorized or issued shares, but it reduces the outstanding shares.

19. (a)

Key Terms

Appropriated retained earnings (p. 526)
Authorized stock (p. 513)
Basic earnings per share (p. 529)
Book value per common share (p. 530)
Book value per preferred share (p. 530)
Call price (p. 523)
Callable preferred stock (p. 523)
Capital stock (p. 513)
Changes in accounting estimates (p. 527)
Common stock (p. 512)
Complex capital structure (p. 529)
Convertible preferred stock (p. 522)
Corporation (p. 510)
Cumulative preferred stock (p. 521)
Date of declaration (p. 517)
Date of payment (p. 517)
Date of record (p. 517)
Diluted earnings per share (p. 529)
Dilutive securities (p. 529)

Discount on stock (p. 515)
Dividend in arrears (p. 521)
Dividend yield (p. 530)
Earnings per share (EPS) (p. 529)
Financial leverage (p. 523)
Large stock dividend (p. 518)
Liquidating cash dividend (p. 518)
Market value per share (p. 513)
Minimum legal capital (p. 513)
Noncumulative preferred stock (p. 521)
Nonparticipating preferred stock (p. 522)
No-par value stock (p. 513)
Organization expenses (p. 511)
Paid-in capital (p. 514)
Paid-in capital in excess of par value (p. 515)
Participating preferred stock (p. 522)
Par value (p. 513)
Par value stock (p. 513)

Preemptive right (p. 512)
Preferred stock (p. 520)
Premium on stock (p. 515)
Price-earnings (PE) ratio (p. 529)
Prior period adjustments (p. 527)
Proxy (p. 511)
Restricted retained earnings (p. 526)
Retained earnings (p. 514)
Retained earnings deficit (p. 517)
Reverse stock split (p. 520)
Simple capital structure (p. 529)
Small stock dividend (p. 518)
Stated value stock (p. 514)
Statement of stockholders' equity (p. 527)
Stock dividend (p. 518)
Stock options (p. 527)
Stock split (p. 520)
Stockholders' equity (p. 514)
Treasury stock (p. 524)

Multiple Choice Quiz   Answers on p. 551   mhhe.com/wildFAP21e

Additional Quiz Questions are available at the book's Website.

1. A corporation issues 6,000 shares of $5 par value common stock for $8 cash per share. The entry to record this transaction includes:
   a. A debit to Paid-In Capital in Excess of Par Value for $18,000.
   b. A credit to Common Stock for $48,000.
   c. A credit to Paid-In Capital in Excess of Par Value for $30,000.
   d. A credit to Cash for $48,000.
   e. A credit to Common Stock for $30,000.

2. A company reports net income of $75,000. Its weighted-average common shares outstanding is 19,000. It has no other stock outstanding. Its earnings per share is:
   a. $4.69
   b. $3.95
   c. $3.75
   d. $2.08
   e. $4.41

3. A company has 5,000 shares of $100 par preferred stock and 50,000 shares of $10 par common stock outstanding. Its total stockholders' equity is $2,000,000. Its book value per common share is:
   a. $100.00
   b. $ 10.00
   c. $ 40.00
   d. $ 30.00
   e. $ 36.36

4. A company paid cash dividends of $0.81 per share. Its earnings per share is $6.95 and its market price per share is $45.00. Its dividend yield is:
   a. 1.8%
   b. 11.7%

   c. 15.4%
   d. 55.6%
   e. 8.6%

5. A company's shares have a market value of $85 per share. Its net income is $3,500,000, and its weighted-average common shares outstanding is 700,000. Its price-earnings ratio is:
   a. 5.9
   b. 425.0
   c. 17.0
   d. 10.4
   e. 41.2

I Icon denotes assignments that involve decision making.

Discussion Questions

1. What are organization expenses? Provide examples.
2. How are organization expenses reported?
3. **I** Who is responsible for directing a corporation's affairs?
4. What is the difference between authorized shares and outstanding shares?
5. What is the preemptive right of common stockholders?
6. List the general rights of common stockholders.
7. What is the difference between the market value per share and the par value per share?
8. What is the difference between the par value and the call price of a share of preferred stock?
9. **I** Why would an investor find convertible preferred stock attractive?
10. Identify and explain the importance of the three dates relevant to corporate dividends.
11. Why is the term *liquidating dividend* used to describe cash dividends debited against paid-in capital accounts?
12. **I** How does declaring a stock dividend affect the corporation's assets, liabilities, and total equity? What are the effects of the eventual distribution of that stock?
13. **I** What is the difference between a stock dividend and a stock split?

14. **I** Courts have ruled that a stock dividend is not taxable income to stockholders. What justifies this decision?
15. How does the purchase of treasury stock affect the purchaser's assets and total equity?
16. **I** Why do laws place limits on treasury stock purchases?
17. How are EPS results computed for a corporation with a simple capital structure?
18. What is a stock option?
19. How is book value per share computed for a corporation with no preferred stock? What is the main limitation of using book value per share to value a corporation?
20. Refer to **Polaris'** 2011 balance sheet in Appendix A. How many shares of common stock are authorized? How many shares of voting common stock are issued? **Polaris**
21. **I** Refer to the 2011 balance sheet for **Arctic Cat** in Appendix A. What is the par value per share of its common stock? Suggest a rationale for the amount of par value it assigned. **Arctic Cat**
22. **I** Refer to the financial statements for **Piaggio** in Appendix A. How much were its cash payments for treasury stock purchases for the year ended December 31, 2011? **PIAGGIO**

Mc Graw Hill connect

Of the following statements, which are true for the corporate form of organization?
1. Ownership rights cannot be easily transferred.
2. Owners have unlimited liability for corporate debts.
3. Capital is more easily accumulated than with most other forms of organization.
4. Corporate income that is distributed to shareholders is usually taxed twice.
5. It is a separate legal entity.
6. It has a limited life.
7. Owners are not agents of the corporation.

QUICK STUDY

QS 13-1
Characteristics of corporations

C1

QS 13-2
Issuance of no-par
common stock

P1

Prepare the journal entry to record Autumn Company's issuance of 63,000 shares of no-par value common stock assuming the shares:

a. Sell for $29 cash per share.

b. Are exchanged for land valued at $1,827,000.

QS 13-3
Issuance of common stock

P1

Prepare the journal entry to record Zende Company's issuance of 75,000 shares of $5 par value common stock assuming the shares sell for:

a. $5 cash per share.

b. $6 cash per share.

QS 13-4
Issuance of par and stated
value common stock

P1

Prepare the journal entry to record Jevonte Company's issuance of 36,000 shares of its common stock assuming the shares have a:

a. $2 par value and sell for $18 cash per share.

b. $2 stated value and sell for $18 cash per share.

QS 13-5
Issuance of common stock

P1

Prepare the issuer's journal entry for each separate transaction. (*a*) On March 1, Atlantic Co. issues 42,500 shares of $4 par value common stock for $297,500 cash. (*b*) On April 1, OP Co. issues no-par value common stock for $70,000 cash. (*c*) On April 6, MPG issues 2,000 shares of $25 par value common stock for $45,000 of inventory, $145,000 of machinery, and acceptance of an $94,000 note payable.

QS 13-6
Issuance of preferred stock

P1 P2

a. Prepare the journal entry to record Tamasine Company's issuance of 5,000 shares of $100 par value 7% cumulative preferred stock for $102 cash per share.

b. Assuming the facts in part 1, if Tamasine declares a year-end cash dividend, what is the amount of dividend paid to preferred shareholders? (Assume no dividends in arrears.)

QS 13-7
Accounting for cash dividends

P2

Prepare journal entries to record the following transactions for Emerson Corporation.

July 15   Declared a cash dividend payable to common stockholders of $165,000.
August 15 Date of record is August 15 for the cash dividend declared on July 15.
August 31 Paid the dividend declared on July 15.

QS 13-8
Accounting for small
stock dividend

P2

The stockholders' equity section of Jun Company's balance sheet as of April 1 follows. On April 2, Jun declares and distributes a 10% stock dividend. The stock's per share market value on April 2 is $20 (prior to the dividend). Prepare the stockholders' equity section immediately after the stock dividend.

Common stock—$5 par value, 375,000 shares authorized, 200,000 shares issued and outstanding	$1,000,000
Paid-in capital in excess of par value, common stock	600,000
Retained earnings	833,000
Total stockholders' equity	$2,433,000

QS 13-9
Dividend allocation between
classes of shareholders

C2

Stockholders' equity of Ernst Company consists of 80,000 shares of $5 par value, 8% cumulative preferred stock and 250,000 shares of $1 par value common stock. Both classes of stock have been outstanding since the company's inception. Ernst did not declare any dividends in the prior year, but it now declares and pays a $110,000 cash dividend at the current year-end. Determine the amount distributed to each class of stockholders for this two-year-old company.

QS 13-10
Purchase and sale of
treasury stock P3

On May 3, Zirbal Corporation purchased 4,000 shares of its own stock for $36,000 cash. On November 4, Zirbal reissued 850 shares of this treasury stock for $8,500. Prepare the May 3 and November 4 journal entries to record Zirbal's purchase and reissuance of treasury stock.

QS 13-11
Accounting for changes in
estimates; error adjustments

C3

Answer the following questions related to a company's activities for the current year:

1. A review of the notes payable files discovers that three years ago the company reported the entire amount of a payment (principal and interest) on an installment note payable as interest expense. This mistake had a material effect on the amount of income in that year. How should the correction be reported in the current year financial statements?

2. After using an expected useful life of seven years and no salvage value to depreciate its office equipment over the preceding three years, the company decided early this year that the equipment will last only two more years. How should the effects of this decision be reported in the current year financial statements?

Murray Company reports net income of $770,000 for the year. It has no preferred stock, and its weighted-average common shares outstanding is 280,000 shares. Compute its basic earnings per share.

QS 13-12
Basic earnings per share A1

Epic Company earned net income of $900,000 this year. The number of common shares outstanding during the entire year was 400,000, and preferred shareholders received a $20,000 cash dividend. Compute Epic Company's basic earnings per share.

QS 13-13
Basic earnings per share A1

Compute Topp Company's price-earnings ratio if its common stock has a market value of $20.54 per share and its EPS is $3.95. Would an analyst likely consider this stock potentially overpriced- or underpriced or neither? Explain.

QS 13-14
Price-earnings ratio A2

Foxburo Company expects to pay a $2.34 per share cash dividend this year on its common stock. The current market value of Foxburo stock is $32.50 per share. Compute the expected dividend yield on the Foxburo stock. Would you classify the Foxburo stock as a growth or an income stock? Explain.

QS 13-15
Dividend yield A3

The stockholders' equity section of Montel Company's balance sheet follows. The preferred stock's call price is $40. Determine the book value per share of the common stock.

QS 13-16
Book value per common share

A4

Preferred stock—5% cumulative, $10 par value,	
20,000 shares authorized, issued and outstanding	$ 200,000
Common stock—$5 par value, 200,000 shares	
authorized, 150,000 shares issued and outstanding	750,000
Retained earnings	900,000
Total stockholders' equity	$1,850,000

Air France-KLM reports the following equity information for its fiscal year ended March 31, 2012 (euros in millions). Prepare its journal entry, using its account titles, to record the issuance of capital stock assuming that its entire par value stock was issued on March 31, 2012, for cash.

QS 13-17
International equity disclosures

P1

March 31	2012
Issued capital	€ 300
Additional paid-in capital	2,971

---

connect

Describe how each of the following characteristics of organizations applies to corporations.

EXERCISES

1. Owner authority and control	5. Duration of life
2. Ease of formation	6. Owner liability
3. Transferability of ownership	7. Legal status
4. Ability to raise large capital amounts	8. Tax status of income

Exercise 13-1
Characteristics of corporations

C1

Rodriguez Corporation issues 19,000 shares of its common stock for $152,000 cash on February 20. Prepare journal entries to record this event under each of the following separate situations.

1. The stock has a $2 par value.

2. The stock has neither par nor stated value.

3. The stock has an $5 stated value.

Exercise 13-2
Accounting for par, stated, and no-par stock issuances

P1

Exercise 13-3
Recording stock issuances

P1

Prepare journal entries to record the following four separate issuances of stock.

1. A corporation issued 4,000 shares of $5 par value common stock for $35,000 cash.

2. A corporation issued 2,000 shares of no-par common stock to its promoters in exchange for their efforts, estimated to be worth $40,000. The stock has a $1 per share stated value.

3. A corporation issued 2,000 shares of no-par common stock to its promoters in exchange for their efforts, estimated to be worth $40,000. The stock has no stated value.

4. A corporation issued 1,000 shares of $50 par value preferred stock for $60,000 cash.

Exercise 13-4
Stock issuance for noncash assets

P1

Sudoku Company issues 7,000 shares of $7 par value common stock in exchange for land and a building. The land is valued at $45,000 and the building at $85,000. Prepare the journal entry to record issuance of the stock in exchange for the land and building.

Exercise 13-5
Identifying characteristics of preferred stock

C2

Match each description 1 through 6 with the characteristic of preferred stock that it best describes by writing the letter of that characteristic in the blank next to each description.

A. Callable   **B.** Convertible   **C.** Cumulative

D. Noncumulative   **E.** Nonparticipating   **F.** Participating

_____ **1.** Holders of the stock are entitled to receive current and all past dividends before common stockholders receive any dividends.

_____ **2.** The issuing corporation can retire the stock by paying a prespecified price.

_____ **3.** Holders of the stock can receive dividends exceeding the stated rate under certain conditions.

_____ **4.** Holders of the stock are not entitled to receive dividends in excess of the stated rate.

_____ **5.** Holders of this stock can exchange it for shares of common stock.

_____ **6.** Holders of the stock lose any dividends that are not declared in the current year.

Exercise 13-6
Stock dividends and splits

P2

On June 30, 2013, Sharper Corporation's common stock is priced at $62 per share before any stock dividend or split, and the stockholders' equity section of its balance sheet appears as follows.

Common stock—$10 par value, 120,000 shares authorized, 50,000 shares issued and outstanding	$ 500,000
Paid-in capital in excess of par value, common stock	200,000
Retained earnings	660,000
Total stockholders' equity	$1,360,000

1. Assume that the company declares and immediately distributes a 50% stock dividend. This event is recorded by capitalizing retained earnings equal to the stock's par value. Answer these questions about stockholders' equity as it exists *after* issuing the new shares.

  a. What is the retained earnings balance?

Check (1b) $1,360,000

  b. What is the amount of total stockholders' equity?

  c. How many shares are outstanding?

2. Assume that the company implements a 3-for-2 stock split instead of the stock dividend in part 1. Answer these questions about stockholders' equity as it exists *after* issuing the new shares.

(2a) $660,000

  a. What is the retained earnings balance?

  b. What is the amount of total stockholders' equity?

  c. How many shares are outstanding?

3. Explain the difference, if any, to a stockholder from receiving new shares distributed under a large stock dividend versus a stock split.

Exercise 13-7
Stock dividends and per share book values

P2

The stockholders' equity of TVX Company at the beginning of the day on February 5 follows:

Common stock—$10 par value, 150,000 shares authorized, 60,000 shares issued and outstanding	$ 600,000
Paid-in capital in excess of par value, common stock	425,000
Retained earnings	550,000
Total stockholders' equity	$1,575,000

On February 5, the directors declare a 20% stock dividend distributable on February 28 to the February 15 stockholders of record. The stock's market value is $40 per share on February 5 before the stock dividend. The stock's market value is $33.40 per share on February 28.

1. Prepare entries to record both the dividend declaration and its distribution.

2. One stockholder owned 800 shares on February 5 before the dividend. Compute the book value per share and total book value of this stockholder's shares immediately before *and* after the stock dividend of February 5.

3. Compute the total market value of the investor's shares in part 2 as of February 5 and February 28.

Check (2) Book value per share: before, $26.250; after, $21.875

York's outstanding stock consists of 80,000 shares of *noncumulative* 7.5% preferred stock with a $5 par value and also 200,000 shares of common stock with a $1 par value. During its first four years of operation, the corporation declared and paid the following total cash dividends:

Exercise 13-8
Dividends on common and noncumulative preferred stock

C2

2013	$ 20,000
2014	28,000
2015	200,000
2016	350,000

Determine the amount of dividends paid each year to each of the two classes of stockholders: preferred and common. Also compute the total dividends paid to each class for the four years combined.

Check 4-year total paid to preferred, $108,000

Use the data in Exercise 13-8 to determine the amount of dividends paid each year to each of the two classes of stockholders assuming that the preferred stock is *cumulative*. Also determine the total dividends paid to each class for the four years combined.

Exercise 13-9
Dividends on common and cumulative preferred stock **C2**

On October 10, the stockholders' equity of Sherman Systems appears as follows:

Exercise 13-10
Recording and reporting treasury stock transactions

P3

Common stock—$10 par value, 72,000 shares authorized, issued, and outstanding	$ 720,000
Paid-in capital in excess of par value, common stock	216,000
Retained earnings	864,000
Total stockholders' equity	$1,800,000

1. Prepare journal entries to record the following transactions for Sherman Systems.

   a. Purchased 5,000 shares of its own common stock at $25 per share on October 11.

   b. Sold 1,000 treasury shares on November 1 for $31 cash per share.

   c. Sold all remaining treasury shares on November 25 for $20 cash per share.

2. Explain how the company's equity section changes after the October 11 treasury stock purchase, and prepare the revised equity section of its balance sheet at that date.

Check (1c) Dr. Retained Earnings, $14,000

The following information is available for Amos Company for the year ended December 31, 2013.

a. Balance of retained earnings, December 31, 2012, prior to discovery of error, $1,375,000.

b. Cash dividends declared and paid during 2013, $43,000.

c. It neglected to record 2011 depreciation expense of $55,500, which is net of $4,500 in income taxes.

d. The company earned $126,000 in 2013 net income.

Prepare a 2013 statement of retained earnings for Amos Company.

Exercise 13-11
Preparing a statement of retained earnings

C3

Ecker Company reports $2,700,000 of net income for 2013 and declares $388,020 of cash dividends on its preferred stock for 2013. At the end of 2013, the company had 678,000 weighted-average shares of common stock.

1. What amount of net income is available to common stockholders for 2013?

2. What is the company's basic EPS for 2013?

Exercise 13-12
Earnings per share

A1

Check (2) $3.41

Exercise 13-13
Earnings per share
A1

Check   (2) $2.10

Kelley Company reports $960,000 of net income for 2013 and declares $120,000 of cash dividends on its preferred stock for 2013. At the end of 2013, the company had 400,000 weighted-average shares of common stock.

1. What amount of net income is available to common stockholders for 2013?

2. What is the company's basic EPS for 2013? Round your answer to the nearest whole cent.

Exercise 13-14
Price-earnings ratio computation and interpretation
A2

Compute the price-earnings ratio for each of these four separate companies. Which stock might an analyst likely investigate as being potentially undervalued by the market? Explain.

Company	Earnings per Share	Market Value per Share
1	$12.00	$176.40
2	10.00	96.00
3	7.50	93.75
4	50.00	250.00

Exercise 13-15
Dividend yield computation and interpretation
A3

Compute the dividend yield for each of these four separate companies. Which company's stock would probably *not* be classified as an income stock? Explain.

Company	Annual Cash Dividend per Share	Market Value per Share
1	$16.06	$220.00
2	13.86	132.00
3	3.96	72.00
4	0.96	80.00

Exercise 13-16
Book value per share
A4

The equity section of Cyril Corporation's balance sheet shows the following:

Preferred stock—6% cumulative, $25 par value, $30 call price, 10,000 shares issued and outstanding	$ 250,000
Common stock—$10 par value, 80,000 shares issued and outstanding	800,000
Retained earnings	535,000
Total stockholders' equity	$1,585,000

Determine the book value per share of the preferred and common stock under two separate situations.

Check   (1) Book value of common, $16.06

1. No preferred dividends are in arrears.

2. Three years of preferred dividends are in arrears.

Exercise 13-17
Accounting for equity under IFRS
C3 P1

Unilever Group reports the following equity information for the years ended December 31, 2009 and 2010 (euros in millions).

December 31	2010	2009
Share capital	€ 484	€ 484
Share premium	134	131
Other reserves	(5,406)	(5,900)
Retained profit	19,273	17,350
Shareholders' equity	€14,485	€12,065

1. For each of the three account titles *share capital, share premium,* and *retained profit,* match it with the usual account title applied under U.S. GAAP from the following options:

   a. Paid-in capital in excess of par value, common stock
   b. Retained earnings
   c. Common stock, par value

2. Prepare Unilever's journal entry, using its account titles, to record the issuance of capital stock assuming that its entire par value stock was issued on December 31, 2009, for cash.

3. What were Unilever's 2010 dividends assuming that only dividends and income impacted retained profit for 2010 and that its 2010 income totaled €4,232?

Alexander Corporation reports the following components of stockholders' equity on December 31, 2013:

Exercise 13-18
Cash dividends, treasury stock, and statement of retained earnings

C3 P2 P3

Common stock—$25 par value, 50,000 shares authorized, 30,000 shares issued and outstanding	$ 750,000
Paid-in capital in excess of par value, common stock	50,000
Retained earnings	340,000
Total stockholders' equity	$1,140,000

In year 2014, the following transactions affected its stockholders' equity accounts.

Jan. 2 Purchased 3,000 shares of its own stock at $25 cash per share.
Jan. 7 Directors declared a $1.50 per share cash dividend payable on Feb. 28 to the Feb. 9 stockholders of record.
Feb. 28 Paid the dividend declared on January 7.
July 9 Sold 1,200 of its treasury shares at $30 cash per share.
Aug. 27 Sold 1,500 of its treasury shares at $20 cash per share.
Sept. 9 Directors declared a $2 per share cash dividend payable on October 22 to the September 23 stockholders of record.
Oct. 22 Paid the dividend declared on September 9.
Dec. 31 Closed the $52,000 credit balance (from net income) in the Income Summary account to Retained Earnings.

Required

1. Prepare journal entries to record each of these transactions for 2014.
2. Prepare a statement of retained earnings for the year ended December 31, 2014.
3. Prepare the stockholders' equity section of the company's balance sheet as of December 31, 2014.

connect

Kinkaid Co. is incorporated at the beginning of this year and engages in a number of transactions. The following journal entries impacted its stockholders' equity during its first year of operations.

PROBLEM SET A

Problem 13-1A
Stockholders' equity transactions and analysis

C2 P1

a.	Cash	300,000	
	Common Stock, $25 Par Value		250,000
	Paid-In Capital in Excess of Par Value, Common Stock		50,000
b.	Organization Expenses	150,000	
	Common Stock, $25 Par Value		125,000
	Paid-In Capital in Excess of Par Value, Common Stock		25,000
c.	Cash	43,000	
	Accounts Receivable	15,000	
	Building	81,500	
	Notes Payable		59,500
	Common Stock, $25 Par Value		50,000
	Paid-In Capital in Excess of Par Value, Common Stock		30,000

[continued on next page]

[continued from previous page]

d.	Cash	120,000	
	Common Stock, $25 Par Value		75,000
	Paid-In Capital in Excess of		
	Par Value, Common Stock		45,000

Required

Check (2) 20,000 shares

(3) $500,000

(4) $650,000

1. Explain the transaction(s) underlying each journal entry (*a*) through (*d*).
2. How many shares of common stock are outstanding at year-end?
3. What is the amount of minimum legal capital (based on par value) at year-end?
4. What is the total paid-in capital at year-end?
5. What is the book value per share of the common stock at year-end if total paid-in capital plus retained earnings equals $695,000?

Problem 13-2A

Cash dividends, treasury stock, and statement of retained earnings

C3 P2 P3

Sage 50

Kohler Corporation reports the following components of stockholders' equity on December 31, 2013:

Common stock—$10 par value, 100,000 shares authorized,	
40,000 shares issued and outstanding	$400,000
Paid-in capital in excess of par value, common stock	60,000
Retained earnings	270,000
Total stockholders' equity	$730,000

In year 2014, the following transactions affected its stockholders' equity accounts.

Jan.	1	Purchased 4,000 shares of its own stock at $20 cash per share.
Jan.	5	Directors declared a $2 per share cash dividend payable on Feb. 28 to the Feb. 5 stockholders of record.
Feb.	28	Paid the dividend declared on January 5.
July	6	Sold 1,500 of its treasury shares at $24 cash per share.
Aug.	22	Sold 2,500 of its treasury shares at $17 cash per share.
Sept.	5	Directors declared a $2 per share cash dividend payable on October 28 to the September 25 stockholders of record.
Oct.	28	Paid the dividend declared on September 5.
Dec.	31	Closed the $388,000 credit balance (from net income) in the Income Summary account to Retained Earnings.

Required

1. Prepare journal entries to record each of these transactions for 2014.
2. Prepare a statement of retained earnings for the year ended December 31, 2014.
3. Prepare the stockholders' equity section of the company's balance sheet as of December 31, 2014.

Check (2) Retained earnings, Dec. 31, 2014, $504,500.

Problem 13-3A

Equity analysis—journal entries and account balances

P2

At September 30, the end of Beijing Company's third quarter, the following stockholders' equity accounts are reported.

Common stock, $12 par value	$360,000
Paid-in capital in excess of par value, common stock	90,000
Retained earnings	320,000

In the fourth quarter, the following entries related to its equity are recorded:

Oct. 2	Retained Earnings	60,000	
	Common Dividend Payable		60,000
Oct. 25	Common Dividend Payable	60,000	
	Cash		60,000
Oct. 31	Retained Earnings	75,000	
	Common Stock Dividend Distributable		36,000
	Paid-In Capital in Excess of		
	Par Value, Common Stock		39,000

[continued on next page]

[continued from previous page]

Nov. 5	Common Stock Dividend Distributable	36,000	
	Common Stock, $12 Par Value		36,000
Dec. 1	Memo—Change the title of the common stock account to reflect the new par value of $4.		
Dec. 31	Income Summary	210,000	
	Retained Earnings		210,000

Required

1. Explain the transaction(s) underlying each journal entry.

2. Complete the following table showing the equity account balances at each indicated date (include the balances from September 30).

	Oct. 2	Oct. 25	Oct. 31	Nov. 5	Dec. 1	Dec. 31
Common stock	$____	$____	$____	$____	$____	$____
Common stock dividend distributable	____	____	____	____	____	____
Paid-in capital in excess of par, common stock	____	____	____	____	____	____
Retained earnings	____	____	____	____	____	____
Total equity	$____	$____	$____	$____	$____	$____

Check Total equity: Oct. 2, $710,000; Dec. 31, $920,000

The equity sections from Atticus Group's 2013 and 2014 year-end balance sheets follow.

Problem 13-4A
Analysis of changes in stockholders' equity accounts

C3 P2 P3

Stockholders' Equity (December 31, 2013)

Common stock—$4 par value, 100,000 shares authorized, 40,000 shares issued and outstanding	$160,000
Paid-in capital in excess of par value, common stock	120,000
Retained earnings	320,000
Total stockholders' equity	$600,000

Stockholders' Equity (December 31, 2014)

Common stock—$4 par value, 100,000 shares authorized, 47,400 shares issued, 3,000 shares in treasury	$189,600
Paid-in capital in excess of par value, common stock	179,200
Retained earnings ($30,000 restricted by treasury stock)	400,000
	768,800
Less cost of treasury stock	(30,000)
Total stockholders' equity	$738,800

The following transactions and events affected its equity during year 2014.

Jan. 5 Declared a $0.50 per share cash dividend, date of record January 10.
Mar. 20 Purchased treasury stock for cash.
Apr. 5 Declared a $0.50 per share cash dividend, date of record April 10.
July 5 Declared a $0.50 per share cash dividend, date of record July 10.
July 31 Declared a 20% stock dividend when the stock's market value is $12 per share.
Aug. 14 Issued the stock dividend that was declared on July 31.
Oct. 5 Declared a $0.50 per share cash dividend, date of record October 10.

Required

1. How many common shares are outstanding on each cash dividend date?
2. What is the total dollar amount for each of the four cash dividends?
3. What is the amount of the capitalization of retained earnings for the stock dividend?
4. What is the per share cost of the treasury stock purchased?
5. How much net income did the company earn during year 2014?

Check (3) $88,800

(4) $10

(5) $248,000

Problem 13-5A
Computation of book values and
dividend allocations

C2 A4

Raphael Corporation's common stock is currently selling on a stock exchange at $85 per share, and its current balance sheet shows the following stockholders' equity section:

Preferred stock—5% cumulative, $___ par value, 1,000 shares authorized, issued, and outstanding	$ 50,000
Common stock—$___ par value, 4,000 shares authorized, issued, and outstanding	80,000
Retained earnings	150,000
Total stockholders' equity	$280,000

Required (Round per share amounts to cents.)

1. What is the current market value (price) of this corporation's common stock?

2. What are the par values of the corporation's preferred stock and its common stock?

3. If no dividends are in arrears, what are the book values per share of the preferred stock and the common stock?

Check (4) Book value of common, $56.25

(5) Book value of common, $55

(6) Dividends per common share, $1.00

4. If two years' preferred dividends are in arrears, what are the book values per share of the preferred stock and the common stock?

5. If two years' preferred dividends are in arrears and the preferred stock is callable at $55 per share, what are the book values per share of the preferred stock and the common stock?

6. If two years' preferred dividends are in arrears and the board of directors declares cash dividends of $11,500, what total amount will be paid to the preferred and to the common shareholders? What is the amount of dividends per share for the common stock?

Analysis Component

7. What are some factors that can contribute to a difference between the book value of common stock and its market value (price)?

PROBLEM SET B

Problem 13-1B
Stockholders' equity
transactions and analysis

C2 P1

Weiss Company is incorporated at the beginning of this year and engages in a number of transactions. The following journal entries impacted its stockholders' equity during its first year of operations.

a.	Cash	120,000	
	Common Stock, $1 Par Value		3,000
	Paid-In Capital in Excess of Par Value, Common Stock		117,000
b.	Organization Expenses	40,000	
	Common Stock, $1 Par Value		1,000
	Paid-In Capital in Excess of Par Value, Common Stock		39,000
c.	Cash	13,300	
	Accounts Receivable	8,000	
	Building	37,000	
	Notes Payable		18,300
	Common Stock, $1 Par Value		800
	Paid-In Capital in Excess of Par Value, Common Stock		39,200
d.	Cash	60,000	
	Common Stock, $1 Par Value		1,200
	Paid-In Capital in Excess of Par Value, Common Stock		58,800

Required

1. Explain the transaction(s) underlying each journal entry (a) through (d).

Check (2) 6,000 shares

(3) $6,000

2. How many shares of common stock are outstanding at year-end?

3. What is the amount of minimum legal capital (based on par value) at year-end?

4. What is the total paid-in capital at year-end?

(4) $260,000

5. What is the book value per share of the common stock at year-end if total paid-in capital plus retained earnings equals $283,000?

Balthus Corp. reports the following components of stockholders' equity on December 31, 2013:

Common stock—$1 par value, 320,000 shares authorized,	
200,000 shares issued and outstanding	$ 200,000
Paid-in capital in excess of par value, common stock	1,400,000
Retained earnings	2,160,000
Total stockholders' equity	$3,760,000

Problem 13-2B
Cash dividends, treasury stock, and statement of retained earnings

C3 P2 P3

It completed the following transactions related to stockholders' equity in year 2014:

Jan. 10 Purchased 40,000 shares of its own stock at $12 cash per share.
Mar. 2 Directors declared a $1.50 per share cash dividend payable on March 31 to the March 15 stockholders of record.
Mar. 31 Paid the dividend declared on March 2.
Nov. 11 Sold 24,000 of its treasury shares at $13 cash per share.
Nov. 25 Sold 16,000 of its treasury shares at $9.50 cash per share.
Dec. 1 Directors declared a $2.50 per share cash dividend payable on January 2 to the December 10 stockholders of record.
Dec. 31 Closed the $1,072,000 credit balance (from net income) in the Income Summary account to Retained Earnings.

Required

1. Prepare journal entries to record each of these transactions for 2014.

2. Prepare a statement of retained earnings for the year ended December 31, 2014.

3. Prepare the stockholders' equity section of the company's balance sheet as of December 31, 2014.

Check (2) Retained earnings, Dec. 31, 2014, $2,476,000

At December 31, the end of Chilton Communication's third quarter, the following stockholders' equity accounts are reported:

Common stock, $10 par value	$ 960,000
Paid-in capital in excess of par value, common stock	384,000
Retained earnings	1,600,000

Problem 13-3B
Equity analysis—journal entries and account balances

P2

In the fourth quarter, the following entries related to its equity are recorded:

Jan. 17	Retained Earnings	96,000	
	Common Dividend Payable...................		96,000
Feb. 5	Common Dividend Payable......................	96,000	
	Cash......................................		96,000
Feb. 28	Retained Earnings	252,000	
	Common Stock Dividend Distributable		120,000
	Paid-In Capital in Excess of Par Value,		
	Common Stock		132,000
Mar. 14	Common Stock Dividend Distributable	120,000	
	Common Stock, $10 Par Value		120,000
Mar. 25	Memo—Change the title of the common stock account to reflect the new par value of $5.		
Mar. 31	Income Summary	720,000	
	Retained Earnings		720,000

Required

1. Explain the transaction(s) underlying each journal entry.
2. Complete the following table showing the equity account balances at each indicated date (include the balances from December 31).

	Jan. 17	Feb. 5	Feb. 28	Mar. 14	Mar. 25	Mar. 31
Common stock	$_____	$_____	$_____	$_____	$_____	$_____
Common stock dividend distributable	_____	_____	_____	_____	_____	_____
Paid-in capital in excess of par, common stock	_____	_____	_____	_____	_____	_____
Retained earnings	_____	_____	_____	_____	_____	_____
Total equity	$_____	$_____	$_____	$_____	$_____	$_____

Check Total equity: Jan. 17, $2,848,000; Mar. 31, $3,568,000

Problem 13-4B
Analysis of changes in stockholders' equity accounts

C3 P2 P3

The equity sections from Hovo Corporation's 2013 and 2014 balance sheets follow.

Stockholders' Equity (December 31, 2013)

Common stock—$20 par value, 30,000 shares authorized, 17,000 shares issued and outstanding	$340,000
Paid-in capital in excess of par value, common stock	60,000
Retained earnings	270,000
Total stockholders' equity	$670,000

Stockholders' Equity (December 31, 2014)

Common stock—$20 par value, 30,000 shares authorized, 19,000 shares issued, 1,000 shares in treasury	$380,000
Paid-in capital in excess of par value, common stock	104,000
Retained earnings ($40,000 restricted by treasury stock)	295,200
	779,200
Less cost of treasury stock	(40,000)
Total stockholders' equity	$739,200

The following transactions and events affected its equity during year 2014.

Feb. 15 Declared a $0.40 per share cash dividend, date of record five days later.
Mar. 2 Purchased treasury stock for cash.
May 15 Declared a $0.40 per share cash dividend, date of record five days later.
Aug. 15 Declared a $0.40 per share cash dividend, date of record five days later.
Oct.   4 Declared a 12.5% stock dividend when the stock's market value is $42 per share.
Oct. 20 Issued the stock dividend that was declared on October 4.
Nov. 15 Declared a $0.40 per share cash dividend, date of record five days later.

Required

1. How many common shares are outstanding on each cash dividend date?
2. What is the total dollar amount for each of the four cash dividends?
3. What is the amount of the capitalization of retained earnings for the stock dividend?
4. What is the per share cost of the treasury stock purchased?
5. How much net income did the company earn during year 2014?

Check (3) $84,000
(4) $40
(5) $136,000

Problem 13-5B
Computation of book values and dividend allocations

C2 A4

Soltech Company's common stock is currently selling on a stock exchange at $90 per share, and its current balance sheet shows the following stockholders' equity section.

Preferred stock—8% cumulative, $___ par value, 1,500 shares authorized, issued, and outstanding	$ 375,000
Common stock—$___ par value, 18,000 shares authorized, issued, and outstanding	900,000
Retained earnings	1,125,000
Total stockholders' equity	$2,400,000

Required (Round per share amounts to cents.)

1. What is the current market value (price) of this corporation's common stock?

2. What are the par values of the corporation's preferred stock and its common stock?

3. If no dividends are in arrears, what are the book values per share of the preferred stock and the common stock? (Round per share values to the nearest cent.)

4. If two years' preferred dividends are in arrears, what are the book values per share of the preferred stock and the common stock? (Round per share values to the nearest cent.)

5. If two years' preferred dividends are in arrears and the preferred stock is callable at $280 per share, what are the book values per share of the preferred stock and the common stock? (Round per share values to the nearest cent.)

6. If two years' preferred dividends are in arrears and the board of directors declares cash dividends of $100,000, what total amount will be paid to the preferred and to the common shareholders? What is the amount of dividends per share for the common stock? (Round per share values to the nearest cent.)

Check (4) Book value of common, $109.17

(5) Book value of common, $106.67

(6) Dividends per common share, $0.56

Analysis Component

7. Discuss why the book value of common stock is not always a good estimate of its market value.

(This serial problem began in Chapter 1 and continues through most of the book. If previous chapter segments were not completed, the serial problem can begin at this point. It is helpful, but not necessary, to use the Working Papers that accompany the book.)

SERIAL PROBLEM
Success Systems
P1 C1 C2

SP 13 Adria Lopez created Success Systems on October 1, 2013. The company has been successful, and Adria plans to expand her business. She believes that an additional $86,000 is needed and is investigating three funding sources.

a. Adria's sister Cicely is willing to invest $86,000 in the business as a common shareholder. Since Adria currently has about $129,000 invested in the business, Cicely's investment will mean that Adria will maintain about 60% ownership, and Cicely will have 40% ownership of Success Systems.

b. Adria's uncle Marcello is willing to invest $86,000 in the business as a preferred shareholder. Marcello would purchase 860 shares of $100 par value, 7% preferred stock.

c. Adria's banker is willing to lend her $86,000 on a 7%, 10-year note payable. She would make monthly payments of $1,000 per month for 10 years.

Required

1. Prepare the journal entry to reflect the initial $86,000 investment under each of the options (a), (b), and (c).

2. Evaluate the three proposals for expansion, providing the pros and cons of each option.

3. Which option do you recommend Adria adopt? Explain.

Beyond the Numbers

BTN 13-1 Refer to **Polaris'** financial statements in Appendix A to answer the following.

REPORTING IN ACTION

C2 A1 A4

Polaris

1. How many shares of common stock are issued and outstanding at December 31, 2011 and 2010? How do these numbers compare with the basic weighted-average common shares outstanding at December 31, 2011 and 2010?

2. What is the book value of its entire common stock at December 31, 2011?

3. What is the total amount of cash dividends paid to common stockholders for the years ended December 31, 2011 and 2010?

4. Identify and compare basic EPS amounts across years 2011, 2010, and 2009. Identify and comment on any notable changes.

5. How many shares does Polaris hold in treasury stock, if any, as of December 31, 2011 and 2010?

Fast Forward

6. Access Polaris' financial statements for fiscal years ending after December 31, 2011, from its Website (**Polaris.com**) or the SEC's EDGAR database (**www.sec.gov**). Has the number of common shares outstanding increased since that date? Has the company increased the total amount of cash dividends paid compared to the total amount for year 2011?

COMPARATIVE ANALYSIS

A1 A2 A3 A4

Polaris
Arctic Cat

BTN 13-2   Key comparative figures for **Polaris** and **Arctic Cat** follow.

Key Figures	Polaris	Arctic Cat
Net income (in thousands)	$227,575	$ 13,007
Cash dividends declared per common share	$ 0.90	$ —
Common shares outstanding (in thousands)	68,430	18,301
Weighted-average common shares outstanding (in thousands)	68,792	18,232
Market value (price) per share	$ 72.10	$ 33.70
Equity applicable to common shares (in thousands)	$500,056	$183,036

Required

1. Compute the book value per common share for each company using these data.
2. Compute the basic EPS for each company using these data.
3. Compute the dividend yield for each company using these data. Does the dividend yield of any of the companies characterize it as an income or growth stock? Explain.
4. Compute, compare, and interpret the price-earnings ratio for each company using these data.

ETHICS CHALLENGE

C3

BTN 13-3   Harriet Moore is an accountant for New World Pharmaceuticals. Her duties include tracking research and development spending in the new product development division. Over the course of the past six months, Harriet notices that a great deal of funds have been spent on a particular project for a new drug. She hears "through the grapevine" that the company is about to patent the drug and expects it to be a major advance in antibiotics. Harriet believes that this new drug will greatly improve company performance and will cause the company's stock to increase in value. Harriet decides to purchase shares of New World in order to benefit from this expected increase.

Required

What are Harriet's ethical responsibilities, if any, with respect to the information she has learned through her duties as an accountant for New World Pharmaceuticals? What are the implications to her planned purchase of New World shares?

COMMUNICATING IN PRACTICE

A1 A2

Hint: Make a transparency of each team's memo for a class discussion.

BTN 13-4   Teams are to select an industry, and each team member is to select a different company in that industry. Each team member then is to acquire the selected company's financial statements (or Form 10-K) from the SEC site (**www.SEC.gov**). Use these data to identify basic EPS. Use the financial press (or **finance.yahoo.com**) to determine the market price of this stock, and then compute the price-earnings ratio. Communicate with teammates via a meeting, e-mail, or telephone to discuss the meaning of this ratio, how companies compare, and the industry norm. The team must prepare a single memorandum reporting the ratio for each company and identifying the team conclusions or consensus of opinion. The memorandum is to be duplicated and distributed to the instructor and teammates.

TAKING IT TO THE NET

C1 C3

BTN 13-5   Access the February 24, 2012, filing of the 2011 calendar-year 10-K report of **McDonald's**, (ticker MCD) from **www.SEC.gov**.

Required

1. Review McDonald's balance sheet and identify how many classes of stock it has issued.
2. What are the par values, number of authorized shares, and issued shares of the classes of stock you identified in part 1?
3. Review its statement of cash flows and identify what total amount of cash it paid in 2011 to purchase treasury stock.
4. What amount did McDonald's pay out in common stock cash dividends for 2011?

TEAMWORK IN ACTION

P3

Hint: Instructor should be sure each team accurately completes part 1 before proceeding.

BTN 13-6   This activity requires teamwork to reinforce understanding of accounting for treasury stock.

1. Write a brief team statement (*a*) generalizing what happens to a corporation's financial position when it engages in a stock "buyback" and (*b*) identifying reasons why a corporation would engage in this activity.
2. Assume that an entity acquires 100 shares of its $100 par value common stock at a cost of $134 cash per share. Discuss the entry to record this acquisition. Next, assign *each* team member to prepare *one* of the following entries (assume each entry applies to all shares):
   a. Reissue treasury shares at cost.
   b. Reissue treasury shares at $150 per share.

c. Reissue treasury shares at $120 per share; assume the paid-in capital account from treasury shares has a $1,500 balance.

d. Reissue treasury shares at $120 per share; assume the paid-in capital account from treasury shares has a $1,000 balance.

e. Reissue treasury shares at $120 per share; assume the paid-in capital account from treasury shares has a zero balance.

3. In sequence, each member is to present his/her entry to the team and explain the *similarities* and *differences* between that entry and the previous entry.

BTN 13-7   Assume that Andrew Mason of **Groupon** decides to launch a new Website to market discount services to consumers. This chain, named Servon, requires $500,000 of start-up capital. Andrew contributes $375,000 of personal assets in return for 15,000 shares of common stock, but he must raise another $125,000 in cash. There are two alternative plans for raising the additional cash. *Plan A* is to sell 3,750 shares of common stock to one or more investors for $125,000 cash. *Plan B* is to sell 1,250 shares of cumulative preferred stock to one or more investors for $125,000 cash (this preferred stock would have a $100 par value, an annual 8% dividend rate, and be issued at par).

ENTREPRENEURIAL DECISION

C2   P2

1. If the new business is expected to earn $72,000 of after-tax net income in the first year, what rate of return on beginning equity will Andrew earn under each alternative plan? Which plan will provide the higher expected return?

2. If the new business is expected to earn $16,800 of after-tax net income in the first year, what rate of return on beginning equity will Andrew earn under each alternative plan? Which plan will provide the higher expected return?

3. Analyze and interpret the differences between the results for parts 1 and 2.

BTN 13-8   Review 30 to 60 minutes of financial news programming on television. Take notes on companies that are catching analysts' attention. You might hear reference to over- and undervaluation of firms and to reports about PE ratios, dividend yields, and earnings per share. Be prepared to give a brief description to the class of your observations.

HITTING THE ROAD

A1   A2   A3

BTN 13-9   Financial information for **KTM Corporation** (**www.KTM.com**) follows:

GLOBAL DECISION

A1   C3

KTM

Net income (in thousands)	€ 20,818
Cash dividends declared (in thousands)	€ 0
Cash dividends declared per share	€ 0.00
Number of shares outstanding (in thousands)*	10,509
Equity applicable to shares (in thousands)	€219,775

* Assume that for KTM the year-end number of shares outstanding approximates the weighted-average shares outstanding.

Required

1. Compute book value per share for KTM.

2. Compute earnings per share (EPS) for KTM.

3. Compare KTM's dividends per share with its EPS. Is KTM paying out a large or small amount of its income as dividends? Explain.

ANSWERS TO MULTIPLE CHOICE QUIZ

1. e; Entry to record this stock issuance is:

Cash (6,000 × $8)	48,000	
Common Stock (6,000 × $5)		30,000
Paid-In Capital in Excess of Par Value,		
Common Stock		18,000

2. b; $75,000/19,000 shares = $3.95 per share

3. d; Preferred stock = 5,000 × $100 = $500,000
Book value per share = ($2,000,000 − $500,000)/50,000 shares = $30 per common share

4. a; $0.81/$45.00 = 1.8%

5. c; Earnings per share = $3,500,000/700,000 shares = $5 per share
PE ratio = $85/$5 = 17.0

Long-Term Liabilities

14

A Look Back

Chapter 13 focused on corporate equity transactions, including stock issuances and dividends. We also explained how to report and analyze income, earnings per share, and retained earnings.

A Look at This Chapter

This chapter describes the accounting for and analysis of bonds and notes. We explain their characteristics, payment patterns, interest computations, retirement, and reporting requirements. An appendix to this chapter introduces leases and pensions.

A Look Ahead

Chapter 15 focuses on how to classify, account for, and report investments in both debt and equity securities. We also describe accounting for transactions listed in a foreign currency.

Learning Objectives

CONCEPTUAL

C1 Explain the types and payment patterns of notes. (p. 564)

C2 *Appendix 14A*—Explain and compute the present value of an amount(s) to be paid at a future date(s). (p. 572)

C3 *Appendix 14C*—Describe interest accrual when bond payment periods differ from accounting periods. (p. 576)

C4 *Appendix 14D*—Describe accounting for leases and pensions. (p. 578)

ANALYTICAL

A1 Compare bond financing with stock financing. (p. 554)

A2 Assess debt features and their implications. (p. 568)

A3 Compute the debt-to-equity ratio and explain its use. (p. 568)

PROCEDURAL

P1 Prepare entries to record bond issuance and interest expense. (p. 556)

P2 Compute and record amortization of bond discount using straight-line method. (p. 557)

P3 Compute and record amortization of bond premium using straight-line method. (p. 560)

P4 Record the retirement of bonds. (p. 563)

P5 Prepare entries to account for notes. (p. 566)

P6 *Appendix 14B*—Compute and record amortization of bond discount using effective interest method. (p. 574)

P7 *Appendix 14B*—Compute and record amortization of bond premium using effective interest method. (p. 575)

Hippie Biz

"I really enjoy the concept of being a modern hippie."

—KYLE SMITLEY

WASHINGTON, DC—"Being a modern hippie is knowing when, where, and how to let both your hippie and modern sides come forth," declares Kyle Smitley. "The eco-friendly world is full of spontaneity and tree-hugging." The hippie in her led Kyle to launch **barley & birch (barleyandbirch.com),** an American-made 100% certified organic clothing line, which pledges to give much of its profits to environmental and social causes. "I started barley & birch to make a difference," insists Kyle. "I wanted to . . . make every single facet of the line carbon neutral."

Kyle is driven to make her business a success. "As a young entrepreneur with no experience, I was a sitting duck," admits Kyle. "There were people that either didn't take me seriously or wanted to take my money." Launching her fledgling business presented challenges. She especially focused on the important task of managing liabilities to suppliers, shippers, and others in the supply chain.

Kyle insists that effective management of liabilities, especially long-term financing from sources such as bonds and notes, is crucial to success. In her case, she launched barley & birch with a loan, or notes payable, from ACCION. "I obtained a $10,000 business loan," explains Kyle. Interest payments,

principal repayments, and operating expenses had to be controlled. "The best advice I ever received was from my father, an accountant," says Kyle. "He told me to be realistic about my budget and that it is easy to spend all of your money on lots of little things that have the risk of killing your business."

Kyle continues to monitor liabilities and their payment patterns, and she is not shy about striving to better learn the accounting side. "I am never done working," says Kyle. "I am always frantically catching up!" She insists that accounting for and monitoring liabilities of long-term financing are important ingredients to a successful start-up. Her company now generates sufficient income to pay for interest and principal on long-term debt and is on target for a goal of $2 million in sales this year.

Still, the larger message of barley & birch is about eco-friendly products and carbon neutrality. "Money only makes me excited if I can give it away," explains Kyle. "The business is only a tool. It is the car, and philanthropy is the engine."

[Sources: *barley & birch Website,* January 2013; *Modern Hippie Mag,* January 2010; *Ladies Who Launch,* June 2010; *YHP Website,* November 2009; *DePauw University News,* March 2011; *The Toledo Times,* May 2012]

Individuals, companies, and governments issue bonds to finance their activities. In return for financing, bonds promise to repay the lender with interest. This chapter explains the basics of bonds and the accounting for their issuance and retirement. The chapter also describes long-term notes as another financing source. We explain how present value concepts impact both the accounting for and reporting of bonds and notes. Appendixes to this chapter discuss present value concepts applicable to liabilities, effective interest amortization, and the accounting for leases and pensions.

Long-Term Liabilities

Bond Basics	Bond Issuances	Bond Retirement	Long-Term Notes
• Bond financing • Bond trading • Issuance procedures	• Issuance at par • Issuance at a discount • Issuance at a premium • Bond pricing	• At maturity • Before maturity • By conversion	• Installment notes • Mortgage terms

BASICS OF BONDS

This section explains the basics of bonds and a company's motivation for issuing them.

Bond Financing

A1 Compare bond financing with stock financing.

Projects that demand large amounts of money often are funded from bond issuances. (Both for-profit and nonprofit companies, as well as governmental units, such as nations, states, cities, and school districts, issue bonds.) A **bond** is its issuer's written promise to pay an amount identified as the par value of the bond with interest. The **par value of a bond,** also called the *face amount* or *face value,* is paid at a specified future date known as the bond's *maturity date.* Most bonds also require the issuer to make semiannual interest payments. The amount of interest paid each period is determined by multiplying the par value of the bond by the bond's contract rate of interest for that same period. This section explains both advantages and disadvantages of bond financing.

Advantages of Bonds   There are three main advantages of bond financing:

1. *Bonds do not affect owner control.* Equity financing reflects ownership in a company, whereas bond financing does not. A person who contributes $1,000 of a company's $10,000 equity financing typically controls one-tenth of all owner decisions. A person who owns a $1,000, 11%, 20-year bond has no ownership right. This person, or bondholder, is to receive from the bond issuer 11% interest, or $110, each year the bond is outstanding and $1,000 when it matures in 20 years.

2. *Interest on bonds is tax deductible.* Bond interest payments are tax deductible for the issuer, but equity payments (distributions) to owners are not. To illustrate, assume that a corporation with no bond financing earns $15,000 in income *before* paying taxes at a 40% tax rate, which amounts to $6,000 ($15,000 × 40%) in taxes. If a portion of its financing is in bonds, however, the resulting bond interest is deducted in computing taxable income. That is, if bond interest expense is $10,000, the taxes owed would be $2,000 ([$15,000 − $10,000] × 40%), which is less than the $6,000 owed with no bond financing.

3. *Bonds can increase return on equity.* A company that earns a higher return with borrowed funds than it pays in interest on those funds increases its return on equity. This process is called *financial leverage* or *trading on the equity.*

Point: Financial leverage reflects issuance of bonds, notes, or preferred stock.

To illustrate the third point, consider Magnum Co., which has $1 million in equity and is planning a $500,000 expansion to meet increasing demand for its product. Magnum predicts the

$500,000 expansion will yield $125,000 in additional income before paying any interest. It currently earns $100,000 per year and has no interest expense. Magnum is considering three plans. Plan A is to not expand. Plan B is to expand and raise $500,000 from equity financing. Plan C is to expand and issue $500,000 of bonds that pay 10% annual interest ($50,000). Exhibit 14.1 shows how these three plans affect Magnum's net income, equity, and return on equity (net income/equity). The owner(s) will earn a higher return on equity if expansion occurs. Moreover, the preferred expansion plan is to issue bonds. Projected net income under Plan C ($175,000) is smaller than under Plan B ($225,000), but the return on equity is larger because of less equity investment. Plan C has another advantage if income is taxable. This illustration reflects a general rule: *Return on equity increases when the expected rate of return from the new assets is higher than the rate of interest expense on the debt financing.*

Example: Compute return on equity for all three plans if Magnum currently earns $150,000 instead of $100,000.
Answer ($ 000s):
Plan A = 15%   ($150/$1,000)
Plan B = 18.3%   ($275/$1,500)
Plan C = 22.5%   ($225/$1,000)

EXHIBIT 14.1

Financing with Bonds versus Equity

	Plan A: Do Not Expand	Plan B: Equity Financing	Plan C: Bond Financing
Income before interest expense	$ 100,000	$ 225,000	$ 225,000
Interest expense	—	—	(50,000)
Net income	**$ 100,000**	**$ 225,000**	**$ 175,000**
Equity	$1,000,000	$1,500,000	$1,000,000
Return on equity	**10.0%**	**15.0%**	**17.5%**

Disadvantages of Bonds   The two main disadvantages of bond financing are these:

1. *Bonds can decrease return on equity.* When a company earns a lower return with the borrowed funds than it pays in interest, it decreases its return on equity. This downside risk of financial leverage is more likely to arise when a company has periods of low income or net losses.

2. *Bonds require payment of both periodic interest and the par value at maturity.* Bond payments can be especially burdensome when income and cash flow are low. Equity financing, in contrast, does not require any payments because cash withdrawals (dividends) are paid at the discretion of the owner (or board).

A company must weigh the risks and returns of the disadvantages and advantages of bond financing when deciding whether to issue bonds to finance operations.

Point: Debt financing is desirable when interest is tax deductible, when owner control is preferred, and when return on equity exceeds the debt's interest rate.

Bond Trading

Bonds are securities that can be readily bought and sold. A large number of bonds trade on both the New York Exchange and the American Exchange. A bond *issue* consists of a number of bonds, usually in denominations of $1,000 or $5,000, and is sold to many different lenders. After bonds are issued, they often are bought and sold by investors, meaning that any particular bond probably has a number of owners before it matures. Since bonds are exchanged (bought and sold) in the market, they have a market value (price). For convenience, bond market values are expressed as a percent of their par (face) value. For example, a company's bonds might be trading at 103½, meaning they can be bought or sold for 103.5% of their par value. Bonds can also trade below par value. For instance, if a company's bonds are trading at 95, they can be bought or sold at 95% of their par value.

Point: The phrase: *debt is cheaper than equity,* refers in part to interest expense on bonds being tax deductible whereas dividends on stock are not.

■ **Decision** Insight

Quotes   The **IBM** bond quote here is interpreted (left to right) as **Bonds,** issuer name; **Rate,** contract interest rate (5.7%); **Mat,** matures in year 2017

Bonds	Rate	Mat	Yld	Vol	Close	Chg
IBM	5.7	17	4.7	130	121.18	+0.24%

when principal is paid; **Yld,** yield rate (4.7%) of bond at current price; **Vol,** daily dollar worth ($130,000) of trades (in 1,000s); **Close,** closing price (121.18) for the day as percentage of par value; **Chg,** change (+0.24%) in closing price from prior day's close. ■

Bond-Issuing Procedures

State and federal laws govern bond issuances. Bond issuers also want to ensure that they do not violate any of their existing contractual agreements when issuing bonds. Authorization of bond issuances includes the number of bonds authorized, their par value, and the contract interest rate. The legal document identifying the rights and obligations of both the bondholders and the

EXHIBIT 14.2

Bond Certificate

Point: *Indenture* refers to a bond's legal contract; *debenture* refers to an unsecured bond.

issuer is called the **bond indenture,** which is the legal contract between the issuer and the bondholders (and specifies how often interest is paid). A bondholder may also receive a bond certificate as evidence of the company's debt. A **bond certificate,** such as that shown in Exhibit 14.2, includes specifics such as the issuer's name, the par value, the contract interest rate, and the maturity date. Many companies reduce costs by not issuing paper certificates to bondholders.[1]

BOND ISSUANCES

This section explains accounting for bond issuances at par, below par (discount), and above par (premium). It also describes how to amortize a discount or premium and record bonds issued between interest payment dates.

Issuing Bonds at Par

P1 Prepare entries to record bond issuance and interest expense.

To illustrate an issuance of bonds at par value, suppose a company receives authorization to issue $800,000 of 9%, 20-year bonds dated January 1, 2013, that mature on December 31, 2032, and pay interest semiannually on each June 30 and December 31. After accepting the bond indenture on behalf of the bondholders, the trustee can sell all or a portion of the bonds to an underwriter. If all bonds are sold at par value, the issuer records the sale as follows.

Assets = Liabilities + Equity
+800,000   +800,000

2013			
Jan. I	Cash	800,000	
	Bonds Payable		800,000
	Sold bonds at par.		

This entry reflects increases in the issuer's cash *and* long-term liabilities.

The issuer records the first semiannual interest payment as follows.

Assets = Liabilities + Equity
−36,000   −36,000

2013			
June 30	Bond Interest Expense	36,000	
	Cash		36,000
	Paid semiannual interest (9% × $800,000 × ½ year).		

Point: The *spread* between the dealer's cost and what buyers pay can be huge. Dealers earn more than $25 billion in annual spread revenue.

Global: In the United Kingdom, government bonds are called *gilts*— short for gilt-edged investments.

[1] The issuing company normally sells its bonds to an investment firm called an *underwriter,* which resells them to the public. An issuing company can also sell bonds directly to investors. When an underwriter sells bonds to a large number of investors, a *trustee* represents and protects the bondholders' interests. The trustee monitors the issuer to ensure that it complies with the obligations in the bond indenture. Most trustees are large banks or trust companies. The trustee writes and accepts the terms of a bond indenture before it is issued. When bonds are offered to the public, called *floating an issue,* they must be registered with the Securities and Exchange Commission (SEC). SEC registration requires the issuer to file certain financial information. Most company bonds are issued in par value units of $1,000 or $5,000. A *baby bond* has a par value of less than $1,000, such as $100.

The issuer pays and records its semiannual interest obligation every six months until the bonds mature. When they mature, the issuer records its payment of principal as follows.

2032			
Dec. 31	Bonds Payable	800,000	
	Cash		800,000
	Paid bond principal at maturity.		

Assets = Liabilities + Equity
−800,000   −800,000

Bond Discount or Premium

The bond issuer pays the interest rate specified in the indenture, the **contract rate,** also referred to as the *coupon rate, stated rate,* or *nominal rate.* The annual interest paid is determined by multiplying the bond par value by the contract rate. The contract rate is usually stated on an annual basis, even if interest is paid semiannually. For example, if a company issues a $1,000, 8% bond paying interest semiannually, it pays annual interest of $80 (8% × $1,000) in two semiannual payments of $40 each.

The contract rate sets the amount of interest the issuer pays in *cash,* which is not necessarily the *bond interest expense* actually incurred by the issuer. Bond interest expense depends on the bond's market value at issuance, which is determined by market expectations of the risk of lending to the issuer. The bond's **market rate** of interest is the rate that borrowers are willing to pay and lenders are willing to accept for a particular bond and its risk level. As the risk level increases, the rate increases to compensate purchasers for the bonds' increased risk. Also, the market rate is generally higher when the time period until the bond matures is longer due to the risk of adverse events occurring over a longer time period.

Many bond issuers try to set a contract rate of interest equal to the market rate they expect as of the bond issuance date. When the contract rate and market rate are equal, a bond sells at par value, but when they are not equal, a bond does not sell at par value. Instead, it is sold at a *premium* above par value or at a *discount* below par value. Exhibit 14.3 shows the relation between the contract rate, market rate, and a bond's issue price.

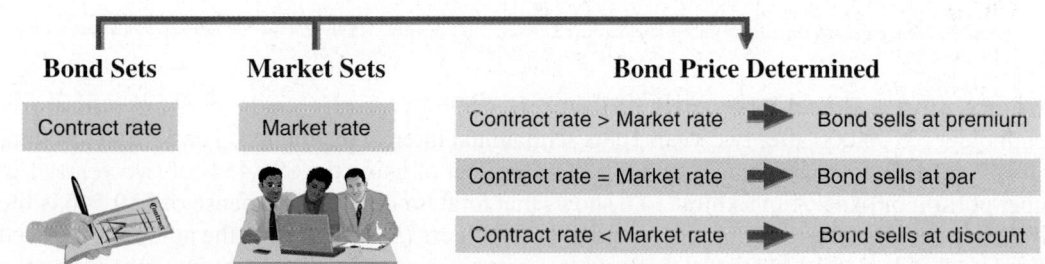

EXHIBIT 14.3

Relation between Bond Issue Price, Contract Rate, and Market Rate

Quick Check

Answers — p. 581

1. A company issues $10,000 of 9%, 5-year bonds dated January 1, 2013, that mature on December 31, 2017, and pay interest semiannually on each June 30 and December 31. Prepare the entry to record this bond issuance and the first semiannual interest payment.
2. How do you compute the amount of interest a bond issuer pays in cash each year?
3. When the contract rate is above the market rate, do bonds sell at a premium or a discount? Do purchasers pay more or less than the par value of the bonds?

Issuing Bonds at a Discount

A **discount on bonds payable** occurs when a company issues bonds with a contract rate less than the market rate. This means that the issue price is less than par value. To illustrate, assume that **Fila** announces an offer to issue bonds with a $100,000 par value, an 8% annual contract rate (paid semiannually), and a two-year life. Also assume that the market rate for Fila bonds is

P2 Compute and record amortization of bond discount.

Point: The difference between the contract rate and the market rate of interest on a new bond issue is usually a fraction of a percent. We use a difference of 2% to emphasize the effects.

10%. These bonds then will sell at a discount since the contract rate is less than the market rate. The exact issue price for these bonds is stated as 96.454 (implying 96.454% of par value, or $96,454); we show how to compute this issue price later in the chapter. These bonds obligate the issuer to pay two separate types of future cash flows:

1. Par value of $100,000 cash at the end of the bonds' two-year life.
2. Cash interest payments of $4,000 (4% × $100,000) at the end of each semiannual period during the bonds' two-year life.

The exact pattern of cash flows for the Fila bonds is shown in Exhibit 14.4.

EXHIBIT 14.4

Cash Flows for Fila Bonds

When Fila accepts $96,454 cash for its bonds on the issue date of December 31, 2013, it records the sale as follows.

Assets = Liabilities + Equity
+96,454   +100,000
           −3,546

Dec. 31	Cash	96,454	
	Discount on Bonds Payable	3,546	
	Bonds Payable		100,000
	Sold bonds at a discount on their issue date.		

Point: Book value at issuance always equals the issuer's cash borrowed.

These bonds are reported in the long-term liability section of the issuer's December 31, 2013, balance sheet as shown in Exhibit 14.5. A discount is deducted from the par value of bonds to yield the **carrying (book) value of bonds.** Discount on Bonds Payable is a contra liability account.

EXHIBIT 14.5

Balance Sheet Presentation of Bond Discount

Point: *Zero-coupon bonds* do not pay periodic interest (contract rate is zero). These bonds always sell at a discount because their 0% contract rate is always below the market rate.

Amortizing a Bond Discount   Fila receives $96,454 for its bonds; in return it must pay bondholders $100,000 after two years (plus semiannual interest payments). The $3,546 discount is paid to bondholders at maturity and is part of the cost of using the $96,454 for two years. The upper portion of panel A in Exhibit 14.6 shows that total bond interest expense of $19,546 is the difference between the total amount repaid to bondholders ($116,000) and the amount borrowed from bondholders ($96,454). Alternatively, we can compute total bond interest expense as the sum of the four interest payments and the bond discount. This alternative computation is shown in the lower portion of panel A.

The total $19,546 bond interest expense must be allocated across the four semiannual periods in the bonds' life, and the bonds' carrying value must be updated at each balance sheet date. This is accomplished using the straight-line method (or the effective interest method in Appendix 14B). Both methods systematically reduce the bond discount to zero over the two-year life. This process is called *amortizing a bond discount*.

> The following section on discount amortization uses the straight-line method. Appendix 14B uses the effective interest method. An instructor can choose to cover either one or both methods. If the straight-line method is skipped, then read Appendix 14B and return to the section (on page 560) titled "Issuing Bonds at a Premium."

Straight-Line Method   The **straight-line bond amortization** method allocates an equal portion of the total bond interest expense to each interest period. To apply the straight-line method to Fila's bonds, we divide the total bond interest expense of $19,546 by 4 (the number of semiannual periods in the bonds' life). This gives a bond interest expense of $4,887 per period, which is $4,886.5 rounded to the nearest dollar per period (all computations, including those for assignments, are rounded to the nearest whole dollar). Alternatively, we can find this

EXHIBIT 14.6

Interest Computation and Entry for Bonds Issued at a Discount

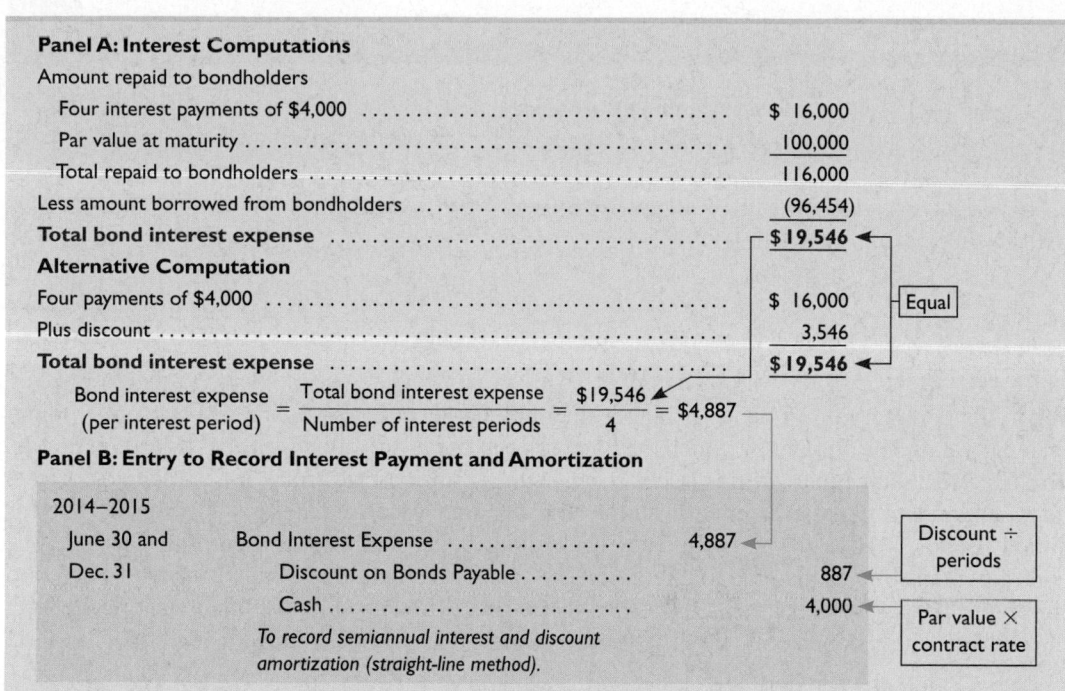

Panel A: Interest Computations

Amount repaid to bondholders	
Four interest payments of $4,000	$ 16,000
Par value at maturity	100,000
Total repaid to bondholders	116,000
Less amount borrowed from bondholders	(96,454)
Total bond interest expense	**$19,546**
Alternative Computation	
Four payments of $4,000	$ 16,000
Plus discount	3,546
Total bond interest expense	**$19,546**

$$\frac{\text{Bond interest expense}}{\text{(per interest period)}} = \frac{\text{Total bond interest expense}}{\text{Number of interest periods}} = \frac{\$19,546}{4} = \$4,887$$

Panel B: Entry to Record Interest Payment and Amortization

2014–2015			
June 30 and Dec. 31	Bond Interest Expense	4,887	
	Discount on Bonds Payable		887
	Cash		4,000
	To record semiannual interest and discount amortization (straight-line method).		

number by first dividing the $3,546 discount by 4, which yields the $887 amount of discount to be amortized each interest period. When the $887 is added to the $4,000 cash payment, the bond interest expense for each period is $4,887. Panel B of Exhibit 14.6 shows how the issuer records bond interest expense and updates the balance of the bond liability account at the end of *each* of the four semiannual interest periods (June 30, 2014, through December 31, 2015).

Exhibit 14.7 shows the pattern of decreases in the Discount on Bonds Payable account and the pattern of increases in the bonds' carrying value. The following points summarize the discount bonds' straight-line amortization:

1. At issuance, the $100,000 par value consists of the $96,454 cash received by the issuer plus the $3,546 discount.

2. During the bonds' life, the (unamortized) discount decreases each period by the $887 amortization ($3,546/4), and the carrying value (par value less unamortized discount) increases each period by $887.

3. At maturity, the unamortized discount equals zero, and the carrying value equals the $100,000 par value that the issuer pays the holder.

EXHIBIT 14.7

Straight-Line Amortization of Bond Discount

	Semiannual Period-End	Unamortized Discount*	Carrying Value†
(0)	12/31/2013	$3,546	$ 96,454
(1)	6/30/2014	2,659	97,341
(2)	12/31/2014	1,772	98,228
(3)	6/30/2015	885	99,115
(4)	12/31/2015	0‡	100,000

* Total bond discount (of $3,546) less accumulated periodic amortization ($887 per semiannual interest period).

† Bond par value (of $100,000) less unamortized discount.

‡ Adjusted for rounding.

The two columns always sum to par value for a discount bond.

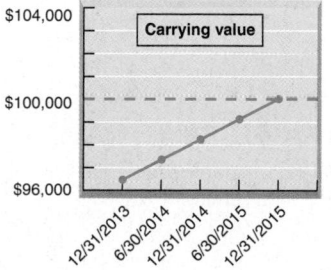

We see that the issuer incurs a $4,887 bond interest expense each period but pays only $4,000 cash. The $887 unpaid portion of this expense is added to the bonds' carrying value. (The total $3,546 unamortized discount is "paid" when the bonds mature; $100,000 is paid at maturity but only $96,454 was received at issuance.)

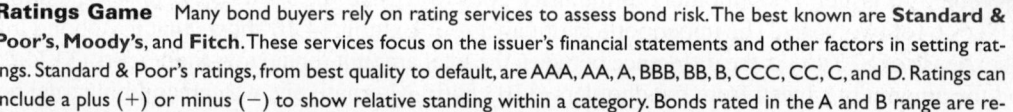

Decision Insight

Ratings Game   Many bond buyers rely on rating services to assess bond risk. The best known are **Standard & Poor's, Moody's,** and **Fitch.** These services focus on the issuer's financial statements and other factors in setting ratings. Standard & Poor's ratings, from best quality to default, are AAA, AA, A, BBB, BB, B, CCC, CC, C, and D. Ratings can include a plus (+) or minus (−) to show relative standing within a category. Bonds rated in the A and B range are referred to as *investment grade;* lower-rated bonds are considered much riskier. ■

Quick Check   Answers — p. 581

Five-year, 6% bonds with a $100,000 par value are issued at a price of $91,893. Interest is paid semiannually, and the bonds' market rate is 8% on the issue date. Use this information to answer the following questions:

4. Are these bonds issued at a discount or a premium? Explain your answer.
5. What is the issuer's journal entry to record the issuance of these bonds?
6. What is the amount of bond interest expense recorded at the first semiannual period using the straight-line method?

Issuing Bonds at a Premium

P3 Compute and record amortization of bond premium.

When the contract rate of bonds is higher than the market rate, the bonds sell at a price higher than par value. The amount by which the bond price exceeds par value is the **premium on bonds.** To illustrate, assume that **Adidas** issues bonds with a $100,000 par value, a 12% annual contract rate, semiannual interest payments, and a two-year life. Also assume that the market rate for Adidas bonds is 10% on the issue date. The Adidas bonds will sell at a premium because the contract rate is higher than the market rate. The issue price for these bonds is stated as 103.546 (implying 103.546% of par value, or $103,546); we show how to compute this issue price later in the chapter. These bonds obligate the issuer to pay out two separate future cash flows:

1. Par value of $100,000 cash at the end of the bonds' two-year life.
2. Cash interest payments of $6,000 (6% × $100,000) at the end of each semiannual period during the bonds' two-year life.

The exact pattern of cash flows for the Adidas bonds is shown in Exhibit 14.8.

EXHIBIT 14.8

Cash Flows for Adidas Bonds

When Adidas accepts $103,546 cash for its bonds on the issue date of December 31, 2013, it records this transaction as follows.

Assets   = Liabilities + Equity
+103,546   +100,000
            +3,546

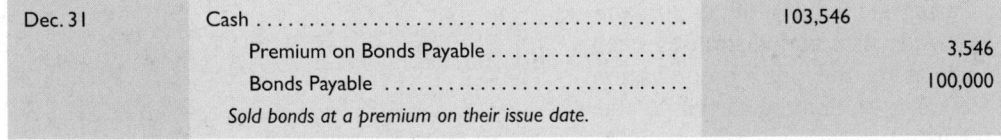

Dec. 31	Cash	103,546	
	Premium on Bonds Payable		3,546
	Bonds Payable		100,000
	Sold bonds at a premium on their issue date.		

These bonds are reported in the long-term liability section of the issuer's December 31, 2013, balance sheet as shown in Exhibit 14.9. A premium is added to par value to yield the carrying (book) value of bonds. Premium on Bonds Payable is an adjunct (also called *accretion*) liability account.

EXHIBIT 14.9

Balance Sheet Presentation of Bond Premium

Long-term liabilities		
Bonds payable, 12%, due December 31, 2015	$100,000	
Plus premium on bonds payable	**3,546**	**$103,546**

Amortizing a Bond Premium   Adidas receives $103,546 for its bonds; in return, it pays bondholders $100,000 after two years (plus semiannual interest payments). The $3,546 premium not repaid to issuer's bondholders at maturity goes to reduce the issuer's expense of using the $103,546 for two years. The upper portion of panel A of Exhibit 14.10 shows that total bond interest expense of $20,454 is the difference between the total amount repaid to bondholders ($124,000) and the amount borrowed from bondholders ($103,546). Alternatively, we can compute total bond

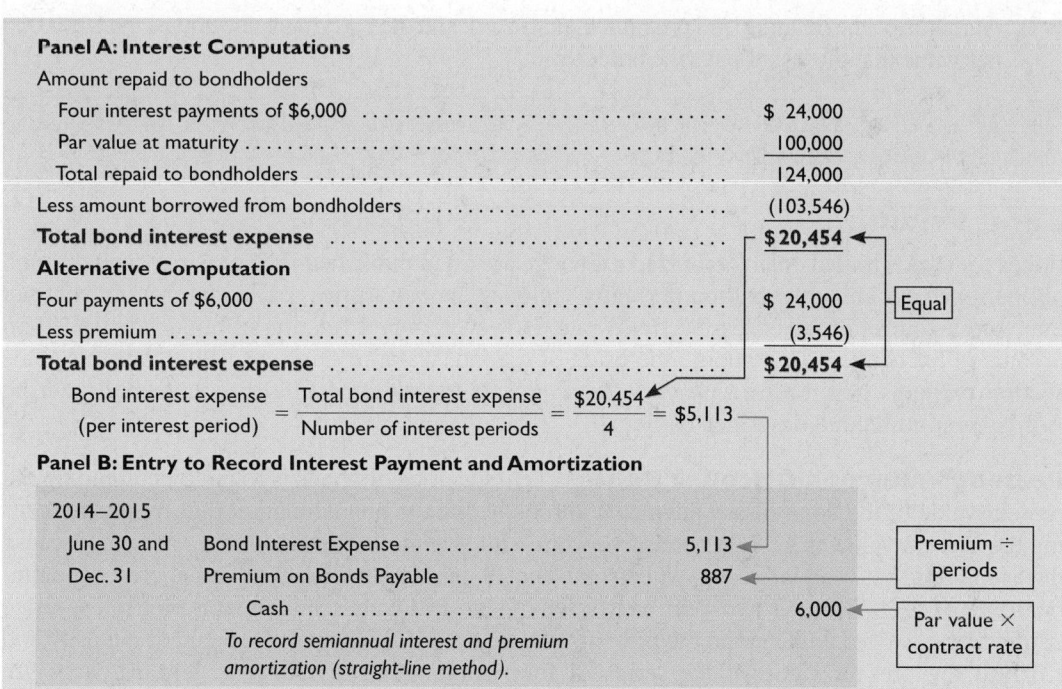

EXHIBIT 14.10

Interest Computation and Entry for Bonds Issued at a Premium

interest expense as the sum of the four interest payments less the bond premium. The premium is subtracted because it will not be paid to bondholders when the bonds mature; see the lower portion of panel A. Total bond interest expense must be allocated over the four semiannual periods using the straight-line method (or the effective interest method in Appendix 14B).

Point: The phrase: *ability to service debt*, refers to making interest and principal payments on time.

> *The following section on premium amortization uses the straight-line method. Appendix 14B uses the effective interest method. An instructor can choose to cover either one or both methods. If the straight-line method is skipped, then read Appendix 14B and return to the section (next page) titled "Bond Pricing."*

Straight-Line Method   The straight-line method allocates an equal portion of total bond interest expense to each of the bonds' semiannual interest periods. To apply this method to Adidas

Point: A premium decreases Bond Interest Expense; a discount increases it.

bonds, we divide the two years' total bond interest expense of $20,454 by 4 (the number of semiannual periods in the bonds' life). This gives a total bond interest expense of $5,113 per period, which is $5,113.5 rounded down so that the journal entry balances and for simplicity in presentation (alternatively, one could carry cents). Panel B of Exhibit 14.10 shows how the issuer records bond interest expense and updates the balance of the bond liability account for *each* semiannual period (June 30, 2014, through December 31, 2015).

Semiannual Period-End	Unamortized Premium*	Carrying Value†
(0) 12/31/2013	$3,546	$103,546
(1) 6/30/2014	2,659	102,659
(2) 12/31/2014	1,772	101,772
(3) 6/30/2015	885	100,885
(4) 12/31/2015	0‡	100,000

* Total bond premium (of $3,546) less accumulated periodic amortization ($887 per semiannual interest period).

† Bond par value (of $100,000) plus unamortized premium.

‡ Adjusted for rounding.

EXHIBIT 14.11

Straight-Line Amortization of Bond Premium

During the bond life, carrying value is adjusted to par and the amortized premium to zero.

Exhibit 14.11 shows the pattern of decreases in the unamortized Premium on Bonds Payable account and in the bonds' carrying value. The following points summarize straight-line amortization of the premium bonds:

1. At issuance, the $100,000 par value plus the $3,546 premium equals the $103,546 cash received by the issuer.

2. During the bonds' life, the (unamortized) premium decreases each period by the $887 amortization ($3,546/4), and the carrying value decreases each period by the same $887.

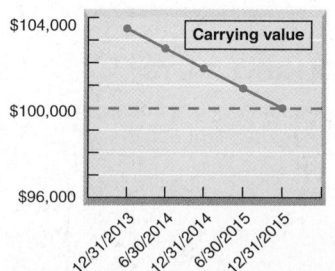

3. At maturity, the unamortized premium equals zero, and the carrying value equals the $100,000 par value that the issuer pays the holder.

> *The next section describes bond pricing. An instructor can choose to cover bond pricing or not. Assignments requiring the next section are Quick Study 14-4 and Exercises 14-9 and 14-10.*

Bond Pricing

Prices for bonds traded on an organized exchange are often published in newspapers and through online services. This information normally includes the bond price (called *quote*), its contract rate, and its current market (called *yield*) rate. However, only a fraction of bonds are traded on organized exchanges. To compute the price of a bond, we apply present value concepts. This section explains how to use *present value concepts* to price the Fila discount bond and the Adidas premium bond described earlier.

Present Value of a Discount Bond   The issue price of bonds is found by computing the present value of the bonds' cash payments, discounted at the bonds' market rate. When computing the present value of the Fila bonds, we work with *semiannual* compounding periods because this is the time between interest payments; the annual market rate of 10% is considered a semiannual rate of 5%. Also, the two-year bond life is viewed as four semiannual periods. The price computation is twofold: (1) Find the present value of the $100,000 par value paid at maturity and (2) find the present value of the series of four semiannual payments of $4,000 each; see Exhibit 14.4. These present values can be found by using *present value tables*. Appendix B at the end of this book shows present value tables and describes their use. Table B.1 at the end of Appendix B is used for the single $100,000 maturity payment, and Table B.3 in Appendix B is used for the $4,000 series of interest payments. Specifically, we go to Table B.1, row 4, and across to the 5% column to identify the present value factor of 0.8227 for the maturity payment. Next, we go to Table B.3, row 4, and across to the 5% column, where the present value factor is 3.5460 for the series of interest payments. We compute bond price by multiplying the cash flow payments by their corresponding present value factors and adding them together; see Exhibit 14.12.

EXHIBIT 14.12

Computing Issue Price for the Fila Discount Bonds

Calculator	
N = 4	PMT = 4,000
I/Yr = 5	FV = 100,000
	PV = 96,454

Cash Flow	Table	Present Value Factor	Amount		Present Value
$100,000 par (maturity) value	B.1	0.8227	× $100,000	=	$ 82,270
$4,000 interest payments	B.3	3.5460	× 4,000	=	14,184
Price of bond					$96,454

Present Value of a Premium Bond   We find the issue price of the Adidas bonds by using the market rate to compute the present value of the bonds' future cash flows. When computing the present value of these bonds, we again work with *semiannual* compounding periods because this is the time between interest payments. The annual 10% market rate is applied as a semiannual rate of 5%, and the two-year bond life is viewed as four semiannual periods. The computation is twofold: (1) Find the present value of the $100,000 par value paid at maturity and (2) find the present value of the series of four payments of $6,000 each; see Exhibit 14.8. These present values can be found by using present value tables. First, go to Table B.1, row 4, and across to the 5% column where the present value factor is 0.8227 for the maturity payment. Second, go to Table B.3, row 4, and across to the 5% column, where the present value factor is 3.5460 for the series of interest payments. The bonds' price is computed by multiplying the cash flow payments by their corresponding present value factors and adding them together; see Exhibit 14.13.

EXHIBIT 14.13

Computing Issue Price for the Adidas Premium Bonds

Calculator	
N = 4	PMT = 6,000
I/Yr = 5	FV = 100,000
	PV = 103,546

Cash Flow	Table	Present Value Factor	Amount		Present Value
$100,000 par (maturity) value	B.1	0.8227	× $100,000	=	$ 82,270
$6,000 interest payments	B.3	3.5460	× 6,000	=	21,276
Price of bond					$103,546

■ Decision Insight

Unreported Liabilities Drove U.S. Financial Crisis?   Many argue that unreported liabilities were a major cause of the financial crisis. They assert that "off-balance-sheet accounting" encouraged bad loans, securitizations, and derivatives that drove much of the crisis. It is argued that balance sheets failed to report many of these liabilities. For example, because bank liabilities used to finance assets were not transparent, the markets failed to penalize banks that used derivatives and variable interest entities (VIEs) to take excessive risks. Arguably, such accounting is fraudulent. ■

Quick Check   Answers — p. 581

On December 31, 2012, a company issues 16%, 10-year bonds with a par value of $100,000. Interest is paid on June 30 and December 31. The bonds are sold to yield a 14% annual market rate at an issue price of $110,592. Use this information to answer questions 7 through 9:

7. Are these bonds issued at a discount or a premium? Explain your answer.

8. Using the straight-line method to allocate bond interest expense, the issuer records the second interest payment (on December 31, 2013) with a debit to Premium on Bonds Payable in the amount of (a) $7,470, (b) $530, (c) $8,000, or (d) $400.

9. How are these bonds reported in the long-term liability section of the issuer's balance sheet as of December 31, 2013?

BOND RETIREMENT

This section describes the retirement of bonds (1) at maturity, (2) before maturity, and (3) by conversion to stock.

P4 Record the retirement of bonds.

Bond Retirement at Maturity

The carrying value of bonds at maturity always equals par value. For example, both Exhibits 14.7 (a discount) and 14.11 (a premium) show that the carrying value of bonds at the end of their lives equals par value ($100,000). The retirement of these bonds at maturity, assuming interest is already paid and entered, is recorded as follows:

2015			
Dec. 31	Bonds Payable	100,000	
	Cash		100,000
	To record retirement of bonds at maturity.		

Assets = Liabilities + Equity
−100,000   −100,000

Bond Retirement before Maturity

Issuers sometimes wish to retire some or all of their bonds prior to maturity. For instance, if interest rates decline greatly, an issuer may wish to replace high-interest-paying bonds with new low-interest bonds. Two common ways to retire bonds before maturity are to (1) exercise a call option or (2) purchase them on the open market. In the first instance, an issuer can reserve the right to retire bonds early by issuing callable bonds. The bond indenture can give the issuer an option to *call* the bonds before they mature by paying the par value plus a *call premium* to bondholders. In the second case, the issuer retires bonds by repurchasing them on the open market at their current price. Whether bonds are called or repurchased, the issuer is unlikely to pay a price that exactly equals their carrying value. When a difference exists between the bonds' carrying value and the amount paid, the issuer records a gain or loss equal to the difference.

To illustrate the accounting for retiring callable bonds, assume that a company issued callable bonds with a par value of $100,000. The call option requires the issuer to pay a call premium of $3,000 to bondholders in addition to the par value. Next, assume that after the June 30, 2013, interest payment, the bonds have a carrying value of $104,500. Then on July 1, 2013, the issuer calls these bonds and pays $103,000 to bondholders. The issuer recognizes a $1,500 gain from

Point: Bond retirement is also referred to as *bond redemption.*

Point: Gains and losses from retiring bonds were *previously* reported as extraordinary items. New standards require that they now be judged by the "unusual and infrequent" criteria for reporting purposes.

the difference between the bonds' carrying value of $104,500 and the retirement price of $103,000. The issuer records this bond retirement as follows.

Assets = Liabilities + Equity
−103,000   −100,000   +1,500
            −4,500

July 1	Bonds Payable	100,000	
	Premium on Bonds Payable	4,500	
	Gain on Bond Retirement		1,500
	Cash		103,000
	To record retirement of bonds before maturity.		

An issuer usually must call all bonds when it exercises a call option. However, to retire as many or as few bonds as it desires, an issuer can purchase them on the open market. If it retires less than the entire class of bonds, it recognizes a gain or loss for the difference between the carrying value of those bonds retired and the amount paid to acquire them.

Bond Retirement by Conversion

Convertible Bond

Assets = Liabilities + Equity
          −100,000   +30,000
                     +70,000

Holders of convertible bonds have the right to convert their bonds to stock. When conversion occurs, the bonds' carrying value is transferred to equity accounts and no gain or loss is recorded. (We further describe convertible bonds in the Decision Analysis section of this chapter.)

To illustrate, assume that on January 1 the $100,000 par value bonds of **Converse**, with a carrying value of $100,000, are converted to 15,000 shares of $2 par value common stock. The entry to record this conversion follows (the market prices of the bonds and stock are *not* relevant to this entry; the material in Chapter 13 is helpful in understanding this transaction):

Jan. 1	Bonds Payable	100,000	
	Common Stock		30,000
	Paid-In Capital in Excess of Par Value		70,000
	To record retirement of bonds by conversion.		

Decision Insight

Junk Bonds   Junk bonds are company bonds with low credit ratings due to a higher than average likelihood of default. On the upside, the high risk of junk bonds can yield high returns if the issuer survives and repays its debt. ■

Quick Check   Answer — p. 581

10. Six years ago, a company issued $500,000 of 6%, eight-year bonds at a price of 95. The current carrying value is $493,750. The company decides to retire 50% of these bonds by buying them on the open market at a price of 102½. What is the amount of gain or loss on the retirement of these bonds?

LONG-TERM NOTES PAYABLE

 C1   Explain the types and payment patterns of notes.

Like bonds, notes are issued to obtain assets such as cash. Unlike bonds, notes are typically transacted with a *single* lender such as a bank. An issuer initially records a note at its selling price—that is, the note's face value minus any discount or plus any premium. Over the note's life, the amount of interest expense allocated to each period is computed by multiplying the market rate (at issuance of the note) by the beginning-of-period note balance. The note's carrying (book) value at any time equals its face value minus any unamortized discount or plus any unamortized premium; carrying value is also computed as the present value of all remaining payments, discounted using the market rate at issuance.

Installment Notes

An **installment note** is an obligation requiring a series of payments to the lender. Installment notes are common for franchises and other businesses when lenders and borrowers agree to spread payments over several periods. To illustrate, assume that Foghog borrows $60,000 from a bank to purchase equipment. It signs an 8% installment note requiring six annual payments of principal plus interest and it records the note's issuance at January 1, 2013, as follows.

Point: Banks sometimes reject loans when risk of default by borrowers is high. Then, bonds can serve as another way borrowers can finance operations or expansion.

Jan. 1	Cash	60,000	
	Notes Payable		60,000
	Borrowed $60,000 by signing an 8%, six-year		
	installment note.		

Assets = Liabilities + Equity
+60,000   +60,000

Payments on an installment note normally include the accrued interest expense plus a portion of the amount borrowed (the *principal*). This section describes an installment note with equal payments.

The equal total payments pattern consists of changing amounts of both interest and principal. To illustrate, assume that Foghog borrows $60,000 by signing a $60,000 note that requires six *equal payments* of $12,979 at the end of each year. (The present value of an annuity of six annual payments of $12,979, discounted at 8%, equals $60,000; we show this computation in footnote 2 on the next page.) The $12,979 includes both interest and principal, the amounts of which change with each payment. Exhibit 14.14 shows the pattern of equal total payments and its two parts, interest and principal. Column A shows the note's beginning balance. Column B shows accrued

Years

2013 2014 2015 2016 2017 2018

Point: Most consumer notes are installment notes that require equal total payments.

EXHIBIT 14.14

Installment Note: Equal Total Payments

		Payments			
Period Ending Date	(A) Beginning Balance	(B) Debit Interest Expense 8% × (A)	+ (C) Debit Notes Payable (D) − (B)	= (D) Credit Cash (computed)	(E) Ending Balance (A) − (C)
(1) 12/31/2013	$60,000	$ 4,800	$ 8,179	$12,979	$51,821
(2) 12/31/2014	51,821	4,146	8,833	12,979	42,988
(3) 12/31/2015	42,988	3,439	9,540	12,979	33,448
(4) 12/31/2016	33,448	2,676	10,303	12,979	23,145
(5) 12/31/2017	23,145	1,852	11,127	12,979	12,018
(6) 12/31/2018	12,018	961	12,018	12,979	0
		$17,874	$60,000	$77,874	

▢ Interest ▢ Principal

Decreasing Accrued Interest

Increasing Principal Component

Equal Total Payments

End of Year		
2013	$4,800	$8,179
2014	$4,146	$8,833
2015	$3,439	$9,540
2016	$2,676	$10,303
2017	$1,852	$11,127
2018	$961	$12,018

0    $2,500 $5,000 $7,500 $10,000 $12,500 $15,000
Cash Payment Pattern

interest for each year at 8% of the beginning note balance. Column C shows the impact on the note's principal, which equals the difference between the total payment in column D and the interest expense in column B. Column E shows the note's year-end balance.

Although the six cash payments arc equal, accrued interest decreases each year because the principal balance of the note declines. As the amount of interest decreases each year, the portion of each payment applied to principal increases. This pattern is graphed in the lower part of Exhibit 14.14. Foghog uses the amounts in Exhibit 14.14 to record its first two payments (for years 2013 and 2014) as follows:

P5 Prepare entries to account for notes.

Assets = Liabilities + Equity
−12,979   −8,179   −4,800

2013			
Dec. 31	Interest Expense	4,800	
	Notes Payable	8,179	
	Cash		12,979
	To record first installment payment.		

Assets = Liabilities + Equity
−12,979   −8,833   −4,146

2014			
Dec. 31	Interest Expense	4,146	
	Notes Payable	8,833	
	Cash		12,979
	To record second installment payment.		

Foghog records similar entries but with different amounts for each of the remaining four payments. After six years, the Notes Payable account balance is zero.[2]

 Decision Insight

Missing Debt   A study reports that 13% of employees in finance and accounting witnessed the falsifying or manipulating of accounting information in the past year (KPMG 2009). This includes nondisclosure of special concern with long-term liabilities. Another study reports that most people committing fraud (36%) work in the finance function of their firm (KPMG 2011). For example, Enron violated GAAP to keep debt off its balance sheet. ■

Mortgage Notes and Bonds

Point: The Truth-in-Lending Act requires lenders to provide information about loan costs including finance charges and interest rate.

A **mortgage** is a legal agreement that helps protect a lender if a borrower fails to make required payments on notes or bonds. A mortgage gives the lender a right to be paid from the cash proceeds of the sale of a borrower's assets identified in the mortgage. A legal document, called a *mortgage contract,* describes the mortgage terms.

Mortgage notes carry a mortgage contract pledging title to specific assets as security for the note. Mortgage notes are especially popular in the purchase of homes and the acquisition of plant assets. Less common *mortgage bonds* are backed by the issuer's assets. Accounting for mortgage notes and bonds is similar to that for unsecured notes and bonds, except that the mortgage agreement must be disclosed. For example, **TIBCO Software** reports that its "mortgage note payable ... is collateralized by the commercial real property acquired [corporate headquarters]."

Global: Countries vary in the preference given to debtholders vs. stockholders when a company is in financial distress. Some countries such as Germany, France, and Japan give preference to stockholders over debtholders.

Example: Suppose the $60,000 installment loan has an 8% interest rate with eight equal annual payments. What is the annual payment? *Answer* (using Table B.3): $60,000/5.7466 = $10,441

---

[2] Table B.3 in Appendix B is used to compute the dollar amount of the six payments that equal the initial note balance of $60,000 at 8% interest. We go to Table B.3, row 6, and across to the 8% column, where the present value factor is 4.6229. The dollar amount is then computed by solving this relation:

Table	Present Value Factor		Dollar Amount		Present Value
B.3	4.6229	×	?	=	$60,000

The dollar amount is computed by dividing $60,000 by 4.6229, yielding $12,979.

Decision Maker

Entrepreneur   You are a furniture retailer planning a Super Bowl sale on a home theater seating that requires no payments for two years. At the end of two years, buyers must pay the full amount. The system's suggested retail price is $4,100, but you are willing to sell it today for $3,000 cash. What is your sale price if payment will not occur for two years and the market interest rate is 10%? ■   [Answer—p. 581]

Quick Check   Answers — p. 581

11. Which of the following is true for an installment note requiring a series of equal total cash payments? (*a*) Payments consist of increasing interest and decreasing principal; (*b*) payments consist of changing amounts of principal but constant interest; or (*c*) payments consist of decreasing interest and increasing principal.

12. How is the interest portion of an installment note payment computed?

13. When a borrower records an interest payment on an installment note, how are the balance sheet and income statement affected?

 # GLOBAL VIEW

This section discusses similarities and differences between U.S. GAAP and IFRS in accounting and reporting for long-term liabilities such as bonds and notes.

Accounting for Bonds and Notes   The definitions and characteristics of bonds and notes are broadly similar for both U.S. GAAP and IFRS. Although slight differences exist, accounting for bonds and notes under U.S. GAAP and IFRS is similar. Specifically, the accounting for issuances (including recording discounts and premiums), market pricing, and retirement of both bonds and notes follows the procedures in this chapter. **Nokia** describes its accounting for bonds, which follows the amortized cost approach explained in this chapter (and in Appendix 14B), as follows: Loans payable [bonds] are recognized initially at fair value, net of transaction costs incurred. In the subsequent periods, they are stated at amortized cost.

NOKIA

Both U.S. GAAP and IFRS allow companies to account for bonds and notes using fair value (different from the amortized value described in this chapter). This method is referred to as the **fair value option.** This method is similar to that applied in measuring and accounting for debt and equity securities. *Fair value* is the amount a company would receive if it settled a liability (or sold an asset) in an orderly transaction as of the balance sheet date. Companies can use several sources of inputs to determine fair value, and those inputs fall into three classes (ranked in order of preference):

Level 1: Observable quoted market prices in active markets for identical items.
Level 2: Observable inputs other than those in Level 1 such as prices from inactive markets or from similar, but not identical, items.
Level 3: Unobservable inputs reflecting a company's assumptions about value.

The procedures for marking liabilities to fair value at each balance sheet date are in advanced courses.

Accounting for Leases and Pensions   Both U.S. GAAP and IFRS require companies to distinguish between operating leases and capital leases; the latter is referred to as *finance leases* under IFRS. The accounting and reporting for leases are broadly similar for both U.S. GAAP and IFRS. The main difference is the criteria for identifying a lease as a capital lease are more general under IFRS. However, the basic approach applies.

Point: Lease accounting is expected to change over the next year or so.

For pensions, both U.S. GAAP and IFRS require companies to record costs of retirement benefits as employees work and earn them. The basic methods are similar in accounting and reporting for pensions.

Decision Analysis Debt Features and the Debt-to-Equity Ratio

Collateral agreements can reduce the risk of loss for both bonds and notes. Unsecured bonds and notes are riskier because the issuer's obligation to pay interest and principal has the same priority as all other unsecured liabilities in the event of bankruptcy. If a company is unable to pay its debts in full, the unsecured creditors (including the holders of debentures) lose all or a portion of their balances. These types of legal agreements and other characteristics of long-term liabilities are crucial for effective business decisions. The first part of this section describes the different types of features sometimes included with bonds and notes. The second part explains and applies the debt-to-equity ratio.

Features of Bonds and Notes

A2 Assess debt features and their implications.

This section describes common features of debt securities.

Secured Debt

Unsecured Debt

Secured or Unsecured   **Secured bonds** (and notes) have specific assets of the issuer pledged (or *mortgaged*) as collateral. This arrangement gives holders added protection against the issuer's default. If the issuer fails to pay interest or par value, the secured holders can demand that the collateral be sold and the proceeds used to pay the obligation. **Unsecured bonds** (and notes), also called *debentures,* are backed by the issuer's general credit standing. Unsecured debt is riskier than secured debt. *Subordinated debentures* are liabilities that are not repaid until the claims of the more senior, unsecured (and secured) liabilities are settled.

Point: More than a million municipal bonds, or "munis," exist, and many are tax exempt. Munis are issued by state, city, town, and county governments to pay for public projects including schools, libraries, roads, bridges, and stadiums.

Term or Serial   **Term bonds** (and notes) are scheduled for maturity on one specified date. **Serial bonds** (and notes) mature at more than one date (often in series) and thus are usually repaid over a number of periods. For instance, $100,000 of serial bonds might mature at the rate of $10,000 each year from 6 to 15 years after they are issued. Many bonds are **sinking fund bonds,** which to reduce the holder's risk require the issuer to create a *sinking fund* of assets set aside at specified amounts and dates to repay the bonds.

Registered or Bearer   Bonds issued in the names and addresses of their holders are **registered bonds.** The issuer makes bond payments by sending checks (or cash transfers) to registered holders. A registered holder must notify the issuer of any ownership change. Registered bonds offer the issuer the practical advantage of not having to actually issue bond certificates. Bonds payable to whoever holds them (the *bearer*) are called **bearer bonds** or *unregistered bonds*. Sales or exchanges might not be recorded, so the holder of a bearer bond is presumed to be its rightful owner. As a result, lost bearer bonds are difficult to replace. Many bearer bonds are also **coupon bonds.** This term reflects interest coupons that are attached to the bonds. When each coupon matures, the holder presents it to a bank or broker for collection. At maturity, the holder follows the same process and presents the bond certificate for collection. Issuers of coupon bonds cannot deduct the related interest expense for taxable income. This is to prevent abuse by taxpayers who own coupon bonds but fail to report interest income on their tax returns.

Convertible Debt

Callable Debt

Convertible and/or Callable   **Convertible bonds** (and notes) can be exchanged for a fixed number of shares of the issuing corporation's common stock. Convertible debt offers holders the potential to participate in future increases in stock price. Holders still receive periodic interest while the debt is held and the par value if they hold the debt to maturity. In most cases, the holders decide whether and when to convert debt to stock. **Callable bonds** (and notes) have an option exercisable by the issuer to retire them at a stated dollar amount before maturity.

▌ Decision Insight ━━━━━━━━━━━━━━━━━━━━━━━━━━━━━

Collateral   Lenders prefer that more liquid assets serve as collateral for loans. These usually are current assets such as accounts receivable or inventory. The reason is if borrowers default and collateral must be seized, then lenders desire assets that are easily sold to recover losses. ▪

A3 Compute the debt-to-equity ratio and explain its use.

Debt-to-Equity Ratio

Beyond assessing different characteristics of debt as just described, we want to know the level of debt, especially in relation to total equity. Such knowledge helps us assess the risk of a company's financing structure. A company financed mainly with debt is more risky because liabilities must be repaid—usually with periodic interest—whereas equity financing does not. A measure to assess the risk of a company's financing structure is the **debt-to-equity ratio** (see Exhibit 14.15).

$$\text{Debt-to-equity} = \frac{\text{Total liabilities}}{\text{Total equity}}$$

EXHIBIT 14.15

Debt-to-Equity Ratio

The debt-to-equity ratio varies across companies and industries. Industries that are more variable and less stable tend to have lower ratios, while more stable industries tend to have higher ratios. To apply the debt-to-equity ratio, let's look at this measure for **Cedar Fair** in Exhibit 14.16.

($ millions)	2011	2010	2009	2008	2007
Total liabilities	$1,915,837	$1,945,308	$2,017.577	$2,079.297	$2,133.576
Total equity	$ 158.720	$ 137.136	$ 127.862	$ 106.786	$ 285.092
Debt-to-equity	**12.1**	**14.2**	**15.8**	**19.5**	**7.5**
Industry debt-to-equity	8.5	9.3	11.4	10.3	5.7

EXHIBIT 14.16

Cedar Fair's Debt-to-Equity Ratio

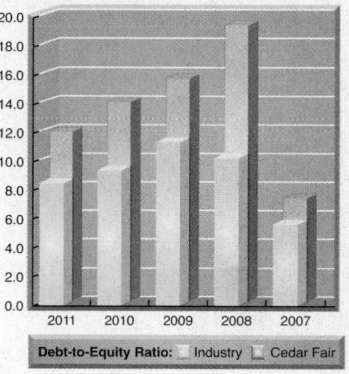

Cedar Fair's 2011 debt-to-equity ratio is 12.1, meaning that debtholders contributed $12.10 for each $1 contributed by equityholders. This implies a fairly risky financing structure for Cedar Fair. A similar concern is drawn from a comparison of Cedar Fair with its competitors, where the 2011 industry ratio is 8.5. Analysis across the years shows that Cedar Fair's financing structure has grown to a risky level in recent years. Given its sluggish revenues and increasing operating expenses in recent years (see its annual report), Cedar Fair is increasingly at risk of financial distress.

 Decision Maker ◄━━━━━━━━━━━━━━━━━━━━━━━━━━━

Bond Investor   You plan to purchase debenture bonds from one of two companies in the same industry that are similar in size and performance. The first company has $350,000 in total liabilities, and $1,750,000 in equity. The second company has $1,200,000 in total liabilities, and $1,000,000 in equity. Which company's debenture bonds are less risky based on the debt-to-equity ratio? ■   [Answer—p. 581]

DEMONSTRATION PROBLEM

Water Sports Company (WSC) patented and successfully test-marketed a new product. To expand its ability to produce and market the new product, WSC needs to raise $800,000 of financing. On January 1, 2013, the company obtained the money in two ways:

a. WSC signed a $400,000, 10% installment note to be repaid with five equal annual installments to be made on December 31 of 2013 through 2017.

b. WSC issued five-year bonds with a par value of $400,000. The bonds have a 12% annual contract rate and pay interest on June 30 and December 31. The bonds' annual market rate is 10% as of January 1, 2013.

Required

1. For the installment note, (*a*) compute the size of each annual payment, (*b*) prepare an amortization table such as Exhibit 14.14, and (*c*) prepare the journal entry for the first payment.

2. For the bonds, (*a*) compute their issue price; (*b*) prepare the January 1, 2013, journal entry to record their issuance; (*c*) prepare an amortization table using the straight-line method; (*d*) prepare the June 30, 2013, journal entry to record the first interest payment; and (*e*) prepare a journal entry to record retiring the bonds at a $416,000 call price on January 1, 2015.

3.[B] Redo parts 2(*c*), 2(*d*), and 2(*e*) assuming the bonds are amortized using the effective interest method.

PLANNING THE SOLUTION

- For the installment note, divide the borrowed amount by the annuity factor (from Table B.3) using the 10% rate and five payments to compute the amount of each payment. Prepare a table similar to Exhibit 14.14 and use the numbers in the table's first line for the journal entry.
- Compute the bonds' issue price by using the market rate to find the present value of their cash flows (use tables found in Appendix B). Then use this result to record the bonds' issuance. Next, prepare an amortization table like Exhibit 14.11 (and Exhibit 14B.11) and use it to get the numbers needed for the journal entry. Also use the table to find the carrying value as of the date of the bonds' retirement that you need for the journal entry.

SOLUTION TO DEMONSTRATION PROBLEM

Part 1: Installment Note

a. Annual payment = Note balance/Annuity factor = $400,000/3.7908 = $105,519 (The annuity factor is for five payments and a rate of 10%.)

b. An amortization table follows.

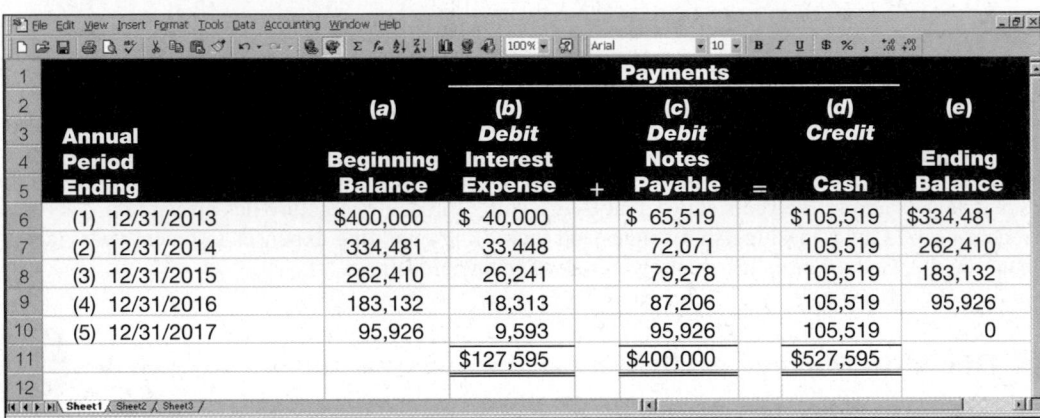

			Payments		
	(a)	**(b)**	**(c)**	**(d)**	**(e)**
Annual		**Debit**	**Debit**	**Credit**	
Period	**Beginning**	**Interest**	**Notes**		**Ending**
Ending	**Balance**	**Expense** +	**Payable** =	**Cash**	**Balance**
(1) 12/31/2013	$400,000	$ 40,000	$ 65,519	$105,519	$334,481
(2) 12/31/2014	334,481	33,448	72,071	105,519	262,410
(3) 12/31/2015	262,410	26,241	79,278	105,519	183,132
(4) 12/31/2016	183,132	18,313	87,206	105,519	95,926
(5) 12/31/2017	95,926	9,593	95,926	105,519	0
		$127,595	$400,000	$527,595	

c. Journal entry for December 31, 2013, payment.

Dec. 31	Interest Expense	40,000	
	Notes Payable	65,519	
	Cash		105,519
	To record first installment payment.		

Part 2: Bonds (Straight-Line Amortization)

a. Compute the bonds' issue price.

Cash Flow	Table	Present Value Factor*	Amount	Present Value
Par (maturity) value	B.1 in App. B (PV of 1)	0.6139	× 400,000	= $245,560
Interest payments	B.3 in App. B (PV of annuity)	7.7217	× 24,000	= 185,321
Price of bond				$430,881

* Present value factors are for 10 payments using a semiannual market rate of 5%.

b. Journal entry for January 1, 2013, issuance.

Jan. 1	Cash	430,881	
	Premium on Bonds Payable		30,881
	Bonds Payable		400,000
	Sold bonds at a premium.		

c. Straight-line amortization table for premium bonds.

Semiannual Period-End	Unamortized Premium	Carrying Value
(0) 1/1/2013	$30,881	$430,881
(1) 6/30/2013	27,793	427,793
(2) 12/31/2013	24,705	424,705
(3) 6/30/2014	21,617	421,617
(4) 12/31/2014	18,529	418,529
(5) 6/30/2015	15,441	415,441
(6) 12/31/2015	12,353	412,353
(7) 6/30/2016	9,265	409,265
(8) 12/31/2016	6,177	406,177
(9) 6/30/2017	3,089	403,089
(10) 12/31/2017	0*	400,000

* Adjusted for rounding.

d. Journal entry for June 30, 2013, bond payment.

June 30	Bond Interest Expense	20,912	
	Premium on Bonds Payable	3,088	
	Cash		24,000
	Paid semiannual interest on bonds.		

e. Journal entry for January 1, 2015, bond retirement.

Jan. 1	Bonds Payable	400,000	
	Premium on Bonds Payable	18,529	
	Cash		416,000
	Gain on Retirement of Bonds		2,529
	To record bond retirement (carrying value as of Dec. 31, 2014).		

Part 3: Bonds (Effective Interest Amortization)[B]

c. The effective interest amortization table for premium bonds.

	(A) Cash Interest Paid 6% × $400,000	(B) Interest Expense 5% × Prior (E)	(C) Premium Amortization (A) − (B)	(D) Unamortized Premium Prior (D) − (C)	(E) Carrying Value $400,000 + (D)
Semiannual Interest Period					
(0) 1/1/2013				$30,881	$430,881
(1) 6/30/2013	$ 24,000	$ 21,544	$ 2,456	28,425	428,425
(2) 12/31/2013	24,000	21,421	2,579	25,846	425,846
(3) 6/30/2014	24,000	21,292	2,708	23,138	423,138
(4) 12/31/2014	24,000	21,157	2,843	20,295	420,295
(5) 6/30/2015	24,000	21,015	2,985	17,310	417,310
(6) 12/31/2015	24,000	20,866	3,134	14,176	414,176
(7) 6/30/2016	24,000	20,709	3,291	10,885	410,885
(8) 12/31/2016	24,000	20,544	3,456	7,429	407,429
(9) 6/30/2017	24,000	20,371	3,629	3,800	403,800
(10) 12/31/2017	24,000	20,200*	3,800	0	400,000
	$240,000	$209,119	$30,881		

* Adjusted for rounding

d. Journal entry for June 30, 2013, bond payment.

June 30	Bond Interest Expense	21,544	
	Premium on Bonds Payable	2,456	
	Cash		24,000
	Paid semiannual interest on bonds.		

e. Journal entry for January 1, 2015, bond retirement.

Jan. 1	Bonds Payable	400,000	
	Premium on Bonds Payable	20,295	
	Cash		416,000
	Gain on Retirement of Bonds		4,295
	To record bond retirement (carrying value		
	as of December 31, 2014).		

APPENDIX

14A Present Values of Bonds and Notes

This appendix explains how to apply present value techniques to measure a long-term liability when it is created and to assign interest expense to the periods until it is settled. Appendix B at the end of the book provides additional discussion of present value concepts.

C2 Explain and compute the present value of an amount(s) to be paid at a future date(s).

Present Value Concepts   The basic present value concept is that cash paid (or received) in the future has less value now than the same amount of cash paid (or received) today. To illustrate, if we must pay $1 one year from now, its present value is less than $1. To see this, assume that we borrow $0.9259 today that must be paid back in one year with 8% interest. Our interest expense for this loan is computed as $0.9259 × 8%, or $0.0741. When the $0.0741 interest is added to the $0.9259 borrowed, we get the $1 payment necessary to repay our loan with interest. This is formally computed in Exhibit 14A.1. The $0.9259 borrowed is the present value of the $1 future payment. More generally, an amount borrowed equals the present value of the future payment. (This same interpretation applies to an investment. If $0.9259 is invested at 8%, it yields $0.0741 in revenue after one year. This amounts to $1, made up of principal and interest.)

EXHIBIT 14A.1

Components of a One-Year Loan

Amount borrowed	**$0.9259**
Interest for one year at 8%	0.0741
Amount owed after 1 year	$ 1.0000

Point: Benjamin Franklin is said to have described compounding as "the money, money makes, makes more money."

To extend this example, assume that we owe $1 two years from now instead of one year, and the 8% interest is compounded annually. *Compounded* means that interest during the second period is based on the total of the amount borrowed plus the interest accrued from the first period. The second period's interest is then computed as 8% multiplied by the sum of the amount borrowed plus interest earned in the first period. Exhibit 14A.2 shows how we compute the present value of $1 to be paid in two years. This amount is $0.8573. The first year's interest of $0.0686 is added to the principal so that the second year's interest is based on $0.9259. Total interest for this two-year period is $0.1427, computed as $0.0686 plus $0.0741.

EXHIBIT 14A.2

Components of a Two-Year Loan

Amount borrowed	**$0.8573**
Interest for first year ($0.8573 × 8%)	0.0686
Amount owed after 1 year	0.9259
Interest for second year ($0.9259 × 8%)	0.0741
Amount owed after 2 years	$ 1.0000

Present Value Tables   The present value of $1 that we must repay at some future date can be computed by using this formula: $1/(1 + i)^n$. The symbol i is the interest rate per period and n is the number of periods until the future payment must be made. Applying this formula to our two-year loan, we get $\$1/(1.08)^2$, or $0.8573. This is the same value shown in Exhibit 14A.2. We can use this formula to find any present value. However, a simpler method is to use a *present value table,* which lists present values computed with this formula for various interest rates and time periods. Many people find it helpful in learning present value concepts to first work with the table and then move to using a calculator.

Exhibit 14A.3 shows a present value table for a future payment of 1 for up to 10 periods at three different interest rates. Present values in this table are rounded to four decimal places. This table is drawn from the larger and more complete Table B.1 in Appendix B at the end of the book. Notice that the first value in the 8% column is 0.9259, the value we computed earlier for the present value of a $1 loan for one year at 8% (see Exhibit 14A.1). Go to the second row in the same 8% column and find the present value of 1 discounted at 8% for two years, or 0.8573. This $0.8573 is the present value of our obligation to repay $1 after two periods at 8% interest (see Exhibit 14A.2).

EXHIBIT 14A.3

Present Value of 1

Periods	Rate		
	6%	8%	10%
1	0.9434	**0.9259**	0.9091
2	0.8900	**0.8573**	0.8264
3	0.8396	0.7938	0.7513
4	0.7921	0.7350	0.6830
5	0.7473	0.6806	0.6209
6	0.7050	0.6302	0.5645
7	0.6651	0.5835	0.5132
8	0.6274	0.5403	0.4665
9	0.5919	0.5002	0.4241
10	0.5584	0.4632	0.3855

Example: Use Exhibit 14A.3 to find the present value of $1 discounted for 2 years at 6%. *Answer:* $0.8900

Applying a Present Value Table   To illustrate how to measure a liability using a present value table, assume that a company plans to borrow cash and repay it as follows: $2,000 after one year, $3,000 after two years, and $5,000 after three years. How much does this company receive today if the interest rate on this loan is 10%? To answer, we need to compute the present value of the three future payments, discounted at 10%. This computation is shown in Exhibit 14A.4 using present values from Exhibit 14A.3. The company can borrow $8,054 today at 10% interest in exchange for its promise to make these three payments at the scheduled dates.

EXHIBIT 14A.4

Present Value of a Series of Unequal Payments

Periods	Payments	Present Value of 1 at 10%	Present Value of Payments
1	$2,000	0.9091	$ 1,818
2	3,000	0.8264	2,479
3	5,000	0.7513	3,757
Present value of all payments			**$8,054**

Present Value of an Annuity   The $8,054 present value for the loan in Exhibit 14A.4 equals the sum of the present values of the three payments. When payments are not equal, their combined present value is best computed by adding the individual present values as shown in Exhibit 14A.4. Sometimes payments follow an **annuity,** which is a series of *equal* payments at equal time intervals. The present value of an annuity is readily computed.

To illustrate, assume that a company must repay a 6% loan with a $5,000 payment at each year-end for the next four years. This loan amount equals the present value of the four payments discounted at 6%. Exhibit 14A.5 shows how to compute this loan's present value of $17,326 by multiplying each payment by its matching present value factor taken from Exhibit 14A.3.

However, the series of $5,000 payments is an annuity, so we can compute its present value with either of two shortcuts. First, the third column of Exhibit 14A.5 shows that the sum of the present values of 1 at 6% for periods 1 through 4 equals 3.4651. One shortcut is to multiply this total of 3.4651 by the $5,000 annual payment to get the combined present value of $17,326. It requires one multiplication instead of four.

EXHIBIT 14A.5

Present Value of a Series of Equal Payments (Annuity) by Discounting Each Payment

Periods	Payments	Present Value of 1 at 6%	Present Value of Payments
1	$5,000	0.9434	$ 4,717
2	5,000	0.8900	4,450
3	5,000	0.8396	4,198
4	5,000	0.7921	3,961
Present value of all payments		**3.4651**	**$17,326**

EXHIBIT 14A.6

Present Value of an Annuity of 1

Periods	Rate		
	6%	8%	10%
1	0.9434	0.9259	0.9091
2	1.8334	1.7833	1.7355
3	2.6730	2.5771	2.4869
4	**3.4651**	3.3121	3.1699
5	4.2124	3.9927	3.7908
6	4.9173	4.6229	4.3553
7	5.5824	5.2064	4.8684
8	6.2098	5.7466	5.3349
9	6.8017	6.2469	5.7590
10	7.3601	6.7101	6.1446

Example: Use Exhibit 14A.6 to find the present value of an annuity of eight $15,000 payments with an 8% interest rate. *Answer:* $15,000 × 5.7466 = $86,199

Example: If this borrower makes five semiannual payments of $8,000, what is the present value of this annuity at a 12% rate? *Answer:* 4.2124 × $8,000 = $33,699

The second shortcut uses an *annuity table* such as the one shown in Exhibit 14A.6, which is drawn from the more complete Table B.3 in Appendix B. We go directly to the annuity table to get the present value factor for a specific number of payments and interest rate. We then multiply this factor by the amount of the payment to find the present value of the annuity. Specifically, find the row for four periods and go across to the 6% column, where the factor is 3.4651. This factor equals the present value of an annuity with four payments of 1, discounted at 6%. We then multiply 3.4651 by $5,000 to get the $17,326 present value of the annuity.

Compounding Periods Shorter Than a Year The present value examples all involved periods of one year. In many situations, however, interest is compounded over shorter periods. For example, the interest rate on bonds is usually stated as an annual rate but interest is often paid every six months (semiannually). This means that the present value of interest payments from such bonds must be computed using interest periods of six months.

Assume that a borrower wants to know the present value of a series of 10 *semiannual payments* of $4,000 made over five years at an *annual interest rate* of 12%. The interest rate is stated as an annual rate of 12%, but it is actually a rate of 6% per semiannual interest period. To compute the present value of this series of $4,000 payments, go to row 10 of Exhibit 14A.6 and across to the 6% column to find the factor 7.3601. The present value of this annuity is $29,440 (7.3601 × $4,000).

Appendix B further describes present value concepts and includes more complete present value tables and assignments.

Quick Check   Answers — p. 581

14. A company enters into an agreement to make four annual year-end payments of $1,000 each, starting one year from now. The annual interest rate is 8%. The present value of these four payments is (*a*) $2,923, (*b*) $2,940, or (*c*) $3,312.

15. Suppose a company has an option to pay either (*a*) $10,000 after one year or (*b*) $5,000 after six months and another $5,000 after one year. Which choice has the lower present value?

APPENDIX

14B

Effective Interest Amortization

P6 Appendix 14B—Compute and record amortization of bond discount using effective interest method.

Point: The effective interest method computes bond interest expense using the market rate at issuance. This rate is applied to a changing carrying value.

Effective Interest Amortization of a Discount Bond   The straight-line method yields changes in the bonds' carrying value while the amount for bond interest expense remains constant. This gives the impression of a changing interest rate when users divide a constant bond interest expense over a changing carrying value. As a result, accounting standards allow use of the straight-line method only when its results do not differ materially from those obtained using the effective interest method. The **effective interest method,** or simply *interest method,* allocates total bond interest expense over the bonds' life in a way that yields a constant rate of interest. This constant rate of interest is the market rate at the issue date. Thus, bond interest expense for a period equals the carrying value of the bond at the beginning of that period multiplied by the market rate when issued.

Exhibit 14B.1 shows an effective interest amortization table for the Fila bonds (as described in Exhibit 14.4). The key difference between the effective interest and straight-line methods lies in computing bond interest expense. Instead of assigning an equal amount of bond interest expense to each period, the effective interest method assigns a bond interest expense amount that increases over the life of a discount bond. **Both methods allocate the** *same* **$19,546 of total bond interest expense to the bonds' life, but in different patterns.** Specifically, the amortization table in Exhibit 14B.1 shows that the balance of the discount (column D) is amortized until it reaches zero. Also, the bonds' carrying value (column E) changes each period until it equals par value at maturity. Compare columns D and E to the corresponding columns in Exhibit 14.7 to see the amortization patterns. Total bond interest expense is $19,546, consisting of $16,000 of semiannual cash payments and $3,546 of the original bond discount, the same for both methods.

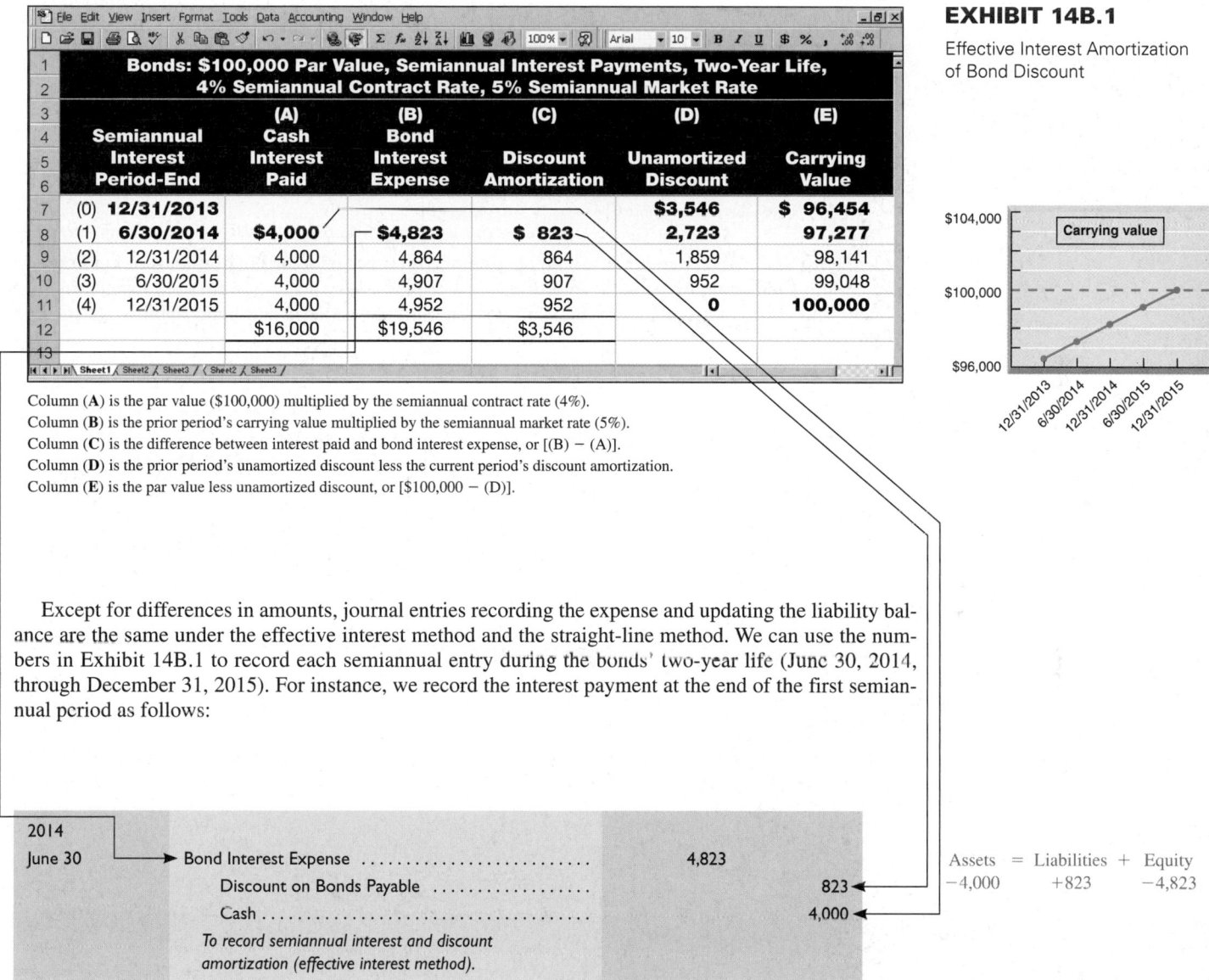

EXHIBIT 14B.1

Effective Interest Amortization of Bond Discount

File Edit View Insert Format Tools Data Accounting Window Help

Bonds: $100,000 Par Value, Semiannual Interest Payments, Two-Year Life, 4% Semiannual Contract Rate, 5% Semiannual Market Rate

Semiannual Interest Period-End	(A) Cash Interest Paid	(B) Bond Interest Expense	(C) Discount Amortization	(D) Unamortized Discount	(E) Carrying Value
(0) 12/31/2013				$3,546	$ 96,454
(1) 6/30/2014	$4,000	$4,823	$ 823	2,723	97,277
(2) 12/31/2014	4,000	4,864	864	1,859	98,141
(3) 6/30/2015	4,000	4,907	907	952	99,048
(4) 12/31/2015	4,000	4,952	952	0	100,000
	$16,000	$19,546	$3,546		

Column (**A**) is the par value ($100,000) multiplied by the semiannual contract rate (4%).
Column (**B**) is the prior period's carrying value multiplied by the semiannual market rate (5%).
Column (**C**) is the difference between interest paid and bond interest expense, or [(B) − (A)].
Column (**D**) is the prior period's unamortized discount less the current period's discount amortization.
Column (**E**) is the par value less unamortized discount, or [$100,000 − (D)].

Except for differences in amounts, journal entries recording the expense and updating the liability balance are the same under the effective interest method and the straight-line method. We can use the numbers in Exhibit 14B.1 to record each semiannual entry during the bonds' two-year life (June 30, 2014, through December 31, 2015). For instance, we record the interest payment at the end of the first semiannual period as follows:

2014			
June 30	Bond Interest Expense	4,823	
	Discount on Bonds Payable		823
	Cash		4,000
	To record semiannual interest and discount amortization (effective interest method).		

Assets = Liabilities + Equity
−4,000   +823   −4,823

Effective Interest Amortization of a Premium Bond   Exhibit 14B.2 shows the amortization table using the effective interest method for the Adidas bonds (as described in Exhibit 14.8). Column A lists the semiannual cash payments. Column B shows the amount of bond interest expense, computed as the 5% semiannual market rate at issuance multiplied by the beginning-of-period carrying value. The amount of cash paid in column A is larger than the bond interest expense because the cash payment is based on the higher 6% semiannual contract rate. The excess cash payment over the interest expense reduces the principal. These amounts are shown in column C. Column E shows the carrying value after

P7 *Appendix 14B*—Compute and record amortization of bond premium using effective interest method.

EXHIBIT 14B.2

Effective Interest Amortization
of Bond Premium

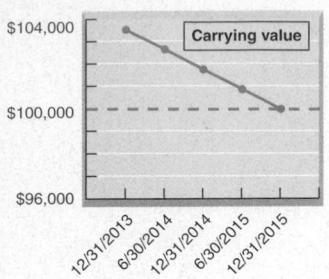

	Bonds: $100,000 Par Value, Semiannual Interest Payments, Two-Year Life, 6% Semiannual Contract Rate, 5% Semiannual Market Rate					
	Semiannual Interest Period-End	**(A) Cash Interest Paid**	**(B) Bond Interest Expense**	**(C) Premium Amortization**	**(D) Unamortized Premium**	**(E) Carrying Value**
(0) 12/31/2013					$3,546	$103,546
(1) 6/30/2014	$6,000	$5,177	$ 823	2,723	102,723
(2) 12/31/2014	6,000	5,136	864	1,859	101,859
(3) 6/30/2015	6,000	5,093	907	952	100,952
(4) 12/31/2015	6,000	5,048	952	0	100,000
	$24,000	$20,454	$3,546		

Column (**A**) is the par value ($100,000) multiplied by the semiannual contract rate (6%).
Column (**B**) is the prior period's carrying value multiplied by the semiannual market rate (5%).
Column (**C**) is the difference between interest paid and bond interest expense, or [(A) − (B)].
Column (**D**) is the prior period's unamortized premium less the current period's premium amortization.
Column (**E**) is the par value plus unamortized premium, or [$100,000 + (D)].

deducting the amortized premium in column C from the prior period's carrying value. Column D shows the premium's reduction by periodic amortization. When the issuer makes the first semiannual interest payment, the effect of premium amortization on bond interest expense and bond liability is recorded as follows:

Assets = Liabilities + Equity
−6,000   −823   −5,177

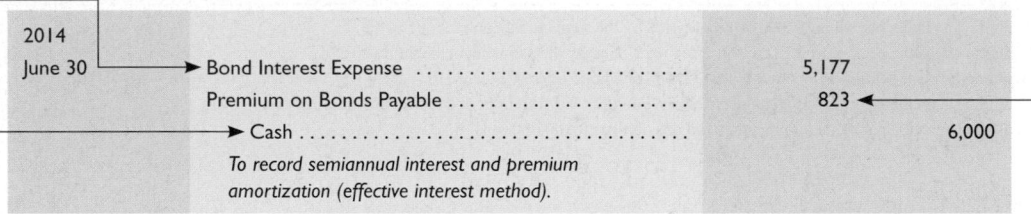

2014 June 30	Bond Interest Expense	5,177	
	Premium on Bonds Payable	823	
	Cash		6,000
	To record semiannual interest and premium amortization (effective interest method).		

Similar entries with different amounts are recorded at each payment date until the bond matures at the end of 2015. The effective interest method yields decreasing amounts of bond interest expense and increasing amounts of premium amortization over the bonds' life.

IFRS

Unlike U.S. GAAP, IFRS requires that interest expense be computed using the effective interest method with *no exemptions*. ∎

APPENDIX

14C

Issuing Bonds between Interest Dates

C3 Describe interest accrual when bond payment periods differ from accounting periods.

An issuer can sell bonds at a date other than an interest payment date. When this occurs, the buyers normally pay the issuer the purchase price plus any interest accrued since the prior interest payment date. This accrued interest is then repaid to these buyers on the next interest payment date. To illustrate, suppose **Avia** sells $100,000 of its 9% bonds at par on March 1, 2013, 60 days after the stated issue date. The interest on Avia bonds is payable semiannually on each June 30 and December 31. Since 60 days have passed, the issuer collects accrued interest from the buyers at the time of issuance. This amount is $1,500 ($100,000 × 9% × $^{60}/_{360}$ year). This case is reflected in Exhibit 14C.1.

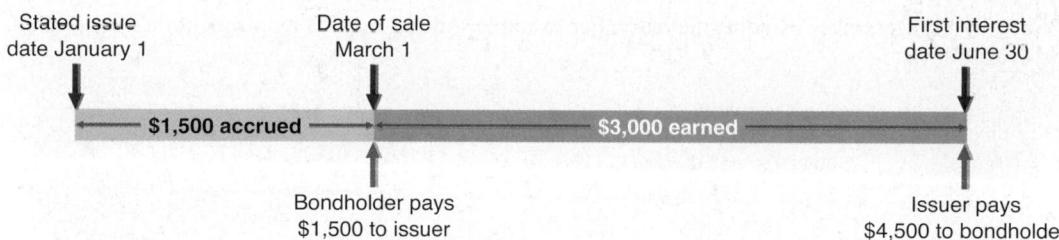

Avia records the issuance of these bonds on March 1, 2013, as follows:

Mar. I	Cash	101,500	
	Interest Payable		1,500
	Bonds Payable..............................		100,000
	Sold bonds at par with accrued interest.		

Assets   =   Liabilities + Equity
+101,500   +100,000
              +1,500

Liabilities for interest payable and bonds payable are recorded in separate accounts. When the June 30, 2013, semiannual interest date arrives, Avia pays the full semiannual interest of $4,500 ($100,000 × 9% × ½ year) to the bondholders. This payment includes the four months' interest of $3,000 earned by the bondholders from March 1 to June 30 *plus* the repayment of the 60 days' accrued interest collected by Avia when the bonds were sold. Avia records this first semiannual interest payment as follows:

Example: How much interest is collected from a buyer of $50,000 of Avia bonds sold at par 150 days after the contract issue date? *Answer:* $1,875 (computed as $50,000 × 9% × $^{150}/_{360}$ year)

June 30	Interest Payable	1,500	
	Bond Interest Expense.........................	3,000	
	Cash		4,500
	Paid semiannual interest on the bonds.		

Assets = Liabilities + Equity
−4,500   −1,500   −3,000

The practice of collecting and then repaying accrued interest with the next interest payment is to simplify the issuer's administrative efforts. To explain, suppose an issuer sells bonds on 15 or 20 different dates between the stated issue date and the first interest payment date. If the issuer does not collect accrued interest from buyers, it needs to pay different amounts of cash to each of them according to the time that passed after purchasing the bonds. The issuer needs to keep detailed records of buyers and the dates they bought bonds. Issuers avoid this recordkeeping by having each buyer pay accrued interest at purchase. Issuers then pay the full semiannual interest to all buyers, regardless of when they bought bonds.

Accruing Bond Interest Expense   If a bond's interest period does not coincide with the issuer's accounting period, an adjusting entry is needed to recognize bond interest expense accrued since the most recent interest payment. To illustrate, assume that the stated issue date for Adidas bonds described in Exhibit 14.10 is September 1, 2013, instead of December 31, 2013, and that the bonds are sold on September 1, 2013. As a result, four months' interest (and premium amortization) accrue before the end of the 2013 calendar year. Interest for this period equals $3,409, or ⅔ of the first six months' interest of $5,113. Also, the premium amortization is $591, or ⅔ of the first six months' amortization of $887. The sum of the bond interest expense and the amortization is $4,000 ($3,409 + $591), which equals ⅔ of the $6,000 cash payment due on February 28, 2014. Adidas records these effects with an adjusting entry at December 31, 2013.

Point: Computation of accrued bond interest may use months instead of days for simplicity purposes. For example, the accrued interest computation for the Adidas bonds is based on months.

Dec. 31	Bond Interest Expense	3,409	
	Premium on Bonds Payable	591	
	Interest Payable		4,000
	To record four months' accrued interest and		
	premium amortization.		

Assets = Liabilities + Equity
              −591   −3,409
              +4,000

Similar entries are made on each December 31 throughout the bonds' two-year life. When the $6,000 cash payment occurs on each February 28 interest payment date, Adidas must recognize bond interest expense and amortization for January and February. It must also eliminate the interest payable liability created by the December 31 adjusting entry. For example, Adidas records its payment on February 28, 2014, as follows:

Assets = Liabilities + Equity
−6,000   −4,000   −1,704
          −296

Feb. 28	Interest Payable	4,000	
	Bond Interest Expense ($5,113 × ⅔)	1,704	
	Premium on Bonds Payable ($887 × ⅔)	296	
	Cash		6,000
	To record 2 months' interest and amortization, and		
	eliminate accrued interest liability.		

The interest payments made each August 31 are recorded as usual because the entire six-month interest period is included within this company's calendar-year reporting period.

Decision Maker

Bond Rater   You work for **Moody's** rating service and its your job to assist in assigning a rating to a bond that reflects its risk to bondholders. Identify factors you consider in assessing bond risk. Indicate the likely levels (relative to the norm) for the factors you identify for a bond that sells at a discount. ■   [Answer—p. 581]

Quick Check   Answer — p. 581

16. On May 1, a company sells 9% bonds with a $500,000 par value that pay semiannual interest on each January 1 and July 1. The bonds are sold at par plus interest accrued since January 1. The issuer records the first semiannual interest payment on July 1 with (*a*) a debit to Interest Payable for $15,000, (*b*) a debit to Bond Interest Expense for $22,500, or (*c*) a credit to Interest Payable for $7,500.

APPENDIX

14D   Leases and Pensions

This appendix briefly explains the accounting and analysis for both leases and pensions.

C4 Describe accounting for leases and pensions.

Lease Liabilities   A **lease** is a contractual agreement between a *lessor* (asset owner) and a *lessee* (asset renter or tenant) that grants the lessee the right to use the asset for a period of time in return for cash (rent) payments. Nearly one-fourth of all equipment purchases are financed with leases. The advantages of lease financing include the lack of an immediate large cash payment and the potential to deduct rental payments in computing taxable income. From an accounting perspective, leases can be classified as either operating or capital leases. (Lease accounting will change over the next few years, whereby operating leases are likely to be accounted for similar to capital leases . . . stay tuned!)

Point: Home Depot reports that its rental expenses from operating leases total more than $900 million.

Operating Leases   **Operating leases** are short-term (or cancelable) leases in which the lessor retains the risks and rewards of ownership. Examples include most car and apartment rental agreements. The lessee records such lease payments as expenses; the lessor records them as revenue. The lessee does not report the leased item as an asset or a liability (it is the lessor's asset). To illustrate, if an employee of Amazon leases a car for $300 at an airport while on company business, Amazon (lessee) records this cost as follows:

Assets = Liabilities + Equity
−300   −300

July 4	Rental Expense	300	
	Cash		300
	To record lease rental payment.		

Capital Leases   **Capital leases** are long-term (or noncancelable) leases by which the lessor transfers substantially all risks and rewards of ownership to the lessee.[3] Examples include most leases of airplanes and department store buildings. The lessee records the leased item as its own asset along with a lease liability at the start of the lease term; the amount recorded equals the present value of all lease payments. To illustrate, assume that K2 Co. enters into a six-year lease of a building in which it will sell sporting equipment. The lease transfers all building ownership risks and rewards to K2 (the present value of its $12,979 annual lease payments is $60,000). K2 records this transaction as follows:

2013			
Jan. 1	Leased Asset—Building	60,000	
	Lease Liability		60,000
	To record leased asset and lease liability.		

Assets = Liabilities + Equity
+60,000   +60,000

K2 reports the leased asset as a plant asset and the lease liability as a long-term liability. The portion of the lease liability expected to be paid in the next year is reported as a current liability.[4] At each year-end, K2 records depreciation on the leased asset (assume straight-line depreciation, six-year lease term, and no salvage value) as follows:

Point: Home Depot reports *"certain locations ... are leased under capital leases."* The net present value of this Lease Liability is about $400 million.

Dec. 31	Depreciation Expense—Building	10,000	
	Accumulated Depreciation—Building		10,000
	To record depreciation on leased asset.		

Assets = Liabilities + Equity
−10,000   −10,000

K2 also accrues interest on the lease liability at each year-end. Interest expense is computed by multiplying the remaining lease liability by the interest rate on the lease. Specifically, K2 records its annual interest expense as part of its annual lease payment ($12,979) as follows (for its first year):

2013			
Dec. 31	Interest Expense	4,800	
	Lease Liability	8,179	
	Cash		12,979
	*To record first annual lease payment.**		

Assets = Liabilities + Equity
−12,979   −8,179   −4,800

* These numbers are computed from a *lease payment schedule*. For simplicity, we use the same numbers from Exhibit 14.14 for this lease payment schedule—with different headings as follows:

			Payments		
	(A)	(B) Debit	(C) Debit	(D) Credit	(E)
Period Ending Date	Beginning Balance of Lease Liability	Interest on Lease Liability 8% × (A)	+ Lease Liability (D) − (B)	= Cash Lease Payment	Ending Balance of Lease Liability (A) − (C)
12/31/2013	$60,000	$ 4,800	$ 8,179	$12,979	$51,821
12/31/2014	51,821	4,146	8,833	12,979	42,988
12/31/2015	42,988	3,439	9,540	12,979	33,448
12/31/2016	33,448	2,676	10,303	12,979	23,145
12/31/2017	23,145	1,852	11,127	12,979	12,018
12/31/2018	12,018	961	12,018	12,979	0
		$17,874	$60,000	$77,874	

[3] A *capital lease* meets any one or more of four criteria: (1) transfers title of leased asset to lessee, (2) contains a bargain purchase option, (3) has a lease term that is 75% or more of the leased asset's useful life, or (4) has a present value of lease payments that is 90% or more of the leased asset's market value.

[4] Most lessees try to keep leased assets and lease liabilities off their balance sheets by failing to meet any one of the four criteria of a capital lease. This is because a lease liability increases a company's total liabilities, making it more difficult to obtain additional financing. The acquisition of assets without reporting any related liabilities (or other asset outflows) on the balance sheet is called **off-balance-sheet financing.**

Pension Liabilities   A **pension plan** is a contractual agreement between an employer and its employees for the employer to provide benefits (payments) to employees after they retire. Most employers pay the full cost of the pension, but sometimes employees pay part of the cost. An employer records its payment into a pension plan with a debit to Pension Expense and a credit to Cash. A *plan administrator* receives payments from the employer, invests them in pension assets, and makes benefit payments to *pension recipients* (retired employees). Insurance and trust companies often serve as pension plan administrators.

Many pensions are known as *defined benefit plans* that define future benefits; the employer's contributions vary, depending on assumptions about future pension assets and liabilities. Several disclosures are necessary in this case. Specifically, a pension liability is reported when the accumulated benefit obligation is *more than* the plan assets, a so-called *underfunded plan*. The accumulated benefit obligation is the present value of promised future pension payments to retirees. *Plan assets* refer to the market value of assets the plan administrator holds. A pension asset is reported when the accumulated benefit obligation is *less than* the plan assets, a so-called *overfunded plan*. An employer reports pension expense when it receives the benefits from the employees' services, which is sometimes decades before it pays pension benefits to employees. (*Other Postretirement Benefits* refer to nonpension benefits such as health care and life insurance benefits. Similar to a pension, costs of these benefits are estimated and liabilities accrued when the employees earn them.)

Summary

C1   **Explain the types and payment patterns of notes.** Notes repaid over a period of time are called *installment notes* and usually follow one of two payment patterns: (1) decreasing payments of interest plus equal amounts of principal or (2) equal total payments. Mortgage notes also are common.

C2ᴬ   **Explain and compute the present value of an amount(s) to be paid at a future date(s).** The basic concept of present value is that an amount of cash to be paid or received in the future is worth less than the same amount of cash to be paid or received today. Another important present value concept is that interest is compounded, meaning interest is added to the balance and used to determine interest for succeeding periods. An annuity is a series of equal payments occurring at equal time intervals. An annuity's present value can be computed using the present value table for an annuity (or a calculator).

C3ᶜ   **Describe interest accrual when bond payment periods differ from accounting periods.** Issuers and buyers of debt record the interest accrued when issue dates or accounting periods do not coincide with debt payment dates.

C4ᴰ   **Describe accounting for leases and pensions.** A lease is a rental agreement between the lessor and the lessee. When the lessor retains the risks and rewards of asset ownership (an *operating lease*), the lessee debits Rent Expense and credits Cash for its lease payments. When the lessor substantially transfers the risks and rewards of asset ownership to the lessee (a *capital lease*), the lessee capitalizes the leased asset and records a lease liability. Pension agreements can result in either pension assets or pension liabilities.

A1   **Compare bond financing with stock financing.** Bond financing is used to fund business activities. Advantages of bond financing versus stock include (1) no effect on owner control, (2) tax savings, and (3) increased earnings due to financial leverage. Disadvantages include (1) interest and principal payments and (2) amplification of poor performance.

A2   **Assess debt features and their implications.** Certain bonds are secured by the issuer's assets; other bonds, called *debentures,* are unsecured. Serial bonds mature at different points in time;

term bonds mature at one time. Registered bonds have each bondholder's name recorded by the issuer; bearer bonds are payable to the holder. Convertible bonds are exchangeable for shares of the issuer's stock. Callable bonds can be retired by the issuer at a set price. Debt features alter the risk of loss for creditors.

A3   **Compute the debt-to-equity ratio and explain its use.** Both creditors and equity holders are concerned about the relation between the amount of liabilities and the amount of equity. A company's financing structure is at less risk when the debt-to-equity ratio is lower, as liabilities must be paid and usually with periodic interest.

P1   **Prepare entries to record bond issuance and interest expense.** When bonds are issued at par, Cash is debited and Bonds Payable is credited for the bonds' par value. At bond interest payment dates (usually semiannual), Bond Interest Expense is debited and Cash credited—the latter for an amount equal to the bond par value multiplied by the bond contract rate.

P2   **Compute and record amortization of bond discount using straight-line method.** Bonds are issued at a discount when the contract rate is less than the market rate, making the issue (selling) price less than par. When this occurs, the issuer records a credit to Bonds Payable (at par) and debits both Discount on Bonds Payable and Cash. The amount of bond interest expense assigned to each period is computed using the straight-line method.

P3   **Compute and record amortization of bond premium using straight-line method.** Bonds are issued at a premium when the contract rate is higher than the market rate, making the issue (selling) price greater than par. When this occurs, the issuer records a debit to Cash and credits both Premium on Bonds Payable and Bonds Payable (at par). The amount of bond interest expense assigned to each period is computed using the straight-line method. The Premium on Bonds Payable is allocated to reduce bond interest expense over the life of the bonds.

P4   **Record the retirement of bonds.** Bonds are retired at maturity with a debit to Bonds Payable and a credit to Cash at par value. The issuer can retire the bonds early by exercising a call option or purchasing them in the market. Bondholders can also re-tire bonds early by exercising a conversion feature on convertible bonds. The issuer recognizes a gain or loss for the difference be-tween the amount paid and the bond carrying value.

P5 **Prepare entries to account for notes.** Interest is allocated to each period in a note's life by multiplying its beginning-period carrying value by its market rate at issuance. If a note is repaid with equal payments, the payment amount is computed by dividing the borrowed amount by the present value of an annuity factor (taken from a present value table) using the market rate and the number of payments.

P6[B] **Compute and record amortization of bond discount using effective interest method.** Bonds are issued at a discount

when the contract rate is less than the market rate, making the issue (selling) price less than par. The amount of bond interest expense assigned to each period, including amortization of the discount, is computed using the effective interest method.

P7[B] **Compute and record amortization of bond premium using effective interest method.** Bonds are issued at a premium when the contract rate is higher than the market rate, making the issue (selling) price greater than par. The amount of bond interest expense assigned to each period, including amortization of the premium, is computed using the effective interest method.

Guidance Answers to Decision Maker

Entrepreneur This is a "present value" question. The market interest rate (10%) and present value ($3,000) are known, but the payment required two years later is unknown. This amount ($3,630) can be computed as $3,000 × 1.10 × 1.10. Thus, the sale price is $3,630 when no payments are received for two years. The $3,630 received two years from today is equivalent to $3,000 cash today.

Bond Investor The debt-to-equity ratio for the first company is 0.2 ($350,000/$1,750,000) and for the second company is 1.2 ($1,200,000/$1,000,000), suggesting that the financing structure of

the second company is more risky than that of the first company. Consequently, as a buyer of unsecured debenture bonds, you prefer the first company (all else equal).

Bond Rater Bonds with longer repayment periods (life) have higher risk. Also, bonds issued by companies in financial difficulties or facing higher than normal uncertainties have higher risk. More-over, companies with higher than normal debt and large fluctuations in earnings are considered of higher risk. Discount bonds are more risky on one or more of these factors.

Guidance Answers to Quick Checks

1.

2013			
Jan. 1	Cash	10,000	
	Bonds Payable		10,000
June 30	Bond Interest Expense	450	
	Cash		450

2. Multiply the bond's par value by its contract rate of interest.

3. Bonds sell at a premium when the contract rate exceeds the market rate and the purchasers pay more than their par value.

4. The bonds are issued at a discount, meaning that issue price is less than par value. A discount occurs because the bond contract rate (6%) is less than the market rate (8%).

5.

Cash	91,893	
Discount on Bonds Payable	8,107	
Bonds Payable		100,000

6. $3,811 (total bond interest expense of $38,107 divided by 10 periods; or the $3,000 semiannual cash payment plus the $8,107 discount divided by 10 periods).

7. The bonds are issued at a premium, meaning issue price is higher than par value. A premium occurs because the bonds' contract rate (16%) is higher than the market rate (14%).

8. (b) For each semiannual period: $10,592/20 periods = $530 premium amortization.

9.

Bonds payable, 16%, due 12/31/2022	$100,000	
Plus premium on bonds payable	9,532*	$109,532

* Original premium balance of $10,592 less $530 and $530 amortized on 6/30/2013 and 12/31/2013, respectively.

10. $9,375 loss, computed as the difference between the repurchase price of $256,250 [50% of ($500,000 × 102.5%)] and the carrying value of $246,875 (50% of $493,750).

11. (c)

12. The interest portion of an installment payment equals the period's beginning loan balance multiplied by the market interest rate at the time of the note's issuance.

13. On the balance sheet, the account balances of the related liability (note payable) and asset (cash) accounts are decreased. On the income statement, interest expense is recorded.

14. (c), computed as 3.3121 × $1,000 = $3,312.

15. The option of paying $10,000 after one year has a lower present value. It postpones paying the first $5,000 by six months. More generally, the present value of a further delayed payment is always lower than a less delayed payment.

16. (a) Reflects payment of accrued interest recorded back on May 1; $500,000 × 9% × 4/12 = $15,000.

Key Terms

Annuity (p. 573)	Debt-to-equity ratio (p. 569)	Pension plan (p. 580)
Bearer bonds (p. 568)	Discount on bonds payable (p. 557)	Premium on bonds (p. 560)
Bond (p. 554)	Effective interest method (p. 574)	Registered bonds (p. 568)
Bond certificate (p. 556)	Fair value option (p. 567)	Secured bonds (p. 568)
Bond indenture (p. 556)	Installment note (p. 565)	Serial bonds (p. 568)
Callable bonds (p. 568)	Lease (p. 578)	Sinking fund bonds (p. 568)
Capital leases (p. 579)	Market rate (p. 557)	Straight-line bond amortization (p. 558)
Carrying (book) value of bonds (p. 558)	Mortgage (p. 566)	Term bonds (p. 568)
Contract rate (p. 557)	Off-balance-sheet financing (p. 579)	Unsecured bonds (p. 568)
Convertible bonds (p. 568)	Operating leases (p. 578)	
Coupon bonds (p. 568)	Par value of a bond (p. 554)	

Multiple Choice Quiz   Answers on p. 595   mhhe.com/wildFAP21e

Additional Quiz Questions are available at the book's Website.

1. A bond traded at 97½ means that
  a. The bond pays 97½% interest.
  b. The bond trades at $975 per $1,000 bond.
  c. The market rate of interest is below the contract rate of interest for the bond.
  d. The bonds can be retired at $975 each.
  e. The bond's interest rate is 2½%.

2. A bondholder that owns a $1,000, 6%, 15-year bond has
  a. The right to receive $1,000 at maturity.
  b. Ownership rights in the bond issuing entity.
  c. The right to receive $60 per month until maturity.
  d. The right to receive $1,900 at maturity.
  e. The right to receive $600 per year until maturity.

3. A company issues 8%, 20-year bonds with a par value of $500,000. The current market rate for the bonds is 8%. The amount of interest owed to the bondholders for each semiannual interest payment is
  a. $40,000.
  b. $0.
  c. $20,000.

  d. $800,000.
  e. $400,000.

4. A company issued 5-year, 5% bonds with a par value of $100,000. The company received $95,735 for the bonds. Using the straight-line method, the company's interest expense for the first semiannual interest period is
  a. $2,926.50.
  b. $5,853.00.
  c. $2,500.00.
  d. $5,000.00.
  e. $9,573.50.

5. A company issued 8-year, 5% bonds with a par value of $350,000. The company received proceeds of $373,745. Interest is payable semiannually. The amount of premium amortized for the first semiannual interest period, assuming straight-line bond amortization, is
  a. $2,698.
  b. $23,745.
  c. $8,750.
  d. $9,344.
  e. $1,484.

B(C,D) *Superscript letter B(C, D) denotes assignments based on Appendix 14B (14C, 14D).*
  Icon denotes assignments that involve decision making.

Discussion Questions

1. What is the main difference between notes payable and bonds payable?

2. What is the main difference between a bond and a share of stock?

3.   What is the advantage of issuing bonds instead of obtaining financing from the company's owners?

4. What is a bond indenture? What provisions are usually included in it?

5. What are the duties of a trustee for bondholders?

6. What are the *contract* rate and the *market* rate for bonds?

7.   What factors affect the market rates for bonds?

8.^B   Does the straight-line or effective interest method produce an interest expense allocation that yields a constant rate of interest over a bond's life? Explain.

9.^C Why does a company that issues bonds between interest dates collect accrued interest from the bonds' purchasers?

10. 🔲 If you know the par value of bonds, the contract rate, and the market rate, how do you compute the bonds' price?

11. What is the issue price of a $2,000 bond sold at 98¼? What is the issue price of a $6,000 bond sold at 101½?

12. Describe the debt-to-equity ratio and explain how creditors and owners would use this ratio to evaluate a company's risk.

13. 🔲 What obligation does an entrepreneur (owner) have to investors that purchase bonds to finance the business?

14. Refer to **Polaris'** annual report in Appendix A. Is there any indication that Polaris has issued long-term debt? **Polaris**

15. By what amount did **KTM**'s long-term interest-bearing loans increase or decrease in 2011? **KTM**

16. Refer to the statement of cash flows for **Piaggio** in Appendix A. For the year ended December 31, 2011, what was the amount for repayment of bank loans? **PIAGGIO**

17. Refer to the statements for **Arctic Cat** in Appendix A. For the year ended March 31, 2011, what is its debt-to-equity ratio? What does this ratio tell us? Arctic Cat

18.^D When can a lease create both an asset and a liability for the lessee?

19.^D Compare and contrast an operating lease with a capital lease.

20.^D Describe the two basic types of pension plans.

Ⓜ connect

| Round dollar amounts to the nearest whole dollar. |

QUICK STUDY

Enviro Company issues 8%, 10-year bonds with a par value of $250,000 and semiannual interest payments. On the issue date, the annual market rate for these bonds is 10%, which implies a selling price of 87½. The straight-line method is used to allocate interest expense.

1. What are the issuer's cash proceeds from issuance of these bonds?

2. What total amount of bond interest expense will be recognized over the life of these bonds?

3. What is the amount of bond interest expense recorded on the first interest payment date?

QS 14-1
Straight-Line: Bond computations
P1 P2

Garcia Company issues 10%, 15-year bonds with a par value of $240,000 and semiannual interest payments. On the issue date, the annual market rate for these bonds is 8%, which implies a selling price of 117¼. The effective interest method is used to allocate interest expense.

1. What are the issuer's cash proceeds from issuance of these bonds?

2. What total amount of bond interest expense will be recognized over the life of these bonds?

3. What amount of bond interest expense is recorded on the first interest payment date?

QS 14-2^B
Effective Interest: Bond computations
P1 P7

Prepare the journal entries for the issuance of the bonds in both QS 14-1 and QS 14-2. Assume that both bonds are issued for cash on January 1, 2013.

QS 14-3
Journalize bond issuance   P1

Using the bond details in both QS 14-1 and QS 14-2, confirm that the bonds' selling prices given in each problem are approximately correct (within $100 of each other). Use the present value tables B.1 and B.3 in Appendix B.

QS 14-4
Computing bond price   P1

Sylvestor Company issues 10%, five-year bonds, on December 31, 2012, with a par value of $100,000 and semiannual interest payments. Use the following bond amortization table and prepare journal entries to record (*a*) the issuance of bonds on December 31, 2012; (*b*) the first interest payment on June 30, 2013; and (*c*) the second interest payment on December 31, 2013.

QS 14-5
Recording bond issuance and discount amortization   P1 P2

Semiannual Period-End	Unamortized Discount	Carrying Value
(0) 12/31/2012	$7,360	$92,640
(1) 6/30/2013	6,624	93,376
(2) 12/31/2013	5,888	94,112

On July 1, 2013, Advocate Company exercises a $8,000 call option (plus par value) on its outstanding bonds that have a carrying value of $416,000 and par value of $400,000. The company exercises the call option after the semiannual interest is paid on June 30, 2013. Record the entry to retire the bonds.

QS 14-6
Bond retirement by call option
P4

On January 1, 2013, the $2,000,000 par value bonds of Spitz Company with a carrying value of $2,000,000 are converted to 1,000,000 shares of $1.00 par value common stock. Record the entry for the conversion of the bonds.

QS 14-7
Bond retirement by stock conversion   P4

QS 14-8
Bond features and terminology
A2

Enter the letter of the description A through H that best fits each term or phrase 1 through 8.

A. Records and tracks the bondholders' names.
B. Is unsecured; backed only by the issuer's credit standing.
C. Has varying maturity dates for amounts owed.
D. Identifies rights and responsibilities of the issuer and the bondholders.
E. Can be exchanged for shares of the issuer's stock.
F. Is unregistered; interest is paid to whoever possesses them.
G. Maintains a separate asset account from which bondholders are paid at maturity.
H. Pledges specific assets of the issuer as collateral.

1. _____ Registered bond   **5.** _____ Convertible bond
2. _____ Serial bond   **6.** _____ Bond indenture
3. _____ Secured bond   **7.** _____ Sinking fund bond
4. _____ Bearer bond   **8.** _____ Debenture

QS 14-9
Computing payments for
an installment note C1

Murray Company borrows $340,000 cash from a bank and in return signs an installment note for five annual payments of equal amount, with the first payment due one year after the note is signed. Use Table B.3 in Appendix B to compute the amount of the annual payment for each of the following annual market rates: (*a*) 4%, (*b*) 8%, and (*c*) 12%.

QS 14-10
Debt-to-equity ratio
A2

Compute the debt-to-equity ratio for each of the following companies. Which company appears to have a riskier financing structure? Explain.

	Atlanta Company	Spokane Company
Total liabilities	$429,000	$ 548,000
Total equity	572,000	1,827,000

QS 14-11[C]
Issuing bonds between
interest dates P1

Madrid Company plans to issue 8% bonds on January 1, 2013, with a par value of $4,000,000. The company sells $3,600,000 of the bonds on January 1, 2013. The remaining $400,000 sells at par on March 1, 2013. The bonds pay interest semiannually as of June 30 and December 31. Record the entry for the March 1 cash sale of bonds.

QS 14-12[D]
Recording operating leases C4

Jin Li, an employee of ETrain.com, leases a car at O'Hare airport for a three-day business trip. The rental cost is $250. Prepare the entry by ETrain.com to record Jin Li's short-term car lease cost.

QS 14-13[D]
Recording capital leases C4

Algoma, Inc., signs a five-year lease for office equipment with Office Solutions. The present value of the lease payments is $15,499. Prepare the journal entry that Algoma records at the inception of this capital lease.

QS 14-14
International liabilities
disclosures
P1

Vodafone Group Plc reports the following information among its bonds payable as of March 31, 2011 (pounds in millions).

Financial Long-Term Liabilities Measured at Amortised Cost			
(£ millions)	Nominal (par) Value	Carrying Value	Fair Value
4.625% (US dollar 500 million) bond due July 2018	£311	£338	£327

a. What is the par value of the 4.625% bond issuance? What is its book (carrying) value?

b. Was the 4.625% bond sold at a discount or a premium? Explain.

Refer to the information in QS 14-14 for **Vodafone Group Plc**. The following price quotes (from Yahoo! Finance Bond Center) relate to its bonds payable. For example, the price quote indicates that the 4.625% bonds have a market price of 98.0 (98.0% of par value), resulting in a yield to maturity of 4.899%.

QS 14-15
International liabilities
disclosures and interpretations

P1

Price	Contract Rate (coupon)	Maturity Date	Market Rate (YTM)
98.0	4.625%	15-Jul-2018	4.899%

a. Assuming that the 4.625% bonds were originally issued at par value, what does the market price reveal about interest rate changes since bond issuance? (Assume that Vodafone's credit rating has remained the same.)

b. Does the change in market rates since the issuance of these bonds affect the amount of interest expense reported on Vodafone's income statement? Explain.

c. How much cash would Vodafone need to pay to repurchase the 4.625% bonds at the quoted market price of 98.0? (Assume no interest is owed when the bonds are repurchased.)

d. Assuming that the 4.625% bonds remain outstanding until maturity, at what market price will the bonds sell on the due date in 2018?

---

connect

> Round dollar amounts to the nearest whole dollar. Assume no reversing entries are used.

EXERCISES

On January 1, 2013, Boston Enterprises issues bonds that have a $3,400,000 par value, mature in 20 years, and pay 9% interest semiannually on June 30 and December 31. The bonds are sold at par.

1. How much interest will Boston pay (in cash) to the bondholders every six months?

2. Prepare journal entries to record (*a*) the issuance of bonds on January 1, 2013; (*b*) the first interest payment on June 30, 2013; and (*c*) the second interest payment on December 31, 2013.

3. Prepare the journal entry for issuance assuming the bonds are issued at (*a*) 98 and (*b*) 102.

Exercise 14-1
Recording bond issuance and interest

P1

Tano issues bonds with a par value of $180,000 on January 1, 2013. The bonds' annual contract rate is 8%, and interest is paid semiannually on June 30 and December 31. The bonds mature in three years. The annual market rate at the date of issuance is 10%, and the bonds are sold for $170,862.

1. What is the amount of the discount on these bonds at issuance?

2. How much total bond interest expense will be recognized over the life of these bonds?

3. Prepare an amortization table like the one in Exhibit 14.7 for these bonds; use the straight-line method to amortize the discount.

Exercise 14-2
Straight-Line: Amortization of bond discount

P2

Stanford issues bonds dated January 1, 2013, with a par value of $500,000. The bonds' annual contract rate is 9%, and interest is paid semiannually on June 30 and December 31. The bonds mature in three years. The annual market rate at the date of issuance is 12%, and the bonds are sold for $463,140.

1. What is the amount of the discount on these bonds at issuance?

2. How much total bond interest expense will be recognized over the life of these bonds?

3. Prepare an amortization table like the one in Exhibit 14B.7 for these bonds; use the effective interest method to amortize the discount.

Exercise 14-3[B]
Effective Interest: Amortization of bond discount

P6

Quatro Co. issues bonds dated January 1, 2013, with a par value of $400,000. The bonds' annual contract rate is 13%, and interest is paid semiannually on June 30 and December 31. The bonds mature in three years. The annual market rate at the date of issuance is 12%, and the bonds are sold for $409,850.

1. What is the amount of the premium on these bonds at issuance?

2. How much total bond interest expense will be recognized over the life of these bonds?

3. Prepare an amortization table like the one in Exhibit 14.11 for these bonds; use the straight-line method to amortize the premium.

Exercise 14-4
Straight-Line: Amortization of bond premium

P3

Effective Interest: Amortization
of bond premium   P7

Refer to the bond details in Exercise 14-4 and prepare an amortization table like the one in Exhibit 14B.2 for these bonds using the effective interest method to amortize the premium.

Exercise 14-6
Recording bond issuance and
discount amortization

P1   P2

Paulson Company issues 6%, four-year bonds, on December 31, 2013, with a par value of $200,000 and semiannual interest payments. Use the following bond amortization table and prepare journal entries to record (*a*) the issuance of bonds on December 31, 2013; (*b*) the first interest payment on June 30, 2014; and (*c*) the second interest payment on December 31, 2014.

Semiannual Period-End	Unamortized Discount	Carrying Value
(0) 12/31/2013	$13,466	$186,534
(1) 6/30/2014	11,782	188,218
(2) 12/31/2014	10,098	189,902

Exercise 14-7
Recording bond issuance and
discount amortization

P1   P2

Dobbs Company issues 5%, two-year bonds, on December 31, 2013, with a par value of $200,000 and semiannual interest payments. Use the following bond amortization table and prepare journal entries to record (*a*) the issuance of bonds on December 31, 2013; (*b*) the first through fourth interest payments on each June 30 and December 31; and (*c*) the maturity of the bond on December 31, 2015.

Semiannual Period-End	Unamortized Discount	Carrying Value
(0) 12/31/2013	$12,000	$188,000
(1) 6/30/2014	9,000	191,000
(2) 12/31/2014	6,000	194,000
(3) 6/30/2015	3,000	197,000
(4) 12/31/2015	0	200,000

Exercise 14-8
Recording bond issuance and
premium amortization

P1   P3

Woodwick Company issues 10%, five-year bonds, on December 31, 2012, with a par value of $200,000 and semiannual interest payments. Use the following bond amortization table and prepare journal entries to record (*a*) the issuance of bonds on December 31, 2012; (*b*) the first interest payment on June 30, 2013; and (*c*) the second interest payment on December 31, 2013.

Semiannual Period-End	Unamortized Premium	Carrying Value
(0) 12/31/2012	$16,222	$216,222
(1) 6/30/2013	14,600	214,600
(2) 12/31/2013	12,978	212,978

Exercise 14-9
Computing bond interest and
price; recording bond issuance

P2

Bringham Company issues bonds with a par value of $800,000 on their stated issue date. The bonds mature in 10 years and pay 6% annual interest in semiannual payments. On the issue date, the annual market rate for the bonds is 8%.

1. What is the amount of each semiannual interest payment for these bonds?

2. How many semiannual interest payments will be made on these bonds over their life?

3. Use the interest rates given to determine whether the bonds are issued at par, at a discount, or at a premium.

4. Compute the price of the bonds as of their issue date.

5. Prepare the journal entry to record the bonds' issuance.

Check   (4) $691,287

Exercise 14-10
Computing bond interest and
price; recording bond issuance

P3

Citywide Company issues bonds with a par value of $150,000 on their stated issue date. The bonds mature in five years and pay 10% annual interest in semiannual payments. On the issue date, the annual market rate for the bonds is 8%.

1. What is the amount of each semiannual interest payment for these bonds?

2. How many semiannual interest payments will be made on these bonds over their life?

3. Use the interest rates given to determine whether the bonds are issued at par, at a discount, or at a premium.

4. Compute the price of the bonds as of their issue date.

Check   (4) $162,172

5. Prepare the journal entry to record the bonds' issuance.

On January 1, 2013, Shay issues $700,000 of 10%, 15-year bonds at a price of 97¾. Six years later, on January 1, 2019, Shay retires 20% of these bonds by buying them on the open market at 104½. All interest is accounted for and paid through December 31, 2018, the day before the purchase. The straight-line method is used to amortize any bond discount.

Exercise 14-11
Straight-Line: Bond computations, amortization, and bond retirement

P2   P4

1. How much does the company receive when it issues the bonds on January 1, 2013?

2. What is the amount of the discount on the bonds at January 1, 2013?

3. How much amortization of the discount is recorded on the bonds for the entire period from January 1, 2013, through December 31, 2018?

4. What is the carrying (book) value of the bonds as of the close of business on December 31, 2018? What is the carrying value of the 20% soon-to-be-retired bonds on this same date?

5. How much did the company pay on January 1, 2019, to purchase the bonds that it retired?

6. What is the amount of the recorded gain or loss from retiring the bonds?

Check   (6) $8,190 loss

7. Prepare the journal entry to record the bond retirement at January 1, 2019.

On May 1, 2013, Brussels Enterprises issues bonds dated January 1, 2013, that have a $3,400,000 par value, mature in 20 years, and pay 9% interest semiannually on June 30 and December 31. The bonds are sold at par plus four months' accrued interest.

Exercise 14-12C
Recording bond issuance with accrued interest

C4   P1

1. How much accrued interest do the bond purchasers pay Brussels on May 1, 2013?

2. Prepare Brussels' journal entries to record (a) the issuance of bonds on May 1, 2013; (b) the first interest payment on June 30, 2013; and (c) the second interest payment on December 31, 2013.

Check   (1) $102,000

Duval Co. issues four-year bonds with a $100,000 par value on June 1, 2013, at a price of $95,948. The annual contract rate is 7%, and interest is paid semiannually on November 30 and May 31.

Exercise 14-13
Straight-Line: Amortization and accrued bond interest expense

P1   P2

1. Prepare an amortization table like the one in Exhibit 14.7 for these bonds. Use the straight-line method of interest amortization.

2. Prepare journal entries to record the first two interest payments and to accrue interest as of December 31, 2013.

On January 1, 2013, Eagle borrows $100,000 cash by signing a four-year, 7% installment note. The note requires four equal total payments of accrued interest and principal on December 31 of each year from 2013 through 2016.

Exercise 14-14
Installment note with equal total payments   C1   P5

Check   (1) $29,523

1. Compute the amount of each of the four equal total payments.

2. Prepare an amortization table for this installment note like the one in Exhibit 14.14.

Use the information in Exercise 14-14 to prepare the journal entries for Eagle to record the loan on January 1, 2013, and the four payments from December 31, 2013, through December 31, 2016.

Exercise 14-15
Installment note entries   P5

Montclair Company is considering a project that will require a $500,000 loan. It presently has total liabilities of $220,000, and total assets of $610,000.

Exercise 14-16
Applying debt-to-equity ratio

A3

1. Compute Montclair's (a) present debt-to-equity ratio and (b) the debt-to-equity ratio assuming it borrows $500,000 to fund the project.

2. Evaluate and discuss the level of risk involved if Montclair borrows the funds to pursue the project.

Indicate whether the company in each separate case 1 through 3 has entered into an operating lease or a capital lease.

Exercise 14-17D
Identifying capital and operating leases

C4

1. The lessor retains title to the asset, and the lease term is three years on an asset that has a five-year useful life.

2. The title is transferred to the lessee, the lessee can purchase the asset for $1 at the end of the lease, and the lease term is five years. The leased asset has an expected useful life of six years.

3. The present value of the lease payments is 95% of the leased asset's market value, and the lease term is 70% of the leased asset's useful life.

Exercise 14-18^D

Accounting for capital lease

C4

Harbor (lessee) signs a five-year capital lease for office equipment with a $10,000 annual lease payment. The present value of the five annual lease payments is $41,000, based on a 7% interest rate.

1. Prepare the journal entry Harbor will record at inception of the lease.

2. If the leased asset has a five-year useful life with no salvage value, prepare the journal entry Harbor will record each year to recognize depreciation expense related to the leased asset.

Exercise 14-19^D

Analyzing lease options

C2   C3   C4

General Motors advertised three alternatives for a 25-month lease on a new Blazer: (1) zero dollars down and a lease payment of $1,750 per month for 25 months, (2) $5,000 down and $1,500 per month for 25 months, or (3) $38,500 down and no payments for 25 months. Use the present value Table B.3 in Appendix B to determine which is the best alternative (assume you have enough cash to accept any alternative and the annual interest rate is 12% compounded monthly).

Exercise 14-20

Accounting for long-term liabilities under IFRS

P1

Heineken N.V. reports the following information for its Loans and Borrowings as of December 31, 2010, including proceeds and repayments for the year ended December 31, 2010 (euros in millions).

Loans and borrowings (noncurrent liabilities)	
Loans and borrowings, December 31, 2010	€ 8,078
Proceeds (cash) from issuances of loans and borrowings	1,920
Repayments (in cash) of loans and borrowings	(3,127)

1. Prepare Heineken's journal entry to record its cash proceeds from issuances of its loans and borrowings for 2010. Assume that the par value of these issuances is €2,000.

2. Prepare Heineken's journal entry to record its cash repayments of its loans and borrowings for 2010. Assume that the par value of these issuances is €3,000, and the premium on them is €32.

3. Compute the discount or premium on its loans and borrowings as of December 31, 2010, assuming that the par value of these liabilities is €8,000.

4. Given the facts in part 3 and viewing the entirety of loans and borrowings as one issuance, was the contract rate on these loans and borrowings higher or lower than the market rate at the time of issuance? Explain. (Assume that Heineken's credit rating has remained the same.)

PROBLEM SET A

> Round dollar amounts to the nearest whole dollar. Assume no reversing entries are used.

Problem 14-1A

Computing bond price and recording issuance

P1

Check (1) Premium, $4,537

(3) Discount, $4,588

Hartford Research issues bonds dated January 1, 2013, that pay interest semiannually on June 30 and December 31. The bonds have a $40,000 par value and an annual contract rate of 10%, and they mature in 10 years.

Required

For each of the following three separate situations, (a) determine the bonds' issue price on January 1, 2013, and (b) prepare the journal entry to record their issuance.

1. The market rate at the date of issuance is 8%.

2. The market rate at the date of issuance is 10%.

3. The market rate at the date of issuance is 12%.

Problem 14-2A

Straight-Line: Amortization of bond discount   P1 P2

mhhe.com/wildFAP21e

Check (3) $4,143,552

(4) 12/31/2014 carrying value, $3,528,920

Hillside issues $4,000,000 of 6%, 15-year bonds dated January 1, 2013, that pay interest semiannually on June 30 and December 31. The bonds are issued at a price of $3,456,448.

Required

1. Prepare the January 1, 2013, journal entry to record the bonds' issuance.

2. For each semiannual period, compute (a) the cash payment, (b) the straight-line discount amortization, and (c) the bond interest expense.

3. Determine the total bond interest expense to be recognized over the bonds' life.

4. Prepare the first two years of an amortization table like Exhibit 14.7 using the straight-line method.

5. Prepare the journal entries to record the first two interest payments.

Refer to the bond details in Problem 14-2A, *except* assume that the bonds are issued at a price of $4,895,980.

Required

1. Prepare the January 1, 2013, journal entry to record the bonds' issuance.
2. For each semiannual period, compute (*a*) the cash payment, (*b*) the straight-line premium amortization, and (*c*) the bond interest expense.
3. Determine the total bond interest expense to be recognized over the bonds' life.
4. Prepare the first two years of an amortization table like Exhibit 14.7 using the straight-line method.
5. Prepare the journal entries to record the first two interest payments.

Problem 14-3A
Straight Line: Amortization of bond premium

P1 P3

Check (3) $2,704,020

(4) 12/31/2014 carrying value, $4,776,516

Ellis issues 6.5%, five-year bonds dated January 1, 2013, with a $250,000 par value. The bonds pay interest on June 30 and December 31 and are issued at a price of $255,333. The annual market rate is 6% on the issue date.

Required

1. Calculate the total bond interest expense over the bonds' life.
2. Prepare a straight-line amortization table like Exhibit 14.11 for the bonds' life.
3. Prepare the journal entries to record the first two interest payments.

Problem 14-4A
Straight-Line: Amortization of bond premium

P1 P3

mhhe.com/wildFAP21e

Check (2) 6/30/2015 carrying value, $252,668

Refer to the bond details in Problem 14-4A.

Required

1. Compute the total bond interest expense over the bonds' life.
2. Prepare an effective interest amortization table like the one in Exhibit 14B.2 for the bonds' life.
3. Prepare the journal entries to record the first two interest payments.
4. Use the market rate at issuance to compute the present value of the remaining cash flows for these bonds as of December 31, 2015. Compare your answer with the amount shown on the amortization table as the balance for that date (from part 2) and explain your findings.

Problem 14-5A[B]
Effective Interest: Amortization of bond premium; computing bond price P1 P7

Check (2) 6/30/2015 carrying value, $252,865

(4) $252,326

Legacy issues $325,000 of 5%, four-year bonds dated January 1, 2013, that pay interest semiannually on June 30 and December 31. They are issued at $292,181 and their market rate is 8% at the issue date.

Required

1. Prepare the January 1, 2013, journal entry to record the bonds' issuance.
2. Determine the total bond interest expense to be recognized over the bonds' life.
3. Prepare a straight-line amortization table like the one in Exhibit 14.7 for the bonds' first two years.
4. Prepare the journal entries to record the first two interest payments.

Analysis Component

5. Assume the market rate on January 1, 2013, is 4% instead of 8%. Without providing numbers, describe how this change affects the amounts reported on Legacy's financial statements.

Problem 14-6A
Straight-Line: Amortization of bond

P1 P2 P3

Check (2) $97,819

(3) 12/31/2014 carrying value, $308,589

Refer to the bond details in Problem 14-6A.

Required

1. Prepare the January 1, 2013, journal entry to record the bonds' issuance.
2. Determine the total bond interest expense to be recognized over the bonds' life.
3. Prepare an effective interest amortization table like the one in Exhibit 14B.1 for the bonds' first two years.
4. Prepare the journal entries to record the first two interest payments.

Problem 14-7A[B]
Effective Interest: Amortization of bond discount P1 P6

Check (2) $97,819

(3) 12/31/2014 carrying value, $307,308

mhhe.com/wildFAP21e

Problem 14-8A[B]

Effective Interest: Amortization of bond; retiring bonds

P1 P4 P6 P7

Check   (3) 6/30/2014 carrying value, $182,448

(5) $5,270 gain

mhhe.com/wildFAP21e

Ike issues $180,000 of 11%, three-year bonds dated January 1, 2013, that pay interest semiannually on June 30 and December 31. They are issued at $184,566. Their market rate is 10% at the issue date.

Required

1. Prepare the January 1, 2013, journal entry to record the bonds' issuance.
2. Determine the total bond interest expense to be recognized over the bonds' life.
3. Prepare an effective interest amortization table like Exhibit 14B.2 for the bonds' first two years.
4. Prepare the journal entries to record the first two interest payments.
5. Prepare the journal entry to record the bonds' retirement on January 1, 2015, at 98.

Analysis Component

6. Assume that the market rate on January 1, 2013, is 12% instead of 10%. Without presenting numbers, describe how this change affects the amounts reported on Ike's financial statements.

Problem 14-9A

Installment notes

C1 P5

Check   (2) 10/31/2017 ending balance, $46,382

On November 1, 2013, Norwood borrows $200,000 cash from a bank by signing a five-year installment note bearing 8% interest. The note requires equal total payments each year on October 31.

Required

1. Compute the total amount of each installment payment.
2. Complete an amortization table for this installment note similar to the one in Exhibit 14.14.
3. Prepare the journal entries in which Leetch records (a) accrued interest as of December 31, 2013 (the end of its annual reporting period), and (b) the first annual payment on the note.

Problem 14-10A

Applying the debt-to-equity ratio

A3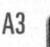

At the end of the current year, the following information is available for both Pulaski Company and Scott Company.

	Pulaski Company	Scott Company
Total assets	$900,000	$450,000
Total liabilities	360,000	240,000
Total equity	540,000	210,000

Required

1. Compute the debt-to-equity ratios for both companies.
2. Comment on your results and discuss the riskiness of each company's financing structure.

Problem 14-11A[D]

Capital lease accounting

C4

Check   (1) $39,927

(3) Year 3 ending balance, $17,833

Rogers Company signs a five-year capital lease with Packer Company for office equipment. The annual lease payment is $10,000, and the interest rate is 8%.

Required

1. Compute the present value of Roger's five-year lease payments.
2. Prepare the journal entry to record Roger's capital lease at its inception.
3. Complete a lease payment schedule for the five years of the lease with the following headings. Assume that the beginning balance of the lease liability (present value of lease payments) is $79,854. (*Hint:* To find the amount allocated to interest in year 1, multiply the interest rate by the beginning-of-year lease liability. The amount of the annual lease payment not allocated to interest is allocated to principal. Reduce the lease liability by the amount allocated to principal to update the lease liability at each year-end.)

Period Ending Date	Beginning Balance of Lease Liability	Interest on Lease Liability	Reduction of Lease Liability	Cash Lease Payment	Ending Balance of Lease Liability

4. Use straight-line depreciation and prepare the journal entry to depreciate the leased asset at the end of year 1. Assume zero salvage value and a five-year life for the office equipment.

| Round dollar amounts to the nearest whole dollar. Assume no reversing entries are used. |

Flagstaff Systems issues bonds dated January 1, 2013, that pay interest semiannually on June 30 and December 31. The bonds have a $90,000 par value and an annual contract rate of 12%, and they mature in five years.

Problem 14-1B
Computing bond price and recording issuance
P1

Required

For each of the following three separate situations, (*a*) determine the bonds' issue price on January 1, 2013, and (*b*) prepare the journal entry to record their issuance.

1. The market rate at the date of issuance is 10%.
2. The market rate at the date of issuance is 12%.
3. The market rate at the date of issuance is 14%.

Check (1) Premium, $6,948

(3) Discount, $6,326

Romero issues $3,400,000 of 10%, 10-year bonds dated January 1, 2013, that pay interest semiannually on June 30 and December 31. The bonds are issued at a price of $3,010,000.

Problem 14-2B
Straight-Line: Amortization of bond discount
P1 P2

Required

1. Prepare the January 1, 2013, journal entry to record the bonds' issuance.
2. For each semiannual period, compute (*a*) the cash payment, (*b*) the straight-line discount amortization, and (*c*) the bond interest expense.
3. Determine the total bond interest expense to be recognized over the bonds' life.
4. Prepare the first two years of an amortization table like Exhibit 14.7 using the straight-line method.
5. Prepare the journal entries to record the first two interest payments.

Check (3) $3,790,000

(4) 6/30/2014 carrying value, $3,068,500

Refer to the bond details in Problem 14-2B, *except* assume that the bonds are issued at a price of $4,192,932.

Problem 14-3B
Straight-line: Amortization of bond premium
P1 P3

Required

1. Prepare the January 1, 2013, journal entry to record the bonds' issuance.
2. For each semiannual period, compute (*a*) the cash payment, (*b*) the straight-line premium amortization, and (*c*) the bond interest expense.
3. Determine the total bond interest expense to be recognized over the bonds' life.
4. Prepare the first two years of an amortization table like Exhibit 14.7 using the straight-line method.
5. Prepare the journal entries to record the first two interest payments.

Check (3) $2,607,068

(4) 6/30/2014 carrying value, 4,073,991

Ripkin Company issues 9%, five-year bonds dated January 1, 2013, with a $320,000 par value. The bonds pay interest on June 30 and December 31 and are issued at a price of $332,988. Their annual market rate is 8% on the issue date.

Problem 14-4B
Straight-Line: Amortization of bond premium
P1 P3

Required

1. Calculate the total bond interest expense over the bonds' life.
2. Prepare a straight-line amortization table like Exhibit 14.11 for the bonds' life.
3. Prepare the journal entries to record the first two interest payments.

Check (2) 6/30/2015 carrying value, $326,493

Refer to the bond details in Problem 14-4B.

Problem 14-5B[B]
Effective Interest: Amortization of bond premium; computing bond price P1 P7

Required

1. Compute the total bond interest expense over the bonds' life.
2. Prepare an effective interest amortization table like the one in Exhibit 14B.2 for the bonds' life.
3. Prepare the journal entries to record the first two interest payments.
4. Use the market rate at issuance to compute the present value of the remaining cash flows for these bonds as of December 31, 2015. Compare your answer with the amount shown on the amortization table as the balance for that date (from part 2) and explain your findings.

Check (2) 6/30/2015 carrying value, $327,136

(4) $325,807

Problem 14-6B
Straight-Line: Amortization of bond discount
P1 P2

Check   (2) $257,506
            (3) 6/30/2014 carrying value, $202,646

Gomez issues $240,000 of 6%, 15-year bonds dated January 1, 2013, that pay interest semiannually on June 30 and December 31. They are issued at $198,494, and their market rate is 8% at the issue date.

Required

1. Prepare the January 1, 2013, journal entry to record the bonds' issuance.
2. Determine the total bond interest expense to be recognized over the life of the bonds.
3. Prepare a straight-line amortization table like the one in Exhibit 14.7 for the bonds' first two years.
4. Prepare the journal entries to record the first two interest payments.

Problem 14-7B[B]
Effective Interest: Amortization of bond discount
P1 P6

Check   (2) $257,506;
            (3) 6/30/2014 carrying value, $200,803

Refer to the bond details in Problem 14-6B.

Required

1. Prepare the January 1, 2013, journal entry to record the bonds' issuance.
2. Determine the total bond interest expense to be recognized over the bonds' life.
3. Prepare an effective interest amortization table like the one in Exhibit 14B.1 for the bonds' first two years.
4. Prepare the journal entries to record the first two interest payments.

Problem 14-8B[B]
Effective Interest: Amortization of bond; retiring bonds
P1 P4 P6 P7

Check   (3) 6/30/2014 carrying value, $479,202

            (5) $3,088 loss

Valdez issues $450,000 of 13%, four-year bonds dated January 1, 2013, that pay interest semiannually on June 30 and December 31. They are issued at $493,608, and their market rate is 10% at the issue date.

Required

1. Prepare the January 1, 2013, journal entry to record the bonds' issuance.
2. Determine the total bond interest expense to be recognized over the bonds' life.
3. Prepare an effective interest amortization table like the one in Exhibit 14B.2 for the bonds' first two years.
4. Prepare the journal entries to record the first two interest payments.
5. Prepare the journal entry to record the bonds' retirement on January 1, 2015, at 106.

Analysis Component

6. Assume that the market rate on January 1, 2013, is 14% instead of 10%. Without presenting numbers, describe how this change affects the amounts reported on Valdez's financial statements.

Problem 14-9B
Installment notes
C1 P5

Check   (2) 9/30/2015 ending balance, $54,836

On October 1, 2013, Gordon Enterprises borrows $150,000 cash from a bank by signing a three-year install-ment note bearing 10% interest. The note requires equal total payments each year on September 30.

Required

1. Compute the total amount of each installment payment.
2. Complete an amortization table for this installment note similar to the one in Exhibit 14.14.
3. Prepare the journal entries to record (*a*) accrued interest as of December 31, 2013 (the end of its annual reporting period) and (*b*) the first annual payment on the note.

Problem 14-10B
Applying the debt-to-equity ratio
A3

At the end of the current year, the following information is available for both Atlas Company and Bryan Company.

	Atlas Company	Bryan Company
Total assets	$180,000	$750,000
Total liabilities	81,000	562,500
Total equity	99,000	187,500

Required

1. Compute the debt-to-equity ratios for both companies.
2. Comment on your results and discuss what they imply about the relative riskiness of these companies.

Braun Company signs a five-year capital lease with Verdi Company for office equipment. The annual lease payment is $20,000, and the interest rate is 10%.

Required

1. Compute the present value of Braun's lease payments.
2. Prepare the journal entry to record Braun's capital lease at its inception.
3. Complete a lease payment schedule for the five years of the lease with the following headings. Assume that the beginning balance of the lease liability (present value of lease payments) is $75,816. (*Hint:* To find the amount allocated to interest in year 1, multiply the interest rate by the beginning-of-year lease liability. The amount of the annual lease payment not allocated to interest is allocated to principal. Reduce the lease liability by the amount allocated to principal to update the lease liability at each year end.)

Period Ending Date	Beginning Balance of Lease Liability	Interest on Lease Liability	Reduction of Lease Liability	Cash Lease Payment	Ending Balance of Lease Liability

4. Use straight-line depreciation and prepare the journal entry to depreciate the leased asset at the end of year 1. Assume zero salvage value and a five-year life for the office equipment.

Problem 14-11B[D]
Capital lease accounting
C4

Check   (1) $75,816

(3) Year 3 ending balance,
$34,712

(This serial problem began in Chapter 1 and continues through most of the book. If previous chapter segments were not completed, the serial problem can begin at this point. It is helpful, but not necessary, to use the Working Papers that accompany the book.)

SP 14   Adria Lopez has consulted with her local banker and is considering financing an expansion of her business by obtaining a long-term bank loan. Selected account balances at March 31, 2014, for Success Systems follow.

Total assets	$129,909	Total liabilities	$875	Total equity	$129,034

Required

1. The bank has offered a long-term secured note to Success Systems. The bank's loan procedures require that a client's debt-to-equity ratio not exceed 0.8. As of March 31, 2014, what is the maximum amount that Success Systems could borrow from this bank (rounded to nearest dollar)?
2. If Success Systems borrows the maximum amount allowed from the bank, what percentage of assets would be financed (*a*) by debt and (*b*) by equity?
3. What are some factors Adria Lopez should consider before borrowing the funds?

SERIAL PROBLEM
Success Systems
A1   A3

Check   (1) $102,352

Beyond the Numbers

BTN 14-1   Refer to **Polaris**' financial statements in Appendix A to answer the following.

1. Identify the items, if any, that make up Polaris' long-term debt as reported on its balance sheet at December 31, 2011.
2. Assume that Polaris has $100,000 thousand in convertible debentures that carry a 4.25% contract rate of interest. How much annual cash interest must be paid on those convertible debentures?
3. How much cash did it generate from issuance of debt for the year-ended December 31, 2011? How much cash did it use for repayments of debt for that same year?

REPORTING IN ACTION
A1   A2

Polaris

Fast Forward

4. Access Polaris' financial statements for the years ending after December 31, 2011, from its Website (**Polaris.com**) or the SEC's EDGAR database (**www.SEC.gov**). Has it issued additional long-term debt since the year-end December 31, 2011? If yes, identify the amount(s).

COMPARATIVE ANALYSIS

A3

Polaris

Arctic Cat

BTN 14-2 Key figures for **Polaris** and **Arctic Cat** follow.

($ thousands)	Polaris		Arctic Cat	
	Current Year	Prior Year	Current Year	Prior Year
Total assets	$1,228,024	$1,061,647	$272,906	$246,084
Total liabilities	727,968	690,656	89,870	78,745
Total equity	500,056	370,991	183,036	167,339

Required

1. Compute the debt-to-equity ratios for Polaris and Arctic Cat for both the current year and the prior year.

2. Use the ratios you computed in part 1 to determine which company's financing structure is least risky. Assume an industry average of 0.64 for debt-to-equity.

ETHICS CHALLENGE

C4 A1

BTN 14-3 Traverse County needs a new county government building that would cost $10 million. The politicians feel that voters will not approve a municipal bond issue to fund the building since it would increase taxes. They opt to have a state bank issue $10 million of tax-exempt securities to pay for the building construction. The county then will make yearly lease payments (of principal and interest) to repay the obligation. Unlike conventional municipal bonds, the lease payments are not binding obligations on the county and, therefore, require no voter approval.

Required

1. Do you think the actions of the politicians and the bankers in this situation are ethical?

2. How do the tax-exempt securities used to pay for the building compare in risk to a conventional municipal bond issued by Traverse County?

COMMUNICATING IN PRACTICE

P3

BTN 14-4 Your business associate mentions that she is considering investing in corporate bonds currently selling at a premium. She says that since the bonds are selling at a premium, they are highly valued and her investment will yield more than the going rate of return for the risk involved. Reply with a memorandum to confirm or correct your associate's interpretation of premium bonds.

TAKING IT TO THE NET

A2

BTN 14-5 Access the March 22, 2012, filing of the 10-K report of **Home Depot** for the year ended January 31, 2012, from **www.sec.gov** (Ticker: HD). Refer to Home Depot's balance sheet, including its note 4 (on debt).

Required

1. Identify Home Depot's long-term liabilities and the amounts for those liabilities from Home Depot's balance sheet at January 31, 2012.

2. Review Home Depot's note 4. The note reports that as of January 31, 2012, it had $2.961 billion of "5.875% Senior Notes; due December 16, 2036; interest payable semiannually on June 16 and December 16." These notes have a face value of $3.0 billion and were originally issued at $2.958 billion.

   a. Why would Home Depot issue $3.0 billion of its notes for only $2.958 billion?

   b. How much cash interest must Home Depot pay each June 16 and December 16 on these notes?

TEAMWORK IN ACTION

P2 P3

BTN 14-6[B] Break into teams and complete the following requirements related to effective interest amortization for a premium bond.

1. Each team member is to independently prepare a blank table with proper headings for amortization of a bond premium. When all have finished, compare tables and ensure that all are in agreement.

Parts 2 and 3 require use of these facts: On January 1, 2013, McElroy issues $100,000, 9%, five-year bonds at 104.1. The market rate at issuance is 8%. McElroy pays interest semiannually on June 30 and December 31.

2. In rotation, *each* team member must explain how to complete *one* line of the bond amortization table, including all computations for his or her line. (Round amounts to the nearest dollar.) All members are to fill in their tables during this process. You need not finish the table; stop after all members have explained a line.

3. In rotation, *each* team member is to identify a separate column of the table and indicate what the final number in that column will be and explain the reasoning.

4. Reach a team consensus as to what the total bond interest expense on this bond issue will be if the bond is not retired before maturity.

Hint: Rotate teams to report on parts 4 and 5. Consider requiring entries for issuance and interest payments.

5. As a team, prepare a list of similarities and differences between the amortization table just prepared and the amortization table if the bond had been issued at a discount.

BTN 14-7   Kyle Smitley is the founder of **barley & birch**. Assume that her company currently has $250,000 in equity, and she is considering a $100,000 expansion to meet increased demand. The $100,000 expansion would yield $16,000 in additional annual income before interest expense. Assume that the business currently earns $40,000 annual income before interest expense of $10,000, yielding a return on equity of 12% ($30,000/$250,000). To fund the expansion, she is considering the issuance of a 10-year, $100,000 note with annual interest payments (the principal due at the end of 10 years).

ENTREPRENEURIAL DECISION

A1

Required

1. Using return on equity as the decision criterion, show computations to support or reject the expansion if interest on the $100,000 note is (*a*) 10%, (*b*) 15%, (*c*) 16%, (*d*) 17%, and (*e*) 20%.

2. What general rule do the results in part 1 illustrate?

BTN 14-8   Visit your city or county library. Ask the librarian to help you locate the recent financial records of your city or county government. Examine those records.

HITTING THE ROAD

A1

Required

1. Determine the amount of long-term bonds and notes currently outstanding.

2. Read the supporting information to your municipality's financial statements and record

   a. The market interest rate(s) when the bonds and/or notes were issued.

   b. The date(s) when the bonds and/or notes will mature.

   c. Any rating(s) on the bonds and/or notes received from **Moody's**, **Standard & Poor's**, or another rating agency.

BTN 14-9   **Piaggio** (**www.piaggio.com**), **Polaris**, and **Arctic Cat** are competitors in the global marketplace. Selected results from these companies follow.

GLOBAL DECISION

A3

PIAGGIO
Polaris
Arctic Cat

Key Figures	Piaggio (Euro thousands) Current Year	Piaggio (Euro thousands) Prior Year	Polaris ($ thousands) Current Year	Polaris ($ thousands) Prior Year	Arctic Cat ($ thousands) Current Year	Arctic Cat ($ thousands) Prior Year
Total assets	€1,520,184	€1,545,722	$1,228,024	$1,061,647	$272,906	$246,084
Total liabilities	1,073,966	1,102,832	727,968	690,656	89,870	78,745
Total equity	446,218	442,890	500,056	370,991	183,036	167,339
Debt-to-equity ratio	?	?	1.46	1.86	0.49	0.47

Required

1. Compute Piaggio's debt-to-equity ratios for the current year and the prior year.

2. Use the data provided and the ratios computed in part 1 to determine which company's financing structure is least risky.

ANSWERS TO MULTIPLE CHOICE QUIZ

1. b

2. a

3. c; $500,000 × 0.08 × ½ year = $20,000

4. a; Cash interest paid = $100,000 × 5% × ½ year = $2,500
Discount amortization = ($100,000 − $95,735)/10 periods = $426.50
Interest expense = $2,500.00 + $426.50 = $2,926.50

5. e; ($373,745 − $350,000)/16 periods = $1,484

Investments and International Operations

15

A Look Back

Chapter 14 focused on long-term liabilities—a main part of most companies' financing. We explained how to value, record, amortize, and report these liabilities in financial statements.

A Look at This Chapter

This chapter focuses on investments in securities. We explain how to identify, account for, and report investments in both debt and equity securities. We also explain accounting for transactions listed in a foreign currency.

A Look Ahead

Chapter 16 focuses on reporting and analyzing a company's cash flows. Special emphasis is directed at the statement of cash flows reported under the indirect method.

Learning Objectives

CONCEPTUAL

C1 Distinguish between debt and equity securities and between short-term and long-term investments. (p. 598)

C2 Describe how to report equity securities with controlling influence. (p. 605)

C3 *Appendix 15A*—Explain foreign exchange rates and record transactions listed in a foreign currency. (p. 612)

ANALYTICAL

A1 Compute and analyze the components of return on total assets. (p. 607)

PROCEDURAL

P1 Account for trading securities. (p. 601)

P2 Account for held-to-maturity securities. (p. 602)

P3 Account for available-for-sale securities. (p. 602)

P4 Account for equity securities with significant influence. (p. 604)

100 Million Dollar Investment

"Never be scared of asking for advice."
—CATHERINE COOK

NEW YORK—"We were relatively new in our high school and we just wanted a better way to get to know our classmates," admits Catherine Cook. "We started brainstorming a general idea of what we wanted: superlatives, profiles, classes, groups . . . and **myYearbook** was born!" Catherine, along with her brother Dave, launched myYearbook aimed at teenagers and young adults. "If you think about Facebook as where you go to connect with people you know," explains Catherine, "myYearbook is where you go to connect with people you want to know."

In 2011, myYearbook was the top site for teenagers, according to the online tracking company comScore, with over 33 million users. Catherine says myYearbook employed more than 100 workers at offices in New York and New Hope, Pennsylvania. She admits, however, that "it is really hard to keep up with the site along with my school work."

The next big step according to Catherine was to take myYearbook to a global audience. "The dream we've had for some time now," she says, "is to become a global brand." This step required Catherine to extend her business into international operations and to deal with intercorporate investments. "I am committed to focus on what we do best," she says, "to make myYearbook the number one site to meet new people."

This broad goal has led to business challenges, involving both investments and international operations. "I want to grow myYearbook as far as I can," insists Catherine. That drive led her into discussions with Quepasa.com, a social network whose users are based mainly in Latin America. Explains Catherine, "With Quepasa, we could end up the leader in social discovery!" However, to make this happen, she had to study their international operations, including their financials and accounting disclosures. Catherine explored various investment deals that she could set up with Quepasa, which required her to learn about accounting for investments.

Catherine recently finalized her investment in Quepasa, which involved a merger of their two operations, whereby she and her brother received $18 million in cash and $82 million in stock. Combined, myYearbook.com and Quepasa.com, now rebranded under the name **Meet Me Inc. (MeetMe.com),** have more than 70 million registered users. Catherine aims to launch translated versions of games, social applications, and mobile platform. "I'm working hard at coming up with interesting and fun features for our members," she said. "I'll be in the office every day working on a full pipeline of new features."

[Sources: *MeetMe Website,* January 2013; *The Star-Ledger,* July 2011; *New Jersey Monthly Magazine,* August 2011; *Smart Business Network,* February 2012]

This chapter's main focus is investments in securities. Many companies have investments, and many of these are in the form of debt and equity securities issued by other companies. We describe investments in these securities and how to account for them. An increasing number of companies also invest in international operations. We explain how to account for and report international transactions listed in foreign currencies.

Investments and International Operations

Basics of Investments
- Motivation for investments
- Short-term versus long-term
- Classification and reporting
- Accounting basics

Noninfluential Investments
- Trading securities
- Held-to-maturity securities
- Available-for-sale securities

Influential Investments
- Securities with significant influence
- Securities with controlling influence
- Accounting summary

BASICS OF INVESTMENTS

C1 Distinguish between debt and equity securities and between short-term and long-term investments.

This section describes the motivation for investments, the distinction between short- and long-term investments, and the different classes of investments.

Motivation for Investments

Companies make investments for at least three reasons. First, companies transfer *excess cash* into investments to produce higher income. Second, some entities, such as mutual funds and pension funds, are set up to produce income from investments. Third, companies make investments for strategic reasons. Examples are investments in competitors, suppliers, and even customers. Exhibit 15.1 shows short-term (S-T) and long-term (L-T) investments as a percent of total assets for several companies.

EXHIBIT 15.1

Investments of Selected Companies

Microsoft	S-T 40% L-T 10%
Pfizer	S-T 12.5% L-T 5%
Starbucks	S-T 12% L-T 6.5%
Coca-Cola	S-T 1.5% L-T 9%

0%   50%
Percent of total assets

Short-Term Investments Cash equivalents are investments that are both readily converted to known amounts of cash and mature within three months. Many investments, however, mature between 3 and 12 months. These investments are **short-term investments,** also called *temporary investments* and *marketable securities.* Specifically, short-term investments are securities that (1) management intends to convert to cash within one year or the operating cycle, whichever is longer, and (2) are readily convertible to cash. Short-term investments are reported under current assets and serve a purpose similar to cash equivalents.

Long-Term Investments **Long-term investments** in securities are defined as those securities that are not readily convertible to cash or are not intended to be converted into cash in the short term. Long-term investments can also include funds earmarked for a special purpose, such as bond sinking funds and investments in land or other assets not used in the company's operations. Long-term investments are reported in the noncurrent section of the balance sheet, often in its own separate line titled *Long-Term Investments*.

Debt Securities versus Equity Securities Investments in securities can include both debt and equity securities. *Debt securities* reflect a creditor relationship such as investments in notes, bonds, and certificates of deposit; they are issued by governments, companies, and individuals. *Equity securities* reflect an owner relationship such as shares of stock issued by companies.

Classification and Reporting

Accounting for investments in securities depends on three factors: (1) security type, either debt or equity, (2) the company's intent to hold the security either short term or long term, and (3) the company's (investor's) percent ownership in the other company's (investee's) equity securities. Exhibit 15.2 identifies five classes of securities using these three factors. It describes each of these five classes of securities and the standard reporting required under each class.

EXHIBIT 15.2

Investments in Securities

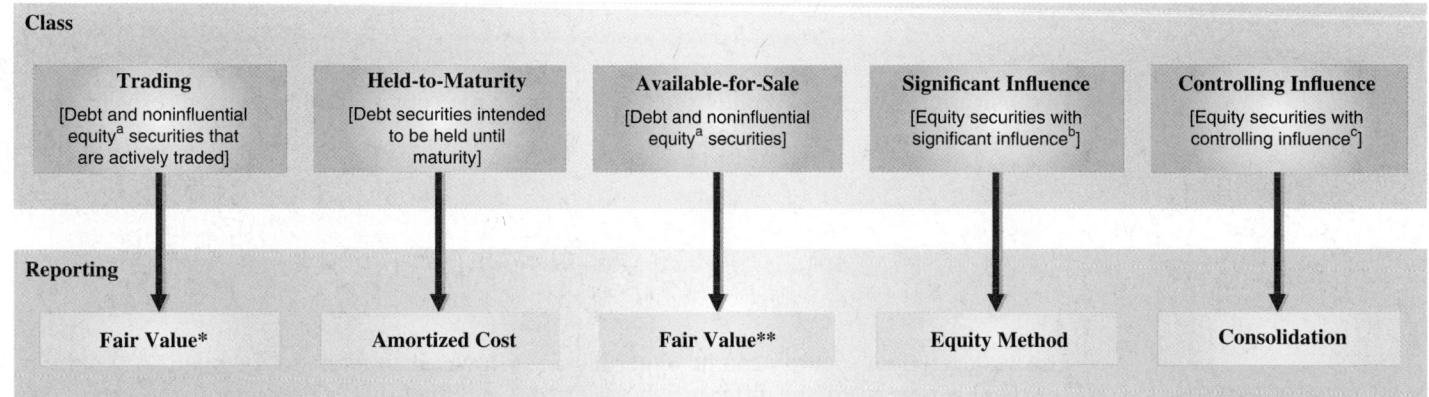

Class

Trading	Held-to-Maturity	Available-for-Sale	Significant Influence	Controlling Influence
[Debt and noninfluential equity[a] securities that are actively traded]	[Debt securities intended to be held until maturity]	[Debt and noninfluential equity[a] securities]	[Equity securities with significant influence[b]]	[Equity securities with controlling influence[c]]

Reporting

Fair Value*	Amortized Cost	Fair Value**	Equity Method	Consolidation

[a] Holding less than 20% of voting stock (equity securities only).   [b] Holding 20% or more, but not more than 50%, of voting stock.   [c] Holding more than 50% of voting stock.
* Unrealized gains and losses reported on the income statement.
** Unrealized gains and losses reported in the equity section of the balance sheet and in comprehensive income.

Debt Securities: Accounting Basics

This section explains the accounting basics for *debt securities,* including that for acquisition, disposition, and any interest.

Acquisition.   Debt securities are recorded at cost when purchased. To illustrate, assume that Music City paid $29,500 plus a $500 brokerage fee on September 1, 2012, to buy Dell's 7%, two-year bonds payable with a $30,000 par value. The bonds pay interest semiannually on August 31 and February 28. Music City intends to hold the bonds until they mature on August 31, 2014; consequently, they are classified as held-to-maturity (HTM) securities. The entry to record this purchase follows. (If the maturity of the securities was short term, and management's intent was to hold them until they mature, then they would be classified as Short-Term Investments—HTM.)

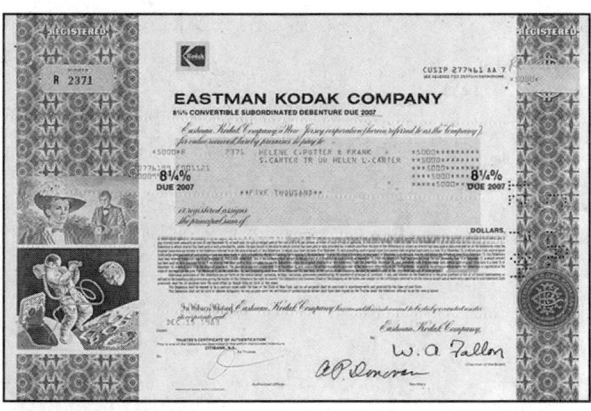

2012			
Sept. 1	Long-Term Investments—HTM (Dell)	30,000	
	Cash		30,000
	Purchased bonds to be held to maturity.		

Assets = Liabilities + Equity
+30,000
−30,000

Interest earned.   Interest revenue for investments in debt securities is recorded when earned. To illustrate, on December 31, 2012, at the end of its accounting period, Music City accrues interest receivable as follows.

Dec. 31	Interest Receivable	700	
	Interest Revenue		700
	Accrued interest earned ($30,000 × 7% × 4/12).		

Assets = Liabilities + Equity
+700   +700

The $700 reflects 4/6 of the semiannual cash receipt of interest—the portion Music City earned as of December 31. Relevant sections of Music City's financial statements at December 31, 2012, are shown in Exhibit 15.3.

EXHIBIT 15.3

Financial Statement Presentation
of Debt Securities

On the income statement for year 2012:

Interest revenue	$ 700

On the December 31, 2012, balance sheet:

Long-term investments—Held-to-maturity securities (at amortized cost)	$30,000

On February 28, 2013, Music City records receipt of semiannual interest.

Assets = Liabilities + Equity
+1,050   +350
−700

Feb. 28	Cash	1,050	
	Interest Receivable		700
	Interest Revenue		350
	Received six months' interest on Dell bonds.		

Disposition.   When the bonds mature, the proceeds (not including the interest entry) are recorded as:

Assets = Liabilities + Equity
+30,000
−30,000

2014			
Aug. 31	Cash	30,000	
	Long-Term Investments—HTM (Dell)		30,000
	Received cash from matured bonds.		

The cost of a debt security can be either higher or lower than its maturity value. When the investment is long term, the difference between cost and maturity value is amortized over the remaining life of the security. We assume for ease of computations that the cost of a long-term debt security equals its maturity value.

Example: What is cost per share?
Answer: Cost per share is the total cost of acquisition, including broker fees, divided by number of shares acquired.

Equity Securities: Accounting Basics

This section explains the accounting basics for *equity securities,* including that for acquisition, dividends, and disposition.

Acquisition.   Equity securities are recorded at cost when acquired, including commissions or brokerage fees paid. To illustrate, assume that Music City purchases 1,000 shares of Intex common stock at par value for $86,000 on October 10, 2012. It records this purchase of available-for-sale (AFS) securities as follows.

Assets = Liabilities + Equity
+86,000
−86,000

Oct. 10	Long-Term Investments—AFS (Intex)	86,000	
	Cash		86,000
	Purchased 1,000 shares of Intex.		

Dividend earned.   Any cash dividends received are credited to Dividend Revenue and reported in the income statement. To illustrate, on November 2, Music City receives a $1,720 quarterly cash dividend on the Intex shares, which it records as:

Assets = Liabilities + Equity
+1,720   +1,720

Nov. 2	Cash	1,720	
	Dividend Revenue		1,720
	Received dividend of $1.72 per share.		

Disposition.   When the securities are sold, sale proceeds are compared with the cost, and any gain or loss is recorded. To illustrate, on December 20, Music City sells 500 of the Intex shares for $45,000 cash and records this sale as:

Assets = Liabilities + Equity
+45,000   +2,000
−43,000

Dec. 20	Cash	45,000	
	Long-Term Investments—AFS (Intex)		43,000
	Gain on Sale of Long-Term Investments		2,000
	Sold 500 Intex shares ($86,000 × 500/1,000).		

REPORTING OF NONINFLUENTIAL INVESTMENTS

Companies must value and report most noninfluential investments at *fair value*. The exact reporting requirements depend on whether the investments are classified as (1) trading, (2) held-to-maturity, or (3) available-for-sale.

Trading Securities

Trading securities are *debt and equity securities* that the company intends to actively manage and trade for profit. Frequent purchases and sales are expected and are made to earn profits on short-term price changes. Trading securities are *always* reported as current assets.

P1	Account for trading securities.

Valuing and reporting trading securities.   The entire portfolio of trading securities is reported at its fair value; this requires a "fair value adjustment" from the cost of the portfolio. The term *portfolio* refers to a group of securities. Any unrealized gain (or loss) from a change in the fair value of the portfolio of trading securities is reported on the income statement. Most users believe accounting reports are more useful when changes in fair value for trading securities are reported in income.

To illustrate, TechCom's portfolio of trading securities had a total cost of $11,500 and a fair value of $13,000 on December 31, 2012, the first year it held trading securities. The difference between the $11,500 cost and the $13,000 fair value reflects a $1,500 gain. It is an unrealized gain because it is not yet confirmed by actual sales. The fair value adjustment for trading securities is recorded with an adjusting entry at the end of each period to equal the difference between the portfolio's cost and its fair value. TechCom records this gain as follows.

Point: '*Unrealized gain (or loss)*' refers to a change in fair value that is not yet realized through actual sale.

Point: 'Fair Value Adjustment—Trading' is a *permanent account*, shown as a deduction or addition to 'Short-Term Investments—Trading.'

Dec. 31	Fair Value Adjustment—Trading	1,500	
	Unrealized Gain—Income		1,500
	To reflect an unrealized gain in fair values of trading securities.		

Assets = Liabilities + Equity
+1,500   +1,500

The **Unrealized Gain (or Loss)** is reported in the Other Revenues and Gains (or Expenses and Losses) section on the income statement. Unrealized Gain (or Loss)—Income is a *temporary* account that is closed to Income Summary at the end of each period. Fair Value Adjustment—Trading is a *permanent* account, which adjusts the reported value of the trading securities portfolio from its prior period fair value to the current period fair value. The total cost of the trading securities portfolio is maintained in one account, and the fair value adjustment is recorded in a separate account. For example, TechCom's investment in trading securities is reported in the current assets section of its balance sheet as follows.

Example: If TechCom's trading securities have a cost of $14,800 and a fair value of $16,100 at Dec. 31, 2013, its adjusting entry is
Unrealized Loss—Income 200
   Fair Value Adj.—Trading 200
This is computed as: $1,500 Beg. Dr. bal. + $200 Cr. = $1,300 End. Dr. bal.

Current Assets		
Short-term investments—Trading (at cost)	$11,500	
Fair Value adjustment—Trading	1,500	
Short-term investments—Trading (at fair value)		$13,000
or simply		
Short-term investments—Trading (at fair value; cost is $11,500)		$13,000

Selling trading securities.   When individual trading securities are sold, the difference between the net proceeds (sale price less fees) and the cost of the individual trading securities that are sold is recognized as a gain or a loss. Any prior period fair value adjustment to the portfolio is *not* used to compute the gain or loss from sale of individual trading securities. For example, if TechCom sold some of its trading securities that had cost $1,000 for $1,200 cash on January 9, 2013, it would record the following.

Point: Reporting securities at fair value is referred to as *mark-to-market* accounting.

Assets = Liabilities + Equity
+1,200   +200
−1,000

Jan. 9	Cash	1,200	
	Short-Term Investments—Trading		1,000
	Gain on Sale of Short-Term Investments		200
	Sold trading securities costing $1,000 for $1,200 cash.		

A gain is reported in the Other Revenues and Gains section on the income statement, whereas a loss is shown in Other Expenses and Losses. When the period-end fair value adjustment for the portfolio of trading securities is computed, it excludes the cost and fair value of any securities sold.

Held-to-Maturity Securities

P2   Account for held-to-maturity securities.

Held-to-maturity (HTM) securities are *debt* securities a company intends and is able to hold until maturity. They are reported in current assets if their maturity dates are within one year or the operating cycle, whichever is longer. HTM securities are reported in long-term assets when the maturity dates extend beyond one year or the operating cycle, whichever is longer. All HTM securities are recorded at cost when purchased, and interest revenue is recorded when earned.

    The portfolio of HTM securities is usually reported at (amortized) cost, which is explained in advanced courses. There is no fair value adjustment to the portfolio of HTM securities—neither to the short-term nor long-term portfolios. The basics of accounting for HTM securities were described earlier in this chapter.

Point: Only debt securities can be classified as *held-to-maturity*; equity securities have no maturity date.

■ Decision Maker

Money Manager   You expect interest rates to sharply fall within a few weeks and remain at this lower rate. What is your strategy for holding investments in fixed-rate bonds and notes? ■   [Answer—p. 615]

Available-for-Sale Securities

P3   Account for available-for-sale securities.

Available-for-sale (AFS) securities are *debt and equity securities* not classified as trading or held-to-maturity securities. AFS securities are purchased to yield interest, dividends, or increases in fair value. They are not actively managed like trading securities. If the intent is to sell AFS securities within the longer of one year or operating cycle, they are classified as short-term investments. Otherwise, they are classified as long-term.

Valuing and reporting available-for-sale securities.   As with trading securities, companies adjust the cost of the portfolio of AFS securities to reflect changes in fair value. This is done with a fair value adjustment to its total portfolio cost. However, any unrealized gain or loss for the portfolio of AFS securities is *not* reported on the income statement. Instead, it is reported in the equity section of the balance sheet (and is part of *comprehensive income,* explained later). To illustrate, assume that Music City had no prior period investments in available-for-sale securities other than those purchased in the current period. Exhibit 15.4 shows both the cost and fair value of those investments on December 31, 2012, the end of its reporting period.

Example: If fair value in Exhibit 15.4 is $70,000 (instead of $74,550), what entry is made? *Answer:*
Unreal. Loss—Equity 3,000
    Fair Value Adj.—AFS. . .   3,000

EXHIBIT 15.4

Cost and Fair Value of Available-for-Sale Securities

	Cost	Fair Value	Unrealized Gain (Loss)
Improv bonds	$30,000	$29,050	$ (950)
Intex common stock, 500 shares	43,000	45,500	2,500
Total	$73,000	$74,550	$1,550

The year-end adjusting entry to record the fair value of these investments follows.

Assets = Liabilities + Equity
+1,550   +1,550

Dec. 31	Fair Value Adjustment—Available-for-Sale (LT)	1,550	
	Unrealized Gain—Equity		1,550
	To record adjustment to fair value of		
	available-for-sale securities.		

Exhibit 15.5 shows the December 31, 2012, balance sheet presentation—it assumes these investments are long term, but they can also be short term. It is also common to combine the cost of investments with the balance in the Fair Value Adjustment account and report the net as a single amount.

Assets		
Long-term investments—Available-for-sale (at cost)	$73,000	
Fair value adjustment—Available-for-sale	1,550	
Long-term investments—Available-for-sale (at fair value)		$74,550
or simply		
Long-term investments—Available-for-sale (at fair value; cost is $73,000)		$74,550
Equity		
...consists of usual equity accounts...		
Add unrealized gain on available-for-sale securities*		$ 1,550

Recorciled

Point: 'Unrealized Loss—Equity' and 'Unrealized Gain—Equity' are *permanent* (balance sheet) equity *accounts.*

EXHIBIT 15.5

Balance Sheet Presentation of Available-for-Sale Securities

* Often included under the caption Accumulated Other Comprehensive Income.

Let's extend this illustration and assume that at the end of its next calendar year (December 31, 2013), Music City's portfolio of long-term AFS securities has an $81,000 cost and an $82,000 fair value. It records the adjustment to fair value as follows.

Point: Income can be window-dressed upward by selling AFS securities with unrealized gains; income is reduced by selling those with unrealized losses.

Dec. 31	Unrealized Gain—Equity	550	
	Fair Value Adjustment—Available-for-Sale (LT).....		550
	To record adjustment to fair value of available-for-sale securities.		

Assets = Liabilities + Equity
−550   −550

The effects of the 2012 and 2013 securities transactions are reflected in the following T-accounts.

Example: If cost is $83,000 and fair value is $82,000 at Dec. 31, 2013, it records the following adjustment:
Unreal. Gain—Equity 1,550
Unreal. Loss—Equity 1,000
    Fair Value Adj.—AFS .. 2,550

Unrealized Gain—Equity				**Fair Value Adjustment—Available-for-Sale (LT)**			
Adj. 12/31/13	550	Bal. 12/31/12	1,550	Bal. 12/31/12	1,550	Adj. 12/31/13	550
		Bal. 12/31/13	1,000	Bal. 12/31/13	1,000		

Amounts reconcile.

Selling available-for-sale securities.   Accounting for the sale of individual AFS securities is identical to that described for the sale of trading securities. When individual AFS securities are sold, the difference between the cost of the individual securities sold and the net proceeds (sale price less fees) is recognized as a gain or loss.

Point: 'Fair Value Adjustment—Available-for-Sale' is a permanent account, shown as a deduction or addition to the Investment account.

Quick Check   Answers — p. 615

1. How are short-term held-to-maturity securities reported (valued) on the balance sheet?
2. How are trading securities reported (valued) on the balance sheet?
3. Where are unrealized gains and losses on available-for-sale securities reported?
4. Where are unrealized gains and losses on trading securities reported?
5. Does the Fair Value Adjustment account have a normal balance?

Alert   *Both U.S. GAAP (and IFRS) permit companies to use fair value in reporting financial assets (referred to as the fair value option). This option allows companies to report any financial asset at fair value and recognize value changes in income. This method was previously reserved only for trading securities, but is now an option for available-for-sale and held-to-maturity securities (and other 'financial assets and liabilities' such as accounts and notes receivable, accounts and notes payable, and bonds). U.S. standards also set a 3-level system to determine fair value:*
—Level 1: Use quoted market values
—Level 2: Use observable values from related assets or liabilities
—Level 3: Use unobservable values from estimates or assumptions
To date, a fairly small set of companies has chosen to broadly apply the fair value option—but, we continue to monitor its use ...

REPORTING OF INFLUENTIAL INVESTMENTS

Investment in Securities with Significant Influence

P4 Account for equity securities with significant influence.

A long-term investment classified as **equity securities with significant influence** implies that the investor can exert significant influence over the investee. An investor that owns 20% or more (but not more than 50%) of a company's voting stock is usually presumed to have a significant influence over the investee. In some cases, however, the 20% test of significant influence is overruled by other, more persuasive, evidence. This evidence can either lower the 20% requirement or increase it. The **equity method** of accounting and reporting is used for long-term investments in equity securities with significant influence, which is explained in this section.

Long-term investments in equity securities with significant influence are recorded at cost when acquired. To illustrate, Micron Co. records the purchase of 3,000 shares (30%) of Star Co. common stock at a total cost of $70,650 on January 1, 2012, as follows.

Assets = Liabilities + Equity
+70,650
−70,650

Jan. 1	Long-Term Investments—Star	70,650	
	Cash		70,650
	To record purchase of 3,000 Star shares.		

The investee's (Star) earnings increase both its net assets and the claim of the investor (Micron) on the investee's net assets. Thus, when the investee reports its earnings, the investor records its share of those earnings in its investment account. To illustrate, assume that Star reports net income of $20,000 for 2012. Micron then records its 30% share of those earnings as follows.

Assets = Liabilities + Equity
+6,000   +6,000

Dec. 31	Long-Term Investments—Star	6,000	
	Earnings from Long-Term Investment		6,000
	To record 30% equity in investee earnings.		

The debit reflects the increase in Micron's equity in Star. The credit reflects 30% of Star's net income. Earnings from Long-Term Investment is a *temporary* account (closed to Income Summary at each period-end) and is reported on the investor's (Micron's) income statement. If the investee incurs a net loss instead of a net income, the investor records its share of the loss and reduces (credits) its investment account. The investor closes this earnings or loss account to Income Summary.

The receipt of cash dividends is not revenue under the equity method because the investor has already recorded its share of the investee's earnings. Instead, cash dividends received by an investor from an investee are viewed as a conversion of one asset to another; that is, dividends reduce the balance of the investment account. To illustrate, Star declares and pays $10,000 in cash dividends on its common stock. Micron records its 30% share of these dividends received on January 9, 2013, as:

Assets = Liabilities + Equity
+3,000
−3,000

Jan. 9	Cash	3,000	
	Long-Term Investments—Star		3,000
	To record share of dividend paid by Star.		

The book value of an investment under the equity method equals the cost of the investment plus (minus) the investor's equity in the *undistributed* (*distributed*) earnings of the investee. Once Micron records these transactions, its Long-Term Investments account appears as in Exhibit 15.6.

EXHIBIT 15.6

Investment in Star Common Stock (Ledger Account)

Long-Term Investment—Star			
1/ 1/2012 Investment acquisition	70,650		
12/31/2012 Share of earnings	6,000		
12/31/2012 Balance	76,650		
		1/ 9/2013 Share of dividend	3,000
1/ 9/2013 Balance	73,650		

EXHIBIT 15.8

Accounting for Investments in Securities

Classification	Accounting
Short-Term Investment in Securities	
Held-to-maturity (debt) securities	Cost (without any discount or premium amortization)
Trading (debt and equity) securities	**Fair value** (with fair value adjustment to income)
Available-for-sale (debt and equity) securities	**Fair value** (with fair value adjustment to equity)
Long-Term Investment in Securities	
Held-to-maturity (debt) securities	Cost (with any discount or premium amortization)
Available-for-sale (debt and equity) securities	**Fair value** (with fair value adjustment to equity)
Equity securities with significant influence	Equity method
Equity securities with controlling influence	Equity method (with consolidation)

Comprehensive Income   **Comprehensive income** is defined as all changes in equity during a period except those from owners' investments and dividends. Specifically, comprehensive income is computed by adding or subtracting *other comprehensive income* to net income:

Net income	$ #
Other comprehensive income	#
Comprehensive income	$ #

Other comprehensive income includes unrealized gains and losses on available-for-sale securities, foreign currency translation adjustments, and certain pension adjustments. (*Accumulated other comprehensive income* is defined as the cumulative impact of *other comprehensive income*.)

Comprehensive income is reported in financial statements in one of two ways (which reflects new FASB guidance as of 2012):

1. On a separate *statement of comprehensive income* that immediately follows the income statement.

2. On the lower section of the income statement (as a single continuous *statement of income and comprehensive income*).

Option 1 is the most common. **KTM,** for example, reports a statement of comprehensive income following its income statement in Appendix A near the end of the book (Piaggio also applies this same presentation in Appendix A). Following is an abbreviated version of the KTM statement using language more common for U.S. GAAP:

KTM

Net income	**20,818**
Foreign currency conversion...................	107
Valuation of cash flow hedges, net of tax	8,545
Other comprehensive income	8,652
Total comprehensive income	**29,470**

Other comprehensive income

Option 2 adds the components of other comprehensive income to net income on the bottom of the income statement to compute a continuous statement of income and comprehensive income. There is no difference in the numbers; it is simply a matter of how those numbers are presented. A third option, which is no longer acceptable, was to include the components of other comprehensive income and its total along with the total of comprehensive income in the statement of equity. Polaris and Arctic Cat show examples of this presentation, which is no longer acceptable for future years.

Point: Some users believe that since AFS securities are not actively traded, reporting fair value changes in income would unnecessarily increase income variability and decrease usefulness.

Quick Check   Answers — p. 615

6. Give at least two examples of assets classified as long-term investments.

7. What are the requirements for an equity security to be listed as a long-term investment?

8. Identify similarities and differences in accounting for long-term investments in debt securities that are held-to-maturity versus those available-for-sale.

9. What are the three possible classifications of long-term equity investments? Describe the criteria for each class and the method used to account for each.

GLOBAL VIEW

This section discusses similarities and differences for the accounting and reporting of investments when financial statements are prepared under U.S. GAAP vis-à-vis IFRS.

Accounting for Noninfluential Securities   The accounting for noninfluential securities is broadly similar between U.S. GAAP and IFRS. *Trading securities* are accounted for using fair values with unrealized gains and losses reported in net income as fair values change. *Available-for-sale securities* are accounted for using fair values with unrealized gains and losses reported in other comprehensive income as fair values change (and later in net income when realized). *Held-to-maturity securities* are accounted for using amortized cost. Similarly, companies have the option under both systems to apply the fair value option for available-for-sale and held-to-maturity securities. Also, both systems review held-to-maturity securities for impairment. There are some differences in terminology under IFRS: (1) trading securities are commonly referred to as *financial assets at fair value through profit and loss,* and (2) available-for-sale securities are commonly referred to as *available-for-sale financial assets.* **NOKIA** reports the following categories for noninfluential securities: (1) *Financial assets at fair value through profit or loss,* consisting of financial assets held for trading and financial assets designated upon initial recognition as at fair value through profit or loss, (2) *Available-for-sale financial assets,* which are measured at fair value.

NOKIA

Accounting for Influential Securities   The accounting for influential securities is broadly similar across U.S. GAAP and IFRS. Specifically, under the *equity method,* the share of investee's net income is reported in the investor's income in the same period the investee earns that income; also, the investment account equals the acquisition cost plus the share of investee income less the share of investee dividends (minus amortization of excess on purchase price above fair value of identifiable, limited-life assets). Under the *consolidation method,* investee and investor revenues and expenses are combined, absent intercompany transactions, and subtracting noncontrolling interests. Also, nonintercompany assets and liabilities are similarly combined (eliminating the need for an investment account), and noncontrolling interests are subtracted from equity. There are some differences in terminology: (1) U.S. GAAP companies commonly refer to earnings from long-term investments as *equity in earnings of affiliates* whereas IFRS companies commonly use *equity in earnings of associated (or associate) companies,* (2) U.S. GAAP companies commonly refer to noncontrolling interests in consolidated subsidiaries as *minority interests* whereas IFRS companies commonly use *noncontrolling interests.*

Components of Return on Total Assets ◻◻◻ **Decision Analysis**

A company's **return on total assets** (or simply *return on assets*) is important in assessing financial performance. The return on total assets can be separated into two components, profit margin and total asset turnover, for additional analyses. Exhibit 15.9 shows how these two components determine return on total assets.

> **A1** Compute and analyze the components of return on total assets.

$$\text{Return on total assets} = \text{Profit margin} \times \text{Total asset turnover}$$

$$\frac{\text{Net income}}{\text{Average total assets}} = \frac{\text{Net income}}{\text{Net sales}} \times \frac{\text{Net sales}}{\text{Average total assets}}$$

EXHIBIT 15.9

Components of Return on Total Assets

Profit margin reflects the percent of net income in each dollar of net sales. Total asset turnover reflects a company's ability to produce net sales from total assets. All companies desire a high return on total assets. By considering these two components, we can often discover strengths and weaknesses not revealed by return on total assets alone. This improves our ability to assess future performance and company strategy.

To illustrate, consider return on total assets and its components for **Gap Inc.** in Exhibit 15.10.

EXHIBIT 15.10

Gap's Components of Return on Total Assets

Fiscal Year	Return on Total Assets	=	Profit Margin	×	Total Asset Turnover
2012	11.5%	=	5.7%	×	2.01
2011	16.0*	=	8.2	×	1.95
2010	14.1*	=	7.7	×	1.83
2009	12.6	=	6.66	×	1.89
2008	10.2*	=	5.28	×	1.92

* Differences due to rounding.

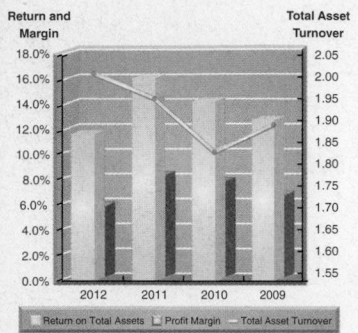

At least three findings emerge. First, Gap's return on total assets improved from 10.2% in 2008 to 11.5% in 2012. Second, total asset turnover has slightly improved over this period, from 1.92 to 2.01. Third, Gap's profit margin steadily increased over this period, from 2008's level of 5.28%. These components reveal the dual role of profit margin and total asset turnover in determining return on total assets. They also reveal that the driver of Gap's recent improvement in return on total assets is not total asset turnover but profit margin.

Generally, if a company is to maintain or improve its return on total assets, it must meet any decline in either profit margin or total asset turnover with an increase in the other. If not, return on assets will decline. Companies consider these components in planning strategies. A component analysis can also reveal where a company is weak and where changes are needed, especially in a competitor analysis. If asset turnover is lower than the industry norm, for instance, a company should focus on raising asset turnover at least to the norm. The same applies to profit margin.

■ **Decision Maker**

Retailer You are an entrepreneur and owner of a retail sporting goods store. The store's recent annual performance reveals (industry norms in parentheses): return on total assets = 11% (11.2%); profit margin = 4.4% (3.5%); and total asset turnover = 2.5 (3.2). What does your analysis of these figures reveal? ■ [Answer—p. 615]

DEMONSTRATION PROBLEM—1

Garden Company completes the following selected transactions related to its short-term investments during 2013.

May 8 Purchased 300 shares of FedEx stock as a short-term investment in available-for-sale securities at $40 per share plus $975 in broker fees.

Sept. 2 Sold 100 shares of its investment in FedEx stock at $47 per share and held the remaining 200 shares; broker's commission was $225.

Oct. 2 Purchased 400 shares of Ajay stock for $60 per share plus $1,600 in commissions. The stock is held as a short-term investment in available-for-sale securities.

Required

1. Prepare journal entries for the above transactions of Garden Company for 2013.

2. Prepare an adjusting journal entry as of December 31, 2013, if the fair values of the equity securities held by Garden Company are $48 per share for FedEx and $55 per share for Ajay. (Year 2013 is the first year Garden Company acquired short-term investments.)

SOLUTION TO DEMONSTRATION PROBLEM—1

1.

May 8	Short-Term Investments—AFS (FedEx)	12,975	
	Cash		12,975
	Purchased 300 shares of FedEx stock		
	(300 × $40) + $975.		

[continued on next page]

[continued from previous page]

Sept. 2	Cash	4,475	
	Gain on Sale of Short-Term Investment		150
	Short-Term Investments—AFS (FedEx)		4,325
	Sold 100 shares of FedEx for $47 per share less		
	a $225 commission. The original cost is		
	($12,975 × 100/300).		
Oct. 2	Short-Term Investments—AFS (Ajay)	25,600	
	Cash		25,600
	Purchased 400 shares of Ajay for $60 per share		
	plus $1,600 in commissions.		

2. Computation of unrealized gain or loss follows.

Short-Term Investments in Available-for-Sale Securities	Shares	Cost per Share	Total Cost	Fair Value per Share	Total Fair Value	Unrealized Gain (Loss)
FedEx	200	$43.25	$ 8,650	$48.00	$ 9,600	
Ajay	400	64.00	25,600	55.00	22,000	
Totals			$34,250		$31,600	$(2,650)

The adjusting entry follows:

Dec. 31	Unrealized Loss—Equity	2,650	
	Fair Value Adjustment—Available-for-Sale (ST)		2,650
	To reflect an unrealized loss in fair values		
	of available-for-sale securities.		

DEMONSTRATION PROBLEM—2

The following transactions relate to Brown Company's long-term investments during 2012 and 2013. Brown did not own any long-term investments prior to 2012. Show (1) the appropriate journal entries and (2) the relevant portions of each year's balance sheet and income statement that reflect these transactions for both 2012 and 2013.

2012

Sept. 9 Purchased 1,000 shares of Packard, Inc., common stock for $80,000 cash. These shares represent 30% of Packard's outstanding shares.

Oct. 2 Purchased 2,000 shares of AT&T common stock for $60,000 cash as a long-term investment. These shares represent less than a 1% ownership in AT&T.

17 Purchased as a long-term investment 1,000 shares of Apple Computer common stock for $40,000 cash. These shares are less than 1% of Apple's outstanding shares.

Nov. 1 Received $5,000 cash dividend from Packard.

30 Received $3,000 cash dividend from AT&T.

Dec. 15 Received $1,400 cash dividend from Apple.

31 Packard's net income for this year is $70,000.

31 Fair values for the investments in equity securities are Packard, $84,000; AT&T, $48,000; and Apple Computer, $45,000.

31 For preparing financial statements, note the following post-closing account balances: Common Stock, $500,000, and Retained Earnings, $350,000.

2013

Jan. 1 Sold Packard, Inc., shares for $108,000 cash.

May 30 Received $3,100 cash dividend from AT&T.

June 15 Received $1,600 cash dividend from Apple.

Aug. 17   Sold the AT&T stock for $52,000 cash.
      19   Purchased 2,000 shares of Coca-Cola common stock for $50,000 cash as a long-term investment. The stock represents less than a 5% ownership in Coca-Cola.
Dec. 15   Received $1,800 cash dividend from Apple.
      31   Fair values of the investments in equity securities are Apple, $39,000, and Coca-Cola, $48,000.
      31   For preparing financial statements, note the following post-closing account balances: Common Stock, $500,000, and Retained Earnings, $410,000.

PLANNING THE SOLUTION

- Account for the investment in Packard under the equity method.
- Account for the investments in AT&T, Apple, and Coca-Cola as long-term investments in available-for-sale securities.
- Prepare the information for the two years' balance sheets by including the relevant asset and equity accounts, and the two years' income statements by identifying the relevant revenues, earnings, gains, and losses.

SOLUTION TO DEMONSTRATION PROBLEM—2

1. Journal entries for 2012.

Sept. 9	Long-Term Investments—Packard	80,000	
	Cash		80,000
	Acquired 1,000 shares, representing a 30% equity in Packard.		
Oct. 2	Long-Term Investments—AFS (AT&T)	60,000	
	Cash		60,000
	Acquired 2,000 shares as a long-term investment in available-for-sale securities.		
Oct. 17	Long-Term Investments—AFS (Apple)	40,000	
	Cash		40,000
	Acquired 1,000 shares as a long-term investment in available-for-sale securities.		
Nov. 1	Cash	5,000	
	Long-Term Investments—Packard		5,000
	Received dividend from Packard.		
Nov. 30	Cash	3,000	
	Dividend Revenue		3,000
	Received dividend from AT&T.		
Dec. 15	Cash	1,400	
	Dividend Revenue		1,400
	Received dividend from Apple.		
Dec. 31	Long-Term Investments—Packard	21,000	
	Earnings from Investment (Packard)		21,000
	To record 30% share of Packard's annual earnings of $70,000.		
Dec. 31	Unrealized Loss—Equity	7,000	
	Fair Value Adjustment—Available-for-Sale (LT)* ...		7,000
	To record change in fair value of long-term available-for-sale securities.		

* Fair value adjustment computations:

	Cost	Fair Value	Unrealized Gain (Loss)
AT&T	$ 60,000	$48,000	$(12,000)
Apple	40,000	45,000	5,000
Total	$100,000	$93,000	$ (7,000)

Required balance of the Fair Value Adjustment—Available-for-Sale (LT) account (credit) .... $(7,000)
Existing balance 0
Necessary adjustment (credit) ...... $(7,000)

2. The December 31, 2012, selected balance sheet items appear as follows.

Assets	
Long-term investments	
Available-for-sale securities (at fair value; cost is $100,000)	$ 93,000
Investment in equity securities	96,000
Total long-term investments	189,000
Stockholders' Equity	
Common stock	500,000
Retained earnings	350,000
Unrealized loss—Equity	(7,000)

The relevant income statement items for the year ended December 31, 2012, follow.

Dividend revenue	$ 4,400
Earnings from investment	21,000

1. Journal entries for 2013.

Jan. 1	Cash	108,000	
	Long-Term Investments—Packard		96,000
	Gain on Sale of Long-Term Investments		12,000
	Sold 1,000 shares for cash.		
May 30	Cash	3,100	
	Dividend Revenue		3,100
	Received dividend from AT&T.		
June 15	Cash	1,600	
	Dividend Revenue		1,600
	Received dividend from Apple.		
Aug. 17	Cash	52,000	
	Loss on Sale of Long-Term Investments	8,000	
	Long-Term Investments—AFS (AT&T)		60,000
	Sold 2,000 shares for cash.		
Aug. 19	Long-Term Investments—AFS (Coca-Cola)	50,000	
	Cash		50,000
	Acquired 2,000 shares as a long-term investment in available-for-sale securities.		
Dec. 15	Cash	1,800	
	Dividend Revenue		1,800
	Received dividend from Apple.		
Dec. 31	Fair Value Adjustment—Available-for-Sale (LT)*	4,000	
	Unrealized Loss—Equity		4,000
	To record change in fair value of long-term available-for-sale securities.		

* Fair value adjustment computations:

	Cost	Fair Value	Unrealized Gain (Loss)		
Apple	$40,000	$39,000	$(1,000)	Required balance of the Fair Value Adjustment—Available-for-Sale (LT) account (credit)............	$(3,000)
Coca-Cola	50,000	48,000	(2,000)	Existing balance (credit)...........	(7,000)
Total	$90,000	$87,000	$(3,000)	Necessary adjustment (debit)	$ 4,000

2. The December 31, 2013, balance sheet items appear as follows.

Assets	
Long-term investments	
Available-for-sale securities (at fair value; cost is $90,000)	$ 87,000
Stockholders' Equity	
Common stock	500,000
Retained earnings	410,000
Unrealized loss—Equity	(3,000)

The relevant income statement items for the year ended December 31, 2013, follow.

Dividend revenue	$ 6,500
Gain on sale of long-term investments..........	12,000
Loss on sale of long-term investments..........	(8,000)

APPENDIX

15A   Investments in International Operations

Many entities from small entrepreneurs to large corporations conduct business internationally. Some entities' operations occur in so many different countries that the companies are called **multinationals.** Many of us think of **Coca-Cola** and **McDonald's**, for example, as primarily U.S. companies, but most of their sales occur outside the United States. Exhibit 15A.1 shows the percent of international sales and income for selected U.S. companies. Managing and accounting for multinationals present challenges. This section describes some of these challenges and how to account for and report these activities.

EXHIBIT 15A.1

International Sales and
Income as a Percent of
Their Totals

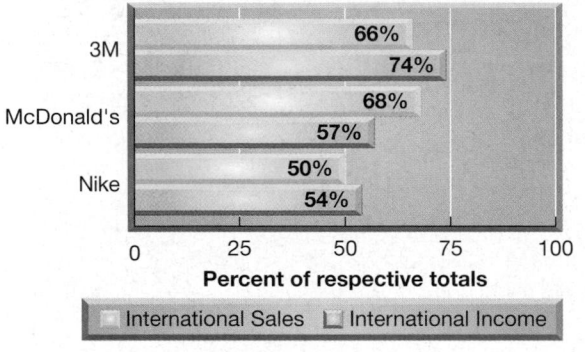

Two major accounting challenges that arise when companies have international operations relate to transactions that involve more than one currency. The first is to account for sales and purchases listed in a foreign currency. The second is to prepare consolidated financial statements with international subsidiaries. For ease in this discussion, we use companies with a U.S. base of operations and assume the need to prepare financial statements in U.S. dollars. This means the *reporting currency* of these companies is the U.S. dollar.

Point: Transactions *listed* or *stated* in a foreign currency are said to be *denominated* in that currency.

C3 Explain foreign exchange rates and record transactions listed in a foreign currency.

Exchange Rates between Currencies   Markets for the purchase and sale of foreign currencies exist all over the world. In these markets, U.S. dollars can be exchanged for Canadian dollars, British pounds, Japanese yen, Euros, or any other legal currencies. The price of one currency stated in terms of another currency is called a **foreign exchange rate.** Exhibit 15A.2 lists recent exchange rates for selected currencies. The exchange rate for British pounds and U.S. dollars is $1.8980, meaning 1 British pound could be purchased for $1.8980. On that same day, the exchange rate between Mexican pesos and U.S. dollars is $0.0925, or 1 Mexican peso can be purchased for $0.0925. Exchange rates fluctuate due to changing economic and political conditions, including the supply and demand for currencies and expectations about future events.

Point: To convert currency, see XE.com

 Decision Insight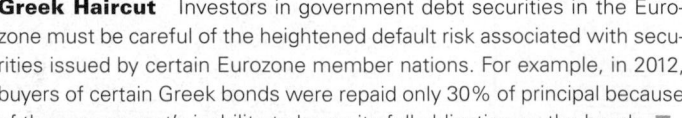

Greek Haircut   Investors in government debt securities in the Eurozone must be careful of the heightened default risk associated with securities issued by certain Eurozone member nations. For example, in 2012, buyers of certain Greek bonds were repaid only 30% of principal because of the government's inability to honor its full obligation on the bonds. ■

Source (unit)	Price in $U.S.	Source (unit)	Price in $U.S.
Britain (pound)	$1.8980	Canada (dollar)	$0.9793
Mexico (peso)	0.0925	Japan (yen)	0.0090
Taiwan (dollar)	0.0305	Europe (Euro)	1.2920

EXHIBIT 15A.2

Foreign Exchange Rates for Selected Currencies*

* Rates will vary over time based on economic, political, and other changes.

Sales and Purchases Listed in a Foreign Currency When a U.S. company makes a credit sale to an international customer, accounting for the sale and the account receivable is straightforward if sales terms require the international customer's payment in U.S. dollars. If sale terms require (or allow) payment in a foreign currency, however, the U.S. company must account for the sale and the account receivable in a different manner.

Sales in a Foreign Currency To illustrate, consider the case of the U.S.-based manufacturer Boston Company, which makes credit sales to London Outfitters, a British retail company. A sale occurs on December 12, 2012, for a price of £10,000 with payment due on February 10, 2013. Boston Company keeps its accounting records in U.S. dollars. To record the sale, Boston Company must translate the sales price from pounds to dollars. This is done using the exchange rate on the date of the sale. Assuming the exchange rate on December 12, 2012, is $1.80, Boston records this sale as follows.

Dec. 12	Accounts Receivable—London Outfitters	18,000	
	Sales*		18,000
	*To record a sale at £10,000, when the exchange rate equals $1.80. * (£10,000 × $1.80/£)*		

Assets = Liabilities + Equity
+18,000   +18,000

When Boston Company prepares its annual financial statements on December 31, 2012, the current exchange rate is $1.84. Thus, the current dollar value of Boston Company's receivable is $18,400 (£10,000 × $1.84/£). This amount is $400 higher than the amount recorded on December 12. Accounting principles require a receivable to be reported in the balance sheet at its current dollar value. Thus, Boston Company must make the following entry to record the increase in the dollar value of this receivable at year-end.

Dec. 31	Accounts Receivable—London Outfitters	400	
	Foreign Exchange Gain		400
	To record the increased value of the British pound for the receivable.		

Assets = Liabilities + Equity
+400   +400

On February 10, 2013, Boston Company receives London Outfitters' payment of £10,000. It immediately exchanges the pounds for U.S. dollars. On this date, the exchange rate for pounds is $1.78. Thus, Boston Company receives only $17,800 (£10,000 × $1.78/£). It records the cash receipt and the loss associated with the decline in the exchange rate as follows.

Point: Foreign exchange gains are credits, and foreign exchange losses are debits.

Feb. 10	Cash	17,800	
	Foreign Exchange Loss	600	
	Accounts Receivable—London Outfitters		18,400
	Received foreign currency payment of an account and converted it into dollars.		

Assets = Liabilities + Equity
+17,800   −600
−18,400

Gains and losses from foreign exchange transactions are accumulated in the Foreign Exchange Gain (or Loss) account. After year-end adjustments, the balance in the Foreign Exchange Gain (or Loss) account is reported on the income statement and closed to the Income Summary account.

Purchases in a Foreign Currency Accounting for credit purchases from an international seller is similar to the case of a credit sale to an international customer. In particular, if the U.S. company is required to make payment in a foreign currency, the account payable must be translated into dollars before the U.S. company can record it. If the exchange rate is different when preparing financial statements and when paying for the purchase, the U.S. company must recognize a foreign exchange gain or loss at those dates. To illustrate, assume NC Imports, a U.S. company, purchases products costing €20,000 (euros) from

Example: Assume that a U.S. company makes a credit purchase from a British company for £10,000 when the exchange rate is $1.62. At the balance sheet date, this rate is $1.72. Does this imply a gain or loss for the U.S. company? *Answer:* A loss.

Hamburg Brewing on January 15, when the exchange rate is $1.20 per euro. NC records this transaction as follows.

Assets = Liabilities + Equity
+24,000   +24,000

Jan. 15	Inventory	24,000	
	Accounts Payable—Hamburg Brewing		24,000
	To record a €20,000 purchase when exchange rate is $1.20 (€20,000 × $1.20/€)		

NC Imports makes payment in full on February 14 when the exchange rate is $1.25 per euro, which is recorded as follows.

Assets = Liabilities + Equity
−25,000   −24,000   −1,000

Feb. 14	Accounts Payable—Hamburg Brewing	24,000	
	Foreign Exchange Loss	1,000	
	Cash		25,000
	To record cash payment towards €20,000 account when exchange rate is $1.25 (€20,000 × $1.25/€).		

Decision Insight

Global Greenback   What do changes in foreign exchange rates mean? A decline in the price of the U.S. dollar against other currencies usually yields increased international sales for U.S. companies, without hiking prices or cutting costs, and puts them on a stronger competitive footing abroad. At home, they can raise prices without fear that foreign rivals will undercut them. ■

Consolidated Statements with International Subsidiaries   A second challenge in accounting for international operations involves preparing consolidated financial statements when the parent company has one or more international subsidiaries. Consider a U.S.-based company that owns a controlling interest in a French subsidiary. The reporting currency of the U.S. parent is the dollar. The French subsidiary maintains its financial records in euros. Before preparing consolidated statements, the parent must translate financial statements of the French company into U.S. dollars. After this translation is complete (including that for accounting differences), it prepares consolidated statements the same as for domestic subsidiaries. Procedures for translating an international subsidiary's account balances depend on the nature of the subsidiary's operations. The process requires the parent company to select appropriate foreign exchange rates and to apply those rates to the foreign subsidiary's account balances. This is described in advanced courses.

Global: A weaker U.S. dollar often increases global sales for U.S. companies.

Decision Maker

Entrepreneur   Assume that Ben and Jerry's purchases milk from dairies in both the U.S. and Canada. The price of the Canadian dollar in terms of the U.S. dollar jumps from US$0.70 to US$0.80. Is the ice cream maker now more or less likely to buy milk from Canadian or U.S. suppliers? ■   [Answer—p. 615]

Summary

C1   **Distinguish between debt and equity securities and between short-term and long-term investments.** *Debt securities* reflect a creditor relationship and include investments in notes, bonds, and certificates of deposit. *Equity securities* reflect an owner relationship and include shares of stock issued by other companies. Short-term investments in securities are current assets that meet two criteria: (1) They are expected to be converted into cash within one year or the current operating cycle of the business, whichever is longer and (2) they are readily convertible to cash, or *marketable*. All other investments in securities are long-term. Long-term investments also include assets not used in operations and those held for special purposes, such as land for expansion. Investments in securities are classified into one of five groups: (1) trading securities, which are always short-term, (2) debt securi-

ties held-to-maturity, (3) debt and equity securities available-for-sale, (4) equity securities in which an investor has a significant influence over the investee, and (5) equity securities in which an investor has a controlling influence over the investee.

C2   **Describe how to report equity securities with controlling influence.** If an investor owns more than 50% of another company's voting stock and controls the investee, the investor's financial reports are prepared on a consolidated basis. These reports are prepared as if the company were organized as one entity.

C3A   **Explain foreign exchange rates and record transactions listed in a foreign currency.** A foreign exchange rate is the price of one currency stated in terms of another. An entity with transactions in a foreign currency when the exchange rate changes between the transaction dates and their settlement will experience exchange gains or losses. When a company makes a credit sale to a foreign customer and sales terms call for payment in a foreign currency, the company must translate the foreign currency into dollars to record the receivable. If the exchange rate changes before payment is received, exchange gains or losses are recognized in the year they occur. The same treatment is used when a company makes a credit purchase from a foreign supplier and is required to make payment in a foreign currency.

A1 **Compute and analyze the components of return on total assets.** Return on total assets has two components: profit margin and total asset turnover. A decline in one component must be met with an increase in another if return on assets is to be maintained. Component analysis is helpful in assessing company performance compared to that of competitors and its own past.

P1 **Account for trading securities.** Investments are initially recorded at cost, and any dividend or interest from these investments is recorded in the income statement. Investments classified as trading securities are reported at fair value. Unrealized gains and losses on trading securities are reported in income. When investments are sold, the difference between the net proceeds from the sale and the cost of the securities is recognized as a gain or loss.

P2 **Account for held-to-maturity securities.** Debt securities held-to-maturity are reported at cost when purchased. Interest revenue is recorded as it accrues. The cost of long-term held-to-maturity securities is adjusted for the amortization of any difference between cost and maturity value.

P3 **Account for available-for-sale securities.** Debt and equity securities available-for-sale are recorded at cost when purchased. Available-for-sale securities are reported at their fair values on the balance sheet with unrealized gains or losses shown in the equity section. Gains and losses realized on the sale of these investments are reported in the income statement.

P4 **Account for equity securities with significant influence.** The equity method is used when an investor has a significant influence over an investee. This usually exists when an investor owns 20% or more of the investee's voting stock but not more than 50%. The equity method means an investor records its share of investee earnings with a debit to the investment account and a credit to a revenue account. Dividends received reduce the investment account balance.

Guidance Answers to Decision Maker

Money Manager   If you have investments in fixed-rate bonds and notes when interest rates fall, the value of your investments increases. This is so because the bonds and notes you hold continue to pay the same (high) rate while the market is demanding a new lower interest rate. Your strategy is to continue holding your investments in bonds and notes, and, potentially, to increase these holdings through additional purchases.

Retailer   Your store's return on assets is 11%, which is similar to the industry norm of 11.2%. However, disaggregation of return on assets reveals that your store's profit margin of 4.4% is much higher than the norm of 3.5%, but your total asset turnover of 2.5 is much lower than the norm of 3.2. These results suggest that, as compared with competitors, you are less efficient in using assets. You need to

focus on increasing sales or reducing assets. You might consider reducing prices to increase sales, provided such a strategy does not reduce your return on assets. For instance, you could reduce your profit margin to 4% to increase sales. If total asset turnover increases to more than 2.75 when profit margin is lowered to 4%, your overall return on assets is improved.

Entrepreneur   You are now less likely to buy Canadian milk products because it takes more U.S. money to buy a Canadian dollar (and milk). For instance, the purchase of milk from a Canadian dairy with a $1,000 (Canadian dollars) price would have cost the U.S. company $700 (U.S. dollars, computed as C$1,000 × US$0.70) before the rate change, and $800 (US dollars, computed as C$1,000 × US$0.80) after the rate change.

Guidance Answers to Quick Checks

1. Short-term held-to-maturity securities are reported at cost.
2. Trading securities are reported at fair value.
3. The equity section of the balance sheet (and in comprehensive income).
4. The income statement.
5. The Fair Value Adjustment account does not have a normal balance. Its balance is a function of market values for securities which move up or down. The balance of this valuation account is determined by market conditions.
6. Long-term investments include (1) long-term funds earmarked for a special purpose, (2) debt and equity securities that do not meet current asset requirements, and (3) long-term assets not used in the regular operations of the business.
7. An equity investment is classified as long term if it is not marketable or, if marketable, it is not held as an available source of cash to meet the needs of current operations.

8. Debt securities held-to-maturity and debt securities available-for-sale are both recorded at cost. Also, interest on both is accrued as earned. However, only long-term securities held-to-maturity require amortization of the difference between cost and maturity value. In addition, only securities available-for-sale require a period-end adjustment to fair value.

9. Long-term equity investments are placed in one of three categories and accounted for as follows: (a) **available-for-sale** (noninfluential, less than 20% of outstanding stock)—fair value; (b) **significant influence** (20% to 50% of outstanding stock)—equity method; and (c) **controlling influence** (holding more than 50% of outstanding stock)—equity method with consolidation.

Key Terms

Available-for-sale (AFS) securities (p. 603)

Comprehensive income (p. 606)

Consolidated financial statements (p. 605)

Equity method (p. 604)

Equity securities with controlling influence (p. 605)

Equity securities with significant influence (p. 604)

Foreign exchange rate (p. 612)

Held-to-maturity (HTM) securities (p. 602)

Long-term investments (p. 598)

Multinational (p. 612)

Other comprehensive income (p. 606)

Parent (p. 605)

Return on total assets (p. 607)

Short-term investments (p. 598)

Subsidiary (p. 605)

Trading securities (p. 601)

Unrealized gain (loss) (p. 601)

Multiple Choice Quiz   Answers on p. 631   mhhe.com/wildFAP21e

Additional Quiz Questions are available at the book's Website.

1. A company purchased $30,000 of 5% bonds for investment purposes on May 1. The bonds pay interest on February 1 and August 1. The amount of interest revenue accrued at December 31 (the company's year-end) is:
   a. $1,500
   b. $1,375
   c. $1,000
   d. $625
   e. $300

2. Earlier this period, Amadeus Co. purchased its only available-for-sale investment in the stock of Bach Co. for $83,000. The period-end fair value of this stock is $84,500. Amadeus records a:
   a. Credit to Unrealized Gain—Equity for $1,500.
   b. Debit to Unrealized Loss—Equity for $1,500.
   c. Debit to Investment Revenue for $1,500.
   d. Credit to Fair Value Adjustment—Available-for-Sale for $3,500.
   e. Credit to Cash for $1,500.

3. Mozart Co. owns 35% of Melody Inc. Melody pays $50,000 in cash dividends to its shareholders for the period. Mozart's entry to record the Melody dividend includes a:
   a. Credit to Investment Revenue for $50,000.
   b. Credit to Long-Term Investments for $17,500.

   c. Credit to Cash for $17,500.
   d. Debit to Long-Term Investments for $17,500.
   e. Debit to Cash for $50,000.

4. A company has net income of $300,000, net sales of $2,500,000, and total assets of $2,000,000. Its return on total assets equals:
   a. 6.7%
   b. 12.0%
   c. 8.3%
   d. 80.0%
   e. 15.0%

5. A company had net income of $80,000, net sales of $600,000, and total assets of $400,000. Its profit margin and total asset turnover are:

	Profit Margin	Total Asset Turnover
a.	1.5%	13.3
b.	13.3%	1.5
c.	13.3%	0.7
d.	7.0%	13.3
e.	10.0%	26.7

A Superscript A denotes assignments based on Appendix 15A.

🔃 Icon denotes assignments that involve decision making.

Discussion Questions

1. Under what two conditions should investments be classified as current assets?

2. 🔃 On a balance sheet, what valuation must be reported for short-term investments in trading securities?

3. If a short-term investment in available-for-sale securities costs $10,000 and is sold for $12,000, how should the difference between these two amounts be recorded?

4. Identify the three classes of noninfluential and two classes of influential investments in securities.

5. Under what conditions should investments be classified as current assets? As long-term assets?

6. For investments in available-for-sale securities, how are unrealized (holding) gains and losses reported?

7. If a company purchases its only long-term investments in available-for-sale debt securities this period and their fair value is below cost at the balance sheet date, what entry is required to recognize this unrealized loss?

8. On a balance sheet, what valuation must be reported for debt securities classified as available-for-sale?

9. Under what circumstances are long-term investments in debt securities reported at cost and adjusted for amortization of any difference between cost and maturity value?

10. In accounting for investments in equity securities, when should the equity method be used?

11. Under what circumstances does a company prepare consolidated financial statements?

12.ᴬ What are two major challenges in accounting for international operations?

13.ᴬ Assume a U.S. company makes a credit sale to a foreign customer that is required to make payment in its foreign currency. In the current period, the exchange rate is $1.40 on the date of the sale and is $1.30 on the date the customer pays the receivable. Will the U.S. company record an exchange gain or loss?

14.ᴬ If a U.S. company makes a credit sale to a foreign customer required to make payment in U.S. dollars, can the U.S. company have an exchange gain or loss on this sale?

15. Refer to **Polaris**' statement of changes in shareholders' equity in Appendix A. What is the amount of foreign currency translation adjustment for the year ended December 31, 2011? Is this adjustment an unrealized gain or an unrealized loss? **Polaris**

16. Refer to **Arctic Cat**'s statement of stockholders' equity. What was the amount of its fiscal 2011 unrealized gain or loss on derivative instruments? **Arctic Cat**

17. Refer to the balance sheet of **KTM** in Appendix A. How can you tell that KTM uses the consolidated method of accounting? **KTM**

18. Refer to the financial statements of **Piaggio** in Appendix A. Compute its return on total assets for the year ended December 31, 2011. **PIAGGIO**

---

connect

On April 18, Riley Co. made a short-term investment in 300 common shares of XLT Co. The purchase price is $42 per share and the broker's fee is $250. The intent is to actively manage these shares for profit. On May 30, Riley Co. receives $1 per share from XLT in dividends. Prepare the April 18 and May 30 journal entries to record these transactions.

QUICK STUDY

QS 15-1
Short-term equity investments

P1

Journ Co. purchased short-term investments in available-for-sale securities at a cost of $50,000 on November 25, 2013. At December 31, 2013, these securities had a fair value of $47,000. This is the first and only time the company has purchased such securities.

1. Prepare the December 31, 2013, year-end adjusting entry for the securities' portfolio.

2. For each account in the entry for part 1, explain how it is reported in financial statements.

3. Prepare the April 6, 2014, entry when Journ sells one-half of these securities for $26,000.

QS 15-2
Available-for-sale securities

P3

Prepare Hertog Company's journal entries to reflect the following transactions for the current year.

May 7   Purchases 200 shares of Kraft stock as a short-term investment in available-for-sale securities at a cost of $50 per share plus $300 in broker fees.

June 6   Sells 200 shares of its investment in Kraft stock at $56 per share. The broker's commission on this sale is $150.

QS 15-3
Available-for-sale securities

P3

Hiker Company completes the following transactions during the current year.

May 9   Purchases 200 shares of Higo stock as a short-term investment in available-for-sale securities at a cost of $25 per share plus $150 in broker fees.

June 2   Sells 100 shares of its investment in Higo stock at $28 per share. The broker's commission on this sale is $90.

Dec. 31   The closing market price (fair value) of the Higo stock is $23 per share.

Prepare the May 9 and June 2 journal entries and the December 31 adjusting entry. This is the first and only time the company purchased such securities.

QS 15-4
Available-for-sale securities

P3

Which of the following statements are true of long-term investments?

a. They are held as an investment of cash available for current operations.

b. They can include funds earmarked for a special purpose, such as bond sinking funds.

c. They can include investments in trading securities.

[continued on next page]

QS 15-5
Identifying long-term investments

C1

    d. They can include debt securities held-to-maturity.

    e. They are always easily sold and therefore qualify as being marketable.

    f. They can include debt and equity securities available-for-sale.

    g. They can include bonds and stocks not intended to serve as a ready source of cash.

QS 15-6
Describing investments
in securities
C1 C2

Complete the following descriptions by filling in the blanks.

1. Equity securities giving an investor significant influence are accounted for using the _____ _____.

2. Available-for-sale debt securities are reported on the balance sheet at _____ _____.

3. Trading securities are classified as _____ assets.

4. Accrual of interest on bonds held as long-term investments requires a credit to _____ _____.

5. The controlling investor (more than 50% ownership) is called the _____, and the investee company is called the _____.

QS 15-7
Debt securities transactions
P2

On February 1, 2013, Garzon purchased 6% bonds issued by PBS Utilities at a cost of $40,000, which is their par value. The bonds pay interest semiannually on July 31 and January 31. For 2013, prepare entries to record Garzon's July 31 receipt of interest and its December 31 year-end interest accrual.

QS 15-8
Recording equity securities
P3

On May 20, 2013, Montero Co. paid $1,000,000 to acquire 25,000 common shares (10%) of ORD Corp. as a long-term investment. On August 5, 2014, Montero sold one-half of these shares for $625,000. What valuation method should be used to account for this stock investment? Prepare entries to record both the acquisition and the sale of these shares.

QS 15-9
Equity method transactions
P4

Assume the same facts as in QS 15-8 except that the stock acquired represents 40% of ORD Corp.'s outstanding stock. Also assume that ORD Corp. paid a $100,000 dividend on November 1, 2013, and reported a net income of $700,000 for 2013. Prepare the entries to record (*a*) the receipt of the dividend and (*b*) the December 31, 2013, year-end adjustment required for the investment account.

QS 15-10
Recording fair value adjustment
for securities
P3

During the current year, Reed Consulting Group acquired long-term available-for-sale securities at a $70,000 cost. At its December 31 year-end, these securities had a fair value of $58,000. This is the first and only time the company purchased such securities.

1. Prepare the necessary year-end adjusting entry related to these securities.

2. Explain how each account used in part 1 is reported in the financial statements.

QS 15-11
Equity securities with
controlling influence
C2

Complete the following descriptions by filling in the blanks.

1. The controlling investor is called the _____, and the investee is called the _____.

2. A long-term investment classified as equity securities with controlling influence implies that the investor can exert a _____ influence over the investee.

QS 15-12
Return on total
assets A1

The return on total assets is the focus of analysts, creditors, and other users of financial statements.

1. How is the return on total assets computed?

2. What does this important ratio reflect?

QS 15-13
Component return on total
assets A1

Return on total assets can be separated into two important components.

1. Write the formula to separate the return on total assets into its two basic components.

2. Explain how these components of the return on total assets are helpful to financial statement users for business decisions.

QS 15-14^A
Foreign currency transactions
C3

A U.S. company sells a product to a British company with the transaction listed in British pounds. On the date of the sale, the transaction total of $14,500 is billed as £10,000, reflecting an exchange rate of 1.45 (that is, $1.45 per pound). Prepare the entry to record (1) the sale and (2) the receipt of payment in pounds when the exchange rate is 1.35.

QS 15-15^A
Foreign currency transactions
C3

On March 1, 2013, a U.S. company made a credit sale requiring payment in 30 days from a Malaysian company, Hamac Sdn. Bhd., in 20,000 Malaysian ringgits. Assuming the exchange rate between Malaysian ringgits and U.S. dollars is $0.4538 on March 1 and $0.4899 on March 31, prepare the entries to record the sale on March 1 and the cash receipt on March 31.

The **Carrefour Group** reports the following description of its trading securities (titled "financial assets reported at fair value in the income statement").

QS 15-16
International accounting
for investments
P1

> These are financial assets held by the Group in order to make a short-term profit on the sale. These assets are valued at their fair value with variations in value recognized in the income statement.

Note 10 to Carrefour's 2010 financial statements reports €7 million in unrealized gains for 2010 and €26 million in unrealized losses for 2010, both included in the fair value of those financial assets held for trading. What amount of these unrealized gains and unrealized losses, if any, are reported in its 2010 income statement? Explain.

connect

Prepare journal entries to record the following transactions involving the short-term securities investments of Duke Co., all of which occurred during year 2013.

EXERCISES

a. On March 22, purchased 1,000 shares of RIP Company stock at $10 per share plus a $80 brokerage fee. These shares are categorized as trading securities.

b. On September 1, received a $1.00 per share cash dividend on the RIP Company stock purchased in transaction *a*.

c. On October 8, sold 500 shares of RIP Co. stock for $15 per share, less a $50 brokerage fee.

Exercise 15-1
Accounting for short-term trading securities
P1

(*c*) Dr. Cash $7,450

Prepare journal entries to record the following transactions involving the short-term securities investments of Natura Co., all of which occurred during year 2013.

Exercise 15-2
Accounting for short-term held-to-maturity securities   P2

a. On June 15, paid $1,000,000 cash to purchase Remedy's 90-day short-term debt securities ($1,000,000 principal), dated June 15, that pay 10% interest (categorized as held-to-maturity securities).

b. On September 16, received a check from Remedy in payment of the principal and 90 days' interest on the debt securities purchased in transaction *a*.

Prepare journal entries to record the following transactions involving the short-term securities investments of Krum Co., all of which occurred during year 2013.

Exercise 15-3
Accounting for short-term available-for-sale securities
P3

a. On August 1, paid $450,000 cash to purchase Houtte's 9% debt securities ($450,000 principal), dated July 30, 2013, and maturing January 30, 2014 (categorized as available-for-sale securities).

b. On October 30, received a check from Houtte for 90 days' interest on the debt securities purchased in transaction *a*.

Complete the following descriptions by filling in the blanks.

1. Debt securities reflect a _____ relationship such as investments in notes, bonds, and certificates of deposit.

2. Equity securities reflect an _____ relationship such as shares of stock issued by companies.

3. Short-term investments are securities that (1) management intends to convert to cash within ___ ___ or the ___ ___ whichever is longer, and (2) are readily convertible to _____.

4. Long-term investments in securities are defined as those securities that are ___ ___ convertible to cash or are ___ ___ to be converted into cash in the short term.

Exercise 15-4
Debt and equity securities and short- and long-term investments
C1

Complete the following descriptions by filling in the blanks.

1. Consolidated _____ _____ show the financial position, results of operations, and cash flows of all entities under the parent's control, including all subsidiaries.

2. The equity method with _____ is used to account for long-term investments in equity securities with controlling influence.

Exercise 15-5
Equity securities with controlling influence
C2

Brooks Co. purchases various investments in trading securities at a cost of $66,000 on December 27, 2013. (This is its first and only purchase of such securities.) At December 31, 2013, these securities had a fair value of $72,000.

1. Prepare the December 31, 2013, year-end adjusting entry for the trading securities' portfolio.

2. Explain how each account in the entry of part 1 is reported in financial statements.

3. Prepare the January 3, 2014, entry when Brooks sells a portion of its trading securities (that had originally cost $33,000) for $35,000.

Exercise 15-6
Accounting for trading securities
P1

Check (3) Gain, $2,000

Exercise 15-7

Adjusting available-for-sale securities to fair value

P3

On December 31, 2013, Reggit Company held the following short-term investments in its portfolio of available-for-sale securities. Reggit had no short-term investments in its prior accounting periods. Prepare the December 31, 2013, adjusting entry to report these investments at fair value.

	Cost	Fair Value
Verrizano Corporation bonds payable	$89,600	$91,600
Preble Corporation notes payable	70,600	62,900
Lucerne Company common stock	86,500	83,100

Check   Unrealized loss, $9,100

Exercise 15-8

Transactions in short-term and long-term investments

P1   P2   P3

Prepare journal entries to record the following transactions involving both the short-term and long-term investments of Cancun Corp., all of which occurred during calendar year 2013. Use the account Short-Term Investments for any transactions that you determine are short term.

a. On February 15, paid $160,000 cash to purchase American General's 90-day short-term notes at par, which are dated February 15 and pay 10% interest (classified as held-to-maturity).

b. On March 22, bought 700 shares of Fran Industries common stock at $51 cash per share plus a $150 brokerage fee (classified as long-term available-for-sale securities).

c. On May 15, received a check from American General in payment of the principal and 90 days' interest on the notes purchased in transaction *a*.

d. On July 30, paid $100,000 cash to purchase MP3 Electronics' 8% notes at par, dated July 30, 2013, and maturing on January 30, 2014 (classified as trading securities).

e. On September 1, received a $1.00 per share cash dividend on the Fran Industries common stock purchased in transaction *b*.

f. On October 8, sold 350 shares of Fran Industries common stock for $64 cash per share, less a $125 brokerage fee.

g. On October 30, received a check from MP3 Electronics for three months' interest on the notes purchased in transaction *d*.

Exercise 15-9

Fair value adjustment to available-for-sale securities

P3

On December 31, 2013, Lujack Co. held the following short-term available-for-sale securities.

	Cost	Fair Value
Nintendo Co. common stock	$44,450	$48,900
Atlantic bonds payable	49,000	47,000
Kellogg Co. notes payable	25,000	23,200
McDonald's Corp. common stock	46,300	44,800

Lujack had no short-term investments prior to the current period. Prepare the December 31, 2013, year-end adjusting entry to record the fair value adjustment for these securities.

Exercise 15-10

Fair value adjustment to available-for-sale securities

P3

Prescrip Co. began operations in 2012. The cost and fair values for its long-term investments portfolio in available-for-sale securities are shown below. Prepare Prescrip's December 31, 2013, adjusting entry to reflect any necessary fair value adjustment for these investments.

	Cost	Fair Value
December 31, 2012	$120,483	$118,556
December 31, 2013	60,120	90,271

Exercise 15-11

Multiyear fair value adjustments to available-for-sale securities

P3

Ticker Services began operations in 2011 and maintains long-term investments in available-for-sale securities. The year-end cost and fair values for its portfolio of these investments follow. Prepare journal entries to record each year-end fair value adjustment for these securities.

	Cost	Fair Value
December 31, 2011	$372,000	$360,860
December 31, 2012	428,500	455,800
December 31, 2013	600,200	700,500
December 31, 2014	876,900	780,200

Information regarding Carperk Company's individual investments in securities during its calendar-year 2013, along with the December 31, 2013, fair values, follows.

a. Investment in Brava Company bonds: $420,500 cost, $457,000 fair value. Carperk intends to hold these bonds until they mature in 2018.

b. Investment in Baybridge common stock: 29,500 shares; $362,450 cost; $391,375 fair value. Carperk owns 32% of Baybridge's voting stock and has a significant influence over Baybridge.

c. Investment in Buffa common stock: 12,000 shares; $165,500 cost; $178,000 fair value. This investment amounts to 3% of Buffa's outstanding shares, and Carperk's goal with this investment is to earn dividends over the next few years.

d. Investment in Newton common stock: 3,500 shares; $90,300 cost; $88,625 fair value. Carperk's goal with this investment is to reap an increase in fair value of the stock over the next three to five years. Newton has 30,000 common shares outstanding.

e. Investment in Farmers common stock: 16,300 shares; $100,860 cost; $111,210 fair value. This stock is marketable and is held as an investment of cash available for operations.

Required

1. Identify whether each investment should be classified as a short-term or long-term investment. For each long-term investment, indicate in which of the long-term investment classifications it should be placed.

2. Prepare a journal entry dated December 31, 2013, to record the fair value adjustment of the long-term investments in available-for-sale securities. Carperk had no long-term investments prior to year 2013.

Exercise 15-12
Classifying investments in securities; recording fair values
C1 P2 P3 P4

Check (2) Unrealized gain, $10,825

Prepare journal entries to record the following transactions and events of Kodax Company.

2013

Jan. 2 Purchased 30,000 shares of Grecco Co. common stock for $408,000 cash plus a broker's fee of $3,000 cash. Bushtex has 90,000 shares of common stock outstanding and its policies will be significantly influenced by Kodax.
Sept. 1 Grecco declared and paid a cash dividend of $1.50 per share.
Dec. 31 Grecco announced that net income for the year is $486,900.

2014

June 1 Grecco declared and paid a cash dividend of $2.10 per share.
Dec. 31 Grecco announced that net income for the year is $702,750.
Dec. 31 Kodax sold 10,000 shares of Grecco for $320,000 cash.

Exercise 15-13
Securities transactions; equity method
P4

The following information is available from the financial statements of Regae Industries. Compute Regae's return on total assets for 2013 and 2014. (Round returns to one-tenth of a percent.) Comment on the company's efficiency in using its assets in 2013 and 2014.

Exercise 15-14
Return on total assets
A1

	2012	2013	2014
Total assets, December 31	$210,000	$340,000	$770,000
Net income	30,200	38,400	60,300

Leigh of New York sells its products to customers in the United States and the United Kingdom. On December 16, 2013, Leigh sold merchandise on credit to Bronson Ltd. of London at a price of 17,000 pounds. The exchange rate on that day for £1 was $1.4583. On December 31, 2013, when Leigh prepared its financial statements, the rate was £1 for $1.4382. Bronson paid its bill in full on January 15, 2014, at which time the exchange rate was £1 for $1.4482. Leigh immediately exchanged the 17,000 pounds for U.S. dollars. Prepare Leigh's journal entries on December 16, December 31, and January 15 (round to the nearest dollar).

Exercise 15-15[A]
Foreign currency transactions
C3

Exercise 15-16[A]
Computing foreign exchange
gains and losses on receivables

C3

On May 8, 2013, Jett Company (a U.S. company) made a credit sale to Lopez (a Mexican company). The terms of the sale required Lopez to pay 800,000 pesos on February 10, 2014. Jett prepares quarterly financial statements on March 31, June 30, September 30, and December 31. The exchange rates for pesos during the time the receivable is outstanding follow.

May 8, 2013	$0.1323
June 30, 2013	0.1352
September 30, 2013	0.1368
December 31, 2013	0.1335
February 10, 2014	0.1386

Compute the foreign exchange gain or loss that Jett should report on each of its quarterly income statements for the last three quarters of 2013 and the first quarter of 2014. Also compute the amount reported on Jett's balance sheets at the end of each of its last three quarters of 2013.

Exercise 15-17
International accounting
for investments

P3

The **Carrefour Group** reports the following description of its financial assets available-for-sale.

> Assets available for sale are . . . valued at fair value. Unrealized . . . gains or losses are recorded as shareholders' equity until they are sold.

Note 10 to Carrefour's 2010 financial statements reports €18 million in *net* unrealized losses (net of unrealized gains) for 2010, which is included in the fair value of its available-for-sale securities reported on the balance sheet.

1. What amount of the €18 million net unrealized losses, if any, is reported in its 2010 income statement? Explain.
2. If the €18 million net unrealized losses are not reported in the income statement, in which statement are they reported, if any? Explain.

connect

PROBLEM SET A

Problem 15-1A
Recording transactions and
fair value adjustments for
trading securities

P1

Sage 50

Carlsville Company, which began operations in 2013, invests its idle cash in trading securities. The following transactions are from its short-term investments in its trading securities.

2013

Jan.	20	Purchased 800 shares of Ford Motor Co. at $26 per share plus a $125 commission.
Feb.	9	Purchased 2,200 shares of Lucent at $44.25 per share plus a $578 commission.
Oct.	12	Purchased 750 shares of Z-Seven at $7.50 per share plus a $200 commission.

2014

Apr.	15	Sold 800 shares of Ford Motor Co. at $29 per share less a $285 commission.
July	5	Sold 750 shares of Z-Seven at $10.25 per share less a $102.50 commission.
July	22	Purchased 1,600 shares of Hunt Corp. at $30 per share plus a $444 commission.
Aug.	19	Purchased 1,800 shares of Donna Karan at $18.25 per share plus a $290 commission.

2015

Feb.	27	Purchased 3,400 shares of HCA at $34 per share plus a $420 commission.
Mar.	3	Sold 1,600 shares of Hunt at $25 per share less a $250 commission.
June	21	Sold 2,200 shares of Lucent at $42 per share less a $420 commission.
June	30	Purchased 1,200 shares of Black & Decker at $47.50 per share plus a $595 commission.
Nov.	1	Sold 1,800 shares of Donna Karan at $18.25 per share less a $309 commission.

Required

1. Prepare journal entries to record these short-term investment activities for the years shown. (Ignore any year-end adjusting entries.)

Check (2) Dr. Fair Value
Adjustment—Trading $985

2. On December 31, 2015, prepare the adjusting entry to record any necessary fair value adjustment for the portfolio of trading securities when HCA's share price is $36 and Black & Decker's share price is $43.50. (Assume the Fair Value Adjustment—Trading account had an unadjusted balance of zero.)

Rose Company had no short-term investments prior to year 2013. It had the following transactions involving short-term investments in available-for-sale securities during 2013.

Apr. 16 Purchased 4,000 shares of Gem Co. stock at $24.25 per share plus a $180 brokerage fee.
May 1 Paid $100,000 to buy 90-day U.S. Treasury bills (debt securities): $100,000 principal amount, 6% interest, securities dated May 1.
July 7 Purchased 2,000 shares of PepsiCo stock at $49.25 per share plus a $175 brokerage fee.
     20 Purchased 1,000 shares of Xerox stock at $16.75 per share plus a $205 brokerage fee.
Aug. 3 Received a check for principal and accrued interest on the U.S. Treasury bills that matured on July 29.
     15 Received an $0.85 per share cash dividend on the Gem Co. stock.
     28 Sold 2,000 shares of Gem Co. stock at $30 per share less a $225 brokerage fee.
Oct. 1 Received a $1.90 per share cash dividend on the PepsiCo shares.
Dec. 15 Received a $1.05 per share cash dividend on the remaining Gem Co. shares.
     31 Received a $1.30 per share cash dividend on the PepsiCo shares.

Required

1. Prepare journal entries to record the preceding transactions and events.
2. Prepare a table to compare the year-end cost and fair values of Rose's short-term investments in available-for-sale securities. The year-end fair values per share are: Gem Co., $26.50; PepsiCo, $46.50; and Xerox, $13.75.
3. Prepare an adjusting entry, if necessary, to record the year-end fair value adjustment for the portfolio of short-term investments in available-for-sale securities.

Analysis Component

4. Explain the balance sheet presentation of the fair value adjustment for Rose's short-term investments.
5. How do these short-term investments affect Rose's (*a*) income statement for year 2013 and (*b*) the equity section of its balance sheet at year-end 2013?

Grass Security, which began operations in 2013, invests in long-term available-for-sale securities. Following is a series of transactions and events determining its long-term investment activity.

2013

Jan. 20 Purchased 1,000 shares of Johnson & Johnson at $20.50 per share plus a $240 commission.
Feb. 9 Purchased 1,200 shares of Sony at $46.20 per share plus a $225 commission.
June 12 Purchased 1,500 shares of Mattel at $27.00 per share plus an $195 commission.
Dec. 31 Per share fair values for stocks in the portfolio are Johnson & Johnson, $21.50; Mattel, $30.90; Sony, $38.

2014

Apr. 15 Sold 1,000 shares of Johnson & Johnson at $23.50 per share less a $525 commission.
July 5 Sold 1,500 shares of Mattel at $23.90 per share less a $235 commission.
July 22 Purchased 600 shares of Sara Lee at $22.50 per share plus a $480 commission.
Aug. 19 Purchased 900 shares of Eastman Kodak at $17 per share plus a $198 commission.
Dec. 31 Per share fair values for stocks in the portfolio are: Kodak, $19.25; Sara Lee, $20.00; Sony, $35.00.

2015

Feb. 27 Purchased 2,400 shares of Microsoft at $67.00 per share plus a $525 commission.
June 21 Sold 1,200 shares of Sony at $48.00 per share less a $880 commission.
June 30 Purchased 1,400 shares of Black & Decker at $36.00 per share plus a $435 commission.
Aug. 3 Sold 600 shares of Sara Lee at $16.25 per share less a $435 commission.
Nov. 1 Sold 900 shares of Eastman Kodak at $22.75 per share less a $625 commission.
Dec. 31 Per share fair values for stocks in the portfolio are: Black & Decker, $39.00; Microsoft, $69.00.

Required

1. Prepare journal entries to record these transactions and events and any year-end fair value adjustments to the portfolio of long-term available-for-sale securities.

[continued on next page]

Problem 15-2A
Recording, adjusting, and reporting short-term available-for-sale securities

P3

Check (2) Cost = $164,220

(3) Dr. Unrealized Loss—
Equity $4,470

Problem 15-3A
Recording, adjusting, and reporting long-term available-for-sale securities

P3

Sage 50

Check   (2b) Fair Value Adjustment bal.: 12/31/13, $(3,650); 12/31/14; $(13,818)

    (3b) Unrealized Gain at 12/31/2015, $8,040

2. Prepare a table that summarizes the (*a*) total cost, (*b*) total fair value adjustment, and (*c*) total fair value of the portfolio of long-term available-for-sale securities at each year-end.

3. Prepare a table that summarizes (*a*) the realized gains and losses and (*b*) the unrealized gains or losses for the portfolio of long-term available-for-sale securities at each year-end.

Problem 15-4A
Long-term investment transactions; unrealized and realized gains and losses
C2 P3 P4

Stoll Co.'s long-term available-for-sale portfolio at December 31, 2012, consists of the following.

Available-for-Sale Securities	Cost	Fair Value
40,000 shares of Company A common stock	$535,300	$490,000
7,000 shares of Company B common stock	159,380	154,000
17,500 shares of Company C common stock	662,750	640,938

Stoll enters into the following long-term investment transactions during year 2013.

Jan. 29   Sold 3,500 shares of Company B common stock for $79,188 less a brokerage fee of $1,500.
Apr. 17   Purchased 10,000 shares of Company W common stock for $197,500 plus a brokerage fee of $2,400. The shares represent a 30% ownership in Company W.
July   6   Purchased 4,500 shares of Company X common stock for $126,562 plus a brokerage fee of $1,750. The shares represent a 10% ownership in Company X.
Aug. 22   Purchased 50,000 shares of Company Y common stock for $375,000 plus a brokerage fee of $1,200. The shares represent a 51% ownership in Company Y.
Nov. 13   Purchased 8,500 shares of Company Z common stock for $267,900 plus a brokerage fee of $2,450. The shares represent a 5% ownership in Company Z.
Dec.   9   Sold 40,000 shares of Company A common stock for $515,000 less a brokerage fee of $4,100.

The fair values of its investments at December 31, 2013, are: B, $81,375; C, $610,312; W, $191,250; X, $118,125; Y, $531,250; and Z, $278,800.

Required

1. Determine the amount Stoll should report on its December 31, 2013, balance sheet for its long-term investments in available-for-sale securities.

Check   (2) Cr. Unrealized Loss— Equity, $20,002

2. Prepare any necessary December 31, 2013, adjusting entry to record the fair value adjustment for the long-term investments in available-for-sale securities.

3. What amount of gains or losses on transactions relating to long-term investments in available-for-sale securities should Stoll report on its December 31, 2013, income statement?

Problem 15-5A
Accounting for long-term investments in securities; with and without significant influence
P3 P4

Selk Steel Co., which began operations on January 4, 2013, had the following subsequent transactions and events in its long-term investments.

2013

Jan.   5   Selk purchased 60,000 shares (20% of total) of Kildaire's common stock for $1,560,000.
Oct. 23   Kildaire declared and paid a cash dividend of $3.20 per share.
Dec. 31   Kildaire's net income for 2013 is $1,164,000, and the fair value of its stock at December 31 is $30.00 per share.

2014

Oct. 15   Kildaire declared and paid a cash dividend of $2.60 per share.
Dec. 31   Kildaire's net income for 2014 is $1,476,000, and the fair value of its stock at December 31 is $32.00 per share.

2015

Jan.   2   Selk sold all of its investment in Kildaire for $1,894,000 cash.

Part 1

Assume that Selk has a significant influence over Kildaire with its 20% share of stock.

Required

1. Prepare journal entries to record these transactions and events for Selk.

Check   (2) Carrying value per share, $29

2. Compute the carrying (book) value per share of Selk's investment in Kildaire common stock as reflected in the investment account on January 1, 2015.

3. Compute the net increase or decrease in Selk's equity from January 5, 2013, through January 2, 2015, resulting from its investment in Kildaire.

Part 2

Assume that although Selk owns 20% of Kildaire's outstanding stock, circumstances indicate that it does not have a significant influence over the investee and that it is classified as an available-for-sale security investment.

Required

1. Prepare journal entries to record the preceding transactions and events for Selk. Also prepare an entry dated January 2, 2015, to remove any balance related to the fair value adjustment.

2. Compute the cost per share of Selk's investment in Kildaire common stock as reflected in the investment account on January 1, 2015.

3. Compute the net increase or decrease in Selk's equity from January 5, 2013, through January 2, 2015, resulting from its investment in Kildaire.

(1) 1/2/2015 Dr. Unrealized Gain—Equity $360,000

(3) Net increase, $682,000

Doering Company, a U.S. corporation with customers in several foreign countries, had the following selected transactions for 2013 and 2014.

Problem 15-6A[A]
Foreign currency transactions

C3

2013

Apr. 8   Sold merchandise to Salinas & Sons of Mexico for $5,938 cash. The exchange rate for pesos is $0.1043 on this day.

July 21   Sold merchandise on credit to Sumito Corp. in Japan. The price of 1.5 million yen is to be paid 120 days from the date of sale. The exchange rate for yen is $0.0094 on this day.

Oct. 14   Sold merchandise for 19,000 pounds to Smithers Ltd. of Great Britain, payment in full to be received in 90 days. The exchange rate for pounds is $1.4566 on this day.

Nov. 18   Received Sumito's payment in yen for its July 21 purchase and immediately exchanged the yen for dollars. The exchange rate for yen is $0.0092 on this day.

Dec. 20   Sold merchandise for 17,000 ringgits to Hamid Albar of Malaysia, payment in full to be received in 30 days. On this day, the exchange rate for ringgits is $0.4501.

Dec. 31   Recorded adjusting entries to recognize exchange gains or losses on Doering's annual financial statements. Rates for exchanging foreign currencies on this day follow.

Pesos (Mexico)	$0.1055
Yen (Japan)	0.0093
Pounds (Britain)	1.4620
Ringgits (Malaysia)	0.4456

2014

Jan. 12   Received full payment in pounds from Smithers for the October 14 sale and immediately exchanged the pounds for dollars. The exchange rate for pounds is $1.4699 on this day.

Jan. 19   Received Hamid Albar's full payment in ringgits for the December 20 sale and immediately exchanged the ringgits for dollars. The exchange rate for ringgits is $0.4420 on this day.

Required

1. Prepare journal entries for the Doering transactions and adjusting entries (round amounts to the nearest dollar).

2. Compute the foreign exchange gain or loss to be reported on Doering's 2013 income statement.

Check   (2) 2013 total foreign exchange loss, $274

Analysis Component

3. What actions might Doering consider to reduce its risk of foreign exchange gains or losses?

Harris Company, which began operations in 2013, invests its idle cash in trading securities. The following transactions relate to its short-term investments in its trading securities.

PROBLEM SET B

Problem 15-1B
Recording transactions and fair value adjustments for trading securities   P1

2013

Mar. 10   Purchased 2,400 shares of AOL at $59.15 per share plus a $1,545 commission.

May 7   Purchased 5,000 shares of MTV at $36.25 per share plus a $2,855 commission.

Sept. 1   Purchased 1,200 shares of UPS at $57.25 per share plus a $1,250 commission.

2014

Apr. 26   Sold 5,000 shares of MTV at $34.50 per share less a $2,050 commission.

Apr. 27   Sold 1,200 shares of UPS at $60.50 per share less an $1,788 commission.

June   2   Purchased 3,600 shares of SPW at $172 per share plus a $3,250 commission.
June 14   Purchased 900 shares of Walmart at $50.25 per share plus a $1,082 commission.

2015

Jan. 28   Purchased 2,000 shares of PepsiCo at $43 per share plus a $2,890 commission.
Jan. 31   Sold 3,600 shares of SPW at $168 per share less a $2,040 commission.
Aug. 22   Sold 2,400 shares of AOL at $56.75 per share less a $2,480 commission.
Sept. 3   Purchased 1,500 shares of Vodaphone at $40.50 per share plus an $1,680 commission.
Oct.   9   Sold 900 shares of Walmart at $53.75 per share less a $1,220 commission.

Required

1. Prepare journal entries to record these short-term investment activities for the years shown. (Ignore any year-end adjusting entries.)

Check   (2) Cr. Fair Value Adjustment—Trading $13,820

2. On December 31, 2015, prepare the adjusting entry to record any necessary fair value adjustment for the portfolio of trading securities when PepsiCo's share price is $41 and Vodaphone's share price is $37. (Assume the Fair Value Adjustment—Trading account had an unadjusted balance of zero.)

Problem 15-2B
Recording, adjusting, and reporting short-term available-for-sale securities

P3

Slip Systems had no short-term investments prior to 2013. It had the following transactions involving short-term investments in available-for-sale securities during 2013.

Feb.   6   Purchased 3,400 shares of Nokia stock at $41.25 per share plus a $3,000 brokerage fee.
     15   Paid $20,000 to buy six-month U.S. Treasury bills (debt securities): $20,000 principal amount, 6% interest, securities dated February 15.
Apr.   7   Purchased 1,200 shares of Dell Co. stock at $39.50 per share plus a $1,255 brokerage fee.
June   2   Purchased 2,500 shares of Merck stock at $72.50 per share plus a $2,890 brokerage fee.
     30   Received a $0.19 per share cash dividend on the Nokia shares.
Aug. 11   Sold 850 shares of Nokia stock at $46 per share less a $1,050 brokerage fee.
     16   Received a check for principal and accrued interest on the U.S. Treasury bills purchased February 15.
     24   Received a $0.10 per share cash dividend on the Dell shares.
Nov.   9   Received a $0.20 per share cash dividend on the remaining Nokia shares.
Dec. 18   Received a $0.15 per share cash dividend on the Dell shares.

Required

1. Prepare journal entries to record the preceding transactions and events.

Check   (2) Cost = $340,232

2. Prepare a table to compare the year-end cost and fair values of the short-term investments in available-for-sale securities. The year-end fair values per share are: Nokia, $40.25; Dell, $40.50; and Merck, $59.

(3) Dr. Unrealized Loss—Equity, $41,494

3. Prepare an adjusting entry, if necessary, to record the year-end fair value adjustment for the portfolio of short-term investments in available-for-sale securities.

Analysis Component

4. Explain the balance sheet presentation of the fair value adjustment to Slip's short-term investments.

5. How do these short-term investments affect (*a*) its income statement for year 2013 and (*b*) the equity section of its balance sheet at the 2013 year-end?

Problem 15-3B
Recording, adjusting, and reporting long-term available-for-sale securities

P3

Paris Enterprises, which began operations in 2013, invests in long-term available-for-sale securities. Following is a series of transactions and events involving its long-term investment activity.

2013

Mar. 10   Purchased 1,200 shares of Apple at $25.50 per share plus $800 commission.
Apr.   7   Purchased 2,500 shares of Ford at $22.50 per share plus $1,033 commission.
Sept. 1   Purchased 600 shares of Polaroid at $47.00 per share plus $890 commission.
Dec. 31   Per share fair values for stocks in the portfolio are: Apple, $27.50; Ford, $21.00; Polaroid, $49.00.

2014

Apr. 26   Sold 2,500 shares of Ford at $20.50 per share less a $1,207 commission.
June   2   Purchased 1,800 shares of Duracell at $19.25 per share plus a $1,050 commission.
June 14   Purchased 1,200 shares of Sears at $21 per share plus a $280 commission.
Nov. 27   Sold 600 shares of Polaroid at $51 per share less a $845 commission.
Dec. 31   Per share fair values for stocks in the portfolio are: Apple, $29.00; Duracell, $18.00; Sears, $23.00.

2015

Jan. 28 Purchased 1,000 shares of Coca-Cola Co. at $40 per share plus a $1,480 commission.
Aug. 22 Sold 1,200 shares of Apple at $21.50 per share less a $1,850 commission.
Sept. 3 Purchased 3,000 shares of Motorola at $28 per share plus a $780 commission.
Oct.   9 Sold 1,200 shares of Sears at $24.00 per share less a $599 commission.
Oct. 31 Sold 1,800 shares of Duracell at $15.00 per share less a $898 commission.
Dec. 31 Per share fair values for stocks in the portfolio are: Coca-Cola, $48.00; Motorola, $24.00.

Required

1. Prepare journal entries to record these transactions and events and any year-end fair value adjustments to the portfolio of long-term available-for-sale securities.

2. Prepare a table that summarizes the (*a*) total cost, (*b*) total fair value adjustment, and (*c*) total fair value for the portfolio of long-term available-for-sale securities at each year-end.

3. Prepare a table that summarizes (*a*) the realized gains and losses and (*b*) the unrealized gains or losses for the portfolio of long-term available-for-sale securities at each year-end.

Check   (2b) Fair Value Adjustment bal.: 12/31/13, ($2,873); 12/31/14, $2,220

(3b) Unrealized Loss at 12/31/2015, $6,260

Troyer's long-term available-for-sale portfolio at December 31, 2012, consists of the following.

Available-for-Sale Securities	Cost	Fair Value
27,500 shares of Company R common stock	$559,125	$599,063
8,500 shares of Company S common stock	308,380	293,250
11,000 shares of Company T common stock	147,295	151,800

Problem 15-4B
Long-term investment transactions; unrealized and realized gains and losses

C2 P3 P4

Troyer enters into the following long-term investment transactions during year 2013.

Jan. 13 Sold 2,125 shares of Company S stock for $72,250 less a brokerage fee of $1,195.
Mar. 24 Purchased 15,500 shares of Company U common stock for $282,875 plus a brokerage fee of $1,980. The shares represent a 62% ownership interest in Company U.
Apr.   5 Purchased 42,500 shares of Company V common stock for $133,875 plus a brokerage fee of $1,125. The shares represent a 10% ownership in Company V.
Sept. 2 Sold 11,000 shares of Company T common stock for $156,750 less a brokerage fee of $2,700.
Sept. 27 Purchased 2,500 shares of Company W common stock for $50,500 plus a brokerage fee of $1,050. The shares represent a 25% ownership interest in Company W.
Oct. 30 Purchased 5,000 shares of Company X common stock for $48,750 plus a brokerage fee of $1,170. The shares represent a 13% ownership interest in Company X.

The fair values of its investments at December 31, 2013, are: R, $568,125; S, $210,375; U, $272,800; V, $134,938; W, $54,689; and X, $45,625.

Required

1. Determine the amount Troyer should report on its December 31, 2013, balance sheet for its long-term investments in available-for-sale securities.

2. Prepare any necessary December 31, 2013, adjusting entry to record the fair value adjustment of the long-term investments in available-for-sale securities.

3. What amount of gains or losses on transactions relating to long-term investments in available-for-sale securities should Troyer report on its December 31, 2013, income statement?

Check   (2) Dr. Unrealized Loss— Equity, $16,267; Cr. Fair Value Adjustment—AFS (LT), $45,580

Brinkley Company, which began operations on January 3, 2013, had the following subsequent transactions and events in its long-term investments.

2013

Jan.   5 Brinkley purchased 20,000 shares (25% of total) of Bloch's common stock for $200,500.
Aug.   1 Bloch declared and paid a cash dividend of $1.05 per share.
Dec. 31 Bloch's net income for 2013 is $82,000, and the fair value of its stock is $11.90 per share.

2014

Aug.   1 Bloch declared and paid a cash dividend of $1.35 per share.
Dec. 31 Bloch's net income for 2014 is $78,000, and the fair value of its stock is $13.65 per share.

Problem 15-5B
Accounting for long-term investments in securities; with and without significant influence

P3 P4

2015

Jan.   8   Brinkley sold all of its investment in Bloch for $375,000 cash.

Part 1

Assume that Brinkley has a significant influence over Bloch with its 25% share.

Required

Check (2) Carrying value per share, $9.63

1. Prepare journal entries to record these transactions and events for Brinkley.

2. Compute the carrying (book) value per share of Brinkley's investment in Bloch common stock as reflected in the investment account on January 7, 2015.

3. Compute the net increase or decrease in Brinkley's equity from January 5, 2013, through January 8, 2015, resulting from its investment in Bloch.

Part 2

Assume that although Brinkley owns 25% of Bloch's outstanding stock, circumstances indicate that it does not have a significant influence over the investee and that it is classified as an available-for-sale security investment.

Required

(1) 1/8/2015 Dr. Unrealized Gain—Equity $72,500

1. Prepare journal entries to record these transactions and events for Brinkley. Also prepare an entry dated January 8, 2015, to remove any balance related to the fair value adjustment.

2. Compute the cost per share of Brinkley's investment in Bloch common stock as reflected in the investment account on January 7, 2015.

(3) Net increase, $222,500

3. Compute the net increase or decrease in Brinkley's equity from January 5, 2013, through January 8, 2015, resulting from its investment in Bloch.

Problem 15-6B^A

Foreign currency transactions

C3

Datamix, a U.S. corporation with customers in several foreign countries, had the following selected transactions for 2013 and 2014.

2013

May 26   Sold merchandise for 6.5 million yen to Fuji Company of Japan, payment in full to be received in 60 days. On this day, the exchange rate for yen is $0.0093.

June   1   Sold merchandise to Fordham Ltd. of Great Britain for $64,800 cash. The exchange rate for pounds is $1.4498 on this day.

July 25   Received Fuji's payment in yen for its May 26 purchase and immediately exchanged the yen for dollars. The exchange rate for yen is $0.0092 on this day.

Oct. 15   Sold merchandise on credit to Martinez Brothers of Mexico. The price of 378,000 pesos is to be paid 90 days from the date of sale. On this day, the exchange rate for pesos is $0.1020.

Dec.   6   Sold merchandise for 250,000 yuans to Chi-Ying Company of China, payment in full to be received in 30 days. The exchange rate for yuans is $0.1439 on this day.

Dec. 31   Recorded adjusting entries to recognize exchange gains or losses on Datamix's annual financial statements. Rates of exchanging foreign currencies on this day follow.

Yen (Japan)	$0.0094
Pounds (Britain)	1.4580
Pesos (Mexico)	0.1060
Yuans (China)	0.1450

2014

Jan.   5   Received Chi-Ying's full payment in yuans for the December 6 sale and immediately exchanged the yuans for dollars. The exchange rate for yuans is $0.1580 on this day.

Jan. 13   Received full payment in pesos from Martinez for the October 15 sale and immediately exchanged the pesos for dollars. The exchange rate for pesos is $0.1039 on this day.

Required

1. Prepare journal entries for the Datamix transactions and adjusting entries.

Check (2) 2013 total foreign exchange gain, $1,137

2. Compute the foreign exchange gain or loss to be reported on Datamix's 2013 income statement.

Analysis Component

3. What actions might Datamix consider to reduce its risk of foreign exchange gains or losses?

(This serial problem began in Chapter 1 and continues through most of the book. If previous chapter segments were not completed, the serial problem can begin at this point. It is helpful, but not necessary, to use the Working Papers that accompany the book.)

SP 15   While reviewing the March 31, 2014, balance sheet of Success Systems, Adria Lopez notes that the business has built a large cash balance of $77,845. Its most recent bank money market statement shows that the funds are earning an annualized return of 0.75%. Adria Lopez decides to make several investments with the desire to earn a higher return on the idle cash balance. Accordingly, in April 2014, Success Systems makes the following investments in trading securities:

April 16   Purchases 400 shares of Johnson & Johnson stock at $50 per share plus $300 commission.
April 30   Purchases 200 shares of Starbucks Corporation at $22 per share plus $250 commission.

On June 30, 2014, the per share market price (fair value) of the Johnson & Johnson shares is $55 and the Starbucks shares is $19.

Required

1. Prepare journal entries to record the April purchases of trading securities by Success Systems.
2. On June 30, 2014, prepare the adjusting entry to record any necessary fair value adjustment to its portfolio of trading securities.

Beyond the Numbers

BTN 15-1   Refer to **Polaris'** financial statements in Appendix A to answer the following.
1. Are Polaris' financial statements consolidated? How can you tell?
2. What is Polaris' *comprehensive income* for the year ended December 31, 2011?
3. Does Polaris have any foreign operations? How can you tell?
4. Compute Polaris' return on total assets for the year ended December 31, 2011.

Fast Forward

5. Access Polaris' annual report for a fiscal year ending after December 31, 2011, from either its Website (**Polaris.com**) or the SEC's database (**www.SEC.gov**). Recompute Polaris' return on total assets for the years subsequent to December 31, 2011.

BTN 15-2   Key figures for **Polaris** and **Arctic Cat** follow.

($ thousands)	Polaris			Arctic Cat		
	Current Year	1 Year Prior	2 Years Prior	Current Year	1 Year Prior	2 Years Prior
Net income	$ 227,575	$ 147,138	$ 101,017	$ 13,007	$ 1,875	($9,508)
Net sales	2,656,949	1,991,139	1,565,887	464,651	450,728	563,613
Total assets	1,228,024	1,061,647	763,653	272,906	246,084	251,165

Required

1. Compute return on total assets for Polaris and Arctic Cat for the two most recent years.
2. Separate the return on total assets computed in part 1 into its components for both companies and both years according to the formula in Exhibit 15.9.
3. Which company has the highest total return on assets? The highest profit margin? The highest total asset turnover? What does this comparative analysis reveal? (Assume an industry average of 10.0% for return on assets.)

BTN 15-3   Kasey Hartman is the controller for Wholemart Company, which has numerous long-term investments in debt securities. Wholemart's investments are mainly in 5-year bonds. Hartman is preparing its year-end financial statements. In accounting for long-term debt securities, she knows that each long-term investment must be designated as a held-to-maturity or an available-for-sale security. Interest rates rose sharply this past year causing the portfolio's fair value to substantially decline. The company does not intend to hold the bonds for the entire 5 years. Hartman also earns a bonus each year, which is computed as a percent of net income.

Required

1. Will Hartman's bonus depend in any way on the classification of the debt securities? Explain.
2. What criteria must Hartman use to classify the securities as held-to-maturity or available-for-sale?
3. Is there likely any company oversight of Hartman's classification of the securities? Explain.

COMMUNICATING IN PRACTICE

P4

BTN 15-4 Assume that you are Jolee Company's accountant. Company owner Mary Jolee has reviewed the 2013 financial statements you prepared and questions the $6,000 loss reported on the sale of its investment in Kemper Co. common stock. Jolee acquired 50,000 shares of Kemper's common stock on December 31, 2011, at a cost of $500,000. This stock purchase represented a 40% interest in Kemper. The 2012 income statement reported that earnings from all investments were $126,000. On January 3, 2013, Jolee Company sold the Kemper stock for $575,000. Kemper did not pay any dividends during 2012 but reported a net income of $202,500 for that year. Mary Jolee believes that because the Kemper stock purchase price was $500,000 and was sold for $575,000, the 2013 income statement should report a $75,000 gain on the sale.

Required

Draft a one-half page memorandum to Mary Jolee explaining why the $6,000 loss on sale of Kemper stock is correctly reported.

TAKING IT TO THE NET

C1

BTN 15-5 Access the July 28, 2011, 10-K filing (for year-end June 30, 2011) of **Microsoft** (MSFT) at **www.SEC.gov**. Review its note 4, "Investments."

Required

1. How does the "cost-basis" total amount for its investments as of June 30, 2011, compare to the prior year-end amount?
2. Identify at least eight types of short-term investments held by Microsoft as of June 30, 2011.
3. What were Microsoft's unrealized gains and its unrealized losses from its investments for 2011?
4. Was the cost or fair value ("recorded basis") of the investments higher as of June 30, 2011?

TEAMWORK IN ACTION

C1 C2 P1 P2 P3 P4

BTN 15-6 Each team member is to become an expert on a specific classification of long-term investments. This expertise will be used to facilitate other teammates' understanding of the concepts and procedures relevent to the classification chosen.

1. Each team member must select an area for expertise by choosing one of the following classifications of long-term investments.
    a. Held-to-maturity debt securities
    b. Available-for-sale debt and equity securities
    c. Equity securities with significant influence
    d. Equity securities with controlling influence
2. Learning teams are to disburse and expert teams are to be formed. Expert teams are made up of those who select the same area of expertise. The instructor will identify the location where each expert team will meet.
3. Expert teams will collaborate to develop a presentation based on the following requirements. Students must write the presentation in a format they can show to their learning teams in part (4).

Requirements for Expert Presentation

   a. Write a transaction for the acquisition of this type of investment security. The transaction description is to include all necessary data to reflect the chosen classification.
   b. Prepare the journal entry to record the acquisition.
   [*Note:* The expert team on equity securities with controlling influence will substitute requirements (*d*) and (*e*) with a discussion of the reporting of these investments.]

c. Identify information necessary to complete the end-of-period adjustment for this investment.

d. Assuming that this is the only investment owned, prepare any necessary year-end entries.

e. Present the relevant balance sheet section(s).

4. Re-form learning teams. In rotation, experts are to present to their teams the presentations they developed in part 3. Experts are to encourage and respond to questions.

BTN 15-7ᴬ Refer to the opening feature in this chapter about Catherine and David Cook and their company, **myYearbook** (now rebranded as **MeetMe**). Assume that they must acquire the Japanese rights to certain games and social applications that will then be produced for presentation on MeetMe's U.S. site. Assume MeetMe acquires those rights on January 1, 2013, from a Japanese distributor and agrees to pay 12,000,000 yen per year for those rights. Quarterly payments are due March 31, June 30, September 30, and December 31 each year. On January 1, 2013, the yen is worth $0.00891.

Required

1. Prepare the journal entry to record the Internet rights purchased on January 1, 2013.

2. Prepare the journal entries to record the payments on March 31, June 30, September 30, and December 31, 2013. The value of the yen on those dates follows.

March 31	$0.00893
June 30	0.00901
September 30	0.00902
December 31	0.00897

3. How can MeetMe protect itself from unanticipated gains and losses from currency translation if all of the payments are specified to be paid in yen?

BTN 15-8ᴬ Assume that you are planning a spring break trip to Europe. Identify three locations where you can find exchange rates for the dollar relative to the Euro or other currencies.

BTN 15-9 **Piaggio**, **Polaris**, and **Arctic Cat** are competitors in the global marketplace. Following are selected data from each company.

Key Figure	Piaggio (Euro thousands) Current Year	One Year Prior	Two Years Prior	Polaris Current Year	Prior Year	Arctic Cat Current Year	Prior Year
Net income	€ 47,053	€ 42,811	€ 46,031	—	—	—	—
Net sales	1,516,463	1,485,351	1,486,882	—	—	—	—
Total assets	1,520,184	1,545,722	1,564,820	—	—	—	—
Profit margin	?	?	—	8.6%	7.4%	2.8%	0.416%
Total asset turnover	?	?	—	2.31	2.18	1.79	1.81

Required

1. Compute Piaggio's return on total assets, and its components of profit margin and total asset turnover, for the most recent two years using the data provided.

2. Which of these three companies has the highest return on total assets? Highest profit margin? Highest total asset turnover? Interpret these results for the (*a*) current year and (*b*) prior year.

ANSWERS TO MULTIPLE CHOICE QUIZ

1. d; $30,000 × 5% × 5/12 = $625

2. a; Unrealized gain = $84,500 − $83,000 = $1,500

3. b; $50,000 × 35% = $17,500

4. e; $300,000/$2,000,000 = 15%

5. b; Profit margin = $80,000/$600,000 = 13.3%
  Total asset turnover = $600,000/$400,000 = 1.5

Reporting the Statement of Cash Flows

A Look Back

Chapter 15 focused on how to identify, account for, and report investments in securities. We also accounted for transactions listed in a foreign currency.

A Look at This Chapter

This chapter focuses on reporting and analyzing cash inflows and cash outflows. We emphasize how to prepare and interpret the statement of cash flows.

A Look Ahead

Chapter 17 focuses on tools to help us analyze financial statements. We also describe comparative analysis and the application of ratios for financial analysis.

Learning Objectives

CONCEPTUAL

C1 Distinguish between operating, investing, and financing activities, and describe how noncash investing and financing activities are disclosed. (p. 635)

ANALYTICAL

A1 Analyze the statement of cash flows and apply the cash flow on total assets ratio. (p. 652)

PROCEDURAL

P1 Prepare a statement of cash flows. (p. 638)

P2 Compute cash flows from operating activities using the indirect method. (p. 641)

P3 Determine cash flows from both investing and financing activities. (p. 647)

P4 *Appendix 16A*—Illustrate use of a spreadsheet to prepare a statement of cash flows. (p. 656)

P5 *Appendix 16B*—Compute cash flows from operating activities using the direct method. (p. 659)

Decision Insight

I'm a Sole Man . . .

Marina del Rey—"Five years ago in Argentina I met some volunteers who were helping children get shoes," explains Blake Mycoskie. "I wanted to help them but I wanted to find a more sustainable way to give them shoes." Later, while "sitting in a field on a farm one day, I had an epiphany," says Blake. "I'm going to start a shoe company, and for every pair I sell, I'm going to give one pair to a kid in need."

With that goal, Blake launched his shoe company named **TOMS (TOMS.com),** which is short for *Tomorrow's Shoes*. "When we first started, we were just trying to learn how to make shoes," admits Blake. Yet he had to be conscious of profits and cash flows. "It's very hard in the first few years because you have so much overhead and start-up cost already, and then you throw in giving away shoes," explains Blake. "It's very tough financially, but it's a sacrifice that we make with a smile because it's why we're here."

Can TOMS be profitable? "I don't think TOMS will ever be a super, super profitable company," admits Blake. "I think it can be profitable, and I think it can do a lot of good, and that's all we really want anyways. So, I think as a profit strategy, it might not make sense, but as a life strategy for me, it definitely makes sense."

Is TOMS sustainable? "Sustainable, to me, means that we are able to sell shoes and have enough profit built in to give a pair away," explains Blake. "Sustainability to us is based on the question: can we continue to give those kids shoes year after

year?" Blake points out that this strategy has cash flow implications, especially for operating and investing cash outflows. He emphasizes the importance of monitoring and tracking cash inflows and cash outflows. "We had some cash flow issues in years two and three," admits Blake. "We went a year where every day someone was calling us, yelling, asking for money."

Blake eventually learned to monitor and control cash flows for each of his operating, investing, and financing activities. "We're [now] very stable, from a cash flow standpoint," he says. His focus on controlling cash flows led him to low cost strategies such as selling online and using free social media for advertising. Analyzing TOMS's statement of cash flows, and its individual cash inflows and outflows, helps him stay on track. "We're not going to make as much . . . and the margins are definitely lower," he admits. "But what we do helps us get publicity . . . [and] we can't find anyone who matches one for one!"

Cash management has not curtailed Blake's approach to life. "I live on a boat in Marina del Rey," exclaims Blake. "I wake up when the sun finds its way into my bedroom. I kind of do my own thing."

[Sources: *TOMS Website*, January 2013; *The Wall Street Journal*, January 2012; *Fast Company*, September 2011; *TIME*, January 2007; *TreeHugger Radio*, September 2008; *INC.*, January 2010; *The Oprah Magazine*, September 2011]]

A company cannot achieve or maintain profits without carefully managing cash. Managers and other users of information pay attention to a company's cash position and the events and transactions affecting cash. This chapter explains how we prepare, analyze, and interpret a statement of cash flows. It also discusses the importance of cash flow information for predicting future performance and making managerial decisions. More generally, effectively using the statement of cash flows is crucial for managing and analyzing the operating, investing, and financing activities of businesses.

Reporting the Statement of Cash Flows

Basics of Cash Flow Reporting	Cash Flows from Operating	Cash Flows from Investing	Cash Flows from Financing
• Purpose • Importance • Measurement • Classification • Noncash activities • Format and preparation	• Indirect and direct methods of reporting • Application of indirect method of reporting • Summary of indirect method adjustments	• Three-stage process of analysis • Analysis of noncurrent assets • Analysis of other assets	• Three-stage process of analysis • Analysis of non-current liabilities • Analysis of equity

BASICS OF CASH FLOW REPORTING

This section describes the basics of cash flow reporting, including its purpose, measurement, classification, format, and preparation.

Purpose of the Statement of Cash Flows

The purpose of the **statement of cash flows** is to report cash receipts (inflows) and cash payments (outflows) during a period. This includes separately identifying the cash flows related to operating, investing, and financing activities. The statement of cash flows does more than simply report changes in cash. It is the detailed disclosure of individual cash flows that makes this statement useful to users. Information in this statement helps users answer questions such as these:

Point: Internal users rely on the statement of cash flows to make investing and financing decisions. External users rely on this statement to assess the amount and timing of a company's cash flows.

● How does a company obtain its cash?
● Where does a company spend its cash?
● What explains the change in the cash balance?

The statement of cash flows addresses important questions such as these by summarizing, classifying, and reporting a company's cash inflows and cash outflows for each period.

Importance of Cash Flows

Information about cash flows can influence decision makers in important ways. For instance, we look more favorably at a company that is financing its expenditures with cash from operations than one that does it by selling its assets. Information about cash flows helps users decide whether a company has enough cash to pay its existing debts as they mature. It is also relied upon to evaluate a company's ability to meet unexpected obligations and pursue unexpected opportunities. External information users especially want to assess a company's ability to take advantage of new business opportunities. Internal users such as managers use cash flow information to plan day-to-day operating activities and make long-term investment decisions.

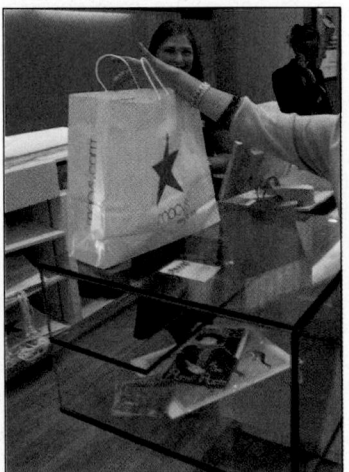

Macy's striking turnaround is an example of how analysis and management of cash flows can lead to improved financial stability. Several years ago Macy's obtained temporary protection from bankruptcy, at which time it desperately needed to improve its cash flows. It did so by engaging in aggressive cost-cutting measures. As a result, Macy's annual cash flow rose to $210 million, up from a negative cash flow of $38.9 million in the prior year. Macy's eventually met its financial obligations and then successfully merged with **Federated Department Stores**.

The case of **W. T. Grant Co.** is a classic example of the importance of cash flow information in predicting a company's future performance and financial strength. Grant reported net income of more than $40 million per year for three consecutive years. At that same time, it was experiencing an alarming decrease in cash provided by operations. For instance, net cash outflow was more than $90 million by the end of that three-year period. Grant soon went bankrupt. Users who relied solely on Grant's income numbers were unpleasantly surprised. This reminds us that cash flows as well as income statement and balance sheet information are crucial in making business decisions.

■ Decision Insight ━━━━━━━━━━━━━━━━━━━━━━━━

Cash Savvy   "A lender must have a complete understanding of a borrower's cash flows to assess both the borrowing needs and repayment sources. This requires information about the major types of cash inflows and outflows. I have seen many companies, whose financial statements indicate good profitability, experience severe financial problems because the owners or managers lacked a good understanding of cash flows."—Mary E. Garza, **Bank of America** ■

Measurement of Cash Flows

Cash flows are defined to include both *cash* and *cash equivalents*. The statement of cash flows explains the difference between the beginning and ending balances of cash and cash equivalents. We continue to use the phrases *cash flows* and the *statement of cash flows,* but we must remember that both phrases refer to cash and cash equivalents. Recall that a cash equivalent must satisfy two criteria: (1) be readily convertible to a known amount of cash and (2) be sufficiently close to its maturity so its market value is unaffected by interest rate changes. In most cases, a debt security must be within three months of its maturity to satisfy these criteria. Companies must disclose and follow a clear policy for determining cash and cash equivalents and apply it consistently from period to period. **American Express**, for example, defines its cash equivalents as "time deposits and other highly liquid investments with original maturities of 90 days or less."

Cash Equivalents

Classification of Cash Flows

Since cash and cash equivalents are combined, the statement of cash flows does not report transactions between cash and cash equivalents such as cash paid to purchase cash equivalents and cash received from selling cash equivalents. However, all other cash receipts and cash payments are classified and reported on the statement as operating, investing, or financing activities. Individual cash receipts and payments for each of these three categories are labeled to identify their originating transactions or events. A net cash inflow (source) occurs when the receipts in a category exceed the payments. A net cash outflow (use) occurs when the payments in a category exceed the receipts.

> **C1** Distinguish between operating, investing, and financing activities, and describe how noncash investing and financing activities are disclosed.

Operating Activities   Operating activities include those transactions and events that determine net income. Examples are the production and purchase of merchandise, the sale of goods and services to customers, and the expenditures to administer the business. Not all items in income, such as unusual gains and losses, are operating activities (we discuss these exceptions later in the chapter). Exhibit 16.1 lists the more common cash inflows and outflows from operating activities. (Although cash receipts and cash payments from buying and selling trading

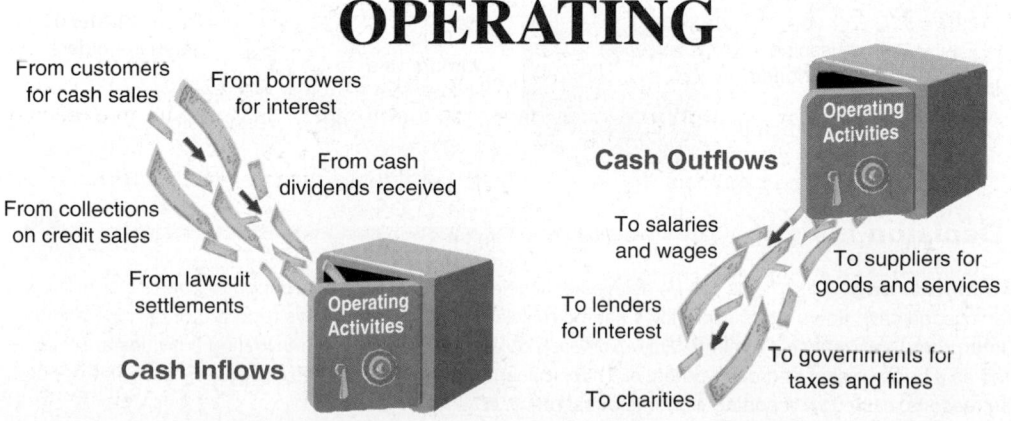

OPERATING

EXHIBIT 16.1

Cash Flows from Operating Activities

securities are often reported under operating activities, new standards require that these receipts and payments be classified based on the nature and purpose of those securities.)

Investing Activities   **Investing activities** generally include those transactions and events that affect long-term assets—namely, the purchase and sale of long-term assets. They also include (1) the purchase and sale of short-term investments in the securities of other entities, other than cash equivalents and trading securities and (2) lending and collecting money for notes receivable. Exhibit 16.2 lists examples of cash flows from investing activities. Proceeds from collecting the principal amounts of notes deserve special mention. If the note results from sales to customers, its cash receipts are classified as operating activities whether short-term or long-term. If the note results from a loan to another party apart from sales, however, the cash receipts from collecting the note principal are classified as an investing activity. The FASB requires that the collection of interest on loans be reported as an operating activity.

Point: The FASB requires that *cash dividends received* and *cash interest received* be reported as operating activities.

EXHIBIT 16.2

Cash Flows from
Investing Activities

INVESTING

Financing Activities   **Financing activities** include those transactions and events that affect long-term liabilities and equity. Examples are (1) obtaining cash from issuing debt and repaying the amounts borrowed and (2) receiving cash from or distributing cash to owners. These activities involve transactions with a company's owners and creditors. They also often involve borrowing and repaying principal amounts relating to both short- and long-term debt. GAAP requires that payments of interest expense be classified as operating activities. Also, cash payments to settle credit purchases of merchandise, whether on account or by note, are operating activities. Exhibit 16.3 lists examples of cash flows from financing activities.

EXHIBIT 16.3

Cash Flows from
Financing Activities

FINANCING

Point: Interest payments on a loan are classified as operating activities, but payments of loan principal are financing activities.

■ **Decision** Insight ▲

Cash Monitoring   Cash flows can be delayed or accelerated at the end of a period to improve or reduce current period cash flows. Also, cash flows can be misclassified. Cash outflows reported under operations are interpreted as expense payments. However, cash outflows reported under investing activities are interpreted as a positive sign of growth potential. Thus, managers face incentives to misclassify cash flows. For these reasons, cash flow reporting warrants our scrutiny. ■

Noncash Investing and Financing

When important investing and financing activities do not affect cash receipts or payments, they are still disclosed at the bottom of the statement of cash flows or in a note to the statement because of their importance and the *full-disclosure principle*. One example of such a transaction is the purchase of long-term assets using a long-term note payable (loan). This transaction involves both investing and financing activities but does not affect any cash inflow or outflow and is not reported in any of the three sections of the statement of cash flows. This disclosure rule also extends to transactions with partial cash receipts or payments.

To illustrate, assume that Goorin purchases land for $12,000 by paying $5,000 cash and trading in used equipment worth $7,000. The investing section of the statement of cash flows reports only the $5,000 cash outflow for the land purchase. The $12,000 investing transaction is only partially described in the body of the statement of cash flows, yet this information is potentially important to users because it changes the makeup of assets. Goorin could either describe the transaction in a footnote or include information at the bottom of its statement that lists the $12,000 land purchase along with the cash financing of $5,000 and a $7,000 trade-in of equipment. As another example, Borg Co. acquired $900,000 of assets in exchange for $200,000 cash and a $700,000 long-term note, which should be reported as follows:

Point: A stock dividend transaction involving a transfer from retained earnings to common stock or a credit to contributed capital is *not* considered a noncash investing and financing activity because the company receives no consideration for shares issued.

Fair value of assets acquired	$900,000
Less cash paid	200,000
Liabilities incurred or assumed	$700,000

Exhibit 16.4 lists transactions commonly disclosed as noncash investing and financing activities.

- Retirement of debt by issuing equity stock.
- Conversion of preferred stock to common stock.
- Lease of assets in a capital lease transaction.
- Purchase of long-term assets by issuing a note or bond.
- Exchange of noncash assets for other noncash assets.
- Purchase of noncash assets by issuing equity or debt.

EXHIBIT 16.4

Examples of Noncash Investing and Financing Activities

Format of the Statement of Cash Flows

Accounting standards require companies to include a statement of cash flows in a complete set of financial statements. This statement must report information about a company's cash receipts and cash payments during the period. Exhibit 16.5 shows the usual format. A company must report cash flows from three activities: operating, investing, and financing. The statement

EXHIBIT 16.5

Format of the Statement of Cash Flows

COMPANY NAME
Statement of Cash Flows
For *period* Ended *date*

Cash flows from operating activities		
[List of individual inflows and outflows]		
Net cash provided (used) by operating activities	$ #	
Cash flows from investing activities		
[List of individual inflows and outflows]		
Net cash provided (used) by investing activities	#	
Cash flows from financing activities		
[List of individual inflows and outflows]		
Net cash provided (used) by financing activities	#	
Net increase (decrease) in cash	$ #	
Cash (and equivalents) balance at prior period-end	#	
Cash (and equivalents) balance at current period-end	$ #	

Separate schedule or note disclosure of any "noncash investing and financing transactions" is required.

Point: Positive cash flows for a section are titled net cash "provided by" or "from." Negative cash flows are labeled as net cash "used by."

explains how transactions and events impact the prior period-end cash (and cash equivalents) balance to produce its current period-end balance.

Decision Maker

Entrepreneur You are considering purchasing a start-up business that recently reported a $110,000 annual net loss and a $225,000 annual net cash inflow. How are these results possible? ■ [Answer—p. 664]

Quick Check   Answers — p. 664

1. Does a statement of cash flows report the cash payments to purchase cash equivalents? Does it report the cash receipts from selling cash equivalents?
2. Identify the three categories of cash flows reported separately on the statement of cash flows.
3. Identify the cash activity category for each transaction: (*a*) purchase equipment for cash, (*b*) cash payment of wages, (*c*) sale of common stock for cash, (*d*) receipt of cash dividends from stock investment, (*e*) cash collection from customers, (*f*) notes issued for cash.

Preparing the Statement of Cash Flows

P1 Prepare a statement of cash flows.

Preparing a statement of cash flows involves five steps: ① compute the net increase or decrease in cash; ② compute and report the net cash provided or used by operating activities (using either the direct or indirect method; both are explained); ③ compute and report the net cash provided or used by investing activities; ④ compute and report the net cash provided or used by financing activities; and ⑤ compute the net cash flow by combining net cash provided or used by operating, investing, and financing activities and then *prove it* by adding it to the beginning cash balance to show that it equals the ending cash balance.

Step ① Compute net increase or decrease in cash

Step ② Compute net cash from operating activities

Step ③ Compute net cash from investing activities

Step ④ Compute net cash from financing activities

Step ⑤ Prove and report beginning and ending cash balances

Computing the net increase or net decrease in cash is a simple but crucial computation. It equals the current period's cash balance minus the prior period's cash balance. This is the *bottom-line* figure for the statement of cash flows and is a check on accuracy. The information we need to prepare a statement of cash flows comes from various sources including comparative balance sheets at the beginning and end of the period, and an income statement for the period. There are two alternative approaches to preparing the statement: (1) analyzing the Cash account and (2) analyzing noncash accounts.

Point: View the change in cash as a *target* number (or check figure) that we will fully explain and prove in the statement of cash flows.

Analyzing the Cash Account A company's cash receipts and cash payments are recorded in the Cash account in its general ledger. The Cash account is therefore a natural place to look for information about cash flows from operating, investing, and financing activities. To illustrate, review the summarized Cash T-account of Genesis, Inc., in Exhibit 16.6. Individual cash transactions are summarized in this Cash account according to the major types of cash receipts and cash payments. For instance, only the total of cash receipts from all customers is listed. Individual cash transactions underlying these totals can number in the thousands. Accounting software is available to provide summarized cash accounts.

Preparing a statement of cash flows from Exhibit 16.6 requires determining whether an individual cash inflow or outflow is an operating, investing, or financing activity, and then listing

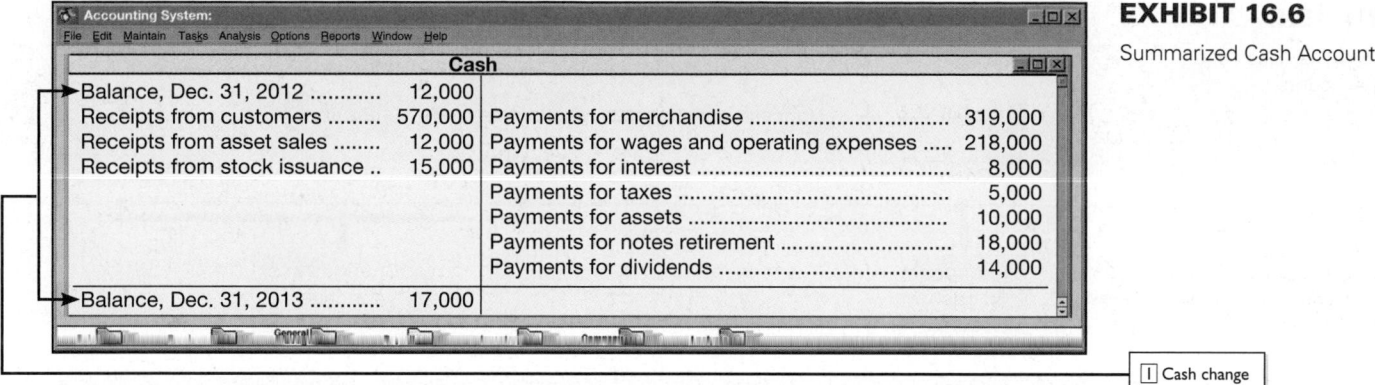

EXHIBIT 16.6

Summarized Cash Account

each by activity. This yields the statement shown in Exhibit 16.7. However, preparing the statement of cash flows from an analysis of the summarized Cash account has two limitations. First, most companies have many individual cash receipts and payments, making it difficult to review them all. Accounting software minimizes this burden, but it is still a task requiring professional judgment for many transactions. Second, the Cash account does not usually carry an adequate description of each cash transaction, making assignment of all cash transactions according to activity difficult.

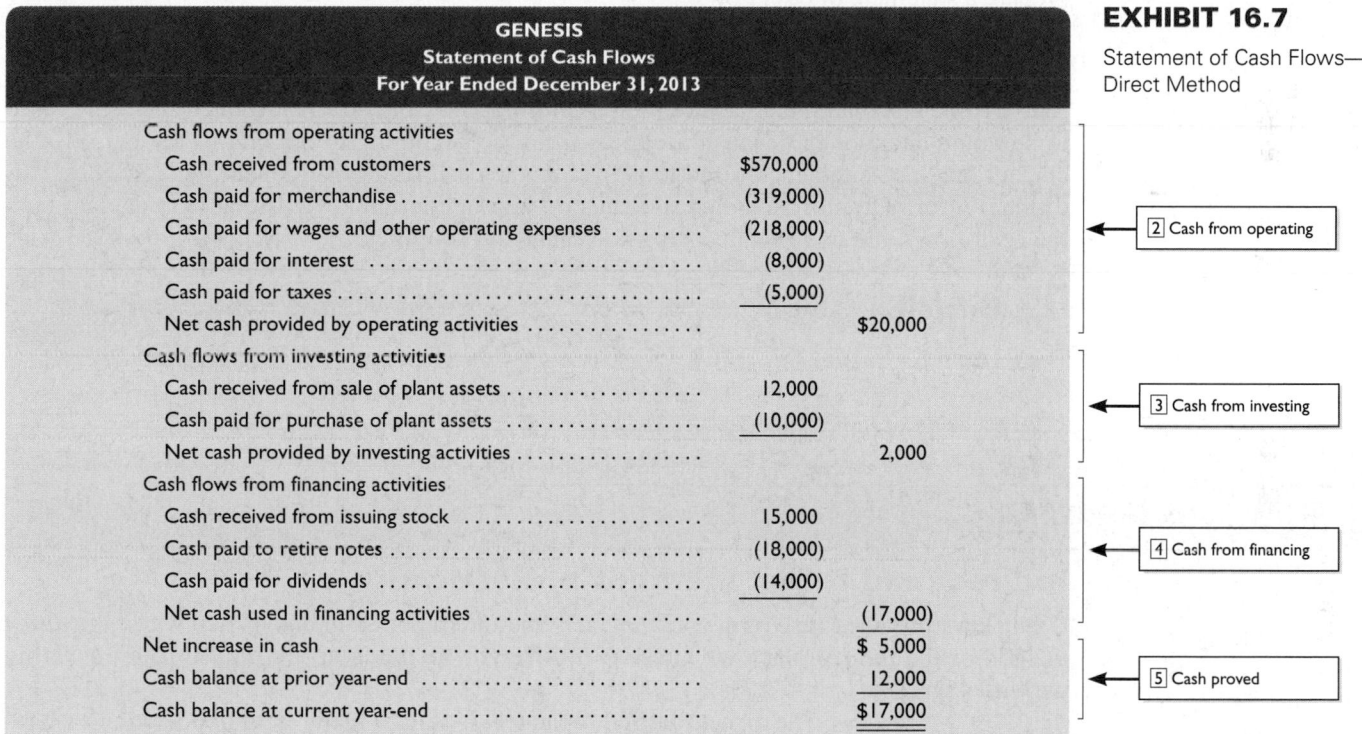

EXHIBIT 16.7

Statement of Cash Flows— Direct Method

Analyzing Noncash Accounts   A second approach to preparing the statement of cash flows is analyzing noncash accounts. This approach uses the fact that when a company records cash inflows and outflows with debits and credits to the Cash account (see Exhibit 16.6), it also records credits and debits in noncash accounts (reflecting double-entry accounting). Many of these noncash accounts are balance sheet accounts—for instance, from the sale of land for cash. Others are revenue and expense accounts that are closed to equity. For instance, the sale of services for cash yields a credit to Services Revenue that is closed to Retained Earnings for a corporation. In sum, *all cash transactions eventually affect noncash balance sheet accounts.* Thus, we can determine cash inflows and outflows by analyzing changes in noncash balance sheet accounts.

Exhibit 16.8 uses the accounting equation to show the relation between the Cash account and the noncash balance sheet accounts. This exhibit starts with the accounting equation at the

EXHIBIT 16.8

Relation between Cash and Noncash Accounts

Information on changes in cash is obtained from analyzing *either* the Cash account *or* the noncash accounts

top. It is then expanded in line (2) to separate cash from noncash asset accounts. Line (3) moves noncash asset accounts to the right-hand side of the equality where they are subtracted. This shows that cash equals the sum of the liability and equity accounts *minus* the noncash asset accounts. Line (4) points out that *changes* on one side of the accounting equation equal *changes* on the other side. It shows that we can explain changes in cash by analyzing changes in the noncash accounts consisting of liability accounts, equity accounts, and noncash asset accounts. By analyzing noncash balance sheet accounts and any related income statement accounts, we can prepare a statement of cash flows.

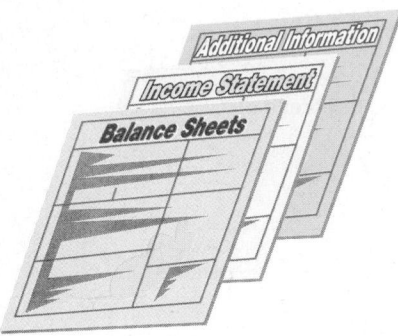

Information to Prepare the Statement Information to prepare the statement of cash flows usually comes from three sources: (1) comparative balance sheets, (2) the current income statement, and (3) additional information. Comparative balance sheets are used to compute changes in noncash accounts from the beginning to the end of the period. The current income statement is used to help compute cash flows from operating activities. Additional information often includes details on transactions and events that help explain both the cash flows and noncash investing and financing activities.

Decision Insight

e-Cash Every credit transaction on the Net leaves a trail that a hacker or a marketer can pick up. Enter e-cash—or digital money. The encryption of e-cash protects your money from snoops and thieves and cannot be traced, even by the issuing bank. ■

CASH FLOWS FROM OPERATING

Indirect and Direct Methods of Reporting

Cash flows provided (used) by operating activities are reported in one of two ways: the *direct method* or the *indirect method*. **These two different methods apply only to the operating activities section.**

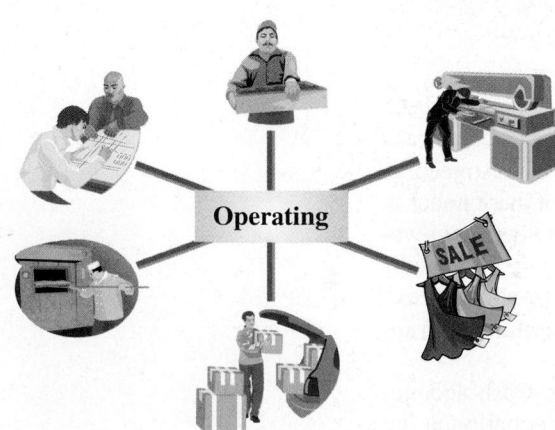

The **direct method** separately lists each major item of operating cash receipts (such as cash received from customers) and each major item of operating cash payments (such as cash paid for merchandise). The cash payments are subtracted from cash receipts to determine the net cash provided (used) by operating activities. The operating activities section of Exhibit 16.7 reflects the direct method of reporting operating cash flows.

The **indirect method** reports net income and then adjusts it for items necessary to obtain net cash provided or used by operating activities. It does *not* report individual items of cash inflows and cash outflows from operating activities. Instead, the indirect method reports the necessary adjustments to reconcile net income to net cash provided or used by operating activities. The operating activities section for Genesis prepared under the indirect method is shown in Exhibit 16.9. **The net cash amount provided by operating activities is *identical* under both the direct and indirect methods.**

Cash flows from operating activities		
Net income	$ 38,000	
Adjustments to reconcile net income to net cash provided by operating activities		
Increase in accounts receivable	(20,000)	
Increase in merchandise inventory	(14,000)	
Increase in prepaid expenses	(2,000)	
Decrease in accounts payable	(5,000)	
Decrease in interest payable	(1,000)	
Increase in income taxes payable	10,000	
Depreciation expense	24,000	
Loss on sale of plant assets	6,000	
Gain on retirement of notes	(16,000)	
Net cash provided by operating activities		**$20,000**

EXHIBIT 16.9

Operating Activities Section—
Indirect Method

This equality always exists. The difference in these methods is with the computation and presentation of this amount. The FASB recommends the direct method, but because it is not required and the indirect method is arguably easier to compute, nearly all companies report operating cash flows using the indirect method.

To illustrate, we prepare the operating activities section of the statement of cash flows for Genesis. Exhibit 16.10 shows the December 31, 2012 and 2013, balance sheets of Genesis along with its 2013 income statement. We use this information to prepare a statement of cash flows that explains the $5,000 increase in cash for 2013 as reflected in its balance sheets. This $5,000 is computed as Cash of $17,000 at the end of 2013 minus Cash of $12,000 at the end of 2012. Genesis discloses additional information on its 2013 transactions:

Point: To better understand the direct and indirect methods of reporting operating cash flows, identify similarities and differences between Exhibits 16.7 and 16.11.

a. The accounts payable balances result from merchandise inventory purchases.

b. Purchased $70,000 in plant assets by paying $10,000 cash and issuing $60,000 of notes payable.

c. Sold plant assets with an original cost of $30,000 and accumulated depreciation of $12,000 for $12,000 cash, yielding a $6,000 loss.

d. Received $15,000 cash from issuing 3,000 shares of common stock.

e. Paid $18,000 cash to retire notes with a $34,000 book value, yielding a $16,000 gain.

f. Declared and paid cash dividends of $14,000.

The next section describes the indirect method. Appendix 16B describes the direct method. An instructor can choose to cover either one or both methods. Neither section depends on the other. If the indirect method is skipped, then read Appendix 16B and return to the section (six pages ahead) titled "Cash Flows from Investing."

Application of the Indirect Method of Reporting

Net income is computed using accrual accounting, which recognizes revenues when earned and expenses when incurred. Revenues and expenses do not necessarily reflect the receipt and payment of cash. The indirect method of computing and reporting net cash flows from operating activities involves adjusting the net income figure to obtain the net cash provided or used by operating activities. This includes subtracting noncash increases (credits) from net income and adding noncash charges (debits) back to net income.

To illustrate, the indirect method begins with Genesis's net income of $38,000 and adjusts it to obtain net cash provided by operating activities of $20,000. Exhibit 16.11 shows the results of the indirect method of reporting operating cash flows, which adjusts net income for three types of adjustments. There are adjustments ① to reflect changes in noncash current assets and current liabilities related to operating activities, ② to income statement items involving operating activities that do not affect cash inflows or outflows, and ③ to eliminate gains and losses resulting from investing and financing activities (not part of operating activities). This section describes each of these adjustments.

P2 Compute cash flows from operating activities using the indirect method.

Point: *Noncash credits* refer to *revenue* amounts reported on the income statement that are *not collected in cash* this period. *Noncash charges* refer to *expense* amounts reported on the income statement that are *not paid* this period.

EXHIBIT 16.10

Financial Statements

GENESIS Income Statement For Year Ended December 31, 2013		
Sales		$590,000
Cost of goods sold	$300,000	
Wages and other operating expenses ..	216,000	
Interest expense	7,000	
Depreciation expense	24,000	(547,000)
		43,000
Other gains (losses)		
Gain on retirement of notes	16,000	
Loss on sale of plant assets	(6,000)	10,000
Income before taxes		53,000
Income taxes expense		(15,000)
Net income		$ 38,000

GENESIS Balance Sheets December 31, 2013 and 2012	2013	2012
Assets		
Current assets		
Cash	$ 17,000	$ 12,000
Accounts receivable	60,000	40,000
Merchandise inventory	84,000	70,000
Prepaid expenses	6,000	4,000
Total current assets	167,000	126,000
Long-term assets		
Plant assets	250,000	210,000
Accumulated depreciation	(60,000)	(48,000)
Total assets	$357,000	$288,000
Liabilities		
Current liabilities		
Accounts payable	$ 35,000	$ 40,000
Interest payable	3,000	4,000
Income taxes payable	22,000	12,000
Total current liabilities	60,000	56,000
Long-term notes payable	90,000	64,000
Total liabilities	150,000	120,000
Equity		
Common stock, $5 par	95,000	80,000
Retained earnings	112,000	88,000
Total equity	207,000	168,000
Total liabilities and equity	$357,000	$288,000

① **Adjustments for Changes in Current Assets and Current Liabilities**   This section describes adjustments for changes in noncash current assets and current liabilities.

Adjustments for changes in noncash current assets.   Changes in noncash current assets normally result from operating activities. Examples are sales affecting accounts receivable and building usage affecting prepaid rent. Decreases in noncash current assets yield the following adjustment:

> **Decreases in noncash current assets are added to net income.**

To see the logic for this adjustment, consider that a decrease in a noncash current asset such as accounts receivable suggests more available cash at the end of the period compared to the beginning. This is so because a decrease in accounts receivable implies higher cash receipts than reflected in sales. We add these higher cash receipts (from decreases in noncash current assets) to net income when computing cash flow from operations.

In contrast, an increase in noncash current assets such as accounts receivable implies less cash receipts than reflected in sales. As another example, an increase in prepaid rent indicates that more cash is paid for rent than is deducted as rent expense. Increases in noncash current assets yield the following adjustment:

> **Increases in noncash current assets are subtracted from net income.**

To illustrate, these adjustments are applied to the noncash current assets in Exhibit 16.10.

Accounts receivable. Accounts receivable *increase* $20,000, from a beginning balance of $40,000 to an ending balance of $60,000. This increase implies that Genesis collects less cash than is reported in sales. That is, some of these sales were in the form of accounts receivable and that amount increased during the period. To see this it is helpful to use *account analysis.* This usually involves setting up a T-account and reconstructing its major entries to compute cash receipts or payments. The following reconstructed Accounts Receivable T-account reveals that cash receipts are less than sales:

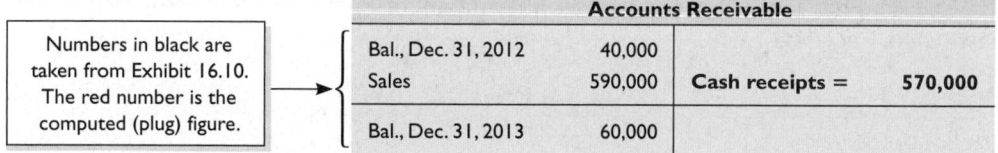

Numbers in black are taken from Exhibit 16.10. The red number is the computed (plug) figure.		**Accounts Receivable**			
	Bal., Dec. 31, 2012	40,000			
	Sales	590,000	**Cash receipts =**	**570,000**	
	Bal., Dec. 31, 2013	60,000			

We see that sales are $20,000 greater than cash receipts. This $20,000—as reflected in the $20,000 increase in Accounts Receivable—is subtracted from net income when computing cash provided by operating activities (see Exhibit 16.11).

Merchandise inventory. Merchandise inventory *increases* by $14,000, from a $70,000 beginning balance to an $84,000 ending balance. This increase implies that Genesis had greater cash purchases than cost of goods sold. This larger amount of cash purchases is in the form of inventory, as reflected in the following account analysis:

Merchandise Inventory			
Bal., Dec. 31, 2012	70,000		
Purchases =	**314,000**	Cost of goods sold	300,000
Bal., Dec. 31, 2013	84,000		

EXHIBIT 16.11

Statement of Cash Flows— Indirect Method

GENESIS Statement of Cash Flows For Year Ended December 31, 2013		
Cash flows from operating activities		
Net income	$ 38,000	
Adjustments to reconcile net income to net cash provided by operating activities		
① ⎰ Increase in accounts receivable.	(20,000)	
Increase in merchandise inventory	(14,000)	
Increase in prepaid expenses	(2,000)	
Decrease in accounts payable.	(5,000)	
Decrease in interest payable.	(1,000)	
Increase in income taxes payable	10,000	
② { Depreciation expense	24,000	
③ ⎰ Loss on sale of plant assets.	6,000	
Gain on retirement of notes.	(16,000)	
Net cash provided by operating activities		$20,000
Cash flows from investing activities		
Cash received from sale of plant assets	12,000	
Cash paid for purchase of plant assets	(10,000)	
Net cash provided by investing activities		2,000
Cash flows from financing activities		
Cash received from issuing stock	15,000	
Cash paid to retire notes	(18,000)	
Cash paid for dividends.	(14,000)	
Net cash used in financing activities		(17,000)
Net increase in cash		$ 5,000
Cash balance at prior year-end.		12,000
Cash balance at current year-end		$17,000

Point: Refer to Exhibit 16.10 and identify the $5,000 change in cash. This change is what the statement of cash flows explains; it serves as a check.

Point: The statement of cash flows is usually the last prepared of the four required financial statements.

The amount by which purchases exceed cost of goods sold—as reflected in the $14,000 increase in inventory—is subtracted from net income when computing cash provided by operating activities (see Exhibit 16.11).

Prepaid expenses. Prepaid Expenses *increase* $2,000, from a $4,000 beginning balance to a $6,000 ending balance, implying that Genesis's cash payments exceed its recorded prepaid expenses. These higher cash payments increase the amount of Prepaid Expenses, as reflected in its reconstructed T-account:

Prepaid Expenses			
Bal., Dec. 31, 2012	4,000		
Cash payments =	**218,000**	Wages and other operating exp.	216,000
Bal., Dec. 31, 2013	6,000		

The amount by which cash payments exceed the recorded operating expenses—as reflected in the $2,000 increase in Prepaid Expenses—is subtracted from net income when computing cash provided by operating activities (see Exhibit 16.11).

Adjustments for changes in current liabilities.   Changes in current liabilities normally result from operating activities. An example is a purchase that affects accounts payable. Increases in current liabilities yield the following adjustment to net income when computing operating cash flows:

Increases in current liabilities are added to net income.

To see the logic for this adjustment, consider that an increase in the Accounts Payable account suggests that cash payments are less than the related (cost of goods sold) expense. As another example, an increase in wages payable implies that cash paid for wages is less than the recorded wages expense. Since the recorded expense is greater than the cash paid, we add the increase in wages payable to net income to compute net cash flow from operations.

Conversely, when current liabilities decrease, the following adjustment is required:

Decreases in current liabilities are subtracted from net income.

To illustrate, these adjustments are applied to the current liabilities in Exhibit 16.10.

Accounts payable. Accounts payable *decrease* $5,000, from a beginning balance of $40,000 to an ending balance of $35,000. This decrease implies that cash payments to suppliers exceed purchases by $5,000 for the period, which is reflected in the reconstructed Accounts Payable T-account:

Accounts Payable			
		Bal., Dec. 31, 2012	40,000
Cash payments =	**319,000**	Purchases	314,000
		Bal., Dec. 31, 2013	35,000

The amount by which cash payments exceed purchases—as reflected in the $5,000 decrease in Accounts Payable—is subtracted from net income when computing cash provided by operating activities (see Exhibit 16.11).

Interest payable. Interest payable *decreases* $1,000, from a $4,000 beginning balance to a $3,000 ending balance. This decrease indicates that cash paid for interest exceeds interest expense by $1,000, which is reflected in the Interest Payable T-account:

Interest Payable			
		Bal., Dec. 31, 2012	4,000
Cash paid for interest =	**8,000**	Interest expense	7,000
		Bal., Dec. 31, 2013	3,000

The amount by which cash paid exceeds recorded expense—as reflected in the $1,000 decrease in Interest Payable—is subtracted from net income (see Exhibit 16.11).

Income taxes payable. Income taxes payable *increase* $10,000, from a $12,000 beginning balance to a $22,000 ending balance. This increase implies that reported income taxes exceed the cash paid for taxes, which is reflected in the Income Taxes Payable T-account:

Income Taxes Payable			
		Bal., Dec. 31, 2012	12,000
Cash paid for taxes =	5,000	Income taxes expense	15,000
		Bal., Dec. 31, 2013	22,000

Summary Adjustments for Changes in Current Assets and Current Liabilities		
Account	Increases	Decreases
Noncash current assets	Deduct from NI	Add to NI
Current liabilities.	Add to NI	Deduct from NI

The amount by which cash paid falls short of the reported taxes expense—as reflected in the $10,000 increase in Income Taxes Payable—is added to net income when computing cash provided by operating activities (see Exhibit 16.11).

② **Adjustments for Operating Items Not Providing or Using Cash**   The income statement usually includes some expenses that do not reflect cash outflows in the period. Examples are depreciation, amortization, depletion, and bad debts expense. The indirect method for reporting operating cash flows requires that

Expenses with no cash outflows are added back to net income.

To see the logic of this adjustment, recall that items such as depreciation, amortization, depletion, and bad debts originate from debits to expense accounts and credits to noncash accounts. These entries have *no* cash effect, and we add them back to net income when computing net cash flows from operations. Adding them back cancels their deductions.

Similarly, when net income includes revenues that do not reflect cash inflows in the period, the indirect method for reporting operating cash flows requires that

Revenues with no cash inflows are subtracted from net income.

We apply these adjustments to the Genesis operating items that do not provide or use cash.

Depreciation.   Depreciation expense is the only Genesis operating item that has no effect on cash flows in the period. We must add back the $24,000 depreciation expense to net income when computing cash provided by operating activities. (We later explain that any cash outflow to acquire a plant asset is reported as an investing activity.)

③ **Adjustments for Nonoperating Items**   Net income often includes losses that are not part of operating activities but are part of either investing or financing activities. Examples are a loss from the sale of a plant asset and a loss from retirement of notes payable. The indirect method for reporting operating cash flows requires that

Nonoperating losses are added back to net income.

To see the logic, consider that items such as a plant asset sale and a notes retirement are normally recorded by recognizing the cash, removing all plant asset or notes accounts, and recognizing any loss or gain. The cash received or paid is not part of operating activities but is part of either investing or financing activities. *No* operating cash flow effect occurs. However, because the nonoperating loss is a deduction in computing net income, we need to add it back to net income when computing cash flow from operations. Adding it back cancels the deduction.

Similarly, when net income includes gains not part of operating activities, the indirect method for reporting operating cash flows requires that

Nonoperating gains are subtracted from net income.

To illustrate these adjustments, we consider the nonoperating items of Genesis.

Point: An income statement reports revenues, gains, expenses, and losses on an accrual basis. The statement of cash flows reports cash received and cash paid for operating, financing, and investing activities.

Loss on sale of plant assets.   Genesis reports a $6,000 loss on sale of plant assets as part of net income. This loss is a proper deduction in computing income, but it is *not part of operating activities*. Instead, a sale of plant assets is part of investing activities. Thus, the $6,000 nonoperating loss is added back to net income (see Exhibit 16.11). Adding it back cancels the loss. We later explain how to report the cash inflow from the asset sale in investing activities.

Gain on retirement of debt.   A $16,000 gain on retirement of debt is properly included in net income, but it is *not part of operating activities*. This means the $16,000 nonoperating gain must be subtracted from net income to obtain net cash provided by operating activities (see Exhibit 16.11). Subtracting it cancels the recorded gain. We later describe how to report the cash outflow to retire debt.

Summary of Adjustments for Indirect Method

Exhibit 16.12 summarizes the most common adjustments to net income when computing net cash provided or used by operating activities under the indirect method.

EXHIBIT 16.12

Summary of Selected Adjustments for Indirect Method

* Excludes current portion of long-term debt and any (nonsales-related) short-term notes payable—both are financing activities.

The computations in determining cash provided or used by operating activities are different for the indirect and direct methods, but the result is identical. Both methods yield the same $20,000 figure for cash from operating activities for Genesis; see Exhibits 16.7 and 16.11.

Decision Insight

Cash or Income   The difference between net income and operating cash flows can be large and sometimes reflects on the quality of earnings. This bar chart shows the net income and operating cash flows of three companies. Operating cash flows can be either higher or lower than net income. ■

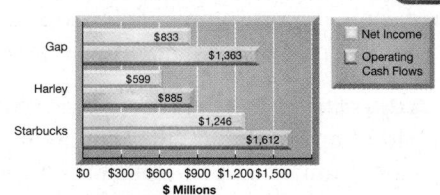

Quick Check   Answers — p. 664

4. Determine the net cash provided or used by operating activities using the following data: net income, $74,900; decrease in accounts receivable, $4,600; increase in inventory, $11,700; decrease in accounts payable, $1,000; loss on sale of equipment, $3,400; payment of cash dividends, $21,500.

5. Why are expenses such as depreciation and amortization added to net income when cash flow from operating activities is computed by the indirect method?

6. A company reports net income of $15,000 that includes a $3,000 gain on the sale of plant assets. Why is this gain subtracted from net income in computing cash flow from operating activities using the indirect method?

CASH FLOWS FROM INVESTING

The third major step in preparing the statement of cash flows is to compute and report cash flows from investing activities. We normally do this by identifying changes in (1) all noncurrent asset accounts and (2) the current accounts for both notes receivable and investments in securities (excluding trading securities). We then analyze changes in these accounts to determine their effect, if any, on cash and report the cash flow effects in the investing activities section of the statement of cash flows. **Reporting of investing activities is identical under the direct method and indirect method.**

Three-Stage Process of Analysis

Information to compute cash flows from investing activities is usually taken from beginning and ending balance sheets and the income statement. We use a three-stage process to determine cash provided or used by investing activities: (1) identify changes in investing-related accounts, (2) explain these changes using reconstruction analysis, and (3) report their cash flow effects.

P3 Determine cash flows from both investing and financing activities.

Analysis of Noncurrent Assets

Information about the Genesis transactions provided earlier reveals that the company both purchased and sold plant assets during the period. Both transactions are investing activities and are analyzed for their cash flow effects in this section.

Plant Asset Transactions The first stage in analyzing the Plant Assets account and its related Accumulated Depreciation is to identify any changes in these accounts from comparative balance sheets in Exhibit 16.10. This analysis reveals a $40,000 increase in plant assets from $210,000 to $250,000 and a $12,000 increase in accumulated depreciation from $48,000 to $60,000.

The second stage is to explain these changes. Items *b* and *c* of the additional information for Genesis (page 641) are relevant in this case. Recall that the Plant Assets account is affected by both asset purchases and sales, while its Accumulated Depreciation account is normally increased from depreciation and decreased from the removal of accumulated depreciation in asset sales. To explain changes in these accounts and to identify their cash flow effects, we prepare *reconstructed entries* from prior transactions; *they are not the actual entries by the preparer.*

To illustrate, item *b* reports that Genesis purchased plant assets of $70,000 by issuing $60,000 in notes payable to the seller and paying $10,000 in cash. The reconstructed entry for analysis of item *b* follows:

Point: Investing activities include (1) purchasing and selling long-term assets, (2) lending and collecting on notes receivable, and (3) purchasing and selling short-term investments other than cash equivalents and trading securities.

Point: Financing and investing info is available in ledger accounts to help explain changes in comparative balance sheets. Post references lead to relevant entries and explanations.

Reconstruction	Plant Assets	70,000	
	Notes Payable		60,000
	Cash		**10,000**

This entry reveals a $10,000 cash outflow for plant assets and a $60,000 noncash investing and financing transaction involving notes exchanged for plant assets.

Next, item *c* reports that Genesis sold plant assets costing $30,000 (with $12,000 of accumulated depreciation) for $12,000 cash, resulting in a $6,000 loss. The reconstructed entry for analysis of item *c* follows:

Reconstruction	**Cash**	**12,000**	
	Accumulated Depreciation	12,000	
	Loss on Sale of Plant Assets	6,000	
	Plant Assets		30,000

Point: When determining cash flows from investing, T-account analysis is key to reconstructing accounts and amounts.

This entry reveals a $12,000 cash inflow from assets sold. The $6,000 loss is computed by comparing the asset book value to the cash received and does not reflect any cash inflow or outflow. We also reconstruct the entry for Depreciation Expense using information from the income statement.

| Reconstruction | Depreciation Expense .... | 24,000 | |
| | Accumulated Depreciation .... | | 24,000 |

This entry shows that Depreciation Expense results in no cash flow effect. These three reconstructed entries are reflected in the following plant asset and related T-accounts.

Plant Assets			
Bal., Dec. 31, 2012	210,000		
Purchase	70,000	Sale	30,000
Bal., Dec. 31, 2013	250,000		

Accumulated Depreciation—Plant Assets			
		Bal., Dec. 31, 2012	48,000
Sale	12,000	Depr. expense	24,000
		Bal., Dec. 31, 2013	60,000

Example: If a plant asset costing $40,000 with $37,000 of accumulated depreciation is sold at a $1,000 loss, what is the cash flow? What is the cash flow if this asset is sold at a gain of $3,000? *Answers:* +$2,000; +$6,000.

This reconstruction analysis is complete in that the change in plant assets from $210,000 to $250,000 is fully explained by the $70,000 purchase and the $30,000 sale. Also, the change in accumulated depreciation from $48,000 to $60,000 is fully explained by depreciation expense of $24,000 and the removal of $12,000 in accumulated depreciation from an asset sale. (Preparers of the statement of cash flows have the entire ledger and additional information at their disposal, but for brevity reasons only the information needed for reconstructing accounts is given.)

The third stage looks at the reconstructed entries for identification of cash flows. The two identified cash flow effects are reported in the investing section of the statement as follows (also see Exhibit 16.7 or 16.11):

Cash flows from investing activities	
Cash received from sale of plant assets	$12,000
Cash paid for purchase of plant assets	(10,000)

The $60,000 portion of the purchase described in item *b* and financed by issuing notes is a non-cash investing and financing activity. It is reported in a note or in a separate schedule to the statement as follows:

Noncash investing and financing activity	
Purchased plant assets with issuance of notes	$60,000

Analysis of Other Assets

Many other asset transactions (including those involving current notes receivable and investments in certain securities) are considered investing activities and can affect a company's cash flows. Since Genesis did not enter into other investing activities impacting assets, we do not need to extend our analysis to these other assets. If such transactions did exist, we would analyze them using the same three-stage process illustrated for plant assets.

Quick Check   Answer — p. 664

7. Equipment costing $80,000 with accumulated depreciation of $30,000 is sold at a loss of $10,000. What is the cash receipt from this sale? In what section of the statement of cash flows is this transaction reported?

CASH FLOWS FROM FINANCING

The fourth major step in preparing the statement of cash flows is to compute and report cash flows from financing activities. We normally do this by identifying changes in all noncurrent liability accounts (including the current portion of any notes and bonds) and the equity accounts. These accounts include long-term debt, notes payable, bonds payable, common stock, and retained earnings. Changes in these accounts are then analyzed using available information to determine their effect, if any, on cash. Results are reported in the financing activities section of the statement. **Reporting of financing activities is identical under the direct method and indirect method.**

Three-Stage Process of Analysis

We again use a three-stage process to determine cash provided or used by financing activities: (1) identify changes in financing-related accounts, (2) explain these changes using reconstruction analysis, and (3) report their cash flow effects.

Analysis of Noncurrent Liabilities

Information about Genesis provided earlier reveals two transactions involving noncurrent liabilities. We analyzed one of those, the $60,000 issuance of notes payable to purchase plant assets. This transaction is reported as a significant noncash investing and financing activity in a footnote or a separate schedule to the statement of cash flows. The other remaining transaction involving noncurrent liabilities is the cash retirement of notes payable.

Point: Financing activities generally refer to changes in the noncurrent liability and the equity accounts. Examples are (1) receiving cash from issuing debt or repaying amounts borrowed and (2) receiving cash from or distributing cash to owners.

Notes Payable Transactions The first stage in analysis of notes is to review the comparative balance sheets from Exhibit 16.10. This analysis reveals an increase in notes payable from $64,000 to $90,000.

The second stage explains this change. Item *e* of the additional information for Genesis (page 641) reports that notes with a carrying value of $34,000 are retired for $18,000 cash, resulting in a $16,000 gain. The reconstructed entry for analysis of item *e* follows:

Reconstruction	Notes Payable	34,000	
	Gain on retirement of debt		16,000
	Cash		**18,000**

This entry reveals an $18,000 cash outflow for retirement of notes and a $16,000 gain from comparing the notes payable carrying value to the cash received. This gain does not reflect any cash inflow or outflow. Also, item *b* of the additional information reports that Genesis purchased plant assets costing $70,000 by issuing $60,000 in notes payable to the seller and paying $10,000 in cash. We reconstructed this entry when analyzing investing activities: It showed a $60,000 increase to notes payable that is reported as a noncash investing and financing transaction. The Notes Payable account reflects (and is fully explained by) these reconstructed entries as follows:

	Notes Payable		
		Bal., Dec. 31, 2012	64,000
Retired notes	34,000	**Issued notes**	**60,000**
		Bal., Dec. 31, 2013	90,000

The third stage is to report the cash flow effect of the notes retirement in the financing section of the statement as follows (also see Exhibit 16.7 or 16.11):

Cash flows from financing activities	
Cash paid to retire notes	$(18,000)

Analysis of Equity

The Genesis information reveals two transactions involving equity accounts. The first is the issuance of common stock for cash. The second is the declaration and payment of cash dividends. We analyze both.

Common Stock Transactions   The first stage in analyzing common stock is to review the comparative balance sheets from Exhibit 16.10, which reveal an increase in common stock from $80,000 to $95,000.

The second stage explains this change. Item *d* of the additional information (page 641) reports that 3,000 shares of common stock are issued at par for $5 per share. The reconstructed entry for analysis of item *d* follows:

Reconstruction	Cash	15,000	
	Common Stock		15,000

This entry reveals a $15,000 cash inflow from stock issuance and is reflected in (and explains) the Common Stock account as follows:

Common Stock		
	Bal., Dec. 31, 2012	80,000
	Issued stock	**15,000**
	Bal., Dec. 31, 2013	95,000

The third stage discloses the cash flow effect from stock issuance in the financing section of the statement as follows (also see Exhibit 16.7 or 16.11):

Cash flows from financing activities	
Cash received from issuing stock	$15,000

Retained Earnings Transactions   The first stage in analyzing the Retained Earnings account is to review the comparative balance sheets from Exhibit 16.10. This reveals an increase in retained earnings from $88,000 to $112,000.

The second stage explains this change. Item *f* of the additional information (page 641) reports that cash dividends of $14,000 are paid. The reconstructed entry follows:

Reconstruction	Retained Earnings	14,000	
	Cash		14,000

This entry reveals a $14,000 cash outflow for cash dividends. Also see that the Retained Earnings account is impacted by net income of $38,000. (Net income was analyzed under the operating section of the statement of cash flows.) The reconstructed Retained Earnings account follows:

Retained Earnings			
		Bal., Dec. 31, 2012	88,000
Cash dividend	**14,000**	**Net income**	**38,000**
		Bal., Dec. 31, 2013	112,000

Point: Financing activities not affecting cash flow include *declaration* of a cash dividend, *declaration* of a stock dividend, payment of a stock dividend, and a stock split.

The third stage reports the cash flow effect from the cash dividend in the financing section of the statement as follows (also see Exhibit 16.7 or 16.11):

Cash flows from financing activities	
Cash paid for dividends.....................	$(14,000)

Global: There are no requirements to separate domestic and international cash flows, leading some users to ask, "Where in the world is cash flow?"

We now have identified and explained all of the Genesis cash inflows and cash outflows and one noncash investing and financing transaction. Specifically, our analysis has reconciled changes in all noncash balance sheet accounts.

Proving Cash Balances

The fifth and final step in preparing the statement is to report the beginning and ending cash balances and prove that the *net change in cash* is explained by operating, investing, and financing cash flows. This step is shown here for Genesis.

Net cash provided by operating activities	$20,000
Net cash provided by investing activities	2,000
Net cash used in financing activities	(17,000)
Net increase in cash	**$ 5,000**
Cash balance at 2012 year-end	12,000
Cash balance at 2013 year-end	$17,000

The preceding table shows that the $5,000 net increase in cash, from $12,000 at the beginning of the period to $17,000 at the end, is reconciled by net cash flows from operating ($20,000 inflow), investing ($2,000 inflow), and financing ($17,000 outflow) activities. This is formally reported at the bottom of the statement of cash flows as shown in both Exhibits 16.7 and 16.11.

Decision Maker

Reporter   Management is in labor contract negotiations and grants you an interview. It highlights a recent $600,000 net loss that involves a $930,000 extraordinary loss and a total net cash outflow of $550,000 (which includes net cash outflows of $850,000 for investing activities and $350,000 for financing activities). What is your assessment of this company? ■   [Answer—p. 664]

 GLOBAL VIEW

The statement of cash flows, which explains changes in cash (including cash equivalents) from period to period, is required under both U.S. GAAP and IFRS. This section discusses similarities and differences between U.S. GAAP and IFRS in reporting that statement.

Reporting Cash Flows from Operating   Both U.S. GAAP and IFRS permit the reporting of cash flows from operating activities using either the direct or indirect method. Further, the basic requirements underlying the application of both methods are fairly consistent across these two accounting systems. Appendix A shows that both **KTM** and **Piaggio** report their cash flows from operating activities using the indirect method, and in a manner similar to that explained in this chapter. Further, the definition of cash and cash equivalents is roughly similar for U.S. GAAP and IFRS.

KTM

PIAGGIO

   There are, however, some differences between U.S. GAAP and IFRS in reporting operating cash flows. We mention two of the more notable. First, U.S. GAAP requires cash inflows from interest revenue and dividend revenue be classified as operating, whereas IFRS permits classification under operating or investing provided that this classification is consistently applied across periods. Nokia reports its cash from interest received under operating, consistent with U.S. GAAP (no mention is made of any dividends received). Second, U.S. GAAP requires cash outflows for interest expense be classified as operating, whereas IFRS again permits classification under operating or financing provided that it is consistently applied across periods. (Some believe that interest payments, like dividends payments, are better classified as financing because they represent payments to financiers.) Piaggio reports cash outflows for interest under operating, which is consistent with U.S. GAAP and acceptable under IFRS.

Reporting Cash Flows from Investing and Financing   U.S. GAAP and IFRS are broadly similar in computing and classifying cash flows from investing and financing activities. A quick review of these two sections for both **KTM**'s and **Piaggio**'s statement of cash flows shows a structure similar to that explained in this chapter. One notable exception is that U.S. GAAP requires cash outflows for income tax be classified as operating, whereas IFRS permits the splitting of those cash flows among operating, investing, and financing depending on the sources of that tax. Both KTM and Piaggio report their cash outflows for income tax under operating, which is similar to U.S. GAAP.

Decision Analysis   Cash Flow Analysis

Analyzing Cash Sources and Uses

A1 Analyze the statement of cash flows and apply the cash flow on total assets ratio.

Most managers stress the importance of understanding and predicting cash flows for business decisions. Creditors evaluate a company's ability to generate cash before deciding whether to lend money. Investors also assess cash inflows and outflows before buying and selling stock. Information in the statement of cash flows helps address these and other questions such as (1) How much cash is generated from or used in operations? (2) What expenditures are made with cash from operations? (3) What is the source of cash for debt payments? (4) What is the source of cash for distributions to owners? (5) How is the increase in investing activities financed? (6) What is the source of cash for new plant assets? (7) Why is cash flow from operations different from income? (8) How is cash from financing used?

To effectively answer these questions, it is important to separately analyze investing, financing, and operating activities. To illustrate, consider data from three different companies in Exhibit 16.13. These companies operate in the same industry and have been in business for several years.

EXHIBIT 16.13

Cash Flows of Competing Companies

($ thousands)	BMX	ATV	Trex
Cash provided (used) by operating activities	$90,000	$40,000	$(24,000)
Cash provided (used) by investing activities			
Proceeds from sale of plant assets			26,000
Purchase of plant assets	(48,000)	(25,000)	
Cash provided (used) by financing activities			
Proceeds from issuance of debt			13,000
Repayment of debt	(27,000)		
Net increase (decrease) in cash	$15,000	$15,000	$ 15,000

Each company generates an identical $15,000 net increase in cash, but its sources and uses of cash flows are very different. BMX's operating activities provide net cash flows of $90,000, allowing it to purchase plant assets of $48,000 and repay $27,000 of its debt. ATV's operating activities provide $40,000 of cash flows, limiting its purchase of plant assets to $25,000. Trex's $15,000 net cash increase is due to selling plant assets and incurring additional debt. Its operating activities yield a net cash outflow of $24,000. Overall, analysis of these cash flows reveals that BMX is more capable of generating future cash flows than is ATV or Trex.

 Decision Insight

Point: CFO (Cash flow from operations)
Less: Capital Expenditures
Less: Debt Repayments
= FCF (free cash flows)

Free Cash Flows Many investors use cash flows to value company stock. However, cash-based valuation models often yield different stock values due to differences in measurement of cash flows. Most models require cash flows that are "free" for distribution to shareholders. These *free cash flows* are defined as cash flows available to shareholders after operating asset reinvestments and debt payments. Knowledge of the statement of cash flows is key to proper computation of free cash flows. A company's growth and financial flexibility depend on adequate free cash flows. ■

Cash Flow on Total Assets

Cash flow information has limitations, but it can help measure a company's ability to meet its obligations, pay dividends, expand operations, and obtain financing. Users often compute and analyze a cash-based ratio similar to return on total assets except that its numerator is net cash flows from operating activities. The **cash flow on total assets** ratio is in Exhibit 16.14.

EXHIBIT 16.14

Cash Flow on Total Assets

$$\text{Cash flow on total assets} = \frac{\text{Cash flow from operations}}{\text{Average total assets}}$$

This ratio reflects actual cash flows and is not affected by accounting income recognition and measurement. It can help business decision makers estimate the amount and timing of cash flows when planning and analyzing operating activities.

To illustrate, the 2011 cash flow on total assets ratio for **Nike** is 12.3%—see Exhibit 16.15. Is a 12.3% ratio good or bad? To answer this question, we compare this ratio with the ratios of prior years (we could also compare its ratio with those of its competitors and the market). Nike's cash flow on total assets ratio for several prior years is in the second column of Exhibit 16.15. Results show that its 12.3% return is the lowest return over the past several years. This is probably reflective of the recent recessionary period.

Year	Cash Flow on Total Assets	Return on Total Assets
2011.........	12.3%	14.5%
2010.........	22.9	13.8
2009.........	13.5	11.6
2008.........	16.7	16.3
2007.........	18.3	14.5

EXHIBIT 16.15

Nike's Cash Flow on Total Assets

As an indicator of *earnings quality,* some analysts compare the cash flow on total assets ratio to the return on total assets ratio. Nike's return on total assets is provided in the third column of Exhibit 16.15. Nike's cash flow on total assets ratio exceeds its return on total assets in four of the five years, leading some analysts to infer that Nike's earnings quality is high for that period because more earnings are realized in the form of cash.

Point: Cash flow ratios are often used by financial analysts.

 Decision Insight

Cash Flow Ratios   Analysts use various other cash-based ratios, including the following two:

(1)
$$\text{Cash coverage of growth} = \frac{\text{Operating cash flow}}{\text{Cash outflow for plant assets}}$$

where a low ratio (less than 1) implies cash inadequacy to meet asset growth, whereas a high ratio implies cash adequacy for asset growth.

(2)
$$\text{Operating cash flow to sales} = \frac{\text{Operating cash flow}}{\text{Net sales}}$$

When this ratio substantially and consistently differs from the operating income to net sales ratio, the risk of accounting improprieties increases. ■

Point: The following ratio helps assess whether operating cash flow is adequate to meet long-term obligations:
Cash coverage of debt = Cash flow from operations ÷ Noncurrent liabilities. A low ratio suggests a higher risk of insolvency; a high ratio suggests a greater ability to meet long-term obligations.

DEMONSTRATION PROBLEM

Umlauf's comparative balance sheets, income statement, and additional information follow.

UMLAUF COMPANY
Balance Sheets
December 31, 2013 and 2012

	2013	2012
Assets		
Cash	$ 43,050	$ 23,925
Accounts receivable	34,125	39,825
Merchandise inventory	156,000	146,475
Prepaid expenses	3,600	1,650
Equipment	135,825	146,700
Accum. depreciation—Equipment	(61,950)	(47,550)
Total assets	$310,650	$311,025
Liabilities and Equity		
Accounts payable	$ 28,800	$ 33,750
Income taxes payable	5,100	4,425
Dividends payable	0	4,500
Bonds payable	0	37,500
Common stock, $10 par	168,750	168,750
Retained earnings	108,000	62,100
Total liabilities and equity	$310,650	$311,025

UMLAUF COMPANY
Income Statement
For Year Ended December 31, 2013

Sales		$446,100
Cost of goods sold	$222,300	
Other operating expenses	120,300	
Depreciation expense	25,500	(368,100)
		78,000
Other gains (losses)		
Loss on sale of equipment	3,300	
Loss on retirement of bonds ..	825	(4,125)
Income before taxes		73,875
Income taxes expense		(13,725)
Net income		$ 60,150

Additional Information

a. Equipment costing $21,375 with accumulated depreciation of $11,100 is sold for cash.

b. Equipment purchases are for cash.

c. Accumulated Depreciation is affected by depreciation expense and the sale of equipment.

d. The balance of Retained Earnings is affected by dividend declarations and net income.

e. All sales are made on credit.

f. All merchandise inventory purchases are on credit.

g. Accounts Payable balances result from merchandise inventory purchases.

h. Prepaid expenses relate to "other operating expenses."

Required

1. Prepare a statement of cash flows using the indirect method for year 2013.

2.ᴮ Prepare a statement of cash flows using the direct method for year 2013.

PLANNING THE SOLUTION

- Prepare two blank statements of cash flows with sections for operating, investing, and financing activities using the (1) indirect method format and (2) direct method format.
- Compute the cash paid for equipment and the cash received from the sale of equipment using the additional information provided along with the amount for depreciation expense and the change in the balances of equipment and accumulated depreciation. Use T-accounts to help chart the effects of the sale and purchase of equipment on the balances of the Equipment account and the Accumulated Depreciation account.
- Compute the effect of net income on the change in the Retained Earnings account balance. Assign the difference between the change in retained earnings and the amount of net income to dividends declared. Adjust the dividends declared amount for the change in the Dividends Payable balance.
- Compute cash received from customers, cash paid for merchandise, cash paid for other operating expenses, and cash paid for taxes as illustrated in the chapter.
- Enter the cash effects of reconstruction entries to the appropriate section(s) of the statement.
- Total each section of the statement, determine the total net change in cash, and add it to the beginning balance to get the ending balance of cash.

SOLUTION TO DEMONSTRATION PROBLEM

Supporting computations for cash receipts and cash payments.

(1)	*Cost of equipment sold	$ 21,375
	Accumulated depreciation of equipment sold	(11,100)
	Book value of equipment sold	10,275
	Loss on sale of equipment	(3,300)
	Cash received from sale of equipment	**$ 6,975**
	Cost of equipment sold	$ 21,375
	Less decrease in the equipment account balance	(10,875)
	Cash paid for new equipment	**$ 10,500**
(2)	Loss on retirement of bonds	$ 825
	Carrying value of bonds retired	37,500
	Cash paid to retire bonds	**$ 38,325**
(3)	Net income	$ 60,150
	Less increase in retained earnings	45,900
	Dividends declared	14,250
	Plus decrease in dividends payable	4,500
	Cash paid for dividends	**$ 18,750**
(4)ᴮ	Sales	$ 446,100
	Add decrease in accounts receivable	5,700
	Cash received from customers	**$451,800**

[continued on next page]

[continued from previous page]

(5)^B Cost of goods sold		$ 222,300
	Plus increase in merchandise inventory	9,525
	Purchases	231,825
	Plus decrease in accounts payable	4,950
	Cash paid for merchandise	**$236,775**
(6)^B Other operating expenses		$ 120,300
	Plus increase in prepaid expenses	1,950
	Cash paid for other operating expenses	**$122,250**
(7)^B Income taxes expense		$ 13,725
	Less increase in income taxes payable	(675)
	Cash paid for income taxes	**$ 13,050**

* Supporting T-account analysis for part 1 follows:

Equipment				
Bal., Dec. 31, 2012	146,700			
Cash purchase	10,500	Sale	21,375	
Bal., Dec. 31, 2013	135,825			

Accumulated Depreciation—Equipment				
		Bal., Dec. 31, 2012	47,550	
Sale	11,100	Depr. expense	25,500	
		Bal., Dec. 31, 2013	61,950	

UMLAUF COMPANY
Statement of Cash Flows (Indirect Method)
For Year Ended December 31, 2013

Cash flows from operating activities		
Net income	$60,150	
Adjustments to reconcile net income to net cash provided by operating activities		
Decrease in accounts receivable	5,700	
Increase in merchandise inventory	(9,525)	
Increase in prepaid expenses	(1,950)	
Decrease in accounts payable	(4,950)	
Increase in income taxes payable	675	
Depreciation expense	25,500	
Loss on sale of plant assets	3,300	
Loss on retirement of bonds	825	
Net cash provided by operating activities		$79,725
Cash flows from investing activities		
Cash received from sale of equipment	6,975	
Cash paid for equipment	(10,500)	
Net cash used in investing activities		(3,525)
Cash flows from financing activities		
Cash paid to retire bonds payable	(38,325)	
Cash paid for dividends	(18,750)	
Net cash used in financing activities		(57,075)
Net increase in cash		$19,125
Cash balance at prior year-end		23,925
Cash balance at current year-end		$43,050

UMLAUF COMPANY
Statement of Cash Flows (Direct Method)
For Year Ended December 31, 2013

Cash flows from operating activities		
Cash received from customers	$451,800	
Cash paid for merchandise	(236,775)	
Cash paid for other operating expenses	(122,250)	
Cash paid for income taxes	(13,050)	
Net cash provided by operating activities		$79,725
Cash flows from investing activities		
Cash received from sale of equipment	6,975	
Cash paid for equipment	(10,500)	
Net cash used in investing activities		(3,525)
Cash flows from financing activities		
Cash paid to retire bonds payable	(38,325)	
Cash paid for dividends	(18,750)	
Net cash used in financing activities		(57,075)
Net increase in cash		$19,125
Cash balance at prior year-end		23,925
Cash balance at current year-end		$43,050

APPENDIX

16A

Spreadsheet Preparation of the Statement of Cash Flows

This appendix explains how to use a spreadsheet to prepare the statement of cash flows under the indirect method.

P4 Illustrate use of a spreadsheet to prepare a statement of cash flows.

Preparing the Indirect Method Spreadsheet   Analyzing noncash accounts can be challenging when a company has a large number of accounts and many operating, investing, and financing transactions. A *spreadsheet,* also called *work sheet* or *working paper,* can help us organize the information needed to prepare a statement of cash flows. A spreadsheet also makes it easier to check the accuracy of our work. To illustrate, we return to the comparative balance sheets and income statement shown in Exhibit 16.10. We use the following identifying letters *a* through *g* to code changes in accounts, and letters *h* through *m* for additional information, to prepare the statement of cash flows:

 a. Net income is $38,000.

 b. Accounts receivable increase by $20,000.

 c. Merchandise inventory increases by $14,000.

 d. Prepaid expenses increase by $2,000.

 e. Accounts payable decrease by $5,000.

 f. Interest payable decreases by $1,000.

 g. Income taxes payable increase by $10,000.

 h. Depreciation expense is $24,000.

 i. Plant assets costing $30,000 with accumulated depreciation of $12,000 are sold for $12,000 cash. This yields a loss on sale of assets of $6,000.

 j. Notes with a book value of $34,000 are retired with a cash payment of $18,000, yielding a $16,000 gain on retirement.

k. Plant assets costing $70,000 are purchased with a cash payment of $10,000 and an issuance of notes payable for $60,000.

l. Issued 3,000 shares of common stock for $15,000 cash.

m. Paid cash dividends of $14,000.

Exhibit 16A.1 shows the indirect method spreadsheet for Genesis. We enter both beginning and ending balance sheet amounts on the spreadsheet. We also enter information in the Analysis of Changes columns (keyed to the additional information items *a* through *m*) to explain changes in the accounts and determine the cash flows for operating, investing, and financing activities. Information about noncash investing and financing activities is reported near the bottom.

EXHIBIT 16A.1

Spreadsheet for Preparing Statement of Cash Flows— Indirect Method

		Dec. 31, 2012	Analysis of Changes Debit		Analysis of Changes Credit		Dec. 31, 2013
	GENESIS Spreadsheet for Statement of Cash Flows—Indirect Method For Year Ended December 31, 2013						
8	**Balance Sheet—Debit Bal. Accounts**						
9	Cash	$ 12,000					$ 17,000
10	Accounts receivable	40,000	(b)	$ 20,000			60,000
11	Merchandise inventory	70,000	(c)	14,000			84,000
12	Prepaid expenses	4,000	(d)	2,000			6,000
13	Plant assets	210,000	(k1)	70,000	(i)	$ 30,000	250,000
14		$336,000					$417,000
16	**Balance Sheet—Credit Bal. Accounts**						
17	Accumulated depreciation	$ 48,000	(i)	12,000	(h)	24,000	$ 60,000
18	Accounts payable	40,000	(e)	5,000			35,000
19	Interest payable	4,000	(f)	1,000			3,000
20	Income taxes payable	12,000			(g)	10,000	22,000
21	Notes payable	64,000	(j)	34,000	(k2)	60,000	90,000
22	Common stock, $5 par value	80,000			(l)	15,000	95,000
23	Retained earnings	88,000	(m)	14,000	(a)	38,000	112,000
24		$336,000					$417,000
26	**Statement of Cash Flows**						
27	Operating activities						
28	Net income		(a)	38,000			
29	Increase in accounts receivable				(b)	20,000	
30	Increase in merchandise inventory				(c)	14,000	
31	Increase in prepaid expenses				(d)	2,000	
32	Decrease in accounts payable				(e)	5,000	
33	Decrease in interest payable				(f)	1,000	
34	Increase in income taxes payable		(g)	10,000			
35	Depreciation expense		(h)	24,000			
36	Loss on sale of plant assets		(i)	6,000			
37	Gain on retirement of notes				(j)	16,000	
38	Investing activities						
39	Receipts from sale of plant assets		(i)	12,000			
40	Payment for purchase of plant assets				(k1)	10,000	
41	Financing activities						
42	Payment to retire notes				(j)	18,000	
43	Receipts from issuing stock		(l)	15,000			
44	Payment of cash dividends				(m)	14,000	
46	**Noncash Investing and Financing Activities**						
47	Purchase of plant assets with notes		(k2)	60,000	(k1)	60,000	
48				$337,000		$337,000	

Entering the Analysis of Changes on the Spreadsheet The following sequence of procedures is used to complete the spreadsheet after the beginning and ending balances of the balance sheet accounts are entered:

① Enter net income as the first item in the Statement of Cash Flows section for computing operating cash inflow (debit) and as a credit to Retained Earnings.

② In the Statement of Cash Flows section, adjustments to net income are entered as debits if they increase cash flows and as credits if they decrease cash flows. Applying this same rule, adjust net income for the change in each noncash current asset and current liability account related to operating activities. For each adjustment to net income, the offsetting debit or credit must help reconcile the beginning and ending balances of a current asset or current liability account.

③ Enter adjustments to net income for income statement items not providing or using cash in the period. For each adjustment, the offsetting debit or credit must help reconcile a noncash balance sheet account.

④ Adjust net income to eliminate any gains or losses from investing and financing activities. Because the cash from a gain must be excluded from operating activities, the gain is entered as a credit in the operating activities section. Losses are entered as debits. For each adjustment, the related debit and/or credit must help reconcile balance sheet accounts and involve reconstructed entries to show the cash flow from investing or financing activities.

⑤ After reviewing any unreconciled balance sheet accounts and related information, enter the remaining reconciling entries for investing and financing activities. Examples are purchases of plant assets, issuances of long-term debt, stock issuances, and dividend payments. Some of these may require entries in the noncash investing and financing section of the spreadsheet (reconciled).

⑥ Check accuracy by totaling the Analysis of Changes columns and by determining that the change in each balance sheet account has been explained (reconciled).

We illustrate these steps in Exhibit 16A.1 for Genesis:

Point: Analysis of the changes on the spreadsheet are summarized here:

1. Cash flows from operating activities generally affect net income, current assets, and current liabilities.

2. Cash flows from investing activities generally affect noncurrent asset accounts.

3. Cash flows from financing activities generally affect noncurrent liability and equity accounts.

Step	Entries
①	(a)
②	(b) through (g)
③	(h)
④	(i) through (j)
⑤	(k) through (m)

Since adjustments *i, j,* and *k* are more challenging, we show them in the following debit and credit format. These entries are for purposes of our understanding; they are *not* the entries actually made in the journals. Changes in the Cash account are identified as sources or uses of cash.

i.	Loss from sale of plant assets	6,000	
	Accumulated depreciation	12,000	
	Receipt from sale of plant assets **(source of cash)**	12,000	
	Plant assets		30,000
	To describe sale of plant assets.		
j.	Notes payable	34,000	
	Payments to retire notes **(use of cash)**		18,000
	Gain on retirement of notes		16,000
	To describe retirement of notes.		
k1.	Plant assets	70,000	
	Payment to purchase plant assets **(use of cash)**		10,000
	Purchase of plant assets financed by notes		60,000
	To describe purchase of plant assets.		
k2.	Purchase of plant assets financed by notes	60,000	
	Notes payable		60,000
	To issue notes for purchase of assets.		

Direct Method of Reporting Operating Cash Flows

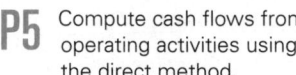
16B

We compute cash flows from operating activities under the direct method by adjusting accrual-based income statement items to the cash basis. The usual approach is to adjust income statement accounts related to operating activities for changes in their related balance sheet accounts as follows:

P5 Compute cash flows from operating activities using the direct method.

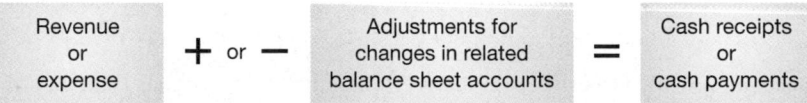

The framework for reporting cash receipts and cash payments for the operating section of the cash flow statement under the direct method follows. We consider cash receipts first and then cash payments.

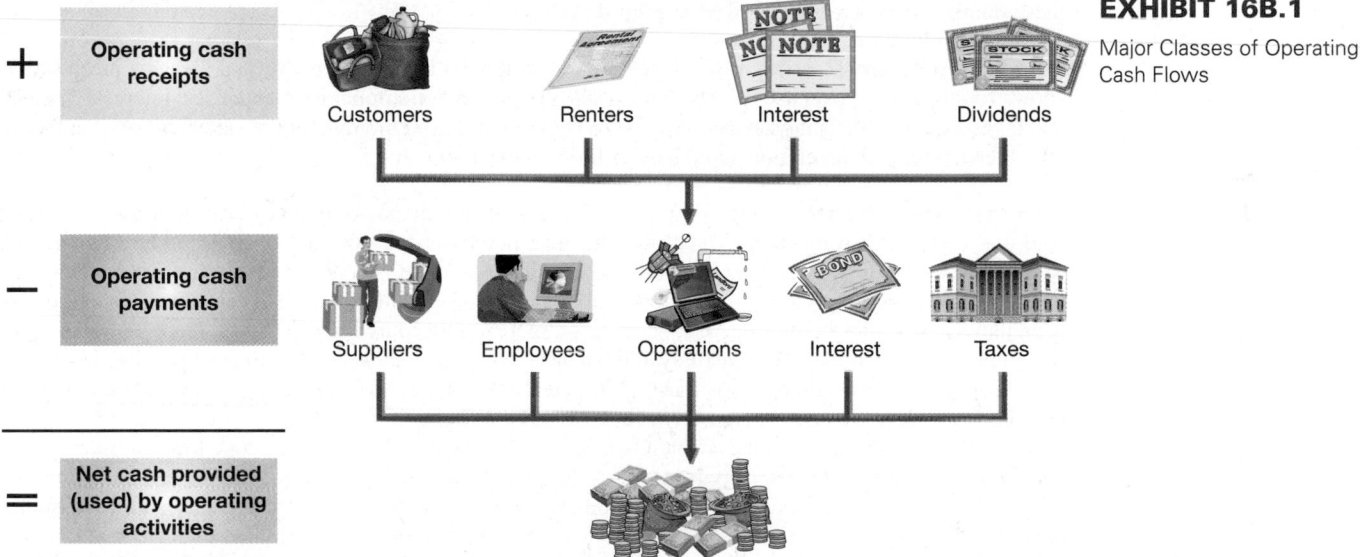

EXHIBIT 16B.1

Major Classes of Operating Cash Flows

Operating Cash Receipts A review of Exhibit 16.10 and the additional information reported by Genesis suggests only one potential cash receipt: sales to customers. This section, therefore, starts with sales to customers as reported on the income statement and then adjusts it as necessary to obtain cash received from customers to report on the statement of cash flows.

Cash Received from Customers If all sales are for cash, the amount received from customers equals the sales reported on the income statement. When some or all sales are on account, however, we must adjust the amount of sales for the change in Accounts Receivable. It is often helpful to use *account analysis* to do this. This usually involves setting up a T-account and reconstructing its major entries, with emphasis on cash receipts and payments. To illustrate, we use a T-account that includes accounts receivable balances for Genesis on December 31, 2012 and 2013. The beginning balance is $40,000 and the ending balance is $60,000. Next, the income statement shows sales of $590,000, which we enter on the debit side of this account. We now can reconstruct the Accounts Receivable account to determine the amount of cash received from customers as follows:

Point: An accounts receivable increase implies that cash received from customers is less than sales (the converse is also true).

Accounts Receivable			
Bal., Dec. 31, 2012	40,000		
Sales	590,000	Cash receipts =	570,000
Bal., Dec. 31, 2013	60,000		

This T-account shows that the Accounts Receivable balance begins at $40,000 and increases to $630,000 from sales of $590,000, yet its ending balance is only $60,000. This implies that cash receipts from customers are $570,000, computed as $40,000 + $590,000 − [?] = $60,000. This computation can be rearranged to express cash received as equal to sales of $590,000 minus a $20,000 increase in accounts receivable. This computation is summarized as a general rule in Exhibit 16B.2. The statement of cash flows in Exhibit 16.7 reports the $570,000 cash received from customers as a cash inflow from operating activities.

EXHIBIT 16B.2

Formula to Compute Cash Received from Customers—Direct Method

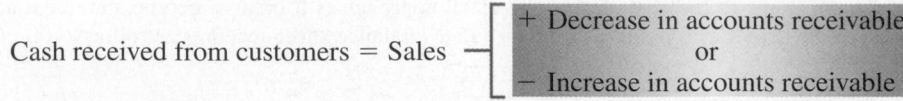

Cash received from customers = Sales − [+ Decrease in accounts receivable / or / − Increase in accounts receivable]

Point: Net income is measured using accrual accounting. Cash flows from operations are measured using cash basis accounting.

Other Cash Receipts   While Genesis's cash receipts are limited to collections from customers, we often see other types of cash receipts, most commonly cash receipts involving rent, interest, and dividends. We compute cash received from these items by subtracting an increase in their respective receivable or adding a decrease. For instance, if rent receivable increases in the period, cash received from renters is less than rent revenue reported on the income statement. If rent receivable decreases, cash received is more than reported rent revenue. The same logic applies to interest and dividends. The formulas for these computations are summarized later in this appendix.

Operating Cash Payments   A review of Exhibit 16.10 and the additional Genesis information shows four operating expenses: cost of goods sold; wages and other operating expenses; interest expense; and taxes expense. We analyze each expense to compute its cash amounts for the statement of cash flows. (We then examine depreciation and the other losses and gains.)

Cash Paid for Merchandise   We compute cash paid for merchandise by analyzing both cost of goods sold and merchandise inventory. If all merchandise purchases are for cash and the ending balance of Merchandise Inventory is unchanged from the beginning balance, the amount of cash paid for merchandise equals cost of goods sold—an uncommon situation. Instead, there normally is some change in the Merchandise Inventory balance. Also, some or all merchandise purchases are often made on credit, and this yields changes in the Accounts Payable balance. When the balances of both Merchandise Inventory and Accounts Payable change, we must adjust the cost of goods sold for changes in both accounts to compute cash paid for merchandise. This is a two-step adjustment.

First, we use the change in the account balance of Merchandise Inventory, along with the cost of goods sold amount, to compute cost of purchases for the period. An increase in merchandise inventory implies that we bought more than we sold, and we add this inventory increase to cost of goods sold to compute cost of purchases. A decrease in merchandise inventory implies that we bought less than we sold, and we subtract the inventory decrease from cost of goods sold to compute purchases. We illustrate the *first step* by reconstructing the Merchandise Inventory account of Genesis:

Merchandise Inventory			
Bal., Dec. 31, 2012	70,000		
Purchases =	**314,000**	Cost of goods sold	300,000
Bal., Dec. 31, 2013	84,000		

The beginning balance is $70,000, and the ending balance is $84,000. The income statement shows that cost of goods sold is $300,000, which we enter on the credit side of this account. With this information, we determine the amount for cost of purchases to be $314,000. This computation can be rearranged to express cost of purchases as equal to cost of goods sold of $300,000 plus the $14,000 increase in inventory.

The second step uses the change in the balance of Accounts Payable, and the amount of cost of purchases, to compute cash paid for merchandise. A decrease in accounts payable implies that we paid for more goods than we acquired this period, and we would then add the accounts payable decrease to cost of purchases to compute cash paid for merchandise. An increase in accounts payable implies that we paid for less than the amount of goods acquired, and we would subtract the accounts payable increase from purchases to compute cash paid for merchandise. The *second step* is applied to Genesis by reconstructing its Accounts Payable account:

Accounts Payable			
	Bal., Dec. 31, 2012		40,000
Cash payments = 319,000	Purchases		314,000
	Bal., Dec. 31, 2013		35,000

Its beginning balance of $40,000 plus purchases of $314,000 minus an ending balance of $35,000 yields cash paid of $319,000 (or $40,000 + $314,000 − [?] = $35,000). Alternatively, we can express cash paid for merchandise as equal to purchases of $314,000 plus the $5,000 decrease in accounts payable. The $319,000 cash paid for merchandise is reported on the statement of cash flows in Exhibit 16.7 as a cash outflow under operating activities.

We summarize this two-step adjustment to cost of goods sold to compute cash paid for merchandise inventory in Exhibit 16B.3.

Example: If the ending balances of Inventory and Accounts Payable are $60,000 and $50,000, respectively (instead of $84,000 and $35,000), what is cash paid for merchandise? *Answer:* $280,000

EXHIBIT 16B.3

Two Steps to Compute Cash Paid for Merchandise—Direct Method

Cash Paid for Wages and Operating Expenses (Excluding Depreciation)   The income statement of Genesis shows wages and other operating expenses of $216,000 (see Exhibit 16.10). To compute cash paid for wages and other operating expenses, we adjust this amount for any changes in their related balance sheet accounts. We begin by looking for any prepaid expenses and accrued liabilities related to wages and other operating expenses in the balance sheets of Genesis in Exhibit 16.10. The balance sheets show prepaid expenses but no accrued liabilities. Thus, the adjustment is limited to the change in prepaid expenses. The amount of adjustment is computed by assuming that all cash paid for wages and other operating expenses is initially debited to Prepaid Expenses. This assumption allows us to reconstruct the Prepaid Expenses account:

Prepaid Expenses			
Bal., Dec. 31, 2012	4,000		
Cash payments = 218,000	Wages and other operating exp.	216,000	
Bal., Dec. 31, 2013	6,000		

Prepaid Expenses increase by $2,000 in the period, meaning that cash paid for wages and other operating expenses exceeds the reported expense by $2,000. Alternatively, we can express cash paid for wages and other operating expenses as equal to its reported expenses of $216,000 plus the $2,000 increase in prepaid expenses.[1]

Exhibit 16B.4 summarizes the adjustments to wages (including salaries) and other operating expenses. The Genesis balance sheet did not report accrued liabilities, but we include them in the formula to explain the adjustment to cash when they do exist. A decrease in accrued liabilities implies that we paid cash for more goods or services than received this period, so we add the decrease in accrued liabilities to the expense amount to obtain cash paid for these goods or services. An increase in accrued liabilities implies that we paid cash for less than what was acquired, so we subtract this increase in accrued liabilities from the expense amount to get cash paid.

Point: A decrease in prepaid expenses implies that reported expenses include an amount(s) that did not require a cash outflow in the period.

---

[1] The assumption that all cash payments for wages and operating expenses are initially debited to Prepaid Expenses is not necessary for our analysis to hold. If cash payments are debited directly to the expense account, the total amount of cash paid for wages and other operating expenses still equals the $216,000 expense plus the $2,000 increase in Prepaid Expenses (which arise from end-of-period adjusting entries).

EXHIBIT 16B.4

Formula to Compute Cash Paid for Wages and Operating Expenses—Direct Method

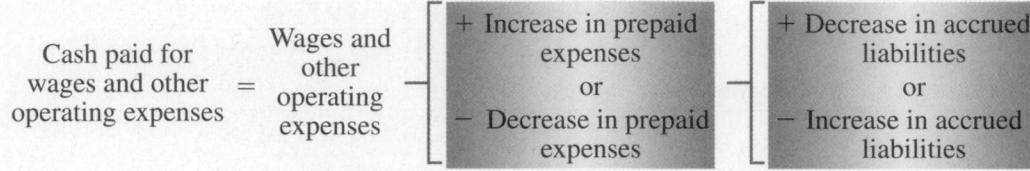

Cash paid for interest and income taxes   Computing operating cash flows for interest and taxes is similar to that for operating expenses. Both require adjustments to their amounts reported on the income statement for changes in their related balance sheet accounts. We begin with the Genesis income statement showing interest expense of $7,000 and income taxes expense of $15,000. To compute the cash paid, we adjust interest expense for the change in interest payable and then the income taxes expense for the change in income taxes payable. These computations involve reconstructing both liability accounts:

Interest Payable		
	Bal., Dec. 31, 2012	4,000
Cash paid for interest = 8,000	Interest expense	7,000
	Bal., Dec. 31, 2013	3,000

Income Taxes Payable		
	Bal., Dec. 31, 2012	12,000
Cash paid for taxes = 5,000	Income taxes expense	15,000
	Bal., Dec. 31, 2013	22,000

These accounts reveal cash paid for interest of $8,000 and cash paid for income taxes of $5,000. The formulas to compute these amounts are in Exhibit 16B.5. Both of these cash payments are reported as operating cash outflows on the statement of cash flows in Exhibit 16.7.

EXHIBIT 16B.5

Formulas to Compute Cash Paid for Both Interest and Taxes—Direct Method

$$\text{Cash paid for interest} = \text{Interest expense} - \begin{bmatrix} + \text{Decrease in interest payable} \\ \text{or} \\ - \text{Increase in interest payable} \end{bmatrix}$$

$$\text{Cash paid for taxes} = \text{Income taxes expenses} - \begin{bmatrix} + \text{Decrease in income taxes payable} \\ \text{or} \\ - \text{Increase in income taxes payable} \end{bmatrix}$$

Analysis of Additional Expenses, Gains, and Losses   Genesis has three additional items reported on its income statement: depreciation, loss on sale of assets, and gain on retirement of debt. We must consider each for its potential cash effects.

Depreciation Expense   Depreciation expense is $24,000. It is often called a *noncash expense* because depreciation has no cash flows. Depreciation expense is an allocation of an asset's depreciable cost. The cash outflow with a plant asset is reported as part of investing activities when it is paid for. Thus, depreciation expense is *never* reported on a statement of cash flows using the direct method; nor is depletion or amortization expense.

Loss on Sale of Assets   Sales of assets frequently result in gains and losses reported as part of net income, but the amount of recorded gain or loss does *not* reflect any cash flows in these transactions. Asset sales result in cash inflow equal to the cash amount received, regardless of whether the asset was sold at a gain or a loss. This cash inflow is reported under investing activities. Thus, the loss or gain on a sale of assets is *never* reported on a statement of cash flows using the direct method.

Gain on Retirement of Debt   Retirement of debt usually yields a gain or loss reported as part of net income, but that gain or loss does *not* reflect cash flow in this transaction. Debt retirement results in cash outflow equal to the cash paid to settle the debt, regardless of whether the debt is retired at a gain or loss.

This cash outflow is reported under financing activities; the loss or gain from retirement of debt is *never* reported on a statement of cash flows using the direct method.

Summary of Adjustments for Direct Method   Exhibit 16B.6 summarizes common adjustments for net income to yield net cash provided (used) by operating activities under the direct method.

Item	From Income Statement	Adjustments to Obtain Cash Flow Numbers	
Receipts			
From sales	Sales Revenue	⌈ +Decrease in Accounts Receivable ⌊ −Increase in Accounts Receivable	
From rent	Rent Revenue	⌈ +Decrease in Rent Receivable ⌊ −Increase in Rent Receivable	
From interest	Interest Revenue	⌈ +Decrease in Interest Receivable ⌊ −Increase in Interest Receivable	
From dividends	Dividend Revenue	⌈ +Decrease in Dividends Receivable ⌊ −Increase in Dividends Receivable	
Payments			
To suppliers	Cost of Goods Sold	⌈ +Increase in Inventory ⌊ −Decrease in Inventory	⌈ +Decrease in Accounts Payable ⌊ −Increase in Accounts Payable
For operations	Operating Expense	⌈ +Increase in Prepaids ⌊ −Decrease in Prepaids	⌈ +Decrease in Accrued Liabilities ⌊ −Increase in Accrued Liabilities
To employees	Wages (Salaries) Expense	⌈ +Decrease in Wages (Salaries) Payable ⌊ −Increase in Wages (Salaries) Payable	
For interest	Interest Expense	⌈ +Decrease in Interest Payable ⌊ −Increase in Interest Payable	
For taxes	Income Tax Expense	⌈ +Decrease in Income Tax Payable ⌊ −Increase in Income Tax Payable	

EXHIBIT 16B.6

Summary of Selected Adjustments for Direct Method

Direct Method Format of Operating Activities Section   Exhibit 16.7 shows the Genesis statement of cash flows using the direct method. Major items of cash inflows and cash outflows are listed separately in the operating activities section. The format requires that operating cash outflows be subtracted from operating cash inflows to get net cash provided (used) by operating activities. The FASB recommends that the operating activities section of the statement of cash flows be reported using the direct method, which is considered more useful to financial statement users. *However, the FASB requires a reconciliation of net income to net cash provided (used) by operating activities when the direct method is used* (which can be reported in the notes). This reconciliation is similar to preparation of the operating activities section of the statement of cash flows using the indirect method.

Point: Some preparers argue that it is easier to prepare a statement of cash flows using the indirect method. This likely explains its greater frequency in financial statements.

 IFRS _____

Currently, U.S. GAAP and IFRS allow cash flows from operating activities to be reported using either the indirect method or the direct method. The IASB and FASB are working on joint guidance that would require the direct method for the operating section with the indirect method's operating section disclosed in the footnotes. Stay tuned . . . ∎

Quick Check   Answers − p. 664

8. Net sales in a period are $590,000, beginning accounts receivable are $120,000, and ending accounts receivable are $90,000. What cash amount is collected from customers in the period?

9. The Merchandise Inventory account balance decreases in the period from a beginning balance of $32,000 to an ending balance of $28,000. Cost of goods sold for the period is $168,000. If the Accounts Payable balance increases $2,400 in the period, what is the cash amount paid for merchandise inventory?

10. This period's wages and other operating expenses total $112,000. Beginning-of-period prepaid expenses totaled $1,200, and its ending balance is $4,200. There were no beginning-of-period accrued liabilities, but end-of-period wages payable equal $5,600. How much cash is paid for wages and other operating expenses?

Summary

C1 **Distinguish between operating, investing, and financing activities, and describe how noncash investing and financing activities are disclosed.** The purpose of the statement of cash flows is to report major cash receipts and cash payments relating to operating, investing, or financing activities. Operating activities include transactions and events that determine net income. Investing activities include transactions and events that mainly affect long-term assets. Financing activities include transactions and events that mainly affect long-term liabilities and equity. Noncash investing and financing activities must be disclosed in either a note or a separate schedule to the statement of cash flows. Examples are the retirement of debt by issuing equity and the exchange of a note payable for plant assets.

A1 **Analyze the statement of cash flows and apply the cash flow on total assets ratio.** To understand and predict cash flows, users stress identification of the sources and uses of cash flows by operating, investing, and financing activities. Emphasis is on operating cash flows since they derive from continuing operations. The cash flow on total assets ratio is defined as operating cash flows divided by average total assets. Analysis of current and past values for this ratio can reflect a company's ability to yield regular and positive cash flows. It is also viewed as a measure of earnings quality.

P1 **Prepare a statement of cash flows.** Preparation of a statement of cash flows involves five steps: (1) Compute the net increase or decrease in cash; (2) compute net cash provided or used by operating activities (*using either the direct or indirect method*); (3) compute net cash provided or used by investing activities; (4) compute net cash

provided or used by financing activities; and (5) report the beginning and ending cash balance and prove that it is explained by net cash flows. Noncash investing and financing activities are also disclosed.

P2 **Compute cash flows from operating activities using the indirect method.** The indirect method for reporting net cash provided or used by operating activities starts with net income and then adjusts it for three items: (1) changes in noncash current assets and current liabilities related to operating activities, (2) revenues and expenses not providing or using cash, and (3) gains and losses from investing and financing activities.

P3 **Determine cash flows from both investing and financing activities.** Cash flows from both investing and financing activities are determined by identifying the cash flow effects of transactions and events affecting each balance sheet account related to these activities. All cash flows from these activities are identified when we can explain changes in these accounts from the beginning to the end of the period.

P4A **Illustrate use of a spreadsheet to prepare a statement of cash flows.** A spreadsheet is a useful tool in preparing a statement of cash flows. Six key steps (see Appendix 16A) are applied when using the spreadsheet to prepare the statement.

P5B **Compute cash flows from operating activities using the direct method.** The direct method for reporting net cash provided or used by operating activities lists major operating cash inflows less cash outflows to yield net cash inflow or outflow from operations.

Guidance Answers to Decision Maker

Entrepreneur   Several factors might explain an increase in net cash flows when a net loss is reported, including (1) early recognition of expenses relative to revenues generated (such as research and development), (2) cash advances on long-term sales contracts not yet recognized in income, (3) issuances of debt or equity for cash to finance expansion, (4) cash sale of assets, (5) delay of cash payments, and (6) cash prepayment on sales. Analysis needs to focus on the components of both the net loss and the net cash flows and their implications for future performance.

Reporter   Your initial reaction based on the company's $600,000 loss with a $550,000 decrease in net cash flows is not positive. However, closer scrutiny reveals a more positive picture of this company's performance. Cash flow from operating activities is $650,000, computed as [?] − $850,000 − $350,000 = $(550,000). You also note that net income *before* the extraordinary loss is $330,000, computed as [?] − $930,000 = $(600,000).

Guidance Answers to Quick Checks

1. No to both. The statement of cash flows reports changes in the sum of cash plus cash equivalents. It does not report transfers between cash and cash equivalents.

2. The three categories of cash inflows and outflows are operating activities, investing activities, and financing activities.

3. **a.** Investing   **c.** Financing   **e.** Operating
   b. Operating   **d.** Operating   **f.** Financing

4. $74,900 + $4,600 − $11,700 − $1,000 + $3,400 = $70,200

5. Expenses such as depreciation and amortization do not require current cash outflows. Therefore, adding these expenses back to

net income eliminates these noncash items from the net income number, converting it to a cash basis.

6. A gain on the sale of plant assets is subtracted from net income because a sale of plant assets is not an operating activity; it is an investing activity for the amount of cash received from its sale. Also, such a gain yields no cash effects.

7. $80,000 − $30,000 − $10,000 = $40,000 cash receipt. The $40,000 cash receipt is reported as an investing activity.

8. $590,000 + ($120,000 − $90,000) = $620,000

9. $168,000 − ($32,000 − $28,000) − $2,400 = $161,600

10. $112,000 + ($4,200 − $1,200) − $5,600 = $109,400

Key Terms

Cash flow on total assets (p. 652)

Direct method (p. 640)

Financing activities (p. 636)

Indirect method (p. 640)

Investing activities (p. 636)

Operating activities (p. 635)

Statement of cash flows (p. 634)

Multiple Choice Quiz   Answers on p. 685   mhhe.com/wildFAP21e

Additional Quiz Questions are available at the book's Website.

1. A company uses the indirect method to determine its cash flows from operating activities. Use the following information to determine its net cash provided or used by operating activities.

Net income	$15,200
Depreciation expense	10,000
Cash payment on note payable	8,000
Gain on sale of land	3,000
Increase in inventory	1,500
Increase in accounts payable	2,850

 a. $23,550 used by operating activities
 b. $23,550 provided by operating activities
 c. $15,550 provided by operating activities
 d. $42,400 provided by operating activities
 e. $20,850 provided by operating activities

2. A machine with a cost of $175,000 and accumulated depreciation of $94,000 is sold for $87,000 cash. The amount reported as a source of cash under cash flows from investing activities is
 a. $81,000.
 b. $6,000.
 c. $87,000.
 d. Zero; this is a financing activity.
 e. Zero; this is an operating activity.

3. A company settles a long-term note payable plus interest by paying $68,000 cash toward the principal amount and $5,440 cash for interest. The amount reported as a use of cash under cash flows from financing activities is
 a. Zero; this is an investing activity.
 b. Zero; this is an operating activity.

 c. $73,440.
 d. $68,000.
 e. $5,440.

4. The following information is available regarding a company's annual salaries and wages. What amount of cash is paid for salaries and wages?

Salaries and wages expense	$255,000
Salaries and wages payable, prior year-end	8,200
Salaries and wages payable, current year-end	10,900

 a. $252,300
 b. $257,700
 c. $255,000
 d. $274,100
 e. $235,900

5. The following information is available for a company. What amount of cash is paid for merchandise for the current year?

Cost of goods sold	$545,000
Merchandise inventory, prior year-end	105,000
Merchandise inventory, current year-end	112,000
Accounts payable, prior year-end	98,500
Accounts payable, current year-end	101,300

 a. $545,000
 b. $554,800
 c. $540,800
 d. $535,200
 e. $549,200

$^{A(B)}$ *Superscript letter A (B) denotes assignments based on Appendix 16A (16B).*

Icon denotes assignments that involve decision making.

Discussion Questions

1. What is the reporting purpose of the statement of cash flows? Identify at least two questions that this statement can answer.

2. What are some investing activities reported on the statement of cash flows?

3. What are some financing activities reported on the statement of cash flows?

4. Describe the direct method of reporting cash flows from operating activities.

5. When a statement of cash flows is prepared using the direct method, what are some of the operating cash flows?

6. Describe the indirect method of reporting cash flows from operating activities.

7. Where on the statement of cash flows is the payment of cash dividends reported?

8. Assume that a company purchases land for $1,000,000, paying $400,000 cash and borrowing the remainder with a long-term note payable. How should this transaction be reported on a statement of cash flows?

9. On June 3, a company borrows $200,000 cash by giving its bank a 90-day, interest-bearing note. On the statement of cash flows, where should this be reported?

10. If a company reports positive net income for the year, can it also show a net cash outflow from operating activities? Explain.

11. Is depreciation a source of cash flow?

12. Refer to **Polaris**' statement of cash flows in Appendix A. (a) Which method is used to compute its net cash provided by operating activities? (b) Its balance sheet shows an increase in accounts (trade) receivables from 2010 to 2011; why is this increase in accounts (trade) receivables subtracted when computing net cash provided by operating activities for the year ended December 31, 2011?

Polaris

13. Refer to **Arctic Cat**'s statement of cash flows in Appendix A. What are its cash flows from financing activities for the year ended March 31, 2011? List the items and amounts.

Arctic Cat

14. Refer to **KTM**'s 2011 statement of cash flows in Appendix A. List its cash flows from operating activities, investing activities, and financing activities.

KTM

15. Refer to **Piaggio**'s statement of cash flows in Appendix A. What investing activities result in cash outflows for the year ended December 31, 2011? List items and amounts.

PIAGGIO

≡ connect

QUICK STUDY

QS 16-1

Statement of cash flows

C1

The statement of cash flows is one of the four primary financial statements.

1. Describe the content and layout of a statement of cash flows, including its three sections.

2. List at least three transactions classified as investing activities in a statement of cash flows.

3. List at least three transactions classified as financing activities in a statement of cash flows.

4. List at least three transactions classified as significant noncash financing and investing activities in the statement of cash flows.

QS 16-2

Transaction classification by activity

C1

Classify the following cash flows as operating, investing, or financing activities.

1. Sold long-term investments for cash.
2. Received cash payments from customers.
3. Paid cash for wages and salaries.
4. Purchased inventories for cash.
5. Paid cash dividends.

6. Issued common stock for cash.
7. Received cash interest on a note.
8. Paid cash interest on outstanding notes.
9. Received cash from sale of land at a loss.
10. Paid cash for property taxes on building.

QS 16-3

Indirect: Computing cash from operations

P2

Use the following information to determine this company's cash flows from operating activities using the indirect method.

MOSS COMPANY
Selected Balance Sheet Information
December 31, 2013 and 2012

	2013	2012
Current assets		
Cash	$84,650	$26,800
Accounts receivable	25,000	32,000
Inventory	60,000	54,100
Current liabilities		
Accounts payable	30,400	25,700
Income taxes payable	2,050	2,200

MOSS COMPANY
Income Statement
For Year Ended December 31, 2013

Sales		$515,000
Cost of goods sold		331,600
Gross profit		183,400
Operating expenses		
Depreciation expense	$ 36,000	
Other expenses	121,500	157,500
Income before taxes		25,900
Income taxes expense		7,700
Net income		$ 18,200

The following selected information is from Ellerby Company's comparative balance sheets.

QS 16-4
Computing cash from asset sales
P3

At December 31	2013	2012
Furniture	$132,000	$ 184,500
Accumulated depreciation—Furniture	(88,700)	(110,700)

The income statement reports depreciation expense for the year of $18,000. Also, furniture costing $52,500 was sold for its book value. Compute the cash received from the sale of furniture.

The following selected information is from the Princeton Company's comparative balance sheets.

QS 16-5
Computing financing cash flows
P3

At December 31	2013	2012
Common stock, $10 par value	$105,000	$100,000
Paid-in capital in excess of par	567,000	342,000
Retained earnings	313,500	287,500

The company's net income for the year ended December 31, 2013, was $48,000.

1. Compute the cash received from the sale of its common stock during 2013.

2. Compute the cash paid for dividends during 2013.

Use the following balance sheets and income statement to answer QS 16-6 through QS 16-11.

QS 16-6
Indirect: Computing cash from operations   P2

CRUZ, INC.
Comparative Balance Sheets
December 31, 2013

	2013	2012
Assets		
Cash	$ 94,800	$ 24,000
Accounts receivable, net	41,000	51,000
Inventory	85,800	95,800
Prepaid expenses	5,400	4,200
Furniture	109,000	119,000
Accum. depreciation—Furniture	(17,000)	(9,000)
Total assets	$319,000	$285,000
Liabilities and Equity		
Accounts payable	$ 15,000	$ 21,000
Wages payable	9,000	5,000
Income taxes payable	1,400	2,600
Notes payable (long-term)	29,000	69,000
Common stock, $5 par value	229,000	179,000
Retained earnings	35,600	8,400
Total liabilities and equity	$319,000	$285,000

CRUZ, INC.
Income Statement
For Year Ended December 31, 2013

Sales		$488,000
Cost of goods sold		314,000
Gross profit		174,000
Operating expenses		
Depreciation expense	$37,600	
Other expenses	89,100	126,700
Income before taxes		47,300
Income taxes expense		17,300
Net income		$ 30,000

Required

Use the indirect method to prepare the cash provided or used from operating activities section only of the statement of cash flows for this company.

Refer to the data in QS 16-6.
Furniture costing $55,000 is sold at its book value in 2013. Acquisitions of furniture total $45,000 cash, on which no depreciation is necessary because it is acquired at year-end. What is the cash inflow related to the sale of furniture?

QS 16-7
Computing cash from asset sales
P3

QS 16-8

Computing financing cash
outflows P3

Refer to the data in QS 16-6.

1. Assume that all common stock is issued for cash. What amount of cash dividends is paid during 2013?
2. Assume that no additional notes payable are issued in 2013. What cash amount is paid to reduce the notes payable balance in 2013?

QS 16-9[B]

Direct: Computing cash
received from customers P5

Refer to the data in QS 16-6.

1. How much cash is received from sales to customers for year 2013?
2. What is the net increase or decrease in cash for year 2013?

QS 16-10[B]

Direct: Computing operating
cash outflows P5

Refer to the data in QS 16-6.

1. How much cash is paid to acquire merchandise inventory during year 2013?
2. How much cash is paid for operating expenses during year 2013?

QS 16-11[B]

Direct: Computing cash from
operations P5

Refer to the data in QS 16-6.
Use the direct method to prepare the cash provided or used from operating activities section only of the statement of cash flows for this company.

QS 16-12

Analyses of sources and uses
of cash A1

Financial data from three competitors in the same industry follow.

1. Which of the three competitors is in the strongest position as shown by its statement of cash flows?
2. Analyze and compare the strength of Moore's cash flow on total assets ratio to that of Sykes.

($ thousands)	Moore	Sykes	Kritch
Cash provided (used) by operating activities	$ 70,000	$ 60,000	$ (24,000)
Cash provided (used) by investing activities			
Proceeds from sale of operating assets			26,000
Purchase of operating assets	(28,000)	(34,000)	
Cash provided (used) by financing activities			
Proceeds from issuance of debt			23,000
Repayment of debt	(6,000)		
Net increase (decrease) in cash	$ 36,000	$ 26,000	$ 25,000
Average total assets	$ 790,000	$ 625,000	$ 300,000

QS 16-13[A]

Noncash accounts
on a spreadsheet P4

When a spreadsheet for a statement of cash flows is prepared, all changes in noncash balance sheet accounts are fully explained on the spreadsheet. Explain how these noncash balance sheet accounts are used to fully account for cash flows on a spreadsheet.

QS 16-14

Indirect: Computing cash flows
from operations

P2

For each of the following separate cases, compute cash flows from operations. The list includes all balance sheet accounts related to operating activities.

	Case X	Case Y	Case Z
Net income	$ 4,000	$100,000	$72,000
Depreciation expense	30,000	8,000	24,000
Accounts receivable increase (decrease)	40,000	20,000	(4,000)
Inventory increase (decrease)	(20,000)	(10,000)	10,000
Accounts payable increase (decrease)	24,000	(22,000)	14,000
Accrued liabilities increase (decrease)	(44,000)	12,000	(8,000)

Compute cash flows from investing activities using the following company information.

Sale of short-term investments	$ 6,000
Cash collections from customers	16,000
Purchase of used equipment	5,000
Depreciation expense	2,000

QS 16-15
Computing cash flows from investing

P3

Compute cash flows from financing activities using the following company information.

Additional short-term borrowings	$20,000
Purchase of short-term investments	5,000
Cash dividends paid	16,000
Interest paid	8,000

QS 16-16
Computing cash flows from financing

P3

Use the following financial statements and additional information to (1) prepare a statement of cash flows for the year ended December 31, 2014, using the *indirect method,* and (2) analyze and briefly discuss the statement prepared in part 1 with special attention to operating activities and to the company's cash level.

QS 16-17
Indirect: Preparation of statement of cash flows

P1

MONTGOMERY INC.
Comparative Balance Sheets
December 31, 2014 and 2013

	2014	2013
Assets		
Cash	$ 30,400	$ 30,550
Accounts receivable, net	10,050	12,150
Inventory	90,100	70,150
Equipment	49,900	41,500
Accum. depreciation—Equipment	(22,500)	(15,300)
Total assets	$157,950	$139,050
Liabilities and Equity		
Accounts payable	$ 23,900	$ 25,400
Salaries payable	500	600
Common stock, no par value	110,000	100,000
Retained earnings	23,550	13,050
Total liabilities and equity	$157,950	$139,050

MONTGOMERY INC.
Income Statement
For Year Ended December 31, 2014

Sales		$45,575
Cost of goods sold		(18,950)
Gross profit		26,625
Operating expenses		
Depreciation expense	$7,200	
Other expenses	5,550	
Total operating expense		12,750
Income before taxes		13,875
Income tax expense		3,375
Net income		$10,500

Additional Information

a. No dividends are declared or paid in 2014.

b. Issued additional stock for $10,000 cash in 2014.

c. Purchased equipment for cash in 2014; no equipment was sold in 2014.

Answer each of the following related to international accounting standards.

1. Which method, indirect or direct, is acceptable for reporting operating cash flows under IFRS?

2. For each of the following four cash flows, identify whether it is reported under the operating, investing, or financing section (or some combination) within the indirect format of the statement of cash flows reported under IFRS and under U.S. GAAP.

QS 16-18
International cash flow disclosures

C1

Cash Flow Source	US GAAP Reporting	IFRS Reporting
a. Interest paid		
b. Dividends paid		
c. Interest received		
d. Dividends received		

connect

EXERCISES

Exercise 16-1

Indirect: Cash flow classification

C1

The following transactions and events occurred during the year. Assuming that this company uses the *indirect method* to report cash provided by operating activities, indicate where each item would appear on its statement of cash flows by placing an *x* in the appropriate column.

	Statement of Cash Flows			Noncash Investing and Financing Activities	Not Reported on Statement or in Notes
	Operating Activities	Investing Activities	Financing Activities		
a. Declared and paid a cash dividend	____	____	____	____	____
b. Recorded depreciation expense	____	____	____	____	____
c. Paid cash to settle long-term note payable	____	____	____	____	____
d. Prepaid expenses increased in the year	____	____	____	____	____
e. Accounts receivable decreased in the year	____	____	____	____	____
f. Purchased land by issuing common stock	____	____	____	____	____
g. Paid cash to purchase inventory	____	____	____	____	____
h. Sold equipment for cash, yielding a loss	____	____	____	____	____
i. Accounts payable decreased in the year	____	____	____	____	____
j. Income taxes payable increased in the year	____	____	____	____	____

Exercise 16-2ᴮ

Direct: Cash flow classification

C1 P5

The following transactions and events occurred during the year. Assuming that this company uses the *direct method* to report cash provided by operating activities, indicate where each item would appear on the statement of cash flows by placing an *x* in the appropriate column.

	Statement of Cash Flows			Noncash Investing and Financing Activities	Not Reported on Statement or in Notes
	Operating Activities	Investing Activities	Financing Activities		
a. Retired long-term notes payable by issuing common stock	____	____	____	____	____
b. Paid cash toward accounts payable	____	____	____	____	____
c. Sold inventory for cash	____	____	____	____	____
d. Paid cash dividend that was declared in a prior period	____	____	____	____	____
e. Accepted six-month note receivable in exchange for plant assets	____	____	____	____	____
f. Recorded depreciation expense	____	____	____	____	____
g. Paid cash to acquire treasury stock	____	____	____	____	____
h. Collected cash from sales	____	____	____	____	____
i. Borrowed cash from bank by signing a nine-month note payable	____	____	____	____	____
j. Paid cash to purchase a patent	____	____	____	____	____

Exercise 16-3

Indirect: Cash flows from operating activities

P2

Fitzpatrick Company's calendar-year 2013 income statement shows the following: Net Income, $374,000; Depreciation Expense, $44,000; Amortization Expense, $7,200; Gain on Sale of Plant Assets, $6,000. An examination of the company's current assets and current liabilities reveals the following changes (all from operating activities): Accounts Receivable decrease, $17,100; Merchandise Inventory decrease, $42,000; Prepaid Expenses increase, $4,700; Accounts Payable decrease, $8,200; Other Payables increase, $1,200. Use the *indirect method* to compute cash flow from operating activities.

Salud Company reports net income of $400,000 for the year ended December 31, 2013. It also reports $80,000 depreciation expense and a $20,000 gain on the sale of machinery. Its comparative balance sheets reveal a $40,000 increase in accounts receivable, $6,000 increase in accounts payable, $12,000 decrease in prepaid expenses, and $2,000 decrease in wages payable.

Exercise 16-4
Indirect: Cash flow from operations
P2

Required

Prepare only the operating activities section of the statement of cash flows for 2013 using the *indirect method.*

For each of the following three separate cases, use the information provided about the calendar-year 2014 operations of Sahim Company to compute the required cash flow information.

Exercise 16-5ᴮ
Direct: Computation of cash flows
P5

Case X: Compute cash received from customers:	
Sales	$515,000
Accounts receivable, December 31, 2013	27,200
Accounts receivable, December 31, 2014	33,600
Case Y: Compute cash paid for rent:	
Rent expense	$139,800
Rent payable, December 31, 2013	7,800
Rent payable, December 31, 2014	6,200
Case Z: Compute cash paid for merchandise:	
Cost of goods sold	$525,000
Merchandise inventory, December 31, 2013	158,600
Accounts payable, December 31, 2013	66,700
Merchandise inventory, December 31, 2014	130,400
Accounts payable, December 31, 2014	82,000

Information: The following income statement and information about changes in noncash current assets and current liabilities are reported.

Exercise 16-6
Indirect: Cash flows from operating activities
P2

SONAD COMPANY **Income Statement** **For Year Ended December 31, 2013**		
Sales		$1,828,000
Cost of goods sold		991,000
Gross profit		837,000
Operating expenses		
Salaries expense	$245,535	
Depreciation expense	44,200	
Rent expense	49,600	
Amortization expenses—Patents	4,200	
Utilities expense	18,125	361,660
		475,340
Gain on sale of equipment		6,200
Net income		$ 481,540

Changes in current asset and current liability accounts for the year that relate to operations follow.

Accounts receivable	$30,500 increase	Accounts payable	$12,500 decrease
Merchandise inventory	25,000 increase	Salaries payable	3,500 decrease

Required

Prepare only the cash flows from operating activities section of the statement of cash flows using the *indirect* method.

Exercise 16-7ᴮ

Direct: Cash flows from operating activities P5

Refer to the information about Sonad Company in Exercise 16-6.
Use the *direct method* to prepare only the cash provided or used by operating activities section of the statement of cash flows for this company.

Exercise 16-8

Cash flows from investing activities

P3

Use the following information to determine this company's cash flows from investing activities.

a. Equipment with a book value of $65,300 and an original cost of $133,000 was sold at a loss of $14,000.

b. Paid $89,000 cash for a new truck.

c. Sold land costing $154,000 for $198,000 cash, yielding a gain of $44,000.

d. Long-term investments in stock were sold for $60,800 cash, yielding a gain of $4,150.

Exercise 16-9

Cash flows from financing activities

P3

Use the following information to determine this company's cash flows from financing activities.

a. Net income was $35,000.

b. Issued common stock for $64,000 cash.

c. Paid cash dividend of $14,600.

d. Paid $50,000 cash to settle a note payable at its $50,000 maturity value.

e. Paid $12,000 cash to acquire its treasury stock.

f. Purchased equipment for $39,000 cash.

Exercise 16-10

Indirect: Preparation of statement of cash flows P1

Information: The following financial statements and additional information are reported.

IKIBAN INC. Income Statement For Year Ended June 30, 2013		
Sales		$678,000
Cost of goods sold		411,000
Gross profit		267,000
Operating expenses		
Depreciation expense	$58,600	
Other expenses	67,000	
Total operating expenses		125,600
		141,400
Other gains (losses)		
Gain on sale of equipment		2,000
Income before taxes		143,400
Income taxes expense		43,890
Net income		$ 99,510

IKIBAN INC. Comparative Balance Sheets June 30, 2013 and 2012		
	2013	**2012**
Assets		
Cash	$ 87,500	$ 44,000
Accounts receivable, net	65,000	51,000
Inventory	63,800	86,500
Prepaid expenses	4,400	5,400
Equipment	124,000	115,000
Accum. depreciation—Equipment	(27,000)	(9,000)
Total assets	$317,700	$292,900
Liabilities and Equity		
Accounts payable	$ 25,000	$ 30,000
Wages payable	6,000	15,000
Income taxes payable	3,400	3,800
Notes payable (long term)	30,000	60,000
Common stock, $5 par value	220,000	160,000
Retained earnings	33,300	24,100
Total liabilities and equity	$317,700	$292,900

Additional Information

a. A $30,000 note payable is retired at its $30,000 carrying (book) value in exchange for cash.

Check (b) Cash dividends, $90,310

b. The only changes affecting retained earnings are net income and cash dividends paid.

c. New equipment is acquired for $57,600 cash.

(d) Cash from equip. sale, $10,000

d. Received cash for the sale of equipment that had cost $48,600, yielding a $2,000 gain.

e. Prepaid Expenses and Wages Payable relate to Other Expenses on the income statement.

f. All purchases and sales of merchandise inventory are on credit.

Required

(1) prepare a statement of cash flows for the year ended June 30, 2013, using the *indirect method,* and

(2) compute the company's cash flow on total assets ratio for its fiscal year 2013.

Refer to the information in Exercise 16-10.

Using the *direct method,* prepare the statement of cash flows for the year ended June 30, 2013.

Exercise 16-11^B

Direct: Preparation of statement of cash flows   P1

Hampton Company reports the following information for its recent calendar year.

Exercise 16-12

Indirect: Reporting cash flows from operations

P2

Sales	$160,000
Expenses	
Cost of goods sold	100,000
Salaries expense	24,000
Depreciation expense	12,000
Net income	$ 24,000
Accounts receivable increase	$ 10,000
Inventory decrease	16,000
Salaries payable increase	1,000

Required

Prepare the operating activities section of the statement of cash flows for Hampton Company using the indirect method.

Arundel Company disclosed the following information for its recent calendar year.

Exercise 16-13

Indirect: Reporting and interpreting cash flows from operations

P2

Revenues	$100,000
Expenses	
Salaries expense	84,000
Utilities expense	14,000
Depreciation expense	14,600
Other expenses	3,400
Net loss	$ (16,000)
Accounts receivable decrease	$ 24,000
Purchased a machine	10,000
Salaries payable increase	18,000
Other accrued liabilities decrease	8,000

Required

1. Prepare the operating activities section of the statement of cash flows using the indirect method.
2. What were the major reasons that this company was able to report a net loss but positive cash flow from operations?
3. Of the potential causes of differences between cash flow from operations and net income, which are the most important to investors?

Complete the following spreadsheet in preparation of the statement of cash flows. (The statement of cash flows is not required.) Prepare the spreadsheet as in Exhibit 16A.1; report operating activities under the indirect method. Identify the debits and credits in the Analysis of Changes columns with letters that correspond to the following transactions and events *a* through *h.*

Exercise 16-14

Indirect: Cash flows spreadsheet

P4

a. Net income for the year was $100,000.
b. Dividends of $80,000 cash were declared and paid.
c. Scoreteck's only noncash expense was $70,000 of depreciation.
d. The company purchased plant assets for $70,000 cash.
e. Notes payable of $20,000 were issued for $20,000 cash.
f. Change in accounts receivable.
g. Change in merchandise inventory.
h. Change in accounts payable.

File Edit View Insert Format Tools Data Accounting Window Help

	SCORETECK CORPORATION				
	Spreadsheet for Statement of Cash Flows—Indirect Method				
	For Year Ended December 31, 2013				
		Dec. 31, 2012	Analysis of Changes		Dec. 31, 2013
			Debit	Credit	
8	**Balance Sheet—Debit Bal. Accounts**				
9	Cash	$ 80,000			$ 60,000
10	Accounts receivable	120,000			190,000
11	Merchandise inventory	250,000			230,000
12	Plant assets	600,000			670,000
13		$1,050,000			$1,150,000
14					
15	**Balance Sheet—Credit Bal. Accounts**				
16	Accumulated depreciation	$100,000			$ 170,000
17	Accounts payable	150,000			140,000
18	Notes payable	370,000			390,000
19	Common stock	200,000			200,000
20	Retained earnings	230,000			250,000
21		$1,050,000			$1,150,000
22					
23	**Statement of Cash Flows**				
24	Operating activities				
25	Net income				
26	Increase in accounts receivable				
27	Decrease in merchandise inventory				
28	Decrease in accounts payable				
29	Depreciation expense				
30	Investing activities				
31	Cash paid to purchase plant assets				
32	Financing activities				
33	Cash paid for dividends				
34	Cash from issuance of notes				

Sheet1 / Sheet2 / Sheet3 /

Exercise 16-15[B]

Direct: Preparation of statement of cash flows and supporting note

P1

Use the following information about the cash flows of Ferron Company to prepare a complete statement of cash flows (*direct method*) for the year ended December 31, 2013. Use a note disclosure for any noncash investing and financing activities.

Cash and cash equivalents balance, December 31, 2012	$ 40,000
Cash and cash equivalents balance, December 31, 2013	148,000
Cash received as interest	3,500
Cash paid for salaries	76,500
Bonds payable retired by issuing common stock (no gain or loss on retirement)	185,500
Cash paid to retire long-term notes payable	100,000
Cash received from sale of equipment	60,250
Cash received in exchange for six-month note payable	35,000
Land purchased by issuing long-term note payable	105,250
Cash paid for store equipment	24,750
Cash dividends paid	10,000
Cash paid for other expenses	20,000
Cash received from customers	495,000
Cash paid for merchandise	254,500

The following summarized Cash T-account reflects the total debits and total credits to the Cash account of Thomas Corporation for calendar year 2013.

(1) Use this information to prepare a complete statement of cash flows for year 2013. The cash provided or used by operating activities should be reported using the *direct method.*

(2) Refer to the statement of cash flows prepared for part 1 to answer the following questions *a* through *d*: (*a*) Which section—operating, investing, or financing—shows the largest cash (i) inflow and (ii) outflow? (*b*) What is the largest individual item among the investing cash outflows? (*c*) Are the cash proceeds larger from issuing notes or issuing stock? (*d*) Does the company have a net cash inflow or outflow from borrowing activities?

Exercise 16-16[B]

Direct: Preparation of statement of cash flows from Cash T-account

P1

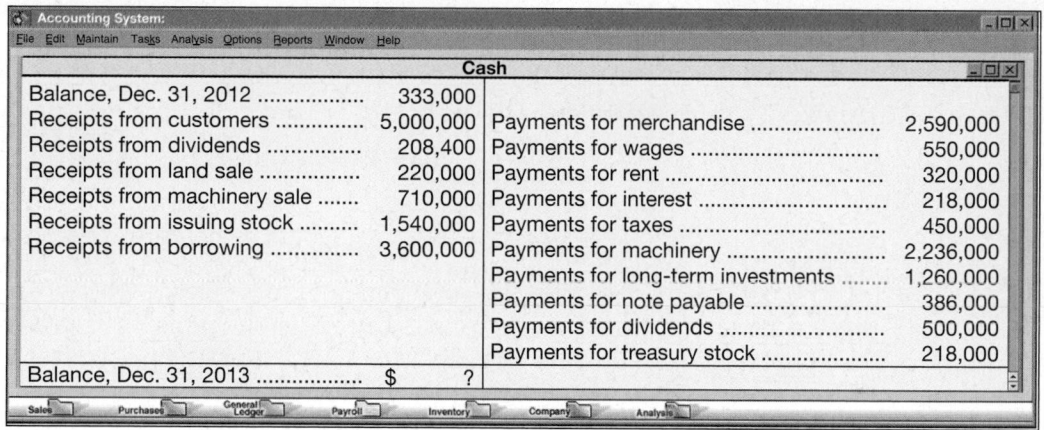

Accounting System:

File   Edit   Maintain   Tasks   Analysis   Options   Reports   Window   Help

Cash			
Balance, Dec. 31, 2012	333,000		
Receipts from customers	5,000,000	Payments for merchandise	2,590,000
Receipts from dividends	208,400	Payments for wages	550,000
Receipts from land sale	220,000	Payments for rent	320,000
Receipts from machinery sale	710,000	Payments for interest	218,000
Receipts from issuing stock	1,540,000	Payments for taxes	450,000
Receipts from borrowing	3,600,000	Payments for machinery	2,236,000
		Payments for long-term investments	1,260,000
		Payments for note payable	386,000
		Payments for dividends	500,000
		Payments for treasury stock	218,000
Balance, Dec. 31, 2013	$?		

Sales   Purchases   General Ledger   Payroll   Inventory   Company   Analysis

---

A company reported average total assets of $1,240,000 in 2012 and $1,510,000 in 2013. Its net operating cash flow in 2012 was $102,920 and $138,920 in 2013. Calculate its cash flow on total assets ratio for both years. Comment on the results and any change in performance.

Exercise 16-17

Analyses of cash flow on total assets   A1

Peugeot S.A. reports the following financial information for the year ended December 31, 2011 (euros in millions). Prepare its statement of cash flows under the indirect method.

Exercise 16-18

Indirect: Statement of cash flows under IFRS

P1

Net income	€ 784	Cash paid for purchase of treasury stock and other	€ (199)
Depreciation and amortization	3,037	Cash paid for other financing activities	(2,282)
Gains on disposals and other	(883)	Cash from disposal of plant assets and intangibles	189
Net decrease in working capital	(1,183)	Cash paid for plant assets and intangibles	(3,921)
Cash paid for dividends	(290)	Cash and cash equivalents, December 31, 2010	10,442

---

connect

Forten Company, a merchandiser, recently completed its calendar-year 2013 operations. For the year, (1) all sales are credit sales, (2) all credits to Accounts Receivable reflect cash receipts from customers, (3) all purchases of inventory are on credit, (4) all debits to Accounts Payable reflect cash payments for inventory, and (5) Other Expenses are paid in advance and are initially debited to Prepaid Expenses. The company's balance sheets and income statement follow.

PROBLEM SET A

Problem 16-1A

Indirect: Statement of cash flows

A1   P1   P2   P3

FORTEN COMPANY
Comparative Balance Sheets
December 31, 2013 and 2012

	2013	2012
Assets		
Cash	$ 49,800	$ 73,500
Accounts receivable	65,810	50,625
Merchandise inventory	275,656	251,800
Prepaid expenses	1,250	1,875
Equipment	157,500	108,000
Accum. depreciation—Equipment	(36,625)	(46,000)
Total assets	$513,391	$439,800
Liabilities and Equity		
Accounts payable	$ 53,141	$114,675
Short-term notes payable	10,000	6,000
Long-term notes payable	65,000	48,750
Common stock, $5 par value	162,750	150,250
Paid-in capital in excess		
of par, common stock	37,500	0
Retained earnings	185,000	120,125
Total liabilities and equity	$513,391	$439,800

FORTEN COMPANY
Income Statement
For Year Ended December 31, 2013

Sales		$582,500
Cost of goods sold		285,000
Gross profit		297,500
Operating expenses		
Depreciation expense	$ 20,750	
Other expenses.................	132,400	153,150
Other gains (losses)		
Loss on sale of equipment		(5,125)
Income before taxes		139,225
Income taxes expense		24,250
Net income		$114,975

Additional Information on Year 2013 Transactions

a. The loss on the cash sale of equipment was $5,125 (details in *b*).

b. Sold equipment costing $46,875, with accumulated depreciation of $30,125, for $11,625 cash.

c. Purchased equipment costing $96,375 by paying $30,000 cash and signing a long-term note payable for the balance.

d. Borrowed $4,000 cash by signing a short-term note payable.

e. Paid $50,125 cash to reduce the long-term notes payable.

f. Issued 2,500 shares of common stock for $20 cash per share.

g. Declared and paid cash dividends of $50,100.

Required

Check Cash from operating activities, $40,900

1. Prepare a complete statement of cash flows; report its operating activities using the *indirect method*. Disclose any noncash investing and financing activities in a note.

Analysis Component

2. Analyze and discuss the statement of cash flows prepared in part 1, giving special attention to the wisdom of the cash dividend payment.

Problem 16-2A[A]
Indirect: Cash flows spreadsheet

P1 P2 P3 P4

Refer to the information reported about Forten Company in Problem 16-1A.

Required

Prepare a complete statement of cash flows using a spreadsheet as in Exhibit 16A.1; report its operating activities using the indirect method. Identify the debits and credits in the Analysis of Changes columns with letters that correspond to the following list of transactions and events.

a. Net income was $114,975.

b. Accounts receivable increased.

c. Merchandise inventory increased.

d. Prepaid expenses decreased.

e. Accounts payable decreased.

f. Depreciation expense was $20,750.

g. Sold equipment costing $46,875, with accumulated depreciation of $30,125, for $11,625 cash. This yielded a loss of $5,125.

h. Purchased equipment costing $96,375 by paying $30,000 cash and **(i.)** by signing a long-term note payable for the balance.

j. Borrowed $4,000 cash by signing a short-term note payable.

k. Paid $50,125 cash to reduce the long-term notes payable.

l. Issued 2,500 shares of common stock for $20 cash per share.

m. Declared and paid cash dividends of $50,100.

Check Analysis of Changes column totals, $600,775

Refer to Forten Company's financial statements and related information in Problem 16-1A.

Required

Prepare a complete statement of cash flows; report its operating activities according to the *direct method*. Disclose any noncash investing and financing activities in a note.

Problem 16-3A[B]
Direct: Statement of cash flows P1 P3 P5

Check Cash used in financing activities, $(46,225)

Golden Corp., a merchandiser, recently completed its 2013 operations. For the year, (1) all sales are credit sales, (2) all credits to Accounts Receivable reflect cash receipts from customers, (3) all purchases of inventory are on credit, (4) all debits to Accounts Payable reflect cash payments for inventory, (5) Other Expenses are all cash expenses, and (6) any change in Income Taxes Payable reflects the accrual and cash payment of taxes. The company's balance sheets and income statement follow.

Problem 16-4A
Indirect: Statement of cash flows

P1 P2 P3

mhhe.com/wildFAP21e

GOLDEN CORPORATION Comparative Balance Sheets December 31, 2013 and 2012		
	2013	**2012**
Assets		
Cash	$ 164,000	$107,000
Accounts receivable	83,000	71,000
Merchandise inventory	601,000	526,000
Equipment.............................	335,000	299,000
Accum. depreciation—Equipment	(158,000)	(104,000)
Total assets	$1,025,000	$899,000
Liabilities and Equity		
Accounts payable	$ 87,000	$ 71,000
Income taxes payable	28,000	25,000
Common stock, $2 par value.............	592,000	568,000
Paid-in capital in excess of par value, common stock.............	196,000	160,000
Retained earnings	122,000	75,000
Total liabilities and equity	$1,025,000	$899,000

GOLDEN CORPORATION Income Statement For Year Ended December 31, 2013		
Sales		$1,792,000
Cost of goods sold		1,086,000
Gross profit		706,000
Operating expenses		
Depreciation expense	$ 54,000	
Other expenses..............	494,000	548,000
Income before taxes		158,000
Income taxes expense		22,000
Net income		$ 136,000

Additional Information on Year 2013 Transactions

a. Purchased equipment for $36,000 cash.

b. Issued 12,000 shares of common stock for $5 cash per share.

c. Declared and paid $89,000 in cash dividends.

Required

Prepare a complete statement of cash flows; report its cash inflows and cash outflows from operating activities according to the *indirect method*.

Check Cash from operating activities, $122,000

Refer to the information reported about Golden Corporation in Problem 16-4A.

Required

Prepare a complete statement of cash flows using a spreadsheet as in Exhibit 16A.1; report operating activities under the indirect method. Identify the debits and credits in the Analysis of Changes columns with letters that correspond to the following list of transactions and events.

a. Net income was $136,000.

b. Accounts receivable increased.

[continued on next page]

Problem 16-5A[A]
Indirect: Cash flows spreadsheet

P1 P2 P3 P4

mhhe.com/wildFAP21e

c. Merchandise inventory increased.

d. Accounts payable increased.

e. Income taxes payable increased.

f. Depreciation expense was $54,000.

g. Purchased equipment for $36,000 cash.

h. Issued 12,000 shares at $5 cash per share.

Check   Analysis of Changes column totals, $481,000

i. Declared and paid $89,000 of cash dividends.

Problem 16-6A[B]

Direct: Statement of cash flows   P1   P3   P5

mhhe.com/wildFAP21e

Check   Cash used in financing activities, $(29,000)

Refer to Golden Corporation's financial statements and related information in Problem 16-4A.

Required

Prepare a complete statement of cash flows; report its cash flows from operating activities according to the *direct method*.

Problem 16-7A

Indirect: Computing cash flows from operations

P2

Lansing Company's 2013 income statement and selected balance sheet data at December 31, 2012 and 2013, follow.

LANSING COMPANY
Selected Balance Sheet Accounts

At December 31	2013	2012
Accounts receivable	$5,600	$5,800
Inventory	1,980	1,540
Accounts payable........	4,400	4,600
Salaries payable	880	700
Utilities payable	220	160
Prepaid insurance	260	280
Prepaid rent	220	180

LANSING COMPANY
Income Statement
For Year Ended December 31, 2013

Sales revenue	$97,200
Expenses	
Cost of goods sold	42,000
Depreciation expense	12,000
Salaries expense	18,000
Rent expense	9,000
Insurance expense	3,800
Interest expense	3,600
Utilities expense	2,800
Net income	$ 6,000

Required

Check   Cash from operating activities, $17,780

Prepare the cash flows from operating activities section only of the company's 2013 statement of cash flows using the indirect method.

Problem 16-8A[B]

Direct: Computing cash flows from operations

P5

Refer to the information in Problem 16-7A.

Required

Prepare the cash flows from operating activities section only of the company's 2013 statement of cash flows using the direct method.

PROBLEM SET B

Problem 16-1B

Indirect: Statement of cash flows

A1   P1   P2   P3

Gazelle Corporation, a merchandiser, recently completed its calendar-year 2013 operations. For the year, (1) all sales are credit sales, (2) all credits to Accounts Receivable reflect cash receipts from customers, (3) all purchases of inventory are on credit, (4) all debits to Accounts Payable reflect cash payments for inventory, and (5) Other Expenses are paid in advance and are initially debited to Prepaid Expenses. The company's balance sheets and income statement follow.

GAZELLE CORPORATION
Comparative Balance Sheets
December 31, 2013 and 2012

	2013	2012
Assets		
Cash	$123,450	$ 61,550
Accounts receivable	77,100	80,750
Merchandise inventory	240,600	250,700
Prepaid expenses	15,100	17,000
Equipment	262,250	200,000
Accum. depreciation—Equipment	(110,750)	(95,000)
Total assets	$607,750	$515,000
Liabilities and Equity		
Accounts payable	$ 17,750	$102,000
Short-term notes payable	15,000	10,000
Long-term notes payable	100,000	77,500
Common stock, $5 par	215,000	200,000
Paid-in capital in excess		
of par, common stock	30,000	0
Retained earnings	230,000	125,500
Total liabilities and equity	$607,750	$515,000

GAZELLE CORPORATION
Income Statement
For Year Ended December 31, 2013

Sales		$1,185,000
Cost of goods sold		595,000
Gross profit		590,000
Operating expenses		
Depreciation expense	$ 38,600	
Other expenses	362,850	
Total operating expenses		401,450
		188,550
Other gains (losses)		
Loss on sale of equipment		(2,100)
Income before taxes		186,450
Income taxes expense		28,350
Net income		$ 158,100

Additional Information on Year 2013 Transactions

a. The loss on the cash sale of equipment was $2,100 (details in *b*).

b. Sold equipment costing $51,000, with accumulated depreciation of $22,850, for $26,050 cash.

c. Purchased equipment costing $113,250 by paying $43,250 cash and signing a long-term note payable for the balance.

d. Borrowed $5,000 cash by signing a short-term note payable.

e. Paid $47,500 cash to reduce the long-term notes payable.

f. Issued 3,000 shares of common stock for $15 cash per share.

g. Declared and paid cash dividends of $53,600.

Required

1. Prepare a complete statement of cash flows; report its operating activities using the *indirect method*. Disclose any noncash investing and financing activities in a note.

Check Cash from operating activities, $130,200

Analysis Component

2. Analyze and discuss the statement of cash flows prepared in part 1, giving special attention to the wisdom of the cash dividend payment.

Refer to the information reported about Gazelle Corporation in Problem 16-1B.

Required

Prepare a complete statement of cash flows using a spreadsheet as in Exhibit 16A.1; report its operating activities using the *indirect method*. Identify the debits and credits in the Analysis of Changes columns with letters that correspond to the following list of transactions and events.

a. Net income was $158,100.

b. Accounts receivable decreased.

c. Merchandise inventory decreased.

d. Prepaid expenses decreased.

e. Accounts payable decreased.

f. Depreciation expense was $38,600.

Problem 16-2B[A]
Indirect: Cash flows spreadsheet

P1 P2 P3 P4

[continued on next page]

g. Sold equipment costing $51,000, with accumulated depreciation of $22,850, for $26,050 cash. This yielded a loss of $2,100.

h. Purchased equipment costing $113,250 by paying $43,250 cash and **(i.)** by signing a long-term note payable for the balance.

j. Borrowed $5,000 cash by signing a short-term note payable.

k. Paid $47,500 cash to reduce the long-term notes payable.

l. Issued 3,000 shares of common stock for $15 cash per share.

Check Analysis of Changes column totals, $681,950

m. Declared and paid cash dividends of $53,600.

Problem 16-3B^B
Direct: Statement of cash flows P1 P3 P5

Refer to Gazelle Corporation's financial statements and related information in Problem 16-1B.

Required

Check Cash used in financing activities, $(51,100)

Prepare a complete statement of cash flows; report its operating activities according to the *direct method.* Disclose any noncash investing and financing activities in a note.

Problem 16-4B
Indirect: Statement of cash flows
P1 P2 P3

Satu Company, a merchandiser, recently completed its 2013 operations. For the year, (1) all sales are credit sales, (2) all credits to Accounts Receivable reflect cash receipts from customers, (3) all purchases of inventory are on credit, (4) all debits to Accounts Payable reflect cash payments for inventory, (5) Other Expenses are cash expenses, and (6) any change in Income Taxes Payable reflects the accrual and cash payment of taxes. The company's balance sheets and income statement follow.

SATU COMPANY
Comparative Balance Sheets
December 31, 2013 and 2012

	2013	2012
Assets		
Cash	$ 58,750	$ 28,400
Accounts receivable	20,222	25,860
Merchandise inventory	165,667	140,320
Equipment	107,750	77,500
Accum. depreciation—Equipment	(46,700)	(31,000)
Total assets	$305,689	$241,080
Liabilities and Equity		
Accounts payable	$ 20,372	$157,530
Income taxes payable	2,100	6,100
Common stock, $5 par value	40,000	25,000
Paid-in capital in excess of par, common stock	68,000	20,000
Retained earnings	175,217	32,450
Total liabilities and equity	$305,689	$241,080

SATU COMPANY
Income Statement
For Year Ended December 31, 2013

Sales		$750,800
Cost of goods sold		269,200
Gross profit		481,600
Operating expenses		
Depreciation expense	$ 15,700	
Other expenses	173,933	189,633
Income before taxes		291,967
Income taxes expense		89,200
Net income		$202,767

Additional Information on Year 2013 Transactions

a. Purchased equipment for $30,250 cash.

b. Issued 3,000 shares of common stock for $21 cash per share.

c. Declared and paid $60,000 of cash dividends.

Required

Check Cash from operating activities, $57,600

Prepare a complete statement of cash flows; report its cash inflows and cash outflows from operating activities according to the *indirect method.*

Refer to the information reported about Satu Company in Problem 16-4B.

Problem 16-5B^A

Indirect: Cash flows spreadsheet

P1   P2   P3   P4

Required

Prepare a complete statement of cash flows using a spreadsheet as in Exhibit 16A.1; report operating activities under the *indirect method*. Identify the debits and credits in the Analysis of Changes columns with letters that correspond to the following list of transactions and events.

a. Net income was $202,767.

b. Accounts receivable decreased.

c. Merchandise inventory increased.

d. Accounts payable decreased.

e. Income taxes payable decreased.

f. Depreciation expense was $15,700.

g. Purchased equipment for $30,250 cash.

h. Issued 3,000 shares at $21 cash per share.

i. Declared and paid $60,000 of cash dividends.

Check Analysis of Changes
column totals, $543,860

Refer to Satu Company's financial statements and related information in Problem 16-4B.

Problem 16-6B^B

Direct: Statement of cash flows

P1   P3   P5

Required

Prepare a complete statement of cash flows; report its cash flows from operating activities according to the *direct method*.

Check Cash provided by financing
activities, $3,000

Salt Lake Company's 2013 income statement and selected balance sheet data at December 31, 2012 and 2013, follow.

Problem 16-7B

Indirect: Computing cash flows
from operations

P2

SALT LAKE COMPANY
Income Statement
For Year Ended December 31, 2013

Sales revenue	$156,000
Expenses	
Cost of goods sold	72,000
Depreciation expense	32,000
Salaries expense	20,000
Rent expense	5,000
Insurance expense	2,600
Interest expense	2,400
Utilities expense	2,000
Net income	$ 20,000

SALT LAKE COMPANY
Selected Balance Sheet Accounts

At December 31	2013	2012
Accounts receivable	$3,600	$3,000
Inventory	860	980
Accounts payable	2,400	2,600
Salaries payable	900	600
Utilities payable	200	0
Prepaid insurance	140	180
Prepaid rent	100	200

Required

Prepare the cash flows from operating activities section only of the company's 2013 statement of cash flows using the indirect method.

Check Cash from operating
activities, $51,960

Refer to the information in Problem 16-7B.

Problem 16-8B^B

Direct: Computing cash flows
from operations

P5

Required

Prepare the cash flows from operating activities section only of the company's 2013 statement of cash flows using the direct method.

SERIAL PROBLEM
Success Systems (Indirect)

P1 P2 P3

(This serial problem began in Chapter 1 and continues through most of the book. If previous chapter segments were not completed, the serial problem can begin at this point. It is helpful, but not necessary, to use the Working Papers that accompany the book.)

SP 16   Adria Lopez, owner of Success Systems, decides to prepare a statement of cash flows for her business. (Although the serial problem allowed for various ownership changes in earlier chapters, we will prepare the statement of cash flows using the following financial data.)

SUCCESS SYSTEMS
Income Statement
For Three Months Ended March 31, 2014

Computer services revenue		$25,160
Net sales		18,693
Total revenue		43,853
Cost of goods sold	$14,052	
Depreciation expense— Office equipment	400	
Depreciation expense— Computer equipment	1,250	
Wages expense	3,250	
Insurance expense	555	
Rent expense	2,475	
Computer supplies expense	1,305	
Advertising expense	600	
Mileage expense	320	
Repairs expense—Computer	960	
Total expenses		25,167
Net income		$18,686

SUCCESS SYSTEMS
Comparative Balance Sheets
December 31, 2013, and March 31, 2014

	2014	2013
Assets		
Cash	$ 77,845	$58,160
Accounts receivable	22,720	5,668
Merchandise inventory	704	0
Computer supplies	2,005	580
Prepaid insurance	1,110	1,665
Prepaid rent	825	825
Office equipment	8,000	8,000
Accumulated depreciation—Office equipment	(800)	(400)
Computer equipment	20,000	20,000
Accumulated depreciation— Computer equipment	(2,500)	(1,250)
Total assets	$129,909	$93,248
Liabilities and Equity		
Accounts payable	$ 0	$ 1,100
Wages payable	875	500
Unearned computer service revenue	0	1,500
Common stock	108,000	83,000
Retained earnings	21,034	7,148
Total liabilities and equity	$129,909	$93,248

Required

Check Cash flows used by operations: $(515)

Prepare a statement of cash flows for Success Systems using the *indirect method* for the three months ended March 31, 2014. Recall that the owner Adria Lopez contributed $25,000 to the business in exchange for additional stock in the first quarter of 2014 and has received $4,800 in cash dividends.

Beyond the Numbers

REPORTING IN ACTION

A1

Polaris

BTN 16-1   Refer to **Polaris'** financial statements in Appendix A to answer the following.

1. Is Polaris' statement of cash flows prepared under the direct method or the indirect method? How do you know?
2. For each year 2011, 2010, and 2009, is the amount of cash provided by operating activities more or less than the cash paid for dividends?
3. What is the largest amount in reconciling the difference between net income and cash flow from operating activities in 2011? In 2010? In 2009?
4. Identify the largest cash inflow and outflow for investing *and* for financing activities in 2012 and in 2010.

Fast Forward

5. Obtain Polaris' financial statements for a year ending after December 31, 2011, from either its Website (**Polaris.com**) or the SEC's database (**www.sec.gov**). Since December 31, 2011, what are Polaris' largest cash outflows and cash inflows in the investing and in the financing sections of its statement of cash flows?

BTN 16-2   Key figures for **Polaris** and **Arctic Cat** follow.

($ thousands)	Polaris			Arctic Cat		
	Current Year	1 Year Prior	2 Years Prior	Current Year	1 Year Prior	2 Years Prior
Operating cash flows	$ 302,530	$ 297,619	$193,201	$ (5,123)	$ 29,315	$ 19,591
Total assets	1,228,024	1,061,647	763,653	272,906	246,084	251,165

COMPARATIVE ANALYSIS

A1

Polaris

Arctic Cat

Required

1. Compute the recent two years' cash flow on total assets ratios for Polaris and Arctic Cat.

2. What does the cash flow on total assets ratio measure?

3. Which company has the highest cash flow on total assets ratio for the periods shown?

4. Does the cash flow on total assets ratio reflect on the quality of earnings? Explain.

BTN 16-3   Katie Murphy is preparing for a meeting with her banker. Her business is finishing its fourth year of operations. In the first year, it had negative cash flows from operations. In the second and third years, cash flows from operations were positive. However, inventory costs rose significantly in year 4, and cash flows from operations will probably be down 25%. Murphy wants to secure a line of credit from her banker as a financing buffer. From experience, she knows the banker will scrutinize operating cash flows for years 1 through 4 and will want a projected number for year 5. Murphy knows that a steady progression upward in operating cash flows for years 1 through 4 will help her case. She decides to use her discretion as owner and considers several business actions that will turn her operating cash flow in year 4 from a decrease to an increase.

ETHICS CHALLENGE

C1   A1

Required

1. Identify two business actions Murphy might take to improve cash flows from operations.

2. Comment on the ethics and possible consequences of Murphy's decision to pursue these actions.

BTN 16-4   Your friend, Diana Wood, recently completed the second year of her business and just received annual financial statements from her accountant. Wood finds the income statement and balance sheet informative but does not understand the statement of cash flows. She says the first section is especially confusing because it contains a lot of additions and subtractions that do not make sense to her. Wood adds, "The income statement tells me the business is more profitable than last year and that's most important. If I want to know how cash changes, I can look at comparative balance sheets."

COMMUNICATING IN PRACTICE

C1

Required

Write a half-page memorandum to your friend explaining the purpose of the statement of cash flows. Speculate as to why the first section is so confusing and how it might be rectified.

BTN 16-5   Access the March 30, 2012, filing of the 10-K report (for year ending December 31, 2011) of **Mendocino Brewing Company, Inc.**, at **WWW.SEC.GOV**.

TAKING IT TO THE NET

A1

Required

1. Does Mendocino Brewing use the direct or indirect method to construct its consolidated statement of cash flows?

2. For the year ended December 31, 2011, what is the largest item in reconciling the net income to net cash provided by operating activities?

3. In the recent two years, has the company been more successful in generating operating cash flows or in generating net income? Identify the figures to support the answer.

4. In the year ended December 31, 2011, what was the largest cash outflow for investing activities *and* for financing activities?

5. What item(s) does Mendocino Brewing report as supplementary cash flow information?

6. Does Mendocino Brewing report any noncash financing activities for 2011? Identify them, if any.

TEAMWORK IN ACTION

C1 A1 P2 P5

BTN 16-6   Team members are to coordinate and independently answer one question within each of the following three sections. Team members should then report to the team and confirm or correct teammates' answers.

1. Answer *one* of the following questions about the statement of cash flows.
   a. What are this statement's reporting objectives?
   b. What two methods are used to prepare it? Identify similarities and differences between them.
   c. What steps are followed to prepare the statement?
   d. What types of analyses are often made from this statement's information?
2. Identify and explain the adjustment from net income to obtain cash flows from operating activities using the indirect method for *one* of the following items.
   a. Noncash operating revenues and expenses.
   b. Nonoperating gains and losses.
   c. Increases and decreases in noncash current assets.
   d. Increases and decreases in current liabilities.
3.ᴮIdentify and explain the formula for computing cash flows from operating activities using the direct method for *one* of the following items.
   a. Cash receipts from sales to customers.
   b. Cash paid for merchandise inventory.
   c. Cash paid for wages and operating expenses.
   d. Cash paid for interest and taxes.

Note: For teams of more than four, some pairing within teams is necessary. Use as an in-class activity or as an assignment. If used in class, specify a time limit on each part. Conclude with reports to the entire class, using team rotation. Each team can prepare responses on a transparency.

ENTREPRENEURIAL DECISION

C1 A1

BTN 16-7   Review the chapter's opener involving **TOMS** and its young entrepreneurial owner, Blake Mycoskie.

Required

1. In a business such as TOMS, monitoring cash flow is always a priority. Even though TOMS now has thousands in annual sales and earns a positive net income, explain how cash flow can lag behind net income.
2. TOMS is a privately owned corporation. What are potential sources of financing for its future expansion?

C1 A1

BTN 16-8   Jenna and Matt Wilder are completing their second year operating Mountain High, a downhill ski area and resort. Mountain High reports a net loss of $(10,000) for its second year, which includes an $85,000 extraordinary loss from fire. This past year also involved major purchases of plant assets for renovation and expansion, yielding a year-end total asset amount of $800,000. Mountain High's net cash outflow for its second year is $(5,000); a summarized version of its statement of cash flows follows:

Net cash flow provided by operating activities	$295,000
Net cash flow used by investing activities	(310,000)
Net cash flow provided by financing activities	10,000

Required

Write a one-page memorandum to the Wilders evaluating Mountain High's current performance and assessing its future. Give special emphasis to cash flow data and their interpretation.

HITTING THE ROAD

C1

BTN 16-9   Visit **The Motley Fool**'s Website (**Fool.com**). Enter the *Fool's School* (at *Fool.com/School*). Identify and select the link *How to Value Stocks*. (Please note the site may ask you to register with your email address. Registration is free and grants access to full articles on the site.)

Required

1. Click on *Introduction to Valuation Methods,* and then *Cash-Flow-Based Valuations*. How does the Fool's school define cash flow? What is the school's reasoning for this definition?
2. Per the school's instruction, why do analysts focus on earnings before interest and taxes (EBIT)?
3. Visit other links at this Website that interest you such as "How to Read a Balance Sheet," or find out what the "Fool's Ratio" is. Write a half-page report on what you find.

BTN 16-10   Key comparative information for **Piaggio** (www.piaggio.com), which manufactures two-, three- and four-wheel vehicles, and is Europe's leading manufacturer of motorcycles and scooters, follows.

GLOBAL DECISION

C1

PIAGGIO
Polaris
Arctic Cat

(Euro in thousands)	Current Year	1 Year Prior	2 Years Prior
Operating cash flows	155,624	122,541	123,237
Total assets	1,520,184	1,545,722	1,564,820

Required

1. Compute the recent two years' cash flow on total assets ratio for Piaggio.
2. How does Piaggio's ratio compare to Polaris' and Arctic Cat's ratios from BTN 16-2?

ANSWERS TO MULTIPLE CHOICE QUIZ

1. b;

Net income	$15,200
Depreciation expense	10,000
Gain on sale of land	(3,000)
Increase in inventory	(1,500)
Increase in accounts payable	2,850
Net cash provided by operations	$23,550

2. c; cash received from sale of machine is reported as an investing activity.

3. d; FASB requires cash interest paid to be reported under operating.
4. a; Cash paid for salaries and wages = $255,000 + $8,200 − $10,900 = $252,300
5. e; Increase in inventory = $112,000 − $105,000 = $7,000
   Increase in accounts payable = $101,300 − $98,500 = $2,800
   Cash paid for merchandise = $545,000 + $7,000 − $2,800 = $549,200

Analysis of Financial Statements

17

A Look Back

Chapter 16 focused on reporting and analyzing cash inflows and cash outflows. We explained how to prepare, analyze, and interpret the statement of cash flows.

A Look at This Chapter

This chapter emphasizes the analysis and interpretation of financial statement information. We learn to apply horizontal, vertical, and ratio analyses to better understand company performance and financial condition.

A Look Ahead

Chapter 18 introduces us to managerial accounting. We discuss its purposes, concepts, and roles in helping managers gather and organize information for decisions. We also explain basic management principles.

Learning Objectives

CONCEPTUAL

C1 Explain the purpose and identify the building blocks of analysis. (p. 688)

C2 Describe standards for comparisons in analysis. (p. 689)

ANALYTICAL

A1 Summarize and report results of analysis. (p. 708)

A2 *Appendix 17A*—Explain the form and assess the content of a complete income statement. (p. 712)

PROCEDURAL

P1 Explain and apply methods of horizontal analysis. (p. 690)

P2 Describe and apply methods of vertical analysis. (p. 695)

P3 Define and apply ratio analysis. (p. 698)

Decision Insight

Motley Fool

"What goes on at The Motley Fool . . . is similar to what goes on in a library."

—**TOM GARDNER** (DAVID GARDNER ON LEFT)

ALEXANDRIA, VA—In Shakespeare's Elizabethan comedy *As You Like It,* only the fool could speak truthfully to the King without getting his head lopped off. Inspired by Shakespeare's stage character, Tom and David Gardner vowed to become modern-day fools who tell it like it is. With under $10,000 in start-up money, the brothers launched **The Motley Fool (Fool.com).** And befitting of a Shakespearean play, the two say they are "dedicated to educating, amusing, and enriching individuals in search of the truth."

The Gardners do not fear the wrath of any King, real or fictional. They are intent on exposing the truth, as they see it, "that the financial world preys on ignorance and fear." As Tom explains, "There is such a great need in the general populace for financial information." Who can argue, given their brilliant success through practically every medium, including their Website, radio shows, newspaper columns, online store, investment newsletters, and global expansion.

Despite the brothers' best efforts, however, ordinary people still do not fully use information available in financial statements.

For instance, discussions keep appearing on The Motley Fool's online bulletin board that can be easily resolved using reliable and published accounting data. So, it would seem that the Fools must continue their work of "educating and enriching" individuals and showing them the advantages of financial statement analysis.

Following The Motley Fool's objectives, this chapter introduces horizontal and vertical analyses—tools used to reveal crucial trends and insights from financial information. It also expands on ratio analysis, which gives insight into a company's financial condition and performance. By arming ourselves with the information contained in this chapter and the investment advice of The Motley Fool, *we* can be sure to not play the fool in today's financial world.

[Sources: *Motley Fool Website,* January 2013; *Washington Business Journal,* January 2011; *What to Do with Your Money Now,* June 2002; *USA Weekend,* July 2004; *Washington Post,* November 2007; *Money after 40,* April 2007]

This chapter shows how we use financial statements to evaluate a company's financial performance and condition. We explain financial statement analysis, its basic building blocks, the information available, standards for comparisons, and tools of analysis. Three major analysis tools are presented: horizontal analysis, vertical analysis, and ratio analysis. We apply each of these tools using **Polaris**'s financial statements, and we introduce comparative analysis using **Arctic Cat** and **KTM** (and sometimes **Piaggio**). This chapter expands and organizes the ratio analyses introduced at the end of each chapter.

Analysis of Financial Statements			
Basics of Analysis	**Horizontal Analysis**	**Vertical Analysis**	**Ratio Analysis**
• Purpose • Building blocks • Information • Standards for comparisons • Tools	• Comparative balance sheets • Comparative income statements • Trend analysis	• Common-size balance sheet • Common-size income statement • Common-size graphics	• Liquidity and efficiency • Solvency • Profitability • Market prospects • Ratio summary

BASICS OF ANALYSIS

C1 Explain the purpose and identify the building blocks of analysis.

Financial statement analysis applies analytical tools to general-purpose financial statements and related data for making business decisions. It involves transforming accounting data into more useful information. Financial statement analysis reduces our reliance on hunches, guesses, and intuition as well as our uncertainty in decision making. It does not lessen the need for expert judgment; instead, it provides us an effective and systematic basis for making business decisions. This section describes the purpose of financial statement analysis, its information sources, the use of comparisons, and some issues in computations.

Purpose of Analysis

Internal users of accounting information are those involved in strategically managing and operating the company. They include managers, officers, internal auditors, consultants, budget directors, and market researchers. The purpose of financial statement analysis for these users is to provide strategic information to improve company efficiency and effectiveness in providing products and services.

Point: Financial statement analysis tools are also used for personal financial investment decisions.

External users of accounting information are *not* directly involved in running the company. They include shareholders, lenders, directors, customers, suppliers, regulators, lawyers, brokers, and the press. External users rely on financial statement analysis to make better and more informed decisions in pursuing their own goals.

We can identify other uses of financial statement analysis. Shareholders and creditors assess company prospects to make investing and lending decisions. A board of directors analyzes financial statements in monitoring management's decisions. Employees and unions use financial statements in labor negotiations. Suppliers use financial statement information in establishing credit terms. Customers analyze financial statements in deciding whether to establish supply relationships. Public utilities set customer rates by analyzing financial statements. Auditors use financial statements in assessing the "fair presentation" of their clients' financial results. Analyst services such as **Dun & Bradstreet**, **Moody's**, and **Standard & Poor's** use financial statements in making buy-sell recommendations and in setting credit ratings. The common goal of these users is to evaluate company performance and financial condition. This includes evaluating (1) past and current performance, (2) current financial position, and (3) future performance and risk.

Point: Financial statement analysis is a topic on the CPA, CMA, CIA, and CFA exams.

Building Blocks of Analysis

Financial statement analysis focuses on one or more elements of a company's financial condition or performance. Our analysis emphasizes four areas of inquiry—with varying degrees of importance. These four areas are described and illustrated in this chapter and are considered the *building blocks* of financial statement analysis:

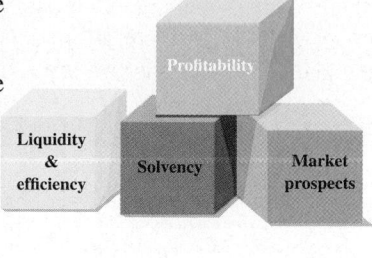

- **Liquidity** and **efficiency**—ability to meet short-term obligations and to efficiently generate revenues.
- **Solvency**—ability to generate future revenues and meet long-term obligations.
- **Profitability**—ability to provide financial rewards sufficient to attract and retain financing.
- **Market prospects**—ability to generate positive market expectations.

Applying the building blocks of financial statement analysis involves determining (1) the objectives of analysis and (2) the relative emphasis among the building blocks. We distinguish among these four building blocks to emphasize the different aspects of a company's financial condition or performance, yet we must remember that these areas of analysis are interrelated. For instance, a company's operating performance is affected by the availability of financing and short-term liquidity conditions. Similarly, a company's credit standing is not limited to satisfactory short-term liquidity but depends also on its profitability and efficiency in using assets. Early in our analysis, we need to determine the relative emphasis of each building block. Emphasis and analysis can later change as a result of evidence collected.

 Decision Insight

Chips and Brokers The phrase *blue chips* refers to stock of big, profitable companies. The phrase comes from poker; where the most valuable chips are blue. The term *brokers* refers to those who execute orders to buy or sell stock. The term comes from wine retailers—individuals who broach (break) wine casks. ■

Information for Analysis

Some users, such as managers and regulatory authorities, are able to receive special financial reports prepared to meet their analysis needs. However, most users must rely on **general-purpose financial statements** that include the (1) income statement, (2) balance sheet, (3) statement of stockholders' equity (or statement of retained earnings), (4) statement of cash flows, and (5) notes to these statements.

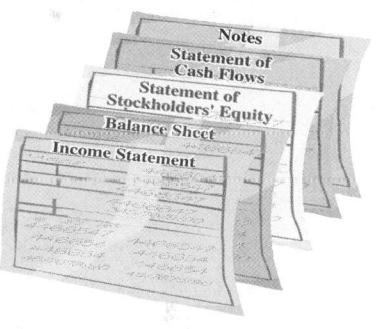

   Financial reporting refers to the communication of financial information useful for making investment, credit, and other business decisions. Financial reporting includes not only general-purpose financial statements but also information from SEC 10-K or other filings, press releases, shareholders' meetings, forecasts, management letters, auditors' reports, and Webcasts.

   Management's Discussion and Analysis (MD&A) is one example of useful information outside traditional financial statements. **Polaris**'s MD&A (available at **Polaris.com**), for example, begins with an overview, followed by critical accounting policies and restatements of previous statements. It then discusses operating results followed by financial condition (liquidity, capital resources, and cash flows). The final few parts discuss legal proceedings, market risk of financial instruments, disclosure controls, and internal controls. The MD&A is an excellent starting point in understanding a company's business activities.

 Decision Insight

Analysis Online Many Websites offer free access and screening of companies by key numbers such as earnings, sales, and book value. For instance, **Investor's Business Daily** has information for more than 10,000 stocks (**www.investors.com**). ■

Standards for Comparisons

When interpreting measures from financial statement analysis, we need to decide whether the measures indicate good, bad, or average performance. To make such judgments, we need standards (benchmarks) for comparisons that include the following:

 C2 Describe standards for comparisons in analysis.

- *Intracompany*—The company under analysis can provide standards for comparisons based on its own prior performance and relations between its financial items. **Polaris**'s current net income, for instance, can be compared with its prior years' net income and in relation to its revenues or total assets.

- *Competitor*—One or more direct competitors of the company being analyzed can provide standards for comparisons. **Coca-Cola**'s profit margin, for instance, can be compared with **PepsiCo**'s profit margin.
- *Industry*—Industry statistics can provide standards of comparisons. Such statistics are available from services such as **Dun & Bradstreet**, **Standard & Poor's**, and **Moody's**.
- *Guidelines (rules of thumb)*—General standards of comparisons can develop from experience. Examples are the 2:1 level for the current ratio or 1:1 level for the acid-test ratio. Guidelines, or rules of thumb, must be carefully applied because context is crucial.

Point: Each chapter's *Reporting in Action* problems engage students in *intracompany* analysis, whereas *Comparative Analysis* problems require competitor analysis (Polaris vs. Arctic Cat vs. KTM).

All of these comparison standards are useful when properly applied, yet measures taken from a selected competitor or group of competitors are often best. Intracompany and industry measures are also important. Guidelines or rules of thumb should be applied with care, and then only if they seem reasonable given past experience and industry norms.

Tools of Analysis

Three of the most common tools of financial statement analysis are

1. **Horizontal analysis**—Comparison of a company's financial condition and performance across time.
2. **Vertical analysis**—Comparison of a company's financial condition and performance to a base amount.
3. **Ratio analysis**—Measurement of key relations between financial statement items.

The remainder of this chapter describes these analysis tools and how to apply them.

■ Decision Insight

Fraud Fighters.   Horizontal, vertical, and ratio analysis tools can uncover fraud by identifying amounts out of line with expectations. One can then follow up and ask questions that can either identify a logical reason for such results or confirm/raise suspicions of fraud. Many past fraud schemes could have been identified much earlier had people applied these tools and pressured management for explanations. ■

Quick Check   Answers — p. 715

1. Who are the intended users of general-purpose financial statements?
2. General-purpose financial statements consist of what information?
3. Which of the following is *least* useful as a basis for comparison when analyzing ratios? (*a*) Company results from a different economic setting. (*b*) Standards from past experience. (*c*) Rule-of-thumb standards. (*d*) Industry averages.
4. What is the preferred basis of comparison for ratio analysis?

HORIZONTAL ANALYSIS

Analysis of any single financial number is of limited value. Instead, much of financial statement analysis involves identifying and describing relations between numbers, groups of numbers, and changes in those numbers. Horizontal analysis refers to examination of financial statement data *across time*. [The term *horizontal analysis* arises from the left-to-right (or right-to-left) movement of our eyes as we review comparative financial statements across time.]

Comparative Statements

P1 Explain and apply methods of horizontal analysis.

Comparing amounts for two or more successive periods often helps in analyzing financial statements. **Comparative financial statements** facilitate this comparison by showing financial amounts in side-by-side columns on a single statement, called a *comparative format*. Using figures from **Polaris**'s financial statements, this section explains how to compute dollar changes and percent changes for comparative statements.

Computation of Dollar Changes and Percent Changes Comparing financial statements over relatively short time periods—two to three years—is often done by analyzing changes in line items. A change analysis usually includes analyzing absolute dollar amount changes and percent changes. Both analyses are relevant because dollar changes can yield large percent changes inconsistent with their importance. For instance, a 50% change from a base figure of $100 is less important than the same percent change from a base amount of $100,000 in the same statement. Reference to dollar amounts is necessary to retain a proper perspective and to assess the importance of changes. We compute the *dollar change* for a financial statement item as follows:

Example: What is a more significant change, a 70% increase on a $1,000 expense or a 30% increase on a $400,000 expense? Answer: The 30% increase.

$$\text{Dollar change} = \text{Analysis period amount} - \text{Base period amount}$$

Analysis period is the point or period of time for the financial statements under analysis, and *base period* is the point or period of time for the financial statements used for comparison purposes. The prior year is commonly used as a base period. We compute the *percent change* by dividing the dollar change by the base period amount and then multiplying this quantity by 100 as follows:

$$\text{Percent change }(\%) = \frac{\text{Analysis period amount} - \text{Base period amount}}{\text{Base period amount}} \times 100$$

We can always compute a dollar change, but we must be aware of a few rules in working with percent changes. To illustrate, look at four separate cases in this chart:

Case	Analysis Period	Base Period	Change Analysis Dollar	Percent
A	$ 1,500	$(4,500)	$ 6,000	—
B	(1,000)	2,000	(3,000)	—
C	8,000	—	8,000	—
D	0	10,000	(10,000)	(100%)

When a negative amount appears in the base period and a positive amount in the analysis period (or vice versa), we cannot compute a meaningful percent change; see cases A and B. Also, when no value is in the base period, no percent change is computable; see case C. Finally, when an item has a value in the base period and zero in the analysis period, the decrease is 100 percent; see case D.

It is common when using horizontal analysis to compare amounts to either average or median values from prior periods (average and median values smooth out erratic or unusual fluctuations).[1] We also commonly round percents and ratios to one or two decimal places, but practice on this matter is not uniform. Computations are as detailed as necessary, which is judged by whether rounding potentially affects users' decisions. Computations should not be excessively detailed so that important relations are lost among a mountain of decimal points and digits.

Example: When there is a value in the base period and zero in the analysis period, the decrease is 100%. Why isn't the reverse situation an increase of 100%? Answer: A 100% increase of zero is still zero.

Comparative Balance Sheets Comparative balance sheets consist of balance sheet amounts from two or more balance sheet dates arranged side by side. Its usefulness is often improved by showing each item's dollar change and percent change to highlight large changes.

Analysis of comparative financial statements begins by focusing on items that show large dollar or percent changes. We then try to identify the reasons for these changes and, if possible, determine whether they are favorable or unfavorable. We also follow up on items with small changes when we expected the changes to be large.

Point: Spreadsheet programs can help with horizontal, vertical, and ratio analyses, including graphical depictions of financial relations.

---

[1] *Median* is the middle value in a group of numbers. For instance, if five prior years' incomes are (in 000s) $15, $19, $18, $20, and $22, the median value is $19. When there are two middle numbers, we can take their average. For instance, if four prior years' sales are (in 000s) $84, $91, $96, and $93, the median is $92 (computed as the average of $91 and $93).

EXHIBIT 17.1

Comparative Balance Sheets

Polaris

POLARIS INDUSTRIES INC. Comparative Balance Sheets December 31, 2011 and 2010				
(in thousands)	2011	2010	Dollar Change	Percent Change
Assets				
Cash and cash equivalents	$ 325,336	$ 393,927	$ (68,591)	(17.4)%
Trade receivables, net	115,302	89,294	26,008	29.1
Inventories, net	298,042	235,927	62,115	26.3
Prepaid expenses and other	37,608	21,628	15,980	73.9
Income taxes receivable..........................	24,723	—	24,723	—
Deferred tax assets	77,665	67,369	10,296	15.3
Total current assets	878,676	808,145	70,531	8.7
Property, plant and equipment, net	213,778	184,011	29,767	16.2
Investments in finance and other affiliates	47,251	38,178	9,073	23.8
Deferred tax assets	10,601	—	10,601	—
Goodwill and other intangible assets, net	77,718	31,313	46,405	148.2
Total assets	$1,228,024	$1,061,647	$166,377	15.7
Liabilities				
Current portion of long-term liablities..............	$ 2,653	$ 100,000	$ (97,347)	(97.3)%
Accounts payable...............................	146,743	113,248	33.495	29.6
Accrued liabilities...............................	465,496	368,358	97,138	26.4
Income taxes payable............................	639	2,604	(1,965)	(75.5)
Total current liabilities	615,531	584,210	31,321	5.4
Long term income taxes payable...................	7,837	5,509	2,328	42.3
Deferred income tax liability......................	—	937	(937)	(100.0)
Capital lease obligations	4,600	—	4,600	—
Long-term debt	100,000	100,000	0	0.0
Total liabilities.................................	727,968	690,656	37,312	5.4
Stockholders' Equity				
Common stock	684	685	(1)	(0.1)
Additional paid-in capital	165,518	79,239	86,279	108.9
Retained earnings	321,831	285,169	36,662	12.9
Accumulated other comprehensive income	12,023	5,898	6,125	103.8
Total stockholders' equity	500,056	370,991	129,065	34.8
Total liabilities and stockholders' equity	$1,228,024	$1,061,647	$166,377	15.7

Point: Business consultants use comparative statement analysis to provide management advice.

Exhibit 17.1 shows comparative balance sheets for **Polaris Industries, Inc. (PII)**. A few items stand out. Accounts receivable and inventories are asset categories showing substantial increases. The inventory build up and accounts receivable increase are likely reflective of the recession. Cash and cash equivalents have decreased substantially. Some of these resources were applied to pay off the long-term debt that came due in 2011. Polaris added property, plant, and equipment, and the increase in Goodwill reflects acquisition activity. Of course, its sizable total asset growth of 15.7% must be accompanied by future income to validate Polaris's growth strategy.

We likewise see substantial increases on the financing side, the most notable ones (in amount) being accounts payable and accrued liabilities totaling $130,633 thousand. The increase in these items is probably related to the recessionary period covering this report. Polaris also reinvested much of its income as reflected in the $36,622 thousand increase in retained earnings. Again, we must monitor these increases in investing and financing activities to be sure they are reflected in increased operating performance.

Comparative Income Statements Comparative income statements are prepared similarly to comparative balance sheets. Amounts for two or more periods are placed side by side, with additional columns for dollar and percent changes. Exhibit 17.2 shows Polaris's comparative income statements.

EXHIBIT 17.2

Comparative Income Statements

Polaris

POLARIS INDUSTRIES INC. Comparative Income Statements For Years Ended December 31, 2011 and 2010				
(in thousands, except per share)	2011	2010	Dollar Change	Percent Change
Sales..........................	$2,656,949	$1,991,139	$665,810	33.4%
Cost of sales	1,916,366	1,460,926	455,440	31.2
Gross profit	740,583	530,213	210,370	39.7
Selling and marketing	178,725	142,353	36,372	25.6
Research and development...........	105,631	84,940	20,691	24.4
General and administrative...........	130,395	99,055	31,340	31.6
Total operating expenses	414,751	326,348	88,403	27.1
Income from financial services	24,092	16,856	7,236	42.9
Operating income	349,924	220,721	129,203	58.5
Non-operating expense, net	3,298	2,180	1,118	51.3
Income before income taxes	346,626	218,541	128,085	58.6
Provision for income taxes	119,051	71,403	47,648	66.7
Net income.......................	$ 227,575	$ 147,138	$ 80,437	54.7
Basic net income per share	$ 3.31	$ 2.20	$ 1.11	50.5
Diluted net income per share	$ 3.20	$ 2.14	$ 1.06	49.5

Polaris has substantial revenue growth of 33.4% in 2011. This finding helps support management's growth strategy as reflected in the comparative balance sheets. Polaris evidences an ability to control cost of goods sold (31.2% increase) and other operating expenses, which all increased but at lower rates than the growth in revenues. Polaris's net income growth of 54.7% on revenue growth of 33.4% is very good.

Point: Percent change can also be computed by dividing the current period by the prior period and subtracting 1.0. For example, the 33.4% revenue increase of Exhibit 17.2 is computed as: ($2,656,949/$1,991,139) − 1.

Trend Analysis

Trend analysis, also called *trend percent analysis* or *index number trend analysis,* is a form of horizontal analysis that can reveal patterns in data across successive periods. It involves computing trend percents for a series of financial numbers and is a variation on the use of percent changes. The difference is that trend analysis does not subtract the base period amount in the numerator. To compute trend percents, we do the following:

1. Select a *base period* and assign each item in the base period a weight of 100%.
2. Express financial numbers as a percent of their base period number.

Specifically, a *trend percent,* also called an *index number,* is computed as follows:

$$\text{Trend percent (\%)} = \frac{\text{Analysis period amount}}{\text{Base period amount}} \times 100$$

Financial Results

Point: *Index* refers to the comparison of the analysis period to the base period. Percents determined for each period are called *index numbers.*

To illustrate trend analysis, we use the **Polaris** data shown in Exhibit 17.3.

EXHIBIT 17.3

Revenue and Expenses

(in thousands)	2011	2010	2009	2008	2007
Sales	$2,656,949	$1,991,139	$1,565,887	$1,948,254	$1,780,009
Cost of sales	1,916,366	1,460,926	1,172,668	1,502,546	1,386,989
Operating expenses	414,751	326,348	245,320	284,114	262,269

These data are from Polaris's current and prior financial statements. The base period is 2007 and the trend percent is computed in each subsequent year by dividing that year's amount by its 2007 amount. For instance, the revenue trend percent for 2011 is 149.3%, computed as $2,656,949/$1,780,009. The trend percents—using the data from Exhibit 17.3—are shown in Exhibit 17.4.

EXHIBIT 17.4

Trend Percents for Revenue and Expenses

	2011	2010	2009	2008	2007
Sales	149.3%	111.9%	88.0%	109.5%	100.0%
Cost of sales	138.2	105.3	84.5	108.3	100.0
Operating expenses	158.1	124.4	93.5	108.3	100.0

Point: Trend analysis expresses a percent of base, not a percent of change.

Graphical depictions often aid analysis of trend percents. Exhibit 17.5 shows the trend percents from Exhibit 17.4 in a *line graph,* which can help us identify trends and detect changes in direction or magnitude. It reveals that the trend line for revenue consistently falls short of that for operating expenses. Moreover, the magnitude of that difference has grown. This result does not bode well for Polaris because profitability of the company will suffer if operating expenses cannot be controlled. Management must try to better control these costs in future years. The trend line for cost of goods sold is much more encouraging since revenue growth outpaces the growth in cost of goods sold for each year from 2008–2011. This trend shows that Polaris is able to increase its gross profit margin in each of these years.

EXHIBIT 17.5

Trend Percent Lines for Revenue and Expenses of Polaris

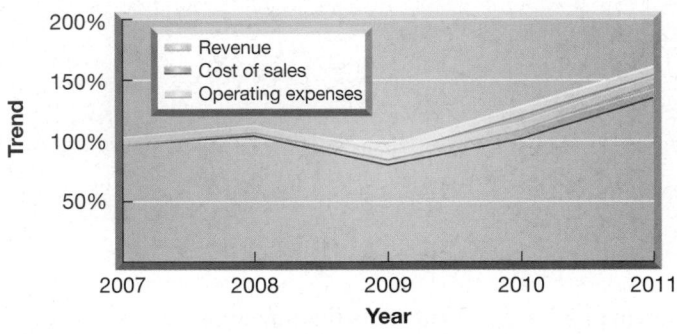

Exhibit 17.6 compares Polaris's revenue trend line to that of Arctic Cat and KTM for this same period. Polaris is able to grow its revenue in each year relative to its base year except for 2008. In this respect Polaris soundly outperforms its competitors, as Arctic Cat's and KTM's revenues fall sharply each year from 2008–2010 before rebounding in 2011. These data indicate that Polaris's products and services have met with greater consumer acceptance.

EXHIBIT 17.6

Trend Percent Lines—Polaris, Arctic Cat and KTM

Polaris

Arctic Cat

KTM

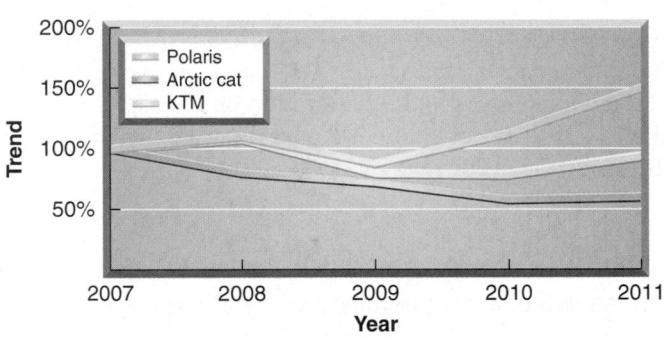

Trend analysis of financial statement items can include comparisons of relations between items on different financial statements. For instance, Exhibit 17.7 compares Polaris's revenue and total assets. The rate of increase in total assets (159.5%) is less than the increase in revenues (723.8%) since 2007. Is this result favorable or not? The answer is that Polaris was *less* efficient in using its assets in 2011. Management has not generated revenues sufficient to compensate for this asset growth.

EXHIBIT 17.7

Revenue and Asset Data for Polaris

(in thousands)	2011	2007	Trend Percent (2011 vs. 2007)
Sales	$2,656,949	$1,780,009	149.3%
Total assets	1,228,024	769,881	159.5

Overall we must remember that an important role of financial statement analysis is identifying questions and areas of interest, which often direct us to important factors bearing on a company's future. Accordingly, financial statement analysis should be seen as a continuous process of refining our understanding and expectations of company performance and financial condition.

■ Decision Maker

Auditor   Your tests reveal a 3% increase in sales from $200,000 to $206,000 and a 4% decrease in expenses from $190,000 to $182,400. Both changes are within your "reasonableness" criterion of ±5%, and thus you don't pursue additional tests. The audit partner in charge questions your lack of follow-up and mentions the *joint relation* between sales and expenses. To what is the partner referring? ■   [Answer—p. 714]

VERTICAL ANALYSIS

Vertical analysis is a tool to evaluate individual financial statement items or a group of items in terms of a specific base amount. We usually define a key aggregate figure as the base, which for an income statement is usually revenue and for a balance sheet is usually total assets. This section explains vertical analysis and applies it to **Polaris**. [The term *vertical analysis* arises from the up-down (or down-up) movement of our eyes as we review common-size financial statements. Vertical analysis is also called *common-size analysis*.]

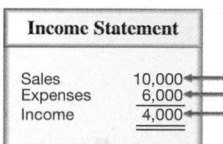

Common-Size Statements

The comparative statements in Exhibits 17.1 and 17.2 show the change in each item over time, but they do not emphasize the relative importance of each item. We use **common-size financial statements** to reveal changes in the relative importance of each financial statement item. All individual amounts in common-size statements are redefined in terms of common-size percents. A *common-size percent* is measured by dividing each individual financial statement amount under analysis by its base amount:

P2 Describe and apply methods of vertical analysis.

$$\text{Common-size percent (\%)} = \frac{\text{Analysis amount}}{\text{Base amount}} \times 100$$

Common-Size Balance Sheets   Common-size statements express each item as a percent of a *base amount,* which for a common-size balance sheet is usually total assets. The base amount is assigned a value of 100%. (This implies that the total amount of liabilities plus equity equals 100% since this amount equals total assets.) We then compute a common-size percent for each asset, liability, and equity item using total assets as the base amount. When we present a company's successive balance sheets in this way, changes in the mixture of assets, liabilities, and equity are apparent.

Exhibit 17.8 shows common-size comparative balance sheets for Polaris. Some relations that stand out on both a magnitude and percentage basis include (1) a 10.6% point decline in cash and equivalents, (2) a 2.1% point increase in inventories, (3) a 3.4% point increase in goodwill and intangibles, (4) a 9.2% point decline in the current portion of long-term liabilities, (5) a 3.2% increase in accrued liabilities, and (6) a 6.0% increase in paid-in capital. Some of these changes reflect a company with reduced cash flow, inventory buildup, and less ability to pay off liabilities. A potential concern is whether Polaris can continue to generate sufficient revenue and income to support its operations and its payment of expenses.

Point: The *base* amount in common-size analysis is an *aggregate* amount from that period's financial statement.

Point: Common-size statements often are used to compare two or more companies in the same industry.

Point: Common-size statements are also useful in comparing firms that report in different currencies.

EXHIBIT 17.8

Common-Size Comparative
Balance Sheets

Polaris

POLARIS INDUSTRIES INC.
Common-Size Comparative Balance Sheets
December 31, 2011 and 2010

(in thousands)	2011	2010	Common-Size Percents* 2011	2010
Assets				
Cash and cash equivalents	$ 325,336	$ 393,927	26.5%	37.1%
Trade receivables, net	115,302	89,294	9.4	8.4
Inventories, net	298,042	235,927	24.3	22.2
Prepaid expenses and other	37,608	21,628	3.1	2.0
Income taxes receivable	24,723	—	2.0	—
Deferred tax assets	77,665	67,369	6.3	6.3
Total current assets	878,676	808,145	71.6	76.1
Property, plant and equipment, net	213,778	184,011	17.4	17.3
Investments in finance and other affiliates	47,251	38,178	3.8	3.6
Deferred tax assets	10,601	—	0.9	0.0
Goodwill and other intangible assets, net	77,718	31,313	6.3	2.9
Total assets	$1,228,024	$1,061,647	100.0%	100.0%
Liabilities				
Current portion of long-term liabilities	$ 2,653	$ 100,000	0.2%	9.4%
Accounts payable	146,743	113,248	11.9	10.7
Accrued liabilities	465,496	368,358	37.9	34.7
Income taxes payable	639	2,604	0.1	0.2
Total current liabilities	615,531	584,210	50.1	55.0
Long term income taxes payable	7,837	5,509	0.6	0.5
Deferred income tax liability	—	937	0.0	0.1
Capital lease obligations	4,600	—	0.4	0.0
Long-term debt	100,000	100,000	8.1	9.4
Total liabilities	727,968	690,656	59.3	65.1
Stockholders' Equity				
Common stock	684	685	0.1	0.1
Additional paid-in capital	165,518	79,239	13.5	7.5
Retained earnings	321,831	285,169	26.2	26.9
Accumulated other comprehensive income	12,023	5,898	1.0	0.6
Total stockholders' equity	500,056	370,991	40.7	34.9
Total liabilities and stockholders' equity	$1,228,024	$1,061,647	100.0%	100.0%

* Percents are rounded to tenths and thus may not exactly sum to totals and subtotals.

Common-Size Income Statements Analysis also benefits from use of a common-size income statement. Revenue is usually the base amount, which is assigned a value of 100%. Each common-size income statement item appears as a percent of revenue. If we think of the 100% revenue amount as representing one sales dollar, the remaining items show how each revenue dollar is distributed among costs, expenses, and income.

Exhibit 17.9 shows common-size comparative income statements for each dollar of Polaris's revenue. The past two years' common-size numbers are similar with a few exceptions. The good news is that Polaris has gained 1.2 cents in earnings per revenue dollar—evidenced by the 7.4% to 8.6% increase in earnings as a percentage of revenue. This implies that management is effectively controlling costs. Much of this is attributed to the decline in operating expenses from 16.4% to 15.6% as a percentage of revenue. Analysis here shows that common-size percents for successive income statements can uncover potentially important changes in a company's expenses. Evidence of no changes, especially when changes are expected, is also informative.

Global: International companies sometimes disclose "convenience" financial statements, which are statements translated in other languages and currencies. However, these statements rarely adjust for differences in accounting principles across countries.

POLARIS INDUSTRIES INC. Common-Size Comparative Income Statements For Years Ended December 31, 2011 and 2010				
			Common-Size Percents*	
(in thousands)	2011	2010	2011	2010
Sales	$2,656,949	$1,991,139	100.0%	100.0%
Cost of sales	1,916,366	1,460,926	72.1	73.4
Gross profit	740,583	530,213	27.9	26.6
Selling and marketing	178,725	142,353	6.7	7.1
Research and development	105,631	84,940	4.0	4.3
General and administrative	130,395	99,055	4.9	5.0
Total operating expenses	414,751	326,348	15.6	16.4
Income from financial services	24,092	16,856	0.9	0.8
Operating income	349,924	220,721	13.2	11.1
Non-operating expenses, net.	3,298	2,180	0.1	0.1
Income before income taxes	346,626	218,541	13.1	11.0
Provision for income taxes	119,051	71,403	4.5	3.6
Net income	$ 227,575	$ 147,138	8.6%	7.4%

EXHIBIT 17.9

Common-Size Comparative Income Statements
Polaris

* Percents are rounded to tenths and thus may not exactly sum to totals and subtotals.

Common-Size Graphics

Two of the most common tools of common-size analysis are trend analysis of common-size statements and graphical analysis. The trend analysis of common-size statements is similar to that of comparative statements discussed under vertical analysis. It is not illustrated here because the only difference is the substitution of common-size percents for trend percents. Instead, this section discusses graphical analysis of common-size statements.

An income statement readily lends itself to common-size graphical analysis. This is so because revenues affect nearly every item in an income statement. Exhibit 17.10 shows **Polaris**'s 2011 common-size income statement in graphical form. This pie chart highlights the contribution of each cost component of revenue for net income (for this graph, financial services income and non-operating expenses are included in general and administrative costs).

EXHIBIT 17.10

Common-Size Graphic of Income Statement

Exhibit 17.11 previews more complex graphical analyses available and the insights they provide. The data for this exhibit are taken from **Polaris**'s *Segments* footnote. Polaris has at least two reportable segments: (1) United States, and (2) outside the United States (titled Non-U.S.).

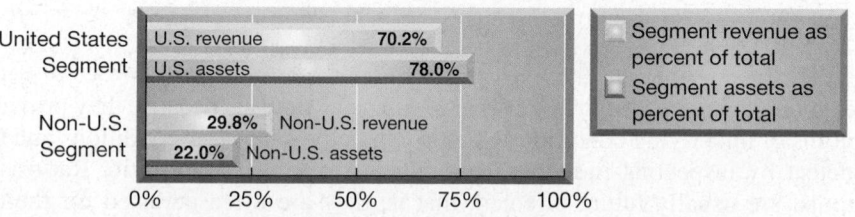

EXHIBIT 17.11

Revenue and Total Asset Breakdown by Segment

EXHIBIT 17.12

Common-Size Graphic of
Asset Components

Cash and cash equivalents
26.5%

Trade receivables,
net 9.4%

Inventories, net 24.3%

Other current assets 5.1%

Deferred tax (current)
asset 6.3%

Investments 3.8%

Property, plant and
equipment 17.4%

Goodwill and other
intangibles 6.3%

Deferred tax (noncurrent)
asset 0.9%

The upper set of bars in Exhibit 17.11 shows the percent of revenues from, and the assets invested in, its U.S. segment. Its U.S. segment generates 70.2% of its revenue, as 78.0% of its assets are in the United States. The lower set of bars shows that 29.8% of its revenue is generated outside the United States, with 22.0% of its assets located outside the United States. This can lead to questions about the revenue generated per assets invested across different countries. This type of information can help users in determining strategic analyses and actions.

Graphical analysis is also useful in identifying (1) sources of financing including the distribution among current liabilities, noncurrent liabilities, and equity capital and (2) focuses of investing activities, including the distribution among current and noncurrent assets. To illustrate, Exhibit 17.12 shows a common-size graphical display of Polaris's assets. Common-size balance sheet analysis can be extended to examine the composition of these subgroups. For instance, in assessing liquidity of current assets, knowing what proportion of *current* assets consists of inventories is usually important, and not simply what proportion inventories are of *total* assets.

Common-size financial statements are also useful in comparing different companies. Exhibit 17.13 shows common-size graphics of **Polaris**, **Arctic Cat** and **KTM** on financing sources. This graphic highlights the larger percent of equity financing for Arctic Cat versus Polaris and KTM. It also highlights the much larger noncurrent (debt) financing of KTM versus Polaris and Arctic Cat. Comparison of a company's common-size statements with competitors' or industry common-size statistics alerts us to differences in the structure or distribution of its financial statements but not to their dollar magnitude.

EXHIBIT 17.13

Common-Size Graphic of Financing
Sources—Competitor Analysis

Polaris

Arctic Cat

KTM

	Polaris	Arctic Cat	KTM
Current liabilities	50.1%	32.0%	22.5%
		0.9%	32.2%
Noncurrent liabilities	9.2%		
		67.1%	
Equity	40.7%		45.3%

Quick Check   Answers — p. 715

5. Which of the following is true for common-size comparative statements? (*a*) Each item is expressed as a percent of a base amount. (*b*) Total assets often are assigned a value of 100%. (*c*) Amounts from successive periods are placed side by side. (*d*) All are true. (*e*) None is true.

6. What is the difference between the percents shown on a comparative income statement and those shown on a common-size comparative income statement?

7. Trend percents are (*a*) shown on comparative income statements and balance sheets, (*b*) shown on common-size comparative statements, or (*c*) also called *index numbers*.

RATIO ANALYSIS

 P3 Define and apply ratio analysis.

Ratios are among the more widely used tools of financial analysis because they provide clues to and symptoms of underlying conditions. A ratio can help us uncover conditions and trends difficult to detect by inspecting individual components making up the ratio. Ratios, like other analysis tools, are usually future oriented; that is, they are often adjusted for their probable future trend and magnitude, and their usefulness depends on skillful interpretation.

A ratio expresses a mathematical relation between two quantities. It can be expressed as a percent, rate, or proportion. For instance, a change in an account balance from $100 to $250 can be expressed as (1) 150% increase, (2) 2.5 times, or (3) 2.5 to 1 (or 2.5:1). Computation of a ratio is a simple arithmetic operation, but its interpretation is not. To be meaningful, a ratio must refer to an economically important relation. For example, a direct and crucial relation exists between an item's sales price and its cost. Accordingly, the ratio of cost of goods sold to sales is meaningful. In contrast, no obvious relation exists between freight costs and the balance of long-term investments.

This section describes an important set of financial ratios and its application. The selected ratios are organized into the four building blocks of financial statement analysis: (1) liquidity and efficiency, (2) solvency, (3) profitability, and (4) market prospects. All of these ratios were explained at relevant points in prior chapters. The purpose here is to organize and apply them under a summary framework. We use four common standards, in varying degrees, for comparisons: intracompany, competitor, industry, and guidelines.

Point: Some sources for industry norms are *Annual Statement Studies* by Robert Morris Associates, *Industry Norms & Key Business Ratios* by Dun & Bradstreet, *Standard & Poor's Industry Surveys*, and Reuters.com/finance.

Liquidity and Efficiency

Liquidity refers to the availability of resources to meet short-term cash requirements. It is affected by the timing of cash inflows and outflows along with prospects for future performance. Analysis of liquidity is aimed at a company's funding requirements. *Efficiency* refers to how productive a company is in using its assets. Efficiency is usually measured relative to how much revenue is generated from a certain level of assets.

Both liquidity and efficiency are important and complementary. If a company fails to meet its current obligations, its continued existence is doubtful. Viewed in this light, all other measures of analysis are of secondary importance. Although accounting measurements assume the company's continued existence, our analysis must always assess the validity of this assumption using liquidity measures. Moreover, inefficient use of assets can cause liquidity problems. A lack of liquidity often precedes lower profitability and fewer opportunities. It can foretell a loss of owner control. To a company's creditors, lack of liquidity can yield delays in collecting interest and principal payments or the loss of amounts due them. A company's customers and suppliers of goods and services also are affected by short-term liquidity problems. Implications include a company's inability to execute contracts and potential damage to important customer and supplier relationships. This section describes and illustrates key ratios relevant to assessing liquidity and efficiency.

Working Capital and Current Ratio The amount of current assets less current liabilities is called **working capital,** or *net working capital.* A company needs adequate working capital to meet current debts, to carry sufficient inventories, and to take advantage of cash discounts. A company that runs low on working capital is less likely to meet current obligations or to continue operating. When evaluating a company's working capital, we must not only look at the dollar amount of current assets less current liabilities, but also at their ratio. The *current ratio* is defined as follows (see Chapter 3 for additional explanation):

$$\text{Current ratio} = \frac{\text{Current assets}}{\text{Current liabilities}}$$

Drawing on information in Exhibit 17.1, **Polaris**'s working capital and current ratio for both 2011 and 2010 are shown in Exhibit 17.14. Also, **Arctic Cat** (2.65), **KTM** (1.77), and the Industry's current ratio (7) are shown in the margin. Polaris's 2011 ratio (1.43) is between the competitors' ratios, and it does not appear in danger of defaulting on loan payments. A high current ratio suggests a strong liquidity position and an ability to meet current obligations. A company can, however, have a current ratio that is too high. An excessively high current ratio means that the company has invested too much in current assets compared to its current

(in thousands)	2011	2010
Current assets	$878,676	$808,145
Current liabilities	615,531	584,210
Working capital	$263,145	$223,935
Current ratio		
$878,676/$615,531 =	1.43 to 1	
$808,145/$584,210 =		1.38 to 1

EXHIBIT 17.14

Polaris's Working Capital and Current Ratio

Current ratio
Arctic Cat = 2.65
KTM = 1.77
Industry = 1.9

obligations. An excessive investment in current assets is not an efficient use of funds because current assets normally generate a low return on investment (compared with long-term assets).

Many users apply a guideline of 2:1 (or 1.5:1) for the current ratio in helping evaluate a company's debt-paying ability. A company with a 2:1 or higher current ratio is generally thought to be a good credit risk in the short run. Such a guideline or any analysis of the current ratio must recognize at least three additional factors: (1) type of business, (2) composition of current assets, and (3) turnover rate of current asset components.

Type of business. A service company that grants little or no credit and carries few inventories can probably operate on a current ratio of less than 1:1 if its revenues generate enough cash to pay its current liabilities. On the other hand, a company selling high-priced clothing or furniture requires a higher ratio because of difficulties in judging customer demand and cash receipts. For instance, if demand falls, inventory may not generate as much cash as expected. Accordingly, analysis of the current ratio should include a comparison with ratios from successful companies in the same industry and from prior periods. We must also recognize that a company's accounting methods, especially choice of inventory method, affect the current ratio. For instance, when costs are rising, a company using LIFO tends to report a smaller amount of current assets than when using FIFO.

Point: When a firm uses LIFO in a period of rising costs, the standard for an adequate current ratio usually is lower than if it used FIFO.

Composition of current assets. The composition of a company's current assets is important to an evaluation of short-term liquidity. For instance, cash, cash equivalents, and short-term investments are more liquid than accounts and notes receivable. Also, short-term receivables normally are more liquid than inventory. Cash, of course, can be used to immediately pay current debts. Items such as accounts receivable and inventory, however, normally must be converted into cash before payment is made. An excessive amount of receivables and inventory weakens a company's ability to pay current liabilities. The acid-test ratio (see below) can help with this assessment.

Turnover rate of assets. Asset turnover measures a company's efficiency in using its assets. One relevant measure of asset efficiency is the revenue generated. A measure of total asset turnover is revenues divided by total assets, but evaluation of turnover for individual assets is also useful. We discuss both receivables turnover and inventory turnover on the next page.

Decision Maker

Banker A company requests a one-year, $200,000 loan for expansion. This company's current ratio is 4:1, with current assets of $160,000. Key competitors carry a current ratio of about 1.9:1. Using this information, do you approve the loan application? Does your decision change if the application is for a 10-year loan? ■ [Answer—p. 715]

Acid-Test Ratio Quick assets are cash, short-term investments, and current receivables. These are the most liquid types of current assets. The *acid-test ratio*, also called *quick ratio,* and introduced in Chapter 5, reflects on a company's short-term liquidity.

$$\text{Acid-test ratio} = \frac{\text{Cash} + \text{Short-term investments} + \text{Current receivables}}{\text{Current liabilities}}$$

Polaris's acid-test ratio is computed in Exhibit 17.15. Polaris's 2011 acid-test ratio (0.72) is between that for Arctic Cat (1.70) and KTM (0.63), but less than the 1:1 common guideline for

EXHIBIT 17.15

Acid-Test Ratio

(in thousands)	2011	2010
Cash and equivalents	$325,336	$393,927
Current receivables	115,302	89,294
Total quick assets	$440,638	$483,221
Current liabilities	$615,531	$584,210
Acid-test ratio		
$440,638/$615,531	0.72 to 1	
$483,221/$584,210		0.83 to 1

Acid-test ratio
Arctic Cat = 1.70
KTM = 0.63
Industry = 0.9

an acceptable acid-test ratio. The ratio for Arctic Cat exceeds the 0.9 industry norm. As with analysis of the current ratio, we need to consider other factors. For instance, the frequency with which a company converts its current assets into cash affects its working capital requirements. This implies that analysis of short-term liquidity should also include an analysis of receivables and inventories, which we consider next.

Global: Ratio analysis helps overcome currency translation problems, but it does *not* overcome differences in accounting principles.

Accounts Receivable Turnover We can measure how frequently a company converts its receivables into cash by computing the *accounts receivable turnover*. This ratio is defined as follows (see Chapter 9 for additional explanation):

$$\text{Accounts receivable turnover} = \frac{\text{Net sales}}{\text{Average accounts receivable, net}}$$

Short-term receivables from customers are often included in the denominator along with accounts receivable. Also, accounts receivable turnover is more precise if credit sales are used for the numerator, but external users generally use net sales (or net revenues) because information about credit sales is typically not reported. Polaris's 2011 accounts receivable turnover is computed as follows ($ millions).

Point: Some users prefer using gross accounts receivable (before subtracting the allowance for doubtful accounts) to avoid the influence of a manager's bad debts estimate.

$$\frac{\$2,656,949}{(\$89,294 + \$115,302)/2} = 26.0 \text{ times}$$

Accounts receivable turnover
Arctic Cat = 17.5
KTM = 9.5
Industry = 15.0

Polaris's value of 26.0 exceeds that of Arctic Cat's 17.5 and KTM's 9.5. Accounts receivable turnover is high when accounts receivable are quickly collected. A high turnover is favorable because it means the company need not commit large amounts of funds to accounts receivable. However, an accounts receivable turnover can be too high; this can occur when credit terms are so restrictive that they negatively affect sales volume.

Point: Ending accounts receivable can be substituted for the average balance in computing accounts receivable turnover if the difference between ending and average receivables is small.

Inventory Turnover How long a company holds inventory before selling it will affect working capital requirements. One measure of this effect is *inventory turnover,* also called *merchandise turnover* or *merchandise inventory turnover,* which is defined as follows (see Chapter 6 for additional explanation):

$$\text{Inventory turnover} = \frac{\text{Cost of goods sold}}{\text{Average inventory}}$$

Using Polaris's cost of goods sold and inventories information, we compute its inventory turnover for 2011 as follows (if the beginning and ending inventories for the year do not represent the usual inventory amount, an average of quarterly or monthly inventories can be used).

Inventory turnover
Arctic Cat = 5.08
KTM = 3.34
Industry = 4.0

$$\frac{\$1,916,366}{(\$235,927 + \$298,042)/2} = 7.18 \text{ times}$$

Polaris's inventory turnover of 7.18 is more than Arctic Cat's 5.08 and KTM's 3.34, and the industry's 4.0. A company with a high turnover requires a smaller investment in inventory than one producing the same sales with a lower turnover. Inventory turnover can be too high, however, if the inventory a company keeps is so small that it restricts sales volume.

Days' Sales Uncollected Accounts receivable turnover provides insight into how frequently a company collects its accounts. Days' sales uncollected is one measure of this activity, which is defined as follows (Chapter 8 provides additional explanation):

$$\text{Days' sales uncollected} = \frac{\text{Accounts receivable, net}}{\text{Net sales}} \times 365$$

Any short-term notes receivable from customers are normally included in the numerator.

Polaris's 2011 days' sales uncollected follows.

Day's sales uncollected
Arctic Cat = 18.6
KTM = 37.1

$$\frac{\$115,302}{\$2,656,949} \times 365 = 15.8 \text{ days}$$

Both Arctic Cat's days' sales uncollected of 18.6 days and KTM's 37.1 days are more than the 15.8 days for Polaris. Days' sales uncollected is more meaningful if we know company credit terms. A rough guideline states that days' sales uncollected should not exceed $1\frac{1}{3}$ times the days in its (1) credit period, *if* discounts are not offered or (2) discount period, *if* favorable discounts are offered.

Days' Sales in Inventory   *Days' sales in inventory* is a useful measure in evaluating inventory liquidity. Days' sales in inventory is linked to inventory in a way that days' sales uncollected is linked to receivables. We compute days' sales in inventory as follows (Chapter 6 provides additional explanation).

$$\text{Days' sales in inventory} = \frac{\text{Ending inventory}}{\text{Cost of goods sold}} \times 365$$

Polaris's days' sales in inventory for 2011 follows.

Days' sales in inventory
Arctic Cat = 61.8
KTM = 111.9
Industry = 75

$$\frac{\$298,042}{\$1,916,366} \times 365 = 56.8 \text{ days}$$

Point: *Average collection period* is estimated by dividing 365 by the accounts receivable turnover ratio. For example, 365 divided by an accounts receivable turnover of 6.1 indicates a 60-day average collection period.

If the products in Polaris's inventory are in demand by customers, this formula estimates that its inventory will be converted into receivables (or cash) in 56.8 days. If all of Polaris's sales were credit sales, the conversion of inventory to receivables in 56.8 days *plus* the conversion of receivables to cash in 15.8 days implies that inventory will be converted to cash in about 72.6 days (56.8 + 15.8).

Total Asset Turnover   *Total asset turnover* reflects a company's ability to use its assets to generate sales and is an important indication of operating efficiency. The definition of this ratio follows (Chapter 10 offers additional explanation).

$$\text{Total asset turnover} = \frac{\text{Net sales}}{\text{Average total assets}}$$

Polaris's total asset turnover for 2011 follows and is greater than that for both Arctic Cat (1.79) and KTM (1.13).

Total asset turnover
Arctic Cat = 1.79
KTM = 1.13
Industry = 1.3

$$\frac{\$2,656,949}{(\$1,061,647 + \$1,228,024)/2} = 2.32 \text{ times}$$

Quick Check   Answers — p. 715

8. Information from Paff Co. at Dec. 31, 2012, follows: cash, $820,000; accounts receivable, $240,000; inventories, $470,000; plant assets, $910,000; accounts payable, $350,000; and income taxes payable, $180,000. Compute its (a) current ratio and (b) acid-test ratio.

9. On Dec. 31, 2013, Paff Company (see question 8) had accounts receivable of $290,000 and inventories of $530,000. During 2013, net sales amounted to $2,500,000 and cost of goods sold was $750,000. Compute (a) accounts receivable turnover, (b) days' sales uncollected, (c) inventory turnover, and (d) days' sales in inventory.

Solvency

Solvency refers to a company's long-run financial viability and its ability to cover long-term obligations. All of a company's business activities—financing, investing, and operating—affect its solvency. Analysis of solvency is long term and uses less precise but more encompassing measures than liquidity. One of the most important components of solvency analysis is the composition of a company's capital structure. *Capital structure* refers to a company's financing sources. It ranges from relatively permanent equity financing to riskier or more temporary short-term financing. Assets represent security for financiers, ranging from loans secured by specific assets to the assets available as general security to unsecured creditors. This section describes the tools of solvency analysis. Our analysis focuses on a company's ability to both meet its obligations and provide security to its creditors *over the long run*. Indicators of this ability include *debt* and *equity* ratios, the relation between *pledged assets and secured liabilities,* and the company's capacity to earn sufficient income to *pay fixed interest charges*.

Debt and Equity Ratios One element of solvency analysis is to assess the portion of a company's assets contributed by its owners and the portion contributed by creditors. This relation is reflected in the debt ratio (also described in Chapter 2). The *debt ratio* expresses total liabilities as a percent of total assets. The **equity ratio** provides complementary information by expressing total equity as a percent of total assets. **Polaris**'s debt and equity ratios follow.

Point: For analysis purposes, Minority Interest is usually included in equity.

(in thousands)	2011	Ratios	
Total liabilities	$ 727,968	59.3%	[Debt ratio]
Total equity	500,056	40.7	[Equity ratio]
Total liabilities and equity	$1,228,024	100.0%	

Debt ratio :: Equity ratio
Arctic Cat = 32.9% :: 67.1%
KTM = 54.8% :: 45.2%
Industry = 45% :: 55%

Polaris's financial statements reveal more debt than equity. A company is considered less risky if its capital structure (equity and long-term debt) contains more equity. One risk factor is the required payment for interest and principal when debt is outstanding. Another factor is the greater the stockholder financing, the more losses a company can absorb through equity before the assets become inadequate to satisfy creditors' claims. From the stockholders' point of view, if a company earns a return on borrowed capital that is higher than the cost of borrowing, the difference represents increased income to stockholders. The inclusion of debt is described as *financial leverage* because debt can have the effect of increasing the return to stockholders. Companies are said to be highly leveraged if a large portion of their assets is financed by debt.

Point: Bank examiners from the FDIC and other regulatory agencies use debt and equity ratios to monitor compliance with regulatory capital requirements imposed on banks and S&Ls.

Debt-to-Equity Ratio The ratio of total liabilities to equity is another measure of solvency. We compute the ratio as follows (Chapter 14 offers additional explanation).

$$\text{Debt-to-equity ratio} = \frac{\text{Total liabilities}}{\text{Total equity}}$$

Polaris's debt-to-equity ratio for 2011 is

$$\$727,968/\$500,056 = 1.46$$

Debt-to-equity
Arctic Cat = 0.49
KTM = 1.21
Industry = 0.8

Polaris's 1.46 debt-to-equity ratio is higher than the 0.49 ratio for Arctic Cat and the industry ratio of 0.8. Consistent with our inferences from the debt ratio, Polaris's capital structure has more debt than equity, which increases risk. Recall that debt must be repaid with interest, while equity does not. These debt requirements can be burdensome when the industry and/or the economy experience a downturn. A larger debt-to-equity ratio also implies less opportunity to expand through use of debt financing.

Times Interest Earned The amount of income before deductions for interest expense and income taxes is the amount available to pay interest expense. The following *times interest earned* ratio reflects the creditors' risk of loan repayments with interest (see Chapter 11 for additional explanation).

$$\text{Times interest earned} = \frac{\text{Income before interest expense and income taxes}}{\text{Interest expense}}$$

The larger this ratio, the less risky is the company for creditors. One guideline says that creditors are reasonably safe if the company earns its fixed interest expense two or more times each year. Polaris's times interest earned ratio follows (Appendix A reveals interest expense of $3,987). Polaris's 87.9 result suggests that its creditors have little risk of nonrepayment.

Times interest earned
Arctic Cat = 2.7
KTM = 3.2

$$\frac{\$227,575 + \$3,987 + \$119,051}{\$3,987} = 87.9 \text{ times}$$

■ **Decision** Insight

Bears and Bulls   A *bear market* is a declining market. The phrase comes from bear-skin jobbers who often sold the skins before the bears were caught. The term *bear* was then used to describe investors who sold shares they did not own in anticipation of a price decline. A *bull market* is a rising market. This phrase comes from the once popular sport of bear and bull baiting. The term *bull* came to mean the opposite of *bear*. ■

Profitability

We are especially interested in a company's ability to use its assets efficiently to produce profits (and positive cash flows). *Profitability* refers to a company's ability to generate an adequate return on invested capital. Return is judged by assessing earnings relative to the level and sources of financing. Profitability is also relevant to solvency. This section describes key profitability measures and their importance to financial statement analysis.

Profit Margin   A company's operating efficiency and profitability can be expressed by two components. The first is *profit margin,* which reflects a company's ability to earn net income from sales (Chapter 3 offers additional explanation). It is measured by expressing net income as a percent of sales (*sales* and *revenues* are similar terms). **Polaris**'s profit margin follows.

Profit margin
Arctic Cat = 2.8%
KTM = 3.9%
Industry = 3%

$$\text{Profit margin} = \frac{\text{Net income}}{\text{Net sales}} = \frac{\$227,575}{\$2,656,949} = 8.6\%$$

To evaluate profit margin, we must consider the industry. For instance, an appliance company might require a profit margin between 10% and 15%; whereas a retail supermarket might require a profit margin of 1% or 2%. Both profit margin and *total asset turnover* make up the two basic components of operating efficiency. These ratios reflect on management because managers are ultimately responsible for operating efficiency. The next section explains how we use both measures to analyze return on total assets.

Return on Total Assets   *Return on total assets* is defined as follows.

$$\text{Return on total assets} = \frac{\text{Net income}}{\text{Average total assets}}$$

Polaris's 2011 return on total assets is

Return on total assets
Arctic Cat = 5.0%
KTM = 4.5%
Industry = 4%

$$\frac{\$227,575}{(\$1,061,647 + \$1,228,024)/2} = 19.9\%$$

Polaris's 19.9% return on total assets is higher than that for many businesses and is higher than Arctic Cat's return of 5.0% and the industry's 4% return. We also should evaluate any trend in the rate of return.

Point: Many analysts add back *Interest expense* × (*1 − Tax rate*) to net income in computing return on total assets.

The following equation shows the important relation between profit margin, total asset turnover, and return on total assets.

$$\textbf{Profit margin} \times \textbf{Total asset turnover} = \textbf{Return on total assets}$$

or

$$\frac{\textbf{Net income}}{\textbf{Net sales}} \times \frac{\textbf{Net sales}}{\textbf{Average total assets}} = \frac{\textbf{Net income}}{\textbf{Average total assets}}$$

Both profit margin and total asset turnover contribute to overall operating efficiency, as measured by return on total assets. If we apply this formula to Polaris, we get

$$8.6\% \times 2.32 = 19.9\% \text{ (with rounding)}$$

Arctic Cat: 2.8% × 1.79 = 5.0% (with rounding)

This analysis shows that Polaris's superior return on assets versus that of Arctic Cat is driven mainly by its higher profit margin.

Return on Common Stockholders' Equity Perhaps the most important goal in operating a company is to earn net income for its owner(s). *Return on common stockholders' equity* measures a company's success in reaching this goal and is defined as follows.

$$\textbf{Return on common stockholders' equity} = \frac{\textbf{Net income} - \textbf{Preferred dividends}}{\textbf{Average common stockholders' equity}}$$

Polaris's 2011 return on common stockholders' equity is computed as follows:

$$\frac{\$227{,}575 - \$0}{(\$370{,}991 + \$500{,}056)/2} = 52.3\%$$

Return on common equity
Arctic Cat = 7.4%
KTM = 10.5%
Industry = 6%

The denominator in this computation is the book value of common equity (minority interest, also called noncontrolling interest, is often included in common equity for this ratio). In the numerator, the dividends on cumulative preferred stock are subtracted whether they are declared or are in arrears. If preferred stock is noncumulative, its dividends are subtracted only if declared. Polaris's return on common stockholders' equity (52.3%) is far superior to Arctic Cat's (7.4%) and KTM's (10.5%).

 Decision Insight

Wall Street *Wall Street* is synonymous with financial markets, but its name comes from the street location of the original New York Stock Exchange. The street's name derives from stockades built by early settlers to protect New York from pirate attacks. ■

Market Prospects

Market measures are useful for analyzing corporations with publicly traded stock. These market measures use stock price, which reflects the market's (public's) expectations for the company. This includes expectations of both company return and risk—as the market perceives it.

Price-Earnings Ratio   Computation of the *price-earnings ratio* follows (Chapter 13 provides additional explanation).

$$\text{Price-earnings ratio} = \frac{\text{Market price per common share}}{\text{Earnings per share}}$$

Predicted earnings per share for the next period is often used in the denominator of this computation. Reported earnings per share for the most recent period is also commonly used. In both cases, the ratio is used as an indicator of the future growth and risk of a company's earnings as perceived by the stock's buyers and sellers.

The market price of Polaris's common stock at the start of fiscal year 2012 was $55.98. Using Polaris's $3.31 basic earnings per share, we compute its price-earnings ratio as follows (some analysts compute this ratio using the median of the low and high stock price).

$$\frac{\$55.98}{\$3.31} = 16.9$$

Polaris's price-earnings ratio is less than that for Arctic Cat, but is slightly higher than the norm for the recessionary period 2009–2012.

Dividend Yield   *Dividend yield* is used to compare the dividend-paying performance of different investment alternatives. We compute dividend yield as follows (Chapter 13 offers additional explanation).

$$\text{Dividend yield} = \frac{\text{Annual cash dividends per share}}{\text{Market price per share}}$$

Polaris's dividend yield, based on its fiscal year-end market price per share of $55.98 and its policy of $0.90 cash dividends per share, is computed as follows.

$$\frac{\$0.90}{\$55.98} = 1.6\%$$

Some companies, such as Arctic Cat, do not declare and pay dividends because they wish to reinvest the cash.

Summary of Ratios

Exhibit 17.16 summarizes the major financial statement analysis ratios illustrated in this chapter and throughout the book. This summary includes each ratio's title, its formula, and the purpose for which it is commonly used.

■ Decision Insight ●━━━━━━━━━━━━━

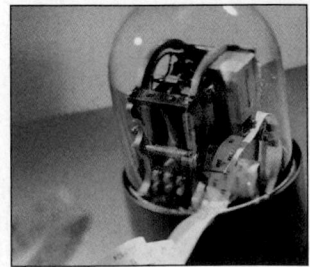

Ticker Prices   *Ticker prices* refer to a band of moving data on a monitor carrying up-to-the-minute stock prices. The phrase comes from *ticker tape*, a 1-inch-wide strip of paper spewing stock prices from a printer that ticked as it ran. Most of today's investors have never seen actual ticker tape, but the phrase survives. ■

EXHIBIT 17.16

Financial Statement Analysis Ratios*

Ratio	Formula	Measure of
Liquidity and Efficiency		
Current ratio	$= \dfrac{\text{Current assets}}{\text{Current liabilities}}$	Short-term debt-paying ability
Acid-test ratio	$= \dfrac{\text{Cash + Short-term investments + Current receivables}}{\text{Current liabilities}}$	Immediate short-term debt-paying ability
Accounts receivable turnover	$= \dfrac{\text{Net sales}}{\text{Average accounts receivable, net}}$	Efficiency of collection
Inventory turnover	$= \dfrac{\text{Cost of goods sold}}{\text{Average inventory}}$	Efficiency of inventory management
Days' sales uncollected	$= \dfrac{\text{Accounts receivable, net}}{\text{Net sales}} \times 365$	Liquidity of receivables
Days' sales in inventory	$= \dfrac{\text{Ending inventory}}{\text{Cost of goods sold}} \times 365$	Liquidity of inventory
Total asset turnover	$= \dfrac{\text{Net sales}}{\text{Average total assets}}$	Efficiency of assets in producing sales
Solvency		
Debt ratio	$= \dfrac{\text{Total liabilities}}{\text{Total assets}}$	Creditor financing and leverage
Equity ratio	$= \dfrac{\text{Total equity}}{\text{Total assets}}$	Owner financing
Debt-to-equity ratio	$= \dfrac{\text{Total liabilities}}{\text{Total equity}}$	Debt versus equity financing
Times interest earned	$= \dfrac{\text{Income before interest expense and income taxes}}{\text{Interest expense}}$	Protection in meeting interest payments
Profitability		
Profit margin ratio	$= \dfrac{\text{Net income}}{\text{Net sales}}$	Net income in each sales dollar
Gross margin ratio	$= \dfrac{\text{Net sales} - \text{Cost of goods sold}}{\text{Net sales}}$	Gross margin in each sales dollar
Return on total assets	$= \dfrac{\text{Net income}}{\text{Average total assets}}$	Overall profitability of assets
Return on common stockholders' equity	$= \dfrac{\text{Net income} - \text{Preferred dividends}}{\text{Average common stockholders' equity}}$	Profitability of owner investment
Book value per common share	$= \dfrac{\text{Shareholders' equity applicable to common shares}}{\text{Number of common shares outstanding}}$	Liquidation at reported amounts
Basic earnings per share	$= \dfrac{\text{Net income} - \text{Preferred dividends}}{\text{Weighted-average common shares outstanding}}$	Net income per common share
Market Prospects		
Price-earnings ratio	$= \dfrac{\text{Market price per common share}}{\text{Earnings per share}}$	Market value relative to earnings
Dividend yield	$= \dfrac{\text{Annual cash dividends per share}}{\text{Market price per share}}$	Cash return per common share

* Additional ratios also examined in previous chapters included credit risk ratio; plant asset useful life; plant asset age; days' cash expense coverage; cash coverage of growth; cash coverage of debt; free cash flow; cash flow on total assets; and payout ratio.

Quick Check   Answers — p. 715

10. Which ratio best reflects a company's ability to meet immediate interest payments? (*a*) Debt ratio. (*b*) Equity ratio. (*c*) Times interest earned.

11. Which ratio best measures a company's success in earning net income for its owner(s)? (*a*) Profit margin. (*b*) Return on common stockholders' equity. (*c*) Price-earnings ratio. (*d*) Dividend yield.

12. If a company has net sales of $8,500,000, net income of $945,000, and total asset turnover of 1.8 times, what is its return on total assets?

GLOBAL VIEW

The analysis and interpretation of financial statements is, of course, impacted by the accounting system in effect. This section discusses similarities and differences for analysis of financial statements when prepared under U.S. GAAP vis-à-vis IFRS.

Horizontal and Vertical Analyses   Horizontal and vertical analyses help eliminate many differences between U.S. GAAP and IFRS when analyzing and interpreting financial statements. Financial numbers are converted to percentages that are, in the best case scenario, consistently applied across and within periods. This enables users to effectively compare companies across reporting regimes. However, when fundamental differences in reporting regimes impact financial statements, such as with certain recognition rule differences, the user must exercise caution when drawing conclusions. Some users will reformulate one set of numbers to be more consistent with the other system to enable comparative analysis. This reformulation process is covered in advanced courses. The important point is that horizontal and vertical analyses help strip away differences between the reporting regimes, but several key differences sometimes remain and require adjustment of the numbers.

Ratio Analysis   Ratio analysis of financial statement numbers has many of the advantages and disadvantages of horizontal and vertical analyses discussed above. Importantly, ratio analysis is useful for business decisions, with some possible changes in interpretation depending on what is and what is not included in accounting measures across U.S. GAAP and IFRS. Still, we must take care in drawing inferences from a comparison of ratios across reporting regimes because what a number measures can differ across regimes. **Piaggio** offers the following example of its own ratio analysis applied to gross margin: "Gross industrial margin, defined as the difference between 'net revenues' and 'cost to sell,' decreased slightly compared to the previous year . . . in relation to net turnover, it was equal to 30.0% (31.1% in the first half of 2010). The decrease as a percentage, due mainly to the different mix of products sold on markets in EMEA and the Americas, and in India and Asia SEA, was within 1.1 percentage points."

■ Decision Insight

Not Created Equal   Financial regulation has several goals. Two of them are to ensure adequate accounting disclosure and to strengthen corporate governance. For disclosure purposes, companies must now provide details of related-party transactions and material off-balance-sheet agreements. This is motivated by several major frauds. For corporate governance, the CEO and CFO must now certify the fairness of financial statements and the effectiveness of internal controls. Yet, concerns remain. A study reports that 23% of management and administrative employees observed activities that posed a conflict of interest in the past year (KPMG 2009). Another 12% witnessed the falsifying or manipulating of accounting information. The bottom line: All financial statements are not of equal quality. ■

Decision Analysis   Analysis Reporting

A1 Summarize and report results of analysis.

Understanding the purpose of financial statement analysis is crucial to the usefulness of any analysis. This understanding leads to efficiency of effort, effectiveness in application, and relevance in focus. The purpose of most financial statement analyses is to reduce uncertainty in business decisions through a rigorous and sound evaluation. A *financial statement analysis report* helps by directly addressing the building blocks of analysis and by identifying weaknesses in inference by requiring explanation: It forces us to organize our reasoning and to verify its flow and logic. A report also serves as a communication link with readers, and the writing process reinforces our judgments and vice versa. Finally, the report helps us (re)evaluate evidence and refine conclusions on key building blocks. A good analysis report usually consists of six sections:

1. **Executive summary**—brief focus on important analysis results and conclusions.
2. **Analysis overview**—background on the company, its industry, and its economic setting.
3. **Evidential matter**—financial statements and information used in the analysis, including ratios, trends, comparisons, statistics, and all analytical measures assembled; often organized under the building blocks of analysis.
4. **Assumptions**—identification of important assumptions regarding a company's industry and economic environment, and other important assumptions for estimates.
5. **Key factors**—list of important favorable and unfavorable factors, both quantitative and qualitative, for company performance; usually organized by areas of analysis.
6. **Inferences**—forecasts, estimates, interpretations, and conclusions drawing on all sections of the report.

We must remember that the user dictates relevance, meaning that the analysis report should include a brief table of contents to help readers focus on those areas most relevant to their decisions. All irrelevant matter must be eliminated. For example, decades-old details of obscure transactions and detailed miscues of the analysis are irrelevant. Ambiguities and qualifications to avoid responsibility or hedging inferences must be eliminated. Finally, writing is important. Mistakes in grammar and errors of fact compromise the report's credibility.

Decision Insight

Short Selling *Short selling* refers to selling stock before you buy it. Here's an example: You borrow 100 shares of Nike stock, sell them at $40 each, and receive money from their sale. You then wait. You hope that Nike's stock price falls to, say, $35 each and you can replace the borrowed stock for less than you sold it for, reaping a profit of $5 each less any transaction costs. ■

DEMONSTRATION PROBLEM

Use the following financial statements of Precision Co. to complete these requirements.

1. Prepare comparative income statements showing the percent increase or decrease for year 2013 in comparison to year 2012.
2. Prepare common-size comparative balance sheets for years 2013 and 2012.
3. Compute the following ratios as of December 31, 2013, or for the year ended December 31, 2013, and identify its building block category for financial statement analysis.
   a. Current ratio
   b. Acid-test ratio
   c. Accounts receivable turnover
   d. Days' sales uncollected
   e. Inventory turnover
   f. Debt ratio
   g. Debt-to-equity ratio
   h. Times interest earned
   i. Profit margin ratio
   j. Total asset turnover
   k. Return on total assets
   l. Return on common stockholders' equity

PRECISION COMPANY
Comparative Income Statements
For Years Ended December 31, 2013 and 2012

	2013	2012
Sales	$2,486,000	$2,075,000
Cost of goods sold	1,523,000	1,222,000
Gross profit	963,000	853,000
Operating expenses		
Advertising expense	145,000	100,000
Sales salaries expense	240,000	280,000
Office salaries expense	165,000	200,000
Insurance expense	100,000	45,000
Supplies expense	26,000	35,000
Depreciation expense	85,000	75,000
Miscellaneous expenses	17,000	15,000
Total operating expenses	778,000	750,000
Operating income	185,000	103,000
Interest expense	44,000	46,000
Income before taxes	141,000	57,000
Income taxes	47,000	19,000
Net income	$ 94,000	$ 38,000
Earnings per share	$ 0.99	$ 0.40

PRECISION COMPANY
Comparative Balance Sheets
December 31, 2013 and 2012

	2013	2012
Assets		
Current assets		
Cash	$ 79,000	$ 42,000
Short-term investments	65,000	96,000
Accounts receivable, net	120,000	100,000
Merchandise inventory	250,000	265,000
Total current assets	514,000	503,000
Plant assets		
Store equipment, net	400,000	350,000
Office equipment, net	45,000	50,000
Buildings, net	625,000	675,000
Land	100,000	100,000
Total plant assets	1,170,000	1,175,000
Total assets	$1,684,000	$1,678,000
Liabilities		
Current liabilities		
Accounts payable	$ 164,000	$ 190,000
Short-term notes payable	75,000	90,000
Taxes payable	26,000	12,000
Total current liabilities	265,000	292,000
Long-term liabilities		
Notes payable (secured by mortgage on buildings)	400,000	420,000
Total liabilities	665,000	712,000
Stockholders' Equity		
Common stock, $5 par value	475,000	475,000
Retained earnings	544,000	491,000
Total stockholders' equity	1,019,000	966,000
Total liabilities and equity	$1,684,000	$1,678,000

PLANNING THE SOLUTION

- Set up a four-column income statement; enter the 2013 and 2012 amounts in the first two columns and then enter the dollar change in the third column and the percent change from 2012 in the fourth column.
- Set up a four-column balance sheet; enter the 2013 and 2012 year-end amounts in the first two columns and then compute and enter the amount of each item as a percent of total assets.
- Compute the required ratios using the data provided. Use the average of beginning and ending amounts when appropriate (see Exhibit 17.16 for definitions).

SOLUTION TO DEMONSTRATION PROBLEM

1.

PRECISION COMPANY
Comparative Income Statements
For Years Ended December 31, 2013 and 2012

			Increase (Decrease) in 2013	
	2013	2012	Amount	Percent
Sales	$2,486,000	$2,075,000	$411,000	19.8%
Cost of goods sold	1,523,000	1,222,000	301,000	24.6
Gross profit	963,000	853,000	110,000	12.9

[continued on next page]

[continued from previous page]

Operating expenses				
Advertising expense	145,000	100,000	**45,000**	**45.0**
Sales salaries expense	240,000	280,000	**(40,000)**	**(14.3)**
Office salaries expense	165,000	200,000	**(35,000)**	**(17.5)**
Insurance expense	100,000	45,000	**55,000**	**122.2**
Supplies expense	26,000	35,000	**(9,000)**	**(25.7)**
Depreciation expense	85,000	75,000	**10,000**	**13.3**
Miscellaneous expenses	17,000	15,000	**2,000**	**13.3**
Total operating expenses	778,000	750,000	**28,000**	**3.7**
Operating income	185,000	103,000	**82,000**	**79.6**
Interest expense	44,000	46,000	**(2,000)**	**(4.3)**
Income before taxes	141,000	57,000	**84,000**	**147.4**
Income taxes	47,000	19,000	**28,000**	**147.4**
Net income	$ 94,000	$ 38,000	**$ 56,000**	**147.4**
Earnings per share	$ 0.99	$ 0.40	**$ 0.59**	**147.5**

2.

PRECISION COMPANY
Common-Size Comparative Balance Sheets
December 31, 2013 and 2012

	December 31		Common-Size Percents	
	2013	**2012**	**2013***	**2012***
Assets				
Current assets				
Cash	$ 79,000	$ 42,000	**4.7%**	**2.5%**
Short-term investments	65,000	96,000	**3.9**	**5.7**
Accounts receivable, net	120,000	100,000	**7.1**	**6.0**
Merchandise inventory	250,000	265,000	**14.8**	**15.8**
Total current assets	514,000	503,000	**30.5**	**30.0**
Plant assets				
Store equipment, net	400,000	350,000	**23.8**	**20.9**
Office equipment, net	45,000	50,000	**2.7**	**3.0**
Buildings, net	625,000	675,000	**37.1**	**40.2**
Land	100,000	100,000	**5.9**	**6.0**
Total plant assets	1,170,000	1,175,000	**69.5**	**70.0**
Total assets	$1,684,000	$1,678,000	**100.0**	**100.0**
Liabilities				
Current liabilities				
Accounts payable	$ 164,000	$ 190,000	**9.7%**	**11.3%**
Short-term notes payable	75,000	90,000	**4.5**	**5.4**
Taxes payable	26,000	12,000	**1.5**	**0.7**
Total current liabilities	265,000	292,000	**15.7**	**17.4**
Long-term liabilities				
Notes payable (secured by mortgage on buildings)	400,000	420,000	**23.8**	**25.0**
Total liabilities	665,000	712,000	**39.5**	**42.4**
Stockholders' equity				
Common stock, $5 par value	475,000	475,000	**28.2**	**28.3**
Retained earnings	544,000	491,000	**32.3**	**29.3**
Total stockholders' equity	1,019,000	966,000	**60.5**	**57.6**
Total liabilities and equity	$1,684,000	$1,678,000	**100.0**	**100.0**

* Columns do not always exactly add to 100 due to rounding.

3. Ratios for 2013:

a. Current ratio: $514,000/$265,000 = 1.9:1 (liquidity and efficiency)

b. Acid-test ratio: ($79,000 + $65,000 + $120,000)/$265,000 = 1.0:1 (liquidity and efficiency)

c. Average receivables: ($120,000 + $100,000)/2 = $110,000
Accounts receivable turnover: $2,486,000/$110,000 = 22.6 times (liquidity and efficiency)

d. Days' sales uncollected: ($120,000/$2,486,000) × 365 = 17.6 days (liquidity and efficiency)

e. Average inventory: ($250,000 + $265,000)/2 = $257,500
Inventory turnover: $1,523,000/$257,500 = 5.9 times (liquidity and efficiency)

f. Debt ratio: $665,000/$1,684,000 = 39.5% (solvency)

g. Debt-to-equity ratio: $665,000/$1,019,000 = 0.65 (solvency)

h. Times interest earned: $185,000/$44,000 = 4.2 times (solvency)

i. Profit margin ratio: $94,000/$2,486,000 = 3.8% (profitability)

j. Average total assets: ($1,684,000 + $1,678,000)/2 = $1,681,000
Total asset turnover: $2,486,000/$1,681,000 = 1.48 times (liquidity and efficiency)

k. Return on total assets: $94,000/$1,681,000 = 5.6% or 3.8% × 1.48 = 5.6% (profitability)

l. Average total common equity: ($1,019,000 + $966,000)/2 = $992,500
Return on common stockholders' equity: $94,000/$992,500 = 9.5% (profitability)

APPENDIX

17A

Sustainable Income

A2	Explain the form and assess the content of a complete income statement.

When a company's revenue and expense transactions are from normal, continuing operations, a simple income statement is usually adequate. When a company's activities include income-related events not part of its normal, continuing operations, it must disclose information to help users understand these events and predict future performance. To meet these objectives, companies separate the income statement into continuing operations, discontinued segments, extraordinary items, comprehensive income, and earnings per share. For illustration, Exhibit 17A.1 shows such an income statement for ComUS. These separate distinctions help us measure *sustainable income,* which is the income level most likely to continue into the future. Sustainable income is commonly used in PE ratios and other market-based measures of performance.

Continuing Operations   The first major section (①) shows the revenues, expenses, and income from continuing operations. Users especially rely on this information to predict future operations. Many users view this section as the most important. Earlier chapters explained the items comprising income from continuing operations.

Discontinued Segments   A **business segment** is a part of a company's operations that serves a particular line of business or class of customers. A segment has assets, liabilities, and financial results of operations that can be distinguished from those of other parts of the company. A company's gain or loss from selling or closing down a segment is separately reported. Section ② of Exhibit 17A.1 reports both (1) income from operating the discontinued segment for the current period prior to its disposal and (2) the loss from disposing of the segment's net assets. The income tax effects of each are reported separately from the income taxes expense in section ①.

Extraordinary Items   Section ③ reports **extraordinary gains and losses,** which are those that are *both unusual* and *infrequent.* An **unusual gain or loss** is abnormal or otherwise unrelated to the company's regular activities and environment. An **infrequent gain or loss** is not expected to recur given the company's operating environment. Reporting extraordinary items in a separate category helps users predict future performance, absent the effects of extraordinary items. Items usually considered extraordinary include (1) expropriation (taking away) of property by a foreign government, (2) condemning of property by a domestic government body, (3) prohibition against using an asset by a newly enacted law, and (4) losses and gains from an unusual and infrequent calamity ("act of God"). Items *not* considered extraordinary include (1) write-downs of inventories and write-offs of receivables, (2) gains and losses from disposing of segments, and (3) financial effects of labor strikes.

EXHIBIT 17A.1

Income Statement (all-inclusive) for a Corporation

ComUS
Income Statement
For Year Ended December 31, 2013

Net sales		$8,478,000
Operating expenses		
Cost of goods sold	$5,950,000	
Depreciation expense	35,000	
Other selling, general, and administrative expenses	515,000	
Interest expense	20,000	
Total operating expenses ①		(6,520,000)
Other gains (losses)		
Loss on plant relocation		(45,000)
Gain on sale of surplus land		72,000
Income from continuing operations before taxes		1,985,000
Income taxes expense		(595,500)
Income from continuing operations		1,389,500
Discontinued segment		
Income from operating Division A (net of $180,000 taxes) ②	420,000	
Loss on disposal of Division A (net of $66,000 tax benefit)	(154,000)	266,000
Income before extraordinary items		1,655,500
Extraordinary items		
Gain on land expropriated by state (net of $85,200 taxes) ③	198,800	
Loss from earthquake damage (net of $270,000 tax benefit)	(630,000)	(431,200)
Net income		$1,224,300
Earnings per common share (200,000 outstanding shares)		
Income from continuing operations		$ 6.95
Discontinued operations		1.33
Income before extraordinary items ④		8.28
Extraordinary items		(2.16)
Net income (basic earnings per share)		$ 6.12

Gains and losses that are neither unusual nor infrequent are reported as part of continuing operations. Gains and losses that are *either* unusual *or* infrequent, but *not* both, are reported as part of continuing operations *but* after the normal revenues and expenses.

Decision Maker

Small Business Owner You own an orange grove near Jacksonville, Florida. A bad frost destroys about one-half of your oranges. You are currently preparing an income statement for a bank loan. Can you claim the loss of oranges as extraordinary? ■ [Answer—p. 715]

Earnings per Share The final section ④ of the income statement in Exhibit 17A.1 reports earnings per share for each of the three subcategories of income (continuing operations, discontinued segments, and extraordinary items) when they exist. Earnings per share is discussed in Chapter 13.

Changes in Accounting Principles The *consistency concept* directs a company to apply the same accounting principles across periods. Yet a company can change from one acceptable accounting principle (such as FIFO, LIFO, or weighted-average) to another as long as the change improves the usefulness of information in its financial statements. A footnote would describe the accounting change and why it is an improvement.

Changes in accounting principles require retrospective application to prior periods' financial statements. *Retrospective application* involves applying a different accounting principle to prior periods as if that principle had always been used. Retrospective application enhances the consistency of financial information between periods, which improves the usefulness of information, especially with comparative

Point: Changes in principles are sometimes required when new accounting standards are issued.

analyses. (Prior to 2005, the cumulative effect of changes in accounting principles was recognized in net income in the period of the change.) Accounting standards also require that *a change in depreciation, amortization, or depletion method for long-term operating assets is accounted for as a change in accounting estimate*—that is, prospectively over current and future periods. This reflects the notion that an entity should change its depreciation, amortization, or depletion method only with changes in estimated asset benefits, the pattern of benefit usage, or information about those benefits.

Quick Check

Answers — p. 715

13. Which of the following is an extraordinary item? (*a*) a settlement paid to a customer injured while using the company's product, (*b*) a loss to a plant from damages caused by a meteorite, or (*c*) a loss from selling old equipment.

14. Identify the four major sections of an income statement that are potentially reportable.

15. A company using FIFO for the past 15 years decides to switch to LIFO. The effect of this event on prior years' net income is (*a*) reported as if the new method had always been used; (*b*) ignored because it is a change in an accounting estimate; or (*c*) reported on the current year income statement.

Summary

C1 **Explain the purpose and identify the building blocks of analysis.** The purpose of financial statement analysis is to help users make better business decisions. Internal users want information to improve company efficiency and effectiveness in providing products and services. External users want information to make better and more informed decisions in pursuing their goals. The common goals of all users are to evaluate a company's (1) past and current performance, (2) current financial position, and (3) future performance and risk. Financial statement analysis focuses on four "building blocks" of analysis: (1) liquidity and efficiency—ability to meet short-term obligations and efficiently generate revenues; (2) solvency—ability to generate future revenues and meet long-term obligations; (3) profitability—ability to provide financial rewards sufficient to attract and retain financing; and (4) market prospects—ability to generate positive market expectations.

C2 **Describe standards for comparisons in analysis.** Standards for comparisons include (1) intracompany—prior performance and relations between financial items for the company under analysis; (2) competitor—one or more direct competitors of the company; (3) industry—industry statistics; and (4) guidelines (rules of thumb)—general standards developed from past experiences and personal judgments.

A1 **Summarize and report results of analysis.** A financial statement analysis report is often organized around the building blocks of analysis. A good report separates interpretations and conclusions of analysis from the information underlying them. An analysis report often consists of six sections: (1) executive summary, (2) analysis overview, (3) evidential matter, (4) assumptions, (5) key factors, and (6) inferences.

A2 **Explain the form and assess the content of a complete income statement.** An income statement has four *potential* sections: (1) continuing operations, (2) discontinued segments, (3) extraordinary items, and (4) earnings per share.

P1 **Explain and apply methods of horizontal analysis.** Horizontal analysis is a tool to evaluate changes in data across time. Two important tools of horizontal analysis are comparative statements and trend analysis. Comparative statements show amounts for two or more successive periods, often with changes disclosed in both absolute and percent terms. Trend analysis is used to reveal important changes occurring from one period to the next.

P2 **Describe and apply methods of vertical analysis.** Vertical analysis is a tool to evaluate each financial statement item or group of items in terms of a base amount. Two tools of vertical analysis are common-size statements and graphical analyses. Each item in common-size statements is expressed as a percent of a base amount. For the balance sheet, the base amount is usually total assets, and for the income statement, it is usually sales.

P3 **Define and apply ratio analysis.** Ratio analysis provides clues to and symptoms of underlying conditions. Ratios, properly interpreted, identify areas requiring further investigation. A ratio expresses a mathematical relation between two quantities such as a percent, rate, or proportion. Ratios can be organized into the building blocks of analysis: (1) liquidity and efficiency, (2) solvency, (3) profitability, and (4) market prospects.

Guidance Answers to Decision Maker

Auditor The *joint relation* referred to is the combined increase in sales and the decrease in expenses yielding more than a 5% increase in income. Both *individual* accounts (sales and expenses) yield percent changes within the ±5% acceptable range. However, a joint analysis suggests a different picture. For example, consider a joint analysis using the profit margin ratio. The client's profit margin is 11.46% ($206,000 − $182,400/$206,000) for the current year compared with 5.0% ($200,000 − $190,000/$200,000) for the prior year—yielding a 129% increase in profit margin! This is what concerns the partner, and it suggests expanding audit tests to verify or refute the client's figures.

Banker   Your decision on the loan application is positive for at least two reasons. First, the current ratio suggests a strong ability to meet short-term obligations. Second, current assets of $160,000 and a current ratio of 4:1 imply current liabilities of $40,000 (one-fourth of current assets) and a working capital excess of $120,000. This working capital excess is 60% of the loan amount. However, if the application is for a 10-year loan, our decision is less optimistic. The

current ratio and working capital suggest a good safety margin, but indications of inefficiency in operations exist. In particular, a 4:1 current ratio is more than double its key competitors' ratio. This is characteristic of inefficient asset use.

Small Business Owner   The frost loss is probably not extraordinary. Jacksonville experiences enough recurring frost damage to make it difficult to argue this event is both unusual and infrequent. Still, you want to highlight the frost loss and hope the bank views this uncommon event separately from continuing operations.

Guidance Answers to Quick Checks

1. General-purpose financial statements are intended for a variety of users interested in a company's financial condition and performance—users without the power to require specialized financial reports to meet their specific needs.

2. General-purpose financial statements include the income statement, balance sheet, statement of stockholders' (owners') equity, and statement of cash flows plus the notes related to these statements.

3. *a*

4. Data from one or more direct competitors are usually preferred for comparative purposes.

5. *d*

6. Percents on comparative income statements show the increase or decrease in each item from one period to the next. On common-size comparative income statements, each item is shown as a percent of net sales for that period.

7. *c*

8. (*a*) ($820,000 + $240,000 + $470,000)/
   ($350,000 + $180,000) = 2.9 to 1.

(*b*) ($820,000 + $240,000)/($350,000 + $180,000) = 2:1.

9. (*a*) $2,500,000/[($290,000 + $240,000)/2] = 9.43 times.
   (*b*) ($290,000/$2,500,000) × 365 = 42 days.
   (*c*) $750,000/[($530,000 + $470,000)/2] = 1.5 times.
   (*d*) ($530,000/$750,000) × 365 = 258 days.

10. *c*

11. *b*

12. $\text{Profit margin} \times \dfrac{\text{Total asset}}{\text{turnover}} = \dfrac{\text{Return on}}{\text{total assets}}$

   $\dfrac{\$945,000}{\$8,500,000} \times 1.8 = 20\%$

13. (*b*)

14. The four (potentially reportable) major sections are income from continuing operations, discontinued segments, extraordinary items, and earnings per share.

15. (*a*); known as retrospective application.

Key Terms

Multiple Choice Quiz   Answers on p. 731   mhhe.com/wildFAP21e

Additional Quiz Questions are available at the book's Website.

1. A company's sales in 2012 were $300,000 and in 2013 were $351,000. Using 2012 as the base year, the sales trend percent for 2013 is:
   a. 17%
   b. 85%
   c. 100%
   d. 117%
   e. 48%

Use the following information for questions 2 through 5.

GALLOWAY COMPANY
Balance Sheet
December 31, 2013

Assets

Cash	$ 86,000
Accounts receivable	76,000
Merchandise inventory	122,000
Prepaid insurance	12,000
Long-term investments	98,000
Plant assets, net	436,000
Total assets	$830,000

Liabilities and Equity

Current liabilities	$124,000
Long-term liabilities	90,000
Common stock	300,000
Retained earnings	316,000
Total liabilities and equity	$830,000

2. What is Galloway Company's current ratio?
   a. 0.69
   b. 1.31
   c. 3.88
   d. 6.69
   e. 2.39

3. What is Galloway Company's acid-test ratio?
   a. 2.39
   b. 0.69
   c. 1.31
   d. 6.69
   e. 3.88

4. What is Galloway Company's debt ratio?
   a. 25.78%
   b. 100.00%
   c. 74.22%
   d. 137.78%
   e. 34.74%

5. What is Galloway Company's equity ratio?
   a. 25.78%
   b. 100.00%
   c. 34.74%
   d. 74.22%
   e. 137.78%

A   *Superscript letter A denotes assignments based on Appendix 17A.*

🔲 Icon denotes assignments that involve decision making.

Discussion Questions

1. Explain the difference between financial reporting and financial statements.

2. What is the difference between comparative financial statements and common-size comparative statements?

3. Which items are usually assigned a 100% value on (*a*) a common-size balance sheet and (*b*) a common-size income statement?

4. 🔲 What three factors would influence your evaluation as to whether a company's current ratio is good or bad?

5. 🔲 Suggest several reasons why a 2:1 current ratio might not be adequate for a particular company.

6. 🔲 Why is working capital given special attention in the process of analyzing balance sheets?

7. 🔲 What does the number of days' sales uncollected indicate?

8. 🔲 What does a relatively high accounts receivable turnover indicate about a company's short-term liquidity?

9. 🔲 Why is a company's capital structure, as measured by debt and equity ratios, important to financial statement analysts?

10. 🔲 How does inventory turnover provide information about a company's short-term liquidity?

11. 🔲 What ratios would you compute to evaluate management performance?

12. 🔲 Why would a company's return on total assets be different from its return on common stockholders' equity?

13. Where on the income statement does a company report an unusual gain not expected to occur more often than once every two years or so?

14. Refer to **Polaris**' financial statements in Appendix A. Compute its profit margin for the years ended December 31, 2011, and December 31, 2010.   **Polaris**

15. Refer to **Arctic Cat**'s financial statements in Appendix A to compute its equity ratio as of March 31, 2011, and March 31, 2010.   **Arctic Cat**

16. Refer to **Piaggio**'s financial statements in Appendix A. Compute its debt ratio as of December 31, 2011, and December 31, 2010.   **PIAGGIO**

17. Use **KTM**'s financial statements in Appendix A to compute its return on total assets for fiscal year ended December 31, 2011.   **KTM**

connect

Which of the following items (*a*) through (*i*) are part of financial reporting but are *not* included as part of general-purpose financial statements? (*a*) balance sheet, (*b*) financial statement notes, (*c*) statement of shareholders' equity, (*d*) prospectus, (*e*) stock price information and analysis, (*f*) statement of cash flows, (*g*) management discussion and analysis of financial performance, (*h*) income statement, (*i*) company news releases.

QUICK STUDY

QS 17-1
Financial reporting C1

Use the following information for Tide Corporation to determine the 2012 and 2013 trend percents for net sales using 2012 as the base year.

($ thousands)	2013	2012
Net sales	$801,810	$453,000
Cost of goods sold	392,887	134,088

QS 17-2
Trend percents

P1

Refer to the information in QS 17-2. Use that information for Tide Corporation to determine the 2012 and 2013 common-size percents for cost of goods sold using net sales as the base.

QS 17-3
Common-size analysis P2

Compute the annual dollar changes and percent changes for each of the following accounts.

	2013	2012
Short-term investments	$374,634	$234,000
Accounts receivable	97,364	101,000
Notes payable	0	88,000

QS 17-4
Horizontal analysis

P1

What are four possible standards of comparison used to analyze financial statement ratios? Which of these is generally considered to be the most useful? Which one is least likely to provide a good basis for comparison?

QS 17-5
Standard of comparison C2

For each ratio listed, identify whether the change in ratio value from 2012 to 2013 is usually regarded as favorable or unfavorable.

QS 17-6
Ratio interpretation

P3

Ratio	2013	2012	Ratio	2013	2012
1. Profit margin	9%	8%	5. Accounts receivable turnover	5.5	6.7
2. Debt ratio	47%	42%	6. Basic earnings per share	$1.25	$1.10
3. Gross margin	34%	46%	7. Inventory turnover	3.6	3.4
4. Acid-test ratio	1.00	1.15	8. Dividend yield	2.0%	1.2%

The following information is available for Morgan Company and Parker Company, similar firms operating in the same industry. Write a half-page report comparing Morgan and Parker using the available information. Your discussion should include their ability to meet current obligations and to use current assets efficiently.

QS 17-7
Analysis of short-term financial condition

A1

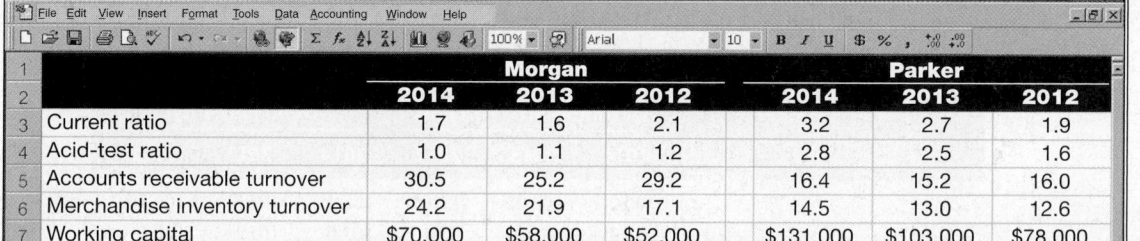

	Morgan			Parker		
	2014	2013	2012	2014	2013	2012
Current ratio	1.7	1.6	2.1	3.2	2.7	1.9
Acid-test ratio	1.0	1.1	1.2	2.8	2.5	1.6
Accounts receivable turnover	30.5	25.2	29.2	16.4	15.2	16.0
Merchandise inventory turnover	24.2	21.9	17.1	14.5	13.0	12.6
Working capital	$70,000	$58,000	$52,000	$131,000	$103,000	$78,000

Team Project: Assume that the two companies apply for a one-year loan from the team. Identify additional information the companies must provide before the team can make a loan decision.

QS 17-8ᴬ
Error adjustments
A2

A review of the notes payable files discovers that three years ago the company reported the entire amount of a payment (principal and interest) on an installment note payable as interest expense. This mistake had a material effect on the amount of income in that year. How should the correction be reported in the current year financial statements?

QS 17-9
International ratio analysis
C2

Answer each of the following related to international accounting and analysis.

a. Identify a limitation to using ratio analysis when examining companies reporting under different accounting systems such as IFRS versus U.S. GAAP.

b. Identify an advantage to using horizontal and vertical analyses when examining companies reporting under different currencies.

EXERCISES

Exercise 17-1
Building blocks of analysis
C1

Match the ratio to the building block of financial statement analysis to which it best relates.

A. Liquidity and efficiency   **C.** Profitability
B. Solvency   **D.** Market prospects

1. _____ Equity ratio   **6.** _____ Accounts receivable turnover
2. _____ Return on total assets   **7.** _____ Debt-to-equity
3. _____ Dividend yield   **8.** _____ Times interest earned
4. _____ Book value per common share **9.** _____ Gross margin ratio
5. _____ Days' sales in inventory   **10.** _____ Acid-test ratio

---

Exercise 17-2
Identifying financial ratios
C2

1. Which two ratios are key components in measuring a company's operating efficiency? Which ratio summarizes these two components?

2. What measure reflects the difference between current assets and current liabilities?

3. Which two short-term liquidity ratios measure how frequently a company collects its accounts?

Exercise 17-3
Computation and analysis of trend percents
P1

Compute trend percents for the following accounts, using 2011 as the base year (round the percents to whole numbers). State whether the situation as revealed by the trends appears to be favorable or unfavorable for each account.

	2015	2014	2013	2012	2011
Sales	$282,880	$270,800	$252,600	$234,560	$150,000
Cost of goods sold	128,200	122,080	115,280	106,440	67,000
Accounts receivable	18,100	17,300	16,400	15,200	9,000

Exercise 17-4
Determination of income effects from common-size and trend percents
P1 P2

Common-size and trend percents for Rustynail Company's sales, cost of goods sold, and expenses follow. Determine whether net income increased, decreased, or remained unchanged in this three-year period.

	Common-Size Percents			Trend Percents		
	2014	2013	2012	2014	2013	2012
Sales	100.0%	100.0%	100.0%	105.4%	104.2%	100.0%
Cost of goods sold	63.4	61.9	59.1	103.0	101.1	100.0
Total expenses	15.3	14.8	15.1	95.0	91.0	100.0

Express the following comparative income statements in common-size percents and assess whether or not this company's situation has improved in the most recent year (round the percents to one decimal).

Exercise 17-5
Common-size percent
computation and interpretation

P2

GOMEZ CORPORATION		
Comparative Income Statements		
For Years Ended December 31, 2013 and 2012		
	2013	**2012**
Sales	$740,000	$625,000
Cost of goods sold	560,300	290,800
Gross profit	179,700	334,200
Operating expenses	128,200	218,500
Net income	$ 51,500	$115,700

Roak Company and Clay Company are similar firms that operate in the same industry. Clay began operations in 2013 and Roak in 2010. In 2015, both companies pay 7% interest on their debt to creditors. The following additional information is available.

Exercise 17-6
Analysis of efficiency and
financial leverage

A1

	Roak Company			Clay Company		
	2015	**2014**	**2013**	**2015**	**2014**	**2013**
Total asset turnover	3.1	2.8	3.0	1.7	1.5	1.1
Return on total assets	9.0%	9.6%	8.8%	5.9%	5.6%	5.3%
Profit margin ratio	2.4%	2.5%	2.3%	2.8%	3.0%	2.9%
Sales	$410,000	$380,000	$396,000	$210,000	$170,000	$110,000

Write a half-page report comparing Roak and Clay using the available information. Your analysis should include their ability to use assets efficiently to produce profits. Also comment on their success in employing financial leverage in 2015.

Simon Company's year-end balance sheets follow. Express the balance sheets in common-size percents. Round amounts to the nearest one-tenth of a percent. Analyze and comment on the results.

Exercise 17-7
Common-size percents

P2

At December 31	2014	2013	2012
Assets			
Cash	$ 31,800	$ 35,625	$ 37,800
Accounts receivable, net	89,500	62,500	50,200
Merchandise inventory	112,500	82,500	54,000
Prepaid expenses	10,700	9,375	5,000
Plant assets, net	278,500	255,000	230,500
Total assets	$523,000	$445,000	$377,500
Liabilities and Equity			
Accounts payable	$129,900	$ 75,250	$ 51,250
Long-term notes payable secured by			
mortgages on plant assets	98,500	101,500	83,500
Common stock, $10 par value	163,500	163,500	163,500
Retained earnings	131,100	104,750	79,250
Total liabilities and equity	$523,000	$445,000	$377,500

Refer to Simon Company's balance sheets in Exercise 17-7. Analyze its year-end short-term liquidity position at the end of 2014, 2013, and 2012 by computing (1) the current ratio and (2) the acid-test ratio. Comment on the ratio results. (Round ratio amounts to two decimals.)

Exercise 17-8
Liquidity analysis

P3

Exercise 17-9
Liquidity analysis and
interpretation
P3

Refer to the Simon Company information in Exercise 17-7. The company's income statements for the years ended December 31, 2014 and 2013, follow. Assume that all sales are on credit and then compute: (1) days' sales uncollected, (2) accounts receivable turnover, (3) inventory turnover, and (4) days' sales in inventory. Comment on the changes in the ratios from 2013 to 2014. (Round amounts to one decimal.)

For Year Ended December 31	2014		2013	
Sales		$673,500		$532,000
Cost of goods sold	$411,225		$345,500	
Other operating expenses	209,550		134,980	
Interest expense	12,100		13,300	
Income taxes	9,525		8,845	
Total costs and expenses		642,400		502,625
Net income		$ 31,100		$ 29,375
Earnings per share		$ 1.90		$ 1.80

Exercise 17-10
Risk and capital structure
analysis P3

Refer to the Simon Company information in Exercises 17-7 and 17-9. Compare the company's long-term risk and capital structure positions at the end of 2014 and 2013 by computing these ratios: (1) debt and equity ratios—percent rounded to one decimal, (2) debt-to-equity ratio—rounded to two decimals, and (3) times interest earned—rounded to one decimal. Comment on these ratio results.

Exercise 17-11
Efficiency and
profitability analysis P3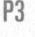

Refer to Simon Company's financial information in Exercises 17-7 and 17-9. Evaluate the company's efficiency and profitability by computing the following for 2014 and 2013: (1) profit margin ratio—percent rounded to one decimal, (2) total asset turnover—rounded to one decimal, and (3) return on total assets—percent rounded to one decimal. Comment on these ratio results.

Exercise 17-12
Profitability analysis
P3

Refer to Simon Company's financial information in Exercises 17-7 and 17-9. Additional information about the company follows. To help evaluate the company's profitability, compute and interpret the following ratios for 2014 and 2013: (1) return on common stockholders' equity—percent rounded to one decimal, (2) price-earnings ratio on December 31—rounded to one decimal, and (3) dividend yield—percent rounded to one decimal.

Common stock market price, December 31, 2014	$30.00
Common stock market price, December 31, 2013	28.00
Annual cash dividends per share in 2014	0.29
Annual cash dividends per share in 2013	0.24

Exercise 17-13^A
Income statement categories
A2

In 2013, Randa Merchandising, Inc., sold its interest in a chain of wholesale outlets, taking the company completely out of the wholesaling business. The company still operates its retail outlets. A listing of the major sections of an income statement follows:

A. Income (loss) from continuing operations

B. Income (loss) from operating, or gain (loss) from disposing, a discontinued segment

C. Extraordinary gain (loss)

Indicate where each of the following income-related items for this company appears on its 2013 income statement by writing the letter of the appropriate section in the blank beside each item.

Section	Item	Debit	Credit
_____	1. Net sales		$2,900,000
_____	2. Gain on state's condemnation of company property (net of tax)		230,000
_____	3. Cost of goods sold	$1,480,000	
_____	4. Income taxes expense	217,000	
_____	5. Depreciation expense	232,500	
_____	6. Gain on sale of wholesale business segment (net of tax)		775,000
_____	7. Loss from operating wholesale business segment (net of tax)	444,000	
_____	8. Salaries expense	640,000	

Use the financial data for Randa Merchandising, Inc., in Exercise 17-13 to prepare its income statement for calendar year 2013. (Ignore the earnings per share section.)

Exercise 17-14^
Income statement presentation
A2

Nintendo Company, Ltd., reports the following financial information as of, or for the year ended, March 31, 2011. Nintendo reports its financial statements in both Japanese yen and U.S. dollars as shown (amounts in millions).

Exercise 17-15
Ratio analysis under different currencies
P3

Current assets	¥1,468,706	$17,695,254
Total assets	1,634,297	19,690,330
Current liabilities	333,301	4,015,683
Net sales	1,014,345	12,221,031
Net income	77,621	935,200

1. Compute Nintendo's current ratio, net profit margin, and sales-to-total-assets using the financial information reported in (a) yen and (b) dollars. Round amounts to two decimals.

2. What can we conclude from a review of the results for part 1?

connect

Selected comparative financial statements of Korbin Company follow.

PROBLEM SET A

Problem 17-1A
Ratios, common-size statements, and trend percents

P1 P2 P3

mhhe.com/wildFAP21e

KORBIN COMPANY			
Comparative Income Statements			
For Years Ended December 31, 2014, 2013, and 2012			
	2014	**2013**	**2012**
Sales	$555,000	$340,000	$278,000
Cost of goods sold	283,500	212,500	153,900
Gross profit	271,500	127,500	124,100
Selling expenses	102,900	46,920	50,800
Administrative expenses	50,668	29,920	22,800
Total expenses	153,568	76,840	73,600
Income before taxes	117,932	50,660	50,500
Income taxes	40,800	10,370	15,670
Net income	$ 77,132	$ 40,290	$ 34,830

KORBIN COMPANY			
Comparative Balance Sheets			
December 31, 2014, 2013, and 2012			
	2014	**2013**	**2012**
Assets			
Current assets	$ 52,390	$ 37,924	$ 51,748
Long-term investments	0	500	3,950
Plant assets, net	100,000	96,000	60,000
Total assets	$152,390	$134,424	$115,698
Liabilities and Equity			
Current liabilities	$ 22,800	$ 19,960	$ 20,300
Common stock	72,000	72,000	60,000
Other paid-in capital	9,000	9,000	6,000
Retained earnings	48,590	33,464	29,398
Total liabilities and equity	$152,390	$134,424	$115,698

Required

1. Compute each year's current ratio. (Round ratio amounts to one decimal.)

2. Express the income statement data in common-size percents. (Round percents to two decimals.)

3. Express the balance sheet data in trend percents with 2012 as the base year. (Round percents to two decimals.)

Analysis Component

4. Comment on any significant relations revealed by the ratios and percents computed.

Problem 17-2A
Calculation and analysis of trend percents

A1 P1

Selected comparative financial statements of Haroun Company follow.

HAROUN COMPANY Comparative Income Statements For Years Ended December 31, 2014–2008							
($ thousands)	2014	2013	2012	2011	2010	2009	2008
Sales	$1,694	$1,496	$1,370	$1,264	$1,186	$1,110	$928
Cost of goods sold	1,246	1,032	902	802	752	710	586
Gross profit	448	464	468	462	434	400	342
Operating expenses	330	256	234	170	146	144	118
Net income	$ 118	$ 208	$ 234	$ 292	$ 288	$ 256	$224

HAROUN COMPANY Comparative Balance Sheets December 31, 2014–2008							
($ thousands)	2014	2013	2012	2011	2010	2009	2008
Assets							
Cash	$ 58	$ 78	$ 82	$ 84	$ 88	$ 86	$ 89
Accounts receivable, net	490	514	466	360	318	302	216
Merchandise inventory	1,838	1,364	1,204	1,032	936	810	615
Other current assets	36	32	14	34	28	28	9
Long-term investments	0	0	0	146	146	146	146
Plant assets, net	2,020	2,014	1,752	944	978	860	725
Total assets	$4,442	$4,002	$3,518	$2,600	$2,494	$2,232	$1,800
Liabilities and Equity							
Current liabilities	$1,220	$1,042	$ 718	$ 614	$ 546	$ 522	$ 282
Long-term liabilities	1,294	1,140	1,112	570	580	620	400
Common stock	1,000	1,000	1,000	850	850	650	650
Other paid-in capital	250	250	250	170	170	150	150
Retained earnings	678	570	438	396	348	290	318
Total liabilities and equity	$4,442	$4,002	$3,518	$2,600	$2,494	$2,232	$1,800

Required

1. Compute trend percents for all components of both statements using 2008 as the base year. (Round percents to one decimal.)

Analysis Component

2. Analyze and comment on the financial statements and trend percents from part 1.

Problem 17-3A
Transactions, working capital, and liquidity ratios

P3

mhhe.com/wildFAP21e

Plum Corporation began the month of May with $700,000 of current assets, a current ratio of 2.50:1, and an acid-test ratio of 1.10:1. During the month, it completed the following transactions (the company uses a perpetual inventory system).

May 2 Purchased $50,000 of merchandise inventory on credit.
   8 Sold merchandise inventory that cost $55,000 for $110,000 cash.
   10 Collected $20,000 cash on an account receivable.
   15 Paid $22,000 cash to settle an account payable.

17   Wrote off a $5,000 bad debt against the Allowance for Doubtful Accounts account.
22   Declared a $1 per share cash dividend on its 50,000 shares of outstanding common stock.
26   Paid the dividend declared on May 22.
27   Borrowed $100,000 cash by giving the bank a 30-day, 10% note.
28   Borrowed $80,000 cash by signing a long-term secured note.
29   Used the $180,000 cash proceeds from the notes to buy new machinery.

Check   May 22: Current ratio, 2.19;
Acid-test ratio, 1.11

May 29: Current ratio, 1.80;
Working capital, $325,000

Required

Prepare a table showing Plum's (1) current ratio, (2) acid-test ratio, and (3) working capital, after each transaction. Round ratios to two decimals.

Selected year-end financial statements of Cabot Corporation follow. (All sales were on credit; selected balance sheet amounts at December 31, 2012, were inventory, $48,900; total assets, $189,400; common stock, $90,000; and retained earnings, $22,748.)

Problem 17-4A
Calculation of financial statement ratios

P3

mhhe.com/wildFAP21e

CABOT CORPORATION Income Statement For Year Ended December 31, 2013	
Sales	$448,600
Cost of goods sold	297,250
Gross profit	151,350
Operating expenses	98,600
Interest expense	4,100
Income before taxes	48,650
Income taxes	19,598
Net income	$ 29,052

CABOT CORPORATION Balance Sheet December 31, 2013			
Assets		**Liabilities and Equity**	
Cash	$ 10,000	Accounts payable	$ 17,500
Short-term investments	8,400	Accrued wages payable	3,200
Accounts receivable, net	29,200	Income taxes payable	3,300
Notes receivable (trade)*	4,500	Long-term note payable, secured	
Merchandise inventory	32,150	by mortgage on plant assets	63,400
Prepaid expenses	2,650	Common stock	90,000
Plant assets, net	153,300	Retained earnings	62,800
Total assets	$240,200	Total liabilities and equity	$240,200

* These are short-term notes receivable arising from customer (trade) sales.

Required

Compute the following: (1) current ratio, (2) acid-test ratio, (3) days' sales uncollected, (4) inventory turnover, (5) days' sales in inventory, (6) debt-to-equity ratio, (7) times interest earned, (8) profit margin ratio, (9) total asset turnover, (10) return on total assets, and (11) return on common stockholders' equity. Round to one decimal place, except for part 6 round to two decimals.

Check   Acid-test ratio, 2.2 to 1:
Inventory turnover, 7.3

Summary information from the financial statements of two companies competing in the same industry follows.

Problem 17-5A
Comparative ratio analysis

A1   P3

	Barco Company	Kyan Company			Barco Company	Kyan Company
Data from the current year-end balance sheets				**Data from the current year's income statement**		
Assets				Sales	$770,000	$880,200
Cash	$ 19,500	$ 34,000		Cost of goods sold	585,100	632,500
Accounts receivable, net	37,400	57,400		Interest expense	7,900	13,000
Current notes receivable (trade)	9,100	7,200		Income tax expense	14,800	24,300
Merchandise inventory	84,440	132,500		Net income	162,200	210,400
Prepaid expenses	5,000	6,950		Basic earnings per share	4.51	5.11
Plant assets, net	290,000	304,400				
Total assets	$445,440	$542,450				
				Beginning-of-year balance sheet data		
Liabilities and Equity				Accounts receivable, net	$ 29,800	$ 54,200
Current liabilities	$ 61,340	$ 93,300		Current notes receivable (trade)	0	0
Long-term notes payable	80,800	101,000		Merchandise inventory	55,600	107,400
Common stock, $5 par value	180,000	206,000		Total assets	398,000	382,500
Retained earnings	123,300	142,150		Common stock, $5 par value	180,000	206,000
Total liabilities and equity	$445,440	$542,450		Retained earnings	98,300	93,600

Required

Check (1) Kyan: Accounts receivable turnover, 14.8; Inventory turnover, 5.3

1. For both companies compute the (*a*) current ratio, (*b*) acid-test ratio, (*c*) accounts (including notes) receivable turnover, (*d*) inventory turnover, (*e*) days' sales in inventory, and (*f*) days' sales uncollected. Identify the company you consider to be the better short-term credit risk and explain why. Round to one decimal place.

(2) Barco: Profit margin, 21.1%; PE, 16.6

2. For both companies compute the (*a*) profit margin ratio, (*b*) total asset turnover, (*c*) return on total assets, and (*d*) return on common stockholders' equity. Assuming that each company paid cash dividends of $3.80 per share and each company's stock can be purchased at $75 per share, compute their (*e*) price-earnings ratios and (*f*) dividend yields. Round to one decimal place. Identify which company's stock you would recommend as the better investment and explain why.

Problem 17-6A[A]
Income statement computations and format

A2

Selected account balances from the adjusted trial balance for Olinda Corporation as of its calendar year-end December 31, 2013, follow.

	Debit	Credit
a. Interest revenue..		$ 14,000
b. Depreciation expense—Equipment......................................	$ 34,000	
c. Loss on sale of equipment..	25,850	
d. Accounts payable		44,000
e. Other operating expenses..	106,400	
f. Accumulated depreciation—Equipment		71,600
g. Gain from settlement of lawsuit		44,000
h. Accumulated depreciation—Buildings..................................		174,500
i. Loss from operating a discontinued segment (pretax)........................	18,250	
j. Gain on insurance recovery of tornado damage (pretax and extraordinary)........		29,120
k. Net sales...		998,500
l. Depreciation expense—Buildings	52,000	
m. Correction of overstatement of prior year's sales (pretax).....................	16,000	
n. Gain on sale of discontinued segment's assets (pretax)........................		34,000
o. Loss from settlement of lawsuit	23,750	
p. Income taxes expense	?	
q. Cost of goods sold	482,500	

Required

Answer each of the following questions by providing supporting computations.

1. Assume that the company's income tax rate is 30% for all items. Identify the tax effects and after-tax amounts of the four items labeled pretax.

2. What is the amount of income from continuing operations before income taxes? What is the amount of the income taxes expense? What is the amount of income from continuing operations?

3. What is the total amount of after-tax income (loss) associated with the discontinued segment?

4. What is the amount of income (loss) before the extraordinary items?

5. What is the amount of net income for the year?

Check   (3) $11,025

(4) $221,375

(5) $241,759

Selected comparative financial statement information of Bluegrass Corporation follows.

PROBLEM SET B

Problem 17-1B
Ratios, common-size statements, and trend percents

P1 P2 P3

BLUEGRASS CORPORATION			
Comparative Income Statements			
For Years Ended December 31, 2014, 2013, and 2012			
	2014	2013	2012
Sales	$198,800	$166,000	$143,800
Cost of goods sold	108,890	86,175	66,200
Gross profit	89,910	79,825	77,600
Selling expenses	22,680	19,790	18,000
Administrative expenses	16,760	14,610	15,700
Total expenses	39,440	34,400	33,700
Income before taxes	50,470	45,425	43,900
Income taxes	6,050	5,910	5,300
Net income	$ 44,420	$ 39,515	$ 38,600

BLUEGRASS CORPORATION			
Comparative Balance Sheets			
December 31, 2014, 2013, and 2012			
	2014	2013	2012
Assets			
Current assets	$ 54,860	$ 32,660	$ 36,300
Long-term investments	0	1,700	10,600
Plant assets, net	112,810	113,660	79,000
Total assets	$167,670	$148,020	$125,900
Liabilities and Equity			
Current liabilities	$ 22,370	$ 19,180	$ 16,500
Common stock	46,500	46,500	37,000
Other paid-in capital	13,850	13,850	11,300
Retained earnings	84,950	68,490	61,100
Total liabilities and equity	$167,670	$148,020	$125,900

Required

1. Compute each year's current ratio. (Round ratio amounts to one decimal.)
2. Express the income statement data in common-size percents. (Round percents to two decimals.)
3. Express the balance sheet data in trend percents with 2012 as the base year. (Round percents to two decimals.)

Check   (3) 2014, Total assets trend, 133.18%

Analysis Component

4. Comment on any significant relations revealed by the ratios and percents computed.

Problem 17-2B
Calculation and analysis of trend percents

A1 P1

Selected comparative financial statements of Tripoly Company follow.

TRIPOLY COMPANY							
Comparative Income Statements							
For Years Ended December 31, 2014–2008							
($ thousands)	2014	2013	2012	2011	2010	2009	2008
Sales	$560	$610	$630	$680	$740	$770	$860
Cost of goods sold	276	290	294	314	340	350	380
Gross profit	284	320	336	366	400	420	480
Operating expenses	84	104	112	126	140	144	150
Net income	$200	$216	$224	$240	$260	$276	$330

TRIPOLY COMPANY							
Comparative Balance Sheets							
December 31, 2014–2008							
($ thousands)	2014	2013	2012	2011	2010	2009	2008
Assets							
Cash	$ 44	$ 46	$ 52	$ 54	$ 60	$ 62	$ 68
Accounts receivable, net	130	136	140	144	150	154	160
Merchandise inventory	166	172	178	180	186	190	208
Other current assets	34	34	36	38	38	40	40
Long-term investments	36	30	26	110	110	110	110
Plant assets, net	510	514	520	412	420	428	454
Total assets	$920	$932	$952	$938	$964	$984	$1,040
Liabilities and Equity							
Current liabilities	$148	$156	$186	$190	$210	$260	$280
Long-term liabilities	92	120	142	148	194	214	260
Common stock	160	160	160	160	160	160	160
Other paid-in capital	70	70	70	70	70	70	70
Retained earnings	450	426	394	370	330	280	270
Total liabilities and equity	$920	$932	$952	$938	$964	$984	$1,040

Required

Check (1) 2014, Total assets trend, 88.5%

1. Compute trend percents for all components of both statements using 2008 as the base year. (Round percents to one decimal.)

Analysis Component

2. Analyze and comment on the financial statements and trend percents from part 1.

Problem 17-3B
Transactions, working capital, and liquidity ratios P3

Koto Corporation began the month of June with $300,000 of current assets, a current ratio of 2.5:1, and an acid-test ratio of 1.4:1. During the month, it completed the following transactions (the company uses a perpetual inventory system).

Check June 1: Current ratio, 2.88; Acid-test ratio, 2.40

June 1 Sold merchandise inventory that cost $75,000 for $120,000 cash.
      3 Collected $88,000 cash on an account receivable.
      5 Purchased $150,000 of merchandise inventory on credit.
      7 Borrowed $100,000 cash by giving the bank a 60-day, 10% note.
     10 Borrowed $120,000 cash by signing a long-term secured note.
     12 Purchased machinery for $275,000 cash.
     15 Declared a $1 per share cash dividend on its 80,000 shares of outstanding common stock.
     19 Wrote off a $5,000 bad debt against the Allowance for Doubtful Accounts account.
     22 Paid $12,000 cash to settle an account payable.
     30 Paid the dividend declared on June 15.

June 30: Working capital, $(10,000); Current ratio, 0.97

Required

Prepare a table showing the company's (1) current ratio, (2) acid-test ratio, and (3) working capital after each transaction. Round ratios to two decimals.

Selected year-end financial statements of Overton Corporation follow. (All sales were on credit; selected balance sheet amounts at December 31, 2012, were inventory, $17,400; total assets, $94,900; common stock, $35,500; and retained earnings, $18,800.)

Problem 17-4B
Calculation of financial statement ratios

P3

OVERTON CORPORATION
Income Statement
For Year Ended December 31, 2013

Sales	$315,500
Cost of goods sold	236,100
Gross profit	79,400
Operating expenses	49,200
Interest expense	2,200
Income before taxes	28,000
Income taxes	4,200
Net income	$ 23,800

OVERTON CORPORATION
Balance Sheet
December 31, 2013

Assets		Liabilities and Equity	
Cash	$ 6,100	Accounts payable	$ 11,500
Short-term investments	6,900	Accrued wages payable	3,300
Accounts receivable, net	12,100	Income taxes payable	2,600
Notes receivable (trade)*	3,000	Long-term note payable, secured	
Merchandise inventory	13,500	by mortgage on plant assets	30,000
Prepaid expenses	2,000	Common stock, $5 par value	35,000
Plant assets, net	73,900	Retained earnings	35,100
Total assets	$117,500	Total liabilities and equity	$117,500

* These are short-term notes receivable arising from customer (trade) sales.

Required

Compute the following: (1) current ratio, (2) acid-test ratio, (3) days' sales uncollected, (4) inventory turnover, (5) days' sales in inventory, (6) debt-to-equity ratio, (7) times interest earned, (8) profit margin ratio, (9) total asset turnover, (10) return on total assets, and (11) return on common stockholders' equity. Round to one decimal place, except for part 6 round to two decimals.

Check Acid-test ratio, 1.6 to 1;
Inventory turnover, 15.3

Summary information from the financial statements of two companies competing in the same industry follows.

Problem 17-5B
Comparative ratio analysis

A1 P3

	Fargo Company	Ball Company		Fargo Company	Ball Company
Data from the current year-end balance sheets			**Data from the current year's income statement**		
Assets			Sales	$393,600	$667,500
Cash	$ 20,000	$ 36,500	Cost of goods sold	290,600	480,000
Accounts receivable, net	77,100	70,500	Interest expense	5,900	12,300
Current notes receivable (trade)	11,600	9,000	Income tax expense	5,700	12,300
Merchandise inventory	86,800	82,000	Net income	33,850	61,700
Prepaid expenses	9,700	10,100	Basic earnings per share	1.27	2.19
Plant assets, net	176,900	252,300			
Total assets	$382,100	$460,400			
			Beginning-of-year balance sheet data		
Liabilities and Equity			Accounts receivable, net	$ 72,200	$ 73,300
Current liabilities	$ 90,500	$ 97,000	Current notes receivable (trade)	0	0
Long-term notes payable	93,000	93,300	Merchandise inventory	105,100	80,500
Common stock, $5 par value	133,000	141,000	Total assets	383,400	443,000
Retained earnings	65,600	129,100	Common stock, $5 par value	133,000	141,000
Total liabilities and equity	$382,100	$460,400	Retained earnings	49,100	109,700

Required

1. For both companies compute the (a) current ratio, (b) acid-test ratio, (c) accounts (including notes) receivable turnover, (d) inventory turnover, (e) days' sales in inventory, and (f) days' sales uncollected. Identify the company you consider to be the better short-term credit risk and explain why. Round to one decimal place.

2. For both companies compute the (a) profit margin ratio, (b) total asset turnover, (c) return on total assets, and (d) return on common stockholders' equity. Assuming that each company paid cash dividends of $1.50 per share and each company's stock can be purchased at $25 per share, compute their (e) price-earnings ratios and (f) dividend yields. Round to one decimal place, except for part b round to two decimals. Identify which company's stock you would recommend as the better investment and explain why.

Problem 17-6B[A]

Income statement computations and format

A2

Selected account balances from the adjusted trial balance for Harbor Corp. as of its calendar year-end December 31, 2013, follow.

	Debit	Credit
a. Accumulated depreciation—Buildings		$ 400,000
b. Interest revenue		20,000
c. Net sales		2,640,000
d. Income taxes expense	$?	
e. Loss on hurricane damage (pretax and extraordinary)	64,000	
f. Accumulated depreciation—Equipment		220,000
g. Other operating expenses	328,000	
h. Depreciation expense—Equipment	100,000	
i. Loss from settlement of lawsuit	36,000	
j. Gain from settlement of lawsuit		68,000
k. Loss on sale of equipment	24,000	
l. Loss from operating a discontinued segment (pretax)	120,000	
m. Depreciation expense—Buildings	156,000	
n. Correction of overstatement of prior year's expense (pretax)		48,000
o. Cost of goods sold	1,040,000	
p. Loss on sale of discontinued segment's assets (pretax)	180,000	
q. Accounts payable		132,000

Required

Answer each of the following questions by providing supporting computations.

1. Assume that the company's income tax rate is 25% for all items. Identify the tax effects and after-tax amounts of the four items labeled pretax.

2. What is the amount of income from continuing operations before income taxes? What is the amount of income taxes expense? What is the amount of income from continuing operations?

3. What is the total amount of after-tax income (loss) associated with the discontinued segment?

4. What is the amount of income (loss) before the extraordinary items?

5. What is the amount of net income for the year?

SERIAL PROBLEM
Success Systems

P3

(This serial problem began in Chapter 1 and continues through most of the book. If previous chapter segments were not completed, the serial problem can begin at this point. It is helpful, but not necessary, to use the Working Papers that accompany the book.)

SP 17   Use the following selected data from Success Systems' income statement for the three months ended March 31, 2014, and from its March 31, 2014, balance sheet to complete the requirements below: computer services revenue, $25,160; net sales (of goods), $18,693; total sales and revenue, $43,853; cost of goods sold, $14,052; net income, $18,686; quick assets, $100,205; current assets, $105,209; total assets, $129,909; current liabilities, $875; total liabilities, $875; and total equity, $129,034.

Required

1. Compute the gross margin ratio (both with and without services revenue) and net profit margin ratio (round the percent to one decimal).

2. Compute the current ratio and acid-test ratio (round to one decimal).

3. Compute the debt ratio and equity ratio (round the percent to one decimal).

4. What percent of its assets are current? What percent are long term (round the percent to one decimal)?

Beyond the Numbers

BTN 17-1   Refer to **Polaris** financial statements in Appendix A to answer the following.

1. Using fiscal 2009 as the base year, compute trend percents for fiscal years 2009, 2010, and 2011 for revenues, cost of sales, operating income, non-operating expenses, income taxes, and net income. (Round percents to one decimal.)

2. Compute common-size percents for fiscal years 2010 and 2011 for the following categories of assets: (*a*) total current assets, (*b*) property and equipment, net, and (*c*) goodwill and other intangible assets. (Round percents to one decimal.)

3. Comment on any notable changes across the years for the income statement trends computed in part 1 and the balance sheet percents computed in part 2.

REPORTING IN ACTION

A1 P1 P2

Polaris

Fast Forward

4. Access Polaris' financial statements for fiscal years ending after December 31, 2011, from its Website (**Polaris.com**) or the SEC database (**www.SEC.gov**). Update your work for parts 1, 2, and 3 using the new information accessed.

BTN 17-2   Key figures for **Polaris** and **Arctic Cat** follow.

($ thousands)	Polaris	Arctic Cat
Cash and equivalents	$ 325,336	$ 14,700
Accounts receivable, net	115,302	23,732
Inventories	298,042	61,478
Retained earnings	321,831	177,493
Cost of sales	1,916,366	363,142
Revenues	2,656,949	464,651
Total assets	1,228,024	272,906

COMPARATIVE ANALYSIS

C2 P2

Polaris

Arctic Cat

Required

1. Compute common-size percents for each of the companies using the data provided. (Round percents to one decimal.)

2. Which company retains a higher portion of cumulative net income in the company?

3. Which company has a higher gross margin ratio on sales?

4. Which company holds a higher percent of its total assets as inventory?

BTN 17-3   As Beacon Company controller, you are responsible for informing the board of directors about its financial activities. At the board meeting, you present the following information.

ETHICS CHALLENGE

A1

	2013	2012	2011
Sales trend percent	147.0%	135.0%	100.0%
Selling expenses to sales	10.1%	14.0%	15.6%
Sales to plant assets ratio	3.8 to 1	3.6 to 1	3.3 to 1
Current ratio	2.9 to 1	2.7 to 1	2.4 to 1
Acid-test ratio	1.1 to 1	1.4 to 1	1.5 to 1
Inventory turnover	7.8 times	9.0 times	10.2 times
Accounts receivable turnover	7.0 times	7.7 times	8.5 times
Total asset turnover	2.9 times	2.9 times	3.3 times
Return on total assets	10.4%	11.0%	13.2%
Return on stockholders' equity.........	10.7%	11.5%	14.1%
Profit margin ratio	3.6%	3.8%	4.0%

After the meeting, the company's CEO holds a press conference with analysts in which she mentions the following ratios.

	2013	2012	2011
Sales trend percent	147.0%	135.0%	100.0%
Selling expenses to sales	10.1%	14.0%	15.6%
Sales to plant assets ratio	3.8 to 1	3.6 to 1	3.3 to 1
Current ratio	2.9 to 1	2.7 to 1	2.4 to 1

Required

1. Why do you think the CEO decided to report 4 ratios instead of the 11 prepared?

2. Comment on the possible consequences of the CEO's reporting of the ratios selected.

COMMUNICATING IN PRACTICE

A1 P3

BTN 17-4   Each team is to select a different industry, and each team member is to select a different company in that industry and acquire its financial statements. Use those statements to analyze the company, including at least one ratio from each of the four building blocks of analysis. When necessary, use the financial press to determine the market price of its stock. Communicate with teammates via a meeting, e-mail, or telephone to discuss how different companies compare to each other and to industry norms. The team is to prepare a single one-page memorandum reporting on its analysis and the conclusions reached.

TAKING IT TO THE NET

P3

BTN 17-5   Access the February 17, 2012, filing of the December 31, 2011, 10-K report of **The Hershey Company** (ticker HSY) at **www.sec.gov** and complete the following requirements.

Required

Compute or identify the following profitability ratios of Hershey for its years ending December 31, 2011, *and* December 31, 2010. Interpret its profitability using the results obtained for these two years.

1. Profit margin ratio (round the percent to one decimal).

2. Gross profit ratio (round the percent to one decimal).

3. Return on total assets (round the percent to one decimal). (Total assets at year-end 2009 were $3,675,031,000.)

4. Return on common stockholders' equity (round the percent to one decimal). (Total shareholders' equity at year-end 2009 was $760,339,000.)

5. Basic net income per common share (round to the nearest cent).

TEAMWORK IN ACTION

P1 P2 P3

Hint: Pairing within teams may be necessary for part 2. Use as an in-class activity or as an assignment. Consider presentations to the entire class using team rotation with transparencies.

BTN 17-6   A team approach to learning financial statement analysis is often useful.

Required

1. Each team should write a description of horizontal and vertical analysis that all team members agree with and understand. Illustrate each description with an example.

2. *Each* member of the team is to select *one* of the following categories of ratio analysis. Explain what the ratios in that category measure. Choose one ratio from the category selected, present its formula, and explain what it measures.

   a. Liquidity and efficiency   **c.** Profitability

   b. Solvency   **d.** Market prospects

3. Each team member is to present his or her notes from part 2 to teammates. Team members are to confirm or correct other teammates' presentation.

ENTREPRENEURIAL DECISION

A1 P1 P2 P3

BTN 17-7   Assume that David and Tom Gardner of **The Motley Fool** (**Fool.com**) have impressed you since you first heard of their rather improbable rise to prominence in financial circles. You learn of a staff opening at The Motley Fool and decide to apply for it. Your resume is successfully screened from the thousands received and you advance to the interview process. You learn that the interview consists of analyzing the following financial facts and answering analysis questions below. (The data are taken from a small merchandiser in outdoor recreational equipment.)

	2012	2011	2010
Sales trend percents	137.0%	125.0%	100.0%
Selling expenses to sales	9.8%	13.7%	15.3%
Sales to plant assets ratio	3.5 to 1	3.3 to 1	3.0 to 1
Current ratio	2.6 to 1	2.4 to 1	2.1 to 1
Acid-test ratio	0.8 to 1	1.1 to 1	1.2 to 1
Merchandise inventory turnover	7.5 times	8.7 times	9.9 times
Accounts receivable turnover	6.7 times	7.4 times	8.2 times
Total asset turnover	2.6 times	2.6 times	3.0 times
Return on total assets	8.8%	9.4%	11.1%
Return on equity	9.75%	11.50%	12.25%
Profit margin ratio	3.3%	3.5%	3.7%

Required

Use these data to answer each of the following questions with explanations.

1. Is it becoming easier for the company to meet its current liabilities on time and to take advantage of any available cash discounts? Explain.
2. Is the company collecting its accounts receivable more rapidly? Explain.
3. Is the company's investment in accounts receivable decreasing? Explain.
4. Is the company's investment in plant assets increasing? Explain.
5. Is the owner's investment becoming more profitable? Explain.
6. Did the dollar amount of selling expenses decrease during the three-year period? Explain.

BTN 17-8   You are to devise an investment strategy to enable you to accumulate $1,000,000 by age 65. Start by making some assumptions about your salary. Next compute the percent of your salary that you will be able to save each year. If you will receive any lump-sum monies, include those amounts in your calculations. Historically, stocks have delivered average annual returns of 10–11%. Given this history, you should probably not assume that you will earn above 10% on the money you invest. It is not necessary to specify exactly what types of assets you will buy for your investments; just assume a rate you expect to earn. Use the future value tables in Appendix B to calculate how your savings will grow. Experiment a bit with your figures to see how much less you have to save if you start at, for example, age 25 versus age 35 or 40. (For this assignment, do not include inflation in your calculations.)

HITTING THE ROAD
C1   P3

BTN 17-9   **KTM (www.KTM.com),** which is a leading manufacturer of offroad and street motorcycles, along with **Polaris** and **Arctic Cat,** are competitors in the global marketplace. Key figures for KTM follow (in Euro thousands).

GLOBAL DECISION
A1

KTM
Polaris
Arctic Cat

Cash and equivalents	14,962
Accounts receivable, net	53,594
Inventories	113,979
Retained earnings	208,987
Cost of sales	371,752
Revenues	526,801
Total assets	485,775

Required

1. Compute common-size percents for KTM using the data provided. (Round percents to one decimal.)
2. Compare the results with Polaris and Arctic Cat from BTN 17-2.

ANSWERS TO MULTIPLE CHOICE QUIZ

1. d; ($351,000/$300,000) × 100 = 117%
2. e; ($86,000 + $76,000 + $122,000 + $12,000)/$124,000 = 2.39
3. c; ($86,000 + $76,000)/$124,000 = 1.31
4. a; ($124,000 + $90,000)/$830,000 = 25.78%
5. d; ($300,000 + $316,000)/$830,000 = 74.22%

Managerial Accounting Concepts and Principles

18

A Look Back

Chapter 17 described the analysis and interpretation of financial statement information. We applied horizontal, vertical, and ratio analyses to better understand company performance and financial condition.

A Look at This Chapter

We begin our study of managerial accounting by explaining its purpose and describing its major characteristics. We also discuss cost concepts and describe how they help managers gather and organize information for making decisions. The reporting of manufacturing activities is also discussed.

A Look Ahead

The remaining chapters discuss the types of decisions managers must make and how managerial accounting helps with those decisions. The first of these chapters, Chapter 19, considers how we measure costs assigned to certain types of projects.

Learning Objectives

CONCEPTUAL

C1 Explain the purpose and nature of, and the role of ethics in, managerial accounting. (p. 734)

C2 Describe accounting concepts useful in classifying costs. (p. 738)

C3 Define product and period costs and explain how they impact financial statements. (p. 740)

C4 Explain how balance sheets and income statements for manufacturing and merchandising companies differ. (p. 743)

C5 Explain manufacturing activities and the flow of manufacturing costs. (p. 746)

C6 Describe trends in managerial accounting. (p. 749)

ANALYTICAL

A1 Assess raw materials inventory management using raw materials inventory turnover and days' sales in raw materials inventory. (p. 752)

PROCEDURAL

P1 Compute cost of goods sold for a manufacturer. (p. 744)

P2 Prepare a manufacturing statement and explain its purpose and links to financial statements. (p. 747)

Fun-guys

"We didn't even know what a good mushroom tasted like."
—**NIKHAIL ARORA**

OAKLAND, CA—Nearing college graduation, Alexandro Velez and Nikhail Arora spurned the glamor of investment banking for a more down-to-earth calling: urban mushroom farming using coffee grounds. Complete strangers, each was intrigued by the idea of turning waste into food (and wages). "We both fell in love with the idea of using coffee waste and started doing research and brainstorming," says Nikhail. After researching mushroom-growing techniques and determining there was a demand for their product, the duo wrote up a business plan, set up a managerial accounting system, and began farming. The result is **Back to the Roots (backtotheroots.com),** a socially conscious company with estimated 2012 revenues of over $5 million.

The company's production process begins with several thousand pounds of used coffee grounds that local coffee shops would typically discard. The company's second key raw material, mushroom seeds, is then added to the coffee grounds. The passage of time and moisture combine with the coffee grounds and mushroom seeds to yield delicious mushrooms in as little as 10 days. Then, the used coffee grounds and mushroom roots are packaged and sold as mulch for landscaping. This simple, sustainable production process "starts with waste and creates delicious food and fertile mulch," explains Alexandro.

Alexandro and Nikhail stress that college is the best time to start a new business. Risk is low, and "if the owners are passionate and have a good plan, someone will provide financing to get the business going," says Nikhail. In Back to the Roots' case, $5,000 of start-up financing was provided by a contest for social

innovation sponsored by their college. In addition to passion and seed money, the owners stress that understanding basic managerial principles, product and period costs, manufacturing statements, and cost flow is critical. Managerial accounting information enables the owners to monitor and control costs and make good decisions. An understanding of costs and a keen eye for demand led the owners to ask, as Alexandro explains, "whether we could take this one step more and enable people to grow mushrooms at home." The company now sells Grow-Your-Own Mushroom Gardens for home use.

Alexandro and Nikhail believe that entrepreneurs fill a void by creating a niche. While financial success depends on monitoring and controlling operations to best meet customers' needs, the owners measure success by more than just profits. "For 2011, we collected and diverted over 1 million pounds of coffee grounds from landfill and enabled families to grow over 250,000 pounds of fresh food. In 2012, we've already been collecting 40,000 lbs. per week," exclaims Nikhail. Now, Alexandro and Nikhail hope to continue to grow their business, while staying focused on sustainability, healthy communities, and green development. Insists Nikhail, "our goal is to show people that you can create a successful company and create a positive impact in the community."

[Sources: *Back to the Roots* Website, January 2013; *Bloomberg Business Week,* http://images.businessweek.com/ss/09/10/1009_entrepreneurs_25_and_under/4.htm; *Whole Foods Market Blog,* August 20, 2011; *White House Champions of Change* blog, August 8, 2011, posted by Ari Matusiak.]

Managerial accounting, like financial accounting, provides information to help users make better decisions. However, managerial accounting and financial accounting differ in important ways, which this chapter explains. This chapter also compares the accounting and reporting practices used by manufacturing and merchandising companies. A merchandising company sells products without changing their condition. A manufacturing company buys raw materials and turns them into finished products for sale to customers. A third type of company earns revenues by providing services rather than products. The skills, tools, and techniques developed for measuring a manufacturing company's activities apply to service companies as well. The chapter concludes by explaining the flow of manufacturing activities and preparing the manufacturing statement.

Managerial Accounting Concepts and Principles

Managerial Accounting Basics
- Purpose of managerial accounting
- Nature of managerial accounting
- Managerial decisions
- Fraud and ethics in managerial accounting

Managerial Cost Concepts
- Types of cost classifications
- Identification of cost classifications
- Cost concepts for service companies

Reporting Manufacturing Activities
- Manufacturer costs
- Balance sheet
- Income statement
- Flow of activities
- Manufacturing statement
- Managerial accounting trends

MANAGERIAL ACCOUNTING BASICS

Managerial accounting is an activity that provides financial and nonfinancial information to an organization's managers and other internal decision makers. This section explains the purpose of managerial accounting (also called *management accounting*) and compares it with financial accounting. The main purpose of the financial accounting system is to prepare general-purpose financial statements. That information is incomplete for internal decision makers who manage organizations.

Purpose of Managerial Accounting

C1 Explain the purpose and nature of, and the role of ethics in, managerial accounting.

The purpose of both managerial accounting and financial accounting is providing useful information to decision makers. They do this by collecting, managing, and reporting information in demand by their users. Both areas of accounting also share the common practice of reporting monetary information, although managerial accounting usually includes the reporting of more nonmonetary information. They even report some of the same information. For instance, a company's financial statements contain information useful for both its managers (insiders) and other persons interested in the company (outsiders).

The remainder of this book looks carefully at managerial accounting information, how to gather it, and how managers use it. We consider the concepts and procedures used to determine the costs of products and services as well as topics such as budgeting, break-even analysis, product costing, profit planning, and cost analysis. Information about the costs of products and services is important for many decisions that managers make. These decisions include predicting the future costs of a product or service. Predicted costs are used in product pricing, profitability analysis, and in deciding whether to make or buy a product or component. More generally, much of managerial accounting involves gathering information about costs for planning and control decisions.

Planning is the process of setting goals and making plans to achieve them. Companies formulate long-term strategic plans that usually span a 5- to 10-year horizon and then refine them with medium-term and short-term plans. Strategic plans usually set a firm's long-term direction by developing a road map based on opportunities such as new products, new markets, and capital investments. A strategic plan's goals and objectives are broadly defined given its long-term

Point: Nonfinancial information, also called nonmonetary information, includes customer and employee satisfaction data, the percentage of on-time deliveries, and product defect rates.

Point: Costs are important to managers because they impact both the financial position and profitability of a business. Managerial accounting assists in analysis, planning, and control of costs.

orientation. Medium- and short-term plans are more operational in nature. They translate the strategic plan into actions. These plans are more concrete and consist of better defined objectives and goals. A short-term plan often covers a one-year period that, when translated in monetary terms, is known as a budget.

Control is the process of monitoring planning decisions and evaluating an organization's activities and employees. It includes the measurement and evaluation of actions, processes, and outcomes. Feedback provided by the control function allows managers to revise their plans. Measurement of actions and processes also allows managers to take corrective actions to avoid undesirable outcomes. For example, managers periodically compare actual results with planned results. Exhibit 18.1 portrays the important management functions of planning and control.

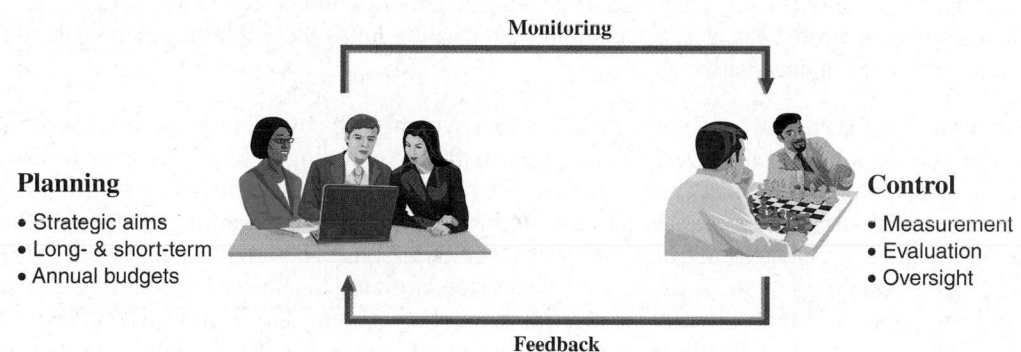

EXHIBIT 18.1

Planning and Control (including monitoring and feedback)

Managers use information to plan and control business activities. In later chapters, we explain how managers also use this information to direct and improve business operations.

Nature of Managerial Accounting

Managerial accounting has its own special characteristics. To understand these characteristics, we compare managerial accounting to financial accounting; they differ in at least seven important ways. These differences are summarized in Exhibit 18.2. This section discusses each of these characteristics.

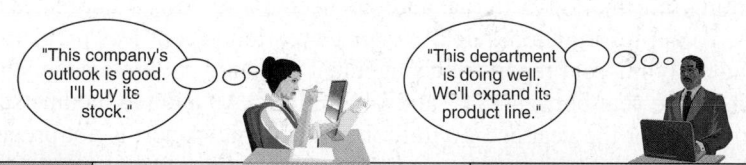

EXHIBIT 18.2

Key Differences between Managerial Accounting and Financial Accounting

	Financial Accounting	Managerial Accounting
1. Users and decision makers	Investors, creditors, and other users external to the organization	Managers, employees, and decision makers internal to the organization
2. Purpose of information	Assist external users in making investment, credit, and other decisions	Assist managers in making planning and control decisions
3. Flexibility of practice	Structured and often controlled by GAAP	Relatively flexible (no GAAP constraints)
4. Timeliness of information	Often available only after an audit is complete	Available quickly without the need to wait for an audit
5. Time dimension	Focus on historical information with some predictions	Many projections and estimates; historical information also presented
6. Focus of information	Emphasis on whole organization	Emphasis on an organization's projects, processes, and subdivisions
7. Nature of information	Monetary information	Mostly monetary; but also nonmonetary information

Users and Decision Makers   Companies accumulate, process, and report financial accounting and managerial accounting information for different groups of decision makers. Financial accounting information is provided primarily to external users including investors, creditors, analysts, and regulators. External users rarely have a major role in managing a company's daily activities. Managerial accounting information is provided primarily to internal users who are responsible for making and implementing decisions about a company's business activities.

Purpose of Information   Investors, creditors, and other external users of financial accounting information must often decide whether to invest in or lend to a company. If they have already done so, they must decide whether to continue owning the company or carrying the loan. Internal decision makers must plan a company's future. They seek to take advantage of opportunities or to overcome obstacles. They also try to control activities and ensure their effective and efficient implementation. Managerial accounting information helps these internal users make both planning and control decisions.

Flexibility of Practice   External users compare companies by using financial reports and need protection against false or misleading information. Accordingly, financial accounting relies on accepted principles that are enforced through an extensive set of rules and guidelines, or GAAP. Internal users need managerial accounting information for planning and controlling their company's activities rather than for external comparisons. They require different types of information depending on the activity. This makes standardizing managerial accounting systems across companies difficult. Instead, managerial accounting systems are flexible. The design of a company's managerial accounting system depends largely on the nature of the business and the arrangement of its internal operations. Managers can decide for themselves what information they want and how they want it reported. Even within a single company, different managers often design their own systems to meet their special needs. The important question a manager must ask is whether the information being collected and reported is useful for planning, decision making, and control purposes.

Timeliness of Information   Formal financial statements reporting past transactions and events are not immediately available to outside parties. Independent certified public accountants often must *audit* a company's financial statements before it provides them to external users. Thus, because audits often take several weeks to complete, financial reports to outsiders usually are not available until well after the period-end. However, managers can quickly obtain managerial accounting information. External auditors need not review it. Estimates and projections are acceptable. To get information quickly, managers often accept less precision in reports. As an example, an early internal report to management prepared right after the year-end could report net income for the year between $4.2 and $4.8 million. An audited income statement could later show net income for the year at $4.6 million. The internal report is not precise, but its information can be more useful because it is available earlier.

    Internal auditing plays an important role in managerial accounting. Internal auditors evaluate the flow of information not only inside but also outside the company. Managers are responsible for preventing and detecting fraudulent activities in their companies.

Time Dimension   To protect external users from false expectations, financial reports deal primarily with results of both past activities and current conditions. While some predictions such as service lives and salvage values of plant assets are necessary, financial accounting avoids predictions whenever possible. Managerial accounting regularly includes predictions of conditions and events. As an example, one important managerial accounting report is a budget, which predicts revenues, expenses, and other items. If managerial accounting reports were restricted to the past and present, managers would be less able to plan activities and less effective in managing and evaluating current activities.

Focus of Information   Companies often organize into divisions and departments, but investors rarely can buy shares in one division or department. Nor do creditors lend money to a company's single division or department. Instead, they own shares in or make loans to the entire company. Financial accounting focuses primarily on a company as a whole as depicted in Exhibit 18.3. The focus of managerial accounting is different. While top-level managers are responsible for managing

Point: It is desirable to accumulate certain information for management reports in a database separate from financial accounting records.

Point: The *Institute of Management Accountants* issues statements that govern the practice of managerial accounting. Accountants who pass a qualifying exam are awarded the CMA.

Point: Financial statements are usually issued several weeks after the period-end. GAAP requires the reporting of important events that occur while the statements are being prepared. These events are called *subsequent events.*

Point: Independent auditors test the integrity of managerial accounting records when they are used in preparing financial statements.

EXHIBIT 18.3

Focus of External Reports

Reports to external users focus on company as a whole

the whole company, most other managers are responsible for much smaller sets of activities. These middle-level and lower-level managers need managerial accounting reports dealing with specific activities, projects, and subdivisions for which they are responsible. For instance, division sales managers are directly responsible only for the results achieved in their divisions. Accordingly, division sales managers need information about results achieved in their own divisions to improve their performance. This information includes the level of success achieved by each individual, product, or department in each division of the whole company as depicted in Exhibit 18.4.

Nature of Information Both financial and managerial accounting systems report monetary information. Managerial accounting systems also report considerable nonmonetary information. Monetary information is an important part of managerial decisions, and nonmonetary information plays a crucial role, especially when monetary effects are difficult to measure. Common examples of nonmonetary information are the quality and delivery criteria of purchasing decisions.

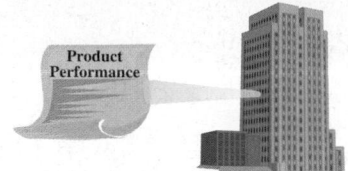

EXHIBIT 18.4

Focus of Internal Reports

Reports to internal users focus on company units and divisions, along with the company as a whole

■ Decision Ethics

Production Manager You invite three friends to a restaurant. When the dinner check arrives, David, a self-employed entrepreneur, picks it up saying, "Here, let me pay. I'll deduct it as a business expense on my tax return." Denise, a salesperson, takes the check from David's hand and says, "I'll put this on my company's credit card. It won't cost us anything." Derek, a factory manager for a company, laughs and says, "Neither of you understands. I'll put this on my company's credit card and call it overhead on a cost-plus contract my company has with a client." (*A cost-plus contract means the company receives its costs plus a percent of those costs.*) Adds Derek, "That way, my company pays for dinner *and* makes a profit." Who should pay the bill? Why? ■ [Answer—p. 757]

Managerial Decision Making

The previous section emphasized differences between financial and managerial accounting, but they are not entirely separate. Similar information is useful to both external and internal users. For instance, information about costs of manufacturing products is useful to all users in making decisions. Also, both financial and managerial accounting affect peoples' actions. For example, **Trek**'s design of a sales compensation plan affects the behavior of its salesforce when selling its manufactured bikes. It also must estimate the dual effects of promotion and sales compensation plans on buying patterns of customers. These estimates impact the equipment purchase decisions for manufacturing and can affect the supplier selection criteria established by purchasing. Thus, financial and managerial accounting systems do more than measure; they also affect people's decisions and actions.

Fraud and Ethics in Managerial Accounting

Fraud, and the role of ethics in reducing fraud, are important factors in running business operations. Fraud involves the use of one's job for personal gain through the deliberate misuse of the employer's assets. Examples include theft of the employer's cash or other assets, overstating reimbursable expenses, payroll schemes, and financial statement fraud. Three factors must exist for a person to commit fraud: opportunity, pressure, and rationalization. This is known as the *fraud triangle*. Fraud affects all business and it is costly: A 2010 *Report to the Nation* from the Association of Certified Fraud Examiners (ACFE) estimates the average U.S. business loses 5% of its annual revenues to fraud. This report also shows that the frequency and average loss from fraud vary by industry; the mining industry has a relatively small number of frauds but a high ($1 million) average loss per fraud. The banking industry has the highest number (16.6%) of the total frauds reported in the current ACFE report.

The most common type of fraud, where employees steal or misuse the employer's resources, results in an average loss of $135,000 per occurrence. For example, in a billing fraud, an employee sets up a bogus supplier. The employee then prepares bills from the supplier and pays these bills from the employer's checking account. The employee cashes the checks sent to the bogus supplier and uses them for his or her own personal benefit.

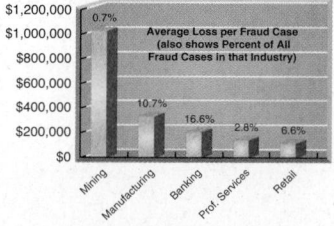

More generally, although there are many types of fraud schemes, all fraud:

- Is done to provide direct or indirect benefit to the employee.
- Violates the employee's obligations to the employer.
- Costs the employer money or loss of other assets.
- Is hidden from the employer.

Implications for Managerial Accounting   Fraud increases a business's costs. Left undetected, these inflated costs can result in poor pricing decisions, an improper product mix, and faulty performance evaluations. Management can develop accounting systems to closely track costs and identify deviations from expected amounts. In addition, managers rely on an **internal control system** to monitor and control business activities. An internal control system is the policies and procedures managers use to:

- Urge adherence to company policies.
- Promote efficient operations.
- Ensure reliable accounting.
- Protect assets.

Combating fraud and other dilemmas requires ethics in accounting. **Ethics** are beliefs that distinguish right from wrong. They are accepted standards of good and bad behavior. Identifying the ethical path can be difficult. The preferred path is a course of action that avoids casting doubt on one's decisions.

The **Institute of Management Accountants** (IMA), the professional association for management accountants, has issued a code of ethics to help accountants involved in solving ethical dilemmas. The IMA's Statement of Ethical Professional Practice requires that management accountants be competent, maintain confidentiality, act with integrity, and communicate information in a fair and credible manner.

The IMA provides a "road map" for resolving ethical conflicts. It suggests that an employee follow the company's policies on how to resolve such conflicts. If the conflict remains unresolved, an employee should contact the next level of management (such as the immediate supervisor) who is not involved in the ethical conflict.

Point: The IMA also issues the Certified Management Accountant (CMA) and the Certified Financial Manager (CFM) certifications. Employees with the CMA or CFM certifications typically earn higher salaries than those without.

Point: The **Sarbanes-Oxley Act** requires each issuer of securities to disclose whether it has adopted a code of ethics for its senior officers and the content of that code.

Quick Check   Answers — p. 758

1. Managerial accounting produces information (*a*) to meet internal users' needs, (*b*) to meet a user's specific needs, (*c*) often focusing on the future, or (*d*) all of these.
2. What is the difference between the intended users of financial and managerial accounting?
3. Do generally accepted accounting principles (GAAP) control and dictate managerial accounting?

MANAGERIAL COST CONCEPTS

 C2 Describe accounting concepts useful in classifying costs.

An organization incurs many different types of costs that are classified differently, depending on management needs (different costs for different purposes). We can classify costs on the basis of their (1) behavior, (2) traceability, (3) controllability, (4) relevance, and (5) function. This section explains each concept for assigning costs to products and services.

Types of Cost Classifications

Classification by Behavior   At a basic level, a cost can be classified as fixed or variable. A **fixed cost** does not change with changes in the volume of activity (within a range of activity known as an activity's *relevant range*). For example, straight-line depreciation on equipment is a fixed cost. A **variable cost** changes in proportion to changes in the volume of activity. Sales commissions computed as a percent of sales revenue are variable costs. Additional examples of fixed and variable costs for a bike manufacturer are provided in Exhibit 18.5. When cost items are combined, total cost can be fixed, variable, or mixed. *Mixed* refers to a combination of fixed and variable costs. Equipment rental often includes a fixed cost for some minimum amount and a variable cost based on amount of usage. Classification of costs by behavior is helpful in cost-volume-profit analyses and short-term decision making. We discuss these in Chapters 21 and 25.

EXHIBIT 18.5

Fixed and Variable Costs

Fixed Cost: Rent for Rocky Mountain Bikes' building is $22,000, and it doesn't change with the number of bikes produced.

Variable Cost: Cost of bicycle tires is variable with the number of bikes produced—this cost is $15 per pair.

Classification by Traceability   A cost is often traced to a **cost object,** which is a product, process, department, or customer to which costs are assigned. **Direct costs** are those traceable to a single cost object. For example, if a product is a cost object, its material and labor costs are usually directly traceable. Direct costs for a bicycle, when it is the cost object, include raw materials such as wheels, brakes, chains, and wages and benefits of employees who work directly on making bikes. **Indirect costs** are those that cannot be easily and cost–beneficially traced to a single cost object. An example of an indirect cost is a maintenance department that benefits two or more departments. Salaries of Rocky Mountain Bikes' maintenance department employees are considered indirect if the cost object is bicycles. However, these salaries are direct if the cost object is the maintenance department. Exhibit 18.6 identifies examples of both direct and indirect costs for the maintenance department, when the maintenance department is considered the cost object. Classification of costs by traceability is useful for cost allocation. This is discussed in Chapter 24.

EXHIBIT 18.6

Direct and Indirect Costs of a Maintenance Department

Direct Costs (to a Maintenance Department)		**Indirect Costs (to a Maintenance Department)**	
• Salaries of maintenance department employees	• Materials purchased by maintenance department	• Factory accounting	• Factory light and heat
• Equipment purchased by maintenance department	• Maintenance department equipment depreciation	• Factory administration • Factory rent • Factory manager's salary	• Factory internal audit • Factory intranet • Insurance on factory

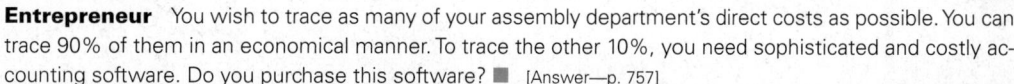

■ Decision Maker

Entrepreneur   You wish to trace as many of your assembly department's direct costs as possible. You can trace 90% of them in an economical manner. To trace the other 10%, you need sophisticated and costly accounting software. Do you purchase this software? ■ [Answer—p. 757]

Classification by Controllability   A cost can be defined as **controllable** or **not controllable.** Whether a cost is controllable or not depends on the employee's responsibilities, as shown in Exhibit 18.7. This is referred to as *hierarchical levels* in management, or *pecking order.* For example, investments in machinery are controllable by upper-level managers but not lower-level managers. Many daily operating expenses such as overtime often are controllable by lower-level managers. Classification of costs by controllability is especially useful for assigning responsibility to and evaluating managers.

EXHIBIT 18.7

Controllability of Costs

Senior Manager
Controls costs of investments in land, buildings, and equipment.

Supervisor
Controls daily expenses such as supplies, maintenance, and overtime.

Classification by Relevance   A cost can be classified by relevance by identifying it as either a sunk cost or an out-of-pocket cost. A **sunk cost** has already been incurred and cannot be avoided or changed. It is irrelevant to future decisions. One example is the cost of a company's office equipment previously purchased. An **out-of-pocket cost** requires a future outlay of cash and is relevant for decision making. Future purchases of equipment involve out-of-pocket costs. A discussion of relevant costs must also consider opportunity costs. An **opportunity cost** is the potential benefit lost by choosing a specific action from two or more alternatives. One example is a student giving up wages from a job to attend evening classes. Consideration of opportunity cost is important when, for example, an insurance company must decide whether to outsource its payroll function or maintain it internally. This is discussed in Chapter 25.

Point: Opportunity costs are not recorded by the accounting system.

C3 Define product and period costs and explain how they impact financial statements.

Classification by Function   Another cost classification (for manufacturers) is capitalization as inventory or to expense as incurred. Costs capitalized as inventory are called **product costs,** which refer to expenditures necessary and integral to finished products. They include direct materials, direct labor, and indirect manufacturing costs called *overhead costs*. Product costs pertain to activities carried out to manufacture the product. Costs expensed are called **period costs,** which refer to expenditures identified more with a time period than with finished products. They include selling and general administrative expenses. Period costs pertain to activities that are not part of the manufacturing process. A distinction between product and period costs is important because period costs are expensed in the income statement and product costs are assigned to inventory on the balance sheet until that inventory is sold. An ability to understand and identify product costs and period costs is crucial to using and interpreting a *manufacturing statement* described later in this chapter.

Point: Only costs of production and purchases are classed as product costs.

Exhibit 18.8 shows the different effects of product and period costs. Period costs flow directly to the current income statement as expenses. They are not reported as assets. Product costs are first assigned to inventory. Their final treatment depends on when inventory is sold or disposed of. Product costs assigned to finished goods that are sold in year 2013 are reported on the 2013 income statement as part of cost of goods sold. Product costs assigned to unsold inventory are carried forward on the balance sheet at the end of year 2013. If this inventory is sold in year 2014, product costs assigned to it are reported as part of cost of goods sold in that year's income statement.

Point: Product costs are either in the income statement as part of cost of goods sold or in the balance sheet as inventory. Period costs appear only on the income statement under operating expenses. See Exhibit 18.8.

The difference between period and product costs explains why the year 2013 income statement does not report operating expenses related to either factory workers' wages or depreciation on factory buildings and equipment. Instead, both costs are combined with the cost of raw materials to compute the product cost of finished goods. A portion of these manufacturing costs

EXHIBIT 18.8

Period and Product Costs in Financial Statements

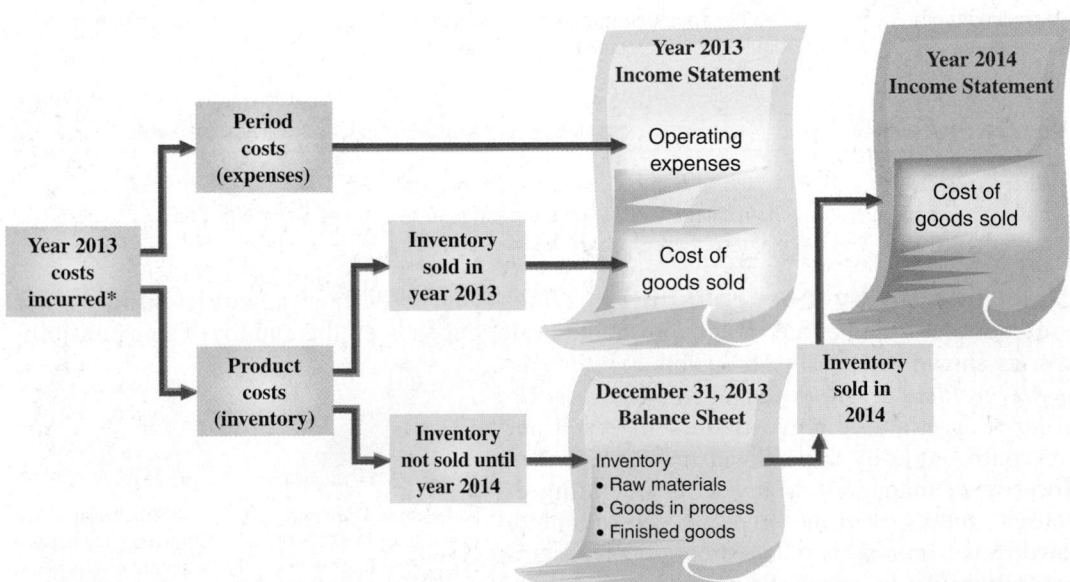

* This diagram excludes costs to acquire assets other than inventory.

(related to the goods sold) is reported in the year 2013 income statement as part of cost of goods sold. The other portion is reported on the balance sheet at the end of that year as part of inventory. The portion assigned to inventory could be included in any or all of raw materials, goods in process, or finished goods inventories.

Exhibit 18.9 summarizes typical managerial decisions for various cost classifications.

Point: For a team approach to identifying period and product costs, see *Teamwork in Action* in the *Beyond the Numbers* section.

Costs Classified By	Example Managerial Decision
Behavior (variable or fixed)	How many units must we sell to break even?
	What will profit be if we raise the selling price?
	Should we add a new line of business?
Traceability (direct or indirect)	How well did our departments perform?
Controllability (controllable or not)	How well did our division managers perform?
Relevance (sunk, out-of-pocket, opportunity)	Should we make or buy a product?
	Should we keep or replace equipment?

EXHIBIT 18.9

Summary of Cost Classifications and Example Managerial Decisions

■ **Decision Maker** ═══════════════════════════════════════

Purchase Manager   You are evaluating two potential suppliers of seats for the manufacturing of motorcycles. One supplier (A) quotes a $145 price per seat and ensures 100% quality standards and on-time delivery. The second supplier (B) quotes a $115 price per seat but does not give any written assurances on quality or delivery. You decide to contract with the second supplier (B), saving $30 per seat. Does this decision have opportunity costs? ■   [Answer—p. 758]

Identification of Cost Classifications

It is important to understand that a cost can be classified using any one (or combination) of the five different means described here. To do this we must understand costs and operations. Specifically, for the five classifications, we must be able to identify the *activity* for behavior, *cost object* for traceability, *management hierarchical level* for controllability, *opportunity cost* for relevance, and *benefit period* for function. Factory rent, for instance, can be classified as a product cost; it is fixed with respect to number of units produced, it is indirect with respect to the product, and it is not controllable by a production supervisor. Potential multiple classifications are shown in Exhibit 18.10 using different cost items incurred in manufacturing mountain bikes. The finished bike is the cost object. Proper allocation of these costs and the managerial decisions based on cost data depend on a correct cost classification.

Cost Item	By Behavior	By Traceability	By Function
Bicycle tires	Variable	Direct	Product
Wages of assembly worker*	Variable	Direct	Product
Advertising	Fixed	Indirect	Period
Production manager's salary	Fixed	Indirect	Product
Office depreciation	Fixed	Indirect	Period

EXHIBIT 18.10

Examples of Multiple Cost Classifications

* Although an assembly worker's wages are classified as variable costs, their actual behavior depends on how workers are paid and whether their wages are based on a union contract (such as piece rate or monthly wages).

Cost Concepts for Service Companies

The cost concepts described are generally applicable to service organizations. For example, consider **Southwest Airlines**. Its cost of beverages for passengers is a variable cost based on number of passengers. The cost of leasing an aircraft is fixed with respect to number of passengers. We can also trace a flight crew's salary to a specific flight whereas we likely cannot trace wages for the ground crew to a specific flight. Classification by function (such as product

Point: All expenses of service companies are period costs because these companies do not have inventory.

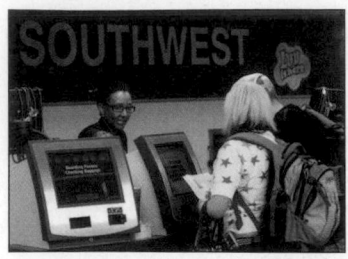

Service Costs
• Beverages and snacks
• Cleaning fees
• Pilot and copilot salaries
• Attendant salaries
• Fuel and oil costs
• Travel agent fees
• Ground crew salaries

versus period costs) is not relevant to service companies because services are not inventoried. Instead, costs incurred by a service firm are expensed in the reporting period when incurred.

Managers in service companies must understand and apply cost concepts. They seek and rely on accurate cost estimates for many decisions. For example, an airline manager must often decide between canceling or rerouting flights. The manager must also be able to estimate costs saved by canceling a flight versus rerouting. Knowledge of fixed costs is equally important. We explain more about the cost requirements for these and other managerial decisions in Chapter 25.

Quick Check   Answers — p. 758

4. Which type of cost behavior increases total costs when volume of activity increases?
5. How could traceability of costs improve managerial decisions?

REPORTING MANUFACTURING ACTIVITIES

Companies with manufacturing activities differ from both merchandising and service companies. The main difference between merchandising and manufacturing companies is that merchandisers buy goods ready for sale while manufacturers produce goods from materials and labor. **Payless** is an example of a merchandising company. It buys and sells shoes without physically changing them. **Adidas** is primarily a manufacturer of shoes, apparel, and accessories. It purchases materials such as leather, cloth, dye, plastic, rubber, glue, and laces and then uses employees' labor to convert these materials to products. **Southwest Airlines** is a service company that transports people and items.

Manufacturer's Costs

Direct Materials   **Direct materials** are tangible components of a finished product. **Direct material costs** are the expenditures for direct materials that are separately and readily traced through the manufacturing process to finished goods. Examples of direct materials in manufactur-

ing a mountain bike include its tires, seat, frame, pedals, brakes, cables, gears, and handlebars. The chart in the margin shows that direct materials generally make up about 45% of manufacturing costs in today's products, but this amount varies across industries and companies.

Direct Labor   **Direct labor** refers to the efforts of employees who physically convert materials to finished product. **Direct labor costs** are the wages and salaries for direct labor that are separately and readily traced through the manufacturing process to finished goods. Examples of direct labor in manufacturing a mountain bike include operators directly involved in converting raw materials into finished products (welding, painting, forming) and assembly workers who attach materials such as tires, seats, pedals, and brakes to the bike frames. Costs of other workers on the assembly line who assist direct laborers are classified as **indirect labor costs. Indirect labor** refers to manufacturing workers' efforts not linked to specific units or batches of the product.

Point: Indirect labor costs are part of factory overhead.

Factory Overhead   **Factory overhead** consists of all manufacturing costs that are not direct materials or direct labor. **Factory overhead costs** cannot be separately or readily traced to finished goods. These costs include indirect materials and indirect labor, costs not directly traceable to the product. Overtime paid to direct laborers is also included in overhead because overtime

Point: Factory overhead is also called *manufacturing overhead.*

is due to delays, interruptions, or constraints not necessarily identifiable to a specific product or batches of product. Factory overhead costs also include maintenance of the mountain bike factory, supervision of its employees, repairing manufacturing equipment, factory utilities (water, gas, electricity), production manager's salary, factory rent, depreciation on factory buildings and equipment, factory insurance, property taxes on factory buildings and equipment, and factory accounting and legal services. Factory overhead does *not* include selling and administrative expenses because they are not incurred in manufacturing products. These expenses are called *period costs* and are recorded as expenses on the income statement when incurred.

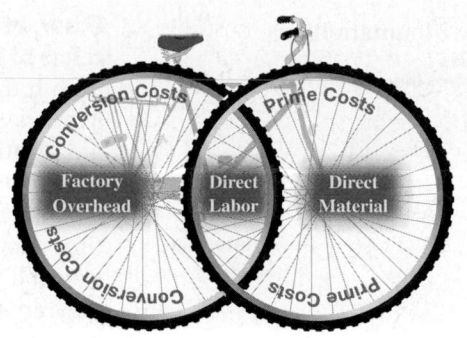

EXHIBIT 18.11

Prime and Conversion Costs and Their Makeup

Prime costs =
Direct materials + Direct labor.
Conversion costs =
Direct labor + Factory overhead.

Prime and Conversion Costs Direct material costs and direct labor costs are also called **prime costs**—expenditures directly associated with the manufacture of finished goods. Direct labor costs and overhead costs are called **conversion costs**—expenditures incurred in the process of converting raw materials to finished goods. Direct labor costs are considered both prime costs and conversion costs. Exhibit 18.11 conveys the relation between prime and conversion costs and their components of direct material, direct labor, and factory overhead.

Since manufacturing activities differ from both selling merchandise and providing services, the financial statements differ slightly between these companies. This section considers some of these differences and compares them to accounting for a merchandising or service company. First we use the cost classification concept of traceability to discuss a manufacturer's costs.

Manufacturer's Balance Sheet

Manufacturers carry several unique assets and usually have three inventories instead of the single inventory that merchandisers carry. Exhibit 18.12 shows three different inventories in the current asset section of the balance sheet for Rocky Mountain Bikes, a manufacturer. The three inventories are raw materials, goods in process, and finished goods.

C4 Explain how balance sheets and income statements for manufacturing and merchandising companies differ.

EXHIBIT 18.12

Balance Sheet for a Manufacturer

ROCKY MOUNTAIN BIKES Balance Sheet December 31, 2013			
Assets		**Liabilities and Equity**	
Current assets		Current liabilities	
Cash	$ 11,000	Accounts payable	$ 14,000
Accounts receivable, net	30,150	Wages payable	540
Raw materials inventory	**9,000**	Interest payable	2,000
Goods in process inventory	**7,500**	Income taxes payable	32,600
Finished goods inventory	**10,300**	Total current liabilities	49,140
Factory supplies	350		
Prepaid insurance	300		
Total current assets	68,600	Long-term liabilities	
Plant assets		Long-term notes payable	50,000
Small tools, net	1,100	Total liabilities	99,140
Delivery equipment, net	5,000		
Office equipment, net	1,300		
Factory machinery, net	65,500	Stockholders' equity	
Factory building, net	86,700	Common stock, $1.2 par	24,000
Land	9,500	Paid-in capital	76,000
Total plant assets, net	169,100	Retained earnings	49,760
Intangible assets (patents), net	11,200	Total stockholders' equity	149,760
Total assets	$248,900	Total liabilities and equity	$248,900

Inventories of Rocky Mountain Bikes

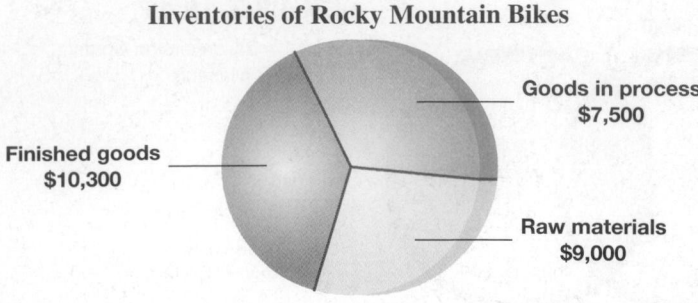

Goods in process
$7,500

Finished goods
$10,300

Raw materials
$9,000

Point: Reducing the size of inventories saves storage costs and frees money for other uses.

Raw Materials Inventory   Raw materials inventory refers to the goods a company acquires to use in making products. It uses raw materials in two ways: directly and indirectly. Most raw materials physically become part of a product and are identified with specific units or batches of a product. Raw materials used directly in a product are called *direct materials.* Other materials used to support production processes are sometimes not as clearly identified with specific units or batches of product. These materials are called **indirect materials** because they are not clearly identified with specific product units or batches. Items used as indirect materials often appear on a balance sheet as factory supplies or are included in raw materials. Some direct materials are classified as indirect materials when their costs are low (insignificant). Examples include screws and nuts used in assembling mountain bikes and staples and glue used in manufacturing shoes. Using the *materiality principle,* individually tracing the costs of each of these materials and classifying them separately as direct materials does not make much economic sense. For instance, keeping detailed records of the amount of glue used to manufacture one shoe is not cost beneficial.

Goods in Process Inventory   Another inventory held by manufacturers is **goods in process inventory,** also called *work in process inventory.* It consists of products in the process of being manufactured but not yet complete. The amount of goods in process inventory depends on the type of production process. If the time required to produce a unit of product is short, the goods in process inventory is likely small; but if weeks or months are needed to produce a unit, the goods in process inventory is usually larger.

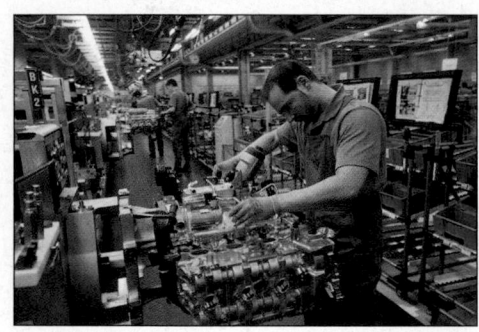

Finished Goods Inventory   A third inventory owned by a manufacturer is **finished goods inventory,** which consists of completed products ready for sale. This inventory is similar to merchandise inventory owned by a merchandising company. Manufacturers also often own unique plant assets such as small tools, factory buildings, factory equipment, and patents to manufacture products. The balance sheet in Exhibit 18.12 shows that Rocky Mountain Bikes owns all of these assets. Some manufacturers invest millions or even billions of dollars in production facilities and patents. **Briggs & Stratton**'s recent balance sheet shows about $1 billion net investment in land, buildings, machinery, and equipment, much of which involves production facilities. It manufactures more racing engines than any other company in the world.

Balance Sheets for Merchandising and Service Companies   The current assets section of the balance sheet will look different for merchandising and service companies as compared to manufacturing companies. A merchandiser will report only merchandise inventory rather than the three types of inventory reported by a manufacturer. A service company's balance sheet does not have any inventory held for sale.

Manufacturer's Income Statement

P1 | Compute cost of goods sold for a manufacturer.

The main difference between the income statement of a manufacturer and that of a merchandiser involves the items making up cost of goods sold. Exhibit 18.13 compares the components of cost of goods sold for a manufacturer and a merchandiser. A merchandiser adds cost of goods purchased to beginning merchandise inventory and then subtracts ending merchandise inventory to get cost of goods sold. A manufacturer adds cost of goods manufactured to beginning finished goods inventory and then subtracts ending finished goods inventory to get cost of goods sold.

A merchandiser often uses the term *merchandise* inventory; a manufacturer often uses the term *finished goods* inventory. A manufacturer's inventories of raw materials and goods in process are not included in finished goods because they are not available for sale. A manufacturer also shows cost of goods *manufactured* instead of cost of goods *purchased.* This difference

EXHIBIT 18.13

Cost of Goods Sold Computation

occurs because a manufacturer produces its goods instead of purchasing them ready for sale. We show later in this chapter how to derive cost of goods manufactured from the manufacturing statement.

The Cost of Goods Sold sections for both a merchandiser (Tele-Mart) and a manufacturer (Rocky Mountain Bikes) are shown in Exhibit 18.14 to highlight these differences. The remaining income statement sections are similar.

EXHIBIT 18.14

Cost of Goods Sold for a
Merchandiser and Manufacturer

Merchandising (Tele-Mart) Company		Manufacturing (Rocky Mtn. Bikes) Company	
Cost of goods sold		Cost of goods sold	
Beginning *merchandise* **inventory**	$ 14,200	**Beginning** *finished goods* **inventory**	$ 11,200
Cost of merchandise *purchased*	234,150	**Cost of goods** *manufactured**	170,500
Goods available for sale	248,350	Goods available for sale	181,700
Less ending *merchandise* **inventory**	12,100	**Less ending** *finished goods* **inventory**	10,300
Cost of goods sold	$236,250	Cost of goods sold	$171,400

* Cost of goods manufactured is reported in the income statement of Exhibit 18.15.

Although the cost of goods sold computations are similar, the numbers in these computations reflect different activities. A merchandiser's cost of goods purchased is the cost of buying products to be sold. A manufacturer's cost of goods manufactured is the sum of direct materials, direct labor, and factory overhead costs incurred in producing products. Next we show a manufacturer's income statement.

Reporting Performance   Exhibit 18.15 shows the income statement for Rocky Mountain Bikes. Its operating expenses include sales salaries, office salaries, and depreciation of delivery and office equipment. Operating expenses do not include manufacturing costs such as factory workers' wages and depreciation of production equipment and the factory buildings. These manufacturing costs are reported as part of cost of goods manufactured and included in cost of goods sold. We explained why and how this is done in the section "Classification by Function."

Point: Manufacturers treat costs such as depreciation and rent as product costs if they are related to manufacturing.

Income Statement for Service Company   Since a service provider does not make or buy inventory to be sold, it does not report cost of goods manufactured or cost of goods sold. Instead, its operating expenses include all of the costs it incurred in providing its service. Southwest Airlines reports large operating expenses for employee pay and benefits, fuel and oil, and depreciation.

EXHIBIT 18.15

Income Statement for a
Manufacturer

ROCKY MOUNTAIN BIKES		
Income Statement		
For Year Ended December 31, 2013		
Sales		$310,000
Cost of goods sold		
Finished goods inventory, Dec. 31, 2012	$ 11,200	
Cost of goods manufactured	**170,500**	
Goods available for sale	181,700	
Less finished goods inventory, Dec. 31, 2013	10,300	
Cost of goods sold		171,400
Gross profit.....................................		138,600
Operating expenses		
Selling expenses		
Sales salaries expense	18,000	
Advertising expense	5,500	
Delivery wages expense	12,000	
Shipping supplies expense	250	
Insurance expense—Delivery equipment	300	
Depreciation expense—Delivery equipment	2,100	
Total selling expenses		38,150
General and administrative expenses		
Office salaries expense	15,700	
Miscellaneous expense	200	
Bad debts expense	1,550	
Office supplies expense	100	
Depreciation expense—Office equipment	200	
Interest expense	4,000	
Total general and administrative expenses		21,750
Total operating expenses		59,900
Income before income taxes		78,700
Income taxes expense		32,600
Net income		$ 46,100

Quick Check   Answers — p. 758

6. What are the three types of inventory on a manufacturing company's balance sheet?

7. How does cost of goods sold differ for merchandising versus manufacturing companies?

Flow of Manufacturing Activities

C5   Explain manufacturing
activities and the flow of
manufacturing costs.

To understand manufacturing and its reports, we must first understand the flow of manufacturing activities and costs. Exhibit 18.16 shows the flow of manufacturing activities for a manufacturer. This exhibit has three important sections: *materials activity, production activity,* and *sales activity.* We explain each activity in this section.

Point: Knowledge of managerial accounting provides us a means of measuring manufacturing costs and is a sound foundation for studying advanced business topics.

Materials Activity   The far left side of Exhibit 18.16 shows the flow of raw materials. Manufacturers usually start a period with some beginning raw materials inventory carried over from the previous period. The company then acquires additional raw materials in the current period. Adding these purchases to beginning inventory gives total raw materials available for use in production. These raw materials are then either used in production in the current period or remain in inventory at the end of the period for use in future periods.

Production Activity   The middle section of Exhibit 18.16 describes production activity. Four factors come together in production: beginning goods in process inventory, direct materials,

EXHIBIT 18.16

Activities and Cost Flows in Manufacturing

direct labor, and overhead. Beginning goods in process inventory consists of partly assembled products from the previous period. Production activity results in products that are either finished or remain unfinished. The cost of finished products makes up the cost of goods manufactured for the current period. Unfinished products are identified as ending goods in process inventory. The cost of unfinished products consists of direct materials, direct labor, and factory overhead, and is reported on the current period's balance sheet. The costs of both finished goods manufactured and goods in process are *product costs*.

Sales Activity The company's sales activity is portrayed in the far right side of Exhibit 18.16. Newly completed units are combined with beginning finished goods inventory to make up total finished goods available for sale in the current period. The cost of finished products sold is reported on the income statement as cost of goods sold. The cost of products not sold is reported on the current period's balance sheet as ending finished goods inventory.

Manufacturing Statement

A company's manufacturing activities are described in a **manufacturing statement,** also called the *schedule of manufacturing activities* or the *schedule of cost of goods manufactured.* The manufacturing statement summarizes the types and amounts of costs incurred in a company's manufacturing process. Exhibit 18.17 shows the manufacturing statement for Rocky Mountain Bikes. The statement is divided into four parts: *direct materials, direct labor, overhead,* and *computation of cost of goods manufactured.* We describe each of these parts in this section.

P2 Prepare a manufacturing statement and explain its purpose and links to financial statements.

① The manufacturing statement begins by computing direct materials used. We start by adding beginning raw materials inventory of $8,000 to the current period's purchases of $86,500. This yields $94,500 of total raw materials available for use. A physical count of inventory shows $9,000 of ending raw materials inventory. This implies a total cost of raw materials used during the period of $85,500 ($94,500 total raw materials available for use − $9,000 ending inventory). (*Note:* All raw materials are direct materials for Rocky Mountain Bikes.)

② The second part of the manufacturing statement reports direct labor costs. Rocky Mountain Bikes had total direct labor costs of $60,000 for the period. This amount includes payroll taxes and fringe benefits.

Point: Direct material and direct labor costs increase with increases in production volume and are called *variable costs.* Overhead can be both variable and fixed. When overhead costs vary with production, they are called *variable overhead.* When overhead costs don't vary with production, they are called *fixed overhead.*

EXHIBIT 18.17

Manufacturing Statement

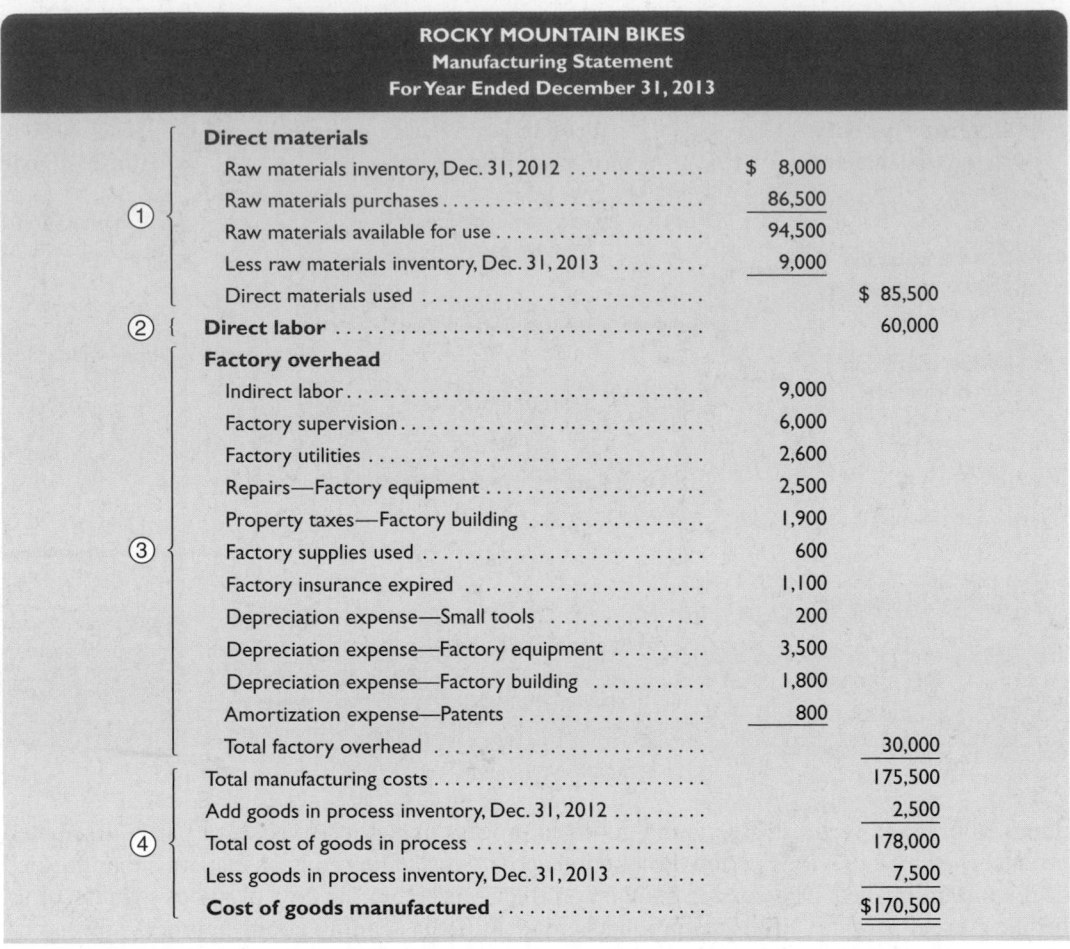

ROCKY MOUNTAIN BIKES
Manufacturing Statement
For Year Ended December 31, 2013

Direct materials		
① Raw materials inventory, Dec. 31, 2012	$ 8,000	
Raw materials purchases	86,500	
Raw materials available for use	94,500	
Less raw materials inventory, Dec. 31, 2013	9,000	
Direct materials used		$ 85,500
② { **Direct labor**		60,000
Factory overhead		
Indirect labor	9,000	
Factory supervision	6,000	
Factory utilities	2,600	
Repairs—Factory equipment	2,500	
Property taxes—Factory building	1,900	
③ Factory supplies used	600	
Factory insurance expired	1,100	
Depreciation expense—Small tools	200	
Depreciation expense—Factory equipment	3,500	
Depreciation expense—Factory building	1,800	
Amortization expense—Patents	800	
Total factory overhead		30,000
Total manufacturing costs		175,500
Add goods in process inventory, Dec. 31, 2012		2,500
④ { Total cost of goods in process		178,000
Less goods in process inventory, Dec. 31, 2013		7,500
Cost of goods manufactured		$170,500

③ The third part of the manufacturing statement reports overhead costs. The statement lists each important factory overhead item and its cost. Total factory overhead cost for the period is $30,000. Some companies report only *total* factory overhead on the manufacturing statement and attach a separate schedule listing individual overhead costs.

④ The final section of the manufacturing statement computes and reports the *cost of goods manufactured.* (Total manufacturing costs for the period are $175,500 [$85,500 + $60,000 + $30,000], the sum of direct materials used and direct labor and overhead costs incurred.) This amount is first added to beginning goods in process inventory. This gives the total goods in process inventory of $178,000 ($175,500 + $2,500). We then compute the current period's cost of goods manufactured of $170,500 by taking the $178,000 total goods in process and subtracting the $7,500 cost of ending goods in process inventory that consists of direct materials, direct labor, and factory overhead. The cost of goods manufactured amount is also called *net cost of goods manufactured* or *cost of goods completed.* Exhibit 18.15 shows that this item and amount are listed in the Cost of Goods Sold section of Rocky Mountain Bikes' income statement and the balance sheet.

A managerial accounting system records costs and reports them in various reports that eventually determine financial statements. Exhibit 18.18 shows how overhead costs flow through the system: from an initial listing of specific costs, to a section of the manufacturing statement, to the reporting on the income statement and the balance sheet.

Management uses information in the manufacturing statement to plan and control the company's manufacturing activities. To provide timely information for decision making, the statement is often prepared monthly, weekly, or even daily. In anticipation of release of its much-hyped iPad, **Apple** grew its inventory of critical components, and its finished goods

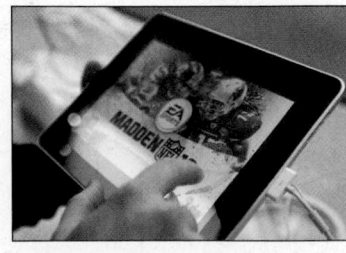

EXHIBIT 18.18

Overhead Cost Flows across Accounting Reports

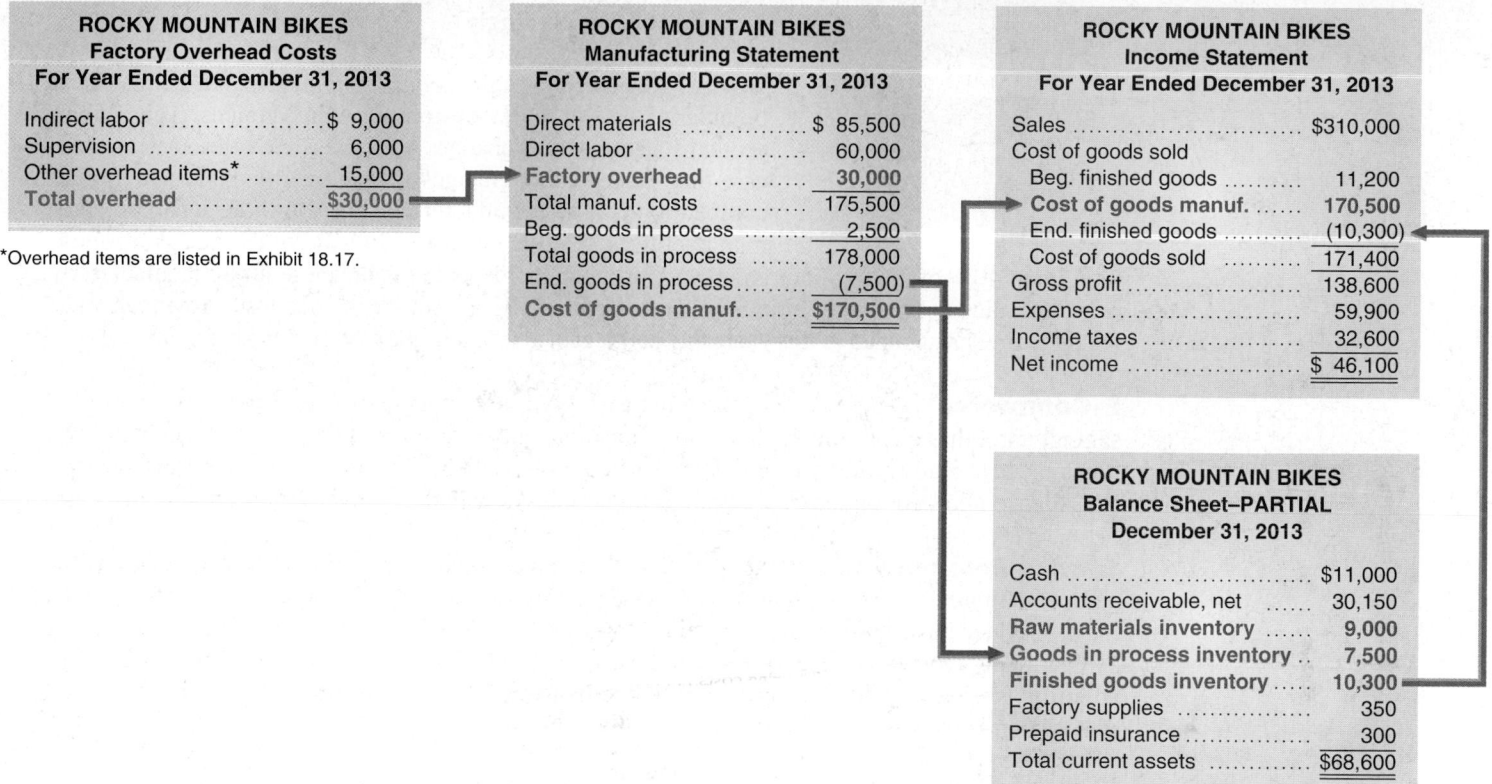

ROCKY MOUNTAIN BIKES
Factory Overhead Costs
For Year Ended December 31, 2013

Indirect labor	$ 9,000
Supervision	6,000
Other overhead items*	15,000
Total overhead	$30,000

*Overhead items are listed in Exhibit 18.17.

ROCKY MOUNTAIN BIKES
Manufacturing Statement
For Year Ended December 31, 2013

Direct materials	$ 85,500
Direct labor	60,000
Factory overhead	30,000
Total manuf. costs	175,500
Beg. goods in process	2,500
Total goods in process	178,000
End. goods in process	(7,500)
Cost of goods manuf.	$170,500

ROCKY MOUNTAIN BIKES
Income Statement
For Year Ended December 31, 2013

Sales	$310,000
Cost of goods sold	
Beg. finished goods	11,200
Cost of goods manuf.	170,500
End. finished goods	(10,300)
Cost of goods sold	171,400
Gross profit	138,600
Expenses	59,900
Income taxes	32,600
Net income	$ 46,100

ROCKY MOUNTAIN BIKES
Balance Sheet–PARTIAL
December 31, 2013

Cash	$11,000
Accounts receivable, net	30,150
Raw materials inventory	9,000
Goods in process inventory	7,500
Finished goods inventory	10,300
Factory supplies	350
Prepaid insurance	300
Total current assets	$68,600

inventory. The manufacturing statement contains information useful to external users but is not a general-purpose financial statement. Companies rarely publish the manufacturing statement because managers view this information as proprietary and potentially harmful to them if released to competitors.

Quick Check   Answers – p. 758

8. A manufacturing statement (*a*) computes cost of goods manufactured for the period, (*b*) computes cost of goods sold for the period, or (*c*) reports operating expenses incurred for the period.

9. Are companies required to report a manufacturing statement?

10. How are both beginning and ending goods in process inventories reported on a manufacturing statement?

Trends in Managerial Accounting

The analytical tools and techniques of managerial accounting have always been useful, and their relevance and importance continue to increase. This is so because of changes in the business environment. This section describes some of these changes and their impact on managerial accounting.

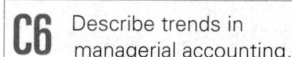

C6   Describe trends in managerial accounting.

Customer Orientation   There is an increased emphasis on *customers* as the most important constituent of a business. Customers expect to derive a certain value for the money they spend to buy products and services. Specifically, they expect that their suppliers will offer them the right service (or product) at the right time and the right price. This implies that companies accept the notion of **customer orientation,** which means that employees understand the changing needs and wants of their customers and align their management and operating practices accordingly.

Global Economy   Our *global economy* expands competitive boundaries and provides customers more choices. The global economy also produces changes in business activities. One notable case that reflects these changes in customer demand and global competition is auto manufacturing. The top three Japanese auto manufacturers (**Honda, Nissan,** and **Toyota**) once controlled more than 40% of the U.S. auto market. Customers perceived that Japanese auto manufacturers provided value not available from other manufacturers. Many European and North American auto manufacturers responded to this challenge and regained much of the lost market share.

E-Commerce   People have become increasingly interconnected via smartphones, text messaging, and other electronic applications. Consumers thus expect and demand to be able to buy items electronically, whenever and wherever they want. Many businesses have enhanced their Websites to allow for online transactions. Online sales now make up over 7% of total retail sales.

Service Economy   Businesses that provide services, such as telecommunications and health care, constitute an ever-growing part of our economy. In developed economies like the United States, service businesses typically account for over 60% to 70% of total economic activity.

Companies must be alert to these and other factors. Many companies have responded by adopting the **lean business model,** whose goal is to *eliminate waste* while "satisfying the customer" and "providing a positive return" to the company.

Lean Practices   **Continuous improvement** rejects the notions of "good enough" or "acceptable" and challenges employees and managers to continuously experiment with new and improved business practices. This has led companies to adopt practices such as total quality management (TQM) and just-in-time (JIT) manufacturing. The philosophy underlying both practices is continuous improvement; the difference is in the focus.

Point: Goals of a TQM process include reduced waste, better inventory control, fewer defects, and continuous improvement. Just-in-time concepts have similar goals.

Total quality management focuses on quality improvement and applies this standard to all aspects of business activities. In doing so, managers and employees seek to uncover waste in business activities including accounting activities such as payroll and disbursements. To encourage an emphasis on quality, the U.S. Congress established the Malcolm Baldrige National Quality Award (MBNQA). Entrants must conduct a thorough analysis and evaluation of their business using guidelines from the Baldrige committee. **Ritz Carlton Hotel** is a recipient of the Baldrige award in the service category. The company applies a core set of values, collectively called *The Gold Standards,* to improve customer service.

Point: The time between buying raw materials and selling finished goods is called *throughput time.*

Just-in-time manufacturing is a system that acquires inventory and produces only when needed. An important aspect of JIT is that companies manufacture products only after they receive an order (a *demand-pull* system) and then deliver the customer's requirements on time. This means that processes must be aligned to eliminate any delays and inefficiencies including inferior inputs and outputs. Companies must also establish good relations and communications with their suppliers. On the downside, JIT is more susceptible to disruption than traditional systems. As one example, several **General Motors** plants were temporarily shut down due to a strike at an assembly division; the plants supplied components *just in time* to the assembly division.

"My boss wants us to appeal to a younger and hipper crowd. So, I'd like to get a tattoo that says-- 'Accounting rules!'"

Value Chain   The **value chain** refers to the series of activities that add value to a company's products or services. Exhibit 18.19 illustrates a possible value chain for a retail cookie company. Companies can use lean practices to increase efficiency and profits.

| Acquire raw materials | Baking | Sales | Service |

EXHIBIT 18.19

Typical Value Chain (Cookie Retailer)

Decision Insight

Global Lean **Toyota Motor Corporation** pioneered lean manufacturing, and it has since spread to other manufacturers throughout the world. The goals include improvements in quality, reliability, inventory turnover, productivity, exports, and—above all—sales and income. ■

Implications for Managerial Accounting Adopting the lean business model can be challenging because to foster its implementation, all systems and procedures that a company follows must be realigned. Managerial accounting has an important role to play by providing accurate cost and performance information. Companies must understand the nature and sources of cost and must develop systems that capture costs accurately. Developing such a system is important to measuring the "value" provided to customers. The price that customers pay for acquiring goods and services is an important determinant of value. In turn, the costs a company incurs are key determinants of price. All else being equal, the better a company is at controlling its costs, the better its performance.

Decision Insight

Balanced Scorecard The *balanced scorecard* aids continuous improvement by augmenting financial measures with information on the "drivers" (indicators) of future financial performance along four dimensions: (1) *financial*—profitability and risk, (2) *customer*—value creation and product and service differentiation, (3) *internal business processes*—business activities that create customer and owner satisfaction, and (4) *learning and growth*—organizational change, innovation, and growth. ■

GLOBAL VIEW

Managerial accounting is more flexible than financial accounting and does not follow a set of strict rules. However, many international businesses use the managerial accounting concepts and principles described in this chapter.

Customer Focus Nestlé, one of the world's leading nutrition and wellness companies, adopts a customer focus and strives to understand its customers' tastes. For example, Nestlé employees spent three days living with people in Lima, Peru, to understand their motivations, routines, buying habits, and everyday lives. This allowed Nestlé to adjust its products to suit local tastes.

Reporting Manufacturing Activities Nestlé must classify and report costs. In reporting inventory, Nestlé includes direct production costs, production overhead, and factory depreciation. A recent Nestlé annual report shows the following:

(in millions of Swiss francs)	Ending Inventory	Beginning Inventory
Raw materials, work in progress, and sundry supplies	3,243	3,175
Finished goods	4,182	4,741

Nestlé managers use this information, along with the more detailed information found in a manufacturing statement, to plan and control manufacturing activities.

A1 Assess raw materials inventory management using raw materials inventory turnover and days' sales in raw materials inventory.

Managerial accounting information helps business managers perform detailed analyses that are not readily available to external users of accounting information. Inventory management is one example. Using publicly available financial statements, an external user can compute the *inventory turnover* ratio. However, a managerial accountant can go much further.

Raw Materials Inventory Turnover

A business manager can assess how effectively a company manages its *raw materials* inventory by computing the **raw materials inventory turnover ratio** as shown in Exhibit 18.20.

EXHIBIT 18.20

Raw Materials Inventory Turnover

> **Raw materials inventory turnover = Raw materials used/Average raw materials inventory**

This ratio reveals how many times a company turns over (uses in production) its raw materials inventory during a period. Generally, a high ratio of raw materials inventory turnover is preferred, as long as raw materials inventory levels are adequate to meet demand. To illustrate, Rocky Mountain Bikes reports direct (raw) materials used of $85,500 for a year, with a beginning raw materials inventory of $8,000 and an ending raw materials inventory of $9,000 (see Exhibit 18.17). Raw materials inventory turnover for Rocky Mountain Bikes for that year is computed as in Exhibit 18.21.

EXHIBIT 18.21

Raw Materials Inventory Turnover Computed

> Raw materials inventory turnover = $85,500/[($8,000 + $9,000)/2] = 10.06 (rounded).

Days' Sales in Raw Materials Inventory

To further assess raw materials inventory management, a manager can measure the adequacy of raw materials inventory to meet production demand. **Days' sales in raw materials inventory** reveals how much raw materials inventory is available in terms of the number of days' sales. It is a measure of how long it takes raw materials to be used in production. It is defined and computed for Rocky Mountain Bikes in Exhibit 18.22.

EXHIBIT 18.22

Days' Sales in Raw Materials Inventory Turnover

> **Days' sales in raw materials inventory = Ending raw materials inventory/Raw materials used × 365**
> = $9,000/$85,500 × 365 = 38.4 days (rounded)

This computation suggests that it will take 38 days for Rocky Mountain Bikes' raw materials inventory to be used in production. Assuming production needs can be met, companies usually prefer a *lower* number of days' sales in raw materials inventory. Just-in-time manufacturing techniques can be useful in lowering days' sales in raw materials inventory; for example, **Dell** keeps less than seven days of production needs in raw materials inventory for most of its computer components.

DEMONSTRATION PROBLEM 1: COST BEHAVIOR AND CLASSIFICATION

Understanding the classification and assignment of costs is important. Consider a company that manufactures computer chips. It incurs the following costs in manufacturing chips and in operating the company.

1. Plastic board used to mount the chip, $3.50 each.
2. Assembly worker pay of $15 per hour to attach chips to plastic board.
3. Salary for factory maintenance workers who maintain factory equipment.
4. Factory supervisor pay of $55,000 per year to supervise employees.
5. Real estate taxes paid on the factory, $14,500.
6. Real estate taxes paid on the company office, $6,000.
7. Depreciation costs on machinery used by workers, $30,000.
8. Salary paid to the chief financial officer, $95,000.
9. Advertising costs of $7,800 paid to promote products.

10. Salespersons' commissions of $0.50 for each assembled chip sold.

11. Management has the option to rent the manufacturing plant to six local hospitals to store medical records instead of producing and assembling chips.

Classify each cost in the following table according to the categories listed in the table header. A cost can be classified under more than one category. For example, the plastic board used to mount chips is classified as a direct material product cost and as a direct unit cost.

Cost	Period Costs: Selling and Administrative	Product Costs: Direct Material (Prime Cost)	Product Costs: Direct Labor (Prime and Conversion)	Product Costs: Factory Overhead (Conversion Cost)	Unit Cost Classification: Direct	Unit Cost Classification: Indirect	Sunk Cost	Opportunity Cost
1. Plastic board used to mount the chip, $3.50 each		✔			✔			

SOLUTION TO DEMONSTRATION PROBLEM 1

Cost*	Period Costs: Selling and Administrative	Product Costs: Direct Material (Prime Cost)	Product Costs: Direct Labor (Prime and Conversion)	Product Costs: Factory Overhead (Conversion Cost)	Unit Cost Classification: Direct	Unit Cost Classification: Indirect	Sunk Cost	Opportunity Cost
1.		✔			✔			
2.			✔		✔			
3.				✔		✔		
4.				✔		✔		
5.				✔		✔		
6.	✔							
7.				✔		✔	✔	
8.	✔							
9.	✔							
10.	✔							
11.								✔

* Costs 1 through 11 refer to the 11 cost items described at the beginning of the problem.

DEMONSTRATION PROBLEM 2: REPORTING FOR MANUFACTURERS

A manufacturing company's balance sheet and income statement differ from those for a merchandising or service company.

Required

1. Fill in the [**BLANK**] descriptors on the partial balance sheets for both the manufacturing company and the merchandising company. Explain why a different presentation is required.

Manufacturing Company

ADIDAS GROUP Partial Balance Sheet December 31, 2013	
Current assets	
Cash	$10,000
[BLANK]	8,000
[BLANK]	5,000
[BLANK]	7,000
Supplies	500
Prepaid insurance	500
Total current assets	$31,000

Merchandising Company

PAYLESS SHOE OUTLET Partial Balance Sheet December 31, 2013	
Current assets	
Cash	$ 5,000
[BLANK]	12,000
Supplies	500
Prepaid insurance	500
Total current assets	$18,000

2. Fill in the [**BLANK**] descriptors on the income statements for the manufacturing company and the merchandising company. Explain why a different presentation is required.

Manufacturing Company

ADIDAS GROUP Partial Income Statement For Year Ended December 31, 2013	
Sales	$200,000
Cost of goods sold	
Finished goods inventory, Dec. 31, 2012	10,000
[BLANK]	120,000
Goods available for sale	130,000
Finished goods inventory, Dec. 31, 2013	(7,000)
Cost of goods sold	123,000
Gross profit	$ 77,000

Merchandising Company

PAYLESS SHOE OUTLET Partial Income Statement For Year Ended December 31, 2013	
Sales	$190,000
Cost of goods sold	
Merchandise inventory, Dec. 31, 2012	8,000
[BLANK]	108,000
Goods available for sale	116,000
Merchandise inventory, Dec. 31, 2013	(12,000)
Cost of goods sold	104,000
Gross profit	$ 86,000

3. A manufacturer's cost of goods manufactured is the sum of (a) _____, (b) _____, and (c) _____ costs incurred in producing the product.

SOLUTION TO DEMONSTRATION PROBLEM 2

1. Inventories for a manufacturer and for a merchandiser.

Manufacturing Company

ADIDAS GROUP Partial Balance Sheet December 31, 2013	
Current assets	
Cash	$10,000
Raw materials inventory	8,000
Goods in process inventory	5,000
Finished goods inventory	7,000
Supplies	500
Prepaid insurance	500
Total current assets	$31,000

Merchandising Company

PAYLESS SHOE OUTLET Partial Balance Sheet December 31, 2013	
Current assets	
Cash	$ 5,000
Merchandise inventory	12,000
Supplies	500
Prepaid insurance	500
Total current assets	$18,000

Explanation: A manufacturing company must control and measure three types of inventories: raw materials, goods in process, and finished goods. In the sequence of making a product, the raw materials move into production—called *goods in process inventory*—and then to finished goods. All raw materials and goods in process inventory at the end of each accounting period are considered current assets. All unsold finished inventory is considered a current asset at the end of each accounting period. The merchandising company must control and measure only one type of inventory, purchased goods.

2. Cost of goods sold for a manufacturer and for a merchandiser.

Manufacturing Company

| **ADIDAS GROUP** |
| Partial Income Statement |
| For Year Ended December 31, 2013 |

Sales	$ 200,000
Cost of goods sold	
Finished goods inventory, Dec. 31, 2012	10,000
Cost of goods manufactured	120,000
Goods available for sale	130,000
Finished goods inventory, Dec. 31, 2013	(7,000)
Cost of goods sold	123,000
Gross profit	$ 77,000

Merchandising Company

| **PAYLESS SHOE OUTLET** |
| Partial Income Statement |
| For Year Ended December 31, 2013 |

Sales	$ 190,000
Cost of goods sold	
Merchandise inventory, Dec. 31, 2012	8,000
Cost of purchases	108,000
Goods available for sale	116,000
Merchandise inventory, Dec. 31, 2013	(12,000)
Cost of goods sold	104,000
Gross profit	$ 86,000

Explanation: Manufacturing and merchandising companies use different reporting terms. In particular, the terms *finished goods* and *cost of goods manufactured* are used to reflect the production of goods, yet the concepts and techniques of reporting cost of goods sold for a manufacturing company and merchandising company are similar.

3. A manufacturer's cost of goods manufactured is the sum of (a) *direct material,* (b) *direct labor,* and (c) *factory overhead* costs incurred in producing the product.

DEMONSTRATION PROBLEM 3: MANUFACTURING STATEMENT

The following account balances and other information are from SUNN Corporation's accounting records for year-end December 31, 2013. Use this information to prepare (1) a table listing factory overhead costs, (2) a manufacturing statement (show only the total factory overhead cost), and (3) an income statement.

Advertising expense	$ 85,000	Goods in process inventory, Dec. 31, 2012	$ 8,000
Amortization expense—Factory Patents	16,000	Goods in process inventory, Dec. 31, 2013	9,000
Bad debts expense	28,000	Income taxes	53,400
Depreciation expense—Office equipment	37,000	Indirect labor	26,000
Depreciation expense—Factory building	133,000	Interest expense	25,000
Depreciation expense—Factory equipment	78,000	Miscellaneous expense	55,000
Direct labor	250,000	Property taxes on factory equipment	14,000
Factory insurance expired	62,000	Raw materials inventory, Dec. 31, 2012	60,000
Factory supervision	74,000	Raw materials inventory, Dec. 31, 2013	78,000
Factory supplies used	21,000	Raw materials purchases	313,000
Factory utilities	115,000	Repairs expense—Factory equipment	31,000
Finished goods inventory, Dec. 31, 2012	15,000	Salaries expense	150,000
Finished goods inventory, Dec. 31, 2013	12,500	Sales	1,630,000

PLANNING THE SOLUTION

- Analyze the account balances and select those that are part of factory overhead costs.
- Arrange these costs in a table that lists factory overhead costs for the year.
- Analyze the remaining costs and select those related to production activity for the year; selected costs should include the materials and goods in process inventories and direct labor.

- Prepare a manufacturing statement for the year showing the calculation of the cost of materials used in production, the cost of direct labor, and the total factory overhead cost. When presenting overhead cost on this statement, report only total overhead cost from the table of overhead costs for the year. Show the costs of beginning and ending goods in process inventory to determine cost of goods manufactured.
- Organize the remaining revenue and expense items into the income statement for the year. Combine cost of goods manufactured from the manufacturing statement with the finished goods inventory amounts to compute cost of goods sold for the year.

SOLUTION TO DEMONSTRATION PROBLEM 3

SUNN CORPORATION
Factory Overhead Costs
For Year Ended December 31, 2013

Amortization expense—Factory patents	$ 16,000
Depreciation expense—Factory building	133,000
Depreciation expense—Factory equipment	78,000
Factory insurance expired	62,000
Factory supervision	74,000
Factory supplies used	21,000
Factory utilities	115,000
Indirect labor	26,000
Property taxes on factory equipment	14,000
Repairs expense—Factory equipment	31,000
Total factory overhead	$570,000

SUNN CORPORATION
Manufacturing Statement
For Year Ended December 31, 2013

Direct materials		
Raw materials inventory, Dec. 31, 2012	$ 60,000	
Raw materials purchase	313,000	
Raw materials available for use	373,000	
Less raw materials inventory, Dec. 31, 2013	78,000	
Direct materials used		295,000
Direct labor		250,000
Factory overhead		570,000
Total manufacturing costs		1,115,000
Goods in process inventory, Dec. 31, 2012		8,000
Total cost of goods in process		1,123,000
Less goods in process inventory, Dec. 31, 2013		9,000
Cost of goods manufactured		$1,114,000

SUNN CORPORATION
Income Statement
For Year Ended December 31, 2013

Sales		$1,630,000
Cost of goods sold		
Finished goods inventory, Dec. 31, 2012	$ 15,000	
Cost of goods manufactured	1,114,000	
Goods available for sale	1,129,000	
Less finished goods inventory, Dec. 31, 2013	12,500	
Cost of goods sold		1,116,500
Gross profit		513,500
Operating expenses		
Advertising expense	85,000	
Bad debts expense	28,000	
Depreciation expense—Office equipment	37,000	
Interest expense	25,000	
Miscellaneous expense	55,000	
Salaries expense	150,000	
Total operating expenses........................		380,000
Income before income taxes		133,500
Income taxes		53,400
Net income		$ 80,100

Summary

C1 **Explain the purpose and nature of, and the role of ethics in, managerial accounting.** The purpose of managerial accounting is to provide useful information to management and other internal decision makers. It does this by collecting, managing, and reporting both monetary and nonmonetary information in a manner useful to internal users. Major characteristics of managerial accounting include (1) focus on internal decision makers, (2) emphasis on planning and control, (3) flexibility, (4) timeliness, (5) reliance on forecasts and estimates, (6) focus on segments and projects, and (7) reporting both monetary and nonmonetary information. Ethics are beliefs that distinguish right from wrong. Ethics can be important in reducing fraud in business operations.

C2 **Describe accounting concepts useful in classifying costs.** We can classify costs on the basis of their (1) behavior—fixed vs. variable, (2) traceability—direct vs. indirect, (3) controllability—controllable vs. uncontrollable, (4) relevance—sunk vs. out of pocket, and (5) function—product vs. period. A cost can be classified in more than one way, depending on the purpose for which the cost is being determined. These classifications help us understand cost patterns, analyze performance, and plan operations.

C3 **Define product and period costs and explain how they impact financial statements.** Costs that are capitalized because they are expected to have future value are called *product costs;* costs that are expensed are called *period costs.* This classification is important because it affects the amount of costs expensed in the income statement and the amount of costs assigned to inventory on the balance sheet. Product costs are commonly made up of direct materials, direct labor, and overhead. Period costs include selling and administrative expenses.

C4 **Explain how balance sheets and income statements for manufacturing and merchandising companies differ.** The main difference is that manufacturers usually carry three inventories on their balance sheets—raw materials, goods in process, and finished goods—instead of one inventory that merchandisers carry. The main difference between income statements of manufacturers and merchandisers is the items making up cost of goods sold. A merchandiser adds beginning merchandise inventory to cost of goods purchased and then subtracts ending merchandise inventory to get cost of goods sold. A manufacturer adds beginning finished goods inventory to cost of goods manufactured and then subtracts ending finished goods inventory to get cost of goods sold.

C5 **Explain manufacturing activities and the flow of manufacturing costs.** Manufacturing activities consist of materials, production, and sales activities. The materials activity consists of the purchase and issuance of materials to production. The production activity consists of converting materials into finished goods. At this stage in the process, the materials, labor, and overhead costs have been incurred and the manufacturing statement is prepared. The sales activity consists of selling some or all of finished goods available for sale. At this stage, the cost of goods sold is determined.

C6 **Describe trends in managerial accounting.** Important trends in managerial accounting include an increased focus on satisfying customers, the impact of a global economy, and the growing presence of e-commerce and service-based businesses. The lean business model, designed to eliminate waste and satisfy customers, can be useful in responding to recent trends. Concepts such as total quality management, just-in-time production, and the value chain often aid in application of the lean business model.

A1 **Assess raw materials inventory management using raw materials inventory turnover and days' sales in raw materials inventory.** A high raw materials inventory turnover suggests a business is more effective in managing its raw materials inventory. We use days' sales in raw materials inventory to assess the likelihood of production being delayed due to inadequate levels of raw materials. We prefer a high raw materials inventory turnover ratio and a small number of days' sales in raw materials inventory, provided that raw materials inventory levels are adequate to keep production steady.

P1 **Compute cost of goods sold for a manufacturer.** A manufacturer adds beginning finished goods inventory to cost of goods manufactured and then subtracts ending finished goods inventory to get cost of goods sold.

P2 **Prepare a manufacturing statement and explain its purpose and links to financial statements.** The manufacturing statement reports computation of cost of goods manufactured for the period. It begins by showing the period's costs for direct materials, direct labor, and overhead and then adjusts these numbers for the beginning and ending inventories of the goods in process to yield cost of goods manufactured.

Guidance Answers to Decision Maker and Decision Ethics

Production Manager It appears that all three friends want to pay the bill with someone else's money. David is using money belonging to the tax authorities, Denise is taking money from her company, and Derek is defrauding the client. To prevent such practices, companies have internal audit mechanisms. Many companies also adopt ethical codes of conduct to help guide employees. We must recognize that some entertainment expenses are justifiable and even encouraged. For example, the tax law allows certain deductions for entertainment that have a business purpose. Corporate policies also sometimes allow and encourage reimbursable spending for social activities, and contracts can include entertainment as allowable costs. Nevertheless, without further details, payment for this bill should be made from personal accounts.

Entrepreneur Tracing all costs directly to cost objects is always desirable, but you need to be able to do so in an economically feasible manner. In this case, you are able to trace 90% of the assembly department's direct costs. It may not be economical to spend more money on a new software to trace the final 10% of costs. You need to make a cost–benefit trade-off. If the software offers benefits beyond tracing the remaining 10% of the assembly department's costs, your decision should consider this.

Purchase Manager   Opportunity costs relate to the potential quality and delivery benefits given up by not choosing supplier (A).

Selecting supplier (B) might involve future costs of poor-quality seats (inspection, repairs, and returns). Also, potential delivery delays could interrupt work and increase manufacturing costs. Your company could also incur sales losses if the product quality of supplier (B) is low. As purchase manager, you are responsible for these costs and must consider them in making your decision.

Guidance Answers to Quick Checks

1. *d*

2. Financial accounting information is intended for users external to an organization such as investors, creditors, and government authorities. Managerial accounting focuses on providing information to managers, officers, and other decision makers within the organization.

3. No, GAAP do not control the practice of managerial accounting. Unlike external users, the internal users need managerial accounting information for planning and controlling business activities rather than for external comparison. Different types of information are required, depending on the activity. Therefore it is difficult to standardize managerial accounting.

4. Variable costs increase when volume of activity increases.

5. By being able to trace costs to cost objects (say, to products and departments), managers better understand the total costs associated with a cost object. This is useful when managers

consider making changes to the cost object (such as when dropping the product or expanding the department).

6. Raw materials inventory, goods in process inventory, and finished goods inventory.

7. The cost of goods sold for merchandising companies includes all costs of acquiring the merchandise; the cost of goods sold for manufacturing companies includes the three costs of manufacturing: direct materials, direct labor, and overhead.

8. *a*

9. No; companies rarely report a manufacturing statement.

10. Beginning goods in process inventory is added to total manufacturing costs to yield total goods in process. Ending goods in process inventory is subtracted from total goods in process to yield cost of goods manufactured for the period.

Key Terms

Continuous improvement (p. 750)

Control (p. 735)

Controllable or **not controllable cost** (p. 739)

Conversion costs (p. 743)

Cost object (p. 739)

Customer orientation (p. 750)

Days' sales in raw materials inventory (p. 752)

Direct costs (p. 739)

Direct labor (p. 742)

Direct labor costs (p. 742)

Direct materials (p. 742)

Direct material costs (p. 742)

Ethics (p. 738)

Factory overhead (p. 742)

Factory overhead costs (p. 742)

Finished goods inventory (p. 744)

Fixed cost (p. 738)

Goods in process inventory (p. 744)

Indirect costs (p. 739)

Indirect labor (p. 742)

Indirect labor costs (p. 742)

Indirect material (p. 744)

Institute of Management Accountants (IMA) (p. 738)

Internal control system (p. 738)

Just-in-time (JIT) manufacturing (p. 750)

Lean business model (p. 750)

Managerial accounting (p. 734)

Manufacturing statement (p. 747)

Opportunity cost (p. 740)

Out-of-pocket cost (p. 740)

Period costs (p. 740)

Planning (p. 734)

Prime costs (p. 743)

Product costs (p. 740)

Raw materials inventory (p. 744)

Raw materials inventory turnover (p. 752)

Sunk cost (p. 740)

Total quality management (TQM) (p. 750)

Value chain (p. 750)

Variable cost (p. 738)

Additional Quiz Questions are available at the book's Website.

1. Continuous improvement
   a. Is used to reduce inventory levels.
   b. Is applicable only in service businesses.
   c. Rejects the notion of "good enough."
   d. Is used to reduce ordering costs.
   e. Is applicable only in manufacturing businesses.

2. A direct cost is one that is
   a. Variable with respect to the cost object.
   b. Traceable to the cost object.
   c. Fixed with respect to the cost object.
   d. Allocated to the cost object.
   e. A period cost.

3. Costs that are incurred as part of the manufacturing process, but are not clearly traceable to the specific unit of product or batches of product, are called
   a. Period costs.
   b. Factory overhead.
   c. Sunk costs.
   d. Opportunity costs.
   e. Fixed costs.

4. The three major cost components of manufacturing a product are
   a. Direct materials, direct labor, and factory overhead.
   b. Period costs, product costs, and sunk costs.
   c. Indirect labor, indirect materials, and fixed expenses.
   d. Variable costs, fixed costs, and period costs.
   e. Opportunity costs, sunk costs, and direct costs.

5. A company reports the following for the current year.

Finished goods inventory, beginning year	$6,000
Finished goods inventory, ending year	3,200
Cost of goods sold	7,500

Its cost of goods manufactured for the current year is
   a. $1,500.
   b. $1,700.
   c. $7,500.
   d. $2,800.
   e. $4,700.

■ Icon denotes assignments that involve decision making.

Discussion Questions

1. Describe the managerial accountant's role in business planning, control, and decision making.

2. Distinguish between managerial and financial accounting on
   a. Users and decision makers.   **b.** Purpose of information.
   c. Flexibility of practice.   **d.** Time dimension.
   e. Focus of information.   **f.** Nature of information.

3. ■ Identify the usual changes that a company must make when it adopts a customer orientation.

4. Distinguish between direct labor and indirect labor.

5. Distinguish between (a) factory overhead and (b) selling and administrative overhead.

6. Distinguish between direct material and indirect material.

7. What product cost is listed as both a prime cost and a conversion cost?

8. ■ Assume that we tour **Polaris**' factory where it makes its products. List three direct costs and three indirect costs that we are likely to see.

9. ■ Should we evaluate a manager's performance on the basis of controllable or noncontrollable costs? Why?

10. ■ Explain why knowledge of cost behavior is useful in product performance evaluation.

11. Explain why product costs are capitalized but period costs are expensed in the current accounting period.

12. ■ Explain how business activities and inventories for a manufacturing company, a merchandising company, and a service company differ.

13. ■ Why does managerial accounting often involve working with numerous predictions and estimates?

14. How do an income statement and a balance sheet for a manufacturing company and a merchandising company differ?

15. Besides inventories, what other assets often appear on manufacturers' balance sheets but not on merchandisers' balance sheets?

16. Why does a manufacturing company require three different inventory categories?

17. Manufacturing activities of a company are described in the _____. This statement summarizes the types and amounts of costs incurred in its manufacturing _____.

18. What are the three categories of manufacturing costs?

19. List several examples of factory overhead.

20. ■ List the four components of a manufacturing statement and provide specific examples of each for **Polaris**.

21. 🔲 Prepare a proper title for the annual "manufacturing statement" of **Arctic Cat**. Does the   Arctic Cat   date match the balance sheet or income statement? Why?

22. 🔲 Describe the relations among the income statement, the manufacturing statement, and a detailed listing of factory overhead costs.

23. 🔲 Define and describe two measures to assess raw materials inventory management.

24. 🔲 Can management of a company such as **Polaris** use cycle time and cycle efficiency as useful measures of performance? Explain.

25. Access **Dell**'s annual report (10-K) for the fiscal year ended February 3, 2012, at the SEC's EDGAR database (**SEC.gov**) or its Website (**Dell.com**). From its financial statement notes, identify the titles and amounts of its inventory components.

QUICK STUDY

QS 18-1
Managerial accounting defined
C1

Managerial accounting (choose one)

1. Is directed at reporting aggregate data on the company as a whole.
2. Provides information that is widely available to all interested parties.
3. Must follow generally accepted accounting principles.
4. Provides information to aid management in planning and controlling business activities.

QS 18-2
Managerial accounting versus financial accounting
C1

Identify whether each description most likely applies to managerial or financial accounting.

1. _____ Its primary users are company managers.
2. _____ Its information is often available only after an audit is complete.
3. _____ Its primary focus is on the organization as a whole.
4. _____ Its principles and practices are very flexible.
5. _____ It is directed at external users in making investment, credit, and other decisions.

QS 18-3
Product and period costs
C3

Which of these statements is true regarding product and period costs?

1. Factory maintenance is a product cost and sales commission is a period cost.
2. Sales commission is a product cost and depreciation on factory equipment is a product cost.
3. Sales commission is a product cost and factory rent is a period cost.
4. Factory wages are a product cost and direct material is a period cost.

QS 18-4
Fixed and variable costs
C2

Which of these statements is true regarding fixed and variable costs?

1. Fixed costs stay the same and variable costs increase in total as activity volume increases.
2. Both fixed and variable costs increase as activity volume increases.
3. Both fixed and variable costs stay the same in total as activity volume increases.
4. Fixed costs increase and variable costs decrease in total as activity volume decreases.

QS 18-5
Direct and indirect costs
C2

Verdi Company produces sporting equipment, including leather footballs. Identify each of the following costs as direct or indirect if the cost object is a football produced by Verdi.

1. Electricity used in the production plant.
2. Labor used on the football production line.
3. Salary of manager who supervises the entire plant.
4. Depreciation on equipment used to produce footballs.
5. Leather used to produce footballs.

Three inventory categories are reported on a manufacturing company's balance sheet: (a) raw materials, (b) goods in process, and (c) finished goods. Identify the usual order in which these inventory items are reported on the balance sheet.

1. (b)(c)(a)   **2.** (c)(b)(a)   **3.** (a)(b)(c)   **4.** (b)(a)(c)

QS 18-6
Inventory reporting for
manufacturers   C4

Compute cost of goods sold for year 2013 using the following information.

Finished goods inventory, Dec. 31, 2012	$345,000
Goods in process inventory, Dec. 31, 2012	83,500
Goods in process inventory, Dec. 31, 2013	72,300
Cost of goods manufactured, year 2013	918,700
Finished goods inventory, Dec. 31, 2013	283,600

QS 18-7
Cost of goods sold
P1

A company has year-end cost of goods manufactured of $4,000, beginning finished goods inventory of $500, and ending finished goods inventory of $750. Its cost of goods sold is

1. $4,250   **2.** $4,000   **3.** $3,750   **4.** $3,900

QS 18-8
Cost of goods sold   P1

Identify the usual sequence of manufacturing activities by filling in the blank (1, 2 or 3) corresponding to its order: _____ Production activities; _____ sales activities; _____ materials activities.

QS 18-9
Manufacturing flows identified
C5

Prepare the 2013 manufacturing statement for Briton Company using the following information.

Direct materials	$190,500
Direct labor	63,150
Factory overhead costs	24,000
Goods in process, Dec. 31, 2012	157,600
Goods in process, Dec. 31, 2013	142,750

QS 18-10
Cost of goods manufactured
P2

Match each lean business concept with its best description by entering its letter in the blank.

1. _____ Just-in-time manufacturing

2. _____ Continuous improvements

3. _____ Customer orientation

4. _____ Total quality management

A. Focuses on quality throughout the production process.

B. Flexible product designs can be modified to accommodate customer choices.

C. Every manager and employee constantly looks for ways to improve company operations.

D. Inventory is acquired or produced only as needed.

QS 18-11
Lean business concepts
C6

Nestlé reports beginning raw materials inventory of 3,243 and ending raw materials inventory of 3,904 (both numbers in millions of Swiss francs). If Nestlé purchased 16,200 (in millions of Swiss francs) of raw materials during the year, what is the amount of raw materials it used during the year?

QS 18-12
Direct materials used
C5

Refer to QS 18-12 and compute raw materials inventory turnover and the number of days' sales in raw materials inventory.

QS 18-13
Raw materials inventory
management   A1

mcGraw connect

EXERCISES

Exercise 18-1
Characteristics of financial accounting and managerial accounting
C1

In the following chart, compare financial accounting and managerial accounting by describing how each differs for the items listed. Be specific in your responses.

	Financial Accounting	Managerial Accounting
1. Time dimension	_____	_____
2. Users and decision makers	_____	_____
3. Timeliness of information	_____	_____
4. Purpose of information	_____	_____
5. Nature of information	_____	_____
6. Flexibility of practice	_____	_____
7. Focus of information	_____	_____

Exercise 18-2
Planning and control descriptions
C1

Complete the following statements by filling in the blanks.

1. _____ _____ usually covers a period of one year.

2. _____ is the process of monitoring planning decisions and evaluating an organization's activities and employees.

3. _____ is the process of setting goals and making plans to achieve them.

4. _____ _____ usually covers a period of 5 to 10 years.

Exercise 18-3
Sources of accounting information
C1

Both managerial accounting and financial accounting provide useful information to decision makers. Indicate in the following chart the most likely source of information for each business decision (a decision can require major input from both sources, in which case both can be marked).

	Primary Information Source	
Business Decision	**Managerial**	**Financial**
1. Determine amount of dividends to pay stockholders	___	___
2. Evaluate a purchasing department's performance	___	___
3. Report financial performance to board of directors	___	___
4. Estimate product cost for a new line of shoes	___	___
5. Plan the budget for next quarter	___	___
6. Measure profitability of all individual stores..............	___	___
7. Prepare financial reports according to GAAP	___	___
8. Determine location and size for a new plant	___	___

Exercise 18-4
Cost classifications C2

(1) Identify each of the five cost classifications discussed in the chapter. (2) List two purposes of identifying these separate cost classifications.

Exercise 18-5
Cost analysis and classification
C2

Listed here are product costs for the production of soccer balls. (1) Classify each cost (a) as either variable or fixed and (b) as either direct or indirect. (2) What pattern do you see regarding the relation between costs classified by behavior and costs classified by traceability?

	Cost by Behavior		Cost by Traceability	
Product Cost	**Variable**	**Fixed**	**Direct**	**Indirect**
1. Leather covers for soccer balls	___	___	___	___
2. Annual flat fee paid for office security	___	___	___	___
3. Coolants for machinery	___	___	___	___
4. Wages of assembly workers	___	___	___	___
5. Lace to hold leather together	___	___	___	___
6. Taxes on factory	___	___	___	___
7. Machinery depreciation	___	___	___	___

Georgia Pacific, a manufacturer, incurs the following costs. (1) Classify each cost as either a product or a period cost. If a product cost, identify it as direct materials, direct labor, or factory overhead, and then as a prime and/or conversion cost. (2) Classify each product cost as either a direct cost or an indirect cost using the product as the cost object.

Exercise 18-6
Cost analysis and identification
C3

| | Product Cost | | | | | | |
| Cost | Prime | | Conversion | | Period Cost | Direct Cost | Indirect Cost |
	Direct Material	Direct Labor	Direct Labor	Overhead			
1. Factory utilities	___	___	___	___	___	___	___
2. Advertising	___	___	___	___	___	___	___
3. Amortization of patents on factory machine	___	___	___	___	___	___	___
4. State and federal income taxes	___	___	___	___	___	___	___
5. Office supplies used	___	___	___	___	___	___	___
6. Bad debts expense	___	___	___	___	___	___	___
7. Small tools used	___	___	___	___	___	___	___
8. Payroll taxes for production supervisor	___	___	___	___	___	___	___
9. Accident insurance on factory workers	___	___	___	___	___	___	___
10. Depreciation—Factory building....................	___	___	___	___	___	___	___
11. Wages to assembly workers	___	___	___	___	___	___	___
12. Direct materials used	___	___	___	___	___	___	___

Current assets for two different companies at calendar year-end 2013 are listed here. One is a manufacturer, Salomon Skis Mfg., and the other, Sun Fresh Foods, is a grocery distribution company. (1) Identify which set of numbers relates to the manufacturer and which to the merchandiser. (2) Prepare the current asset section for each company from this information. Discuss why the current asset section for these two companies is different.

Exercise 18-7
Balance sheet identification and preparation
C4

Account	Company 1	Company 2
Cash	$ 7,000	$ 5,000
Raw materials inventory	—	42,000
Merchandise inventory	45,000	—
Goods in process inventory	—	30,000
Finished goods inventory	—	50,000
Accounts receivable, net	62,000	75,000
Prepaid expenses	1,500	900

Using the following data, compute (1) the cost of goods manufactured and (2) the cost of goods sold for both Garcia Company and Culpepper Company.

Exercise 18-8
Cost of goods manufactured and cost of goods sold computation
P1 P2

	Garcia Company	Culpepper Company
Beginning finished goods inventory	$12,000	$16,450
Beginning goods in process inventory	14,500	19,950
Beginning raw materials inventory	7,250	9,000
Rental cost on factory equipment	27,000	22,750
Direct labor.............................	19,000	35,000
Ending finished goods inventory	17,650	13,300
Ending goods in process inventory	22,000	16,000
Ending raw materials inventory	5,300	7,200
Factory utilities	9,000	12,000
Factory supplies used	8,200	3,200
General and administrative expenses	21,000	43,000
Indirect labor...........................	1,250	7,660
Repairs—Factory equipment	4,780	1,500
Raw materials purchases	33,000	52,000
Sales salaries	50,000	46,000

Check   Garcia COGS, $91,030

Exercise 18-9

Cost of goods sold computation

P1

Compute cost of goods sold for each of these two companies for the year ended December 31, 2013.

		Viking Retail	Log Homes Manufacturing
1			
2			
3	Beginning inventory		
4	Merchandise	$275,000	
5	Finished goods		$450,000
6	Cost of purchases	500,000	
7	Cost of goods manufactured		900,000
8	Ending inventory		
9	Merchandise	115,000	
10	Finished goods		375,000

Check   Viking COGS, $660,000

Exercise 18-10

Cost flows in manufacturing

C5

The following chart shows how costs flow through a business as a product is manufactured. Some boxes in the flowchart show cost amounts. Compute the cost amounts for the boxes that contain question marks.

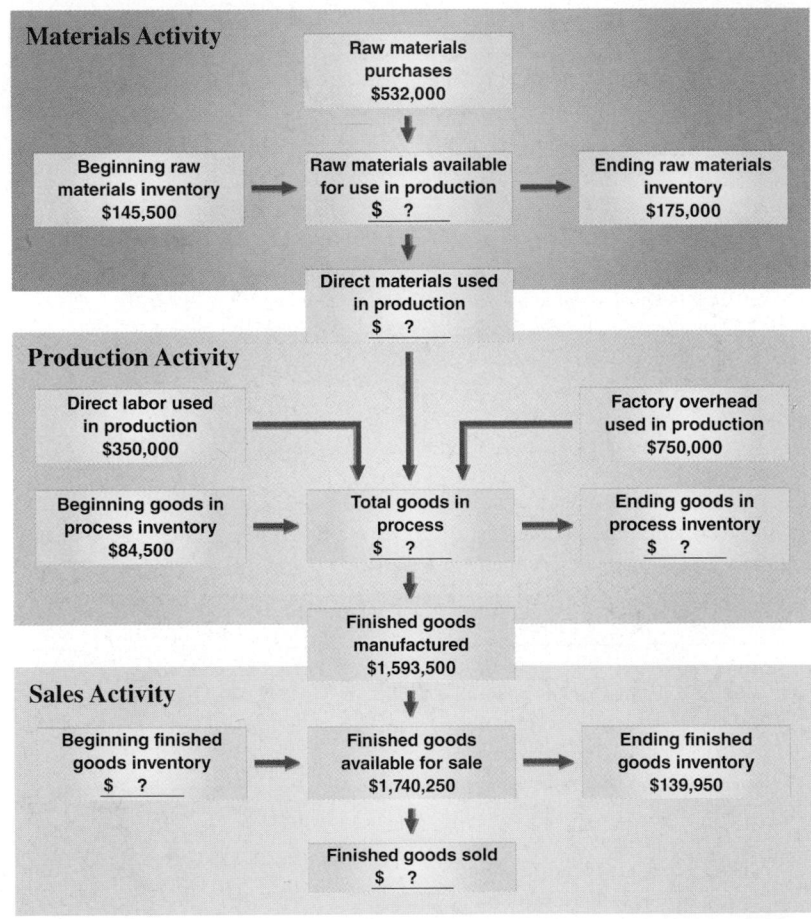

Exercise 18-11

Components of accounting reports

P2

For each of the following accounts for a manufacturing company, place a ✔ in the appropriate column indicating that it appears on the balance sheet, the income statement, the manufacturing statement, and/or a detailed listing of factory overhead costs. Assume that the income statement shows the calculation of cost of goods sold and the manufacturing statement shows only the total amount of factory overhead. (An account can appear on more than one report.)

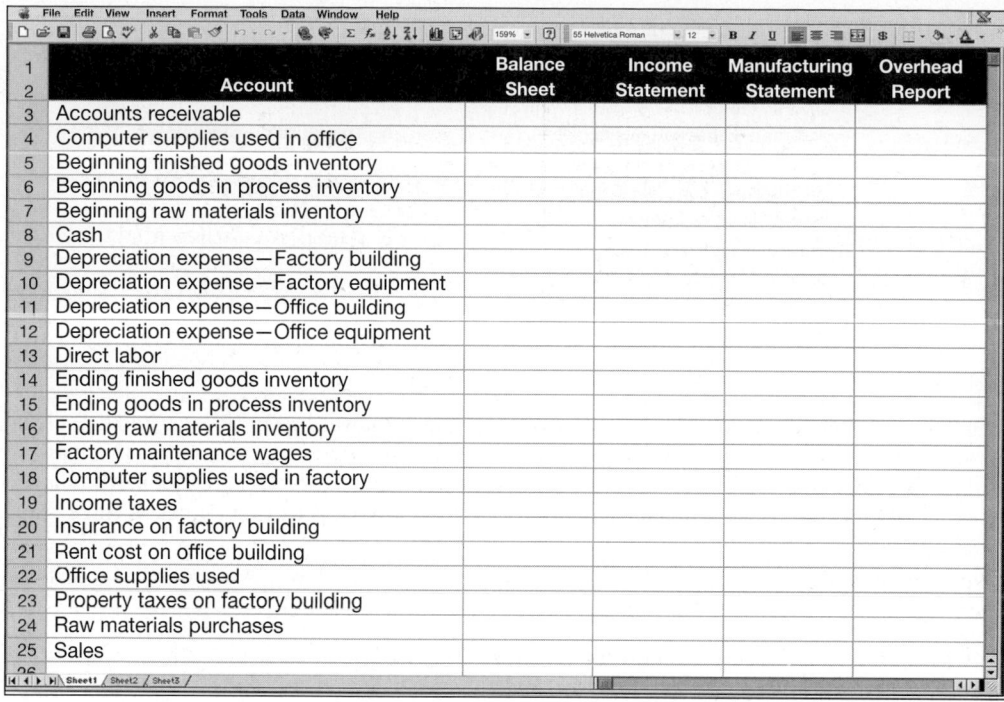

Account	Balance Sheet	Income Statement	Manufacturing Statement	Overhead Report
3 Accounts receivable				
4 Computer supplies used in office				
5 Beginning finished goods inventory				
6 Beginning goods in process inventory				
7 Beginning raw materials inventory				
8 Cash				
9 Depreciation expense—Factory building				
10 Depreciation expense—Factory equipment				
11 Depreciation expense—Office building				
12 Depreciation expense—Office equipment				
13 Direct labor				
14 Ending finished goods inventory				
15 Ending goods in process inventory				
16 Ending raw materials inventory				
17 Factory maintenance wages				
18 Computer supplies used in factory				
19 Income taxes				
20 Insurance on factory building				
21 Rent cost on office building				
22 Office supplies used				
23 Property taxes on factory building				
24 Raw materials purchases				
25 Sales				

Given the following selected account balances of Shanta Company, prepare its manufacturing statement for the year ended on December 31, 2013. Include a listing of the individual overhead account balances in this statement.

Sales	$1,250,000
Raw materials inventory, Dec. 31, 2012	37,000
Goods in process inventory, Dec. 31, 2012	53,900
Finished goods inventory, Dec. 31, 2012	62,750
Raw materials purchases	175,600
Direct labor	225,000
Factory computer supplies used	17,840
Indirect labor	47,000
Repairs—Factory equipment	5,250
Rent cost of factory building	57,000
Advertising expense	94,000
General and administrative expenses	129,300
Raw materials inventory, Dec. 31, 2013	42,700
Goods in process inventory, Dec. 31, 2013	41,500
Finished goods inventory, Dec. 31, 2013	67,300

Exercise 18-12
Manufacturing statement preparation

P2

Check Cost of goods manufactured, $534,390

Use the information in Exercise 18-12 to prepare an income statement for Shanta Company (a manufacturer). Assume that its cost of goods manufactured is $534,390.

Exercise 18-13
Income statement preparation

P2

Following are three separate events affecting the managerial accounting systems for different companies. Match the management concept(s) that the company is likely to adopt for the event identified. There is some overlap in the meaning of customer orientation and total quality management and, therefore, some responses can include more than one concept.

Exercise 18-14
Management concepts

C6

Event	Management Concept
____ 1. The company starts reporting measures such as the percent of defective products and the number of units scrapped.	a. Continuous improvement (CI)
____ 2. The company starts reporting measures on customer complaints and product returns from customers.	b. Total quality management (TQM)
____ 3. The company starts measuring inventory turnover and discontinues elaborate inventory records. Its new focus is to pull inventory through the system.	c. Just-in-time (JIT) system
	d. Customer orientation (CO)

Exercise 18-15

Customer orientation in practice

C6

Customer orientation means that a company's managers and employees respond to customers' changing wants and needs. A manufacturer of metal parts has created a customer satisfaction survey that it asks each of its customers to complete. The survey asks about the following factors: (A) product performance; (B) price; (C) lead time; (D) delivery. Each factor is to be rated as unsatisfactory, marginal, average, satisfactory, or very satisfied.

a. Match the competitive forces 1 through 4 to the factors on the survey. A factor can be matched to more than one competitive force.

Survey Factor	Competitive Force
A. Product performance	____ **1.** Time
B. Price	____ **2.** Quality
C. Lead time	____ **3.** Cost
D. Delivery	____ **4.** Flexibility of service

b. How can managers of this company use the information from this customer satisfaction survey to better meet competitive forces and satisfy their customers?

Exercise 18-16

Cost classifications for a service company

C2

Listed below are costs of providing an airline service. Classify each cost as (a) either variable or fixed and (b) as either direct or indirect. Consider the cost object to be a flight.

Cost	Cost by Behavior		Cost by Traceability	
	Variable	Fixed	Direct	Indirect
1. Advertising............................	____	____	____	____
2. Beverages and snacks....................	____	____	____	____
3. Regional vice-president salary.............	____	____	____	____
4. Depreciation on ground equipment........	____	____	____	____
5. Fuel and oil used in planes..............	____	____	____	____
6. Flight attendant salaries..................	____	____	____	____
7. Pilot salaries...........................	____	____	____	____
8. Ground crew wages.....................	____	____	____	____
9. Travel agent salaries....................	____	____	____	____

PROBLEM SET A

Problem 18-1A

Managerial accounting role

C1

This chapter explained the purpose of managerial accounting in the context of the current business environment. Review the *automobile* section of your local newspaper; the Sunday paper is often best. Review advertisements of sport-utility vehicles and identify the manufacturers that offer these products and the factors on which they compete.

Required

Discuss the potential contributions and responsibilities of the managerial accounting professional in helping an automobile manufacturer succeed. (*Hint:* Think about information and estimates that a managerial accountant might provide new entrants into the sport-utility market.)

Refer to *Decision Maker,* **Purchase Manager,** in this chapter. Assume that you are the motorcycle manufacturer's managerial accountant. The purchasing manager asks you about preparing an estimate of the related costs for buying motorcycle seats from supplier (B). She tells you this estimate is needed because unless dollar estimates are attached to nonfinancial factors, such as lost production time, her supervisor will not give it full attention. The manager also shows you the following information.

Problem 18-2A
Opportunity cost
estimation and application

C1 C2

- Production output is 1,000 motorcycles per year based on 250 production days a year.
- Production time per day is 8 hours at a cost of $2,000 per hour to run the production line.
- Lost production time due to poor quality is 1%.
- Satisfied customers purchase, on average, three motorcycles during a lifetime.
- Satisfied customers recommend the product, on average, to 5 other people.
- Marketing predicts that using seat (B) will result in 5 lost customers per year from repeat business and referrals.
- Average gross profit per motorcycle is $3,000.

Required

Estimate the costs (including opportunity costs) of buying motorcycle seats from supplier (B). This problem requires that you think creatively and make reasonable estimates; thus there could be more than one correct answer. (*Hint:* Reread the answer to *Decision Maker* and compare the cost savings for buying from supplier [B] to the sum of lost customer revenue from repeat business and referrals and the cost of lost production time.)

Check   Estimated cost of lost production time, $40,000

Listed here are the total costs associated with the 2013 production of 1,000 drum sets manufactured by DrumBeat. The drum sets sell for $500 each.

Problem 18-3A
Cost computation, classification, and analysis

C2 C3

Costs	Cost by Behavior		Cost by Function	
	Variable	Fixed	Product	Period
1. Plastic for casing—$17,000..........................	$17,000	____	$17,000	____
2. Wages of assembly workers—$82,000..................	____	____	____	____
3. Property taxes on factory—$5,000	____	____	____	____
4. Accounting staff salaries—$35,000	____	____	____	____
5. Drum stands (1,000 stands outsourced)—$26,000	____	____	____	____
6. Rent cost of equipment for sales staff—$10,000	____	____	____	____
7. Upper management salaries—$125,000	____	____	____	____
8. Annual flat fee for maintenance service—$10,000	____	____	____	____
9. Sales commissions—$15 per unit	____	____	____	____
10. Machinery depreciation, straight-line—$40,000	____	____	____	____

Required

1. Classify each cost and its amount as (*a*) either variable or fixed and (*b*) either product or period. (The first cost is completed as an example.)

2. Compute the manufacturing cost per drum set.

Check   (1) Total variable production cost, $125,000

Analysis Component

3. Assume that 1,200 drum sets are produced in the next year. What do you predict will be the total cost of plastic for the casings and the per unit cost of the plastic for the casings? Explain.

4. Assume that 1,200 drum sets are produced in the next year. What do you predict will be the total cost of property taxes and the per unit cost of the property taxes? Explain.

Assume that you must make a presentation to the marketing staff explaining the difference between product and period costs. Your supervisor tells you the marketing staff would also like clarification regarding prime and conversion costs and an explanation of how these terms fit with product and period cost. You are told that many on the staff are unable to classify costs in their merchandising activities.

Problem 18-4A
Cost classification
and explanation

C2 C3

Required

Prepare a one-page memorandum to your supervisor outlining your presentation to the marketing staff.

Problem 18-5A
Ending inventory computation and evaluation

C4

Notaro's Boot Company makes specialty boots for the rodeo circuit. On December 31, 2012, the company had (a) 300 pairs of boots in finished goods inventory and (b) 1,200 heels at a cost of $8 each in raw materials inventory. During 2013, the company purchased 35,000 additional heels at $8 each and manufactured 16,600 pairs of boots.

Required

1. Determine the unit and dollar amounts of raw materials inventory in heels at December 31, 2013.

Analysis Component

2. Write a one-half page memorandum to the production manager explaining why a just-in-time inventory system for heels should be considered. Include the amount of working capital that can be reduced at December 31, 2013, if the ending heel raw material inventory is cut by half.

Problem 18-6A
Inventory computation and reporting

C4 P1

mhhe.com/wildFAP21e

Shown here are annual financial data at December 31, 2013, taken from two different companies.

	Sports World Retail	Sno-Board Manufacturing
Beginning inventory		
Merchandise	$200,000	
Finished goods		$500,000
Cost of purchases	300,000	
Cost of goods manufactured		875,000
Ending inventory		
Merchandise	175,000	
Finished goods		225,000

Required

1. Compute the cost of goods sold section of the income statement at December 31, 2013, for each company. Include the proper title and format in the solution.

2. Write a half-page memorandum to your instructor (a) identifying the inventory accounts and (b) describing where each is reported on the income statement and balance sheet for both companies.

Problem 18-7A
Manufacturing and income statements; inventory analysis

P2 A1

The following calendar year-end information is taken from the December 31, 2013, adjusted trial balance and other records of DeLeon Company.

Advertising expense	$ 28,750	Direct labor	$ 675,480
Depreciation expense—Office equipment	7,250	Income taxes expense	233,725
Depreciation expense—Selling equipment	8,600	Indirect labor	56,875
Depreciation expense—Factory equipment	33,550	Miscellaneous production costs	8,425
Factory supervision	102,600	Office salaries expense	63,000
Factory supplies used	7,350	Raw materials purchases	925,000
Factory utilities	33,000	Rent expense—Office space	22,000
Inventories		Rent expense—Selling space	26,100
Raw materials, December 31, 2012	166,850	Rent expense—Factory building	76,800
Raw materials, December 31, 2013	182,000	Maintenance expense—Factory equipment	35,400
Goods in process, December 31, 2012	15,700	Sales	4,525,000
Goods in process, December 31, 2013...........	19,380	Sales discounts	62,500
Finished goods, December 31, 2012	167,350	Sales salaries expense	392,560
Finished goods, December 31, 2013	136,490		

Required

1. Prepare the company's 2013 manufacturing statement.
2. Prepare the company's 2013 income statement that reports separate categories for (*a*) selling expenses and (*b*) general and administrative expenses.

Check (1) Cost of goods manufactured, $1,935,650

Analysis Component

3. Compute the (*a*) inventory turnover, defined as cost of goods sold divided by average inventory, and (*b*) days' sales in inventory, defined as 365 times ending inventory divided by cost of goods sold, for both its raw materials inventory and its finished goods inventory. (To compute turnover and days' sales in inventory for raw materials, use raw materials used rather than cost of goods sold.) Discuss some possible reasons for differences between these ratios for the two types of inventories. Round answers to one decimal place.

Many fast-food restaurants compete on lean business concepts. Match each of the following activities at a fast-food restaurant with the lean business concept it strives to achieve. Some activities might relate to more than one lean business concept.

Problem 18-8A
Lean business concepts

C6

_____ **1.** Courtcous employees
_____ **2.** Food produced to order
_____ **3.** Clean tables and floors
_____ **4.** Orders filled within three minutes
_____ **5.** Standardized food making processes
_____ **6.** New product development
_____ **7.** Customer satisfaction surveys
_____ **8.** Standardized menus from location to location
_____ **9.** Drive-through windows
_____ **10.** Continually changing menus

a. Just-in-time (JIT)
b. Continuous improvement (CI)
c. Total quality management (TQM)

This chapter described the purpose of managerial accounting in the context of the current business environment. Review the *home electronics* section of your local newspaper; the Sunday paper is often best. Review advertisements of home electronics and identify the manufacturers that offer these products and the factors on which they compete.

PROBLEM SET B

Problem 18-1B
Managerial accounting role

C1

Required

Discuss the potential contributions and responsibilities of the managerial accounting professional in helping a home electronics manufacturer succeed. (*Hint:* Think about information and estimates that a managerial accountant might provide new entrants into the home electronics market.)

Refer to *Decision Maker,* **Purchase Manager,** in this chapter. Assume that you are the motorcycle manufacturer's managerial accountant. The purchasing manager asks you about preparing an estimate of the related costs for buying motorcycle seats from supplier (B). She tells you this estimate is needed because unless dollar estimates are attached to nonfinancial factors such as lost production time, her supervisor will not give it full attention. The manager also shows you the following information.

Problem 18-2B
Opportunity cost estimation and application

C1 C2

● Production output is 1,000 motorcycles per year based on 250 production days a year.
● Production time per day is 8 hours at a cost of $500 per hour to run the production line.
● Lost production time due to poor quality is 1%.
● Satisfied customers purchase, on average, three motorcycles during a lifetime.
● Satisfied customers recommend the product, on average, to four other people.
● Marketing predicts that using seat (B) will result in four lost customers per year from repeat business and referrals.
● Average gross profit per motorcycle is $4,000.

Required

Estimate the costs (including opportunity costs) of buying motorcycle seats from supplier (B). This problem requires that you think creatively and make reasonable estimates; thus there could be more than one correct answer. (*Hint:* Reread the answer to *Decision Maker,* and compare the cost savings for buying from supplier [B] to the sum of lost customer revenue from repeat business and referrals and the cost of lost production time.)

Problem 18-3B

Cost computation, classification, and analysis

C2   C3

Listed here are the total costs associated with the 2013 production of 15,000 Blu-ray Discs (BDs) manufactured by Nextgen. The BDs sell for $18 each.

	Cost by Behavior		Cost by Function	
Costs	Variable	Fixed	Product	Period
1. Plastic for BDs—$1,500	$1,500		$1,500	
2. Wages of assembly workers—$30,000				
3. Cost of factory rent—$6,750				
4. Systems staff salaries—$15,000				
5. Labeling (12,000 outsourced)—$3,750				
6. Cost of office equipment rent—$1,050				
7. Upper management salaries—$120,000				
8. Annual fixed fee for cleaning service—$4,520				
9. Sales commissions—$0.50 per BD				
10. Machinery depreciation, straight-line—$18,000				

Required

1. Classify each cost and its amount as (*a*) either variable or fixed and (*b*) either product or period. (The first cost is completed as an example.)

2. Compute the manufacturing cost per BD.

Analysis Component

3. Assume that 10,000 BDs are produced in the next year. What do you predict will be the total cost of plastic for the BDs and the per unit cost of the plastic for the BDs? Explain.

4. Assume that 10,000 BDs are produced in the next year. What do you predict will be the total cost of factory rent and the per unit cost of the factory rent? Explain.

Problem 18-4B

Cost classification and explanation

C2   C3

Assume that you must make a presentation to a client explaining the difference between prime and conversion costs. The client makes and sells 200,000 cookies per week. The client tells you that her sales staff also would like a clarification regarding product and period costs. She tells you that most of the staff lack training in managerial accounting.

Required

Prepare a one-page memorandum to your client outlining your planned presentation to her sales staff.

Problem 18-5B

Ending inventory computation and evaluation

C4

Sharp Edges makes specialty skates for the ice skating circuit. On December 31, 2012, the company had (*a*) 1,500 skates in finished goods inventory and (*b*) 2,500 blades at a cost of $20 each in raw materials inventory. During 2013, Sharp Edges purchased 45,000 additional blades at $20 each and manufactured 20,750 pairs of skates.

Required

1. Determine the unit and dollar amounts of raw materials inventory in blades at December 31, 2013.

Check (1) Ending (blade) inventory, 6,000 units; $120,000

Analysis Component

2. Write a one-half page memorandum to the production manager explaining why a just-in-time inventory system for blades should be considered. Include the amount of working capital that can be reduced at December 31, 2013, if the ending blade raw materials inventory is cut in half.

Shown here are annual financial data at December 31, 2013, taken from two different companies.

	Badger (Retail)	Naima (Manufacturing)
Beginning inventory		
Merchandise	$100,000	
Finished goods		$300,000
Cost of purchases	250,000	
Cost of goods manufactured		586,000
Ending inventory		
Merchandise	150,000	
Finished goods		200,000

Problem 18-6B
Inventory computation and reporting

C4 P1

Required

1. Compute the cost of goods sold section of the income statement at December 31, 2013, for each company. Include the proper title and format in the solution.

Check (1) Badger cost of goods sold, $200,000

2. Write a half-page memorandum to your instructor (*a*) identifying the inventory accounts and (*b*) identifying where each is reported on the income statement and balance sheet for both companies.

The following calendar year-end information is taken from the December 31, 2013, adjusted trial balance and other records of Elegant Furniture.

Problem 18-7B
Manufacturing and income statements; analysis of inventories P2 A1

Advertising expense	$ 20,250	Direct labor	$ 562,500
Depreciation expense—Office equipment	8,440	Income taxes expense	136,700
Depreciation expense—Selling equipment	10,125	Indirect labor	59,000
Depreciation expense—Factory equipment	35,400	Miscellaneous production costs	8,440
Factory supervision	121,500	Office salaries expense	70,875
Factory supplies used	6,060	Raw materials purchases	894,375
Factory utilities	37,500	Rent expense—Office space	23,625
Inventories		Rent expense—Selling space	27,000
Raw materials, December 31, 2012	40,375	Rent expense—Factory building	93,500
Raw materials, December 31, 2013	70,430	Maintenance expense—Factory equipment	30,375
Goods in process, December 31, 2012	12,500	Sales	5,000,000
Goods in process, December 31, 2013	14,100	Sales discounts	57,375
Finished goods, December 31, 2012	177,200	Sales salaries expense	295,300
Finished goods, December 31, 2013	141,750		

Required

1. Prepare the company's 2013 manufacturing statement.
2. Prepare the company's 2013 income statement that reports separate categories for (*a*) selling expenses and (*b*) general and administrative expenses.

Check (1) Cost of goods manufactured, $1,816,995

Analysis Component

3. Compute the (*a*) inventory turnover, defined as cost of goods sold divided by average inventory, and (*b*) days' sales in inventory, defined as 365 times ending inventory divided by cost of goods sold, for both its raw materials inventory and its finished goods inventory. (To compute turnover and days' sales in inventory for raw materials, use raw materials used rather than cost of goods sold.) Discuss some possible reasons for differences between these ratios for the two types of inventories. Round answers to one decimal place.

Problem 18-8B
Lean business concepts
C6

Canon manufactures digital cameras and must compete on lean manufacturing concepts. Match each of the following activities that it engages in with the lean manufacturing concept it strives to achieve. (Some activities might relate to more than one lean manufacturing concept.)

_____ **1.** Manufacturing facilities are arranged to reduce move time and wait time.

_____ **2.** Canon conducts focus groups to determine new features that customers want in digital cameras.

_____ **3.** Canon monitors the market to determine what features its competitors are offering on digital cameras.

_____ **4.** Canon asks production workers for ideas to improve production.

_____ **5.** The manufacturing process is standardized and documented.

_____ **6.** Cameras are produced in small lots, and only to customer order.

_____ **7.** Lenses are received daily based on customer orders.

_____ **8.** Customers receive a satisfaction survey with each camera purchased.

_____ **9.** Orders received are filled within two business days.

_____ **10.** Canon works with suppliers to reduce inspection time of incoming materials.

a. Just-in-time (JIT)
b. Continuous improvement (CI)
c. Total quality management (TQM)

SERIAL PROBLEM
Success Systems
C2 C4 P2

(This serial problem begins in Chapter 1 and continues through most of the book. If previous chapter segments were not completed, the serial problem can begin at this point. It is helpful, but not necessary, to use the Working Papers that accompany the book.)

SP 18 Adria Lopez, owner of Success Systems, decides to diversify her business by also manufacturing computer workstation furniture.

Required

1. Classify the following manufacturing costs of Success Systems by behavior and traceability.

Product Costs	Cost by Behavior		Cost by Traceability	
	Variable	Fixed	Direct	Indirect
1. Monthly flat fee to clean workshop.........	___	___	___	___
2. Laminate coverings for desktops...........	___	___	___	___
3. Taxes on assembly workshop.............	___	___	___	___
4. Glue to assemble workstation component parts...................	___	___	___	___
5. Wages of desk assembler...............	___	___	___	___
6. Electricity for workshop................	___	___	___	___
7. Depreciation on tools.................	___	___	___	___

2. Prepare a manufacturing statement for Success Systems for the month ended January 31, 2014. Assume the following manufacturing costs:

Direct materials: $2,200

Factory overhead: $490

Direct labor: $900

Beginning goods in process: none (December 31, 2013)

Ending goods in process: $540 (January 31, 2014)

Beginning finished goods inventory: none (December 31, 2013)

Ending finished goods inventory: $350 (January 31, 2014)

3. Prepare the cost of goods sold section of a partial income statement for Success Systems for the month ended January 31, 2014.

Check (3) COGS, $2,700

Beyond the Numbers

BTN 18-1   Managerial accounting is more than recording, maintaining, and reporting financial results. Managerial accountants must provide managers with both financial and nonfinancial information including estimates, projections, and forecasts. An important estimate for **Polaris** is its reserve for warranty claims, and the company must provide shareholders information on these estimates.

REPORTING IN ACTION

C1

Polaris

Required

1. Access and read Polaris' "Product warranties" section of the "Organization and Significant Accounting Policies" footnote to its financial statements, from Appendix A. What is the warranty period for Polaris' products? How does management establish and adjust the warranty reserve? What are some of the effects if the company's actual results differ from its estimates?

2. What is the management accountant's role in determining those estimates?

3. What are some factors that could impact the warranty accrual in a given year?

Fast Forward

4. Access **Polaris**' annual report for a fiscal year ending after December 31, 2011, from either its Website [Polaris.com] or the SEC's EDGAR database [www.sec.gov]. Answer the questions in parts (1), (2), and (3) after reading the current "Organization and Significant Accounting Policies". Identify any major changes.

BTN 18-2   Both **Polaris** and **Arctic Cat** provide warranties on the products they sell. Accurate estimates of these future warranty claims are important. Access the annual report or 10-K for both Polaris (from Appendix A) and Arctic Cat. The Polaris report is for the year ended December 31, 2011, and the Arctic Cat report is for the year ended March 31, 2011.

COMPARATIVE ANALYSIS

C2

Polaris

Arctic Cat

Required

1. Read the "Product warranties" section of the "Organization and Significant Accounting Policies" footnote for Polaris. For each of the three years reported, compare the dollar amounts of the annual warranty expense and actual warranty claims paid. Is Polaris' warranty expense higher, lower, or about the same as its warranty claims paid?

2. Read the "Product Warranties" section of the "Summary of Significant Accounting Policies" footnote for Arctic Cat. For each of the three years reported, compare the dollar amounts of the annual warranty expense and actual warranty claims paid. Is Arctic Cat's warranty expense higher, lower, or about the same as its warranty claims paid?

3. Using the answers from parts (1) and (2), which company made more accurate estimates of warranty costs over the most recent three years?

BTN 18-3   Assume that you are the managerial accountant at Infostore, a manufacturer of hard drives, CDs, and DVDs. Its reporting year-end is December 31. The chief financial officer is concerned about having enough cash to pay the expected income tax bill because of poor cash flow management. On November 15, the purchasing department purchased excess inventory of CD raw materials in anticipation of rapid growth of this product beginning in January. To decrease the company's tax liability, the chief financial officer tells you to record the purchase of this inventory as part of supplies and expense it in the current year; this would decrease the company's tax liability by increasing expenses.

ETHICS CHALLENGE

C1 C3

Required

1. In which account should the purchase of CD raw materials be recorded?
2. How should you respond to this request by the chief financial officer?

COMMUNICATING IN PRACTICE

C6

BTN 18-4   Write a one-page memorandum to a prospective college student about salary expectations for graduates in business. Compare and contrast the expected salaries for accounting (including different subfields such as public, corporate, tax, audit, and so forth), marketing, management, and finance majors. Prepare a graph showing average starting salaries (and those for experienced professionals in those fields if available). To get this information, stop by your school's career services office; libraries also have this information. The Website **JobStar.org** (click on *Salary Info*) also can get you started.

TAKING IT TO THE NET

C1

BTN 18-5   Managerial accounting professionals follow a code of ethics. As a member of the Institute of Management Accountants, the managerial accountant must comply with Standards of Ethical Conduct.

Required

1. Identify, print, and read the *Statement of Ethical Professional Practice* posted at **www.IMAnet.org**. (Search using "statement of ethical professional practice and select the Ethics Center and Helpline link. Under Ethical Practices, select Learn More.")
2. What four overarching ethical principles underlie the IMA's statement?
3. Describe the courses of action the IMA recommends in resolving ethical conflicts.

TEAMWORK IN ACTION

C5 P2

BTN 18-6   The following calendar-year information is taken from the December 31, 2013, adjusted trial balance and other records of Dahlia Company.

Advertising expense	$ 19,125	Direct labor	$ 650,750
Depreciation expense—Office equipment	8,750	Indirect labor	60,000
Depreciation expense—Selling equipment	10,000	Miscellaneous production costs	8,500
Depreciation expense—Factory equipment	32,500	Office salaries expense	100,875
Factory supervision	122,500	Raw materials purchases	872,500
Factory supplies used	15,750	Rent expense—Office space	21,125
Factory utilities	36,250	Rent expense—Selling space	25,750
Inventories		Rent expense—Factory building	79,750
Raw materials, December 31, 2012	177,500	Maintenance expense—Factory equipment	27,875
Raw materials, December 31, 2013	168,125	Sales	3,275,000
Goods in process, December 31, 2012	15,875	Sales discounts	57,500
Goods in process, December 31, 2013	14,000	Sales salaries expense	286,250
Finished goods, December 31, 2012	164,375		
Finished goods, December 31, 2013	129,000		

Required

1. *Each* team member is to be responsible for computing **one** of the following amounts. You are not to duplicate your teammates' work. Get any necessary amounts from teammates. Each member is to explain the computation to the team in preparation for reporting to class.

   a. Materials used.   **d.** Total cost of goods in process.
   b. Factory overhead.   **e.** Cost of goods manufactured.
   c. Total manufacturing costs.

2. Check your cost of goods manufactured with the instructor. If it is correct, proceed to part (3).

3. *Each* team member is to be responsible for computing **one** of the following amounts. You are not to duplicate your teammates' work. Get any necessary amounts from teammates. Each member is to explain the computation to the team in preparation for reporting to class.

   a. Net sales.   **d.** Total operating expenses.

   b. Cost of goods sold.   **e.** Net income or loss before taxes.

   c. Gross profit.

Point: Provide teams with transparencies and markers for presentation purposes.

BTN 18-7   Alexandro Velez and Nikhail Arora of **Back to the Roots** must understand manufacturing costs to effectively operate and succeed as a profitable and efficient business.

Required

1. What are the three main categories of manufacturing costs the owners must monitor and control? Provide examples of each.

2. What are four goals of a total quality management process? How can Back to the Roots use TQM to improve its business activities?

ENTREPRENEURIAL DECISION

C1 C2 C6

BTN 18-8   Visit your favorite fast-food restaurant. Observe its business operations.

Required

1. Describe all business activities from the time a customer arrives to the time that customer departs.

2. List all costs you can identify with the separate activities described in part 1.

3. Classify each cost from part 2 as fixed or variable, and explain your classification.

HITTING THE ROAD

C1 C2

BTN 18-9   Access **Piaggio**'s Website (**www.piaggiogroup.com**) and select "Governance" and then select "Company boards." Read the section dealing with the role of its board of directors.

Required

1. Identify the role of Piaggio's board of directors.

2. How would management accountants be involved in assisting the board of directors in carrying out their responsibilities? Explain.

GLOBAL DECISION

C1

PIAGGIO

ANSWERS TO MULTIPLE CHOICE QUIZ

1. c

2. b

3. b

4. a

5. Beginning finished goods + Cost of goods manufactured (COGM) −
Ending finished goods = Cost of goods sold
$6,000 + COGM − $3,200 = $7,500
COGM = $4,700

Job Order Cost Accounting

A Look Back

Chapter 18 introduced managerial accounting and explained basic cost concepts. We also described the lean business model and the reporting of manufacturing activities, including the manufacturing statement.

A Look at This Chapter

We begin this chapter by describing a cost accounting system. We then explain the procedures used to determine costs using a job order costing system. We conclude with a discussion of over- and underapplied overhead.

A Look Ahead

Chapter 20 focuses on measuring costs in process production companies. We explain process production, describe how to assign costs to processes, and compute and analyze cost per equivalent unit.

Learning Objectives

CONCEPTUAL

C1 Describe important features of job order production. (p. 778)

C2 Explain job cost sheets and how they are used in job order cost accounting. (p. 780)

ANALYTICAL

A1 Apply job order costing in pricing services. (p. 791)

PROCEDURAL

P1 Describe and record the flow of materials costs in job order cost accounting. (p. 782)

P2 Describe and record the flow of labor costs in job order cost accounting. (p. 784)

P3 Describe and record the flow of overhead costs in job order cost accounting. (p. 785)

P4 Determine adjustments for overapplied and underapplied factory overhead. (p. 790)

Decision Insight

Suit Yourself!

"Be fearless!"

—DAVID SCHOTTENSTEIN

COLUMBUS, OH—Watching Italian tailors hand-sew high-quality men's suits, David Schottenstein decided to start his own men's clothing store. David's aspirations were high: Sell custom-made mens' suits, hand-sewn and made from the finest fabrics, at prices up to 80 percent less than competitor's clothes. David recalls thinking, "If I have to crawl around on my hands and knees to measure people's inseams to get this business started, I'm going to do it." The result is **Astor and Black (AstorandBlack.com),** a startup international company with sales in 2010 of over $20 million.

David's employees travel to customers' homes, offices, and clubs around the world to do personal fittings. Customers select the fabrics, buttons, stitching, and other details, and then tailors hand-sew each suit to exact customer specifications. "I like to pick out my own stuff, and it's easier than going to a store," says Malcolm Jenkins, All-Pro NFL cornerback and owner of over 30 Astor and Black suits. David stresses that "customer service and satisfying each customer's individual needs" are what drive success.

David's business model is based on selling a higher volume of suits than competitors, but at lower margins per suit. This requires David to carefully monitor costs. Astor and Black, like other makers of custom products, uses a state-of-the-art job order cost accounting system to track costs. Such a system tracks the cost of materials, labor, and overhead for each suit, enabling David to make quick business decisions regarding costs and selling prices. Job order costing allows entrepreneurs like David to better isolate costs and avoid the run away costs often experienced by startups that fail to use such costing techniques. "We keep our fixed costs low by not stocking inventory," explains David, "and we use minimal office space as our sales mainly occur in customer's homes or offices."

David encourages young entrepreneurs to believe in themselves. "People have great ideas all the time but find all the [wrong] reasons not to do it. You have to be fearless," says David. In David's case, that fearlessness began with selling rare cigars and trading stocks as a teenager. "It was bizarre," says his father Tom. "He was a kid on a mission." With attention to detail and insights gained from job order costing information, David's business continues to expand, now offering women's suits and online tailoring, allowing customers to create a simulated version of the outfit they want. "Be brazen or you will be done on the day you start," says David.

[Sources: *Astor and Black* Website, January 2013; *Yourhiddenpotential.co.uk* Website, May 8, 2011; *The Columbus Dispatch*, June 22, 2008; *Forbes*, May 9, 2011; *Smart Business Online*, www.sbonline.com, June 2009.]

This chapter introduces a system for assigning costs to the flow of goods through a production process. We then describe the details of a *job order cost accounting system*. Job order costing is frequently used by manufacturers of custom products or providers of custom services. Manufacturers that use job order costing typically base it on a perpetual inventory system, which provides a continuous record of materials, goods in process, and finished goods inventories.

Job Order Cost Accounting

Job Order Cost Accounting	**Job Order Cost Flows and Reports**	**Adjusting Factory Overhead**
• Cost accounting system • Job order production • Job order costing of services • Events in job order costing • Job cost sheet	• Materials cost flows and documents • Labor cost flows and documents • Overhead cost flows and documents • Summary of cost flows	• Factory overhead T-account • Underapplied or overapplied overhead

JOB ORDER COST ACCOUNTING

This section describes a cost accounting system and job order production and costing.

Cost Accounting System

An ever-increasing number of companies use a cost accounting system to generate timely and accurate inventory information. A **cost accounting system** records manufacturing activities using a *perpetual* inventory system, which continuously updates records for costs of materials, goods in process, and finished goods inventories. A cost accounting system also provides timely information about inventories and manufacturing costs per unit of product. This is especially helpful for managers' efforts to control costs and determine selling prices. (A **general accounting system** records manufacturing activities using a *periodic* inventory system. Some companies still use a general accounting system, but its use is declining as competitive forces and customer demands have increased pressures on companies to better manage inventories.)

C1 Describe important features of job order production.

The two basic types of cost accounting systems are *job order cost accounting* and *process cost accounting*. We describe job order cost accounting in this chapter. Process cost accounting is explained in the next chapter.

Job Order Production

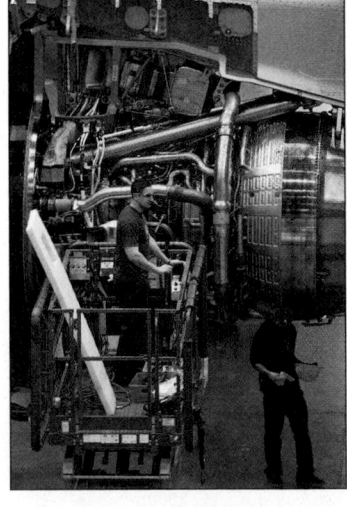

Many companies produce products individually designed to meet the needs of a specific customer. Each customized product is manufactured separately and its production is called **job order production,** or *job order manufacturing* (also called *customized production,* which is the production of products in response to special orders). Examples of such products include synthetic football fields, special-order machines, a factory building, custom jewelry, wedding invitations, and artwork. The production activities for a customized product represent a **job.**

Boeing's aerospace division is one example of a job order production system. Its primary business is twofold: (1) design, develop, and integrate space carriers and (2) provide systems engineering and integration of Department of Defense (DoD) systems. Many of its orders are customized and produced through job order operations.

When a job involves producing more than one unit of a custom product, it is often called a **job lot.** Products produced as job lots could include benches for a church, imprinted T-shirts for a 10K race or company picnic, or advertising signs for a chain of stores. Although these orders involve more than one unit, the volume of production is typically low, such as 50 benches, 200 T-shirts, or 100 signs. Another feature of job order production is the diversity, often called *heterogeneity,* of the products produced. Namely, each customer order is likely to differ from another in some important respect. These variations can be minor or major.

 Decision Insight

Custom Design Managers once saw companies as the center of a solar system orbited by suppliers and customers. Now the customer has become the center of the business universe. **Nike** allows custom orders over the Internet, enabling customers to select materials, colors, and to personalize their shoes with letters and numbers. Soon consumers may be able to personalize almost any product, from cellular phones to appliances to furniture. ■

Job Order Costing of Services

The principle of customization is equally applicable to both manufacturing *and* service companies. Most service companies meet customers' needs by performing a custom service for a specific customer. Examples of such services include an accountant auditing a client's financial statements, an interior designer remodeling an office, a wedding consultant planning and supervising a reception, and a lawyer defending a client. Whether the setting is manufacturing or services, job order operations involve meeting the needs of customers by producing or performing custom jobs. We show an example of job order costing for an advertising service in the Decision Analysis section of this chapter.

Events in Job Order Costing

The initial event in a normal job order operation is the receipt of a customer order for a custom product. This causes the company to begin work on a job. A less common case occurs when management decides to begin work on a job before it has a signed contract. This is referred to as *jobs produced on speculation.*

Step 1: Predict the cost to complete the job. This cost depends on the product design prepared by either the customer or the producer.

Step 2: Negotiate price and decide whether to pursue the job. Other than for government or other cost-plus contracts, the selling price is determined by market factors. Producers evaluate the market price, compare it to cost, and determine whether the profit on the job is reasonable. If the profit is not reasonable, the producer would determine a desired **target cost.**

Point: Some jobs are priced on a *cost-plus basis:* The customer pays the manufacturer for costs incurred on the job plus a negotiated amount or rate of profit.

Step 3: Schedule production of the job. This must meet the customer's needs and fit within the company's own production constraints. Preparation of this work schedule should consider workplace facilities including equipment, personnel, and supplies. Once this schedule is complete, the producer can place orders for raw materials. Production occurs as materials and labor are applied to the job.

An overview of job order production activity is shown in Exhibit 19.1. This exhibit shows the March production activity of Road Warriors, which installs security devices into cars and trucks. The company converts any vehicle by adding alarms, reinforced exterior, bulletproof glass, and bomb detectors. The company began by catering to high-profile celebrities, but it now caters to anyone who desires added security in a vehicle.

Job order production for Road Warriors requires materials, labor, and overhead costs. Recall that direct materials are goods used in manufacturing that are clearly identified with a particular job. Similarly, direct labor is effort devoted to a particular job. Overhead costs support production of more than one job. Common overhead items are depreciation on factory buildings and equipment, factory supplies, supervision, maintenance, cleaning, and utilities.

Exhibit 19.1 shows that materials, labor, and overhead are added to Jobs B15, B16, B17, B18, and B19, which were started during March. Special tires and bulletproof glass are added to Jobs B15 and B16, while Job B17 receives a reinforced exterior and bulletproof glass. Road Warriors completed Jobs B15, B16, and B17 in March and delivered Jobs B15 and B16 to

Point: Many professional examinations including the CPA and CMA exams require knowledge of job order and process cost accounting.

EXHIBIT 19.1

Job Order Production Activities

customers. At the end of March, Jobs B18 and B19 remain in goods in process inventory and Job B17 is in finished goods inventory. Both labor and materials costs are also separated into their direct and indirect components. Their indirect amounts are added to overhead. Total overhead cost is then allocated to the various jobs.

■ **Decision** Insight

Target Costing   Many producers determine a target cost for their jobs. Target cost is determined as follows: Expected selling price − Desired profit = Target cost. If the projected target cost of the job as determined by job costing is too high, the producer can apply *value engineering,* which is a method of determining ways to reduce job cost until the target cost is met. ■

Job Cost Sheet

C2   Explain job cost sheets and how they are used in job order cost accounting.

General ledger accounts usually do not provide the accounting information that managers of job order cost operations need to plan and control production activities. This is so because the needed information often requires more detailed data. Such detailed data are usually stored in subsidiary records controlled by general ledger accounts. Subsidiary records store information about raw materials, overhead costs, jobs in process, finished goods, and other items. This section describes the use of these records.

A major aim of a **job order cost accounting system** is to determine the cost of producing each job or job lot. In the case of a job lot, the system also aims to compute the cost per unit. The accounting system must include separate records for each job to accomplish this, and it must capture information about costs incurred and charge these costs to each job.

A **job cost sheet** is a separate record maintained for each job. Exhibit 19.2 shows a job cost sheet for an alarm system that Road Warriors produced for a customer. This job cost sheet identifies the customer, the job number assigned, the product, and key dates. Costs incurred on the job are immediately recorded on this sheet. When each job is complete, the supervisor enters the date of completion, records any remarks, and signs the sheet. The job cost sheet in Exhibit 19.2 classifies costs as direct materials, direct labor, or overhead. It shows that a total of $600 in direct materials is added to Job B15 on four different dates. It also shows seven entries for direct labor costs that total $1,000. Road Warriors *allocates* (also termed *applies, assigns,* or *charges*) factory overhead costs of $1,600 to this job using an allocation rate of 160% of direct labor cost (160% × $1,000)—we discuss overhead allocation later in this chapter.

Point: Factory overhead consists of costs (other than direct materials and direct labor) that ensure the production activities are carried out.

Cost Flows: During Production   While a job is being produced, its accumulated costs are kept in **Goods in Process Inventory.** The collection of job cost sheets for all jobs in process makes up a subsidiary ledger controlled by the Goods in Process Inventory account in the general ledger. Managers use job cost sheets to monitor costs incurred to date and to predict and control costs for each job.

EXHIBIT 19.2

Job Cost Sheet

Accounting System: Exhibit 19-2   _ □ ☒

File   Edit   Maintain   Tasks   Analysis   Options   Reports   Window   Help

Road Warriors, Los Angeles, California   **JOB COST SHEET**

| Customer's Name | Carroll Connor | Job No. | B15 |

| Address | 1542 High Point Dr. | City & State | Malibu, California |

| Job Description | Level 1 Alarm System on Ford Expedition |

| Date promised | March 15 | Date started | March 3 | Date completed | March 11 |

Direct Materials			Direct Labor			Overhead		
Date	**Requisition**	**Cost**	**Date**	**Time Ticket**	**Cost**	**Date**	**Rate**	**Cost**
3/3/2013	R-4698	100.00	3/3/2013	L-3393	120.00	3/11/2013	160% of	1,600.00
3/7/2013	R-4705	225.00	3/4/2013	L-3422	150.00		Direct	
3/9/2013	R-4725	180.00	3/5/2013	L-3456	180.00		Labor	
3/10/2013	R-4777	95.00	3/8/2013	L-3479	60.00		Cost	
			3/9/2013	L-3501	90.00			
			3/10/2013	L-3535	240.00			
			3/11/2013	L-3559	160.00			
	Total	600.00		**Total**	1,000.00		**Total**	1,600.00

REMARKS: Completed job on March 11, and shipped to customer	SUMMARY:	
on March 15. Met all specifications and requirements.	Materials	600.00
	Labor	1,000.00
	Overhead	1,600.00
Signed: *C. Luther, Supervisor*	Total cost	3,200.00

Cost Flows: Job Completion   When a job is finished, its job cost sheet is completed and moved from the jobs in process file to the finished jobs file. This latter file acts as a subsidiary ledger controlled by the **Finished Goods Inventory** account.

Cost Flows: Job Delivery   When a finished job is delivered to a customer, the job cost sheet is moved to a permanent file supporting the total cost of goods sold. This permanent file contains records from both current and prior periods. When the job is finished, the company also prepares a journal entry that credits Sales and debits Cash (or Accounts Receivable).

Point: Documents (electronic and paper) are crucial in a job order system, and the job cost sheet is a cornerstone. Understanding it aids in grasping concepts of capitalizing product costs and product cost flow.

Decision Maker

Management Consultant   One of your tasks is to control and manage costs for a consulting company. At the end of a recent month, you find that three consulting jobs were completed and two are 60% complete. Each unfinished job is estimated to cost $10,000 and to earn a revenue of $12,000. You are unsure how to recognize goods in process inventory and record costs and revenues. Do you recognize any inventory? If so, how much? How much revenue is recorded for unfinished jobs this month? ■   [Answer—p. 795]

Quick Check
Answers — p. 795

1. Which of these products is likely to involve job order production? (*a*) inexpensive watches, (*b*) racing bikes, (*c*) bottled soft drinks, or (*d*) athletic socks.
2. What is the difference between a job and a job lot?
3. Which of these statements is correct? (*a*) The collection of job cost sheets for unfinished jobs makes up a subsidiary ledger controlled by the Goods in Process Inventory account, (*b*) Job cost sheets are financial statements provided to investors, or (*c*) A separate job cost sheet is maintained in the general ledger for each job in process.
4. What three costs are normally accumulated on job cost sheets?

JOB ORDER COST FLOWS AND REPORTS

P1 Describe and record the flow of materials costs in job order cost accounting.

Materials

Materials Cost Flows and Documents

This section focuses on the flow of materials costs and the related documents in a job order cost accounting system. We begin analysis of the flow of materials costs by examining Exhibit 19.3. When materials are first received from suppliers, the employees count and inspect them and record the items' quantity and cost on a receiving report. The receiving report serves as the *source document* for recording materials received in both a materials ledger card and in the general ledger. In nearly all job order cost systems, **materials ledger cards** (or files) are perpetual records that are updated each time units are purchased and each time units are issued for use in production.

Point: Some companies certify certain suppliers based on the quality of their materials. Goods received from these suppliers are not always inspected by the purchaser to save costs.

To illustrate the purchase of materials, Road Warriors acquired $450 of wiring and related materials on March 4, 2013. This purchase is recorded as follows.

Assets = Liabilities + Equity
+450   +450

Mar. 4	Raw Materials Inventory—M-347	450	
	Accounts Payable		450
	To record purchase of materials for production.		

EXHIBIT 19.3

Materials Cost Flows through Subsidiary Records

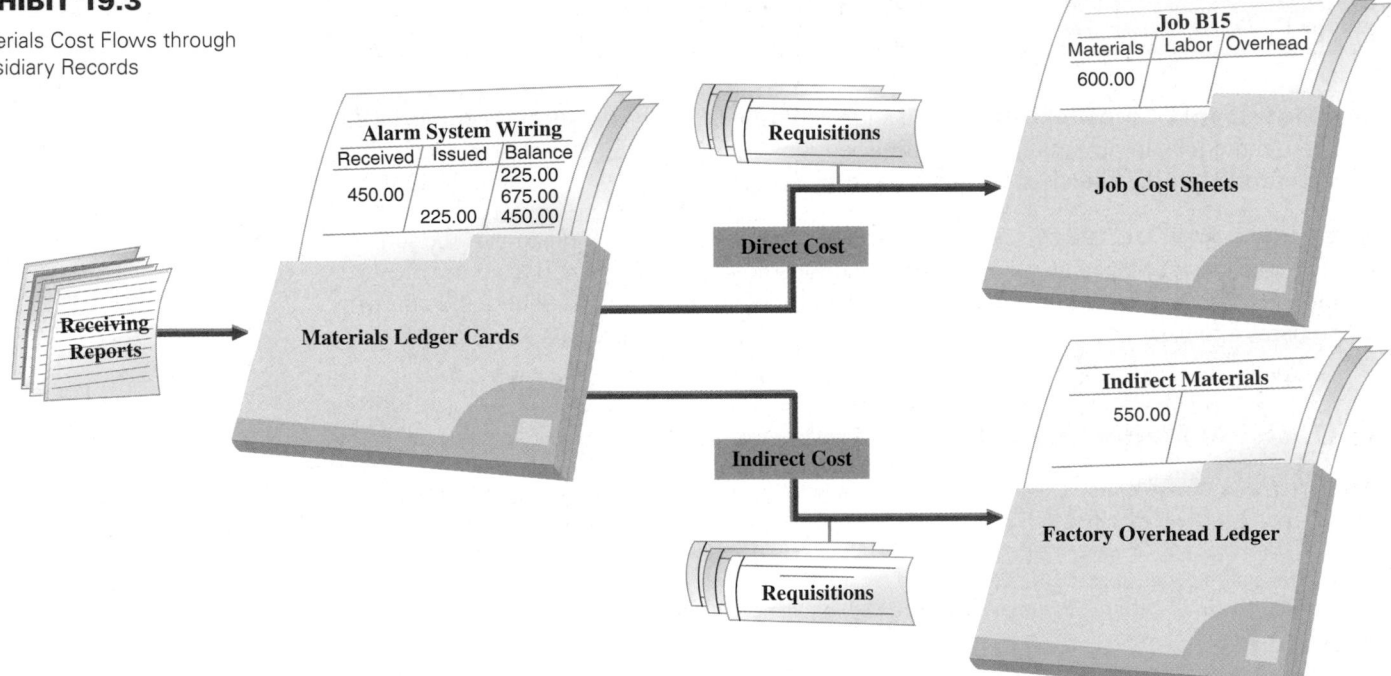

Exhibit 19.3 shows that materials can be requisitioned for use either on a specific job (direct materials) or as overhead (indirect materials). Cost of direct materials flows from the materials ledger card to the job cost sheet. The cost of indirect materials flows from the materials ledger card to the Indirect Materials account in the factory overhead ledger, which is a subsidiary ledger controlled by the Factory Overhead account in the general ledger.

Exhibit 19.4 shows a materials ledger card for material received and issued by Road Warriors. The card identifies the item as alarm system wiring and shows the item's stock number, its location in the storeroom, information about the maximum and minimum quantities that should be available, and the reorder quantity. For example, alarm system wiring is issued

EXHIBIT 19.4

Materials Ledger Card

and recorded on March 7, 2013. The job cost sheet in Exhibit 19.2 showed that Job B15 used this wiring.

When materials are needed in production, a production manager prepares a **materials requisition** and sends it to the materials manager. The requisition shows the job number, the type of material, the quantity needed, and the signature of the manager authorized to make the requisition. Exhibit 19.5 shows the materials requisition for alarm system wiring for Job B15. To see how this requisition ties to the flow of costs, compare the information on the requisition with the March 7, 2013, data in Exhibits 19.2 and 19.4.

Point: Requisitions are often accumulated and recorded in one entry. The frequency of entries depends on the job, the industry, and management procedures.

MATERIALS REQUISITION   No. R–4705

Road Warriors
Los Angeles, California

Job No. _____ B15 _____	Date _____ 3/7/2013 _____
Material Stock No. ____ M–347 ____	Material Description ____ Alarm system wiring ____
Quantity Requested ____ 1 ____	Requested By ____ C. Luther ____
Quantity Provided ____ 1 ____	Date Provided ____ 3/7/2013 ____
Filled By ____ M. Bateman ____	Material Received By ____ C. Luther ____
Remarks _____	

EXHIBIT 19.5

Materials Requisition

The use of alarm system wiring on Job B15 yields the following entry (locate this cost item in the job cost sheet shown in Exhibit 19.2).

Mar. 7	Goods in Process Inventory—Job B15	225	
	Raw Materials Inventory—M-347		225
	To record use of material on Job B15.		

Assets = Liabilities + Equity
+225
−225

This entry is posted both to its general ledger accounts and to subsidiary records. Posting to subsidiary records includes a debit to a job cost sheet and a credit to a materials ledger card. (*Note:* An entry to record use of indirect materials is the same as that for direct materials *except* the debit is to Factory Overhead. In the subsidiary factory overhead ledger, this entry is posted to Indirect Materials.)

Point: Exhibit 19.12 shows this entry.

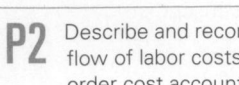

P2 Describe and record the flow of labor costs in job order cost accounting.

Labor

Labor Cost Flows and Documents

Exhibit 19.6 shows the flow of labor costs from clock cards and the Factory Payroll account to subsidiary records of the job order cost accounting system. Recall that costs in subsidiary records give detailed information needed to manage and control operations.

EXHIBIT 19.6

Labor Cost Flows through Subsidiary Records

Point: In the accounting equation, we treat accounts such as Factory Payroll and Factory Overhead as temporary accounts, which hold various expenses until they are allocated to balance sheet or income statement accounts.

The flow of costs in Exhibit 19.6 begins with **clock cards.** Employees commonly use these cards to record the number of hours worked, and they serve as source documents for entries to record labor costs. Clock card data on the number of hours worked is used at the end of each pay period to determine total labor cost. This amount is then debited to the Factory Payroll account, a temporary account containing the total payroll cost (both direct and indirect). Payroll cost is later allocated to both specific jobs and overhead.

According to clock card data, workers earned $1,500 for the week ended March 5. Illustrating the flow of labor costs, the accrual and payment of these wages are recorded as follows.

Assets = Liabilities + Equity
−1,500   −1,500

Mar. 6	Factory Payroll	1,500	
	Cash		1,500
	To record the weekly payroll.		

Point: Many employee fraud schemes involve payroll, including overstated hours on clock cards.

To assign labor costs to specific jobs and to overhead, we must know how each employee's time is used and its costs. Source documents called **time tickets** usually capture these data. Employees regularly fill out time tickets to report how much time they spent on each job. An employee who works on several jobs during a day completes a separate time ticket for each job. Tickets are also prepared for time charged to overhead as indirect labor. A supervisor signs an employee's time ticket to confirm its accuracy.

Exhibit 19.7 shows a time ticket reporting the time a Road Warrior employee spent working on Job B15. The employee's supervisor signed the ticket to confirm its accuracy. The hourly rate and total labor cost are computed after the time ticket is turned in. To see the effect of this time ticket on the job cost sheet, look at the entry dated March 8, 2013, in Exhibit 19.2.

EXHIBIT 19.7
Time Ticket

Road Warriors
Los Angeles, California

TIME TICKET   No. L–3479

Date .....March 8..... 20 ...13...

Employee Name	Employee Number	Job No.
T. Zeller	3969	B15

TIME AND RATE INFORMATION:

Remarks
....
....
....
....

Start Time	Finish Time	Elapsed Time	Hourly Rate
9:00	12:00	3.0	$20.00

Approved By ....*C. Luther*.......... **Total Cost** $60.00

When time tickets report labor used on a specific job, this cost is recorded as direct labor. The following entry records the data from the time ticket in Exhibit 19.7.

Mar. 8	Goods in Process Inventory—Job B15	60	
	Factory Payroll		60
	To record direct labor used on Job B15.		

Assets = Liabilities + Equity
+60   +60

The debit in this entry is posted both to the general ledger account and to the appropriate job cost sheet. (*Note:* An entry to record indirect labor is the same as for direct labor *except* that it debits Factory Overhead and credits Factory Payroll. In the subsidiary factory overhead ledger, the debit in this entry is posted to the Indirect Labor account.)

Point: Exhibit 19.12 shows this entry.

Overhead Cost Flows and Documents

Factory overhead (or simply overhead) cost flows are shown in Exhibit 19.8. Factory overhead includes all production costs other than direct materials and direct labor. Two sources of overhead costs are indirect materials and indirect labor. These costs are recorded from requisitions for indirect materials and time tickets for indirect labor. Two other sources of overhead are (1) vouchers authorizing payments for items such as supplies or utilities and (2) adjusting entries for costs such as depreciation on factory assets.

Overhead

P3 Describe and record the flow of overhead costs in job order cost accounting.

Factory overhead usually includes many different costs and, thus, a separate account for each is often maintained in a subsidiary factory overhead ledger. This ledger is controlled by the Factory Overhead account in the general ledger. Factory Overhead is a temporary account that accumulates costs until they are allocated to jobs.

Recording Overhead   Recall that overhead costs are recorded with debits to the Factory Overhead account and with credits to other accounts such as Cash, Accounts Payable, and

Point: Companies also incur *nonmanufacturing* costs, such as advertising, salesperson's salaries, and depreciation on assets not used in production. These types of costs are not considered overhead, but instead are treated as period costs and charged directly to the income statement. These period costs can be relevant to managers' pricing decisions.

EXHIBIT 19.8
Overhead Cost Flows through Subsidiary Records

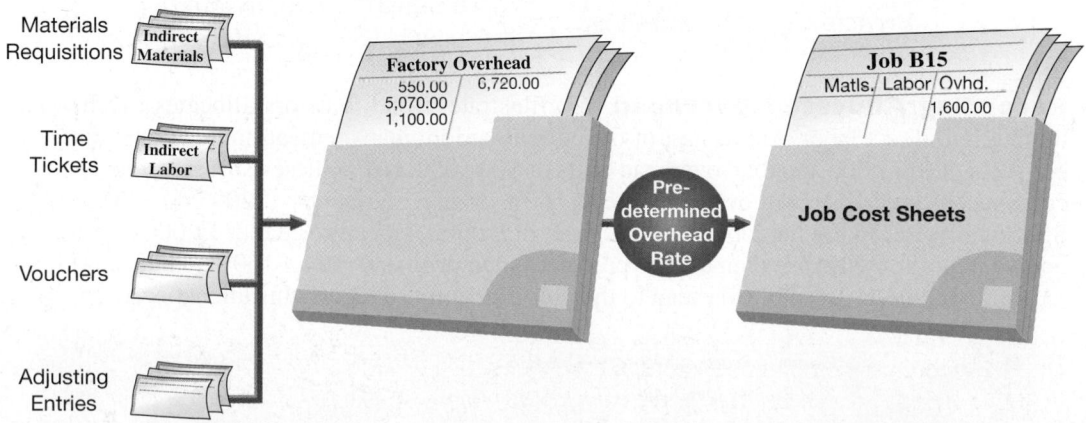

Accumulated Depreciation—Equipment. In the subsidiary factory overhead ledger, the debits are posted to their respective accounts such as Depreciation Expense—Equipment, Insurance Expense—Warehouse, or Amortization Expense—Patents.

To illustrate the recording of overhead, the following two entries reflect the depreciation of factory equipment and the accrual of utilities, respectively, for the week ended March 6.

Assets = Liabilities + Equity
−600   −600

Assets = Liabilities + Equity
              +250   −250

Mar. 6	Factory Overhead	600	
	Accumulated Depreciation—Equipment		600
	To record depreciation on factory equipment.		
Mar. 6	Factory Overhead	250	
	Utilities Payable		250
	To record the accrual of factory utilities.		

Entries to record indirect materials and indirect labor follow:

Factory Overhead .... $
    Raw Materials Inventory .... $

Factory Overhead .... $
    Factory Payroll .... $

In the subsidiary factory overhead ledger, these entries are posted to Indirect Materials and Indirect Labor, respectively.

Point: The predetermined overhead rate is computed at the start of the period and is used throughout the period to allocate overhead to jobs. Predetermined overhead rates can be estimated using mathematical equations, statistical analysis, or professional experience.

EXHIBIT 19.9

Predetermined Overhead Allocation Rate Formula

Example: If management predicts total direct labor costs of $100,000 and total overhead costs of $200,000, what is its predetermined overhead rate? *Answer:* 200% of direct labor cost.

Assets = Liabilities + Equity
+1,600   +1,600

Exhibit 19.8 shows that overhead costs flow from the Factory Overhead account to job cost sheets. Because overhead is made up of costs not directly associated with specific jobs or job lots, we cannot determine the dollar amount incurred on a specific job. We know, however, that overhead costs represent a necessary part of business activities. If a job cost is to include all costs needed to complete the job, some amount of overhead must be included. Given the difficulty in determining the overhead amount for a specific job, however, we allocate overhead to individual jobs in some reasonable manner.

Overhead Allocation Bases   We generally allocate overhead by linking it to another factor used in production, such as direct labor or machine hours. The factor to which overhead costs are linked is known as the *allocation base*. A manager must think carefully about how many and which allocation bases to use. This managerial decision influences the accuracy with which overhead costs are allocated to individual jobs. In turn, the cost of individual jobs might impact a manager's decisions for pricing or performance evaluation. In Exhibit 19.2, overhead is expressed as 160% of direct labor. We then allocate overhead by multiplying 160% by the estimated amount of direct labor on the jobs.

Overhead Allocation Rates   We cannot wait until the end of a period to allocate overhead to jobs because perpetual inventory records are part of the job order costing system (demanding up-to-date costs). Instead, we must predict overhead in advance and assign it to jobs so that a job's total costs can be estimated prior to its completion. This estimated cost is useful for managers in many decisions including setting prices and identifying costs that are out of control. Being able to estimate overhead in advance requires a **predetermined overhead rate,** also called *predetermined overhead allocation* (or *application*) *rate*. This rate requires an estimate of total overhead cost and an allocation factor such as total direct labor cost before the start of the period. Exhibit 19.9 shows the usual formula for computing a predetermined overhead rate (estimates are commonly based on annual amounts). This rate is used during the period to allocate overhead to jobs. It is common for companies to use multiple activity (allocation) bases and multiple predetermined overhead rates for different types of products and services.

$$\text{Predetermined overhead rate} = \frac{\text{Estimated}}{\text{overhead costs}} \div \frac{\text{Estimated}}{\text{activity base}}$$

Recording Allocated Overhead   To illustrate, Road Warriors allocates overhead by linking it to direct labor. At the start of the current period, management predicts total direct labor costs of $125,000 and total overhead costs of $200,000. Using these estimates, management computes its predetermined overhead rate as 160% of direct labor cost ($200,000 ÷ $125,000). Specifically, reviewing the job order cost sheet in Exhibit 19.2, we see that $1,000 of direct labor went into Job B15. We then use the predetermined overhead rate of 160% to allocate $1,600 (equal to $1,000 × 1.60) of overhead to this job. The entry to record this allocation is

Mar. 11	Goods in Process Inventory—Job B15..............	1,600	
	Factory Overhead		1,600
	To assign overhead to Job B15.		

Since the allocation rate for overhead is estimated at the start of a period, the total amount assigned to jobs during a period rarely equals the amount actually incurred. We explain how this difference is treated later in this chapter.

■ Decision Ethics

Web Consultant   You are working on seven client engagements. Two clients reimburse your firm for actual costs plus a 10% markup. The other five pay a fixed fee for services. Your firm's costs include overhead allocated at $47 per labor hour. The managing partner of your firm instructs you to record as many labor hours as possible to the two markup engagements by transferring labor hours from the other five. What do you do? ■ [Answer—p. 795]

Summary of Cost Flows

We showed journal entries for charging Goods in Process Inventory (Job B15) with the cost of (1) direct materials requisitions, (2) direct labor time tickets, and (3) factory overhead. We made separate entries for each of these costs, but they are usually recorded in one entry. Specifically, materials requisitions are often collected for a day or a week and recorded with a single entry summarizing them. The same is done with labor time tickets. When summary entries are made, supporting schedules of the jobs charged and the types of materials used provide the basis for postings to subsidiary records.

Point: Study the flow of manufacturing costs through general ledger accounts and job cost sheets. Use Exhibit 19.11 as reinforcement.

To show all production cost flows for a period and their related entries, we again look at Road Warriors' activities. Exhibit 19.10 shows costs linked to all of Road Warriors' production activities for March. Road Warriors did not have any jobs in process at the beginning of March, but it did apply materials, labor, and overhead costs to five new jobs in March. Jobs B15 and B16 are completed and delivered to customers in March, Job B17 is completed but not delivered, and Jobs B18 and B19 are still in process. Exhibit 19.10 also shows purchases of raw materials for $2,750, labor costs incurred for $5,300, and overhead costs of $6,720.

EXHIBIT 19.10

Job Order Costs of All Production Activities

Explanation	Materials	Labor	Overhead Incurred	Overhead Allocated	Goods in Process	Finished Goods	Cost of Goods Sold
Job B15	$ 600	$1,000		$1,600			$3,200
Job B16	300	800		1,280			2,380
Job B17	500	1,100		1,760		$3,360	
Job B18	150	700		1,120	$1,970		
Job B19	250	600		960	1,810		
Total job costs	1,800	4,200		$6,720	$3,780	$3,360	$5,580
Indirect materials	550		$ 550				
Indirect labor		1,100	1,100				
Other overhead			5,070				
Total costs used in production	2,350	$5,300	$6,720				
Ending materials inventory	1,400						
Materials available	3,750						
Less beginning materials inventory	(1,000)						
Materials purchased	$2,750						

(Table title: ROAD WARRIORS / Job Order Manufacturing Costs / For Month Ended March 31, 2013)

The upper part of Exhibit 19.11 shows the flow of these costs through general ledger accounts and the end-of-month balances in key subsidiary records. Arrow lines are numbered to show the flows of costs for March. Each numbered cost flow reflects several entries made in March. The lower part of Exhibit 19.11 shows summarized job cost sheets and their status at the end of March. The sum of costs assigned to the jobs in process ($1,970 + $1,810) equals the

EXHIBIT 19.11

Job Order Cost Flows and Ending Job Cost Sheets

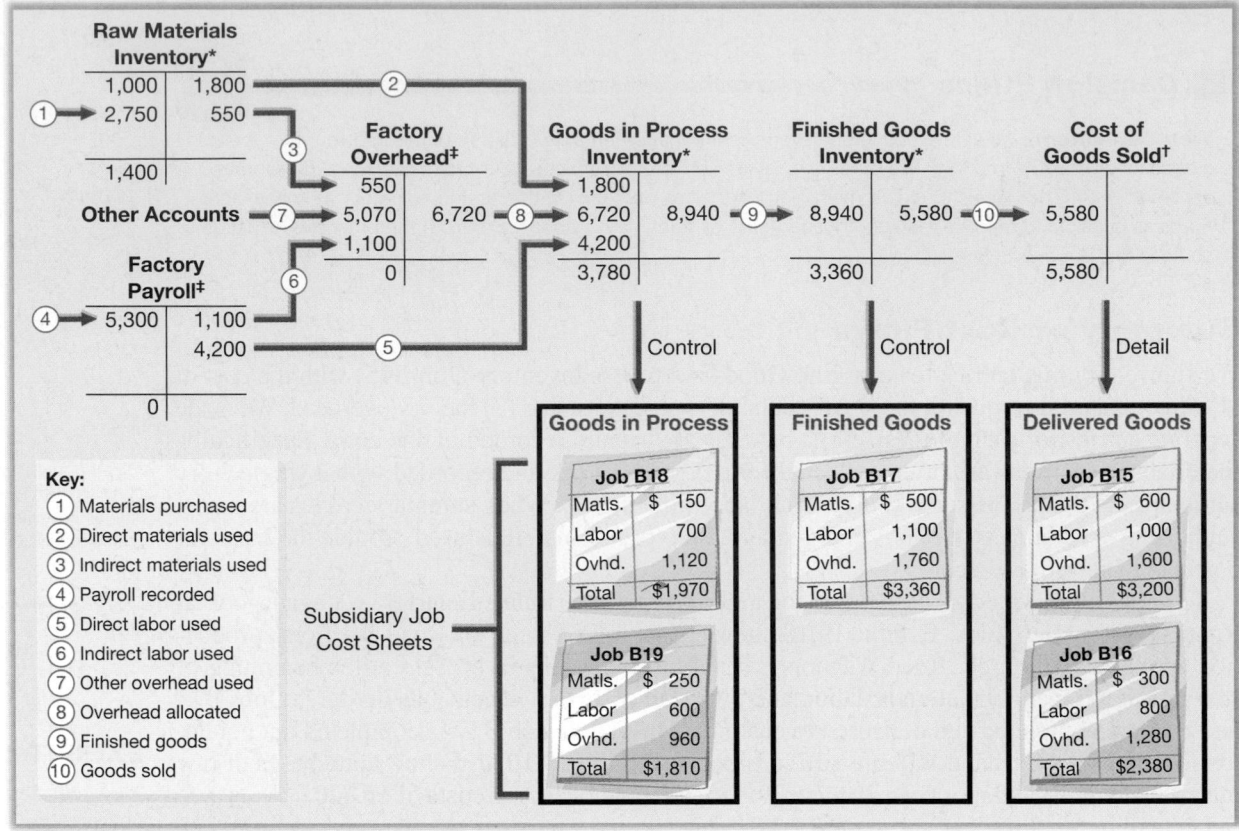

* The ending balances in the inventory accounts are carried to the balance sheet.

† The Cost of Goods Sold balance is carried to the income statement.

‡ Factory Payroll and Factory Overhead are considered temporary accounts; when these costs are allocated to jobs, the balances in these accounts are reduced.

$3,780 balance in Goods in Process Inventory shown in Exhibit 19.10. Also, costs assigned to Job B17 equal the $3,360 balance in Finished Goods Inventory. The sum of costs assigned to Jobs B15 and B16 ($3,200 + $2,380) equals the $5,580 balance in Cost of Goods Sold.

Exhibit 19.12 shows each cost flow with a single entry summarizing the actual individual entries made in March. Each entry is numbered to link with the arrow lines in Exhibit 19.11.

Decision Maker

Entrepreneur Competitors' prices on one of your product segments are lower than yours. Of the total product cost used in setting your prices, 53% is overhead allocated using direct labor hours. You believe that product costs are distorted and wonder whether there is a better way to allocate overhead and to set product price. What do you suggest? ■ [Answer—p. 795]

Quick Check   Answers — p. 795

5. In job order cost accounting, which account is debited in recording a raw materials requisition? (a) Raw Materials Inventory, (b) Raw Materials Purchases, (c) Goods in Process Inventory if for a job, or (d) Goods in Process Inventory if they are indirect materials.

6. What are four sources of information for recording costs in the Factory Overhead account?

7. Why does job order cost accounting require a predetermined overhead rate?

8. What events result in a debit to Factory Payroll? What events result in a credit?

EXHIBIT 19.12

Entries for Job Order Production Costs*

①	Raw Materials Inventory	2,750	
	Accounts Payable		2,750
	Acquired materials on credit for factory use.		
②	Goods in Process Inventory	1,800	
	Raw Materials Inventory		1,800
	To assign costs of direct materials used.		
③	Factory Overhead	550	
	Raw Materials Inventory		550
	To record use of indirect materials.		
④	Factory Payroll	5,300	
	Cash (and other accounts)		5,300
	To record salaries and wages of factory workers (including various payroll liabilities).		
⑤	Goods in Process Inventory	4,200	
	Factory Payroll		4,200
	To assign costs of direct labor used.		
⑥	Factory Overhead	1,100	
	Factory Payroll		1,100
	To record indirect labor costs as overhead.		
⑦	Factory Overhead	5,070	
	Cash (and other accounts)		5,070
	To record factory overhead costs such as insurance, utilities, rent, and depreciation.		
⑧	Goods in Process Inventory	6,720	
	Factory Overhead		6,720
	To apply overhead at 160% of direct labor.		
⑨	Finished Goods Inventory	8,940	
	Goods in Process Inventory		8,940
	To record completion of Jobs B15, B16, and B17.		
⑩	Cost of Goods Sold	5,580	
	Finished Goods Inventory		5,580
	To record sale of Jobs B15 and B16.		

* Exhibit 19.12 provides summary journal entries. *Actual* overhead is debited to Factory Overhead. *Allocated* overhead is credited to Factory Overhead.

ADJUSTING FACTORY OVERHEAD

Refer to the debits in the Factory Overhead account in Exhibit 19.11 (or Exhibit 19.12). The total cost of factory overhead incurred during March is $6,720 ($550 + $5,070 + $1,100). The $6,720 exactly equals the amount assigned to goods in process inventory (see ⑧). Therefore, the overhead incurred equals the overhead applied in March. The amount of overhead incurred rarely equals the amount of overhead applied, however, because estimates rarely equal the exact amounts actually incurred. This section explains what we do when too much or too little overhead is applied to jobs.

Factory Overhead T-Account

Exhibit 19.13 shows a Factory Overhead T-account. The company applies overhead using a predetermined rate estimated at the beginning of the period. At the end of the period, the company receives bills for its actual overhead costs.

EXHIBIT 19.13

Factory Overhead T-account

Exhibit 19.14 shows what to do when actual overhead does not equal applied overhead. When less overhead is applied than is actually incurred, the remaining debit balance in the Factory Overhead account is called **underapplied overhead.** When the overhead applied in a period exceeds the overhead incurred, the resulting credit balance in the Factory Overhead account is called **overapplied overhead.** In either case, a journal entry is needed to adjust Factory Overhead and Cost of Goods Sold. Exhibit 19.14 summarizes this entry.

EXHIBIT 19.14

Adjusting Factory Overhead

Overhead Costs	Factory Overhead Balance Is	Overhead Is	Journal Entry Required		
Actual > Applied	Debit	Underapplied	Cost of Goods Sold	#	
			Factory Overhead		#
Actual < Applied	Credit	Overapplied	Factory Overhead	#	
			Cost of Goods Sold		#

Underapplied or Overapplied Overhead

To illustrate, assume that Road Warriors actually incurred *other overhead costs* of $5,550 instead of the $5,070 shown in Exhibit 19.11. This yields an actual total overhead cost of $7,200 in March. Since the amount of overhead applied was only $6,720, the Factory Overhead account is left with a $480 debit balance as shown in the ledger account in Exhibit 19.15.

EXHIBIT 19.15

Underapplied Overhead in the Factory Overhead Ledger Account

Factory Overhead				Acct. No. 540
Date	Explanation	Debit	Credit	Balance
Mar. 31	Indirect materials cost	550		550 Dr.
31	Indirect labor cost	1,100		1,650 Dr.
31	Other overhead cost	5,550		7,200 Dr.
31	Overhead costs applied to jobs		6,720	480 Dr.

The $480 debit balance reflects manufacturing costs not assigned to jobs. This means that the balances in Goods in Process Inventory, Finished Goods Inventory, and Cost of Goods Sold do not include all production costs incurred. When the underapplied overhead amount is immaterial, it is allocated (closed) to the Cost of Goods Sold account with the following adjusting entry.

Example: If we do not adjust for underapplied overhead, will net income be overstated or understated? *Answer:* Overstated.

Assets = Liabilities + Equity
             −480
             +480

Mar. 31	Cost of Goods Sold.............................	480	
	Factory Overhead		480
	To adjust for underapplied overhead costs.		

The $480 debit (increase) to Cost of Goods Sold reduces income by $480. (When the underapplied (or overapplied) overhead is material, the amount is normally allocated to the Cost of Goods Sold, Finished Goods Inventory, and Goods in Process Inventory accounts. This process is covered in advanced courses.)

We treat overapplied overhead at the end of the period in the same way we treat underapplied overhead, except that we debit Factory Overhead and credit Cost of Good Sold for the amount.

Decision Insight

Job Order Learning   Many companies invest in their employees, and the demand for executive education is strong. Annual spending on training and education exceeds $20 billion. Annual revenues for providers of executive education continue to rise, with about 40% of revenues coming from custom programs designed for one or a select group of companies. ■

Quick Check   Answers — p. 796

9. In a job order cost accounting system, why does the Factory Overhead account usually have an overapplied or underapplied balance at period-end?

10. When the Factory Overhead account has a debit balance at period-end, does this reflect overapplied or underapplied overhead?

 GLOBAL VIEW

Porsche AG manufactures high-performance cars. Each car is built according to individual customer specifications. Customers can use the Internet to place orders for their dream cars. Porsche employs just-in-time inventory techniques to ensure a flexible production process that can respond rapidly to customer orders. For a recent year, Porsche reported €33,781 million in costs of materials and €9,038 million in personnel costs, which helped generate €57,081 million in revenue.

The chapter described job order costing mainly using a manufacturing setting. However, these concepts and procedures are applicable to a service setting. Consider AdWorld, an advertising agency that develops Web-based ads for small firms. Each of its customers has unique requirements, so costs for each individual job must be tracked separately.

A1 Apply job order costing in pricing services.

AdWorld uses two types of labor: Web designers ($65 per hour) and computer staff ($50 per hour). It also incurs overhead costs that it assigns using two different predetermined overhead allocation rates: $125 per designer hour and $96 per staff hour. For each job, AdWorld must estimate the number of designer and staff hours needed. Then total costs pertaining to each job are determined using the procedures in the chapter. (*Note:* Most service firms have neither the category of materials cost nor inventory.)

To illustrate, a manufacturer of golf balls requested a quote from AdWorld for an advertising engagement. AdWorld estimates that the job will require 43 designer hours and 61 staff hours, with the following total estimated cost for this job.

Direct Labor		
Designers (43 hours × $65)	$ 2,795	
Staff (61 hours × $50)	3,050	
Total direct labor		$ 5,845
Overhead		
Designer related (43 hours × $125)	5,375	
Staff related (61 hours × $96)	5,856	
Total overhead		11,231
Total estimated job cost		$17,076

AdWorld can use this cost information to help determine the price quote for the job (see *Decision Maker*, **Sales Manager,** scenario in this chapter).

Another source of information that AdWorld must consider is the market, that is, how much competitors will quote for this job. Competitor information is often unavailable; therefore, AdWorld's managers must use estimates based on their assessment of the competitive environment.

◼ **Decision Maker**

Sales Manager As AdWorld's sales manager, assume that you estimate costs pertaining to a proposed job as $17,076. Your normal pricing policy is to apply a markup of 18% from total costs. However, you learn that three other agencies are likely to bid for the same job, and that their quotes will range from $16,500 to $22,000. What price should you quote? What factors other than cost must you consider? ◼ [Answer—p. 795]

DEMONSTRATION PROBLEM—JOB ORDER COSTING

The following information reflects Walczak Company's job order production activities for May.

Raw materials purchases	$16,000
Factory payroll cost	15,400
Overhead costs incurred	
Indirect materials	5,000
Indirect labor	3,500
Other factory overhead	9,500

Walczak's predetermined overhead rate is 150% of direct labor cost. Costs are allocated to the three jobs worked on during May as follows.

	Job 401	Job 402	Job 403
In-process balances on April 30			
Direct materials	$3,600		
Direct labor	1,700		
Applied overhead	2,550		
Costs during May			
Direct materials	3,550	$3,500	$1,400
Direct labor	5,100	6,000	800
Applied overhead	?	?	?
Status on May 31	**Finished (sold)**	**Finished (unsold)**	**In process**

Required

1. Determine the total cost of:

   a. The April 30 inventory of jobs in process.

   b. Materials used during May.

   c. Labor used during May.

   d. Factory overhead incurred and applied during May and the amount of any over- or underapplied overhead on May 31.

   e. Each job as of May 31, the May 31 inventories of both goods in process and finished goods, and the goods sold during May.

2. Prepare summarized journal entries for the month to record:

   a. Materials purchases (on credit), the factory payroll (paid with cash), indirect materials, indirect labor, and the other factory overhead (paid with cash).

   b. Assignment of direct materials, direct labor, and overhead costs to the Goods in Process Inventory account. (Use separate debit entries for each job.)

   c. Transfer of each completed job to the Finished Goods Inventory account.

   d. Cost of goods sold.

   e. Removal of any underapplied or overapplied overhead from the Factory Overhead account. (Assume the amount is not material.)

3. Prepare a manufacturing statement for May.

PLANNING THE SOLUTION

- Determine the cost of the April 30 goods in process inventory by totaling the materials, labor, and applied overhead costs for Job 401.
- Compute the cost of materials used and labor by totaling the amounts assigned to jobs and to overhead.
- Compute the total overhead incurred by summing the amounts for the three components. Compute the amount of applied overhead by multiplying the total direct labor cost by the predetermined overhead rate. Compute the underapplied or overapplied amount as the difference between the actual cost and the applied cost.
- Determine the total cost charged to each job by adding the costs incurred in April (if any) to the cost of materials, labor, and overhead applied during May.
- Group the costs of the jobs according to their completion status.
- Record the direct materials costs assigned to the three jobs, using a separate Goods in Process Inventory account for each job; do the same for the direct labor and the applied overhead.
- Transfer costs of Jobs 401 and 402 from Goods in Process Inventory to Finished Goods.
- Record the costs of Job 401 as cost of goods sold.
- Record the transfer of underapplied overhead from the Factory Overhead account to the Cost of Goods Sold account.
- On the manufacturing statement, remember to include the beginning and ending goods in process inventories and to deduct the underapplied overhead.

SOLUTION TO DEMONSTRATION PROBLEM

1. Total cost of

a. April 30 inventory of jobs in process (Job 401).

Direct materials..........	$3,600
Direct labor.............	1,700
Applied overhead	2,550
Total cost	$7,850

b. Materials used during May.

Direct materials		
Job 401..................	$ 3,550	
Job 402..................	3,500	
Job 403..................	1,400	
Total direct materials	8,450	
Indirect materials	5,000	
Total materials used	$13,450	

c. Labor used during May.

Direct labor	
Job 401..............	$ 5,100
Job 402..............	6,000
Job 403..............	800
Total direct labor	11,900
Indirect labor	3,500
Total labor used	$15,400

d. Factory overhead incurred in May.

Actual overhead	
Indirect materials......................	$ 5,000
Indirect labor	3,500
Other factory overhead	9,500
Total actual overhead	18,000
Overhead applied (150% × $11,900)	17,850
Underapplied overhead	$ 150

e. Total cost of each job.

	401	402	403
In-process costs from April			
Direct materials................	$ 3,600		
Direct labor	1,700		
Applied overhead*.............	2,550		
Cost incurred in May			
Direct materials................	3,550	$ 3,500	$1,400
Direct labor	5,100	6,000	800
Applied overhead*.............	7,650	9,000	1,200
Total costs	$24,150	$18,500	$3,400

* Equals 150% of the direct labor cost.

Total cost of the May 31 inventory of goods in process (Job 403) = $3,400

Total cost of the May 31 inventory of finished goods (Job 402) = $18,500

Total cost of goods sold during May (Job 401) = $24,150

2. Journal entries.

a.

Raw Materials Inventory	16,000	
Accounts Payable		16,000
To record materials purchases.		
Factory Payroll...................................	15,400	
Cash		15,400
To record factory payroll.		
Factory Overhead	5,000	
Raw Materials Inventory		5,000
To record indirect materials.		
Factory Overhead	3,500	
Factory Payroll		3,500
To record indirect labor.		
Factory Overhead	9,500	
Cash		9,500
To record other factory overhead.		

b. Assignment of costs to Goods in Process Inventory.

Goods in Process Inventory (Job 401)	3,550	
Goods in Process Inventory (Job 402)	3,500	
Goods in Process Inventory (Job 403)	1,400	
Raw Materials Inventory		8,450
To assign direct materials to jobs.		
Goods in Process Inventory (Job 401)	5,100	
Goods in Process Inventory (Job 402)	6,000	
Goods in Process Inventory (Job 403)	800	
Factory Payroll		11,900
To assign direct labor to jobs.		
Goods in Process Inventory (Job 401)	7,650	
Goods in Process Inventory (Job 402)	9,000	
Goods in Process Inventory (Job 403)	1,200	
Factory Overhead		17,850
To apply overhead to jobs.		

c. Transfer of completed jobs to Finished Goods Inventory.

Finished Goods Inventory	42,650	
Goods in Process Inventory (Job 401)		24,150
Goods in Process Inventory (Job 402)		18,500
To record completion of jobs.		

d.

Cost of Goods Sold	24,150	
Finished Goods Inventory		24,150
To record sale of Job 401.		

e.

Cost of Goods Sold	150	
Factory Overhead		150
To assign underapplied overhead.		

3.

WALCZAK COMPANY
Manufacturing Statement
For Month Ended May 31

Direct materials		$ 8,450
Direct labor		11,900
Factory overhead		
Indirect materials	$5,000	
Indirect labor	3,500	
Other factory overhead	9,500	18,000
Total production costs		38,350
Add goods in process, April 30		7,850
Total cost of goods in process		46,200
Less goods in process, May 31		3,400
Less underapplied overhead		150
Cost of goods manufactured		$42,650

> Note how underapplied overhead is reported. Overapplied overhead is similarly reported, but is added.

Summary

C1 **Describe important features of job order production.** Certain companies called *job order manufacturers* produce custom-made products for customers. These customized products are produced in response to a customer's orders. A job order manufacturer produces products that usually are different and, typically, produced in low volumes. The production systems of job order companies are flexible and are not highly standardized.

C2 **Explain job cost sheets and how they are used in job order cost accounting.** In a job order cost accounting system, the costs of producing each job are accumulated on a separate job cost sheet. Costs of direct materials, direct labor, and overhead are accumulated separately on the job cost sheet and then added to determine the total cost of a job. Job cost sheets for jobs in process, finished jobs, and jobs sold make up subsidiary records controlled by general ledger accounts.

A1 **Apply job order costing in pricing services.** Job order costing can usefully be applied to a service setting. The resulting job cost estimate can then be used to help determine a price for services.

P1 **Describe and record the flow of materials costs in job order cost accounting.** Costs of materials flow from receiving reports to materials ledger cards and then to either job cost sheets or the Indirect Materials account in the factory overhead ledger.

P2 **Describe and record the flow of labor costs in job order cost accounting.** Costs of labor flow from clock cards to the Factory Payroll account and then to either job cost sheets or the Indirect Labor account in the factory overhead ledger.

P3 **Describe and record the flow of overhead costs in job order cost accounting.** Overhead costs are accumulated in the Factory Overhead account that controls the subsidiary factory overhead ledger. Then, using a predetermined overhead rate, overhead costs are charged to jobs.

P4 **Determine adjustments for overapplied and underapplied factory overhead.** At the end of each period, the Factory Overhead account usually has a residual debit (underapplied overhead) or credit (overapplied overhead) balance. If the balance is not material, it is transferred to Cost of Goods Sold, but if it is material, it is allocated to Goods in Process Inventory, Finished Goods Inventory, and Cost of Goods Sold.

Guidance Answers to Decision Maker and Decision Ethics

Management Consultant Service companies (such as this consulting firm) do not recognize goods in process inventory or finished goods inventory—an important difference between service and manufacturing companies. For the two jobs that are 60% complete, you could recognize revenues and costs at 60% of the total expected amounts. This means you could recognize revenue of $7,200 (0.60 × $12,000) and costs of $6,000 (0.60 × $10,000), yielding net income of $1,200 from each job.

Web Consultant The partner has a monetary incentive to *manage* the numbers and assign more costs to the two cost-plus engagements. This also would reduce costs on the fixed-price engagements. To act in such a manner is unethical. As a professional and an honest person, it is your responsibility to engage in ethical behavior. You must not comply with the partner's instructions. If the partner insists you act in an unethical manner, you should report the matter to a higher authority in the organization.

Entrepreneur An inadequate cost system can distort product costs. You should review overhead costs in detail. Once you know the different cost elements in overhead, you can classify them into groups such as material related, labor related, or machine related. Other groups can also be formed (we discuss this in Chapter 21). Once you have classified overhead items into groups, you can better establish overhead allocation bases and use them to compute predetermined overhead rates. These multiple rates and bases can then be used to assign overhead costs to products. This will likely improve product pricing.

Sales Manager The price based on AdWorld's normal pricing policy is $20,150 ($17,076 × 1.18), which is within the price range offered by competitors. One option is to apply normal pricing policy and quote a price of $20,150. On the other hand, assessing the competition, particularly in terms of their service quality and other benefits they might offer, would be useful. Although price is an input customers use to select suppliers, factors such as quality and timeliness (responsiveness) of suppliers are important. Accordingly, your price can reflect such factors.

Guidance Answers to Quick Checks

1. *b*

2. A job is a special order for a custom product. A job lot consists of a quantity of identical, special-order items.

3. *a*

4. Three costs normally accumulated on a job cost sheet are direct materials, direct labor, and factory overhead.

5. *c*

6. Four sources of factory overhead are materials requisitions, time tickets, vouchers, and adjusting entries.

7. Since a job order cost accounting system uses perpetual inventory records, overhead costs must be assigned to jobs before the end of a period. This requires the use of a predetermined overhead rate.

8. Debits are recorded when wages and salaries of factory employees are paid or accrued. Credits are recorded when direct labor costs are assigned to jobs and when indirect labor costs are transferred to the Factory Overhead account.

9. Overapplied or underapplied overhead usually exists at the end of a period because application of overhead is based on

estimates of overhead and another variable such as direct labor. Estimates rarely equal actual amounts incurred.

10. A debit balance reflects underapplied factory overhead.

Key Terms

Clock card (p. 784)	Job cost sheet (p. 780)	Materials requisition (p. 783)
Cost accounting system (p. 778)	Job lot (p. 778)	Overapplied overhead (p. 789)
Finished Goods Inventory (p. 781)	Job order cost accounting	Predetermined overhead rate (p. 786)
General accounting system (p. 778)	system (p. 780)	Target cost (p. 779)
Goods in Process Inventory (p. 780)	Job order production (p. 778)	Time ticket (p. 784)
Job (p. 778)	Materials ledger card (p. 782)	Underapplied overhead (p. 789)

Multiple Choice Quiz   Answers on p. 813   mhhe.com/wildFAP21e

Additional Quiz Questions are available at the book's Website.

1. A company's predetermined overhead allocation rate is 150% of its direct labor costs. How much overhead is applied to a job that requires total direct labor costs of $30,000?
   a. $15,000
   b. $30,000
   c. $45,000
   d. $60,000
   e. $75,000

2. A company's cost accounting system uses direct labor costs to apply overhead to goods in process and finished goods inventories. Its production costs for the period are: direct materials, $45,000; direct labor, $35,000; and overhead applied, $38,500. What is its predetermined overhead allocation rate?
   a. 10%
   b. 110%
   c. 86%
   d. 91%
   e. 117%

3. A company's ending inventory of finished goods has a total cost of $10,000 and consists of 500 units. If the overhead applied to these goods is $4,000, and the predetermined overhead rate is 80% of direct labor costs, how much direct materials cost was incurred in producing these 500 units?
   a. $10,000
   b. $ 6,000
   c. $ 4,000
   d. $ 5,000
   e. $ 1,000

4. A company's Goods in Process Inventory T-account follows.

Goods in Process Inventory			
Beginning balance	9,000		
Direct materials	94,200		
Direct labor	59,200		
Overhead applied	31,600	?	Finished goods
Ending balance	17,800		

The cost of units transferred to Finished Goods inventory is
   a. $193,000
   b. $211,800
   c. $185,000
   d. $144,600
   e. $176,200

5. At the end of its current year, a company learned that its overhead was underapplied by $1,500 and that this amount is not considered material. Based on this information, the company should
   a. Close the $1,500 to Finished Goods Inventory.
   b. Close the $1,500 to Cost of Goods Sold.
   c. Carry the $1,500 to the next period.
   d. Do nothing about the $1,500 because it is not material and it is likely that overhead will be overapplied by the same amount next year.
   e. Carry the $1,500 to the Income Statement as "Other Expense."

🔵 Icon denotes assignments that involve decision making.

Discussion Questions

1. Why must a company estimate the amount of factory overhead assigned to individual jobs or job lots?

2. 🔵 The chapter used a percent of labor cost to assign factory overhead to jobs. Identify another factor (or base) a company might reasonably use to assign overhead costs.

3. [icon] What information is recorded on a job cost sheet? How do management and employees use job cost sheets?

4. In a job order cost accounting system, what records serve as a subsidiary ledger for Goods in Process Inventory? For Finished Goods Inventory?

5. What journal entry is recorded when a materials manager receives a materials requisition and then issues materials (both direct and indirect) for use in the factory?

6. [icon] How does the materials requisition help safeguard a company's assets?

7. **Polaris** uses a "time ticket" for some employees.   **Polaris**
What is the difference between a clock card and a
time ticket?

8. What events cause debits to be recorded in the Factory Overhead account? What events cause credits to be recorded in the Factory Overhead account?

9. **Piaggio** applies overhead to product costs. What
account(s) is(are) used to eliminate overapplied   **PIAGGIO**

or underapplied overhead from the Factory Overhead account, assuming the amount is not material?

10. [icon] Assume that **Arctic Cat** produces a batch
of 1,000 snowmobile helmets. Does it account   **Arctic Cat**
for this as 1,000 individual jobs or as a job lot? Explain (consider costs and benefits).

11. Why must a company prepare a predetermined overhead rate when using job order cost accounting?

12. [icon] How would a hospital apply job order costing? Explain.

13. [icon] **Harley-Davidson** manufactures 30 custom-   **Harley-**
made, luxury-model motorcycles. Does it account for   **Davidson**
these motorcycles as 30 individual jobs or as a job
lot? Explain.

14. Assume **Sprint** will install and service a server to link
all of a customer's employees' smartphones to a cen-   **Sprint**
tralized company server, for an upfront flat price. How can Sprint
use a job order costing system?

[McGraw Hill] connect

Determine which products are most likely to be manufactured as a job and which as a job lot.

1. Hats imprinted with company logo.
2. Little League trophies.
3. A hand-crafted table.
4. A 90-foot motor yacht.
5. Wedding dresses for a chain of stores.
6. A custom-designed home.

QUICK STUDY

QS 19-1
Jobs and job lots   C1

List the three types of costs that are typically recorded on a job cost sheet. How can managers use job cost sheets?

QS 19-2
Job cost sheets   C2

Clemens Cars' job cost sheet for job A40 shows that the cost to add security features to a car was $10,500. The car was delivered to the customer, who paid $14,900 in cash for the added features. What journal entries should Clemens record for the completion and delivery of job A40?

QS 19-3
Job cost sheets   C2

During the current month, a company that uses a job order cost accounting system purchases $50,000 in raw materials for cash. It then uses $12,000 of raw materials indirectly as factory supplies and uses $32,000 of raw materials as direct materials. Prepare entries to record these three transactions.

QS 19-4
Direct materials journal entries
P1

During the current month, a company that uses a job order cost accounting system incurred a monthly factory payroll of $180,000, paid in cash. Of this amount, $40,000 is classified as indirect labor and the remainder as direct. Prepare entries to record these transactions.

QS 19-5
Direct labor journal entries   P2

During the current month, a company that uses a job order cost accounting system incurred a monthly factory payroll of $175,000, paid in cash. Of this amount, $44,000 is classified as indirect labor and the remainder as direct for the production of Job 65A. Factory overhead is applied at 90% of direct labor. Prepare the entry to apply factory overhead to this job lot.

QS 19-6
Factory overhead journal entries
P3

A company incurred the following manufacturing costs this period: direct labor, $468,000; direct materials, $354,000; and factory overhead, $117,000. Compute its overhead cost as a percent of (1) direct labor and (2) direct materials. Express your answers as percents, rounded to the nearest whole number.

QS 19-7
Factory overhead rates   P3

A company's Factory Overhead T-account shows total debits of $624,000 and total credits of $646,000 at the end of a period. Prepare the journal entry to close the balance in the Factory Overhead account to Cost of Goods Sold.

QS 19-8
Entry for over- or underapplied overhead   P4

QS 19-9
Entry for over- or
underapplied overhead   P4

A company allocates overhead at a rate of 150% of direct labor cost. Actual overhead cost for the current period is $950,000, and direct labor cost is $600,000. Prepare the entry to close over- or underapplied overhead to cost of goods sold.

QS 19-10
Predetermined overhead rate
P3

At the beginning of a period a company predicts total direct materials costs of $900,000 and total overhead costs of $1,170,000. If the company uses direct materials costs as its activity base to allocate overhead, what is the predetermined overhead rate it should use during the period?

QS 19-11
Pricing services   A1

An advertising agency is estimating costs for advertising a music festival. The job will require 200 direct labor hours at a cost of $50 per hour. Overhead costs are applied at a rate of $65 per direct labor hour. What is the total estimated cost for this job?

QS 19-12
Job order production   C1

Refer to this chapter's Global View. **Porsche AG** is the manufacturer of the Porsche automobile line. Does Porsche produce in jobs or in job lots? Explain.

connect

EXERCISES

Exercise 19-1
Job order production
C1

Match the terms below with their definitions.

1. Cost accounting system
2. Target cost
3. General accounting system
4. Job
5. Job order production
6. Job lot

a. Production of products in response to customer orders.
b. A system that records manufacturing costs using a periodic inventory system.
c. A system that records manufacturing costs using a perpetual inventory system.
d. The expected selling price of a job minus its desired profit.
e. Production of more than one unit of a custom product.
f. Production activities for a customized product.

Exercise 19-2
Job cost computation
C2

The following information is from the materials requisitions and time tickets for Job 9-1005 completed by Great Bay Boats. The requisitions are identified by code numbers starting with the letter Q and the time tickets start with W. At the start of the year, management estimated that overhead cost would equal 110% of direct labor cost for each job. Determine the total cost on the job cost sheet for Job 9-1005.

Date	Document	Amount
7/1/2013..........	Q-4698	$1,250
7/1/2013..........	W-3393	600
7/5/2013..........	Q-4725	1,000
7/5/2013..........	W-3479	450
7/10/2013.........	W-3559	300

Exercise 19-3
Documents in job order
cost accounting
P1 P2 P3

The left column lists the titles of documents and accounts used in job order cost accounting. The right column presents short descriptions of the purposes of the documents. Match each document in the left column to its numbered description in the right column.

A. Time ticket
B. Materials ledger card
C. Factory Payroll account
D. Clock card
E. Materials requisition
F. Factory Overhead account
G. Voucher

_____ **1.** Shows amount of time an employee works on a job.
_____ **2.** Temporarily accumulates the cost of incurred overhead until the cost is assigned to specific jobs.
_____ **3.** Temporarily accumulates incurred labor costs until they are assigned to specific jobs or to overhead.
_____ **4.** Communicates the need for materials to complete a job.
_____ **5.** Shows only total time an employee works each day.
_____ **6.** Shows amount approved for payment of an overhead or other cost.
_____ **7.** Perpetual inventory record of raw materials received, used, and available for use.

As of the end of June, the job cost sheets at Racing Wheels, Inc., show the following total costs accumulated on three custom jobs.

Exercise 19-4
Analysis of cost flows

C2 P1 P2 P3

	Job 102	Job 103	Job 104
Direct materials.........	$15,000	$33,000	$27,000
Direct labor............	8,000	14,200	21,000
Overhead..............	4,000	7,100	10,500

Job 102 was started in production in May and the following costs were assigned to it in May: direct materials, $6,000, direct labor, $1,000, and overhead, $900. Jobs 103 and 104 are started in June. Overhead cost is applied with a predetermined rate based on direct labor cost. Jobs 102 and 103 are finished in June, and Job 104 is expected to be finished in July. No raw materials are used indirectly in June. Using this information, answer the following questions. (Assume this company's predetermined overhead rate did not change across these months).

1. What is the cost of the raw materials requisitioned in June for each of the three jobs?

2. How much direct labor cost is incurred during June for each of the three jobs?

3. What predetermined overhead rate is used during June?

4. How much total cost is transferred to finished goods during June?

Check   (4) $81,300

In December 2012, Shire Computer's management establishes the year 2013 predetermined overhead rate based on direct labor cost. The information used in setting this rate includes estimates that the company will incur $747,500 of overhead costs and $575,000 of direct labor cost in year 2013. During March 2013, Shire began and completed Job No. 13-56.

Exercise 19-5
Overhead rate; costs assigned to jobs

P3

1. What is the predetermined overhead rate for year 2013?

2. Use the information on the following job cost sheet to determine the total cost of the job.

Check   (2) $22,710

JOB COST SHEET

| **Customer's Name** | Keiser Co. | | **Job No.** 13-56 | | | |
| **Job Description** | 5 plasma monitors—61 inch | | | | | |

	Direct Materials			**Direct Labor**		**Overhead Costs Applied**	
Date	Requisition No.	Amount		Time-Ticket No.	Amount	Rate	Amount
Mar. 8	4-129	$5,000		T-306	$ 700		
Mar. 11	4-142	7,020		T-432	1,250		
Mar. 18	4-167	3,330		T-456	1,250		
Totals							

Lorenzo Company uses a job order cost accounting system that charges overhead to jobs on the basis of direct material cost. At year-end, the Goods in Process Inventory account shows the following.

Exercise 19-6
Analysis of costs assigned to goods in process

P3

Accounting System
File Edit Maintain Tasks Analysis Options Reports Window Help

Goods in Process Inventory   Acct. No. 121

Date	Explanation	Debit	Credit	Balance
2013				
Dec. 31	Direct materials cost	1,500,000		1,500,000
31	Direct labor cost	300,000		1,800,000
31	Overhead costs	600,000		2,400,000
31	To finished goods		2,350,000	50,000

Sales   Purchases   General Ledger   Payroll   Inventory   Company   Analysis

1. Determine the overhead rate used (based on direct material cost).

2. Only one job remained in the goods in process inventory at December 31, 2013. Its direct materials cost is $30,000. How much direct labor cost and overhead cost are assigned to it?

Check   (2) Direct labor cost, $8,000

Exercise 19-7
Cost flows in a job order
cost system

P1   P2   P3   P4

The following information is available for Lock-Safe Company, which produces special-order security products and uses a job order cost accounting system.

	April 30	May 31
Inventories		
Raw materials	$43,000	$ 52,000
Goods in process	10,200	21,300
Finished goods	63,000	35,600
Activities and information for May		
Raw materials purchases (paid with cash)		210,000
Factory payroll (paid with cash)		345,000
Factory overhead		
Indirect materials...		15,000
Indirect labor		80,000
Other overhead costs		120,000
Sales (received in cash)		1,400,000
Predetermined overhead rate based on direct labor cost		70%

Compute the following amounts for the month of May.

1. Cost of direct materials used.

4. Cost of goods sold.*

2. Cost of direct labor used.

5. Gross profit.

Check   (3) $625,400

3. Cost of goods manufactured.

6. Overapplied or underapplied overhead.

*Do not consider any underapplied or overapplied overhead.

Exercise 19-8
Journal entries for materials

P1

Use information in Exercise 19-7 to prepare journal entries for the following events for the month of May.

1. Raw materials purchases for cash.   **3.** Indirect materials usage.

2. Direct materials usage.

Exercise 19-9
Journal entries for labor

P2

Use information in Exercise 19-7 to prepare journal entries for the following events for the month of May.

1. Factory payroll costs in cash.   **3.** Indirect labor usage.

2. Direct labor usage.

Exercise 19-10
Journal entries for overhead

P3

Use information in Exercise 19-7 to prepare journal entries for the following events for the month of May.

1. Factory overhead excluding indirect materials and indirect labor (record credit to Other Accounts).

2. Application of overhead to goods in process.

Exercise 19-11
Adjusting factory overhead   P4

Refer to information in Exercise 19-7. Prepare the journal entry to allocate (close) overapplied or underapplied overhead to Cost of Goods Sold.

Exercise 19-12
Adjusting factory overhead

P4

Record the journal entry to close over- or underapplied factory overhead to Cost of Goods Sold for each of the independent cases below.

	Marsh Concert Promotions	Ellis Home Builders
Actual indirect materials costs	$22,000	$ 12,500
Actual indirect labor costs	46,000	46,500
Other overhead costs	17,000	47,000
Overhead applied	88,200	105,200

Exercise 19-13
Recording events in job order
costing

P1   P2   P3   P4

Using Exhibit 19.12 as a guide, prepare summary journal entries to record the following transactions and events *a* through *h* for a company in its first month of operations.

a. Raw materials purchased on account, $90,000.

b. Direct materials used in production, $36,500. Indirect materials used in production, $19,200.

c. Paid cash for factory payroll, $50,000. Of this total, $38,000 is for direct labor and $12,000 is for indirect labor.

d. Paid cash for other actual overhead costs, $11,475.

e. Applied overhead at the rate of 125 percent of direct labor cost.

f. Transferred cost of jobs completed to finished goods, $56,800.

g. Sold jobs on account for $82,000. The jobs had a cost of $56,800.

h. Close underapplied or overapplied overhead to cost of goods sold.

In December 2012, Infovision established its predetermined overhead rate for movies produced during year 2013 by using the following cost predictions: overhead costs, $1,680,000, and direct labor costs, $480,000. At year end 2013, the company's records show that actual overhead costs for the year are $1,652,000. Actual direct labor cost had been assigned to jobs as follows.

Exercise 19-14
Factory overhead computed, applied, and adjusted
P3 P4

Movies completed and released	$425,000
Movies still in production	50,000
Total actual direct labor cost	$475,000

1. Determine the predetermined overhead rate for year 2013.

2. Set up a T-account for overhead and enter the overhead costs incurred and the amounts applied to movies during the year using the predetermined overhead rate.

3. Determine whether overhead is overapplied or underapplied (and the amount) during the year.

Check   (3) $10,500 overapplied

4. Prepare the adjusting entry to allocate any over- or underapplied overhead to Cost of Goods Sold.

In December 2012, Cardozo Company established its predetermined overhead rate for jobs produced during year 2013 by using the following cost predictions: overhead costs, $750,000, and direct labor costs, $625,000. At year end 2013, the company's records show that actual overhead costs for the year are $830,000. Actual direct labor cost had been assigned to jobs as follows.

Exercise 19-15
Factory overhead computed, applied, and adjusted
P3 P4

Jobs completed and sold	$513,750
Jobs in finished goods inventory	102,750
Jobs in goods in process inventory	68,500
Total actual direct labor cost	$685,000

1. Determine the predetermined overhead rate for year 2013.

2. Set up a T-account for Factory Overhead and enter the overhead costs incurred and the amounts applied to jobs during the year using the predetermined overhead rate.

3. Determine whether overhead is overapplied or underapplied (and the amount) during the year.

Check   (3) $8,000 underapplied

4. Prepare the adjusting entry to allocate any over- or underapplied overhead to Cost of Goods Sold.

Sunrise Company applies factory overhead based on direct labor costs. The company incurred the following costs during 2013: direct materials costs, $650,000; direct labor costs, $3,000,000; and factory overhead costs applied, $1,800,000.

Exercise 19-16
Overhead rate calculation, allocation, and analysis
P3

1. Determine the company's predetermined overhead rate for year 2013.

2. Assuming that the company's $71,000 ending Goods in Process Inventory account for year 2013 had $20,000 of direct labor costs, determine the inventory's direct materials costs.

3. Assuming that the company's $490,000 ending Finished Goods Inventory account for year 2013 had $250,000 of direct materials costs, determine the inventory's direct labor costs and its overhead costs.

Check   (3) $90,000 overhead costs

Deschamps Company's ending Goods in Process Inventory account consists of 5,000 units of partially completed product, and its Finished Goods Inventory account consists of 12,000 units of product. The factory manager determines that Goods in Process Inventory includes direct materials cost of $10 per unit and direct labor cost of $7 per unit. Finished goods are estimated to have $12 of direct materials cost per unit and $9 of direct labor cost per unit. The company established the predetermined overhead rate using the following predictions: estimated direct labor cost, $300,000, and estimated factory overhead, $375,000. The company allocates factory overhead to its goods in process and finished goods inventories based on direct labor cost. During the period, the company incurred these costs: direct materials, $535,000; direct labor, $290,000; and factory overhead applied, $362,500.

Exercise 19-17
Costs allocated to ending inventories
P1 P2 P3

1. Determine the predetermined overhead rate.

2. Compute the total cost of the two ending inventories.

3. Compute cost of goods sold for the year (assume no beginning inventories and no underapplied or overapplied overhead).

Check   (3) Cost of goods sold, $671,750

Exercise 19-18
Cost-based pricing

A1

Hansel Corporation has requested bids from several architects to design its new corporate headquarters. Frey Architects is one of the firms bidding on the job. Frey estimates that the job will require the following direct labor.

	Labor	Estimated Hours	Hourly Rate
1			
2	Architects	150	$300
3	Staff	300	75
4	Clerical	500	20

Frey applies overhead to jobs at 175% of direct labor cost. Frey would like to earn at least $80,000 profit on the architectural job. Based on past experience and market research, it estimates that the competition will bid between $285,000 and $350,000 for the job.

Check (1) $213,125

1. What is Frey's estimated cost of the architectural job?

2. What bid would you suggest that Frey submit?

Exercise 19-19
Direct materials journal entries

P1

A recent balance sheet for **Porsche AG** shows beginning raw materials inventory of €83 million and ending raw materials inventory of €85 million. Assume the company purchased raw materials (on account) for €3,108 million during the year. (1) Prepare journal entries to record (a) the purchase of raw materials and (b) the use of raw materials in production. (2) What do you notice about the € amounts in your journal entries?

PROBLEM SET A

Problem 19-1A
Production costs computed and recorded; reports prepared

C2 P1 P2 P3 P4

Sage 50 QB

Ciolino Co.'s March 31 inventory of raw materials is $80,000. Raw materials purchases in April are $500,000, and factory payroll cost in April is $363,000. Overhead costs incurred in April are: indirect materials, $50,000; indirect labor, $23,000; factory rent, $32,000; factory utilities, $19,000; and factory equipment depreciation, $51,000. The predetermined overhead rate is 50% of direct labor cost. Job 306 is sold for $635,000 cash in April. Costs of the three jobs worked on in April follow.

	Job 306	Job 307	Job 308
Balances on March 31			
Direct materials.............	$ 29,000	$ 35,000	
Direct labor.................	20,000	18,000	
Applied overhead............	10,000	9,000	
Costs during April			
Direct materials.............	135,000	220,000	$100,000
Direct labor.................	85,000	150,000	105,000
Applied overhead............	?	?	?
Status on April 30............	Finished (sold)	Finished (unsold)	In process

Required

1. Determine the total of each production cost incurred for April (direct labor, direct materials, and applied overhead), and the total cost assigned to each job (including the balances from March 31).

2. Prepare journal entries for the month of April to record the following.

    a. Materials purchases (on credit), factory payroll (paid in cash), and actual overhead costs including indirect materials and indirect labor. (Factory rent and utilities are paid in cash.)

    b. Assignment of direct materials, direct labor, and applied overhead costs to the Goods in Process Inventory.

    c. Transfer of Jobs 306 and 307 to the Finished Goods Inventory.

    d. Cost of goods sold for Job 306.

    e. Revenue from the sale of Job 306.

Check (2f) $5,000 underapplied

    f. Assignment of any underapplied or overapplied overhead to the Cost of Goods Sold account. (The amount is not material.)

(3) Cost of goods
   manufactured, $828,500

3. Prepare a manufacturing statement for April (use a single line presentation for direct materials and show the details of overhead cost).

4. Compute gross profit for April. Show how to present the inventories on the April 30 balance sheet.

Analysis Component

5. The over- or underapplied overhead is closed to Cost of Goods Sold. Discuss how this adjustment impacts business decision making regarding individual jobs or batches of jobs.

Farina Bay's computer system generated the following trial balance on December 31, 2013. The company's manager knows something is wrong with the trial balance because it does not show any balance for Goods in Process Inventory but does show balances for the Factory Payroll and Factory Overhead accounts.

Problem 19-2A
Source documents, journal entries, overhead, and financial reports

P1 P2 P3 P4

Sage 50

	Debit	Credit
Cash	$102,000	
Accounts receivable	75,000	
Raw materials inventory	80,000	
Goods in process inventory	0	
Finished goods inventory	15,000	
Prepaid rent	3,000	
Accounts payable		$ 17,000
Notes payable		25,000
Common stock		50,000
Retained earnings		271,000
Sales		373,000
Cost of goods sold	218,000	
Factory payroll	68,000	
Factory overhead	115,000	
Operating expenses	60,000	
Totals	$736,000	$736,000

After examining various files, the manager identifies the following six source documents that need to be processed to bring the accounting records up to date.

Materials requisition 21-3010:	$10,200 direct materials to Job 402
Materials requisition 21-3011:	$18,600 direct materials to Job 404
Materials requisition 21-3012:	$5,600 indirect materials
Labor time ticket 6052:	$36,000 direct labor to Job 402
Labor time ticket 6053:	$23,800 direct labor to Job 404
Labor time ticket 6054:	$8,200 indirect labor

Jobs 402 and 404 are the only units in process at year-end. The predetermined overhead rate is 200% of direct labor cost.

Required

1. Use information on the six source documents to prepare journal entries to assign the following costs.
   a. Direct materials costs to Goods in Process Inventory.
   b. Direct labor costs to Goods in Process Inventory.
   c. Overhead costs to Goods in Process Inventory.
   d. Indirect materials costs to the Factory Overhead account.
   e. Indirect labor costs to the Factory Overhead account.

2. Determine the revised balance of the Factory Overhead account after making the entries in part 1. Determine whether there is any under- or overapplied overhead for the year. Prepare the adjusting entry to allocate any over- or underapplied overhead to Cost of Goods Sold, assuming the amount is not material.

3. Prepare a revised trial balance.

4. Prepare an income statement for year 2013 and a balance sheet as of December 31, 2013.

Check (2) $9,200 underapplied overhead

(3) T. B. totals, $736,000

(4) Net income, $85,800

Analysis Component

5. Assume that the $5,600 on materials requisition 21-3012 should have been direct materials charged to Job 404. Without providing specific calculations, describe the impact of this error on the income statement for 2013 and the balance sheet at December 31, 2013.

Problem 19-3A

Source documents, journal entries, and accounts in job order cost accounting

P1 P2 P3

Widmer Watercraft's predetermined overhead rate for year 2013 is 200% of direct labor. Information on the company's production activities during May 2013 follows.

a. Purchased raw materials on credit, $200,000.

b. Paid $126,000 cash for factory wages.

c. Paid $15,000 cash to a computer consultant to reprogram factory equipment.

d. Materials requisitions record use of the following materials for the month.

Job 136......................	$ 48,000
Job 137......................	32,000
Job 138......................	19,200
Job 139......................	22,400
Job 140......................	6,400
Total direct materials.........	128,000
Indirect materials............	19,500
Total materials used..........	$147,500

e. Time tickets record use of the following labor for the month.

Job 136	$ 12,000
Job 137	10,500
Job 138	37,500
Job 139	39,000
Job 140	3,000
Total direct labor	102,000
Indirect labor............	24,000
Total	$126,000

f. Applied overhead to Jobs 136, 138, and 139.

g. Transferred Jobs 136, 138, and 139 to Finished Goods.

h. Sold Jobs 136 and 138 on credit at a total price of $525,000.

i. The company incurred the following overhead costs during the month (credit Prepaid Insurance for expired factory insurance).

Depreciation of factory building	$68,000
Depreciation of factory equipment	36,500
Expired factory insurance	10,000
Accrued property taxes payable	35,000

j. Applied overhead at month-end to the Goods in Process (Jobs 137 and 140) using the predetermined overhead rate of 200% of direct labor cost.

Required

1. Prepare a job cost sheet for each job worked on during the month. Use the following simplified form.

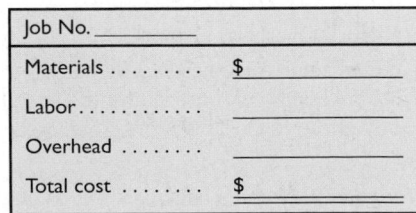

Job No. _____

Materials .... $ _____

Labor............ _____

Overhead .... _____

Total cost .... $ _____

Check (2f) Cr. Factory Overhead, $177,000

2. Prepare journal entries to record the events and transactions *a* through *j*.

3. Set up T-accounts for each of the following general ledger accounts, each of which started the month with a zero balance: Raw Materials Inventory; Goods in Process Inventory; Finished Goods Inventory;

Factory Payroll; Factory Overhead; Cost of Goods Sold. Then post the journal entries to these T-accounts and determine the balance of each account.

4. Prepare a report showing the total cost of each job in process and prove that the sum of their costs equals the Goods in Process Inventory account balance. Prepare similar reports for Finished Goods Inventory and Cost of Goods Sold.

Check (4) Finished Goods Inventory, $139,400

In December 2012, Yerbury Company's manager estimated next year's total direct labor cost assuming 50 persons working an average of 2,000 hours each at an average wage rate of $25 per hour. The manager also estimated the following manufacturing overhead costs for year 2013.

Problem 19-4A
Overhead allocation and adjustment using a predetermined overhead rate
P3 P4

mhhe.com/wildFAP21e

Indirect labor	$ 319,200
Factory supervision	240,000
Rent on factory building	140,000
Factory utilities	88,000
Factory insurance expired	68,000
Depreciation—Factory equipment	480,000
Repairs expense—Factory equipment	60,000
Factory supplies used	68,800
Miscellaneous production costs	36,000
Total estimated overhead costs	$1,500,000

At the end of 2013, records show the company incurred $1,520,000 of actual overhead costs. It completed and sold five jobs with the following direct labor costs: Job 201, $604,000; Job 202, $563,000; Job 203, $298,000; Job 204, $716,000; and Job 205, $314,000. In addition, Job 206 is in process at the end of 2013 and had been charged $17,000 for direct labor. No jobs were in process at the end of 2012. The company's predetermined overhead rate is based on direct labor cost.

Required

1. Determine the following.

 a. Predetermined overhead rate for year 2013.

 b. Total overhead cost applied to each of the six jobs during year 2013.

 c. Over- or underapplied overhead at year-end 2013.

2. Assuming that any over- or underapplied overhead is not material, prepare the adjusting entry to allocate any over- or underapplied overhead to Cost of Goods Sold at the end of year 2013.

Check (1c) 12,800 underapplied

(2) Cr. Factory Overhead $12,800

Sager Company manufactures variations of its product, a technopress, in response to custom orders from its customers. On May 1, the company had no inventories of goods in process or finished goods but held the following raw materials.

Problem 19-5A
Production transactions, subsidiary records, and source documents
P1 P2 P3 P4

Material M	200 units @ $250 =	$50,000
Material R	95 units @ 180 =	17,100
Paint	55 units @ 75 =	4,125
Total cost		$71,225

On May 4, the company began working on two technopresses: Job 102 for Worldwide Company and Job 103 for Reuben Company.

Required

Using Exhibit 19.2 as a guide, prepare job cost sheets for jobs 102 and 103. Using Exhibit 19.4 as a guide, prepare materials ledger cards for Material M, Material R, and paint. Enter the beginning raw materials inventory dollar amounts for each of these materials on their respective ledger cards. Then, follow the instructions in this list of activities.

a. Purchased raw materials on credit and recorded the following information from receiving reports and invoices.

Receiving Report No. 426, Material M, 250 units at $250 each.
Receiving Report No. 427, Material R, 90 units at $180 each.

Instructions: Record these purchases with a single journal entry. Enter the receiving report information on the materials ledger cards.

b. Requisitioned the following raw materials for production.

> Requisition No. 35, for Job 102, 135 units of Material M.
> Requisition No. 36, for Job 102, 72 units of Material R.
> Requisition No. 37, for Job 103, 70 units of Material M.
> Requisition No. 38, for Job 103, 38 units of Material R.
> Requisition No. 39, for 15 units of paint.

Instructions: Enter amounts for direct materials requisitions on the materials ledger cards and the job cost sheets. Enter the indirect material amount on the materials ledger card. Do not record a journal entry at this time.

c. Received the following employee time tickets for work in May.

> Time tickets Nos. 1 to 10 for direct labor on Job 102, $90,000.
> Time tickets Nos. 11 to 30 for direct labor on Job 103, $65,000.
> Time tickets Nos. 31 to 36 for equipment repairs, $19,250.

Instructions: Record direct labor from the time tickets on the job cost sheets. Do not record a journal entry at this time.

d. Paid cash for the following items during the month: factory payroll, $174,250, and miscellaneous overhead items, $102,000.

Instructions: Record these payments with journal entries.

e. Finished Job 102 and transferred it to the warehouse. The company assigns overhead to each job with a predetermined overhead rate equal to 80% of direct labor cost.

Instructions: Enter the allocated overhead on the cost sheet for Job 102, fill in the cost summary section of the cost sheet, and then mark the cost sheet "Finished." Prepare a journal entry to record the job's completion and its transfer to Finished Goods.

f. Delivered Job 102 and accepted the customer's promise to pay $400,000 within 30 days.

Instructions: Prepare journal entries to record the sale of Job 102 and the cost of goods sold.

g. Applied overhead to Job 103 based on the job's direct labor to date.

Instructions: Enter overhead on the job cost sheet but do not make a journal entry at this time.

Check (h) Dr. Goods in Process Inventory, $71,050

h. Recorded the total direct and indirect materials costs as reported on all the requisitions for the month.

Instructions: Prepare a journal entry to record these costs.

i. Recorded the total direct and indirect labor costs as reported on all time tickets for the month.

Instructions: Prepare a journal entry to record these costs.

Check Balance in Factory Overhead, $1,625 Cr., overapplied

j. Recorded the total overhead costs applied to jobs.

Instructions: Prepare a journal entry to record the allocation of these overhead costs.

k. Compute the balance in the Factory Overhead account as of the end of May.

PROBLEM SET B

Problem 19-1B
Production costs computed and recorded; reports prepared

C2 P1 P2 P3 P4

Tavella Co.'s August 31 inventory of raw materials is $150,000. Raw materials purchases in September are $400,000, and factory payroll cost in September is $232,000. Overhead costs incurred in September are: indirect materials, $30,000; indirect labor, $14,000; factory rent, $20,000; factory utilities, $12,000; and factory equipment depreciation, $30,000. The predetermined overhead rate is 50% of direct labor cost. Job 114 is sold for $380,000 cash in September. Costs for the three jobs worked on in September follow.

	Job 114	Job 115	Job 116
Balances on August 31			
Direct materials..............	$ 14,000	$ 18,000	
Direct labor.................	18,000	16,000	
Applied overhead............	9,000	8,000	
Costs during September			
Direct materials..............	100,000	170,000	$ 80,000
Direct labor.................	30,000	68,000	120,000
Applied overhead............	?	?	?
Status on September 30	Finished (sold)	Finished (unsold)	In process

Required

1. Determine the total of each production cost incurred for September (direct labor, direct materials, and applied overhead), and the total cost assigned to each job (including the balances from August 31).

2. Prepare journal entries for the month of September to record the following.

    a. Materials purchases (on credit), factory payroll (paid in cash), and actual overhead costs including indirect materials and indirect labor. (Factory rent and utilities are paid in cash.)

    b. Assignment of direct materials, direct labor, and applied overhead costs to Goods in Process Inventory.

    c. Transfer of Jobs 114 and 115 to the Finished Goods Inventory.

    d. Cost of Job 114 in the Cost of Goods Sold account.

    e. Revenue from the sale of Job 114.

    f. Assignment of any underapplied or overapplied overhead to the Cost of Goods Sold account. (The amount is not material.)

    Check (2f) $3,000 overapplied

3. Prepare a manufacturing statement for September (use a single line presentation for direct materials and show the details of overhead cost).

    (3) Cost of goods manufactured, $500,000

4. Compute gross profit for September. Show how to present the inventories on the September 30 balance sheet.

Analysis Component

5. The over- or underapplied overhead adjustment is closed to Cost of Goods Sold. Discuss how this adjustment impacts business decision making regarding individual jobs or batches of jobs.

Swisher Company's computer system generated the following trial balance on December 31, 2013. The company's manager knows that the trial balance is wrong because it does not show any balance for Goods in Process Inventory but does show balances for the Factory Payroll and Factory Overhead accounts.

Problem 19-2B
Source documents, journal entries, overhead, and financial reports

P1 P2 P3 P4

	Debit	Credit
Cash............................	$ 48,000	
Accounts receivable	42,000	
Raw materials inventory	26,000	
Goods in process inventory	0	
Finished goods inventory	9,000	
Prepaid rent	3,000	
Accounts payable		$ 10,500
Notes payable		13,500
Common stock		30,000
Retained earnings		87,000
Sales		180,000
Cost of goods sold	105,000	
Factory payroll	16,000	
Factory overhead	27,000	
Operating expenses	45,000	
Totals	$321,000	$321,000

After examining various files, the manager identifies the following six source documents that need to be processed to bring the accounting records up to date.

Materials requisition 94-231:	$4,600 direct materials to Job 603
Materials requisition 94-232:	$7,600 direct materials to Job 604
Materials requisition 94-233:	$2,100 indirect materials
Labor time ticket 765:	$5,000 direct labor to Job 603
Labor time ticket 766:	$8,000 direct labor to Job 604
Labor time ticket 777:	$3,000 indirect labor

Jobs 603 and 604 are the only units in process at year-end. The predetermined overhead rate is 200% of direct labor cost.

Required

1. Use information on the six source documents to prepare journal entries to assign the following costs.
   a. Direct materials costs to Goods in Process Inventory.
   b. Direct labor costs to Goods in Process Inventory.
   c. Overhead costs to Goods in Process Inventory.
   d. Indirect materials costs to the Factory Overhead account.
   e. Indirect labor costs to the Factory Overhead account.

Check (2) $6,100 underapplied overhead

2. Determine the revised balance of the Factory Overhead account after making the entries in part 1. Determine whether there is under- or overapplied overhead for the year. Prepare the adjusting entry to allocate any over- or underapplied overhead to Cost of Goods Sold, assuming the amount is not material.

(3) T. B. totals, $321,000

3. Prepare a revised trial balance.

(4) Net income, $23,900

4. Prepare an income statement for year 2013 and a balance sheet as of December 31, 2013.

Analysis Component

5. Assume that the $2,100 indirect materials on materials requisition 94-233 should have been direct materials charged to Job 604. Without providing specific calculations, describe the impact of this error on the income statement for 2013 and the balance sheet at December 31, 2013.

Problem 19-3B
Source documents, journal entries, and accounts in job order cost accounting
P1 P2 P3

Prescott Company's predetermined overhead rate is 200% of direct labor. Information on the company's production activities during September 2013 follows.

a. Purchased raw materials on credit, $125,000.
b. Paid $84,000 cash for factory wages.
c. Paid $11,000 cash for miscellaneous factory overhead costs.
d. Materials requisitions record use of the following materials for the month.

Job 487	$30,000
Job 488	20,000
Job 489	12,000
Job 490	14,000
Job 491	4,000
Total direct materials	80,000
Indirect materials	12,000
Total materials used	$92,000

e. Time tickets record use of the following labor for the month.

Job 487	$ 8,000
Job 488	7,000
Job 489	25,000
Job 490	26,000
Job 491	2,000
Total direct labor	68,000
Indirect labor	16,000
Total	$84,000

f. Allocated overhead to Jobs 487, 489, and 490.

g. Transferred Jobs 487, 489, and 490 to Finished Goods.

h. Sold Jobs 487 and 489 on credit for a total price of $340,000.

i. The company incurred the following overhead costs during the month (credit Prepaid Insurance for expired factory insurance).

Depreciation of factory building	$37,000
Depreciation of factory equipment	21,000
Expired factory insurance	7,000
Accrued property taxes payable	31,000

j. Applied overhead at month-end to the Goods in Process (Jobs 488 and 491) using the predetermined overhead rate of 200% of direct labor cost.

Required

1. Prepare a job cost sheet for each job worked on in the month. Use the following simplified form.

Job No. _____	
Materials	$ _____
Labor	_____
Overhead	_____
Total cost	$ _____

2. Prepare journal entries to record the events and transactions *a* through *j*.

3. Set up T-accounts for each of the following general ledger accounts, each of which started the month with a zero balance: Raw Materials Inventory, Goods in Process Inventory, Finished Goods Inventory, Factory Payroll, Factory Overhead, Cost of Goods Sold. Then post the journal entries to these T-accounts and determine the balance of each account.

4. Prepare a report showing the total cost of each job in process and prove that the sum of their costs equals the Goods in Process Inventory account balance. Prepare similar reports for Finished Goods Inventory and Cost of Goods Sold.

Check (2f) Cr. Factory Overhead, $118,000

(3) Finished goods inventory, $92,000 bal.

In December 2012, Pavelka Company's manager estimated next year's total direct labor cost assuming 50 persons working an average of 2,000 hours each at an average wage rate of $15 per hour. The manager also estimated the following manufacturing overhead costs for year 2013.

Problem 19-4B
Overhead allocation and adjustment using a predetermined overhead rate

P3 P4

Indirect labor	$159,600
Factory supervision	120,000
Rent on factory building	70,000
Factory utilities	44,000
Factory insurance expired	34,000
Depreciation—Factory equipment	240,000
Repairs expense—Factory equipment	30,000
Factory supplies used	34,400
Miscellaneous production costs	18,000
Total estimated overhead costs	$750,000

At the end of 2013, records show the company incurred $725,000 of actual overhead costs. It completed and sold five jobs with the following direct labor costs: Job 625, $354,000; Job 626, $330,000; Job 627, $175,000; Job 628, $420,000; and Job 629, $184,000. In addition, Job 630 is in process at the end of 2013 and had been charged $10,000 for direct labor. No jobs were in process at the end of 2012. The company's predetermined overhead rate is based on direct labor cost.

Required

1. Determine the following.

   a. Predetermined overhead rate for year 2013.

   b. Total overhead cost applied to each of the six jobs during year 2013.

   c. Over- or underapplied overhead at year-end 2013.

2. Assuming that any over- or underapplied overhead is not material, prepare the adjusting entry to allocate any over- or underapplied overhead to Cost of Goods Sold at the end of year 2013.

Problem 19-5B
Production transactions,
subsidiary records, and
source documents

P1   P2   P3   P4

King Company produces variations of its product, a megatron, in response to custom orders from its customers. On June 1, the company had no inventories of goods in process or finished goods but held the following raw materials.

Material M	120 units @ $200 =	$24,000
Material R	80 units @ 160 =	12,800
Paint	44 units @ 72 =	3,168
Total cost		$39,968

On June 3, the company began working on two megatrons: Job 450 for Encinita Company and Job 451 for Fargo, Inc.

Required

Using Exhibit 19.2 as a guide, prepare job cost sheets for jobs 20 and 21. Using Exhibit 19.4 as a guide, prepare materials ledger cards for Material M, Material R, and paint. Enter the beginning raw materials inventory dollar amounts for each of these materials on their respective ledger cards. Then, follow instructions in this list of activities.

a. Purchased raw materials on credit and recorded the following information from receiving reports and invoices.

> Receiving Report No. 20, Material M, 150 units at $200 each.
> Receiving Report No. 21, Material R, 70 units at $160 each.

Instructions: Record these purchases with a single journal entry. Enter the receiving report information on the materials ledger cards.

b. Requisitioned the following raw materials for production.

> Requisition No. 223, for Job 450, 80 units of Material M.
> Requisition No. 224, for Job 450, 60 units of Material R.
> Requisition No. 225, for Job 451, 40 units of Material M.
> Requisition No. 226, for Job 451, 30 units of Material R.
> Requisition No. 227, for 12 units of paint.

Instructions: Enter amounts for direct materials requisitions on the materials ledger cards and the job cost sheets. Enter the indirect material amount on the materials ledger card. Do not record a journal entry at this time.

c. Received the following employee time tickets for work in June.

> Time tickets Nos. 1 to 10 for direct labor on Job 450, $40,000.
> Time tickets Nos. 11 to 20 for direct labor on Job 451, $32,000.
> Time tickets Nos. 21 to 24 for equipment repairs, $12,000.

Instructions: Record direct labor from the time tickets on the job cost sheets. Do not record a journal entry at this time.

d. Paid cash for the following items during the month: factory payroll, $84,000, and miscellaneous overhead items, $36,800.

Instructions: Record these payments with journal entries.

e. Finished Job 450 and transferred it to the warehouse. The company assigns overhead to each job with a predetermined overhead rate equal to 70% of direct labor cost.

Instructions: Enter the allocated overhead on the cost sheet for Job 450, fill in the cost summary section of the cost sheet, and then mark the cost sheet "Finished." Prepare a journal entry to record the job's completion and its transfer to Finished Goods.

f. Delivered Job 450 and accepted the customer's promise to pay $290,000 within 30 days.

Instructions: Prepare journal entries to record the sale of Job 450 and the cost of goods sold.

g. Applied overhead cost to Job 451 based on the job's direct labor used to date.

Instructions: Enter overhead on the job cost sheet but do not make a journal entry at this time.

h. Recorded the total direct and indirect materials costs as reported on all the requisitions for the month.

Instructions: Prepare a journal entry to record these.

i. Recorded the total direct and indirect labor costs as reported on all time tickets for the month.

Instructions: Prepare a journal entry to record these costs.

j. Recorded the total overhead costs applied to jobs.

Instructions: Prepare a journal entry to record the allocation of these overhead costs.

k. Compute the balance in the Factory Overhead account as of the end of June.

Check (h) Dr. Goods in Process Inventory, $38,400

Check Balance in Factory Overhead, $736 Cr., overapplied

(This serial problem began in Chapter 1 and continues through most of the book. If previous chapter segments were not completed, the serial problem can begin at this point. It is helpful, but not necessary, to use the Working Papers that accompany the book.)

SERIAL PROBLEM
Success Systems
P1 P2 P3

SP 19 The computer workstation furniture manufacturing that Adria Lopez started in January is progressing well. As of the end of June, Success Systems' job cost sheets show the following total costs accumulated on three furniture jobs.

	Job 6.02	Job 6.03	Job 6.04
Direct materials.........	$1,500	$3,300	$2,700
Direct labor............	800	1,420	2,100
Overhead..............	400	710	1,050

Job 6.02 was started in production in May, and these costs were assigned to it in May: direct materials, $600; direct labor, $180; and overhead, $90. Jobs 6.03 and 6.04 were started in June. Overhead cost is applied with a predetermined rate based on direct labor costs. Jobs 6.02 and 6.03 are finished in June, and Job 6.04 is expected to be finished in July. No raw materials are used indirectly in June. (Assume this company's predetermined overhead rate did not change over these months).

Required

1. What is the cost of the raw materials used in June for each of the three jobs and in total?

Check (1) Total materials, $6,900

2. How much total direct labor cost is incurred in June?

3. What predetermined overhead rate is used in June?

(3) 50%

4. How much cost is transferred to finished goods inventory in June?

Beyond the Numbers

BTN 19-1 **Polaris'** financial statements and notes in Appendix A provide evidence of growth potential in its sales.

REPORTING IN ACTION

C1

Polaris

Required

1. Identify at least two types of costs that will predictably increase as a percent of sales with growth in sales.

2. Explain why you believe the types of costs identified for part 1 will increase, and describe how you might assess Polaris' success with these costs. (*Hint:* You might consider the gross margin ratio.)

Fast Forward

3. Access Polaris' annual report for a fiscal year ending after December 31, 2011, from its Website [**Polaris.com**] or the SEC's EDGAR database [**www.sec.gov**]. Review and report its growth in sales along with its cost and income levels (including its gross margin ratio).

COMPARATIVE ANALYSIS

C1

Polaris

Arctic Cat

BTN 19-2   Manufacturers and merchandisers can apply just-in-time (JIT) to their inventory management. Both **Polaris** and **Arctic Cat** want to know the impact of a JIT inventory system for their operating cash flows. Review each company's statement of cash flows in Appendix A to answer the following.

Required

1. Identify the impact on operating cash flows (increase or decrease) for changes in inventory levels (increase or decrease) for both companies for each of the three most recent years.

2. What impact would a JIT inventory system have on both Polaris' and Arctic Cat's operating income? Link the answer to your response for part 1.

3. Would the move to a JIT system have a one-time or recurring impact on operating cash flow?

ETHICS CHALLENGE

P3

Point: Students could compare responses and discuss differences in concerns with allocating overhead.

BTN 19-3   An accounting professional requires at least two skill sets. The first is to be technically competent. Knowing how to capture, manage, and report information is a necessary skill. Second, the ability to assess manager and employee actions and biases for accounting analysis is another skill. For instance, knowing how a person is compensated helps anticipate information biases. Draw on these skills and write a one-half page memo to the financial officer on the following practice of allocating overhead.

Background: Assume that your company sells portable housing to both general contractors and the government. It sells jobs to contractors on a bid basis. A contractor asks for three bids from different manufacturers. The combination of low bid and high quality wins the job. However, jobs sold to the government are bid on a cost-plus basis. This means price is determined by adding all costs plus a profit based on cost at a specified percent, such as 10%. You observe that the amount of overhead allocated to government jobs is higher than that allocated to contract jobs. These allocations concern you and motivate your memo.

COMMUNICATING IN PRACTICE

C1   C2

Point: Have students present a mock interview, one assuming the role of the president of the company and the other the applicant.

BTN 19-4   Assume that you are preparing for a second interview with a manufacturing company. The company is impressed with your credentials but has indicated that it has several qualified applicants. You anticipate that in this second interview, you must show what you offer over other candidates. You learn the company currently uses a periodic inventory system and is not satisfied with the timeliness of its information and its inventory management. The company manufactures custom-order holiday decorations and display items. To show your abilities, you plan to recommend that it use a cost accounting system.

Required

In preparation for the interview, prepare notes outlining the following:

1. Your cost accounting system recommendation and why it is suitable for this company.

2. A general description of the documents that the proposed cost accounting system requires.

3. How the documents in part 2 facilitate the operation of the cost accounting system.

TAKING IT TO THE NET

C1

BTN 19-5   Many contractors work on custom jobs that require a job order costing system.

Required

Access the Website **AMSI.com** and click on *Construction Management Software,* and then on STARBUILDER. Prepare a one-page memorandum for the CEO of a construction company providing information about the job order costing software this company offers. Would you recommend that the company purchase this software?

BTN 19-6   Consider the activities undertaken by a medical clinic in your area.

TEAMWORK IN ACTION

C1

Required

1. Do you consider a job order cost accounting system appropriate for the clinic?

2. Identify as many factors as possible to lead you to conclude that it uses a job order system.

BTN 19-7   Refer to the chapter opener regarding David Schottenstein and his company, **Astor and Black**. All successful businesses track their costs, and it is especially important for start-up businesses to monitor and control costs.

ENTREPRENEURIAL DECISION

C1 C2

Required

1. Assume that Astor and Black uses a job order costing system. For the basic cost category of direct materials, explain how a job cost sheet for Astor and Black would differ from a job cost sheet for a service company.

2. For the basic cost categories of direct labor and overhead, provide examples of the types of costs that would fall into each category for Astor and Black.

BTN 19-8   Job order cost accounting is frequently used by home builders.

HITTING THE ROAD

C2 P1 P2 P3

Required

1. You (or your team) are to prepare a job cost sheet for a single-family home under construction. List four items of both direct materials and direct labor. Explain how you think overhead should be applied.

2. Contact a builder and compare your job cost sheet to this builder's job cost sheet. If possible, speak to that company's accountant. Write your findings in a short report.

BTN 19-9   **KTM** and **Piaggio** are competitors in the global marketplace. KTM's and Piaggio's financial statements are in Appendix A.

GLOBAL DECISION

C1

KTM

PIAGGIO

Required

1. Determine the change in KTM's and Piaggio's inventories for the most recent year reported. Then identify the impact on net resources generated by operating activities (increase or decrease) for the change in inventory level (increase or decrease) for KTM and Piaggio for that same year.

2. How would the move to a just-in-time (JIT) system likely impact future operating cash flows and operating income?

3. Would a move to a JIT system likely impact KTM more than it would Piaggio? Explain.

ANSWERS TO MULTIPLE CHOICE QUIZ

1. c; $30,000 × 150% = $\underline{\$45,000}$

2. b; $38,500/$35,000 = $\underline{110\%}$

3. e; Direct materials + Direct labor + Overhead = Total cost;
   Direct materials + ($4,000/.80) + $4,000 = $10,000
   Direct materials = $\underline{\$1,000}$

4. e; $9,000 + $94,200 + $59,200 + $31,600 − Finished goods = $17,800
   Thus, finished goods = $\underline{\$176,200}$

5. b

Process Cost Accounting

20

A Look Back

Chapter 18 introduced managerial accounting and described cost concepts and the reporting of manufacturing activities. Chapter 19 explained job order costing—an important cost accounting system for customized products and services.

A Look at This Chapter

This chapter focuses on how to measure and account for costs in process operations. We explain process production, describe how to assign costs to processes, and compute cost per equivalent unit for a process.

A Look Ahead

Chapter 21 looks at cost behavior and explains how its identification is useful to managers in performing cost-volume-profit analyses. It also shows how to apply cost-volume-profit analysis.

Learning Objectives

CONCEPTUAL

C1 Explain process operations and the way they differ from job order operations. (p. 816)

C2 Define and compute equivalent units and explain their use in process cost accounting. (p. 823)

C3 Describe accounting for production activity and preparation of a process cost summary using weighted average. (p. 824)

C4 *Appendix 20A*—Describe accounting for production activity and preparation of a process cost summary using FIFO. (p. 833)

ANALYTICAL

A1 Compare process cost accounting and job order cost accounting. (p. 819)

A2 Explain and illustrate a hybrid costing system. (p. 831)

PROCEDURAL

P1 Record the flow of direct materials costs in process cost accounting. (p. 820)

P2 Record the flow of direct labor costs in process cost accounting. (p. 821)

P3 Record the flow of factory overhead costs in process cost accounting. (p. 821)

P4 Record the transfer of completed goods to Finished Goods Inventory and Cost of Goods Sold. (p. 829)

Sweet Success

"Anyone can do it!"

—NEAL GOTTLIEB

SAN FRANCISCO—After returning from a stint in the Peace Corps, Neal Gottlieb wanted to start the "most Earth-friendly business I could think of." Using the $70,000 he saved from delivering newspapers and other boyhood jobs, Neal started **Three Twins Ice Cream (ThreeTwinsIceCream.com),** a manufacturer and seller of organic ice cream. Business started slowly, with Neal as the lone employee in a single ice cream shop. "I made ice cream in the morning, ran the shop all day, then cleaned up and did paperwork at night," recalls Neal.

Working 166 straight days without a day off and recording gross sales of $49 on one cold, rainy Monday, Neal decided he had to expand into the wholesale ice cream business or abandon his dreams. Neal's gamble paid off—today Three Twins Ice Cream is certified organic in more ice cream flavors than any ice cream company in the world, and as Neal says, "I'm happy to say I don't mop floors anymore."

In addition to using only organic ingredients, Neal strives to make his entire operation Earth-friendly. "Everything we give the customer can be composted," explains Neal. Cups and spoons are made from pressed sugar cane, potatoes, and corn starch. His production strategy adds overhead costs; for example, spoons cost 4 cents each instead of 1 cent each for plastic spoons. Neal explains that "using organic ingredients isn't the cheapest option, but it's the best." With costly raw materials and overhead costs, Neal must be adept at interpreting product cost reports. Without good cost and production process controls, his income would quickly melt away.

With costly raw materials and overhead costs, Neal relies on process cost summary reports to enable him to monitor and control costs of materials, labor, and overhead in his production processes. Accurate costing is especially useful in companies like Neal's, where different products require different processes and costs. Traditional flavors like vanilla, chocolate, and strawberry can be made in large quantities in large production runs, while treats like Peanut Butter Confetti Crunch and The Chocolate Project are made in small quantities.

Neal's recipe is working. Three Twins recently built a 4,200 square foot manufacturing facility to expand its business and reduce costs. Neal's factory allows him to produce larger quantities of ice cream at lower cost because he now makes his own mix. "We used to pay $15 per gallon for our mix; we can now make mix for less than $7 per gallon," explains Neal. Neal responded to these cost savings by lowering his selling prices and saw demand for his products grow.

From humble beginnings, Three Twins' sales are growing at almost 100 percent per year. "We want to be a national brand," says Neal. "We believe we have the potential to find a huge market." Still, Neal advises would-be entrepreneurs to "enjoy what they do, work hard, and give back."

[Sources: *Three Twins Ice Cream Company* Website, January 2013; *Marin Independent Journal*, July 2010; sf.eater.com, April 2010; *North Bay Business* Journal, April 2010; *Napa Valley Register*, April 2007]

The type of product or service a company offers determines its cost accounting system. Job order costing is used to account for custom products and services that meet the demands of a particular customer. Not all products are manufactured in this way; many carry standard designs so that one unit is no different than any other unit. Such a system often produces large numbers of units on a continuous basis, all of which pass through similar processes. This chapter describes how to use a process cost accounting system to account for these types of products. It also explains how costs are accumulated for each process and then assigned to units passing through those processes. This information helps us understand and estimate the cost of each process as well as find ways to reduce costs and improve processes.

Process Cost Accounting

Process Operations
- Comparing job order and process operations
- Organization of process operations
- GenX Company—an illustration

Process Cost Accounting
- Job order versus process cost systems
- Direct and indirect costs
- Accounting for materials costs
- Accounting for labor costs
- Accounting for factory overhead

Equivalent Units of Production (EUP)
- Accounting for goods in process
- Differences between EUP for materials, labor, and overhead

Process Costing Illustration
- Physical flow of units
- EUP
- Cost per EUP
- Cost reconciliation
- Process cost summary
- Transfers to finished goods and to cost of goods sold
- Trends in process operations

PROCESS OPERATIONS

C1 Explain process operations and the way they differ from job order operations.

Process operations, also called *process manufacturing* or *process production,* is the mass production of products in a continuous flow of steps. This means that products pass through a series of sequential processes. Petroleum refining is a common example of process operations. Crude oil passes through a series of steps before it is processed into different grades of petroleum. **Exxon Mobil's** oil activities reflect a process operation. An important characteristic of process operations is the high level of standardization necessary if the system is to produce large volumes of products. Process operations also extend to services. Examples include mail sorting in large post offices and order processing in large mail-order firms such as **L.L. Bean**. The common feature in these service organizations is that operations are performed in a sequential manner using a series of standardized processes. Other companies using process operations include:

Company*	Product or Service	Company	Product or Service
Kellogg	Cereals	Heinz	Ketchup
Pfizer	Pharmaceuticals	Penn	Tennis balls
Proctor & Gamble	Household products	Hershey	Chocolate
Coca-Cola	Soft drinks	Jiffy Lube	Oil changes

*For virtual tours of process operations visit PennRacquet.com/factory.html (tennis balls) and Hersheys.com/ads-and-videos/how-we-make-chocolate.aspx (chocolate).

Each of these examples of products and services involves operations having a series of *processes,* or steps. Each process involves a different set of activities. A production operation that processes chemicals, for instance, might include the four steps shown in Exhibit 20.1. Understanding such processes for companies with process operations is crucial for measuring their costs. Increasingly, process operations use machines and automation to control product quality and reduce manufacturing costs.

EXHIBIT 20.1
Process Operations: Chemicals

| Preparing the chemicals | → | Mixing the chemicals | → | Bottling the chemical mix | → | Packaging the bottles |

EXHIBIT 20.1
Process Operations: Chemicals

Comparing Job Order and Process Operations

Job order and process operations can be considered as two ends of a continuum. Important features of both systems are shown in Exhibit 20.2. We often describe job order and process operations with manufacturing examples, but both also apply to service companies. In a job order costing system, the measurement focus is on the individual job or batch. In a process costing system, the measurement focus is on the process itself and the standardized units produced.

Job Order Operations	Process Operations
• Custom orders	• Repetitive procedures
• Heterogeneous products and services	• Homogeneous products and services
• Low production volume	• High production volume
• High product flexibility	• Low product flexibility
• Low to medium standardization	• High standardization

EXHIBIT 20.2
Comparing Job Order and Process Operations

Organization of Process Operations

In a process operation, each process is identified as a separate *production department, workstation,* or *work center.* With the exception of the first process or department, each receives the output from the prior department as a partially processed product. Depending on the nature of the process, a company applies direct labor, overhead, and, perhaps, additional direct materials to move the product toward completion. Only the final process or department in the series produces finished goods ready for sale to customers.

Tracking costs for several related departments can seem complex. Yet because process costing procedures are applied to the activity of each department or process separately, we need to consider only one process at a time. This simplifies the procedures.

When the output of one department becomes an input to another department, as is the case in sequential processing, we simply transfer the costs associated with those units from the first department into the next. We repeat these steps from department to department until the final process is complete. At that point the accumulated costs are transferred with the product from Goods in Process Inventory to Finished Goods Inventory. The next section illustrates a company with a single process, but the methods illustrated apply to a multiprocess scenario as each department's costs are handled separately for each department.

Decision Insight

Processing Health   Many service companies use process departments to perform specific tasks for consumers. Hospitals, for instance, have radiology and physical therapy facilities with special equipment and trained employees. When patients need services, they are processed through departments to receive prescribed care. Service companies need process cost accounting information as much as manufacturers to estimate costs of services, to plan future operations, to control costs, and to determine customer charges. ■

GenX Company—An Illustration

The GenX Company illustrates process operations. It produces Profen®, an over-the-counter pain reliever for athletes. GenX sells Profen to wholesale distributors, who in turn sell it to

EXHIBIT 20.3

Floor Plan of GenX's Factory

retailers. Profen is produced by mixing its active ingredient, Profelene, with flavorings and preservatives, molding it into Profen tablets, and packaging the tablets. Exhibit 20.3 shows a summary floor plan of the GenX factory, which has five areas.

The first step in process manufacturing is to decide when to produce a product. Management determines the types and quantities of materials and labor needed and then schedules the work. Unlike a job order process, where production often begins only after receipt of a custom order, managers of companies with process operations often forecast the demand expected for their products. Based on these plans, production begins. The flowchart in Exhibit 20.4 shows the production steps for GenX. The following sections explain how GenX uses a process cost accounting system to compute these costs. Many of the explanations refer to this exhibit and its numbered cost flows ① through ⑩. (*Hint:* The amounts for the numbered cost flows in Exhibit 20.4 are summarized in Exhibit 20.21. Those amounts are explained in the following pages, but it can help to refer to Exhibit 20.21 as we proceed through the explanations.)

Point: Electronic monitoring of operations is common in factories.

EXHIBIT 20.4

Process Operations and Costs: GenX

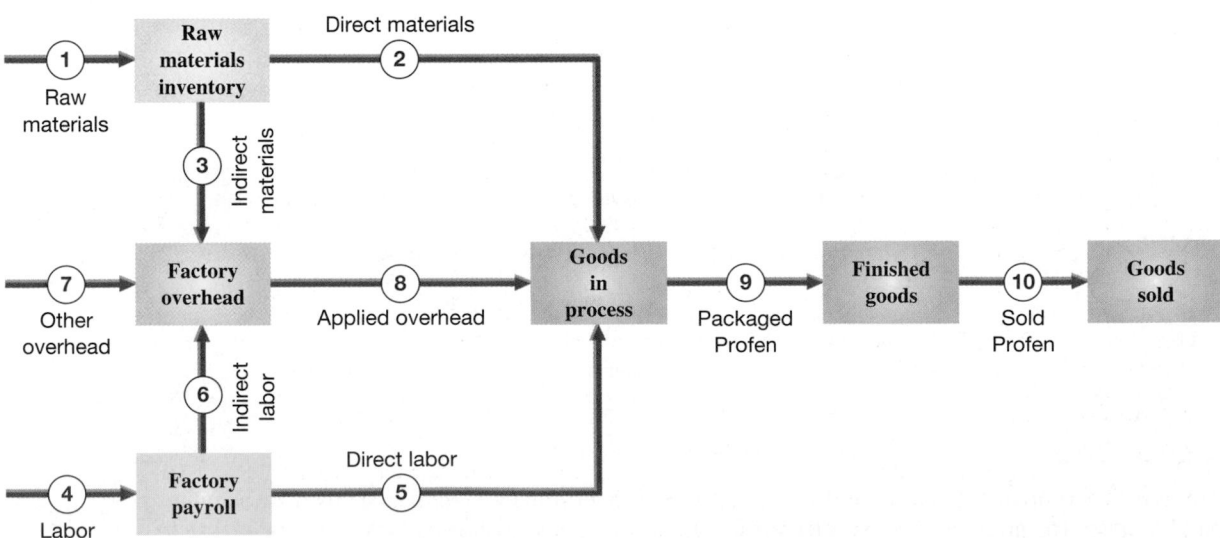

PROCESS COST ACCOUNTING

Comparing Job Order and Process Cost Accounting Systems

A1 Compare process cost accounting and job order cost accounting.

Process and job order operations are similar in that both combine materials, labor, and overhead in the process of producing products. They differ in how they are organized and managed. The measurement focus in a job order costing system is on the individual job or batch, whereas in a process costing system, it is on the individual process. Regardless of the measurement focus, we are ultimately interested in determining the cost per unit of product (or service) resulting from either system.

Both **job order cost accounting systems** and **process cost accounting systems** track direct materials, direct labor, and overhead costs. However, these two accounting systems differ in terms of measuring unit costs. A job order system measures cost per unit upon completion of a job, by dividing the total cost for that job by the number of units in that job. A process costing system measures unit costs at the end of a period (for example, a month) by dividing the total costs for that process by the number of units passing through that process to determine the cost per equivalent unit (defined later in the chapter). Differences in the way these two systems apply materials, labor, and overhead costs are highlighted in Exhibit 20.5.

Point: The cost object in a job order system is the specific job; the cost object in a process costing system is the process.

Job order systems

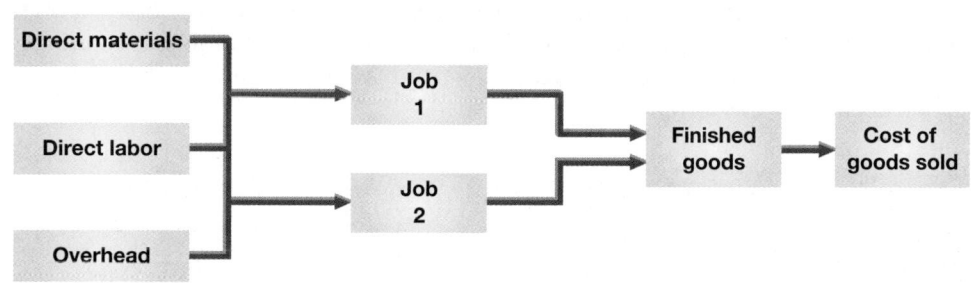

EXHIBIT 20.5

Comparing Job Order and Process Cost Accounting Systems

Process systems

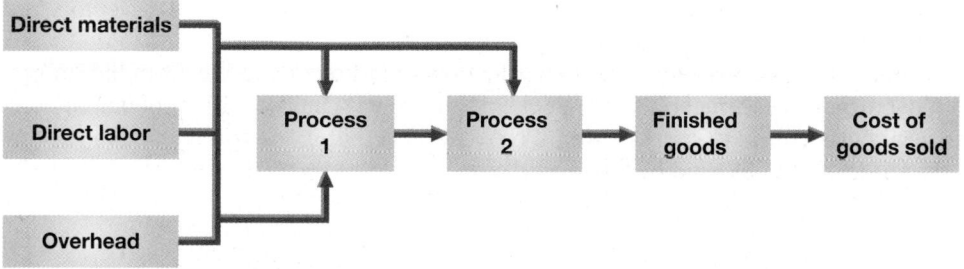

Direct and Indirect Costs

Like job order operations, process cost accounting systems use the concepts of direct and indirect costs. If a cost can be traced to the cost object, it is direct; if it cannot, it is indirect. Materials and labor that can be traced to specific processes are assigned to those processes as direct costs. Materials and labor that cannot be traced to a specific process are indirect costs and are assigned to overhead. Some costs classified as overhead in a job order system may be classified as direct costs in process cost accounting. For example, depreciation of a machine used entirely by one process is a direct cost of that process.

▓ **Decision** Insight ━━━━━━━━━━━━━━━━━━━━━━━━━━━━━━

JIT Boon to Process Operations   Companies that adopt JIT manufacturing often organize their production system as a series of sequential processes. One survey found 60% of companies that converted to JIT used process operations; this compares to only 20% before converting to JIT. ■

Accounting for Materials Costs

In Exhibit 20.4, arrow line ① reflects the arrival of materials at GenX's factory. These materials include Profelene, flavorings, preservatives, and packaging. They also include supplies for the production support office. GenX uses a perpetual inventory system and makes all purchases on credit. The summary entry for receipts of raw materials in April follows (dates in journal entries numbered ① through ⑩ are omitted because they are summary entries, often reflecting two or more transactions or events).

Assets   =   Liabilities   +   Equity
+11,095   +11,095

①	Raw Materials Inventory	11,095	
	Accounts Payable		11,095
	Acquired materials on credit for factory use.		

Arrow line ② in Exhibit 20.4 reflects the flow of direct materials to production, where they are used to produce Profen. Most direct materials are physically combined into the finished product; the remaining direct materials include those used and clearly linked with a specific process. The manager of a process usually obtains materials by submitting a *materials requisition* to the materials storeroom manager. In some situations, materials move continuously from raw materials inventory through the manufacturing process. **Pepsi Bottling**, for instance, uses a process in which inventory moves continuously through the system. In these cases, a **materials consumption report** summarizes the materials used by a department during a reporting period and replaces materials requisitions. The entry to record the use of direct materials by GenX's production department in April follows.

Assets   =   Liabilities   +   Equity
+9,900
−9,900

②	Goods in Process Inventory	9,900	
	Raw Materials Inventory		9,900
	To assign costs of direct materials used in production.		

This entry transfers costs from one asset account to another asset account. (When two or more production departments exist, a company uses two or more Goods in Process Inventory accounts to separately accumulate costs incurred by each.)

In Exhibit 20.4, the arrow line ③ reflects the flow of indirect materials from the storeroom to factory overhead. These materials are not clearly linked with any specific production process or department but are used to support overall production activity. The following entry records the cost of indirect materials used by GenX in April.

Example: What types of materials might the flow of arrow line ③ in Exhibit 20.4 reflect? *Answer:* Goggles, gloves, protective clothing, recordkeeping supplies, and cleaning supplies.

Assets   =   Liabilities   +   Equity
−1,195   −1,195

③	Factory Overhead	1,195	
	Raw Materials Inventory		1,195
	To record indirect materials used in April.		

After the entries for both direct and indirect materials are posted, the Raw Materials Inventory account appears as shown in Exhibit 20.6. The April 30 balance sheet reports the $4,000 Raw Materials Inventory account as a current asset.

EXHIBIT 20.6

Raw Materials Inventory

Raw Materials Inventory				Acct. No. 132
Date	Explanation	Debit	Credit	Balance
Mar. 31	Balance			4,000
Apr. 30	Materials purchases	11,095		15,095
30	Direct materials usage		9,900	5,195
30	Indirect materials usage		1,195	4,000

Accounting for Labor Costs

Exhibit 20.4 shows GenX factory payroll costs as reflected in arrow line ④. Total labor costs of $8,920 are paid in cash and are recorded in the Factory Payroll account.

④	Factory Payroll	8,920	
	Cash		8,920
	To record factory wages for April.		

P2 Record the flow of direct labor costs in process cost accounting.

Assets = Liabilities + Equity
−8,920   −8,920

Time reports from the production department and the production support office triggered this entry. (For simplicity, we do not separately identify withholdings and additional payroll taxes for employees.) In a process operation, the direct labor of a production department includes all labor used exclusively by that department. This is the case even if the labor is not applied to the product itself. If a production department in a process operation, for instance, has a full-time manager and a full-time maintenance worker, their salaries are direct labor costs of that process and are not factory overhead.

Arrow line ⑤ in Exhibit 20.4 shows GenX's use of direct labor in the production department. The following entry transfers April's direct labor costs from the Factory Payroll account to the Goods in Process Inventory account.

⑤	Goods in Process Inventory	5,700	
	Factory Payroll		5,700
	To assign costs of direct labor used in production.		

Assets = Liabilities + Equity
+5,700   +5,700

Arrow line ⑥ in Exhibit 20.4 reflects GenX's indirect labor costs. These employees provide clerical, maintenance, and other services that help produce Profen efficiently. For example, they order materials, deliver them to the factory floor, repair equipment, operate and program computers used in production, keep payroll and other production records, clean up, and move the finished goods to the warehouse. The following entry charges these indirect labor costs to factory overhead.

Point: A department's indirect labor cost might include an allocated portion of the salary of a manager who supervises two or more departments. Allocation of costs between departments is discussed in a later chapter.

⑥	Factory Overhead	3,220	
	Factory Payroll		3,220
	To record indirect labor as overhead.		

Assets = Liabilities + Equity
                        −3,220
                        +3,220

After these entries for both direct and indirect labor are posted, the Factory Payroll account appears as shown in Exhibit 20.7. The temporary Factory Payroll account is now closed to another temporary account, Factory Overhead, and is ready to receive entries for May. Next we show how to apply overhead to production and close the temporary Factory Overhead account.

Factory Payroll				Acct. No. 530		
Date		Explanation	Debit	Credit	Balance	
Mar.	31	Balance			0	
Apr.	30	Total payroll for April	8,920		8,920	
	30	Direct labor costs		5,700	3,220	
	30	Indirect labor costs		3,220	0	

EXHIBIT 20.7

Factory Payroll

Accounting for Factory Overhead

Overhead costs other than indirect materials and indirect labor are reflected by arrow line ⑦ in Exhibit 20.4. These overhead items include the costs of insuring production assets, renting the factory building, using factory utilities, and depreciating equipment not directly related to a specific process. The following entry records overhead costs for April.

P3 Record the flow of factory overhead costs in process cost accounting.

Assets = Liabilities + Equity
−180   +645   −2,425
−750
−850

(7)	Factory Overhead		2,425	
	Prepaid Insurance			180
	Utilities Payable			645
	Cash			750
	Accumulated Depreciation—Factory Equipment ...			850
	To record overhead items incurred in April.			

After this entry is posted, the Factory Overhead account balance is $6,840, comprising indirect materials of $1,195, indirect labor of $3,220, and $2,425 of other overhead.

Arrow line ⑧ in Exhibit 20.4 reflects the application of factory overhead to production. Factory overhead is applied to processes by relating overhead cost to another variable such as direct labor hours or machine hours used. With increasing automation, companies with process operations are more likely to use machine hours to allocate overhead. In some situations, a single allocation basis such as direct labor hours (or a single rate for the entire plant) fails to provide useful allocations. As a result, management can use different rates for different production departments. Based on an analysis of its operations, GenX applies its April overhead at a rate of 120% of direct labor cost, as shown in Exhibit 20.8.

Point: The time it takes to process (cycle) products through a process is sometimes used to allocate costs.

EXHIBIT 20.8

Applying Factory Overhead (Production Department)

Overhead applied = Direct labor cost × Predetermined rate
$6,840   = $5,700   ×   120%

GenX records its applied overhead with the following entry.

Assets = Liabilities + Equity
+6,840   +6,840

⑧	Goods in Process Inventory		6,840	
	Factory Overhead			6,840
	Allocated overhead costs to production at 120% of direct labor cost.			

After posting this entry, the Factory Overhead account appears as shown in Exhibit 20.9. For GenX, the amount of overhead applied equals the actual overhead incurred during April. In most cases, using a predetermined overhead rate leaves an overapplied or underapplied balance in the Factory Overhead account. At the end of the period, this overapplied or underapplied balance should be closed to the Cost of Goods Sold account, as described in the job order costing chapter.

EXHIBIT 20.9

Factory Overhead

Example: If applied overhead results in a $6,940 credit to the factory overhead account, does it yield an over- or underapplied overhead amount?
Answer: $100 overapplied overhead

| Factory Overhead | | | | | Acct. No. 540 |
Date		Explanation	Debit	Credit	Balance
Mar.	31	Balance			0
Apr.	30	Indirect materials usage	1,195		1,195
	30	Indirect labor costs	3,220		4,415
	30	Other overhead costs	2,425		6,840
	30	Applied to production departments		6,840	0

■ Decision Ethics

Budget Officer   You are working to identify the direct and indirect costs of a new processing department that has several machines. This department's manager instructs you to classify a majority of the costs as indirect to take advantage of the direct labor-based overhead allocation method so it will be charged a lower amount of overhead (because of its small direct labor cost). This would penalize other departments with higher allocations. It also will cause the performance ratings of managers in these other departments to suffer. What action do you take? ■   [Answer—p. 840]

Quick Check   Answers – p. 840

1. A process operation (*a*) is another name for a job order operation, (*b*) does not use the concepts of direct materials or direct labor, or (*c*) typically produces large quantities of homogeneous products or services.
2. Under what conditions is a process cost accounting system more suitable for measuring production costs than a job order cost accounting system?
3. When direct materials are assigned and used in production, the entry to record their use includes (*a*) a credit to Goods in Process Inventory, (*b*) a debit to Goods in Process Inventory, or (*c*) a debit to Raw Materials Inventory.
4. What are the three cost categories incurred by both job order and process operations?
5. How many Goods in Process Inventory accounts are needed in a process cost system?

EQUIVALENT UNITS OF PRODUCTION

We explained how materials, labor, and overhead costs for a period are accumulated in the Goods in Process Inventory account, but we have not explained the arrow lines labeled ⑨ and ⑩ in Exhibit 20.4. These lines reflect the transfer of products from the production department to finished goods inventory, and from finished goods inventory to cost of goods sold. To determine the costs recorded for these flows, we must first determine the cost per unit of product and then apply this result to the number of units transferred.

C2 Define and compute equivalent units and explain their use in process cost accounting.

Accounting for Goods in Process

If a process has *no beginning and no ending goods in process inventory,* the unit cost of goods transferred out of a process is computed as follows:

> **Total cost assigned to the process (direct materials, direct labor, and overhead)**
> **Total number of units started and finished in the period**

If a process has a beginning or ending inventory of partially processed units (or both), then the total cost assigned to the process must be allocated to all completed and incomplete units worked on during the period. Therefore, the denominator must measure the entire production activity of the process for the period, called **equivalent units of production** (or **EUP**), a phrase that refers to the number of units that could have been started *and* completed given the cost incurred during a period. This measure is then used to compute the cost per equivalent unit and to assign costs to finished goods and goods in process inventory.

To illustrate, assume that GenX adds (or introduces) 100 units into its process during a period. Suppose at the end of that period, the production supervisor determines that those 100 units are 60% of the way through the process. Therefore, equivalent units of production for that period total 60 EUP (100 units × 60%). This means that with the resources used to put 100 units 60% of the way through the process, GenX could have started and completed 60 whole units.

Point: For GenX, "units" might refer to individual Profen tablets. For a juice maker, units might refer to gallons.

Differences in Equivalent Units for Materials, Labor, and Overhead

In many processes, the equivalent units of production for direct materials are not the same with respect to direct labor and overhead. To illustrate, consider a five-step process operation shown in Exhibit 20.10.

EXHIBIT 20.10

An Illustrative Five-Step Process
Operation

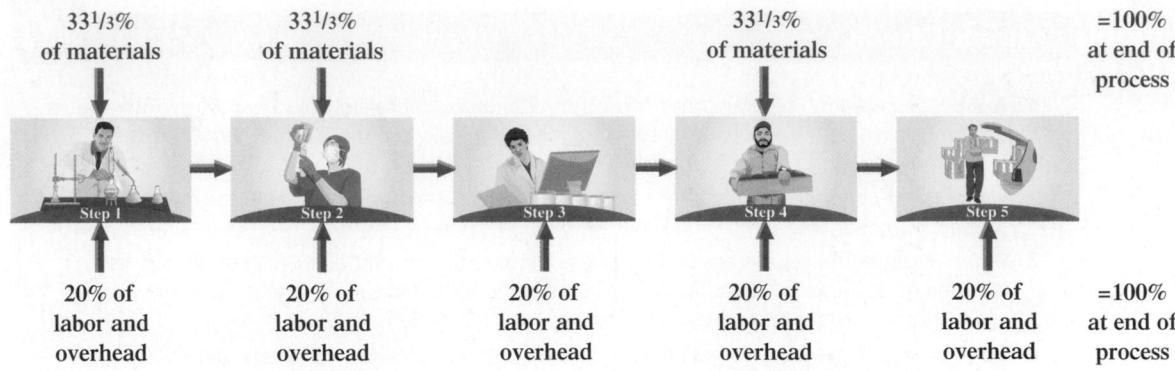

This exhibit shows that one-third of the direct material cost is added at each of three steps: 1, 2, and 4. One-fifth of the direct labor cost is added at each of the five steps. One-fifth of the overhead also is added at each step because overhead is applied as a percent of direct labor for this company.

When units finish step 1, they are one-third complete with respect to direct materials but only one-fifth complete with respect to direct labor and overhead. When they finish step 2, they are two-thirds complete with respect to direct materials but only two-fifths complete with respect to direct labor and overhead. When they finish step 3, they remain two-thirds complete with respect to materials but are now three-fifths complete with respect to labor and overhead. When they finish step 4, they are 100% complete with respect to materials (all direct materials have been added) but only four-fifths complete with respect to labor and overhead.

For example, if 300 units of product are started and processed through step 1 of Exhibit 20.10, they are said to be one-third complete *with respect to materials*. Expressed in terms of equivalent finished units, the processing of these 300 units is equal to finishing 100 EUP with respect to materials (300 units × 33⅓%). However, only one-fifth of direct labor and overhead has been applied to the 300 units at the end of step 1. This means that the equivalent units of production *with respect to labor and overhead* total 60 EUP (300 units × 20%).

Decision Insight

Process Services   Customer interaction software is a hot item in customer service processes. Whether in insurance, delivery, or technology services, companies are finding that this software can turn their customer service process into an asset. How does it work? For starters, it cuts time spent on service calls because a customer describes a problem only once. It also yields a database of customer questions and complaints that gives insights into needed improvements. It recognizes incoming phone numbers and accesses previous interactions. ■

PROCESS COSTING ILLUSTRATION

This section applies process costing concepts and procedures to GenX. **This illustration uses the weighted-average method for inventory costs. The FIFO method is illustrated in Appendix 20A.** (Assume a weighted-average cost flow for all computations and assignments in this chapter unless explicitly stated differently. When using a just-in-time inventory system, different inventory methods yield similar results because inventories are immaterial.)

Exhibit 20.11 shows selected information from the production department for the month of April. Accounting for a department's activity for a period includes four steps involving analysis of (1) physical flow, (2) equivalent units, (3) cost per equivalent unit, and (4) cost assignment and reconciliation. The next sections describe each step.

C3 Describe accounting for production activity and preparation of a process cost summary using weighted average.

EXHIBIT 20.11

Production Data

Beginning goods in process inventory (March 31)	
Units of product	30,000 units
Percentage of completion—Direct materials..................	100%
Percentage of completion—Direct labor	65%
Direct materials costs	$ 3,300
Direct labor costs	$ 600
Factory overhead costs applied (120% of direct labor)	$ 720
Activities during the current period (April)	
Units started this period	90,000 units
Units transferred out (completed)	100,000 units
Direct materials costs....................................	$ 9,900
Direct labor costs	$ 5,700
Factory overhead costs applied (120% of direct labor)	$ 6,840
Ending goods in process inventory (April 30)	
Units of product	20,000 units
Percentage of completion—Direct materials	100%
Percentage of completion—Direct labor....................	25%

Step 1: Determine the Physical Flow of Units

A *physical flow reconciliation* is a report that reconciles (1) the physical units started in a period with (2) the physical units completed in that period. A physical flow reconciliation for GenX is shown in Exhibit 20.12 for April.

EXHIBIT 20.12

Physical Flow Reconciliation

Units to Account For		Units Accounted For	
Beginning goods in process inventory	30,000 units	Units completed and transferred out	100,000 units
Units started this period	90,000 units	Ending goods in process inventory.....	20,000 units
Total units to account for	**120,000 units**	Total units accounted for	**120,000 units**

reconciled

The weighted-average method does not require us to separately track the units in beginning work in process from those units started this period. Instead, the units are treated as part of a large pool with an average cost per unit.

Step 2: Compute Equivalent Units of Production

The second step is to compute *equivalent units of production* for direct materials, direct labor, and factory overhead for April. Overhead is applied using direct labor as the allocation base for GenX. This also implies that equivalent units are the same for both labor and overhead.

   GenX used its direct materials, direct labor, and overhead to make finished units of Profen and to begin processing some units that are not yet complete. We must convert the physical units measure to equivalent units based on how each input has been used. Equivalent units are computed by multiplying the number of physical units by the percentage of completion for each input—see Exhibit 20.13.

EXHIBIT 20.13

Equivalent Units of Production—
Weighted Average

Equivalent Units of Production	Direct Materials	Direct Labor	Factory Overhead
Equivalent units completed and transferred out (100,000 × 100%)	100,000 EUP	100,000 EUP	100,000 EUP
Equivalent units for ending goods in process			
Direct materials (20,000 × 100%).................	20,000		
Direct labor (20,000 × 25%)		5,000	
Factory overhead (20,000 × 25%)			5,000
Equivalent units of production	120,000 EUP	105,000 EUP	105,000 EUP

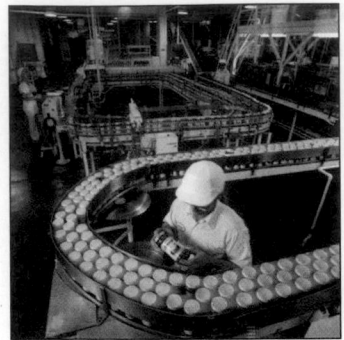

The first row of Exhibit 20.13 reflects units transferred out in April. The production department entirely completed its work on the 100,000 units transferred out. These units have 100% of the materials, labor, and overhead required, or 100,000 equivalent units of each input (100,000 × 100%).

The second row references the ending goods in process, and rows three, four, and five break it down by materials, labor, and overhead. For direct materials, the units in ending goods in process inventory (20,000 physical units) include all materials required, so there are 20,000 equivalent units (20,000 × 100%) of materials in the unfinished physical units. Regarding labor, the units in ending goods in process inventory include 25% of the labor required, which implies 5,000 equivalent units of labor (20,000 × 25%). These units are only 25% complete and labor is used uniformly through the process. Overhead is applied on the basis of direct labor for GenX, so equivalent units for overhead are computed identically to labor (20,000 × 25%).

The final row reflects the whole units of product that could have been manufactured with the amount of inputs used to create some complete and some incomplete units. For GenX, the amount of inputs used to produce 100,000 complete units and to start 20,000 additional units is equivalent to the amount of direct materials in 120,000 whole units, the amount of direct labor in 105,000 whole units, and the amount of overhead in 105,000 whole units.

Step 3: Compute the Cost per Equivalent Unit

Equivalent units of production for each product (from step 2) is used to compute the average cost per equivalent unit. Under the **weighted-average method,** the computation of EUP does not separate the units in beginning inventory from those started this period; similarly, this method combines the costs of beginning goods in process inventory with the costs incurred in the current period. This process is illustrated in Exhibit 20.14.

EXHIBIT 20.14

Cost per Equivalent Unit of Production—Weighted Average

Cost per Equivalent Unit of Production	Direct Materials	Direct Labor	Factory Overhead
Costs of beginning goods in process inventory	$ 3,300	$ 600	$ 720
Costs incurred this period	9,900	5,700	6,840
Total costs	$13,200	$6,300	$7,560
÷ Equivalent units of production (from Step 2)	120,000 EUP	105,000 EUP	105,000 EUP
= Cost per equivalent unit of production	$0.11 per EUP*	$0.06 per EUP†	$0.072 per EUP‡

*$13,200 ÷ 120,000 EUP   †$6,300 ÷ 105,000 EUP   ‡$7,560 ÷ 105,000 EUP

For direct materials, the cost averages $0.11 per EUP, computed as the sum of direct materials cost from beginning goods in process inventory ($3,300) and the direct materials cost incurred in April ($9,900), and this sum ($13,200) is then divided by the 120,000 EUP for materials (from step 2). The costs per equivalent unit for labor and overhead are similarly computed. Specifically, direct labor cost averages $0.06 per EUP, computed as the sum of labor cost in beginning goods in process inventory ($600) and the labor costs incurred in April ($5,700), and this sum ($6,300) divided by 105,000 EUP for labor. Overhead costs averages $0.072 per EUP, computed as the sum of overhead cost in the beginning goods in process inventory ($720) and the overhead costs applied in April ($6,840), and this sum ($7,560) divided by 105,000 EUP for overhead.

Step 4: Assign and Reconcile Costs

The EUP from step 2 and the cost per EUP from step 3 are used in step 4 to assign costs to (a) units that production completed and transferred to finished goods and (b) units that remain in process. This is illustrated in Exhibit 20.15.

EXHIBIT 20.15

Report of Costs Accounted
For—Weighted Average

Cost of units completed and transferred out

Direct materials (100,000 EUP × $0.11 per EUP)	$11,000	
Direct labor (100,000 EUP × $0.06 per EUP)	6,000	
Factory overhead (100,000 EUP × $0.072 per EUP)	7,200	
Cost of units completed this period		$ 24,200

Cost of ending goods in process inventory

Direct materials (20,000 EUP × $0.11 per EUP)	2,200	
Direct labor (5,000 EUP × $0.06 per EUP)	300	
Factory overhead (5,000 EUP × $0.072 per EUP)	360	
Cost of ending goods in process inventory		2,860
Total costs accounted for		**$27,060**

Cost of Units Completed and Transferred The 100,000 units completed and transferred to finished goods inventory required 100,000 EUP of direct materials. Thus, we assign $11,000 (100,000 EUP × $0.11 per EUP) of direct materials cost to those units. Similarly, those units had received 100,000 EUP of direct labor and 100,000 EUP of factory overhead (recall Exhibit 20.13). Thus, we assign $6,000 (100,000 EUP × $0.06 per EUP) of direct labor and $7,200 (100,000 EUP × $0.072 per EUP) of overhead to those units. The total cost of the 100,000 completed and transferred units is $24,200 ($11,000 + $6,000 + $7,200) and their average cost per unit is $0.242 ($24,200 ÷ 100,000 units).

Cost of Units for Ending Goods in Process There are 20,000 incomplete units in goods in process inventory at period-end. For direct materials, those units have 20,000 EUP of material (from step 2) at a cost of $0.11 per EUP (from step 3), which yields the materials cost of goods in process inventory of $2,200 (20,000 EUP × $0.11 per EUP). For direct labor, the in-process units have 25% of the required labor, or 5,000 EUP (from step 2). Using the $0.06 labor cost per EUP (from step 3) we obtain the labor cost of goods in process inventory of $300 (5,000 EUP × $0.06 per EUP). For overhead, the in-process units reflect 5,000 EUP (from step 2). Using the $0.072 overhead cost per EUP (from step 3) we obtain overhead costs with in-process inventory of $360 (5,000 EUP × $0.072 per EUP). Total cost of goods in process inventory at period-end is $2,860 ($2,200 + $300 + $360).

As a check, management verifies that total costs assigned to those units completed and transferred plus the costs of those in process (from Exhibit 20.15) equal the costs incurred by production. Exhibit 20.16 shows the costs incurred by production this period. We then reconcile the *costs accounted for* in Exhibit 20.15 with the *costs to account for* in Exhibit 20.16.

EXHIBIT 20.16

Report of Costs to Account
For—Weighted Average

Cost of beginning goods in process inventory

Direct materials	$3,300	
Direct labor	600	
Factory overhead	720	$ 4,620

Cost incurred this period

Direct materials	9,900	
Direct labor	5,700	
Factory overhead	6,840	22,440
Total costs to account for		**$27,060**

At GenX, the production department manager is responsible for $27,060 in costs: $4,620 that is assigned to the goods in process at the start of the period plus $22,440 of materials, labor, and overhead incurred in the period. At period-end, that manager must show where these costs are assigned. The manager for GenX reports that $2,860 are assigned to units in process and $24,200 are assigned to units completed (per Exhibit 20.15). The sum of these amounts equals $27,060. Thus, the total *costs to account for* equal the total *costs accounted for* (minor differences can sometimes occur from rounding).

Process Cost Summary   An important managerial accounting report for a process cost accounting system is the **process cost summary** (also called *production report*), which is prepared separately for each process or production department. Three reasons for the summary are to (1) help department managers control and monitor their departments, (2) help factory managers evaluate department managers' performances, and (3) provide cost information for financial statements. A process cost summary achieves these purposes by describing the costs charged to each department, reporting the equivalent units of production achieved by each department, and determining the costs assigned to each department's output. For our purposes, it is prepared using a combination of Exhibits 20.13, 20.14, 20.15, and 20.16.

The process cost summary for GenX is shown in Exhibit 20.17. The report is divided into three sections. Section ① lists the total costs charged to the department, including direct materials, direct labor, and overhead costs incurred, as well as the cost of the beginning goods in process inventory. Section ② describes the equivalent units of production for the department. Equivalent units for materials, labor, and overhead are in separate columns. It also reports direct

Point: The key report in a job order costing system is a job cost sheet, which reports manufacturing costs per job. A process cost summary reports manufacturing costs per equivalent unit of a process or department.

EXHIBIT 20.17

Process Cost Summary

GenX COMPANY
Process Cost Summary (Weighted-Average Method)
For Month Ended April 30, 2013

Costs Charged to Production

Costs of beginning goods in process

Direct materials	$3,300	
Direct labor	600	
Factory overhead	720	$ 4,620

① Costs incurred this period

Direct materials	9,900	
Direct labor	5,700	
Factory overhead	6,840	22,440
Total costs to account for		**$27,060**

Unit Cost Information

Units to account for:		Units accounted for:	
Beginning goods in process	30,000	Completed and transferred out	100,000
Units started this period	90,000	Ending goods in process	20,000
Total units to account for	120,000	Total units accounted for	120,000

Equivalent Units of Production (EUP)	Direct Materials	Direct Labor	Factory Overhead
Units completed and transferred out	100,000 EUP	100,000 EUP	100,000 EUP
Units of ending goods in process			
Direct materials (20,000 × 100%)	20,000		
② Direct labor (20,000 × 25%)		5,000	
Factory overhead (20,000 × 25%)			5,000
Equivalent units of production	120,000 EUP	105,000 EUP	105,000 EUP

Cost per EUP	Direct Materials	Direct Labor	Factory Overhead
Costs of beginning goods in process	$ 3,300	$ 600	$ 720
Costs incurred this period	9,900	5,700	6,840
Total costs	$13,200	$6,300	$7,560
÷ EUP	120,000 EUP	105,000 EUP	105,000 EUP
Cost per EUP	$0.11 per EUP	$0.06 per EUP	$0.072 per EUP

Cost Assignment and Reconciliation

Costs transferred out (cost of goods manufactured)

Direct materials (100,000 EUP × $0.11 per EUP)	$11,000	
Direct labor (100,000 EUP × $0.06 per EUP)	6,000	
Factory overhead (100,000 EUP × $0.072 per EUP)	7,200	$ 24,200

③ Costs of ending goods in process

Direct materials (20,000 EUP × $0.11 per EUP)	2,200	
Direct labor (5,000 EUP × $0.06 per EUP)	300	
Factory overhead (5,000 EUP × $0.072 per EUP)	360	2,860
Total costs accounted for		**$27,060**

reconciled

materials, direct labor, and overhead costs per equivalent unit. Section ③ allocates total costs among units worked on in the period. The $24,200 is the total cost of goods transferred out of the department, and the $2,860 is the cost of partially processed ending inventory units. The assigned costs are then added to show that the total $27,060 cost charged to the department in section ① is now assigned to the units in section ③.

Quick Check

Answers – p. 840

6. Equivalent units are (a) a measure of a production department's productivity in using direct materials, direct labor, or overhead; (b) units of a product produced by a foreign competitor that are similar to units produced by a domestic company; or (c) generic units of a product similar to brand name units of a product.

7. Interpret the meaning of a department's equivalent units with respect to direct labor.

8. A department began the period with 8,000 units that were one-fourth complete with respect to direct labor. It completed 58,000 units, and ended with 6,000 units that were one-third complete with respect to direct labor. What were its direct labor equivalent units for the period using the weighted-average method?

9. A process cost summary for a department has three sections. What information is presented in each of them?

Transfers to Finished Goods Inventory and Cost of Goods Sold

> **P4** Record the transfer of completed goods to Finished Goods Inventory and Cost of Goods Sold.

Arrow line ⑨ in Exhibit 20.4 reflects the transfer of completed products from production to finished goods inventory. The process cost summary shows that the 100,000 units of finished Profen are assigned a cost of $24,200. The entry to record this transfer follows.

⑨	Finished Goods Inventory	24,200	
	Goods in Process Inventory		24,200
	To record transfer of completed units.		

Assets = Liabilities + Equity
+24,200
24,200

The credit to Goods in Process Inventory reduces that asset balance to reflect that 100,000 units are no longer in production. The cost of these units has been transferred to Finished Goods Inventory, which is recognized as a $24,200 increase in this asset. After this entry is posted, there remains a balance of $2,860 in the Goods in Process Inventory account, which is the amount computed in Step 4 previously. The cost of units transferred from Goods in Process Inventory to Finished Goods Inventory is called the **cost of goods manufactured.** Exhibit 20.18 reveals the activities in the Goods in Process Inventory account for this period. The ending balance of this account equals the cost assigned to the partially completed units in section ③ of Exhibit 20.17.

		Goods in Process Inventory		Acct. No. 134	
Date		**Explanation**	**Debit**	**Credit**	**Balance**
Mar.	31	Balance			4,620
Apr.	30	Direct materials usage	9,900		14,520
	30	Direct labor costs incurred	5,700		20,220
	30	Factory overhead applied	6,840		27,060
	30	Transfer completed product to warehouse		24,200	2,860

EXHIBIT 20.18

Goods in Process Inventory

Arrow line ⑩ in Exhibit 20.4 reflects the sale of finished goods. Assume that GenX sold 106,000 units of Profen this period, and that its beginning inventory of finished goods consisted of 26,000 units with a cost of $6,292. Also assume that its ending finished goods inventory consists of 20,000 units at a cost of $4,840. Using this information, we can compute its cost of goods sold for April as shown in Exhibit 20.19.

Point: We omit the journal entry for sales, but it totals the number of units sold times price per unit. The Accounts Receivable (or Cash) account is debited and the Sales Revenue account is credited.

EXHIBIT 20.19

Cost of Goods Sold

Beginning finished goods inventory	$ 6,292
+ Cost of goods manufactured this period	24,200
= Cost of goods available for sale	$30,492
− Ending finished goods inventory	4,840
= Cost of goods sold	$25,652

The summary entry to record cost of goods sold for this period follows:

Assets = Liabilities + Equity
−25,652   −25,652

⑩	Cost of Goods Sold	25,652	
	Finished Goods Inventory		25,652
	To record cost of goods sold for April.		

The Finished Goods Inventory account now appears as shown in Exhibit 20.20.

EXHIBIT 20.20

Finished Goods Inventory

Date		Explanation	Debit	Credit	Balance
Mar.	31	Balance			6,292
Apr.	30	Transfer in cost of goods manufactured	24,200		30,492
	30	Cost of goods sold		25,652	4,840

Finished Goods Inventory   Acct. No. 135

Summary of Cost Flows   Exhibit 20.21 shows GenX's manufacturing cost flows for
April. Each of these cost flows and the entries to record them have been explained. The flow
of costs through the accounts reflects the flow of production activities and products.

EXHIBIT 20.21*

Cost Flows through GenX

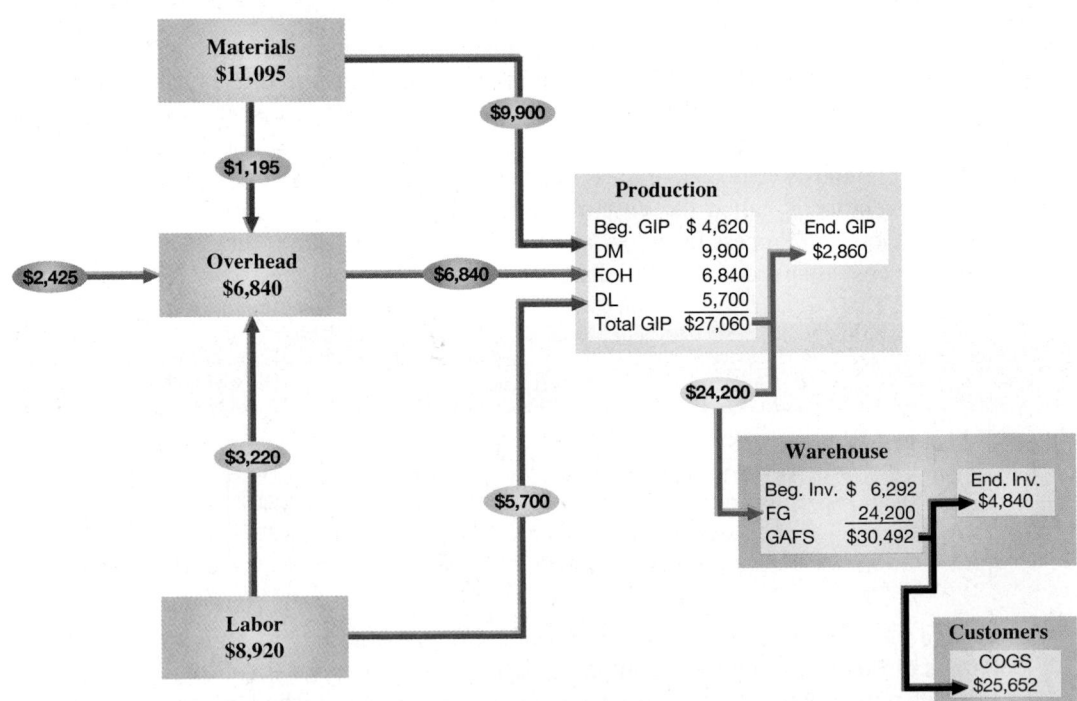

*Abbreviations: GIP (goods in process); DM (direct materials); DL (direct labor); FOH (factory overhead);
FG (finished goods); GAFS (goods available for sale); COGS (cost of goods sold).

Trends in Process Operations

Some of the recent trends in process operations are discussed in the following paragraphs.

Process Design Management concerns with production efficiency can lead companies to entirely reorganize production processes. For example, instead of producing different types of computers in a series of departments, a separate work center for each computer can be established in one department. The process cost system is then changed to account for each work center's costs.

Just-in-Time Production Companies are increasingly adopting just-in-time techniques. With a just-in-time inventory system, inventory levels can be minimal. If raw materials are not ordered or received until needed, a Raw Materials Inventory account might be unnecessary. Instead, materials cost is immediately debited to the Goods in Process Inventory account. Similarly, a Finished Goods Inventory account may not be needed. Instead, cost of finished goods may be immediately debited to the Cost of Goods Sold account.

Automation Advances in technology increasingly enable companies to automate their production processes. This allows them to reduce direct labor costs. Reflecting this, some companies focus on **conversion costs per equivalent unit,** which is the combined costs of direct labor and factory overhead per equivalent unit.

Services Service-based businesses are increasingly prevalent. For routine, standardized services like oil changes and simple tax returns, computing costs based on the process is simpler and more useful than a cost per individual job.

Customer Orientation Focus on customer orientation also leads to improved processes. A manufacturer of control devices improved quality and reduced production time by forming teams to study processes and suggest improvements. An ice cream maker studied customer tastes to develop a more pleasing ice cream texture.

 GLOBAL VIEW

As part of a series of global environmental goals, the international giant **Anheuser-Busch InBev** set targets to reduce its water usage. The company uses massive amounts of water in beer production and in its cleaning and cooling processes. To meet these goals, the company followed recent trends in process operations. These included extensive redesign of production processes and the use of advanced technology to increase efficiency at wastewater treatment plants. As a result water usage decreased by almost 37 percent in its global operations.

Hybrid Costing System **Decision Analysis**

This chapter explained the process costing system and contrasted it with the job order costing system. Many organizations use a *hybrid system* that contains features of both process and job order operations. A recent survey of manufacturers revealed that a majority use hybrid systems (also called *operation cost systems*).

> **A2** Explain and illustrate a hybrid costing system.

To illustrate, consider a car manufacturer's assembly line. On one hand, the line resembles a process operation in that the assembly steps for each car are nearly identical. On the other hand, the specifications of most cars have several important differences. At the **Ford** Mustang plant, each car assembled on a given day can be different from the previous car and the next car. This means that the costs of materials (subassemblies or components) for each car can differ. Accordingly, while the conversion costs (direct labor and overhead) can be accounted for using a process costing system, the component costs (direct materials) are accounted for using a job order system (separately for each car or type of car).

A hybrid system of processes requires a *hybrid costing system* to properly cost products or services. In the Ford plant, the assembly costs per car are readily determined using process costing. The costs of additional components can then be added to the assembly costs to determine each car's total cost (as in job order costing). To illustrate, consider the following information for a daily assembly process at Ford.

Assembly process costs	
Direct materials	$10,600,000
Direct labor	$5,800,000
Factory overhead	$6,200,000
Number of cars assembled	1,000
Costs of three different types of steering wheels	$240, $330, $480
Costs of three different types of seats	$620, $840, $1,360

The assembly process costs $22,600 per car. Depending on the type of steering wheel and seats the customer requests, the cost of a car can range from $23,460 to $24,440 (a $980 difference).

Today companies are increasingly trying to standardize processes while attempting to meet individual customer needs. To the extent that differences among individual customers' requests are large, understanding the costs to satisfy those requests is important. Thus, monitoring and controlling both process and job order costs are important.

■ Decision Ethics

Entrepreneur You operate a process production company making similar products for three different customers. One customer demands 100% quality inspection of products at your location before shipping. The added costs of that inspection are spread across all customers, not just the one demanding it. If you charge the added costs to that customer, you could lose that customer and experience a loss. Moreover, your other two customers have agreed to pay 110% of full costs. What actions (if any) do you take? ■ [Answer—p. 840]

DEMONSTRATION PROBLEM

Pennsylvania Company produces a product that passes through a single production process. Then completed products are transferred to finished goods in its warehouse. Information related to its manufacturing activities for July follows.

Raw Materials

Beginning inventory	$100,000
Raw materials purchased on credit	211,400
Direct materials used	(190,000)
Indirect materials used	(51,400)
Ending inventory	$ 70,000

Factory Payroll

Direct labor incurred	$ 55,500
Indirect labor incurred	50,625
Total payroll (paid in cash)	$106,125

Factory Overhead

Indirect materials used	$ 51,400
Indirect labor used	50,625
Other overhead costs	71,725
Total factory overhead incurred	$173,750

Factory Overhead Applied

Overhead applied (200% of direct labor)	$111,000

Production Department

Beginning goods in process inventory (units)	5,000
Percentage completed—Materials	100%
Percentage completed—Labor and overhead	60%
Beginning goods in process inventory (costs)	
Direct materials used	$ 20,000
Direct labor incurred	9,600
Overhead applied (200% of direct labor)	19,200
Total costs of beginning goods in process	$ 48,800
Units started this period	20,000
Units completed this period	17,000
Ending goods in process inventory (units)	8,000
Percentage completed—Materials	100%
Percentage completed—Labor and overhead	20%

Finished Goods Inventory

Beginning finished goods inventory	$ 96,400
Cost transferred in from production	321,300
Cost of goods sold	(345,050)
Ending finished goods inventory	$ 72,650

Required

1. Prepare a physical flow reconciliation for July as illustrated in Exhibit 20.12.

2. Compute the equivalent units of production in July for direct materials, direct labor, and factory overhead.

3. Compute the costs per equivalent units of production in July for direct materials, direct labor, and factory overhead.

4. Prepare a report of costs accounted for and a report of costs to account for.

5. Prepare summary journal entries to record the transactions and events of July for (a) raw materials purchases, (b) direct materials usage, (c) indirect materials usage, (d) factory payroll costs, (e) direct labor usage, (f) indirect labor usage, (g) other overhead costs (credit Other Accounts), (h) application of overhead to production, (i) transfer of finished goods from production, and (j) the cost of goods sold.

PLANNING THE SOLUTION

● Track the physical flow to determine the number of units completed in July.

● Compute the equivalent unit of production for direct materials, direct labor, and factory overhead.

● Compute the costs per equivalent unit of production with respect to direct materials, direct labor, and overhead; and determine the cost per unit for each.

● Compute the total cost of the goods transferred to production by using the equivalent units and unit costs. Determine (a) the cost of the beginning in-process inventory, (b) the materials, labor, and overhead costs added to the beginning in-process inventory, and (c) the materials, labor, and overhead costs added to the units started and completed in the month.

● Determine the cost of goods sold using balances in finished goods and cost of units completed this period.

● Use the information to record the summary journal entries for July.

SOLUTION TO DEMONSTRATION PROBLEM

1. Physical flow reconciliation.

Units to Account For		Units Accounted For	
Beginning goods in process inventory	5,000 units	Units completed and transferred out	17,000 units
Units started this period	20,000 units	Ending goods in process inventory......	8,000 units
Total units to account for	**25,000 units**	Total units accounted for	**25,000 units**

reconciled

2. Equivalent units of production.

Equivalent Units of Production	Direct Materials	Direct Labor	Factory Overhead
Equivalent units completed and transferred out	17,000 EUP	17,000 EUP	17,000 EUP
Equivalent units in ending goods in process			
Direct materials (8,000 × 100%)	8,000		
Direct labor (8,000 × 20%)		1,600	
Factory overhead (8,000 × 20%)			1,600
Equivalent units of production	25,000 EUP	18,600 EUP	18,600 EUP

3. Costs per equivalent unit of production.

Costs per Equivalent Unit of Production	Direct Materials	Direct Labor	Factory Overhead
Costs of beginning goods in process	$ 20,000	$ 9,600	$ 19,200
Costs incurred this period	190,000	55,500	111,000*
Total costs	$210,000	$65,100	$130,200
÷ Equivalent units of production (from part 2) ..	25,000 EUP	18,600 EUP	18,600 EUP
= Costs per equivalent unit of production	$8.40 per EUP	$3.50 per EUP	$7.00 per EUP

*Factory overhead applied

4. Reports of costs accounted for and of costs to account for

Report of Costs Accounted For

Cost of units transferred out (cost of goods manufactured)

Direct materials ($8.40 per EUP × 17,000 EUP)	$142,800	
Direct labor ($3.50 per EUP × 17,000 EUP)	59,500	
Factory overhead ($7.00 per EUP × 17,000 EUP)	119,000	
Cost of units completed this period		$ 321,300

Cost of ending goods in process inventory

Direct materials ($8.40 per EUP × 8,000 EUP)	67,200	
Direct labor ($3.50 per EUP × 1,600 EUP)	5,600	
Factory overhead ($7.00 per EUP × 1,600 EUP)	11,200	
Cost of ending goods in process inventory		84,000
Total costs accounted for		**$405,300**

Report of Costs to Account For

Cost of beginning goods in process inventory

Direct materials	$ 20,000	
Direct labor	9,600	
Factory overhead	19,200	$ 48,800

Cost incurred this period

Direct materials	190,000	
Direct labor	55,500	
Factory overhead	111,000	356,500
Total costs to account for		**$405,300**

reconciled

5. Summary journal entries for the transactions and events in July.

a.	Raw Materials Inventory	211,400	
	Accounts Payable		211,400
	To record raw materials purchases.		
b.	Goods in Process Inventory	190,000	
	Raw Materials Inventory		190,000
	To record direct materials usage.		
c.	Factory Overhead	51,400	
	Raw Materials Inventory		51,400
	To record indirect materials usage.		
d.	Factory Payroll............................	106,125	
	Cash...................................		106,125
	To record factory payroll costs.		
e.	Goods in Process Inventory	55,500	
	Factory Payroll		55,500
	To record direct labor usage.		
f.	Factory Overhead	50,625	
	Factory Payroll		50,625
	To record indirect labor usage.		

g.	Factory Overhead	71,725	
	Other Accounts........................		71,725
	To record other overhead costs.		
h.	Goods in Process Inventory	111,000	
	Factory Overhead		111,000
	To record application of overhead.		
i.	Finished Goods Inventory...................	321,300	
	Goods in Process Inventory		321,300
	To record transfer of finished goods *from production.*		
j.	Cost of Goods Sold........................	345,050	
	Finished Goods Inventory..............		345,050
	To record cost of goods sold.		

FIFO Method of Process Costing

20A

C4 *Appendix 20A—Describe accounting for production activity and preparation of a process cost summary using FIFO.*

The **FIFO method** of process costing assigns costs to units assuming a first-in, first-out flow of product. The objectives, concepts, and journal entries (not amounts) are the same as for the weighted-average method, but computation of equivalent units of production and cost assignment are slightly different.

Exhibit 20A.11 shows selected information from GenX's production department for the month of April. Accounting for a department's activity for a period includes four steps. (1) determine physical flow, (2) compute equivalent units, (3) compute cost per equivalent unit, and (4) determine cost assignment and reconciliation. This appendix describes each of these steps using the FIFO method for process costing.

EXHIBIT 20A.11

Production Data

Beginning goods in process inventory (March 31)	
Units of product	30,000 units
Percentage of completion—Direct materials	100%
Percentage of completion—Direct labor	65%
Direct materials costs	$ 3,300
Direct labor costs	$ 600
Factory overhead costs applied (120% of direct labor)	$ 720
Activities during the current period (April)	
Units started this period	90,000 units
Units transferred out (completed)	100,000 units
Direct materials costs	$ 9,900
Direct labor costs	$ 5,700
Factory overhead costs applied (120% of direct labor)	$ 6,840
Ending goods in process inventory (April 30)	
Units of product	20,000 units
Percentage of completion—Direct materials	100%
Percentage of completion—Direct labor	25%

Step 1: Determine Physical Flow of Units A *physical flow reconciliation* is a report that reconciles (1) the physical units started in a period with (2) the physical units completed in that period. The physical flow reconciliation for GenX is shown in Exhibit 20A.12 for April.

EXHIBIT 20A.12

Physical Flow Reconciliation

Units to Account For		Units Accounted For	
Beginning goods in process inventory	30,000 units	Units completed and transferred out	100,000 units
Units started this period	90,000 units	Ending goods in process inventory	20,000 units
Total units to account for	**120,000 units**	Total units accounted for	**120,000 units**

reconciled

FIFO assumes that the 100,000 units transferred to finished goods during April include the 30,000 units from the beginning goods in process inventory. The remaining 70,000 units transferred out are from units started in April. Of the total 90,000 units started in April, 70,000 were completed, leaving 20,000 units unfinished at period-end.

Step 2: Compute Equivalent Units of Production—FIFO GenX used its direct materials, direct labor, and overhead both to make complete units of Profen and to start some units that are not yet complete. We need to convert the physical measure of units to equivalent units based on how much of each input has been used. We do this by multiplying the number of physical units by the percentage of processing applied to those units in the current period; this is done for each input (materials, labor, and overhead). The FIFO method accounts for cost flow in a sequential manner—earliest costs are the first to flow out. (This is different from the weighted-average method, which combines prior period costs—those in beginning Goods in Process Inventory—with costs incurred in the current period.)

Three distinct groups of units must be considered in determining the equivalent units of production under the FIFO method: (a) units in beginning Goods in Process Inventory that were completed this period, (b) units started *and* completed this period, and (c) units in ending Goods in Process Inventory. We must determine how much material, labor, and overhead are used for each of these unit groups. These computations are shown in Exhibit 20A.13. The remainder of this section explains these computations.

EXHIBIT 20A.13

Equivalent Units of Production—FIFO

Equivalent Units of Production	Direct Materials	Direct Labor	Factory Overhead
(a) Equivalent units to complete beginning goods in process			
Direct materials (30,000 × 0%)	0 EUP		
Direct labor (30,000 × 35%)		10,500 EUP	
Factory overhead (30,000 × 35%)			10,500 EUP
(b) Equivalent units started and completed*	70,000	70,000	70,000
(c) Equivalent units in ending goods in process			
Direct materials (20,000 × 100%)	20,000		
Direct labor (20,000 × 25%)		5,000	
Factory overhead (20,000 × 25%)			5,000
Equivalent units of production	90,000 EUP	85,500 EUP	85,500 EUP

*Units completed this period	100,000 units	
Less units in beginning goods in process	30,000	
Units started and completed this period	70,000 units	

(a) Beginning Goods in Process   Under FIFO, we assume that production first completes any units started in the prior period. There were 30,000 physical units in beginning goods in process inventory. Those units were 100% complete with respect to direct materials as of the end of the prior period. This means that no materials (0%) are needed in April to complete those 30,000 units. So the equivalent units of *materials* to complete beginning goods in process are zero (30,000 × 0%)—see first row under row "(a)" in Exhibit 20A.13. The units in process as of April 1 had already been through 65% of production prior to this period and need only go through the remaining 35% of production. The equivalent units of *labor* to complete the beginning goods in process are 10,500 (30,000 × 35%)—see the second row under row "(a)." This implies that the amount of labor required this period to complete the 30,000 units started in the prior period is the amount of labor needed to make 10,500 units, start-to-finish. Finally, overhead is applied based on direct labor costs, so GenX computes equivalent units for overhead as it would for direct labor.

(b) Units Started and Completed This Period   After completing any beginning goods in process, FIFO assumes that production begins on newly started units. GenX began work on 90,000 new units this period. Of those units, 20,000 remain incomplete at period-end. This means that 70,000 of the units started in April were completed in April. These complete units have received 100% of materials, labor, and overhead. Exhibit 20A.13 reflects this by including 70,000 equivalent units (70,000 × 100%) of materials, labor, and overhead in its equivalent units of production—see row "(b)."

(c) Ending Goods in Process   The 20,000 units started in April that GenX was not able to complete by period-end consumed materials, labor, and overhead. Specifically, those 20,000 units received 100% of materials and, therefore, the equivalent units of materials in ending goods in process inventory are 20,000 (20,000 × 100%)—see the first row under row "(c)." For labor and overhead, the units in ending goods in process were 25% complete in production. This means the equivalent units of labor and overhead for those units are 5,000 (20,000 × 25%) as GenX incurs labor and overhead costs uniformly throughout its production process. Finally, for each input (direct materials, direct labor, and factory overhead), the equivalent units for each of the unit groups (a), (b), and (c) are added to determine the total equivalent units of production with respect to each—see the final row in Exhibit 20A.13.

Step 3: Compute Cost per Equivalent Unit—FIFO   To compute cost per equivalent unit, we take the product costs (for each of direct materials, direct labor, and factory overhead from Exhibit 20A.11) added in April and divide by the equivalent units of production from step 2. Exhibit 20A.14 illustrates these computations.

EXHIBIT 20A.14

Cost per Equivalent Unit of Production—FIFO

Cost per Equivalent Unit of Production	Direct Materials	Direct Labor	Factory Overhead
Costs incurred this period	$9,900	$5,700	$6,840
÷ Equivalent units of production (from Step 2)	90,000 EUP	85,500 EUP	85,500 EUP
Cost per equivalent unit of production	$0.11 per EUP	$0.067 per EUP	$0.08 per EUP

It is essential to compute costs per equivalent unit for *each* input because production inputs are added at different times in the process. The FIFO method computes the cost per equivalent unit based solely on this period's EUP and costs (unlike the weighted-average method, which adds in the costs of the beginning goods in process inventory).

Step 4: Assign and Reconcile Costs The equivalent units determined in step 2 and the cost per equivalent unit computed in step 3 are both used to assign costs (1) to units that the production department completed and transferred to finished goods and (2) to units that remain in process at period-end.

In Exhibit 20A.15, under the section for cost of units transferred out, we see that the cost of units completed in April includes the $4,620 cost carried over from March for work already applied to the 30,000 units that make up beginning Goods in Process Inventory, plus the $1,544 incurred in April to complete those units. This section also includes the $17,990 of cost assigned to the 70,000 units started and completed this period. Thus, the total cost of goods manufactured in April is $24,154 ($4,620 + $1,544 + $17,990). The average cost per unit for goods completed in April is $0.242 ($24,154 ÷ 100,000 completed units).

EXHIBIT 20A.15

Report of Costs Accounted For—FIFO

Cost of units transferred out (cost of goods manufactured)		
Cost of beginning goods in process inventory		$ 4,620
Cost to complete beginning goods in process		
Direct materials ($0.11 per EUP × 0 EUP)	$ 0	
Direct labor ($0.067 per EUP × 10,500 EUP)	704	
Factory overhead ($0.08 per EUP × 10,500 EUP)	840	1,544
Cost of units started and completed this period		
Direct materials ($0.11 per EUP × 70,000 EUP)	7,700	
Direct labor ($0.067 per EUP × 70,000 EUP)	4,690	
Factory overhead ($0.08 per EUP × 70,000 EUP)	5,600	17,990
Total cost of units finished this period		24,154
Cost of ending goods in process inventory		
Direct materials ($0.11 per EUP × 20,000 EUP)	2,200	
Direct labor ($0.067 per EUP × 5,000 EUP)	335	
Factory overhead ($0.08 per EUP × 5,000 EUP)	400	
Total cost of ending goods in process inventory		2,935
Total costs accounted for		**$27,089**

The computation for cost of ending goods in process inventory is in the lower part of Exhibit 20A.15. The cost of units in process includes materials, labor, and overhead costs corresponding to the percentage of these resources applied to those incomplete units in April. That cost of $2,935 ($2,200 + $335 + $400) also is the ending balance for the Goods in Process Inventory account.

Management verifies that the total costs assigned to units transferred out and units still in process equal the total costs incurred by production. We reconcile the costs accounted for (in Exhibit 20A.15) to the costs that production was charged for as shown in Exhibit 20A.16.

EXHIBIT 20A.16

Report of Costs to Account For—FIFO

Cost of beginning goods in process inventory		
Direct materials	$3,300	
Direct labor	600	
Factory overhead	720	$ 4,620
Costs incurred this period		
Direct materials	9,900	
Direct labor.	5,700	
Factory overhead	6,840	22,440
Total costs to account for		**$27,060**

The production manager is responsible for $27,060 in costs: $4,620 that had been assigned to the department's Goods in Process Inventory as of April 1 plus $22,440 of materials, labor, and overhead costs the department incurred in April. At period-end, the manager must identify where those costs were assigned. The production manager can report that $24,154 of cost was assigned to units completed in April and $2,935 was assigned to units still in process at period-end. The sum of these amounts is $29 different from the $27,060 total costs incurred by production due to rounding in step 3—rounding errors are common and not a concern.

The final report is the process cost summary, which summarizes key information from Exhibits 20A.13, 20A.14, 20A.15, and 20A.16. Reasons for the summary are to (1) help managers control and monitor costs, (2) help upper management assess department manager performance, and (3) provide cost information for financial reporting. The process cost summary, using FIFO, for GenX is in Exhibit 20A.17. Section ◇ lists

EXHIBIT 20A.17

Process Cost Summary

	GenX COMPANY **Process Cost Summary (FIFO Method)** **For Month Ended April 30, 2013**		

Costs charged to production

Costs of beginning goods in process inventory

Direct materials	$3,300	
Direct labor	600	
Factory overhead	720	$ 4,620

Costs incurred this period

Direct materials	9,900	
Direct labor	5,700	
Factory overhead	6,840	22,440
Total costs to account for		$27,060

Unit cost information

Units to account for		Units accounted for	
Beginning goods in process	30,000	Transferred out	100,000
Units started this period	90,000	Ending goods in process	20,000
Total units to account for	120,000	Total units accounted for	120,000

Equivalent units of production	**Direct Materials**	**Direct Labor**	**Factory Overhead**
Equivalent units to complete beginning goods in process			
Direct materials (30,000 × 0%)	0 EUP		
Direct labor (30,000 × 35%)		10,500 EUP	
Factory overhead (30,000 × 35%)			10,500 EUP
Equivalent units started and completed	70,000	70,000	70,000
Equivalent units in ending goods in process			
Direct materials (20,000 × 100%)	20,000		
Direct labor (20,000 × 25%)		5,000	
Factory overhead (20,000 × 25%)			5000
Equivalent units of production	90,000 EUP	85,500 EUP	85,500 EUP

Cost per equivalent unit of production	**Direct Materials**	**Direct Labor**	**Factory Overhead**
Costs incurred this period	$9,900	$5,700	$6,840
÷ Equivalent units of production	90,000 EUP	85,500 EUP	85,500 EUP
Cost per equivalent unit of production	$0.11 per EUP	$0.067 per EUP	$0.08 per EUP

Cost assignment and reconciliation

(cost of units completed and transferred out)

Cost of beginning goods in process		$ 4,620
Cost to complete beginning goods in process		
Direct materials ($0.11 per EUP × 0 EUP)	$ 0	
Direct labor ($0.067 per EUP × 10,500 EUP)	704	
Factory overhead ($0.08 per EUP × 10,500 EUP)	840	1,544
Cost of units started and completed this period		
Direct materials ($0.11 per EUP × 70,000 EUP)	7,700	
Direct labor ($0.067 per EUP × 70,000 EUP)	4,690	
Factory overhead ($0.08 per EUP × 70,000 EUP)	5,600	17,990
Total cost of units finished this period		24,154
Cost of ending goods in process		
Direct materials ($0.11 per EUP × 20,000 EUP)	2,200	
Direct labor ($0.067 per EUP × 5,000 EUP)	335	
Factory overhead ($0.08 per EUP × 5,000 EUP)	400	
Total cost of ending goods in process		2,935
Total costs accounted for		$27,089*

reconciled

*$29 difference due to rounding

the total costs charged to the department, including direct materials, direct labor, and overhead costs incurred, as well as the cost of the beginning goods in process inventory. Section ◇2◇ describes the equivalent units of production for the department. Equivalent units for materials, labor, and overhead are in separate columns. It also reports direct materials, direct labor, and overhead costs per equivalent unit. Section ◇3◇ allocates total costs among units worked on in the period.

■ Decision Maker

Cost Manager As cost manager for an electronics manufacturer, you apply a process costing system using FIFO. Your company plans to adopt a just-in-time system and eliminate inventories. What is the impact of the use of FIFO (versus the weighted-average method) given these plans? ■ [Answer—p. 840]

Summary

C1 Explain process operations and the way they differ from job order operations. Process operations produce large quantities of similar products or services by passing them through a series of processes, or steps, in production. Like job order operations, they combine direct materials, direct labor, and overhead in the operations. Unlike job order operations that assign the responsibility for each job to a manager, process operations assign the responsibility for each *process* to a manager.

C2 Define and compute equivalent units and explain their use in process cost accounting. Equivalent units of production measure the activity of a process as the number of units that would be completed in a period if all effort had been applied to units that were started and finished. This measure of production activity is used to compute the cost per equivalent unit and to assign costs to finished goods and goods in process inventory. To compute equivalent units, determine the number of units that would have been finished if all materials (or labor or overhead) had been used to produce units that were started and completed during the period. The costs incurred by a process are divided by its equivalent units to yield cost per unit.

C3 Describe accounting for production activity and preparation of a process cost summary using weighted average. A process cost summary reports on the activities of a production process or department for a period. It describes the costs charged to the department, the equivalent units of production for the department, and the costs assigned to the output. The report aims to (1) help managers control their departments, (2) help factory managers evaluate department managers' performances, and (3) provide cost information for financial statements. A process cost summary includes the physical flow of units, equivalent units of production, costs per equivalent unit, and a cost reconciliation. It reports the units and costs to account for during the period and how they were accounted for during the period. In terms of units, the summary includes the beginning goods in process inventory and the units started during the month. These units are accounted for in terms of the goods completed and transferred out, and the ending goods in process inventory. With respect to costs, the summary includes materials, labor, and overhead costs assigned to the process during the period. It shows how these costs are assigned to goods completed and transferred out, and to ending goods in process inventory.

C4 *Appendix 20A*—Describe accounting for production activity and preparation of a process cost summary using FIFO.

The FIFO method for process costing is applied and illustrated to (1) report the physical flow of units, (2) compute the equivalent units of production, (3) compute the cost per equivalent unit of production, and (4) assign and reconcile costs.

A1 Compare process cost accounting and job order cost accounting. Process and job order manufacturing operations are similar in that both combine materials, labor, and factory overhead to produce products or services. They differ in the way they are organized and managed. In job order operations, the job order cost accounting system assigns materials, labor, and overhead to specific jobs. In process operations, the process cost accounting system assigns materials, labor, and overhead to specific processes. The total costs associated with each process are then divided by the number of units passing through that process to get cost per equivalent unit. The costs per equivalent unit for all processes are added to determine the total cost per unit of a product or service.

A2 Explain and illustrate a hybrid costing system. A hybrid costing system contains features of both job order and process costing systems. Generally, certain direct materials are accounted for by individual products as in job order costing, but direct labor and overhead costs are accounted for similar to process costing.

P1 Record the flow of direct materials costs in process cost accounting. Materials purchased are debited to a Raw Materials Inventory account. As direct materials are issued to processes, they are separately accumulated in a Goods in Process Inventory account for that process.

P2 Record the flow of direct labor costs in process cost accounting. Direct labor costs are initially debited to the Factory Payroll account. The total amount in it is then assigned to the Goods in Process Inventory account pertaining to each process.

P3 Record the flow of factory overhead costs in process cost accounting. The different factory overhead items are first accumulated in the Factory Overhead account and are then allocated, using a predetermined overhead rate, to the different processes. The allocated amount is debited to the Goods in Process Inventory account pertaining to each process.

P4 Record the transfer of completed goods to Finished Goods Inventory and Cost of Goods Sold. As units complete the final process and are eventually sold, their accumulated cost is transferred to Finished Goods Inventory and finally to Cost of Goods Sold.

Guidance Answers to Decision Maker and Decision Ethics

Budget Officer   By instructing you to classify a majority of costs as indirect, the manager is passing some of his department's costs to a common overhead pool that other departments will partially absorb. Since overhead costs are allocated on the basis of direct labor for this company and the new department has a relatively low direct labor cost, the new department will be assigned less overhead. Such action suggests unethical behavior by this manager. You must object to such reclassification. If this manager refuses to comply, you must inform someone in a more senior position.

Entrepreneur   By spreading the added quality-related costs across three customers, the entrepreneur is probably trying to remain competitive with respect to the customer that demands the 100%

quality inspection. Moreover, the entrepreneur is partly covering the added costs by recovering two-thirds of them from the other two customers who are paying 110% of total costs. This act likely breaches the trust placed by the two customers in this entrepreneur's application of its costing system. The costing system should be changed, and the entrepreneur should consider renegotiating the pricing and/or quality test agreement with this one customer (at the risk of losing this currently loss-producing customer).

Cost Manager   Differences between the FIFO and weighted-average methods are greatest when large work in process inventories exist and when costs fluctuate. The method used if inventories are eliminated does not matter; both produce identical costs.

Guidance Answers to Quick Checks

1. *c*

2. When a company produces large quantities of similar products/ services, a process cost system is often more suitable.

3. *b*

4. The costs are direct materials, direct labor, and overhead.

5. A goods in process inventory account is needed for *each* production department.

6. *a*

7. Equivalent units with respect to direct labor are the number of units that would have been produced if all labor had been used on units that were started and finished during the period.

8.

Units completed and transferred out	58,000 EUP
Units of ending goods in process	
Direct labor (6,000 × 1/3)	2,000 EUP
Units of production	60,000 EUP

9. The first section shows the costs charged to the department. The second section describes the equivalent units produced by the department. The third section shows the assignment of total costs to units worked on during the period.

Key Terms

Conversion costs per equivalent unit (p. 831)

Cost of goods manufactured (p. 829)

Equivalent units of production
(EUP) (p. 823)

FIFO method (p. 835)

Job order cost accounting
system (p. 819)

Materials consumption report (p. 820)

Process cost accounting system (p. 819)

Process cost summary (p. 828)

Process operations (p. 816)

Weighted-average method (p. 826)

Multiple Choice Quiz   Answers on p. 859   mhhe.com/wildFAP21e

Additional Quiz Questions are available at the book's Website.

1. Equivalent units of production are equal to
  a. Physical units that were completed this period from all effort being applied to them.
  b. The number of units introduced into the process this period.
  c. The number of finished units actually completed this period.
  d. The number of units that could have been started and completed given the cost incurred.
  e. The number of units in the process at the end of the period.

2. Recording the cost of raw materials purchased for use in a process costing system includes a
  a. Credit to Raw Materials Inventory.
  b. Debit to Goods in Process Inventory.

  c. Debit to Factory Overhead.
  d. Credit to Factory Overhead.
  e. Debit to Raw Materials Inventory.

3. The production department started the month with a beginning goods in process inventory of $20,000. During the month, it was assigned the following costs: direct materials, $152,000; direct labor, $45,000; overhead applied at the rate of 40% of direct labor cost. Inventory with a cost of $218,000 was transferred to finished goods. The ending balance of goods in process inventory is
  a. $330,000.   **d.** $112,000.
  b. $ 17,000.   **e.** $118,000.
  c. $220,000.

4. A company's beginning work in process inventory consists of 10,000 units that are 20% complete with respect to direct labor costs. A total of 40,000 units are completed this period. There are 15,000 units in goods in process, one-third complete for direct labor, at period-end. The equivalent units of production (EUP) with respect to direct labor at period-end, assuming the weighted-average method, are

a. 45,000 EUP.
b. 40,000 EUP.
c. 5,000 EUP.
d. 37,000 EUP.
e. 43,000 EUP.

5. Assume the same information as in question 4. Also assume that beginning work in process had $6,000 in direct labor cost and that $84,000 in direct labor is added during this period. What is the cost per EUP for labor?

a. $0.50 per EUP
b. $1.87 per EUP
c. $2.00 per EUP
d. $2.10 per EUP
e. $2.25 per EUP

🏃 Icon denotes assignments that involve decision making.

Discussion Questions

1. 🏃 What is the main factor for a company in choosing between the job order costing and process costing accounting systems? Give two likely applications of each system.

2. The focus in a job order costing system is the job or batch. Identify the main focus in process costing.

3. 🏃 Can services be delivered by means of process operations? Support your answer with an example.

4. Are the journal entries that match cost flows to product flows in process costing primarily the same or much different than those in job order costing? Explain.

5. Identify the control document for materials flow when a materials requisition slip is not used.

6. 🏃 Explain in simple terms the notion of equivalent units of production (EUP). Why is it necessary to use EUP in process costing?

7. 🏃 What are the two main inventory methods used in process costing? What are the differences between these methods?

8. 🏃 Why is it possible for direct labor in process operations to include the labor of employees who do not work directly on products or services?

9. Assume that a company produces a single product by processing it first through a single production department. Direct labor costs flow through what accounts in this company's process cost system?

10. After all labor costs for a period are allocated, what balance should remain in the Factory Payroll account?

11. 🏃 Is it possible to have under- or overapplied overhead costs in a process cost accounting system? Explain.

12. Explain why equivalent units of production for both direct labor and overhead can be the same as, and why they can be different from, equivalent units for direct materials.

13. Companies such as **Piaggio** apply process operations. List the four steps in accounting for production activity in a reporting period (for process operations). **PIAGGIO**

14. Companies such as **KTM** commonly prepare a process cost summary. What purposes does a process cost summary serve? **KTM**

15. 🏃 Are there situations where **Polaris** can use process costing? Identify at least one and explain it. **Polaris**

16. 🏃 **Arctic Cat** produces snowmobiles with a multiple process production line. Identify and list some of its production processing steps and departments. **Arctic Cat**

Ⓜ connect _____

For each of the following products and services, indicate whether it is most likely produced in a process operation or in a job order operation.

1. Tennis courts
2. Apple juice
3. Vanilla ice cream
4. Luxury cars

QUICK STUDY

QS 20-1
Process vs. job order operations
C1

Blanche's Boxes makes cardboard shipping cartons in a single operation. This period, Blanche purchased $62,000 in raw materials. Its production department requisitioned $50,000 of those materials for use in producing cartons. Prepare journal entries to record its (1) purchase of raw materials and (2) requisition of direct materials.

QS 20-2
Recording costs of direct
materials   P1

QS 20-3
Recording costs of direct labor
P2

Refer to the information in QS 20-2. Blanche's Boxes incurred $135,000 in factory payroll costs, of which $125,000 was direct labor. Prepare journal entries to record its (1) total factory payroll incurred and (2) direct labor used in production.

QS 20-4
Recording costs of factory overhead
P3

Refer to the information in QS 20-2 and QS 20-3. Blanche's Boxes requisitioned $9,000 of indirect materials from its raw materials and used $10,000 of indirect labor in its production of boxes. Also, it incurred $156,000 of other factory overhead costs. It applies factory overhead at the rate of 140% of direct labor costs. Prepare journal entries to record its (1) indirect materials requisitioned, (2) indirect labor used in production, (3) other factory overhead costs incurred, and (4) application of overhead to production.

QS 20-5
Recording transfer of costs to finished goods   P4

Refer to the information in QS 20-2, QS 20-3, and QS 20-4. Blanche's Boxes completed 20,000 boxes costing $275,000 and transferred them to finished goods. Prepare its journal entry to record the transfer of the boxes from production to finished goods inventory.

QS 20-6
Weighted average: Computing equivalent units of production
C2

The following refers to units processed in Sunfllower Printing's binding department in March. Compute the total equivalent units of production with respect to labor for March using the weighted-average inventory method.

	Units of Product	Percent of Labor Added
Beginning goods in process	150,000	80%
Goods started	310,000	100
Goods completed	340,000	100
Ending goods in process	120,000	25

QS 20-7
Computing EUP cost   C2

The cost of beginning inventory plus the costs added during the period should equal the cost of units _____ plus the cost of _____.

QS 20-8
Hybrid costing   A2

Explain how a car maintenance and repair garage might use a hybrid costing system.

QS 20-9[A]
FIFO: Computing equivalent units   C4

Refer to QS 20-6 and compute the total equivalent units of production with respect to labor for March using the FIFO inventory method.

QS 20-10
Steps in process costing
C3

Put the four steps in accounting for production activities in the order in which they would occur.
a. Determine physical flow of units
b. Compute the cost per equivalent unit
c. Compute equivalent units of production
d. Assign and reconcile costs

QS 20-11
Process cost summary   C3

List the headings of the three major sections of a process cost summary. Refer to Exhibit 20.17.

QS 20-12
Process cost summary   C3

Anheuser-Busch InBev is attempting to reduce its water usage. How could a company manager use a process cost summary to determine if the program to reduce water usage is successful?

Label each statement below as either true ("T") or false ("F").

1. The cost per equivalent unit is computed as the total costs of a process divided by the number of equivalent units passing through that process.

2. Service companies are not able to use process costing.

3. Costs per job are computed in both job order and process costing systems.

4. Job order and process operations both combine materials, labor, and overhead in producing products or services.

QS 20-13
Process vs. job order costing
A1

The following refers to units processed by an ice cream maker in July. Compute the total equivalent units of production with respect to labor for July using the weighted-average inventory method.

	Gallons of Product	Percent of Labor Added
Beginning goods in process	320,000	25%
Goods started	620,000	100
Goods completed	680,000	100
Ending goods in process	240,000	75

QS 20-14
Weighted average: Computing equivalent units of production
C2

Refer to QS 20-14 and compute the total equivalent units of production with respect to labor for July using the FIFO inventory method.

QS 20-15[A]
FIFO: Computing equivalent units C4

Mc Graw Hill connect

Match each of the following items A through G with the best numbered description of its purpose.

A. Factory Overhead account
B. Process cost summary
C. Equivalent units of production
D. Goods in Process Inventory account
E. Raw Materials Inventory account
F. Materials requisition
G. Finished Goods Inventory account

EXERCISES

Exercise 20-1
Terminology in process cost accounting
C1 A1 P1 P2 P3

_____ 1. Notifies the materials manager to send materials to a production department.

_____ 2. Holds costs of indirect materials, indirect labor, and similar costs until assigned to production.

_____ 3. Holds costs of direct materials, direct labor, and applied overhead until products are transferred from production to finished goods (or another department).

_____ 4. Standardizes partially completed units into equivalent completed units.

_____ 5. Holds costs of finished products until sold to customers.

_____ 6. Describes the activity and output of a production department for a period.

_____ 7. Holds costs of materials until they are used in production or as factory overhead.

Prepare journal entries to record the following production activities.

1. Purchased $80,000 of raw materials on credit.
2. Used $42,000 of direct materials in production.
3. Used $22,500 of indirect materials.

Exercise 20-2
Recording costs of materials
P1

Prepare journal entries to record the following production activities.

1. Incurred total labor cost of $95,000, which is paid in cash.
2. Used $75,000 of direct labor in production.
3. Used $20,000 of indirect labor.

Exercise 20-3
Recording costs of labor
P2

Refer to information in Exercise 20-3. Prepare journal entries to record the following production activities.

1. Paid overhead costs (other than indirect materials and indirect labor) of $38,750.
2. Applied overhead at 110% of direct labor costs.

Exercise 20-4
Recording overhead costs
P3

Exercise 20-5
Recording cost of completed goods P4

Prepare journal entries to record the following production activities.

1. Transferred completed products with a cost of $135,600 to finished goods inventory.
2. Sold $315,000 of products on credit. Their cost is $175,000.

Exercise 20-6
Recording cost flows in a process cost system
P1 P2 P3 P4

Laffer Lumber produces bagged bark for use in landscaping. Production involves packaging bark chips in plastic bags in a bagging department. The following information describes production operations for October.

	Bagging Department
Direct materials used	$ 522,000
Direct labor used	$ 130,000
Predetermined overhead rate (based on direct labor)	175%
Goods transferred from bagging to finished goods	$(595,000)

The company's revenue for the month totaled $950,000 from credit sales, and its cost of goods sold for the month is $540,000. Prepare summary journal entries dated October 31 to record its October production activities for (1) direct material usage, (2) direct labor usage, (3) overhead allocation, (4) goods transfer from production to finished goods, and (5) credit sales.

Check (3) Cr. Factory Overhead, $227,500

Exercise 20-7
Interpretation of journal entries in process cost accounting
P1 P2 P3 P4

The following journal entries are recorded in Kiesha Co.'s process cost accounting system. Kiesha produces apparel and accessories. Overhead is applied to production based on direct labor cost for the period. Prepare a brief explanation (including any overhead rates applied) for each journal entry *a* through *j*.

a.	Raw Materials Inventory	52,000			g.	Factory Overhead	6,000	
	Accounts Payable		52,000			Factory Payroll		6,000
b.	Goods in Process Inventory	42,000			h.	Goods in Process Inventory	33,600	
	Raw Materials Inventory		42,000			Factory Overhead		33,600
c.	Factory Payroll	26,000			i.	Finished Goods Inventory	88,000	
	Cash		26,000			Goods in Process Inventory		88,000
d.	Goods in Process Inventory	32,000			j.	Accounts Receivable	250,000	
	Factory Payroll		32,000			Sales		250,000
e.	Factory Overhead	10,000				Cost of Goods Sold	100,000	
	Cash		10,000			Finished Goods Inventory		100,000
f.	Factory Overhead	10,000						
	Raw Materials Inventory		10,000					

Exercise 20-8
Weighted average: Computing equivalent units of production
C2

During April, the production department of a process manufacturing system completed a number of units of a product and transferred them to finished goods. Of these transferred units, 60,000 were in process in the production department at the beginning of April and 240,000 were started and completed in April. April's beginning inventory units were 60% complete with respect to materials and 40% complete with respect to labor. At the end of April, 82,000 additional units were in process in the production department and were 80% complete with respect to materials and 30% complete with respect to labor.

1. Compute the number of units transferred to finished goods.
2. Compute the number of equivalent units with respect to both materials used and labor used in the production department for April using the weighted-average method.

Check (2) EUP for materials, 365,600

Exercise 20-9
Weighted average: Costs assigned to output and inventories
C2 P4

The production department described in Exercise 20-8 had $850,000 of direct materials and $650,000 of direct labor cost charged to it during April. Also, its beginning inventory included $118,840 of direct materials cost and $47,890 of direct labor.

1. Compute the direct materials cost and the direct labor cost per equivalent unit for the department.
2. Using the weighted-average method, assign April's costs to the department's output—specifically, its units transferred to finished goods and its ending goods in process inventory.

Check (1) $2.65 per EUP of direct materials

Refer to the information in Exercise 20-8 to compute the number of equivalent units with respect to both materials used and labor used in the production department for April using the FIFO method.

Exercise 20-10[A]
FIFO: Computing equivalent units of production C4

Refer to the information in Exercise 20-9 and complete its parts (1) and (2) using the FIFO method. (Round cost per equivalent unit to two decimal places.)

Exercise 20-11[A]
FIFO: Costs assigned to output

C4 P4

The production department in a process manufacturing system completed 80,000 units of product and transferred them to finished goods during a recent period. Of these units, 24,000 were in process at the beginning of the period. The other 56,000 units were started and completed during the period. At period-end, 16,000 units were in process. Compute the department's equivalent units of production with respect to direct materials under each of three separate assumptions:

Exercise 20-12
Weighted average: Equivalent units computed

C2

1. All direct materials are added to products when processing begins.

2. Direct materials are added to products evenly throughout the process. Beginning goods in process inventory was 50% complete, and ending goods in process inventory was 75% complete.

3. One-half of direct materials is added to products when the process begins and the other half is added when the process is 75% complete as to direct labor. Beginning goods in process inventory is 40% complete as to direct labor, and ending goods in process inventory is 60% complete as to direct labor.

Check (3) EUP for materials, 88,000

Refer to the information in Exercise 20-12 and complete it for each of the three separate assumptions using the FIFO method for process costing.

Exercise 20-13[A]
FIFO: Equivalent units computed C4

Check (3) EUP for materials, 76,000

The following flowchart shows the August production activity of the Spalding Company. Use the amounts shown on the flowchart to compute the missing four numbers identified by blanks.

Exercise 20-14
Flowchart of costs for a process operation P1 P2 P3 P4

Exercise 20-15
Weighted average: Completing a process cost summary

C3

The following partially completed process cost summary describes the July production activities of Ashad Company. Its production output is sent to its warehouse for shipping. All direct materials are added to products when processing begins. Beginning goods in process inventory is 20% complete with respect to direct labor and overhead. Prepare its process cost summary using the weighted-average method.

Equivalent Units of Production	Direct Materials	Direct Labor	Factory Overhead
Units transferred out	32,000	32,000	32,000
Units of ending goods in process	2,500	1,500	1,500
Equivalent units of production	34,500	33,500	33,500

Costs per EUP	Direct Materials	Direct Labor	Factory Overhead
Costs of beginning goods in process	$ 18,550	$ 760	$ 1,520
Costs incurred this period	357,500	62,890	125,780
Total costs	$376,050	$63,650	$127,300

Units in beginning goods in process (all completed during July)	2,000
Units started this period	32,500
Units completed and transferred out	32,000
Units in ending goods in process	2,500

Exercise 20-16^A
FIFO: Completing a process cost summary   C3   C4

Refer to the information in Exercise 20-15. Prepare a process cost summary using the FIFO method. (Round cost per equivalent unit calculations to two decimal places.)

Exercise 20-17
Matching of product to cost accounting system

C1

For each of the following products and services, indicate whether it is most likely produced in a process operation or in a job order operation.

1. Beach towels
2. Bolts and nuts
3. Lawn chairs
4. Headphones
5. Designed patio
6. Door hardware
7. Cut flower arrangements
8. House paints
9. Concrete swimming pools
10. Custom tailored dresses
11. Grand pianos
12. Table lamps

Exercise 20-18
Compare process and job order operations

C1

Label each item *a* through *h* below as a feature of either a job order or process operation.
a. Heterogeneous products and services
b. Custom orders
c. Low production volume
d. Routine, repetitive procedures
e. Focus on individual batch
f. Low product standardization
g. Low product flexibility
h. Focus on standardized units

Exercise 20-19
Hybrid costing system   A2

Explain a hybrid costing system. Identify a product or service operation that might well fit a hybrid costing system.

Exercise 20-20
Weighted average: Equivalent units computed

C2

ProChem manufactures aspirin in a process operation. Details on production activity follow. Compute the department's equivalent units of production with respect to direct materials under each of two separate assumptions.

Beginning goods in process	31,500
Goods started	189,500
Goods completed	191,500

1. All direct materials are added to products when processing begins.

Check   (2) EUP for materials, 206,250

2. One-half of direct materials is added to products when the process begins and the other half is added when the process is 75% complete as to direct labor. Beginning goods in process is 20% complete as to direct labor, and ending goods in process inventory is 45% complete as to direct labor.

Refer to the information in Exercise 20-20 and complete it for each of the two separate assumptions using the FIFO method for process costing.

Exercise 20-21[A]

FIFO: Equivalent units computed C4

Check (2) EUP for materials, 190,500

Hi-Test Company uses the weighted-average method of process costing to assign production costs to its products. Information for September follows. Assume that all materials are added at the beginning of its production process, and that direct labor and factory overhead are added uniformly throughout the process.

Exercise 20-22

Weighted average: Process cost summary C3

Goods in process inventory, September 1 (2,000 units, 100% complete with respect to direct materials, 80% complete with respect to direct labor and overhead; includes $45,000 of direct material cost, $25,600 in direct labor cost, $30,720 overhead cost)	$101,320
Units started in April	28,000
Units completed and transferred to finished goods inventory	23,000
Goods in process inventory, September 30 (__?__ units, 100% complete with respect to direct materials, 40% complete with respect to direct labor and overhead)	?
Costs incurred in September	
Direct materials	$375,000
Direct labor	$155,000
Overhead applied at 120% of direct labor cost	?

Required

Fill in the blanks labeled *a* through *uu* in the following process cost summary.

HI-TEST COMPANY
Process Cost Summary
For Month Ended September 30

Costs Charged to Production

Costs of beginning goods in process

Direct materials	$ 45,000	
Direct labor	25,600	
Factory overhead	30,720	$101,320

Costs incurred this period

Direct materials	$375,000	
Direct labor	155,000	
Factory overhead	(a)_____	(b)_____
Total costs to account for		(c)_____

Check (c) $817,320

Unit Cost Information

Units to account for		Units accounted for	
Beginning goods in process	2,000	Completed and transferred out	23,000
Units started this period	28,000	Ending goods in process	(d)_____
Total units to account for	(e)_____	Total units accounted for	(f)_____

Equivalent Units of Production (EUP)				**Direct Materials**	**Direct Labor**	**Factory Overhead**
Units completed and transferred out				(g)_____EUP	(h)_____EUP	(i)_____EUP
Units of ending goods in process						
Materials	(j)_____	×	100%	(k)_____EUP		
Direct labor	(l)_____	×	40%		(m)_____EUP	
Factory overhead	(n)_____	×	40%			(o)_____EUP
Equivalent units of production (EUP)				(p)_____EUP	(q)_____EUP	(r)_____EUP

[continued on next page]

[continued from previous page]

Cost per EUP		Direct Materials	Direct Labor	Factory Overhead
Costs of beginning goods in process		$ 45,000	$ 25,600	$30,720
Costs incurred this period		375,000	155,000	(s)_____
Total costs		$420,000	$180,600	(t)_____
÷ EUP		(u)_____	(v)_____	(w)_____
Cost per EUP		(x)_____	(y)_____	(z)_____

Check   (z) $8.40 per EUP

Cost Assignment and Reconciliation

Costs transferred out	Cost/EUP	×	EUP		
Direct materials	(aa)_____	×	(bb)_____	(cc)_____	
Direct labor	(dd)_____	×	(ee)_____	(ff)_____	
Factory overhead	(gg)_____	×	(hh)_____	(ii)_____	
Costs of goods completed and transferred out					(jj)_____
Costs of ending goods in process					
Direct materials	(kk)_____	×	(ll)_____	(mm)_____	
Direct labor	(nn)_____	×	(oo)_____	(pp)_____	
Factory overhead	(qq)_____	×	(rr)_____	(ss)_____	
Costs of ending goods in process					(tt)_____
Total costs accounted for					(uu)_____

PROBLEM SET A

Problem 20-1A
Production cost flow and measurement; journal entries

P1 P2 P3 P4

Sierra Company manufactures woven blankets and accounts for product costs using process costing. The following information is available regarding its May inventories.

	Beginning Inventory	Ending Inventory
Raw materials inventory	$ 60,000	$ 92,500
Goods in process inventory	435,000	515,000
Finished goods inventory	633,000	605,000

The following additional information describes the company's production activities for May.

Raw materials purchases (on credit)	$ 250,000
Factory payroll cost (paid in cash)	1,530,000
Other overhead cost (Other Accounts credited)	87,000
Materials used	
Direct	$ 157,500
Indirect	60,000
Labor used	
Direct	$ 780,000
Indirect	750,000
Overhead rate as a percent of direct labor	115%
Sales (on credit)	$2,500,000

Required

Check (1b) Cost of goods sold $1,782,500

1. Compute the cost of (a) products transferred from production to finished goods, and (b) goods sold.

2. Prepare summary journal entries dated May 31 to record the following production activities during May: (a) raw materials purchases, (b) direct materials usage, (c) indirect materials usage, (d) payroll costs, (e) direct labor costs, (f) indirect labor costs, (g) other overhead costs, (h) overhead applied, (i) goods transferred from production to finished goods, and (j) sale of finished goods.

Victory Company uses weighted-average process costing to account for its production costs. Direct labor is added evenly throughout the process. Direct materials are added at the beginning of the process. During November, the company transferred 700,000 units of product to finished goods. At the end of November, the goods in process inventory consists of 180,000 units that are 30% complete with respect to labor. Beginning inventory had $420,000 of direct materials and $139,000 of direct labor cost. The direct material cost added in November is $2,220,000, and the direct labor cost added is $3,254,000.

Required

1. Determine the equivalent units of production with respect to (a) direct labor and (b) direct materials.
2. Compute both the direct labor cost and the direct materials cost per equivalent unit.
3. Compute both direct labor cost and direct materials cost assigned to (a) units completed and transferred out, and (b) ending goods in process inventory.

Analysis Component

4. The company sells and ships all units to customers as soon as they are completed. Assume that an error is made in determining the percentage of completion for units in ending inventory. Instead of being 30% complete with respect to labor, they are actually 60% complete. Write a one-page memo to the plant manager describing how this error affects its November financial statements.

Beginning goods in process consisted of 60,000 units that were 100% complete with respect to direct materials and 80% complete with respect to direct labor. Of the 700,000 units completed, 60,000 were from beginning goods in process and 640,000 units were started and completed during the period.

Problem 20-2A
Weighted average: Cost per equivalent unit; costs assigned to products

C2   C3

mhhe.com/wildFAP21e

Check (2) Direct labor cost per equivalent unit, $4.50

(3b) $783,000

Elliott Company produces large quantities of a standardized product. The following information is available for its production activities for March.

Raw materials		Factory overhead incurred	
Beginning inventory	$ 16,000	Indirect materials used	$ 70,000
Raw materials purchased (on credit)	250,000	Indirect labor used	45,000
Direct materials used	(168,000)	Other overhead costs	164,790
Indirect materials used	(70,000)	Total factory overhead incurred	$279,790
Ending inventory	$ 28,000		
		Factory overhead applied	
Factory payroll		**(140% of direct labor cost)**	
Direct labor used	$199,850	Total factory overhead applied	$279,790
Indirect labor used	45,000		
Total payroll cost (paid in cash)	$244,850		

Problem 20-3A
Weighted average: Journalizing in process costing; equivalent units and costs

C2 P1 P2 P3

Sage 50
QB

Additional information about units and costs of production activities follows.

Units		Costs		
Beginning goods in process inventory	2,000	Beginning goods in process inventory		
Started	20,000	Direct materials	$2,500	
Ending goods in process inventory	5,000	Direct labor	2,650	
		Factory overhead	3,710	$ 8,860
Status of ending goods in process inventory		Direct materials added		168,000
Materials—Percent complete	100%	Direct labor added		199,850
Labor and overhead—Percent complete	35%	Overhead applied (140% of direct labor)		279,790
		Total costs		$656,500
		Ending goods in process inventory		$ 84,110

During March, 10,000 units of finished goods are sold for $120 cash each. Cost information regarding finished goods follows.

Beginning finished goods inventory	$150,000
Cost transferred in	572,390
Cost of goods sold	(592,390)
Ending finished goods inventory	$130,000

Required

1. Prepare journal entries dated March 31 to record the following March activities: (a) purchase of raw materials, (b) direct materials usage, (c) indirect materials usage, (d) factory payroll costs, (e) direct labor costs used in production, (f) indirect labor costs, (g) other overhead costs—credit Other Accounts, (h) overhead applied, (i) goods transferred to finished goods, and (j) sale of finished goods.

2. Prepare a process cost summary report for this company, showing costs charged to production, units cost information, equivalent units of production, cost per EUP, and its cost assignment and reconciliation.

Analysis Component

3. The company provides incentives to its department managers by paying monthly bonuses based on their success in controlling costs per equivalent unit of production. Assume that the production department underestimates the percentage of completion for units in ending inventory with the result that its equivalent units of production in ending inventory for March are understated. What impact does this error have on the March bonuses paid to the production managers? What impact, if any, does this error have on April bonuses?

Problem 20-4A
Weighted Average: Process cost summary; equivalent units

C2 C3 P4

mhhe.com/wildFAP21e

Fast Co. produces its product through a single processing department. Direct materials are added at the start of production, and direct labor and overhead are added evenly throughout the process. The company uses monthly reporting periods for its weighted-average process cost accounting system. Its Goods in Process Inventory account follows after entries for direct materials, direct labor, and overhead costs for October.

Goods in Process Inventory				Acct. No. 133	
Date		Explanation	Debit	Credit	Balance
Oct.	1	Balance			335,930
	31	Direct materials	102,050		437,980
	31	Direct labor	408,200		846,180
	31	Applied overhead	244,920		1,091,100

Its beginning goods in process consisted of $59,450 of direct materials, $172,800 of direct labor, and $103,680 of factory overhead. During October, the company started 140,000 units and transferred 150,000 units to finished goods. At the end of the month, the goods in process inventory consisted of 20,000 units that were 80% complete with respect to direct labor and factory overhead.

Required

1. Prepare the company's process cost summary for October using the weighted-average method.

2. Prepare the journal entry dated October 31 to transfer the cost of the completed units to finished goods inventory.

Problem 20-5A
Weighted average: Process cost summary, equivalent units, cost estimates

C2 C3 P4

Tamar Co. manufactures a single product in one department. All direct materials are added at the beginning of the manufacturing process. Direct labor and overhead are added evenly throughout the process. The company uses monthly reporting periods for its weighted-average process cost accounting. During May, the company completed and transferred 22,200 units of product to finished goods inventory. Its 3,000 units of beginning goods in process consisted of $19,800 of direct materials, $123,300 of direct labor, and $98,640 of factory overhead. It has 2,400 units (100% complete with respect to direct materials and 80% complete with respect to direct labor and overhead) in process at month-end. After entries to record direct materials, direct labor, and overhead for May, the company's Goods in Process Inventory account follows.

Goods in Process Inventory				Acct. No. 133	
Date		Explanation	Debit	Credit	Balance
May	1	Balance			241,740
	31	Direct materials	496,800		738,540
	31	Direct labor	1,203,300		1,941,840
	31	Applied overhead	962,640		2,904,480

Required

1. Prepare the company's process cost summary for May using the weighted-average method.

2. Prepare the journal entry dated May 31 to transfer the cost of completed units to finished goods inventory.

Analysis Components

3. The cost accounting process depends on numerous estimates.

a. Identify two major estimates that determine the cost per equivalent unit.

b. In what direction might you anticipate a bias from management for each estimate in part 3a (assume that management compensation is based on maintaining low inventory amounts)? Explain your answer.

Refer to the data in Problem 20-5A. Assume that Tamar uses the FIFO method to account for its process costing system. The following additional information is available:

- Beginning goods in process consisted of 3,000 units that were 100% complete with respect to direct materials and 40% complete with respect to direct labor and overhead.
- Of the 22,200 units completed, 3,000 were from beginning goods in process. The remaining 19,200 were units started and completed during May.

Required

1. Prepare the company's process cost summary for May using FIFO.

2. Prepare the journal entry dated May 31 to transfer the cost of completed units to finished goods inventory.

Problem 20-6A[A]

FIFO: Process cost summary; equivalent units; cost estimates

C3 C4 P4

Check (1) EUP for both labor and overhead, 22,920 EUP

(2) Cost transferred out to finished goods, $2,667,840

During May, the production department of a process manufacturing system completed a number of units of a product and transferred them to finished goods. Of these transferred units, 37,500 were in process in the production department at the beginning of May and 150,000 were started and completed in May. May's beginning inventory units were 60% complete with respect to materials and 40% complete with respect to labor. At the end of May, 51,250 additional units were in process in the production department and were 60% complete with respect to materials and 20% complete with respect to labor. The production department had $505,035 of direct materials and $396,568 of direct labor cost charged to it during May. Its beginning inventory included $74,075 of direct materials cost and $28,493 of direct labor cost.

1. Compute the number of units transferred to finished goods.

2. Compute the number of equivalent units with respect to both materials used and labor used in the production department for May using the FIFO method.

3. Compute the direct materials cost and the direct labor cost per equivalent unit for the department.

4. Using the FIFO method, assign May's costs to the units transferred to finished goods and assign costs to its ending goods in process inventory.

Problem 20-7A

FIFO: Costs per equivalent unit; costs assigned to products

C2 C4

Check (2) EUP for materials, 195,750

Refer to the information in Problem 20-2A and complete its parts (1) through (4) using the FIFO method of process costing. Round cost per equivalent unit calculations to two decimal places.

Problem 20-8A[A]

FIFO: Cost per equivalent unit; costs assigned to products

C2 C3 C4

Check (2) $4.61 direct labor cost per EUP; $2.71 direct materials cost per EUP

Dengo Co. manufactures a single product in one department. Direct labor and overhead are added evenly throughout the process, while direct materials are added at the beginning of the process. The company uses the FIFO method of process costing. During October, the company completed and transferred 22,200 units to finished goods inventory. Of the units completed, 3,000 were from beginning inventory and the remaining 19,200 were started and completed during the month. Beginning goods in process were 100% complete with respect to direct materials and 40% complete with respect to direct labor and overhead. The company has 2,400 units (100% complete with respect to direct materials and 80% complete with respect to direct labor and overhead) in process at month-end. Information on costs of beginning inventory and costs added during the month follows.

Problem 20-9A[A]

FIFO: Process cost summary, equivalent units, cost estimates

C2 C3 C4 P4

Cost	Raw Materials	Direct Labor	Overhead
Of beginning inventory	$ 9,900	$ 61,650	$ 49,320
Added during the month.........	248,400	601,650	481,320

Required

1. Prepare the company's process cost summary for October using the FIFO method.
2. Prepare the journal entry dated October 31 to transfer the cost of completed units to finished good inventory.

Analysis Component

3. The company provides incentives to department managers by paying monthly bonuses based on their success in controlling costs per equivalent unit of production. Assume that the production department underestimates the percentage of completion for units in ending inventory with the result that its equivalent units of production for October are understated. What impact does this error have on the October bonuses paid to the production managers? What impact, if any, does this error have on November bonuses?

PROBLEM SET B

Problem 20-1B
Production cost flow and measurement; journal entries

P1 P2 P3 P4

Dream Toys Company manufactures video game consoles and accounts for product costs using process costing. The following information is available regarding its June inventories.

	Beginning Inventory	Ending Inventory
Raw materials inventory	$ 72,000	$110,000
Goods in process inventory	156,000	250,000
Finished goods inventory	160,000	198,000

The following additional information describes the company's production activities for June.

Raw materials purchases (on credit)	$200,000
Factory payroll cost (paid in cash)	400,000
Other overhead cost (Other Accounts credited)	170,500
Materials used	
Direct	$120,000
Indirect	42,000
Labor used	
Direct	$350,000
Indirect	50,000
Overhead rate as a percent of direct labor	75%
Sales (on credit)	$1,000,000

Required

1. Compute the cost of (a) products transferred from production to finished goods, and (b) goods sold.
2. Prepare journal entries dated June 30 to record the following production activities during June: (a) raw materials purchases, (b) direct materials usage, (c) indirect materials usage, (d) payroll costs, (e) direct labor costs, (f) indirect labor costs, (g) other overhead costs, (h) overhead applied, (i) goods transferred from production to finished goods, and (j) sale of finished goods.

Problem 20-2B
Weighted average: Cost per equivalent unit; costs assigned to products

C2 C3

Abraham Company uses process costing to account for its production costs. Direct labor is added evenly throughout the process. Direct materials are added at the beginning of the process. During September, the production department transferred 80,000 units of product to finished goods. Beginning goods in process consisted of 2,000 units that were 100% complete with respect to direct materials and 85% complete with respect to direct labor. Of the 40,000 units completed, 2,000 were from beginning goods in process and 78,000 units were started and completed during the period. Beginning goods in process had $58,000 of direct materials and $86,400 of direct labor cost. At the end of September, the goods in process inventory consists of 8,000 units that are 25% complete with respect to labor. The direct materials cost added in September is $712,000, and direct labor cost added is $1,980,000.

Required

1. Determine the equivalent units of production with respect to (a) direct labor and (b) direct materials.

2. Compute both the direct labor cost and the direct materials cost per equivalent unit.

3. Compute both direct labor cost and direct materials cost assigned to (a) units completed and transferred out, and (b) ending goods in process inventory.

Check   (2) Direct labor cost per equivalent unit, $25.20

(3b) $120,400

Analysis Component

4. The company sells and ships all units to customers as soon as they are completed. Assume that an error is made in determining the percentage of completion for units in ending inventory. Instead of being 25% complete with respect to labor, they are actually 75% complete. Write a one-page memo to the plant manager describing how this error affects its September financial statements.

Oslo Company produces large quantities of a standardized product. The following information is available for its production activities for May.

Problem 20-3B
Weighted Average: Journalizing in process costing; equivalent units and costs

C2 P1 P2 P3 P4

Raw materials		Factory overhead incurred	
Beginning inventory	$ 32,000	Indirect materials used	$ 40,560
Raw materials purchased (on credit)	221,120	Indirect labor used	36,320
Direct materials used	(197,120)	Other overhead costs	34,432
Indirect materials used	(40,560)	Total factory overhead incurred	$111,312
Ending inventory	$ 15,440		
		Factory overhead applied	
Factory payroll		**(90% of direct labor cost)**	
Direct labor used	$123,680	Total factory overhead applied	$111,312
Indirect labor used	36,320		
Total payroll cost (paid in cash)	$160,000		

Additional information about units and costs of production activities follows.

Units		Costs		
Beginning goods in process inventory	4,000	Beginning goods in process inventory		
Started	12,000	Direct materials	$2,880	
Ending goods in process inventory	3,000	Direct labor	2,820	
		Factory overhead	2,538	$ 8,238
Status of ending goods in process inventory		Direct materials added		197,120
Materials—Percent complete	100%	Direct labor added		123,680
Labor and overhead—Percent complete	25%	Overhead applied (90% of direct labor) . . .		111,312
		Total costs		$440,350
		Ending goods in process inventory		$ 50,610

During May, 10,000 units of finished goods are sold for $120 cash each. Cost information regarding finished goods follows.

Beginning finished goods inventory	$148,400
Cost transferred in from production	389,740
Cost of goods sold	(474,540)
Ending finished goods inventory	$ 63,600

Required

1. Prepare journal entries dated May 31 to record the following May activities: (a) purchase of raw materials, (b) direct materials usage, (c) indirect materials usage, (d) factory payroll costs, (e) direct labor costs used in production, (f) indirect labor costs, (g) other overhead costs—credit Other Accounts, (h) overhead applied, (i) goods transferred to finished goods, and (j) sale of finished goods.

2. Prepare a process cost summary report for this company, showing costs charged to production, unit cost information, equivalent units of production, cost per EUP, and its cost assignment and reconciliation.

Check   (2) Cost per equivalent unit: materials, $12.50; labor, $9.20; overhead, $8.28

Analysis Component

3. This company provides incentives to its department managers by paying monthly bonuses based on their success in controlling costs per equivalent unit of production. Assume that production over-estimates the percentage of completion for units in ending inventory with the result that its equivalent units of production in ending inventory for May are overstated. What impact does this error have on bonuses paid to the managers of the production department? What impact, if any, does this error have on these managers' June bonuses?

Problem 20-4B
Weighted average: Process cost summary; equivalent units

C2 C3 P4

Braun Company produces its product through a single processing department. Direct materials are added at the beginning of the process. Direct labor and overhead are added to the product evenly throughout the process. The company uses monthly reporting periods for its weighted-average process cost accounting. Its Goods in Process Inventory account follows after entries for direct materials, direct labor, and overhead costs for November.

Goods in Process Inventory			Debit	Credit	Acct. No. 133
Date		Explanation	Debit	Credit	Balance
Nov.	1	Balance			21,300
	30	Direct materials	116,400		137,700
	30	Direct labor	426,800		564,500
	30	Applied overhead	640,200		1,204,700

The 7,500 units of beginning goods in process consisted of $6,800 of direct materials, $5,800 of direct labor, and $8,700 of factory overhead. During November, the company finished and transferred 100,000 units of its product to finished goods. At the end of the month, the goods in process inventory consisted of 12,000 units that were 100% complete with respect to direct materials and 25% complete with respect to direct labor and factory overhead.

Required

1. Prepare the company's process cost summary for November using the weighted-average method.
2. Prepare the journal entry dated November 30 to transfer the cost of the completed units to finished goods inventory.

Problem 20-5B
Weighted average: Process cost summary; equivalent units; cost estimates

C2 C3 P4

Switch Co. manufactures a single product in one department. Direct labor and overhead are added evenly throughout the process. Direct materials are added as needed. The company uses monthly reporting periods for its weighted-average process cost accounting. During January, Switch completed and transferred 220,000 units of product to finished goods inventory. Its 10,000 units of beginning goods in process consisted of $7,500 of direct materials, $14,240 of direct labor, and $35,600 of factory overhead. 40,000 units (50% complete with respect to direct materials and 30% complete with respect to direct labor and overhead) are in process at month-end. After entries for direct materials, direct labor, and overhead for January, the company's Goods in Process Inventory account follows.

Goods in Process Inventory			Debit	Credit	Acct. No. 133
Date		Explanation	Debit	Credit	Balance
Jan.	1	Balance			57,340
	31	Direct materials	112,500		169,840
	31	Direct labor	176,000		345,840
	31	Applied overhead	440,000		785,840

Required

1. Prepare the company's process cost summary for January using the weighted-average method.
2. Prepare the journal entry dated January 31 to transfer the cost of completed units to finished goods inventory.

Analysis Components

3. The cost accounting process depends on several estimates.

    a. Identify two major estimates that affect the cost per equivalent unit.

    b. In what direction might you anticipate a bias from management for each estimate in part 3a (assume that management compensation is based on maintaining low inventory amounts)? Explain your answer.

Refer to the information in Problem 20-5B. Assume that Switch uses the FIFO method to account for its process costing system. The following additional information is available.

- Beginning goods in process consists of 10,000 units that were 75% complete with respect to direct materials and 60% complete with respect to direct labor and overhead.
- Of the 220,000 units completed, 10,000 were from beginning goods in process; the remaining 210,000 were units started and completed during January.

Required

1. Prepare the company's process cost summary for January using FIFO. Round cost per EUP to one-tenth of a cent.

2. Prepare the journal entry dated January 31 to transfer the cost of completed units to finished goods inventory.

Problem 20-6B[A]

FIFO: Process cost summary; equivalent units; cost estimates

C3 C4 P4

Check (1) Labor and overhead EUP, 226,000

(2) Cost transferred out, $743,554

During May, the production department of a process manufacturing system completed a number of units of a product and transferred them to finished goods. Of these transferred units, 62,500 were in process in the production department at the beginning of May and 175,000 were started and completed in May. May's beginning inventory units were 40% complete with respect to materials and 80% complete with respect to labor. At the end of May, 76,250 additional units were in process in the production department and were 80% complete with respect to materials and 20% complete with respect to labor. The production department had $683,750 of direct materials and $446,050 of direct labor cost charged to it during May. Its beginning inventory included $99,075 of direct materials cost and $53,493 of direct labor cost.

1. Compute the number of units transferred to finished goods.

2. Compute the number of equivalent units with respect to both materials used and labor used in the production department for May using the FIFO method.

3. Compute the direct materials cost and the direct labor cost per equivalent unit for the department.

4. Using the FIFO method, assign May's costs to the units transferred to finished goods and assign costs to its ending goods in process inventory.

Problem 20-7B

FIFO: Costs per equivalent unit; costs assigned to products

C2 C4

Check (2) EUP for materials, 273,500

Refer to the information in Problem 20-2B and complete its parts (1) through (4) using the FIFO method of process costing. Round cost per equivalent unit calculations to two decimal places.

Problem 20-8B[A]

FIFO: Cost per equivalent unit; costs assigned to products

C2 C3 C4

Check (2) $24.66 direct labor cost per EUP; $8.28 direct materials cost per EUP

Belda Co. manufactures a single product in one department. Direct labor and overhead are added evenly throughout the process. Direct materials are added as needed. The company uses the FIFO method of process costing. During March, the company completed and transferred 220,000 units to finished goods inventory. Of the units completed, 10,000 were from beginning inventory and the remaining 210,000 were started and completed during the month. Beginning goods in process were 75% complete with respect to direct materials and 60% complete with respect to direct labor and overhead. The company has 40,000 units (50% complete with respect to direct materials and 30% complete with respect to direct labor and

Problem 20-9B[A]

FIFO: Process cost summary, equivalent units, cost estimates

C2 C3 C4 P4

overhead) in process at month-end. Information on costs of beginning inventory and costs added during the month follows.

Cost	Raw Materials	Direct Labor	Overhead
Of beginning inventory	$ 16,800	$ 27,920	$ 69,800
Added during the month	223,200	352,560	881,400

Required

1. Prepare the company's process cost summary for March using the FIFO method.
2. Prepare the journal entry dated March 31 to transfer the cost of completed units to finished good inventory.

Analysis Component

3. The company provides incentives to department managers by paying monthly bonuses based on their success in controlling costs per equivalent unit of production. Assume that the production department overestimates the percentage of completion for units in ending inventory with the result that its equivalent units of production for March are overstated. What impact does this error have on bonuses paid to the managers of the production department? What impact, if any, does this error have on these managers' April bonuses?

SERIAL PROBLEM

Success Systems

C1 A1

(This serial problem began in Chapter 1 and continues through most of the book. If previous chapter segments were not completed, the serial problem can begin at this point.)

SP 20 The computer workstation furniture manufacturing that Adria Lopez started is progressing well. At this point, Adria is using a job order costing system to account for the production costs of this product line. Adria has heard about process costing and is wondering whether process costing might be a better method for her to keep track of and monitor her production costs.

Required

1. What are the features that distinguish job order costing from process costing?
2. Do you believe that Adria should continue to use job order costing or switch to process costing for her workstation furniture manufacturing? Explain.

COMPREHENSIVE PROBLEM

Major League Bat Company

Weighted average: Review of Chapters 2, 5, 18, 20

CP 20 Major League Bat Company manufactures baseball bats. In addition to its goods in process inventories, the company maintains inventories of raw materials and finished goods. It uses raw materials as direct materials in production and as indirect materials. Its factory payroll costs include direct labor for production and indirect labor. All materials are added at the beginning of the process, and direct labor and factory overhead are applied uniformly throughout the production process.

Required

You are to maintain records and produce measures of inventories to reflect the July events of this company. Set up the following general ledger accounts and enter the June 30 balances: Raw Materials Inventory, $25,000; Goods in Process Inventory, $8,135 ($2,660 of direct materials, $3,650 of direct labor, and $1,825 of overhead); Finished Goods Inventory, $110,000; Sales, $0; Cost of Goods Sold, $0; Factory Payroll, $0; and Factory Overhead, $0.

1. Prepare journal entries to record the following July transactions and events.
   a. Purchased raw materials for $125,000 cash (the company uses a perpetual inventory system).
   b. Used raw materials as follows: direct materials, $52,440; and indirect materials, $10,000.
   c. Incurred factory payroll cost of $227,250 paid in cash (ignore taxes).
   d. Assigned factory payroll costs as follows: direct labor, $202,250; and indirect labor, $25,000.
   e. Incurred additional factory overhead costs of $80,000 paid in cash.
   f. Allocated factory overhead to production at 50% of direct labor costs.

2. Information about the July inventories follows. Use this information with that from part 1 to prepare a process cost summary, assuming the weighted-average method is used.

Check (2) EUP for overhead, 14,200

Units	
Beginning inventory	5,000 units
Started	14,000 units
Ending inventory	8,000 units
Beginning inventory	
Materials—Percent complete	100%
Labor and overhead—Percent complete	75%
Ending inventory	
Materials—Percent complete	100%
Labor and overhead—Percent complete	40%

3. Using the results from part 2 and the available information, make computations and prepare journal entries to record the following:

g. Total costs transferred to finished goods for July (label this entry g).

h. Sale of finished goods costing $265,700 for $625,000 in cash (label this entry h).

(3g) $271,150

4. Post entries from parts 1 and 3 to the ledger accounts set up at the beginning of the problem.

5. Compute the amount of gross profit from the sales in July. (*Note:* Add any underapplied overhead to, or deduct any overapplied overhead from, the cost of goods sold. Ignore the corresponding journal entry.)

Beyond the Numbers

BTN 20-1 **Polaris** reports in notes to its financial statements that, in addition to its products sold, it includes the following costs (among others) in cost of sales: customer shipping and handling expenses, warranty expenses, and depreciation expense on assets used in manufacturing.

REPORTING IN ACTION

C2

Polaris

Required

1. Why do you believe Polaris includes these costs in its cost of sales?

2. What effect does this cost accounting policy for its cost of sales have on Polaris' financial statements and any analysis of those statements? Explain.

Fast Forward

3. Access Polaris' financial statements for the years after December 31, 2011, from its Website (**Polaris.com**) or the SEC's EDGAR Website (**sec.gov**). Review its footnote relating to Organization and Significant Accounting Policies. Has Polaris' changed its policy with respect to what costs are included in the cost of sales? Explain.

BTN 20-2 Manufacturers such as **Polaris** and **Arctic Cat** usually work to maintain a high-quality and low-cost operation. One ratio routinely computed for this assessment is the cost of goods sold divided by total expenses. A decline in this ratio can mean that the company is spending too much on selling and administrative activities. An increase in this ratio beyond a reasonable level can mean that the company is not spending enough on selling activities. (Assume for this analysis that total expenses equal the cost of goods sold plus total operating expenses.)

COMPARATIVE ANALYSIS

C1

Polaris

Arctic Cat

Required

1. For Polaris and Arctic Cat refer to Appendix A and compute the ratios of cost of goods sold to total expenses for their two most recent fiscal years. (Record answers as percents, rounded to one decimal.)

2. Comment on the similarities or differences in the ratio results across both years between the companies.

ETHICS CHALLENGE

C1

BTN 20-3 Many accounting and accounting-related professionals are skilled in financial analysis, but most are not skilled in manufacturing. This is especially the case for process manufacturing environments (for example, a bottling plant or chemical factory). To provide professional accounting and financial services, one must understand the industry, product, and processes. We have an ethical responsibility to develop this understanding before offering services to clients in these areas.

Required

Write a one-page action plan, in memorandum format, discussing how you would obtain an understanding of key business processes of a company that hires you to provide financial services. The memorandum should specify an industry, a product, and one selected process and should draw on at least one reference, such as a professional journal or industry magazine.

COMMUNICATING IN PRACTICE

A1 C1 P1 P2

BTN 20-4 You hire a new assistant production manager whose prior experience is with a company that produced goods to order. Your company engages in continuous production of homogeneous products that go through various production processes. Your new assistant e-mails you questioning some cost classifications on an internal report—specifically why the costs of some materials that do not actually become part of the finished product, including some labor costs not directly associated with producing the product, are classified as direct costs. Respond to this concern via memorandum.

TAKING IT TO THE NET

C1

BTN 20-5 Many companies acquire software to help them monitor and control their costs and as an aid to their accounting systems. One company that supplies such software is **proDacapo** (**prodacapo.com**). There are many other such vendors. Access proDacapo's Website, click on "Prodacapo Process Management," and review the information displayed.

Required

How is process management software helpful to businesses? Explain with reference to costs, efficiency, and examples, if possible.

TEAMWORK IN ACTION

C1 P1 P2 P3 P4

BTN 20-6 The purpose of this team activity is to ensure that each team member understands process operations and the related accounting entries. Find the activities and flows identified in Exhibit 20.4 with numbers ①–⑩. Pick a member of the team to start by describing activity number ① in this exhibit, then verbalizing the related journal entry, and describing how the amounts in the entry are computed. The other members of the team are to agree or disagree; discussion is to continue until all members express understanding. Rotate to the next numbered activity and next team member until all activities and entries have been discussed. If at any point a team member is uncertain about an answer, the team member may pass and get back in the rotation when he or she can contribute to the team's discussion.

ENTREPRENEURIAL DECISION

C3 A2

BTN 20-7 This chapter's opener featured Neal Gottlieb and his company **Three Twins Ice Cream**.

Required

1. Neal recently built a large manufacturing facility. Explain how his company's process cost summary report would differ after his new manufacturing facility is operating.
2. How does holding raw materials inventories increase costs? If the items are not used in production, how can they impact profits? Explain.
3. Suppose Three Twins Ice Cream decides to allow customers to make their own unique ice cream flavors. Why might the company then use a hybrid costing system?

BTN 20-8 In process costing, the process is analyzed first and then a unit measure is computed in the form of equivalent units for direct materials, direct labor, overhead, and all three combined. The same analysis applies to both manufacturing and service processes.

HITTING THE ROAD

C2

Required

Visit your local **U.S. Mail** center. Look into the back room, and you will see several ongoing processes. Select one process, such as sorting, and list the costs associated with this process. Your list should include materials, labor, and overhead; be specific. Classify each cost as fixed or variable. At the bottom of your list, outline how overhead should be assigned to your identified process. The following format (with an example) is suggested.

Point: The class can compare and discuss the different processes studied and the answers provided.

Cost Description	Direct Material	Direct Labor	Overhead	Variable Cost	Fixed Cost
Manual sorting		X		X	
. . .					
Overhead allocation suggestions:					

BTN 20-9 **Piaggio**, **Polaris**, and **Arctic Cat** are competitors in the global marketplace. Selected data for Piaggio follow.

GLOBAL DECISION

C1

PIAGGIO
Polaris
Arctic Cat

(millions of euros)	Current Year	Prior Year
Cost of goods sold	€1,061.9	€1,023.1
Operating expenses	349.1	351.2
Total expenses	€1,411.0	€1,374.3

Required

1. Review the discussion of the importance of the cost of goods sold divided by total expenses ratio in BTN 20-2. Compute the cost of goods sold to total expenses ratio for Piaggio for the two years of data provided. (Record answers as percents, rounded to one decimal.)
2. Comment on the similarities or differences in the ratio results calculated in part *1* and in BTN 20-2 across years and companies. (Record answers as percents, rounded to one decimal.)

ANSWERS TO MULTIPLE CHOICE QUIZ

1. d

2. e

3. b; $20,000 + $152,000 + $45,000 + $18,000 − $218,000 = $17,000

4. a; 40,000 + (15,000 × 1/3) = 45,000 EUP

5. c; ($6,000 + $84,000) ÷ 45,000 EUP = $2 per EUP

Cost-Volume-Profit Analysis

21

A Look Back

Chapter 20 focused on how to measure and account for costs in process operations. It explained process production, described how to assign costs to processes, and computed cost per equivalent unit.

A Look at This Chapter

This chapter shows how information on both costs and sales behavior is useful to managers in performing cost-volume-profit analysis. This analysis is an important part of successful management and sound business decisions.

A Look Ahead

Chapter 22 introduces and describes the budgeting process and its importance to management. It also explains the master budget and its usefulness to the planning of future company activities.

Learning Objectives

CONCEPTUAL

C1 Describe different types of cost behavior in relation to production and sales volume. (p. 862)

C2 Describe several applications of cost-volume-profit analysis. (p. 873)

ANALYTICAL

A1 Compute the contribution margin and describe what it reveals about a company's cost structure. (p. 869)

A2 Analyze changes in sales using the degree of operating leverage. (p. 879)

PROCEDURAL

P1 Determine cost estimates using the scatter diagram, high-low, and regression methods of estimating costs. (p. 865)

P2 Compute the break-even point for a single product company. (p. 869)

P3 Graph costs and sales for a single product company. (p. 871)

P4 Compute the break-even point for a multiproduct company. (p. 877)

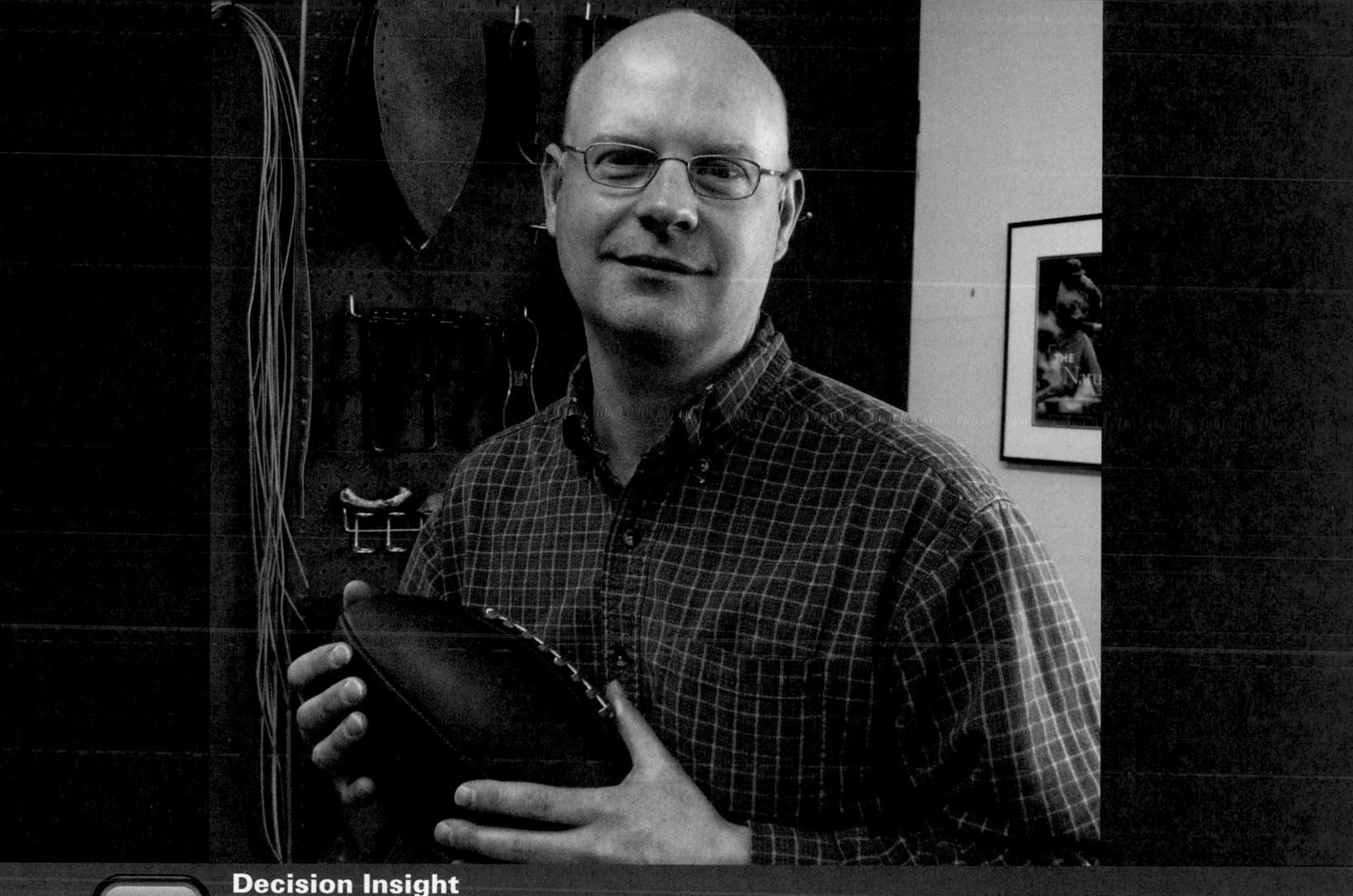

Touchdown!

"Put passion into your work."

—PAUL CUNNINGHAM

GLEN ROCK, NJ—Most quarterbacks in backyard football games have a glaring weakness: They can't throw good passes. Paul Cunningham, lifelong sports fan and master craftsman, set out to make "an exceptional quality football, slightly smaller than an NFL ball, so that the average person can throw it." As a result, what started as a side project in his home workshop turned into a full-fledged business, **Leather Head Sports (Leather-headsports.com)**. As Paul notes, "I've been able to leave the corporate world and do this full-time."

Paul's forays began when he crafted leather baseballs for the Major League Baseball Hall of Fame to use in recreating 19th century baseball games. Now, Paul makes leather baseballs, which he sells as Lemon Balls™, along with a line of Leather Head™ footballs and medicine balls. Paul makes every Leather Head™ ball himself. "I want someone to look at my football and see the passion that went into it," says Paul.

Paul stresses that he, like many entrepreneurs, had to learn through a process of trial and error. "Every hide is different, and I tried many different approaches to making a football." Now, upon receiving an order, Paul begins his production process by grabbing a side of top-quality leather. Using custom-made cutting dies, he hand cuts the leather panels. He then sews the leather panels together, inserts a rubber bladder, and laces the ball with rawhide lace. The result is what Paul calls the "official football of collegiate tailgating."

Operating at a small scale and using expensive, top-quality materials require Paul to understand and control his costs. Successful entrepreneurs must understand cost behavior to succeed. Identifying fixed and variable costs is key to understanding break-even points and maintaining the right product mix. Paul's small but diverse product line has considerably different selling prices and costs. Contribution margin income statements, which separate fixed and variable costs, enable entrepreneurs like Paul to quickly see how changes in selling prices, variable costs, or fixed costs impact profit. Understanding contribution margins and cost-volume-profit analyses enables small businesses to profit and grow.

Paul encourages young entrepreneurs to get out and make it happen. His sights are set on growing his company, possibly by bringing in additional craftsmen. Scaling his business in this way would make understanding how costs relate to volume and profit even more important. "I work hard," says Paul, "but I love working with my hands and creating things." Sounds like a perfect pass.

[Sources: *Leather Head Sports Website,* January 2013; http://www. youtube.com/watch?v=GaL3qxV4UzQ; http://video.foxbusiness.com/ v/1404850982001/investors-consider-adding-fine-art-to-portfoliomix/ ?playlist_id=87185; http://video.foxbusiness.com/v/3972553/]

This chapter describes different types of costs and shows how changes in a company's operating volume affect these costs. The chapter also analyzes a company's costs and sales to explain how different operating strategies affect profit or loss. Managers use this type of analysis to forecast what will happen if changes are made to costs, sales volume, selling prices, or product mix. They then use these forecasts to select the best business strategy for the company.

Cost-Volume-Profit Analysis

Identifying Cost Behavior	Measuring Cost Behavior	Using Break-Even Analysis	Applying Cost-Volume-Profit Analysis
• Fixed costs • Variable costs • Mixed costs • Step-wise costs • Curvilinear costs	• Scatter diagrams • High-low method • Least-squares regression • Comparison of cost estimation methods	• Computing contribution margin • Computing break-even • Computing margin of safety • Preparing a cost-volume-profit chart • Assumptions in cost-volume-profit analysis	• Computing income from sales and costs • Computing sales for target income • Using sensitivity analysis • Computing multiproduct break-even

IDENTIFYING COST BEHAVIOR

Planning a company's future activities and events is crucial to successful management. One of the first steps in planning is to predict the volume of activity, the costs to be incurred, sales to be made, and profit to be received. An important tool to help managers carry out this step is **cost-volume-profit (CVP) analysis,** which helps them predict how changes in costs and sales levels affect income. In its basic form, CVP analysis involves computing the sales level at which a company neither earns an income nor incurs a loss, called the *break-even point.* For this reason, this basic form of cost-volume-profit analysis is often called *break-even analysis.* Managers use variations of CVP analysis to answer questions like:

Point: *Profit* is another term for *income.*

- What sales volume is needed to earn a target income?
- What is the change in income if selling prices decline and sales volume increases?
- How much does income increase if we install a new machine to reduce labor costs?
- How will income change if we change the sales mix of our products or services?

Consequently, cost-volume-profit analysis is useful in a wide range of business decisions.

Conventional cost-volume-profit analysis requires management to classify all costs as either *fixed* or *variable* with respect to production or sales volume. The remainder of this section discusses the concepts of fixed and variable cost behavior as they relate to CVP analysis.

■ **Decision Insight**

No Free Lunch   Hardly a week goes by without a company advertising a free product with the purchase of another. Examples are a free printer with a digital camera purchase or a free monitor with a computer purchase. Can these companies break even, let alone earn profits? We are reminded of the *no-free-lunch* adage, meaning that companies expect profits from the companion or add-on purchase to make up for the free product. ■

 C1 Describe different types of cost behavior in relation to production and sales volume.

Fixed Costs

A *fixed cost* remains unchanged in amount when the volume of activity varies from period to period within a relevant range. For example, $32,000 in monthly rent paid for a factory building remains the same whether the factory operates with a single eight-hour shift or around the clock with three shifts. This means that rent cost is the same each month at any level of output from zero to the plant's full productive capacity. Notice that while *total* fixed cost does not change as the level of production changes, the fixed cost *per unit* of output decreases as volume increases. For instance, if 200 units are produced when monthly rent is $32,000, the average rent cost per unit is $160 (computed as $32,000/200 units); and when 100 units are produced, the average rent cost per unit is $320 (computed as $32,000/100 units). When production increases to 1,000 units per month, the average rent cost per unit decreases to $32 (computed as $32,000/1,000 units). The average rent cost decreases to $16 per unit if production increases to 2,000 units per month. Common examples of fixed costs include depreciation, property taxes, office salaries, and many service department costs.

When production volume and costs are graphed, units of product are usually plotted on the *horizontal axis* and dollars of cost are plotted on the *vertical axis*. Fixed costs then are represented as a horizontal line because they remain constant at all levels of production. To illustrate, the top graph in Exhibit 21.1 shows that fixed costs remain at $32,000 at all production levels up to the company's monthly capacity of 2,000 units of output. The bottom graph in Exhibit 21.1 shows that fixed costs per unit fall as production levels increase. This drop in costs per unit as production levels increase is known as *economies of scale*. The *relevant range* for fixed costs in Exhibit 21.1 is 0 to 2,000 units. If the relevant range changes (that is, production capacity extends beyond this range), the amount of fixed costs will likely change.

Example: If the fixed cost line in Exhibit 21.1 is shifted upward, does the total cost line shift up, down, or remain in the same place? *Answer:* It shifts up by the same amount.

EXHIBIT 21.1

Relations of Total and Per-Unit Costs to Volume

Relation of Total Fixed and Variable Costs to Volume

Monthly Capacity

- Fixed Costs, $32,000
- Variable Costs, $20 per unit
- Total (Mixed) Costs

Example: If the level of fixed costs in Exhibit 21.1 changes, does the slope of the total cost line change? *Answer:* No, the slope doesn't change. The total cost line is simply shifted upward or downward.

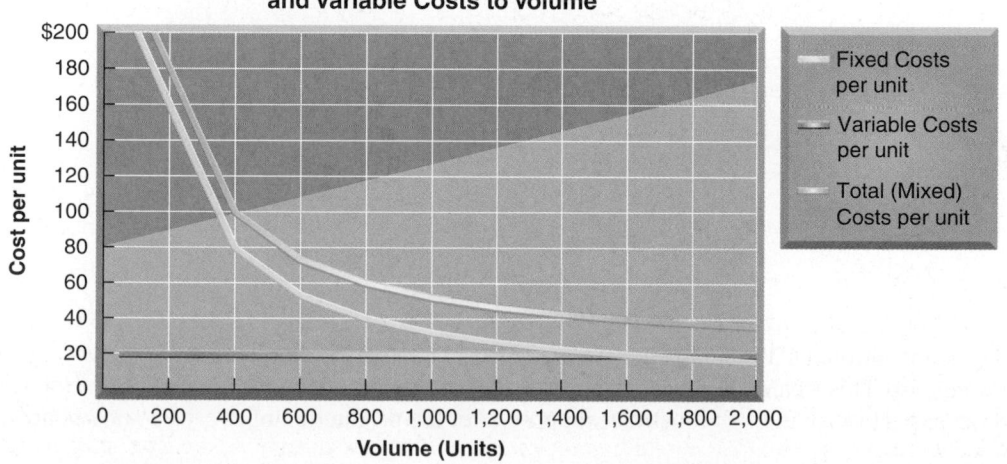

Relations of Per-Unit Fixed and Variable Costs to Volume

- Fixed Costs per unit
- Variable Costs per unit
- Total (Mixed) Costs per unit

Variable Costs

A *variable cost* changes in proportion to changes in volume of activity. The direct materials cost of a product is one example of a variable cost. If one unit of product requires materials costing $20, total materials costs are $200 when 10 units of product are manufactured, $400 for 20 units, $600 for 30 units, and so on. Notice that variable cost *per unit* remains constant but the *total* amount of variable cost changes with the level of production. In addition to direct materials, common variable costs include direct labor (if employees are paid per unit), sales commissions, shipping costs, and some overhead costs.

When variable costs are plotted on a graph of cost and volume, they appear as a straight line starting at the zero cost level. This straight line is upward (positive) sloping. The line rises as volume of activity increases. A variable cost line using a $20 per unit cost is graphed in Exhibit 21.1. The bottom graph in Exhibit 21.1 shows that variable cost per unit is constant as production levels change.

Mixed Costs

A **mixed cost** includes both fixed and variable cost components. For example, compensation for sales representatives often includes a fixed monthly salary and a variable commission based on sales. Like a fixed cost, a mixed cost is greater than zero when volume is zero; but unlike a fixed cost, it increases steadily in proportion to increases in volume. The mixed cost line in the top graph Exhibit 21.1 starts on the vertical axis at the $32,000 fixed cost point. Thus, at the zero volume level, total (mixed) cost equals the fixed costs. As the activity level increases, the mixed cost line increases at an amount equal to the variable cost per unit. This line is highest when the volume of activity is at 2,000 units (the end point of the relevant range). In CVP analysis, mixed costs are often separated into fixed and variable components. The fixed component is added to other fixed costs, and the variable component is added to other variable costs.

Step-Wise Costs

A **step-wise cost** reflects a step pattern in costs. Salaries of production supervisors often behave in a step-wise manner in that their salaries are fixed within a *relevant range* of the current production volume. However, if production volume expands significantly (for example, with the addition of another shift), additional supervisors must be hired. This means that the total cost for supervisory salaries goes up by a lump-sum amount. Similarly, if volume takes another significant step up, supervisory salaries will increase by another lump sum. This behavior reflects a step-wise cost, also known as a *stair-step cost,* which is graphed in Exhibit 21.2. See how the step-wise cost line is flat within ranges (steps). Then, when volume significantly changes, it shifts to another level for that range (step).

EXHIBIT 21.2

Step-Wise and
Curvilinear Costs

In a conventional CVP analysis, a step-wise cost is usually treated as either a fixed cost or a variable cost. This treatment involves manager judgment and depends on the width of the range and the expected volume. To illustrate, suppose after the production of every 25 snowboards, an operator lubricates the finishing machine. The cost of this lubricant reflects a step-wise pattern. Also, suppose that after the production of every 1,000 units, the snowboard cutting tool is replaced. Again, this is a step-wise cost. Note that the range of 25 snowboards is much narrower than the range of 1,000 snowboards. Some managers might treat the lubricant cost as a variable cost and the cutting tool cost as a fixed cost.

Point: Computer spreadsheets are important and effective tools for CVP analysis and for analyzing alternative "what-if" strategies.

Curvilinear Costs

A variable cost, as explained, is a *linear* cost; that is, it increases at a constant rate as volume of activity increases. A **curvilinear cost,** also called a *nonlinear cost,* increases at a nonconstant rate as volume increases. When graphed, curvilinear costs appear as a curved line. Exhibit 21.2 shows a curvilinear cost beginning at zero when production is zero and then increasing at different rates.

An example of a curvilinear cost is total direct labor cost when workers are paid by the hour. At low to medium levels of production, adding more employees allows each of them to specialize by doing certain tasks repeatedly instead of doing several different tasks. This often yields additional units of output at lower costs. A point is eventually reached at which adding more employees creates inefficiencies. For instance, a large crew demands more time and effort in communicating and coordinating their efforts. While adding employees in this case increases output, the labor cost per unit increases, and the total labor cost goes up at a steeper slope. This pattern is seen in Exhibit 21.2 where the curvilinear cost curve starts at zero, rises, flattens out, and then increases at a faster rate as output nears the maximum.

Point: Cost-volume-profit analysis helped Rod Canion, Jim Harris, and Bill Murto raise start-up capital of $20 million to launch **Compaq Computer.** They showed that break-even volumes were attainable within the first year.

Quick Check   Answers — p. 883

1. Which of the following statements is typically true? (*a*) Variable cost per unit increases as volume increases, (*b*) fixed cost per unit decreases as volume increases, or (*c*) a curvilinear cost includes both fixed and variable elements.
2. Describe the behavior of a fixed cost.
3. If cost per unit of activity remains constant (fixed), why is it called a variable cost?

MEASURING COST BEHAVIOR

Identifying and measuring cost behavior requires careful analysis and judgment. An important part of this process is to identify costs that can be classified as either fixed or variable, which often requires analysis of past cost behavior. Three methods are commonly used to analyze past costs: scatter diagrams, the high-low method, and least-squares regression. Each method is discussed in this section using the unit and cost data shown in Exhibit 21.3, which

P1 Determine cost estimates using the scatter diagram, high-low, and regression methods of estimating costs.

Month	Units Produced	Total Cost
January	27,500	$21,500
February	17,500	20,500
March	25,000	25,000
April	35,000	21,500
May	47,500	25,500
June	22,500	18,500
July	30,000	23,500
August	52,500	28,500
September	37,500	26,000
October	67,500	29,000
November	62,500	31,000
December	57,500	26,000

EXHIBIT 21.3

Data for Estimating Cost Behavior

are taken from a start-up company that uses units produced as the activity base in estimating cost behavior.

Scatter Diagrams

Scatter diagrams display past cost and unit data in graphical form. In preparing a scatter diagram, units are plotted on the horizontal axis and cost is plotted on the vertical axis. Each individual point on a scatter diagram reflects the cost and number of units for a prior period. In Exhibit 21.4, the prior 12 months' costs and numbers of units are graphed. Each point reflects total costs incurred and units produced for one of those months. For instance, the point labeled March had units produced of 25,000 and costs of $25,000.

EXHIBIT 21.4

Scatter Diagram

The **estimated line of cost behavior** is drawn on a scatter diagram to reflect the relation between cost and unit volume. This line best visually "fits" the points in a scatter diagram. Fitting this line demands judgment. The line drawn in Exhibit 21.4 intersects the vertical axis at approximately $16,000, which reflects fixed cost. To compute variable cost per unit, or the slope, we perform three steps. First, we select any two points on the horizontal axis (units), say 0 and 40,000. Second, we draw a vertical line from each of these points to intersect the estimated line of cost behavior. The point on the vertical axis (cost) corresponding to the 40,000 units point that intersects the estimated line is roughly $24,000. Similarly, the cost corresponding to zero units is $16,000 (the fixed cost point). Third, we compute the slope of the line, or variable cost, as the change in cost divided by the change in units. Exhibit 21.5 shows this computation.

EXHIBIT 21.5

Variable Cost per Unit
(Scatter Diagram)

$$\frac{\textbf{Change in cost}}{\textbf{Change in units}} = \frac{\$24,000 - \$16,000}{40,000 - 0} = \frac{\$8,000}{40,000} = \$0.20 \text{ per unit}$$

Example: In Exhibits 21.4 and 21.5, if units are projected at 30,000, what is the predicted cost? *Answer:* Approximately $22,000.

Variable cost is $0.20 per unit. Thus, the cost equation that management will use to estimate costs for different unit levels is **$16,000 plus $0.20 per unit**.

High-Low Method

The **high-low method** is a way to estimate the cost equation by graphically connecting the two cost amounts at the highest and lowest unit volumes. In our case, the lowest number of units is 17,500, and the highest is 67,500. The costs corresponding to these unit volumes are $20,500 and $29,000, respectively (see the data in Exhibit 21.3). The estimated line of cost behavior for the high-low method is then drawn by connecting these two points on the scatter diagram corresponding to the lowest and highest unit volumes as follows.

Point: Note that the high-low method identifies the high and low points of the volume (activity) base, and the costs linked with those extremes—which may not be the highest and lowest costs.

The variable cost per unit is determined as the change in cost divided by the change in units and uses the data from the high and low unit volumes. This results in a slope, or variable cost per unit, of $0.17 as computed in Exhibit 21.6.

$$\frac{\text{Change in cost}}{\text{Change in units}} = \frac{\$29,000 - \$20,500}{67,500 - 17,500} = \frac{\$8,500}{50,000} = \$0.17 \text{ per unit}$$

EXHIBIT 21.6

Variable Cost per Unit (High-Low Method)

To estimate the fixed cost for the high-low method, we use the knowledge that total cost equals fixed cost plus variable cost per unit times the number of units. Then we pick either the high or low point to determine the fixed cost. This computation is shown in Exhibit 21.7—where we use the high point (67,500 units) in determining the fixed cost of $17,525. Use of the low point (17,500 units) yields the same fixed cost estimate: $20,500 = Fixed cost + ($0.17 per unit × 17,500), or Fixed cost = $17,525.

Total cost = Fixed cost + (Variable cost × Units)

$29,000 = Fixed cost + ($0.17 per unit × 67,500 units)

Then,   Fixed cost = $17,525

EXHIBIT 21.7

Fixed Cost (High-Low Method)

Thus, the cost equation used to estimate costs at different units is **$17,525 plus $0.17 per unit**. This cost equation differs slightly from that determined from the scatter diagram method. A deficiency of the high-low method is that it ignores all cost points except the highest and lowest. The result is less precision because the high-low method uses the most extreme points rather than the more usual conditions likely to recur.

Least-Squares Regression

Least-squares regression is a statistical method for identifying cost behavior. For our purposes, we use the cost equation estimated from this method but leave the computational details for more advanced courses. Such computations for least-squares regression are readily done using most spreadsheet programs or calculators. We illustrate this using Excel® in Appendix 21A.

The regression cost equation for the data presented in Exhibit 21.3 is **$16,947 plus $0.19 per unit**; that is, the fixed cost is estimated as $16,947 and the variable cost at $0.19 per unit. Both costs are reflected in the following graph.

Comparison of Cost Estimation Methods

The three cost estimation methods result in slightly different estimates of fixed and variable costs as summarized in Exhibit 21.8. Estimates from the scatter diagram are based on a visual fit of the cost line and are subject to interpretation. Estimates from the high-low method use only two sets of values corresponding to the lowest and highest unit volumes. Estimates from least-squares regression use a statistical technique and all available data points.

EXHIBIT 21.8

Comparison of Cost
Estimation Methods

Estimation Method	Fixed Cost	Variable Cost
Scatter diagram	$16,000	$0.20 per unit
High-low method	17,525	0.17 per unit
Least-squares regression	16,947	0.19 per unit

We must remember that all three methods use *past data*. Thus, cost estimates resulting from these methods are only as good as the data used for estimation. Managers must establish that the data are reliable in deriving cost estimates for the future. If the data are reliable, the use of more data points, as in the regression or scatter diagram methods, should yield more accurate estimates than the high-low method. However, the high-low method is easier to apply than the regression method and less subject to interpretation than the scatter diagram approach.

Quick Check   Answers — p. 883

4. Which of the following methods is likely to yield the most precise estimated line of cost behavior? (a) High-low, (b) least-squares regression, or (c) scatter diagram.
5. What is the primary weakness of the high-low method?
6. Using conventional CVP analysis, a mixed cost should be (a) disregarded, (b) treated as a fixed cost, or (c) separated into fixed and variable components.

USING BREAK-EVEN ANALYSIS

Break-even analysis is a special case of cost-volume-profit analysis. This section describes break-even analysis by computing the break-even point and preparing a CVP (or break-even) chart.

Contribution Margin and Its Measures

We explained how managers classify costs by behavior. This often refers to classifying costs as being fixed or variable with respect to volume of activity. In manufacturing companies, volume of activity usually refers to the number of units produced. We then classify a cost as either fixed or variable, depending on whether total cost changes as the number of units produced changes. Once we separate costs by behavior, we can then compute a product's contribution margin. **Contribution margin per unit,** or *unit contribution margin,* is the amount by which a product's unit selling price exceeds its total variable cost per unit. This excess amount contributes to covering fixed costs and generating profits on a per unit basis. Exhibit 21.9 shows the contribution margin per unit formula.

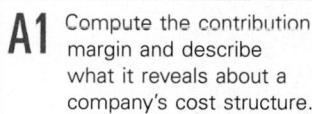

A1   Compute the contribution margin and describe what it reveals about a company's cost structure.

Contribution margin per unit = Sales price per unit − Total variable cost per unit

EXHIBIT 21.9

Contribution Margin per Unit

The **contribution margin ratio,** which is the percent of a unit's selling price that exceeds total unit variable cost, is also useful for business decisions. It can be interpreted as the percent of each sales dollar that remains after deducting the total unit variable cost. Exhibit 21.10 shows the formula for the contribution margin ratio.

$$\text{Contribution margin ratio} = \frac{\text{Contribution margin per unit}}{\text{Sales price per unit}}$$

EXHIBIT 21.10

Contribution Margin Ratio

To illustrate the use of contribution margin, let's consider **Rydell,** which sells footballs for $100 each and incurs variable costs of $70 per football sold. Its fixed costs are $24,000 per month with monthly capacity of 1,800 units (footballs). Rydell's contribution margin per unit is $30, which is computed as follows.

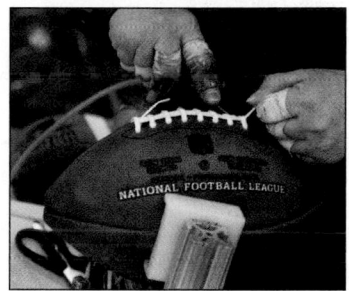

Selling price per unit	$100
Variable cost per unit	70
Contribution margin per unit	$ 30

Its contribution margin ratio is 30%, computed as $30/$100. This reveals that for each unit sold, Rydell has $30 that contributes to covering fixed cost and profit. If we consider sales in dollars, a contribution margin of 30% implies that for each $1 in sales, Rydell has $0.30 that contributes to fixed cost and profit.

■ **Decision Maker** ━━━━━━━━━━━━━━━━━━━━━━━━━━━━

Sales Manager   You are evaluating orders from two customers but can accept only one of the orders because of your company's limited capacity. The first order is for 100 units of a product with a contribution margin ratio of 60% and a selling price of $1,000. The second order is for 500 units of a product with a contribution margin ratio of 20% and a selling price of $800. The incremental fixed costs are the same for both orders. Which order do you accept? ■ [Answer—p. 882]

Computing the Break-Even Point

The **break-even point** is the sales level at which a company neither earns a profit nor incurs a loss. The concept of break-even is applicable to nearly all organizations, activities, and events. One of the most important items of information when launching a project is whether it will break even—that is, whether sales will at least cover total costs. The break-even point can be expressed in either units or dollars of sales.

P2   Compute the break-even point for a single product company.

To illustrate break-even analysis, let's again look at Rydell, which sells footballs for $100 per unit and incurs $70 of variable costs per unit sold. Its fixed costs are $24,000 per month. Rydell breaks even for the month when it sells 800 footballs (sales volume of $80,000). We compute this break-even point using the formula in Exhibit 21.11. This formula uses the contribution margin per unit, which for Rydell is $30 ($100 − $70). From this we can compute the break-even sales volume as $24,000/$30, or 800 units per month.

EXHIBIT 21.11

Formula for Computing
Break-Even Sales (in Units)

$$\text{Break-even point in units} = \frac{\text{Fixed costs}}{\text{Contribution margin per unit}}$$

At a price of $100 per unit, monthly sales of 800 units yield sales dollars of $80,000 (called *break-even sales dollars*). This $80,000 break-even sales can be computed directly using the formula in Exhibit 21.12.

EXHIBIT 21.12

Formula for Computing
Break-Even Sales (in Dollars)

$$\text{Break-even point in dollars} = \frac{\text{Fixed costs}}{\text{Contribution margin ratio}}$$

Point: Even if a company operates at a level in excess of its break-even point, management may decide to stop operating because it is not earning a reasonable return on investment.

Rydell's break-even point in dollars is computed as $24,000/0.30, or $80,000 of monthly sales. To verify that Rydell's break-even point equals $80,000 (or 800 units), we prepare a simplified income statement in Exhibit 21.13. It shows that the $80,000 revenue from sales of 800 units exactly equals the sum of variable and fixed costs.

EXHIBIT 21.13

Contribution Margin
Income Statement for
Break-Even Sales

RYDELL COMPANY	
Contribution Margin Income Statement (at Break-Even)	
For Month Ended January 31, 2013	
Sales (800 units at $100 each)	$80,000
Variable costs (800 units at $70 each)	56,000
Contribution margin	24,000
Fixed costs	24,000
Net income	$ 0

Point: A contribution margin income statement is also referred to as a *variable costing income statement*. This differs from the traditional *absorption costing* approach where all product costs are assigned to units sold and to units in ending inventory. Recall that variable costing expenses all fixed product costs. Thus, income for the two approaches differs depending on the level of finished goods inventory; the lower inventory is, the more similar the two approaches are.

The statement in Exhibit 21.13 is called a *contribution margin income statement*. It differs in format from a conventional income statement in two ways. First, it separately classifies costs and expenses as variable or fixed. Second, it reports contribution margin (Sales − Variable costs). The contribution margin income statement format is used in this chapter's assignment materials because of its usefulness in CVP analysis.

Computing the Margin of Safety

All companies wish to sell more than the break-even number of units. The excess of expected sales over the break-even sales level is called a company's **margin of safety,** the amount that sales can drop before the company incurs a loss. It can be expressed in units, dollars, or even as a percent of the predicted level of sales. To illustrate, if Rydell's expected sales are $100,000, the margin of safety is $20,000 above break-even sales of $80,000. As a percent, the margin of safety is 20% of expected sales as shown in Exhibit 21.14.

EXHIBIT 21.14

Computing Margin of Safety
(in Percent)

$$\text{Margin of safety (in percent)} = \frac{\text{Expected sales} - \text{Break-even sales}}{\text{Expected sales}}$$

$$= \frac{\$100,000 - \$80,000}{\$100,000} = 20\%$$

Management must assess whether the margin of safety is adequate in light of factors such as sales variability, competition, consumer tastes, and economic conditions.

Preparing a Cost-Volume-Profit Chart

Exhibit 21.15 is a graph of Rydell's cost-volume-profit relations. This graph is called a **cost-volume-profit (CVP) chart,** or a *break-even chart* or *break-even graph*. The horizontal axis is the number of units produced and sold and the vertical axis is dollars of sales and costs. The lines in the chart depict both sales and costs at different output levels.

P3 Graph costs and sales for a single product company.

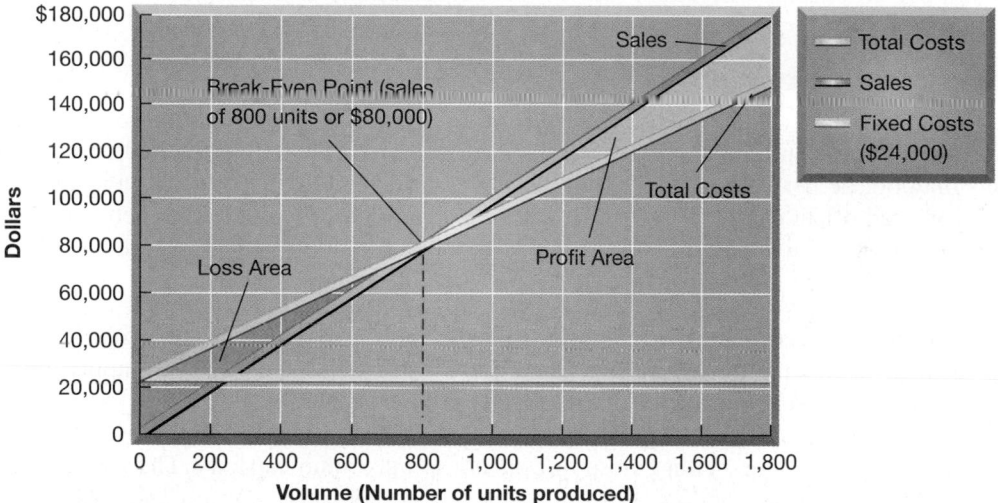

EXHIBIT 21.15

Cost-Volume-Profit Chart

We follow three steps to prepare a CVP chart, which can also be drawn with computer programs that convert numeric data to graphs:

1. Plot fixed costs on the vertical axis ($24,000 for Rydell). Draw a horizontal line at this level to show that fixed costs remain unchanged regardless of output volume (drawing this fixed cost line is not essential to the chart).

2. Draw the total (variable plus fixed) cost line for a relevant range of volume levels. This line starts at the fixed costs level on the vertical axis because total costs equal fixed costs at zero volume. The slope of the total cost line equals the variable cost per unit ($70). To draw the line, compute the total costs for any volume level, and connect this point with the vertical axis intercept ($24,000). Do not draw this line beyond the productive capacity for the planning period (1,800 units for Rydell).

3. Draw the sales line. Start at the origin (zero units and zero dollars of sales) and make the slope of this line equal to the selling price per unit ($100). To sketch the line, compute dollar sales for any volume level and connect this point with the origin. Do not extend this line beyond the productive capacity. Total sales will be at the highest level at maximum capacity.

Point: CVP analysis is often based on *sales volume*, using either units sold or dollar sales. Other output measures, such as the number of units produced, can also be used.

The total cost line and the sales line intersect at 800 units in Exhibit 21.15, which is the break-even point—the point where total dollar sales of $80,000 equals the sum of both fixed and variable costs ($80,000).

On either side of the break-even point, the vertical distance between the sales line and the total cost line at any specific volume reflects the profit or loss expected at that point. At volume levels to the left of the break-even point, this vertical distance is the amount of the expected loss because the total costs line is above the total sales line. At volume levels to the right of the break-even point, the vertical distance represents the expected profit because the total sales line is above the total cost line.

Example: In Exhibit 21.15, the sales line intersects the total cost line at 800 units. At what point would the two lines intersect if selling price is increased by 20% to $120 per unit? *Answer:* $24,000/($120 − $70) = 480 units

 Decision Maker ━━━━━━━━━━━━━━━━━━━━━

Operations Manager As a start-up manufacturer, you wish to identify the behavior of manufacturing costs to develop a production cost budget. You know three methods can be used to identify cost behavior from past data, but past data are unavailable because this is a start-up. What do you do? ■ [Answer—p. 883]

Making Assumptions in Cost-Volume-Profit Analysis

Cost-volume-profit analysis assumes that relations can normally be expressed as simple lines similar to those in Exhibits 21.4 and 21.15. CVP analysis assumes that selling prices per unit, variable costs per unit, and total fixed costs are all held constant. If the expected costs and sales behavior differ from the assumptions, the results of CVP analysis can be limited. While the behavior of individual costs and sales may not be perfectly consistent with CVP assumptions, we can still perform useful analyses in spite of these assumptions' limitations, for reasons we describe next.

Working with Assumptions

Summing costs can offset individual deviations.   Deviations from assumptions with individual costs are often minor when these costs are summed. That is, individual variable cost items may not be perfectly variable, but when we sum these variable costs, their individual deviations can offset each other. This means the assumption of variable cost behavior can be proper for total variable costs. Similarly, an assumption that total fixed costs are constant can be proper even when individual fixed cost items are not exactly constant.

CVP is applied to a relevant range of operations.   Sales, variable costs, and fixed costs often are reasonably reflected in straight lines on a graph when the assumptions are applied over a relevant range. The **relevant range of operations** is the normal operating range for a business. Except for unusually difficult or prosperous times, management typically plans for operations within a range of volume neither close to zero nor at maximum capacity. The relevant range excludes extremely high and low operating levels that are unlikely to occur. The validity of assuming that a specific cost is fixed or variable is more acceptable when operations are within the relevant range. As shown in Exhibit 21.2, a curvilinear cost can be treated as variable and linear if the relevant range covers volumes where it has a nearly constant slope. If the normal range of activity changes, some costs might need reclassification.

Example: If the selling price declines, what happens to the break-even point? *Answer:* It increases.

CVP analysis yields estimates.   CVP analysis yields approximate answers to questions about costs, volumes, and profits. These answers do not have to be precise because the analysis makes rough estimates about the future. For example, to simplify analysis, we sometimes assume that the production level is the same as the sales level. That is, inventory levels do not change. This often is justified by arguing that CVP analysis provides only approximations. With just-in-time inventory systems, production levels should approximate sales levels, thus CVP estimates should be more accurate. As long as managers understand that CVP analysis gives estimates, it can be a useful tool for starting the planning process. Other qualitative factors also must be considered.

Quick Check   Answers — p. 883

7. Fixed cost divided by the contribution margin ratio yields the (*a*) break-even point in dollars, (*b*) contribution margin per unit, or (*c*) break-even point in units.

8. A company sells a product for $90 per unit with variable costs of $54 per unit. What is the contribution margin ratio?

9. Refer to Quick Check (8). If fixed costs for the period are $90,000, what is the break-even point in dollars?

10. What is a company's margin of safety?

11. What three basic assumptions are used in CVP analysis?

Working with Changes in Estimates   Because CVP analysis uses estimates, knowing how changes in those estimates impact break-even is useful. For example, a manager might form three estimates for each of the components of break-even: optimistic, most likely, and pessimistic. Then ranges of break-even points in units can be computed using the formula in Exhibit 21.11.

To illustrate, assume Rydell's managers provide the set of estimates in Exhibit 21.16.

	Selling Price per Unit	Variable Cost per Unit	Total Fixed Costs
Optimistic	$105	$68	$21,000
Most likely	100	70	24,000
Pessimistic	95	72	27,000

EXHIBIT 21.16

Alternative Estimates for Break-Even Analysis

If, for example, Rydell's managers believe they can raise the selling price of a football to $105, without any change in unit variable or total fixed costs, then the revised contribution margin per football is $35, and the revised break-even in units follows in Exhibit 21.17.

EXHIBIT 21.17

Revised Break-Even in Units

$$\text{Revised break-even point in units} = \frac{\$24,000}{\$35} = 686 \text{ units (rounded)}$$

Repeating this calculation using each of the other eight separate estimates above, and graphing the results, yields the three scatter diagrams in Exhibit 21.18.

EXHIBIT 21.18

Scatter Diagrams—Break-Even Points for Alternative Estimates

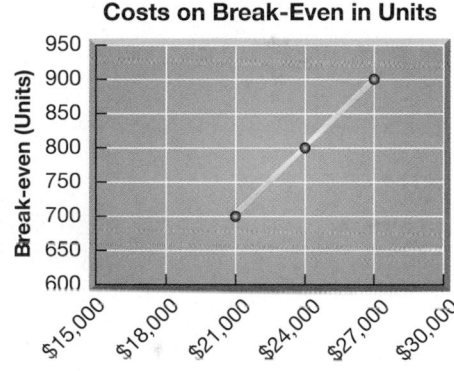

These scatter diagrams show how changes in selling prices, variable costs, and fixed costs impact break-even. When selling prices can be increased without impacting unit variable costs or total fixed costs, break-even decreases. When competition drives selling prices down, and the company cannot reduce costs, break-even increases. Increases in either variable or fixed costs, if they cannot be passed on to customers via higher selling prices, will increase break-even. If costs can be reduced and selling prices held constant, the break-even decreases.

Point: This analysis changed only one estimate at a time; managers can examine how combinations of changes in estimates will impact break-even.

APPLYING COST-VOLUME-PROFIT ANALYSIS

Managers consider a variety of strategies in planning business operations. Cost-volume-profit analysis is useful in helping managers evaluate the likely effects of these strategies, which is the focus of this section.

Computing Income from Sales and Costs

An important question managers often ask is "What is the predicted income from a predicted level of sales?" To answer this, we look at four variables in CVP analysis. These variables and their relations to income (pretax) are shown in Exhibit 21.19. We use these relations to compute expected income from predicted sales and cost levels.

 C2 Describe several applications of cost-volume-profit analysis.

EXHIBIT 21.19

Income Relations in
CVP Analysis

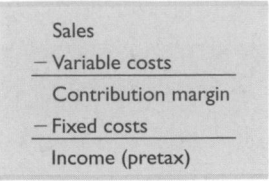

Sales
− Variable costs
Contribution margin
− Fixed costs
Income (pretax)

To illustrate, let's assume that Rydell's management expects to sell 1,500 units in January 2013. What is the amount of income if this sales level is achieved? Following Exhibit 21.19, we compute Rydell's expected income in Exhibit 21.20.

EXHIBIT 21.20

Computing Expected Pretax
Income from Expected Sales

RYDELL COMPANY Contribution Margin Income Statement For Month Ended January 31, 2013	
Sales (1,500 units at $100 each)	$150,000
Variable costs (1,500 units at $70 each)	105,000
Contribution margin	45,000
Fixed costs	24,000
Income (pretax)	$ 21,000

The $21,000 income is pretax. To find the amount of *after-tax* income from selling 1,500 units, management must apply the proper tax rate. Assume that the tax rate is 25%. Then we can prepare the after-tax income statement shown in Exhibit 21.21. We can also compute pretax income as after-tax income divided by (1 − tax rate); for Rydell, this is $15,750/(1 − 0.25), or $21,000.

EXHIBIT 21.21

Computing Expected After-Tax
Income from Expected Sales

RYDELL COMPANY Contribution Margin Income Statement For Month Ended January 31, 2013	
Sales (1,500 units at $100 each)	$150,000
Variable costs (1,500 units at $70 each)	105,000
Contribution margin	45,000
Fixed costs	24,000
Pretax income	21,000
Income taxes (25%)	5,250
Net income (after tax)	$ 15,750

Management then assesses whether this income is an adequate return on assets invested. Management should also consider whether sales and income can be increased by raising or lowering prices. CVP analysis is a good tool for addressing these kinds of "what-if" questions.

Computing Sales for a Target Income

"How many units must we sell to earn $50,000?"

Many companies' annual plans are based on certain income targets (sometimes called *budgets*). Rydell's income target for this year is to increase income by 10% over the prior year. When prior year income is known, Rydell easily computes its target income. CVP analysis helps to determine the sales level needed to achieve the target income. Planning for the year is then based on this level.

We use the formula shown in Exhibit 21.22 to compute sales for a target *after-tax* income. To illustrate, Rydell has monthly fixed costs of $24,000 and a 30% contribution margin ratio. Assume that it sets a target monthly after-tax income of $9,000 when the tax rate is 25%. This means the pretax income is targeted at $12,000 [$9,000/(1 − 0.25)] with a tax expense of $3,000. Using the formula in Exhibit 21.22, we find that $120,000 of sales are needed to produce a $9,000 after-tax income.

$$\text{Dollar sales at target after-tax income} = \frac{\text{Fixed costs} + \text{Target pretax income}}{\text{Contribution margin ratio}}$$

$$= \frac{\$24,000 + \$12,000}{30\%} = \$120,000$$

EXHIBIT 21.22

Computing Sales (Dollars) for a Target After-Tax Income

We can alternatively compute *unit sales* instead of dollar sales. To do this, we substitute *contribution margin per unit* for the contribution margin ratio in the denominator. This gives the number of units to sell to reach the target after-tax income. Exhibit 21.23 illustrates this for Rydell. The two computations in Exhibits 21.22 and 21.23 are equivalent because sales of 1,200 units at $100 per unit equal $120,000 of sales.

Point: Break-even is a special case of the formulas in Exhibits 21.22 and 21.23; simply set target pretax income to $0 and the formulas reduce to those in Exhibits 21.11 and 21.12.

EXHIBIT 21.23

Computing Sales (Units) for a Target After-Tax Income

$$\text{Unit sales at target after-tax income} = \frac{\text{Fixed costs} + \text{Target pretax income}}{\text{Contribution margin per unit}}$$

$$= \frac{\$24,000 + \$12,000}{\$30} = 1,200 \text{ units}$$

■ Decision Ethics

Supervisor Your team is conducting a cost-volume-profit analysis for a new product. Different sales projections have different incomes. One member suggests picking numbers yielding favorable income because any estimate is "as good as any other." Another member points to a scatter diagram of 20 months' production on a comparable product and suggests dropping unfavorable data points for cost estimation. What do you do? ■ [Answer—p. 883]

We can also use the contribution margin income statement approach to compute sales for a target income. In step 1, we insert the fixed costs ($24,000) and the desired after tax profit level ($9,000) into a contribution margin income statement, as shown in Exhibit 21.24. To achieve an after tax profit of $9,000, Rydell's pretax income must be $12,000, computed as $9,000/(1 − 0.25). We insert this as step 2 in the pretax income row in the contribution margin income statement and solve for Rydell's income taxes ($12,000 − $9,000), or $3,000. To cover its fixed costs of $24,000 and yield a pretax income of $12,000, Rydell must generate a contribution margin of $36,000 (computed as $24,000 plus $12,000). We enter this in the contribution margin row as step 3. With a contribution margin ratio of 30%, sales must be $120,000, computed as $36,000/0.30, to yield a contribution margin of $36,000. We enter this in the sales row of the contribution margin income statement as step 3 and solve for variable costs of $84,000 (computed as $120,000 − $36,000). At a selling price of $100 per unit, Rydell must sell 1,200 units ($120,000/$100) to earn after tax net income of $9,000.

EXHIBIT 21.24

Using the Contribution Margin Income Statement to Find Target Sales

RYDELL COMPANY			
Contribution Margin Income Statement			
For Month Ended January 31, 2013			
	Step 1	**Step 2**	**Step 3**
Sales	?	?	$120,000
Variable costs	?	?	84,000
Contribution margin	?	?	36,000
Fixed costs	24,000	24,000	24,000
Income (pretax)	?	12,000	12,000
Incomes taxes (25%)	?	3,000	3,000
Net income (after tax)	$ 9,000	$ 9,000	$ 9,000

$9,000/(1 − 0.25)	$24,000 + $12,000	$36,000/0.30

Using Sensitivity Analysis

Earlier we showed how changing one of the estimates in a CVP analysis impacts break-even. We can also examine strategies that impact several estimates in the CVP analysis. For instance, we might want to know what happens to income if we automate a currently manual process. We can use CVP analysis to predict income if we can describe how these changes affect a company's fixed costs, variable costs, selling price, and volume.

To illustrate, assume that Rydell Company is looking into buying a new machine that would increase monthly fixed costs from $24,000 to $30,000 but decrease variable costs from $70 per unit to $60 per unit. The machine is used to produce output whose selling price will remain unchanged at $100. This results in increases in both the unit contribution margin and the contribution margin ratio. The revised contribution margin per unit is $40 ($100 − $60), and the revised contribution margin ratio is 40% of selling price ($40/$100). Using CVP analysis, Rydell's revised break-even point in dollars would be $75,000 as computed in Exhibit 21.25.

Example: If fixed costs decline, what happens to the break-even point? *Answer:* It decreases.

EXHIBIT 21.25

Revising Break-even When Changes Occur

$$\text{Revised break-even point in dollars} = \frac{\text{Revised fixed costs}}{\text{Revised contribution margin ratio}} = \frac{\$30,000}{40\%} = \$75,000$$

We can also use the contribution margin income statement approach in sensitivity analysis, as we show in Exhibit 21.26. The revised fixed costs and the revised contribution margin ratio can be used to address other issues including computation of (1) expected income for a given sales level and (2) the sales level needed to earn a target income. Once again, we can use sensitivity analysis to generate different sets of revenue and cost estimates that are *optimistic, pessimistic,* and *most likely.* Different CVP analyses based on these estimates provide different scenarios that management can analyze and use in planning business strategy.

EXHIBIT 21.26

Using the Contribution Margin Income Statement in Sensitivity Analysis

RYDELL COMPANY
Contribution Margin Income Statement
For Month Ended January 31, 2013

	Step 1	Step 2	Step 3
Sales	?	?	$75,000
Variable costs	?	?	45,000
Contribution margin	?	30,000	30,000
Fixed costs	30,000	30,000	30,000
Income (pretax)	$ 0	$ 0	$ 0

$30,000 + $0 $30,000/0.40

Decision Insight

RFID-CVP Companies are increasingly using radio-frequency identification (RFID) tags to control inventory. Affixed to products, RFID tags enable companies to reduce costs of inventory theft and scanning errors. Are RFID systems economically feasible? Railroad companies have long used RFID tags on rail cars. While expensive, these tags can be reused thousands of times, thus the cost per tag falls as railroad traffic increases. Such economies of scale and other cost savings make RFID a better-than break-even investment for railroad companies. ∎

Quick Check

Answers — p. 883

12. A company has fixed costs of $50,000 and a 25% contribution margin ratio. What dollar sales are necessary to achieve an after-tax net income of $120,000 if the tax rate is 20%? (*a*) $800,000, (*b*) $680,000, or (*c*) $600,000.

13. If a company's contribution margin ratio decreases from 50% to 25%, what can be said about the unit sales needed to achieve the same target income level?

Computing a Multiproduct Break-Even Point

To this point, we have looked only at cases where the company sells a single product or service. This was to keep the basic CVP analysis simple. However, many companies sell multiple products or services, and we can modify the CVP analysis for use in these cases. An important assumption in a multiproduct setting is that the sales mix of different products is known and remains constant during the planning period. **Sales mix** is the ratio (proportion) of the sales volumes for the various products. For instance, if a company normally sells 10,000 footballs, 5,000 softballs, and 4,000 basketballs per month, its sales mix can be expressed as 10:5:4 for footballs, softballs, and basketballs.

P4 Compute the break-even point for a multiproduct company.

To apply multiproduct CVP analysis, we can estimate the break-even point by using a **composite unit,** which consists of a specific number of units of each product in proportion to their expected sales mix. Multiproduct CVP analysis treats this composite unit as a single product. To illustrate, let's look at Hair-Today, a styling salon that offers three cuts: basic, ultra, and budget in the ratio of 4 basic units to 2 ultra units to 1 budget unit (expressed as 4:2:1). Management wants to estimate its break-even point for next year. Unit selling prices for these three cuts are basic, $20; ultra, $32; and budget, $16. Using the 4:2:1 sales mix, the selling price of a composite unit of the three products is computed as follows.

4 units of basic @ $20 per unit	$ 80
2 units of ultra @ $32 per unit	64
1 unit of budget @ $16 per unit	16
Selling price of a composite unit	**$160**

Hair-Today's fixed costs are $192,000 per year, and its variable costs of the three products are basic, $13; ultra, $18.00; and budget, $8.00. Variable costs for a composite unit of these products follow.

Point: Selling prices and variable costs are usually expressed in per unit amounts. Fixed costs are usually expressed in total amounts.

4 units of basic @ $13 per unit	$52
2 units of ultra @ $18 per unit	36
1 unit of budget @ $8 per unit	8
Variable costs of a composite unit	**$96**

Hair-Today's $64 contribution margin for a composite unit is computed by subtracting the variable costs of a composite unit ($96) from its selling price ($160). We then use the contribution margin to determine Hair-Today's break-even point in composite units in Exhibit 21.27.

$$\text{Break-even point in composite units} = \frac{\text{Fixed costs}}{\text{Contribution margin per composite unit}}$$

$$= \frac{\$192,000}{\$64} = 3,000 \text{ composite units}$$

EXHIBIT 21.27

Break-Even Point in Composite Units

This computation implies that Hair-Today breaks even when it sells 3,000 composite units. To determine how many units of each product it must sell to break even, we multiply the number of units of each product in the composite by 3,000 as follows.

Point: The break-even point in dollars for Exhibit 21.27 is $192,000/($64/$160) = $480,000.

Basic:	4 × 3,000	. . . .	12,000 units
Ultra:	2 × 3,000	. . . .	6,000 units
Budget:	1 × 3,000	. . . .	3,000 units

Instead of computing contribution margin per composite unit, a company can compute a **weighted-average contribution margin.** Given the 4:2:1 product mix, basic cuts comprise 57.14% (computed as 4/7) of the company's haircuts, ultra makes up 28.57% of its business, and budget cuts comprise 14.29%. The weighted-average contribution margin follows in Exhibit 21.28.

EXHIBIT 21.28

Weighted-Average
Contribution Margin

	Unit contribution margin	× Percentage of sales mix	= Weighted unit contribution margin
Basic	$ 7	57.14%	$4.000
Ultra	14	28.57	4.000
Budget	8	14.29	1.143
Weighted-average contribution margin			$9.143

The company's break-even point in units is computed in Exhibit 21.29 as follows:

EXHIBIT 21.29

Break-Even in Units using
Weighted-Average
Contribution Margin

$$\text{Break-even point in units} = \frac{\text{Fixed costs}}{\text{Weighted-average contribution margin}}$$

$$= \frac{\$192,000}{\$9.143} = 21,000 \text{ units}$$

We see that the weighted-average contribution margin method yields 21,000 whole units as the break-even amount, the same total as the composite unit approach.

Exhibit 21.30 verifies the results for composite units by showing Hair-Today's sales and costs at this break-even point using a contribution margin income statement.

EXHIBIT 21.30

Multiproduct Break-Even
Income Statement

HAIR-TODAY Forecasted Contribution Margin Income Statement (at Break-Even)				
	Basic	Ultra	Budget	Totals
Sales				
Basic (12,000 @ $20)	$240,000			
Ultra (6,000 @ $32)		$192,000		
Budget (3,000 @ $16)			$48,000	
Total sales				$480,000
Variable costs				
Basic (12,000 @ $13)	156,000			
Ultra (6,000 @ $18)		108,000		
Budget (3,000 @ $8)			24,000	
Total variable costs				288,000
Contribution margin	$ 84,000	$ 84,000	$24,000	192,000
Fixed costs				192,000
Net income				$ 0

A CVP analysis using composite units can be used to answer a variety of planning questions. Once a product mix is set, all answers are based on the assumption that the mix remains constant at all relevant sales levels as other factors in the analysis do. We also can vary the sales mix to see what happens under alternative strategies.

Point: Enterprise resource planning (ERP) systems can quickly generate multiproduct break-even analyses.

■ Decision Maker

Entrepreneur A CVP analysis indicates that your start-up, which markets electronic products, will break even with the current sales mix and price levels. You have a target income in mind. What analysis might you perform to assess the likelihood of achieving this income? ■ [Answer—p. 883]

Quick Check   Answers — p. 883 ☑

14. The sales mix of a company's two products, X and Y, is 2:1. Unit variable costs for both products are $2, and unit sales prices are $5 for X and $4 for Y. What is the contribution margin per composite unit? (a) $5, (b) $10, or (c) $8.

15. What additional assumption about sales mix must be made in doing a conventional CVP analysis for a company that produces and sells more than one product?

GLOBAL VIEW

Survey evidence shows that many German companies have elaborate and detailed cost accounting systems. Over 90 percent of companies surveyed report their systems focus on *contribution margin*. This focus helps German companies like **Volkswagen** control costs and plan their production levels. Recently, Volkswagen announced it expects its Spanish brand *Seat* to break even within five years. For 2010, the *Seat* brand lost €311 million on revenue of €5.038 billion (349,000 units).

Degree of Operating Leverage   **Decision Analysis**

CVP analysis is especially useful when management begins the planning process and wishes to predict outcomes of alternative strategies. These strategies can involve changes in selling prices, fixed costs, variable costs, sales volume, and product mix. Managers are interested in seeing the effects of changes in some or all of these factors.

> **A2** Analyze changes in sales using the degree of operating leverage.

One goal of all managers is to get maximum benefits from their fixed costs. Managers would like to use 100% of their output capacity so that fixed costs are spread over the largest number of units. This would decrease fixed cost per unit and increase income. The extent, or relative size, of fixed costs in the total cost structure is known as **operating leverage.** Companies having a higher proportion of fixed costs in their total cost structure are said to have higher operating leverage. An example of this is a company that chooses to automate its processes instead of using direct labor, increasing its fixed costs and lowering its variable costs. A useful managerial measure to help assess the effect of changes in the level of sales on income is the **degree of operating leverage (DOL)** defined in Exhibit 21.31.

> **DOL = Total contribution margin (in dollars)/Pretax income**

EXHIBIT 21.31

Degree of Operating Leverage

To illustrate, let's return to Rydell Company. At a sales level of 1,200 units, Rydell's total contribution margin is $36,000 (1,200 units × $30 contribution margin per unit). Its pretax income, after subtracting fixed costs of $24,000, is $12,000 ($36,000 − $24,000). Rydell's degree of operating leverage at this sales level is 3.0, computed as contribution margin divided by pretax income ($36,000/$12,000). We then use DOL to measure the effect of changes in the level of sales on pretax income. For instance, suppose Rydell expects sales to increase by 10%. If this increase is within the relevant range of operations, we can expect this 10% increase in sales to result in a 30% increase in pretax income computed as DOL multiplied by the increase in sales (3.0 × 10%). Similar analyses can be done for expected decreases in sales.

DEMONSTRATION PROBLEM

Sport Caps Co. manufactures and sells caps for different sporting events. The fixed costs of operating the company are $150,000 per month, and the variable costs for caps are $5 per unit. The caps are sold for $8 per unit. The fixed costs provide a production capacity of up to 100,000 caps per month.

Required

1. Use the formulas in the chapter to compute the following:

   a. Contribution margin per cap.

   b. Break-even point in terms of the number of caps produced and sold.

   c. Amount of net income at 30,000 caps sold per month (ignore taxes).

   d. Amount of net income at 85,000 caps sold per month (ignore taxes).

   e. Number of caps to be produced and sold to provide $45,000 of after-tax income, assuming an income tax rate of 25%.

2. Draw a CVP chart for the company, showing cap output on the horizontal axis. Identify (*a*) the break-even point and (*b*) the amount of pretax income when the level of cap production is 70,000. (Omit the fixed cost line.)

3. Use the formulas in the chapter to compute the

    a. Contribution margin ratio.

    b. Break-even point in terms of sales dollars.

    c. Amount of net income at $250,000 of sales per month (ignore taxes).

    d. Amount of net income at $600,000 of sales per month (ignore taxes).

    e. Dollars of sales needed to provide $45,000 of after-tax income, assuming an income tax rate of 25%.

PLANNING THE SOLUTION

- Identify the formulas in the chapter for the required items expressed in units and solve them using the data given in the problem.
- Draw a CVP chart that reflects the facts in the problem. The horizontal axis should plot the volume in units up to 100,000, and the vertical axis should plot the total dollars up to $800,000. Plot the total cost line as upward sloping, starting at the fixed cost level ($150,000) on the vertical axis and increasing until it reaches $650,000 at the maximum volume of 100,000 units. Verify that the break-even point (where the two lines cross) equals the amount you computed in part 1.
- Identify the formulas in the chapter for the required items expressed in dollars and solve them using the data given in the problem.

SOLUTION TO DEMONSTRATION PROBLEM

1. a. Contribution margin per cap

$$= \text{Selling price per unit} - \text{Variable cost per unit}$$
$$= \$8 - \$5 = \underline{\$3}$$

   b. Break-even point in caps

$$= \frac{\text{Fixed costs}}{\text{Contribution margin per cap}} = \frac{\$150,000}{\$3} = \underline{50,000 \text{ caps}}$$

   c. Net income at 30,000 caps sold

$$= (\text{Units} \times \text{Contribution margin per unit}) - \text{Fixed costs}$$
$$= (30,000 \times \$3) - \$150,000 = \underline{\$(60,000) \text{ loss}}$$

   d. Net income at 85,000 caps sold

$$= (\text{Units} \times \text{Contribution margin per unit}) - \text{Fixed costs}$$
$$= (85,000 \times \$3) - \$150,000 = \underline{\$105,000 \text{ profit}}$$

   e. Pretax income

$$= \$45,000/(1 - 0.25) = \$60,000$$

      Income taxes

$$= \$60,000 \times 25\% = \$15,000$$

      Units needed for $45,000 income

$$= \frac{\text{Fixed costs} + \text{Target pretax income}}{\text{Contribution margin per cap}}$$
$$= \frac{\$150,000 + \$60,000}{\$3} = \underline{70,000 \text{ caps}}$$

2. CVP chart.

3. a. Contribution margin ratio $= \dfrac{\text{Contribution margin per unit}}{\text{Selling price per unit}} = \dfrac{\$3}{\$8} = 0.375, \text{ or } 37.5\%$

b. Break-even point in dollars $= \dfrac{\text{Fixed costs}}{\text{Contribution margin ratio}} = \dfrac{\$150,000}{37.5\%} = \underline{\$400,000}$

c. Net income at sales of \$250,000 $= (\text{Sales} \times \text{Contribution margin ratio}) - \text{Fixed costs}$
$= (\$250,000 \times 37.5\%) - \$150,000 = \underline{\$(56,250) \text{ loss}}$

d. Net income at sales of \$600,000 $= (\text{Sales} \times \text{Contribution margin ratio}) - \text{Fixed costs}$
$= (\$600,000 \times 37.5\%) - \$150,000 = \underline{\$75,000 \text{ income}}$

e. Dollars of sales to yield
$45,000 after-tax income $= \dfrac{\text{Fixed costs} + \text{Target pretax income}}{\text{Contribution margin ratio}}$
$= \dfrac{\$150,000 + \$60,000}{37.5\%} = \underline{\$560,000}$

APPENDIX

Using Excel to Estimate Least-Squares Regression

21A

Microsoft Excel® and other spreadsheet software can be used to perform least-squares regressions to identify cost behavior. In Excel®, the INTERCEPT and SLOPE functions are used. The following screen shot reports the data from Exhibit 21.3 in cells Al through C13 and shows the cell contents to find the intercept (cell B15) and slope (cell B16). Cell B15 uses Excel® to find the intercept from a least-squares regression of total cost (shown as C2:C13 in cell B15) on units produced (shown as B2:B13 in cell B15). Spreadsheet software is useful in understanding cost behavior when many data points (such as monthly total costs and units produced) are available.

	A	B	C
1	**Month**	**Units Produced**	**Total Cost**
2	January	27500	21500
3	February	17500	20500
4	March	25000	25000
5	April	35000	21500
6	May	47500	25500
7	June	22500	18500
8	July	30000	23500
9	August	52500	28500
10	September	37500	26000
11	October	67500	29000
12	November	62500	31000
13	December	57500	26000
14			
15	**Intercept**	=INTERCEPT(C2:C13, B2:B13)	
16	**Slope**	=SLOPE(C2:C13,B2:B13)	

Excel® can also be used to create scatter diagrams such as that in Exhibit 21.4. In contrast to visually drawing a line that "fits" the data, Excel® more precisely fits the regression line. To draw a scatter diagram with a line of fit, follow these steps:

1. Highlight the data cells you wish to diagram; in this example, start from cell C13 and highlight through cell B2.

2. Then select "Insert" and "Scatter" from the drop-down menus. Selecting the chart type in the upper left corner of the choices under Scatter will produce a diagram that looks like that in Exhibit 21.4, without a line of fit.

3. To add a line of fit (also called trend line), select "Layout" and "Trendline" from the drop-down menus. Selecting "Linear Trendline" will produce a diagram that looks like that in Exhibit 21.4, including the line of fit.

Summary

C1   Describe different types of cost behavior in relation to production and sales volume. Cost behavior is described in terms of how its amount changes in relation to changes in volume of activity within a relevant range. Fixed costs remain constant to changes in volume. Total variable costs change in direct proportion to volume changes. Mixed costs display the effects of both fixed and variable components. Step-wise costs remain constant over a small volume range, then change by a lump sum and remain constant over another volume range, and so on. Curvilinear costs change in a nonlinear relation to volume changes.

C2   Describe several applications of cost-volume-profit analysis. Cost-volume-profit analysis can be used to predict what can happen under alternative strategies concerning sales volume, selling prices, variable costs, or fixed costs. Applications include "what-if" analysis, computing sales for a target income, and break-even analysis.

A1   Compute the contribution margin and describe what it reveals about a company's cost structure. Contribution margin per unit is a product's sales price less its total variable costs. Contribution margin ratio is a product's contribution margin per unit divided by its sales price. Unit contribution margin is the amount received from each sale that contributes to fixed costs and income. The contribution margin ratio reveals what portion of each sales dollar is available as contribution to fixed costs and income.

A2   Analyze changes in sales using the degree of operating leverage. The extent, or relative size, of fixed costs in a company's total cost structure is known as *operating leverage*. One tool useful in assessing the effect of changes in sales on income is the degree of operating leverage, or DOL. DOL is the ratio of the contribution margin divided by pretax income. This ratio can be used to determine the expected percent change in income given a percent change in sales.

P1   Determine cost estimates using the scatter diagram, high-low, and regression methods of estimating costs. Three different methods used to estimate costs are the scatter diagram, the high-low method, and least-squares regression. All three methods use past data to estimate costs. Cost estimates from a scatter diagram are based on a visual fit of the cost line. Estimates from the high-low method are based only on costs corresponding to the lowest and highest sales. The least-squares regression method is a statistical technique and uses all data points.

P2   Compute the break-even point for a single product company. A company's break-even point for a period is the sales volume at which total revenues equal total costs. To compute a break-even point in terms of sales units, we divide total fixed costs by the contribution margin per unit. To compute a break-even point in terms of sales dollars, divide total fixed costs by the contribution margin ratio.

P3   Graph costs and sales for a single product company. The costs and sales for a company can be graphically illustrated using a CVP chart. In this chart, the horizontal axis represents the number of units sold and the vertical axis represents dollars of sales or costs. Straight lines are used to depict both costs and sales on the CVP chart.

P4   Compute the break-even point for a multiproduct company. CVP analysis can be applied to a multiproduct company by expressing sales volume in terms of composite units. A composite unit consists of a specific number of units of each product in proportion to their expected sales mix. Multiproduct CVP analysis treats this composite unit as a single product.

Guidance Answers to Decision Maker and Decision Ethics

Sales Manager   The contribution margin per unit for the first order is $600 (60% of $1,000); the contribution margin per unit for the second order is $160 (20% of $800). You are likely tempted to accept the first order based on its high contribution margin per unit, but you must compute the total contribution margin based on the number of units sold for each order. Total contribution margin is $60,000 ($600 per unit × 100 units) and $80,000 ($160 per unit × 500 units) for the two orders, respectively. The second order provides the largest return in absolute dollars and is the order you would accept. Another factor to consider in your selection is the potential for a long-term relationship with these customers including repeat sales and growth.

Operations Manager   Without the availability of past data, none of the three methods described in the chapter can be used to measure cost behavior. Instead, the manager must investigate whether data from similar manufacturers can be accessed. This is likely difficult due to the sensitive nature of such data. In the absence of data, the manager should develop a list of the different production inputs and identify input-output relations. This provides guidance to the manager in measuring cost behavior. After several months, actual cost data will be available for analysis.

Supervisor   Your dilemma is whether to go along with the suggestions to "manage" the numbers to make the project look like it will achieve sufficient profits. You should not succumb to these suggestions. Many people will likely be affected negatively if you manage the predicted numbers and the project eventually is unprofitable. Moreover, if it does fail, an investigation would likely reveal that data in the proposal were "fixed" to make it look good. Probably the only benefit from managing the numbers is the short-term payoff of pleasing those who proposed the product. One way to deal with this dilemma is to prepare several analyses showing results under different assumptions and then let senior management make the decision.

Entrepreneur   You must first compute the level of sales required to achieve the desired net income. Then you must conduct sensitivity analysis by varying the price, sales mix, and cost estimates. Results from the sensitivity analysis provide information you can use to assess the possibility of reaching the target sales level. For instance, you might have to pursue aggressive marketing strategies to push the high-margin products, or you might have to cut prices to increase sales and profits, or another strategy might emerge.

Guidance Answers to Quick Checks

1. *b*

2. A fixed cost remains unchanged in total amount regardless of output levels. However, fixed *cost per unit* declines with increased output.

3. Such a cost is considered variable because the *total* cost changes in proportion to volume changes.

4. *b*

5. The high-low method ignores all costs and sales (activity base) volume data points except the costs corresponding to the high-est and lowest (most extreme) sales (activity base) volume.

6. *c*

7. *a*

8. ($90 − $54)/$90 = 40%

9. $90,000/40% = $225,000

10. A company's margin of safety is the excess of the predicted sales level over its break-even sales level.

11. Three basic CVP assumptions are that (1) selling price per unit is constant, (2) variable costs per unit are constant, and (3) total fixed costs are constant.

12. *a*; Two steps are required for explanation:
(1) Pretax income = $120,000/(1 − 0.20) = $150,000
(2) $\dfrac{\$50,000 + \$150,000}{25\%}$ = $800,000

13. If the contribution margin ratio decreases from 50% to 25%, unit sales would have to double.

14. *c*; Selling price of a composite unit:

2 units of X @ $5 per unit	$10
1 unit of Y @ $4 per unit	4
Selling price of a composite unit	$14

Variable costs of a composite unit:

2 units of X @ $2 per unit	$4
1 unit of Y @ $2 per unit	2
Variable costs of a composite unit	$6

Therefore, the contribution margin per composite unit is $8.

15. It must be assumed that the sales mix remains unchanged at all sales levels in the relevant range.

Key Terms

Absorption costing (p. 870)

Break-even point (p. 869)

Composite unit (p. 877)

Contribution margin per unit (p. 869)

Contribution margin ratio (p. 869)

Cost-volume-profit (CVP) analysis (p. 871)

Cost-volume-profit (CVP) chart (p. 862)

Curvilinear cost (p. 865)

Degree of operating leverage (DOL) (p. 879)

Estimated line of cost behavior (p. 866)

High-low method (p. 866)

Least-squares regression (p. 867)

Margin of safety (p. 870)

Mixed cost (p. 864)

Operating leverage (p. 879)

Relevant range of operations (p. 872)

Sales mix (p. 877)

Scatter diagram (p. 866)

Step-wise cost (p. 864)

Variable costing income statement (p. 870)

Weighted-average contribution margin (p. 877)

Additional Quiz Questions are available at the book's Website.

1. A company's only product sells for $150 per unit. Its variable costs per unit are $100, and its fixed costs total $75,000. What is its contribution margin per unit?
   a. $50
   b. $250
   c. $100
   d. $150
   e. $25

2. Using information from question 1, what is the company's contribution margin ratio?
   a. 66⅔%
   b. 100%
   c. 50%
   d. 0%
   e. 33⅓%

3. Using information from question 1, what is the company's break-even point in units?
   a. 500 units
   b. 750 units
   c. 1,500 units
   d. 3,000 units
   e. 1,000 units

4. A company's forecasted sales are $300,000 and its sales at break-even are $180,000. Its margin of safety in dollars is
   a. $180,000.
   b. $120,000.
   c. $480,000.
   d. $60,000.
   e. $300,000.

5. A product sells for $400 per unit and its variable costs per unit are $260. The company's fixed costs are $840,000. If the company desires $70,000 pretax income, what is the required dollar sales?
   a. $2,400,000
   b. $200,000
   c. $2,600,000
   d. $2,275,000
   e. $1,400,000

A Superscript letter A denotes assignments based on Appendix 21A
[I] Icon denotes assignments that involve decision making.

Discussion Questions

1. What is a variable cost? Identify two variable costs.
2. [I] When output volume increases, do variable costs per unit increase, decrease, or stay the same within the relevant range of activity? Explain.
3. [I] When output volume increases, do fixed costs per unit increase, decrease, or stay the same within the relevant range of activity? Explain.
4. [I] How is cost-volume-profit analysis useful?
5. How do step-wise costs and curvilinear costs differ?
6. Describe the contribution margin ratio in layperson's terms.
7. Define and explain the *contribution margin ratio*.
8. Define and describe *contribution margin* per unit.
9. In performing CVP analysis for a manufacturing company, what simplifying assumption is usually made about the volume of production and the volume of sales?
10. What two arguments tend to justify classifying all costs as either fixed or variable even though individual costs might not behave exactly as classified?
11. [I] How does assuming that operating activity occurs within a relevant range affect cost-volume-profit analysis?
12. List three methods to measure cost behavior.
13. How is a scatter diagram used to identify and measure the behavior of a company's costs?
14. In cost-volume-profit analysis, what is the estimated profit at the break-even point?

15. [I] Assume that a straight line on a CVP chart intersects the vertical axis at the level of fixed costs and has a positive slope that rises with each additional unit of volume by the amount of the variable costs per unit. What does this line represent?
16. **KTM** has both fixed and variable costs. Why are fixed costs depicted as a horizontal line on a CVP chart? **KTM**
17. [I] Each of two similar companies has sales of $20,000 and total costs of $15,000 for a month. Company A's total costs include $10,000 of variable costs and $5,000 of fixed costs. If Company B's total costs include $4,000 of variable costs and $11,000 of fixed costs, which company will enjoy more profit if sales double?
18. _____ of _____ reflects expected sales in excess of the level of break-even sales.
19. [I] **Arctic Cat** produces snowmobiles for sale. Identify some of the variable and fixed product costs associated with that production. **Arctic Cat**
   [*Hint:* Limit costs to product costs.]
20. [I] Should **Polaris** use single product or multi-product break-even analysis? Explain. **Polaris**
21. [I] **Piaggio** is thinking of expanding sales of its most popular scooter model by 65%. Should **PIAGGIO** we expect its variable and fixed costs for this model to stay within the relevant range? Explain.

connect

Listed here are four series of separate costs measured at various volume levels. Examine each series and identify whether it is best described as a fixed, variable, step-wise, or curvilinear cost. (It can help to graph the cost series.)

QUICK STUDY

QS 21-1
Cost behavior identification
C1

Volume (Units)	Series 1	Series 2	Series 3	Series 4
0	$ 0	$450	$ 800	$100
100	800	450	800	105
200	1,600	450	800	120
300	2,400	450	1,600	143
400	3,200	450	1,600	190
500	4,000	450	2,400	250
600	4,800	450	2,400	320

Determine whether each of the following is best described as a fixed, variable, or mixed cost with respect to product units.

1. Rubber used to manufacture athletic shoes.
2. Maintenance of factory machinery.
3. Packaging expense.
4. Wages of an assembly-line worker paid on the basis of acceptable units produced.
5. Factory supervisor's salary.
6. Taxes on factory building.
7. Depreciation expense of warehouse.

QS 21-2
Cost behavior identification
C1

The following information is available for a company's maintenance cost over the last seven months. Using the high-low method, estimate both the fixed and variable components of its maintenance cost.

QS 21-3
Cost behavior estimation—
high-low method
P1

Month	Maintenance Hours	Maintenance Cost
June............	9	$5,450
July.............	18	6,900
August..........	12	5,100
September........	15	6,000
October..........	21	6,900
November........	24	8,100
December........	6	3,600

This scatter diagram reflects past maintenance hours and their corresponding maintenance costs.

QS 21-4
Cost behavior estimation—
scatter diagram
P1

1. Draw an estimated line of cost behavior.
2. Estimate the fixed and variable components of maintenance costs.

Compute and interpret the contribution margin ratio using the following data: sales, $5,000; total variable cost, $3,000.

QS 21-5
Contribution margin ratio
A1

QS 21-6

Contribution margin per unit and break-even units   P2

SBD Phone Company sells its cordless phone for $90 per unit. Fixed costs total $162,000, and variable costs are $36 per unit. Determine the (1) contribution margin per unit and (2) break-even point in units.

QS 21-7

Assumptions in CVP analysis

C2

Refer to the information from QS 21-6. How will the break-even point in units change in response to each of the following independent changes in selling price per unit, variable cost per unit, or total fixed costs? Use I for increase and D for decrease. (It is not necessary to compute new break-even points.)

Change	Break-even in Units Will
1. Total fixed cost to $190,000	_____
2. Variable cost to $34 per unit	_____
3. Selling price per unit to $80	_____
4. Variable cost to $67 per unit	_____
5. Total fixed cost to $150,000	_____
6. Selling price per unit to $120	_____

QS 21-8

Contribution margin ratio and break-even dollars   P2

Refer to QS 21-6. Determine the (1) contribution margin ratio and (2) break-even point in dollars.

QS 21-9

CVP analysis and target income

P2

Refer to QS 21-6. Assume that SBD Phone Co. is subject to a 30% income tax rate. Compute the units of product that must be sold to earn after-tax income of $140,000. (Round to the nearest whole unit.)

QS 21-10

CVP assumptions

C2

Which one of the following is an assumption that underlies cost-volume-profit analysis?
1. The selling price per unit must change in proportion to the number of units sold.
2. All costs have approximately the same relevant range.
3. For costs classified as variable, the costs per unit of output must change constantly.
4. For costs classified as fixed, the costs per unit of output must remain constant.

QS 21-11

Operating leverage analysis   A2

A high proportion of Company A's total costs are variable with respect to units sold; a high proportion of Company B's total costs are fixed with respect to units sold. Which company is likely to have a higher degree of operating leverage (DOL)? Explain.

QS 21-12

Multiproduct break-even   P4

US-Mobile Company manufactures and sells two products, conventional phones and smart phones, in the ratio of 5:3. Fixed costs are $105,000, and the contribution margin per composite unit is $125. What number of both conventional and smart phones is sold at the break-even point?

QS 21-13

CVP graph   P3

Corme Company expects sales of $34 million (400,000 units). The company's total fixed costs are $17.5 million and its variable costs are $35 per unit. Prepare a CVP chart from this information.

QS 21-14

Contribution margin   A1

A recent income statement for **Volkswagen** reports the following (in € millions). Assume 75 percent of the cost of sales and 75 percent of the selling and administrative costs are variable costs, and the remaining 25 percent of each is fixed. Compute the contribution margin (in € millions). (Round computations using percentages to the nearest whole euro.)

Sales	€126,875
Cost of sales	105,431
Selling and administrative expenses	15,500

■ connect

A company reports the following information about its sales and its cost of sales. Each unit of its product sells for $500. Use these data to prepare a scatter diagram. Draw an estimated line of cost behavior and determine whether the cost appears to be variable, fixed, or mixed.

EXERCISES

Exercise 21-1
Measurement of cost behavior using a scatter diagram
P1

Period	Sales	Cost of Sales	Period	Sales	Cost of Sales
1	$22,500	$15,150	4	11,250	8,250
2	17,250	11,250	5	13,500	9,000
3	15,750	10,500	6	18,750	14,250

Following are five graphs representing various cost behaviors. (1) Identify whether the cost behavior in each graph is mixed, step-wise, fixed, variable, or curvilinear. (2) Identify the graph (by number) that best illustrates each cost behavior: (a) Factory policy requires one supervisor for every 30 factory workers; (b) real estate taxes on factory; (c) electricity charge that includes the standard monthly charge plus a charge for each kilowatt hour; (d) commissions to salespersons; and (e) costs of hourly paid workers that provide substantial gains in efficiency when a few workers are added but gradually smaller gains in efficiency when more workers are added.

Exercise 21-2
Cost behavior in graphs
C1

The left column lists several cost classifications. The right column presents short definitions of those costs. In the blank space beside each of the numbers in the right column, write the letter of the cost best described by the definition.

Exercise 21-3
Cost behavior defined
C1

A. Total cost

B. Mixed cost

C. Variable cost

D. Curvilinear cost

E. Step-wise cost

F. Fixed cost

_____ **1.** This cost is the combined amount of all the other costs.

_____ **2.** This cost remains constant over a limited range of volume; when it reaches the end of its limited range, it changes by a lump sum and remains at that level until it exceeds another limited range.

_____ **3.** This cost has a component that remains the same over all volume levels and another component that increases in direct proportion to increases in volume.

_____ **4.** This cost increases when volume increases, but the increase is not constant for each unit produced.

_____ **5.** This cost remains constant over all volume levels within the productive capacity for the planning period.

_____ **6.** This cost increases in direct proportion to increases in volume; its amount is constant for each unit produced.

Following are five series of costs A through E measured at various volume levels. Examine each series and identify which is fixed, variable, mixed, step-wise, or curvilinear.

Exercise 21-4
Cost behavior identification
C1

File Edit View Insert Format Tools Data Window Help

	Volume (Units)	Series A	Series B	Series C	Series D	Series E
1	0	$ 0	$2,500	$ 0	$1,000	$5,000
2	400	3,600	3,100	6,000	1,000	5,000
3	800	7,200	3,700	6,600	2,000	5,000
4	1,200	10,800	4,300	7,200	2,000	5,000
5	1,600	14,400	4,900	8,200	3,000	5,000
6	2,000	18,000	5,500	9,600	3,000	5,000
7	2,400	21,600	6,100	13,500	4,000	5,000

Sheet1 / Sheet2 / Sheet3 /

Exercise 21-5
Predicting sales and variable costs
using contribution margin   C2

Bloom Company management predicts that it will incur fixed costs of $160,000 and earn pretax income of $164,000 in the next period. Its expected contribution margin ratio is 25%. Use this information to compute the amounts of (1) total dollar sales and (2) total variable costs.

Exercise 21-6
Scatter diagram and
measurement of cost behavior

P1

Use the following information about sales and costs to prepare a scatter diagram. Draw a cost line that reflects the behavior displayed by this cost. Determine whether the cost is variable, step-wise, fixed, mixed, or curvilinear.

Period	Sales	Costs	Period	Sales	Costs
1.............	$760	$590	9.............	$580	$390
2.............	800	560	10.............	320	240
3.............	200	230	11.............	240	230
4.............	400	400	12.............	720	550
5.............	480	390	13.............	280	260
6.............	620	550	14.............	440	410
7.............	680	590	15.............	380	260
8.............	540	430			

Exercise 21-7
Cost behavior estimation—
scatter diagram and high-low

P1

Felix & Co. reports the following information about its sales and cost of sales. Draw an estimated line of cost behavior using a scatter diagram, and compute fixed costs and variable costs per unit sold. Then use the high-low method to estimate the fixed and variable components of the cost of sales.

Period	Units Sold	Cost of Sales	Period	Units Sold	Cost of Sales
1.............	0	$2,500	6.............	2,000	5,500
2.............	400	3,100	7.............	2,400	6,100
3.............	800	3,700	8.............	2,800	6,700
4.............	1,200	4,300	9.............	3,200	7,300
5.............	1,600	4,900	10.............	3,600	7,900

Exercise 21-8[A]
Measurement of cost behavior
using regression   P1

Refer to the information from Exercise 21-7. Use spreadsheet software to use ordinary least-squares regression to estimate the cost equation, including fixed and variable cost amounts.

Exercise 21-9
Contribution margin
A2

A jeans maker is designing a new line of jeans called the Slims. The jeans will sell for $205 per pair and cost $164 per pair in variable costs to make. (1) Compute the contribution margin per pair. (2) Compute the contribution margin ratio. (3) Describe what the contribution margin ratio reveals about this new jeans line.

Exercise 21-10
Contribution margin and
break-even   P2

Blanchard Company manufactures a single product that sells for $180 per unit and whose total variable costs are $135 per unit. The company's annual fixed costs are $562,500. (1) Use this information to compute the company's (a) contribution margin, (b) contribution margin ratio, (c) break-even point in units, and (d) break-even point in dollars of sales.

Exercise 21-11
CVP chart   P3

Refer to the information in Exercise 21-10. Prepare a CVP chart for the company.

Exercise 21-12
Income reporting and
break-even analysis   C2

Refer to Exercise 21-10. (1) Prepare a contribution margin income statement for Blanchard Company showing sales, variable costs, and fixed costs at the break-even point. (2) If the company's fixed costs increase by $135,000, what amount of sales (in dollars) is needed to break even? Explain.

Exercise 21-13
Computing sales to achieve
target income   C2

Blanchard Company management (in Exercise 21-10) targets an annual after-tax income of $810,000. The company is subject to a 20% income tax rate. Assume that fixed costs remain at $562,500. Compute the (1) unit sales to earn the target after-tax net income and (2) dollar sales to earn the target after-tax net income.

Blanchard Company's sales manager (in Exercise 21-10) predicts that annual sales of the company's product will soon reach 40,000 units and its price will increase to $200 per unit. According to the production manager, the variable costs are expected to increase to $140 per unit but fixed costs will remain at $562,500. The income tax rate is 20%. What amounts of pretax and after-tax income can the company expect to earn from these predicted changes? (*Hint:* Prepare a forecasted contribution margin income statement as in Exhibit 21.21.)

Exercise 21-14
Forecasted income statement
C2

Check Forecasted income, $1,470,000

Nombre Company management predicts $390,000 of variable costs, $430,000 of fixed costs, and a pretax income of $155,000 in the next period. Management also predicts that the contribution margin per unit will be $9. Use this information to compute the (1) total expected dollar sales for next period and (2) number of units expected to be sold next period.

Exercise 21-15
Predicting unit and dollar sales
C2

Cooper Company expects to sell 200,000 units of its product next year, which would generate total sales of $17 million. Management predicts that pretax net income for next year will be $1,250,000 and that the contribution margin per unit will be $25. Use this information to compute next year's total expected (a) variable costs and (b) fixed costs.

Exercise 21-16
Computation of variable and fixed costs
C2

Handy Home sells windows and doors in the ratio of 8:2 (windows:doors). The selling price of each window is $200 and of each door is $500. The variable cost of a window is $125 and of a door is $350. Fixed costs are $900,000. Use this information to determine the (1) selling price per composite unit, (2) variable costs per composite unit, (3) break-even point in composite units, and (4) number of units of each product that will be sold at the break-even point.

Exercise 21-17
CVP analysis using composite units P4

Check (3) 1,000 composite units

Refer to the information from Exercise 21-17. Use the information to determine the (1) weighted-average contribution margin, (2) break-even point in units, and (3) number of units of each product that will be sold at the break-even point.

Exercise 21-18
CVP analysis using weighted-average contribution margin
P4

R&R Tax Service offers tax and consulting services to individuals and small businesses. Data for fees and costs of three types of tax returns follow. R&R provides services in the ratio of 5:3:2 (easy, moderate, business). Fixed costs total $18,000 for the tax season. Use this information to determine the (1) selling price per composite unit, (2) variable costs per composite unit, (3) break-even point in composite units, and (4) number of units of each product that will be sold at the break-even point.

Exercise 21-19
CVP analysis using composite units
P4

Type of Return	Fee Charged	Variable Cost per Return
Easy (form 1040EZ)	$ 50	$ 30
Moderate (form 1040)	125	75
Business	275	100

Refer to the information from Exercise 21-19. Use the information to determine the (1) weighted-average contribution margin, (2) break-even point in units, and (3) number of units of each product that will be sold at the break-even point.

Exercise 21-20
CVP analysis using weighted-average contribution margin
P4

Company A is a manufacturer with current sales of $6,000,000 and a 60% contribution margin. Its fixed costs equal $2,600,000. Company B is a consulting firm with current service revenues of $4,500,000 and a 25% contribution margin. Its fixed costs equal $375,000. Compute the degree of operating leverage (DOL) for each company. Identify which company benefits more from a 20% increase in sales and explain why.

Exercise 21-21
Operating leverage computed and applied
A2

PROBLEM SET A

Problem 21-1A
Contribution margin income statement and contribution margin ratio

A1

The following costs result from the production and sale of 1,000 drum sets manufactured by Tom Thompson Company for the year ended December 31, 2013. The drum sets sell for $500 each. The company has a 25% income tax rate.

Variable production costs	
Plastic for casing	$ 17,000
Wages of assembly workers	82,000
Drum stands	26,000
Variable selling costs	
Sales commissions	15,000
Fixed manufacturing costs	
Taxes on factory	5,000
Factory maintenance	10,000
Factory machinery depreciation	40,000
Fixed selling and administrative costs	
Lease of equipment for sales staff	10,000
Accounting staff salaries	35,000
Administrative management salaries	125,000

Required

Check (1) Net income, $101,250

1. Prepare a contribution margin income statement for the company.

2. Compute its contribution margin per unit and its contribution margin ratio.

Analysis Component

3. Interpret the contribution margin and contribution margin ratio from part 2.

Problem 21-2A
CVP analysis and charting

P2 P3

mhhe.com/wildFAP21e

Check (1) Break-even sales, 4,500 units

Xcite Equipment Co. manufactures and markets a number of rope products. Management is considering the future of Product XT, a special rope for hang gliding, that has not been as profitable as planned. Since Product XT is manufactured and marketed independently of the other products, its total costs can be precisely measured. Next year's plans call for a $200 selling price per 100 yards of XT rope. Its fixed costs for the year are expected to be $270,000, up to a maximum capacity of 700,000 yards of rope. Forecasted variable costs are $140 per 100 yards of XT rope.

Required

1. Estimate Product XT's break-even point in terms of (a) sales units and (b) sales dollars.

2. Prepare a CVP chart for Product XT like that in Exhibit 21.15. Use 7,000 units (700,000 yards/100 yards) as the maximum number of sales units on the horizontal axis of the graph, and $1,400,000 as the maximum dollar amount on the vertical axis.

3. Prepare a contribution margin income statement showing sales, variable costs, and fixed costs for Product XT at the break-even point.

Problem 21-3A
Scatter diagram and cost behavior estimation

P1

Alden Co.'s monthly sales and cost data for its operating activities of the past year follow. Management wants to use these data to predict future fixed and variable costs.

Month	Sales	Total Cost	Month	Sales	Total Cost
1	$320,000	$160,000	7	$340,000	$220,000
2	160,000	100,000	8	280,000	160,000
3	280,000	220,000	9	80,000	64,000
4	200,000	100,000	10	160,000	140,000
5	300,000	230,000	11	100,000	100,000
6	200,000	120,000	12	110,000	80,000

Required

1. Prepare a scatter diagram for these data with sales volume (in $) plotted on the horizontal axis and total cost plotted on the vertical axis.

2. Estimate both the variable costs per sales dollar and the total monthly fixed costs using the high-low method. Draw the total costs line on the scatter diagram in part 1.

3. Use the estimated line of cost behavior and results from part 2 to predict future total costs when sales volume is (a) $200,000 and (b) $300,000.

Check (2) Variable costs, $0.60 per sales dollar; fixed costs, $16,000

Astro Co. sold 20,000 units of its only product and incurred a $50,000 loss (ignoring taxes) for the current year as shown here. During a planning session for year 2014's activities, the production manager notes that variable costs can be reduced 50% by installing a machine that automates several operations. To obtain these savings, the company must increase its annual fixed costs by $200,000. The maximum output capacity of the company is 40,000 units per year.

Problem 21-4A
Break-even analysis; income targeting and forecasting
C2 P2 A1

ASTRO COMPANY Contribution Margin Income Statement For Year Ended December 31, 2013	
Sales	$1,000,000
Variable costs	800,000
Contribution margin	200,000
Fixed costs	250,000
Net loss	$ (50,000)

Required

1. Compute the break-even point in dollar sales for year 2013.

2. Compute the predicted break-even point in dollar sales for year 2014 assuming the machine is installed and there is no change in the unit sales price.

3. Prepare a forecasted contribution margin income statement for 2014 that shows the expected results with the machine installed. Assume that the unit sales price and the number of units sold will not change, and no income taxes will be due.

Check (3) Net income, $150,000

4. Compute the sales level required in both dollars and units to earn $140,000 of after-tax income in 2014 with the machine installed and no change in the unit sales price. Assume that the income tax rate is 30%. (*Hint:* Use the procedures in Exhibits 21.22 and 21.23.) (Round answers to whole dollars or units.)

(4) Required sales, $1,083,333 or 21,667 units

5. Prepare a forecasted contribution margin income statement that shows the results at the sales level computed in part 4. Assume an income tax rate of 30%.

Vanna Co. produces and sells two products, T and O. It manufactures these products in separate factories and markets them through different channels. They have no shared costs. This year, the company sold 50,000 units of each product. Sales and costs for each product follow.

Problem 21-5A
Break-even analysis, different cost structures, and income calculations
C2 A1 P4

	Product T	Product O
Sales	$2,000,000	$2,000,000
Variable costs	1,600,000	250,000
Contribution margin	400,000	1,750,000
Fixed costs	125,000	1,475,000
Income before taxes	275,000	275,000
Income taxes (32% rate)	88,000	88,000
Net income	$ 187,000	$ 187,000

Required

1. Compute the break-even point in dollar sales for each product. (Round the answer to whole dollars.)

2. Assume that the company expects sales of each product to decline to 30,000 units next year with no change in unit sales price. Prepare forecasted financial results for next year following the format of the contribution margin income statement as just shown with columns for each of the two products (assume a 32% tax rate). Also, assume that any loss before taxes yields a 32% tax savings.

3. Assume that the company expects sales of each product to increase to 60,000 units next year with no change in unit sales price. Prepare forecasted financial results for next year following the format of the contribution margin income statement shown with columns for each of the two products (assume a 32% tax rate).

Analysis Component

4. If sales greatly decrease, which product would experience a greater loss? Explain.

5. Describe some factors that might have created the different cost structures for these two products.

Problem 21-6A

Analysis of price, cost, and volume changes for contribution margin and net income

P2   A1

mhhe.com/wildFAP21e

This year Bertrand Company sold 40,000 units of its only product for $25 per unit. Manufacturing and selling the product required $200,000 of fixed manufacturing costs and $325,000 of fixed selling and administrative costs. Its per unit variable costs follow.

Material	$8.00
Direct labor (paid on the basis of completed units)..........	5.00
Variable overhead costs	1.00
Variable selling and administrative costs	0.50

Next year the company will use new material, which will reduce material costs by 50% and direct labor costs by 60% and will not affect product quality or marketability. Management is considering an increase in the unit sales price to reduce the number of units sold because the factory's output is nearing its annual output capacity of 45,000 units. Two plans are being considered. Under plan 1, the company will keep the price at the current level and sell the same volume as last year. This plan will increase income because of the reduced costs from using the new material. Under plan 2, the company will increase price by 20%. This plan will decrease unit sales volume by 10%. Under both plans 1 and 2, the total fixed costs and the variable costs per unit for overhead and for selling and administrative costs will remain the same.

Required

1. Compute the break-even point in dollar sales for both (a) plan 1 and (b) plan 2.

2. Prepare a forecasted contribution margin income statement with two columns showing the expected results of plan 1 and plan 2. The statements should report sales, total variable costs, contribution margin, total fixed costs, income before taxes, income taxes (30% rate), and net income.

Problem 21-7A

Break-even analysis with composite units

P4

Patriot Co. manufactures and sells three products: red, white, and blue. Their unit sales prices are red, $20; white, $35; and blue, $65. The per unit variable costs to manufacture and sell these products are red, $12; white, $22; and blue, $50. Their sales mix is reflected in a ratio of 5:4:2 (red:white:blue). Annual fixed costs shared by all three products are $250,000. One type of raw material has been used to manufacture all three products. The company has developed a new material of equal quality for less cost. The new material would reduce variable costs per unit as follows: red, by $6; white, by $12; and blue, by $10. However, the new material requires new equipment, which will increase annual fixed costs by $50,000. (Round answers to whole composite units.)

Required

1. If the company continues to use the old material, determine its break-even point in both sales units and sales dollars of each individual product.

2. If the company uses the new material, determine its new break-even point in both sales units and sales dollars of each individual product.

Analysis Component

3. What insight does this analysis offer management for long-term planning?

The following costs result from the production and sale of 12,000 CD sets manufactured by Gilmore Company for the year ended December 31, 2013. The CD sets sell for $18 each. The company has a 25% income tax rate.

Variable manufacturing costs	
Plastic for CD sets	$ 1,500
Wages of assembly workers	30,000
Labeling	3,000
Variable selling costs	
Sales commissions	6,000
Fixed manufacturing costs	
Rent on factory	6,750
Factory cleaning service	4,520
Factory machinery depreciation	20,000
Fixed selling and administrative costs	
Lease of office equipment	1,050
Systems staff salaries	15,000
Administrative management salaries	120,000

Required

1. Prepare a contribution margin income statement for the company.
2. Compute its contribution margin per unit and its contribution margin ratio.

Analysis Component

3. Interpret the contribution margin and contribution margin ratio from part 2.

PROBLEM SET B

Problem 21-1B
Contribution margin income statement and contribution margin ratio

A1

Check (1) Net income, $6,135

Hip-Hop Co. manufactures and markets several products. Management is considering the future of one product, electronic keyboards, that has not been as profitable as planned. Since this product is manufactured and marketed independently of the other products, its total costs can be precisely measured. Next year's plans call for a $350 selling price per unit. The fixed costs for the year are expected to be $42,000, up to a maximum capacity of 700 units. Forecasted variable costs are $210 per unit.

Required

1. Estimate the keyboards' break-even point in terms of (a) sales units and (b) sales dollars.
2. Prepare a CVP chart for keyboards like that in Exhibit 21.15. Use 700 keyboards as the maximum number of sales units on the horizontal axis of the graph, and $250,000 as the maximum dollar amount on the vertical axis.
3. Prepare a contribution margin income statement showing sales, variable costs, and fixed costs for keyboards at the break-even point.

Problem 21-2B
CVP analysis and charting

P2 P3

Check (1) Break-even sales, 300 units

Kyo Co.'s monthly sales and costs data for its operating activities of the past year follow. Management wants to use these data to predict future fixed and variable costs. (Dollar amounts are in thousands.)

Month	Sales	Total Cost	Month	Sales	Total Cost
1	$195	$ 97	7	$145	$ 93
2	125	87	8	185	105
3	105	73	9	135	85
4	155	89	10	85	58
5	95	81	11	175	95
6	215	110	12	115	79

Problem 21-3B
Scatter diagram and cost behavior estimation

P1

Required

1. Prepare a scatter diagram for these data with sales volume (in $) plotted on the horizontal axis and total costs plotted on the vertical axis.

2. Estimate both the variable costs per sales dollar and the total monthly fixed costs using the high-low method. Draw the total costs line on the scatter diagram in part 1.

3. Use the estimated line of cost behavior and results from part 2 to predict future total costs when sales volume is (a) $100 and (b) $170.

Problem 21-4B
Break-even analysis; income targeting and forecasting

C2 P2 A1

Rivera Co. sold 20,000 units of its only product and incurred a $50,000 loss (ignoring taxes) for the current year as shown here. During a planning session for year 2014's activities, the production manager notes that variable costs can be reduced 50% by installing a machine that automates several operations. To obtain these savings, the company must increase its annual fixed costs by $150,000. The maximum output capacity of the company is 40,000 units per year.

RIVERA COMPANY	
Contribution Margin Income Statement	
For Year Ended December 31, 2013	
Sales	$750,000
Variable costs..............	600,000
Contribution margin	150,000
Fixed costs................	200,000
Net loss	$ (50,000)

Required

1. Compute the break-even point in dollar sales for year 2013.

2. Compute the predicted break-even point in dollar sales for year 2014 assuming the machine is installed and no change occurs in the unit sales price. (Round the change in variable costs to a whole number.)

3. Prepare a forecasted contribution margin income statement for 2014 that shows the expected results with the machine installed. Assume that the unit sales price and the number of units sold will not change, and no income taxes will be due.

4. Compute the sales level required in both dollars and units to earn $140,000 of after-tax income in 2014 with the machine installed and no change in the unit sales price. Assume that the income tax rate is 30%. (*Hint:* Use the procedures in Exhibits 21.22 and 21.23.) (Round sales in dollars to whole dollars and round sales in units to the next whole unit.)

5. Prepare a forecasted contribution margin income statement that shows the results at the sales level computed in part 4. Assume an income tax rate of 30%.

Problem 21-5B
Break-even analysis, different cost structures, and income calculations

C2 P4 A1

Mingei Co. produces and sells two products, BB and TT. It manufactures these products in separate factories and markets them through different channels. They have no shared costs. This year, the company sold 50,000 units of each product. Sales and costs for each product follow.

	Product BB	Product TT
Sales	$800,000	$800,000
Variable costs.................	560,000	100,000
Contribution margin	240,000	700,000
Fixed costs....................	100,000	560,000
Income before taxes	140,000	140,000
Income taxes (32% rate)	44,800	44,800
Net income	$ 95,200	$ 95,200

Required

1. Compute the break-even point in dollar sales for each product. (Round the answer to the next whole dollar.)

2. Assume that the company expects sales of each product to decline to 33,000 units next year with no change in the unit sales price. Prepare forecasted financial results for next year following the format of the contribution margin income statement as shown here with columns for each of the two products (assume a 32% tax rate, and that any loss before taxes yields a 32% tax savings).

3. Assume that the company expects sales of each product to increase to 64,000 units next year with no change in the unit sales prices. Prepare forecasted financial results for next year following the format of the contribution margin income statement as shown here with columns for each of the two products (assume a 32% tax rate).

Analysis Component

4. If sales greatly increase, which product would experience a greater increase in profit? Explain.

5. Describe some factors that might have created the different cost structures for these two products.

This year Best Company earned a disappointing 5.6% after-tax return on sales (net income/sales) from marketing 100,000 units of its only product. The company buys its product in bulk and repackages it for resale at the price of $20 per unit. Best incurred the following costs this year.

Total variable unit costs.............	$800,000
Total variable packaging costs	$100,000
Fixed costs......................	$950,000
Income tax rate	25%

The marketing manager claims that next year's results will be the same as this year's unless some changes are made. The manager predicts the company can increase the number of units sold by 80% if it reduces the selling price by 20% and upgrades the packaging. This change would increase variable packaging costs by 20%. Increased sales would allow the company to take advantage of a 25% quantity purchase discount on the cost of the bulk product. Neither the packaging change nor the volume discount would affect fixed costs, which provide an annual output capacity of 200,000 units.

Required

1. Compute the break-even point in dollar sales under the (a) existing business strategy and (b) new strategy that alters both unit sales price and variable costs. (Round answers to the next whole dollar.)

2. Prepare a forecasted contribution margin income statement with two columns showing the expected results of (a) the existing strategy and (b) changing to the new strategy. The statements should report sales, total variable costs (unit and packaging), contribution margin, fixed costs, income before taxes, income taxes, and net income. Also determine the after-tax return on sales for these two strategies.

Problem 21-6B
Analysis of price, cost, and volume changes for contribution margin and net income

A1 P2

Check (1) Break-even sales for new strategy, $1,727,273

(2) Net income: Existing strategy, $112,500; new strategy, $475,500

Milano Co. manufactures and sells three products: product 1, product 2, and product 3. Their unit sales prices are product 1, $40; product 2, $30; and product 3, $20. The per unit variable costs to manufacture and sell these products are product 1, $30; product 2, $15; and product 3, $8. Their sales mix is reflected in a ratio of 6:4:2. Annual fixed costs shared by all three products are $270,000. One type of raw material has been used to manufacture products 1 and 2. The company has developed a new material of equal quality for less cost. The new material would reduce variable costs per unit as follows: product 1 by $10, and product 2, by $5. However, the new material requires new equipment, which will increase annual fixed costs by $50,000.

Required

1. If the company continues to use the old material, determine its break-even point in both sales units and sales dollars of each individual product.

2. If the company uses the new material, determine its new break-even point in both sales units and sales dollars of each individual product.

Analysis Component

3. What insight does this analysis offer management for long-term planning?

Problem 21-7B
Break-even analysis with composite units

P4

Check (1) Old plan break-even, 1,875 composite units (rounded)

(2) New plan break-even, 1,429 composite units (rounded)

(This serial problem began in Chapter 1 and continues through most of the book. If previous chapter segments were not completed, the serial problem can begin at this point. It is helpful, but not necessary, to use the working papers that accompany the book.)

SP 21 Success Systems sells upscale modular desk units and office chairs in the ratio of 3:2 (desk unit:chair). The selling prices are $1,250 per desk unit and $500 per chair. The variable costs are $750 per desk unit and $250 per chair. Fixed costs are $120,000.

Required

1. Compute the selling price per composite unit.

2. Compute the variable costs per composite unit.

3. Compute the break-even point in composite units.

4. Compute the number of units of each product that would be sold at the break-even point.

SERIAL PROBLEM
Success Systems

P4

Check (3) 60 composite units

Beyond the Numbers

REPORTING IN ACTION

C1

Polaris

BTN 21-1   **Polaris** offers extended service contracts that provide repair and maintenance coverage over its products. As you complete the following requirements, assume that the Polaris services department uses many of Polaris' existing resources such as its facilities, repair machinery, and computer systems.

Required

1. Identify several of the variable, mixed, and fixed costs that the Polaris services department is likely to incur in carrying out its services.
2. Assume that Polaris's services revenues are expected to grow by 25% in the next year. How would we expect the costs identified in part 1 to change, if at all?
3. Based on the answer to part 2, can Polaris use the contribution margin ratio to predict how income will change in response to increases in Polaris's services revenues?

COMPARATIVE ANALYSIS

P2 A2

Polaris

Arctic Cat

BTN 21-2   Both **Polaris** and **Arctic Cat** sell motorized vehicles, and each of these companies has a different product mix.

Required

1. Assume the following data are available for both companies. Compute each company's break-even point in unit sales. (Each company sells many motorized vehicles at many different selling prices, and each has its own variable costs. This assignment assumes an *average* selling price per unit and an *average* cost per item.)

	Polaris	Arctic Cat
Average selling price per item sold	$10,500	$11,200
Average variable cost per item sold	$4,200	$5,100
Total fixed costs ($ in thousands)	$146,570	$133,570

2. If unit sales were to decline, which company would experience the larger decline in operating profit? Explain.

ETHICS CHALLENGE

C1

BTN 21-3   Labor costs of an auto repair mechanic are seldom based on actual hours worked. Instead, the amount paid a mechanic is based on an industry average of time estimated to complete a repair job. The repair shop bills the customer for the industry average amount of time at the repair center's billable cost per hour. This means a customer can pay, for example, $120 for two hours of work on a car when the actual time worked was only one hour. Many experienced mechanics can complete repair jobs faster than the industry average. The average data are compiled by engineering studies and surveys conducted in the auto repair business. Assume that you are asked to complete such a survey for a repair center. The survey calls for objective input, and many questions require detailed cost data and analysis. The mechanics and owners know you have the survey and encourage you to complete it in a way that increases the average billable hours for repair work.

Required

Write a one-page memorandum to the mechanics and owners that describes the direct labor analysis you will undertake in completing this survey.

COMMUNICATING IN PRACTICE

C2

BTN 21-4   Several important assumptions underlie CVP analysis. Assumptions often help simplify and focus our analysis of sales and costs. A common application of CVP analysis is as a tool to forecast sales, costs, and income.

Required

Assume that you are actively searching for a job. Prepare a one-half page report identifying (1) three assumptions relating to your expected revenue (salary) and (2) three assumptions relating to your expected costs for the first year of your new job. Be prepared to discuss your assumptions in class.

BTN 21-5 Access and review the entrepreneurial information at **Business Owner's Toolkit** [**Toolkit.com**]. Access and review its *New Business Cash Needs Checklist* under the Start Up menu bar or similar worksheets related to controls of cash and costs.

TAKING IT TO THE NET

C1

Required

Write a one-half page report that describes the information and resources available at the Business Owner's Toolkit to help the owner of a start-up business to control and monitor its cash flows and costs.

BTN 21-6 A local movie theater owner explains to you that ticket sales on weekends and evenings are strong, but attendance during the weekdays, Monday through Thursday, is poor. The owner proposes to offer a contract to the local grade school to show educational materials at the theater for a set charge per student during school hours. The owner asks your help to prepare a CVP analysis listing the cost and sales projections for the proposal. The owner must propose to the school's administration a charge per child. At a minimum, the charge per child needs to be sufficient for the theater to break even.

TEAMWORK IN ACTION

C2

Required

Your team is to prepare two separate lists of questions that enable you to complete a reliable CVP analysis of this situation. One list is to be answered by the school's administration, the other by the owner of the movie theater.

BTN 21-7 **Leather Head Sports**, launched by entrepreneur Paul Cunningham, produces balls for various sports. Selling prices typically range from $40 per ball to $295 per ball.

ENTREPRENEURIAL DECISION

C1 A1

Required

1. Identify at least two fixed costs that will not change regardless of how many footballs Leather Head Sports produces.
2. How could overly optimistic sales estimates potentially hurt Paul Cunningham's business?
3. Explain how cost-volume-profit analysis can help Paul Cunningham manage Leather Head Sports.

BTN 21-8 Multiproduct break-even analysis is often viewed differently when actually applied in practice. You are to visit a local fast-food restaurant and count the number of items on the menu. To apply multiproduct break-even analysis to the restaurant, similar menu items must often be fit into groups. A reasonable approach is to classify menu items into approximately five groups. We then estimate average selling price and average variable cost to compute average contribution margin. (*Hint:* For fast-food restaurants, the highest contribution margin is with its beverages, at about 90%.)

HITTING THE ROAD

P4

Required

1. Prepare a one-year multiproduct break-even analysis for the restaurant you visit. Begin by establishing groups. Next, estimate each group's volume and contribution margin. These estimates are necessary to compute each group's contribution margin. Assume that annual fixed costs in total are $500,000 per year. (*Hint:* You must develop your own estimates on volume and contribution margin for each group to obtain the break-even point and sales.)
2. Prepare a one-page report on the results of your analysis. Comment on the volume of sales necessary to break even at a fast-food restaurant.

BTN 21-9 Access and review **Piaggio**'s Website (**www.piaggio.com**) to answer the following questions.

GLOBAL DECISION

P4

Required

1. Do you believe that Piaggio's managers use single product CVP analysis or multiproduct break-even analysis? Explain.
2. How does the addition of a new product line affect Piaggio's CVP analysis?

PIAGGIO

ANSWERS TO MULTIPLE CHOICE QUIZ

1. a; $150 − $100 = $50
2. e; ($150 − $100)/$150 = 33⅓%
3. c; $75,000/$50 CM per unit = 1,500 units
4. b; $300,000 − $180,000 = $120,000
5. c; Contribution margin ratio = ($400 − $260)/$400 = 0.35
   Targeted sales = ($840,000 + $70,000)/0.35 = $2,600,000

Master Budgets and Planning

22

◀ A Look Back

Chapter 21 looked at cost behavior and its use by managers in performing cost-volume-profit analysis. It also illustrated the application of cost-volume-profit analysis.

▼ A Look at This Chapter

This chapter explains the importance of budgeting and describes the master budget and its preparation. It also discusses the value of the master budget to the planning of future business activities.

▶ A Look Ahead

Chapter 23 focuses on flexible budgets, standard costs, and variance reporting. It explains the usefulness of these procedures and reports for business decisions.

Learning Objectives

CONCEPTUAL

C1 Describe the importance and benefits of budgeting and the process of budget administration. (p. 900)

C2 Describe a master budget and the process of preparing it. (p. 904)

ANALYTICAL

A1 Analyze expense planning using activity-based budgeting. (p. 914)

PROCEDURAL

P1 Prepare each component of a master budget and link each to the budgeting process. (p. 906)

P2 Link both operating and capital expenditures budgets to budgeted financial statements. (p. 910)

P3 *Appendix 22A*—Prepare production and manufacturing budgets. (p. 920)

Decision Insight

Fresh Profits

"Talk is cheap . . . execution sets you apart."
—MATTHEW CORRIN

CHICAGO, IL—Matthew Corrin was tired of eating typical lunch fare. Stuck in a greasy deli, Matthew realized "the service and food was lackluster. I needed an alternative." The then 22-year-old budding entrepreneur set off to build a restaurant based on fresh, healthy foods served in an environmentally sustaining environment. Today, Matthew's company, **Freshii (Freshii.com),** has over 60 stores across several countries.

Matthew admits he was "totally naïve. Restaurants are one of the hardest businesses. A thousand things have to go right every day." Unfortunately, many things did go wrong at the beginning. "The first day we ran out of food at lunch. We ordered more but ran out again on the second day," recalls Matt. Making accurate sales forecasts is one of the most important, but most difficult, parts of preparing business budgets. Sales forecasts are especially challenging for new businesses. Through hard work and help from his girlfriend (now wife), Matthew's business broke sales records every day for its first six months. "Those first days were a turning point for me. I realized if I could get through that, I could survive anything" says Matthew.

Matthew learned his business by doing "whatever needed to be done." "This isn't rocket science," he says, "just hard work." In addition to learning the nuances of the restaurant business, Matthew had to learn budgeting and cost concepts. As Matthew explains, the perishability of food items is a key variable. Food

costs can vary due to weather, supply disruptions, and other factors. Matthew updates his budgets frequently to factor in changing costs and customer tastes.

Matthew advises young entrepreneurs to "go for it." "Some might say starting a restaurant with no previous food or retail experience wasn't the smartest move. But, isn't that the entrepreneurial spirit, to just jump in and figure it out on the fly?" As his company continues to grow, the budgeting process and master budgets become even more important. Budgets help formalize plans and goals, and help direct and monitor employees. Matthew also uses budgeted income statements to determine how changes in the cost of food, labor, and overhead will impact his bottom line.

While linking budgeted data to budgeted financial statements and using that information to control costs is important, Matthew stresses "you have to execute every day and generate a buzz." From humble beginnings, Freshii has over 400 new locations in development, forecasted sales of $50 million, and, in Matthew's words, "a vision to be the Starbucks of the fresh food business." Bold and fresh.

[Sources: *Freshii Website,* January 2013; *Inc.com,* March 16, 2011, and June 27, 2011; *Canada Restaurant News,* January 31, 2011; *Under30ceo. com,* October 25, 2010.]

Management seeks to turn its strategies into action plans. These action plans include financial details that are compiled in a master budget. The budgeting process serves several purposes, including motivating employees and communicating with them. The budget process also helps coordinate a company's activities toward common goals and is useful in evaluating results and management performance. This chapter explains how to prepare a master budget and use it as a formal plan of a company's future activities. The ability to prepare this type of plan is of enormous help in starting and operating a company. Such planning gives managers a glimpse into the future, and it can help translate ideas into actions.

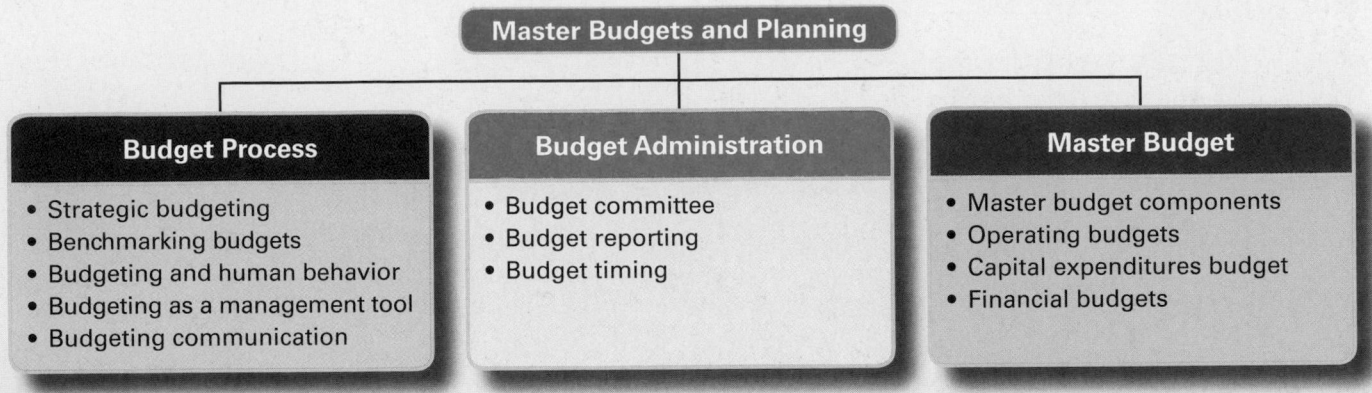

Master Budgets and Planning

Budget Process	Budget Administration	Master Budget
• Strategic budgeting • Benchmarking budgets • Budgeting and human behavior • Budgeting as a management tool • Budgeting communication	• Budget committee • Budget reporting • Budget timing	• Master budget components • Operating budgets • Capital expenditures budget • Financial budgets

BUDGET PROCESS

Strategic Budgeting

C1 Describe the importance and benefits of budgeting and the process of budget administration.

Most companies prepare long-term strategic plans spanning 5 to 10 years. They then fine-tune them in preparing medium-term and short-term plans. Strategic plans usually set a company's long-term direction. They provide a road map for the future about potential opportunities such as new products, markets, and investments. The strategic plan can be inexact, given its long-term focus. Medium- and short-term plans are more operational and translate strategic plans into actions. These action plans are fairly concrete and consist of defined objectives and goals.

Short-term financial plans are called *budgets* and typically cover a one-year period. A **budget** is a formal statement of a company's future plans. It is usually expressed in monetary terms because the economic or financial aspects of the business are the primary factors driving management's decisions. All managers should be involved in **budgeting,** the process of planning future business actions and expressing them as formal plans. Managers who plan carefully and formalize plans in a budgeting process increase the likelihood of both personal and company success. (Although most firms prepare annual budgets, it is not unusual for organizations to prepare three-year and five-year budgets that are revised at least annually.)

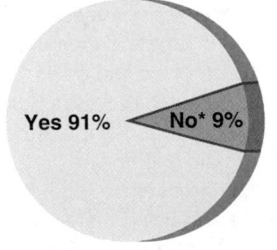

Companies Performing Annual Budgeting

Yes 91%   No* 9%

*Most of the 9% have eliminated annual budgeting in favor of rolling or continual budgeting.

The relevant focus of a budgetary analysis is the future. Management must focus on future transactions and events and the opportunities available. A focus on the future is important because the pressures of daily operating problems often divert management's attention and take precedence over planning. A good budgeting system counteracts this tendency by formalizing the planning process and demanding relevant input. Budgeting makes planning an explicit management responsibility.

Benchmarking Budgets

The control function requires management to evaluate (benchmark) business operations against some norm. Evaluation involves comparing actual results against one of two usual alternatives: (1) past performance or (2) expected performance.

An evaluation assists management in identifying problems and taking corrective actions if necessary. Evaluation using expected, or budgeted, performance is potentially superior to using past performance to decide whether actual results trigger a need for corrective actions. This is so because past performance fails to consider several changes that can affect current and future activities. Changes in economic conditions, shifts in competitive advantages within the industry, new product developments, increased or decreased advertising, and other factors reduce the usefulness of comparisons with past results. In hi-tech industries, for instance, increasing competition, technological advances, and other innovations often reduce the usefulness of performance comparisons across years.

Budgeted performance is computed after careful analysis and research that attempts to anticipate and adjust for changes in important company, industry, and economic factors. Therefore, budgets usually provide management an effective control and monitoring system.

Budgeting and Human Behavior

Budgeting provides standards for evaluating performance and can affect the attitudes of employees evaluated by them. It can be used to create a positive effect on employees' attitudes, but it can also create negative effects if not properly applied. Budgeted levels of performance, for instance, must be realistic to avoid discouraging employees. Personnel who will be evaluated should be consulted and involved in preparing the budget to increase their commitment to meeting it. Performance evaluations must allow the affected employees to explain the reasons for apparent performance deficiencies.

The budgeting process has three important guidelines: (1) Employees affected by a budget should be consulted when it is prepared (*participatory budgeting*), (2) goals reflected in a budget should be attainable, and (3) evaluations should be made carefully with opportunities to explain any failures. Budgeting can be a positive motivating force when these guidelines are followed. Budgeted performance levels can provide goals for employees to attain or even exceed as they carry out their responsibilities. This is especially important in organizations that consider the annual budget a "sacred" document.

Managers must also be aware of potential negative outcomes of budgeting. Under participatory budgeting, some employees might understate sales budgets and overstate expense budgets to allow them a cushion, or *budgetary slack*, to aid in meeting targets. For some businesses, pressure to meet budgeted results might lead employees to engage in unethical behavior or commit fraud. Finally, some employees might always spend their budgeted amounts, even on unnecessary items, to ensure their budgets aren't reduced for the next period.

Point: The practice of involving employees in the budgeting process is known as *participatory budgeting*.

Example: Assume a company's sales force receives a bonus when sales exceed the budgeted amount. How would this arrangement affect the participatory sales forecasts? *Answer:* Sales reps may understate their budgeted sales.

■ Decision Ethics

Budget Staffer   Your company's earnings for the current period will be far below the budgeted amount reported in the press. One of your superiors, who is aware of the upcoming earnings shortfall, has accepted a management position with a competitor. This superior is selling her shares of the company. What are your ethical concerns, if any? ■   [Answer—p. 922]

Budgeting as a Management Tool

An important management objective in large companies is to ensure that activities of all departments contribute to meeting the company's overall goals. This requires coordination. Budgeting helps to achieve this coordination.

We describe later in this chapter that a company's budget, or operating plan, is based on its objectives. This operating plan starts with the sales budget, which drives all other budgets including production, materials, labor, and overhead. The budgeting process coordinates the activities of these various departments to meet the company's overall goals.

Budgeting Communication

Managers of small companies can adequately explain business plans directly to employees through conversations and other informal communications. However, conversations can create uncertainty and confusion if not supported by clear documentation of the plans. A written budget is preferred and can inform employees in all types of organizations about management's plans. The budget can also communicate management's specific action plans for the employees in the budget period.

 Decision Insight

Budgets Exposed When companies go public and their securities trade on an organized stock exchange, management usually develops specific future plans and budgets. For this purpose, companies often develop detailed six- to twelve-month budgets and less-detailed budgets spanning two to five years. ■

BUDGET ADMINISTRATION

Budget Committee

The task of preparing a budget should not be the sole responsibility of any one department. Similarly, the budget should not be simply handed down as top management's final word. Instead, budget figures and budget estimates developed through a *bottom-up* process

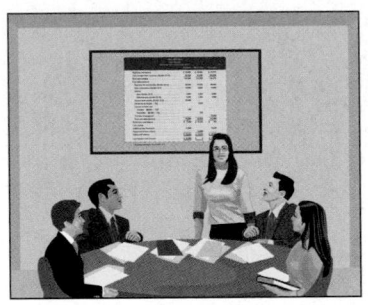

usually are more useful. This includes, for instance, involving the sales department in preparing sales estimates. Likewise, the production department should have initial responsibility for preparing its own expense budget. Without active employee involvement in preparing budget figures, there is a risk these employees will feel that the numbers fail to reflect their special problems and needs.

Most budgets should be developed by a bottom-up process, but the budgeting system requires central guidance. This guidance is supplied by a budget committee of department heads and other executives responsible for seeing that budgeted amounts are realistic and coordinated. If a de-

Point: In a large company, developing a budget through a bottom-up process can involve hundreds of employees and take several weeks to finalize.

partment submits initial budget figures not reflecting efficient performance, the budget committee should return them with explanatory comments on how to improve them. Then the originating department must either adjust its proposals or explain why they are acceptable. Communication between the originating department and the budget committee should continue as needed to ensure that both parties accept the budget as reasonable, attainable, and desirable.

The concept of continuous improvement applies to budgeting as well as production. For example, one of the world's largest energy companies streamlined its monthly budget report from a one-inch-thick stack of monthly control reports to a tidy, two-page flash report on monthly earnings and key production statistics. The key to this efficiency gain was the integration of new budgeting and cost allocation processes with its strategic planning process. Its controller explained the new role of the finance department with respect to the budgetary control process as follows: "there's less of an attitude that finance's job is to control. People really have come to see that our job is to help attain business objectives."

Budget Reporting

The budget period usually coincides with the accounting period. Most companies prepare at least an annual budget, which reflects the objectives for the next year. To provide specific guidance, the annual budget usually is separated into quarterly or monthly budgets. These short-term budgets allow management to periodically evaluate performance and take needed corrective action.

Managers can compare actual results to budgeted amounts in a report such as that shown in Exhibit 22.1. This report shows actual amounts, budgeted amounts, and their differences. A difference is called a *variance*. Management examines variances, particularly large ones, to identify areas for improvement and corrective action.

EXHIBIT 22.1

Comparing Actual Performance with Budgeted Performance

ECCENTRIC MUSIC Income Statement with Variances from Budget For Month Ended April 30, 2013	Actual	Budget	Variance
Net sales	$60,500	$57,150	$+3,350
Cost of goods sold	41,350	39,100	+2,250
Gross profit	19,150	18,050	+1,100
Operating expenses			
Selling expenses			
Sales salaries	6,250	6,000	+250
Advertising	900	800	+100
Store supplies	550	500	+50
Depreciation—Store equipment	1,600	1,600	
Total selling expenses	9,300	8,900	+400
General and administrative expenses			
Office salaries	2,000	2,000	
Office supplies used	165	150	+15
Rent	1,100	1,100	
Insurance	200	200	
Depreciation—Office equipment	100	100	
Total general and administrative expenses	3,565	3,550	+15
Total operating expenses	12,865	12,450	+415
Net income	$ 6,285	$ 5,600	$ +685

Example: Assume that you must explain variances to top management. Which variances in Exhibit 22.1 would you research and why? *Answer:* Sales and cost of goods sold—due to their large variances.

Budget Timing

The time period required for the annual budgeting process can vary considerably. For example, budgeting for 2014 can begin as early as January 2013 or as late as December 2013. Large, complex organizations usually require a longer time to prepare their budgets than do smaller organizations. This is so because considerable effort is required to coordinate the different units (departments) within large organizations.

Many companies apply **continuous budgeting** by preparing **rolling budgets.** As each monthly or quarterly budget period goes by, these companies revise their entire set of budgets for the months or quarters remaining and add new monthly or quarterly budgets to replace the ones that have lapsed. At any point in time, monthly or quarterly budgets are available for the next 12 months or four quarters. Exhibit 22.2 shows rolling budgets prepared at the end of five consecutive

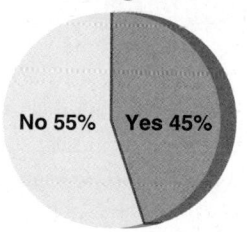

Companies Using Rolling Budgets

No 55%   Yes 45%

EXHIBIT 22.2

Rolling Budgets

periods. The first set (at top) is prepared in December 2012 and covers the four calendar quarters of 2013. In March 2013, the company prepares another rolling budget for the next four quarters through March 2014. This same process is repeated every three months. As a result, management is continuously planning ahead.

Exhibit 22.2 reflects an annual budget composed of four quarters prepared four times per year using the most recent information available. For example, the budget for the fourth quarter of 2013 is prepared in December 2012 and revised in March, June, and September of 2013. When continuous budgeting is not used, the fourth-quarter budget is nine months old and perhaps out of date when applied.

Decision Insight

Budget Calendar   Many companies use long-range operating budgets. For large companies, three groups usually determine or influence the budgets: creditors, directors, and management. All three are interested in the companies' future cash flows and earnings. The annual budget process often begins six months or more before the budget is due to the board of directors. A typical budget calendar, shown here, provides insight into the budget process during a typical calendar year. ■

Quick Check

Answers — p. 922

1. What are the major benefits of budgeting?
2. What is the main responsibility of the budget committee?
3. What is the usual time period covered by a budget?
4. What are rolling budgets?

MASTER BUDGET

C2 Describe a master budget and the process of preparing it.

A **master budget** is a formal, comprehensive plan for a company's future. It contains several individual budgets that are linked with each other to form a coordinated plan.

Master Budget Components

The master budget typically includes individual budgets for sales, purchases, production, various expenses, capital expenditures, and cash. Managers often express the expected financial results of these planned activities with both a budgeted income statement for the budget period and a budgeted balance sheet for the end of the budget period. The usual number and types of budgets included in a master budget depend on the company's size and complexity. A master budget should include, at a minimum, the budgets listed in Exhibit 22.3. In addition to these individual budgets, managers often include supporting calculations and additional tables with the master budget.

Some budgets require the input of other budgets. For example, the merchandise purchases budget cannot be prepared until the sales budget has been prepared because the number of units

Operating budgets
- *Sales budget*
- For merchandisers add: *Merchandise purchases budget* (units to be purchased)
- For manufacturers add: *Production budget* (units to be produced)
  Manufacturing budget (manufacturing costs)
- *Selling expense budget*
- *General and administrative expense budget*

Capital expenditures budget (expenditures for plant assets)

Financial budgets
- *Cash budget* (cash receipts and disbursements)
- *Budgeted income statement*
- *Budgeted balance sheet*

to be purchased depends on how many units are expected to be sold. As a result, we often must sequentially prepare budgets within the master budget.

A typical sequence for a master budget consists of the five steps in Exhibit 22.4. Any stage in this budgeting process might reveal undesirable outcomes, so changes often must be made to prior budgets by repeating the previous steps. For instance, an early version of the cash budget could show an insufficient amount of cash unless cash outlays are reduced. This could yield a reduction in planned equipment purchases. A preliminary budgeted balance sheet could also reveal too much debt from an ambitious capital expenditures budget. Findings such as these often result in revised plans and budgets.

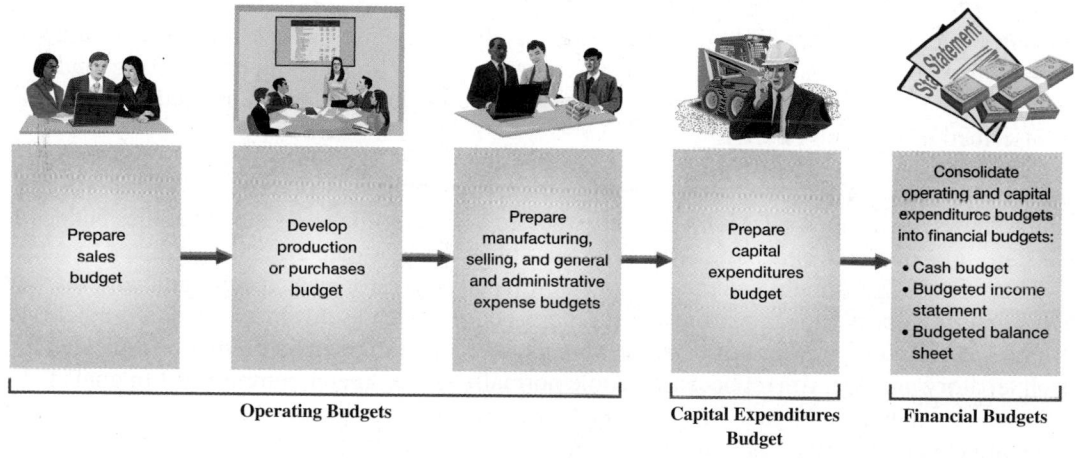

EXHIBIT 22.4

Master Budget Sequence

Prepare sales budget → Develop production or purchases budget → Prepare manufacturing, selling, and general and administrative expense budgets → Prepare capital expenditures budget → Consolidate operating and capital expenditures budgets into financial budgets: • Cash budget • Budgeted income statement • Budgeted balance sheet

Operating Budgets   **Capital Expenditures Budget**   **Financial Budgets**

The remainder of this section explains how Hockey Den (HD), a retailer of youth hockey sticks, prepares its master budget. Its master budget includes operating, capital expenditures, and cash budgets for each month in each quarter. It also includes a budgeted income statement for each quarter and a budgeted balance sheet as of the last day of each quarter. We show how HD prepares budgets for October, November, and December 2013. Exhibit 22.5 presents HD's balance sheet at the start of this budgeting period, which we often refer to as we prepare the component budgets.

 Decision Insight

Incentive Pay   Budgets are important in determining managers' pay. A recent survey shows that 82% of large companies tie managers' bonus payments to beating budget goals. For these companies, bonus payments are frequently more than 20% of total manager pay. ■

EXHIBIT 22.5

Balance Sheet Prior to the
Budgeting Periods

HOCKEY DEN
Balance Sheet
September 30, 2013

Assets

Cash		$ 20,000
Accounts receivable		42,000
Inventory (900 units @ $60)		54,000
Equipment*	$200,000	
Less accumulated depreciation	36,000	164,000
Total assets		$280,000

Liabilities and Equity

Liabilities		
Accounts payable	$ 58,200	
Income taxes payable (due 10/31/2013)	20,000	
Note payable to bank	10,000	$ 88,200
Stockholders' equity		
Common stock	150,000	
Retained earnings	41,800	191,800
Total liabilities and equity		$280,000

* Equipment is depreciated on a straight-line basis over 10 years (salvage value is $20,000).

Operating Budgets

P1 Prepare each component of a master budget and link each to the budgeting process.

This section explains HD's preparation of operating budgets. Its operating budgets consist of the sales budget, merchandise purchases budget, selling expense budget, and general and administrative expense budget. HD does not prepare production and manufacturing budgets because it is a merchandiser. (The preparation of production budgets and manufacturing budgets is described in Appendix 22A.)

Sales Budget   The first step in preparing the master budget is planning the **sales budget,** which shows the planned sales units and the expected dollars from these sales. The sales budget is the starting point in the budgeting process because plans for most departments are linked to sales.

The sales budget should emerge from a careful analysis of forecasted economic and market conditions, business capacity, proposed selling expenses (such as advertising), and predictions of unit sales. A company's sales personnel are usually asked to develop predictions of sales for each territory and department because people normally feel a greater commitment to goals they help set. Another advantage to this participatory budgeting approach is that it draws on knowledge and experience of people involved in the activity.

To illustrate, in September 2013, HD sold 700 hockey sticks at $100 per unit. After considering sales predictions and market conditions, HD prepares its sales budget for the next quarter (three months) plus one extra month (see Exhibit 22.6). The sales budget includes

EXHIBIT 22.6

Sales Budget for Planned Unit and Dollar Sales

HOCKEY DEN
Monthly Sales Budget
October 2013–January 2014

	Budgeted Unit Sales	Budgeted Unit Price	Budgeted Total Sales
September 2013 (actual)	700	$100	$ 70,000
October 2013	1,000	$100	$100,000
November 2013	800	100	80,000
December 2013	1,400	100	140,000
Totals for the quarter	3,200	100	$320,000
January 2014	900	100	$ 90,000

January 2014 because the purchasing department relies on estimated January sales to decide on December 2013 inventory purchases. The sales budget in Exhibit 22.6 includes forecasts of both unit sales and unit prices. Some sales budgets are expressed only in total sales dollars, but most are more detailed. Management finds it useful to know budgeted units and unit prices for many different products, regions, departments, and sales representatives.

■ Decision Maker

Entrepreneur You run a start-up that manufactures designer clothes. Business is seasonal, and fashions and designs quickly change. How do you prepare reliable annual sales budgets? ■   (Answer—p. 922)

Merchandise Purchases Budget   Companies use various methods to help managers make inventory purchasing decisions. These methods recognize that the number of units added to inventory depends on budgeted sales volume. Whether a company manufactures or purchases the product it sells, budgeted future sales volume is the primary factor in most inventory management decisions. A company must also consider its inventory system and other factors that we discuss next.

Just-in-time inventory systems.   Managers of *just-in-time* (JIT) inventory systems use sales budgets for short periods (often as few as one or two days) to order just enough merchandise or materials to satisfy the immediate sales demand. This keeps the amount of inventory to a minimum (or zero in an ideal situation). A JIT system minimizes the costs of maintaining inventory, but it is practical only if customers are content to order in advance or if managers can accurately determine short-term sales demand. Suppliers also must be able and willing to ship small quantities regularly and promptly.

Point: Accurate estimates of future sales are crucial in a JIT system.

Safety stock inventory systems.   Market conditions and manufacturing processes for some products do not allow use of a just-in-time system. Companies in these cases maintain sufficient inventory to reduce the risk and cost of running short. This practice requires enough purchases to satisfy the budgeted sales amounts and to maintain a **safety stock,** a quantity of inventory that provides protection against lost sales caused by unfulfilled demands from customers or delays in shipments from suppliers.

Merchandise purchases budget preparation.   A merchandiser usually expresses a **merchandise purchases budget** in both units and dollars. Exhibit 22.7 shows the general layout for this budget in equation form. If this formula is expressed in units and only one product is involved, we can compute the number of dollars of inventory to be purchased for the budget by multiplying the units to be purchased by the cost per unit.

Inventory to be purchased	=	Budgeted ending inventory	+	Budgeted cost of sales for the period	−	Budgeted beginning inventory

EXHIBIT 22.7

General Formula for a Merchandise Purchases Budget

To illustrate, after assessing the cost of keeping inventory along with the risk and cost of inventory shortages, HD decided that the number of units in its inventory at each month-end should equal 90% of next month's predicted sales. For example, inventory at the end of October should equal 90% of budgeted November sales, and the November ending inventory should equal 90% of budgeted December sales, and so on. Also, HD's suppliers expect the September 2013 per unit cost of $60 to remain unchanged through January 2014. This information along with knowledge of 900 units in inventory at September 30 (see Exhibit 22.5) allows the company to prepare the merchandise purchases budget shown in Exhibit 22.8.

The first three lines of HD's merchandise purchases budget determine the required ending inventories (in units). Budgeted unit sales are then added to the desired ending inventory to give the required units of available merchandise. We then subtract beginning inventory to

Example: Assume Hockey Den adopts a JIT system in purchasing merchandise. How will its sales budget differ from its merchandise purchases budget? *Answer:* The two budgets will be similar because future inventory should be near zero.

EXHIBIT 22.8

Merchandise Purchases Budget

HOCKEY DEN Merchandise Purchases Budget October 2013–December 2013			
	October	November	December
Next month's budgeted sales (units)	800	1,400	900
Ratio of inventory to future sales	× 90%	× 90%	× 90%
Budgeted ending inventory (units)	720	1,260	810
Add budgeted sales (units)	1,000	800	1,400
Required units of available merchandise	1,720	2,060	2,210
Deduct beginning inventory (units)	900	720	1,260
Units to be purchased	820	1,340	950
Budgeted cost per unit	$ 60	$ 60	$ 60
Budgeted cost of merchandise purchases	$49,200	$80,400	$57,000

Example: If ending inventory in Exhibit 22.8 is required to equal 80% of next month's predicted sales, how many units must be purchased each month? *Answer:* Budgeted ending inventory: Oct. = 640 units; Nov. = 1,120 units; Dec. = 720 units. Required purchases: Oct. = 740 units; Nov. = 1,280 units; Dec. = 1,000 units.

determine the budgeted number of units to be purchased. The last line is the budgeted cost of the purchases, computed by multiplying the number of units to be purchased by the predicted cost per unit.

We already indicated that some budgeting systems describe only the total dollars of budgeted sales. Likewise, a system can express a merchandise purchases budget only in terms of the total cost of merchandise to be purchased, omitting the number of units to be purchased. This method assumes a constant relation between sales and cost of goods sold. HD, for instance, might assume the expected cost of goods sold to be 60% of sales, computed from the budgeted unit cost of $60 and the budgeted sales price of $100. However, it still must consider the effects of changes in beginning and ending inventories in determining the amounts to be purchased.

Selling Expense Budget   The **selling expense budget** is a plan listing the types and amounts of selling expenses expected during the budget period. Its initial responsibility usually rests with the vice president of marketing or an equivalent sales manager. The selling expense budget is normally created to provide sufficient selling expenses to meet sales goals reflected in the sales budget. Predicted selling expenses are based on both the sales budget and the experience of previous periods. After some or all of the master budget is prepared, management might decide that projected sales volume is inadequate. If so, subsequent adjustments in the sales budget can require corresponding adjustments in the selling expense budget.

To illustrate, HD's selling expense budget is in Exhibit 22.9. The firm's selling expenses consist of commissions paid to sales personnel and a $2,000 monthly salary paid to the sales manager. Sales commissions equal 10% of total sales and are paid in the month sales occur. Sales commissions are variable with respect to sales volume, but the sales manager's salary is fixed. No advertising expenses are budgeted for this particular quarter.

EXHIBIT 22.9

Selling Expense Budget

HOCKEY DEN Selling Expense Budget October 2013–December 2013				
	October	November	December	Totals
Budgeted sales	$100,000	$80,000	$140,000	$320,000
Sales commission percent	× 10%	× 10%	× 10%	× 10%
Sales commissions	10,000	8,000	14,000	32,000
Salary for sales manager	2,000	2,000	2,000	6,000
Total selling expenses	$ 12,000	$10,000	$ 16,000	$ 38,000

Example: If sales commissions in Exhibit 22.9 are increased, which budgets are affected? *Answer:* Selling expenses budget, cash budget, and budgeted income statement.

General and Administrative Expense Budget   The **general and administrative expense budget** plans the predicted operating expenses not included in the selling expenses budget. General and administrative expenses can be either variable or fixed with respect to sales volume. The office manager responsible for general administration often is responsible for preparing the initial general and administrative expense budget.

Exhibit 22.10 shows HD's general and administrative expense budget. It includes salaries of $54,000 per year, or $4,500 per month (paid each month when they are earned). Using information in Exhibit 22.5, the depreciation on equipment is computed as $18,000 per year [($200,000 − $20,000)/10 years], or $1,500 per month ($18,000/12 months).

HOCKEY DEN General and Administrative Expense Budget October 2013–December 2013				
	October	November	December	Totals
Administrative salaries	$4,500	$4,500	$4,500	$13,500
Depreciation of equipment	1,500	1,500	1,500	4,500
Total general and administrative expenses	$6,000	$6,000	$6,000	$18,000

EXHIBIT 22.10

General and Administrative Expense Budget

Interest expense and income tax expense are often classified as general and administrative expenses in published income statements but normally cannot be planned at this stage of the budgeting process. The prediction of interest expense follows the preparation of the cash budget and the decisions regarding debt. The predicted income tax expense depends on the budgeted amount of pretax income. Both interest and income taxes are usually beyond the control of the office manager. As a result, they are not used in comparison to the budget to evaluate that person's performance.

Example: In Exhibit 22.10, how would a rental agreement of $5,000 per month plus 1% of sales affect the general and administrative expense budget? (Budgeted sales are in Exhibit 22.6.) *Answer: Rent expense:* Oct. = $6,000; Nov. = $5,800; Dec. = $6,400; Total = $18,200; *Revised total general and administrative expenses:* Oct. = $12,000; Nov. = $11,800; Dec. = $12,400; Total = $36,200.

Decision Insight

No Biz Like Snow Biz   Ski resorts' costs of making snow are in the millions of dollars for equipment alone. Snowmaking involves spraying droplets of water into the air, causing them to freeze and come down as snow. Making snow can cost more than $2,000 an hour. Snowmaking accounts for 40 to 50 percent of the operating budgets for many ski resorts. ■

Quick Check   Answers — p. 922

5. What is a master budget?

6. A master budget (*a*) always includes a manufacturing budget specifying the units to be produced; (*b*) is prepared with a process starting with the operating budgets and continues with the capital expenditures budget and then financial budgets; or (*c*) is prepared with a process ending with the sales budget.

7. What are the three primary categories of budgets in the master budget?

8. In preparing monthly budgets for the third quarter, a company budgeted sales of 120 units for July and 140 units for August. Management wants each month's ending inventory to be 60% of next month's sales. The June 30 inventory consists of 50 units. How many units of product for July acquisition should the merchandise purchases budget specify for the third quarter? (*a*) 84, (*b*) 120, (*c*) 154, or (*d*) 204.

9. How do the operating budgets for merchandisers and manufacturers differ?

10. How does a just-in-time inventory system differ from a safety stock system?

Capital Expenditures Budget

The **capital expenditures budget** lists dollar amounts to be both received from plant asset disposals and spent to purchase additional plant assets to carry out the budgeted business activities. It is usually prepared after the operating budgets. Since a company's plant assets determine its productive capacity, this budget is usually affected by long-range plans for the business. Yet the process of preparing a sales or purchases budget can reveal that the company requires more (or less) capacity, which implies more (or less) plant assets.

Capital budgeting is the process of evaluating and planning for capital (plant asset) expenditures. This is an important management task because these expenditures often involve long-run commitments of large amounts, affect predicted cash flows, and impact future debt and equity financing. This means that the capital expenditures budget is often linked with management's evaluation of the company's ability to take on more debt. We describe capital budgeting in Chapter 25.

Hockey Den does not anticipate disposal of any plant assets through December 2013, but it does plan to acquire additional equipment for $25,000 cash near the end of December 2013. This is the only budgeted capital expenditure from October 2013 through January 2014. Thus, no separate budget is shown. Hockey Den's cash budget will reflect this $25,000 planned expenditure.

Financial Budgets

After preparing its operating and capital expenditures budgets, a company uses information from these budgets to prepare at least three financial budgets: the cash budget, budgeted income statement, and budgeted balance sheet.

P2 Link both operating and capital expenditures budgets to budgeted financial statements.

Cash Budget After developing budgets for sales, merchandise purchases, expenses, and capital expenditures, the next step is to prepare the **cash budget,** which shows expected cash inflows and outflows during the budget period. It is especially important to maintain a cash balance necessary to meet ongoing obligations. By preparing a cash budget, management can prearrange loans to cover anticipated cash shortages before they are needed. A cash budget also helps management avoid a cash balance that is too large. Too much cash is undesirable because it earns a relatively low (if any) return. Exhibit 22.11 shows the general formula for the cash budget.

EXHIBIT 22.11

General Formula for
Cash Budget

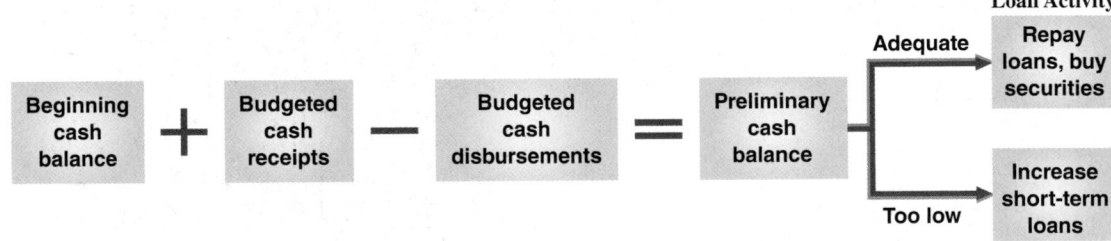

When preparing a cash budget, we add expected cash receipts to the beginning cash balance and deduct expected cash disbursements. If the expected (preliminary) ending cash balance is too low, additional cash requirements appear in the budget as planned increases from short-term loans. If the expected ending cash balance exceeds the desired balance, the excess is used to repay loans or to acquire short-term investments. Information for preparing the cash budget is mainly taken from the operating and capital expenditures budgets.

Cash Receipts from Sales To illustrate, Exhibit 22.12 presents HD's budgeted cash receipts.

EXHIBIT 22.12

Computing Budgeted Cash
Receipts

	September	October	November	December
Sales	$70,000	$100,000	$80,000	$140,000
Less ending accounts receivable (60%)	42,000	60,000	48,000	84,000
Cash receipts from				
Cash sales (40% of sales)		40,000	32,000	56,000
Collections of prior month's receivables		42,000	60,000	48,000
Total cash receipts		$ 82,000	$92,000	$104,000

We begin with reference to HD's budgeted sales (Exhibit 22.6). Analysis of past sales indicates that 40% of the firm's sales are for cash. The remaining 60% are credit sales; these customers are expected to pay in full in the month following the sales. We now can compute the budgeted cash receipts from customers as shown in Exhibit 22.12. October's budgeted cash receipts consist of $40,000 from expected cash sales ($100,000 × 40%) plus the anticipated collection of $42,000 of accounts receivable from the end of September.

Cash Disbursements for Merchandise   Next, we see that HD's merchandise purchases are entirely on account. It makes full payment during the month following its purchases. Therefore, cash disbursements for purchases can be computed from the September 30, 2013, balance sheet (Exhibit 22.5), for October disbursements, and the merchandise purchases budget (Exhibit 22.8), for November and December disbursements. This is shown in Exhibit 22.13.

	October	November	December
Purchases (from Exhibit 22.8)	$49,200	$80,400	$57,000
Cash disbursements for			
Current month purchases (0%)	0	0	0
Prior month purchases (100%)	58,200*	49,200	80,400
Total cash disbursements for purchases	$58,200	$49,200	$80,400

EXHIBIT 22.13

Computing Cash Disbursements for Purchases

*From September 30 balance sheet (Exhibit 22.5)

The schedule above can be modified for alternative payment timing. For example, if Hockey Den paid for 20% of its purchases in the month of purchase, and paid the remaining 80% of a month's purchases in the following month, its cash disbursements in December would equal $75,720, computed as (20% × $57,000) plus (80% × $80,400).

Exhibit 22.14 shows the full cash budget for Hockey Den, beginning with information on budgeted cash receipts from Exhibit 22.13 and budgeted cash purchases for merchandise from Exhibit 22.13. Next we discuss HD's other cash disbursements and loan activity on its cash budget.

EXHIBIT 22.14

Cash Budget

HOCKEY DEN Cash Budget October 2013–December 2013	October	November	December
Beginning cash balance	$ 20,000	$ 20,000	$ 22,272
Cash receipts from customers (Exhibit 22.12)	82,000	92,000	104,000
Total cash available	102,000	112,000	126,272
Cash disbursements			
Payments for merchandise (Exhibit 22.13)	58,200	49,200	80,400
Sales commissions (Exhibit 22.9)	10,000	8,000	14,000
Salaries			
Sales (Exhibit 22.9)	2,000	2,000	2,000
Administrative (Exhibit 22.10)	4,500	4,500	4,500
Income taxes payable (Exhibit 22.5)	20,000		
Dividends ($150,000 × 2%)			3,000
Interest on bank loan			
October ($10,000 × 1%)*	100		
November ($22,800 × 1%)		228	
Purchase of equipment			25,000
Total cash disbursements	94,800	66,928	125,900
Preliminary cash balance	$ 7,200	$ 45,072	$ 372
Loan activity			
Additional loan from bank	12,800		19,628
Repayment of loan to bank		22,800	
Ending cash balance	$ 20,000	$ 22,272	$ 20,000
Loan balance, end of month	$ 22,800	$ 0	$ 19,628

* Beginning loan balance from Exhibit 22.5

Example: If the minimum ending cash balance in Exhibit 22.14 is changed to $25,000 for each month, what is the projected loan balance at Dec. 31, 2013?
Answer:

Loan balance, Oct. 31	$27,800
November interest	278
November payment	25,022
Loan balance, Nov. 30	2,778
December interest	28
Additional loan in Dec.	21,928
Loan balance, Dec. 31	$24,706

The monthly budgeted cash disbursements for sales commissions and salaries are taken from the selling expense budget (Exhibit 22.9) and the general and administrative expense budget (Exhibit 22.10). The cash budget is unaffected by depreciation as reported in the general and administrative expenses budget.

Cash Disbursements for Other Items   Income taxes are due and payable in October as shown in the September 30, 2013, balance sheet (Exhibit 22.5). The cash budget in Exhibit 22.14 shows this $20,000 expected payment in October. Predicted income tax expense for the quarter ending December 31 is 40% of net income and is due in January 2014. It is therefore not reported in the October–December 2013 cash budget but in the budgeted income statement as income tax expense and on the budgeted balance sheet as income tax liability.

Hockey Den also pays a cash dividend equal to 2% of the par value of common stock in the second month of each quarter. The cash budget in Exhibit 22.14 shows a November payment of $3,000 for this purpose (2% of $150,000; see Exhibit 22.5).

Loan Activity   Analyzing Hockey Den's loan activity is necessary in computing its budgeted cash disbursements for interest. Hockey Den has an agreement with its bank that promises additional loans at each month-end, if necessary, to keep a minimum cash balance of $20,000. If the cash balance exceeds $20,000 at a month-end, HD uses the excess to repay loans. Interest is paid at each month-end at the rate of 1% of the beginning balance of these loans. For October, this payment is 1% of the $10,000 amount reported in the balance sheet of Exhibit 22.5. For November, HD expects to pay interest of $228, computed as 1% of the $22,800 expected loan balance at October 31. No interest is budgeted for December because the company expects to repay the loans in full at the end of November. Exhibit 22.14 shows that the October 31 cash balance declines to $7,200 (before any loan-related activity). This amount is less than the $20,000 minimum. Hockey Den will bring this balance up to the minimum by borrowing $12,800 with a short-term note. At the end of November, the budget shows an expected cash balance of $45,072 before any loan activity. This means that HD expects to repay $22,800 of debt. The equipment purchase budgeted for December reduces the expected cash balance to $372, far below the $20,000 minimum. The company expects to borrow $19,628 in that month to reach the minimum desired ending balance.

■ **Decision** Insight ●━━━━━━━━━━━━━━━━━━━━━━

Cash Cushion   Why do some companies maintain a minimum cash balance when the budget shows extra cash is not needed? For example, iPhone sales have pushed Apple's cash and investments balance to over $97 billion. For Apple's CEO Tim Cook the cushion provides "flexibility and security," important in navigating uncertain economic times. ■

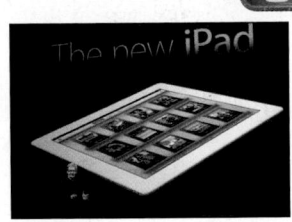

Budgeted Income Statement   One of the final steps in preparing the master budget is to summarize the income effects. The **budgeted income statement** is a managerial accounting report showing predicted amounts of sales and expenses for the budget period. Information needed for preparing a budgeted income statement is primarily taken from already prepared budgets. The volume of information summarized in the budgeted income statement is so large for some companies that they often use spreadsheets to accumulate the budgeted transactions and classify them by their effects on income. We condense HD's budgeted income statement and show it in Exhibit 22.15. All information in this exhibit is taken from earlier budgets. Also, we now can predict the amount of income tax expense for the quarter, computed as 40% of the budgeted pretax income. This amount is included in the cash budget and/or the budgeted balance sheet as necessary.

Budgeted Balance Sheet   The final step in preparing the master budget is summarizing the company's financial position. The **budgeted balance sheet** shows predicted amounts for the

Point: Lenders often require potential borrowers to provide cash budgets, budgeted income statements, and budgeted balance sheets, as well as data on past performance.

EXHIBIT 22.15

Budgeted Income Statement

HOCKEY DEN
Budgeted Income Statement
For Three Months Ended December 31, 2013

Sales (Exhibit 22.6, 3,200 units @ $100)		$320,000
Cost of goods sold (3,200 units @ $60)		192,000
Gross profit		128,000
Operating expenses		
Sales commissions (Exhibit 22.9)	$32,000	
Sales salaries (Exhibit 22.9)	6,000	
Administrative salaries (Exhibit 22.10)	13,500	
Depreciation on equipment (Exhibit 22.10)	4,500	
Interest expense (Exhibit 22.14)	328	56,328
Income before income taxes		71,672
Income tax expense ($71,672 × 40%)		28,669
Net income		$ 43,003

company's assets, liabilities, and equity as of the end of the budget period. HD's budgeted balance sheet in Exhibit 22.16 is prepared using information from the other budgets. The sources of amounts are reported in the notes to the budgeted balance sheet.[1]

EXHIBIT 22.16

Budgeted Balance Sheet

HOCKEY DEN
Budgeted Balance Sheet
December 31, 2013

Assets

Cash[a]		$ 20,000
Accounts receivable[b]		84,000
Inventory[c]		48,600
Equipment[d]	$225,000	
Less accumulated depreciation[e]	40,500	184,500
Total assets		$337,100

Liabilities and Equity

Liabilities		
Accounts payable[f]	$ 57,000	
Income taxes payable[g]	28,669	
Bank loan payable[h]	19,628	$105,297
Stockholders' equity		
Common stock[i]	150,000	
Retained earnings[j]	81,803	231,803
Total liabilities and equity		$337,100

[a] Ending balance for December from the cash budget in Exhibit 22.14.

[b] 60% of $140,000 sales budgeted for December from the sales budget in Exhibit 22.6.

[c] 810 units in budgeted December ending inventory at the budgeted cost of $60 per unit (from the purchases budget in Exhibit 22.8).

[d] September 30 balance of $200,000 from the beginning balance sheet in Exhibit 22.5 plus $25,000 cost of new equipment from the cash budget in Exhibit 22.14.

[e] September 30 balance of $36,000 from the beginning balance sheet in Exhibit 22.5 plus $4,500 expense from the general and administrative expense budget in Exhibit 22.10.

[f] Budgeted cost of purchases for December from the purchases budget in Exhibit 22.8.

[g] Income tax expense from the budgeted income statement for the fourth quarter in Exhibit 22.15.

[h] Budgeted December 31 balance from the cash budget in Exhibit 22.14.

[i] Unchanged from the beginning balance sheet in Exhibit 22.5.

[j] September 30 balance of $41,800 from the beginning balance sheet in Exhibit 22.5 plus budgeted net income of $43,003 from the budgeted income statement in Exhibit 22.15 minus budgeted cash dividends of $3,000 from the cash budget in Exhibit 22.14.

---

[1] An eight-column spreadsheet, or work sheet, can be used to prepare a budgeted balance sheet (and income statement). The first two columns show the ending balance sheet amounts from the period prior to the budget period. The budgeted transactions and adjustments are entered in the third and fourth columns in the same manner as adjustments are entered on an ordinary work sheet. After all budgeted transactions and adjustments have been entered, the amounts in the first two columns are combined with the budget amounts in the third and fourth columns and sorted to the proper Income Statement (fifth and sixth columns) and Balance Sheet columns (seventh and eighth columns). Amounts in these columns are used to prepare the budgeted income statement and balance sheet.

Decision Insight

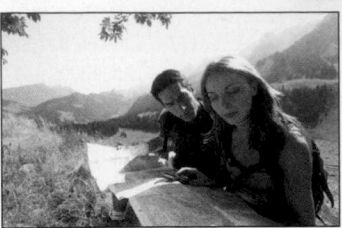

Strategic Planning   Most companies allocate dollars based on budgets submitted by department managers. These managers verify the numbers and monitor the budget. Managers must remember, however, that a budget is judged by its success in helping achieve the company's mission. One analogy is that a hiker must know the route to properly plan a hike and monitor hiking progress. ■

Quick Check

Answers — p. 922

11. In preparing a budgeted balance sheet, (*a*) plant assets are determined by analyzing the capital expenditures budget and the balance sheet from the beginning of the budget period, (*b*) liabilities are determined by analyzing the general and administrative expense budget, or (*c*) retained earnings are determined from information contained in the cash budget and the balance sheet from the beginning of the budget period.

12. What sequence is followed in preparing the budgets that constitute the master budget?

GLOBAL VIEW

Royal Phillips Electronics of the Netherlands is a diversified company. Preparing budgets and evaluating progress helps the company achieve its goals. In a recent annual report the company reports that it budgets sales to grow at a faster pace than overall economic growth. Based on this sales target, company managers prepare detailed operating, capital expenditure, and financial budgets.

Budgeted and actual results of companies that do global business are impacted by changes in foreign currency exchange rates. While most of Royal Phillips' cash disbursements are in euros, the company's sales are in euros, U.S. dollars, Chinese yuan, Brazilian real, and other currencies. Forecasting future exchange rates and their impact on sales budgets is difficult. In addition, global economic and political uncertainties add to budgeting challenges.

Decision Analysis   Activity-Based Budgeting

A1	Analyze expense planning using activity-based budgeting.

Activity-based budgeting (ABB) is a budget system based on expected activities. Knowledge of expected activities and their levels for the budget period enables management to plan for resources required to perform the activities. To illustrate, we consider the budget of a company's accounting department. Traditional budgeting systems list items such as salaries, supplies, equipment, and utilities. Such an itemized budget informs management of the use of the funds budgeted (for example, salaries), but management cannot assess the basis for increases or decreases in budgeted amounts as compared to prior periods. Accordingly, management often makes across-the-board cuts or increases. In contrast, ABB requires management to list activities performed by, say, the accounting department such as auditing, tax reporting, financial reporting, and cost accounting. Exhibit 22.17 contrasts a traditional budget with an activity-based

EXHIBIT 22.17

Activity-Based Budgeting versus Traditional Budgeting (for an accounting department)

Activity-Based Budget		Traditional Budget	
Auditing	$ 58,000	Salaries	$152,000
Tax reporting	71,000	Supplies	22,000
Financial reporting	63,000	Depreciation	36,000
Cost accounting	32,000	Utilities	14,000
Total	$224,000	Total	$224,000

budget for a company's accounting department. An understanding of the resources required to perform the activities, the costs associated with these resources, and the way resource use changes with changes in activity levels allows management to better assess how expenses will change to accommodate changes in activity levels. Moreover, by knowing the relation between activities and costs, management can attempt to reduce costs by eliminating nonvalue-added activities.

 Decision Maker

Environmental Manager You hold the new position of environmental control manager for a chemical company. You are asked to develop a budget for your job and identify job responsibilities. How do you proceed? ■ [Answer—p. 922]

DEMONSTRATION PROBLEM

Wild Wood Company's management asks you to prepare its master budget using the following information. The budget is to cover the months of April, May, and June of 2013.

WILD WOOD COMPANY			
Balance Sheet			
March 31, 2013			
Assets		**Liabilities and Equity**	
Cash	$ 50,000	Accounts payable	$156,000
Accounts receivable	175,000	Short-term notes payable	12,000
Inventory	126,000	Total current liabilities	168,000
Total current assets	351,000	Long-term note payable	200,000
Equipment, gross	480,000	Total liabilities	368,000
Accumulated depreciation	(90,000)	Common stock	235,000
Equipment, net	390,000	Retained earnings	138,000
		Total stockholders' equity	373,000
Total assets	$741,000	Total liabilities and equity	$741,000

Additional Information

a. Sales for March total 10,000 units. Each month's sales are expected to exceed the prior month's results by 5%. The product's selling price is $25 per unit.

b. Company policy calls for a given month's ending inventory to equal 80% of the next month's expected unit sales. The March 31 inventory is 8,400 units, which complies with the policy. The purchase price is $15 per unit.

c. Sales representatives' commissions are 12.5% of sales and are paid in the month of the sales. The sales manager's monthly salary will be $3,500 in April and $4,000 per month thereafter.

d. Monthly general and administrative expenses include $8,000 administrative salaries, $5,000 depreciation, and 0.9% monthly interest on the long-term note payable.

e. The company expects 30% of sales to be for cash and the remaining 70% on credit. Receivables are collected in full in the month following the sale (none is collected in the month of the sale).

f. All merchandise purchases are on credit, and no payables arise from any other transactions. One month's purchases are fully paid in the next month.

g. The minimum ending cash balance for all months is $50,000. If necessary, the company borrows enough cash using a short-term note to reach the minimum. Short-term notes require an interest payment of 1% at each month-end (before any repayment). If the ending cash balance exceeds the minimum, the excess will be applied to repaying the short-term notes payable balance.

h. Dividends of $100,000 are to be declared and paid in May.

i. No cash payments for income taxes are to be made during the second calendar quarter. Income taxes will be assessed at 35% in the quarter.

j. Equipment purchases of $55,000 are scheduled for June.

Required

Prepare the following budgets and other financial information as required:

  1. Sales budget, including budgeted sales for July.

  2. Purchases budget, the budgeted cost of goods sold for each month and quarter, and the cost of the June 30 budgeted inventory.

  3. Selling expense budget.

  4. General and administrative expense budget.

  5. Expected cash receipts from customers and the expected June 30 balance of accounts receivable.

  6. Expected cash payments for purchases and the expected June 30 balance of accounts payable.

  7. Cash budget.

  8. Budgeted income statement.

  9. Budgeted statement of retained earnings.

10. Budgeted balance sheet.

PLANNING THE SOLUTION

- The sales budget shows expected sales for each month in the quarter. Start by multiplying March sales by 105% and then do the same for the remaining months. July's sales are needed for the purchases budget. To complete the budget, multiply the expected unit sales by the selling price of $25 per unit.

- Use these results and the 80% inventory policy to budget the size of ending inventory for April, May, and June. Add the budgeted sales to these numbers and subtract the actual or expected beginning inventory for each month. The result is the number of units to be purchased each month. Multiply these numbers by the per unit cost of $15. Find the budgeted cost of goods sold by multiplying the unit sales in each month by the $15 cost per unit. Compute the cost of the June 30 ending inventory by multiplying the expected units available at that date by the $15 cost per unit.

- The selling expense budget has only two items. Find the amount of the sales representatives' commissions by multiplying the expected dollar sales in each month by the 12.5% commission rate. Then include the sales manager's salary of $3,500 in April and $4,000 in May and June.

- The general and administrative expense budget should show three items. Administrative salaries are fixed at $8,000 per month, and depreciation is $5,000 per month. Budget the monthly interest expense on the long-term note by multiplying its $200,000 balance by the 0.9% monthly interest rate.

- Determine the amounts of cash sales in each month by multiplying the budgeted sales by 30%. Add to this amount the credit sales of the prior month (computed as 70% of prior month's sales). April's cash receipts from collecting receivables equals the March 31 balance of $175,000. The expected June 30 accounts receivable balance equals 70% of June's total budgeted sales.

- Determine expected cash payments on accounts payable for each month by making them equal to the merchandise purchases in the prior month. The payments for April equal the March 31 balance of accounts payable shown on the beginning balance sheet. The June 30 balance of accounts payable equals merchandise purchases for June.

- Prepare the cash budget by combining the given information and the amounts of cash receipts and cash payments on account that you computed. Complete the cash budget for each month by either borrowing enough to raise the preliminary balance to the minimum or paying off short-term debt as much as the balance allows without falling below the minimum. Show the ending balance of the short-term note in the budget.

- Prepare the budgeted income statement by combining the budgeted items for all three months. Determine the income before income taxes and multiply it by the 35% rate to find the quarter's income tax expense.

- The budgeted statement of retained earnings should show the March 31 balance plus the quarter's net income minus the quarter's dividends.

- The budgeted balance sheet includes updated balances for all items that appear in the beginning balance sheet and an additional liability for unpaid income taxes. Amounts for all asset, liability, and equity accounts can be found either in the budgets, other calculations, or by adding amounts found there to the beginning balances.

SOLUTION TO DEMONSTRATION PROBLEM

1. Sales budget

	April	May	June	July
Prior period's unit sales	10,000	→10,500	→11,025	→11,576
Plus 5% growth	500	525	551	579
Projected unit sales	10,500	11,025	11,576	12,155

	April	May	June	Quarter
Projected unit sales	10,500	11,025	11,576	
Selling price per unit	× $25	× $25	× $25	
Projected sales	$262,500	$275,625	$289,400	$827,525

2. Purchases budget

	April	May	June	Quarter
Next period's unit sales (part 1)	11,025	11,576	12,155	
Ending inventory percent	× 80%	× 80%	× 80%	
Desired ending inventory	8,820	9,261	9,724	
Current period's unit sales (part 1)	10,500	11,025	11,576	
Units to be available	19,320	20,286	21,300	
Less beginning inventory	8,400	8,820	9,261	
Units to be purchased	10,920	11,466	12,039	
Budgeted cost per unit	× $15	× $15	× $15	
Projected purchases	$163,800	$171,990	$180,585	$516,375

Budgeted cost of goods sold

	April	May	June	Quarter
This period's unit sales (part 1)	10,500	11,025	11,576	
Budgeted cost per unit	× $15	× $15	× $15	
Projected cost of goods sold	$157,500	$165,375	$173,640	$496,515

Budgeted inventory for June 30

Units (part 2)	9,724
Cost per unit	× $15
Total	$145,860

3. Selling expense budget

	April	May	June	Quarter
Budgeted sales (part 1)	$262,500	$275,625	$289,400	$827,525
Commission percent	× 12.5%	× 12.5%	× 12.5%	× 12.5%
Sales commissions	32,813	34,453	36,175	103,441
Manager's salary	3,500	4,000	4,000	11,500
Projected selling expenses	$ 36,313	$ 38,453	$ 40,175	$114,941

4. General and administrative expense budget

	April	May	June	Quarter
Administrative salaries	$ 8,000	$ 8,000	$ 8,000	$24,000
Depreciation	5,000	5,000	5,000	15,000
Interest on long-term note payable (0.9% × $200,000)	1,800	1,800	1,800	5,400
Projected expenses	$14,800	$14,800	$14,800	$44,400

5. Expected cash receipts from customers

	April	May	June	Quarter
Budgeted sales (part 1)	$262,500	$275,625	$289,400	
Ending accounts receivable (70%)	$183,750	$192,938	$202,580	
Cash receipts				
Cash sales (30% of budgeted sales)	$ 78,750	$ 82,687	$ 86,820	$248,257
Collections of prior month's receivables	175,000	183,750	192,938	551,688
Total cash to be collected	$253,750	$266,437	$279,758	$799,945

6. Expected cash payments to suppliers

	April	May	June	Quarter
Cash payments (equal to prior month's purchases)	$156,000	$163,800	$171,990	$491,790
Expected June 30 balance of accounts payable (June purchases)			$180,585	

7. Cash budget

	April	May	June
Beginning cash balance	$ 50,000	$ 89,517	$ 50,000
Cash receipts (part 5)	253,750	266,437	279,758
Total cash available	303,750	355,954	329,758
Cash payments			
Payments for merchandise (part 6)	156,000	163,800	171,990
Sales commissions (part 3)	32,813	34,453	36,175
Salaries			
Sales (part 3)	3,500	4,000	4,000
Administrative (part 4)	8,000	8,000	8,000
Interest on long-term note (part 4)	1,800	1,800	1,800
Dividends		100,000	
Equipment purchase			55,000
Interest on short-term notes			
April ($12,000 × 1.0%)	120		
June ($6,099 × 1.0%)			61
Total cash payments	202,233	312,053	277,026
Preliminary balance	101,517	43,901	52,732
Loan activity			
Additional loan		6,099	
Loan repayment	(12,000)		(2,732)
Ending cash balance	$ 89,517	$ 50,000	$ 50,000
Ending short-term notes	$ 0	$ 6,099	$ 3,367

8.

WILD WOOD COMPANY Budgeted Income Statement For Quarter Ended June 30, 2013		
Sales (part 1)		$827,525
Cost of goods sold (part 2)		496,515
Gross profit		331,010
Operating expenses		
Sales commissions (part 3)	$103,441	
Sales salaries (part 3)	11,500	
Administrative salaries (part 4)	24,000	
Depreciation (part 4)	15,000	
Interest on long-term note (part 4)	5,400	
Interest on short-term notes (part 7)	181	
Total operating expenses		159,522
Income before income taxes		171,488
Income taxes (35%)		60,021
Net income		$111,467

9.

WILD WOOD COMPANY Budgeted Statement of Retained Earnings For Quarter Ended June 30, 2013	
Beginning retained earnings (given)	$138,000
Net income (part 8)	111,467
	249,467
Less cash dividends (given)	100,000
Ending retained earnings	$149,467

10.

WILD WOOD COMPANY Budgeted Balance Sheet June 30, 2013		
Assets		
Cash (part 7)		$ 50,000
Accounts receivable (part 5)		202,580
Inventory (part 2)		145,860
Total current assets		398,440
Equipment (given plus purchase)	$535,000	
Less accumulated depreciation (given plus expense)	105,000	430,000
Total assets		$828,440
Liabilities and Equity		
Accounts payable (part 6)		$180,585
Short-term notes payable (part 7)		3,367
Income taxes payable (part 8)		60,021
Total current liabilities		243,973
Long-term note payable (given)		200,000
Total liabilities		443,973
Common stock (given)		235,000
Retained earnings (part 9)		149,467
Total stockholders' equity		384,467
Total liabilities and equity		$828,440

22A

Production and Manufacturing Budgets

P3 Prepare production and manufacturing budgets.

Unlike a merchandising company, a manufacturer must prepare a **production budget** instead of a merchandise purchases budget. A production budget, which shows the number of units to be produced each month, is similar to merchandise purchases budgets except that the number of units to be purchased each month (as shown in Exhibit 22.8) is replaced by the number of units to be manufactured each month. A production budget does not show costs; it is *always expressed in units of product*. Exhibit 22A.1 shows the production budget for **Toronto Sticks Company (TSC),** a manufacturer of hockey sticks. TSC is an exclusive supplier of hockey sticks to Hockey Den, meaning that TSC uses HD's budgeted sales figures (Exhibit 22.6) to determine its production and manufacturing budgets.

EXHIBIT 22A.1

Production Budget

TSC Production Budget October 2013–December 2013	October	November	December
Next period's budgeted sales (units)	800	1,400	900
Ratio of inventory to future sales	× 90%	× 90%	× 90%
Budgeted ending inventory (units)	720	1,260	810
Add budgeted sales for the period (units)	1,000	800	1,400
Required units of available production	1,720	2,060	2,210
Deduct beginning inventory (units)	(900)	(720)	(1,260)
Units to be produced	820	1,340	950

A **manufacturing budget** shows the budgeted costs for direct materials, direct labor, and overhead. It is based on the budgeted production volume from the production budget. The manufacturing budget for most companies consists of three individual budgets: direct materials budget, direct labor budget, and overhead budget. Exhibits 22A.2–22A.4 show these three manufacturing budgets for TSC. These budgets yield the total expected cost of goods to be manufactured in the budget period.

The *direct materials budget* is driven by the budgeted materials needed to satisfy each month's production requirement. To this we must add the desired ending inventory requirements. The desired ending inventory of direct materials as shown in Exhibit 22A.2 is 50% of next month's budgeted materials requirements of wood. For instance, in October 2013, an ending inventory of 335 units of material is desired (50% of November's 670 units). The desired ending inventory for December 2013 is 225 units, computed from the direct material requirement of 450 units for a production level of 900 units in January 2014. The total materials requirements are computed by adding the desired ending inventory figures to that month's budgeted production material requirements. For October 2013, the total materials requirement is 745 units (335 + 410). From the total materials requirement, we then subtract the units of

EXHIBIT 22A.2

Direct Materials Budget

TSC Direct Materials Budget October 2013–December 2013	October	November	December
Budget production (units)	820	1,340	950
Materials requirements per unit	× 0.5	× 0.5	× 0.5
Materials needed for production (units)	410	670	475
Add budgeted ending inventory (units)	335	237.5	225
Total materials requirements (units)	745	907.5	700
Deduct beginning inventory (units)	(205)	(335)	(237.5)
Materials to be purchased (units)	540	572.5	462.5
Material price per unit	$ 20	$ 20	$ 20
Total cost of direct materials purchases	$10,800	$11,450	$9,250

materials available in beginning inventory. For October 2013, the materials available from September 2013 are computed as 50% of October's materials requirements to satisfy production, or 205 units (50% of 410). Therefore, direct materials purchases in October 2013 are budgeted at 540 units (745 − 205). See Exhibit 22A.2.

TSC's *direct labor budget* is shown in Exhibit 22A.3. About 15 minutes of labor time is required to produce one unit. Labor is paid at the rate of $12 per hour. Budgeted labor hours are computed by multiplying the budgeted production level for each month by one-quarter (0.25) of an hour. Direct labor cost is then computed by multiplying budgeted labor hours by the labor rate of $12 per hour.

TSC Direct Labor Budget October 2013–December 2013	October	November	December
Budgeted production (units)	820	1,340	950
Labor requirements per unit (hours)	× 0.25	× 0.25	× 0.25
Total labor hours needed	205	335	237.5
Labor rate (per hour)	$ 12	$ 12	$ 12
Labor dollars	$2,460	$4,020	$2,850

EXHIBIT 22A.3

Direct Labor Budget

TSC's *factory overhead budget* is shown in Exhibit 22A.4. The variable portion of overhead is assigned at the rate of $2.50 per unit of production. The fixed portion stays constant at $1,500 per month. The budget in Exhibit 22A.4 is in condensed form; most overhead budgets are more detailed, listing each overhead cost item. We explain these more detailed overhead budgets in the next chapter.

TSC Factory Overhead Budget October 2013–December 2013	October	November	December
Budgeted production (units)	820	1,340	950
Variable factory overhead rate	× $2.50	× $2.50	× $2.50
Budgeted variable overhead	2,050	3,350	2,375
Budgeted fixed overhead	1,500	1,500	1,500
Budgeted total overhead	$3,550	$4,850	$3,875

EXHIBIT 22A.4

Factory Overhead Budget

Summary

C1 **Describe the importance and benefits of budgeting and the process of budget administration.** Planning is a management responsibility of critical importance to business success. Budgeting is the process management uses to formalize its plans. Budgeting promotes management analysis and focuses its attention on the future. Budgeting also provides a basis for evaluating performance, serves as a source of motivation, is a means of coordinating activities, and communicates management's plans and instructions to employees. Budgeting is a detailed activity that requires administration. At least three aspects are important: budget committee, budget reporting, and budget timing. A budget committee oversees the budget preparation. The budget period pertains to the time period for which the budget is prepared such as a year or month.

C2 **Describe a master budget and the process of preparing it.** A master budget is a formal overall plan for a company. It consists of plans for business operations and capital expenditures, plus the financial results of those activities. The budgeting process begins with a sales budget. Based on expected sales volume, companies can budget purchases, selling expenses, and administrative expenses. Next, the capital expenditures budget is prepared, followed by the cash budget and budgeted financial statements. Manufacturers also must budget production quantities, materials purchases, labor costs, and overhead.

A1 **Analyze expense planning using activity-based budgeting.** Activity-based budgeting requires management to identify activities performed by departments, plan necessary activity levels, identify resources required to perform these activities, and budget the resources.

P1 **Prepare each component of a master budget and link each to the budgeting process.** The term *master budget* refers to a collection of individual component budgets. Each component budget is designed to guide persons responsible for activities covered by that component. A master budget must reflect the components of a company and their interaction in pursuit of company goals.

P2 **Link both operating and capital expenditures budgets to budgeted financial statements.** The operating budgets, capital expenditures budget, and cash budget contain much of the information to prepare a budgeted income statement for the budget period and a budgeted balance sheet at the end of the budget period. Budgeted financial statements show the expected financial consequences of the planned activities described in the budgets.

P3 **Prepare production and manufacturing budgets.** A manufacturer must prepare a *production budget* instead of a purchases budget. A *manufacturing budget* shows the budgeted production costs for direct materials, direct labor, and overhead.

Guidance Answers to Decision Maker and Decision Ethics

Budget Staffer Your superior's actions appear unethical because she is using private information for personal gain. As a budget staffer, you are low in the company's hierarchical structure and probably unable to confront this superior directly. You should inform an individual with a position of authority within the organization about your concerns.

Entrepreneur You must deal with two issues. First, because fashions and designs frequently change, you cannot heavily rely on previous budgets. As a result, you must carefully analyze the market to understand what designs are in vogue. This will help you plan the product mix and estimate demand. The second issue is the budgeting

period. An annual sales budget may be unreliable because tastes can quickly change. Your best bet might be to prepare monthly and quarterly sales budgets that you continuously monitor and revise.

Environmental Manager You are unlikely to have data on this new position to use in preparing your budget. In this situation, you can use activity-based budgeting. This requires developing a list of activities to conduct, the resources required to perform these activities, and the expenses associated with these resources. You should challenge yourself to be absolutely certain that the listed activities are necessary and that the listed resources are required.

Guidance Answers to Quick Checks

1. Major benefits include promoting a focus on the future; providing a basis for evaluating performance; providing a source of motivation; coordinating the departments of a business; and communicating plans and instructions.

2. The budget committee's responsibility is to provide guidance to ensure that budget figures are realistic and coordinated.

3. Budget periods usually coincide with accounting periods and therefore cover a month, quarter, or a year. Budgets can also be prepared for longer time periods, such as five years.

4. Rolling budgets are budgets that are periodically revised in the ongoing process of continuous budgeting.

5. A master budget is a comprehensive or overall plan for the company that is generally expressed in monetary terms.

6. *b*

7. The master budget includes operating budgets, the capital expenditures budget, and financial budgets.

8. *c*; Computed as (60% × 140) + 120 − 50 = 154.

9. Merchandisers prepare merchandise purchases budgets; manufacturers prepare production and manufacturing budgets.

10. A just-in-time system keeps the level of inventory to a minimum and orders merchandise or materials to meet immediate sales demand. A safety stock system maintains an inventory that is large enough to meet sales demands plus an amount to satisfy unexpected sales demands and an amount to cover delayed shipments from suppliers.

11. *a*

12. (a) Operating budgets (such as sales, selling expense, and administrative budgets), (b) capital expenditures budget, (c) financial budgets: cash budget, budgeted income statement, and budgeted balance sheet.

Key Terms

Multiple Choice Quiz   Answers on p. 945   mhhe.com/wildFAP21e

Additional Quiz Questions are available at the book's Website.

1. A plan that reports the units or costs of merchandise to be purchased by a merchandising company during the budget period is called a
   a. Capital expenditures budget.
   b. Cash budget.
   c. Merchandise purchases budget.
   d. Selling expenses budget.
   e. Sales budget.

2. A hardware store has budgeted sales of $36,000 for its power tool department in July. Management wants to have $7,000 in power tool inventory at the end of July. Its beginning inventory of power tools is expected to be $6,000. What is the budgeted dollar amount of merchandise purchases?
   a. $36,000
   b. $43,000
   c. $42,000
   d. $35,000
   e. $37,000

3. A store has the following budgeted sales for the next five months.

May	$210,000
June	186,000
July	180,000
August	220,000
September	240,000

   Cash sales are 25% of total sales and all credit sales are expected to be collected in the month following the sale. The total amount of cash expected to be received from customers in September is

   a. $240,000
   b. $225,000
   c. $ 60,000
   d. $165,000
   e. $220,000

4. A plan that shows the expected cash inflows and cash outflows during the budget period, including receipts from loans needed to maintain a minimum cash balance and repayments of such loans, is called
   a. A rolling budget.
   b. An income statement.
   c. A balance sheet.
   d. A cash budget.
   e. An operating budget.

5.[A] The following sales are predicted for a company's next four months.

	September	October	November	December
Unit sales ..	480	560	600	480

   Each month's ending inventory of finished goods should be 30% of the next month's sales. At September 1, the finished goods inventory is 140 units. The budgeted production of units for October is
   a. 572 units.
   b. 560 units.
   c. 548 units.
   d. 600 units.
   e. 180 units.

[A] *Superscript letter A denotes assignments based on Appendix 22A.*

🚹 Icon denotes assignments that involve decision making.

Refer to Appendix 22A for assignments relating to production, direct materials, direct labor, and factory overhead budgets.

Discussion Questions

1. 🚹 Identify at least three roles that budgeting plays in helping managers control and monitor a business.

2. What two common benchmarks can be used to evaluate actual performance? Which of the two is generally more useful?

3. 🚹 What is the benefit of continuous budgeting?

4. Identify three usual time horizons for short-term planning and budgets.

5. 🚹 Why should each department participate in preparing its own budget?

6. 🚹 How does budgeting help management coordinate and plan business activities?

7. 🚹 Why is the sales budget so important to the budgeting process?

8. What is a selling expense budget? What is a capital expenditures budget?

9. Budgeting promotes good decision making by requiring managers to conduct _____ and by focusing their attention on the _____.

10. **Piaggio** prepares a cash budget. What is a cash budget? Why must operating budgets and the capital expenditures budget be prepared before the cash budget?   **PIAGGIO**

11. **KTM** regularly uses budgets. What is the difference between a production budget and a manufacturing budget?   **KTM**

12. 🚹 Would a manager of an **Apple** retail store participate more in budgeting than a manager at the corporate offices? Explain.   **Apple**

13. 🚹 Does the manager of a **Arctic Cat** distribution center participate in long-term budgeting? Explain.   **Arctic Cat**

14. 🚹 Assume that **Polaris'** snowmobile division is charged with preparing a master budget. Identify the participants—for example, the sales manager for the sales budget—and describe the information each person provides in preparing the master budget.   **Polaris**

QUICK STUDY

QS 22-1

Components of a master budget

C2

Which one of the following sets of items are all necessary components of the master budget?

1. Operating budgets, historical income statement, and budgeted balance sheet.
2. Prior sales reports, capital expenditures budget, and financial budgets.
3. Sales budget, operating budgets, and historical financial budgets.
4. Operating budgets, financial budgets, and capital expenditures budget.

QS 22-2

Budget motivation   C1

The motivation of employees is one goal of budgeting. Identify three guidelines that organizations should follow if budgeting is to serve effectively as a source of motivation for employees.

QS 22-3

Merchandising: Purchases budget   P1

Montel Company's July sales budget calls for sales of $600,000. The store expects to begin July with $50,000 of inventory and to end the month with $40,000 of inventory. Gross margin is typically 40% of sales. Determine the budgeted cost of merchandise purchases for July.

QS 22-4

Budgeting process   C1

Good management includes good budgeting. (1) Explain why the bottom-up approach to budgeting is considered a more successful management technique than a top-down approach. (2) Provide an example of implementation of the bottom-up approach to budgeting.

QS 22-5

Computing budgeted accounts receivable

P2

Lighthouse Company anticipates total sales for June and July of $420,000 and $398,000, respectively. Cash sales are normally 60% of total sales. Of the credit sales, 20% are collected in the same month as the sale, 70% are collected during the first month after the sale, and the remaining 10% are collected in the second month. Determine the amount of accounts receivable reported on the company's budgeted balance sheet as of July 31.

QS 22-6

Cash budget

P1

Use the following information to prepare a cash budget for the month ended on March 31 for Gado Merchandising Company. The budget should show expected cash receipts and cash disbursements for the month of March and the balance expected on March 31.

a. Beginning cash balance on March 1, $72,000.
b. Cash receipts from sales, $300,000.
c. Budgeted cash disbursements for purchases, $140,000.
d. Budgeted cash disbursements for salaries, $80,000.
e. Other budgeted cash expenses, $45,000.
f. Cash repayment of bank loan, $20,000.

QS 22-7

Activity-based budgeting

A1

Activity-based budgeting is a budget system based on *expected activities*. (1) Describe activity-based budgeting, and explain its preparation of budgets. (2) How does activity-based budgeting differ from traditional budgeting?

QS 22-8ᴬ

Manufacturing: Production budget

P3

Forrest Company manufactures watches and has a JIT policy that ending inventory must equal 10% of the next month's sales. It estimates that October's actual ending inventory will consist of 40,000 watches. November and December sales are estimated to be 400,000 and 350,000 watches, respectively. Compute the number of watches to be produced that would appear on the company's production budget for the month of November.

QS 22-9ᴬ

Manufacturing: Factory overhead budget   P3

Refer to information from QS 22-8. Forrest Company assigns variable overhead at the rate of $1.50 per unit of production. Fixed overhead equals $4,600,000 per month. Prepare a factory overhead budget for November.

QS 22-10

Sales budget   P1

Grace sells miniature digital cameras for $250 each. 1,000 units were sold in May, and it forecasts 4% growth in unit sales each month. Determine (a) the number of camera sales and (b) the dollar amount of camera sales for the month of June.

Refer to information from QS 22-10. Grace pays a sales manager a monthly salary of $6,000 and a commission of 8% of camera sales (in dollars). Prepare a selling expense budget for the month of June.

QS 22-11
Selling expense budget P1

Refer to information from QS 22-10. Assume 60% of Grace's sales are for cash. The remaining 40% are credit sales; these customers pay in the month following the sale. Compute the budgeted cash receipts for June.

QS 22-12
Cash budget P1

Following are selected accounts for a company. For each account, indicate whether it will appear on a budgeted income statement (BIS) or a budgeted balance sheet (BBS). If an item will not appear on either budgeted financial statement, label it NA.

QS 22-13
Budgeted financial statements
P2

Sales	_____	Interest paid on note payable	_____
Office salaries paid	_____	Cash dividends paid	_____
Accumulated depreciation	_____	Bank loan owed	_____
Amortization expense	_____	Cost of goods sold	_____

The Candle Shoppe reports the following sales forecast: August, $150,000; September, $170,000. Cash sales are normally 40% of total sales and all credit sales are expected to be collected in the month following the date of sale. Prepare a schedule of cash receipts for September.

QS 22-14
Cash receipts P1

Wells Company reports the following sales forecast: September, $55,000; October, $66,000; and November, $80,000. All sales are on account. Collections of credit sales are received as follows: 20% in the month of sale, 70% in the first month after sale, and 10% in the second month after sale. Prepare a schedule of cash receipts for November.

QS 22-15
Cash receipts P1

Gordands purchased $600,000 of merchandise in August and expects to purchase $720,000 in September. Merchandise purchases are paid as follows: 25% in the month of purchase and 75% in the following month. Compute cash disbursements for merchandise for September.

QS 22-16
Merchandising: Cash disbursements for merchandise
P1

Meyer Co. forecasts merchandise purchases of $15,800 in January, $18,600 in February, and $20,200 in March; 40% of purchases are paid in the month of purchase and 60% are paid in the following month. At December 31 of the prior year, the balance of Accounts Payable (for December purchases) is $22,000. Prepare a schedule of cash disbursements for merchandise for each of the months of January, February, and March.

QS 22-17
Merchandising: Cash disbursements for merchandise
P1

Raider-X Company forecasts sales of 18,000 units for April. Beginning inventory is 3,000 units. The desired ending inventory is 30% higher than the beginning inventory. How many units should Raider-X purchase in April?

QS 22-18
Merchandising: Computing purchases
P1

Lexi Company forecasts unit sales of 1,040,000 in April, 1,220,000 in May, 980,000 in June, and 1,020,000 in July. Beginning inventory on April 1 is 280,000 units, and the company wants to have 30% of next month's sales in inventory at the end of each month. Prepare a merchandise purchases budget for the months of April, May, and June.

QS 22-19
Merchandising: Computing purchases
P1

Champ, Inc. predicts the following sales in units for the coming three months:

QS 22-20ᴬ
Manufacturing: Production budget
P3

	May	June	July
Sales in units	180	200	240

Each month's ending inventory of finished units should be 60% of the next month's sales. The April 30 finished goods inventory is 50 units. Compute Champ's budgeted production (in units) for May.

Zortek Corp. budgets production of 400 units in January and 200 units in February. Each finished unit requires five pounds of raw material Z, which costs $2 per pound. Each month's ending inventory of raw materials should be 40% of the following month's budgeted production. The January 1 raw materials inventory has 130 pounds of Z. Prepare a direct materials budget for January.

QS 22-21ᴬ
Manufacturing: Direct materials budget P3

QS 22-22ᴬ
Manufacturing: Direct labor budget   P3

Tora Co. plans to produce 1,020 units in July. Each unit requires two hours of direct labor. The direct labor rate is $20 per hour. Prepare a direct labor budget for July.

QS 22-23
Sales budget   P1

Scora, Inc., is preparing its master budget for the quarter ending March 31. It sells a single product for $50 per unit. Budgeted sales for the next four months follow. Prepare a sales budget for the months of January, February, and March.

	January	February	March	April
Sales in units	1,200	2,000	1,600	1,400

QS 22-24
Cash receipts budget   P1

Refer to information in QS 22-23. In addition, sales are 40% cash and 60% on credit. All credit sales are collected in the month following the sale. The January 1 balance in accounts receivable is $15,000. Prepare a schedule of budgeted cash receipts for January, February, and March.

QS 22-25
Selling expense budget   P1

Refer to information in QS 22-23. In addition, sales commissions are 10% of sales and the company pays a sales manager a salary of $6,000 per month. Sales commissions and salaries are paid in the month incurred. Prepare a selling expense budget for January, February, and March.

QS 22-26
Budgeted loan activity

P1

Messers Company is preparing a cash budget for February. The company has $20,000 cash at the beginning of February and anticipates $75,000 in cash receipts and $100,250 in cash disbursements during February. What amount, if any, must the company borrow during February to maintain a $5,000 cash balance? The company has no loans outstanding on February 1.

QS 22-27
Operating budgets

P1

Royal Phillips Electronics of the Netherlands reports sales of €25,400 million for a recent year. Assume that the company expects sales growth of 3 percent for the next year. Also assume that selling expenses are typically 20 percent of sales, while general and administrative expenses are 4 percent of sales.

Required

1. Compute budgeted sales for the next year.
2. Assume budgeted sales for next year is €26,000 million, and then compute budgeted selling expenses and budgeted general and administrative expenses for the next year.

connect

EXERCISES

Exercise 22-1
Preparation of cash budgets (for three periods)

P1

Kayak Co. budgeted the following cash receipts (excluding cash receipts from loans received) and cash disbursements (excluding cash disbursements for loan and interest payments) for the first three months of next year.

	Cash Receipts	Cash Disbursements
January	$525,000	$475,000
February.	400,000	350,000
March	450,000	525,000

Check   January ending cash balance, $30,000

According to a credit agreement with the company's bank, Kayak promises to have a minimum cash balance of $30,000 at each month-end. In return, the bank has agreed that the company can borrow up to $150,000 at an annual interest rate of 12%, paid on the last day of each month. The interest is computed based on the beginning balance of the loan for the month. The company has a cash balance of $30,000 and a loan balance of $60,000 at January 1. Prepare monthly cash budgets for each of the first three months of next year.

Exercise 22-2
Merchandising: Preparation of purchases budgets (for three periods)

P1

Walker Company prepares monthly budgets. The current budget plans for a September ending inventory of 30,000 units. Company policy is to end each month with merchandise inventory equal to a specified percent of budgeted sales for the following month. Budgeted sales and merchandise purchases for the three most recent months follow. (1) Prepare the merchandise purchases budget for the months of July, August, and September. (2) Compute the ratio of ending inventory to the next month's sales for each budget prepared in part 1. (3) How many units are budgeted for sale in October?

	Sales (Units)	Purchases (Units)
July	180,000	200,250
August	315,000	308,250
September	270,000	259,500

Use the following information to prepare the July cash budget for Acco Co. It should show expected cash receipts and cash disbursements for the month and the cash balance expected on July 31.

a. Beginning cash balance on July 1: $50,000.

b. Cash receipts from sales: 30% is collected in the month of sale, 50% in the next month, and 20% in the second month after sale (uncollectible accounts are negligible and can be ignored). Sales amounts are: May (actual), $1,720,000; June (actual), $1,200,000; and July (budgeted), $1,400,000.

c. Payments on merchandise purchases: 60% in the month of purchase and 40% in the month following purchase. Purchases amounts are: June (actual), $700,000; and July (budgeted), $750,000.

d. Budgeted cash disbursements for salaries in July: $275,000.

e. Budgeted depreciation expense for July: $36,000.

f. Other cash expenses budgeted for July: $200,000.

g. Accrued income taxes due in July: $80,000.

h. Bank loan interest due in July: $6,600.

Exercise 22-3

Merchandising: Preparation of a cash budget

P1

Check   Ending cash balance, $122,400

Use the information in Exercise 22-3 and the following additional information to prepare a budgeted income statement for the month of July and a budgeted balance sheet for July 31.

a. Cost of goods sold is 55% of sales.

b. Inventory at the end of June is $80,000 and at the end of July is $60,000.

c. Salaries payable on June 30 are $50,000 and are expected to be $60,000 on July 31.

d. The equipment account balance is $1,600,000 on July 31. On June 30, the accumulated depreciation on equipment is $280,000.

e. The $6,600 cash payment of interest represents the 1% monthly expense on a bank loan of $660,000.

f. Income taxes payable on July 31 are $30,720, and the income tax rate applicable to the company is 30%.

g. The only other balance sheet accounts are: Common Stock, with a balance of $600,000 on June 30; and Retained Earnings, with a balance of $964,000 on June 30.

Exercise 22-4

Merchandising: Preparing a budgeted income statement and balance sheet

P2

Check   Net income, $71,680; Total assets, $2,686,400

Hardy Company's cost of goods sold is consistently 60% of sales. The company plans to carry ending merchandise inventory for each month equal to 20% of the next month's budgeted cost of good sold. All merchandise is purchased on credit, and 50% of the purchases made during a month is paid for in that month. Another 35% is paid for during the first month after purchase, and the remaining 15% is paid for during the second month after purchase. Expected sales are: August (actual), $325,000; September (actual), $320,000; October (estimated), $250,000; November (estimated), $310,000. Use this information to determine October's expected cash payments for purchases. (*Hint:* Use the layout of Exhibit 22.8, but revised for the facts given here.)

Exercise 22-5

Merchandising: Computing budgeted cash payments for purchases

P1

Check   Budgeted purchases: August, $194,400; October, $157,200

Quick Dollar Company purchases all merchandise on credit. It recently budgeted the following month-end accounts payable balances and merchandise inventory balances. Cash payments on accounts payable during each month are expected to be: May, $1,600,000; June, $1,490,000; July, $1,425,000; and August, $1,495,000. Use the available information to compute the budgeted amounts of (1) merchandise purchases for June, July, and August and (2) cost of goods sold for June, July, and August.

Exercise 22-6

Merchandising: Computing budgeted purchases and costs of goods sold

P1

	Accounts Payable	Merchandise Inventory
May 31	$150,000	$250,000
June 30	200,000	400,000
July 31	235,000	300,000
August 31	195,000	330,000

Check   June purchases, $1,540,000; June cost of goods sold, $1,390,000

Exercise 22-7
Merchandising: Computing budgeted accounts payable and purchases—sales forecast in dollars

P1 P2

Check July purchases, $236,600; Sept. payments on accts. pay., $214,235

Big Sound, a merchandising company specializing in home computer speakers, budgets its monthly cost of goods sold to equal 70% of sales. Its inventory policy calls for ending inventory in each month to equal 20% of the next month's budgeted cost of goods sold. All purchases are on credit, and 25% of the purchases in a month is paid for in the same month. Another 60% is paid for during the first month after purchase, and the remaining 15% is paid for in the second month after purchase. The following sales budgets are set: July, $350,000; August, $290,000; September, $320,000; October, $275,000; and November, $265,000. Compute the following: (1) budgeted merchandise purchases for July, August, September, and October; (2) budgeted payments on accounts payable for September and October; and (3) budgeted ending balances of accounts payable for September and October. (*Hint:* For part 1, refer to Exhibits 22.7 and 22.8 for guidance, but note that budgeted sales are in dollars for this assignment.)

Exercise 22-8ᴬ
Manufacturing: Preparing production budgets (for two periods) P3

Check Second quarter production, 480,000 units

Electro Company manufactures an innovative automobile transmission for electric cars. Management predicts that ending inventory for the first quarter will be 75,000 units. The following unit sales of the transmissions are expected during the rest of the year: second quarter, 450,000 units; third quarter, 525,000 units; and fourth quarter, 475,000 units. Company policy calls for the ending inventory of a quarter to equal 20% of the next quarter's budgeted sales. Prepare a production budget for both the second and third quarters that shows the number of transmissions to manufacture.

Exercise 22-9ᴬ
Manufacturing: Direct materials budget

P3

Refer to information from Exercise 22-8. Each transmission requires 0.80 pounds of a key raw material. Electro Company aims to end each quarter with an ending inventory of direct materials equal to 50% of next quarter's budgeted materials requirements. Direct materials cost $170 per unit. Prepare a direct materials budget for the second quarter.

Exercise 22-10ᴬ
Manufacturing: Direct labor budget P3

Refer to information from Exercise 22-8. Each transmission requires 4 direct labor hours, at a cost of $12 per hour. Prepare a direct labor budget for the second quarter.

Exercise 22-11
Merchandising: Budgeted cash disbursements

P1

Hector Company reports the following:

	July	August	September
Sales	$50,000	$72,000	$66,000
Purchases	14,400	19,200	21,600

Payments for purchases are made in the month after purchase. Selling expenses are 10% of sales, administrative expenses are 8% of sales, and both are paid in the month of sale. Rent expense of $7,400 is paid monthly. Depreciation expense is $2,300 per month. Prepare a schedule of budgeted cash disbursements for August and September.

Exercise 22-12
Budgeted cash receipts

P1

Jasper Company has sales on account and for cash. Specifically, 70% of its sales are on account and 30% are for cash. Credit sales are collected in full in the month following the sale. The company forecasts sales of $525,000 for April, $535,000 for May, and $560,000 for June. The beginning balance of Accounts Receivable is $400,000 on April 1. Prepare a schedule of budgeted cash receipts for April, May, and June.

Exercise 22-13
Cash budget

P1

Karim Corp. requires a minimum $8,000 cash balance. If necessary, loans are taken to meet this requirement at a cost of 1% interest per month (paid monthly). Any excess cash is used to repay loans at month-end. The cash balance on July 1 is $8,400 and the company has no outstanding loans. Forecasted cash receipts (other than for loans received) and forecasted cash payments (other than for loan or interest payments) are:

	July	August	September
Cash receipts	$20,000	$26,000	$40,000
Cash disbursements	28,000	30,000	22,000

Prepare a cash budget for July, August, and September. Round interest payments to the nearest whole dollar.

Foyert Corp. requires a minimum $30,000 cash balance. If necessary, loans are taken to meet this requirement at a cost of 1% interest per month (paid monthly). Any excess cash is used to repay loans at month-end. The cash balance on October 1 is $30,000 and the company has an outstanding loan of $10,000. Forecasted cash receipts (other than for loans received) and forecasted cash payments (other than for loan or interest payments) follow. Prepare a cash budget for October, November, and December. Round interest payments to the nearest whole dollar.

Exercise 22-14
Cash budget
P1

	October	November	December
Cash receipts	$110,000	$80,000	$100,000
Cash disbursements	120,000	75,000	80,000

Castor, Inc. is preparing its master budget for the quarter ended June 30. Budgeted sales and cash payments for merchandise for the next three months follow:

Exercise 22-15
Merchandising: Cash budget
P1

	April	May	June
Budgeted sales	$32,000	$40,000	$24,000
Budgeted cash payments for merchandise...................	20,200	16,800	17,200

Sales are 50% cash and 50% on credit. All credit sales are collected in the month following the sale. The March 30 balance sheet includes balances of $12,000 in cash, $12,000 in accounts receivable, $11,000 in accounts payable, and a $2,000 balance in loans payable. A minimum cash balance of $12,000 is required. Loans are obtained at the end of any month when a cash shortage occurs. Interest is 1% per month based on the beginning of the month loan balance and is paid at each month-end. If an excess balance of cash exists, loans are repaid at the end of the month. Operating expenses are paid in the month incurred and consist of sales commissions (10% of sales), shipping (2% of sales), office salaries ($5,000 per month) and rent ($3,000 per month). Prepare a cash budget for each of the months of April, May, and June (round all dollar amounts to the nearest whole dollar).

Kelsey is preparing its master budget for the quarter ended September 30. Budgeted sales and cash payments for merchandise for the next three months follow:

Exercise 22-16
Merchandising: Cash budget
P1

	July	August	September
Budgeted sales	$64,000	$80,000	$48,000
Budgeted cash payments for merchandise...................	40,400	33,600	34,400

Sales are 20% cash and 80% on credit. All credit sales are collected in the month following the sale. The June 30 balance sheet includes balances of $15,000 in cash; $45,000 in accounts receivable; $4,500 in accounts payable; and a $5,000 balance in loans payable. A minimum cash balance of $15,000 is required. Loans are obtained at the end of any month when a cash shortage occurs. Interest is 1% per month based on the beginning of the month loan balance and is paid at each month-end. If an excess balance of cash exists, loans are repaid at the end of the month. Operating expenses are paid in the month incurred and consist of sales commissions (10% of sales), office salaries ($4,000 per month), and rent ($6,500 per month). (1) Prepare a cash receipts budget for July, August, and September. (2) Prepare a cash budget for each of the months of July, August, and September. (Round all dollar amounts to the nearest whole dollar.)

Exercise 22-17
Merchandising: Budgeted balance sheet
P2

The following information is available for Zetrov Company:

a. The cash budget for March shows an ending bank loan of $10,000 and an ending cash balance of $50,000.

b. The sales budget for March indicates sales of $140,000. Accounts receivable are expected to be 70% of the current-month sales.

c. The merchandise purchases budget indicates that $89,000 in merchandise will be purchased on account in March. Purchases on account are paid 100% in the month following the purchase. Ending inventory for March is predicted to be 600 units at a cost of $35 each.

d. The budgeted income statement for March shows net income of $48,000. Depreciation expense of $1,000 and $26,000 in income tax expense were used in computing net income for March. Accrued taxes will be paid in April.

e. The balance sheet for February shows equipment of $84,000 with accumulated depreciation of $46,000, common stock of $25,000, and ending retained earnings of $8,000. There are no changes budgeted in the equipment or common stock accounts.

Prepare a budgeted balance sheet for March.

Exercise 22-18
Merchandising: Budgeted income statement
P2

Fortune, Inc., is preparing its master budget for the first quarter. The company sells a single product at a price of $25 per unit. Sales (in units) are forecasted at 45,000 for January, 55,000 for February, and 50,000 for March. Cost of goods sold is $14 per unit. Other expense information for the first quarter follows. Prepare a budgeted income statement for this first quarter.

Commissions	8% of sales
Rent	$14,000 per month
Advertising	15% of sales
Office salaries	$75,000 per month
Depreciation	$40,000 per month
Interest	15% annually on a $250,000 note payable
Tax rate.	30%

Exercise 22-19^A
Manufacturing: Direct labor budget
P3

The production budget for Manner Company shows units to be produced as follows: July, 620; August, 680; September, 540. Each unit produced requires two hours of direct labor. The direct labor rate is currently $20 per hour but is predicted to be $21 per hour in September. Prepare a direct labor budget for the months July, August, and September.

Exercise 22-20^A
Manufacturing: Production budget
P3

Hospitable Co. provides the following sales forecast for the next four months:

	April	May	June	July
Sales (units)	500	580	540	620

The company wants to end each month with ending finished goods inventory equal to 25% of next month's sales. Finished goods inventory on April 1 is 190 units. Assume July's budgeted production is 540 units. Prepare a production budget for the months of April, May, and June.

Exercise 22-21^A
Manufacturing: Direct materials budget   P3

Refer to the information in Exercise 22-20. In addition, assume each finished unit requires five pounds of raw materials and the company wants to end each month with raw materials inventory equal to 30% of next month's production needs. Beginning raw materials inventory for April was 663 pounds.
Prepare a direct materials budget for April, May, and June.

Match the definitions 1 through 9 with the term or phrase a through i.

A. Budget

B. Merchandise purchases budget

C. Cash budget

D. Safety stock

E. Budgeted income statement

F. General and administrative expense budget

G. Sales budget

H. Master budget

I. Budgeted balance sheet

_____ **1.** A comprehensive business plan that includes specific plans for expected sales, the units of product to be produced, the merchandise or materials to be purchased, the expenses to be incurred, the long-term assets to be purchased, and the amounts of cash to be borrowed or loans to be repaid, as well as a budgeted income statement and balance sheet.

_____ **2.** A quantity of inventory or materials over the minimum to reduce the risk of running short.

_____ **3.** A plan showing the units of goods to be sold and the sales to be derived; the usual starting point in the budgeting process.

_____ **4.** An accounting report that presents predicted amounts of the company's revenues and expenses for the budgeting period.

_____ **5.** An accounting report that presents predicted amounts of the company's assets, liabilities, and equity balances at the end of the budget period.

_____ **6.** A plan that shows the units or costs of merchandise to be purchased by a merchandising company during the budget period.

_____ **7.** A formal statement of a company's future plans, usually expressed in monetary terms.

_____ **8.** A plan that shows predicted operating expenses not included in the selling expenses budget.

_____ **9.** A plan that shows the expected cash inflows and cash outflows during the budget period, including receipts from any loans needed to maintain a minimum cash balance and repayments of such loans.

Exercise 22-22
Master budget definitions
C2

Participatory budgeting can sometimes lead to negative consequences. Identify three potential negative outcomes that can arise from participatory budgeting.

Exercise 22-23
Budget consequences C1

Render Co. CPA is preparing activity-based budgets for 2013. The partners expect the firm to generate billable hours for the year as follows:

Data entry	2,200 hours
Auditing	4,800 hours
Tax	4,300 hours
Consulting	750 hours

The company pays $10 per hour to data-entry clerks, $40 per hour to audit personnel, $50 per hour to tax personnel, and $50 per hour to consulting personnel. Prepare a schedule of budgeted labor costs for 2013 using activity-based budgeting.

Exercise 22-24
Activity-based budgeting
A1

Rida, Inc., a manufacturer in a seasonal industry, is preparing its direct materials budget for the second quarter. It forecasts sales of 225,000 units in the second quarter and 262,500 units in the third quarter. It also plans production of 52,500 units for the third quarter. Based on this information, the company plans to produce 240,000 units in the second quarter. Other information is as follows:

Direct materials	Each unit requires 0.60 pounds of a key raw material, priced at $175 per pound. The company plans to end each quarter with an ending inventory of materials equal to 50% of next quarter's budgeted materials requirements.
Direct labor	Each finished unit requires 4 direct labor hours, at a cost of $9 per hour.
Variable overhead	Applied at the rate of $11 per direct labor hour.
Fixed overhead	Budgeted at $450,000 per quarter

Prepare a direct materials budget for the second quarter.

Exercise 22-25
Manufacturing: Direct materials budget
P3

Exercise 22-26
Manufacturing: Direct labor
and factory overhead budgets

P3

Refer to Exercise 22-25. For the second quarter, prepare (1) a direct labor budget and (2) a factory overhead budget.

Exercise 22-27
Manufacturing: Direct
materials budget

P3

Rad Co. provides the following sales forecast and production budget for the next four months:

	April	May	June	July
Sales (units)	500	580	530	600
Budgeted production (units)	442	570	544	540

The company plans for finished goods inventory of 120 units at the end of June. In addition, each finished unit requires five pounds of raw materials and the company wants to end each month with raw materials inventory equal to 30% of next month's production needs. Beginning raw materials inventory for April was 663 pounds. Each finished unit requires 0.50 hours of direct labor at the rate of $16 per hour. The company budgets variable overhead at the rate of $20 per direct labor hour and budgets fixed overhead of $8,000 per month. Prepare a raw materials budget for April, May, and June.

Exercise 22-28
Manufacturing: Direct labor
and factory overhead budgets

P3

Refer to Exercise 22-27. For April, May, and June, prepare (1) a direct labor budget and (2) a factory overhead budget.

---

 connect

PROBLEM SET A

Problem 22-1A
Merchandising: Preparation
and analysis of purchases
budgets

C2   P1

mhhe.com/wildFAP21e

Keggler's Supply is a merchandiser of three different products. The company's February 28 inventories are footwear, 20,000 units; sports equipment, 80,000 units; and apparel, 50,000 units. Management believes that excessive inventories have accumulated for all three products. As a result, a new policy dictates that ending inventory in any month should equal 30% of the expected unit sales for the following month. Expected sales in units for March, April, May, and June follow.

	Budgeted Sales in Units			
	March	April	May	June
Footwear	15,000	25,000	32,000	35,000
Sports equipment	70,000	90,000	95,000	90,000
Apparel	40,000	38,000	37,000	25,000

Check (1) March budgeted
purchases Footwear, 2,500; Sports
equip., 17,000; Apparel, 1,400

Required

1. Prepare a merchandise purchases budget (in units) for each product for each of the months of March, April, and May.

Analysis Component

2. The purchases budgets in part 1 should reflect fewer purchases of all three products in March compared to those in April and May. What factor caused fewer purchases to be planned? Suggest business conditions that would cause this factor to both occur and impact the company in this way.

Problem 22-2A
Merchandising: Preparation of
cash budgets (for three periods)

C2   P2

mhhe.com/wildFAP21e

During the last week of August, Oneida Company's owner approaches the bank for an $100,000 loan to be made on September 2 and repaid on November 30 with annual interest of 12%, for an interest cost of $3,000. The owner plans to increase the store's inventory by $80,000 during September and needs the loan to pay for inventory acquisitions. The bank's loan officer needs more information about Oneida's ability to repay the loan and asks the owner to forecast the store's November 30 cash position. On September 1, Oneida is expected to have a $5,000 cash balance, $148,000 of accounts receivable, and $125,000 of accounts payable. Its budgeted sales, merchandise purchases, and various cash disbursements for the next three months follow.

File   Edit   View   Insert   Format   Tools   Data   Window   Help

	Budgeted Figures*	September	October	November
1				
2	Sales	$250,000	$375,000	$400,000
3	Merchandise purchases	240,000	225,000	200,000
4	Cash disbursements			
5	Payroll	20,000	22,000	24,000
6	Rent	10,000	10,000	10,000
7	Other cash expenses	35,000	30,000	20,000
8	Repayment of bank loan			100,000
9	Interest on the bank loan			3,000

Sheet1 / Sheet2 / Sheet3 /

* Operations began in August, August sales were $215,000 and purchases were $125,000.

The budgeted September merchandise purchases include the inventory increase. All sales are on account. The company predicts that 25% of credit sales is collected in the month of the sale, 45% in the month following the sale, 20% in the second month, 9% in the third, and the remainder is uncollectible. Applying these percents to the August credit sales, for example, shows that $96,750 of the $215,000 will be collected in September, $43,000 in October, and $19,350 in November. All merchandise is purchased on credit; 80% of the balance is paid in the month following a purchase, and the remaining 20% is paid in the second month. For example, of the $125,000 August purchases, $100,000 will be paid in September and $25,000 in October.

Required

Prepare a cash budget for September, October, and November for Oneida Company. Show supporting calculations as needed.

Check   Budgeted cash balance: September, $99,250; October, $69,500; November, $22,600

Aztec Company sells its product for $180 per unit. Its actual and projected sales follow.

	Units	Dollars
April (actual)	4,000	$ 720,000
May (actual)	2,000	360,000
June (budgeted)	6,000	1,080,000
July (budgeted).............	5,000	900,000
August (budgeted)	3,800	684,000

Problem 22-3A

Merchandising: Preparation and analysis of cash budgets with supporting inventory and purchases budgets

C2   P2

All sales are on credit. Recent experience shows that 20% of credit sales is collected in the month of the sale, 50% in the month after the sale, 28% in the second month after the sale, and 2% proves to be uncollectible. The product's purchase price is $110 per unit. All purchases are payable within 12 days. Thus, 60% of purchases made in a month is paid in that month and the other 40% is paid in the next month. The company has a policy to maintain an ending monthly inventory of 20% of the next month's unit sales plus a safety stock of 100 units. The April 30 and May 31 actual inventory levels are consistent with this policy. Selling and administrative expenses for the year are $1,320,000 and are paid evenly throughout the year in cash. The company's minimum cash balance at month-end is $100,000. This minimum is maintained, if necessary, by borrowing cash from the bank. If the balance exceeds $100,000, the company repays as much of the loan as it can without going below the minimum. This type of loan carries an annual 12% interest rate. On May 31, the loan balance is $25,000, and the company's cash balance is $100,000. (Round amounts to the nearest dollar.)

Required

1. Prepare a table that shows the computation of cash collections of its credit sales (accounts receivable) in each of the months of June and July.

2. Prepare a table that shows the computation of budgeted ending inventories (in units) for April, May, June, and July.

3. Prepare the merchandise purchases budget for May, June, and July. Report calculations in units and then show the dollar amount of purchases for each month.

4. Prepare a table showing the computation of cash payments on product purchases for June and July.

5. Prepare a cash budget for June and July, including any loan activity and interest expense. Compute the loan balance at the end of each month.

Check   (1) Cash collections: June, $597,600; July, $820,800

(3) Budgeted purchases: May, $308,000; June, $638,000

(5) Budgeted ending loan balance: June, $43,650; July, $0

Analysis Component

6. Refer to your answer to part 5. Aztec's cash budget indicates the company will need to borrow more than $18,000 in June. Suggest some reasons that knowing this information in May would be helpful to management.

Problem 22-4A
Merchandising: Preparation and analysis of budgeted income statements

C2 P2

Merline, a one-product mail-order firm, buys its product for $75 per unit and sells it for $150 per unit. The sales staff receives a 10% commission on the sale of each unit. Its December income statement follows.

MERLINE COMPANY Income Statement For Month Ended December 31, 2013	
Sales	$2,250,000
Cost of goods sold	1,125,000
Gross profit	1,125,000
Expenses	
Sales commissions (10%)	225,000
Advertising	250,000
Store rent	30,000
Administrative salaries	45,000
Depreciation	50,000
Other expenses	10,000
Total expenses	610,000
Net income	$ 515,000

Management expects December's results to be repeated in January, February, and March of 2014 without any changes in strategy. Management, however, has an alternative plan. It believes that unit sales will increase at a rate of 10% *each* month for the next three months (beginning with January) if the item's selling price is reduced to $125 per unit and advertising expenses are increased by 15% and remain at that level for all three months. The cost of its product will remain at $75 per unit, the sales staff will continue to earn a 10% commission, and the remaining expenses will stay the same.

Required

Check (1) Budgeted net income: January, $196,250; February, $258,125; March, $326,187

1. Prepare budgeted income statements for each of the months of January, February, and March that show the expected results from implementing the proposed changes. Use a three-column format, with one column for each month.

Analysis Component

2. Use the budgeted income statements from part 1 to recommend whether management should implement the proposed changes. Explain.

Problem 22-5A
Merchandising: Preparation of a complete master budget

C2 P1 P2

Near the end of 2013, the management of Dimsdale Sports Co., a merchandising company, prepared the following estimated balance sheet for December 31, 2013.

DIMSDALE SPORTS COMPANY Estimated Balance Sheet December 31, 2013					
Assets			**Liabilities and Equity**		
Cash	$ 36,000		Accounts payable	$360,000	
Accounts receivable	525,000		Bank loan payable	15,000	
Inventory	150,000		Taxes payable (due 3/15/2014) . . .	90,000	
Total current assets		$ 711,000	Total liabilities		$465,000
Equipment	540,000		Common stock	472,500	
Less accumulated depreciation . . .	67,500		Retained earnings	246,000	
Equipment, net		472,500	Total stockholders' equity		718,500
Total assets		$1,183,500	Total liabilities and equity		$1,183,500

To prepare a master budget for January, February, and March of 2014, management gathers the following information.

a. Dimsdale Sports' single product is purchased for $30 per unit and resold for $55 per unit. The expected inventory level of 5,000 units on December 31, 2013, is more than management's desired level for 2014, which is 20% of the next month's expected sales (in units). Expected sales are: January, 7,000 units; February, 9,000 units; March, 11,000 units; and April, 10,000 units.

b. Cash sales and credit sales represent 25% and 75%, respectively, of total sales. Of the credit sales, 60% is collected in the first month after the month of sale and 40% in the second month after the month of sale. For the December 31, 2013, accounts receivable balance, $125,000 is collected in January and the remaining $400,000 is collected in February.

c. Merchandise purchases are paid for as follows: 20% in the first month after the month of purchase and 80% in the second month after the month of purchase. For the December 31, 2013, accounts payable balance, $80,000 is paid in January and the remaining $280,000 is paid in February.

d. Sales commissions equal to 20% of sales are paid each month. Sales salaries (excluding commissions) are $60,000 per year.

e. General and administrative salaries are $144,000 per year. Maintenance expense equals $2,000 per month and is paid in cash.

f. Equipment reported in the December 31, 2013, balance sheet was purchased in January 2013. It is being depreciated over eight years under the straight-line method with no salvage value. The following amounts for new equipment purchases are planned in the coming quarter: January, $36,000; February, $96,000; and March, $28,800. This equipment will be depreciated under the straight-line method over eight years with no salvage value. A full month's depreciation is taken for the month in which equipment is purchased.

g. The company plans to acquire land at the end of March at a cost of $150,000, which will be paid with cash on the last day of the month.

h. Dimsdale Sports has a working arrangement with its bank to obtain additional loans as needed. The interest rate is 12% per year, and interest is paid at each month-end based on the beginning balance. Partial or full payments on these loans can be made on the last day of the month. The company has agreed to maintain a minimum ending cash balance of $25,000 in each month.

i. The income tax rate for the company is 40%. Income taxes on the first quarter's income will not be paid until April 15.

Required

Prepare a master budget for each of the first three months of 2014; include the following component budgets (show supporting calculations as needed, and round amounts to the nearest dollar):

1. Monthly sales budgets (showing both budgeted unit sales and dollar sales).

2. Monthly merchandise purchases budgets.

3. Monthly selling expense budgets.

4. Monthly general and administrative expense budgets.

5. Monthly capital expenditures budgets.

6. Monthly cash budgets.

7. Budgeted income statement for the entire first quarter (not for each month).

8. Budgeted balance sheet as of March 31, 2014.

Check (2) Budgeted purchases: January, $114,000; February, $282,000
(3) Budgeted selling expenses: January, $82,000; February, $104,000
(6) Ending cash bal.: January, $30,100; February, $210,300
(8) Budgeted total assets at March 31, $1,568,650

Black Diamond Company produces snow skis. Each ski requires 2 pounds of carbon fiber. The company's management predicts that 5,000 skis and 6,000 pounds of carbon fiber will be in inventory on June 30 of the current year and that 150,000 skis will be sold during the next (third) quarter. A set of two skis sells for $300. Management wants to end the third quarter with 3,500 skis and 4,000 pounds of carbon fiber in inventory. Carbon fiber can be purchased for $15 per pound. Each ski requires 0.5 hours of direct labor at $20 per hour. Variable overhead is applied at the rate of $8 per direct labor hour. The company budgets fixed overhead of $1,782,000 for the quarter.

Problem 22-6A^A
Manufacturing: Preparing production and manufacturing budgets

C2 P3

Required

1. Prepare the third-quarter production budget for skis.

2. Prepare the third-quarter direct materials (carbon fiber) budget; include the dollar cost of purchases.

[continued on next page]

Check (1) Units manuf., 148,500;
(2) Cost of carbon fiber purchases, $4,425,000

3. Prepare the direct labor budget for the third quarter.

4. Prepare the factory overhead budget for the third quarter.

Problem 22-7A

Manufacturing: Preparation of a complete master budget

C2 P1 P2 P3

The management of Zigby Manufacturing prepared the following estimated balance sheet for March, 2013:

ZIGBY MANUFACTURING				
Estimated Balance Sheet				
March 31, 2013				
Assets		**Liabilities and Equity**		
Cash	$ 40,000	Accounts payable	$ 200,500	
Accounts receivable	342,248	Short-term notes payable	12,000	
Raw materials inventory...........	98,500	Total current liabilities	212,500	
Finished goods inventory	325,540	Long-term note payable	500,000	
Total current assets.............	806,288	Total liabilities	712,500	
Equipment, gross.................	600,000	Common stock	335,000	
Accumulated depreciation	(150,000)	Retained earnings	208,788	
Equipment, net	450,000	Total stockholders' equity	543,788	
Total assets	$1,256,288	Total liabilities and equity	$1,256,288	

To prepare a master budget for April, May, and June of 2013, management gathers the following information:

a. Sales for March total 20,500 units. Forecasted sales in units are as follows: April, 20,500; May, 19,500; June, 20,000; July, 20,500. Sales of 240,000 units are forecasted for the entire year. The product's selling price is $23.85 per unit and its total product cost is $19.85 per unit.

b. Company policy calls for a given month's ending raw materials inventory to equal 50% of the next month's materials requirements. The March 31 raw materials inventory is 4,925 units, which complies with the policy. The expected June 30 ending raw materials inventory is 4,000 units. Raw materials cost $20 per unit. Each finished unit requires 0.50 units of raw materials.

c. Company policy calls for a given month's ending finished goods inventory to equal 80% of the next month's expected unit sales. The March 31 finished goods inventory is 16,400 units, which complies with the policy.

d. Each finished unit requires 0.50 hours of direct labor at a rate of $15 per hour.

e. Overhead is allocated based on direct labor hours. The predetermined variable overhead rate is $2.70 per direct labor hour. Depreciation of $20,000 per month is treated as fixed factory overhead.

f. Sales representatives' commissions are 8% of sales and are paid in the month of the sales. The sales manager's monthly salary is $3,000 per month.

g. Monthly general and administrative expenses include $12,000 administrative salaries and 0.9% monthly interest on the long-term note payable.

h. The company expects 30% of sales to be for cash and the remaining 70% on credit. Receivables are collected in full in the month following the sale (none is collected in the month of the sale).

i. All raw materials purchases are on credit, and no payables arise from any other transactions. One month's raw materials purchases are fully paid in the next month.

j. The minimum ending cash balance for all months is $40,000. If necessary, the company borrows enough cash using a short-term note to reach the minimum. Short-term notes require an interest payment of 1% at each month-end (before any repayment). If the ending cash balance exceeds the minimum, the excess will be applied to repaying the short-term notes payable balance.

k. Dividends of $10,000 are to be declared and paid in May.

l. No cash payments for income taxes are to be made during the second calendar quarter. Income tax will be assessed at 35% in the quarter and paid in the third calendar quarter.

m. Equipment purchases of $130,000 are budgeted for the last day of June.

Required

Prepare the following budgets and other financial information as required. All budgets and other financial information should be prepared for the second calendar quarter, except as otherwise noted below. Round calculations up to the nearest whole dollar, except for the amount of cash sales, which should be rounded down to the nearest whole dollar.:

1. Sales budget.
2. Production budget.
3. Raw materials budget.
4. Direct labor budget.
5. Factory overhead budget.
6. Selling expense budget.
7. General and administrative expense budget.
8. Cash budget.
9. Budgeted income statement for the entire first quarter (not for each month separately).
10. Budgeted statement of retained earnings.
11. Budgeted balance sheet as of the end of the second calendar quarter.

Check (2) Units to produce: April, 19,700; May, 19,900
(3) Cost of raw materials purchases, April, $198,000
(5) Total overhead cost, May, $46,865

(8) Ending cash balance: April, $83,346; May, $124,295

(10) Budgeted total assets, June 30: $1,299,440

H20 Sports Company is a merchandiser of three different products. The company's March 31 inventories are water skis, 40,000 units; tow ropes, 90,000 units; and life jackets, 150,000 units. Management believes that excessive inventories have accumulated for all three products. As a result, a new policy dictates that ending inventory in any month should equal 10% of the expected unit sales for the following month. Expected sales in units for April, May, June, and July follow.

PROBLEM SET B

Problem 22-1B
Merchandising: Preparation and analysis of purchases budgets

C2 P1

| | Budgeted Sales in Units | | | |
	April	May	June	July
Water skis	70,000	90,000	130,000	100,000
Tow ropes	100,000	90,000	110,000	100,000
Life jackets	160,000	190,000	200,000	120,000

Required

1. Prepare a merchandise purchases budget (in units) for each product for each of the months of April, May, and June.

Check (1) April budgeted purchases: Water skis, 39,000; Tow ropes, 19,000; Life jackets, 29,000

Analysis Component

2. The purchases budgets in part 1 should reflect fewer purchases of all three products in April compared to those in May and June. What factor caused fewer purchases to be planned? Suggest business conditions that would cause this factor to both occur and affect the company as it has.

During the last week of March, Sony Stereo's owner approaches the bank for a $80,000 loan to be made on April 1 and repaid on June 30 with annual interest of 12%, for an interest cost of $2,400. The owner plans to increase the store's inventory by $60,000 in April and needs the loan to pay for inventory acquisitions. The bank's loan officer needs more information about Sony Stereo's ability to repay the loan and asks the owner to forecast the store's June 30 cash position. On April 1, Sony Stereo is expected to have a $3,000 cash balance, $135,000 of accounts receivable, and $100,000 of accounts

Problem 22-2B
Merchandising: Preparation of cash budgets (for three periods)

C2 P2

payable. Its budgeted sales, merchandise purchases, and various cash disbursements for the next three months follow.

Budgeted Figures*	April	May	June
Sales	$220,000	$300,000	$380,000
Merchandise purchases	210,000	180,000	220,000
Cash disbursements			
Payroll	16,000	17,000	18,000
Rent	6,000	6,000	6,000
Other cash expenses	64,000	8,000	7,000
Repayment of bank loan			80,000
Interest on the bank loan.........			2,400

*Operations began in March; March sales were $180,000 and purchases were $100,000.

The budgeted April merchandise purchases include the inventory increase. All sales are on account. The company predicts that 25% of credit sales is collected in the month of the sale, 45% in the month following the sale, 20% in the second month, 9% in the third, and the remainder is uncollectible. Applying these percents to the March credit sales, for example, shows that $81,000 of the $180,000 will be collected in April, $36,000 in May, and $16,200 in June. All merchandise is purchased on credit; 80% of the balance is paid in the month following a purchase and the remaining 20% is paid in the second month. For example, of the $100,000 March purchases, $80,000 will be paid in April and $20,000 in May.

Check Budgeted cash balance: April, $53,000; May, $44,000; June, $34,800

Required

Prepare a cash budget for April, May, and June for Sony Stereo. Show supporting calculations as needed.

Problem 22-3B

Merchandising: Preparation and analysis of cash budgets with supporting inventory and purchases budgets

C2 P2

Connick Company sells its product for $22 per unit. Its actual and projected sales follow.

	Units	Dollars
January (actual)	18,000	$396,000
February (actual)	22,500	495,000
March (budgeted)	19,000	418,000
April (budgeted)	18,750	412,500
May (budgeted)	21,000	462,000

All sales are on credit. Recent experience shows that 40% of credit sales is collected in the month of the sale, 35% in the month after the sale, 23% in the second month after the sale, and 2% proves to be uncollectible. The product's purchase price is $12 per unit. All purchases are payable within 21 days. Thus, 30% of purchases made in a month is paid in that month and the other 70% is paid in the next month. The company has a policy to maintain an ending monthly inventory of 20% of the next month's unit sales plus a safety stock of 100 units. The January 31 and February 28 actual inventory levels are consistent with this policy. Selling and administrative expenses for the year are $1,920,000 and are paid evenly throughout the year in cash. The company's minimum cash balance for month-end is $50,000. This minimum is maintained, if necessary, by borrowing cash from the bank. If the balance exceeds $50,000, the company repays as much of the loan as it can without going below the minimum. This type of loan carries an annual 12% interest rate. At February 28, the loan balance is $12,000, and the company's cash balance is $50,000.

Required

Check (1) Cash collections: March, $431,530; April, $425,150

1. Prepare a table that shows the computation of cash collections of its credit sales (accounts receivable) in each of the months of March and April.
2. Prepare a table showing the computations of budgeted ending inventories (units) for January, February, March, and April.

(3) Budgeted purchases: February, $261,600; March, $227,400

3. Prepare the merchandise purchases budget for February, March, and April. Report calculations in units and then show the dollar amount of purchases for each month.
4. Prepare a table showing the computation of cash payments on product purchases for March and April.

(5) Ending cash balance: March, $58,070, April, $94,920

5. Prepare a cash budget for March and April, including any loan activity and interest expense. Compute the loan balance at the end of each month.

Analysis Component

6. Refer to your answer to part 5. Connick's cash budget indicates whether the company must borrow additional funds at the end of March. Suggest some reasons that knowing the loan needs in advance would be helpful to management.

Comp-Media buys its product for $60 and sells it for $130 per unit. The sales staff receives a 10% commission on the sale of each unit. Its June income statement follows.

Problem 22-4B

Merchandising: Preparation and analysis of budgeted income statements

C2   P2

COMP-MEDIA COMPANY	
Income Statement	
For Month Ended June 30, 2013	
Sales	$1,300,000
Cost of goods sold	600,000
Gross profit	700,000
Expenses	
Sales commissions (10%)	130,000
Advertising	200,000
Store rent	24,000
Administrative salaries	40,000
Depreciation	50,000
Other expenses	12,000
Total expenses	456,000
Net income	$ 244,000

Management expects June's results to be repeated in July, August, and September without any changes in strategy. Management, however, has another plan. It believes that unit sales will increase at a rate of 10% *each* month for the next three months (beginning with July) if the item's selling price is reduced to $115 per unit and advertising expenses are increased by 25% and remain at that level for all three months. The cost of its product will remain at $60 per unit, the sales staff will continue to earn a 10% commission, and the remaining expenses will stay the same.

Required

1. Prepare budgeted income statements for each of the months of July, August, and September that show the expected results from implementing the proposed changes. Use a three-column format, with one column for each month.

Check   Budgeted net income: July, $102,500; August, $150,350; September, $202,985

Analysis Component

2. Use the budgeted income statements from part 1 to recommend whether management should implement the proposed plan. Explain.

Near the end of 2013, the management of Isle Corp., a merchandising company, prepared the following estimated balance sheet for December 31, 2013.

Problem 22-5B

Merchandising: Preparation of a complete master budget

C2   P1   P2

ISLE CORPORATION				
Estimated Balance Sheet				
December 31, 2013				
Assets			**Liabilities and Equity**	
Cash	$ 36,000		Accounts payable	$360,000
Accounts receivable	525,000		Bank loan payable	15,000
Inventory	150,000		Taxes payable (due 3/15/2014)	90,000
Total current assets		$ 711,000	Total liabilities	$ 465,000
Equipment	540,000		Common stock	472,500
Less accumulated depreciation	67,500		Retained earnings	246,000
Equipment, net		472,500	Total stockholders' equity	718,500
Total assets		$1,183,500	Total liabilities and equity	$1,183,500

To prepare a master budget for January, February, and March of 2014, management gathers the following information.

a. Isle Corp.'s single product is purchased for $30 per unit and resold for $45 per unit. The expected inventory level of 5,000 units on December 31, 2013, is more than management's desired level for 2014, which is 25% of the next month's expected sales (in units). Expected sales are: January, 6,000 units; February, 8,000 units; March, 10,000 units; and April, 9,000 units.

b. Cash sales and credit sales represent 25% and 75%, respectively, of total sales. Of the credit sales, 60% is collected in the first month after the month of sale and 40% in the second month after the month of sale. For the $525,000 accounts receivable balance at December 31, 2013, $315,000 is collected in January 2014 and the remaining $210,000 is collected in February 2014.

c. Merchandise purchases are paid for as follows: 20% in the first month after the month of purchase and 80% in the second month after the month of purchase. For the $360,000 accounts payable balance at December 31, 2013, $72,000 is paid in January 2014 and the remaining $288,000 is paid in February 2014.

d. Sales commissions equal to 20% of sales are paid each month. Sales salaries (excluding commissions) are $90,000 per year.

e. General and administrative salaries are $144,000 per year. Maintenance expense equals $3,000 per month and is paid in cash.

f. Equipment reported in the December 31, 2013, balance sheet was purchased in January 2013. It is being depreciated over 8 years under the straight-line method with no salvage value. The following amounts for new equipment purchases are planned in the coming quarter: January, $72,000; February, $96,000; and March, $28,800. This equipment will be depreciated using the straight-line method over 8 years with no salvage value. A full month's depreciation is taken for the month in which equipment is purchased.

g. The company plans to acquire land at the end of March at a cost of $150,000, which will be paid with cash on the last day of the month.

h. Isle Corp. has a working arrangement with its bank to obtain additional loans as needed. The interest rate is 12% per year, and interest is paid at each month-end based on the beginning balance. Partial or full payments on these loans can be made on the last day of the month. Isle has agreed to maintain a minimum ending cash balance of $36,000 in each month.

i. The income tax rate for the company is 40%. Income taxes on the first quarter's income will not be paid until April 15.

Required

Prepare a master budget for each of the first three months of 2014; include the following component budgets (show supporting calculations as needed, and round amounts to the nearest dollar):

1. Monthly sales budgets (showing both budgeted unit sales and dollar sales).
2. Monthly merchandise purchases budgets.
3. Monthly selling expense budgets.
4. Monthly general and administrative expense budgets.
5. Monthly capital expenditures budgets.
6. Monthly cash budgets.
7. Budgeted income statement for the entire first quarter (not for each month).
8. Budgeted balance sheet as of March 31, 2014.

Check   (2) Budgeted purchases: January, $90,000; February, $255,000;
(3) Budgeted selling expenses: January, $61,500; February, $79,500

(6) Ending cash bal.: January, $182,500; February, $107,850

(8) Budgeted total assets at March 31, $1,346,875

Problem 22-6B[A]

Manufacturing: Preparing production and manufacturing budgets

C2 P3

NSA Company produces baseball bats. Each bat requires 3 pounds of aluminum alloy. Management predicts that 8,000 bats and 15,000 pounds of aluminum alloy will be in inventory on March 31 of the current year and that 250,000 bats will be sold during this year's second quarter. Bats sell for $80 each. Management wants to end the second quarter with 6,000 finished bats and 12,000 pounds of aluminum alloy in inventory. Aluminum alloy can be purchased for $4 per pound. Each bat requires 0.5 hours of direct labor at $18 per hour. Variable overhead is applied at the rate of $12 per direct labor hour. The company budgets fixed overhead of $1,776,000 for the quarter.

Required

1. Prepare the second-quarter production budget for bats.

2. Prepare the second-quarter direct materials (aluminum alloy) budget; include the dollar cost of purchases.

3. Prepare the direct labor budget for the second quarter.

4. Prepare the factory overhead budget for the second quarter.

Check   (1) Units manuf., 248,000;
(2) Cost of materials
purchases, $2,964,000

The management of Nabar Manufacturing prepared the following estimated balance sheet for June, 2013:

Problem 22-7B
Manufacturing: Preparation of a complete master budget

C2   P1   P2   P3

NABAR MANUFACTURING
Estimated Balance Sheet
June 30, 2013

Assets		Liabilities and Equity	
Cash	$ 40,000	Accounts payable	$ 51,400
Accounts receivable	249,900	Income taxes payable............	10,000
Raw materials inventory...........	35,000	Short-term notes payable	24,000
Finished goods inventory	241,080	Total current liabilities	85,400
Total current assets.............	565,980	Long-term note payable	300,000
Equipment, gross.................	720,000	Total liabilities	385,400
Accumulated depreciation	(240,000)	Common stock	600,000
Equipment, net	480,000	Retained earnings	60,580
		Total stockholders' equity	660,580
Total assets	$1,045,980	Total liabilities and equity	$1,045,980

To prepare a master budget for July, August, and September of 2013, management gathers the following information:

a. Sales were 20,000 units in June. Forecasted sales in units are as follows: July, 21,000; August, 19,000; September, 20,000; October, 24,000. The product's selling price is $17 per unit and its total product cost is $14.35 per unit.

b. Company policy calls for a given month's ending finished goods inventory to equal 70% of the next month's expected unit sales. The June 30 finished goods inventory is 16,800 units, which does not comply with the policy.

c. Company policy calls for a given month's ending raw materials inventory to equal 20% of the next month's materials requirements. The June 30 raw materials inventory is 4,375 units (which also fails to meet the policy). The budgeted September 30 raw materials inventory is 1,980 units. Raw materials cost $8 per unit. Each finished unit requires 0.50 units of raw materials.

d. Each finished unit requires 0.50 hours of direct labor at a rate of $16 per hour.

e. Overhead is allocated based on direct labor hours. The predetermined variable overhead rate is $1.35 per direct labor hour. Depreciation of $20,000 per month is treated as fixed factory overhead.

f. Monthly general and administrative expenses include $9,000 administrative salaries and 0.9% monthly interest on the long-term note payable.

g. Sales representatives' commissions are 10% of sales and are paid in the month of the sales. The sales manager's monthly salary is $3,500 per month.

h. The company expects 30% of sales to be for cash and the remaining 70% on credit. Receivables are collected in full in the month following the sale (none is collected in the month of the sale).

i. All raw materials purchases are on credit, and no payables arise from any other transactions. One month's raw materials purchases are fully paid in the next month.

j. Dividends of $20,000 are to be declared and paid in August.

k. Income taxes payable at June 30 will be paid in July. Income tax expense will be assessed at 35% in the quarter and paid in October.

l. Equipment purchases of $100,000 are budgeted for the last day of September.

m. The minimum ending cash balance for all months is $40,000. If necessary, the company borrows enough cash using a short-term note to reach the minimum. Short-term notes require an interest payment of 1% at each month-end (before any repayment). If the ending cash balance exceeds the minimum, the excess will be applied to repaying the short-term notes payable balance.

Required

Prepare the following budgets and other financial information as required. All budgets and other financial information should be prepared for the second calendar quarter, except as otherwise noted below. Round calculations to the nearest whole dollar:

Check   (2) Units to produce:
July, 17,500; August, 19,700
    (3) Cost of raw materials
purchases, July, $50,760
    (5) Total overhead cost,
August, $46,595

    (8) Ending cash balance:
July, $96,835; August, $141,180

    (10) Budgeted total assets,
Sept. 30: $1,054,920

1. Sales budget.
2. Production budget.
3. Raw materials budget.
4. Direct labor budget.
5. Factory overhead budget.
6. Selling expense budget.
7. General and administrative expense budget.
8. Cash budget.
9. Budgeted income statement for the entire quarter (not for each month separately).
10. Budgeted statement of retained earnings for the quarter.
11. Budgeted balance sheet as of September 30, 2013.

SERIAL PROBLEM
Success Systems

P2

(This serial problem began in Chapter 1 and continues through most of the book. If previous chapter segments were not completed, the serial problem can begin at this point. It is helpful, but not necessary, to use the Working Papers that accompany the book.)

SP 22   Adria Lopez expects second quarter 2014 sales of her new line of computer furniture to be the same as the first quarter's sales (reported below) without any changes in strategy. Monthly sales averaged 40 desk units (sales price of $1,250) and 20 chairs (sales price of $500).

SUCCESS SYSTEMS Segment Income Statement* For Quarter Ended March 31, 2014	
Sales†	$180,000
Cost of goods sold‡	115,000
Gross profit	65,000
Expenses	
Sales commissions (10%)	18,000
Advertising expenses	9,000
Other fixed expenses	18,000
Total expenses	45,000
Net income	$ 20,000

* Reflects revenue and expense activity only related to the computer furniture segment.

† Revenue: (120 desks × $1,250) + (60 chairs × $500) = $150,000 + $30,000 = $180,000

‡ Cost of goods sold: (120 desks × $750) + (60 chairs × $250) + $10,000 = $115,000

Adria Lopez believes that sales will increase each month for the next three months (April, 48 desks, 32 chairs; May, 52 desks, 35 chairs; June, 56 desks, 38 chairs) *if* selling prices are reduced to $1,150 for desks and $450 for chairs, and advertising expenses are increased by 10% and remain at that level for all three months. The products' variable cost will remain at $750 for desks and $250 for chairs. The sales staff will continue to earn a 10% commission, the fixed manufacturing costs per month will remain at $10,000 and other fixed expenses will remain at $6,000 per month.

Required

1. Prepare budgeted income statements for each of the months of April, May, and June that show the expected results from implementing the proposed changes. Use a three-column format, with one column for each month.

2. Use the budgeted income statements from part 1 to recommend whether Adria Lopez should implement the proposed changes. Explain.

Check (1) Budgeted income (loss): April, $(660); May, $945

Beyond the Numbers

BTN 22-1 Financial statements often serve as a starting point in formulating budgets. Review **Polaris'** financial statements to determine its cash paid for acquisitions of property and equipment in the current year and the budgeted cash needed for such acquisitions in the next year.

REPORTING IN ACTION

P2

Polaris

Required

1. Which financial statement reports the amount of cash paid for acquisitions of property and equipment? Explain where on the statement this information is reported.

2. Indicate the amount of cash (a) paid for acquisitions of property and equipment in the year ended December 31, 2011, and (b) to be paid (budgeted for) next year under the assumption that annual acquisitions of property and equipment equal 40% of the prior year's net income.

Fast Forward

3. Access Polaris' financial statements for a year ending after December 31, 2011, from either its Website [**Polaris.com**] or the SEC's EDGAR database [**www.sec.gov**]. Compare your answer for part 2 with actual cash paid for acquisitions of property and equipment for that fiscal year. Compute the error, if any, in your estimate. Speculate as to why cash paid for acquisitions of property and equipment was higher or lower than your estimate.

BTN 22-2 One source of cash savings for a company is improved management of inventory. To illustrate, assume that **Polaris** and **Arctic Cat** both have $1,000,000 per month in sales of one model of snowmobiles in Canada, and both forecast this level of sales per month for the next 24 months. Also assume that both Polaris and Arctic Cat have a 20% contribution margin, their fixed costs are equal, and that cost of goods sold is the only variable cost. Assume that the main difference between Polaris and Arctic Cat is the distribution system. Polaris uses a just-in-time system and requires ending inventory of only 10% of next month's sales in inventory at each month-end. However, Arctic Cat is building an improved distribution system and currently requires 30% of next month's sales in inventory at each month-end.

COMPARATIVE ANALYSIS

P2

Polaris

Arctic Cat

Required

1. Compute the amount by which Arctic Cat can reduce its inventory level if it can match Polaris' system of maintaining an inventory equal to 10% of next month's sales. (*Hint:* Focus on the facts given and only on the Canadian market.)

2. Explain how the analysis in part 1 that shows ending inventory levels for both the 30% and 10% required inventory policies can help justify a just-in-time inventory system. Assume a 15% interest cost for resources that are tied up in ending inventory.

ETHICS CHALLENGE

C1

BTN 22-3   Both the budget process and budgets themselves can impact management actions, both positively and negatively. For instance, a common practice among not-for-profit organizations and government agencies is for management to spend any amounts remaining in a budget at the end of the budget period, a practice often called "use it or lose it." The view is that if a department manager does not spend the budgeted amount, top management will reduce next year's budget by the amount not spent. To avoid losing budget dollars, department managers often spend all budgeted amounts regardless of the value added to products or services. All of us pay for the costs associated with this budget system.

Required

Write a one-half page report to a local not-for-profit organization or government agency offering a solution to the "use it or lose it" budgeting problem.

COMMUNICATING IN PRACTICE

C2

BTN 22-4   The sales budget is usually the first and most crucial of the component budgets in a master budget because all other budgets usually rely on it for planning purposes.

Required

Assume that your company's sales staff provides information on expected sales and selling prices for items making up the sales budget. Prepare a one-page memorandum to your supervisor outlining concerns with the sales staff's input in the sales budget when its compensation is at least partly tied to these budgets. More generally, explain the importance of assessing any potential bias in information provided to the budget process.

TAKING IT TO THE NET

C1

BTN 22-5   Access information on e-budgets through The Manage Mentor:
http://www.themanagementor.com/kuniverse/kmailers_universe/finance_kmailers/cfa/budgeting2.htm
Read the information provided.

Required

1. Assume the role of a senior manager in a large, multidivision company. What are the benefits of using e-budgets?
2. As a senior manager, what concerns do you have with the concept and application of e-budgets?

TEAMWORK IN ACTION

A1

BTN 22-6   Your team is to prepare a budget report outlining the costs of attending college (full-time) for the next two semesters (30 hours) or three quarters (45 hours). This budget's focus is solely on attending college; do not include personal items in the team's budget. Your budget must include tuition, books, supplies, club fees, food, housing, and all costs associated with travel to and from college. This budgeting exercise is similar to the initial phase in activity-based budgeting. Include a list of any assumptions you use in completing the budget. Be prepared to present your budget in class.

ENTREPRENEURIAL DECISION

C1

BTN 22-7   **Freshii** sells fresh foods with a focus on healthy fare. Company founder Matthew Corrin stresses the importance of planning and budgeting for business success.

Required

1. How can budgeting help Matthew Corrin efficiently develop and operate his business?
2. Why would sales forecasts and purchases budgets be particularly important for a business like Freshii?

BTN 22-8   To help understand the factors impacting a sales budget, you are to visit three businesses with the same ownership or franchise membership. Record the selling prices of two identical products at each location, such as regular and premium gas sold at **Chevron** stations. You are likely to find a difference in prices for at least one of the three locations you visit.

HITTING THE ROAD

C2   P1

Required

1. Identify at least three external factors that must be considered when setting the sales budget. (*Note:* There is a difference between internal and external factors that impact the sales budget.)
2. What factors might explain any differences identified in the prices of the businesses you visited?

BTN 22-9   Access **KTM**'s income statement (in Appendix A) for the business year 2011.

GLOBAL DECISION

P1

KTM

Required

1. Is KTM's infrastructure and administration expense budget likely to be an important budget in its master budgeting process? Explain.
2. Identify three types of expenses that would be reported as infrastructure and administration expenses on KTM's income statement.
3. Who likely has the initial responsibility for KTM's infrastructure and administration expense budget? Explain.

ANSWERS TO MULTIPLE CHOICE QUIZ

1. c

2. e; Budgeted purchases = $36,000 + $7,000 − $6,000 = $37,000

3. b; Cash collected = 25% of September sales + 75% of August sales = (0.25 × $240,000) + (0.75 × $220,000) = $225,000

4. d

5. a; 560 units + (0.30 × 600 units) − (0.30 × 560 units) = 572 units

Flexible Budgets and Standard Costs

23

Learning Objectives

CONCEPTUAL

C1 Define *standard costs* and explain how standard cost information is useful for management by exception. (p. 953)

C2 Describe variances and what they reveal about performance. (p. 955)

ANALYTICAL

A1 Analyze changes in sales from expected amounts. (p. 963)

PROCEDURAL

P1 Prepare a flexible budget and interpret a flexible budget performance report. (p. 950)

P2 Compute materials and labor variances. (p. 956)

P3 Compute overhead variances. (p. 960)

P4 *Appendix 23A*—Prepare journal entries for standard costs and account for price and quantity variances. (p. 970)

Decision Insight

Whoosh!

"Skiing is not just a sport, it's a life-long choice."
—MIKE McCABE

BOULDER, CO—Self-described "ski bum" Jordan Grano wanted a pair of skis that could handle more than one ski season. Frustrated by the quality and performance of "off-the-rack" skis, Jordan began researching how to build better skis. The result is **Folsom Custom Skis (folsomskis.com),** the company he founded in 2007. In addition to building custom skis to precise customer specifications, the company also builds "semi-custom" skis which allow customers fewer choices.

Master Builder and current company President Mike McCabe says customers can "take their favorite skis and alter them to suit their needs and wants. We come up with a finished ski built exactly to customer specifications." The company's manufacturing process demands precision. "Design elements like ski turn radius, camber, and taper interact in complex ways and require careful measurement," says Mike. The result is a better-quality and more durable ski as Mike, a professional skier, can attest to. "I was hired to break a set of skis. I failed."

Manufacturers like Folsom Custom Skis must control materials, labor, and overhead costs. Determining standard costs helps. For example, Mike estimates it takes 12 hours to go from design to a complete ski. "We make them as fast as we can but we don't cut corners; we make sure we put an equal amount of time into every one of our skis," explains Mike. Putting too much time into a ski could waste the company's productive capacity,

but putting too little time into a ski could result in an inferior product. Attention to variances from standards can keep the manufacturing process on track.

The company uses only the highest quality poplar and bamboo in their skis. Here too, Mike analyzes materials price and quantity variances to control costs. Mike stresses the importance of "having precise specifications and controls to detect problems; we don't use any material that does not meet our requirements." Unfavorable materials price variances could result from rising raw materials prices, which could cause the company to consider alternative suppliers or raising prices.

At an average price of about $1,300 per pair, the company reports revenue of about $300,000 per year. While currently operating at about a break-even level, Mike hopes to double the company's output and ultimately make profits. The use of flexible budgets, reflecting cost estimates at different production levels, can be useful in making business decisions. While attention to budgeting, standards, and variances is important, Mike encourages entrepreneurs to "build a business on something you feel passionate about."

[Sources: *Folsom Custom Skis website*, January 2013; *Boulder County Business Report*, November 13, 2009; *Skiing mag* (*www.skinet.com*), July 2009.]

Budgeting helps organize and formalize management's planning activities. This chapter extends the study of budgeting to look more closely at the use of budgets to evaluate performance. Evaluations are important for controlling and monitoring business activities. This chapter also describes and illustrates the use of standard costs and variance analyses. These managerial tools are useful for both evaluating and controlling organizations and for the planning of future activities.

Flexible Budgets

Budgetary Process	Flexible Budget Reports
• Control and reporting • Fixed budget performance report • Budget reports for evaluation	• Purpose • Preparation • Flexible budget performance report

Standard Costs

Materials and Labor Standards	Cost Variances	Overhead Standards and Variances
• Identifying standard costs • Setting standard costs	• Analysis • Computation • Computing materials and labor variances	• Setting overhead standards • Predicting activity levels • Computing overhead variances

Section 1—Flexible Budgets

This section introduces fixed budgets and fixed budget performance reports. It then introduces flexible budgets and flexible budget performance reports and illustrates their advantages.

BUDGETARY PROCESS

A master budget reflects management's planned objectives for a future period. The preparation of a master budget is based on a predicted level of activity such as sales volume for the budget period. This section discusses the effects on the usefulness of budget reports when the actual level of activity differs from the predicted level.

Budgetary Control and Reporting

Budgetary control refers to management's use of budgets to monitor and control a company's operations. This includes using budgets to see that planned objectives are met. **Budget reports** contain relevant information that compares actual results to planned activities. This comparison is motivated by a need to both monitor performance and control activities. Budget reports are sometimes viewed as progress reports, or *report cards,* on management's performance in achieving planned objectives. These reports can be prepared at any time and for any period. Three common periods for a budget report are a month, quarter, and year.

Point: Budget reports are often used to determine bonuses of managers.

The budgetary control process involves at least four steps: (1) develop the budget from planned objectives, (2) compare actual results to budgeted amounts and analyze any differences, (3) take corrective and strategic actions, and (4) establish new planned objectives and prepare a new budget. Exhibit 23.1 shows this continual process of budgetary control. Budget reports and

EXHIBIT 23.1

Process of Budgetary Control

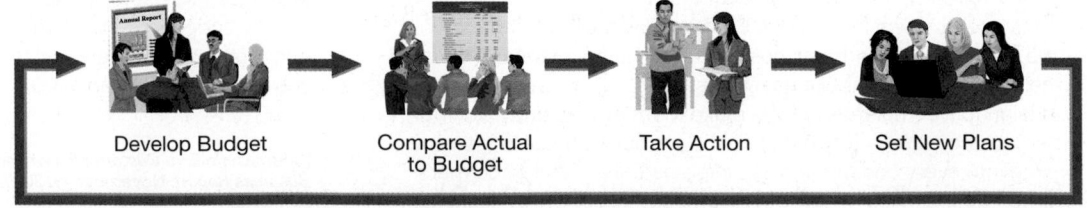

Develop Budget → Compare Actual to Budget → Take Action → Set New Plans

related documents are effective tools for managers to obtain the greatest benefits from this budgetary process.

Fixed Budget Performance Report

In a fixed budgetary control system, the master budget is based on a single prediction for sales volume or other activity level. The budgeted amount for each cost essentially assumes that a specific (or *fixed*) amount of sales will occur. A **fixed budget,** also called a *static budget,* is based on a single predicted amount of sales or other measure of activity.

One benefit of a budget is its usefulness in comparing actual results with planned activities. Information useful for analysis is often presented for comparison in a performance report. As shown in Exhibit 23.2, a **fixed budget performance report** for **Optel** compares actual results for January 2013 with the results expected under its fixed budget that predicted 10,000 (composite) units of sales. Optel manufactures inexpensive eyeglasses, frames, contact lens, and related supplies. For this report, its production volume equals sales volume (its inventory level did not change).

EXHIBIT 23.2

Fixed Budget Performance Report

OPTEL Fixed Budget Performance Report For Month Ended January 31, 2013	Fixed Budget	Actual Results	Variances*
Sales (in units)	10,000	12,000	
Sales (in dollars)	$100,000	$125,000	$25,000 F
Cost of goods sold			
Direct materials	10,000	13,000	3,000 U
Direct labor	15,000	20,000	5,000 U
Overhead			
Factory supplies	2,000	2,100	100 U
Utilities	3,000	4,000	1,000 U
Depreciation—machinery	8,000	8,000	0
Supervisory salaries	11,000	11,000	0
Selling expenses			
Sales commissions	9,000	10,800	1,800 U
Shipping expenses	4,000	4,300	300 U
General and administrative expenses			
Office supplies	5,000	5,200	200 U
Insurance expenses	1,000	1,200	200 U
Depreciation—office equipment	7,000	7,000	0
Administrative salaries	13,000	13,000	0
Total expenses	88,000	99,600	11,600 U
Income from operations	$ 12,000	$ 25,400	$13,400 F

* F = Favorable variance; U = Unfavorable variance.

This type of performance report designates differences between budgeted and actual results as variances. We see the letters *F* and *U* located beside the numbers in the third number column of this report. Their meanings are as follows:

F = **Favorable variance**   When compared to budget, the actual cost or revenue contributes to a *higher* income. That is, actual revenue is higher than budgeted revenue, or actual cost is lower than budgeted cost.

U = **Unfavorable variance**   When compared to budget, the actual cost or revenue contributes to a *lower* income; actual revenue is lower than budgeted revenue, or actual cost is higher than budgeted cost.

This convention is common in practice and is used throughout this chapter.

Example: How is it that the favorable sales variance in Exhibit 23.2 is linked with so many unfavorable cost and expense variances? *Answer:* Costs have increased with the increase in sales.

Budget Reports for Evaluation

A primary use of budget reports is as a tool for management to monitor and control operations. Evaluation by Optel management is likely to focus on a variety of questions that might include these:

- Why is actual income from operations $13,400 higher than budgeted?
- Are amounts paid for each expense item too high?
- Is manufacturing using too much direct material?
- Is manufacturing using too much direct labor?

The performance report in Exhibit 23.2 provides little help in answering these questions because actual sales volume is 2,000 units higher than budgeted. A manager does not know if this higher level of sales activity is the cause of variations in total dollar sales and expenses or if other factors have influenced these amounts. This inability of fixed budget reports to adjust for changes in activity levels is a major limitation of a fixed budget performance report. That is, it fails to show whether actual costs are out of line due to a change in actual sales volume or some other factor.

Cruise Control   Budget reporting and evaluation are used at service providers such as **Royal Carribbean Cruises Ltd.** It regularly prepares performance plans and budget requests for its fleet of cruise ships, which describe performance goals, measure outcomes, and analyze variances. ■

FLEXIBLE BUDGET REPORTS

Purpose of Flexible Budgets

To help address limitations with the fixed budget performance report, particularly from the effects of changes in sales volume, management can use a flexible budget. A **flexible budget,** also called a *variable budget,* is a report based on predicted amounts of revenues and expenses corresponding to the actual level of output. Flexible budgets are useful both before and after the period's activities are complete.

A flexible budget prepared before the period is often based on several levels of activity. Budgets for those different levels can provide a "what-if" look at operations. The different levels often include both a best case and worst case scenario. This allows management to make adjustments to avoid or lessen the effects of the worst case scenario.

Point: A flexible budget yields an "apples to apples" comparison because budgeted activity levels are the same as the actual.

A flexible budget prepared after the period helps management evaluate past performance. It is especially useful for such an evaluation because it reflects budgeted revenues and costs based on the actual level of activity. Thus, comparisons of actual results with budgeted performance are more likely to identify the causes of any differences. This can help managers focus attention on real problem areas and implement corrective actions. This is in contrast to a fixed budget, whose primary purpose is to assist managers in planning future activities and whose numbers are based on a single predicted amount of budgeted sales or production.

Preparation of Flexible Budgets

P1 Prepare a flexible budget and interpret a flexible budget performance report.

A flexible budget is designed to reveal the effects of volume of activity on revenues and costs. To prepare a flexible budget, management relies on the distinctions between fixed and variable costs. Recall that the cost per unit of activity remains constant for variable costs so that the total amount of a variable cost changes in direct proportion to a change in activity level. The total amount of fixed cost remains unchanged regardless of changes in the level of activity within a relevant (normal) operating range. (Assume that costs can be reasonably classified as variable or fixed within a relevant range.)

When we create the numbers constituting a flexible budget, we express each variable cost as either a constant amount per unit of sales or as a percent of a sales dollar. In the case of a fixed cost, we express its budgeted amount as the total amount expected to occur at any sales volume within the relevant range.

Exhibit 23.3 shows a set of flexible budgets for Optel for January 2013. Seven of its expenses are classified as variable costs. Its remaining five expenses are fixed costs. These classifications result from management's investigation of each expense. Variable and fixed expense categories are *not* the same for every company, and we must avoid drawing conclusions from specific cases. For example, depending on the nature of a company's operations, office supplies expense can be either fixed or variable with respect to sales.

Point: The usefulness of a flexible budget depends on valid classification of variable and fixed costs. Some costs are mixed and must be analyzed to determine their variable and fixed portions.

EXHIBIT 23.3

Flexible Budgets

	Flexible Budget		Flexible Budget for Unit Sales of		
	Variable Amount per Unit	Total Fixed Cost	10,000	12,000	14,000
Sales	$10.00		$100,000	$120,000	$140,000
Variable costs					
Direct materials	1.00		10,000	12,000	14,000
Direct labor	1.50		15,000	18,000	21,000
Factory supplies	0.20		2,000	2,400	2,800
Utilities	0.30		3,000	3,600	4,200
Sales commissions	0.90		9,000	10,800	12,600
Shipping expenses	0.40		4,000	4,800	5,600
Office supplies	0.50		5,000	6,000	7,000
Total variable costs	4.80		48,000	57,600	67,200
Contribution margin	$ 5.20		$ 52,000	$ 62,400	$ 72,800
Fixed costs					
Depreciation—machinery		$ 8,000	8,000	8,000	8,000
Supervisory salaries		11,000	11,000	11,000	11,000
Insurance expense		1,000	1,000	1,000	1,000
Depreciation—office equipment		7,000	7,000	7,000	7,000
Administrative salaries		13,000	13,000	13,000	13,000
Total fixed costs		$40,000	40,000	40,000	40,000
Income from operations			$ 12,000	$ 22,400	$ 32,800

OPTEL
Flexible Budgets
For Month Ended January 31, 2013

The layout for the flexible budgets in Exhibit 23.3 follows a *contribution margin format*—beginning with sales followed by variable costs and then fixed costs. Both the expected individual and total variable costs are reported and then subtracted from sales. The difference between sales and variable costs equals contribution margin. The expected amounts of fixed costs are listed next, followed by the expected income from operations before taxes.

The first and second number columns of Exhibit 23.3 show the flexible budget amounts for variable costs per unit and each fixed cost for any volume of sales in the relevant range. The third, fourth, and fifth columns show the flexible budget amounts computed for three different sales volumes. For instance, the third column's flexible budget is based on 10,000 units. These numbers are the same as those in the fixed budget of Exhibit 23.2 because the expected volumes are the same for these two budgets.

Recall that Optel's actual sales volume for January is 12,000 units. This sales volume is 2,000 units more than the 10,000 units originally predicted in the master budget. When differences between actual and predicted volume arise, the usefulness of a flexible budget is apparent. For instance, compare the flexible budget for 10,000 units in the third column (which is the same as the fixed budget in Exhibit 23.2) with the flexible budget for 12,000 units in the fourth

Example: Using Exhibit 23.3, what is the budgeted income from operations for unit sales of (a) 11,000 and (b) 13,000? *Answers:* $17,200 for unit sales of 11,000; $27,600 for unit sales of 13,000.

Point: Flexible budgeting allows a budget to be prepared at the *actual* output level. Performance reports are then prepared comparing the flexible budget to actual revenues and costs.

column. The higher levels for both sales and variable costs reflect nothing more than the increase in sales activity. Any budget analysis comparing actual with planned results that ignores this information is less useful to management.

To illustrate, when we evaluate Optel's performance, we need to prepare a flexible budget showing actual and budgeted values at 12,000 units. As part of a complete profitability analysis, managers could compare the actual income of $25,400 (from Exhibit 23.2) with the $22,400 income expected at the actual sales volume of 12,000 units (from Exhibit 23.3). This results in a total favorable income variance of $3,000 to be explained and interpreted. This variance is markedly lower from the $13,400 favorable variance identified in Exhibit 23.2 using a fixed budget, but still suggests good performance. After receiving the flexible budget based on January's actual volume, management must determine what caused this $3,000 difference. The next section describes a flexible budget performance report that provides guidance in this analysis.

■ Decision Maker ●━━━━━━━━━━━━━━━━━━━━━━━━━━━━

Entrepreneur The heads of both the strategic consulting and tax consulting divisions of your financial services firm complain to you about the unfavorable variances on their performance reports. "We worked on more consulting assignments than planned. It's not surprising our costs are higher than expected. To top it off, this report characterizes our work as *poor!*" How do you respond? ■ [Answer—p. 972]

Flexible Budget Performance Report

A **flexible budget performance report** lists differences between actual performance and budgeted performance based on actual sales volume or other activity level. This report helps direct management's attention to those costs or revenues that differ substantially from budgeted amounts. Exhibit 23.4 shows Optel's flexible budget performance report for January. We prepare this report after the actual volume is known to be 12,000 units. This report shows a $5,000 favorable variance in total dollar sales. Because actual and budgeted volumes are both 12,000 units, the $5,000 sales variance must have resulted from a higher than expected selling price.

EXHIBIT 23.4

Flexible Budget Performance Report

OPTEL Flexible Budget Performance Report For Month Ended January 31, 2013	Flexible Budget	Actual Results	Variances*
Sales (12,000 units)	$120,000	$125,000	$5,000 F
Variable costs			
Direct materials	12,000	13,000	1,000 U
Direct labor	18,000	20,000	2,000 U
Factory supplies	2,400	2,100	300 F
Utilities	3,600	4,000	400 U
Sales commissions	10,800	10,800	0
Shipping expenses	4,800	4,300	500 F
Office supplies	6,000	5,200	800 F
Total variable costs	57,600	59,400	1,800 U
Contribution margin	62,400	65,600	3,200 F
Fixed costs			
Depreciation—machinery	8,000	8,000	0
Supervisory salaries	11,000	11,000	0
Insurance expense	1,000	1,200	200 U
Depreciation—office equipment	7,000	7,000	0
Administrative salaries	13,000	13,000	0
Total fixed costs	40,000	40,200	200 U
Income from operations	$ 22,400	$ 25,400	$3,000 F

* F = Favorable variance; U = Unfavorable variance.

Further analysis of the facts surrounding this $5,000 sales variance reveals a favorable sales variance per unit of nearly $0.42 as shown here:

Actual average price per unit (rounded to cents)	$125,000/12,000 = $10.42
Budgeted price per unit	$120,000/12,000 = 10.00
Favorable sales variance per unit	$5,000/12,000 = $ 0.42

The other variances in Exhibit 23.4 also direct management's attention to areas where corrective actions can help control Optel's operations. Each expense variance is analyzed as the sales variance was. We can think of each expense as the joint result of using a given number of units of input and paying a specific price per unit of input. Optel's expense variances total $2,000 unfavorable, suggesting poor control of some costs, particularly direct materials and direct labor.

Each variance in Exhibit 23.4 is due in part to a difference between *actual price* per unit of input and *budgeted price* per unit of input. This is a **price variance.** Each variance also can be due in part to a difference between *actual quantity* of input used and *budgeted quantity* of input. This is a **quantity variance.** We explain more about this breakdown, known as **variance analysis,** next in the standard costs section of this chapter.

Quick Check

Answers — p. 973

1. A flexible budget (*a*) shows fixed costs as constant amounts of cost per unit of activity, (*b*) shows variable costs as constant amounts of cost per unit of activity, or (*c*) is prepared based on one expected amount of budgeted sales or production.
2. What is the initial step in preparing a flexible budget?
3. What is the main difference between a fixed and a flexible budget?
4. What is the contribution margin?

Section 2—Standard Costs

Standard costs are preset costs for delivering a product or service under normal conditions. These costs are established by personnel, engineering, and accounting studies using past experiences and data. Management uses these costs to assess the reasonableness of actual costs incurred for producing the product or providing the service. When actual costs vary from standard costs, management follows up to identify potential problems and take corrective actions. **Management by exception** means that managers focus attention on the most significant differences between actual costs and standard costs and give less attention to areas where performance is reasonably close to standard. Management by exception is especially useful when directed at controllable items, enabling top management to affect the actions of lower-level managers responsible for the company's revenues and costs.

Standard costs are often used in preparing budgets because they are the anticipated costs incurred under normal conditions. Terms such as *standard materials cost, standard labor cost,* and *standard overhead cost* are often used to refer to amounts budgeted for direct materials, direct labor, and overhead.

While many managers use standard costs to investigate manufacturing costs, standard costs can also help control *nonmanufacturing* costs. Companies providing services instead of products can also benefit from the use of standard costs. For example, while quality medical service is paramount, efficiency in providing that service is also important to medical professionals. The use of budgeting and standard costing is touted as an effective means to control and monitor medical costs, especially overhead.

C1 Define *standard costs* and explain how standard cost information is useful for management by exception.

Point: Business practice often uses the word *budget* when speaking of total amounts and *standard* when discussing per unit amounts.

■ Decision Ethics

Internal Auditor   You discover a manager who always spends exactly what is budgeted. About 30% of her budget is spent just before the period-end. She admits to spending what is budgeted, whether or not it is needed. She offers three reasons: (1) she doesn't want her budget cut, (2) "management by exception" focuses on budget deviations; and (3) she believes the money is budgeted to be spent. What action do you take? ■   [Answer—p. 972]

MATERIALS AND LABOR STANDARDS

This section explains how to set materials and labor standards and how to prepare a standard cost card.

Identifying Standard Costs

Managerial accountants, engineers, personnel administrators, and other managers combine their efforts to set standard costs. To identify standards for direct labor costs, we can conduct time and motion studies for each labor operation in the process of providing a product or service. From these studies, management can learn the best way to perform the operation and then set the standard labor time required for the operation under normal conditions. Similarly, standards for materials are set by studying the quantity, grade, and cost of each material used. Standards for overhead costs are explained later in the chapter.

Regardless of the care used in setting standard costs and in revising them as conditions change, actual costs frequently differ from standard costs, often as a result of one or more factors. For instance, the actual quantity of material used can differ from the standard, or the price paid per unit of material can differ from the standard. Quantity and price differences from standard amounts can also occur for labor. That is, the actual labor time and actual labor rate can vary from what was expected. The same analysis applies to overhead costs.

Example: What factors might be considered when deciding whether to revise standard costs? *Answer:* Changes in the processes and/or resources needed to carry out the processes.

■ Decision Insight

Cruis'n Standards   The **Corvette** consists of hundreds of parts for which engineers set standards. Various types of labor are also involved in its production, including machining, assembly, painting, and welding, and standards are set for each. Actual results are periodically compared with standards to assess performance. ■

Setting Standard Costs

To illustrate the setting of a standard cost, we consider a professional league baseball bat manufactured by **ProBat.** Its engineers have determined that manufacturing one bat requires 0.90 kg. of high-grade wood. They also expect some loss of material as part of the process because of inefficiencies and waste. This results in adding an *allowance* of 0.10 kg., making the standard requirement 1.0 kg. of wood for each bat.

The 0.90 kg. portion is called an *ideal standard;* it is the quantity of material required if the process is 100% efficient without any loss or waste. Reality suggests that some loss of material usually occurs with any process. The standard of 1.0 kg. is known as the *practical standard,* the quantity of material required under normal application of the process.

Point: Companies promoting continuous improvement strive to achieve ideal standards by eliminating inefficiencies and waste.

High-grade wood can be purchased at a standard price of $25 per kg. The purchasing department sets this price as the expected price for the budget period. To determine this price, the purchasing department considers factors such as the quality of materials, future economic conditions, supply factors (shortages and excesses), and any available discounts. The engineers also decide that two hours of labor time (after including allowances) are required to manufacture a bat. The wage rate is $20 per hour (better than average skilled labor is required). ProBat assigns all overhead at the rate of $10 per labor hour. The standard costs of direct materials, direct labor, and overhead for one bat are shown in Exhibit 23.5 in what is called a *standard cost card.* These cost amounts are then used to prepare manufacturing budgets for a budgeted level of production.

EXHIBIT 23.5

Standard Cost Card

STANDARD COST CARD		▢□✕
Production factor	**Cost factor**	**Total**
Direct materials (wood)	1 kg. @ $25 per kg.	$25
Direct labor	2 hours @ $20 per hour	40
Overhead	2 labor hours @ $10 per hour	20
	Total	**$85**

REMARKS:	SUMMARY:	
Based on standard costs of direct materials, direct labor, and overhead for a single ProBat	Materials	$25
	Labor	40
	Overhead	20
	Total cost	$85

COST VARIANCES

A **cost variance,** also simply called a *variance,* is the difference between actual and standard costs. A cost variance can be favorable or unfavorable. A variance from standard cost is considered favorable if actual cost is less than standard cost. It is considered unfavorable if actual cost is more than standard cost.[1] This section discusses variance analysis.

 C2 Describe variances and what they reveal about performance.

Cost Variance Analysis

Variances are usually identified in performance reports. When a variance occurs, management wants to determine the factors causing it. This often involves analysis, evaluation, and explanation. The results of these efforts should enable management to assign responsibility for the variance and then to take actions to correct the situation.

To illustrate, ProBat's standard materials cost for producing 500 bats is $12,500. Assume that its actual materials cost for those 500 bats is $13,000. The $500 unfavorable variance raises questions that call for answers that, in turn, can lead to changes to correct the situation and eliminate this variance in the next period. A performance report often identifies the existence of a problem, but we must follow up with further investigation to see what can be done to improve future performance.

Exhibit 23.6 shows the flow of events in the effective management of variance analysis. It shows four steps: (1) preparing a standard cost performance report, (2) computing and analyzing variances, (3) identifying questions and their explanations, and (4) taking corrective and strategic actions. These variance analysis steps are interrelated and are frequently applied in good organizations.

Prepare Reports   Analyze Variances   Questions and Answers   Take Action

EXHIBIT 23.6

Variance Analysis

Cost Variance Computation

Management needs information about the factors causing a cost variance, but first it must properly compute the variance. In its most simple form, a cost variance (CV) is computed as the difference between actual cost (AC) and standard cost (SC) as shown in Exhibit 23.7.

---

[1] Short-term favorable variances can sometimes lead to long-term unfavorable variances. For instance, if management spends less than the budgeted amount on maintenance or insurance, the performance report would show a favorable variance. Cutting these expenses can lead to major losses in the long run if machinery wears out prematurely or insurance coverage proves inadequate.

EXHIBIT 23.7

Cost Variance Formulas

> **Cost Variance (CV) = Actual Cost (AC) − Standard Cost (SC)**
>
> where:
>
> **Actual Cost (AC) = Actual Quantity (AQ) × Actual Price (AP)**
>
> **Standard Cost (SC) = Standard Quantity (SQ) × Standard Price (SP)**

A cost variance is further defined by its components. Actual quantity (AQ) is the input (material or labor) used to manufacture the quantity of output. Standard quantity (SQ) is the expected input for the quantity of output. Actual price (AP) is the amount paid to acquire the input (material or labor), and standard price (SP) is the expected price.

Two main factors cause a cost variance: (1) the difference between actual price and standard price results in a *price* (or rate) *variance* and (2) the difference between actual quantity and standard quantity results in a *quantity* (or usage or efficiency) *variance*. To assess the impacts of these two factors in a cost variance, we use the formulas in Exhibit 23.8.

Point: Price and quantity variances for direct labor are nearly always referred to as *rate* and *efficiency variances*, respectively.

EXHIBIT 23.8

Price Variance and Quantity Variance Formulas

In computing a price variance, the quantity (actual) is held constant. In computing a quantity variance, the price (standard) is held constant. The cost variance, or total variance, is the sum of the price and quantity variances. These formulas identify the sources of the cost variance. Managers sometimes find it useful to apply an alternative (but equivalent) computation for the price and quantity variances as shown in Exhibit 23.9.

EXHIBIT 23.9

Alternative Price Variance and Quantity Variance Formulas

> **Price Variance (PV) = [Actual Price (AP) − Standard Price (SP)] × Actual Quantity (AQ)**
>
> **Quantity Variance (QV) = [Actual Quantity (AQ) − Standard Quantity (SQ)] × Standard Price (SP)**

The results from applying the formulas in Exhibits 23.8 and 23.9 are identical.

Computing Materials and Labor Variances

P2 Compute materials and labor variances.

We illustrate the computation of the materials and labor cost variances using data from **G-Max,** a company that makes specialty golf equipment and accessories for individual customers. This company has set the following standard quantities and costs for materials and labor per unit for one of its hand-crafted golf clubheads:

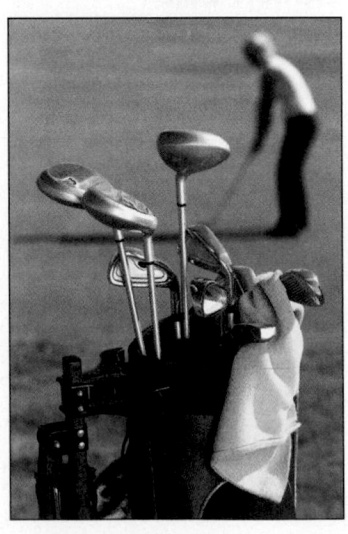

Direct materials (0.5 lb. per unit at $20 per lb.)	$10.00
Direct labor (1 hr. per unit at $8 per hr.)	8.00
Total standard direct cost per unit	$18.00

Materials Cost Variances   During May 2013, G-Max budgeted to produce 4,000 clubheads (units). It actually produced only 3,500 units. It used 1,800 pounds of direct materials (titanium) costing $21.00 per pound, meaning its total materials cost was $37,800. This information allows us to compute both actual and standard direct materials costs for G-Max's 3,500 units and its direct materials cost variance as follows:

Actual cost	1,800 lbs. @ $21.00 per lb. =	$37,800
Standard cost	1,750 lbs. @ $20.00 per lb. =	35,000
Direct materials cost variance (unfavorable)	=	$ 2,800

To better isolate the causes of this $2,800 unfavorable total direct materials cost variance, the materials price and quantity variances for these G-Max clubheads are computed and shown in Exhibit 23.10.

EXHIBIT 23.10

Materials Price and Quantity Variances*

*AQ is actual quantity; AP is actual price; SP is standard price; SQ is standard quantity allowed for actual output.

The $1,800 unfavorable price variance results from paying $1 more per unit than the standard price, computed as 1,800 lbs. × $1. The $1,000 unfavorable quantity variance is due to using 50 lbs. more materials than the standard quantity, computed as 50 lbs. × $20. The total direct materials variance is $2,800 and it is unfavorable. This information allows management to ask the responsible individuals for explanations and corrective actions.

The purchasing department is usually responsible for the price paid for materials. Responsibility for explaining the price variance in this case rests with the purchasing manager if a price higher than standard caused the variance. The production department is usually responsible for the amount of material used and in this case is responsible for explaining why the process used more than the standard amount of materials.

Variance analysis presents challenges. For instance, the production department could have used more than the standard amount of material because its quality did not meet specifications and led to excessive waste. In this case, the purchasing manager is responsible for explaining why inferior materials were acquired. However, the production manager is responsible for explaining what happened if analysis shows that waste was due to inefficiencies, not poor quality material.

In evaluating price variances, managers must recognize that a favorable price variance can indicate a problem with poor product quality. **Redhook Ale**, a micro brewery in the Pacific Northwest, can probably save 10% to 15% in material prices by buying six-row barley malt instead of the better two-row from Washington's Yakima valley. Attention to quality, however, has helped Redhook Ale increase its sales. Redhook's purchasing activities are judged on both the quality of the materials and the purchase price variance.

Example: Identify at least two factors that might have caused the unfavorable quantity variance and the unfavorable price variance in Exhibit 23.10. *Answer:* Poor quality materials or untrained workers for the former; poor price negotiation or higher-quality materials for the latter.

Labor Cost Variances   Labor cost for a specific product or service depends on the number of hours worked (quantity) and the wage rate paid to employees (price). When actual amounts for a task differ from standard, the labor cost variance can be divided into a rate (price) variance and an efficiency (quantity) variance.

To illustrate, G-Max's direct labor standard for 3,500 units of its hand-crafted clubheads is one hour per unit, or 3,500 hours at $8 per hour. Since only 3,400 hours at $8.30 per hour were actually used to complete the units, the actual and standard labor costs are

Actual cost	3,400 hrs. @ $8.30 per hr.	= $28,220
Standard cost	3,500 hrs. @ $8.00 per hr.	= 28,000
Direct labor cost variance (unfavorable)		= $ 220

This analysis shows that actual cost is merely $220 over the standard and suggests no immediate concern. Computing both the labor rate and efficiency variances reveals a different picture, however, as shown in Exhibit 23.11.

EXHIBIT 23.11

Labor Rate and
Efficiency Variances*

* AH is actual direct labor hours; AR is actual wage rate; SH is standard direct labor hours allowed for actual output; SR is standard wage rate.

Example: Compute the rate variance and the efficiency variance for Exhibit 23.11 if 3,700 actual hours are used at an actual price of $7.50 per hour. *Answer:* $1,850 favorable labor rate variance and $1,600 unfavorable labor efficiency variance.

The analysis in Exhibit 23.11 shows that an $800 favorable efficiency variance results from using 100 fewer direct labor hours than standard for the units produced, but this favorable variance is more than offset by a wage rate that is $0.30 per hour higher than standard. The personnel administrator or the production manager needs to explain why the wage rate is higher than expected. The production manager should also explain how the labor hours were reduced. If this experience can be repeated and transferred to other departments, more savings are possible.

One possible explanation of these labor rate and efficiency variances is the use of workers with different skill levels. If this is the reason, senior management must discuss the implications with the production manager who has the responsibility to assign workers to tasks with the appropriate skill level. In this case, an investigation might show that higher-skilled workers were used to produce 3,500 units of hand-crafted clubheads. As a result, fewer labor hours might be required for the work, but the wage rate paid these workers is higher than standard because of their greater skills. The effect of this strategy is a higher than standard total cost, which would require actions to remedy the situation or adjust the standard.

Decision Maker

Production Manager   You receive the manufacturing variance report for June and discover a large unfavorable labor efficiency (quantity) variance. What factors do you investigate to identify its possible causes? ■   [Answer—p. 972]

Quick Check   Answers — p. 973

5. A standard cost (*a*) changes in direct proportion to changes in the level of activity, (*b*) is an amount incurred at the actual level of production for the period, or (*c*) is an amount incurred under normal conditions to provide a product or service.

6. What is a cost variance?

7. The following information is available for York Company.

Actual direct labor hours per unit	2.5 hours
Standard direct labor hours per unit	2.0 hours
Actual production (units)	2,500 units
Budgeted production (units)	3,000 units
Actual rate per hour	$3.10
Standard rate per hour	$3.00

The labor efficiency variance is (*a*) $3,750 U, (*b*) $3,750 F, or (*c*) $3,875 U.

8. Refer to Quick Check 7; the labor rate variance is (*a*) $625 F or (*b*) $625 U.

9. If a materials quantity variance is favorable and a materials price variance is unfavorable, can the total materials cost variance be favorable?

OVERHEAD STANDARDS AND VARIANCES

When standard costs are used, a predetermined overhead rate is used to assign standard overhead costs to products or services produced. This predetermined rate is often based on some overhead allocation base (such as standard labor cost, standard labor hours, or standard machine hours).

Setting Overhead Standards

Standard overhead costs are the amounts expected to occur at a certain activity level. Unlike direct materials and direct labor, overhead includes fixed costs and variable costs. This results in the average overhead cost per unit changing as the predicted volume changes. Since standard costs are also budgeted costs, they must be established before the reporting period begins. Standard overhead costs are therefore average per unit costs based on the predicted activity level.

To establish the standard overhead cost rate, management uses the same cost structure it used to construct a flexible budget at the end of a period. This cost structure identifies the different overhead cost components and classifies them as variable or fixed. To get the standard overhead rate, management selects a level of activity (volume) and predicts total overhead cost. It then divides this total by the allocation base to get the standard rate. Standard direct labor hours expected to be used to produce the predicted volume is a common allocation base and is used in this section.

To illustrate, Exhibit 23.12 shows the overhead cost structure used to develop G-Max's flexible overhead budgets for May 2013. The predetermined standard overhead rate for May is set before the month begins. The first two number columns list the per unit amounts of variable costs and the monthly amounts of fixed costs. The four right-most columns show the costs expected to occur at four different levels of production activity. The predetermined overhead rate per labor hour is smaller as volume of activity increases because total fixed costs remain constant.

Point: With increased automation, machine hours are frequently used in applying overhead instead of labor hours.

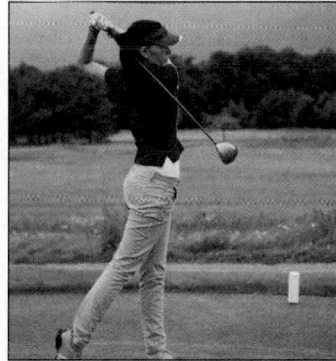

EXHIBIT 23.12

Flexible Overhead Budgets

G-MAX Flexible Overhead Budgets For Month Ended May 31, 2013	Flexible Budget		Flexible Budget at Capacity Level of			
	Variable Amount per Unit	Total Fixed Cost	70%	80%	90%	100%
Production (in units)	1 unit		3,500	4,000	4,500	5,000
Factory overhead						
Variable costs						
Indirect labor	$0.40/unit		$1,400	$1,600	$1,800	$2,000
Indirect materials	0.30/unit		1,050	1,200	1,350	1,500
Power and lights	0.20/unit		700	800	900	1,000
Maintenance	0.10/unit		350	400	450	500
Total variable overhead costs	$1.00/unit		3,500	4,000	4,500	5,000
Fixed costs (per month)						
Building rent		$1,000	1,000	1,000	1,000	1,000
Depreciation—machinery		1,200	1,200	1,200	1,200	1,200
Supervisory salaries		1,800	1,800	1,800	1,800	1,800
Total fixed overhead costs		$4,000	4,000	4,000	4,000	4,000
Total factory overhead			$7,500	$8,000	$8,500	$9,000
Standard direct labor hours 1 hr./unit . .			3,500 hrs.	4,000 hrs.	4,500 hrs.	5,000 hrs.
Predetermined overhead rate per standard direct labor hour			$ 2.14	$ 2.00	$ 1.89	$ 1.80

Predicting Activity Levels

When choosing the predicted activity level, management considers many factors. The level can be set as high as 100% of capacity, but this is rare. Factors causing the activity level to be less than full capacity include difficulties in scheduling work, equipment under repair or maintenance, and insufficient product demand. Good long-run management practices often call for some plant capacity in excess of current operating needs to allow for special opportunities and demand changes.

G-Max managers predicted an 80% activity level for May, or a production volume of 4,000 clubheads. At this volume, they budget $8,000 as the May total overhead. This choice implies a $2 per unit (labor hour) average overhead cost ($8,000/4,000 units). Since G-Max has a standard of one direct labor hour per unit, the predetermined standard overhead rate for May is $2 per standard direct labor hour. The variable overhead rate remains constant at $1 per direct labor hour regardless of the budgeted production level. The fixed overhead rate changes according to the budgeted production volume. For instance, for the predicted level of 4,000 units of production, the fixed rate is $1 per hour ($4,000 fixed costs/4,000 units). For a production level of 5,000 units, however, the fixed rate is $0.80 per hour ($4,000 fixed costs/5,000 units).

Point: Variable costs per unit remain constant, but fixed costs per unit decline with increases in volume. This means the average total overhead cost per unit declines with increases in volume.

 Decision Insight

Measuring Up   In the spirit of continuous improvement, competitors compare their processes and performance standards against benchmarks established by industry leaders. Those that use **benchmarking** include Jiffy Lube, All Tune and Lube, and Speedee Oil Change and Tune-Up. ■

P3 Compute overhead variances.

Computing Overhead Cost Variances

EXHIBIT 23.13

Overhead Cost Variance

When standard costs are used, the cost accounting system applies overhead to the good units produced using the predetermined standard overhead rate. At period-end, the difference between the total overhead cost applied to products and the total overhead cost actually incurred is called an **overhead cost variance** (total overhead variance), which is defined in Exhibit 23.13.

> **Overhead cost variance (OCV) = Actual overhead incurred (AOI) − Standard overhead applied (SOA)**

The standard overhead applied is based on the predetermined overhead rate (at the predicted activity level) and the standard number of hours that should have been used, based on the actual production. To illustrate, G-Max produced 3,500 units during the month, which should have used 3,500 direct labor hours. From Exhibit 23.12, G-Max's predetermined overhead rate at the predicted capacity level of 4,000 units was $2.00 per direct labor hour, so the standard overhead applied is $7,000 (computed as 3,500 direct labor hours × $2.00). Additional data from cost reports show that the actual overhead cost incurred in the month is $7,650. G-Max's total overhead variance is thus $650, computed as:

Actual total overhead (given)	$7,650
Standard overhead applied (3,500 DLH × $2.00)	7,000
Total overhead variance (unfavorable).	$ 650

This variance is unfavorable, as G-Max's actual overhead was higher than it should have been based on budgeted amounts.

Controllable and Volume Variances   To help identify factors causing the overhead cost variance, managers analyze this variance separately for controllable and volume variances, as illustrated in Exhibit 23.14. The results provide information useful for taking strategic actions to improve company performance.

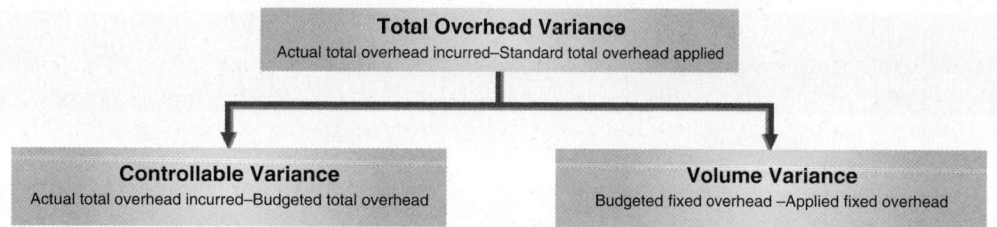

EXHIBIT 23.14

Framework for Understanding Total Overhead Variance

The **controllable variance** is the difference between actual overhead costs incurred and the budgeted overhead costs based on a flexible budget. The controllable variance is so named because it refers to activities usually under management control. A **volume variance** occurs when there is a difference between the actual volume of production and the standard volume of production. The volume variance is based solely on *fixed* overhead. The budgeted fixed overhead amount is the same regardless of the volume of production (within the relevant range). The applied fixed overhead is based, however, on the standard direct labor hours allowed for the actual volume of production, using the flexible budget. When a company operates at a capacity level different from what it expected, the volume variance will differ from zero. We next compute the controllable and volume variances for G-Max.

Returning to the G-Max data, the flexible budget in Exhibit 23.12 shows budgeted factory overhead of $7,500 at the production volume of 3,500 units during the month. The controllable variance is then computed as:

Controllable Variance	
Actual total overhead (given)	$7,650
Applied total overhead (from flexible budget)	7,500
Controllable variance (unfavorable)	$ 150

We then compute the volume variance. G-Max's budgeted fixed overhead at the predicted capacity level for the month was $4,000. Recall from Exhibit 23.12 that G-Max's predetermined fixed overhead at the predicted capacity level of 4,000 units was $1 per hour. Thus, G-Max's applied fixed overhead was $3,500, computed as 3,500 direct labor hours × $1.00 per unit. G-Max's volume variance is then computed as:

Volume Variance	
Budgeted fixed overhead (at predicted capacity)	$4,000
Applied fixed overhead (3,500 DLH × $1.00)	3,500
Volume variance (unfavorable)	$ 500

Analyzing Controllable and Volume Variances How should the top management of G-Max interpret the unfavorable controllable and volume variances? An unfavorable volume variance means that the company did not reach its predicted operating level. In this case, 80% of manufacturing capacity was budgeted but only 70% was used. Management needs to know why the actual level of production differs from the expected level. The main purpose of the volume variance is to identify what portion of the total overhead variance is caused by failing to meet the expected production level. Often the reasons for failing to meet this expected production level are due to factors, for example customer demand, that are beyond employees' control. This information permits management to focus on explanations for the controllable variance, as we discuss next.

Overhead Variance Reports To help management isolate the reasons for the $150 unfavorable controllable variance, an *overhead variance report* can be prepared. A complete overhead variance report provides managers information about specific overhead costs and how they differ from budgeted amounts. Exhibit 23.15 shows G-Max's overhead variance report for May. It reveals that (1) fixed costs and maintenance costs were incurred as expected, (2) costs for indirect labor and power and lights were higher than expected, and (3) indirect materials cost was less than expected.

EXHIBIT 23.15

Overhead Variance Report

G-MAX
Overhead Variance Report
For Month Ended May 31, 2013

Volume Variance

Expected production level	80% of capacity
Production level achieved	70% of capacity
Volume variance	**$500 (unfavorable)**

Controllable Variance	Flexible Budget	Actual Results	Variances*
Variable overhead costs			
Indirect labor	$1,400	$1,525	$125 U
Indirect materials	1,050	1,025	25 F
Power and lights	700	750	50 U
Maintenance	350	350	0
Total variable overhead costs	3,500	3,650	150 U
Fixed overhead costs			
Building rent	1,000	1,000	0
Depreciation—machinery	1,200	1,200	0
Supervisory salaries	1,800	1,800	0
Total fixed overhead costs	4,000	4,000	0
Total overhead costs	$7,500	$7,650	$150 U

* F = Favorable variance; U = Unfavorable variance.

The total controllable variance amount ($150 unfavorable) is also readily available from Exhibit 23.15. The overhead variance report shows the total volume variance as $500 unfavorable (shown at the top) and the $150 unfavorable controllable variance (reported at the bottom right). The sum of the controllable variance and the volume variance equals the total overhead variance of $650 unfavorable.

Appendix 23A describes an expanded analysis of overhead variances.

Quick Check   Answers — p. 973

10. Under what conditions is an overhead volume variance considered favorable?

11. To use management by exception, a company (a) need not study fixed overhead variances, (b) should compute variances from flexible budget amounts to allow management to focus its attention on significant differences between actual and budgeted results, or (c) should analyze only variances for direct materials and direct labor.

 GLOBAL VIEW

BMW, a German automobile manufacturer, uses concepts of standard costing and variance analysis. Production begins with huge rolls of steel and aluminum, which are then cut and pressed by large machines. Material must meet high quality standards, and the company sets standards for each of its machine operations. In the Assembly department, highly-trained employees complete the assembly of the painted car chassis, often to customer specifications. Again, BMW sets standards for how much labor should be used and monitors its employee performance. The company then computes and analyzes materials price and quantity variances and labor rate and efficiency variances and takes action as needed.

This chapter explained the computation and analysis of cost variances. A similar variance analysis can be applied to sales. To illustrate, consider the following sales data from G-Max for two of its golf products, Excel golf balls and Big Bert® drivers.

> **A1** Analyze changes in sales from expected amounts.

	Budgeted	Actual
Sales of Excel golf balls (units)	1,000 units	1,100 units
Sales price per Excel golf ball	$10	$10.50
Sales of Big Bert® drivers (units)	150 units	140 units
Sales price per Big Bert® driver	$200	$190

Using this information, we compute both the *sales price variance* and the *sales volume variance* as shown in Exhibit 23.16. The total sales price variance is $850 unfavorable, and the total sales volume variance is $1,000 unfavorable. Neither total variance implies anything positive about these two products. However, further analysis of these total sales variances reveals that both the sales price and sales volume variances for Excel golf balls are favorable, meaning that both the unfavorable total sales price variance and the unfavorable total sales volume variance are due to the Big Bert driver.

EXHIBIT 23.16

Computing Sales Variances*

* AS = actual sales units; AP = actual sales price; BP = budgeted sales price; BS = budgeted sales units (fixed budget).

Managers use sales variances for planning and control purposes. The sales variance information is used to plan future actions to avoid unfavorable variances. G-Max sold 90 total combined units (both balls and drivers) more than planned, but these 90 units were not sold in the proportion budgeted. G-Max sold fewer than the budgeted quantity of the higher-priced driver, which contributed to the unfavorable total sales variances. Managers use such detail to question what caused the company to sell more golf balls and fewer drivers. Managers also use this information to evaluate and even reward their salespeople. Extra compensation is paid to salespeople who contribute to a higher profit margin. Finally, with multiple products, the sales volume variance can be separated into a *sales mix variance* and a *sales quantity variance*. The sales mix variance is the difference between the actual and budgeted sales mix of the products. The sales quantity variance is the difference between the total actual and total budgeted quantity of units sold.

Decision Maker

Sales Manager   The current performance report reveals a large favorable sales volume variance but an unfavorable sales price variance. You did not expect to see a large increase in sales volume. What steps do you take to analyze this situation? ■   [Answer—p. 972]

DEMONSTRATION PROBLEM

Pacific Company provides the following information about its budgeted and actual results for June 2013. Although the expected June volume was 25,000 units produced and sold, the company actually produced and sold 27,000 units as detailed here:

	Budget (25,000 units)	Actual (27,000 units)
Selling price	$5.00 per unit	$5.23 per unit
Variable costs (per unit)		
Direct materials	1.24 per unit	1.12 per unit
Direct labor	1.50 per unit	1.40 per unit
Factory supplies*	0.25 per unit	0.37 per unit
Utilities*	0.50 per unit	0.60 per unit
Selling costs	0.40 per unit	0.34 per unit
Fixed costs (per month)		
Depreciation—machinery*	$3,750	$3,710
Depreciation—building*	2,500	2,500
General liability insurance	1,200	1,250
Property taxes on office equipment	500	485
Other administrative expense	750	900

* Indicates factory overhead item; $0.75 per unit or $3 per direct labor hour for variable overhead, and $0.25 per unit or $1 per direct labor hour for fixed overhead.

Standard costs based on expected output of 25,000 units

	Per Unit of Output	Quantity to Be Used	Total Cost
Direct materials, 4 oz. @ $0.31/oz.	$1.24/unit	100,000 oz.	$31,000
Direct labor, 0.25 hrs. @ $6.00/hr.	1.50/unit	6,250 hrs.	37,500
Overhead	1.00/unit		25,000

Actual costs incurred to produce 27,000 units

	Per Unit of Output	Quantity Used	Total Cost
Direct materials, 4 oz. @ $0.28/oz.	$1.12/unit	108,000 oz.	$30,240
Direct labor, 0.20 hrs. @ $7.00/hr.	1.40/unit	5,400 hrs.	37,800
Overhead	1.20/unit		32,400

Standard costs based on expected output of 27,000 units

	Per Unit of Output	Quantity to Be Used	Total Cost
Direct materials, 4 oz. @ $0.31/oz.	$1.24/unit	108,000 oz.	$33,480
Direct labor, 0.25 hrs. @ $6.00/hr.	1.50/unit	6,750 hrs.	40,500
Overhead			26,500

Required

1. Prepare June flexible budgets showing expected sales, costs, and net income assuming 20,000, 25,000, and 30,000 units of output produced and sold.

2. Prepare a flexible budget performance report that compares actual results with the amounts budgeted if the actual volume had been expected.

3. Apply variance analysis for direct materials and direct labor.

4. Compute the total overhead variance, and the controllable and volume variances.

5. Compute spending and efficiency variances for overhead. (Refer to Appendix 23A.)

6. Prepare journal entries to record standard costs, and price and quantity variances, for direct materials, direct labor, and factory overhead. (Refer to Appendix 23A.)

PLANNING THE SOLUTION

● Prepare a table showing the expected results at the three specified levels of output. Compute the variable costs by multiplying the per unit variable costs by the expected volumes. Include fixed costs at the given amounts. Combine the amounts in the table to show total variable costs, contribution margin, total fixed costs, and income from operations.

● Prepare a table showing the actual results and the amounts that should be incurred at 27,000 units. Show any differences in the third column and label them with an *F* for favorable if they increase income or a *U* for unfavorable if they decrease income.

● Using the chapter's format, compute these total variances and the individual variances requested:
  ● Total materials variance (including the direct materials quantity variance and the direct materials price variance).
  ● Total direct labor variance (including the direct labor efficiency variance and rate variance).
  ● Total overhead variance (including both controllable and volume overhead variances and their component variances).

SOLUTION TO DEMONSTRATION PROBLEM

1.

PACIFIC COMPANY Flexible Budgets For Month Ended June 30, 2013					
	Flexible Budget		**Flexible Budget for Unit Sales of 20,000**	**Flexible Budget for Unit Sales of 25,000**	**Flexible Budget for Unit Sales of 30,000**
	Variable Amount per Unit	**Total Fixed Cost**			
Sales	$5.00		$100,000	$125,000	$150,000
Variable costs					
Direct materials......................	1.24		24,800	31,000	37,200
Direct labor	1.50		30,000	37,500	45,000
Factory supplies	0.25		5,000	6,250	7,500
Utilities	0.50		10,000	12,500	15,000
Selling costs	0.40		8,000	10,000	12,000
Total variable costs	3.89		77,800	97,250	116,700
Contribution margin	$1.11		22,200	27,750	33,300
Fixed costs					
Depreciation—machinery		$3,750	3,750	3,750	3,750
Depreciation—building		2,500	2,500	2,500	2,500
General liability insurance		1,200	1,200	1,200	1,200
Property taxes on office equipment		500	500	500	500
Other administrative expense		750	750	750	750
Total fixed costs		$8,700	8,700	8,700	8,700
Income from operations			$ 13,500	$ 19,050	$ 24,600

2.

PACIFIC COMPANY Flexible Budget Performance Report For Month Ended June 30, 2013	Flexible Budget	Actual Results	Variance*
Sales (27,000 units)	$135,000	$141,210	$6,210 F
Variable costs			
Direct materials	33,480	30,240	3,240 F
Direct labor	40,500	37,800	2,700 F
Factory supplies	6,750	9,990	3,240 U
Utilities.	13,500	16,200	2,700 U
Selling costs	10,800	9,180	1,620 F
Total variable costs	105,030	103,410	1,620 F
Contribution margin	29,970	37,800	7,830 F
Fixed costs			
Depreciation—machinery	3,750	3,710	40 F
Depreciation—building	2,500	2,500	0
General liability insurance	1,200	1,250	50 U
Property taxes on office equipment	500	485	15 F
Other administrative expense	750	900	150 U
Total fixed costs	8,700	8,845	145 U
Income from operations	$ 21,270	$ 28,955	$7,685 F

* F = Favorable variance; U = Unfavorable variance.

3. Variance analysis of materials and labor costs.

Materials cost variances

Actual cost	108,000 oz. @ $0.28	$30,240
Standard cost	108,000 oz. @ $0.31	33,480
Direct materials cost variance (favorable)		$ 3,240

Price and quantity variances (based on formulas in Exhibit 23.10):

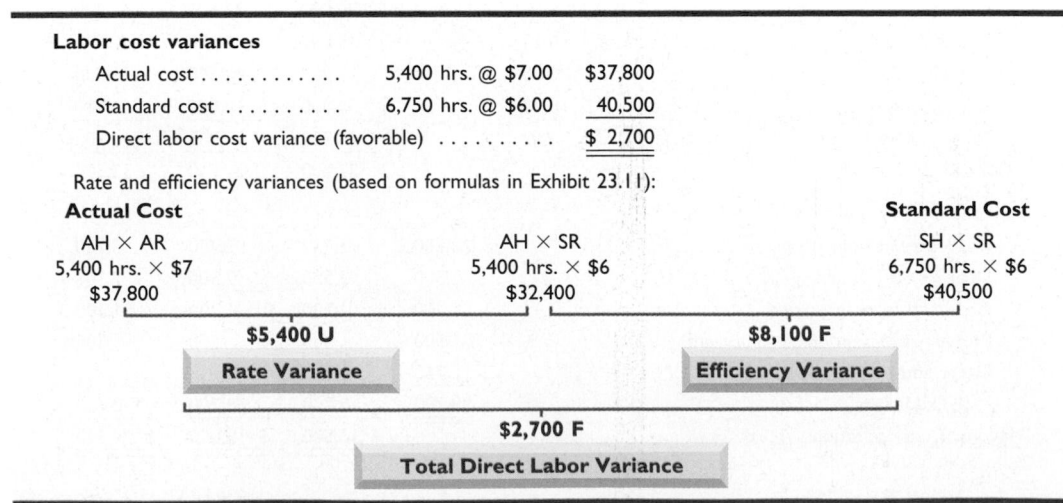

Labor cost variances

Actual cost	5,400 hrs. @ $7.00	$37,800
Standard cost	6,750 hrs. @ $6.00	40,500
Direct labor cost variance (favorable)		$ 2,700

Rate and efficiency variances (based on formulas in Exhibit 23.11):

Actual Cost

AH × AR	AH × SR	SH × SR
5,400 hrs. × $7	5,400 hrs. × $6	6,750 hrs. × $6
$37,800	$32,400	$40,500

$5,400 U
Rate Variance

$8,100 F
Efficiency Variance

$2,700 F
Total Direct Labor Variance

4. Total, controllable, and volume variances for overhead.

Overhead cost variances

Total overhead cost incurred	27,000 units @ $1.20	$32,400
Total overhead applied	27,000 units @ $1.00	27,000
Overhead cost variance (unfavorable)		$ 5,400

Controllable variance

Actual overhead (given)	$32,400
Applied overhead (from flexible budget for 27,000 units)	26,500
Controllable variance (unfavorable)	$ 5,900

Volume variance

Budgeted fixed overhead (at predicted capacity)	$ 6,250
Applied fixed overhead (6,750 × $1.00)	6,750
Volume variance (favorable).	$ 500

5. Variable and fixed overhead spending and efficiency variances.

Variable overhead variance (factory supplies and utilities)

Variable overhead cost incurred	($9,990 + $16,200)	$26,190
Variable overhead cost applied	6,750 hrs. @ $3/hr.	20,250
Variable overhead cost variance (unfavorable)		$ 5,940

Spending and efficiency variances (based on formulas in Exhibit 23A.2):

Actual Overhead		**Applied Overhead**
AH × AVR	AH × SVR	SH × SVR
	5,400 × $3	6,750 × $3
$26,190	$16,200	$20,250

$9,990 U — **Spending Variance**

$4,050 F — **Efficiency Variance**

$5,940 U — **Total Variable Overhead Variance**

Fixed overhead (depreciation on machinery and building)

Fixed overhead cost incurred	($3,710 + $2,500)	$ 6,210
Fixed overhead cost applied	6,750 hrs. @ $1/hr.	6,750
Fixed overhead cost variance (favorable)		$ 540

Spending and volume variances (based on formulas in Exhibit 23A.2):

Actual Overhead	**Budgeted Overhead**	**Applied Overhead**
		6,750 × $1
$6,210	$6,250	$6,750

$40 F — **Spending Variance**

$500 F — **Volume Variance**

$540 F — **Total Fixed Overhead Variance**

We can also compute

Controllable variance:	$5,900 U (both spending variances plus efficiency variance)
Volume variance:	500 F (identified as above)

6.

Goods in Process Inventory	33,480	
Direct Materials Price Variance		3,240
Raw Materials Inventory		30,240
Goods in Process Inventory	40,500	
Direct Labor Rate Variance	5,400	
Direct Labor Efficiency Variance		8,100
Factory Payroll		37,800
Goods in Process Inventory*	27,000	
Variable Overhead Spending Variance	9,990	
Variable Overhead Efficiency Variance		4,050
Fixed Overhead Spending Variance		40
Fixed Overhead Volume Variance		500
Factory Overhead†		32,400

* $20,250 + $6,750   †$26,190 + $6,210

APPENDIX

23A

Expanded Overhead Variances and Standard Cost Accounting System

Expanded Overhead Variances   Similar to analysis of direct materials and direct labor, overhead variances can be more completely analyzed. Exhibit 23A.1 shows an expanded framework for understanding these component overhead variances. This framework uses classifications of overhead costs as

EXHIBIT 23A.1

Expanded Framework for Total Overhead Variance

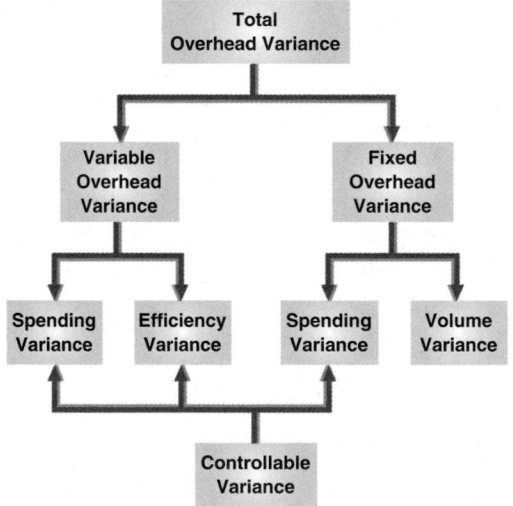

either variable or fixed. A **spending variance** occurs when management pays an amount different than the standard price to acquire an item. For instance, the actual wage rate paid to indirect labor might be higher than the standard rate. Similarly, actual supervisory salaries might be different than expected. Spending variances such as these cause management to investigate the reasons that the amount paid differs from the standard. Both variable and fixed overhead costs can yield their own spending variances. Analyzing variable overhead includes computing an **efficiency variance,** which occurs when standard direct labor hours (the allocation base) expected for actual production differ from the actual direct labor hours used. This efficiency variance reflects on the cost-effectiveness in using the overhead allocation base (such as direct labor).

Exhibit 23A.1 shows that we can combine the variable overhead spending variance, the fixed overhead spending variance, and the variable overhead efficiency variance to get the controllable variance.

Computing Variable and Fixed Overhead Cost Variances   To illustrate the computation of more detailed overhead cost variances, we return to the G-Max data. We know that G-Max produced 3,500 units when 4,000 units were budgeted. Additional data from cost reports show that the actual overhead cost incurred is $7,650 (the variable portion of $3,650 and the fixed portion of $4,000). Recall from Exhibit 23.12 that each unit requires 1 hour of direct labor, that variable overhead is applied at a rate of $1.00 per direct labor hour, and that the predetermined fixed overhead rate is $1.00 per direct labor hour. Using this information, we can compute overhead variances for both variable and fixed overhead as follows:

Actual variable overhead (given)	$3,650
Applied variable overhead (3,500 × $1.00)	3,500
Variable overhead variance (unfavorable)	$ 150

Actual fixed overhead (given)	$4,000
Applied fixed overhead (3,500 × $1.00)	3,500
Fixed overhead variance (unfavorable)	$ 500

Management should seek to determine the causes of these unfavorable variances and take corrective action. To help better isolate the causes of these variances, more detailed overhead variances can be used, as shown in the next section.

Expanded Overhead Variance Formulas Exhibit 23A.2 shows formulas to use in computing detailed overhead variances that can better identify reasons for variable and fixed overhead variances.

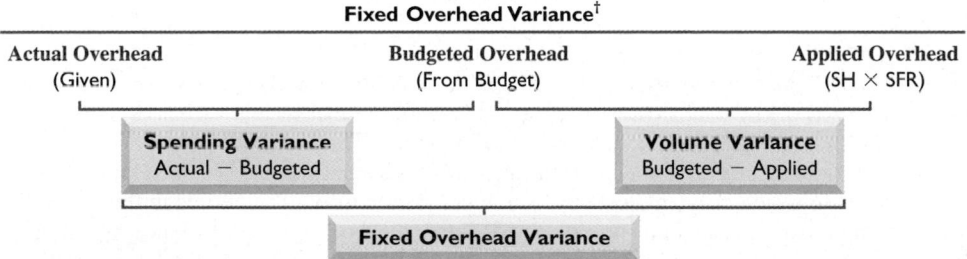

EXHIBIT 23A.2

Variable and Fixed Overhead Variances

Variable Overhead Cost Variances Using these formulas, Exhibit 23A.3 offers insight into the causes of G-Max's $150 unfavorable variable overhead cost variance. Recall that G-Max applies overhead based on direct labor hours as the allocation base. We know that it used 3,400 direct labor hours to produce 3,500 units. This compares favorably to the standard requirement of 3,500 direct labor hours at one labor hour per unit. At a standard variable overhead rate of $1.00 per direct labor hour, this should have resulted in variable overhead costs of $3,400 (middle column of Exhibit 23A.3).

EXHIBIT 23A.3

Computing Variable Overhead Cost Variances

G-Max's cost records, however, report actual variable overhead of $3,650, or $250 higher than expected. This means G-Max has an unfavorable variable overhead spending variance of $250 ($3,650 − $3,400). On the other hand, G-Max used 100 fewer labor hours than expected to make 3,500 units, and its actual variable overhead is lower than its applied variable overhead. Thus, G-Max has a favorable variable overhead efficiency variance of $100 ($3,400 − $3,500).

Fixed Overhead Cost Variances   Exhibit 23A.4 provides insight into the causes of G-Max's $500 unfavorable fixed overhead variance. G-Max reports that it incurred $4,000 in actual fixed overhead; this amount equals the budgeted fixed overhead for May at the expected production level of 4,000 units (see Exhibit 23.12). Thus, the fixed overhead spending variance is zero, suggesting good control of fixed overhead costs. G-Max's budgeted fixed overhead application rate is $1 per hour ($4,000/4,000 direct labor hours), but the actual production level is only 3,500 units. Using this information, we can compute the fixed overhead volume variance shown in Exhibit 23A.4. The applied fixed overhead is computed by multiplying 3,500 standard hours allowed for the actual production by the $1 fixed overhead allocation rate. The volume variance of $500 occurs because 500 fewer units are produced than budgeted; namely, 80% of the manufacturing capacity is budgeted but only 70% is used.

EXHIBIT 23A.4

Computing Fixed Overhead
Cost Variances

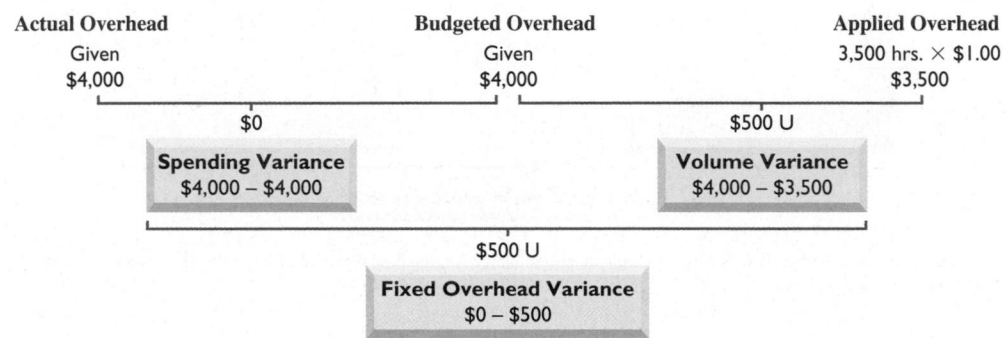

Standard Cost Accounting System   We have shown how companies use standard costs in management reports. Most standard cost systems also record these costs and variances in accounts. This practice simplifies recordkeeping and helps in preparing reports. Although we do not need knowledge of standard cost accounting practices to understand standard costs and their use, we must know how to interpret the accounts in which standard costs and variances are recorded. The entries in this section briefly illustrate the important aspects of this process for G-Max's standard costs and variances for May.

The first of these entries records standard materials cost incurred in May in the Goods in Process Inventory account. This part of the entry is similar to the usual accounting entry, but the amount of the debit equals the standard cost ($35,000) instead of the actual cost ($37,800). This entry credits Raw Materials Inventory for actual cost. The difference between standard and actual direct materials costs is recorded with debits to two separate materials variance accounts (recall Exhibit 23.10). Both the materials price and quantity variances are recorded as debits because they reflect additional costs higher than the standard cost (if actual costs were less than the standard, they are recorded as credits). This treatment (debit) reflects their unfavorable effect because they represent higher costs and lower income.

P4 Prepare journal entries for standard costs and account for price and quantity variances.

Assets	=	Liabilities	+	Equity
+35,000				−1,000
−37,800				−1,800

May 31			
	Goods in Process Inventory	35,000	
	Direct Materials Price Variance*	1,800	
	Direct Materials Quantity Variance	1,000	
	Raw Materials Inventory		37,800
	To charge production for standard quantity of		
	materials used (1,750 lbs.) at the standard		
	price ($20 per lb.), and to record material price		
	and material quantity variances.		

* Many companies record the materials price variance when materials are purchased. For simplicity, we record both the materials price and quantity variances when materials are issued to production.

The second entry debits Goods in Process Inventory for the standard labor cost of the goods manufactured during May ($28,000). Actual labor cost ($28,220) is recorded with a credit to the Factory Payroll account. The difference between standard and actual labor costs is explained by two variances (see Exhibit 23.11). The direct labor rate variance is unfavorable and is debited to that account. The direct labor efficiency variance is favorable and that account is credited. The direct labor efficiency variance is favorable because it represents a lower cost and a higher net income.

May 31	Goods in Process Inventory	28,000	
	Direct Labor Rate Variance	**1,020**	
	Direct Labor Efficiency Variance		**800**
	Factory Payroll		28,220
	To charge production with 3,500 standard hours of direct labor at the standard $8 per hour rate, and to record the labor rate and efficiency variances.		

Assets = Liabilities + Equity
+28,000   +28,220
                                   − 1,020
                                   +   800

The entry to assign standard predetermined overhead to the cost of goods manufactured must debit the $7,000 predetermined amount to the Goods in Process Inventory account. Actual overhead costs of $7,650 were debited to Factory Overhead during the period (entries not shown here). Thus, when Factory Overhead is applied to Goods in Process Inventory, the actual amount is credited to the Factory Overhead account. To account for the difference between actual and standard overhead costs, the entry includes a $250 debit to the Variable Overhead Spending Variance, a $100 credit to the Variable Overhead Efficiency Variance, and a $500 debit to the Volume Variance (recall Exhibits 23A.3 and 23A.4). An alternative (simpler) approach is to record the difference with a $150 debit to the Controllable Variance account and a $500 debit to the Volume Variance account (recall from Exhibit 23A.1 that controllable variance is the sum of both variable overhead variances and the fixed overhead spending variance).

May 31	Goods in Process Inventory	7,000	
	Volume Variance	**500**	
	Variable Overhead Spending Variance	**250**	
	Variable Overhead Efficiency Variance		**100**
	Factory Overhead		7,650
	To apply overhead at the standard rate of $2 per standard direct labor hour (3,500 hours), and to record overhead variances.		

Assets = Liabilities + Equity
+7,000   +7,650
                                   − 250
                                   − 500
                                   + 100

The balances of these different variance accounts accumulate until the end of the accounting period. As a result, the unfavorable variances of some months can offset the favorable variances of other months.

These ending variance account balances, which reflect results of the period's various transactions and events, are closed at period-end. If the amounts are *immaterial,* they are added to or subtracted from the balance of the Cost of Goods Sold account. This process is similar to that shown in the job order costing chapter for eliminating an underapplied or overapplied balance in the Factory Overhead account. (*Note:* These variance balances, which represent differences between actual and standard costs, must be added to or subtracted from the materials, labor, and overhead costs recorded. In this way, the recorded costs equal the actual costs incurred in the period; a company must use actual costs in external financial statements prepared in accordance with generally accepted accounting principles.)

Point: If variances are material they can be allocated between Goods in Process Inventory, Finished Goods Inventory, and Cost of Goods Sold. This closing process is explained in advanced courses.

Quick Check   Answers − p. 973

12. A company uses a standard cost accounting system. Prepare the journal entry to record these direct materials variances:

Direct materials cost actually incurred.................	$73,200
Direct materials quantity variance (favorable)	3,800
Direct materials price variance (unfavorable)	1,300

13. If standard costs are recorded in the manufacturing accounts, how are recorded variances treated at the end of an accounting period?

Summary

C1 **Define *standard costs* and explain how standard cost information is useful for management by exception.** Standard costs are the normal costs that should be incurred to produce a product or perform a service. They should be based on a careful examination of the processes used to produce a product or perform a service as well as the quantities and prices that should be incurred in carrying out those processes. On a performance report, standard costs (which are flexible budget amounts) are compared to actual costs, and the differences are presented as variances. Standard cost accounting provides management information about costs that differ from budgeted (expected) amounts. Performance reports disclose the costs or areas of operations that have significant variances from budgeted amounts. This allows managers to focus attention on the exceptions and less attention on areas proceeding normally.

C2 **Describe variances and what they reveal about performance.** Management can use variances to monitor and control activities. Total cost variances can be broken into price and quantity variances to direct management's attention to those responsible for quantities used and prices paid.

A1 **Analyze changes in sales from expected amounts.** Actual sales can differ from budgeted sales, and managers can investigate this difference by computing both the sales price and sales volume variances. The *sales price variance* refers to that portion of total variance resulting from a difference between actual and budgeted selling prices. The *sales volume variance* refers to that portion of total variance resulting from a difference between actual and budgeted sales quantities.

P1 **Prepare a flexible budget and interpret a flexible budget performance report.** A flexible budget expresses variable costs in per unit terms so that it can be used to develop budgeted amounts for any volume level within the relevant range. Thus, managers compute budgeted amounts for evaluation after a period for the volume that actually occurred. To prepare a flexible budget, we express each variable cost as a constant amount per unit of sales (or as a percent of sales dollars). In contrast, the budgeted amount of each fixed cost is expressed as a total amount expected to occur at any sales volume within the relevant range. The flexible budget is then determined using these computations and amounts for fixed and variable costs at the expected sales volume.

P2 **Compute materials and labor variances.** Materials and labor variances are due to differences between the actual costs incurred and the budgeted costs. The price (or rate) variance is computed by comparing the actual cost with the flexible budget amount that should have been incurred to acquire the actual quantity of resources. The quantity (or efficiency) variance is computed by comparing the flexible budget amount that should have been incurred to acquire the actual quantity of resources with the flexible budget amount that should have been incurred to acquire the standard quantity of resources.

P3 **Compute overhead variances.** Overhead variances are due to differences between the actual overhead costs incurred and the overhead applied to production. An overhead spending variance arises when the actual amount incurred differs from the budgeted amount of overhead. An overhead efficiency (or volume) variance arises when the flexible overhead budget amount differs from the overhead applied to production. It is important to realize that overhead is assigned using an overhead allocation base, meaning that an efficiency variance (in the case of variable overhead) is a result of the overhead application base being used more or less efficiently than planned.

P4^A **Prepare journal entries for standard costs and account for price and quantity variances.** When a company records standard costs in its accounts, the standard costs of materials, labor, and overhead are debited to the Goods in Process Inventory account. Based on an analysis of the material, labor, and overhead costs, each quantity variance, price variance, volume variance, and controllable variance is recorded in a separate account. At period-end, if the variances are material, they are allocated among the balances of the Goods in Process Inventory, Finished Goods Inventory, and Cost of Goods Sold accounts. If they are not material, they are simply debited or credited to the Cost of Goods Sold account.

Guidance Answers to Decision Maker and Decision Ethics

Entrepreneur From the complaints, this performance report appears to compare actual results with a fixed budget. This comparison is useful in determining whether the amount of work actually performed was more or less than planned, but it is not useful in determining whether the divisions were more or less efficient than planned. If the two consulting divisions worked on more assignments than expected, some costs will certainly increase. Therefore, you should prepare a flexible budget using the actual number of consulting assignments and then compare actual performance to the flexible budget.

Internal Auditor Although the manager's actions might not be unethical, this action is undesirable. The internal auditor should report this behavior, possibly recommending that for the purchase of such discretionary items, the manager must provide budgetary requests using an activity-based budgeting process. The internal auditor would then be given full authority to verify this budget request.

Production Manager As production manager, you should investigate the causes for any labor-related variances although you may not be responsible for them. An unfavorable labor efficiency variance occurs because more labor hours than standard were used during the period. There are at least three possible reasons for this: (1) materials quality could be poor, resulting in more labor consumption due to rework; (2) unplanned interruptions (strike, breakdowns, accidents) could have occurred during the period; and (3) a different labor mix might have occurred for a strategic reason such as to expedite orders. This new labor mix could have consisted of a larger proportion of untrained labor, which resulted in more labor hours.

Sales Manager The unfavorable sales price variance suggests that actual prices were lower than budgeted prices. As the sales manager, you want to know the reasons for a lower than expected price. Perhaps your salespeople lowered the price of certain products by offering quantity discounts. You then might want to know what prompted them to offer the quantity dis counts (perhaps competitors were offering discounts). You want to break the sales volume variance into both the sales mix and sales quantity variances. You could find that although the sales quantity variance is favorable, the sales mix variance is not. Then you need to investigate why the actual sales mix differs from the budgeted sales mix.

Guidance Answers to Quick Checks

1. *b*

2. The first step is classifying each cost as variable or fixed.

3. A fixed budget is prepared using an expected volume of sales or production. A flexible budget is prepared using the actual volume of activity.

4. The contribution margin equals sales less variable costs.

5. *c*

6. It is the difference between actual cost and standard cost.

7. *a*; Total actual hours: 2,500 × 2.5 = 6,250
   Total standard hours: 2,500 × 2.0 = 5,000
   Efficiency variance = (6,250 − 5,000) × $3.00
                       = $3,750 U

8. *b*; Rate variance = ($3.10 − $3.00) × 6,250 = $625 U

9. Yes, this will occur when the materials quantity variance is more than the materials price variance.

10. The overhead volume variance is favorable when the actual operating level is higher than the expected level.

11. *b*

12.

Goods in Process Inventory	75,700	
Direct Materials Price Variance	1,300	
Direct Materials Quantity Variance		3,800
Raw Materials Inventory		73,200

13. If the variances are material, they should be prorated among the Goods in Process Inventory, Finished Goods Inventory, and Cost of Goods Sold accounts. If they are not material, they can be closed to Cost of Goods Sold.

Key Terms

Benchmarking (p. 960)

Budget report (p. 948)

Budgetary control (p. 948)

Controllable variance (p. 961)

Cost variance (p. 955)

Efficiency variance (p. 968)

Favorable variance (p. 949)

Fixed budget (p. 949)

Fixed budget performance report (p. 949)

Flexible budget (p. 950)

Flexible budget performance report (p. 952)

Management by exception (p. 953)

Overhead cost variance (p. 960)

Price variance (p. 953)

Quantity variance (p. 953)

Spending variance (p. 968)

Standard costs (p. 953)

Unfavorable variance (p. 949)

Variance analysis (p. 953)

Volume variance (p. 961)

Multiple Choice Quiz   Answers on p. 991   mhhe.com/wildFAP21e

Additional Quiz Questions are available at the book's Website.

1. A company predicts its production and sales will be 24,000 units. At that level of activity, its fixed costs are budgeted at $300,000, and its variable costs are budgeted at $246,000. If its activity level declines to 20,000 units, what will be its fixed costs and its variable costs?
   a. Fixed, $300,000; variable, $246,000
   b. Fixed, $250,000; variable, $205,000
   c. Fixed, $300,000; variable, $205,000
   d. Fixed, $250,000; variable, $246,000
   e. Fixed, $300,000; variable, $300,000

2. Using the following information about a single product company, compute its total actual cost of direct materials used.
   • Direct materials standard cost: 5 lbs. × $2 per lb. = $10.
   • Total direct materials cost variance: $15,000 unfavorable.
   • Actual direct materials used: 300,000 lbs.
   • Actual units produced: 60,000 units.

   a. $585,000
   b. $600,000
   c. $300,000
   d. $315,000
   e. $615,000

3. A company uses four hours of direct labor to produce a product unit. The standard direct labor cost is $20 per hour. This period the company produced 20,000 units and used 84,160 hours of direct labor at a total cost of $1,599,040. What is its labor rate variance for the period?
   a. $83,200 F
   b. $84,160 U
   c. $84,160 F
   d. $83,200 U
   e. $ 960 F

4. A company's standard for a unit of its single product is $6 per unit in variable overhead (4 hours × $1.50 per hour). Actual data for the period show variable overhead costs of $150,000 and production of 24,000 units. Its total variable overhead cost variance is
  a. $ 6,000 F.
  b. $ 6,000 U.
  c. $114,000 U.
  d. $114,000 F.
  e. $ 0.

5. A company's standard for a unit of its single product is $4 per unit in fixed overhead ($24,000 total/6,000 units budgeted). Actual data for the period show total actual fixed overhead of $24,100 and production of 4,800 units. Its volume variance is
  a. $4,800 U.
  b. $4,800 F.
  c. $ 100 U.
  d. $ 100 F.
  e. $4,900 U.

A *Superscript letter A denotes assignments based on Appendix 23A.*

🎲 Icon denotes assignments that involve decision making.

Discussion Questions

1. 🎲 What limits the usefulness to managers of fixed budget performance reports?

2. 🎲 Identify the main purpose of a flexible budget for managers.

3. Prepare a flexible budget performance report title (in proper form) for Spalding Company for the calendar year 2013. Why is a proper title important for this or any report?

4. 🎲 What type of analysis does a flexible budget performance report help management perform?

5. In what sense can a variable cost be considered constant?

6. 🎲 What department is usually responsible for a direct labor rate variance? What department is usually responsible for a direct labor efficiency variance? Explain.

7. What is a price variance? What is a quantity variance?

8. 🎲 What is the purpose of using standard costs?

9. **KTM** monitors its fixed overhead. In an analysis of fixed overhead cost variances, what is the volume variance? **KTM**

10. What is the predetermined standard overhead rate? How is it computed?

11. In general, variance analysis is said to provide information about _____ and _____ variances.

12. 🎲 **Polaris** monitors its overhead. In an analysis of overhead cost variances, what is the controllable variance and what causes it? **Polaris**

13. What are the relations among standard costs, flexible budgets, variance analysis, and management by exception?

14. 🎲 How can the manager of snowmobile sales at **Arctic Cat** use flexible budgets to enhance performance? **Arctic Cat**

15. 🎲 Is it possible for a retail store such as **Apple** to use variances in analyzing its operating performance? Explain. **Apple**

16. 🎲 Assume that **Piaggio** is budgeted to operate at 80% of capacity but actually operates at 75% of capacity. What effect will the 5% deviation have on its controllable variance? Its volume variance? **PIAGGIO**

🔲 connect

QUICK STUDY

QS 23-1
Flexible budget performance report
P1

Beech Company sold 105,000 units of its product in May. For the level of production achieved in May, the budgeted amounts were: sales, $1,300,000; variable costs, $750,000; and fixed costs, $300,000. The following actual financial results are available for May. Prepare a flexible budget performance report for May.

Sales (105,000 units)	$1,275,000
Variable costs.	712,500
Fixed costs	300,000

QS 23-2
Standard cost card   C1

BatCo makes metal baseball bats. Each bat requires 1 kg. of aluminum at $18 per kg. and 0.25 direct labor hours at $20 per hour. Overhead is assigned at the rate of $40 per labor hour. What amounts would appear on a standard cost card for BatCo?

QS 23-3
Cost variances   C2

Refer to information in QS 23-2. Assume the actual cost to manufacture one metal bat was $40. Compute the cost variance and classify it as favorable or unfavorable.

QS 23-4
Management by exception

C1 🎲

Managers use *management by exception* for control purposes. (1) Describe the concept of management by exception. (2) Explain how standard costs help managers apply this concept to monitor and control costs.

Juan Company's output for the current period was assigned a $150,000 standard direct materials cost. The direct materials variances included a $12,000 favorable price variance and a $2,000 favorable quantity variance. What is the actual total direct materials cost for the current period?

QS 23-5
Materials cost variances   P2

Frontera Company's output for the current period results in a $20,000 unfavorable direct labor rate variance and a $10,000 unfavorable direct labor efficiency variance. Production for the current period was assigned an $400,000 standard direct labor cost. What is the actual total direct labor cost for the current period?

QS 23-6
Labor cost variances   P2

For the current period, Kayenta Company's manufacturing operations yield a $4,000 unfavorable price variance on its direct materials usage. The actual price per pound of material is $78; the standard price is $77.50. How many pounds of material are used in the current period?

QS 23-7
Materials cost variances   P2

Alvarez Company's output for the current period yields a $20,000 favorable overhead volume variance and a $60,400 unfavorable overhead controllable variance. Standard overhead charged to production for the period is $225,000. What is the actual total overhead cost incurred for the period?

QS 23-8
Overhead cost variances   P3

Refer to the information in QS 23-8. Alvarez records standard costs in its accounts. Prepare the journal entry to charge overhead costs to the Goods in Process Inventory account and to record any variances.

QS 23-9[A]
Preparing overhead entries   P4

Mosaic Company applies overhead using machine hours and reports the following information. Compute the total variable overhead cost variance.

Actual machine hours used	4,700 hours
Standard machine hours	5,000 hours
Actual variable overhead rate per hour	$4.15
Standard variable overhead rate per hour	$4.00

QS 23-10
Total overhead cost variance
P3

Refer to the information from QS 23-10. Compute the variable overhead spending variance and the variable overhead efficiency variance.

QS 23-11[A]
Overhead spending and efficiency variances   P3

Farad, Inc. specializes in selling used SUVs. During the first six months of 2013, the dealership sold 50 trucks at an average price of $9,000 each. The budget for the first six months of 2013 was to sell 45 trucks at an average price of $9,500 each. Compute the dealership's sales price variance and sales volume variance for the first six months of 2013.

QS 23-12
Computing sales price and volume variances   A1

Based on predicted production of 24,000 units, a company anticipates $300,000 of fixed costs and $246,000 of variable costs. If the company actually produces 20,000 units, what are the flexible budget amounts of fixed and variable costs?

QS 23-13
Flexible budget   P1

Brodrick Company expects to produce 20,000 units for the year ending December 31. A flexible budget for 20,000 units of production reflects sales of $400,000; variable costs of $80,000; and fixed costs of $150,000. If the company instead produces and sells 26,000 units for the year, calculate the expected level of income from operations.

QS 23-14
Flexible budget
P1

Refer to information in QS 23-14. Assume that actual sales are $480,000, actual variable costs for the year are $112,000, and actual fixed costs for the year are $145,000. Prepare a flexible budget performance report for the year.

QS 23-15
Flexible budget performance report   P1

Tercer reports the following on one of its products. Compute the direct materials price and quantity variances.

Direct materials standard (4 lbs. @ $2/lb.)	$8 per finished unit
Actual direct materials used	300,000 lbs.
Actual finished units produced	60,000 units
Actual cost of direct materials used	$535,000

QS 23-16
Materials variances
P2

QS 23-17

Direct labor variances

P2

The following information describes a company's usage of direct labor in a recent period. Compute the direct labor rate and efficiency variances for the period.

Actual direct labor hours used	65,000
Actual direct labor rate per hour	$15
Standard direct labor rate per hour	$14
Standard direct labor hours for units produced	67,000

QS 23-18

Controllable overhead variance

P3

Fogel Co. expects to produce 116,000 units for the year. The company's flexible budget for 116,000 units of production shows variable overhead costs of $162,400 and fixed overhead costs of $124,000. For the year, the company incurred actual overhead costs of $262,800 while producing 110,000 units. Compute the controllable overhead variance.

QS 23-19

Controllable overhead variance

P3

AirPro Corp. reports the following for November. Compute the controllable overhead variance for November.

Actual total factory overhead incurred	$28,175
Standard factory overhead:	
Variable overhead	$3.10 per unit produced
Fixed overhead	
($12,000/12,000 predicted units to be produced)	$1 per unit
Predicted units produced	12,000 units
Actual units produced	9,800 units

QS 23-20

Volume variance   P3

Refer to information in QS 23-19. Compute the overhead volume variance for November.

QS 23-21

Sales variances   A1

In a recent year, **BMW** sold 216,944 of its 1 Series cars. Assume the company expected to sell 225,944 of these cars during the year. Also assume the budgeted sales price for each car was $30,000, and the actual sales price for each car was $30,200. Compute the sales price variance and the sales volume variance.

Mc Graw Hill **connect**

EXERCISES

Exercise 23-1

Classification of costs as fixed or variable

P1

JPAK Company manufactures and sells mountain bikes. It normally operates eight hours a day, five days a week. Using this information, classify each of the following costs as fixed or variable. If additional information would affect your decision, describe the information.

a. Bike frames   **e.** Bike tires   **i.** Office supplies

b. Screws for assembly   **f.** Gas used for heating   **j.** Depreciation on tools

c. Repair expense for tools   **g.** Incoming shipping expenses   **k.** Management salaries

d. Direct labor   **h.** Taxes on property

Exercise 23-2

Preparation of flexible budgets

P1

Tempo Company's fixed budget for the first quarter of calendar year 2013 reveals the following. Prepare flexible budgets following the format of Exhibit 23.3 that show variable costs per unit, fixed costs, and three different flexible budgets for sales volumes of 6,000, 7,000, and 8,000 units.

Sales (7,000 units)		$2,800,000
Cost of goods sold		
Direct materials	$280,000	
Direct labor	490,000	
Production supplies	175,000	
Plant manager salary	65,000	1,010,000
Gross profit		1,790,000
Selling expenses		
Sales commissions	140,000	
Packaging	154,000	
Advertising	125,000	419,000
Administrative expenses		
Administrative salaries	85,000	
Depreciation—office equip.	35,000	
Insurance	20,000	
Office rent	36,000	176,000
Income from operations		$1,195,000

Check   Income (at 6,000 units), $972,000

Solitaire Company's fixed budget performance report for June follows. The $315,000 budgeted expenses include $294,000 variable expenses and $21,000 fixed expenses. Actual expenses include $27,000 fixed expenses. Prepare a flexible budget performance report showing any variances between budgeted and actual results. List fixed and variable expenses separately.

Exercise 23-3
Preparation of a flexible budget performance report
P1

	Fixed Budget	Actual Results	Variances
Sales (in units)	8,400	10,800	
Sales (in dollars)	$420,000	$540,000	$120,000 F
Total expenses	315,000	378,000	63,000 U
Income from operations	$105,000	$162,000	$ 57,000 F

Check Income variance, $21,000 F

Bay City Company's fixed budget performance report for July follows. The $647,500 budgeted expenses include $487,500 variable expenses and $160,000 fixed expenses. Actual expenses include $158,000 fixed expenses. Prepare a flexible budget performance report that shows any variances between budgeted results and actual results. List fixed and variable expenses separately.

Exercise 23-4
Preparation of a flexible budget performance report
P1

	Fixed Budget	Actual Results	Variances
Sales (in units)	7,500	7,200	
Sales (in dollars)	$750,000	$737,000	$13,000 U
Total expenses	647,500	641,000	6,500 F
Income from operations	$102,500	$ 96,000	$ 6,500 U

Check Income variance, $4,000 F

After evaluating Null Company's manufacturing process, management decides to establish standards of 3 hours of direct labor per unit of product and $15 per hour for the labor rate. During October, the company uses 16,250 hours of direct labor at a $247,000 total cost to produce 5,600 units of product. In November, the company uses 22,000 hours of direct labor at a $335,500 total cost to produce 6,000 units of product. (1) Compute the rate variance, the efficiency variance, and the total direct labor cost variance for each of these two months. (2) Interpret the October direct labor variances.

Exercise 23-5
Computation and interpretation of labor variances P2

Check (1) October rate variance, $3,250 U

Sedona Company set the following standard costs for one unit of its product for 2013.

Exercise 23-6
Computation of total variable and fixed overhead variances
P3

Direct material (20 lbs. @ $2.50 per lb.)	$ 50.00
Direct labor (10 hrs. @ $8.00 per hr.)	80.00
Factory variable overhead (10 hrs. @ $4.00 per hr.)	40.00
Factory fixed overhead (10 hrs. @ $1.60 per hr.)	16.00
Standard cost	$186.00

The $5.60 ($4.00 + $1.60) total overhead rate per direct labor hour is based on an expected operating level equal to 75% of the factory's capacity of 50,000 units per month. The following monthly flexible budget information is also available.

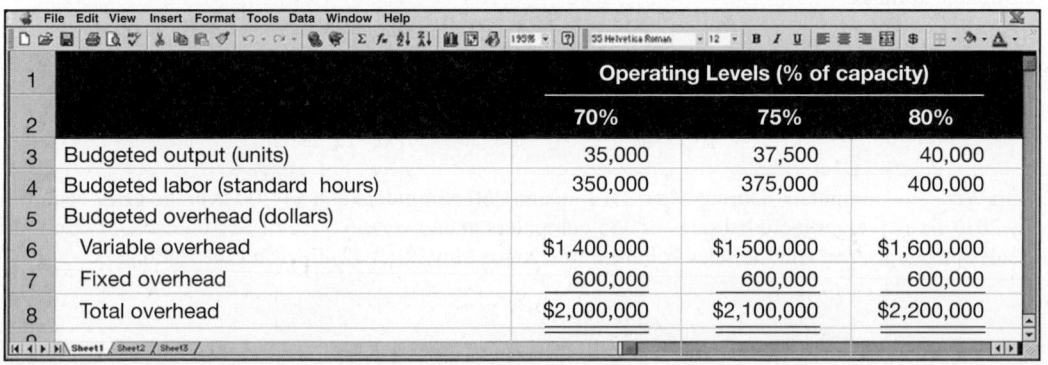

	Operating Levels (% of capacity)		
	70%	75%	80%
Budgeted output (units)	35,000	37,500	40,000
Budgeted labor (standard hours)	350,000	375,000	400,000
Budgeted overhead (dollars)			
Variable overhead	$1,400,000	$1,500,000	$1,600,000
Fixed overhead	600,000	600,000	600,000
Total overhead	$2,000,000	$2,100,000	$2,200,000

During the current month, the company operated at 70% of capacity, employees worked 340,000 hours, and the following actual overhead costs were incurred.

Variable overhead costs	$1,375,000
Fixed overhead costs	628,600
Total overhead costs	$2,003,600

Check (2) Variable overhead cost variance, $25,000 F

(1) Show how the company computed its predetermined overhead application rate per hour for total overhead, variable overhead, and fixed overhead. (2) Compute the total variable and total fixed overhead variances.

Exercise 23-7^A

Computation and interpretation of overhead spending, efficiency, and volume variances P3

Check (1) Variable overhead: Spending, $15,000 U; Efficiency, $40,000 F

Refer to the information from Exercise 23-6. Compute and interpret the following.
1. Variable overhead spending and efficiency variances.
2. Fixed overhead spending and volume variances.
3. Controllable variance.

Exercise 23-8

Computation and interpretation of materials variances P2

Check Price variance, $2,200 U

Hart Company made 3,000 bookshelves using 22,000 board feet of wood costing $266,200. The company's direct materials standards for one bookshelf are 8 board feet of wood at $12 per board foot. (1) Compute the direct materials variances incurred in manufacturing these bookshelves. (2) Interpret the direct materials variances.

Exercise 23-9^A

Materials variances recorded and closed

P4

Check (2) Cr. to Cost of Goods Sold, $21,800

Refer to Exercise 23-8. Hart Company records standard costs in its accounts and its material variances in separate accounts when it assigns materials costs to the Goods in Process Inventory account. (1) Show the journal entry that both charges the direct materials costs to the Goods in Process Inventory account and records the materials variances in their proper accounts. (2) Assume that Hart's material variances are the only variances accumulated in the accounting period and that they are immaterial. Prepare the adjusting journal entry to close the variance accounts at period-end. (3) Identify the variance that should be investigated according to the management by exception concept. Explain.

Exercise 23-10

Computation of total overhead rate and total overhead variance

P3

Check (1) Variable overhead rate, $11.00 per hour

World Company expects to operate at 80% of its productive capacity of 50,000 units per month. At this planned level, the company expects to use 25,000 standard hours of direct labor. Overhead is allocated to products using a predetermined standard rate based on direct labor hours. At the 80% capacity level, the total budgeted cost includes $50,000 fixed overhead cost and $275,000 variable overhead cost. In the current month, the company incurred $305,000 actual overhead and 22,000 actual labor hours while producing 35,000 units. (1) Compute the overhead application rate for total overhead. (2) Compute the total overhead variance.

Exercise 23-11

Computation of volume and controllable overhead variances

P3

Check (2) $14,375 U

Refer to the information from Exercise 23-10. Compute the (1) overhead volume variance and (2) overhead controllable variance.

Exercise 23-12

Computing and interpreting sales variances

A1

Comp Wiz sells computers. During May 2013, it sold 350 computers at a $1,200 average price each. The May 2013 fixed budget included sales of 365 computers at an average price of $1,100 each. (1) Compute the sales price variance and the sales volume variance for May 2013. (2) Interpret the findings.

Match the terms a–e with their correct definition 1–5.

a. Standard cost card

b. Management by exception

c. Standard cost

d. Ideal standard

e. Practical standard

1. Quantity of input required under normal conditions.

2. Quantity of input required if a production process is 100% efficient.

3. Managing by focusing on large differences from standard costs.

4. Record that accumulates standard cost information.

5. Preset cost for delivering a product or service under normal conditions.

Exercise 23-13
Standard costs

C1

Presented below are terms preceded by letters a through j and a list of definitions 1 through 10. Enter the letter of the term with the definition, using the space preceding the definition.

a. Fixed budget

b. Standard costs

c. Price variance

d. Quantity variance

e. Volume variance

f. Controllable variance

g. Cost variance

h. Flexible budget

i. Variance analysis

j. Management by exception

_____ **1.** The difference between actual and budgeted sales or cost caused by the difference between the actual price per unit and the budgeted price per unit.

_____ **2.** A planning budget based on a single predicted amount of sales or production volume; unsuitable for evaluations if the actual volume differs from the predicted volume.

_____ **3.** Preset costs for delivering a product, component, or service under normal conditions.

_____ **4.** A process of examining the differences between actual and budgeted sales or costs and describing them in terms of the amounts that resulted from price and quantity differences.

_____ **5.** The difference between the total budgeted overhead cost and the overhead cost that was allocated to products using the predetermined fixed overhead rate.

_____ **6.** A budget prepared based on predicted amounts of revenues and expenses corresponding to the actual level of output.

_____ **7.** The difference between actual and budgeted cost caused by the difference between the actual quantity and the budgeted quantity.

_____ **8.** The combination of both overhead spending variances (variable and fixed) and the variable overhead efficiency variance.

_____ **9.** A management process to focus on significant variances and give less attention to areas where performance is close to the standard.

_____ **10.** The difference between actual cost and standard cost, made up of a price variance and a quantity variance.

Exercise 23-14
Cost variances

C2

Resset Co. provides the following results of April's operations: F indicates favorable and U indicates unfavorable. Applying the management by exception approach, which of the variances are of greatest concern? Why?

Direct materials price variance	$ 300 F
Direct materials quantity variance	3,000 U
Direct labor rate variance	100 U
Direct labor efficiency variance	2,200 F
Controllable overhead variance	400 U
Fixed overhead volume variance	500 F

Exercise 23-15
Analyzing variances

C1

The following information describes production activities of Mercer Manufacturing for the year:

Actual raw materials used	16,000 lbs. at $4.05 per lb.
Actual factory payroll	5,545 hours for a total of $105,355
Actual units produced	30,000

Exercise 23-16
Direct materials and direct labor variances

P2

Budgeted standards for each unit produced are 0.50 pounds of raw material at $4.00 per pound and 10 minutes of direct labor at $20 per hour. (1) Compute the direct materials price and quantity variances. (2) Compute the direct labor rate and efficiency variances. Indicate whether each variance is favorable or unfavorable.

PROBLEM SET A

Problem 23-1A
Computation of materials, labor, and overhead variances

P2 P3

mhhe.com/wildFAP21e

Trico Company set the following standard unit costs for its single product.

Direct materials (30 lbs. @ $4 per lb.)	$120.00
Direct labor (5 hrs. @ $14 per hr.)	70.00
Factory overhead—variable (5 hrs. @ $8 per hr.)	40.00
Factory overhead—fixed (5 hrs. @ $10 per hr.)	50.00
Total standard cost	$280.00

The predetermined overhead rate is based on a planned operating volume of 80% of the productive capacity of 60,000 units per quarter. The following flexible budget information is available.

	Operating Levels		
	70%	80%	90%
Production in units	42,000	48,000	54,000
Standard direct labor hours	210,000	240,000	270,000
Budgeted overhead			
Fixed factory overhead	$2,400,000	$2,400,000	$2,400,000
Variable factory overhead	$1,680,000	$1,920,000	$2,160,000

During the current quarter, the company operated at 90% of capacity and produced 54,000 units of product; actual direct labor totaled 265,000 hours. Units produced were assigned the following standard costs:

Direct materials (1,620,000 lbs. @ $4 per lb.)	$ 6,480,000
Direct labor (270,000 hrs. @ $14 per hr.)	3,780,000
Factory overhead (270,000 hrs. @ $18 per hr.)	4,860,000
Total standard cost	$15,120,000

Actual costs incurred during the current quarter follow:

Direct materials (1,615,000 lbs. @ $4.10)	$ 6,621,500
Direct labor (265,000 hrs. @ $13.75)	3,643,750
Fixed factory overhead costs	2,350,000
Variable factory overhead costs	2,200,000
Total actual costs	$14,815,250

Required

1. Compute the direct materials cost variance, including its price and quantity variances.
2. Compute the direct labor variance, including its rate and efficiency variances.
3. Compute the overhead controllable and volume variances.

Problem 23-2A[A]
Expanded overhead variances

P3

Refer to information in Problem 23-1A.

Required

Compute these variances: (a) variable overhead spending and efficiency, (b) fixed overhead spending and volume, and (c) total overhead controllable.

Phoenix Company's 2013 master budget included the following fixed budget report. It is based on an expected production and sales volume of 15,000 units.

Problem 23-3A
Preparation and analysis
of a flexible budget   P1

PHOENIX COMPANY		
Fixed Budget Report		
For Year Ended December 31, 2013		
Sales		$3,000,000
Cost of goods sold		
Direct materials	$975,000	
Direct labor	225,000	
Machinery repairs (variable cost)	60,000	
Depreciation—plant equipment	300,000	
Utilities ($45,000 is variable)	195,000	
Plant management salaries	200,000	1,955,000
Gross profit		1,045,000
Selling expenses		
Packaging	75,000	
Shipping	105,000	
Sales salary (fixed annual amount)	250,000	430,000
General and administrative expenses		
Advertising expense	125,000	
Salaries	241,000	
Entertainment expense	90,000	456,000
Income from operations		$ 159,000

Required

1. Classify all items listed in the fixed budget as variable or fixed. Also determine their amounts per unit or their amounts for the year, as appropriate.

2. Prepare flexible budgets (see Exhibit 23.3) for the company at sales volumes of 14,000 and 16,000 units.

3. The company's business conditions are improving. One possible result is a sales volume of approximately 18,000 units. The company president is confident that this volume is within the relevant range of existing capacity. How much would operating income increase over the 2013 budgeted amount of $159,000 if this level is reached without increasing capacity?

4. An unfavorable change in business is remotely possible; in this case, production and sales volume for 2013 could fall to 12,000 units. How much income (or loss) from operations would occur if sales volume falls to this level?

Check   (2) Budgeted income at
16,000 units, $260,000

(4) Potential operating loss,
$(144,000)

Refer to the information in Problem 23-3A. Phoenix Company's actual income statement for 2013 follows.

Problem 23-4A
Preparation and analysis
of a flexible budget
performance report

P1 P2 A1

mhhe.com/wildFAP21e

PHOENIX COMPANY		
Statement of Income from Operations		
For Year Ended December 31, 2013		
Sales (18,000 units)		$3,648,000
Cost of goods sold		
Direct materials	$1,185,000	
Direct labor	278,000	
Machinery repairs (variable cost)	63,000	
Depreciation—plant equipment	300,000	
Utilities (fixed cost is $147,500)	200,500	
Plant management salaries...............	210,000	2,236,500
Gross profit		1,411,500
Selling expenses		
Packaging	87,500	
Shipping	118,500	
Sales salary (annual)....................	268,000	474,000
General and administrative expenses		
Advertising expense	132,000	
Salaries	241,000	
Entertainment expense	93,500	466,500
Income from operations		$ 471,000

Required

1. Prepare a flexible budget performance report for 2013.

Analysis Component

2. Analyze and interpret both the (a) sales variance and (b) direct materials variance.

Problem 23-5A
Flexible budget preparation;
computation of materials, labor,
and overhead variances; and
overhead variance report

P1 P2 P3 C2

Antuan Company set the following standard costs for one unit of its product.

Direct materials (6 lbs. @ $5 per lb.).........	$ 30
Direct labor (2 hrs. @ $17 per hr.)	34
Overhead (2 hrs. @ $18.50 per hr.)..........	37
Total standard cost.......................	$101

The predetermined overhead rate ($18.50 per direct labor hour) is based on an expected volume of 75% of the factory's capacity of 20,000 units per month. Following are the company's budgeted overhead costs per month at the 75% level.

Overhead Budget (75% Capacity)		
Variable overhead costs		
Indirect materials	$ 45,000	
Indirect labor	180,000	
Power	45,000	
Repairs and maintenance	90,000	
Total variable overhead costs		$360,000
Fixed overhead costs		
Depreciation—building	24,000	
Depreciation—machinery	80,000	
Taxes and insurance	12,000	
Supervision	79,000	
Total fixed overhead costs		195,000
Total overhead costs		$555,000

The company incurred the following actual costs when it operated at 75% of capacity in October.

Direct materials (91,000 lbs. @ $5.10 per lb.)		$ 464,100
Direct labor (30,500 hrs. @ $17.25 per hr.)		526,125
Overhead costs		
Indirect materials	$ 44,250	
Indirect labor	177,750	
Power	43,000	
Repairs and maintenance	96,000	
Depreciation—building	24,000	
Depreciation—machinery	75,000	
Taxes and insurance	11,500	
Supervision	89,000	560,500
Total costs		$1,550,725

Required

1. Examine the monthly overhead budget to (a) determine the costs per unit for each variable overhead item and its total per unit costs, and (b) identify the total fixed costs per month.

2. Prepare flexible overhead budgets (as in Exhibit 23.12) for October showing the amounts of each variable and fixed cost at the 65%, 75%, and 85% capacity levels.

3. Compute the direct materials cost variance, including its price and quantity variances.

4. Compute the direct labor cost variance, including its rate and efficiency variances.
5. Prepare a detailed overhead variance report (as in Exhibit 23.15) that shows the variances for individual items of overhead.

(4) Labor variances: Rate, $7,625 U; Efficiency, $8,500 U

Kegler Company has set the following standard costs per unit for the product it manufactures.

Problem 23-6A[A]

Materials, labor, and overhead variances; overhead variance report

C2   P2   P3

Direct materials (15 lbs. @ $4 per lb.)	$ 60.00
Direct labor (3 hrs. @ $15 per hr.)	45.00
Overhead (3 hrs. @ $3.85 per hr.)	11.55
Total standard cost	$116.55

The predetermined overhead rate is based on a planned operating volume of 80% of the productive capacity of 10,000 units per month. The following flexible budget information is available.

	Operating Levels		
	70%	**80%**	**90%**
Production in units	7,000	8,000	9,000
Standard direct labor hours	21,000	24,000	27,000
Budgeted overhead			
Variable overhead costs			
Indirect materials	$13,125	$15,000	$16,875
Indirect labor	21,000	24,000	27,000
Power	5,250	6,000	6,750
Maintenance	2,625	3,000	3,375
Total variable costs	42,000	48,000	54,000
Fixed overhead costs			
Rent of factory building	15,000	15,000	15,000
Depreciation machinery	10,000	10,000	10,000
Supervisory salaries	19,400	19,400	19,400
Total fixed costs	44,400	44,400	44,400
Total overhead costs	$86,400	$92,400	$98,400

During May, the company operated at 90% of capacity and produced 9,000 units, incurring the following actual costs.

Direct materials (138,000 lbs. @ $3.75 per lb.)		$ 517,500
Direct labor (31,000 hrs. @ $15.10 per hr.)		468,100
Overhead costs		
Indirect materials	$15,000	
Indirect labor	26,500	
Power	6,750	
Maintenance	4,000	
Rent of factory building	15,000	
Depreciation—machinery	10,000	
Supervisory salaries	22,000	99,250
Total costs		$1,084,850

Required

1. Compute the direct materials variance, including its price and quantity variances.
2. Compute the direct labor variance, including its rate and efficiency variances.

[continued on next page]

Check   (1) Materials variances: Price, $34,500 F; Quantity, $12,000 U (2) Labor variances: Rate, $3,100 U; Efficiency, $60,000 U

3. Compute these variances: (a) variable overhead spending and efficiency, (b) fixed overhead spending and volume, and (c) total overhead controllable.

4. Prepare a detailed overhead variance report (as in Exhibit 23.15) that shows the variances for individual items of overhead.

Problem 23-7A[A]
Materials, labor, and overhead variances recorded and analyzed

C1   P4

Boss Company's standard cost accounting system recorded this information from its December operations.

Standard direct materials cost	$100,000
Direct materials quantity variance (unfavorable)	3,000
Direct materials price variance (favorable)	500
Actual direct labor cost	90,000
Direct labor efficiency variance (favorable).............	7,000
Direct labor rate variance (unfavorable)	1,200
Actual overhead cost	375,000
Volume variance (unfavorable)........................	12,000
Controllable variance (unfavorable)...................	9,000

Required

Check (1) Dr. Goods in Process
Inventory (for overhead), $354,000

1. Prepare December 31 journal entries to record the company's costs and variances for the month. (Do not prepare the journal entry to close the variances.)

Analysis Component

2. Identify the areas that would attract the attention of a manager who uses management by exception. Explain what action(s) the manager should consider.

PROBLEM SET B

Problem 23-1B
Computation of materials, labor, and overhead variances

P2   P3

Kryll Company set the following standard unit costs for its single product.

Direct materials (25 lbs. @ $4 per lb.)	$100.00
Direct labor (6 hrs. @ $8 per hr.)......................	48.00
Factory overhead—variable (6 hrs. @ $5 per hr.)	30.00
Factory overhead—fixed (6 hrs. @ $7 per hr.)	42.00
Total standard cost	$220.00

The predetermined overhead rate is based on a planned operating volume of 80% of the productive capacity of 60,000 units per quarter. The following flexible budget information is available.

	Operating Levels		
	70%	80%	90%
Production in units	42,000	48,000	54,000
Standard direct labor hours	252,000	288,000	324,000
Budgeted overhead			
Fixed factory overhead	$2,016,000	$2,016,000	$2,016,000
Variable factory overhead	1,260,000	1,440,000	1,620,000

During the current quarter, the company operated at 70% of capacity and produced 42,000 units of product; direct labor hours worked were 250,000. Units produced were assigned the following standard costs:

Direct materials (1,050,000 lbs. @ $4 per lb.)	$4,200,000
Direct labor (252,000 hrs. @ $8 per hr.)	2,016,000
Factory overhead (252,000 hrs. @ $12 per hr.)	3,024,000
Total standard cost	$9,240,000

Actual costs incurred during the current quarter follow:

Direct materials (1,000,000 lbs. @ $4.25).	$4,250,000
Direct labor (250,000 hrs. @ $7.75).	1,937,500
Fixed factory overhead costs	1,960,000
Variable factory overhead costs	1,200,000
Total actual costs.	$9,347,500

Required

1. Compute the direct materials cost variance, including its price and quantity variances.
2. Compute the direct labor variance, including its rate and efficiency variances.
3. Compute the total overhead controllable and volume variances.

Check (1) Materials variances: Price, $250,000 U; Quantity, $200,000 F (2) Labor variances: Rate, $62,500 F; Efficiency, $16,000 F

Refer to information in Problem 23-1B.

Problem 23-2B[A]
Expanded overhead variances

P3

Required

Compute these variances: (a) variable overhead spending and efficiency, (b) fixed overhead spending and volume, and (c) total overhead controllable.

Tohono Company's 2013 master budget included the following fixed budget report. It is based on an expected production and sales volume of 20,000 units.

Problem 23-3B
Preparation and analysis of a flexible budget P1 A1

TOHONO COMPANY Fixed Budget Report For Year Ended December 31, 2013		
Sales		$3,000,000
Cost of goods sold		
Direct materials	$1,200,000	
Direct labor	260,000	
Machinery repairs (variable cost)	57,000	
Depreciation—machinery	250,000	
Utilities (25% is variable cost)	200,000	
Plant manager salaries	140,000	2,107,000
Gross profit		893,000
Selling expenses		
Packaging	80,000	
Shipping	116,000	
Sales salary (fixed annual amount)	160,000	356,000
General and administrative expenses		
Advertising	81,000	
Salaries	241,000	
Entertainment expense	90,000	412,000
Income from operations		$ 125,000

Required

1. Classify all items listed in the fixed budget as variable or fixed. Also determine their amounts per unit or their amounts for the year, as appropriate.
2. Prepare flexible budgets (see Exhibit 23.3) for the company at sales volumes of 18,000 and 24,000 units.
3. The company's business conditions are improving. One possible result is a sales volume of approximately 28,000 units. The company president is confident that this volume is within the relevant range of existing capacity. How much would operating income increase over the 2013 budgeted amount of $125,000 if this level is reached without increasing capacity?
4. An unfavorable change in business is remotely possible; in this case, production and sales volume for 2013 could fall to 14,000 units. How much income (or loss) from operations would occur if sales volume falls to this level?

Check (2) Budgeted income at 24,000 units, $372,400

(4) Potential operating loss, $(246,100)

Problem 23-4B

Preparation and analysis
of a flexible budget
performance report

P1 A1

Refer to the information in Problem 23-3B. Tohono Company's actual income statement for 2013 follows.

TOHONO COMPANY		
Statement of Income from Operations		
For Year Ended December 31, 2013		
Sales (24,000 units)		$3,648,000
Cost of goods sold		
Direct materials	$1,400,000	
Direct labor	360,000	
Machinery repairs (variable cost)	60,000	
Depreciation—machinery	250,000	
Utilities (variable cost, $64,000)	218,000	
Plant manager salaries	155,000	2,443,000
Gross profit		1,205,000
Selling expenses		
Packaging	90,000	
Shipping	124,000	
Sales salary (annual)	162,000	376,000
General and administrative expenses		
Advertising expense	104,000	
Salaries	232,000	
Entertainment expense	100,000	436,000
Income from operations		$ 393,000

Required

Check (1) Variances: Fixed costs,
$45,000 U; Income, $20,600 F

1. Prepare a flexible budget performance report for 2013.

Analysis Component

2. Analyze and interpret both the (a) sales variance and (b) direct materials variance.

Problem 23-5B

Flexible budget preparation;
computation of materials, labor,
and overhead variances; and
overhead variance report

P1 P2 P3 C2

Suncoast Company set the following standard costs for one unit of its product.

Direct materials (4.5 lb. @ $6 per kg.)	$27
Direct labor (1.5 hrs. @ $12 per hr.)	18
Overhead (1.5 hrs. @ $16 per hr.)	24
Total standard cost........................	$69

The predetermined overhead rate ($16.00 per direct labor hour) is based on an expected volume of 75% of the factory's capacity of 20,000 units per month. Following are the company's budgeted overhead costs per month at the 75% level.

Overhead Budget (75% Capacity)	
Variable overhead costs	
Indirect materials	$22,500
Indirect labor.....................	90,000
Power	22,500
Repairs and maintenance	45,000
Total variable overhead costs	$180,000
Fixed overhead costs	
Depreciation—building	24,000
Depreciation—machinery............	72,000
Taxes and insurance	18,000
Supervision	66,000
Total fixed overhead costs...........	180,000
Total overhead costs	$360,000

The company incurred the following actual costs when it operated at 75% of capacity in December.

Direct materials (69,000 lbs. @ $6.10)		$ 420,900
Direct labor (22,800 hrs. @ $12.30)		280,440
Overhead costs		
Indirect materials	$21,600	
Indirect labor	82,260	
Power	23,100	
Repairs and maintenance	46,800	
Depreciation—building	24,000	
Depreciation—machinery	75,000	
Taxes and insurance	16,500	
Supervision	66,000	355,260
Total costs		$1,056,600

Required

1. Examine the monthly overhead budget to (a) determine the costs per unit for each variable overhead item and its total per unit costs, and (b) identify the total fixed costs per month.

2. Prepare flexible overhead budgets (as in Exhibit 23.12) for December showing the amounts of each variable and fixed cost at the 65%, 75%, and 85% capacity levels.

3. Compute the direct materials cost variance, including its price and quantity variances.

4. Compute the direct labor cost variance, including its rate and efficiency variances.

5. Prepare a detailed overhead variance report (as in Exhibit 23.15) that shows the variances for individual items of overhead.

Check   (2) Budgeted total overhead at 17,000 units, $384,000

(3) Materials variances: Price, $6,900 U; Quantity, $9,000 U

(4) Labor variances: Rate, $6,840 U; Efficiency, $3,600 U

Guadelupe Company has set the following standard costs per unit for the product it manufactures.

Direct materials (10 lbs. @ $3.00 per lb.)	$30.00
Direct labor (1 hr. @ $6 per hr.)	24.00
Overhead (4 hr. @ $2.50 per hr.)	10.00
Total standard cost	$64.00

Problem 23-6B[A]
Materials, labor, and overhead variances; overhead variance report

C2   P2   P3

The predetermined overhead rate is based on a planned operating volume of 80% of the productive capacity of 10,000 units per month. The following flexible budget information is available.

	Operating Levels		
	70%	80%	90%
Production in units	7,000	8,000	9,000
Standard direct labor hours	28,000	32,000	36,000
Budgeted overhead			
Variable overhead costs			
Indirect materials	$ 8,750	$10,000	$11,250
Indirect labor	14,000	16,000	18,000
Power	3,500	4,000	4,500
Maintenance	1,750	2,000	2,250
Total variable costs	28,000	32,000	36,000
Fixed overhead costs			
Rent of factory building	12,000	12,000	12,000
Depreciation—machinery	20,000	20,000	20,000
Taxes and insurance	2,400	2,400	2,400
Supervisory salaries	13,600	13,600	13,600
Total fixed costs	48,000	48,000	48,000
Total overhead costs	$76,000	$80,000	$84,000

During March, the company operated at 90% of capacity and produced 9,000 units, incurring the following actual costs.

Direct materials (92,000 lbs. @ 2.95 per lb.)		$271,400
Direct labor (37,600 hrs. @ $6.05 per hr.)		227,480
Overhead costs		
Indirect materials.	$10,000	
Indirect labor.	16,000	
Power.	4,500	
Maintenance.	3,000	
Rent of factory building	12,000	
Depreciation—machinery	19,200	
Taxes and insurance.	3,000	
Supervisory salaries.	14,000	81,700
Total costs		$580,580

Required

Check (1) Materials variances: Price, $4,600 F; Quantity, $6,000 U

　　　　　(2) Labor variances: Rate, $1,880 U; Efficiency, $9,600 U

1. Compute the direct materials cost variance, including its price and quantity variances.
2. Compute the direct labor variance, including its rate and efficiency variances.
3. Compute these variances: (a) variable overhead spending and efficiency, (b) fixed overhead spending and volume, and (c) total overhead controllable.
4. Prepare a detailed overhead variance report (as in Exhibit 23.15) that shows the variances for individual items of overhead.

Problem 23-7B[A]

Materials, labor, and overhead variances recorded and analyzed

C1 P4

Kenya Company's standard cost accounting system recorded this information from its June operations.

Standard direct materials cost	$130,000
Direct materials quantity variance (favorable)	5,000
Direct materials price variance (favorable)	1,500
Actual direct labor cost	65,000
Direct labor efficiency variance (favorable)	3,000
Direct labor rate variance (unfavorable)	500
Actual overhead cost	250,000
Volume variance (unfavorable)	12,000
Controllable variance (unfavorable).	8,000

Required

Check (1) Dr. Goods in Process Inventory (for overhead), $230,000

1. Prepare journal entries dated June 30 to record the company's costs and variances for the month. (Do not prepare the journal entry to close the variances.)

Analysis Component

2. Identify the areas that would attract the attention of a manager who uses management by exception. Describe what action(s) the manager should consider.

SERIAL PROBLEM

Success Systems

P1

(This serial problem began in Chapter 1 and continues through most of the book. If previous chapter segments were not completed, the serial problem can begin at this point. It is helpful, but not necessary, to use the working papers that accompany the book.)

SP 23 Success Systems' second quarter 2014 fixed budget performance report for its computer furniture operations follows. The $156,000 budgeted expenses include $108,000 in variable expenses for desks and $18,000 in variable expenses for chairs, as well as $30,000 fixed expenses. The actual expenses include

$31,000 fixed expenses. Prepare a flexible budget performance report that shows any variances between budgeted results and actual results. List fixed and variable expenses separately.

	Fixed Budget	Actual Results	Variances
Desk sales (in units).............	144	150	
Chair sales (in units)	72	80	
Desk sales (in dollars)	$180,000	$186,000	$6,000 F
Chair sales (in dollars)...........	$ 36,000	$ 41,200	$5,200 F
Total expenses.................	$156,000	$163,880	$7,880 U
Income from operations	$ 60,000	$ 63,320	$3,320 F

Check Variances: Fixed expenses, $1,000 U

Beyond the Numbers

BTN 23-1   Analysis of flexible budgets and standard costs emphasizes the importance of a similar unit of measure for meaningful comparisons and evaluations. When **Polaris** compiles its financial reports in compliance with GAAP, it applies the same unit of measurement, U.S. dollars, for most measures of business operations. One issue for Polaris is how best to adjust account values for its subsidiaries that compile financial reports in currencies other than the U.S. dollar.

REPORTING IN ACTION

C1

Polaris

Required

1. Read Polaris' Note 1 in Appendix A and identify the financial statement where it reports the annual adjustment (remeasurement) for foreign currency translation.
2. Translating financial statements requires the use of a currency exchange rate. For each of the following three financial statement items, explain the exchange rate the company would apply to translate into U.S. dollars.
   a. Cash
   b. Sales revenue
   c. Property, plant and equipment

BTN 23-2   The usefulness of budgets, variances, and related analyses often depends on the accuracy of management's estimates of future sales activity.

COMPARATIVE ANALYSIS

A1

Polaris

Arctic Cat

Required

1. Identify and record the prior three years' sales (in dollars) for **Polaris** and for **Arctic Cat** using their financial statements in Appendix A.
2. Using the data in part *1*, predict both companies' sales activity for the next two to three years. (If possible, compare your predictions to actual sales figures for those years.)

BTN 23-3   Setting materials, labor, and overhead standards is challenging. If standards are set too low, companies might purchase inferior products and employees might not work to their full potential. If standards are set too high, companies could be unable to offer a quality product at a profitable rate and employees could be overworked. The ethical challenge is to set a high but reasonable standard. Assume that as a manager, you are asked to set the standard materials price and quantity for the new 1,000 CKB Mega-Max chip, a technically advanced product. To properly set the price and quantity standards, you assemble a team of specialists to provide input.

ETHICS CHALLENGE

C1

Required

Identify four types of specialists that you would assemble to provide information to help set the materials price and quantity standards. Briefly explain why you chose each individual.

COMMUNICATING IN PRACTICE

P4 C2

BTN 23-4 The reason we use the words *favorable* and *unfavorable* when evaluating variances is made clear when we look at the closing of accounts. To see this, consider that (1) all variance accounts are closed at the end of each period (temporary accounts), (2) a favorable variance is always a credit balance, and (3) an unfavorable variance is always a debit balance. Write a one-half page memorandum to your instructor with three parts that answer the three following requirements. (Assume that variance accounts are closed to Cost of Goods Sold.)

Required

1. Does Cost of Goods Sold increase or decrease when closing a favorable variance? Does gross margin increase or decrease when a favorable variance is closed to Cost of Goods Sold? Explain.
2. Does Cost of Goods Sold increase or decrease when closing an unfavorable variance? Does gross margin increase or decrease when an unfavorable variance is closed to Cost of Goods Sold? Explain.
3. Explain the meaning of a favorable variance and an unfavorable variance.

TAKING IT TO THE NET

C1

BTN 23-5 Access **iSixSigma**'s Website (**iSixSigma.com**) to search for and read information about *benchmarking* to complete the following requirements. (*Hint:* Look in the "dictionary" link.)

Required

1. Write a one-paragraph explanation (in layperson's terms) of benchmarking.
2. How does standard costing relate to benchmarking?

TEAMWORK IN ACTION

C2

BTN 23-6 Many service industries link labor rate and time (quantity) standards with their processes. One example is the standard time to board an aircraft. The reason time plays such an important role in the service industry is that it is viewed as a competitive advantage: best service in the shortest amount of time. Although the labor rate component is difficult to observe, the time component of a service delivery standard is often readily apparent—for example, "Lunch will be served in less than five minutes, or it is free."

Required

Break into teams and select two service industries for your analysis. Identify and describe all the time elements each industry uses to create a competitive advantage.

ENTREPRENEURIAL DECISION

C1 C2

BTN 23-7 Folsom Custom Skis, as discussed in the chapter opener, uses a costing system with standard costs for direct materials, direct labor, and overhead costs. Two comments frequently are mentioned in relation to standard costing and variance analysis: "Variances are not explanations" and "Management's goal is not to minimize variances."

Required

Write a short memo to Mike McCabe, Folsom Custom Skis' President, (no more than 1 page) interpreting these two comments in the context of his business.

HITTING THE ROAD

C1

BTN 23-8 Training employees to use standard amounts of materials in production is common. Typically large companies invest in this training but small organizations do not. One can observe these different practices in a trip to two different pizza businesses. Visit both a local pizza business and a national pizza chain business and then complete the following.

Required

1. Observe and record the number of raw material items used to make a typical cheese pizza. Also observe how the person making the pizza applies each item when preparing the pizza.
2. Record any differences in how items are applied between the two businesses.
3. Estimate which business is more profitable from your observations. Explain.

BTN 23-9   Access the annual report of **Piaggio** (at www.piaggio.com) for the year ended December 31, 2011. The usefulness of its budgets, variances, and related analyses depends on the accuracy of management's estimates of future sales activity.

GLOBAL DECISION

A1

PIAGGIO

Required

1. Identify and record the prior two years' sales (in € thousands) for Piaggio from its income statement.
2. Using the data in part *1*, predict sales activity for Piaggio for the next two years. Explain your prediction process.

ANSWERS TO MULTIPLE CHOICE QUIZ

1. c; Fixed costs remain at $300,000; Variable costs = ($246,000/24,000 units) × 20,000 units = $205,000.

2. e; Budgeted direct materials + Unfavorable variance = Actual cost of direct materials used; or, 60,000 units × $10 per unit = $600,000 + $15,000 U = $615,000.

3. c; (AH × AR) − (AH × SR) = $1,599,040 − (84,160 hours × $20 per hour) = $84,160 F.

4. b; Actual variable overhead − Variable overhead applied to production = Variable overhead cost variance; or $150,000 − (96,000 hours × $1.50 per hour) = $6,000 U.

5. a; Budgeted fixed overhead − Fixed overhead applied to production = Volume variance; or $24,000 − (4,800 units × $4 per unit) = $4,800 U.

Performance Measurement and Responsibility Accounting

24

A Look Back

Chapter 23 explained the master budget and its component budgets as well as their usefulness for planning and monitoring company activities.

A Look at This Chapter

This chapter identifies managerial reports useful in directing a company's activities. It describes responsibility accounting, measuring departmental and investment center performance, transfer pricing, and allocating common costs across departments.

A Look Ahead

Chapter 25 focuses on capital budgeting decisions. It also explains and illustrates several procedures used in evaluating short-term managerial decisions.

Learning Objectives

CONCEPTUAL

C1 Distinguish between direct and indirect expenses and identify bases for allocating indirect expenses to departments. (p. 997)

C2 *Appendix 24A*—Explain transfer pricing and methods to set transfer prices. (p. 1013)

C3 *Appendix 24B*—Describe allocation of joint costs across products. (p. 1014)

ANALYTICAL

A1 Analyze investment centers using return on assets and residual income. (p. 1005)

A2 Analyze investment centers using profit margin and investment turnover. (p. 1006)

A3 Analyze investment centers using the balanced scorecard. (p. 1007)

A4 Compute cycle time and cycle efficiency, and explain their importance to production management. (p. 1009)

PROCEDURAL

P1 Prepare a responsibility report for a cost center. (p. 996)

P2 Allocate indirect expenses to departments (p. 998)

P3 Prepare departmental income statements and contribution reports. (p. 999)

Go Blue!

"Do the dirty work yourself."

—BRIAN LINTON

PHILADELPHIA, PA—Brian Linton has a passion for oceans. Growing up in Singapore, Brian spent time scuba diving and tending to his 30 fish tanks. Traveling the world enabled Brian to see the "good, the bad, and the ugly of oceans and waterways." Combining his love of the water with an entrepreneurial spirit, Brian started his company **United By Blue (UnitedByBlue.com),** an apparel and jewelry company that removes one pound of trash in oceans and waterways for every product sold. As Brian notes, the company's unique business model was driven by "a quest for concrete ways to contribute to real and significant conservation efforts."

Building off Brian's college experiences selling jewelry he imported from Thailand, United By Blue sells men's and women's clothing, bags, and jewelry. The company uses organic cotton and creative designs to make products that elicit a fun vibe associated with oceans and harbor villages. Offering a diverse product line requires Brian to pay attention to cost management and departmental profits. The Sand Shack, a product in the company's jewelry department, "is a line of jewelry with chunky turquoise stones that generates much of the profits the company runs on," says Brian. His managers monitor direct, indirect, and controllable costs; allocate indirect costs to departments; and "measure return on investment (ROI)," explains Brian.

While focusing on controlling costs, United By Blue also strives to remove plastic from its packaging. "The number one material we collect during cleanups is plastic debris. We try to eliminate as much plastic as we can from our supply chain," says Brian. Apparel tags are made from biodegradable substances, infused with flower seeds. T-shirts are packaged in banana fiber paper. "We use things that go back to the earth in a very natural way and actually grow life." While these materials are more costly than plastic, they better fit the company's philosophy and, Brian believes, help generate new business. "We have customers that double their orders the next season because of the cleanups," Brian notes.

As United By Blue continues to grow, Brian focuses on financial *and* nonfinancial performance measures. Revenues were $330,000 in 2010, and were projected to exceed $800,000 in 2011. A focus on departmental contribution margins enables the company to operate efficiently to finance future growth. Likewise, more revenues mean the company collects more trash, over 80,000 pounds by the end of 2011 and a goal of over a million pounds by the end of 2012. As company founder and chief trash collector, this nonfinancial indicator measures progress toward Brian's vision of "doing the most good possible."

Brian encourages young entrepreneurs to "leave a positive impact on this world" by focusing on what you love. "My heart is in the ocean, so whatever I am doing is going to be in that realm. Whatever your passion is, leave that positive impact."

[Sources: *United By Blue* Website, January 2013; *Bloomberg Businessweek*, January 9, 2012; *MO.com* interview, *http://www.mo.com/brian-linton-united-by-blue*; *Philadelphia Magazine*, July 2011; *PRweb.com*, January 2012.]

This chapter describes how to measure performance when organizations are split into separate departments. It discusses responsibility accounting and how to allocate indirect costs of shared items such as utilities, advertising, and rent. This knowledge helps managers better measure and evaluate departmental performance. The chapter also introduces additional managerial accounting reports useful in managing a company's activities and explains how and why management divides companies into departments.

Performance Measurement and Responsibility Accounting

Responsibility Accounting	Cost Centers	Profit Centers	Investment Centers
• Motivation for departmentalization • Departmental evaluation • Controllable versus uncontrollable costs	• Responsibility accounting system • Evaluating cost center performance	• Direct and indirect expenses • Allocation of indirect expenses • Departmental income statements • Departmental contribution to overhead	• Financial performance measures • Nonfinancial performance measures • Transfer pricing

RESPONSIBILITY ACCOUNTING

Companies are divided into *departments*, also called *subunits*, when they are too large to be managed effectively as a single unit. The use of departments creates a need for performance measures to evaluate department performance. A **responsibility accounting system** can be set up to control costs and expenses and evaluate department managers' performance by assigning costs and expenses to the managers responsible for controlling them. This chapter introduces responsibility accounting and departmental performance measures.

Motivation for Departmentalization

Many companies are so large and complex that they are broken into separate divisions for efficiency and/or effectiveness purposes. Divisions then are usually organized into separate departments. When a company is departmentalized, each department is often placed under the direction of a manager. As a company grows, management often divides departments into new departments so that responsibilities for a department's activities do not overwhelm the manager's ability to oversee and control them. A company also creates departments to take advantage of the skills of individual managers. Departments are broadly classified as either operating or service departments.

Operating departments perform an organization's main functions. For example, an accounting firm's main functions usually include auditing, tax, and advisory services. Similarly, the production and selling departments of a manufacturing firm perform its main functions and serve as operating departments. *Service departments* provide support to an organization's operating departments. Examples of service departments are payroll, human resource management, accounting, and executive management. Service departments do not engage in activities that generate revenues, yet their support is crucial for the operating departments' success.

Departmental Evaluation

When a company is divided into departments, managers need to know how each department is performing. The accounting system must supply information about resources used and outputs achieved by each department. This requires a system to measure and accumulate revenue and expense information for each department whenever possible.

Departmental information is rarely distributed publicly because of its potential usefulness to competitors. Information about departments is prepared for internal managers to help control operations, appraise performance, allocate resources, and plan strategy. If a department is highly profitable, management may decide to expand its operations, or if a department is performing poorly, information about revenues or expenses can suggest useful changes.

More companies are emphasizing customer satisfaction as a main responsibility of many departments. This has led to changes in the measures reported. Increasingly, financial measurements are being supplemented with quality and customer satisfaction indexes. **Motorola**, for instance, uses two key measures: the number of defective parts per million parts produced and the percent of orders delivered on time to customers. (Note that some departments have only "internal customers.")

Financial information used to evaluate a department depends on whether it is evaluated as a profit center, cost center, or investment center. A **profit center** incurs costs and generates revenues; selling departments are often evaluated as profit centers. A **cost center** incurs costs without directly generating revenues. An **investment center** incurs costs and generates revenues, and is responsible for effectively using center assets. The manufacturing departments of a manufacturer and its service departments such as accounting, advertising, and purchasing, are all cost centers.

Evaluating managers' performance depends on whether they are responsible for profit centers, cost centers, or investment centers. Profit center managers are judged on their abilities to generate revenues in excess of the department's costs. They are assumed to influence both revenue generation and cost incurrence. Cost center managers are judged on their abilities to control costs by keeping them within a satisfactory range under an assumption that only they influence costs. Investment center managers are evaluated on their use of center assets to generate income.

> **Point:** Selling departments are often treated as *revenue centers*; their managers are responsible for maximizing sales revenues.

Controllable versus Uncontrollable Costs

We often evaluate a manager's performance using responsibility accounting reports that describe a department's activities in terms of **controllable costs.**[1] A cost is controllable if a manager has the power to determine or at least significantly affect the amount incurred. **Uncontrollable costs** are not within the manager's control or influence. For example, department managers often have little or no control over depreciation expense because they cannot affect the amount of equipment assigned to their departments. Also, department managers rarely control their own salaries. However, they can control or influence items such as the cost of supplies used in their department. When evaluating managers' performances, we should use data reflecting their departments' outputs along with their controllable costs and expenses.

Distinguishing between controllable and uncontrollable costs depends on the particular manager and time period under analysis. For example, the cost of property insurance is usually not controllable at the department manager's level but by the executive responsible for obtaining the company's insurance coverage. Likewise, this executive might not control costs resulting from insurance policies already in force. However, when a policy expires, this executive can renegotiate a replacement policy and then controls these costs. Therefore, all costs are controllable at some management level if the time period is sufficiently long. We must use good judgment in identifying controllable costs.

Quick Check   Answers — p. 1017

1. Service departments (*a*) manufacture products, (*b*) make sales directly to customers, (*c*) produce revenues, (*d*) assist operating departments.
2. Explain the difference between a cost center and a profit center. Cite an example of each.
3. Performance reports to evaluate managers should [select *a*, *b* or *c*] (*a*) include data about controllable expenses, (*b*) compare actual results with budgeted levels, or (*c*) both (*a*) and (*b*).

---

[1] The terms *cost* and *expense* are often used interchangeably in managerial accounting, but they are not necessarily the same. *Cost* often refers to the monetary outlay to acquire some resource that can have present and future benefit. *Expense* usually refers to an expired cost. That is, as the benefit of a resource expires, a portion of its cost is written off as an expense.

COST CENTERS

Responsibility Accounting System

P1 Prepare a responsibility accounting report for a cost center

A *responsibility accounting system* uses the concept of controllable costs to assign managers the responsibility for costs and expenses under their control. Prior to each reporting period, a company prepares plans that identify costs and expenses under each manager's control. These **responsibility accounting budgets** are typically based on the flexible budgeting approach we showed in Chapter 23. To ensure the cooperation of managers and the reasonableness of budgets, managers should be involved in preparing their budgets.

EXHIBIT 24.1

Organizational Responsibility Chart

A responsibility accounting system also involves performance reports. A **responsibility accounting performance report** accumulates and reports costs and expenses that a manager is responsible for and their budgeted amounts. Management's analysis of differences between budgeted amounts and actual costs and expenses often results in corrective or strategic managerial actions. Upper-level management uses performance reports to evaluate the effectiveness of lower-level managers in controlling costs and expenses and keeping them within budgeted amounts.

A responsibility accounting system recognizes that control over costs and expenses belongs to several levels of management. We illustrate this by considering the organization chart in Exhibit 24.1. The lines in this chart connecting the managerial positions reflect channels of authority. For example, the four department managers of this consulting firm (benchmarking, cost management, outsourcing, and service) are responsible for controllable costs and expenses incurred in their departments, but these same costs are subject to the overall control of the vice president (VP) for operational consulting. Similarly, this VP's costs are subject to the control of the executive vice president (EVP) for operations, the president, and, ultimately, the board of directors.

Point: Responsibility accounting does not place blame. Instead, responsibility accounting is used to identify opportunities for improving performance.

At lower levels, managers have limited responsibility and relatively little control over costs and expenses. Performance reports for low-level management typically cover few controllable costs. Responsibility and control broaden for higher-level managers; therefore, their reports span a wider range of costs. However, reports to higher-level managers seldom contain the details reported to their subordinates but are summarized for two reasons: (1) lower-level managers are often responsible for these detailed costs and (2) detailed reports can obscure broader, more important issues facing a company.

Evaluating Cost Center Performance

Exhibit 24.2 shows summarized performance reports for the three management levels identified in Exhibit 24.1. Exhibit 24.2 shows that costs under the control of the benchmarking department manager are totaled and included among controllable costs of the VP for operational consulting. Also, costs under the control of the VP are totaled and included among controllable costs of the EVP for operations. In this way, a responsibility accounting system provides relevant information for each management level.

Point: Responsibility accounting usually divides a company into subunits, or *responsibility centers*. A center manager is evaluated on how well the center performs, as reported in responsibility accounting reports.

Technological advances increase our ability to produce vast amounts of information that often exceed our ability to use it. Good managers select relevant data for planning and controlling the areas under their responsibility. A good responsibility accounting system makes every effort to provide relevant information to the right person (the one who controls the cost) at the right time (before a cost is out of control).

EXHIBIT 24.2

Responsibility Accounting Performance Reports for Cost Centers

Executive Vice President, Operations

Controllable Costs	For July Budgeted Amount	Actual Amount	Over (Under) Budget
Salaries, VPs	$ 80,000	$ 80,000	$ 0
Quality control costs	21,000	22,400	1,400
Office costs	29,500	28,800	(700)
Operational consulting	**276,700**	**279,500**	**2,800** ◄
Strategic consulting	390,000	380,600	(9,400)
Totals	$ 797,200	$ 791,300	$ (5,900)

Vice President, Operational Consulting

Controllable Costs	For July Budgeted Amount	Actual Amount	Over (Under) Budget
Salaries, department managers	$ 75,000	$ 78,000	$ 3,000
Depreciation	10,600	10,600	0
Insurance	6,800	6,300	(500)
Benchmarking department	**79,600**	**79,900**	**300**
Cost management department	61,500	60,200	(1,300)
Outsourcing department	24,300	24,700	400
Service department	18,900	19,800	900
Totals	**$276,700**	**$279,500**	**$2,800**

Manager, Benchmarking Department

Controllable Costs	For July Budgeted Amount	Actual Amount	Over (Under) Budget
Salaries	$ 51,600	$ 52,500	$ 900
Supplies	8,000	7,800	(200)
Other controllable costs	20,000	19,600	(400)
Totals	**$ 79,600**	**$ 79,900**	**$ 300**

PROFIT CENTERS

When departments are organized as profit centers, responsibility accounting focuses on how well each department controlled costs and generated revenues. This leads to **departmental income statements** as a common way to report profit center performance. When a company computes departmental profits, it confronts some accounting challenges that involve allocating expenses across its operating departments. We next illustrate these allocations and departmental income statement reporting.

C1 Distinguish between direct and indirect expenses and identify bases for allocating indirect expenses to departments.

Direct and Indirect Expenses

Direct expenses are costs readily traced to a department because they are incurred for that department's sole benefit. They require no allocation across departments. For example, the salary of an employee who works in only one department is a direct expense of that one department. Direct expenses are often, but not always, controllable costs.

    Indirect expenses are costs that are incurred for the joint benefit of more than one department and cannot be readily traced to only one department. For example, if two or more departments share a single building, all enjoy the benefits of the expenses for rent, heat, and light. Indirect expenses are allocated across departments benefiting from them when we need information about departmental profits. Ideally, we allocate indirect expenses by using a cause-effect relation. When we cannot identify cause-effect relations, we allocate each indirect expense on a

Point: Utility expense has elements of both direct and indirect expenses.

basis approximating the relative benefit each department receives. Measuring the benefit for each department from an indirect expense can be difficult. Indirect expenses are typically considered uncontrollable costs when evaluating a department manager's performance.

Illustration of Indirect Expense Allocation   To illustrate how to allocate an indirect expense, we consider a retail store that purchases janitorial services from an outside company. Management allocates this cost across the store's three departments according to the floor space each occupies. Costs of janitorial services for a recent month are $300. Exhibit 24.3 shows the square feet of floor space each department occupies. The store computes the percent of total square feet allotted to each department and uses it to allocate the $300 cost.

EXHIBIT 24.3

Indirect Expense Allocation

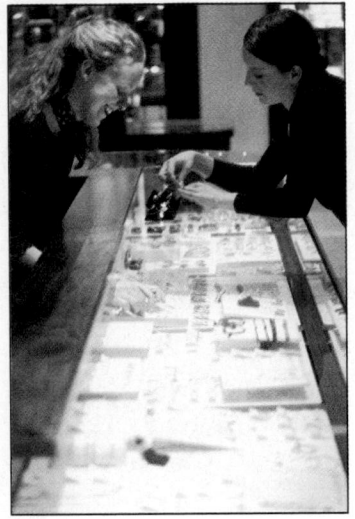

Department	Square Feet	Percent of Total	Allocated Cost
Jewelry	2,400	60%	$180
Watch repair	600	15	45
China and silver	1,000	25	75
Totals	4,000	100%	$300

Specifically, because the jewelry department occupies 60% of the floor space, 60% of the total $300 cost is assigned to it. The same procedure is applied to the other departments. When the allocation process is complete, these and other allocated costs are deducted from the gross profit for each department to determine net income for each. One consideration in allocating costs is to motivate managers and employees to behave as desired. As a result, a cost incurred in one department might be best allocated to other departments when one of the other departments caused the cost.

Allocation of Indirect Expenses

This section describes how to identify the bases used to allocate indirect expenses across departments. No standard rule identifies the best basis because expense allocation involves several factors, and the relative importance of these factors varies across departments and organizations. Judgment is required, and people do not always agree. Employee morale suffers when allocations are perceived as unfair. Thus, it is important to carefully design and explain the allocation of service department costs. In our discussion, note the parallels between activity-based costing and the departmental expense allocation procedures described here.

P2   Allocate indirect expenses to departments.

Wages and Salaries   Employee wages and salaries can be either direct or indirect expenses. If their time is spent entirely in one department, their wages are direct expenses of that department. However, if employees work for the benefit of more than one department, their wages are indirect expenses and must be allocated across the departments benefited. An employee's contribution to a department usually depends on the number of hours worked in contributing to that department. Thus, a reasonable basis for allocating employee wages and salaries is the *relative amount of time spent in each department*. In the case of a supervisor who manages more than one department, recording the time spent in each department may not always be practical. Instead, a company can allocate the supervisor's salary to departments on the basis of the number of employees in each department—a reasonable basis if a supervisor's main task is managing people. Another basis of allocation is on sales across departments, also a reasonable basis if a supervisor's job reflects on departmental sales.

Point: Some companies ask supervisors to estimate time spent supervising specific departments for purposes of expense allocation.

Rent and Related Expenses   Rent expense for a building is reasonably allocated to a department on the basis of floor space it occupies. Location can often make some floor space more valuable than other space. Thus, the allocation method can charge departments that occupy more valuable space a higher expense per square foot. Ground floor retail space, for instance, is often more valuable than basement or upper-floor space because all customers pass departments near the entrance but fewer go beyond the first floor. When no precise measures of floor space values exist, basing allocations on data such as customer traffic and real estate assessments is helpful. When a company owns its building, its expenses for depreciation, taxes, insurance, and other related building expenses are allocated like rent expense.

Advertising Expenses Effective advertising of a department's products increases its sales and customer traffic. Moreover, advertising products for some departments usually helps other departments' sales because customers also often buy unadvertised products. Thus, many stores treat advertising as an indirect expense allocated on the basis of each department's proportion of total sales. For example, a department with 10% of a store's total sales is assigned 10% of advertising expense. Another method is to analyze each advertisement to compute the Web/newspaper space or TV/radio time devoted to the products of a department and charge that department for the proportional costs of advertisements. Management must consider whether this more detailed and costly method is justified.

Equipment and Machinery Depreciation Depreciation on equipment and machinery used only in one department is a direct expense of that department. Depreciation on equipment and machinery used by more than one department is an indirect expense to be allocated across departments. Accounting for each department's depreciation expense requires a company to keep records showing which departments use specific assets. The number of hours that a department uses equipment and machinery is a reasonable basis for allocating depreciation.

Utilities Expenses Utilities expenses such as heating and lighting are usually allocated on the basis of floor space occupied by departments. This practice assumes their use is uniform across departments. When this is not so, a more involved allocation can be necessary, although there is often a trade-off between the usefulness of more precise allocations and the effort to compute them. Manufacturers often allocate electricity cost to departments on the basis of the horsepower of equipment located in each department.

Service Department Expenses To generate revenues, operating departments require support services provided by departments such as personnel, payroll, advertising, and purchasing. Such service departments are typically evaluated as cost centers because they do not produce revenues. (Evaluating them as profit centers requires the use of a system that "charges" user departments a price that then serves as the "revenue" generated by service departments.) A departmental accounting system can accumulate and report costs incurred directly by each service department for this purpose. The system then allocates a service department's expenses to operating departments benefiting from them. Exhibit 24.4 shows some commonly used bases for allocating service department expenses to operating departments.

Point: When a service department "charges" its user departments within a company, a *transfer pricing system* must be set up to determine the "revenue" from its services provided.

Service Department	Common Allocation Bases
Office expenses	Number of employees or sales in each department
Personnel expenses	Number of employees in each department
Payroll expenses	Number of employees in each department
Advertising expenses	Sales or amount of advertising charged directly to each department
Purchasing costs	Dollar amounts of purchases or number of purchase orders processed
Cleaning expenses	Square feet of floor space occupied
Maintenance expenses	Square feet of floor space occupied

EXHIBIT 24.4

Bases for Allocating Service Department Expenses

Departmental Income Statements

An income statement can be prepared for each operating department once expenses have been assigned to it. Its expenses include both direct expenses and its share of indirect expenses. For this purpose, compiling all expenses incurred in service departments before assigning them to

P3 Prepare departmental income statements and contribution reports.

operating departments is useful. We illustrate the steps to prepare departmental income statements using **A-1 Hardware** and its five departments. Two of them (office and purchasing) are service departments and the other three (hardware, housewares, and appliances) are operating (selling) departments. Allocating costs to operating departments and preparing departmental income statements involves four steps.

Step 1: Accumulating revenues and direct expenses by department.

Step 2: Allocating indirect expenses across departments.

Step 3: Allocating service department expenses to operating departments.

Step 4: Preparing departmental income statements.

Exhibit 24.5 summarizes the steps in preparing departmental performance reports for cost centers and profit centers. A-1 Hardware's service departments (general office and purchasing) are cost centers, so their performance will be based on how well they controlled total service department expenses. The company's operating departments (hardware, housewares, and appliances) are profit centers, and their performance will be based on how well they generated departmental net income.

EXHIBIT 24.5

Departmental Performance Reporting

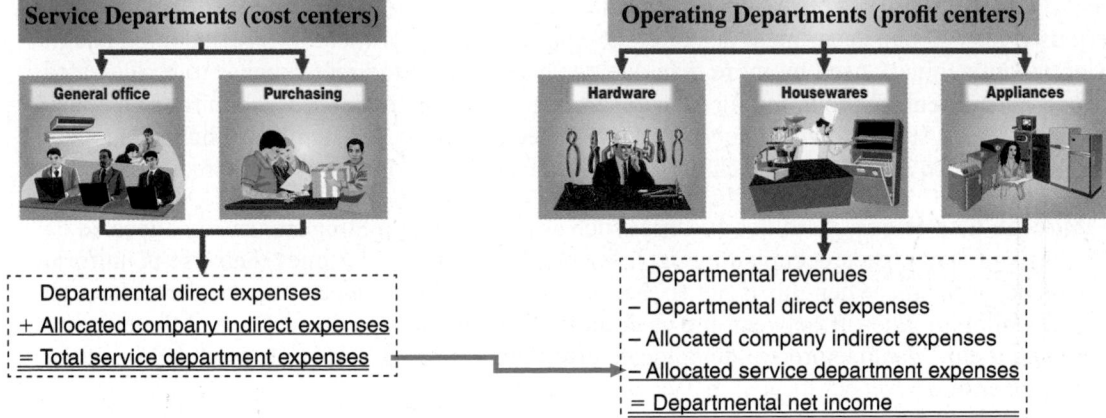

Step 1:   Step 1 accumulates revenues and direct expenses in departmental accounts for each department. As cost centers, the service departments do not generate revenues. Direct expenses include salaries, wages, and other expenses that each department incurs but does not share with any other department.

Step 2:   Step 2 allocates indirect company expenses across all service and operating departments. Indirect expenses can include items such as depreciation, rent, advertising, and any other expenses that cannot be directly assigned to a department. Indirect expenses are recorded in *company* accounts, an allocation base is identified for each expense, and costs are allocated using a *departmental expense allocation spreadsheet* described next.

Point: We sometimes allocate service department costs across other service departments before allocating them to operating departments. This "step-wise" process is in advanced courses.

Step 3:   Step 3 allocates service department expenses to operating departments. Service department expenses are not allocated to other service departments.[2] Exhibit 24.6 reflects the allocation of service department expenses using the allocation base(s). All of the direct and indirect expenses of service departments are allocated to operating departments.

Computations for both steps 2 and 3 are commonly made using a departmental expense allocation spreadsheet as shown in Exhibit 24.6. The first two sections of this spreadsheet list direct expenses and indirect expenses by department. The third section lists the service department expenses and their allocations to operating departments. The allocation bases are identified in the second column, and total expense amounts are reported in the third column.

---

[2] In some cases we allocate a service department's expenses to other service departments when they use its services. For example, expenses of a payroll office benefit all service and operating departments and can be assigned to all departments. Nearly all examples and assignment materials in this book allocate service expenses only to operating departments for simplicity.

EXHIBIT 24.6

Departmental Expense Allocation Spreadsheet

	File Edit View Insert Format Tools Data Window Help								

A-1 HARDWARE
Departmental Expense Allocations
For Year Ended December 31, 2013

	Allocation Base	Expense Account Balance	Allocation of Expenses to Departments				
			General Office Dept.	Purchas- ing Dept.	Hard- ware Dept.	House- wares Dept.	Appli- ances Dept.
Direct expenses							
Salaries expense...................	Payroll records......................	$51,900	$13,300	$8,200	$15,600	$ 7,000	$ 7,800
Depreciation—Equipment......	Depreciation records............	1,500	500	300	400	100	200
Supplies expense..................	Requisitions..........................	900	200	100	300	200	100
Indirect expenses							
Rent expense	Amount and value of space..	12,000	600	600	4,860	3,240	2,700
Utilities expense....................	Floor space...........................	2,400	300	300	810	540	450
Advertising expense..............	Sales.....................................	1,000			500	300	200
Insurance expense................	Value of insured assets	2,500	400	200	900	600	400
Total department expenses		72,200	15,300	9,700	23,370	11,980	11,850
Service department expenses							
General office department.....	Sales.....................................		(15,300)		→7,650	→4,590	→3,060
Purchasing department	Purchase orders....................			(9,700)	→3,880	→2,630	→3,190
Total expenses allocated to operating departments............................		$72,200	$ 0	$ 0	$34,900	$19,200	$18,100

Sheet1 / Sheet2 / Sheet3 /

Second (step 2), the four indirect expenses of rent, utilities, advertising, and insurance are allocated to all departments using the allocation bases identified. For example, consider rent allocation. Exhibit 24.7 lists the five departments' square footage of space occupied.

EXHIBIT 24.7

Departments' Allocation Bases

Department	Floor Space (Square Feet)	Value of Insured Assets ($)	Sales ($)	Number of Purchase Orders
General office	1,500	$ 38,000		—
Purchasing	1,500	19,000		—*
Hardware	4,050	85,500	$119,500	394
Housewares	2,700	57,000	71,700	267
Appliances	2,250	38,000	47,800	324
Total	12,000	$237,500	$239,000	985

* Purchasing department tracks purchase orders by department.

The two service departments (office and purchasing) occupy 25% of the total space (3,000 sq. feet/ 12,000 sq. feet). However, they are located near the back of the building, which is of lower value than space near the front that is occupied by operating departments. Management esti- mates that space near the back accounts for $1,200 of the total rent expense of $12,000. Exhibit 24.8 shows how we allocate the $1,200 rent expense between these two service departments in proportion to their square footage. Exhibit 24.8 shows a simple rule for cost

EXHIBIT 24.8

Allocating Indirect (Rent) Expense to Service Departments

Department	Square Feet	Percent of Total	Allocated Cost
General office	1,500	50.0%	$ 600
Purchasing	1,500	50.0	600
Totals	3,000	100.0%	$1,200

allocations: Allocated cost = Percentage of allocation base × Total cost. We then allocate the remaining $10,800 of rent expense to the three operating departments as shown in Exhibit 24.9.

EXHIBIT 24.9

Allocating Indirect (Rent) Expense to Operating Departments

Department	Square Feet	Percent of Total	Allocated Cost
Hardware	4,050	45.0%	$ 4,860
Housewares	2,700	30.0	3,240
Appliances	2,250	25.0	2,700
Totals	9,000	100.0%	$10,800

We continue step 2 by allocating the $2,400 of utilities expense to all departments based on the square footage occupied as shown in Exhibit 24.10.

EXHIBIT 24.10

Allocating Indirect (Utilities) Expense to All Departments

Department	Square Feet	Percent of Total	Allocated Cost
General office	1,500	12.50%	$ 300
Purchasing	1,500	12.50	300
Hardware	4,050	33.75	810
Housewares	2,700	22.50	540
Appliances	2,250	18.75	450
Totals	12,000	100.00%	$2,400

Exhibit 24.11 shows the allocation of $1,000 of advertising expense to the three operating departments on the basis of sales dollars. We exclude service departments from this allocation because they do not generate sales.

EXHIBIT 24.11

Allocating Indirect (Advertising) Expense to Operating Departments

Department	Sales	Percent of Total	Allocated Cost
Hardware	$119,500	50.0%	$ 500
Housewares	71,700	30.0	300
Appliances	47,800	20.0	200
Totals	$239,000	100.0%	$1,000

To complete step 2 we allocate insurance expense to each service and operating department as shown in Exhibit 24.12.

EXHIBIT 24.12

Allocating Indirect (Insurance) Expense to All Departments

Department	Value of Insured Assets	Percent of Total	Allocated Cost
General office	$ 38,000	16.0%	$ 400
Purchasing	19,000	8.0	200
Hardware	85,500	36.0	900
Housewares	57,000	24.0	600
Appliances	38,000	16.0	400
Total	$237,500	100.0%	$2,500

Third (step 3), total expenses of the two service departments are allocated to the three operating departments as shown in Exhibits 24.13 and 24.14.

EXHIBIT 24.13

Allocating Service Department (General Office) Expenses to Operating Departments

Department	Sales	Percent of Total	Allocated Cost
Hardware	$119,500	50.0%	$ 7,650
Housewares	71,700	30.0	4,590
Appliances	47,800	20.0	3,060
Total	$239,000	100.0%	$15,300

Department	Number of Purchase Orders	Percent of Total	Allocated Cost
Hardware	394	40.00%	$3,880
Housewares	267	27.11	2,630
Appliances	324	32.89	3,190
Total	985	100.00%	$9,700

EXHIBIT 24.14

Allocating Service Department (Purchasing) Expenses to Operating Departments

Step 4: The departmental expense allocation spreadsheet can now be used to prepare performance reports for the company's service and operating departments. The general office and purchasing departments are cost centers, and their managers will be evaluated on their control of costs. Actual amounts of service department expenses can be compared to budgeted amounts to help assess cost center manager performance.

Amounts in the operating department columns are used to prepare departmental income statements as shown in Exhibit 24.15. This exhibit uses the spreadsheet for its operating expenses; information on sales and cost of goods sold comes from departmental records.

Example: If the $15,300 general office expenses in Exhibit 24.6 are allocated equally across departments, what is net income for the hardware department and for the combined company? *Answer:* Hardware income, $13,350; combined income, $19,000.

EXHIBIT 24.15

Departmental Income Statements (Operating Departments)

A-1 HARDWARE
Departmental Income Statements
For Year Ended December 31, 2013

	Hardware Department	Housewares Department	Appliances Department	Combined	
Sales	$119,500	$71,700	$47,800	$239,000	
Cost of goods sold	73,800	43,800	30,200	147,800	
Gross profit	45,700	27,900	17,600	91,200	
Operating expenses					
Salaries expense	15,600	7,000	7,800	30,400	⎤
Depreciation expense—Equipment	400	100	200	700	Direct expenses
Supplies expense	300	200	100	600	⎦
Rent expense........................	4,860	3,240	2,700	10,800	⎤
Utilities expense	810	540	450	1,800	Allocated indirect
Advertising expense	500	300	200	1,000	expenses
Insurance expense....................	900	600	400	1,900	⎦
Share of general office expenses	7,650	4,590	3,060	15,300	⎤ Allocated service
Share of purchasing expenses	3,880	2,630	3,190	9,700	⎦ department expenses
Total operating expenses	34,900	19,200	18,100	72,200	
Net income (loss)	$10,800	$8,700	$(500)	$19,000	

Departmental Contribution to Overhead

Data from departmental income statements are not always best for evaluating each profit center's performance, especially when indirect expenses are a large portion of total expenses and when weaknesses in assumptions and decisions in allocating indirect expenses can markedly affect net income. Also, operating department managers might have no control over the level of service department services they use. In these and other cases, we might better evaluate profit center performance using the **departmental contribution to overhead,** which is a report of the amount of sales less *direct* expenses.[3] (We can also examine cost center performance by focusing on control of direct expenses.)

---

[3] A department's contribution is said to be "to overhead" because of the practice of considering all indirect expenses as overhead. Thus, the excess of a department's sales over direct expenses is a contribution toward at least a portion of its total overhead.

EXHIBIT 24.16

Departmental Contribution
to Overhead

A-1 HARDWARE Income Statement Showing Departmental Contribution to Overhead For Year Ended December 31, 2013				
	Hardware Department	Housewares Department	Appliances Department	Combined
Sales	$119,500	$ 71,700	$47,800	$239,000
Cost of goods sold	73,800	43,800	30,200	147,800
Gross profit	45,700	27,900	17,600	91,200
Direct expenses				
Salaries expense	15,600	7,000	7,800	30,400
Depreciation expense—Equipment	400	100	200	700
Supplies expense	300	200	100	600
Total direct expenses	16,300	7,300	8,100	31,700
Departmental contributions				
to overhead	$29,400	$20,600	$ 9,500	$59,500
Indirect expenses				
Rent expense				10,800
Utilities expense				1,800
Advertising expense				1,000
Insurance expense				1,900
General office department expense				15,300
Purchasing department expense				9,700
Total indirect expenses				40,500
Net income				$19,000
Contribution as percent of sales	24.6%	28.7%	19.9%	24.9%

Point: Net income is the same in Exhibits 24.15 and 24.16. The method of reporting indirect expenses in Exhibit 24.16 does not change total net income but does identify each operating department's contribution to overhead and net income.

The upper half of Exhibit 24.16 shows a departmental (profit center) contribution to overhead as part of an expanded income statement. This format is common when reporting departmental contributions to overhead. Using the information in Exhibits 24.15 and 24.16, we can evaluate the profitability of the three profit centers. For instance, let's compare the performance of the appliances department as described in these two exhibits. Exhibit 24.15 shows a $500 net loss resulting from this department's operations, but Exhibit 24.16 shows a $9,500 positive contribution to overhead, which is 19.9% of the appliance department's sales. The contribution of the appliances department is not as large as that of the other selling departments, but a $9,500 contribution to overhead is better than a $500 loss. This tells us that the appliances department is not a money loser. On the contrary, it is contributing $9,500 toward defraying total indirect expenses of $40,500.

Quick Check   Answers — p. 1017

4. If a company has two operating (selling) departments (shoes and hats) and two service departments (payroll and advertising), which of the following statements is correct? (a) Wages incurred in the payroll department are direct expenses of the shoe department, (b) Wages incurred in the payroll department are indirect expenses of the operating departments, or (c) Advertising department expenses are allocated to the other three departments.

5. Which of the following bases can be used to allocate supervisors' salaries across operating departments? (a) Hours spent in each department, (b) number of employees in each department, (c) sales achieved in each department, or (d) any of the above, depending on which information is most relevant and accessible.

6. What three steps are used to allocate expenses to operating departments?

7. An income statement showing departmental contribution to overhead, (a) subtracts indirect expenses from each department's revenues, (b) subtracts only direct expenses from each department's revenues, or (c) shows net income for each department.

EVALUATING INVESTMENT CENTER PERFORMANCE

This section introduces both financial and nonfinancial measures of investment center performance.

Financial Performance Evaluation Measures

Investment center managers are typically evaluated using performance measures that combine income and assets. Consider the following data for ZTel, a company which operates two divisions: LCD and S-Phone. The LCD division manufactures liquid crystal display (LCD) touch-screen monitors and sells them for use in computers, cellular phones, and other products. The S-Phone division sells smartphones, mobile phones that also function as personal computers, MP3 players, cameras, and global positioning satellite (GPS) systems. Exhibit 24.17 shows current year income and assets for those divisions.

A1 Analyze investment centers using return on assets and residual income.

	LCD	S-Phone
Net income	$ 526,500	$ 417,600
Average invested assets	2,500,000	1,850,000

EXHIBIT 24.17

Investment Center Income and Assets

Investment Center Return on (Assets) Investment One measure to evaluate division performance is the **investment center return on total assets,** commonly called *return on investment* (ROI) or *return on assets* (ROA). This measure is computed as follows:

$$\text{Return on investment} = \frac{\text{Investment center net income}}{\text{Investment center average invested assets}}$$

The return on investment for the LCD division is 21% (rounded), computed as $526,500/$2,500,000. The S-Phone division's return on investment is 23% (rounded), computed as $417,600/$1,850,000. Though the LCD division earned more dollars of net income, it was less efficient in using its assets to generate income compared to the S-Phone division.

Investment Center Residual Income Another way to evaluate division performance is to compute **investment center residual income,** which is computed as follows:

$$\text{Residual income} = \frac{\text{Investment center}}{\text{net income}} - \frac{\text{Target investment center}}{\text{net income}}$$

Assume ZTel's top management sets target net income at 8% of divisional assets. For an investment center, this **hurdle rate** is typically the cost of obtaining financing. Applying this hurdle rate using the data from Exhibit 24.17 yields the residual income for ZTel's divisions in Exhibit 24.18.

	LCD	S-Phone
Net income	$526,500	$417,600
Less: Target net income		
$2,500,000 × 8%	200,000	
$1,850,000 × 8%		148,000
Investment center residual income	$326,500	$269,600

EXHIBIT 24.18

Investment Center Residual Income

Unlike return on assets, residual income is expressed in dollars. The LCD division outperformed the S-Phone division on the basis of residual income. However, this result is due in part to the LCD division having a larger asset base than the S-Phone division.

Using residual income to evaluate division performance encourages division managers to accept all opportunities that return more than the target net income, thus increasing company value. For example, the S-Phone division might not want to accept a new customer that will provide a 15% return on investment, since that will reduce the S-Phone division's overall return on investment (23% as shown above). However, the S-Phone division should accept this opportunity because the new customer would increase residual income by providing net income above the target net income.

Issues in Computing Return on (Assets) Investment and Residual Income

Evaluations of investment center performance using return on assets and residual income can be impacted by how a company answers the questions below:

1. How do you compute average invested assets? It is common to compute the average by adding the year's beginning amount of invested assets to the year's ending amount of invested assets, and dividing that sum by 2. Averages based on monthly or quarterly asset amounts are also acceptable.

2. How do you measure invested assets? It is common to measure invested assets using their *net* book values. For example, depreciable assets would be measured at their cost minus accumulated depreciation. As net book value declines over a depreciable asset's useful life, the result is that return on assets and residual income would increase over that asset's life. This might cause managers not to invest in new assets. In addition, in measuring invested assets, companies commonly exclude assets that are not used in generating investment center net income such as land held for resale.

3. How do you measure investment center income? It is common to exclude both interest expense and tax expense from investment center income. Interest expense reflects a company's financing decisions, and tax expense is typically considered outside the control of an investment center manager. Excluding interest and taxes in these calculations enables more meaningful comparisons of return on assets and residual income across investment centers and companies.

Point: *Economic Value Added* (EVA®), developed and trademarked by Stern, Stewart, and Co., is an approach to address issues in computing residual income. This method uses a variety of adjustments to compute income, assets, and the hurdle rate.

■ Decision Insight ━━━━━━━━━━━━━━

In-the-Money Executive pay is often linked to performance measures. Bonus payments are often based on exceeding a target return on investment or certain balanced scorecard indicators. Stock awards, such as stock options and restricted stock, reward executives when their company's stock price rises. The goal of bonus plans and stock awards is to encourage executives to make decisions that increase company performance and value. ■

A2 Analyze investment centers using profit margin and investment turnover.

Investment Center Profit Margin and Investment Turnover We can further examine investment center (division) performance by splitting return on investment into **profit margin** and **investment turnover** as follows

| Return on investment | = | Profit margin | × | Investment turnover |

$$\frac{\text{Investment center net income}}{\text{Investment center average assets}} = \frac{\text{Investment center net income}}{\text{Investment center sales}} \times \frac{\text{Investment center sales}}{\text{Investment center average assets}}$$

Profit margin measures the income earned per dollar of sales. **Investment turnover** measures how efficiently an investment center generates sales from its invested assets. Profit margin is expressed as a percent, while investment turnover is interpreted as the number of times assets were converted into sales. Higher profit margin and higher investment turnover indicate better performance. To illustrate, consider **Best Buy** which reports in Exhibit 24.19 results for two divisions (segments): Domestic and International.

($ millions)	Domestic	International
Sales........................	$37,186	$13,086
Net income	2,031	83
Average invested assets	10,021	8,055

EXHIBIT 24.19

Best Buy Division Sales, Income, and Assets

Profit margin and investment turnover for its Domestic and International divisions are computed and shown in Exhibit 24.20:

($ millions)	Domestic	International
Profit Margin		
$2,031/$37,186	5.55%	
$83/$13,086		0.6%
Investment Turnover		
$37,186/$10,021	3.71	
$13,086/$8,055		1.62
Return on Investment		
5.55% × 3.71	20.59%	
0.6% × 1.62		1.01%

EXHIBIT 24.20

Best Buy Division Profit Margin and Investment Turnover

Best Buy's Domestic division generates 5.55 cents of profit per $1 of sales, while its International division generates less than 1 cent of profit per dollar of sales. Its Domestic division also uses its assets more efficiently; its investment turnover of 3.71 is over twice that of its International division's 1.62. Alternatively, if Best Buy's Domestic division instead had sales of $40 billion, net income of $3 billion, and average invested assets of $4 billion, its profit margin, investment turnover, and return on assets would be 7.5%, 4%, and 30%, respectively. Top management can use profit margin and investment turnover to evaluate the performance of division managers. The measures can also aid management when considering further investment in its divisions. As a result of both a much higher profit margin and a more rapid investment turnover, the Domestic division's return on investment (20.59%) is much greater than that of the International division (0.97%).

Decision Maker

Division Manager   You manage a division in a highly competitive industry. You will receive a cash bonus if your division achieves an ROI above 12%. Your division's profit margin is 7%, equal to the industry average, and your division's investment turnover is 1.5. What actions can you take to increase your chance of receiving the bonus? ■   [Answer—p. 1017]

Quick Check   Answers — p. 1017

8. A division reports sales of $50,000, income of $2,000, and average invested assets of $10,000. Compute the division's (a) profit margin, (b) investment turnover, and (c) return on investment.

Nonfinancial Performance Evaluation Measures

Evaluating performance solely on financial measures such as return on investment or residual income has limitations. For example, some investment center managers might forgo profitable opportunities to keep their return on investment high. Also, residual income is less useful when comparing investment centers of different size. And, both return on investment and residual income can encourage managers to focus too heavily on short-term financial goals.

A3 Analyze investment centers using the balanced scorecard.

In response to these limitations, companies consider nonfinancial measures. For example, a delivery company such as **FedEx** might track the percentage of on-time deliveries. The percentage of defective tennis balls manufactured can be used to assess performance of **Penn**'s production managers. **Walmart**'s credit card screens commonly ask customers at check-out whether the cashier was friendly or the store was clean. This kind of information can help division managers run their divisions and help top management evaluate division manager performance.

Balanced Scorecard   The **balanced scorecard** is a system of performance measures, including nonfinancial measures, used to assess company and division manager performance. The balanced scorecard requires managers to think of their company from four perspectives:

1. **Customer:** What do customers think of us?
2. **Internal processes:** Which of our operations are critical to meeting customer needs?
3. **Innovation and learning:** How can we improve?
4. **Financial:** What do our owners think of us?

Point: One survey indicates that nearly 60% of global companies use some form of a balanced scorecard.

The balanced scorecard collects information on several key performance indicators within each of the four perspectives. These key indicators vary across companies. Exhibit 24.21 lists common performance measures.

EXHIBIT 24.21

Balanced Scorecard Performance Indicators

Customer	Internal Process	Innovation/Learning	Financial
• Customer satisfaction rating	• Defect rates	• Employee satisfaction	• Net income
• # of new customers acquired	• Cycle time	• Employee turnover	• ROI
• % of on-time deliveries	• Product costs	• $ spent on training	• Sales growth
• % of sales from new products	• Labor hours per order	• # of new products	• Cash flow
• Time to fill orders	• Production days without an accident	• # of patents	• Residual income
• % of sales returned		• $ spent on research	• Stock price

After selecting key performance indicators, companies collect data on each indicator and compare actual amounts to expected amounts to assess performance. For example, a company might have a goal of filling 98% of customer orders within two hours. Balanced scorecard reports are often presented in graphs or tables that can be updated frequently. Such timely information aids division managers in their decisions, and can be used by top management to evaluate division manager performance.

Exhibit 24.22 is an example of balanced scorecard reporting on the customer perspective for an Internet retailer. This scorecard reports for example that the retailer is getting 62% of its potential customers successfully through the checkout process, and that 2.2% of all orders are returned. The *color* of the arrows in the right-most column reveals whether the company is exceeding its goal (green), barely meeting the goal (yellow), or not meeting the goal (red). The *direction* of the arrows reveals any trend in performance: an upward arrow indicates improvement, a downward arrow indicates declining performance, and an arrow pointing sideways indicates no change. A

EXHIBIT 24.22

Balanced Scorecard Reporting: Internet Retailer

Customer Perspective	Actual	Goal
Checkout success	62%	↑
Orders returned	2.2%	↔
Customer satisfaction rating	9.5	↑
Number of customer complaints	142	↓

review of these arrows' color and direction suggests the retailer is meeting or exceeding its goals on checkout success, orders returned, and customer satisfaction. Further, checkout success and customer satisfaction are improving. The red arrow shows the company has received more customer complaints than was hoped for; however, the number of customer complaints is declining. A manager would combine this information with similar information on the internal process, innovation and learning, and financial perspectives to get an overall view of division performance.

■ Decision Maker

Center Manager   Your center's usual return on total assets is 19%. You are considering two new investments for your center. The first requires a $250,000 average investment and is expected to yield annual net income of $50,000. The second requires a $1 million average investment with an expected annual net income of $175,000. Do you pursue either? ■   [Answer—p. 1017]

 GLOBAL VIEW

L'Oreal is an international cosmetics company incorporated in France. With multiple brands and operations in over 100 countries, the company uses concepts of departmental accounting and controllable costs to evaluate performance. For example, its 2010 annual report shows the following for the major divisions in its Cosmetics branch:

Division	Operating Profit (€ millions)	
Consumer products	€1,765	
Professional products	552	
Luxury products	791	
Active cosmetics	277	€3,385 ← Similar to "Departmental contributions to overhead" in Exhibit 24.16
Nonallocated costs		(513)
Cosmetics branch total		€2,872 ← Similar to "Net income" in Exhibit 24.16

For L'Oreal, nonallocated costs include costs that are not controllable by division managers, including fundamental research and development and costs of service operations like insurance and banking. Excluding noncontrollable costs enables L'Oreal to prepare more meaningful division performance evaluations.

Cycle Time and Cycle Efficiency   **Decision Analysis**

Manufacturing companies commonly use nonfinancial measures to evaluate the performance of their production processes. For example, as lean manufacturing practices help companies move toward just-in-time manufacturing, it is important for these companies to reduce the time to manufacture their products and to improve manufacturing efficiency. One metric that measures that time element is **cycle time (CT)**. A definition of cycle time is in Exhibit 24.23.

> **A4** Compute cycle time and cycle efficiency, and explain their importance to production management.

> **Cycle time = Process time + Inspection time + Move time + Wait time**

EXHIBIT 24.23
Cycle Time

Process time is the time spent producing the product. *Inspection time* is the time spent inspecting (1) raw materials when received, (2) goods in process while in production, and (3) finished goods prior to shipment. *Move time* is the time spent moving (1) raw materials from storage to production and (2) goods in process from one factory location to another factory location. *Wait time* is the time that an order or job sits with no production applied to it; this can be due to order delays, bottlenecks in production, and poor scheduling.

Process time is considered **value-added time** because it is the only activity in cycle time that adds value to the product from the customer's perspective. The other three time activities are considered **non-value-added time** because they add no value to the customer.

Companies strive to reduce non-value-added time to improve **cycle efficiency (CE).** Cycle efficiency is the ratio of value-added time to total cycle time—see Exhibit 24.24.

EXHIBIT 24.24

Cycle Efficiency

$$\text{Cycle efficiency} = \frac{\text{Value-added time}}{\text{Cycle time}}$$

To illustrate, assume that Rocky Mountain Bikes receives and produces an order for 500 Tracker® mountain bikes. Assume that the following times were measured during production of this order.

Process time... 1.8 days   Inspection time... 0.5 days   Move time... 0.7 days   Wait time... 3.0 days

In this case, cycle time is 6.0 days, computed as 1.8 days + 0.5 days + 0.7 days + 3.0 days. Also, cycle efficiency is 0.3, or 30%, computed as 1.8 days divided by 6.0 days. This means that Rocky Mountain Bikes spends 30% of its time working on the product (value-added time). The other 70% is spent on non-value-added activities.

If a company has a CE of 1, it means that its time is spent entirely on value-added activities. If the CE is low, the company should evaluate its production process to see if it can identify ways to reduce non-value-added activities. The 30% CE for Rocky Mountain Bikes is low and its management should look for ways to reduce non-value-added activities.

DEMONSTRATION PROBLEM

Management requests departmental income statements for Hacker's Haven, a computer store that has five departments. Three are operating departments (hardware, software, and repairs) and two are service departments (general office and purchasing).

	General Office	Purchasing	Hardware	Software	Repairs
Sales	—	—	$960,000	$600,000	$840,000
Cost of goods sold	—	—	500,000	300,000	200,000
Direct expenses					
Payroll	$60,000	$45,000	80,000	25,000	325,000
Depreciation	6,000	7,200	33,000	4,200	9,600
Supplies	15,000	10,000	10,000	2,000	25,000

The departments incur several indirect expenses. To prepare departmental income statements, the indirect expenses must be allocated across the five departments. Then the expenses of the two service departments must be allocated to the three operating departments. Total cost amounts and the allocation bases for each indirect expense follow.

Indirect Expense	Total Cost	Allocation Basis
Rent	$150,000	Square footage occupied
Utilities	50,000	Square footage occupied
Advertising	125,000	Dollars of sales
Insurance	30,000	Value of assets insured
Service departments		
General office	?	Number of employees
Purchasing	?	Dollars of cost of goods sold

The following additional information is needed for indirect expense allocations.

Department	Square Feet	Sales	Insured Assets	Employees	Cost of Goods Sold
General office	500		$ 60,000		
Purchasing	500		72,000		
Hardware.............	4,000	$ 960,000	330,000	5	$ 500,000
Software.............	3,000	600,000	42,000	5	300,000
Repairs..............	2,000	840,000	96,000	10	200,000
Totals	10,000	$2,400,000	$600,000	20	$1,000,000

Required

1. Prepare a departmental expense allocation spreadsheet for Hacker's Haven.
2. Prepare a departmental income statement reporting net income for each operating department and for all operating departments combined.

PLANNING THE SOLUTION

- Set up and complete four tables to allocate the indirect expenses—one each for rent, utilities, advertising, and insurance.
- Allocate the departments' indirect expenses using a spreadsheet like the one in Exhibit 24.6. Enter the given amounts of the direct expenses for each department. Then enter the allocated amounts of the indirect expenses that you computed.
- Complete two tables for allocating the general office and purchasing department costs to the three operating departments. Enter these amounts on the spreadsheet and determine the total expenses allocated to the three operating departments.
- Prepare departmental income statements like the one in Exhibit 24.15. Show sales, cost of goods sold, gross profit, individual expenses, and net income for each of the three operating departments and for the combined company.

SOLUTION TO DEMONSTRATION PROBLEM

Allocations of the four indirect expenses across the five departments.

Rent	Square Feet	Percent of Total	Allocated Cost
General office	500	5.0%	$ 7,500
Purchasing	500	5.0	7,500
Hardware.............	4,000	40.0	60,000
Software	3,000	30.0	45,000
Repairs	2,000	20.0	30,000
Totals	10,000	100.0%	$150,000

Utilities	Square Feet	Percent of Total	Allocated Cost
General office	500	5.0%	$ 2,500
Purchasing	500	5.0	2,500
Hardware.............	4,000	40.0	20,000
Software	3,000	30.0	15,000
Repairs	2,000	20.0	10,000
Totals	10,000	100.0%	$50,000

Advertising	Sales Dollars	Percent of Total	Allocated Cost
Hardware...........	$ 960,000	40.0%	$ 50,000
Software............	600,000	25.0	31,250
Repairs.............	840,000	35.0	43,750
Totals	$2,400,000	100.0%	$125,000

Insurance	Assets Insured	Percent of Total	Allocated Cost
General office	$ 60,000	10.0%	$ 3,000
Purchasing	72,000	12.0	3,600
Hardware	330,000	55.0	16,500
Software	42,000	7.0	2,100
Repairs..............	96,000	16.0	4,800
Totals	$600,000	100.0%	$30,000

1. Allocations of service department expenses to the three operating departments.

General Office Allocations to	Employees	Percent of Total	Allocated Cost
Hardware..............	5	25.0%	$23,500
Software..............	5	25.0	23,500
Repairs...............	10	50.0	47,000
Totals	20	100.0%	$94,000

Purchasing Allocations to	Cost of Goods Sold	Percent of Total	Allocated Cost
Hardware..............	$ 500,000	50.0%	$37,900
Software..............	300,000	30.0	22,740
Repairs...............	200,000	20.0	15,160
Totals	$1,000,000	100.0%	$75,800

HACKER'S HAVEN
Departmental Expense Allocations
For Year Ended December 31, 2013

	Allocation Base	Expense Account Balance	General Office Dept.	Purchasing Dept.	Hardware Dept.	Software Dept.	Repairs Dept.
Direct Expenses							
Payroll...............................		$ 535,000	$ 60,000	$ 45,000	$ 80,000	$ 25,000	$ 325,000
Depreciation		60,000	6,000	7,200	33,000	4,200	9,600
Supplies		62,000	15,000	10,000	10,000	2,000	25,000
Indirect Expenses							
Rent	Square ft.	150,000	7,500	7,500	60,000	45,000	30,000
Utilities.............................	Square ft.	50,000	2,500	2,500	20,000	15,000	10,000
Advertising..........................	Sales	125,000	—	—	50,000	31,250	43,750
Insurance	Assets	30,000	3,000	3,600	16,500	2,100	4,800
Total expenses........................		1,012,000	94,000	75,800	269,500	124,550	448,150
Service Department Expenses							
General office	Employees		(94,000)		23,500	23,500	47,000
Purchasing	Goods sold			(75,800)	37,900	22,740	15,160
Total expenses allocated to operating departments		$1,012,000	$ 0	$ 0	$330,900	$170,790	$510,310

2. Departmental income statements for Hacker's Haven.

HACKER'S HAVEN
Departmental Income Statements
For Year Ended December 31, 2013

	Hardware	Software	Repairs	Combined
Sales	$ 960,000	$ 600,000	$ 840,000	$2,400,000
Cost of goods sold	500,000	300,000	200,000	1,000,000
Gross profit	460,000	300,000	640,000	1,400,000
Expenses				
Payroll	80,000	25,000	325,000	430,000
Depreciation	33,000	4,200	9,600	46,800
Supplies	10,000	2,000	25,000	37,000
Rent	60,000	45,000	30,000	135,000
Utilities	20,000	15,000	10,000	45,000
Advertising..................	50,000	31,250	43,750	125,000
Insurance	16,500	2,100	4,800	23,400
Share of general office	23,500	23,500	47,000	94,000
Share of purchasing	37,900	22,740	15,160	75,800
Total expenses	330,900	170,790	510,310	1,012,000
Net income	$129,100	$129,210	$129,690	$ 388,000

Transfer Pricing

24A

Divisions in decentralized companies sometimes do business with one another. For example, a separate division of **Harley-Davidson** manufactures its plastic and fiberglass parts used in the company's motorcycles. **Anheuser-Busch**'s metal container division makes cans and lids used in its brewing operations, and also sells cans and lids to soft-drink companies. A division of **Prince** produces strings used in tennis rackets made by Prince and other manufacturers.

Determining the price that should be used to record transfers between divisions in the same company is the focus of this appendix. Because these transactions are transfers within the same company, the price to record them is called the **transfer price.** In decentralized organizations, division managers have input on or decide those prices. Transfer prices can be used in cost, profit, and investment centers. Since these transfers are not with customers outside the company, the transfer price has no direct impact on the company's overall profits. However, transfer prices can impact performance evaluations and, if set incorrectly, lead to bad decisions.

C2 Explain transfer pricing and methods to set transfer prices.

Point: Transfer pricing can impact company profits when divisions are located in countries with different tax rates; this is covered in advanced courses.

Alternative Transfer Prices Exhibit 24A.1 reports data on the LCD division of ZTel. LCD manufactures liquid crystal display (LCD) touch-screen monitors for use in ZTel's S-Phone division's smartphones, which sell for $400 each. The monitors can also be used in other products. So, LCD can sell its monitors to buyers other than S-Phone. Likewise, the S-Phone division can purchase monitors from suppliers other than LCD.

EXHIBIT 24A.1

LCD Division Manufacturing Information—Monitors

Production capacity . . . . 100,000 units
Selling price per unit to outside customers $80
Variable manufacturing costs per unit $40
Fixed manufacturing costs $2,000,000

Exhibit 24A.1 reveals the range of transfer prices for transfers of monitors from LCD to S-Phone. The manager of LCD wants to report a division profit; thus, this manager will not accept a transfer price less than $40 (variable manufacturing cost per unit) because doing so would cause the division to lose money on each monitor transferred. The LCD manager will only consider transfer prices of $40 or more. On the other hand, the S-Phone division manager also wants to report a division profit. Thus, this manager will not pay more than $80 per monitor because similar monitors can be bought from outside suppliers at that price. The S-Phone manager will only consider transfer prices of $80 or less. As any transfer price between $40 and $80 per monitor is possible, how does ZTel determine the transfer price? The answer depends in part on whether the LCD division has excess capacity to manufacture monitors.

No Excess Capacity　Assume the LCD division can sell every monitor it produces, and thus is producing 100,000 units. In that case, a **market-based transfer price** of $80 per monitor is preferred. At that price, the LCD division manager is willing to either transfer monitors to S-Phone or sell to outside customers. The S-Phone manager cannot buy monitors for less than $80 from outside suppliers, so the $80 price is acceptable. Further, with a transfer price of $80 per monitor, top management of ZTel is indifferent to S-Phone buying from LCD or buying similar-quality monitors from outside suppliers.

With no excess capacity, the LCD manager will not accept a transfer price less than $80 per monitor. For example, suppose the S-Phone manager suggests a transfer price of $70 per monitor. At that price the LCD manager incurs an unnecessary *opportunity cost* of $10 per monitor (computed as $80 market price minus $70 transfer price). This would lower the LCD division's income and hurt its performance evaluation.

Excess Capacity　Assume that the LCD division has excess capacity. For example, the LCD division might currently be producing only 80,000 units. Because LCD has $2,000,000 of fixed manufacturing costs, both LCD and the top management of ZTel prefer that S-Phone purchases its monitors from LCD. For example, if S-Phone purchases its monitors from an outside supplier at the market price of $80 each, LCD manufactures no units. Then, LCD reports a division loss equal to its fixed costs, and ZTel overall reports a lower net income as its costs are higher. Consequently, with excess capacity, LCD should accept any transfer price of $40 per unit or greater and S-Phone should purchase monitors from LCD. This will allow LCD to recover some (or all) of its fixed costs and increase ZTel's overall profits. For example, if a transfer price of $50 per monitor is used, the S-Phone manager is pleased to buy from LCD, since that price is below the market price of $80. For each monitor transferred from LCD to S-Phone at $50, the LCD division receives a *contribution margin* of $10 (computed as $50 transfer price less $40 variable cost) to contribute towards recovering its fixed costs. This form of transfer pricing is called **cost-based transfer pricing.** Under this approach the transfer price might be based on variable costs, total costs, or variable costs plus a markup. Determining the transfer price under excess capacity is complex and is covered in advanced courses.

Transfer Pricing Approaches Used by Companies

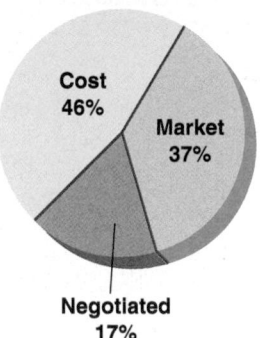

Cost 46%

Market 37%

Negotiated 17%

Additional Issues in Transfer Pricing　Several additional issues arise in determining transfer prices which include the following:

- **No market price exists.** Sometimes there is no market price for the product being transferred. The product might be a key component that requires additional conversion costs at the next stage and is not easily replicated by an outside company. For example, there is no market for a console for a **Nissan** Maxima and there is no substitute console **Nissan** can use in assembling a Maxima. In this case a market-based transfer price cannot be used.
- **Cost control.** To provide incentives for cost control, transfer prices might be based on standard, rather than actual costs. For example, if a transfer price of actual variable costs plus a markup of $20 per unit is used in the case above, LCD has no incentive to control its costs.
- **Division managers' negotiation.** With excess capacity, division managers will often negotiate a transfer price that lies between the variable cost per unit and the market price per unit. In this case, the **negotiated transfer price** and resulting departmental performance reports reflect, in part, the negotiating skills of the respective division managers. This might not be best for overall company performance.
- **Nonfinancial factors.** Factors such as quality control, reduced lead times, and impact on employee morale can be important factors in determining transfer prices.

APPENDIX

24B　Joint Costs and Their Allocation

C3 Describe allocation of joint costs across products.

Most manufacturing processes involve **joint costs,** which refer to costs incurred to produce or purchase two or more products at the same time. A joint cost is like an indirect expense in the sense that more than one cost object share it. For example, a sawmill company incurs a joint cost when it buys logs that it cuts into lumber as shown in Exhibit 24B.1. The joint cost includes the logs (raw material) and its cutting (conversion) into boards classified as Clear, Select, No. 1 Common, No. 2 Common, No. 3 Common, and other types of lumber and by-products.

When a joint cost is incurred, a question arises as to whether to allocate it to different products resulting from it. The answer is that when management wishes to estimate the costs of individual products, joint costs are included and must be allocated to these joint products. However, when management needs information to help decide whether to sell a product at a certain point in the production process or to process it further, the joint costs are ignored.

Financial statements prepared according to GAAP must assign joint costs to products. To do this, management must decide how to allocate joint costs across products benefiting from these costs. If some products are sold and others remain in inventory, allocating joint costs involves assigning costs to both cost of goods sold and ending inventory.

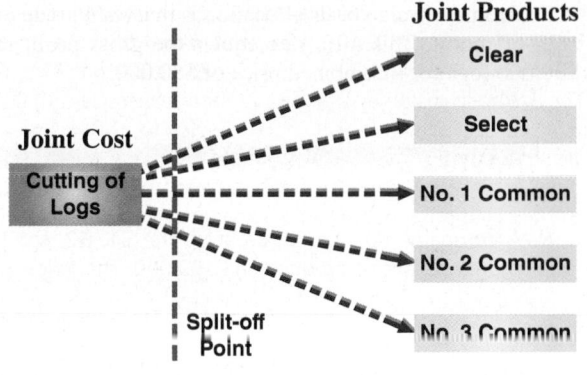

Joint Products

EXHIBIT 24B.1

Joint Products from Logs

The two usual methods to allocate joint costs are the (1) *physical basis* and (2) the *value basis*. The physical basis typically involves allocating joint cost using physical characteristics such as the ratio of pounds, cubic feet, or gallons of each joint product to the total pounds, cubic feet, or gallons of all joint products flowing from the cost. This method is not preferred because the resulting cost allocations do not reflect the relative market values the joint cost generates. The preferred approach is the value basis, which allocates joint cost in proportion to the sales value of the output produced by the process at the "split-off point"; see Exhibit 24B.1.

Physical Basis Allocation of Joint Cost   To illustrate the physical basis of allocating a joint cost, we consider a sawmill that bought logs for $30,000. When cut, these logs produce 100,000 board feet of lumber in the grades and amounts shown in Exhibit 24B.2. The logs produce 20,000 board feet of No. 3 Common lumber, which is 20% of the total. With physical allocation, the No. 3 Common lumber is assigned 20% of the $30,000 cost of the logs, or $6,000 ($30,000 × 20%). Because this low-grade lumber sells for $4,000, this allocation gives a $2,000 loss from its production and sale. The physical basis for allocating joint costs does not reflect the extra value flowing into some products or the inferior value flowing into others. That is, the portion of a log that produces Clear and Select grade lumber is worth more than the portion used to produce the three grades of common lumber, but the physical basis fails to reflect this.

Grade of Lumber	Board Feet Produced	Percent of Total	Allocated Cost	Sales Value	Gross Profit
Clear and Select............	10,000	10.0%	$ 3,000	$12,000	$ 9,000
No. 1 Common	30,000	30.0	9,000	18,000	9,000
No. 2 Common	40,000	40.0	12,000	16,000	4,000
No. 3 Common	20,000	20.0	6,000	4,000	(2,000)
Totals	100,000	100.0%	$30,000	$50,000	$20,000

EXHIBIT 24B.2

Allocating Joint Costs on a Physical Basis

Value Basis Allocation of Joint Cost   Exhibit 24B.3 illustrates the value basis method of allocation. It determines the percents of the total costs allocated to each grade by the ratio of each grade's sales value to the total sales value of $50,000 (sales value is the unit selling price multiplied by the number of units produced). The Clear and Select lumber grades receive 24% of the total cost ($12,000/$50,000) instead of the 10% portion using a physical basis. The No. 3 Common lumber receives only 8% of the total cost, or $2,400, which is much less than the $6,000 assigned to it using the physical basis.

Grade of Lumber	Sales Value	Percent of Total	Allocated Cost	Gross Profit
Clear and Select	$12,000	24.0%	$ 7,200	$ 4,800
No. 1 Common	18,000	36.0	10,800	7,200
No. 2 Common	16,000	32.0	9,600	6,400
No. 3 Common	4,000	8.0	2,400	1,600
Totals	$50,000	100.0%	$30,000	$20,000

EXHIBIT 24B.3

Allocating Joint Costs on a Value Basis

Example: Refer to Exhibit 24B.3. If the sales value of Clear and Select lumber is changed to $10,000, what is the revised ratio of the market value of No. 1 Common to the total?
Answer: $18,000/$48,000 = 37.5%

An outcome of value basis allocation is that *each* grade produces exactly the same 40% gross profit at the split-off point. This 40% rate equals the gross profit rate from selling all the lumber made from the $30,000 logs for a combined price of $50,000.

Quick Check
Answers — p. 1017

9. A company produces three products, B1, B2, and B3. The joint cost incurred for the current month for these products is $180,000. The following data relate to this month's production:

Product	Units Produced	Unit Sales Value
B1	96,000	$3.00
B2	64,000	6.00
B3	32,000	9.00

The amount of joint cost allocated to product B3 using the value basis allocation is (*a*) $30,000, (*b*) $54,000, or (*c*) $90,000.

Summary

C1 **Distinguish between direct and indirect expenses and identify bases for allocating indirect expenses to departments.** Direct expenses are traced to a specific department and are incurred for the sole benefit of that department. Indirect expenses benefit more than one department. Indirect expenses are allocated to departments when computing departmental net income. Ideally, we allocate indirect expenses by using a cause-effect relation for the allocation base. When a cause-effect relation is not identifiable, each indirect expense is allocated on a basis reflecting the relative benefit received by each department.

C2 **Explain transfer pricing and methods to set transfer prices.** Transfer prices are used to record transfers of items between divisions of the same company. Transfer prices can be based on costs or market prices, or can be negotiated by division managers.

C3 **Describe allocation of joint costs across products.** A joint cost refers to costs incurred to produce or purchase two or more products at the same time. When income statements are prepared, joint costs are usually allocated to the resulting joint products using either a physical or value basis.

A1 **Analyze investment centers using return on assets and residual income.** A financial measure often used to evaluate an investment center manager is the *investment center return on total assets,* also called *return on investment.* This measure is computed as the center's net income divided by the center's average total assets. Residual income, computed as investment center net income minus a target net income is an alternative financial measure of investment center performance.

A2 **Analyze investment centers using profit margin and investment turnover.** Return on investment can also be computed as profit margin times investment turnover. Profit margin (equal to net income/sales) measures the income earned per dollar of sales and investment turnover (equal to sales/assets) measures how efficiently a division uses its assets.

A3 **A balanced scorecard uses a combination of financial and nonfinancial measures to evaluate performance.** Customer, internal process, and innovation and learning are the three primary perspectives of nonfinancial measures used in balanced scorecards.

A4 **Compute cycle time and cycle efficiency, and explain their importance to production management.** It is important for companies to reduce the time to produce their products and to improve manufacturing efficiency. One measure of that time is cycle time (CT), defined as Process time + Inspection time + Move time + Wait time. Process time is value-added time; the others are non-value-added time. Cycle efficiency (CE) is the ratio of value-added time to total cycle time. If CE is low, management should evaluate its production process to see if it can reduce non-value-added activities.

P1 **Prepare a responsibility report for a cost center.** Responsibility accounting systems provide information for evaluating the performance of department managers. A responsibility accounting system's performance reports for evaluating department managers should include only the expenses (and revenues) that each manager controls.

P2 **Allocate indirect expenses to departments.** Indirect expenses include items like depreciation, rent, advertising, and other expenses that cannot be assigned directly to departments. Indirect expenses are recorded in company accounts, an allocation base is identified for each expense, and costs are allocated to departments. Departmental expense allocation spreadsheets are often used in allocating indirect expenses to departments.

P3 **Prepare departmental income statements and contribution reports.** Each profit center (department) is assigned its expenses to yield its own income statement. These costs include its direct expenses and its share of indirect expenses. The departmental income statement lists its revenues and costs of goods sold to determine gross profit. Its operating expenses (direct expenses and its indirect expenses allocated to the department) are deducted from gross profit to yield departmental net income. The departmental contribution report is similar to the departmental income statement in terms of computing the gross profit for each department. Then the direct operating expenses for each department are deducted from gross profit to determine the contribution generated by each department. Indirect operating expenses are deducted *in total* from the company's combined contribution.

Guidance Answers to Decision Maker and Decision Ethics

Division Manager   Your division's ROI without further action is 10.5% (equal to 7% × 1.5). In a highly competitive industry, it is difficult to increase profit margins by raising prices. Your division might be better able to control its costs to increase its profit margin. In addition, you might engage in a marketing program to increase sales without increasing your division's invested assets. Investment turnover and thus ROI will increase if the marketing campaign attracts customers.

Center Manager   We must first realize that the two investment opportunities are not comparable on the basis of absolute dollars of

income or on assets. For instance, the second investment provides a higher income in absolute dollars but requires a higher investment. Accordingly, we need to compute return on total assets for each alternative: (1) $50,000 ÷ $250,000 = 20%, and (2) $175,000 ÷ $1 million = 17.5%. Alternative 1 has the higher return and is preferred over alternative 2. Do you pursue one, both, or neither? Because alternative 1's return is higher than the center's usual return of 19%, it should be pursued, assuming its risks are acceptable. Also, since alternative 1 requires a small investment, top management is likely to be more agreeable to pursuing it. Alternative 2's return is lower than the usual 19% and is not likely to be acceptable.

Guidance Answers to Quick Checks

1. *d*

2. A cost center, such as a service department, incurs costs without directly generating revenues. A profit center, such as a product division, incurs costs but also generates revenues.

3. *c*

4. *b*

5. *d*

6. (1) Assign the direct expenses to each department. (2) Allocate indirect expenses to all departments. (3) Allocate the service department expenses to the operating departments.

7. *b*

8. a) $2,000/50,000 = 4%; b) $50,000/10,000 = 5; $2,000/10,000 = 20%.

9. *b*; $180,000 × ([32,000 × $9]/[96,000 × $3 + 64,000 × $6 + 32,000 × $9]) = $54,000.

Key Terms

Balanced scorecard (p. 1008)
Controllable costs (p. 995)
Cost-based transfer pricing (p. 1014)
Cost center (p. 995)
Cycle efficiency (p. 1010)
Cycle Time (CT) (p. 1009)
Departmental contribution to overhead (p. 1003)
Departmental income statements (p. 997)
Direct expenses (p. 997)
Hurdle rate (p. 1005)

Indirect expenses (p. 997)
Investment center (p. 995)
Investment center residual income (p. 1005)
Investment center return on total assets (p. 1005)
Investment turnover (p. 1006)
Joint cost (p. 1014)
Market-based transfer price (p. 1014)
Negotiated transfer price (p. 1014)
Non-value-added time (p. 1010)

Profit center (p. 995)
Profit margin (p. 1006)
Responsibility accounting budget (p. 996)
Responsibility accounting performance report (p. 996)
Responsibility accounting system (p. 994)
Transfer price (p. 1013)
Uncontrollable costs (p. 995)
Value-added time (p. 1010)

Multiple Choice Quiz   Answers on p. 1035   mhhe.com/wildFAP21e

Additional Quiz Questions are available at the book's Website.

1. A retailer has three departments—housewares, appliances, and clothing—and buys advertising that benefits all departments. Advertising expense is $150,000 for the year, and departmental sales for the year follow: housewares, $356,250; appliances, $641,250; clothing, $427,500. How much advertising expense is allocated to appliances if allocation is based on departmental sales?

a. $37,500
b. $67,500
c. $45,000
d. $150,000
e. $641,250

2. Indirect expenses
   a. Cannot be readily traced to one department.
   b. Are allocated to departments based on the relative benefit each department receives.
   c. Are the same as uncontrollable expenses.
   d. a, b, and c above are all true.
   e. a and b above are true.

3. A division reports the information below. What is the division's investment (asset) turnover?

Sales	$500,000
Income	75,000
Average assets	200,000

   a. 37.5%
   b. 15
   c. 2.5
   d. 2.67
   e. 4

4. A company operates three retail departments as profit centers, and the following information is available for each. Which department has the largest dollar amount of departmental contribution to overhead and what is the dollar amount contributed?

Department	Sales	Cost of Goods Sold	Direct Expenses	Allocated Indirect Expenses
X	$500,000	$350,000	$50,000	$40,000
Y	200,000	75,000	20,000	50,000
Z	350,000	150,000	75,000	10,000

   a. Department Y, $ 55,000
   b. Department Z, $125,000
   c. Department X, $500,000
   d. Department Z, $200,000
   e. Department X, $ 60,000

5. Using the data in question 4, Department X's contribution to overhead as a percentage of sales is
   a. 20%
   b. 30%
   c. 12%
   d. 48%
   e. 32%

A(B) *Superscript letter A (B) denotes assignments based on Appendix 24A (24B).*
   🔲 Icon denotes assignments that involve decision making.

Discussion Questions

1. Why are many companies divided into departments?

2. What is the difference between operating departments and service departments?

3. 🔲 What are controllable costs?

4. Controllable and uncontrollable costs must be identified with a particular _____ and a definite _____ period.

5. 🔲 Why should managers be closely involved in preparing their responsibility accounting budgets?

6. 🔲 What are two main goals in managerial accounting for reporting on and analyzing departments?

7. 🔲 Is it possible to evaluate a cost center's profitability? Explain.

8. What is the difference between direct and indirect expenses?

9. 🔲 Suggest a reasonable basis for allocating each of the following indirect expenses to departments: (a) salary of a supervisor who manages several departments, (b) rent, (c) heat, (d) electricity for lighting, (e) janitorial services, (f) advertising, (g) expired insurance on equipment, and (h) property taxes on equipment.

10. **Piaggio** has many departments. How is a department's contribution to overhead measured? **PIAGGIO**

11. 🔲 **KTM** aims to give its managers timely cost reports. In responsibility accounting, who receives timely cost reports and specific cost information? Explain. **KTM**

12.A What is a transfer price? Under what conditions is a market-based transfer price most likely to be used?

13.B What is a joint cost? How are joint costs usually allocated among the products produced from them?

14.B 🔲 Give two examples of products with joint costs.

15. 🔲 Each retail store of **Apple** has several departments. Why is it useful for its management to (a) collect accounting information about each department and (b) treat each department as a profit center? **Apple**

16. 🔲 **Polaris** delivers its products to locations around the world. List three controllable and three uncontrollable costs for its delivery department. **Polaris**

17. 🔲 Define and describe *cycle time* and identify the components of cycle time.

18. 🔲 Explain the difference between value-added time and non-value-added time.

19. Define and describe *cycle efficiency*.

20. 🔲 Can management of a company such as **Arctic Cat** use cycle time and cycle efficiency as useful measures of performance? Explain. **Arctic Cat**

connect

In each blank next to the following terms, place the identifying letter of its best description.

1. _____ Cost center
2. _____ Investment center
3. _____ Departmental accounting system
4. _____ Operating department
5. _____ Profit center
6. _____ Responsibility accounting system
7. _____ Service department

A. Incurs costs without directly yielding revenues.
B. Provides information used to evaluate the performance of a department.
C. Holds manager responsible for revenues, costs, and investments.
D. Engages directly in manufacturing or in making sales directly to customers.
E. Does not directly manufacture products but contributes to profitability of the entire company.
F. Incurs costs and also generates revenues.
G. Provides information used to evaluate the performance of a department manager.

QUICK STUDY

QS 24-1
Allocation and measurement terms
C1

For each of the following types of indirect expenses and service department expenses, identify one allocation basis that could be used to distribute it to the departments indicated.

1. Computer service expenses of production scheduling for operating departments.
2. General office department expenses of the operating departments.
3. Maintenance department expenses of the operating departments.
4. Electric utility expenses of all departments.

QS 24-2
Basis for cost allocation

C1

In each blank next to the following terms, place the identifying letter of its best description.

1. _____ Indirect expenses
2. _____ Controllable costs
3. _____ Direct expenses
4. _____ Uncontrollable costs

A. Costs not within a manager's control or influence
B. Costs that can be readily traced to a department
C. Cost that a manager has the ability to affect
D. Costs incurred for the joint benefit of more than one department

QS 24-3
Responsibility accounting terms

C1

Use the information in the following table to compute each department's contribution to overhead (both in dollars and as a percent). Which department contributes the largest dollar amount to total overhead? Which contributes the highest percent (as a percent of sales)? Round percents to one decimal.

QS 24-4
Departmental contribution to overhead

P3

	Dept. A	Dept. B	Dept. C
Sales	$53,000	$180,000	$84,000
Cost of goods sold	34,185	103,700	49,560
Gross profit	18,815	76,300	34,440
Total direct expenses	3,660	37,060	7,386
Contribution to overhead	$	$	$
Contribution percent	%	%	%

Compute return on assets for each of the divisions below (each is an investment center). Comment on the relative performance of each investment center.

QS 24-5
Computing investment center return on assets

A1

Investment Center	Net Income	Average Assets	Return on Assets
Cameras and camcorders	$4,500,000	$20,000,000	_____
Phones and communications	1,500,000	12,500,000	_____
Computers and accessories	800,000	10,000,000	_____

Refer to information in QS 24-5. Assume a target income of 12% of average invested assets. Compute residual income for each division.

QS 24-6
Computing residual income

A1

QS 24-7
Computing profit margin and
investment turnover   A2

A company's shipping division (an investment center) has sales of $2,420,000, net income of $516,000, and average invested assets of $2,250,000. Compute the division's profit margin and investment turnover.

QS 24-8
Performance measures

A1   A2

Fill in the blanks in the schedule below for two separate investment centers A and B. Round answers to the nearest whole percent.

	Investment Center	
	A	B
Sales	$_____	$10,400,000
Net income	$ 352,000	$_____
Average invested assets	$1,400,000	_____
Profit margin	8%	_____%
Investment turnover	_____	1.5
Return on (assets) investment	_____%	12%

QS 24-9
Performance measures—
balanced scorecard

A3

Classify each of the performance measures below into the most likely balanced scorecard perspective it relates to. Label your answers using C (customer), P (internal process), I (innovation and growth), or F (financial).

1. Customer wait time   _____
2. Number of days of employee absences   _____
3. Profit margin   _____
4. Number of new products introduced   _____
5. Change in market share   _____
6. Employee training sessions attended   _____
7. Length of time raw materials are in inventory _____
8. Customer satisfaction index   _____

QS 24-10
Performance measures—
balanced scorecard

A3

Walt Disney reports the following information for its two Parks and Resorts divisions.

	East Coast		West Coast	
	Current year	Prior year	Current year	Prior year
Hotel occupancy rates	89%	86%	92%	93%

Assume Walt Disney uses a balanced scorecard and sets a target of 90% occupancy in its resorts. Using Exhibit 24.22 as a guide, show how the company's performance on hotel occupancy would appear on a balanced scorecard report.

QS 24-11[A]
Determining transfer prices
without excess capacity

C2

The Windshield division of Fast Car Co. makes windshields for use in Fast Car's Assembly division. The Windshield division incurs variable costs of $200 per windshield and has capacity to make 500,000 windshields per year. The market price is $450 per windshield. The Windshield division incurs total fixed costs of $3,000,000 per year. If the Windshield division is operating at full capacity, what transfer price should be used on transfers between the Windshield and Assembly divisions? Explain.

QS 24-12[A]
Determining transfer prices with
excess capacity   C2

Refer to information in QS 24-11. If the Windshield division has excess capacity, what is the range of possible transfer prices that could be used on transfers between the Windshield and Assembly divisions? Explain.

QS 24-13[B]
Joint cost allocation

C3

A company purchases a 10,020 square foot commercial building for $325,000 and spends an additional $50,000 to divide the space into two separate rental units and prepare it for rent. Unit A, which has the desirable location on the corner and contains 3,340 square feet, will be rented for $1.00 per square foot. Unit B contains 6,680 square feet and will be rented for $0.75 per square foot. How much of the joint cost should be assigned to Unit B using the value basis of allocation?

Car Mart pays $130,000 rent each year for its two-story building. The space in this building is occupied by five departments as specified here.

Paint department	1,440 square feet of first-floor space
Engine department	3,360 square feet of first-floor space
Window department	2,016 square feet of second-floor space
Electrical department	960 square feet of second-floor space
Accessory department	1,824 square feet of second-floor space

The company allocates 65% of total rent expense to the first floor and 35% to the second floor, and then allocates rent expense for each floor to the departments occupying that floor on the basis of space occupied. Determine the rent expense to be allocated to each department. (Round percents to the nearest one-tenth and dollar amounts to the nearest whole dollar.)

QS 24-14
Rent expense allocated
to departments

P2

Check Allocated to Paint Dept.,
$25,350

For a recent year **L'Oreal** reported operating profit of €3,385 (in millions) for its Cosmetics division. Total assets were €12,888 at the beginning of the year and €13,099 (in millions) at the end of the year. Compute return on investment for the year. State your answer as a percent, rounded to one decimal.

QS 24-15
Return on investment

A1

Compute and interpret (a) manufacturing cycle time and (b) manufacturing cycle efficiency using the following information from a manufacturing company.

Process time	15 minutes
Inspection time	2 minutes
Move time	6.4 minutes
Wait time	36.6 minutes

QS 24-16
Manufacturing cycle time
and efficiency

A4

connect

Woh Che Co. has four departments: materials, personnel, manufacturing, and packaging. In a recent month, the four departments incurred three shared indirect expenses. The amounts of these indirect expenses and the bases used to allocate them follow.

Indirect Expense	Cost	Allocation Base
Supervision	$ 82,500	Number of employees
Utilities	50,000	Square feet occupied
Insurance	22,500	Value of assets in use
Total	$155,000	

EXERCISES

Exercise 24-1
Departmental expense
allocations

P2

Departmental data for the company's recent reporting period follow.

Department	Employees	Square Feet	Asset Values
Materials	27	25,000	$ 6,000
Personnel............	9	5,000	1,200
Manufacturing	63	55,000	37,800
Packaging	51	15,000	15,000
Total	150	100,000	$60,000

(1) Use this information to allocate each of the three indirect expenses across the four departments.
(2) Prepare a summary table that reports the indirect expenses assigned to each of the four departments.

Check (2) Total of $29,600 assigned
to Materials Dept.

Exercise 24-2
Managerial performance evaluation

P1

Maryanne Dinardo manages an auto dealership's service department. The recent month's income statement for his department follows. (1) Analyze the items on the income statement and identify those that definitely should be included on a performance report used to evaluate Dinardo's performance. List them and explain why you chose them. (2) List and explain the items that should definitely be excluded. (3) List the items that are not definitely included or excluded and explain why they fall into that category.

Revenues		
Sales of parts	$ 72,000	
Sales of services........................	105,000	$177,000
Costs and expenses		
Cost of parts sold	30,000	
Building depreciation	9,300	
Income taxes allocated to department.........	8,700	
Interest on long-term debt	7,500	
Manager's salary..........................	12,000	
Payroll taxes............................	8,100	
Supplies	15,900	
Utilities................................	4,400	
Wages (hourly)...........................	16,000	
Total costs and expenses		111,900
Departmental net income		$ 65,100

Exercise 24-3
Departmental contribution report

P3

Below are departmental income statements for a guitar manufacturer. The manufacturer is considering dropping its electric guitar department since it has a net loss. The company classifies advertising, rent, and utilities expenses as indirect. (1) Prepare a departmental contribution report that shows each department's contribution to overhead. (2) Based on contribution to overhead, should the electric guitar department be eliminated?

WHOLESALE GUITARS		
Departmental Income Statements		
For Year Ended December 31, 2013		
	Acoustic	**Electric**
Sales	$111,500	$105,500
Cost of goods sold	55,675	66,750
Gross profit	56,825	38,750
Operating expenses		
Advertising expense..................	8,075	6,250
Depreciation expense-equipment	10,150	9,000
Salaries expense.....................	17,300	13,500
Supplies expense	2,030	1,700
Rent expense	6,105	5,950
Utilities expense.....................	3,045	2,550
Total operating expenses...............	46,705	38,950
Net income (loss)	**$ 10,120**	**($200)**

Exercise 24-4
Departmental expense allocation spreadsheet

P2

Marathon Running Shop has two service departments (advertising and administration) and two operating departments (shoes and clothing). During 2013, the departments had the following direct expenses and occupied the following amount of floor space.

Department	Direct Expenses	Square Feet
Advertising	$ 18,000	1,120
Administrative	25,000	1,400
Shoes	103,000	7,140
Clothing	15,000	4,340

The advertising department developed and distributed 120 advertisements during the year. Of these, 90 promoted shoes and 30 promoted clothing. The store sold $350,000 of merchandise during the year. Of this amount, $273,000 is from the shoes department, and $77,000 is from the clothing department. The utilities expense of $64,000 is an indirect expense to all departments. Prepare a departmental expense allocation spreadsheet for Marathon Running Shop. The spreadsheet should assign (1) direct expenses to each of the four departments, (2) the $64,000 of utilities expense to the four departments on the basis of floor space occupied, (3) the advertising department's expenses to the two operating departments on the basis of the number of ads placed that promoted a department's products, and (4) the administrative department's expenses to the two operating departments based on the amount of sales. Provide supporting computations for the expense allocations.

Check Total expenses allocated to Shoes Dept., $177,472

The following is a partially completed lower section of a departmental expense allocation spreadsheet for Cozy Bookstore. It reports the total amounts of direct and indirect expenses allocated to its five departments. Complete the spreadsheet by allocating the expenses of the two service departments (advertising and purchasing) to the three operating departments.

Exercise 24-5
Service department expenses allocated to operating departments P2

			Allocation of Expenses to Departments				
	Allocation Base	Expense Account Balance	Advertising Dept.	Purchasing Dept.	Books Dept.	Magazines Dept.	Newspapers Dept.
5 Total department expenses..........		$698,000	$24,000	$34,000	$425,000	$90,000	$125,000
6 **Service department expenses**							
7 Advertising department............ Sales			?		?	?	?
8 Purchasing department............ Purch. orders				?	?	?	?
9 Total expenses allocated to							
10 operating departments..............		?	$ 0	$ 0	?	?	?

Advertising and purchasing department expenses are allocated to operating departments on the basis of dollar sales and purchase orders, respectively. Information about the allocation bases for the three operating departments follows.

Department	Sales	Purchase Orders
Books..............	$495,000	516
Magazines...........	198,000	360
Newspapers..........	207,000	324
Total..............	$900,000	1,200

Check Total expenses allocated to Books Dept., $452,820

Jessica Porter works in both the jewelry department and the hosiery department of a retail store. Porter assists customers in both departments and arranges and stocks merchandise in both departments. The store allocates Porter's $30,000 annual wages between the two departments based on a sample of the time worked in the two departments. The sample is obtained from a diary of hours worked that Porter kept in a randomly chosen two-week period. The diary showed the following hours and activities spent in the two departments. Allocate Porter's annual wages between the two departments.

Exercise 24-6
Indirect payroll expense allocated to departments
P2

Selling in jewelry department..	51 hours
Arranging and stocking merchandise in jewelry department........................	6 hours
Selling in hosiery department	12 hours
Arranging and stocking merchandise in hosiery department	7 hours
Idle time spent waiting for a customer to enter one of the selling departments	4 hours

Check Assign $7,500 to Hosiery

Exercise 24-7

Investment center analysis

A1

You must prepare a return on investment analysis for the regional manager of Fast & Great Burgers. This growing chain is trying to decide which outlet of two alternatives to open. The first location (A) requires a $1,000,000 investment and is expected to yield annual net income of $160,000. The second location (B) requires a $600,000 investment and is expected to yield annual net income of $108,000. Compute the return on investment for each Fast & Great Burgers alternative and then make your recommendation in a one-half page memorandum to the regional manager. (The chain currently generates an 18% return on total assets.)

Exercise 24-8

Computing return on assets and residual income; investing decision

A1

Megamart, a retailer of consumer goods, provides the following information on two of its departments (each considered an investment center).

Investment Center	Sales	Net Income	Average Invested Assets
Electronics	$40,000,000	$2,880,000	$16,000,000
Sporting goods	20,000,000	2,040,000	12,000,000

(1) Compute return on investment for each department. Using return on investment, which department is most efficient at using assets to generate returns for the company? (2) Assume a target income level of 12% of average invested assets. Compute residual income for each department. Which department generated the most residual income for the company? (3) Assume the Electronics department is presented with a new investment opportunity that will yield a 15% return on assets. Should the new investment opportunity be accepted? Explain.

Exercise 24-9

Computing margin and turnover; department efficiency   A2

Refer to information in Exercise 24-8. Compute profit margin and investment turnover for each department. Which department generates the most net income per dollar of sales? Which department is most efficient at generating sales from average invested assets?

Exercise 24-10

Performance measures—balanced scorecard

A3

USA Airlines uses the following performance measures. Classify each of the performance measures below into the most likely balanced scorecard perspective it relates to. Label your answers using C (customer), P (internal process), I (innovation and growth), or F (financial).

  1. Cash flow from operations   _____
  2. Number of reports of mishandled or lost baggage   _____
  3. Percentage of on-time departures   _____
  4. On-time flight percentage   _____
  5. Percentage of ground crew trained   _____
  6. Return on investment   _____
  7. Market value   _____
  8. Accidents or safety incidents per mile flown _____
  9. Customer complaints   _____
  10. Flight attendant training sessions attended   _____
  11. Time airplane is on ground between flights   _____
  12. Airplane miles per gallon of fuel   _____
  13. Revenue per seat   _____
  14. Cost of leasing airplanes   _____

Exercise 24-11^A

Determining transfer prices

C2

The Trailer department of Baxter Bicycles makes bike trailers that attach to bicycles and can carry children or cargo. The trailers have a retail price of $200 each. Each trailer incurs $80 of variable manufacturing costs. The Trailer department has capacity for 40,000 trailers per year, and incurs fixed costs of $1,000,000 per year.

Required

  1. Assume the Assembly division of Baxter Bicycles wants to buy 15,000 trailers per year from the Trailer division. If the Trailer division can sell all of the trailers it manufactures to outside customers, what price should be used on transfers between Baxter Bicycle's divisions? Explain.

2. Assume the Trailer division currently only sells 20,000 trailers to outside customers, and the Assembly division wants to buy 15,000 trailers per year from the Trailer division. What is the range of acceptable prices that could be used on transfers between Baxter Bicycle's divisions? Explain.

3. Assume transfer prices of either $80 per trailer or $140 per trailer are being considered. Comment on the preferred transfer prices from the perspectives of the Trailer division manager, the Assembly division manager, and the top management of Baxter Bicycles.

Heart & Home Properties is developing a subdivision that includes 600 home lots. The 450 lots in the Canyon section are below a ridge and do not have views of the neighboring canyons and hills; the 150 lots in the Hilltop section offer unobstructed views. The expected selling price for each Canyon lot is $55,000 and for each Hilltop lot is $110,000. The developer acquired the land for $4,000,000 and spent another $3,500,000 on street and utilities improvements. Assign the joint land and improvement costs to the lots using the value basis of allocation and determine the average cost per lot.

Exercise 24-12ᴮ
Joint real estate costs assigned
C3

Check Total Hilltop cost, $3,000,000

Pirate Seafood Company purchases lobsters and processes them into tails and flakes. It sells the lobster tails for $21 per pound and the flakes for $14 per pound. On average, 100 pounds of lobster are processed into 52 pounds of tails and 22 pounds of flakes, with 26 pounds of waste. Assume that the company purchased 2,400 pounds of lobster for $4.50 per pound and processed the lobsters with an additional labor cost of $1,800. No materials or labor costs are assigned to the waste. If 1,096 pounds of tails and 324 pounds of flakes are sold, what is (1) the allocated cost of the sold items and (2) the allocated cost of the ending inventory? The company allocates joint costs on a value basis. (Round the dollar cost per pound to the nearest thousandth.)

Exercise 24-13ᴮ
Joint product costs assigned
C3

Check (2) Inventory cost, $2,268

L'Oreal reports the following for a recent year for the major divisions in its Cosmetics branch.

Exercise 24-14
Profit margin and investment turnover
A2

(€ millions)	Sales	Income	Total Assets End of Year	Total Assets Beginning of Year
Professional products	€ 2,717	€ 552	€ 2,624	€ 2,516
Consumer products	9,530	1,765	5,994	5,496
Luxury products	4,507	791	3,651	4,059
Active cosmetics	1,386	278	830	817
Total	€18,140	€3,386	€13,099	€12,888

1. Compute profit margin for each division. State your answers as percents, rounded to two decimal places. Which L'Oreal division has the highest profit margin?

2. Compute investment turnover for each division. Round your answers to two decimal places. Which L'Oreal division has the best investment turnover?

≣ connect

National Bank has several departments that occupy both floors of a two-story building. The departmental accounting system has a single account, Building Occupancy Cost, in its ledger. The types and amounts of occupancy costs recorded in this account for the current period follow.

Depreciation—Building	$18,000
Interest—Building mortgage	27,000
Taxes—Building and land	9,000
Gas (heating) expense	3,000
Lighting expense	3,000
Maintenance expense	6,000
Total occupancy cost	$66,000

PROBLEM SET A

Problem 24-1A
Allocation of building occupancy costs to departments
P2 ♟

mhhe.com/wildFAP21e

The building has 4,000 square feet on each floor. In prior periods, the accounting manager merely divided the $66,000 occupancy cost by 8,000 square feet to find an average cost of $8.25 per square foot and then charged each department a building occupancy cost equal to this rate times the number of square feet that it occupied.

Diane Linder manages a first-floor department that occupies 1,000 square feet, and Juan Chiro manages a second-floor department that occupies 1,800 square feet of floor space. In discussing the departmental reports, the second-floor manager questions whether using the same rate per square foot for all departments makes sense because the first-floor space is more valuable. This manager also references a recent real estate study of average local rental costs for similar space that shows first-floor space worth $30 per square foot and second-floor space worth $20 per square foot (excluding costs for heating, lighting, and maintenance).

Required

Check (1) Total allocated to Linder and Chiro, $23,100 (2) Total occupancy cost to Linder, $9,600

1. Allocate occupancy costs to the Linder and Chiro departments using the current allocation method.
2. Allocate the depreciation, interest, and taxes occupancy costs to the Linder and Chiro departments in proportion to the relative market values of the floor space. Allocate the heating, lighting, and maintenance costs to the Linder and Chiro departments in proportion to the square feet occupied (ignoring floor space market values).

Analysis Component

3. Which allocation method would you prefer if you were a manager of a second-floor department? Explain.

Problem 24-2A

Departmental income statements; forecasts

P3

mhhe.com/wildFAP21e

Williams Company began operations in January 2013 with two operating (selling) departments and one service (office) department. Its departmental income statements follow.

WILLIAMS COMPANY Departmental Income Statements For Year Ended December 31, 2013			
	Clock	Mirror	Combined
Sales	$130,000	$55,000	$185,000
Cost of goods sold	63,700	34,100	97,800
Gross profit	66,300	20,900	87,200
Direct expenses			
Sales salaries	20,000	7,000	27,000
Advertising	1,200	500	1,700
Store supplies used	900	400	1,300
Depreciation—Equipment	1,500	300	1,800
Total direct expenses	23,600	8,200	31,800
Allocated expenses			
Rent expense	7,020	3,780	10,800
Utilities expense	2,600	1,400	4,000
Share of office department expenses	10,500	4,500	15,000
Total allocated expenses	20,120	9,680	29,800
Total expenses	43,720	17,880	61,600
Net income	$ 22,580	$ 3,020	$ 25,600

Williams plans to open a third department in January 2014 that will sell paintings. Management predicts that the new department will generate $50,000 in sales with a 55% gross profit margin and will require the following direct expenses: sales salaries, $8,000; advertising, $800; store supplies, $500; and equipment depreciation, $200. It will fit the new department into the current rented space by taking some square footage from the other two departments. When opened the new painting department will fill one-fifth of the space presently used by the clock department and one-fourth used by the mirror department. Management does not predict any increase in utilities costs, which are allocated to the departments in proportion to occupied space (or rent expense). The company allocates office department expenses to the operating departments in proportion to their sales. It expects the painting department to increase total office department expenses by $7,000. Since the painting department will bring new customers into the store, management expects sales in both the clock and mirror departments to increase by 8%. No changes for those departments' gross profit percents or their direct expenses are expected except for store supplies used, which will increase in proportion to sales.

Required

Prepare departmental income statements that show the company's predicted results of operations for calendar year 2014 for the three operating (selling) departments and their combined totals. (Round percents to the nearest one-tenth and dollar amounts to the nearest whole dollar.)

Check   2014 forecasted combined net income (sales), $43,472 ($249,800)

Billie Whitehorse, the plant manager of Travel Free's Indiana plant, is responsible for all of that plant's costs other than her own salary. The plant has two operating departments and one service department. The camper and trailer operating departments manufacture different products and have their own managers. The office department, which Whitehorse also manages, provides services equally to the two operating departments. A budget is prepared for each operating department and the office department. The company's responsibility accounting system must assemble information to present budgeted and actual costs in performance reports for each operating department manager and the plant manager. Each performance report includes only those costs that a particular operating department manager can control: raw materials, wages, supplies used, and equipment depreciation. The plant manager is responsible for the department managers' salaries, utilities, building rent, office salaries other than her own, and other office costs plus all costs controlled by the two operating department managers. The annual departmental budgets and actual costs for the two operating departments follow.

Problem 24-3A
Responsibility accounting performance reports; controllable and budgeted costs
P1

	Budget			Actual		
	Campers	**Trailers**	**Combined**	**Campers**	**Trailers**	**Combined**
Raw materials	$195,000	$275,000	$ 470,000	$194,200	$273,200	$ 467,400
Employee wages	104,000	205,000	309,000	106,600	206,400	313,000
Dept. manager salary	43,000	52,000	95,000	44,000	53,500	97,500
Supplies used	33,000	90,000	123,000	31,700	91,600	123,300
Depreciation—Equip.	60,000	125,000	185,000	60,000	125,000	185,000
Utilities....................	3,600	5,400	9,000	3,300	5,000	8,300
Building rent	5,700	9,300	15,000	5,300	8,700	14,000
Office department costs	68,750	68,750	137,500	67,550	67,550	135,100
Totals	$513,050	$830,450	$1,343,500	$512,650	$830,950	$1,343,600

The office department's annual budget and its actual costs follow.

	Budget	Actual
Plant manager salary	$ 80,000	$ 82,000
Other office salaries	32,500	30,100
Other office costs	25,000	23,000
Totals	$137,500	$135,100

Required

1. Prepare responsibility accounting performance reports like those in Exhibit 24.2 that list costs controlled by the following:

  a. Manager of the camper department.

  b. Manager of the trailer department.

  c. Manager of the Indiana plant.

In each report, include the budgeted and actual costs and show the amount that each actual cost is over or under the budgeted amount.

Check   (1a) $500 total over budget

(1c) Indiana plant controllable costs, $1,900 total under budget

Analysis Component

2. Did the plant manager or the operating department managers better manage costs? Explain.

Problem 24-4A[B]

Allocation of joint costs

C3

Georgia Orchards produced a good crop of peaches this year. After preparing the following income statement, the company believes it should have given its No. 3 peaches to charity and saved its efforts.

	GEORGIA ORCHARDS **Income Statement** **For Year Ended December 31, 2013**			
	No. 1	**No. 2**	**No. 3**	**Combined**
Sales (by grade)				
No. 1: 300,000 lbs. @ $1.50/lb	$450,000			
No. 2: 300,000 lbs. @ $1.00/lb		$300,000		
No. 3: 750,000 lbs. @ $0.25/lb			$ 187,500	
Total sales				$937,500
Costs				
Tree pruning and care @ $0.30/lb	90,000	90,000	225,000	405,000
Picking, sorting, and grading @ $0.15/lb	45,000	45,000	112,500	202,500
Delivery costs	15,000	15,000	37,500	67,500
Total costs	150,000	150,000	375,000	675,000
Net income (loss)	$300,000	$150,000	$(187,500)	$262,500

In preparing this statement, the company allocated joint costs among the grades on a physical basis as an equal amount per pound. The company's delivery cost records show that $30,000 of the $67,500 relates to crating the No. 1 and No. 2 peaches and hauling them to the buyer. The remaining $37,500 of delivery costs is for crating the No. 3 peaches and hauling them to the cannery.

Required

Check (1) $129,600 tree pruning and care costs allocated to No. 2

1. Prepare reports showing cost allocations on a sales value basis to the three grades of peaches. Separate the delivery costs into the amounts directly identifiable with each grade. Then allocate any shared delivery costs on the basis of the relative sales value of each grade.

(2) Net income from No. 1 & No. 2 peaches, $140,400 & $93,600

2. Using your answers to part 1, prepare an income statement using the joint costs allocated on a sales value basis.

Analysis Component

3. Do you think delivery costs fit the definition of a joint cost? Explain.

Problem 24-5A

Manufacturing cycle time and efficiency

A4

Oakwood Company produces maple bookcases to customer order. It received an order from a customer to produce 5,000 bookcases. The following information is available for the production of the bookcases.

Process time	6.0 days
Inspection time	0.8 days
Move time	3.2 days
Wait time	5.0 days

Required

1. Compute the company's manufacturing cycle time.

Check (2) Manufacturing cycle efficiency, 0.40

2. Compute the company's manufacturing cycle efficiency. Interpret your answer.

Analysis Component

3. Assume that Oakwood wishes to increase its manufacturing cycle efficiency to 0.75. What are some ways that it can accomplish this?

Harmon's has several departments that occupy all floors of a two-story building that includes a basement floor. Harmon rented this building under a long-term lease negotiated when rental rates were low. The departmental accounting system has a single account, Building Occupancy Cost, in its ledger. The types and amounts of occupancy costs recorded in this account for the current period follow.

PROBLEM SET B

Problem 24-1B
Allocation of building occupancy costs to departments

P2

Building rent	$400,000
Lighting expense	25,000
Cleaning expense	40,000
Total occupancy cost	$465,000

The building has 7,500 square feet on each of the upper two floors but only 5,000 square feet in the basement. In prior periods, the accounting manager merely divided the $465,000 occupancy cost by 20,000 square feet to find an average cost of $23.25 per square foot and then charged each department a building occupancy cost equal to this rate times the number of square feet that it occupies.

Jordan Style manages a department that occupies 2,000 square feet of basement floor space. In discussing the departmental reports with other managers, she questions whether using the same rate per square foot for all departments makes sense because different floor space has different values. Style checked a recent real estate report of average local rental costs for similar space that shows first-floor space worth $40 per square foot, second-floor space worth $20 per square foot, and basement space worth $10 per square foot (excluding costs for lighting and cleaning).

Required

1. Allocate occupancy costs to Style's department using the current allocation method.
2. Allocate the building rent cost to Style's department in proportion to the relative market value of the floor space. Allocate to Style's department the lighting and cleaning costs in proportion to the square feet occupied (ignoring floor space market values). Then, compute the total occupancy cost allocated to Style's department.

Analysis Component

3. Which allocation method would you prefer if you were a manager of a basement department?

Check   Total costs allocated to Style's Dept., (1) $46,500; (2) Total occupancy cost to Style $22,500

Bonanza Entertainment began operations in January 2013 with two operating (selling) departments and one service (office) department. Its departmental income statements follow.

Problem 24-2B
Departmental income statements; forecasts   P3

BONANZA ENTERTAINMENT Departmental Income Statements For Year Ended December 31, 2013	Movies	Video Games	Combined
Sales	$600,000	$200,000	$800,000
Cost of goods sold	420,000	154,000	574,000
Gross profit	180,000	46,000	226,000
Direct expenses			
Sales salaries	37,000	15,000	52,000
Advertising	12,500	6,000	18,500
Store supplies used	4,000	1,000	5,000
Depreciation—Equipment	4,500	3,000	7,500
Total direct expenses	58,000	25,000	83,000
Allocated expenses			
Rent expense	41,000	9,000	50,000
Utilities expense	7,380	1,620	9,000
Share of office department expenses	56,250	18,750	75,000
Total allocated expenses	104,630	29,370	134,000
Total expenses	162,630	54,370	217,000
Net income (loss)	$ 17,370	$ (8,370)	$ 9,000

The company plans to open a third department in January 2014 that will sell compact discs. Management predicts that the new department will generate $300,000 in sales with a 35% gross profit margin and will require the following direct expenses: sales salaries, $18,000; advertising, $10,000; store supplies, $2,000; and equipment depreciation, $1,200. The company will fit the new department into the current rented space by taking some square footage from the other two departments. When opened, the new compact disc department will fill one-fourth of the space presently used by the movie department and one-third of the space used by the video game department. Management does not predict any increase in utilities costs, which are allocated to the departments in proportion to occupied space (or rent expense). The company allocates office department expenses to the operating departments in proportion to their sales. It expects the compact disc department to increase total office department expenses by $10,000. Since the compact disc department will bring new customers into the store, management expects sales in both the movie and video game departments to increase by 8%. No changes for those departments' gross profit percents or for their direct expenses are expected, except for store supplies used, which will increase in proportion to sales.

Required

Check 2014 forecasted movies net income (sales), $52,450 ($648,000)

Prepare departmental income statements that show the company's predicted results of operations for calendar year 2014 for the three operating (selling) departments and their combined totals. (Round percents to the nearest one-tenth and dollar amounts to the nearest whole dollar.)

Problem 24-3B
Responsibility accounting performance reports; controllable and budgeted costs
P1

Britney Brown, the plant manager of LMN Co.'s Chicago plant, is responsible for all of that plant's costs other than her own salary. The plant has two operating departments and one service department. The refrigerator and dishwasher operating departments manufacture different products and have their own managers. The office department, which Brown also manages, provides services equally to the two operating departments. A monthly budget is prepared for each operating department and the office department. The company's responsibility accounting system must assemble information to present budgeted and actual costs in performance reports for each operating department manager and the plant manager. Each performance report includes only those costs that a particular operating department manager can control: raw materials, wages, supplies used, and equipment depreciation. The plant manager is responsible for the department managers' salaries, utilities, building rent, office salaries other than her own, and other office costs plus all costs controlled by the two operating department managers. The April departmental budgets and actual costs for the two operating departments follow.

	Budget			Actual		
	Refrigerators	**Dishwashers**	**Combined**	**Refrigerators**	**Dishwashers**	**Combined**
Raw materials	$400,000	$200,000	$ 600,000	$385,000	$202,000	$ 587,000
Employee wages	170,000	80,000	250,000	174,700	81,500	256,200
Dept. manager salary	55,000	49,000	104,000	55,000	46,500	101,500
Supplies used	15,000	9,000	24,000	14,000	9,700	23,700
Depreciation—Equip.	53,000	37,000	90,000	53,000	37,000	90,000
Utilities	30,000	18,000	48,000	34,500	20,700	55,200
Building rent	63,000	17,000	80,000	65,800	16,500	82,300
Office department costs	70,500	70,500	141,000	75,000	75,000	150,000
Totals	$856,500	$480,500	$1,337,000	$857,000	$488,900	$1,345,900

The office department's budget and its actual costs for April follow.

	Budget	Actual
Plant manager salary	$ 80,000	$ 85,000
Other office salaries	40,000	35,200
Other office costs	21,000	29,800
Totals	$141,000	$150,000

Required

1. Prepare responsibility accounting performance reports like those in Exhibit 24.2 that list costs controlled by the following:

   a. Manager of the refrigerator department.

   b. Manager of the dishwasher department.

   c. Manager of the Chicago plant.

In each report, include the budgeted and actual costs for the month and show the amount by which each actual cost is over or under the budgeted amount.

Check   (1a) $11,300 total under budget

(1c) Chicago plant controllable costs, $3,900 total over budget

Analysis Component

2. Did the plant manager or the operating department managers better manage costs? Explain.

Rita and Rick Redding own and operate a tomato grove. After preparing the following income statement, Rita believes they should have offered the No. 3 tomatoes to the public for free and saved themselves time and money.

Problem 24-4B[B]
Allocation of joint costs

C3

RITA AND RICK REDDING Income Statement For Year Ended December 31, 2013				
	No. 1	No. 2	No. 3	Combined
Sales (by grade)				
No. 1: 500,000 lbs. @ $1.80/lb	$900,000			
No. 2: 400,000 lbs. @ $1.25/lb		$500,000		
No. 3: 100,000 lbs. @ $0.40/lb			$ 40,000	
Total sales				$1,440,000
Costs				
Land preparation, seeding, and cultivating @ $0.70/lb	350,000	280,000	70,000	700,000
Harvesting, sorting, and grading @ $0.04/lb	20,000	16,000	4,000	40,000
Delivery costs	10,000	7,000	3,000	20,000
Total costs	380,000	303,000	77,000	760,000
Net income (loss)	$520,000	$197,000	$(37,000)	$ 680,000

In preparing this statement, Rita and Rick allocated joint costs among the grades on a physical basis as an equal amount per pound. Also, their delivery cost records show that $17,000 of the $20,000 relates to crating the No. 1 and No. 2 tomatoes and hauling them to the buyer. The remaining $3,000 of delivery costs is for crating the No. 3 tomatoes and hauling them to the cannery.

Required

1. Prepare reports showing cost allocations on a sales value basis to the three grades of tomatoes. Separate the delivery costs into the amounts directly identifiable with each grade. Then allocate any shared delivery costs on the basis of the relative sales value of each grade. (Round percents to the nearest one-tenth and dollar amounts to the nearest whole dollar.)

2. Using your answers to part 1, prepare an income statement using the joint costs allocated on a sales value basis.

Check   (1) $1,120 harvesting, sorting and grading costs allocated to No. 3

(2) Net income from No. 1 & No. 2 tomatoes, $426,569 & $237,151

Analysis Component

3. Do you think delivery costs fit the definition of a joint cost? Explain.

Best Ink produces ink-jet printers for personal computers. It received an order for 500 printers from a customer. The following information is available for this order.

Problem 24-5B
Manufacturing cycle time and efficiency

A4

Process time	16.0 hours
Inspection time	3.5 hours
Move time	9.0 hours
Wait time	21.5 hours

Required

1. Compute the company's manufacturing cycle time.
2. Compute the company's manufacturing cycle efficiency. Interpret your answer.

Analysis Component

3. Assume that Best Ink wishes to increase its manufacturing cycle efficiency to 0.80. What are some ways that it can accomplish this?

SERIAL PROBLEM

Success Systems

A3

(This serial problem began in Chapter 1 and continues through most of the book. If previous chapter segments were not completed, the serial problem can begin at this point. It is helpful, but not necessary, to use the Working Papers that accompany the book.)

SP 24   Adria Lopez's two departments, computer consulting services and computer workstation furniture manufacturing, have each been profitable. Adria has heard of the balanced scorecard and wants you to provide details on how it could be used to measure performance of her departments.

Required

1. Explain the four performance perspectives included in a balanced scorecard.
2. For each of the four performance perspectives included in a balanced scorecard, provide examples of measures Adria could use to measure performance of her departments.

Beyond the Numbers

REPORTING IN ACTION

C1

Polaris

BTN 24-1   Review **Polaris'** income statement in Appendix A and identify its revenues for the years ended December 31, 2011, December 31, 2010, and December 31, 2009. For the year ended December 31, 2011, Polaris reports the following product revenue mix. (Assume that its product revenue mix is the same for each of the three years reported when answering the requirements.)

Off-Road Vehicles	Snowmobiles	On-Road Vehicles	Parts, Garments, & Accessories
69%	11%	5%	15%

Required

1. Compute the amount of revenue from each of its product lines for the years ended December 31, 2011, December 31, 2010, and December 31, 2009.
2. If Polaris wishes to evaluate each of its product lines, how can it allocate its operating expenses to each of them to determine each product line's profitability?

Fast Forward

3. Access Polaris' annual report for a fiscal year ending after December 31, 2011, from its Website (**Polaris.com**) or the SEC's EDGAR database (**sec.gov**). Compute its revenues for its product lines for the most recent year(s). Compare those results to those from part 1. How has its product mix changed?

COMPARATIVE ANALYSIS

A2

Polaris

Arctic Cat

BTN 24-2   **Polaris** and **Arctic Cat** compete in several on-road and off-road motorized vehicle categories. Sales, income, and asset information is provided for each company below.

(in thousands)	Polaris	Arctic Cat
Sales.................................	$2,656,949	$464,651
Net income	227,575	13,007
Invested assets, beginning of year	1,061,647	246,084
Invested assets, end of year..............	1,228,024	272,906

Required

1. Compute profit margin for each company.

2. Compute investment turnover for each company.

Analysis Component

3. Using your answers to the questions above, compare the companies' performance during the most recent year.

BTN 24-3   Senior Security Co. offers a range of security services for senior citizens. Each type of service is considered within a separate department. Mary Pincus, the overall manager, is compensated partly on the basis of departmental performance by staying within the quarterly cost budget. She often revises operations to make sure departments stay within budget. Says Pincus, "I will not go over budget even if it means slightly compromising the level and quality of service. These are minor compromises that don't significantly affect my clients, at least in the short term."

ETHICS CHALLENGE

P3

Required

1. Is there an ethical concern in this situation? If so, which parties are affected? Explain.

2. Can Mary Pincus take action to eliminate or reduce any ethical concerns? Explain.

3. What is Senior Security's ethical responsibility in offering professional services?

BTN 24-4   Improvement Station is a national home improvement chain with more than 100 stores throughout the country. The manager of each store receives a salary plus a bonus equal to a percent of the store's net income for the reporting period. The following net income calculation is on the Denver store manager's performance report for the recent monthly period.

COMMUNICATING IN PRACTICE

P2

Sales	$2,500,000
Cost of goods sold	800,000
Wages expense	500,000
Utilities expense	200,000
Home office expense	75,000
Net income	$ 925,000
Manager's bonus (0.5%)	$ 4,625

In previous periods, the bonus had also been 0.5%, but the performance report had not included any charges for the home office expense, which is now assigned to each store as a percent of its sales.

Required

Assume that you are the national office manager. Write a one-half page memorandum to your store managers explaining why home office expense is in the new performance report.

BTN 24-5   This chapter described and used spreadsheets to prepare various managerial reports (see Exhibit 24-6). You can download from Websites various tutorials showing how spreadsheets are used in managerial accounting and other business applications.

TAKING IT TO THE NET

P2

Required

1. Link to the Website **Lacher.com**. Select "Excel Examples." Identify and list three tutorials for review.

2. Describe in a one-half page memorandum to your instructor how the applications described in each tutorial are helpful in business and managerial decision making.

TEAMWORK IN ACTION

P1

Polaris

Arctic Cat

BTN 24-6 **Polaris**, and **Arctic Cat** compete across the world in several markets.

Required

1. Design a three-tier responsibility accounting organizational chart assuming that you have available internal information for both companies. Use Exhibit 24.1 as an example. The goal of this assignment is to design a reporting framework for the companies; numbers are not required. Limit your reporting framework to sales activity only.

2. Explain why it is important to have similar performance reports when comparing performance within a company (and across different companies). Be specific in your response.

ENTREPRENEURIAL DECISION

P3

BTN 24-7 Brian Linton's company, **United By Blue**, sells jewelry and apparel. His company's plans call for continued expansion into other types of products.

Required

1. How can United By Blue use departmental income statements to assist in understanding and controlling operations?

2. Are departmental income statements always the best measure of a department's performance? Explain.

3. Provide examples of nonfinancial performace indicators United By Blue might use as part of a balanced scorecard system of performance evaluation.

HITTING THE ROAD

C1 P1

BTN 24-8 Visit a local movie theater and check out both its concession area and its showing areas. The manager of a theater must confront questions such as:

- How much return do we earn on concessions?
- What types of movies generate the greatest sales?
- What types of movies generate the greatest net income?

Required

Assume that you are the new accounting manager for a 16-screen movie theater. You are to set up a responsibility accounting reporting framework for the theater.

1. Recommend how to segment the different departments of a movie theater for responsibility reporting.

2. Propose an expense allocation system for heat, rent, insurance, and maintenance costs of the theater.

GLOBAL DECISION

P3

PIAGGIO

BTN 24-9 Selected product data from **Piaggio** (www.piaggio.com) follow.

Product Segment for Year Ended (millions)	Net Sales		Gross Margin	
	December 31, 2011	December 31, 2010	December 31, 2011	December 31, 2010
Two-wheeler vehicles............	€1,025.3	€988.1	€337.1	€330.7
Commercial vehicles	491.1	497.3	117.5	131.6

Required

1. Compute the percentage growth in net sales for each product line from fiscal year 2010 to 2011. Round percents to one decimal.

2. Which product line's net sales grew the fastest?

3. Which segment was the most profitable?

4. How can Piaggio's managers use this information?

ANSWERS TO MULTIPLE CHOICE QUIZ

1. b; [$641,250/($356,250 + $641,250 + $427,500)] × $150,000 = $67,500

2. d;

3. c; $500,000/200,000 = 2.5

4. b;

	Department X	Department Y	Department Z
Sales	$500,000	$200,000	$350,000
Cost of goods sold	350,000	75,000	150,000
Gross profit	150,000	125,000	200,000
Direct expenses.	50,000	20,000	75,000
Departmental contribution.	$100,000	$105,000	$125,000

5. a; $100,000/$500,000 = 20%

Capital Budgeting and Managerial Decisions

25

A Look Back

Chapter 24 focused on cost allocations and performance measurement. We identified ways to measure and analyze company activities, its departments, and its managers.

A Look at This Chapter

This chapter focuses on evaluating capital budgeting decisions. It also explains several tools and procedures used in making and evaluating short-term managerial decisions.

Learning Objectives

CONCEPTUAL

C1 Describe the importance of relevant costs for short-term decisions. (p. 1048)

ANALYTICAL

A1 Evaluate short-term managerial decisions using relevant costs. (p. 1049)

A2 Analyze a capital investment project using break-even time. (p. 1056)

PROCEDURAL

P1 Compute payback period and describe its use. (p. 1039)

P2 Compute accounting rate of return and explain its use. (p. 1041)

P3 Compute net present value and describe its use. (p. 1042)

P4 Compute internal rate of return and explain its use. (p. 1045)

Decision Insight

Sweet Success

"Put all of your love into your product."

—CHARLIE FYFFE

LOS ANGELES—Noticing long lines and an inadequate supply of sweets to satisfy his high school friends' cravings, Charlie Fyffe began making brownies and selling them at school. His brownies were an instant hit, and as his clientele and passion for baking grew, so did his desire to start his own business. "I started **Charlie's Brownies (CharliesBrownies.com)** because sweets make people happy and baking is a fun industry," explains Charlie. "I developed a quality original recipe and started selling brownies in simple cake boxes. Staying simple and consistent opened the door to a viable business."

After six months of professional baking classes to sharpen his skills, Charlie turned to the business side. "I had a lot to learn," admits Charlie. "I read entrepreneurial books and did internships to learn how to run a business. Becoming an entrepreneur was hard work, but it allows me a life of freedom outside the cubicle and the opportunity to pursue my dreams and visions." Charlie had to learn how to use accounting information to make important business decisions. For example, attention to contribution margins enables Charlie to decide if adding new product lines, like vegan and gluten-free brownies, would increase profits. Focusing on contribution margins, his own and his competition's, also helps Charlie decide whether to eliminate certain products because they are not profitable.

Charlie applies high standards to his production process. Unlike some companies that can rework substandard materials

into a viable product, Charlie explains that "raw materials that don't meet our standards never enter the baking process." Further, although expensive, exotic ingredients like "Chardonnay-infused sea salts create a pop and that undeniable urge to eat another brownie. It isn't heavy, and you want another one." Charlie has also managed to control overhead costs by doing much of the baking, marketing, and delivery himself. "I do whatever it takes to get the job done" he says. "There is never a dull moment!"

Much of Charlie's Brownies business is done online. To meet Charlie's goal of developing the company into a "nationwide and global Brownie Experience," he must increase the scale of his operations. Charlie sees food trucks and storefront locations as central to his vision, and explains that "we need to upgrade our space and add to our capacity." Assessing payback periods, rates of return, and net present values helps Charlie with these and other long-term capital budgeting decisions.

Charlie advises young entrepreneurs to follow their passion. "Hang out with other overachievers and young entrepreneurs to stay one step ahead," he says. "Stay focused, work hard, and seek guidance from other successful business people." Sounds like a recipe for success.

[Sources: *Charlie's Brownies* Website, January 2013; *JaredSurnamer.com*, August 2011; *PopularFinesse.tumblr.com*, October 2011; *Twentity.com*, February 2011.]

Making business decisions involves choosing between alternative courses of action. Many factors affect business decisions, yet analysis typically focuses on finding the alternative that offers the highest return on investment or the greatest reduction in costs. Some decisions are based on little more than an intuitive understanding of the situation because available information is too limited to allow a more systematic analysis. In other cases, intangible factors such as convenience, prestige, and environmental considerations are more important than strictly quantitative factors. In all situations, managers can reach a sounder decision if they identify the consequences of alternative choices in financial terms. This chapter explains several methods of analysis that can help managers make those business decisions.

Capital Budgeting		Managerial Decisions	
Nonpresent Value Methods	**Present Value Methods**	**Decisions and Information**	**Decision Scenarios**
• Payback period • Accounting rate of return	• Net present value • Internal rate of return • Comparison of methods	• Decision making • Relevant costs	• Additional business • Make or buy • Scrap or rework • Sell or process • Sales mix selection • Segment elimination • Keep or replace

Section 1—Capital Budgeting

The capital expenditures budget is management's plan for acquiring and selling plant assets. **Capital budgeting** is the process of analyzing alternative long-term investments and deciding which assets to acquire or sell. These decisions can involve developing a new product or process, buying a new machine or a new building, or acquiring an entire company. An objective for these decisions is to earn a satisfactory return on investment.

Capital budgeting decisions require careful analysis because they are usually the most difficult and risky decisions that managers make. These decisions are difficult because they require predicting events that will not occur until well into the future. Many of these predictions are tentative and potentially unreliable. Specifically, a capital budgeting decision is risky because (1) the outcome is uncertain, (2) large amounts of money are usually involved, (3) the investment involves a long-term commitment, and (4) the decision could be difficult or impossible to reverse, no matter how poor it turns out to be. Risk is especially high for investments in technology due to innovations and uncertainty.

Managers use several methods to evaluate capital budgeting decisions. Nearly all of these methods involve predicting cash inflows and cash outflows of proposed investments, assessing the risk of and returns on those flows, and then choosing the investments to make. Management often restates future cash flows in terms of their present value. This approach applies the time value of money: A dollar today is worth more than a dollar tomorrow. Similarly, a dollar tomorrow is worth less than a dollar today. The process of restating future cash flows in terms of their present value is called *discounting*. The time value of money is important when evaluating capital investments, but managers sometimes apply evaluation methods that ignore present value. This section describes four methods for comparing alternative investments.

Point: The nature of capital spending has changed with the business environment. Budgets for information technology have increased from about 25% of corporate capital spending 20 years ago to an estimated 35% today.

METHODS NOT USING TIME VALUE OF MONEY

All investments, whether they involve the purchase of a machine or another long-term asset, are expected to produce net cash flows. *Net cash flow* is cash inflows minus cash outflows. Sometimes managers perform simple analyses of the financial feasibility of an investment's net cash flow without using the time value of money. This section explains two of the most common methods in this category: (1) payback period and (2) accounting rate of return.

Payback Period

An investment's **payback period (PBP)** is the expected time period to recover the initial investment amount. Managers prefer investing in assets with shorter payback periods to reduce the risk of an unprofitable investment over the long run. Acquiring assets with short payback periods reduces a company's risk from potentially inaccurate long-term predictions of future cash flows.

P1 Compute payback period and describe its use.

Computing Payback Period with Even Cash Flows To illustrate use of the payback period for an investment with even cash flows, we look at data from FasTrac, a manufacturer of exercise equipment and supplies. (*Even cash flows* are cash flows that are the same each and every year; *uneven cash flows* are cash flows that are not all equal in amount.) FasTrac is considering several different capital investments, one of which is to purchase a machine to use in manufacturing a new product. This machine costs $16,000 and is expected to have an eight-year life with no salvage value. Management predicts this machine will produce 1,000 units of product each year and that the new product will be sold for $30 per unit. Exhibit 25.1 shows the expected annual net cash flows for this asset over its life as well as the expected annual revenues and expenses (including depreciation and income taxes) from investing in the machine.

EXHIBIT 25.1

Cash Flow Analysis

FASTRAC Cash Flow Analysis—Machinery Investment January 15, 2013		
	Expected Accrual Income	Expected Net Cash Flow
Annual sales of new product	$30,000	$30,000
Deduct annual expenses		
Cost of materials, labor, and overhead (except depreciation)	15,500	15,500
Depreciation—Machinery	2,000	
Additional selling and administrative expenses....................	9,500	9,500
Annual pretax accrual income	3,000	
Income taxes (30%)	900	900
Annual net income	$ 2,100	
Annual net cash flow		**$ 4,100**

The amount of net cash flow from the machinery is computed by subtracting expected cash outflows from expected cash inflows. The cash flows column of Exhibit 25.1 excludes all noncash revenues and expenses. Depreciation is FasTrac's only noncash item. Alternatively, managers can adjust the projected net income for revenue and expense items that do not affect cash flows. For FasTrac, this means taking the $2,100 net income and adding back the $2,000 depreciation.

The formula for computing the payback period of an investment that yields even net cash flows is in Exhibit 25.2.

Point: Annual net cash flow in Exhibit 25.1 equals net income plus depreciation (a noncash expense).

$$\text{Payback period} = \frac{\text{Cost of investment}}{\text{Annual net cash flow}}$$

EXHIBIT 25.2

Payback Period Formula with Even Cash Flows

The payback period reflects the amount of time for the investment to generate enough net cash flow to return (or pay back) the cash initially invested to purchase it. FasTrac's payback period for this machine is just under four years:

$$\text{Payback period} = \frac{\$16,000}{\$4,100} = 3.9 \text{ years}$$

Example: If an alternative machine (with different technology) yields a payback period of 3.5 years, which one does a manager choose? Answer: The alternative (3.5 is less than 3.9).

The initial investment is fully recovered in 3.9 years, or just before reaching the halfway point of this machine's useful life of eight years.

Decision Insight

e-Payback Health-care providers are increasingly using electronic systems to improve their operations. With *e-charting*, doctor's orders and notes are saved electronically. Such systems allow for more personalized care plans, more efficient staffing, and reduced costs. Investments in such systems must be evaluated on the basis of payback periods and other financial measures. ■

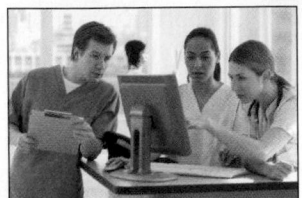

Computing Payback Period with Uneven Cash Flows Computing the payback period in the prior section assumed even net cash flows. What happens if the net cash flows are uneven? In this case, the payback period is computed using the *cumulative total of net cash flows*. The word *cumulative* refers to the addition of each period's net cash flows as we progress through time. To illustrate, consider data for another investment that FasTrac is considering. This machine is predicted to generate uneven net cash flows over the next eight years. The relevant data and payback period computation are shown in Exhibit 25.3.

EXHIBIT 25.3

Payback Period Calculation with Uneven Cash Flows

Period*	Expected Net Cash Flows	Cumulative Net Cash Flows
Year 0	$(16,000)	$(16,000)
Year 1	3,000	(13,000)
Year 2	4,000	(9,000)
Year 3............	4,000	(5,000)
Year 4	4,000	(1,000)
Year 5	5,000	4,000
Year 6	3,000	7,000
Year 7	2,000	9,000
Year 8	2,000	11,000
		Payback period = 4.2 years

* All cash inflows and outflows occur uniformly during the year.

Example: Find the payback period in Exhibit 25.3 if net cash flows for the first 4 years are:
Year 1 = $6,000; Year 2 = $5,000; Year 3 = $4,000; Year 4 = $3,000.
Answer: 3.33 years

Year 0 refers to the period of initial investment in which the $16,000 cash outflow occurs at the end of year 0 to acquire the machinery. By the end of year 1, the cumulative net cash flow is reduced to $(13,000), computed as the $(16,000) initial cash outflow plus year 1's $3,000 cash inflow. This process continues throughout the asset's life. The cumulative net cash flow amount changes from negative to positive in year 5. Specifically, at the end of year 4, the cumulative net cash flow is $(1,000). As soon as FasTrac receives net cash inflow of $1,000 during the fifth year, it has fully recovered the investment. If we assume that cash flows are received uniformly *within* each year, receipt of the $1,000 occurs about one-fifth of the way through the year. This is computed as $1,000 divided by year 5's total net cash flow of $5,000, or 0.20. This yields a payback period of 4.2 years, computed as 4 years plus 0.20 of year 5.

Using the Payback Period Companies desire a short payback period to increase return and reduce risk. The more quickly a company receives cash, the sooner it is available for other uses and the less time it is at risk of loss. A shorter payback period also improves the company's ability to respond to unanticipated changes and lowers its risk of having to keep an unprofitable investment.

Payback period should never be the only consideration in evaluating investments. This is so because it ignores at least two important factors. First, it fails to reflect differences in the timing of net cash flows within the payback period. In Exhibit 25.3, FasTrac's net cash flows in the first five years were $3,000, $4,000, $4,000, $4,000, and $5,000. If another investment had predicted cash flows of $9,000, $3,000, $2,000, $1,800, and $1,000 in these five years, its payback period would also be 4.2 years, but this second alternative could be more desirable because it provides cash more quickly. The second important factor is that the payback period ignores *all* cash flows after the point where its costs are fully recovered. For example, one investment might pay back its cost in 3 years but stop producing cash after 4 years. A second investment might require 5 years to pay back its cost yet continue to produce net cash flows for another 15 years. A focus on only the payback period would mistakenly lead management to choose the first investment over the second.

Quick Check

Answers — p. 1061

1. Capital budgeting is (a) concerned with analyzing alternative sources of capital, including debt and equity, (b) an important activity for companies when considering what assets to acquire or sell, or (c) best done by intuitive assessments of the value of assets and their usefulness.

2. Why are capital budgeting decisions often difficult?

3. A company is considering purchasing equipment costing $75,000. Future annual net cash flows from this equipment are $30,000, $25,000, $15,000, $10,000, and $5,000. The payback period is (a) 4 years, (b) 3.5 years, or (c) 3 years.

4. If depreciation is an expense, why is it added back to an investment's net income to compute the net cash flow from that investment?

5. If two investments have the same payback period, are they equally desirable? Explain.

Accounting Rate of Return

The **accounting rate of return,** also called *return on average investment*, is computed by dividing a project's after-tax net income by the average amount invested in it. To illustrate, we return to FasTrac's $16,000 machinery investment described in Exhibit 25.1. We first compute (1) the after-tax net income and (2) the average amount invested. The $2,100 after-tax net income is already available from Exhibit 25.1.

If a company uses straight-line depreciation, we can find the average amount invested by using the formula in Exhibit 25.4. Because FasTrac uses straight-line depreciation, its average amount invested for the eight years equals the sum of the book value at the beginning of the asset's investment period and the book value at the end of its investment period, divided by 2, as shown in Exhibit 25.4.

P2 Compute accounting rate of return and explain its use.

Point: Amount invested includes all costs that must be incurred to get the asset in its location and ready for use.

$$\text{Annual average investment} = \frac{\text{Beginning book value} + \text{Ending book value}}{2}$$
(straight-line case only)
$$= \frac{\$16,000 + \$0}{2} = \$8,000$$

EXHIBIT 25.4

Computing Average Amount Invested under Straight-Line Depreciation

If an investment has a salvage value, the average amount invested when using straight-line depreciation is computed as (Beginning book value + Salvage value)/2.

If a company uses a depreciation method other than straight-line, the calculation of average book value is more complicated. In this case, the book value of the asset is computed for *each year* of its life. The general formula for the annual average investment is shown in Exhibit 25.5.

$$\text{Annual average investment} = \frac{\text{Sum of individual years' average book values}}{\text{Number of years of the planned investment}}$$
(general case)

EXHIBIT 25.5

General Formula for Average Amount Invested

Once we determine the after-tax net income and the average amount invested, the accounting rate of return on the investment can be computed from the annual after-tax net income divided by the average amount invested, as shown in Exhibit 25.6.

EXHIBIT 25.6

Accounting Rate of Return Formula

$$\text{Accounting rate of return} = \frac{\text{Annual after-tax net income}}{\text{Annual average investment}}$$

This yields an accounting rate of return of 26.25% ($2,100/$8,000). FasTrac management must decide whether a 26.25% accounting rate of return is satisfactory. To make this decision, we must factor in the investment's risk. For instance, we cannot say an investment with a 26.25% return is preferred over one with a lower return unless we consider any differences in risk. Thus, an investment's return is satisfactory or unsatisfactory only when it is related to returns from other investments with similar lives and risk.

When accounting rate of return is used to choose among capital investments, the one with the least risk, the shortest payback period, and the highest return for the longest time period is often identified as the best. However, use of accounting rate of return to evaluate investment opportunities is limited because it bases the amount invested on book values (not predicted market values) in future periods. Accounting rate of return is also limited when an asset's net incomes are expected to vary from year to year. This requires computing the rate using *average* annual net incomes, yet this accounting rate of return fails to distinguish between two investments with the same average annual net income but different amounts of income in early years versus later years or different levels of income variability.

Quick Check
Answers — p. 1062

6. The following data relate to a company's decision on whether to purchase a machine:

Cost	$180,000
Salvage value	15,000
Annual after-tax net income	40,000

The machine's accounting rate of return, assuming the even receipt of its net cash flows during the year and use of straight-line depreciation, is (a) 22%, (b) 41%, or (c) 21%.

7. Is a 15% accounting rate of return for a machine a good rate?

METHODS USING TIME VALUE OF MONEY

Methods using Time Value of Money

P3 Compute net present value and describe its use.

This section describes two methods that help managers with capital budgeting decisions and that use the time value of money: (1) net present value and (2) internal rate of return. *(To apply these methods, you need a basic understanding of the concept of present value. An expanded explanation of present value concepts is in Appendix B near the end of the book. You can use the present value tables at the end of Appendix B to solve many of this chapter's assignments that use the time value of money.)*

Net Present Value

Net present value analysis applies the time value of money to future cash inflows and cash outflows so management can evaluate a project's benefits and costs at one point in time. Specifically, **net present value (NPV)** is computed by discounting the future net cash flows from the investment at the project's required rate of return and then subtracting the initial amount invested. A company's required return, often called its hurdle rate, is typically its **cost of capital**, which is the rate the company must pay to its long-term creditors and shareholders.

To illustrate, let's return to FasTrac's proposed machinery purchase described in Exhibit 25.1. Does this machine provide a satisfactory return while recovering the amount invested? Recall that the machine requires a $16,000 investment and is expected to provide $4,100 annual net cash inflows for the next eight years. If we assume that net cash flows from this machine are received at each year-end and that FasTrac requires a 12% annual return, net present value can be computed as in Exhibit 25.7.

	Net Cash Flows*	Present Value of 1 at 12%[†]	Present Value of Net Cash Flows
Year 1	$ 4,100	0.8929	$ 3,661
Year 2	4,100	0.7972	3,269
Year 3	4,100	0.7118	2,918
Year 4	4,100	0.6355	2,606
Year 5	4,100	0.5674	2,326
Year 6	4,100	0.5066	2,077
Year 7	4,100	0.4523	1,854
Year 8	4,100	0.4039	1,656
Totals	$32,800		20,367
Amount invested			(16,000)
Net present value			$ 4,367

EXHIBIT 25.7

Net Present Value Calculation with Equal Cash Flows

* Cash flows occur at the end of each year.

[†] Present value of 1 factors are taken from Table B.1 in Appendix B.

The first number column of Exhibit 25.7 shows the annual net cash flows. Present value of 1 factors, also called *discount factors,* are shown in the second column. Taken from Table B.1 in Appendix B, they assume that net cash flows are received at each year-end. *(To simplify present value computations and for assignment material at the end of this chapter, we assume that net cash flows are received at each year-end.)* Annual net cash flows from the first column of Exhibit 25.7 are multiplied by the discount factors in the second column to give present values shown in the third column. The last three lines of this exhibit show the final NPV computations. The asset's $16,000 initial cost is deducted from the $20,367 total present value of all future net cash flows to give this asset's NPV of $4,367. The machine is thus expected to (1) recover its cost, (2) provide a 12% compounded return, and (3) generate $4,367 above cost. We summarize this analysis by saying the present value of this machine's future net cash flows to FasTrac exceeds the $16,000 investment by $4,367.

Point: The assumption of end-of-year cash flows simplifies computations and is common in practice.

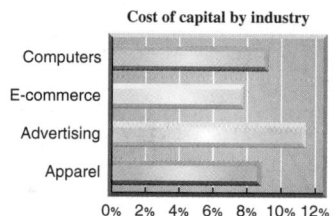

Cost of capital by industry

Example: What is the net present value in Exhibit 25.7 if a 10% return is applied? *Answer:* $5,873

Net Present Value Decision Rule   The decision rule in applying NPV is as follows: When an asset's expected cash flows are discounted at the required rate and yield a *positive* net present value, the asset should be acquired. This decision rule is reflected in the graphic below. When comparing several investment opportunities of about the same cost and same risk, we prefer the one with the highest positive net present value.

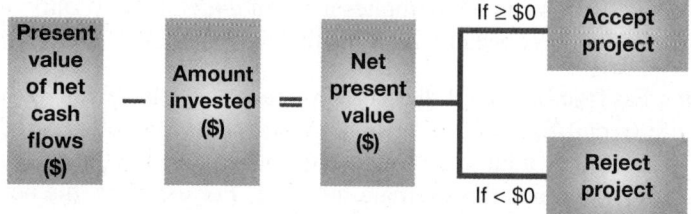

Simplifying Computations   The computations in Exhibit 25.7 use separate present value of 1 factors for each of the eight years. Each year's net cash flow is multiplied by its present value of 1 factor to determine its present value. The individual present values for each of the eight net cash flows are added to give the asset's total present value. This computation can be simplified in two ways if annual net cash flows are equal in amount. A series of cash flows of equal dollar amount is called an **annuity.** One way is to add the eight annual present value of 1 factors for a total of 4.9676 and multiply this amount by the annual $4,100 net cash flow to get the $20,367 total present value of net cash flows.[1] A second simplification is to use a calculator

Example: Why does the net present value of an investment increase when a lower discount rate is used? *Answer:* The present value of net cash flows increases.

---

[1] We can simplify this computation using Table B.3, which gives the present value of 1 to be received periodically for a number of periods. To determine the present value of these eight annual receipts discounted at 12%, go down the 12% column of Table B.3 to the factor on the eighth line. This cumulative discount factor, also known as an *annuity* factor, is 4.9676. We then compute the $20,367 present value for these eight annual $4,100 receipts, computed as 4.9676 × $4,100.

with compound interest functions or a spreadsheet program. We show how to use Excel functions to compute net present value in this chapter's Appendix. Whatever procedure you use, it is important to understand the concepts behind these computations.

■ **Decision Ethics**

Systems Manager   Top management adopts a policy requiring purchases in excess of $5,000 to be submitted with cash flow projections to the cost analyst for capital budget approval. As systems manager, you want to upgrade your computers at a $25,000 cost. You consider submitting several orders all under $5,000 to avoid the approval process. You believe the computers will increase profits and wish to avoid a delay. What do you do? ■   [Answer—p. 1061]

Uneven Cash Flows   Net present value analysis can also be applied when net cash flows are uneven (unequal). To illustrate, assume that FasTrac can choose only one capital investment from among projects A, B, and C. Each project requires the same $12,000 initial investment. Future net cash flows for each project are shown in the first three number columns of Exhibit 25.8.

EXHIBIT 25.8

Net Present Value Calculation with Uneven Cash Flows

	Net Cash Flows			Present Value of 1 at 10%	Present Value of Net Cash Flows		
	A	**B**	**C**		**A**	**B**	**C**
Year 1...............	$ 5,000	$ 8,000	$ 1,000	0.9091	$ 4,546	$ 7,273	$ 909
Year 2...............	5,000	5,000	5,000	0.8264	4,132	4,132	4,132
Year 3...............	5,000	2,000	9,000	0.7513	3,757	1,503	6,762
Totals	$15,000	$15,000	$15,000		12,435	12,908	11,803
Amount invested					(12,000)	(12,000)	(12,000)
Net present value					$ 435	$ 908	$ (197)

Example: If 12% is the required return in Exhibit 25.8, which project is preferred? *Answer:* Project B. Net present values are: A = $10; B = $553; C = $(715).

Example: Will the rankings of Projects A, B, and C change with the use of different discount rates, assuming the same rate is used for all projects? *Answer:* No; only the NPV amounts will change.

Point: Projects with higher cash flows in earlier years generally yield higher net present values.

The three projects in Exhibit 25.8 have the same expected total net cash flows of $15,000. Project A is expected to produce equal amounts of $5,000 each year. Project B is expected to produce a larger amount in the first year. Project C is expected to produce a larger amount in the third year. The fourth column of Exhibit 25.8 shows the present value of 1 factors from Table B.1 assuming 10% required return.

Computations in the right-most columns show that Project A has a $435 positive NPV. Project B has the largest NPV of $908 because it brings in cash more quickly. Project C has a $(197) *negative* NPV because its larger cash inflows are delayed. If FasTrac requires a 10% return, it should reject Project C because its NPV implies a return *under* 10%. If only one project can be accepted, project B appears best because it yields the highest NPV.

Salvage Value   FasTrac predicted the $16,000 machine to have zero salvage value at the end of its useful life (recall Exhibit 25.1). In many cases, assets are expected to have salvage values. If so, this amount is an additional net cash inflow received at the end of the final year of the asset's life. All other computations remain the same. For example, the net present value of the $16,000 investment that yields $4,100 of net cash flows for eight years is $4,367, as shown in Exhibit 25.7. If that machine is expected to have a $1,500 salvage value at the end of its eight-year life, the present value of this salvage amount is $606 (computed as $1,500 × 0.4039). The net present value of the machine, including the present value of its expected salvage amount, is $4,973 (computed as $4,367 + $606).

Accelerated Depreciation   Depreciation computations also affect net present value analysis. FasTrac computes depreciation using the straight-line method. Accelerated depreciation is also commonly used, especially for income tax reports. Accelerated depreciation produces larger depreciation deductions in the early years of an asset's life and smaller deductions in later years. This pattern results in smaller income tax payments in early years and larger payments in later years. Accelerated depreciation does not change the basics of a present value analysis, but it can change the result. Using accelerated depreciation for tax reporting affects the NPV of an asset's cash flows because it produces larger net cash inflows in the early years

Point: Tax savings from depreciation is called: **depreciation tax shield.**

of the asset's life and smaller ones in later years. Being able to use accelerated depreciation for tax reporting always makes an investment more desirable because early cash flows are more valuable than later ones.

Use of Net Present Value   In deciding whether to proceed with a capital investment project, we approve the proposal if the NPV is positive but reject it if the NPV is negative. When considering several projects of similar investment amounts and risk levels, we can compare the different projects' NPVs and rank them on the basis of their NPVs. However, if the amount invested differs substantially across projects, the NPV is of limited value for comparison purposes. One means to compare projects, especially when a company cannot fund all positive net present value projects, is to use the **profitability index,** which is computed as:

Example: When is it appropriate to use different discount rates for different projects? *Answer:* When risk levels are different.

$$\text{Profitability index} = \frac{\text{Net present value of cash flows}}{\text{Investment}}$$

A higher profitability index suggests a more desirable project. To illustrate, suppose that Project X requires a $1 million investment and provides a $100,000 NPV. Project Y requires an investment of only $100,000 and returns a $75,000 NPV. Ranking on the basis of NPV puts Project X ahead of Y, yet X's profitability index is only 0.10 ($100,000/$1,000,000) whereas Y's profitability index is 0.75. We must also remember that when reviewing projects with different risks, we computed the NPV of individual projects using different discount rates. The higher the risk, the higher the discount rate.

Inflation   Large price-level increases should be considered in NPV analyses. Hurdle rates should already include inflation forecasts. Net cash flows can be adjusted for inflation by using *future value* computations. For example, if the expected net cash inflow in year 1 is $4,100 and 5% inflation is expected, then the expected net cash inflow in year 2 is $4,305, computed as $4,100 × 1.05 (1.05 is the future value of $1 (Table B.2) for 1 period with a 5% rate).

Internal Rate of Return

Another means to evaluate capital investments is to use the **internal rate of return (IRR),** which equals the rate that yields an NPV of zero for an investment. This means that if we compute the total present value of a project's net cash flows using the IRR as the discount rate and then subtract the initial investment from this total present value, we get a zero NPV.

P4 Compute internal rate of return and explain its use.

To illustrate, we use the data for FasTrac's Project A from Exhibit 25.8 to compute its IRR. Exhibit 25.9 shows the two-step process in computing IRR.

EXHIBIT 25.9

Computing Internal Rate of Return (with even cash flows)

Step 1: Compute the present value factor for the investment project.

$$\text{Present value factor} = \frac{\text{Amount invested}}{\text{Net cash flows}} = \frac{\$12,000}{\$5,000} = 2.4000$$

Step 2: Identify the discount rate (IRR) yielding the present value factor

Search Table B.3 for a present value factor of 2.4000 in the three-year row (equaling the 3-year project duration). The 12% discount rate yields a present value factor of 2.4018. This implies that the IRR is approximately 12%.*

* Since the present value factor of 2.4000 is not exactly equal to the 12% factor of 2.4018, we can more precisely estimate the IRR as follows:

Discount rate	Present Value Factor from Table B.3
12%	2.4018
15%	2.2832
	0.1186 = difference

Then, $\text{IRR} = 12\% + \left[(15\% - 12\%) \times \dfrac{2.4018 - 2.4000}{0.1186} \right] = \underline{\underline{12.05\%}}$

When cash flows are equal, as with Project A, we compute the present value factor (as shown in Exhibit 25.9) by dividing the initial investment by its annual net cash flows. We then use an annuity table to determine the discount rate equal to this present value factor. For FasTrac's Project A, we look across the three-period row of Table B.3 and find that the discount rate corresponding to the present value factor of 2.4000 roughly equals the 2.4018 value for the 12% rate. This row is reproduced here:

| | Present Value of an Annuity of 1 for Three Periods | | | | |
| | | | Discount Rate | | |
Periods	1%	5%	10%	12%	15%
3	2.9410	2.7232	2.4869	2.4018	2.2832

The 12% rate is the Project's IRR. A more precise IRR estimate can be computed following the procedure shown in the note to Exhibit 25.9. Spreadsheet software and calculators can also compute this IRR. We show how to use an Excel function to compute IRR in this chapter's appendix.

Uneven Cash Flows   If net cash flows are uneven, we must use trial and error to compute the IRR. We do this by selecting any reasonable discount rate and computing the NPV. If the amount is positive (negative), we recompute the NPV using a higher (lower) discount rate. We continue these steps until we reach a point where two consecutive computations result in NPVs having different signs (positive and negative). Because the NPV is zero using IRR, we know that the IRR lies between these two discount rates. We can then estimate its value. Spreadsheet programs and calculators can also do these computations.

Decision Insight

CEO-IRR   A survey reported that 41% of top managers would reject a project with an internal rate of return *above* the cost of capital *if* the project would cause the firm to miss its earnings forecast. The roles of benchmarks and manager compensation plans must be considered in capital budgeting decisions. ■

Use of Internal Rate of Return   When we use the IRR to evaluate a project, we compare it to a predetermined **hurdle rate,** which is a minimum acceptable rate of return and is applied as follows.

Example: How can management evaluate the risk of an investment? *Answer:* It must assess the uncertainty of future cash flows.

Top management selects the hurdle rate to use in evaluating capital investments. Financial formulas aid in this selection, but the choice of a minimum rate is subjective and left to management. For projects financed from borrowed funds, the hurdle rate must exceed the interest rate paid on these funds. The return on an investment must cover its interest and provide an additional profit to reward the company for its risk. For instance, if money is borrowed at 10%, an average risk investment often requires an after-tax return of 15% (or 5% above the borrowing rate). Remember that lower-risk investments require a lower rate of return compared with higher-risk investments.

If the project is internally financed, the hurdle rate is often based on actual returns from comparable projects. If the IRR is higher than the hurdle rate, the project is accepted. Multiple projects are often ranked by the extent to which their IRR exceeds the hurdle rate. The hurdle rate for individual projects is often different, depending on the risk involved. IRR is not subject to the limitations of NPV when comparing projects with different amounts invested because the IRR is expressed as a percent rather than as an absolute dollar value in NPV.

Decision Maker

Entrepreneur You are developing a new product and you use a 12% discount rate to compute its NPV. Your banker, from whom you hope to obtain a loan, expresses concern that your discount rate is too low. How do you respond? ■ [Answer—p. 1061]

Comparison of Capital Budgeting Methods

We explained four methods that managers use to evaluate capital investment projects. How do these methods compare with each other? Exhibit 25.10 addresses that question. Neither the payback period nor the accounting rate of return considers the time value of money. On the other hand, both the net present value and the internal rate of return do.

EXHIBIT 25.10

Comparing Capital Budgeting Methods

	Payback Period	Accounting Rate of Return	Net Present Value	Internal Rate of Return
Measurement basis	● Cash flows	● Accrual income	● Cash flows ● Profitability	● Cash flows ● Profitability
Measurement unit	● Years	● Percent	● Dollars	● Percent
Strengths	● Easy to understand	● Easy to understand	● Reflects time value of money	● Reflects time value of money
	● Allows comparison of projects	● Allows comparison of projects	● Reflects varying risks over project's life	● Allows comparisons of dissimilar projects
Limitations	● Ignores time value of money	● Ignores time value of money	● Difficult to compare dissimilar projects	● Ignores varying risks over life of project
	● Ignores cash flows after payback period	● Ignores annual rates over life of project		

The payback period is probably the simplest method. It gives managers an estimate of how soon they will recover their initial investment. Managers sometimes use this method when they have limited cash to invest and a number of projects to choose from. The accounting rate of return yields a percent measure computed using accrual income instead of cash flows. The accounting rate of return is an average rate for the entire investment period. Net present value considers all estimated net cash flows for the project's expected life. It can be applied to even and uneven cash flows and can reflect changes in the level of risk over a project's life. Since it yields a dollar measure, comparing projects of unequal sizes is more difficult. The profitability index, based on each project's net present value, can be used in this case. The internal rate of return considers all cash flows from a project. It is readily computed when the cash flows are even but requires some trial and error or use of a computer estimation when cash flows are uneven. Because the IRR is a percent measure, it is readily used to compare projects with different investment amounts. However, IRR does not reflect changes in risk over a project's life.

Decision Insight

And the Winner Is . . . How do we choose among the methods for evaluating capital investments? Management surveys consistently show the internal rate of return (IRR) as the most popular method followed by the payback period and net present value (NPV). Few companies use the accounting rate of return (ARR), but nearly all use more than one method. ■

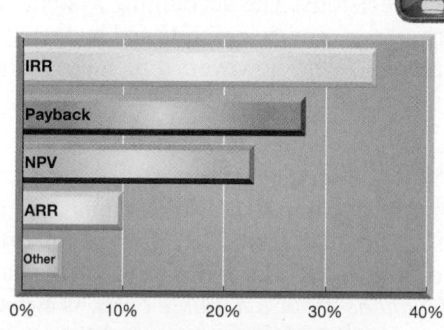

Company Usage of Capital Budgeting Methods

Quick Check   Answers — p. 1062

8. A company can invest in only one of two projects, A or B. Each project requires a $20,000 investment and is expected to generate end-of-period, annual cash flows as follows:

	Year 1	Year 2	Year 3	Total
Project A	$12,000	$8,500	$4,000	$24,500
Project B	4,500	8,500	13,000	26,000

Assuming a discount rate of 10%, which project has the higher net present value?

9. Two investment alternatives are expected to generate annual cash flows with the same net present value (assuming the same discount rate applied to each). Using this information, can you conclude that the two alternatives are equally desirable?

10. When two investment alternatives have the same total expected cash flows but differ in the timing of those flows, which method of evaluating those investments is superior, (a) accounting rate of return or (b) net present value?

Section 2—Managerial Decisions

This section focuses on methods that use accounting information to make several important managerial decisions. Most of these involve short-term decisions. This differs from methods used for longer-term managerial decisions that are described in the first section of this chapter and in several other chapters of this book.

DECISIONS AND INFORMATION

This section explains how managers make decisions and the information relevant to those decisions.

Decision Making

Managerial decision making involves five steps: (1) define the decision task, (2) identify alternative courses of action, (3) collect relevant information and evaluate each alternative, (4) select the preferred course of action, and (5) analyze and assess decisions made. These five steps are illustrated in Exhibit 25.11.

EXHIBIT 25.11

Managerial Decision Making

| Define Task and Goal | Identify Alternative Actions | Collect Relevant Information | Select Course of Action | Analyze and Assess Decision |

Both managerial and financial accounting information play an important role in most management decisions. The accounting system is expected to provide primarily *financial* information such as performance reports and budget analyses for decision making. *Nonfinancial* information is also relevant, however; it includes information on environmental effects, political sensitivities, and social responsibility.

Relevant Costs

C1 Describe the importance of relevant costs for short-term decisions.

Most financial measures of revenues and costs from accounting systems are based on historical costs. Although historical costs are important and useful for many tasks such as product pricing and the control and monitoring of business activities, we sometimes find that an analysis of *relevant costs,* or *avoidable costs,* is especially useful. Three types of costs are pertinent to our discussion of relevant costs: sunk costs, out-of-pocket costs, and opportunity costs.

A *sunk cost* arises from a past decision and cannot be avoided or changed; it is irrelevant to future decisions. An example is the cost of computer equipment previously purchased by a company. Most of a company's allocated costs, including fixed overhead items such as depreciation and administrative expenses, are sunk costs.

An *out-of-pocket cost* requires a future outlay of cash and is relevant for current and future decision making. These costs are usually the direct result of management's decisions. For instance, future purchases of computer equipment involve out-of-pocket costs. Depreciation and amortization are allocations of the original cost of plant and intangible assets. They are sunk costs, not out-of-pocket costs.

An *opportunity cost* is the potential benefit lost by taking a specific action when two or more alternative choices are available. An example is a student giving up wages from a job to attend summer school. Companies continually must choose from alternative courses of action. For instance, a company making standardized products might be approached by a customer to supply a special (nonstandard) product. A decision to accept or reject the special order must consider not only the profit to be made from the special order but also the profit given up by devoting time and resources to this order instead of pursuing an alternative project. The profit given up is an opportunity cost. Consideration of opportunity costs is important. The implications extend to internal resource allocation decisions. For instance, a computer manufacturer must decide between internally manufacturing a chip versus buying it externally. In another case, management of a multidivisional company must decide whether to continue operating or close a particular division.

"Sunk costs are not relevant to my decision."

"I must consider out-of-pocket and opportunity costs."

Point: Opportunity costs are not entered in accounting records. This does not reduce their relevance for managerial decisions.

Besides relevant costs, management must also consider the relevant benefits associated with a decision. **Relevant benefits** refer to the additional or *incremental* revenue generated by selecting a particular course of action over another. For instance, a student must decide the relevant benefits of taking one course over another. In sum, both relevant costs and relevant benefits are crucial to managerial decision making.

MANAGERIAL DECISION SCENARIOS

Managers experience many different scenarios that require analyzing alternative actions and making a decision. We describe several different types of decision scenarios in this section. We set these tasks in the context of FasTrac, an exercise supplies and equipment manufacturer introduced earlier. *We treat each of these decision tasks as separate from each other.*

A1 Evaluate short-term managerial decisions using relevant costs.

Additional Business

FasTrac is operating at its normal level of 80% of full capacity. At this level, it produces and sells approximately 100,000 units of product annually. Its per unit and annual total sales and costs are shown in Exhibit 25.12.

	Per Unit	Annual Total
Sales (100,000 units)	$10.00	$1,000,000
Direct materials	(3.50)	(350,000)
Direct labor	(2.20)	(220,000)
Overhead	(1.10)	(110,000)
Selling expenses	(1.40)	(140,000)
Administrative expenses	(0.80)	(80,000)
Total costs and expenses	(9.00)	(900,000)
Operating income	$ 1.00	$ 100,000

EXHIBIT 25.12

Selected Operating Income Data

A current buyer of FasTrac's products wants to purchase additional units of its product and export them to another country. This buyer offers to buy 10,000 units of the product at $8.50 per unit, or $1.50 less than the current price. The offer price is low, but FasTrac is considering the proposal because this sale would be several times larger than any single previous sale and it would use idle capacity. Also, the units will be exported, so this new business will not affect current sales.

To determine whether to accept or reject this order, management needs to know whether accepting the offer will increase net income. The analysis in Exhibit 25.13 shows that if management relies incorrectly on per unit historical costs, it would reject the sale because the selling price ($8.50) per unit is less than the total costs per unit ($9.00), and it thus yields a loss. However, historical costs are *not* relevant to this decision. Instead, the relevant costs are the additional costs, called **incremental costs.** These costs, also called *differential costs,* are the additional costs incurred if a company pursues a certain course of action. FasTrac's incremental costs are those related to the added volume that this new order would bring.

EXHIBIT 25.13

Analysis of Additional Business Using Historical Costs

	Per Unit	Total
Sales (10,000 additional units)	$ 8.50	$ 85,000
Total costs and expenses	(9.00)	(90,000)
Operating loss	$(0.50)	$(5,000)

To correctly make its decision, FasTrac must analyze the costs of this new business in a different manner. The following information regarding the order is available:

- Manufacturing 10,000 additional units requires direct materials of $3.50 per unit and direct labor of $2.20 per unit (same as for all other units).
- Manufacturing 10,000 additional units adds $5,000 of incremental overhead costs for power, packaging, and indirect labor (all variable costs).
- Incremental commissions and selling expenses from this sale of 10,000 additional units would be $2,000 (all variable costs).
- Incremental administrative expenses of $1,000 for clerical efforts are needed (all fixed costs) with the sale of 10,000 additional units.

We use this information, as shown in Exhibit 25.14, to assess how accepting this new business will affect FasTrac's income.

EXHIBIT 25.14

Analysis of Additional Business Using Relevant Costs

	Additional Business	Current Business	Combined
Sales	$ 85,000	$1,000,000	$1,085,000
Direct materials	(35,000)	(350,000)	(385,000)
Direct labor	(22,000)	(220,000)	(242,000)
Overhead	(5,000)	(110,000)	(115,000)
Selling expenses	(2,000)	(140,000)	(142,000)
Administrative expense	(1,000)	(80,000)	(81,000)
Total costs and expenses	(65,000)	(900,000)	(965,000)
Operating income	$ 20,000	$ 100,000	$ 120,000

The analysis of relevant costs in Exhibit 25.14 suggests that the additional business be accepted. It would provide $85,000 of added revenue while incurring only $65,000 of added costs. This would yield $20,000 of additional pretax income, or a pretax profit margin of 23.5%. More generally, FasTrac would increase its income with any price that exceeded $6.50 per unit ($65,000 incremental cost/10,000 additional units). The key point is that *management must not blindly use historical costs, especially allocated overhead costs.* Instead, the accounting system needs to provide information about the incremental costs to be incurred if the additional business is accepted.

Other Factors   An analysis of the incremental costs pertaining to the additional volume is always relevant for this type of decision. We must proceed cautiously, however, when the additional volume approaches or exceeds the factory's existing available capacity. If the additional volume requires the company to expand its capacity by obtaining more equipment, more space, or more personnel, the incremental costs could quickly exceed the incremental revenue. Another cautionary note is the effect on existing sales. All new units of the extra business will be sold outside FasTrac's normal domestic sales channels. If accepting additional business would cause existing sales to decline, this information must be included in our analysis. The contribution margin lost from a decline in sales is an opportunity cost. If future cash flows over several time periods are affected, their net present value also must be computed and used in this analysis.

Example: Exhibit 25.14 uses quantitative information. Suggest some qualitative factors to be considered when deciding whether to accept this project. *Answer:* (1) Impact on relationships with other customers and (2) Improved relationship with customer buying additional units.

Decision Maker

Partner   You are a partner in a small accounting firm that specializes in keeping the books and preparing taxes for clients. A local restaurant is interested in obtaining these services from your firm. Identify factors that are relevant in deciding whether to accept the engagement. ■   [Answer   p. 1061]

Make or Buy

The managerial decision to make or buy a component for one of its current products is common and depends on incremental costs. To illustrate, FasTrac has excess productive capacity it can use to manufacture Part 417, a component of the main product it sells. The part is currently purchased and delivered to the plant at a cost of $1.20 per unit. FasTrac estimates that making Part 417 would cost $0.45 for direct materials, $0.50 for direct labor, and an undetermined amount for overhead. The task is to determine how much overhead to add to these costs so we can decide whether to make or buy Part 417. If FasTrac's normal predetermined overhead application rate is 100% of direct labor cost, we might be tempted to conclude that overhead cost is $0.50 per unit, computed as 100% of the $0.50 direct labor cost. We would then mistakenly conclude that total cost is $1.45 per unit ($0.45 of materials + $0.50 of labor + $0.50 of overhead). A wrong decision in this case would be to conclude that the company is better off buying the part at $1.20 each than making it for $1.45 each.

Instead, as we explained earlier, only incremental overhead costs are relevant in this situation. Thus, we must compute an *incremental overhead rate*. Incremental overhead costs might include, for example, additional power for operating machines, extra supplies, added cleanup costs, materials handling, and quality control. We can prepare a per unit analysis in this case as shown in Exhibit 25.15.

	Make	Buy
Direct materials	$0.45	—
Direct labor	0.50	—
Overhead costs	[?]	—
Purchase price	—	$1.20
Total incremental costs	$0.95 + [?]	$1.20

EXHIBIT 25.15

Make or Buy Analysis

We can see that if incremental overhead costs are less than $0.25 per unit, ($1.20 − $0.95) the total cost of making the component is less than the purchase price of $1.20 and FasTrac should make the part. FasTrac's decision rule in this case is that any amount of overhead less than $0.25 per unit yields a total cost for Part 417 that is less than the $1.20 purchase price. FasTrac must consider several nonfinancial factors in the make or buy decision, including product quality, timeliness of delivery (especially in a just-in-time setting), reactions of customers and suppliers, and other intangibles such as employee morale and workload. It must also consider whether making the part requires incremental fixed costs to expand plant capacity. When these added factors are considered, small cost differences may not matter.

Decision Insight

Make or Buy IT   Companies apply make or buy decisions to their services. Many now outsource their information technology activities. Information technology companies provide infrastructure and services to enable businesses to focus on their key activities. It is argued that outsourcing saves money and streamlines operations, and without the headaches. ■

Scrap or Rework

Managers often must make a decision on whether to scrap or rework products in process. Remember that costs already incurred in manufacturing the units of a product that do not meet quality standards are sunk costs that have been incurred and cannot be changed. Sunk costs are irrelevant in any decision on whether to sell the substandard units as scrap or to rework them to meet quality standards.

To illustrate, assume that FasTrac has 10,000 defective units of a product that have already cost $1 per unit to manufacture. These units can be sold as is (as scrap) for $0.40 each, or they can be reworked for $0.80 per unit and then sold for their full price of $1.50 each. Should FasTrac sell the units as scrap or rework them?

To make this decision, management must recognize that the already incurred manufacturing costs of $1 per unit are sunk (unavoidable). These costs are *entirely irrelevant* to the decision. In addition, we must be certain that all costs of reworking defects, including interfering with normal operations, are accounted for in our analysis. For instance, reworking the defects means that FasTrac is unable to manufacture 10,000 *new* units with an incremental cost of $1 per unit and a selling price of $1.50 per unit, meaning it incurs an *opportunity cost* equal to the lost $5,000 net return from making and selling 10,000 new units. This opportunity cost is the difference between the $15,000 revenue (10,000 units × $1.50) from selling these new units and their $10,000 manufacturing costs (10,000 units × $1). Our analysis is reflected in Exhibit 25.16.

EXHIBIT 25.16

Scrap or Rework Analysis

	Scrap	Rework
Sale of scrapped/reworked units (10,000 units)	$ 4,000	$ 15,000
Less out-of-pocket costs to rework defects ($0.80 per unit)		(8,000)
Less opportunity cost of not making new units		**(5,000)**
Incremental net income	**$4,000**	**$ 2,000**

The analysis yields a $2,000 difference in favor of scrapping the defects, yielding a total incremental net income of $4,000. If we had failed to include the opportunity costs of $5,000, the rework option would have shown an income of $7,000 instead of $2,000, mistakenly making reworking appear more favorable than scrapping.

Quick Check   Answers — p. 1062

11. A company receives a special order for 200 units that requires stamping the buyer's name on each unit, yielding an additional fixed cost of $400 to its normal costs. Without the order, the company is operating at 75% of capacity and produces 7,500 units of product at the following costs:

Direct materials	$37,500
Direct labor	60,000
Overhead (30% variable)	20,000
Selling expenses (60% variable)	25,000

The special order will not affect normal unit sales and will not increase fixed overhead and selling expenses. Variable selling expenses on the special order are reduced to one-half the normal amount. The price per unit necessary to earn $1,000 on this order is (a) $14.80, (b) $15.80, (c) $19.80, (d) $20.80, or (e) $21.80.

12. What are the incremental costs of accepting additional business?

Sell or Process

The managerial decision to sell partially completed products as is or to process them further for sale depends significantly on relevant costs. To illustrate, suppose that FasTrac has 40,000 units of partially finished Product Q. It has already spent $0.75 per unit to manufacture these 40,000 units at a $30,000 total cost. FasTrac can sell the 40,000 units to another manufacturer as raw material for $50,000. Alternatively, it can process them further and produce finished products X, Y, and Z at an incremental cost of $2 per unit. The added processing yields the products and revenues shown in Exhibit 25.17. FasTrac must decide whether the added revenues from selling finished products X, Y, and Z exceed the costs of finishing them.

EXHIBIT 25.17

Revenues from
Processing Further

Product	Price	Units	Revenues
Product X	$4.00	10,000	$ 40,000
Product Y..........	6.00	22,000	132,000
Product Z	8.00	6,000	48,000
Spoilage	—	2,000	0
Totals		40,000	$220,000

Exhibit 25.18 shows the two-step analysis for this decision. First, FasTrac computes its incremental revenue from further processing Q into products X, Y, and Z. This amount is the difference between the $220,000 revenue from the further processed products and the $50,000 FasTrac will give up by not selling Q as is (a $50,000 opportunity cost). Second, FasTrac computes its incremental costs from further processing Q into X, Y, and Z. This amount is $80,000 (40,000 units × $2 incremental cost). The analysis shows that FasTrac can earn incremental net income of $90,000 from a decision to further process Q. (Notice that the earlier incurred $30,000 manufacturing cost for the 40,000 units of Product Q does not appear in Exhibit 25.18 because it is a sunk cost and as such is irrelevant to the decision.)

Example: Does the decision change if incremental costs in Exhibit 25.18 increase to $4 per unit and the opportunity cost increases to $95,000? *Answer:* Yes. There is now an incremental net loss of $35,000.

EXHIBIT 25.18

Sell or Process Analysis

Revenue if processed...............	$220,000
Revenue if sold as is................	(50,000)
Incremental revenue	170,000
Incremental cost to process	(80,000)
Incremental net income	**$ 90,000**

Quick Check

Answers — p. 1062

13. A company has already incurred a $1,000 cost in partially producing its four products. Their selling prices when partially and fully processed follow with additional costs necessary to finish these partially processed units:

Product	Unfinished Selling Price	Finished Selling Price	Further Processing Costs
Alpha.............	$300	$600	$150
Beta..............	450	900	300
Gamma	275	425	125
Delta.............	150	210	75

Which product(s) should *not* be processed further, (*a*) Alpha, (*b*) Beta, (*c*) Gamma, or (*d*) Delta?

14. Under what conditions is a sunk cost relevant to decision making?

Sales Mix Selection

When a company sells a mix of products, some are likely to be more profitable than others. Management is often wise to concentrate sales efforts on more profitable products. If production facilities or other factors are limited, an increase in the production and sale of one product usually requires reducing the production and sale of others. In this case, management must identify the most profitable combination, or *sales mix* of products. To identify the best sales mix, management must know the contribution margin of each product, the facilities required to produce each product, any constraints on these facilities, and its markets.

Point: A method called *linear programming* is useful for finding the optimal sales mix for several products subject to many market and production constraints. This method is described in advanced courses.

To illustrate, assume that FasTrac makes and sells two products, A and B. The same machines are used to produce both products. A and B have the following selling prices and variable costs per unit:

	Product A	Product B
Selling price per unit	$5.00	$7.50
Variable costs per unit	3.50	5.50
Contribution margin per unit	$1.50	$2.00

The variable costs are included in the analysis because they are the incremental costs of producing these products within the existing capacity of 100,000 machine hours per month. We consider three separate cases.

Demand Is Unlimited and Products Use Same Inputs   Assume that (1) each product requires 1 machine hour per unit for production and (2) the demand for these products is unlimited. Under these conditions, FasTrac should produce as much of Product B as it can because of its larger contribution margin of $2 per unit. At full capacity, FasTrac would produce $200,000 of total contribution margin per month, computed as $2 per unit times 100,000 machine hours.

Demand Is Unlimited and Products Use Different Inputs   Assume that (1) Product A requires 1 machine hour per unit, (2) Product B requires 2 machine hours per unit, and (3) the demand for these products is unlimited. Under these conditions, FasTrac should produce as much of Product A as it can because it has a contribution margin of $1.50 per machine hour compared with only $1 per machine hour for Product B. Exhibit 25.19 shows the relevant analysis.

EXHIBIT 25.19

Sales Mix Analysis

	Product A	Product B
Selling price per unit	$5.00	$7.50
Variable costs per unit	3.50	5.50
Contribution margin per unit	$1.50	$2.00
Machine hours per unit	1.0	2.0
Contribution margin per machine hour	**$1.50**	**$1.00**

At its full capacity of 100,000 machine hours, FasTrac would produce 100,000 units of Product A, yielding $150,000 of total contribution margin per month. In contrast, if it uses all 100,000 hours to produce Product B, only 50,000 units would be produced yielding a contribution margin of $100,000. These results suggest that when a company faces unlimited demand and limited capacity, only the most profitable product per input should be manufactured.

Example: If Product B's variable costs per unit increase to $6, Product A's variable costs per unit decrease to $3, and the same machine hours per unit are used, which product should FasTrac produce? *Answer:* Product A. Its contribution margin of $2 per machine hour is higher than B's $.75 per machine hour.

Point: FasTrac might consider buying another machine to reduce the constraint on production. A strategy designed to reduce the impact of constraints or bottlenecks, on production, is called the *theory of constraints*.

Demand Is Limited and Products Use Different Inputs   The need for a mix of different products arises when market demand is not sufficient to allow a company to sell all that it produces. For instance, assume that (1) Product A requires 1 machine hour per unit, (2) Product B requires 2 machine hours per unit, and (3) the market for Product A is limited to 80,000 units. Under these conditions, FasTrac should produce no more than 80,000 units of Product A. This would leave another 20,000 machine hours of capacity for making Product B. FasTrac should use this spare capacity to produce 10,000 units of Product B. This sales mix would maximize FasTrac's total contribution margin per month at an amount of $140,000. In this case, the company first produces its most profitable product, up to the point of total demand (or its capacity constraint). It then uses remaining capacity to produce its next most profitable product.

■ **Decision** Insight ━━━━━━━━━━━━━━━━━━━━━━━━━━

Companies such as **Gap**, **Abercrombie & Fitch**, and **American Eagle** must continuously monitor and manage the sales mix of their product lists. Selling their products in hundreds of countries and territories further complicates their decision process. The contribution margin of each product is crucial to their product mix strategies. ■

Segment Elimination

When a segment such as a department or division is performing poorly, management must consider eliminating it. Segment information on either net income (loss) or its contribution to overhead is not sufficient for this decision. Instead, we must look at the segment's avoidable expenses and unavoidable expenses. **Avoidable expenses,** also called *escapable expenses,* are amounts the company would not incur if it eliminated the segment. **Unavoidable expenses,** also called *inescapable expenses,* are amounts that would continue even if the segment is eliminated.

To illustrate, FasTrac considers eliminating its treadmill division because its $48,300 total expenses are higher than its $47,800 sales. Classification of this division's operating expenses into avoidable or unavoidable expenses is shown in Exhibit 25.20.

	Total	Avoidable Expenses	Unavoidable Expenses
Cost of goods sold	$ 30,000	$ 30,000	—
Direct expenses			
Salaries expense	7,900	7,900	—
Depreciation expense—Equipment	200	—	$ 200
Indirect expenses			
Rent and utilities expense	3,150	—	3,150
Advertising expense	400	400	—
Insurance expense	400	300	100
Service department costs			
Share of office department expenses	3,060	2,200	860
Share of purchasing expenses	3,190	1,000	2,190
Total	**$48,300**	**$41,800**	**$6,500**

EXHIBIT 25.20

Classification of Segment Operating Expenses for Analysis

FasTrac's analysis shows that it can avoid $41,800 expenses if it eliminates the treadmill division. Because this division's sales are $47,800, eliminating it will cause FasTrac to lose $6,000 of income. *Our decision rule is that a segment is a candidate for elimination if its revenues are less than its avoidable expenses.* Avoidable expenses can be viewed as the costs to generate this segment's revenues.

When considering elimination of a segment, we must assess its impact on other segments. A segment could be unprofitable on its own, but it might still contribute to other segments' revenues and profits. It is possible then to continue a segment even when its revenues are less than its avoidable expenses. Similarly, a profitable segment might be discontinued if its space, assets, or staff can be more profitably used by expanding existing segments or by creating new ones. Our decision to keep or eliminate a segment requires a more complex analysis than simply looking at a segment's performance report. Such reports provide useful information, but they do not provide all the information necessary for this decision.

Keep or Replace Equipment

Businesses periodically must decide whether to keep using equipment or replace it. Advances in technology typically mean newer equipment can operate more efficiently and at lower cost than older equipment. In making the decision to keep or replace equipment, managers must decide whether the reduction in *variable* manufacturing costs with the new equipment over its useful life is greater than the net purchase price of the equipment. In this setting, the net purchase price of the equipment is its total cost minus any trade-in allowance or cash receipt for the old equipment.

For example, FasTrac has a piece of manufacturing equipment with a book value (cost minus accumulated depreciation) of $20,000 and a remaining useful life of four years. At the end of four years the equipment will have a salvage value of zero. The market value of the equipment is currently $25,000.

FasTrac can purchase a new machine for $100,000 and receive $25,000 in return for trading in its old machine. The new machine will reduce FasTrac's variable manufacturing costs by $18,000 per year over the four-year life of the new machine. FasTrac's incremental analysis is shown in Exhibit 25.21.

EXHIBIT 25.21

Keep or Replace Analysis

	Increase or (Decrease) in Net Income
Cost to buy new machine	$(100,000)
Cash received to trade in old machine	25,000
Reduction in variable manufacturing costs*	72,000
Total increase (decrease) in net income	$ (3,000)

*18,000 × 4 years

The analysis in Exhibit 25.21 shows that FasTrac should not replace the old equipment with this newer version as it will decrease income by $3,000. Note, the book value of the old equipment ($20,000) is not relevant to this analysis. Book value is a sunk cost, and it cannot be changed regardless of whether FasTrac keeps or replaces this equipment.

Qualitative Decision Factors

Managers must consider qualitative factors in making managerial decisions. Consider a decision on whether to buy a component from an outside supplier or continue to make it. Several qualitative decision factors must be considered. For example, the quality, delivery, and reputation of the proposed supplier are important. The effects from deciding not to make the component can include potential layoffs and impaired worker morale. Consider another situation in which a company is considering a one-time sale to a new customer at a special low price. Qualitative factors to consider in this situation include the effects of a low price on the company's image and the threat that regular customers might demand a similar price. The company must also consider whether this customer is really a one-time customer. If not, can it continue to offer this low price in the long run? Clearly, management cannot rely solely on financial data to make such decisions.

Quick Check   Answers — p. 1062

15. What is the difference between avoidable and unavoidable expenses?

16. A segment is a candidate for elimination if (a) its revenues are less than its avoidable expenses, (b) it has a net loss, (c) its unavoidable expenses are higher than its revenues.

GLOBAL VIEW

Siemens AG is a global electrical engineering and electronics company headquartered in Germany. Recently, the company announced plans to invest £80 million to build a wind turbine plant in the United Kingdom. Net present value analyses support such decisions. In this case, Siemens foresees strong future cash flows based on increased demand for clean sources of energy, like wind power.

Decision Analysis   Break-Even Time

A2 Analyze a capital investment project using break-even time.

The first section of this chapter explained several methods to evaluate capital investments. Break-even time of an investment project is a variation of the payback period method that overcomes the limitation of not using the time value of money. **Break-even time (BET)** is a time-based measure used to evaluate a capital investment's acceptability. Its computation yields a measure of expected time, reflecting the time period until the *present value* of the net cash flows from an investment equals the initial cost of the investment. In basic terms, break-even time is computed by restating future cash flows in terms of present values and then determining the payback period using these present values.

To illustrate, we return to the FasTrac case described in Exhibit 25.1 involving a $16,000 investment in machinery. The annual net cash flows from this investment are projected at $4,100 for eight years. Exhibit 25.22 shows the computation of break-even time for this investment decision.

Year	Cash Flows	Present Value of 1 at 10%	Present Value of Cash Flows	Cumulative Present Value of Cash Flows
0	$(16,000)	1.0000	$(16,000)	$(16,000)
1	4,100	0.9091	3,727	(12,273)
2	4,100	0.8264	3,388	(8,885)
3	4,100	0.7513	3,080	(5,805)
4	4,100	0.6830	2,800	(3,005)
5	4,100	0.6209	2,546	(459)
6	4,100	0.5645	2,314	1,855
7	4,100	0.5132	2,104	3,959
8	4,100	0.4665	1,913	5,872

EXHIBIT 25.22

Break-Even Time Analysis*

* The time of analysis is the start of year 1 (same as end of year 0). All cash flows occur at the end of each year.

The right-most column of this exhibit shows that break-even time is between 5 and 6 years, or about 5.2 years—also see margin graph (where the line crosses the zero point). This is the time the project takes to break even after considering the time value of money (recall that the payback period computed without considering the time value of money was 3.9 years). We interpret this as cash flows earned after 5.2 years contribute to a positive net present value that, in this case, eventually amounts to $5,872.

Break-even time is a useful measure for managers because it identifies the point in time when they can expect the cash flows to begin to yield net positive returns. Managers expect a positive net present value from an investment if break-even time is less than the investment's estimated life. The method allows managers to compare and rank alternative investments, giving the project with the shortest break-even time the highest rank.

Decision Maker

Investment Manager Management asks you, the investment manager, to evaluate three alternative investments. Investment recovery time is crucial because cash is scarce. The time value of money is also important. Which capital budgeting method(s) do you use to assess the investments? ■   [Answer—p. 1061]

DEMONSTRATION PROBLEM

Determine the appropriate action in each of the following managerial decision situations.

1. Packer Company is operating at 80% of its manufacturing capacity of 100,000 product units per year. A chain store has offered to buy an additional 10,000 units at $22 each and sell them to customers so as not to compete with Packer Company. The following data are available.

Costs at 80% Capacity	Per Unit	Total
Direct materials	$ 8.00	$ 640,000
Direct labor	7.00	560,000
Overhead (fixed and variable)	12.50	1,000,000
Totals	$27.50	$2,200,000

In producing 10,000 additional units, fixed overhead costs would remain at their current level but incremental variable overhead costs of $3 per unit would be incurred. Should the company accept or reject this order?

2. Green Company uses Part JR3 in manufacturing its products. It has always purchased this part from a supplier for $40 each. It recently upgraded its own manufacturing capabilities and has enough excess capacity (including trained workers) to begin manufacturing Part JR3 instead of buying it. The company prepares the following cost projections of making the part, assuming that overhead is allocated to the part at the normal predetermined rate of 200% of direct labor cost.

Direct materials	$11
Direct labor	15
Overhead (fixed and variable) (200% of direct labor)	30
Total	$56

The required volume of output to produce the part will not require any incremental fixed overhead. Incremental variable overhead cost will be $17 per unit. Should the company make or buy this part?

3. Gold Company's manufacturing process causes a relatively large number of defective parts to be produced. The defective parts can be (a) sold for scrap, (b) melted to recover the recycled metal for reuse, or (c) reworked to be good units. Reworking defective parts reduces the output of other good units because no excess capacity exists. Each unit reworked means that one new unit cannot be produced. The following information reflects 500 defective parts currently available.

Proceeds of selling as scrap	$2,500
Additional cost of melting down defective parts	400
Cost of purchases avoided by using recycled metal from defects	4,800
Cost to rework 500 defective parts	
Direct materials	0
Direct labor	1,500
Incremental overhead	1,750
Cost to produce 500 new parts	
Direct materials	6,000
Direct labor	5,000
Incremental overhead	3,200
Selling price per good unit	40

Should the company melt the parts, sell them as scrap, or rework them?

4. White Company can invest in one of two projects, TD1 or TD2. Each project requires an initial investment of $100,000 and produces the year-end cash inflows shown in the following table. Use net present values to determine which project, if any, should be chosen. Assume that the company requires a 10% return from its investments.

	Net Cash Flows	
	TD1	**TD2**
Year 1	$ 20,000	$ 40,000
Year 2	30,000	40,000
Year 3	70,000	40,000
Totals	$120,000	$120,000

PLANNING THE SOLUTION

- Determine whether Packer Company should accept the additional business by finding the incremental costs of materials, labor, and overhead that will be incurred if the order is accepted. Omit fixed costs that the order will not increase. If the incremental revenue exceeds the incremental cost, accept the order.

- Determine whether Green Company should make or buy the component by finding the incremental cost of making each unit. If the incremental cost exceeds the purchase price, the component should be purchased. If the incremental cost is less than the purchase price, make the component.

- Determine whether Gold Company should sell the defective parts, melt them down and recycle the metal, or rework them. To compare the three choices, examine all costs incurred and benefits received from the alternatives in working with the 500 defective units versus the production of 500 new units. For the scrapping alternative, include the costs of producing 500 new units and subtract the $2,500 proceeds from selling the old ones. For the melting alternative, include the costs of melting the defective units, add the net cost of new materials in excess over those obtained from recycling, and add the direct labor and overhead costs. For the reworking alternative, add the costs of direct labor and incremental overhead. Select the alternative that has the lowest cost. The cost assigned to the 500 defective units is sunk and not relevant in choosing among the three alternatives.

- Compute White Company's net present value of each investment using a 10% discount rate.

SOLUTION TO DEMONSTRATION PROBLEM

1. This decision involves accepting additional business. Since current unit costs are $27.50, it appears initially as if the offer to sell for $22 should be rejected, but the $27.50 cost includes fixed costs. When the analysis includes only *incremental* costs, the per unit cost is as shown in the following table. The offer should be accepted because it will produce $4 of additional profit per unit (computed as $22 price less $18 incremental cost), which yields a total profit of $40,000 for the 10,000 additional units.

Direct materials	$ 8.00
Direct labor	7.00
Variable overhead (given)	3.00
Total incremental cost	$18.00

2. For this make or buy decision, the analysis must not include the $13 nonincremental overhead per unit ($30 − $17). When only the $17 incremental overhead is included, the relevant unit cost of manufacturing the part is shown in the following table. It would be better to continue buying the part for $40 instead of making it for $43.

Direct materials	$11.00
Direct labor	15.00
Variable overhead	17.00
Total incremental cost	$43.00

3. The goal of this scrap or rework decision is to identify the alternative that produces the greatest net benefit to the company. To compare the alternatives, we determine the net cost of obtaining 500 marketable units as follows:

Incremental Cost to Produce 500 Marketable Units	Sell as Is	Melt and Recycle	Rework Units
Direct materials			
New materials	$ 6,000	$6,000	
Recycled metal materials.......................................		(4,800)	
Net materials cost...		1,200	
Melting costs		400	
Total direct materials cost	6,000	1,600	
Direct labor	5,000	5,000	$1,500
Incremental overhead	3,200	3,200	1,750
Cost to produce 500 marketable units	14,200	9,800	3,250
Less proceeds of selling defects as scrap	(2,500)		
Opportunity costs*			5,800
Net cost	$11,700	$9,800	$9,050

* The $5,800 opportunity cost is the lost contribution margin from not being able to produce and sell 500 units because of reworking, computed as ($40 − [$14,200/500 units]) × 500 units.

The incremental cost of 500 marketable parts is smallest if the defects are reworked.

4. TD1:

	Net Cash Flows	Present Value of 1 at 10%	Present Value of Net Cash Flows
Year 1	$ 20,000	0.9091	$ 18,182
Year 2	30,000	0.8264	24,792
Year 3	70,000	0.7513	52,591
Totals	$120,000		95,565
Amount invested			(100,000)
Net present value			**$ (4,435)**

TD2:

	Net Cash Flows	Present Value of 1 at 10%	Present Value of Net Cash Flows
Year 1....................	$ 40,000	0.9091	$ 36,364
Year 2	40,000	0.8264	33,056
Year 3	40,000	0.7513	30,052
Totals	$120,000		99,472
Amount invested			(100,000)
Net present value			**$ (528)**

White Company should not invest in either project. Both are expected to yield a negative net present value, and it should invest only in positive net present value projects.

25A
Using Excel to Compute Net Present Value and Internal Rate of Return

Computing present values and internal rates of return for projects with uneven cash flows is tedious and error prone. These calculations can be performed simply and accurately by using functions built into Excel. Many calculators and other types of spreadsheet software can perform them too. To illustrate, consider FasTrac, a company that is considering investing in a new machine with the expected cash flows shown in the following spreadsheet. Cash outflows are entered as negative numbers, and cash inflows are entered as positive numbers. Assume FasTrac requires a 12% annual return, entered as 0.12 in cell C1.

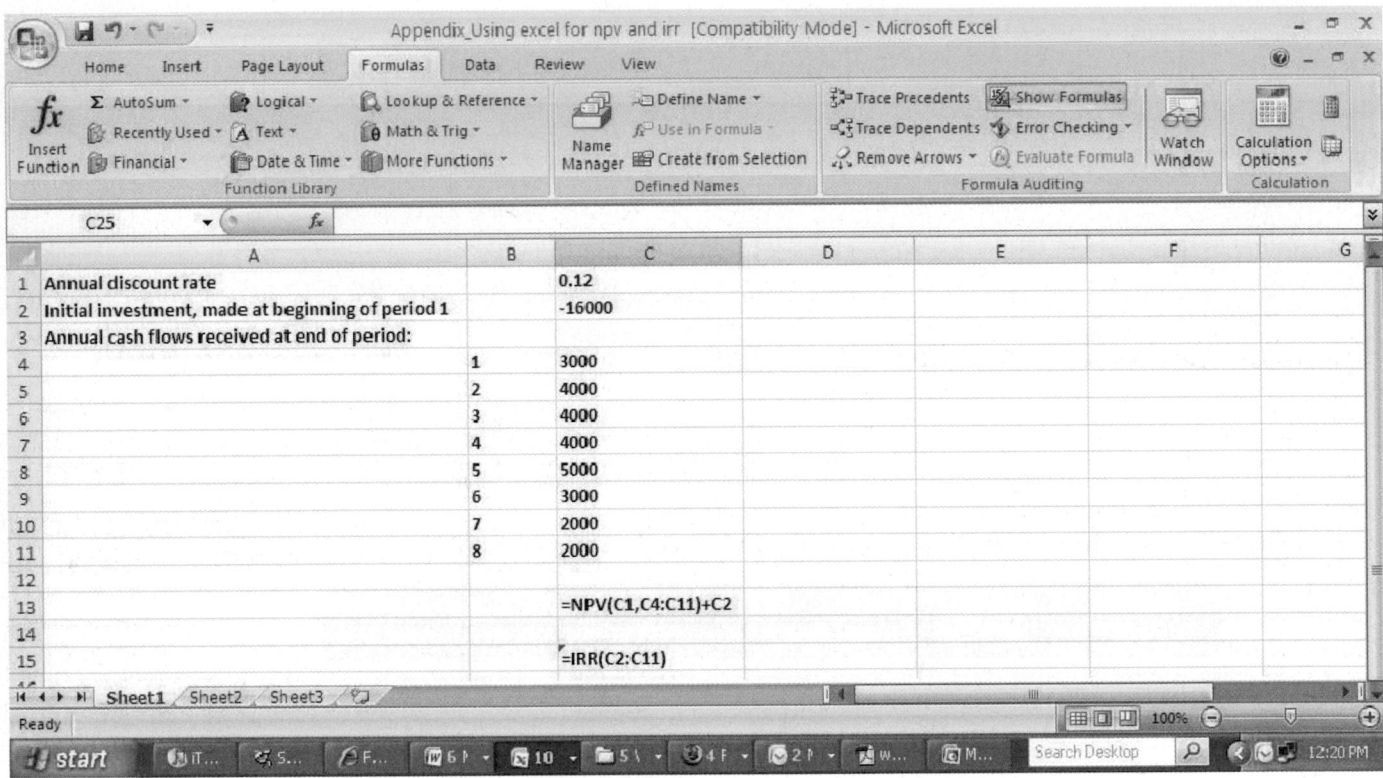

To compute the net present value of this project, the following is entered into cell C13:

$$=\text{NPV(C1,C4:C11)}+\text{C2}.$$

This instructs Excel to use its NPV function to compute the present value of the cash flows in cells C4 through C11, using the discount rate in cell C1, and then add the amount of the (negative) initial investment. For this stream of cash flows and a discount rate of 12%, the net present value is $1,326.03.
To compute the internal rate of return for this project, the following is entered into cell C15:

$$=\text{IRR(C2:C11)}.$$

This instructs Excel to use its IRR function to compute the internal rate of return of the cash flows in cells C2 through C11. By default, Excel starts with a guess of 10%, and then uses trial and error to find the IRR. The IRR equals 14% for this project.

Summary

C1 **Describe the importance of relevant costs for short-term decisions.** A company must rely on relevant costs pertaining to alternative courses of action rather than historical costs. Out-of-pocket expenses and opportunity costs are relevant because these are avoidable; sunk costs are irrelevant because they result from past decisions and are therefore unavoidable. Managers must also consider the relevant benefits associated with alternative decisions.

A1 **Evaluate short-term managerial decisions using relevant costs.** Relevant costs are useful in making decisions such as to accept additional business, make or buy, and sell as is or process further. For example, the relevant factors in deciding whether to produce and sell additional units of product are incremental costs and incremental revenues from the additional volume.

A2 **Analyze a capital investment project using break-even time.** Break-even time (BET) is a method for evaluating capital investments by restating future cash flows in terms of their present values (discounting the cash flows) and then calculating the payback period using these present values of cash flows.

P1 **Compute payback period and describe its use.** One way to compare potential investments is to compute and compare their payback periods. The payback period is an estimate of the expected time before the cumulative net cash inflow from the investment equals its initial cost. A payback period analysis fails to reflect risk of the cash flows, differences in the timing of cash flows within the payback period, and cash flows that occur after the payback period.

P2 **Compute accounting rate of return and explain its use.** A project's accounting rate of return is computed by dividing the expected annual after-tax net income by the average amount of investment in the project. When the net cash flows are received evenly throughout each period and straight-line depreciation is used, the average investment is computed as the average of the investment's initial book value and its salvage value.

P3 **Compute net present value and describe its use.** An investment's net present value is determined by predicting the future cash flows it is expected to generate, discounting them at a rate that represents an acceptable return, and then by subtracting the investment's initial cost from the sum of the present values. This technique can deal with any pattern of expected cash flows and applies a superior concept of return on investment.

P4 **Compute internal rate of return and explain its use.** The internal rate of return (IRR) is the discount rate that results in a zero net present value. When the cash flows are equal, we can compute the present value factor corresponding to the IRR by dividing the initial investment by the annual cash flows. We then use the annuity tables to determine the discount rate corresponding to this present value factor.

Guidance Answers to Decision Maker and Decision Ethics

Systems Manager   Your dilemma is whether to abide by rules designed to prevent abuse or to bend them to acquire an investment that you believe will benefit the firm. You should not pursue the latter action because breaking up the order into small components is dishonest and there are consequences of being caught at a later stage. Develop a proposal for the entire package and then do all you can to expedite its processing, particularly by pointing out its benefits. When faced with controls that are not working, there is rarely a reason to overcome its shortcomings by dishonesty. A direct assault on those limitations is more sensible and ethical.

Entrepreneur   The banker is probably concerned because new products are risky and should therefore be evaluated using a higher rate of return. You should conduct a thorough technical analysis and obtain detailed market data and information about any similar products available in the market. These factors might provide sufficient information to support the use of a lower return. You must convince yourself that the risk level is consistent with the discount rate used.

You should also be confident that your company has the capacity and the resources to handle the new product.

Partner   You should identify the differences between existing clients and this potential client. A key difference is that the restaurant business has additional inventory components (groceries, vegetables, meats, etc.) and is likely to have a higher proportion of depreciable assets. These differences imply that the partner must spend more hours auditing the records and understanding the business, regulations, and standards that pertain to the restaurant business. Such differences suggest that the partner must use a different "formula" for quoting a price to this potential client vis-à-vis current clients.

Investment Manager   You should probably focus on either the payback period or break-even time because both the time value of money and recovery time are important. Break-even time method is superior because it accounts for the time value of money, which is an important consideration in this decision.

Guidance Answers to Quick Checks

1. *b*

2. A capital budgeting decision is difficult because (1) the outcome is uncertain, (2) large amounts of money are usually involved, (3) a long-term commitment is required, and (4) the decision could be difficult or impossible to reverse.

3. *b*

4. Depreciation expense is subtracted from revenues in computing net income but does not use cash and should be added back to net income to compute net cash flows.

5. Not necessarily. One investment can continue to generate cash flows beyond the payback period for a longer time period than the other. The timing of their cash flows within the payback period also can differ.

6. *b*; Annual average investment = ($180,000 + $15,000)/2
= $97,500

Accounting rate of return = $40,000/$97,500 = 41%

7. For this determination, we need to compare it to the returns expected from alternative investments with similar risk.

8. Project A has the higher net present value as follows:

Year	Present Value of 1 at 10%	Project A Net Cash Flows	Project A Present Value of Net Cash Flows	Project B Net Cash Flows	Project B Present Value of Net Cash Flows
1	0.9091	$12,000	$10,909	$ 4,500	$ 4,091
2	0.8264	8,500	7,024	8,500	7,024
3	0.7513	4,000	3,005	13,000	9,767
Totals		$24,500	$20,938	$26,000	$20,882
Amount invested			(20,000)		(20,000)
Net present value			**$ 938**		**$ 882**

9. No, the information is too limited to draw that conclusion. For example, one investment could be riskier than the other, or one could require a substantially larger initial investment.

10. *b*

11. *e*; Variable costs per unit for this order of 200 units follow:

Direct materials ($37,500/7,500)	$ 5.00
Direct labor ($60,000/7,500)	8.00
Variable overhead [(0.30 × $20,000)/7,500]	0.80
Variable selling expenses [(0.60 × $25,000 × 0.5)/7,500]	1.00
Total variable costs per unit	$14.80

Cost to produce special order: (200 × $14.80) + $400
= $3,360.

Price per unit to earn $1,000: ($3,360 + $1,000)/200 = 21.80.

12. They are the additional (new) costs of accepting new business.

13. *d*;

	Incremental benefits		Incremental costs
Alpha	$300 ($600 − $300)	>	$150 (given)
Beta	$450 ($900 − $450)	>	$300 (given)
Gamma	$150 ($425 − $275)	>	$125 (given)
Delta	$ 60 ($210 − $150)	<	$ 75 (given)

14. A sunk cost is *never* relevant because it results from a past decision and is already incurred.

15. Avoidable expenses are ones a company will not incur by eliminating a segment; unavoidable expenses will continue even after a segment is eliminated.

16. *a*

Multiple Choice Quiz   Answers on p. 1078   mhhe.com/wildFAP21e

Additional Quiz Questions are available at the book's Website.

1. A company inadvertently produced 3,000 defective MP3 players. The players cost $12 each to produce. A recycler offers to purchase the defective players as they are for $8 each. The production manager reports that the defects can be corrected for $10 each, enabling them to be sold at their regular market price of $19 each. The company should:
a. Correct the defect and sell them at the regular price.
b. Sell the players to the recycler for $8 each.
c. Sell 2,000 to the recycler and repair the rest.
d. Sell 1,000 to the recycler and repair the rest.
e. Throw the players away.

2. A company's productive capacity is limited to 480,000 machine hours. Product X requires 10 machine hours to produce; and Product Y requires 2 machine hours to produce. Product X

sells for $32 per unit and has variable costs of $12 per unit; Product Y sells for $24 per unit and has variable costs of $10 per unit. Assuming that the company can sell as many of either product as it produces, it should:
a. Produce X and Y in the ratio of 57% and 43%.
b. Produce X and Y in the ratio of 83% X and 17% Y.
c. Produce equal amounts of Product X and Product Y.
d. Produce only Product X.
e. Produce only Product Y.

3. A company receives a special one-time order for 3,000 units of its product at $15 per unit. The company has excess capacity and it currently produces and sells the units at $20 each to its regular customers. Production costs are $13.50 per unit, which includes $9 of variable costs. To produce the special order, the company must incur additional fixed costs of $5,000. Should the company accept the special order?

  a. Yes, because incremental revenue exceeds incremental costs.

  b. No, because incremental costs exceed incremental revenue.

  c. No, because the units are being sold for $5 less than the regular price.

  d. Yes, because incremental costs exceed incremental revenue.

  e. No, because incremental cost exceeds $15 per unit when total costs are considered.

4. A company is considering the purchase of equipment for $270,000. Projected annual cash inflow from this equipment is $61,200 per year. The payback period is:

  a. 0.2 years

  b. 5.0 years

  c. 4.4 years

  d. 2.3 years

  e. 3.9 years

5. A company buys a machine for $180,000 that has an expected life of nine years and no salvage value. The company expects an annual net income (after taxes of 30%) of $8,550. What is the accounting rate of return?

  a. 4.75%

  b. 42.75%

  c. 2.85%

  d. 9.50%

  e. 6.65%

I Icon denotes assignments that involve decision making.

Discussion Questions

1. Capital budgeting decisions require careful analysis because they are generally the _____ _____ and _____ decisions that management faces.

2. What is capital budgeting?

3. **I** Identify four reasons that capital budgeting decisions by managers are risky.

4. Identify two disadvantages of using the payback period for comparing investments.

5. **I** Why is an investment more attractive to management if it has a shorter payback period?

6. What is the average amount invested in a machine during its predicted five-year life if it costs $200,000 and has a $20,000 salvage value? Assume that net income is received evenly throughout each year and straight-line depreciation is used.

7. If the present value of the expected net cash flows from a machine, discounted at 10%, exceeds the amount to be invested, what can you say about the investment's expected rate of return? What can you say about the expected rate of return if the present value of the net cash flows, discounted at 10%, is less than the investment amount?

8. Why is the present value of $100 that you expect to receive one year from today worth less than $100 received today? What is the present value of $100 that you expect to receive one year from today, discounted at 12%?

9. **I** Why should managers set the required rate of return higher than the rate at which money can be borrowed when making a typical capital budgeting decision?

10. **I** Why does the use of the accelerated depreciation method (instead of straight line) for income tax reporting increase an investment's value?

11. **Arctic Cat** has many types of costs. What is an out-of-pocket cost? What is an opportunity cost? Arctic Cat Are opportunity costs recorded in the accounting records?

12. **I** **Piaggio** must confront sunk costs. Why are sunk costs irrelevant in deciding whether to **PIAGGIO** sell a product in its present condition or to make it into a new product through additional processing?

13. **I** Identify the incremental costs incurred by **Apple** for shipping one additional iPod from a warehouse to **Apple** a retail store along with the store's normal order of 75 iPods.

14. **I** **KTM** is considering expanding a store. Identify three methods management can use to evaluate **KTM** whether to expand.

15. **I** Assume that **Polaris** manufactures and sells 60,000 units of a product at $11,000 per unit in **Polaris** domestic markets. It costs $6,000 per unit to manufacture ($4,000 variable cost per unit, $2,000 fixed cost per unit). Can you describe a situation under which the company is willing to sell an additional 8,000 units of the product in an international market at $5,000 per unit?

---

connect

Freeman Brothers Co. is considering an investment that requires immediate payment of $27,000 and provides expected cash inflows of $9,000 annually for four years. What is the investment's payback period?

QUICK STUDY

QS 25-1
Payback period   P1

QS 25-2

Analyzing payback periods   P1

Park Company is considering two alternative investments. The payback period is 3.5 years for investment A and 4 years for investment B. (1) If management relies on the payback period, which investment is preferred? (2) Why might Park's analysis of these two alternatives lead to the selection of B over A?

QS 25-3

Computation of

accounting rate of return   P2

Peng Company is considering an investment expected to generate an average net income after taxes of $1,950 for three years. The investment costs $45,000 and has an estimated $6,000 salvage value. Compute the accounting rate of return for this investment; assume the company uses straight-line depreciation. Hint: Use the formula in Exhibit 25.4 when computing the average annual investment.

QS 25-4

Computation of

net present value   P3

If Quail Company invests $50,000 today, it can expect to receive $10,000 at the end of each year for the next seven years, plus an extra $6,000 at the end of the seventh year. What is the net present value of this investment assuming a required 10% return on investments?

QS 25-5

Profitability index

P3

Yokam Company is considering two alternative projects. Project 1 requires an initial investment of $400,000 and has a net present value of cash flows of $1,100,000. Project 2 requires an initial investment of $3,500,000 and has a net present value of cash flows of $2,500,000. Compute the profitability index for each project. Based on the profitability index, which project should the company prefer? Explain.

QS 25-6

Internal rate of return   P4

A company is considering investing in a new machine that requires a cash payment of $47,946 today. The machine will generate annual cash flows of $21,000 for the next three years. What is the internal rate of return if the company buys this machine?

QS 25-7

Relevant costs

C1

Label each of the following statements as either true ("T") or false ("F").

1. Relevant costs are also known as unavoidable costs.
2. Incremental costs are also known as differential costs.
3. An out-of-pocket cost requires a current and/or future outlay of cash.
4. An opportunity cost is the potential benefit that is lost by taking a specific action when two or more alternative choices are available.
5. A sunk cost will change with a future course of action.

QS 25-8

Analysis of incremental costs

A1

Kando Company incurs a $9 per unit cost for Product A, which it currently manufactures and sells for $13.50 per unit. Instead of manufacturing and selling this product, the company can purchase Product B for $5 per unit and sell it for $12 per unit. If it does so, unit sales would remain unchanged and $5 of the $9 per unit costs assigned to Product A would be eliminated. Should the company continue to manufacture Product A or purchase Product B for resale?

QS 25-9

Selection of sales mix

A1

Excel Memory Company can sell all units of computer memory X and Y that it can produce, but it has limited production capacity. It can produce two units of X per hour *or* three units of Y per hour, and it has 4,000 production hours available. Contribution margin is $5 for product X and $4 for product Y. What is the most profitable sales mix for this company?

QS 25-10

Sell or process decision

A1

Holmes Company produces a product that can either be sold as is or processed further. Holmes has already spent $50,000 to produce 1,250 units that can be sold now for $67,500 to another manufacturer. Alternatively, Holmes can process the units further at an incremental cost of $250 per unit. If Holmes processes further, the units can be sold for $375 each. Compute the incremental income if Holmes processes further.

QS 25-11

Scrap or rework

A1

Signal mistakenly produced 10,000 defective cell phones. The phones cost $60 each to produce. A salvage company will buy the defective phones as they are for $30 each. It would cost Signal $80 per phone to rework the phones. If the phones are reworked, Signal could sell them for $110 each. Compute the incremental net income from reworking the phones.

Radar Company sells bikes for $300 each. The company currently sells 3,750 bikes per year and could make as many as 5,000 bikes per year. The bikes cost $225 each to make; $150 in variable costs per bike and $75 of fixed costs per bike. Radar received an offer from a potential customer who wants to buy 750 bikes for $250 each. Incremental fixed costs to make this order are $50,000. No other costs will change if this order is accepted. Compute Radar's additional income (ignore taxes) if it accepts this order.

QS 25-12
Decision to accept additional business
A1

A guitar manufacturer is considering eliminating its electric guitar division because its $76,000 expenses are higher than its $72,000 sales. The company reports the following expenses for this division. Should the division be eliminated?

QS 25-13
Segment elimination
A1

	Avoidable Expenses	Unavoidable Expenses
Cost of goods sold	$56,000	
Direct expenses	9,250	$1,250
Indirect expenses	470	1,600
Service department costs	6,000	1,430

Rory Company has a machine with a book value of $75,000 and a remaining five-year useful life. A new machine is available at a cost of $112,500, and Rory can also receive $60,000 for trading in its old machine. The new machine will reduce variable manufacturing costs by $12,000 per year over its five-year useful life. Should the machine be replaced?

QS 25-14
Keep or replace decision
A1

Heels, a shoe manufacturer, is evaluating the costs and benefits of new equipment that would custom fit each pair of athletic shoes. The customer would have his or her foot scanned by digital computer equipment; this information would be used to cut the raw materials to provide the customer a perfect fit. The new equipment costs $90,000 and is expected to generate an additional $35,000 in cash flows for five years. A bank will make a $90,000 loan to the company at a 10% interest rate for this equipment's purchase. Use the following table to determine the break-even time for this equipment. (Round the present value of cash flows to the nearest dollar.)

QS 25-15
Computation of break-even time
A2

Year	Cash Flows*	Present Value of 1 at 10%	Present Value of Cash Flows	Cumulative Present Value of Cash Flows
0	$(90,000)	1.0000		
1	35,000	0.9091		
2	35,000	0.8264		
3	35,000	0.7513		
4	35,000	0.6830		
5	35,000	0.6209		

* All cash flows occur at year-end.

Siemens AG invests €80 million to build a manufacturing plant to build wind turbines. The company predicts net cash flows of €16 million per year for the next 8 years. Assume the company requires an 8% rate of return from its investments. (1) What is the payback period of this investment? (2) What is the net present value of this investment?

QS 25-16
Capital budgeting methods
P1 P3

connect

Beyer Company is considering the purchase of an asset for $180,000. It is expected to produce the following net cash flows. The cash flows occur evenly throughout each year. Compute the payback period for this investment (round years to two decimals).

EXERCISES

Exercise 25-1
Payback period computation; uneven cash flows
P1

Check 3.08 years

	Year 1	Year 2	Year 3	Year 4	Year 5	Total
Net cash flows	$60,000	$40,000	$70,000	$125,000	$35,000	$330,000

Exercise 25-2

Payback period computation; declining-balance depreciation

P1

A machine can be purchased for $150,000 and used for 5 years, yielding the following net incomes. In project-ing net incomes, double-declining balance depreciation is applied, using a 5-year life and a zero salvage value. Compute the machine's payback period (ignore taxes). (Round the payback period to three decimals.)

	Year 1	Year 2	Year 3	Year 4	Year 5
Net incomes	$10,000	$25,000	$50,000	$37,500	$100,000

Check 2.265 years

Exercise 25-3

Payback period computation; even cash flows

P1

Compute the payback period for each of these two separate investments (round the payback period to two decimals):

a. A new operating system for an existing machine is expected to cost $520,000 and have a useful life of six years. The system yields an incremental after-tax income of $150,000 each year after de-ducting its straight-line depreciation. The predicted salvage value of the system is $10,000.

b. A machine costs $380,000, has a $20,000 salvage value, is expected to last eight years, and will generate an after-tax income of $60,000 per year after straight-line depreciation.

Exercise 25-4

Accounting rate of return   P2

A machine costs $700,000 and is expected to yield an after-tax net income of $52,000 each year. Management predicts this machine has a 10-year service life and a $100,000 salvage value, and it uses straight-line depreciation. Compute this machine's accounting rate of return.

Exercise 25-5

Payback period and accounting rate of return on investment

P1 P2

B2B Co. is considering the purchase of equipment that would allow the company to add a new product to its line. The equipment is expected to cost $360,000 with a 6-year life and no salvage value. It will be depreciated on a straight-line basis. The company expects to sell 144,000 units of the equipment's product each year. The expected annual income related to this equipment follows. Compute the (1) payback period and (2) accounting rate of return for this equipment.

Sales	$225,000
Costs	
Materials, labor, and overhead (except depreciation)	120,000
Depreciation on new equipment	30,000
Selling and administrative expenses	22,500
Total costs and expenses...............................	172,500
Pretax income	52,500
Income taxes (30%)	15,750
Net income	$ 36,750

Check (1) 5.39 years (2) 20.42%

Exercise 25-6

Computing net present value   P3

After evaluating the risk of the investment described in Exercise 25-5, B2B Co. concludes that it must earn at least a 8% return on this investment. Compute the net present value of this investment. (Round the net present value to the nearest dollar.)

Exercise 25-7

Computation and interpretation of net present value and internal rate of return

P3 P4

Phoenix Company can invest in each of three cheese-making projects: C1, C2, and C3. Each project requires an initial investment of $228,000 and would yield the following annual cash flows.

	C1	C2	C3
Year 1.........	$ 12,000	$ 96,000	$180,000
Year 2	108,000	96,000	60,000
Year 3	168,000	96,000	48,000
Totals	$288,000	$288,000	$288,000

Check (3) IRR = 13%

(1) Assuming that the company requires a 12% return from its investments, use net present value to determine which projects, if any, should be acquired. (2) Using the answer from part 1, explain whether the internal rate of return is higher or lower than 12% for project C2. (3) Compute the internal rate of return for project C2.

Exercise 25-8

NPV and profitability index   P3

Following is information on two alternative investments being considered by Jolee Company. The company requires a 10% return from its investments.

	Project A	Project B
Initial investment	$(160,000)	$(105,000)
Expected net cash flows in year:		
1	40,000	32,000
2	56,000	50,000
3	80,295	66,000
4	90,400	72,000
5	65,000	24,000

For each alternative project compute the (a) net present value, and (b) profitability index. If the company can only select one project, which should it choose? Explain.

Refer to the information in Exercise 25-8. Create an Excel spreadsheet to compute the internal rate of return for each of the projects. Round the percentage return to two decimals.

Exercise 25-9ᴬ
Using Excel to compute IRR P4

Fill in each of the blanks below with the correct term.

1. A _____ arises from a past decision and cannot be avoided or changed; it is irrelevant to future decisions.

2. _____ refer to the incremental revenue generated from taking one particular action over another.

3. Relevant costs are also known as _____.

4. An _____ requires a future outlay of cash and is relevant for current and future decision making.

5. An _____ is the potential benefit lost by taking a specific action when two or more alternative choices are available.

Exercise 25-10
Relevant costs

C1

Xinhong Company is considering replacing one of its manufacturing machines. The machine has a book value of $45,000 and a remaining useful life of 5 years, at which time its salvage value will be zero. It has a current market value of $52,000. Variable manufacturing costs are $36,000 per year for this machine. Information on two alternative replacement machines follows. Should Xinhong keep or replace its manufacturing machine? If the machine should be replaced, which alternative new machine should Xinhong purchase?

Exercise 25-11
Keep or replace

A1

	Alternative A	Alternative B
Cost.......................................	$115,000	$125,000
Variable manufacturing costs per year.........	19,000	15,000

A company must decide between scrapping or reworking units that do not pass inspection. The company has 22,000 defective units that cost $6 per unit to manufacture. The units can be sold as is for $2.50 each, or they can be reworked for $4.50 each and then sold for the full price of $8.50 each. If the units are sold as is, the company will have to build 22,000 replacement units at a cost of $6 each, and sell them at the full price of $8.50 each. (1) What is the incremental income from selling the units as scrap? (2) What is the incremental income from reworking and selling the units? (3) Should the company sell the units as scrap or rework them?

Exercise 25-12
Scrap or rework

A1

Farrow Co. expects to sell 150,000 units of its product in the next period with the following results.

Exercise 25-13
Decision to accept additional business or not

A1

Sales (150,000 units)	$2,250,000
Costs and expenses	
Direct materials................	300,000
Direct labor....................	600,000
Overhead.....................	150,000
Selling expenses................	225,000
Administrative expenses	385,500
Total costs and expenses...........	1,660,500
Net income	$ 589,500

The company has an opportunity to sell 15,000 additional units at $12 per unit. The additional sales would not affect its current expected sales. Direct materials and labor costs per unit would be the same for the additional units as they are for the regular units. However, the additional volume would create the following incremental costs: (1) total overhead would increase by 15% and (2) administrative expenses would increase by $64,500. Prepare an analysis to determine whether the company should accept or reject the offer to sell additional units at the reduced price of $12 per unit.

Check Income increase, $3,000

Exercise 25-14
Make or buy decision
A1

Check $35,750 increased costs to buy

Gilberto Company currently manufactures one of its crucial parts at a cost of $4.45 per unit. This cost is based on a normal production rate of 65,000 units per year. Variable costs are $1.95 per unit, fixed costs related to making this part are $65,000 per year, and allocated fixed costs are $58,500 per year. Allocated fixed costs are unavoidable whether the company makes or buys the part. Gilberto is considering buying the part from a supplier for a quoted price of $3.50 per unit guaranteed for a three-year period. Should the company continue to manufacture the part, or should it buy the part from the outside supplier? Support your answer with analyses.

Exercise 25-15
Sell or process decision
A1

Cobe Company has already manufactured 28,000 units of Product A at a cost of $28 per unit. The 28,000 units can be sold at this stage for $700,000. Alternatively, the units can be further processed at a $420,000 total additional cost and be converted into 5,600 units of Product B and 11,200 units of Product C. Per unit selling price for Product B is $105 and for Product C is $70. Prepare an analysis that shows whether the 28,000 units of Product A should be processed further or not.

Exercise 25-16
Analysis of income effects from eliminating departments
A1

Suresh Co. expects its five departments to yield the following income for next year.

	Dept. M	Dept. N	Dept. O	Dept. P	Dept. T
Sales	$63,000	$35,000	$56,000	$42,000	$ 28,000
Expenses					
Avoidable	9,800	36,400	22,400	14,000	37,800
Unavoidable	51,800	12,600	4,200	29,400	9,800
Total expenses	61,600	49,000	26,600	43,400	47,600
Net income (loss)	$ 1,400	$(14,000)	$29,400	$(1,400)	$ (19,600)

Check Total income (loss)
(2) $(21,000), (3) $7,000

Recompute and prepare the departmental income statements (including a combined total column) for the company under each of the following separate scenarios: Management (1) does not eliminate any department, (2) eliminates departments with expected net losses, and (3) eliminates departments with sales dollars that are less than avoidable expenses. Explain your answers to parts 2 and 3.

Exercise 25-17
Sales mix determination and analysis
A1

Colt Company owns a machine that can produce two specialized products. Production time for Product TLX is two units per hour and for Product MTV is five units per hour. The machine's capacity is 2,750 hours per year. Both products are sold to a single customer who has agreed to buy all of the company's output up to a maximum of 4,700 units of Product TLX and 2,500 units of Product MTV. Selling prices and variable costs per unit to produce the products follow. Determine (1) the company's most profitable sales mix and (2) the contribution margin that results from that sales mix.

	Product TLX	Product MTV
Selling price per unit	$15.00	$9.50
Variable costs per unit	4.80	5.50

Check (2) $55,940

Exercise 25-18
Comparison of payback and BET
P1 A2

This chapter explained two methods to evaluate investments using recovery time, the payback period and break-even time (BET). Refer to QS 25-15 and (1) compute the recovery time for both the payback period and break-even time, (2) discuss the advantage(s) of break-even time over the payback period, and (3) list two conditions under which payback period and break-even time are similar.

connect

Factor Company is planning to add a new product to its line. To manufacture this product, the company needs to buy a new machine at a $480,000 cost with an expected four-year life and a $20,000 salvage value. All sales are for cash, and all costs are out of pocket except for depreciation on the new machine. Additional information includes the following.

Expected annual sales of new product	$1,840,000
Expected annual costs of new product	
Direct materials	480,000
Direct labor	672,000
Overhead excluding straight-line depreciation on new machine	336,000
Selling and administrative expenses	160,000
Income taxes	30%

Required

1. Compute straight-line depreciation for each year of this new machine's life. (Round depreciation amounts to the nearest dollar.)
2. Determine expected net income and net cash flow for each year of this machine's life. (Round answers to the nearest dollar.)
3. Compute this machine's payback period, assuming that cash flows occur evenly throughout each year. (Round the payback period to two decimals.)
4. Compute this machine's accounting rate of return, assuming that income is earned evenly throughout each year. (Round the percentage return to two decimals.)
5. Compute the net present value for this machine using a discount rate of 7% and assuming that cash flows occur at each year-end. (*Hint:* Salvage value is a cash inflow at the end of the asset's life. Round the net present value to the nearest dollar.)

Most Company has an opportunity to invest in one of two new projects. Project Y requires a $350,000 investment for new machinery with a four-year life and no salvage value. Project Z requires a $350,000 investment for new machinery with a three-year life and no salvage value. The two projects yield the following predicted annual results. The company uses straight-line depreciation, and cash flows occur evenly throughout each year.

	Project Y	Project Z
Sales	$350,000	$280,000
Expenses		
Direct materials	49,000	35,000
Direct labor...........................	70,000	42,000
Overhead including depreciation	126,000	126,000
Selling and administrative expenses	25,000	25,000
Total expenses	270,000	228,000
Pretax income	80,000	52,000
Income taxes (30%)	24,000	15,600
Net income	$ 56,000	$ 36,400

Required

1. Compute each project's annual expected net cash flows. (Round the net cash flows to the nearest dollar.)
2. Determine each project's payback period. (Round the payback period to two decimals.)
3. Compute each project's accounting rate of return. (Round the percentage return to one decimal.)
4. Determine each project's net present value using 8% as the discount rate. For part 4 only, assume that cash flows occur at each year-end. (Round the net present value to the nearest dollar.)

Analysis Component

5. Identify the project you would recommend to management and explain your choice.

Problem 25-3A
Computation of cash flows
and net present values with
alternative depreciation
methods

P3

Manning Corporation is considering a new project requiring a $90,000 investment in test equipment with
no salvage value. The project would produce $66,000 of pretax income before depreciation at the end of
each of the next six years. The company's income tax rate is 40%. In compiling its tax return and computing its income tax payments, the company can choose between the two alternative depreciation schedules
shown in the table.

	Straight-Line Depreciation	MACRS Depreciation*
Year 1.........	$ 9,000	$18,000
Year 2.........	18,000	28,800
Year 3.........	18,000	17,280
Year 4.........	18,000	10,368
Year 5.........	18,000	10,368
Year 6.........	9,000	5,184
Totals	$90,000	$90,000

* The modified accelerated cost recovery system (MACRS) for
depreciation is discussed in Chapter 10.

Required

1. Prepare a five-column table that reports amounts (assuming use of straight-line depreciation) for each
of the following for each of the six years: (a) pretax income before depreciation, (b) straight-line depreciation expense, (c) taxable income, (d) income taxes, and (e) net cash flow. Net cash flow equals the
amount of income before depreciation minus the income taxes. (Round answers to the nearest dollar.)

2. Prepare a five-column table that reports amounts (assuming use of MACRS depreciation) for each of
the following for each of the six years: (a) pretax income before depreciation, (b) MACRS depreciation expense, (c) taxable income, (d) income taxes, and (e) net cash flow. Net cash flow equals the income amount before depreciation minus the income taxes. (Round answers to the nearest dollar.)

Check Net present value:
    (3) $108,518
    (4) $110,303

3. Compute the net present value of the investment if straight-line depreciation is used. Use 10% as the
discount rate. (Round the net present value to the nearest dollar.)

4. Compute the net present value of the investment if MACRS depreciation is used. Use 10% as the discount rate. (Round the net present value to the nearest dollar.)

Analysis Component

5. Explain why the MACRS depreciation method increases this project's net present value.

Problem 25-4A
Analysis of income effects of
additional business

A1

mhhe.com/wildFAP21e

Jones Products manufactures and sells to wholesalers approximately 400,000 packages per year of under-
water markers at $6 per package. Annual costs for the production and sale of this quantity are shown in the
table.

Direct materials................	$576,000
Direct labor	144,000
Overhead.....................	320,000
Selling expenses...............	150,000
Administrative expenses	100,000
Total costs and expenses........	$1,290,000

A new wholesaler has offered to buy 50,000 packages for $5.20 each. These markers would be marketed
under the wholesaler's name and would not affect Jones Products' sales through its normal channels.
A study of the costs of this additional business reveals the following:

● Direct materials costs are 100% variable.
● Per unit direct labor costs for the additional units would be 50% higher than normal because their production would require overtime pay at one-and-one-half times the usual labor rate.
● 25% of the normal annual overhead costs are fixed at any production level from 350,000 to 500,000
units. The remaining 75% of the annual overhead cost is variable with volume.

- Accepting the new business would involve no additional selling expenses.
- Accepting the new business would increase administrative expenses by a $5,000 fixed amount.

Required

Prepare a three-column comparative income statement that shows the following:

1. Annual operating income without the special order (column 1).
2. Annual operating income received from the new business only (column 2).
3. Combined annual operating income from normal business and the new business (column 3).

Check Operating income:
(1) $1,110,000

(2) $126,000

Edgerron Company is able to produce two products, G and B, with the same machine in its factory. The following information is available.

Problem 25-5A
Analysis of sales mix strategies

A1

	Product G	Product B
Selling price per unit	$120	$160
Variable costs per unit.................	40	90
Contribution margin per unit	$ 80	$ 70
Machine hours to produce 1 unit	0.4 hours	1.0 hours
Maximum unit sales per month...........	600 units	200 units

The company presently operates the machine for a single eight-hour shift for 22 working days each month. Management is thinking about operating the machine for two shifts, which will increase its productivity by another eight hours per day for 22 days per month. This change would require $15,000 additional fixed costs per month.

Required

1. Determine the contribution margin per machine hour that each product generates.
2. How many units of Product G and Product B should the company produce if it continues to operate with only one shift? How much total contribution margin does this mix produce each month?
3. If the company adds another shift, how many units of Product G and Product B should it produce? How much total contribution margin would this mix produce each month? Should the company add the new shift? Explain.
4. Suppose that the company determines that it can increase Product G's maximum sales to 700 units per month by spending $12,000 per month in marketing efforts. Should the company pursue this strategy and the double shift? Explain.

Check Units of Product G:
(2) 440

(3) 600

(4) 700

Elegant Decor Company's management is trying to decide whether to eliminate Department 200, which has produced losses or low profits for several years. The company's 2013 departmental income statement shows the following.

Problem 25-6A
Analysis of possible elimination of a department

A1

ELEGANT DECOR COMPANY
Departmental Income Statements
For Year Ended December 31, 2013

	Dept. 100	Dept. 200	Combined
Sales	$436,000	$290,000	$726,000
Cost of goods sold	262,000	207,000	469,000
Gross profit	174,000	83,000	257,000
Operating expenses			
Direct expenses			
Advertising......................	17,000	12,000	29,000
Store supplies used	4,000	3,800	7,800
Depreciation—Store equipment.........	5,000	3,300	8,300
Total direct expenses	26,000	19,100	45,100

[continued on next page]

[continued from previous page]

Allocated expenses			
Sales salaries	65,000	39,000	104,000
Rent expense	9,440	4,720	14,160
Bad debts expense	9,900	8,100	18,000
Office salary	18,720	12,480	31,200
Insurance expense	2,000	1,100	3,100
Miscellaneous office expenses	2,400	1,600	4,000
Total allocated expenses	107,460	67,000	174,460
Total expenses	133,460	86,100	219,560
Net income (loss)	$ 40,540	$ (3,100)	$ 37,440

In analyzing whether to eliminate Department 200, management considers the following:

a. The company has one office worker who earns $600 per week, or $31,200 per year, and four sales-clerks who each earn $500 per week, or $26,000 per year for each salesclerk.

b. The full salaries of two salesclerks are charged to Department 100. The full salary of one salesclerk is charged to Department 200. The salary of the fourth clerk, who works half-time in both departments, is divided evenly between the two departments.

c. Eliminating Department 200 would avoid the sales salaries and the office salary currently allocated to it. However, management prefers another plan. Two salesclerks have indicated that they will be quitting soon. Management believes that their work can be done by the other two clerks if the one office worker works in sales half-time. Eliminating Department 200 will allow this shift of duties. If this change is implemented, half the office worker's salary would be reported as sales salaries and half would be reported as office salary.

d. The store building is rented under a long-term lease that cannot be changed. Therefore, Department 100 will use the space and equipment currently used by Department 200.

e. Closing Department 200 will eliminate its expenses for advertising, bad debts, and store supplies; 70% of the insurance expense allocated to it to cover its merchandise inventory; and 25% of the miscellaneous office expenses presently allocated to it.

Required

Check   (1) Total expenses:
(a) $688,560, (b) $284,070

1. Prepare a three-column report that lists items and amounts for (a) the company's total expenses (including cost of goods sold)—in column 1, (b) the expenses that would be eliminated by closing Department 200—in column 2, and (c) the expenses that will continue—in column 3.

(2) Forecasted net income without Department 200, $31,510

2. Prepare a forecasted annual income statement for the company reflecting the elimination of Department 200 assuming that it will not affect Department 100's sales and gross profit. The statement should reflect the reassignment of the office worker to one-half time as a salesclerk.

Analysis Component

3. Reconcile the company's combined net income with the forecasted net income assuming that Department 200 is eliminated (list both items and amounts). Analyze the reconciliation and explain why you think the department should or should not be eliminated.

PROBLEM SET B

Problem 25-1B
Computation of payback period, accounting rate of return, and net present value

P1   P2   P3

Cortino Company is planning to add a new product to its line. To manufacture this product, the company needs to buy a new machine at a $300,000 cost with an expected four-year life and a $20,000 salvage value. All sales are for cash and all costs are out of pocket, except for depreciation on the new machine. Additional information includes the following.

Expected annual sales of new product	$1,150,000
Expected annual costs of new product	
Direct materials	300,000
Direct labor	420,000
Overhead excluding straight-line depreciation on new machine	210,000
Selling and administrative expenses	100,000
Income taxes	30%

Required

1. Compute straight-line depreciation for each year of this new machine's life. (Round depreciation amounts to the nearest dollar.)

2. Determine expected net income and net cash flow for each year of this machine's life. (Round answers to the nearest dollar.)

3. Compute this machine's payback period, assuming that cash flows occur evenly throughout each year. (Round the payback period to two decimals.)

4. Compute this machine's accounting rate of return, assuming that income is earned evenly throughout each year. (Round the percentage return to two decimals.)

5. Compute the net present value for this machine using a discount rate of 7% and assuming that cash flows occur at each year-end. (*Hint:* Salvage value is a cash inflow at the end of the asset's life.)

Check (4) 21.88%

(5) $70,915

Aikman Company has an opportunity to invest in one of two projects. Project A requires a $240,000 investment for new machinery with a four-year life and no salvage value. Project B also requires a $240,000 investment for new machinery with a three-year life and no salvage value. The two projects yield the following predicted annual results. The company uses straight-line depreciation, and cash flows occur evenly throughout each year.

Problem 25-2B
Analysis and computation of payback period, accounting rate of return, and net present value

P1 P2 P3

	Project A	Project B
Sales	$250,000	$200,000
Expenses		
Direct materials	35,000	25,000
Direct labor	50,000	30,000
Overhead including depreciation	90,000	90,000
Selling and administrative expenses	18,000	18,000
Total expenses	193,000	163,000
Pretax income	57,000	37,000
Income taxes (30%)	17,100	11,100
Net income	$ 39,900	$ 25,900

Required

1. Compute each project's annual expected net cash flows. (Round net cash flows to the nearest dollar.)

2. Determine each project's payback period. (Round the payback period to two decimals.)

3. Compute each project's accounting rate of return. (Round the percentage return to one decimal.)

4. Determine each project's net present value using 8% as the discount rate. For part 4 only, assume that cash flows occur at each year-end. (Round net present values to the nearest dollar.)

Check For Project A: (2) 2.4 years

(3) 33.3%

(4) $90,879

Analysis Component

5. Identify the project you would recommend to management and explain your choice.

Grossman Corporation is considering a new project requiring a $30,000 investment in an asset having no salvage value. The project would produce $12,000 of pretax income before depreciation at the end of each of the next six years. The company's income tax rate is 40%. In compiling its tax return and computing its income tax payments, the company can choose between two alternative depreciation schedules as shown in the table.

Problem 25-3B
Computation of cash flows and net present values with alternative depreciation methods

P3

	Straight-Line Depreciation	MACRS Depreciation*
Year 1	$ 3,000	$ 6,000
Year 2	6,000	9,600
Year 3	6,000	5,760
Year 4	6,000	3,456
Year 5	6,000	3,456
Year 6	3,000	1,728
Totals	$30,000	$30,000

* The modified accelerated cost recovery system (MACRS) for depreciation is discussed in Chapter 10.

Required

1. Prepare a five-column table that reports amounts (assuming use of straight-line depreciation) for each of the following items for each of the six years: (a) pretax income before depreciation, (b) straight-line depreciation expense, (c) taxable income, (d) income taxes, and (e) net cash flow. Net cash flow equals the amount of income before depreciation minus the income taxes. (Round answers to the nearest dollar.)

2. Prepare a five-column table that reports amounts (assuming use of MACRS depreciation) for each of the following items for each of the six years: (a) income before depreciation, (b) MACRS depreciation expense, (c) taxable income, (d) income taxes, and (e) net cash flow. Net cash flow equals the amount of income before depreciation minus the income taxes. (Round answers to the nearest dollar.)

Check Net present value:
(3) $10,041
(4) $10,635

3. Compute the net present value of the investment if straight-line depreciation is used. Use 10% as the discount rate. (Round the net present value to the nearest dollar.)

4. Compute the net present value of the investment if MACRS depreciation is used. Use 10% as the discount rate. (Round the net present value to the nearest dollar.)

Analysis Component

5. Explain why the MACRS depreciation method increases the net present value of this project.

Problem 25-4B
Analysis of income effects of additional business
A1

Windmire Company manufactures and sells to local wholesalers approximately 300,000 units per month at a sales price of $4 per unit. Monthly costs for the production and sale of this quantity follow.

Direct materials	$384,000
Direct labor	96,000
Overhead	288,000
Selling expenses	120,000
Administrative expenses	80,000
Total costs and expenses	$968,000

A new out-of-state distributor has offered to buy 50,000 units next month for $3.44 each. These units would be marketed in other states and would not affect Windtrax's sales through its normal channels. A study of the costs of this new business reveals the following:

- Direct materials costs are 100% variable.
- Per unit direct labor costs for the additional units would be 50% higher than normal because their production would require overtime pay at one and one half times their normal rate to meet the distributor's deadline.
- Twenty-five percent of the normal annual overhead costs are fixed at any production level from 250,000 to 400,000 units. The remaining 75% is variable with volume.
- Accepting the new business would involve no additional selling expenses.
- Accepting the new business would increase administrative expenses by a $4,000 fixed amount.

Required

Prepare a three-column comparative income statement that shows the following:

Check Operating income:
(1) $232,000, (2) $44,000

1. Monthly operating income without the special order (column 1).

2. Monthly operating income received from the new business only (column 2).

3. Combined monthly operating income from normal business and the new business (column 3).

Problem 25-5B
Analysis of sales mix strategies
A1

Sung Company is able to produce two products, R and T, with the same machine in its factory. The following information is available.

	Product R	Product T
Selling price per unit	$60	$80
Variable costs per unit	20	45
Contribution margin per unit	$40	$35
Machine hours to produce 1 unit	0.4 hours	1.0 hours
Maximum unit sales per month	550 units	175 units

The company presently operates the machine for a single eight-hour shift for 22 working days each month. Management is thinking about operating the machine for two shifts, which will increase its productivity by another eight hours per day for 22 days per month. This change would require $3,250 additional fixed costs per month.

Required

1. Determine the contribution margin per machine hour that each product generates.

2. How many units of Product R and Product T should the company produce if it continues to operate with only one shift? How much total contribution margin does this mix produce each month?

3. If the company adds another shift, how many units of Product R and Product T should it produce? How much total contribution margin would this mix produce each month? Should the company add the new shift? Explain.

4. Suppose that the company determines that it can increase Product R's maximum sales to 675 units per month by spending $4,500 per month in marketing efforts. Should the company pursue this strategy and the double shift? Explain.

Check Units of Product R: (2) 440

(3) 550

(4) 675

Esme Company's management is trying to decide whether to eliminate Department Z, which has produced low profits or losses for several years. The company's 2013 departmental income statement shows the following.

Problem 25-6B
Analysis of possible elimination of a department

A1

ESME COMPANY Departmental Income Statements For Year Ended December 31, 2013			
	Dept. A	Dept. Z	Combined
Sales	$700,000	$175,000	$875,000
Cost of goods sold	461,300	125,100	586,400
Gross profit	238,700	49,900	288,600
Operating expenses			
Direct expenses			
Advertising	27,000	3,000	30,000
Store supplies used	5,600	1,400	7,000
Depreciation—Store equipment	14,000	7,000	21,000
Total direct expenses	46,600	11,400	58,000
Allocated expenses			
Sales salaries	70,200	23,400	93,600
Rent expense	22,080	5,520	27,600
Bad debts expense	21,000	4,000	25,000
Office salary	20,800	5,200	26,000
Insurance expense	4,200	1,400	5,600
Miscellaneous office expenses	1,700	2,500	4,200
Total allocated expenses	139,980	42,020	182,000
Total expenses	186,580	53,420	240,000
Net income (loss)	$ 52,120	$ (3,520)	$ 48,600

In analyzing whether to eliminate Department Z, management considers the following items:

a. The company has one office worker who earns $500 per week or $26,000 per year and four salesclerks who each earn $450 per week or $23,400 per year for each salesclerk.

b. The full salaries of three salesclerks are charged to Department A. The full salary of one salesclerk is charged to Department Z.

c. Eliminating Department Z would avoid the sales salaries and the office salary currently allocated to it. However, management prefers another plan. Two salesclerks have indicated that they will be quitting soon. Management believes that their work can be done by the two remaining clerks if the one office worker works in sales half-time. Eliminating Department Z will allow this shift of duties. If this change is implemented, half the office worker's salary would be reported as sales salaries and half would be reported as office salary.

d. The store building is rented under a long-term lease that cannot be changed. Therefore, Department A will use the space and equipment currently used by Department Z.

e. Closing Department Z will eliminate its expenses for advertising, bad debts, and store supplies; 65% of the insurance expense allocated to it to cover its merchandise inventory; and 30% of the miscellaneous office expenses presently allocated to it.

Required

1. Prepare a three-column report that lists items and amounts for (a) the company's total expenses (including cost of goods sold)—in column 1, (b) the expenses that would be eliminated by closing Department Z—in column 2, and (c) the expenses that will continue—in column 3.

2. Prepare a forecasted annual income statement for the company reflecting the elimination of Department Z assuming that it will not affect Department A's sales and gross profit. The statement should reflect the reassignment of the office worker to one-half time as a salesclerk.

Analysis Component

3. Reconcile the company's combined net income with the forecasted net income assuming that Department Z is eliminated (list both items and amounts). Analyze the reconciliation and explain why you think the department should or should not be eliminated.

SERIAL PROBLEM
Success Systems

P1 P2

(This serial problem began in Chapter 1 and continues through most of the book. If previous chapter segments were not completed, the serial problem can begin at this point. It is helpful, but not necessary, to use the Working Papers that accompany the book.)

SP 25 Adria Lopez is considering the purchase of equipment for Success Systems that would allow the company to add a new product to its computer furniture line. The equipment is expected to cost $300,000 and to have a six-year life and no salvage value. It will be depreciated on a straight-line basis. Success Systems expects to sell 100 units of the equipment's product each year. The expected annual income related to this equipment follows.

Sales	$375,000
Costs	
Materials, labor, and overhead (except depreciation)	200,000
Depreciation on new equipment	50,000
Selling and administrative expenses	37,500
Total costs and expenses	287,500
Pretax income	87,500
Income taxes (30%)	26,250
Net income	$ 61,250

Required

Compute the (1) payback period and (2) accounting rate of return for this equipment. (Record answers as percents, rounded to one decimal.)

Beyond the Numbers

REPORTING IN ACTION

P3

Polaris

BTN 25-1 Assume **Polaris** invested $2.12 million to expand its manufacturing capacity. Assume that these assets have a ten-year life, and that Polaris requires a 10% internal rate of return on these assets.

Required

1. What is the amount of annual cash flows that Polaris must earn from these projects to have a 10% internal rate of return? (*Hint:* Identify the ten-period, 10% factor from the present value of an annuity table, and then divide $2.12 million by this factor to get the annual cash flows necessary.)

Fast Forward

2. Access Polaris' financial statements for fiscal years ended after December 31, 2011, from its Website (**Polaris.com**) or the SEC's Website (**SEC.gov**).

   a. Determine the amount that Polaris invested in capital assets for the most recent year. (*Hint:* Refer to the statement of cash flows.)

   b. Assume a ten-year life and a 10% internal rate of return. What is the amount of cash flows that Polaris must earn on these new projects?

BTN 25-2   **Polaris** and **Arctic Cat** sell several different products; most are profitable but some are not. Teams of employees in each company make advertising, investment, and product mix decisions. A certain portion of advertising for both companies is on a local basis to a target audience.

COMPARATIVE ANALYSIS

A1

Polaris

Arctic Cat

Required

1. Contact the local newspaper and ask the approximate cost of ad space (for example, cost of one page or one-half page of advertising) for a company's product or group of products (such as Polaris ATVs).

2. Estimate how many products this advertisement must sell to justify its cost. Begin by taking the product's sales price advertised for each company and assume a 20% contribution margin.

3. Prepare a one-half page memorandum explaining the importance of effective advertising when making a product mix decision. Be prepared to present your ideas in class.

BTN 25-3   A consultant commented that "too often the numbers look good but feel bad." This comment often stems from estimation error common to capital budgeting proposals that relate to future cash flows. Three reasons for this error often exist. First, reliably predicting cash flows several years into the future is very difficult. Second, the present value of cash flows many years into the future (say, beyond 10 years) is often very small. Third, it is difficult for personal biases and expectations not to unduly influence present value computations.

ETHICS CHALLENGE

P3

Required

1. Compute the present value of $100 to be received in 10 years assuming a 12% discount rate.

2. Why is understanding the three reasons mentioned for estimation errors important when evaluating investment projects? Link this response to your answer for part 1.

BTN 25-4   Payback period, accounting rate of return, net present value, and internal rate of return are common methods to evaluate capital investment opportunities. Assume that your manager asks you to identify the type of measurement basis and unit that each method offers and to list the advantages and disadvantages of each. Present your response in memorandum format of less than one page.

COMMUNICATING IN PRACTICE

P1 P2 P3 P4

BTN 25-5   Many companies must determine whether to internally produce their component parts or to outsource them. Further, some companies now outsource key components or business processes to international providers. Access the Website **BizBrim.com** and review the available information on business process outsourcing.

TAKING IT TO THE NET

A1

Required

1. What types of processes are commonly outsourced, according to Bizbrim?

2. What are some of the benefits listed for business process outsourcing?

BTN 25-6   Break into teams and identify four reasons that an international airline such as **Southwest** or **Delta** would invest in a project when its direct analysis using both payback period and net present value indicate it to be a poor investment. (*Hint:* Think about qualitative factors.) Provide an example of an investment project supporting your answer.

TEAMWORK IN ACTION

P1 P3

ENTREPRENEURIAL DECISION

P1 P2 P3 P4

BTN 25-7   Read the chapter opener about Charlie Fyffe and his company, **Charlie's Brownies**. Suppose Charlie's business grows and he considers building a new, massive bakery and warehousing center to make his business more efficient and reduce costs.

Required

1. What are some of the management tools that Charlie can use to evaluate whether the new bakery and warehousing center will be a good investment?
2. What information does Charlie need to use the tools that you identified in your answer to part 1?
3. What are some of the advantages and disadvantages of each tool identified in your answer to part 1?

HITTING THE ROAD

P3

BTN 25-8   Visit or call a local auto dealership and inquire about leasing a car. Ask about the down payment and the required monthly payments. You will likely find the salesperson does not discuss the cost to purchase this car but focuses on the affordability of the monthly payments. This chapter gives you the tools to compute the cost of this car using the lease payment schedule in present dollars and to estimate the profit from leasing for an auto dealership.

Required

1. Compare the cost of leasing the car to buying it in present dollars using the information from the dealership you contact. (Assume you will make a final payment at the end of the lease and then own the car.)
2. Is it more costly to lease or buy the car? Support your answer with computations.

GLOBAL DECISION

C1

KTM

BTN 25-9   Access **KTM**'s 2011 annual report dated December 31, 2011, from its Website **www.KTM.com**. Identify and read the section in the Group Status Report—2011, section 12, regarding Sustainability.

Required

KTM reports that they developed a special KTM motorcycle logistics system on reusable metal plates. This special system eliminates additional packaging materials. These sustainability efforts are costly. Why would a company like KTM pursue these costly efforts?

ANSWERS TO MULTIPLE CHOICE QUIZ

1. a; Reworking provides incremental revenue of $11 per unit ($19 − $8); and, it costs $10 to rework them. The company is better off by $1 per unit when it reworks these products and sells them at the regular price.

2. e; Product X has a $2 contribution margin per machine hour [($32 − $12)/ 10 MH]; Product Y has a $7 contribution margin per machine hour [($24 − $10)/2 MH]. It should produce as much of Product Y as possible.

3. a; Total revenue from the special order = 3,000 units × $15 per unit = $45,000; and, Total costs for the special order = (3,000 units × $9 per unit) + $5,000 = $32,000. Net income from the special order = $45,000 − $32,000 = $13,000. Thus, yes, it should accept the order.

4. c; Payback = $270,000/$61,200 per year = 4.4 years.

5. d; Accounting rate of return = $8,550/[($180,000 + $0)/2] = 9.5%.

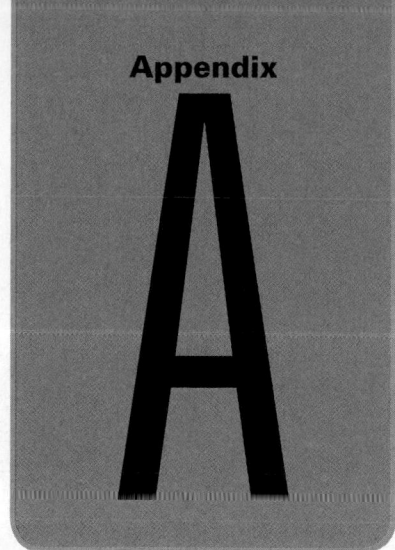

Financial Statement Information

This appendix includes financial information for (1) **Polaris**, (2) **Arctic Cat**, (3) **KTM**, and (4) **Piaggio**. This information is taken from their annual 10-K reports (or annual reports for KTM and Piaggio) filed with the SEC or other regulatory agency. An **annual report** is a summary of a company's financial results for the year along with its current financial condition and future plans. This report is directed to external users of financial information, but it also affects the actions and decisions of internal users.

A company often uses an annual report to showcase itself and its products. Many annual reports include photos, diagrams, and illustrations related to the company. The primary objective of annual reports, however, is the *financial section,* which communicates much information about a company, with most data drawn from the accounting information system. The layout of an annual report's financial section is fairly established and typically includes the following:

- Letter to Shareholders
- Financial History and Highlights
- Management Discussion and Analysis
- Management's Report on Financial Statements and on Internal Controls
- Report of Independent Accountants (Auditor's Report) and on Internal Controls
- Financial Statements
- Notes to Financial Statements
- List of Directors and Officers

This appendix provides the financial statements for Polaris (plus selected notes), Arctic Cat, KTM, and Piaggio. The appendix is organized as follows:

- **Polaris A-2** through **A-9**
- **Arctic Cat A-10** through **A-13**
- **KTM A-14** through **A-17**
- **Piaggio A-18** through **A-21**

Polaris
Arctic Cat
KTM
PIAGGIO

Many assignments at the end of each chapter refer to information in this appendix. We encourage readers to spend time with these assignments; they are especially useful in showing the relevance and diversity of financial accounting and reporting.

Special note: The SEC maintains the EDGAR (**E**lectronic **D**ata **G**athering, **A**nalysis, and **R**etrieval) database at **www.sec.gov** for U.S. filers. The **Form 10-K** is the annual report form for most companies. It provides electronically accessible information. The **Form 10-KSB** is the annual report form filed by small businesses. It requires slightly less information than the Form 10-K. One of these forms must be filed within 90 days after the company's fiscal year-end. (Forms 10-K405, 10-KT, 10-KT405, and 10-KSB405 are slight variations of the usual form due to certain regulations or rules.)

POLARIS

POLARIS INDUSTRIES INC.
CONSOLIDATED BALANCE SHEETS

December 31 (In thousands, except per share data)	2011	2010
ASSETS		
Current Assets		
Cash and cash equivalents	$ 325,336	$ 393,927
Trade receivables, net	115,302	89,294
Inventories, net	298,042	235,927
Prepaid expenses and other	37,608	21,628
Income taxes receivable	24,723	—
Deferred tax assets	77,665	67,369
Total current assets	878,676	808,145
Property and Equipment		
Land, buildings and improvements	123,771	118,831
Equipment and tooling	524,382	488,562
	648,153	607,393
Less accumulated depreciation	(434,375)	(423,382)
Property and equipment, net	213,778	184,011
Investments in finance affiliate	42,251	37,169
Investments in other affiliates	5,000	1,009
Deferred tax assets	10,601	—
Goodwill and other intangible assets, net	77,718	31,313
Total Assets	$1,228,024	$1,061,647
LIABILITIES AND SHAREHOLDERS' EQUITY		
Current Liabilities		
Current portion of long-term borrowings under credit agreement	—	$ 100,000
Current portion of capital lease obligations	$ 2,653	—
Accounts payable	146,743	113,248
Accrued expenses		
Compensation	187,671	126,781
Warranties	44,355	32,651
Sales promotions and incentives	81,228	75,494
Dealer holdback	76,512	79,688
Other	75,730	53,744
Income taxes payable	639	2,604
Total current liabilities	615,531	584,210
Long term income taxes payable	7,837	5,509
Deferred income taxes	—	937
Capital lease obligations	4,600	—
Long-term debt	100,000	100,000
Total liabilities	727,968	690,656
Shareholders' Equity		
Preferred stock $0.01 par value, 20,000 shares authorized, no shares issued and outstanding	—	—
Common stock $0.01 par value, 160,000 shares authorized, 68,430 and 68,468 shares issued and outstanding	684	685
Additional paid-in capital	165,518	79,239
Retained earnings	321,831	285,169
Accumulated other comprehensive income, net	12,023	5,898
Total shareholders' equity	500,056	370,991
Total Liabilities and Shareholders' Equity	$1,228,024	$1,061,647

Shares outstanding, common stock, additional paid-in-capital, retained earnings and per share data
have been adjusted to give effect to the two-for-one stock split declared on July 20, 2011, paid on
September 12, 2011 to shareholders of record on September 2, 2011.

POLARIS INDUSTRIES INC.
CONSOLIDATED STATEMENTS OF INCOME

For the Years Ended December 31 (In thousands, except per share data)	2011	2010	2009
Sales	$2,656,949	$1,991,139	$1,565,887
Cost of sales	1,916,366	1,460,926	1,172,668
Gross profit	740,583	530,213	393,219
Operating expenses			
Selling and marketing	178,725	142,353	111,137
Research and development	105,631	84,940	62,999
General and administrative	130,395	99,055	71,184
Total operating expenses	414,751	326,348	245,320
Income from financial services	24,092	16,856	17,071
Operating income	349,924	220,721	164,970
Non-operating expense (income)			
Interest expense	3,987	2,680	4,111
(Gain) loss on securities available for sale	—	(825)	8,952
Other expense (income), net	(689)	325	733
Income before income taxes	346,626	218,541	151,174
Provision for income taxes	119,051	71,403	50,157
Net income	$ 227,575	$ 147,138	$ 101,017
Basic net income per share	$ 3.31	$ 2.20	$ 1.56
Diluted net income per share	$ 3.20	$ 2.14	$ 1.53
Weighted average shares outstanding:			
Basic	68,792	66,900	64,798
Diluted	71,057	68,765	66,148

Shares outstanding and per share data have been adjusted to give effect to the two-for-one stock split declared on
July 20, 2011, paid on September 12, 2011 to shareholders of record on September 2, 2011.

POLARIS INDUSTRIES INC.
CONSOLIDATED STATEMENTS OF SHAREHOLDERS' EQUITY AND COMPREHENSIVE INCOME

(In thousands, except per share data)	Number of Shares	Common Stock	Additional Paid-In Capital	Retained Earnings	Accumulated Other Comprehensive Income (Loss)	Total
Balance, December 31, 2008	64,984	$650	—	$ 140,234	$ (3,857)	$ 137,027
Employee stock compensation	62	1	10,225			10,226
Proceeds from stock issuances under employee plans	472	4	4,729			4,733
Tax effect of exercise of stock options			(410)			(410)
Cash dividends declared ($0.78 per share)				(50,177)		(50,177)
Repurchase and retirement of common shares	(222)	(2)	(4,554)			(4,556)
Comprehensive income:						
Net Income				101,017		
Foreign currency translation adjustments, net of tax of $69					115	
Reclassification of unrealized loss on available for sale securities to the income statement, net of tax of $2,277					6,675	
Unrealized loss on available for sale securities, net of tax benefit of $230					(382)	
Unrealized gain on derivative instruments, net of tax of $165					273	
Total comprehensive income						107,698
Balance, December 31, 2009	65,296	653	9,990	191,074	2,824	204,541
Employee stock compensation	308	3	18,049			18,052
Proceeds from stock issuances under employee plans	4,066	41	68,064			68,105
Tax effect of exercise of stock options			10,610			10,610
Cash dividends declared ($0.80 per share)				(53,043)		(53,043)
Repurchase and retirement of common shares	(1,202)	(12)	(27,474)			(27,486)
Comprehensive income:						
Net Income				147,138		
Foreign currency translation adjustments, net of tax of $222					3,131	
Unrealized gain on available for sale securities, net of tax benefit of $230					382	
Unrealized loss on derivative instruments, net of tax benefit of $256					(439)	
Total comprehensive income						150,212
Balance, December 31, 2010	68,468	685	79,239	285,169	5,898	370,991
Employee stock compensation	290	3	20,545			20,548
Proceeds from stock issuances under employee plans	2,280	22	45,632			45,654
Tax effect of exercise of stock options			23,120			23,120
Cash dividends declared ($0.90 per share)				(61,585)		(61,585)
Repurchase and retirement of common shares	(2,608)	(26)	(3,018)	(129,328)		(132,372)
Comprehensive income:						
Net Income				227,575		
Foreign currency translation adjustments, net of tax benefit of $6,782					2,554	
Unrealized gain/(loss) on derivative instruments, net of tax of $2,125					3,571	
Total comprehensive income						233,700
Balance, December 31, 2011	68,430	$684	$165,518	$ 321,831	$12,023	$ 500,056

Shares outstanding, common stock, additional paid-in-capital, retained earnings and per share data
have been adjusted to give effect to the two-for-one stock split declared on July 20, 2011, paid on
September 12, 2011 to shareholders of record on September 2, 2011.

POLARIS INDUSTRIES INC.
CONSOLIDATED STATEMENTS OF CASH FLOWS

For the Year Ended December 31 (In thousands)	2011	2010	2009
Operating Activities			
Net income	$ 227,575	$147,138	$ 101,017
Adjustments to reconcile net income to net cash provided by operating activities:			
(Gain) loss on securities available for sale	—	(825)	8,952
Depreciation and amortization	66,390	66,519	64,593
Noncash compensation	20,548	18,052	10,226
Noncash income from financial services	(4,444)	(4,574)	(4,021)
Noncash expense from other affiliates	133	1,376	382
Deferred income taxes	(16,946)	(16,888)	13,573
Tax effect of share-based compensation exercises	(23,120)	(10,610)	410
Changes in current operating items:			
Trade receivables	(23,115)	1,111	8,192
Inventories	(49,973)	(56,612)	42,997
Accounts payable	27,232	37,580	(40,329)
Accrued expenses	80,668	107,363	(24,759)
Income taxes payable/receivable	(1,343)	7,033	7,325
Prepaid expenses and others, net	(1,075)	956	4,643
Net cash provided by operating activities	302,530	297,619	193,201
Investing Activities			
Purchase of property and equipment	(84,484)	(55,718)	(43,932)
Investments in finance affiliate	(12,588)	(9,173)	(3,007)
Distributions from finance affiliate	11,950	17,910	17,261
Investment in other affiliates	(5,000)	—	—
Proceeds from sale of investments	876	9,061	—
Acquisition of businesses, net of cash acquired	(51,899)	(4,738)	—
Net cash used for investment activities	(141,145)	(42,118)	(29,678)
Financing Activities			
Borrowings under credit agreement / senior notes	100,000	—	364,000
Repayments under credit agreement	(202,333)	—	(364,000)
Repurchase and retirement of common shares	(132,372)	(27,486)	(4,556)
Cash dividends to shareholders	(61,585)	(53,043)	(50,177)
Tax effect of proceeds from share-based compensation exercises	23,120	10,610	(410)
Proceeds from stock issuances under employee plans	45,654	68,105	4,733
Net cash used for financing activities	(227,516)	(1,814)	(50,410)
Impact of currency exchange rates on cash balances	(2,460)	—	—
Net increase (decrease) in cash and cash equivalents	(68,591)	253,687	113,113
Cash and cash equivalents at beginning of period	393,927	140,240	27,127
Cash and cash equivalents at end of period	$ 325,336	$393,927	$ 140,240
Supplemental Cash Flow Information:			
Interest paid on debt borrowings	$ 3,350	$ 2,813	$ 3,966
Income taxes paid	$ 132,088	$ 81,142	$ 29,039

POLARIS

POLARIS INDUSTRIES INC.
<u>SELECTED</u> NOTES TO CONSOLIDATED FINANCIAL STATEMENTS

Note 1. Organization and Significant Accounting Policies

Polaris Industries Inc. ("Polaris" or the "Company") a Minnesota corporation, and its subsidiaries, are engaged in the design, engineering, manufacturing and marketing of innovative, high-quality, high-performance Off-Road Vehicles ("ORV"), Snowmobiles, and On-Road Vehicles, including motorcycles and Small Electric Vehicles. Polaris products, together with related parts, garments and accessories are sold worldwide through a network of dealers, distributors and its subsidiaries located in the United States, Canada, France, the United Kingdom, Australia, Norway, Sweden, Germany, Spain, China, India and Brazil.

Basis of presentation: The accompanying consolidated financial statements include the accounts of Polaris and its wholly-owned subsidiaries. All inter-company transactions and balances have been eliminated in consolidation. Income from financial services is reported as a component of operating income to better reflect income from ongoing operations, of which financial services has a significant impact.

During the 2011 third quarter, the Board of Directors declared a two-for-one split of the Company's outstanding shares of Common Stock. On September 12, 2011, Polaris shareholders received one additional share of Common Stock for each share they held of record at the close of business on September 2, 2011. All amounts, including shares and per share information, have been adjusted to give effect to the two-for-one stock split.

Investment in finance affiliate: The caption Investment in finance affiliate in the consolidated balance sheets represents Polaris' 50 percent equity interest in Polaris Acceptance, a partnership agreement between GE Commercial Distribution Finance Corporation ("GECDF") and one of Polaris' wholly-owned subsidiaries. Polaris Acceptance provides floor plan financing to Polaris dealers in the United States. Polaris' investment in Polaris Acceptance is accounted for under the equity method, and is recorded as investments in finance affiliate in the consolidated balance sheets.

Investment in other affiliates: The caption Investments in other affiliates in the consolidated balance sheets for the period ended December 31, 2011 represents the Company's October 2011 investment in Brammo, Inc., a privately held manufacturer of electric motorcycles. This investment represents a minority interest in Brammo and is accounted for under the cost method.

(Gain) Loss on Securities Available for Sale: The net gain of $825,000 in 2010 on securities available for sale resulted from a $1,594,000 gain on the sale of our remaining investment in KTM during the 2010 third quarter offset by a related non-cash impairment charge of $769,000 during the 2010 second quarter. In the first quarter 2009, we recorded a non-cash impairment charge on securities held for sales of $8,952,000 from the decline in the fair value of the KTM shares owned by Polaris as of March 31, 2009, when it was determined that the decline in the fair value of the KTM shares owned by the Company was other than temporary.

Use of estimates: The preparation of financial statements in conformity with accounting principles generally accepted in the United States requires management to make estimates and assumptions that affect the reported amounts of assets and liabilities and disclosure of contingent assets and liabilities at the date of the financial statements and the reported amounts of revenues and expenses during the reporting period. Ultimate results could differ from those estimates.

Cash equivalents: Polaris considers all highly liquid investments purchased with an original maturity of 90 days or less to be cash equivalents. Cash equivalents are stated at cost, which approximates fair value. Such investments consist principally of money market mutual funds.

Allowance for doubtful accounts: Polaris' financial exposure to collection of accounts receivable is limited due to its agreements with certain finance companies. For receivables not serviced through these finance companies, the Company provides a reserve for doubtful accounts based on historical rates and trends. This reserve is adjusted periodically as information about specific accounts becomes available.

Inventories: Inventories are stated at the lower of cost (first-in, first-out method) or market. The major components of inventories are as follows (in thousands):

December 31	2011	2010
Raw materials and purchased components	$ 61,296	$ 35,580
Service parts, garments and accessories	77,437	60,813
Finished goods	175,252	155,744
Less: reserves	(15,943)	(16,210)
Inventories	$298,042	$235,927

Property and equipment: Property and equipment is stated at cost. Depreciation is provided using the straight-line method over the estimated useful life of the respective assets, ranging from 10–40 years for buildings and improvements and from 1–7 years for equipment and tooling. Fully depreciated tooling is eliminated from the accounting records annually.

Research and Development Expenses: Polaris records research and development expenses in the period in which they are incurred as a component of operating expenses. In the years ended December 31, 2011, 2010, and 2009, Polaris incurred $105,631,000, $84,940,000, and $62,999,000, respectively.

Advertising Expenses: Polaris records advertising expenses as a component of selling and marketing expenses in the period in which they are incurred. In the years ended December 31, 2011, 2010, and 2009, Polaris incurred $48,877,000, $40,833,000 and $37,433,000, respectively.

Shipping and Handling Costs: Polaris records shipping and handling costs as a component of cost of sales at the time the product is shipped.

Product warranties: Polaris provides a limited warranty for its ORVs for a period of six months and for a period of one year for its snowmobiles and motorcycles and a two year period for SEVs. Polaris provides longer warranties in certain geographical markets as determined by local regulations and market conditions and may provide longer warranties related to certain promotional programs.

Polaris' standard warranties require the Company or its dealers to repair or replace defective products during such warranty periods at no cost to the consumer. The warranty reserve is established at the time of sale to the dealer or distributor based on management's best estimate using historical rates and trends. Adjustments to the warranty reserve are made from time to time as actual claims become known in order to properly estimate the amounts necessary to settle future and existing claims on products sold as of the balance sheet date. Factors that could have an impact on the warranty accrual in any given year include the following: improved manufacturing quality, shifts in product mix, changes in warranty coverage periods, snowfall and its impact on snowmobile usage, product recalls and any significant changes in sales volume. The activity in the warranty reserve during the years presented is as follows (in thousands):

For the Year Ended December 31	2011	2010	2009
Balance at beginning of year	$ 32,651	$ 25,520	$ 28,631
Additions to warranty reserve through acquisitions	2,727	—	—
Additions charged to expense	46,217	43,721	40,977
Warranty claims paid	(37,240)	(36,590)	(44,088)
Balance at end of year	$ 44,355	$ 32,651	$ 25,520

Sales promotions and incentives: Polaris provides for estimated sales promotion and incentive expenses, which are recognized as a reduction to sales, at the time of sale to the dealer or distributor. Polaris recorded accrued liabilities of $81,228,000 and $75,494,000 related to various sales promotions and incentive programs as of December 31, 2011 and 2010, respectively.

Dealer holdback programs: Dealer holdback represents a portion of the invoiced sales price that is expected to be subsequently returned to the dealer or distributor as a sales incentive upon the ultimate retail sale of the product. Polaris recorded accrued liabilities of $76,512,000 and $79,688,000, for dealer holdback programs in the consolidated balance sheets as of December 31, 2011 and 2010, respectively.

Foreign currency translation: The functional currency for each of the Polaris foreign subsidiaries is their respective local currencies. The assets and liabilities in all Polaris foreign entities are translated at the foreign exchange rate in effect at the balance sheet date. Translation gains and losses are reflected as a component of Accumulated other comprehensive income in the shareholders' equity section of the accompanying consolidated balance sheets. Revenues and expenses in all of Polaris' foreign entities are translated at the average foreign exchange rate in effect for each month of the quarter. Transaction gains and losses including intercompany transactions denominated in a currency other than the functional currency of the entity involved are included in "Other income (expense), net" on our Consolidated statements of income. The net Accumulated other comprehensive income related to translation gains and losses was a net gain of $9,545,000 and $6,991,000 at December 31, 2011 and 2010, respectively.

Revenue recognition: Revenues are recognized at the time of shipment to the dealer or distributor or other customers. Product returns, whether in the normal course of business or resulting from repossession under its customer financing program, have not been material. Polaris sponsors certain sales incentive programs and accrues liabilities for estimated sales promotion expenses and estimated holdback amounts that are recognized as reductions to sales when products are sold to the dealer or distributor customer.

Comprehensive income: Components of comprehensive income include net income, foreign currency translation adjustments, unrealized gains or losses on derivative instruments, and unrealized gains or losses on securities held for sale, net of tax. The Company has chosen to disclose comprehensive income in the accompanying consolidated statements of shareholders' equity and comprehensive income.

Note 3. Financing

The following summarizes activity under Polaris' credit arrangements (dollars in thousands):

	2011	2010	2009
Total borrowings at December 31, ...	$100,000	$200,000	$200,000
Average outstanding borrowings during year	$133,800	$200,000	$268,100
Maximum outstanding borrowings during year. . . .	$200,000	$200,000	$345,000
Interest rate at December 31	4.40%	0.65%	0.79%

The carrying amounts of the Company's long-term debt approximates its fair vale as December 31, 2011 and 2010.

Note 4. Goodwill and Other Intangible Assets

Goodwill and other intangible assets: ASC Topic 350 prohibits the amortization of goodwill and intangible assets with indefinite useful lives. Topic 350 requires that these assets be reviewed for impairment at least annually. An impairment charge for goodwill is recognized only when the estimated fair value of a reporting unit, including goodwill, is less than its carrying amount. The results of the analyses indicated that no goodwill or intangible impairment existed. In accordance with Topic 350, the Company will continue to complete an impairment analysis on an annual basis. Goodwill and other intangible assets, net, consist of $44,668,000 and $28,354,000 of goodwill and $33,050,000 and $2,959,000 of intangible assets, net of accumulated amortization, for the periods ended December 31, 2011 and December 31, 2010, respectively. Amortization expense for intangible assets during 2011 and 2010 was $1,018,000 and $188,000, respectively.

Note 9. Commitments and Contingencies

Product liability: Polaris is subject to product liability claims in the normal course of business. Polaris is currently self-insured for all product liability claims. The estimated costs resulting from any losses are charged to operating expenses when it is probable a loss has been incurred and the amount of the loss is reasonably determinable. The Company utilizes historical trends and actuarial analysis tools, along with an analysis of current claims, to assist in determining the appropriate loss reserve levels. At December 31, 2011, the Company had an accrual of $16,861,000 for the probable payment of pending claims related to product liability litigation associated with Polaris products. This accrual is included as a component of Other Accrued expenses in the accompanying consolidated balance sheets.

Leases: Polaris leases buildings and equipment under non-cancelable operating leases. Total rent expense under all operating lease agreements was $9,184,000, $5,553,000 and $4,999,000 for 2011, 2010 and 2009, respectively. Future minimum annual lease payments under capital and operating leases with non-cancelable terms in excess of one year as of December 31, 2011, including payments for the Monterrey, Mexico facility operating lease were as follows (in thousands):

Lease Obligations	Capital Leases	Operating Leases
2012	$2,653	$ 7,184
2013	2,190	5,845
2014	1,444	4,857
2015	701	3,899
2016	222	3,460
Thereafter	43	11,644
Total future minimum lease obligation	$7,253	$36,889

Note 12. Segment Reporting

Polaris has reviewed ASC Topic 280 and determined that the Company meets the aggregation criteria outlined since the Company's segments have similar (1) economic characteristics, (2) product and services, (3) production processes, (4) customers, (5) distribution channels, and (6) regulatory environments. Therefore, the Company reports as a single reportable business segment. The following data relates to Polaris' foreign operations:

For the Year Ended December 31 (In thousands)	2011	2010	2009
Canadian subsidiary:			
Sales	$368,487	$279,309	$239,240
Identifiable assets	18,008	42,936	35,462
Other foreign countries:			
Sales	$424,363	$305,864	$252,419
Identifiable assets	252,519	145,528	97,771

POLARIS INDUSTRIES INC.
SCHEDULE II—VALUATION AND QUALIFYING ACCOUNTS

(In thousands) Allowance for Doubtful Accounts	Balance at Beginning of Period	Additions Charged to Costs and Expenses	Additions Through Acquisition	Other Changes Add (Deduct)	Balance at End of Period
2009: Deducted from asset accounts—Allowance for doubtful accounts receivable	$6,098	$5,741	—	$(2,246)[1]	$9,593
2010: Deducted from asset accounts—Allowance for doubtful accounts receivable	$9,593	$1,599	—	$(4,823)[1]	$6,369
2011: Deducted from asset accounts—Allowance for doubtful accounts receivable	$6,369	$ 25	$532	$(2,453)[1]	$4,473
Inventory Reserve					
2009: Deducted from asset accounts—Allowance for obsolete inventory	$17,216	$6,400	—	$(8,023)[2]	$15,593
2010: Deducted from asset accounts—Allowance for obsolete inventory	$15,593	$5,840	—	$(5,223)[2]	$16,210
2011: Deducted from asset accounts—Allowance for obsolete inventory	$16,210	$4,611	$725	$(5,603)[2]	$15,943

[1] Uncollectible accounts receivable written off, net of recoveries.

[2] Inventory disposals, net of recoveries

POLARIS INDUSTRIES INC.

Selected Financial Data

(Dollars in millions, except per-share data)	For the Years Ended December 31					
	2011	2010	2009	2008	2007	2006
Statement of Operations Data						
Sales Data:						
Total sales	$2,656.9	$1,991.1	$1,565.9	$1,948.3	$1,780.0	$1,656.5
Percent change from prior year	33%	27%	-20%	9%	7%	-11%
Sales mix by product:						
Off-Road Vehicles	69%	69%	65%	67%	67%	67%
Snowmobiles	11%	10%	12%	10%	10%	10%
On-Road Vehicles	5%	4%	3%	5%	6%	7%
Parts, Garments and Accessories	15%	17%	20%	18%	17%	16%
Gross Profit Data:						
Total gross profit	$ 740.6	$ 530.2	$ 393.2	$ 445.7	$ 393.0	$ 359.4
Percent of sales	27.9%	26.6%	25.1%	22.9%	22.1%	21.7%
Operating Expense Data:						
Total operating expenses	$ 414.7	$ 326.3	$ 245.3	$ 284.1	$ 262.3	$ 238.4
Percent of sales	15.6%	16.4%	15.7%	14.6%	14.7%	14.4%
Operating Income Data:						
Total operating income	$ 349.9	$ 220.7	$ 165.0	$ 182.8	$ 176.0	$ 168.1
Percent of sales	13.2%	11.1%	10.5%	9.4%	9.9%	10.1%
Net Income Data:						
Net income from continuing operations	$ 227.6	$ 147.1	$ 101.0	$ 117.4	$ 112.6	$ 112.8
Percent of sales	8.6%	7.4%	6.5%	6.0%	6.3%	6.8%
Diluted net income per share from continuing operations	$ 3.20	$ 2.14	$ 1.53	$ 1.75	$ 1.55	$ 1.36
Net income	$ 227.6	$ 147.1	$ 101.0	$ 117.4	$ 111.7	$ 107.0
Diluted net income per share	$ 3.20	$ 2.14	$ 1.53	$ 1.75	$ 1.54	$ 1.29
Cash Flow Data:						
Cash flow provided by continuing operations	$ 302.5	$ 297.9	$ 193.2	$ 176.2	$ 213.2	$ 152.8
Purchase of property and equipment for continuing operations	84.5	55.7	43.9	76.6	63.7	52.6
Repurchase and retirement of common stock	132.4	27.5	4.6	107.2	103.1	307.6
Cash dividends to shareholders	61.6	53.0	50.2	49.6	47.7	50.2
Cash dividends per share	$ 0.90	$ 0.80	$ 0.78	$ 0.76	$ 0.68	$ 0.62
Balance Sheet Data (at end of year):						
Cash and cash equivalents	$ 325.3	$ 393.9	$ 140.2	$ 27.2	$ 63.3	$ 19.6
Current assets	878.7	808.1	491.5	443.6	447.6	393.0
Total assets	1,228.0	1,061.6	763.7	751.1	769.9	778.8
Current liabilities	615.5	584.2	343.1	404.8	388.2	361.4
Long-term debt	104.6	100.0	200.0	200.0	200.0	250.0
Shareholders' equity	500.1	371.0	204.5	137.0	173.0	167.4

POLARIS

ARCTIC CAT INC.

CONSOLIDATED BALANCE SHEETS

March 31	2011	2010
ASSETS		
Current Assets		
Cash and cash equivalents	$ 14,700,000	$ 31,811,000
Short term investments	110,413,000	39,251,000
Accounts receivable, less allowances	23,732,000	29,227,000
Inventories	61,478,000	81,361,000
Prepaid expenses	4,048,000	4,384,000
Deferred income taxes	17,669,000	14,981,000
Total current assets	232,040,000	201,015,000
Property and Equipment		
Machinery, equipment and tooling	195,189,000	185,023,000
Land, building and improvements	28,924,000	28,937,000
	224,113,000	213,960,000
Less accumulated depreciation	184,883,000	170,644,000
	39,230,000	43,316,000
Other Assets	1,636,000	1,753,000
	$272,906,000	$246,084,000
LIABILITIES AND SHAREHOLDERS' EQUITY		
Current Liabilities		
Accounts payable	$ 41,666,000	$ 37,303,000
Accrued expenses	44,398,000	35,042,000
Income taxes payable	1,380,000	2,975,000
Total current liabilities	87,444,000	75,320,000
Deferred Income Taxes	2,426,000	3,425,000
Commitments and Contingencies	—	—
Shareholders' Equity		
Preferred stock, par value $1.00; 2,050,000 shares authorized; none issued	—	—
Preferred stock—Series A Junior Participating, par value $1.00; 450,000 shares authorized; none issued	—	—
Common stock, par value $.01; 37,440,000 shares authorized; shares issued and outstanding: 12,199,271 in 2011 and 12,125,985 in 2010	122,000	121,000
Class B common stock, par value $.01; 7,560,000 shares authorized; shares issued and outstanding: 6,102,000 in 2011 and 2010	61,000	61,000
Additional paid-in-capital	7,280,000	5,053,000
Accumulated other comprehensive loss	(1,920,000)	(2,382,000)
Retained earnings	177,493,000	164,486,000
Total shareholders' equity	183,036,000	167,339,000
	$272,906,000	$246,084,000

ARCTIC CAT INC.

CONSOLIDATED STATEMENTS OF OPERATIONS

Years ended March 31	2011	2010	2009
Net sales			
Snowmobile & ATV units	$363,015,000	$350,871,000	$454,589,000
Parts, garments, & accessories	101,636,000	99,857,000	109,024,000
Total net sales	464,651,000	450,728,000	563,613,000
Cost of goods sold			
Snowmobile & ATV units	302,783,000	309,217,000	411,776,000
Parts, garments, & accessories	60,359,000	58,275,000	68,665,000
Total cost of goods sold	363,142,000	367,492,000	480,441,000
Gross profit	101,509,000	83,236,000	83,172,000
Operating expenses			
Selling & marketing	33,540,000	33,929,000	43,971,000
Research & development	15,029,000	12,926,000	18,404,000
General & administrative	34,805,000	35,045,000	33,904,000
Goodwill impairment charge	—	—	1,750,000
Total operating expenses	83,374,000	81,900,000	98,029,000
Operating profit (loss)	18,135,000	1,336,000	(14,857,000)
Other income (expense)			
Interest income	107,000	12,000	117,000
Interest expense	(11,000)	(250,000)	(1,015,000)
Total other income (expense)	96,000	(238,000)	(898,000)
Earnings (loss) before Incomes taxes	18,231,000	1,098,000	(15,755,000)
Income tax expense (benefit)	5,224,000	(777,000)	(6,247,000)
Net earnings (loss)	$ 13,007,000	$ 1,875,000	$ (9,508,000)
Net earnings (loss) per share			
Basic	$ 0.71	$ 0.10	$ (0.53)
Diluted	$ 0.70	$ 0.10	$ (0.53)
Weighted average share outstanding			
Basic	18,232,000	18,220,000	18,070,000
Diluted	18,539,000	18,291,000	18,070,000

ARCTIC CAT

ARCTIC CAT INC.

CONSOLIDATED STATEMENTS OF SHAREHOLDERS' EQUITY

Years ended March 31	Common Stock		Class B Common Stock		Additional Paid-in Capital	Accumulated Other Comprehensive Income (Loss)	Retained Earnings	Total
	Shares	Amount	Shares	Amount				
Balances at March 31, 2008	11,833,485	$118,000	6,102,000	$61,000	$ —	$ 4,768,000	$175,915,000	$180,862,000
Restricted stock awards	163,500	2,000	—	—	(2,000)	—	—	—
Restricted stock forfeited	(9,500)	—	—	—	—	—	—	—
Stock based compensation expense	—	—	—	—	2,570,000	—	—	2,570,000
Comprehensive loss:								
Net loss	—	—	—	—	—	—	(9,508,000)	(9,508,000)
Unrealized loss on derivative instruments, net of tax	—	—	—	—	—	(133,000)	—	(133,000)
Foreign currency adjustment	—	—	—	—	—	(5,147,000)	—	(5,147,000)
Total comprehensive loss								(14,788,000)
Dividends ($.21 per share)	—	—	—	—	—	—	(3,796,000)	(3,796,000)
Balances at March 31, 2009	11,987,485	120,000	6,102,000	61,000	2,568,000	(512,000)	162,611,000	164,848,000
Restricted stock awards	140,500	1,000	—	—	(1,000)	—	—	—
Restricted stock forfeited	(2,000)	—	—	—	—	—	—	—
Stock based compensation expense	—	—	—	—	2,486,000	—	—	2,486,000
Comprehensive income:								
Net earnings	—	—	—	—	—	—	1,875,000	1,875,000
Unrealized gain on derivative instruments, net of tax	—	—	—	—	—	244,000	—	244,000
Foreign currency adjustment	—	—	—	—	—	(2,114,000)	—	(2,114,000)
Total comprehensive income								5,000
Balances at March 31, 2010	12,125,985	121,000	6,102,000	61,000	5,053,000	(2,382,000)	164,486,000	167,339,000
Exercise of stock options	184,869	2,000	—	—	726,000	—	—	728,000
Tax benefits from stock options exercised	—	—	—	—	745,000	—	—	745,000
Repurchase of common stock	(183,953)	(2,000)	—	—	(2,417,000)	—	—	(2,419,000)
Restricted stock awards	78,500	1,000	—	—	(1,000)	—	—	—
Restricted stock forfeited	(6,130)	—	—	—	—	—	—	—
Stock based compensation expense	—	—	—	—	3,174,000	—	—	3,174,000
Comprehensive income:								
Net earnings	—	—	—	—	—	—	13,007,000	13,007,000
Unrealized loss on derivative instruments, net of tax	—	—	—	—	—	(1,147,000)	—	(1,147,000)
Foreign currency adjustment	—	—	—	—	—	1,609,000	—	1,609,000
Total comprehensive income								13,469,000
Balances at March 31, 2011	12,199,271	$122,000	6,102,000	$61,000	$ 7,280,000	$(1,920,000)	$177,493,000	$183,036,000

ARCTIC CAT INC.

CONSOLIDATED STATEMENTS OF CASH FLOWS

Years ended March 31	2011	2010	2009
Cash flows from operating activities			
Net earnings (loss)	$ 13,007,000	$ 1,875,000	$ (9,508,000)
Adjustments to reconcile net earnings to net cash provided by (used in) operating activities			
Depreciation and amortization	15,816,000	22,779,000	28,981,000
Loss on the disposal of assets	105,000	144,000	252,000
Impairment of goodwill	—	—	1,750,000
Deferred income taxes benefit	(3,194,000)	(3,577,000)	(6,379,000)
Stock based compensation expense	3,174,000	2,486,000	2,570,000
Changes in operating assets and liabilities			
Trading securities	(71,162,000)	(39,082,000)	24,837,000
Accounts receivable, less allowances	5,543,000	9,400,000	(437,000)
Inventories	20,587,000	40,003,000	2,798,000
Prepaid expenses	345,000	205,000	(1,246,000)
Accounts payable	2,879,000	(7,668,000)	(29,615,000)
Accrued expenses	9,238,000	(585,000)	(3,392,000)
Income taxes	(1,461,000)	3,335,000	8,980,000
Net cash provided by (used in) operating activities	(5,123,000)	29,315,000	19,591,000
Cash flows from investing activities			
Purchases of property and equipment	(11,761,000)	(6,540,000)	(14,226,000)
Proceeds from the sale of assets	87,000	—	—
Net cash used in investing activities	(11,674,000)	(6,540,000)	(14,226,000)
Cash flows from financing activities			
Checks written in excess of bank balance	—	221,000	—
Proceeds from short-term borrowings	1,012,000	73,429,000	227,230,000
Payments on short-term borrowings	(1,012,000)	(73,429,000)	(227,230,000)
Proceeds from issuance of common stock	728,000	—	—
Tax benefit from stock option exercises	745,000	—	—
Repurchase of common stock	(2,419,000)	—	—
Dividends paid	—	—	(3,796,000)
Net cash provided by (used in) financing activities	(946,000)	221,000	(3,796,000)
Effect of exchange rate changes on cash and cash equivalents	632,000	(2,429,000)	(382,000)
Net increase (decrease) in cash and cash equivalents	(17,111,000)	20,567,000	1,187,000
Cash and cash equivalents at beginning of year	31,811,000	11,244,000	10,057,000
Cash and cash equivalents at end of year	$ 14,700,000	$ 31,811,000	$ 11,244,000
Supplemental disclosure of cash payments for:			
Income taxes	$ 9,179,000	$ 1,935,000	$ 409,000
Interest	$ 11,000	$ 250,000	$ 987,000

Supplemental disclosure of non-cash investing and financing activities:

As of March 31, 2011 and 2010, the unrealized gain (loss) on derivative instruments, net of tax was ($1,147,000) and $244,000.

KTM POWER SPORTS AG
CONSOLIDATED INCOME STATEMENT
FOR BUSINESS YEAR 2011

(In thousands of Euro)	2011
Net sales	526,801
Cost of goods sold	(371,752)
Gross margin	**155,049**
Selling and sport-activity expenses	(71,952)
R&D expenses	(23,099)
Infrastructure and administration expenses	(20,870)
Other operating expenses	(9,206)
Other operating Income	1,088
Operating result	**31,009**
Interest income	768
Interest expenses	(9,693)
Other financial and participation result	(2,975)
Pre-tax result	**19,109**
Tax on income and earnings	1,709
NET RESULT	**20,818**
Thereof net result to owners	*20,719*
Thereof net result to non-controlling shareholders	*99*
EARNINGS PER SHARE (EUR)	
Basic	2.003
Diluted	1.968

KTM POWER SPORTS AG
CONSOLIDATED STATEMENT OF COMPREHENSIVE INCOME
FOR BUSINESS YEAR 2011

(In thousands of Euro)	2011
Net result of the business year	**20,818**
Currency conversion	107
Valuation of cash flow hedges	11,393
Deferred tax on the valuation of cash flow hedges	(2,848)
Other income	**8,652**
TOTAL INCOME	**29,470**
Thereof net result to owners	*29,371*
Thereof net result to non-controlling shareholders	*99*

KTM POWER SPORTS AG
CONSOLIDATED BALANCE SHEET
AS AT DECEMBER 31

ASSETS

(In thousands of Euro)	12/31/2011	12/31/2010
SHORT-TERM ASSETS		
Liquid assets	14,962	8,946
Accounts receivable − trade to third parties	49,924	53,087
Accounts receivable − trade to affiliated companies	1,443	1,040
Accounts receivable − trade to associated companies	2,227	3,130
Inventory	113,979	108,910
Prepayments	1,649	1,169
Other short-term assets	9,701	7,231
	193,885	**183,513**
LONG-TERM ASSETS		
Financial fixed assets	7,458	6,222
Tangible fixed assets	84,256	63,204
Goodwill	78,793	78,492
Intangible fixed assets	118,202	110,118
Deferred taxes	3,132	3,725
Other long-term assets	49	51
	291,890	**261,812**
ASSETS	**485,775**	**445,325**

EQUITY AND LIABILITIES

(In thousands of Euro)	12/31/2011	12/31/2010
SHORT-TERM LIABILITIES		
Bank loans	5,415	14,061
Accounts payable − trade to third parties	54,578	37,725
Accounts payable − trade to affiliated companies	11,062	7,979
Accounts payable − trade to associated companies	2,600	2,895
Provisions	4,238	3,993
Liabilities − corporate tax	1,470	33
Prepayments	735	1,614
Other short-term liabilities	29,256	33,926
	109,353	**102,226**
LONG-TERM LIABILITIES		
Interest-bearing loans	132,898	129,957
Liabilities for personnel	7,699	6,479
Liabilities from deferred taxes	14,560	15,851
Liabilities to affiliated companies	0	13,021
Other long-term liabilities	1,490	1,005
	156,648	**166,313**
SHAREHOLDER'S EQUITY		
Share capital	10,509	10,109
Reserves including retained earnings	208,987	166,593
Non-controlling shares	279	84
	219,775	**176,786**
EQUITY AND LIABILITIES	**485,775**	**445,325**

KTM

KTM POWER SPORTS AG
CONSOLIDATED CASH FLOW STATEMENT
FOR BUSINESS YEAR 2011

(In thousands of Euro)	2011
CONSOLIDATED CASH FLOW FROM OPERATING ACTIVITIES	
+(−) Profit (loss) of the business year	20,818
+(−) Profit (loss) of non-controlling shareholders	(99)
+(−) Depreciation (write-up) of fixed assets	33,368
+(−) Depreciation (write-up) to financial assets	118
+(−) Deferred taxes	(3,352)
− Results from consolidation not affecting income	(649)
− Results from companies validated at-equity not affecting income	(657)
+(−) Addition (disposal) of liabilities for personnel	1,432
−(+) Profit (loss) from the sale of fixed assets	(59)
Consolidated cash flow from earnings	**50,919**
−(+) Increase (decrease) in inventories including prepayments	(5,069)
−(+) Increase (decrease) in accounts receiveable − trade, prepayments, other short- and longterm assets	831
−(+) Increase (decrease) in accounts receivable − trade from affiliated companies	430
−(+) Increase (decrease) in accounts receivable − trade from associated companies	903
(+)− Increase (decrease) in accounts payable − trade, prepayments and other short-term and long-term liabilities	16,346
(+)− Increase (decrease) in accounts payable − trade from affiliated companies	3,083
(+)− Increase (decrease) in accounts payable − trade from associated companies	(295)
(+)− Increase (decrease) from corporate taxes, deferred taxes and other provisions	3,201
	19,429
Cash flow from operating activities	**70,348**
CONSOLIDATED CASH FLOW FROM INVESTMENT ACTIVITIES	
− Investments in fixed assets (outflow of funds for investments)	(37,705)
− Investments in financial assets	(697)
(+)− Changes from first/final consolidation	273
+ Disposal of fixed assets (inflow of funds from sales: book value + profit (− loss) from the disposal of fixed assets)	871
(+)− Currency rate differences from fixed assets	(13)
Consolidated cash flow from investment activities	**(37,271)**
CONSOLIDATED CASH FLOW FROM FINANCING ACTIVITIES	
(+)− Currency rate differences	33
+ Capital increase	1,095
(+)− Increase (decrease) of short-term bank loans	(8,646)
(+)− Change in liabilities to affiliated and associated companies	(259)
(+)− Increase (decrease) in long-term interest bearing loans	(19,479)
+(−) Changes in non-controlling interests	196
+(−) Change deconsolidation Cost Plus subsidiaries	0
Consolidated cash flow from financing activities	**(27,060)**
CONSOLIDATED CASH FLOW	
+(−) Consolidated cash flow from operating activities	70,348
+(−) Consolidated cash flow from investment activities	(37,271)
+(−) Consolidated cash flow from financing activities	(27,060)
Change in the liquidity of the group	**6,017**
+ Starting cash and cash equivalents of the group	8,946
CASH AND CASH EQUIVALENTS OF THE GROUP AS AT DECEMBER 31	**14,962**
Consisting of cash in hand. cheques, cash at bank and term deposits	*14,962*
Interest paid	10,052
Taxes paid	547

KTM POWER SPORTS AG
DEVELOPMENT OF THE GROUP'S EQUITY CAPITAL
FOR BUSINESS YEAR 2011

(In thousands of Euro)	Nominal capital	Reserves incl. net result for the business year	Revaluation reserve	Cash flow hedge reserve	Currency translation adjustments	Total	Shares of non-controlling Interests	Total share capital
As at December 31, 2010	10,109	163,106	17,235	(13,648)	(100)	176,702	84	176,786
Currency conversion	0	0	0	0	105	105	0	105
Financial instruments	0	0	0	8,545	0	8,545	0	8,545
Profit and loss directly recognized in equity	0	0	0	8,545	105	8,650	0	8,650
Result of the business year	0	20,719	0	0	0	20,719	99	20,819
Total profit and loss recognized in equity	0	20,719	0	8,545	105	29,369	99	29,469
Capital increase	400	13,600	0	0	0	14,000	0	14,000
Cost of capital increase	0	(480)	0	0	0	(480)	0	(480)
Change in non-controlling interests	0	(96)	0	0	0	(96)	96	0
AS AT DECEMBER 31, 2011	10,509	196,849	17,235	(5,103)	5	219,495	279	219,775

KTM

Piaggio Group
Consolidated Income Statement

For Year Ended December 31 (In thousands of Euro)	2011	2010
Net revenues	1,516,463	1,485,351
Cost for materials	904,060	881,075
Cost for services and leases and rentals	266,484	258,358
Employee costs	247,600	240,115
Depreciation of property, plant and equipment	35,219	35,879
Amortisation of intangible assets	59,794	50,127
Other operating income	122,562	121,128
Other operating costs	20,323	29,821
Operating income	105,545	111,104
Income/(loss) from investments	2,481	5,252
Financial income	4,087	2,891
Borrowing Costs	31,853	33,905
Net exchange gains/(losses)	(932)	(1,518)
Earnings before tax	79,328	83,824
Taxation for the period	32,305	40,983
Earnings from continuing activities	47,023	42,841
Assets held for disposal:		
Profits or losses arising from assets held for disposal		
Net Income (Loss) for the period	47,023	42,841
Attributable to:		
Shareholders of the Parent Company	47,053	42,811
Non-controlling interests	(30)	30
Earnings per share (figures in €)	0.126	0.113
Diluted earnings per share (figures in €)	0.126	0.112

Piaggio Group
Consolidated Statement of Comprehensive Income

For Year Ended December 31 (In thousands of Euro)	2011	2010
Profit (loss) for the period (A)	47,023	42,841
Effective portion of profits (losses) on cash flow hedges	(1,283)	(354)
Profit (loss) deriving from the translation of financial statements of foreign companies denominated in foreign currency	(11,262)	3,060
Total Other Profits (and losses) for the period (B)	(12,545)	2,706
Total Profit (loss) for the period (A + B)	34,478	45,547
Attributable to:		
Shareholders of the Parent Company	34,533	45,531
Non-controlling interests	(55)	16

Piaggio Group
Consolidated Statement of Financial Position

As of December 31 (In thousands of Euro)	2011	2010
Assets		
Non-current assets		
Intangible assets	649,420	652,622
Property, plant and equipment	274,871	256,759
Investment property		
Investments	2,482	194
Other financial assets	11,836	334
Long-term tax receivables	976	967
Deferred tax assets	55,726	46,294
Trade receivables		
Other receivables	15,165	12,655
Total non-current assets	**1,010,476**	**969,825**
Assets held for sale		
Current assets		
Trade receivables	65,560	90,421
Other receivables	28,028	23,300
Short-term tax receivables	27,245	44,200
Inventories	236,988	240,066
Other financial assets	0	23,051
Cash and cash equivalents	151,887	154,859
Total current assets	**509,708**	**575,897**
Total assets	**1,520,184**	**1,545,722**
Shareholders' equity and liabilities		
Shareholders' equity		
Share capital and reserves attributable to the shareholders of the Parent Company	445,036	441,277
Share capital and reserves attributable to non-controlling interests	1,182	1,613
Total shareholders' equity	**446,218**	**442,890**
Non-current liabilities		
Financial liabilities falling due after one year	329,200	371,048
Trade payables	235	88
Other long-term provisions	12,429	16,993
Deferred tax liabilities	32,735	32,338
Retirement funds and employee benefits	46,603	58,636
Tax payables	2,539	3,361
Other long-term payables	5,948	4,202
Total non-current liabilities	**429,689**	**486,666**
Current liabilities		
Financial liabilities falling due within one year	170,261	156,800
Trade payables	375,263	352,627
Tax payables	20,920	19,290
Other short-term payables	64,718	69,503
Current portion of other long-term provisions	13,115	17,946
Total current liabilities	**644,277**	**616,166**
Total shareholders' equity and liabilities	**1,520,184**	**1,545,722**

Piaggio Group
Consolidated Cash Flow Statement

For Year Ended December 31 (In thousands of Euro)	2011	2010
Operating activities		
Consolidated net income	47,053	42,811
Allocation of profit to non-controlling interests	(30)	30
Taxation for the period	32,305	40,983
Depreciation of property, plant and equipment	35,219	35,879
Amortisation of intangible assets	59,794	50,127
Non-monetary costs for stock options	771	2,650
Allocations for risks and retirement funds and employee benefits	21,134	29,243
Write-downs / (Reversals)	(1,192)	1,755
Losses / (Gains) on the disposal of property, plants and equipment	(6,012)	(2,240)
Losses / (Gains) on the disposal of intangible assets	0	0
Financial income	(3,910)	(2,891)
Dividend income	(193)	(12)
Borrowing Costs	25,558	29,744
Income from public grants	(3,492)	(4,164)
Portion of earnings of affiliated companies	0	45
Change in working capital:		
(Increase)/Decrease in trade receivables	24,861	12,743
(Increase)/Decrease in other receivables	(18,740)	(1,157)
(Increase)/Decrease in inventories	3,078	12,430
Increase/(Decrease) in trade payables	22,783	6,640
Increase/(Decrease) in other payables	8,636	(12,347)
Increase/(Decrease) in provisions for risks	(21,782)	(26,974)
Increase/(Decrease) in retirement funds and employee benefits	(20,795)	(13,028)
Other changes	5,265	(43,774)
Cash generated from operating activities	**210,311**	**158,493**
Interest paid	(22,825)	(23,178)
Taxes paid	(31,862)	(12,774)
Cash flow from operating activities (A)	**155,624**	**122,541**
Investment activities		
Investment in property, plant and equipment	(61,790)	(37,132)
Sale price, or repayment value, of property, plant and equipment	6,542	3,823
Investment in intangible assets	(64,300)	(59,063)
Sale price, or repayment value, of intangible assets	122	261
Purchase of financial assets	0	(23,051)
Sale price of financial assets	23,051	4,127
Collected interests	11,666	2,360
Cash flow from investment activities (B)	**(84,709)**	**(108,675)**
Financing activities		
Exercise of stock options	2,843	
Purchase of treasury shares	(9,080)	(3,344)
Outflow for dividends paid	(25,684)	(25,765)
Loans received	71,400	37,652
Outflow for repayment of loans	(112,727)	(65,174)
Financing received for leases	227	0
Repayment of finance leases	(850)	(758)
Cash flow from funding activities (C)	**(73,871)**	**(57,389)**
Increase / (Decrease) in cash and cash equivalents (A+B+C)	(2,956)	(43,523)
Opening balance	**154,758**	**198,281**
Exchange differences		
Closing balance	**151,802**	**154,758**

Piaggio Group
Changes in Consolidated Shareholders' Equity

Movements from 1 January 2011 / 31 December 2011

In thousands of Euro	Share capital	Share premium reserve	Legal reserve	Reserve for measurement of financial instruments	IAS transition reserve	Group consolidation reserve	Group conversion reserve	Stock option reserve	Performance reserve	Consolidated Group shareholders' equity	Non-controlling interests capital and reserves	Total shareholders' equity
As of 1 January 2011	203,348	3,493	11,299	(227)	(5,859)	993	(1,850)	11,929	218,151	441,277	1,613	442,890
Charges for the period for stock option plans								771		771		771
Allocation of profits			942						(942)	0		0
Distribution of dividends									(25,684)	25,684		(25,684)
Purchase of treasury shares	(2,382)								(6,698)	(9,080)		(9,080)
Exercise of stock options	1,243								1,600	2,843		2,843
Reacquisiton of the Simest investment									376	376	(376)	0
Total overall profit (loss)				(1,283)			(11,237)		47,053	34,533	(55)	34,478
As of 31 December 2011	202,209	3,493	12,241	(1,510)	(5,859)	993	(13,087)	12,700	233,856	445,036	1,182	446,218

Movements from 1 January 2010 / 31 December 2010

In thousands of Euro	Share capital	Share premium reserve	Legal reserve	Reserve for measurement of financial instruments	IAS transition reserve	Group consolidation reserve	Group conversion reserve	Stock option reserve	Performance reserve	Consolidated Group shareholders' equity	Non-controlling interests capital and reserves	Total shareholders' equity
As of 1 January 2010	191,616	3,493	8,996	127	(5,859)	993	(5,468)	9,279	218,484	421,661	2,141	423,802
Charges for the period for stock option plans								2,650		2,650		2,650
Allocation of profits			2,303						(2,303)	0		0
Distribution of dividends									(25,765)	(25,765)		(25,765)
Cancellation of treasury shares	12,608								(12,608)	0		0
Purchase of treasury shares	(876)								(2,468)	(3,344)		(3,344)
Total overall profit (loss)				(354)			3,618		42,811	46,075	(528)	45,547
As of 31 December 2010	203,348	3,493	11,299	(227)	(5,859)	993	(1,850)	11,929	218,151	441,277	1,613	442,890

Time Value of Money

Learning Objectives

CONCEPTUAL

C1 Describe the earning of interest and the concepts of present and future values. (p. B-1)

PROCEDURAL

P1 Apply present value concepts to a single amount by using interest tables. (p. B-3)

P2 Apply future value concepts to a single amount by using interest tables. (p. B-4)

P3 Apply present value concepts to an annuity by using interest tables. (p. B-5)

P4 Apply future value concepts to an annuity by using interest tables. (p. B-6)

The concepts of present and future values are important to modern business, including the preparation and analysis of financial statements. The purpose of this appendix is to explain, illustrate, and compute present and future values. This appendix applies these concepts with reference to both business and everyday activities.

Time Value of Money

Present and Future Value Concepts	Value of a Single Amount	Value of an Annuity
• Time is money • Concept of interest	• Present value of a single amount • Future value of a single amount	• Present value of an annuity • Future value of an annuity

PRESENT AND FUTURE VALUE CONCEPTS

The old saying "Time is money" reflects the notion that as time passes, the values of our assets and liabilities change. This change is due to *interest*, which is a borrower's payment to the owner of an asset for its use. The most common example of interest is a savings account asset. As we keep a balance of cash in the account, it earns interest that the financial institution pays us. An example of a liability is a car loan. As we carry the balance of the loan, we accumulate interest costs on it. We must ultimately repay this loan with interest.

Present and future value computations enable us to measure or estimate the interest component of holding assets or liabilities over time. The present value computation is important when we want to know the value of future-day assets *today*. The future value computation is important when we want to know the value of present-day assets *at a future date*. The first section focuses on the present value of a single amount. The second section focuses on the future value of a single amount. Then both the present and future values of a series of amounts (called an *annuity*) are defined and explained.

C1 Describe the earning of interest and the concepts of present and future values.

Decision Insight

Working for Lotto Winnings Lottery winners often never work again. Kenny Dukes, a recent Georgia lottery winner, doesn't have that option. He is serving parole for burglary charges, and Georgia requires its parolees to be employed (or in school). For his lottery winnings, Dukes had to choose between $31 million in 30 annual payments or $16 million in one lump sum ($10.6 million after-tax); he chose the latter. ■

PRESENT VALUE OF A SINGLE AMOUNT

We graphically express the present value, called *p*, of a single future amount, called *f*, that is received or paid at a future date in Exhibit B.1.

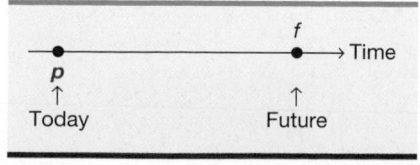

EXHIBIT B.1

Present Value of a Single Amount Diagram

The formula to compute the present value of a single amount is shown in Exhibit B.2, where p = present value; f = future value; i = rate of interest per period; and n = number of periods. (Interest is also called the *discount,* and an interest rate is also called the *discount rate.*)

EXHIBIT B.2

Present Value of a Single
Amount Formula

$$p = \frac{f}{(1 + i)^n}$$

To illustrate present value concepts, assume that we need $220 one period from today. We want to know how much we must invest now, for one period, at an interest rate of 10% to provide for this $220. For this illustration, the p, or present value, is the unknown amount—the specifics are shown graphically as follows:

$$(i = 0.10) \qquad f = \$220$$
$$p = ?$$

Conceptually, we know p must be less than $220. This is obvious from the answer to this question: Would we rather have $220 today or $220 at some future date? If we had $220 today, we could invest it and see it grow to something more than $220 in the future. Therefore, we would prefer the $220 today. This means that if we were promised $220 in the future, we would take less than $220 today. But how much less? To answer that question, we compute an estimate of the present value of the $220 to be received one period from now using the formula in Exhibit B.2 as follows:

$$p = \frac{f}{(1 + i)^n} = \frac{\$220}{(1 + 0.10)^1} = \$200$$

We interpret this result to say that given an interest rate of 10%, we are indifferent between $200 today or $220 at the end of one period.

We can also use this formula to compute the present value for *any number of periods.* To illustrate, consider a payment of $242 at the end of two periods at 10% interest. The present value of this $242 to be received two periods from now is computed as follows:

$$p = \frac{f}{(1 + i)^n} = \frac{\$242}{(1 + 0.10)^2} = \$200$$

I will pay your allowance at the end of the month. Do you want to wait or receive its present value today?

Together, these results tell us we are indifferent between $200 today, or $220 one period from today, or $242 two periods from today given a 10% interest rate per period.

The number of periods (n) in the present value formula does not have to be expressed in years. Any period of time such as a day, a month, a quarter, or a year can be used. Whatever period is used, the interest rate (i) must be compounded for the same period. This means that if a situation expresses n in months and i equals 12% per year, then i is transformed into interest earned per month (or 1%). In this case, interest is said to be *compounded monthly.*

A present value table helps us with present value computations. It gives us present values (factors) for a variety of both interest rates (i) and periods (n). Each present value in a present value table assumes that the future value (f) equals 1. When the future value (f) is different from 1, we simply multiply the present value (p) from the table by that future value to give us the estimate. The formula used to construct a table of present values for a single future amount of 1 is shown in Exhibit B.3.

EXHIBIT B.3

Present Value of 1 Formula

$$p = \frac{1}{(1 + i)^n}$$

This formula is identical to that in Exhibit B.2 except that f equals 1. Table B.1 at the end of this appendix is such a present value table. It is often called a **present value of 1 table**. A present value table involves three factors: p, i, and n. Knowing two of these three factors allows us to compute the third. (A fourth is f, but as already explained, we need only multiply the 1 used in the formula by f.) To illustrate the use of a present value table, consider three cases.

P1 Apply present value concepts to a single amount by using interest tables.

Case 1 (solve for p when knowing i and n). To show how we use a present value table, let's look again at how we estimate the present value of $220 (the f value) at the end of one period ($n = 1$) where the interest rate (i) is 10%. To solve this case, we go to the present value table (Table B.1) and look in the row for 1 period and in the column for 10% interest. Here we find a present value (p) of 0.9091 based on a future value of 1. This means, for instance, that $1 to be received one period from today at 10% interest is worth $0.9091 today. Since the future value in this case is not $1 but $220, we multiply the 0.9091 by $220 to get an answer of $200.

Case 2 (solve for n when knowing p and i). To illustrate, assume a $100,000 future value ($f$) that is worth $13,000 today ($p$) using an interest rate of 12% (i) but where n is unknown. In particular, we want to know how many periods (n) there are between the present value and the future value. To put this in context, it would fit a situation in which we want to retire with $100,000 but currently have only $13,000 that is earning a 12% return and we will be unable to save any additional money. How long will it be before we can retire? To answer this, we go to Table B.1 and look in the 12% interest column. Here we find a column of present values (p) based on a future value of 1. To use the present value table for this solution, we must divide $13,000 ($p$) by $100,000 ($f$), which equals 0.1300. This is necessary because *a present value table defines* f *equal to 1, and* p *as a fraction of 1*. We look for a value nearest to 0.1300 (p), which we find in the row for 18 periods (n). This means that the present value of $100,000 at the end of 18 periods at 12% interest is $13,000; alternatively stated, we must work 18 more years.

Case 3 (solve for i when knowing p and n). In this case, we have, say, a $120,000 future value ($f$) worth $60,000 today ($p$) when there are nine periods (n) between the present and future values, but the interest rate is unknown. As an example, suppose we want to retire with $120,000, but we have only $60,000 and we will be unable to save any additional money, yet we hope to retire in nine years. What interest rate must we earn to retire with $120,000 in nine years? To answer this, we go to the present value table (Table B.1) and look in the row for nine periods. To use the present value table, we must divide $60,000 ($p$) by $120,000 ($f$), which equals 0.5000. Recall that this step is necessary because a present value table defines f equal to 1 and p as a fraction of 1. We look for a value in the row for nine periods that is nearest to 0.5000 (p), which we find in the column for 8% interest (i). This means that the present value of $120,000 at the end of nine periods at 8% interest is $60,000 or, in our example, we must earn 8% annual interest to retire in nine years.

Quick Check   Answer — p. B-7

1. A company is considering an investment expected to yield $70,000 after six years. If this company demands an 8% return, how much is it willing to pay for this investment?

FUTURE VALUE OF A SINGLE AMOUNT

We must modify the formula for the present value of a single amount to obtain the formula for the future value of a single amount. In particular, we multiply both sides of the equation in Exhibit B.2 by $(1 + i)^n$ to get the result shown in Exhibit B.4.

$$f = p \times (1 + i)^n$$

EXHIBIT B.4

Future Value of a Single Amount Formula

The future value (f) is defined in terms of p, i, and n. We can use this formula to determine that \$200 (p) invested for 1 (n) period at an interest rate of 10% (i) yields a future value of \$220 as follows:

$$f = p \times (1 + i)^n$$
$$= \$200 \times (1 + 0.10)^1$$
$$= \$220$$

P2 Apply future value concepts to a single amount by using interest tables.

This formula can also be used to compute the future value of an amount for *any number of periods* into the future. To illustrate, assume that \$200 is invested for three periods at 10%. The future value of this \$200 is \$266.20, computed as follows:

$$f = p \times (1 + i)^n$$
$$= \$200 \times (1 + 0.10)^3$$
$$= \$266.20$$

A future value table makes it easier for us to compute future values (f) for many different combinations of interest rates (i) and time periods (n). Each future value in a future value table assumes the present value (p) is 1. As with a present value table, if the future amount is something other than 1, we simply multiply our answer by that amount. The formula used to construct a table of future values (factors) for a single amount of 1 is in Exhibit B.5.

EXHIBIT B.5

Future Value of 1 Formula

$$f = (1 + i)^n$$

Table B.2 at the end of this appendix shows a table of future values for a current amount of 1. This type of table is called a **future value of 1 table**.

There are some important relations between Tables B.1 and B.2. In Table B.2, for the row where $n = 0$, the future value is 1 for each interest rate. This is so because no interest is earned when time does not pass. We also see that Tables B.1 and B.2 report the same information but in a different manner. In particular, one table is simply the *inverse* of the other. To illustrate this inverse relation, let's say we invest \$100 for a period of five years at 12% per year. How much do we expect to have after five years? We can answer this question using Table B.2 by finding the future value (f) of 1, for five periods from now, compounded at 12%. From that table we find $f = 1.7623$. If we start with \$100, the amount it accumulates to after five years is \$176.23 (\$100 × 1.7623). We can alternatively use Table B.1. Here we find that the present value (p) of 1, discounted five periods at 12%, is 0.5674. Recall the inverse relation between present value and future value. This means that $p = 1/f$ (or equivalently, $f = 1/p$). We can compute the future value of \$100 invested for five periods at 12% as follows: $f = \$100 \times (1/0.5674) = \$176.24$ (which equals the \$176.23 just computed, except for a 1 cent rounding difference).

A future value table involves three factors: f, i, and n. Knowing two of these three factors allows us to compute the third. To illustrate, consider these three possible cases.

Case 1 (solve for f when knowing i and n). Our preceding example fits this case. We found that \$100 invested for five periods at 12% interest accumulates to \$176.24.

Case 2 (solve for n when knowing f and i). In this case, we have, say, \$2,000 (p) and we want to know how many periods (n) it will take to accumulate to \$3,000 (f) at 7% (i) interest. To answer this, we go to the future value table (Table B.2) and look in the 7% interest column. Here we find a column of future values (f) based on a present value of 1. To use a future value table, we must divide \$3,000 (f) by \$2,000 (p), which equals 1.500. This is necessary because *a future value table defines* p *equal to 1, and* f *as a multiple of 1.* We look for a value nearest to 1.50 (f), which we find in the row for six periods (n). This means that \$2,000 invested for six periods at 7% interest accumulates to \$3,000.

Case 3 (solve for i when knowing f and n). In this case, we have, say, \$2,001 (p), and in nine years (n) we want to have \$4,000 (f). What rate of interest must we earn to accomplish this? To answer that, we go to Table B.2 and search in the row for nine periods. To use a future value table, we must divide \$4,000 (f) by \$2,001 (p), which equals 1.9990. Recall that this is necessary because a future value table defines p equal to 1 and f as a multiple of 1. We look for a value nearest to 1.9990 (f), which we find in the column for 8% interest (i). This means that $2,001 invested for nine periods at 8% interest accumulates to $4,000.

Quick Check   Answer — p. B-7

2. Assume that you win a $150,000 cash sweepstakes. You decide to deposit this cash in an account earning 8% annual interest, and you plan to quit your job when the account equals $555,000. How many years will it be before you can quit working?

PRESENT VALUE OF AN ANNUITY

An *annuity* is a series of equal payments occurring at equal intervals. One example is a series of three annual payments of $100 each. An *ordinary annuity* is defined as equal end-of-period payments at equal intervals. An ordinary annuity of $100 for three periods and its present value (p) are illustrated in Exhibit B.6.

EXHIBIT B.6

Present Value of an Ordinary Annuity Diagram

One way to compute the present value of an ordinary annuity is to find the present value of each payment using our present value formula from Exhibit B.3. We then add each of the three present values. To illustrate, let's look at three $100 payments at the end of each of the next three periods with an interest rate of 15%. Our present value computations are

P3 Apply present value concepts to an annuity by using interest tables.

$$p = \frac{\$100}{(1 + 0.15)^1} + \frac{\$100}{(1 + 0.15)^2} + \frac{\$100}{(1 + 0.15)^3} = \$228.32$$

This computation is identical to computing the present value of each payment (from Table B.1) and taking their sum or, alternatively, adding the values from Table B.1 for each of the three payments and multiplying their sum by the $100 annuity payment.

A more direct way is to use a present value of annuity table. Table B.3 at the end of this appendix is one such table. This table is called a **present value of an annuity of 1 table**. If we look at Table B.3 where $n = 3$ and $i = 15\%$, we see the present value is 2.2832. This means that the present value of an annuity of 1 for three periods, with a 15% interest rate, equals 2.2832.

A present value of an annuity formula is used to construct Table B.3. It can also be constructed by adding the amounts in a present value of 1 table. To illustrate, we use Tables B.1 and B.3 to confirm this relation for the prior example:

From Table B.1		From Table B.3	
$i = 15\%, n = 1$	0.8696		
$i = 15\%, n = 2$	0.7561		
$i = 15\%, n = 3$	0.6575		
Total	2.2832	$i = 15\%, n = 3$	2.2832

We can also use business calculators or spreadsheet programs to find the present value of an annuity.

Decision Insight

Blessed Winnings   "I don't have good luck—I'm blessed," proclaimed Andrew "Jack" Whittaker, 55, a sewage treatment contractor, after winning the largest ever undivided jackpot in a U.S. lottery. Whittaker had to choose between $315 million in 30 annual installments or $170 million in one lump sum ($112 million after-tax). ∎

Quick Check   Answer — p. B-7

3. A company is considering an investment paying $10,000 every six months for three years. The first payment would be received in six months. If this company requires an 8% annual return, what is the maximum amount it is willing to pay for this investment?

FUTURE VALUE OF AN ANNUITY

The future value of an *ordinary annuity* is the accumulated value of each annuity payment with interest as of the date of the final payment. To illustrate, let's consider the earlier annuity of three annual payments of $100. Exhibit B.7 shows the point in time for the future value (f). The first payment is made two periods prior to the point when future value is determined, and the final payment occurs on the future value date.

EXHIBIT B.7

Future Value of an Ordinary
Annuity Diagram

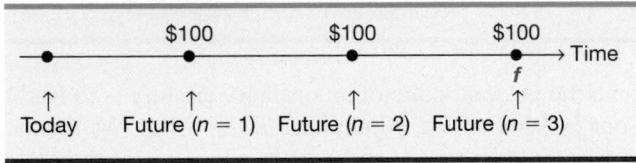

One way to compute the future value of an annuity is to use the formula to find the future value of *each* payment and add them. If we assume an interest rate of 15%, our calculation is

$$f = \$100 \times (1 + 0.15)^2 + \$100 \times (1 + 0.15)^1 + \$100 \times (1 + 0.15)^0 = \$347.25$$

This is identical to using Table B.2 and summing the future values of each payment, or adding the future values of the three payments of 1 and multiplying the sum by $100.

A more direct way is to use a table showing future values of annuities. Such a table is called a **future value of an annuity of 1 table**. Table B.4 at the end of this appendix is one such table. Note that in Table B.4 when $n = 1$, the future values equal 1 ($f = 1$) for all rates of interest. This is so because such an annuity consists of only one payment and the future value is determined on the date of that payment—no time passes between the payment and its future value. The future value of an annuity formula is used to construct Table B.4. We can also construct it by adding the amounts from a future value of 1 table. To illustrate, we use Tables B.2 and B.4 to confirm this relation for the prior example:

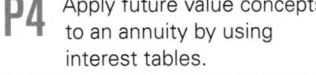

From Table B.2		From Table B.4	
$i = 15\%, n = 0$	1.0000		
$i = 15\%, n = 1$	1.1500		
$i = 15\%, n = 2$	1.3225		
Total	3.4725	$i = 15\%, n = 3$	3.4725

Note that the future value in Table B.2 is 1.0000 when $n = 0$, but the future value in Table B.4 is 1.0000 when $n = 1$. Is this a contradiction? No. When $n = 0$ in Table B.2, the future value is determined on the date when a single payment occurs. This means that no interest is earned because no time has passed, and the future value equals the payment. Table B.4 describes annuities with equal payments occurring at the end of each period. When $n = 1$, the annuity has one payment, and its future value equals 1 on the date of its final and only payment. Again, no time passes between the payment and its future value date.

Quick Check   Answer – p. B-7

4. A company invests $45,000 per year for five years at 12% annual interest. Compute the value of this annuity investment at the end of five years.

Summary

C1   **Describe the earning of interest and the concepts of present and future values.** Interest is payment by a borrower to the owner of an asset for its use. Present and future value computations are a way for us to estimate the interest component of holding assets or liabilities over a period of time.

P1   **Apply present value concepts to a single amount by using interest tables.** The present value of a single amount received at a future date is the amount that can be invested now at the specified interest rate to yield that future value.

P2   **Apply future value concepts to a single amount by using interest tables.** The future value of a single amount invested

at a specified rate of interest is the amount that would accumulate by the future date.

P3   **Apply present value concepts to an annuity by using interest tables.** The present value of an annuity is the amount that can be invested now at the specified interest rate to yield that series of equal periodic payments.

P4   **Apply future value concepts to an annuity by using interest tables.** The future value of an annuity invested at a specific rate of interest is the amount that would accumulate by the date of the final payment.

Guidance Answers to Quick Checks

1. $70,000 × 0.6302 = $44,114 (use Table B.1, $i = 8\%$, $n = 6$).

2. $555,000/$150,000 = 3.7000; Table B.2 shows this value is not achieved until after 17 years at 8% interest.

3. $10,000 × 5.2421 = $52,421 (use Table B.3, $i = 4\%$, $n = 6$).

4. $45,000 × 6.3528 = $285,876 (use Table B.4, $i = 12\%$, $n = 5$).

---

connect

Assume that you must make future value estimates using the *future value of 1 table* (Table B.2). Which interest rate column do you use when working with the following rates?

1. 8% annual rate, compounded quarterly

2. 12% annual rate, compounded annually

3. 6% annual rate, compounded semiannually

4. 12% annual rate, compounded monthly

QUICK STUDY

QS B-1
Identifying interest rates in tables
C1

Ken Francis is offered the possibility of investing $2,745 today and in return to receive $10,000 after 15 years. What is the annual rate of interest for this investment? (Use Table B.1.)

QS B-2
Interest rate on an investment   P1

Megan Brink is offered the possibility of investing $6,651 today at 6% interest per year in a desire to accumulate $10,000. How many years must Brink wait to accumulate $10,000? (Use Table B.1.)

QS B-3
Number of periods
of an investment   P1

Flaherty is considering an investment that, if paid for immediately, is expected to return $140,000 five years from now. If Flaherty demands a 9% return, how much is she willing to pay for this investment?

QS B-4
Present value of an amount   P1

CII, Inc., invests $630,000 in a project expected to earn a 12% annual rate of return. The earnings will be reinvested in the project each year until the entire investment is liquidated 10 years later. What will the cash proceeds be when the project is liquidated?

QS B-5
Future value of an amount   P2

Beene Distributing is considering a project that will return $150,000 annually at the end of each year for the next six years. If Beene demands an annual return of 7% and pays for the project immediately, how much is it willing to pay for the project?

QS B-6
Present value
of an annuity   P3

QS B-7 Future value of an annuity P4	Claire Fitch is planning to begin an individual retirement program in which she will invest $1,500 at the end of each year. Fitch plans to retire after making 30 annual investments in the program earning a return of 10%. What is the value of the program on the date of the last payment (30 years from the present)?

━━━ **connect**

EXERCISES

Exercise B-1 Number of periods of an investment P2	Bill Thompson expects to invest $10,000 at 12% and, at the end of a certain period, receive $96,463. How many years will it be before Thompson receives the payment? (Use Table B.2.)
Exercise B-2 Interest rate on an investment P2	Ed Summers expects to invest $10,000 for 25 years, after which he wants to receive $108,347. What rate of interest must Summers earn? (Use Table B.2.)
Exercise B-3 Interest rate on an investment P3	Jones expects an immediate investment of $57,466 to return $10,000 annually for eight years, with the first payment to be received one year from now. What rate of interest must Jones earn? (Use Table B.3.)
Exercise B-4 Number of periods of an investment P3	Keith Riggins expects an investment of $82,014 to return $10,000 annually for several years. If Riggins earns a return of 10%, how many annual payments will he receive? (Use Table B.3.)
Exercise B-5 Interest rate on an investment P4	Algoe expects to invest $1,000 annually for 40 years to yield an accumulated value of $154,762 on the date of the last investment. For this to occur, what rate of interest must Algoe earn? (Use Table B.4.)
Exercise B-6 Number of periods of an investment P4	Kate Beckwith expects to invest $10,000 annually that will earn 8%. How many annual investments must Beckwith make to accumulate $303,243 on the date of the last investment? (Use Table B.4.)
Exercise B-7 Present value of an annuity P3	Sam Weber finances a new automobile by paying $6,500 cash and agreeing to make 40 monthly payments of $500 each, the first payment to be made one month after the purchase. The loan bears interest at an annual rate of 12%. What is the cost of the automobile?
Exercise B-8 Present value of bonds P1 P3	Spiller Corp. plans to issue 10%, 15-year, $500,000 par value bonds payable that pay interest semiannually on June 30 and December 31. The bonds are dated December 31, 2013, and are issued on that date. If the market rate of interest for the bonds is 8% on the date of issue, what will be the total cash proceeds from the bond issue?
Exercise B-9 Present value of an amount P1	McAdams Company expects to earn 10% per year on an investment that will pay $606,773 six years from now. Use Table B.1 to compute the present value of this investment. (Round the amount to the nearest dollar.)
Exercise B-10 Present value of an amount and of an annuity P1 P3	Compute the amount that can be borrowed under each of the following circumstances: **1.** A promise to repay $90,000 seven years from now at an interest rate of 6%. **2.** An agreement made on February 1, 2013, to make three separate payments of $20,000 on February 1 of 2014, 2015, and 2016. The annual interest rate is 10%.
Exercise B-11 Present value of an amount P1	On January 1, 2013, a company agrees to pay $20,000 in three years. If the annual interest rate is 10%, determine how much cash the company can borrow with this agreement.
Exercise B-12 Practical applications of the time value of money P1 P2 P3 P4	**a.** How much would you have to deposit today if you wanted to have $60,000 in 4 years? Annual interest rate is 9%. **b.** Assume that you are saving up for a trip around the world when you graduate in 2 years. If you can earn 8% on your investments, how much would you have to deposit today to have $15,000 when you graduate?

c. Would you rather have $463 now or $1,000 ten years from now? Assume that you can earn 9% on your investments.

d. Assume that a college parking sticker today costs $90. If the cost of parking is increasing at the rate of 5% per year, how much will a college parking sticker cost in 8 years?

e. Assume that the average price of a new home is $158,500. If new homes are increasing at a rate of 10% per year, how much will a new home cost in 8 years?

f. An investment will pay you $10,000 in 10 years, and it will also pay you $400 at the end of *each* of the next 10 years (years 1 thru 10). If the annual interest rate is 6%, how much would you be willing to pay today for this type of investment?

g. A college student is reported in the newspaper as having won $10,000,000 in the Kansas State Lottery. However, as is often the custom with lotteries, she does *not* actually receive the entire $10 million now. Instead she will receive $500,000 at the end of the year for *each* of the next 20 years. If the annual interest rate is 6%, what is the present value (today's amount) that she won? (Ignore taxes.)

C&H Ski Club recently borrowed money and agrees to pay it back with a series of six annual payments of $5,000 each. C&H subsequently borrows more money and agrees to pay it back with a series of four annual payments of $7,500 each. The annual interest rate for both loans is 6%.

Exercise B-13
Present values of annuities
P3

1. Use Table B.1 to find the present value of these two separate annuities. (Round amounts to the nearest dollar.)

2. Use Table B.3 to find the present value of these two separate annuities. (Round amounts to the nearest dollar.)

Otto Co. borrows money on April 30, 2013, by promising to make four payments of $13,000 each on November 1, 2013; May 1, 2014; November 1, 2014; and May 1, 2015.

Exercise B-14
Present value with semiannual compounding
C1 P3

1. How much money is Otto able to borrow if the interest rate is 8%, compounded semiannually?

2. How much money is Otto able to borrow if the interest rate is 12%, compounded semiannually?

3. How much money is Otto able to borrow if the interest rate is 16%, compounded semiannually?

Mark Welsch deposits $7,200 in an account that earns interest at an annual rate of 8%, compounded quarterly. The $7,200 plus earned interest must remain in the account 10 years before it can be withdrawn. How much money will be in the account at the end of 10 years?

Exercise B-15
Future value
of an amount   P2

Kelly Malone plans to have $50 withheld from her monthly paycheck and deposited in a savings account that earns 12% annually, compounded monthly. If Malone continues with her plan for two and one-half years, how much will be accumulated in the account on the date of the last deposit?

Exercise B-16
Future value
of an annuity   P4

Starr Company decides to establish a fund that it will use 10 years from now to replace an aging production facility. The company will make a $100,000 initial contribution to the fund and plans to make quarterly contributions of $50,000 beginning in three months. The fund earns 12%, compounded quarterly. What will be the value of the fund 10 years from now?

Exercise B-17
Future value of
an amount plus
an annuity P2 P4

Catten, Inc., invests $163,170 today earning 7% per year for nine years. Use Table B.2 to compute the future value of the investment nine years from now. (Round the amount to the nearest dollar.)

Exercise B-18
Future value of an amount   P2

For each of the following situations, identify (1) the case as either (*a*) a present or a future value and (*b*) a single amount or an annuity, (2) the table you would use in your computations (but do not solve the problem), and (3) the interest rate and time periods you would use.

Exercise B-19
Using present and future
value tables
C1 P1 P2 P3 P4

a. You need to accumulate $10,000 for a trip you wish to take in four years. You are able to earn 8% compounded semiannually on your savings. You plan to make only one deposit and let the money accumulate for four years. How would you determine the amount of the one-time deposit?

b. Assume the same facts as in part (*a*) except that you will make semiannual deposits to your savings account.

c. You want to retire after working 40 years with savings in excess of $1,000,000. You expect to save $4,000 a year for 40 years and earn an annual rate of interest of 8%. Will you be able to retire with more than $1,000,000 in 40 years? Explain.

d. A sweepstakes agency names you a grand prize winner. You can take $225,000 immediately or elect to receive annual installments of $30,000 for 20 years. You can earn 10% annually on any investments you make. Which prize do you choose to receive?

TABLE B.1

Present Value of 1

$$p = 1/(1 + i)^n$$

Periods	1%	2%	3%	4%	5%	6%	7%	8%	9%	10%	12%	15%
1	0.9901	0.9804	0.9709	0.9615	0.9524	0.9434	0.9346	0.9259	0.9174	0.9091	0.8929	0.8696
2	0.9803	0.9612	0.9426	0.9246	0.9070	0.8900	0.8734	0.8573	0.8417	0.8264	0.7972	0.7561
3	0.9706	0.9423	0.9151	0.8890	0.8638	0.8396	0.8163	0.7938	0.7722	0.7513	0.7118	0.6575
4	0.9610	0.9238	0.8885	0.8548	0.8227	0.7921	0.7629	0.7350	0.7084	0.6830	0.6355	0.5718
5	0.9515	0.9057	0.8626	0.8219	0.7835	0.7473	0.7130	0.6806	0.6499	0.6209	0.5674	0.4972
6	0.9420	0.8880	0.8375	0.7903	0.7462	0.7050	0.6663	0.6302	0.5963	0.5645	0.5066	0.4323
7	0.9327	0.8706	0.8131	0.7599	0.7107	0.6651	0.6227	0.5835	0.5470	0.5132	0.4523	0.3759
8	0.9235	0.8535	0.7894	0.7307	0.6768	0.6274	0.5820	0.5403	0.5019	0.4665	0.4039	0.3269
9	0.9143	0.8368	0.7664	0.7026	0.6446	0.5919	0.5439	0.5002	0.4604	0.4241	0.3606	0.2843
10	0.9053	0.8203	0.7441	0.6756	0.6139	0.5584	0.5083	0.4632	0.4224	0.3855	0.3220	0.2472
11	0.8963	0.8043	0.7224	0.6496	0.5847	0.5268	0.4751	0.4289	0.3875	0.3505	0.2875	0.2149
12	0.8874	0.7885	0.7014	0.6246	0.5568	0.4970	0.4440	0.3971	0.3555	0.3186	0.2567	0.1869
13	0.8787	0.7730	0.6810	0.6006	0.5303	0.4688	0.4150	0.3677	0.3262	0.2897	0.2292	0.1625
14	0.8700	0.7579	0.6611	0.5775	0.5051	0.4423	0.3878	0.3405	0.2992	0.2633	0.2046	0.1413
15	0.8613	0.7430	0.6419	0.5553	0.4810	0.4173	0.3624	0.3152	0.2745	0.2394	0.1827	0.1229
16	0.8528	0.7284	0.6232	0.5339	0.4581	0.3936	0.3387	0.2919	0.2519	0.2176	0.1631	0.1069
17	0.8444	0.7142	0.6050	0.5134	0.4363	0.3714	0.3166	0.2703	0.2311	0.1978	0.1456	0.0929
18	0.8360	0.7002	0.5874	0.4936	0.4155	0.3503	0.2959	0.2502	0.2120	0.1799	0.1300	0.0808
19	0.8277	0.6864	0.5703	0.4746	0.3957	0.3305	0.2765	0.2317	0.1945	0.1635	0.1161	0.0703
20	0.8195	0.6730	0.5537	0.4564	0.3769	0.3118	0.2584	0.2145	0.1784	0.1486	0.1037	0.0611
25	0.7798	0.6095	0.4776	0.3751	0.2953	0.2330	0.1842	0.1460	0.1160	0.0923	0.0588	0.0304
30	0.7419	0.5521	0.4120	0.3083	0.2314	0.1741	0.1314	0.0994	0.0754	0.0573	0.0334	0.0151
35	0.7059	0.5000	0.3554	0.2534	0.1813	0.1301	0.0937	0.0676	0.0490	0.0356	0.0189	0.0075
40	0.6717	0.4529	0.3066	0.2083	0.1420	0.0972	0.0668	0.0460	0.0318	0.0221	0.0107	0.0037

TABLE B.2

Future Value of 1

$$f = (1 + i)^n$$

Periods	1%	2%	3%	4%	5%	6%	7%	8%	9%	10%	12%	15%
0	1.0000	1.0000	1.0000	1.0000	1.0000	1.0000	1.0000	1.0000	1.0000	1.0000	1.0000	1.0000
1	1.0100	1.0200	1.0300	1.0400	1.0500	1.0600	1.0700	1.0800	1.0900	1.1000	1.1200	1.1500
2	1.0201	1.0404	1.0609	1.0816	1.1025	1.1236	1.1449	1.1664	1.1881	1.2100	1.2544	1.3225
3	1.0303	1.0612	1.0927	1.1249	1.1576	1.1910	1.2250	1.2597	1.2950	1.3310	1.4049	1.5209
4	1.0406	1.0824	1.1255	1.1699	1.2155	1.2625	1.3108	1.3605	1.4116	1.4641	1.5735	1.7490
5	1.0510	1.1041	1.1593	1.2167	1.2763	1.3382	1.4026	1.4693	1.5386	1.6105	1.7623	2.0114
6	1.0615	1.1262	1.1941	1.2653	1.3401	1.4185	1.5007	1.5869	1.6771	1.7716	1.9738	2.3131
7	1.0721	1.1487	1.2299	1.3159	1.4071	1.5036	1.6058	1.7138	1.8280	1.9487	2.2107	2.6600
8	1.0829	1.1717	1.2668	1.3686	1.4775	1.5938	1.7182	1.8509	1.9926	2.1436	2.4760	3.0590
9	1.0937	1.1951	1.3048	1.4233	1.5513	1.6895	1.8385	1.9990	2.1719	2.3579	2.7731	3.5179
10	1.1046	1.2190	1.3439	1.4802	1.6289	1.7908	1.9672	2.1589	2.3674	2.5937	3.1058	4.0456
11	1.1157	1.2434	1.3842	1.5395	1.7103	1.8983	2.1049	2.3316	2.5804	2.8531	3.4785	4.6524
12	1.1268	1.2682	1.4258	1.6010	1.7959	2.0122	2.2522	2.5182	2.8127	3.1384	3.8960	5.3503
13	1.1381	1.2936	1.4685	1.6651	1.8856	2.1329	2.4098	2.7196	3.0658	3.4523	4.3635	6.1528
14	1.1495	1.3195	1.5126	1.7317	1.9799	2.2609	2.5785	2.9372	3.3417	3.7975	4.8871	7.0757
15	1.1610	1.3459	1.5580	1.8009	2.0789	2.3966	2.7590	3.1722	3.6425	4.1772	5.4736	8.1371
16	1.1726	1.3728	1.6047	1.8730	2.1829	2.5404	2.9522	3.4259	3.9703	4.5950	6.1304	9.3576
17	1.1843	1.4002	1.6528	1.9479	2.2920	2.6928	3.1588	3.7000	4.3276	5.0545	6.8660	10.7613
18	1.1961	1.4282	1.7024	2.0258	2.4066	2.8543	3.3799	3.9960	4.7171	5.5599	7.6900	12.3755
19	1.2081	1.4568	1.7535	2.1068	2.5270	3.0256	3.6165	4.3157	5.1417	6.1159	8.6128	14.2318
20	1.2202	1.4859	1.8061	2.1911	2.6533	3.2071	3.8697	4.6610	5.6044	6.7275	9.6463	16.3665
25	1.2824	1.6406	2.0938	2.6658	3.3864	4.2919	5.4274	6.8485	8.6231	10.8347	17.0001	32.9190
30	1.3478	1.8114	2.4273	3.2434	4.3219	5.7435	7.6123	10.0627	13.2677	17.4494	29.9599	66.2118
35	1.4166	1.9999	2.8139	3.9461	5.5160	7.6861	10.6766	14.7853	20.4140	28.1024	52.7996	133.1755
40	1.4889	2.2080	3.2620	4.8010	7.0400	10.2857	14.9745	21.7245	31.4094	45.2593	93.0510	267.8635

$$p = \left[1 - \frac{1}{(1 + i)^n}\right]/i$$

TABLE B.3

Present Value of an Annuity of 1

Periods	1%	2%	3%	4%	5%	6%	7%	8%	9%	10%	12%	15%
1	0.9901	0.9804	0.9709	0.9615	0.9524	0.9434	0.9346	0.9259	0.9174	0.9091	0.8929	0.8696
2	1.9704	1.9416	1.9135	1.8861	1.8594	1.8334	1.8080	1.7833	1.7591	1.7355	1.6901	1.6257
3	2.9410	2.8839	2.8286	2.7751	2.7232	2.6730	2.6243	2.5771	2.5313	2.4869	2.4018	2.2832
4	3.9020	3.8077	3.7171	3.6299	3.5460	3.4651	3.3872	3.3121	3.2397	3.1699	3.0373	2.8550
5	4.8534	4.7135	4.5797	4.4518	4.3295	4.2124	4.1002	3.9927	3.8897	3.7908	3.6048	3.3522
6	5.7955	5.6014	5.4172	5.2421	5.0757	4.9173	4.7665	4.6229	4.4859	4.3553	4.1114	3.7845
7	6.7282	6.4720	6.2303	6.0021	5.7864	5.5824	5.3893	5.2064	5.0330	4.8684	4.5638	4.1604
8	7.6517	7.3255	7.0197	6.7327	6.4632	6.2098	5.9713	5.7466	5.5348	5.3349	4.9676	4.4873
9	8.5660	8.1622	7.7861	7.4353	7.1078	6.8017	6.5152	6.2469	5.9952	5.7590	5.3282	4.7716
10	9.4713	8.9826	8.5302	8.1109	7.7217	7.3601	7.0236	6.7101	6.4177	6.1446	5.6502	5.0188
11	10.3676	9.7868	9.2526	8.7605	8.3064	7.8869	7.4987	7.1390	6.8052	6.4951	5.9377	5.2337
12	11.2551	10.5753	9.9540	9.3851	8.8633	8.3838	7.9427	7.5361	7.1607	6.8137	6.1944	5.4206
13	12.1337	11.3484	10.6350	9.9856	9.3936	8.8527	8.3577	7.9038	7.4869	7.1034	6.4235	5.5831
14	13.0037	12.1062	11.2961	10.5631	9.8986	9.2950	8.7455	8.2442	7.7862	7.3667	6.6282	5.7245
15	13.8651	12.8493	11.9379	11.1184	10.3797	9.7122	9.1079	8.5595	8.0607	7.6061	6.8109	5.8474
16	14.7179	13.5777	12.5611	11.6523	10.8378	10.1059	9.4466	8.8514	8.3126	7.8237	6.9740	5.9542
17	15.5623	14.2919	13.1661	12.1657	11.2741	10.4773	9.7632	9.1216	8.5436	8.0216	7.1196	6.0472
18	16.3983	14.9920	13.7535	12.6593	11.6896	10.8276	10.0591	9.3719	8.7556	8.2014	7.2497	6.1280
19	17.2260	15.6785	14.3238	13.1339	12.0853	11.1581	10.3356	9.6036	8.9501	8.3649	7.3658	6.1982
20	18.0456	16.3514	14.8775	13.5903	12.4622	11.4699	10.5940	9.8181	9.1285	8.5136	7.4694	6.2593
25	22.0232	19.5235	17.4131	15.6221	14.0939	12.7834	11.6536	10.6748	9.8226	9.0770	7.8431	6.4641
30	25.8077	22.3965	19.6004	17.2920	15.3725	13.7648	12.4090	11.2578	10.2737	9.4269	8.0552	6.5660
35	29.4086	24.9986	21.4872	18.6646	16.3742	14.4982	12.9477	11.6546	10.5668	9.6442	8.1755	6.6166
40	32.8347	27.3555	23.1148	19.7928	17.1591	15.0463	13.3317	11.9246	10.7574	9.7791	8.2438	6.6418

$$f = [(1 + i)^n - 1]/i$$

TABLE B.4

Future Value of an Annuity of 1

Periods	1%	2%	3%	4%	5%	6%	7%	8%	9%	10%	12%	15%
1	1.0000	1.0000	1.0000	1.0000	1.0000	1.0000	1.0000	1.0000	1.0000	1.0000	1.0000	1.0000
2	2.0100	2.0200	2.0300	2.0400	2.0500	2.0600	2.0700	2.0800	2.0900	2.1000	2.1200	2.1500
3	3.0301	3.0604	3.0909	3.1216	3.1525	3.1836	3.2149	3.2464	3.2781	3.3100	3.3744	3.4725
4	4.0604	4.1216	4.1836	4.2465	4.3101	4.3746	4.4399	4.5061	4.5731	4.6410	4.7793	4.9934
5	5.1010	5.2040	5.3091	5.4163	5.5256	5.6371	5.7507	5.8666	5.9847	6.1051	6.3528	6.7424
6	6.1520	6.3081	6.4684	6.6330	6.8019	6.9753	7.1533	7.3359	7.5233	7.7156	8.1152	8.7537
7	7.2135	7.4343	7.6625	7.8983	8.1420	8.3938	8.6540	8.9228	9.2004	9.4872	10.0890	11.0668
8	8.2857	8.5830	8.8923	9.2142	9.5491	9.8975	10.2598	10.6366	11.0285	11.4359	12.2997	13.7268
9	9.3685	9.7546	10.1591	10.5828	11.0266	11.4913	11.9780	12.4876	13.0210	13.5795	14.7757	16.7858
10	10.4622	10.9497	11.4639	12.0061	12.5779	13.1808	13.8164	14.4866	15.1929	15.9374	17.5487	20.3037
11	11.5668	12.1687	12.8078	13.4864	14.2068	14.9716	15.7836	16.6455	17.5603	18.5312	20.6546	24.3493
12	12.6825	13.4121	14.1920	15.0258	15.9171	16.8699	17.8885	18.9771	20.1407	21.3843	24.1331	29.0017
13	13.8093	14.6803	15.6178	16.6268	17.7130	18.8821	20.1406	21.4953	22.9534	24.5227	28.0291	34.3519
14	14.9474	15.9739	17.0863	18.2919	19.5986	21.0151	22.5505	24.2149	26.0192	27.9750	32.3926	40.5047
15	16.0969	17.2934	18.5989	20.0236	21.5786	23.2760	25.1290	27.1521	29.3609	31.7725	37.2797	47.5804
16	17.2579	18.6393	20.1569	21.8245	23.6575	25.6725	27.8881	30.3243	33.0034	35.9497	42.7533	55.7175
17	18.4304	20.0121	21.7616	23.6975	25.8404	28.2129	30.8402	33.7502	36.9737	40.5447	48.8837	65.0751
18	19.6147	21.4123	23.4144	25.6454	28.1324	30.9057	33.9990	37.4502	41.3013	45.5992	55.7497	75.8364
19	20.8109	22.8406	25.1169	27.6712	30.5390	33.7600	37.3790	41.4463	46.0185	51.1591	63.4397	88.2118
20	22.0190	24.2974	26.8704	29.7781	33.0660	36.7856	40.9955	45.7620	51.1601	57.2750	72.0524	102.4436
25	28.2432	32.0303	36.4593	41.6459	47.7271	54.8645	63.2490	73.1059	84.7009	98.3471	133.3339	212.7930
30	34.7849	40.5681	47.5754	56.0849	66.4388	79.0582	94.4608	113.2832	136.3075	164.4940	241.3327	434.7451
35	41.6603	49.9945	60.4621	73.6522	90.3203	111.4348	138.2369	172.3168	215.7108	271.0244	431.6635	881.1702
40	48.8864	60.4020	75.4013	95.0255	120.7998	154.7620	199.6351	259.0565	337.8824	442.5926	767.0914	1,779.0903

Activity-Based Costing

Learning Objectives

CONCEPTUAL

C1 Explain cost flows for activity-based costing (p. C-2)

ANALYTICAL

A1 Identify and assess advantages and disadvantages of activity-based costing (p. C-5)

PROCEDURAL

P1 Assign overhead costs using the plantwide overhead rate method. (p. C-1)

P2 Assign overhead costs using activity-based costing. (p. C-2)

This appendix describes how to allocate costs shared by more than one product across those different products. The appendix first illustrates overhead allocation using a single plantwide overhead rate. The appendix also describes activity-based costing and how it traces the costs of individual activities. The appendix then compares the plantwide and activity-based methods and discusses their use in managerial decisions.

Activity-Based Costing

Overhead Cost Allocation Methods

- Plantwide overhead rate method
- Activity-based cost allocation
- Comparison of allocation methods

OVERHEAD COST ALLOCATION METHODS

We previously explained how to assign overhead costs to jobs (and processes) by using a predetermined overhead rate per unit of an allocation base such as direct labor cost. When a single overhead rate is used on a companywide basis, all overhead is lumped together, and a predetermined overhead rate per unit of an allocation base is computed and used to assign overhead to jobs (and processes). The use of a single predetermined overhead rate suggests that this allocation process is simple. In reality, it can be complicated. This appendix reviews the traditional plantwide cost allocation procedure and then introduces the activity-based cost allocation procedure.

Plantwide Overhead Rate Method

Cost Flows under Plantwide Overhead Rate Method The *single plantwide overhead rate method,* or simply the *plantwide overhead rate method,* uses one overhead rate to allocate overhead costs to products. For this method, the target of the cost assignment, or **cost object,** is the unit of product   see Exhibit C.1. The rate is determined using volume-related measures such as direct labor hours, direct labor cost dollars, or machine hours, which are readily available in most manufacturing settings. In some industries, overhead costs are closely related to these volume-related measures. In such cases it is logical to use this method as a basis for assigning indirect manufacturing costs to products.

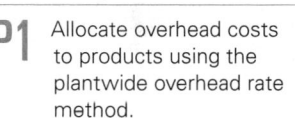

P1 Allocate overhead costs to products using the plantwide overhead rate method.

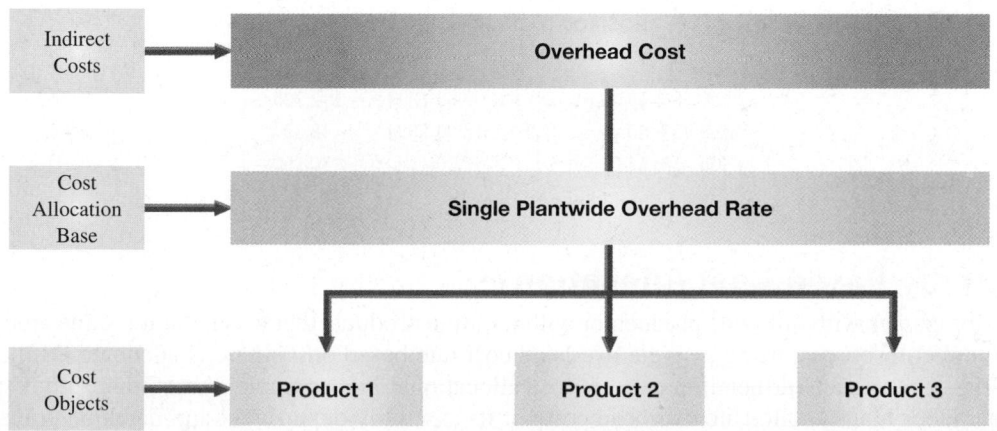

EXHIBIT C.1

Plantwide Overhead Rate Method

Applying the Plantwide Overhead Rate Method   Under the single plantwide overhead rate method, total budgeted overhead costs are combined into one overhead cost pool. This cost pool is then divided by the chosen allocation base, such as total direct labor hours, to arrive at a single plantwide overhead rate. This rate then is applied to assign costs to all products based on the allocation base such as direct labor hours required to manufacture each product.

To illustrate, consider data from **AutoGrand,** a custom automobile manufacturer. AutoGrand applies overhead on the basis of direct labor hours. For its three jobs, AutoGrand reports the budgeted direct labor hours in Exhibit C.2.

EXHIBIT C.2

AutoGrand's Budgeted Direct Labor Hours

Total Direct Labor Hours	
Job 236.........	4,000
Job 237.........	6,000
Job 238.........	10,000
Total..........	20,000

AutoGrand has five manufacturing-related departments that generate overhead costs: janitorial, maintenance, factory accounting, machining, and assembly. Expenses incurred by each of these departments (provided in Exhibit C.3) are considered product costs.

EXHIBIT C.3

AutoGrand's Overhead Costs

Department	Budgeted Overhead Cost
Janitorial...........................	$10,000
Maintenance.......................	15,000
Factory accounting..................	8,000
Machining..........................	10,000
Assembly	18,000
Total budgeted overhead cost.........	$61,000

The single plantwide overhead rate for AutoGrand is computed as follows:

$$\begin{array}{ccc} \textbf{Plantwide} & = & \textbf{Total budgeted} & \div & \textbf{Total budgeted direct} \\ \textbf{overhead rate} & & \textbf{overhead cost} & & \textbf{labor hours} \\ & = & \$61,000 & \div & 20,000 \text{ DLH} \\ & = & \$3.05 \text{ per DLH} \end{array}$$

This plantwide overhead rate is then used to allocate overhead cost to products based on the number of direct labor hours required to produce each unit as follows:

Overhead allocated to each product unit = Plantwide overhead rate × DLH per unit

For AutoGrand, overhead cost is allocated to its three products as follows:

Job 236: $3.05 per DLH × 4,000 DLH = $12,200	
Job 237: $3.05 per DLH × 6,000 DLH = 18,300	
Job 238: $3.05 per DLH × 10,000 DLH = 30,500	
Total $61,000	

Activity-Based Cost Allocation

C1 Explain cost flows for activity-based costing.

For companies with only one product, or with multiple products that use about the same amount of indirect resources, using a single overhead cost rate based on volume is adequate. Multiple overhead rates can further improve on cost allocations. For example, AutoGrand might use direct labor hours to allocate overhead costs of its assembly department and machine hours to allocate costs of its machining department. This could result in more accurate overhead cost

EXHIBIT C.4

Activity-Based Cost Allocation

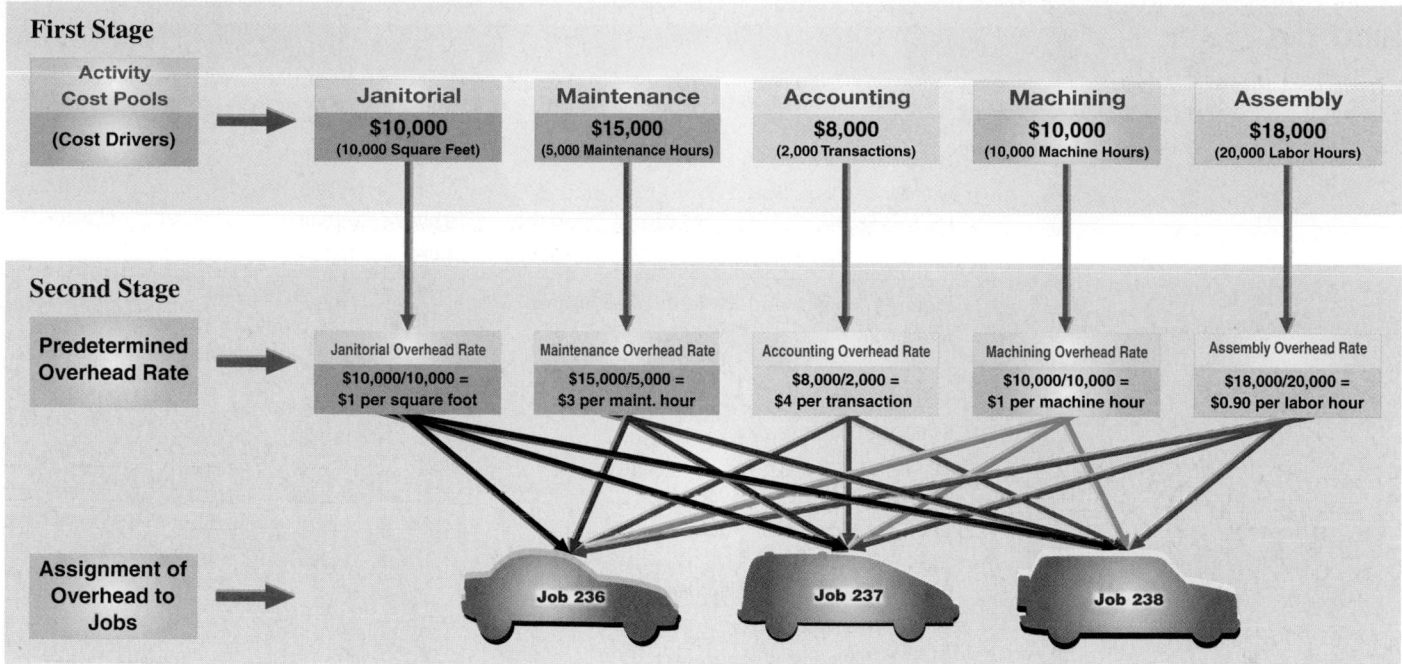

allocations, if different products use different amounts of direct labor and machine hours. Yet, when a company has many products that consume different amounts of indirect resources, even the multiple overhead rate system based on volume is often inadequate. Such a system usually fails to reflect the products' different uses of indirect resources and often distorts products costs.

Specifically, low-volume complex products are usually undercosted, whereas high-volume simpler products are overcosted. This can cause companies to believe that their complex products are more profitable than they really are, which can lead those companies to focus on them to the detriment of high-volume simpler products. This creates a demand for a better cost allocation system for these indirect (overhead) costs.

Activity-based costing (ABC) attempts to better allocate costs to the proper users of overhead by focusing on *activities*. Costs are traced to individual activities and then allocated to cost objects. Exhibit C.4 shows the (two-stage) activity-based cost allocation method. The first stage identifies the activities involved in processing Jobs 236, 237, and 238 and forms activity cost *pools* by combining those activities. The second stage involves computing predetermined overhead cost rates for each cost pool and then assigning costs to jobs.

We begin our explanation at the top of Exhibit C.4. The first stage identifies individual activities, which are pooled in a logical manner into homogenous groups, or *cost pools*. A homogenous cost pool consists of activities that belong to the same process and/or are caused by the same cost driver. An **activity cost driver,** or simply *cost driver,* is a factor that causes the cost of an activity to go up or down. For example, preparing an invoice, checking it, and dispatching it are activities of the "invoicing" process and can therefore be grouped in a single cost pool. Moreover, the number of invoices processed likely drives the costs of these activities.

An **activity cost pool** is a temporary account accumulating the costs a company incurs to support an identified set of activities. Costs accumulated in an activity cost pool include the variable and fixed costs of the activities in the pool. Variable costs pertain to resources acquired as needed (such as materials); fixed costs pertain to resources acquired in advance (such as equipment). An activity cost pool account is handled like a factory overhead account.

In the second stage, after all activity costs are accumulated in an activity cost pool account, overhead rates are computed. Then, costs are allocated to cost objects (users) based on cost drivers (allocation bases).

Point: Activity based costing is used in many settings. A study found that activity-based costing improves health care costing accuracy, enabling improved profitability analysis and decision making. However, identifying cost drivers in a health care setting is challenging.

P2 Assign overhead costs using activity-based costing.

Point: A cost driver is different from an allocation base. An allocation base is used as a basis for assigning overhead but need not have a cause-effect relation with the costs assigned. However, a cost driver has a cause-effect relation with the cost assigned.

Illustration of Activity-Based Costing   To illustrate, let's return to AutoGrand's three jobs. Assume that resources used to complete Jobs 236, 237, and 238 are shown in panel A at the top of Exhibit C.5.

EXHIBIT C.5

Activity Resource Use and Assignment of Overhead to Output

	Job 236	Job 237	Job 238	Activity Totals
Panel A: Resources Used				
Square feet of space	5,000	3,000	2,000	
Maintenance hours	2,500	1,500	1,000	
Number of transactions	500	700	800	
Machine hours	2,000	3,000	5,000	
Direct labor hours	4,000	6,000	10,000	
Panel B: Assignment of overhead to output				
Janitorial				
$1.00 × 5,000 sq. ft.	$ 5,000			
$1.00 × 3,000 sq. ft.		$ 3,000		
$1.00 × 2,000 sq. ft.			$ 2,000	$10,000
Maintenance				
$3.00 × 2,500 maint. hrs.	7,500			
$3.00 × 1,500 maint. hrs.		4,500		
$3.00 × 1,000 maint. hrs.			3,000	15,000
Factory Accounting				
$4.00 × 500 transactions	2,000			
$4.00 × 700 transactions		2,800		
$4.00 × 800 transactions			3,200	8,000
Machining				
$1.00 × 2,000 machine hrs.	2,000			
$1.00 × 3,000 machine hrs.		3,000		
$1.00 × 5,000 machine hrs.			5,000	10,000
Assembly				
$0.90 × 4,000 labor hrs.	3,600			
$0.90 × 6,000 labor hrs.		5,400		
$0.90 × 10,000 labor hrs.			9,000	18,000
Total overhead assigned	$20,100	$18,700	$22,200	$61,000

The $61,000 of total costs are assigned to these three jobs using activity-based costing as shown in panel B at the bottom of Exhibit C.5 (*rates are taken from the second stage of Exhibit C.4*).

From Exhibit C.6, we see that the costs assigned to the three jobs vary markedly depending on which allocation method is used. Costs assigned to Job 236 go from $12,200 under plant-wide cost allocation to $20,100 under activity-based costing. Costs assigned to Job 238 decline from $30,500 to $22,200. These differences in assigned amounts result from more accurately tracing costs to each job using activity-based costing where the allocation bases reflect actual cost drivers.

EXHIBIT C.6

Comparing Overhead Costs Assigned under Alternative Methods

Overhead Assigned	Job 236	Job 237	Job 238	Total
Plantwide cost allocation	$12,200	$18,300	$30,500	$61,000
Activity-based costing (Exhibit C.5)	20,100	18,700	22,200	61,000

Decision Maker

Director of Operations   Two department managers at your ad agency complain to you that overhead costs assigned to them are too high. Overhead is assigned on the basis of labor hours for designers. These managers argue that overhead depends not only on designers' hours but on many activities unrelated to these hours. What is your response? ■   [Answer—p. C-6]

Comparison of Plantwide and Activity-Based Cost Allocation

Traditional cost systems capture overhead costs by individual department (or function) and accumulate these costs in one or more overhead accounts. Companies then assign these overhead costs using a single allocation base such as direct labor or multiple volume-based allocation bases. Unfortunately, traditional cost systems have tended to use allocation bases that are often not closely related to the way these costs are actually incurred.

In contrast, activity-based cost systems capture costs by individual activity. These activities and their costs are then accumulated into activity cost pools. A company selects a cost driver (allocation base) for each activity pool. It uses this cost driver to assign the accumulated activity costs to cost objects (such as jobs or products) benefiting from the activity. As shown in Exhibit C.6, the activity-based costing (ABC) system can more accurately trace costs to individual jobs. More generally, we can conclude the following:

A1 Identify and assess advantages and disadvantages of activity-based costing.

- ABC uses more allocation bases than a traditional cost system. For example, a Chicago-based manufacturer currently uses nearly 20 different activity cost drivers to assign overhead costs to its products. Exhibit C.7 lists common examples of overhead cost pools and their usual cost drivers.

- ABC is especially effective when the same department or departments produce many different types of products. For instance, more complex products often require more help from service departments such as engineering, maintenance, and materials handling. If the same amount of direct labor is applied to the complex and simple products, a traditional overhead allocation system assigns the same overhead cost to both. With activity-based costing, however, the complex products are assigned a larger portion of overhead. The difference in overhead assigned can affect product pricing, make-or-buy, and other managerial decisions.

- ABC encourages managers to focus on *activities* as well as the use of those activities. For instance, assume AutoGrand can reduce the number of transactions processed in Factory Accounting to 1,500 (375 transactions for Job 236, 525 transactions for Job 237, and 600 transactions for Job 238) and that through continuous improvement it can reduce costs of processing those transactions to $4,500. The resulting rate to process a transaction is $3 per transaction ($4,500/1,500 transactions—down from $4 per Exhibit C.4). The cost of transaction processing is reduced for all jobs (Job 236, $1,125; Job 237, $1,575; Job 238, $1,800). However, if those accounting costs were grouped in a single overhead cost pool, it is more difficult to identify cost savings and understand their effects on product costs.

- ABC requires managers to look at each item and encourages them to manage each cost to increase the benefit from each dollar spent. It also encourages managers to cooperate because it shows how their efforts are interrelated. This results in *activity-based management*.

Activity Cost Pool	Cost Driver
Materials purchasing	Number of purchase orders
Materials handling	Number of materials requisitions
Personnel processing	Number of employees hired or laid off
Equipment depreciation	Number of products produced or hours of use
Quality inspection	Number of units inspected
Indirect labor in setting up equipment	Number of setups required
Engineering costs for product modifications	Number of modifications (engineering change orders)

EXHIBIT C.7

Cost Pools and Cost Drivers in Activity-Based Costing

■ **Decision Ethics**

Accounting Officer   Your company produces expensive garments, whose production involves many complex and specialized activities. Your general manager recently learned about activity-based costing (ABC) and asks your advice. However, your supervisor does not want to disturb the existing cost system and instructs you to prepare a report stating that "implementation of ABC is a complicated process involving too many steps and not worth the effort." You believe ABC will actually help the company identify sources of costs and control them. What action do you take? ■   [Answer—p. C-6]

Quick Check	Answers — p. C-6

1. What is a cost driver?
2. When activity-based costing is used rather than traditional allocation methods [select one], (*a*) managers must identify cost drivers for various items of overhead cost, (*b*) individual cost items in service departments are allocated directly to products or services, (*c*) managers can direct their attention to the activities that drive overhead cost, or (*d*) all of the above.

Summary

C1   **Explain cost flows for activity-based costing.** With ABC, overhead costs are first traced to the activities that cause them, and then cost pools are formed combining costs caused by the same activity. Overhead rates based on these activities are then used to assign overhead to products in proportion to the amount of activity required to produce them.

A1   **Identify and assess advantages and disadvantages of activity-based costing.** ABC improves product costing accuracy and draws management attention to relevant factors to control. The cost of constructing and maintaining an ABC system can sometimes outweigh its value.

P1   **Allocate overhead costs to products using the plantwide overhead rate method.** The plantwide overhead rate equals total budgeted overhead divided by budgeted plant volume, the latter often measured in direct labor hours or machine hours. This rate multiplied by the number of direct labor hours (or machine hours) required for each product provides the overhead assigned to each product.

P2   **Assign overhead costs using activity-based costing.** In activity-based costing, the costs of related activities are collected and then pooled in some logical manner into activity cost pools. After all activity costs have been accumulated in an activity cost pool account, users of the activity, termed *cost objects*, are assigned a portion of the total activity cost using a cost driver (allocation base).

Guidance Answers to Decision Maker and Decision Ethics	

Director of Operations   You should collect details on overhead items and review them to see whether direct labor drives these costs. If it does not, overhead might be improperly assigned to departments. The situation also provides an opportunity to consider other overhead allocation bases, including use of activity-based costing.

Accounting Officer   You should not author a report that you disagree with. You are responsible for ascertaining all the facts of ABC (implementation procedures, advantages and disadvantages, and costs). You should then approach your supervisor with these facts and suggest that you would like to modify the report to request, for example, a pilot test. The pilot test will allow you to further assess the suitability of ABC. Your suggestion might be rejected, at which time you may wish to speak with a more senior-level manager.

Guidance Answers to Quick Checks	

1. Cost drivers are the factors that have a cause-effect relation with costs (or activities that pertain to costs).
2. *d*

Key Terms

Activity-based costing (ABC) (p. C-3)   Activity cost driver (C-3)   Activity cost pool (C-3)

Discussion Questions

1. Why are overhead costs allocated to products and not traced to products as direct materials and direct labor are?

2. Complete the following for a traditional two-stage allocation system: In the first stage, service department costs are assigned to _____ departments. In the second stage, a predetermined overhead rate is computed for each operating department and used to assign overhead to _____.

3. What is the difference between operating departments and service departments?

4. What is activity-based costing? What is its goal?

5. What is a cost object?

6. What is an activity cost driver?

7. 🛈 What company circumstances especially encourage use of activity-based costing?

8. 🛈 Identify at least four typical cost pools for activity-based costing in most organizations.

9. In activity-based costing, costs in a cost pool are allocated to _____ using predetermined overhead rates.

10. **Polaris** must assign overhead costs to its prod-   **Polaris** ucts. Activity-based costing is generally considered more accurate than other methods of assigning overhead. If this is so, why do all manufacturers not use it?

11. **Arctic Cat** is a manufacturer. It is said that: **Arctic Cat** "Activity-based costing is only useful for manufacturing companies." Is this a true statement? Explain.

---

connect

In the blank next to the following terms, place the letter A through D corresponding to the best description of that term.

1. _____ Activity
2. _____ Activity driver
3. _____ Cost pool
4. _____ Cost object

A. Measurement associated with an activity.
B. A group of costs that have the same activity drivers.
C. Anything to which costs will be assigned.
D. A task that causes a cost to be incurred.

QUICK STUDY

QS C-1
Costing terminology
A1

Chan Company identified the following activities, costs, and activity drivers. The company manufactures two types of go-karts: Fast and Standard. Production volume is 10,000 units of the Fast model and 30,000 units of the Standard model.

Activity	Expected Costs	Expected Activity
Handling materials	$625,000	100,000 parts in stock
Inspecting product	900,000	1,500 batches
Processing purchase orders	105,000	700 orders
Paying suppliers	175,000	500 invoices
Insuring the factory	300,000	40,000 square feet
Designing packaging	375,000	10 models

QS C-2
Compute plantwide overhead rates
P1

Required

1. Compute a single plantwide overhead rate assuming that the company assigns overhead based on 100,000 budgeted direct labor hours.

2. Assign overhead costs to each model assuming the Fast model requires 25,000 direct labor hours and the Standard model requires 60,000 direct labor hours. What is the overhead cost per unit for each model?

QS C-3
Compute overhead rates
under ABC   P2

Refer to the information in QS C-2. Compute the activity rate for each activity, assuming the company uses activity-based costing.

QS C-4
Assigning costs using ABC

P2

Refer to the data in QS C-2. Assume that the following information is available for the company's two products.

	Fast Model	Standard Model
Production volume.......	10,000 units	30,000 units
Parts required	20,000 parts	30,000 parts
Batches made...........	250 batches	100 batches
Purchase orders	50 orders	20 orders
Invoices	50 invoices	10 invoices
Space occupied	10,000 sq. ft.	7,000 sq. ft.
Models	1 model	1 model

Required

Assign overhead costs to each product model using activity-based costing (ABC). What is the overhead cost per unit of each model?

QS C-5
Assigning costs using ABC

P2

Qinto Company sells two types of products, Basic and Deluxe. The company provides technical support for users of its products, at an expected cost of $250,000 per year. The company expects to process 10,000 customer service calls per year.

Required

1. Determine the company's cost of technical support per customer service call.
2. During the month of January, Qinto received 650 calls for customer service on its Deluxe model, and 150 calls for customer service on its Basic model. Assign technical support costs to each model using activity-based costing (ABC).

QS C-6
Multiple choice overhead
questions

A1

1. Which costing method tends to overstate the cost of high-volume products?
   a. Traditional volume-based costing   **c.** Job order costing
   b. Activity-based costing   **d.** Differential costing
2. If management wants the most accurate product cost, which of the following costing methods should be used?
   a. Volume-based costing using direct labor hours to allocate overhead
   b. Volume-based costing using a plantwide overhead rate
   c. Normal costing using a plantwide overhead rate
   d. Activity-based costing
3. Disadvantages of activity-based costing include
   a. It is not acceptable under GAAP for external reporting.   **c.** It can be used in an activity-based management.
   b. It can be costly to implement.   **d.** Both a. and b.

QS C-7
Activity-based costing and
overhead cost allocation

P2

The following is taken from Mortan Co.'s internal records of its factory with two operating departments. The cost driver for indirect labor and supplies is direct labor costs, and the cost driver for the remaining overhead items is number of hours of machine use. Compute the total amount of overhead cost allocated to Operating Department 1 using activity-based costing.

	Direct Labor	Machine Use Hours
Operating department 1	$18,800	2,000
Operating department 2	13,200	1,200
Totals	$32,000	3,200
Factory overhead costs		
Rent and utilities		$12,200
Indirect labor		5,400
General office expense		4,000
Depreciation—Equipment		3,000
Supplies		2,600
Total factory overhead		$27,200

Check   Dept. 1 allocation, $16,700

A company uses activity-based costing to determine the costs of its three products: A, B, and C. The budgeted cost and cost driver activity for each of the company's three activity cost pools follow.

QS C-8
Computing activity rates

P2

		Budgeted Activity of Cost Driver		
Activity Cost Pool	**Budgeted Cost**	**Product A**	**Product B**	**Product C**
Activity 1	$70,000	6,000	9,000	20,000
Activity 2	45,000	7,000	15,000	8,000
Activity 3	82,000	2,500	1,000	1,625

Compute the activity rates for each of the company's three activities.

A company has two products: standard and deluxe. The company expects to produce 34,300 standard units and 69,550 deluxe units. It uses activity-based costing and has prepared the following analysis showing budgeted cost and cost driver activity for each of its three activity cost pools.

QS C-9
Activity-based costing rates and allocations

P2

		Budgeted Activity of Cost Driver	
Activity Cost Pool	**Budgeted Cost**	**Standard**	**Deluxe**
Activity 1	$87,000	3,000	2,800
Activity 2	62,000	4,500	5,500
Activity 3	93,000	2,500	5,250

Required

1. What is the overhead cost per unit for the standard units?
2. What is the overhead cost per unit for the deluxe units?

The following is taken from Antuan Co.'s internal records of its factory with two operating departments. The cost driver for indirect labor and supplies is direct labor costs, and the cost driver for the remaining overhead items is number of hours of machine use. Compute the total amount of overhead cost allocated to Operating Department 1 using activity-based costing.

QS C-10
Activity-based costing and overhead cost allocation

P1

	Direct Labor	Machine Use Hours
Operating department 1	$ 9,400	1,200
Operating department 2	6,600	2,000
Totals	$16,000	3,200
Factory overhead costs		
Rent and utilities		$ 6,100
Indirect labor		2,700
General office expense		2,000
Depreciation—Equipment		1,500
Supplies		1,300
Total factory overhead		$13,600

Check   Dept. 1 allocation, $5,950

EXERCISES

Exercise C-1
Using the plantwide overhead rate to assess prices

P1

Real Cool produces two different models of air conditioners. The company produces the mechanical systems in their components department. The mechanical systems are combined with the housing assembly in its finishing department. The activities, costs, and drivers associated with these two manufacturing processes and the production support process follow.

Process	Activity	Overhead Cost	Driver	Quantity
Components	Changeover	$ 500,000	Number of batches	800
	Machining	279,000	Machine hours	6,000
	Setups	225,000	Number of setups	120
		$1,004,000		
Finishing	Welding	$ 180,300	Welding hours	3,000
	Inspecting	210,000	Number of inspections	700
	Rework	75,000	Rework orders	300
		$ 465,300		
Support	Purchasing	$ 135,000	Purchase orders	450
	Providing space	32,000	Number of units	5,000
	Providing utilities	65,000	Number of units	5,000
		$ 232,000		

Additional production information concerning its two product lines follows.

	Model 145	Model 212
Units produced	1,500	3,500
Welding hours	800	2,200
Batches	400	400
Number of inspections	400	300
Machine hours	1,800	4,200
Setups	60	60
Rework orders	160	140
Purchase orders	300	150

Required

1. Using a plantwide overhead rate based on machine hours, compute the overhead cost per unit for each product line.
2. Determine the total cost per unit for each product line if the direct labor and direct materials costs per unit are $250 for Model 145 and $180 for Model 212.

Check   (3) Model 212, $(50.26) per unit loss

3. If the market price for Model 145 is $800 and the market price for Model 212 is $470, determine the profit or loss per unit for each model. Comment on the results.

Exercise C-2
Using ABC to assess prices

P2

Refer to the information in Exercise C-1 to answer the following requirements.

Required

1. Using ABC, compute the overhead cost per unit for each product line.
2. Determine the total cost per unit for each product line if the direct labor and direct materials costs per unit are $250 for Model 145 and $180 for Model 212.

Check   (3) Model 212, $24.88 per unit profit

3. If the market price for Model 145 is $800 and the market price for Model 212 is $470, determine the profit or loss per unit for each model. Comment on the results.

Singh and Smythe is an architectural firm that provides services for residential construction projects. The following data pertain to a recent reporting period.

Exercise C-3
Using ABC in a service company
P2

	Activities	Costs
Design department		
Client consultation	1,500 contact hours	$270,000
Drawings	2,000 design hours	115,000
Modeling	40,000 square feet	30,000
Project management department		
Supervision	600 days	$120,000
Billings	8 jobs	10,000
Collections	8 jobs	12,000

Required

1. Using ABC, compute the firm's activity overhead rates. Form activity cost pools where appropriate.
2. Assign costs to a 9,200 square foot job that requires 450 contact hours, 340 design hours, and 200 days to complete.

Check (2) $150,200

Consider the following data for two products of Vigano Manufacturing.

Exercise C-4
Using ABC for strategic decisions
P1 P2

	Overhead Cost	Product A	Product B
Number of units produced		10,000 units	2,000 units
Direct labor cost (@$24 per DLH)		0.20 DLH per unit	0.25 DLH per unit
Direct materials cost.		$2 per unit	$3 per unit
Activity			
Machine setup	$121,000		
Materials handling	48,000		
Quality control	80,000		
	$249,000		

Required

1. Using direct labor hours as the basis for assigning overhead costs, determine the total production cost per unit for each product line.
2. If the market price for Product A is $20 and the market price for Product B is $60, determine the profit or loss per unit for each product. Comment on the results.
3. Consider the following additional information about these two product lines. If ABC is used for assigning overhead costs to products, what is the cost per unit for Product A and for Product B?

Check (2) Product B, $26.10 per unit profit

	Product A	Product B
Number of setups required for production	10 setups	12 setups
Number of parts required.	1 part/unit	3 parts/unit
Inspection hours required	40 hours	210 hours

4. Determine the profit or loss per unit for each product. Should this information influence company strategy? Explain.

(4) Product B, ($24.60) per unit loss

Exercise C-5

Activity-based costing

P2 A1

Northwest Company produces two types of glass shelving, rounded edge and squared edge, on the same production line. For the current period, the company reports the following data.

	Rounded Edge	Squared Edge	Total
Direct materials	$19,000	$ 43,200	$ 62,200
Direct labor	12,200	23,800	36,000
Overhead (300% of direct labor cost)	36,600	71,400	108,000
Total cost	$67,800	$138,400	$206,200
Quantity produced	10,500 ft.	14,100 ft.	
Average cost per ft. (rounded)	$ 6.46	$ 9.82	

Northwest's controller wishes to apply activity-based costing (ABC) to allocate the $108,000 of overhead costs incurred by the two product lines to see whether cost per foot would change markedly from that reported above. She has collected the following information.

Overhead Cost Category (Activity Cost Pool)	Cost
Supervision	$ 5,400
Depreciation of machinery	56,600
Assembly line preparation.............................	46,000
Total overhead	$108,000

She has also collected the following information about the cost drivers for each category (cost pool) and the amount of each driver used by the two product lines.

Overhead Cost Category (Activity Cost Pool)	Driver	Usage		
		Rounded Edge	Squared Edge	Total
Supervision	Direct labor cost ($)	$12,200	$23,800	$36,000
Depreciation of machinery	Machine hours	500 hours	1,500 hours	2,000 hours
Assembly line preparation	Setups (number)	40 times	210 times	250 times

Required

Check   (2) Rounded edge, $5.19;
Squared edge, $10.76

1. Assign these three overhead cost pools to each of the two products using ABC.
2. Determine average cost per foot for each of the two products using ABC.
3. Compare the average cost per foot under ABC with the average cost per foot under the current method for each product. Explain why a difference between the two cost allocation methods exists.

Exercise C-6

Activity-based costing

P2

Health Co-op is an outpatient surgical clinic that wants to better understand its costs. It decides to prepare an activity-based cost analysis, including an estimate of the average cost of both general surgery and orthopedic surgery. The clinic's three cost centers and their cost drivers follow.

Cost Center	Cost	Cost Driver	Driver Quantity
Professional salaries................	$1,600,000	Professional hours	10,000
Patient services and supplies	27,000	Number of patients	600
Building cost	150,000	Square feet	1,500

The two main surgical units and their related data follow.

Service	Hours	Square Feet*	Patients
General surgery............	2,500	600	400
Orthopedic surgery.........	7,500	900	200

* Orthopedic surgery requires more space for patients, supplies, and equipment.

Required

1. Assume costs are allocated based on number of patients. Compute the average cost per patient. (Round to the nearest whole dollar.)
2. Compute the cost per cost driver for each of the three cost centers.
3. Use the results from part 1 to allocate costs from each of the three cost centers to the general surgery unit. Compute total cost and average cost per patient for the general surgery unit.

Check (3) Average cost of general surgery, $1,195 per patient

connect

Healthy Day Company produces two beverages, PowerPunch and SlimLife. Data about these products follow.

PROBLEM SET A

Problem C-1A
Evaluating product line costs and prices using ABC

P2

	PowerPunch	SlimLife
Production volume	12,500 bottles	180,000 bottles
Liquid materials	1,400 gallons	37,000 gallons
Dry materials	620 pounds	12,000 pounds
Bottles	12,500 bottles	180,000 bottles
Labels	3 labels per bottle	1 label per bottle
Machine setups	500 setups	300 setups
Machine hours	200 MH	3,750 MH

Additional data from its two production departments follow.

Department	Driver	Cost
Mixing department		
Liquid materials	Gallons	$ 2,304
Dry materials............	Pounds	6,941
Utilities................	Machine hours	1,422
Bottling department		
Bottles	Units	$77,000
Labeling	Labels per bottle	6,525
Machine setup	Setups	20,000

Required

1. Determine the cost of each product line using ABC.
2. What is the cost per bottle for PowerPunch? What is the cost per bottle of SlimLife? (*Hint:* Your answer should draw on the total cost for each product line computed in requirement 1.)
3. If PowerPunch sells for $3.75 per bottle, how much profit does the company earn per bottle of PowerPunch that it sells?
4. What is the minimum price that the company should set per bottle of SlimLife? Explain.

Check (3) $2.22 profit per bottle

Problem C-2A

Applying activity-based costing

P1 P2 A1

Craftmore Machining produces machine tools for the construction industry. The following details about overhead costs were taken from its company records.

Production Activity	Indirect Labor	Indirect Materials	Other Overhead
Grinding	$320,000		
Polishing		$135,000	
Product modification	600,000		
Providing power.			$255,000
System calibration	500,000		

Additional information on the drivers for its production activities follows.

Grinding	13,000 machine hours
Polishing	13,000 machine hours
Product modification	1,500 engineering hours
Providing power.	17,000 direct labor hours
System calibration	400 batches

Required

1. Compute the activity overhead rates using ABC. Form cost pools as appropriate.
2. Determine overhead costs to assign to the following jobs using ABC.

	Job 3175	Job 4286
Number of units	200 units	2,500 units
Machine hours	550 MH	5,500 MH
Engineering hours	26 eng. hours	32 eng. hours
Batches	30 batches	90 batches
Direct labor hours	500 DLH	4,375 DLH

Check   (3) Job 3175, $373.25 per unit

3. What is the overhead cost per unit for Job 3175? What is the overhead cost per unit for Job 4286?
4. If the company used a plantwide overhead rate based on direct labor hours, what is the overhead cost for each unit of Job 3175? Of Job 4286?
5. Compare the overhead costs per unit computed in requirements 4 and 5 for each job. Which method more accurately assigns overhead costs?

Problem C-3A

Assessing impacts of using a plantwide overhead rate versus ABC

A1 A2

Maxlon Company manufactures custom-made furniture for its local market and produces a line of home furnishings sold in retail stores across the country. The company uses traditional volume-based methods of assigning direct materials and direct labor to its product lines. Overhead has always been assigned by using a plantwide overhead rate based on direct labor hours. In the past few years, management has seen its line of retail products continue to sell at high volumes, but competition has forced it to lower prices on these items. The prices are declining to a level close to its cost of production.

Meanwhile, its custom-made furniture is in high demand and customers have commented on its favorable (lower) prices compared to its competitors. Management is considering dropping its line of retail products and devoting all of its resources to custom-made furniture.

Required

1. What reasons could explain why competitors are forcing the company to lower prices on its high-volume retail products?

2. Why do you believe the company charges less for custom-order products than its competitors?

3. Does a company's costing method have any effect on its pricing decisions? Explain.

4. Aside from the differences in volume of output, what production differences do you believe exist between making custom-order furniture and mass-market furnishings?

5. What information might the company obtain from using ABC that it might not obtain using volume-based costing methods?

The following data are for the two products produced by Shakti Company.

Problem C-4A
Comparing costs using ABC with the plantwide overhead rate

P1 P2 A1

	Product A	Product B
Direct materials	$15 per unit	$24 per unit
Direct labor hours	0.3 DLH per unit	1.6 DLH per unit
Machine hours	0.1 MH per unit	1.2 MH per unit
Batches	125 batches	225 batches
Volume	10,000 units	2,000 units
Engineering modifications	12 modifications	58 modifications
Number of customers	500 customers	400 customers
Market price	$30 per unit	$120 per unit

The company's direct labor rate is $20 per direct labor hour (DLH). Additional information follows.

	Costs	Driver
Indirect manufacturing		
Engineering support	$24,500	Engineering modifications
Electricity	34,000	Machine hours
Setup costs	52,500	Batches
Nonmanufacturing		
Customer service	81,000	Number of customers

Required

1. Compute the manufacturing cost per unit using the plantwide overhead rate based on direct labor hours. What is the gross profit per unit?

2. How much gross profit is generated by each customer of Product A using the plantwide overhead rate? How much gross profit is generated by each customer of Product B using the plantwide overhead rate? What is the cost of providing customer service to each customer? What information is provided by this comparison?

3. Determine the manufacturing cost per unit of each product line using ABC. What is the gross profit per unit?

4. How much gross profit is generated by each customer of Product A using ABC? How much gross profit is generated by each customer of Product B using ABC? Is the gross profit per customer adequate?

5. Which method of product costing gives better information to managers of this company? Explain why.

Check (1) Product A, $26.37 per unit manufacturing cost

(3) Product A, $24.30 per unit manufacturing cost

Problem C-5A
Pricing analysis with ABC and a plantwide overhead rate

A1 P1 P2

Tent Master produces two lines of tents sold to outdoor enthusiasts. The tents are cut to specifications in department A. In department B the tents are sewn and folded. The activities, costs, and drivers associated with these two manufacturing processes and its production support activities follow.

Process	Activity	Overhead Cost	Driver	Quantity
Department A	Pattern alignment	$ 64,400	Batches	560
	Cutting	50,430	Machine hours	12,300
	Moving product	100,800	Moves	2,400
		$215,630		
Department B	Sewing	$327,600	Direct labor hours	4,200
	Inspecting	24,000	Inspections	600
	Folding	47,880	Units	22,800
		$399,480		
Support	Design	$280,000	Modification orders	280
	Providing space	51,600	Square feet	8,600
	Materials handling	184,000	Square yards	920,000
		$515,600		

Additional production information on the two lines of tents follows.

	Pup Tent	Pop-Up Tent
Units produced	15,200 units	7,600 units
Moves.	800 moves	1,600 moves
Batches.	140 batches	420 batches
Number of inspections	240 inspections	360 inspections
Machine hours	7,000 MH	5,300 MH
Direct labor hours.	2,600 DLH	1,600 DLH
Modification orders	70 modification orders	210 modification orders
Space occupied	4,300 square feet	4,300 square feet
Material required	450,000 square yards	470,000 square yards

Required

1. Using a plantwide overhead rate based on direct labor hours, compute the overhead cost that is assigned to each pup tent and each pop-up tent.

2. Using the plantwide overhead rate, determine the total cost per unit for the two products if the direct materials and direct labor cost is $25 per pup tent and $32 per pop-up tent.

3. If the market price of the pup tent is $65 and the market price of the pop-up tent is $200, determine the gross profit per unit for each tent. What might management conclude about the pup tent?

Check (4) Pup tent, $58.46 per unit cost

4. Using ABC, compute the total cost per unit for each tent if the direct labor and direct materials cost is $25 per pup tent and $32 per pop-up tent.

5. If the market price is $65 per pup tent and $200 per pop-up tent, determine the gross profit per unit for each tent. Comment on the results.

6. Would your pricing analysis be improved if the company used, instead of ABC, departmental rates determined using machine hours in Department A and direct labor hours in Department B? Explain.

Problem C-6A
Activity-based costing

P2

Patient Health is an outpatient surgical clinic that was profitable for many years, but Medicare has cut its reimbursements by as much as 50%. As a result, the clinic wants to better understand its costs. It decides to prepare an activity-based cost analysis, including an estimate of the average cost of both general surgery and orthopedic surgery. The clinic's three cost centers and their cost drivers follow.

Cost Center	Cost	Cost Driver	Driver Quantity
Professional salaries................	$2,000,000	Professional hours	10,000
Patient services and supplies........	37,500	Number of patients	500
Building cost	300,000	Square feet	2,000

The two main surgical units and their related data follow.

Service	Hours	Square Feet*	Patients
General surgery............	2,500	720	400
Orthopedic surgery.........	7,500	1,280	100

* Orthopedic surgery requires more space for patients, supplies, and equipment.

Required

1. Compute the cost per cost driver for each of the three cost centers.
2. Use the results from part 1 to allocate costs from each of the three cost centers to both the general surgery and the orthopedic surgery units. Compute total cost and average cost per patient for both the general surgery and the orthopedic surgery units.

Check (2) Average cost of general (orthopedic) surgery, $1,595 ($16,995) per patient

Analysis Component

3. Without providing computations, would the average cost of general surgery be higher or lower if all center costs were allocated based on the number of patients? Explain.

MathGames produces two electronic, handheld educational games: *Fun with Fractions* and *Count Calculus*. Data on these products follow.

PROBLEM SET B

Problem C-1B
Evaluating product line costs and prices using ABC

P2

	Fun with Fractions	Count Calculus
Production volume	150,000 units	10,000 units
Components	450,000 parts	100,000 parts
Direct labor hours	15,000 DLH	2,000 DLH
Packaging materials	150,000 boxes	10,000 boxes
Shipping cartons	100 units per carton	25 units per carton
Machine setups	52 setups	52 setups
Machine hours	5,000 MH	2,000 MH

Additional data from its two production departments follow.

Department	Driver	Cost
Assembly department		
Component cost	Parts	$495,000
Assembly labor.............	Direct labor hours	244,800
Maintenance	Machine hours	100,800
Wrapping department		
Packaging materials	Boxes	$460,800
Shipping	Cartons	27,360
Machine setup	Setups	187,200

Required

1. Using ABC, determine the cost of each product line.
2. What is the cost per unit for Fun with Fractions? What is the cost per unit of Count Calculus?
3. If Count Calculus sells for $59.95 per unit, how much profit does the company earn per unit of Count Calculus sold?
4. What is the minimum price that the company should set per unit of Fun with Fractions? Explain.

Check (3) $32.37 profit per unit

Problem C-2B
Applying activity-based costing
P1 P2 A1

Fancy Foods produces gourmet gift baskets that it distributes online as well as from its small retail store. The following details about overhead costs are taken from its records.

Production Activity	Indirect Labor	Indirect Materials	Other Overhead
Wrapping....................	$300,000	$200,000	
Assembling	400,000		
Product design	180,000		
Obtaining business licenses			$100,000
Cooking	150,000	120,000	

Additional information on the drivers for its production activities follows.

Wrapping......................	100,000 units
Assembling.....................	20,000 direct labor hours
Product design..................	3,000 design hours
Obtaining business licenses........	20,000 direct labor hours
Cooking	1,000 batches

Required

1. Compute the activity overhead rates using ABC. Form cost pools as appropriate.
2. Determine the overhead cost to assign to the following jobs using ABC.

	Holiday Basket	Executive Basket
Number of units	8,000 units	1,000 units
Direct labor hours.........	2,000 DLH	500 DLH
Design hours	40 design hours	40 design hours
Batches..................	80 batches	200 batches

Check (3) Holiday Basket, $14.25 per unit

(4) Holiday Basket, $18.13 per unit

3. What is the overhead cost per unit for the Holiday Basket? What is the overhead cost per unit for the Executive Basket?
4. If the company used a plantwide overhead rate based on direct labor hours, what is the overhead cost for each Holiday Basket unit? What would be the overhead cost for each Executive Basket unit if a single plantwide overhead rate is used?
5. Compare the overhead costs per unit computed in requirements 4 and 5 for each job. Which cost assignment method provides the most accurate cost? Explain.

Problem C-3B
Assessing impacts of using a plantwide overhead rate versus ABC
A1 A2

Lakeside Paper produces cardboard boxes. The boxes require designing, cutting, and printing. (The boxes are shipped flat and customers fold them as necessary.) Lakeside has a reputation for providing high-quality products and excellent service to customers, who are major U.S. manufacturers. Costs are assigned to products based on the number of machine hours required to produce them.

Three years ago, a new marketing executive was hired. She suggested the company offer custom design and manufacturing services to small specialty manufacturers. These customers required boxes for their products and were eager to have Lakeside as a supplier. Within one year Lakeside found that it was so busy with orders from small customers, that it had trouble supplying boxes to all its customers on a timely basis. Large, long-time customers began to complain about slow service and several took their business elsewhere. Within another 18 months, Lakeside was in financial distress with a backlog of orders to be filled.

Required

1. What do you believe are the major costs of making its boxes? How are those costs related to the volume of boxes produced?
2. How did Lakeside's new customers differ from its previous customers?
3. Would the unit cost to produce a box for new customers be different from the unit cost to produce a box for its previous customers? Explain.
4. Could Lakeside's fate have been different if it had used ABC for determining the cost of its boxes?
5. What information would have been available with ABC that might have been overlooked using a traditional volume-based costing method?

Vargo Company makes two distinct products with the following information available for each.

	Standard	Deluxe
Direct materials	$4 per unit	$8 per unit
Direct labor hours	4 DLH per unit	5 DLH per unit
Machine hours	3 MH per unit	3 MH per unit
Batches	175 batches	75 batches
Volume......................	40,000 units	10,000 units
Engineering modifications	50 modifications	25 modifications
Number of customers...........	1,000 customers	1,000 customers
Market price	$92 per unit	$125 per unit

The company's direct labor rate is $20 per direct labor hour (DLH). Additional information follows.

	Costs	Driver
Indirect manufacturing		
Engineering support	$ 56,250	Engineering modifications
Electricity.................	112,500	Machine hours
Setup costs...............	41,250	Batches
Nonmanufacturing		
Customer service	250,000	Number of customers

Problem C-4B

Comparing costs using ABC with the plantwide overhead rate

A1 P1 P2

Required

1. Compute the manufacturing cost per unit using the plantwide overhead rate based on machine hours. What is the gross profit per unit?

2. How much gross profit is generated by each customer of the standard product using the plantwide overhead rate? How much gross profit is generated by each customer of the deluxe product using the plantwide overhead rate? What is the cost of providing customer service to each customer? What information is provided by this comparison?

3. Determine the manufacturing cost per unit of each product line using ABC. What is the gross profit per unit?

4. How much gross profit is generated by each customer of the standard product using ABC? How much gross profit is generated by each customer of the deluxe product using ABC? Is the gross profit per customer adequate?

5. Which method of product costing gives better information to managers of this company? Explain.

Check (1) Gross profit per unit: Standard, $3.80; Deluxe, $12.80

(3) Gross profit per unit: Standard, $4.09; Deluxe, $11.64

Spicy Salsa Company produces its condiments in two types: Extra Fine for restaurant customers and Family Style for home use. Salsa is prepared in department 1 and packaged in department 2. The activities, overhead costs, and drivers associated with these two manufacturing processes and its production support activities follow.

Problem C-5B

Pricing analysis with ABC and a plantwide overhead rate

A1 P1 P2

Process	Activity	Overhead Cost	Driver	Quantity
Department 1	Mixing	$ 4,500	Machine hours	1,500
	Cooking	11,250	Machine hours	1,500
	Product testing	112,500	Batches	600
		$128,250		
Department 2	Machine calibration	$250,000	Production runs	400
	Labeling	12,000	Cases of output	120,000
	Defects	6,000	Cases of output	120,000
		$268,000		
Support	Recipe formulation	$ 90,000	Focus groups	45
	Heat, lights, and water	27,000	Machine hours	1,500
	Materials handling	65,000	Container types	8
		$182,000		

Additional production information about its two product lines follows.

	Extra Fine	Family Style
Units produced	20,000 cases	100,000 cases
Batches.	200 batches	400 batches
Machine hours	500 MH	1,000 MH
Focus groups	30 groups	15 groups
Container types	5 containers	3 containers
Production runs	200 runs	200 runs

Required

Check (2) Cost per case: Extra Fine, $10.82; Family Style, $9.82

1. Using a plantwide overhead rate based on cases, compute the overhead cost that is assigned to each case of Extra Fine Salsa and each case of Family Style Salsa.

2. Using the plantwide overhead rate, determine the total cost per unit for the two products if the direct materials and direct labor cost is $6 per case of Extra Fine and $5 per case of Family Style.

3. If the market price of Extra Fine Salsa is $18 per case and the market price of Family Style Salsa is $9 per case, determine the gross profit per case for each product. What might management conclude about each product line?

(4) Cost per case: Extra Fine, $20.02; Family Style, $7.98

4. Using ABC, compute the total cost per case for each product type if the direct labor and direct materials cost is $6 per case of Extra Fine and $5 per case of Family Style.

5. If the market price is $18 per case of Extra Fine and $9 per case of Family Style, determine the gross profit per case for each product. How should management interpret the market prices given your computations?

6. Would your pricing analysis be improved if the company used departmental rates based on machine hours in department 1 and number of cases in department 2, instead of ABC? Explain.

Problem C-6B
Activity-based costing

P2

Wooddale Landscaping has enjoyed profits for many years, but new competition has cut service revenue by as much as 30%. As a result, the company wants to better understand its costs. It decides to prepare an activity-based cost analysis, including an estimate of the average cost of both general landscaping services and custom design landscaping services. The company's three cost centers and their cost drivers follow.

Cost Center	Cost	Cost Driver	Driver Quantity
Professional salaries	$600,000	Professional hours	10,000
Customer supplies	150,000	Number of customers	800
Building cost	240,000	Square feet	2,500

The two main landscaping units and their related data follow.

Service	Hours	Square Feet*	Customers
General landscaping.	2,500	1,000	600
Custom design landscaping	7,500	1,500	200

* Custom design landscaping requires more space for equipment, supplies, and planning.

Required

1. Compute the cost per cost driver for each of the three cost centers.

Check (2) Average cost of general (custom) landscaping, $597.50 ($3,157.50) per customer

2. Use the results from part 1 to allocate costs from each of the three cost centers to both the general landscaping and the custom design landscaping units. Compute total cost and average cost per customer for both the general landscaping and the custom design landscaping units.

Analysis Component

3. Without providing computations, would the average cost of general landscaping be higher or lower if all center costs were allocated based on the number of customers? Explain.

(This serial problem began in Chapter 1 and continues through most of the book. If previous chapter seg-ments were not completed, the serial problem can begin at this point. It is helpful, but not necessary, to use the Working Papers that accompany the book.)

SP C   After reading an article about activity-based costing in a trade journal for the furniture industry, Adria Lopez wondered if it was time to critically analyze overhead costs at Success Systems. In a recent month, Lopez found that setup costs, inspection costs, and utility costs made up most of its overhead. Additional information about overhead follows.

Activity	Cost	Driver
Setting up machines............	$20,000	25 batches
Inspecting components	$ 7,500	5,000 parts
Providing utilities	$10,000	5,000 machine hours

Overhead has been applied to output at a rate of 50% of direct labor costs. The following data pertain to Job 6.15.

Direct materials..........	$2,500	Number of parts.........	400 parts
Direct labor.............	$3,500	Machine hours...........	600 machine hours
Batches................	2 batches		

Required

1. What is the total cost of Job 6.15 if Success Systems applies overhead at 50% of direct labor cost?
2. What is the total cost of Job 6.15 if Success Systems uses activity-based costing?
3. Which approach to assigning overhead gives a better representation of the costs incurred to produce Job 6.15? Explain.

Glossary

Absorption costing Costing method that assigns both variable and fixed costs to products. *(p. 870)*

Accelerated depreciation method Method that produces larger depreciation charges in the early years of an asset's life and smaller charges in its later years. *(p. 402)*

Account Record within an accounting system in which increases and decreases are entered and stored in a specific asset, liability, equity, revenue, or expense. *(p. 51)*

Account balance Difference between total debits and total credits (including the beginning balance) for an account. *(p. 55)*

Account form balance sheet Balance sheet that lists assets on the left side and liabilities and equity on the right. *(p. 18)*

Account payable Liability created by buying goods or services on credit; backed by the buyer's general credit standing. *(p. 50)*

Accounting Information and measurement system that identifies, records, and communicates relevant information about a company's business activities. *(p. 4)*

Accounting cycle Recurring steps performed each accounting period, starting with analyzing transactions and continuing through the post-closing trial balance (or reversing entries). *(p. 148)*

Accounting equation Equality involving a company's assets, liabilities, and equity; Assets = Liabilities + Equity; also called *balance sheet equation*. *(p. 15)*

Accounting information system People, records, and methods that collect and process data from transactions and events, organize them in useful forms, and communicate results to decision makers. *(p. 278)*

Accounting period Length of time covered by financial statements; also called *reporting period*. *(p. 94)*

Accounting rate of return Rate used to evaluate the acceptability of an investment; equals the after-tax periodic income from a project divided by the average investment in the asset; also called *rate of return on average investment*. *(p. 1041)*

Accounts payable ledger Subsidiary ledger listing individual creditor (supplier) accounts. *(p. 283)*

Accounts receivable Amounts due from customers for credit sales; backed by the customer's general credit standing. *(p. 362)*

Accounts receivable ledger Subsidiary ledger listing individual customer accounts. *(p. 283)*

Accounts receivable turnover Measure of both the quality and liquidity of accounts receivable; indicates how often receivables are received and collected during the period; computed by dividing net sales by average accounts receivable. *(p. 377)*

Accrual basis accounting Accounting system that recognizes revenues when earned and expenses when incurred; the basis for GAAP. *(p. 95)*

Accrued expenses Costs incurred in a period that are both unpaid and unrecorded; adjusting entries for recording accrued expenses involve increasing expenses and increasing liabilities. *(p. 101)*

Accrued revenues Revenues earned in a period that are both unrecorded and not yet received in cash (or other assets); adjusting entries for recording accrued revenues involve increasing assets and increasing revenues. *(p. 103)*

Accumulated depreciation Cumulative sum of all depreciation expense recorded for an asset. *(p. 99)*

Acid-test ratio Ratio used to assess a company's ability to settle its current debts with its most liquid assets; defined as quick assets (cash, short-term investments, and current receivables) divided by current liabilities. *(p. 198)*

Activity-based budgeting (ABB) Budget system based on expected activities. *(p. 914)*

Activity-based costing (ABC) Cost allocation method that focuses on activities performed; traces costs to activities and then assigns them to cost objects. *(p. C-3)*

Activity cost driver Variable that causes an activity's cost to go up or down; a causal factor. *(p. C-3)*

Activity cost pool Temporary account that accumulates costs a company incurs to support an activity. *(p. C-3)*

Adjusted trial balance List of accounts and balances prepared after period-end adjustments are recorded and posted. *(p. 106)*

Adjusting entry Journal entry at the end of an accounting period to bring an asset or liability account to its proper amount and update the related expense or revenue account. *(p. 97)*

Aging of accounts receivable Process of classifying accounts receivable by how long they are past due for purposes of estimating uncollectible accounts. *(p. 370)*

Allowance for Doubtful Accounts Contra asset account with a balance approximating uncollectible accounts receivable; also called *Allowance for Uncollectible Accounts*. *(p. 367)*

Allowance method Procedure that (a) estimates and matches bad debts expense with its sales for the period and/or (b) reports accounts receivable at estimated realizable value. *(p. 367)*

Amortization Process of allocating the cost of an intangible asset to expense over its estimated useful life. *(p. 411)*

Annual financial statements Financial statements covering a one-year period; often based on a calendar year, but any consecutive 12-month (or 52-week) period is acceptable. *(p. 94)*

Annual report Summary of a company's financial results for the year with its current financial condition and future plans; directed to external users of financial information. *(p. A-1)*

Annuity Series of equal payments at equal intervals. *(pp. 573 & 1043)*

Appropriated retained earnings Retained earnings separately reported to inform stockholders of funding needs. *(p. 526)*

Asset book value (See *book value*.)

Assets Resources a business owns or controls that are expected to provide current and future benefits to the business. *(p. 15)*

Audit Analysis and report of an organization's accounting system, its records, and its reports using various tests. *(p. 13)*

Auditors Individuals hired to review financial reports and information systems. *Internal auditors* of a company are employed to assess and evaluate its system of internal controls, including the resulting reports. *External auditors* are independent of a company and are hired to assess and evaluate the "fairness" of financial statements (or to perform other contracted financial services). *(p. 13)*

Authorized stock Total amount of stock that a corporation's charter authorizes it to issue. *(p. 513)*

Available-for-sale (AFS) securities Investments in debt and equity securities that are not classified as trading securities or held-to-maturity securities. *(p. 603)*

Average cost See *weighted average*.

Avoidable expense Expense (or cost) that is relevant for decision making; expense that is not incurred if a department, product, or service is eliminated. *(p. 1055)*

Bad debts Accounts of customers who do not pay what they have promised to pay; an expense of selling on credit; also called *uncollectible accounts*. *(p. 366)*

Balance column account Account with debit and credit columns for recording entries and another column for showing the balance of the account after each entry. *(p. 58)*

Balance sheet Financial statement that lists types and dollar amounts of assets, liabilities, and equity at a specific date. *(p. 20)*

Balance sheet equation (See *accounting equation*.)

Balanced scorecard A system of performance measurement that collects information on several key performance indicators within each of four perspectives: customer, internal processes, innovation and learning, and financial. *(p. 1008)*

Bank reconciliation Report that explains the difference between the book (company) balance of cash and the cash balance reported on the bank statement. *(p. 333)*

Bank statement Bank report on the depositor's beginning and ending cash balances, and a listing of its changes, for a period. *(p. 332)*

Basic earnings per share Net income less any preferred dividends and then divided by weighted-average common shares outstanding. *(p. 529)*

Batch processing Accumulating source documents for a period of time and then processing them all at once such as once a day, week, or month. *(p. 292)*

Bearer bonds Bonds made payable to whoever holds them (the *bearer*); also called *unregistered bonds*. *(p. 568)*

Benchmarking Practice of comparing and analyzing company financial performance or position with other companies or standards. *(p. 960)*

Betterments Expenditures to make a plant asset more efficient or productive; also called *improvements*. *(p. 407)*

Bond Written promise to pay the bond's par (or face) value and interest at a stated contract rate; often issued in denominations of $1,000. *(p. 554)*

Bond certificate Document containing bond specifics such as issuer's name, bond par value, contract interest rate, and maturity date. *(p. 556)*

Bond indenture Contract between the bond issuer and the bondholders; identifies the parties' rights and obligations. *(p. 556)*

Book value Asset's acquisition costs less its accumulated depreciation (or depletion, or amortization); also sometimes used synonymously as the *carrying value* of an account. *(pp. 100 & 401)*

Book value per common share Recorded amount of equity applicable to common shares divided by the number of common shares outstanding. *(p. 530)*

Book value per preferred share Equity applicable to preferred shares (equals its call price [or par value if it is not callable] plus any cumulative dividends in arrears) divided by the number of preferred shares outstanding. *(p. 530)*

Bookkeeping (See *recordkeeping*.)

Break-even point Output level at which sales equals fixed plus variable costs; where income equals zero. *(p. 869)*

Break-even time (BET) Time-based measurement used to evaluate the acceptability of an investment; equals the time expected to pass before the present value of the net cash flows from an investment equals its initial cost. *(p. 1056)*

Budget Formal statement of future plans, usually expressed in monetary terms. *(p. 900)*

Budget report Report comparing actual results to planned objectives; sometimes used as a progress report. *(p. 948)*

Budgetary control Management use of budgets to monitor and control company operations. *(p. 948)*

Budgeted balance sheet Accounting report that presents predicted amounts of the company's assets, liabilities, and equity balances as of the end of the budget period. *(p. 912)*

Budgeted income statement Accounting report that presents predicted amounts of the company's revenues and expenses for the budget period. *(p. 912)*

Budgeting Process of planning future business actions and expressing them as formal plans. *(p. 900)*

Business An organization of one or more individuals selling products and/or services for profit. *(p. 12)*

Business entity assumption Principle that requires a business to be accounted for separately from its owner(s) and from any other entity. *(p. 12)*

Business segment Part of a company that can be separately identified by the products or services that it provides or by the geographic markets that it serves; also called *segment*. *(p. 712)*

C corporation Corporation that does not qualify for nor elect to be treated as a proprietorship or partnership for income tax purposes and therefore is subject to income taxes; also called *C corp*. *(p. 484)*

Call price Amount that must be paid to call and retire a callable preferred stock or a callable bond. *(p. 523)*

Callable bonds Bonds that give the issuer the option to retire them at a stated amount prior to maturity. *(p. 568)*

Callable preferred stock Preferred stock that the issuing corporation, at its option, may retire by paying the call price plus any dividends in arrears. *(p. 523)*

Canceled checks Checks that the bank has paid and deducted from the depositor's account. *(p. 332)*

Capital budgeting Process of analyzing alternative investments and deciding which assets to acquire or sell. *(p. 1038)*

Capital expenditures Additional costs of plant assets that provide material benefits extending beyond the current period; also called *balance sheet expenditures*. *(p. 406)*

Capital expenditures budget Plan that lists dollar amounts to be both received from disposal of plant assets and spent to purchase plant assets. *(p. 910)*

Capital leases Long-term leases in which the lessor transfers substantially all risk and rewards of ownership to the lessee. *(p. 579)*

Capital stock General term referring to a corporation's stock used in obtaining capital (owner financing). *(p. 513)*

Capitalize Record the cost as part of a permanent account and allocate it over later periods. *(p. 406)*

Carrying (book) value of bonds Net amount at which bonds are reported on the balance sheet; equals the par value of the bonds less any unamortized discount or plus any unamortized premium; also called *carrying amount or book value*. *(p. 558)*

Cash Includes currency, coins, and amounts on deposit in bank checking or savings accounts. *(p. 323)*

Cash basis accounting Accounting system that recognizes revenues when cash is received and records expenses when cash is paid. *(p. 95)*

Cash budget Plan that shows expected cash inflows and outflows during the budget period, including receipts from loans needed to maintain a minimum cash balance and repayments of such loans. *(p. 910)*

Cash disbursements journal Special journal normally used to record all payments of cash; also called *cash payments journal*. *(p. 290)*

Cash discount Reduction in the price of merchandise granted by a seller to a buyer when payment is made within the discount period. *(p. 185)*

Cash equivalents Short-term, investment assets that are readily convertible to a known cash amount or sufficiently close to their maturity date (usually within 90 days) so that market value is not sensitive to interest rate changes. *(p. 323)*

Cash flow on total assets Ratio of operating cash flows to average total assets; not sensitive to income recognition and measurement; partly reflects earnings quality. *(p. 652)*

Cash Over and Short Income statement account used to record cash overages and cash shortages arising from errors in cash receipts or payments. *(p. 325)*

Cash receipts journal Special journal normally used to record all receipts of cash. *(p. 287)*

Change in an accounting estimate Change in an accounting estimate that results from new information, subsequent developments, or improved judgment that impacts current and future periods. *(pp. 405 & 527)*

Chart of accounts List of accounts used by a company; includes an identification number for each account. *(p. 54)*

Check Document signed by a depositor instructing the bank to pay a specified amount to a designated recipient. *(p. 331)*

Check register Another name for a cash disbursements journal when the journal has a column for check numbers. *(pp. 290 & 342)*

Classified balance sheet Balance sheet that presents assets and liabilities in relevant subgroups, including current and noncurrent classifications. *(p. 149)*

Clock card Source document used to record the number of hours an employee works and to determine the total labor cost for each pay period. *(p. 784)*

Closing entries Entries recorded at the end of each accounting period to transfer end-of-period balances in revenue, gain, expense, loss, and withdrawal (dividend for a corporation) accounts to the capital account (to retained earnings for a corporation). *(p. 145)*

Closing process Necessary end-of-period steps to prepare the accounts for recording the transactions of the next period. *(p. 144)*

Columnar journal Journal with more than one column. *(p. 284)*

Committee of Sponsoring Organizations (COSO) Committee of Sponsoring Organizations of the Treadway Commission (or COSO) is a joint initiative of five private sector organizations and is dedicated to providing thought leadership through the development of frameworks and guidance on enterprise risk management, internal control, and fraud deterrence. *(p. 319)*

Common stock Corporation's basic ownership share; also generically called *capital stock*. *(pp. 13 & 512)*

Common-size financial statement Statement that expresses each amount as a percent of a base amount. In the balance sheet, total assets is usually the base and is expressed as 100%. In the income statement, net sales is usually the base. *(p. 695)*

Comparative financial statement Statement with data for two or more successive periods placed in side-by-side columns, often with changes shown in dollar amounts and percents. *(p. 690)*

Compatibility principle Information system principle that prescribes an accounting system to conform with a company's activities, personnel, and structure. *(p. 279)*

Complex capital structure Capital structure that includes outstanding rights or options to purchase common stock, or securities that are convertible into common stock. *(p. 529)*

Components of accounting systems Five basic components of accounting systems are source documents, input devices, information processors, information storage, and output devices. *(p. 279)*

Composite unit Generic unit consisting of a specific number of units of each product; unit comprised in proportion to the expected sales mix of its products. *(p. 877)*

Compound journal entry Journal entry that affects at least three accounts. *(p. 61)*

Comprehensive income Net change in equity for a period, excluding owner investments and distributions. *(p. 606)*

Computer hardware Physical equipment in a computerized accounting information system. *(p. 280)*

Computer network Linkage giving different users and different computers access to common databases and programs. *(p. 292)*

Computer software Programs that direct operations of computer hardware. *(p. 280)*

Conceptual framework The basic concepts that underlie the preparation and presentation of financial statements for external users; can serve as a guide in developing future standards and to resolve accounting issues that are not addressed directly in current standards using the definitions, recognition criteria, and measurement concepts for assets, liabilities, revenues, and expenses. *(p. 10)*

Conservatism constraint Principle that prescribes the less optimistic estimate when two estimates are about equally likely. *(p. 240)*

Consignee Receiver of goods owned by another who holds them for purposes of selling them for the owner. *(p. 230)*

Consignor Owner of goods who ships them to another party who will sell them for the owner. *(p. 230)*

Consistency concept Principle that prescribes use of the same accounting method(s) over time so that financial statements are comparable across periods. *(p. 239)*

Consolidated financial statements Financial statements that show all (combined) activities under the parent's control, including those of any subsidiaries. *(p. 605)*

Contingent liability Obligation to make a future payment if, and only if, an uncertain future event occurs. *(p. 450)*

Continuous budgeting Practice of preparing budgets for a selected number of future periods and revising those budgets as each period is completed. *(p. 903)*

Continuous improvement Concept requiring every manager and employee continually to look to improve operations. *(p. 750)*

Contra account Account linked with another account and having an opposite normal balance; reported as a subtraction from the other account's balance. *(p. 99)*

Contract rate Interest rate specified in a bond indenture (or note); multiplied by the par value to determine the interest paid each period; also called *coupon rate, stated rate,* or *nominal rate. (p. 557)*

Contributed capital Total amount of cash and other assets received from stockholders in exchange for stock; also called *paid-in capital. (p. 514)*

Contributed capital in excess of par value Difference between the par value of stock and its issue price when issued at a price above par. *(p. 514)*

Contribution margin Sales revenue less total variable costs. *(p. 869)*

Contribution margin income statement Income statement that separates variable and fixed costs; highlights the contribution margin, which is sales less variable expenses. *(p. 870)*

Contribution margin per unit Amount that the sale of one unit contributes toward recovering fixed costs and earning profit; defined as sales price per unit minus variable expense per unit. *(p. 869)*

Contribution margin ratio Product's contribution margin divided by its sale price. *(p. 869)*

Control Process of monitoring planning decisions and evaluating the organization's activities and employees. *(p. 735)*

Control principle Information system principle that prescribes an accounting system to aid managers in controlling and monitoring business activities. *(p. 278)*

Controllable costs Costs that a manager has the power to control or at least strongly influence. *(pp. 739 & 995)*

Controllable variance Combination of both overhead spending variances (variable and fixed) and the variable overhead efficiency variance. *(p. 961)*

Controlling account General ledger account, the balance of which (after posting) equals the sum of the balances in its related subsidiary ledger. *(p. 283)*

Conversion costs Expenditures incurred in converting raw materials to finished goods; includes direct labor costs and overhead costs. *(p. 743)*

Conversion costs per equivalent unit The combined costs of direct labor and factory overhead per equivalent unit. *(p. 831)*

Convertible bonds Bonds that bondholders can exchange for a set number of the issuer's shares. *(p. 568)*

Convertible preferred stock Preferred stock with an option to exchange it for common stock at a specified rate. *(p. 522)*

Copyright Right giving the owner the exclusive privilege to publish and sell musical, literary, or artistic work during the creator's life plus 70 years. *(p. 412)*

Corporation Business that is a separate legal entity under state or federal laws with owners called *shareholders* or *stockholders. (pp. 12 & 510)*

Cost All normal and reasonable expenditures necessary to get an asset in place and ready for its intended use. *(pp. 397 & 399)*

Cost accounting system Accounting system for manufacturing activities based on the perpetual inventory system. *(p. 778)*

Cost-based transfer pricing A transfer pricing system based on the cost of goods or services being transferred across divisions within the same company. *(p. 1014)*

Cost-benefit constraint The notion that the benefit of a disclosure exceeds the cost of that disclosure. *(p. 13)*

Cost-benefit principle Information system principle that prescribes the benefits from an activity in an accounting system to outweigh the costs of that activity. *(pp. 11 & 279)*

Cost center Department that incurs costs but generates no revenues; common example is the accounting or legal department. *(p. 995)*

Cost object Product, process, department, or customer to which costs are assigned. *(p. 739)*

Cost of capital Rate the company must pay to its long-term creditors and shareholders. *(p. 1042)*

Cost of goods available for sale Consists of beginning inventory plus net purchases of a period. *(p. 183)*

Cost of goods manufactured Total manufacturing costs (direct materials, direct labor, and factory overhead) for the period plus beginning goods in process less ending goods in process; also called *net cost of goods manufactured* and *cost of goods completed. (p. 829)*

Cost of goods sold Cost of inventory sold to customers during a period; also called *cost of sales. (p. 182)*

Cost principle Accounting principle that prescribes financial statement information to be based on actual costs incurred in business transactions. *(p. 11)*

Cost variance Difference between the actual incurred cost and the standard cost. *(p. 955)*

Cost-volume-profit (CVP) analysis Planning method that includes predicting the volume of activity, the costs incurred, sales earned, and profits received. *(p. 871)*

Cost-volume-profit (CVP) chart Graphic representation of cost-volume-profit relations. *(p. 862)*

Coupon bonds Bonds with interest coupons attached to their certificates; bondholders detach coupons when they mature and present them to a bank or broker for collection. *(p. 568)*

Credit Recorded on the right side; an entry that decreases asset and expense accounts, and increases liability, revenue, and most equity accounts; abbreviated Cr. *(p. 55)*

Credit memorandum Notification that the sender has credited the recipient's account in the sender's records. *(p. 191)*

Credit period Time period that can pass before a customer's payment is due. *(p. 185)*

Credit terms Description of the amounts and timing of payments that a buyer (debtor) agrees to make in the future. *(p. 185)*

Creditors Individuals or organizations entitled to receive payments. *(p. 52)*

Cumulative preferred stock Preferred stock on which undeclared dividends accumulate until paid; common stockholders cannot receive dividends until cumulative dividends are paid. *(p. 521)*

Current assets Cash and other assets expected to be sold, collected, or used within one year or the company's operating cycle, whichever is longer. *(p. 150)*

Current liabilities Obligations due to be paid or settled within one year or the company's operating cycle, whichever is longer. *(pp. 151 & 439)*

Current portion of long-term debt Portion of long-term debt due within one year or the operating cycle, whichever is longer; reported under current liabilities. *(p. 447)*

Current ratio Ratio used to evaluate a company's ability to pay its short-term obligations, calculated by dividing current assets by current liabilities. *(p. 152)*

Curvilinear cost Cost that changes with volume but not at a constant rate. *(p. 865)*

Customer orientation Company position that its managers and employees be in tune with the changing wants and needs of consumers. *(p. 750)*

Cycle efficiency (CE) A measure of production efficiency, which is defined as value-added (process) time divided by total cycle time. *(p. 1010)*

Cycle time (CT) A measure of the time to produce a product or service, which is the sum of process time, inspection time, move time, and wait time; also called *throughput time*. *(p. 1009)*

Date of declaration Date the directors vote to pay a dividend. *(p. 517)*

Date of payment Date the corporation makes the dividend payment. *(p. 517)*

Date of record Date directors specify for identifying stockholders to receive dividends. *(p. 517)*

Days' sales in inventory Estimate of number of days needed to convert inventory into receivables or cash; equals ending inventory divided by cost of goods sold and then multiplied by 365; also called *days' stock on hand*. *(p. 243)*

Days' sales in raw materials inventory Measure of how much raw materials inventory is available in terms of the number of days' sales; defined as Ending raw materials inventory divided by Raw materials used and that quotient multiplied by 365 days. *(p. 752)*

Days' sales uncollected Measure of the liquidity of receivables computed by dividing the current balance of receivables by the annual credit (or net) sales and then multiplying by 365; also called *days' sales in receivables*. *(p. 337)*

Debit Recorded on the left side; an entry that increases asset and expense accounts, and decreases liability, revenue, and most equity accounts; abbreviated Dr. *(p. 55)*

Debit memorandum Notification that the sender has debited the recipient's account in the sender's records. *(p. 186)*

Debt ratio Ratio of total liabilities to total assets; used to reflect risk associated with a company's debts. *(p. 69)*

Debt-to-equity ratio Defined as total liabilities divided by total equity; shows the proportion of a company financed by non-owners (creditors) in comparison with that financed by owners. *(p. 569)*

Debtors Individuals or organizations that owe money. *(p. 51)*

Declining-balance method Method that determines depreciation charge for the period by multiplying a depreciation rate (often twice the straight-line rate) by the asset's beginning-period book value. *(p. 402)*

Deferred income tax liability Corporation income taxes that are deferred until future years because of temporary differences between GAAP and tax rules. *(p. 462)*

Degree of operating leverage (DOL) Ratio of contribution margin divided by pretax income; used to assess the effect on income of changes in sales. *(p. 879)*

Departmental accounting system Accounting system that provides information useful in evaluating the profitability or cost effectiveness of a department. *(p. 999)*

Departmental contribution to overhead Amount by which a department's revenues exceed its direct expenses. *(p. 1003)*

Depletion Process of allocating the cost of natural resources to periods when they are consumed and sold. *(p. 410)*

Departmental income statements Income statements prepared for each operating department within a decentralized organization. *(p. 997)*

Deposit ticket Lists items such as currency, coins, and checks deposited and their corresponding dollar amounts. *(p. 341)*

Deposits in transit Deposits recorded by the company but not yet recorded by its bank. *(p. 334)*

Depreciable cost Cost of a plant asset less its salvage value. *(p. 400)*

Depreciation Expense created by allocating the cost of plant and equipment to periods in which they are used; represents the expense of using the asset. *(pp. 99 & 399)*

Diluted earnings per share Earnings per share calculation that requires dilutive securities be added to the denominator of the basic EPS calculation. *(p. 529)*

Dilutive securities Securities having the potential to increase common shares outstanding; examples are options, rights, convertible bonds, and convertible preferred stock. *(p. 529)*

Direct costs Costs incurred for the benefit of one specific cost object. *(p. 739)*

Direct expenses Expenses traced to a specific department (object) that are incurred for the sole benefit of that department. *(p. 997)*

Direct labor Efforts of employees who physically convert materials to finished product. *(p. 742)*

Direct labor costs Wages and salaries for direct labor that are separately and readily traced through the production process to finished goods. *(p. 742)*

Direct material Raw material that physically becomes part of the product and is clearly identified with specific products or batches of product. *(p. 742)*

Direct material costs Expenditures for direct material that are separately and readily traced through the production process to finished goods. *(p. 742)*

Direct method Presentation of net cash from operating activities for the statement of cash flows that lists major operating cash receipts less major operating cash payments. *(p. 640)*

Direct write-off method Method that records the loss from an uncollectible account receivable at the time it is determined to be uncollectible; no attempt is made to estimate bad debts. *(p. 366)*

Discount on bonds payable Difference between a bond's par value and its lower issue price or carrying value; occurs when the contract rate is less than the market rate. *(p. 557)*

Discount on note payable Difference between the face value of a note payable and the (lesser) amount borrowed; reflects the added interest to be paid on the note over its life. *(p. 564)*

Discount on stock Difference between the par value of stock and its issue price when issued at a price below par value. *(p. 515)*

Discount period Time period in which a cash discount is available and the buyer can make a reduced payment. *(p. 185)*

Discount rate Expected rate of return on investments; also called *cost of capital, hurdle rate,* or *required rate of return. (p. B-2)*

Discounts lost Expenses resulting from not taking advantage of cash discounts on purchases. *(p. 343)*

Dividend in arrears Unpaid dividend on cumulative preferred stock; must be paid before any regular dividends on preferred stock and before any dividends on common stock. *(p. 521)*

Dividend yield Ratio of the annual amount of cash dividends distributed to common shareholders relative to the common stock's market value (price). *(p. 530)*

Dividends Corporation's distributions of assets to its owners. *(p. 53)*

Double-declining-balance (DDB) depreciation Depreciation equals beginning book value multiplied by 2 times the straight-line rate. *(p. 402)*

Double-entry accounting Accounting system in which each transaction affects at least two accounts and has at least one debit and one credit. *(p. 55)*

Double taxation Corporate income is taxed and then its later distribution through dividends is normally taxed again for shareholders. *(p. 13)*

Earnings (See *net income.*)

Earnings per share (EPS) Amount of income earned by each share of a company's outstanding common stock; also called *net income per share. (p. 529)*

Effective interest method Allocates interest expense over the bond life to yield a constant rate of interest; interest expense for a period is found by multiplying the balance of the liability at the beginning of the period by the bond market rate at issuance; also called *interest method. (p. 574)*

Efficiency Company's productivity in using its assets; usually measured relative to how much revenue a certain level of assets generates. *(p. 689)*

Efficiency variance Difference between the actual quantity of an input and the standard quantity of that input. *(p. 968)*

Electronic funds transfer (EFT) Use of electronic communication to transfer cash from one party to another. *(p. 331)*

Employee benefits Additional compensation paid to or on behalf of employees, such as premiums for medical, dental, life, and disability insurance, and contributions to pension plans. *(p. 447)*

Employee earnings report Record of an employee's net pay, gross pay, deductions, and year-to-date payroll information. *(p. 458)*

Enterprise resource planning (ERP) software Programs that manage a company's vital operations, which range from order taking to production to accounting. *(p. 293)*

Entity Organization that, for accounting purposes, is separate from other organizations and individuals. *(p. 12)*

EOM Abbreviation for *end of month;* used to describe credit terms for credit transactions. *(p. 185)*

Equity Owner's claim on the assets of a business; equals the residual interest in an entity's assets after deducting liabilities; also called *net assets. (p. 15)*

Equity method Accounting method used for long-term investments when the investor has "significant influence" over the investee. *(p. 604)*

Equity ratio Portion of total assets provided by equity, computed as total equity divided by total assets. *(p. 703)*

Equity securities with controlling influence Long-term investment when the investor is able to exert controlling influence over the investee; investors owning 50% or more of voting stock are presumed to exert controlling influence. *(p. 605)*

Equity securities with significant influence Long-term investment when the investor is able to exert significant influence over the investee; investors owning 20 percent or more (but less than 50 percent) of voting stock are presumed to exert significant influence. *(p. 604)*

Equivalent units of production (EUP) Number of units that would be completed if all effort during a period had been applied to units that were started and finished. *(p. 823)*

Estimated liability Obligation of an uncertain amount that can be reasonably estimated. *(p. 447)*

Estimated line of cost behavior Line drawn on a graph to visually fit the relation between cost and sales. *(p. 866)*

Ethics Codes of conduct by which actions are judged as right or wrong, fair or unfair, honest or dishonest. *(pp. 7 & 738)*

Events Happenings that both affect an organization's financial position and can be reliably measured. *(p. 16)*

Expanded accounting equation Assets = Liabilities + Equity; Equity equals [Owner capital − Owner withdrawals + Revenues − Expenses] for a noncorporation; Equity equals [Contributed capital + Retained earnings + Revenues − Expenses] for a corporation where dividends are subtracted from retained earnings. *(p. 15)*

Expense recognition (or **matching**) **principle** (See *matching principle.*)

Expenses Outflows or using up of assets as part of operations of a business to generate sales. *(p. 15)*

External transactions Exchanges of economic value between one entity and another entity. *(p. 16)*

External users Persons using accounting information who are not directly involved in running the organization. *(p. 5)*

Extraordinary gains or losses Gains or losses reported separately from continuing operations because they are both unusual and infrequent. *(p. 712)*

Extraordinary repairs Major repairs that extend the useful life of a plant asset beyond prior expectations; treated as a capital expenditure. *(p. 407)*

Factory overhead Factory activities supporting the production process that are not direct material or direct labor; also called *overhead* and *manufacturing overhead*. *(p. 742)*

Factory overhead costs Expenditures for factory overhead that cannot be separately or readily traced to finished goods; also called *overhead costs*. *(p. 742)*

Fair value option Fair Value Option (FVO) refers to an option to measure eligible items at fair value; eligible items include *financial assets,* such as HTM, AFS, and equity method investments, and *financial liabilities*. FVO is applied "instrument by instrument" and is elected when the eligible item is "first recognized"; once FVO is elected the decision is "irrevocable." When FVO is elected, it is measured at "fair value" and unrealized gains and losses are recognized in earnings. *(p. 567)*

Favorable variance Difference in actual revenues or expenses from the budgeted amount that contributes to a higher income. *(p. 949)*

Federal depository bank Bank authorized to accept deposits of amounts payable to the federal government. *(p. 455)*

Federal Insurance Contributions Act (FICA) Taxes Taxes assessed on both employers and employees; for Social Security and Medicare programs. *(p. 444)*

Federal Unemployment Taxes (FUTA) Payroll taxes on employers assessed by the federal government to support its unemployment insurance program. *(p. 446)*

FIFO method (See *first-in, first-out*.)

Financial accounting Area of accounting aimed mainly at serving external users. *(p. 5)*

Financial Accounting Standards Board (FASB) Independent group of full-time members responsible for setting accounting rules. *(p. 9)*

Financial leverage Earning a higher return on equity by paying dividends on preferred stock or interest on debt at a rate lower than the return earned with the assets from issuing preferred stock or debt; also called *trading on the equity*. *(p. 523)*

Financial reporting Process of communicating information relevant to investors, creditors, and others in making investment, credit, and business decisions. *(p. 689)*

Financial statement analysis Application of analytical tools to general-purpose financial statements and related data for making business decisions. *(p. 688)*

Financial statements Includes the balance sheet, income statement, statement of owner's (or stockholders') equity, and statement of cash flows. *(p. 20)*

Financing activities Transactions with owners and creditors that include obtaining cash from issuing debt, repaying amounts borrowed, and obtaining cash from or distributing cash to owners. *(p. 636)*

Finished goods inventory Account that controls the finished goods files, which acts as a subsidiary ledger (of the Inventory account) in which the costs of finished goods that are ready for sale are recorded. *(pp. 744 & 781)*

First-in, first-out (FIFO) Method to assign cost to inventory that assumes items are sold in the order acquired; earliest items purchased are the first sold. *(pp. 235 & 835)*

Fiscal year Consecutive 12-month (or 52-week) period chosen as the organization's annual accounting period. *(p. 95)*

Fixed budget Planning budget based on a single predicted amount of volume; unsuitable for evaluations if the actual volume differs from predicted volume. *(p. 949)*

Fixed budget performance report Report that compares actual revenues and costs with fixed budgeted amounts and identifies the differences as favorable or unfavorable variances. *(p. 949)*

Fixed cost Cost that does not change with changes in the volume of activity. *(p. 738)*

Flexibility principle Information system principle that prescribes an accounting system be able to adapt to changes in the company, its operations, and needs of decision makers. *(p. 279)*

Flexible budget Budget prepared (using actual volume) once a period is complete that helps managers evaluate past performance; uses fixed and variable costs in determining total costs. *(p. 950)*

Flexible budget performance report Report that compares actual revenues and costs with their variable budgeted amounts based on actual sales volume (or other level of activity) and identifies the differences as variances. *(p. 952)*

FOB Abbreviation for *free on board*; the point when ownership of goods passes to the buyer; *FOB shipping point* (or *factory*) means the buyer pays shipping costs and accepts ownership of goods when the seller transfers goods to carrier; *FOB destination* means the seller pays shipping costs and buyer accepts ownership of goods at the buyer's place of business. *(p. 187)*

Foreign exchange rate Price of one currency stated in terms of another currency. *(p. 612)*

Form 940 IRS form used to report an employer's federal unemployment taxes (FUTA) on an annual filing basis. *(p. 455)*

Form 941 IRS form filed to report FICA taxes owed and remitted. *(p. 455)*

Form 10-K (or 10-KSB) Annual report form filed with SEC by businesses (small businesses) with publicly traded securities. *(p. A-1)*

Form W-2 Annual report by an employer to each employee showing the employee's wages subject to FICA and federal income taxes along with amounts withheld. *(p. 457)*

Form W-4 Withholding allowance certificate, filed with the employer, identifying the number of withholding allowances claimed. *(p. 460)*

Franchises Privileges granted by a company or government to sell a product or service under specified conditions. *(p. 413)*

Full disclosure principle Principle that prescribes financial statements (including notes) to report all relevant information about an entity's operations and financial condition. *(p. 11)*

GAAP (See *generally accepted accounting principles*.)

General accounting system Accounting system for manufacturing activities based on the *periodic* inventory system. *(p. 778)*

General and administrative expenses Expenses that support the operating activities of a business. *(p. 195)*

General and administrative expense budget Plan that shows predicted operating expenses not included in the selling expenses budget. *(p. 909)*

General journal All-purpose journal for recording the debits and credits of transactions and events. *(p. 282)*

General ledger (See *ledger.*)

General partner Partner who assumes unlimited liability for the debts of the partnership; responsible for partnership management. *(p. 483)*

General partnership Partnership in which all partners have mutual agency and unlimited liability for partnership debts. *(p. 483)*

Generally accepted accounting principles (GAAP) Rules that specify acceptable accounting practices. *(p. 9)*

Generally accepted auditing standards (GAAS) Rules that specify acceptable auditing practices.

General-purpose financial statements Statements published periodically for use by a variety of interested parties; includes the income statement, balance sheet, statement of owner's equity (or statement of retained earnings for a corporation), statement of cash flows, and notes to these statements. *(p. 689)*

Going-concern assumption Principle that prescribes financial statements to reflect the assumption that the business will continue operating. *(p. 12)*

Goods in process inventory Account in which costs are accumulated for products that are in the process of being produced but are not yet complete; also called *work in process inventory.* *(pp. 744 & 780)*

Goodwill Amount by which a company's (or a segment's) value exceeds the value of its individual assets less its liabilities. *(p. 413)*

Gross margin (See *gross profit.*)

Gross margin ratio Gross margin (net sales minus cost of goods sold) divided by net sales; also called *gross profit ratio. (p. 193)*

Gross method Method of recording purchases at the full invoice price without deducting any cash discounts. *(p. 343)*

Gross pay Total compensation earned by an employee. *(p. 443)*

Gross profit Net sales minus cost of goods sold; also called *gross margin. (pp. 182 & 183)*

Gross profit method Procedure to estimate inventory by using the past gross profit rate to estimate cost of goods sold, which is then subtracted from the cost of goods available for sale. *(p. 255)*

Held-to-maturity (HTM) securities Debt securities that a company has the intent and ability to hold until they mature. *(p. 602)*

High-low method Procedure that yields an estimated line of cost behavior by graphically connecting costs associated with the highest and lowest sales volume. *(p. 866)*

Horizontal analysis Comparison of a company's financial condition and performance across time. *(p. 690)*

Hurdle rate Minimum acceptable rate of return (set by management) for an investment. *(pp. 1005 & 1046)*

Impairment Diminishment of an asset value. *(pp. 406 & 412)*

Imprest system Method to account for petty cash; maintains a constant balance in the fund, which equals cash plus petty cash receipts. *(p. 328)*

Inadequacy Condition in which the capacity of plant assets is too small to meet the company's production demands. *(p. 399)*

Income (See *net income.*)

Income statement Financial statement that subtracts expenses from revenues to yield a net income or loss over a specified period of time; also includes any gains or losses. *(p. 20)*

Income summary Temporary account used only in the closing process to which the balances of revenue and expense accounts (including any gains or losses) are transferred; its balance is transferred to the capital account (or retained earnings for a corporation). *(p. 145)*

Incremental cost Additional cost incurred only if a company pursues a specific course of action. *(p. 1050)*

Indefinite life Asset life that is not limited by legal, regulatory, contractual, competitive, economic, or other factors. *(p. 411)*

Indirect costs Costs incurred for the benefit of more than one cost object. *(p. 739)*

Indirect expenses Expenses incurred for the joint benefit of more than one department (or cost object). *(p. 997)*

Indirect labor Efforts of production employees who do not work specifically on converting direct materials into finished products and who are not clearly identified with specific units or batches of product. *(p. 742)*

Indirect labor costs Labor costs that cannot be physically traced to production of a product or service; included as part of overhead. *(p. 742)*

Indirect material Material used to support the production process but not clearly identified with products or batches of product. *(p. 744)*

Indirect method Presentation that reports net income and then adjusts it by adding and subtracting items to yield net cash from operating activities on the statement of cash flows. *(p. 640)*

Information processor Component of an accounting system that interprets, transforms, and summarizes information for use in analysis and reporting. *(p. 280)*

Information storage Component of an accounting system that keeps data in a form accessible to information processors. *(p. 280)*

Infrequent gain or loss Gain or loss not expected to recur given the operating environment of the business. *(p. 712)*

Input device Means of capturing information from source documents that enables its transfer to information processors. *(p. 280)*

Installment note Liability requiring a series of periodic payments to the lender. *(p. 565)*

Institute of Management Accountants (IMA) A professional association of management accountants. *(p. 738)*

Intangible assets Long-term assets (resources) used to produce or sell products or services; usually lack physical form and have uncertain benefits. *(pp. 151 & 411)*

Interest Charge for using money (or other assets) loaned from one entity to another. *(p. 372)*

Interim financial statements Financial statements covering periods of less than one year; usually based on one-, three-, or six-month periods. *(pp. 94 & 254)*

Interim statements (See *interim financial statements.*)

Internal controls or **Internal control system** All policies and procedures used to protect assets, ensure reliable accounting, promote efficient operations, and urge adherence to company policies. *(pp. 278, 318, & 738)*

Internal rate of return (IRR) Rate used to evaluate the acceptability of an investment; equals the rate that yields a net present value of zero for an investment. *(p. 1045)*

Internal transactions Activities within an organization that can affect the accounting equation. *(p. 16)*

Internal users Persons using accounting information who are directly involved in managing the organization. *(p. 6)*

International Accounting Standards Board (IASB) Group that identifies preferred accounting practices and encourages global acceptance; issues International Financial Reporting Standards (IFRS). *(p. 9)*

International Financial Reporting Standards (IFRS) Set of international accounting standards explaining how types of transactions and events are reported in financial statements; IFRS are issued by the International Accounting Standards Board *(p. 9)*

Inventory Goods a company owns and expects to sell in its normal operations. *(p. 183)*

Inventory turnover Number of times a company's average inventory is sold during a period; computed by dividing cost of goods sold by average inventory; also called *merchandise turnover*. *(p. 243)*

Investing activities Transactions that involve purchasing and selling of long-term assets; includes making and collecting notes receivable and investments in other than cash equivalents. *(p. 636)*

Investment center Center of which a manager is responsible for revenues, costs, and asset investments. *(p. 995)*

Investment center residual income The net income an investment center earns above a target return on average invested assets. *(p. 1005)*

Investment center return on total assets Center net income divided by average total assets for the center. *(p. 1005)*

Investment turnover The efficiency with which a company generates sales from its available assets; computed as sales divided by average invested assets. *(p. 1006)*

Invoice Itemized record of goods prepared by the vendor that lists the customer's name, items sold, sales prices, and terms of sale. *(p. 341)*

Invoice approval Document containing a checklist of steps necessary for approving the recording and payment of an invoice; also called *check authorization*. *(p. 341)*

Job Production of a customized product or service. *(p. 778)*

Job cost sheet Separate record maintained for each job. *(p. 780)*

Job lot Production of more than one unit of a customized product or service. *(p. 778)*

Job order cost accounting system Cost accounting system to determine the cost of producing each job or job lot. *(pp. 780 & 819)*

Job order production Production of special-order products; also called *customized production*. *(p. 778)*

Joint cost Cost incurred to produce or purchase two or more products at the same time. *(p. 1014)*

Journal Record in which transactions are entered before they are posted to ledger accounts; also called *book of original entry*. *(p. 56)*

Journalizing Process of recording transactions in a journal. *(p. 56)*

Just-in-time (JIT) manufacturing Process of acquiring or producing inventory only when needed. *(p. 750)*

Known liabilities Obligations of a company with little uncertainty; set by agreements, contracts, or laws; also called *definitely determinable liabilities*. *(p. 440)*

Land improvements Assets that increase the benefits of land, have a limited useful life, and are depreciated. *(p. 398)*

Large stock dividend Stock dividend that is more than 25% of the previously outstanding shares. *(p. 518)*

Last-in, first-out (LIFO) Method for assigning cost to inventory that assumes costs for the most recent items purchased are sold first and charged to cost of goods sold. *(p. 235)*

Lean business model Practice of eliminating waste while meeting customer needs and yielding positive company returns. *(p. 750)*

Lease Contract specifying the rental of property. *(pp. 413 & 578)*

Leasehold Rights the lessor grants to the lessee under the terms of a lease. *(p. 413)*

Leasehold improvements Alterations or improvements to leased property such as partitions and storefronts. *(p. 414)*

Least-squares regression Statistical method for deriving an estimated line of cost behavior that is more precise than the high-low method and the scatter diagram. *(p. 867)*

Ledger Record containing all accounts (with amounts) for a business; also called *general ledger*. *(p. 51)*

Lessee Party to a lease who secures the right to possess and use the property from another party (the lessor). *(p. 413)*

Lessor Party to a lease who grants another party (the lessee) the right to possess and use its property. *(p. 413)*

Liabilities Creditors' claims on an organization's assets; involves a probable future payment of assets, products, or services that a company is obligated to make due to past transactions or events. *(p. 15)*

Licenses (See *franchises*.)

Limited liability Owner can lose no more than the amount invested. *(p. 12)*

Limited liability company Organization form that combines select features of a corporation and a limited partnership; provides limited liability to its members (owners), is free of business tax, and allows members to actively participate in management. *(p. 484)*

Limited liability partnership Partnership in which a partner is not personally liable for malpractice or negligence unless that partner is responsible for providing the service that resulted in the claim. *(p. 483)*

Limited life (See *useful life*.)

Limited partners Partners who have no personal liability for partnership debts beyond the amounts they invested in the partnership. *(p. 483)*

Limited partnership Partnership that has two classes of partners, limited partners and general partners. *(p. 483)*

Liquid assets Resources such as cash that are easily converted into other assets or used to pay for goods, services, or liabilities. *(p. 323)*

Liquidating cash dividend Distribution of assets that returns part of the original investment to stockholders; deducted from contributed capital accounts. *(p. 518)*

Liquidation Process of going out of business; involves selling assets, paying liabilities, and distributing remainder to owners.

Liquidity Availability of resources to meet short-term cash requirements. *(pp. 323 & 689)*

List price Catalog (full) price of an item before any trade discount is deducted. *(p. 184)*

Long-term investments Long-term assets not used in operating activities such as notes receivable and investments in stocks and bonds. *(pp. 151 & 598)*

Long-term liabilities Obligations not due to be paid within one year or the operating cycle, whichever is longer. *(pp. 151 & 439)*

Lower of cost or market (LCM) Required method to report inventory at market replacement cost when that market cost is lower than recorded cost. *(p. 239)*

Maker of the note Entity who signs a note and promises to pay it at maturity. *(p. 372)*

Management by exception Management process to focus on significant variances and give less attention to areas where performance is close to the standard. *(p. 953)*

Managerial accounting Area of accounting aimed mainly at serving the decision-making needs of internal users; also called *management accounting*. *(pp. 6 & 734)*

Manufacturer Company that uses labor and operating assets to convert raw materials to finished goods. *(p. 13)*

Manufacturing budget Plan that shows the predicted costs for direct materials, direct labor, and overhead to be incurred in manufacturing units in the production budget. *(p. 920)*

Manufacturing statement Report that summarizes the types and amounts of costs incurred in a company's production process for a period; also called *cost of goods manufacturing statement*. *(p. 747)*

Margin of safety Excess of expected sales over the level of break-even sales. *(p. 870)*

Market-based transfer price A transfer pricing system based on the market price of the goods or services being transferred across divisions within the same company. *(p. 1014)*

Market prospects Expectations (both good and bad) about a company's future performance as assessed by users and other interested parties. *(p. 689)*

Market rate Interest rate that borrowers are willing to pay and lenders are willing to accept for a specific lending agreement given the borrowers' risk level. *(p. 557)*

Market value per share Price at which stock is bought or sold. *(p. 513)*

Master budget Comprehensive business plan that includes specific plans for expected sales, product units to be produced, merchandise (or materials) to be purchased, expenses to be incurred, plant assets to be purchased, and amounts of cash to be borrowed or loans to be repaid, as well as a budgeted income statement and balance sheet. *(p. 904)*

Matching (or expense recognition) principle Prescribes expenses to be reported in the same period as the revenues that were earned as a result of the expenses. *(pp. 11, 96, & 366)*

Materiality constraint Prescribes that accounting for items that significantly impact financial statement and any inferences from them adhere strictly to GAAP. *(pp. 13 & 366)*

Materials consumption report Document that summarizes the materials a department uses during a reporting period; replaces materials requisitions. *(p. 820)*

Materials ledger card Perpetual record updated each time units are purchased or issued for production use. *(p. 782)*

Materials requisition Source document production managers use to request materials for production; used to assign materials costs to specific jobs or overhead. *(p. 783)*

Maturity date of a note Date when a note's principal and interest are due. *(p. 372)*

Measurement principle Principle that prescribes financial statement information, and its underlying transactions and events, be based on relevant measures of valuation; also called the *cost principle*. *(p. 11)*

Merchandise (See *merchandise inventory*.) *(p. 182)*

Merchandise inventory Goods that a company owns and expects to sell to customers; also called *merchandise* or *inventory*. *(p. 183)*

Merchandise purchases budget Plan that shows the units or costs of merchandise to be purchased by a merchandising company during the budget period. *(p. 907)*

Merchandiser Entity that earns net income by buying and selling merchandise. *(p. 182)*

Merit rating Rating assigned to an employer by a state based on the employer's record of employment. *(p. 446)*

Minimum legal capital Amount of assets defined by law that stockholders must (potentially) invest in a corporation; usually defined as par value of the stock; intended to protect creditors. *(p. 513)*

Mixed cost Cost that behaves like a combination of fixed and variable costs. *(p. 864)*

Modified Accelerated Cost Recovery System (MACRS) Depreciation system required by federal income tax law. *(p. 404)*

Monetary unit assumption Principle that assumes transactions and events can be expressed in money units. *(p. 12)*

Mortgage Legal loan agreement that protects a lender by giving the lender the right to be paid from the cash proceeds from the sale of a borrower's assets identified in the mortgage. *(p. 566)*

Multinational Company that operates in several countries. *(p. 612)*

Multiple-step income statement Income statement format that shows subtotals between sales and net income, categorizes expenses, and often reports the details of net sales and expenses. *(p. 195)*

Mutual agency Legal relationship among partners whereby each partner is an agent of the partnership and is able to bind the partnership to contracts within the scope of the partnership's business. *(p. 482)*

Natural business year Twelve-month period that ends when a company's sales activities are at their lowest point. *(p. 95)*

Natural resources Assets physically consumed when used; examples are timber, mineral deposits, and oil and gas fields; also called *wasting assets*. *(p. 410)*

Negotiated transfer price A system where division managers negotiate to determine the price to use to record transfers of goods or services across divisions within the same company. *(p. 1014)*

Net assets (See *equity*.)

Net income Amount earned after subtracting all expenses necessary for and matched with sales for a period; also called *income, profit*, or *earnings*. *(p. 15)*

Net loss Excess of expenses over revenues for a period. *(p. 15)*

Net method Method of recording purchases at the full invoice price less any cash discounts. *(p. 343)*

Net pay Gross pay less all deductions; also called *take-home pay.* *(p. 444)*

Net present value (NPV) Dollar estimate of an asset's value that is used to evaluate the acceptability of an investment; computed by discounting future cash flows from the investment at a satisfactory rate and then subtracting the initial cost of the investment. *(p. 1042)*

Net realizable value Expected selling price (value) of an item minus the cost of making the sale. *(p. 230)*

Noncumulative preferred stock Preferred stock on which the right to receive dividends is lost for any period when dividends are not declared. *(p. 521)*

Noninterest-bearing note Note with no stated (contract) rate of interest; interest is implicitly included in the note's face value.

Nonparticipating preferred stock Preferred stock on which dividends are limited to a maximum amount each year. *(p. 522)*

No-par value stock Stock class that has not been assigned a par (or stated) value by the corporate charter. *(p. 513)*

Nonsufficient funds (NSF) check Maker's bank account has insufficient money to pay the check; also called *hot check.* *(p. 334)*

Non-value-added time The portion of cycle time that is not directed at producing a product or service; equals the sum of inspection time, move time, and wait time. *(p. 1010)*

Not controllable costs Costs that a manager does not have the power to control or strongly influence. *(p. 739)*

Note (See *promissory note.*)

Note payable Liability expressed by a written promise to pay a definite sum of money on demand or on a specific future date(s). *(p. 52)*

Note receivable Asset consisting of a written promise to receive a definite sum of money on demand or on a specific future date(s). *(p. 51)*

Objectivity Concept that prescribes independent, unbiased evidence to support financial statement information. *(p. 11)*

Obsolescence Condition in which, because of new inventions and improvements, a plant asset can no longer be used to produce goods or services with a competitive advantage. *(p. 399)*

Off-balance-sheet financing Acquisition of assets by agreeing to liabilities not reported on the balance sheet. *(p. 579)*

Online processing Approach to inputting data from source documents as soon as the information is available. *(p. 292)*

Operating activities Activities that involve the production or purchase of merchandise and the sale of goods or services to customers, including expenditures related to administering the business. *(p. 635)*

Operating cycle Normal time between paying cash for merchandise or employee services and receiving cash from customers. *(p. 149)*

Operating leases Short-term (or cancelable) leases in which the lessor retains risks and rewards of ownership. *(p. 578)*

Operating leverage Extent, or relative size, of fixed costs in the total cost structure. *(p. 879)*

Opportunity cost Potential benefit lost by choosing a specific action from two or more alternatives. *(p. 740)*

Ordinary repairs Repairs to keep a plant asset in normal, good operating condition; treated as a revenue expenditure and immediately expensed. *(p. 407)*

Organization expenses (costs) Costs such as legal fees and promoter fees to bring an entity into existence. *(p. 511)*

Other comprehensive income (See *comprehensive income.*)

Out-of-pocket cost Cost incurred or avoided as a result of management's decisions. *(p. 740)*

Output devices Means by which information is taken out of the accounting system and made available for use. *(p. 281)*

Outsourcing Manager decision to buy a product or service from another entity; part of a *make-or-buy* decision; also called *make or buy.* *(p. 1051)*

Outstanding checks Checks written and recorded by the depositor but not yet paid by the bank at the bank statement date. *(p. 334)*

Outstanding stock Corporation's stock held by its shareholders. *(p. 513)*

Overapplied overhead Amount by which the overhead applied to production in a period using the predetermined overhead rate exceeds the actual overhead incurred in a period. *(p. 789)*

Overhead cost variance Difference between the total overhead cost applied to products and the total overhead cost actually incurred. *(p. 960)*

Owner, Capital Account showing the owner's claim on company assets; equals owner investments plus net income (or less net losses) minus owner withdrawals since the company's inception; also referred to as *equity.* *(p. 15)*

Owner investment Assets put into the business by the owner. *(p. 15)*

Owner's equity (See *equity.*)

Owner, Withdrawals Account used to record asset distributions to the owner. *(See also withdrawals.) (p. 15)*

Paid-in capital (See *contributed capital.*)

Paid-in capital in excess of par value Amount received from issuance of stock that is in excess of the stock's par value. *(p. 515)*

Par value Value assigned a share of stock by the corporate charter when the stock is authorized. *(p. 513)*

Par value of a bond Amount the bond issuer agrees to pay at maturity and the amount on which cash interest payments are based; also called *face amount* or *face value* of a bond. *(p. 554)*

Par value stock Class of stock assigned a par value by the corporate charter. *(p. 513)*

Parent Company that owns a controlling interest in a corporation (requires more than 50% of voting stock). *(p. 605)*

Participating preferred stock Preferred stock that shares with common stockholders any dividends paid in excess of the percent stated on preferred stock. *(p. 522)*

Partner return on equity Partner net income divided by average partner equity for the period. *(p. 494)*

Partnership Unincorporated association of two or more persons to pursue a business for profit as co-owners. *(pp. 12 & 482)*

Partnership contract Agreement among partners that sets terms under which the affairs of the partnership are conducted; also called *articles of partnership.* *(p. 482)*

Partnership liquidation Dissolution of a partnership by (1) selling noncash assets and allocating any gain or loss according to partners' income-and-loss ratio, (2) paying liabilities, and (3) distributing any remaining cash according to partners' capital balances. *(p. 491)*

Patent Exclusive right granted to its owner to produce and sell an item or to use a process for 17 years. *(p. 412)*

Payback period (PBP) Time-based measurement used to evaluate the acceptability of an investment; equals the time expected to pass before an investment's net cash flows equal its initial cost. *(p. 1039)*

Payee of the note Entity to whom a note is made payable. *(p. 372)*

Payroll bank account Bank account used solely for paying employees; each pay period an amount equal to the total employees' net pay is deposited in it and the payroll checks are drawn on it. *(p. 460)*

Payroll deductions Amounts withheld from an employee's gross pay; also called *withholdings*. *(p. 444)*

Payroll register Record for a pay period that shows the pay period dates, regular and overtime hours worked, gross pay, net pay, and deductions. *(p. 457)*

Pension plan Contractual agreement between an employer and its employees for the employer to provide benefits to employees after they retire; expensed when incurred. *(p. 580)*

Period costs Expenditures identified more with a time period than with finished products costs; includes selling and general administrative expenses. *(p. 740)*

Periodic inventory system Method that records the cost of inventory purchased but does not continuously track the quantity available or sold to customers; records are updated at the end of each period to reflect the physical count and costs of goods available. *(p. 184)*

Permanent accounts Accounts that reflect activities related to one or more future periods; balance sheet accounts whose balances are not closed; also called *real accounts*. *(p. 144)*

Perpetual inventory system Method that maintains continuous records of the cost of inventory available and the cost of goods sold. *(p. 184)*

Petty cash Small amount of cash in a fund to pay minor expenses; accounted for using an imprest system. *(p. 328)*

Planning Process of setting goals and preparing to achieve them. *(p. 734)*

Plant asset age Plant asset age is an approximation of the age of plant assets, which is estimated by dividing accumulated depreciation by depreciation expense. *(p. 415)*

Plant assets Tangible long-lived assets used to produce or sell products and services; also called *property, plant and equipment (PP&E)* or *fixed assets*. *(pp. 99 & 396)*

Pledged assets to secured liabilities Ratio of the book value of a company's pledged assets to the book value of its secured liabilities. *(p. 703)*

Post-closing trial balance List of permanent accounts and their balances from the ledger after all closing entries are journalized and posted. *(p. 146)*

Posting Process of transferring journal entry information to the ledger; computerized systems automate this process. *(p. 56)*

Posting reference (PR) column A column in journals in which individual ledger account numbers are entered when entries are posted to those ledger accounts. *(p. 58)*

Predetermined overhead rate Rate established prior to the beginning of a period that relates estimated overhead to another variable, such as estimated direct labor, and is used to assign overhead cost to production. *(p. 786)*

Preemptive right Stockholders' right to maintain their proportionate interest in a corporation with any additional shares issued. *(p. 512)*

Preferred stock Stock with a priority status over common stockholders in one or more ways, such as paying dividends or distributing assets. *(p. 520)*

Premium on bonds Difference between a bond's par value and its higher carrying value; occurs when the contract rate is higher than the market rate; also called *bond premium*. *(p. 560)*

Premium on stock (See *contributed capital in excess of par value*.) *(p. 515)*

Prepaid expenses Items paid for in advance of receiving their benefits; classified as assets. *(p. 97)*

Price-earnings (PE) ratio Ratio of a company's current market value per share to its earnings per share; also called *price-to-earnings*. *(p. 529)*

Price variance Difference between actual and budgeted revenue or cost caused by the difference between the actual price per unit and the budgeted price per unit. *(p. 953)*

Prime costs Expenditures directly identified with the production of finished goods; include direct materials costs and direct labor costs. *(p. 743)*

Principal of a note Amount that the signer of a note agrees to pay back when it matures, not including interest. *(p. 372)*

Principles of internal control Principles prescribing management to establish responsibility, maintain records, insure assets, separate record-keeping from custody of assets, divide responsibility for related transactions, apply technological controls, and perform reviews. *(p. 319)*

Prior period adjustment Correction of an error in a prior year that is reported in the statement of retained earnings (or statement of stockholders' equity) net of any income tax effects. *(p. 527)*

Pro forma financial statements Statements that show the effects of proposed transactions and events as if they had occurred. *(p. 144)*

Process cost accounting system System of assigning direct materials, direct labor, and overhead to specific processes; total costs associated with each process are then divided by the number of units passing through that process to determine the cost per equivalent unit. *(p. 819)*

Process cost summary Report of costs charged to a department, its equivalent units of production achieved, and the costs assigned to its output. *(p. 828)*

Process operations Processing of products in a continuous (sequential) flow of steps; also called *process manufacturing* or *process production*. *(p. 816)*

Product costs Costs that are capitalized as inventory because they produce benefits expected to have future value; include direct materials, direct labor, and overhead. *(p. 740)*

Production budget Plan that shows the units to be produced each period. *(p. 920)*

Profit (See *net income*.)

Profit center Business unit that incurs costs and generates revenues. *(p. 995)*

Profit margin Ratio of a company's net income to its net sales; the percent of income in each dollar of revenue; also called *net profit margin*. *(pp. 109 & 1006)*

Profitability Company's ability to generate an adequate return on invested capital. *(p. 689)*

Profitability index A measure of the relation between the expected benefits of a project and its investment, computed as the present value of expected future cash flows from the investment divided by the cost of the investment; a higher value indicates a more desirable investment, and a value below 1 indicates an unacceptable project. *(p. 1045)*

Promissory note (or note) Written promise to pay a specified amount either on demand or at a definite future date; is a *note receivable* for the lender but a *note payable* for the lendee. *(p. 372)*

Proprietorship (See *sole proprietorship.*)

Proxy Legal document giving a stockholder's agent the power to exercise the stockholder's voting rights. *(p. 511)*

Purchase discount Term used by a purchaser to describe a cash discount granted to the purchaser for paying within the discount period. *(p. 185)*

Purchase order Document used by the purchasing department to place an order with a seller (vendor). *(p. 340)*

Purchase requisition Document listing merchandise needed by a department and requesting it be purchased. *(p. 340)*

Purchases journal Journal normally used to record all purchases on credit. *(p. 289)*

Quantity variance Difference between actual and budgeted revenue or cost caused by the difference between the actual number of units and the budgeted number of units. *(p. 953)*

Ratio analysis Determination of key relations between financial statement items as reflected in numerical measures. *(p. 690)*

Raw materials inventory Goods a company acquires to use in making products. *(p. 744)*

Raw materials inventory turnover Measure of how many times a company turns over (uses in production) its raw materials inventory during a period; defined as Raw materials used divided by Average raw materials inventory. *(p. 752)*

Realizable value Expected proceeds from converting an asset into cash. *(p. 367)*

Receiving report Form used to report that ordered goods are received and to describe their quantity and condition. *(p. 341)*

Recordkeeping Part of accounting that involves recording transactions and events, either manually or electronically; also called *bookkeeping. (p. 4)*

Registered bonds Bonds owned by investors whose names and addresses are recorded by the issuer; interest payments are made to the registered owners. *(p. 568)*

Relevance principle Information system principle prescribing that its reports be useful, understandable, timely, and pertinent for decision making. *(p. 278)*

Relevant benefits Additional or incremental revenue generated by selecting a particular course of action over another. *(p. 1049)*

Relevant range of operations Company's normal operating range; excludes extremely high and low volumes not likely to occur. *(p. 872)*

Report form balance sheet Balance sheet that lists accounts vertically in the order of assets, liabilities, and equity. *(p. 22)*

Responsibility accounting budget Report of expected costs and expenses under a manager's control. *(p. 996)*

Responsibility accounting performance report Responsibility report that compares actual costs and expenses for a department with budgeted amounts. *(p. 996)*

Responsibility accounting system System that provides information that management can use to evaluate the performance of a department's manager. *(p. 994)*

Restricted retained earnings Retained earnings not available for dividends because of legal or contractual limitations. *(p. 526)*

Retail inventory method Method for estimating ending inventory based on the ratio of the amount of goods for sale at cost to the amount of goods for sale at retail. *(p. 254)*

Retailer Intermediary that buys products from manufacturers or wholesalers and sells them to consumers. *(p. 182)*

Retained earnings Cumulative income less cumulative losses and dividends. *(p. 514)*

Retained earnings deficit Debit (abnormal) balance in Retained Earnings; occurs when cumulative losses and dividends exceed cumulative income; also called *accumulated deficit. (p. 517)*

Return Monies received from an investment; often in percent form. *(p. 27)*

Return on assets (See *return on total assets.*)

Return on equity Ratio of net income to average equity for the period.

Return on total assets Ratio reflecting operating efficiency; defined as net income divided by average total assets for the period; also called *return on assets* or *return on investment. (pp. 24 & 607)*

Revenue expenditures Expenditures reported on the current income statement as an expense because they do not provide benefits in future periods. *(p. 406)*

Revenue recognition principle The principle prescribing that revenue is recognized when earned. *(p. 11)*

Revenues Gross increase in equity from a company's business activities that earn income; also called *sales. (p. 15)*

Reverse stock split Occurs when a corporation calls in its stock and replaces each share with less than one new share; increases both market value per share and any par or stated value per share. *(p. 520)*

Reversing entries Optional entries recorded at the beginning of a period that prepare the accounts for the usual journal entries as if adjusting entries had not occurred in the prior period. *(p. 156)*

Risk Uncertainty about an expected return. *(p. 27)*

Rolling budget New set of budgets a firm adds for the next period (with revisions) to replace the ones that have lapsed. *(p. 903)*

S corporation Corporation that meets special tax qualifications so as to be treated like a partnership for income tax purposes. *(p. 483)*

Safety stock Quantity of inventory or materials over the minimum needed to satisfy budgeted demand. *(p. 907)*

Sales (See *revenues.*)

Sales budget Plan showing the units of goods to be sold or services to be provided; the starting point in the budgeting process for most departments. *(p. 906)*

Sales discount Term used by a seller to describe a cash discount granted to buyers who pay within the discount period. *(p. 185)*

Sales journal Journal normally used to record sales of goods on credit. *(p. 284)*

Sales mix Ratio of sales volumes for the various products sold by a company. *(p. 877)*

Salvage value Estimate of amount to be recovered at the end of an asset's useful life; also called *residual value* or *scrap value*. *(p. 399)*

Sarbanes-Oxley Act (SOX) Created the *Public Company Accounting Oversight Board,* regulates analyst conflicts, imposes corporate governance requirements, enhances accounting and control disclosures, impacts insider transactions and executive loans, establishes new types of criminal conduct, and expands penalties for violations of federal securities laws. *(pp. 13 & 318)*

Scatter diagram Graph used to display data about past cost behavior and sales as points on a diagram. *(p. 866)*

Schedule of accounts payable List of the balances of all accounts in the accounts payable ledger and their totals. *(p. 290)*

Schedule of accounts receivable List of the balances of all accounts in the accounts receivable ledger and their totals. *(p. 285)*

Section 404 (of SOX) Section 404 of SOX requires management and the external auditor to report on the adequacy of the company's internal control on financial reporting, which is the most costly aspect of SOX for companies to implement as documenting and testing important financial manual and automated controls require enormous efforts. Section 404 also requires management to produce an "internal control report" as part of each annual SEC report that affirms "the responsibility of management for establishing and maintaining an adequate internal control structure and procedures for financial reporting." *(p. 319)*

Secured bonds Bonds that have specific assets of the issuer pledged as collateral. *(p. 568)*

Securities and Exchange Commission (SEC) Federal agency Congress has charged to set reporting rules for organizations that sell ownership shares to the public. *(p. 9)*

Segment return on assets Segment operating income divided by segment average (identifiable) assets for the period. *(p. 295)*

Selling expense budget Plan that lists the types and amounts of selling expenses expected in the budget period. *(p. 908)*

Selling expenses Expenses of promoting sales, such as displaying and advertising merchandise, making sales, and delivering goods to customers. *(p. 195)*

Serial bonds Bonds consisting of separate amounts that mature at different dates. *(p. 568)*

Service company Organization that provides services instead of tangible products.

Shareholders Owners of a corporation; also called *stockholders*. *(p. 13)*

Shares Equity of a corporation divided into ownership units; also called *stock*. *(p. 13)*

Short-term investments Debt and equity securities that management expects to convert to cash within the next 3 to 12 months (or the operating cycle if longer); also called *temporary investments* or *marketable securities*. *(p. 598)*

Short-term note payable Current obligation in the form of a written promissory note. *(p. 441)*

Shrinkage Inventory losses that occur as a result of theft or deterioration. *(p. 192)*

Signature card Includes the signatures of each person authorized to sign checks on the bank account. *(p. 331)*

Simple capital structure Capital structure that consists of only common stock and nonconvertible preferred stock; consists of no dilutive securities. *(p. 529)*

Single-step income statement Income statement format that includes cost of goods sold as an expense and shows only one subtotal for total expenses. *(p. 196)*

Sinking fund bonds Bonds that require the issuer to make deposits to a separate account; bondholders are repaid at maturity from that account. *(p. 568)*

Small stock dividend Stock dividend that is 25% or less of a corporation's previously outstanding shares. *(p. 518)*

Social responsibility Being accountable for the impact that one's actions might have on society. *(p. 8)*

Sole proprietorship Business owned by one person that is not organized as a corporation; also called *proprietorship*. *(p. 12)*

Solvency Company's long-run financial viability and its ability to cover long-term obligations. *(p. 689)*

Source documents Source of information for accounting entries that can be in either paper or electronic form; also called *business papers*. *(p. 50)*

Special journal Any journal used for recording and posting transactions of a similar type. *(p. 288)*

Specific identification Method for assigning cost to inventory when the purchase cost of each item in inventory is identified and used to compute cost of inventory. *(pp. 233 & 250)*

Spending variance Difference between the actual price of an item and its standard price. *(p. 968)*

Spreadsheet Computer program that organizes data by means of formulas and format; also called *electronic work sheet*. *(p. 140)*

Standard costs Costs that should be incurred under normal conditions to produce a product or component or to perform a service. *(p. 953)*

State Unemployment Taxes (SUTA) State payroll taxes on employers to support its unemployment programs. *(p. 446)*

Stated value stock No-par stock assigned a stated value per share; this amount is recorded in the stock account when the stock is issued. *(p. 514)*

Statement of cash flows A financial statement that lists cash inflows (receipts) and cash outflows (payments) during a period; arranged by operating, investing, and financing. *(pp. 20 & 634)*

Statement of owner's equity Report of changes in equity over a period; adjusted for increases (owner investment and net income) and for decreases (withdrawals and net loss). *(p. 20)*

Statement of partners' equity Financial statement that shows total capital balances at the beginning of the period, any additional investment by partners, the income or loss of the period, the partners' withdrawals, and the partners' ending capital balances; also called *statement of partners' capital*. *(p. 487)*

Statement of retained earnings Report of changes in retained earnings over a period; adjusted for increases (net income), for decreases (dividends and net loss), and for any prior period adjustment. *(p. 526)*

Statement of stockholders' equity Financial statement that lists the beginning and ending balances of each major equity account and describes all changes in those accounts. *(p. 527)*

Statements of Financial Accounting Standards (SFAS) FASB publications that establish U.S. GAAP.

Step-wise cost Cost that remains fixed over limited ranges of volumes but changes by a lump sum when volume changes occur outside these limited ranges. *(p. 864)*

Stock (See *shares*) *(p. 13)*

Stock dividend Corporation's distribution of its own stock to its stockholders without the receipt of any payment. *(p. 518)*

Stock options Rights to purchase common stock at a fixed price over a specified period of time. *(p. 527)*

Stock split Occurs when a corporation calls in its stock and replaces each share with more than one new share; decreases both the market value per share and any par or stated value per share. *(p. 520)*

Stock subscription Investor's contractual commitment to purchase unissued shares at future dates and prices.

Stockholders (See *shareholders*.) *(p. 13)*

Stockholders' equity A corporation's equity; also called *shareholders' equity* or *corporate capital*. *(p. 514)*

Straight-line depreciation Method that allocates an equal portion of the depreciable cost of plant asset (cost minus salvage) to each accounting period in its useful life. *(pp. 99 & 400)*

Straight-line bond amortization Method allocating an equal amount of bond interest expense to each period of the bond life. *(p. 558)*

Subsidiary Entity controlled by another entity (parent) in which the parent owns more than 50% of the subsidiary's voting stock. *(p. 605)*

Subsidiary ledger List of individual subaccounts and amounts with a common characteristic; linked to a controlling account in the general ledger. *(p. 282)*

Sunk cost Cost already incurred and cannot be avoided or changed. *(p. 740)*

Supplementary records Information outside the usual accounting records; also called *supplemental records*. *(p. 188)*

Supply chain Linkages of services or goods extending from suppliers, to the company itself, and on to customers.

T-account Tool used to show the effects of transactions and events on individual accounts. *(p. 54)*

Target cost Maximum allowable cost for a product or service; defined as expected selling price less the desired profit. *(p. 779)*

Temporary accounts Accounts used to record revenues, expenses, and withdrawals (dividends for a corporation); they are closed at the end of each period; also called *nominal accounts*. *(p. 144)*

Term bonds Bonds scheduled for payment (maturity) at a single specified date. *(p. 568)*

Throughput time (See *cycle time*.)

Time period assumption Assumption that an organization's activities can be divided into specific time periods such as months, quarters, or years. *(pp. 12 & 94)*

Time ticket Source document used to report the time an employee spent working on a job or on overhead activities and then to determine the amount of direct labor to charge to the job or the amount of indirect labor to charge to overhead. *(p. 784)*

Times interest earned Ratio of income before interest expense (and any income taxes) divided by interest expense; reflects risk of covering interest commitments when income varies. *(p. 452)*

Total asset turnover Measure of a company's ability to use its assets to generate sales; computed by dividing net sales by average total assets. *(p. 415)*

Total quality management (TQM) Concept calling for all managers and employees at all stages of operations to strive toward higher standards and reduce number of defects. *(p. 750)*

Trade discount Reduction from a list or catalog price that can vary for wholesalers, retailers, and consumers. *(p. 184)*

Trademark or **Trademark** or **trade (brand) name** Symbol, name, phrase, or jingle identified with a company, product, or service. *(p. 413)*

Trading on the equity (See *financial leverage*.)

Trading securities Investments in debt and equity securities that the company intends to actively trade for profit. *(p. 601)*

Transfer price The price used to record transfers of goods or services across divisions within the same company. *(p. 1013)*

Transaction Exchange of economic consideration affecting an entity's financial position that can be reliably measured. *(p. 16)*

Treasury stock Corporation's own stock that it reacquired and still holds. *(p. 524)*

Trial balance List of accounts and their balances at a point in time; total debit balances equal total credit balances. *(p. 65)*

Unadjusted trial balance List of accounts and balances prepared before accounting adjustments are recorded and posted. *(p. 106)*

Unavoidable expense Expense (or cost) that is not relevant for business decisions; an expense that would continue even if a department, product, or service is eliminated. *(p. 1055)*

Unclassified balance sheet Balance sheet that broadly groups assets, liabilities, and equity accounts. *(p. 149)*

Uncontrollable costs Costs that a manager does not have the power to determine or strongly influence. *(p. 995)*

Underapplied overhead Amount by which overhead incurred in a period exceeds the overhead applied to that period's production using the predetermined overhead rate. *(p. 789)*

Unearned revenue Liability created when customers pay in advance for products or services; earned when the products or services are later delivered. *(p. 100)*

Unfavorable variance Difference in revenues or costs, when the actual amount is compared to the budgeted amount, that contributes to a lower income. *(p. 949)*

Unit contribution margin Amount a product's unit selling price exceeds its total unit variable cost. *(p. 869)*

Units-of-production depreciation Method that charges a varying amount to depreciation expense for each period of an asset's useful life depending on its usage. *(p. 401)*

Unlimited liability Legal relationship among general partners that makes each of them responsible for partnership debts if the other partners are unable to pay their shares. *(p. 483)*

Unrealized gain (loss) Gain (loss) not yet realized by an actual transaction or event such as a sale. *(p. 601)*

Unsecured bonds Bonds backed only by the issuer's credit standing; almost always riskier than secured bonds; also called *debentures*. *(p. 568)*

Unusual gain or loss Gain or loss that is abnormal or unrelated to the company's ordinary activities and environment. *(p. 712)*

Useful life Length of time an asset will be productively used in the operations of a business; also called *service life* or *limited life*. *(pp. 399 & 411)*

Value-added time The portion of cycle time that is directed at producing a product or service; equals process time. *(p. 1010)*

Value chain Sequential activities that add value to an entity's products or services; includes design, production, marketing, distribution, and service. *(p. 750)*

Variable cost Cost that changes in proportion to changes in the activity output volume. *(p. 738)*

Variable costing income statement An income statement in which costs are classified as variable or fixed; also called *contribution margin income statement*. *(p. 870)*

Variance analysis Process of examining differences between actual and budgeted revenues or costs and describing them in terms of price and quantity differences. *(p. 953)*

Vendee Buyer of goods or services. *(p. 341)*

Vendor Seller of goods or services. *(p. 340)*

Vertical analysis Evaluation of each financial statement item or group of items in terms of a specific base amount. *(p. 690)*

Volume variance Difference between two dollar amounts of fixed overhead cost; one amount is the total budgeted overhead cost, and the other is the overhead cost allocated to products using the predetermined fixed overhead rate. *(p. 961)*

Voucher Internal file used to store documents and information to control cash disbursements and to ensure that a transaction is properly authorized and recorded. *(p. 327)*

Voucher register Journal (referred to as *book of original entry*) in which all vouchers are recorded after they have been approved. *(p. 342)*

Voucher system Procedures and approvals designed to control cash disbursements and acceptance of obligations. *(p. 326)*

Wage bracket withholding table Table of the amounts of income tax withheld from employees' wages. *(p. 460)*

Warranty Agreement that obligates the seller to correct or replace a product or service when it fails to perform properly within a specified period. *(p. 448)*

Weighted average Method for assigning inventory cost to sales; the cost of available-for-sale units is divided by the number of units available to determine per unit cost prior to each sale that is then multiplied by the units sold to yield the cost of that sale. *(pp. 236, 252, & 826)*

Weighted-average contribution margin The contribution margin per composite unit for a company that provides multiple goods or services; also called *contribution margin per composite unit*. *(p. 877)*

Weighted-average method (See *weighted average*.)

Wholesaler Intermediary that buys products from manufacturers or other wholesalers and sells them to retailers or other wholesalers. *(p. 182)*

Withdrawals Payment of cash or other assets from a proprietorship or partnership to its owner or owners. *(p. 15)*

Work sheet Spreadsheet used to draft an unadjusted trial balance, adjusting entries, adjusted trial balance, and financial statements. *(p. 140)*

Working capital Current assets minus current liabilities at a point in time. *(p. 699)*

Working papers Analyses and other informal reports prepared by accountants and managers when organizing information for formal reports and financial statements. *(p. 140)*

Credits

Index

Note: Page numbers followed by *n* indicate information found in footnotes; **boldface** entries indicate defined terms.

interest revenue, 104, 288, 335, 599–600
miscellaneous, 325–326
other revenues and gains, 195–196
received in sales, 189
unearned (*See* **Unearned revenue(s)**)
for unfinished jobs, 781, 795
Revenue accounts, 53, 114–115, 145, 146, 147
Revenue expenditures, 406, 407, 420
Revenue recognition, 11, 108, A-7
Revenue recognition principle, 11, 53, 61, 96, 101, 103
Reverse stock split, 520
Reversing entries, 156, 150, 191
accounting with, 149, 156–157
accounting without, 156
Reward (loyalty) programs, 441
RFID tags, 190, 320, 876
Rights of stockholders, 512, 525
Rihanna, 441
Ripken, Cal, Jr., 448
Risk, 27, 28, 1038, 1042
The Risk Management Association, 24
Ritz-Carlton Hotel, 750
ROA. *See* **Return on assets (ROA)**
Robbery prevention, 325
Rodgers, Aaron, 230
Rogue insiders, 322
ROI. *See* **Return on assets**
Rolling budgets, 903–904
Rounding, 68, 561
Royal Caribbean Cruises Ltd., 950
Royal Phillips Electronics, 914
Rules-based accounting, 22, 109

Safety stock, 907
Safety stock inventory systems, 907
Salaries, 7, 60, 102, 444, 454, 998
"Salary allowances," 485–486
Sales
on account (*See* Credit sales)
cash sales, 17, 288
computing for target income, 874–875, 880, 881
cost of (*See* **Cost of goods sold**)
credit cards (*See* Credit card(s))
expenses allocated on proportion of, 999
in foreign currency, 613
gift card sales, 441
internal control and, 319
joint relation with expenses, 695
of merchandise, accounting for, 189–191, 208
under periodic inventory system, 204
returns and allowances, 190–191
sales discounts, 190
under perpetual inventory system, 189–191
seasonal variations in, 95
Sales activity, 747, 879, 951–952
Sales allowances, 190, 191, 286
Sales budget, 905, 906–907, 917
Sales commissions, 738–739, 908, 912
Sales discount(s), 185, 190, 204
Sales invoices, 51, 286, 319, 341
Sales journal, 284–286
additional issues with, 285–286
demonstration of, 297
journalizing in, 284–285

posting, 285
proving ledgers, 285
Sales mix, 877, 1053, 1054
Sales mix selection, 1053–1054
Sales mix variance, 963
Sales on account, 51, 362–364
Sales price variance, 963, 972
Sales promotions and incentives, 104, 116, 567, 581, A-7
Sales quantity variance, 963
Sales returns, 190–191, 204, 286
Sales taxes, 286, 440–441, 441*n*
Sales volume, 871
Sales volume variance, 963, 972
Salvage value of asset, **399**
annual review of, 409
in computing ARR, 1041
net present value and, 1044
Sam's Club, 184
SAP, 293
Sarbanes-Oxley Act (SOX), 13–14, **318**–319, 738
code of ethics mandated by, 7
e-communications, 279
exemption from Section 404(b) of, 14
filing requirements of, 106
internal control report mandated by, 319
Section 404 requirements, 319
Satyam Computers, 9
SBA (Small Business Administration), 484
SBA.gov, 484
Scanners, 280
Scatter diagrams, 866, 867, 868
for changes in estimates, 873
creating with Excel®, 882
manipulation of, 875, 883
Schedule of accounts payable, 290, 299
Schedule of accounts receivable, 285, 299, 363
Schedule of cost of goods manufactured, 747–749
Schedule of manufacturing activities, 747–749
Schottenstein, David, 777
Scope of business, 482–483
S corporations, 13, 483–484
Scrap or rework decision, 1052, 1058, 1059
Sea Ray, 605
Sears, 364
Seasonal businesses, 907, 922
Seasonal variations in sales, 95
SEC. *See* **Securities and Exchange Commission (SEC)**
sec.gov/investor/pubs/cyberfraud.htm, 321
Section 404 (of SOX), 319
Secured bonds, 568
Securities and Exchange Commission (SEC), 9
annual reports filed with, A-1
bond registration requirements, 556*n*
EDGAR database, 16, A-1
financial statements filed with, 106
fines paid to, for accounting fraud, 327
Form 10–K requirements, 689
required to pay some whistle-blowers, 14
SEC databases, 281
Segment elimination decision, 1055
Segment reporting, A-8
Segment return on assets, 295, 299, 300
Selling departments, 995
Selling expense budget, 908, 917
Selling expenses, 195

Selling price, 184
Sell or process decision, 1052–1053
Semiannual compounding, 562, 574
Sensitivity analysis, 876
Separate legal entity, 510
Separation of duties, 231, 320, 321, 323
Serial bonds, 568
Service businesses, 16
account titles for, 53*n*
analyst services, 688
bond rating services, 559, 578, 581
budget reporting and evaluation, 950
cost concepts for, 741–742
cost of sales in, 182
current ratios of, 700
job order cost accounting for, 781, 791, 795
manufacturing activities different from, 742
process cost accounting for, 817
process operations in, 816, 831
Service charges/fees, 332, 334
Service department(s), 994
Service department expenses, 999, 1000*n*, 1000–1003
Service economy, 750
Service life of plant asset, 396, 399, 400, 405, 409, 415
Services, 17, 18, 51
capital, and stated ratio method, 486–487
Services revenue, 103–104
Shareholders. *See* **Stockholder(s)**
Shareholders' equity. *See* **Stockholders' equity**
Shares. *See* **Stock**
Sharing agreement loss, 486
Shipping and handling costs, A-6
Shoplifting, 192
Short selling, 706, 709
Short-term investments, 324, 598, 608–609, 636
Short-term liabilities. *See* **Current liabilities**
Short-term notes payable, 441–443, 462
to borrow from bank, 442–443, 454
end-of-period interest adjustment, 443
to extend credit period, 442, 454
Short-term planning, 734, 735
Short-term receivables, 701
Shrinkage, 192, 254
Siemens AG, 1056
Signature card, 331
Significant accounting policies, A-6–A-7
Significant influence, 599, 604–605, 615
Simple capital structure, 529*n*
Single-step income statement, 196, 201, 208
Sinking fund bonds, 568
Siri (Speech Interpretation and Recognition Interface), 280
Six Flags, 439
Skechers, 70
Small Business Administration (SBA), 484
Small businesses, 8
Small stock dividend, 518, 519
SmartIT Staffing, 437
SmartIT-Staffing.com, 437
Smitley, Kyle, 553
Snowmaking costs, 909
Social responsibility, 8
Social Security Administration (SSA), 457
Social Security benefits, 444
Social Security taxes, 444

A Rose by Any Other Name

The same financial statement sometimes receives different titles. Following are some of the more common aliases.*

Balance Sheet	Statement of Financial Position Statement of Financial Condition
Income Statement	Statement of Income Operating Statement Statement of Operations Statement of Operating Activity Earnings Statement Statement of Earnings Profit and Loss (P&L) Statement
Statement of Cash Flows	Statement of Cash Flow Cash Flows Statement Statement of Changes in Cash Position Statement of Changes in Financial Position
Statement of Owner's Equity	Statement of Changes in Owner's Equity Statement of Changes in Owner's Capital Statement of Shareholders' Equity[†] Statement of Changes in Shareholders' Equity[†] Statement of Stockholders' Equity and Comprehensive Income[†] Statement of Changes in Capital Accounts[†]

*The term **Consolidated** often precedes or follows these statement titles to reflect the combination of different entities, such as a parent company and its subsidiaries.

[†] For corporations only.

We thank Dr. Louella Moore from Arkansas State University for suggesting this listing.

Chart of Accounts

Following is a typical chart of accounts, which is used in several assignments. Every company has its own unique accounts and numbering system.

Assets

Current Assets

101 Cash
102 Petty cash
103 Cash equivalents
104 Short-term investments
105 Fair value adjustment, _____ securities (S-T)
106 Accounts receivable
107 Allowance for doubtful accounts
108 Legal fees receivable
109 Interest receivable
110 Rent receivable
111 Notes receivable
119 Merchandise inventory
120 _____ inventory
121 _____ inventory
124 Office supplies
125 Store supplies
126 _____ supplies
128 Prepaid insurance
129 Prepaid interest
131 Prepaid rent
132 Raw materials inventory
133 Goods in process inventory, _____
134 Goods in process inventory, _____
135 Finished goods inventory

Long-Term Investments

141 Long-term investments
142 Fair value adjustment, _____ securities (L-T)
144 Investment in _____
145 Bond sinking fund

Plant Assets

151 Automobiles
152 Accumulated depreciation—Automobiles
153 Trucks
154 Accumulated depreciation—Trucks
155 Boats
156 Accumulated depreciation—Boats
157 Professional library
158 Accumulated depreciation—Professional library
159 Law library
160 Accumulated depreciation—Law library
161 Furniture
162 Accumulated depreciation—Furniture
163 Office equipment
164 Accumulated depreciation—Office equipment
165 Store equipment

166 Accumulated depreciation—Store equipment
167 _____ equipment
168 Accumulated depreciation—_____ equipment
169 Machinery
170 Accumulated depreciation—Machinery
173 Building _____
174 Accumulated depreciation—Building _____
175 Building _____
176 Accumulated depreciation—Building _____
179 Land improvements _____
180 Accumulated depreciation—Land improvements _____
181 Land improvements _____
182 Accumulated depreciation—Land improvements _____
183 Land

Natural Resources

185 Mineral deposit
186 Accumulated depletion—Mineral deposit

Intangible Assets

191 Patents
192 Leasehold
193 Franchise
194 Copyrights
195 Leasehold improvements
196 Licenses
197 Accumulated amortization—_____

Liabilities

Current Liabilities

201 Accounts payable
202 Insurance payable
203 Interest payable
204 Legal fees payable
207 Office salaries payable
208 Rent payable
209 Salaries payable
210 Wages payable
211 Accrued payroll payable
214 Estimated warranty liability
215 Income taxes payable
216 Common dividend payable
217 Preferred dividend payable
218 State unemployment taxes payable
219 Employee federal income taxes payable
221 Employee medical insurance payable

222 Employee retirement program payable
223 Employee union dues payable
224 Federal unemployment taxes payable
225 FICA taxes payable
226 Estimated vacation pay liability

Unearned Revenues

230 Unearned consulting fees
231 Unearned legal fees
232 Unearned property management fees
233 Unearned _____ fees
234 Unearned _____ fees
235 Unearned janitorial revenue
236 Unearned _____ revenue
238 Unearned rent

Notes Payable

240 Short-term notes payable
241 Discount on short-term notes payable
245 Notes payable
251 Long-term notes payable
252 Discount on long-term notes payable

Long-Term Liabilities

253 Long-term lease liability
255 Bonds payable
256 Discount on bonds payable
257 Premium on bonds payable
258 Deferred income tax liability

Equity

Owner's Equity

301 _____, Capital
302 _____, Withdrawals
303 _____, Capital
304 _____, Withdrawals
305 _____, Capital
306 _____, Withdrawals

Paid-In Capital

307 Common stock, $ _____ par value
308 Common stock, no-par value
309 Common stock, $ _____ stated value
310 Common stock dividend distributable
311 Paid-in capital in excess of par value, Common stock

312 Paid-in capital in excess of stated value,
     No-par common stock
313 Paid-in capital from retirement of common stock
314 Paid-in capital, Treasury stock
315 Preferred stock
316 Paid-in capital in excess of par value,
     Preferred stock

Retained Earnings

318 Retained earnings
319 Cash dividends (or Dividends)
320 Stock dividends

Other Equity Accounts

321 Treasury stock, Common
322 Unrealized gain—Equity
323 Unrealized loss—Equity

Revenues

401 _____ fees earned
402 _____ fees earned
403 _____ services revenue
404 _____ services revenue
405 Commissions earned
406 Rent revenue (or Rent earned)
407 Dividends revenue (or Dividend earned)
408 Earnings from investment in _____
409 Interest revenue (or Interest earned)
410 Sinking fund earnings
413 Sales
414 Sales returns and allowances
415 Sales discounts

Cost of Sales

Cost of Goods Sold

502 Cost of goods sold
505 Purchases
506 Purchases returns and allowances
507 Purchases discounts
508 Transportation-in

Manufacturing

520 Raw materials purchases
521 Freight-in on raw materials
530 Factory payroll
531 Direct labor
540 Factory overhead
541 Indirect materials
542 Indirect labor
543 Factory insurance expired
544 Factory supervision
545 Factory supplies used
546 Factory utilities
547 Miscellaneous production costs
548 Property taxes on factory building
549 Property taxes on factory equipment
550 Rent on factory building
551 Repairs, factory equipment
552 Small tools written off
560 Depreciation of factory equipment
561 Depreciation of factory building

Standard Cost Variance

580 Direct material quantity variance
581 Direct material price variance
582 Direct labor quantity variance
583 Direct labor price variance
584 Factory overhead volume variance
585 Factory overhead controllable variance

Expenses

Amortization, Depletion, and Depreciation

601 Amortization expense—_____
602 Amortization expense—_____
603 Depletion expense—_____
604 Depreciation expense—Boats
605 Depreciation expense—Automobiles
606 Depreciation expense—Building _____
607 Depreciation expense—Building _____
608 Depreciation expense—Land
     improvements _____
609 Depreciation expense—Land
     improvements _____
610 Depreciation expense—Law library
611 Depreciation expense—Trucks
612 Depreciation expense _____ equipment
613 Depreciation expense—_____ equipment
614 Depreciation expense—_____
615 Depreciation expense—_____

Employee-Related Expenses

620 Office salaries expense
621 Sales salaries expense
622 Salaries expense
623 _____ wages expense
624 Employees' benefits expense
625 Payroll taxes expense

Financial Expenses

630 Cash over and short
631 Discounts lost
632 Factoring fee expense
633 Interest expense

Insurance Expenses

635 Insurance expense—Delivery equipment
636 Insurance expense—Office equipment
637 Insurance expense—_____

Rental Expenses

640 Rent expense
641 Rent expense—Office space
642 Rent expense—Selling space
643 Press rental expense
644 Truck rental expense
645 _____ rental expense

Supplies Expenses

650 Office supplies expense
651 Store supplies expense
652 _____ supplies expense
653 _____ supplies expense

Miscellaneous Expenses

655 Advertising expense
656 Bad debts expense
657 Blueprinting expense
658 Boat expense
659 Collection expense
661 Concessions expense
662 Credit card expense
663 Delivery expense
664 Dumping expense
667 Equipment expense
668 Food and drinks expense
671 Gas and oil expense
672 General and administrative expense
673 Janitorial expense
674 Legal fees expense
676 Mileage expense
677 Miscellaneous expenses
678 Mower and tools expense
679 Operating expense
680 Organization expense
681 Permits expense
682 Postage expense
683 Property taxes expense
684 Repairs expense—_____
685 Repairs expense—_____
687 Selling expense
688 Telephone expense
689 Travel and entertainment expense
690 Utilities expense
691 Warranty expense
695 Income taxes expense

Gains and Losses

701 Gain on retirement of bonds
702 Gain on sale of machinery
703 Gain on sale of investments
704 Gain on sale of trucks
705 Gain on _____
706 Foreign exchange gain or loss
801 Loss on disposal of machinery
802 Loss on exchange of equipment
803 Loss on exchange of _____
804 Loss on sale of notes
805 Loss on retirement of bonds
806 Loss on sale of investments
807 Loss on sale of machinery
808 Loss on _____
809 Unrealized gain—Income
810 Unrealized loss—Income
811 Impairment gain
812 Impairment loss

Clearing Accounts

901 Income summary
902 Manufacturing summary

SELECTED TRANSACTIONS AND RELATIONS

① Merchandising Transactions Summary

Merchandising Transactions	Merchandising Entries	Dr.	Cr.
Purchases — Purchasing merchandise for resale.	• Merchandise Inventory	#	
	Cash or Accounts Payable		#
Paying freight costs on purchases; FOB shipping point.	• Merchandise Inventory	#	
	Cash		#
Paying within discount period.	• Accounts Payable	#	
	Merchandise Inventory		#
	Cash		#
Recording purchase returns or allowances.	• Cash or Accounts Payable	#	
	Merchandise Inventory		#
Sales — Selling merchandise.	• Cash or Accounts Receivable	#	
	Sales		#
	• Cost of Goods Sold..................	#	
	Merchandise Inventory		#
Receiving payment within discount period.	• Cash	#	
	Sales Discounts	#	
	Accounts Receivable...............		#
Granting sales returns or allowances.	• Sales Returns and Allowances...........	#	
	Cash or Accounts Receivable		#
	• Merchandise Inventory	#	
	Cost of Goods Sold		#
Paying freight costs on sales; FOB destination.	• Delivery Expense	#	
	Cash		#

Merchandising Events	Adjusting and Closing Entries	Dr.	Cr.
Adjusting — Adjusting due to shrinkage (occurs when recorded amount larger than physical inventory).	Cost of Goods Sold	#	
	Merchandise Inventory		#
Closing — Closing temporary accounts with credit balances.	Sales	#	
	Income Summary		#
Closing temporary accounts with debit balances.	Income Summary	#	
	Sales Returns and Allowances		#
	Sales Discounts		#
	Cost of Goods Sold		#
	Delivery Expense		#
	"Other Expenses"		#

② Merchandising Cash Flows

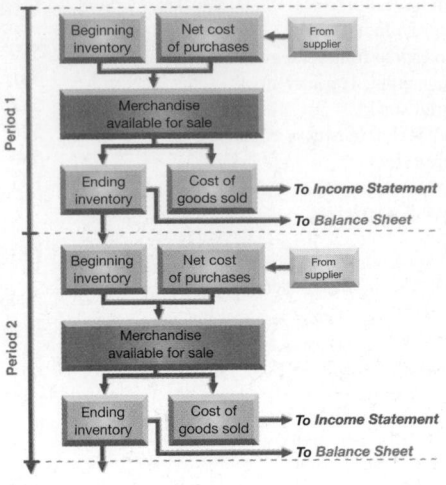

③ Credit Terms and Amounts

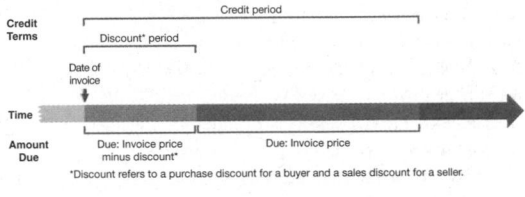

*Discount refers to a purchase discount for a buyer and a sales discount for a seller.

④ Bad Debts Estimation

Bad Debts Estimation
or

Income Statement Focus
- **Percent of Sales** [Emphasis on Matching]
  - Sales × Rate = Bad Debts Expense

Balance Sheet Focus
or
- **Percent of Receivables** [Emphasis on Realizable Value]
  - Accounts Receivable × Rate = Allowance for Doubtful Accounts
- **Aging of Receivables** [Emphasis on Realizable Value]
  - Accounts Receivable (by Age) × Rates (by Age) = Allowance for Doubtful Accounts

⑤ Bond Valuation

Bond Sets — Contract rate
Market Sets — Market rate

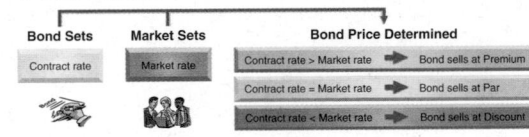

Bond Price Determined

Contract rate > Market rate	➡	Bond sells at Premium
Contract rate = Market rate	➡	Bond sells at Par
Contract rate < Market rate	➡	Bond sells at Discount

⑦ Dividend Transactions

Account Affected	Cash Dividend	Stock Dividend	Stock Split
Cash.............	Decrease	—	—
Common Stock	—	Increase	—
Retained Earnings ..	Decrease	Decrease	—

⑥ Stock Transactions Summary

Stock Transactions	Stock Entries	Dr.	Cr.
Issue Common Stock — Issue par value common stock at par (par stock recorded at par).	Cash	#	
	Common Stock		#
Issue par value common stock at premium (par stock recorded at par).	Cash	#	
	Common Stock		#
	Paid-In Capital in Excess of Par Value, Common Stock		#
Issue no-par value common stock (no-par stock recorded at amount received).	Cash	#	
	Common Stock		#
Issue stated value common stock at stated value (stated stock recorded at stated value).	Cash	#	
	Common stock		#
Issue stated value common stock at premium (stated stock recorded at stated value).	Cash	#	
	Common stock		#
	Paid-In Capital in Excess of Stated Value, Common Stock		#
Issue Preferred Stock — Issue par value preferred stock at par (par stock recorded at par).	Cash	#	
	Preferred Stock		#
Issue par value preferred stock at premium (par stock recorded at par).	Cash	#	
	Preferred Stock		#
	Paid-In Capital in Excess of Par Value, Preferred Stock		#
Reacquire Common Stock — Reacquire its own common stock (treasury stock recorded at cost).	Treasury Stock, Common	#	
	Cash		#
Reissue Common Stock — Reissue its treasury stock at cost (treasury stock removed at cost).	Cash	#	
	Treasury Stock, Common		#
Reissue its treasury stock above cost (treasury stock removed at cost).	Cash	#	
	Treasury Stock, Common		#
	Paid-In Capital, Treasury		#
Reissue its treasury stock below cost (treasury stock removed at cost; if paid-in capital is insufficient to cover amount below cost, retained earnings is debited for remainder).	Cash	#	
	Paid-In Capital, Treasury	#	
	Treasury Stock, Common		#
	Retained Earnings (if necessary) ...		#

⑧ A Rose by Any Other Name

The same financial statement sometimes receives different titles. Following are some of the more common aliases.*

Balance Sheet	Statement of Financial Position Statement of Financial Condition
Income Statement	Statement of Income Operating Statement Statement of Operations Statement of Operating Activity Earnings Statement Statement of Earnings Profit and Loss (P&L) Statement
Statement of Cash Flows	Statement of Cash Flow Cash Flows Statement Statement of Changes in Cash Position Statement of Changes in Financial Position
Statement of Owner's Equity	Statement of Changes in Owner's Equity Statement of Changes in Owner's Capital Statement of Shareholders' Equity† Statement of Changes in Shareholders' Equity† Statement of Stockholders' Equity and Comprehensive Income† Statement of Changes in Capital Accounts†

*The term **Consolidated** often precedes or follows these statement titles to reflect the combination of different entities, such as a parent company and its subsidiaries.
† Corporation only.

MANAGERIAL ANALYSES AND REPORTS

① Cost Types
Variable costs: Total cost changes in proportion to volume of activity
Fixed costs: Total cost does not change in proportion to volume of activity
Mixed costs: Cost consists of both a variable and a fixed element

② Cost Sources
Direct materials: Raw materials costs directly linked to finished product
Direct labor: Employee costs directly linked to finished product
Overhead: Costs indirectly linked to finished product

③ Costing Systems
Job order costing: Costs assigned to each unique unit or batch of units
Process costing: Costs assigned to similar products that are mass-produced in a continuous manner

④ Costing Ratios
Contribution margin ratio = (Net sales − Variable costs)/Net sales
Predetermined overhead rate = Estimated overhead costs/Estimated activity base
Break-even point in units = Total fixed costs/Contribution margin per unit

⑤ Planning and Control Metrics
Cost variance = Actual cost − Standard (budgeted) cost
Sales (revenue) variance = Actual sales − Standard (budgeted) sales

⑥ Capital Budgeting
Payback period = Time expected to recover investment cost
Accounting rate of return = Expected annual net income/Average annual investment
Net present value (NPV) = Present value of future cash flows − Investment cost
NPV rule: 1. Compute net present value (NPV in $)
2. If NPV ≥ 0, then accept project; If NPV < 0, then reject project
Internal rate 1. Compute internal rate of return (IRR in %)
of return rule: 2. If IRR ≥ hurdle rate, accept project; If IRR < hurdle rate, reject project

⑦ Costing Terminology
Relevant range: Organization's normal range of operating activity.
Direct cost: Cost incurred for the benefit of one cost object.
Indirect cost: Cost incurred for the benefit of more than one cost object.
Product cost: Cost that is necessary and integral to finished products.
Period cost: Cost identified more with a time period than with finished products.
Overhead cost: Cost not separately or directly traceable to a cost object.
Relevant cost: Cost that is pertinent to a decision.
Opportunity cost: Benefit lost by choosing an action from two or more alternatives.
Sunk cost: Cost already incurred that cannot be avoided or changed.
Standard cost: Cost computed using standard price and standard quantity.
Budget: Formal statement of an organization's future plans.
Break-even point: Sales level at which an organization earns zero profit.
Incremental cost: Cost incurred only if the organization undertakes a certain action.
Transfer price: Price on transactions between divisions within a company.

⑧ Standard Cost Variances

Total materials variance − | Materials price variance + Materials quantity variance

Total labor variance = | Labor (rate) variance + Labor efficiency (quantity) variance

Total overhead variance = | Overhead controllable variance + Fixed overhead volume variance

Overhead controllable variance = Actual total overhead − Applied total overhead from flexible budget

Fixed overhead volume variance = Budgeted fixed overhead − Applied fixed overhead

Variable overhead variance = Variable overhead spending variance + Variable overhead efficiency variance
Fixed overhead variance = Fixed overhead spending variance + Fixed overhead volume variance
} = Total overhead variance

Materials price variance = [AQ × AP] − [AQ × SP]

Materials quantity variance = [AQ × SP] − [SQ × SP]

Labor (rate) variance = [AH × AR] − [AH × SR]

Labor efficiency (quantity) variance = [AH × SR] − [SH × SR]

Variable overhead spending variance = [AH × AVR] − [AH × SVR]
Variable overhead efficiency variance = [AH × SVR] − [SH × SVR]
Fixed overhead spending variance = Actual fixed overhead − Budgeted fixed overhead

where AQ is actual quantity of materials; AP is actual price of materials; AH is actual hours of labor; AR is actual rate of wages; AVR is actual variable rate of overhead; SQ is standard quantity of materials; SP is standard price of materials; SH is standard hours of labor; SR is standard rate of wages; SVR is standard variable rate of overhead.

⑨ Sales Variances

Sales price variance = [AS × AP] − [AS × BP]

Sales volume variance = [AS × BP] − [BS × BP]

where AS = actual sales units; AP = actual sales price; BP = budgeted sales price; BS = budgeted sales units (fixed budget)

Manufacturing Statement
For _period_ Ended _date_

Direct materials		
Raw materials inventory, Beginning	$	#
Raw materials purchases		#
Raw materials available for use		#
Raw materials inventory, Ending		(#)
Direct materials used		#
Direct labor		#
Overhead costs		
Total overhead costs		#
Total manufacturing costs		#
Add goods in process inventory, Beginning		#
Total cost of goods in process		#
Deduct goods in process inventory, Ending		(#)
Cost of goods manufactured	$	#

Contribution Margin Income Statement
For _period_ Ended _date_

Net sales (revenues)	$	#
Total variable costs		#
Contribution margin		#
Total fixed costs		#
Net income	$	#

Flexible Budget
For _period_ Ended _date_

	Flexible Budget		Flexible Budget for Unit Sales of #
	Variable Amount per Unit	Fixed Cost	
Sales (revenues)	$ #		$ #
Variable costs			
Examples: Direct materials, Direct labor,			
Other variable costs	#		#
Total variable costs	#		#
Contribution margin	$ #		#
Fixed costs			
Examples: Depreciation, Manager		$ #	#
salaries, Administrative salaries		#	#
Total fixed costs		$ #	#
Income from operations			$ #

Budget Performance Report*
For _period_ Ended _date_

	Budget	Actual Performance	Variances†
Sales: In units	#	#	
In dollars	$ #	$ #	$ # F or U
Cost of sales			
Direct costs	#	#	# F or U
Indirect costs	#	#	# F or U
Selling expenses			
Examples: Commissions	#	#	# F or U
Shipping expenses	#	#	# F or U
General and administrative expenses			
Examples: Administrative salaries	#	#	# F or U
Total expenses	$ #	$ #	$ # F or U
Income from operations	$ #	$ #	$ # F or U

† F = Favorable variance; U = Unfavorable variance. * Applies to both flexible and fixed budgets.

Master Budget Sequence

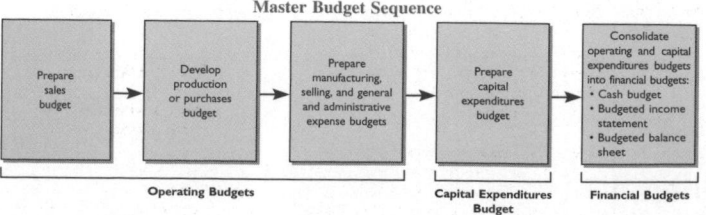

Prepare sales budget → Develop production or purchases budget → Prepare manufacturing, selling, and general and administrative expense budgets → Prepare capital expenditures budget → Consolidate operating and capital expenditures budgets into financial budgets: • Cash budget • Budgeted income statement • Budgeted balance sheet

Operating Budgets | **Capital Expenditures Budget** | **Financial Budgets**

FUNDAMENTALS

① Accounting Equation

Assets	=	Liabilities	+	Equity

Debit for increases	Credit for decreases	Debit for decreases	Credit for increases	Debit for decreases	Credit for increases

Owner's Capital*	−	Owner's Withdrawals*	+	Revenues	−	Expenses

Dr. for decreases	Cr. for increases	Dr. for increases	Cr. for decreases	Dr. for decreases	Cr. for increases	Dr. for increases	Cr. for decreases

Indicates normal balance.

*Comparable corporate accounts are Common Stock (Paid-In Capital) and Dividends.

② Accounting Cycle

1. Analyze transactions
2. Journalize
3. Post
4. Prepare unadjusted trial balance
5. Adjust
6. Prepare adjusted trial balance
7. Prepare statements
8. Close
9. Prepare post-closing trial balance
10. Reverse (Optional)

Accounting Cycle

③ Adjustments and Entries

Type	Adjusting Entry	
Prepaid Expenses	Dr. Expense	Cr. Asset*
Unearned Revenues	Dr. Liability	Cr. Revenue
Accrued Expenses	Dr. Expense	Cr. Liability
Accrued Revenues	Dr. Asset	Cr. Revenue

*For depreciation, credit Accumulated Depreciation (contra asset).

④ 4-Step Closing Process

1. Transfer revenue and gain account balances to Income Summary.
2. Transfer expense and loss account balances to Income Summary.
3. Transfer Income Summary balance to Owner's Capital.
4. Transfer Withdrawals balance to Owner's Capital.

⑤ Accounting Concepts

Characteristics	Assumptions	Principles	Constraints
Relevance	Business entity	Measurement (historical cost)	Cost-benefit
Reliability	Going concern	Revenue recognition	Materiality
Comparability	Monetary unit	Expense recognition	Industry practice
Consistency	Periodicity	Full disclosure	Conservatism

⑥ Ownership of Inventory

	Ownership Transfers When Goods Passed To	Transportation Costs Paid By
FOB Shipping Point	Carrier	Buyer
FOB Destination	Buyer	Seller

⑦ Inventory Costing Methods

- Specific Identification
- First-In, First-Out (FIFO)
- Weighted-Average
- Last-In, First-Out (LIFO)

⑧ Depreciation and Depletion

Straight-Line: $\dfrac{\text{Cost} - \text{Salvage value}}{\text{Useful life in periods}} \times \text{Periods expired}$

Units-of-Production: $\dfrac{\text{Cost} - \text{Salvage value}}{\text{Useful life in units}} \times \text{Units produced}$

Declining-Balance: Rate* × Beginning-of-period book value
*Rate is often double the straight-line rate, or 2 × (1/Useful life)

Depletion: $\dfrac{\text{Cost} - \text{Salvage value}}{\text{Total capacity in units}} \times \text{Units extracted}$

⑨ Interest Computation

Interest = Principal (face) × Rate × Time

⑩ Accounting for Investment Securities

Classification*	Accounting
Short-Term Investment in Securities	
Held-to-maturity (debt) securities	**Cost** (without any discount or premium amortization)
Trading (debt and equity) securities	**Fair value** (with fair value adjustment to income)
Available-for-sale (debt and equity) securities	**Fair value** (with fair value adjustment to equity)
Long-Term Investment in Securities	
Held-to-maturity (debt) securities	**Cost** (with any discount or premium amortization)
Available-for-sale (debt and equity) securities	**Fair value** (with fair value adjustment to equity)
Equity securities with significant influence	Equity method
Equity securities with controlling influence	Equity method (with consolidation)

*A *fair value option* allows companies to report HTM and AFS securities much like trading securities.

ANALYSES

① Liquidity and Efficiency

Current ratio $= \dfrac{\text{Current assets}}{\text{Current liabilities}}$ — p. 152

Working capital = Current assets − Current liabilities — p. 699

Acid-test ratio $= \dfrac{\text{Cash} + \text{Short-term investments} + \text{Current receivables}}{\text{Current liabilities}}$ — p. 198

Accounts receivable turnover $= \dfrac{\text{Net sales}}{\text{Average accounts receivable, net}}$ — p. 377

Credit risk ratio $= \dfrac{\text{Allowance for doubtful accounts}}{\text{Accounts receivable, net}}$ — p. 377

Inventory turnover $= \dfrac{\text{Cost of goods sold}}{\text{Average inventory}}$ — p. 243

Days' sales uncollected $= \dfrac{\text{Accounts receivable, net}}{\text{Net sales}} \times 365*$ — p. 337

Days' sales in inventory $= \dfrac{\text{Ending inventory}}{\text{Cost of goods sold}} \times 365*$ — p. 243

Total asset turnover $= \dfrac{\text{Net sales}}{\text{Average total assets}}$ — p. 415

Plant asset useful life $= \dfrac{\text{Plant asset cost}}{\text{Depreciation expense}}$ — p. 415

Plant asset age $= \dfrac{\text{Accumulated depreciation}}{\text{Depreciation expense}}$ — p. 415

Days' cash expense coverage $= \dfrac{\text{Cash and cash equivalents}}{\text{Average daily cash expenses}}$ — p. 324

*360 days is also commonly used.

② Solvency

Debt ratio $= \dfrac{\text{Total liabilities}}{\text{Total assets}}$ Equity ratio $= \dfrac{\text{Total equity}}{\text{Total assets}}$ — pp. 69 & 707

Debt-to-equity $= \dfrac{\text{Total liabilities}}{\text{Total equity}}$ — p. 569

Times interest earned $= \dfrac{\text{Income before interest expense and income taxes}}{\text{Interest expense}}$ — p. 452

Cash coverage of growth $= \dfrac{\text{Cash flow from operations}}{\text{Cash outflow for plant assets}}$ — p. 653

Cash coverage of debt $= \dfrac{\text{Cash flow from operations}}{\text{Total noncurrent liabilities}}$ — p. 653

③ Profitability

Profit margin ratio $= \dfrac{\text{Net income}}{\text{Net sales}}$ — p. 109

Gross margin ratio $= \dfrac{\text{Net sales} - \text{Cost of goods sold}}{\text{Net sales}}$ — p. 198

Return on total assets $= \dfrac{\text{Net income}}{\text{Average total assets}}$ — p. 24

$= \text{Profit margin ratio} \times \text{Total asset turnover}$ — p. 705

Return on common stockholders' equity $= \dfrac{\text{Net income} - \text{Preferred dividends}}{\text{Average common stockholders' equity}}$ — p. 707

Book value per common share $= \dfrac{\text{Stockholders' equity applicable to common shares}}{\text{Number of common shares outstanding}}$ — p. 530

Basic earnings per share $= \dfrac{\text{Net income} - \text{Preferred dividends}}{\text{Weighted-average common shares outstanding}}$ — p. 529

Cash flow on total assets $= \dfrac{\text{Cash flow from operations}}{\text{Average total assets}}$ — p. 652

Payout ratio $= \dfrac{\text{Cash dividends declared on common stock}}{\text{Net income}}$ — p. 530

④ Market

Price-earnings ratio $= \dfrac{\text{Market value (price) per share}}{\text{Earnings per share}}$ — p. 529

Dividend yield $= \dfrac{\text{Annual cash dividends per share}}{\text{Market price per share}}$ — p. 530

Residual income = Net income − Target net income